IFRS® Standards

issued at 1 January 2021,
reflecting changes not yet required

This edition is issued in three parts

PART C

contains the bases for conclusions that accompany the Standards, the *Conceptual Framework for Financial Reporting* and IFRS practice statements, together with the *Constitution* and *Due Process Handbook* of the IFRS Foundation

See also Parts A and B of this edition:

Part A

contains the text of IFRS Standards including IAS® Standards, IFRIC® Interpretations and SIC® Interpretations, together with the Conceptual Framework for Financial Reporting

Part B

contains the illustrative examples and implementation guidance that accompany the Standards, together with IFRS practice statements

❀IFRS®

Contents

continued...

IFRIC Interpretations

continued...

...continued

Conceptual Framework for Financial Reporting

Conceptual Framework for Financial Reporting (Conceptual Framework) (issued March 2018) was issued by the International Accounting Standards Board (Board).

The text of the Conceptual Framework is contained in Part A of this edition. This part presents the following accompanying document:

BASIS FOR CONCLUSIONS

CONTENTS

Basis for Conclusions on
Conceptual Framework for Financial Reporting

This Basis for Conclusions accompanies, but is not part of the Conceptual Framework for Financial Reporting *(Conceptual Framework). It summarises the considerations of the* International Accounting Standards Board *(Board) in developing the* Conceptual Framework. *Individual Board members gave greater weight to some factors than to others.*

Contents

History of the project

BC0.1   In 1989, the Board's predecessor body, the International Accounting Standards Committee, issued the *Framework for the Preparation and Presentation of Financial Statements* (1989 *Framework*).

BC0.2   In 2004, the Board and the US national standard-setter, the Financial Accounting Standards Board (FASB), started a joint project to revise their conceptual frameworks.

BC0.3   The first phase of the project was to develop chapters that describe the objective of general purpose financial reporting and the qualitative characteristics of useful financial information. In developing these chapters, the Board and the FASB published a Discussion Paper in 2006 (2006 Discussion Paper) and an Exposure Draft in 2008 (2008 Exposure Draft).[1] After considering feedback on those documents and information gained from outreach, in 2010 the Board and the FASB issued two chapters of a revised *Conceptual Framework for Financial Reporting* (2010 *Conceptual Framework*). The chapters on the objective of general purpose financial reporting and qualitative characteristics of useful financial information came into effect as soon as they were issued. The remaining text of the 1989 *Framework* was carried forward to the 2010 *Conceptual Framework* unchanged.

BC0.4   In addition to finalising the chapters on the objective of general purpose financial reporting and qualitative characteristics of useful financial information, the Board and the FASB:

(a)   published a Discussion Paper and then an Exposure Draft (2010 Exposure Draft) on the concept of a reporting entity;[2]

(b)   discussed the definitions of the elements of financial statements; and

(c)   discussed and held public round-table meetings about measurement.

BC0.5   This work did not lead to further revisions at that time because in 2010 the Board and the FASB suspended work on the *Conceptual Framework* to concentrate on other projects.

BC0.6   In 2011, the Board carried out a public consultation on its agenda. Most respondents to that consultation identified the Conceptual Framework as a priority project for the Board. Consequently, in 2012 the Board restarted its Conceptual Framework project.

BC0.7   Before 2010, the Board and the FASB had planned to complete the project in eight separate phases, but completed only one phase—on objectives and qualitative characteristics. On restarting the project in 2012, the Board decided to develop a complete set of proposals for a revised *Conceptual*

---

1   See the Discussion Paper *Preliminary Views on an Improved Conceptual Framework for Financial Reporting: The Objective of Financial Reporting and Qualitative Characteristics of Decision-useful Financial Reporting Information* published in 2006 and the Exposure Draft *An Improved Conceptual Framework for Financial Reporting: Chapters 1 and 2* published in 2008.

2   See the Discussion Paper *Preliminary Views on an Improved Conceptual Framework for Financial Reporting—The Reporting Entity* published in 2008 and the Exposure Draft *Conceptual Framework for Financial Reporting—The Reporting Entity* published in 2010.

Framework instead of continuing with the phased approach. Developing the *Conceptual Framework* as a whole enabled the Board and stakeholders to see more clearly the links between different aspects of the *Conceptual Framework*.

BC0.8 In developing the revised *Conceptual Framework*, the Board published a Discussion Paper in 2013 (2013 Discussion Paper) and an Exposure Draft in 2015 (2015 Exposure Draft).[3] After considering feedback on these documents and information gained from outreach, in 2018 the Board completed its Conceptual Framework project when it issued the revised *Conceptual Framework for Financial Reporting* (2018 *Conceptual Framework*).

BC0.9 The work since restarting the project in 2012 was not conducted jointly with the FASB. The 2018 *Conceptual Framework* includes limited changes to the chapters on the objective of general purpose financial reporting and qualitative characteristics of useful financial information. The FASB did not make corresponding changes to its Statements of Financial Accounting Concepts.

Revision in 2018—approach and scope

BC0.10 Although the 2010 *Conceptual Framework* had helped the Board when developing IFRS Standards (Standards):

(a) some important areas were not covered;

(b) the guidance in some areas was unclear; and

(c) some aspects were out of date.

BC0.11 In developing the 2018 *Conceptual Framework*, the Board built on the 2010 *Conceptual Framework*—filling in gaps, as well as clarifying and updating it, but not fundamentally reconsidering all aspects of the 2010 *Conceptual Framework*. In particular, although the Board reconsidered some aspects of chapters on the objective of financial reporting and qualitative characteristics of useful financial information, it did not reconsider those chapters fundamentally. In selecting that approach, the Board noted that these chapters went through extensive due process during the development of the 2010 *Conceptual Framework*.

BC0.12 The Board normally establishes a consultative group for major projects. For the Conceptual Framework project, the Board used the Accounting Standards Advisory Forum (ASAF) as its consultative group. The ASAF is an advisory group to the Board. It comprises national accounting standard-setters and regional bodies with an interest in financial reporting. The Board discussed a range of topics with the ASAF during the development of the 2018 *Conceptual Framework*.

BC0.13 In developing the 2018 *Conceptual Framework*, the Board sought a balance between providing high-level concepts and providing enough detail for the 2018 *Conceptual Framework* to be useful to the Board and others. Some stakeholders stated that in some areas the Board's proposals merely described

---

3 See the Discussion Paper *A Review of the Conceptual Framework for Financial Reporting* published in 2013 and the Exposure Draft *Conceptual Framework for Financial Reporting* published in 2015.

the factors that the Board would consider in making judgements when developing Standards. They expressed the view that, as a result, the proposals did not examine fundamental concepts and were not sufficiently aspirational. The Board did not share that view. The Board viewed the *Conceptual Framework* as a practical tool to help it to develop Standards. The Board concluded that a *Conceptual Framework* would not fulfil this role if it described concepts without explaining the factors the Board needs to consider in making judgements when the application of concepts does not lead to a single answer, or leads to conflicting answers.

BC0.14   In developing the 2018 *Conceptual Framework*, the Board drew on some concepts developed in recent standard-setting projects. The Board's aim in doing so was to reflect the Board's most developed thinking on these matters, not to justify its standard-setting decisions or current practice.

BC0.15   The 2018 *Conceptual Framework* does not address classification of financial instruments with characteristics of both liabilities and equity because the Board did not want to delay other much-needed improvements to the *Conceptual Framework*. The Board is exploring how to distinguish liabilities from equity in its research project on Financial Instruments with Characteristics of Equity. If necessary, the *Conceptual Framework* will be updated as one possible outcome of that project (see paragraph BC4.45).

BC0.16   The discussion of capital and capital maintenance in the 2018 *Conceptual Framework* is unchanged from the 2010 *Conceptual Framework*. That discussion originally appeared in the 1989 *Framework* (see paragraphs BC8.1–BC8.4). The Board may consider revising that discussion in the future if it considers that necessary.

BC0.17   In developing the 2018 *Conceptual Framework*, the Board did not address the equity method of accounting, the translation of amounts denominated in foreign currency or the restatement of the measuring unit in hyperinflation. The Board concluded that these issues would best be dealt with if it were to carry out projects to consider revising Standards on these topics.

Purpose (paragraph SP1.1)

BC0.18   The 2010 *Conceptual Framework* included a long list of possible uses of the *Conceptual Framework*. In 2018, the Board streamlined the list, identifying three main uses of the *Conceptual Framework*: assisting the Board in developing Standards, assisting preparers in developing accounting policies when no Standard applies to a particular transaction or other event (or when a Standard allows a choice of accounting policy) and assisting all parties in understanding and interpreting Standards.

BC0.19   The Board considered whether to focus the stated purpose of the *Conceptual Framework* by stating that its primary purpose would be only to assist the Board in developing Standards. The Board rejected this approach because acknowledging the assistance the *Conceptual Framework* can give to other parties would not prevent the Board from developing focused and consistent concepts that will help it to develop Standards.

BC0.20   Although preparers apply the *Conceptual Framework* in developing accounting policies when no Standard applies to a particular transaction or other event or when a Standard allows a choice of accounting policy, a few aspects of the *Conceptual Framework* can only be applied by the Board. In such cases, the 2018 *Conceptual Framework* indicates that the Board may make particular decisions in developing Standards (for example, see paragraph 7.17).

Status (paragraphs SP1.2–SP1.3)

BC0.21   The 1989 *Framework* and the 2010 *Conceptual Framework* stated that the *Conceptual Framework* is not a Standard and does not override any specific Standards. In the 2018 *Conceptual Framework*, the Board reconfirmed this status.

BC0.22   The Board found that the status of the *Conceptual Framework* has worked well in practice. Also, an explicit statement that the *Conceptual Framework* does not override any requirements in a Standard prevents entities from attempting to override inappropriately Standards those entities might view as contradicting the *Conceptual Framework*.

BC0.23   In some stakeholders' view, the Board should never develop Standards that depart from the *Conceptual Framework*. The Board disagreed with this view. In some circumstances, the Board might need to depart from aspects of the *Conceptual Framework*. It is helpful for the *Conceptual Framework* to acknowledge this, and to specify that such departures are appropriate only if needed to meet the objective of general purpose financial reporting. That need might arise because conceptual thinking or the economic environment may change, and new or revised Standards might need to reflect these changes.

BC0.24   Some respondents to the 2015 Exposure Draft expressed concerns about the implications of the proposals for future Standards. In particular, they expressed concerns about proposed changes to the definitions of an asset and a liability. In response, the Board tested the revised definitions of an asset and a liability and the guidance supporting those definitions (see paragraphs BC4.19–BC4.22). One of the aims of this test was to enable both the Board and stakeholders to assess implications of the revised concepts for future Standards. In addition, the Board tested for inconsistencies between the revised concepts and existing Standards.

BC0.25   The aim of these tests was not to identify whether the Board should develop proposals to amend any Standards following the revision of the *Conceptual Framework*. Amending a Standard is not an automatic consequence of that revision. Changes to Standards are made to address deficiencies in financial reporting. Any changes to the *Conceptual Framework* that highlight inconsistencies in the Standards must be considered by the Board in the light of other priorities when developing its work plan.[4]

---

4   See paragraph 4.23 of the IFRS Foundation *Due Process Handbook*.

BC0.26   The *IFRS for SMEs®* Standard includes a section on the concepts and basic principles underlying the financial statements of small and medium-sized entities. That section is based on the 1989 *Framework*. The Board will consider whether it should amend this section of the *IFRS for SMEs* Standard when it next reviews that Standard.

Transition to the 2018 *Conceptual Framework*

BC0.27   The Board and the IFRS Interpretations Committee will start using the 2018 *Conceptual Framework* immediately once it is issued. If, when developing a draft IFRIC® Interpretation, the IFRS Interpretation Committee is faced with an inconsistency between a Standard (including any Standard developed on the basis of the 1989 *Framework* or the 2010 *Conceptual Framework*) and the concepts in the 2018 *Conceptual Framework*, it will refer the issue to the Board, as required by the IFRS Foundation *Due Process Handbook*.[5]

BC0.28   The revised concepts will guide the Board when it develops or revises Standards. However, changes to the *Conceptual Framework* will not automatically lead to changes in existing Standards (see paragraph BC0.25). Accordingly, changes to the *Conceptual Framework* will have no immediate effect on the financial statements of most reporting entities. Preparers of financial statements could be directly affected by the changes only if they need to use the *Conceptual Framework* to develop an accounting policy when no Standard applies to a particular transaction or other event or when a Standard allows a choice of accounting policy.[6] To achieve transition to the 2018 *Conceptual Framework* for such entities, the Board issued *Amendments to References to the Conceptual Framework in IFRS Standards* in 2018. Where appropriate, that document replaces references in Standards to the 1989 *Framework* with references to the 2018 *Conceptual Framework* and updates related quotations.

Business activities

BC0.29   In developing the 2018 *Conceptual Framework*, the Board concluded that the nature of an entity's business activities can affect the relevance of some types of financial information and that the Board may need to consider that factor when developing or revising Standards.

BC0.30   The Board disagreed with the view expressed by some stakeholders that considering the nature of an entity's business activities necessarily leads to subjectivity and impairs comparability of financial statements. An entity's business activities are a matter of fact that can in most cases be determined

---

5   See paragraph 7.8 of the IFRS Foundation *Due Process Handbook*.

6   If no Standard specifically applies to a transaction, other event or condition, paragraph 11 of IAS 8 *Accounting Policies, Changes in Accounting Estimates and Errors* requires entities to consider the *Conceptual Framework* in developing and applying an accounting policy for that transaction. If a Standard permits a choice of accounting policy, entities select an accounting policy subject to an overall requirement in IAS 1 *Presentation of Financial Statements* that financial statements must provide a fair presentation of the entity's financial position, financial performance and cash flows. The link between fair presentation and the concepts in the *Conceptual Framework* is described in paragraph 15 of IAS 1.

objectively. Hence, if entities conduct the same type of business activities, the Board expects that those activities would be reflected in a similar manner in the entities' financial statements.

BC0.31 The Board considered whether the nature of business activities should be considered in all areas of standard-setting and should be embedded in the *Conceptual Framework* as an overarching concept. The Board concluded that the nature of an entity's business activities does not affect all areas of financial reporting in the same way and to the same extent and so it should not be included as an overarching concept. Accordingly, the 2018 *Conceptual Framework* does not include a general discussion of how an entity's business activities affect financial reporting decisions. Instead, the 2018 *Conceptual Framework* describes that factor in the context of:

(a) the selection of the unit of account (see paragraph 4.51(a)(iv)).

(b) the selection of a measurement basis for an asset or liability and for related income and expenses (see paragraphs 6.54–6.57). In some cases, this would lead to some items of income or expenses being included in other comprehensive income (see the discussion of more than one measurement basis in paragraphs 6.83–6.86).

(c) classification of assets, liabilities, equity, income or expenses (see paragraph 7.7).

BC0.32 The concept of business activities is discussed in the 2018 *Conceptual Framework* to assist the Board in developing Standards. In a particular Standard, the concept of business activities can be further explained and developed. The discussion of business model in IFRS 9 *Financial Instruments* is one example of how the Board has applied the concept of business activities.

BC0.33 The Board decided to use the term 'business activities' rather than the term 'business model' in the 2018 *Conceptual Framework*. The term 'business model' is used with a range of different meanings by various organisations, for example, the International Integrated Reporting Council, the Enhanced Disclosure Task Force of the Financial Stability Board and various regulators. Adopting the term 'business model' in the 2018 *Conceptual Framework* could have led to confusion with those definitions.

Implications of long-term investment

BC0.34 The subject of long-term investment has attracted a great deal of attention from governments and others. Governments have indicated that encouraging long-term investment is an important tool for promoting economic growth.

BC0.35 The Board considered the role of its Standards in promoting long-term investment and noted that:

(a) the Board makes an important contribution to the promotion of investment, including long-term investment, by producing Standards that require transparent financial reporting. This is a precondition for the healthy and efficient functioning of financial markets. Transparent financial reporting helps market participants to make more efficient and informed resource allocation and other economic decisions and thus makes investment more attractive to capital providers (investors and lenders). It also provides useful inputs for an assessment of stewardship.

(b)   it is not, however, the role of the Standards to encourage or discourage any type of investments. Instead, standard-setting decisions are driven by the need for entities to provide useful information.

BC0.36   When developing the 2018 *Conceptual Framework*, the Board considered whether the *Conceptual Framework* will provide the Board with sufficient and appropriate tools to enable it, when developing Standards, to consider:

(a)   the business activity of long-term investment (see paragraphs BC0.37–BC0.39); and

(b)   the information needs of long-term investors (see paragraphs BC0.40–BC0.43).

Long-term investment as a business activity

BC0.37   The Board considered a suggestion made by some stakeholders that it should identify long-term investment as a particular type of business activity (or business model) and develop specific measurement and presentation and disclosure requirements for entities conducting that business activity. Some stakeholders expressing those views suggested that:

(a)   entities should not use a current value measurement basis for their long-term investments and for their liabilities; or

(b)   if a current value measurement basis is used for those investments and liabilities, income and expenses resulting from remeasurements should be included in other comprehensive income, not in the statement of profit or loss.

BC0.38   As discussed in paragraphs 6.54–6.57 of the 2018 *Conceptual Framework*, the nature of the business activities being conducted affects how an asset or liability contributes to future cash flows. Thus, the nature of an entity's business activities is considered in selecting a measurement basis for an asset or liability and for related income and expenses. Moreover, in some cases, considering the nature of an entity's activities may lead to some items of income and expenses being included in other comprehensive income (see paragraphs 6.85–6.86). The Board concluded that the discussion on this factor in the 2018 *Conceptual Framework* provides sufficient tools for the Board to make appropriate standard-setting decisions if future projects consider how to account for the long-term investments of entities whose business activities include long-term investment or for their liabilities.

BC0.39   For the following reasons, the Board decided that the 2018 *Conceptual Framework* should not refer explicitly to the business activity of long-term investment:

(a)   referring explicitly to any particular business activity would, inappropriately, embed excessive detail in the *Conceptual Framework*; and

(b)   the *Conceptual Framework* does not refer to any other business activity.

Information needs of long-term investors

BC0.40   Some stakeholders suggested that the *Conceptual Framework* should emphasise the information needs of long-term investors and that their information needs may differ from those of short-term investors. Views expressed by these stakeholders included the following:

(a)   the Board focuses too much on the needs of short-term investors.

(b)   the Board gives too much weight to the needs of potential investors and not enough weight to the needs of existing long-term investors. Existing long-term investors own the reporting entity and bear the residual risks of ownership. Hence, these stakeholders argue that long-term investors need information that helps them to assess management's stewardship of the entity's economic resources.

(c)   the Board makes excessive use of current value measurement bases, particularly those reflecting market-participant assumptions, such as fair value, and those measurement bases provide information more relevant to short-term investors than to investors who are interested in long-term value creation.

(d)   excessive use of current value measurement bases (especially for long-term investments) and recognition of unrealised gains in the statement of profit or loss may:

(i)   lead to excessive and volatile dividend distributions that are not in the best interest of long-term investors;

(ii)   lead to inflated management remuneration (including bonuses); and

(iii)   encourage short-termism and financial engineering and discourage long-term investment.

BC0.41   For the following reasons, the Board disagreed with the views expressed in paragraph BC0.40:

(a)   the Board does not place more emphasis on the needs of short-term investors than on the needs of long-term investors. The Board considers both long-term investors and short-term investors to be primary users of financial statements. Moreover, the Board believes that there is no reason why short-term investors would need information that is not also needed by long-term investors.

(b)   the *Conceptual Framework* identifies both existing and potential investors as primary users of financial statements. The Board's discussions with users in its project on the *Conceptual Framework* and in many other projects have identified no reasons why existing investors would need information that differs from the information needed by potential investors. Furthermore, the changes made by the 2018 *Conceptual Framework* to the discussion of the objective of general purpose financial reporting highlight the importance of providing information to help investors to assess management's stewardship of the entity's economic resources. The 2018 *Conceptual Framework* states explicitly that decisions relating to providing resources to the entity include decisions about exercising rights to vote on, or otherwise influence, management's actions that affect the use of the entity's economic resources. Thus, the 2018 *Conceptual Framework* clarifies that the needs of existing investors (including long-term investors) are considered when making decisions about the usefulness of financial information (see paragraphs BC1.36–BC1.37).

(c)   when the Board has decided to require or permit current value measurement bases, that has not been because of a belief that those measurement bases would be particularly useful to short-term investors. Instead, the Board's decisions have been driven by an assessment of what information is most likely to be useful to the primary users of financial statements, including both long-term and short-term investors. Under the concepts in Chapter 6—*Measurement* of the 2018 *Conceptual Framework*, this will continue to be the case.

(d)   in the Board's view, accounting information (such as reported profit) is not, and should not be, the sole determinant of distributions of dividends and bonuses. Distribution policy is affected by many other factors, for example, the entity's financing needs, current and projected liquidity, the risks faced by the entity, legal constraints and (in the case of bonus decisions) remuneration policy and incentive arrangements. These factors differ by entity, by country and over time. It would be neither desirable nor feasible for the Board to consider them in standard-setting decisions.

BC0.42   For these reasons, the Board concluded that the 2018 *Conceptual Framework* contains sufficient and appropriate discussion of primary users and their information needs, and of the objective of general purpose financial reporting, to address appropriately the needs of long-term investors.

BC0.43   Conceivably, long-term investors may need entities to provide some information that is not also needed by short-term investors; for example, long-term investors may have more extensive needs for information to support decisions to vote on, or otherwise influence, management's actions. However, the Board concluded that to help it to identify what information particular Standards should require entities to provide, there is no need for the *Conceptual Framework* to contain a specific reference to the needs of long-term investors. When the Board develops Standards, it routinely seeks input and feedback from investors, including long-term investors, to help ensure that it understands what information they need.

Contents

In 2018, the Board made limited changes to Chapter 1 of the Conceptual Framework. A description of the Board's considerations in developing those changes was added to the original Basis for Conclusions on this chapter. The Board added a date to the heading of each section of the Basis for Conclusions to indicate when that section was developed. Sections of the Basis for Conclusions that reflect the Board's considerations at the time of developing the chapter in 2010 were not updated in 2018 except to add and update cross-references and to make minor necessary editorial changes.

Introduction

BC1.1   The first version of Chapter 1 was developed jointly with the FASB and issued in 2010 (see paragraph BC0.3). Consequently, this Basis for Conclusions includes some references to the FASB's literature.

Revision in 2018

BC1.2   When the Board restarted its work on the Conceptual Framework project in 2012, it did not reconsider Chapter 1 fundamentally (see paragraph BC0.11). Although some respondents to the 2013 Discussion Paper agreed with this approach, many stated that the Board should reconsider one or more aspects of Chapter 1. In the light of these comments, the Board considered whether to make changes in the following areas:

(a)   primary users (see paragraphs BC1.18–BC1.20); and

(b)   stewardship (see paragraphs BC1.32–BC1.41).

BC1.3   The FASB has not made any changes to its Concepts Statement No. 8 *Conceptual Framework for Financial Reporting – Chapter 1*, The Objective of General Purpose Financial Reporting corresponding to the limited changes made by the Board in 2018. The Board concluded that the clarity achieved by its improvements to Chapter 1 outweighs the disadvantages of divergence in those respects from the FASB's version.

General purpose financial reporting (2010)

BC1.4   Consistently with the Board's responsibilities, the *Conceptual Framework* establishes an objective of financial reporting and not just of financial statements. Financial statements are a central part of financial reporting, and most of the issues that the Board addresses involve financial statements. Although the scope of FASB Concepts Statement No. 1 *Objectives of Financial Reporting by Business Enterprises* was financial reporting, the other FASB concepts statements focused on financial statements. The scope of the Board's *Framework for the Preparation and Presentation of Financial Statements*, which was published by the Board's predecessor body in 1989 (1989 *Framework*), dealt with financial statements only. Therefore, for both boards the scope of the 2010 *Conceptual Framework* is broader than the scopes of their previous frameworks.[7]

---

7   With the exception of Chapters 1 and 2, the 2018 *Conceptual Framework* focuses on (general purpose) financial statements rather than on (general purpose) financial reports (see paragraph 3.1).

BC1.5   Some stakeholders suggested that advances in technology may make general purpose financial reporting obsolete. New technologies, for example the use of eXtensible Business Reporting Language (XBRL), may make it practicable in the future for reporting entities either to prepare or to make available the information necessary for different users to assemble different financial reports to meet their individual information needs.

BC1.6   To provide different reports for different users, or to make available all of the information that users would need to assemble their own custom-designed reports, would be expensive. Requiring users of financial information to assemble their own reports might also be unreasonable, because many users would need to have a greater understanding of accounting than they have now. Therefore, the Board concluded that for now a general purpose financial report is still the most efficient and effective way to meet the information needs of a variety of users.

BC1.7   In the 2006 Discussion Paper, the Board used the term 'general purpose external financial reporting'. External was intended to convey that internal users such as management were not the intended beneficiaries for general purpose financial reporting as established by the Board. During redeliberations, the Board concluded that this term was redundant. Therefore, Chapter 1 uses 'general purpose financial reporting'.

Financial reporting of the reporting entity (2010)

BC1.8   Some respondents to the 2008 Exposure Draft said that the reporting entity is not separate from its equity investors or a subset of those equity investors. This view has its roots in the days when most businesses were sole proprietorships and partnerships that were managed by their owners who had unlimited liability for the debts incurred in the course of the business. Over time, the separation between businesses and their owners has grown. The vast majority of today's businesses have legal substance separate from their owners by virtue of their legal form of organisation, numerous investors with limited legal liability and professional managers separate from the owners. Consequently, the Board concluded that financial reports should reflect that separation by accounting for the entity (and its economic resources and claims) rather than its primary users and their interests in the reporting entity.[8]

Primary users (paragraphs 1.5, 1.8–1.10)

Primary users (2010)

BC1.9   The objective of financial reporting in paragraph 1.2 refers to existing and potential investors, lenders and other creditors. The description of the primary users in paragraph 1.5 refers to existing and potential investors, lenders and other creditors who cannot require reporting entities to provide information directly to them. Paragraph 1.10 states that 'regulators and members of the public other than investors, lenders and other creditors' may

---

8   See also paragraph 3.8 of the 2018 *Conceptual Framework* and paragraphs BC3.9–BC3.10.

find information in general purpose financial reports useful but states that those are not the parties to whom general purpose financial reports are primarily directed.

BC1.10   Paragraph 9 of the 1989 *Framework* stated that users included 'present and potential investors, employees, lenders, suppliers and other trade creditors' (and later added advisers in the discussion of investors' needs), all of which are intended to be encompassed by the phrase in paragraph 1.2. Paragraph 9 of the 1989 *Framework* also included a list of other potential users such as customers, governments and their agencies, and the public, which is similar to the list in paragraph 1.10 of those who may be interested in financial reports but are not primary users.

BC1.11   Paragraph 10 of the 1989 *Framework* stated that 'as investors are providers of risk capital to the entity, the provision of financial statements that meet their needs will also meet most of the needs of other users that financial statements can satisfy', which might have been read to narrow the focus to investors only. However, paragraph 12 explicitly stated that the objective of financial statements is to provide information 'that is useful to a wide range of users in making economic decisions.' Thus, the 1989 *Framework* focused on investors' needs as representative of the needs of a wide range of users but did not explicitly identify a group of primary users.

BC1.12   FASB Concepts Statement 1 referred to 'present and potential investors and creditors and other users in making rational investment, credit, and similar decisions' (paragraph 34). It also stated that 'major groups of investors are equity securityholders and debt securityholders' and 'major groups of creditors are suppliers of goods and services who extend credit, customers and employees with claims, lending institutions, individual lenders, and debt securityholders' (paragraph 35). One difference in emphasis from the 1989 *Framework*, which emphasised providers of risk capital, is that Concepts Statement 1 referred to 'both those who desire safety of investment and those who are willing to accept risk to obtain high rates of return' (paragraph 35). However, like the 1989 *Framework*, Concepts Statement 1 stated that the terms investors and creditors 'also may comprehend security analysts and advisors, brokers, lawyers, regulatory agencies, and others who advise or represent the interests of investors and creditors or who otherwise are interested in how investors and creditors are faring' (paragraph 35).

BC1.13   Paragraphs 1.3, 1.5 and 1.10 differ from the 1989 *Framework* and Concepts Statement 1 for two reasons—to eliminate differences between the 1989 *Framework* and Concepts Statement 1 and to be more direct by focusing on users making decisions relating to providing resources (but not to exclude advisers). The reasons are discussed in paragraphs BC1.15–BC1.17 and BC1.21–BC1.26.

Should there be a primary user group? (2010)

BC1.14   The 2006 Discussion Paper and the 2008 Exposure Draft proposed identifying a group of primary users of financial reports. Some respondents to the 2008 Exposure Draft said that other users who have not provided, and are not considering providing, resources to the entity, use financial reports for a variety of reasons. The Board sympathised with their information needs but concluded that without a defined group of primary users, the *Conceptual Framework* would risk becoming unduly abstract or vague.

Why are existing and potential investors, lenders and other creditors considered the primary users? (2010)

BC1.15   Some respondents to the 2006 Discussion Paper and the 2008 Exposure Draft suggested that the primary user group should be limited to existing shareholders or the controlling entity's majority shareholders. Others said that the primary users should be existing shareholders and creditors, and that financial reports should focus on their needs.

BC1.16   The reasons why the Board concluded that the primary user group should be the existing and potential investors, lenders and other creditors of a reporting entity are:

(a)   Existing and potential investors, lenders and other creditors have the most critical and immediate need for the information in financial reports and many cannot require the entity to provide the information to them directly.

(b)   The Board's and the FASB's responsibilities require them to focus on the needs of participants in capital markets, which include not only existing investors but also potential investors and existing and potential lenders and other creditors.

(c)   Information that meets the needs of the specified primary users is likely to meet the needs of users both in jurisdictions with a corporate governance model defined in the context of shareholders and those with a corporate governance model defined in the context of all types of stakeholders.

BC1.17   Some respondents expressed the view that the specified primary user group was too broad and that it would result in too much information in the financial reports. However, too much is a subjective judgement. In developing financial reporting requirements that meet the objective of financial reporting, the boards will rely on the qualitative characteristics of, and the cost constraint on, useful financial information to provide discipline to avoid providing too much information.

Primary user group (2018)

BC1.18   Views expressed by respondents to the 2013 Discussion Paper and to the 2015 Exposure Draft about the description of the primary user group were similar to those expressed by stakeholders and considered by the Board when it originally developed Chapter 1:

(a) some respondents commented that the primary user group is defined too narrowly. They argued that it should be expanded to include, for example, employees, customers, suppliers, regulators and others.

(b) in contrast, others said that the primary user group is defined too broadly. These respondents stated that the Board should describe primary users as holders of equity claims against the entity (or perhaps as the holders of the most residual equity claims against the entity). The respondents argued that holders of equity claims have different (and perhaps more extensive) information needs than other capital providers because they are exposed to more extensive risks.

BC1.19 In the light of views expressed by respondents, the Board reconsidered the description of the primary user group. Nevertheless, it concluded that its reasons for describing the primary user group as the existing and potential investors, lenders and other creditors of a reporting entity were still valid (see paragraph BC1.16). In addition, as explained in paragraph 1.8 of the 2018 *Conceptual Framework*, focusing on the common information needs of the primary users does not prevent a reporting entity from including additional information that is most useful to a particular subset of primary users. Consequently, the Board concluded that no changes to the description of the primary user group were needed.

BC1.20 In addition, the Board decided that there was no need for the 2018 *Conceptual Framework* to identify long-term investors as a particular subset of primary users with specific information needs (see paragraphs BC0.40–BC0.41).

Should there be a hierarchy of users? (2010)

BC1.21 Some respondents to the 2008 Exposure Draft who supported the composition of the primary user group also recommended that the Board should establish a hierarchy of primary users because investors, lenders and other creditors have different information needs. However, the Board observed that individual users may have information needs and desires that are different from, and possibly conflict with, those of other users with the same type of interest in the reporting entity. General purpose financial reports are intended to provide common information to users and cannot accommodate every request for information. The Board will seek the information set that is intended to meet the needs of the maximum number of users in cost-beneficial ways.

Information needs of other users who are not within the primary user group (2010)

Management's information needs (2010)

BC1.22 Some stakeholders questioned the interaction between general purpose financial reporting and management's needs. The Board stated that some of the information directed to the primary users is likely to meet some of management's needs but not all of them. However, management has the ability to access additional financial information, and consequently, general purpose financial reporting need not be explicitly directed to management.

Regulators' information needs (2010)

BC1.23   Some stakeholders said that maintaining financial stability in capital markets (the stability of a country's or region's economy or financial systems) should be an objective of financial reporting. They stated that financial reporting should focus on the needs of regulators and fiscal policy decision-makers who are responsible for maintaining financial stability.

BC1.24   Other stakeholders opposed establishing an objective to maintain financial stability. They said that financial statements should present the economic reality of the reporting entity with as little bias as possible, but that such a presentation is not necessarily inconsistent with a financial stability objective. By presenting economic reality, financial statements could lead to more informed decision-making and thereby support financial stability even if that is not the primary aim.[9]

BC1.25   However, advocates of a financial stability objective had a different outcome in mind. They did not encourage the Board to require reporting entities to provide information for use by regulators and fiscal policy decision-makers. Instead, they recommended that the Board consider the consequences of new Standards for the stability of the world's economies and financial systems and, at least at times, assign greater weight to that objective than to the information needs of investors, lenders and other creditors.

BC1.26   The Board acknowledged that the interests of investors, lenders and other creditors often overlap with those of regulators. However, expanding the objective of financial reporting to include maintaining financial stability could at times create conflicts between the objectives that the Board is not well-equipped to resolve. For example, some may take the view that the best way to maintain financial stability is to require entities not to report, or to delay reporting, some changes in asset or liability values. That requirement would almost certainly result in depriving investors, lenders and other creditors of information that they need. The only way to avoid conflicts would be to eliminate or de-emphasise the existing objective of providing information to investors, lenders and other creditors. The Board concluded that eliminating that objective would be inconsistent with its basic mission, which is to serve the information needs of participants in capital markets. The Board also noted that providing financial information that is relevant and faithfully represents what it purports to represent can improve users' confidence in the information, and thus contribute to promoting financial stability.[10]

---

9   One group expressing that view was the Financial Crisis Advisory Group (FCAG). The FCAG comprised approximately 20 senior leaders with broad experience in international financial markets and an interest in the transparency of financial reporting information. The FCAG was formed in 2009 to advise the Board and the FASB about the standard-setting implications of the financial crisis and of potential changes in the global regulatory environment.

10   See also paragraphs BC0.34–BC0.43 for the Board's 2018 discussion on the role of Standards in promoting long-term investment and paragraph SP1.5 of the 2018 Conceptual Framework for an explanation of the Conceptual Framework's contribution to the mission of the IFRS Foundation and of the Board, which is to develop Standards that bring transparency, accountability and efficiency to financial markets.

Usefulness for making decisions (paragraphs 1.2–1.4)

Usefulness for making decisions (2010)

BC1.27 Both the Board's and the FASB's previous frameworks focused on providing information that is useful in making economic decisions as the fundamental objective of financial reporting. Those frameworks also stated that financial information that is useful in making economic decisions would also be helpful in assessing how management has fulfilled its stewardship responsibility.

BC1.28 The 2006 Discussion Paper that led to Chapter 1 stated that the objective of financial reporting should focus on resource allocation decisions. Although most respondents to the 2006 Discussion Paper agreed that providing useful information for decision-making was the appropriate objective, they said that investors, lenders and other creditors make other decisions that are aided by financial reporting information in addition to resource allocation decisions. For example, shareholders who vote on whether to retain directors or replace them, and on how members of management should be remunerated for their services, need information on which to base their decisions. Shareholders' decision-making process may include evaluating how management of the entity performed against management in competing entities in similar circumstances.

BC1.29 The Board agreed with these respondents and noted that, in most cases, information designed for resource allocation decisions would also be useful for assessing management's performance. Therefore, in the 2008 Exposure Draft leading to Chapter 1, the Board proposed that the objective of financial reporting is to provide financial information about the reporting entity that is useful to present and potential investors, lenders and other creditors in making decisions in their capacity as capital providers. The 2008 Exposure Draft also described the role financial statements can have in supporting decisions related to the stewardship of an entity's resources.

BC1.30 The 2008 Exposure Draft discussed the *Objective of Financial Reporting and Decision-usefulness* in separate sections. The Board combined those two sections in Chapter 1 because usefulness in making decisions is the objective of financial reporting. Consequently, both sections addressed the same points and provided more detail than was necessary. Combining those two sections resulted in eliminating the separate subsections on usefulness in assessing cash flow prospects and usefulness in assessing stewardship. The Board did not intend to imply that assessing prospects for future cash flow or assessing the quality of management's stewardship is more important than the other. Both are important for making decisions about providing resources to an entity, and information about stewardship is also important for resource providers who have the ability to vote on, or otherwise influence, management's actions.

BC1.31 The Board decided not to use the term 'stewardship' in the 2010 *Conceptual Framework* because there would be difficulties in translating it into other languages. Instead, the Board described what stewardship encapsulates. Accordingly, the objective of financial reporting in the 2010 *Conceptual*

Framework acknowledged that users make resource allocation decisions as well as decisions as to whether management has made efficient and effective use of the resources provided.

Stewardship (2018)

BC1.32 After Chapter 1 was issued in 2010, some stakeholders interpreted the chapter, and in particular the removal from it of the term 'stewardship', as neglecting the fact that users of financial statements need information to help them to assess management's stewardship. As mentioned in paragraph BC1.30, the Board had not intended to neglect that need. Nevertheless, the Board concluded subsequently that the wording in the 2010 *Conceptual Framework* was not clear enough.

BC1.33 Thus, in the 2018 *Conceptual Framework* the Board improved the wording to clarify its original intention. The Board reintroduced the term 'stewardship' and, in describing the objective of general purpose financial reporting, gave more prominence to the importance of providing information needed to assess management's stewardship of the entity's economic resources. That extra prominence contributes to highlighting management's accountability to users for economic resources entrusted to their care.

BC1.34 To provide that greater prominence, the 2018 *Conceptual Framework* identifies information needed to assess management's stewardship as possibly partly separate from the information needed to help users to assess the prospects for future net cash inflows to the entity. Both types of information are needed to meet the overall objective of financial reporting—that is to provide information that is useful for making decisions relating to providing resources to the entity (resource allocation decisions).

BC1.35 The Board also considered other approaches suggested by some stakeholders. Those approaches would have identified the provision of information to help to assess management's stewardship as part of the objective of financial reporting or as an additional and equally prominent objective. The Board rejected those approaches because:

(a) assessing management's stewardship is not an end in itself; it is an input needed in making resource allocation decisions. For example, a conclusion that management's stewardship is unsatisfactory may lead to a decision to replace management with the aim of increasing future returns.

(b) introducing an additional objective of financial reporting could be confusing.

BC1.36 Further, in the 2018 *Conceptual Framework* the Board clarified how the assessment of management's stewardship contributed to resource allocation decisions. The Board did this by expanding the explanation of resource allocation decisions. The feedback on the 2015 Exposure Draft indicated that some respondents interpreted resource allocation decisions as referring solely to buying, selling or holding decisions. Thus, in their view, resource allocation decisions excluded decisions made while holding an investment, for example, decisions to reappoint or replace management, to assess the adequacy of management's remuneration or to approve a business strategy proposed by management.

BC1.37 The Board did not intend resource allocation decisions to be interpreted narrowly as referring solely to buying, selling or holding decisions. Consequently, the 2018 *Conceptual Framework* states explicitly that resource allocation decisions involve decisions about:

(a) buying, selling or holding equity and debt instruments;

(b) providing or settling loans and other forms of credit; or

(c) exercising rights to vote on, or otherwise influence, management's[11] actions that affect the use of the entity's economic resources.

Users of financial statements need to assess both the amount, timing and uncertainty of future net cash inflows and management's stewardship of the entity's economic resources to make any of these decisions.

BC1.38 Paragraph BC1.37(c) refers to management's actions that affect the use of the entity's economic resources. One example of a decision about such actions is a decision in voting on the membership of the Board of directors. That vote will ultimately influence the Board of directors' subsequent actions affecting the use of the entity's economic resources. However, financial reporting is not designed to provide information that will help the primary users of that information to exercise their rights to vote on other actions by management, such as developing a statement on an issue of a public policy that does not directly affect the use of the entity's economic resources.

BC1.39 Some respondents to the 2015 Exposure Draft suggested that in some cases the information needed to assess management's stewardship differs from the information needed to assess prospects for future net cash inflows to the entity. In particular, these respondents focused on the selection of a measurement basis:

(a) some respondents suggested that, in some cases, historical cost measures are more useful than current value measures for assessing stewardship because, in their opinion, historical cost measures are more verifiable and provide a more direct link to the transactions actually undertaken by management; and

(b) in contrast, other respondents argued that, in some cases, current value measures may be more useful for assessing stewardship because, in their opinion, such measures can provide information about how well management has performed in comparison with other courses of action currently available.

---

11 The term 'management' refers to management and the governing board of an entity (see paragraph 1.4(b) of the 2018 *Conceptual Framework*).

BC1.40   In giving more prominence to stewardship within the description of the objective of financial reporting in the 2018 *Conceptual Framework*, the Board did not intend to imply a preference for any particular measurement basis. Factors to be considered in the selection of a measurement basis are discussed in Chapter 6—*Measurement* of the 2018 *Conceptual Framework*.

The term 'stewardship' (2018)

BC1.41   The revised Chapter 1 reintroduces the term 'stewardship' and explains that the assessment of management's stewardship involves assessing how efficiently and effectively the entity's management and governing board have discharged their responsibilities to use the entity's economic resources (see paragraphs 1.4 and 1.22–1.23). That assessment enables users of financial statements to hold management to account for its actions. The Board's use of the term 'stewardship' is consistent with the general understanding of that term: the careful and responsible management of something entrusted to one's care.[12] These improvements to Chapter 1 provide increased clarity and the Board concluded that this outweighs the translation difficulties identified in 2010.

The objective of financial reporting for different types of entities (2010)

BC1.42   The Board considered whether the objective of general purpose financial reporting should differ for different types of entities. Possibilities include:

(a)   smaller entities versus larger entities;

(b)   entities with listed (publicly traded) debt or equity financial instruments versus those without such instruments; and

(c)   closely held entities versus those with widely dispersed ownership.

BC1.43   External users of financial reporting have similar objectives, irrespective of the type of entities in which they invest. Therefore, the Board concluded that the objective of general purpose financial reports is the same for all entities. However, cost constraints and differences in activities among entities may sometimes lead the Board to permit or require differences in reporting for different types of entities.

---

12 This definition of stewardship is provided in the Merriam-Webster online dictionary (https://www.merriam-webster.com/dictionary/stewardship).

Information about a reporting entity's economic resources, claims against the entity and changes in resources and claims (paragraphs 1.12–1.21)

The significance of information about financial performance (2010)

BC1.44   A long-standing assertion by many stakeholders is that a reporting entity's financial performance as represented by comprehensive income and its components is the most important information.[13] Concepts Statement 1 (paragraph 43) stated:

> The primary focus of financial reporting is information about an enterprise's performance provided by measures of comprehensive income and its components. Investors, creditors, and others who are concerned with assessing the prospects for enterprise net cash inflows are especially interested in that information.

In contrast, the 1989 *Framework* considered information on the reporting entity's financial position and financial performance of equal importance.

BC1.45   To be useful for decision-making, financial reports must provide information about a reporting entity's economic resources and claims, and the change during a period in economic resources and claims. A reporting entity cannot provide reasonably complete information about its financial performance (as represented by comprehensive income, profit or loss or other similar terms) without identifying and measuring its economic resources and the claims. Consequently, the Board concluded that to designate one type of information as the primary focus of financial reporting would be inappropriate.

BC1.46   In discussing the financial position of an entity, the 2008 Exposure Draft referred to 'economic resources and claims on them'. The chapter uses the phrase 'the entity's economic resources and the claims against the reporting entity' (see paragraph 1.12). The reason for the change is that in many cases, claims against an entity are not claims on specific resources. In addition, many claims will be satisfied using resources that will result from future net cash inflows. Thus, while all claims are claims against the entity, not all are claims against the entity's existing resources.

Financial position and solvency (2010)

BC1.47   Some stakeholders have suggested that the main purpose of the statement of financial position should be to provide information that helps assess the reporting entity's solvency. The question is not whether information provided in the financial reports should be helpful in assessing solvency; clearly, it should. Assessing solvency is of interest to investors, lenders and other creditors, and the objective of general purpose financial reporting is to provide information that is useful to them for making decisions.

---

13   Concepts Statement 1 referred to 'earnings and its components'. However, FASB Concepts Statement No. 6 *Elements of Financial Statements* substituted the term 'comprehensive income' for the term 'earnings'. The latter term is reserved for a component of comprehensive income.

BC1.48   However, some have suggested that the statement of financial position should be directed towards the information needs of lenders, other creditors and regulators, possibly to the detriment of investors and other users. To do so would be inconsistent with the objective of serving the common information needs of the primary user group. Therefore, the Board rejected the notion of directing the statement of financial position (or any other particular financial statement) towards the needs of a particular subset of users.

CONTENTS

In 2018, the Board made limited changes to Chapter 2 of the Conceptual Framework. A description of the Board's considerations in developing those changes was added to the original Basis for Conclusions on this chapter. The Board added a date to the heading of each section of the Basis for Conclusions to indicate when that section was developed. Sections of the Basis for Conclusions that reflect the Board's considerations at the time of developing the chapter in 2010 were not updated in 2018 except to add and update cross-references and to make minor necessary editorial changes.

Introduction

BC2.1   The first version of this chapter was developed jointly with the FASB and issued in 2010 as Chapter 3 of the 2010 Conceptual Framework (see paragraph BC0.3). Consequently, this Basis for Conclusions includes some references to the FASB's literature.

Revision in 2018

BC2.2   When the Board restarted its work on the Conceptual Framework project in 2012, it did not reconsider fundamentally the chapter on the qualitative characteristics of useful financial information (see paragraph BC0.11). Although some respondents to the 2013 Discussion Paper agreed with this approach, many stated that the Board should reconsider one or more aspects of this chapter. In the light of these comments, the Board considered whether to make changes in the following areas:

(a)   materiality (see paragraph BC2.20);

(b)   reliability and measurement uncertainty (see paragraphs BC2.28–BC2.31 and BC2.46–BC2.49);

(c)   substance over form (see paragraph BC2.33);

(d)   prudence (see paragraphs BC2.37–BC2.45); and

(e)   applying the fundamental qualitative characteristics (see paragraphs BC2.52–BC2.57).

BC2.3   In addition, the Board renumbered the chapter on qualitative characteristics of useful financial information as Chapter 2. The Board also made some editorial changes to Chapter 2, mainly to use the term 'faithful representation' more precisely by discussing whether financial information faithfully represents what it purports to represent (for example, an economic phenomenon), rather than by discussing whether financial information itself is faithfully represented.

BC2.4   The FASB has not made any changes to its Concepts Statement No. 8 Conceptual Framework for Financial Reporting—Chapter 3, Qualitative Characteristics of Useful Financial Information corresponding to the limited changes made by the Board in 2018. The Board concluded that the clarity achieved by its improvements to Chapter 2 outweigh the disadvantages of divergence in those respects from the FASB's version.

The objective of financial reporting and the qualitative characteristics of useful financial information (2010)

BC2.5   Alternatives are available for all aspects of financial reporting, including recognition, derecognition, measurement, classification, presentation and disclosure. When developing Standards, the Board will choose the alternative that goes furthest towards achieving the objective of financial reporting. Preparers of financial information will also have to choose among the alternatives in a way that achieves the objective of financial reporting if no Standards apply or if application of a particular Standard requires judgements or provides options.

BC2.6   Chapter 1 specifies that the objective of general purpose financial reporting is to provide financial information about the reporting entity that is useful to existing and potential investors, lenders and other creditors in making decisions about providing resources to the entity. The decision-makers on which this *Conceptual Framework* focuses are existing and potential investors, lenders and other creditors.

BC2.7   That objective by itself leaves a great deal to judgement and provides little guidance on how to exercise that judgement. Chapter 2 describes the first step in making the judgements needed to apply that objective. It identifies and describes the qualitative characteristics that financial information should have if it is to meet the objective of financial reporting. It also discusses cost, which is a pervasive constraint on financial reporting.

BC2.8   Subsequent chapters use the qualitative characteristics to help guide choices about recognition, measurement and the other aspects of financial reporting.

Fundamental and enhancing qualitative characteristics (2010) (paragraph 2.4)

BC2.9   Chapter 2 distinguishes between the fundamental qualitative characteristics that are the most critical and the enhancing qualitative characteristics that are less critical but still highly desirable. The 2006 Discussion Paper did not explicitly distinguish between those qualitative characteristics. The Board made the distinction later because of confusion among respondents to the 2006 Discussion Paper about how the qualitative characteristics relate to each other.

BC2.10   Some respondents to the 2008 Exposure Draft stated that all of the qualitative characteristics should be considered equal, and that the distinction between fundamental and enhancing qualitative characteristics was arbitrary. Others said that the most important qualitative characteristic differs depending on the circumstances; therefore, differentiating qualitative characteristics was not appropriate.

BC2.11   The Board does not agree that the distinction is arbitrary. Financial information without the two fundamental qualitative characteristics of relevance and faithful representation is not useful, and it cannot be made useful by being more comparable, verifiable, timely or understandable. However, financial information that is relevant and faithfully represents what it purports to represent may still be useful even if it does not have any of the enhancing qualitative characteristics.

Fundamental qualitative characteristics (paragraphs 2.5–2.22)

Relevance (paragraphs 2.6–2.11)

BC2.12   It is self-evident that financial information is useful for making a decision only if it is capable of making a difference in that decision. 'Relevance' is the term used in the *Conceptual Framework* to describe that capability. It is a fundamental qualitative characteristic of useful financial information.

BC2.13   The definition of relevance in the *Conceptual Framework* is consistent with the definition in FASB Concepts Statement No. 2 *Qualitative Characteristics of Accounting Information*. The 1989 *Framework* definition of relevance was that information is relevant only if it actually makes a difference in users' decisions. However, users consider a variety of information from many sources, and the extent to which a decision is affected by information about a particular economic phenomenon is difficult, if not impossible, to determine, even after the fact.

BC2.14   In contrast, whether information is capable of making a difference in a decision (relevance as defined in the 2010 *Conceptual Framework*) can be determined. One of the primary purposes of publishing exposure drafts and other due process documents is to seek the views of users on whether information that would be required by proposed Standards is capable of making a difference in their decisions. The Board also assesses relevance by meeting users to discuss proposed Standards, potential agenda decisions, effects on reported information of applying recently implemented Standards and other matters.

Predictive and confirmatory value (2010) (paragraphs 2.7–2.10)

BC2.15   Many decisions by investors, lenders and other creditors are based on implicit or explicit predictions about the amount and timing of the return on an equity investment, loan or other debt instrument. Consequently, information is capable of making a difference in one of those decisions only if it will help users to make new predictions, confirm or correct prior predictions or both (which is the definition of predictive or confirmatory value).

BC2.16   The 1989 *Framework* identified predictive value and confirmatory value as components of relevance, and Concepts Statement 2 referred to predictive value and feedback value. The Board concluded that confirmatory value and feedback value were intended to have the same meaning. The Board and the FASB agreed that both boards would use the same term (confirmatory value) to avoid giving the impression that the two frameworks were intended to be different.

The difference between predictive value and related statistical terms (2010)

BC2.17   Predictive value, as used in the *Conceptual Framework*, is not the same as predictability and persistence as used in statistics. Information has predictive value if it can be used in making predictions about the eventual outcomes of past or current events. In contrast, statisticians use predictability to refer to the accuracy with which it is possible to foretell the next number in a series and persistence to refer to the tendency of a series of numbers to continue to change as it has changed in the past.

Materiality (2010) (paragraph 2.11)

BC2.18   Concepts Statement 2 and the 1989 *Framework* discussed materiality and defined it similarly. Concepts Statement 2 described materiality as a constraint on financial reporting that can be considered only together with the qualitative characteristics, especially relevance and faithful representation. The 1989 *Framework*, on the other hand, discussed materiality as an aspect of relevance and did not indicate that materiality has a role in relation to the other qualitative characteristics.

BC2.19   The 2006 Discussion Paper and the 2008 Exposure Draft proposed that materiality is a pervasive constraint in financial reporting because it is pertinent to all of the qualitative characteristics. However, some respondents to the 2008 Exposure Draft agreed that although materiality is pervasive, it is not a constraint on a reporting entity's ability to report information. Rather, materiality is an aspect of relevance, because immaterial information does not affect a user's decision. Furthermore, a standard-setter does not consider materiality when developing standards because it is an entity-specific consideration. The boards agreed with those views and concluded that materiality is an aspect of relevance that applies at the individual entity level.

Materiality (2018)

BC2.20   In revising the *Conceptual Framework* in 2018, the Board concluded that the concept of materiality is described clearly in the 2010 *Conceptual Framework*. Hence, the Board did not amend that description of materiality, except to clarify that the users mentioned in the description are the primary users of general purpose financial reports, as described in paragraph 1.5 of the *Conceptual Framework*. This clarification emphasises that decisions about materiality are intended to reflect the needs of the primary users, not the needs of any other group.

Materiality (October 2018)

BC2.20A   The definition of material in the *Conceptual Framework* was amended to include a reference to 'obscuring information' and to replace the phrase 'could influence decisions' with 'could reasonably be expected to influence decisions'. Paragraphs BC13A–BC13T of the Basis for Conclusions on IAS 1 explains the reasons for those amendments.

Faithful representation (paragraphs 2.12–2.19)

BC2.21　The discussion of faithful representation in Chapter 3 of the 2010 *Conceptual Framework* differed from that in the previous frameworks in two significant ways. First, it used the term 'faithful representation' instead of the term 'reliability'. Second, substance over form, prudence (conservatism) and verifiability, which had been aspects of reliability in Concepts Statement 2 and the 1989 *Framework*, were not considered aspects of faithful representation in the 2010 *Conceptual Framework*. References to substance over form and prudence were removed in 2010 for the reasons described in paragraphs BC2.32 and BC2.34, but they were reinstated, with clarifications, in the 2018 *Conceptual Framework*. Since 2010, verifiability has been described as an enhancing qualitative characteristic rather than as part of this fundamental qualitative characteristic (see paragraphs 2.30–2.32).

Replacement of the term 'reliability' (2010)

BC2.22　Concepts Statement 2 and the 1989 *Framework* used the term 'reliability' to describe what is now called faithful representation.

BC2.23　Concepts Statement 2 listed representational faithfulness, verifiability and neutrality as aspects of reliability and discussed completeness as part of representational faithfulness.

BC2.24　The 1989 *Framework* said:

> Information has the quality of reliability when it is free from material error and bias and can be depended upon by users to represent faithfully that which it either purports to represent or could reasonably be expected to represent.

The 1989 *Framework* also discussed substance over form, neutrality, prudence and completeness as aspects of faithful representation.

BC2.25　Unfortunately, neither framework clearly conveyed the meaning of reliability. The comments of respondents to numerous proposed standards indicated a lack of a common understanding of the term 'reliability'. Some focused on verifiability or free from material error to the virtual exclusion of faithful representation. Others focused more on faithful representation, perhaps combined with neutrality. Some apparently think that reliability refers primarily to precision.

BC2.26　Because attempts to explain what reliability was intended to mean in this context have proved unsuccessful, the Board sought a different term that would more clearly convey the intended meaning. The term 'faithful representation', the faithful depiction in financial reports of economic phenomena, was the result of that search. That term encompasses the main characteristics that the previous frameworks included as aspects of reliability.

BC2.27　Many respondents to the 2006 Discussion Paper and the 2008 Exposure Draft opposed the Board's preliminary decision to replace 'reliability' with 'faithful representation'. Some said that the Board could have better explained what reliable means rather than replacing the term. However, many respondents who made those comments assigned a different meaning to reliability from what the Board meant. In particular, many respondents' descriptions of reliability more closely resembled the Board's notion of verifiability than its notion of reliability. Those comments led the Board to affirm its decision to replace the term 'reliability' with 'faithful representation'.

Retention of the term 'faithful representation' (2018)

BC2.28   In developing the 2018 *Conceptual Framework*, the Board considered whether to reinstate the term 'reliability' as a label for the qualitative characteristic now called 'faithful representation'. Arguments given for such a reinstatement by some stakeholders included:

(a)   the term 'reliability' is clearer and better understood than the term 'faithful representation'.

(b)   the 2010 *Conceptual Framework* implies that anything can be faithfully represented if sufficient explanatory information is given. This interpretation of faithful representation would allow the recognition of items that cannot be measured reliably. Consequently, the qualitative characteristic of faithful representation does not act as an effective filter when identifying the types of information to be included in financial statements.

(c)   the 1989 *Framework* acknowledged a trade-off between the qualitative characteristics of relevance and reliability. More relevant information may lack reliability and more reliable information may lack relevance. Some respondents expressed the view that this trade-off was missing in the 2010 *Conceptual Framework* (see paragraphs BC2.52–BC2.57).

(d)   the idea that financial statements should be credible, that is, that users need assurance that they can depend on financial statements to faithfully represent what they purport to represent, is a key concept that should be acknowledged in the *Conceptual Framework*. Treating that concept solely as an enhancing qualitative characteristic (verifiability, see paragraphs BC2.60–BC2.62) gives it too little weight.

BC2.29   The Board noted that the notion of reliability was used in two different ways in Standards:

(a)   to mean that the level of measurement uncertainty is tolerable. This use of the word reflects the recognition criteria included in the 1989 *Framework* (and not reviewed in amending the 1989 *Framework* in 2010) —an item that meets the definition of an element is recognised only if it is probable there will be a flow of economic benefits and it has a cost or value that can be measured with reliability.

(b)   to refer to a qualitative characteristic of useful financial information— the characteristic previously called 'reliability' and now called 'faithful representation'. This use of reliability is much less frequent in Standards.

BC2.30   The decision to change from the term 'reliability' to the term 'faithful representation' was made to avoid confusion between the two uses of the word 'reliability' described in paragraph BC2.29. The responses both to the 2013 Discussion Paper and the 2015 Exposure Draft seemed to confirm that many respondents continue to equate the word 'reliability' with a tolerable level of measurement uncertainty, not with the qualitative characteristic described in the 1989 *Framework*. Hence, the Board retained the term 'faithful representation' as the label for the qualitative characteristic previously called 'reliability'. However, to address concerns that the 2010 *Conceptual Framework* did not adequately discuss the role of measurement uncertainty in financial reporting, the Board included in the 2018 *Conceptual Framework* a discussion of how measurement uncertainty affects the usefulness of financial information (see paragraphs 2.19, 2.22 and BC2.46–BC2.49). Furthermore, the 2018 *Conceptual Framework* discusses the role of measurement uncertainty in decisions about recognition and measurement (see paragraphs 5.19–5.23 and 6.60).

BC2.31 Following the 2018 amendments to the discussion of prudence and substance over form (see paragraphs BC2.37–BC2.45 and BC2.33), the description of the qualitative characteristic of reliability in the 1989 *Framework* and the description of the qualitative characteristic of faithful representation in the 2018 *Conceptual Framework* are substantially aligned. Table 2.1 compares those descriptions.

Table 2.1—Reliability in the 1989 *Framework* and faithful representation in the 2018 *Conceptual Framework*

1989 *Framework* Reliability	2018 *Conceptual Framework* Faithful representation
Can be depended on by users to faithfully represent what it purports to represent	Faithfully represents the phenomena that it purports to represent (see paragraph 2.12)
Complete	Complete (see paragraph 2.14)
Neutral	Neutral (see paragraph 2.15)
Free from material error or bias	Free from error and neutral (see paragraphs 2.18 and 2.15)
Substance over form	Substance over form (see paragraph 2.12)
Prudence	Prudence (see paragraphs 2.16–2.17)

Substance over form (2010) (paragraph 2.12)

BC2.32 In the 2010 *Conceptual Framework*, substance over form was not considered a separate component of faithful representation because the Board concluded that it would be redundant. Faithful representation means that financial information represents the substance of an economic phenomenon rather than merely representing its legal form. Representing a legal form that differs from the economic substance of the underlying economic phenomenon could not result in a faithful representation.

Substance over form (2018)

BC2.33   In developing the 2018 *Conceptual Framework*, the Board noted that some stakeholders had inferred that the 2010 deletion of the reference to substance over form meant that the Board was no longer committed to depicting the substance of an economic phenomenon. The Board did not intend to imply such a change. Accordingly, to avoid any further misunderstandings and to highlight the Board's intention, the Board reinstated in paragraph 2.12 of the 2018 *Conceptual Framework* an explicit reference to the need to faithfully represent the substance of an economic phenomenon. The Board explained further how to provide a faithful representation of the substance of contractual rights and contractual obligations in paragraphs 4.59–4.62 of the 2018 *Conceptual Framework*.

Prudence and neutrality (2010) (paragraph 2.15)

BC2.34   Chapter 2 of the 2010 *Conceptual Framework* did not include prudence or conservatism as an aspect of faithful representation because the Board concluded then that including either would be inconsistent with neutrality. Some respondents to the 2006 Discussion Paper and the 2008 Exposure Draft disagreed with that view. They said that the framework should include conservatism, prudence or both. They said that bias should not always be assumed to be undesirable, especially in circumstances when bias, in their view, produces information that is more relevant to some users.

BC2.35   Deliberately reflecting conservative estimates of assets, liabilities, income or equity has sometimes been considered desirable to counteract the effects of some management estimates that have been perceived as excessively optimistic. However, even with the prohibitions against deliberate misstatement that appeared in the 1989 *Framework*, an admonition to be prudent is likely to lead to a bias. Understating assets or overstating liabilities in one period frequently leads to overstating financial performance in later periods—a result that cannot be described as prudent or neutral.

BC2.36   Other respondents to the 2008 Exposure Draft said that neutrality is impossible to achieve. In their view, relevant information must have purpose, and information with a purpose is not neutral. In other words, because financial reporting is a tool to influence decision-making, it cannot be neutral. Obviously, reported financial information is expected to influence the actions of users of that information, and the mere fact that many users take similar actions on the basis of reported information does not demonstrate a lack of neutrality. The Board does not attempt to encourage or predict specific actions of users. If financial information is biased in a way that encourages users to take or avoid predetermined actions, that information is not neutral.

Prudence (2018) (paragraphs 2.16–2.17)

BC2.37   In developing the 2018 *Conceptual Framework*, the Board noted that different stakeholders apply the term 'prudence' to mean different things. In particular:

(a)   some use it to refer to being cautious when making judgements under conditions of uncertainty, but without employing more caution in judgements relating to income or assets than in those relating to expenses or liabilities ('cautious prudence'—see paragraphs BC2.39–BC2.40).

(b)   others use it to refer to applying systematic asymmetry—expenses are recognised at an earlier stage than is income ('asymmetric prudence'—see paragraphs BC2.41–BC2.45). Stakeholders expressed a range of views on how to achieve such asymmetry and to what extent it should be achieved. For example, some advocate a concept of prudence that would:

> (i)   require more persuasive evidence to support the recognition of income or assets than the recognition of expenses or liabilities; or

> (ii)   require the selection of measurement bases that recognise losses at an earlier stage than gains.

BC2.38   An understanding of prudence is linked to an understanding of the term 'neutrality'. The Board has identified two aspects of neutrality:

(a)   the neutral application of accounting policies—applying the selected accounting policies in a neutral (ie unbiased) manner (see paragraph BC2.39); and

(b)   the selection of neutral accounting policies—selecting accounting policies in order to provide relevant information that faithfully represents the items that it purports to represent (see paragraph BC2.44). A faithful representation requires that the depiction is neutral.

Financial information is neutral if it is not slanted, weighted, emphasised, de-emphasised or otherwise manipulated to increase the probability that the information will be received favourably or unfavourably by users.[14]

BC2.39   The Board was persuaded by the arguments made by some stakeholders that applying prudence (defined as the exercise of caution when making judgements under conditions of uncertainty) can help to achieve neutrality in applying accounting policies. Thus, 'cautious prudence' (see paragraph BC2.37(a)) can help to achieve a faithful representation of assets, liabilities, equity, income and expenses. Setting out that message clearly is expected to:

(a)   help preparers, auditors and regulators to counter a natural bias that management may have towards optimism; for example, the message underlines the need to exercise care in selecting the inputs used in estimating a measure that cannot be observed directly; and

---

14 See paragraph 2.15 of the 2018 *Conceptual Framework*.

(b) help the Board to develop rigorous Standards that would reduce the risk of management bias in applying the reporting entity's accounting policies.

BC2.40 The Board found that the removal of the term 'prudence' in the 2010 revisions had led to confusion and had perhaps exacerbated the diversity in use of this term. People continued to use the term, but did not always say clearly what they meant by it. In addition, some stakeholders said that, because the term had been removed, financial information prepared using IFRS Standards was not neutral but was, in fact, imprudent. The Board concluded that it would reduce the confusion by reintroducing the term with a clear explanation that caution works both ways, so that assets and liabilities are neither overstated nor understated. Therefore, the Board reintroduced the term 'prudence', defined as the exercise of caution when making judgements under conditions of uncertainty, in the 2018 *Conceptual Framework*.

BC2.41 Some respondents to the 2015 Exposure Draft suggested that the Board should go further and identify 'asymmetric prudence' (see paragraph BC2.37(b)) as a necessary qualitative characteristic of useful financial information for these reasons:

(a) asymmetric prudence reflects the view that investors are more interested in downside risk than upside potential;

(b) asymmetric prudence is inherent in many Standards and the *Conceptual Framework* should acknowledge this fact so that asymmetric prudence could be applied consistently when developing Standards;

(c) by limiting distributions to shareholders, asymmetric prudence minimises the risk that today's shareholders would benefit at the expense of future shareholders; and

(d) by limiting management remuneration, asymmetric prudence would reduce management's opportunism and encourage long-term growth.

BC2.42 The Board did not include asymmetric prudence in the 2018 *Conceptual Framework* because a systematic requirement for asymmetry in the accounting treatment of assets and liabilities or of income and expenses could sometimes conflict with the need for financial information to be relevant and provide a faithful representation. The Board noted that, depending on its exact nature, the requirement to apply asymmetric prudence in all circumstances might:

(a) prohibit the recognition of all unrealised gains. In some circumstances, for example, in the measurement of many financial instruments, recognising unrealised gains is necessary to provide relevant information to users of financial reports.

(b) prohibit the recognition of all unrealised gains not supported by observable market prices. In some circumstances, measuring an asset or liability at a current value (which may require the recognition of unrealised gains) provides relevant information to users of financial reports even if the current value cannot be determined directly by observing prices in an active market.

(c)   permit an entity to measure an asset at an amount lower than an unbiased estimate using the measurement basis selected for that asset or to measure a liability at an amount higher than such an estimate. Such an approach cannot result in relevant information and cannot provide a faithful representation.

BC2.43   Further, the Board noted that information in financial reports may be used as an input in determining distributions to shareholders and management remuneration, but such information is only one of the factors to be considered (see paragraph BC0.41(d)).

BC2.44   However, although the Board rejected a requirement for systematic asymmetry, the Board also concluded that not all asymmetry is inconsistent with neutrality. The selection of neutral accounting policies means selecting accounting policies in a manner that is not intended to increase the probability that financial information will be received favourably or unfavourably by users. The selection of neutral accounting policies:

(a)   does not require an entity to recognise the value of the entity in the statement of financial position. Paragraph 1.7 of the 2018 *Conceptual Framework* states that general purpose financial reports are not designed to show the value of a reporting entity.

(b)   does not require the recognition of all assets and liabilities. Chapter 5 —*Recognition and derecognition* of the 2018 *Conceptual Framework* discusses recognition criteria for assets and liabilities.

(c)   does not require the measurement of all assets and liabilities at a current value. Chapter 6—*Measurement* of the 2018 *Conceptual Framework* discusses factors to consider when selecting a measurement basis. Considering those factors would not lead to such a requirement.

(d)   does not prohibit impairment tests on assets measured at historical cost. Measurement at historical cost, including an impairment test, is consistent with neutrality if that measurement basis is selected without bias. The absence of bias means that the measurement basis is selected without slanting, weighting, emphasising, de-emphasising or otherwise manipulating information to increase the probability that it will be received favourably or unfavourably by users.

BC2.45   Hence, the 2018 *Conceptual Framework* acknowledges that Standards may contain asymmetric requirements. This would be the consequence of the Board taking decisions that it believes require entities to produce the most relevant information that faithfully represents what it purports to represent, rather than a consequence of applying asymmetric prudence. Such decisions are reflected in several Standards developed before the 2018 *Conceptual Framework*. For example, IAS 37 *Provisions, Contingent Liabilities and Contingent Assets* requires one recognition threshold for contingent liabilities and a different recognition threshold for contingent assets.

Measurement uncertainty (2018) (paragraph 2.19)

BC2.46   As mentioned in paragraph BC2.28(b), some respondents to the 2013 Discussion Paper expressed concern that the qualitative characteristic of faithful representation did not act as an effective filter when identifying the types of information to be included in financial statements. These respondents said that the 2010 *Conceptual Framework* did not convey the idea that a high level of measurement uncertainty can make financial information less useful.

BC2.47   Paragraph QC16 of the 2010 *Conceptual Framework* already set out the idea that an estimate might not provide useful information if the level of uncertainty in the estimate is too large:

> A faithful representation, by itself, does not necessarily result in useful information. For example, a reporting entity may receive property, plant and equipment through a government grant. Obviously, reporting that an entity acquired an asset at no cost would faithfully represent its cost, but that information would probably not be very useful. A slightly more subtle example is an estimate of the amount by which an asset's carrying amount should be adjusted to reflect an impairment in the asset's value. That estimate can be a faithful representation if the reporting entity has properly applied an appropriate process, properly described the estimate and explained any uncertainties that significantly affect the estimate. However, if the level of uncertainty in such an estimate is sufficiently large, that estimate will not be particularly useful. In other words, the relevance of the asset being faithfully represented is questionable. If there is no alternative representation that is more faithful, that estimate may provide the best available information.

BC2.48   Nevertheless, it was apparent that the link between the level of uncertainty in an estimate and its usefulness was not very visible and many readers of the 2010 *Conceptual Framework* seemed to overlook it. Consequently, the 2015 Exposure Draft discussed how measurement uncertainty could affect the relevance of financial information. Respondents to the 2015 Exposure Draft welcomed the discussion of measurement uncertainty. However, some argued that measurement uncertainty is an aspect of the fundamental qualitative characteristic of faithful representation rather than an aspect of relevance. The Board agreed with these arguments noting that:

(a)   measurement uncertainty makes information less verifiable. As explained in paragraph 2.30 of the 2018 *Conceptual Framework*, verifiability helps to assure users of financial statements that information faithfully represents what it purports to represent. The higher the level of measurement uncertainty, the less assurance users have that a particular estimate provides a faithful representation of the phenomenon. Thus, measurement uncertainty affects whether economic phenomena can be faithfully represented.

(b)   paragraphs 2.20–2.21 of the 2018 *Conceptual Framework* describe the most efficient and effective process of applying the fundamental qualitative characteristics. In line with that description, the qualitative characteristic of relevance is concerned with what particular piece of information is capable of being useful to users. On the other hand, the qualitative characteristic of faithful representation is concerned with whether that information can provide a faithful representation. Thus, measurement uncertainty associated with the estimation process does not affect relevance; it affects whether that measure can be provided in a way that produces a faithful representation.

(c)   even if information is subject to a high level of measurement uncertainty, it can be relevant. For example, if the underlying phenomenon is subject to significant risks and uncertainties, a highly uncertain measure may provide the only relevant information about that phenomenon.

BC2.49   Hence, the 2018 *Conceptual Framework* describes measurement uncertainty as a factor that can affect whether it is possible to provide a faithful representation. In addition, the Board noted that addressing measurement uncertainty in the discussion of faithful representation is more consistent with a notion of a trade-off between the two fundamental qualitative characteristics—relevance and faithful representation (see paragraphs 2.22 and BC2.52–BC2.56).

Can faithful representation be empirically measured? (2010)

BC2.50   Empirical accounting researchers have accumulated considerable evidence, through correlation with changes in the market prices of entities' equity or debt instruments, supporting financial information that is relevant and provides a faithful representation. However, such studies have not provided techniques for empirically measuring faithful representation apart from relevance.

BC2.51   Both previous frameworks discussed the desirability of providing statistical information about how faithfully a financial measure is represented. That would not be unprecedented. Other statistical information is sometimes reflected in financial reports. For example, some entities disclose value at risk from derivative financial instruments and similar positions. The Board expects that the use of statistical concepts for financial reporting in some situations will continue to be important. Unfortunately, the Board and the FASB have not identified any way to quantify the faithfulness of the representations in a financial report.

Applying the fundamental qualitative characteristics (2018) (paragraphs 2.20–2.22)

BC2.52   In developing the 2018 *Conceptual Framework*, the Board discussed whether a trade-off may need to be made in applying the fundamental qualitative characteristics.

BC2.53   The notion of a trade-off between relevance and reliability—then both identified as qualitative characteristics of useful financial information—was present in the 1989 *Framework*. The 2010 *Conceptual Framework* did not mention such a trade-off but referred to the need for both characteristics—relevance and faithful representation—to be present for information to be useful. It further stated that neither a faithful representation of an irrelevant phenomenon nor an unfaithful representation of a relevant phenomenon helps users to make useful decisions. The discussion in paragraph QC16 of the

2010 *Conceptual Framework* of uncertainty in estimates[15] implied that a trade-off may need to be made between relevance and faithful representation (see paragraph BC2.47).

BC2.54 Some respondents to the 2013 Discussion Paper expressed concern about the lack of discussion of the notion of a trade-off between qualitative characteristics in the 2010 *Conceptual Framework*. Their main concern seemed to relate to the relationship between the relevance of information and the tolerable level of measurement uncertainty for that information.

BC2.55 As explained in paragraphs BC2.48–BC2.49, in the 2018 *Conceptual Framework* the Board described measurement uncertainty as a factor that can affect whether it is possible to provide a faithful representation. Further, the Board clarified in paragraph 2.22 that following the process described in paragraphs 2.20–2.21 a trade-off may need to be made between relevance and faithful representation. One case when such a trade-off may need to be made is when a high level of measurement uncertainty makes it questionable whether an estimate would provide a sufficiently faithful representation of an economic phenomenon. The material in paragraph 2.22 builds on the discussion of measurement uncertainty in paragraph QC16 of the 2010 *Conceptual Framework* (see paragraph BC2.47).

BC2.56 The Board concluded that an explicit acknowledgement of the trade-off between relevance and measurement uncertainty would help to explain why, in some cases, an estimate with a high level of measurement uncertainty might, nevertheless, provide useful information — for example, in cases when the only relevant information is a highly uncertain estimate.

BC2.57 In addition, the Board updated the terminology used in the description of the process of applying fundamental qualitative characteristics. To be consistent with the description of relevance in paragraph 2.6 of the 2018 *Conceptual Framework* and to avoid confusion with the use of the term 'potential' in the definition of an economic resource (see paragraphs BC4.8–BC4.9), the Board replaced the phrase 'has the potential to be' with 'is capable of being' in paragraph 2.21.

Enhancing qualitative characteristics

Comparability (2010) (paragraphs 2.24–2.29)

BC2.58 Comparability was an important concept in both the 1989 *Framework* and Concepts Statement 2, but the two previous frameworks disagreed on its importance. The 1989 *Framework* stated that comparability is as important as relevance and faithful representation.[16] Concepts Statement 2 described comparability as a quality of the relationship between two or more pieces of information that, although important, is secondary to relevance and faithful representation.

---

15 In the context of paragraph QC16 of the 2010 *Conceptual Framework*, uncertainty of estimates refers to what the 2018 *Conceptual Framework* calls measurement uncertainty.

16 The term 'reliability' was used instead of 'faithful representation', but the meaning was intended to be similar.

BC2.59   Relevant information that provides a faithful representation is most useful if it can be readily compared with similar information reported by other entities and by the same entity in other periods. One of the most important reasons that Standards are needed is to increase the comparability of reported financial information. However, even if it is not readily comparable, information that is relevant and faithfully represents what it purports to represent is still useful. Comparable information, however, is not useful if it is not relevant and may mislead if it does not faithfully represent what it purports to represent. Therefore, comparability is considered an enhancing qualitative characteristic instead of a fundamental qualitative characteristic.

Verifiability (2010) (paragraphs 2.30–2.32)

BC2.60   Verifiable information can be used with confidence. Lack of verifiability does not necessarily render information useless, but users are likely to be more cautious because there is a greater risk that the information does not faithfully represent what it purports to represent.

BC2.61   The 1989 *Framework* did not explicitly include verifiability as an aspect of reliability, but Concepts Statement 2 did. However, the two frameworks are not as different as it might appear because the definition of reliability in the 1989 *Framework* contained the phrase 'and can be depended upon by users', which implies that users need assurance on the information.

BC2.62   The 2006 Discussion Paper stated that reported financial information should be verifiable to assure users that it is free from material error and bias and can be depended on to represent what it purports to represent. Therefore, verifiability was considered an aspect of faithful representation. Some respondents pointed out that including verifiability as an aspect of faithful representation could result in excluding information that is not readily verifiable. Those respondents recognised that many forward-looking estimates that are very important in providing relevant financial information (for example, expected cash flows, useful lives and residual values) cannot be directly verified. However, excluding information about those estimates would make the financial reports much less useful. The Board agreed and repositioned verifiability as an enhancing qualitative characteristic, very desirable but not necessarily required.

Timeliness (2010) (paragraph 2.33)

BC2.63   The 1989 *Framework* discussed timeliness as a constraint that could rob information of relevance. Concepts Statement 2 described timeliness as an aspect of relevance. However, the substance of timeliness as discussed in those two previous frameworks was essentially the same.

BC2.64   The 2006 Discussion Paper described timeliness as an aspect of relevance. However, some respondents pointed out that timeliness is not part of relevance in the same sense that predictive and confirmatory value are. The Board was persuaded that timeliness is different from the other components of relevance.

BC2.65　Timeliness is very desirable, but it is not as critical as relevance and faithful representation. Timely information is useful only if it is relevant and faithfully represents what it purports to represent. In contrast, relevant information that provides a faithful representation may still be useful (especially for confirmatory purposes) even if it is not reported in as timely a manner as would be desirable.

Understandability (2010) (paragraphs 2.34–2.36)

BC2.66　Both the 1989 *Framework* and Concepts Statement 2 included understandability, a qualitative characteristic that enables users to comprehend the information and therefore make it useful for making decisions. Both frameworks also similarly described that for financial information to be understandable, users should have a reasonable degree of financial knowledge and a willingness to study the information with reasonable diligence.

BC2.67　Despite those discussions of understandability and users' responsibilities for understanding financial reports, misunderstanding persists. For example, some have expressed the view that a new accounting method should not be implemented because some users might not understand it, even though the new accounting method would result in reporting financial information that is useful for decision-making. They imply that understandability is more important than relevance.

BC2.68　If understandability considerations were fundamental, it might be appropriate to avoid reporting information about very complicated things even if the information is relevant and provides a faithful representation. Classifying understandability as an enhancing qualitative characteristic is intended to indicate that information that is difficult to understand should be presented and explained as clearly as possible.

BC2.69　To clarify another frequently misunderstood point, since 2010 the *Conceptual Framework* has explained that users are responsible for actually studying reported financial information with reasonable diligence rather than only being willing to do so (which was the statement in the previous frameworks). In addition, since 2010 the *Conceptual Framework* has stated that users may need to seek the aid of advisers to understand economic phenomena that are particularly complex.

Qualitative characteristics not included (2010)

BC2.70　Transparency, high quality, internal consistency, true and fair view or fair presentation and credibility have been suggested as desirable qualitative characteristics of financial information. However, transparency, high quality, internal consistency, true and fair view or fair presentation are different words to describe information that has the qualitative characteristics of relevance and representational faithfulness enhanced by comparability, verifiability, timeliness and understandability. Credibility is similar but also implies trustworthiness of a reporting entity's management.

BC2.71   Interested parties sometimes suggested other criteria for standard-setting decisions, and the Board has at times cited some of those criteria as part of the rationale for some decisions. Those criteria include simplicity, operationality, practicability or practicality, and acceptability.

BC2.72   Those criteria are not qualitative characteristics. Instead, they are part of the overall weighing of benefits and costs of providing useful financial information. For example, a simpler method may be less costly to apply than a more complex method. In some circumstances, a simpler method may result in information that is essentially the same as, but somewhat less precise than, information produced by a more complex method. In that situation, a standard-setter would include the decrease in faithful representation and the decrease in implementation cost in weighing benefits against costs.

The cost constraint on useful financial reporting (2010) (paragraphs 2.39–2.43)

BC2.73   Cost is a pervasive constraint that standard-setters, as well as providers and users of financial information, should keep in mind when considering the benefits of a possible new financial reporting requirement. Cost is not a qualitative characteristic of information. It is a characteristic of the process used to provide the information.

BC2.74   The Board has attempted and continues to attempt to develop more structured methods of obtaining information about the cost of gathering and processing the information that proposed Standards would require entities to provide. The primary method used is to request interested parties, sometimes formally (such as by field tests and questionnaires), to submit cost and benefit information for a specific proposal that is quantified to the extent feasible. Those requests have resulted in helpful information and have led directly to changes to proposed requirements to reduce the costs without significantly reducing the related benefits.

CONTENTS

Focus on financial statements (paragraph 3.1)

BC3.1   Chapter 1 sets the objective of general purpose financial reporting. Chapter 2 discusses the qualitative characteristics of financial information that is useful for achieving that objective. Those qualitative characteristics apply to both financial information provided in financial statements and financial information provided in other financial reports.

BC3.2   Financial statements are a central part of financial reporting and most issues that the Board addresses involve financial statements. Moreover, addressing issues related to other forms of financial reporting could have substantially delayed completion of the 2018 *Conceptual Framework*, thus delaying the improvements it brought. Consequently, Chapters 3–8 of the 2018 *Conceptual Framework* focus on information provided in financial statements and do not address other forms of financial reporting, for example, management commentary, interim financial reports, press releases and supplementary material provided for analysis.[17]

Objective and scope of financial statements (paragraphs 3.2–3.3)

BC3.3   The Board based the description of the objective of financial statements in the 2018 *Conceptual Framework* on the description of the objective of general purpose financial reporting (see paragraph 1.2 of the 2018 *Conceptual Framework*) and the description of the objective of financial statements in paragraph 9 of IAS 1 *Presentation of Financial Statements*, which states:

> Financial statements are a structured representation of the financial position and financial performance of an entity. The objective of financial statements is to provide information about the financial position, financial performance and cash flows of an entity that is useful to a wide range of users in making economic decisions. Financial statements also show the results of the management's stewardship of the resources entrusted to it. To meet this objective...

BC3.4   The description of the objective of financial statements in the 2018 *Conceptual Framework* differs from the description of their objective in IAS 1 in the following ways:

(a)   to provide a link to the elements of financial statements, the description of the objective in the 2018 *Conceptual Framework* refers to:

(i)   assets, liabilities and equity instead of financial position; and

(ii)   income and expenses instead of financial performance.

(b)   the description of the objective in the 2018 *Conceptual Framework* does not refer to providing information about cash flows. Although information about cash flows is important to users of financial statements, the 2018 *Conceptual Framework* does not identify cash inflows and cash outflows as elements of financial statements.

---

17 In 2010, the Board issued IFRS Practice Statement 1 *Management Commentary*—a broad, non-binding framework for the presentation of management commentary to accompany financial statements prepared in accordance with the Standards.

(c)   the description of the objective in the 2018 *Conceptual Framework* expands on what makes information useful to primary users of financial statements in making decisions relating to providing resources to the entity. Information needs to be useful in assessing the prospects for future net cash inflows to the reporting entity and in assessing management's stewardship of the entity's economic resources.

BC3.5   The description of the information provided in financial statements refers to the statement of financial position and the statement(s) of financial performance. A few respondents to the 2015 Exposure Draft suggested that this description should also refer to the statement of cash flows and the statement of changes in equity. They argued that making explicit references only to the statement of financial position and the statement(s) of financial performance could be interpreted as implying that these two statements are more important than statements providing information about cash flows or about contributions from holders of equity claims and distributions to those holders.

BC3.6   Paragraph 3.3(c) of the 2018 *Conceptual Framework* refers to information about cash flows and about contributions from holders of equity claims and distributions to them. The Board does not view that information as less important than information provided in the statement of financial position and the statement(s) of financial performance. Nevertheless, the 2018 *Conceptual Framework* refers only to those statements because only those statements provide a summary of recognised elements — assets, liabilities, equity, income and expenses. In addition, it is necessary to identify those statements as the place where recognition occurs because otherwise it would not be possible to describe recognition clearly. In contrast, because cash inflows and cash outflows and contributions from holders of equity claims and distributions to them are not elements of financial statements, statements providing information about those items do not provide a summary of recognised elements.

Information about risks (paragraphs 3.3(c)(i)–3.3(c)(ii))

BC3.7   The 2018 *Conceptual Framework* states that financial statements provide information about the risks arising from recognised and unrecognised items that meet the definitions of an element of financial statements. Some respondents to the 2013 Discussion Paper expressed a concern that the term 'risk' was not explicitly defined. Hence, they argued that 'information about risks' could be understood to include almost any type of information, including information that would be best reported outside financial statements. Indeed, some argued that the information about how an entity manages risks belongs outside financial statements.

BC3.8   However, the Board noted that information about the risks associated with an entity's recognised and unrecognised assets and liabilities is likely to be useful in assessing the entity's ability to generate cash flows and in assessing management's stewardship of the entity's economic resources. Thus, this information contributes to meeting the objective of financial statements.

Perspective adopted in financial statements (paragraph 3.8)

BC3.9 The 2018 *Conceptual Framework* states that financial statements provide information from the perspective of the reporting entity as a whole (often referred to as 'the entity perspective'), not from the perspective of any particular group of the entity's existing or potential investors, lenders or other creditors. This reflects the Board's view that the reporting entity is separate from its investors, lenders and other creditors (see paragraph BC1.8).

BC3.10 The Board adopted the entity perspective because it is consistent with the objective of general purpose financial reporting set out in paragraph 1.2. This objective is to provide useful information to existing and potential investors, lenders and other creditors rather than to provide information to a particular subset of those capital providers. If information were to be directed towards the needs of a particular subset of primary users, it might be necessary to provide different sets of financial statements for each subset. That could cause confusion and undermine confidence in financial reporting. In addition, as mentioned in paragraph BC1.6, providing different reports for different subsets of primary users could be expensive.

Going concern assumption (paragraph 3.9)

BC3.11 The description of the going concern assumption is brought forward from the 2010 *Conceptual Framework* largely unchanged, except that the phrase 'cease trading' replaces the phrase 'curtail materially the scale of its operations'. This change aligned the description more closely with that used in IAS 1 *Presentation of Financial Statements* and IAS 10 *Events after the Reporting Period*.

The reporting entity (paragraphs 3.10–3.18)

BC3.12 The 2010 *Conceptual Framework* did not discuss what a reporting entity is; nor did it describe how to determine what a reporting entity comprises. In developing concepts on the reporting entity for the 2018 *Conceptual Framework*, the Board considered comments received on the 2010 Exposure Draft developed jointly with the FASB[18] and comments received on the 2015 Exposure Draft.

Description and boundary of the reporting entity (paragraphs 3.10 and 3.13–3.14)

BC3.13 The 2018 *Conceptual Framework* provides a general description of a reporting entity, rather than stating who must, should or could prepare general purpose financial statements. The Board has no authority to determine who must, should or could prepare such statements.

---

18 See the Exposure Draft *Conceptual Framework for Financial Reporting—The Reporting Entity* published in March 2010.

BC3.14   When developing the description of a reporting entity for the 2018 *Conceptual Framework*, the Board considered whether that description could be improved by including material that described some key features of a reporting entity from the 2010 Exposure Draft. In particular, in the 2010 Exposure Draft the Board:

(a)   described a reporting entity as a circumscribed area of economic activities whose financial information has the potential to be useful to existing and potential equity investors, lenders and other creditors who cannot directly obtain the information they need in making decisions about providing resources to an entity and in assessing whether management and the governing board of that entity have made efficient and effective use of the resources provided; and

(b)   set out three features that are necessary—but not always sufficient—for identifying a reporting entity:

(i)   economic activities of an entity are being conducted, have been conducted or will be conducted;

(ii)   economic activities of the entity can be objectively distinguished from those of other entities and from the economic environment in which the entity exists; and

(iii)   financial information about the economic activities of that entity has the potential to be useful in making decisions about providing resources to the entity and in assessing whether the management and the governing board have made efficient and effective use of the resources provided.

BC3.15   The Board concluded that the feature mentioned in paragraph BC3.14(b)(iii) plays a role in determining the boundary of the reporting entity (see paragraph BC3.18). However, the Board did not use other material from the 2010 Exposure Draft to expand the description of the reporting entity in the 2018 *Conceptual Framework* for the following reasons:

(a)   the financial statements of an entity that has never conducted and will never conduct economic activities are unlikely to provide useful information to users of financial statements; and

(b)   the terms 'circumscribed area' and 'objectively distinguished' are vague and unclear, so they would not provide clear guidance on what constitutes a reporting entity.

BC3.16   In the 2015 Exposure Draft the Board proposed that the boundary of a reporting entity would be set in such a way that its financial statements provide relevant information to existing and potential investors, lenders and other creditors and faithfully represent the economic activities of the entity. It further proposed that financial statements should describe the set of economic activities included within the reporting entity.

BC3.17   Some respondents to the 2015 Exposure Draft expressed concern that the proposal would not sufficiently restrict what can constitute a reporting entity and that, as a result, financial statements could be prepared for any arbitrary collection of assets and liabilities and thus provide incomplete and therefore misleading information. In particular, they were concerned that a reporting entity that is a portion of an entity could choose to report on an incomplete set of economic activities, for example, by excluding from its financial statements the reporting entity's share of overheads. In addition, there may be difficulties in identifying which claims should be included in financial statements if the reporting entity is a portion of an entity.

BC3.18   In the light of those concerns, the Board revised the discussion of the determination of the boundary of a reporting entity. The 2018 *Conceptual Framework* explains that, in determining the boundary of a reporting entity that is not a legal entity and does not comprise only legal entities all linked by a parent-subsidiary relationship, the focus is on users' information needs. As stated in paragraph 2.4, users need information that is relevant and faithfully represents what it purports to represent. The Board concluded that the completeness and neutrality aspects of the qualitative characteristic of faithful representation are particularly important in determining the boundary of a reporting entity. For example, if the boundary of a reporting entity were determined in such a way that the boundary contains an arbitrary or incomplete set of economic activities, financial information provided in that reporting entity's financial statements would be incomplete and may also lack neutrality. Thus, if the boundary were to be determined in such a way, the resulting information would not meet users' information needs. The Board also concluded that to help users to understand what is included in a set of financial statements, those financial statements need to describe how the boundary of the reporting entity was determined and what constitutes the reporting entity.

BC3.19   Determining the boundary of a reporting entity is normally straightforward if that entity is a legal entity or if that entity comprises only legal entities all linked by a parent-subsidiary relationship. In those cases, the boundary of the legal entity or legal entities determines the boundary of the reporting entity. Determining the boundary in this way meets users' information needs.

Combined financial statements (paragraph 3.12)

BC3.20   The 2010 Exposure Draft stated that combined financial statements might provide useful information about a reporting entity that comprises entities under common control. Many of those who commented welcomed a discussion of this issue, but disagreed with restricting the preparation of combined financial statements to entities under common control.

BC3.21   The Board concluded that combined financial statements can provide useful information to users of financial statements in some circumstances. Accordingly, paragraph 3.12 of the 2018 *Conceptual Framework* acknowledges the concept of combined financial statements. However, the 2018 *Conceptual Framework* does not discuss when or how entities could prepare combined financial statements. The Board concluded that such discussion would be best developed if the Board decides in the future to develop a Standard on this topic.

Consolidated and unconsolidated financial statements (paragraphs 3.11 and 3.15–3.18)

BC3.22 The 2018 *Conceptual Framework* discusses the usefulness of financial information provided in consolidated and unconsolidated financial statements. As stated in paragraph 3.2, the objective of financial statements is to provide useful financial information to primary users of those financial statements. In the case of consolidated financial statements, the information needs of primary users may differ depending on whether their focus is on the parent (see paragraphs BC3.23–BC3.24) or on the subsidiaries (see paragraph BC3.25).

BC3.23 In developing the 2018 *Conceptual Framework*, the Board concluded that information about the assets, liabilities, equity, income and expenses of the parent with its subsidiaries is useful to existing and potential investors, lenders and other creditors of the parent (see paragraph 3.15). Consolidated financial statements provide that information.

BC3.24 The Board also concluded that information about assets, liabilities, equity, income and expenses of the parent alone is another type of information that may be useful to existing and potential investors, lenders and other creditors of the parent (see paragraph 3.17). Hence, the 2018 *Conceptual Framework* states that a parent may be required, or choose, to:

(a) prepare unconsolidated financial statements in addition to consolidated financial statements it prepares; or

(b) provide information about the assets, liabilities, equity, income and expenses of the parent alone in consolidated financial statements, in the notes.

BC3.25 Financial statements are designed to meet the common information needs of the maximum number of primary users, so they do not necessarily include some information that is useful to only a particular subset of primary users, such as investors, lenders and other creditors of a subsidiary. For example, some information about a subsidiary's assets, liabilities, equity, income and expenses may be material to the financial statements of the subsidiary, but may not be material to the consolidated financial statements of the parent. The subsidiary's own financial statements are designed to provide the primary users of its financial statements with information about the subsidiary's assets, liabilities, equity, income and expenses.

Joint control and significant influence

BC3.26 In developing the 2018 *Conceptual Framework*, the Board considered whether the *Conceptual Framework* should explain the notions of joint control and significant influence. The 2010 Exposure Draft stated that joint control and significant influence do not give rise to control. The Board still agrees with that conclusion, but sees no need to embed the notions of joint control and significant influence in the *Conceptual Framework*. Hence, the 2018 *Conceptual Framework* does not refer to these notions. In developing the 2018 *Conceptual Framework*, the Board did not discuss whether these notions should continue to play a role in standard-setting.

Contents

Introduction

BC4.1 The 2010 *Conceptual Framework*, and previously the 1989 *Framework*, defined the following elements of financial statements:

(a) an asset—as a resource controlled by the entity as a result of past events and from which future economic benefits are expected to flow to the entity;

(b) a liability—as a present obligation of the entity arising from past events, the settlement of which is expected to result in an outflow from the entity of resources embodying economic benefits;

(c) equity—as the residual interest in the assets of the entity after deducting all its liabilities;

(d) income—as increases in economic benefits during the accounting period in the form of inflows or enhancements of assets or decreases of liabilities that result in increases in equity, other than those relating to contributions from equity participants; and

(e) expenses—as decreases in economic benefits during the accounting period in the form of outflows or depletions of assets or incurrences of liabilities that result in decreases in equity, other than those relating to distributions to equity participants.

BC4.2 In the 2018 *Conceptual Framework* the Board amended these definitions.

Definitions—issues common to both assets and liabilities

BC4.3 The Board found the definitions of an asset and a liability in the 2010 *Conceptual Framework* to be useful for solving many issues in standard-setting. However, some aspects of those definitions caused confusion in practice because:

(a) the explicit reference in the definitions of an asset and a liability to the flows of economic benefits blurred the distinction between the economic resource or obligation and the resulting flows of economic benefits; and

(b) some readers interpreted the term 'expected' as a probability threshold. In addition, some readers were unclear about the relationship between the terms 'expected' in the definitions and 'probable' in the recognition criteria.

BC4.4 To address these issues, and for the reasons given in paragraphs BC4.6–BC4.18, the Board revised the definitions to read as follows:

(a) an asset is a present economic resource controlled by the entity as a result of past events;

(b) a liability is a present obligation of the entity to transfer an economic resource as a result of past events; and

(c)   an economic resource is a right that has the potential to produce economic benefits.

BC4.5   Supporting guidance for the definition of an asset is discussed in paragraphs BC4.23–BC4.43 and for the definition of a liability in paragraphs BC4.44–BC4.68.

Separate definition of an economic resource (paragraph 4.4)

BC4.6   The main structural change from the 2010 *Conceptual Framework* definitions is the introduction of a separate definition of an economic resource. This moved the references to future flows of economic benefits so that they now appear in the supporting definition of an economic resource instead of in the definitions of an asset and a liability.

BC4.7   The Board concluded that this separation would help to remove the confusion mentioned in paragraph BC4.3(a). It emphasises more clearly that an asset (or liability) is an economic resource (or obligation) and that it is not the ultimate inflow (or outflow) of economic benefits that the economic resource (or obligation) may produce. This approach also streamlines the definitions and shows more clearly the parallels between assets and liabilities.

Deletion of the notion of an expected flow (paragraphs 4.14 and 4.37)

BC4.8   The 2018 *Conceptual Framework* replaces the notion used in the 2010 *Conceptual Framework* that an inflow or outflow of resources is 'expected' with the concept that an asset (or liability) 'has the potential to produce economic benefits' (or 'has the potential to require a transfer of an economic resource'). References to that concept appear in the definition of an economic resource and in the guidance supporting the definition of a liability.

BC4.9   The Board replaced the notion of an expected inflow or outflow of resources for the following reasons:

(a)   removal of 'expected' appropriately focuses the definition on the economic resource or obligation. To retain a notion of expected or probable outflows or inflows could exclude many items that are clearly assets and liabilities, for example, out-of-the money purchased and written options, insurance contracts and obligations to transfer an economic resource if a specified uncertain future event occurs (see paragraph BC4.63).

(b)   the notion of expected flows is unhelpful because interpretations of this term can vary widely and are often tied to a notion of a threshold level of probability.

BC4.10   The 2013 Discussion Paper used the term 'capable of' producing economic benefits rather than 'has the potential to'. However, 'capable of' is already used in the discussion of relevance in paragraphs 2.6–2.7 of the 2018 *Conceptual Framework*. It could be confusing to use the term 'capable' with one meaning describing what information is relevant and with a different meaning in defining an economic resource. To avoid such confusion, the Board introduced the phrase 'has the potential to' in the definition of an economic resource.

BC4.11 The phrase 'has the potential to produce economic benefits' (or similarly 'has the potential to require a transfer of an economic resource') captures the following points:

(a) it is not sufficient that the economic benefits may arise in the future. Those economic benefits must arise from some feature that already exists within the economic resource. For example, a purchased option has the potential to produce economic benefits for the holder, but only because the option already contains a right that will permit the holder to exercise the option.

(b) the definition is not intended to impose a minimum probability threshold. The important thing is that in at least one circumstance the economic resource will produce economic benefits.

BC4.12 Some stakeholders stated that the Board should retain the notion of an expected inflow or outflow of resources. They stated that users and preparers of financial statements do not regard an item as an asset if inflows of economic benefits are not expected or are not at least reasonably possible. Those respondents argued that the revised definitions would considerably widen the range of items identified as assets and liabilities, which might lead to:

(a) pressure to identify every possible asset and liability, imposing a significant operational burden for little benefit if ultimately the asset or liability is not recognised or is measured at nil;

(b) recognition as assets and liabilities of more items that are uncertain, improbable or hard to measure, unless the recognition criteria are made more robust;

(c) a presumption that, in principle, all assets and liabilities should be recognised even if inflows or outflows are not expected; and

(d) pressure to provide in the notes irrelevant information about unrecognised assets and liabilities for which inflows or outflows are unlikely.

BC4.13 The Board concluded that removing the notion of 'expected'—interpreted by some as a probability threshold—would not impose a significant operational burden. In practice, an entity considers the definitions of an asset and a liability and recognition criteria at the same time to identify those assets and liabilities that the entity might need to recognise, or about which it might need to provide information in the notes.

BC4.14 In addition, the Board concluded that stakeholders' concerns about recognising assets or liabilities when the probability of an inflow or outflow of economic benefits is low are best addressed in decisions about recognition, not in the definitions (see paragraphs 4.15, 4.38, 5.15–5.17 and BC5.15–BC5.20).

This approach is consistent with how the Board had applied the 2010 *Conceptual Framework* definitions for several years.

Past event (paragraphs 4.26 and 4.42–4.47)

BC4.15   In the 2018 *Conceptual Framework*:

(a)   the phrase 'as a result of past events' remains in the definitions of an asset and a liability; and

(b)   the word 'present' remains in the definition of a liability and is inserted in the definition of an asset.

BC4.16   In developing the 2018 *Conceptual Framework* the Board considered whether references to both 'present' and 'as a result of past events' are needed in the definitions of an asset and a liability.

BC4.17   The Board did not identify any significant problems that had arisen from including the phrase 'as a result of past events' in the definitions of an asset and a liability. Moreover, by identifying the past event, an entity can determine how to report that event in its financial statements; for example, how to classify and present income, expenses or cash flows arising from that event. Paragraphs BC4.64–BC4.68 discuss why the phrase 'as a result of past events' is particularly important to the revised definition of a liability. Hence, the Board retained that phrase in the definitions.

BC4.18   If a past event created an asset or liability, that fact alone does not confirm that the asset or liability still exists: it is also necessary to consider whether the entity still controls a present economic resource or is still bound by a present obligation. Thus, the Board also retained the reference to 'present' in the definition of a liability and added it to the definition of an asset. That addition emphasises the parallels between the two definitions.

Testing of revised definitions

BC4.19   In 2016, the Board analysed the effects of changes to the definitions of an asset and a liability proposed in the 2015 Exposure Draft. This exercise had two objectives:

(a)   to enable both the Board and stakeholders to assess implications of the proposals for future Standards; and

(b)   to help to identify any problems with the proposed definitions and supporting guidance.

BC4.20   This exercise involved:

(a)   analysing the outcome of applying the proposed definitions and supporting guidance to 23 illustrative examples;

(b)   identifying ways in which the proposed definitions and supporting guidance could help the Board to reach decisions in some of its current projects; and

(c)   discussing the illustrative examples with participants at the meeting of World Standard-setters in September 2016.

BC4.21   The examples were selected and developed to examine questions raised by respondents to the 2015 Exposure Draft. These examples included rights and obligations that meet the definitions of an asset or a liability but have a low probability of inflows or outflows of economic benefits or have highly uncertain outcomes. The analysis of those examples explained not only why an asset or liability exists, but also why, applying the recognition criteria in Chapter 5, that asset or liability would not necessarily be recognised in the financial statements. The examples also included transactions for which respondents to the 2015 Exposure Draft thought the implications of the proposed definitions and supporting guidance were unclear and were possibly inconsistent with requirements in Standards. The analysis of those examples illustrated how and why applying the proposed definitions and supporting guidance could, in many cases, lead to conclusions consistent with the requirements in the Standards.

BC4.22   Feedback from the participants at the World Standards-setters meeting in September 2016 highlighted a few areas in which the wording of the proposed guidance was not sufficiently clear. In developing the revised definitions and supporting guidance, the Board considered this feedback together with other feedback received on the proposals.

Definition of an asset

BC4.23   This section discusses the following aspects of the definition of an asset:

(a)   economic resource (see paragraphs BC4.24–BC4.27);

(b)   focus on rights (see paragraphs BC4.28–BC4.39); and

(c)   control (see paragraphs BC4.40–BC4.43).

Economic resource (paragraphs 4.4 and 4.14–4.18)

BC4.24   Paragraphs BC4.6–BC4.7 explain the Board's decision to introduce a separate definition of an economic resource and paragraphs BC4.8–BC4.14 discuss the Board's decision to remove the notion of expected flows from the definition of an asset and not to include that notion in the definition of an economic resource.

BC4.25   The Board concluded that the definition of an asset should refer to the economic resource, not to the resulting economic benefits. Although an asset derives its value from its potential to produce future economic benefits, what the entity controls is the present right that contains that potential. The entity does not control the future economic benefits.

BC4.26   The Board considered whether to use the term 'resource' instead of 'economic resource'. Some respondents to the 2013 Discussion Paper suggested that the term 'economic resource' is too limiting and would cover only resources that have a market value. The Board intended that the term 'economic resource' cover all resources that have the potential to produce economic benefits rather than be limited to resources for which a market currently exists. The Board chose the term 'economic resource' because it helps to emphasise that the resource in question is not, for example, a physical object, but rights over a physical object, as discussed in paragraphs 4.11–4.12 of the 2018 *Conceptual Framework*.

BC4.27 In some jurisdictions, the Board's *Conceptual Framework* is applied in the public sector and in other settings outside the financial markets, including the not-for-profit sector. Consequently, some stakeholders stated that the definition of an asset should include resources that produce benefits other than cash flows, for example, social or environmental services or benefits to the reporting entity, to other parties or to wider society. Similarly, the definition of a liability should, some stakeholders suggested, include obligations to transfer such benefits as well as obligations entered into for prudential or moral purposes, to meet expectations of a broader group of stakeholders or to maintain public support. However, the Board focuses currently on for-profit entities, and, therefore, concluded that the definition of an asset should continue to focus on resources that have the potential to produce economic benefits and that the definition of a liability should continue to focus on obligations to transfer an economic resource.

Focus on rights (paragraphs 4.6–4.13)

BC4.28 Prior to the publication of the 2018 *Conceptual Framework*, the definition of an asset included the term 'resource'. The 2018 *Conceptual Framework* uses the term 'economic resource' and defines an economic resource and, hence, an asset as a right. To illustrate the effect of this change in emphasis, the 2018 *Conceptual Framework* states that, for a physical object, such as an item of property, plant and equipment, the economic resource is not the physical object but a set of rights over that object. Examples of such rights are listed in paragraph 4.11.

BC4.29 In developing the 2018 *Conceptual Framework*, the Board considered a suggestion made by some respondents to the 2013 Discussion Paper and a few respondents to the 2015 Exposure Draft that an asset should be defined as a right or resource, not merely as a right. These respondents argued that:

(a) some assets, for example, tangible assets, are best described as resources instead of rights. The concept of accounting for tangible assets as a set of rights is inconsistent with practice, they argued, especially when that concept is combined with the idea of 'unbundling' rights and recognising them as separate assets.

(b) unless the *Conceptual Framework* explains what factors drive the identification of the unit of account, it would be difficult to explain consistently for a single asset comprising several rights whether to recognise that single asset as a whole or to recognise some of those rights separately.

(c)   a focus on rights within a larger set of rights would put more pressure on the recognition and derecognition criteria and the unit of account. Entities would need to ask themselves numerous questions in order to confirm whether new assets or liabilities exist, without providing any clear benefit to users of financial statements. These respondents argued that the rights approach has caused challenges in developing Standards and also in applying them, particularly in relation to derecognition decisions.

BC4.30   The Board noted that many assets are rights that are established by contract, legislation or similar means, for example, financial assets, a lessee's rights of use of a leased machine, and many intangible assets, such as patents. It is equally true that ownership of a physical object arises because of rights conferred by law. Furthermore, although they differ in extent, the rights conferred by full legal ownership of a physical object and by a contract to use an object for 99% (or 50% or even 1%) of its useful life are all rights of one kind or another. In addition, because of legal differences or changes, a particular set of rights may constitute full legal ownership in one jurisdiction but not in another jurisdiction, or at one date but not at another date.

BC4.31   Hence, the Board saw no advantage in defining two separate types of asset, one described in financial statements as a resource (for example, in cases of full legal ownership of a physical object) and the other described as a right (all other rights over all or part of a resource). Nevertheless, the 2018 *Conceptual Framework* notes in paragraph 4.12 that describing the set of rights as the physical object will often provide a faithful representation of those rights in the most concise and understandable way.

Goodwill

BC4.32   In developing the 2018 *Conceptual Framework*, the Board did not reconsider the conclusions in paragraphs BC313–BC323 of the Basis for Conclusions on IFRS 3 *Business Combinations*. Those paragraphs explain what constitutes 'core' goodwill and state that core goodwill meets the definition of an asset.

BC4.33   In finalising the 2018 *Conceptual Framework*, the Board concluded that including in the *Conceptual Framework* a reference to one particular asset — goodwill — was not appropriate. Accordingly, the 2018 *Conceptual Framework* does not mention goodwill.

Identifiability and separability

BC4.34   IAS 38 *Intangible Assets* requires an intangible asset to be identifiable, so as to distinguish it from goodwill. IAS 38 states that an asset is identifiable if it either is separable from the entity, or arises from contractual or other legal rights. Therefore, in developing the 2018 *Conceptual Framework*, the Board discussed whether the definition of an asset should require an asset to be identifiable and whether that definition should require an asset to be separable. The Board concluded that if an asset is separable or arises from contractual or other legal rights, it is likely to be easier to identify, measure and describe the asset. This may affect whether recognising the asset would provide relevant information and whether it is possible to represent it faithfully. However, the Board concluded that identifiability and separability should not form part of the definition of an asset.

Other sources of value

BC4.35 In developing the 2018 *Conceptual Framework*, the Board discussed items, such as know-how, that an entity obtains in ways other than by contract, legislation and similar means. The Board concluded that such items can be assets. It considered whether the term 'right' was broad enough to capture such items, or whether the Board should instead define an economic resource by reference to a 'right or other source of value'.

BC4.36 The Board concluded that the notion of 'other sources of value' was too vague to be useful in a formal definition. Instead, the 2018 *Conceptual Framework* explains that the term 'right' captures not merely rights obtained by contract, legislation and similar means, but also rights obtained in other ways, for example, by acquiring or creating know-how that is not in the public domain. Paragraph 4.22 further explains why the entity could control the right to use such know-how even if that know-how is not protected by a registered patent. This explanation of the concept is not new—it builds on material in paragraph 4.12 of the 2010 *Conceptual Framework*.

Goods or services that are immediately consumed (paragraph 4.8)

BC4.37 The 2018 *Conceptual Framework* clarifies that goods or services that are received and immediately consumed create a momentary right to obtain the economic benefits produced by those goods or services. That right exists momentarily until the goods or services are consumed, at which point the consumption is recognised as an expense. This is consistent with IFRS 2 *Share-based Payment*, which treats employees' services received as an asset that is immediately consumed.

Economic benefits available to all other parties (paragraph 4.9)

BC4.38 The 2018 *Conceptual Framework* explains that if rights are available to all other parties without significant cost, those rights are typically not assets for the entities that hold them. The Board included this explanation in the 2018 *Conceptual Framework* to clarify that defining an asset as a right would not compel entities to identify and recognise as assets their holdings of a possibly large array of rights.

BC4.39 There are various ways to explain why rights available to all other parties are typically not assets of a particular entity. One reason could be that such rights, for example, public rights of way over land, do not have a potential to produce for that entity economic benefits beyond those available to all other parties. An alternative or additional reason could be that such rights are not controlled by the entity—the entity cannot deny other parties access to any economic benefits that may flow from those rights.

Control (paragraphs 4.19–4.25)

BC4.40   The 2018 *Conceptual Framework* kept in the definition of an asset the requirement for the economic resource to be 'controlled by the entity'. It also introduced a definition of control. The Board built that definition on the definitions of control in IFRS 15 *Revenue from Contracts with Customers*, which defines control of an asset, and in IFRS 10 *Consolidated Financial Statements*, which defines control of an entity.[19] Although the definitions in these Standards differ, they are based on the same basic concepts—that the entity has the ability to direct the use of the asset (or of the entity) and to obtain economic benefits (or returns). The 2018 *Conceptual Framework* uses the concept of control both in the definition of an asset and in its description of a parent's control of its subsidiaries.

Risks and rewards of ownership

BC4.41   The Board considered whether the definition of an asset should incorporate the notion of exposure to risks and rewards of ownership. Some Standards identify that exposure (or the related notion of exposure to variable returns) as either an aspect of control or an indicator of control:

(a)   IFRS 10 states that 'an investor controls an investee when it is exposed, or has rights, to variable returns from its involvement with the investee and has the ability to affect those returns through its power over the investee'.

(b)   IFRS 15 states that one of the indicators that control of an asset has been transferred to a customer is that 'the customer has the significant risks and rewards of ownership of the asset'. The Basis for Conclusions on IFRS 15 explains that exposure to the risks and rewards of ownership of an asset may indicate control.

BC4.42   The 2018 *Conceptual Framework* explains in general terms the relationship between control and exposure to the risks and rewards of ownership. However, instead of using the phrase 'risks and rewards of ownership', the 2018 *Conceptual Framework* refers to 'exposure to significant variations in the amount of economic benefits' (see paragraph 4.24).

Rejected suggestions

BC4.43   In developing the 2018 *Conceptual Framework*, the Board considered and rejected other suggested changes to the definition and treatment of control:

(a)   a suggestion to exclude a reference to control from the definition of an asset because it is implicit in the definition of an economic resource as a right that the entity controls the resource. The Board agreed that this is implicit in the definition of an economic resource but decided that explicitly referring to control is a helpful way of structuring the definition and supporting guidance.

---

19   See paragraph 33 of IFRS 15 and paragraphs 5–7 of IFRS 10.

(b)   a suggestion that the requirement for control to exist should be a recognition criterion, instead of part of the definition of an asset. A few stakeholders argued that this approach would separate two questions that are independent of each other (namely: does an asset exist? and to whom does the asset belong?). The Board did not move the reference to control into the asset recognition criteria because such a move would be unlikely to change which assets would be recognised and because the Board has identified no problems in practice that would be addressed by such a move.

(c)   a suggestion that the Board should amend the definition of control to refer to 'substantially all' economic benefits. The Board noted that the reference to 'substantially all' economic benefits would be redundant, and possibly confusing, if an entity recognises only the rights it controls. For example, if an entity controls the right to obtain 20% of the economic benefits from a building, its asset is the right to obtain 20% of the economic benefits from the building. The entity would not need the right to obtain all, or even substantially all, the economic benefits from the building because its asset is not a right over the whole building. The question of whether to include a threshold such as 'substantially all' may arise when developing Standards, for example, if a Standard requires an entity to account for a group of rights as a single asset (a single unit of account).

Definition of a liability (paragraphs 4.26–4.47)

BC4.44   The 2018 *Conceptual Framework* defines a liability as a present obligation of the entity to transfer an economic resource as a result of past events. The main changes from the previous definition are as follows:

(a)   deletion of the reference to an expected outflow of economic benefits. For reasons discussed in paragraphs BC4.8–BC4.14, that reference was replaced by supporting guidance explaining that an obligation to transfer an economic resource must have the potential to require the entity to transfer an economic resource to another party (see paragraph 4.37).

(b)   replacement of the phrase 'resources embodying economic benefits' with the new defined term 'economic resource' (see paragraphs BC4.6–BC4.7).

BC4.45   As mentioned in paragraph BC0.15, the 2018 *Conceptual Framework* does not address classification of financial instruments with characteristics of both liabilities and equity. The Board is exploring how to distinguish liabilities from equity in its research project on Financial Instruments with Characteristics of Equity. If necessary, the *Conceptual Framework* will be updated as one possible outcome of that project. In finalising the 2018 *Conceptual Framework*, the Board sought not to add new concepts and new guidance that it may need to revisit after that research project.

BC4.46   In developing the 2018 *Conceptual Framework*, the Board concluded that for a liability to exist, three criteria must all be satisfied:

(a)   the entity has an obligation (see paragraphs BC4.47–BC4.61);

(b)   the obligation is to transfer an economic resource (see paragraphs BC4.62–BC4.63); and

(c)   the obligation is a present obligation that exists as a result of past events (see paragraphs BC4.64–BC4.68).

Obligation (paragraphs 4.28–4.35)

BC4.47   In applying the previous definition of a liability, it was generally accepted that an entity has a present obligation to transfer an economic resource when that obligation is unconditional and legally enforceable – in such situations, the entity clearly has no ability to avoid the transfer. However, in some other situations an entity has some limited ability to avoid a future transfer. Both in developing Standards and in applying them, problems had arisen because it was unclear how limited that ability must be for an entity to have a 'present obligation'.

BC4.48   The 2018 *Conceptual Framework* defines an obligation as a duty or responsibility, as did the 2010 *Conceptual Framework*. However, to clarify the meaning of the term 'obligation', the 2018 *Conceptual Framework* states that an entity has an obligation if it has a duty or responsibility that it has no practical ability to avoid.

No practical ability to avoid (paragraphs 4.29–4.34)

BC4.49   The Board developed the 'no practical ability to avoid' criterion by considering the problems arising when:

(a)   an entity does not have a legally enforceable obligation to transfer an economic resource, but its ability to avoid the transfer is limited by its customary practices, published policies or specific statements (such obligations are sometimes referred to as 'constructive obligations'); or

(b)   a requirement already exists for an entity to transfer an economic resource, but the outcome of that requirement is conditional on the action that the entity itself may take.

BC4.50   Although the 2013 Discussion Paper considered those two situations separately, some respondents noted that the underlying issues are similar in both situations – the entity's ability to avoid a transfer is limited. In the 2018 *Conceptual Framework*, the 'no practical ability to avoid' criterion applies in both situations. However, the factors used to assess whether an entity has the practical ability to avoid a particular transfer would depend on the nature of the entity's duty or responsibility and would be considered when developing Standards.

BC4.51 Different Standards required different approaches to situations in which an entity can avoid a transfer of economic resources through its future action. The Board identified three views applied at that time in Standards to determine when a present obligation to transfer an economic resource has arisen:

(a) View 1—an entity must have no ability to avoid the future transfer. For example, IAS 37 *Provisions, Contingent Liabilities and Contingent Assets*, as it had been interpreted in IFRIC 21 *Levies*, required that for a present obligation to exist, the entity must have no ability, even in theory, to avoid the future transfer.

(b) View 2—an entity must have no practical ability to avoid the future transfer. For example, IAS 34 *Interim Financial Reporting* specified that, if a lease provides for variable lease payments based on the entity achieving a specified level of annual sales, an obligation can arise before that level has been achieved if that level is expected to be achieved and the entity therefore has no realistic alternative but to make the future lease payments.

(c) View 3—there need be no limits on an entity's ability to avoid the future transfer. It is sufficient that, as a consequence of a past event, the entity may have to transfer an economic resource if further conditions are met. For example, IAS 19 *Employee Benefits* required a liability to be recognised for benefits that are conditional on future employment (unvested benefits) if those benefits are given in exchange for service already provided by employees. IAS 19 did not require an entity to assess whether it has the practical ability to avoid paying those benefits.

BC4.52 In the 2018 *Conceptual Framework* the Board adopted View 2 for the following reasons:

(a) the Board rejected View 1 because when an entity has the theoretical ability to avoid transferring an economic resource but no practical ability to avoid that transfer, omitting from a list of the entity's obligations the requirement to make that transfer would exclude information that many users of financial statements would find useful. That omission would place too much emphasis on legal form and not enough weight on faithfully representing the substance of obligations that are, in practice, as binding as obligations that are legally enforceable. Moreover, if an entity has a theoretical right to take action that would avoid an obligation, but has no practical ability to exercise that right, that obligation binds the entity as effectively as if it did not have that theoretical right.

(b) the Board rejected View 3 because the term 'obligation' implies some limit on the entity's ability to avoid the transfer of an economic resource.

BC4.53 The Board rejected a suggestion made by several stakeholders to apply a threshold based on the probability of future outflows. Those respondents suggested that an entity should be regarded as having an obligation if it were probable or, perhaps, reasonably certain that the entity would transfer an economic resource. They argued that such a threshold would provide the most relevant measure of the expenses in the period. Nevertheless, in the 2018 *Conceptual Framework* the definition of a liability focuses on the existence of an obligation for the reasons set out in paragraphs BC4.9(a), BC4.52(b) and BC4.94(d). The supporting guidance focuses on what an entity is obliged to do — not on the likelihood of the possible outcomes.

Interpreting 'no practical ability to avoid'

BC4.54 The Board concluded that the factors used to assess whether an entity has the practical ability to avoid a particular transfer should depend on the nature of the entity's duty or responsibility. Applying the criterion of 'no practical ability to avoid' will require judgement. Some stakeholders were concerned that allowing preparers of financial statements to apply this criterion would lead to diverse practice and that in some circumstances entities would recognise a liability when, in the view of some of those stakeholders, the entity does not have a genuine obligation. However, the Board noted that preparers of financial statements will rarely be required to apply that criterion without further requirements and guidance. The Board will, if necessary, develop guidance on applying that criterion to particular cases as it develops Standards.

BC4.55 Paragraph 4.34 of the 2018 *Conceptual Framework* refers to actions that would have economic consequences significantly more adverse than a transfer of economic resources as an example of when an entity may have no practical ability to avoid a transfer. This is intended to mean not just that it would be economically advantageous to make the transfer. Rather, the adverse economic consequences of not making the transfer are so severe that the entity has no practical ability to avoid the transfer. Although the entity has the theoretical right to avoid the transfer, it has no practical ability to exercise that right.

Terminology

BC4.56 The Board considered whether phrases such as the following could be easier to interpret than 'no practical ability to avoid':

(a) 'no realistic alternative'; or

(b) 'little or no discretion (in practice) to avoid'.

BC4.57 These two phrases have a meaning similar to 'no practical ability to avoid'. The Board chose the phrase 'no practical ability to avoid' because it most effectively conveys the need to identify what an entity is obliged to do, instead of focusing on the probable outcome. Furthermore, it mirrors the term 'practical ability', which is applied in some Standards in assessing whether an entity controls an asset, and the term 'present ability' used for a similar purpose in paragraphs 4.20 and 4.22 of the 2018 *Conceptual Framework*.

BC4.58   Some Standards developed before the 2018 *Conceptual Framework* use the term 'constructive obligation' to refer to some circumstances that give rise to an obligation or the term 'economic compulsion' to refer to some circumstances that give rise to no obligation. The 2018 *Conceptual Framework* does not use those terms to distinguish circumstances when an obligation exists from circumstances when an obligation does not exist because the Board concluded that those terms have not proved helpful for that purpose and are not necessary.

An obligation for one party is a right for another party

BC4.59   Paragraph 4.30 of the 2018 *Conceptual Framework* states that if one party has an obligation to transfer an economic resource, it follows that another party (or parties) has a right to receive that economic resource. The Board decided that this statement would help entities to apply the definition of a liability because it may sometimes be easier to identify whether that other party (or parties) has a right than to identify whether the first party has an obligation.

BC4.60   The Board considered whether another party has any asset that it controls if the reporting entity's obligation is not legally enforceable but arises from the reporting entity's customary practices, published policies or specific statements, or is conditional on the entity's own future actions. The Board concluded that the counterparty does control an asset in such cases. According to paragraph 4.23, if an entity is the party that will obtain economic benefits produced by an economic resource, that entity controls the economic resource.

BC4.61   In developing the 2018 *Conceptual Framework*, the Board discussed whether environmental obligations are an exception to the general principle that for every obligation, a corresponding right to receive the economic resource exists. It concluded that in the case of such obligations a corresponding right is controlled by society at large—the people living in the area. They have the right to receive the services required to restore their environment. Therefore, the 2018 *Conceptual Framework* identifies no exception to the general principle.

Transfer of an economic resource (paragraphs 4.36–4.41)

BC4.62   The 2018 *Conceptual Framework* states that the second criterion for a liability is that the obligation must have the potential to require the entity to transfer an economic resource. Paragraphs BC4.8–BC4.14 explain why the Board replaced the notion that an outflow of resources is expected with the concept that a liability has the potential to require a transfer of an economic resource.

BC4.63   An obligation to transfer an economic resource if a specified uncertain future event occurs has the potential to require a transfer of an economic resource and hence can give rise to a liability. That would be the case if the obligation is a present obligation that has arisen as a result of the past events discussed in paragraphs BC4.64–BC4.68. Such obligations are sometimes referred to as 'stand-ready obligations'. The 2018 *Conceptual Framework* does not use that term because the Board considered it unnecessary.

Present obligation as a result of past events (paragraphs 4.42–4.47)

BC4.64   The definition of a liability in the 2010 *Conceptual Framework* required a present obligation to be the result of past events but did not specify how to identify which event results in creation of a present obligation (sometimes referred to as the 'obligating event'). The 2018 *Conceptual Framework*, however, explains how to interpret the phrase 'as a result of past events'.

BC4.65   Some obligations arise from a single obligating event, for example, receiving goods. Other obligations build up over time through a continuous obligating event, for example, conducting a continuous activity.

BC4.66   In some cases, a chain of events creates an obligation. For example, an obligation may arise if a minimum threshold is reached in a period (such as a minimum amount of revenue, a minimum number of employees or a minimum amount of assets) and if the reporting entity is still operating on a specified later date. In such cases, identifying which of those events (reaching the threshold or operating on the specified date) is the obligating event can be particularly difficult. If the definition of obligations encompassed only unconditional obligations (View 1 discussed in paragraph BC4.51(a)), the explicit reference to a past event would, arguably, have been redundant. That is because under View 1 the obligating event would be the event that makes the obligation unconditional. In the example given in this paragraph that event is operating on the specified later date.

BC4.67   However, the Board adopted a broader 'no practical ability to avoid' approach (View 2 discussed in paragraph BC4.51(b)). Applying this concept, an entity may have an obligation if only some of the events in the chain have occurred: an entity could have an obligation if it has no practical ability to avoid the events that have not yet occurred. Therefore, it is important to explain which of the events in the chain must have occurred for an entity to have a present obligation 'as a result of past events'.

BC4.68   The Board concluded that the concept 'as a result of past events' means that:

(a)   an entity has obtained economic benefits or taken an action.

(b)   as a consequence, the entity will or may have to transfer an economic resource that it would not otherwise have had to transfer. The activity increases the magnitude of the economic resources that the entity will or may have to transfer.

Assets and liabilities

Non-reciprocal transactions

BC4.69   The Board considered whether the 2018 *Conceptual Framework* should explicitly discuss assets and liabilities that arise in non-reciprocal transactions, for example, donations, income taxes and other taxes and levies. It noted that the guidance in the 2018 *Conceptual Framework* had been developed without assuming that all transactions are reciprocal exchanges. Indeed, some guidance—in particular, the guidance supporting the liability definition—was developed with significant thought given to non-reciprocal transactions.

BC4.70   The Board concluded that its guidance supporting the definitions of an asset and a liability is equally suitable for reciprocal exchange transactions and non-reciprocal transactions. In both cases, the starting point is to identify the rights and obligations arising from the transaction. Therefore, the 2018 *Conceptual Framework* does not contain guidance that specifically addresses non-reciprocal transactions.

Contingent liabilities and contingent assets

BC4.71   The 2018 *Conceptual Framework* does not use the terms 'contingent liability' and 'contingent asset'. In IAS 37 *Provisions, Contingent Liabilities and Contingent Assets*, developed before the 2018 *Conceptual Framework*, the term 'contingent liability' is used as a collective label encompassing three categories of items that fail to meet that Standard's recognition criteria:

(a)   the first category is possible obligations whose existence is uncertain and will be confirmed only by the occurrence or non-occurrence of uncertain future events not wholly within the control of the entity. Paragraphs 4.35 and 5.14 of the 2018 *Conceptual Framework* analyse such items as cases of existence uncertainty—it is uncertain whether a liability exists.

(b)   the second category is present obligations that arise from past events but are not recognised because it is not probable that an outflow of economic resources will be required to settle them. Paragraphs 4.37–4.38 and 5.15–5.17 of the 2018 *Conceptual Framework* analyse these items as cases of liabilities with a low probability of an outflow of economic benefits.

(c)   the last category is present obligations that arise from past events but are not recognised because their amount cannot be measured with sufficient reliability. Paragraphs 2.19, 2.22 and 5.19–5.23 of the 2018 *Conceptual Framework* analyse these items as cases of liabilities that are subject to a high level of measurement uncertainty.

BC4.72   The term 'contingent liability' is not used in the 2018 *Conceptual Framework* because:

(a)   the three categories of item encompassed by the IAS 37 definition do not form a single natural class. The items in category (a) may be liabilities but are subject to existence uncertainty. The items in categories (b) and (c) are liabilities but might or might not be recognised after applying the recognition criteria described in Chapter 5—*Recognition and derecognition*.

(b)   contingent liabilities are not a further element of financial statements, additional to liabilities and equity. Moreover, some 'contingent liabilities' are liabilities, but others are not.

(c)   in common usage, the term 'contingent liability' is not used in the same way as in IAS 37. It often refers to an item that may give rise to an outflow of economic resources if some uncertain future event occurs. Depending on the circumstances, an obligating event might or might not have occurred. If an obligating event has occurred, the item might be a liability subject to existence uncertainty, outcome uncertainty, measurement uncertainty or any combination of those uncertainties. The liability might be recognised or unrecognised.

BC4.73   Similar considerations apply for 'contingent assets'.

Unit of account (paragraphs 4.48–4.55)

BC4.74   It would be impossible to set out recognition requirements or a measurement basis for a particular item without selecting a unit of account to which those requirements apply. Likewise, selecting a unit of account without considering how recognition or measurement requirements would apply may not result in useful information. Therefore, the 2018 *Conceptual Framework* explains that the unit of account and recognition and measurement requirements for a particular item are all considered at the same time.

BC4.75   In developing the 2018 *Conceptual Framework*, the Board considered whether the unit of account for recognition could differ from the unit of account for measurement. In the Board's view, it is possible for items to qualify for recognition on an individual basis and to be measured on a group basis. For example, a collection of items qualifying for recognition on an individual basis:

(a)   could be measured as a single unit of account when estimating their recoverable amount; or

(b)   may sometimes, as a practical expedient, be measured as a portfolio.

Hence, the Board concluded that sometimes it might be appropriate to select one unit of account for recognition and a different unit of account for measurement.

BC4.76   Decisions about the unit of account are linked to decisions about recognition and measurement that are made in developing Standards. Hence, the Board concluded that decisions about selecting a unit of account will need to be made in developing Standards, not in the *Conceptual Framework*.

BC4.77   The 2018 *Conceptual Framework* includes a discussion of the factors to consider when determining which unit of account to use. The Board did not rank the factors by priority because their relative importance depends on the specific features of the item for which the entity is accounting. In the Board's view, no single ranking could be used to determine the most useful unit of account consistently for a broad range of Standards.

Executory contracts (paragraphs 4.56–4.58)

BC4.78   The 2018 *Conceptual Framework* provides revised and more extensive supporting guidance on executory contracts. It clarifies that:

(a)   an executory contract establishes a combined right and obligation to exchange economic resources;

(b)   that combined right and obligation to exchange economic resources are interdependent and cannot be separated; and

(c)   the combined right and obligation constitute a single asset or liability.

BC4.79   Although some stakeholders expressed a view that executory contracts give rise to a right (to receive one economic resource) and a separate obligation (to transfer a second economic resource), the Board noted that the right and obligation are highly interdependent: the right to receive the first resource is conditional on fulfilling the obligation to transfer the second resource and the obligation to transfer the second resource is conditional on receiving the first resource.

BC4.80   The Board further noted that even if the parties transfer economic resources at different times, a simultaneous exchange occurs at the time of the first transfer. For example, an entity might have a contract to sell goods to a customer and receive payment from the customer at a later date. When the entity transfers the goods to the customer, it simultaneously receives a right to receive payment from the customer. At that time, the customer receives the goods and incurs an obligation to pay for them. Each party's combined right and obligation to exchange economic resources is satisfied at the time of the first transfer and replaced at that time by a new right (in this example to receive payment) or obligation (in this example to make payment).

BC4.81   The Board therefore concluded that an executory contract contains a combined right and obligation to exchange economic resources, not a right to receive one economic resource and a separate obligation to transfer another economic resource.

BC4.82   The Board considered whether the combined right and obligation to exchange economic resources could give a reporting entity both a separate asset (a right to exchange resources, equivalent to a purchased option) and a separate liability (the obligation to exchange resources, equivalent to a written option).

BC4.83   A purchased option to exchange economic resources gives the holder the right either to make an exchange or to withdraw from the exchange without penalty. Conversely, the issuer of the written option undertakes the obligation to make the exchange, if the holder exercises its right. However, if an entity is both the holder of a purchased option and the issuer of an identical written option for the same underlying exchange of economic resources:

(a)   the entity's right under its purchased option to withdraw from the exchange is nullified by its obligation to exchange if the counterparty exercises its right under the entity's written option; and

(b)   the counterparty's right under the entity's written option to withdraw from the exchange is nullified by its obligation to exchange if the entity exercises its right under its purchased option.

BC4.84   Consequently, if an entity is both the holder of a purchased option and the issuer of a written option for the same underlying exchange on the same terms, neither party has the right to avoid exchanging economic resources. It follows that for an executory contract, the terms of the contract provide for only one outcome—the exchange will occur unless both parties agree to terminate the contract. Moreover, the entity's right and obligation to exchange economic resources are so interdependent that they cannot be separated. Hence, the contract cannot be separated into more than a single asset or liability. If the exchange is on terms that are currently favourable to the reporting entity, the contract is an asset; if it is on terms that are currently unfavourable, it is a liability.

BC4.85   Some respondents to the 2015 Exposure Draft asked how the Board's conclusion on executory contracts could affect the treatment of assets and liabilities arising in a lease contract or could affect trade date accounting for financial assets:

(a)   as explained in the Basis for Conclusions on IFRS 16 *Leases*, at the commencement date, a lessee has obtained the right to use an underlying asset for a period of time and the lessor has delivered that right by making the asset available for use by the lessee. Once the lessor has performed its obligation to deliver that right, the lease contract is no longer an executory contract. The lessee controls the right-of-use asset and has a liability for the lease payments.

(b)   IFRS 9 *Financial Instruments* permits 'trade date accounting' for a 'regular way' purchase or sale of a financial asset. Trade date accounting treats the financial asset as having already been delivered at the commitment (trade) date, instead of accounting for the purchase or sale contract as a derivative until settlement. IFRS 9 permits trade date accounting as a simple and practical method of managing and recording transactions that have only a short duration. In other words, permitting this method results from considering the cost constraint— from considering the relative costs and benefits of trade date accounting and settlement date accounting (the other method permitted by IFRS 9).

BC4.86   The 2018 *Conceptual Framework* does not specifically discuss recognition of executory contract assets and liabilities because it does not set out specific recognition requirements for any other types of assets and liabilities. The Board will set recognition requirements for executory contracts in developing Standards in the same way it sets recognition requirements for other assets and liabilities.

BC4.87   In the light of stakeholders' concerns, the Board considered whether the revised concepts on executory contracts could result in more assets and liabilities arising from executory contracts being recognised. In many cases in current practice, an asset or liability is not recognised for an executory contract. The Board expects that this will continue to be so. The same measurement considerations that apply to all other assets and liabilities (see Chapter 6—*Measurement*) apply also to the single asset or liability that arises from an executory contract. When a historical cost measurement basis is applied to an executory contract, the contract is typically measured at zero (which has the same practical effect as not recognising the contract) unless it is onerous. For example, the historical cost of an executory contract for the purchase of inventories is zero (assuming no transaction costs) unless the contract is onerous.

Reporting the substance of contractual rights and obligations (paragraphs 4.59–4.62)

BC4.88   As explained in paragraph 2.12, the 2018 *Conceptual Framework* explicitly states that, to provide a faithful representation of an economic phenomenon, an entity should report the substance of that phenomenon. The 2018 *Conceptual Framework* includes concepts for reporting the substance of contractual rights and contractual obligations. Those concepts drew on concepts developed by the Board in standard-setting projects. The Board decided that including the underlying concepts in the 2018 *Conceptual Framework* would help to ensure that these concepts are applied more consistently in Standards.

Definition of equity (paragraphs 4.63–4.67)

BC4.89   The 2018 *Conceptual Framework* continues:

(a)   to make a binary distinction between liabilities and equity;

(b)   to define equity as the residual interest in the assets of the entity after deducting all its liabilities; and

(c)   not to discuss what forms of presentation and disclosure are appropriate if an entity's equity comprises different classes of equity claims and different components of equity (see paragraphs 7.12–7.13).

BC4.90   The Board considered whether continuing to make a binary distinction between liabilities and equity is sufficient to provide users of financial statements with useful information about claims against the entity. The inherent limitation of a binary distinction between liabilities and equity is that it attempts to make a single distinction between claims that have various characteristics in varying degrees. Eliminating that binary distinction and defining a single element for all claims would allow the accounting for each type of claim to be determined individually to depict its specific characteristics. However, unless all claims are measured directly, any approach would need to identify at least one residual class of claim that would be measured indirectly by reference to the carrying amounts of assets and liabilities. Moreover, it is not possible to measure all claims directly without valuing the entire entity, which goes beyond the stated objective of general purpose financial reports. Thus, dividing claims into at least two classes is unavoidable.

BC4.91   Some respondents to the 2013 Discussion Paper suggested that defining equity directly and introducing another element (a third class of claim) may better depict claims that have some characteristics of both liabilities and equity. However, the Board concluded that introducing another element would make the classification and resulting accounting more complex. In addition, it would be necessary to determine whether changes in this third class of claim should meet the definition of income or expenses. An outcome similar to introducing a new element could instead be achieved by separately presenting different classes within liabilities or within equity.

BC4.92   The Board will further explore how to distinguish liabilities from equity in its research project on Financial Instruments with Characteristics of Equity. That research project:

(a)   will consider approaches to distinguishing liabilities from equity, including approaches that could require changes to the definitions of a liability or equity in the *Conceptual Framework*. The Board will use the output from that project when it decides, in due course, whether to add to its active agenda a project to amend the relevant Standards, the *Conceptual Framework*, or both. Any decision to start an active project would require the Board to go through its due process for adding a project to its agenda.

(b)   is unlikely to result in changes to the supporting guidance in paragraphs 4.28–4.35 that focuses on identifying whether the reporting entity has an obligation to transfer an economic resource. That guidance was not designed to help to distinguish liabilities from equity (see paragraph BC4.45).

Definitions of income and expenses (paragraphs 4.68–4.72)

Income and expenses defined in terms of changes in assets and liabilities

BC4.93   The 2010 *Conceptual Framework* defined income and expenses in terms of changes in assets and liabilities. A few respondents to the 2013 Discussion Paper questioned this approach. They argued that it gives undue primacy to the statement of financial position over the statement(s) of financial performance and insufficiently acknowledges the importance of accounting for transactions in the statement(s) of financial performance or of matching income and expenses.

BC4.94   The Board disagreed with these arguments, concluding that:

(a)   it is incorrect to assume that the Board focuses solely or primarily on the statement of financial position. Financial statements are intended to provide information about an entity's financial position and its financial performance (see paragraph 3.3). Hence, when making decisions about recognition, measurement and presentation and disclosure, the Board considers whether the resulting information provides useful information about both an entity's financial position and its financial performance. The Board has not designated one type of information — about financial position or about financial performance — as the primary focus of financial reporting.

(b)   information about transactions is relevant to users of financial statements. Hence, much of financial reporting is currently based on transactions and will continue to be so.

(c)   transactions that result in income and expenses also cause changes in assets and liabilities. Consequently, identifying income and expenses necessarily leads to identifying which assets and liabilities have changed. The Board and other standard-setters have found over many years that it is more effective, efficient and rigorous to define assets and liabilities first and to define income and expenses as changes in assets and liabilities, instead of trying to define income and expenses first and then describe assets and liabilities as by-products of the recognition of income and expenses.

(d)   the definitions of an asset and a liability are not merely accounting technicalities. They refer to real economic phenomena (economic resources and obligations to transfer economic resources). A statement of financial position depicting assets, liabilities and equity provides users with more relevant and understandable information about an entity's financial position than does a mere summary of amounts that have arisen as by-products of a matching process. Those amounts do not necessarily depict economic phenomena.

(e)   an approach based on matching income and expenses does not define the period to which the income and expenses relate. As explained in paragraph 5.5 of the 2018 *Conceptual Framework*, if income and expenses relate to each other, they will often be recognised simultaneously because of simultaneous changes in related assets and liabilities. However, an intention to match income and expenses does not justify the recognition in the statement of financial position of items that do not meet the definitions of an asset or a liability.

BC4.95   The Board noted that no major problems had been identified with the definitions of income and expenses. Hence, the only changes made in the 2018 *Conceptual Framework* were those necessary to make the definitions of income and expenses consistent with the revised definitions of an asset and a liability.

Types of income and expenses

BC4.96   Much of the discussion of income and expenses in the 2010 *Conceptual Framework* related to their presentation and disclosure. Presentation and disclosure are discussed in Chapter 7 — *Presentation and disclosure* of the 2018 *Conceptual Framework*. The rest of the discussion in the 2010 *Conceptual Framework* referred to various types of income and expenses, for example, revenue, gains and losses. That material was not included in the 2018 *Conceptual Framework*. The material was originally included to emphasise that income includes revenue and gains and that expenses include losses. The Board decided that that emphasis is now unnecessary and the implication that the *Conceptual Framework* defines subclasses of income and expenses is unhelpful. The Board does not expect the removal of that material to cause any changes in practice.

Other possible definitions

BC4.97   In developing the 2018 *Conceptual Framework*, the Board considered whether to define as elements of financial statements contributions from holders of equity claims and distributions to holders of equity claims, and cash inflows and cash outflows. Because the Board concluded that the absence of such definitions had not caused major problems, it did not include such definitions in the 2018 *Conceptual Framework*.

CONTENTS

Recognition (paragraphs 5.6–5.25)

BC5.1 The recognition criteria in the 2010 *Conceptual Framework* stated that an entity recognises an item that meets the definition of an element if:

(a) it is probable that any future economic benefit associated with the item will flow to or from the entity; and

(b) the item has a cost or value that can be measured with reliability.

BC5.2 The recognition criteria created the following problems:

(a) some Standards developed before the 2018 *Conceptual Framework* applied a probability recognition criterion, but they did not use it consistently. They used different probability thresholds which included 'probable', 'more likely than not', 'virtually certain' and 'reasonably possible'.

(b) the application of the probability criterion to some recognition questions could lead to loss of relevant information or a misleading representation of the entity's financial position or financial performance. For example, applying the criterion could prevent the recognition of some derivative financial instruments. Moreover, it could result in a gain being recognised for a transaction when no economic gain has occurred. For example, suppose that, in exchange for receiving cash, an entity incurs a liability to pay a fixed amount if some unlikely event occurs in the future. If the liability is not recognised because an outflow of economic benefits is not considered probable when the entity receives the cash, the entity will recognise an immediate gain at that time. To avoid such problems, some Standards developed before the 2018 *Conceptual Framework*, for example, IFRS 9 *Financial Instruments*, applied no probability recognition criterion.

(c) the reference to reliability was unclear and could result in inappropriate outcomes. Although reliability was identified as a qualitative characteristic in the 1989 *Framework*, in the 2010 *Conceptual Framework*, the term 'reliability' was no longer used to refer to a qualitative characteristic and was not defined (see paragraphs BC2.21–BC2.31). In practice, a 'reliable' measure was usually interpreted as one with a tolerable level of measurement uncertainty and perhaps also as verifiable and free from error. Hence, a recognition criterion referring to reliable measurement could be interpreted as one prohibiting recognition of any item that has a high level of measurement uncertainty, even if recognising such an item would provide useful information.

BC5.3 The 2018 *Conceptual Framework* states that an asset or liability is recognised only if such recognition provides users of financial statements with useful information, namely:

(a) relevant information about the asset or liability and about any resulting income, expenses or changes in equity; and

(b)   a faithful representation of the asset or liability and of any resulting income, expenses or changes in equity.

BC5.4   The approaches in the 2010 *Conceptual Framework* and the 2018 *Conceptual Framework* have similar objectives but sought to achieve them by different means:

(a)   the 2010 *Conceptual Framework* set up practical, but subjective filters for cases where recognition is not likely to provide information with the qualitative characteristics of useful financial information. Those filters referred to probability and reliability.

(b)   the 2018 *Conceptual Framework* refers directly to the qualitative characteristics and then provides guidance on how to apply them. That guidance explains when recognition might produce information that lacks those qualitative characteristics—including some (but not necessarily all) cases where applying the 2010 *Conceptual Framework* might have led to a conclusion that a flow of economic benefits is not probable or that reliable measurement is not possible.

BC5.5   The Board considered whether the 2018 *Conceptual Framework* should include a presumption (or overarching principle) that every item meeting the definition of an asset or a liability is recognised. This would have meant that if the Board had decided that recognition of a particular item would not provide useful information, it would have had to include an exception to this principle in particular Standards.

BC5.6   The Board rejected that approach because it expects that in some circumstances it will continue to conclude that recognising particular assets or particular liabilities will not provide useful information or that the costs of recognising them would exceed the benefits of doing so. To be useful to the Board, the *Conceptual Framework* needs to give guidance on how to approach decisions about setting recognition requirements in Standards. A presumption or overarching principle that every item meeting the definition of an asset or a liability should be recognised would be too restrictive and would not provide such guidance.

BC5.7   Some stakeholders expressed a concern that the approach now included in the 2018 *Conceptual Framework* would not provide enough direction because it is too abstract and subjective. These stakeholders suggested that the Board needs more concrete and robust recognition criteria to ensure that it develops Standards with consistent requirements that result in useful information.

BC5.8   In considering that concern, the Board noted that the 1989 *Framework* and the 2010 *Conceptual Framework* also set abstract and subjective criteria—probability and reliability. The revised approach in the 2018 *Conceptual Framework* is linked directly to the qualitative characteristics of useful financial information and provides clearer and more developed guidance than the previous approach. In the Board's view, setting more rigid recognition criteria in the *Conceptual Framework* would not help the Board to set recognition requirements in Standards that result in useful information to users of financial statements at a cost that does not exceed the benefits.

BC5.9 Some stakeholders disagreed with the revised approach to recognition because they were concerned that it could increase the range of recognised assets and liabilities.

BC5.10 In developing the revised recognition criteria, the Board aimed to develop tools that would help it to base decisions on a more coherent set of principles. It did not have an objective of either increasing or decreasing the range of assets and liabilities recognised. Paragraphs BC5.15–BC5.20 provide the Board's responses to specific concerns in relation to situations when probability of inflows or outflows of economic benefits is low and paragraphs BC5.21–BC5.22 provide the Board's responses to specific concerns in relation to measurement uncertainty.

BC5.11 Further, the Board noted that, as explained in paragraph SP1.2 of the 2018 *Conceptual Framework*, the *Conceptual Framework* does not override requirements in Standards, so the 2018 revision of recognition criteria will not affect how preparers of financial statements apply recognition criteria developed in Standards issued before the 2018 *Conceptual Framework*.

Relevance (paragraphs 5.12–5.17)

BC5.12 The guidance supporting the revised recognition criteria provides examples of factors that may indicate when recognising an asset or liability may fail to provide users of financial statements with relevant information. Two of those factors relate to cases in which:

(a) it is uncertain whether an asset or liability exists (see paragraphs BC5.13–BC5.14); or

(b) an asset or liability exists, but the probability of an inflow or outflow of economic benefits is low (see paragraphs BC5.15–BC5.20).

Existence uncertainty (paragraph 5.14)

BC5.13 It is sometimes uncertain whether an asset or liability exists (existence uncertainty). The Board concluded that it is helpful to consider existence uncertainty separately from outcome uncertainty and separately from measurement uncertainty. Although existence uncertainty may contribute to outcome uncertainty and measurement uncertainty, conceptually it is different and could affect recognition decisions differently. Distinguishing different types of uncertainty makes it easier to decide what information is most likely to be relevant to users of financial statements and how to provide that information in a way that provides a faithful representation.

BC5.14 The 2018 *Conceptual Framework* does not provide detailed guidance on how to consider existence uncertainty in making recognition decisions because the appropriate approach will depend on facts and circumstances.

Low probability of an inflow or outflow of economic benefits (paragraphs 5.15–5.17)

BC5.15   Many respondents both to the 2013 Discussion Paper and to the 2015 Exposure Draft argued that the recognition criteria should continue to refer to probability. They argued that:

    (a)   the probability criterion had proved to be a practical way of applying the qualitative characteristics. The proposed supporting guidance on items with a low probability of generating a flow of economic benefits was not clear enough and would lead to doubt and inconsistency.

    (b)   the removal of the probability criterion, in combination with the removal of the reference to 'expected' from the definitions of an asset and a liability, could lead to requirements for entities to recognise more assets and liabilities with a low probability of inflows or outflows of economic benefits. Recognising such assets and liabilities would not provide useful information. In addition, preparers of financial statements might have to search extensively for rights and obligations. (The deletion of the notion of an 'expected' flow is discussed in paragraphs BC4.8–BC4.14.)

    (c)   if assets and liabilities with a low probability of future inflows and outflows were recognised, they might have to be measured at amounts based on expected value. Such measurement is difficult and puts a burden on preparers of financial statements. Sometimes, providing information about the range and distribution of possible outcomes is more useful than providing a measure based on expected value. Such measures may provide an illusion of precision that does not exist.

BC5.16   Some respondents suggested applying a probability filter for some assets or liabilities (for example, for patents or research and development), but not for all (for example, not for derivative financial assets), or for some transactions but not for others (for example, not for the acquisition of an asset for cash). Those respondents suggested it is not reasonable to remove the probability requirement from the recognition criteria simply to permit the recognition of some financial instruments. Including an exception for particular financial instruments in a Standard would be sufficient to achieve that result.

BC5.17   The Board acknowledged that a probability threshold could be a practical way to filter out assets and liabilities whose recognition might not provide relevant information. However, this approach would lead to not recognising assets and liabilities in some cases when recognition could provide relevant information. It would also be difficult to set a probability threshold that could be applied across all Standards and in all recognition events.

BC5.18   The Board also noted that, whatever measurement basis is used for an asset or liability with a low probability of an inflow or outflow of economic benefits, that basis would be likely to reflect that low probability—it is unlikely that a required measurement basis would reflect only the maximum inflow or maximum outflow of economic benefits.

BC5.19   The 2018 *Conceptual Framework*, therefore, does not include a probability threshold. Instead, the low probability of an inflow or outflow of economic benefits is discussed as an indicator that, in some cases, recognition may not provide relevant information, for the reasons discussed in paragraphs 5.16–5.17.

BC5.20   Some stakeholders expressed a concern that the term 'low probability' is too subjective to be interpreted consistently. However, the Board's objective in discussing situations of low probability was to indicate that in some such situations, the Board might conclude that some information may not be relevant. The Board's objective was not to identify a threshold above which information would always be relevant and below which it would always be irrelevant.

Faithful representation (paragraphs 5.18–5.25)

BC5.21   As discussed in paragraphs BC5.2–BC5.4, the recognition criteria in the 2018 *Conceptual Framework* do not include a requirement to recognise an asset or liability only if it has a cost or value that can be measured with reliability. The Board concluded that a high level of measurement uncertainty would not necessarily preclude a measure from providing useful information about an asset or liability, so it would be difficult to set a single threshold based on measurement uncertainty that could be applied across all Standards and in all recognition events. Hence, the 2018 *Conceptual Framework* discusses measurement uncertainty as a factor that may affect whether faithful representation can be provided by recognition of an asset or liability, supported, if necessary, by explanatory information. This discussion is based on the discussion of measurement uncertainty in Chapter 2—*Qualitative characteristics of useful financial information* (see paragraphs 2.19, 2.22 and BC2.46–BC2.49).

BC5.22   Some respondents to the 2013 Discussion Paper and to the 2015 Exposure Draft suggested that a higher level of measurement uncertainty is tolerable when recognising liabilities or expenses than when recognising assets or income. They described this as an application of prudence (asymmetric prudence, applying the terminology used in paragraph BC2.37). The Board concluded that the level of measurement uncertainty beyond which a measure does not provide a faithful representation depends on facts and circumstances and so can be determined only when developing Standards (see paragraph 5.9). Paragraphs BC2.44–BC2.45 provide further discussion of symmetry in decisions about recognition and measurement.

Derecognition (paragraphs 5.26–5.33)

BC5.23   The 2010 *Conceptual Framework* did not define derecognition; nor did it describe when derecognition occurs.

BC5.24   Discussions about derecognition have typically contrasted two approaches to derecognition:

   (a)   a control approach—derecognition is the mirror image of recognition. Thus, an entity derecognises an asset or liability when it no longer meets the criteria for recognition (or no longer exists, or is no longer an asset or liability of the entity).

   (b)   a risks-and-rewards approach—an entity continues to recognise an asset or liability until the entity is no longer exposed to most of the risks and rewards generated by that asset or liability. This continued recognition would apply even if that asset or liability would not qualify for recognition at the date when the entity disposed of the transferred component, if at that date it acquired only the retained component and had not previously recognised the retained component.[20]

BC5.25   To address some apparent conflicts between the control approach and the risks-and-rewards approach, the Board explained in the 2018 *Conceptual Framework* that:

   (a)   if an entity has apparently transferred an asset but retains exposure to significant positive or negative variations in the amount of economic benefits that may be produced by the asset, this sometimes indicates that the entity might continue to control that asset; and

   (b)   if an entity has transferred an asset to another party that holds the asset as an agent for the entity, the transferor still controls the asset.

BC5.26   In developing the 2018 *Conceptual Framework*, the Board concluded that accounting requirements for derecognition should aim to faithfully represent both:

   (a)   any assets and liabilities retained after the transaction or other event that led to the derecognition (including any asset or liability acquired, incurred or created as part of the transaction or other event); and

   (b)   the change in the entity's assets and liabilities as a result of that transaction or other event.

BC5.27   In the Board's view, the control approach focuses more on the aim described in paragraph BC5.26(a) and the risks-and-rewards approach focuses more on the aim described in paragraph BC5.26(b). If an entity transfers an entire asset or an entire liability and retains no exposure to that asset or liability, the control approach and the risks-and-rewards approach both lead to the same outcome. Moreover, in such cases, achieving both aims described in paragraph BC5.26 is straightforward.

---

20   Paragraph 5.28 of the 2018 *Conceptual Framework* explains what is included in the transferred component and the retained component.

BC5.28 In contrast, the Board has encountered difficulties in standard-setting when an entity transfers only part of an asset or liability or retains some exposure to variations. In those cases, the control approach does not always lead to the same outcome as the risks-and-rewards approach and the two aims described in paragraph BC5.26 sometimes conflict. The Board views both aims as valid. Accordingly, in the 2018 *Conceptual Framework* the Board did not specify the use of the control approach or the risks-and-rewards approach.

BC5.29 Instead, the Board adopted an approach that involves:

(a) derecognising the transferred component.

(b) continuing to recognise the retained component, if any.

(c) applying one or more of the following procedures if necessary to achieve one or both of the aims described in paragraph BC5.26:

(i) present any retained component separately in the statement of financial position;

(ii) present separately in the statement(s) of financial performance any income and expenses recognised as a result of derecognition of the transferred component; and

(iii) provide explanatory information.

(d) as a last resort, if derecognition of the transferred component is not sufficient to achieve both aims described in paragraph BC5.26 even when supported by separate presentation or by explanatory information, considering whether continuing to recognise the transferred component would achieve those aims. That continued recognition would need to be supported by separate presentation or explanatory information because financial statements would include as assets and liabilities, and as related income and expenses, items that do not meet the definition of an element of financial statements.

BC5.30 The Board considered whether the description of aims of accounting requirements for derecognition should explicitly refer to the qualitative characteristic of relevance in addition to the qualitative characteristic of faithful representation. The Board noted that the aims described in paragraph BC5.26 identify what economic phenomena need to be represented faithfully when derecognition is being considered. In the Board's view, information about those economic phenomena is what would be relevant to users of financial statements. Therefore, the Board concluded that adding an explicit reference to relevance would not change how it would seek to achieve the two aims.

CONTENTS

Introduction

BC6.1 In developing the 2018 *Conceptual Framework*, the Board did not provide detailed guidance on when a particular measurement basis would be suitable because the suitability of particular measurement bases will vary depending on facts and circumstances. Instead, the 2018 *Conceptual Framework*:

(a) describes measurement bases and the information they provide; and

(b) discusses the factors to consider when selecting a measurement basis.

BC6.2 Some respondents to the 2015 Exposure Draft questioned whether simply describing the measurement bases and discussing the factors to consider when selecting a measurement basis would provide the Board with sufficient guidance to develop measurement requirements in Standards. These respondents suggested that the Board should undertake further research on measurement and either:

(a) delay issuing a revised *Conceptual Framework* until that research is completed;

(b) issue a revised *Conceptual Framework* without a measurement section; or

(c) develop high-level interim guidance on measurement for use until more complete concepts and principles can be developed.

BC6.3 The Board rejected these suggestions. The 2010 *Conceptual Framework* provided little guidance on measurement. This lack of guidance was a significant gap in the 2010 *Conceptual Framework* that needed to be addressed. The Board concluded that the guidance in the 2018 *Conceptual Framework* will help it to develop measurement requirements in Standards.

BC6.4 Further, the Board considered whether the 2018 *Conceptual Framework* needs to identify a separate overall objective for measurement. The Board concluded that a separate measurement objective is unlikely to provide useful additional guidance to help it to develop measurement requirements. Instead, the 2018 *Conceptual Framework* describes how measurement contributes to the objective of general purpose financial statements—see paragraph 6.45.

Mixed measurement (paragraph 6.2)

BC6.5 In developing the 2018 *Conceptual Framework*, the Board considered whether the *Conceptual Framework* should advocate using a single measurement basis. The main advantages of using a single measurement basis would be:

(a) the amounts included in the financial statements could be more meaningfully added, subtracted and compared; and

(b) the financial statements would be less complex and, arguably, more understandable.

BC6.6 In addition, if the Board were to identify a concept of wealth or capital that would meet the information needs of users of financial statements, a single measurement basis would be required in order to produce a measure of that wealth or capital. However, as discussed in paragraphs BC8.1–BC8.4 the Board decided not to update the discussion of capital and capital maintenance and not to seek to identify a concept of wealth or capital that would meet the information needs of users of financial statements.

BC6.7   Both the 2013 Discussion Paper and the 2015 Exposure Draft suggested that a single measurement basis for all assets, liabilities, income and expenses might not always provide the most relevant information to users of financial statements. Nearly all respondents who commented on this issue supported the suggested approach.

BC6.8   However, a few respondents disagreed and proposed one of the following as a single measurement basis:

(a)   historical cost;

(b)   fair value;

(c)   current entry value (for example, current cost, see paragraphs 6.21–6.22 of the 2018 Conceptual Framework); or

(d)   deprival (relief) value (see paragraph BC6.29(a)).

BC6.9   Most of the respondents who suggested the use of a single measurement basis conceded that this could not be achieved in practice, at least in the short term. However, they said that the Board should describe a default measurement basis that it would use when developing Standards. The Board should then commit to explaining any decisions to use any other measurement basis.

BC6.10   The Board concluded that in different circumstances different measurement bases may provide information relevant to users of financial statements. In addition, in different circumstances, a particular measurement basis may be:

(a)   easier to understand and implement than another;

(b)   more verifiable, less prone to error or subject to a lower level of measurement uncertainty than another; or

(c)   less costly to implement than another.

BC6.11   Hence, the 2018 Conceptual Framework states that consideration of the qualitative characteristics of useful financial information and of the cost constraint is likely to result in the selection of different measurement bases for different assets, liabilities, income and expenses.

Measurement bases and the information they provide (paragraphs 6.4–6.42)

BC6.12   The 2018 Conceptual Framework identifies two categories of measurement bases. Paragraphs BC6.19–BC6.22 discuss historical cost measurement bases and paragraphs BC6.23–BC6.29 discuss current value measurement bases.

BC6.13   The 2013 Discussion Paper identified cash-flow-based measurements as a separate category of measurement bases. The 2018 Conceptual Framework does not do so because the Board concluded that cash-flow-based measurements are not measurement bases in their own right. Instead, cash-flow-based measurement techniques can be used to estimate a measure in applying a specified measurement basis. Paragraphs 6.91–6.95 of the 2018 *Conceptual Framework* discuss how those techniques can be used in this way.

BC6.14   The Board considered and rejected the idea of categorising measurement bases according to whether they provide information about the cost of inputs to an entity's business activities—entry values such as historical cost and current cost—or information about the cost of outputs from an entity's business activities—exit values such as fair value, value in use and fulfilment value. The Board did not find such a distinction useful when describing or selecting a measurement basis for use in a particular Standard because the difference between entry and exit values in the same market is often small, except for transaction costs (see paragraphs BC6.30–BC6.33).

BC6.15   The 2018 *Conceptual Framework* describes the measurement bases the Board is likely to consider selecting when developing Standards. It acknowledges in paragraph 6.3 that a Standard may need to describe how to implement the measurement basis selected in that Standard.

BC6.16   In addition, the 2018 *Conceptual Framework* discusses the information provided by particular measurement bases. Identifying that information will help to identify whether a particular measurement basis is likely to provide useful information to the users of financial statements in particular circumstances.

BC6.17   A few respondents to the 2015 Exposure Draft said the discussion of measurement bases is biased: some suggested that the discussion is biased against historical cost; conversely, others perceived a bias against current values. In developing the 2018 *Conceptual Framework*, the Board sought to provide a balanced description of the measurement bases and the information that they provide. The Board did not intend to favour one measurement basis over the others.

BC6.18   In the measurement chapter, the term 'value' is used to refer in general terms to an economic value of an asset or liability, rather than its carrying amount (see paragraph 5.1) and rather than a specific current value such as fair value. That term is used, for example, when that economic value may differ from the amount of a future cash payment or future cash receipt, for example, because of factors such as the time value of money.

Historical cost (paragraphs 6.4–6.9 and 6.24–6.31)

BC6.19   The 2018 *Conceptual Framework* explains that the historical cost of an asset is initially the value of the costs incurred in acquiring or creating the asset, comprising the consideration paid to acquire or create the asset plus transaction costs. The historical cost of a liability when it is incurred or taken on is initially the value of the consideration received to incur or take on the liability minus transaction costs. When developing Standards, the Board will decide whether to specify how those initial values are determined.

BC6.20 Consumption of all or part of an asset leads to derecognition of the part of the asset that is consumed. If the asset is measured at historical cost, this derecognition is reflected through depreciation or amortisation of the asset. Similarly, fulfilment of all or part of a liability leads to derecognition of the part of the liability that is fulfilled.

BC6.21 If an asset has become impaired or a liability has become onerous, the cost determined at initial recognition is unlikely to provide relevant information if it is not updated. Consequently, the 2018 *Conceptual Framework* describes the historical cost of an asset as being updated to reflect the fact that part of the historical cost is no longer recoverable, that is, the carrying amount of the asset is updated to reflect impairment. Similarly, the historical cost of a liability is updated to reflect changes that result in the liability becoming onerous, that is, the consideration received to incur or take on the liability is no longer sufficient to depict the obligation to fulfil the liability. However, historical cost does not reflect changes in value of an asset that is not impaired or of a liability that is not onerous.

BC6.22 The amortised cost of a financial asset or financial liability reflects estimates of future cash flows discounted at a rate that is not updated after initial recognition, unless the asset or liability bears interest at a variable rate. For loans given or received, if interest is receivable or payable regularly, the amortised cost of the loan typically approximates the amount originally paid or received. In addition, the carrying amount of a loan given is reduced if it is impaired. Therefore, the 2018 *Conceptual Framework* categorises amortised cost of financial assets and financial liabilities as a form of historical cost.

Current value (paragraphs 6.10–6.22 and 6.32–6.42)

BC6.23 The 2018 *Conceptual Framework* identifies current value measures as providing monetary information about assets, liabilities and related income and expenses using information updated to reflect conditions at the measurement date. It states that current measurement bases include fair value, value in use (for assets), fulfilment value (for liabilities) and current cost.

BC6.24 The description of fair value in the 2018 *Conceptual Framework* is consistent with its description in IFRS 13 *Fair Value Measurement*. The descriptions of value in use and fulfilment value are derived from the definition of value in use in IAS 36 *Impairment of Assets*, which is the most explicit of the various definitions of entity-specific value in Standards developed before the 2018 *Conceptual Framework*. The description of current cost is derived from descriptions of current cost in various academic sources.

BC6.25 Some Standards developed before the 2018 *Conceptual Framework* use value in use, but not as a separate measurement basis. In those Standards, value in use is used in determining the recoverable amount of an asset that is measured at historical cost and may be impaired. Within that context, if value in use is used to determine the recoverable amount of an impaired asset, immediately after the impairment loss has been recognised, the carrying amount of the asset equals its value in use. Nevertheless, the 2018 *Conceptual Framework* identifies value in use as a separate measurement basis because:

(a)   it differs conceptually from historical cost, even though value in use is used in determining recoverable historical cost; and

(b)   the Board might decide that in some circumstances an entity should measure an asset using an entity-specific current value (ie value in use) instead of fair value.

BC6.26   The 2018 *Conceptual Framework* explains that value in use and fulfilment value reflect the same factors as fair value, but using entity-specific assumptions, not assumptions by market participants.

BC6.27   Value in use and fulfilment value, therefore, reflect the price for bearing the uncertainty inherent in the cash flows — a risk premium. Including such a risk premium produces information that can be relevant because it reflects the economic difference between items subject to different levels of uncertainty. The inclusion of a risk premium is implicit in how value in use is described in IAS 36.[21]

BC6.28   Although current cost is not widely used in IFRS Standards, there is a significant body of academic literature that advocates the use of current cost in financial reporting. Consequently, the 2018 *Conceptual Framework* describes current cost.

BC6.29   The 2018 *Conceptual Framework* does not describe the following current value measurement bases:

(a)   deprival value for assets or relief value for liabilities. The deprival value of an asset is the loss that an entity would suffer if it were deprived of the asset being measured. Similarly, the relief value of a liability is the benefit that an entity would enjoy if it were relieved of the liability being measured. The Board did not include a discussion of deprival value or relief value because they are more complex than other measurement bases and have been used in few jurisdictions. Hence, the Board concluded that it is unlikely to use deprival value or relief value when developing Standards.

(b)   net realisable value. Net realisable value depicts the estimated consideration from the sale of the asset reduced by the estimated costs of sale. The Board concluded that it is unnecessary to describe net realisable value separately, because it is derived from another current measure.

(c)   cost of release. Cost of release depicts the estimated cost (including transaction costs) of obtaining release from a liability by negotiation with the counterparty. Because it is relatively unusual for entities to obtain release from liabilities, instead of fulfilling them, the Board concluded that it is unnecessary to describe this measurement basis in the 2018 *Conceptual Framework*.

---

21   See paragraphs 55–56, A1 and A15–A21 of IAS 36 *Impairment of Assets*.

Transaction costs

BC6.30   Transaction costs can arise both when:

(a)   an asset is acquired or a liability is incurred or taken on; and

(b)   an asset is sold or disposed of or a liability is settled or transferred.

BC6.31   Defining which costs are transaction costs is beyond the scope of the *Conceptual Framework*. They have normally been defined in particular Standards as incremental costs, other than the transaction price, that would not have been incurred if the particular asset (or liability) being measured had not been acquired (incurred) or sold or disposed of (transferred or settled).

BC6.32   Transaction costs incurred in acquiring an asset or incurring a liability are a feature of the transaction in which the asset was acquired or the liability was incurred. Hence:

(a)   the historical cost and current cost of an asset or liability reflect those transaction costs. Although the transaction costs are not part of the transaction price, the entity could not have acquired the asset or incurred the liability without incurring those transaction costs.

(b)   if the measure is intended to depict the fair value, fulfilment value or value in use of an asset or liability, the measure does not reflect those transaction costs. Those costs do not affect the current value of that asset or liability.

BC6.33   Transaction costs that would be incurred in selling or disposing of an asset or in settling or transferring a liability are a feature of a possible future transaction. Hence:

(a)   value in use and fulfilment value reflect those transaction costs if the entity expects to incur them;

(b)   fair value does not reflect those transaction costs; and

(c)   historical cost and current cost do not reflect transaction costs that would be incurred in selling or disposing of an asset or in settling or transferring a liability because these measurement bases are entry values—they reflect the costs of acquiring the asset or incurring the liability.

Factors to consider when selecting a measurement basis (paragraphs 6.43–6.86)

BC6.34   To meet the objective of financial statements, information provided by a particular measurement basis must be useful to users of financial statements. A measurement basis achieves this if it provides information that is relevant and faithfully represents what it purports to represent. The 2018 *Conceptual Framework* discusses how relevance and faithful representation affect the selection of a measurement basis.

BC6.35   The Board considered whether to prescribe the order in which factors should be considered in selecting a measurement basis (for example, using a hierarchy or decision tree). However, the Board concluded that this would not be possible or desirable. The relative importance of the factors will depend on facts and circumstances. Indeed, in many cases it will be important to consider several factors when selecting a measurement basis.

Effect on both the statement of financial position and the statement(s) of financial performance (paragraph 6.43)

BC6.36   The 2018 *Conceptual Framework* states that when selecting a measurement basis it is necessary to consider the nature of the information that the measurement basis will produce in both the statement of financial position and the statement(s) of financial performance. Some respondents to the 2015 Exposure Draft stated that the *Conceptual Framework* should give more weight to the effect that a particular measure would have on the statement(s) of financial performance. In their view, the statement(s) of financial performance is more useful than the statement of financial position to users of financial statements. However, the Board concluded that the relative importance of the information produced in those statements will depend on how users will use the resulting information in their analysis, which will, in turn, depend on facts and circumstances.

Relevance (paragraphs 6.49–6.57)

BC6.37   The 2018 *Conceptual Framework* discusses the following factors that can affect the relevance of the information provided by a measurement basis:

(a)   characteristics of the asset or liability; and

(b)   contribution to future cash flows (see paragraphs BC6.38–BC6.42).

BC6.38   Paragraph 1.14 notes that some economic resources produce cash flows directly, whereas other economic resources are used in combination to produce cash flows. Building on this idea, the 2018 *Conceptual Framework* identifies as one factor in the selection of a measurement basis the way in which an asset or liability contributes to future cash flows.

BC6.39   The 2018 *Conceptual Framework* states that the way in which an asset or liability contributes to future cash flows depends, in part, on the nature of the business activities conducted by the entity. For example, depending on the nature of an entity's business activities, the same asset could be sold as inventory, leased to another entity or used in the entity's business. The Board acknowledged that measuring in the same way assets or liabilities that contribute to cash flows differently could reduce comparability by making different things appear the same.[22]

---

22 Paragraph 2.27 of the 2018 *Conceptual Framework* states: 'Comparability is not uniformity. For information to be comparable, like things must look alike and different things must look different.'

BC6.40 Although some respondents to the 2015 Exposure Draft expressed a concern that subjectivity could result if the nature of an entity's business activities were to be considered when selecting a measurement basis, many supported this approach. In addition, the Board noted that, in many cases, the nature of an entity's business activities is a matter of fact, not an opinion or management intent. When this is not the case, the Board will need to consider how to address any subjectivity.

BC6.41 The 2018 *Conceptual Framework* does not refer explicitly to any particular business activity, for example, long-term investment, for the reasons set out in paragraph BC0.39.

BC6.42 To help in the selection of a measurement basis, the 2018 *Conceptual Framework* also provides guidance on when historical cost or current value measurement bases might provide relevant information about financial assets and financial liabilities. That guidance builds on concepts identified by the Board in developing IFRS 9 *Financial Instruments*. The Basis for Conclusions on IFRS 9 explains why the Board decided to use those concepts.

Faithful representation (paragraphs 6.58–6.62)

BC6.43 The 2018 *Conceptual Framework* identifies the following as factors that can affect whether the information provided by a particular measurement basis provides a faithful representation of the economic phenomena that are being depicted:

(a) whether the assets and liabilities are related in some way; and

(b) measurement uncertainty (see paragraphs BC6.44–BC6.45).

BC6.44 Some respondents to the 2013 Discussion Paper suggested that one factor to be considered in selecting a measurement basis is the level of measurement uncertainty associated with that measurement basis. Some respondents used the term 'reliability' to describe that factor. As discussed in paragraphs BC2.28–BC2.31, the Board did not reintroduce the term 'reliability'. Paragraph 2.22 of the 2018 *Conceptual Framework* explains that if a high level of measurement uncertainty is involved in making an estimate, that may indicate that different information about the economic phenomenon might be more useful (see paragraphs BC2.55–BC2.56). In addition, Chapter 6—*Measurement* discusses how measurement uncertainty can affect the selection of a measurement basis.

BC6.45 Some respondents to the 2015 Exposure Draft stated that applying prudence as they understand the term would imply that the tolerable level of measurement uncertainty would always be higher for liabilities than for assets (see paragraphs BC2.37(b), BC2.41–BC2.45 and BC2.55–BC2.56). The Board disagreed with this view, concluding that the tolerable level of measurement uncertainty depends on facts and circumstances and can be decided only when developing Standards.

Enhancing qualitative characteristics (paragraphs 6.63–6.76)

BC6.46 The 2018 *Conceptual Framework* identifies four 'enhancing qualitative characteristics' that make financial information more useful—comparability, verifiability, timeliness and understandability. In developing the 2018 *Conceptual Framework*, the Board identified no specific implications of timeliness for selection of a measurement basis beyond those discussed in Chapter 2—*Qualitative characteristics of useful financial information*. The 2018 *Conceptual Framework* discusses the general implications that comparability, verifiability and understandability have for the selection of a measurement basis.

BC6.47 In developing the 2018 *Conceptual Framework*, the Board considered these suggestions made by respondents:

(a) verifiability should play a more significant role in selecting a measurement basis; and

(b) comparability could be enhanced if the Board, when developing Standards, prevented preparers of financial statements from choosing between measurement bases.

BC6.48 The Board concluded that the discussion of verifiability appropriately reflects the role of verifiability as a factor to consider when selecting a measurement basis. Further, the Board concluded that additional discussion of the disadvantages of developing Standards that allow preparers to choose between alternative measurement bases is unnecessary because paragraph 2.29 acknowledges that permitting alternative accounting methods for the same economic phenomenon diminishes comparability.

Factors specific to initial measurement (paragraphs 6.77–6.82)

BC6.49 The 2015 Exposure Draft discussed both exchanges of items of similar value and exchanges of items of different value. Respondents to the 2015 Exposure Draft commented that the meaning of the terms 'similar value' and 'different value' was unclear. To respond to such concerns, the 2018 *Conceptual Framework* refers instead to whether the terms of a transaction are market terms.

More than one measurement basis (paragraphs 6.83–6.86)

BC6.50 The 2018 *Conceptual Framework* discusses situations in which more than one measurement basis is needed for an asset or liability and for related income and expenses to provide users of financial statements with useful information.

BC6.51 One way in which such information could be provided is to use a current measurement basis for an asset or liability in the statement of financial position and to use a different measurement basis for the related income or expenses in the statement of profit or loss. In such cases, the difference between the income or expenses included in the statement of profit or loss and the change in current value of the asset or liability is included in other comprehensive income. As discussed in paragraph 7.17, the Board would decide to require information to be provided in this way only in exceptional circumstances—and only if doing so would result in the statement of profit or loss providing more relevant information or providing a more faithful representation of the entity's financial performance for the period.

Measurement of equity (paragraphs 6.87–6.90)

BC6.52   Although total equity is not measured directly, it may be appropriate to measure directly individual classes of equity or components of equity to provide useful information. The 2018 *Conceptual Framework* discusses this idea.

BC6.53   A few respondents to the 2015 Exposure Draft disagreed with the proposal that some individual classes or components of equity could be measured directly. The respondents said they disagreed because:

(a)   measuring a class of equity or a component of equity directly would be inappropriate because equity is defined as a residual interest; and

(b)   it would be inconsistent with the reporting entity perspective because dividing total equity between classes and into components would result in the reporting of items that do not have a financial effect on the reporting entity as a whole.

BC6.54   Although the total carrying amount of equity (total equity) is measured as a residual, the Board noted that equity is defined as a type of claim—a residual interest in the assets of the entity after deducting all its liabilities. Measuring some classes of equity, or some components of equity, directly does not contradict that definition and differs from measuring total equity directly. Even if some individual classes or components of equity are measured directly, total equity will continue to equal the total of the carrying amounts of all recognised assets minus the total of the carrying amounts of all recognised liabilities. Consequently, if an entity has more than one class of equity or more than one component of equity, at least one of them is measured as a residual.

BC6.55   The Board also concluded that the direct measurement of some individual classes of equity or components of equity would not contradict the entity perspective adopted in financial statements. Those direct measures might provide users of financial statements with information useful in making decisions relating to providing resources to the entity. This information would be provided from the perspective of the entity and reflect the equity claims held against the entity. Such information would not be provided from the perspective of a particular claimholder.

CONTENTS

Introduction

BC7.1   The topic of presentation and disclosure was not addressed in the 2010 *Conceptual Framework*. Respondents to the Board's public consultation on its agenda in 2011 identified this topic as a priority. A particular issue identified was providing information about an entity's financial performance, including the use of other comprehensive income.

BC7.2   In response to that feedback, the 2018 *Conceptual Framework* introduces for the first time:

(a)   concepts that describe how information should be presented and disclosed in financial statements. Those concepts will guide the Board in setting presentation and disclosure requirements in Standards and may guide entities in providing information in financial statements.

(b)   guidance on classifying income and expenses for the Board to use when it decides whether they are included in the statement of profit or loss or are included outside the statement of profit or loss, in other comprehensive income (see paragraphs 7.15–7.18).

(c)   guidance for the Board on whether and when income and expenses included in other comprehensive income should subsequently be reclassified into the statement of profit or loss (paragraph 7.19).

BC7.3   When it issued the 2018 *Conceptual Framework*, the Board was undertaking:

(a)   a Disclosure Initiative, a collection of implementation and research projects aimed at improving disclosure in financial statements by providing additional guidance that builds on the presentation and disclosure concepts set out in the *Conceptual Framework*.

(b)   a research project on primary financial statements. That project was examining potential targeted improvements to the structure and content of the statement(s) of financial performance and the statement of cash flows and perhaps also the statement of financial position and the statement of changes in equity.

Classification of equity (paragraphs 7.12–7.13)

BC7.4   The 2018 *Conceptual Framework* provides only high-level guidance on when it may be appropriate to present separately different classes of equity claims, and different components of equity. This guidance is based on the concepts for classification in paragraphs 7.7–7.8.

BC7.5   The Board may explore enhancements to the statement of changes in equity or other enhancements to presentation or disclosure requirements as part of its research project on Financial Instruments with Characteristics of Equity. Such enhancements might include some approaches the Board explored in the 2013 Discussion Paper.

Classification of income and expenses (paragraphs 7.14–7.19)

Terminology

BC7.6　The 2018 *Conceptual Framework* introduced the term 'statement(s) of financial performance' to refer to the statement or section of profit or loss together with the statement or section showing other comprehensive income.

BC7.7　The 2018 *Conceptual Framework* uses that term because it is consistent with the term 'statement of financial position' used in Standards and is clearer than the term 'statement of comprehensive income' sometimes used by the Board.

BC7.8　In 2007, the Board introduced a requirement to present all income and expenses recognised outside profit or loss in a statement of comprehensive income. The Board also introduced the term 'other comprehensive income' at that point. That term refers to income and expenses not included in the statement of profit of loss. Some respondents suggested that the term 'other comprehensive income' is neither particularly descriptive nor well understood by users of financial statements. Nonetheless, the Board concluded that avoiding the use of that term or using a different term could be confusing. Hence, the 2018 *Conceptual Framework* uses that term.

Approach to guidance on presentation and disclosure of income and expenses

BC7.9　Over the years, the Board has decided that several items of income and expenses may or must be recognised outside profit or loss. Those decisions were made for particular reasons in particular projects, not for a single consistently applied conceptual reason.

BC7.10　The 1989 *Framework* and the 2010 *Conceptual Framework* contained no reference to income or expenses presented outside the statement of profit or loss and no reference to other comprehensive income.

BC7.11　The Board decided it was important for the *Conceptual Framework* to include some discussion of this topic. However, the Board decided that the *Conceptual Framework* should not discuss whether income and expenses should be presented in a single statement of financial performance or in two statements, viewing this as a decision to be made when developing Standards. Since 2007, that decision has been set out in IAS 1 *Presentation of Financial Statements*.

BC7.12　In developing the 2018 *Conceptual Framework*, the Board considered the following questions:

(a)　how to define or describe profit or loss (see paragraphs BC7.15–BC7.20);

(b)　how to decide which income and expenses are included in the statement of profit or loss and which income and expenses are included in other comprehensive income (see paragraphs BC7.21–BC7.25); and

(c)   whether and when the amounts included in other comprehensive income should be reclassified into the statement of profit or loss (see paragraphs BC7.26–BC7.33).

BC7.13   Many respondents to the 2013 Discussion Paper and to the 2015 Exposure Draft expressed a view that the proposed guidance on presentation of income and expenses was insufficient and would not provide the Board with a clear basis for standard-setting. Many respondents asked the Board to do further work on reporting financial performance.

BC7.14   However, the Board decided that the lack of guidance on the presentation of income and expenses was a significant gap in the 2010 *Conceptual Framework*. The Board concluded that it had made significant progress in developing high-level guidance on presentation of income and expenses and that this guidance would help the Board to develop presentation requirements in Standards. Hence, the Board decided to include such guidance in the 2018 *Conceptual Framework*, rather than to explore the use of the statement of profit or loss and other comprehensive income in a separate project. That decision will not preclude further work on reporting financial performance.

Describing profit or loss (paragraph 7.16)

BC7.15   The 2018 *Conceptual Framework* describes:

(a)   the statement of profit or loss as the primary source of information about an entity's financial performance for the reporting period; and

(b)   the total or subtotal for profit or loss as a highly summarised depiction of the entity's financial performance for the period.

BC7.16   Those descriptions are consistent with the fact that many users of financial statements incorporate the total or subtotal for profit or loss in their analysis, either as a starting point or as the main indicator of an entity's financial performance.

BC7.17   Merely describing the statement of profit or loss in the manner set out in paragraph 7.16 will be unlikely to satisfy those who asked for a definition of 'profit or loss' or for a more precise description. However, on the basis of its previous work the Board concluded that no single characteristic, or small number of characteristics, is shared by all items included in the statement of profit or loss but not shared by items that are most appropriately included in other comprehensive income. Consequently, the Board concluded that it is not possible to produce a robust conceptual definition of profit or loss or of other comprehensive income.

BC7.18   The Board also concluded that it could not create a prescriptive list of all categories of items that are most appropriately included in the statement of profit or loss. Such a list could never be complete and would inevitably lead to reporting in other comprehensive income some, perhaps many, items that would generally be regarded as being more appropriately included in the statement of profit or loss.

BC7.19　A number of stakeholders repeatedly asked the Board to define profit or loss. A few of them provided suggestions for how to develop such a definition or for distinguishing income and expenses to be included in the statement of profit or loss from income and expenses to be included in other comprehensive income. However, no consensus on a viable approach emerged.

BC7.20　As discussed in paragraphs BC7.17–BC7.19 of this Basis for Conclusions, the Board concluded that it was not possible to develop a robust conceptual definition of profit or loss or of other comprehensive income or a prescriptive list of all categories of items that are most appropriately included in the statement of profit or loss. Nevertheless, the 2018 *Conceptual Framework* introduces for the first time guidance on when it might be appropriate for the Board to include income or expenses in other comprehensive income. The Board concluded that introducing guidance on this topic was a significant improvement.

Profit or loss and other comprehensive income (paragraph 7.17)

BC7.21　As mentioned in paragraph BC7.17, the Board did not identify a single characteristic or a single set of characteristics shared by all items that are most appropriately included in the statement of profit or loss.

BC7.22　Further, the Board explored whether it might be possible to define a small number of categories of items that would or might be included in other comprehensive income. The Board described one approach to doing that in the 2013 Discussion Paper, but that approach did not attract significant support from respondents.

BC7.23　For the 2018 *Conceptual Framework*, the Board developed an approach to classifying income and expenses that is based on the description of the statement of profit or loss. As mentioned in paragraph BC7.15, that description states that the statement of profit or loss is the primary source of information about an entity's financial performance for the reporting period. If that statement is the primary source of that information, excluding income and expenses from that statement without compelling reasons could make that statement less useful.

BC7.24　Accordingly, the 2018 *Conceptual Framework* sets out a principle that all income and expenses are included in the statement of profit or loss. The Board's intention in establishing this principle was to emphasise that the statement of profit or loss is the default location for income and expenses. Thus, decisions to exclude any income and expenses from the statement of profit or loss and to include them in other comprehensive income can be made only in exceptional circumstances. Those exceptional circumstances would be when the Board concludes that requiring or permitting the exclusion of particular items of income or expenses from the statement of profit or loss would result in the statement of profit or loss providing more relevant information or providing a more faithful representation of an entity's financial performance for that period.

BC7.25   The 2018 *Conceptual Framework* does not include specific guidance on how the Board might reach that conclusion. The Board expects to take that decision when developing Standards and to explain its reasons in the bases for conclusions on those Standards. Entities cannot take that decision (see paragraph 88 of IAS 1).

Reclassifying items into the statement of profit or loss (paragraph 7.19)

BC7.26   The Board considered whether items of income and expenses included in other comprehensive income should be subsequently reclassified into the statement of profit or loss. Such reclassification is sometimes referred to as 'recycling'.

BC7.27   Some of the Standards developed before the 2018 *Conceptual Framework* require such reclassification; other Standards prohibit reclassification. The differences between these requirements arose because the Board had taken different approaches to the issue at different times. Sometimes, the Board's approach was to view the statement(s) of financial performance as a single performance statement so that each item of income or expenses should appear only once in that statement. To be consistent with that approach, the Board generally prohibited reclassification in Standards it developed at those times. At other times, the Board's approach was that all income and expenses should be included in the statement of profit or loss at some point. To achieve that objective, reclassification would be necessary.

BC7.28   It would have been undesirable for the Board's decisions on reclassification to continue to fluctuate over time in line with changes in the composition of the Board and in the Board's approach. Accordingly, the 2018 *Conceptual Framework* sets out the principle that the Board will apply in making decisions about reclassification.

BC7.29   The Board concluded that if the statement of profit or loss is the primary source of information about an entity's financial performance for the period, the cumulative amounts included in that statement over time need to be as complete as possible. Hence, income and expenses can be permanently excluded from the statement of profit or loss only if there is a compelling reason in that particular case.

BC7.30   Accordingly, the 2018 *Conceptual Framework* includes a principle that income and expenses included in other comprehensive income are subsequently reclassified into the statement of profit or loss. The reporting period in which reclassification takes place is the period when doing so results in the statement of profit or loss providing more relevant information or providing a more faithful representation of the entity's financial performance for that period.

BC7.31   Paragraphs 6.83–6.86 describe an approach that uses one measurement basis in the statement of financial position and a different measurement basis in the statement of profit or loss. When this approach is used, reclassification is the only way to ensure that, over the holding period of the asset or liability, the cumulative amount of income or expenses included in the statement of profit or loss for that asset or liability is the amount determined using the measurement basis selected for that statement.

BC7.32 In some cases, it might not be possible to identify any period when reclassifying income and expenses into the statement of profit or loss would have the result described in paragraph BC7.30. In such cases, without an appropriate, non-arbitrary basis for reclassification, reclassification would not provide useful information.

BC7.33 The 2018 *Conceptual Framework* does not include specific guidance on when reclassification would not provide useful information. The Board expects to take that decision when developing Standards and to explain its reasons in the bases for conclusions on those Standards. Entities cannot take that decision.

CHAPTER 8—CONCEPTS OF CAPITAL AND CAPITAL MAINTENANCE

BC8.1   The Board decided that updating the discussion of capital and capital maintenance was not feasible when it developed the 2018 *Conceptual Framework* and could have delayed the completion of the 2018 *Conceptual Framework* significantly.

BC8.2   The Board decided that it would be inappropriate for the 2018 *Conceptual Framework* to exclude a discussion of capital and capital maintenance altogether. Those concepts are important to financial reporting and influence the definitions of income and expenses, the selection of measurement bases, and presentation and disclosure decisions.

BC8.3   Therefore, the material in Chapter 8 — *Concepts of capital and capital maintenance* of the 2018 *Conceptual Framework* has been carried forward unchanged from the 2010 *Conceptual Framework*. That material originally appeared in the 1989 *Framework*.

BC8.4   The Board may decide to revisit the concepts of capital and capital maintenance in the future if it considers such a revision necessary.

IASB documents published to accompany

IFRS 1

First-time Adoption of International Financial Reporting Standards

The text of the unaccompanied standard, IFRS 1, is contained in Part A of this edition. Its effective date when issued was 1 July 2009. The text of the Accompanying Guidance on IFRS 1 is contained in Part B of this edition. This part presents the following documents:

BASIS FOR CONCLUSIONS

APPENDIX TO THE BASIS FOR CONCLUSIONS

Amendments to Basis for Conclusions on other IFRSs

CONTENTS

Basis for Conclusions on
IFRS 1 *First-time Adoption of International Financial Reporting Standards*

This Basis for Conclusions accompanies, but is not part of, IFRS 1.

In this Basis for Conclusions the terminology has not been amended to reflect the changes made by IAS 1 Presentation of Financial Statements *(as revised in 2007).*

This Basis for Conclusions has not been revised to reflect the restructuring of IFRS 1 in November 2008, but cross-references have been updated.

Introduction

BC1   This Basis for Conclusions summarises the International Accounting Standards Board's considerations in reaching the conclusions in IFRS 1 *First-time Adoption of International Financial Reporting Standards*. Individual Board members gave greater weight to some factors than to others.

BC2   SIC-8 *First-time Application of IASs as the Primary Basis of Accounting*, issued in 1998, dealt with matters that arose when an entity first adopted IASs. In 2001, the Board began a project to review SIC-8. In July 2002, the Board published ED 1 *First-time Application of International Financial Reporting Standards*, with a comment deadline of 31 October 2002. The Board received 83 comment letters on ED 1. IFRS 1 was issued by the Board in June 2003.

BC2A   IFRS 1 replaced SIC-8. The Board developed the IFRS to address concerns that:

   (a)   some aspects of SIC-8's requirement for full retrospective application caused costs that exceeded the likely benefits for users of financial statements. Moreover, although SIC-8 did not require retrospective application when this would be impracticable, it did not explain whether a first-time adopter should interpret impracticability as a high hurdle or a low hurdle and it did not specify any particular treatment in cases of impracticability.

   (b)   SIC-8 could require a first-time adopter to apply two different versions of a standard if a new version were introduced during the periods covered by its first financial statements prepared under IASs and the new version prohibited retrospective application.

   (c)   SIC-8 did not state clearly whether a first-time adopter should use hindsight in applying recognition and measurement decisions retrospectively.

   (d)   there was some doubt about how SIC-8 interacted with specific transitional provisions in individual standards.

BC2B   Like SIC-8, IFRS 1 requires retrospective application in most areas. Unlike SIC-8, it:

(a)   includes targeted exemptions to avoid costs that would be likely to exceed the benefits to users of financial statements, and a small number of other exceptions for practical reasons.

(b)   clarifies that an entity applies the latest version of IFRSs.

(c)   clarifies how a first-time adopter's estimates in accordance with IFRSs relate to the estimates it made for the same date in accordance with previous GAAP.

(d)   specifies that the transitional provisions in other IFRSs do not apply to a first-time adopter.

(e)   requires enhanced disclosure about the transition to IFRSs.

BC3   The project took on added significance because of the requirement for listed European Union companies to adopt IFRSs in their consolidated financial statements from 2005. Several other countries announced that they would permit or require entities to adopt IFRSs in the next few years. Nevertheless, the Board's aim in developing the IFRS was to find solutions that would be appropriate for any entity, in any part of the world, regardless of whether adoption occurs in 2005 or at a different time.

Restructuring of the IFRS

BC3A   Since it was issued in 2003, IFRS 1 has been amended many times to accommodate first-time adoption requirements resulting from new or amended IFRSs. Because of the way IFRS 1 was structured, those amendments made the IFRS more complex and less clear. As more amendments become necessary, this problem will become worse.

BC3B   As part of its improvements project in 2007, therefore, the Board proposed to change the structure of IFRS 1 without amending its substance. Respondents to the exposure draft published in October 2007 supported the restructuring. The revised structure of the IFRS issued in November 2008 is easier for the reader to understand and is better designed to accommodate future changes. The focus of the restructuring was to move to appendices all specific exemptions and exceptions from the requirements of IFRSs. Exemptions are categorised into business combinations, exemptions and short-term exemptions. Exemptions are applicable to all first-time adopters regardless of their date of transition to IFRSs. Short-term exemptions are those exemptions applicable to users for a short time. Once those exemptions have become out of date, they will be deleted.

Scope

BC4   The IFRS applies to an entity that presents its first IFRS financial statements (a first-time adopter). Some suggested that an entity should not be regarded as a first-time adopter if its previous financial statements contained an explicit statement of compliance with IFRSs, except for specified (and explicit) departures. They argued that an explicit statement of compliance establishes that an entity regards IFRSs as its basis of accounting, even if the entity does not comply with every requirement of every IFRS. Some regarded this argument as especially strong if an entity previously complied with all recognition and measurement requirements of IFRSs, but did not give some required disclosures—for example, segmental disclosures that IAS 14 *Segment Reporting*[1] requires or the explicit statement of compliance with IFRSs that IAS 1 *Presentation of Financial Statements* requires.

BC5　To implement that approach, it would be necessary to establish how many departures are needed—and how serious they must be—before an entity would conclude that it has not adopted IFRSs. In the Board's view, this would lead to complexity and uncertainty. Also, an entity should not be regarded as having adopted IFRSs if it does not give all disclosures required by IFRSs, because that approach would diminish the importance of disclosures and undermine efforts to promote full compliance with IFRSs. Therefore, the IFRS contains a simple test that gives an unambiguous answer: an entity has adopted IFRSs if, and only if, its financial statements contain an explicit and unreserved statement of compliance with IFRSs (paragraph 3 of the IFRS).

BC6　If an entity's financial statements in previous years contained that statement, any material disclosed or undisclosed departures from IFRSs are errors. The entity applies IAS 8 *Accounting Policies, Changes in Accounting Estimates and Errors* in correcting them.

Repeated application of IFRS 1

BC6A　In *Annual Improvements 2009–2011 Cycle* (issued in May 2012) the Board addressed a request to clarify whether an entity may apply IFRS 1:

(a)　if the entity meets the criteria for applying IFRS 1 and has applied IFRS 1 in a previous reporting period; or

(b)　if the entity meets the criteria for applying IFRS 1 and has applied IFRSs in a previous reporting period when IFRS 1 did not exist.

For example, an entity may have applied IFRS 1 in a previous reporting period to meet listing requirements in a foreign jurisdiction. The entity then delists and no longer presents financial statements in accordance with IFRSs. In a subsequent reporting period, the reporting requirements in the entity's local jurisdiction may change from national GAAP to IFRSs. Consequently, the entity is again required to present its financial statements in accordance with IFRSs.

BC6B　The Board noted that the scope of IFRS 1 focuses on whether an entity's financial statements are its first IFRS financial statements (a term defined in Appendix A). If an entity's financial statements meet the definition of 'first IFRS financial statements', the entity is required to apply IFRS 1 in accordance with paragraph 2(a). However, use of the term 'first' raises the question whether IFRS 1 can be applied more than once.

1　In 2006 IAS 14 was replaced by IFRS 8 *Operating Segments*.

BC6C   In the June 2011 exposure draft the Board proposed to clarify that an entity is required to apply IFRS 1 when the entity's most recent previous annual financial statements do not contain an explicit and unreserved statement of compliance with IFRSs, even if the entity has applied IFRS 1 in a reporting period before the period reported in the most recent previous annual financial statements. However, in the light of respondents' comments on the June 2011 exposure draft, the Board decided that an entity that meets the criteria for applying IFRS 1 and that has applied IFRSs in a previous reporting period (regardless of whether it used IFRS 1 or SIC-8 *First-Time Application of IASs*, if either, when previously adopting) may choose to apply IFRS 1 when it re-adopts IFRSs. The Board decided that the entity should be allowed, rather than required, to apply IFRS 1 because, as explained in paragraph IN5 of IFRS 1, IFRS 1 grants limited exemptions from some requirements of IFRSs on the assumption that the cost of complying with some IFRSs would be likely to exceed the benefits to users of financial statements. However, the costs of applying IFRSs in full might not exceed the benefits of doing so for an entity that had previously applied IFRSs. Consequently, the Board concluded that an entity returning to IFRSs might determine that the benefits of applying IFRSs as if it had continued to do so without interruption would exceed the costs of preparing such information, and that an entity should not be prohibited from following that approach. In applying such an approach, an entity should apply IFRSs retrospectively in accordance with IAS 8 *Accounting Policies, Changes in Estimates and Errors* as if the entity had never stopped applying IFRSs. The Board noted that hindsight is not applied by an entity in preparing IFRS financial statements, whether that entity is applying IFRS 1, or whether that entity applies IFRSs retrospectively as if the entity had never stopped applying them in accordance with IAS 8. The Board noted that paragraphs 14–17 of IFRS 1 and paragraph 53 of IAS 8 provide guidance in this regard.

BC6D   The Board also noted that, in accordance with paragraph 2 of IFRS 1, an entity that has never applied IFRSs in the past would continue to be required to apply IFRS 1 in its first IFRS financial statements.

BC6E   The Board also decided that the entity shall disclose the reason why it stopped applying IFRSs and the reason why it is resuming reporting in accordance with IFRSs. The Board thinks that this disclosure requirement provides users with useful information and would discourage the intentional omission of the statement of compliance with IFRSs solely to allow an entity to take advantage of the exemptions in IFRS 1. The Board also decided that an entity that does not elect to apply IFRS 1 shall explain the reasons why it has elected to apply IFRSs as if it had never stopped applying them. The Board believes that this disclosure ensures that useful information will be provided to users.

Basic concepts

Useful information for users

BC7 In developing recognition and measurement requirements for an entity's opening IFRS balance sheet, the Board referred to the objective of financial statements, as set out in the *Framework for the Preparation and Presentation of Financial Statements*. The *Framework*[2] states that the objective of financial statements is to provide information about the financial position, performance and changes in financial position of an entity that is useful to a wide range of users in making economic decisions.

BC8 The *Framework* identifies four qualitative characteristics that make information in financial statements useful to users. In summary, the information should be:

 (a) readily understandable by users.

 (b) relevant to the decision-making needs of users.

 (c) reliable, in other words financial statements should:

  (i) represent faithfully the transactions and other events they either purport to represent or could reasonably be expected to represent;

  (ii) represent transactions and other events in accordance with their substance and economic reality and not merely their legal form;

  (iii) be neutral, that is to say, free from bias;

  (iv) contend with the uncertainties that inevitably surround many events and circumstances by the exercise of prudence; and

  (v) be complete within the bounds of materiality and cost.

 (d) comparable with information provided by the entity in its financial statements through time and with information provided in the financial statements of other entities.

Comparability

BC9 The previous paragraph notes the need for comparability. Ideally, a regime for first-time adoption of IFRSs would achieve comparability:

 (a) within an entity over time;

 (b) between different first-time adopters; and

 (c) between first-time adopters and entities that already apply IFRSs.

---

2 References to the *Framework* in this Basis for Conclusions are to the IASC's *Framework for the Preparation and Presentation of Financial Statements*, adopted by the Board in 2001 and in effect when the Standard was developed.

BC10   SIC-8 gave priority to ensuring comparability between a first-time adopter and entities that already applied IASs. It was based on the principle that a first-time adopter should comply with the same standards as an entity that already applied IASs. However, the Board decided that it is more important to achieve comparability over time within a first-time adopter's first IFRS financial statements and between different entities adopting IFRSs for the first time at a given date; achieving comparability between first-time adopters and entities that already apply IFRSs is a secondary objective.

Current version of IFRSs

BC11   Paragraphs 7–9 of the IFRS require a first-time adopter to apply the current version of IFRSs, without considering superseded or amended versions.[3] This:

(a)   enhances comparability, because the information in a first-time adopter's first IFRS financial statements is prepared on a consistent basis over time;

(b)   gives users comparative information prepared using later versions of IFRSs that the Board regards as superior to superseded versions; and

(c)   avoids unnecessary costs.

BC11A   Paragraph 7 requires an entity to use the IFRSs that are effective at the end of its first IFRS reporting period. Paragraph 8 allows a first-time adopter to apply a new IFRS that is not yet mandatory if that IFRS permits early application. Notwithstanding the advantages, set out in paragraph BC11, of applying a more recent version of an IFRS, paragraphs 7–8 permit an entity to use either the IFRS that is currently mandatory or the new IFRS that is not yet mandatory, if that new IFRS permits early application. Paragraph 7 requires an entity to apply the same version of the IFRS throughout the periods covered by the entity's first IFRS financial statements. Consequently, if a first-time adopter chooses to early apply a new IFRS, that new IFRS will be applied throughout all the periods presented in its first IFRS financial statements on a retrospective basis, unless IFRS 1 provides an exemption or an exception that permits or requires otherwise.

BC12   In general, the transitional provisions in other IFRSs do not apply to a first-time adopter (paragraph 9 of the IFRS). Some of these transitional provisions require or permit an entity already reporting in accordance with IFRSs to apply a new requirement prospectively. These provisions generally reflect a conclusion that one or both of the following factors are present in a particular case:

(a)   Retrospective application may be difficult or involve costs exceeding the likely benefits. The IFRS permits prospective application in specific cases where this could occur (paragraphs BC30–BC73).

---

3   *Annual Improvements Cycle 2011–2013* clarified that this paragraph does not require an entity to use a more recent version of an IFRS. It only explains the advantages of applying a more recent version of an IFRS. See paragraph BC11A for further details.

(b) There is a danger of abuse if retrospective application would require judgements by management about past conditions after the outcome of a particular transaction is already known. The IFRS prohibits retrospective application in some areas where this could occur (paragraphs BC74–BC84).

BC13 Some have suggested three further reasons for permitting or requiring prospective application in some cases:

(a) to alleviate unforeseen consequences of a new IFRS if another party uses financial statements to monitor compliance with a contract or agreement. However, in the Board's view, it is up to the parties to an agreement to determine whether to insulate the agreement from the effects of a future IFRS and, if not, how they might renegotiate it so that it reflects changes in the underlying financial condition rather than changes in reporting (paragraph 21[4] of the *Preface to International Financial Reporting Standards*).

(b) to give a first-time adopter the same accounting options as an entity that already applies IFRSs. However, permitting prospective application by a first-time adopter would conflict with the Board's primary objective of comparability within an entity's first IFRS financial statements (paragraph BC10). Therefore, the Board did not adopt a general policy of giving first-time adopters the same accounting options of prospective application that existing IFRSs give to entities that already apply IFRSs. Paragraphs BC20–BC23 discuss one specific case, namely derecognition of financial assets and financial liabilities.

(c) to avoid difficult distinctions between changes in estimates and changes in the basis for making estimates. However, a first-time adopter need not make this distinction in preparing its opening IFRS balance sheet, so the IFRS does not include exemptions on these grounds. If an entity becomes aware of errors made under previous GAAP, the IFRS requires it to disclose the correction of the errors (paragraph 26 of the IFRS).

BC14 The Board will consider case by case when it issues a new IFRS whether a first-time adopter should apply that IFRS retrospectively or prospectively. The Board expects that retrospective application will be appropriate in most cases, given its primary objective of comparability over time within a first-time adopter's first IFRS financial statements. However, if the Board concludes in a particular case that prospective application by a first-time adopter is justified, it will amend the IFRS on first-time adoption of IFRSs. As a result, IFRS 1 will contain all material on first-time adoption of IFRSs and other IFRSs will not refer to first-time adopters (except, when needed, in the Basis for Conclusions and consequential amendments).

---

4   Amended to paragraph 13 when the *Preface to IFRS Standards* was revised and renamed in December 2018.

BC15   Under the proposals in ED 1, a first-time adopter could have elected to apply IFRSs as if it had always applied IFRSs. This alternative approach was intended mainly to help an entity that did not wish to use any of the exemptions proposed in ED 1 because it had already been accumulating information in accordance with IFRSs without presenting IFRS financial statements. To enable an entity using this approach to use the information it had already accumulated, ED 1 would have required it to consider superseded versions of IFRSs if more recent versions required prospective application. However, as explained in paragraphs BC28 and BC29, the Board abandoned ED 1's all-or-nothing approach to exemptions. Because this eliminated the reason for the alternative approach, the Board deleted it in finalising the IFRS.

Opening IFRS balance sheet

BC16   An entity's opening IFRS balance sheet is the starting point for its accounting in accordance with IFRSs. The following paragraphs explain how the Board used the *Framework* in developing recognition and measurement requirements for the opening IFRS balance sheet.

Recognition

BC17   The Board considered a suggestion that the IFRS should not require a first-time adopter to investigate transactions that occurred before the beginning of a 'look back' period of, say, three to five years before the date of transition to IFRSs. Some argued that this would be a practical way for a first-time adopter to give a high level of transparency and comparability, without incurring the cost of investigating very old transactions. They noted two particular precedents for transitional provisions that have permitted an entity to omit some assets and liabilities from its balance sheet:

(a)   A previous version of IAS 39 *Financial Instruments: Recognition and Measurement*[5] prohibited restatement of securitisation, transfer or other derecognition transactions entered into before the beginning of the financial year in which it was initially applied.

(b)   Some national accounting standards and IAS 17 *Accounting for Leases* (superseded in 1997 by IAS 17 *Leases*) permitted prospective application of a requirement for lessees to capitalise finance leases. Under this approach, a lessee would not be required to recognise finance lease obligations and the related leased assets for leases that began before a specified date.

BC18   However, limiting the look back period could lead to the omission of material assets or liabilities from an entity's opening IFRS balance sheet. Material omissions would undermine the understandability, relevance, reliability and comparability of an entity's first IFRS financial statements. Therefore, the Board concluded that an entity's opening IFRS balance sheet should:

---

5   IFRS 9 *Financial Instruments* replaced IAS 39. IFRS 9 applies to all items that were previously within the scope of IAS 39.

(a)   include all assets and liabilities whose recognition is required by IFRSs, except:

    (i)   some financial assets or financial liabilities derecognised in accordance with previous GAAP before the date of transition to IFRSs (paragraphs BC20–BC23); and

    (ii)   goodwill and other assets acquired, and liabilities assumed, in a past business combination that were not recognised in the acquirer's consolidated balance sheet in accordance with previous GAAP and also would not qualify for recognition in accordance with IFRSs in the balance sheet of the acquiree (paragraphs BC31–BC40).

(b)   not report items as assets or liabilities if they do not qualify for recognition in accordance with IFRSs.

BC19   Some financial instruments may be classified as equity in accordance with previous GAAP but as financial liabilities in accordance with IAS 32 *Financial Instruments: Presentation*. Some respondents to ED 1 requested an extended transitional period to enable the issuer of such instruments to renegotiate contracts that refer to debt-equity ratios. However, although a new IFRS may have unforeseen consequences if another party uses financial statements to monitor compliance with a contract or agreement, that possibility does not, in the Board's view, justify prospective application (paragraph BC13(a)).

Derecognition in accordance with previous GAAP

BC20   An entity may have derecognised financial assets or financial liabilities in accordance with its previous GAAP that do not qualify for derecognition in accordance with IAS 39.[6] ED 1 proposed that a first-time adopter should recognise those assets and liabilities in its opening IFRS balance sheet. Some respondents to ED 1 requested the Board to permit or require a first-time adopter not to restate past derecognition transactions, on the following grounds:

(a)   Restating past derecognition transactions would be costly, especially if restatement involves determining the fair value of retained servicing assets and liabilities and other components retained in a complex securitisation. Furthermore, it may be difficult to obtain information on financial assets held by transferees that are not under the transferor's control.

(b)   Restatement undermines the legal certainty expected by parties who entered into transactions on the basis of the accounting rules in effect at the time.

---

6   IFRS 9 *Financial Instruments* replaced IAS 39. IFRS 9 applies to all items that were previously within the scope of IAS 39.

(c) IAS 39 did not, before the improvements proposed in June 2002, require (or even permit) entities to restate past derecognition transactions. Without a similar exemption, first-time adopters would be unfairly disadvantaged.

(d) Retrospective application would not result in consistent measurement, as entities would need to recreate information about past transactions with the benefit of hindsight.

BC21 The Board had considered these arguments in developing ED 1. The Board's reasons for the proposal in ED 1 were as follows:

(a) The omission of material assets or liabilities would undermine the understandability, relevance, reliability and comparability of an entity's financial statements. Many of the transactions under discussion are large and will have effects for many years.

(b) Such an exemption would be inconsistent with the June 2002 exposure draft of improvements to IAS 39.

(c) The Board's primary objective is to achieve comparability over time within an entity's first IFRS financial statements. Prospective application by a first-time adopter would conflict with that primary objective, even if prospective application were available to entities already applying IFRSs.

(d) Although a new IFRS may have unforeseen consequences if another party uses financial statements to monitor compliance with a contract or agreement, that possibility does not justify prospective application (paragraph BC13(a)).

BC22 Nevertheless, in finalising the IFRS, the Board concluded that it would be premature to require a treatment different from the current version of IAS 39 before completing the proposed improvements to IAS 39. Accordingly, the IFRS originally required the same treatment as the then current version of IAS 39 for derecognition transactions before the effective date of the then current version of IAS 39, namely that any financial assets or financial liabilities derecognised in accordance with previous GAAP before financial years beginning on 1 January 2001 remain derecognised. The Board agreed that when it completed the improvements to IAS 39, it might amend or delete this exemption.

BC22A The Board reconsidered this issue in completing the revision of IAS 39 in 2003. The Board decided to retain the transition requirements as set out in IFRS 1, for the reasons given in paragraph BC20. However, the Board amended the date from which prospective application was required to transactions that occur on or after 1 January 2004 in order to overcome the practical difficulties of restating transactions that had been derecognised before that date. In 2010 the Board was asked to reconsider whether 1 January 2004 is the appropriate date from which a first-time adopter should be required to restate past derecognition transactions. Constituents were concerned that, as time passes, the fixed transition date of 1 January 2004 becomes more remote and increasingly less relevant to the financial reports as additional jurisdictions adopt IFRSs. The Board accepted that the cost of reconstructing transactions back in time to 1 January 2004 was likely to outweigh the benefit to be achieved in doing so. It therefore amended the fixed date of 1 January 2004 in paragraph B2 to 'the date of transition to IFRSs'. The Board also amended the wording of the illustration in paragraph B2, in order to clarify that it is providing an example.

BC22B   The Board also noted that financial statements that include financial assets and financial liabilities that would otherwise be omitted under the provisions of the IFRS would be more complete and therefore more useful to users of financial statements. The Board therefore decided to permit retrospective application of the derecognition requirements. It also decided that retrospective application should be limited to cases when the information needed to apply the IFRS to past transactions was obtained at the time of initially accounting for those transactions. This limitation prevents the unacceptable use of hindsight.

BC23   The Board removed from IAS 39 the following consequential amendments to IAS 39 made when IFRS 1 was issued, because, for first-time adopters, these clarifications are clear in paragraphs IG26–IG31 and IG53 of the guidance on implementing IFRS 1. These were:

(a)   the clarification that an entity is required to apply IAS 39 to all derivatives or other interests retained after a derecognition transaction, even if the transaction occurred before the effective date of IAS 39; and

(b)   the confirmation that there are no exemptions for special purpose entities[7] that existed before the date of transition to IFRSs.

Measurement

BC24   The Board considered whether it should require a first-time adopter to measure all assets and liabilities at fair value in the opening IFRS balance sheet. Some argued that this would result in more relevant information than an aggregation of costs incurred at different dates, or of costs and fair values. However, the Board concluded that a requirement to measure all assets and liabilities at fair value at the date of transition to IFRSs would be unreasonable, given that an entity may use an IFRS-compliant cost-based measurement before and after that date for some items.

BC25   The Board decided as a general principle that a first-time adopter should measure all assets and liabilities recognised in its opening IFRS balance sheet on the basis required by the relevant IFRSs. This is needed for an entity's first IFRS financial statements to present understandable, relevant, reliable and comparable information.

---

7   SIC-12 Consolidation – Special Purpose Entities was withdrawn and superseded by IFRS 10 Consolidated Financial Statements issued in May 2011. There is no longer specific accounting guidance for special purpose entities because IFRS 10 applies to all types of entities.

Benefits and costs

BC26   The *Framework* acknowledges that the need for a balance between the benefits of information and the cost of providing it may constrain the provision of relevant and reliable information. The Board considered these cost-benefit constraints and developed targeted exemptions from the general principle described in paragraph BC25. SIC-8 did not include specific exemptions of this kind, although it provided general exemptions from:

(a)   retrospective adjustments to the opening balance of retained earnings 'when the amount of the adjustment relating to prior periods cannot be reasonably determined'.

(b)   provision of comparative information when it is 'impracticable' to provide such information.

BC27   The Board expects that most first-time adopters will begin planning on a timely basis for the transition to IFRSs. Accordingly, in balancing benefits and costs, the Board took as its benchmark an entity that plans the transition well in advance and can collect most information needed for its opening IFRS balance sheet at, or very soon after, the date of transition to IFRSs.

BC28   ED 1 proposed that a first-time adopter should use either all the exemptions in ED 1 or none. However, some respondents disagreed with this all-or-nothing approach for the following reasons:

(a)   Many of the exemptions are not interdependent, so there is no conceptual reason to condition use of one exemption on use of other exemptions.

(b)   Although it is necessary to permit some exemptions on pragmatic grounds, entities should be encouraged to use as few exemptions as possible.

(c)   Some of the exemptions proposed in ED 1 were implicit options because they relied on the entity's own judgement of undue cost or effort and some others were explicit options. Only a few exemptions were really mandatory.

(d)   Unlike the other exceptions to retrospective application, the requirement to apply hedge accounting prospectively was not intended as a pragmatic concession on cost-benefit grounds. Retrospective application in an area that relies on designation by management would not be acceptable, even if an entity applied all other aspects of IFRSs retrospectively.

BC29   The Board found these comments persuasive. In finalising the IFRS, the Board grouped the exceptions to retrospective application into two categories:

(a)   Some exceptions consist of optional exemptions (paragraphs BC30–BC63E).

(b)   The other exceptions prohibit full retrospective application of IFRSs to some aspects of derecognition (paragraphs BC20–BC23), hedge accounting (paragraphs BC75–BC80), and estimates (paragraph BC84).

Exemptions from other IFRSs

BC30   An entity may elect to use one or more of the following exemptions:

(a)   business combinations (paragraphs BC31–BC40);

(b)   deemed cost (paragraphs BC41–BC47K);

(c)   employee benefits (paragraphs BC48–BC52);

(d)   cumulative translation differences (paragraphs BC53–BC55C);

(e)   compound financial instruments (paragraphs BC56–BC58);

(f)   investments in subsidiaries, jointly controlled entities[8] and associates (paragraphs BC58A–BC58M);

(g)   assets and liabilities of subsidiaries, associates and joint ventures (paragraphs BC59–BC63);

(h)   designation of previously recognised financial instruments (paragraph BC63A);

(i)   share-based payment transactions (paragraph BC63B);

(j)   changes in existing decommissioning, restoration and similar liabilities included in the cost of property, plant and equipment (paragraphs BC63C and BC63CA);

(k)   leases (paragraphs BC63D–BC63DB);

(l)   borrowing costs (paragraph BC63E);

(m)   severe hyperinflation (paragraphs BC63F–BC63J); and

(n)   joint arrangements (paragraphs BC63K and BC63L).

Business combinations[9]

BC31   The following paragraphs discuss various aspects of accounting for business combinations that an entity recognised in accordance with previous GAAP before the date of transition to IFRSs:

(a)   whether retrospective restatement of past business combinations should be prohibited, permitted or required (paragraphs BC32–BC34).

(b)   whether an entity should recognise assets acquired and liabilities assumed in a past business combination if it did not recognise them in accordance with previous GAAP (paragraph BC35).

(c)   whether an entity should restate amounts assigned to the assets and liabilities of the combining entities if previous GAAP brought forward unchanged their pre-combination carrying amounts (paragraph BC36).

---

8   'Jointly controlled entities' were defined in IAS 31 *Interests in Joint Ventures*. IFRS 11 *Joint Arrangements*, issued in May 2011, replaced IAS 31 and changed the terminology.

9   In October 2012 the Board issued *Investment Entities* (Amendments to IFRS 10, IFRS 12 and IAS 27), which stated that Appendix C of IFRS 1 should only apply to business combinations within the scope of IFRS 3 *Business Combinations*.

(d)   whether an entity should restate goodwill for adjustments made in its opening IFRS balance sheet to the carrying amounts of assets acquired and liabilities assumed in past business combinations (paragraphs BC37–BC40).

BC32   Retrospective application of IFRS 3 *Business Combinations* could require an entity to recreate data that it did not capture at the date of a past business combination and make subjective estimates about conditions that existed at that date. These factors could reduce the relevance and reliability of the entity's first IFRS financial statements. Therefore, ED 1 would have prohibited restatement of past business combinations (unless an entity used the proposed alternative approach, discussed in paragraph BC15, of applying IFRSs as if it had always applied IFRSs). Some respondents agreed, arguing that restatement of past business combinations would involve subjective, and potentially selective, use of hindsight that would diminish the relevance and reliability of financial statements.

BC33   Other respondents disagreed. They argued that:

(a)   effects of business combination accounting can last for many years. Previous GAAP may differ significantly from IFRSs, and in some countries there are no accounting requirements at all for business combinations. Previous GAAP balances might not result in decision-useful information in these countries.

(b)   restatement is preferable and may not involve as much cost or effort for more recent business combinations.

BC34   In the light of these comments, the Board concluded that restatement of past business combinations is conceptually preferable, although for cost-benefit reasons this should be permitted but not required. The Board decided to place some limits on this election and noted that information is more likely to be available for more recent business combinations. Therefore, if a first-time adopter restates any business combination, the IFRS requires it to restate all later business combinations (paragraph C1 of the IFRS).

BC35   If an entity did not recognise a particular asset or liability in accordance with previous GAAP at the date of the business combination, ED 1 proposed that its deemed cost in accordance with IFRSs would be zero. As a result, the entity's opening IFRS balance sheet would not have included that asset or liability if IFRSs permit or require a cost-based measurement. Some respondents to ED 1 argued that this would be an unjustifiable departure from the principle that the opening IFRS balance sheet should include all assets and liabilities. The Board agreed with that conclusion. Therefore, paragraph C4(f) of the IFRS requires that the acquirer should recognise those assets and liabilities and measure them on the basis that IFRSs would require in the separate balance sheet of the acquiree.

BC36   In accordance with previous GAAP, an entity might have brought forward unchanged the pre-combination carrying amounts of the combining entities' assets and liabilities. Some argued that it would be inconsistent to use these carrying amounts as deemed cost in accordance with IFRSs, given that the

IFRS does not permit the use of similar carrying amounts as deemed cost for assets and liabilities that were not acquired in a business combination. However, the Board identified no specific form of past business combination, and no specific form of accounting for past business combinations, for which it would not be acceptable to bring forward cost-based measurements made in accordance with previous GAAP.

BC37   Although the IFRS treats amounts assigned in accordance with previous GAAP to goodwill and other assets acquired and liabilities assumed in a past business combination as their deemed cost in accordance with IFRSs at the date of the business combination, an entity needs to adjust their carrying amounts in its opening IFRS balance sheet, as follows.

(a)   Assets and liabilities measured in accordance with IFRSs at fair value[10] or other forms of current value: remeasure to fair value or that other current value.

(b)   Assets (other than goodwill) and liabilities for which IFRSs apply a cost-based measurement: adjust the accumulated depreciation or amortisation since the date of the business combination if it does not comply with IFRSs. Depreciation is based on deemed cost, which is the carrying amount in accordance with previous GAAP immediately following the business combination.

(c)   Assets (other than goodwill) and liabilities not recognised in accordance with previous GAAP: measure on the basis that IFRSs would require in the separate balance sheet of the acquiree.

(d)   Items that do not qualify for recognition as assets and liabilities in accordance with IFRSs: eliminate from the opening IFRS balance sheet.

BC38   The Board considered whether a first-time adopter should recognise the resulting adjustments by restating goodwill. Because intangible assets and goodwill are closely related, the Board decided that a first-time adopter should restate goodwill when it:

(a)   eliminates an item that was recognised in accordance with previous GAAP as an intangible asset but does not qualify for separate recognition in accordance with IFRSs; or

(b)   recognises an intangible asset that was subsumed within goodwill in accordance with previous GAAP.

However, to avoid costs that would exceed the likely benefits to users, the IFRS prohibits restatement of goodwill for most other adjustments reflected in the opening IFRS balance sheet, unless a first-time adopter elects to apply IFRS 3 retrospectively (paragraph C4(g) of the IFRS).

---

10 IFRS 13 *Fair Value Measurement*, issued in May 2011, defines fair value and contains the requirements for measuring fair value.

BC39　To minimise the possibility of double-counting an item that was included in goodwill in accordance with previous GAAP, and is included in accordance with IFRSs either within the measurement of another asset or as a deduction from a liability, the IFRS requires an entity to test goodwill recognised in its opening IFRS balance sheet for impairment (paragraph C4(g)(ii) of the IFRS). This does not prevent the implicit recognition of internally generated goodwill that arose after the date of the business combination. However, the Board concluded that an attempt to exclude such internally generated goodwill would be costly and lead to arbitrary results.

BC40　Some respondents to ED 1 suggested that a formal impairment test should be required only if there is a possibility of double-counting—ie when additional, previously unrecognised, assets relating to a past business combination are recognised in the opening IFRS balance sheet (or an indicator of impairment is present). However, the Board decided that a first-time adopter should carry out a formal impairment test of all goodwill recognised in its opening IFRS balance sheet, as previous GAAP might not have required a test of comparable rigour.

Deemed cost

BC41　Some measurements in accordance with IFRSs are based on an accumulation of past costs or other transaction data. If an entity has not previously collected the necessary information, collecting or estimating it retrospectively may be costly. To avoid excessive cost, ED 1 proposed that an entity could use the fair value of an item of property, plant and equipment at the date of transition to IFRSs as its deemed cost at that date if determining a cost-based measurement in accordance with IFRSs would involve undue cost or effort.

BC42　In finalising the IFRS, the Board noted that reconstructed cost data might be less relevant to users, and less reliable, than current fair value data. Furthermore, the Board concluded that balancing costs and benefits was a task for the Board when it sets accounting requirements rather than for entities when they apply those requirements. Therefore, the IFRS permits an entity to use fair value as deemed cost in some cases without any need to demonstrate undue cost or effort.

BC43　Some expressed concerns that the use of fair value would lead to lack of comparability. However, cost is generally equivalent to fair value at the date of acquisition. Therefore, the use of fair value as the deemed cost of an asset means that an entity will report the same cost data as if it had acquired an asset with the same remaining service potential at the date of transition to IFRSs. If there is any lack of comparability, it arises from the aggregation of costs incurred at different dates, rather than from the targeted use of fair value as deemed cost for some assets. The Board regarded this approach as justified to solve the unique problem of introducing IFRSs in a cost-effective way without damaging transparency.

BC44　The IFRS restricts the use of fair value as deemed cost to those assets for which reconstructing costs is likely to be of limited benefit to users and particularly onerous: property, plant and equipment, investment property (if an entity elects to use the cost method in IAS 40 *Investment Property*) and intangible assets that meet restrictive criteria (paragraphs D5 and D7 of the IFRS).

BC45   Under the revaluation model in IAS 16 *Property, Plant and Equipment*, if an entity revalues an asset, it must revalue all assets in that class. This restriction prevents selective revaluation of only those assets whose revaluation would lead to a particular result. Some suggested a similar restriction on the use of fair value as deemed cost. However, IAS 36 *Impairment of Assets* requires an impairment test if there is any indication that an asset is impaired. Thus, if an entity uses fair value as deemed cost for assets whose fair value is above cost, it cannot ignore indications that the recoverable amount of other assets may have fallen below their carrying amount. Therefore, the IFRS does not restrict the use of fair value as deemed cost to entire classes of asset.

BC46   Some revaluations in accordance with previous GAAP might be more relevant to users than original cost. If so, it would not be reasonable to require time-consuming and expensive reconstruction of a cost that complies with IFRSs. In consequence, the IFRS permits an entity to use amounts determined using previous GAAP as deemed cost for IFRSs in the following cases:

(a)   if an entity revalued one of the assets described in paragraph BC44 using its previous GAAP and the revaluation met specified criteria (paragraphs D6 and D7 of the IFRS).

(b)   if an entity established a deemed cost in accordance with previous GAAP for some or all assets and liabilities by measuring them at their fair value at one particular date because of an event such as a privatisation or initial public offering (paragraph D8 of the IFRS).

BC46A   In *Improvements to IFRSs* issued in May 2010, the Board extended the scope of paragraph D8 for the use of the deemed cost exemption for an event-driven fair value. In some jurisdictions, local law requires an entity to revalue its assets and liabilities to fair value for a privatisation or initial public offering (IPO) and to treat the revalued amounts as deemed cost for the entity's previous GAAP. Before the amendment made in May 2010, if that revaluation occurred after the entity's date of transition to IFRSs, the entity could not have used that revaluation as deemed cost for IFRSs. Therefore, the entity would have had to prepare two sets of measurements for its assets and liabilities — one to comply with IFRSs, and one to comply with local law. The Board considered this unduly onerous. Therefore, the Board amended paragraph D8 to allow an entity to recognise an event-driven fair value measurement as deemed cost when the event occurs, provided that this is during the periods covered by its first IFRS financial statements. In addition, the Board concluded that the same relief should apply to an entity that adopted IFRSs in periods before the effective date of IFRS 1 or applied IFRS 1 in a previous period, provided the measurement date is within the period covered by its first IFRS financial statements.

BC46B   The Board also decided to require the entity to present historical costs or other amounts already permitted by IFRS 1 for the periods before that date. In this regard, the Board considered an approach where an entity could 'work back' to the deemed cost on the date of transition, using the revaluation amounts obtained on the measurement date, adjusted to exclude any depreciation, amortisation or impairment between the two dates. Although some believed that this presentation would have provided greater comparability throughout the first IFRS reporting period, the Board rejected it because making such adjustments would require hindsight and the computed carrying amounts on the date of transition to IFRSs would be neither the historical costs of the revalued assets nor their fair values on that date.

BC47   Paragraph D6 of the IFRS refers to revaluations that are broadly comparable to fair value or reflect an index applied to a cost that is broadly comparable to cost determined in accordance with IFRSs. It may not always be clear whether a previous revaluation was intended as a measure of fair value or differs materially from fair value. The flexibility in this area permits a cost-effective solution for the unique problem of transition to IFRSs. It allows a first-time adopter to establish a deemed cost using a measurement that is already available and is a reasonable starting point for a cost-based measurement.

BC47A   Under their previous GAAP many oil and gas entities accounted for exploration and development costs for properties in development or production in cost centres that include all properties in a large geographical area. (In some jurisdictions, this is referred to as full cost accounting.) Those entities will in most cases have to determine the carrying amounts for oil and gas assets at the date of transition to IFRSs. Information about oil and gas assets recorded in an accounting system using this method of accounting will almost always be at a larger unit of account than the unit of account that is acceptable under IFRSs. Amortisation at the IFRS unit of account level would also have to be calculated (on a unit of production basis) for each year, using a reserves base that has changed over time because of changes in factors such as geological understanding and prices for oil and gas. In many cases, particularly for older assets, this information may not be available. The Board was advised that even if such information is available the effort and associated cost to determine the opening balances at the date of transition would usually be very high.

BC47B   IFRS 1 permits an entity to measure an item of property, plant and equipment at its fair value at the date of transition to IFRSs and to use that fair value as the item's deemed cost at that date. Determining the fair value of oil and gas assets is a complex process that begins with the difficult task of estimating the volume of reserves and resources. When the fair value amounts must be audited, determining significant inputs to the estimates generally requires the use of qualified external experts. For entities with many oil and gas assets, the use of this fair value as deemed cost alternative would not meet the Board's stated intention of avoiding excessive cost (see paragraph BC41).

BC47C   The Board decided that for oil and gas assets in the development or production phases, it would permit entities that used the method of accounting described in paragraph BC47A under their previous GAAP to determine the deemed cost at the date of transition to IFRSs using an allocation of the amount determined for a cost centre under the entity's previous GAAP on the basis of the reserves associated with the oil and gas assets in that cost centre.

BC47D   The deemed cost of oil and gas assets determined in this way may include amounts that would not have been capitalised in accordance with IFRSs, such as some overhead costs, costs that were incurred before the entity obtained legal rights to explore a specific area (and cannot be capitalised in accordance with IAS 38 *Intangible Assets*) and, most significantly, unsuccessful exploration costs. This is a consequence of having included these costs in the single carrying amount under the method of accounting described in paragraph BC47A. To avoid the use of deemed costs resulting in an oil and gas asset being measured at more than its recoverable amount, the Board decided that oil and gas assets should be tested for impairment at the date of transition to IFRSs.

BC47E   Not all oil and gas entities used the method of accounting described in paragraph BC47A under their previous GAAP. Some used a method of accounting that requires a unit of account that is generally consistent with IFRSs and does not cause similar transition issues. Therefore, the Board decided that the exemption would apply only to entities that used the method of accounting described in paragraph BC47A under their previous GAAP.

BC47F   In *Improvements to IFRSs* issued in May 2010, the Board extended the use of the deemed cost exemption to entities with operations subject to rate regulation. An entity might have items of property, plant and equipment or intangible assets that it holds for use in operations subject to rate regulation, or that it once used for this purpose and now holds for other purposes. Under previous GAAP, an entity might have capitalised, as part of the carrying amount of items of property, plant and equipment or intangible assets held for use in operations subject to rate regulation, amounts that do not qualify for capitalisation under IFRSs. For example, when setting rates regulators often permit entities to capitalise, as part of the cost of property, plant and equipment or intangible assets acquired, constructed or produced over time, an allowance for the cost of financing the asset's acquisition, construction or production. This allowance typically includes an imputed cost of equity. IFRSs do not permit an entity to capitalise an imputed cost of equity.

BC47G   Before this amendment, an entity with such items whose carrying amounts include amounts that do not qualify for capitalisation under IFRSs would have had either to restate those items retrospectively to remove the non-qualifying amounts, or to use the exemption in paragraph D5 (fair value as deemed cost). Both of those alternatives pose significant practical challenges, the cost of which can often outweigh the benefit.

BC47H   Typically, once amounts are included in the total cost of an item of property, plant and equipment, they are no longer tracked separately. The restatement of property, plant and equipment to remove amounts not in compliance with IFRSs would require historical information that, given the typical age of some of the assets involved, is probably no longer available and would be difficult to estimate. Obtaining the fair value information necessary to use the exemption in paragraph D5 may not be a practical alternative, given the lack of readily available fair value information for those assets.

BC47I   The Board decided it would permit entities with operations subject to rate regulation to use as deemed cost at the date of transition to IFRSs the carrying amount of the items of property, plant and equipment or intangible assets determined under the entity's previous GAAP. The Board views this exemption as consistent with the exemptions already included in IFRS 1 in that it avoids excessive costs while meeting the objectives of the IFRS.

BC47J   The Board understands that most first-time adopters with operations subject to rate regulation have previously accounted for property, plant and equipment largely in accordance with a historical cost model consistent with IAS 16. The Board concluded that the cost and effort required to achieve total compliance in this area for the purposes of preparing an entity's first IFRS financial statements is not warranted to meet the objective of providing a suitable starting point for accounting under IFRSs. IFRS 1 requires that each item for which the exemption is used is tested for impairment, either individually or at the cash-generating unit to which the item belongs in accordance with IAS 36, at the date of transition. This requirement provides further assurance that this objective is met.

BC47K   Consistent with the Board's rationale for the use of fair value as deemed cost in paragraphs BC43 and BC44, this exemption means that an entity will report the same cost data as if it had acquired an asset with the same remaining service potential for that amount at the date of transition to IFRSs. An entity's use of this exemption results in a new cost basis for the item and previous GAAP depreciation methods and capitalisation policies are not relevant. Thus, if an entity uses this exemption for items of property, plant and equipment or intangible assets, it does not also apply the exemption for borrowing costs provided in paragraph D23.

Employee benefits

BC48   [Deleted]

BC49   The revision of IAS 19 in 1998 increased the reported employee benefit liabilities of some entities. IAS 19 permitted entities to amortise that increase over up to five years. Some suggested a similar transitional treatment for first-time adopters. However, the Board has no general policy of exempting transactions occurring before a specific date from the requirements of new IFRSs (paragraph 21[11] of the *Preface to International Financial Reporting Standards*). Therefore, the Board did not include a similar transitional provision for first-time adopters.

BC50   An entity's first IFRS financial statements may reflect measurements of pension liabilities at three dates: the reporting date, the end of the comparative year and the date of transition to IFRSs. Some suggested that obtaining three separate actuarial valuations for a single set of financial statements would be costly. Therefore, they proposed that the Board should permit an entity to use a single actuarial valuation, based, for example, on

---

11 Amended to paragraph 13 when the *Preface to IFRS Standards* was revised and renamed in December 2018.

assumptions valid at the reporting date, with service costs and interest costs based on those assumptions for each of the periods presented.

BC51　However, the Board concluded that a general exemption from the principle of measurement at each date would conflict with the objective of providing understandable, relevant, reliable and comparable information for users. If an entity obtains a full actuarial valuation at one or two of these dates and rolls that (those) valuation(s) forward or back to the other date(s), any such roll forward or roll back needs to reflect material transactions and other material events (including changes in market prices and interest rates) between those dates (IAS 19 paragraph 57).

BC52　[Deleted]

Cumulative translation differences

BC53　IAS 21 *The Effects of Changes in Foreign Exchange Rates* requires an entity to classify some cumulative translation differences (CTDs) relating to a net investment in a foreign operation as a separate component of equity. The entity transfers the CTDs to the income statement on subsequent disposal of the foreign operation. The proposals in ED 1 would have permitted a first-time adopter to use the CTDs in accordance with previous GAAP as the deemed CTDs in accordance with IFRSs if reconstructing CTDs would have involved undue cost or effort.

BC54　Some respondents to ED 1 argued that it would be more transparent and comparable to exempt an entity from the requirement to identify CTDs at the date of transition to IFRSs, for the following reasons:

(a)　An entity might know the aggregate CTDs, but might not know the amount for each subsidiary. If so, it could not transfer that amount to the income statement on disposal of that subsidiary. This would defeat the objective of identifying CTDs as a separate component of equity.

(b)　The amount of CTDs in accordance with previous GAAP might be inappropriate as it might be affected by adjustments made on transition to IFRSs to assets and liabilities of foreign entities.

BC55　The Board found these arguments persuasive. Therefore, a first-time adopter need not identify the CTDs at the date of transition to IFRSs (paragraphs D12 and D13 of the IFRS). The first-time adopter need not show that identifying the CTDs would involve undue cost or effort.

Subsidiary as a First-time Adopter (Annual Improvements to IFRS Standards 2018–2020)

BC55A　Paragraph D16(a) provides a subsidiary that becomes a first-time adopter later than its parent with an exemption relating to the measurement of its assets and liabilities. Paragraphs BC59–BC60 explain that the Board provided this exemption so that a subsidiary would not have to keep two parallel sets of accounting records based on different dates of transition to IFRSs.

BC55B   The exemption in paragraph D16(a) does not apply to components of equity. Accordingly, before the amendment that added paragraph D13A, a subsidiary that became a first-time adopter later than its parent might have been required to keep two parallel sets of accounting records for cumulative translation differences based on different dates of transition to IFRSs. Following the rationale in paragraphs BC59–BC60, the Board decided to extend the exemption in paragraph D16(a) to cumulative translation differences to reduce costs for first-time adopters. The Board noted that IFRS 1 already provides an exemption relating to cumulative translation differences. Extending the exemption in paragraph D16(a) would therefore not diminish the relevance of information reported by a subsidiary that becomes a first-time adopter later than its parent.

BC55C   Entities that apply paragraph D16(a) could in some situations find it burdensome to measure cumulative translation differences using the amount reported by the parent. The Board therefore decided to permit, but not require, a subsidiary applying paragraph D16(a) to use that exemption for cumulative translation differences. The amendment also applies to an associate or joint venture that uses the exemption in paragraph D16(a).

Compound financial instruments

BC56   IAS 32 requires an entity to split a compound financial instrument at inception into separate liability and equity components. Even if the liability component is no longer outstanding, retrospective application of IAS 32 would involve separating two portions of equity. The first portion is in retained earnings and represents the cumulative interest accreted on the liability component. The other portion represents the original equity component of the instrument.

BC57   Some respondents to ED 1 argued that separating these two portions would be costly if the liability component of the compound instrument is no longer outstanding at the date of transition to IFRSs. The Board agreed with those comments. Therefore, if the liability component is no longer outstanding at the date of transition to IFRSs, a first-time adopter need not separate the cumulative interest on the liability component from the equity component (paragraph D18 of the IFRS).

BC58   Some respondents requested an exemption for compound instruments even if still outstanding at the date of transition to IFRSs. One possible approach would be to use the fair value of the components at the date of transition to IFRSs as deemed cost. However, as the IFRS does not include any exemptions for financial liabilities, the Board concluded that it would be inconsistent to create such an exemption for the liability component of a compound instrument.

Investments in subsidiaries, jointly controlled entities[12] and associates

BC58A IAS 27 *Consolidated and Separate Financial Statements* requires an entity, in its separate financial statements, to account for investments in subsidiaries, jointly controlled entities and associates either at cost or in accordance with IAS 39.[13,14] For those investments that are measured at cost, the previous version of IAS 27 (before *Cost of an Investment* in a *Subsidiary, Jointly Controlled Entity or Associate* was issued in May 2008) required an entity to recognise income from the investment only to the extent the entity received distributions from post-acquisition retained earnings (the 'cost method'). Distributions received in excess of such profits were regarded as a recovery of investment and were recognised as a reduction in the cost of the investment.

BC58B For some jurisdictions, these aspects of IAS 27 led to practical difficulties on transition to IFRSs. In order to apply IAS 27 retrospectively, it would be necessary:

(a) to measure the fair value of the consideration given at the date of acquisition; and

(b) to determine whether any dividends received from a subsidiary after its acquisition were paid out of pre-acquisition retained earnings, which would reduce the carrying amount of the investment in the subsidiary in the parent's separate financial statements.

BC58C If a parent held an investment in a subsidiary for many years, such an exercise might be difficult, or even impossible, and perhaps costly. For example, in some jurisdictions, entities accounted for some previous acquisitions that were share-for-share exchanges using so-called 'merger relief' or 'group reconstruction relief'. In this situation, the carrying amount of the investment in the parent's separate financial statements was based on the nominal value of the shares given rather than the value of the purchase consideration. This might make it difficult or impossible to measure the fair value of the shares given.

BC58D The Board published *Cost of an Investment in a Subsidiary*, an exposure draft of proposed amendments to IFRS 1, in January 2007. In response to the issues outlined in paragraphs BC58A–BC58C, the Board proposed two exemptions from applying the requirements of IAS 27 retrospectively upon first-time adoption of IFRSs:

(a) an alternative approach for determining the cost of an investment in a subsidiary in the separate financial statements of a parent; and

(b) simplification of the process for determining the pre-acquisition retained earnings of that subsidiary.

---

12 'Jointly controlled entities' were defined in IAS 31 *Interests in Joint Ventures*. IFRS 11 *Joint Arrangements*, issued in May 2011, replaced IAS 31 and changed the terminology.

13 The consolidation guidance was removed from IAS 27 and the Standard was renamed *Separate Financial Statements* by IFRS 10 *Consolidated Financial Statements* issued in May 2011. The accounting requirements for separate financial statements were not changed.

14 IFRS 9 *Financial Instruments* replaced IAS 39. IFRS 9 applies to all items that were previously within the scope of IAS 39.

BC58E   In developing that exposure draft, the Board considered three ways of determining a deemed cost of an investment in a subsidiary at the parent's date of transition to IFRSs in its separate financial statements. These were:

(a)   the previous GAAP cost of the investment (previous GAAP deemed cost).

(b)   the parent's interest in the subsidiary's assets less liabilities, using the carrying amounts that IFRSs would require in the subsidiary's statement of financial position (net asset deemed cost).

(c)   the fair value of the investment (fair value deemed cost).

BC58F   The Board decided that the net asset deemed cost option would provide relevant information to users about the subsidiary's financial position at the date of transition to IFRSs and would be relatively easy to determine. The fair value deemed cost option would provide relevant information at the date of transition to IFRSs, but might be more costly and difficult to determine.

BC58G   In some situations, the cost of an investment in a subsidiary determined using the previous GAAP carrying amount might bear little resemblance to cost determined in accordance with IAS 27. Therefore, the Board rejected the use of a deemed cost based on the previous GAAP carrying amount. The Board proposed to allow entities a choice between the net asset deemed cost and the fair value deemed cost.

BC58H   Respondents to the exposure draft stated that the previous GAAP carrying amount is a more appropriate deemed cost. They argued that:

(a)   a net asset deemed cost would not include goodwill or other intangible assets that might be present in a carrying amount determined in accordance with previous GAAP. When this is the case, the net asset deemed cost option would understate the assets of the entities for which it is used. The resulting reduction in the carrying amount of the investment could reduce the distributable profits of the parent.

(b)   it was difficult to see why, in the light of the exemption in IFRS 1 from applying IFRS 3 retrospectively, the Board did not propose to permit the cost of the investment in a subsidiary in accordance with previous GAAP to be used as a deemed cost. When an entity had chosen not to apply IFRS 3 retrospectively to a past business combination, it would be logical not to require it to restate the cost of the related investment in the separate financial statements of the parent.

BC58I   In the light of respondents' comments, the Board observed that, in many instances, neither the previous GAAP carrying amount nor the net asset deemed cost represents 'cost'—both numbers could be viewed as being equally arbitrary.

BC58J   In order to reduce the cost of adopting IFRSs in the parent entity's separate financial statements without significantly reducing the benefits of those statements, the Board decided to allow entities a choice between the previous GAAP carrying amount and the fair value as deemed cost.

BC58K   The Board also agreed with respondents that similar issues arise for investments in associates and jointly controlled entities.[15] As a result, paragraph D15 of the IFRS applies to such investments.

BC58L   The Board published its revised proposals in *Cost of an Investment in a Subsidiary, Jointly Controlled Entity or Associate*, an exposure draft of proposed amendments to IFRS 1 and IAS 27, in December 2007. Respondents generally supported the proposed amendments to IFRS 1. The Board included the amendments in *Cost of an Investment in a Subsidiary, Jointly Controlled Entity or Associate* issued in May 2008.

BC58M   In developing the December 2007 exposure draft, the Board decided to address the simplification of the process for determining the pre-acquisition retained earnings of a subsidiary more generally through an amendment to IAS 27 (see paragraph 38A of IAS 27 and paragraphs BC66D–BC66J[16] of the Basis for Conclusions on IAS 27).

Assets and liabilities of subsidiaries, associates and joint ventures

BC59   A subsidiary may have reported to its parent in the previous period using IFRSs without presenting a full set of financial statements in accordance with IFRSs. If the subsidiary subsequently begins to present financial statements that contain an explicit and unreserved statement of compliance with IFRSs, it becomes a first-time adopter at that time. This might compel the subsidiary to keep two parallel sets of accounting records based on different dates of transition to IFRSs, because some measurements in accordance with the IFRS depend on the date of transition to IFRSs.

BC60   In developing ED 1, the Board concluded that a requirement to keep two parallel sets of records would be burdensome and not be beneficial to users. Therefore, ED 1 proposed that a subsidiary would not be treated as a first-time adopter for recognition and measurement purposes if the subsidiary was consolidated in IFRS financial statements for the previous period and all owners of the minority interests consented.[17]

BC61   Some respondents to ED 1 opposed the exemption, on the following grounds:

    (a)   The exemption would not eliminate all differences between the group reporting package and the subsidiary's own financial statements. The reporting package does not constitute a full set of financial statements, the parent may have made adjustments to the reported numbers (for example, if pension cost adjustments were made centrally), and the group materiality threshold may be higher than for the subsidiary.

---

15 'Jointly controlled entities' were defined in IAS 31 *Interests in Joint Ventures*. IFRS 11 *Joint Arrangements*, issued in May 2011, replaced IAS 31 and changed the terminology.

16 renumbered to paragraphs 12 and BC16–BC22 when IAS 27 was amended in May 2011.

17 In January 2008 the IASB issued an amended IAS 27 *Consolidated and Separate Financial Statements*, which amended 'minority interests' to 'non-controlling interests'. The consolidation requirements in IAS 27 were superseded by IFRS 10 *Consolidated Financial Statements* issued in May 2011. The term 'non-controlling interests' and the requirements for non-controlling interests were not changed.

(b)   The Board's objective of comparability between different entities adopting IFRSs for the first time at the same date (paragraph BC10) should apply equally to any entity, including subsidiaries, particularly if the subsidiary's debt or equity securities are publicly traded.

BC62   However, the Board retained the exemption because it will ease some practical problems. Although the exemption does not eliminate all differences between the subsidiary's financial statements and a group reporting package, it does reduce them. Furthermore, the exemption does not diminish the relevance and reliability of the subsidiary's financial statements because it permits a measurement that is already acceptable in accordance with IFRSs in the consolidated financial statements of the parent. Therefore, the Board also eliminated the proposal in ED 1 that the exemption should be conditional on the consent of minorities.

BC63   In finalising the IFRS, the Board simplified the description of the exemption for a subsidiary that adopts IFRSs after its parent. In accordance with the IFRS, the subsidiary may measure its assets and liabilities at the carrying amounts that would be included in the parent's consolidated financial statements, based on the parent's date of transition to IFRSs, if no adjustments were made for consolidation procedures and for the effects of the business combination in which the parent acquired the subsidiary.[18] Alternatively, it may elect to measure them at the carrying amounts required by the rest of the IFRS, based on the subsidiary's date of transition to IFRSs. The Board also extended the exemption to an associate or joint venture that becomes a first-time adopter later than an entity that has significant influence or joint control over it (paragraph D16 of the IFRS). However, if a parent adopts IFRSs later than a subsidiary, the parent cannot, in its consolidated financial statements, elect to change IFRS measurements that the subsidiary has already used in its financial statements, except to adjust for consolidation procedures and for the effects of the business combination in which the parent acquired the subsidiary[19] (paragraph D17 of the IFRS).

Designation of previously recognised financial instruments

BC63A   IAS 39[20] permits an entity to designate, on initial recognition only, a financial instrument as (a) available for sale[21] (for a financial asset) or (b) a financial asset or financial liability at fair value through profit or loss (provided the asset or liability qualifies for such designation in accordance with paragraph 9(b)(i), 9(b)(ii)). Despite this requirement, an entity that had already applied IFRSs before the effective date of IAS 39 (as revised in March 2004) may (a) designate a previously recognised financial asset as available for sale

---

18   In October 2012 the Board issued *Investment Entities* (Amendments to IFRS 10, IFRS 12 and IAS 27), which removed option D16(a) for investments in subsidiaries of investment entities, as defined in IFRS 10 *Consolidated Financial Statements*, required to be measured at fair value through profit or loss.

19   In October 2012 the Board issued *Investment Entities* (Amendments to IFRS 10, IFRS 12 and IAS 27), which amended paragraph D17 to clarify its application to investment entities, as defined in IFRS 10.

20   IFRS 9 *Financial Instruments* replaced IAS 39. IFRS 9 applies to all items that were previously within the scope of IAS 39.

21   IFRS 9 *Financial Instruments* eliminated the category of available-for-sale financial assets.

on initial application of IAS 39 (as revised in March 2004), or (b) designate a previously recognised financial instrument as at fair value through profit or loss in the circumstances specified in paragraph 105B of IAS 39. The Board decided that the same considerations apply to first-time adopters as to entities that already apply IFRSs. Accordingly, a first-time adopter of IFRSs may similarly designate a previously recognised financial instrument in accordance with paragraph D19 of the IFRS. Such an entity shall disclose the fair value of the financial assets or financial liabilities designated into each category at the date of designation and their classification and carrying amount in the previous financial statements.

Share-based payment transactions

BC63B   IFRS 2 *Share-based Payment* contains various transitional provisions. For example, for equity-settled share-based payment arrangements, IFRS 2 requires an entity to apply IFRS 2 to shares, share options or other equity instruments that were granted after 7 November 2002 and had not vested at the effective date of IFRS 2. IFRS 2 is effective for annual periods beginning on or after 1 January 2005. There are also transitional arrangements for liabilities arising from cash-settled share-based payment transactions, and for modifications of the terms or conditions of a grant of equity instruments to which IFRS 2 has not been applied, if the modification occurs after the effective date of IFRS 2. The Board decided that, in general, first-time adopters should be treated in the same way as entities that already apply IFRSs. For example, a first-time adopter should not be required to apply IFRS 2 to equity instruments that were granted on or before 7 November 2002. Similarly, a first-time adopter should not be required to apply IFRS 2 to equity instruments that were granted after 7 November 2002 if those equity instruments vested before 1 January 2005. In addition, the Board decided that a first-time adopter should not be required to apply IFRS 2 to equity instruments that were granted after 7 November 2002 if those equity instruments vested before the date of transition to IFRSs. Similarly, the Board decided that a first-time adopter should not be required to apply IFRS 2 to liabilities arising from cash-settled share-based payment transactions if those liabilities were settled before the date of transition to IFRSs.

Changes in existing decommissioning, restoration and similar liabilities included in the cost of property, plant and equipment

BC63C   IFRIC 1 *Changes in Existing Decommissioning, Restoration and Similar Liabilities* requires specified changes in decommissioning, restoration and similar liabilities to be added to, or deducted from, the cost of the assets to which they relate, and the adjusted depreciable amount to be depreciated prospectively over the remaining useful life of those assets. Retrospective application of this requirement at the date of transition would require an entity to construct a historical record of all such adjustments that would have been made in the past. In many cases this will not be practicable. The Board agreed that, as an alternative to complying with this requirement, an entity should be permitted to include in the depreciated cost of the asset, at the date of transition to IFRSs, an amount calculated by discounting the liability at that date back to, and depreciating it from, when the liability was first incurred.

BC63CA   Paragraph D21 of the IFRS exempts from the requirements of IFRIC 1 *Changes in Existing Decommissioning, Restoration and Similar Liabilities* changes in decommissioning costs incurred before the date of transition to IFRSs. Use of this exemption would require detailed calculations that would not be practicable for entities that used the method of accounting described in paragraph BC47A under their previous GAAP. The Board noted that adjustments to liabilities as a result of initial adoption of IFRSs arise from events and transactions before the date of transition to IFRSs and are generally recognised in retained earnings. Therefore, the Board decided that, for entities that used the method of accounting described in paragraph BC47A, any adjustment for a difference between decommissioning, restoration and similar liabilities measured in accordance with IAS 37 and the liability determined under the entity's previous GAAP should be accounted for in the same manner.

Leases

BC63D   IFRIC 4 *Determining whether an Arrangement contains a Lease* contains transitional provisions because the IFRIC acknowledged the practical difficulties raised by full retrospective application of the Interpretation, in particular the difficulty of going back potentially many years and making a meaningful assessment of whether the arrangement satisfied the criteria at that time. The Board decided to treat first-time adopters in the same way as entities that already apply IFRSs.

BC63DA   IFRIC 4 permits an entity to apply its requirements to arrangements existing at the start of the earliest period for which comparative information is presented on the basis of facts and circumstances existing at the start of that period. Before adopting IFRSs, a jurisdiction might adopt a national standard having the same effect as the requirements of IFRIC 4, including the same transitional provisions. An entity in that jurisdiction might then apply requirements having the same effect as the requirements of IFRIC 4 to some or all arrangements (even if the wording of those requirements is not identical). However, the entity might apply the requirements at a date different from the date in the transitional provisions of IFRIC 4. IFRS 1 would require such an entity to reassess that accounting retrospectively on first-time adoption. This might result in additional costs, with no obvious benefits. Accordingly, the Board decided that if a first-time adopter made the same determination under previous GAAP as that required by IFRIC 4 but at a date other than that required by IFRIC 4, the first-time adopter need not reassess that determination when it adopts IFRSs.

BC63DB   The Board considered a more general modification to IFRS 1. It considered whether to modify IFRS 1 so that entities need not reassess, at the date of transition to IFRSs, prior accounting if that prior accounting permitted the same prospective application as IFRSs with the only difference from IFRSs being the effective date from when that accounting was applied. In this regard, the Board noted that any such proposal must apply to assessments resulting in the *same* determination, rather than *similar* determinations, because it would be too difficult to determine and enforce what constitutes a sufficient degree of similarity. The Board noted that many of the circumstances in which this situation might arise have been dealt with in IFRS 1 or other IFRSs. Accordingly, the Board decided to focus on IFRIC 4 only.

Borrowing costs

BC63E   IAS 23 *Borrowing Costs* (as revised in 2007) contains transitional provisions because the Board acknowledged that if an entity has been following the accounting policy of immediately recognising borrowing costs as an expense and has not previously gathered the necessary information for capitalisation of borrowing costs, getting the information retrospectively may be costly. First-time adopters of IFRSs face problems similar to those facing entities that already apply IFRSs. Moreover, although first-time adopters have the option of using fair value as the deemed cost of an asset at the date of transition to IFRSs, this option is not applicable to all qualifying assets, such as inventories. Furthermore, the Board concluded that the existence of the deemed cost option is not sufficient to justify a more stringent requirement for the application of IAS 23 for first-time adopters than for entities that already apply IFRSs. A more stringent requirement for the adoption of the capitalisation treatment could be justified when IFRS 1 was originally issued because capitalisation was then an option. The requirements for the application of mandatory capitalisation, on the other hand, should be the same for entities that already apply IFRSs and for first-time adopters. Therefore, the Board decided to amend IFRS 1, allowing first-time adopters transitional provisions equivalent to those available to entities that already apply IFRSs in paragraphs 27 and 28 of IAS 23, as revised in 2007.

BC63EA   In *Annual Improvements 2009–2011 Cycle* (issued in May 2012) the Board addressed some concerns that were raised by first-time adopters about the transitional provisions for borrowing costs relating to qualifying assets for which the commencement date for capitalisation was before the date of transition to IFRSs. Interested parties found it unclear whether borrowing costs capitalised in accordance with previous GAAP should be retained, restated or eliminated in the opening statement of financial position. Interested parties also questioned the accounting, after the date of transition, for borrowing costs that relate to such qualifying assets when these qualifying assets are under construction at the date of transition. They wanted clarification as to whether the first-time adopter should apply the requirements of IAS 23 *Borrowing Costs* or whether it should continue applying its previous GAAP even if that previous GAAP is not consistent with IAS 23.

BC63EB   The Board clarified that when the entity chooses to apply the exemption in paragraph D23 of IFRS 1, the borrowing costs that were capitalised in accordance with previous GAAP should be carried forward in the opening statement of financial position. This is because gathering the information for capitalisation of borrowing costs under IAS 23 and identifying and eliminating the amounts (if any) capitalised in past years under previous GAAP may be costly. In addition, the Board clarified that an entity should account for borrowing costs that are incurred after the date of transition and that relate to qualifying assets under construction at the date of transition in accordance with IAS 23, regardless of whether the entity capitalised or recognised in profit and loss borrowing costs under previous GAAP. The Board determined that this requirement would ensure useful information to users of financial statements. A first-time adopter could also choose to apply the requirements of IAS 23 from a date earlier than the date of transition, in which case it should account for borrowing costs in accordance with IAS 23 on or after the earlier date selected.

Severe hyperinflation

BC63F   In 2010 the Board was asked to clarify how an entity should resume presenting financial statements in accordance with IFRSs after a period of severe hyperinflation, during which the entity had been unable to comply with IAS 29 *Financial Reporting in Hyperinflationary Economies*. An entity would be unable to comply with IAS 29 if a reliable general price index is not available to all entities with that same functional currency, and exchangeability between the currency and a relatively stable foreign currency does not exist. However, once the functional currency changes to a non-hyperinflationary currency, or the currency ceases to be severely hyperinflationary, an entity would be able to start applying IFRSs to subsequent transactions.

BC63G   The Board noted that IFRSs did not provide sufficient guidance in these circumstances. The Board therefore decided to amend IFRS 1 to provide guidance on how an entity can present IFRS financial statements after its currency ceases to be severely hyperinflationary, by presenting an opening IFRS statement of financial position on or after the functional currency normalisation date. The Board believed that allowing an entity to apply the exemption when presenting an opening IFRS statement of financial position after, and not just on, the functional currency normalisation date, would address practical concerns that may arise if the functional currency normalisation date and the entity's date of transition to IFRSs are different. The Board decided that this amendment would also be available to entities that were emerging from a period of severe hyperinflation but had not applied IFRSs in the past.

BC63H   The Board decided to permit an entity emerging from a period of severe hyperinflation to elect to measure its assets and liabilities at fair value. That fair value could then be used as the deemed cost in its opening IFRS statement of financial position. The Board believed that this approach would expand the scope of the deemed cost exemptions in IFRS 1 to enable them to be applied in these specific circumstances. However, because severe hyperinflation is a specific set of circumstances, the Board wanted to ensure that the fair value measurement option was applied only to those assets and liabilities that were held before the functional currency normalisation date, and not to other assets and liabilities held by the entity at the time it made the transition to IFRSs. Furthermore, where a parent entity's functional currency has been subject to severe hyperinflation, but its subsidiary company's functional currency has not been subject to severe hyperinflation, the Board decided it was inappropriate for such a subsidiary company to be able to apply this exemption.

BC63I   The Board decided that any adjustments arising on electing to measure assets and liabilities at fair value in the opening IFRS statement of financial position arise from events and transactions before the date of transition to IFRSs. Consequently, those adjustments should be accounted for in accordance with paragraph 11 of IFRS 1, and an entity should recognise those adjustments directly in retained earnings (or, if appropriate, in another category of equity) at the date of transition to IFRSs.

BC63J   The Board observed that entities are required to apply paragraph 21 of IFRS 1 and prepare and present comparative information in accordance with IFRSs. The Board noted that preparation of information in accordance with IFRSs for periods before the functional currency normalisation date may not be possible; hence the exemption refers to a date of transition on or after the functional currency normalisation date. This may lead to a comparative period of less than 12 months. The Board identified that entities should consider whether disclosure of non-IFRS comparative information and historical summaries, in accordance with paragraph 22 of IFRS 1, would provide useful information to users of financial statements. The Board also noted that an entity should clearly explain the transition to IFRSs in accordance with paragraphs 23–28.

Joint arrangements

BC63K   During its redeliberation of the exposure draft ED 9 *Joint Arrangements* the Board decided not to require entities changing from proportionate consolidation to the equity method to adjust any differences between the two accounting methods retrospectively. Instead an entity should determine the opening balance of the investment relating to its interest in a joint venture as the aggregate of the carrying amounts of the assets and liabilities that the entity had been previously proportionately consolidated, including any goodwill arising from acquisition as at the beginning of the earliest period presented. The Board decided to treat first-time adopters in the same way as entities that already apply IFRSs with the following exception.

BC63L   A first-time adopter is required to test for impairment the opening investment in accordance with IAS 36 at the earliest period presented, regardless of whether there is any indication that the investment may be impaired. The Board noted that this is a more stringent requirement for the application of IFRS 11 *Joint Arrangements* by first-time adopters, but is aligned with the requirement for first-time adopters to apply IAS 36 in testing goodwill for impairment at the date of transition to IFRSs regardless of whether there is any indication that the goodwill may be impaired.

BC63M   *Consolidated Financial Statements, Joint Arrangements and Disclosure of Interests in Other Entities: Transition Guidance* (Amendments to IFRS 10, IFRS 11 and IFRS 12), issued in June 2012, amended IFRS 11 to require the transition adjustments of that IFRS to be recognised at the beginning of the annual period immediately preceding the first annual period for which IFRS 11 is applied (the 'immediately preceding period') instead of the beginning of the earliest period presented. The Board agreed that IFRS 1 should not be amended to reflect those amendments because the adjustments required on transition to IFRS should be reflected at the date of transition, which may be earlier than the beginning of the immediately preceding period. Consequently, paragraph D31 was amended to clarify that, when a first-time adopter is applying the transition guidance of IFRS 11, they shall apply the requirements at the date of transition, which is the same as the beginning of the earliest IFRS period presented.

Other possible exemptions rejected

BC64   The Board considered and rejected suggestions for other exemptions. Each such exemption would have moved the IFRS away from a principle-based approach, diminished transparency for users, decreased comparability over time within an entity's first IFRS financial statements and created additional complexity. In the Board's view, any cost savings generated would not have outweighed these disadvantages. Paragraphs BC65–BC73 discuss some of the specific suggestions the Board considered for embedded derivatives, hyperinflation, intangible assets and transaction costs on financial instruments.

Embedded derivatives

BC65   IAS 39[22] requires an entity to account separately for some embedded derivatives at fair value. Some respondents to ED 1 argued that retrospective application of this requirement would be costly. Some suggested either an exemption from retrospective application of this requirement, or a requirement or option to use the fair value of the host instrument at the date of transition to IFRSs as its deemed cost at that date.

BC66   The Board noted that US GAAP provides an option in this area. Under the transitional provisions of SFAS 133 *Accounting for Derivative Instruments and Hedging Activities*, an entity need not account separately for some pre-existing embedded derivatives. Nevertheless, the Board concluded that the failure to measure embedded derivatives at fair value would diminish the relevance and reliability of an entity's first IFRS financial statements. The Board also observed that IAS 39 addresses an inability to measure an embedded derivative and the host contract separately. In such cases, IAS 39 requires an entity to measure the entire combined contract at fair value.

Hyperinflation

BC67   Some argued that the cost of restating financial statements for the effects of hyperinflation in periods before the date of transition to IFRSs would exceed the benefits, particularly if the currency is no longer hyperinflationary. However, the Board concluded that such restatement should be required, because hyperinflation can make unadjusted financial statements meaningless or misleading.

---

22   The Board amended the requirements in IAS 39 to identify and separately account for embedded derivatives and relocated them to IFRS 9 *Financial Instruments*. This Basis for Conclusions has not been updated for changes in requirements since IFRIC 9 *Reassessment of Embedded Derivatives* was issued in March 2006.

Intangible assets

BC68 For the following reasons, some proposed that a first-time adopter's opening IFRS balance sheet should exclude intangible assets that it did not recognise in accordance with previous GAAP:

(a) Using hindsight to assess retrospectively when the recognition criteria for intangible assets were met could be subjective, open up possibilities for manipulation and involve costs that might exceed the benefits to users.

(b) The benefits expected from intangible assets are often not related directly to the costs incurred. Therefore, capitalising the costs incurred is of limited benefit to users, particularly if the costs were incurred in the distant past.

(c) Such an exclusion would be consistent with the transitional provisions in IAS 38 *Intangible Assets*. These encourage (but do not require) the recognition of intangible assets acquired in a previous business combination that was an acquisition and prohibit the recognition of all other previously unrecognised intangible assets.

BC69 In many cases, internally generated intangible assets do not qualify for recognition in accordance with IAS 38 at the date of transition to IFRSs because an entity did not, in accordance with previous GAAP, accumulate cost information or did not carry out contemporaneous assessments of future economic benefits. In these cases, there is no need for a specific requirement to exclude those assets. Furthermore, when these assets do not qualify for recognition, first-time adopters will not generally, in the Board's view, need to perform extensive work to reach this conclusion.

BC70 In other cases, an entity may have accumulated and retained sufficient information about costs and future economic benefits to determine which intangible assets (whether internally generated or acquired in a business combination or separately) qualify in accordance with IAS 38 for recognition in its opening IFRS balance sheet. If that information is available, no exclusion is justified.

BC71 Some argued that fair value should be used as deemed cost for intangible assets in the opening IFRS balance sheet (by analogy with a business combination). ED 1 would not have permitted this. However, in finalising the IFRS, the Board concluded that this approach should be available for those intangible assets for which IFRSs already permit fair value measurements. Therefore, in accordance with the IFRS, a first-time adopter may elect to use fair value or some previous GAAP revaluations of intangible assets as deemed cost for IFRSs, but only if the intangible assets meet:

(a) the recognition criteria in IAS 38 (including reliable measurement of original cost); and

(b) the criteria in IAS 38 for revaluation (including the existence of an active market) (paragraph D7 of the IFRS).

Transaction costs: financial instruments

BC72 To determine the amortised cost of a financial asset or financial liability using the effective interest method, it is necessary to determine the transaction costs incurred when the asset or liability was originated. Some respondents to ED 1 argued that determining these transaction costs could involve undue cost or effort for financial assets or financial liabilities originated long before the date of transition to IFRSs. They suggested that the Board should permit a first-time adopter:

(a) to use the fair value of the financial asset or financial liability at the date of transition to IFRSs as its deemed cost at that date; or

(b) to determine amortised cost without considering transaction costs.

BC73 In the Board's view, the unamortised portion of transaction costs at the date of transition to IFRSs is unlikely to be material for most financial assets and financial liabilities. Even when the unamortised portion is material, reasonable estimates should be possible. Therefore, the Board created no exemption in this area.

Retrospective designation

BC74 The Board considered practical implementation difficulties that could arise from the retrospective application of aspects of IAS 39:[23]

(a) hedge accounting (paragraphs BC75–BC80);

(b) government loans (paragraphs BC80A–BC80E);

(c) the treatment of cumulative fair value changes on available-for-sale financial assets[24] at the date of transition to IFRSs (paragraphs BC81–BC83); and

(d) 'day 1' gain or loss recognition (paragraph BC83A).

Hedge accounting[25]

BC75 Before beginning their preparations for adopting IAS 39 (or a local standard based on IAS 39), it is unlikely that most entities would have adopted IAS 39's criteria for (a) documenting hedges at their inception and (b) testing the hedges for effectiveness, even if they intended to continue the same hedging strategies after adopting IAS 39. Furthermore, retrospective designation of hedges (or retrospective reversal of their designation) could lead to selective designation of some hedges to report a particular result.

---

23 IFRS 9 *Financial Instruments* replaced IAS 39. IFRS 9 applies to all items that were previously within the scope of IAS 39.

24 IFRS 9 *Financial Instruments* eliminated the category of available-for-sale financial assets.

25 IFRS 9 *Financial Instruments* replaced the hedge accounting requirements in IAS 39.

BC76   To overcome these problems, the transitional requirements in IAS 39 require an entity already applying IFRSs to apply the hedging requirements prospectively when it adopts IAS 39. As the same problems arise for a first-time adopter, the IFRS requires prospective application by a first-time adopter.

BC77   ED 1 included a redrafted version of the transitional provisions in IAS 39 and related *Questions and Answers* (Q&As) developed by the IAS 39 Implementation Guidance Committee. The Board confirmed in the Basis for Conclusions published with ED 1 that it did not intend the redrafting to create substantive changes. However, in the light of responses to ED 1, the Board decided in finalising IFRS 1 that the redrafting would not make it easier for first-time adopters and others to understand and apply the transitional provisions and Q&As. However, the project to improve IAS 32 and IAS 39 resulted in certain amendments to the transition requirements. In addition, this project incorporated selected other Q&As (ie not on transition) into IAS 39. The Board therefore took this opportunity to consolidate all the guidance for first-time adopters in one place, by incorporating the Q&As on transition into IFRS 1.

BC78   Some respondents to ED 1 asked the Board to clarify what would happen if hedge accounting in accordance with previous GAAP involved hedging relationships of a type that does not qualify for hedge accounting in accordance with IAS 39. The problem can be seen most clearly for a hedge of a net position (macro hedge). If a first-time adopter were to use hedge accounting in its opening IFRS balance sheet for a hedge of a net position, this would involve either:

(a)   recognising deferred debits and credits that are not assets and liabilities (for a fair value hedge); or

(b)   deferring gains or losses in equity when there is, at best, a weak link to an underlying item that defines when they should be transferred to the income statement (for a cash flow hedge).

BC79   As either of these treatments would diminish the relevance and reliability of an entity's first IFRS financial statements, the Board decided that an entity should not apply hedge accounting in its opening IFRS balance sheet to a hedge of a net position that does not qualify as a hedged item in accordance with IAS 39. However, the Board concluded that it would be reasonable (and consistent with IAS 39 paragraph 133[26]) to permit a first-time adopter to designate an individual item as a hedged item within the net position, provided that it does so no later than the date of transition to IFRSs, to prevent selective designation. For similar reasons, the Board prohibited hedge accounting in the opening IFRS balance sheet for any hedging relationship of a type that does not qualify for hedge accounting in accordance with IAS 39 (see paragraph B5 of the IFRS).

26   In IAS 39, as revised in 2003, paragraph 133 was replaced by paragraphs 84 and AG101.

BC80   Some respondents to ED 1 suggested that an entity adopting IFRSs for the first time in 2005 could not meet IAS 39's documentation and effectiveness criteria by the date of transition to IFRSs (1 January 2004 for many entities). Some requested an exemption from these criteria until the beginning of the latest period covered by the first IFRS financial statements (1 January 2005 for many entities). However, for the following reasons, the Board did not create an exemption in this area:

     (a)   The Board's primary objective is comparability within a first-time adopter's first IFRS financial statements and between different first-time adopters switching to IFRSs at the same time (paragraph BC10).

     (b)   The continuation of previous GAAP hedge accounting practices could permit the non-recognition of derivatives or the recognition of deferred debits and credits that are not assets and liabilities.

     (c)   The Board's benchmark for cost-benefit assessments was an entity that has planned the transition to IFRSs and is able to collect the necessary information at, or very soon after, the date of transition to IFRSs (paragraph BC27). Entities should not be 'rewarded' by concessions if they failed to plan for transition, nor should that failure be allowed to undermine the integrity of their opening IFRS balance sheet. Entities switching to IFRSs in 2005 need to have their hedge accounting systems in place by the beginning of 2004. In the Board's view, that is a challenging but achievable timetable. Entities preparing to switch to IFRSs in 2004 should have been aware of the implications of IAS 39 already and the exposure draft of improvements to IAS 39, published in June 2002, proposed very few changes in this area, so delayed transition is not justified for these entities either.

Government loans

BC80A   IAS 20 *Accounting for Government Grants and Disclosure of Government Assistance* (as revised in May 2008) introduced a requirement that government loans with a below-market rate of interest shall be measured at fair value on initial recognition. At the time this requirement was added, the Board recognised that applying it retrospectively may require entities to measure the fair value of loans at an earlier date. Accordingly, the Board decided that entities should apply this requirement in IAS 20 prospectively, with earlier application permitted.

BC80B   In 2011 the application of this requirement by first-time adopters was brought to the Board's attention. The Board noted that the general requirement in IFRS 1 for first-time adopters to apply IFRSs retrospectively at the date of transition to IFRSs could require some entities to measure such government loans at fair value at a date before the date of transition to IFRSs. This may lead to an entity applying hindsight if it must derive a fair value that needs significant unobservable inputs. Accordingly, the Board decided to add an exception to the retrospective application of IFRSs to require that first-time adopters shall apply the requirements of IAS 20 prospectively to government loans existing at the date of transition to IFRSs, unless the necessary information was obtained at the time of initially accounting for that loan. As a result of not applying IAS 20 and IFRS 9 retrospectively to government loans at the date of transition, the corresponding benefit of the government loan at a below-market rate of interest is not recognised as a government grant.

BC80C   The Board proposed the exception in October 2011 in the exposure draft *Government Loans* (proposed amendments to IFRS 1). In recognition of comments on the exposure draft, the Board revised paragraph B10 to specify that an entity applies IAS 32 *Financial Instruments: Presentation* to classify the government loans as a financial liability or an equity instrument, and to limit the scope of the exemption to matters of recognition and measurement. This will give first-time adopters the same relief as existing preparers and will mean that if a first-time adopter had classified government loans in equity under its previous GAAP, it will reclassify those loans as liabilities, if those loans meet the definition of a financial liability in IAS 32. The Board also clarified that an entity should use its previous GAAP carrying amount of such loans at the date of transition to IFRSs as the carrying amount in the opening IFRS statement of financial position. IFRS 9 should be applied to such loans subsequently.

BC80D   Some respondents to the exposure draft asked why the retrospective application of IAS 20 should be optional, rather than mandatory, if the information needed to apply IFRS 9 had been obtained. The Board thought that mandatory restatement could require an onerous search to determine whether this information had been obtained when initially accounting for loans that were received many years ago.

BC80E   The Board noted that prohibiting the application of this option on a loan-by-loan basis might introduce further complexity into IFRS 1. This is because it may raise further questions, such as whether the retrospective application would be permitted for all the loans for which the information needed was obtained at the time, even if there are other similar loans for which the fair value information was not obtained at that time; and whether the retrospective application should be restricted to all loans received after a certain date and for which all necessary information was obtained to enable retrospective application. The Board concluded that the exception proposed in paragraph B11 should be available on a loan-by-loan basis.

BC80F   In November 2013 the Board amended the examples in the guidance on hedge accounting so that they conformed to IFRS 9, which replaced the hedge accounting requirements in IAS 39.

Available-for-sale financial assets[27]

BC81   Retrospective application of IAS 39[28] to available-for-sale financial assets requires a first-time adopter to recognise the cumulative fair value changes in a separate component of equity in the opening IFRS balance sheet, and transfer those fair value changes to the income statement on subsequent

---

27   IFRS 9 *Financial Instruments* eliminated the category of available-for-sale financial assets.

28   IFRS 9 *Financial Instruments* replaced IAS 39. IFRS 9 applies to all items that were previously within the scope of IAS 39.

disposal or impairment of the asset. This could allow, for example, selective classification of assets with cumulative gains as available for sale (with subsequent transfers to the income statement on disposal) and assets with cumulative losses as held for trading (with no transfers on disposal).

BC82　IAS 39 confirmed the proposal in the exposure draft of June 2002 to give an entity that already applies IFRSs an option to designate any financial asset as at fair value through profit or loss when it first applies the proposed improvements. Although this requirement could increase the risk of selective classification by first-time adopters of the kind discussed in the previous paragraph, the Board noted that an entity could achieve a similar result by selective disposal of some assets before the date of transition to IFRSs. Therefore, the Board concluded that it should treat first-time adopters in the same way as entities that already apply IFRSs by requiring retrospective application.

BC83　Some respondents to ED 1 commented that the cost of determining the amount to be included in a separate component of equity would exceed the benefits. However, the Board noted that these costs would be minimal if a first-time adopter carried the available-for-sale financial assets in accordance with previous GAAP at cost or the lower of cost and market value. These costs might be more significant if it carried them at fair value, but in that case it might well classify the assets as held for trading. Therefore, the Board made no changes to ED 1's proposal that a first-time adopter should apply IAS 39 retrospectively to available-for-sale financial assets.

BC83A　IFRS 1 originally required retrospective application of the 'day 1' gain or loss recognition requirements in IAS 39 paragraph AG76. After the revised IAS 39 was issued, constituents raised concerns that retrospective application would diverge from the requirements of US GAAP, would be difficult and expensive to implement, and might require subjective assumptions about what was observable and what was not. In response to these concerns, the Board decided to permit entities to apply the requirements in the last sentence of IAS 39 paragraph AG76 and in paragraph AG76A, in any one of the following ways:

(a)　retrospectively;

(b)　prospectively to transactions entered into after 25 October 2002; or

(c)　prospectively to transactions entered into after 1 January 2004.

In 2010 the Board was asked to reconsider whether the fixed dates of 25 October 2002 and 1 January 2004 continued to be appropriate for first-time adopters. Constituents were concerned that, as time passes, these fixed dates become more remote and increasingly less relevant to the financial reports as additional jurisdictions adopt IFRSs. The Board accepted that the cost of reconstructing transactions back in time to 25 October 2002 or 1 January 2004 was likely to outweigh the benefit to be achieved in doing so. It therefore amended the fixed dates included in paragraph D20 of IFRS 1 to permit a first-time adopter to apply the 'day 1' gain or loss recognition requirement in

IAS 39 paragraphs AG76 and AG76A prospectively from 'the date of transition to IFRSs'.[29]

Estimates

BC84   An entity will have made estimates in accordance with previous GAAP at the date of transition to IFRSs. Events between that date and the reporting date for the entity's first IFRS financial statements might suggest a need to change those estimates. Some of those events might qualify as adjusting events in accordance with IAS 10 *Events after the Balance Sheet Date*.[30] However, if the entity made those estimates on a basis consistent with IFRSs, the Board concluded that it would be more helpful to users—and more consistent with IAS 8—to recognise the revision of those estimates as income or expense in the period when the entity made the revision, rather than in preparing the opening IFRS balance sheet (paragraphs 14–17 of the IFRS).

Presentation and disclosure

Comparative information

BC85   IAS 1 requires an entity to disclose comparative information (in accordance with IFRSs) for the previous period. Some suggested that a first-time adopter should disclose comparative information for more than one previous period. For entities that already apply IFRSs, users normally have access to financial statements prepared on a comparable basis for several years. However, this is not the case for a first-time adopter.

BC86   Nevertheless, the Board did not require a first-time adopter to present more comparative information than IAS 1 requires, because such a requirement would impose costs out of proportion to the benefits to users, and increase the risk that preparers might need to make arbitrary assumptions in applying hindsight.

BC87   ED 1 proposed that if the first IFRS financial statements include more than one year of comparative information, the additional comparative information should comply with IFRSs. Some respondents to ED 1 noted that some regulators require entities to prepare more than two years of comparatives. They argued the following:

(a)   A requirement to restate two years of comparatives would impose excessive costs and lead to arbitrary restatements that might be biased by hindsight.

---

29   IFRS 9 *Financial Instruments* replaced IAS 39. Paragraphs AG76 and AG76A of IAS 39 were relocated to IFRS 9 as paragraphs B5.4.8 and B5.4.9. However, in May 2011, IFRS 13 deleted paragraphs B5.4.8 and B5.4.9 of IFRS 9. In 2014 the requirements for amortised cost measurement and impairment were added to IFRS 9 as Sections 5.4 and 5.5. Paragraphs B5.4.8 and B5.4.9 of IFRS 9 now contains requirements related to amortised cost measurement.

30   In September 2007 the IASB amended the title of IAS 10 *Events after the Balance Sheet Date* to *Events after the Reporting Period* as a consequence of the revision of IAS 1 *Presentation of Financial Statements* in 2007.

(b)   Consider an entity adopting IFRSs in 2005 and required by its regulator to give two years of comparatives. Its date of transition to IFRSs would be 1 January 2003 — several months before the publication of the IFRS and of the standards resulting from the improvements project. This could contradict the Board's assertion in paragraph BC27 above that most preparers could gather most information they need for their opening IFRS balance sheet at, or soon after, the date of transition to IFRSs.

BC88   In response to these comments, the Board deleted this proposal. Instead, if a first-time adopter elects to give more than one year of comparative information, the additional comparative information need not comply with IFRSs, but the IFRS requires the entity:

(a)   to label previous GAAP information prominently as not being prepared in accordance with IFRSs.

(b)   to disclose the nature of the main adjustments that would make it comply with IFRSs (paragraph 22 of the IFRS).

BC89   Some respondents to ED 1 suggested that it would be onerous to prepare comparative information in accordance with IAS 32 and IAS 39[31] about financial instruments. They suggested that an entity should be able to apply IAS 39 prospectively from the beginning of the year of its first IFRS financial statements (eg 1 January 2005 for many first-time adopters). They noted that US companies were not required to restate comparatives on the introduction of SFAS 133 *Accounting for Derivative Instruments and Hedging Activities*. However, given the Board's emphasis on comparability within the first IFRS financial statements (paragraph BC10) and the assumption of timely planning (paragraph BC27), the Board introduced no general exemption in this area.

BC89A   Nevertheless, the Board noted that the revised IAS 32 and IAS 39[32] were not issued until December 2003. Additionally, the Board's decision to re-expose its proposals for portfolio hedges of interest rate risk had the effect that some of the requirements will not be finalised until early 2004. The Board was sympathetic to concerns that entities that will be required to comply with IFRSs for the first time in 2005 could not make a timely transition to IFRSs because IAS 39 will not be issued in final form until after the start of 2004. Therefore, the Board decided to exempt entities adopting IFRSs for the first time before 1 January 2006 from producing comparative information that complies with IAS 32 and IAS 39, as revised in 2003, in their first IFRS financial statements.

BC89B   In the light of respondents' comments on the June 2011 exposure draft *Improvements to IFRSs*, the Board amended paragraph 21 as part of *Annual Improvements 2009–2011 Cycle* (issued in May 2012) because it considered that the requirements for comparative information for a first-time adopter should be different from the requirements for comparative information for an

---

31 IFRS 9 *Financial Instruments* replaced IAS 39. IFRS 9 applies to all items that were previously within the scope of IAS 39.

32 IFRS 9 *Financial Instruments* replaced IAS 39. IFRS 9 applies to all items that were previously within the scope of IAS 39.

existing preparer. The Board noted that a first-time adopter should not be exempted from presenting three statements of financial position and related notes because it might not have presented this information previously on a basis consistent with IFRSs.

BC89C   In addition, the Board considered that a first-time adopter may provide additional comparative information that is presented in accordance with previous GAAP to help the user understand the effects of the transition to IFRSs in accordance with paragraph 22 of IFRS 1. For example, a law or a regulator requires an entity to present the first comparative financial statements in accordance with both IFRSs and previous GAAP and the second comparative in accordance with previous GAAP only. The presentation of this information is an exception from the requirement in paragraph 38C of IAS 1 (to allow an entity to present comparative information in addition to the minimum comparative information required by IFRSs).

Historical summaries

BC90   Some entities choose, or are required, to present in their financial statements historical summaries of selected data covering periods before the first period for which they present full comparative information. Some argued that an entity should present this information in accordance with IFRSs, to ensure comparability over time. However, the Board concluded that such a requirement would cause costs out of proportion to the benefit to users. The IFRS requires disclosure of the nature of the main adjustments needed to make historical summaries included in financial statements or interim financial reports comply with IFRSs (paragraph 22 of the IFRS). Historical summaries published outside financial statements or interim financial reports are beyond the scope of the IFRS.

Explanation of transition to IFRSs

BC91   The IFRS requires disclosures about the effect of the transition from previous GAAP to IFRSs. The Board concluded that such disclosures are essential, in the first (annual) IFRS financial statements as well as in interim financial reports (if any), because they help users understand the effect and implications of the transition to IFRSs and how they need to change their analytical models to make the best use of information presented using IFRSs. The required disclosures relate to both:

(a)   the most recent information published in accordance with previous GAAP, so that users have the most up-to-date information; and

(b)   the date of transition to IFRSs. This is an important focus of attention for users, preparers and auditors because the opening IFRS balance sheet is the starting point for accounting in accordance with IFRSs.

BC92   Paragraph 24(a) and (b) of the IFRS requires reconciliations of equity and total comprehensive income. The Board concluded that users would also find it helpful to have information about the other adjustments that affect the opening IFRS balance sheet but do not appear in these reconciliations. Because a reconciliation could be voluminous, the IFRS requires disclosure of narrative information about these adjustments, as well as about adjustments to the cash flow statement (paragraph 25 of the IFRS).

BC92A   The Board decided to require a first-time adopter to include in its first IFRS financial statements a reconciliation of total comprehensive income (or, if an entity did not report such a total, profit or loss) in accordance with previous GAAP to total comprehensive income in accordance with IFRSs for the latest period reported in accordance with previous GAAP.

BC92B   The Board observed that the amendments to IAS 1 in 2007 regarding the presentation of income and expense might result in users having to change their analytical models to include both income and expense that are recognised in profit or loss and those recognised outside profit or loss. Accordingly, the Board concluded that it would be helpful to those users to provide information on the effect and implication of the transition to IFRSs on all items of income and expense, not only those recognised in profit or loss.

BC92C   The Board acknowledged that GAAP in other jurisdictions might not have a notion of total comprehensive income. Accordingly, it decided that an entity should reconcile to total comprehensive income in accordance with IFRSs from the previous GAAP equivalent of total comprehensive income. The previous GAAP equivalent might be profit or loss.

BC93   Paragraph 26 of the IFRS states that the reconciliations should distinguish changes in accounting policies from the correction of errors. Some respondents to ED 1 argued that complying with this requirement could be difficult or costly. However, the Board concluded that both components are important and their disclosure should be required because:

(a)   information about changes in accounting policies helps explain the transition to IFRSs.

(b)   information about errors helps users assess the reliability of financial information. Furthermore, a failure to disclose the effect of material errors would obscure the 'results of the stewardship of management, or the accountability of management for the resources entrusted to it' (*Framework*, paragraph 14).

BC94   For impairment losses (and reversals) recognised in preparing the opening IFRS balance sheet, paragraph 24(c) of the IFRS requires the disclosures that IAS 36 would require if those impairment losses (and reversals) were recognised during the period beginning with the date of transition to IFRSs. The rationale for this requirement is that there is inevitably subjectivity about impairment losses. This disclosure provides transparency about impairment losses recognised on transition to IFRSs. These losses might otherwise receive less attention than impairment losses recognised in earlier or later periods.

BC95   Paragraph 30 of the IFRS requires disclosures about the use of fair value as deemed cost. Although the adjustment arising from the use of this exemption appears in the reconciliations discussed above, this more specific disclosure highlights it. Furthermore, this exemption differs from the other exemptions that might apply for property, plant and equipment (previous GAAP revaluation or event-driven fair value measurement). The latter two exemptions do not lead to a restatement on transition to IFRSs because they apply only if the measurement was already used in previous GAAP financial statements.

Interim financial reports

BC96   IAS 34 *Interim Financial Reporting* states that the interim financial report is 'intended to provide an update on the latest complete set of annual financial statements' (paragraph 6). Thus, IAS 34 requires less disclosure in interim financial statements than IFRSs require in annual financial statements. However, an entity's interim financial report in accordance with IAS 34 is less helpful to users if the entity's latest annual financial statements were prepared using previous GAAP than if they were prepared in accordance with IFRSs. Therefore, the Board concluded that a first-time adopter's first interim financial report in accordance with IAS 34 should include sufficient information to enable users to understand how the transition to IFRSs affected previously reported annual, as well as interim, figures (paragraphs 32 and 33 of the IFRS).

Accounting policy changes in the year of adoption

BC97   In *Improvements to IFRSs* issued in May 2010, the Board clarified unclear wording concerning how changes in accounting policies should be addressed by a first-time adopter when those changes occur after the publication of the entity's first interim financial report. The Board decided that a first-time adopter is exempt from all the requirements of IAS 8 for the interim financial report it presents in accordance with IAS 34 for part of the period covered by its first IFRS financial statements and for its first IFRS financial statements. The Board concluded that to comply with IFRS 1's requirement to explain its transition to IFRSs, an entity should be required to explain any changes in its accounting policies or the IFRS 1 exemptions it applied between its first IFRS interim financial report and its first IFRS financial statements. The Board decided that the most useful information it could require was updated reconciliations between previous GAAP and IFRSs.

Short-term exemptions from IFRSs

BC98   [Deleted][33]

Deletion of short-term exemptions (amendments issued in December 2016)

BC99   In *Annual Improvements to IFRS Standards 2014–2016 Cycle*, the Board deleted the short-term exemptions in paragraphs E3–E7 and the related effective date paragraphs. The Board noted that the reliefs provided in those paragraphs were no longer applicable. The reliefs provided had been available to entities only for reporting periods that had passed.

---

33 *Annual Improvements to IFRS Standards 2014–2016 Cycle*, issued in December 2016, deleted some short-term exemptions for first-time adopters (see paragraph BC99), and as a consequence deleted paragraph BC98.

Appendix
Amendments to Basis for Conclusions on other IFRSs

This appendix contains amendments to the Basis for Conclusions on other IFRSs that are necessary to ensure consistency with IFRS 1 (as revised in 2008).

* * * * *

The amendments contained in this appendix when the revised IFRS 1 was issued in 2008 have been incorporated into the text of the Basis for Conclusions on IFRS 6 and IASs 27 and 39 as issued at 27 November 2008.

IASB documents published to accompany

IFRS 2

Share-based Payment

The text of the unaccompanied standard, IFRS 2, is contained in Part A of this edition. Its effective date when issued was 1 January 2005. The text of the Accompanying Guidance on IFRS 2 is contained in Part B of this edition. This part presents the following document:

BASIS FOR CONCLUSIONS

Contents

continued...

...continued

Basis for Conclusions on
IFRS 2 *Share-based Payment*

This Basis for Conclusions accompanies, but is not part of, IFRS 2.

Introduction

BC1　This Basis for Conclusions summarises the International Accounting Standards Board's considerations in reaching the conclusions in IFRS 2 *Share-based Payment*. Individual Board members gave greater weight to some factors than to others.

BC2　Entities often issue[1] shares or share options to pay employees or other parties. Share plans and share option plans are a common feature of employee remuneration, not only for directors and senior executives, but also for many other employees. Some entities issue shares or share options to pay suppliers, such as suppliers of professional services.

BC3　Until the issue of IFRS 2, there has been no International Financial Reporting Standard (IFRS) covering the recognition and measurement of these transactions. Concerns have been raised about this gap in international standards. For example, the International Organization of Securities Commissions (IOSCO), in its 2000 report on international standards, stated that IASC (the IASB's predecessor body) should consider the accounting treatment of share-based payment.

BC4　Few countries have standards on the topic. This is a concern in many countries, because the use of share-based payment has increased in recent years and continues to spread. Various standard-setting bodies have been working on this issue. At the time the IASB added a project on share-based payment to its agenda in July 2001, some standard-setters had recently published proposals. For example, the German Accounting Standards Committee published a draft accounting standard *Accounting for Share Option Plans and Similar Compensation Arrangements* in June 2001. The UK Accounting Standards Board led the development of the Discussion Paper *Accounting for Share-based Payment*, published in July 2000 by IASC, the ASB and other bodies represented in the G4+1.[2] The Danish Institute of State Authorised Public Accountants issued a Discussion Paper *The Accounting Treatment of Share-based Payment* in April 2000. More recently, in December 2002, the Accounting Standards Board of Japan published a Summary Issues Paper on share-based payment. In March 2003, the US Financial Accounting Standards Board (FASB) added to its agenda a project to review US accounting requirements on

---

1　The word 'issue' is used in a broad sense. For example, a transfer of shares held in treasury (own shares held) to another party is regarded as an 'issue' of equity instruments. Some argue that if options or shares are granted with vesting conditions, they are not 'issued' until those vesting conditions have been satisfied. However, even if this argument is accepted, it does not change the Board's conclusions on the requirements of the IFRS, and therefore the word 'issue' is used broadly, to include situations in which equity instruments are conditionally transferred to the counterparty, subject to the satisfaction of specified vesting conditions.

2　The G4+1 comprised members of the national accounting standard-setting bodies of Australia, Canada, New Zealand, the UK and the US, and IASC.

share-based payment. Also, the Canadian Accounting Standards Board (AcSB) recently completed its project on share-based payment. The AcSB standard requires recognition of all share-based payment transactions, including transactions in which share options are granted to employees (discussed further in paragraphs BC281 and BC282).

BC5   Users of financial statements and other commentators are calling for improvements in the accounting treatment of share-based payment. For example, the proposal in the IASC/G4+1 Discussion Paper and ED 2 *Share-based Payment*, that share-based payment transactions should be recognised in the financial statements, resulting in an expense when the goods or services are consumed, received strong support from investors and other users of financial statements. Recent economic events have emphasised the importance of high quality financial statements that provide neutral, transparent and comparable information to help users make economic decisions. In particular, the omission of expenses arising from share-based payment transactions with employees has been highlighted by investors, other users of financial statements and other commentators as causing economic distortions and corporate governance concerns.

BC6   As noted above, the Board began a project to develop an IFRS on share-based payment in July 2001. In September 2001, the Board invited additional comment on the IASC/G4+1 Discussion Paper, with a comment deadline of 15 December 2001. The Board received over 270 letters. During the development of ED 2, the Board was also assisted by an Advisory Group, consisting of individuals from various countries and with a range of backgrounds, including persons from the investment, corporate, audit, academic, compensation consultancy, valuation and regulatory communities. The Board received further assistance from other experts at a panel discussion held in New York in July 2002. In November 2002, the Board published an Exposure Draft, ED 2 *Share-based Payment*, with a comment deadline of 7 March 2003. The Board received over 240 letters. The Board also worked with the FASB after that body added to its agenda a project to review US accounting requirements on share-based payment. This included participating in meetings of the FASB's Option Valuation Group and meeting the FASB to discuss convergence issues.

BC6A In 2007 the Board added to its agenda a project to clarify the scope and accounting for group cash-settled share-based payment transactions in the separate or individual financial statements of the entity receiving the goods or services when that entity has no obligation to settle the share-based payment. In December 2007 the Board published *Group Cash-settled Share-based Payment Transactions* (proposed amendments to IFRS 2). The resulting amendments issued in June 2009 also incorporate the requirements of two Interpretations —IFRIC 8 *Scope of IFRS 2* and IFRIC 11 *IFRS 2—Group and Treasury Share Transactions*. As a consequence, the Board withdrew both Interpretations.

Scope

BC7 Much of the controversy and complexity surrounding the accounting for share-based payment relates to employee share options. However, the scope of IFRS 2 is broader than that. It applies to transactions in which shares or other equity instruments are granted to employees. It also applies to transactions with parties other than employees, in which goods or services are received as consideration for the issue of shares, share options or other equity instruments. The term 'goods' includes inventories, consumables, property, plant and equipment, intangible assets and other non-financial assets. Lastly, the IFRS applies to payments in cash (or other assets) that are 'share-based' because the amount of the payment is based on the price of the entity's shares or other equity instruments, eg cash share appreciation rights.

Broad-based employee share plans, including employee share purchase plans

BC8 Some employee share plans are described as 'broad-based' or 'all-employee' plans, in which all (or virtually all) employees have the opportunity to participate, whereas other plans are more selective, covering individual or specific groups of employees (eg senior executives). Employee share purchase plans are often broad-based plans. Typically, employee share purchase plans provide employees with an opportunity to buy a specific number of shares at a discounted price, ie at an amount that is less than the fair value of the shares. The employee's entitlement to discounted shares is usually conditional upon specific conditions being satisfied, such as remaining in the service of the entity for a specified period.

BC9 The issues that arise with respect to employee share purchase plans are:

(a) are these plans somehow so different from other employee share plans that a different accounting treatment is appropriate?

(b) even if the answer to the above question is 'no', are there circumstances, such as when the discount is very small, when it is appropriate to exempt employee share purchase plans from an accounting standard on share-based payment?

BC10 Some respondents to ED 2 argued that broad-based employee share plans should be exempt from an accounting standard on share-based payment. The reason usually given was that these plans are different from other types of employee share plans and, in particular, are not a part of remuneration for employee services. Some argued that requiring the recognition of an expense in respect of these types of plans was perceived to be contrary to government policy to encourage employee share ownership. In contrast, other respondents saw no difference between employee share purchase plans and other employee share plans, and argued that the same accounting requirements should therefore apply. However, some suggested that there should be an exemption if the discount is small.

BC11   The Board concluded that, in principle, there is no reason to treat broad-based employee share plans, including broad-based employee share purchase plans, differently from other employee share plans (the issue of 'small' discounts is considered later). The Board noted that the fact that these schemes are available only to employees is in itself sufficient to conclude that the benefits provided represent employee remuneration. Moreover, the term 'remuneration' is not limited to remuneration provided as part of an individual employee's contract: it encompasses all benefits provided to employees. Similarly, the term services encompasses all benefits provided by the employees in return, including increased productivity, commitment or other enhancements in employee work performance as a result of the incentives provided by the share plan.

BC12   Moreover, distinguishing regular employee services from the additional benefits received from broad-based employee share plans would not change the conclusion that it is necessary to account for such plans. No matter what label is placed on the benefits provided by employees—or the benefits provided by the entity—the transaction should be recognised in the financial statements.

BC13   Furthermore, that governments in some countries have a policy of encouraging employee share ownership is not a valid reason for according these types of plans a different accounting treatment, because it is not the role of financial reporting to give favourable accounting treatment to particular transactions to encourage entities to enter into them. For example, governments might wish to encourage entities to provide pensions to their employees, to lessen the future burden on the state, but that does not mean that pension costs should be excluded from the financial statements. To do so would impair the quality of financial reporting. The purpose of financial reporting is to provide information to users of financial statements, to assist them in making economic decisions. The omission of expenses from the financial statements does not change the fact that those expenses have been incurred. The omission of expenses causes reported profits to be overstated and hence the financial statements are not neutral, are less transparent and comparable, and are potentially misleading to users.

BC14   There remains the question whether there should be an exemption for some plans, when the discount is small. For example, FASB Statement of Financial Accounting Standards No. 123 *Accounting for Stock-Based Compensation* contains an exemption for employee share purchase plans that meet specified criteria, of which one is that the discount is small.

BC15   On the one hand, it seems reasonable to exempt an employee share purchase plan if it has substantially no option features and the discount is small. In such situations, the rights given to the employees under the plan probably do not have a significant value, from the entity's perspective.

BC16   On the other hand, even if one accepts that an exemption is appropriate, specifying its scope is problematic, eg deciding what constitutes a small discount. Some argue that a 5 per cent discount from the market price (as specified in SFAS 123) is too high, noting that a block of shares can be sold on the market at a price close to the current share price. Furthermore, it could be argued that it is unnecessary to exempt these plans from the standard. If the rights given to the employees do not have a significant value, this suggests that the amounts involved are immaterial. Because it is not necessary to include immaterial information in the financial statements, there is no need for a specific exclusion in an accounting standard.

BC17   For the reasons given in the preceding paragraph, the Board concluded that broad-based employee share plans, including broad-based employee share purchase plans, should not be exempted from the IFRS.

BC18   However, the Board noted that there might be instances when an entity engages in a transaction with an employee in his/her capacity as a holder of equity instruments, rather than in his/her capacity as an employee. For example, an entity might grant all holders of a particular class of its equity instruments the right to acquire additional equity instruments of the entity at a price that is less than the fair value of those equity instruments. If an employee receives such a right because he/she is a holder of that particular class of equity instruments, the Board concluded that the granting or exercise of that right should not be subject to the requirements of the IFRS, because the employee has received that right in his/her capacity as a shareholder, rather than as an employee.

Transactions in which an entity cannot identify some or all of the goods or services received (paragraph 2)[3]

BC18A   The Board incorporated into IFRS 2 the consensus of IFRIC 8 in *Group Cash-settled Share-based Payment Transactions* issued in June 2009. This section summarises the IFRIC's considerations in reaching that consensus, as approved by the Board.

BC18B   IFRS 2 applies to share-based payment transactions in which the entity receives or acquires goods or services. However, in some situations it might be difficult to demonstrate that the entity has received goods or services. This raises the question of whether IFRS 2 applies to such transactions. In addition, if the entity has made a share-based payment and the identifiable consideration received (if any) appears to be less than the fair value of the share-based payment, does this situation indicate that goods or services have been received, even though those goods or services are not specifically identified, and therefore that IFRS 2 applies?

BC18C   When the Board developed IFRS 2, it concluded that the directors of an entity would expect to receive some goods or services in return for equity instruments issued (paragraph BC37). This implies that it is not necessary to identify the specific goods or services received in return for the equity instruments granted to conclude that goods or services have been (or will be) received. Furthermore, paragraph 8 of the IFRS establishes that it is not necessary for the goods or services received to qualify for recognition as an asset in order for the share-based payment to be within the scope of IFRS 2. In

---

3   Paragraphs BC18A–BC18D are added as a consequence of *Group Cash-settled Share-based Payment Transactions* (Amendments to IFRS 2) issued in June 2009.

this case, the IFRS requires the cost of the goods or services received or receivable to be recognised as expenses.

BC18D   Accordingly, the Board concluded that the scope of IFRS 2 includes transactions in which the entity cannot identify some or all of the specific goods or services received. If the value of the identifiable consideration received appears to be less than the fair value of the equity instruments granted or liability incurred, typically,[4] this circumstance indicates that other consideration (ie unidentifiable goods or services) has been (or will be) received.

Transfers of equity instruments to employees (paragraphs 3 and 3A)[5]

BC19   In some situations, an entity might not issue shares or share options to employees (or other parties) direct. Instead, a shareholder (or shareholders) might transfer equity instruments to the employees (or other parties).

BC20   Under this arrangement, the entity has received services (or goods) that were paid for by its shareholders. The arrangement could be viewed as being, in substance, two transactions—one transaction in which the entity has reacquired equity instruments for nil consideration, and a second transaction in which the entity has received services (or goods) as consideration for equity instruments issued to the employees (or other parties).

BC21   The second transaction is a share-based payment transaction. Therefore, the Board concluded that the entity should account for transfers of equity instruments by shareholders to employees or other parties in the same way as other share-based payment transactions. The Board reached the same conclusion with respect to transfers of equity instruments of the entity's parent, or of another entity within the same group as the entity, to the entity's employees or other suppliers.

BC22   However, such a transfer is not a share-based payment transaction if the transfer of equity instruments to an employee or other party is clearly for a purpose other than payment for goods or services supplied to the entity. This would be the case, for example, if the transfer is to settle a shareholder's personal obligation to an employee that is unrelated to employment by the entity, or if the shareholder and employee are related and the transfer is a personal gift because of that relationship.

BC22A   In December 2007 the Board published an exposure draft *Group Cash-settled Share-based Payment Transactions* proposing amendments to IFRS 2 and IFRIC 11 to clarify the accounting for such transactions in the separate or individual financial statements of the entity receiving goods or services. The Board

---

4   In some cases, the reason for the transfer would explain why no goods or services have been or will be received. For example, a principal shareholder, as part of estate planning, transfers some of his shares to a family member. In the absence of factors that indicate that the family member has provided, or is expected to provide, any goods or services to the entity in return for the shares, such a transaction would be outside the scope of IFRS 2.

5   Paragraphs BC22A—BC22G are added as a consequence of *Group Cash-settled Share-based Payment Transactions* (Amendments to IFRS 2) issued in June 2009.

proposed to include specified types of such transactions within the scope of IFRS 2 (not IAS 19 *Employee Benefits*), regardless of whether the group share-based payment transaction is cash-settled or equity-settled.

BC22B   Nearly all of the respondents to the exposure draft agreed that the group cash-settled transactions between a parent and a subsidiary described in the exposure draft should be within the scope of IFRS 2. Respondents generally believed that including these transactions is consistent with IFRS 2's main principle that the entity should recognise the goods or services that it receives in a share-based transaction. However, respondents also expressed concerns that the proposed scope:

(a)   adopted a case-by-case approach and was inconsistent with the definitions of share-based payment transactions in IFRS 2.

(b)   was unclear and increased the inconsistency in the scope requirements among the applicable IFRSs, including IFRIC 11.

BC22C   Many respondents expressed concerns that similar transactions would continue to be treated differently. Because no amendments to the definitions of share-based payment transactions were proposed, some transactions might not be included within the scope of IFRS 2 because they did not meet those definitions. The Board agreed with respondents that the proposals did not achieve the objective of including all share-based payment transactions within the scope of IFRS 2 as intended.

BC22D   When finalising the amendments issued in June 2009, the Board reaffirmed the view it had intended to convey in the proposed amendments, namely that the entity receiving the goods or services should account for group share-based payment transactions in accordance with IFRS 2. Consequently, IFRS 2 applies even when the entity receiving the goods or services has no obligation to settle the transaction and regardless of whether the payments to the suppliers are equity-settled or cash-settled. To avoid the need for further guidance on the scope of IFRS 2 for group transactions, the Board decided to amend some of the defined terms and to supersede paragraph 3 by a new paragraph 3A to state clearly the principles applicable to those transactions.

BC22E   During its redeliberations of the proposed amendments, the Board agreed with respondents' comments that, as proposed, the scope of IFRS 2 remained unclear and inconsistent between the standard and related Interpretations. For example, the terms 'shareholder' and 'parent' have different meanings: a shareholder is not necessarily a parent, and a parent does not have to be a shareholder. The Board noted that share-based payment transactions among group entities are often directed by the parent, indicating a level of control. Therefore, the Board clarified the boundaries of a 'group' by adopting the same definition as in paragraph 4 of IAS 27 *Consolidated and Separate Financial Statements*, which includes only a parent and its subsidiaries.[6]

---

6   The consolidation requirements in IAS 27 were superseded by IFRS 10 *Consolidated Financial Statements* issued in May 2011. The definition of control changed but the definition of a group was not substantially changed.

BC22F   Some respondents to the exposure draft questioned whether the proposals should apply to joint ventures. Before the Board's amendments, the guidance in paragraph 3 (now superseded by paragraph 3A) stated that when a shareholder transferred equity instruments of the entity (or another group entity), the transaction would be within the scope of IFRS 2 for the entity receiving the goods or services. However, that guidance did not specify the accounting by a shareholder transferor. The Board noted that the defined terms in Appendix A, as amended, would clearly state that any entity (including a joint venture) that receives goods or services in a share-based payment transaction should account for the transaction in accordance with the IFRS, regardless of whether that entity also settles the transaction.

BC22G   Furthermore, the Board noted that the exposure draft and related discussions focused on clarifying guidance for transactions involving group entities in the separate or individual financial statements of the entity receiving the goods or services. Addressing transactions involving related parties outside a group structure in their separate or individual financial statements would significantly expand the scope of the project and change the scope of IFRS 2. Therefore, the Board decided not to address transactions between entities not in the same group that are similar to share-based payment transactions but outside the definitions as amended. This carries forward the existing guidance of IFRS 2 for entities not in the same group and the Board does not intend to change that guidance.

Transactions within the scope of IFRS 3 *Business Combinations*

BC23   An entity might acquire goods (or other non-financial assets) as part of the net assets acquired in a business combination for which the consideration paid included shares or other equity instruments issued by the entity. Because IFRS 3 applies to the acquisition of assets and issue of shares in connection with a business combination, that is the more specific standard that should be applied to that transaction.

BC24   Therefore, equity instruments issued in a business combination in exchange for control of the acquiree are not within the scope of IFRS 2. However, equity instruments granted to employees of the acquiree in their capacity as employees, eg in return for continued service, are within the scope of IFRS 2. Also, the cancellation, replacement, or other modifications to share-based payment arrangements because of a business combination or other equity restructuring should be accounted for in accordance with IFRS 2.

BC24A   IFRS 3 (as revised in 2008) changed the definition of a business combination. The previous definition of a business combination was 'the bringing together of separate entities or businesses into one reporting entity'. The revised definition of a business combination is 'a transaction or other event in which an acquirer obtains control of one or more businesses'.

BC24B   The Board was advised that the changes to that definition caused the accounting for the contribution of a business in exchange for shares issued on formation of a joint venture by the venturers to be within the scope of IFRS 2. The Board noted that common control transactions may also be within the scope of IFRS 2 depending on which level of the group reporting entity is assessing the combination.

BC24C   The Board noted that during the development of revised IFRS 3 it did not discuss whether it intended IFRS 2 to apply to these types of transactions. The Board also noted that the reason for excluding common control transactions and the accounting by a joint venture upon its formation from the scope of revised IFRS 3 was to give the Board more time to consider the relevant accounting issues. When the Board revised IFRS 3, it did not intend to change existing practice by bringing such transactions within the scope of IFRS 2, which does not specifically address them.

BC24D   Accordingly, in *Improvements to IFRSs* issued in April 2009, the Board amended paragraph 5 of IFRS 2 to confirm that the contribution of a business on the formation of a joint venture and common control transactions are not within the scope of IFRS 2.

Transactions within the scope of IAS 32 *Financial Instruments: Presentation* and IAS 39 *Financial Instruments: Recognition and Measurement*[7]

BC25   The IFRS includes consequential amendments to IAS 32 and IAS 39 (both as revised in 2003)[8] to exclude from their scope transactions within the scope of IFRS 2.

BC26   For example, suppose the entity enters into a contract to purchase cloth for use in its clothing manufacturing business, whereby it is required to pay cash to the counterparty in an amount equal to the value of 1,000 of the entity's shares at the date of delivery of the cloth. The entity will acquire goods and pay cash at an amount based on its share price. This meets the definition of a share-based payment transaction. Moreover, because the contract is to purchase cloth, which is a non-financial item, and the contract was entered into for the purpose of taking delivery of the cloth for use in the entity's manufacturing business, the contract is not within the scope of IAS 32 and IAS 39.

BC27   The scope of IAS 32 and IAS 39 includes contracts to buy non-financial items that can be settled net in cash or another financial instrument, or by exchanging financial instruments, with the exception of contracts that were entered into and continue to be held for the purpose of the receipt or delivery of a non-financial item in accordance with the entity's expected purchase, sale or usage requirements. A contract that can be settled net in cash or another financial instrument or by exchanging financial instruments includes (a) when the terms of the contract permit either party to settle it net in cash

---

7   IFRS 9 *Financial Instruments* replaced IAS 39. IFRS 9 applies to all items that were previously within the scope of IAS 39. Paragraphs BC25–BC28 refer to matters relevant when IFRS 2 was issued.

8   The title of IAS 32 was amended in 2005.

or another financial instrument or by exchanging financial instruments; (b) when the ability to settle net in cash or another financial instrument, or by exchanging financial instruments, is not explicit in the terms of the contract, but the entity has a practice of settling similar contracts net in cash or another financial instrument, or by exchanging financial instruments (whether with the counterparty, by entering into offsetting contracts, or by selling the contract before its exercise or lapse); (c) when, for similar contracts, the entity has a practice of taking delivery of the underlying and selling it within a short period after delivery for the purpose of generating a profit from short-term fluctuations in price or dealer's margin; and (d) when the non-financial item that is the subject of the contract is readily convertible to cash (IAS 32, paragraphs 8–10 and IAS 39, paragraphs 5–7).

BC28   The Board concluded that the contracts discussed in paragraph BC27 should remain within the scope of IAS 32 and IAS 39 and they are therefore excluded from the scope of IFRS 2.

Recognition of equity-settled share-based payment transactions

BC29   When it developed ED 2, the Board first considered conceptual arguments relating to the recognition of an expense arising from equity-settled share-based payment transactions, including arguments advanced by respondents to the Discussion Paper and other commentators. Some respondents who disagreed with the recognition of an expense arising from particular share-based payment transactions (ie those involving employee share options) did so for practical, rather than conceptual, reasons. The Board considered those practical issues later (see paragraphs BC294–BC310).

BC30   The Board focused its discussions on employee share options, because that is where most of the complexity and controversy lies, but the question of whether expense recognition is appropriate is broader than that—it covers all transactions involving the issue of shares, share options or other equity instruments to employees or suppliers of goods and services. For example, the Board noted that arguments made by respondents and other commentators against expense recognition are directed solely at employee share options. However, if conceptual arguments made against recognition of an expense in relation to employee share options are valid (eg that there is no cost to the entity), those arguments ought to apply equally to transactions involving other equity instruments (eg shares) and to equity instruments issued to other parties (eg suppliers of professional services).

BC31   The rationale for recognising all types of share-based payment transactions— irrespective of whether the equity instrument is a share or a share option, and irrespective of whether the equity instrument is granted to an employee or to some other party—is that the entity has engaged in a transaction that is in essence the same as any other issue of equity instruments. In other words, the entity has received resources (goods or services) as consideration for the issue of shares, share options or other equity instruments. It should therefore account for the inflow of resources (goods or services) and the increase in equity. Subsequently, either at the time of receipt of the goods or services or at some later date, the entity should also account for the expense arising from the consumption of those resources.

BC32 Many respondents to ED 2 agreed with this conclusion. Of those who disagreed, some disagreed in principle, some disagreed for practical reasons, and some disagreed for both reasons. The arguments against expense recognition in principle were considered by the Board when it developed ED 2, as were the arguments against expense recognition for practical reasons, as explained below and in paragraphs BC294–BC310.

BC33 Arguments commonly made against expense recognition include:

(a) the transaction is between the shareholders and the employees, not the entity and the employees.

(b) the employees do not provide services for the options.

(c) there is no cost to the entity, because no cash or other assets are given up; the shareholders bear the cost, in the form of dilution of their ownership interests, not the entity.

(d) the recognition of an expense is inconsistent with the definition of an expense in the conceptual frameworks used by accounting standard-setters, including the IASB's *Framework for the Preparation and Presentation of Financial Statements*.[9]

(e) the cost borne by the shareholders is recognised in the dilution of earnings per share (EPS); if the transaction is recognised in the entity's accounts, the resulting charge to the income statement would mean that EPS is 'hit twice'.

(f) requiring the recognition of a charge would have adverse economic consequences, because it would discourage entities from introducing or continuing employee share plans.

'The entity is not a party to the transaction'

BC34 Some argue that the effect of employee share plans is that the existing shareholders transfer some of their ownership interests to the employees and that the entity is not a party to this transaction.

BC35 The Board did not accept this argument. Entities, not shareholders, set up employee share plans and entities, not shareholders, issue share options to their employees. Even if that were not the case, eg if shareholders transferred shares or share options direct to the employees, this would not mean that the entity is not a party to the transaction. The equity instruments are issued in return for services rendered by the employees and the entity, not the shareholders, receives those services. Therefore, the Board concluded that the entity should account for the services received in return for the equity instruments issued. The Board noted that this is no different from other

---

9 References to the *Framework* in this Basis for Conclusions are to the IASC's *Framework for the Preparation and Presentation of Financial Statements*, adopted by the Board in 2001 and in effect when the Standard was developed.

situations in which equity instruments are issued. For example, if an entity issues warrants for cash, the entity recognises the cash received in return for the warrants issued. Although the effect of an issue, and subsequent exercise, of warrants might be described as a transfer of ownership interests from the existing shareholders to the warrant holders, the entity nevertheless is a party to the transaction because it receives resources (cash) for the issue of warrants and further resources (cash) for the issue of shares upon exercise of the warrants. Similarly, with employee share options, the entity receives resources (employee services) for the issue of the options and further resources (cash) for the issue of shares on the exercise of options.

'The employees do not provide services'

BC36   Some who argue that the entity is not a party to the transaction counter the points made above with the argument that employees do not provide services for the options, because the employees are paid in cash (or other assets) for their services.

BC37   Again, the Board was not convinced by this argument. If it were true that employees do not provide services for their share options, this would mean that entities are issuing valuable share options and getting nothing in return. Employees do not pay cash for the share options they receive. Hence, if they do not provide services for the options, the employees are providing nothing in return. If this were true, by issuing such options the entity's directors would be in breach of their fiduciary duties to their shareholders.

BC38   Typically, shares or share options granted to employees form one part of their remuneration package. For example, an employee might have a remuneration package consisting of a basic cash salary, company car, pension, healthcare benefits, and other benefits including shares and share options. It is usually not possible to identify the services received in respect of individual components of that remuneration package, eg the services received in respect of healthcare benefits. But that does not mean that the employee does not provide services for those healthcare benefits. Rather, the employee provides services for the entire remuneration package.

BC39   In summary, shares, share options or other equity instruments are granted to employees because they are employees. The equity instruments granted form a part of their total remuneration package, regardless of whether that represents a large part or a small part.

'There is no cost to the entity, therefore there is no expense'

BC40   Some argue that because share-based payments do not require the entity to sacrifice any cash or other assets, there is no cost to the entity, and therefore no expense should be recognised.

BC41   The Board regards this argument as unsound, because it overlooks that:

(a)   every time an entity receives resources as consideration for the issue of equity instruments, there is no outflow of cash or other assets, and on every other occasion the resources received as consideration for the issue of equity instruments are recognised in the financial statements; and

(b)   the expense arises from the consumption of those resources, not from an outflow of assets.

BC42   In other words, irrespective of whether one accepts that there is a cost to the entity, an accounting entry is required to recognise the resources received as consideration for the issue of equity instruments, just as it is on other occasions when equity instruments are issued. For example, when shares are issued for cash, an entry is required to recognise the cash received. If a non-monetary asset, such as plant and machinery, is received for those shares instead of cash, an entry is required to recognise the asset received. If the entity acquires another business or entity by issuing shares in a business combination, the entity recognises the net assets acquired.

BC43   The recognition of an expense arising out of such a transaction represents the consumption of resources received, ie the 'using up' of the resources received for the shares or share options. In the case of the plant and machinery mentioned above, the asset would be depreciated over its expected life, resulting in the recognition of an expense each year. Eventually, the entire amount recognised for the resources received when the shares were issued would be recognised as an expense (including any residual value, which would form part of the measurement of the gain or loss on disposal of the asset). Similarly, if another business or entity is acquired by an issue of shares, an expense is recognised when the assets acquired are consumed. For example, inventories acquired will be recognised as an expense when sold, even though no cash or other assets were disbursed to acquire those inventories.

BC44   The only difference in the case of employee services (or other services) received as consideration for the issue of shares or share options is that usually the resources received are consumed immediately upon receipt. This means that an expense for the consumption of resources is recognised immediately, rather than over a period of time. The Board concluded that the timing of consumption does not change the principle; the financial statements should recognise the receipt and consumption of resources, even when consumption occurs at the same time as, or soon after, receipt. This point is discussed further in paragraphs BC45–BC53.

'Expense recognition is inconsistent with the definition of an expense'

BC45   Some have questioned whether recognition of an expense arising from particular share-based payment transactions is consistent with accounting standard-setters' conceptual frameworks, in particular, the *Framework*, which states:

© IFRS Foundation

> Expenses are decreases in economic benefits during the accounting period in the form of outflows or *depletions of assets* or incurrences of liabilities that result in decreases in equity, other than those relating to distributions to equity participants. (paragraph 70, emphasis added)

BC46 Some argue that if services are received in a share-based payment transaction, there is no transaction or event that meets the definition of an expense. They contend that there is no outflow of assets and that no liability is incurred. Furthermore, because services usually do not meet the criteria for recognition as an asset, it is argued that the consumption of those services does not represent a depletion of assets.

BC47 The *Framework* defines an asset and explains that the term 'asset' is not limited to resources that can be recognised as assets in the balance sheet (*Framework*, paragraphs 49 and 50). Although services to be received in the future might not meet the definition of an asset,[10] services are assets when received. These assets are usually consumed immediately. This is explained in FASB Statement of Financial Accounting Concepts No. 6 *Elements of Financial Statements*:

> Services provided by other entities, including personal services, cannot be stored and are received and used simultaneously. They can be assets of an entity only momentarily—as the entity receives and uses them—although their use may create or add value to other assets of the entity … (paragraph 31)

BC48 This applies to all types of services, eg employee services, legal services and telephone services. It also applies irrespective of the form of payment. For example, if an entity purchases services for cash, the accounting entry is:

Dr   Services received

  Cr   Cash paid

BC49 Sometimes, those services are consumed in the creation of a recognisable asset, such as inventories, in which case the debit for services received is capitalised as part of a recognised asset. But often the services do not create or form part of a recognisable asset, in which case the debit for services received is charged immediately to the income statement as an expense. The debit entry above (and the resulting expense) does not represent the cash outflow— that is what the credit entry was for. Nor does it represent some sort of balancing item, to make the accounts balance. The debit entry above represents the resources received, and the resulting expense represents the consumption of those resources.

BC50 The same analysis applies if the services are acquired with payment made in shares or share options. The resulting expense represents the consumption of services, ie a depletion of assets.

BC51 To illustrate this point, suppose that an entity has two buildings, both with gas heating, and the entity issues shares to the gas supplier instead of paying cash. Suppose that, for one building, the gas is supplied through a pipeline, and so is consumed immediately upon receipt. Suppose that, for the other building, the gas is supplied in bottles, and is consumed over a period of time.

---

10 For example, the entity might not have control over future services.

In both cases, the entity has received assets as consideration for the issue of equity instruments, and should therefore recognise the assets received, and a corresponding contribution to equity. If the assets are consumed immediately (the gas received through the pipeline), an expense is recognised immediately; if the assets are consumed later (the gas received in bottles), an expense is recognised later when the assets are consumed.

BC52　Therefore, the Board concluded that the recognition of an expense arising from share-based payment transactions is consistent with the definition of an expense in the *Framework*.

BC53　The FASB considered the same issue and reached the same conclusion in SFAS 123:

> Some respondents pointed out that the definition of expenses in FASB Concepts Statement No. 6, *Elements of Financial Statements*, says that expenses result from outflows or using up of assets or incurring of liabilities (or both). They asserted that because the issuance of stock options does not result in the incurrence of a liability, no expense should be recognised. The Board agrees that employee stock options are not a liability—like stock purchase warrants, employee stock options are equity instruments of the issuer. However, equity instruments, including employee stock options, are valuable financial instruments and thus are issued for valuable consideration, which…for employee stock options is employee services. Using in the entity's operations the benefits embodied in the asset received results in an expense … (Concepts Statement 6, paragraph 81, footnote 43, notes that, in concept most expenses decrease assets. However, if receipt of an asset, such as services, and its use occur virtually simultaneously, the asset often is not recorded.) [paragraph 88]

'Earnings per share is "hit twice"'

BC54　Some argue that any cost arising from share-based payment transactions is already recognised in the dilution of earnings per share (EPS). If an expense were recognised in the income statement, EPS would be 'hit twice'.

BC55　However, the Board noted that this result is appropriate. For example, if the entity paid the employees in cash for their services and the cash was then returned to the entity, as consideration for the issue of share options, the effect on EPS would be the same as issuing those options direct to the employees.

BC56　The dual effect on EPS simply reflects the two economic events that have occurred: the entity has issued shares or share options, thereby increasing the number of shares included in the EPS calculation—although, in the case of options, only to the extent that the options are regarded as dilutive—and it has also consumed the resources it received for those options, thereby decreasing earnings. This is illustrated by the plant and machinery example mentioned in paragraphs BC42 and BC43. Issuing shares affects the number of shares in the EPS calculation, and the consumption (depreciation) of the asset affects earnings.

BC57　In summary, the Board concluded that the dual effect on diluted EPS is not double-counting the effects of a share or share option grant—the same effect is not counted twice. Rather, two different effects are each counted once.

'Adverse economic consequences'

BC58　Some argue that to require recognition (or greater recognition) of employee share-based payment would have adverse economic consequences, in that it might discourage entities from introducing or continuing employee share plans.

BC59　Others argue that if the introduction of accounting changes did lead to a reduction in the use of employee share plans, it might be because the requirement for entities to account properly for employee share plans had revealed the economic consequences of such plans. They argue that this would correct the present economic distortion, whereby entities obtain and consume resources by issuing valuable shares or share options without accounting for those transactions.

BC60　In any event, the Board noted that the role of accounting is to report transactions and events in a neutral manner, not to give 'favourable' treatment to particular transactions to encourage entities to engage in those transactions. To do so would impair the quality of financial reporting. The omission of expenses from the financial statements does not change the fact that those expenses have been incurred. Hence, if expenses are omitted from the income statement, reported profits are overstated. The financial statements are not neutral, are less transparent and are potentially misleading to users. Comparability is impaired, given that expenses arising from employee share-based payment transactions vary from entity to entity, from sector to sector, and from year to year. More fundamentally, accountability is impaired, because the entities are not accounting for transactions they have entered into and the consequences of those transactions.

Measurement of equity-settled share-based payment transactions

BC61　To recognise equity-settled share-based payment transactions, it is necessary to decide how the transactions should be measured. The Board began by considering how to measure share-based payment transactions in principle. Later, it considered practical issues arising from the application of its preferred measurement approach. In terms of accounting principles, there are two basic questions:

(a)　which measurement basis should be applied?

(b)　when should that measurement basis be applied?

BC62　To answer these questions, the Board considered the accounting principles applying to equity transactions. The *Framework* states:

> Equity is the residual interest in the assets of the enterprise after deducting all of its liabilities ... The amount at which equity is shown in the balance sheet is dependent upon the measurement of assets and liabilities. Normally, the aggregate amount of equity only by coincidence corresponds with the aggregate market value of the shares of the enterprise ... (paragraphs 49 and 67)

BC63　The accounting equation that corresponds to this definition of equity is:

> assets minus liabilities equals equity

BC64   Equity is a residual interest, dependent on the measurement of assets and liabilities. Therefore, accounting focuses on recording changes in the left side of the equation (assets minus liabilities, or net assets), rather than the right side. Changes in equity arise from changes in net assets. For example, if an entity issues shares for cash, it recognises the cash received and a corresponding increase in equity. Subsequent changes in the market price of the shares do not affect the entity's net assets and therefore those changes in value are not recognised.

BC65   Hence, the Board concluded that, when accounting for an equity-settled share-based payment transaction, the primary accounting objective is to account for the goods or services received as consideration for the issue of equity instruments. Therefore, equity-settled share-based payment transactions should be accounted for in the same way as other issues of equity instruments, by recognising the consideration received (the change in net assets), and a corresponding increase in equity.

BC66   Given this objective, the Board concluded that, in principle, the goods or services received should be measured at their fair value at the date when the entity obtains those goods or as the services are received. In other words, because a change in net assets occurs when the entity obtains the goods or as the services are received, the fair value of those goods or services at that date provides an appropriate measure of the change in net assets.

BC67   However, for share-based payment transactions with employees, it is usually difficult to measure directly the fair value of the services received. As noted earlier, typically shares or share options are granted to employees as one component of their remuneration package. It is usually not possible to identify the services rendered in respect of individual components of that package. It might also not be possible to measure independently the fair value of the total package, without measuring directly the fair value of the equity instruments granted. Furthermore, options or shares are sometimes granted as part of a bonus arrangement, rather than as a part of basic remuneration, eg as an incentive to the employees to remain in the entity's employ, or to reward them for their efforts in improving the entity's performance. By granting share options, in addition to other remuneration, the entity is paying additional remuneration to obtain additional benefits. Estimating the fair value of those additional benefits is likely to be difficult.

BC68   Given these practical difficulties in measuring directly the fair value of the employee services received, the Board concluded that it is necessary to measure the other side of the transaction, ie the fair value of the equity instruments granted, as a surrogate measure of the fair value of the services received. In this context, the Board considered the same basic questions, as mentioned above:

(a)   which measurement basis should be applied?

(b)   when should that measurement basis be applied?

Measurement basis

BC69   The Board discussed the following measurement bases, to decide which should be applied in principle:

(a)   historical cost

(b)   intrinsic value

(c)   minimum value

(d)   fair value.

Historical cost

BC70   In jurisdictions where legislation permits, entities commonly repurchase their own shares, either directly or through a vehicle such as a trust, which are used to fulfil promised grants of shares to employees or the exercise of employee share options. A possible basis for measuring a grant of options or shares would be the historical cost (purchase price) of its own shares that an entity holds (own shares held), even if they were acquired before the award was made.

BC71   For share options, this would entail comparing the historical cost of own shares held with the exercise price of options granted to employees. Any shortfall would be recognised as an expense. Also, presumably, if the exercise price exceeded the historical cost of own shares held, the excess would be recognised as a gain.

BC72   At first sight, if one simply focuses on the cash flows involved, the historical cost basis appears reasonable: there is a cash outflow to acquire the shares, followed by a cash inflow when those shares are transferred to the employees (the exercise price), with any shortfall representing a cost to the entity. If the cash flows related to anything other than the entity's own shares, this approach would be appropriate. For example, suppose ABC Ltd bought shares in another entity, XYZ Ltd, for a total cost of CU500,000,[11] and later sold the shares to employees for a total of CU400,000. The entity would recognise an expense for the CU100,000 shortfall.

---

11   All monetary amounts in this Basis for Conclusions are denominated in 'currency units (CU)'.

BC73　But when this analysis is applied to the entity's own shares, the logic breaks down. The entity's own shares are not an asset of the entity.[12] Rather, the shares are an interest in the entity's assets. Hence, the distribution of cash to buy back shares is a return of capital to shareholders, and should therefore be recognised as a decrease in equity. Similarly, when the shares are subsequently reissued or transferred, the inflow of cash is an increase in shareholders' capital, and should therefore be recognised as an increase in equity. It follows that no revenue or expense should be recognised. Just as the issue of shares does not represent revenue to the entity, the repurchase of those shares does not represent an expense.

BC74　Therefore, the Board concluded that historical cost is not an appropriate basis upon which to measure equity-settled share-based payment transactions.

Intrinsic value

BC75　An equity instrument could be measured at its intrinsic value. The intrinsic value of a share option at any point in time is the difference between the market price of the underlying shares and the exercise price of the option.

BC76　Often, employee share options have zero intrinsic value at the date of grant—commonly the exercise price is at the market value of the shares at grant date. Therefore, in many cases, valuing share options at their intrinsic value at grant date is equivalent to attributing no value to the options.

BC77　However, the intrinsic value of an option does not fully reflect its value. Options sell in the market for more than their intrinsic value. This is because the holder of an option need not exercise it immediately and benefits from any increase in the value of the underlying shares. In other words, although the ultimate benefit realised by the option holder is the option's intrinsic value at the date of exercise, the option holder is able to realise that future intrinsic value because of having held the option. Thus, the option holder benefits from the right to participate in future gains from increases in the share price. In addition, the option holder benefits from the right to defer payment of the exercise price until the end of the option term. These benefits are commonly referred to as the option's 'time value'.

12　The Discussion Paper discusses this point: Accounting practice in some jurisdictions may present own shares acquired as an asset, but they lack the essential feature of an asset—the ability to provide future economic benefits. The future economic benefits usually provided by an interest in shares are the right to receive dividends and the right to gain from an increase in value of the shares. When a company has an interest in its own shares, it will receive dividends on those shares only if it elects to pay them, and such dividends do not represent a gain to the company, as there is no change in net assets: the flow of funds is simply circular. Whilst it is true that a company that holds its own shares in treasury may sell them and receive a higher amount if their value has increased, a company is generally able to issue shares to third parties at (or near) the current market price. Although there may be legal, regulatory or administrative reasons why it is easier to sell shares that are held as treasury shares than it would be to issue new shares, such considerations do not seem to amount to a fundamental contrast between the two cases. (Footnote to paragraph 4.7)

BC78   For many options, time value represents a substantial part of their value. As noted earlier, many employee share options have zero intrinsic value at grant date, and hence the option's value consists entirely of time value. In such cases, ignoring time value by applying the intrinsic value method at grant date understates the value of the option by 100 per cent.

BC79   The Board concluded that, in general, the intrinsic value measurement basis is not appropriate for measuring share-based payment transactions, because omitting the option's time value ignores a potentially substantial part of an option's total value. Measuring share-based payment transactions at such an understated value would fail to represent those transactions faithfully in the financial statements.

Minimum value

BC80   A share option could be measured at its minimum value. Minimum value is based on the premise that someone who wants to buy a call option on a share would be willing to pay at least (and the option writer would demand at least) the value of the right to defer payment of the exercise price until the end of the option's term. Therefore, minimum value can be calculated using a present value technique. For a dividend-paying share, the calculation is:

    (a)   the current price of the share, minus

    (b)   the present value of expected dividends on that share during the option term (if the option holder does not receive dividends), minus

    (c)   the present value of the exercise price.

BC81   Minimum value can also be calculated using an option pricing model with an expected volatility of effectively zero (not exactly zero, because some option pricing models use volatility as a divisor, and zero cannot be a divisor).

BC82   The minimum value measurement basis captures part of the time value of options, being the value of the right to defer payment of the exercise price until the end of the option's term. It does not capture the effects of volatility. Option holders benefit from volatility because they have the right to participate in gains from increases in the share price during the option term without having to bear the full risk of loss from decreases in the share price. By ignoring volatility, the minimum value method produces a value that is lower, and often much lower, than values produced by methods designed to estimate the fair value of an option.

BC83   The Board concluded that minimum value is not an appropriate measurement basis, because ignoring the effects of volatility ignores a potentially large part of an option's value. As with intrinsic value, measuring share-based payment transactions at the option's minimum value would fail to represent those transactions faithfully in the financial statements.

Fair value

BC84 Fair value is already used in other areas of accounting, including other transactions in which non-cash resources are acquired through the issue of equity instruments. For example, consideration transferred in a business combination is measured at fair value, including the fair value of any equity instruments issued by the entity.

BC85 Fair value, which is the amount at which an equity instrument granted could be exchanged between knowledgeable, willing parties in an arm's length transaction, captures both intrinsic value and time value and therefore provides a measure of the share option's total value (unlike intrinsic value or minimum value). It is the value that reflects the bargain between the entity and its employees, whereby the entity has agreed to grant share options to employees for their services to the entity. Hence, measuring share-based payment transactions at fair value ensures that those transactions are represented faithfully in the financial statements, and consistently with other transactions in which the entity receives resources as consideration for the issue of equity instruments.

BC86 Therefore, the Board concluded that shares, share options or other equity instruments granted should be measured at their fair value.

BC87 Of the respondents to ED 2 who addressed this issue, many agreed with the proposal to measure the equity instruments granted at their fair value. Some respondents who disagreed with the proposal, or who agreed with reservations, expressed concerns about measurement reliability, particularly in the case of smaller or unlisted entities. The issues of measurement reliability and unlisted entities are discussed in paragraphs BC294–BC310 and BC137–BC144, respectively.

Measurement date

BC88 The Board first considered at which date the fair value of equity instruments should be determined for the purpose of measuring share-based payment transactions with employees (and others providing similar services).[13] The possible measurement dates discussed were grant date, service date, vesting date and exercise date. Much of this discussion was in the context of share options rather than shares or other equity instruments, because only options have an exercise date.

---

13 When the Board developed the proposals in ED 2, it focused on the measurement of equity-settled transactions with employees and with parties other than employees. ED 2 did not propose a definition of the term 'employees'. When the Board reconsidered the proposals in ED 2 in the light of comments received, it discussed whether the term might be interpreted too narrowly. This could result in a different accounting treatment of services received from individuals who are regarded as employees (eg for legal or tax purposes) and substantially similar services received from other individuals. The Board therefore concluded that the requirements of the IFRS for transactions with employees should also apply to transactions with other parties providing similar services. This includes services received from (1) individuals who work for the entity under its direction in the same way as individuals who are regarded as employees for legal or tax purposes and (2) individuals who are not employees but who render personal services to the entity similar to those rendered by employees. All references to employees therefore include other parties providing similar services.

BC89   In the context of an employee share option, grant date is when the entity and the employee enter into an agreement, whereby the employee is granted rights to the share option, provided that specified conditions are met, such as the employee's remaining in the entity's employ for a specified period. Service date is the date when the employee renders the services necessary to become entitled to the share option.[14] Vesting date is the date when the employee has satisfied all the conditions necessary to become entitled to the share option. For example, if the employee is required to remain in the entity's employ for three years, vesting date is at the end of that three-year period. Exercise date is when the share option is exercised.

BC90   To help determine the appropriate measurement date, the Board applied the accounting concepts in the *Framework* to each side of the transaction. For transactions with employees, the Board concluded that grant date is the appropriate measurement date, as explained in paragraphs BC91–BC105. The Board also considered some other issues, as explained in paragraphs BC106–BC118. For transactions with parties other than employees, the Board concluded that delivery date is the appropriate measurement date (ie the date the goods or services are received, referred to as service date in the context of transactions with employees), as explained in paragraphs BC119–BC128.

The debit side of the transaction

BC91   Focusing on the debit side of the transaction means focusing on measuring the fair value of the resources received. This measurement objective is consistent with the primary objective of accounting for the goods or services received as consideration for the issue of equity instruments (see paragraphs BC64–BC66). The Board therefore concluded that, in principle, the goods or services received should be measured at their fair value at the date when the entity obtains those goods or as the services are received.

BC92   However, if the fair value of the services received is not readily determinable, then a surrogate measure must be used, such as the fair value of the share options or shares granted. This is the case for employee services.

BC93   If the fair value of the equity instruments granted is used as a surrogate measure of the fair value of the services received, both vesting date and exercise date measurement are inappropriate because the fair value of the services received during a particular accounting period is not affected by subsequent changes in the fair value of the equity instrument. For example, suppose that services are received during years 1–3 as the consideration for share options that are exercised at the end of year 5. For services received in year 1, subsequent changes in the value of the share option in years 2–5 are unrelated to, and have no effect on, the fair value of those services when received.

---

14 Service date measurement theoretically requires the entity to measure the fair value of the share option at each date when services are received. For pragmatic reasons, an approximation would probably be used, such as the fair value of the share option at the end of each accounting period, or the value of the share option measured at regular intervals during each accounting period.

BC94 Service date measurement measures the fair value of the equity instrument at the same time as the services are received. This means that changes in the fair value of the equity instrument during the vesting period affect the amount attributed to the services received. Some argue that this is appropriate, because, in their view, there is a correlation between changes in the fair value of the equity instrument and the fair value of the services received. For example, they argue that if the fair value of a share option falls, so does its incentive effects, which causes employees to reduce the level of services provided for that option, or demand extra remuneration. Some argue that when the fair value of a share option falls because of a general decline in share prices, remuneration levels also fall, and therefore service date measurement reflects this decline in remuneration levels.

BC95 The Board concluded, however, that there is unlikely to be a high correlation between changes in the fair value of an equity instrument and the fair value of the services received. For example, if the fair value of a share option doubles, it is unlikely that the employees work twice as hard, or accept a reduction in the rest of their remuneration package. Similarly, even if a general rise in share prices is accompanied by a rise in remuneration levels, it is unlikely that there is a high correlation between the two. Furthermore, it is likely that any link between share prices and remuneration levels is not universally applicable to all industry sectors.

BC96 The Board concluded that, at grant date, it is reasonable to presume that the fair value of both sides of the contract are substantially the same, ie the fair value of the services expected to be received is substantially the same as the fair value of the equity instruments granted. This conclusion, together with the Board's conclusion that there is unlikely to be a high correlation between the fair value of the services received and the fair value of the equity instruments granted at later measurement dates, led the Board to conclude that grant date is the most appropriate measurement date for the purposes of providing a surrogate measure of the fair value of the services received.

The credit side of the transaction

BC97 Although focusing on the debit side of the transaction is consistent with the primary accounting objective, some approach the measurement date question from the perspective of the credit side of the transaction, ie the issue of an equity instrument. The Board therefore considered the matter from this perspective too.

Exercise date

BC98 Under exercise date measurement, the entity recognises the resources received (eg employee services) for the issue of share options, and also recognises changes in the fair value of the option until it is exercised or lapses. Thus, if the option is exercised, the transaction amount is ultimately 'trued up' to equal the gain made by the option holder on exercise of the option. However, if the option lapses at the end of the exercise period, any amounts previously recognised are effectively reversed, hence the transaction amount is ultimately trued up to equal zero. The Board rejected exercise date measurement because it requires share options to be treated as liabilities, which is inconsistent with the definition of liabilities in the *Framework*. Exercise date measurement requires share options to be treated as liabilities because it requires the remeasurement of share options after initial recognition, which is inappropriate if the share options are equity instruments. A share option does not meet the definition of a liability, because it does not contain an obligation to transfer cash or other assets.

Vesting date, service date and grant date

BC99　The Board noted that the IASC/G4+1 Discussion Paper supported vesting date measurement, and rejected grant date and service date measurement, because it concluded that the share option is not issued until vesting date. It noted that the employees must perform their side of the arrangement by providing the necessary services and meeting any other performance criteria before the entity is obliged to perform its side of the arrangement. The provision of services by the employees is not merely a condition of the arrangement, it is the consideration they use to 'pay' for the share option. Therefore, the Discussion Paper concluded, in economic terms the share option is not issued until vesting date. Because the entity performs its side of the arrangement on vesting date, that is the appropriate measurement date.

BC100　The Discussion Paper also proposed recognising an accrual in equity during the vesting period to ensure that the services are recognised when they are received. It proposed that this accrual should be revised on vesting date to equal the fair value of the share option at that date. This means that amounts credited to equity during the vesting period will be subsequently remeasured to reflect changes in the value of that equity interest before vesting date. That is inconsistent with the *Framework* because equity interests are not subsequently remeasured, ie any changes in their value are not recognised. The Discussion Paper justified this remeasurement by arguing that because the share option is not issued until vesting date, the option is not being remeasured. The credit to equity during the vesting period is merely an interim measure that is used to recognise the partially completed transaction.

BC101　However, the Board noted that even if one accepts that the share option is not issued until vesting date, this does not mean that there is no equity interest until then. If an equity interest exists before vesting date, that interest should not be remeasured. Moreover, the conversion of one type of equity interest into another should not, in itself, cause a change in total equity, because no change in net assets has occurred.

BC102　Some supporters of vesting date suggest that the accrual during the performance period meets the definition of a liability. However, the basis for this conclusion is unclear. The entity is not required to transfer cash or other assets to the employees. Its only commitment is to issue equity instruments.

BC103　The Board concluded that vesting date measurement is inconsistent with the *Framework*, because it requires the remeasurement of equity.

BC104   Service date measurement does not require remeasurement of equity interests after initial recognition. However, as explained earlier, the Board concluded that incorporating changes in the fair value of the share option into the transaction amount is unlikely to produce an amount that fairly reflects the fair value of the services received, which is the primary objective.

BC105   The Board therefore concluded that, no matter which side of the transaction one focuses upon (ie the receipt of resources or the issue of an equity instrument), grant date is the appropriate measurement date under the *Framework*, because it does not require remeasurement of equity interests and it provides a reasonable surrogate measure of the fair value of the services received from employees.

Other issues

IAS 32 Financial Instruments: Disclosure and Presentation[15]

BC106   As discussed above, under the definitions of liabilities and equity in the *Framework*, both shares and share options are equity instruments, because neither instrument requires the entity to transfer cash or other assets. Similarly, all contracts or arrangements that will be settled by the entity issuing shares or share options are classified as equity. However, this differs from the distinction between liabilities and equity applied in IAS 32. Although IAS 32 also considers, in its debt/equity distinction, whether an instrument contains an obligation to transfer cash or other assets, this is supplemented by a second criterion, which considers whether the number of shares to be issued (and cash to be received) on settlement is fixed or variable. IAS 32 classifies a contract that will or may be settled in the entity's own equity instruments as a liability if the contract is a non-derivative for which the entity is or may be obliged to deliver a variable number of the entity's own equity instruments; or a derivative that will or may be settled other than by the exchange of a fixed amount of cash or another financial asset for a fixed number of the entity's own equity instruments.

BC107   In some cases, the number of share options to which employees are entitled varies. For example, the number of share options to which the employees will be entitled on vesting date might vary depending on whether, and to the extent that, a particular performance target is exceeded. Another example is share appreciation rights settled in shares. In this situation, a variable number of shares will be issued, equal in value to the appreciation of the entity's share price over a period of time.

BC108   Therefore, if the requirements of IAS 32 were applied to equity-settled share-based payment transactions, in some situations an obligation to issue equity instruments would be classified as a liability. In such cases, final measurement of the transaction would be at a measurement date later than grant date.

---

15 In August 2005 IAS 32 was amended as IAS 32 *Financial Instruments: Presentation*.

BC109　The Board concluded that different considerations applied in developing IFRS 2. For example, drawing a distinction between fixed and variable option plans and requiring a later measurement date for variable option plans has undesirable consequences, as discussed in paragraphs BC272–BC275.

BC110　The Board concluded that the requirements in IAS 32, whereby some obligations to issue equity instruments are classified as liabilities, should not be applied in the IFRS on share-based payment. The Board recognises that this creates a difference between IFRS 2 and IAS 32. Before deciding whether and how that difference should be eliminated, the Board concluded that it is necessary to address this issue in a broader context, as part of a fundamental review of the definitions of liabilities and equity in the *Framework*, particularly because this is not the only debt/equity classification issue that has arisen in the share-based payment project, as explained below.

Suggestions to change the definitions of liabilities and equity

BC111　In concluding that, for transactions with employees, grant date is the appropriate measurement date under the *Framework*, the Board noted that some respondents to ED 2 and the Discussion Paper support other measurement dates because they believe that the definitions of liabilities and equity in the *Framework* should be revised.

BC112　For example, some supporters of vesting date argue that receipt of employee services between grant date and vesting date creates an obligation for the entity to pay for those services, and that the method of settlement should not matter. In other words, it should not matter whether that obligation is settled in cash or in equity instruments—both ought to be treated as liabilities. Therefore, the definition of a liability should be modified so that all types of obligations, however settled, are included in liabilities. But it is not clear that this approach would necessarily result in vesting date measurement. A share option contains an obligation to issue shares. Hence, if all types of obligations are classified as liabilities, then a share option would be a liability, which would result in exercise date measurement.

BC113　Some support exercise date measurement on the grounds that it produces the same accounting result as 'economically similar' cash-settled share-based payments. For example, it is argued that share appreciation rights (SARs) settled in cash are substantially similar to SARs settled in shares, because in both cases the employee receives consideration to the same value. Also, if the SARs are settled in shares and the shares are immediately sold, the employee ends up in exactly the same position as under a cash-settled SAR, ie with cash equal to the appreciation in the entity's share price over the specified period. Similarly, some argue that share options and cash-settled SARs are economically similar. This is particularly true when the employee realises the gain on the exercise of share options by selling the shares immediately after exercise, as commonly occurs. Either way, the employee ends up with an amount of cash that is based on the appreciation of the share price over a period of time. If cash-settled transactions and equity-settled transactions are economically similar, the accounting treatment should be the same.

BC114   However, it is not clear that changing the distinction between liabilities and equity to be consistent with exercise date measurement is the only way to achieve the same accounting treatment. For example, the distinction could be changed so that cash-settled employee share plans are measured at grant date, with the subsequent cash payment debited directly to equity, as a distribution to equity participants.

BC115   Others who support exercise date measurement do not regard share option holders as part of the ownership group, and therefore believe that options should not be classified as equity. Option holders, some argue, are only potential owners of the entity. But it is not clear whether this view is held generally, ie applied to all types of options. For example, some who support exercise date measurement for employee share options do not necessarily advocate the same approach for share options or warrants issued for cash in the market. However, any revision to the definitions of liabilities and equity in the *Framework* would affect the classification of all options and warrants issued by the entity.

BC116   Given that there is more than one suggestion to change the definitions of liabilities and equity, and these suggestions have not been fully explored, it is not clear exactly what changes to the definitions are being proposed.

BC117   Moreover, the Board concluded that these suggestions should not be considered in isolation, because changing the distinction between liabilities and equity affects all sorts of financial interests, not just those relating to employee share plans. All of the implications of any suggested changes should be explored in a broader project to review the definitions of liabilities and equity in the *Framework*. If such a review resulted in changes to the definitions, the Board would then consider whether the IFRS on share-based payment should be revised.

BC118   Therefore, after considering the issues discussed above, the Board confirmed its conclusion that grant date is the appropriate date at which to measure the fair value of the equity instruments granted for the purposes of providing a surrogate measure of the fair value of services received from employees.

Share-based payment transactions with parties other than employees

BC119   In many share-based payment transactions with parties other than employees, it should be possible to measure reliably the fair value of the goods or services received. The Board therefore concluded that the IFRS should require an entity to presume that the fair value of the goods or services received can be measured reliably.[16] However, in rare cases in which the presumption is rebutted, it is necessary to measure the transaction at the fair value of the equity instruments granted.

BC120　Some measurement issues that arise in respect of share-based payment transactions with employees also arise in transactions with other parties. For example, there might be performance (ie vesting) conditions that must be met before the other party is entitled to the shares or share options. Therefore, any conclusions reached on how to treat vesting conditions in the context of share-based payment transactions with employees also apply to transactions with other parties.

BC121　Similarly, performance by the other party might take place over a period of time, rather than on one specific date, which again raises the question of the appropriate measurement date.

BC122　SFAS 123 does not specify a measurement date for share-based payment transactions with parties other than employees, on the grounds that this is usually a minor issue in such transactions. However, the date at which to estimate the fair value of equity instruments issued to parties other than employees is specified in the US interpretation EITF 96-18 *Accounting for Equity Instruments That Are Issued to Other Than Employees for Acquiring, or in Conjunction with Selling, Goods or Services*:

> [The measurement date is] the earlier of the following:
>
> (a)　The date at which a commitment for performance by the counterparty to earn the equity instruments is reached (a "performance commitment"), or
>
> (b)　The date at which the counterparty's performance is complete. (extract from Issue 1, footnotes excluded)

BC123　The second of these two dates corresponds to vesting date, because vesting date is when the other party has satisfied all the conditions necessary to become unconditionally entitled to the share options or shares. The first of the two dates does not necessarily correspond to grant date. For example, under an employee share plan, the employees are (usually) not committed to providing the necessary services, because they are usually able to leave at any time. Indeed, EITF 96-18 makes it clear that the fact that the equity instrument will be forfeited if the counterparty fails to perform is not

---

16　ED 2 proposed that equity-settled share-based payment transactions should be measured at the fair value of the goods or services received, or by reference to the fair value of the equity instruments granted, whichever fair value is more readily determinable. For transactions with parties other than employees, ED 2 proposed that there should be a rebuttable presumption that the fair value of the goods or services received is the more readily determinable fair value. The Board reconsidered these proposed requirements when finalising the IFRS. It concluded that it would be more consistent with the primary accounting objective (explained in paragraphs BC64–BC66) to require equity-settled share-based payment transactions to be measured at the fair value of the goods or services received, unless that fair value cannot be estimated reliably (eg in transactions with employees). For transactions with parties other than employees, the Board concluded that, in many cases, it should be possible to measure reliably the fair value of the goods or services received, as noted above. Hence, the Board concluded that the IFRS should require an entity to presume that the fair value of the goods or services received can be measured reliably.

sufficient evidence of a performance commitment (Issue 1, footnote 3). Therefore, in the context of share-based payment transactions with parties other than employees, if the other party is not committed to perform, there would be no performance commitment date, in which case the measurement date would be vesting date.

BC124   Accordingly, under SFAS 123 and EITF 96-18, the measurement date for share-based payment transactions with employees is grant date, but for transactions with other parties the measurement date could be vesting date, or some other date between grant date and vesting date.

BC125   In developing the proposals in ED 2, the Board concluded that for transactions with parties other than employees that are measured by reference to the fair value of the equity instruments granted, the equity instruments should be measured at grant date, the same as for transactions with employees.

BC126   However, the Board reconsidered this conclusion during its redeliberations of the proposals in ED 2. The Board considered whether the delivery (service) date fair value of the equity instruments granted provided a better surrogate measure of the fair value of the goods or services received from parties other than employees than the grant date fair value of those instruments. For example, some argue that if the counterparty is not firmly committed to delivering the goods or services, the counterparty would consider whether the fair value of the equity instruments at the delivery date is sufficient payment for the goods or services when deciding whether to deliver the goods or services. This suggests that there is a high correlation between the fair value of the equity instruments at the date the goods or services are received and the fair value of those goods or services. The Board noted that it had considered and rejected a similar argument in the context of transactions with employees (see paragraphs BC94 and BC95). However, the Board found the argument more compelling in the case of transactions with parties other than employees, particularly for transactions in which the counterparty delivers the goods or services on a single date (or over a short period of time) that is substantially later than grant date, compared with transactions with employees in which the services are received over a continuous period that typically begins on grant date.

BC127   The Board was also concerned that permitting entities to measure transactions with parties other than employees on the basis of the fair value of the equity instruments at grant date would provide opportunities for entities to structure transactions to achieve a particular accounting result, causing the carrying amount of the goods or services received, and the resulting expense for the consumption of those goods or services, to be understated.

BC128   The Board therefore concluded that for transactions with parties other than employees in which the entity cannot measure reliably the fair value of the goods or services received at the date of receipt, the fair value of those goods or services should be measured indirectly, based on the fair value of the equity instruments granted, measured at the date the goods or services are received.

Transactions in which the entity cannot identify specifically some or all of the goods or services received (paragraph 13A)[17]

BC128A   The Board incorporated into IFRS 2 the consensus of IFRIC 8 in *Group Cash-settled Share-based Payment Transactions* issued in June 2009. This section summarises the IFRIC's considerations in reaching that consensus, as approved by the Board.

BC128B   IFRS 2 presumes that the consideration received for share-based payments is consistent with the fair value of those share-based payments. For example, if the entity cannot estimate reliably the fair value of the goods or services received, paragraph 10 of the IFRS requires the entity to measure the fair value of the goods or services received by reference to the fair value of the share-based payment made to acquire those goods or services.

BC128C   The Board noted that it is neither necessary nor appropriate to measure the fair value of goods or services as well as the fair value of the share-based payment for every transaction in which the entity receives goods or non-employee services. However, when the value of the identifiable consideration received appears to be less than the fair value of the share-based payment, measurement of both the goods or the services received and the share-based payment may be necessary in order to measure the value of the unidentifiable goods or services received.

BC128D   Paragraph 13 of the IFRS stipulates a rebuttable presumption that the value of identifiable goods or services received can be reliably measured. The Board noted that goods or services that are unidentifiable cannot be reliably measured and that this rebuttable presumption is relevant only for identifiable goods or services.

BC128E   The Board noted that when the goods or services received are identifiable, the measurement principles in the IFRS should be applied. When the goods or services received are unidentifiable, the Board concluded that the grant date is the most appropriate date for the purposes of providing a surrogate measure of the value of the unidentifiable goods or services received (or to be received).

BC128F   The Board noted that some transactions include identifiable and unidentifiable goods or services. In this case, it would be necessary to measure at the grant date the fair value of the unidentifiable goods or services received and to measure the value of the identifiable goods or services in accordance with the IFRS.

BC128G   For cash-settled transactions in which unidentifiable goods or services are received, it is necessary to remeasure the liability at each subsequent reporting date in order to be consistent with the IFRS.

BC128H   The Board noted that the IFRS's requirements in respect of the recognition of the expense arising from share-based payments would apply to identifiable and unidentifiable goods or services. Therefore, the Board decided not to issue additional guidance on this point.

---

17   Paragraphs BC128A–BC128H are added as a consequence of amendments to IFRS 2 *Group Cash-settled Share-based Payment Transactions* issued in June 2009.

Fair value of employee share options

BC129   The Board spent much time discussing how to measure the fair value of employee share options, including how to take into account common features of employee share options, such as vesting conditions and non-transferability. These discussions focused on measuring fair value at grant date, not only because the Board regarded grant date as the appropriate measurement date for transactions with employees, but also because more measurement issues arise at grant date than at later measurement dates. In reaching its conclusions in ED 2, the Board received assistance from the project's Advisory Group and from a panel of experts. During its redeliberations of the proposals in ED 2, the Board considered comments by respondents and advice received from valuation experts on the FASB's Option Valuation Group.

BC130   Market prices provide the best evidence of the fair value of share options. However, share options with terms and conditions similar to employee share options are seldom traded in the markets. The Board therefore concluded that, if market prices are not available, it will be necessary to apply an option pricing model to estimate the fair value of share options.

BC131   The Board decided that it is not necessary or appropriate to prescribe the precise formula or model to be used for option valuation. There is no particular option pricing model that is regarded as theoretically superior to the others, and there is the risk that any model specified might be superseded by improved methodologies in the future. Entities should select whichever model is most appropriate in the circumstances. For example, many employee share options have long lives, are usually exercisable during the period between vesting date and the end of the option's life, and are often exercised early. These factors should be considered when estimating the grant date fair value of share options. For many entities, this might preclude the use of the Black-Scholes-Merton formula, which does not take into account the possibility of exercise before the end of the share option's life and may not adequately reflect the effects of expected early exercise. This is discussed further below (paragraphs BC160–BC162).

BC132   All option pricing models take into account the following option features:

- the exercise price of the option

- the current market price of the share

- the expected volatility of the share price

- the dividends expected to be paid on the shares

- the rate of interest available in the market

- the term of the option.

BC133   The first two items define the intrinsic value of a share option; the remaining four are relevant to the share option's time value. Expected volatility, dividends and interest rate are all based on expectations over the option term. Therefore, the option term is an important part of calculating time value, because it affects the other inputs.

BC134   One aspect of time value is the value of the right to participate in future gains, if any. The valuation does not attempt to predict what the future gain will be, only the amount that a buyer would pay at the valuation date to obtain the right to participate in any future gains. In other words, option pricing models estimate the value of the share option at the measurement date, not the value of the underlying share at some future date.

BC135   The Board noted that some argue that any estimate of the fair value of a share option is inherently uncertain, because it is not known what the ultimate outcome will be, eg whether the share option will expire worthless or whether the employee (or other party) will make a large gain on exercise. However, the valuation objective is to measure the fair value of the rights granted, not to predict the outcome of having granted those rights. Hence, irrespective of whether the option expires worthless or the employee makes a large gain on exercise, that outcome does not mean that the grant date estimate of the fair value of the option was unreliable or wrong.

BC136   A similar analysis applies to the argument that share options do not have any value until they are in the money, ie the share price is greater than the exercise price. This argument refers to the share option's intrinsic value only. Share options also have a time value, which is why they are traded in the markets at prices greater than their intrinsic value. The option holder has a valuable right to participate in any future increases in the share price. So even share options that are at the money have a value when granted. The subsequent outcome of that option grant, even if it expires worthless, does not change the fact that the share option had a value at grant date.

Application of option pricing models to unlisted and newly listed entities

BC137   As explained above, two of the inputs to an option pricing model are the entity's share price and the expected volatility of its share price. For an unlisted entity, there is no published share price information. The entity would therefore need to estimate the fair value of its shares (eg based on the share price of similar entities that are listed, or on a net assets or earnings basis). It would also need to estimate the expected volatility of that value.

BC138   The Board considered whether unlisted entities should be permitted to use the minimum value method instead of a fair value measurement method. The minimum value method is explained earlier, in paragraphs BC80–BC83. Because it excludes the effects of expected volatility, the minimum value method produces a value that is lower, often much lower, than that produced by methods designed to estimate the fair value of an option. Therefore, the Board discussed how an unlisted entity could estimate expected volatility.

BC139   An unlisted entity that regularly issues share options or shares to employees (or other parties) might have an internal market for its shares. The volatility of the internal market share prices provides a basis for estimating expected volatility. Alternatively, an entity could use the historical or implied volatility of similar entities that are listed, and for which share price or option price information is available, as the basis for an estimate of expected volatility.

This would be appropriate if the entity has estimated the value of its shares by reference to the share prices of these similar listed entities. If the entity has instead used another methodology to value its shares, the entity could derive an estimate of expected volatility consistent with that methodology. For example, the entity might value its shares on the basis of net asset values or earnings, in which case it could use the expected volatility of those net asset values or earnings as a basis for estimating expected share price volatility.

BC140 The Board acknowledged that these approaches for estimating the expected volatility of an unlisted entity's shares are somewhat subjective. However, the Board thought it likely that, in practice, the application of these approaches would result in underestimates of expected volatility, rather than overestimates, because entities were likely to exercise caution in making such estimates, to ensure that the resulting option values are not overstated. Therefore, estimating expected volatility is likely to produce a more reliable measure of the fair value of share options granted by unlisted entities than an alternative valuation method, such as the minimum value method.

BC141 Newly listed entities would not need to estimate their share price. However, like unlisted entities, newly listed entities could have difficulties in estimating expected volatility when valuing share options, because they might not have sufficient historical share price information upon which to base an estimate of expected volatility.

BC142 SFAS 123 requires such entities to consider the historical volatility of similar entities during a comparable period in their lives:

> For example, an entity that has been publicly traded for only one year that grants options with an average expected life of five years might consider the pattern and level of historical volatility of more mature entities in the same industry for the first six years the stock of those entities were publicly traded. (paragraph 285b)

BC143 The Board concluded that, in general, unlisted and newly listed entities should not be exempt from a requirement to apply fair value measurement and that the IFRS should include implementation guidance on estimating expected volatility for the purposes of applying an option pricing model to share options granted by unlisted and newly listed entities.

BC144 However, the Board acknowledged that there might be some instances in which an entity—such as (but not limited to) an unlisted or newly listed entity—cannot estimate reliably the grant date fair value of share options granted. In this situation, the Board concluded that the entity should measure the share option at its intrinsic value, initially at the date the entity obtains the goods or the counterparty renders service and subsequently at each reporting date until the final settlement of the share-based payment arrangement, with the effects of the remeasurement recognised in profit or loss. For a grant of share options, the share-based payment arrangement is finally settled when the options are exercised, forfeited (eg upon cessation of employment) or lapse (eg at the end of the option's life). For a grant of shares, the share-based payment arrangement is finally settled when the shares vest or are forfeited.

Application of option pricing models to employee share options

BC145 Option pricing models are widely used in, and accepted by, the financial markets. However, there are differences between employee share options and traded share options. The Board considered the valuation implications of these differences, with assistance from its Advisory Group and other experts, including experts in the FASB's Option Valuation Group, and comments made by respondents to ED 2. Employee share options usually differ from traded options in the following ways, which are discussed further below:

(a) there is a vesting period, during which time the share options are not exercisable;

(b) the options are non-transferable;

(c) there are conditions attached to vesting which, if not satisfied, cause the options to be forfeited; and

(d) the option term is significantly longer.

Inability to exercise during the vesting period

BC146 Typically, employee share options have a vesting period, during which the options cannot be exercised. For example, a share option might be granted with a ten-year life and a vesting period of three years, so the option is not exercisable for the first three years and can then be exercised at any time during the remaining seven years. Employee share options cannot be exercised during the vesting period because the employees must first 'pay' for the options, by providing the necessary services. Furthermore, there might be other specified periods during which an employee share option cannot be exercised (eg during a closed period).

BC147 In the finance literature, employee share options are sometimes called Bermudian options, being partly European and partly American. An American share option can be exercised at any time during the option's life, whereas a European share option can be exercised only at the end of the option's life. An American share option is more valuable than a European share option, although the difference in value is not usually significant.

BC148 Therefore, other things being equal, an employee share option would have a higher value than a European share option and a lower value than an American share option, but the difference between the three values is unlikely to be significant.

BC149 If the entity uses the Black-Scholes-Merton formula, or another option pricing model that values European share options, there is no need to adjust the model for the inability to exercise an option in the vesting period (or any other period), because the model already assumes that the option cannot be exercised during that period.

BC150 If the entity uses an option pricing model that values American share options, such as the binomial model, the inability to exercise an option during the vesting period can be taken into account in applying such a model.

BC151　Although the inability to exercise the share option during the vesting period does not, in itself, have a significant effect on the value of the option, there is still the question whether this restriction has an effect when combined with non-transferability. This is discussed in the following section.

BC152　The Board therefore concluded that:

(a)　if the entity uses an option pricing model that values European share options, such as the Black-Scholes-Merton formula, no adjustment is required for the inability to exercise the options during the vesting period, because the model already assumes that they cannot be exercised during that period.

(b)　if the entity uses an option pricing model that values American share options, such as a binomial model, the application of the model should take account of the inability to exercise the options during the vesting period.

Non-transferability

BC153　From the option holder's perspective, the inability to transfer a share option limits the opportunities available when the option has some time yet to run and the holder wishes either to terminate the exposure to future price changes or to liquidate the position. For example, the holder might believe that over the remaining term of the share option the share price is more likely to decrease than to increase. Also, employee share option plans typically require employees to exercise vested options within a fixed period of time after the employee leaves the entity, or to forfeit the options.

BC154　In the case of a conventional share option, the holder would sell the option rather than exercise it and then sell the shares. Selling the share option enables the holder to receive the option's fair value, including both its intrinsic value and remaining time value, whereas exercising the option enables the holder to receive intrinsic value only.

BC155　However, the option holder is not able to sell a non-transferable share option. Usually, the only possibility open to the option holder is to exercise it, which entails forgoing the remaining time value. (This is not always true. The use of other derivatives, in effect, to sell or gain protection from future changes in the value of the option is discussed later.)

BC156　At first sight, the inability to transfer a share option could seem irrelevant from the entity's perspective, because the entity must issue shares at the exercise price upon exercise of the option, no matter who holds it. In other words, from the entity's perspective, its commitments under the contract are unaffected by whether the shares are issued to the original option holder or to someone else. Therefore, in valuing the entity's side of the contract, from the entity's perspective, non-transferability seems irrelevant.

BC157　However, the lack of transferability often results in early exercise of the share option, because that is the only way for the employees to liquidate their position. Therefore, by imposing the restriction on transferability, the entity has caused the option holder to exercise the option early, thereby resulting in the loss of time value. For example, one aspect of time value is the value of the right to defer payment of the exercise price until the end of the option term. If the option is exercised early because of non-transferability, the entity receives the exercise price much earlier than it would otherwise have done.

BC158　Non-transferability is not the only reason why employees might exercise share options early. Other reasons include risk aversion, lack of wealth diversification, and termination of employment (typically, employees must exercise vested options soon after termination of employment; otherwise the options are forfeited).

BC159　Recent accounting standards and proposed standards (including ED 2) address the issue of early exercise by requiring the expected life of a non-transferable share option to be used in valuing it, rather than the contractual option term. Expected life can be estimated either for the entire share option plan or for subgroups of employees participating in the plan. The estimate takes into account factors such as the length of the vesting period, the average length of time similar options have remained outstanding in the past and the expected volatility of the underlying shares.

BC160　However, comments from respondents to ED 2 and advice received from valuation experts during the Board's redeliberations led the Board to conclude that using a single expected life as an input into an option pricing model (eg the Black-Scholes-Merton formula) was not the best solution for reflecting in the share option valuation the effects of early exercise. For example, such an approach does not take into account the correlation between the share price and early exercise. It would also mean that the share option valuation does not take into account the possibility that the option might be exercised at a date that is later than the end of its expected life. Therefore, in many instances, a more flexible model, such as a binomial model, that uses the share option's contractual life as an input and takes into account the possibility of early exercise on a range of different dates in the option's life, allowing for factors such as the correlation between the share price and early exercise and expected employee turnover, is likely to produce a more accurate estimate of the option's fair value.

BC161　Binomial lattice and similar option pricing models also have the advantage of permitting the inputs to the model to vary over the share option's life. For example, instead of using a single expected volatility, a binomial lattice or similar option pricing model can allow for the possibility that volatility might change over the share option's life. This would be particularly appropriate when valuing share options granted by entities experiencing higher than usual volatility, because volatility tends to revert to its mean over time.

BC162　For these reasons, the Board considered whether it should require the use of a more flexible model, rather than the more commonly used Black-Scholes-Merton formula. However, the Board concluded that it was not necessary to prohibit the use of the Black-Scholes-Merton formula, because there might be instances in which the formula produces a sufficiently reliable estimate of the fair value of the share options granted. For example, if the entity has not granted many share options, the effects of applying a more flexible model might not have a material impact on the entity's financial statements. Also, for share options with relatively short contractual lives, or share options that must be exercised within a short period of time after vesting date, the issues discussed in paragraph BC160 may not be relevant, and hence the Black-Scholes-Merton formula may produce a value that is substantially the same as that produced by a more flexible option pricing model. Therefore, rather than prohibit the use of the Black-Scholes-Merton formula, the Board concluded that the IFRS should include guidance on selecting the most appropriate model to apply. This includes the requirement that the entity should consider factors that knowledgeable, willing market participants would consider in selecting the option pricing model to apply.

BC163　Although non-transferability often results in the early exercise of employee share options, some employees can mitigate the effects of non-transferability, because they are able, in effect, to sell the options or protect themselves from future changes in the value of the options by selling or buying other derivatives. For example, the employee might be able, in effect, to sell an employee share option by entering into an arrangement with an investment bank whereby the employee sells a similar call option to the bank, ie an option with the same exercise price and term. A zero-cost collar is one means of obtaining protection from changes in the value of an employee share option, by selling a call option and buying a put option.

BC164　However, it appears that such arrangements are not always available. For example, the amounts involved have to be sufficiently large to make it worthwhile for the investment bank, which would probably exclude many employees (unless a collective arrangement was made). Also, it appears that investment banks are unlikely to enter into such an arrangement unless the entity is a top listed company, with shares traded in a deep and active market, to enable the investment bank to hedge its own position.

BC165　It would not be feasible to stipulate in an accounting standard that an adjustment to take account of non-transferability is necessary only if the employees cannot mitigate the effects of non-transferability through the use of other derivatives. However, using expected life as an input into an option pricing model, or modelling early exercise in a binomial or similar model, copes with both situations. If employees were able to mitigate the effects of non-transferability by using derivatives, this would often result in the employee share options being exercised later than they would otherwise have been. By taking this factor into account, the estimated fair value of the share option would be higher, which makes sense, given that non-transferability is not a constraint in this case. If the employees cannot mitigate the effects of non-transferability through the use of derivatives, they are likely to exercise the share options much earlier than is optimal. In this case, allowing for the effects of early exercise would significantly reduce the estimated value of the share option.

BC166　This still leaves the question whether there is a need for further adjustment for the combined effect of being unable to exercise or transfer the share option during the vesting period. In other words, the inability to exercise a share option does not, in itself, appear to have a significant effect on its value.

But if the share option cannot be transferred and cannot be exercised, and assuming that other derivatives are not available, the holder is unable to extract value from the share option or protect its value during the vesting period.

BC167 However, it should be noted why these restrictions are in place: the employee has not yet 'paid' for the share option by providing the required services (and fulfilling any other performance conditions). The employee cannot exercise or transfer a share option to which he/she is not yet entitled. The share option will either vest or fail to vest, depending on whether the vesting conditions are satisfied. The possibility of forfeiture resulting from failure to fulfil the vesting conditions is taken into account through the application of the modified grant date method (discussed in paragraphs BC170–BC184).

BC168 Moreover, for accounting purposes, the objective is to estimate the fair value of the share option, not the value from the employee's perspective. The fair value of any item depends on the expected amounts, timing, and uncertainty of the future cash flows relating to the item. The share option grant gives the employee the right to subscribe to the entity's shares at the exercise price, provided that the vesting conditions are satisfied and the exercise price is paid during the specified period. The effect of the vesting conditions is considered below. The effect of the share option being non-exercisable during the vesting period has already been considered above, as has the effect of non-transferability. There does not seem to be any additional effect on the expected amounts, timing or uncertainty of the future cash flows arising from the combination of non-exercisability and non-transferability during the vesting period.

BC169 After considering all of the above points, the Board concluded that the effects of early exercise, because of non-transferability and other factors, should be taken into account when estimating the fair value of the share option, either by modelling early exercise in a binomial or similar model, or using expected life rather than contracted life as an input into an option pricing model, such as the Black-Scholes-Merton formula.

Vesting conditions

BC170 Employee share options usually have vesting conditions. The most common condition is that the employee must remain in the entity's employ for a specified period, say three years. If the employee leaves during that period, the options are forfeited. There might also be other performance conditions, eg that the entity achieves a specified growth in share price or earnings.

BC171 Vesting conditions ensure that the employees provide the services required to 'pay' for their share options. For example, the usual reason for imposing service conditions is to retain staff; the usual reason for imposing other performance conditions is to provide an incentive for the employees to work towards specified performance targets.

BC171A   In 2005 the Board decided to take on a project to clarify the definition of vesting conditions and the accounting treatment of cancellations. In particular, the Board noted that it is important to distinguish between non-vesting conditions, which need to be satisfied for the counterparty to become entitled to the equity instrument, and vesting conditions such as performance conditions. In February 2006 the Board published an exposure draft *Vesting Conditions and Cancellations*, which proposed to restrict vesting conditions to service conditions and performance conditions. Those are the only conditions that determine whether *the entity receives the services* that entitle the counterparty to the share-based payment, and therefore whether the share-based payment vests. In particular, a share-based payment may vest even if some non-vesting conditions have not been met. The feature that distinguishes a performance condition from a non-vesting condition is that the former has an explicit or implicit service requirement and the latter does not.

BC171B   In general, respondents to the exposure draft agreed with the Board's proposals but asked for clarification of whether particular restrictive conditions, such as 'non-compete provisions', are vesting conditions. The Board noted that a share-based payment vests when the counterparty's entitlement to it is no longer conditional on future service or performance conditions. Therefore, conditions such as non-compete provisions and transfer restrictions, which apply after the counterparty has become entitled to the share-based payment, are not vesting conditions. The Board revised the definition of 'vest' accordingly.

BC172   Some argue that the existence of vesting conditions does not necessarily imply that the value of employee share options is significantly less than the value of traded share options. The employees have to satisfy the vesting conditions to fulfil their side of the arrangement. In other words, the employees' performance of their side of the arrangement is what they do to pay for their share options. Employees do not pay for the options with cash, as do the holders of traded share options; they pay with their services. Having to pay for the share options does not make them less valuable. On the contrary, it proves that the share options are valuable.

BC173   Others argue that the possibility of forfeiture without compensation for part-performance suggests that the share options are less valuable. The employees might partly perform their side of the arrangement, eg by working for part of the period, then have to leave for some reason, and forfeit the share options without compensation for that part performance. If there are other performance conditions, such as achieving a specified growth in the share price or earnings, the employees might work for the entire vesting period, but fail to meet the vesting conditions and therefore forfeit the share options.

BC174   Similarly, some argue that the entity would take into account the possibility of forfeiture when entering into the agreement at grant date. In other words, in deciding how many share options to grant in total, the entity would allow for expected forfeitures. Hence, if the objective is to estimate at grant date the fair value of the entity's commitments under the share option agreement, that valuation should take into account that the entity's commitment to fulfil its side of the option agreement is conditional upon the vesting conditions being satisfied.

BC175 In developing the proposals in ED 2, the Board concluded that the valuation of rights to share options or shares granted to employees (or other parties) should take into account all types of vesting conditions, including both service conditions and performance conditions. In other words, the grant date valuation should be reduced to allow for the possibility of forfeiture due to failure to satisfy the vesting conditions.

BC176 Such a reduction might be achieved by adapting an option pricing model to incorporate vesting conditions. Alternatively, a more simplistic approach might be applied. One such approach is to estimate the possibility of forfeiture at grant date, and reduce the value produced by an option pricing model accordingly. For example, if the valuation calculated using an option pricing model was CU15, and the entity estimated that 20 per cent of the share options would be forfeited because of failure to satisfy the vesting conditions, allowing for the possibility of forfeiture would reduce the grant date value of each option granted from CU15 to CU12.

BC177 The Board decided against proposing detailed guidance on how the grant date value should be adjusted to allow for the possibility of forfeiture. This is consistent with the Board's objective of setting principles-based standards. The measurement objective is to estimate fair value. That objective might not be achieved if detailed, prescriptive rules were specified, which would probably become outdated by future developments in valuation methodologies.

BC178 However, respondents to ED 2 raised a variety of concerns about the inclusion of vesting conditions in the grant date valuation. Some respondents were concerned about the practicality and subjectivity of including non-market performance conditions in the share option valuation. Some were also concerned about the practicality of including service conditions in the grant date valuation, particularly in conjunction with the units of service method proposed in ED 2 (discussed further in paragraphs BC203–BC217).

BC179 Some respondents suggested the alternative approach applied in SFAS 123, referred to as the modified grant date method. Under this method, service conditions and non-market performance conditions are excluded from the grant date valuation (ie the possibility of forfeiture is not taken into account when estimating the grant date fair value of the share options or other equity instruments, thereby producing a higher grant date fair value), but are instead taken into account by requiring the transaction amount to be based on the number of equity instruments that eventually vest. Under this method, on a cumulative basis, no amount is recognised for goods or services received if the equity instruments granted do not vest because of failure to satisfy a vesting condition (other than a market condition), eg the counterparty fails to complete a specified service period, or a performance condition (other than a market condition) is not satisfied.

BC180   After considering respondents' comments and obtaining further advice from valuation experts, the Board decided to adopt the modified grant date method applied in SFAS 123. However, the Board decided that it should not permit the choice available in SFAS 123 to account for the effects of expected or actual forfeitures of share options or other equity instruments because of failure to satisfy a service condition. For a grant of equity instruments with a service condition, SFAS 123 permits an entity to choose at grant date to recognise the services received based on an estimate of the number of share options or other equity instruments expected to vest, and to revise that estimate, if necessary, if subsequent information indicates that actual forfeitures are likely to differ from previous estimates. Alternatively, an entity may begin recognising the services received as if all the equity instruments granted that are subject to a service requirement are expected to vest. The effects of forfeitures are then recognised when those forfeitures occur, by reversing any amounts previously recognised for services received as consideration for equity instruments that are forfeited.

BC181   The Board decided that the latter method should not be permitted. Given that the transaction amount is ultimately based on the number of equity instruments that vest, it is appropriate to estimate the number of expected forfeitures when recognising the services received during the vesting period. Furthermore, by ignoring expected forfeitures until those forfeitures occur, the effects of reversing any amounts previously recognised might result in a distortion of remuneration expense recognised during the vesting period. For example, an entity that experiences a high level of forfeitures might recognise a large amount of remuneration expense in one period, which is then reversed in a later period.

BC182   Therefore, the Board decided that the IFRS should require an entity to estimate the number of equity instruments expected to vest and to revise that estimate, if necessary, if subsequent information indicates that actual forfeitures are likely to differ from previous estimates.

BC183   Under SFAS 123, market conditions (eg a condition involving a target share price, or specified amount of intrinsic value on which vesting or exercisability is conditioned) are included in the grant date valuation, without subsequent reversal. That is to say, when estimating the fair value of the equity instruments at grant date, the entity takes into account the possibility that the market condition may not be satisfied. Having allowed for that possibility in the grant date valuation of the equity instruments, no adjustment is made to the number of equity instruments included in the calculation of the transaction amount, irrespective of the outcome of the market condition. In other words, the entity recognises the goods or services received from a counterparty that satisfies all other vesting conditions (eg services received from an employee who remains in service for the specified service period), irrespective of whether that market condition is satisfied. The treatment of market conditions therefore contrasts with the treatment of other types of vesting conditions. As explained in paragraph BC179, under the modified grant date method, vesting conditions are not taken into account when estimating the fair value of the equity instruments at grant date, but are instead taken into account by requiring the transaction amount to be based on the number of equity instruments that eventually vest.

BC184　The Board considered whether it should apply the same approach to market conditions as is applied in SFAS 123. It might be argued that it is not appropriate to distinguish between market conditions and other types of performance conditions, because to do so could create opportunities for arbitrage, or cause an economic distortion by encouraging entities to favour one type of performance condition over another. However, the Board noted that it is not clear what the result would be. On the one hand, some entities might prefer the 'truing up' aspect of the modified grant date method, because it permits a reversal of remuneration expense if the condition is not met. On the other hand, if the performance condition is met, and it has not been incorporated into the grant date valuation (as is the case when the modified grant date method is used), the expense will be higher than it would otherwise have been (ie if the performance condition had been incorporated into the grant date valuation). Furthermore, some entities might prefer to avoid the potential volatility caused by the truing up mechanism. Therefore, it is not clear whether having a different treatment for market and non-market performance conditions will necessarily cause entities to favour market conditions over non-market performance conditions, or vice versa. Furthermore, the practical difficulties that led the Board to conclude that non-market performance conditions should be dealt with via the modified grant date method rather than being included in the grant date valuation do not apply to market conditions, because market conditions can be incorporated into option pricing models. Moreover, it is difficult to distinguish between market conditions, such as a target share price, and the market condition that is inherent in the option itself, ie that the option will be exercised only if the share price on the date of exercise exceeds the exercise price. For these reasons, the Board concluded that the IFRS should apply the same approach as is applied in SFAS 123.

Option term

BC185　Employee share options often have a long contractual life, eg ten years. Traded options typically have short lives, often only a few months. Estimating the inputs required by an option pricing model, such as expected volatility, over long periods can be difficult, giving rise to the possibility of significant estimation error. This is not usually a problem with traded share options, given their much shorter lives.

BC186　However, some share options traded over the counter have long lives, such as ten or fifteen years. Option pricing models are used to value them. Therefore, contrary to the argument sometimes advanced, option pricing models can be (and are being) applied to long-lived share options.

BC187　Moreover, the potential for estimation error is mitigated by using a binomial or similar model that allows for changes in model inputs over the share option's life, such as expected volatility, and interest and dividend rates, that could occur and the probability of those changes occurring during the term of the share option. The potential for estimation error is further mitigated by taking into account the possibility of early exercise, either by using expected life rather than contracted life as an input into an option pricing model or by modelling exercise behaviour in a binomial or similar model, because this reduces the expected term of the share option. Because employees often exercise their share options relatively early in the share option's life, the expected term is usually much shorter than contracted life.

Other features of employee share options

BC188 Whilst the features discussed above are common to most employee share options, some might include other features. For example, some share options have a reload feature. This entitles the employee to automatic grants of additional share options whenever he/she exercises previously granted share options and pays the exercise price in the entity's shares rather than in cash. Typically, the employee is granted a new share option, called a reload option, for each share surrendered when exercising the previous share option. The exercise price of the reload option is usually set at the market price of the shares on the date the reload option is granted.

BC189 When SFAS 123 was developed, the FASB concluded that, ideally, the value of the reload feature should be included in the valuation of the original share option at grant date. However, at that time the FASB believed that it was not possible to do so. Accordingly, SFAS 123 does not require the reload feature to be included in the grant date valuation of the original share option. Instead, reload options granted upon exercise of the original share options are accounted for as a new share option grant.

BC190 However, recent academic research indicates that it is possible to value the reload feature at grant date, eg Saly, Jagannathan and Huddart (1999).[18] However, if significant uncertainties exist, such as the number and timing of expected grants of reload options, it might not be practicable to include the reload feature in the grant date valuation.

BC191 When it developed ED 2, the Board concluded that the reload feature should be taken into account, where practicable, when measuring the fair value of the share options granted. However, if the reload feature was not taken into account, then when the reload option is granted, it should be accounted for as a new share option grant.

BC192 Many respondents to ED 2 agreed with the proposals in ED 2. However, some disagreed. For example, some disagreed with there being a choice of treatments. Some respondents supported always treating reload options granted as new grants whereas others supported always including the reload feature in the grant date valuation. Some expressed concerns about the practicality of including the reload feature in the grant date valuation. After reconsidering this issue, the Board concluded that the reload feature should not be included in the grant date valuation and therefore all reload options granted should be accounted for as new share option grants.

---

18 P J Saly, R Jagannathan and S J Huddart. 1999. Valuing the Reload Features of Executive Stock Options. *Accounting Horizons* 13 (3): 219–240.

BC193   There may be other features of employee (and other) share options that the Board has not yet considered. But even if the Board were to consider every conceivable feature of employee (and other) share options that exist at present, new features might be developed in the future.

BC194   The Board therefore concluded that the IFRS should focus on setting out clear principles to be applied to share-based payment transactions, and provide guidance on the more common features of employee share options, but should not prescribe extensive application guidance, which would be likely to become outdated.

BC195   Nevertheless, the Board considered whether there are share options with such unusual or complex features that it is too difficult to make a reliable estimate of their fair value and, if so, what the accounting treatment should be.

BC196   SFAS 123 states that 'it should be possible to reasonably estimate the fair value of most stock options and other equity instruments at the date they are granted' (paragraph 21). However, it states that, 'in unusual circumstances, the terms of the stock option or other equity instrument may make it virtually impossible to reasonably estimate the instrument's fair value at the date it is granted'. The standard requires that, in such situations, measurement should be delayed until it is possible to estimate reasonably the instrument's fair value. It notes that this is likely to be the date at which the number of shares to which the employee is entitled and the exercise price are determinable. This could be vesting date. The standard requires that estimates of compensation expense for earlier periods (ie until it is possible to estimate fair value) should be based on current intrinsic value.

BC197   The Board thought it unlikely that entities could not reasonably determine the fair value of share options at grant date, particularly after excluding vesting conditions[19] and reload features from the grant date valuation. The share options form part of the employee's remuneration package, and it seems reasonable to presume that an entity's management would consider the value of the share options to satisfy itself that the employee's remuneration package is fair and reasonable.

BC198   When it developed ED 2, the Board concluded that there should be no exceptions to the requirement to apply a fair value measurement basis, and therefore it was not necessary to include in the proposed IFRS specific accounting requirements for share options that are difficult to value.

BC199   However, after considering respondents' comments, particularly with regard to unlisted entities, the Board reconsidered this issue. The Board concluded that, in rare cases only, in which the entity could not estimate reliably the grant date fair value of the equity instruments granted, the entity should measure the equity instruments at intrinsic value, initially at grant date and subsequently at each reporting date until the final settlement of the share-based payment arrangement, with the effects of the remeasurement recognised in profit or loss. For a grant of share options, the share-based payment arrangement is finally settled when the share options are exercised,

---

19 ie vesting conditions other than market conditions.

are forfeited (eg upon cessation of employment) or lapse (eg at the end of the option's life). For a grant of shares, the share-based payment arrangement is finally settled when the shares vest or are forfeited. This requirement would apply to all entities, including listed and unlisted entities.

Recognition and measurement of services received in an equity-settled share-based payment transaction

During the vesting period

BC200   In an equity-settled share-based payment transaction, the accounting objective is to recognise the goods or services received as consideration for the entity's equity instruments, measured at the fair value of those goods or services when received. For transactions in which the entity receives employee services, it is often difficult to measure directly the fair value of the services received. In this case, the Board concluded that the fair value of the equity instruments granted should be used as a surrogate measure of the fair value of the services received. This raises the question how to use that surrogate measure to derive an amount to attribute to the services received. Another related question is how the entity should determine when the services are received.

BC201   Starting with the latter question, some argue that shares or share options are often granted to employees for past services rather than future services, or mostly for past services, irrespective of whether the employees are required to continue working for the entity for a specified future period before their rights to those shares or share options vest. Conversely, some argue that shares or share options granted provide a future incentive to the employees and those incentive effects continue after vesting date, which implies that the entity receives services from employees during a period that extends beyond vesting date. For share options in particular, some argue that employees render services beyond vesting date, because employees are able to benefit from an option's time value between vesting date and exercise date only if they continue to work for the entity (since usually a departing employee must exercise the share options within a short period, otherwise they are forfeited).

BC202   However, the Board concluded that if the employees are required to complete a specified service period to become entitled to the shares or share options, this requirement provides the best evidence of when the employees render services in return for the shares or share options. Consequently, the Board concluded that the entity should presume that the services are received during the vesting period. If the shares or share options vest immediately, it should be presumed that the entity has already received the services, in the absence of evidence to the contrary. An example of when immediately vested shares or share options are not for past services is when the employee concerned has only recently begun working for the entity, and the shares or share options are granted as a signing bonus. But in this situation, it might nevertheless be necessary to recognise an expense immediately, if the future employee services do not meet the definition of an asset.

BC203　Returning to the first question in paragraph BC200, when the Board developed ED 2 it developed an approach whereby the fair value of the shares or share options granted, measured at grant date and allowing for all vesting conditions, is divided by the number of units of service expected to be received to determine the deemed fair value of each unit of service subsequently received.

BC204　For example, suppose that the fair value of share options granted, before taking into account the possibility of forfeiture, is CU750,000. Suppose that the entity estimates the possibility of forfeiture because of failure of the employees to complete the required three-year period of service is 20 per cent (based on a weighted average probability), and hence it estimates the fair value of the options granted at CU600,000 (CU750,000 × 80%). The entity expects to receive 1,350 units of service over the three-year vesting period.

BC205　Under the units of service method proposed in ED 2, the deemed fair value per unit of service subsequently received is CU444.44 (CU600,000/1,350). If everything turns out as expected, the amount recognised for services received is CU600,000 (CU444.44 × 1,350).

BC206　This approach is based on the presumption that there is a fairly bargained contract at grant date. Thus the entity has granted share options valued at CU600,000 and expects to receive services valued at CU600,000 in return. It does not expect all share options granted to vest because it does not expect all employees to complete three years' service. Expectations of forfeiture because of employee departures are taken into account when estimating the fair value of the share options granted, and when determining the fair value of the services to be received in return.

BC207　Under the units of service method, the amount recognised for services received during the vesting period might exceed CU600,000, if the entity receives more services than expected. This is because the objective is to account for the services subsequently received, not the fair value of the share options granted. In other words, the objective is not to estimate the fair value of the share options granted and then spread that amount over the vesting period. Rather, the objective is to account for the services subsequently received, because it is the receipt of those services that causes a change in net assets and hence a change in equity. Because of the practical difficulty of valuing those services directly, the fair value of the share options granted is used as a surrogate measure to determine the fair value of each unit of service subsequently received, and therefore the transaction amount is dependent upon the number of units of service actually received. If more are received than expected, the transaction amount will be greater than CU600,000. If fewer services are received, the transaction amount will be less than CU600,000.

BC208　Hence, a grant date measurement method is used as a practical expedient to achieve the accounting objective, which is to account for the services actually received in the vesting period. The Board noted that many who support grant date measurement do so for reasons that focus on the entity's commitments under the contract, not the services received. They take the view that the entity has conveyed to its employees valuable equity instruments at grant date and that the accounting objective should be to account for the equity instruments conveyed. Similarly, supporters of vesting date measurement argue that the entity does not convey valuable equity instruments to the employees until vesting date, and that the accounting objective should be to account for the equity instruments conveyed at vesting date. Supporters of exercise date measurement argue that, ultimately, the valuable equity instruments conveyed by the entity to the employees are the shares issued on exercise date and the objective should be to account for the value given up by the entity by issuing equity instruments at less than their fair value.

BC209 Hence all of these arguments for various measurement dates are focused entirely on what the entity (or its shareholders) has given up under the share-based payment arrangement, and accounting for that sacrifice. Therefore, if 'grant date measurement' were applied as a matter of principle, the primary objective would be to account for the value of the rights granted. Depending on whether the services have already been received and whether a prepayment for services to be received in the future meets the definition of an asset, the other side of the transaction would either be recognised as an expense at grant date, or capitalised as a prepayment and amortised over some period of time, such as over the vesting period or over the expected life of the share option. Under this view of grant date measurement, there would be no subsequent adjustment for actual outcomes. No matter how many share options vest or how many share options are exercised, that does not change the value of the rights given to the employees at grant date.

BC210 Therefore, the reason why some support grant date measurement differs from the reason why the Board concluded that the fair value of the equity instruments granted should be measured at grant date. This means that some will have different views about the consequences of applying grant date measurement. Because the units of service method is based on using the fair value of the equity instruments granted, measured at grant date, as a surrogate measure of the fair value of the services received, the total transaction amount is dependent upon the number of units of service received.

BC211 Some respondents to ED 2 disagreed with the units of service method in principle, because they did not accept that the fair value of the services received should be the accounting focus. Rather, the respondents focused on accounting for the 'cost' of the equity instruments issued (ie the credit side of the transaction rather than the debit side), and took the view that if the share options or shares are forfeited, no cost was incurred, and thus any amounts recognised previously should be reversed, as would happen with a cash-settled transaction.

BC212 Some respondents also disagreed with the treatment of performance conditions under the units of service method, because if the employee completes the required service period but the equity instruments do not vest because of the performance condition not being satisfied, there is no reversal of amounts recognised during the vesting period. Some argue that this result is unreasonable because, if the performance condition is not satisfied, then the employee did not perform as required, hence it is inappropriate to recognise an expense for services received or consumed, because the entity did not receive the specified services.

BC213 The Board considered and rejected the above arguments made against the units of service method in principle. For example, the Board noted that the objective of accounting for the services received, rather than the cost of the equity instruments issued, is consistent with the accounting treatment of other issues of equity instruments, and with the IASB *Framework*. With regard to performance conditions, the Board noted that the strength of the argument in paragraph BC212 depends on the extent to which the employee has control or influence over the achievement of the performance target. One cannot necessarily conclude that the non-attainment of the performance target is a good indication that the employee has failed to perform his/her side of the arrangement (ie failed to provide services).

BC214 Therefore, the Board was not persuaded by those respondents who disagreed with the units of service method in principle. However, the Board also noted that some respondents raised practical concerns about the method. Some respondents regarded the units of service method as too complex and burdensome to apply in practice. For example, if an entity granted share options to a group of employees but did not grant the same number of share options to each employee (eg the number might vary according to their salary or position in the entity), it would be necessary to calculate a different deemed fair value per unit of service for each individual employee (or for each subgroup of employees, if there are groups of employees who each received the same number of options). Then the entity would have to track each employee, to calculate the amount to recognise for each employee. Furthermore, in some circumstances, an employee share or share option scheme might not require the employee to forfeit the shares or share options if the employee leaves during the vesting period in specified circumstances. Under the terms of some schemes, employees can retain their share options or shares if they are classified as a 'good leaver', eg a departure resulting from circumstances not within the employee's control, such as compulsory retirement, ill health or redundancy. Therefore, in estimating the possibility of forfeiture, it is not simply a matter of estimating the possibility of employee departure during the vesting period. It is also necessary to estimate whether those departures will be 'good leavers' or 'bad leavers'. And because the share options or shares will vest upon departure of 'good leavers', the expected number of units to be received and the expected length of the vesting period will be shorter for this group of employees. These factors would need to be incorporated into the application of the units of service method.

BC215 Some respondents also raised practical concerns about applying the units of service method to grants with performance conditions. These concerns include the difficulty of incorporating non-market and complex performance conditions into the grant date valuation, the additional subjectivity that this introduces, and that it was unclear how to apply the method when the length of the vesting period is not fixed, because it depends on when a performance condition is satisfied.

BC216   The Board considered the practical concerns raised by respondents, and obtained further advice from valuation experts concerning the difficulties highlighted by respondents of including non-market performance conditions in the grant date valuation. Because of these practical considerations, the Board concluded that the units of service method should not be retained in the IFRS. Instead, the Board decided to adopt the modified grant date method applied in SFAS 123. Under this method, service conditions and non-market performance conditions are excluded from the grant date valuation (ie the possibility of forfeiture is not taken into account when estimating the grant date fair value of the share options or other equity instruments, thereby producing a higher grant date fair value), but are instead taken into account by requiring that the transaction amount be based on the number of equity instruments that eventually vest.[20] Under this method, on a cumulative basis, no amount is recognised for goods or services received if the equity instruments granted do not vest because of failure to satisfy a vesting condition (other than a market condition), eg the counterparty fails to complete a specified service period, or a performance condition (other than a market condition) is not satisfied.

BC217   However, as discussed earlier (paragraphs BC180–BC182), the Board decided that it should not permit the choice available in SFAS 123 to account for the effects of expected or actual forfeitures of share options or other equity instruments because of failure to satisfy a service condition. The Board decided that the IFRS should require an entity to estimate the number of equity instruments expected to vest and to revise that estimate, if necessary, if subsequent information indicates that actual forfeitures are likely to differ from previous estimates.

Share options that are forfeited or lapse after the end of the vesting period

BC218   Some share options might not be exercised. For example, a share option holder is unlikely to exercise a share option if the share price is below the exercise price throughout the exercise period. Once the last date for exercise is passed, the share option will lapse.

BC219   The lapse of a share option at the end of the exercise period does not change the fact that the original transaction occurred, ie goods or services were received as consideration for the issue of an equity instrument (the share option). The lapsing of the share option does not represent a gain to the entity, because there is no change to the entity's net assets. In other words, although some might see such an event as being a benefit to the remaining shareholders, it has no effect on the entity's financial position. In effect, one type of equity interest (the share option holders' interest) becomes part of another type of equity interest (the shareholders' interest). The Board

---

20   The treatment of market conditions is discussed in paragraphs BC183 and BC184. As noted in paragraph BC184, the practical difficulties that led the Board to conclude that non-market conditions should be dealt with via the modified grant date method rather than being included in the grant date valuation do not apply to market conditions, because market conditions can be incorporated into option pricing models.

therefore concluded that the only accounting entry that might be required is a movement within equity, to reflect that the share options are no longer outstanding (ie as a transfer from one type of equity interest to another).

BC220   This is consistent with the treatment of other equity instruments, such as warrants issued for cash. When warrants subsequently lapse unexercised, this is not treated as a gain; instead the amount previously recognised when the warrants were issued remains within equity.[21]

BC221   The same analysis applies to equity instruments that are forfeited after the end of the vesting period. For example, an employee with vested share options typically must exercise those options within a short period after cessation of employment, otherwise the options are forfeited. If the share options are not in the money, the employee is unlikely to exercise the options and hence they will be forfeited. For the same reasons as are given in paragraph BC219, no adjustment is made to the amounts previously recognised for services received as consideration for the share options. The only accounting entry that might be required is a movement within equity, to reflect that the share options are no longer outstanding.

Modifications to the terms and conditions of share-based payment arrangements

BC222   An entity might modify the terms of or conditions under which the equity instruments were granted. For example, the entity might reduce the exercise price of share options granted to employees (ie reprice the options), which increases the fair value of those options. During the development of ED 2, the Board focused mainly on the repricing of share options.

BC223   The Board noted that the IASC/G4+1 Discussion Paper argued that if the entity reprices its share options it has, in effect, replaced the original share option with a more valuable share option. The entity presumably believes that it will receive an equivalent amount of benefit from doing so, because otherwise the directors would not be acting in the best interests of the entity or its shareholders. This suggests that the entity expects to receive additional or enhanced employee services equivalent in value to the incremental value of the repriced share options. The Discussion Paper therefore proposed that the incremental value given (ie the difference between the value of the original share option and the value of the repriced share option, as at the date of repricing) should be recognised as additional remuneration expense. Although the Discussion Paper discussed repricing in the context of vesting date measurement, SFAS 123, which applies a grant date measurement basis for employee share-based payment, contains reasoning similar to that in the Discussion Paper.

---

21   However, an alternative approach is followed in some jurisdictions (eg Japan and the UK), where the entity recognises a gain when warrants lapse. But under the *Framework*, recognising a gain on the lapse of warrants would be appropriate only if warrants were liabilities, which they are not.

BC224　This reasoning seems appropriate if grant date measurement is applied on the grounds that the entity made a payment to the employees on grant date by granting them valuable rights to equity instruments of the entity. If the entity is prepared to replace that payment with a more valuable payment, it must believe it will receive an equivalent amount of benefit from doing so.

BC225　The same conclusion is drawn if grant date measurement is applied on the grounds that some type of equity interest is created at grant date, and thereafter changes in the value of that equity interest accrue to the option holders as equity participants, not as employees. Repricing is inconsistent with the view that share option holders bear changes in value as equity participants. Hence it follows that the incremental value has been granted to the share option holders in their capacity as employees (rather than equity participants), as part of their remuneration for services to the entity. Therefore additional remuneration expense arises in respect of the incremental value given.

BC226　It could be argued that if (a) grant date measurement is used as a surrogate measure of the fair value of the services received and (b) the repricing occurs between grant date and vesting date and (c) the repricing merely restores the share option's original value at grant date, then the entity may not receive additional services. Rather, the repricing might simply be a means of ensuring that the entity receives the services it originally expected to receive when the share options were granted. Under this view, it is not appropriate to recognise additional remuneration expense to the extent that the repricing restores the share option's original value at grant date.

BC227　Some argue that the effect of a repricing is to create a new deal between the entity and its employees, and therefore the entity should estimate the fair value of the repriced share options at the date of repricing to calculate a new measure of the fair value of the services received subsequent to repricing. Under this view, the entity would cease using the grant date fair value of the share options when measuring services received after the repricing date, but without reversal of amounts recognised previously. The entity would then measure the services received between the date of repricing and the end of the vesting period by reference to the fair value of the modified share options, measured at the date of repricing. If the repricing occurs after the end of the vesting period, the same process applies. That is to say, there is no adjustment to previously recognised amounts, and the entity recognises—either immediately or over the vesting period, depending on whether the employees are required to complete an additional period of service to become entitled to the repriced share options—an amount equal to the fair value of the modified share options, measured at the date of repricing.

BC228　In the context of measuring the fair value of the equity instruments as a surrogate measure of the fair value of the services received, after considering the above points, the Board concluded when it developed ED 2 that the incremental value granted on repricing should be taken into account when measuring the services received, because:

(a)   there is an underlying presumption that the fair value of the equity instruments, at grant date, provides a surrogate measure of the fair value of the services received. That fair value is based on the share option's original terms and conditions. Therefore, if those terms or conditions are modified, the modification should be taken into account when measuring the services received.

(b)   a share option that will be repriced if the share price falls is more valuable than one that will not be repriced. Therefore, by presuming at grant date that the share option will not be repriced, the entity underestimated the fair value of that option. The Board concluded that, because it is impractical to include the possibility of repricing in the estimate of fair value at grant date, the incremental value granted on repricing should be taken into account as and when the repricing occurs.

BC229   Many of the respondents to ED 2 who addressed the issue of repricing agreed with the proposed requirements. After considering respondents' comments, the Board decided to retain the approach to repricing as proposed in ED 2, ie recognise the incremental value granted on repricing, in addition to continuing to recognise amounts based on the fair value of the original grant.

BC230   The Board also discussed situations in which repricing might be effected by cancelling share options and issuing replacement share options. For example, suppose an entity grants at-the-money share options with an estimated fair value of CU20 each. Suppose the share price falls, so that the share options become significantly out of the money, and are now worth CU2 each. Suppose the entity is considering repricing, so that the share options are again at the money, which would result in them being worth, say, CU10 each. (Note that the share options are still worth less than at grant date, because the share price is now lower. Other things being equal, an at-the-money option on a low priced share is worth less than an at-the-money option on a high priced share.)

BC231   Under ED 2's proposed treatment of repricing, the incremental value given on repricing (CU10 − CU2 = CU8 increment in fair value per share option) would be accounted for when measuring the services rendered, resulting in the recognition of additional expense, ie additional to any amounts recognised in the future in respect of the original share option grant (valued at CU20). If the entity instead cancelled the existing share options and then issued what were, in effect, replacement share options, but treated the replacement share options as a new share option grant, this could reduce the expense recognised. Although the new grant would be valued at CU10 rather than incremental value of CU8, the entity would not recognise any further expense in respect of the original share option grant, valued at CU20. Although some regard such a result as appropriate (and consistent with their views on repricing, as explained in paragraph BC227), it is inconsistent with the Board's treatment of repricing.

BC232   By this means, the entity could, in effect, reduce its remuneration expense if the share price falls, without having to increase the expense if the share price rises (because no repricing would be necessary in this case). In other words, the entity could structure a repricing so as to achieve a form of service date measurement if the share price falls and grant date measurement if the share price rises, ie an asymmetrical treatment of share price changes.

BC233   When it developed ED 2, the Board concluded that if an entity cancels a share or share option grant during the vesting period (other than cancellations because of employees' failing to satisfy the vesting conditions), it should nevertheless continue to account for services received, as if that share or share option grant had not been cancelled. In the Board's view, it is very unlikely that a share or share option grant would be cancelled without some compensation to the counterparty, either in the form of cash or replacement share options. Moreover, the Board saw no difference between a repricing of share options and a cancellation of share options followed by the granting of replacement share options at a lower exercise price, and therefore concluded that the accounting treatment should be the same. If cash is paid on the cancellation of the share or share option grant, the Board concluded that the payment should be accounted for as the repurchase of an equity interest, ie as a deduction from equity.

BC234   The Board noted that its proposed treatment means that an entity would continue to recognise services received during the remainder of the original vesting period, even though the entity might have paid cash compensation to the counterparty upon cancellation of the share or share option grant. The Board discussed an alternative approach applied in SFAS 123: if an entity settles unvested shares or share options in cash, those shares or share options are treated as having immediately vested. The entity is required to recognise immediately an expense for the amount of compensation expense that would otherwise have been recognised during the remainder of the original vesting period. Although the Board would have preferred to adopt this approach, it would have been difficult to apply in the context of the proposed accounting method in ED 2, given that there is not a specific amount of unrecognised compensation expense—the amount recognised in the future would have depended on the number of units of service received in the future.

BC235   Many respondents who commented on the treatment of cancellations disagreed with the proposals in ED 2. They commented that it was inappropriate to continue recognising an expense after a grant has been cancelled. Some suggested other approaches, including the approach applied in SFAS 123. After considering these comments, and given that the Board had decided to replace the units of service method with the modified grant date method in SFAS 123, the Board concluded that it should adopt the same approach as applied in SFAS 123 to cancellations and settlements. Under SFAS 123, a settlement (including a cancellation) is regarded as resulting in the immediate vesting of the equity instruments. The amount of remuneration expense measured at grant date but not yet recognised is recognised immediately at the date of settlement or cancellation.

BC236   In addition to the above issues, during its redeliberation of the proposals in ED 2 the Board also considered more detailed issues relating to modifications and cancellations. Specifically, the Board considered:

(a)   a modification that results in a decrease in fair value (ie the fair value of the modified instrument is less than the fair value of the original instrument, measured at the date of the modification).

(b)   a change in the number of equity instruments granted (increase and decrease).

(c)   a change in services conditions, thereby changing the length of the vesting period (increase and decrease).

(d)   a change in performance conditions, thereby changing the probability of vesting (increase and decrease).

(e)   a change in the classification of the grant, from equity to liabilities.

BC237   The Board concluded that having adopted a grant date measurement method, the requirements for modifications and cancellations should ensure that the entity cannot, by modifying or cancelling the grant of shares or share options, avoid recognising remuneration expense based on the grant date fair values. Therefore, the Board concluded that, for arrangements that are classified as equity-settled arrangements (at least initially), the entity must recognise the grant date fair value of the equity instruments over the vesting period, unless the employee fails to vest in those equity instruments under the terms of the original vesting conditions.

BC237A   During the deliberations of its proposals in the exposure draft *Vesting Conditions and Cancellations* published in February 2006, the Board considered how failure to meet a non-vesting condition should be treated. The Board concluded that in order to be consistent with the grant date measurement method, failure to meet a non-vesting condition should have no accounting effect when neither the entity nor the counterparty can choose whether that condition is met. The entity should continue to recognise the expense, based on the grant date fair value, over the vesting period unless the employee fails to meet a vesting condition.

BC237B   However, the Board concluded that the entity's failure to meet a non-vesting condition is a cancellation if the entity can choose whether that non-vesting condition is met. Furthermore, the Board noted that no non-arbitrary or unambiguous criteria exist to distinguish between a decision by the counterparty not to meet a non-vesting condition and a cancellation by the entity. The Board considered establishing a rebuttable presumption that a counterparty's failure to meet a non-vesting condition is (or is not) a cancellation, unless it can be demonstrated that the entity had no (or had some) influence over the counterparty's decision. The Board did not believe that the information about the entity's decision-making processes that is publicly available would be sufficient to determine whether the presumption has been rebutted. Therefore, the Board concluded that a failure to meet a non-vesting condition should be treated as a cancellation when either the entity or the counterparty can choose whether that non-vesting condition is met.

Accounting for a modification of a share-based payment transaction that changes its classification from cash-settled to equity-settled (2016 amendments)[22]

BC237C   This section summarises the Board's considerations when finalising its proposals to address the accounting for a modification to the terms and conditions of a share-based payment that changes the classification of the transaction from cash-settled to equity-settled. These changes were proposed in the Exposure Draft *Classification and Measurement of Share-based Payment Transactions* (Proposed amendments to IFRS 2) published in November 2014 (November 2014 ED).

BC237D   The Board was informed that there are situations in which a cash-settled share-based payment is modified by cancelling it and replacing it with a new equity-settled share-based payment, and, at the replacement date, the fair value of the replacement award is different from the recognised value of the original award. Interested parties told the Board that there is diversity in practice because IFRS 2 does not provide specific requirements for these situations and asked the Board to clarify the accounting.

BC237E   The Board decided that paragraphs 27 and B42–B44 of IFRS 2, which set out the requirements for modifications to the terms and conditions of equity-settled share-based payments, should not be applied by analogy to account for the fact patterns raised. This is because the requirement in paragraph 27 of IFRS 2 to recognise a minimum amount for the equity-settled share-based payment following a modification is inconsistent with the requirement in paragraph 30 of IFRS 2 to remeasure the liability for a cash-settled share-based payment at fair value at the end of each reporting date until the liability is settled.

BC237F   Accordingly, the Board decided to require that the equity-settled share-based payment transaction be recognised in equity to the extent to which goods or services have been received at the modification date. The Board required this measurement to be made by reference to the modification-date fair value of the equity instruments granted. The Board noted that, at the original grant date, there was a shared understanding that the entity would pay cash for services to be rendered by the counterparty. However, at the modification date, the entity and the counterparty have a new shared understanding that the entity will issue equity instruments to the counterparty. Therefore, the Board concluded that the modification-date fair value should be used to measure the modified equity-settled share-based payment.

---

22   Paragraphs BC237C–BC237L are added as a consequence of amendments to IFRS 2 *Classification and Measurement of Share-based Payment Transactions*, issued in June 2016.

BC237G   Furthermore, the Board noted that the liability for the original cash-settled share-based payment is derecognised on the modification date as it is considered to be settled when the entity grants the replacement equity-settled share-based payment. This is because, at the modification date, the entity is no longer obliged to transfer cash (or other assets) to the counterparty.

BC237H   The Board observed that any difference between the carrying amount of the derecognised liability and the amount of recognised equity on the modification date is recognised immediately in profit or loss. The Board observed that this is consistent with how cash-settled share-based payments are measured in accordance with paragraph 30 of IFRS 2. The Board further observed that recognising the difference in value between the original and the replacement award in profit or loss is also consistent with the requirements for the extinguishment of a financial liability (that has been extinguished fully or partially by the issue of equity instruments) in paragraph 3.3.3 of IFRS 9 *Financial Instruments* and with paragraph 9 of IFRIC *Interpretation 19 Extinguishing Financial Liabilities with Equity Instruments*.

BC237I   Respondents to the November 2014 ED questioned whether the guidance in paragraph B44A would also apply to a situation in which the modification changes the vesting period of the share-based payment transaction. The Board confirmed in paragraph B44B that the guidance in paragraph B44A is applied when the modification occurs during or after the vesting period, and when the vesting period is extended or shortened.

BC237J   The Board provided guidance in paragraph B44C to account for a grant of equity instruments that has been identified as a replacement for a cancelled cash-settled share-based payment. The Board observed that if an entity does not identify a grant of equity instruments as a replacement, the entity would have to reverse the expense recognised for the cash-settled share-based payment and recognise an expense for the new equity-settled share-based payment. The Board noted that this accounting treatment is different from the accounting for modifications of equity-settled awards when the entity does not identify new equity instruments granted as replacement equity instruments for the cancelled equity instrument (as set out in paragraph 28(c) of IFRS 2). In that case, the entity does not reverse the expense recognised for the cancelled original equity-settled award and recognises an expense for the new grant of equity instruments.

BC237K   Some respondents to the November 2014 ED suggested that the Board add examples to the implementation guidance of IFRS 2 to illustrate the accounting for other types of modifications of share-based payments (for example, a modification from equity-settled to cash-settled). The Board decided that it was not necessary to include additional examples (other than adding paragraph IG19B and IG Example 12C which illustrates the application of paragraphs B44A–B44C), because the existing implementation guidance in IFRS 2 could be applied by analogy. For example, Example 9 illustrates a grant of shares to which a cash settlement alternative is subsequently added.

Effective date and transition (2016 amendments)

BC237L In response to the comments received on the November 2014 ED, the Board decided to provide specific transition requirements in paragraph 59A of IFRS 2 for each of the amendments. The Board also decided to permit an entity to apply all of the amendments retrospectively if, (and only if), the necessary information to do so is available without the use of hindsight.

Share appreciation rights settled in cash

BC238 Some transactions are 'share-based', even though they do not involve the issue of shares, share options or any other form of equity instrument. Share appreciation rights (SARs) settled in cash are transactions in which the amount of cash paid to the employee (or another party) is based upon the increase in the share price over a specified period, usually subject to vesting conditions, such as the employee's remaining with the entity during the specified period. (Note that the following discussion focuses on SARs granted to employees, but also applies to SARs granted to other parties.)

BC239 In terms of accounting concepts, share-based payment transactions involving an outflow of cash (or other assets) are different from transactions in which goods or services are received as consideration for the issue of equity instruments.

BC240 In an equity-settled transaction, only one side of the transaction causes a change in assets, ie an asset (services) is received but no assets are disbursed. The other side of the transaction increases equity; it does not cause a change in assets. Accordingly, not only is it not necessary to remeasure the transaction amount upon settlement, it is not appropriate, because equity interests are not remeasured.

BC241 In contrast, in a cash-settled transaction, both sides of the transaction cause a change in assets, ie an asset (services) is received and an asset (cash) is ultimately disbursed. Therefore, no matter what value is attributed to the first asset (services received), eventually it will be necessary to recognise the change in assets when the second asset (cash) is disbursed. Thus, no matter how the transaction is accounted for between the receipt of services and the settlement in cash, it will be 'trued up' to equal the amount of cash paid out, to account for both changes in assets.

BC242 Because cash-settled SARs involve an outflow of cash (rather than the issue of equity instruments) cash SARs should be accounted for in accordance with the usual accounting for similar liabilities. That sounds straightforward, but there are some questions to consider:

(a) should a liability be recognised before vesting date, ie before the employees have fulfilled the conditions to become unconditionally entitled to the cash payment?

(b) if so, how should that liability be measured?

(c) how should the expense be presented in the income statement?

Is there a liability before vesting date?

BC243   It could be argued that the entity does not have a liability until vesting date, because the entity does not have a present obligation to pay cash to the employees until the employees fulfil the conditions to become unconditionally entitled to the cash; between grant date and vesting date there is only a contingent liability.

BC244   The Board noted that this argument applies to all sorts of employee benefits settled in cash, not just SARs. For example, it could be argued that an entity has no liability for pension payments to employees until the employees have met the specified vesting conditions. This argument was considered by IASC in IAS 19 *Employee Benefits*. The Basis for Conclusions states:

> Paragraph 54 of the new IAS 19 summarises the recognition and measurement of liabilities arising from defined benefit plans ... Paragraph 54 of the new IAS 19 is based on the definition of, and recognition criteria for, a liability in IASC's *Framework* ... The Board believes that an enterprise has an obligation under a defined benefit plan when an employee has rendered service in return for the benefits promised under the plan ... The Board believes that an obligation exists even if a benefit is not vested, in other words if the employee's right to receive the benefit is conditional upon future employment. For example, consider an enterprise that provides a benefit of 100 to employees who remain in service for two years. At the end of the first year, the employee and the enterprise are not in the same position as at the beginning of the first year, because the employee will only need to work for one year, instead of two, before becoming entitled to the benefit. Although there is a possibility that the benefit may not vest, that difference is an obligation and, in the Board's view, should result in the recognition of a liability at the end of the first year. The measurement of that obligation at its present value reflects the enterprise's best estimate of the probability that the benefit may not vest. (IAS 19, Basis for Conclusions, paragraphs BC11–BC14)[23]

BC245   Therefore, the Board concluded that, to be consistent with IAS 19, which covers other cash-settled employee benefits, a liability should be recognised in respect of cash-settled SARs during the vesting period, as services are rendered by the employees. Thus, no matter how the liability is measured, the Board concluded that it should be accrued over the vesting period, to the extent that the employees have performed their side of the arrangement. For example, if the terms of the arrangement require the employees to perform services over a three-year period, the liability would be accrued over that three-year period, consistently with the treatment of other cash-settled employee benefits.

How should the liability be measured?

BC246   A simple approach would be to base the accrual on the entity's share price at the end of each reporting period. If the entity's share price increased over the vesting period, expenses would be larger in later reporting periods compared with earlier reporting periods. This is because each reporting period will include the effects of (a) an increase in the liability in respect of the employee

---

23 IAS 19 *Employee Benefits* (as amended in June 2011) renumbered and amended paragraphs BC11–BC14 as paragraphs BC52–BC55. The amendments changed the terminology for consistency with IAS 19.

services received during that reporting period and (b) an increase in the liability attributable to the increase in the entity's share price during the reporting period, which increases the amount payable in respect of past employee services received.

BC247   This approach is consistent with SFAS 123 (paragraph 25) and FASB Interpretation No. 28 *Accounting for Stock Appreciation Rights and Other Variable Stock Option or Award Plans.*

BC248   However, this is not a fair value approach. Like share options, the fair value of SARs includes both their intrinsic value (the increase in the share price to date) and their time value (the value of the right to participate in future increases in the share price, if any, that may occur between the valuation date and the settlement date). An option pricing model can be used to estimate the fair value of SARs.

BC249   Ultimately, however, no matter how the liability is measured during the vesting period, the liability—and therefore the expense—will be remeasured, when the SARs are settled, to equal the amount of the cash paid out. The amount of cash paid will be based on the SARs' intrinsic value at the settlement date. Some support measuring the SAR liability at intrinsic value for this reason, and because intrinsic value is easier to measure.

BC250   The Board concluded that measuring SARs at intrinsic value would be inconsistent with the fair value measurement basis applied, in most cases, in the rest of the IFRS. Furthermore, although a fair value measurement basis is more complex to apply, it was likely that many entities would be measuring the fair value of similar instruments regularly, eg new SAR or share option grants, which would provide much of the information required to remeasure the fair value of the SAR at each reporting date. Moreover, because the intrinsic value measurement basis does not include time value, it is not an adequate measure of either the SAR liability or the cost of services consumed.

BC251   The question of how to measure the liability is linked with the question how to present the associated expense in the income statement, as explained below.

How should the associated expense be presented in the income statement?

BC252   SARs are economically similar to share options. Hence some argue that the accounting treatment of SARs should be the same as the treatment of share options, as discussed earlier (paragraph BC113). However, as noted in paragraphs BC240 and BC241, in an equity-settled transaction there is one change in net assets (the goods or services received) whereas in a cash-settled transaction there are two changes in net assets (the goods or services received and the cash or other assets paid out). To differentiate between the effects of each change in net assets in a cash-settled transaction, the expense could be separated into two components:

- an amount based on the fair value of the SARs at grant date, recognised over the vesting period, in a manner similar to accounting for equity-settled share-based payment transactions, and

- changes in estimate between grant date and settlement date, ie all changes required to remeasure the transaction amount to equal the amount paid out on settlement date.

BC253   In developing ED 2, the Board concluded that information about these two components would be helpful to users of financial statements. For example, users of financial statements regard the effects of remeasuring the liability as having little predictive value. Therefore, the Board concluded that there should be separate disclosure, either on the face of the income statement or in the notes, of that portion of the expense recognised during each accounting period that is attributable to changes in the estimated fair value of the liability between grant date and settlement date.

BC254   However, some respondents to ED 2 disagreed with the proposed disclosure, arguing that it was burdensome and inappropriate to require the entity to account for the transaction as a cash-settled transaction and also calculate, for the purposes of the disclosure, what the transaction amount would have been if the arrangement was an equity-settled transaction.

BC255   The Board considered these comments and also noted that its decision to adopt the SFAS 123 modified grant date method will make it more complex for entities to determine the amount to disclose, because it will be necessary to distinguish between the effects of forfeitures and the effects of fair value changes when calculating the amount to disclose. The Board therefore concluded that the disclosure should not be retained as a mandatory requirement, but instead should be given as an example of an additional disclosure that entities should consider providing. For example, entities with a significant amount of cash-settled arrangements that experience significant share price volatility will probably find that the disclosure is helpful to users of their financial statements.

Share-based payment transactions with a net settlement feature for withholding tax obligations (2016 amendments)[24]

BC255A   This section summarises the Board's considerations when it finalised its proposals to address the classification of a share-based payment transaction with a net settlement feature for withholding tax obligations, contained in the November 2014 ED.

BC255B   Some jurisdictions have tax laws or regulations that oblige an entity to withhold an amount for an employee's tax obligation associated with a share-based payment and to transfer that amount, normally in cash, to the tax authority on the employee's behalf. Those tax withholding obligations vary from jurisdiction to jurisdiction. To fulfill this obligation, many plans include a net settlement feature that permits or requires the entity to deduct from the

---

24   Paragraphs BC255A–BC255P are added as a consequence of amendments to IFRS 2 *Classification and Measurement of Share-based Payment Transactions*, issued in June 2016.

total number of equity instruments that it otherwise would deliver to the employee, the number of equity instruments needed to equal the monetary value of the tax obligation that the employee incurs as a result of the share-based payment transaction. The entity transfers the amount withheld to the tax authority in cash or other assets.

BC255C   The Board received a request to address the classification of such a share-based payment transaction. Specifically, the Board was asked whether the portion of the share-based payment that the entity withholds to satisfy the employee's tax obligation should be classified as cash-settled or equity-settled, if the transaction would otherwise have been classified as an equity-settled share-based payment transaction.

BC255D   There were two views on this issue:

(a)   View 1—The share-based payment has two components and each component is accounted for consistently with its manner of settlement. The portion that the entity withholds, and for which it incurs a liability to transfer cash (or other assets) to the tax authority, should be accounted for as a cash-settled share-based payment transaction. The portion of the share-based payment that the entity settles by issuing equity instruments to the employee is accounted for as an equity-settled share-based payment.

(b)   View 2—The entire share-based payment transaction should be classified as an equity-settled share-based payment transaction, because the net settlement should be viewed as if the entity had repurchased some of the equity instruments issued to the employee (ie the entity would apply the requirements in paragraph 29 of IFRS 2 for a repurchase of vested equity instruments).

BC255E   View 1 is based on the view that the entity is settling part of the share-based payment transaction in cash; ie the entity has an obligation to transfer cash (or other assets) to the tax authority to settle the employee's tax obligation on the employee's behalf. Paragraph 34 of IFRS 2 requires a share-based payment transaction, or components of that transaction, to be classified as cash-settled if, and to the extent that, the entity has incurred a liability to settle in cash or other assets.

BC255F   View 2 is based on the view that the entity is acting as an agent when it transfers cash to the tax authority because the employee has the tax obligation. Under this view, it is as if the entity settles the share-based payment transaction in its entirety by issuing equity instruments to the employee. As a separate (yet simultaneous) transaction, the entity repurchases a portion of those equity instruments from the employee. The entity then remits the cash value of the repurchased equity instruments to the tax authority on behalf of the employee to settle the employee's tax obligation in relation to the share-based payment.

BC255G   The Board observed that paragraph 34 of IFRS 2 indicates that a share-based payment transaction, or components of that transaction, should be classified as a cash-settled share-based payment transaction if, and to the extent that, the entity has incurred a liability to settle in cash or other assets. Consequently a transaction with such a net settlement feature would be divided into two components and each component would be accounted for consistently with how it is settled (View 1). Consequently, the component that reflects the entity's obligation to pay cash to the tax authority would be accounted for as a cash-settled share-based payment and the component that reflects the entity's obligation to issue equity instruments to the employee would be accounted for as an equity-settled share-based payment.

BC255H   The Board observed that the entity's payment to the tax authority represents, in substance, a payment to the counterparty (ie the employee) for the services received from the counterparty, despite the fact that the entity transfers the cash to the tax authority. This is because:

(a)   when the entity pays the amount withheld to the tax authority on behalf of the employee, the entity is acting as an agent for the employee; however,

(b)   the entity is also acting as a principal because it is fulfilling its obligation to the employee (ie the counterparty in the share-based payment transaction) to transfer cash (or other assets) for the goods or services received.

BC255I   Nevertheless, despite the requirements in paragraph 34, the Board decided to make an exception with the result that the transaction would be classified as equity-settled in its entirety if it would have been so classified had it not included the net settlement feature. The Board decided that this exception should be limited to the share-based payment transaction described in paragraph 33E.

BC255J   The Board decided to make the exception because it observed that dividing the specific transaction described in paragraph 33E into two components could be a significant operational challenge for preparers and thus impose cost in excess of the benefit of distinguishing the two components. This is because dividing the transaction into two components requires an entity to estimate changes that affect the amount that the entity is required to withhold and remit to the tax authority on the employee's behalf in respect of the share-based payment. As that estimate changes, the entity would need to reclassify a portion of the share-based payment between cash-settled and equity-settled.

BC255K   Respondents to the November 2014 ED observed that this ED did not specifically address the accounting for the amount paid by the entity to the tax authority. In response to these concerns the Board decided to explain how the requirements of paragraph 29 of IFRS 2 would be applied. Paragraph 33G explains that the accounting for the amount transferred to the tax authority in respect of the employee's tax obligation associated with the share-based payment is consistent with the accounting described in paragraph 29 of this Standard (ie as if the entity had repurchased the vested equity instruments).

This amendment does not address the recognition and measurement of any liability to the tax authority.

BC255L The Board observed that withholding shares to fund the payment (in cash or other assets) to the tax authority could result in a significant difference between the amount paid and the amount at which the share-based payment was measured. This is because the amount payable to the tax authority may reflect settlement-date fair value, whereas the amount recognised for the equity-settled share-based payment during the vesting period would reflect grant-date fair value.

BC255M The Board further observed that it could be necessary to inform users about the future cash flow effects associated with the share-based payment arrangement as the settlement of the tax payment to the tax authority approaches. Therefore, the Board decided to require an entity to disclose the estimated amount that it expects to transfer to the tax authority when this disclosure is needed to inform users about the future cash-flow effects associated with the share-based payment. The Board did not specify the basis for calculating such an estimate.

BC255N The Board also received questions about the accounting when the number of equity instruments withheld exceeds the number of equity instruments needed to equal the monetary value of the employee's tax obligation in respect of the share-based payment. The Board observed that the classification exception (in paragraph 33F) for the classification of a share-based payment award with a net settlement feature would not apply to any equity instruments withheld in excess of the number required to equal the monetary value of the employee's tax obligation. Consequently, when that excess amount is paid to the employee in cash (or other assets), and consistent with existing requirements, the excess number of equity instruments withheld should be separated and accounted for as a cash-settled share-based payment.

BC255O Some respondents to the November 2014 ED asked the Board to clarify whether the exception in paragraph 33F (ie relief from dividing the share-based payment into its different components) applies to arrangements other than those in which an entity is obliged by tax laws or regulations to withhold an employee's tax obligation. For example, an entity may not be obliged by tax laws or regulations to withhold an amount for an employee's tax obligation but it is the entity's normal practice to withhold such an amount. The Board noted that its intent is to limit the exception to circumstances in which the tax laws or regulations impose the obligation on the entity to withhold an amount for the employee's tax obligation associated with a share-based payment for the exception in paragraph 33F to apply.

BC255P Furthermore, the Board added paragraph IG19A and IG Example 12B to the Guidance on Implementing IFRS 2 to illustrate a share-based payment transaction with a net settlement feature for withholding tax obligations.

Share-based payment transactions with cash alternatives

BC256   Under some employee share-based payment arrangements the employees can choose to receive cash instead of shares or share options, or instead of exercising share options. There are many possible variations of share-based payment arrangements under which a cash alternative may be paid. For example, the employees may have more than one opportunity to elect to receive the cash alternative, eg the employees may be able to elect to receive cash instead of shares or share options on vesting date, or elect to receive cash instead of exercising the share options. The terms of the arrangement may provide the entity with a choice of settlement, ie whether to pay the cash alternative instead of issuing shares or share options on vesting date or instead of issuing shares upon the exercise of the share options. The amount of the cash alternative may be fixed or variable and, if variable, may be determinable in a manner that is related, or unrelated, to the price of the entity's shares.

BC257   The IFRS contains different accounting methods for cash-settled and equity-settled share-based payment transactions. Hence, if the entity or the employee has the choice of settlement, it is necessary to determine which accounting method should be applied. The Board considered situations when the terms of the arrangement provide (a) the employee with a choice of settlement and (b) the entity with a choice of settlement.

The terms of the arrangement provide the employee with a choice of settlement

BC258   Share-based payment transactions without cash alternatives do not give rise to liabilities under the *Framework*, because the entity is not required to transfer cash or other assets to the other party. However, this is not so if the contract between the entity and the employee gives the employee the contractual right to demand the cash alternative. In this situation, the entity has an obligation to transfer cash to the employee and hence a liability exists. Furthermore, because the employee has the right to demand settlement in equity instead of cash, the employee also has a conditional right to equity instruments. Hence, on grant date the employee was granted rights to a compound financial instrument, ie a financial instrument that includes both debt and equity components.

BC259   It is common for the alternatives to be structured so that the fair value of the cash alternative is always the same as the fair value of the equity alternative, eg where the employee has a choice between share options and SARs. However, if this is not so, then the fair value of the compound financial instrument will usually exceed both the individual fair value of the cash alternative (because of the possibility that the shares or share options may be more valuable than the cash alternative) and that of the shares or options (because of the possibility that the cash alternative may be more valuable than the shares or options).

BC260　Under IAS 32, a financial instrument that is accounted for as a compound instrument is separated into its debt and equity components, by allocating the proceeds received for the issue of a compound instrument to its debt and equity components. This entails determining the fair value of the liability component and then assigning the remainder of the proceeds received to the equity component. This is possible if those proceeds are cash or non-cash consideration whose fair value can be reliably measured. If that is not the case, it will be necessary to estimate the fair value of the compound instrument itself.

BC261　The Board concluded that the compound instrument should be measured by first valuing the liability component (the cash alternative) and then valuing the equity component (the equity instrument)—with that valuation taking into account that the employee must forfeit the cash alternative to receive the equity instrument—and adding the two component values together. This is consistent with the approach adopted in IAS 32, whereby the liability component is measured first and the residual is allocated to equity. If the fair value of each settlement alternative is always the same, then the fair value of the equity component of the compound instrument will be zero and hence the fair value of the compound instrument will be the same as the fair value of the liability component.

BC262　The Board concluded that the entity should separately account for the services rendered in respect of each component of the compound financial instrument, to ensure consistency with the IFRS's requirements for equity-settled and cash-settled share-based payment transactions. Hence, for the debt component, the entity should recognise the services received, and a liability to pay for those services, as the employees render services, in the same manner as other cash-settled share-based payment transactions (eg SARs). For the equity component (if any), the entity should recognise the services received, and an increase in equity, as the employees render services, in the same way as other equity-settled share-based payment transactions.

BC263　The Board concluded that the liability should be remeasured to its fair value as at the date of settlement, before accounting for the settlement of the liability. This ensures that, if the entity settles the liability by issuing equity instruments, the resulting increase in equity is measured at the fair value of the consideration received for the equity instruments issued, being the fair value of the liability settled.

BC264　The Board also concluded that, if the entity pays cash rather than issuing equity instruments on settlement, any contributions to equity previously recognised in respect of the equity component should remain in equity. By electing to receive cash rather than equity instruments, the employee has surrendered his/her rights to receive equity instruments. That event does not cause a change in net assets and hence there is no change in total equity. This is consistent with the Board's conclusions on other lapses of equity instruments (see paragraphs BC218–BC221).

The terms of the arrangement provide the entity with a choice of settlement

BC265   For share-based payment transactions in which the terms of the arrangement provide the entity with a choice of whether to settle in cash or by issuing equity instruments, the entity would need first to determine whether it has an obligation to settle in cash and therefore does not, in effect, have a choice of settlement. Although the contract might specify that the entity can choose whether to settle in cash or by issuing equity instruments, the Board concluded that the entity will have an obligation to settle in cash if the choice of settlement in equity has no commercial substance (eg because the entity is legally prohibited from issuing shares), or if the entity has a past practice or a stated policy of settling in cash, or generally settles in cash whenever the counterparty asks for cash settlement. The entity will also have an obligation to settle in cash if the shares issued (including shares issued upon the exercise of share options) are redeemable, either mandatorily (eg upon cessation of employment) or at the counterparty's option.

BC266   During its redeliberations of the proposals in ED 2, the Board noted that the classification as liabilities or equity of arrangements in which the entity appears to have the choice of settlement differs from the classification under IAS 32, which requires such an arrangement to be classified either wholly as a liability (if the contract is a derivative contract) or as a compound instrument (if the contract is a non-derivative contract). However, consistently with its conclusions on the other differences between IFRS 2 and IAS 32 (see paragraphs BC106–BC110), the Board decided to retain this difference, pending the outcome of its longer-term Concepts project, which includes reviewing the definitions of liabilities and equity.

BC267   Even if the entity is not obliged to settle in cash until it chooses to do so, at the time it makes that election a liability will arise for the amount of the cash payment. This raises the question how to account for the debit side of the entry. It could be argued that any difference between (a) the amount of the cash payment and (b) the total expense recognised for services received and consumed up to the date of settlement (which would be based on the grant date value of the equity settlement alternative) should be recognised as an adjustment to the employee remuneration expense. However, given that the cash payment is to settle an equity interest, the Board concluded that it is consistent with the *Framework* to treat the cash payment as the repurchase of an equity interest, ie as a deduction from equity. In this case, no adjustment to remuneration expense is required on settlement.

BC268   However, the Board concluded that an additional expense should be recognised if the entity chooses the settlement alternative with the higher fair value because, given that the entity has voluntarily paid more than it needed to, presumably it expects to receive (or has already received) additional services from the employees in return for the additional value given.

Share-based payment transactions among group entities (2009 amendments)[25]

BC268A This section summarises the Board's considerations when finalising its proposals contained in the exposure draft *Group Cash-settled Share-based Payment Transactions* published in December 2007. Until the Board amended IFRS 2 in 2009, IFRIC 11 provided guidance on how an entity that received the goods or services from its suppliers should account for some specific group equity-settled share-based payment transactions in its separate or individual financial statements. Therefore, the amendments issued in June 2009 incorporated substantially the same consensus contained in IFRIC 11. The relevant matters the IFRIC considered when reaching the consensus contained in IFRIC 11, as approved by the Board, are also carried forward in this section.

BC268B The exposure draft published in December 2007 addressed two arrangements in which the parent (not the entity itself) has an obligation to make the required cash payments to the suppliers of the entity:

(a) Arrangement 1 – the supplier of the entity will receive cash payments that are linked to the price of the equity instruments of the entity.

(b) Arrangement 2 – the supplier of the entity will receive cash payments that are linked to the price of the equity instruments of the parent of the entity.

BC268C The Board noted that like those group equity-settled share-based payment transactions originally addressed in IFRIC 11, the two arrangements described in paragraph BC268B did not meet the definition of either an equity-settled or a cash-settled share-based payment transaction. The Board considered whether a different conclusion should be reached for such arrangements merely because they are cash-settled rather than equity-settled. Paragraphs BC22A–BC22F explain the Board's considerations in finalising the amendments to clarify the scope of IFRS 2. The section below summarises the Board's considerations in finalising the amendments relating to the measurement of such transactions.

BC268D The Board noted that the arrangements described in paragraph BC268B are

(a) for the purpose of providing benefits to the employees of the subsidiary in return for employee services, and

(b) share-based and cash-settled.

In addition, the Board noted that the guidance in paragraph 3 (now superseded by paragraph 3A) already stated that when a shareholder transferred equity instruments of the entity (or another group entity), the transaction would be within the scope of IFRS 2 for the entity receiving the goods or services.

---

25 Paragraphs BC268A–BC268O are added as a consequence of amendments to IFRS 2 *Group Cash-settled Share-based Payment Transactions* issued in June 2009.

BC268E　For these reasons, in the exposure draft published in December 2007 the Board proposed to amend IFRS 2 and IFRIC 11 to require that, in the separate or individual financial statements of the entity receiving the goods or services, the entity should measure the employee services in accordance with the requirements applicable to cash-settled share-based payment transactions on the basis of the fair value of the corresponding liability incurred by the parent. Specifically, until the liability incurred by the parent is settled, the entity should recognise any changes in the fair value of the liability in profit or loss and changes in the entity's equity as adjustments to contributions from the parent.

BC268F　Because group cash-settled share-based payment transactions did not meet the definition of either an equity-settled or a cash-settled share-based payment transaction, some respondents did not object to measuring them as cash-settled on the basis that the accounting reflects the form of the payment received by the entity's suppliers. However, many respondents questioned the basis for the conclusions reached, citing reasons that included:

(a)　the lack of a 'push-down' accounting concept in current IFRSs that would require the parent's costs incurred on behalf of the subsidiary to be attributed to the subsidiary,

(b)　conflicts with the *Framework* and with other IFRSs that prohibit remeasurement of equity, and

(c)　conflicts with the rationale in the Basis for Conclusions on IFRS 2 related to the remeasurement of cash-settled share-based payment transactions when the entity itself has no obligation to its suppliers.

BC268G　The Board agreed with respondents that the entity receiving goods or services has no obligation to distribute assets and that the parent's settlement is an equity contribution to the entity. The Board noted that regardless of how such group transactions are structured or accounted for in the separate or individual financial statements of the group entities, the accounting measurement in the consolidated financial statements of the group will be the same. The Board also noted that the share-based payment expense measured on grant date results in the same fair value for both the entity receiving goods or services and the entity settling the transaction, regardless of whether it is measured as equity-settled or as cash-settled.

BC268H　To address the comments received from respondents, the Board reviewed two issues to determine the appropriate subsequent measurement in the separate or individual financial statements of the entity receiving the goods or services. The first issue was whether the entity should recognise in its separate or individual financial statements:

(a)　Approach 1 – an expense of the same amount as in the consolidated financial statements, or

(b)　Approach 2 – an expense measured by classifying the transaction as equity-settled or cash-settled evaluated from its own perspective, which may not always be the same as the amount recognised by the consolidated group.

BC268I   The Board noted that IFRSs have no broad-based guidance to address push-down accounting or the accounting in separate or individual financial statements for the allocation of costs among group entities. When addressing defined benefit plans that share risks between entities under common control, IAS 19 requires an expense to be recognised by the subsidiary on the basis of the cash amount charged by the group plan. When there are no repayment arrangements, in the separate or individual financial statements, the subsidiary should recognise a cost equal to its contribution payable for the period. This is consistent with Approach 2 described in paragraph BC268H.

BC268J   The Board therefore decided to adopt Approach 2. However, the approach adopted in IFRS 2 is different from that in IAS 19 in that the entity receiving goods or services in a share-based payment transaction recognises an expense even when it has no obligation to pay cash or other assets. The Board concluded that this approach is consistent with the expense attribution principles underlying IFRS 2.

BC268K   The Board noted that Approach 2 is consistent with the rationale that the information provided by general purpose financial reporting should 'reflect the perspective of the entity rather than the perspective of the entity's equity investors ....' because the reporting entity is deemed to have substance of its own, separate from that of its owners. Approach 1 reflects the perspective of the entity's owners (the group) rather than the rights and obligations of the entity itself.

BC268L   The Board also noted that the consensus reached in IFRIC 11 reflected Approach 1 described in paragraph BC268H for some scenarios and Approach 2 for others. The Board concluded that this was undesirable and decided that there should be a single approach to measurement that would apply in all situations.

BC268M   The second issue the Board considered was identifying the criteria for classifying group share-based payment transactions as equity-settled or cash-settled. How a transaction is classified determines the subsequent measurement in the separate or individual financial statements of both the entity receiving the goods or services and the entity settling the transaction, if different. The Board reviewed the two classification criteria set out in the consensus in IFRIC 11 for group equity-settled transactions:

(a)   based on the nature of the award given to the employees—therefore, classified as *equity-settled* if the entity's own equity instruments are given, regardless of which entity grants or settles it; otherwise classified as *cash-settled* even when the entity receiving the goods or services has no obligation.

(b)   based on the entity's own rights and obligations—therefore, classified as *cash-settled* if the entity has an obligation to settle, regardless of the nature of the consideration; otherwise classified as *equity-settled*.

BC268N   The Board noted that, on its own, either of the two criteria described above would not consistently reflect the entity's perspective when assessing the appropriate classification for transactions described in paragraph BC268B. The Board concluded that the entity should consider both criteria in IFRIC 11, ie *equity-settled* when suppliers are given the entity's own equity instruments or when the entity receiving the goods or services has no obligation to settle and *cash-settled* in all other circumstances. The Board also noted that when the entity receiving goods or services has no obligation to deliver cash or other assets to its suppliers, accounting for the transaction as cash-settled in its separate or individual financial statements is not appropriate. The equity-settled basis is more consistent with the principles and rationales in both IFRS 2 and IFRIC 11. Therefore, the Board decided that the entity receiving the goods or services should classify both of the group cash-settled share-based payment transactions described in paragraph BC268B as *equity-settled* in its separate or individual financial statements.

BC268O   This conclusion is the main change to the proposals in the exposure draft. The Board concluded that the broader principles it developed during its redeliberations addressed the three main concerns expressed by respondents described in paragraph BC268F. Those principles apply to all group share-based payment transactions, whether they are cash-settled or equity-settled. The Board's conclusions do not result in any changes to the guidance in IFRIC 11 that addressed similar group equity-settled share-based payment transactions. Other than the change described above, the Board reaffirmed the proposals in the exposure draft. Therefore, the Board concluded that it was not necessary to re-expose the amendments before finalising them.

Transfers of employees between group entities (paragraphs B59–B61)

BC268P   When it developed the consensus in IFRIC 11, the IFRIC noted that some share-based payment arrangements involve a parent granting rights to the employees of more than one subsidiary with a vesting condition that requires the employees to work for the group for a particular period. Sometimes, an employee of one subsidiary transfers employment to another subsidiary during the vesting period, without the employee's rights under the original share-based payment arrangements being affected.

BC268Q   The IFRIC noted that the terms of the original share-based payment arrangement require the employees to work for the group, rather than for a particular group entity. Thus, the IFRIC concluded that the change of employment should not result in a new grant of equity instruments in the financial statements of the subsidiary to which the employees transferred employment. The subsidiary to which the employee transfers employment should measure the fair value of the services received from the employee by reference to the fair value of the equity instruments at the date those equity instruments were originally granted to the employee by the parent. For the same reason, the IFRIC concluded that the transfer itself should not be treated as an employee's failure to satisfy a vesting condition. Thus, the transfer should not trigger any reversal of the charge previously recognised in respect of the services received from the employee in the separate or individual financial statements of the subsidiary from which the employee transfers employment.

BC268R   The IFRIC noted that paragraph 19 of the IFRS requires the cumulative amount recognised for goods or services as consideration for the equity instruments granted to be based on the number of equity instruments that eventually vest. Accordingly, on a cumulative basis, no amount is recognised for goods or services if the equity instruments do not vest because of failure to satisfy a vesting condition other than a market condition as defined in Appendix A. Applying the principles in paragraph 19, the IFRIC concluded that when the employee fails to satisfy a vesting condition other than a market condition, the services from that employee recognised in the financial statements of each group entity during the vesting period should be reversed.

BC268S   When finalising the 2009 amendments to IFRS 2 for group share-based payment transactions, the Board concluded that the guidance in IFRIC 11 should apply to all group share-based payment transactions classified as equity-settled in the entity's separate or individual financial statements in accordance with paragraphs 43A–43C.

Overall conclusions on accounting for employee share options

BC269   The Board first considered all major issues relating to the recognition and measurement of share-based payment transactions, and reached conclusions on those issues. It then drew some overall conclusions, particularly on the treatment of employee share options, which is one of the most controversial aspects of the project. In arriving at those conclusions, the Board considered the following issues:

- convergence with US GAAP
- recognition versus disclosure of expenses arising from employee share-based payment transactions
- reliability of measurement of the fair value of employee share options.

Convergence with US GAAP

BC270   Some respondents to the Discussion Paper and ED 2 urged the Board to develop an IFRS that was based on existing requirements under US generally accepted accounting principles (US GAAP).

BC271   More specifically, respondents urged the Board to develop a standard based on SFAS 123. However, given that convergence of accounting standards was commonly given as a reason for this suggestion, the Board considered US GAAP overall, not just one aspect of it. The main pronouncements of US GAAP on share-based payment are Accounting Principles Board Opinion No. 25 *Accounting for Stock Issued to Employees*, and SFAS 123.

APB 25

BC272　APB 25 was issued in 1972. It deals with employee share plans only, and draws a distinction between non-performance-related (fixed) plans and performance-related and other variable plans.

BC273　For fixed plans, an expense is measured at intrinsic value (ie the difference between the share price and the exercise price), if any, at grant date. Typically, this results in no expense being recognised for fixed plans, because most share options granted under fixed plans are granted at the money. For performance-related and other variable plans, an expense is measured at intrinsic value at the measurement date. The measurement date is when both the number of shares or share options that the employee is entitled to receive and the exercise price are fixed. Because this measurement date is likely to be much later than grant date, any expense is subject to uncertainty and, if the share price is increasing, the expense for performance-related plans would be larger than for fixed plans.

BC274　In SFAS 123, the FASB noted that APB 25 is criticised for producing anomalous results and for lacking any underlying conceptual rationale. For example, the requirements of APB 25 typically result in the recognition of an expense for performance-related share options but usually no expense is recognised for fixed share options. This result is anomalous because fixed share options are usually more valuable at grant date than performance-related share options. Moreover, the omission of an expense for fixed share options impairs the quality of financial statements:

> The resulting financial statements are less credible than they could be, and the financial statements of entities that use fixed employee share options extensively are not comparable to those of entities that do not make significant use of fixed options. (SFAS 123, paragraph 56)

BC275　The Discussion Paper, in its discussion of US GAAP, noted that the different accounting treatments for fixed and performance-related plans also had the perverse effect of discouraging entities from setting up performance-related employee share plans.

SFAS 123

BC276　SFAS 123 was issued in 1995. It requires recognition of share-based payment transactions with parties other than employees, based on the fair value of the shares or share options issued or the fair value of the goods or services received, whichever is more reliably measurable. Entities are also encouraged, but not required, to apply the fair value accounting method in SFAS 123 to share-based payment transactions with employees. Generally speaking, SFAS 123 draws no distinction between fixed and performance-related plans.

BC277　If an entity applies the accounting method in APB 25 rather than that in SFAS 123, SFAS 123 requires disclosures of pro forma net income and earnings per share in the annual financial statements, as if the standard had been applied. Recently, a significant number of major US companies have voluntarily adopted the fair value accounting method in SFAS 123 for transactions with employees.

BC278   The FASB regards SFAS 123 as superior to APB 25, and would have preferred recognition based on the fair value of employee options to be mandatory, not optional. SFAS 123 makes it clear that the FASB decided to permit the disclosure-based alternative for political reasons, not because it thought that it was the best accounting solution:

> ... the Board ... continues to believe that disclosure is not an adequate substitute for recognition of assets, liabilities, equity, revenues and expenses in financial statements ... The Board chose a disclosure-based solution for stock-based employee compensation to bring closure to the divisive debate on this issue—not because it believes that solution is the best way to improve financial accounting and reporting.

> (SFAS 123, paragraphs 61 and 62)

BC279   Under US GAAP, the accounting treatment of share-based payment transactions differs, depending on whether the other party to the transaction is an employee or non-employee, and whether the entity chooses to apply SFAS 123 or APB 25 to transactions with employees. Having a choice of accounting methods is generally regarded as undesirable. Indeed, the Board recently devoted much time and effort to developing improvements to existing international standards, one of the objectives of which is to eliminate choices of accounting methods.

BC280   Research in the US demonstrates that choosing one accounting method over the other has a significant impact on the reported earnings of US entities. For example, research by Bear Stearns and Credit Suisse First Boston on the S&P 500 shows that, had the fair value measurement method in SFAS 123 been applied for the purposes of recognising an expense for employee stock-based compensation, the earnings of the S&P 500 companies would have been significantly lower, and that the effect is growing. The effect on reported earnings is substantial in some sectors, where companies make heavy use of share options.

BC281   The Canadian Accounting Standards Board (AcSB) recently completed its project on share-based payment. In accordance with the AcSB's policy of harmonising Canadian standards with those in the US, the AcSB initially proposed a standard that was based on US GAAP, including APB 25. After considering respondents' comments, the AcSB decided to delete the guidance drawn from APB 25. The AcSB reached this decision for various reasons, including that, in its view, the intrinsic value method is flawed. Also, incorporating the requirements of APB 25 into an accounting standard would result in preparers of financial statements incurring substantial costs for which users of financial statements would derive no benefit—entities would spend a great deal of time and effort on understanding the rules and then redesigning option plans, usually by deleting existing performance conditions, to avoid recognising an expense in respect of such plans, thereby producing no improvement in the accounting for share option plans.

BC282   The Canadian standard was initially consistent with SFAS 123. That included permitting a choice between fair value-based accounting for employee stock-based compensation expense in the income statement and disclosure of pro forma amounts in the notes to both interim and annual financial statements. However, the AcSB recently amended its standard to remove the choice between recognition and disclosure, and therefore expense recognition is mandatory for financial periods beginning on or after 1 January 2004.

BC283 Because APB 25 contains serious flaws, the Board concluded that basing an IFRS on it is unlikely to represent much, if any, improvement in financial reporting. Moreover, the perverse effects of APB 25, particularly in discouraging performance-related share option plans, may cause economic distortions. Accounting standards are intended to be neutral, not to give favourable or unfavourable accounting treatments to particular transactions to encourage or discourage entities from entering into those transactions. APB 25 fails to achieve that objective. Performance-related employee share plans are common in Europe (performance conditions are often required by law) and in other parts of the world outside the US, and investors are calling for greater use of performance conditions. Therefore, the Board concluded that introducing an accounting standard based on APB 25 would be inconsistent with its objective of developing high quality accounting standards.

BC284 That leaves SFAS 123. Comments from the FASB, in the SFAS 123 Basis for Conclusions, and from the Canadian AcSB when it developed a standard based on SFAS 123, indicate that both standard-setters regard it as inadequate, because it permits a choice between recognition and disclosure. (This issue is discussed further below.) The FASB added to its agenda in March 2003 a project to review US accounting requirements on share-based payment, including removing the disclosure alternative in SFAS 123, so that expense recognition is mandatory. The Chairman of the FASB commented:

> Recent events have served as a reminder to all of us that clear, credible and comparable financial information is essential to the health and vitality of our capital market system. In the wake of the market meltdown and corporate reporting scandals, the FASB has received numerous requests from individual and institutional investors, financial analysts and many others urging the Board to mandate the expensing of the compensation cost relating to employee stock options ... While a number of major companies have voluntarily opted to reflect these costs as an expense in reporting their earnings, other companies continue to show these costs in the footnotes to their financial statements. In addition, a move to require an expense treatment would be consistent with the FASB's commitment to work toward convergence between U.S. and international accounting standards. In taking all of these factors into consideration, the Board concluded that it was critical that it now revisit this important subject. (FASB News Release, 12 March 2003)

BC285 During the Board's redeliberations of the proposals in ED 2, the Board worked with the FASB to achieve convergence of international and US standards, to the extent possible, bearing in mind that the FASB was at an earlier stage in its project—the FASB was developing an Exposure Draft to revise SFAS 123 whereas the IASB was finalising its IFRS. The Board concluded that, although convergence is an important objective, it would not be appropriate to delay the issue of the IFRS, because of the pressing need for a standard on share-based payment, as explained in paragraphs BC2–BC5. In any event, at the time the IASB concluded its deliberations, a substantial amount of convergence had been achieved. For example, the FASB agreed with the IASB that all share-based payment transactions should be recognised in the financial statements, measured on a fair value measurement basis, including transactions in which share options are granted to employees. Hence, the FASB agreed that the disclosure alternative in SFAS 123 should be eliminated.

BC286　The IASB and FASB also agreed that, once both boards have issued final standards on share-based payment, the two boards will consider undertaking a convergence project, with the objective of eliminating any remaining areas of divergence between international and US standards on this topic.

Recognition versus disclosure

BC287　A basic accounting concept is that disclosure of financial information is not an adequate substitute for recognition in the financial statements. For example, the *Framework* states:

> Items that meet the recognition criteria should be recognised in the balance sheet or income statement. The failure to recognise such items is not rectified by disclosure of the accounting policies used nor by notes or explanatory material. (paragraph 82)

BC288　A key aspect of the recognition criteria is that the item can be measured with reliability. This issue is discussed further below. Therefore, this discussion focuses on the 'recognition versus disclosure' issue in principle, not on measurement reliability. Once it has been determined that an item meets the criteria for recognition in the financial statements, failing to recognise it is inconsistent with the basic concept that disclosure is not an adequate substitute for recognition.

BC289　Some disagree with this concept, arguing that it makes no difference whether information is recognised in the financial statements or disclosed in the notes. Either way, users of financial statements have the information they require to make economic decisions. Hence, they believe that note disclosure of expenses arising from particular employee share-based payment transactions (ie those involving awards of share options to employees), rather than recognition in the income statement, is acceptable.

BC290　The Board did not accept this argument. The Board noted that if note disclosure is acceptable, because it makes no difference whether the expense is recognised or disclosed, then recognition in the financial statements must also be acceptable for the same reason. If recognition is acceptable, and recognition rather than mere disclosure accords with the accounting principles applied to all other expense items, it is not acceptable to leave one particular expense item out of the income statement.

BC291　The Board also noted that there is significant evidence that there is a difference between recognition and disclosure. First, academic research indicates that whether information is recognised or merely disclosed affects market prices (eg Barth, Clinch and Shibano, 2003).[26] If information is disclosed only in the notes, users of financial statements have to expend time

---

26　M E Barth, G Clinch and T Shibano. 2003. Market Effects of Recognition and Disclosure. *Journal of Accounting Research* 41(4): 581–609.

and effort to become sufficiently expert in accounting to know (a) that there are items that are not recognised in the financial statements, (b) that there is information about those items in the notes, and (c) how to assess the note disclosures. Because gaining that expertise comes at a cost, and not all users of financial statements will become accounting experts, information that is merely disclosed may not be fully reflected in share prices.

BC292　Second, both preparers and users of financial statements appear to agree that there is an important difference between recognition and disclosure. Users of financial statements have strongly expressed the view that all forms of share-based payment, including employee share options, should be recognised in the financial statements, resulting in the recognition of an expense when the goods or services received are consumed, and that note disclosure alone is inadequate. Their views have been expressed by various means, including:

(a)　users' responses to the Discussion Paper and ED 2.

(b)　the 2001 survey by the Association for Investment Management and Research of analysts and fund managers—83 per cent of survey respondents said the accounting method for all share-based payment transactions should require recognition of an expense in the income statement.

(c)　public comments by users of financial statements, such as those reported in the press or made at recent US Senate hearings.

BC293　Preparers of financial statements also see a major difference between recognition and disclosure. For example, some preparers who responded to the Discussion Paper and ED 2 were concerned that unless expense recognition is required in all countries, entities that are required to recognise an expense would be at a competitive disadvantage compared with entities that are permitted a choice between recognition and disclosure. Comments such as these indicate that preparers of financial statements regard expense recognition as having consequences that are different from those of disclosure.

Reliability of measurement

BC294　One reason commonly given by those who oppose the recognition of an expense arising from transactions involving grants of share options to employees is that it is not possible to measure those transactions reliably.

BC295　The Board discussed these concerns about reliability, after first putting the issue into context. For example, the Board noted that when estimating the fair value of share options, the objective is to measure that fair value at the measurement date, not the value of the underlying share at some future date. Some regard the fair value estimate as inherently uncertain because it is not known, at the measurement date, what the final outcome will be, ie how much the gain on exercise (if any) will be. However, the valuation does not attempt to estimate the future gain, only the amount that the other party would pay to obtain the right to participate in any future gains. Therefore, even if the share option expires worthless or the employee makes a large gain on exercise, this does not mean that the grant date estimate of the fair value of that option was unreliable or wrong.

BC296 The Board also noted that accounting often involves making estimates, and therefore reporting an estimated fair value is not objectionable merely because that amount represents an estimate rather than a precise measure. Examples of other estimates made in accounting, which may have a material effect on the income statement and the balance sheet, include estimates of the collectability of doubtful debts, estimates of the useful life of fixed assets and the pattern of their consumption, and estimates of employee pension liabilities.

BC297 However, some argue that including in the financial statements an estimate of the fair value of employee share options is different from including other estimates, because there is no subsequent correction of the estimate. Other estimates, such as employee pension costs, will ultimately be revised to equal the amount of the cash paid out. In contrast, because equity is not remeasured, if the estimated fair value of employee share options is recognised, there is no remeasurement of the fair value estimate—unless exercise date measurement is used—so any estimation error is permanently embedded in the financial statements.

BC298 The FASB considered and rejected this argument in developing SFAS 123. For example, for employee pension costs, the total cost is never completely trued up unless the scheme is terminated, the amount attributed to any particular year is never trued up, and it can take decades before the amounts relating to particular employees are trued up. In the meantime, users of financial statements have made economic decisions based on the estimated costs.

BC299 Moreover, the Board noted that if no expense (or an expense based on intrinsic value only, which is typically zero) is recognised in respect of employee share options, that also means that there is an error that is permanently embedded in the financial statements. Reporting zero (or an amount based on intrinsic value, if any) is never trued up.

BC300 The Board also considered the meaning of reliability. Arguments about whether estimates of the fair value of employee share options are sufficiently reliable focus on one aspect of reliability only—whether the estimate is free from material error. The *Framework*, in common with the conceptual frameworks of other accounting standard-setters, makes it clear that another important aspect of reliability is whether the information can be depended upon by users of financial statements to represent faithfully what it purports to represent. Therefore, in assessing whether a particular accounting method produces reliable financial information, it is necessary to consider whether that information is representationally faithful. This is one way in which reliability is linked to another important qualitative characteristic of financial information, relevance.

BC301 For example, in the context of share-based payment, some commentators advocate measuring employee share options at intrinsic value rather than fair value, because intrinsic value is regarded as a much more reliable measure. Whether intrinsic value is a more reliable measure is doubtful—it is certainly less subject to estimation error, but is unlikely to be a representationally faithful measure of remuneration. Nor is intrinsic value a relevant measure, especially when measured at grant date. Many employee share options are issued at the money, so have no intrinsic value at grant date. A share option with no intrinsic value consists entirely of time value. If a share option is measured at intrinsic value at grant date, zero value is attributed to the share option. Therefore, by ignoring time value, the amount attributed to the share option is 100 per cent understated.

BC302   Another qualitative characteristic is comparability. Some argue that, given the uncertainties relating to estimating the fair value of employee share options, it is better for all entities to report zero, because this will make financial statements more comparable. They argue that if, for example, for two entities the 'true' amount of expense relating to employee share options is CU500,000, and estimation uncertainties cause one entity to report CU450,000 and the other to report CU550,000, the two entities' financial statements would be more comparable if both reported zero, rather than these divergent figures.

BC303   However, it is unlikely that any two entities will have the same amount of employee share-based remuneration expense. Research (eg by Bear Stearns and Credit Suisse First Boston) indicates that the expense varies widely from industry to industry, from entity to entity, and from year to year. Reporting zero rather than an estimated amount is likely to make the financial statements much less comparable, not more comparable. For example, if the estimated employee share-based remuneration expense of Company A, Company B and Company C is CU10,000, CU100,000 and CU1,000,000 respectively, reporting zero for all three companies will not make their financial statements comparable.

BC304   In the context of the foregoing discussion of reliability, the Board addressed the question whether transactions involving share options granted to employees can be measured with sufficient reliability for the purpose of recognition in the financial statements. The Board noted that many respondents to the Discussion Paper asserted that this is not possible. They argue that option pricing models cannot be applied to employee share options, because of the differences between employee options and traded options.

BC305   The Board considered these differences, with the assistance of the project's Advisory Group and other experts, and has reached conclusions on how to take account of these differences when estimating the fair value of employee share options, as explained in paragraphs BC145–BC199. In doing so, the Board noted that the objective is to measure the fair value of the share options, ie an estimate of what the price of those equity instruments would have been on grant date in an arm's length transaction between knowledgeable, willing parties. The valuation methodology applied should therefore be consistent with valuation methodologies that market participants would use for pricing similar financial instruments, and should incorporate all factors and assumptions that knowledgeable, willing market participants would consider in setting the price.

BC306   Hence, factors that a knowledgeable, willing market participant would not consider in setting the price of an option are not relevant when estimating the fair value of shares, share options or other equity instruments granted. For example, for share options granted to employees, factors that affect the value of the option from the individual employee's perspective only are not relevant to estimating the price that would be set by a knowledgeable, willing market participant. Many respondents' comments about measurement reliability, and the differences between employee share options and traded options, often focused on the value of the option from the employee's perspective. Therefore, the Board concluded that the IFRS should emphasise that the objective is to estimate the fair value of the share option, not an employee-specific value.

BC307   The Board noted that there is evidence to support a conclusion that it is possible to make a reliable estimate of the fair value of employee share options. First, there is academic research to support this conclusion (eg Carpenter 1998, Maller, Tan and Van De Vyver 2002).[27] Second, users of financial statements regard the estimated fair values as sufficiently reliable for recognition in the financial statements. Evidence of this can be found in a variety of sources, such as the comment letters received from users of financial statements who responded to the Discussion Paper and ED 2. Users' views are important, because the objective of financial statements is to provide high quality, transparent and comparable information to help users make economic decisions. In other words, financial statements are intended to meet the needs of users, rather than preparers or other interest groups. The purpose of setting accounting standards is to ensure that, wherever possible, the information provided in the financial statements meets users' needs. Therefore, if the people who use the financial statements in making economic decisions regard the fair value estimates as sufficiently reliable for recognition in the financial statements, this provides strong evidence of measurement reliability.

BC308   The Board also noted that, although the FASB decided to permit a choice between recognition and disclosure of expenses arising from employee share-based payment transactions, it did so for non-technical reasons, not because it agreed with the view that reliable measurement was not possible:

> The Board continues to believe that use of option-pricing models, as modified in this statement, will produce estimates of the fair value of stock options that are sufficiently reliable to justify recognition in financial statements. Imprecision in those estimates does not justify failure to recognize compensation cost stemming from employee stock options. That belief underlies the Board's encouragement to entities to adopt the fair value based method of recognizing stock-based employee compensation cost in their financial statements. (SFAS 123, Basis for Conclusions, paragraph 117)

---

27 J N Carpenter. 1998. The exercise and valuation of executive stock options. *Journal of Financial Economics* 48: 127–158. R A Maller, R Tan and M Van De Vyver. 2002. How Might Companies Value ESOs? *Australian Accounting Review* 12 (1): 11–24.

BC309   In summary, if expenses arising from grants of share options to employees are omitted from the financial statements, or recognised using the intrinsic value method (which typically results in zero expense) or the minimum value method, there will be a permanent error embedded in the financial statements. So the question is, which accounting method is more likely to produce the smallest amount of error and the most relevant, comparable information—a fair value estimate, which might result in some understatement or overstatement of the associated expense, or another measurement basis, such as intrinsic value (especially if measured at grant date), that will definitely result in substantial understatement of the associated expense?

BC310   Taking all of the above into consideration, the Board concluded that, in virtually all cases, the estimated fair value of employee share options at grant date can be measured with sufficient reliability for the purposes of recognising employee share-based payment transactions in the financial statements. The Board therefore concluded that, in general, the IFRS on share-based payment should require a fair value measurement method to be applied to all types of share-based payment transactions, including all types of employee share-based payment. Hence, the Board concluded that the IFRS should not allow a choice between a fair value measurement method and an intrinsic value measurement method, and should not permit a choice between recognition and disclosure of expenses arising from employee share-based payment transactions.

Transitional provisions

Share-based payment transactions among group entities

BC310A   The Board noted a potential difficulty when an entity retrospectively applies the amendments made by *Group Cash-settled Share-based Payment Transactions* issued in June 2009. An entity might not have accounted for some group share-based payment transactions in accordance with IFRS 2 in its separate or individual financial statements. In a few cases, an entity that settles a group share-based payment transaction may have to apply hindsight to measure the fair value of awards now required to be accounted for as cash-settled. However, the Board noted that such transactions would have been accounted for in accordance with IFRS 2 in the group's consolidated financial statements. For these reasons and those outlined in paragraph BC268G, if the information necessary for retrospective application is not available, the Board decided to require an entity to use amounts previously recognised in the group's consolidated financial statements when applying the new requirements retrospectively in the entity's separate or individual financial statements.

Consequential amendments to other Standards

Tax effects of share-based payment transactions

BC311   Whether expenses arising from share-based payment transactions are deductible, and if so, whether the amount of the tax deduction is the same as the reported expense and whether the tax deduction arises in the same accounting period, varies from country to country.

BC312   If the amount of the tax deduction is the same as the reported expense, but the tax deduction arises in a later accounting period, this will result in a deductible temporary difference under IAS 12 *Income Taxes*. Temporary differences usually arise from differences between the carrying amount of assets and liabilities and the amount attributed to those assets and liabilities for tax purposes. However, IAS 12 also deals with items that have a tax base but are not recognised as assets and liabilities in the balance sheet. It gives an example of research costs that are recognised as an expense in the financial statements in the period in which the costs are incurred, but are deductible for tax purposes in a later accounting period. The Standard states that the difference between the tax base of the research costs, being the amount that will be deductible in a future accounting period, and the carrying amount of nil is a deductible temporary difference that results in a deferred tax asset (IAS 12, paragraph 9).

BC313   Applying this guidance indicates that if an expense arising from a share-based payment transaction is recognised in the financial statements in one accounting period and is tax-deductible in a later accounting period, this should be accounted for as a deductible temporary difference under IAS 12. Under that Standard, a deferred tax asset is recognised for all deductible temporary differences to the extent that it is probable that taxable profit will be available against which the deductible temporary difference can be used (IAS 12, paragraph 24).

BC314   Whilst IAS 12 does not discuss reverse situations, the same logic applies. For example, suppose the entity is able to claim a tax deduction for the total transaction amount at the date of grant but the entity recognises an expense arising from that transaction over the vesting period. Applying the guidance in IAS 12 suggests that this should be accounted for as a taxable temporary difference, and hence a deferred tax liability should be recognised.

BC315   However, the amount of the tax deduction might differ from the amount of the expense recognised in the financial statements. For example, the measurement basis applied for accounting purposes might not be the same as that used for tax purposes, eg intrinsic value might be used for tax purposes and fair value for accounting purposes. Similarly, the measurement date might differ. For example, US entities receive a tax deduction based on intrinsic value at the date of exercise in respect of some share options, whereas for accounting purposes an entity applying SFAS 123 would recognise an expense based on the option's fair value, measured at the date of grant. There could also be other differences in the measurement method applied for accounting and tax purposes, eg differences in the treatment of forfeitures or different valuation methodologies applied.

BC316 SFAS 123 requires that, if the amount of the tax deduction exceeds the total expense recognised in the financial statements, the tax benefit for the excess deduction should be recognised as additional paid-in capital, ie as a direct credit to equity. Conversely, if the tax deduction is less than the total expense recognised for accounting purposes, the write-off of the related deferred tax asset in excess of the benefits of the tax deduction is recognised in the income statement, except to the extent that there is remaining additional paid-in capital from excess tax deductions from previous share-based payment transactions (SFAS 123, paragraph 44).

BC317 At first sight, it may seem questionable to credit or debit directly to equity amounts that relate to differences between the amount of the tax deduction and the total recognised expense. The tax effects of any such differences would ordinarily flow through the income statement. However, some argue that the approach in SFAS 123 is appropriate if the reason for the difference between the amount of the tax deduction and the recognised expense is that a different measurement date is applied.

BC318 For example, suppose grant date measurement is used for accounting purposes and exercise date measurement is used for tax purposes. Under grant date measurement, any changes in the value of the equity instrument after grant date accrue to the employee (or other party) in their capacity as equity participants. Therefore, some argue that any tax effects arising from those valuation changes should be credited to equity (or debited to equity, if the value of the equity instrument declines).

BC319 Similarly, some argue that the tax deduction arises from an equity transaction (the exercise of options), and hence the tax effects should be reported in equity. It can also be argued that this treatment is consistent with the requirement in IAS 12 to account for the tax effects of transactions or events in the same way as the entity accounts for those transactions or events themselves. If the tax deduction relates to both an income statement item and an equity item, the associated tax effects should be allocated between the income statement and equity.

BC320 Others disagree, arguing that the tax deduction relates to employee remuneration expense, ie an income statement item only, and therefore all of the tax effects of the deduction should be recognised in the income statement. The fact that the taxing authority applies a different method in measuring the amount of the tax deduction does not change this conclusion. A further argument is that this treatment is consistent with the *Framework*, because reporting amounts directly in equity would be inappropriate, given that the government is not an owner of the entity.

BC321 The Board noted that, if one accepts that it might be appropriate to debit/credit to equity the tax effect of the difference between the amount of the tax deduction and the total recognised expense where that difference relates to changes in the value of equity interests, there could be other reasons why the amount of the tax deduction differs from the total recognised expense. For example, grant date measurement may be used for both tax and accounting purposes, but the valuation methodology used for tax purposes might produce a higher value than the methodology used for accounting purposes (eg the effects of early exercise might be ignored when valuing an option for tax purposes). The Board saw no reason why, in this situation, the excess tax benefits should be credited to equity.

BC322 In developing ED 2, the Board concluded that the tax effects of share-based payment transactions should be recognised in the income statement by being taken into account in the determination of tax expense. It agreed that this should be explained in the form of a worked example in a consequential amendment to IAS 12.

BC323 During the Board's redeliberation of the proposals in ED 2, the Board reconsidered the points above, and concluded that the tax effects of an equity-settled share-based payment transaction should be allocated between the income statement and equity. The Board then considered how this allocation should be made and related issues, such as the measurement of the deferred tax asset.

BC324 Under IAS 12, the deferred tax asset for a deductible temporary difference is based on the amount the taxation authorities will permit as a deduction in future periods. Therefore, the Board concluded that the measurement of the deferred tax asset should be based on an estimate of the future tax deduction. If changes in the share price affect that future tax deduction, the estimate of the expected future tax deduction should be based on the current share price.

BC325 These conclusions are consistent with the proposals in ED 2 concerning the measurement of the deferred tax asset. However, this approach differs from SFAS 123, which measures the deferred tax asset on the basis of the cumulative recognised expense. The Board rejected the SFAS 123 method of measuring the deferred tax asset because it is inconsistent with IAS 12. As noted above, under IAS 12, the deferred tax asset for a deductible temporary difference is based on the amount the taxation authorities will permit as a deduction in future periods. If a later measurement date is applied for tax purposes, it is very unlikely that the tax deduction will ever equal the cumulative expense, except by coincidence. For example, if share options are granted to employees, and the entity receives a tax deduction measured as the difference between the share price and the exercise price at the date of exercise, it is extremely unlikely that the tax deduction will ever equal the cumulative expense. By basing the measurement of the deferred tax asset on the cumulative expense, the SFAS 123 method is likely to result in the understatement or overstatement of the deferred tax asset. In some situations, such as when share options are significantly out of the money, SFAS 123 requires the entity to continue to recognise a deferred tax asset even when the possibility of the entity recovering that asset is remote. Continuing to recognise a deferred tax asset in this situation is not only inconsistent with IAS 12, it is inconsistent with the definition of an asset in the *Framework*, and the requirements of other IFRSs for the recognition and measurement of assets, including requirements to assess impairment.

BC326   The Board also concluded that:

(a)   if the tax deduction received (or expected to be received, measured as described in paragraph BC324) is less than or equal to the cumulative expense, the associated tax benefits received (or expected to be received) should be recognised as tax income and included in profit or loss for the period.

(b)   if the tax deduction received (or expected to be received, measured as described in paragraph BC324) exceeds the cumulative expense, the excess associated tax benefits received (or expected to be received) should be recognised directly in equity.

BC327   The above allocation method is similar to that applied in SFAS 123, with some exceptions. First, the above allocation method ensures that the total tax benefits recognised in the income statement in respect of a particular share-based payment transaction do not exceed the tax benefits ultimately received. The Board disagreed with the approach in SFAS 123, which sometimes results in the total tax benefits recognised in the income statement exceeding the tax benefits ultimately received because, in some situations, SFAS 123 permits the unrecovered portion of the deferred tax asset to be written off to equity.

BC328   Second, the Board concluded that the above allocation method should be applied irrespective of why the tax deduction received (or expected to be received) differs from the cumulative expense. The SFAS 123 method is based on US tax legislation, under which the excess tax benefits credited to equity (if any) arise from the use of a later measurement date for tax purposes. The Board agreed with respondents who commented that the accounting treatment must be capable of being applied in various tax jurisdictions. The Board was concerned that requiring entities to examine the reasons why there is a difference between the tax deduction and the cumulative expense, and then account for the tax effects accordingly, would be too complex to be applied consistently across a wide range of different tax jurisdictions.

BC329   The Board noted that it might need to reconsider its conclusions on accounting for the tax effects of share-based payment transactions in the future, for example, if the Board reviews IAS 12 more broadly.

Accounting for own shares held

BC330   IAS 32 requires the acquisition of treasury shares to be deducted from equity, and no gain or loss is to be recognised on the sale, issue or cancellation of treasury shares. Consideration received on the subsequent sale or issue of treasury shares is credited to equity.

BC331   This is consistent with the *Framework*. The repurchase of shares and their subsequent reissue or transfer to other parties are transactions with equity participants that should be recognised as changes in equity. In accounting terms, there is no difference between shares that are repurchased and cancelled, and shares that are repurchased and held by the entity. In both cases, the repurchase involves an outflow of resources to shareholders (ie a distribution), thereby reducing shareholders' investment in the entity. Similarly, there is no difference between a new issue of shares and an issue of shares previously repurchased and held in treasury. In both cases, there is an inflow of resources from shareholders, thereby increasing shareholders' investment in the entity. Although accounting practice in some jurisdictions treats own shares held as assets, this is not consistent with the definition of assets in the *Framework* and the conceptual frameworks of other standard-setters, as explained in the Discussion Paper (footnote to paragraph 4.7 of the Discussion Paper, reproduced earlier in the footnote to paragraph BC73).

BC332   Given that treasury shares are treated as an asset in some jurisdictions, it will be necessary to change that accounting treatment when this IFRS is applied, because otherwise an entity would be faced with two expense items—an expense arising from the share-based payment transaction (for the consumption of goods and services received as consideration for the issue of an equity instrument) and another expense arising from the write-down of the 'asset' for treasury shares issued or transferred to employees at an exercise price that is less than their purchase price.

BC333   Hence, the Board concluded that the requirements in the relevant paragraphs of IAS 32 regarding treasury shares should also be applied to treasury shares purchased, sold, issued or cancelled in connection with employee share plans or other share-based payment arrangements.

Definition of vesting condition (2013 amendments)

BC334   The Board decided to clarify the definition of 'vesting conditions' in IFRS 2 to ensure the consistent classification of conditions attached to a share-based payment. Previously, this Standard did not separately define 'performance condition' or 'service condition', but instead described both concepts within the definition of vesting conditions.

BC335   The Board decided to separate the definitions of performance condition and service condition from the definition of vesting condition to make the description of each condition clearer.

BC336   In response to the comments received on the Exposure Draft *Annual Improvements to IFRSs 2010–2012 Cycle* (Proposed amendments to International Financial Reporting Standards) (the 'ED'), published in May 2012, the Board addressed the following concerns that had been raised about the definitions of performance condition, service condition and market condition:

(a)   whether a performance target can be set by reference to the price (or value) of another entity (or entities) that is (are) within the group;

(b)   whether a performance target that refers to a longer period than the required service period may constitute a performance condition;

(c)   whether the specified period of service that the counterparty is required to complete can be either implicit or explicit;

(d)   whether a performance target needs to be influenced by an employee;

(e) whether a share market index target may constitute a performance condition or a non-vesting condition;

(f) whether the definition of performance condition should indicate that it includes a market condition;

(g) whether a definition of non-vesting condition is needed; and

(h) whether the employee's failure to complete a required service period due to termination of employment is considered to be a failure to satisfy a service condition.

Whether a performance target can be set by reference to the price (or value) of another entity (or entities) that is (are) within the group

BC337 The Board decided to clarify that within the context of a share-based payment transaction that involves entities in the same group, a performance target can be defined by the price (or value) of the equity instruments of another entity in that group. This amendment is consistent with the guidance in paragraphs 3A and 43A–43D of IFRS 2. Paragraph 3A, which provides guidance about the scope of IFRS 2, states that "a share-based payment transaction may be settled by another group entity (or a shareholder of any group entity) on behalf of the entity receiving or acquiring the goods or services".

BC338 The Board decided to make a similar amendment to the definition of market condition to indicate that a market condition can be based on the market price of the entity's equity instruments or the equity instruments of another entity in the same group.

Whether a performance target that refers to a longer period than the required service period may constitute a performance condition

BC339 The Board observed that IFRS 2 was not clear about the duration of a performance target relative to the duration of the related service condition. Some understood IFRS 2 to require that the duration of the performance has to be wholly within the period of the related service requirement; others understood that a performance target could be achieved over a period that extends beyond the period for which the employee is required to provide a service.

BC340 During its deliberations prior to the issue of the ED, the Board decided to clarify that the duration of the performance condition needed to be wholly within the period of the related service requirement. This meant that the period of achieving the performance target could not start before, or end after, the service period. This requirement was reflected in the ED.

BC341 Some respondents to the ED disagreed with the requirement that the duration of the performance condition needed to be wholly within the period of the related service, because they asserted that it was common for a performance target to start before the service period. For example, a performance target could be set as a measure of the growth in earnings per share (the 'EPS target') between the most recently published financial statements on the grant date and the most recently published financial statements before the vesting date.

BC342　Other respondents noted that if the beginning of the period for achieving the performance target was restricted, then a relatively minor difference in the way that the awards are structured could lead to a different classification of the performance target (ie as either a non-vesting condition or a performance (vesting) condition), which could consequently lead to differences in the way in which the award would be accounted for in accordance with the guidance in IFRS 2.

BC343　In response to the comments received on the ED, the Board decided to revise the proposed definition of performance condition. In this revision, the Board decided to ease the restriction on when the period for a performance target could start. It therefore decided to clarify that the start of the period of achieving the performance target could be before the service period, provided that the commencement date of the performance target is not substantially before the commencement of the service period.

BC344　However, the Board decided to retain the proposal in the ED that the period over which the performance target is achieved should not extend beyond the service period. It thought that this decision was consistent with the definition of a performance condition, which was previously included within the definition of a vesting condition. The definition of a performance condition requires the counterparty to complete a specified period of service and to meet the performance target(s) while the counterparty is rendering the service required. The definition of performance condition reflects the principle in paragraph 7 of IFRS 2, which states that "An entity shall recognise the goods or services received or acquired in a share-based payment transaction when it obtains the goods or as the services are received".

BC345　The Board also decided to add the words "ie a **service condition**" to criterion (a) of the definition of performance condition in order to create a cross-reference to the definition of service condition.

Whether the specified period of service that the counterparty is required to complete can be either implicit or explicit

BC346　In the definition of performance condition, the Board decided to highlight a feature that distinguishes a performance condition from a non-vesting condition in accordance with paragraph BC171A of IFRS 2; namely, that a performance condition has an explicit or implicit service requirement and a non-vesting condition does not. This is so that, in order to constitute a performance condition, a performance target needs to be accompanied by a service requirement, which can be implicit or explicit. The Board observed that if the share-based payment arrangement does not contain an explicit requirement to provide services, the arrangement may still contain an implicit service condition.

Whether a performance target needs to be influenced by an employee

BC347   During its deliberations the Board observed that for a target to constitute a performance condition it needs to be both 'within the influence' of the employee and in the interest of the entity. Consequently, the Board proposed that the definition of performance condition should make clear that a performance target is defined by reference to the entity's own operations (or activities) or the price (or value) of its equity instruments (including shares and share options).

BC348   In response to the ED, some respondents indicated that the reason why the performance target needed to be within the influence of the employee was unclear and found it to be contradictory to the proposed definition of performance condition. This is because in the proposed definition, the performance target was defined by reference to the performance of the entity, that is, by reference to the entity's own operations (or activities) or the price (or value) of its equity instruments. Some other respondents also raised some difficulties that they expected to encounter when applying the proposed guidance. In this respect, the respondents stated that determining whether a performance target is within the influence of the employee would be difficult to apply in the case of a group of entities; for example, the profit or share price of a group of companies could be seen to be 'remote from the influence of' an employee of a particular subsidiary of the group.

BC349   The Board observed that requiring a performance target to be within the influence of the employee could be misinterpreted as meaning that the Board's intention was to challenge management to explain how the performance of the employee affects the performance target. The Board confirmed that it was not its intention to do so. It observed that the link between the employee's service/performance against a given performance target is management's responsibility. It noted that each employee has, in varying degrees, an influence over an entity's (or group's) overall performance, that is, over an entity's (or group's) own operations (or activities) or the price (or value) of its equity instruments. Consequently, the Board decided to omit the requirement that the target "needs to be within the influence of the employee" to avoid further confusion.

BC350   In its review of the definition of performance condition the Board also considered what, if any, level of correlation is required between an employee's responsibility and the performance target. Potential diversity in practice had emerged because some were of the view that if share based payment awards are granted to employees conditional on the entity-wide profit, it is not clear that the profit target constitutes a performance condition on the basis that the employee might have so little influence on the entity-wide profit that it is not clear whether the target is able to sufficiently incentivise an individual employee's actions. Others held the view that because the entity is in business in order to make a profit, it is reasonable to assume that all employees contribute directly or indirectly to the entity-wide profit, ie that the whole body of employees contribute towards the entity-wide profit.

BC351   In the ED the Board observed that it is reasonable to assume that the performance target that is set by management for an employee's share-based payment appropriately incentivises the employee to provide an increased quality and/or quantity of service to benefit the entity. Consequently, the Board decided that the definition of performance condition should make clear that a performance target may relate either to the performance of the entity as a whole or to some part of it, such as a division or an individual employee.

BC352   Respondents to the ED questioned whether it was the Board's intention to require an entity to demonstrate, or provide evidence of, the correlation between an employee's responsibility and the performance target in order for that target to be a performance condition. During its deliberations, the Board confirmed that it was not its intention to require an entity to prove this correlation.

Whether a share market index target may constitute a performance condition or a non-vesting condition

BC353   The Board analysed the case in which a share-based payment is conditional on a share market index target and whether it would be considered a performance condition or a non-vesting condition. For example, a grant might be conditional on a stock exchange index (of which the entity's shares are a part) reaching a specified target and the employee remaining in service up to the date that the target is met.

BC354   The Board observed that some might argue that the share market index target with the implicit service requirement constitutes a performance condition, because an employee is required to provide service to the entity, and that the time estimated to affect the share market index target implicitly determines how long the entity receives the required service. Others might argue that the share market index target is a non-vesting condition because it is not related to the performance of the entity (ie instead it is related to, or based on, not only the entity's share price but also the share price of other unrelated entities).

BC355   In the ED the Board observed that the share market index target would be considered a non-vesting condition because it is not related to the performance of the entity or of another entity in the same group, even if the shares of the entity or of another entity in the same group form part of that index. The Board also observed that a share market index target may be predominantly affected by many external variables or factors involved in its determination, including macroeconomic factors such as the risk-free interest rate or foreign exchange rates and, consequently, it is remote from the influence of the employee.

BC356   Respondents to the ED agreed that it would be reasonable to assume that the share market index target is a non-vesting condition but some thought that it should not be based on the level of influence exercised by an employee over the performance target or on whether the target is affected by external variables or factors. This is because, in their view, the level of influence and the effect of external variables are subjective reasons that are difficult to measure.

BC357　The Board decided to reaffirm its position that a share market index is a non-vesting condition but, on the basis of the comments received, it is clarifying that the reason why it is a non-vesting condition is because a share market index not only reflects the performance of an entity but, in addition, also reflects the performance of other entities outside the group.

BC358　The Board also considered a similar case in which the entity's share price makes up a substantial part of the share market index. The Board determined that even in such a case the condition should still be considered a non-vesting condition because it reflects the performance of other entities that are outside the group.

Whether the definition of performance condition should indicate that it includes a market condition

BC359　A respondent to the ED noted that the final sentence of the definition of vesting conditions, which states that "a performance condition might include a market condition", is contradictory. This is because a market condition:

(a)　is a target that is related to the market price of the entity's equity instruments; and

(b)　includes no explicit requirement for the counterparty to complete a specified period of service.

BC360　The Board observed that, on the basis of the definition of performance condition, a performance target that is related to the market price of an entity's equity instruments and to the completion of a specified period of service is considered a market (performance) condition. Consequently, the Board disagreed that an inconsistency existed in the definitions of performance condition and market condition. To avoid confusion in the definitions of performance condition and market condition, the Board decided to:

(a)　delete the last sentence in the definition of vesting condition (ie "a performance condition might include a market condition"); and

(b)　indicate within the definition of performance condition that performance conditions are either market conditions or non-market conditions.

BC361　The Board decided to confirm that a market condition is a type of performance condition. The Board considered that a condition that is not subject to a service requirement is not a performance condition, and instead, is considered a non-vesting condition. In making this clarification, the Board did not change the measurement requirements in IFRS 2 for a market condition.

Whether a definition of 'non-vesting condition' is needed

BC362   Respondents to the ED thought that clarity could be further improved in IFRS 2 by defining a 'non-vesting condition'.

BC363   The Board noted that there is no formal definition of non-vesting condition in IFRS 2, but Implementation Guidance on the split between vesting and non-vesting conditions is provided in a flowchart in paragraph IG24 of IFRS 2.

BC364   The Board determined that the creation of a stand-alone definition of non-vesting condition would not be the best alternative for providing clarity on this issue. This is because the Board observed that the concept of a non-vesting condition can be inferred from paragraphs BC170–BC184 of IFRS 2, which clarify the definition of vesting conditions. In accordance with this guidance it can be inferred that a non-vesting condition is any condition that does not determine whether the entity receives the services that entitle the counterparty to receive cash, other assets or equity instruments of the entity under a share-based payment arrangement. In other words, a non-vesting condition is any condition that is not a vesting condition. On the basis of its analysis the Board decided to not add a definition of non-vesting condition.

Whether the employee's failure to complete a required service period due to termination of employment is considered to be a failure to satisfy a service condition

BC365   When considering a possible revision of the definition of service condition, the Board observed that in IFRS 2 there is no specific guidance on how to account for a share-based payment award when the entity terminates an employee's employment.

BC366   The Board noted, however, that paragraph 19 of this Standard regards the employee's failure to complete a specified service period as a failure to satisfy a service condition. In the ED the Board proposed to clarify within the definition of service condition that if the employee fails to complete a specified service period, the employee thereby fails to satisfy a service condition, regardless of the reason for that failure. The Board also noted that the accounting consequence is that the compensation expense would be reversed if an employee fails to complete a specified service period.

BC367   Some respondents to the ED thought that more clarity could be provided in the proposed guidance. This is because they noted that in some circumstances in which an employee is unable to perform the service condition by completing the stipulated service period (such as when the employee is ill or dies in service), it would normally be expected that part of the award would vest and that the related compensation expense should not be reversed. They noted that, to the extent that a portion of the award vests, that portion should be recognised as an expense.

BC368   In response to the comments received, the Board noted that the objective of the proposed amendment to the definition of service condition is to clarify that the termination of an employee's employment is a situation in which the employee fails to complete a specified service period and, consequently, is considered a situation in which the service condition is not met.

BC369   The Board observed that in circumstances in which equity instruments do not vest because of failure to satisfy a vesting condition, paragraph 19 of IFRS 2 states that "on a cumulative basis, no amount is recognised for goods or services received if the equity instruments granted do not vest because of a failure to satisfy a vesting condition". The Board observed that in circumstances in which the equity instruments either partly or fully vest on cessation of employment, paragraph 23 of IFRS 2 states that "the entity shall make no subsequent adjustment to total equity after vesting date". The Board also noted that, in accordance with paragraph 28, "if a grant of equity instruments is cancelled or settled during the vesting period (other than a grant cancelled by forfeiture when the vesting conditions are not satisfied) the entity shall account for the cancellation or settlement as an acceleration of vesting, and shall therefore recognise immediately the amount that otherwise would have been recognised for services received over the remainder of the vesting period". Noting the guidance already provided in IFRS 2, the Board concluded that further guidance was not necessary.

Transition provisions

BC370   The Board considered the transition provisions and effective date of the amendment to IFRS 2. The Board noted that the changes to the definitions of vesting conditions and market condition and the addition of performance condition and service condition might result in changes to the grant-date fair value of share-based payment transactions for which the grant date was in previous periods. To avoid the use of hindsight, it decided that an entity would apply the amendments to IFRS 2 prospectively to share-based payment transactions for which the grant date is on or after 1 July 2014. Earlier application should be permitted.

Effects of vesting conditions on the measurement of a cash-settled share-based payment (2016 amendments)[28]

BC371   This section summarises the Board's considerations when it finalised its proposals to address the accounting for the effects of vesting conditions on the measurement of a cash-settled share-based payment, contained in the November 2014 ED.

BC372   The Board received a request regarding the measurement requirements in IFRS 2 for cash-settled share-based payment transactions that include a performance condition.

---

28 Paragraphs BC371–BC382 are added as a consequence of amendments to IFRS 2 *Classification and Measurement of Share-based Payment Transactions* issued in June 2016.

BC373   The Board noted that IFRS 2 requires the use of fair value as a principle in measuring share-based payment transactions. The Board observed that paragraphs 19–21A of IFRS 2 provide the requirements for measuring the fair value of equity-settled share-based payment transactions that include vesting and non-vesting conditions. The Board also observed that, in the case of cash-settled share-based payment transactions, paragraph 33 of IFRS 2 requires an entity to measure the liability, initially and at the end of each reporting period until settled, at fair value. The entity is required to apply an option pricing model, taking into account the terms and conditions on which the cash-settled share-based payments were granted and the extent to which the employees have rendered service to date.

BC374   However, IFRS 2 does not specifically address the impact of vesting and non-vesting conditions on the measurement of the fair value of the liability incurred in a cash-settled share-based payment transaction. Specifically, it was unclear whether an entity should apply, by analogy, the requirements in paragraphs 19–21A of IFRS 2 for measuring equity-settled share-based payment transactions when measuring cash-settled share-based payment transactions that include vesting and non-vesting conditions.

BC375   The Board observed that, in accordance with paragraph 6A, IFRS 2 uses the term 'fair value' in a way that differs in some respects from the definition of fair value in IFRS 13 *Fair Value Measurement*. When applying IFRS 2, an entity is required to measure fair value in accordance with that Standard (and not in accordance with IFRS 13) for cash-settled and equity-settled awards. Consequently, the Board decided to add paragraphs 33A–33D on how market and non-market vesting conditions and non-vesting conditions should be reflected in the measurement of a cash-settled share-based payment transaction. The Board decided that those conditions should be reflected in the measurement of cash-settled share-based payments in a manner consistent with how they are reflected in the measurement of an equity-settled share-based payment transaction.

BC376   The Board further observed that measuring the fair value of the liability incurred in a cash-settled share-based payment transaction by analogy to the requirements for equity-settled share-based payment transactions would avoid the practical difficulties of measuring the effects of vesting conditions (other than market conditions) on the fair value of the awards. Those practical difficulties were identified by the Board when it originally issued IFRS 2, and are explained in paragraph BC184 of IFRS 2.

BC377   Consequently the Board decided to amend paragraphs 30–31, and 33 and added paragraphs 33A–33D to clarify the effect that market and non-market vesting conditions and non-vesting conditions have on the measurement of the liability incurred in a cash-settled share-based payment transaction.

BC378   The Board observed that if an employee does not receive the payment because of a failure to satisfy any condition, this should result in remeasuring the liability to zero. The amendments make clear that the cumulative amount ultimately recognised for goods or services received as consideration for a cash-settled share-based payment will be equal to the amount of cash (or other assets) that is paid.

BC379   Furthermore, the Board amended paragraph IG19 and added IG Example 12A to the Guidance on Implementing IFRS 2 to illustrate the impact of a performance condition on the measurement of a cash-settled share-based payment transaction.

BC380   Respondents to the November 2014 ED questioned the meaning of 'best available estimate', as that notion was used in the proposal, for estimating the fair value of a cash-settled share-based payment. The Board noted that the term 'best available estimate' is already used in IFRS 2 and is not a new notion. This term is also used in paragraph 20 of IFRS 2 for estimating the number of equity instruments expected to vest of an equity-settled share-based payment. The Board further observed that analysing such a notion would potentially involve examining similar notions in other Standards and observed that such notions would be better examined as part of a broader project.

BC381   Respondents to the November 2014 ED suggested that the Board should add an explicit requirement for the disclosure of a contingent liability when vesting is not probable (and thus no liability is recognised, as illustrated in Year 1 of Example 12A). The Board observed that adding such a requirement is not necessary because the general requirement in paragraph 50 of IFRS 2 already requires entities to

> ...disclose information that enables users of the financial statements to understand the effect of share-based payment transactions on the entity's profit or loss for the period and on its financial position.

BC382   Some respondents to the November 2014 ED suggested that the Board should add other examples to the Guidance on Implementing IFRS 2 to illustrate the effects of vesting and non-vesting conditions on the measurement of cash-settled awards. The Board did not think this was necessary because of the existing examples in the implementation guidance that illustrate the effects of market and non-market vesting conditions and of non-vesting conditions on equity-settled awards. These examples also serve to illustrate the effects of such conditions on cash-settled awards because the amendments require consistent treatment for both types of awards.

Amended quotation from the *Conceptual Framework*

BC383   In Appendix A, the footnote to the definition of an equity instrument quoted the definition of a liability from the *Conceptual Framework for Financial Reporting* issued in 2010. Following the issue of the revised *Conceptual Framework for Financial Reporting* in 2018 (2018 *Conceptual Framework*), *Amendments to References to the Conceptual Framework in IFRS Standards* amended the footnote to quote the revised definition of a liability from the 2018 *Conceptual Framework*.

BC384   The 2018 *Conceptual Framework* did not address classification of financial instruments with characteristics of both liabilities and equity. In addition, *Amendments to References to the Conceptual Framework in IFRS Standards* did not amend the guidance on classification of financial instruments in IFRS 2. Therefore the Board does not expect the amendment to the footnote in IFRS 2 to have a significant effect on the application of this Standard.

IASB documents published to accompany

IFRS 3

Business Combinations

The text of the unaccompanied standard, IFRS 3, is contained in Part A of this edition. Its effective date when issued was 1 July 2009. The text of the Accompanying Guidance on IFRS 3 is contained in Part B of this edition. This part presents the following documents:

BASIS FOR CONCLUSIONS

APPENDIX TO THE BASIS FOR CONCLUSIONS
Amendments to the Basis for Conclusions on other IFRSs

DISSENTING OPINIONS

Contents

...continued

Basis for Conclusions on
IFRS 3 *Business Combinations*

This Basis for Conclusions and its appendix accompany, but are not part of, IFRS 3.

Background information

In 2001 the International Accounting Standards Board began a project to review IAS 22 *Business Combinations* (revised in 1998) as part of its initial agenda, with the objective of improving the quality of, and seeking international convergence on, the accounting for business combinations. The Board decided to address the accounting for business combinations in two phases.

As part of the first phase, the Board published in December 2002 ED 3 *Business Combinations*, together with an exposure draft of proposed related amendments to IAS 36 *Impairment of Assets* and IAS 38 *Intangible Assets*, with a comment deadline of 4 April 2003. The Board received 136 comment letters.

The Board concluded the first phase in March 2004 by issuing simultaneously IFRS 3 *Business Combinations* and revised versions of IAS 36 and IAS 38. The Board's primary conclusion in the first phase was that virtually all business combinations are acquisitions. Accordingly, the Board decided to require the use of one method of accounting for business combinations – the acquisition method.

The US Financial Accounting Standards Board (FASB) also conducted a project on business combinations in multiple phases. The FASB concluded its first phase in June 2001 by issuing FASB Statements No. 141 *Business Combinations* (SFAS 141) and No. 142 *Goodwill and Other Intangible Assets*. The scope of that first phase was similar to IFRS 3 and the FASB reached similar conclusions on the major issues.

The two boards began deliberating the second phase of their projects at about the same time. They decided that a significant improvement could be made to financial reporting if they had similar standards for accounting for business combinations. They therefore agreed to conduct the second phase of the project as a joint effort with the objective of reaching the same conclusions.

The second phase of the project addressed the guidance for applying the acquisition method. In June 2005 the boards published an exposure draft of revisions to IFRS 3 and SFAS 141, together with exposure drafts of related amendments to IAS 27 *Consolidated and Separate Financial Statements* and Accounting Research Bulletin No. 51 *Consolidated Financial Statements*, with a comment deadline of 28 October 2005. The boards received more than 280 comment letters.

The boards concluded the second phase of the project by issuing their revised standards, IFRS 3 *Business Combinations* (as revised in 2008) and FASB Statement No. 141 (revised 2007) *Business Combinations* and the related amendments to IAS 27 and FASB Statement No. 160 *Noncontrolling Interests in Consolidated Financial Statements*.

Introduction

BC1   This Basis for Conclusions summarises the considerations of the International Accounting Standards Board (IASB) and the US Financial Accounting Standards Board (FASB) in reaching the conclusions in their revised standards, IFRS 3 *Business Combinations* (as revised in 2008) and FASB Statement No. 141 (revised 2007) *Business Combinations* (SFAS 141(R)). It includes the reasons why each board accepted particular approaches and rejected others. Individual board members gave greater weight to some factors than to others.

BC2   The revised IFRS 3 and SFAS 141(R) carry forward without reconsideration the primary conclusions each board reached in IFRS 3 (issued in 2004) and FASB Statement No. 141 (SFAS 141, issued in 2001), both of which were titled *Business Combinations*. The conclusions carried forward include, among others, the requirement to apply the *purchase method* (which the revised standards refer to as the *acquisition method*) to account for all business combinations and the identifiability criteria for recognising an intangible asset separately from goodwill. This Basis for Conclusions includes the reasons for those conclusions, as well as the reasons for the conclusions the boards reached in their joint deliberations that led to the revised standards. Because the provisions of the revised standards on applying the acquisition method represent a more extensive change to SFAS 141 than to the previous version of IFRS 3, this Basis for Conclusions includes more discussion of the FASB's conclusions than of the IASB's in the second phase of their respective business combinations projects.

BC3   In discussing the boards' consideration of comments on exposure drafts, this Basis for Conclusions refers to the exposure draft that preceded the previous version of IFRS 3 as *ED 3* and to the one that preceded SFAS 141 as the *1999 Exposure Draft*; it refers to the joint exposure draft that preceded the revised standards as the *2005 Exposure Draft*. Other exposure drafts published by each board in developing IFRS 3 or SFAS 141 are explained in the context of the issues they addressed. As used in this Basis for Conclusions, *the revised IFRS 3, SFAS 141(R)* and *the revised standards* refer to the revised versions of IFRS 3 and SFAS 141; references to *IFRS 3* and *SFAS 141* are to the original versions of those standards.

BC4   The IASB and the FASB concurrently deliberated the issues in the second phase of the project and reached the same conclusions on most of them. The table of differences between the revised IFRS 3 and SFAS 141(R) (presented after the illustrative examples) describes the substantive differences that remain; the most significant difference is the measurement of a non-controlling interest in an acquiree (see paragraphs BC205–BC221).[1] In addition, the application of some provisions of the revised standards on which the boards reached the same conclusions may differ because of differences in:

---

1   [Editor's note: The table of differences between IFRS 3, as revised in 2008, and SFAS 141 (R) has not been updated since it was issued in 2008. This outdated table appeared in the Bound Volume up to 2018 and was removed in 2019.]

(a) other accounting standards of the boards to which the revised standards refer. For example, recognition and measurement requirements for a few particular assets acquired (eg a deferred tax asset) and liabilities assumed (eg an employee benefit obligation) refer to existing IFRSs or US generally accepted accounting principles (GAAP) rather than fair value measures.

(b) disclosure practices of the boards. For example, the FASB requires particular supplementary information or particular disclosures by public entities only. The IASB has no similar requirements for supplementary information and does not distinguish between listed and unlisted entities.

(c) particular transition provisions for changes to past accounting practices of US and non-US companies that previously differed.

Definition of a business combination

BC5 The FASB's 1999 Exposure Draft proposed that a *business combination* should be defined as occurring when one entity acquires net assets that constitute a business or acquires equity interests in one or more other entities and thereby obtains control over that entity or entities. Many respondents who commented on the proposed definition said that it would exclude certain transactions covered by APB Opinion No. 16 *Business Combinations* (APB Opinion 16), in particular, transactions in which none of the former shareholder groups of the combining entities obtained control over the combined entity (such as roll-ups, put-togethers and so-called mergers of equals). During its redeliberations of the 1999 Exposure Draft, the FASB concluded that those transactions should be included in the definition of a business combination and in the scope of SFAS 141. Therefore, paragraph 10 of SFAS 141 indicated that it also applied to business combinations in which none of the owners of the combining entities as a group retain or receive a majority of the voting rights of the combined entity. However, the FASB acknowledged at that time that some of those business combinations might not be acquisitions and said that it intended to consider in another project whether business combinations that are not acquisitions should be accounted for using the fresh start method rather than the purchase method.

BC6 IFRS 3 defined a business combination as 'the bringing together of separate entities or businesses into one reporting entity.' In developing IFRS 3, the IASB considered adopting the definition of a business combination in SFAS 141. It did not do so because that definition excluded some forms of combinations encompassed in IAS 22 *Business Combinations* (which IFRS 3 replaced), such as those described in paragraph BC5 in which none of the former shareholder groups of the combining entities obtained control over the combined entity. Accordingly, IFRS 3 essentially retained the definition of a business combination from IAS 22.

BC7   The definition of a business combination was an item of divergence between IFRS 3 and SFAS 141. In addition, the definition in SFAS 141 excluded combinations in which control is obtained by means other than acquiring net assets or equity interests. An objective of the second phase of the FASB's project leading to SFAS 141(R) was to reconsider whether the accounting for a change in control resulting in the acquisition of a business should differ because of the way in which control is obtained.

BC8   The FASB considered several alternatives for improving the definition of a business combination, including adopting the definition of a business combination in IFRS 3. That definition would encompass all transactions or other events that are within the scope of the revised standards. The FASB concluded, however, that the definition of a business combination in IFRS 3 was too broad for its purposes because it would allow for the inclusion in a business combination of one or more businesses that the acquirer does not control.

BC9   Because the FASB considers all changes of control in which an entity acquires a business to be economically similar transactions or events, it decided to expand the definition of a business combination to include all transactions or other events in which an entity obtains control of a business. Application of the expanded definition will improve the consistency of accounting guidance and the relevance, completeness and comparability of the resulting information about the assets, liabilities and activities of an acquired business.

BC10   The IASB also reconsidered the definition of a business combination. The result was that the IASB and the FASB adopted the same definition. The IASB observed that the IFRS 3 definition could be read to include circumstances in which there may be no triggering economic event or transaction and thus no change in an economic entity, per se. For example, under the IFRS 3 definition, an individual's decision to prepare combined financial statements for all or some of the entities that he or she controls could qualify as a business combination. The IASB concluded that a business combination should be described in terms of an economic event rather than in terms of consolidation accounting and that the definition in the revised standards satisfies that condition.

BC11   The IASB also observed that, although the IFRS 3 definition of a business combination was sufficiently broad to include them, formations of joint ventures were excluded from the scope of IFRS 3. Because joint ventures are also excluded from the scope of the revised standards, the revised definition of a business combination is intended to include all of the types of transactions and other events initially included in the scope of IFRS 3.

BC12   Some respondents to the 2005 Exposure Draft who consider particular combinations of businesses to be 'true mergers' said that the definition of a business combination as a transaction or other event in which an acquirer obtains control of one or more businesses seemed to exclude true mergers. The boards concluded that the most straightforward way of indicating that the scope of the revised standards, and the definition of a business combination, is intended to include true mergers, if any occur, is simply to state that fact.

BC13　Some respondents to the 2005 Exposure Draft also said that it was not clear that the definition of a business combination, and thus the scope of the revised standards, includes reverse acquisitions and perhaps other combinations of businesses. The boards observed that in a reverse acquisition, one entity—the one whose equity interests are acquired—obtains economic (although not legal) control over the other and is therefore the acquirer, as indicated in paragraph B15 of the revised IFRS 3. Therefore, the boards concluded that it is unnecessary to state explicitly that reverse acquisitions are included in the definition of a business combination and thus within the scope of the revised standards.

Change in terminology

BC14　As defined in the revised standards, a business combination could occur in the absence of a purchase transaction. Accordingly, the boards decided to replace the term *purchase method*, which was previously used to describe the method of accounting for business combinations that the revised standards require, with the term *acquisition method*. To avoid confusion, this Basis for Conclusions uses that term throughout, including when it refers to IFRS 3 and SFAS 141 (and earlier exposure drafts or other documents), which used the term *purchase method*.

Definition of a business

BC15　The definition of a business combination in the revised standards provides that a transaction or other event is a business combination only if the assets acquired and liabilities assumed constitute a business (an acquiree), and Appendix A defines a *business*.

BC16　SFAS 141 did not include a definition of a business. Instead, it referred to EITF Issue No. 98-3 *Determining Whether a Nonmonetary Transaction Involves Receipt of Productive Assets or of a Business* for guidance on whether a group of net assets constitutes a business. Some constituents said that particular aspects of the definition and the related guidance in EITF Issue 98-3 were both unnecessarily restrictive and open to misinterpretation. They suggested that the FASB should reconsider that definition and guidance as part of this phase of the project, and it agreed to do so. In addition to considering how its definition and guidance might be improved, the FASB, in conjunction with the IASB, decided that the boards should strive to develop a joint definition of a business.

BC17　Before issuing IFRS 3, the IASB did not have a definition of a business or guidance similar to that in EITF Issue 98-3. Consistently with the suggestions of respondents to ED 3, the IASB decided to provide a definition of a business in IFRS 3. In developing that definition, the IASB also considered the guidance in EITF Issue 98-3. However, the definition in IFRS 3 benefited from deliberations in this project to that date, and it differed from EITF Issue 98-3 in some aspects. For example, the definition in IFRS 3 did not include either of the following factors, both of which were in EITF Issue 98-3:

(a)   a requirement that a business be self-sustaining; or

(b)   a presumption that a transferred set of activities and assets in the development stage that has not commenced planned principal operations cannot be a business.

BC18   In the second phase of their business combinations projects, both boards considered the suitability of their existing definitions of a business in an attempt to develop an improved, common definition. To address the perceived deficiencies and misinterpretations, the boards modified their respective definitions of a business and clarified the related guidance. The more significant modifications, and the reasons for them, are:

(a)   to continue to exclude self-sustaining as the definition in IFRS 3 did, and instead, provide that the integrated set of activities and assets must be **capable** of being conducted and managed for the purpose of providing a return in the form of dividends, lower costs or other economic benefits directly to investors or other owners, members or participants. Focusing on the capability to achieve the purposes of the business helps avoid the unduly restrictive interpretations that existed in accordance with the former guidance.

(b)   to clarify the meanings of the terms *inputs*, *processes* and *outputs* that were used in both EITF Issue 98-3 and IFRS 3. Clarifying the meanings of those terms, together with other modifications, helps eliminate the need for extensive detailed guidance and the misinterpretations that sometimes stem from such guidance.

(c)   to clarify that inputs and processes applied to those inputs are essential and that although the resulting outputs are normally present, they need not be present. Therefore, an integrated set of assets and activities could qualify as a business if the integrated set is capable of being conducted and managed to produce the resulting outputs. Together with item (a), clarifying that outputs need not be present for an integrated set to be a business helps avoid the unduly restrictive interpretations of the guidance in EITF Issue 98-3.

(d)   to clarify that a business need not include all of the inputs or processes that the seller used in operating that business if a market participant is capable of continuing to produce outputs, for example, by integrating the business with its own inputs and processes. This clarification also helps avoid the need for extensive detailed guidance and assessments about whether a missing input or process is minor.

(e)   to continue to exclude a presumption that an integrated set in the development stage is not a business merely because it has not yet begun its planned principal operations, as IFRS 3 did. Eliminating that presumption is consistent with focusing on assessing the capability to achieve the purposes of the business (item (a)) and helps avoid the unduly restrictive interpretations that existed with the former guidance.

BC19 The boards also considered whether to include in the revised standards a presumption similar to the one in EITF Issue 98-3 that an asset group is a business if goodwill is present. Some members of the FASB's resource group suggested that that presumption results in circular logic that is not especially useful guidance in practice. Although the boards had some sympathy with those views, they noted that such a presumption could be useful in avoiding interpretations of the definition of a business that would hinder the stated intention of applying the revised standards' guidance to economically similar transactions. The presumption might also simplify the assessment of whether a particular set of activities and assets meets the definition of a business. Therefore, the revised standards' application guidance retains that presumption.

BC20 The boards considered whether to expand the scope of the revised standards to all acquisitions of groups of assets. They noted that doing so would avoid the need to distinguish between those groups that are businesses and those that are not. However, both boards noted that broadening the scope of the revised standards beyond acquisitions of businesses would require further research and deliberation of additional issues and delay the implementation of the revised standards' improvements to practice. The boards therefore did not extend the scope of the revised standards to acquisitions of all asset groups. Paragraph 2(b) of the revised IFRS 3 describes the typical accounting for an asset acquisition.

BC21 SFAS 141(R) amends FASB Interpretation No. 46 (revised December 2003) *Consolidation of Variable Interest Entities* (FASB Interpretation 46(R)) to clarify that the initial consolidation of a variable interest entity that is a business is a business combination. Therefore, the assets, liabilities and non-controlling interests of the variable interest entity should be measured in accordance with the requirements of SFAS 141(R). Previously, FASB Interpretation 46(R) required assets, liabilities and non-controlling interests of variable interest entities that are businesses to be measured at fair value. The FASB concluded that variable interest entities that are businesses should be afforded the same exceptions to fair value measurement and recognition that are provided for assets and liabilities of acquired businesses. The FASB also decided that upon the initial consolidation of a variable interest entity that is not a business, the assets (other than goodwill), liabilities and non-controlling interests should be recognised and measured in accordance with the requirements of SFAS 141(R), rather than at fair value as previously required by FASB Interpretation 46(R). The FASB reached that decision for the same reasons described above, ie if SFAS 141(R) allows an exception to fair value measurement for a particular asset or liability, it would be inconsistent to require the same type of asset or liability to be measured at fair value. Except for that provision, the FASB did not reconsider the requirements in FASB Interpretation 46(R) for the initial consolidation of a variable interest entity that is not a business.

Clarifying the definition of a business

BC21A   Following a Post-implementation Review (PIR) of IFRS 3, the Board noted that many stakeholders had concerns about how to interpret and apply the definition of a business. Stakeholders indicated that these concerns arose for one or more of the following main reasons:

    (a)   IFRS 3 requires a fact-driven assessment that adopts the perspective of market participants and does not consider the business rationale, strategic considerations and objectives of the acquirer (see paragraph BC21G);

    (b)   some sets of activities and assets might have been considered a business from the perspective of particular market participants who could integrate the set in their processes. However, the same sets of activities and assets might not have been considered a business from the perspective of other market participants (see paragraphs BC21H–BC21I);

    (c)   the definition of a business used the wording 'capable of being conducted and managed for the purpose of providing' a return. That wording did not help in determining whether a transaction includes a business (see paragraphs BC21J–BC21K);

    (d)   it was difficult to assess:

        (i)   whether the processes acquired are sufficient to constitute one of the elements required for an acquired set of activities and assets to be a business, and whether any missing processes are so significant that the set is not a business; and

        (ii)   how to apply the definition of a business if the acquired set of activities and assets does not generate revenue (see paragraphs BC21L–BC21R); and

    (e)   the definition of a business was broad and IFRS 3 had no guidance identifying when an acquired set of activities and assets is not a business (see paragraphs BC21S–BC21AC).

BC21B   To consider those concerns, the Board added to its agenda a project to clarify the definition of a business, with the objective of assisting entities to determine whether a transaction should be accounted for as a business combination or as an asset acquisition. In 2016 the Board published an exposure draft *Definition of a Business and Accounting for Previously Held Interests* (2016 Exposure Draft). The 2016 Exposure Draft attracted 80 comment letters. The Board reviewed those comment letters and consulted the Accounting Standards Advisory Forum (ASAF), the Capital Markets Advisory Committee and the Global Preparers Forum. In 2018 the Board issued *Definition of a Business* (2018 Amendments). In the 2018 Amendments, the Board:

    (a)   clarified that to be considered a business, an acquired set of activities and assets must include, at a minimum, an input and a substantive process that together significantly contribute to the ability to create outputs (see paragraph BC21F);

(b)   removed the assessment of whether market participants are capable of replacing any missing inputs or processes and continuing to produce outputs (see paragraphs BC21H–BC21I);

(c)   added guidance and illustrative examples to help entities assess whether a substantive process has been acquired (see paragraphs BC21L–BC21R);

(d)   narrowed the definitions of a business and of outputs by focusing on goods and services provided to customers and by removing the reference to an ability to reduce costs (see paragraph BC21S);

(e)   added an optional concentration test that permits a simplified assessment of whether an acquired set of activities and assets is not a business (see paragraphs BC21T–BC21AC); and

(f)   decided that an entity is permitted but not required to apply the amendments to transactions that occurred before the effective date of the amendments. Retrospective application of the amendments to earlier transactions is not required because it is unlikely to provide useful information to users of financial statements, could have been costly and could have been impracticable if hindsight were to be needed. Retrospective application was not prohibited because there may be instances when it would provide useful information and because when it is used it would not deprive users of useful information.

BC21C   The 2016 Exposure Draft also dealt with a second topic, accounting for previously held interests. The Board finalised its work on that topic, among others, in 2017 by issuing *Annual Improvements to IFRS Standards 2015–2017 Cycle*.

BC21D   IFRS 3 is the result of a joint project between the Board and the FASB and it contained the same definition of a business as the definition in US GAAP. The PIR of IFRS 3 and a PIR of SFAS 141(R) identified similar difficulties in applying the definition of a business. Moreover, the FASB received feedback from many stakeholders that the definition of a business in US GAAP was, in practice, viewed as capturing a broader range of transactions than the identical definition in IFRS 3. Consequently, the FASB amended US GAAP in 2017 by issuing Accounting Standards Update No. 2017-01 *Clarifying the Definition of a Business* (FASB 2017 Amendments). The 2018 Amendments addressed the issues identified during the PIR of IFRS 3 and, though worded differently, are based on conclusions similar to those reached by the FASB. The Board concluded that its 2018 Amendments and the FASB 2017 Amendments could together be expected to lead to more consistency in applying the definition of a business across entities applying US GAAP and entities applying IFRS Standards.

BC21E   The 2018 Amendments differ in some respects from the FASB 2017 Amendments. Before finalising the 2018 Amendments, the Board discussed those differences with ASAF. The differences are as follows:

(a)   the concentration test set out in paragraphs B7A–B7B of IFRS 3 is optional. The corresponding test in the FASB 2017 Amendments is mandatory. The guidance on how to identify concentration of fair value is substantially the same, but the Board added confirmation of the calculations normally needed (see paragraph B7B(b)) and an illustrative example (Example I).

(b)   the Board concluded that an acquired outsourcing contract may give access to an organised workforce that performs a substantive process, even if the acquired set of activities and assets has no outputs. In some cases, that may lead to a conclusion that a business was acquired. In contrast, the FASB concluded that when outputs are not present, a business has been acquired only if the acquired set includes an organised workforce made up of employees.

(c)   the Board clarified in paragraph B12D that difficulties in replacing an organised workforce may indicate that the organised workforce performs a process that is critical to the ability to create outputs. The FASB 2017 Amendments do not include this clarification.

(d)   the FASB 2017 Amendments include a statement that the presence of more than an insignificant amount of goodwill may be an indicator that an acquired process is substantive. The Board did not include such a statement in the 2018 Amendments (see paragraph BC21R(d)).

(e)   the Board clarified in paragraph B7(c) of IFRS 3 that the narrowed definition of outputs includes other income from ordinary activities. An example of such other income is income from contracts outside the scope of IFRS 15 *Revenue from Contracts with Customers*. The FASB expressed a similar view as an observation in its Basis for Conclusions.

(f)   the Board aligned the definition of a business with the revised definition of outputs in paragraph B7(c) of IFRS 3. The FASB did not align the two definitions, but its definition of a business refers explicitly to supporting guidance, including guidance on outputs.

Minimum requirements to be a business

BC21F   The existence of a process (or processes) is what distinguishes a business from a set of activities and assets that is not a business. Consequently, the Board decided that to be considered a business, an acquired set of activities and assets must include, at a minimum, an input and a substantive process that together significantly contribute to the ability to create outputs. The Board incorporated this requirement in paragraph B8. To clarify that a business can exist without including all of the inputs and processes needed to create outputs, the Board replaced the term 'ability to create outputs' with 'ability to contribute to the creation of outputs' in paragraph B7 of IFRS 3.

Market participant's perspective

BC21G   Paragraph B11 of IFRS 3 adopts a market participant's perspective in determining whether an acquired set of activities and assets is a business. Some participants in the PIR of IFRS 3 noted that adopting that perspective requires a fact-driven assessment that does not consider the business rationale, strategic considerations and objectives of the acquirer. They expressed concerns that excluding those factors would not result in the most useful information for users of financial statements. Nevertheless, the Board concluded that the assessment should continue to be made from a market participant's perspective and to be driven by facts that indicate the current state and condition of what has been acquired, rather than by considering what the acquirer might intend to do with the acquired set of activities and assets. Basing this determination on facts, rather than on the intentions of the acquirer, helps to prevent similar transactions being accounted for differently. In the Board's view, bringing the business rationale, strategic considerations and objectives of the acquirer into the determination would have made the determination more subjective and thus would have increased diversity in practice. Consequently, the Board did not change paragraph B11 in this regard.

Market participant's ability to replace missing elements

BC21H   Before the 2018 Amendments, paragraph B8 of IFRS 3 stated that a business need not include all of the inputs or processes that the seller used in operating that business 'if market participants are capable of acquiring the business and continuing to produce outputs, for example, by integrating the business with their own inputs and processes'. Many participants in the PIR of IFRS 3 stated that it can be challenging to assess whether market participants are capable of performing such an integration, especially if only some market participants are capable of performing such an integration.

BC21I   In the light of those comments, the Board decided to base the assessment on what has been acquired in its current state and condition, rather than on whether market participants would be capable of replacing any missing inputs or processes, for example by integrating the acquired activities and assets. Therefore, the Board deleted the reference to such integration. Instead, as discussed in paragraph BC21F, the 2018 Amendments focus on whether acquired inputs and acquired substantive processes together significantly contribute to the ability to create outputs.

The term 'capable of' in the definition of a business

BC21J   The definition of a business includes the phrase 'capable of being conducted and managed for the purpose of providing' a return. Many participants in the PIR indicated that this phrase was too broad in scope to be helpful in distinguishing businesses from assets. However, the Board concluded that it was not necessary to change or clarify this phrase because the 2018 Amendments:

(a)   removed the assessment of whether market participants are capable of integrating the acquired activities and assets;

(b)   clarified that the acquired processes need to be substantive;

(c)   narrowed the definition of output; and

(d)   added more robust guidance and illustrative examples supporting various aspects of the definition.

BC21K   The Board considered whether additional guidance was needed regarding the acquisition of suppliers. In some cases, the acquirer integrates an acquired business with the result that it no longer generates revenue. For example, an entity may acquire a supplier and subsequently consume all the output from the supplier. The acquired inputs and processes are still 'capable of' generating revenue at the acquisition date and so could qualify as a business, if the criteria in paragraph B12C are met. The Board concluded that this outcome was appropriate because the assessment focuses on what the acquirer acquired, not on what the acquirer intends to do with what it acquired. Accordingly, the Board retained the term 'capable of' as the basis for assessment.

Assessing whether an acquired process is substantive

BC21L   Many participants in the PIR of IFRS 3 stated that it is difficult to assess:

(a)   whether the processes acquired are sufficient to constitute one of the elements required for an acquired set of activities and assets to be a business;

(b)   whether any processes missing from that set are so significant that the set is not a business; and

(c)   how to apply the definition of a business when the acquired set of assets does not generate revenue.

BC21M   To address these concerns, the 2018 Amendments added guidance to help entities to assess whether an acquired process is substantive. That guidance seeks more persuasive evidence when there are no outputs because the existence of outputs already provides some evidence that the acquired set of activities and assets is a business. In particular, if the set has no outputs at the acquisition date, the inputs acquired must include:

(a)   an organised workforce that meets specified criteria (see paragraphs BC21N–BC21P); and

(b)   other inputs that the organised workforce could develop or convert into outputs (see paragraph BC21Q)

BC21N   The Board concluded that the presence of an organised workforce is an indicator of a substantive process. Consequently, the Board decided that, except in limited circumstances, an organised workforce is required in order to conclude that the set of activities and assets is a business. The limited circumstances are when the acquired set both:

(a)   has outputs; and

      (b)   includes a process (or a group of processes) that is unique or scarce, or cannot be replaced without significant cost, effort, or delay in the ability to continue producing outputs. The Board concluded that such processes are usually valuable and that this would often indicate that the processes are substantive, even if no organised workforce is acquired.

BC21O   The Board concluded that although an organised workforce is an input to a business, it is not in itself a business. To conclude otherwise would mean that hiring a skilled employee without acquiring any other inputs could be considered to be acquiring a business. The Board decided that such an outcome would be inconsistent with the definition of a business.

BC21P   Although the Board concluded that an organised workforce is an input, paragraph B7(b) indicates that the intellectual capacity of an organised workforce having the necessary skills and experience following rules and conventions may provide the necessary processes that are capable of being applied to inputs to create outputs. The Board concluded that this is the case even if the processes are not documented. The Board inserted the phrase 'intellectual capacity' to provide clarity.

BC21Q   For an acquired set of activities and assets to be considered a business if the set has no outputs, the Board concluded that the set should include not only a substantive process but also both an organised workforce and other inputs that the acquired organised workforce could develop or convert into outputs. Entities will need to evaluate the nature of those inputs to assess whether that process is substantive. The Board observed that many entities in the development stage will meet this criterion because technology, intellectual property, or other assets are being developed into a good or service. Conversely, if a set is producing outputs at the acquisition date, the set already contains inputs that are being converted into outputs, and, therefore, there is no need to consider specifically the type of inputs to which the acquired process is applied.

BC21R   In finalising the 2018 Amendments, the Board also:

      (a)   specified in paragraph B12D(a) that an acquired contract is not a substantive process, in order to clarify that a contract that provides a continuing revenue stream (eg a lease contract) is not itself a process.

      (b)   clarified in paragraph B12D(a) that an acquired outsourcing agreement may give access to an organised workforce and that an entity should assess whether an organised workforce accessed through an outsourcing arrangement performs a substantive process that the entity controls, and thus has acquired. The Board added this paragraph because some IFRS Interpretations Committee members observed that IFRS 3 did not provide guidance on whether an outsourced process should be considered in assessing whether a set of activities and assets is a business.

(c)   clarified in paragraph B12D(b) that difficulties in replacing an acquired organised workforce may indicate that the organised workforce performs a process that is critical to the ability to create outputs, because the Board expected that it would normally be more difficult to replace a workforce that performs a critical process than to replace a workforce that performs, for example, an ancillary process. The Board provided this indicator because some respondents to the 2016 Exposure Draft commented that the proposed guidance on substantive processes would require too much judgement.

(d)   removed the presumption, proposed in the 2016 Exposure Draft, that the presence of more than an insignificant amount of goodwill may be an indicator that an acquired process is substantive. Responses to the 2016 Exposure Draft showed that this proposal created more confusion than clarity. For example, some respondents were unclear whether this proposal referred to 'core goodwill' that is economically present in a business, or to the accounting measurement of goodwill that is determined in accounting for business combinations. Some respondents wondered whether this proposal would, in effect, force entities to apply business combination accounting to measure goodwill in order to assess whether what was acquired was in fact a business.

(e)   deleted paragraph B10 of IFRS 3, which described factors to consider when assessing an integrated set of activities and assets in the development stage. The Board deleted that paragraph because the 2018 Amendments provide a more general discussion of acquired sets of activities and assets that do not have outputs.

(f)   added illustrative examples in paragraphs IE73–IE123 to assist with the interpretation of what is considered a business. The draft illustrative examples in the 2016 Exposure Draft also included an example on the acquisition of oil and gas operations. To be consistent with the FASB 2017 Amendments, the Board did not include that example in the 2018 Amendments.

Narrowed definition of outputs

BC21S   In the 2018 Amendments, the Board narrowed the definition of outputs to focus on goods and services provided to customers, investment returns and other income from ordinary activities and to exclude returns in the form of lower costs, and other economic benefits provided directly to investors or other owners, members, or participants. The Board also amended the definition of a business to make it consistent with the narrowed definition of outputs. The Board made these changes because:

(a)   IFRS 15 *Revenue from Contracts with Customers* focuses on goods or services that are an output of an entity's ordinary activities. Nevertheless, because not all businesses have revenue within the scope of IFRS 15, the revised definition also includes outputs that are investment income or other income from ordinary activities.

(b)   the previous definition of outputs referred to lower costs and economic benefits provided directly to investors. This reference did not help to distinguish between an asset and a business, because it confused motives for acquiring an asset with the characteristics of the activities and assets acquired. Many asset acquisitions (for example, the purchase of new manufacturing equipment) may be made with the motive of lowering costs but may not involve acquiring a substantive process.

Concentration test

BC21T   Many participants in the PIR of IFRS 3 noted that applying the definition of a business involves significant judgements and that IFRS 3 provided little or no guidance that identifies situations in which an acquired set of activities and assets is not a business. To address these concerns, in the 2018 Amendments the Board added a concentration test that is designed to reduce cost and complexity by avoiding the need for a detailed assessment in some circumstances. If substantially all of the fair value of the gross assets acquired is concentrated in a single identifiable asset, or group of similar identifiable assets, the concentration test is met and the set of activities and assets is considered not to be a business. If the concentration test is met, no further assessment is needed.

BC21U   The Board designed the concentration test with the aim of making it easy to understand and—in some straightforward cases that are easy to explain—simple to operate and less costly than applying the detailed assessment otherwise required by paragraphs B8–B12D. To target that aim, the concentration test focuses on a single identifiable asset or a single group of similar identifiable assets. The Board did not expect entities to carry out detailed calculations to apply the test, because detailed calculations would have frustrated the purpose of the test, which is to permit a simplified assessment. In addition, the Board wanted the test to have the same outcome in most circumstances as the detailed assessment and wanted to minimise the risk that the outcome of applying the concentration test could deprive users of financial statements of useful information.

BC21V   To confirm that the Board did not expect detailed calculations, paragraph B7B(b) clarifies how the fair value of the gross assets acquired may normally be determined by reference to the fair value of the consideration transferred. In finalising the 2018 Amendments, the Board added an illustrative example showing that calculation (Example I).

BC21W   The Board concluded that whether a set of activities and assets includes a substantive process does not depend on how the set is financed. Consequently, the concentration test is based on the gross assets acquired, not on net assets. Thus, the existence of debt (for example, a mortgage loan financing a building) or other liabilities does not alter the conclusion on whether an acquisition is a business combination. In addition, in response to requests from respondents, the Board specified, in finalising the 2018 Amendments, that the gross assets considered in the concentration test exclude cash and cash equivalents acquired, deferred tax assets, and goodwill resulting from the effects of deferred tax liabilities. These exclusions were made because cash acquired, and the tax base of the assets and liabilities acquired, are independent of whether the acquired set of activities and assets includes a substantive process.

BC21X   In finalising the 2018 Amendments, the Board made the concentration test optional. This change enables entities to assess whether they have acquired a substantive process when, for example, such an assessment would be more efficient than applying the concentration test, or would result in a conclusion that more faithfully represents the economics of a particular transaction. In line with the purpose of the concentration test, the 2018 Amendments:

(a)   specify that the election to carry out that test is available transaction by transaction; and

(b)   do not prohibit an entity from carrying out the detailed assessment required by paragraphs B8–B12D if the entity has carried out the concentration test and concluded that the acquired set of activities and assets is not a business. The Board decided that such a prohibition was unnecessary, because if an entity intended to disregard the outcome of the concentration test, it could have elected not to apply it.

BC21Y   In making the concentration test optional, the Board considered the accounting consequences that would occur if, when applied to a particular transaction, the concentration test does not achieve the same outcome as the detailed assessment otherwise required by paragraphs B8–B12D. The concentration test identifies some transactions as an asset acquisition. For all other transactions, the entity must go on to perform the detailed assessment. The concentration test never determines that a transaction is a business combination.

BC21Z   In theory, the concentration test might sometimes identify a transaction as an asset acquisition when the detailed assessment would identify it as a business combination. That outcome would be a false positive. The Board designed the concentration test to minimise the risk that a false positive could deprive users of financial statements of useful information. A false positive has two consequences:

(a)   the entity fails to recognise 'core goodwill' that is economically present in a business combination but is not present in an asset acquisition.[2] Nevertheless, if substantially all of the fair value of the gross assets acquired (including core goodwill) is concentrated in a single identifiable asset (or a group of similar identifiable assets), the fair value of the core goodwill cannot be a substantial part of the total fair value of the gross assets acquired. Thus, information about the value of that core goodwill is unlikely to be material. Moreover, if the fair value of the processes acquired is not significant, the detailed assessment required by paragraphs B8–B12D would be unlikely to conclude that the processes are substantive.

---

2   Paragraphs BC313–BC318 describe 'core goodwill'. Those paragraphs also note that, because goodwill is measured as a residual, the carrying amount of goodwill includes several other factors as well as core goodwill.

(b) there are some other differences between the accounting required for a business combination and the accounting required for an asset acquisition, including differences relating to deferred tax, contingent consideration, acquisition-related costs, and gains on bargain purchases. Those differences in accounting requirements are not driven by differences between the economics of a business combination and the economics of an asset acquisition. Therefore, the Board did not expect a false positive to result in a loss of information about the economics of a business combination.

BC21AA The concentration test might not identify an asset acquisition that would be identified by the detailed assessment required by paragraphs B8–B12D. That outcome would be a false negative. An entity is required to carry out the detailed assessment in such a case and is expected to reach the same conclusion as if it had not applied the concentration test. Thus, a false negative has no accounting consequences.

BC21AB In finalising the 2018 Amendments, the Board also clarified some aspects of the guidance on a single identifiable asset and on similar identifiable assets (see paragraphs B7B(c)–(f) and B7C).

BC21AC In finalising the 2018 Amendments, the Board did not:

(a) make the concentration test an indicator, rather than determinative. Such a change would have been inconsistent with the objective of reducing the costs of applying IFRS 3 by providing a test that is designed to be simple in some straightforward cases that are easy to explain.

(b) provide further guidance on the term 'substantially all' because that term is already used in several IFRS Standards.

Method of accounting for business combinations

BC22 Both IAS 22 and APB Opinion 16 permitted use of either the acquisition method or the pooling of interests (pooling) method of accounting for a business combination, although the two methods were not intended as alternatives for the same set of facts and circumstances. ED 3 and the 1999 Exposure Draft proposed, and IFRS 3 and SFAS 141 required, use of the acquisition method to account for all business combinations. The boards did not redeliberate that conclusion during the project that led to the revised standards.

BC23 In developing IFRS 3 and SFAS 141, the IASB and the FASB considered three possible methods of accounting for business combinations — the pooling method, the acquisition method and the fresh start method. In assessing those methods, both boards were mindful of the disadvantages of having more than one method of accounting for business combinations, as evidenced by the experience with IAS 22 and APB Opinion 16. The boards concluded that having more than one method could be justified only if the alternative method (or methods) could be demonstrated to produce information that is more decision-useful and if unambiguous and non-arbitrary boundaries could be established that unequivocally distinguish when one method is to be applied instead of another. The boards also concluded that most business combinations are acquisitions and, for the reasons discussed in paragraphs BC24–BC28, that the acquisition method is the appropriate method for those business combinations. Respondents to ED 3 and the 1999 Exposure Draft generally agreed. Therefore, neither the pooling method nor the fresh start method could be appropriately used for all business combinations.

Reasons for adopting the acquisition method

BC24 Both boards concluded that the acquisition method is the appropriate method of accounting for all business combinations in which one entity obtains control of one or more other businesses[3] because that method is consistent with how the accounting model generally accounts for transactions in which assets are acquired and liabilities are assumed or incurred. Therefore, it produces information that is comparable with other accounting information.

BC25 The acquisition method views a combination from the perspective of the acquirer—the entity that obtains control of the other combining businesses. The acquirer purchases or otherwise obtains control over net assets and recognises in its financial statements the assets acquired and liabilities assumed, including those not previously recognised by the acquiree. Consequently, users of financial statements are better able to assess the initial investments made and the subsequent performance of those investments and compare them with the performance of other entities. In addition, by initially recognising almost all of the assets acquired and liabilities assumed at their fair values, the acquisition method includes in the financial statements more information about the market's expectation of the value of the future cash flows associated with those assets and liabilities, which enhances the relevance of that information.

BC26 Most of the respondents to ED 3 supported the proposal to eliminate the pooling method and to require all business combinations to be accounted for by applying the acquisition method, pending the IASB's future consideration of whether the fresh start method might be applied to some combinations. Respondents to the 1999 Exposure Draft generally agreed that most business combinations are acquisitions, and many said that all combinations involving only two entities are acquisitions. Respondents also agreed that the acquisition method is the appropriate method of accounting for business combinations in which one of the combining entities obtains control over the other combining entities. However, some qualified their support for the acquisition method as contingent upon the FASB's decisions about some aspects of applying that method, particularly the accounting for goodwill.

---

3 In October 2012 the Board issued *Investment Entities* (Amendments to IFRS 10, IFRS 12 and IAS 27), which removed from the scope of IFRS 3 *Business Combinations* the acquisition by an investment entity, as defined in IFRS 10 *Consolidated Financial Statements*, of an investment in a subsidiary required to be measured at fair value through profit or loss.

BC27   The boards concluded that most business combinations, both two-party transactions and those involving three or more entities (multi-party combinations), are acquisitions. The boards acknowledged that some multi-party combinations (in particular, those that are commonly referred to as roll-up or put-together transactions) might not be acquisitions; however, they noted that the acquisition method has generally been used to account for them. The boards decided not to change that practice at this time. Consequently, the revised standards require the acquisition method to be used to account for all business combinations, including those that some might not consider acquisitions.

BC28   Both boards considered assertions that exceptions to the acquisition method should be provided for circumstances in which identifying the acquirer is difficult. Respondents taking that view generally said that the pooling method would provide better information in those circumstances. Although acknowledging that identifying the acquirer sometimes may be difficult, the boards concluded that it would be practicable to identify an acquirer in all business combinations. Moreover, in some jurisdictions an acquirer must be identified for tax purposes, regardless of how difficult it may be to do so. Both boards also concluded that in no circumstances does the pooling method provide better information than the acquisition method.

Reasons for rejecting the pooling method

Mergers and acquisitions are economically similar

BC29   Some observers, including some respondents to the ED 3 and to the 1999 Exposure Draft, argued that business combinations in which the predominant form of consideration is equity interests, generally referred to as *mergers*, are different from acquisitions and should be accounted for differently. They said that the pooling method is appropriate for a merger because ownership interests are continued (either completely or substantially), no new capital is invested and no assets are distributed, post-combination ownership interests are proportional to those before the combination, and the intention is to unite commercial strategies. Those respondents said that a merger should be accounted for in terms of the carrying amounts of the assets and liabilities of the combining entities because, unlike acquisitions in which only the acquirer survives the combination, all of the combining entities effectively survive a merger.

BC30   Most respondents who favoured retaining the pooling method also supported limiting its application. Many of those respondents suggested limiting use of the pooling method to 'true mergers' or 'mergers of equals', which they described as combinations of entities of approximately equal size or those in which it is difficult to identify an acquirer.

BC31   The boards also considered the assertion that the pooling method properly portrays true mergers as a transaction between the owners of the combining entities rather than between the combining entities. The boards rejected that assertion, noting that business combinations are initiated by, and take place because of, a transaction between the combining entities themselves. The entities — not their owners — engage in the negotiations necessary to carry out the combination, although the owners must eventually participate in and approve the transaction.

BC32   Many respondents agreed with the boards that although ownership interests are continued in a combination effected by an exchange of equity instruments, those interests **change** as a result of the combination. The former owners of each entity no longer have an exclusive interest in the net assets of the pre-combination entities. Rather, after the business combination, the owners of the combining entities have a residual interest in the net assets of the combined entity. The information provided by the pooling method fails to reflect that and is therefore not a faithful representation.

BC33   Both boards observed that all business combinations entail some bringing together of commercial strategies. Accordingly, the intention to unite commercial strategies is not unique to mergers and does not support applying a different accounting method to some combinations from that applied to others.

BC34   Some respondents said that, economically, mergers are virtually identical to acquisitions, making them in-substance acquisitions. Some noted that shares could have been issued for cash and that cash then used to effect the combination, with the result being economically the same as if shares had been used to effect the combination.

BC35   Both boards concluded that 'true mergers' or 'mergers of equals' in which none of the combining entities obtains control of the others are so rare as to be virtually non-existent, and many respondents agreed. Other respondents stated that even if a true merger or merger of equals did occur, it would be so rare that a separate accounting treatment is not warranted. The boards also observed that respondents and other constituents were unable to suggest an unambiguous and non-arbitrary boundary for distinguishing true mergers or mergers of equals from other business combinations and concluded that developing such an operational boundary would not be feasible. Moreover, even if those mergers could feasibly be distinguished from other combinations, both boards noted that it does not follow that mergers should be accounted for on a carry-over basis. If they were to be accounted for using a method other than the acquisition method, the fresh start method would be better than the pooling method.

Information provided is not decision-useful

BC36   Some proponents of the pooling method argued that it provides decision-useful information for the business combinations for which they favour its use. They said that the information is a more faithful representation than the information that the acquisition method would provide for those combinations. However, other respondents said that the information provided by the acquisition method is more revealing than that provided by the pooling method. Respondents also noted that the pooling method does not hold management accountable for the investment made and the subsequent performance of that investment. In contrast, the accountability that results from applying the acquisition method forces management to examine business combination deals carefully to see that they make economic sense.

BC37   Both boards observed that an important part of decision-useful information is information about cash-generating abilities and cash flows generated. The IASB's *Framework[4] for the Preparation and Presentation of Financial Statements* says that 'The economic decisions that are taken by users of financial statements require an evaluation of the ability of an entity to generate cash and cash equivalents and of the timing and certainty of their generation' (paragraph 15). FASB Concepts Statement No. 1 *Objectives of Financial Reporting by Business Enterprises* indicates that '... financial reporting should provide information to help investors, creditors, and others assess the amounts, timing, and uncertainty of prospective net cash inflows to the related enterprise' (paragraph 37; footnote reference omitted). Neither the cash-generating abilities of the combined entity nor its future cash flows generally are affected by the method used to account for the combination. However, fair values reflect the expected cash flows associated with acquired assets and assumed liabilities. Because the pooling method records the net assets acquired at their carrying amounts rather than at their fair values, the information that the pooling method provides about the cash-generating abilities of those net assets is less useful than that provided by the acquisition method.

BC38   Both boards also concluded that the information provided by the pooling method is less relevant because it has less predictive value and feedback value than the information that is provided by other methods. It is also less complete because it does not reflect assets acquired or liabilities assumed that were not included in the pre-combination financial statements of the combining entities. The pooling method also provides a less faithful representation of the combined entity's performance in periods after the combination. For example, by recording assets and liabilities at the carrying amounts of predecessor entities, post-combination revenues may be overstated (and expenses understated) as the result of embedded gains that were generated by predecessor entities but not recognised by them.

BC39   The *Framework* and FASB Concepts Statement No. 2 *Qualitative Characteristics of Accounting Information* describe comparability as an important characteristic of decision-useful information. Use of different accounting methods for the same set of facts and circumstances makes the resulting information less comparable and thus less useful for making economic decisions. As discussed in paragraphs BC29–BC35, the boards concluded that all business combinations are economically similar. Accordingly, use of the same method to account for all combinations enhances the comparability of the resulting financial reporting information. Both boards observed that the acquisition method, but not the pooling method, could reasonably be applied to all business combinations in which one party to the combination obtains control over the combined entity.

---

4   References to the *Framework* in this Basis for Conclusions are to the IASC's *Framework for the Preparation and Presentation of Financial Statements*, adopted by the IASB in 2001 and in effect when the Standard was developed.

BC40　　Opponents of the pooling method generally said that eliminating that method would enhance the comparability of financial statements of entities that grow by means of acquisitions. Both boards agreed.

Inconsistent with historical cost accounting model

BC41　　Both boards observed that the pooling method is an exception to the general concept that exchange transactions are accounted for in terms of the fair values of the items exchanged. Because the pooling method records the combination in terms of the pre-combination carrying amounts of the parties to the transaction, it fails to record and thus to hold management accountable for the investment made in the combination.

BC42　　Some respondents to the FASB's 1999 Exposure Draft who advocated use of the pooling method asserted that it is consistent with the historical cost model and that eliminating the pooling method would be a step towards adopting a fair value model. They argued that before eliminating the pooling method, the FASB should resolve the broad issue of whether to adopt a fair value model in place of the historical cost model. The FASB disagreed, noting that, regardless of the merits of a fair value model, the pooling method is an aberration that is inconsistent with the historical cost model.

BC43　　Although the historical cost model is frequently described as being 'transaction based', the fair value model also records all transactions. In both models, transactions are recognised on the basis of the fair values exchanged at the transaction date. In contrast, the pooling method does not result in recognising in the records of the combined entity the values exchanged; instead, only the carrying amounts of the predecessor entities are recognised. Failure to record those values can adversely affect the relevance and reliability of the combined entity's financial statements for years—and even decades—to come. For those reasons, both boards concluded that the pooling method is inconsistent with the historical cost model. Requiring use of the acquisition method is not a step towards adopting a fair value accounting model. Rather, it eliminates an exception to the historical cost model and requires accounting for assets acquired and liabilities assumed in a business combination consistently with other acquisitions of assets and incurrences of liabilities.

Disclosure not an adequate response

BC44　　In urging that the pooling method should be retained, a few respondents to the 1999 Exposure Draft said that any perceived problems with having two methods of accounting could be addressed by enhanced disclosures in the notes to the financial statements. However, they generally did not specify what those disclosures should be and how they would help overcome the comparability problems that inevitably result from having two methods.

BC45　　The FASB considered whether enhanced disclosures might compensate for the deficiencies of the pooling method but doubted the usefulness of almost any disclosures short of disclosing what the results would have been had the acquisition method been used to account for the business combination. Providing disclosures that would enable users of financial statements to determine what the results would have been had the transaction been accounted for by the acquisition method would be a costly solution that begs the question of why the acquisition method was not used to account for the transaction in the first place. Thus, the FASB rejected enhanced disclosures as a viable alternative.

Not cost-beneficial

BC46   Some of the boards' constituents cited cost-benefit considerations as a reason for retaining the pooling method. They argued that the pooling method is a quicker and less expensive way to account for a business combination because it does not require an entity to hire valuation experts to value assets for accounting purposes.

BC47   Other constituents favoured eliminating the pooling method for cost-benefit reasons. Some argued that the pooling method causes preparers of financial statements, auditors, regulators and others to spend unproductive time dealing with the detailed criteria required by IAS 22 or APB Opinion 16 in attempts to qualify some business combinations for the pooling method. Others noted that using the acquisition method of accounting for all business combinations would eliminate the enormous amount of interpretative guidance necessary to accommodate the pooling method. They also said that the benefits derived from making the acquisition method the only method of accounting for business combinations would significantly outweigh any issues that might arise from accounting for the very rare true merger or merger of equals by the acquisition method.

BC48   Both boards concluded that requiring a single method of accounting is preferable because having more than one method would lead to higher costs associated with applying, auditing, enforcing and analysing the information produced by the different methods. The IASB's conclusions on benefits and costs are more fully discussed in paragraphs BC435–BC439.

Perceived economic consequences not a valid reason for retention

BC49   Some of the respondents to ED 3 and the 1999 Exposure Draft who favoured retaining the pooling method cited public policy considerations or other perceived economic consequences of eliminating it. Some argued that eliminating the pooling method would require some investors to adjust to different measures of performance, potentially affecting market valuations adversely in some industries during the transition period. Others argued that it would impede desirable consolidation in some industries, reduce the amount of capital flowing into those industries, slow the development of new technology and adversely affect entrepreneurial culture. Some argued that eliminating the pooling method would reduce the options available to some regulatory agencies and possibly require regulated entities to maintain a second set of accounting records.

BC50   Other respondents did not share those views. Some said that because business combinations are (or should be) driven by economic rather than accounting considerations, economically sound deals would be completed regardless of the method used to account for them. Others noted that the financial community values business combinations in terms of their fair values rather than book values; therefore, those transactions should initially be recognised in the financial statements at fair value.

BC51 Both boards have long held that accounting standards should be neutral; they should not be slanted to favour one set of economic interests over another. Neutrality is the absence of bias intended to attain a predetermined result or to induce a particular behaviour. Neutrality is an essential aspect of decision-useful financial information because biased financial reporting information cannot faithfully represent economic phenomena. The consequences of a new financial reporting standard may indeed be negative for some interests in either the short term or the long term. But the dissemination of unreliable and potentially misleading information is, in the long run, harmful for all interests.

BC52 Both boards rejected the view that the pooling method should be retained because eliminating it could have adverse consequences for some economic interests. Accounting requirements for business combinations should seek neither to encourage nor to discourage business combinations. Instead, those standards should produce unbiased information about those combinations that is useful to investors, creditors and others in making economic decisions about the combined entity.

Acquisition method flaws remedied

BC53 Some respondents to ED 3 or to the 1999 Exposure Draft supported retaining the pooling method because of perceived problems associated with the acquisition method. Most of those comments focused on the effects of goodwill amortisation.

BC54 Both boards concluded that the pooling method is so fundamentally flawed that it does not warrant retention, regardless of perceived problems with the acquisition method. The boards also observed that the most frequently cited concern is remedied by the requirement of IAS 36 *Impairment of Assets* and FASB Statement No. 142 *Goodwill and Other Intangible Assets* (SFAS 142) to test goodwill for impairment and recognise a loss if it is impaired rather than to amortise goodwill.

The fresh start method

BC55 In the fresh start method, none of the combining entities is viewed as having survived the combination as an independent reporting entity. Rather, the combination is viewed as the transfer of the net assets of the combining entities to a new entity that assumes control over them. The history of that new entity, by definition, begins with the combination.

BC56 In the first part of their respective business combinations projects, both the IASB and the FASB acknowledged that a case could be made for using the fresh start method to account for the relatively rare business combination that does not clearly qualify as an acquisition. Such a combination might be defined either as one in which an acquirer cannot be identified or as one in which the acquirer is substantially modified by the transaction. However, the boards observed that those transactions have been accounted for by the acquisition method and they decided not to change that practice.

BC57 Neither the IASB nor the FASB has on its agenda a project to consider the fresh start method. However, both boards have expressed interest in considering whether joint venture formations and some formations of new entities in multi-party business combinations should be accounted for by the fresh start method. Depending on the relative priorities of that topic and other topics competing for their agendas when time becomes available, the boards might undertake a joint project to consider those issues at some future date.

Scope

BC58 The revised standards exclude from their scope some transactions that were also excluded from the scope of both IFRS 3 and SFAS 141. However, the revised standards include within their scope combinations involving only mutual entities and combinations achieved by contract alone, which were excluded from the scope of IFRS 3 and SFAS 141. Paragraphs BC59–BC79 discuss the boards' reasons for those conclusions.

Joint ventures and combinations of entities under common control

BC59 Formations of joint ventures and combinations of entities under common control are excluded from the scope of the revised standards. Those transactions were also excluded from the scope of both IFRS 3 and SFAS 141, and the boards continue to believe that issues related to such combinations are appropriately excluded from the scope of this project. The boards are aware of nothing that has happened since IFRS 3 and SFAS 141 were issued to suggest that the revised standards should be delayed to address the accounting for those events.

BC60 In developing IFRS 3, the IASB considered whether it should amend the definition of joint control in IAS 31 *Interests in Joint Ventures*[5] because it was concerned that its decision to eliminate the pooling method would create incentives for business combinations to be structured to meet the definition of a joint venture. After considering comments on the definition proposed in ED 3, the IASB revised the definition of joint control in IAS 31 to clarify that:

(a) unanimous consent on **all** financial and operating decisions is not necessary for an arrangement to satisfy the definition of a joint venture—unanimous consent on only strategic decisions is sufficient.

(b) in the absence of a contractual agreement requiring unanimous consent to strategic financial and operating decisions, a transaction in which the owners of multiple businesses agree to combine their businesses into a new entity (sometimes referred to as a roll-up transaction) should be accounted for by the acquisition method. Majority consent on such decisions is not sufficient.

---

5   IFRS 11 *Joint Arrangements*, issued in May 2011, replaced IAS 31.

BC61   In developing SFAS 141, the FASB noted that constituents consider the guidance in paragraph 3(d) of APB Opinion No. 18 *The Equity Method of Accounting for Investments in Common Stock* in assessing whether an entity is a joint venture, and it decided not to change that practice in its project on business combinations.

Annual Improvements Cycle 2011–2013

BC61A   The IASB observed that there was uncertainty about whether paragraph 2(a) of IFRS 3, which excludes the formation of joint ventures from the scope of IFRS 3, should have been amended to refer to joint arrangements when IFRS 11 was issued. IFRS 11 had changed the use of the term 'joint venture' from having a general meaning that included 'jointly controlled operations', 'jointly controlled assets' and 'jointly controlled entities', to meaning a specific type of joint arrangement, which does not include 'joint operations'. The IASB did not change the wording of the scope exclusion in paragraph 2(a) of IFRS 3 for 'the formation of a joint venture' when it replaced IAS 31 with IFRS 11 *Joint Arrangements*, although it had not intended to change the scope of IFRS 3.

BC61B   There was also uncertainty about whether the scope exclusion in paragraph 2(a) of IFRS 3 addresses:

(a)   the accounting by the joint arrangements themselves in their financial statements only; or also

(b)   the accounting by the parties to the joint arrangement for their interests in the joint arrangement.

BC61C   The IASB noted that paragraph 2(a) of IFRS 3 should exclude formations of every type of joint arrangement (ie joint ventures and joint operations) from the scope of IFRS 3. It also noted that paragraph 2(a) of IFRS 3 excludes, from the scope of IFRS 3, only the accounting by the joint arrangements themselves in their financial statements.

BC61D   The IASB concluded that paragraph 2(a) of IFRS 3 should be amended to address all types of joint arrangements and to remove uncertainty about the financial statements to which it applies.

BC61E   Consequently, the IASB amended paragraph 2(a) of IFRS 3 to:

(a)   exclude the formation of all types of joint arrangements from the scope of IFRS 3 by replacing 'joint venture' with 'joint arrangement'; and

(b)   clarify that the only scope exclusion needed from the scope of IFRS 3 is the accounting for the formation of a joint arrangement in the financial statements of the joint arrangement itself.

Not-for-profit organisations

BC62 The FASB also decided to exclude from the scope of SFAS 141(R) business combinations of not-for-profit organisations and acquisitions of for-profit businesses by not-for-profit organisations. Some aspects of combinations of not-for-profit organisations are different from combinations of business entities. For example, it cannot be presumed that combinations of organisations that serve a public interest are necessarily exchange transactions in which willing parties exchange equal values. For that reason, the FASB is addressing the accounting for combinations of not-for-profit organisations in a separate project. It published an exposure draft in October 2006 that addresses accounting for combinations of not-for-profit organisations.

BC63 IFRSs generally do not have scope limitations for not-for-profit activities in the private or public sector. Although IFRSs are developed for profit-oriented entities, a not-for-profit entity might be required, or choose, to apply IFRSs. A scope exclusion for combinations of not-for-profit organisations is not necessary.

Combinations of mutual entities

BC64 During its deliberations leading to SFAS 141, the FASB concluded that combinations involving only mutual entities should also be accounted for using the acquisition method but decided not to mandate its use until the FASB had considered implementation questions raised about the application of that method. Similarly, IFRS 3 did not require use of the acquisition method for combinations of mutual entities, although the IASB had also concluded that the acquisition method was appropriate for those combinations. Instead, as part of the first phase of its business combinations project, the IASB published an exposure draft of proposed amendments to IFRS 3—*Combinations by Contract Alone or Involving Mutual Entities*, which proposed an interim approach for accounting for those combinations until the IASB had considered related implementation issues in the second phase of its project. In the light of respondents' comments, the IASB decided not to proceed with the proposals in the exposure draft, primarily for reasons of timing and impending consideration of those issues in the second phase of this project.

BC65 After SFAS 141 was issued, the FASB began a joint project with the Canadian Accounting Standards Board (AcSB). The objective of that project was to develop guidance for combinations of two or more mutual entities. In October 2001 the FASB and the AcSB held a round-table discussion with representatives of mutual banks, credit unions, co-operatives and other mutual entities. In January 2004 the FASB met representatives of organisations of co-operative and other mutual entities to discuss its tentative conclusions and specific concerns raised by constituents. In addition, the FASB conducted field visits to three mutual entities in 2004.

BC66   A few participants in those meetings indicated a preference for the fresh start method as an alternative to the acquisition method for particular mergers, especially for those in which it is difficult to identify the acquirer. On both occasions, however, those participants acknowledged the costs and practical difficulties that a fresh start alternative would impose, especially on entities with recurring combinations. After considering those views, the FASB concluded that any potential advantages of using the fresh start method for some combinations of mutual entities would be outweighed by the disadvantages of having two methods of accounting.

BC67   During the deliberations leading to the 2005 Exposure Draft, some representatives of mutual entities reiterated concerns expressed during the development of SFAS 141 about requiring all combinations of mutual entities to be accounted for using the acquisition method. Many of those constituents reiterated public policy concerns similar to those discussed in paragraphs BC49–BC52. For example, some said that eliminating the pooling method could impede desirable combinations and reduce the amount of capital flowing into their industries. They suggested, for example, that the requirement to identify an acquirer could impede mergers of neighbouring mutual entities when both the fact and appearance of a merger of equals are of paramount importance to their directors, members and communities. The boards did not find those arguments persuasive for the same reasons discussed in paragraphs BC49–BC52.

BC68   Although mutual entities have particular characteristics that distinguish them from other business entities, the boards noted that the two types of entities also have many common characteristics. The boards also observed that the economic motivations for combinations of mutual entities, such as to provide their constituents with a broader range of, or access to, services and cost savings through economies of scale, are similar to those for combinations of other business entities. For example:

(a)   although mutual entities generally do not have shareholders in the traditional sense of investor-owners, they are in effect 'owned' by their members and are in business to serve their members or other stakeholders. Like other businesses, mutual entities strive to provide their members with a financial return or benefits. A mutual entity generally does that by focusing on providing its members with its products and services at lower prices. For example, the benefit provided by a credit union may be a lower interest rate on a borrowing than might be obtainable through an investor-owned financial institution. In a wholesale buying co-operative, the benefit might be lower net costs, after reflecting patronage dividends.

(b)   members' interests in a mutual entity are generally not transferable like other ownership interests. However, they usually include a right to share in the net assets of the mutual entity in the event of its liquidation or conversion to another form of entity.

(c)   a higher percentage of combinations of mutual entities than of combinations of other business entities occur without an exchange of cash or other readily measurable consideration, but such combinations are not unique to mutual entities. Business combinations of other entities, particularly private entities, also take place without an exchange of cash or other readily measurable consideration.

BC69   Thus, the boards concluded that the attributes of mutual entities are not sufficiently different from those of other entities to justify different accounting for business combinations. The boards also concluded that the benefits of requiring combinations of mutual entities to be accounted for by the acquisition method would justify the related costs. Therefore, combinations of mutual entities were included within the scope of the 2005 Exposure Draft.

BC70   Many of the respondents to the 2005 Exposure Draft who commented on combinations of mutual entities objected to including them in the scope of the revised standards and thus requiring them to be accounted for by the acquisition method. Respondents objected to the use of the acquisition method for conceptual, practical and cost-benefit reasons. For example, some said that a combination involving only mutual entities is a 'true pooling of interests' and that the acquisition method would not reflect the economics of the transactions. Some also said that it would often be difficult to identify an acquirer. Some also noted the absence of readily measurable consideration transferred in many combinations of mutual entities, which would make it necessary to use other valuation techniques to develop the fair values needed to apply the acquisition method. For those reasons, respondents also said that using the acquisition method for combinations of mutual entities would not be cost-beneficial. Respondents proposed other methods of accounting for mutual entities, including the pooling method, the fresh start method and a net asset method that was the same as the modified version of the acquisition method proposed by the IASB in its exposure draft mentioned in paragraph BC64.

BC71   In considering those comments, the boards noted that respondents' reasons for their objections to the acquisition method were generally the same as the factors discussed in paragraphs BC67 and BC68. For the same reasons discussed in those paragraphs, the boards affirmed their conclusion that the attributes of mutual entities are not sufficiently different from those of investor-owned entities to justify a different method of accounting for combinations of mutual entities. The boards also noted that, regardless of the intentions of the combining entities, the general result of a combination involving only mutual entities is that one entity obtains control of the other entity (or entities). Thus, combinations involving only mutual entities are included in the scope of the revised standards.

BC72   Some representatives of mutual entities suggested that the revised standards should permit an acquisition of a mutual entity to be reported as an increase in the retained earnings of the acquirer (combined entity) as had been the practice in accordance with the pooling method of accounting. The boards observed that in a combination of two investor-owned entities in which the acquirer issues its equity shares as consideration for all of the acquiree's equity shares, the fair value of the acquiree's equity is recognised as an addition to the acquirer's equity—generally as an increase to the acquirer's ordinary shares and capital. Thus, the equity (net assets) of the combined entity is increased from the acquisition of the acquiree (and the fair value of its net assets), but retained earnings of the acquirer are unaffected. The boards concluded that business combinations of two investor-owned entities are economically similar to those of two mutual entities in which the acquirer issues member interests for all the member interests of the acquiree. Thus, the boards concluded that those similar transactions should be similarly reported. Therefore, the revised standards clarify that if the only consideration exchanged is the member interests of the acquiree for the member interests of the acquirer (or the member interests of the newly combined entity), the amount of the acquiree's net assets is recognised as a direct addition to capital or equity, not retained earnings (paragraph B47 of the revised IFRS 3).

BC73 During the boards' redeliberations of the 2005 Exposure Draft, some representatives of mutual entities also proposed that the entire amount of the acquiree's net assets recognised in accordance with the revised standards should be considered a gain on a bargain purchase. They contended that the exchange of member interests in at least some forms of mutual entities does not constitute consideration because the interests the acquirer transfers have no economic value. The boards disagreed, noting that one mutual entity—the acquiree—would presumably not be willing to transfer its net assets to the control of another—the acquirer—in exchange for nothing of value.

BC74 The FASB also considered more specific concerns of representatives of credit unions about adverse economic consequences for those entities. Those representatives argued that requiring the application of the acquisition method would impede consolidation within that industry and might misrepresent the financial soundness and regulatory capital of two credit unions that combine their operations. They noted that in the United States, applicable federal law defines net worth for credit unions as the 'retained earnings balance of the credit union, as determined under generally accepted accounting principles.' Because the regulatory definition of net worth is narrower than equity under US GAAP, they expressed concern that the exclusion of the equity of an acquired credit union from retained earnings of the combined entity could make a financially sound combined entity appear to be financially unsound. Thus, they suggested that credit unions should be permitted to continue to report the equity of an acquired mutual entity as an addition to retained earnings of the combined entity. The FASB was not persuaded by those arguments; it believes that Statement 141(R) will not affect the ability of credit unions to restructure and combine with other credit unions.

BC75 Additionally, constituents told the FASB that the number of combinations of credit unions in which the regulatory net worth calculation could be significantly affected is relatively small in any given year. The FASB also noted that the regulatory filings of credit unions and other entities and the needs of their regulators are separate matters beyond the purpose of financial statements. The FASB's Concepts Statement 2 states that a necessary and important characteristic of accounting information is neutrality. In the context of business combinations, neutrality means that accounting standards should neither encourage nor discourage business combinations but rather provide information about those combinations that is fair and even-handed. The FASB observed that its public policy goal is to issue accounting standards that result in neutral and representationally faithful financial information. Eliminating use of the pooling method for all entities and requiring all entities, including mutual entities, to report the resulting increase directly in equity other than retained earnings is consistent with that public policy goal.

BC76 Some respondents to the 2005 Exposure Draft said that co-operatives do not fit within the definition of a mutual entity and that co-operatives are sufficiently different from other entities to justify a different method of accounting for combinations involving only co-operatives. To support their view, they cited factors such as differences in legal characteristics and different purposes of co-operatives in addition to providing economic benefits to members.

BC77 The boards considered the differences between, for example, a co-operative that provides electricity to its members in a rural area and other types of mutual entities, such as a mutual insurance company. The boards acknowledged particular differences between the two types of entities, for example, the co-operative issues member shares and the mutual insurance company does not. In addition, the objective of the co-operative may include providing more social and cultural benefits to its community in addition to the economic benefits provided to its members than does another type of mutual entity. However, the boards concluded that co-operatives generally provide direct and indirect economic benefits such as dividends and lower costs of services, including credit, or other products directly to its members. The boards concluded that differences in the amount of social and cultural benefits an entity seeks to provide do not justify a conclusion that co-operatives are sufficiently different from other mutual entities that they do not fit within the definition of a mutual entity in the revised standards. Thus, co-operatives are included in the definition of a mutual entity in the revised standards.

Combinations achieved by contract alone

BC78 Both boards also concluded that business combinations achieved by contract alone should be included in the scope of the revised standards. Those combinations were not included in the scope of either IFRS 3 or SFAS 141, although the boards understand that practice in the United States generally was to account for them in accordance with SFAS 141. For example, in EITF Issue No. 97-2 *Application of FASB Statement No. 94 and APB Opinion No. 16 to Physician Practice Management Entities and Certain Other Entities with Contractual Management Arrangements*, the Task Force reached a consensus that a transaction in which a physician practice management entity executes a management agreement with the physician practice should be accounted for as a business combination. Technically, that transaction would not meet the definition of a business combination in APB Opinion 16 or SFAS 141 because the physician practice management entity does not acquire either equity interests in, or the net assets of, the physician practice.

BC79   The boards understand that difficulties may arise in applying the acquisition method to combinations achieved by contract alone. In particular, such business combinations normally do not involve the payment of readily measurable consideration and in rare circumstances it might be difficult to identify the acquirer. However, as for combinations of mutual entities and for the reasons discussed above, the boards concluded that the acquisition method can and should be applied in accounting for such business combinations. In reaching that conclusion, the boards also concluded that in a business combination achieved by contract alone:

(a)   difficulties in identifying the acquirer are not a sufficient reason to justify a different accounting treatment, and no further guidance is necessary for identifying the acquirer for combinations by contract alone.

(b)   in the United States, these transactions are already being accounted for by the acquisition method and insurmountable issues have not been encountered.

(c)   determining the fair value of the identifiable assets acquired and liabilities assumed and calculating the related goodwill should be consistent with decisions reached in the second phase of the project.

Applying the acquisition method

BC80   The 2005 Exposure Draft identified four steps in applying the acquisition method, and it discussed the requirements for applying the acquisition method in terms of those steps:

(a)   identifying the acquirer;

(b)   determining the acquisition date;

(c)   measuring the fair value of the acquiree; and

(d)   measuring and recognising the assets acquired and the liabilities assumed.

BC80A   In contrast, the revised standards indicate (paragraph 5 of the revised IFRS 3) that applying the acquisition method requires:

(a)   identifying the acquirer;

(b)   determining the acquisition date;

(c)   recognising and measuring the identifiable assets acquired, liabilities assumed and any non-controlling interest in the acquiree; and

(d)   recognising and measuring goodwill or a gain from a bargain purchase.

BC81 The main changes to the list of steps in applying the acquisition method are to eliminate measuring the fair value of the acquiree as a whole and to add recognising and measuring goodwill as a separate step. The primary reason for those changes is the boards' decision to focus on measuring the components of the business combination, including any non-controlling interest in the acquiree, rather than measuring the fair value of the acquiree as a whole. The boards observed that neither the requirements of the 2005 Exposure Draft nor those of the revised standards for applying the acquisition method result in a fair value measure of either the acquiree as a whole or the acquirer's interest in the acquiree. For example, the revised standards do not provide for recognising a loss if the acquirer overpays for the acquiree, ie if the acquisition-date fair value of the consideration transferred exceeds the acquisition-date fair value of the acquirer's interest in the acquiree. The IASB's decision to allow an acquirer to choose to measure any non-controlling interest in the acquiree at fair value or on the basis of its proportionate interest in the acquiree's identifiable net assets adds another potential difference between the results of applying the requirements of the revised IFRS 3 and measuring the acquisition-date fair value of the acquiree as a whole. (See paragraphs BC209–BC221 for discussion of the reasons why the IASB provided that choice.) Paragraphs BC330 and BC331 discuss the reasons why the revised standards also eliminate the related presumption in the 2005 Exposure Draft that the consideration transferred in exchange for the acquiree measures the fair value of the acquirer's interest in the acquiree.

Identifying the acquirer

BC82 The boards' decision that all business combinations within the scope of the revised standards should be accounted for by the acquisition method means that the acquirer must be identified in every business combination.

BC83 The IASB and the FASB separately developed the guidance on identifying the acquirer that appeared in IFRS 3 and SFAS 141, respectively. Paragraphs BC84–BC92 discuss the FASB's development of the guidance in SFAS 141 and paragraphs BC93–BC101 discuss the IASB's development of the guidance in IFRS 3. Paragraphs BC102–BC105 discuss the boards' joint consideration of how to identify the acquirer in a business combination in the second phase of their projects on business combinations.

Developing the guidance in SFAS 141

BC84 SFAS 141's guidance on identifying the acquirer focused on the types of business combinations included in its scope, which excluded transactions in which one entity obtains control over one or more other entities by means other than transferring assets, incurring liabilities or issuing equity securities. Thus, SFAS 141 did not include the general guidance that the entity that obtains control is the acquirer, although that was the effect of the guidance for the combinations within its scope.

BC85   In developing its 1999 Exposure Draft, the FASB affirmed the guidance in APB Opinion 16 that in a business combination effected primarily through the distribution of cash or other assets or by incurring liabilities, the acquirer is generally the entity that distributes cash or other assets or assumes or incurs liabilities. The FASB considered a variety of suggestions on factors that should be considered in identifying the acquirer in a business combination effected through an exchange of equity interests. The guidance proposed in the 1999 Exposure Draft reflected the FASB's conclusion that all pertinent facts and circumstances should be considered when identifying the acquirer, particularly the relative voting rights in the combined entity after the combination. That proposed guidance said that the existence of unusual or special voting arrangements and options, warrants or convertible securities should be considered in determining which shareholder group retained or received the larger portion of the voting rights in the combined entity. In addition, factors related to the composition of the board of directors and senior management of the combined entity should be considered and should be weighted equally with the factors related to voting rights.

BC86   Respondents to the 1999 Exposure Draft who commented on the proposed criteria for identifying the acquirer generally agreed that they were appropriate. Some respondents said that the proposed guidance was an improvement over APB Opinion 16 because it provided additional factors to consider in determining which shareholder group retained or received the larger share of the voting rights in the combined entity. However, many respondents suggested improvements to the proposed criteria, and some suggested that the FASB should consider other criteria.

BC87   Several respondents suggested that the FASB should retain the presumptive approach in APB Opinion 16 for identifying the acquirer in transactions effected through an exchange of equity interests. That approach presumes that, in the absence of evidence to the contrary, the acquirer is the combining entity whose owners as a group retain or receive the larger share of the voting rights in the combined entity. Other respondents suggested that the factors to be considered in identifying the acquirer should be provided in the form of a hierarchy. Some of those respondents also suggested that the FASB should provide additional guidance explaining how factors relating to voting rights (unusual special voting arrangements and options, warrants or convertible securities) would affect the determination of the acquirer.

BC88   In considering those suggestions, the FASB observed, as it did in developing the 1999 Exposure Draft, that because each business combination is unique, the facts and circumstances relevant to identifying the acquirer in one combination may be less relevant in another. Therefore, SFAS 141 did not retain the presumptive approach in APB Opinion 16 nor did it provide hierarchical guidance because to do so would have implied that some factors are always more important than others in identifying the acquirer. However, as suggested by respondents, the FASB modified the proposed guidance to explain how some of the factors influence the identification of the acquirer.

BC89   The 1999 Exposure Draft did not propose requiring consideration of the payment of a premium over the market value of the equity securities acquired as evidence of the identity of the acquirer. Some respondents to the 1999 Exposure Draft said that the payment of a premium is a strong indicator of the identity of the acquirer. Upon reconsideration, the FASB decided to include in SFAS 141 the payment of a premium as a criterion to be considered in identifying the acquirer.

BC90   In developing SFAS 141, the FASB observed that identifying the acquirer might be difficult in some multi-party business combinations, particularly those that might not be acquisitions but are required to be accounted for as such. The FASB noted that in those circumstances it might be helpful to consider additional factors such as which of the entities initiated the combination and whether the reported amounts of assets, revenues and earnings of one of the combining entities significantly exceed those of the others. Respondents to the 1999 Exposure Draft generally agreed, and SFAS 141 included that guidance.

BC91   In addition, as suggested by respondents, the FASB decided that SFAS 141 should explicitly state that in some business combinations, such as reverse acquisitions, the entity that issues the equity interests may not be the acquirer. In a reverse acquisition, one entity (Entity A) obtains ownership of the equity instruments of another entity (Entity B), but Entity A issues enough of its own voting equity instruments as consideration in the exchange transaction for control of the combined entity to pass to the owners of Entity B.

BC92   If a new entity is formed to issue equity instruments to effect a business combination, SFAS 141 required that one of the combining entities that existed before the combination must be identified as the acquirer for essentially the same reasons as those discussed in paragraphs BC98–BC101 in the context of IFRS 3's similar requirement.

Developing the guidance in IFRS 3

BC93   As proposed in ED 3, IFRS 3 carried forward from IAS 22 the principle that in a business combination accounted for using the acquisition method the acquirer is the combining entity that obtains control of the other combining entities or businesses. The IASB observed that using the control concept as the basis for identifying the acquirer is consistent with using the control concept in IAS 27 *Consolidated and Separate Financial Statements* to define the boundaries of the reporting entity and to provide the basis for establishing the existence of a parent-subsidiary relationship.[6] IFRS 3 also carried forward the guidance in IAS 22 that control is the power to govern the financial and operating policies of the other entity so as to obtain benefits from its activities. IFRS 3 also provided the same guidance as IAS 22 for identifying the acquirer if one of the combining entities might have obtained control even if it does not acquire more than one-half of the voting rights of another combining entity.

---

6   The consolidation requirements in IAS 27 were superseded, and the definition of control was revised, by IFRS 10 *Consolidated Financial Statements* issued in May 2011.

Identifying an acquirer in a business combination effected through an exchange of equity interests

BC94   In developing ED 3 and IFRS 3, the IASB decided not to carry forward the guidance in IAS 22 on identifying which of the combining entities is the acquirer in a reverse acquisition. IAS 22 required the entity whose owners control the combined entity to be treated as the acquirer. That approach presumed that in a business combination effected through an exchange of equity interests, the entity whose owners control the combined entity is always the entity with the power to govern the financial and operating policies of the other entity so as to obtain benefits from its activities. The IASB observed that because the presumption is not always accurate, carrying it forward would in effect override the control concept for identifying the acquirer.

BC95   The IASB observed that the control concept focuses on the relationship between two entities, in particular, whether one entity has the power to govern the financial and operating policies of another so as to obtain benefits from its activities. Therefore, determining which of the combining entities has, as a consequence of the combination, the power to govern the financial and operating policies of the other so as to obtain benefits from its activities is fundamental to identifying the acquirer, regardless of the form of the consideration.

BC96   The IASB also observed that in some reverse acquisitions, the acquirer may be the entity whose equity interests have been acquired and the acquiree is the issuing entity. For example, a private entity might arrange to have itself 'acquired' by a smaller public entity through an exchange of equity interests as a means of obtaining a stock exchange listing. As part of the agreement, the directors of the public entity resign and are replaced by directors appointed by the private entity and its former owners. The IASB observed that in such circumstances, the private entity, which is the legal subsidiary, has the power to govern the financial and operating policies of the combined entity so as to obtain benefits from its activities. Treating the legal subsidiary as the acquirer in such circumstances is thus consistent with applying the control concept for identifying the acquirer. Treating the legal parent as the acquirer in such circumstances would place the form of the transaction over its substance, thereby providing less useful information than would be provided using the control concept to identify the acquirer.

BC97   Therefore, the IASB proposed in ED 3 that the acquirer in a business combination effected through an issue of equity interests should be identified by considering all pertinent facts and circumstances to determine which of the combining entities has the power to govern the financial and operating policies of the other so as to obtain benefits from its activities. Pertinent facts and circumstances include, but are not limited to, the relative ownership interests of the owners of the combining entities. Respondents to ED 3 generally supported that requirement, which was consistent with the requirement of SFAS 141.

Identifying an acquirer if a new entity is formed to effect a business combination

BC98   If a new entity is formed to issue equity instruments to effect a business combination, ED 3 proposed and IFRS 3 required one of the combining entities that existed before the combination to be identified as the acquirer on the basis of the evidence available. In considering that requirement, the IASB identified two approaches to applying the acquisition method that had been applied in various jurisdictions. The first approach viewed business combinations from the perspective of one of the combining entities that existed before the combination. Under that approach, the acquirer must be one of the combining entities that existed before the combination and therefore cannot be a new entity formed to issue equity instruments to effect a combination. The second approach viewed business combinations from the perspective of the entity providing the consideration, which could be a newly formed entity. Under that approach, the acquirer must be the entity providing the consideration. Some jurisdictions interpreted IAS 22 as requiring the first approach; other jurisdictions interpreted IAS 22 as requiring the second approach.

BC99   If a new entity is formed to issue equity instruments to effect a business combination involving two or more other entities, viewing the combination from the perspective of the entity providing the consideration would result in the newly formed entity applying the acquisition method to each of the other combining entities. The IASB noted that the result would be the same as applying the fresh start method to account for the business combination, which would potentially provide users of the financial statements with more relevant information than requiring one of the pre-existing entities to be treated as the acquirer.

BC100   The IASB also considered whether treating a new entity formed to issue equity instruments to effect a business combination as the acquirer would place the form of the transaction over its substance, because the new entity may have no economic substance. The formation of such entities is often related to legal, tax or other business considerations that do not affect the identification of the acquirer. For example, a combination of two entities that is structured so that one entity directs the formation of a new entity to issue equity instruments to the owners of both of the combining entities is, in substance, no different from a transaction in which one of the combining entities directly acquires the other. Therefore, the transaction should be accounted for in the same way as a transaction in which one of the combining entities directly acquires the other. To do otherwise would impair both the comparability and the reliability of the information.

BC101   The IASB concluded that the users of an entity's financial statements are provided with more useful information about a business combination when that information faithfully represents the transaction it purports to represent. Therefore, IFRS 3 required the acquirer to be one of the combining entities that existed before the combination.

Convergence and clarification of SFAS 141's and IFRS 3's guidance for identifying the acquirer

BC102   The deliberations of the FASB and the IASB described in paragraphs BC84–BC101 resulted in similar but not identical guidance for identifying the acquirer in SFAS 141 and IFRS 3. But the guidance was worded differently, and the boards were concerned that differences in identifying the acquirer could arise. Therefore, as part of the effort to develop a common standard on accounting for business combinations, the boards decided to develop common guidance for identifying the acquirer that could be applied internationally. For example, the FASB adopted the IASB's definition of an acquirer as the entity that obtains control of the other combining entities, and both boards decided to include in the revised standards an explicit reference to their other standards that provide guidance for identifying the acquirer. That guidance, although previously implicit, was not in SFAS 141. The intention of the boards is to conform and clarify their guidance but not to change the substance of the provisions for identifying an acquirer previously provided in SFAS 141 and IFRS 3.

BC103   Some respondents to the 2005 Exposure Draft noted that the existing IASB and FASB definitions of control in their respective consolidations standards are somewhat different and, in rare instances, may lead to identifications of different acquirers. The boards agreed with that observation, but they affirmed their conclusion in developing the 2005 Exposure Draft that developing a common definition of control is outside the scope of the business combinations project.

Identifying the acquirer in business combinations involving only mutual entities

BC104   The boards considered whether differences between mutual entities and investor-owned entities or differences between combinations of mutual entities and combinations of investor-owned entities result in a need for different or additional guidance for identifying the acquirer in combinations of mutual entities. The boards did not note any such differences. As a result, the boards concluded that an acquirer must be identified for all business combinations, including those involving only mutual entities.

BC105   The boards also concluded that the indicators for identifying the acquirer in a business combination are applicable to mutual entities and that no additional indicators are needed to identify the acquirer in those combinations. Both boards acknowledged that difficulties may arise in identifying the acquirer in combinations of two virtually equal mutual entities but observed that those difficulties also arise in combinations of two virtually equal investor-owned entities. The boards concluded that those difficulties, which are not unique to mutual entities, could be resolved in practice.

Determining the acquisition date

BC106   IFRS 3 and SFAS 141 carried forward without reconsideration the provisions of IAS 22 and APB Opinion 16, respectively, on determining the acquisition date. With one exception that applies only to SFAS 141 (see paragraphs BC108–BC110), that guidance resulted in the same acquisition date as the guidance in the revised standards.

BC107   In both IFRS 3 and SFAS 141, the guidance on the acquisition date, which IFRS 3 also referred to as the *exchange date*, was incorporated within the guidance on determining the cost of the acquisition rather than being stated separately. The revised standards clarify the acquisition-date guidance to make explicit that the acquisition date is the date that the acquirer obtains control of the acquiree. Paragraphs BC338–BC342 discuss the related issue of the measurement date for equity securities transferred as consideration in a business combination and the changes the revised standards make to the previous requirements on that issue.

BC108   The FASB also eliminated the 'convenience' exception that SFAS 141 carried forward from APB Opinion 16 and the reporting alternative permitted by Accounting Research Bulletin No. 51 *Consolidated Financial Statements* (ARB 51). SFAS 141, paragraph 48, permitted an acquirer to designate an effective date other than the date that assets or equity interests are transferred or liabilities are assumed or incurred (the acquisition date) if it also reduced the cost of the acquiree and net income as required by that paragraph to compensate for recognising income before consideration was transferred. Paragraph 11 of ARB 51 permitted an acquirer to include a subsidiary that was purchased during the year in the consolidation as though it had been acquired at the beginning of the year and to deduct the pre-acquisition earnings at the bottom of the consolidated income statement.

BC109   The FASB concluded that to represent faithfully an acquirer's financial position and results of operations, the acquirer should account for all business combinations at the acquisition date. In other words, its financial position should reflect the assets acquired and liabilities assumed at the acquisition date—not before or after they are obtained or assumed. Moreover, the acquirer's financial statements for the period should include only the cash inflows and outflows, revenues and expenses and other effects of the acquiree's operations after the acquisition date.

BC110   Very few respondents to the 2005 Exposure Draft commented on the proposed guidance on determining the acquisition date. Those who did so generally raised practicability issues related to eliminating the ability to designate an effective date other than the acquisition date. The boards concluded that the financial statement effects of eliminating that exception were rarely likely to be material. For example, for convenience an entity might wish to designate an acquisition date of the end (or the beginning) of a month, the date on which it closes its books, rather than the actual acquisition date during the month. Unless events between the 'convenience' date and the actual acquisition date result in material changes in the amounts recognised, that entity's practice would comply with the requirements of the revised standards. Therefore, the boards decided to retain the guidance in the 2005 Exposure Draft about determining the acquisition date.

Recognising and measuring the identifiable assets acquired, the liabilities assumed and any non-controlling interest in the acquiree

Recognition

BC111 The revised standards' recognition principle is stated in paragraph 10 of the revised IFRS 3. Paragraphs BC112–BC130 discuss the recognition conditions the acquirer is to use in applying the recognition principle. The revised standards also provide guidance for recognising particular assets and liabilities, which is discussed in paragraphs BC131–BC184. The revised standards' guidance on classifying and designating assets acquired and liabilities assumed is discussed in paragraphs BC185–BC188, and the limited exceptions to the recognition principle provided in the revised standards are discussed in paragraphs BC263–BC303.

Conditions for recognition

BC112 The boards decided that to achieve a reasonably high degree of consistency in practice and to resolve existing inconsistencies, the revised standards should provide guidance on applying the recognition principle. That guidance emphasises two fundamental conditions. To measure and recognise an item as part of applying the acquisition method, the item acquired or assumed must be:

(a) an asset or liability at the acquisition date; and

(b) part of the business acquired (the acquiree) rather than the result of a separate transaction.

An asset or a liability at the acquisition date

BC113 In determining whether an item should be recognised at the acquisition date as part of the business combination, the boards decided that the appropriate first step is to apply the definitions of assets and liabilities in the IASB's *Framework* or FASB Concepts Statement No. 6 *Elements of Financial Statements*, respectively.

BC114 The boards observed that in accordance with both IFRS 3 and SFAS 141, and their predecessors and the related interpretative guidance, particular items were recognised as if they were assets acquired or liabilities assumed at the acquisition date even though they did not meet the definition of an asset or a liability. That practice was related to the previous emphasis on measuring the cost of (or investment in) the acquiree rather than the acquisition-date fair values of the assets acquired and liabilities assumed. For example, as discussed in paragraphs BC365–BC370, some expenses for services received in connection with a business combination were capitalised as part of the cost of the acquiree (and recognised as part of goodwill) as if they were an asset at the acquisition date. In addition, some future costs that an acquirer expected to incur often were viewed as a cost of the acquiree and recognised as if they were a liability at the acquisition date—expected restructuring costs were an example. The boards concluded that the representational faithfulness, consistency and understandability of financial reporting would be improved by eliminating such practices.

BC114A   Paragraph 11 of IFRS 3 referred to the definitions of an asset and a liability in the *Framework for the Preparation and Presentation of Financial Statements* (*Framework*). It required those definitions to be used when deciding whether to recognise assets and liabilities as part of a business combination. In developing the revised *Conceptual Framework for Financial Reporting*, issued in 2018 (2018 *Conceptual Framework*), the IASB considered whether it should replace that reference with a reference to the revised definitions in the 2018 *Conceptual Framework*. In some cases, applying the revised definitions could change which assets and liabilities qualify for recognition in a business combination. In some such cases, the post-acquisition accounting required by other IFRS Standards could then lead to immediate derecognition of assets or liabilities recognised in a business combination, resulting in so-called *Day 2 gains or losses* that do not depict an economic gain or loss.

BC114B   Although the IASB intended to replace all references to the *Framework* with references to the 2018 *Conceptual Framework*, the IASB did not intend to make significant changes to the requirements of IFRS Standards containing those references. Consequently, the IASB decided to retain the reference to the *Framework* in paragraph 11 of IFRS 3 until it had completed an analysis of the possible consequences of referring in that paragraph to the revised definitions of an asset and a liability.

BC114C   The IASB's analysis led it to conclude that the problem of *Day 2 gains or losses* would be significant in practice only for liabilities that an acquirer accounts for after the acquisition date by applying IAS 37 *Provisions, Contingent Liabilities and Contingent Assets* or IFRIC 21 *Levies*. To avoid the problem, the IASB decided to add a further exception to the recognition principle in IFRS 3. The reasons for making this exception are explained in paragraphs BC264A–BC264E. The IASB noted that adding this exception to the recognition principle would not only avoid *Day 2 gains or losses*; it would also avoid any changes to the assets and liabilities recognised in a business combination ahead of any future amendments to align IAS 37 and IFRIC 21 with the 2018 *Conceptual Framework*.

BC114D   The IASB replaced the reference to the *Framework* and added the exception to its recognition principle in May 2020. At the same time, the IASB made two other amendments to clarify aspects of IFRS 3 that it concluded would not be affected by replacing the reference to the *Framework*:

    (a)   the IASB added paragraph 23A to IFRS 3 to clarify the requirements for contingent assets—that is, possible assets whose existence is uncertain. IFRS 3 prohibits the recognition of contingent assets acquired in a business combination. This prohibition can be inferred from the recognition principle and is confirmed in paragraph BC276 of this Basis for Conclusions. However, the prohibition was not stated explicitly in IFRS 3 itself, and questions arose as to how it would be affected by replacing the reference to the *Framework*. The IASB concluded it would be unaffected—the 2018 *Conceptual Framework* specifies criteria for recognising assets and liabilities, and paragraph 5.14 says that these criteria might not be met if it is uncertain whether an asset exists. The IASB added paragraph 23A to IFRS 3 to make its requirements for contingent assets explicit and clarify that replacing the reference to the *Framework* does not change them.

(b)   the IASB deleted paragraph BC125 from this Basis for Conclusions. In applying any IFRS Standard, an entity should apply only the recognition criteria specified in that Standard. However, paragraph BC125 referred to the *Framework* in a way that could be read to mean that, in applying IFRS 3, an acquirer of a business should apply both the recognition criteria specified in IFRS 3 and other recognition criteria discussed in the *Framework*. The IASB deleted paragraph BC125 because of its potential to cause misunderstanding. The IASB does not usually amend the basis for its previous conclusions, but decided that, in this instance, the importance of reducing the risk of misunderstanding warranted the deletion.

Part of the business combination

BC115   The second condition for recognising an asset acquired or a liability assumed or incurred in a business combination is that the asset or liability must be part of the business combination transaction rather than an asset or a liability resulting from a separate transaction. Making that distinction requires an acquirer to identify the components of a transaction in which it obtains control over an acquiree. The objective of the condition and the guidance on identifying the components of a business combination is to ensure that each component is accounted for in accordance with its economic substance.

BC116   The boards decided to provide application guidance to help address concerns about the difficulty of determining whether a part of the consideration transferred is for the acquiree or is for another purpose. The boards observed that parties directly involved in the negotiations of an impending business combination may take on the characteristics of related parties. Therefore, they may be willing to enter into other agreements or include as part of the business combination agreement some arrangements that are designed primarily for the benefit of the acquirer or the combined entity, for example, to achieve more favourable financial reporting outcomes after the business combination. Because of those concerns the boards decided to develop a principle for determining whether a particular transaction or arrangement entered into by the parties to the combination is part of what the acquirer and acquiree exchange in the business combination or is a separate transaction.

BC117   The boards concluded that a transaction that is designed primarily for the economic benefit of the acquirer or the combined entity (rather than the acquiree or its former owners before the business combination) is not part of the exchange for the acquiree. Those transactions should be accounted for separately from the business combination. The boards acknowledge that judgement may be required to determine whether part of the consideration paid or the assets acquired and liabilities assumed stems from a separate transaction. Accordingly, the 2005 Exposure Draft included both a general principle and implementation guidance for applying that principle, including several examples.

BC118　Respondents' comments on the proposed guidance on identifying the components of a business combination transaction were mixed. For example, some respondents said that the general principle was clear and provided adequate guidance; others said that the proposed principle was not clear. Several respondents said that the focus on determining whether a transaction benefits the acquiree or the acquirer was not clear because a transaction or event that benefits the acquiree would also benefit the combined entity because the acquiree is part of the combined entity.

BC119　The boards agreed with respondents that the proposed principle for distinguishing between components of a business combination needed improvement. Accordingly, they revised the principle to focus on whether a transaction is entered into by or on behalf of the acquirer or **primarily** for the benefit of the acquirer or the combined entity, rather than **primarily** for the benefit of the acquiree or its former owners **before the combination** (paragraph 52 of the revised IFRS 3).

BC120　The boards also concluded that the focus of the principle should be on identifying whether a business combination includes separate transactions that should be accounted for separately in accordance with their economic substance rather than solely on assessing whether a transaction is part of the exchange for the acquiree (paragraph 51 of the revised IFRS 3). Focusing solely on whether assets or liabilities are part of the exchange for the acquiree might not result in all transactions being accounted for in accordance with their economic substance. For example, if an acquirer asks the acquiree to pay some or all of the acquisition-related costs on its behalf and the acquiree has paid those costs before the acquisition date, at the acquisition date the acquiree will show no liability for those costs. Therefore, some might think that the principle as stated in the 2005 Exposure Draft does not apply to the transactions giving rise to the acquisition-related costs. The boards concluded that focusing instead on whether a transaction is separate from the business combination will more clearly convey the intention of the principle and thus will provide users with more relevant information about the financial effects of transactions and events entered into by the acquirer. The acquirer's financial statements will reflect the financial effects of all transactions for which the acquirer is responsible in accordance with their economic substance.

BC121　To help in applying the principle, paragraph 52 of the revised IFRS 3 includes three examples of transactions that are separate from the transaction in which an acquirer obtains control over an acquiree, and Appendix B provides additional application guidance.

BC122   The first example in paragraph 52 is directed at ensuring that a transaction that in effect settles a pre-existing relationship between the acquirer and the acquiree is excluded from the accounting for the business combination. Assume, for example, that a potential acquiree has an asset (receivable) for an unresolved claim against the potential acquirer. The acquirer and the acquiree's owners agree to settle that claim as part of an agreement to sell the acquiree to the acquirer. The boards concluded that if the acquirer makes a lump sum payment to the seller-owner, part of that payment is to settle the claim and is not part of the consideration transferred to acquire the business. Thus, the portion of the payment that relates to the claim settlement should be excluded from the accounting for the business combination and accounted for separately. In effect, the acquiree relinquished its claim (receivable) against the acquirer by transferring it (as a dividend) to the acquiree's owner. Thus, at the acquisition date the acquiree has no receivable (asset) to be acquired as part of the combination, and the acquirer would account for its settlement payment separately. The FASB observed that the conclusion that a transaction that settles a pre-existing relationship is not part of applying the acquisition method is consistent with the conclusion in EITF Issue No. 04-1 *Accounting for Preexisting Relationships between the Parties to a Business Combination*, which is incorporated into SFAS 141(R) and therefore superseded.

BC123   The second and third examples are also directed at ensuring that payments that are not part of the consideration transferred for the acquiree are excluded from the business combination accounting. The boards concluded that the payments for such transactions or arrangements should be accounted for separately in accordance with the applicable requirements for those transactions. Paragraph BC370 also discusses potential abuses related to the third example—payments to reimburse the acquiree or its former owners for paying the acquirer's costs incurred in connection with the business combination.

BC124   To provide additional help in identifying the components of a business combination, paragraph B50 of the revised IFRS 3 includes three factors to be considered in assessing a business combination transaction: (a) the reason for the transaction, (b) who initiated the transaction and (c) the timing of the transaction. Although those factors are neither mutually exclusive nor individually conclusive, the boards decided that the factors could help in considering whether a transaction or event is arranged primarily for the economic benefit of the acquirer or the combined entity or primarily for the benefit of the acquiree and its former owners before the business combination.

BC125   [Deleted][7]

---

7   See paragraph BC114D(b).

IFRS 3's criterion on probability of an inflow or outflow of benefits

BC126   IFRS 3 provided that an acquirer should recognise the acquiree's identifiable assets (other than intangible assets) and liabilities (other than contingent liabilities) only if it is probable that the asset or liability will result in an inflow or outflow of economic benefits. The revised IFRS 3 does not contain that probability recognition criterion and thus it requires the acquirer to recognise identifiable assets acquired and liabilities assumed regardless of the degree of probability of an inflow or outflow of economic benefits.

BC127   The recognition criteria in the *Framework* include the concept of probability to refer to the degree of uncertainty that the future economic benefits associated with an asset or liability will flow to or from the entity.

BC128   During the development of the revised IFRS 3, the IASB reconsidered items described in IAS 37 *Provisions, Contingent Liabilities and Contingent Assets* as contingent assets and contingent liabilities. Analysing the rights or obligations in such items to determine which are conditional and which are unconditional clarifies the question of whether the entity has an asset or a liability at the acquisition date.[8] As a result, the IASB concluded that many items previously described as contingent assets or contingent liabilities meet the definition of an asset or a liability in the *Framework* because they contain unconditional rights or obligations as well as conditional rights or obligations. Once the unconditional right in an asset (the unconditional obligation in a liability) is identified, the question to be addressed becomes what is the inflow (outflow) of economic benefits relating to that unconditional right (unconditional obligation).

BC129   The IASB noted that the *Framework* articulates the probability recognition criterion in terms of a flow of economic benefits rather than just direct cash flows. If an entity has an unconditional obligation, it is certain that an outflow of economic benefits from the entity is required, even if there is uncertainty about the timing and the amount of the outflow of benefits associated with a related conditional obligation. Hence, the IASB concluded that the liability (the unconditional obligation) satisfies the *Framework*'s probability recognition criterion. That conclusion applies equally to unconditional rights. Thus, if an entity has an unconditional right, it is certain that it has the right to an inflow of economic benefits, and the probability recognition criterion is satisfied.

BC130   Therefore, the IASB decided that inclusion of the probability criterion in the revised IFRS 3 is unnecessary because an unconditional right or obligation will always satisfy the criterion. In addition, the IASB made consequential amendments to paragraphs 25 and 33 of IAS 38 *Intangible Assets* to clarify the reason for its conclusion that the probability recognition criterion is always considered to be satisfied for intangible assets that are acquired separately or in a business combination. Specifically, the amendment indicates that an entity expects there to be an inflow of economic benefits embodied in an intangible asset acquired separately or in a business combination, even if there is uncertainty about the timing and the amount of the inflow.

---

8   Paragraphs BC11–BC17 and BC22–BC26 of the Basis for Conclusions on the draft amendments to IAS 37, published for comment in June 2005, discuss this issue in more detail.

Recognising particular identifiable assets acquired and liabilities assumed

BC131   To help ensure the consistent application of the requirements of the revised standards, the boards decided to provide specific recognition guidance for particular types of identifiable assets acquired and liabilities assumed in a business combination. That guidance and the reasons for it are discussed in the following paragraphs.

Liabilities associated with restructuring or exit activities of the acquiree

BC132   The revised standards explain that an acquirer recognises liabilities for restructuring or exit activities acquired in a business combination only if they meet the definition of a liability at the acquisition date (paragraph 11 of the revised IFRS 3). Costs associated with restructuring or exiting an acquiree's activities that are not liabilities at that date are recognised as post-combination activities or transactions of the combined entity when the costs are incurred. In considering acquired restructuring or exit activities the FASB and the IASB began at different points because the requirements of SFAS 141 and IFRS 3 on the issue differed.

BC133   In applying SFAS 141, acquirers looked to EITF Issue No. 95-3 *Recognition of Liabilities in Connection with a Purchase Business Combination* for guidance on recognising liabilities associated with restructuring or exit activities of an acquirer. EITF Issue 95-3 provided that the costs of an acquirer's plan (a) to exit an activity of an acquired company, (b) to involuntarily terminate the employment of employees of an acquired company or (c) to relocate employees of an acquired company should be recognised as liabilities assumed in a purchase business combination if specified conditions were met. Those conditions did not require the existence of a present obligation to another party. In developing the 2005 Exposure Draft, the FASB concluded, as it did in FASB Statement No. 146 *Accounting for Costs Associated with Exit or Disposal Activities* (SFAS 146), that only present obligations to others are liabilities under the definition in the FASB's Concepts Statement 6. An exit or disposal plan, by itself, does not create a present obligation to others for costs an entity expects to incur under the plan. Thus, an entity's commitment to an exit or disposal plan, by itself, is not a sufficient condition for recognition of a liability. Consistently with that conclusion, SFAS 141(R) nullifies the guidance in EITF Issue 95-3, which was not consistent with SFAS 146.

BC134   Before the IASB issued IFRS 3, IAS 22, like EITF Issue 95-3, required the acquirer to recognise as part of allocating the cost of a combination a provision for terminating or reducing the activities of the acquiree (*a restructuring provision*) that was not a liability of the acquiree at the acquisition date, provided that the acquirer had satisfied specified criteria. The criteria in IAS 22 were similar to those in EITF Issue 95-3. In developing ED 3 and IFRS 3, the IASB considered the view that a restructuring provision that was not a liability of the acquiree at the acquisition date should nonetheless be recognised by the acquirer as part of allocating the cost of the combination if the specified conditions were met. Those supporting this view, including some respondents to ED 3, argued that:

(a)   the estimated cost of terminating or reducing the activities of the acquiree would have influenced the price paid by the acquirer for the acquiree and therefore should be taken into account in measuring goodwill.

(b)   the acquirer is committed to the costs of terminating or reducing the activities of the acquiree because of the business combination. In other words, the combination is the past event that gives rise to a present obligation to terminate or reduce the activities of the acquiree.

BC135   In developing IFRS 3, the IASB rejected those arguments, noting that the price paid by the acquirer would also be influenced by future losses and other 'unavoidable' costs that relate to the future conduct of the business, such as costs of investing in new systems. IFRS 3 did not provide for recognising those costs as liabilities because they do not represent liabilities of the acquiree at the acquisition date, although the expected future outflows may affect the value of existing recognised assets. The IASB concluded that it would be inconsistent to recognise 'unavoidable' restructuring costs that arise in a business combination but to prohibit recognition of a liability for other 'unavoidable' costs to be incurred as a result of the combination.

BC136   The IASB's general criteria for identifying and recognising restructuring provisions are set out in IAS 37. IAS 37 states that a constructive obligation to restructure (and therefore a liability) arises only when the entity has developed a detailed formal plan for the restructuring and either raised a valid expectation in those affected that it will carry out the restructuring by publicly announcing details of the plan or begun implementing the plan. IAS 37 requires such a liability to be recognised when it becomes probable that an outflow of resources embodying economic benefits will be required to settle the obligation and the amount of the obligation can be reliably estimated.

BC137   IFRS 3 reflected the IASB's conclusion that if the criteria in paragraph 31 of IAS 22 for the recognition of a restructuring provision were carried forward, similar items would be accounted for differently. The timing of the recognition of restructuring provisions would differ, depending on whether a plan to restructure arises in connection with, or in the absence of, a business combination. The IASB decided that such a difference would impair the usefulness of the information provided to users about an entity's plans to restructure because both comparability and reliability would be diminished. Accordingly, IFRS 3 contained the same requirements as the revised IFRS 3 for recognising liabilities associated with restructuring or exit activities.

BC138   Few of the comments on the 2005 Exposure Draft from respondents who apply IFRSs in preparing their financial statements addressed its proposal on accounting for costs to restructure or exit activities of an acquiree (restructuring costs). Those who did so generally agreed with its proposal to carry forward the requirement of IFRS 3 for recognising liabilities associated with restructuring or exit activities of an acquiree. But the provisions of the 2005 Exposure Draft on that issue represented a change to GAAP in the United States, and the FASB received several responses objecting to the proposed change. It also received some responses that agreed with them, generally for the same reasons that the boards proposed the provisions in the 2005 Exposure Draft.

BC139 Respondents who disagreed with the proposed accounting for liabilities associated with restructuring or exit activities of an acquiree generally cited one or more of the following reasons in support of their view:

(a) Acquirers factor restructuring costs into the amount they are willing to pay for the acquiree. Therefore, those costs should be included in accounting for the business combination.

(b) It is not clear why the boards decided that restructuring costs should not be recognised as liabilities assumed in the business combination when those costs are more likely to be incurred than some of the liabilities related to contingencies that the boards proposed to recognise as liabilities assumed in a combination.

(c) Capitalising restructuring costs as part of a business combination would be consistent with the accounting for other asset acquisitions in which the amount capitalised is equal to the amount paid to acquire and place the asset in service.

BC140 The boards were not persuaded by those views. They observed that the view described in paragraph BC139(a) is essentially the same as the view of some respondents to ED 3 discussed in paragraph BC134(a). In addition, the boards noted that the acquirer does not pay the acquiree or its owners for the anticipated costs to restructure or exit activities and the acquirer's plans to do so do not give rise to an obligation and associated liability at the acquisition date. The acquirer ordinarily incurs a liability associated with such costs after it gains control of the acquiree's business.

BC141 The boards also disagreed with the view that the accounting for costs to restructure or exit some of an acquiree's activities is inconsistent with the requirements of the revised standards on contingencies. On the contrary, the two requirements are consistent with each other because both require recognition of a liability only if an obligation that meets the definition of a liability exists at the acquisition date.

BC142 The boards also observed that the requirements of the revised standards on restructuring costs are consistent with current practice in accounting for many similar costs expected to be incurred in conjunction with other acquisitions of assets. For example, one airline might acquire an aircraft from another airline. The acquirer was likely to consider the costs of changing the logo on the aircraft and making any other intended changes to its configuration in deciding what it was willing to pay for the aircraft. Other airlines bidding for the aircraft might also have plans to change the aircraft if they were the successful bidders. The nature and extent of the changes each airline expected to make and the costs each would incur were likely to differ.

BC143 In accordance with both US GAAP and IFRSs, the airline would recognise none of those expected, post-acquisition costs at the date the aircraft is acquired. Instead, those costs are accounted for after control of the aircraft is obtained. If the costs add to the value of the aircraft and meet the related requirements of US GAAP or IFRSs, they will be recognised as assets (probably as an addition to the carrying amount of the aircraft). Otherwise, those additional costs are likely to be charged to expense when incurred.

Operating leases

BC144 In accordance with both FASB Statement No. 13 *Accounting for Leases* (SFAS 13) and IAS 17 *Leases*, an acquiree that is the lessee in an operating lease does not recognise separately the rights and obligations embodied in operating leases. The boards considered whether to require, for example, the separate recognition of an asset acquired for an acquiree's rights to use property for the specified period and related renewal options or other rights and a liability assumed for an acquiree's obligations to make required lease payments for an operating lease acquired in a business combination. However, at the time they considered how to account for operating leases in a business combination, they were considering adding to their agendas a joint project on accounting for leases. That project was added in 2006. Accordingly, the boards concluded that the revised standards should be consistent with the existing accounting requirements on accounting for leases. Therefore, the revised standards provide that the acquirer recognises no assets or liabilities related to an operating lease in which the acquiree is the lessee other than those referred to in paragraphs B29 and B30 of the revised IFRS 3, which are discussed in the following paragraphs.

BC145 The 2005 Exposure Draft proposed that the amount by which the terms of an operating lease are favourable or unfavourable in relation to market terms should be recognised as a separate intangible asset, regardless of whether the acquiree is the lessee or the lessor. For the FASB, that proposal would have carried forward the related guidance in SFAS 141 for leases in which the acquiree is the lessee. Some respondents suggested that, instead, the measure of the fair value of an asset subject to an operating lease in which the acquiree is the lessor should take into account the favourable or unfavourable aspect of the lease terms.

BC146 The boards considered this issue in the context of their respective guidance in other standards on how to determine the fair value of an asset. As noted above, the proposal in the 2005 Exposure Draft was generally consistent with US GAAP for business combinations. However, FASB Statement No. 157 *Fair Value Measurements* (SFAS 157) does not provide guidance on the *unit of valuation* —the level at which an asset or liability is aggregated or disaggregated to determine what is being measured. The IASB also does not have general guidance on determining the unit of valuation. However, IAS 40 *Investment Property* provides that the fair value of investment property takes into account rental income from current leases, and the IASB understands that practice in measuring the fair value of investment property is to take into account the contractual terms of the leases and other contracts in place relating to the asset.

BC147   The FASB concluded that SFAS 141 should retain the guidance in the 2005 Exposure Draft that the favourable or unfavourable aspect of an operating lease in which the acquiree is the lessor should be separately recognised as an intangible asset or liability. It concluded that separately reporting that amount rather than embedding an aspect of a lease contract in the fair value of the leased asset would provide more complete information to users of the post-combination financial statements. In addition, the FASB noted that reporting the favourable or unfavourable aspect of the lease contract separately would facilitate appropriate amortisation of that amount over the term of the lease rather than over the remaining life of the leased asset. Unlike IAS 16 *Property, Plant and Equipment*, US GAAP does not require an item of property, plant or equipment to be separated into components, with the components depreciated or amortised over different useful lives.

BC148   The IASB decided to require the acquirer in a business combination to follow the guidance in IAS 40 for assets subject to operating leases in which the acquiree is the lessor. The IASB observed that, for lessors who choose the cost option in IAS 40, both IAS 16 and IAS 38 require use of a depreciation or amortisation method that reflects the pattern in which the entity expects to consume the asset's future economic benefits. In addition, IAS 16 requires each part of an item of property, plant and equipment that has a cost that is significant in relation to the total cost of the item to be depreciated separately. Thus, an entity would be required to adjust the depreciation or amortisation method for the leased asset to reflect the timing of cash flows attributable to the underlying leases. Therefore, although the presentation of operating leases and the underlying leased assets in the statement of financial position will differ depending on whether an entity applies IFRSs or US GAAP, the IASB observed that the identifiable net assets and the depreciation or amortisation recognised in the post-combination financial statements will be the same.

Research and development assets

BC149   The revised standards require an acquirer to recognise all tangible and intangible research and development assets acquired in a business combination, as was proposed in the 2005 Exposure Draft. Previously, FASB Interpretation No. 4 *Applicability of FASB Statement No. 2 to Business Combinations Accounted for by the Purchase Method* (FASB Interpretation 4) required an acquirer to measure and immediately recognise as expense tangible and intangible assets to be used in research and development that had no alternative future use. A research and development asset was recognised as such only if it had an alternative future use. In contrast, IFRS 3 did not require a research and development asset to have an alternative future use for it to be recognised. The revised standards therefore do not change the provisions of IFRS 3 on that issue. Accordingly, most of the discussion in paragraphs BC150–BC156 pertains to the FASB's consideration of this issue.

BC150   The FASB concluded that the requirement to write off assets to be used in research and development activities immediately if they have no alternative future use resulted in information that was not representationally faithful. In addition, eliminating that requirement furthers the goal of international convergence of accounting standards. Therefore, SFAS 141(R) supersedes FASB

Interpretation 4 and requires research and development assets acquired in a business combination to be recognised regardless of whether they have an alternative future use.

BC151 Relatively few respondents to the 2005 Exposure Draft commented on the proposed accounting for research and development assets. Those who did so generally disagreed with those proposals (they also generally applied US GAAP rather than IFRSs), citing either or both of the following concerns as support for their view:

(a) In-process research and development may not meet the definition of an asset in the FASB's Concepts Statement 6 because its low likelihood of success does not represent **probable** future economic benefits.

(b) The fair value of in-process research and development may not be measurable with sufficient reliability for recognition in financial statements.

The boards rejected both of those views for the reasons explained in the following paragraphs.

BC152 The boards agreed with respondents that the likelihood that an individual research and development project will result in a profitable product is often low. However, the boards also noted that the use of the word *probable* in the FASB's Concepts Statement 6 refers only to something that is not certain. The definition does not use that term as a recognition criterion that specifies the degree of probability of the inflow or outflow of future economic benefits that must be present for an item to qualify for recognition. Therefore, the boards concluded that in-process research and development acquired in a business combination will generally satisfy the definition of an asset because the observable exchange at the acquisition date provides evidence that the parties to the exchange expect future economic benefits to result from that research and development. Uncertainty about the outcome of an individual project is reflected in measuring its fair value.

BC153 The boards also agreed that determining the fair value of in-process research and development requires the use of estimates and judgement, and the resulting amount will generally not be as reliable as the fair values of other assets for which quoted prices in active markets are available. However, the boards observed that use of estimates and judgement, by itself, does not mean that information is unreliable; reliability does not require precision or certainty. For example, paragraph 86 of the IASB's *Framework* says that 'In many cases, cost or value must be estimated; the use of reasonable estimates is an essential part of the preparation of financial statements and does not undermine their reliability.' The boards also noted that the requirement to measure the fair value of in-process research and development assets acquired in a business combination is not new—not even in US GAAP. In accordance with FASB Interpretation 4, that amount was measured but immediately written off. Moreover, respondents to the 2005 Exposure Draft that apply IFRSs generally did not mention any problems with complying with the provisions of IFRS 3 on research and development assets, which are the same as those in the revised standards.

BC154   In developing the 2005 Exposure Draft, the FASB also considered whether it could make further improvements by extending the recognition provisions of SFAS 141(R) for research and development assets to purchases of in-process research and development assets outside a business combination. At that time, the FASB decided not to do so because the additional time needed to deliberate the related issues would have unduly delayed the revised standards.

BC155   Some respondents to the 2005 Exposure Draft objected to the resulting inconsistent US GAAP requirements for research and development assets acquired in a business combination and those acquired in another type of transaction. The FASB agreed with respondents that inconsistent accounting for research and development assets depending on how they are acquired is undesirable. Therefore, the FASB expects to reconsider the accounting for research and development assets acquired by means other than in a business combination separately from its project on business combinations.

BC156   The FASB also decided to provide guidance on the impairment testing of in-process research and development projects that are temporarily idled or abandoned. It did that by means of an amendment to SFAS 142.

Distinguishing identifiable intangible assets from goodwill

BC157   Early in their respective projects on accounting for business combinations, the IASB and the FASB both observed that intangible assets make up an increasing proportion of the assets of many (if not most) entities. The boards also observed that intangible assets acquired in a business combination were often included in the amount recognised as goodwill.

BC158   Both the IASB and the FASB decided that they needed to provide explicit criteria for determining whether an acquired intangible asset should be recognised separately from goodwill. The FASB provided such criteria in SFAS 141 and the IASB provided similar, although not identical, criteria in IAS 38.[9] One reason for providing such criteria was the boards' conclusion that the decision-usefulness of financial statements would be enhanced if intangible assets acquired in a business combination were distinguished from goodwill. For example, the FASB's Concepts Statement No. 5 *Recognition and Measurement in Financial Statements of Business Enterprises* says that classification in financial statements facilitates analysis by grouping items with essentially similar characteristics and separating items with essentially different characteristics. Analysis aimed at objectives such as predicting amounts, timing and uncertainty of future cash flows requires financial information segregated into reasonably homogeneous groups.

BC159   In developing its 1999 Exposure Draft, the FASB considered various characteristics that might distinguish other intangible assets from goodwill. Because the FASB concluded that identifiability is the characteristic that conceptually distinguishes other intangible assets from goodwill, the 1999 Exposure Draft proposed that intangible assets that are identifiable and reliably measurable should be recognised as assets separately from goodwill.

---

9   More detailed information about the IASB's reasoning in developing the criteria in IAS 38 is available in its Basis for Conclusions.

Most respondents to the 1999 Exposure Draft agreed that many intangible assets are identifiable and that various intangible assets are reliably measurable. However, respondents' views on the proposed recognition criteria varied. Many of those respondents suggested alternative recognition criteria and many urged the FASB to clarify the term *reliably measurable*.

BC160 The FASB considered those suggestions and decided to modify the proposed recognition criteria to provide a clearer distinction between intangible assets that should be recognised separately from goodwill and those that should be subsumed into goodwill. The FASB then published a revised exposure draft *Business Combinations and Intangible Assets—Accounting for Goodwill* (2001 Exposure Draft) which proposed that an intangible asset should be recognised separately from goodwill if either:

(a) control over the future economic benefits of the asset results from contractual or other legal rights (the contractual-legal criterion); or

(b) the intangible asset is capable of being separated or divided and sold, transferred, licensed, rented or exchanged (either separately or as part of a group of assets) (the separability criterion).

The FASB concluded that sufficient information should exist to measure reliably the fair value of an asset that satisfies either of those criteria. Thus, the change in the recognition criteria eliminated the need explicitly to include *reliably measurable* as a recognition criterion or to clarify the meaning of that term.

BC161 IAS 38 (as issued by the IASB's predecessor body in 1998) clarified that the definition of an intangible asset required an intangible asset to be identifiable to distinguish it from goodwill. However, it did not define the term *identifiable*. Instead, IAS 38 stated that an intangible asset could be distinguished from goodwill if the asset was separable, though separability was not a necessary condition for identifiability.

BC162 In developing IFRS 3, the IASB affirmed the conclusion in IAS 38 that identifiability is the characteristic that conceptually distinguishes other intangible assets from goodwill. In addition, the IASB concluded that to provide a definitive basis for identifying and recognising intangible assets separately from goodwill, the concept of identifiability needed to be articulated more clearly. As a result of that consideration, which is discussed in paragraphs BC163–BC165, the IASB developed more definitive criteria for distinguishing between identifiable intangible assets and goodwill and included those criteria in both IFRS 3 and IAS 38 (as revised in 2004).

Reasons for the contractual-legal criterion

BC163 In developing IFRS 3 and SFAS 141, the IASB and the FASB observed that many intangible assets arise from rights conveyed legally by contract, statute or similar means. For example, franchises are granted to car dealers, fast food outlets and professional sports teams. Trademarks and service marks may be registered with the government. Contracts are often negotiated with customers or suppliers. Technological innovations are often protected by patents. In contrast, goodwill arises from the collection of assembled assets that make up an acquiree or the value created by assembling a collection of assets through a business combination, such as the synergies that are expected to result from combining two or more businesses. Therefore, both boards concluded that the fact that an intangible asset arises from contractual or other legal rights is an important characteristic that distinguishes many intangible assets from goodwill and an acquired intangible asset with that characteristic should be recognised separately from goodwill.

Reasons for the separability criterion

BC164   As already noted (paragraph BC161), the original version of IAS 38 included separability as a characteristic that helps to distinguish intangible assets from goodwill. In developing IFRS 3, the IASB affirmed that conclusion for the reasons discussed in the following paragraphs.

BC165   In developing IFRS 3 and SFAS 141, the IASB and the FASB observed that some intangible assets that do not arise from rights conveyed by contract or other legal means are nonetheless capable of being separated from the acquiree and exchanged for something else of value. Others, like goodwill, cannot be separated from an entity and sold or otherwise transferred. Both boards thus concluded that separability is another important characteristic that distinguishes many intangible assets from goodwill. An acquired intangible asset with that characteristic should be recognised separately from goodwill.

BC166   The FASB's 2001 Exposure Draft proposed that an intangible asset that was not separable individually would meet the separability criterion if it could be sold, transferred, licensed, rented or exchanged along with a group of related assets or liabilities. Some respondents suggested that the FASB should eliminate that requirement, arguing that unless the asset is separable individually it should be included in the amount recognised as goodwill. Others asked the FASB to clarify the meaning of the term *group of related assets*, noting that even goodwill can be separated from the acquiree if the asset group sold constitutes a business.

BC167   The FASB noted that some intangible assets are so closely related to another asset or liability that they are usually sold as a 'package' (eg deposit liabilities and the related depositor relationship intangible asset). If those intangible assets were subsumed into goodwill, gains might be inappropriately recognised if the intangible asset was later sold along with the related asset or obligation. However, the FASB agreed that the proposed requirement to recognise an intangible asset separately from goodwill if it could be sold or transferred as part of an asset group was a broader criterion than it had intended. For those reasons, SFAS 141 provided, as do the revised standards, that an intangible asset that is not separable individually meets the separability criterion if it can be separated from the entity and sold, transferred, licensed, rented or exchanged in combination with a related contract, other identifiable asset or other liability.

BC168   Some respondents to the 2001 Exposure Draft suggested limiting the separability criterion to intangible assets that are separable **and** are traded in observable exchange transactions. Although the FASB agreed that exchange transactions provide evidence of an asset's separability, it concluded that those transactions were not necessarily the only evidence of separability and it did not adopt that suggestion.

BC169 Other respondents suggested that the separability criterion should be modified to require recognition of an intangible asset separately from goodwill only if management of the entity **intends** to sell, lease or otherwise exchange the asset. The FASB rejected that suggestion because it concluded that the asset's **capability** of being separated from the entity and exchanged for something else of value is the pertinent characteristic of an intangible asset that distinguishes it from goodwill. In contrast, management's intentions are not a characteristic of an asset.

The FASB's reasons for rejecting other recognition criteria suggested for SFAS 141

BC170 Some respondents suggested that the FASB should eliminate the requirement to recognise intangible assets separately from goodwill. Others suggested that all intangible assets with characteristics similar to goodwill should be included in the amount recorded as goodwill. The FASB rejected those suggestions because they would diminish rather than improve the decision-usefulness of reported financial information.

BC171 Some respondents doubted their ability to measure reliably the fair values of many intangible assets. They suggested that the only intangible assets that should be recognised separately from goodwill are those that have direct cash flows and those that are bought and sold in observable exchange transactions. The FASB rejected that suggestion. Although the fair value measures of some identifiable intangible assets might lack the precision of the measures for other assets, the FASB concluded that the information that will be provided by recognising intangible assets at their estimated fair values is a more faithful representation than that which would be provided if those intangible assets were subsumed into goodwill. Moreover, including finite-lived intangible assets in goodwill that is not being amortised would further diminish the representational faithfulness of financial statements.

Convergence of criteria in SFAS 141 and IFRS 3

BC172 The criteria in IFRS 3 for determining if an intangible asset is identifiable and thus should be recognised separately from goodwill included the same contractual or legal and separability conditions as SFAS 141. However, IFRS 3 also included a requirement that the fair value of an identifiable intangible asset should be reliably measurable to be recognised separately. In developing the 2005 Exposure Draft, the boards considered how best to achieve convergence of their respective recognition criteria for intangible assets.

BC173 In developing IFRS 3, the IASB noted that the fair value of identifiable intangible assets acquired in a business combination is normally measurable with sufficient reliability to be recognised separately from goodwill. The effects of uncertainty because of a range of possible outcomes with different probabilities are reflected in measuring the asset's fair value; the existence of such a range does not demonstrate an inability to measure fair value reliably. IAS 38 (before amendment by the revised IFRS 3) included a rebuttable presumption that the fair value of an intangible asset with a finite useful life acquired in a business combination can be measured reliably. The IASB had concluded that it might not always be possible to measure reliably the fair value of an asset that has an underlying contractual or legal basis. However, IAS 38 provided that the only circumstances in which it might not be possible to measure reliably the fair value of an intangible asset that arises from legal or other contractual rights acquired in a business combination were if it either:

(a)   is not separable; or

(b)   is separable, but there is no history or evidence of exchange transactions for the same or similar assets, and otherwise estimating fair value would depend on immeasurable variables.

BC174   In developing the 2005 Exposure Draft, the IASB concluded that separate recognition of intangible assets, on the basis of an estimate of fair value, rather than subsuming them in goodwill, provides better information to the users of financial statements even if a significant degree of judgement is required to estimate fair value. For that reason, the IASB decided to propose consequential amendments to IAS 38 to remove the reliability of measurement criterion for intangible assets acquired in a business combination. In redeliberating the proposals in the 2005 Exposure Draft, the IASB affirmed those amendments to IAS 38.

Illustrative list of intangible assets

BC175   The illustrative examples that accompanied IFRS 3 included a list of examples of identifiable intangible assets that might be acquired in a business combination. A similar list accompanies the revised IFRS 3 (see the illustrative examples). The list reflects various changes to similar lists in the exposure drafts that the boards published earlier in their respective projects on business combinations. The boards observed that the list is not exhaustive, and a particular type of intangible asset that was included on an earlier list might not be mentioned in the illustrative examples. That does not necessarily mean that the intangible asset does not qualify as identifiable in accordance with the criteria in the revised standards. An acquirer must consider the nature of each acquired intangible asset in determining whether those criteria are met.

Assembled workforce

BC176   In developing SFAS 141, the FASB did not consider whether an assembled workforce met either the contractual-legal or the separability criterion for recognition as an identifiable intangible asset. Instead, SFAS 141 precluded separate recognition of an assembled workforce because of the FASB's conclusion that techniques to measure the value of an assembled workforce with sufficient reliability were not currently available. IFRS 3 and IAS 38, on the other hand, did not explicitly preclude separate recognition of an assembled workforce. However, paragraph 15 of IAS 38 noted that an entity would not usually have sufficient control over the expected future economic benefits arising from an assembled workforce for it to meet the definition of a separate intangible asset.

BC177   In developing the 2005 Exposure Draft, the boards concluded that an acquirer should not recognise an assembled workforce as a separate intangible asset because it meets neither the contractual-legal nor the separability criterion. The views of respondents who commented on recognition of an assembled workforce were mixed. Some agreed with its proposed recognition prohibition. Others suggested that the boards should reconsider that prohibition; they generally said that an assembled workforce is already valued in many situations for the purpose of calculating a 'contributory asset charge' in determining the fair value of some intangible assets. (In using an 'excess earnings' income valuation technique, a contributory asset charge is required to isolate the cash flows generated by the intangible asset being valued from the contribution to those cash flows made by other assets, including other intangible assets. Contributory asset charges are hypothetical 'rental' charges for the use of those other contributing assets.) Those respondents opposed a prohibition on recognising an assembled workforce as a separate intangible asset; they favoured permitting acquirers to assess whether an assembled workforce is separable in each situation and to recognise those that are separable.

BC178   In reconsidering the proposal in the 2005 Exposure Draft, the boards concluded that the prohibition of recognising an assembled workforce should be retained. Because an assembled workforce is a collection of employees rather than an individual employee, it does not arise from contractual or legal rights. Although individual employees might have employment contracts with the employer, the collection of employees, as a whole, does not have such a contract. In addition, an assembled workforce is not separable, either as individual employees or together with a related contract, identifiable asset or liability. An assembled workforce cannot be sold, transferred, licensed, rented or otherwise exchanged without causing disruption to the acquirer's business. In contrast, an entity could continue to operate after transferring an identifiable asset. Therefore, an assembled workforce is not an identifiable intangible asset to be recognised separately from goodwill.

BC179   The boards observed that neither IAS 38 nor SFAS 141 defined an assembled workforce, and that inconsistencies have resulted in practice. In addition, some who objected to the recognition prohibition in the 2005 Exposure Draft apparently consider that an assembled workforce represents the intellectual capital of the skilled workforce — the (often specialised) knowledge and experience that employees of an acquiree bring to their jobs. However, the boards view an assembled workforce as an existing collection of employees that permits an acquirer to continue to operate an acquired business from the acquisition date and they decided to include that definition in the revised standards (paragraph B37 of the revised IFRS 3).

BC180   The boards observed that the value of intellectual capital is, in effect, recognised because it is part of the fair value of the entity's other intangible assets, such as proprietary technologies and processes and customer contracts and relationships. In that situation, a process or methodology can be documented and followed to the extent that the business would not be materially affected if a particular employee left the entity. In most jurisdictions, the employer usually 'owns' the intellectual capital of an employee. Most employment contracts stipulate that the employer retains the rights to and ownership of any intellectual property created by the employee. For example, a software program created by a particular employee (or group of employees) would be documented and generally would be the property of the entity. The particular programmer who created the program could be replaced by another software programmer with equivalent expertise without significantly affecting the ability of the entity to continue to operate. But the intellectual property created in the form of a software program is part of the fair value of that program and is an identifiable intangible asset if it is separable from the entity. In other words, the prohibition of recognising an assembled workforce as an intangible asset does not apply to intellectual property; it applies only to the value of having a workforce in place on the acquisition date so that the acquirer can continue the acquiree's operations without having to hire and train a workforce.

Reacquired rights

BC181 As part of a business combination, an acquirer may reacquire a right that it had previously granted to the acquiree to use the acquirer's recognised or unrecognised intangible assets. Examples of such rights include a right to use the acquirer's trade name under a franchise agreement or a right to use the acquirer's technology under a technology licensing agreement. The 2005 Exposure Draft proposed, and the revised standards require, an acquirer to recognise such a reacquired right as an identifiable intangible asset (paragraph B35 of the revised IFRS 3). The fair value of a reacquired right is to be amortised over the remaining term of the contract that gave rise to the right. For entities applying US GAAP, that guidance is not new; it is the same as the related guidance in EITF Issue 04-1. (Paragraphs BC308–BC310 discuss the measurement of reacquired rights.)

BC182 A few respondents to the 2005 Exposure Draft disagreed with recognising a reacquired right as an identifiable intangible asset because they considered that doing so was the same as recognising an internally generated intangible asset. Some suggested recognising a reacquired right as the settlement of a pre-existing relationship; others said that a reacquired right should be recognised as part of goodwill.

BC183 The boards rejected the alternative of treating a reacquired right as the termination of a pre-existing relationship because reacquisition of, for example, a franchise right does not terminate the right. After a business combination, the right to operate a franchised outlet in a particular region continues to exist. The difference is that the acquirer, rather than the acquiree by itself, now controls the franchise right.

BC184 The boards also rejected recognising a reacquired right as part of goodwill. Supporters of that alternative consider that such a right differs from other identifiable intangible assets recognised in a business combination because, from the perspective of the combined entity, a franchising relationship with an outside party no longer exists. As already noted, however, the reacquired right and the related cash flows continue to exist. The boards concluded that recognising that right separately from goodwill provides users of the financial statements of the combined entity with more decision-useful information than subsuming the right into goodwill. The boards also observed that a reacquired right meets the contractual-legal and the separability criteria and therefore qualifies as an identifiable intangible asset.

Classifying and designating assets acquired and liabilities assumed

BC185   In some situations, IFRSs and US GAAP provide for different accounting depending on how a particular asset or liability is classified or designated. For example, in accordance with both IAS 39 *Financial Instruments: Recognition and Measurement*[10] and FASB Statement No. 115 *Accounting for Certain Investments in Debt and Equity Securities*, the accounting for particular financial instruments differs depending on how the instrument is classified, for example, as at fair value through profit or loss, available for sale or held to maturity. Another example is the accounting for a derivative instrument in accordance with either IAS 39[11] or FASB Statement No.133 *Accounting for Derivative Instruments and Hedging Activities* (SFAS 133), which depends on whether the derivative is designated as a hedge, and if so, the type of hedge designated.

BC186   The 2005 Exposure Draft proposed that the classification of an acquired lease would not change from the acquiree's classification at lease inception unless the terms of the lease were modified as a result of the business combination in a way that would require a different classification in accordance with IAS 17 or SFAS 13. But that exposure draft did not address classification or designation issues pertaining to other types of contracts. Some respondents and others asked the boards to provide additional guidance on when the acquirer in a business combination should reconsider and perhaps change the classification or designation of a contract for the purpose of applying other accounting requirements.

BC187   The boards decided that providing a general principle for classifying or designating contracts acquired in a business combination would facilitate consistent implementation of the revised standards. They observed that application of the acquisition method results in the initial recognition in the acquirer's financial statements of the assets acquired and liabilities assumed in a business combination. Therefore, in concept, the acquirer should classify and designate all items acquired in a business combination at the acquisition date in the context of the contractual terms, economic conditions and other pertinent factors at that date. That concept underlies the classification and designation principle (paragraph 15 of the revised IFRS 3).

BC188   In the two situations described in paragraph 17[12] of the revised IFRS 3, classification of a lease contract as an operating lease or a finance lease and classification of a contract as an insurance or reinsurance contract or a deposit contract, other IFRSs and US GAAP require an entity to classify a contract only

---

10   IFRS 9 *Financial Instruments* replaced IAS 39. IFRS 9 applies to all items that were previously within the scope of IAS 39.

11   IFRS 9 *Financial Instruments* replaced the hedge accounting requirements in IAS 39.

12   IFRS 17 *Insurance Contracts*, issued in May 2017, replaced IFRS 4 and amended paragraph 17 of IFRS 3 for consistency with the requirements in IFRS 17.

at its inception, on the basis of contractual terms and other factors at that date. Because those requirements apply to specific types of contracts regardless of the identity of the parties to the contract, the boards concluded that such requirements should also apply in accounting for a business combination. Thus, the revised standards provide an exception to the principle for classifying and designating assets acquired and liabilities assumed in a business combination for the two types of contracts identified in paragraph 17.

Recognition, classification and measurement guidance for insurance and reinsurance contracts[13]

BC189   SFAS 141(R) provides guidance specific to insurance and reinsurance contracts acquired or assumed in a business combination, primarily by means of amendments to other insurance-related standards. Paragraphs BC190–BC195 discuss that guidance. Paragraph BC196 discusses the IASB's guidance on recognition and measurement of insurance contracts in a business combination, which is provided in IFRS 4 *Insurance Contracts*.

BC190   The FASB decided that insurance and reinsurance contracts acquired in a business combination should be accounted for on a fresh start (new contract) basis. Accordingly, all assets and liabilities arising from the rights and obligations of insurance and reinsurance contracts acquired in a business combination are recognised at the acquisition date, measured at their acquisition-date fair values. That recognition and measurement might include a reinsurance recoverable, a liability to pay future contract claims and claims expenses on the unexpired portion of the acquired contracts and a liability to pay incurred contract claims and claims expenses. However, those assets acquired and liabilities assumed would not include the acquiree's insurance and reinsurance contract accounts such as deferred acquisition costs and unearned premiums that do not represent future cash flows. The FASB considers that model the most consistent with the acquisition method and with the accounting for other types of contracts acquired in a business combination.

BC191   The FASB also decided to require the acquirer to carry forward the acquiree's classification of a contract as an insurance or reinsurance contract (rather than a deposit) on the basis of the terms of the acquired contract and any related contracts or agreements at the inception of the contract. If the terms of those contracts or agreements have been modified in a manner that would change the classification, the acquirer determines the classification of the contract on the basis of its terms and other pertinent factors as of the modification date, which may be the acquisition date. Consideration of related contracts and arrangements is important in assessing whether a contract qualifies as insurance or reinsurance because they can significantly affect the amount of risk transferred.

---

13   IFRS 17, issued in 2017, replaced IFRS 4. The requirements for insurance contracts acquired in a business combination are provided in IFRS 17 and are discussed in paragraphs BC323–BC327 of the Basis for Conclusions of IFRS 17.

BC192   SFAS 141(R) also requires the fair value of the insurance and reinsurance contracts acquired in a business combination to be separated into (a) insurance and reinsurance US GAAP accounting balances using the acquirer's accounting policies and (b) an intangible asset (or, at times that are expected to be rare, another liability). That guidance permits the acquirer to report the acquired business subsequently on the same basis as its written business (with the exception of the amortisation of the intangible asset). Other contracts providing for third-party contingent commissions would be accounted for in the same way as other contingencies, and contracts that provide guarantees of the adequacy of claims liabilities would be accounted for as indemnifications.

BC193   The FASB concluded that the intangible asset should be amortised on a basis consistent with the measurement of the liability. For example, for most short-duration contracts such as property and liability insurance contracts, US GAAP claims liabilities are not discounted, so amortising the intangible asset like a discount using an interest method could be an appropriate method. For particular long-duration contracts such as most traditional life insurance contracts, using a basis consistent with the measurement of the liability would be similar to the guidance provided in paragraph 31 of FASB Statement No. 60 *Accounting and Reporting by Insurance Enterprises* (SFAS 60).

BC194   The FASB considered several implementation issues identified by respondents to the 2005 Exposure Draft but decided that specifying the fresh start model for acquired insurance and reinsurance contracts and providing limited guidance on subsequent accounting, including requiring the intangible asset to be amortised on a basis consistent with the liability, should be sufficient to resolve most practice issues. That level of guidance is also consistent with the limited guidance provided by IFRS 4.

BC195   The FASB decided to provide the guidance on recognition and measurement, including subsequent measurement, of insurance and reinsurance contracts acquired in a business combination by means of an amendment to SFAS 60. That parallels the location of the IASB's business combination guidance for insurance contracts in IFRS 4 and will make it easier to address any changes in that guidance that might result if the FASB and the IASB eventually undertake a joint project to reconsider comprehensively the accounting for insurance contracts.

BC196   Paragraphs 31–33 of IFRS 4 deal with limited aspects of insurance contracts acquired in a business combination. That guidance was developed in phase I of the IASB's project on insurance contracts. The IASB decided not to amend those paragraphs in phase II of the business combinations project, so as not to pre-empt phase II of the IASB's project on insurance contracts. In May 2007 the IASB published its initial thoughts for phase II of that project in a discussion paper *Preliminary Views on Insurance Contracts*.

Measurement

BC197   Paragraph 18 of the revised IFRS 3 establishes the principle that the identifiable assets acquired and liabilities assumed should be measured at their acquisition-date fair values. The reasons for that principle and its application to contingencies and non-controlling interests are discussed in paragraphs BC198–BC245, and the definition of fair value[14] is discussed in paragraphs BC246–BC251. The revised standards provide guidance on determining the acquisition-date fair value of particular types of assets acquired, which is discussed in paragraphs BC252–BC262. The exceptions to the measurement principle are discussed in paragraphs BC279–BC311.

Why establish fair value as the measurement principle?

Identifiable assets acquired and liabilities assumed

BC198   In developing the measurement principle in the revised standards, the boards concluded that fair value is the most relevant attribute for assets acquired and liabilities assumed in a business combination. Measurement at fair value also provides information that is more comparable and understandable than measurement at cost or on the basis of allocating the total cost of an acquisition. Both IFRS 3 and SFAS 141 required allocation of that cost on the basis of the fair value of the assets acquired and the liabilities assumed. However, other guidance in those standards required measurements that were other than fair value. Moreover, SFAS 141's requirements for measuring identifiable assets acquired and liabilities assumed in an acquisition achieved in stages (a step acquisition) and in acquisitions of less than all of the equity interests in the acquiree resulted in another difference between fair value measurement of identifiable assets and liabilities and the process of accumulating and allocating costs. Those requirements were the same as the benchmark treatment in IAS 22, which IFRS 3 replaced. The following paragraphs discuss both the IASB's reasons for that change to IAS 22 and the FASB's reasons for the change to SFAS 141's requirements for step acquisitions, as well as providing additional discussion of the reasons for the fair value measurement principle in the revised standards.

BC199   In developing IFRS 3 and SFAS 141(R), respectively, the boards examined the inconsistencies that resulted from applying the benchmark treatment in IAS 22 and the provisions of SFAS 141, and the related implementation guidance, to acquisitions of businesses. For a step acquisition, that process involved accumulating the costs or carrying amounts of earlier purchases of interests in an entity, which may have occurred years or decades ago. Those amounts were added to the current costs to purchase incremental interests in the acquiree on the acquisition date. The accumulated amounts of those purchases were then allocated to the assets acquired and liabilities assumed. Allocating the accumulated amounts generally resulted in recognising the identifiable assets and liabilities of the acquiree at a mixture of current exchange prices and carry-forward book values for each earlier purchase rather than at their acquisition-date fair values. Users of financial statements have long criticised those practices as resulting in information that lacks consistency, understandability and usefulness. For example, in response to the September 1991 FASB Discussion Memorandum *Consolidation Policy and Procedures*, an organisation representing lending officers said:

---

14 IFRS 13 *Fair Value Measurement*, issued in May 2011, defines fair value and contains the requirements for measuring fair value.

> [We believe] that the assets and liabilities of the subsidiary [acquiree] reported in the consolidation should reflect the full values established by the exchange transaction in which they were purchased. ... [We believe] the current practice of reporting individual assets and liabilities at a mixture of some current exchange prices and some carry-forward book values is **dangerously misleading**. [emphasis added]

BC200　The boards concluded that no useful purpose is served by reporting the assets or liabilities of a newly acquired business using a mixture of their fair values at the date acquired and the acquirer's historical costs or carrying amounts. Amounts that relate to transactions and events occurring before the business is included in the acquirer's financial statements are not relevant to users of those financial statements.

BC201　The boards also observed the criticisms of the information resulting from application of the cost accumulation and allocation process to acquisitions of businesses that resulted in ownership of less than all of the equity interests in the acquiree. In those circumstances, application of the cost accumulation and allocation process also resulted in identifiable assets and liabilities being assigned amounts that were generally not their acquisition-date fair values. For example, in its 1993 Position Paper *Financial Reporting in the 1990s and Beyond* the Association for Investment Management and Research (AIMR)[15] said:

> An even more difficult situation arises when Firm B acquires less than total ownership of Firm A. Under current practice, only the proportionate share of Firm A's assets and liabilities owned by Firm B are re-valued, but all of Firm A's assets and liabilities — partially re-valued, partially not — are consolidated with those of Firm B, none of whose assets and liabilities have been re-valued. What a mélange! **The result is a combination of historic and current values that only a mystic could sort out with precision.** [page 28, emphasis added]

BC202　In contrast, if all of the interests in the business were acquired in a single purchase, the process of assigning that current purchase price generally resulted in the assets and liabilities being measured and recognised at their acquisition-date fair values. Thus, the reported amounts of assets and liabilities differed depending on whether an acquirer purchased all of the equity interests in an acquiree in one transaction or in multiple transactions.

BC203　The boards concluded that measuring assets acquired or liabilities assumed at amounts other than their fair values at the acquisition date does not faithfully represent their economic values or the acquirer's economic circumstances resulting from the business combination. As discussed in paragraph BC37, an important purpose of financial statements is to provide users with relevant and reliable information about the performance of the entity and the resources under its control. That applies regardless of the extent of the ownership interest a parent holds in a particular subsidiary. The boards concluded that measurement at fair value enables users to make a better assessment of the cash-generating abilities of the identifiable net assets acquired in the business combination and the accountability of management

---

15　Subsequently, the AIMR changed its name to the CFA Institute. References to the organisation in this Basis for Conclusions use its name at the date it published a particular paper.

　© IFRS Foundation

for the resources entrusted to it. Thus, the fair value measurement principle in the revised standards will improve the completeness, reliability and relevance of the information reported in an acquirer's financial statements. The boards also concluded that application of that measurement principle should not impose undue incremental costs on entities because it was also necessary to measure the fair values of assets acquired and liabilities assumed under the provisions of IFRS 3 and SFAS 141, even though those fair values were not always the amounts at which assets and liabilities were recognised.

BC204 Thus, the revised standards reflect the decisions of the IASB and the FASB to develop a standard (and related application guidance) for measuring assets acquired and liabilities assumed in a business combination that:

(a) is consistent with the general principle of initially measuring assets acquired and liabilities assumed at their fair values, thereby improving the relevance and comparability of the resulting information about the assets acquired and liabilities assumed;

(b) eliminates inconsistencies and other deficiencies of the purchase price allocation process, including those in acquisitions of businesses that occur in stages and those in which the acquirer obtains a business without purchasing all, or perhaps any, of the acquiree's equity interests on the acquisition date; and

(c) can be applied in practice with a reasonably high degree of consistency and without imposing undue costs.

Non-controlling interests

BC205 The 2005 Exposure Draft proposed that a non-controlling interest in an acquiree should be determined as the sum of the non-controlling interest's proportional interest in the identifiable assets acquired and liabilities assumed plus the non-controlling interest's share of goodwill. Thus, because goodwill is measured as a residual, the amount recognised for a non-controlling interest in an acquiree would also have been a residual. Also, an important issue in deciding how to measure a non-controlling interest was whether its share of goodwill should be recognised (often referred to as the 'full goodwill versus partial goodwill issue'). In developing the 2005 Exposure Draft, the boards concluded that it should be recognised (in other words, they selected the 'full goodwill' alternative).

BC206 In redeliberating the 2005 Exposure Draft, the boards observed that they had specified the mechanics of determining the reported amount of a non-controlling interest but had not identified its measurement attribute. The result of those mechanics would have been that the non-controlling interest was effectively measured as the 'final residual' in a business combination. That is to say, the reported amount of the non-controlling interest depended on the amount of goodwill attributed to it, and goodwill is measured as a residual. Thus, in a sense, a non-controlling interest would have been the residual after allocating the residual, or the residual of a residual.

BC207   The boards concluded that, in principle, it is undesirable to have two residual amounts in accounting for a business combination. They also observed that goodwill cannot be measured as other than as a residual; measuring the fair value of goodwill directly would not be possible. In contrast, an acquirer can measure the fair value of a non-controlling interest, for example, on the basis of market prices for the shares held by non-controlling shareholders or by applying another valuation technique. The non-controlling interest in the acquiree is a component of a business combination in which less than 100 per cent of the equity interests are acquired, and the boards concluded that, in concept, the non-controlling interest, like other components of the combination, should be measured at fair value. The boards concluded that the decision-usefulness of information about a non-controlling interest would be improved if the revised standards specified a measurement attribute for a non-controlling interest rather than merely mechanics for determining that amount. They also concluded that, in principle, the measurement attribute should be fair value. The boards also understand from consultation with some constituents who use financial statements for making (or making recommendations about) investment decisions that information about the acquisition-date fair value of a non-controlling interest would be helpful in estimating the value of shares of the parent company, not only at the acquisition date but also at future dates.

BC208   The boards also observed that a non-controlling interest is a component of equity in the acquirer's consolidated financial statements and that measuring a non-controlling interest at its acquisition-date fair value is consistent with the way in which other components of equity are measured. For example, outstanding shares of the parent company, including shares issued to former owners of an acquiree to effect a business combination, were measured in the financial statements at their fair value (market price) on the date they were issued. Accordingly, the fair value measurement principle in SFAS 141(R) applies to a non-controlling interest in an acquiree, and the revised IFRS 3 permits an acquirer to measure a non-controlling interest in an acquiree at its acquisition-date fair value.

IFRS 3's choice of measurement basis for a non-controlling interest

BC209   The IASB concluded that, in principle, an acquirer should measure all components of a business combination, including any non-controlling interest in an acquiree, at their acquisition-date fair values. However, the revised IFRS 3 permits an acquirer to choose whether to measure any non-controlling interest in an acquiree at its fair value or as the non-controlling interests' proportionate share of the acquiree's identifiable net assets.

BC210   Introducing a choice of measurement basis for non-controlling interests was not the IASB's first preference. In general, the IASB believes that alternative accounting methods reduce the comparability of financial statements. However, the IASB was not able to agree on a single measurement basis for non-controlling interests because neither of the alternatives considered (fair value and proportionate share of the acquiree's identifiable net assets) was supported by enough board members to enable a revised business combinations standard to be issued. The IASB decided to permit a choice of measurement basis for non-controlling interests because it concluded that the benefits of the other improvements to, and the convergence of, the accounting for business combinations developed in this project outweigh the disadvantages of allowing this particular option.

BC211　The following sections (a) provide additional information about the measurement alternatives considered by the IASB, (b) summarise the main effects of permitting a choice in measurement basis and (c) discuss the effect on convergence.

Measurement alternatives

BC212　Although the IASB supports the principle of measuring all components of a business combination at fair value, support for that principle was not unanimous. Some IASB members did not support that principle because it would require measuring non-controlling interests at fair value. For that reason, those IASB members supported making an exception to the measurement principle for the non-controlling interest in an acquiree.

BC213　Some other IASB members supported an exception for the non-controlling interest for different reasons. Some advocated an exception on the basis that they did not have sufficient evidence to assess the marginal benefits of reporting the acquisition-date fair value of non-controlling interests. Those members concluded that, generally, the fair value of the non-controlling interest could be measured reliably, but they noted that it would be more costly to do so than measuring it at its proportionate share of the acquiree's identifiable net assets. Those members observed that many respondents had indicated that they saw little information of value in the reported non-controlling interest, no matter how it is measured.

BC214　Those IASB members who did not support making an exception concluded that the marginal benefits of reporting the acquisition-date fair value of non-controlling interests exceed the marginal costs of measuring it.

BC215　The IASB considered making it a requirement to measure non-controlling interests at fair value unless doing so would impose undue cost or effort on the acquirer. However, feedback from constituents and staff research indicated that it was unlikely that the term *undue cost or effort* would be applied consistently. Therefore, such a requirement would be unlikely to increase appreciably the consistency with which different entities measured non-controlling interests.

BC216　The IASB reluctantly concluded that the only way the revised IFRS 3 would receive sufficient votes to be issued was if it permitted an acquirer to measure a non-controlling interest either at fair value or at its proportionate share of the acquiree's identifiable net assets, on a transaction-by-transaction basis.

Effects of the optional measurement of non-controlling interests

BC217　The IASB noted that there are likely to be three main differences in outcome that occur when the non-controlling interest is measured as its proportionate share of the acquiree's identifiable net assets, rather than at fair value. First, the amounts recognised in a business combination for non-controlling interests and goodwill are likely to be lower (and these should be the only two items affected on initial recognition). Second, if a cash-generating unit is subsequently impaired, any resulting impairment of goodwill recognised through income is likely to be lower than it would have been if the non-controlling interest had been measured at fair value (although it does not affect the impairment loss attributable to the controlling interest).

BC218   The third difference arises if the acquirer subsequently purchases some (or all) of the shares held by the non-controlling shareholders. If the non-controlling interests are acquired, presumably at fair value, the equity of the group is reduced by the non-controlling interests' share of any unrecognised changes in the fair value of the net assets of the business, including goodwill. If the non-controlling interest is measured initially as a proportionate share of the acquiree's identifiable net assets, rather than at fair value, that reduction in the reported equity attributable to the acquirer is likely to be larger. This matter was considered further in the IASB's deliberations on the proposed amendments to IAS 27.[16]

Convergence

BC219   Both boards decided that, although they would have preferred to have a common measurement attribute for non-controlling interests, they had considered and removed as many differences between IFRS 3 and SFAS 141 as was practicable.

BC220   The boards were unable to achieve convergence of their respective requirements in several areas because of existing differences between IFRSs and US GAAP requirements outside a business combination. The boards observed that the accounting for impairments in IFRSs is different from that in US GAAP. This means that even if the boards converged on the initial measurement of non-controlling interests, and therefore goodwill, the subsequent accounting for goodwill would not have converged. Although this is not a good reason for allowing divergence in the initial measurement of non-controlling interests, it was a mitigating factor.

BC221   Because most business combinations do not involve a non-controlling interest, the boards also observed that the revised standards will align most of the accounting for most business combinations regardless of the different accounting for non-controlling interests in the revised standards.

Subsequent improvements to IFRS 3

BC221A In *Improvements to IFRSs* issued in May 2010, the Board addressed a concern that permitting the measurement choice for certain components of non-controlling interest might result in inappropriate measurement of those components in some circumstances. The Board decided to limit the choice to non-controlling interests that are present ownership instruments and entitle their holders to a proportionate share of the entity's net assets in the event of liquidation. The amendment requires the acquirer to measure all other

---

16   The consolidation requirements in IAS 27 were superseded by IFRS 10 *Consolidated Financial Statements* issued in May 2011. The requirements with respect to transactions between owners in their capacity as owners did not change.

components of non-controlling interest at the acquisition-date fair value, unless IFRSs require another measurement basis. For example, if a share-based payment transaction is classified as equity, an entity measures it in accordance with IFRS 2 *Share-based Payment*. Without this amendment, if the acquirer chose to measure non-controlling interest at its proportionate share of the acquiree's identifiable net assets, the acquirer might have measured some equity instruments at nil. In the Board's view, this would result in not recognising economic interests that other parties have in the acquiree. Therefore, the Board amended IFRS 3 to limit the scope of the measurement choice.

Measuring assets and liabilities arising from contingencies, including subsequent measurement

BC222   FASB Statement No. 5 *Accounting for Contingencies* (SFAS 5) defines a *contingency* as an existing condition, situation or set of circumstances involving uncertainty as to possible gain or loss to an entity that will ultimately be resolved when one or more future events occur or fail to occur. SFAS 141(R) refers to the assets and liabilities to which contingencies relate as *assets and liabilities arising from contingencies*. For ease of discussion, this Basis for Conclusions also uses that term to refer broadly to the issues related to contingencies, including the issues that the IASB considered in developing its requirements on recognising and measuring contingent liabilities in a business combination (paragraphs BC242–BC245 and BC272–BC278).

BC223   The revised standards require the assets and liabilities arising from contingencies that are recognised as of the acquisition date to be measured at their acquisition-date fair values. That requirement is generally consistent with the measurement requirements of IFRS 3, but it represents a change in the way entities generally applied SFAS 141. In addition, the IASB's measurement guidance on contingent liabilities carries forward the related guidance in IFRS 3, pending completion of the project to revise IAS 37 (paragraphs BC272–BC276). Accordingly, the FASB's and the IASB's conclusions on measuring assets and liabilities arising from contingencies are discussed separately.

The FASB's conclusions on measuring assets and liabilities arising from contingencies

BC224   The amount of an asset or a liability arising from a contingency recognised in accordance with SFAS 141 was seldom the acquisition-date fair value. Rather, it was often the settlement amount or a best estimate of the expected settlement amount on the basis of circumstances existing at a date after the acquisition date.

BC225   In developing the 2005 Exposure Draft, the FASB considered whether to require a strict SFAS 5 approach for the initial measurement and recognition of all contingencies in a business combination. That would mean that contingencies that did not meet the SFAS 5 'probability' criterion would be measured at zero (or at a minimum amount that qualifies as probable) rather than at fair value. Some constituents said that applying SFAS 5 in accounting for a business combination might be a practical way to reduce the costs and measurement difficulties involved in obtaining the information and legal counsel needed to measure the fair value of numerous contingencies that the acquiree had not recognised in accordance with SFAS 5.

BC226　The FASB observed that paragraph 17(a) of SFAS 5 states that 'Contingencies that might result in gains usually are not reflected in the accounts since to do so might be to recognize revenue prior to its realization.' Thus, to apply SFAS 5 in accounting for a business combination in the same way it is applied in other situations was likely to result in non-recognition of gain contingencies, including those for which all of the needed information is available at the acquisition date. The FASB concluded that that would be a step backwards; SFAS 141 already required the recognition of gain contingencies at the acquisition date and for which fair value is determinable (paragraphs 39 and 40(a) of SFAS 141). Also, in accordance with SFAS 5's requirements, contingent losses that arise outside a business combination are not recognised unless there is a high likelihood of a future outflow of resources. In addition, because goodwill is calculated as a residual, omitting an asset for an identifiable contingent gain would also result in overstating goodwill. Similarly, omitting a liability for a contingent loss would result in understating goodwill. Thus, the FASB rejected the SFAS 5 approach in accounting for a business combination.

BC227　The FASB also considered but rejected retaining existing practice based on FASB Statement No. 38 *Accounting for Preacquisition Contingencies of Purchased Enterprises* (SFAS 38), which SFAS 141 carried forward without reconsideration. For the reasons described in the preceding paragraph, the FASB concluded that continuing to permit the delayed recognition of most assets and liabilities arising from contingencies that occurred in applying SFAS 141 and the related guidance would fail to bring about needed improvements in the accounting for business combinations. The FASB decided that requiring an acquirer to measure at fair value and recognise any assets and liabilities arising from contingencies that meet the conceptual elements definition would help bring about those needed improvements, in particular, improvements in the completeness of reported financial information.

BC228　Some respondents to the 2005 Exposure Draft were concerned about the ability to measure reliably the fair value of assets and liabilities arising from contingencies at the acquisition date. The FASB concluded that measuring the fair value of an asset or a liability arising from a contractual contingency with sufficient reliability as of the acquisition date should not be more difficult than measuring the fair value of many other assets and liabilities that the revised standards require to be measured at fair value as of that date. The terms of the contract, together with information developed during the acquisition process, for example, to determine the price to be paid, should provide the needed information. Sufficient information is also likely to be available to measure the acquisition-date fair value of assets and liabilities arising from non-contractual contingencies that satisfy the more-likely-than-not criterion (see paragraphs BC270 and BC271). The FASB acknowledges that non-contractual assets and liabilities that do not meet that criterion at the acquisition date are most likely to raise difficult measurement issues and concerns about the reliability of those measures. To address those reliability concerns, the FASB decided that an acquirer should not measure and recognise such assets and liabilities. Rather, assets and liabilities arising from non-contractual contingencies that do not satisfy the more-likely-than-not criterion at the acquisition date are accounted for in accordance with other US GAAP, including SFAS 5.

BC229   The FASB also observed that respondents who are concerned about the reliability with which the fair values of assets and liabilities arising from contingencies can be measured may be interpreting *reliable measurement* differently from the FASB. To determine a reliable measure of the fair value of a contingency, the acquirer need not be able to determine, predict or otherwise know the ultimate settlement amount of that contingency at the acquisition date (or within the measurement period) with certainty or precision.

BC230   In 2006 the FASB and the IASB published for comment the first discussion paper in their joint project to improve their respective conceptual frameworks. Paragraph QC21 of that paper—*Preliminary Views on an improved Conceptual Framework for Financial Reporting: The Objective of Financial Reporting and Qualitative Characteristics of Decision-useful Financial Reporting Information*—discusses the relationship between faithful representation, the quality of decision-useful financial reporting information that pertains to the reliability of information, and precision. It says that accuracy of estimates is desirable and some minimum level of accuracy is necessary for an estimate to be a faithful representation of an economic phenomenon. However, faithful representation implies neither absolute precision in the estimate nor certainty about the outcome.

BC231   The FASB concluded that the fair values of assets and liabilities arising from contingencies meeting the recognition criteria of SFAS 141(R) are measurable with sufficient reliability as of the acquisition date for recognition in accounting for a business combination if the estimates are based on the appropriate inputs and each input reflects the best available information about that factor. The FASB acknowledges that the fair value measured at the acquisition date will not be the amount for which the asset or liability is ultimately settled, but it provides information about the current value of an asset or a liability by incorporating uncertainty into the measure.

Subsequent measurement of assets and liabilities arising from contingencies

BC232   The FASB observed that applying SFAS 5 in the post-combination period to a recognised liability or asset arising from a contingency that did not meet the SFAS 5 probability threshold at the acquisition date would result in derecognising that liability or asset and reporting a gain or loss in income of the post-combination period. That result would not faithfully represent the economic events occurring in that period. The FASB noted that similar concerns about the potential for misleading reporting consequences do not exist for many financial instruments arising from contingencies, such as options, forward contracts and other derivatives. Such assets and liabilities generally would continue to be measured at fair value in accordance with other applicable US GAAP, which also provides guidance on how to report subsequent changes in the fair values of financial instruments in earnings or comprehensive income. Thus, the FASB decided that it must address the subsequent measurement of assets and liabilities arising from contingencies recognised in a business combination. However, it limited the scope of that effort to assets and liabilities that would be subsequently subject to SFAS 5.

BC233 The FASB considered five alternatives for subsequent measurement of assets and liabilities arising from contingencies that would be subject to SFAS 5 if not acquired or assumed in a business combination:

> Alternative 1— Subsequently measuring at fair value
>
> Alternative 2—Subsequently reporting amounts initially recognised in a business combination at their acquisition-date fair values until the acquirer obtains new information about the possible outcome of the contingency. When new information is obtained the acquirer evaluates that new information and measures a liability at the **higher** of its acquisition-date fair value or the amount that would be recognised if applying SFAS 5 and an asset at the **lower** of its acquisition-date fair value or the best estimate of its future settlement amount
>
> Alternative 3—'Freezing' amounts initially recognised in a business combination
>
> Alternative 4—Applying an interest allocation method (similar to the model in FASB Statement No. 143 *Accounting for Asset Retirement Obligations* (SFAS 143))
>
> Alternative 5—Applying a deferred revenue method, but only to those items that relate to revenue-generating activities.

BC234 Paragraphs BC224–BC231 discuss the reasons for the FASB's decision to require fair value measurement for initial recognition of assets and liabilities arising from contingencies. For many of those same reasons, the FASB considered requiring Alternative 1—subsequent measurement at fair value. For a variety of reasons, the FASB ultimately rejected that alternative. Adopting this alternative would mean that for some entities (maybe many entities) assets and liabilities arising from contingencies acquired in a business combination would be reported at fair value, while other similar assets and liabilities would be reported at SFAS 5 amounts—different measurement of similar assets and liabilities would make financial reports more difficult to understand. The FASB noted that a project on business combinations would not be the appropriate place to address broadly perceived deficiencies in SFAS 5. Moreover, at the same time as SFAS 141(R) was finalised, the FASB was considering adding a project to its technical agenda to reconsider comprehensively the accounting for contingencies in SFAS 5. (The FASB added a project to reconsider the accounting for contingencies to its agenda in September 2007.) The FASB concluded that requiring assets and liabilities arising from contingencies to be subsequently measured at fair value was premature and might prejudge the outcome of its deliberations in that project.

BC235   The FASB decided, as a practical alternative, to require Alternative 2. In accordance with that approach, the acquirer continues to report an asset or liability arising from a contingency recognised as of the acquisition date at its acquisition-date fair value in the absence of new information about the possible outcome of the contingency. When such new information is obtained, the acquirer evaluates that information and measures the asset or liability as follows:

(a)   a liability is measured at the **higher** of:

    (i)   its acquisition-date fair value; and

    (ii)   the amount that would be recognised if applying SFAS 5.

(b)   an asset is measured at the **lower** of:

    (i)   its acquisition-date fair value; and

    (ii)   the best estimate of its future settlement amount.

BC236   The FASB concluded that this alternative was a practical bridge between improved reporting at the acquisition date and subsequent accounting under the existing requirements of SFAS 5. It would not prejudge the outcome of deliberations that the FASB will have in a project to reconsider SFAS 5. It also addressed the concerns of some constituents that requiring contingencies to be subsequently measured at fair value would result in contingencies acquired or assumed in a business combination being measured differently from contingencies that arise outside of a business combination.

BC237   The FASB observed that this alternative provides slightly different guidance for liabilities from its guidance for assets. Unlike liabilities, it could not require assets to be measured at the lower of their acquisition-date fair values or *the amounts that would be recognised if applying* SFAS 5. Because SFAS 5 does not allow recognition of gain contingencies, the amount that would be recognised by applying SFAS 5 to an asset would be zero. Thus, the FASB decided that an asset arising from a contingency should be measured at the lower of its acquisition-date fair value or *the best estimate of its future settlement amount.* The FASB believes that that measure is similar to the measure required by SFAS 5 for liabilities (loss contingencies). The FASB also observed that the approach for assets allows for the recognition of impairments to the asset; it requires an asset to be decreased to the current estimate of the amount the acquirer expects to collect.

BC238   The FASB rejected Alternative 3—freezing the amounts initially recognised. The FASB observed that this alternative results in less relevant information than Alternative 2. Because the FASB views Alternative 2 as a practical and operational solution, it saw no compelling reason to adopt a less optimal alternative. The FASB also rejected Alternative 4—the interest allocation method. In accordance with that method, the contingency would be remeasured using a convention similar to SFAS 143 whereby interest rates are held constant for initial cash flow assumptions. The FASB noted that the reasons for selecting the interest allocation method in SFAS 143 for long-term asset retirement obligations, including concerns about income statement volatility, are not compelling for contingencies such as warranties and pending litigation that generally have shorter lives.

BC239 In accordance with Alternative 5—the deferred revenue method—the acquisition-date fair value of a deferred revenue liability (performance obligation) would be amortised after the acquisition date, like the approach for separately priced extended warranties and product maintenance contracts acquired outside a business combination. Accruals would be added to the contingency for subsequent direct costs. The FASB acknowledged that the costs to apply that measurement approach would be lower than other measurement approaches. However, the FASB concluded that the potential reduction in costs does not justify (a) creating inconsistencies in the subsequent accounting for particular classes of contingencies acquired or assumed in a business combination and (b) the diminished relevance of the resulting information. Thus, the FASB also rejected Alternative 5. Some respondents to the 2005 Exposure Draft supported recognition of subsequent changes in the amounts recognised for assets and liabilities arising from contingencies either as adjustments to goodwill or in comprehensive income rather than in earnings. Some who favoured reporting such changes as adjustments to goodwill did so at least in part because of the difficulties they see in distinguishing between changes that result from changes in circumstances after the acquisition date and changes that pertain more to obtaining better information about circumstances that existed at that date. They noted that the latter are measurement period adjustments, many of which result in adjustments to goodwill.

BC240 The FASB understands that distinguishing between measurement period adjustments and other changes in the amounts of assets and liabilities arising from contingencies will sometimes be difficult. It observed, however, that similar difficulties exist for other assets acquired and liabilities assumed in a business combination; changes in the amounts of those assets and liabilities after the acquisition date are included in earnings. The FASB saw no compelling reason to treat items arising from contingencies differently.

BC241 Those who favoured reporting subsequent changes in the amounts recognised for assets and liabilities arising from contingencies in other comprehensive income rather than in earnings generally analogised to the present accounting for available-for-sale securities. They said that items arising from contingencies were not 'realised' until the contingency is resolved. The FASB rejected that alternative because it saw no compelling reason to add to the category of items that are initially recognised as other comprehensive income and later 'recycled' to earnings. The FASB considers reporting subsequent changes in the amounts of items arising from contingencies in earnings not only conceptually superior to reporting those changes only in comprehensive income but also consistent with the way in which other changes in amounts of items acquired or assumed in a business combination are recognised.

The IASB's conclusions on initial and subsequent measurement of contingent liabilities

BC242   As noted in paragraph BC223, the IASB's measurement guidance on contingencies carries forward the related guidance in IFRS 3 (except for clarifying that an acquirer cannot recognise a contingency that is not a liability), pending completion of the project to revise IAS 37. Accordingly, contingent liabilities recognised in a business combination are initially measured at their acquisition-date fair values.

BC243   In developing IFRS 3, the IASB observed that not specifying the subsequent accounting for contingent liabilities recognised in a business combination might result in inappropriately derecognising some or all of those contingent liabilities immediately after the combination.

BC244   In ED 3 the IASB proposed that a contingent liability recognised in a business combination should be excluded from the scope of IAS 37 and subsequently measured at fair value with changes in fair value recognised in profit or loss until the liability is settled or the uncertain future event described in the definition of a contingent liability is resolved. In considering respondents' comments on this issue, the IASB noted that subsequently measuring such contingent liabilities at fair value would be inconsistent with the conclusions it reached on the accounting for financial guarantees and commitments to provide loans at below-market interest rates when it revised IAS 39.[17]

BC245   The IASB decided to revise the proposal in ED 3 for consistency with IAS 39. Therefore, the revised IFRS 3 requires contingent liabilities recognised in a business combination to be measured after their initial recognition at the higher of:

(a)   the amount that would be recognised in accordance with IAS 37; and

(b)   the amount initially recognised less, when appropriate, cumulative amortisation recognised in accordance with IAS 18 *Revenue*.[18]

Definition of fair value[19]

BC246   The revised IFRS 3 and SFAS 141(R) each use the same definition of fair value that the IASB and the FASB respectively use in their other standards. Specifically, IAS 39[20] and other IFRSs define fair value as 'the amount for which an asset could be exchanged, or a liability settled, between knowledgeable, willing parties in an arm's length transaction' and the revised IFRS 3 uses that definition. SFAS 157, on the other hand, defines fair value as 'the price that would be received to sell an asset or paid to transfer a liability

---

17   IFRS 9 *Financial Instruments* relocated to IFRS 9 the requirements on the accounting for financial guarantees and commitments to provide loans at below-market interest rates.

18   IFRS 15 *Revenue from Contracts with Customers*, issued in May 2014, replaced IAS 18 *Revenue* and amended paragraph 56 of IFRS 3 for consistency with the requirements in IFRS 15.

19   IFRS 13, issued in May 2011, defines fair value.

20   IFRS 9 *Financial Instruments* replaced IAS 39. IFRS 9 applies to all items that were previously within the scope of IAS 39.

in an orderly transaction between market participants at the measurement date' and that definition is used in SFAS 141(R).[21]

BC247 The IASB considered also using the definition of fair value from SFAS 157 but decided that to do so would prejudge the outcome of its project on fair value measurements. Similarly, the FASB considered using the definition of fair value from IFRS 3 but decided that to do so would be inappropriate in the light of SFAS 157, which it intends for use in all situations in which a new standard requires measurement at fair value.

BC248 The boards acknowledge that the differing definitions of fair value might result in measuring the fair values of assets acquired and liabilities assumed in a business combination differently depending on whether the combination is accounted for in accordance with the revised IFRS 3 or SFAS 141(R). However, the boards consulted valuation experts on the likely effects of the differing definitions of fair value. As a result of that consultation, the boards understand that such differences are unlikely to occur often. The boards also observed that the definitions use different words to articulate essentially the same concepts in two general areas—the non-performance risk and credit standing of financial liabilities and the market-based measurement objective.

BC249 SFAS 157 defines non-performance risk as the risk that an obligation will not be fulfilled and indicates that it affects the fair value of a liability. Non-performance risk includes but may not be limited to the reporting entity's own credit risk. In comparison, IFRSs do not use the term *non-performance risk* in discussing the fair value of a liability. However, IAS 39 requires the fair value of a financial liability to reflect its credit risk. Although the words are different, the boards believe that the underlying concepts are essentially the same.

BC250 The definition of fair value from SFAS 157 indicates that it is a price in an orderly transaction between market participants. In comparison, IFRSs indicate that fair value reflects an arm's length transaction between knowledgeable, willing parties. Paragraphs 42–44 of IAS 40 discuss what a *transaction between knowledgeable, willing parties* means:

> ... In this context, 'knowledgeable' means that both the willing buyer and the willing seller are reasonably informed about the nature and characteristics of the investment property, its actual and potential uses, and market conditions at the end of the reporting period ...

> ... The willing seller is motivated to sell the investment property at market terms for the best price obtainable. The factual circumstances of the actual investment property owner are not a part of this consideration because the willing seller is a hypothetical owner (eg a willing seller would not take into account the particular tax circumstances of the investment property owner).

---

21 IFRS 13, issued in May 2011, is the result of the IASB's and the FASB's joint project on fair value measurement. As a result, the definition of fair value in IFRSs is identical to the definition in US GAAP (Topic 820 *Fair Value Measurement* in the *FASB Accounting Standards Codification* codified SFAS 157).

The definition of fair value refers to an arm's length transaction. An arm's length transaction is one between parties that do not have a particular or special relationship that makes prices of transactions uncharacteristic of market conditions. The transaction is presumed to be between unrelated parties, each acting independently.

Thus, although the two definitions use different words, the concept is the same — fair value is a market-based measure in a transaction between unrelated parties.

BC251 However, differences in the results of applying the different definitions of fair value may occur in particular areas. For example, SFAS 157 defines fair value as an exit price between market participants and IFRSs define fair value as an exchange price in an arm's length transaction. Most valuation experts the boards consulted said that, because transaction costs are not a component of fair value in either definition, an exit price for an asset or liability acquired or assumed in a business combination would differ from an exchange price (entry or exit) only (a) if the asset is acquired for its defensive value or (b) if a liability is measured on the basis of settling it with the creditor rather than transferring it to a third party. However, the boards understand that ways of measuring assets on the basis of their defensive value in accordance with paragraph A12 of SFAS 157 are developing, and it is too early to tell the significance of any differences that might result. It is also not clear that entities will use different methods of measuring the fair value of liabilities assumed in a business combination.

Measuring the acquisition-date fair values of particular assets acquired

Assets with uncertain cash flows (valuation allowances)

BC252 Both IFRS 3 and SFAS 141 required receivables to be measured at the present values of amounts to be received determined at appropriate current interest rates, less allowances for uncollectibility and collection costs, if necessary. The boards considered whether an exception to the fair value measurement principle is necessary for assets such as trade receivables and other short-term and long-term receivables acquired in a business combination. Several of the boards' constituents suggested that an exception should be permitted for practical and other reasons, including concerns about comparing credit losses on loans acquired in a business combination with those on originated loans. In developing the 2005 Exposure Draft, however, the boards saw no compelling reason for such an exception. The boards observed that using an acquiree's carrying basis and including collection costs is inconsistent with the revised standards' fair value measurement requirement and the underlying notion that the acquirer's initial measurement, recognition and classification of the assets acquired and liabilities assumed begins on the acquisition date. Because uncertainty about collections and future cash flows is included in the fair value measure of a receivable, the 2005 Exposure Draft proposed that the acquirer should not recognise a separate valuation allowance for acquired assets measured at fair value.

BC253   In developing the 2005 Exposure Draft, the FASB acknowledged that including uncertainties about future cash flows in a fair value measure, with no separate allowance for uncollectible amounts, differed from the current practice for SEC registrants. That practice was established in SEC Staff Accounting Bulletin Topic 2.A.5 *Adjustments to Allowances for Loan Losses in Connection with Business Combinations* which states that generally the acquirer's estimation of the uncollectible portion of the acquiree's loans should not change from the acquiree's estimation before the acquisition. However, the FASB also observed that fair value measurement is consistent with guidance in AICPA Statement of Position 03-3 *Accounting for Certain Loans or Debt Securities Acquired in a Transfer* (AICPA SOP 03-3), which prohibits 'carrying over' or creating valuation allowances in the initial accounting of all loans acquired in transfers that are within its scope, including business combinations accounted for as an acquisition.

BC254   In developing the 2005 Exposure Draft, the boards also acknowledged that the fair value measurement approach has implications for the capital requirements for financial institutions, particularly banks. The boards noted, however, that regulatory reporting requirements are a separate matter that is beyond the scope of general purpose financial reporting.

BC255   Some respondents to the 2005 Exposure Draft who commented on this issue agreed with the proposal, but many who commented on it disagreed with not recognising a separate valuation allowance for receivables and similar assets. Some of those respondents favoured retaining the guidance in IFRS 3 and SFAS 141. They said that the costs of measuring the fair value of trade receivables, loans, receivables under financing leases and the like would be high; they did not think the related benefits would justify those costs. Some also said that software systems currently available for loans and other receivables do not provide for separate accounting for acquired and originated loans; they have to account manually for loans to which AICPA SOP 03-3 applies, incurring significant costs to do so.

BC256   As they did in developing the 2005 Exposure Draft, the boards acknowledged that the requirement to measure receivables and similar assets at fair value with no separate valuation allowance may lead to additional costs for some entities. However, the boards observed that entities that apply IAS 39[22] are required to measure financial assets acquired outside a business combination, as well as those originated, at fair value on initial recognition. The boards do not think financial or other assets should be measured differently because of the nature of the transaction in which they are acquired. Because the boards saw no compelling reason to provide an exception to the measurement principle for receivables or other assets with credit risk, they affirmed their conclusion that the benefits of measuring receivables and similar assets at fair value justify the related costs.

---

22   IFRS 9 *Financial Instruments* replaced IAS 39. IFRS 9 applies to all items that were previously within the scope of IAS 39.

BC257   Some respondents to the 2005 Exposure Draft said that separate recognition of valuation allowances for loans and similar assets was important to users in evaluating the credit assumptions built into loan valuations. They suggested that the fair value of receivables should be split into three components: (a) the gross contractual amounts, (b) a separate discount or premium for changes in interest rates and (c) a valuation allowance for the credit risk, which would be based on the contractual cash flows expected to be uncollectible. In evaluating that alternative presentation, the boards noted that the valuation allowance presented would differ from the valuation allowance for receivables under IAS 39 and SFAS 5, each of which is determined on the basis of incurred, rather than expected, losses. Thus, how to determine the valuation allowance on an ongoing basis would be problematic. For example, if requirements for other receivables were applied, an immediate gain would be recognised for the difference between incurred losses and expected losses. In contrast, if the valuation allowance for receivables acquired by transfer, including in a business combination, rather than by origination was determined subsequently on an expected loss basis, the result would be a new accounting model for those receivables. The boards concluded that this project is not the place to consider the broader issues of how best to determine the valuation allowances for receivables, regardless of the manner in which the receivables are acquired.

Disclosure of information about receivables acquired

BC258   Some constituents asked the boards to consider requiring additional disclosures about receivables measured at fair value to help in assessing considerations of credit quality included in the fair value measures, including expectations about receivables that will be uncollectible. Those constituents were concerned that without additional disclosure, it would be impossible to determine the contractual cash flows and the amount of the contractual cash flows not expected to be collected if receivables were recognised at fair value. In response to those comments, the boards decided to require disclosure of the fair value of receivables acquired, the gross contractual amounts receivable and the best estimate at the acquisition date of the contractual cash flows not expected to be collected. The disclosures are required for each major class of receivable.

BC259   In January 2007 the FASB added a project to its technical agenda to improve disclosures relating to the allowance for credit losses associated with financing receivables. As part of that project, the FASB is considering potential new disclosures and enhanced current disclosures about the credit quality of an entity's portfolio, the entity's credit risk exposures, its accounting policies on valuation allowances and possibly other areas.

BC260   The boards observed that the work involved in developing a complete set of credit quality disclosures to be made for receivables acquired in a business combination would be similar to that required in the FASB's disclosure project related to valuation allowances. Combining those efforts would be a more efficient use of resources. Accordingly, the FASB decided to include disclosures that should be made in a business combination in the scope of its project on disclosures related to valuation allowances and credit quality, and the IASB will monitor that project. In the interim, the disclosures required by the revised standards (paragraph B64(h) of the revised IFRS 3) will provide at least some, although perhaps not all, of the information users need to evaluate the credit quality of receivables acquired.

Assets that the acquirer intends not to use or to use in a way that is different from the way other market participants would use them

BC261   While the revised standards were being developed, the FASB received enquiries about inconsistencies in practice in accordance with SFAS 141 related to measuring particular intangible assets that an acquirer intends not to use or intends to use in a way different from the way other market participants would use them. For example, if the acquirer did not intend to use a brand name acquired in a business combination, some entities assigned no value to the asset and other entities measured it at the amount at which market participants could be expected to exchange the asset, ie at its fair value.

BC262   To avoid such inconsistencies in practice, the boards decided to clarify the measurement of assets that an acquirer intends not to use (paragraph B43 of the revised IFRS 3). The intention of both IFRS 3 and SFAS 141 was that assets, both tangible and intangible, should be measured at their fair values regardless of how or whether the acquirer intends to use them. The FASB observed that measuring such assets in accordance with their highest and best use is consistent with SFAS 157. Paragraph A12 of SFAS 157 illustrates determining the fair value of an in-process research and development project acquired in a business combination that the acquirer does not intend to complete. The IASB understands from its consultation with preparers, valuation experts and auditors that IFRS 3 was applied in the way the revised standards require.[23]

Exceptions to the recognition or measurement principle

BC263   As indicated in paragraphs 14 and 20 of the revised IFRS 3, the revised standards include limited exceptions to its recognition and measurement principles. Paragraphs BC265–BC311 discuss the types of identifiable assets and liabilities for which exceptions are provided and the reasons for those exceptions.

BC264   It is important to note that not every item that falls into a particular type of asset or liability is an exception to either the recognition or the measurement principle (or both). For example, contingent liabilities are identified as an exception to the recognition principle because the revised IFRS 3 includes a recognition condition for them in addition to the recognition conditions in paragraphs 11 and 12. Although applying that additional condition will result in not recognising some contingent liabilities, those that meet the additional condition will be recognised in accordance with the recognition principle. Another example is employee benefits, which are identified as a type of asset or liability for which exceptions to both the recognition and the measurement

---

23   IFRS 13, issued in May 2011, describes the concept of highest and best use and provides examples of its application in a business combination.

principles are provided. As discussed further in paragraphs BC296–BC300, the acquirer is required to recognise and measure liabilities and any related assets resulting from the acquiree's employee benefit arrangements in accordance with IAS 19 *Employee Benefits* rather than by applying the recognition and measurement principles in the revised IFRS 3. Applying the requirements of IAS 19 will result in recognising many, if not most, types of employee benefit liabilities in the same way as would result from applying the recognition principle (see paragraph BC297). However, others, for example withdrawal liabilities from multi-employer plans for entities applying US GAAP, are not necessarily consistent with the recognition principle. In addition, applying the requirements of IAS 19 generally will result in measuring liabilities for employee benefits (and any related assets) on a basis other than their acquisition-date fair values. However, applying the requirements of SFAS 146 to one-off termination benefits results in measuring liabilities for those benefits at their acquisition-date fair values.

Exceptions to the recognition principle

Liabilities and contingent liabilities within the scope of IAS 37 or IFRIC 21 (paragraphs 21A–21C)

BC264A   Paragraph 11 of IFRS 3 specifies that, to qualify for recognition at the acquisition date, the identifiable assets acquired and liabilities assumed must meet the definitions of assets and liabilities in the 2018 *Conceptual Framework*. Paragraph 54 of IFRS 3 specifies that after the acquisition date, an entity generally accounts for those assets and liabilities in accordance with other applicable IFRS Standards for those items.

BC264B   As a result of applying the definition of a liability in the 2018 *Conceptual Framework*, an acquirer might recognise at the acquisition date a liability to pay a levy that it would not recognise subsequently when applying IFRIC 21 *Levies*. This difference arises because an entity might recognise a liability earlier applying the 2018 *Conceptual Framework*. Applying IFRIC 21, an entity recognises a liability to pay a levy only when it conducts the activity that triggers the payment of the levy, whereas applying the 2018 *Conceptual Framework*, an entity recognises a liability when it conducts an earlier activity if:

(a)   conducting that earlier activity means the entity may have to pay a levy it would not otherwise have had to pay; and

(b)   the entity has no practical ability to avoid the later activity that will trigger payment of the levy.

BC264C   If an acquirer recognised a liability to pay a levy at the acquisition date when applying the 2018 *Conceptual Framework* and derecognised the liability immediately afterwards when applying IFRIC 21, it would recognise a so-called *Day 2 gain*. This recognised gain would not depict an economic gain, so would not faithfully represent any aspect of the entity's financial performance.

BC264D   The IASB noted that IFRIC 21 is an interpretation of IAS 37, and so concluded that the problem of *Day 2 gains* could arise not only for levies within the scope of IFRIC 21 but also for other obligations within the scope of IAS 37. To avoid this problem, the IASB added paragraph 21B to IFRS 3. This paragraph makes an exception from the requirements of paragraph 11 for liabilities and contingent liabilities that would be within the scope of IAS 37 or IFRIC 21 if incurred separately, rather than assumed in a business combination. The exception requires an entity to apply criteria in IAS 37 or IFRIC 21 respectively to determine whether a present obligation exists at the acquisition date. The exception refers to IFRIC 21 as well as IAS 37 because, although IFRIC 21 is an interpretation of IAS 37, it also applies to levies whose timing and amount are certain and so are outside the scope of IAS 37.

BC264E   A present obligation identified applying the exception in paragraph 21B of IFRS 3 might meet the definition of a contingent liability. This will be the case if it is not probable that an outflow of resources embodying economic benefits will be required to settle the obligation, or if the amount of the obligation cannot be measured with sufficient reliability. The IASB added paragraph 21C to IFRS 3 to clarify that, if the present obligation identified applying paragraph 21B meets the definition of a contingent liability, paragraph 23 of IFRS 3 also applies to that contingent liability.

Assets and liabilities arising from contingencies (paragraphs 22–23A)

BC265   Both the FASB's conclusions on recognising assets and liabilities arising from contingencies and the IASB's conclusions on recognising contingent liabilities resulted in exceptions to the recognition principle in the revised standards because both will result in some items being unrecognised at the acquisition date. However, the details of the exceptions differ. The reasons for those exceptions and the differences between them are discussed in paragraphs BC266–BC278.

The FASB's conclusions on assets and liabilities arising from contingencies

BC266   SFAS 141 carried forward without reconsideration the requirements of SFAS 38, which required an acquirer to include in the purchase price allocation the fair value of an acquiree's contingencies if their fair value could be determined during the allocation period. For those contingencies whose fair value could not be determined during the allocation period, SFAS 141 required the acquirer to recognise the contingency in earnings when the occurrence of the contingency became probable and its amount could be reasonably estimated.

BC267   Members of its resource group and others told the FASB that in practice acquirers often did not recognise an acquiree's assets and liabilities arising from contingencies at the acquisition date. Instead, contingencies were recognised after the acquisition date at an amount determined at that later date either because their amount could not be 'reasonably estimated' or because the contingency was determined not to meet the SFAS 5 'probability' criterion for recognition.

BC268   The 2005 Exposure Draft proposed that an acquirer should recognise all assets and liabilities arising from an acquiree's contingencies if they meet the definition of an asset or a liability in the FASB's Concepts Statement 6 regardless of whether a contingency meets the recognition criteria in SFAS 5. The FASB, like the IASB, concluded that to represent faithfully the economic circumstances at the acquisition date, in principle, all identifiable assets acquired and liabilities assumed should be recognised separately from goodwill, including assets and liabilities arising from contingencies at the acquisition date.

BC269   Respondents to the 2005 Exposure Draft that apply US GAAP expressed concern about how to deal with uncertainty about whether and when a contingency gives rise to an asset or a liability that meets the definition in the FASB's Concepts Statement 6, referred to as *element uncertainty*. An example cited by some respondents involved an acquiree's negotiations with another party at the acquisition date for reimbursement of costs incurred on the other party's behalf. How should the acquirer determine whether that contingency gave rise to an asset that should be recognised as part of the accounting for the business combination? Respondents suggested several means of dealing with element uncertainty, which generally involved introducing a threshold either for all contingencies or for the non-contractual contingencies an acquirer is required to recognise at the acquisition date. Other respondents suggested requiring recognition of only those assets and liabilities arising from contingencies whose fair values can be reliably determined, which would be similar to the requirements of SFAS 141.

BC270   The FASB understands the potential difficulty of resolving element uncertainty, especially for assets or liabilities arising from non-contractual contingencies. It considered whether to deal with element uncertainty by requiring assets and liabilities arising from contingencies to be recognised only if their fair values are reliably measurable. The FASB concluded that applying the guidance in SFAS 157 on measuring fair value should result in an estimate of the fair value of assets and liabilities arising from contingencies that is sufficiently reliable for recognition. The FASB also observed that adding a measurement condition is an indirect way of dealing with uncertainty involving recognition; it would be better to deal with such uncertainty more directly.

BC271   The FASB concluded that most cases of significant uncertainty about whether a potential asset or liability arising from a contingency meets the pertinent definition (element uncertainty) are likely to involve non-contractual contingencies. To help preparers and their auditors deal with element uncertainty, the FASB decided to add a requirement for the acquirer to assess whether it is **more likely than not** that the contingency gives rise to an asset or a liability as defined in the FASB's Concepts Statement 6. For an asset arising from a contingency, applying that criterion focuses on whether it is more likely than not that the acquirer has obtained control of a future economic benefit as a result of a past transaction or other event. For a liability, the more-likely-than-not criterion focuses on whether the acquirer has a present obligation to sacrifice future economic benefits as a result of a past transaction or other event. If that criterion is met at the acquisition date, the acquirer recognises the asset or liability, measured at its acquisition-date fair value, as part of the accounting for the business combination. If that criterion is not met at the acquisition date, the acquirer accounts for the non-contractual contingency in accordance with other US GAAP, including SFAS 5, as appropriate. The FASB concluded that adding the more-likely-than-not criterion would permit acquirers to focus their efforts on the more readily identifiable contingencies of acquirees, thereby avoiding spending disproportionate amounts of time searching for contingencies that, even if identified, would have less significant effects.

The IASB's conclusions on contingent liabilities and contingent assets

BC272 In developing the 2005 Exposure Draft, the IASB concluded that an asset or a liability should be recognised separately from goodwill if it satisfies the definitions in the *Framework*. In some cases, the amount of the future economic benefits embodied in the asset or required to settle the liability is contingent (or conditional) on the occurrence or non-occurrence of one or more uncertain future events. That uncertainty is reflected in measurement. The FASB reached a consistent conclusion.

BC273 At the same time as it published the 2005 Exposure Draft, the IASB also published for comment a separate exposure draft containing similar proposals on the accounting for contingent assets and contingent liabilities within the scope of IAS 37. At that time, the IASB expected that the effective date of the revised IAS 37 would be the same as the effective date of the revised IFRS 3. However, the IASB now expects to issue a revised IAS 37 at a later date. Accordingly, except for clarifying that an acquirer should not recognise a so-called contingent liability that is not an obligation at the acquisition date, the IASB decided to carry forward the related requirements in the original IFRS 3. The IASB expects to reconsider and, if necessary, amend the requirements in the revised IFRS 3 when it issues the revised IAS 37.

BC274 The IASB concluded that an acquirer should recognise a contingent liability assumed in a business combination only if it satisfies the definition of a liability in the *Framework*. This is consistent with the overall objective of the second phase of the project on business combinations in which an acquirer recognises the assets acquired and liabilities assumed at the date control is obtained.

BC275 However, the IASB observed that the definition of a contingent liability in IAS 37 includes both (a) 'possible obligations' and (b) present obligations for which either it is not probable that an outflow of resources embodying economic benefits will be required to settle the obligation or the amount of the obligation cannot be measured reliably. The IASB concluded that a contingent liability assumed in a business combination should be recognised only if it is a present obligation. Therefore, unlike the previous version of IFRS 3, the revised IFRS 3 does not permit the recognition of 'possible obligations'.

BC276   Like its decision on the recognition of contingent liabilities assumed in a business combination, the IASB concluded that an acquirer should recognise a contingent asset acquired in a business combination only if it satisfies the definition of an asset in the *Framework*. However, the IASB observed that the definition of a contingent asset in IAS 37 includes only 'possible assets'. A contingent asset arises when it is uncertain whether an entity has an asset at the end of the reporting period, but it is expected that some future event will confirm whether the entity has an asset. Accordingly, the IASB concluded that contingent assets should not be recognised, even if it is virtually certain that they will become unconditional or non-contingent. If an entity determines that an asset exists at the acquisition date (ie that it has an unconditional right at the acquisition date), that asset is not a contingent asset and should be accounted for in accordance with the appropriate IFRS.

BC276A   In May 2020 the IASB added paragraph 23A to IFRS 3 to clarify the requirements for contingent assets. This amendment is explained further in paragraph BC114D(a).

BC276B   The requirements for recognising contingent liabilities and contingent assets include both applications of and exceptions to the recognition principle. The IASB located all these requirements in the section headed 'exceptions to the recognition principle' because it concluded the requirements are clearest if they are all located together.

Convergence

BC277   The result of the FASB's and the IASB's conclusions on recognising assets and liabilities arising from contingencies is that the criteria for determining which items to recognise at the acquisition date differ, at least for the short term. That lack of convergence is inevitable at this time, given the status of the IASB's redeliberations on its revision of IAS 37 and the fact that the FASB had no project on its agenda to reconsider the requirements of SFAS 5 while the boards were developing the revised standards. (The FASB added a project to reconsider the accounting for contingencies to its agenda in September 2007.) To attempt to converge on guidance for recognising assets and liabilities arising from contingencies in a business combination now would run the risk of establishing requirements for a business combination that would be inconsistent with the eventual requirements for assets and liabilities arising from contingencies acquired or incurred by means other than a business combination.

BC278   However, the boards observed that the assets or liabilities arising from contingencies that are recognised in accordance with the FASB's recognition guidance and the contingent liabilities recognised in accordance with the IASB's recognition guidance will be measured consistently. In other words, the initial measurement requirements for assets and liabilities arising from contingencies recognised at the acquisition date have converged. However, the boards acknowledge that the subsequent measurement requirements differ because SFAS 5's measurement guidance differs from that in IAS 37. The reasons for the boards' conclusion on measuring those assets and liabilities are discussed in paragraphs BC224–BC245.

Exceptions to both the recognition and measurement principles

Income taxes

BC279 The 2005 Exposure Draft proposed, and the revised standards require, that a deferred tax asset or liability should be recognised and measured in accordance with either IAS 12 *Income Taxes* or FASB Statement No. 109 *Accounting for Income Taxes* (SFAS 109) respectively. IAS 12 and SFAS 109 establish requirements for recognising and measuring deferred tax assets and liabilities—requirements that are not necessarily consistent with the recognition and measurement principles in the revised standards.

BC280 The boards considered identifying deferred tax assets and liabilities as an exception to only the measurement principle because most, if not all, of the requirements of IAS 12 and SFAS 109 are arguably consistent with the revised standards' recognition principle. The recognition principle requires the acquirer to recognise at the acquisition date the assets acquired and liabilities assumed that meet the conceptual definition of an asset or a liability at that date. However, the boards concluded that exempting deferred tax assets and liabilities from both the recognition and the measurement principles would more clearly indicate that the acquirer should apply the recognition and measurement provisions of IAS 12 and SFAS 109 and their related interpretations or amendments.

BC281 Deferred tax assets or liabilities generally are measured at undiscounted amounts in accordance with IAS 12 and SFAS 109. The boards decided not to require deferred tax assets or liabilities acquired in a business combination to be measured at fair value because they observed that:

(a) if those assets and liabilities were measured at their acquisition-date fair values, their subsequent measurement in accordance with IAS 12 or SFAS 109 would result in reported post-combination gains or losses in the period immediately following the acquisition even though the underlying economic circumstances did not change. That would not faithfully represent the results of the post-combination period and would be inconsistent with the notion that a business combination that is a fair value exchange should not give rise to the recognition of immediate post-combination gains or losses.

(b) to measure those assets and liabilities at their acquisition-date fair values and overcome the reporting problem noted in (a) would require a comprehensive consideration of whether and how to modify the requirements of IAS 12 and SFAS 109 for the subsequent measurement of deferred tax assets or liabilities acquired in a business combination. Because of the complexities of IAS 12 and SFAS 109 and the added complexities that would be involved in tracking deferred tax assets acquired and liabilities assumed in a business combination, the boards concluded that the benefits of applying the revised standards' fair value measurement principle would not warrant the costs or complexities that would cause.

Respondents to the 2005 Exposure Draft generally supported that exception to the fair value measurement requirements.

BC282 To align IAS 12 and SFAS 109 more closely and to make the accounting more consistent with the principles in the revised standards, the boards decided to address four specific issues pertaining to the acquirer's income tax accounting in connection with a business combination:

(a) accounting for a change in the acquirer's recognised deferred tax asset that results from a business combination;

(b) accounting for a change after the acquisition date in the deferred tax benefits for the acquiree's deductible temporary differences or operating loss or tax credit carryforwards acquired in a business combination;

(c) accounting for tax benefits arising from tax-deductible goodwill in excess of goodwill for financial reporting; and

(d) accounting for changes after the acquisition date in the uncertainties pertaining to acquired tax positions.

BC283 The boards addressed the first issue because the existing requirements of IAS 12 and SFAS 109 differed, with IAS 12 accounting for a change in recognised deferred tax assets separately from the business combination and SFAS 109 including a change in the acquirer's valuation allowance for its deferred tax asset in the business combination accounting. The FASB decided to converge with the IAS 12 requirement on the first issue, which the IASB decided to retain. Thus, the acquirer would recognise the change in its recognised deferred tax assets as income or expense (or a change in equity), as required by IAS 12, in the period of the business combination.

BC284 Because the boards considered the first issue primarily in an attempt to achieve convergence, they limited their consideration to the requirements of IAS 12 and SFAS 109. The FASB acknowledged that both alternatives are defensible on conceptual grounds. However, it concluded that on balance the benefits of converging with the IAS 12 method outweigh the costs related to a change in the accounting in accordance with SFAS 109. SFAS 141(R) therefore amends SFAS 109 accordingly.

BC285 Most of the respondents to the 2005 Exposure Draft supported its proposal on accounting for changes to the acquirer's own deferred taxes in conjunction with a business combination. But some disagreed; they said that an acquirer factors its expected tax synergies into the price it is willing to pay for the acquiree, and therefore those tax synergies constitute goodwill. Those respondents were concerned about the potential for double-counting the synergies once in the consideration and a second time by separately recognising the changes in the acquirer's income taxes.

BC286 The boards acknowledged that in some situations a portion of the tax synergies might be factored into the price paid in the business combination. However, they concluded that it would be difficult, if not impossible, to identify that portion. In addition, an acquirer would not pay more for an acquiree because of tax synergies unless another bidder would also pay more; an acquirer would not knowingly pay more than necessary for the acquiree. Therefore, in some situations none (or only a very small portion) of the tax synergies are likely to be factored into the price paid. The boards also observed that the revised standards (paragraph 51 of the revised IFRS 3) require only the portion of the consideration transferred for the acquiree and the assets acquired and liabilities assumed in the exchange for the acquiree to be included in applying the acquisition method. Excluding effects on the acquirer's ability to utilise its deferred tax asset is consistent with that requirement. Therefore, the boards decided to retain the treatment of changes in an acquirer's tax assets and liabilities proposed in the 2005 Exposure Draft.

BC287　The revised standards also amend IAS 12 and SFAS 109 to require disclosure of the amount of the deferred tax benefit (or expense) recognised in income in the period of the acquisition for the reduction (or increase) of the acquirer's valuation allowance for its deferred tax asset that results from a business combination. The boards decided that disclosure of that amount is necessary to enable users of the acquirer's financial statements to evaluate the nature and financial effect of a business combination.

BC288　The second issue listed in paragraph BC282 relates to changes after the acquisition date in the amounts recognised for deferred tax benefits acquired in a business combination. IAS 12 and SFAS 109 both required subsequent recognition of acquired tax benefits to reduce goodwill. However, IAS 12 and SFAS 109 differed in that:

(a)　IAS 12 did not permit the reduction of other non-current intangible assets, which SFAS 109 required; and

(b)　IAS 12 required the recognition of offsetting income and expense in the acquirer's profit or loss when subsequent changes are recognised.

BC289　In developing the 2005 Exposure Draft, the FASB concluded that the fair value of other long-lived assets acquired in a business combination should no longer be reduced for changes in a valuation allowance after the acquisition date. That decision is consistent with the boards' decision not to adjust other acquired assets or assumed liabilities, with a corresponding adjustment to goodwill, for the effects of other events occurring after the acquisition date.

BC290　Few respondents to the 2005 Exposure Draft addressed this issue, and the views of those who commented differed. Some favoured providing for reduction of goodwill indefinitely because they view the measurement exception for deferred tax assets as resulting in a measure that is drastically different from fair value. Those who supported not permitting the indefinite reduction of goodwill said that, conceptually, changes in estimates pertaining to deferred taxes recognised in a business combination should be treated the same as other revisions to the amounts recorded at acquisition. The boards agreed with those respondents that a measurement exception should not result in potentially indefinite adjustments to goodwill. The revised standards provide other limited exceptions to the recognition and measurement principles, for example, for employee benefits—none of which result in indefinite adjustments to goodwill for subsequent changes.

BC291   The 2005 Exposure Draft proposed a rebuttable presumption that the subsequent recognition of acquired tax benefits within one year of the acquisition date should be accounted for by reducing goodwill. The rebuttable presumption could have been overcome if the subsequent recognition of the tax benefits resulted from a discrete event or circumstance occurring after the acquisition date. Recognition of acquired tax benefits after the one-year period would be accounted for in profit or loss (or, if IAS 12 or SFAS 109 so requires, outside profit or loss). Respondents suggested particular modifications to that proposal, including removing the rebuttable presumption about subsequent recognition of acquired tax benefits within one year of the acquisition date and treating increases and decreases in deferred tax assets consistently. (IAS 12 and SFAS 109 provided guidance on accounting for decreases.) The boards agreed with those suggestions and revised the requirements of the revised standards accordingly.

BC292   As described in paragraph BC282(c), the boards considered whether a deferred tax asset should be recognised in a business combination for any excess amount of tax-deductible goodwill over the goodwill for financial reporting purposes (excess tax goodwill). From a conceptual standpoint, the excess tax goodwill meets the definition of a temporary difference. Not recognising the tax benefit of that temporary difference at the date of the business combination would be inappropriate and inconsistent with IAS 12 and SFAS 109; it would also be inconsistent with the recognition principle in the revised standards. Thus, the revised IFRS 3 clarifies IAS 12 and SFAS 141(R) amends SFAS 109 accordingly.

BC293   On the issue in paragraph BC282(d), respondents to the 2005 Exposure Draft suggested that the revised standards should address how to account for subsequent adjustments to amounts recognised for acquired income tax uncertainties. Respondents supported accounting for subsequent adjustments to amounts recognised for tax uncertainties using the same approach as the accounting for subsequent adjustments to acquired deferred tax benefits.

BC294   The FASB agreed with respondents' suggestion that an acquirer should recognise changes to acquired income tax uncertainties after the acquisition in the same way as changes in acquired deferred tax benefits. Therefore, SFAS 141(R) amends FASB Interpretation No. 48 *Accounting for Uncertainty in Income Taxes* (FASB Interpretation 48) to require a change to an acquired income tax uncertainty within the measurement period that results from new information about facts and circumstances that existed at the acquisition date to be recognised through a corresponding adjustment to goodwill. If that reduces goodwill to zero, an acquirer would recognise any additional increases of the recognised income tax uncertainty as a reduction of income tax expense. All other changes in the acquired income tax uncertainties would be accounted for in accordance with FASB Interpretation 48.

BC295   The IASB also considered whether to address the accounting for changes in acquired income tax uncertainties in a business combination. IAS 12 is silent on income tax uncertainties. The IASB is considering tax uncertainties as part of the convergence income tax project. Therefore, the IASB decided not to modify IAS 12 as part of this project to address specifically the accounting for changes in acquired income tax uncertainties in a business combination.

Employee benefits

BC296 The revised standards provide exceptions to both the recognition and measurement principles for liabilities and any related assets resulting from the employee benefit arrangements of an acquiree. The acquirer is required to recognise and measure those assets and liabilities in accordance with IAS 19 or applicable US GAAP.

BC297 As with deferred tax assets and liabilities, the boards considered identifying employee benefits as an exception only to the measurement principle. The boards concluded that essentially the same considerations discussed in paragraph BC280 for deferred tax assets and liabilities also apply to employee benefits. In addition, the FASB observed that FASB Statements No. 43 *Accounting for Compensated Absences* and 112 *Employers' Accounting for Postemployment Benefits* require recognition of a liability for compensated absences or post-employment benefits, respectively, only if payment is probable. Arguably, a liability for those benefits exists, at least in some circumstances, regardless of whether payment is probable. Accordingly, to make it clear that the acquirer should apply the recognition and measurement requirements of IAS 19 or applicable US GAAP without separately considering the extent to which those requirements are consistent with the principles in the revised standards, the boards exempted employee benefit obligations from both the recognition and the measurement principles.

BC298 The FASB decided to amend FASB Statements No. 87 *Employers' Accounting for Pensions* (SFAS 87) and 106 *Employers' Accounting for Postretirement Benefits Other Than Pensions* (SFAS 106) to require the acquirer to exclude from the liability it recognises for a single-employer pension or other post-retirement benefit plan the effects of expected plan amendments, terminations or curtailments that it has no obligation to make at the acquisition date. However, those amendments also require the acquirer to include in the liability it recognises at the acquisition date the expected withdrawal liability for a multi-employer plan if it is probable at that date that the acquirer will withdraw from the plan. For a pension or other post-retirement benefit plan, the latter requirement brings into the authoritative literature a provision that previously appeared only in the Basis for Conclusions on SFASs 87 and 106. The FASB acknowledges that the provisions for single-employer and multi-employer plans are not necessarily consistent, and it considered amending SFASs 87 and 106 to require recognition of withdrawal liabilities not yet incurred in post-combination financial statements of the periods in which withdrawals occur. However, it observed that the liability recognised upon withdrawal from a multi-employer plan represents the previously unrecognised portion of the accumulated benefits obligation, which is recognised as it arises for a single-employer plan. In addition, the FASB observed that some might consider the employer's contractual obligation upon withdrawal from a multi-employer plan an unconditional obligation to 'stand ready' to pay if withdrawal occurs and therefore a present obligation. Therefore, the FASB decided not to require the same accounting for expected withdrawals from a multi-employer plan as it requires for expected terminations or curtailments of a single-employer plan.

BC299 The effect of the revised standards' measurement exception for liabilities and any related assets resulting from the acquiree's employee benefit plans is more significant than the related recognition exception. The boards concluded that it was not feasible to require all employee benefit obligations assumed in a business combination to be measured at their acquisition-date fair values. To do so would effectively require the boards to reconsider comprehensively the relevant standards for those employee benefits as a part of their business combinations projects. Given the complexities in accounting for employee benefit obligations in accordance with existing requirements, the boards decided that the only practicable alternative is to require those obligations, and any related assets, to be measured in accordance with their applicable standards.

BC300 The 2005 Exposure Draft proposed exempting only employee benefits subject to SFASs 87 and 106 from its fair value measurement requirement. Some respondents observed that existing measurement requirements for other types of employee benefits are not consistent with fair value and said that those benefits should also be exempted. The FASB agreed and modified the measurement exception for employee benefits accordingly.

Indemnification assets

BC301 A few constituents asked about the potential inconsistency if an asset for an indemnification is measured at fair value at the acquisition date and the related liability is measured using a different measurement attribute. Members of the FASB's resource group raised the issue primarily in the context of FASB Interpretation 48, which requires an entity to measure a tax position that meets the more-likely-than-not recognition threshold at the largest amount of tax benefit that is more than 50 per cent likely to be realised upon ultimate settlement with a taxing authority.

BC302 The boards understand that a business combination sometimes includes an indemnification agreement under which the former owners of the acquiree are required to reimburse the acquirer for any payments the acquirer eventually makes upon settlement of a particular liability. If the indemnification pertains to uncertainty about a position taken in the acquiree's tax returns for prior years or to another item for which the revised standards provide a recognition or measurement exception, not providing a related exception for the indemnification asset would result in recognition or measurement anomalies. For example, for an indemnification pertaining to a deferred tax liability, the acquirer would recognise at the acquisition date a liability to the taxing authority for the deferred taxes and an asset for the indemnification due from the former owners of the acquiree. In the absence of an exception, the asset would be measured at fair value, and the liability would be measured in accordance with the pertinent income tax accounting requirements, such as FASB Interpretation 48 for an entity that applies US GAAP, because income taxes are an exception to the fair value measurement principle. Those two amounts would differ. The boards agreed with constituents that an asset representing an indemnification related to a specific liability should be recognised and measured on the same basis as that liability.

BC303   The boards also provided an exception to the recognition principle for indemnification assets. The reasons for that exception are much the same as the reasons why the boards exempted deferred tax assets and liabilities and employee benefits from that principle. Providing an exception to the recognition principle for indemnification assets clarifies that the acquirer does not apply that principle in determining whether or when to recognise such an asset. Rather, the acquirer recognises the asset when it recognises the related liability. Therefore, the revised standards provide an exception to the recognition and measurement principles for indemnification assets.

Exceptions to the measurement principle

BC304   In addition to the exceptions to both the recognition and measurement principles discussed above, the revised standards provide exceptions to the measurement principle for particular types of assets acquired or liabilities assumed in a business combination. Those exceptions are discussed in paragraphs BC305–BC311.

Temporary exception for assets held for sale

BC305   The 2005 Exposure Draft proposed that non-current assets qualifying as held for sale at the acquisition date under IFRS 5 *Non-current Assets Held for Sale and Discontinued Operations* or FASB Statement No. 144 *Accounting for the Impairment or Disposal of Long-Lived Assets* (SFAS 144) should be measured as those standards require—at fair value less costs to sell. The purpose of that proposed exception was to avoid the need to recognise a loss for the selling costs immediately after a business combination (referred to as a *Day 2 loss* because in theory it would be recognised on the day after the acquisition date). That Day 2 loss would result if the assets were initially measured at fair value but the acquirer then applied either IFRS 5 or SFAS 144, requiring measurement at fair value less costs to sell, for subsequent accounting. Because that loss would stem entirely from different measurement requirements for assets held for sale acquired in a business combination and for assets already held that are classified as held for sale, the reported loss would not faithfully represent the activities of the acquirer.

BC306   After considering responses to the 2005 Exposure Draft, the boards decided that the exception to the measurement principle for assets held for sale should be eliminated. The definitions of fair value[24] in the revised standards, and their application in other areas focuses on market data. Costs that a buyer (acquirer) incurs to purchase or expects to incur to sell an asset are excluded from the amount at which an asset is measured. The boards concluded that disposal costs should also be excluded from the measurement of assets held for sale.

---

24   IFRS 13, issued in May 2011, defines fair value and describes the effect that transaction costs have on a fair value measurement.

BC307   However, avoiding the Day 2 loss described in paragraph BC305 will require the boards to amend IFRS 5 and SFAS 144 to require assets classified as held for sale to be measured at fair value rather than at fair value less costs to sell. The boards decided to do that, but their respective due process procedures require those amendments to be made in separate projects to give constituents the opportunity to comment on the proposed changes. Although the boards intend the amendments of IFRS 5 and SFAS 144 to be effective at the same time as the revised standards, they decided as an interim step to include a measurement exception until completion of the amendments.

Reacquired rights

BC308   The revised standards (paragraph 29 of the revised IFRS 3) require the fair value of a reacquired right recognised as an intangible asset to be measured on the basis of the remaining contractual term of the contract that gave rise to the right, without taking into account potential renewals of that contract. In developing the 2005 Exposure Draft, the boards observed that a reacquired right is no longer a contract with a third party. An acquirer who controls a reacquired right could assume indefinite renewals of its contractual term, effectively making the reacquired right an intangible asset with an indefinite life. (The boards understood that some entities had been classifying reacquired rights in that way.) The boards concluded that a right reacquired from an acquiree has in substance a finite life; a renewal of the contractual term after the business combination is not part of what was acquired in the business combination. Accordingly, the 2005 Exposure Draft proposed, and the revised standards require, limiting the period over which the intangible asset is amortised (its useful life) to the remaining contractual term of the contract from which the reacquired right stems.

BC309   The 2005 Exposure Draft did not include guidance on determining the fair value of a reacquired right. Some constituents indicated that determining that value is a problem in practice, and the boards agreed that the revised standards should include guidance on that point. To be consistent with the requirement for determining the useful life of a reacquired right, the boards concluded that the fair value of the right should be based on the remaining term of the contract giving rise to the right. The boards acknowledge that market participants would generally reflect expected renewals of the term of a contractual right in the fair value of a right traded in the market. The boards decided, however, that determining the fair value of a reacquired right in that manner would be inconsistent with amortising its value over the remaining contractual term. The boards also observed that a contractual right transferred to a third party (traded in the market) is not a **reacquired** right. Accordingly, the boards decided that departing from the assumptions that market participants would use in measuring the fair value of a reacquired right is appropriate.

BC310   A few constituents asked for guidance on accounting for the sale of a reacquired right after the business combination. The boards concluded that the sale of a reacquired right is in substance the sale of an intangible asset, and the revised standards require the sale of a reacquired right to be accounted for in the same way as sales of other assets (paragraph 55 of the revised IFRS 3). Thus, the carrying amount of the right is to be included in determining the gain or loss on the sale.

Share-based payment awards

BC311 FASB Statement No. 123 (revised 2004) *Share-Based Payment* (SFAS 123(R)) requires measurement of share-based payment awards using what it describes as the *fair-value-based method*. IFRS 2 *Share-based Payment* requires essentially the same measurement method, which the revised IFRS 3 refers to as the *market-based measure*. For reasons identified in those standards, application of the measurement methods they require generally does not result in the amount at which market participants would exchange an award at a particular date—its fair value at that date. Therefore, the revised standards provide an exception to the measurement principle for share-based payment awards. The reasons for that exception are essentially the same as the reasons already discussed for other exceptions to its recognition and measurement principles that the revised standards provide. For example, as with both deferred tax assets and liabilities and assets and liabilities related to employee benefit arrangements, initial measurement of share-based payment awards at their acquisition-date fair values would cause difficulties with the subsequent accounting for those awards in accordance with IFRS 2 or SFAS 123(R).

Un-replaced and voluntarily replaced share-based payment transactions

BC311A In *Improvements to IFRSs* issued in May 2010, the Board addressed a concern that there was insufficient application guidance for share-based payment transactions that are replaced in the context of a business combination. After the revised IFRS 3 was issued in 2008, some constituents raised concerns about the lack of explicit guidance with respect to share-based payment transactions of the acquiree that the acquirer chooses to replace, even though either they are unaffected by the business combination or vesting is accelerated as a consequence of the business combination. In addition, some were concerned that the measurement guidance for share-based payment transactions applies only to replacement awards but not to acquiree awards that the acquirer chooses not to replace. In response to those concerns, the Board added explicit guidance in paragraphs B56 and B62A to clarify that those awards should be accounted for in the same way as acquiree awards that the acquirer is obliged to replace.

BC311B Employee share-based payment awards might expire in the event of a business combination. When this occurs, the acquirer may choose to grant a new award to those employees voluntarily. The new award granted in such circumstances can only be for future services, because the acquirer has no obligation to the employees in respect of past services that they provided to the acquiree. Accordingly, paragraph B56 requires the whole of the market-based value of the new award to be accounted for as a post-combination expense, which is recognised in accordance with IFRS 2. This accounting treatment is different from that required in circumstances when the employee share-based payment award does not expire in the event of a business combination. When an unexpired award is replaced by the acquirer, part of the market-based value of the replacement award reflects the acquiree's obligation that remains outstanding at the date of the business combination, and is accounted for as part of the consideration transferred in the business combination. The balance of the market-based value of the replacement award is accounted for as a post-combination expense for the services to be received over the period to when the replacement award vests, in accordance with IFRS 2. The accounting for the replacement of unexpired awards is the same for awards that are replaced voluntarily by the acquirer and those that the acquirer is obliged to replace because the substance is the same in both circumstances.

Recognising and measuring goodwill or a gain from a bargain purchase

BC312 Consistently with IFRS 3 and SFAS 141, the revised standards require the acquirer to recognise goodwill as an asset and to measure it as a residual.

Goodwill qualifies as an asset

BC313 The FASB's 1999 and 2001 Exposure Drafts listed six components of the amount that in practice, under authoritative guidance in effect at that time, had been recognised as goodwill. The IASB's ED 3 included a similar, but not identical, discussion. The components and their descriptions, taken from the FASB's exposure drafts, were:

Component 1 — The excess of the fair values over the book values of the acquiree's net assets at the date of acquisition.

Component 2 — The fair values of other net assets that the acquiree had not previously recognised. They may not have been recognised because they failed to meet the recognition criteria (perhaps because of measurement difficulties), because of a requirement that prohibited their recognition, or because the acquiree concluded that the costs of recognising them separately were not justified by the benefits.

Component 3 — The fair value of the *going concern* element of the acquiree's existing business. The going concern element represents the ability of the established business to earn a higher rate of return on an assembled collection of net assets than would be expected if those net assets had to be acquired separately. That value stems from the synergies of the net assets of the business, as well as from other benefits (such as factors related to market imperfections, including the ability to earn monopoly profits and barriers to market entry — either legal or because of transaction costs — by potential competitors).

Component 4 — The fair value of the expected synergies and other benefits from combining the acquirer's and acquiree's net assets and businesses. Those synergies and other benefits are unique to each combination, and different combinations would produce different synergies and, hence, different values.

Component 5—Overvaluation of the consideration paid by the acquirer stemming from errors in valuing the consideration tendered. Although the purchase price in an all-cash transaction would not be subject to measurement error, the same may not necessarily be said of a transaction involving the acquirer's equity interests. For example, the number of ordinary shares being traded daily may be small relative to the number of shares issued in the combination. If so, imputing the current market price to all of the shares issued to effect the combination may produce a higher value than those shares would command if they were sold for cash and the cash then used to effect the combination.

Component 6—Overpayment or underpayment by the acquirer. Overpayment might occur, for example, if the price is driven up in the course of bidding for the acquiree; underpayment may occur in a distress sale (sometimes termed a fire sale).

BC314 The boards observed that the first two components, both of which relate to the acquiree, are conceptually not part of goodwill. The first component is not itself an asset; instead, it reflects gains that the acquiree had not recognised on its net assets. As such, that component is part of those assets rather than part of goodwill. The second component is also not part of goodwill conceptually; it primarily reflects intangible assets that might be recognised as individual assets.

BC315 The fifth and sixth components, both of which relate to the acquirer, are also not conceptually part of goodwill. The fifth component is not an asset in and of itself or even part of an asset but, rather, is a measurement error. The sixth component is also not an asset; conceptually it represents a loss (in the case of overpayment) or a gain (in the case of underpayment) to the acquirer. Thus, neither of those components is conceptually part of goodwill.

BC316 The boards also observed that the third and fourth components are part of goodwill. The third component relates to the acquiree and reflects the excess assembled value of the acquiree's net assets. It represents the pre-existing goodwill that was either internally generated by the acquiree or acquired by it in prior business combinations. The fourth component relates to the acquiree and the acquirer jointly and reflects the excess assembled value that is created by the combination—the synergies that are expected from combining those businesses. The boards described the third and fourth components collectively as 'core goodwill'.

BC317 The revised standards try to avoid subsuming the first, second and fifth components of goodwill into the amount initially recognised as goodwill. Specifically, an acquirer is required to make every effort:

(a) to measure the consideration accurately (eliminating or reducing component 5);

(b) to recognise the identifiable net assets acquired at their fair values rather than their carrying amounts (eliminating or reducing component 1); and

(c)   to recognise all acquired intangible assets meeting the criteria in the revised standards (paragraph B31 of the revised IFRS 3) so that they are not subsumed into the amount initially recognised as goodwill (reducing component 2).

BC318   In developing IFRS 3 and SFAS 141, the IASB and the FASB both considered whether 'core goodwill' (the third and fourth components) qualifies as an asset under the definition in their respective conceptual frameworks. (That consideration was based on the existing conceptual frameworks. In 2004, the IASB and the FASB began work on a joint project to develop an improved conceptual framework that, among other things, would eliminate both substantive and wording differences between their existing frameworks. Although the asset definition is likely to change as a result of that project, the boards observed that nothing in their deliberations to date indicates that any such changes are likely to call into question whether goodwill continues to qualify as an asset.)

Asset definition in the FASB's Concepts Statement 6

BC319   Paragraph 172 of the FASB's Concepts Statement 6 says that an item that has future economic benefits has the capacity to serve the entity by being exchanged for something else of value to the entity, by being used to produce something of value to the entity or by being used to settle its liabilities.

BC320   The FASB noted that goodwill cannot be exchanged for something else of value to the entity and it cannot be used to settle the entity's liabilities. Goodwill also lacks the capacity singly to produce future net cash inflows, although it can—in combination with other assets—produce cash flows. Thus, the future benefit associated with goodwill is generally more nebulous and may be less certain than the benefit associated with most other assets. Nevertheless, goodwill generally provides future economic benefit. The FASB's Concepts Statement 6 observes that 'Anything that is commonly bought and sold has future economic benefit, including the individual items that a buyer obtains and is willing to pay for in a "basket purchase" of several items or in a business combination' (paragraph 173).

BC321   For the future economic benefit embodied in goodwill to qualify as an asset, the acquirer must control that benefit. The FASB observed that the acquirer's control is demonstrated by means of its ability to direct the policies and management of the acquiree. The FASB also observed that the past transaction or event necessary for goodwill to qualify as the acquirer's asset is the transaction in which it obtained the controlling interest in the acquiree.

Asset definition in the IASB's Framework

BC322   Paragraph 53 of the IASB's *Framework* explains that 'The future economic benefit embodied in an asset is the potential to contribute, directly or indirectly, to the flow of cash and cash equivalents to the entity.'

BC323   The IASB concluded that core goodwill represents resources from which future economic benefits are expected to flow to the entity. In considering whether core goodwill represents a resource **controlled** by the entity, the IASB considered the assertion that core goodwill arises, at least in part, through factors such as a well-trained workforce, loyal customers and so on, and that these factors cannot be regarded as controlled by the entity because the workforce could leave and the customers could go elsewhere. However, the IASB, like the FASB, concluded that control of core goodwill is provided by means of the acquirer's power to direct the policies and management of the acquiree. Therefore, both the IASB and the FASB concluded that core goodwill meets the conceptual definition of an asset.

Relevance of information about goodwill

BC324 In developing SFAS 141, the FASB also considered the relevance of information about goodwill. Although the IASB's Basis for Conclusions on IFRS 3 did not explicitly discuss the relevance of information about goodwill, the FASB's analysis of that issue was available to the IASB members as they developed IFRS 3, and they saw no reason not to accept that analysis.

BC325 More specifically, in developing SFAS 141, the FASB considered the views of users as reported by the AICPA Special Committee[25] and as expressed by the Financial Accounting Policy Committee (FAPC) of the Association for Investment Management and Research (AIMR) in its 1993 position paper *Financial Reporting in the 1990s and Beyond*. The FASB observed that users have mixed views about whether goodwill should be recognised as an asset. Some are troubled by the lack of comparability between internally generated goodwill and acquired goodwill that results under present standards, but others do not appear to be particularly bothered by it. However, users appear to be reluctant to give up information about goodwill acquired in a business combination. In the view of the AICPA Special Committee, users want to retain the option of being able to use that information. Similarly, the FAPC said that goodwill should be recognised in financial statements.

BC326 The FASB also considered the growing use of 'economic value added' (EVA)[26] and similar measures, which are increasingly being employed as means of assessing performance. The FASB observed that such measures commonly incorporate goodwill, and in business combinations accounted for by the pooling method, an adjustment was commonly made to incorporate a measure of the goodwill that was not recognised under that method. As a result, the aggregate amount of goodwill is included in the base that is subject to a capital charge that is part of the EVA measure and management is held accountable for the total investment in the acquiree.

---

25 AICPA Special Committee on Financial Reporting, *Improving Business Reporting—A Customer Focus* (New York: AICPA, 1994).

26 EVA was developed by the consulting firm of Stern Stewart & Company (and is a registered trademark of Stern Stewart) as a financial performance measure that improves management's ability to make decisions that enhance shareholder value.

BC327   The FASB also considered evidence about the relevance of goodwill provided by a number of research studies that empirically examined the relationship between goodwill and the market value of business entities.[27] Those studies generally found a positive relationship between the reported goodwill of entities and their market values, thereby indicating that investors in the markets behave as if they view goodwill as an asset.

Measuring goodwill as a residual

BC328   The revised standards require the acquirer to measure goodwill as the excess of one amount (described in paragraph 32(a) of the revised IFRS 3) over another (described in paragraph 32(b) of the revised IFRS 3). Therefore, goodwill is measured as a residual, which is consistent with IFRS 3 and SFAS 141, in which the IASB and the FASB, respectively, concluded that direct measurement of goodwill is not possible. The boards did not reconsider measuring goodwill as a residual in the second phase of the business combinations project. However, the boards simplified the measurement of goodwill acquired in a business combination achieved in stages (a step acquisition). In accordance with IFRS 3 and SFAS 141, an entity that acquired another entity in a step acquisition measured goodwill by reference to the cost of each step and the related fair value of the underlying identifiable net assets acquired. This process was costly because it required the acquirer in a step acquisition to determine the amounts allocated to the identifiable net assets acquired at the date of each acquisition, even if those steps occurred years or decades earlier. In contrast, the revised standards require goodwill to be measured once—at the acquisition date. Thus, the revised standards reduce the complexity and costs of accounting for step acquisitions.

BC329   Both boards decided that all assets acquired and liabilities assumed, including those of an acquiree (subsidiary) that is not wholly-owned, as well as, in principle, any non-controlling interest in the acquiree, should be measured at their acquisition-date fair values (or in limited situations, their amounts determined in accordance with other US GAAP or IFRSs). Thus, SFAS 141(R) eliminates the past practice of not recognising the portion of goodwill related to the non-controlling interests in subsidiaries that are not wholly-owned. However, as discussed in paragraphs BC209–BC211, the IASB concluded that the revised IFRS 3 should permit entities to measure any non-controlling interest in an acquiree as its proportionate share of the acquiree's identifiable net assets. If an entity chooses that alternative, only the goodwill related to the acquirer is recognised.

---

27   Refer to, for example, Eli Amir, Trevor S Harris and Elizabeth K Venuti, 'A Comparison of the Value-Relevance of U.S. versus Non-U.S. GAAP Accounting Measures Using Form 20-F Reconciliations', *Journal of Accounting Research*, Supplement (1993): 230–264; Mary Barth and Greg Clinch, 'International Accounting Differences and Their Relation to Share Prices: Evidence from U.K., Australian and Canadian Firms', *Contemporary Accounting Research* (spring 1996): 135–170; Keith W Chauvin and Mark Hirschey, 'Goodwill, Profitability, and the Market Value of the Firm', *Journal of Accounting and Public Policy* (summer 1994): 159–180; Ross Jennings, John Robinson, Robert B Thompson and Linda Duvall, 'The Relation between Accounting Goodwill Numbers and Equity Values', *Journal of Business Finance and Accounting* (June 1996): 513–533; and Mark G McCarthy and Douglas K Schneider, 'Market Perception of Goodwill: Some Empirical Evidence', *Accounting and Business Research* (winter 1995): 69–81.

Using the acquisition-date fair value of consideration to measure goodwill

BC330   As discussed in paragraph BC81, the revised standards do not focus on measuring the acquisition-date fair value of either the acquiree as a whole or the acquirer's interest in the acquiree as the 2005 Exposure Draft did. Consistently with that change, the boards also eliminated the presumption in the 2005 Exposure Draft that, in the absence of evidence to the contrary, the acquisition-date fair value of the consideration transferred is the best evidence of the fair value of the acquirer's interest in the acquiree at that date. Therefore, the revised standards describe the measurement of goodwill in terms of the recognised amount of the consideration transferred — generally its acquisition-date fair value (paragraph 32 of the revised IFRS 3) — and specify how to measure goodwill if the fair value of the acquiree is more reliably measurable than the fair value of the consideration transferred or if no consideration is transferred (paragraph 33 of the revised IFRS 3).

BC331   Because business combinations are generally exchange transactions in which knowledgeable, unrelated willing parties exchange equal values, the boards continue to believe that the acquisition-date fair value of the consideration transferred provides the best evidence of the acquisition-date fair value of the acquirer's interest in the acquiree in many, if not most, situations. However, that is not the case if the acquirer either makes a bargain purchase or pays more than the acquiree is worth at the acquisition date if the acquirer underpays or overpays. The revised standards provide for recognising a gain in the event of a bargain purchase, but they do not provide for recognising a loss in the event of an overpayment (paragraph BC382). Therefore, the boards concluded that focusing directly on the fair value of the consideration transferred rather than on the fair value of the acquirer's interest in the acquiree, with a presumption that the two amounts are usually equal, would be a more straightforward way of describing how to measure goodwill. (The same conclusion applies to measuring the gain on a bargain purchase, which is discussed in paragraphs BC371–BC381.) That change in focus will also avoid unproductive disputes in practice about whether the consideration transferred or another valuation technique provides the best evidence for measuring the acquirer's interest in the acquiree in a particular situation.

Using the acquirer's interest in the acquiree to measure goodwill

BC332   The boards acknowledge that in the absence of measurable consideration, the acquirer is likely to incur costs to measure the acquisition-date fair value of its interest in the acquiree and incremental costs to have that measure independently verified. The boards observed that in many of those circumstances companies already incur such costs as part of their due diligence procedures. For example, an acquisition of a privately held entity by another privately held entity is often accomplished by an exchange of equity shares that do not have observable market prices. To determine the exchange ratio, those entities generally engage advisers and valuation experts to assist them in valuing the acquiree as well as the equity transferred by the acquirer in exchange for the acquiree. Similarly, a combination of two mutual entities is often accomplished by an exchange of member interests of the acquirer for all of the member interests of the acquiree. In many, but not necessarily all, of those cases the directors and managers of the entities also assess the relative fair values of the combining entities to ensure that the exchange of member interests is equitable to the members of both entities.

BC333   The boards concluded that the benefits in terms of improved financial information resulting from the revised standards outweigh the incremental measurement costs that the revised standards may require. Those improvements include the increased relevance and understandability of information resulting from applying the revised standards' measurement principle and guidance on recognising and measuring goodwill, which are consistent with reflecting the change in economic circumstances that occurs at that date.

BC334   The 2005 Exposure Draft included illustrative guidance for applying the fair value measurement requirement if no consideration is transferred or the consideration transferred is not the best evidence of the acquisition-date fair value of the acquiree. That illustrative guidance drew on related guidance in the FASB's exposure draft that preceded SFAS 157. Because SFAS 157 provides guidance on using valuation techniques such as the market approach and the income approach for measuring fair value, the FASB decided that it is unnecessary for SFAS 141(R) to provide the same guidance.

BC335   The IASB decided not to include in the revised IFRS 3 guidance on using valuation techniques to measure the acquisition-date fair value of the acquirer's interest in the acquiree. The IASB has on its agenda a project to develop guidance on measuring fair value. While deliberations on that project are in progress, the IASB considers it inappropriate to include fair value measurement guidance in IFRSs.

BC336   The FASB, on the other hand, completed its project on fair value measurement when it issued SFAS 157. SFAS 141(R), together with SFAS 157, provides broadly applicable measurement guidance that is relevant and useful in measuring the acquirer's interest in the acquiree. However, both boards were concerned that without some discussion of special considerations for measuring the fair value of mutual entities, some acquirers might neglect to consider relevant assumptions that market participants would make about future member benefits when using a valuation technique. For example, the acquirer of a co-operative entity should consider the value of the member discounts in its determination of the fair value of its interest in the acquiree. Therefore, the boards decided to include a discussion of special considerations in measuring the fair value of mutual entities (paragraphs B47–B49 of the revised IFRS 3).[28]

---

28   The combination of IFRS 3 and IFRS 13, issued in May 2011, provides guidance for measuring the fair value of an acquirer's interest in the acquiree (including mutual entities).

Measuring consideration and determining whether particular items are part of the consideration transferred for the acquiree

BC337 Paragraphs BC338–BC360 discuss the boards' conclusions on measuring specific items of consideration that are often transferred by acquirers. Paragraphs BC361–BC370 then discuss whether particular replacement awards of share-based remuneration and acquisition-related costs incurred by acquirers are part of the consideration transferred for the acquiree.

Measurement date for equity securities transferred

BC338 The guidance in IFRS 3 and SFAS 141 on the measurement date for equity securities transferred as consideration in a business combination differed, and SFAS 141's guidance on that issue was contradictory. Paragraph 22 of SFAS 141, which was carried forward from APB Opinion 16, said that the market price for a reasonable period before and after the date that the terms of the acquisition are agreed to and announced should be considered in determining the fair value of the securities issued. That effectively established the agreement date as the measurement date for equity securities issued as consideration. However, paragraph 49 of SFAS 141, which was also carried forward from APB Opinion 16, said that the cost of an acquiree should be determined as of the acquisition date. IFRS 3, on the other hand, required measuring the consideration transferred in a business combination at its fair value on the exchange date, which was the acquisition date for a combination in which control is achieved in a single transaction. (IFRS 3, like SFAS 141, included special guidance on determining the cost of a business combination in which control is achieved in stages.) In their deliberations leading to the 2005 Exposure Draft, the boards decided that the fair value of equity securities issued as consideration in a business combination should be measured at the acquisition date.

BC339 In reaching their conclusions on this issue, the boards considered the reasons for the consensus reached in EITF Issue No. 99-12 *Determination of the Measurement Date for the Market Price of Acquirer Securities Issued in a Purchase Business Combination*. That consensus states that the value of the acquirer's marketable equity securities issued to effect a business combination should be determined on the basis of the market price of the securities over a reasonable period before and after the terms of the acquisition are agreed to and announced. The arguments for that consensus are based on the view that the announcement of a transaction, and the related agreements, normally bind the parties to the transaction so that the acquirer is obliged at that point to issue the equity securities at the closing date. If the parties are bound to the transaction at the agreement (announcement) date, the value of the underlying securities on that date best reflects the value of the bargained exchange. The boards did not find those arguments compelling. The boards observed that to make the announcement of a recommended transaction binding generally requires shareholders' authorisation or another binding event, which also gives rise to the change in control of the acquiree.

BC340   Additionally, the boards noted that measuring the fair value of equity securities issued on the agreement date (or on the basis of the market price of the securities for a short period before and after that date) did not result in a consistent measure of the consideration transferred. The fair values of all other forms of consideration transferred are measured at the acquisition date. The boards decided that all forms of consideration transferred should be valued on the same date, which should also be the same date as when the assets acquired and liabilities assumed are measured. The boards also observed that negotiations between an acquirer and an acquiree typically provide for share adjustments in the event of material events and circumstances between the agreement date and acquisition date. In addition, ongoing negotiations after announcement of agreements, which are not unusual, provide evidence that agreements are generally not binding at the date they are announced. Lastly, the boards also observed that the parties typically provide for cancellation options if the number of shares to be issued at the acquisition date would not reflect an exchange of approximately equal fair values at that date.

BC341   Respondents to the 2005 Exposure Draft expressed mixed views on the measurement date for equity securities. Some supported the proposal to measure equity securities at their fair value on the acquisition date, generally for the same reasons given in that exposure draft. Others, however, favoured use of the agreement date. They generally cited one or more of the following as support for their view:

    (a)   An acquirer and a target entity both consider the fair value of a target entity on the agreement date in negotiating the amount of consideration to be paid. Measuring equity securities issued as consideration at fair value on the agreement date reflects the values taken into account in negotiations.

    (b)   Changes in the fair value of the acquirer's equity securities between the agreement date and the acquisition date may be caused by factors unrelated to the business combination.

    (c)   Changes in the fair value of the acquirer's equity securities between the agreement date and the acquisition date may result in inappropriate recognition of either a bargain purchase or artificially inflated goodwill if the fair value of those securities is measured at the acquisition date.

BC342   In considering those comments, the boards observed, as they did in the 2005 Exposure Draft, that valid conceptual arguments can be made for both the agreement date and the acquisition date. However, they also observed that the parties to a business combination are likely to take into account expected changes between the agreement date and the acquisition date in the fair value of the acquirer and the market price of the acquirer's securities issued as consideration. The argument against acquisition date measurement of equity securities noted in paragraph BC341(a) is mitigated if acquirers and targets generally consider their best estimates at the agreement date of the fair values of the amounts to be exchanged on the acquisition dates. The boards also noted that measuring the equity securities on the acquisition date avoids the complexities of dealing with situations in which the number of shares or other consideration transferred can change between the agreement date and the acquisition date. The boards therefore concluded that equity instruments issued as consideration in a business combination should be measured at their fair values on the acquisition date.

Contingent consideration, including subsequent measurement

BC343   In accordance with the guidance in SFAS 141, which was carried forward from APB Opinion 16 without reconsideration, an acquirer's obligations to make payments conditional on the outcome of future events (often called *contingent consideration*) were not usually recognised at the acquisition date. Rather, acquirers usually recognised those obligations when the contingency was resolved and consideration was issued or became issuable. In general, issuing additional securities or distributing additional cash or other assets upon resolving contingencies on the basis of reaching particular earnings levels resulted in delayed recognition of an additional element of cost of an acquiree. In contrast, issuing additional securities or distributing additional assets upon resolving contingencies on the basis of security prices did not change the recognised cost of an acquiree.

BC344   The IASB carried forward in IFRS 3 the requirements for contingent consideration from IAS 22 without reconsideration. In accordance with IFRS 3, an acquirer recognised consideration that is contingent on future events at the acquisition date only if it is probable and can be measured reliably. If the required level of probability or reliability for recognition was reached only after the acquisition date, the additional consideration was treated as an adjustment to the accounting for the business combination and to goodwill at that later date.

BC345   Therefore, in accordance with both SFAS 141 and IFRS 3, unlike other forms of consideration, an obligation for contingent consideration was not always measured at its acquisition-date fair value and its remeasurement either sometimes (SFAS 141) or always (IFRS 3) resulted in an adjustment to the business combination accounting.

BC346   In developing the 2005 Exposure Draft, both boards concluded that the delayed recognition of contingent consideration in their previous standards on business combinations was unacceptable because it ignored that the acquirer's agreement to make contingent payments is the obligating event in a business combination transaction. Although the amount of the future payments the acquirer will make is conditional on future events, the obligation to make them if the specified future events occur is unconditional. The same is true for a right to the return of previously transferred consideration if specified conditions are met. Failure to recognise that obligation or right at the acquisition date would not faithfully represent the economic consideration exchanged at that date. Thus, both boards concluded that obligations and rights associated with contingent consideration arrangements should be measured and recognised at their acquisition-date fair values.

BC347   The boards considered arguments that it might be difficult to measure the fair value of contingent consideration at the acquisition date. The boards acknowledged that measuring the fair value of some contingent payments may be difficult, but they concluded that to delay recognition of, or otherwise ignore, assets or liabilities that are difficult to measure would cause financial reporting to be incomplete and thus diminish its usefulness in making economic decisions.

BC348   Moreover, a contingent consideration arrangement is inherently part of the economic considerations in the negotiations between the buyer and seller. Such arrangements are commonly used by buyers and sellers to reach an agreement by sharing particular specified economic risks related to uncertainties about future outcomes. Differences in the views of the buyer and seller about those uncertainties are often reconciled by their agreeing to share the risks in such ways that favourable future outcomes generally result in additional payments to the seller and unfavourable outcomes result in no or lower payments. The boards observed that information used in those negotiations will often be helpful in estimating the fair value of the contingent obligation assumed by the acquirer.

BC349   The boards noted that most contingent consideration obligations are financial instruments, and many are derivative instruments. Reporting entities that use such instruments extensively, auditors and valuation professionals are familiar with the use of valuation techniques for estimating the fair values of financial instruments. The boards concluded that acquirers should be able to use valuation techniques to develop estimates of the fair values of contingent consideration obligations that are sufficiently reliable for recognition. The boards also observed that an effective estimate of zero for the acquisition-date fair value of contingent consideration, which was often the result under IFRS 3 and SFAS 141, was unreliable.

BC350   Some respondents to the 2005 Exposure Draft were especially concerned about the reliability with which the fair value of performance-based contingent consideration can be measured. The IASB and the FASB considered those concerns in the context of related requirements in their standards on share-based payments (IFRS 2 and SFAS 123(R), respectively), neither of which requires performance conditions that are not market conditions to be included in the market-based measure of an award of share-based payment at the grant date. For example, remuneration cost is recognised for a share option with vesting requirements that depend on achievement of an earnings target based on the number of equity instruments expected to vest and any such cost recognised during the vesting period is reversed if the target is not achieved. Both IFRS 2 and SFAS 123(R) cite constituents' concerns about the measurability at the grant date of the expected outcomes associated with performance conditions as part of the reason for that treatment.

BC351   The boards concluded that the requirements for awards of share-based payment subject to performance conditions should not determine the requirements for contingent (or conditional) consideration in a business combination. In addition, the boards concluded that the negotiations between buyer and seller inherent in a contingent consideration arrangement in a business combination provide better evidence of its fair value than is likely to be available for most share-based payment arrangements with performance conditions.

BC352   The boards also noted that some contingent consideration arrangements oblige the acquirer to deliver its equity securities if specified future events occur. The boards concluded that the classification of such instruments as either equity or a liability should be based on existing IFRSs or US GAAP, as indicated in paragraph 40 of the revised IFRS 3.

Subsequent measurement of contingent consideration

BC353   For reasons similar to those discussed in the context of contingent liabilities (paragraphs BC232 and BC243), the boards concluded that the revised standards must address subsequent accounting for contingent consideration. For consistency with the accounting for other obligations that require an entity to deliver its equity shares, the boards concluded that obligations for contingent payments that are classified as equity should not be remeasured after the acquisition date.

BC354   The boards observed that many obligations for contingent consideration that qualify for classification as liabilities meet the definition of derivative instruments in IAS 39[29] or SFAS 133. To improve transparency in reporting particular instruments, the boards concluded that all contracts that would otherwise be within the scope of those standards (if not issued in a business combination) should be subject to their requirements if issued in a business combination. Therefore, the boards decided to eliminate their respective provisions (paragraph 2(f) of IAS 39 and paragraph 11(c) of SFAS 133) that excluded contingent consideration in a business combination from the scope of those standards. Accordingly, liabilities for payments of contingent consideration that are subject to the requirements of IAS 39 or SFAS 133 would subsequently be measured at fair value at the end of each reporting period, with changes in fair value recognised in accordance with whichever of those standards an entity applies in its financial statements.

BC355   In considering the subsequent accounting for contingent payments that are liabilities but are not derivatives, the boards concluded that, in concept, all liabilities for contingent payments should be accounted for similarly. Therefore, liabilities for contingent payments that are not derivative instruments should also be remeasured at fair value after the acquisition date. The boards concluded that applying those provisions would faithfully represent the fair value of the liability for the contingent payment of consideration that remains a liability until settled.

BC356   The boards also considered whether subsequent changes in the fair values of liabilities for contingent consideration should be reflected as adjustments to the consideration transferred in the business combination (usually in goodwill). Some respondents to the 2005 Exposure Draft favoured that alternative because they thought that changes in the fair value of contingent

---

29   IFRS 9 *Financial Instruments* replaced IAS 39. IFRS 9 applies to all items that were previously within the scope of IAS 39.

consideration effectively resolve differing views of the acquirer and the former owners of the acquiree about the acquisition-date fair value of the acquiree. The boards acknowledged that a conclusive determination at the acquisition date of the fair value of a liability for contingent consideration might not be practicable in the limited circumstances in which particular information is not available at that date. As discussed in more detail in paragraphs BC390–BC400, the boards decided that the revised standards should provide for provisional measurement of the fair value of assets acquired or liabilities assumed or incurred, including liabilities for contingent payments, in those circumstances.

BC357   Except for adjustments during the measurement period to provisional estimates of fair values at the acquisition date, the boards concluded that subsequent changes in the fair value of a liability for contingent consideration do not affect the acquisition-date fair value of the consideration transferred. Rather, those subsequent changes in value are generally directly related to post-combination events and changes in circumstances related to the combined entity. Thus, subsequent changes in value for post-combination events and circumstances should not affect the measurement of the consideration transferred or goodwill on the acquisition date. (The boards acknowledge that some changes in fair value might result from events and circumstances related in part to a pre-combination period. But that part of the change is usually indistinguishable from the part related to the post-combination period and the boards concluded that the benefits in those limited circumstances that might result from making such fine distinctions would not justify the costs that such a requirement would impose.)

BC358   The boards also considered arguments that the results of the requirements of the revised standards for recognition of changes in the fair value of contingent consideration after the acquisition date are counter-intuitive because they will result in:

(a)   recognising gains if the specified milestone or event requiring the contingent payment is not met. For example, the acquirer would recognise a gain on the reversal of the liability if an earnings target in an earn-out arrangement is not achieved.

(b)   recognising losses if the combined entity is successful and the amount paid exceeds the estimated fair value of the liability at the acquisition date.

BC359   The boards accept the consequence that recognising the fair value of a liability for payment of contingent consideration is likely to result subsequently in a gain if smaller or no payments are required or result in a loss if greater payments are required. That is a consequence of entering into contingent consideration arrangements related to future changes in the value of a specified asset or liability or earnings of the acquiree after the acquisition date. For example, if a contingent consideration arrangement relates to the level of future earnings of the combined entity, higher earnings in the specified periods may be partially offset by increases in the liability to make contingent payments based on earnings because the acquirer has agreed to share those increases with former owners of the acquiree.

BC360   The boards also observed that liabilities for contingent payments may be related to contingencies surrounding an outcome for a particular asset or another liability. In those cases, the effect on income of the period of a change in the fair value of the liability for the contingent payment may be offset by a change in the value of the asset or other liability. For example, after an acquisition the combined entity might reach a favourable settlement of pending litigation of the acquiree for which it had a contingent consideration arrangement. If the combined entity is thus required to make a contingent payment to the seller of the acquiree that exceeds the initially estimated fair value of the liability for contingent consideration, the effect of the increase in that liability may be offset in part by the reduction in the liability to the litigation claimant. Similarly, if the acquirer is not required to make a contingent payment to the seller because an acquired research and development project failed to result in a viable product, the gain from the elimination of the liability may be offset, in whole or in part, by an impairment charge to the asset acquired.

Clarification on the accounting for contingent consideration in a business combination

BC360A   The IASB clarified the accounting for contingent consideration arising from business combinations.

Classification of contingent consideration in a business combination

BC360B   The IASB noted that the classification requirements in paragraph 40 of IFRS 3 were unclear as to when, if ever, "other applicable IFRSs" would need to be used to determine the classification of contingent consideration as a financial liability or as an equity instrument. Consequently, the IASB deleted the reference to "other applicable IFRSs" in paragraph 40.

Subsequent measurement of contingent consideration in a business combination

BC360C   The IASB also noted that the requirements for subsequent measurement in paragraph 58 require contingent consideration, other than that which meets the definition of equity in accordance with IAS 32 *Financial Instruments: Presentation*, to be subsequently measured at fair value. However, paragraph 58 then refers to IFRS 9 *Financial Instruments* (or IAS 39, if IFRS 9 has not yet been applied), IAS 37 or other IFRSs as appropriate, which may not require subsequent measurement at fair value.

Subsequent measurement of contingent consideration that is a financial instrument

BC360D   The IASB noted that the requirements for subsequent measurement in paragraph 58 for contingent consideration that is a financial instrument within the scope of IFRS 9 (or IAS 39[30]) were inconsistent with the accounting requirements of IFRS 9 (or IAS 39). Because paragraph 58 referred to IFRS 9 (or IAS 39), which allows amortised cost measurement in some circumstances, contingent consideration that is a financial liability might be classified as being measured at amortised cost. This would conflict with the requirement in paragraph 58 that such contingent consideration should be subsequently measured at fair value. Consequently, the IASB amended the classification requirements of IFRS 9 (and IAS 39) to ensure that the subsequent measurement requirement for contingent consideration that is a financial liability is fair value. The IASB thinks that this clarifies the original intention for subsequent measurement of contingent consideration as explained in paragraph BC355.

BC360E   In redeliberating this issue, the IASB decided that it would not be possible for contingent consideration that is a financial asset that meets the requirements in IFRS 9 to be subsequently measured at amortised cost (because the contractual terms of contingent consideration that is a financial asset would not give rise on specified dates to cash flows that are solely payments of principal and interest on the principal amount outstanding). Consequently, the IASB decided that the proposed amendments to paragraph 4.1.2 of IFRS 9 in the Exposure Draft *Annual Improvements to IFRSs 2010–2012 Cycle* were not needed.

BC360F   The IASB also decided that changes in fair value of any contingent consideration that is a financial asset or a financial liability should be recognised in profit or loss. Consequently, the IASB decided to amend paragraph 5.7.5 of IFRS 9 to ensure that any change in the fair value of investments in equity instruments that are contingent consideration in a business combination should be presented in profit or loss. The IASB noted that it was unlikely that contingent consideration that is an asset would meet the definition of equity. However, it decided to amend the paragraph to ensure that all contingent consideration that is made up of financial instruments is accounted for consistently.

Subsequent measurement of contingent consideration that is a non-financial asset or a non-financial liability

BC360G   The IASB also noted that the subsequent measurement requirements in paragraph 58(b) for contingent consideration that is a non-financial asset or a non-financial liability may conflict with the measurement requirements in other applicable Standards. The conflict arises because paragraph 58 refers to changes in the fair value of contingent consideration but paragraph 58(b) refers to Standards that do not require fair value as a measurement basis, for example, IAS 37. Consequently, the IASB deleted the reference to "IAS 37 or

---

30   IFRS 9 *Financial Instruments* replaced IAS 39. IFRS 9 applies to all items that were previously within the scope of IAS 39.

other IFRSs as appropriate" from paragraph 58(b). This, therefore, maintains fair value as the subsequent measurement basis for all non equity contingent consideration to which IFRS 3 applies. The IASB thinks that this clarifies the original intention for subsequent measurement of contingent consideration as explained in paragraph BC355.

BC360H   The IASB also decided that the full change in the fair value of any contingent consideration that is a non-financial asset or a non-financial liability should be recognised in profit or loss.

Other considerations given to subsequent measurement of contingent consideration

BC360I   The IASB considered alternatives for the subsequent measurement requirements for contingent consideration. It considered whether all references to other Standards, including references to IFRS 9 (or IAS 39[31]), should be removed and instead all necessary guidance for the subsequent measurement of contingent consideration should be included in IFRS 3. It decided, however, to amend IFRS 9 (and IAS 39) as a consequential amendment derived from the amendment to IFRS 3 and to retain the link to IFRS 9 (or IAS 39) so that the general guidance in IFRS 9 (or IAS 39) applies to contingent consideration that is within the scope of IFRS 9 (or IAS 39). The IASB also considered whether some liability contingent consideration should be measured at fair value with some fair value changes being presented in other comprehensive income. It decided that it was preferable that the guidance was consistent for all liability contingent consideration and, consequently, it decided that all liability contingent consideration should be subsequently measured at fair value with any resulting gain or loss, including gain or loss attributable to changes in own credit risk, being recognised in profit or loss.

Disclosure

BC360J   Some stakeholders had asked whether the IASB had intended the disclosure requirements in IFRS 7 *Financial Instruments: Disclosures* to apply to contingent consideration, noting that there are disclosure requirements for contingent consideration in IFRS 3. The IASB thinks that it is appropriate for the disclosure requirements of IFRS 7 to apply to contingent consideration that is a financial instrument within the scope of IFRS 7. Consequently, the IASB decided not to make any changes to the scope of IFRS 7 to exclude such financial instruments.

Replacement awards

BC361   An acquirer sometimes issues replacement awards to benefit the employees of the acquiree for past services, for future services or for both. Accordingly, the 2005 Exposure Draft included guidance for determining the extent to which replacement awards are for past services (and thus part of the consideration transferred in the business combination) or future services (and thus not part

---

31 IFRS 9 *Financial Instruments* replaced IAS 39. IFRS 9 applies to all items that were previously within the scope of IAS 39.

of the consideration transferred). In developing that guidance, the boards' objective was, as far as possible, to be consistent with the guidance in their respective standards on share-based payments.

BC362 Few respondents to the 2005 Exposure Draft commented on this issue, and those who did so generally agreed with the proposals, at least as they related to entities that apply IFRS 2 in accounting for share-based payment awards granted otherwise than in a business combination. However, in redeliberating the 2005 Exposure Draft, the FASB observed that some of its proposals on share-based payment awards were not consistent with SFAS 123(R), which was published after the related deliberations in the second phase of its business combinations project. For example, the 2005 Exposure Draft proposed that the excess, if any, of the fair value of replacement awards over the fair value of the replaced acquiree awards should be immediately recognised as remuneration cost in the post-combination financial statements even if employees were required to render future service to earn the rights to the replacement awards. SFAS 123(R), on the other hand, requires recognition of additional remuneration cost arising in a modification of the terms of an award (which is the same as the replacement of one award with another) over the requisite service period. The FASB concluded that, in general, the requirements of SFAS 141(R) on accounting for replacements of share-based payment awards should be consistent with the requirements for other share-based payment awards in SFAS 123(R). To achieve that goal the FASB modified the guidance in SFAS 141(R) on accounting for any excess of the fair value of replacement awards over the fair value of the replaced awards.

BC363 In addition, the FASB's constituents raised questions about other aspects of the guidance on accounting for the replacement of share-based payment awards. Those questions generally related to interpretative guidance that SFAS 123(R) superseded or nullified without providing comparable guidance—specifically, FASB Interpretation No. 44 *Accounting for Certain Transactions involving Stock Compensation* and EITF Issue No. 00-23 *Issues Related to the Accounting for Stock Compensation under APB Opinion No. 25 and FASB Interpretation No. 44*. Paragraphs B56–B62 of the revised IFRS 3 provide guidance to help in resolving those implementation questions. In developing that guidance, the FASB sought to apply the same principles to the replacement of share-based payment awards in a business combination that are applied to share-based payment awards in other situations. The IASB agreed with that goal, and it decided that the guidance on accounting for replacement awards of share-based payment is consistent with the guidance in IFRS 2 on accounting for modification of share-based payment awards.

BC364 The boards concluded that the guidance in the revised standards is consistent with the objective that the consideration transferred for an acquired business includes those payments that are for the business and excludes those payments that are for other purposes. Remuneration for future services to be rendered to the acquirer by former owners or other employees of the acquiree is not, in substance, consideration for the business acquired.

Acquisition-related costs

BC365 The boards considered whether acquisition-related costs are part of the consideration transferred in exchange for the acquiree. Those costs include an acquirer's costs incurred in connection with a business combination (a) for the services of lawyers, investment bankers, accountants and other third parties and (b) for issuing debt or equity instruments used to effect the business combination (issue costs). Generally, acquisition-related costs are charged to expense as incurred, but the costs to issue debt or equity securities are an exception. Currently, the accounting for issue costs is mixed and conflicting practices have developed in the absence of clear accounting guidance. The FASB is addressing issue costs in its project on liabilities and equity and has tentatively decided that those costs should be recognised as expenses as incurred. Some FASB members would have preferred to require issue costs to effect a business combination to be recognised as expenses, but they did not think that the business combinations project was the place to make that decision. Therefore, the FASB decided to allow mixed practices for accounting for issue costs to continue until the project on liabilities and equity resolves the issue broadly.

BC366 The boards concluded that acquisition-related costs are not part of the fair value exchange between the buyer and seller for the business. Rather, they are separate transactions in which the buyer pays for the fair value of services received. The boards also observed that those costs, whether for services performed by external parties or internal staff of the acquirer, do not generally represent assets of the acquirer at the acquisition date because the benefits obtained are consumed as the services are received.

BC367 Thus, the 2005 Exposure Draft proposed, and the revised standards require, the acquirer to exclude acquisition-related costs from the measurement of the fair value of both the consideration transferred and the assets acquired or liabilities assumed as part of the business combination. Those costs are to be accounted for separately from the business combination, and generally recognised as expenses when incurred. The revised standards therefore resolve inconsistencies in accounting for acquisition-related costs in accordance with the cost-accumulation approach in IFRS 3 and SFAS 141, which provided that the cost of an acquiree included *direct* costs incurred for an acquisition of a business but excluded *indirect* costs. Direct costs included out-of-pocket or incremental costs, for example, finder's fees and fees paid to outside consultants for accounting, legal or valuation services for a successful acquisition, but direct costs incurred in unsuccessful negotiations were recognised as expenses as incurred. Indirect costs included recurring internal costs, such as maintaining an acquisition department. Although those costs also could be directly related to a successful acquisition, they were recognised as expenses as incurred.

BC368 Some respondents to the 2005 Exposure Draft said that acquisition-related costs, including costs of due diligence, are unavoidable costs of the investment in a business. They suggested that, because the acquirer intends to recover its due diligence cost through the post-acquisition operations of the business, that transaction cost should be capitalised as part of the total investment in the business. Some also argued that the buyer specifically considers those costs in determining the amount that it is willing to pay for the acquiree. The boards rejected those arguments. They found no persuasive evidence indicating that the seller of a particular business is willing to accept less than fair value as consideration for its business merely because a particular buyer may incur more (or less) acquisition-related costs than other potential buyers for that business. Furthermore, the boards concluded that the intentions of a particular buyer, including its plans to recover such costs, are a separate matter that is distinct from the fair value measurement objective in the revised standards.

BC369 The boards acknowledge that the cost-accumulation models in IFRS 3 and SFAS 141 included some acquisition-related costs as part of the carrying amount of the assets acquired. The boards also acknowledge that all asset acquisitions are similar transactions that, in concept, should be accounted for similarly, regardless of whether assets are acquired separately or as part of a group of assets that may meet the definition of a business. However, as noted in paragraph BC20, the boards decided not to extend the scope of the revised standards to all acquisitions of groups of assets. Therefore, the boards accept that, at this time, accounting for most acquisition-related costs separately from the business combination, generally as an expense as incurred for services received in connection with a combination, differs from some standards or accepted practices that require or permit particular acquisition-related costs to be included in the cost of an asset acquisition. The boards concluded, however, that the revised standards improve financial reporting by eliminating inconsistencies in accounting for acquisition-related costs in connection with a business combination and by applying the fair value measurement principle to all business combinations. The boards also observed that in practice under IFRS 3 and SFAS 141, most acquisition-related costs were subsumed in goodwill, which was also not consistent with accounting for asset acquisitions.

BC370 The boards also considered concerns about the potential for abuse. Some constituents, including some respondents to the 2005 Exposure Draft, said that if acquirers could no longer capitalise acquisition-related costs as part of the cost of the business acquired, they might modify transactions to avoid recognising those costs as expenses. For example, some said that a buyer might ask a seller to make payments to the buyer's vendors on its behalf. To facilitate the negotiations and sale of the business, the seller might agree to make those payments if the total amount to be paid to it upon closing of the business combination is sufficient to reimburse the seller for payments it made on the buyer's behalf. If the disguised reimbursements were treated as part of the consideration transferred for the business, the acquirer might not recognise those expenses. Rather, the measure of the fair value of the business and the amount of goodwill recognised for that business might be overstated. To mitigate such concerns, the revised standards require any payments to an acquiree (or its former owners) in connection with a business combination that are payments for goods or services that are not part of the acquired business to be assigned to those goods or services and accounted for as a separate transaction. The revised standards specifically require an acquirer to determine whether any portion of the amounts transferred by the acquirer are separate from the consideration exchanged for the acquiree and the assets acquired and liabilities assumed in the business combination. The revised standards (see paragraphs 51–53 and B50 of the revised IFRS 3) provide guidance for making that determination.

Bargain purchases

BC371   Paragraphs 34–36 of the revised IFRS 3 set out the accounting requirements for a bargain purchase. The boards consider bargain purchases anomalous transactions — business entities and their owners generally do not knowingly and willingly sell assets or businesses at prices below their fair values. However, bargain purchases have occurred and are likely to continue to occur. Circumstances in which they occur include a forced liquidation or distress sale (eg after the death of a founder or key manager) in which owners need to sell a business quickly, which may result in a price that is less than fair value.

BC372   The boards observed that an economic gain is inherent in a bargain purchase. At the acquisition date, the acquirer is better off by the amount by which the fair value of what is acquired exceeds the fair value of the consideration transferred (paid) for it. The boards concluded that, in concept, the acquirer should recognise that gain at the acquisition date. However, the boards acknowledged that although the reasons for a forced liquidation or distress sale are often apparent, sometimes clear evidence might not exist, for example, if a seller uses a closed (private) process for the sale and to maintain its negotiating position is unwilling to reveal the main reason for the sale. The appearance of a bargain purchase without evidence of the underlying reasons would raise concerns in practice about the existence of measurement errors.

BC373   Constituents, including some respondents to the 2005 Exposure Draft, expressed concerns about recognising gains upon the acquisition of a business, particularly if it is difficult to determine whether a particular acquisition is in fact a bargain purchase. They also suggested that an initial determination of an excess of the acquisition-date fair value (or other recognised amounts) of the identifiable net assets acquired over the fair value of the consideration paid by the acquirer plus the recognised amount of any non-controlling interest in the acquiree might arise from other factors, including:

(a)   errors in measuring the fair values of (i) the consideration paid for the business, (ii) the assets acquired or (iii) the liabilities assumed; and

(b)   using measures in accordance with IFRSs or US GAAP that are not fair values.

Distinguishing a bargain purchase from measurement errors

BC374   The boards acknowledged concerns raised by constituents that a requirement to recognise gains on a bargain purchase might provide an opportunity for inappropriate gain recognition from intentional errors resulting from the acquirer's:

(a) understating or failing to identify the value of items of consideration that it transferred;

(b) overstating values attributed to particular assets acquired; or

(c) understating or failing to identify and recognise particular liabilities assumed.

BC375   The boards think that problems surrounding intentional measurement errors by acquirers are generally best addressed by means other than setting standards specifically intended to avoid abuse. Strong internal control systems and the use of independent valuation experts and external auditors are among the means by which both intentional and unintentional measurement errors are minimised. Standards specifically designed to avoid abuse would inevitably lack neutrality. (See paragraph BC51 for a discussion of the need for neutrality in accounting and accounting standards.) However, the boards share constituents' concerns about the potential for inappropriate gain recognition resulting from measurement bias or undetected measurement errors. Thus, the boards decided (see paragraph 36 of the revised IFRS 3) to require the acquirer to reassess whether it has correctly identified all of the assets acquired and all of the liabilities assumed before recognising a gain on a bargain purchase. The acquirer must then review the procedures used to measure the amounts the revised standards require to be recognised at the acquisition date for all of the following:

(a) the identifiable assets acquired and liabilities assumed;

(b) the non-controlling interest in the acquiree, if any;

(c) for a business combination achieved in stages, the acquirer's previously held equity interest in the acquiree; and

(d) the consideration transferred.

The objective of that review is to ensure that appropriate consideration has been given to all available information in identifying the items to be measured and recognised and in determining their fair values. The boards believe that the required review will mitigate, if not eliminate, undetected errors that might have existed in the initial measurements.

BC376   The boards acknowledged, however, that the required review might be insufficient to eliminate concerns about unintentional measurement bias. They decided to address that concern by limiting the extent of gain that can be recognised. Thus, the revised standards provide that a gain on a bargain purchase is measured as the excess of:

(a) the net of the acquisition-date amounts of the identifiable assets acquired and liabilities assumed; over

(b) the acquisition-date fair value of the consideration transferred plus the recognised amount of any non-controlling interest in the acquiree and, if the transaction is an acquisition achieved in stages, the acquisition-date fair value of the acquirer's previously held equity interest in the acquiree.

That means that a gain on a bargain purchase and goodwill cannot both be recognised for the same business combination. The 2005 Exposure Draft defined a bargain purchase as a transaction in which the fair value of the acquirer's interest in the acquiree exceeds the consideration transferred for it, but it would have required that any resulting goodwill should be written off before a gain was recognised. The result of the revised standards' requirement is the same, but there will be no goodwill to write off if the gain is measured with reference to the identifiable net assets acquired rather than the fair value of the acquirer's interest in the acquiree. In addition, the revised standards require (paragraph B64(n) of the revised IFRS 3) the acquirer to disclose information about a gain recognised on a bargain purchase.

BC377 The main purpose of the limitation on gain recognition is to mitigate the potential for inappropriate gain recognition through measurement errors, particularly those that might result from unintended measurement bias. The main purpose of the disclosure requirement is to provide information that enables users of an acquirer's financial statements to evaluate the nature and financial effect of business combinations that occur during the period. The boards acknowledged, however, that the limitation and disclosure requirements may also help to mitigate constituents' concerns about potential abuse, although that is not their primary objective.

BC378 Moreover, the boards believe that concerns about abuse resulting from the opportunity for gain recognition may be overstated. Financial analysts and other users have often told the boards that they give little weight to one-off or unusual gains, such as those resulting from a bargain purchase transaction. In addition, the boards noted that managers of entities generally have no incentive to overstate assets acquired or understate liabilities assumed in a business combination because that would generally result in higher post-combination expenses—when the assets are used or become impaired or liabilities are remeasured or settled.

Distinguishing a bargain purchase from a 'negative goodwill result'

BC379 The boards acknowledged that a so-called negative goodwill result remains a possibility (although in most situations, a remote possibility) because the revised standards continue to require particular assets acquired and liabilities assumed to be measured at amounts other than their acquisition-date fair values. The boards observed, however, that the revised standards address most deficiencies in past requirements on accounting for business combinations that previously led to negative goodwill results—ie a result that had the appearance but not the economic substance of a bargain purchase. For example, often no liability was recognised for some contingent payment arrangements (eg earn-outs) at the acquisition date, which could result in the appearance of a bargain purchase by understating the consideration paid. The revised standards, in contrast, require the measurement and recognition of substantially all liabilities at their fair values on the acquisition date.

BC380   The boards also considered concerns raised by some constituents that a buyer's expectations of future losses and its need to incur future costs to make a business viable might give rise to a negative goodwill result. In other words, a buyer would be willing to pay a seller only an amount that is, according to that view, less than the fair value of the acquiree (or its identifiable net assets) because to make a fair return on the business the buyer would need to make further investments in that business to bring its condition to fair value. The boards disagreed with that view for the reasons noted in paragraphs BC134–BC143 in the context of liabilities associated with restructuring or exit activities of the acquiree, as well as those that follow.

BC381   Fair values are measured by reference to unrelated buyers and sellers that are knowledgeable and have a common understanding about factors relevant to the business and the transaction and are also willing and able to transact business in the same market(s) and have the legal and financial ability to do so. The boards are aware of no compelling reason to believe that, in the absence of duress, a seller would willingly and knowingly sell a business for an amount less than its fair value. Thus, the boards concluded that careful application of the revised standards' fair value measurement requirements will mitigate concerns that negative goodwill might result and be misinterpreted as a bargain purchase transaction.

Overpayments

BC382   The boards considered whether the revised standards should include special provisions to account for a business combination in which a buyer overpays for its interest in the acquiree. The boards acknowledged that overpayments are possible and, in concept, an overpayment should lead to the acquirer's recognition of an expense (or loss) in the period of the acquisition. However, the boards believe that in practice any overpayment is unlikely to be detectable or known at the acquisition date. In other words, the boards are not aware of instances in which a buyer knowingly overpays or is compelled to overpay a seller to acquire a business. Even if an acquirer thinks it might have overpaid in some sense, the amount of overpayment would be difficult, if not impossible, to quantify. Thus, the boards concluded that in practice it is not possible to identify and reliably measure an overpayment at the acquisition date. Accounting for overpayments is best addressed through subsequent impairment testing when evidence of a potential overpayment first arises.

Additional guidance for particular types of business combinations

BC383   To help entities apply the acquisition method as required by the revised standards, the boards decided to provide additional guidance for business combinations achieved in stages and those achieved without the transfer of consideration. Paragraphs BC384–BC389 discuss the guidance provided on business combinations achieved in stages. The guidance on combinations achieved without the transfer of consideration merely responds to a question about how to report the acquiree's net assets in the equity section of the acquirer's post-combination statement of financial position, and this Basis for Conclusions does not discuss that guidance further.

Business combinations achieved in stages

BC384   In a business combination achieved in stages, the acquirer remeasures its previously held equity interest at its acquisition-date fair value and recognises the related gain or loss in profit or loss (paragraph 42 of the revised IFRS 3). The boards concluded that a change from holding a non-controlling investment in an entity to obtaining control of that entity is a significant change in the nature of and economic circumstances surrounding that investment. That change warrants a change in the classification and measurement of that investment. Once it obtains control, the acquirer is no longer the owner of a non-controlling investment asset in the acquiree. As in present practice, the acquirer ceases its accounting for an investment asset and begins reporting in its financial statements the underlying assets, liabilities and results of operations of the acquiree.[32] In effect, the acquirer exchanges its status as an owner of an investment asset in an entity for a controlling financial interest in all of the underlying assets and liabilities of that entity (acquiree) and the right to direct how the acquiree and its management use those assets in its operations.

BC385   In August 2003 the FASB held a round-table meeting with members of its resource group on business combinations and other constituents to discuss, among other things, the decision to require an acquirer to remeasure any previously held equity investment in an acquiree at its acquisition-date fair value and to recognise in earnings any gain or loss. The users of financial statements indicated they did not have significant concerns with that change to present practice, as long as the amount of the gain or loss is clearly disclosed in the financial statements or in the notes. Paragraph B64(p) of the revised IFRS 3 requires that disclosure.

BC386   The boards rejected the view expressed by some constituents that the carrying amount of any pre-acquisition investment should be retained in the initial accounting for the cost of the business acquired. The boards concluded that cost-accumulation practices led to many of the inconsistencies and deficiencies in financial reporting as required by SFAS 141 and, to a lesser extent, by IFRS 3 (see paragraphs BC198–BC202).

BC387   Some constituents also expressed concern about what they described as allowing an opportunity for gain recognition on a purchase transaction. The boards noted that the required remeasurement could also result in loss recognition. Moreover, the boards rejected the characterisation that the result is to recognise a gain or loss on a purchase. Rather, under today's mixed attribute accounting model, economic gains and losses are recognised as they occur for some, but not all, financial instruments. If an equity interest in an entity is not required to be measured at its fair value, the recognition of a gain or loss at the acquisition date is merely a consequence of the delayed recognition of the economic gain or loss that is present in that financial instrument. If the investment asset had been measured at fair value at the end

---

32   In October 2012 the Board issued *Investment Entities* (Amendments to IFRS 10, IFRS 12 and IAS 27), which required investment entities, as defined in IFRS 10, to measure their investments in subsidiaries, other than those providing investment-related services or activities, at fair value through profit or loss.

of each reporting period, the gain or loss would have been recognised as it occurred and measurement of the asset at its acquisition-date fair value would result in no further gain or loss.

BC388   Some respondents who agreed that an acquirer should remeasure its previously held equity interest at fair value would recognise any resulting gain or loss in other comprehensive income rather than in profit or loss. Those respondents said that the accounting for previously held equity interests is similar to the accounting for available-for-sale securities. Changes in the value of available-for-sale securities are recognised in other comprehensive income. They view each step in a step acquisition as a transaction in which the acquirer only obtains more shares in the acquiree. Because the shares that the acquirer previously held have not been exchanged or sold, they think that the recognition of profit or loss is not appropriate.

BC389   The boards understand that the required treatment of a previously held equity investment in a step acquisition is different from the initial recognition of gains or losses on available-for-sale securities.[33] However, the boards noted that changes in the value of available-for-sale securities are recognised in profit or loss when the securities are derecognised. In a business combination achieved in stages, the acquirer derecognises its investment asset in an entity in its consolidated financial statements when it achieves control. Thus, the boards concluded that it is appropriate to recognise any resulting gain or loss in profit or loss at the acquisition date.

Previously held interest in a joint operation (amendments issued in December 2017)

BC389A   The IASB was informed that entities, on obtaining control of a business that is a joint operation, accounted for their previously held interest in the joint operation differently. In particular, there were different views on whether the term 'equity interest' in paragraphs 41–42 of IFRS 3 applied to such a previously held interest.

BC389B   The IASB concluded that the transaction described in paragraph BC389A is a business combination achieved in stages. This transaction results in a significant change in the nature of, and economic circumstances surrounding, any interest in the joint operation; remeasuring the previously held interest at fair value is therefore warranted. Accordingly, the IASB added paragraph 42A to clarify that, when obtaining control of a business that is a joint operation, the acquirer applies the requirements for a business combination achieved in stages, including remeasuring its previously held interest in the joint operation at its acquisition-date fair value.

BC389C   Some respondents to the exposure draft of the proposed amendments to IFRS 3 suggested that the IASB clarify whether an acquirer would be required to remeasure its entire previously held interest in a joint operation or only the assets and liabilities relating to the joint operation it had recognised before obtaining control. In response, the IASB clarified that an entity remeasures its entire previously held interest in the joint operation. IFRS 3 views a business

---

33   IFRS 9 *Financial Instruments* eliminated the category of available-for-sale financial assets.

combination achieved in stages as a transaction in which an acquirer exchanges its status as an owner of a non-controlling interest in a business for a controlling interest in all of the underlying assets and liabilities of that business. Accordingly, when an acquirer obtains control of a business that is a joint operation, it effectively (a) derecognises its previously held interest (ie non-controlling interest) in the joint operation, and (b) recognises a controlling interest in all of the assets and liabilities of the former joint operation. The IASB observed that remeasuring the entire previously held interest would result in an entity recognising the same gain or loss on remeasurement that it would have recognised had it otherwise disposed of its previously held interest in the joint operation in an exchange transaction.

Measurement period

BC390   The revised standards provide an acquirer with a reasonable period after the acquisition date, a *measurement period*, during which to obtain the information necessary to identify and measure the items specified in paragraph 46 of the revised IFRS 3 as of the acquisition date in accordance with the requirements of the revised standards. If sufficient information is not available at the acquisition date to measure those amounts, the acquirer determines and recognises provisional amounts until the necessary information becomes available.

BC391   The boards concluded that providing for retrospective adjustments during the measurement period should help to resolve concerns about the quality and availability of information at the acquisition date for measuring the fair values of particular items at that date. Constituents especially indicated such concerns about contingent liabilities and contingent consideration arrangements, which also affect the amount of goodwill or the gain recognised on a bargain purchase.

BC392   The boards decided to place constraints on the period for which it is deemed reasonable to be seeking information necessary to complete the accounting for a business combination. The measurement period ends as soon as the acquirer receives the necessary information about facts and circumstances that existed as of the acquisition date or learns that the information is not obtainable. However, in no circumstances may the measurement period exceed one year from the acquisition date. The boards concluded that allowing a measurement period longer than one year would not be especially helpful; obtaining reliable information about circumstances and conditions that existed more than a year ago is likely to become more difficult as time passes. Of course, the outcome of some contingencies and similar matters may not be known within a year. But the objective of the measurement period is to provide time to obtain the information necessary to measure the fair value of the item as of the acquisition date. Determining the ultimate settlement amount of a contingency or other item is not necessary. Uncertainties about the timing and amount of future cash flows are part of the measure of the fair value of an asset or liability.

BC393   The boards also concluded that acquirers should provide users of their financial statements with relevant information about the status of items that have been measured only provisionally. Thus, paragraph B67(a) of the revised IFRS 3 specifies particular disclosures about those items.

BC394   Both IFRS 3 and SFAS 141 included a period during which an acquirer might measure particular amounts provisionally if the necessary information was not available at the acquisition date. Neither of those provisions was identical to the measurement period guidance in the revised standards, although IFRS 3's was quite similar. However, the measurement period provisions in the revised standards differ in important ways from the allocation period guidance of SFAS 141 and its cost-allocation method. The revised standards emphasise the principle that assets acquired, liabilities assumed and any non-controlling interest in the acquiree should be measured at their acquisition-date fair values. SFAS 141's allocation period and its post-combination adjustments delayed the recognition of assets and liabilities, and those assets and liabilities were not measured at their acquisition-date fair values when they were recognised. Therefore, the FASB decided to replace the SFAS 141 term *allocation period* and its guidance with the measurement period guidance in the revised standards.

BC395   The FASB also decided that to improve the quality of comparative information reported in financial statements and to converge with the requirements of IFRS 3, SFAS 141(R) should require an acquirer:

   (a)   to recognise adjustments made during the measurement period to the provisional values of the assets acquired and liabilities assumed as if the accounting for the business combination had been completed at the acquisition date.

   (b)   to adjust comparative information in previously issued financial statements, including any change in depreciation, amortisation or other income effect recognised as a result of completing the initial accounting.

BC396   SFAS 141 was silent about whether adjustments during its allocation period were to be reported retrospectively, but the FASB noted that in practice the effects of those adjustments were typically reported in the post-combination period, not retrospectively. The FASB acknowledged concerns that retrospective adjustments and adjusting previously issued comparative information are more costly. The FASB observed, however, that applying measurement period adjustments retrospectively would result in at least two significant benefits: (a) improvements in comparative period information and (b) avoidance of divergent accounting between US entities and others and the reduction of reconciling items and their attendant costs. The FASB concluded, as had the IASB in developing IFRS 3, that those overall benefits outweigh the potential costs of retrospective application.

BC397   Some respondents to the 2005 Exposure Draft (generally those who apply US GAAP rather than IFRSs) disagreed with retrospective application of measurement period adjustments. They regarded measurement period adjustments as similar to changes in estimates, which are accounted for prospectively. They noted that FASB Statement No. 154 *Accounting Changes and Error Corrections* (SFAS 154) and IAS 8 *Accounting Policies, Changes in Accounting Estimates and Errors* both require retrospective adjustment only for changes in accounting policy or restatement for errors.

BC398   In considering those responses, the boards observed that measurement period adjustments in a business combination differ from the changes in estimates dealt with by SFAS 154 and IAS 8. Measurement period adjustments result from information about assets, liabilities and non-controlling interests as of the acquisition date that becomes available only after that date. In contrast, adjustments for changes in estimates generally result from changes in facts and circumstances that affect an estimate, for example, a change in technology that affects the useful life of an asset.

BC399   The boards concluded that adjustments during the measurement period following a business combination are more analogous to adjusting events after the end of the reporting period (IAS 10 *Events after the Reporting Period*) than to changes in estimates. The effects of events that occur after the end of an accounting period but before the financial statements for the period are authorised for issue and provide evidence of a condition that existed at the date of the financial statements are reflected in financial statements as of that date. Similarly, the effects of information that first becomes available during the measurement period and provides evidence of conditions or circumstances that existed at the acquisition date should be reflected in the accounting as of that date.

BC400   To recognise measurement period adjustments only prospectively would be inconsistent with the recognition and measurement principles in the revised standards. Thus, although the boards understand the practical and other difficulties with retrospective adjustments, on balance, they concluded that requiring such adjustments in this situation is appropriate.

Disclosures

BC401   Because a business combination often results in a significant change to an entity's operations, the nature and extent of the information disclosed about the transaction bear on users' abilities to assess the effects of such changes on post-combination profit or loss and cash flows. Accordingly, as part of their respective projects that led to IFRS 3 and SFAS 141, the IASB and the FASB both considered the usefulness of the disclosure requirements required by IAS 22 and APB Opinion 16, respectively, for the acquisition method. IFRS 3 and SFAS 141 carried forward disclosures from the earlier requirements for business combinations that remained relevant, eliminated those that did not and modified those that were affected by changes in the recognition or measurement requirements. In the second phase of their projects on business combinations, the boards undertook essentially the same sort of reconsideration of the disclosure requirements in IFRS 3 and SFAS 141, and they also considered particular disclosures requested by respondents to the 2005 Exposure Draft.

BC402   The remainder of this section first reviews the changes that SFAS 141 and IFRS 3 made to the disclosure requirements of APB Opinion 16 and IAS 22 respectively (paragraphs BC403–BC418). Paragraphs BC419–BC428 then discuss the changes the revised standards make to the disclosure requirements of SFAS 141 and IFRS 3.

Disclosure requirements of SFAS 141

Disclosure of information about the purchase price allocation and pro forma sales and earnings

BC403   The 1999 Exposure Draft would have required tabular disclosure of the fair values allocated to each of the major classes of assets and liabilities presented in the statement of financial position and the acquiree's related carrying amounts immediately before its acquisition. That exposure draft also proposed eliminating the pro forma sales and earnings disclosures required by APB Opinion 16.

BC404   Approximately half of the respondents who commented on the proposed requirement to disclose information about the purchase price allocation agreed that the information would be useful in assessing post-acquisition earnings and cash flows of the acquirer. However, some respondents questioned the usefulness of the proposed disclosure of information about the acquiree's carrying amounts of assets acquired and liabilities assumed, particularly if the financial statements of the acquiree were not audited or were prepared on a basis other than US GAAP. After considering those views, the FASB affirmed its conclusion that information about the allocation of the purchase price to major classes of assets and liabilities in the statement of financial position would be useful in assessing the amount and timing of future cash flows. However, it agreed that information about the related carrying amounts might be of limited usefulness. Thus, SFAS 141 required disclosure of information about the allocation of the purchase price to each major class of asset and liability in the acquiree's statement of financial position but not their previous carrying amounts.

BC405   After considering respondents' views, the FASB included in SFAS 141 the pro forma disclosure requirements from APB Opinion 16. However, the FASB also continued the exemption of non-public entities from the pro forma disclosure requirements. Preparers and auditors of financial statements of non-public entities urged the FASB to continue that exemption, which was initially provided by FASB Statement No. 79 *Elimination of Certain Disclosures for Business Combinations by Nonpublic Enterprises*.

Disclosures related to goodwill

BC406   The FASB's 2001 Exposure Draft (see paragraph BC160 for a discussion of that exposure draft) would have required the acquirer to disclose (a) the reasons for the acquisition, including a description of the factors that led to a purchase price that resulted in goodwill and (b) the amount of goodwill assigned to each reportable segment. The requirement to disclose goodwill by reportable segment was limited to entities that are within the scope of FASB Statement

No. 131 *Disclosures about Segments of an Enterprise and Related Information*. That exposure draft also proposed requiring disclosure of the amount of goodwill expected to be deductible for tax purposes if the goodwill initially recognised in a material business combination was significant in relation to the total cost of the acquiree. After considering the comments of respondents, the FASB affirmed its conclusion that the information would be useful in estimating the amount and timing of future impairment losses, and SFAS 141 required that disclosure.

Disclosure of information about intangible assets other than goodwill

BC407   If the amount assigned to intangible assets was significant in relation to the total cost of an acquiree, SFAS 141 required disclosure of the following information to help users of financial statements assess the amount and timing of future cash flows:

(a)   the total amount assigned to intangible assets subject to amortisation and the total amount assigned to those that are not subject to amortisation;

(b)   the amount assigned to each major intangible asset class;

(c)   for intangible assets subject to amortisation, the weighted average amortisation period in total and for each major intangible asset class; and

(d)   the amount of any significant residual value assumed, both in total and for each major class of intangible asset.

Other disclosure requirements

BC408   The 1999 Exposure Draft proposed, and SFAS 141 required, disclosure of specified information for a series of immaterial business combinations that are material in the aggregate completed in a reporting period:

(a)   the number of entities acquired and a brief description of them;

(b)   the aggregate cost of the acquired entities, the number of equity interests issued or issuable and the value assigned to them;

(c)   the aggregate amount of any contingent payments, options or commitments and the accounting treatment that will be followed should any such contingency occur (if potentially significant in relation to the aggregate cost of the acquired entities); and

(d)   the information about goodwill required for a material acquisition if the aggregate amount assigned to goodwill or to other intangible assets acquired was significant in relation to the aggregate cost of the acquired entities.

BC409   In addition, the 1999 Exposure Draft proposed, and SFAS 141 required, that the information required to be disclosed for a completed business combination would also be disclosed for a material business combination completed after the balance sheet date but before the financial statements are authorised for issue (unless disclosure of such information was not practicable). That requirement was consistent with auditing standards on subsequent events.

Disclosures in interim financial information

BC410   Several analysts and other users recommended that the FASB should require disclosure of supplemental pro forma revenues and earnings in interim financial information because that information would be more useful if it was available earlier. SFAS 141 amended APB Opinion No. 28 *Interim Financial Reporting* to require disclosure of that information.

Disclosure requirements of IFRS 3

BC411   IFRS 3 identified three objectives that its disclosure requirements were intended to meet, specifically, to provide the users of an acquirer's financial statements with information that enables them to evaluate:

(a)   the nature and financial effect of business combinations that were effected during the reporting period or after the balance sheet date but before the financial statements were authorised for issue.

(b)   the financial effects of gains, losses, error corrections and other adjustments recognised in the current period that relate to business combinations that were effected in the current period or in previous periods.

(c)   changes in the carrying amount of goodwill during the period.

BC412   The IASB began its discussion of the disclosure requirements necessary to meet the objectives by assessing the disclosure requirements in SIC-28 *Business Combinations — "Date of Exchange" and Fair Value of Equity Instruments* and IAS 22. The IASB concluded that information disclosed in accordance with SIC-28 about equity instruments issued as part of the cost of a business combination helped to meet the first of the three objectives outlined above. Therefore, IFRS 3 carried forward the disclosure requirements in SIC-28.

BC413   The IASB also concluded that information previously disclosed in accordance with IAS 22 about business combinations classified as acquisitions and goodwill helped to meet the objectives in paragraph BC411. Therefore, IFRS 3 carried forward the related disclosure requirements in IAS 22, amended as necessary to reflect changes IFRS 3 made to the provisions of IAS 22. For example, IAS 22 required disclosure of the amount of any adjustment during the period to goodwill or 'negative goodwill' resulting from subsequent identification or changes in value of the acquiree's identifiable assets and liabilities. IFRS 3 required an acquirer, with specified exceptions, to adjust the initial accounting for a combination after that accounting was complete only to correct an error. Thus, IFRS 3 revised the IAS 22 disclosure requirement to require disclosure of information about error corrections required to be disclosed by IAS 8.

BC414　The IASB then assessed whether any additional disclosure requirements should be included in IFRS 3 to ensure that the three disclosure objectives were met and considered the disclosure requirements in the corresponding standards of its partner standard-setters. As a result, and after considering respondents' comments on ED 3, the IASB identified, and IFRS 3 required, the following additional disclosures to help meet the first of the three disclosure objectives in paragraph BC411:

    (a)　For each business combination effected during the period:

        (i)　the amounts recognised at the acquisition date for each class of the acquiree's assets, liabilities and contingent liabilities and, if practicable, the carrying amounts of each of those classes, determined in accordance with IFRSs, immediately before the combination. If such disclosure was impracticable, an entity disclosed that fact, together with an explanation of why disclosure was impracticable.

        (ii)　a description of the factors that contributed to the recognition of goodwill—including a description of each intangible asset that was not recognised separately from goodwill and an explanation of why the intangible asset's fair value could not be measured reliably. If the acquirer's interest in the acquiree's identifiable net assets exceeded the cost, the acquirer was required to describe the nature of that excess.

        (iii)　the amount of the acquiree's profit or loss since the acquisition date included in the acquirer's profit or loss for the period, unless disclosure was impracticable. If such disclosure was impracticable, the acquirer disclosed that fact, together with an explanation of why disclosure was impracticable.

    (b)　The information required to be disclosed for each business combination that was effected during the period in aggregate for business combinations that are individually immaterial.

    (c)　The revenue and profit or loss of the combined entity for the period as though the acquisition date for all business combinations that were effected during the period had been the beginning of that period, unless such disclosure was impracticable.

BC415　To aid in meeting the second disclosure objective in paragraph BC411, IFRS 3 also required disclosure of the amount and an explanation of any gain or loss recognised in the current period that both:

    (a)　related to the identifiable assets acquired or liabilities or contingent liabilities assumed in a business combination that was effected in the current or a previous period; and

    (b)　was of such size, nature or incidence that disclosure was relevant to an understanding of the combined entity's financial performance.

BC416   To help achieve the third disclosure objective in paragraph BC411, the IASB concluded that the previous requirement to disclose a reconciliation of the carrying amount of goodwill at the beginning and end of the period should be amended to require separate disclosure of net exchange rate differences arising during the period in accordance with IAS 21 *The Effects of Changes in Foreign Exchange Rates*.

BC417   The IASB observed that there might be situations in which the information disclosed under the specific requirements would not completely satisfy IFRS 3's three disclosure objectives. In that situation, IFRS 3 required disclosure of any additional information necessary to meet those objectives.

BC418   IFRS 3 also required the acquirer to disclose the number of equity instruments issued or issuable as part of the cost of a business combination, the fair value of those instruments and the basis for determining that fair value. Although IAS 22 did not explicitly require disclosure of that information, the IASB concluded that the acquirer should have provided it as part of disclosing the cost of acquisition and a description of the purchase consideration paid or contingently payable in accordance with paragraph 87(b) of IAS 22. The IASB decided that to avoid inconsistent application, IFRS 3 should explicitly require disclosure of that information.

Disclosure requirements of the revised standards

BC419   The boards decided that the revised standards should include overall objectives for the disclosure of information that would be useful to investors, creditors and others in evaluating the financial effects of a business combination. The objectives, which are stated in paragraphs 59 and 61 of the revised IFRS 3, are, in substance, the same as those in IFRS 3 and the 2005 Exposure Draft. Respondents to the 2005 Exposure Draft who discussed the proposed disclosures generally agreed with the disclosure objectives. In reconsidering that exposure draft, however, the boards noted that the third objective in IFRS 3, to provide information that enables users of an entity's financial statements to evaluate changes in the carrying amount of goodwill during the period, is effectively included in the objective in paragraph 61. Thus, the boards combined those two objectives.

BC420   In addition, both boards concluded, as the IASB did in developing IFRS 3, that it is not necessary (or possible) to identify all of the specific information that may be necessary to meet those objectives for all business combinations. Rather, the revised standards specify particular disclosures that are generally required to meet those objectives and require acquirers to disclose any additional information about the circumstances surrounding a particular business combination that they consider necessary to meet those objectives (paragraph 63 of the revised IFRS 3).

BC421   Changes to the disclosure requirements of IFRS 3 and SFAS 141 include the elimination of disclosures of amounts or information that was based on applying the cost allocation (purchase price) method for assigning amounts to assets and liabilities that is replaced by the revised standards' fair value measurement principle. Some of those disclosures are modified to retain the information but conform the amounts to be disclosed with the fair value measurement principle.

BC422   The boards added some disclosure requirements to those in IFRS 3, SFAS 141 or both and modified or eliminated others. Those changes are described below, together with an indication of how the changes relate to each board's previous requirements and references to related discussions in other parts of this Basis for Conclusions where pertinent.[34]

(a)   In response to requests from some commentators on the 2005 Exposure Draft, the boards added to both IFRS 3 and SFAS 141 disclosure of information about receivables acquired. (paragraphs BC258–BC260)

(b)   The boards modified both IFRS 3's and SFAS 141's disclosures about contingent consideration in a business combination to make them consistent with the revised standards' requirements for contingent consideration. Paragraph B64(g) of the revised IFRS 3 describes the specific disclosures now required.

(c)   The FASB added to SFAS 141 disclosure of the revenue and earnings of the acquiree, if practicable, for a minimum of the period from the acquisition date to the end of the current year. The disclosure is required only from public business entities for the current year, the current interim period and cumulative interim periods from the acquisition date to the end of the current year. IFRS 3 already required disclosure of the amount of the acquiree's profit or loss included in the acquirer's profit or loss for the period, unless that was impracticable; the IASB added revenues to that disclosure. (paragraphs BC423–BC428)

(d)   The FASB modified SFAS 141's disclosure of supplemental pro forma information about results of operations for the comparable prior period presented to focus on revenue and earnings of the combined entity for the comparable prior reporting period as though the acquisition date for all business combinations during the current year had been the beginning of the comparable prior annual reporting period. The disclosure is required only from public entities and only if practicable. The IASB decided not to add that disclosure. (paragraph BC428)

(e)   The FASB replaced SFAS 141's disclosure of the period for which the results of operations of the acquiree are included in the income statement of the combined entity with disclosure of the acquisition date—a disclosure that IFRS 3 already required. SFAS 141(R) no longer permits the alternative practice of reporting revenues and expenses of the acquiree as if the acquisition occurred as of the beginning of the year (or a designated date) with a reduction to eliminate the acquiree's pre-acquisition period earnings. (paragraphs BC108–BC110)

---

34   IFRS 13, issued in May 2011, requires disclosures about fair value measurements after initial recognition. Although the disclosures required by IFRS 13 are not required for IFRS 3, the wording has been aligned.

(f)　The boards revised both IFRS 3's and SFAS 141's disclosures about contingencies, at the acquisition date and subsequently, to make them consistent with the requirement of the revised standards on assets and liabilities arising from contingencies. The IASB's and the FASB's disclosures on contingencies differ because the recognition requirements to which they relate differ. (paragraphs BC265–BC278)

(g)　The FASB added to SFAS 141 disclosure of the amount of acquisition-related costs, which IFRS 3 already required, and the boards added to both IFRS 3 and SFAS 141 disclosure of the amount of acquisition-related costs recognised as expense and the statement of comprehensive income line item in which that expense is reported.

(h)　The FASB eliminated SFAS 141's requirement to disclose the amount of in-process research and development acquired that had been measured and immediately written off to expense in accordance with FASB Interpretation 4. SFAS 141(R) no longer permits that practice. (paragraphs BC149–BC155)

(i)　The boards added to both IFRS 3 and SFAS 141 disclosure of the acquisition-date fair value or other recognised amount of the non-controlling interest in the acquiree and the valuation techniques and key model inputs used for determining that value. An entity that prepares its financial statements in accordance with IFRSs also discloses the measurement basis selected for the non-controlling interest.

(j)　For a business combination achieved in stages, the boards added to both IFRS 3 and SFAS 141 disclosure of the fair value of the acquirer's previously held equity interest in the acquiree, the amount of gain or loss recognised in accordance with paragraph 42 of the revised IFRS 3 and the line item in the statement of comprehensive income in which that gain or loss is recognised.

(k)　The FASB replaced SFAS 141's disclosure of extraordinary gains recognised for 'negative goodwill' with disclosure of the amount of any gain recognised in the period for a bargain purchase, the line item in the statement of comprehensive income in which it is recognised and a description of the reasons why the transaction resulted in a gain (paragraphs BC371–BC381). IFRS 3 already required disclosure of that amount (although it was not called a gain on a bargain purchase).

(l)　The boards added to both IFRS 3 and SFAS 141 the disclosures described in paragraph B64(l) of the revised IFRS 3 about transactions that are separate from the acquisition of assets and assumption of liabilities in the exchange for the acquiree. The 2005 Exposure Draft proposed requiring disclosures about only pre-existing relationships between the acquirer and acquiree. The boards broadened the disclosure to all separate transactions in response to comments on the exposure draft.

(m) The boards revised the disclosures in IFRS 3 and SFAS 141 about aspects of the purchase price allocation not yet completed to make them consistent with the requirements of the revised standards about the measurement period. The specific disclosures required are in paragraph B67(a) of the revised IFRS 3.

(n) The IASB eliminated IFRS 3's required disclosure of the acquiree's carrying amounts in accordance with IFRSs for each class of its assets and liabilities immediately before the combination. The IASB concluded that providing that disclosure could often involve significant costs because the acquiree might not be applying IFRSs and that those costs might exceed the benefits of the information to users.

Disclosure of information about post-combination revenue and profit or loss of the acquiree

BC423 Paragraph B64(q) of the revised IFRS 3 requires an entity to disclose, for each business combination (and for individually immaterial business combinations that are material collectively), the amounts of revenue and profit or loss of the acquiree since the acquisition date included in the consolidated statement of comprehensive income for the period. At its August 2003 round-table discussion with users of financial statements, the FASB discussed the potential usefulness of information about increases or decreases in post-combination revenues and earnings from acquired businesses versus revenues and earnings from the operations already owned by the acquirer (organic growth). The FASB also asked whether that information would be preferable to the pro forma supplemental disclosure of revenue and results of operations of the combined entity for the current period as though the acquisition date for all business combinations during the year had been as of the beginning of the annual reporting period. SFAS 141 carried that disclosure forward from APB Opinion 16 and IFRS 3 required a similar disclosure.

BC424 The FASB also questioned whether those disclosures are directed at similar objectives and, if so, whether one may be preferable. The FASB observed that making post-combination distinctions might be too costly or impossible if the operations of the acquiree are integrated with those of the acquirer. Although users acknowledged that point, they indicated that information about actual post-combination revenues and earnings is preferable to the pro forma disclosures and should be required whenever possible. Some also said that distinguishing acquired revenues from organic revenues is most important and suggested that acquirers should be required to provide that information for a twelve-month period following an acquisition rather than only to the end of the annual period.

BC425 The boards agreed with users that the information about post-combination revenues and profit or loss of the acquiree is useful. However, for practical reasons, the boards concluded that the revised standards should provide an exception to that requirement if distinguishing the post-combination earnings of the acquiree from earnings of the combined entity is impracticable. The boards also decided that in those circumstances the acquirer should disclose that fact and the reasons why it is impracticable to provide the post-combination information. The period for that disclosure is limited to the end of the current annual period because the boards concluded that the information needed to provide the disclosure during that period will generally be available. A short period is often required to integrate an acquiree's operations fully with those of the acquirer. The boards also observed that the usefulness of the separate information diminishes as the operations of the acquiree are integrated with the combined entity.

BC426   The FASB proposed in its version of the 2005 Exposure Draft that the post-combination disclosures should focus on *results of operations* rather than on revenues and earnings. *Results of operations* was defined as revenue, income before extraordinary items and the cumulative effect of accounting changes, earnings and earnings per share. In considering the responses to the exposure draft and opportunities for further convergence, the FASB decided to revise its disclosures to focus on revenues and earnings, which is consistent with the related requirements of the IASB. The boards observed that the term *results of operations* is not used or defined in IFRSs; it would thus have been more difficult for the IASB to converge with the disclosures initially proposed by the FASB.

BC427   The FASB considered expanding the disclosure of post-combination revenues and earnings of an acquiree to all entities because the information would be valuable to any investor, not merely investors in public business entities. To do so would also converge with the requirements of the IASB. However, the FASB was concerned about imposing the additional costs on non-public entities because it believes that the benefits to users of those entities would not be sufficient to warrant imposing those costs. The FASB also observed that the IASB has not completed its separate deliberations on its small and medium-sized entities project and thus does not have an established practice of differential disclosure for circumstances in which it is clear that the benefits would be sufficient for some entities but not so clear for all entities. Because of those cost-benefit concerns, the FASB decided not to extend this disclosure requirement to all entities.

BC428   If comparative financial statements are presented, the FASB decided to require disclosure of supplemental pro forma information about the revenue and earnings of the combined entity for the comparable prior reporting period as though the acquisition date for all business combinations during the current year had been the beginning of the comparable prior annual reporting period. The disclosure is required only for public entities and only if practicable. The IASB considered also requiring that disclosure, but it observed that the needed information would be particularly difficult and costly to obtain in the international environment. An entity that prepares its financial statements in accordance with IFRSs might in a given year acquire other entities that had previously applied the domestic reporting requirements of several different countries. Because the IASB did not consider it feasible to require the disclosure in the international environment, the revised IFRS 3 requires only disclosure of revenues and profit or loss for the current reporting period determined as though the acquisition date for all combinations during the period had been as of the beginning of the annual reporting period.

Effective date and transition

BC429   SFAS 141(R) is effective for business combinations for which the acquisition date is on or after the beginning of the first annual reporting period beginning on or after 15 December 2008, ie for 2009 financial statements. The IASB decided to provide a slightly later effective date. The revised IFRS 3 is effective for business combinations for which the acquisition date is on or after the beginning of the first annual reporting period beginning on or after 1 July 2009. The IASB made a commitment to its constituents that there would be a transition period of approximately 18 months between the publication date and the effective date of the revised IFRS 3 as part of its commitment to have a period of stability following the initial transition to IFRSs. The FASB decided to make SFAS 141(R) effective as soon as practicable, ie for 2009 financial statements. The FASB believes that that effective date provides sufficient time for entities and their auditors to analyse, interpret and prepare for implementation of the provisions of SFAS 141(R).

BC430   The boards also concluded that the effective date of the revised standards should be the same as that of the amendments to their respective consolidation standards (FASB Statement No. 160 *Noncontrolling Interests in Consolidated Financial Statements* and the IASB's amendments to IAS 27). Particular provisions in those amendments, which address the subsequent accounting for an acquiree in consolidated financial statements, are related to provisions in the revised standards that address the initial accounting for an acquiree at the acquisition date.[35] The boards concluded that linking the timing of the changes in accounting required by those amendments to those required by the revised standards would minimise disruptions to practice, which benefits both preparers and users of financial statements.

BC431   SFAS 141(R) prohibits early application and the revised IFRS 3 permits early application. The FASB's Investors Technical Advisory Committee and other users of financial statements told the FASB that providing alternatives for when entities adopt a new standard impairs comparability. The IASB observed, however, that the changes to IFRS 3 are less extensive than the changes to SFAS 141. In addition, the IASB observed that IAS 27 is silent on the accounting for changes in controlling ownership interests in a subsidiary and it wanted entities to be able to adopt the guidance in the amended IAS 27 as soon as it is published. Accordingly, the IASB retained the proposal in the 2005 Exposure Draft to permit entities to adopt the revised IFRS 3 early if they so choose.

BC432   The IASB and the FASB also concluded that the revised standards should be applied prospectively. As with most other requirements that relate to particular types of transactions, applying the revised standards retrospectively would not be feasible.

---

35   The consolidation requirements in IAS 27 were superseded by IFRS 10 *Consolidated Financial Statements* issued in May 2011. The requirements for the subsequent accounting for an acquiree in consolidated financial statements were not changed.

Effective date and transition for combinations of mutual entities or by contract alone

BC433   IFRS 3 excluded from its scope combinations of mutual entities and those achieved by contract alone. In developing IFRS 3, the IASB decided that these combinations should be excluded from its scope until the IASB published interpretative guidance for the application of the acquisition method to those transactions. The revised IFRS 3 provides that guidance. The effective date for combinations of mutual entities and those achieved by contract alone is the same as the effective date for all other entities applying the revised IFRS 3.

BC434   For the reasons outlined in paragraph BC180 of IFRS 3 the IASB concluded that the transitional provisions for combinations involving mutual entities only or those achieved by contract alone should be prospective. Given that these combinations were not within the scope of IFRS 3, they may have been accounted for differently from what IFRS 3 required. The transitional provisions in IFRS 3 took into consideration that entities may have used a range of alternatives in accounting for combinations in the past. The IASB concluded that the transitional provisions for these combinations should incorporate the transitional provisions in IFRS 3 for other business combinations. In addition, the IASB concluded that the transitional provisions should provide that an entity should continue to classify prior combinations in accordance with its previous accounting for such combinations. This is consistent with the prospective approach. Those provisions are contained in paragraphs B68 and B69 of the revised IFRS 3.

Transition requirements for contingent consideration from a business combination that occurred before the effective date of IFRS 3 (as revised in 2008)

BC434A   In *Improvements to IFRSs* issued in May 2010, the Board addressed a perceived conflict in the guidance on accounting for contingent consideration in a business combination. The perceived conflict related to the transition guidance for contingent consideration arising from business combinations that had been accounted for in accordance with IFRS 3 (as issued in 2004). Before their deletion in January 2008, paragraph 3(c) of IFRS 7, paragraph 4(c) of IAS 32 and paragraph 2(f) of IAS 39[36] excluded contingent consideration arrangements from the scope of those IFRSs. To allow the acquirer to account for contingent consideration as required by IFRS 3 (revised 2008), the Board deleted those scope exceptions in the second phase of its project on business combinations.

BC434B   Some interpreted the deletion of the scope exception as meaning that IAS 39 would apply to all contingent consideration, including contingent consideration from business combinations with an acquisition date earlier than the application date of IFRS 3 (revised 2008). However, this interpretation is inconsistent with the transition guidance in paragraph 65 of IFRS 3 (revised 2008).

---

36   IFRS 9 *Financial Instruments* replaced IAS 39. IFRS 9 applies to all items that were previously within the scope of IAS 39.

BC434C   Therefore, the Board reproduced paragraphs 32–35 of IFRS 3 (as issued in 2004) as paragraphs 65B–65E in IFRS 3 (revised 2008) and made the conforming changes to IFRS 7, IAS 32 and IAS 39. The Board did this to clarify that the requirements in IAS 39 do not apply to contingent consideration that arose from a business combination whose acquisition date preceded the application of IFRS 3 (revised 2008) and to provide guidance on how to account for such balances. The Board believes that the amendments will not cause IFRS 3 to diverge from FASB ASC Topic 805 *Business Combinations* (SFAS 141(R) *Business Combinations*).

Effective date and transition for clarifications of the accounting for contingent consideration that arises from business combinations

BC434D   *Annual Improvements to IFRSs 2010–2012 Cycle*, issued in December 2013, clarifies the accounting for contingent consideration that arises from business combinations. The IASB considered whether the transition provisions of paragraph 19 in IAS 8 should apply, which require retrospective application. The IASB considered that the amendments required fair value measurement, and that some entities might not have previously applied fair value measurement for the subsequent measurement of contingent consideration. Retrospective application might therefore require the determination of fair value for contingent consideration, which might not have been previously measured at fair value following initial recognition. It may be impracticable for an entity to determine the fair value of such contingent consideration without using hindsight. Consequently, the IASB decided to require prospective application to avoid the risk of hindsight being applied. The IASB also decided on a 1 July 2014 mandatory effective date for the amendments to IFRS 3 and the consequential amendments to IAS 37 as well as to IFRS 9 and IAS 39, depending on the financial instruments Standard that is applied by the entity at the time that this amendment becomes effective.

Scope exceptions for joint ventures

BC434E   *Annual Improvements Cycle 2011–2013* issued in December 2013 amended paragraph 2(a) and added paragraph 64J to clarify the scope exception in paragraph 2(a) of IFRS 3. It took into consideration the transition provisions and effective date of the amendment to IFRS 3. In order to be consistent with the prospective initial application of IFRS 3, the IASB decided that an entity shall apply the amendment to IFRS 3 prospectively for annual periods beginning on or after 1 July 2014.

Previously held interest in a joint operation (amendments issued in December 2017)

BC434F   The IASB decided that an entity applies paragraph 42A to business combinations occurring on or after the date it first applies the amendments. Applying the amendments to business combinations occurring before that date may have required the use of hindsight to remeasure the entity's previously held interest.

Amendments issued in May 2020

BC434G *Reference to the Conceptual Framework*, issued in May 2020, updated paragraph 11 of IFRS 3, replacing a reference to the *Framework* with a reference to the 2018 *Conceptual Framework*. It made further amendments to avoid unintended consequences of updating the reference.

BC434H Paragraph 64Q of IFRS 3 requires an entity to apply these amendments prospectively. It also permits an entity to apply the amendments before their effective date, without disclosing that it has done so. The IASB concluded that no significant benefits would be gained from requiring either retrospective application or disclosure of early application. The IASB reached this conclusion because it did not expect the amendments to change significantly the population of assets and liabilities recognised in a business combination.

Benefits and costs

BC435 The objective of financial statements is to provide information about the financial position, performance and changes in financial position of an entity that is useful to a wide range of users in making economic decisions. However, the benefits derived from information should exceed the cost of providing it. The evaluation of benefits and costs is substantially a judgemental process. Furthermore, the costs do not necessarily fall on those who enjoy the benefits. For these reasons, it is difficult to apply a cost-benefit test in any particular case. In making its judgement, the IASB considers:

(a) the costs incurred by preparers of financial statements;

(b) the costs incurred by users of financial statements when information is not available;

(c) the comparative advantage that preparers have in developing information, when compared with the costs that users would incur to develop surrogate information; and

(d) the benefit of better economic decision-making as a result of improved financial reporting.

In the second phase of the business combinations project the IASB also considered the costs and benefits of the revised IFRS 3 relative to IFRS 3.

BC436 The IASB concluded that the revised IFRS 3 benefits both preparers and users of financial statements by converging to common high quality, understandable and enforceable accounting standards for business combinations in IFRSs and US GAAP. This improves the comparability of financial information around the world and it also simplifies and reduces the costs of accounting for entities that issue financial statements in accordance with both IFRSs and US GAAP.

BC437 The revised IFRS 3 builds on the core principles established by IFRS 3. However, the IASB sought to improve the understandability, relevance, reliability and comparability of information provided to users of financial statements as follows:

(a) **Scope**

The revised IFRS 3 has a broader scope than IFRS 3. Those entities that will now be required to apply the acquisition method might incur additional costs to obtain valuations and account for intangible assets and goodwill after the acquisition date. However, the IASB observes that much of the information required to account for a business combination by applying the acquisition method is already prepared by those entities that are currently applying the pooling of interests method. There might be additional costs associated with presenting this information within the financial statements, such as audit costs, but much of the information will already be available to management. The IASB concluded therefore that the benefits of improved comparability and faithful representation outweigh the costs that those entities will incur.

(b) **Non-controlling interest**

Paragraph 19 of the revised IFRS 3 provides preparers of financial statements with a choice for each business combination to measure initially a non-controlling interest either at fair value or as the non-controlling interest's proportionate share of the acquiree's identifiable net assets. Paragraphs BC209–BC221 discuss the benefits and costs associated with granting a choice on how non-controlling interests should be measured.

(c) **Contingent consideration**

Paragraph 58 of the revised IFRS 3 requires contingent consideration that is classified as a liability and is within the scope of IAS 39[37] to be remeasured to fair value (or for those within the scope of IAS 37 or another IFRS, to be accounted for in accordance with that IFRS)[38] and that contingent consideration classified as equity is not remeasured. The IASB understands that remeasuring the fair value of contingent consideration after the acquisition date results in additional costs to preparers. Preparers will need to measure the fair value of these arrangements or will need to obtain external valuations at the end of each reporting period. However, users have stated that the information they receive under IFRS 3 is too late to be useful. The IASB concluded therefore that the benefits of relevance and representational faithfulness and the increased information that would be provided to users outweigh the costs.

---

37 IFRS 9 *Financial Instruments* replaced IAS 39. IFRS 9 applies to all items that were previously within the scope of IAS 39.

38 *Annual Improvements to IFRSs 2010–2012 Cycle*, issued in December 2013, amended IFRS 3, IFRS 9, IAS 37 and IAS 39 to clarify that contingent consideration in a business combination that is classified as an asset or a liability shall be subsequently measured at fair value with changes in fair value recognised in profit or loss.

(d)   **Acquisition-related costs**

Paragraph 53 of the revised IFRS 3 requires the costs the acquirer incurs in connection with a business combination to be accounted for separately from the business combination. The IASB concluded that this treatment would improve the understandability of the information provided to users of financial statements. The IASB observed that the new requirement does not create significant additional costs for preparers of financial statements because paragraph 67(d) of IFRS 3 already required disclosure of acquisition-related costs.

(e)   **Business combinations achieved in stages**

The revised IFRS 3 establishes the acquisition date as the single measurement date for all assets acquired, liabilities assumed and any non-controlling interest in the acquiree.

In a business combination achieved in stages, the acquirer also remeasures its previously held equity interest in the acquiree at its acquisition-date fair value and recognises the resulting gain or loss, if any, in profit or loss. In contrast, IFRS 3 required that for a business combination achieved in stages each exchange transaction should be treated separately by the acquirer, using the cost of the transaction and fair value information at the date of each exchange transaction, to determine the amount of any goodwill associated with that transaction. Therefore, the previous treatment required a comparison of the cost of the individual investments with the acquirer's interest in the fair values of the acquiree's identifiable assets and liabilities at each step. The IASB concluded that the revised treatment of business combinations achieved in stages would improve understandability and relevance of the information provided as well as reduce the cost of accounting for such transactions.

BC438   The IASB concluded that the guidance in the revised IFRS 3 is not unduly complex. Indeed, it eliminates guidance that many have found to be complex, costly and arbitrary and that has been the source of considerable uncertainties and costs in the marketplace. Moreover, the revised IFRS 3 does not introduce a new method of accounting but rather expands the use of the acquisition-method of accounting that is familiar, has been widely used and for which there is a substantial base of experience. However, the IASB also sought to reduce the costs of applying the revised IFRS 3 by:

(a)   requiring particular assets and liabilities (eg those related to deferred taxes and employee benefits) to continue to be measured in accordance with existing accounting standards rather than at fair value;

(b)   carrying over the basic requirements of IFRS 3 on contingent liabilities assumed in a business combination into the revised IFRS 3 until the IASB has comprehensively reconsidered the accounting for contingencies in its liabilities project; and

(c)   requiring the revised IFRS 3 to be applied prospectively rather than retrospectively.

BC439   The IASB acknowledges that those steps may result in some sacrifice to the benefits of improved information in financial statements in accordance with the revised IFRS 3. However, the IASB concluded that the complexities and related costs that would result from applying the fair value measurement requirement to all assets and liabilities, at this time, and requiring retrospective application are not justified.

Appendix
Amendments to the Basis for Conclusions on other IFRSs

This appendix contains amendments to the Basis for Conclusions on other IFRSs that are necessary in order to ensure consistency with IFRS 3 (as revised in 2008) and the related amendments to other IFRSs. Amended paragraphs are shown with new text underlined and deleted text struck through.

* * * * *

The amendments contained in this appendix when the revised IFRS 3 was issued in 2008 have been incorporated into the text of the Basis for Conclusions on IFRSs 2, 4 and 5 and on IASs 36 and 38 as issued at 10 January 2008.

Dissenting opinions

Dissent of Mary E Barth, Robert P Garnett and John T Smith

DO1 Professor Barth and Messrs Garnett and Smith dissent from the publication of IFRS 3 *Business Combinations* (as revised in 2008), for the reasons set out below.

Measurement of non-controlling interest

DO2 Professor Barth and Mr Smith disagree with the Board's decision to make an exception to the IFRS's measurement principle and permit acquirers a free choice, acquisition by acquisition, to measure any non-controlling interest in an acquiree as the non-controlling interest's proportionate share of the acquiree's identifiable net assets, rather than at fair value (paragraph 19 of the IFRS).

DO3 Professor Barth and Mr Smith agree with the measurement principle as explained in paragraph BC207 that the acquirer should recognise the identifiable assets acquired, the liabilities assumed and any non-controlling interest in the acquiree at their acquisition-date fair values. Paragraph BC209 indicates that the Board also supports this principle, but decided to make an exception. Professor Barth and Mr Smith support the Board's general view that exceptions should be avoided because they undermine principle-based standards, but understand that they are necessary in well-justified circumstances. Professor Barth and Mr Smith do not believe that an exception to this principle, with a free choice in applying it, is justified in this situation.

DO4 First, Professor Barth and Mr Smith are among those Board members mentioned in paragraph BC213 who believe that non-controlling interests can be measured reliably. Second, Professor Barth and Mr Smith believe that the benefits of consistently measuring all assets acquired and liabilities assumed outweigh the costs involved in conducting the measurement. To address concerns about costs exceeding benefits in particular acquisitions, they would have supported an exception to the principle based on undue cost or effort. Such an exception would not have been a free choice, but would have required assessment of the facts and circumstances associated with the acquisition. Professor Barth and Mr Smith disagree with the Board's decision to permit a free choice, rather than to adopt such an exception. They also disagree with the Board's decision not to require fair value measurement even for acquisitions of listed acquirees, for which the cost would be nil. Third, a consequence of failure to measure non-controlling interests at fair value is that acquired goodwill is not measured at fair value. In addition to being an exception to the IFRS's measurement principle, this has several undesirable effects beyond the initial accounting for goodwill. The Board acknowledges these in paragraphs BC217 and BC218. In particular, if goodwill is impaired the impairment loss is understated, and if the acquirer subsequently purchases more of the non-controlling interests equity is reduced more than it would be had goodwill been measured initially at fair value. Fourth, based on staff research, the choice will benefit only a minority of acquirers because most acquisitions are for 100 per cent of the acquiree. As noted above, any benefit is reduced if such acquirers subsequently impair goodwill or acquire more of the non-controlling interest because of the resulting anomalous accounting results.

DO5   Professor Barth and Mr Smith agree with the Board that permitting entities a choice between alternative accounting methods impairs comparability, as noted in paragraph BC210. They disagree with the Board's decision not to support a single method, particularly a method consistent with the IFRS's measurement principle. However, Professor Barth and Mr Smith disagree with the Board that the benefits of other changes to the IFRS outweigh the disadvantages of permitting entities that acquire less than 100 per cent of an acquiree a free choice as to how to account for the acquisition. Although Professor Barth and Mr Smith agree with the other changes to IFRS 3, they believe that these changes are not as important as having a consistent measurement principle.

DO6   In addition to improving the accounting for business combinations, a primary goal of the business combinations project was to achieve convergence between IFRS 3 and FASB Statement No. 141 (revised 2007) *Business Combinations* (SFAS 141(R)). Professor Barth and Mr Smith strongly support that goal. The Board's decision to make the exception to the measurement principle for non-controlling interests creates a divergence from SFAS 141(R). Both the FASB and the IASB made compromises to achieve a converged result in other aspects of the IFRS, and the FASB made a number of changes to its standard that conform to IFRS 3 (as issued in 2004). Professor Barth and Mr Smith believe that the Board's compromise on this particular issue diminishes the importance of convergence, establishes a precedent for allowing a choice when the two boards cannot reach agreement and may suggest that full convergence in the long term cannot be achieved. This is particularly concerning for this decision given that the Board supports the principle underlying the FASB's answer, there are comparability costs inherent in a free choice of accounting methods and there are likely to be few benefits arising from the exception.

DO7   Mr Garnett dissents from the issue of the IFRS because it both establishes a measurement principle for non-controlling interests with which he disagrees, and permits an exception to that principle. Whilst the exception permits the accounting that he considers appropriate, the use of alternative accounting methods reduces the comparability of financial statements.

DO8   Mr Garnett observes that the application of the measurement principle that an acquirer should measure the components of a business combination, including non-controlling interests, at their acquisition-date fair values results in the recognition of not only the purchased goodwill attributable to the acquirer as a result of the acquisition transaction, but also the goodwill attributable to the non-controlling interest in the acquiree. This is often referred to as the 'full goodwill' method.

DO9   Mr Garnett considers that goodwill is unlike other assets since it cannot be identified separately, or measured directly. Purchased goodwill is a residual resulting from a calculation that absorbs the effects of recognition and measurement exceptions made in the IFRS (such as the accounting for employee benefit plans and deferred taxes) and any differences between an entry price used in valuing the business as a whole and the valuation of the individual assets and liabilities acquired.

DO10   Mr Garnett notes that the 'parent-only' approach to goodwill in the previous version of IFRS 3 (as issued in 2004) avoids this difficulty by measuring goodwill as the difference between the fair value of the consideration paid by the parent for the acquiree and its share of the fair value of the identifiable net assets of the acquiree. Thus, purchased goodwill is the amount implicit in the acquisition transaction and excludes any goodwill attributable to non-controlling interests. This method gives rise to more reliable measurement because it is based on the purchase consideration, which can usually be reliably measured, and it reflects faithfully the acquisition transaction to which the non-controlling interests were not a party.

A business combination achieved in stages

DO11   Mr Garnett disagrees with the requirement in a business combination achieved in stages to recognise the effect of remeasuring any previously-held equity interest in the acquiree to fair value through profit or loss (paragraph 42 of the IFRS), because that investment was not part of the exchange. Mr Garnett agrees that gaining control is a significant economic event that warrants a change from investment accounting to consolidation. However, the previous investment has not been sold. Under current IFRSs, gains and losses on cost method, available-for-sale and equity method investments are recognised in profit or loss only when the investment is sold (other than impairment). Mr Garnett would have recognised the effect of those remeasurements as a separate component of other comprehensive income instead of profit or loss.

IASB documents published to accompany

IFRS 5

Non-current Assets Held for Sale and Discontinued Operations

The text of the unaccompanied standard, IFRS 5, is contained in Part A of this edition. Its effective date when issued was 1 January 2005. The text of the Accompanying Guidance on IFRS 5 is contained in Part B of this edition. This part presents the following documents:

BASIS FOR CONCLUSIONS

DISSENTING OPINIONS

Contents

Basis for Conclusions on
IFRS 5 *Non-current Assets Held for Sale and Discontinued Operations*

This Basis for Conclusions accompanies, but is not part of, IFRS 5.

Introduction

BC1　This Basis for Conclusions summarises the International Accounting Standards Board's considerations in reaching the conclusions in IFRS 5 *Non-current Assets Held for Sale and Discontinued Operations*. Individual Board members gave greater weight to some factors than to others.

BC2　In September 2002 the Board agreed to add a short-term convergence project to its active agenda. The objective of the project is to reduce differences between IFRSs and US GAAP that are capable of resolution in a relatively short time and can be addressed outside major projects. The project is a joint project with the US Financial Accounting Standards Board (FASB).

BC3　As part of the project, the two boards agreed to review each other's deliberations on each of the selected possible convergence topics, and choose the highest quality solution as the basis for convergence. For topics recently considered by either board, there is an expectation that whichever board has more recently deliberated that topic will have the higher quality solution.

BC4　As part of the review of topics recently considered by the FASB, the Board discussed the requirements of SFAS 144 *Accounting for the Impairment or Disposal of Long-Lived Assets*, as they relate to assets held for sale and discontinued operations. The Board did not consider the requirements of SFAS 144 relating to the impairment of assets held for use. Impairment of such assets is an issue that is being addressed in the IASB research project on measurement being led by the Canadian Accounting Standards Board.

BC5　Until the issue of IFRS 5, the requirements of SFAS 144 on assets held for sale and discontinued operations differed from IFRSs in the following ways:

(a)　if specified criteria are met, SFAS 144 requires non-current assets that are to be disposed of to be classified as held for sale. Such assets are remeasured at the lower of carrying amount and fair value less costs to sell and are not depreciated or amortised. IFRSs did not require non-current assets that are to be disposed of to be classified separately or measured differently from other non-current assets.

(b)　the definition of discontinued operations in SFAS 144 was different from the definition of discontinuing operations in IAS 35 *Discontinuing Operations* and the presentation of such operations required by the two standards was also different.

BC6　As discussed in more detail below, the Board concluded that introducing a classification of assets that are held for sale would substantially improve the information available to users of financial statements about assets to be sold.

BC7   The Board published its proposals in an Exposure Draft, ED 4 *Disposal of Non-current Assets and Presentation of Discontinued Operations*, in July 2003 with a comment deadline of 24 October 2003. The Board received over 80 comment letters on the Exposure Draft.

Scope of the IFRS

BC8   In ED 4, the Board proposed that the IFRS should apply to all non-current assets except:

(a)   goodwill,

(b)   financial instruments within the scope of IAS 39 *Financial Instruments: Recognition and Measurement*,[1]

(c)   financial assets under leases, and

(d)   deferred tax assets and assets arising from employee benefits.

BC9   In reconsidering the scope, the Board noted that the use of the term 'non-current' caused the following problems:

(a)   assets that are acquired with the intention of resale were clearly intended to be within the scope of ED 4, but would also be within the definition of current assets and so might be thought to be excluded. The same was true for assets that had been classified as non-current but were now expected to be realised within twelve months.

(b)   it was not clear how the scope would apply to assets presented in accordance with a liquidity presentation.

BC10   The Board noted that it had not intended that assets classified as non-current in accordance with IAS 1 *Presentation of Financial Statements* would be reclassified as current assets simply because of management's intention to sell or because they reached their final twelve months of expected use by the entity. The Board decided to clarify in IFRS 5 that assets classified as non-current are not reclassified as current assets until they meet the criteria to be classified as held for sale in accordance with the IFRS. Further, assets of a class that an entity would normally regard as non-current and are acquired exclusively with a view to resale are not classified as current unless they meet the criteria to be classified as held for sale in accordance with the IFRS.

BC11   In relation to assets presented in accordance with a liquidity presentation, the Board decided that non-current should be taken to mean assets that include amounts expected to be recovered more than twelve months after the balance sheet date.

BC12   These clarifications ensure that all assets of the type normally regarded by the entity as non-current will be within the scope of the IFRS.

---

1   IFRS 9 *Financial Instruments* replaced IAS 39. IFRS 9 applies to all items that were previously within the scope of IAS 39. This paragraph refers to matters relevant when IFRS 5 was issued.

BC13   The Board also reconsidered the exclusions from the scope proposed in ED 4. The Board noted that the classification and presentation requirements of the IFRS are applicable to all non-current assets and concluded that any exclusions should relate only to the measurement requirements. In relation to the measurement requirements, the Board decided that non-current assets should be excluded only if (i) they are already carried at fair value with changes in fair value recognised in profit or loss or (ii) there would be difficulties in determining their fair value less costs to sell. The Board therefore concluded that only the following non-current assets should be excluded from the measurement requirements of the IFRS:

Assets already carried at fair value with changes in fair value recognised in profit or loss:

(a)   financial assets within the scope of IAS 39.[2]

(b)   non-current assets that have been accounted for using the fair value model in IAS 40 *Investment Property*.

(c)   non-current assets that have been measured at fair value less estimated point-of-sale costs in accordance with IAS 41 *Agriculture*.[3]

Assets for which there might be difficulties in determining their fair value:

(a)   deferred tax assets.

(b)   assets arising from employee benefits.

(c)   assets arising from insurance contracts.[4]

BC14   The Board acknowledged that the scope of the IFRS would differ from that of SFAS 144 but noted that SFAS 144 covers the impairment of non-current assets held for use as well as those held for sale. Furthermore, other requirements in US GAAP affect the scope of SFAS 144. The Board therefore concluded that convergence with the scope of SFAS 144 would not be possible.

BC14A   The Board identified a need to clarify the disclosure requirements for non-current assets (or disposal groups) classified as held for sale or discontinued operations in accordance with IFRS 5. Some believed that IFRS 5 and other IFRSs that specifically refer to non-current assets (or disposal groups) classified as held for sale or discontinued operations set out all the disclosures required in respect of those assets or operations. Others believed that all disclosures required by IFRSs whose scope does not specifically exclude non-current assets (or disposal groups) classified as held for sale or discontinued operations apply to such assets (or disposal groups).[5]

---

2   IFRS 9 *Financial Instruments* replaced IAS 39. IFRS 9 applies to all items that were previously within the scope of IAS 39. This paragraph refers to matters relevant when IFRS 5 was issued.

3   In *Improvements to IFRSs* issued in May 2008 the Board amended IAS 41: the term 'estimated point-of-sale costs' was replaced by 'costs to sell'. IFRS 13 *Fair Value Measurement*, issued in May 2011, defines fair value and contains the requirements for measuring fair value.

4   IFRS 17 *Insurance Contracts*, issued in May 2017, replaced IFRS 4. In developing IFRS 17, the Board concluded that fair value could be determined for insurance contracts. Nonetheless, groups of insurance contracts within the scope of IFRS 17 that are assets are excluded from the measurement requirements of IFRS 5.

5   Paragraphs BC14A–BC14E were added as a consequence of amendments to IFRS 5 by *Improvements to IFRSs* issued in April 2009.

BC14B   The Board noted that paragraph 30 of IFRS 5 requires an entity to 'present and disclose information that enables users of the financial statements to evaluate the financial effects of discontinued operations and disposals of non-current assets (or disposal groups).' Paragraph BC17 below states that 'the Board concluded that providing information about assets and groups of assets and liabilities to be disposed of is of benefit to users of financial statements. Such information should assist users in assessing the timing, amount and uncertainty of future cash flows.'

BC14C   The Board noted that some IFRSs other than IFRS 5 require specific disclosures for non-current assets (or disposal groups) classified as held for sale or discontinued operations. For instance, paragraph 68 of IAS 33 *Earnings per Share* requires an entity to disclose the amount per share for discontinued operations. The Board also noted that the requirements of IAS 1 on fair presentation and materiality also apply to such assets (or disposal groups).

BC14D   The Board also noted that when a disposal group includes assets and liabilities that are not within the scope of the measurement requirements of IFRS 5, disclosures about measurement of those assets and liabilities are normally provided in the other notes to the financial statements and do not need to be repeated, unless they better enable users of the financial statements to evaluate the financial effects of discontinued operations and disposals of non-current assets (or disposal groups).

BC14E   Consequently, in *Improvements to IFRSs* issued in April 2009, the Board clarified that IFRS 5 and other IFRSs that specifically refer to non-current assets (or disposal groups) classified as held for sale or discontinued operations set out all the disclosures required in respect of those assets or operations. Additional disclosures about non-current assets (or disposal groups) classified as held for sale may be necessary to comply with the general requirements of IAS 1, in particular paragraphs 15 and 125 of that Standard.

Classification of non-current assets to be disposed of as held for sale

BC15   Under SFAS 144, long-lived assets are classified as either (i) held and used or (ii) held for sale. Before the issue of this IFRS, no distinction was made in IFRSs between non-current assets held and used and non-current assets held for sale, except in relation to financial instruments.

BC16   The Board considered whether a separate classification for non-current assets held for sale would create unnecessary complexity in IFRSs and introduce an element of management intent into the accounting. Some commentators suggested that the categorisation 'assets held for sale' is unnecessary, and that if the focus were changed to 'assets *retired* from active use' much of the complexity could be eliminated, because the latter classification would be based on actuality rather than what they perceive as management intent. They assert that it is the potential abuse of the classification that necessitates many of the detailed requirements in SFAS 144. Others suggested that, if existing IFRSs were amended to specify that assets retired from active use are measured at fair value less costs to sell and to require additional disclosure, some convergence with SFAS 144 could be achieved without creating a new IFRS.

BC17 However, the Board concluded that providing information about assets and groups of assets and liabilities to be disposed of is of benefit to users of financial statements. Such information should assist users in assessing the timing, amount and uncertainty of future cash flows. The Board understands that this was also the assessment underpinning SFAS 144. Therefore the Board concluded that introducing the notion of assets and disposal groups held for sale makes IFRSs more complete.

BC18 Furthermore, although the held for sale classification begins from an intention to sell the asset, the other criteria for this classification are tightly drawn and are significantly more objective than simply specifying an intention or commitment to sell. Some might argue that the criteria are too specific. However, the Board believes that the criteria should be specific to achieve comparability of classification between entities. The Board does not believe that a classification 'retired from active use' would necessarily require fewer criteria to support it. For example, it would be necessary to establish a distinction between assets retired from active use and those that are held as back-up spares or are temporarily idle.

BC19 Lastly, if the classification and measurement of assets held for sale in IFRSs are the same as in US GAAP, convergence will have been achieved in an area of importance to users of financial statements.

BC20 Most respondents to ED 4 agreed that a separate classification for non-current assets that are no longer held to be used is desirable. However, the proposals in ED 4 were criticised for the following reasons:

(a) the criteria were too restrictive and rules-based.

(b) a commitment to sell needs to be demonstrated, consistently with the requirements of IAS 37 *Provisions, Contingent Liabilities and Contingent Assets* relating to restructuring provisions.

(c) the classification should be for assets retired from active use.

(d) assets to be abandoned should be treated in the same way as assets to be sold.

BC21 The Board noted that a more flexible definition would be open to abuse. Further, changing the criteria for classification could cause divergence from US GAAP. The Board has, however, reordered the criteria to highlight the principles.

BC22 The Board also noted that the requirements of IAS 37 establish when a liability is incurred, whereas the requirements of the IFRS relate to the measurement and presentation of assets that are already recognised.

BC23 Finally, the Board reconfirmed the principle behind the classification proposals in ED 4, which is that the carrying amount of the assets will be recovered principally through sale. Applying this principle to assets retired from active use, the Board decided that assets retired from active use that do not meet the criteria for classification as assets held for sale should not be presented separately because the carrying amount of the asset may not be recovered principally through sale. Conversely, the Board decided that assets that meet the criteria to be classified as held for sale and are being used should not be precluded from being separately classified. This is because, if a non-current asset is available for immediate sale, the remaining use of the asset is incidental to its recovery through sale and the carrying amount of the asset will be recovered principally through sale.

BC24 Applying the same principle to assets to be abandoned, the Board noted that their carrying value will never be recovered principally through sale.

Plan to sell the controlling interest in a subsidiary[6]

BC24A In 2007 the Board considered situations in which an entity is committed to a plan to sell the controlling interest in a subsidiary and, after the sale, retains a non-controlling interest in its former subsidiary, taking the form of an investment in an associate, an investment in a joint venture or a financial asset. The Board considered how the classification as held for sale applies to the subsidiary in the consolidated financial statements of the entity.

BC24B The Board noted that paragraph 6 states that 'An entity shall classify a non-current asset (or disposal group) as held for sale if its carrying amount will be recovered principally through a sale transaction rather than through continuing use.' The Board also noted that IAS 27 *Consolidated and Separate Financial Statements* (as amended in January 2008) defines control and requires a parent to consolidate a subsidiary until control is lost.[7] At the date control is lost, all the subsidiary's assets and liabilities are derecognised and any investment retained in the former subsidiary is recognised. Loss of control is a significant economic event that changes the nature of an investment. The parent-subsidiary relationship ceases to exist and an investor-investee relationship begins that differs significantly from the former parent-subsidiary relationship. Therefore, the new investor-investee relationship is recognised and measured initially at the date when control is lost.

BC24C The Board concluded that, under the sale plan described above, the controlling interest in the subsidiary is, in substance, exchanged for a non-controlling interest. Therefore, in the Board's view, being committed to a plan involving loss of control of a subsidiary should trigger classification as held for sale. The Board also noted that this conclusion is consistent with IAS 27.

---

6 This section and paragraphs BC77A and BC79A were added as a consequence of amendments to IFRS 5 by *Improvements to IFRSs* issued in May 2008.

7 The consolidation requirements in IAS 27 were superseded, and the definition of control was consequently revised, by IFRS 10 *Consolidated Financial Statements* issued in May 2011. The requirement to consolidate a subsidiary until control is lost did not change. In October 2012 the Board issued *Investment Entities* (Amendments to IFRS 10, IFRS 12 and IAS 27), which required investment entities, as defined in IFRS 10 *Consolidated Financial Statements*, to measure their investments in subsidiaries, other than those providing investment-related services or activities, at fair value through profit or loss.

BC24D   The Board noted that the subsidiary's assets and liabilities meet the definition of a disposal group in accordance with paragraph 4. Therefore, the Board concluded that all the subsidiary's assets and liabilities should be classified as held for sale, not only the portion of the interest to be disposed of, regardless of whether the entity will retain a non-controlling interest.

BC24E   The Board considered the comments received on the proposal set out in its exposure draft of October 2007. In response to comments from some respondents, the Board clarified in the amendment that the criteria for classification as held for sale need to be met.

Assets to be exchanged for other non-current assets

BC25   Under SFAS 144, long-lived assets that are to be exchanged for similar productive assets cannot be classified as held for sale. They are regarded as disposed of only when exchanged. The Basis for Conclusions on SFAS 144 explains that this is because the exchange of such assets is accounted for at amounts based on the carrying amount of the assets, not at fair value, and that using the carrying amount is more consistent with the accounting for a long-lived asset to be held and used than for a long-lived asset to be sold.

BC26   Under IAS 16 *Property, Plant and Equipment*, as revised in 2003, an exchange of assets is normally measured at fair value. The SFAS 144 reasoning for the classification of such assets as held for sale does not, therefore, apply. Consistently with IAS 16, the IFRS treats an exchange of assets as a disposal and acquisition of assets unless the exchange has no commercial substance.

BC27   The FASB has published an exposure draft proposing to converge with the requirements in IAS 16 for an exchange of assets to be measured at fair value. The exposure draft also proposes a consequential amendment to SFAS 144 that would make exchanges of assets that have commercial substance eligible for classification as held for sale.

Measurement of non-current assets held for sale

BC28   SFAS 144 requires a long-lived asset or a disposal group classified as held for sale to be measured at the lower of its carrying amount and fair value less costs to sell. A long-lived asset classified as held for sale (or included within a disposal group) is not depreciated, but interest and other expenses attributable to the liabilities of a disposal group are recognised.

BC29   As explained in the Basis for Conclusions on SFAS 144, the remaining use in operations of an asset that is to be sold is incidental to the recovery of the carrying amount through sale. The accounting for such an asset should therefore be a process of valuation rather than allocation.

BC30   The FASB further observed that once the asset is remeasured, to depreciate the asset would reduce its carrying amount below its fair value less costs to sell. It also noted that should there be a decline in the value of the asset after initial classification as held for sale and before eventual sale, the loss would be recognised in the period of decline because the fair value less costs to sell is evaluated each period.

BC31   The counter-argument is that, although classified as held for sale, the asset is still being used in operations, and hence cessation of depreciation is inconsistent with the basic principle that the cost of an asset should be allocated over the period during which benefits are obtained from its use. Furthermore, although the decline in the value of the asset through its use would be reflected in the recognised change in fair value, it might also be masked by an increase arising from changes in the market prices of the asset.

BC32   However, the Board noted that IAS 16 requires an entity to keep the expected useful life and residual values of property, plant and equipment up to date, and IAS 36 *Impairment of Assets* requires an immediate write-down to the higher of value in use and fair value less costs to sell. An entity should, therefore, often achieve a measurement effect for individual assets that are about to be sold under other IFRSs similar to that required by this IFRS as follows. Under other IFRSs, if the fair value less costs to sell is higher than carrying amount there will be no impairment and no depreciation (because the residual value will have been updated). If fair value less costs to sell is lower than carrying amount, there will be an impairment loss that reduces the carrying amount to fair value less costs to sell and then no depreciation (because the residual value will have been updated), unless value in use is higher than fair value less costs to sell. If value in use is higher than fair value less costs to sell, there would be small differences between the treatment that would arise under other IFRSs and the treatment under IFRS 5. Under other IFRSs there would be an impairment loss to the extent that the carrying amount exceeds value in use rather than to the extent that the carrying amount exceeds fair value less costs to sell. Under other IFRSs, there would also then be depreciation of the excess of value in use (the new carrying amount of the asset) over fair value less costs to sell (its residual value). However, for assets classified as held for sale, value in use will differ from fair value less costs to sell only to the extent of the net cash flows expected to arise before the sale. If the period to sale is short, this amount will usually be relatively small. The difference in impairment loss recognised and subsequent depreciation under other IFRSs compared with the impairment loss and no subsequent depreciation under IFRS 5 would, therefore, also be small.

BC33   The Board concluded that the measurement requirements of IFRS 5 for individual assets would often not involve a significant change from the requirements of other IFRSs. Furthermore, the Board agreed with the FASB that the cash flows arising from the asset's remaining use were incidental to the recovery of the asset through sale and, hence, concluded that individual assets classified as held for sale should be measured at the lower of carrying amount and fair value less costs to sell and should not be depreciated.

BC34   For disposal groups, there could be greater differences between the requirements in other IFRSs and the requirements of IFRS 5. For example, the fair value less costs to sell of a disposal group may reflect internally generated goodwill to the extent that it is higher than the carrying value of the net assets in the disposal group. The residual value of the non-current assets in the disposal group may, nonetheless, be such that, if they were accounted for in accordance with IAS 16, those assets would be depreciated.

BC35   In such a situation, some might view the requirements in IFRS 5 as allowing internally generated goodwill to stop the depreciation of non-current assets. However, the Board does not agree with that view. Rather, the Board believes that the internally generated goodwill provides a buffer against the recognition of an impairment loss on the disposal group. The same effect arises from the impairment requirements in IAS 36. The non-depreciation of the non-current assets in the disposal group is, as with individual assets, a consequence of the basic principle underlying the separate classification, that the carrying amount of the asset will be recovered principally through sale, not continuing use, and that amounts recovered through continuing use will be incidental.

BC36   In addition, it is important to emphasise that IFRS 5 permits only an asset (or disposal group) that is to be *sold* to be classified as held for sale. Assets to be abandoned are classified as held and used until disposed of, and thus are depreciated. The Board agrees with the FASB's observation that a distinction can be drawn between an asset that is to be sold and an asset that is to be abandoned, because the former will be recovered principally through sale and the latter through its continuing use. Therefore, it is logical that depreciation should cease in the former but not the latter case.

BC37   When an asset or a disposal group held for sale is part of a foreign operation with a functional currency that is different from the presentation currency of the group, an exchange difference will have been recognised in equity[8] arising from the translation of the asset or disposal group into the presentation currency of the group. IAS 21 *The Effects of Changes in Foreign Exchange Rates* requires the exchange difference to be 'recycled' from equity to profit or loss on disposal of the operation. The question arises whether classification as held for sale should trigger the recycling of any exchange differences. Under US GAAP (EITF 01-5 *Application of FASB Statement No. 52 to an Investment Being Evaluated for Impairment That Will Be Disposed Of*) the accumulated foreign currency translation adjustments previously recognised in other comprehensive income that are expected to be recycled in income at the time of sale are included in the carrying amount of the asset (or disposal group) being tested for impairment.

BC38   In its project on reporting comprehensive income, the Board may reconsider the issue of recycling. Therefore, it did not wish to make any interim changes to the requirements in IAS 21. Hence, the IFRS does not permit any exchange differences to be recycled on the classification of an asset or a disposal group as held for sale. The recycling will take place when the asset or disposal group is sold.

---

8   As a consequence of the revision of IAS 1 *Presentation of Financial Statements* (as revised in 2007) such a difference is recognised in other comprehensive income.

The allocation of an impairment loss to a disposal group

BC39   Under SFAS 144 and the proposals in ED 4, assets within the disposal group that are not within the scope of the IFRS are adjusted in accordance with other standards before measuring the fair value less costs to sell of the disposal group. Any loss or gain recognised on adjusting the carrying amount of the disposal group is allocated to the carrying amount of the long-lived assets of the group.

BC40   This is different from the requirements of IAS 36 for the allocation of an impairment loss arising on a cash-generating unit. IAS 36 requires an impairment loss on a cash-generating unit to be allocated first to reduce the carrying amount of goodwill and then to reduce pro rata the carrying amounts of the other assets in the unit.

BC41   The Board considered whether the allocation of an impairment loss for a disposal group should be consistent with the requirements of IAS 36 or with the requirements of SFAS 144. The Board concluded that it would be simplest to require the same allocation as is required by IAS 36 for cash-generating units. Although this is different from SFAS 144, the disposal group as a whole will be measured at the same amount.

Newly acquired assets

BC42   SFAS 144 requires, and ED 4 proposed, newly acquired assets that meet the criteria to be classified as held for sale to be measured at fair value less costs to sell on initial recognition. So, in those instances, other than in a business combination, in which an entity acquires a non-current asset that meets the criteria to be classified as held for sale, a loss is recognised in profit or loss if the cost of the asset exceeds its fair value less costs to sell. In the more common cases in which an entity acquires, as part of a business combination, a non-current asset (or disposal group) that meets the criteria to be classified as held for sale, the difference between fair value and fair value less costs to sell is recognised in goodwill.

BC43   Some respondents to ED 4 noted that measuring newly acquired assets not part of a business combination at fair value less costs to sell was inconsistent with the general proposal that assets classified as held for sale should be measured at *the lower of carrying amount* and fair value less costs to sell. The Board agreed and amended the requirement so that it is clear that the newly acquired assets (or disposal groups) are measured on initial recognition at the lower of what their carrying amount would be were they not classified as held for sale (ie cost) and fair value less costs to sell.

BC44   In relation to business combinations, the Board noted that conceptually the assets should be recognised initially at fair value and then immediately classified as held for sale, with the result that the costs to sell are recognised in profit or loss, not goodwill. In theory, if the entity had factored the costs to sell into the purchase price, the reduced price would lead to the creation of negative goodwill, the immediate recognition of which in profit or loss would offset the loss arising from the costs to sell. Of course, in practice, the reduced price will usually result in lower net positive goodwill rather than negative goodwill to be recognised in profit or loss. For that reason, and for the sake of convergence, the Board concluded that in a business combination non-current assets that meet the criteria to be classified as held for sale on acquisition should be measured at fair value less costs to sell on initial recognition.

BC45 The Board and the FASB are considering which items should form part of the business combination transaction more generally in their joint project on the application of the purchase method. This consideration includes whether the assets and liabilities recognised in the transaction should be based on the acquirer's or the acquiree's perspective. The outcome of those deliberations may affect the decision discussed in paragraph BC44.[9]

Recognition of subsequent increases in fair value less costs to sell

BC46 The Board considered whether a subsequent increase in fair value less costs to sell should be recognised to the extent that it reversed previous impairments. SFAS 144 requires the recognition of a subsequent increase in fair value less costs to sell, but not in excess of the cumulative loss previously recognised for a write-down to fair value less costs to sell. The Board decided that, under IFRSs, a gain should be recognised to the extent that it reverses any impairment of the asset, either in accordance with the IFRS or previously in accordance with IAS 36. Recognising a gain for the reversal of an impairment that occurred before the classification of the asset as held for sale is consistent with the requirement in IAS 36 to recognise reversals of impairment.

Recognition of impairment losses and subsequent gains for assets that, before classification as held for sale, were measured at revalued amounts in accordance with another IFRS

BC47 ED 4 proposed that impairment losses and subsequent gains for assets that, before classification as held for sale, were measured at revalued amounts in accordance with another IFRS should be treated as revaluation decreases and increases according to the standard under which the assets had previously been revalued, consistently with the requirements of IAS 36, except to the extent that the losses and gains are caused by the initial recognition of, or changes in, costs to sell. ED 4 also proposed that costs to sell should always be recognised in profit or loss.

BC48 Many respondents disagreed with these proposals, because of their complexity and because of the resulting inconsistent treatment of assets classified as held for sale. The Board considered the issues raised and decided that assets that were already carried at fair value with changes in fair value recognised in profit or loss should not be subject to the measurement requirements of the IFRS. The Board believes that, for such assets, continued measurement at fair

---

9   In their joint project on the application of the acquisition method, the Board and the FASB clarified that the classification of assets acquired in a business combination as held for sale should be based on the acquirer's perspective. Therefore, the acquirer would have to satisfy the criteria in paragraphs 6–11 of IFRS 5 at the acquisition date in order to classify assets acquired as held for sale on initial recognition.

value gives better information than measurement at the lower of carrying amount and fair value less costs to sell. The Board did not, however, believe that such treatment was appropriate for assets that had been revalued in accordance with IAS 16 and IAS 38, because those standards require depreciation to continue and the revaluation change would not necessarily be recognised in profit or loss. The Board concluded that assets that had been revalued in accordance with IAS 16 and IAS 38 should be treated in the same way as any assets that, before classification as held for sale, had not been revalued. Such an approach results in a consistent treatment for assets that are within the scope of the measurement requirements of the IFRS and, hence, a simpler standard.

Measurement of assets reclassified as held for use

BC49 Under SFAS 144, when an entity changes its plan to sell the asset and reclassifies a long-lived asset from held for sale to held and used, the asset is measured at the lower of (a) the carrying amount before the asset (or disposal group) was classified as held for sale, adjusted for any depreciation (or amortisation) that would have been recognised had the asset (or disposal group) been continuously classified as held and used and (b) its fair value at the date of the decision not to sell.

BC50 The underlying principle is to restore the carrying value of the asset to what it would have been had it never been classified as held for sale, taking into account any impairments that may have occurred. In fact, SFAS 144 requires that, for held and used assets, an impairment is recognised only if the carrying amount of the asset exceeds the sum of the undiscounted cash flows expected to result from its use and eventual disposal. Thus, the carrying amount of the asset if it had never been classified as held for sale might exceed its fair value. As a result, SFAS 144 does not necessarily lead to the asset reverting to its original carrying amount. However, the Basis for Conclusions on SFAS 144 notes that the FASB concluded it would be inappropriate to write up the carrying amount of the asset to an amount greater than its fair value solely on the basis of an undiscounted cash flow test. Hence, it arrived at the requirement for measurement at the lower of (a) the asset's carrying amount had it not been classified as held for sale and (b) fair value at the date of the decision not to sell the asset.

BC51 IAS 36 has a different measurement basis for impaired assets, ie recoverable amount. The Board concluded that to be consistent with the principle of SFAS 144 and also to be consistent with the requirements of IAS 36, an asset that ceases to be classified as held for sale should be measured at the lower of (a) the carrying amount that would have been recognised had the asset not been classified as held for sale and (b) its recoverable amount at the date of reclassification. Whilst this is not full convergence, the difference arises from differences in the US GAAP and IFRS impairment models.

Removal of exemption from consolidation for subsidiaries acquired and held exclusively with a view to resale

BC52   SFAS 144 removed the exemption from consolidation in US GAAP for subsidiaries held on a temporary basis on the grounds that all assets held for sale should be treated in the same way, ie as required by SFAS 144 rather than having some assets consolidated and some not.

BC53   The Board agreed that all subsidiaries should be consolidated and that all assets (and disposal groups) that meet the criteria to be classified as held for sale should be treated in the same way. The exemption from consolidation in IAS 27 *Consolidated and Separate Financial Statements* for subsidiaries acquired and held exclusively with a view to resale prevents those assets and disposal groups within such subsidiaries that meet the criteria to be classified as held for sale from being treated consistently with other assets and disposal groups. ED 4 therefore proposed that the exemption in IAS 27 should be removed.[10]

BC54   Some respondents disagreed with this proposal, on the grounds that the information provided by consolidation of such subsidiaries would be less useful than that provided by the current requirement to measure the investment in such subsidiaries at fair value. The Board noted that the impact of the proposals in ED 4 would be limited to the following:

(a)   the measurement of a subsidiary that currently is within the scope of the exemptions would change from fair value as required by IAS 39[11] to the lower of cost and fair value less costs to sell.

(b)   any change in fair value of the investment in the subsidiary would, in accordance with the current requirements in IAS 27, be presented as a single amount in profit or loss as a held-for-trading financial asset[12] in accordance with IAS 39. As discussed in paragraph BC72, the subsidiary would be a discontinued operation and, in accordance with the IFRS's requirements (see paragraphs BC73–BC76), any recognised change in the value of the disposal group that comprises the subsidiary would be presented as a single amount in profit or loss.

(c)   the presentation in the balance sheet would change from a single amount for the investment in the subsidiary to two amounts—one for the assets and one for the liabilities of the disposal group that is the subsidiary.[13]

---

10   The consolidation requirements in IAS 27 were superseded by IFRS 10 *Consolidated Financial Statements* issued in May 2011. IFRS 10 does not contain an exception from consolidation for subsidiaries acquired and held exclusively with a view to resale.

11   IFRS 9 *Financial Instruments* replaced IAS 39. IFRS 9 applies to all items that were previously within the scope of IAS 39. This paragraph refers to matters relevant when IFRS 5 was issued.

12   IFRS 9 *Financial Instruments* eliminated the category of held-for-trading financial assets. This paragraph refers to matters relevant when IFRS 5 was issued.

13   Greater disaggregation of the disposal group in the statement of financial position is permitted but not required.

BC55   The Board reaffirmed its conclusion set out in paragraph BC53. However, it noted that the limited impact of the proposals apply only to the amounts required to be presented on the face of the balance sheet and the income statement. Providing the required analyses of those amounts in the notes could potentially involve the entity having to obtain significantly more information. The Board therefore decided not to require the disclosure of the analyses of the amounts presented on the face of the balance sheet and income statement for newly acquired subsidiaries and to clarify in an example the computational short cuts that could be used to arrive at the amounts to be presented on the face of the balance sheet and income statement.

Presentation of non-current assets held for sale

BC56   SFAS 144 requires an entity to present:

(a)   a long-lived asset classified as held for sale separately in the balance sheet; and

(b)   the assets and liabilities of a disposal group classified as held for sale separately in the asset and liability sections of the balance sheet. The major classes of those assets and liabilities are separately disclosed either on the face of the balance sheet or in the notes.

BC57   In the Basis for Conclusions on SFAS 144 the FASB noted that information about the nature of both assets and liabilities of a disposal group is useful to users. Separately presenting those items in the balance sheet provides information that is relevant. Separate presentation also distinguishes those assets that are not being depreciated from those that are being depreciated. The Board agreed with the FASB's views.

BC58   Respondents to ED 4 noted that the separate presentation within equity of amounts relating to assets and disposal groups classified as held for sale (such as, for example, unrealised gains and losses on available-for-sale assets[14] and foreign currency translation adjustments) would also provide useful information. The Board agreed and has added such a requirement to the IFRS.

Timing of classification as, and definition of, discontinued operations

BC59   With the introduction of SFAS 144, the FASB broadened the scope of a discontinued operation from a 'segment of a business' to a 'component of an entity'. A component is widely drawn, the criterion being that it comprises 'operations and cash flows that can be clearly distinguished, operationally and for financial reporting purposes, from the rest of the entity'. SFAS 144 states that a component may be a segment, a reporting unit, a subsidiary or an asset group.

---

14   IFRS 9 *Financial Instruments* eliminated the category of available-for-sale financial assets. This paragraph refers to matters relevant when IFRS 5 was issued.

BC60　　However, at the same time, the FASB specified more restrictive criteria for determining *when* the component is classified as discontinued and hence when its results are presented as discontinued. SFAS 144 requires a component to be classified as discontinued only if it has been disposed of or if it meets the criteria for classification as an asset 'held for sale'.

BC61　　The definition of a discontinuing operation in IAS 35 as a 'major line of business' or 'geographical area of operations' is closer to the former, and narrower, US GAAP definition. The trigger in IAS 35 for classifying the operation as discontinuing is the earlier of (a) the entity entering into a binding sale agreement and (b) the board of directors approving and announcing a formal disposal plan. Although IAS 35 refers to IAS 37 for further guidance on what constitutes a plan, the criteria are less restrictive than those in SFAS 144.

BC62　　Paragraph 12 of the *Framework*[15] states that the objective of financial statements is to provide information about the financial position, performance and changes in financial position of an entity that is useful to a wide range of users in making economic decisions. Paragraph 15 of the *Framework* goes on to state that the economic decisions that are taken by users of financial statements require an evaluation of the ability of an entity to generate cash and cash equivalents. Separately highlighting the results of discontinued operations provides users with information that is relevant in assessing the ongoing ability of the entity to generate cash flows.

BC63　　In terms of the timing of classifying an operation as discontinued, the Board considered whether more useful information is provided by making the classification conditional upon a firm decision to discontinue an operation (the current IAS 35 approach) or conditional upon the classification of an operation as held for sale.

BC64　　The Board decided that, to be consistent with the presentation of assets held for disposal and in the interests of convergence, an operation should be classified as discontinued when it is disposed of or classified as held for sale.

BC65　　IAS 35 also adopts a different approach from US GAAP when criteria for classification as discontinued are met after the period-end but before the financial statements are issued. SFAS 144 requires some disclosure; however, the component is *not* presented as a discontinued operation. IAS 35 requires the component to be classified as discontinuing.

BC66　　The Board believes that, consistently with IAS 10 *Events after the Balance Sheet Date*,[16] a component should not be classified as discontinued in the financial statements unless it meets the criteria to be so classified at the balance sheet date.

15　References to the *Framework* in this Basis for Conclusions are to the IASC's *Framework for the Preparation and Presentation of Financial Statements*, adopted by the Board in 2001 and in effect when the Standard was developed.

16　In September 2007 the title of IAS 10 was amended from *Events after the Balance Sheet Date* to *Events after the Reporting Period* as a consequence of the revision of IAS 1 *Presentation of Financial Statements* in 2007.

BC67　In terms of the definition of a discontinued operation, ED 4 proposed adopting the SFAS 144 definition of a discontinued operation. The Board argued that under existing IAS 35 there may be disposal transactions that, although likely to have an impact on the ongoing operations of the entity, do not meet the criteria for classification as a discontinuing activity. For example, an entity might dispose of a significant portion, but not all, of its cash-generating units operating in a particular geographical area. Under IAS 35, that might not meet the definition of a discontinuing operation. Under SFAS 144, if the relevant criteria were met, it would.

BC68　However, a substantial majority of respondents to ED 4 disagreed with this proposal. They preferred instead to retain the IAS 35 criterion that a discontinued operation should be a major line of business or geographical area of operations.

BC69　The Board reconsidered the issue in the light of the comments received and concluded that the size of unit that could be classified as discontinued in accordance with SFAS 144 was too small, with the result that the information provided by separately presenting discontinued operations may not be as useful as it could be.

BC70　The Board also noted that the FASB Emerging Issues Task Force (EITF) is considering practical problems that have arisen in implementing the criteria for discontinued operations in SFAS 144. Specifically, the EITF is considering (a) the cash flows of the component that should be considered in the determination of whether cash flows have been or will be eliminated from the ongoing operations of the entity and (b) the types of continuing involvement that constitute significant continuing involvement in the operations of the disposal component. As a result of these practical problems, the Board further concluded that it was not appropriate to change the definition of a discontinued operation in a way that was likely to cause the same problems in practice as have arisen under SFAS 144.

BC71　The Board therefore decided that it would retain the requirement in IAS 35 that a discontinued operation should be a major line of business or geographical area of operations, noting that this will include operations that would have been excluded from the US definition before SFAS 144, which was based on a reporting segment. However, the Board regards this as an interim measure and intends to work with the FASB to arrive at a converged definition within a relatively short time.

BC72　Lastly, the Board considered whether newly acquired subsidiaries that meet the criteria to be classified as held for sale should always be classified as discontinued. The Board concluded that they should be so classified because they are being disposed of for one of the following reasons:

(a)　the subsidiary is in a different line of business from the entity, so disposing of it is similar to disposing of a major line of business.

(b)   the subsidiary is required to be disposed of by regulators because the entity would otherwise have too much of a particular type of operation in a particular geographical area. In such a case the subsidiary must be a significant operation.

Changes to a plan of sale (amendment 2011)

BC72A   During its redeliberation of the exposure draft ED 9 *Joint Arrangements* the Board decided that if a disposal group or non-current asset that ceases to be classified as held for sale is a subsidiary, a joint operation, a joint venture, an associate, or a portion of an interest in a joint venture or associate, an entity should amend its financial statements for the periods since the classification as held for sale was made.

Changes to a plan of sale or to a plan of distribution to owners

BC72B   The Board received a request to clarify the accounting for a change in a disposal plan from a plan to sell to a plan to distribute a dividend in kind to its shareholders. Paragraph 26 of IFRS 5 was interpreted by some, but not all, as requiring this change to be considered as a change to a plan of sale that would be accounted for in accordance with paragraphs 27–29 of IFRS 5

BC72C   In analysing this issue the Board observed that there was no specific guidance in IFRS 5 for the discontinuation of held-for-distribution accounting, when an entity determines that the asset (or disposal group) is no longer available for immediate distribution to owners or that the distribution to owners is no longer 'highly probable', in accordance with paragraph 12A of IFRS 5.

BC72D   The Board observed that IFRIC 17 *Distribution of Non-cash Assets to Owners* amended IFRS 5 by adding paragraphs 5A, 12A and 15A to provide guidance for the held-for-distribution classification. However, this amendment did not provide guidance for when an entity reclassifies an asset (or disposal group) from held for sale to held for distribution to owners (or vice versa), or when held-for-distribution accounting is discontinued. The Board noted that paragraphs 27–29 of IFRS 5 should have been considered for amendment by IFRIC 17 and the fact that they were not amended at the time was an oversight.

BC72E   The Board observed that the current guidance in IFRS 5 could be read in a way that a change from a plan to sell a non-current asset (or disposal group) to a plan to distribute a non-current asset (or disposal group) automatically results in a change to a plan of sale and that the guidance in paragraphs 27–29 of IFRS 5 should be applied.

BC72F   The Board observed that, consistently with paragraphs 5A of IFRS 5 and BC60 of IFRIC 17, it was the intention of the Board to have consistent criteria and accounting requirements for an asset (or disposal group) classified as held for sale and for an asset (or disposal group) classified as held for distribution to owners. In addition:

(a)   the conditions required by paragraph 8 of IFRS 5 for a sale to be considered highly probable are similar to the conditions required by paragraph 12A of IFRS 5 for a distribution to owners to be considered highly probable, so they should be accounted for in the same way; and

(b)   paragraph 5A of IFRS 5 confirms that the classification, presentation and measurement requirements in IFRS 5 that are applicable for an asset (or disposal group) that is classified as held for sale also apply to an asset (or disposal group) that is classified as held for distribution to owners.

BC72G   The Board noted that, on the basis of the current guidance in paragraphs 5A, 8 and 12A of IFRS 5 and the explanations in the Basis for Conclusions on IFRIC 17, the change from being held for sale to held for distribution to owners (or vice versa) when an entity reclassifies an asset (or disposal group) directly from one method of disposal to the other should not be considered a new plan (to sell or distribute). Instead, it should be treated as a continuation of the original plan. This means that an entity moves from one method of disposal to the other without any time lag, so that there is no interruption of the application of the requirements in IFRS 5. This would involve applying the classification, presentation and measurement requirements required for each type of disposal in IFRS 5.

BC72H   Consequently, when an entity reclassifies an asset (or disposal group) directly from held for sale to held for distribution to owners (or vice versa), the Board decided to clarify that such a reclassification shall not be treated as a change to a plan of sale (or distribution to owners) and an entity shall not follow the guidance in paragraphs 27–29 of IFRS 5 to account for this change.

BC72I   In response to the comments received on the Exposure Draft *Annual Improvements to IFRSs 2012–2014 Cycle* (the '2013 Annual Improvements Exposure Draft'), published in December 2013, the Board clarified that at the time of the change in the disposal plan, an entity would need to measure the non-current asset (or disposal group) in accordance with paragraph 15 or 15A of IFRS 5, and recognise any write-down in value (impairment loss) or gain for the subsequent increase in the fair value less costs to sell/costs to distribute a non-current asset (or disposal group) in accordance with paragraphs 20–25 of IFRS 5.

BC72J   In response to the comments received on the 2013 Annual Improvements Exposure Draft, the Board further clarified that a change from being held for sale to held for distribution to owners (or vice versa) via a direct reclassification is not a new plan of disposal and does not change the requirements in IFRS 5 to determine whether a sale (or a distribution to owners) is highly probable, in accordance with paragraph 8 (or 12A) of IFRS 5. Consequently, the determination of the 12-month period should not restart when such a change in the method of disposal occurs, but should instead continue to be the same as initially determined by management in its assessment of whether the sale and/or distribution to owners is highly probable. The Board also noted that the period required to complete a sale or distribution to owners can be extended if the conditions in paragraph 9 of

IFRS 5 are met. The Board noted that when an entity changes its planned method of disposal via a direct reclassification, it does not restate prior periods to reflect the new method of disposal.

BC72K To address the lack of guidance in circumstances when an asset no longer meets the criteria for held for distribution to owners (without meeting the held-for-sale criteria), the Board decided to clarify that an entity should cease to apply held-for-distribution accounting in the same way as it ceases to apply the held-for-sale accounting when it no longer meets the held-for-sale criteria.

BC72L In response to the comments received on the 2013 Annual Improvements Exposure Draft, the Board concluded that the amendments to IFRS 5 are required to be applied, on a prospective basis, to changes in the method of disposal that occur after the first application of the amendments. This is because this requirement is consistent with the transition requirements provided by IFRIC 17 when it amended IFRS 5 (see paragraph 44D of IFRS 5). The Board considered that prospective application is also required to avoid the potential use of hindsight, because an entity might not have collected all the relevant information at the time of the change in the plan to allow the entity to account for this change.

Presentation of discontinued operations

BC73 SFAS 144 requires the results of a discontinued operation to be presented as a separate component in the income statement (net of income tax) for all periods presented.

BC74 IAS 35 did not require the results of a discontinuing operation to be presented as a net amount on the face of the income statement. Instead, specified items are disclosed either in the notes or on the face of the income statement.

BC75 In ED 4, the Board noted that it was considering the presentation of discontinued operations in the income statement in its project on reporting comprehensive income and that it did not wish to prejudge the outcome of that project by changing the requirements of IAS 35 in respect of the components to be disclosed. Given that the project on reporting comprehensive income will not be completed as soon as previously expected, the Board decided to proceed with its decisions on the presentation of discontinued operations in this IFRS.

BC76 The Board believes that discontinued operations should be shown in a section of the income statement separately from continuing operations because of the different cash flows expected to arise from the two types of operations. The Board concluded that it is sufficient to show a single net figure for discontinued operations on the face of the income statement because of the limited future cash flows expected to arise from the operations. The IFRS therefore permits an analysis of the single net amount to be presented either in the notes or in the income statement.[17]

---

17 IAS 1 *Presentation of Financial Statements* (as revised in 2007) requires an entity to present all income and expense items in one statement of comprehensive income or in two statements (a separate income statement and a statement of comprehensive income).

BC77   A substantial majority of the respondents to ED 4 supported such a presentation.

BC77A   The Board considered the comments received on the draft amendments in the 2007 exposure draft of proposed *Improvements to International Financial Reporting Standards*. Some respondents asked the Board to clarify the effects of the proposed amendment on the income statement when the disposal group meets the definition of a discontinued operation. The Board concluded that when a subsidiary is a disposal group that meets the definition of a discontinued operation in accordance with paragraph 32, an entity that is committed to a sale plan involving loss of control of the subsidiary should disclose the information required by paragraphs 33–36. The Board agreed with respondents that presentation should not differ simply because of the form of the disposal group.

Transitional arrangements

BC78   Some respondents to ED 4 noted that there could be difficulties in obtaining the information necessary to apply the IFRS retrospectively. The Board agreed that hindsight might be involved in determining at what date assets or disposal groups met the criteria to be classified as held for sale and their fair value at that date. Problems might also arise in separating the results of operations that would have been classified as discontinued operations in prior periods and that had been derecognised in full before the effective date of the IFRS.

BC79   The Board therefore decided to require application of the IFRS prospectively and allow retrospective application only when the necessary information had been obtained in the prior periods in question.

BC79A   The Board concluded that the effective date of the amendments in paragraphs 8A and 36A for presentation purposes should be 1 July 2009 to be consistent with the effective date of the amendments to IAS 27 (as amended in January 2008) for measurement purposes. Because paragraph 45(c) of IAS 27 provides an exception to retrospective application of the amendments relating to the loss of control of a subsidiary for measurement purposes, the Board required an entity to consider the applicable transitional provisions in IAS 27 when implementing the amendments in paragraphs 8A and 36A.[18]

Terminology

BC80   Two issues of terminology arose in developing the IFRS:

       (a)   the use of the term 'probable' and

       (b)   the use of the term 'fair value less costs to sell'.[19]

---

18   The consolidation requirements in IAS 27 were superseded by IFRS 10 *Consolidated Financial Statements* issued in May 2011. Paragraph 45(c) in IAS 27 was moved to paragraph C6(c) of IFRS 10; however, the transition provisions were not changed.

19   IFRS 13, issued in May 2011, defines fair value and contains the requirements for measuring fair value.

                © IFRS Foundation

BC81   In SFAS 144, the term *probable* is described as referring to a future sale that is 'likely to occur'. For the purposes of IFRSs, probable is defined as 'more likely than not'. To converge on the same meaning as SFAS 144 and to avoid using the term 'probable' with different meanings in IFRSs, this IFRS uses the phrase 'highly probable'. The Board regards 'highly probable' as implying a significantly higher probability than 'more likely than not' and as implying the same probability as the FASB's phrase 'likely to occur'. This is consistent with the Board's use of 'highly probable' in IAS 39.[20]

BC82   The measurement basis 'fair value less costs to sell' used in SFAS 144 is the same as the measurement 'net selling price' used in IAS 36 (as issued in 1998). SFAS 144 defines fair value of an asset as 'the amount at which that asset could be bought or sold in a current transaction between willing parties, that is, other than in a forced or liquidation sale', and costs to sell as 'the incremental direct costs to transact a sale, that is, the costs that result directly from and are essential to a sale transaction and that would not have been incurred by the entity had the decision to sell not been made.' IAS 36 defines net selling price as the amount obtainable from the sale of an asset in an arm's length transaction between knowledgeable, willing parties, less the costs of disposal. Costs of disposal are incremental costs directly attributable to the disposal of an asset, excluding finance costs and income tax expenses.

BC83   The Board considered using the phrase 'net selling price' to be consistent with IAS 36. However, it noted that 'fair value' is used in many IFRSs. The Board concluded that it would be preferable to use the same phrase as SFAS 144 so that it is clear that convergence on this point had been achieved and to amend IAS 36 so that the terminology in IAS 36 is consistent with other IFRSs. Therefore, a consequential amendment made by IFRS 5 replaces 'net selling price' with 'fair value less costs to sell' throughout IAS 36.

Summary of changes from ED 4

BC84   The major changes from the proposals in ED 4 are:

    (a)   clarification that assets classified as non-current are not reclassified as current until they meet the criteria to be classified as held for sale (paragraph BC10).

    (b)   goodwill and financial assets under leases are included in the scope of the measurement provisions of the IFRS (paragraphs BC8–BC14).

    (c)   non-current assets carried at fair value with changes recognised in profit or loss are excluded from the measurement provisions of the IFRS (paragraphs BC8–BC14).

    (d)   assets that are revalued in accordance with IAS 16 or IAS 38 are, when classified as held for sale, treated consistently with assets that had not previously been revalued (paragraphs BC47 and BC48).

---

20   IFRS 9 *Financial Instruments* replaced IAS 39. IFRS 9 applies to all items that were previously within the scope of IAS 39. This paragraph refers to matters relevant when IFRS 5 was issued.

(e)   the allocation of an impairment loss on a disposal group is consistent with the order of allocation of impairment losses in IAS 36 (paragraphs BC39–BC41).

(f)   the criterion in IAS 35 that a discontinued operation should be a major line of business or area of geographical operations has been added (paragraphs BC67–BC71).

(g)   discontinued operations can be presented on the face of the income statement as a single amount (paragraphs BC73–BC77).

Comparison with relevant aspects of SFAS 144

BC85   The following table sets out the extent of convergence with SFAS 144:

Requirement	Extent of convergence with SFAS 144
Scope	Some differences in scope arising from other differences between IFRSs and US GAAP.
Criteria for classification as held for sale	Fully converged.
Treatment of assets to be exchanged	Fully converged if FASB proposals on exchanges of non-monetary assets are finalised.
Treatment of assets to be abandoned	Fully converged.
Measurement on initial classification	Converged, other than cumulative exchange differences recognised directly in equity[(a)] that are included in the carrying amount of the asset (or disposal group) under US GAAP but are not under IFRS 5.
Subsequent measurement	Converged on the principles, but some differences arising from different requirements on reversals of previous impairments.
Changes to a plan to sell	Converged on reclassification and on measurement, except for differences arising from different requirements on reversals of previous impairments.
Presentation of assets classified as held for sale	Fully converged.

continued...

...continued

Requirement	Extent of convergence with SFAS 144
Definition of a discontinued operation	Not converged but the Board intends to work with the FASB to arrive at a converged definition within a relatively short time.
Timing of classification of an operation as discontinued	Fully converged.
Presentation of a discontinued operation	Converged except that SFAS 144 requires the presentation of pre- and post-tax profits on the face of the income statement and IFRS 5 requires the presentation of post-tax profit only (although disaggregation is permitted).

(a) As a consequence of the revision of IAS 1 *Presentation of Financial Statements* (as revised in 2007) such differences are recognised in other comprehensive income.

Dissenting opinions

Dissent of Anthony T Cope and Harry K Schmid

DO1   Messrs Cope and Schmid dissent from the issue of IFRS 5.

Dissent of Anthony T Cope

DO2   Mr Cope dissents because, in his view, the IFRS fails to meet fully the needs of users in this important area.

DO3   In deciding to undertake this project, the Board had two objectives – to improve users' ability to assess the amount, timing and uncertainty of future cash flows, and to converge with US GAAP. The ability to identify assets (or asset groups) whose value will be recovered principally through sale rather than through operations has significant implications for future cash flows. Similarly, separate presentation of discontinued operations enables users to distinguish those parts of a business that will not contribute to future cash flows.

DO4   The importance of identifying and disaggregating these components was emphasised in the 1994 report of the Special Committee on Financial Reporting of the American Institute of Certified Public Accountants (the AICPA Jenkins Committee). The Jenkins Committee report, arguably the most extensive and authoritative survey of user needs ever undertaken, recommended that:

> [The definition of discontinued operations] should be broadened to include all significant discontinued operations whose assets and results of operations and activities can be distinguished physically and operationally and for business reporting purposes.

The sections of SFAS 144 dealing with discontinued operations were the direct response of the FASB to this recommendation.

DO5   Indeed, the Board appeared to agree in its initial deliberations. In ED 4, the Board stated:

> [The Board] further concluded that the definition of discontinued operations in SFAS 144 leads to more useful information being presented and disclosed for a wider range of operations than did the existing definition in IAS 35. That information is important to users in their assessment of the amount, timing and uncertainty of future cash flows.

Mr Cope continues to agree with that statement.

DO6   However, the Board ultimately has decided to retain the definition in IAS 35, thus failing to gain convergence on an important point in a project designed to achieve such convergence, and failing to respond to the stated needs of users.

DO7   The reason given for the Board's action is that implementation problems with SFAS 144 have emerged in the US. (Most of these problems seem to be with the guidance concerning the definition in SFAS 144, rather than the definition itself.) In paragraph BC71, the Board describes its action as an interim measure, and plans to work with the FASB to arrive promptly at a converged solution. In Mr Cope's view, it would have been much preferable to have converged first, and then dealt with any implementation problems jointly with the FASB.

Dissent of Harry K Schmid

DO8   The main reasons for Mr Schmid's dissent are:

(a)   depreciation/amortisation of non-current assets that are still in active use should not cease only because of a management decision to sell the assets that has not yet been fully carried out; and

(b)   measurement of assets should not be based on a management decision that has not yet been fully carried out, requiring a very rule-based Standard.

DO9   Mr Schmid believes that not depreciating/amortising assets classified as held for sale but still in active use is conceptually wrong and is especially problematic for discontinued operations because such operations represent a separate major line of business or geographical area of operations. Mr Schmid does not accept that measurement at the lower of carrying amount and fair value less costs to sell acts as a proxy for depreciation because, in most such cases, the fair value less costs to sell will be higher than the carrying amount as the fair value of such disposal groups will often reflect internally generated goodwill. Therefore, non-current assets in such disposal groups will simply remain at their carrying amounts even though they are still actively used, up to one year or even longer. In addition, the net profit shown separately in the income statement for discontinued operations will not be meaningful because depreciation/amortisation charges are not deducted for the continued use of the assets and this profit cannot be compared with the information restated in comparative periods where depreciation had been charged.

DO10   The proposed classification 'held for sale' and resulting measurement of non-current assets (or disposal groups) so classified is based on a management decision that has not yet been fully carried out and demands detailed (anti-abuse) rules to define the classification and to fix the time boundaries during which these assets can remain within the classification. The final result is, in Mr Schmid's view, an excessively detailed and rule-based Standard.

DO11   Mr Schmid believes that a more simple and straightforward solution would have been possible by creating a special category of non-current assets retired from active use. The concept 'retired from active use' would have been simple to apply and management intentions would be removed from the Standard. The classification would equally apply to any form of disposal (sale, abandonment, exchange, spin-off etc); no detailed (anti-abuse) rules and no illustrations would be necessary and the Standard would be simple and based on a clear and unambiguous principle. Mr Schmid, on this point, does not agree with the conclusions in paragraph BC18 that a classification 'retired from active use' would not require fewer criteria to support it than the category 'assets held for sale'.

DO12   Mr Schmid agrees with paragraph BC17 of the Basis for Conclusions, but in order to provide information of intended sales of non-current assets, especially discontinued operations, disclosure could have been required to take effect as soon as such assets are likely to be sold, even if they are still in active use.

DO13   Mr Schmid is fully in favour of seeking, whenever possible, convergence with US GAAP, but only if the converged solution is of high quality. He is of the opinion that this is not the case for this Standard for the reasons given.

IASB documents published to accompany

IFRS 6

Exploration for and Evaluation of Mineral Resources

The text of the unaccompanied standard, IFRS 6, is contained in Part A of this edition. Its effective date when issued was 1 January 2013. This part presents the following documents:

BASIS FOR CONCLUSIONS

DISSENTING OPINIONS

Contents

Basis for Conclusions on
IFRS 6 *Exploration for and Evaluation of Mineral Resources*

This Basis for Conclusions accompanies, but is not part of, IFRS 6.

Introduction

BC1   This Basis for Conclusions summarises the International Accounting Standards Board's considerations in reaching the conclusions in IFRS 6 *Exploration for and Evaluation of Mineral Resources*. Individual Board members gave greater weight to some factors than to others.

Reasons for issuing the IFRS

BC2   Paragraphs 10–12 of IAS 8 *Accounting Policies, Changes in Accounting Estimates and Errors* specify a hierarchy of criteria that an entity should use in developing an accounting policy if no IFRS applies specifically to an item. Without the exemption in IFRS 6, an entity adopting IFRSs in 2005 would have needed to assess whether its accounting policies for the exploration for and evaluation of mineral resources complied with those requirements. In the absence of guidance, there might have been uncertainty about what would be acceptable. Establishing what would be acceptable could have been costly and some entities might have made major changes in 2005 followed by further significant changes once the Board completes its comprehensive review of accounting for extractive activities.

BC3   To avoid unnecessary disruption for both users and preparers at this time, the Board proposed to limit the need for entities to change their existing accounting policies for exploration and evaluation assets. The Board did this by:

(a)   creating a temporary exemption from parts of the hierarchy in IAS 8 that specify the criteria an entity uses in developing an accounting policy if no IFRS applies specifically.

(b)   limiting the impact of that exemption from the hierarchy by identifying expenditures to be included in and excluded from exploration and evaluation assets and requiring all exploration and evaluation assets to be assessed for impairment.

BC4   The Board published its proposals in January 2004. ED 6 *Exploration for and Evaluation of Mineral Resources* had a comment deadline of 16 April 2004. The Board received 55 comment letters.

BC5   In April 2004 the Board approved a research project to be undertaken by staff from the national standard-setters in Australia, Canada, Norway and South Africa that will address accounting for extractive activities generally. The research project team is assisted by an advisory panel, which includes members from industry (oil and gas and mining sectors), accounting firms, users and securities regulators from around the world.

Scope

BC6 In the Board's view, even though no IFRS has addressed extractive activities directly, all IFRSs (including International Accounting Standards and Interpretations) are applicable to entities engaged in the exploration for and evaluation of mineral resources that make an unreserved statement of compliance with IFRSs in accordance with IAS 1 *Presentation of Financial Statements*. Consequently, each IFRS must be applied by all such entities.

BC7 Some respondents to ED 6 encouraged the Board to develop standards for other stages in the process of exploring for and evaluating mineral resources, including pre-exploration activities (ie activities preceding the exploration for and evaluation of mineral resources) and development activities (ie activities after the technical feasibility and commercial viability of extracting a mineral resource are demonstrable). The Board decided not to do this for two reasons. First, it did not want to prejudge the comprehensive review of the accounting for such activities. Second, the Board concluded that an appropriate accounting policy for pre-exploration activities could be developed from an application of existing IFRSs, from the *Framework*'s[1] definitions of assets and expenses, and by applying the general principles of asset recognition in IAS 16 *Property, Plant and Equipment* and IAS 38 *Intangible Assets*.

BC8 The Board also decided not to expand the scope of IFRS 6 beyond that proposed in ED 6 because to do so would require additional due process, possibly including another exposure draft. In view of the many entities engaged in extractive activities that would be required to apply IFRSs from 1 January 2005, the Board decided that it should not delay issuing guidance by expanding the scope of the IFRS beyond the exploration for and evaluation of mineral resources.

Definition of exploration and evaluation assets

BC9 Most respondents to ED 6 agreed with the Board's proposed definition of exploration and evaluation assets, but asked for changes or clarifications to make the Board's intentions clearer:

(a) some respondents asked the Board to distinguish between exploration and pre-exploration expenditures.

(b) others asked the Board to define exploration and evaluation activities separately, reflecting the different risk profiles of such activities or the requirements of other jurisdictions.

(c) other respondents asked for further guidance on what constitute mineral resources, principally examples of what constitutes a mineral reserve.

---

1 References to the *Framework* in this Basis for Conclusions are to the IASC's *Framework for the Preparation and Presentation of Financial Statements*, adopted by the Board in 2001 and in effect when the Standard was developed.

Expenditures incurred before the exploration for and evaluation of mineral resources

BC10   Respondents seemed to be concerned that the Board was extending the scope of the proposals to include expenditures incurred before the acquisition of legal rights to explore in a specific area in the definition of exploration and evaluation expenditure. Some were concerned that such an extension would open the way for the recognition of such expenditures as assets; others preferred this result. In drafting IFRS 6, the Board could not identify any reason why the *Framework* was not applicable to such expenditures.

BC11   The Board decided not to define pre-acquisition or pre-exploration expenditures. However, the IFRS clarifies that expenditures before the entity has obtained legal rights to explore in a specific area are not exploration and evaluation expenditures and are therefore outside the scope of the IFRS.

BC12   The Board noted that an appropriate application of IFRSs might require pre-acquisition expenditures related to the acquisition of an intangible asset (eg expenditures directly attributable to the acquisition of an exploration licence) to be recognised as part of the intangible asset in accordance with IAS 38. Paragraph 27(a) of IAS 38 states that the cost of a separately acquired intangible asset comprises its purchase price, including import duties and non-refundable purchase taxes, and some directly attributable costs.

BC13   Similarly, the Board understands that expenditures incurred before the exploration for and evaluation of mineral resources cannot usually be associated with any specific mineral property and thus are likely to be recognised as an expense as incurred. However, such expenditures need to be distinguished from expenditures on infrastructure—for example access roads—necessary for the exploration work to proceed. Such expenditures should be recognised as property, plant and equipment in accordance with paragraph 3 of IAS 16.

Separate definitions of 'exploration' and 'evaluation'

BC14   Some respondents asked the Board to provide separate definitions of exploration and evaluation. The Board considered using the definitions provided in the Issues Paper *Extractive Industries* published by its predecessor, the Board of the International Accounting Standards Committee, in November 2000, because those definitions would be acceptable to many respondents, particularly because they are based on definitions that have been used for a number of years in both the mining and the oil and gas sectors.

BC15   The Board concluded that distinguishing between evaluation and exploration would not improve the IFRS. Exploration and evaluation are accounted for in the same way.

Mineral resources

BC16   Some respondents asked the Board to define mineral resources more precisely. The Board concluded that, for the purposes of the IFRS, elaboration was unnecessary. The items listed in the definition of exploration for and evaluation of mineral resources were sufficient to convey the Board's intentions.

Recognition of exploration and evaluation assets

Temporary exemption from IAS 8 paragraphs 11 and 12

BC17   A variety of accounting practices are followed by entities engaged in the exploration for and evaluation of mineral resources. These practices range from deferring on the balance sheet nearly all exploration and evaluation expenditure to recognising all such expenditure in profit or loss as incurred. The IFRS permits these various accounting practices to continue. Given this diversity, some respondents to ED 6 opposed any exemption from paragraphs 11 and 12 of IAS 8. These respondents were concerned that entities could give the appearance of compliance with IFRSs while being inconsistent with the stated objectives of the IASB, ie to provide users of financial statements with financial information that was of high quality, transparent and comparable. The Board did not grant the exemption from parts of IAS 8 lightly, but took this step to minimise disruption, especially in 2006 (or 2005, for those entities that adopt the IFRS early), both for users (eg lack of continuity of trend data) and for preparers (eg systems changes).

BC18   IFRS 4 *Insurance Contracts* provides a temporary exemption from paragraphs 10–12 of IAS 8. That exemption is broader than in IFRS 6 because IFRS 4 leaves many significant aspects of accounting for insurance contracts until phase II of the Board's project on that topic. A requirement to apply paragraph 10 of IAS 8 to insurance contracts would have had much more pervasive effects and insurers would have needed to address matters such as completeness, substance over form and neutrality. In contrast, IFRS 6 leaves a relatively narrow range of issues unaddressed and the Board did not think that an exemption from paragraph 10 of IAS 8 was necessary.

BC19   ED 6 made it clear that the Board intended to suspend only paragraphs 11 and 12 of IAS 8, implying that paragraph 10 should be followed when an entity was determining its accounting policies for exploration and evaluation assets. However, it was apparent from some comments received that the Board's intention had not been understood clearly. Consequently, the IFRS contains a specific statement that complying with paragraph 10 of IAS 8 is mandatory.

BC20   Respondents who objected to the Board's proposal in ED 6 to permit some accounting practices to continue found it difficult to draw a meaningful distinction between the exploration for and evaluation of mineral resources and scientific research. Both activities can be costly and have significant risks of failure. These respondents would support bringing the exploration for and evaluation of mineral resources within the scope of IAS 16 and IAS 38. The Board is similarly concerned that existing accounting practices might result in the inappropriate recognition of exploration and evaluation assets. However, it is also concerned that accounting for exploration and evaluation expenditures in accordance with IAS 38 might result in the overstatement of expenses. In the absence of internationally accepted standards for such expenditures, the Board concluded that it could not make an informed judgement in advance of the comprehensive review of accounting for extractive activities.

BC21   Some suggested that the Board should require an entity to follow its national accounting requirements (ie national GAAP) in accounting for the exploration for and evaluation of mineral resources until the Board completes its comprehensive review of accounting for extractive activities, to prevent the selection of accounting policies that do not form a comprehensive basis of accounting. Consistently with its conclusions in IFRS 4, the Board concluded that defining national GAAP would have posed problems. Further definitional problems could have arisen because some entities do not apply the national GAAP of their own country. For example, some non-US entities with extractive activities in the oil and gas sector apply US GAAP. Moreover, it is unusual and, arguably, beyond the Board's mandate to impose requirements set by another body.

BC22   Therefore, the Board decided that an entity could continue to follow the accounting policies that it was using when it first applied the IFRS's requirements, provided they satisfy the requirements of paragraph 10 of IAS 8 and with some exceptions noted below. An entity could also improve those accounting policies if specified criteria are met (see paragraphs 13 and 14 of the IFRS).

BC23   The Board acknowledges that it is difficult to make piecemeal changes to recognition and measurement practices at this time because many aspects of accounting for extractive activities are interrelated with aspects that will not be considered until the Board completes its comprehensive review of accounting for extractive activities. However, not imposing the requirements in the IFRS would detract from the relevance and reliability of an entity's financial statements to an unacceptable degree.

BC23A   In 2008, as part of its annual improvements project, the Board considered the guidance on the treatment in IAS 7 Statement of Cash Flows of some types of expenditures incurred with the objective of generating future cash flows when those expenditures are not recognised as assets in accordance with IFRSs. Some entities classify such expenditures as cash flows from operating activities and others classify them as investing activities. Examples of such expenditures are those for exploration and evaluation activities, which can be recognised according to IFRS 6 as either an asset or an expense.[2]

---

2   Paragraphs BC23A and BC23B were added as a consequence of an amendment to IAS 7 included in Improvements to IFRSs issued in April 2009.

BC23B   The Board noted that the exemption in IFRS 6 applies only to recognition and measurement of exploration and evaluation assets, not to the classification of related expenditures in the statement of cash flows. Consequently, the Board amended paragraph 16 of IAS 7 to state that only an expenditure that results in a recognised asset can be classified as a cash flow from investing activities.

Elements of cost of exploration and evaluation assets

BC24   ED 6 paragraph 7 listed examples of expenditures related to the exploration for and evaluation of mineral resources that might be included in the cost of an exploration and evaluation asset. ED 6 paragraph 8 listed expenditures that could not be recognised as an exploration and evaluation asset. Respondents expressed a desire for greater clarity with respect to these paragraphs and more examples of types of expenditures that would be included or excluded.

BC25   In the light of the responses, the Board decided to redraft the guidance to state that the list is not exhaustive and that the items noted are examples of expenditures that might, but need not always, satisfy the definition of exploration and evaluation expenditure. In addition, the Board noted that IFRSs require that expenditures should be treated consistently for comparable activities and between reporting periods. Any change in what is deemed to be an expenditure qualifying for recognition as an exploration and evaluation asset should be treated as a change in an accounting policy accounted for in accordance with IAS 8. Pending the comprehensive review of accounting for extractive activities, the Board does not think that it is feasible to define what expenditures should be included or excluded.

BC26   ED 6 paragraph 8 proposed to prohibit expenditure related to the development of a mineral resource from being recognised as an exploration and evaluation asset. Respondents expressed difficulty identifying expenditures on 'development'. The Board did not define 'development of a mineral resource' because this is beyond the scope of the IFRS.

BC27   However, the Board noted that development of a mineral resource once the technical feasibility and commercial viability of extracting the mineral resource had been determined was an example of the development phase of an internal project. Paragraph 57 of IAS 38 provides guidance that should be followed in developing an accounting policy for this activity.

BC28   ED 6 proposed that administration and other general overhead costs should be excluded from the initial measurement of exploration and evaluation assets. Several respondents suggested that general and administrative and overhead costs *directly attributable* to the exploration and evaluation activities should qualify for inclusion in the carrying amount of the asset. These respondents saw this treatment as consistent with the treatment of such costs with respect to inventory (paragraph 11 of IAS 2 *Inventories*) and intangible assets (paragraph 67(a) of IAS 38). However, the Board noted that such a treatment would seem to be inconsistent with paragraph 19(d) of IAS 16. The IFRS was not regarded as the appropriate Standard in which to resolve this inconsistency, and the Board decided to delete the reference in the IFRS to administrative and other general overheads. The treatment of such expenditures would be an accounting policy choice; the chosen policy should be consistent with one of the treatments available under IFRSs.

Measurement after recognition

BC29   The IFRS permits an entity recognising exploration and evaluation assets to measure such assets, after recognition, using either the cost model or the revaluation model in IAS 16 and IAS 38. The model chosen should be consistent with how the entity classifies the exploration and evaluation assets. Those revaluation models permit the revaluation of assets when specified requirements are met (see paragraphs 31–42 of IAS 16 and paragraphs 72–84 of IAS 38). The revaluation model in IAS 38 can be used only if the asset's fair value can be determined by reference to an active market; the revaluation model in IAS 16 refers only to 'market-based evidence'. The Board was troubled by this inconsistency and was concerned that entities might choose accounting policies to achieve a more advantageous measurement of exploration and evaluation assets.

BC30   A few respondents were also concerned with the option proposed in ED 6. Some did not agree that exploration and evaluation assets should be revalued, preferring an arbitrary prohibition of remeasurement. Others were concerned about the reliability of the measure. The Board concluded that no substantive reasons had been presented for reaching a conclusion different from that in ED 6. Although the revaluation of an exploration asset in accordance with IAS 16 or IAS 38 might not be widespread, it was not appropriate to prohibit remeasurement of specific types of IAS 16 or IAS 38 assets on a selective basis.

BC31   Exploration and evaluation assets may arise as a result of a business combination. The Board noted that IFRS 3 *Business Combinations* applies to all entities asserting compliance with IFRSs and that any exploration and evaluation assets acquired in a business combination should be accounted for in accordance with IFRS 3.

Presentation of exploration and evaluation assets

BC32   ED 6 noted that the Board had not yet considered whether exploration and evaluation assets are tangible or intangible. Several respondents suggested that the Board should give some direction on this issue.

BC33   Some exploration and evaluation assets are treated as intangible assets (eg drilling rights), whereas others are clearly tangible (eg vehicles and drilling rigs). A tangible asset may be used in the development of an intangible one. For example, a portable drilling rig may be used to drill test wells or take core samples, clearly part of the exploration activity. To the extent that the tangible asset is consumed in developing an intangible asset, the amount reflecting that consumption is part of the cost of the intangible asset. However, using the drilling rig to develop an intangible asset does not change a tangible asset into an intangible asset.

BC34   Pending completion of the comprehensive review of accounting practices for extractive activities, the Board did not wish to decide whether and which exploration and evaluation assets should be classified as tangible or intangible. However, the Board concluded that an entity should classify the elements of exploration and evaluation assets as tangible or intangible according to their nature and apply this classification consistently. This classification is the foundation for other accounting policy choices as described in paragraphs BC29–BC31 and for the disclosures required by the IFRS.

Impairment of exploration and evaluation assets

BC35   When it developed ED 6, the Board decided that an entity recognising exploration and evaluation assets should test those assets for impairment, and that the impairment test to be applied should be that in IAS 36 *Impairment of Assets*. Respondents accepted the general proposition that exploration and evaluation assets should be tested for impairment. However, the Board's proposals for a special 'cash-generating unit for exploration and evaluation assets' (the special CGU) were not thought appropriate or useful.

Assessment of impairment

BC36   In some cases, and particularly in exploration-only entities, exploration and evaluation assets do not generate cash flows and there is insufficient information about the mineral resources in a specific area for an entity to make reasonable estimates of exploration and evaluation assets' recoverable amount. This is because the exploration for and evaluation of the mineral resources has not reached a stage at which information sufficient to estimate future cash flows is available to the entity. Without such information, it is not possible to estimate either fair value less costs to sell or value in use, the two measures of recoverable amount in IAS 36. Respondents noted that this would lead to an immediate write-off of exploration assets in many cases.

BC37   The Board was persuaded by respondents' arguments that recognising impairment losses on this basis was potentially inconsistent with permitting existing methods of accounting for exploration and evaluation assets to continue. Therefore, pending completion of the comprehensive review of accounting for extractive activities, the Board decided to change the approach to recognition of impairment; the assessment of impairment should be triggered by changes in facts and circumstances. However, it also confirmed that, once an entity had determined that an exploration and evaluation asset was impaired, IAS 36 should be used to measure, present and disclose that impairment in the financial statements, subject to special requirements with respect to the level at which impairment is assessed.

BC38   Paragraph 12 of ED 6 proposed that an entity that had recognised exploration and evaluation assets should assess those assets for impairment annually and recognise any resulting impairment loss in accordance with IAS 36. Paragraph 13 proposed a set of indicators of impairment that an entity would consider in addition to those in IAS 36. Respondents stated that these indicators would not achieve the Board's intended result, especially in circumstances in which the information necessary for an assessment of mineral reserves was not available.

BC39 The Board replaced the proposals in paragraphs 12 and 13 of ED 6 with an exception to the recognition requirements in IAS 36. The Board decided that, until the entity had sufficient data to determine technical feasibility and commercial viability, exploration and evaluation assets need not be assessed for impairment. However, when such information becomes available, or other facts and circumstances suggest that the asset might be impaired, the exploration and evaluation assets must be assessed for impairment. The IFRS suggests possible indicators of impairment.

The level at which impairment is assessed

BC40 When it developed ED 6, the Board decided that there was a need for consistency between the level at which costs were accumulated and the level at which impairment was assessed. Without this consistency, there was a danger that expenditures that would form part of the cost of an exploration and evaluation asset under one of the common methods of accounting for the exploration for and evaluation of mineral resources would need to be recognised in profit or loss in accordance with IAS 36. Consequently, ED 6 proposed that an entity recognising exploration and evaluation assets should make a one-time election to test those assets either at the level of the IAS 36 cash-generating unit (CGU) or at the level of a special CGU. ED 6 explained that any assets other than exploration and evaluation assets included within the special CGU should continue to be subject to separate impairment testing in accordance with IAS 36, and that impairment test should be performed before the special CGU was tested for impairment.

BC41 Respondents disagreed with the Board's proposal. In particular, and for various reasons, they did not accept that the special CGU would provide the relief it was intended to provide, because:

(a) small, start-up or exploration-only entities might not have adequate cash flows to support exploration and evaluation assets that were not cash-generating.

(b) entities applying the successful efforts method of accounting typically conduct impairment tests property by property. However, because of the way in which the special CGU was defined in ED 6 such entities would be forced to carry out impairment tests at the CGU level.

(c) the special CGU permitted management extensive discretion.

In addition, there was concern that, because the exploration and evaluation assets could be aggregated with other assets in the special CGU, there would be confusion about the appropriate measurement model to apply (fair value less costs to sell or value in use). As a result, many respondents to ED 6 did not think that the Board had achieved its intention in this respect, and said that they preferred to apply IAS 36 without the special CGU.

BC42   Although the Board disagreed with some of the arguments put forward by respondents, it acknowledged that the special CGU seemed to be more confusing than helpful. This suggested that it was not needed. Paragraph BC20 of the Basis for Conclusions on ED 6 noted the Board's reluctance to introduce a special CGU. Removing the special CGU would eliminate much of the complexity in the proposed IFRS and the confusion among constituents. It would also mean that entities with extractive activities would assess their assets for impairment at the same level as other entities – providing a higher level of comparability than might otherwise be the case.

BC43   Board members noted that paragraph 22 of IAS 36 requires impairment to be assessed at the individual asset level 'unless the asset does not generate cash inflows that are largely independent of those from other assets or groups of assets'. In addition, paragraph 70 of IAS 36 requires that 'if an active market exists for the output produced by an asset or group of assets, that asset or group of assets shall be identified as a cash-generating unit'. In some cases in which exploration and evaluation assets are recognised, eg in the petroleum sector, each well is potentially capable of producing cash inflows that are observable and capable of reliable measurement because there is an active market for crude oil. The Board was concerned that removing the special CGU would cause entities recognising exploration and evaluation assets to test for impairment at a very low level.

BC44   The issue was highlighted in the July 2004 issue of *IASB Update*, in the project summary and in the *Effect of Redeliberations* documents available on the IASB's Website. These documents were also sent to the Board's research project team and others with a request to encourage their constituents to respond to the issues raised. The Board received 16 comment letters.

BC45   The majority of respondents continued to support the elimination of the special CGU. They also supported the notion that entities should test impairment at the level of the cost centre and suggested that the Board should consider defining an 'asset' as it applied to exploration and evaluation assets. The respondents argued that such an approach would reflect more accurately the way in which the industry manages its operations. The Board was persuaded by these arguments and decided that it should permit entities some flexibility in allocating exploration and evaluation assets to cash-generating units or groups of units, subject to an upper limit on the size of the units or groups of units.

BC46   The Board decided that its approach to the impairment of goodwill in the 2004 revisions to IAS 36 paragraphs 80–82 offered the best model available within IFRSs to accomplish its objective. It noted that entities might be able to monitor exploration and evaluation assets for internal management purposes at the level of an oilfield or a contiguous ore body. The Board did not intend to require impairment to be assessed at such a low level. Consequently, the IFRS permits CGUs to be aggregated. However, the Board decided to require the level at which impairment was assessed to be no larger than a segment, based on either the entity's primary or the entity's secondary segment reporting format in accordance with IAS 14 *Segment Reporting*. The Board concluded, consistently with the approach to goodwill in IAS 36, that this approach was necessary to ensure that entities managed on a matrix basis could test exploration and evaluation assets for impairment at the level of reporting that reflects the way they manage their operations. This requirement is no less rigorous than ED 6's requirement that the special CGU should 'be no larger than a segment'.[3]

BC47 Consequently, the Board decided to remove the proposed special CGU. In doing so, it noted that eliminating this requirement would have the following benefits:

(a) once an impairment was identified, the measurement, presentation and disclosure of impairment would be more consistent across entities recognising exploration and evaluation assets.

(b) it would remove the confusion about what practices entities recognising exploration and evaluation assets for the first time should follow.

(c) it would remove the risk noted in some comment letters that the special CGU could become the 'industry norm', limiting the Board's options when the comprehensive review of accounting for extractive activities is completed.

Reversal of impairment losses

BC48 The reversal of impairment losses when specified requirements (ie those set out in paragraphs 109–123 of IAS 36) are met is required of all entities for all assets (excluding goodwill and equity investments classified as available for sale). Respondents to ED 6 who commented on this issue and who disagreed with the ability to reverse impairment losses advanced no new arguments why the Board should prohibit reversal of impairment losses in the case of exploration and evaluation assets. Consequently, the Board reaffirmed its conclusion that it would not be appropriate to propose an exemption from the requirement to reverse impairment losses for exploration and evaluation assets.

Changes in accounting policies

BC49 IAS 8 prohibits a change in accounting policies that is not required by an IFRS, unless the change will result in the provision of reliable and more relevant information. Although the Board wished to avoid imposing unnecessary changes in this IFRS, it did not believe it should exempt entities from the requirement to justify changes in accounting policies. Consistently with its conclusions in IFRS 4, the Board decided to permit changes in accounting policies for exploration and evaluation assets if they make the financial statements more relevant and no less reliable, or more reliable and no less relevant judged by the criteria in IAS 8.

---

3 In 2006 IAS 14 was replaced by IFRS 8 *Operating Segments*, which does not require the identification of primary and secondary segments. See paragraph BC150A of the Basis for Conclusions on IAS 36 *Impairment of Assets*.

Disclosures

BC50   The disclosure requirements in the IFRS are based on a principle that an entity should disclose information that identifies and explains the amounts recognised in its financial statements that arise from the exploration for and evaluation of mineral resources, supplemented by specified disclosures to meet that objective.

BC51   Although respondents agreed that entities should be allowed flexibility in determining the levels of aggregation and amount of disclosure, they suggested that the Board should introduce more specific and standardised disclosure requirements. Some respondents were concerned that the variety of accounting for the exploration for and evaluation of mineral resources could reduce comparability.

BC52   The Board concluded that the ED 6 approach was superior to requiring a long list of detailed and prescriptive disclosures because concentrating on the underlying principle:

   (a)   makes it easier for entities to understand the rationale for the requirements, which promotes compliance.

   (b)   avoids requiring specific disclosures that may not be needed to meet the underlying objectives in the circumstances of every entity and could lead to information overload that obscures important information in a mass of detail.

   (c)   gives entities flexibility to decide on an appropriate level of aggregation that enables users to see the overall picture, but without combining information that has different characteristics.

   (d)   permits reporting exploration and evaluation expenditure by segment on either an annual basis or an accumulated basis.

BC53   Some respondents suggested that the Board should require disclosures similar to those in paragraphs 73 and 74 of IAS 16 or in paragraphs 118–125 of IAS 38. Both IAS 16 and IAS 38 contain scope exclusions for exploration and evaluation assets. Therefore, entities recognising these assets could claim that the requirements were not applicable. The Board decided that, although the scope of those standards excludes exploration and evaluation assets, their required disclosures would provide information relevant to an understanding of the financial statements and useful to users. Consequently, the Board concluded that the IFRS should confirm that the disclosures of IASs 16 and 38 are required consistently with how the entity classifies its exploration and evaluation assets (ie tangible (IAS 16) or intangible (IAS 38)).

BC54   In addition, some respondents suggested that the Board should require disclosure of non-financial information, including:

   (a)   commercial reserve quantities;

   (b)   rights to explore for, develop and produce wasting resources;

   (c)   disclosures about stages after exploration and evaluation; and

(d) the number of years since exploration started, and an estimation of the time remaining until a decision could be made about the technical feasibility and commercial viability of extracting the mineral resource.

Commercial reserves

BC55 The Board acknowledged that information about commercial reserve quantities is, perhaps, the most important disclosure for an entity with extractive activities. However, it noted that commercial reserves are usually determined after the exploration and evaluation stage has ended and it concluded that such disclosure was beyond the stated scope of the IFRS.

Stages after exploration and evaluation

BC56 As with commercial reserves, the Board concluded that, although information about stages after exploration and evaluation would be useful to users of financial statements, such disclosure is beyond the scope of the IFRS.

Project timing

BC57 The Board also concluded that disclosure of the number of years since exploration started and the estimated time remaining until a decision could be made about development would apply only to large scale exploration activities. It noted that if the project is significant, paragraph 112(c) of IAS 1 already requires its disclosure, ie as additional information that is necessary for an understanding of the financial statements.

Effective date

BC58 ED 6 proposed that the IFRS should be effective for annual periods beginning on or after 1 January 2005. The Board decided to change the effective date to 1 January 2006 to allow entities more time to make the transition to the IFRS. It also decided to permit an entity that wishes or is required to adopt IFRSs before 1 January 2006 to adopt IFRS 6 early.

Transition

BC59 The Board did not propose any special transition in ED 6. Consequently, paragraphs 14–27 of IAS 8 would apply to any changes in accounting that are necessary as a result of the IFRS.

BC60 Some respondents expressed concern about the application of the proposals to prior periods—especially those related to impairment and the inclusion or exclusion of some expenditures from exploration and evaluation assets. In particular, respondents requested that if the Board were to require restatement, it should give transitional guidance on how to identify elements previously recognised as exploration and evaluation assets now outside the definition.

BC61   IAS 8 would require entities recognising exploration and evaluation assets to determine whether there were any facts and circumstances indicating impairment in prior periods. The Board concluded that retrospective application was not likely to involve the use of hindsight because the facts and circumstances identified in the IFRS are generally objective indicators and whether they existed at a particular date should be a question of fact. However, the Board noted that it provided transitional relief in IFRS 4 for applying the liability adequacy test to comparative periods on the basis of impracticability, principally because the liability adequacy test involves the use of current estimates of future cash flows from an entity's insurance contracts. The Board does not expect that IFRS 6's approach to impairment will involve current estimates of future cash flows and other variables to the same extent. However, it is aware that the variety of approaches to assessing recoverability means that current estimates of future cash flows and other variables are likely to be in use by some entities.

BC62   Therefore, consistently with IFRS 4, the Board concluded that if it is impracticable to apply the impairment test to comparative information that relates to annual periods beginning before 1 January 2006, an entity should disclose that fact.

BC63   Some respondents were concerned that entities would have difficulty in compiling the information necessary for 2004 comparative figures, and suggested that entities should be exempted from restating comparatives on transition, given that the IFRS would be introduced close to 1 January 2005, and could result in substantial changes.

BC64   The Board considered a similar issue when it developed ED 7 *Financial Instruments: Disclosures*, in which it concluded that entities that apply the requirements proposed in ED 7 only when they become mandatory should be required to provide comparative disclosures because such entities will have enough time to prepare the information.

BC65   In ED 7, the Board decided to propose that an entity that both (a) adopts IFRSs for the first time before 1 January 2006 and (b) applies the IFRS before that date should be exempt from the requirement to produce comparative information in the first year of application. The Board compared the concerns raised by constituents in response to ED 6 and the issues it considered in developing ED 7 and decided that its conclusions in ED 7 were also appropriate for the IFRS.

BC65A   [Deleted][4]

---

4   Paragraph BC65A was deleted as a result of revisions to IFRS 1 *First-time Adoption of International Financial Reporting Standards* in November 2008 as it was no longer applicable.

Summary of changes from ED 6

BC66   The following is a summary of the main changes from ED 6 to the IFRS. The Board:

(a)   deleted the specific prohibition against including administration and other general overhead costs in the initial measurement of an exploration and evaluation asset (paragraph BC28).

(b)   introduced a requirement for the entity to classify exploration and evaluation assets as either tangible or intangible according to the nature of the asset acquired and to apply this classification consistently (paragraphs BC32–BC34).

(c)   amended the impairment principle so that an impairment is recognised on the basis of an assessment of facts and circumstances and measured, presented and disclosed in accordance with IAS 36, subject to the modification of the level at which the impairment is assessed (paragraphs BC36–BC39).

(d)   deleted the indicators of impairment proposed in ED 6 and replaced them with examples of facts and circumstances that would suggest that an exploration and evaluation asset was impaired (paragraphs BC36–BC39).

(e)   deleted the special cash-generating unit for exploration and evaluation assets and instead required that the entity determine an accounting policy for allocating exploration and evaluation assets to a cash-generating unit or units for the purpose of the impairment test (paragraphs BC40–BC47).

(f)   amended the effective date of the IFRS so that the IFRS is effective for annual periods beginning on or after 1 January 2006 (paragraph BC58).

(g)   provided transitional relief for entities adopting IFRSs for the first time and adopting the IFRS before 1 January 2006 (paragraphs BC59–BC65).

Amended reference to the *Conceptual Framework*

BC67   Following the issue of the revised *Conceptual Framework for Financial Reporting* in 2018 (2018 *Conceptual Framework*), the Board issued *Amendments to References to the Conceptual Framework in IFRS Standards*. In IFRS 6, that document replaced a reference in paragraph 10 to the *Framework* with a reference to the 2018 *Conceptual Framework*. The Board does not expect that replacement to have a significant effect on the application of the Standard for the following reasons:

(a)   The Board does not expect the application of the revised definition of an asset, together with the revised recognition criteria, to lead to significant changes in practice for entities that applied the *Framework* when developing their accounting policies for recognition of assets arising from development of mineral resources. Although the Board replaced the probability and reliability recognition criteria with recognition criteria based on the qualitative characteristics of useful financial information, the 2018 *Conceptual Framework* specifies low probability of an inflow or outflow of economic benefits and measurement uncertainty as factors to be considered in decisions about recognition.

(b)   Entities that apply IAS 38 to develop their accounting policies for recognition of assets arising from development of mineral resources will not be affected by the amendment of the reference to the *Framework* in IFRS 6.

Dissenting opinions

Dissent of Robert P Garnett, James J Leisenring, Warren J McGregor and John T Smith

DO1   Messrs Garnett, Leisenring, McGregor and Smith dissent from the issue of IFRS 6.

DO2   These four Board members dissent because they would not permit entities the alternative of continuing their existing accounting treatment for exploration and evaluation assets. In particular, they believe that all entities should be required to apply paragraphs 11 and 12 of IAS 8 *Accounting Policies, Changes in Accounting Estimates and Errors* when developing an accounting policy for exploration and evaluation assets. These Board members believe that the requirements in IAS 8 have particular relevance and applicability when an IFRS lacks specificities, as is the case for entities recognising exploration and evaluation assets. This is especially true because the IFRS allows the continuation of a variety of measurement bases for these items and, because of the failure to consider the *Framework*,[5] may result in the inappropriate recognition of assets. In the view of these Board members, if an entity cannot meet those requirements, it should not be allowed to describe its financial statements as being in accordance with International Financial Reporting Standards.

DO3   Messrs Garnett and McGregor also disagree with the modifications to the requirements of IAS 36 for the purpose of assessing exploration and evaluation assets for impairment contained in paragraphs 18–22 of the IFRS. They think that the requirements of IAS 36 should be applied in their entirety to exploration and evaluation assets. Failure to do so could result in exploration and evaluation assets continuing to be carried forward when such assets are not known to be recoverable. This could result in the exclusion of relevant information from the financial statements because of the failure to recognise impairment losses on a timely basis and the inclusion of unreliable information because of the inclusion of assets that do not faithfully represent the transactions and other events that they purport to represent.

DO4   The four Board members' concerns are heightened by the absence as yet from the Board's main agenda of a project on accounting for exploration for and evaluation of mineral resources generally. Although a research project has begun, it is unlikely that the Board will be able to develop financial reporting standards in the medium term. Accordingly, it is likely that the concession referred to in paragraph DO2 and, in Messrs Garnett and McGregor's cases, in paragraph DO3, will remain in place for some time.

---

5   The reference to the *Framework* is to the IASC's *Framework for the Preparation and Presentation of Financial Statements*, adopted by the Board in 2001 and in effect when the Standard was developed.

IASB documents published to accompany

IFRS 7

Financial Instruments: Disclosures

The text of the unaccompanied standard, IFRS 7, is contained in Part A of this edition. Its effective date when issued was 1 January 2007. The text of the Accompanying Guidance on IFRS 7 is contained in Part B of this edition. This part presents the following documents:

BASIS FOR CONCLUSIONS

APPENDIX TO THE BASIS FOR CONCLUSIONS
Amendments to Basis for Conclusions on other IFRSs

Contents

Basis for Conclusions on
IFRS 7 *Financial Instruments: Disclosures*

This Basis for Conclusions accompanies, but is not part of, IFRS 7.

In this Basis for Conclusions the terminology has not been amended to reflect the changes made by IAS 1 Presentation of Financial Statements *(as revised in 2007).*

The requirements of IAS 39 relating to classification and measurement of items within the scope of IAS 39 were relocated to IFRS 9 Financial Instruments, *and IFRS 7 was amended accordingly. The text of this Basis for Conclusions has been amended for consistency with those changes.*

Introduction

BC1 This Basis for Conclusions summarises the International Accounting Standards Board's considerations in reaching the conclusions in IFRS 7 *Financial Instruments: Disclosures*. Individual Board members gave greater weight to some factors than to others.

BC2 During the late 1990s, the need for a comprehensive review of IAS 30 *Disclosures in the Financial Statements of Banks and Similar Financial Institutions* became apparent. The Board's predecessor, the International Accounting Standards Committee (IASC), issued a number of Standards that addressed, more comprehensively, some of the topics previously addressed only for banks in IAS 30. Also, fundamental changes were taking place in the financial services industry and in the way in which financial institutions manage their activities and risk exposures. This made it increasingly difficult for users of banks' financial statements to assess and compare their financial position and performance, their associated risk exposures, and their processes for measuring and managing those risks.

BC3 In 1999 IASC added a project to its agenda to revise IAS 30 and in 2000 it appointed a steering committee.

BC4 In 2001 the Board added this project to its agenda. To assist and advise it, the Board retained the IAS 30 steering committee, renamed the Financial Activities Advisory Committee (FAAC), as an expert advisory group. FAAC members had experience and expertise in banks, finance companies and insurance companies and included auditors, financial analysts, preparers and regulators. The FAAC's role was:

(a) to provide input from the perspective of preparers and auditors of financial statements of entities that have significant exposures to financial instruments; and

(b) to assist the Board in developing a standard and implementation guidance for risk disclosures arising from financial instruments and for other related disclosures.

BC5   The Board published its proposals in July 2004 as ED 7 *Financial Instruments: Disclosures*. The deadline for comments was 27 October 2004. The Board received 105 comment letters. After reviewing the responses, the Board issued IFRS 7 in August 2005.

BC5A   In October 2008 the Board published an exposure draft *Improving Disclosures about Financial Instruments* (proposed amendments to IFRS 7). The aim of the proposed amendments was to enhance disclosures about fair value and liquidity risk. The Board received 89 comment letters. After reviewing the responses, the Board issued amendments to IFRS 7 in March 2009. The Board decided to require application of the amendments for periods beginning on or after 1 January 2009. The Board noted that, although the effective date of IFRSs and amendments to IFRSs is usually 6–18 months after issue, the urgent need for enhanced disclosures about financial instruments demanded earlier application.

BC5B   In January 2011 the IASB and the US national standard-setter, the Financial Accounting Standards Board (FASB), published the exposure draft *Offsetting Financial Assets and Financial Liabilities*. This was in response to requests from users of financial statements and recommendations from the Financial Stability Board to achieve convergence of the boards' requirements for offsetting financial assets and financial liabilities. The different requirements result in a significant difference between amounts presented in statements of financial position prepared in accordance with IFRSs and amounts presented in statements of financial position prepared in accordance with US GAAP, particularly for entities that have large amounts of derivative activities. The proposals in the exposure draft would have replaced the requirements for offsetting financial assets and financial liabilities and would have established a common approach with the FASB. After considering the responses to the exposure draft, the boards decided to maintain their respective offsetting models. However, to meet the needs of users of financial statements, the boards agreed jointly on additional disclosures to enable users of financial statements to evaluate the effect or potential effect of netting arrangements, including rights of set-off associated with an entity's recognised financial assets and recognised financial liabilities, on the entity's financial position. *Disclosures – Offsetting Financial Assets and Financial Liabilities* (Amendments to IFRS 7) was issued in December 2011 and is effective for annual periods beginning on or after 1 January 2013 and interim periods within those annual periods.

Scope (paragraphs 3–5)

The entities to which the IFRS applies

BC6   Although IFRS 7 arose from a project to revise IAS 30 (a Standard that applied only to banks and similar financial institutions), it applies to all entities that have financial instruments. The Board observed that the reduction in regulatory barriers in many countries and increasing competition between banks, non-bank financial services firms, and financial conglomerates have resulted in many entities providing financial services that were traditionally provided only by entities regulated and supervised as banks. The Board concluded that this development would make it inappropriate to limit this project to banks and similar financial institutions.

BC7　The Board considered whether entities that undertake specified activities commonly undertaken by banks and other financial institutions, namely deposit-taking, lending and securities activities, face unique risks that would require a standard specific to them. However, the Board decided that the scope of this project should include disclosures about risks arising from financial instruments in all entities for the following reasons:

(a)　disclosures about risks associated with financial instruments are useful to users of the financial statements of all entities.

(b)　the Board found it could not satisfactorily define deposit-taking, lending, and securities activities. In particular, it could not satisfactorily differentiate an entity with securities activities from an entity holding a portfolio of financial assets for investment and liquidity management purposes.

(c)　responses to the Exposure Draft of Improvements to IAS 32 *Financial Instruments: Disclosure and Presentation*, published in June 2002, indicated that IAS 32's risk disclosure requirements, applicable to all entities, could be improved.

(d)　the exclusion of some financial instruments would increase the danger that risk disclosures could be incomplete and possibly misleading. For example, a debt instrument issued by an entity could significantly affect its exposures to liquidity risk, interest rate risk and currency risk even if that instrument is not held as part of deposit-taking, lending and securities activities.

(e)　users of financial statements need to be able to compare similar activities, transactions and events of different entities on a consistent basis. Hence, the disclosure principles that apply to regulated entities should not differ from those that apply to non-regulated, but otherwise similar, entities.

BC8　The Board decided that the scope of the IFRS should be the same as that of IAS 32 with one exception. The Board concluded that the IFRS should not apply to derivatives based on interests in subsidiaries, associates or joint ventures if the derivatives meet the definition of an equity instrument in IAS 32. This is because equity instruments are not remeasured and hence:

(a)　they do not expose the issuer to balance sheet and income statement risk; and

(b)　the disclosures about the significance of financial instruments for financial position and performance are not relevant to equity instruments.

Although these instruments are excluded from the scope of IFRS 7, they are within the scope of IAS 32 for the purpose of determining whether they meet the definition of equity instruments.

Exemptions considered by the Board

Insurers

BC9   The Board considered whether the IFRS should apply to entities that both have financial instruments and issue insurance contracts. The Board did not exempt these entities because financial instruments expose all entities to risks regardless of what other assets and liabilities they have. Accordingly, an entity that both issues insurance contracts and has financial instruments applies IFRS 4 *Insurance Contracts*[1] to its insurance contracts and IFRS 7 to its financial assets and financial liabilities. However, many of the disclosure requirements in IFRS 4 were applications of, or relatively straightforward analogies with, existing requirements in IAS 32. Therefore, the Board also updated the disclosures required by IFRS 4 to make them consistent with IFRS 7, with modifications that reflect the interim nature of IFRS 4.

Small and medium-sized entities

BC10   The Board considered whether it should exempt small and medium-sized entities from the scope of the IFRS. The Board noted that the extent of disclosures required by the IFRS will depend on the extent to which the entity uses financial instruments and the extent to which it has assumed associated risks. The IFRS requires entities with few financial instruments and few risks to give few disclosures. Also, many of the requirements in the IFRS are based on information provided internally to the entity's key management personnel. This helps to avoid unduly onerous requirements that would not be appropriate for smaller entities. Accordingly, the Board decided not to exempt such entities from the scope of IFRS 7. However, it will keep this decision under review in its project on financial reporting for small and medium-sized entities.

Subsidiaries

BC11   Some respondents to ED 7 stated that there is little public interest in the financial statements of some entities, such as a wholly-owned subsidiary whose parent issues publicly available financial statements. These respondents stated that such subsidiaries should be exempt from some of the requirements of IFRS 7 in their individual financial statements. However, deciding whether such an entity should prepare general purpose financial statements is a matter for the entity and local legislators and regulators. If such an entity prepares financial statements in accordance with IFRSs, users of those statements should receive information of the same quality as users of any general purpose financial statements prepared in accordance with IFRSs. The Board confirmed its view that no exemptions from the general requirements of any Standard should be given for the financial statements of subsidiaries.

---

1   IFRS 17 *Insurance Contracts*, issued in May 2017, replaced IFRS 4.

Disclosures about the significance of financial instruments for financial position and performance (paragraphs 7–30, B4 and B5)[2]

BC12   The Board relocated disclosures from IAS 32 to IFRS 7, so that all disclosure requirements for financial instruments are in one Standard. Many of the disclosure requirements about the significance of financial instruments for an entity's financial position and performance were previously in IAS 32. For these disclosures, the relevant paragraphs from the Basis for Conclusions on IAS 32 have been incorporated into this Basis for Conclusions. This Basis for Conclusions does not discuss requirements that the Board did not reconsider either in revising IAS 32 in 2003 or in developing IFRS 7.

The principle (paragraph 7)

BC13   The Board decided that the disclosure requirements of IFRS 7 should result from the explicit disclosure principle in paragraph 7. The Board also decided to specify disclosures to satisfy this principle. In the Board's view, entities could not satisfy the principle in paragraph 7 unless they disclose the information required by paragraphs 8–30.

Balance sheet disclosures (paragraphs 8–19 and B4)[3]

Categories of financial assets and financial liabilities (paragraph 8)

BC14   Paragraph 8 requires entities to disclose financial assets and financial liabilities by the measurement categories in IFRS 9 *Financial Instruments*. The Board concluded that disclosures for each measurement category would assist users in understanding the extent to which accounting policies affect the amounts at which financial assets and financial liabilities are recognised.

BC15   The Board also concluded that separate disclosure of the carrying amounts of financial assets and financial liabilities that are designated upon initial recognition as financial assets and financial liabilities at fair value through profit or loss and those mandatorily measured at fair value is useful because such designation is at the discretion of the entity.

Financial assets or financial liabilities at fair value through profit or loss (paragraphs 9–11, B4 and B5)[4]

BC16   IFRS 9 permits entities to designate a non-derivative financial liability as at fair value through profit or loss, if specified conditions are met. If entities do so, they are required to provide the disclosures in paragraphs 10–11. The Board's reasons for these disclosures are set out in the Basis for Conclusions on IFRS 9, paragraphs BCZ5.29–BCZ5.34.

---

2   IFRS 9 *Financial Instruments* deleted paragraph B4 of IFRS 7.
3   IFRS 9 *Financial Instruments* deleted paragraph B4 of IFRS 7.
4   IFRS 9 *Financial Instruments* deleted paragraph B4 of IFRS 7.

BC17   The requirements in paragraphs 9, 11 and B5(a) are related to the Amendments to IAS 39 Financial Instruments: Recognition and Measurement —*The Fair Value Option*, issued in June 2005.[5] The reasons for those requirements are discussed in the Basis for Conclusions on those Amendments.

BC18   Paragraph 10(a) requires disclosure of the change in fair value of a financial liability designated as at fair value through profit or loss that is attributable to changes in the liability's credit risk. The Board previously considered this disclosure in its deliberations on the fair value measurement of financial liabilities in IAS 39.

BC19   Although quantifying such changes might be difficult in practice, the Board concluded that disclosure of such information would be useful to users of financial statements and would help alleviate concerns that users may misinterpret the profit or loss effects of changes in credit risk, especially in the absence of disclosures. Therefore, in finalising the revisions to IAS 32 in 2003, it decided to require disclosure of the change in fair value of the financial liability that is not attributable to changes in a benchmark interest rate. The Board believed that this is often a reasonable proxy for the change in fair value that is attributable to changes in the liability's credit risk, in particular when such changes are large, and would provide users with information with which to understand the profit or loss effect of such a change in credit risk.

BC20   However, some respondents to ED 7 stated that they did not agree that the IAS 32 disclosure provided a reasonable proxy, except for straightforward debt instruments. In particular, there could be other factors involved in the change in an instrument's fair value unrelated to the benchmark interest rate, such as the effect of an embedded derivative. Respondents also cited difficulties for unit-linked insurance contracts, for which the amount of the liability reflects the performance of a defined pool of assets. The Board noted that the proxy that was developed in IAS 32 assumed that it is not practicable for entities to determine directly the change in fair value arising from changes in credit risk. However, the Board acknowledged and shared these concerns.

BC21   As a result, the Board amended this requirement to focus directly on the objective of providing information about the effects of changes in credit risk:

(a)   by permitting entities to provide a more faithful representation of the amount of change in fair value that is attributable to changes in credit risk if they could do so. However, such entities are also required to disclose the methods used and provide their justification for concluding that those methods give a more faithful representation than the proxy in paragraph 10(a)(i).

---

5   IFRS 9 *Financial Instruments* replaced IAS 39. IFRS 9 applies to all items that were previously within the scope of IAS 39. This paragraph refers to matters relevant when IFRS 7 was issued.

(b)   by amending the proxy disclosure to be the amount of change in fair value that is not attributable to changes in market conditions that give rise to market risk. For example, some entities may be able to identify part of the change in the fair value of the liability as attributable to a change in an index. In these cases, the proxy disclosure would exclude the amount of change attributable to a change in an index. Similarly, excluding the amount attributable to a change in an internal or external investment fund makes the proxy more suitable for unit-linked insurance contracts.

BC22   The Board decided that when an entity has designated a financial liability as at fair value through profit or loss, it should disclose the difference between the carrying amount and the amount the entity would contractually be required to pay at maturity to the holders of the liability (see paragraph 10(b)). The fair value may differ significantly from the settlement amount, in particular for financial liabilities with a long duration when an entity has experienced a significant deterioration in creditworthiness since their issue. The Board concluded that knowledge of this difference would be useful to users of financial statements. Also, the settlement amount is important to some financial statement users, particularly creditors.

Reclassification (paragraphs 12B–12D)

BC23   IAS 32 required disclosure of the reason for reclassification of financial assets at cost or amortised cost rather than at fair value. The Board extended this requirement to include disclosure of the reason for reclassifications and of the amount reclassified into and out of each category. As noted in paragraph BC14, the Board regards such information as useful because the categorisation of financial instruments has a significant effect on their measurement.

BC23A   In October and November 2008 the Board amended IAS 39[6] to permit reclassification of particular financial assets in some circumstances. The Board decided to require additional disclosures about the situations in which any such reclassification is made, and the effects on the financial statements. The Board regards such information as useful because the reclassification of a financial asset can have a significant effect on the financial statements.

BC23B   The Board issued the requirements relating to the reclassification of financial assets in IFRS 9 *Financial Instruments* and revised accordingly the disclosure requirements relating to the reclassification of financial assets.

BC24   [Deleted]

---

6   IFRS 9 *Financial Instruments* replaced IAS 39. IFRS 9 applies to all items that were previously within the scope of IAS 39. This paragraph refers to matters relevant when IFRS 7 was issued.

Offsetting financial assets and financial liabilities

Background

BC24A Following requests from users of financial statements and recommendations from the Financial Stability Board, in June 2010 the IASB and the FASB added a project to their respective agendas to improve and potentially achieve convergence of the requirements for offsetting financial assets and financial liabilities. The different requirements result in a significant difference between amounts presented in statements of financial position prepared in accordance with IFRSs and amounts presented in statements of financial position prepared in accordance with US GAAP, particularly for entities that have large amounts of derivative activities.

BC24B Consequently, in January 2011 the IASB and the FASB published the exposure draft *Offsetting Financial Assets and Financial Liabilities*. The exposure draft proposed common offsetting requirements for IFRSs and US GAAP and proposed disclosures about financial assets and financial liabilities that are subject to rights of set-off and related arrangements.

BC24C Most respondents to the exposure draft supported the boards' efforts towards achieving convergence, but their responses to the proposals varied. Many IFRS preparers agreed with the proposals, stating that the underlying principle and proposed criteria were similar to those in IAS 32 and reflect an entity's credit and liquidity exposure to such instruments. Some US GAAP preparers indicated that offsetting in the statement of financial position in accordance with the proposed criteria provided more relevant information than the current model, except for derivatives and repurchase or reverse repurchase agreements.

BC24D There was no consensus among users of financial statements regarding if, or when, to present gross or net information in the statement of financial position. However, there was consensus that both gross and net information are useful and necessary for analysing financial statements. Users of financial statements supported achieving convergence of the IFRS and US GAAP requirements, and also supported improving disclosures so that financial statements prepared in accordance with IFRSs and US GAAP would be more comparable. Comparable information is important to investors for calculating their ratios and performing their analyses.

BC24E As a result of the feedback received on the exposure draft, the IASB and the FASB decided to maintain their respective offsetting models. However, the boards noted that requiring common disclosures of gross and net amounts of recognised financial instruments that are (a) set off in the statement of financial position and (b) subject to enforceable master netting arrangements and similar agreements, even if not set off in the statement of financial position, would be helpful for users of financial statements. Accordingly, the boards agreed on common disclosure requirements by amending and finalising the disclosures initially proposed in the exposure draft.

Scope (paragraph 13A)

BC24F   The disclosures in the exposure draft would have applied to all recognised financial assets and recognised financial liabilities subject to a right of set-off, and/or for which an entity had either received or pledged cash or other financial instruments as collateral.

BC24G   Respondents to the exposure draft noted that paragraphs 14, 15 and 36(b) of IFRS 7 already require disclosures of financial instrument collateral received and pledged and other credit enhancements. US GAAP has similar disclosure requirements. Consequently, if an entity has no financial assets or financial liabilities subject to a right of set-off (other than collateral agreements or credit enhancements), the boards concluded that there would be no incremental value in providing additional disclosure information for such instruments.

BC24H   For example, some respondents were concerned that providing disclosure of conditional rights to set off loans and customer deposits at the same financial institution would be a significant operational burden. Such rights are often a result of statute, and entities do not typically manage their credit risk related to such amounts based on these rights of set-off. In addition, entities that have contractual rights to set off customer deposits with loans only in situations such as events of default see these rights as a credit enhancement and not as the primary source of credit mitigation. Respondents argued that the cost of including these amounts in the amended disclosures would outweigh the benefit because users of financial statements did not request information related to these instruments when discussing the offsetting disclosure requirements.

BC24I   The boards agreed and decided to limit the scope of the disclosures to all financial instruments that meet the boards' respective offsetting models and recognised financial assets and recognised financial liabilities that are subject to an enforceable master netting arrangement or a similar agreement. The boards specifically excluded loans and customer deposits with the same financial institution from the scope of these requirements (except in the limited cases when the respective offsetting model is satisfied). This reduced scope still responds to the needs of users of financial statements for information about amounts that have been set off in accordance with IFRSs and amounts that have been set off in accordance with US GAAP. The types of instruments that fall within the scope of these disclosures include the instruments that cause significant differences between amounts presented in statements of financial position prepared in accordance with IFRSs and amounts presented in statements of financial position prepared in accordance with US GAAP.

BC24J   If there is an associated collateral agreement for such instruments, an entity would disclose amounts subject to such agreements in order to provide full information about its exposure in the normal course of business, as well as in the events of default and insolvency or bankruptcy.

BC24K   Other respondents requested that the scope of the proposed disclosures be further amended to exclude financial instruments for which the lender has the right to set off the related non-financial collateral in the event of default. Although non-financial collateral agreements may exist for some financial instruments, those preparers do not necessarily manage the credit risk related to such financial instruments on the basis of the non-financial collateral held.

BC24L   The disclosures focus on the effects of recognised financial instruments and financial instrument set-off agreements on an entity's financial position. The boards also noted that a comprehensive reconsideration of credit risk disclosures was not within the scope of this project. They therefore restricted the scope of the disclosures to exclude financial instruments with rights of set-off only for non-financial collateral.

BC24M   A few respondents were concerned that the proposals seem to be designed for financial institutions and would impose requirements on non-financial institutions. They questioned the benefit that such disclosures would provide to investors in non-financial entities.

BC24N   Although the boards acknowledged that financial institutions would be among those most affected, they did not agree that the disclosures are only relevant for financial institutions. Other industries have similar financial instrument activities and use enforceable master netting arrangements and similar agreements to mitigate exposure to credit risks. Consequently, the boards concluded that the required disclosures provide useful information about an entity's arrangements, irrespective of the nature of the entity's business.

Disclosure of quantitative information for recognised financial assets and recognised financial liabilities within the scope of paragraph 13A (paragraph 13C)

BC24O   The boards understood that recognised financial instruments included in the disclosure requirements in paragraph 13C of IFRS 7 may be subject to different measurement requirements. For example, a payable related to a repurchase agreement may be measured at amortised cost, while a derivative asset or derivative liability subject to the same disclosure requirements (for example, in paragraph 13C(a) of IFRS 7) will be measured at fair value. In addition, the fair value amount of any financial instrument collateral received or pledged and subject to paragraph 13C(d)(ii) of IFRS 7 should be included in the disclosures to provide users of financial statements with the best information about an entity's exposure. Consequently, a financial asset or financial liability disclosure table may include financial instruments measured at different amounts. To provide users of financial statements with the information they need to evaluate the amounts disclosed in accordance with paragraph 13C of IFRS 7, the boards decided that an entity should describe any resulting measurement differences in the related disclosures.

Disclosure of the net amounts presented in the statement of financial position (paragraph 13C(c))

BC24P   When providing feedback on the proposals in the exposure draft, users of financial statements emphasised that information in the notes should be clearly reconciled back to the amounts in the statement of financial position. The boards therefore decided that if an entity determines that the aggregation or disaggregation of individual financial statement line item amounts provides more relevant information when disclosing amounts in accordance with paragraph 13C of IFRS 7, the entity must still reconcile the amounts disclosed in paragraph 13C(c) of IFRS 7 back to the individual line item amounts in the statement of financial position.

Disclosure of the amounts subject to an enforceable master netting arrangement or similar agreement that are not otherwise included in paragraph 13C(b) (paragraph 13C(d))

BC24Q   Paragraph 13C(d)(i) of IFRS 7 requires disclosure of amounts related to recognised financial instruments that do not meet some or all of the offsetting criteria in paragraph 42 of IAS 32. This may include current rights of set-off that do not meet the criterion in paragraph 42(b) of IAS 32, or conditional rights of set-off that are enforceable and exercisable only in the event of default, or only in the event of insolvency or bankruptcy of any of the counterparties. Although such rights do not qualify for set-off in accordance with IAS 32, users of financial statements are interested in arrangements that an entity has entered into that mitigate the entity's exposure to such financial instruments in the normal course of business and/or in the events of default and insolvency or bankruptcy.

BC24R   Paragraph 13C(d)(ii) of IFRS 7 requires disclosure of amounts of cash and financial instrument collateral (whether recognised or unrecognised) that do not meet the criteria for offsetting in the statement of financial position but that relate to financial instruments within the scope of these disclosure requirements. Depending on the terms of the collateral arrangement, collateral will often reduce an entity's exposure in the events of default and insolvency or bankruptcy of a counterparty to the contract. Collateral received or pledged against financial assets and financial liabilities may often be liquidated immediately upon an event of default. Consequently, the boards concluded that the amounts of collateral that are not set off in the statement of financial position but that are associated with other netting arrangements should be included in the amounts disclosed as required by paragraph 13C(d) (ii) of IFRS 7.

Limits on the amounts disclosed in paragraph 13C(d) (paragraph 13D)

BC24S   The boards concluded that an aggregate disclosure of the amount of cash collateral and/or the fair value of collateral in the form of other financial instruments would be misleading when some financial assets and financial liabilities are over-collateralised and others have insufficient collateral. To prevent an entity from inappropriately obscuring under-collateralised financial instruments with others that are over-collateralised, paragraph 13D of IFRS 7 restricts the amounts of cash and/or financial instrument collateral to be disclosed in respect of a recognised financial instrument to more accurately reflect an entity's exposure. However, if rights to collateral can be enforced across financial instruments, such rights can be included in the disclosure provided in accordance with paragraph 13D of IFRS 7. At no point in time should under-collateralisation be obscured.

Disclosure by type of financial instrument or by counterparty

BC24T   The exposure draft proposed disclosures by class of financial instrument. An entity would have been required to group financial assets and financial liabilities separately into classes that were appropriate to the nature of the information disclosed, taking into account the characteristics of those financial instruments and the applicable rights of set-off. Many preparers were concerned that the cost of disclosing amounts related to rights of set-off in the events of default and insolvency or bankruptcy by class of financial instrument would outweigh the benefit. They also indicated that they often manage credit exposure by counterparty and not necessarily by class of financial instrument.

BC24U   Many users of financial statements indicated that disclosure of recognised amounts subject to enforceable master netting arrangements and similar agreements (including financial collateral) that were not set off in the statement of financial position would be useful irrespective of whether the amounts are disclosed by counterparty or by type or by class of financial instrument, as long as they can reconcile these amounts back to the statement of financial position. In evaluating whether the disclosures should be provided by type or by class of financial instrument or by counterparty, the boards noted that the objective of these disclosures (paragraph 13B of IFRS 7) is that an entity should disclose information to enable users of its financial statements to evaluate the effect or potential effect of netting arrangements on the entity's financial position.

BC24V   The boards decided to reduce the burden on preparers by requiring disclosure by type of financial instrument rather than by class. Disclosure by type of financial instrument may (or may not) differ from the class of financial instrument used for other disclosures in IFRS 7, but is appropriate in circumstances where a difference would better achieve the objective of the disclosures required by these amendments. The boards also decided to provide flexibility as to whether the information required by paragraph 13C(c)–(e) of IFRS 7 is presented by type of financial instrument or by counterparty. This would allow preparers to present the disclosures in the same way that they manage their credit exposure.

BC24W   The Board also noted that paragraph 31 of IFRS 7 requires an entity to disclose information that enables users of its financial statements to evaluate the nature and extent of risks arising from financial instruments to which the entity is exposed at the end of the reporting period. In addition, paragraph 34 of IFRS 7 requires the disclosure of concentrations of risk for each type of risk. Consequently, the Board noted that, irrespective of whether the disclosures were required to be provided by type or by class of financial instrument or by counterparty, entities are already required to disclose information about risks and how they are managed, including information about concentrations of credit risk.

Other considerations

Reconciliation between IFRSs and US GAAP

BC24X   Some users of financial statements asked for information to help them reconcile between the amounts set off in accordance with IFRSs and the amounts set off in accordance with US GAAP. The boards recognised that the amounts disclosed in accordance with paragraph 13C(b), (c) and (d) of IFRS 7 will probably be different for financial statements prepared in accordance with IFRSs and those prepared in accordance with US GAAP. However, the amounts disclosed in accordance with paragraph 13C(a) and (e) of IFRS 7 are generally not affected by the offsetting criteria applied in the statement of financial position. These amounts are important for users of financial statements to understand the effects of netting arrangements on an entity's financial position in the normal course of business and in the events of default and insolvency or bankruptcy.

BC24Y   Consequently, while the amended disclosure requirements do not directly reconcile the IFRS and US GAAP amounts, they provide both gross and net information on a comparable basis. The boards considered that requiring a full reconciliation between IFRSs and US GAAP was unnecessary, particularly given the relative costs and benefits. Such reconciliation would have required preparers to apply two sets of accounting requirements and to track any changes to the related accounting standards and to contracts in the related jurisdictions.

Tabular information

BC24Z   The disclosures require amounts to be presented in a tabular format (ie a table) unless another format is more appropriate. The boards believe that a tabular format best conveys an overall understanding of the effect of any rights of set-off and other related arrangements on an entity's financial position and improves the transparency of such information.

Transition and effective date

BC24AA   The boards identified two transition approaches in the exposure draft — prospective and retrospective.

BC24AB   Prospective transition is generally appropriate only in situations where it is not practicable to apply a standard to all prior periods. The boards did not believe that this was the case with the proposed disclosure requirements. Retrospective transition would require an entity to apply the new requirements to all periods presented. This would maximise consistency of financial information between periods. Retrospective transition would enable analysis and understanding of comparative accounting information among entities. In addition, the scope of the disclosures was reduced and the disclosures amended to require less detailed information than originally proposed, which would make them less burdensome for preparers to apply retrospectively.

BC24AC   The exposure draft did not propose an effective date, but instead asked respondents for information about the time and effort that would be involved in implementing the proposed requirements. The boards indicated that they would use such feedback, as well as the responses in their *Request for Views on Effective Dates and Transition Methods*, and the timing of other planned accounting and reporting standards, to determine an appropriate effective date for the proposals in the exposure draft.

BC24AD   Some respondents suggested that the offsetting proposals should have the same effective date as the other components of the IASB's project to replace IAS 39 with IFRS 9 *Financial Instruments*. If an earlier date was required, it was suggested that application should be restricted only to the accounting period being presented, rather than providing comparative information, because of the potential burden of applying the proposed disclosure requirements.

BC24AE   At the time the amended disclosure requirements were issued (December 2011), IFRS 9 was not yet mandatorily effective. However, the Board did not believe that the IFRS 9 project would change the offsetting disclosures. Aligning the effective date of these amendments with the effective date of the financial instruments project could result in postponing the effective date of the common disclosure requirements, which would mean a delay in providing users of financial statements the information that they need. For users of financial statements to benefit from the increased comparability, and because the offsetting and IFRS 9 projects are independent of one another, the boards decided that common disclosures should be effective as early as possible.

BC24AF   In addition, the boards did not think that a long transition period was needed, because the amended disclosures had a reduced scope and less detailed information than originally proposed in the exposure draft and were related to the presentation of instruments that entities have already recognised and measured. The boards therefore decided that the effective date for the amended disclosures should be for annual periods beginning on or after 1 January 2013, and interim periods within those annual periods.

BC24AG   As described in greater detail in other sections of this Basis for Conclusions, the disclosures required by paragraphs 13B–13E of IFRS 7 are a result of requests from users of financial statements for information to enable them to compare statements of financial position prepared in accordance with IFRSs with statements of financial position prepared in accordance with US GAAP, particularly for entities that have large amounts of derivative activities.

BC24AH   The information required in paragraphs 13B–13E of IFRS 7 will enable users of financial statements to evaluate the effect or potential effect of netting arrangements, including rights of set-off associated with an entity's recognised financial assets and recognised financial liabilities, on the entity's financial position for financial statements presented in accordance with IFRSs and those presented in accordance with US GAAP.

BC24AI   The Board noted that paragraph 10(f) of IAS 1 *Presentation of Financial Statements* requires an entity to provide a statement of financial position as at the beginning of the earliest comparative period when an entity applies an accounting policy retrospectively or makes a retrospective restatement of items in its financial statements, or when it reclassifies items in its financial statements. In the case of *Disclosures — Offsetting Financial Assets and Financial Liabilities* (Amendments to IFRS 7), because the change relates only to disclosures and there is no associated change in accounting policy, or a resulting restatement or reclassification, it was noted that paragraph 10(f) of IAS 1 does not apply for these amendments to IFRS 7.

Cost-benefit considerations

BC24AJ   Before issuing an IFRS or an amendment to an IFRS, the Board seeks to ensure that it will meet a significant need and that the overall benefits of the resulting information justify the costs of providing it. As described in greater detail in other sections of this Basis for Conclusions on *Disclosures — Offsetting Financial Assets and Financial Liabilities* (Amendments to IFRS 7), the Board considered that there is significant benefit to market participants in providing these disclosures. The disclosures address a significant difference between the amounts presented in statements of financial position prepared in accordance with IFRSs and amounts presented in statements of financial position prepared in accordance with US GAAP, particularly for entities that have large amounts of derivative activities. The disclosures therefore make the amounts presented in accordance with both sets of standards more comparable.

BC24AK   During redeliberations, the Board considered feedback related to the costs of providing the disclosures proposed in the exposure draft. As described in greater detail in other sections of this Basis for Conclusions, the Board decided to limit the scope of the disclosures because these changes would reduce the cost to preparers while still providing the information that users of financial statements had requested.

BC24AL   On the basis of the considerations described in the Basis for Conclusions on these amendments, and summarised in paragraphs BC24AJ and BC24AK, the Board concluded that the benefits of *Disclosures — Offsetting Financial Assets and Financial Liabilities* (Amendments to IFRS 7) outweigh the costs to preparers of applying these amendments.

Collateral (paragraphs 14 and 15)

BC25   Paragraph 15 requires disclosures about collateral that the entity holds if it is permitted to sell or repledge the collateral in the absence of default by the owner. Some respondents to ED 7 argued for an exemption from this disclosure if it is impracticable to obtain the fair value of the collateral held. However, the Board concluded that it is reasonable to expect an entity to know the fair value of collateral that it holds and can sell even if there is no default.

Allowance account for credit losses (paragraph 16)[7]

BC26   When a separate account is used to record impairment losses (such as an allowance account or similar account used to record a collective impairment of assets), paragraph 16 requires a reconciliation of that account to be disclosed. The Board was informed that analysts and other users find this information useful in assessing the adequacy of the allowance for impairment losses for such entities and when comparing one entity with another. However, the Board decided not to specify the components of the reconciliation. This allows entities flexibility in determining the most appropriate format for their needs.

BC27   Respondents to ED 7 asked the Board to require entities to provide equivalent information if they do not use an allowance account. The Board decided not to add this disclosure in finalising the IFRS. It concluded that, for virtually all entities, IAS 39's requirement to consider impairment on a group basis would necessitate the use of an allowance or similar account. The accounting policy disclosures required by paragraph B5(d) also include information about the use of direct adjustments to carrying amounts of financial assets.

Compound financial instruments with multiple embedded derivatives (paragraph 17)

BC28   IAS 32 requires the separation of the liability and equity components of a compound financial instrument. The Board notes that this is more complicated for compound financial instruments with multiple embedded derivative features whose values are interdependent (for example, a convertible debt instrument that gives the issuer a right to call the instrument back from the holder, or the holder a right to put the instrument back to the issuer) than for those without such features. If the embedded equity and non-equity derivative features are interdependent, the sum of the separately determined values of the liability and equity components will not equal the value of the compound financial instrument as a whole.

BC29   For example, the values of an embedded call option feature and an equity conversion option feature in a callable convertible debt instrument depend in part on each other if the holder's equity conversion option is extinguished when the entity exercises the call option or vice versa. The following diagram illustrates the joint value arising from the interaction between a call option and an equity conversion option in a callable convertible bond. Circle L represents the value of the liability component, ie the value of the straight debt and the embedded call option on the straight debt, and Circle E represents the value of the equity component, ie the equity conversion option on the straight debt.

---

7   IFRS 9 *Financial Instruments* replaced IAS 39. IFRS 9 applies to all items that were previously within the scope of IAS 9. This paragraph refers to matters relevant when IFRS 7 was issued.

L   E

The total area of the two circles represents the value of the callable convertible bond. The difference between the value of the callable convertible bond as a whole and the sum of the separately determined values for the liability and equity components is the joint value attributable to the interdependence between the call option feature and the equity conversion feature. It is represented by the intersection between the two circles.

BC30 Under the approach in IAS 32, the joint value attributable to the interdependence between multiple embedded derivative features is included in the liability component. A numerical example is set out as Illustrative Example 10 accompanying IAS 32.

BC31 Even though this approach is consistent with the definition of equity as a residual interest, the Board recognises that the allocation of the joint value to either the liability component or the equity component is arbitrary because it is, by its nature, joint. Therefore, the Board concluded that it is important to disclose the existence of issued compound financial instruments with multiple embedded derivative features that have interdependent values. Such disclosure highlights the effect of multiple embedded derivative features on the amounts recognised as liabilities and equity.

Defaults and breaches (paragraphs 18 and 19)

BC32 Paragraphs 18 and 19 require disclosures about defaults and breaches of loans payable and other loan agreements. The Board concluded that such disclosures provide relevant information about the entity's creditworthiness and its prospects of obtaining future loans.

Income statement and equity (paragraph 20)

Items of income, expenses, gains or losses (paragraph 20(a))

BC33 Paragraph 20(a) requires disclosure of income statement gains and losses by the measurement classifications in IFRS 9 (which complement the balance sheet disclosure requirement described in paragraph BC14). The Board concluded that the disclosure is needed for users to understand the financial performance of an entity's financial instruments, given the different measurement bases in IFRS 9.

BC34　　Some entities include interest and dividend income in gains and losses on financial assets and financial liabilities measured at fair value through profit or loss and others do not. To assist users in comparing income arising from financial instruments across different entities, the Board decided that an entity should disclose how the income statement amounts are determined. For example, an entity should disclose whether net gains and losses on financial assets or financial liabilities measured at fair value through profit or loss include interest and dividend income (see Appendix B, paragraph B5(e)).

Fee income and expense (paragraph 20(c))

BC35　　Paragraph 20(c) requires disclosure of fee income and expense (other than amounts included in determining the effective interest rate) arising from financial assets or financial liabilities and from trust and other fiduciary activities that result in the entity holding or placing assets on behalf of individuals, trusts, retirement benefit plans, and other institutions. This information indicates the level of such activities and helps users to estimate possible future income of the entity.

Other Disclosures—Hedge Accounting

BC35A　　The Board divided its project to replace IAS 39 into three phases. As the Board completed each phase, it deleted the relevant portions in IAS 39 and replaced it with chapters in IFRS 9. The third phase of the project to replace IAS 39 related to hedge accounting. As a consequence of the decisions the Board made when it replaced the hedge accounting guidance in IAS 39, the Board also considered changes to the disclosure requirements related to hedge accounting contained in IFRS 7.

BC35B　　During its deliberations, the Board engaged in outreach activities with users of financial statements. This outreach included soliciting views on presentation and disclosures. The Board used the responses received from those outreach activities to develop the proposed hedge accounting disclosures.

BC35C　　The Board was told that many users did not find the hedge accounting disclosures in financial statements helpful. Many also think that the hedge accounting disclosures that were originally in IFRS 7 did not provide transparency on an entity's hedging activities.

BC35D　　To provide relevant information that enhances the transparency on an entity's hedging activities, the Board proposes hedge accounting disclosures that meet particular objectives. Clear disclosure objectives allow an entity to apply its judgement when it provides information that is useful and relevant to users of financial statements.

BC35E　　The following sub-sections set out the Board's considerations regarding the proposed hedge accounting disclosures.

General considerations

Scope of the hedge accounting disclosures

BC35F An entity might enter into a transaction to manage an exposure to a particular risk that might not qualify for hedge accounting (for various reasons), for example, an item that is not eligible to be designated as a hedged item or hedging instrument. Information on such transactions might enable users to understand why an entity has entered into a transaction and how it manages the particular risk, even though those transactions do not qualify for hedge accounting.

BC35G However, the Board thought that mandating such disclosures would require it to determine the part of an entity's risk management that was relevant for the purpose of this disclosure and then define that part to make the disclosure requirement operational. The Board did not believe that this would be feasible as part of its hedge accounting project as it requires a much wider scope because the disclosures would not depend on the accounting treatment.

BC35H Furthermore, users of financial statements can often obtain information on an entity's hedging activities from information in management reports and sources outside the financial reporting context. That often gives a reasonable overview of why hedge accounting might be difficult to achieve. Consequently, the Board decided not to propose in its 2010 Exposure Draft *Hedge Accounting* (the '2010 Hedge Accounting Exposure Draft') disclosures about hedging when hedge accounting does not apply.

BC35I Most respondents to the 2010 Hedge Accounting Exposure Draft agreed with the Board's proposed scope for hedge accounting disclosures (ie to provide information about risk exposures that an entity hedges and for which hedge accounting is applied). However, some did raise concerns about the potential lack of information that will be available to users of financial statements about those risk exposures an entity hedges but for which hedge accounting is not applied.

BC35J The Board noted that IFRS 7 requires entities to provide qualitative and quantitative disclosure about the nature and extent of risks arising from financial instruments to which the entity is exposed at the end of the reporting period and how those risks are being managed. The Board believes that, as part of these disclosures, entities would provide information for users of financial statements to understand how it manages risk exposures for which hedge accounting is not applied.

BC35K Consequently, the Board decided to retain the scope of the hedge accounting disclosures as proposed in the 2010 Hedge Accounting Exposure Draft, that is, to provide information to users of financial statements on exposures that an entity hedges and for which hedge accounting is applied.

Location of disclosures

BC35L   The Board decided that all hedge accounting disclosures should be presented in one location within an entity's financial statements. However, if such information is already presented elsewhere the Board decided that, in order to avoid duplication, an entity should be allowed to incorporate that information by cross-reference, which is similar to the approach used by IFRS 7 for some disclosures that can be incorporated by reference. The Board thinks that the information will be more transparent and easier to understand if it is presented in one location within the entity's financial statements.

Disclosures by risk category

BC35M   The Board noted that recognition and measurement requirements allow for only a partial reflection of the economic hedging activities in the financial statements, which results in a limitation of an entity's reporting of its hedging activities. Hence, the Board considered that the transparency of an entity's hedging activities could be enhanced by an approach that considers:

(a)   information that provides a clear picture of those risk management activities of an entity that are captured by hedge accounting (this information is not necessarily provided in the primary financial statements); and

(b)   information that is included in the primary financial statements.

BC35N   To provide information that is useful to users of financial statements, there should be a clear link between the hedge accounting information that is outside the primary financial statements and the hedge accounting within those. To provide such a link, the Board decided that an entity should provide hedge accounting disclosures by risk category. Consequently, an entity should disclose by risk category:

(a)   information that is not included in the primary financial statements (see paragraphs BC35P–BC35BB); and

(b)   information that is included in the primary financial statements (see paragraphs BC35CC–BC35SS).

BC35O   The Board decided not to prescribe the risk categories by which the disclosures need to be disaggregated. In the Board's view an entity should apply judgement and categorise risks on the basis of how it manages its risks through hedging. For example, an entity manages its floating interest rate risk using interest rate swaps (to change it to a fixed interest rate) for some hedging relationships (cash flow hedges), while it also uses cross-currency interest rate swaps to manage both the floating interest rate and foreign exchange risk of other hedging relationships (cash flow hedges). Consequently, the entity would have one risk category for floating interest rate risk and another risk category for foreign exchange risk combined with floating interest rate risk. However, an entity should apply its risk categories consistently throughout all the proposed hedge accounting disclosures.

The risk management strategy

BC35P Users of financial statements need to understand how an entity's risk management strategy is applied. Understanding an entity's risk management strategy for each risk helps users to understand the accounting information disclosed.

BC35Q Consequently, in its 2010 Hedge Accounting Exposure Draft, the Board proposed that an entity should provide an explanation of its risk management strategy for each category of risk.

BC35R Most respondents to the 2010 Hedge Accounting Exposure Draft agreed with this proposal. However, some raised concerns that the 2010 Hedge Accounting Exposure Draft was not clear enough on how much detail should be provided by entities to comply with the disclosure requirement.

BC35S The Board noted that an entity will identify and ultimately describe their risk management strategies based on how it manages risk. Because entities manage risk in different ways, the Board did not think that users of financial statements would necessarily understand an entity's risk management strategy if it required a specific list of information to be disclosed. Instead, the Board decided to add additional guidance on the type of information that should be included in a risk management description.

The amount, timing and uncertainty of future cash flows

BC35T The Board decided that, in order to meet the objectives of hedge accounting disclosures, an entity would have to provide sufficient quantitative information to help users of financial statements understand how its risk management strategy for each particular risk affects the amount, timing and uncertainty of future cash flows. In this context, risk exposure refers only to risks that the entity has decided to hedge and for which hedge accounting is applied.

BC35U Consequently, in its 2010 Hedge Accounting Exposure Draft, the Board proposed that an entity should provide:

(a) quantitative information on the risk exposure that the entity manages and the extent to which the entity hedges that exposure; and

(b) a breakdown of that information for each future period that a hedging relationship (which exists at the reporting date) covers.

BC35V The Board also proposed that an entity should disclose information about the sources of hedge ineffectiveness of hedging relationships for each particular risk category. In the Board's view this would assist users in identifying the reasons for hedge ineffectiveness that is recognised in profit or loss. It would also help users to determine how hedging relationships will affect profit or loss.

BC35W Most respondents disagreed with the Board's proposal to require entities to disclose information on the risk exposure and the hedged rate. They commented that this would result in the disclosure of commercially sensitive information (ie the risk exposure and the hedged rate). They believed that those who do not elect to apply hedge accounting would potentially have an unfair advantage because although they do not have to disclose anything, they could nonetheless gain insight into their competitor's hedge positions. Commercial sensitivity was also of concern to those entities whose competitors are not listed companies or who do not report under IFRSs.

BC35X   The Board noted that the proposal in the 2010 Hedge Accounting Exposure Draft focused on the hedged risk (ie the hedged item). Consequently, it would result in disclosures about forward looking information and the rates at which future transactions are hedged. The Board acknowledged that this would potentially provide competitors with insight into an entity's costing structure. Consequently, the Board decided not to require information to be disclosed about the total risk exposure because of the potential forward looking nature of this information. The Board also decided to change the focus of the proposed disclosure from the hedged item to the hedging instrument. In other words, the disclosure would require information on some of the terms and conditions of the hedging instrument to be provided. The Board believes that this information will still be relevant and useful for users of financial statements in inferring the exposure that an entity is exposed to and what the effects will be on future cash flows as a result of how the entity manages the particular risk.

BC35Y   The Board also discussed situations in which an entity uses a 'dynamic' hedging process, ie a situation in which entities assess their overall exposure to a particular risk and then designate hedging relationships for constantly evolving exposures that require frequent discontinuations and restarts of hedging relationships. This is particularly the case for hedges of open portfolios. The Board noted that, because the general hedge accounting model allows hedge accounting for hedges of groups and net positions in relation to closed portfolios, entities need to use a 'dynamic' hedging process for an open portfolio. This means that entities designate hedging relationships for an open portfolio as if it were a closed portfolio for a short period and at the end of that period look at the open portfolio as the next closed portfolio for another short period. The dynamic nature of this process involves frequent discontinuations and restarts of hedging relationships.

BC35Z   The Board considered that, in those circumstances, providing information about the terms and conditions of the hedging instruments would not be useful given that the hedging instruments are part of a particular hedging relationship for only a short period at a time and are then designated into a new hedging relationship or left undesignated. In contrast, the disclosure requirement related to the terms and conditions of the hedging instrument was designed to provide information for situations in which an entity hedges a risk that remains broadly the same over the entire hedged period. Consequently, the Board decided to exempt entities from the requirement to disclose the terms and conditions of the hedging instruments in situations in which they use a 'dynamic' hedging process that involves frequent discontinuations and restarts of hedging relationships.

BC35AA   The Board was of the view that it was more important for users to understand why entities use hedge accounting in the context of 'dynamic' hedging processes than to provide users with information about the terms and conditions of a hedging instrument that is part of a hedging relationship for only a short period at a time (and the designation of which changes frequently). Consequently, the Board decided that, in such circumstances, an entity should expand its discussion of the risk management strategy by providing the following information about how the entity uses hedge accounting to reflect its risk management strategy:

(a)   information about what the ultimate risk management strategy is (for the dynamic hedging process);

(b)   a description of how it reflects its risk management strategy by using hedge accounting and designating the particular hedging relationships; and

(c)   an indication of how frequently the hedging relationships are discontinued and restarted as part of the dynamic hedging process.

BC35BB   The Board also noted that, because the designated hedging relationships change frequently, the specific relationships at the reporting date might not be representative of the normal volumes during the period. The Board therefore decided to require entities to disclose when the volumes at the reporting date are unrepresentative of normal volumes during the period (similar to the disclosure requirement on sensitivity analyses for market risk in paragraph 42).

BC35CC   One function of hedge accounting is to mitigate the recognition and measurement anomalies between the accounting for hedging instruments and the accounting for hedged items. Hedge accounting disclosures should therefore increase the transparency of how an entity has mitigated these recognition and measurement anomalies. Doing so will help users identify how hedge accounting has affected the entity's statement of profit or loss and other comprehensive income and statement of financial position.

The effects of hedge accounting on financial position and performance

BC35DD   To provide information on the effects of hedge accounting on the statement of profit or loss and other comprehensive income and the statement of financial position, the Board proposed disclosures that should be presented in a tabular format that separates the information by risk category and by type of hedge. Providing disclosures in a tabular format allows users to identify clearly the relevant numbers and their effects on the entity's statement of profit or loss and other comprehensive income and statement of financial position.

BC35EE   During the Board's initial outreach, users said that they do not analyse an entity's hedging activities by type of hedging relationship (for example, a cash flow hedge or a fair value hedge). They said that it is more important to understand the risks that the entity manages and the results after hedging. However, to provide information effectively on the effects of hedge accounting on the statement of profit or loss and other comprehensive income and the statement of financial position, the information should reflect the accounting that was applied (for example, cash flow hedge accounting or fair value hedge accounting). The Board believed that if the proposed table is prepared by risk category and by type of hedge, the table would provide sufficient links between the accounting information and the risk management information.

BC35FF   The Board did not propose prescribing levels of aggregation or disaggregation for the information that should be disclosed in a tabular format. An entity should apply judgement when it determines the appropriate level of aggregation or disaggregation. However, the Board proposed that an entity should consider other disclosure requirements in IFRS 7 when it considers the appropriate level of aggregation or disaggregation. For example, users should be able to take amounts that are disclosed and measured at fair value and make comparisons between the fair value disclosures and the proposed hedge accounting disclosures.

BC35GG   Cash flow hedge accounting requires an entity to defer gains or losses on the hedging instrument in other comprehensive income. The deferred amounts are reflected in the statement of changes in equity in the cash flow hedge reserve. IAS 1 requires an entity to prepare a reconciliation for each component of equity between the carrying amount at the beginning and at the end of the period. In conformity with its objectives for hedge accounting disclosures, the Board proposed that the reconciliation required by IAS 1 should have the same level of detail as the information that identifies the effects of hedge accounting on the statement of profit or loss and other comprehensive income. The Board also proposed that the reconciliation should be by type of risk. The Board considered that such a disclosure would allow users of financial statements to evaluate the effects of hedge accounting on equity and the statement of profit or loss and other comprehensive income.

BC35HH   Many respondents to the 2010 Hedge Accounting Exposure Draft agreed with the Board's proposal to explain the effects of hedge accounting disclosures using a tabular disclosure format. However, some respondents raised concerns that the proposal seems too prescriptive. Some also commented that they did not think that the tabular disclosure, as proposed, provided a clear enough link between hedged items and hedging instruments for the purpose of explaining hedge ineffectiveness. A few respondents also commented that the disclosures did not allow them to differentiate between financial instruments that have been designated as hedging instruments and those that have not. These respondents believe that it is helpful to understand the purpose and effect of financial instruments if their designation is made clear through disclosures.

BC35II   The Board thinks that providing a tabular disclosure format separated by type of hedge (ie fair value hedges or cash flow hedge), risk category and by risk management strategy provides a sufficient link between the accounting information and the risk management information.

BC35JJ The Board did not propose any more specific format other than requiring information to be disclosed in a tabular format. The Board thought that entities should have the freedom to present the disclosures that require a tabular format however they feel is best in order to provide users with the most useful information.

BC35KK While the 2010 Hedge Accounting Exposure Draft was open for public comment, the Board issued IFRS 13 *Fair Value Measurement*. As a consequence of issuing that IFRS, the Board moved the fair value disclosures in IFRS 7 to IFRS 13. To improve the usefulness of the hedge accounting disclosures, the Board decided to require entities to use the same level of aggregation or disaggregation it used for other IFRS 7 or IFRS 13 disclosures related to the same underlying information.

BC35LL In its redeliberations of the 2010 Hedge Accounting Exposure Draft, the Board also considered a disclosure that would allow understanding how the hedge ineffectiveness that is recognised in the statement of comprehensive income relates to the changes in the values of the hedging instruments and the hedged items. The Board decided to require disclosure of the change in fair value of the hedging instruments and the change in the value of the hedged items on the basis that is used to calculate the hedge ineffectiveness that is recognised in the statement of comprehensive income. Those are the changes in value during the period (after taking into account the effect of the 'lower of' test for cash flow hedges and hedges of a net investment in a foreign operation). This means that the difference between the amount included in the table for hedged items and the amount included in the table for hedging instruments equals the hedge ineffectiveness recognised in the statement of comprehensive income.

BC35MM The Board also did not think that it was necessary to provide a specific disclosure that indicates which financial instruments have been designated as hedging instruments and which have not. The Board thought that such a disclosure would provide potentially misleading information to users of financial statements. This is because users of financial statements might think that all financial instruments not designated as hedging instruments might be held for speculative purposes. This is not necessarily the case. Entities might hold financial instruments for hedging purposes but may decide not to elect hedge accounting. In addition to this, the Board thought that, because entities need to provide the information that requires a tabular format based on the same level of aggregation or disaggregation as in IFRS 13, users of financial statements should be able to identify the financial instruments not designated as hedging instruments by simply comparing the disclosures with each other. In addition, users should be able to understand how an entity manages the risks it is exposed to as a result of financial instruments using the disclosure requirements in IFRS 7 that are not related to the hedge accounting disclosures.

Time value of options accumulated through other comprehensive income

BC35NN   The Board proposed accounting requirements that involve other comprehensive income for the time value of an option when an entity elects to separate the time value of the option and designate (as the hedging instrument) only its intrinsic value. Consequently, the Board also considered disclosures regarding the amounts that would be recognised in other comprehensive income under these proposals.

BC35OO   The Board noted that IAS 1 requires an entity to prepare a reconciliation for each component of equity between the carrying amount at the beginning and at the end of the period. Consequently, as a result of IAS 1, an entity would disclose the amounts in relation to the time value of options that would be accumulated in other comprehensive income and the movements in that balance.

BC35PP   However, in its 2010 Hedge Accounting Exposure Draft, the Board proposed that an entity should differentiate between transaction related hedged items and time-period related hedged items when providing the reconciliation of the accumulated other comprehensive income. This disaggregation would provide additional information about what cumulative amount in other comprehensive income would become an expense item over time and what amount would be transferred when a particular transaction occurs.

BC35QQ   Most respondents agreed with the Board's proposal and consequently, the Board decided to retain the proposal from its 2010 Hedge Accounting Exposure Draft. However, as a consequence of the Board's decision to also allow an alternative accounting treatment for forward elements and foreign currency basis spreads, the Board also required that for the purpose of the IAS 1, amounts recognised in accumulated other comprehensive income that relate to forward elements and foreign currency basis spreads should be reconciled separately from amounts in relation to time value of options.

Hedging credit risk using credit derivatives

BC35RR   For situations in which entities hedge credit risk using credit derivatives the Board decided to mitigate accounting mismatches in relation to credit derivatives accounted for at fair value through profit or loss by also using fair value through profit or loss accounting for the hedged credit exposure. Consequently, the Board also considered disclosures to provide transparency when entities apply that accounting.

BC35SS   The Board considered that the following information would be useful for understanding the accounting in such situations:

(a)   a reconciliation of amounts at the beginning and end of the period for the nominal amount and for the fair value of the credit derivatives;

(b)   the gain or loss recognised in profit or loss as a result of changing the accounting for a credit exposure to fair value through profit or loss; and

(c)   when an entity discontinues fair value through profit or loss accounting for credit exposures, the fair value that becomes the new deemed cost or amortisable amount (for loan commitments) and the related nominal or principal amount.

Uncertainty arising from interest rate benchmark reform

BC35TT   In May 2019 the Board published the Exposure Draft *Interest Rate Benchmark Reform* (2019 Exposure Draft), which proposed exceptions to specific hedge accounting requirements in IFRS 9 and IAS 39 to provide relief in the period before the reform of interest rate benchmarks. The Board issued the final amendments to IFRS 9 and IAS 39 in September 2019. Paragraphs BC6.546–BC6.603 of the Basis for Conclusions on IFRS 9 and paragraphs BC223–BC288 of the Basis for Conclusions on IAS 39 provide the background to these amendments.

BC35UU   In the 2019 Exposure Draft, the Board proposed that entities applying the exceptions provide disclosure about the magnitude of the hedging relationships to which the exceptions apply. As explained in paragraph BC44 of the Basis for Conclusions on the 2019 Exposure Draft, the Board noted that IFRS 7 already requires specific disclosures about hedge accounting. The Board proposed that for some specifically identified disclosures, information be provided separately for hedging relationships to which the proposed exceptions apply. Specifically, the Board proposed that an entity provide separately the information required by paragraphs 24A(a), 24A(c)–(d), 24B(a)(i)–(ii), 24B(a)(iv) and 24B(b) of IFRS 7 for hedging relationships affected by interest rate benchmark reform.

BC35VV   Most respondents to the 2019 Exposure Draft agreed that information about the magnitude of the hedging relationships to which the proposed exceptions apply would be useful to users of financial statements. However, respondents had mixed views on whether the proposed disclosure requirements struck the right balance between the expected benefits for users of financial statements and the expected cost for preparers. As a result, these respondents suggested simplifying the proposed disclosure requirements.

BC35WW   In addition, users of financial statements told the Board that, since the proposed amendments to IFRS 9 and IAS 39 would be mandatory, information about the extent to which an entity's hedging relationships are within the scope of the exceptions would provide useful information. Such information could be provided by requiring entities to disclose the nominal amounts of hedging instruments in hedging relationships in the scope of the amendments, supplemented with an explanation about how the entity is managing the process to transition to alternative benchmark rates. These disclosures would help users of financial statements understand how an entity's hedging relationships are affected by the uncertainty arising from interest rate benchmark reform.

BC35XX   On the basis of respondents' comments and feedback from users of financial statements, the Board decided to require entities to provide the disclosures set out in paragraph 24H of IFRS 7 for hedging relationships directly affected by interest rate benchmark reform.

BC35YY   Specific to the disclosure requirement in paragraph 24H(d) of IFRS 7, the Board acknowledged that given the objective and specificity of the amendments to IFRS 9 and IAS 39, there may be limited additional assumptions or judgements in the context of applying those exceptions. For example, the exceptions specify the assumptions to make about the interest rate benchmark-based cash flows. Nevertheless, the Board observed that if an entity makes significant assumptions or judgements in applying the exceptions in those amendments (for example, to determine when the uncertainty arising from interest rate benchmark reform is no longer present), that would be useful information for the users of financial statements. Accordingly, the Board decided to require entities to disclose information about any significant assumptions or judgements that the entity makes in applying the exceptions in the amendments.

BC35ZZ   The Board noted that the requirement in paragraph 24H(e) of IFRS 7 is intended to provide users of financial statements with information about the quantum of hedging relationships which are directly affected by the uncertainties arising from the reform. That paragraph requires disclosure of the nominal amount of the hedging instruments in a hedging relationship directly affected by the uncertainties arising from the reform so that the information is disclosed on a gross basis rather than on a net basis (that is, offsetting hedging instruments in a liability position against those in an asset position).

BC35AAA   Some respondents to the 2019 Exposure Draft raised concerns about the disclosure requirement in paragraph 28(f) of IAS 8 *Accounting Policies, Changes in Accounting Estimates and Errors*. This paragraph requires an entity, on the initial application of an IFRS (or amendments to an IFRS), to disclose, for the current period and each prior period presented, the amount of any adjustment for each financial statement line item affected.

BC35BBB   These respondents said that requiring such disclosure for the amendments to IFRS 9 and IAS 39 would not provide useful information to users of financial statements and also would be onerous for preparers. This is because it would require an entity to maintain parallel systems in order to determine the amount of the adjustment for each financial statement line item affected. Furthermore, disclosing this information would be inconsistent with the Board's observation in paragraph BC6.550 of IFRS 9 and paragraph BC227 of IAS 39, that discontinuing hedge accounting solely due to uncertainties arising from the reform would not provide useful information to users of financial statements.

BC35CCC   The Board agreed with these comments and decided to exempt entities from the requirement in paragraph 28(f) of IAS 8 in the reporting period in which an entity first applies the amendments to IFRS 9 and IAS 39.

Other Disclosures—Additional disclosures related to interest rate benchmark reform

BC35DDD In April 2020 the Board published the Exposure Draft *Interest Rate Benchmark Reform—Phase 2* (2020 Exposure Draft), which proposed amendments to specific requirements in IFRS 9, IAS 39, IFRS 7, IFRS 4 and IFRS 16 to address issues that might affect financial reporting during the reform of an interest rate benchmark, including the replacement of an interest rate benchmark with an alternative benchmark rate. The term 'interest rate benchmark reform' refers to the market-wide reform of an interest rate benchmark as described in paragraph 6.8.2 of IFRS 9 (the reform). The Board issued the final amendments to IFRS 9, IAS 39, IFRS 7, IFRS 4 and IFRS 16 in August 2020 (Phase 2 amendments). Paragraphs BC5.287–BC5.320, BC6.604–BC6.660 and BC7.86–BC7.99 of the Basis for Conclusions on IFRS 9 and paragraphs BC289–BC371 of the Basis for Conclusions on IAS 39 discuss the background to these amendments.

BC35EEE In deciding whether disclosures should accompany the Phase 2 amendments, the Board acknowledged that it was important to balance the benefits of providing useful information to users of financial statements with the costs for preparers to provide the information. To achieve this balance, the Board sought to develop disclosure requirements that would provide useful information to users of financial statements about the effects of the reform on an entity's financial instruments and risk management strategy without requiring disclosures for which the cost of providing that information would outweigh the benefits of the amendments. Consequently, the Board decided not to require quantitative disclosures of what the effects of the reform would have been in the absence of the Phase 2 amendments because the cost of providing such information could outweigh the benefits provided by the amendments. For the same reason, the Board decided not to require entities to provide the disclosure that would otherwise be required by paragraph 28(f) of IAS 8.

BC35FFF In the 2020 Exposure Draft the Board proposed limited additional disclosure requirements by setting out the proposed disclosure objectives and the disclosure requirements to meet those objectives. Most respondents to the 2020 Exposure Draft supported the proposed disclosure objectives and broadly agreed with the proposed disclosures. However, respondents suggested that the Board should simplify aspects of the disclosure required by paragraph 24J(b) of IFRS 7. Furthermore, respondents asked the Board to reconsider whether disclosure of information about how an entity applied the requirements in paragraphs 5.4.6–5.4.8 of IFRS 9 would provide useful information to users of financial statements.

BC35GGG Paragraph 24J(b) of IFRS 7 in the 2020 Exposure Draft proposed requiring that entities disclose the carrying amount of non-derivative financial assets, non-derivative financial liabilities and the nominal amount of derivatives, that continue to reference interest rate benchmarks subject to the reform. Respondents to the 2020 Exposure Draft agreed that providing quantitative information about the magnitude of remaining financial instruments that still need to transition to alternative benchmark rates would be useful for understanding the entity's progress towards completing the implementation of the reform. However, respondents said that the requirement to provide this quantitative information based on the carrying amounts of the relevant non-derivative financial instruments may require an entity to make costly enhancements to its reporting systems and implement additional controls and reconciliations. In the light of a limited time frame, this would be challenging for preparers, in particular those preparers that plan to early apply the Phase 2 amendments. These respondents asked the Board to permit entities to disclose quantitative information on alternative bases—for example, if information about the carrying amounts of relevant non-derivative financial instruments is not available without undue cost or effort, an entity would be able to disclose the quantitative information on the basis that is reported internally to management as part of implementing the reform.

BC35HHH During outreach on the proposed disclosure requirements, users of financial statements told the Board that, while the quantitative information proposed in the 2020 Exposure Draft is a useful measure of an entity's progress in implementing the reform, they acknowledge the quantitative information for non-derivative financial assets and non-derivative financial liabilities is only a subset of the amounts already presented in the relevant line items of the entity's financial statements and therefore such quantitative information does not reconcile. These users of financial statements said that quantitative information would still be useful even if an entity selected another representative basis on which to disclose it.

BC35III The Board considered that the underlying objective of the disclosure required by paragraph 24J(b) of IFRS 7 is to enable users of financial statements to understand the entity's progress towards completing the transition to alternative benchmark rates. Quantitative information about financial assets and financial liabilities that—as at the end of the reporting period—reference interest rate benchmarks that are subject to the reform would therefore assist users of financial statements to assess an entity's progress towards implementing the reform. The Board also considered that for this disclosure to be useful, the quantitative information about non-derivative financial assets, non-derivative financial liabilities and derivatives that continue to reference interest rate benchmarks subject to the reform should be provided in the context of the total non-derivative financial assets, total non-derivative financial liabilities and total derivatives as at the end of the reporting period.

BC35JJJ The Board agreed that an entity could still meet the underlying objective of this disclosure requirement by providing the relevant quantitative information in different ways. Furthermore, the Board considered that permitting entities to select a basis on which to provide relevant quantitative information to achieve the disclosure objective would allow entities to leverage information that is already available and therefore would reduce the costs of providing the information.

BC35KKK Accordingly, the Board amended paragraph 24J(b) of IFRS7 to require an entity to disclose quantitative information that enables users of financial statements to understand the extent of financial assets and financial liabilities that, as at the end of the reporting period, have yet to transition to alternative benchmark rates. This information would be disaggregated by significant interest rate benchmark. An entity would select the basis for disclosing the quantitative information and explain which basis was applied. For example, the quantitative information may be based on:

(a) the carrying amounts of non-derivative financial assets, the carrying amount of non-derivative financial liabilities and the nominal amount of derivatives;

(b) the amounts related to recognised financial instruments (for example, the contractual par amount of non-derivative financial assets and non-derivative financial liabilities, and nominal amounts of derivatives); or

(c) the amounts provided internally to key management personnel (as defined in IAS 24) of the entity about these financial instruments, for example, the entity's board of directors or chief executive officer.

BC35LLL Furthermore, the Board clarified that the disclosure in paragraph 24J(b) of IFRS 7 does not require disclosure of financial instruments that are referenced to an interest rate benchmark subject to the reform at the reporting date, but which will expire prior to transitioning to an alternative benchmark rate. This is because, to meet the objective of this disclosure requirement (see paragraph BC35III), an entity is required to provide information about financial instruments that would be required to transition to alternative benchmark rates (ie before their maturity).

BC35MMM The 2020 Exposure Draft proposed requiring a description of how an entity determined the base rate and relevant adjustments to that rate, including any significant judgements the entity made to assess whether the conditions for applying the practical expedient in paragraph 5.4.7 of IFRS 9 were met. Respondents to the 2020 Exposure Draft said that in the light of the regulatory nature of the reform, entities might be unable to provide this information in a way that would be sufficiently detailed and entity-specific for it to be useful to users of financial statements. Respondents often described the potential challenges in disclosing this information in a meaningful way by reference to multinational entities that are exposed to different alternative benchmark rates. These respondents said that if the proposed disclosure was intended to confirm that the changes were economically equivalent, then the disclosure was unnecessary. The fact that an entity has applied the practical expedient would automatically inform users of financial statements that the entity has assessed that the conditions for applying the practical expedient were met. These respondents also said that, if applying those conditions required significant judgement, paragraph 122 of IAS 1 would require an entity to disclose those judgements.

BC35NNN During outreach on the proposed disclosure requirements in the 2020 Exposure Draft, users of financial statements expressed mixed views on this proposed disclosure requirement. While some users of financial statements said the proposed disclosure could be useful for understanding the extent of changes to financial instruments to which the practical expedient is being applied, others were sceptical about whether entities would be able to disclose information in sufficient detail for it to be meaningful. In particular, they highlighted the risk that the disclosures would be summarised at such an aggregated level that the information would not be useful. They also said that they would regard a requirement for an entity to explain how it has determined that it met the conditions to apply the practical expedient in paragraph 5.4.7 of IFRS 9 to be an audit or regulatory enforcement matter, rather than a matter for disclosure in the financial statements. The Board therefore decided to omit this proposed disclosure requirement from the final amendments to IFRS 7.

BC35OOO Some respondents to the 2020 Exposure Draft asked the Board to clarify whether paragraphs 24I and 24J of IFRS 7 are required for comparative periods, ie periods before the date of initial application of these amendments, even if the entity does not restate prior periods. The Board noted that the transition requirements for the Phase 2 amendments to IFRS 9, IAS 39, IFRS 4 and IFRS 16 specify that an entity is not required (but is permitted if, and only if, it is possible without the use of hindsight) to restate prior periods to reflect the application of these amendments. Therefore, if the entity does not restate prior periods, paragraphs 24I and 24J of IFRS 7 need not be applied to prior reporting periods.

Other disclosures—fair value (paragraphs 25–30)[8]

BC36 Many entities use fair value information internally in determining their overall financial position and in making decisions about individual financial instruments. It is also relevant to many decisions made by users of financial statements because, in many circumstances, it reflects the judgement of the financial markets about the present value of expected future cash flows relating to an instrument. Fair value information permits comparisons of financial instruments having substantially the same economic characteristics, regardless of why they are held and when and by whom they were issued or acquired. Fair values provide a neutral basis for assessing management's stewardship by indicating the effects of its decisions to buy, sell or hold financial assets and to incur, maintain or discharge financial liabilities. The Board decided that when an entity does not measure a financial asset or financial liability in its balance sheet at fair value, it should provide fair value information through supplementary disclosures to assist users to compare entities on a consistent basis.

---

8 IFRS 13 *Fair Value Measurement*, issued in May 2011, defines fair value and contains requirements for measuring fair value and for disclosing information about fair value measurements. As a consequence paragraphs 27–27B of IFRS 7 have been deleted.

BC37   Disclosure of fair value is not required for investments in unquoted equity instruments[9] and derivatives linked to such equity instruments if their fair value cannot be measured reliably.[10] Similarly, IFRS 4[11] does not specify the accounting required for contracts containing a discretionary participation feature pending phase II of the Board's project on insurance contracts. Accordingly, disclosure of fair value is not required for contracts containing a discretionary participation feature, if the fair value of that feature cannot be measured reliably. For all other financial assets and financial liabilities, it is reasonable to expect that fair value can be determined with sufficient reliability within constraints of timeliness and cost. Therefore, the Board concluded that there should be no other exception from the requirement to disclose fair value information for financial assets or financial liabilities.

BC38   To provide users of financial statements with a sense of the potential variability of fair value estimates, the Board decided that information about the use of valuation techniques should be disclosed, in particular the sensitivities of fair value estimates to the main valuation assumptions.[12] In forming this conclusion, the Board considered the view that disclosure of sensitivities could be difficult, particularly when there are many assumptions to which the disclosure would apply and these assumptions are interdependent. However, the Board noted that a detailed quantitative disclosure of sensitivity to all assumptions is not required (only those that could result in a significantly different estimate of fair value are required) and that the disclosure does not require the entity to reflect interdependencies between assumptions when making the disclosure. Additionally, the Board considered whether this disclosure might imply that a fair value established by a valuation technique is less reliable than one established by other means. However, the Board noted that fair values estimated by valuation techniques are more subjective than those established from an observable market price, and concluded that users need information to help them assess the extent of this subjectivity.

BC39   Paragraph 28 requires disclosure about the difference that arises if the transaction price differs from the fair value of a financial instrument that is determined in accordance with paragraph B5.4.8 of IFRS 9.[13] Those disclosures relate to matters addressed in the December 2004 amendment to IAS 39 *Transition and Initial Recognition of Financial Assets and Financial*

---

9   IFRS 13, issued in May 2011, defines a Level 1 input as a quoted price in an active market for an identical asset or liability. Level 2 inputs include quoted prices for identical assets or liabilities in markets that are not active. As a result IAS 39 and IFRS 9 refer to such equity instruments as 'an equity instrument that does not have a quoted price in an active market for an identical instrument (ie a Level 1 input)'.

10   IFRS 9 changed the measurement requirements for investments in equity instruments.

11   In developing IFRS 17, the Board concluded that fair value could be determined for such financial instruments. The disclosure requirements for contracts within the scope of IFRS 17 are provided in IFRS 17.

12   IFRS 13, issued in May 2011, resulted in paragraph 27B(e) of IFRS 7 being deleted.

13   IFRS 13, issued in May 2011, contains the requirements for measuring fair value. As a consequence of issuing that IFRS, paragraph B5.4.8 of IFRS 9 was deleted. However, in 2014 the requirements for amortised cost measurement and impairment were added to IFRS 9 as Sections 5.4 and 5.5. Paragraph B5.4.8 of IFRS 9 now contains requirements related to amortised cost measurement.

Liabilities. That amendment does not specify how entities should account for those initial differences in subsequent periods. The disclosures required by paragraph 28 inform users about the amount of gain or loss that will be recognised in profit or loss in future periods. The Board noted that the information required to provide these disclosures would be readily available to the entities affected.

BC39A   Statement of Financial Accounting Standards No. 157 *Fair Value Measurements* (SFAS 157) issued by the US Financial Accounting Standards Board requires disclosures that are based on a three-level fair value hierarchy for the inputs used in valuation techniques to measure fair value. The Board was asked by some users of financial statements to include similar disclosure requirements in IFRS 7 to provide more information about the relative reliability of the inputs to fair value measurements. The Board concluded that such a hierarchy would improve comparability between entities about the effects of fair value measurements as well as increase the convergence of IFRSs and US generally accepted accounting principles (GAAP). Therefore, the Board decided to require disclosures for financial instruments on the basis of a fair value hierarchy.[14]

BC39B   Because its own fair value measurement project was not yet completed, the Board decided not to propose a fair value hierarchy for measurement but only for disclosures. The fair value hierarchy for disclosures is the same as that in SFAS 157 but uses IFRS language pending completion of the fair value measurement project. Although the implicit fair value hierarchy for measurement in IFRS 9 is different from the fair value hierarchy in SFAS 157, the Board recognised the importance of using a three-level hierarchy for disclosures that is the same as that in SFAS 157.

BC39C   The Board noted the following three-level measurement hierarchy implicit in IFRS 9:

(a)   financial instruments quoted in an active market;

(b)   financial instruments whose fair value is evidenced by comparison with other observable current market transactions in the same instrument (ie without modification or repackaging) or based on a valuation technique whose variables include only data from observable markets; and

(c)   financial instruments whose fair value is determined in whole or in part using a valuation technique based on assumptions that are not supported by prices from observable current market transactions in the same instrument (ie without modification or repackaging) and not based on available observable market data.

BC39D   For example, the Board acknowledged that some financial instruments that, for measurement purposes, are considered to have an active market in accordance with paragraphs B5.4.3–B5.4.5 of IFRS 9 might be in Level 2 for disclosure purposes. Also, the application of paragraph B5.4.9 of IFRS 9 might

---

14 IFRS 13, issued in May 2011, contains a three-level fair value hierarchy for the inputs used in the valuation techniques used to measure fair value and for the related disclosures.

result in no gain or loss being recognised on the initial recognition of a financial instrument that is in Level 2 for disclosure purposes.[15]

BC39E The introduction of the fair value disclosure hierarchy does not affect any measurement or recognition requirements of other IFRSs. In particular, the Board noted that the recognition of gains or losses at inception of a financial instrument (as required by paragraph B5.4.8 of IFRS 9[16]) would not change as a result of the fair value disclosure hierarchy.

BC39F The Board decided to require additional disclosures for instruments with fair value measurements that are in Level 3 of the fair value hierarchy.[17] These disclosures inform users of financial statements about the effects of those fair value measurements that use the most subjective inputs.

BC39G After reviewing comments received on the exposure draft, the Board decided not to require disclosure by level of the fair value hierarchy for financial instruments that are not measured at fair value in the statement of financial position. The Board noted that paragraphs 25 and 27 of IFRS 7, which require the disclosure of the fair value of each class of assets and liabilities in a way that permits it to be compared with its carrying amount, and the methods and assumptions applied in determining fair values, were retained.[18]

Disclosures about the nature and extent of risks arising from financial instruments (paragraphs 31–42 and B6–B28)

BC40 The Board was informed that users of financial statements value information about the risks arising from financial instruments, such as credit risk, liquidity risk and market risk, to which entities are exposed, and the techniques used to identify, measure, monitor and control those risks. Therefore, the Board decided to require disclosure of this information. The Board also decided to balance two objectives:

(a) consistent requirements should apply to all entities so that users receive comparable information about the risks to which entities are exposed.

---

15 IFRS 13, issued in May 2011, contains the requirements for measuring fair value. As a consequence of issuing that IFRS, paragraphs B5.4.3–B5.4.5 of IFRS 9 were deleted and paragraph B5.4.9 of IFRS 9 was relocated to paragraphs B5.1.2A and B5.2.2A. However, in 2014 the requirements for amortised cost measurement and impairment were added to IFRS 9 as Sections 5.4 and 5.5. Paragraphs B5.4.3–B5.4.5 and paragraph B5.4.9 of IFRS 9 now contain requirements related to amortised cost measurement.

16 IFRS 13, issued in May 2011, contains the requirements for measuring fair value. As a consequence of issuing that IFRS, paragraph B5.4.8 of IFRS 9 was deleted. However, in 2014 the requirements for amortised cost measurement and impairment were added to IFRS 9 as Sections 5.4 and 5.5. Paragraph B5.4.8 of IFRS 9 now contains requirements related to amortised cost measurement.

17 IFRS 13, issued in May 2011, requires disclosures about fair value measurements. As a consequence paragraphs 27–27B of IFRS 7 have been deleted.

18 IFRS 13, issued in May 2011, resulted in paragraph 27 of IFRS 7 being deleted.

(b) the disclosures provided should depend on the extent of an entity's use of financial instruments and the extent to which it assumes associated risks. Entities with many financial instruments and related risks should provide more disclosure to communicate those risks to users of financial statements. Conversely, entities with few financial instruments and related risks may provide less extensive disclosure.

BC41 The Board decided to balance these two objectives by developing an IFRS that sets out principles and minimum requirements applicable to all entities, supported by guidance on implementing the IFRS. The requirements in paragraphs 33–42 combine qualitative disclosures of the entity's exposure to risks arising from financial instruments, and the way in which management views and manages these risks, with quantitative disclosures about material risks arising from financial instruments. The extent of disclosure depends on the extent of the entity's exposure to risks arising from financial instruments. The guidance on implementing the IFRS illustrates how an entity might apply the IFRS. This guidance is consistent with the disclosure requirements for banks developed by the Basel Committee (known as Pillar 3), so that banks can prepare, and users receive, a single co-ordinated set of disclosures about financial risk.

BC42 The Board noted that because entities view and manage risk in different ways, disclosures based on how an entity manages risk are unlikely to be comparable between entities. In addition, for an entity that undertakes limited management of risks arising from financial instruments, such disclosures would convey little or no information about the risks the entity has assumed. To overcome these limitations, the Board decided to specify disclosures about risk exposures applicable to all entities. These disclosures provide a common benchmark for financial statement users when comparing risk exposures across different entities and are expected to be relatively easy for entities to prepare. Entities with more developed risk management systems would provide more detailed information.

Interaction between qualitative and quantitative disclosures (paragraph 32A)

BC42A In *Improvements to IFRSs* issued in May 2010, the Board addressed a perceived lack of clarity in the intended interaction between the qualitative and quantitative disclosures of the nature and extent of risks arising from financial instruments. The Board emphasised the interaction between qualitative and quantitative disclosures about the nature and extent of risks arising from financial instruments. This enables users to link related disclosures and hence form an overall picture of the nature and extent of risks arising from financial instruments. The Board concluded that an explicit emphasis on the interaction between qualitative and quantitative disclosures will contribute to disclosure of information in a way that better enables users to evaluate an entity's exposure.

Location of disclosures of risks arising from financial instruments (paragraph B6)

BC43 Many respondents to ED 7 argued that disclosures about risks in paragraphs 31–42 should not be part of the financial statements for the following reasons:

(a) the information would be difficult and costly to audit.

(b) the information is different from information generally included in financial statements because it is subjective, forward-looking and based on management's judgement. Thus, the information does not meet the criteria of comparability, faithful representation and completeness.

(c) inclusion of such information in a management commentary section outside the financial statements would be consistent with practice in other jurisdictions, including the US. Having this information in the financial statements would put IFRS preparers at a disadvantage relative to their US peers.

BC44 Respondents raised concerns that the disclosure of sensitivity analysis in particular should not be part of the financial statements. Respondents stated that sensitivity analysis cannot be prepared with the degree of reliability expected of information in the financial statements, and that the subjectivity in the sensitivity analysis and the hypothetical alternative values could undermine the credibility of the fair values recognised in the financial statements.

BC45 The Board considered whether the disclosures should be part of the information provided by management outside the financial statements. The Board noted that respondents generally regarded the disclosures proposed in ED 7 as useful, even if they did not agree that they should be located in the financial statements. The Board's view is that financial statements would be incomplete and potentially misleading without disclosures about risks arising from financial instruments. Hence, it concluded that such disclosures should be part of the financial statements. The Board rejected the argument that increased transparency puts an entity at a disadvantage; greater certainty on the part of investors can provide a significant advantage by lowering the entity's cost of capital.

BC46 The Board also noted that some entities might prefer to present the information required by the IFRS together with material such as a management commentary or risk report that is not part of the financial statements. Some entities might be required by regulatory authorities to provide in a separate report information similar to that required by the IFRS. Accordingly, the Board decided these disclosures should be given in the financial statements or incorporated by cross-reference from the financial statements to some other statement that is available to users of the financial statements on the same terms as the financial statements and at the same time.

Quantitative disclosures (paragraphs 34–42 and B7–B28)

Information based on how the entity manages risk (paragraphs 34 and B7)

BC47   The Board concluded that disclosures about an entity's exposure to risks arising from financial instruments should be required, and should be based on how the entity views and manages its risks, ie using the information provided to key management personnel (for example, its board of directors or chief executive officer). This approach:

(a)   provides a useful insight into how the entity views and manages risk;

(b)   results in information that has more predictive value than information based on assumptions and methods that management does not use, for instance, in considering the entity's ability to react to adverse situations;

(c)   is more effective in adapting to changes in risk measurement and management techniques and developments in the external environment;

(d)   has practical advantages for preparers of financial statements, because it allows them to use the data they use in managing risk; and

(e)   is consistent with the approach used in IAS 14 *Segment Reporting*.[19]

BC47A   In *Improvements to IFRSs* issued in May 2010, the Board removed the reference to materiality from paragraph 34(b) of IFRS 7. The Board noted that the reference could imply that disclosures in IFRS 7 are required even if those disclosures are not material, which was not the Board's intention.

Information on averages

BC48   The Board considered whether it should require quantitative information about average risk exposures during the period. It noted that information about averages is more informative if the risk exposure at the reporting date is not typical of the exposure during the period. However, information about averages is also more onerous to prepare. On balance, the Board decided to require disclosure of the exposures at the reporting date in all cases and to require additional information only if the information provided at the reporting date is unrepresentative of the entity's exposure to risk during the period.

Credit risk (paragraphs 36–38, B9 and B10)

Disclosure objectives

BC48A   In developing the impairment disclosure requirements in this IFRS, the Board sought to supplement the existing disclosures to meet the additional information needs of users of financial statements that will arise specifically from an impairment model based on expected credit losses. When relevant,

---

19   In 2006 IAS 14 was replaced by IFRS 8 *Operating Segments*.

the Board has considered the comments received on the disclosure requirements proposed in the original Exposure Draft *Financial Instruments: Amortised Cost and Impairment* (the '2009 Impairment Exposure Draft') and the Board-only appendix to the Supplementary Document *Financial Instruments: Impairment*.

BC48B   During the development of the expected credit loss requirements, the Board acknowledged that any approach that attempts to reflect expected credit losses will be subject to measurement uncertainty and will place greater emphasis on management's judgement and the quality of the information used.

BC48C   However, the Board believes that this level of judgement is necessary given the differences in how entities approach credit risk management. The Board considered that information is useful and relevant when it enables users of financial statements to predict the likely amounts, timing and uncertainty of future cash flows. Accordingly, the Board identified three objectives for the disclosure requirements and this IFRS requires both qualitative and quantitative disclosures to assist users of financial statements to understand and identify:

(a)   an entity's credit risk management practices and how they relate to the recognition and measurement of expected credit losses;

(b)   the amounts in the financial statements that arise from expected credit losses that are measured in accordance with IFRS 9, including the changes in the estimate of expected credit losses and the reasons for the changes; and

(c)   an entity's credit risk profile (ie the credit risk inherent in an entity's financial instruments), including significant credit concentrations at the reporting date.

Credit risk management practices

BC48D   Requiring entities to estimate expected credit losses will increase the significance of forecasts and the use of an entity's judgement. In addition, IFRS 9 requires entities to incorporate new types of information into the measurement of expected credit losses as compared to IAS 39. In the Board's view it is helpful for users of financial statements to understand the information entities use to estimate expected credit losses.

BC48E   When developing the proposals in the 2013 Exposure Draft *Financial Instruments: Expected Credit Losses* (the '2013 Impairment Exposure Draft') the Board noted that disclosures about the methods, assumptions and information used to estimate expected credit losses have been a core part of the disclosure package since the 2009 Impairment Exposure Draft, and are important for understanding how an entity applies the expected credit loss requirements. However, the Board acknowledges that different entities will use different information and techniques for assessing whether they should recognise lifetime expected credit losses. The information and techniques that an entity uses will depend on the nature of its financial instruments and other factors.

BC48F   The 2013 Impairment Exposure Draft acknowledged and permitted this. The Board considered that to understand how an entity has applied the proposed expected credit loss requirements, the following information would be relevant and useful:

(a)   how significant increases in credit risk are assessed and identified;

(b)   how default is defined and the reasons for selecting that definition;

(c)   how an entity assesses that financial assets are credit-impaired; and

(d)   the write-off policy applied.

BC48G   Respondents to the 2013 Impairment Exposure Draft supported the disclosure of that qualitative information, with a few respondents requesting the disclosure of more qualitative information about the modification of financial instruments and how an entity has incorporated macroeconomic information in its estimates of expected credit losses.

BC48H   As noted in paragraph BC5.252 of IFRS 9, the notion of default is fundamental to the application of the impairment model, particularly because it affects the population that is subject to the 12-month expected credit loss measure. The Board noted during redeliberations on the 2013 Impairment Exposure Draft that default can be interpreted in various ways, ranging from broad judgemental definitions based on qualitative factors to narrower non-judgemental definitions focusing only on non-payment. The appropriate definition also depends on the nature of the financial instrument in question. Given the various interpretations of default, the Board decided to require the disclosure of an entity's definition of default and the reasons for its selection.

BC48I   The Board considered that an explanation of how forward-looking information, including macroeconomic information, has been incorporated in the measurement of expected credit losses would provide relevant and useful information, given the requirement in IFRS 9 to consider all reasonable and supportable information that is available without undue cost and effort when determining whether there has been a significant increase in credit risk since initial recognition. The Board also considered that an explanation of how an entity has applied the requirements in paragraph 5.5.12 of IFRS 9 for the modification of contractual cash flows of financial assets, including how an entity determines whether the credit risk of modified financial assets has improved so that is not considered to be significantly increased compared to initial recognition, would enhance the understanding of how an entity manages credit risk through modifications and restructurings.

BC48J   The 2013 Impairment Exposure Draft proposed that an entity should disclose the nominal amount of financial assets that have been written off but that are still subject to enforcement activity. This was included because feedback from users of financial statements indicated users would like to understand the extent to which recoveries of written off assets are still possible. The Board acknowledged this desire, however it determined that the disclosure of the aggregate amount of financial assets that have been written off but that remain subject to enforcement activity would not provide the most relevant information for this purpose. For example, the nominal amount could be very high (particularly as time passes, if the asset legally continues to accrue interest) even though the prospect of recovering any amounts outstanding might be extremely low. In addition, the Board received feedback from preparers that tracking these amounts for an extended period would be operationally burdensome. As a result, the Board decided to modify the disclosure and require that entities disclose the amount of financial assets that have been written off during the period, while narrative information is provided about financial assets that have previously been written off but that are still subject to enforcement activity.

BC48K   The Board also proposed narrative disclosures to complement the quantitative disclosures. In the Board's view, users of financial statements would further benefit from a qualitative explanation of changes in estimates of expected credit losses. Estimates of expected credit losses may change, for example, because of changes in the volume of financial instruments, changes in overall market conditions or as a result of a significant event (for example, a sovereign debt crisis, weather-related events or other disasters). The disclosures should therefore include a qualitative narrative describing how significant events have affected the entity's estimate of expected credit losses.

Financial instruments evaluated on an individual basis

BC48L   Previously paragraph 37(b) of IFRS 7 required an analysis of financial instruments that are individually determined to be credit-impaired as at the end of the reporting period, including an analysis of the factors that the entity considered when determining that those financial instruments are credit-impaired. Many entities already disclose the loan balance and loss allowance amount for both collectively and individually assessed credit-impaired loans. Consequently, the 2013 Impairment Exposure Draft proposed amendments to those requirements to limit them to financial instruments that an entity assesses individually for recognition of lifetime expected credit losses.

BC48M   During outreach activities, users of financial statements noted that it is important for them to understand which financial instruments an entity assesses on an individual basis, especially when that individual assessment is because of an increase in credit risk and closer management of the instrument. While these financial instruments may not have experienced an increase in credit risk greater than those evaluated on a group basis, the Board concluded that this distinction helps users of financial statements to understand how an entity is monitoring and managing credit risk, so it is useful even when the difference is not attributable to differences in credit risk.

BC48N   However, several respondents to the 2013 Impairment Exposure Draft argued that a disclosure of the gross carrying amount of financial assets (and the amount recognised as a loss allowance for loan commitments and financial guarantee contracts) that are assessed on an individual basis is not relevant in an impairment model based on expected credit losses. These respondents argued that unlike in IAS 39, the loss allowance does not result from objective evidence of impairment on an individual asset.

BC48O   The Board noted that conceptually, an assessment on an individual or collective basis should render the same result. However, as noted in paragraph B5.5.2 of IFRS 9, an entity may not have access to reasonable and supportable information that enables it to identify significant increases in credit on an individual basis prior to financial assets becoming past due. Furthermore, an entity may only be able to incorporate forward-looking information in its estimates of expected credit losses on a collective basis. The Board therefore decided instead to require the disclosure of information about how an entity has grouped financial instruments if they are assessed or measured on a collective basis.

Amounts arising from expected credit losses

Reconciliation of the gross carrying amount and loss allowance

BC48P   The Supplementary Document proposed the mandatory use of a loss allowance account for credit losses, with separate disclosure of reconciliations for the two groups of financial assets that an entity would distinguish for the purpose of determining the loss allowance (ie assets in the 'good book' and assets in the 'bad book'). Almost all respondents supported the mandatory use of a loss allowance account. Consequently, the 2013 Impairment Exposure Draft retained that proposal.

BC48Q   The 2013 Impairment Exposure Draft also retained the proposal in the Supplementary Document to show a reconciliation of the gross carrying amount of financial assets separately for each of the groups of financial assets that an entity would distinguish between for the purpose of determining the loss allowance (ie 12-month expected credit losses and lifetime expected credit losses) and each of the related loss allowances. Respondents (including preparers) generally supported disclosing a reconciliation (ie flow information) of changes in the loss allowance and stated that it was operational and useful. However, similar to the feedback received on the Supplementary Document, respondents to the 2013 Impairment Exposure Draft commented that showing separate reconciliations of the gross carrying amount of financial assets was onerous, especially when they were required to disclose the effect of the change of financial assets between those with loss allowances measured at amounts equal to 12-month and lifetime expected credit losses. They noted that when loss allowances are determined on a collective (ie portfolio) basis, an entity does not allocate loss allowances to individual financial assets. Preparers also stated that the costs associated with the disclosure, and any disclosure about flow information, would be substantial. In order to provide this information for open portfolios, an entity would be required to track changes in the credit risk of individual financial instruments and calculate the change in the loss allowance that results from new loans, derecognised assets, changes between 12-month and lifetime loss allowances and changes in estimates of credit losses. They noted that this would be contrary to the requirement in IFRS 9 which requires lifetime expected credit losses to be recognised even if a significant increase in credit risk cannot be identified on an individual financial instrument basis.

BC48R   During outreach, users of financial statements have consistently and strongly expressed the view that the change in the gross carrying amount of financial assets and the effect on the loss allowance are critical elements in understanding the credit quality of an entity's financial instruments and its credit risk management practices. They held the view that the reconciliation of the gross carrying amount of financial instruments would greatly enhance transparency of an entity's financial asset portfolio. While these disclosures would require systems changes and the cost of providing the information would be high, the Board noted that such reconciliations provide key information about movements between 12-month and lifetime loss allowances and about the causes of changes in expected credit losses and about the effect of changes in volume and credit quality.

BC48S   The Board therefore decided to retain the requirement to provide a reconciliation of the changes in the loss allowance. However, in the light of the feedback about the operational burden of reconciling the changes in the gross carrying amount of financial assets, the Board clarified that the objective of that reconciliation is to provide information about the key drivers for changes in the gross carrying amount to the extent that it contributes to changes in the loss allowance during the period. Examples of such key drivers for change could include new originations and purchases, deterioration of existing financial instruments resulting in the loss allowance changing to lifetime expected credit losses and financial assets being written off during the period. The Board also acknowledged that although the most relevant and useful information will be provided by disclosing the gross movements between loss allowance measurement categories, in some circumstances, or for some types of financial assets, information will be more useful if the movements are disclosed on a net basis (for example trade receivables accounted for in accordance with the general approach in IFRS 9).

Loan commitments and financial guarantee contracts

BC48T   The 2013 Impairment Exposure Draft proposed that expected credit losses on loan commitments and financial guarantee contracts should be recognised as a provision in the statement of financial position. The Board noted that it would be inappropriate to recognise a loss allowance for such financial instruments because there is no corresponding asset with which to present that loss allowance.

BC48U   The Board noted feedback on the 2013 Impairment Exposure Draft that indicated that for most loan commitments and financial guarantee contracts, entities estimate expected credit losses on an instrument (facility) level and are therefore not able to distinguish the expected credit losses related to the drawn component (the financial asset) and the undrawn component (the loan commitment). Consequently, it would not seem appropriate to attempt to allocate expected credit losses to each of these components for the purposes of presenting the loss allowance on each component separately and any allocation would probably be arbitrary.

BC48V The Board therefore decided that the loss allowance on a loan commitment or a financial guarantee contract should be presented together with the loss allowance for expected credit losses on the associated financial asset, if an entity cannot separately identify the expected credit losses related to the separate components. To the extent that the amount of expected credit losses on a loan commitment or a financial guarantee contract exceeds the carrying amount of the associated financial asset recognised in the statement of financial position, the remaining balance should be presented as a provision.

Purchased or originated credit-impaired assets

BC48W The Board sought to enhance the comparability of financial assets that are credit-impaired on initial recognition with those that are not. Consequently, the Board decided that an entity should disclose the undiscounted expected credit losses that are implicit in the pricing at initial recognition for purchased or originated credit-impaired financial assets. Users of financial statements have indicated that such a disclosure would be helpful in alleviating some of the complexity in this area of accounting and would allow them to see the possible contractual cash flows that an entity could collect if there was a favourable change in expectations of credit losses for such assets.

Modifications

BC48X Throughout the Impairment project, users of financial statements have noted that an area in which current disclosures and information is insufficient is that of restructurings and modifications. Particularly during the global financial crisis, users have expressed frustration at the difficulty of understanding the extent of restructuring activity that entities are undertaking in respect of their financial assets.

BC48Y The 2013 Impairment Exposure Draft proposed to require the disclosure of the gross carrying amount of financial assets that have been modified during their life at a time when the loss allowance was measured at lifetime expected credit losses and for which the measurement of the loss allowance had subsequently changed back to 12-month expected credit losses. This proposed requirement resulted from users of financial statements requesting information to enable them to understand the amount of financial assets that have been modified and that have subsequently improved in credit quality. During redeliberations the Board noted operational concerns raised in feedback from preparers about the need to meet such a requirement by tracking individual financial assets, particularly even long after such assets have returned to a performing status and are no longer closely monitored for credit risk management purposes. The Board noted that the usefulness of the information would decrease over time as an increasing number of assets are required to be included in the disclosure. The Board therefore decided to limit the requirement to financial assets that have previously been modified at a time when the loss allowance was measured at lifetime expected credit losses and for which the loss allowance has changed back to 12-month expected credit losses during the reporting period.

BC48Z   During redeliberations of the 2013 Impairment Exposure Draft the Board received feedback that the modification guidance in IFRS 9 should be limited to modifications of credit-impaired assets or modifications undertaken for credit risk management purposes. The Board rejected these views and confirmed that the scope of this guidance applies to all modifications of contractual cash flows, regardless of the reason for the modification. In making this decision, the Board noted that an amortised cost carrying amount equates to the present value of the expected contractual cash flows, discounted at the effective interest rate. Consequently, the carrying amount should reflect changes in those contractual cash flows, irrespective of the reason for the modification occurring. In addition, it was noted that any change in contractual terms will have an impact on credit risk, even if small. Furthermore, the Board noted that it has been told previously that identifying those modifications that have been performed for credit risk management (ie non-commercial) purposes is operationally challenging. Consequently, the disclosures in paragraph 35J of IFRS 7 apply to all modifications of contractual cash flows.

Collateral and credit risk mitigation disclosures

BC48AA   Collateral and other credit risk mitigants are important factors in an entity's estimate of expected credit losses. For instance, an entity with more heavily collateralised loans will, all other things being equal, record a smaller loss allowance for credit losses than an entity with unsecured loans. The previous requirements of paragraph 36(b) of IFRS 7 required the disclosure of information similar to that proposed in the 2013 Impairment Exposure Draft. However, the Board received feedback that these collateral disclosures were too onerous and costly to prepare, and therefore proposed to limit the quantitative collateral disclosure requirements to those financial instruments that become credit-impaired subsequent to initial recognition.

BC48BB   Feedback on the 2013 Impairment Exposure Draft indicated that respondents remained concerned about the disclosure of quantitative information about collateral for financial instruments that become credit-impaired subsequent to initial recognition. The Board maintained the view that information about the financial effect of collateral is useful. However, the Board noted that it did not intend to require providing information about the fair value of collateral. In addition, the Board decided that qualitative information should be disclosed about how collateral and other credit enhancements have been incorporated into the measurement of expected credit losses on all financial instruments.

Credit risk exposure

BC48CC   Because the recognition of lifetime expected credit losses is based on a significant increase in credit risk since initial recognition, there could be a wide range of initial credit risk for which 12-month expected credit losses is recognised (for example, loans that are originated with a high credit risk but have not increased in credit risk subsequently would have a loss allowance based on 12-month expected credit losses as would high quality loans that have not significantly increased in credit risk since initial recognition). To provide users of financial statements with information about the changes in the loss allowance and the entity's exposure to credit risk on financial instruments, the 2013 Impairment Exposure Draft proposed a disaggregation of the carrying amounts of financial instruments into credit risk categories, for both 12-month and lifetime expected credit losses.

BC48DD   Disaggregating by credit risk shows the entity's exposure to credit risk and its credit risk profile at a given point in time (ie the reporting date). Users of financial statements indicated that they were concerned about the relative nature of the disclosure that is based on the range of credit risk relevant to the entity's portfolio and that it would lack comparability as a result (ie a high risk for one entity may only be a medium risk for another). Furthermore, without vintage information, a user would not be able to determine whether changes in the risk profile are a result of changes in the credit risk of existing financial instruments or a result of the credit risk of new instruments recognised during the period. However, they believed that risk disaggregation would still provide insight into an entity's exposure to credit risk and were therefore in favour of including it in the notes to the financial statements. The Board required the disclosure because changes in risk will affect the measurement of expected credit losses and it would therefore provide users of financial statements with information about the drivers of the change in the measurement. The Board also noted that this disclosure, particularly when considered together with the reconciliation of the gross carrying amount and loss allowance, provides relevant and useful information about credit risk migration and changes in overall credit risk over time.

BC48EE   The Board considered adding language to the proposed disclosure that would have required an entity to reconcile this disclosure to internal credit rating grades. However, responses to the Supplementary Document considered this internal risk-rating information to be proprietary and therefore objected to this level of specificity. Consequently, the Board decided not to propose this reconciliation.

BC48FF   Some respondents to the 2013 Impairment Exposure Draft also commented that the disclosure was incompatible with the credit risk management practices for some asset classes and for non-financial entities, and noted that the disclosure should be aligned with an entity's internal credit risk approach. In the light of this feedback the Board decided to remove the requirement to provide a disaggregation across a minimum of three credit risk rating grades, and instead require that the disaggregation to be aligned with how credit risk is managed internally. The Board additionally decided to permit the use of an ageing analysis for financial assets for which delinquency information is the only borrower-specific information available to assess significant increases in credit risk.

Simplified approach for trade receivables, contract assets and lease receivables

BC48GG   This IFRS includes exceptions to the general disclosures for trade receivables, contract assets and lease receivables when an entity applies the simplified approach. The Board noted that these exemptions provide relief that is consistent with the intention to simplify the application of the impairment model for these categories of financial assets to alleviate some of the practical concerns of tracking changes in credit risk.

Maximum exposure to credit risk (paragraphs 36(a), B9 and B10)

BC49   Paragraph 36(a) requires disclosure of an entity's maximum exposure to credit risk at the reporting date. Some respondents to ED 7 stated that these disclosures would not provide useful information when there are no identified problems in a loan portfolio, and it is not likely that collateral would be called on. However, the Board disagreed because it believes that such information:

(a)   provides users of financial statements with a consistent measure of an entity's exposure to credit risk; and

(b)   takes into account the possibility that the maximum exposure to loss may differ from the amount recognised in the balance sheet.

BC49A   In *Improvements to IFRSs* issued in May 2010, the Board enhanced consistency within IFRS 7 by clarifying that the disclosure requirement in paragraph 36(a) applies only to financial assets whose carrying amounts do not show the reporting entity's maximum exposure to credit risk. Such an approach is consistent with the approach taken in paragraph 29(a), which states that disclosure of fair value is not required when the carrying amount is a reasonable approximation of fair value. Moreover, the Board concluded that the requirement might be duplicative for assets that are presented in the statement of financial position because the carrying amount of these assets often represents the maximum exposure to credit risk. In the Board's view, the disclosure requirement should focus on the entity's exposure to credit risk that is not already reflected in the statement of financial position.

BC50   Some respondents to ED 7 questioned whether the maximum exposure to credit risk for a derivative contract is its carrying amount because fair value does not always reflect potential future exposure to credit risk (see paragraph B10(b)). However, the Board noted that paragraph 36(a) requires disclosure of the amount that best represents the maximum exposure to credit risk *at the reporting date*, which is the carrying amount.

Collateral held as security and other credit enhancements (paragraphs 36(b) and 37(c))

BC51   ED 7 proposed that, unless impracticable, the entity should disclose the fair value of collateral held as security and other credit enhancements, to provide information about the loss the entity might incur in the event of default. However, many respondents to ED 7 disagreed with this proposal on cost/benefit grounds. Respondents indicated that fair value information might not be available for:

(a)   small entities and entities other than banks, which may find it onerous to acquire information about collateral;

(b)   banks that collect precise information on the value of collateral only on origination, for loans whose payments are made on time and in full (for example a mortgage portfolio secured by properties, for which valuations are not kept up to date on an asset-by-asset basis);

(c)   particular types of collateral, such as a floating charge on all the assets of an entity; and

(d)   insurers that hold collateral for which fair value information is not readily available.

BC52   The Board also noted respondents' concerns that an aggregate disclosure of the fair value of collateral held would be misleading when some loans in a portfolio are over-collateralised, and other loans have insufficient collateral. In these circumstances, netting the fair value of the two types of collateral would under-report the amount of credit risk. The Board agreed with respondents that the information useful to users is not the total amount of credit exposure less the total amount of collateral, but rather is the amount of credit exposure that is left after available collateral is taken into account.

BC53   Therefore, the Board decided not to require disclosure of the fair value of collateral held, but to require disclosure of only a description of collateral held as security and other credit enhancements. The Board noted that such disclosure does not require an entity to establish fair values for all its collateral (in particular when the entity has determined that the fair value of some collateral exceeds the carrying amount of the loan) and, thus, would be less onerous for entities to provide than fair values.

Credit quality of financial assets that are neither past due nor impaired (paragraph 36(c))[20]

BC54   The Board noted that information about credit quality gives a greater insight into the credit risk of assets and helps users assess whether such assets are more or less likely to become impaired in the future. Because this information will vary between entities, the Board decided not to specify a particular method for giving this information, but rather to allow each entity to devise a method that is appropriate to its circumstances.

Financial assets with renegotiated terms (paragraph 36(d))

BC54A   In *Improvements to IFRSs* issued in May 2010, the Board addressed a practical concern relating to the disclosure requirements for renegotiated financial assets. The Board deleted the requirement in paragraph 36(d) to disclose the carrying amount of financial assets that would otherwise be past due or impaired whose terms have been renegotiated. The Board considered the difficulty in identifying financial assets whose terms have been renegotiated to avoid becoming past due or impaired (rather than for other commercial reasons). The Board noted that the original requirement was unclear about whether the requirement applies only to financial assets that were

---

20   IFRS 9 *Financial Instruments* deleted paragraph 36(c) of IFRS 7.

© IFRS Foundation

renegotiated in the current reporting period or whether past negotiations of those assets should be considered. Moreover, the Board was informed that commercial terms of loans are often renegotiated regularly for reasons that are not related to impairment. In practice it is difficult, especially for a large portfolio of loans, to ascertain which loans were renegotiated to avoid becoming past due or impaired.

Financial assets that are either past due or impaired (paragraph 37)[21]

BC55   The Board decided to require separate disclosure of financial assets that are past due or impaired to provide users with information about financial assets with the greatest credit risk (paragraph 37). This includes:

(a)   an analysis of the age of financial assets, including trade receivables, that are past due at the reporting date, but not impaired (paragraph 37(a)). This information provides users with information about those financial assets that are more likely to become impaired and helps users to estimate the level of future impairment losses.

(b)   an analysis of financial assets that are individually determined to be impaired at the reporting date, including the factors the entity considered in determining that the financial assets are impaired (paragraph 37(b)). The Board concluded that an analysis of impaired financial assets by factors other than age (eg nature of the counterparty, or geographical analysis of impaired assets) would be useful because it helps users to understand why the impairment occurred.

BC55A   In *Improvements to IFRSs* issued in May 2010, the Board addressed a concern that the disclosure of the fair value of collateral was potentially misleading. Within a class of assets some might be over-collateralised while others might be under-collateralised. Hence, aggregate disclosure of the fair value might be misleading. Therefore, the Board removed from paragraph 37(c) the requirement to disclose the fair value of collateral and other credit enhancements. However, the Board believes that information on the financial effect of such assets is useful to users. Hence, the Board included in paragraph 36(b) a requirement to disclose a description of collateral held as security and of other credit enhancements and to disclose their financial effect.

Collateral and other credit enhancements obtained (paragraph 38)

BC56   Paragraph 38 requires the entity to disclose the nature and carrying amount of assets obtained by taking possession of collateral held as security or calling on other credit enhancements and its policy for disposing of such assets. The Board concluded that this information is useful because it provides information about the frequency of such activities and the entity's ability to obtain and realise the value of the collateral. ED 7 had proposed that the entity should disclose the fair value of the assets obtained less the cost of

---

21 IFRS 9 *Financial Instruments* deleted paragraph 37 of IFRS 7.

selling them, rather than the carrying amount. The Board noted that this amount might be more relevant in the case of collateral obtained that is expected to be sold. However, it also noted that such an amount would be included in the impairment calculation that is reflected in the amount recognised in the balance sheet and the purpose of the disclosure is to indicate the amount recognised in the balance sheet for such assets.

BC56A   In *Improvements to IFRSs* issued in May 2010, the Board enhanced consistency within IFRS 7 by clarifying that paragraph 38 requires entities to disclose the amount of foreclosed collateral held at the reporting date. This is consistent with the objective in IFRS 7 to disclose information that enables users to evaluate the nature and extent of risks arising from financial instruments to which the entity is exposed at the end of the reporting period.

Liquidity risk (paragraphs 34(a), 39, B10A and B11A–B11F)

BC57   The Board decided to require disclosure of a maturity analysis for financial liabilities showing the remaining earliest contractual maturities (paragraph 39(a) and paragraphs B11–B16 of Appendix B).[22] Liquidity risk, ie the risk that the entity will encounter difficulty in meeting commitments associated with financial liabilities, arises because of the possibility (which may often be remote) that the entity could be required to pay its liabilities earlier than expected. The Board decided to require disclosure based on the earliest contractual maturity date because this disclosure shows a worst case scenario.

BC58   Some respondents expressed concerns that such a contractual maturity analysis does not reveal the expected maturity of liabilities, which, for some entities – eg banks with many demand deposits – may be very different. They suggested that a contractual maturity analysis alone does not provide information about the conditions expected in normal circumstances or how the entity manages deviations from expected maturity. Therefore, the Board decided to require a description of how the entity manages the liquidity risk portrayed by the contractual maturity analysis.

BC58A   In March 2009 the Board amended the disclosure requirements on the nature and extent of liquidity risk by:

(a)   amending the definition of liquidity risk to clarify that paragraph 39 applies only to financial liabilities that will result in the outflow of cash or another financial asset. This clarifies that the disclosure requirements would not apply to financial liabilities that will be settled in the entity's own equity instruments and to liabilities within the scope of IFRS 7 that are settled with non-financial assets.

---

22   Amendments to IFRS 7 issued in March 2009 amended paragraph 39 and paragraphs B11–B16. The paragraph references in paragraph BC57 have not been amended as a result of these amendments.

(b)   emphasising that an entity must provide summary quantitative data about its exposure to liquidity risk based on information provided internally to key management personnel of the entity as required by paragraph 34(a). This reinforces the principles of IFRS 7.

(c)   amending the requirement in paragraph 39 to disclose a contractual maturity analysis.

BC58B   The requirements in paragraph 39(a) and (b) relate to minimum benchmark disclosures as set out in paragraph 34(b) and are expected to be relatively easy to apply. However, the Board noted that the requirement to provide disclosures based on the remaining contractual maturities was difficult to apply for some derivative financial liabilities and did not always result in information that reflects how many entities manage liquidity risk for such instruments. Hence, for some circumstances the Board eliminated the previous requirement to disclose contractual maturity information for derivative financial liabilities. However, the Board retained minimum contractual maturity disclosures for non-derivative financial liabilities (including issued financial guarantee contracts within the scope of the IFRS) and for some derivative financial liabilities.

BC58C   The Board noted that for non-derivative financial liabilities (including issued financial guarantee contracts within the scope of the IFRS) and some derivative financial liabilities, contractual maturities are essential for an understanding of the timing of cash flows associated with the liabilities. Therefore, this information is useful to users of financial statements. The Board concluded that disclosures based on the remaining contractual maturities of these financial liabilities should continue to be required.

BC58D   The Board also emphasised the existing requirement to disclose a maturity analysis for financial assets held for managing liquidity risk, if that information is required to enable users of its financial statements to evaluate the nature and extent of liquidity risk. The Board also emphasised that an entity must explain the relationship between qualitative and quantitative disclosures about liquidity risk so that users of financial statements can evaluate the nature and extent of liquidity risk.

Market risk (paragraphs 40–42 and B17–B28)

BC59   The Board decided to require disclosure of a sensitivity analysis for each type of market risk (paragraph 40) because:

(a)   users have consistently emphasised the fundamental importance of sensitivity analysis;

(b)   a sensitivity analysis can be disclosed for all types of market risk and by all entities, and is relatively easy to understand and calculate; and

(c)   it is suitable for all entities – including non-financial entities – that have financial instruments. It is supported by disclosures of how the entity manages the risk. Thus, it is a simpler and more suitable disclosure than other approaches, including the disclosures of terms and conditions and the gap analysis of interest rate risk previously required by IAS 32.

The Board noted that information provided by a simple sensitivity analysis would not be comparable across entities. This is because the methodologies used to prepare the sensitivity analysis and the resulting disclosures would vary according to the nature of the entity and the complexity of its risk management systems.

BC60   The Board acknowledged that a simple sensitivity analysis that shows a change in only one variable has limitations. For example, the analysis may not reveal non-linearities in sensitivities or the effects of interdependencies between variables. The Board decided to meet the first concern by requiring additional disclosure when the sensitivity analysis is unrepresentative of a risk inherent in a financial instrument (paragraph 42). The Board noted that it could meet the second concern by requiring a more complex sensitivity analysis that takes into account the interdependencies between risks. Although more informative, such an analysis is also more complex and costly to prepare. Accordingly, the Board decided not to require such an analysis, but to permit its disclosure as an alternative to the minimum requirement when it is used by management to manage risk.

BC61   Respondents to ED 7 noted that a value-at-risk amount would not show the effect on profit or loss or equity. However, entities that manage on the basis of value at risk would not want to prepare a separate sensitivity analysis solely for the purpose of this disclosure. The Board's objective was to require disclosures about sensitivity, not to mandate a particular form of sensitivity disclosure. Therefore, the Board decided not to require disclosure of the effects on profit or loss and equity if an alternative disclosure of sensitivity is made.

BC62   Respondents to ED 7 requested the Board to provide more guidance and clarification about the sensitivity analysis, in particular:

(a)   what is a reasonably possible change in the relevant risk variable?

(b)   what is the appropriate level of aggregation in the disclosures?

(c)   what methodology should be used in preparing the sensitivity analysis?

BC63   The Board concluded that it would not be possible to provide comprehensive guidance on the methodology to be used in preparing the sensitivity analysis. The Board noted that more comparable information would be obtained if it imposed specific requirements about the inputs, process and methodology of the analysis, for example disclosure of the effects of a parallel shift of the yield curve by 100 basis points. However, the Board decided against such a specific requirement because a reasonably possible change in a relevant risk variable (such as interest rates) in one economic environment may not be reasonably possible in another (such as an economy with higher inflation). Moreover, the effect of a reasonably possible change will vary depending on the entity's risk exposures. As a result, entities are required to judge what those reasonably possible changes are.

BC64   However, the Board decided that it would provide high level application guidance about how the entity should assess what is a reasonably possible change and on the appropriate level of aggregation in the disclosures. In response to comments received on ED 7, the Board also decided to clarify that:

(a)   an entity should not aggregate information about material exposures to risk from significantly different economic environments. However, if it has exposure to only one type of market risk in only one economic environment, it might not show disaggregated information.

(b)   the sensitivity analysis does not require entities to determine what the profit or loss for the period would have been had the relevant risk variable been different. The sensitivity analysis shows the effect on current period profit or loss and equity if a reasonably possible change in the relevant risk variable had applied to the risk exposures in existence at the balance sheet date.

(c)   a reasonably possible change is judged relative to the economic environments in which the entity operates, and does not include remote or 'worst case' scenarios or 'stress tests'.

(d)   entities are required to disclose only the effects of the changes at the limits of the reasonably possible range of the relevant risk variable, rather than all reasonably possible changes.

(e)   the time frame for which entities should make an assessment about what is reasonably possible is the period until the entity next presents these disclosures, usually its next annual reporting period.

The Board also decided to add a simple example of what a sensitivity analysis might look like.

Operational risk

BC65   The Board discussed whether it should require disclosure of information about operational risk. However, the Board noted that the definition and measurement of operational risk are in their infancy and are not necessarily related to financial instruments. It also decided that such disclosures would be more appropriately located outside the financial statements. Therefore, the Board decided to defer this issue to its research project on management commentary.

Disclosures relating to transfers of financial assets

Background

BC65A   In March 2009, in conjunction with the Memorandum of Understanding between the IASB and the US Financial Accounting Standards Board (FASB) to improve and achieve convergence of IFRS and US standards for derecognition, the IASB published an exposure draft to replace the derecognition requirements of IAS 39[23] and to improve the disclosure requirements in IFRS 7 relating to the transfer of financial assets and liabilities. In response to feedback received on the exposure draft the IASB developed more fully the alternative model described in the exposure draft and the boards discussed the alternative model.

BC65B   In May 2010 the boards reconsidered their strategies and plans for the derecognition project in the light of:

(a)   their joint discussions of the alternative derecognition model described in the exposure draft;

(b)   the June 2009 amendments to the US GAAP derecognition guidance by the FASB, which reduced the differences between IFRSs and US GAAP by improving requirements relating to derecognition of financial assets and liabilities; and

(c)   the feedback the IASB received from national standard-setters on the largely favourable effects of the IFRS derecognition requirements during the financial crisis.

BC65C   As a result, in June 2010 the IASB and the FASB agreed that their near-term priority was on increasing the transparency and comparability of their standards by improving and aligning the disclosure requirements in IFRSs and US GAAP for financial assets transferred to another entity. The boards also decided to conduct additional research and analysis, including a post-implementation review of some of the FASB's recently amended requirements, as a basis for assessing the nature and direction of any further efforts to improve or align IFRSs and US GAAP.

BC65D   As a result, the Board decided to finalise the derecognition disclosures and related objectives, proposed in the exposure draft. Accordingly, in October 2010 the Board issued *Disclosures – Transfers of Financial Assets* (Amendments to IFRS 7), requiring disclosures to help users of financial statements:

(a)   to understand the relationship between transferred financial assets that are not derecognised in their entirety and the associated liabilities; and

(b)   to evaluate the nature of and risks associated with the entity's continuing involvement in derecognised financial assets.

Transferred financial assets that are not derecognised in their entirety

BC65E   When financial assets are transferred but not derecognised, there has been an exchange transaction that is not reflected as such in the financial statements as a result of the accounting requirements. The Board concluded that in those situations, users of financial statements need to understand the relationship between those transferred financial assets and the associated liabilities that an entity recognises. Understanding that relationship helps users of financial

---

23   IFRS 9 *Financial Instruments* replaced IAS 39. IFRS 9 applies to all items that were previously within the scope of IAS 39.

statements in assessing an entity's cash flow needs and the cash flows available to the entity from its assets.

BC65F   The Board observed that IFRS 7 required disclosures about transferred financial assets that are not derecognised in their entirety. The Board decided to continue requiring those disclosures because they provide information that is useful in understanding the relationship between transferred financial assets that are not derecognised and associated liabilities.

BC65G   However, the Board also decided that the following additional disclosures were necessary:

(a)   a qualitative description of the nature of the relationship between transferred assets and associated liabilities, including restrictions arising from the transfer on the reporting entity's use of the transferred assets; and

(b)   a schedule that sets out the fair value of the transferred financial assets, the associated liabilities and the net position when the counterparty to the associated liabilities has recourse only to the transferred assets.

BC65H   The Board concluded that these disclosures would provide information that is useful in assessing the extent to which the economic benefits generated by assets of an entity cannot be used in an unrestricted manner, as is implied when assets are recognised in an entity's statement of financial position. In addition, the disclosures would provide information about liabilities that will be settled entirely from the proceeds received from the transferred assets, and thus identify liabilities for which the counterparties do not have claims on the assets of the entity in general. For those assets for which the underlying cash flows are committed to be used to satisfy related liabilities, the Board noted that a schedule that sets out the fair value of the transferred financial assets, the associated liabilities and the net position (in addition to showing the cash flow relationship between those assets and liabilities) also provides a means of understanding the net exposure of an entity following a transfer transaction that fails derecognition.

Transferred financial assets that are derecognised in their entirety

BC65I   The Board was asked by users of financial statements, regulators and others to review the disclosure requirements for what are often described as 'off balance sheet' activities. Transfers of financial assets, particularly securitisation of financial assets, were identified as forming part of such activities.

BC65J   The Board concluded that when an entity retains continuing involvement in financial assets that it has derecognised, users of financial statements would benefit from information about the risks to which the entity remains exposed. Such information is relevant in assessing the amount, timing and uncertainty of the entity's future cash flows.

BC65K   The Board observed that IFRS 7 already requires certain disclosures by class of financial instrument or by type of risk. However, the IFRS requires the information at an aggregated level, so information specific to derecognition transactions is often not available. In response to requests from users and others the Board concluded that disclosures specific to derecognition transactions were necessary.

BC65L   The Board concluded that the disclosures should focus on the risk exposure of an entity, and should provide information about the timing of the return and the cash outflow that would or may be required to repurchase the derecognised financial assets in the future. The Board reasoned that a combination of disclosures about the strike price or repurchase price to repurchase assets, the fair value of its continuing involvement, the maximum exposure to loss and qualitative information about an entity's obligations to provide financial support are relevant in understanding an entity's exposure to risks.

BC65M   In addition, the Board concluded that information about an entity's gain or loss on derecognition and the timing of recognition of that gain or loss provides information about the proportion of an entity's profit or loss that arises from transferring financial assets in which the entity also retains continuing involvement. Such information is useful in assessing the extent to which an entity generates profits from transferring financial assets while retaining some form of continuing involvement and thus exposure to risk.

BC65N   The Board observed that the total amount of proceeds from transfer activity (that qualifies for derecognition) in a reporting period may not be evenly distributed throughout the reporting period (eg if a substantial proportion of the total amount of transfer activity takes place in the closing days of a reporting period). The Board decided that if transfer activity is concentrated around the end of reporting periods, disclosure of this fact provides an indication of whether transfer transactions are undertaken for the purpose of altering the appearance of the statement of financial position rather than for an ongoing commercial or financing purpose. In such cases, the amendments require disclosure of when the greatest transfer activity took place within that reporting period, the amount recognised from the transfer activity in that part of the reporting period, and the total amount of proceeds from transfer activity in that part of the reporting period.

Application of the disclosure requirements to a servicing contract

BC65O   Paragraphs 42A–42H of IFRS 7 require an entity to provide disclosures for all transferred financial assets that are not derecognised in their entirety and for any continuing involvement in a transferred asset that is derecognised in its entirety, existing at the reporting date, irrespective of when the related transfer transaction occurred.

BC65P   The Board received a request to clarify whether servicing contracts constitute continuing involvement for the purposes of applying the disclosure requirements in paragraphs 42E–42H of IFRS 7. The question raised was whether paragraph 42C(c) of IFRS 7 excludes servicing contracts from the scope of those disclosure requirements.

BC65Q   The Board observed that paragraph 42C(c) of IFRS 7 discusses arrangements whereby an entity retains the contractual rights to receive the cash flows of a financial asset but assumes a contractual obligation to pay the cash flows to one or more entities and the conditions in paragraph 3.2.5(a)–(c) of IFRS 9 are met; ie it is a 'pass-through arrangement'.[24] Paragraph 42C(c) of IFRS 7 confirms that the cash flows collected to be passed through are not themselves continuing involvement for the purposes of the transfer disclosure requirements. Consequently, the Board observed that the servicer's obligation to pass through to one or more entities the cash flows that it collects from a transferred financial asset is not in itself continuing involvement for the purposes of the disclosure requirements, because the activity of passing through cash flows does not in itself constitute an interest in the future performance of the transferred financial asset. The Board observed, however, that a servicing contract is generally continuing involvement for the purposes of the transfer disclosure requirements because, in most cases, the servicer has an interest in the future performance of the transferred financial assets as a result of that contract. That would be the case if the amount and/or timing of the servicing fee depended on the amount and/or timing of the cash flows collected from the transferred financial asset. This would be true irrespective of how the servicer receives its servicing fee; ie whether the servicer retains a portion of the cash flows collected from the transferred financial asset as its fee or it passes through all of the cash flows collected and receives its fee separately from the transferee or another entity.

BC65R   On the basis of these observations, the Board noted that paragraphs 42C and B30 of IFRS 7 are considered to determine whether a servicing contract gives rise to continuing involvement for the purposes of the transfer disclosure requirements. The Board decided to add guidance to the Application Guidance of IFRS 7 to clarify how the guidance in paragraph 42C of IFRS 7 is applied to servicing contracts.

BC65S   During its discussions on this issue, the Board noted that for the purpose of applying the disclosure requirements in paragraphs 42E–42H of IFRS 7, continuing involvement as described in paragraph 42C of IFRS 7 has a different meaning from that used in paragraphs 3.2.6(c)(ii) and 3.2.16 of IFRS 9.[25] The Board considered, but decided against, making a clarification in respect of this point because it thought that this difference was already clear from the description of continuing involvement in the two IFRSs.

Effective date and transition (paragraphs 43–44A)

BC66   The Board is committed to maintaining a 'stable platform' of substantially unchanged Standards for annual periods beginning on or before 1 January 2005, when many entities will adopt IFRSs for the first time. In addition, some preparers will need time to make the system changes necessary to comply with the IFRS. Therefore, the Board decided that the effective date of IFRS 7

---

24   If IFRS 9 has not been applied early, the equivalent reference is paragraph 19(a)–(c) of IAS 39.

25   If IFRS 9 has not been applied early, the equivalent references are paragraphs 20(c)(ii) and 30 of IAS 39.

should be annual periods beginning on or after 1 January 2007, with earlier application encouraged.

BC67   The Board noted that entities that apply IFRS 7 only when it becomes mandatory will have sufficient time to prepare comparative information. This conclusion does not apply to entities that apply IFRS 7 early. In particular, the time would be extremely short for those entities that would like to apply IFRS 7 when they first adopt IFRSs in 2005, to avoid changing from local GAAP to IAS 32 and IAS 30 when they adopt IFRSs and then changing again to IFRS 7 only one or two years later. Therefore, the Board gave an exemption from providing comparative disclosure in the first year of application of IFRS 7 to any entity that both (a) is a first-time adopter of IFRSs and (b) applies IFRS 7 before 1 January 2006. The Board noted that such an exemption for first-time adopters exists in IAS 32 and IFRS 4 and that the reasons for providing the exemption apply equally to IFRS 7.

BC68   The Board also considered whether it should provide an exemption from presenting all or some of the comparative information to encourage early adoption of IFRS 7 by entities that already apply IFRSs.

BC69   The Board noted that IFRS 7 contains two types of disclosures: accounting disclosures (in paragraphs 7–30) that are based on requirements previously in IAS 32 and new risk disclosures (in paragraphs 31–42). The Board concluded that existing users of IFRSs already will have complied with the requirements of IAS 32 and will not encounter difficulty in providing comparative information for the accounting disclosures.

BC70   The Board noted that most of the risk disclosures, in particular those about market risk, are based on information collected at the end of the reporting period. The Board concluded that although IFRS 7 was published in August 2005, it will still be possible for entities to collect the information that they require to comply with IFRS 7 for accounting periods beginning in 2005. However, it would not always be possible to collect the information needed to provide comparative information about accounting periods that began in 2004. As a result, the Board decided that entities that apply IFRS 7 for accounting periods beginning in 2005 (ie before 1 January 2006) need not present comparative information about the risk disclosures.

BC71   The Board also noted that comparative disclosures about risk are less relevant because these disclosures are intended to have predictive value. As a result information about risk loses relevance more quickly than other types of disclosure, and any disclosures required by previous GAAP are unlikely to be comparable with those required by IFRS 7. Accordingly, the Board decided that an entity that is not a first-time adopter and applies IFRS 7 for annual periods beginning before 1 January 2006 need not present comparative disclosures about the nature and extent of risks arising from financial instruments. In reaching this conclusion, the Board noted that the advantages of encouraging more entities to apply IFRS 7 early outweighed the disadvantage of the reduced information provided.

BC72   The Board considered and rejected arguments that it should extend the exemption:

(a) from providing comparative information to first-time adopters that applied IFRS 7 before 1 January 2007 (rather than only those that applied IFRS 7 before 1 January 2006). The Board concluded that an entity that intends to adopt IFRSs for the first time on or after 1 January 2006 will have sufficient time to collect information for its accounting period beginning on or after 1 January 2005 and, thus, should not have difficulty in providing the comparative disclosures for accounting periods beginning on or after 1 January 2006.

(b) from providing comparative disclosures about the significance of financial instruments to all entities adopting the IFRS for annual periods beginning before 1 January 2006 (rather than only to first-time adopters). The Board concluded that only first-time adopters warranted special relief so that they would be able to adopt IFRS 7 early without first having to adopt IAS 32 and IAS 30 for only one period. Entities that are not first-time adopters already apply IAS 32 and IAS 30 and have no particular need to adopt IFRS 7 before 1 January 2007.

(c) from providing comparative disclosures about risk to periods beginning before 1 January 2007 (rather than 2006). The Board noted that entities adopting IFRS 7 after 1 January 2006 would have a full calendar year to prepare after the publication of the IFRS.

BC72A   *Annual Improvements to IFRSs 2012–2014 Cycle*, issued in September 2014, amended paragraph B30 and added paragraph B30A of IFRS 7. The Board considered whether the amendment should apply to any period presented that begins before the annual period for which the entity first applies the amendment. The Board noted that paragraph 42E(b) of IFRS 7 requires disclosure of the fair value of the assets and liabilities that represent the entity's continuing involvement in the derecognised financial assets. Application of the amendment to such a period might therefore require an entity to determine the fair value as at the end of the period for a servicing asset or servicing liability, which the entity might not have previously determined. It might be impracticable for an entity to determine the fair value of such a servicing asset or servicing liability without using hindsight. The Board also noted that paragraph 44M of IFRS 7 provides transition relief by which the entity need not apply the transfer disclosure requirements to comparative periods. Consequently, to avoid the risk of hindsight being applied, the Board decided to require the application of the amendment only to annual periods beginning on or after the beginning of the annual period for which the amendment is applied for the first time. Furthermore, for the same reason, the Board observed that those transition provisions should be available to first-time adopters. The Board has characterised the transition provisions in paragraph 44AA of IFRS 7 as retrospective despite this relief, because entities are required to look back to past derecognition events to determine whether a servicing asset or servicing liability needs to be disclosed.[26]

---

26 *Annual Improvements to IFRS Standards 2014–2016 Cycle*, issued in December 2016, amended IFRS 1 *First-time Adoption of International Financial Reporting Standards* by deleting the short-term exemption for first-time adopters (see paragraph BC99 of IFRS 1), because it was no longer applicable.

Applicability of the offsetting amendments to IFRS 7 to condensed interim financial statements (paragraph 44R)

BC72B   The Board was asked to clarify the applicability of the amendments to IFRS 7 *Disclosure–Offsetting Financial Assets and Financial Liabilities* (the 'amendments to IFRS 7 concerning offsetting'), issued in December 2011, to condensed interim financial statements. It was asked to clarify the meaning of the reference to 'interim periods within those annual periods', used in paragraph 44R of IFRS 7. There was uncertainty about whether the disclosures required by paragraphs 13A–13F and B40–B53 of IFRS 7 were required to be included in condensed interim financial statements prepared in accordance with IFRS and, if so, whether those disclosures should be presented in every set of condensed interim financial statements, or only in those interim financial statements presented in the first year in which the disclosure requirements are effective or for which disclosure would be required under the principles in IAS 34 *Interim Financial Reporting*.

BC72C   The Board noted that IAS 34 was not consequentially amended upon issue of the amendments to IFRS 7 concerning offsetting and that when the Board intends to require an entity to provide a disclosure in condensed interim financial statements in all circumstances it amends IAS 34. Consequently, the Board decided to amend paragraph 44R of IFRS 7 within the *Annual Improvements to IFRSs 2012–2014 Cycle* in order to clarify that the additional disclosure required by the amendments to IFRS 7 concerning offsetting is not specifically required for all interim periods. However, when considering this amendment, the Board noted that the additional disclosure is required to be given in condensed interim financial statements prepared in accordance with IAS 34 when its inclusion would be required in accordance with the general requirements of that IFRS. IAS 34 requires the disclosure of information in condensed interim financial statements when its omission would make the condensed interim financial statements misleading. The Board noted that in accordance with paragraph 15 of IAS 34 "an entity shall include in its interim financial report an explanation of events and transactions that are significant to an understanding of the changes in financial position and performance of the entity since the end of the last annual reporting period". The Board further noted that in accordance with paragraph 25 of IAS 34: "The overriding goal is to ensure that an interim financial report includes all information that is relevant to understanding an entity's financial position and performance during the interim period".

Summary of main changes from the Exposure Draft

BC73   The main changes to the proposals in ED 7 are:

(a)   ED 7 proposed disclosure of the amount of change in the fair value of a financial liability designated as at fair value through profit or loss that is not attributable to changes in a benchmark interest rate as a proxy for the amount of change in fair value attributable to changes in the instrument's credit risk. The IFRS permits entities to determine the amount of change in fair value attributable to changes in the instrument's credit risk using an alternative method if the entity believes that its alternative method gives more faithful representation. The proxy disclosure has been amended to be the amount of change in fair value that is not attributable to changes in market conditions that give rise to market risk. As a result, entities may exclude factors other than a change in a benchmark interest rate when calculating the proxy.

(b)   a requirement has been added for disclosures about the difference between the transaction price at initial recognition (used as fair value in accordance with paragraph B5.4.8[27] of IFRS 9) and the results of a valuation technique that will be used for subsequent measurement.

(c)   no disclosure is required of the fair value of collateral pledged as security and other credit enhancements as was proposed in ED 7.

(d)   the sensitivity analysis requirements have been clarified.

(e)   the exemption from presenting comparatives has been widened.

(f)   the capital disclosures are a stand-alone amendment to IAS 1, rather than part of the IFRS. No disclosure is required of whether the entity has complied with capital targets set by management and of the consequences of any non-compliance with those targets.

(g)   the amendments to IFRS 4 related to IFRS 7 have been modified to reduce systems changes for insurers.

---

27 IFRS 13, issued in May 2011, contains the requirements for measuring fair value. As a consequence of issuing that IFRS, paragraph B5.4.8 of IFRS 9 was deleted. However, in 2014 the requirements for amortised cost measurement and impairment were added to IFRS 9 as Sections 5.4 and 5.5. Paragraph B5.4.8 of IFRS 9 now contains requirements related to amortised cost measurement.

Appendix
Amendments to Basis for Conclusions on other IFRSs

This appendix contains amendments to the Basis for Conclusions on other IFRSs that are necessary in order to ensure consistency with IFRS 7. In the amended paragraphs, new text is underlined and deleted text is struck through.

* * * * * *

The amendments contained in this appendix when IFRS 7 was issued in 2005 have been incorporated into the text of the Basis of Conclusions on IFRS 4 and on IASs 32, 39 and 41 as issued at 18 August 2005.

IASB documents published to accompany

IFRS 8

Operating Segments

The text of the unaccompanied standard, IFRS 8, is contained in Part A of this edition. Its effective date when issued was 1 January 2009. The text of the Accompanying Guidance on IFRS 8 is contained in Part B of this edition. This part presents the following documents:

BASIS FOR CONCLUSIONS

APPENDICES TO THE BASIS FOR CONCLUSIONS

A Background information and basis for conclusions of the US Financial Accounting Standards Board on SFAS 131

B Amendments to the Basis for Conclusions on other IFRSs

DISSENTING OPINIONS

Contents

Basis for Conclusions on
IFRS 8 *Operating Segments*

This Basis for Conclusions and its appendices accompany, but are not part of, IFRS 8.

Introduction

BC1 This Basis for Conclusions summarises the International Accounting Standards Board's considerations in reaching the conclusions in IFRS 8 *Operating Segments*. Individual Board members gave greater weight to some factors than to others.

BC2 In September 2002 the Board decided to add a short-term convergence project to its active agenda. The project is being conducted jointly with the United States standard-setter, the Financial Accounting Standards Board (FASB). The objective of the project is to reduce differences between IFRSs and US generally accepted accounting principles (US GAAP) that are capable of resolution in a relatively short time and can be addressed outside major projects.

BC3 As part of the project, the Board identified differences between IAS 14 *Segment Reporting* and the US standard SFAS 131 *Disclosures about Segments of an Enterprise and Related Information*, reviewed academic research findings on segment reporting, in particular relating to the implementation of SFAS 131, and had meetings with users of financial statements.

Differences between IAS 14 and SFAS 131

BC4 The requirements of SFAS 131 are based on the way that management regards an entity, focusing on information about the components of the business that management uses to make decisions about operating matters. In contrast, IAS 14 requires the disaggregation of the entity's financial statements into segments based on related products and services, and on geographical areas.

BC5 The requirements of SFAS 14 *Financial Reporting for Segments of a Business Enterprise*, the predecessor to SFAS 131, were similar to those of IAS 14. In particular, both standards required the accounting policies underlying the disaggregated information to be the same as those underlying the entity information, since segment information was regarded as a disaggregation of the entity information. The approach to segment disclosures in SFAS 14 was criticised for not providing information about segments based on the structure of an entity's internal organisation that could enhance a user's ability to predict actions or reactions of management that could significantly affect the entity's future cash flow prospects.

Academic research findings

BC6 Most of the academic research findings on segment reporting indicated that application of SFAS 131 resulted in more useful information than its predecessor, SFAS 14. According to the research, the management approach of SFAS 131:

(a)   increased the number of reported segments and provided more information;

(b)   enabled users to see an entity through the eyes of management;

(c)   enabled an entity to provide timely segment information for external interim reporting with relatively low incremental cost;

(d)   enhanced consistency with the management discussion and analysis or other annual report disclosures; and

(e)   provided various measures of segment performance.

Meetings with users

BC7   The Board discussed segment reporting at several meetings with users of financial statements. Most of the users supported the management approach of SFAS 131 for the reasons mentioned in the previous paragraph. In particular, they supported an approach that would enable more segment information to be provided in interim financial reports.

BC8   Consequently the Board decided to adopt the US approach and published its proposals as an exposure draft in ED 8 *Operating Segments* in January 2006. The deadline for comments was 19 May 2006. The Board received 182 comment letters. After reviewing the responses, the Board issued IFRS 8 in November 2006.

Adoption of management approach

BC9   In the Basis for Conclusions on ED 8, the Board noted that the primary benefits of adopting the management approach in SFAS 131 are that:

(a)   entities will report segments that correspond to internal management reports;

(b)   entities will report segment information that will be more consistent with other parts of their annual reports;

(c)   some entities will report more segments; and

(d)   entities will report more segment information in interim financial reports.

In addition, the Board noted that the proposed IFRS would reduce the cost of providing disaggregated information for many entities because it uses segment information that is generated for management's use.

BC10   Most respondents to the Exposure Draft supported the adoption of the management approach. They considered the management approach appropriate, and superior to the approach of IAS 14. These respondents observed that the management approach for segment reporting allows users to review an entity's operations from the same perspective as management. They noted that although the IAS 14 approach would enhance comparability by requiring entities to report segment information that is consistent with

IFRSs, the disclosures will not necessarily correspond to segment information that is reported to management and is used for making decisions.

BC11 Other respondents disagreed with the management approach. They argued that convergence should instead be achieved by changing SFAS 131 to IAS 14. In their view the latter approach is superior because it provides comparability of information across entities by defining measures of segment revenue, segment expense, segment result, segment assets and segment liabilities.

BC12 Yet other respondents agreed with the management approach for the identification of segment assets, but disagreed with the management approach for the measurement of the various segment disclosures. In particular, they doubted whether the publication of internally reported amounts would generate significant benefit for investors if those amounts differ from IFRS amounts.

BC13 The Board noted that if IFRS amounts could be prepared reliably and on a timely basis for segments identified using the management approach, that approach would provide the most useful information. However, the Board observed that IFRS amounts for segments cannot always be prepared on a sufficiently timely basis for interim reporting.

BC14 The Board also noted the requirements in the IFRS for an explanation of the measurements of segment profit or loss and segment assets and for reconciliations of the segment amounts to the amounts recognised in the entity's financial statements. The Board was satisfied that users would be able to understand and judge appropriately the basis on which the segment amounts were determined.

BC15 The Board concluded that the advantages of the management approach, in particular the ability of entities to prepare segment information on a sufficiently timely basis for inclusion in interim financial reports, outweighed any disadvantages arising from the potential for segments to be reported in accordance with non-IFRS accounting policies.

BC16 Given the Board's support for the principles of the management approach required by SFAS 131 and the objectives of the short-term convergence project, the Board decided that the simplest and most complete way to achieve convergence would be to use the text of SFAS 131 for the IFRS.

BC17 The FASB's thinking behind the management approach of SFAS 131 is presented in its Background Information and Basis for Conclusions. Because the Board has adopted that approach, the FASB's Background Information and Basis for Conclusions are reproduced in Appendix A to this Basis for Conclusions. The few differences from SFAS 131 that the Board has included in the IFRS are noted in paragraph BC60 below.

Scope of the standard

BC18   In ED 8, the Board proposed extending the scope of the IFRS to all entities that have public accountability rather than just entities whose securities are publicly traded. The Board noted that it was premature to adopt the proposed definition of public accountability that is being considered in a separate Board project on small and medium-sized entities (SMEs). However, the Board decided that the scope of the standard should be extended to include entities that hold assets in a fiduciary capacity for a broad group of outsiders. The Board concluded that the SMEs project is the most appropriate context in which to decide whether to extend the scope of the requirements on segment reporting to other entities.

BC19   Some respondents to ED 8 commented that the scope of the IFRS should not be extended until the Board has reached a conclusion on the definitions of 'fiduciary capacity' and 'public accountability' in the SMEs project. They argued that the terms needed clarification and definition.

BC20   The Board accepted these concerns and decided that the IFRS should not apply to entities that hold assets in a fiduciary capacity. However, the Board decided that publicly accountable entities should be within the scope of the IFRS, and that a future amendment of the scope of the IFRS should be proposed to include publicly accountable entities once the definition has been properly developed in the SMEs project. The proposed amendment will therefore be exposed at the same time as the exposure draft of the proposed IFRS for SMEs.

BC21   A number of respondents to ED 8 suggested that the scope exemption of paragraph 6 of IAS 14 should be included in the IFRS. This paragraph provided an exemption from segment reporting in the separate financial statements of the parent when a financial report contains both consolidated financial statements and the parent's separate financial statements. The Board agreed that on practical grounds such an exemption was appropriate.

BC22   In ED 8 the Board proposed that if an entity not required to apply the IFRS chooses to disclose segment information in financial statements that comply with IFRSs, that entity would be required to comply with the requirements of the IFRS. Respondents commented that this was unnecessarily restrictive. For example, they observed that requiring full compliance with the IFRS would prevent an entity outside its scope from voluntarily disclosing sales information for segments without also disclosing segment profit or loss. The Board concluded that an entity should be able to provide segment information on a voluntary basis without triggering the need to comply fully with the IFRS, so long as the disclosure is not referred to as segment information.

BC23　A respondent to ED 8 asked for clarification on whether the scope of the proposed IFRS included the consolidated financial statements of a group whose parent has no listed financial instruments, but includes a listed minority interest[1] or a subsidiary with listed debt. The Board decided that such consolidated financial statements should not be included in the scope and that the scope should be clarified accordingly. The Board also noted that the same clarification should be made to the scope of IAS 33 *Earnings per Share*.

Aspects of the management approach

Specific measurement requirements for some items

BC24　In ED 8, the Board invited comments on whether the proposed IFRS should depart from the management approach in SFAS 131 by setting measurement requirements for specified items. Some respondents to ED 8 supported an approach that would define the measurement of the key terms such as segment revenues, segment expenses, segment results, segment assets and segment liabilities in order to enhance comparability between reporting entities. Other respondents disagreed with any departure from SFAS 131 on the grounds that defined measurements for specified items would eliminate the major benefits of the management approach.

BC25　The IFRS requires the entity to explain the measurements of segment profit or loss and segment assets and liabilities and to provide reconciliations of the total segment amounts to the amounts recognised in the entity's financial statements. The Board believes that such reconciliations will enable users to understand and judge the basis on which the segment amounts were determined. The Board also noted that to define the measurement of such amounts would be a departure from the requirements of SFAS 131 that would involve additional time and cost for entities and would be inconsistent with the management perspective on segment information.

BC26　Therefore, the Board decided not to require defined measures of segment revenues, segment expenses, segment result, segment assets and segment liabilities.

Matrix form of organisations

BC27　In ED 8 the Board proposed that when more than one set of segments could be identified, for example when entities use a matrix form of organisation, the components based on products and services should be the basis for the operating segments. Some respondents noted that matrix organisational structures are commonly used for large complex organisations and that mandating the use of components based on products and services was inconsistent with the management approach. The Board agreed with this

---

1　In January 2008 the IASB issued an amended IAS 27 *Consolidated and Separate Financial Statements*, which amended 'minority interest' to 'non-controlling interests'. The consolidation requirements in IAS 27 were superseded by IFRS 10 *Consolidated Financial Statements* issued in May 2011. The term 'non-controlling interests' and the requirements for non-controlling interests were not changed.

view. Accordingly, the IFRS requires the identification of operating segments to be made by reference to the core principle of the IFRS.

Quantitative thresholds

BC28   In ED 8 the Board proposed quantitative thresholds for identifying reportable segments. Some respondents argued that such requirements represent adoption of a rule-based, rather than a principle-based, approach. In addition, some respondents commented that the inclusion of a 10 per cent threshold could create a precedent for determining materiality in other areas.

BC29   The Board considered an approach whereby any material operating segment would be required to be disclosed separately. However, the Board was concerned that there might be uncertainty about the meaning of materiality in relation to disclosure. Furthermore, such a requirement would be a significant change from the wording of SFAS 131. Thus, the Board was concerned that the change would be from an easily understandable and familiar set of words that converges with SFAS 131 to a potentially confusing principle. Accordingly, the Board decided to retain the quantitative thresholds.

Interaction of aggregation criteria and quantitative thresholds

BC30   One respondent commented that the ranking of the aggregation criteria for operating segments and the quantitative thresholds for determining reportable segments was unclear in ED 8. However, the flow chart in paragraph IG7 of the implementation guidance indicates that the aggregation criteria take precedence over the quantitative thresholds. The Board also noted that the wording in SFAS 131 was clear because the paragraph on aggregation refers to aggregation into a 'single operating segment'. The quantitative thresholds then determine which operating segments are reportable segments. The term 'operating' has been inserted in paragraph 12 of the IFRS.

Aggregation of operating segments

BC30A   The Board received a request to consider including a disclosure in paragraph 22 that would require a description of the operating segments that have been aggregated and the economic indicators that have been assessed to decide whether operating segments have 'similar economic characteristics' in accordance with paragraph 12. The Board observed that:

(a)   paragraph 12 does not elaborate upon the meaning of "similar economic characteristics" except to say that operating segments that share similar economic characteristics would be expected to exhibit a similar long term financial performance. In addition, determining whether operating segments have similar economic characteristics requires the use of judgement.

(b)   paragraph 22(a) currently contains a requirement to disclose the factors used to identify the entity's reportable segments, including the basis of organisation, and suggests, as an example, disclosing whether operating segments have been aggregated. However, there is no explicit, or indeed apparent, requirement in paragraph 22(a) to disclose the aggregation of operating segments.

BC30B   The Board noted that the disclosure is complementary to the information required by paragraph 22(a). The Board thinks that including a disclosure requirement in paragraph 22 would provide users of financial statements with an understanding of the judgements made by management on how (and the reasons why) operating segments have been aggregated. The judgements made by management may relate to the application of any of the criteria in paragraph 12, which states that two or more operating segments may be aggregated into a single operating segment if aggregation is consistent with the core principle of IFRS 8, the segments have similar economic characteristics and the segments are similarly based on the factors listed in paragraph 12(a)–(e). Consequently, the Board added paragraph 22(aa) to complement the disclosure required in paragraph 22(a). The requirements in paragraph 22(b) remain the same and its wording has not been modified.

Inclusion of US guidance

BC31   The Board discussed the extent to which the IFRS should address the practical problems that have arisen from applying SFAS 131 in the US. The Board considered the FASB *Q&A 131 Segment Information: Guidance on Applying Statement 131* and Emerging Issues Task Force (EITF) 04-10 *Determining Whether to Aggregate Operating Segments that do not Meet the Quantitative Threshold.*

BC32   EITF 04-10 addresses the issue of whether to aggregate operating segments that do not meet the quantitative thresholds. It requires quantitative thresholds to be aggregated only if aggregation is consistent with the objective and core principles of SFAS 131, the segments have similar economic characteristics, and the segments share a majority of the aggregation criteria listed in paragraph 17(a)–(e) of SFAS 131. The Board agreed with the approach adopted in EITF 04-10 and concluded that the same requirement should be included in the IFRS.

BC33   FASB *Q&A 131 — Segment Information: Guidance on Applying Statement 131* is an implementation guide that provides the views of the FASB staff on certain questions on SFAS 131. Because it was not issued by the FASB itself, the Board decided not to include this material in the IFRS.

Information about segment assets

BC34   Several respondents noted that, whilst a measure of segment profit or loss can be expected in every entity's internal reporting, a measure of segment assets is not always available, particularly in service industries or other industries with low utilisation of physical assets. Respondents suggested that in such circumstances a measure of segment assets should be disclosed only if those amounts were regularly provided to the chief operating decision maker.

BC35   ~~The Board noted that requiring disclosure of a measure of segment assets only when such a measure is reviewed by the chief operating decision maker would create divergence from SFAS 131. The Board also supported a minimum disclosure of segment profit or loss and segment assets. The Board therefore concluded that measures of segment profit or loss and total segment assets should be disclosed for all segments regardless of whether those measures are reviewed by the chief operating decision maker.[2]~~

BC35A   After IFRS 8 was issued, the Board was informed that the reasons originally set out in paragraph BC35 contradict long-standing interpretations published in the US for the application of SFAS 131 and create an unintended difference from practice in the US under SFAS 131. After reconsideration and discussion of the interaction between the disclosure and measurement requirements in the IFRS (paragraphs 23 and 25), the Board concluded that those reasons no longer reflected its thinking. Therefore, the Board amended paragraph 23 by *Improvements to IFRSs* issued in April 2009 to clarify that a measure of segment assets should be disclosed only if that amount is regularly provided to the chief operating decision maker.

Reconciliation of segment assets

BC35B   The Board received a request to clarify in paragraph 28(c) that a reconciliation of the total of the reportable segments' assets to the entity's assets should only be disclosed if that amount is regularly provided to the chief operating decision maker. This clarification would make this paragraph consistent with paragraphs 23 and 28(d). The Board agreed with the request and decided to modify paragraph 28(c) to achieve this.

Information about segment liabilities

BC36   ED 8 did not propose disclosure of segment liabilities because there is no such requirement in SFAS 131. The reasons for this are set out in paragraph 96 of the Basis for Conclusions on SFAS 131, included as Appendix A to this Basis for Conclusions.

BC37   Some respondents proposed adding a requirement for each entity to disclose information about segment liabilities, if such information is regularly provided to the chief operating decision maker. They argued that information about segment liabilities would be helpful to users. Other respondents favoured information about net segment assets rather than gross segment assets.

BC38   The Board noted that if segment liabilities are considered in assessing the performance of, and allocating resources to, the segments of an entity, such disclosure would be consistent with the management approach. The Board also noted support for this disclosure from some commentators, particularly users of financial statements. Accordingly the Board decided to require disclosure of a measure of segment liabilities if those amounts are regularly

---

2   Paragraph BC35 was deleted and paragraph BC35A added as a consequence of *Improvements to IFRSs* issued in April 2009.

provided to the chief operating decision maker notwithstanding that such a requirement would create divergence from SFAS 131.

Level of reconciliations

BC39 ED 8 proposed that an entity should provide reconciliations of total reportable segment amounts for specified items to amounts the entity recognised in accordance with IFRSs. It did not propose such reconciliations for individual reportable segments.

BC40 Several respondents expressed concern about the level of detail provided by the proposed reconciliations. They argued that if the IFRS allows segment information to be measured on the basis of management information, it should require reconciliations for individual reportable segments between the segment amounts and the equivalent amounts measured in accordance with an entity's IFRS accounting policies. They added that reconciling only total reportable segment amounts to amounts presented in the financial statements does not provide useful information.

BC41 Other respondents supported the proposed reconciliations on the grounds that more detailed reconciliations would not be more understandable to users and might be confusing. They believed that the additional costs to reporting entities were not justified.

BC42 The Board noted that a requirement to provide reconciliations at the individual reportable segment level would effectively lead to two complete segment reports—one according to internal measures and the other according to IFRSs. The Board concluded that the cost of providing two sets of segment information would outweigh the benefits.

Lack of a competitive harm exemption

BC43 The Board discussed whether entities should be exempt from aspects of the IFRS if disclosure could cause competitive damage or erosion of shareholder value. The Board considered an alternative approach whereby entities could be required to provide reasons for non-disclosure on a 'comply or explain' basis.

BC44 The Board concluded that a 'competitive harm' exemption would be inappropriate because it would provide a means for broad non-compliance with the IFRS. The Board noted that entities would be unlikely to suffer competitive harm from the required disclosures since most competitors have sources of detailed information about an entity other than its financial statements.

BC45 Respondents also commented that the requirements of the IFRS would place small listed companies at a disadvantage to non-listed companies, which are outside the scope of the IFRS. The Board noted that the relative advantage/disadvantage of an entity being publicly listed is not a matter for the Board to consider.

Adoption of the term 'impracticable'

BC46 Some respondents to ED 8 expressed concern that entities were to be allowed not to give entity-wide disclosures about products and services and geographical areas if '... the necessary information is not available and the cost to develop it would be excessive.' They argued that the test to be applied for non-disclosure should be that of impracticability as defined in IAS 1 *Presentation of Financial Statements.*

BC47 The Board noted that the wording in ED 8 ensures convergence with SFAS 131. Using the term 'impracticable' as defined in IAS 1 would change the requirement and create divergence from SFAS 131. Therefore, the Board decided to retain the wording of ED 8.

Entity-wide disclosures

Geographical information

BC48 The IFRS requires an entity to disclose geographical information about non-current assets, excluding specified items. The Board considered comments made by some respondents who advocated country-by-country disclosure, others who requested specific items of geographical information to be disclosed, and some who expressed reservations with the proposed requirement relating to disclosure of country of domicile.

BC49 A coalition of over 300 organisations from more than 50 countries known as the Publish What You Pay campaign requested that the scope of the IFRS should be extended to require additional disclosure on a country-by-country basis. The objective of such additional disclosure would be to promote greater transparency in the management of amounts paid by the oil, gas and mining industries to governments in developing or transitional countries that are resource-rich. The view of these campaigners was that publication of specific payments made by those companies to governments is in the interest of all users of financial statements.

BC50 Because the IFRS is being developed in a short-term convergence project to converge with SFAS 131, the Board decided that issues raised by the Publish What You Pay campaign relating to country-by-country disclosures should not be addressed in the IFRS. The Board was of the view that such issues merit further discussion with bodies that are currently engaged in similar issues, for example the United Nations, International Public Sector Accounting Standards Board, International Monetary Fund, World Bank, regional development banks and Financial Stability Forum.

Exemption from entity-wide disclosures

BC51 Several respondents suggested different geographical disclosures from those proposed in ED 8. For example, some preferred disclosures by geographical areas rather than by individual country. Others favoured geographical disclosure of profit or loss as well as non-current assets. Several respondents expressed the view that disclosure of total assets would be more relevant than non-current assets. Some took the view that disclosures should be made of both current and non-current assets. Other respondents recommended that financial assets should be disclosed as well as non-current assets. Some respondents expressed the view that disclosure of non-current assets should not be required if those amounts are not reviewed by the chief operating decision maker.

BC52 In developing ED 8, the Board decided to adopt the requirements in SFAS 131. Paragraphs 104–107 of the Basis for Conclusions on SFAS 131 provide the rationale for the geographical disclosures required.

BC53 None of the suggested alternative disclosures was broadly supported by the user responses. The Board noted that entities that wish to give additional information are free to do so. The Board therefore concluded that the disclosure requirement taken from SFAS 131 should not be changed.

Country of domicile

BC54 Some respondents asserted that disclosures relating to the country of domicile were inappropriate for many entities. They expressed the view that such information would be relevant when a large proportion of an entity's business is carried out in its country of domicile. They noted, however, that in many circumstances the country of domicile represents a small proportion of the entity's business and in these cases the information required would not be relevant. In addition, they argued that SFAS 131 had been designed for entities in the US, for whom the 'country of domicile' is in itself a significant geographical area. These respondents suggested that disclosures should instead be required about the country of principal activities.

BC55 The IFRS requires disclosures for any country that is individually material. The Board noted that identifying the country of principal activities may be difficult and subjective. Accordingly, the Board decided not to require entities to identify the country of principal activities.

Subtotal for tangible non-current assets

BC56 Paragraphs 14 and 15 of the Basis for Conclusions on ED 8 highlighted a potential difference from SFAS 131. SFAS 131 requires disclosure of 'long-lived assets' excluding intangible assets, whereas ED 8 proposed disclosure of 'non-current assets' including intangible assets. The Board reconsidered whether, in the interest of convergence, the IFRS should require disclosure of the subtotal of tangible non-current assets.

BC57 The Board concluded that a separate disclosure of a subtotal of tangible non-current assets was unnecessary on the grounds that the incremental benefit does not justify such disclosure. However, the Board noted that entities that wish to provide that information are free to do so.

Information about major customers

BC58   ED 8 proposed that, in respect of the disclosures about major customers, a group of entities known to be under common control should be treated as a single customer. Some respondents noted that this could be difficult when entities are state-controlled. The Board noted that it was considering proposals to amend IAS 24 *Related Party Disclosures* with regard to state-controlled entities, and a consequential amendment to the IFRS on reporting segments might result from those proposals. In the meantime, the Board decided to require in the IFRS that a government (whether national, state, provincial, territorial, local or foreign) and entities known to the reporting entity to be controlled by that government should be treated as a single customer. This makes the requirements relating to government-controlled entities the same as those relating to privately controlled entities.

Interim financial information

BC59   The Board decided that the changes to IAS 34 *Interim Financial Reporting* proposed in ED 8 should be amended to clarify that interim disclosure of information on segment profit or loss items is required only if the specified amounts are included in the measure of segment profit or loss reviewed by the chief operating decision maker. The Board reached this conclusion because it noted that such disclosure is consistent with the management approach.

Differences from SFAS 131

BC60   In developing the IFRS, the Board included the following differences from SFAS 131:

(a)   The FASB *Guidance on Applying Statement 131* indicates that the FASB staff believe that 'long-lived assets', as that phrase is used in paragraph 38 of SFAS 131, implies hard assets that cannot be readily removed, which would appear to exclude intangibles. Non-current assets in the IFRS include intangibles (see paragraphs BC56 and BC57).

(b)   SFAS 131 does not require disclosure of a measure of segment liabilities. The IFRS requires disclosure of segment liabilities if such a measure is regularly provided to the chief operating decision maker (see paragraphs BC36–BC38).

(c)   SFAS 131 requires an entity with a matrix form of organisation to determine operating segments based on products and services. The IFRS requires such an entity to determine operating segments by reference to the core principle of the IFRS (see paragraph BC27).

Transitional provisions

BC61   Under its transitional provisions, SFAS 131 was not required to be applied to interim financial statements in the initial year of its application. However, in the second year of application, comparative information relating to interim periods in the initial year of application was required. The Basis for Conclusions on SFAS 131 explained that the reason for these transitional requirements was that some of the information that is required to be reported for interim periods is based on information reported in the most recent annual financial statements. Interim segment information would not be as meaningful without a full set of annual segment information to use as a comparison and to provide an understanding of the basis on which it is provided.

BC62   The Board did not agree with the transitional provision for interim financial statements in SFAS 131. The Board noted that the IFRS is not effective until 2009, giving entities adequate time to prepare. Furthermore, the Board was aware that some entities adopting IFRSs for the first time may wish to present comparative information in accordance with the IFRS rather than IAS 14.

CONTENTS

Background information and basis for conclusions of the US Financial Accounting Standards Board on SFAS 131

Introduction

41.   This appendix summarizes considerations that were deemed significant by Board members in reaching the conclusions in this Statement. It includes reasons for accepting certain approaches and rejecting others. Individual Board members gave greater weight to some factors than to others.

Background Information

42.   FASB Statement No. 14, *Financial Reporting for Segments of a Business Enterprise*, was issued in 1976. That Statement required that business enterprises report segment information on two bases: by industry and by geographic area. It also required disclosure of information about export sales and major customers.

43.   The Board concluded at the time it issued Statement 14 that information about components of an enterprise, the products and services that it offers, its foreign operations, and its major customers is useful for understanding and making decisions about the enterprise as a whole. Financial statement users observe that the evaluation of the prospects for future cash flows is the central element of investment and lending decisions. The evaluation of prospects requires assessment of the uncertainty that surrounds both the timing and the amount of the expected cash flows to the enterprise, which in turn affect potential cash flows to the investor or creditor. Users also observe that uncertainty results in part from factors related to the products and services an enterprise offers and the geographic areas in which it operates.

44.   In its 1993 position paper, *Financial Reporting in the 1990s and Beyond*, the Association for Investment Management and Research (AIMR) said:

> [Segment data] is vital, essential, fundamental, indispensable, and integral to the investment analysis process. Analysts need to know and understand how the various components of a multifaceted enterprise behave economically. One weak member of the group is analogous to a section of blight on a piece of fruit; it has the potential to spread rot over the entirety. Even in the absence of weakness, different segments will generate dissimilar streams of cash flows to which are attached disparate risks and which bring about unique values. Thus, without disaggregation, there is no sensible way to predict the overall amounts, timing, or risks of a complete enterprise's future cash flows. There is little dispute over the analytic usefulness of disaggregated financial data. [pages 59 and 60]

45.   Over the years, financial analysts consistently requested that financial statement data be disaggregated to a much greater degree than it is in current practice. Many analysts said that they found Statement 14 helpful but inadequate. In its 1993 position paper, the AIMR emphasized that:

> There is no disagreement among AIMR members that segment information is totally vital to their work. There also is general agreement among them that the current segment reporting standard, Financial Accounting Standard No. 14, is inadequate. Recent work by a subcommittee of the [Financial Accounting Policy Committee] has confirmed that a substantial majority of analysts seek and, when it is available, use quarterly segment data. [page 5]

46. The Canadian Institute of Chartered Accountants (CICA) published a Research Study, *Financial Reporting for Segments*, in August 1992. An FASB Research Report, *Reporting Disaggregated Information*, was published in February 1993. In March 1993, the FASB and the Accounting Standards Board (AcSB) of the CICA agreed to pursue their projects jointly.

47. In May 1993, the FASB and the AcSB jointly issued an Invitation to Comment, *Reporting Disaggregated Information by Business Enterprises*. That Invitation to Comment identified certain issues related to disclosure of information about segments, solicited comments on those issues, and asked readers to identify additional issues. The boards received 129 comment letters from U.S. and Canadian respondents.

48. In late 1993, the FASB and the AcSB formed the Disaggregated Disclosures Advisory Group to advise and otherwise support the two boards in their efforts to improve disaggregated disclosures. The members of the group included financial statement issuers, auditors, financial analysts, and academics from both the United States and Canada. In January 1994, the FASB and the AcSB began discussing changes to Statement 14 and *CICA Handbook* Section 1700, "Segmented Information." The two boards met with and otherwise actively solicited the views of analysts and preparers of financial statements about possible improvements to the current segment reporting requirements. FASB and AcSB members and staff also discussed disaggregated disclosures at meetings of several groups of analysts, including the AIMR's Financial Accounting Policy Committee.

49. In 1991, the AICPA formed the Special Committee on Financial Reporting (the Special Committee) to make recommendations to improve the relevance and usefulness of business reporting. The Special Committee, which comprised financial statement auditors and preparers, established focus groups of credit analysts and equity analysts to assist in formulating its recommendations. The Special Committee issued its report, *Improving Business Reporting—A Customer Focus*, in 1994. That report listed improvements in disclosures of business segment information as its first recommendation and included the following commentary:

> ... for users analyzing a company involved in diverse businesses, financial information about business segments often is as important as information about the company as a whole. Users suggest that standard setters assign the highest priority to improving segment reporting because of its importance to their work and the perceived problems with current reporting of segment information. [page 68]

50. The report of the Special Committee listed the following as among the most important improvements needed:

    (a)   Disclosure of segment information in interim financial reports

    (b)   Greater number of segments for some enterprises

    (c)   More information about segments

    (d)   Segmentation that corresponds to internal management reports

(e)   Consistency of segment information with other parts of an annual report.

Similar recommendations had been made in each of the last 20 years in evaluations of corporate reporting conducted by the AIMR.

51.   The two boards reached tentative conclusions about an approach to segment reporting that was substantially different from the approach in Statement 14 and Section 1700. Key characteristics of the new approach were that (a) information would be provided about segments of the enterprise that corresponded to the structure of the enterprise's internal organization, that is, about the divisions, departments, subsidiaries, or other internal units that the chief operating decision maker uses to make operating decisions and to assess an enterprise's performance, (b) specific amounts would be allocated to segments only if they were allocated in reports used by the chief operating decision maker for evaluation of segment performance, and (c) accounting policies used to produce the disaggregated information would be the same as those used in the reports used by the chief operating decision maker in allocating resources and assessing segment performance.

52.   In February 1995, the staffs of the FASB and the CICA distributed a paper, "Tentative Conclusions on Financial Reporting for Segments" (Tentative Conclusions), to selected securities analysts, the FASB Task Force on Consolidations and Related Matters, the Disaggregated Disclosures Advisory Group, the FASB's Emerging Issues Task Force, the Financial Accounting Standards Advisory Council, the AcSB's list of Associates,[3] and members of representative organizations that regularly work with the boards. The paper also was announced in FASB and CICA publications and was sent to anyone who requested a copy. Board and staff members discussed the Tentative Conclusions with various analyst and preparer groups. Approximately 80 comment letters were received from U.S. and Canadian respondents.

53.   In January 1996, the FASB and the AcSB issued virtually identical Exposure Drafts, *Reporting Disaggregated Information about a Business Enterprise*. The FASB received 221 comment letters and the AcSB received 73 comment letters in response to the Exposure Drafts. A field test of the proposals was conducted in March 1996. A public meeting was held in Toronto in October 1996 to discuss results and concerns with field test participants. Other interested parties attended a public meeting in Norwalk in October 1996 to discuss their concerns about the proposals in the Exposure Drafts. The FASB decided that it could reach an informed decision on the project without holding a public hearing.

54.   The FASB and the AcSB exchanged information during the course of redeliberating the proposals in their respective Exposure Drafts. AcSB members and CICA staff attended FASB meetings, and FASB members and staff attended AcSB meetings in late 1996 and in 1997 to discuss the issues raised by respondents. Both boards reached agreement on all of the

---

3   Associates are individuals and organizations with a particular interest in financial reporting issues that have volunteered to provide an outside reaction to AcSB positions at an early stage in the AcSB's deliberations.

substantive issues to achieve virtually identical standards for segment reporting in the United States and Canada. Members of the Segment Disclosures Advisory Group (formerly the Disaggregated Disclosures Advisory Group) discussed a draft of the standards section in March 1997.

55. The International Accounting Standards Committee (IASC) issued an Exposure Draft of a proposed International Accounting Standard that would replace International Accounting Standard IAS 14, *Reporting Financial Information by Segment*, in December 1995. Although many of its provisions are similar to those of the FASB and AcSB Exposure Drafts, the IASC's proposal is based on different objectives and is different from those Exposure Drafts. A member of the IASC Segments Steering Committee participated in FASB meetings during the redeliberations of the Exposure Draft, and members of the FASB participated in meetings of the IASC Segments Steering Committee. Many of the respondents to the Exposure Drafts encouraged the FASB and the AcSB to work closely with the IASC to achieve similar standards for segment reporting. The IASC expects to issue a standard on segment reporting later in 1997. Although there likely will be differences between the IASC's requirements for segment reporting and those of this Statement, the boards expect that it will be possible to prepare one set of segment information that complies with both the IASC requirements and those of this Statement.

56. This Statement addresses the following key issues:

(a) What is the appropriate basis for defining segments?

(b) What accounting principles and allocations should be used?

(c) What specific items of information should be reported?

(d) Should segment information be reported in condensed financial statements for interim periods?

Defining Operating Segments of an Enterprise

57. The Board concluded that the *industry approach* to segment disclosures in Statement 14 was not providing the information required by financial statement users and that disclosure of disaggregated information should be based on operating segments. This Statement defines an operating segment as a component of an enterprise (a) that engages in business activities from which it may earn revenues and incur expenses, (b) whose operating results are regularly reviewed by the enterprise's chief operating decision maker to make decisions about resources to be allocated to the segment and to assess its performance, and (c) for which discrete financial information is available.

58. The AIMR's 1993 position paper and the report of the AICPA Special Committee criticized Statement 14's industry segment approach to reporting segment information. The AIMR's position paper included the following:

> FAS 14 requires disclosure of line-of-business information classified by "industry segment." Its definition of segment is necessarily imprecise, recognizing that there are numerous practical problems in applying that definition to different business entities operating under disparate circumstances. That weakness in FAS 14 has been exploited by many enterprises to suit their own financial reporting

purposes. As a result, we have seen one of the ten largest firms in the country report all of its operations as being in a single, very broadly defined industry segment. [page 60]

The report of the Special Committee said that "[financial statement users] believe that many companies define industry segments too broadly for business reporting and thus report on too few industry segments" (page 69).

59.   The report of the AICPA Special Committee also said that "... the primary means to improving industry segment reporting should be to align business reporting with internal reporting" (page 69), and the AIMR's 1993 position paper recommended that:

> ... priority should be given to the production and dissemination of financial data that reflects and reports sensibly the operations of specific enterprises. If we could obtain reports showing the details of how an individual business firm is organized and managed, we would assume more responsibility for making meaningful comparisons of those data to the unlike data of other firms that conduct their business differently. [pages 60 and 61]

Almost all of the users and many other constituents who responded to the Exposure Draft or who met with Board and staff members agreed that defining segments based on the structure of an enterprise's internal organization would result in improved information. They said that not only would enterprises be likely to report more detailed information but knowledge of the structure of an enterprise's internal organization is valuable in itself because it highlights the risks and opportunities that management believes are important.

60.   Segments based on the structure of an enterprise's internal organization have at least three other significant advantages. First, an ability to see an enterprise "through the eyes of management" enhances a user's ability to predict actions or reactions of management that can significantly affect the enterprise's prospects for future cash flows. Second, because information about those segments is generated for management's use, the incremental cost of providing information for external reporting should be relatively low. Third, practice has demonstrated that the term *industry* is subjective. Segments based on an existing internal structure should be less subjective.

61.   The AIMR and other users have commented that segment information is more useful if it is consistent with explanatory information provided elsewhere in the annual report. They note that the business review section and the chairman's letter in an annual report frequently discuss the enterprise's operations on a basis different from that of the segment information in the notes to the financial statements and the management's discussion and analysis section, which is required by SEC rules to correspond to the segment information provided to comply with Statement 14. That appears to occur if the enterprise is not managed in a way that corresponds to the way it defines segments under the requirements of Statement 14. Segmentation based on the structure of an enterprise's internal organization should facilitate consistent discussion of segment financial results throughout an enterprise's annual report.

62. Some respondents to the Exposure Draft opposed the Board's approach for several reasons. Segments based on the structure of an enterprise's internal organization may not be comparable between enterprises that engage in similar activities and may not be comparable from year to year for an individual enterprise. In addition, an enterprise may not be organized based on products and services or geographic areas, and thus the enterprise's segments may not be susceptible to analysis using macroeconomic models. Finally, some asserted that because enterprises are organized strategically, the information that would be reported may be competitively harmful to the reporting enterprise.

63. The Board acknowledges that comparability of accounting information is important. The summary of principal conclusions in FASB Concepts Statement No. 2, *Qualitative Characteristics of Accounting Information*, says: "Comparability between enterprises and consistency in the application of methods over time increases the informational value of comparisons of relative economic opportunities or performance. The significance of information, especially quantitative information, depends to a great extent on the user's ability to relate it to some benchmark." However, Concepts Statement 2 also notes a danger:

> Improving comparability may destroy or weaken relevance or reliability if, to secure comparability between two measures, one of them has to be obtained by a method yielding less relevant or less reliable information. Historically, extreme examples of this have been provided in some European countries in which the use of standardized charts of accounts has been made mandatory in the interest of interfirm comparability but at the expense of relevance and often reliability as well. That kind of uniformity may even adversely affect comparability of information if it conceals real differences between enterprises. [paragraph 116]

64. The Board was concerned that segments defined using the approach in Statement 14 may appear to be more comparable between enterprises than they actually are. Statement 14 included the following:

> Information prepared in conformity with [Statement 14] may be of limited usefulness for comparing an industry segment of one enterprise with a similar industry segment of another enterprise (i.e., for interenterprise comparison). Interenterprise comparison of industry segments would require a fairly detailed prescription of the basis or bases of disaggregation to be followed by all enterprises, as well as specification of the basis of accounting for intersegment transfers and methods of allocating costs common to two or more segments. [paragraph 76]

65. Statement 14 explained why the Board chose not to develop a detailed prescription of the bases of disaggregation:

> ... differences among enterprises in the nature of their operations and in the extent to which components of the enterprise share common facilities, equipment, materials and supplies, or labor force make unworkable the prescription of highly detailed rules and procedures that must be followed by all enterprises. Moreover, ... differences in the accounting systems of business enterprises are a practical constraint on the degree of specificity with which standards of financial accounting and reporting for disaggregated information can be established. [paragraph 74]

Those same considerations persuaded the Board not to adopt more specific requirements in this Statement. Both relevance and comparability will not be achievable in all cases, and relevance should be the overriding concern.

66. The AICPA Special Committee, some respondents to the Exposure Draft, and other constituents recommended that the Board require that an enterprise use an alternative method of segmentation for external reporting if its internal organization is not based on differences in products and services or geography. Some specifically recommended adoption of the proposal in the IASC Exposure Draft that was commonly referred to as a "safety net." The IASC Exposure Draft approach to identifying primary and secondary operating segments calls for review of management's organization of segments, but both primary and secondary segments are required to be defined either on the basis of related products and services or on the basis of geography. That is, regardless of management's organization, segments must be grouped either by related products and services or by geographic areas, and one set must be presented as primary segments and the other as secondary segments.

67. The Board recognizes that an enterprise may not be divided into components with similar products and services or geographic areas for internal purposes and that some users of financial statements have expressed a desire for information organized on those bases. However, instead of an alternative method of segmentation, which would call for multiple sets of segment information in many circumstances, the Board chose to require disclosure of additional information about products and services and about geographic areas of operations for the enterprise as a whole if the basic segment disclosures do not provide it.

68. One reason for not prescribing segmentation along bases of only related products and services or geography is that it is difficult to define clearly the circumstances in which an alternative method that differs from the management approach would be applied consistently. An enterprise with a relatively narrow product line may not consider two products to be similar, while an enterprise with a broad product line may consider those same two products to be similar. For example, a highly diversified enterprise may consider all consumer products to be similar if it has other businesses such as financial services and road construction. However, an enterprise that sells only consumer products might consider razor blades to be different from toasters.

69. A second reason for rejecting that approach is that an alternative method of segmentation would increase the cost to some enterprises to prepare the information. A management approach to defining segments allows enterprises to present the information that they use internally and facilitates consistent descriptions of the components of an enterprise from one part of the annual report to another. An enterprise could be organized by its products and services, geography, a mixture of both products and services and geography, or other bases, such as customer type, and the segment information required by this Statement would be consistent with that method of organization. Furthermore, the enterprise-wide disclosures about products and services will provide information about the total revenues from related products and

services, and the enterprise-wide disclosures about geography will provide information about the revenues and assets of an enterprise both inside and outside its home country. If material, individual foreign country information also is required.

70. The Board recognizes that some enterprises organize their segments on more than one basis. Other enterprises may produce reports in which their activities are presented in a variety of ways. In those situations, reportable segments are to be determined based on a review of other factors to identify the enterprise's operating segments, including the nature of the activities of each component, the existence of managers responsible for them, and the information provided to the board of directors. In many enterprises, only one set of data is provided to the board of directors. That set of data generally is indicative of how management views the enterprise's activities.

Reportable Segments

71. The Board included a notion of reportable segments, a subset of operating segments, in this Statement by defining aggregation criteria and quantitative thresholds for determining which operating segments should be reported separately in the financial statements.

72. A so-called pure management approach to segment reporting might require that an enterprise report all of the information that is reviewed by the chief operating decision maker to make decisions about resource allocations and to assess the performance of the enterprise. However, that level of detail may not be useful to readers of external financial statements, and it also may be cumbersome for an enterprise to present. Therefore, this Statement uses a modified management approach that includes both aggregation criteria and quantitative thresholds for determining reportable operating segments. However, an enterprise need not aggregate similar segments, and it may present segments that fall below the quantitative thresholds.

Aggregation of Similar Operating Segments

73. The Board believes that separate reporting of segment information will not add significantly to an investor's understanding of an enterprise if its operating segments have characteristics so similar that they can be expected to have essentially the same future prospects. The Board concluded that although information about each segment may be available, in those circumstances the benefit would be insufficient to justify its disclosure. For example, a retail chain may have 10 stores that individually meet the definition of an operating segment, but each store may be essentially the same as the others.

74. Most respondents commented on the aggregation criteria in the Exposure Draft. Many said that the criteria were unreasonably strict, to the extent that nearly identical segments might not qualify for aggregation. Some respondents linked their concerns about competitive harm and too many segments directly to the aggregation criteria, indicating that a relaxation of the criteria would significantly reduce those concerns. To better convey its intent, the Board revised the wording of the aggregation criteria and the

introduction to them. However, the Board rejected recommendations that the criteria be indicators rather than tests and that the guidance require only the expectation of similar long-term performance of segments to justify aggregation because those changes might result in a level of aggregation that would cause a loss of potentially valuable information. For the same reason, the Board also rejected suggestions that segments need be similar in only a majority of the characteristics in paragraph 17 to justify aggregation. The Board recognizes that determining when two segments are sufficiently similar to justify aggregating them is difficult and subjective. However, the Board notes that one of the reasons that the information provided under Statement 14 did not satisfy financial statement users' needs is that segments with different characteristics in important areas were at times aggregated.

Quantitative Thresholds

75. In developing the Exposure Draft, the Board had concluded that quantitative criteria might interfere with the determination of operating segments and, if anything, might unnecessarily reduce the number of segments disclosed. Respondents to the Exposure Draft and others urged the Board to include quantitative criteria for determining which segments to report because they said that some enterprises would be required to report too many segments unless specific quantitative guidelines allowed them to omit small segments. Some respondents said that the Exposure Draft would have required disclosure of as many as 25 operating segments, which was not a result anticipated by the Board in its deliberations preceding the Exposure Draft. Others said that enterprises would report information that was too highly aggregated unless quantitative guidelines prevented it. The Board decided that the addition of quantitative thresholds would be a practical way to address respondents' concerns about competitive harm and proliferation of segments without fundamentally changing the management approach to segment definition.

76. Similar to the requirements in Statement 14, the Board decided to require that any operating segment that constitutes 10 percent or more of reported revenues, assets, or profit or loss be reported separately and that reportable segments account for at least 75 percent of an enterprise's external revenues. The Board decided to retain that guidance for the quantitative thresholds because it can be objectively applied and because preparers and users of financial statements already understand it.

77. Inclusion of quantitative thresholds similar to those in Statement 14 necessitates guidance on how to report operating segments that do not meet the thresholds. The Board concluded that enterprises should be permitted to aggregate information about operating segments that do not meet the thresholds with information about other operating segments that do not meet the thresholds if a majority of the aggregation criteria in paragraph 17 are met. That is a more liberal aggregation provision than that for individually material operating segments, but it prohibits aggregation of segments that are dissimilar.

78.   Paragraph 125 of Concepts Statement 2 states that "... magnitude by itself, without regard to the nature of the item and the circumstances in which the judgment has to be made, will not generally be a sufficient basis for a materiality judgment." That guidance applies to segment information. An understanding of the material segments of an enterprise is important for understanding the enterprise as a whole, and individual items of segment information are important for understanding the segments. Thus, an item of segment information that, if omitted, would change a user's decision about that segment so significantly that it would change the user's decision about the enterprise as a whole is material even though an item of a similar magnitude might not be considered material if it were omitted from the consolidated financial statements. Therefore, enterprises are encouraged to report information about segments that do not meet the quantitative thresholds if management believes that it is material. Those who are familiar with the particular circumstances of each enterprise must decide what constitutes *material*.

Vertically Integrated Enterprises

79.   The Board concluded that the definition of an operating segment should include components of an enterprise that sell primarily or exclusively to other operating segments of the enterprise if the enterprise is managed that way. Information about the components engaged in each stage of production is particularly important for understanding vertically integrated enterprises in certain businesses, for example, oil and gas enterprises. Different activities within the enterprise may have significantly different prospects for future cash flows, and users of financial statements have asserted that they need to know results of each operation.

80.   Some respondents to the Exposure Draft opposed the requirement to report vertically integrated segments separately. They said that the segment results may not be comparable between enterprises and that transfer prices are not sufficiently reliable for external reporting purposes. The Board considered an approach that would have required separate reporting of vertically integrated segments only if transfer prices were based on quoted market prices and if there was no basis for combining the selling segment and the buying segment. However, that would have been a significant departure from the management approach to defining segments. The Board also was concerned that the criteria would be unworkable. Therefore, the Board decided to retain the Exposure Draft's provisions for vertically integrated segments.

Accounting Principles and Allocations

81.   The Board decided that the information to be reported about each segment should be measured on the same basis as the information used by the chief operating decision maker for purposes of allocating resources to segments and assessing segments' performance. That is a management approach to measuring segment information as proposed in the Exposure Draft. The Board does not think that a separate measure of segment profit or loss or assets should have to be developed solely for the purpose of disclosing segment information. For example, an enterprise that accounts for inventory using a

specialized valuation method for internal purposes should not be required to restate inventory amounts for each segment, and an enterprise that accounts for pension expense only on a consolidated basis should not be required to allocate pension expense to each operating segment.

82. The report of the AICPA Special Committee said that the Board "should allow companies to report a statistic on the same basis it is reported for internal purposes, if the statistic is reported internally. The usefulness of information prepared only for [external] reporting is questionable. Users want to understand management's perspective on the company and the implications of key statistics." It also said that "key statistics to be reported [should] be limited to statistics a company has available..." (page 72).

83. Respondents to the Exposure Draft had mixed reactions to its measurement guidance. Very few suggested that the Board require allocations solely for external reporting purposes. Most agreed that allocations are inherently arbitrary and may not be meaningful if they are not used for management purposes. No respondents suggested that intersegment transfers should be reported on any basis other than that used internally. However, some respondents recommended that information about each segment be provided based on the accounting principles used in the enterprise's general-purpose financial statements. Some observed that unadjusted information from internal sources would not necessarily comply with generally accepted accounting principles and, for that reason, might be difficult for users to understand. Other respondents argued that comparability between enterprises would be improved if the segment information were provided on the basis of generally accepted accounting principles. Finally, a few questioned the verifiability of the information.

84. The Board decided not to require that segment information be provided in accordance with the same generally accepted accounting principles used to prepare the consolidated financial statements for several reasons. Preparing segment information in accordance with the generally accepted accounting principles used at the consolidated level would be difficult because some generally accepted accounting principles are not intended to apply at a segment level. Examples include allocation of the cost of an acquisition to individual assets and liabilities of a subsidiary using the purchase method of accounting, accounting for the cost of enterprise-wide employee benefit plans, accounting for income taxes in an enterprise that files a consolidated income tax return, and accounting for inventory on a last-in, first-out basis if the pools include items in more than one segment. In addition, there are no generally accepted accounting principles for allocating joint costs, jointly used assets, or jointly incurred liabilities to segments or for pricing intersegment transfers. As a consequence, it generally is not feasible to present segment profitability in accordance with generally accepted accounting principles.

85. The Board recognizes that segment information is subject to certain limitations and that some of that information may not be susceptible to the same degree of verifiability as some other financial information. However, verifiability is not the only important qualitative characteristic of accounting information. Verifiability is a component of reliability, which is one of two

characteristics that contribute to the usefulness of accounting information. The other is relevance, which is equally important. Concepts Statement 2 states:

> Although financial information must be both relevant and reliable to be useful, information may possess both characteristics to varying degrees. It may be possible to trade relevance for reliability or vice versa, though not to the point of dispensing with one of them altogether. ... trade-offs between characteristics may be necessary or beneficial.
>
> In a particular situation, the importance attached to relevance in relation to the importance of other decision specific qualities of accounting information (for example, reliability) will be different for different information users, and their willingness to trade one quality for another will also differ. [paragraphs 42 and 45]

86. It is apparent that users are willing to trade a degree of reliability in segment information for more relevant information. The AIMR's 1993 position paper states:

> Analysts need financial statements structured so as to be consistent with how the business is organized and managed. That means that two different companies in the same industry may have to report segment data differently because they are structured differently themselves. [page 20]

But, as previously noted, the position paper says that, under those circumstances, analysts "would assume more responsibility for making meaningful comparisons of those data to the unlike data of other firms that conduct their business differently" (page 61).

87. The Board believes that the information required by this Statement meets the objective of reliability of which both representational faithfulness and verifiability are components. An auditor can determine whether the information reported in the notes to the financial statements came from the required source by reviewing management reports or minutes from meetings of the board of directors. The information is not required to be provided on a specified basis, but the enterprise is required to explain the basis on which it is provided and to reconcile the segment information to consolidated enterprise totals. Adequate explanation and an appropriate reconciliation will enable a user to understand the information and its limitations in the context of the enterprise's financial statements. The auditor can test both the explanation of segment amounts and the reconciliations to consolidated totals. Furthermore, because management uses that information in its decision-making processes, that information is likely to be highly reliable. The information provided to comply with Statement 14 was more difficult to verify in many situations and was less reliable. Because it was prepared solely for external reporting purposes, it required allocations that may have been arbitrary, and it was based on accounting principles that may have been difficult to apply at the segment level.

88. Paragraph 29 requires amounts allocated to a segment to be allocated on a reasonable basis. However, the Board believes that the potential increased reliability that might have been achieved by requiring allocation of consolidated amounts is illusory because expenses incurred at the

consolidated level could be allocated to segments in a variety of ways that could be considered "reasonable." For example, an enterprise could use either the number of employees in each segment or the segment's total salary expense in relation to the consolidated amounts as a basis for allocating pension expense to segments. Those two approaches to allocation could result in significantly different measures of segment profit or loss. However, both the number of employees and the total salary expense might be reasonable bases on which to allocate total pension expense. In contrast, it would not seem reasonable for an enterprise to allocate pension expense to a segment that had no employees eligible for the pension plan. Because of the potential for misleading information that may result from such allocations, the Board decided that it is appropriate for this Statement to require that amounts allocated to a segment be allocated on a reasonable basis.

89. The Board also considered explicitly requiring that revenues and expenses directly incurred by or directly attributable to an operating segment be reported by that segment. However, it decided that, in some cases, whether an item of revenue or expense is attributable to an operating segment is a matter of judgment. Further, such an explicit requirement would be an additional modification of the management approach to measurement. While the Board decided not to include an explicit requirement, it believes that many items of revenue or expense clearly relate to a particular segment and that it would be unlikely that the information used by management would omit those items.

90. To assist users of financial statements in understanding segment disclosures, this Statement requires that enterprises provide sufficient explanation of the basis on which the information was prepared. That disclosure must include any differences in the basis of measurement between the consolidated amounts and the segment amounts. It also must indicate whether allocations of items were made symmetrically. An enterprise may allocate an expense to a segment without allocating the related asset; however, disclosure of that fact is required. Enterprises also are required to reconcile to the consolidated totals in the enterprise's financial statements the totals of reportable segment assets, segment revenues, segment profit or loss, and any other significant segment information that is disclosed.

91. In addition, the advantages of reporting unadjusted management information are significant. That practice is consistent with defining segments based on the structure of the enterprise's internal organization. It imposes little incremental cost on the enterprise and requires little incremental time to prepare. Thus, the enterprise can more easily report segment information in condensed financial statements for interim periods and can report more information about each segment in annual financial statements. Information used by management also highlights for a user of financial statements the risks and opportunities that management considers important.

Information to Be Disclosed about Segments

92.   The items of information about each reportable operating segment that must be disclosed as described in paragraphs 25–31 represent a balance between the needs of users of financial statements who may want a complete set of financial statements for each segment and the costs to preparers who may prefer not to disclose any segment information. Statement 14 required disclosure of internal and external revenues; profit or loss; depreciation, depletion, and amortization expense; and unusual items as defined in APB Opinion No. 30, *Reporting the Results of Operations — Reporting the Effects of Disposal of a Segment of a Business, and Extraordinary, Unusual and Infrequently Occurring Events and Transactions*, for each segment. Statement 14 also required disclosure of total assets, equity in the net income of investees accounted for by the equity method, the amount of investment in equity method investees, and total expenditures for additions to long-lived assets. Some respondents to the Exposure Draft objected to disclosing any information that was not required by Statement 14, while others recommended disclosure of additional items that are not required by this Statement. This Statement calls for the following additional disclosures only if the items are included in the measure of segment profit or loss that is reviewed by the chief operating decision maker: significant noncash items, interest revenue, interest expense, and income tax expense.

93.   Some respondents to the Exposure Draft expressed concern that the proposals would increase the sheer volume of information compared to what was required to be reported under Statement 14. The Board considers that concern to be overstated for several reasons. Although this Statement requires disclosure of more information about an individual operating segment than Statement 14 required for an industry segment, this Statement requires disclosure of information about only one type of segment—reportable operating segments — while Statement 14 required information about two types of segments — industry segments and geographic segments. Moreover, Statement 14 required that many enterprises create information solely for external reporting, while almost all of the segment information that this Statement requires is already available in management reports. The Board recognizes, however, that some enterprises may find it necessary to create the enterprise-wide information about products and services, geographic areas, and major customers required by paragraphs 36–39.

94.   The Board decided to require disclosure of significant noncash items included in the measure of segment profit or loss and information about total expenditures for additions to long-lived segment assets (other than financial instruments, long-term customer relationships of a financial institution, mortgage and other servicing rights, deferred policy acquisition costs, and deferred tax assets) if that information is reported internally because it improves financial statement users' abilities to estimate cash-generating potential and cash requirements of operating segments. As an alternative, the Board considered requiring disclosure of operating cash flow for each operating segment. However, many respondents said that disclosing operating cash flow in accordance with FASB Statement No. 95, *Statement of Cash Flows*,

would require that they gather and process information solely for external reporting purposes. They said that management often evaluates cash generated or required by segments in ways other than by calculating operating cash flow in accordance with Statement 95. For that reason, the Board decided not to require disclosure of cash flow by segment.

95. Disclosure of interest revenue and interest expense included in reported segment profit or loss is intended to provide information about the financing activities of a segment. The Exposure Draft proposed that an enterprise disclose gross interest revenue and gross interest expense for all segments in which reported profit or loss includes those items. Some respondents said that financial services segments generally are managed based on net interest revenue, or the "spread," and that management looks only to that data in its decision-making process. Therefore those segments should be required to disclose only the net amount and not both gross interest revenue and expense. Those respondents noted that requiring disclosure of both gross amounts would be analogous to requiring nonfinancial services segments to disclose both sales and cost of sales. The Board decided that segments that derive a majority of revenue from interest should be permitted to disclose net interest revenue instead of gross interest revenue and gross interest expense if management finds that amount to be more relevant in managing the segment. Information about interest is most important if a single segment comprises a mix of financial and nonfinancial operations. If a segment is primarily a financial operation, interest revenue probably constitutes most of segment revenues and interest expense will constitute most of the difference between reported segment revenues and reported segment profit or loss. If the segment has no financial operations or only immaterial financial operations, no information about interest is required.

96. The Board decided not to require the disclosure of segment liabilities. The Exposure Draft proposed that an enterprise disclose segment liabilities because the Board believed that liabilities are an important disclosure for understanding the financing activities of a segment. The Board also noted that the requirement in FASB Statement No. 94, *Consolidation of All Majority-Owned Subsidiaries*, to disclose assets, liabilities, and profit or loss about previously unconsolidated subsidiaries was continued from APB Opinion No. 18, *The Equity Method of Accounting for Investments in Common Stock*, pending completion of the project on disaggregated disclosures. However, in commenting on the disclosures that should be required by this Statement, many respondents said that liabilities are incurred centrally and that enterprises often do not allocate those amounts to segments. The Board concluded that the value of information about segment liabilities in assessing the performance of the segments of an enterprise was limited.

97. The Board decided not to require disclosure of research and development expense included in the measure of segment profit or loss. The Exposure Draft would have required that disclosure to provide financial statement users with information about the operating segments in which an enterprise is focusing its product development efforts. Disclosure of research and development expense was requested by a number of financial statement users and was

specifically requested in both the report of the AICPA's Special Committee and the AIMR's 1993 position paper. However, respondents said that disclosing research and development expense by segment may result in competitive harm by providing competitors with early insight into the strategic plans of an enterprise. Other respondents observed that research and development is only one of a number of items that indicate where an enterprise is focusing its efforts and that it is much more significant in some enterprises than in others. For example, costs of employee training and advertising were cited as items that often are more important to some enterprises than research and development, calling into question the relevance of disclosing only research and development expense. Additionally, many respondents said that research and development expense often is incurred centrally and not allocated to segments. The Board therefore decided not to require the disclosure of research and development expense by segment.

Interim Period Information

98.   This Statement requires disclosure of limited segment information in condensed financial statements that are included in quarterly reports to shareholders, as was proposed in the Exposure Draft. Statement 14 did not apply to those condensed financial statements because of the expense and the time required for producing segment information under Statement 14. A few respondents to the Exposure Draft said that reporting segment information in interim financial statements would be unnecessarily burdensome. However, users contended that, to be timely, segment information is needed more often than annually and that the difficulties of preparing it on an interim basis could be overcome by an approach like the one in this Statement. Managers of many enterprises agree and have voluntarily provided segment information for interim periods.

99.   The Board decided that the condensed financial statements in interim reports issued to shareholders should include disclosure of segment revenues from external customers, intersegment revenues, a measure of segment profit or loss, material changes in segment assets, differences in the basis of segmentation or the way segment profit or loss was measured in the previous annual period, and a reconciliation to the enterprise's total profit or loss. That decision is a compromise between the needs of users who want the same segment information for interim periods as that required in annual financial statements and the costs to preparers who must report the information. Users will have some key information on a timely basis. Enterprises should not incur significant incremental costs to provide the information because it is based on information that is used internally and therefore already available.

Restatement of Previously Reported Information

100.   The Board decided to require restatement of previously reported segment information following a change in the composition of an enterprise's segments unless it is impracticable to do so. Changes in the composition of segments interrupt trends, and trend analysis is important to users of financial statements. Some financial statement issuers have said that their policy is to restate one or more prior years for internal trend analysis. Many

reorganizations result in discrete profit centers' being reassigned from one segment to another and lead to relatively simple restatements. However, if an enterprise undergoes a fundamental reorganization, restatement may be very difficult and expensive. The Board concluded that in those situations restatement may be impracticable and, therefore, should not be required. However, if an enterprise does not restate its segment information, the enterprise is required to provide current-period segment information on both the old and new bases of segmentation in the year in which the change occurs unless it is impracticable to do so.

Enterprise-Wide Disclosures

101. Paragraphs 36–39 require disclosure of information about an enterprise's products and services, geographic areas, and major customers, regardless of the enterprise's organization. The required disclosures need be provided only if they are not included as part of the disclosures about segments. The Exposure Draft proposed requiring additional disclosures about products and services and geographic areas *by segment*. Many respondents said that that proposal would have resulted in disclosure of excessive amounts of information. Some enterprises providing a variety of products and services throughout many countries, for example, would have been required to present a large quantity of information that would have been time-consuming to prepare and of questionable benefit to most financial statement users. The Board decided that additional disclosures provided on an enterprise-wide basis rather than on a segment basis would be appropriate and not unduly burdensome. The Board also agreed that those enterprise-wide disclosures are appropriate for all enterprises including those that have a single operating segment if the enterprise offers a range of products and services, derives revenues from customers in more than one country, or both.

102. Based on reviews of published information about public enterprises, discussions with constituents, and a field test of the Exposure Draft, the Board believes that most enterprises are organized by products and services or by geography and will report one or both of those types of information in their reportable operating segment disclosures. However, some enterprises will be required by paragraphs 36–39 to report additional information because the enterprise-wide disclosures are required for all enterprises, even those that have a single reportable segment.

Information about Products and Services

103. This Statement requires that enterprises report revenues from external customers for each product and service or each group of similar products and services for the enterprise as a whole. Analysts said that an analysis of trends in revenues from products and services is important in assessing both past performance and prospects for future growth. Those trends can be compared to benchmarks such as industry statistics or information reported by competitors. Information about the assets that are used to produce specific products and deliver specific services also might be useful. However, in many enterprises, assets are not dedicated to specific products and services and reporting assets by products and services would require arbitrary allocations.

Information about Geographic Areas

104.   This Statement requires disclosure of information about both revenues and assets by geographic area. Analysts said that information about revenues from customers in different geographic areas assists them in understanding concentrations of risks due to negative changes in economic conditions and prospects for growth due to positive economic changes. They said that information about assets located in different areas assists them in understanding concentrations of risks (for example, political risks such as expropriation).

105.   Statement 14 requires disclosure of geographic information by geographic region, whereas this Statement requires disclosure of individually material countries as well as information for the enterprise's country of domicile and all foreign countries in the aggregate. This Statement's approach has two significant benefits. First, it will reduce the burden on preparers of financial statements because most enterprises are likely to have material operations in only a few countries or perhaps only in their country of domicile. Second, and more important, it will provide information that is more useful in assessing the impact of concentrations of risk. Information disclosed by country is more useful because it is easier to interpret. Countries in contiguous areas often experience different rates of growth and other differences in economic conditions. Under the requirements of Statement 14, enterprises often reported information about broad geographic areas that included groupings such as Europe, Africa, and the Middle East. Analysts and others have questioned the usefulness of that type of broad disclosure.

106.   Respondents to the Exposure Draft questioned how revenues should be allocated to individual countries. For example, guidance was requested for situations in which products are shipped to one location but the customer resides in another location. The Board decided to provide flexibility concerning the basis on which enterprises attribute revenues to individual countries rather than requiring that revenues be attributed to countries according to the location of customers. The Board also decided to require that enterprises disclose the basis they have adopted for attributing revenues to countries to permit financial statement users to understand the geographic information provided.

107.   As a result of its decision to require geographic information on an enterprise-wide basis, the Board decided not to require disclosure of capital expenditures on certain long-lived assets by geographic area. Such information on an enterprise-wide basis is not necessarily helpful in forecasting future cash flows of operating segments.

Information about Major Customers

108.   The Board decided to retain the requirement in Statement 14, as amended by FASB Statement No. 30, *Disclosure of Information about Major Customers*, to report information about major customers because major customers of an enterprise represent a significant concentration of risk. The 10 percent threshold is arbitrary; however, it has been accepted practice since Statement 14 was issued, and few have suggested changing it.

Competitive Harm

109. A number of respondents to the Exposure Draft noted the potential for competitive harm as a result of disclosing segment information in accordance with this Statement. The Board considered adopting special provisions to reduce the potential for competitive harm from certain segment information but decided against it. In the Invitation to Comment, the Tentative Conclusions, and the Exposure Draft, the Board asked constituents for specific illustrations of competitive harm that has resulted from disclosing segment information. Some respondents said that public enterprises may be at a disadvantage to nonpublic enterprises or foreign competitors that do not have to disclose segment information. Other respondents suggested that information about narrowly defined segments may put an enterprise at a disadvantage in price negotiations with customers or in competitive bid situations.

110. Some respondents said that if a competitive disadvantage exists, it is a consequence of an obligation that enterprises have accepted to gain greater access to capital markets, which gives them certain advantages over nonpublic enterprises and many foreign enterprises. Other respondents said that enterprises are not likely to suffer competitive harm because most competitors have other sources of more detailed information about an enterprise than that disclosed in the financial statements. In addition, the information that is required to be disclosed about an operating segment is no more detailed or specific than the information typically provided by a smaller enterprise with a single operation.

111. The Board was sympathetic to specific concerns raised by certain constituents; however, it decided that a competitive-harm exemption was inappropriate because it would provide a means for broad noncompliance with this Statement. Some form of relief for single-product or single-service segments was explored; however, there are many enterprises that produce a single product or a single service that are required to issue general-purpose financial statements. Those statements would include the same information that would be reported by single-product or single-service segments of an enterprise. The Board concluded that it was not necessary to provide an exemption for single-product or single-service segments because enterprises that produce a single product or service that are required to issue general-purpose financial statements have that same exposure to competitive harm. The Board noted that concerns about competitive harm were addressed to the extent feasible by four changes made during redeliberations: (a) modifying the aggregation criteria, (b) adding quantitative materiality thresholds for identifying reportable segments, (c) eliminating the requirements to disclose research and development expense and liabilities by segment, and (d) changing the second-level disclosure requirements about products and services and geography from a segment basis to an enterprise-wide basis.

Cost-Benefit Considerations

112. One of the precepts of the Board's mission is to promulgate standards only if the expected benefits of the resulting information exceed the perceived costs. The Board strives to determine that a proposed standard will fill a significant need and that the costs incurred to satisfy that need, as compared with other alternatives, are justified in relation to the overall benefits of the resulting information. The Board concluded that the benefits that will result from this Statement will exceed the related costs.

113. The Board believes that the primary benefits of this Statement are that enterprises will report segment information in interim financial reports, some enterprises will report a greater number of segments, most enterprises will report more items of information about each segment, enterprises will report segments that correspond to internal management reports, and enterprises will report segment information that will be more consistent with other parts of their annual reports.

114. This Statement will reduce the cost of providing disaggregated information for many enterprises. Statement 14 required that enterprises define segments by both industry and by geographical area, ways that often did not match the way that information was used internally. Even if the reported segments aligned with the internal organization, the information required was often created solely for external reporting because Statement 14 required certain allocations of costs, prohibited other cost allocations, and required allocations of assets to segments. This Statement requires that information about operating segments be provided on the same basis that it is used internally. The Board believes that most of the enterprise-wide disclosures in this Statement about products and services, geography, and major customers typically are provided in current financial statements or can be prepared with minimal incremental cost.

Applicability to Nonpublic Enterprises and Not-for-Profit Organizations

115. The Board decided to continue to exempt nonpublic enterprises from the requirement to report segment information. Few users of nonpublic enterprises' financial statements have requested that the Board require that those enterprises provide segment information.

116. At the time the Board began considering improvements to disclosures about segment information, FASB Statement No. 117, *Financial Statements of Not-for-Profit Organizations*, had not been issued and there were no effective standards for consolidated financial statements of not-for-profit organizations. Most not-for-profit organizations provided financial information for each of their funds, which is a form of disaggregated information. The situation in Canada was similar. Thus, when the two boards agreed to pursue a joint project, they decided to limit the scope to public business enterprises.

117. The Board provided a limited form of disaggregated information in paragraph 26 of Statement 117, which requires disclosure of expense by functional classification. However, the Board acknowledges that the application of that Statement may increase the need for disaggregated information about not-for-profit organizations. A final Statement expected to result from the FASB Exposure Draft, *Consolidated Financial Statements: Policy and Procedures*, also may increase that need by requiring aggregation of information about more entities in the financial statements of not-for-profit organizations.

118. The general approach of providing information based on the structure of an enterprise's internal organization may be appropriate for not-for-profit organizations. However, the Board decided not to add not-for-profit organizations to the scope of this Statement. Users of financial statements of not-for-profit organizations have not urged the Board to include those organizations, perhaps because they have not yet seen the effects of Statement 117 and the Exposure Draft on consolidations. Furthermore, the term *not-for-profit organizations* applies to a wide variety of entities, some of which are similar to business enterprises and some of which are very different. There are likely to be unique characteristics of some of those entities or special user needs that require special provisions, which the Board has not studied. In addition, the AcSB has recently adopted standards for reporting by not-for-profit organizations that are different from Statement 117. In the interest of completing this joint project in a timely manner, the Board decided not to undertake the research and deliberations that would be necessary to adapt the requirements of this Statement to not-for-profit organizations at this time. Few respondents to the Exposure Draft disagreed with the Board's position.

Effective Date and Transition

119. The Board concluded that this Statement should be effective for financial statements issued for fiscal years beginning after December 15, 1997. In developing the Exposure Draft, the Board had decided on an effective date of December 15, 1996. The Board believed that that time frame was reasonable because almost all of the information that this Statement requires is generated by systems already in place within an enterprise and a final Statement was expected to be issued before the end of 1996. However, respondents said that some enterprises may need more time to comply with the requirements of this Statement than would have been provided under the Exposure Draft.

120. The Board also decided not to require that segment information be reported in financial statements for interim periods in the initial year of application. Some of the information that is required to be reported for interim periods is based on information that would have been reported in the most recent annual financial statements. Without a full set of segment information to use as a comparison and to provide an understanding of the basis on which it is provided, interim information would not be as meaningful.

Appendix B
Amendments to Basis for Conclusions on other IFRSs

This appendix contains amendments to the Basis for Conclusions on other IFRSs that are necessary in order to note the replacement of IAS 14 by IFRS 8.

* * * * *

The amendments contained in this appendix when IFRS 8 was issued in 2006 have been incorporated into the text of the Basis for Conclusions on IFRSs 1, 6 and 7 and IASs 27 and 36 as issued at 30 November 2006.

© IFRS Foundation

Dissenting opinions

Dissent of Gilbert Gélard and James J Leisenring

DO1 Messrs Gélard and Leisenring dissent from the issue of the IFRS because it does not require a defined measure of segment profit or loss to be disclosed and does not require the measure of profit or loss reported to be consistent with the attribution of assets to reportable segments.

DO2 By not defining segment profit or loss, the IFRS allows the reporting of any measure of segment profit or loss as long as that measure is reviewed by the chief operating decision maker. Items of revenue and expense directly attributable to a segment need not be included in the reported profit or loss of that segment, and allocation of items not directly attributable to any given segment is not required. Messrs Gélard and Leisenring believe that the IFRS should require amounts directly incurred by or directly attributable to a segment to be included in that segment's profit or loss, and measurement of a segment's profit or loss to be consistent with the attribution of assets to the segment.

DO3 Messrs Gélard and Leisenring support the disclosure of information to enable users of financial statements to evaluate the activities of an entity and the economic environment in which it operates. However, they believe that the IFRS will not meet this objective, even with the required disclosures and reconciliation to the entity's annual financial statements, because it does not define segment profit or loss and does not require consistent attribution of assets and profit or loss to segments.

DO4 Messrs Gélard and Leisenring support the management approach for defining reportable segments and support requiring disclosure of selected segment information in interim financial reports. They believe, however, that the definitions of segment revenue, expense, result, assets and liabilities in paragraph 16 of IAS 14 *Segment Reporting* should be retained in the IFRS and applied to segments identified by the management approach. They believe that proper external reporting of segment information should not permit the use of non-GAAP measures because they might mislead users.

DO5 Messrs Gélard and Leisenring also believe that the changes from IAS 14 are not justified by the need for convergence with US GAAP. IAS 14 is a disclosure standard and therefore does not affect the reconciliation of IFRS amounts to US GAAP, though additional disclosure from what is required now by IAS 14 might be needed to comply with US GAAP.

Dissent of Stephen Cooper from the amendment issued in April 2009

DO1   Mr Cooper dissents from the amendment to IFRS 8 *Operating Segments* made by *Improvements to IFRSs* issued in April 2009.

DO2   In his view the changes are unnecessary considering that the provisions in the *Framework*[4] regarding materiality already enable a reporting entity not to disclose segment assets when those assets are small relative to segment profit and not relevant to the understanding of the business. Mr Cooper believes that allowing a reporting entity not to disclose segment assets merely because this is not reported to the chief operating decision maker weakens IFRS 8, and may result in segment assets not being disclosed even when they are important to understanding the performance and financial position of that business.

---

4   The reference to the *Framework* is to the IASC's *Framework for the Preparation and Presentation of Financial Statements*, adopted by the Board in 2001 and in effect when the Standard was amended.

IASB documents published to accompany

IFRS 9

Financial Instruments

The text of the unaccompanied standard, IFRS 9, is contained in Part A of this edition. Its effective date when issued was 1 January 2018. The text of the Accompanying Guidance on IFRS 9 is contained in Part B of this edition. This part presents the following documents:

BASIS FOR CONCLUSIONS

DISSENTING OPINIONS

APPENDIX A

Previous dissenting opinions

APPENDIX B

Amendments to the Basis for Conclusions on other Standards

CONTENTS

Basis for Conclusions on
IFRS 9 *Financial Instruments*

This Basis for Conclusions accompanies, but is not part of, IFRS 9.

IFRS 9 replaced IAS 39 Financial Instruments: Recognition and Measurement. *When revised in 2003 IAS 39 was accompanied by a Basis for Conclusions summarising the considerations of the IASB as constituted at the time, in reaching some of its conclusions in that Standard. That Basis for Conclusions was subsequently updated to reflect amendments to the Standard. For convenience the IASB has incorporated into its Basis for Conclusions on IFRS 9 material from the Basis for Conclusions on IAS 39 that discusses matters that the IASB has not reconsidered. That material is contained in paragraphs denoted by numbers with the prefix BCZ. In those paragraphs cross-references to the Standard have been updated accordingly and minor necessary editorial changes have been made. In 2003 and later some IASB members dissented from the issue of IAS 39 and subsequent amendments, and portions of their dissenting opinions relate to requirements that have been carried forward to IFRS 9. Those dissenting opinions are set out in an appendix after this Basis for Conclusions.*

Paragraphs describing the IASB's considerations in reaching its own conclusions on IFRS 9 are numbered with the prefix BC.

Introduction

BCIN.1   This Basis for Conclusions summarises the considerations of the International Accounting Standards Board (IASB) when developing IFRS 9 *Financial Instruments*. Individual IASB members gave greater weight to some factors than to others.

BCIN.2   The IASB has long acknowledged the need to improve the requirements for financial reporting of financial instruments to enhance the relevance and understandability of information about financial instruments for users of financial statements. That need became more urgent in the light of the global financial crisis that started in 2007 ('the global financial crisis'), so the IASB decided to replace IAS 39 *Financial Instruments: Recognition and Measurement* in its entirety as expeditiously as possible. To do this the IASB divided the project into several phases. In adopting this approach, the IASB acknowledged the difficulties that might be created by differences in timing between this project and others, in particular the project on insurance contracts.

Classification and measurement

BCIN.3   IFRS 9 is a new Standard that deals with the accounting for financial instruments. When developing IFRS 9, the IASB considered the responses to its 2009 Exposure Draft *Financial Instruments: Classification and Measurement* (the '2009 Classification and Measurement Exposure Draft').

BCIN.4   That 2009 Classification and Measurement Exposure Draft contained proposals for all items within the scope of IAS 39. However, some respondents said that the IASB should finalise its proposals on the classification and measurement of financial assets while retaining the existing requirements for financial liabilities (including the requirements for embedded derivatives and the fair value option) until the IASB had more fully considered the issues relating to financial liabilities. Those respondents pointed out that the IASB had accelerated its project on financial instruments because of the global financial crisis, which had placed more emphasis on issues in the accounting for financial assets than for financial liabilities. They suggested that the IASB should consider issues related to financial liabilities more closely before finalising the requirements for classification and measurement of financial liabilities.

BCIN.5 The IASB noted those concerns and, as a result, in November 2009 it finalised the first chapters of IFRS 9, dealing with the classification and measurement of financial assets. In the IASB's view, requirements for classification and measurement are the foundation for a financial reporting standard on accounting for financial instruments, and the requirements on associated matters (for example, on impairment and hedge accounting) have to reflect those requirements. In addition, the IASB noted that many of the application issues that arose in the global financial crisis were related to the classification and measurement of financial assets in accordance with IAS 39.

BCIN.6 Thus, financial liabilities, including derivative liabilities, initially remained within the scope of IAS 39. Taking that course enabled the IASB to obtain further feedback on the accounting for financial liabilities, including how best to address accounting for changes in own credit risk.

BCIN.7 Immediately after issuing IFRS 9, the IASB began an extensive outreach programme to gather feedback on the classification and measurement of financial liabilities. The IASB obtained information and views from its Financial Instruments Working Group (FIWG) and from users of financial statements, regulators, preparers, auditors and others from a range of industries across different geographical regions. The primary messages that the IASB received were that the requirements in IAS 39 for classifying and measuring financial liabilities were generally working well but that the effects of the changes in a liability's credit risk ought not to affect profit or loss unless the liability is held for trading. As a result of the feedback received, the IASB decided to retain almost all of the requirements in IAS 39 for the classification and measurement of financial liabilities and carry them forward to IFRS 9 (see paragraphs BC4.46–BC4.53).

BCIN.8 By taking that course, the issue of accounting for the effects of changes in credit risk does not arise for most liabilities and would remain only in the context of financial liabilities designated as measured at fair value under the fair value option. Thus, in May 2010, the IASB published the Exposure Draft *Fair Value Option for Financial Liabilities* (the '2010 Own Credit Risk Exposure Draft'), which proposed that the effects of changes in the credit risk of liabilities designated under the fair value option would be presented in other comprehensive income. The IASB considered the responses to the 2010 Own Credit Risk Exposure Draft and finalised the requirements, which were then added to IFRS 9 in October 2010.

BCIN.9   In November 2012 the IASB published the Exposure Draft *Classification and Measurement: Limited Amendments to IFRS 9* (Proposed amendments to IFRS 9 (2010)) (the '2012 Limited Amendments Exposure Draft'). In that Exposure Draft, the IASB proposed limited amendments to the classification and measurement requirements in IFRS 9 for financial assets with the aims of:

(a)   considering the interaction between the classification and measurement of financial assets and the accounting for insurance contract liabilities;

(b)   addressing specific application questions that had been raised by some interested parties since IFRS 9 was issued; and

(c)   seeking to reduce key differences with the US national standard-setter, the Financial Accounting Standards Board's (FASB) tentative classification and measurement model for financial instruments.

BCIN.10   Accordingly, the 2012 Limited Amendments Exposure Draft proposed limited amendments to clarify the application of the existing classification and measurement requirements for financial assets and to introduce a fair value through other comprehensive income measurement category for particular debt investments. Most respondents to the 2012 Limited Amendments Exposure Draft—as well as participants in the IASB's outreach programme—generally supported the proposed limited amendments. However, many asked the IASB for clarifications or additional guidance on particular aspects of the proposals. The IASB considered the responses in the comment letters and the information received during its outreach activities when it finalised the limited amendments in July 2014.

Amortised cost and impairment methodology

BCIN.11   In October 2008, as part of a joint approach to dealing with the financial reporting issues arising from the global financial crisis, the IASB and the FASB set up the Financial Crisis Advisory Group (FCAG). The FCAG considered how improvements in financial reporting could help to enhance investor confidence in financial markets. In its report, published in July 2009, the FCAG identified weaknesses in the current accounting standards for financial instruments and their application. Those weaknesses included the delayed recognition of credit losses on loans (and other financial instruments) and the complexity of multiple impairment approaches. One of the FCAG's recommendations was to explore alternatives to the incurred credit loss model that would use more forward looking information.

BCIN.12   Following a Request for Information that the IASB posted on its website in June 2009, the IASB published, in November 2009, the Exposure Draft *Financial Instruments: Amortised Cost and Impairment* (the '2009 Impairment Exposure Draft'). Comments received on the 2009 Impairment Exposure Draft and during outreach indicated support for the concept of such an impairment model, but highlighted the operational difficulties of applying it.

BCIN.13   In response, the IASB decided to modify the impairment model proposed in the 2009 Impairment Exposure Draft to address those operational difficulties while replicating the outcomes of that model that it proposed in that Exposure Draft as closely as possible. These simplifications were published in the Supplementary Document *Financial Instruments: Impairment* in January 2011, however the IASB did not receive strong support on these proposals.

BCIN.14   The IASB started developing an impairment model that would reflect the general pattern of deterioration in the credit quality of financial instruments and in which the amount of the expected credit losses recognised as a loss allowance or provision would depend on the level of deterioration in the credit quality of financial instruments since initial recognition.

BCIN.15   In 2013 the IASB published the Exposure Draft *Financial Instruments: Expected Credit Losses* (the '2013 Impairment Exposure Draft'), which proposed to recognise a loss allowance or provision at an amount equal to lifetime expected credit losses if there was a significant increase in credit risk after initial recognition of a financial instrument and at 12-month expected credit losses for all other instruments.

BCIN.16   Most respondents to the 2013 Impairment Exposure Draft—as well as participants in the IASB's outreach and field work programme—generally supported the proposed impairment model. However, many asked the IASB for clarifications or additional guidance on particular aspects of the proposals. The IASB considered the responses in the comment letters and the information received during its outreach activities when it finalised the impairment requirements in July 2014.

Hedge accounting

BCIN.17   In December 2010 the IASB published the Exposure Draft *Hedge Accounting* (the '2010 Hedge Accounting Exposure Draft'). That Exposure Draft contained an objective for hedge accounting that aimed to align accounting more closely with risk management and to provide useful information about the purpose and effect of hedging instruments. It also proposed requirements for:

(a)   what financial instruments qualify for designation as hedging instruments;

(b)   what items (existing or expected) qualify for designation as hedged items;

(c)   an objective-based hedge effectiveness assessment;

(d)   how an entity should account for a hedging relationship (fair value hedge, cash flow hedge or a hedge of a net investment in a foreign operation as defined in IAS 21 *The Effects of Changes in Foreign Exchange Rates*); and

(e)   hedge accounting presentation and disclosures.

BCIN.18 After the publication of the 2010 Hedge Accounting Exposure Draft, the IASB began an extensive outreach programme to gather feedback on the hedge accounting proposals. The IASB obtained information and views from users of financial statements, preparers, treasurers, risk management experts, auditors, standard-setters and regulators from a range of industries across different geographical regions.

BCIN.19 The views from participants in the IASB's outreach activities were largely consistent with the views in the comment letters to the 2010 Hedge Accounting Exposure Draft. The IASB received strong support for the objective of aligning accounting more closely with risk management. However, many asked the IASB for added clarification on some of the fundamental changes proposed in the 2010 Hedge Accounting Exposure Draft.

BCIN.20 The IASB considered the responses in the comment letters to the 2010 Hedge Accounting Exposure Draft and the information received during its outreach activities when it finalised the requirements for hedge accounting that were then added to IFRS 9 in November 2013.

Scope (Chapter 2)

BC2.1 The scope of IAS 39 was not raised as a matter of concern during the global financial crisis and, hence, the IASB decided that the scope of IFRS 9 should be based on that of IAS 39. Consequently, the scope of IAS 39 was carried forward to IFRS 9. It has been changed only as a consequence of other new requirements, such as to reflect the changes to the accounting for expected credit losses on loan commitments that an entity issues (see paragraph BC2.8). As a result, most of paragraphs in this section of the Basis for Conclusions were carried forward from the Basis for Conclusion on IAS 39 and describe the IASB's rationale when it set the scope of that Standard.

Loan commitments

BCZ2.2 Loan commitments are firm commitments to provide credit under pre-specified terms and conditions. In the IAS 39 implementation guidance process, the question was raised whether a bank's loan commitments are derivatives accounted for at fair value under IAS 39. This question arises because a commitment to make a loan at a specified rate of interest during a fixed period of time meets the definition of a derivative. In effect, it is a written option for the potential borrower to obtain a loan at a specified rate.

BCZ2.3 To simplify the accounting for holders and issuers of loan commitments, the IASB decided to exclude particular loan commitments from the scope of IAS 39. The effect of the exclusion is that an entity will not recognise and measure changes in fair value of these loan commitments that result from changes in market interest rates or credit spreads. This is consistent with the measurement of the loan that results if the holder of the loan commitment exercises its right to obtain financing, because changes in market interest rates do not affect the measurement of an asset measured at amortised cost (assuming it is not designated in a category other than loans and receivables).[1]

BCZ2.4 However, the IASB decided that an entity should be permitted to measure a loan commitment at fair value with changes in fair value recognised in profit or loss on the basis of designation at inception of the loan commitment as a financial liability through profit or loss. This may be appropriate, for example, if the entity manages risk exposures related to loan commitments on a fair value basis.

BCZ2.5 The IASB further decided that a loan commitment should be excluded from the scope of IAS 39 only if it cannot be settled net. If the value of a loan commitment can be settled net in cash or another financial instrument, including when the entity has a past practice of selling the resulting loan assets shortly after origination, it is difficult to justify its exclusion from the requirement in IAS 39 to measure at fair value similar instruments that meet the definition of a derivative.

BCZ2.6 Some comments received on the Exposure Draft that preceded the issuance of these requirements in IAS 39 disagreed with the IASB's proposal that an entity that has a past practice of selling the assets resulting from its loan commitments shortly after origination should apply IAS 39 to all of its loan commitments. The IASB considered this concern and agreed that the words in that Exposure Draft did not reflect the IASB's intention. Thus, the IASB clarified that if an entity has a past practice of selling the assets resulting from its loan commitments shortly after origination, it applies IAS 39 only to its loan commitments in the same class.

BCZ2.7 Finally, in developing the requirements in IAS 39, the IASB decided that commitments to provide a loan at a below-market interest rate should be initially measured at fair value, and subsequently measured at the higher of (a) the amount that would be recognised under IAS 37 and (b) the amount initially recognised less, where appropriate, cumulative amortisation recognised in accordance with IAS 18 *Revenue*.[2] It noted that without such a requirement, liabilities that result from such commitments might not be recognised in the balance sheet, because in many cases no cash consideration is received.

BC2.8 In developing IFRS 9, the IASB decided to retain the accounting in IAS 39 for loan commitments, except to reflect the new impairment requirements. Consequently, in accordance with Section 5.5 of IFRS 9, an entity must apply the impairment requirements of IFRS 9 to loan commitments that are not otherwise within the scope of that Standard. Additionally, IFRS 9 requires that an issuer of a loan commitment to provide a loan at a below-market interest rate must measure it at the higher of (a) the amount of the loss allowance determined in accordance with Section 5.5 of that Standard and (b) the amount initially recognised less, when appropriate, the cumulative amount of

---

1 IFRS 9 eliminated the category of loans and receivables.

2 IFRS 15 *Revenue from Contracts with Customers*, issued in May 2014, replaced IAS 18.

income recognised in accordance with the principles of IFRS 15. The IASB did not change the accounting for loan commitments held by potential borrowers.

Financial guarantee contracts

BCZ2.9 In finalising IFRS 4 *Insurance Contracts*[3] in early 2004, the IASB reached the following conclusions:

(a) Financial guarantee contracts can have various legal forms, such as that of a guarantee, some types of letter of credit, a credit default contract or an insurance contract. However, although this difference in legal form may in some cases reflect differences in substance, the accounting for these instruments should not depend on their legal form.

(b) If a financial guarantee contract is not an insurance contract, as defined in IFRS 4, it should be within the scope of IAS 39. This was the case before the IASB finalised IFRS 4.

(c) As required before the IASB finalised IFRS 4, if a financial guarantee contract was entered into or retained on transferring to another party financial assets or financial liabilities within the scope of IAS 39, the issuer should apply IAS 39 to that contract even if it is an insurance contract, as defined in IFRS 4.

(d) Unless (c) applies, the following treatment is appropriate for a financial guarantee contract that meets the definition of an insurance contract:

(i) At inception, the issuer of a financial guarantee contract has a recognisable liability and should measure it at fair value. If a financial guarantee contract was issued in a stand-alone arm's length transaction to an unrelated party, its fair value at inception is likely to equal the premium received, unless there is evidence to the contrary.

(ii) Subsequently, the issuer should measure the contract at the higher of the amount determined in accordance with IAS 37 *Provisions, Contingent Liabilities and Contingent Assets* and the amount initially recognised less, when appropriate, cumulative amortisation recognised in accordance with IAS 18.[4]

BCZ2.10 Mindful of the need to develop a 'stable platform' of Standards for 2005, the IASB finalised IFRS 4 in early 2004 without specifying the accounting for these contracts and then published an Exposure Draft *Financial Guarantee Contracts and Credit Insurance* in July 2004 to expose for public comment the conclusion set out in paragraph BCZ2.9(d). The IASB set a comment deadline of 8 October 2004 and received more than 60 comment letters. Before reviewing the comment letters, the IASB held a public education session at which it received

---

3   The Board completed its insurance project with the issuance of IFRS 17. IFRS 17, issued in May 2017, replaced IFRS 4. IFRS 17 did not change the scope requirements relating to financial guarantee contracts.

4   IFRS 15, issued in May 2014, replaced IAS 18.

briefings from representatives of the International Credit Insurance & Surety Association and of the Association of Financial Guaranty Insurers.

BCZ2.11 Some respondents to the Exposure Draft of July 2004 argued that there were important economic differences between credit insurance contracts and other forms of contract that met the proposed definition of a financial guarantee contract. However, both in developing the Exposure Draft of July 2004 and in subsequently discussing the comments received, the IASB was unable to identify differences that would justify differences in accounting treatment.

BCZ2.12 Some respondents to the Exposure Draft of July 2004 noted that some credit insurance contracts contain features, such as cancellation and renewal rights and profit-sharing features, that the IASB will not address until Phase II of its project on insurance contracts. They argued that the Exposure Draft did not give enough guidance to enable them to account for these features. The IASB concluded it could not address such features in the short term. The IASB noted that when credit insurers issue credit insurance contracts, they typically recognise a liability measured as either the premium received or an estimate of the expected losses. However, the IASB was concerned that some other issuers of financial guarantee contracts might argue that no recognisable liability existed at inception. To provide a temporary solution that balances these competing concerns, the IASB decided the following:

(a) If the issuer of financial guarantee contracts has previously asserted explicitly that it regards such contracts as insurance contracts and has used accounting applicable to insurance contracts, the issuer may elect to apply either IAS 39 or IFRS 4 to such financial guarantee contracts.

(b) In all other cases, the issuer of a financial guarantee contract should apply IAS 39.

BCZ2.13 The IASB does not regard criteria such as those described in paragraph BCZ2.12(a) as suitable for the long term, because they can lead to different accounting for contracts that have similar economic effects. However, the IASB could not find a more compelling approach to resolve its concerns for the short term. Moreover, although the criteria described in paragraph BCZ2.12(a) may appear imprecise, the IASB believes that the criteria would provide a clear answer in the vast majority of cases. Paragraph B2.6 in IFRS 9 gives guidance on the application of those criteria.

BCZ2.14 The IASB considered convergence with US generally accepted accounting principles (GAAP). In US GAAP, the requirements for financial guarantee contracts (other than those covered by US Standards specific to the insurance sector) are in FASB Interpretation 45 *Guarantor's Accounting and Disclosure Requirements for Guarantees, Including Indirect Guarantees of Indebtedness of Others* (FIN 45). The recognition and measurement requirements of FIN 45 do not apply to guarantees issued between parents and their subsidiaries, between entities under common control, or by a parent or subsidiary on behalf of a subsidiary or the parent. Some respondents to the Exposure Draft of July 2004 asked the IASB to provide a similar exemption. They argued that the requirement to recognise these financial guarantee contracts in separate or individual financial statements would cause costs disproportionate to the likely benefits, given that intragroup transactions are eliminated on consolidation. However, to avoid the omission of material liabilities from separate or individual financial statements, the IASB did not create such an exemption.

BCZ2.15 The IASB issued the amendments for financial guarantee contracts in August 2005. After those amendments, the recognition and measurement requirements for financial guarantee contracts within the scope of IAS 39 were consistent with FIN 45 in some areas, but differed in others:

(a) Like FIN 45, IAS 39 requires initial recognition at fair value.

(b) IAS 39 requires systematic amortisation, in accordance with IAS 18[5], of the liability recognised initially. This is compatible with FIN 45, though FIN 45 contains less prescriptive requirements on subsequent measurement. Both IAS 39 and FIN 45 include a liability adequacy (or loss recognition) test, although the tests differ because of underlying differences in the Standards to which those tests refer (IAS 37 and Statement of Financial Accounting Standards No. 5 *Accounting for Contingencies*).

(c) Like FIN 45, IAS 39 permits a different treatment for financial guarantee contracts issued by insurers.

(d) Unlike FIN 45, IAS 39 does not contain exemptions for parents, subsidiaries or other entities under common control. However, any differences are reflected only in the separate or individual financial statements of the parent, subsidiaries or common control entities.

BCZ2.16 Some respondents to the Exposure Draft of July 2004 asked for guidance on the treatment of financial guarantee contracts by the holder. However, this was beyond the limited scope of the project.

BC2.17 In developing IFRS 9, the IASB decided to retain the accounting in IAS 39 for financial guarantee contracts, except to reflect the new impairment requirements. Consequently, financial guarantee contracts that are within the scope of IFRS 9 and that are not measured at fair value through profit or loss, are measured at the higher of (a) the amount of the loss allowance determined in accordance with Section 5.5 of that Standard and (b) the amount initially recognised less, when appropriate, the cumulative amount of income recognised in accordance with the principles of IFRS 15.

Contracts to buy or sell a non-financial item

BCZ2.18 Before the amendments in 2003, IAS 39 and IAS 32 were not consistent with respect to the circumstances in which a commodity-based contract meets the definition of a financial instrument and is accounted for as a derivative. The IASB concluded that the amendments should make them consistent on the basis of the notion that a contract to buy or sell a non-financial item should be accounted for as a derivative when it (i) can be settled net or by exchanging financial instruments and (ii) is not held for the purpose of receipt or delivery

---

5 IFRS 15, issued in May 2014, replaced IAS 18.

of the non-financial item in accordance with the entity's expected purchase, sale or usage requirements (a 'normal' purchase or sale). In addition, the IASB concluded that the notion of when a contract can be settled net should include contracts:

(a)   where the entity has a practice of settling similar contracts net in cash or another financial instrument or by exchanging financial instruments;

(b)   for which the entity has a practice of taking delivery of the underlying and selling it within a short period after delivery for the purpose of generating a profit from short-term fluctuations in price or dealer's margin; and

(c)   in which the non-financial item that is the subject of the contract is readily convertible to cash.

Because practices of settling net or taking delivery of the underlying and selling it within a short period after delivery also indicate that the contracts are not 'normal' purchases or sales, such contracts are within the scope of IAS 39 and are accounted for as derivatives. The IASB also decided to clarify that a written option that can be settled net in cash or another financial instrument, or by exchanging financial instruments, is within the scope of the Standard and cannot qualify as a 'normal' purchase or sale.

Accounting for a contract to buy or sell a non-financial item as a derivative

BCZ2.19   In the third phase of its project to replace IAS 39 with IFRS 9, the IASB considered replacing the hedge accounting requirements in IAS 39. As part of those deliberations, the IASB considered the accounting for executory contracts that gives rise to accounting mismatches in some situations. The IASB's decision is discussed in more detail below.

BCZ2.20   Contracts accounted for in accordance with IAS 39 include those contracts to buy or sell a non-financial item that can be settled net in cash (including net settlement in another financial instrument or by exchanging financial instruments), as if the contracts were financial instruments. In addition, IAS 39 specifies that there are various ways in which a contract to buy or sell a non-financial item can be settled net in cash. For example, a contract is considered to be settleable net in cash even if it is not explicit in the terms of the contract, but the entity has a practice of settling similar contracts net in cash.

BCZ2.21   However, such contracts are excluded from the scope of IAS 39 if they were entered into and continue to be held for the purpose of the receipt or delivery of a non-financial item in accordance with the entity's expected purchase, sale or usage requirements. This is commonly referred to as the 'own use' scope exception of IAS 39. The own use scope exception in IAS 39 mostly applies to contracts for commodity purchases or sales.

BCZ2.22   It is not uncommon for a commodity contract to be within the scope of IAS 39 and meet the definition of a derivative. Many commodity contracts meet the criteria for net settlement in cash because in many instances commodities are readily convertible to cash. When such a contract is accounted for as a derivative, it is measured at fair value with changes in the fair value recognised in profit or loss. If an entity enters into a derivative to hedge the change in the fair value of the commodity contract, that derivative is also measured at fair value with changes in fair value recognised in profit or loss. Because the changes in the fair value of the commodity contract and the derivative are recognised in profit or loss, an entity does not need hedge accounting.

BCZ2.23   However, in situations in which a commodity contract is not within the scope of IAS 39, it is accounted for as a normal sale or purchase contract ('executory contract'). Consequently, if an entity enters into a derivative contract to hedge changes in the fair value arising from a commodity supply contract that is not within the scope of IAS 39, an accounting mismatch is created. This is because the change in the fair value of the derivative is recognised in profit or loss while the change in the fair value of the commodity supply contract is not recognised (unless the contract is onerous).

BCZ2.24   To eliminate this accounting mismatch, an entity could apply hedge accounting. It could designate the commodity supply contracts (which meet the definition of a firm commitment) as a hedged item in a fair value hedge relationship. Consequently, the commodity supply contracts would be measured at fair value and the fair value changes would offset the changes in the fair value of the derivative instruments (to the extent that those are effective hedges). However, hedge accounting in these circumstances is administratively burdensome and often produces a less meaningful result than fair value accounting. Furthermore, entities enter into large volumes of commodity contracts and some positions may offset each other. An entity would therefore typically hedge on a net basis. Moreover, in many business models, this net position also includes physical long positions such as commodity inventory. That net position as a whole is then managed using derivatives to achieve a net position (after hedging) of nil (or close to nil). The net position is typically monitored, managed and adjusted daily. Because of the frequent movement of the net position and therefore the frequent adjustment of the net position to nil or close to nil by using derivatives, an entity would have to adjust the fair value hedge relationships frequently if the entity were to apply hedge accounting.

BCZ2.25   The IASB noted that in such situations hedge accounting would not be an efficient solution because entities manage a net position of derivatives, executory contracts and physical long positions in a dynamic way. Consequently, the IASB considered amending the scope of IAS 39 so that it would allow a commodity contract to be accounted for as a derivative in such situations. The IASB considered two alternatives for amending the scope of IAS 39:

(a)   allowing an entity to elect to account for commodity contracts as derivatives (ie a free choice); or

(b)   accounting for a commodity contract as a derivative if that is in accordance with the entity's fair value-based risk management strategy.

BCZ2.26   The IASB noted that giving an entity the choice to account for commodity contracts as derivatives would be tantamount to an elective 'own use' scope exception, which would have outcomes that would be similar to the accounting treatment in US GAAP. This approach would, in effect, allow an entity to elect the own use scope exception instead of derivative accounting at inception or a later date. Once the entity had elected to apply the scope exception it would not be able to change its election and switch to derivative accounting.

BCZ2.27   However, the IASB noted that such an approach would not be consistent with the approach in IAS 39 because:

(a)   the accounting treatment in accordance with IAS 39 is dependent on, and reflects, the purpose (ie whether it is for 'own use') for which the contracts to buy or sell non-financial items are entered into and continue to be held for. This is different from a free choice, which would allow, but not require, the accounting treatment to reflect the purpose of the contract.

(b)   in accordance with IAS 39, if similar contracts have been settled net, a contract to buy or sell non-financial items that can be settled net in cash must be accounted for as a derivative. Hence, a free choice would allow an entity to account for a commodity contract as a derivative regardless of whether similar contracts have been settled net in cash.

Consequently, in the Exposure Draft *Hedge Accounting* (the '2010 Hedge Accounting Exposure Draft'), the IASB decided not to propose that entities can elect to account for commodity contracts as derivatives.

BCZ2.28   Alternatively, the IASB considered applying derivative accounting to commodity contracts if that is in accordance with the entity's underlying business model and how the contracts are managed. Consequently, the actual type of settlement (ie whether settled net in cash) would not be conclusive for the evaluation of the appropriate accounting treatment. Instead, an entity would consider not only the purpose (based solely on the actual type of settlement) but also how the contracts are managed. As a result, if an entity's underlying business model changes and the entity no longer manages its commodity contracts on a fair value basis, the contracts would revert to the own use scope exception. This would be consistent with the criteria for using the fair value option for financial instruments (ie eliminating an accounting mismatch or if the financial instruments are managed on a fair value basis).

BCZ2.29   Consequently, the IASB proposed that derivative accounting would apply to contracts that would otherwise meet the own use scope exception if that is in accordance with the entity's fair value-based risk management strategy. The IASB believed that this approach would faithfully represent the financial position and the performance of entities that manage their entire business on a fair value basis, provide more useful information to users of financial statements, and be less onerous for entities than applying hedge accounting.

BCZ2.30 Most respondents to the 2010 Hedge Accounting Exposure Draft supported the IASB's approach of using fair value accounting for resolving the accounting mismatch that arises when a commodity contract that is outside the scope of IAS 39 is hedged with a derivative. Those who supported the proposal thought that it would facilitate a better presentation of the overall economic effects of entering into such hedging transactions.

BCZ2.31 However, some respondents were concerned that the proposal would have unintended consequences by creating an accounting mismatch for some entities. They argued that in scenarios in which there are other items that are managed within a fair value-based risk management strategy and those other items are not measured at fair value under IFRS, applying derivative accounting to 'own use contracts' would introduce (instead of eliminate) an accounting mismatch. For example, in the electricity industry the risk management for some power plants and the related electricity sales is on a fair value basis. If these entities had to apply derivative accounting for customer sales contracts it would create an accounting mismatch. This accounting mismatch would result in artificial profit or loss volatility if the power plant is measured at cost under IAS 16 *Property, Plant and Equipment*. Another example raised by respondents was that of entities risk-managing the own use contracts, inventory and derivatives on a fair value basis. An accounting mismatch would arise if the inventory is measured in accordance with IAS 2 *Inventories* at the lower of cost and net realisable value while the own use contracts are measured at fair value.

BCZ2.32 Some respondents also requested that the IASB remove the precondition that an entity achieves a nil or close to nil net risk position in order to qualify for accounting for executory contracts as derivatives. They argued that if the condition was not removed it would limit the benefits of the proposal. This is because some entities, while generally seeking to maintain a net risk position close to nil, may sometimes take an open position depending on market conditions. These respondents noted that, from an entity's perspective, whether it takes a position or manages its exposure close to nil, it is still employing a fair value-based risk management strategy and that the financial statements should reflect the nature of its risk management activities.

BCZ2.33 Some also requested that the IASB clarify whether the proposal required that a fair value-based risk management strategy is adopted at an entity level or whether the business model can be assessed at a level lower than the entity level. These respondents commented that within an entity, a part of the business may be risk-managed on a fair value basis while other businesses within the entity may be managed differently.

BCZ2.34 In the light of the arguments raised by respondents to the 2010 Hedge Accounting Exposure Draft, the IASB discussed whether an alternative would be extending the fair value option in IFRS 9 (for situations in which it eliminates or significantly reduces an accounting mismatch) to contracts that meet the own use scope exception. The IASB noted that because the fair value option would be an election by the entity, it would address the concerns raised about creating unintended accounting mismatches (see paragraph BCZ2.31) while still providing an efficient solution to the problem that the IASB wanted to address through its 2010 Hedge Accounting Exposure Draft.

BCZ2.35 The IASB considered that the disadvantage of providing an election (ie different accounting outcomes as the result of the entity's choice) by extending the fair value option in IFRS 9 was outweighed by the benefits of this alternative because:

(a) it is consistent with the IASB's objective to represent more faithfully the financial position and performance of entities that risk-manage an entire business on a fair value basis;

(b) it provides operational relief for entities that risk-manage an entire business on a dynamic fair value basis (ie it is less onerous than applying hedge accounting); and

(c) it does not have the unintended consequences of creating an accounting mismatch in some situations.

BCZ2.36 The IASB also considered whether specific transition requirements were needed for this amendment to IAS 39. Without those, the amendment would, by default, apply retrospectively. However, the IASB noted that because the decision is to be made at inception of a contract, the transition to the amended scope of IAS 39 would in effect be prospective in that the election would not be available for contracts that already exist on the date on which an entity applies the amendment for the first time.

BCZ2.37 The IASB considered that this transition would detrimentally affect financial statements because of the co-existence of two different accounting treatments (derivative and executory contract accounting) for similar contracts until all own use contracts that existed on transition would have matured. The IASB also noted that this effect may create a practical disincentive that would dissuade entities from making the election for new contracts. This could result in a failure to achieve the benefit of reducing accounting mismatches that the changes were designed to address.

BCZ2.38 Consequently, the IASB decided to provide entities with an option to elect accounting as at fair value through profit or loss for own use contracts that already exist on the date on which an entity applies the amendment for the first time. The IASB decided that that option would apply on an 'all-or-none basis' for all similar contracts in order to prevent selective use of this option for similar contracts. The IASB also noted that because these contracts would previously have been outside the scope of IFRS 7 *Financial Instruments: Disclosures*, entities would not have measured the fair value of these contracts for measurement or disclosure purposes. Consequently, restating comparatives would be impracticable because it would involve hindsight.

Business combination forward contracts

BCZ2.39   The IASB was advised that there was diversity in practice regarding the application of the exemption in paragraph 2(g) of IAS 39 (now paragraph 2.1(f) of IFRS 9).[6] That paragraph applies to particular contracts associated with a business combination and results in those contracts not being accounted for as derivatives while, for example, necessary regulatory and legal processes are being completed.

BCZ2.40   As part of the *Improvements to IFRSs* issued in April 2009, the IASB concluded that that paragraph should be restricted to forward contracts between an acquirer and a selling shareholder to buy or sell an acquiree in a business combination at a future acquisition date and should not apply to option contracts, whether or not currently exercisable, that on exercise will result in control of an entity.

BCZ2.41   The IASB concluded that the purpose of paragraph 2(g) is to exempt from the provisions of IAS 39 contracts for business combinations that are firmly committed to be completed. Once the business combination is consummated, the entity follows the requirements of IFRS 3. Paragraph 2(g) applies only when completion of the business combination is not dependent on further actions of either party (and only the passage of a normal period of time is required). Option contracts allow one party to control the occurrence or non-occurrence of future events depending on whether the option is exercised.

BCZ2.42   Several respondents to the Exposure Draft that proposed the amendment expressed the view that it should also apply to contracts to acquire investments in associates, referring to paragraph 20 of IAS 28. However, the acquisition of an interest in an associate represents the acquisition of a financial instrument. The acquisition of an interest in an associate does not represent an acquisition of a business with subsequent consolidation of the constituent net assets. The IASB noted that paragraph 20 of IAS 28 explains only the methodology used to account for investments in associates. This should not be taken to imply that the principles for business combinations and consolidations can be applied by analogy to accounting for investments in associates and joint ventures. The IASB concluded that paragraph 2(g) should not be applied by analogy to contracts to acquire investments in associates and similar transactions. This conclusion is consistent with the conclusion the IASB reached regarding impairment losses on investments in associates as noted in the *Improvements to IFRSs* issued in May 2008 and stated in paragraph BC27 of the Basis for Conclusions on IAS 28.

BCZ2.43   Some respondents to the Exposure Draft that proposed the amendment raised concerns about the proposed transition requirement. The IASB noted that determining the fair value of a currently outstanding contract when its inception was before the effective date of this amendment would require the use of hindsight and might not achieve comparability. Accordingly, the IASB

---

6   In October 2012 the IASB issued *Investment Entities* (Amendments to IFRS 10, IFRS 12 and IAS 27), which amended paragraph 2(g) of IAS 39 (now paragraph 2.1(f) of IFRS 9) to clarify that the exception should only apply to forward contracts that result in a business combination within the scope of IFRS 3 *Business Combinations*.

decided not to require retrospective application. The IASB also rejected applying the amendment prospectively only to new contracts entered into after the effective date because that would create a lack of comparability between contracts outstanding as of the effective date and contracts entered into after the effective date. Consequently, the IASB concluded that the amendment to paragraph 2(g) should be applied prospectively to all unexpired contracts for annual periods beginning on or after 1 January 2010.

Recognition and derecognition (Chapter 3)

Derecognition of a financial asset

The original IAS 39[7]

BCZ3.1 Under the original IAS 39, several concepts governed when a financial asset should be derecognised. It was not always clear when and in what order to apply those concepts. As a result, the derecognition requirements in the original IAS 39 were not applied consistently in practice.

BCZ3.2 As an example, the original IAS 39 was unclear about the extent to which risks and rewards of a transferred asset should be considered for the purpose of determining whether derecognition is appropriate and how risks and rewards should be assessed. In some cases (eg transfers with total returns swaps or unconditional written put options), the Standard specifically indicated whether derecognition was appropriate, whereas in others (eg credit guarantees) it was unclear. Also, some questioned whether the assessment should focus on risks and rewards or only risks and how different risks and rewards should be aggregated and weighed.

BCZ3.3 To illustrate, assume an entity sells a portfolio of short-term receivables of CU100[8] and provides a guarantee to the buyer for credit losses up to a specified amount (say CU20) that is less than the total amount of the receivables, but higher than the amount of expected losses (say CU5). In this case, should (a) the entire portfolio continue to be recognised, (b) the portion that is guaranteed continue to be recognised or (c) the portfolio be derecognised in full and a guarantee be recognised as a financial liability? The original IAS 39 did not give a clear answer and the IAS 39 Implementation Guidance Committee—a group set up by the IASB's predecessor body to resolve interpretative issues raised in practice—was unable to reach an agreement on how IAS 39 should be applied in this case. In developing proposals for improvements to IAS 39, the IASB concluded that it was important that IAS 39 should provide clear and consistent guidance on how to account for such a transaction.

---

7   In this Basis for Conclusions, the phrase 'the original IAS 39' refers to the Standard issued by the IASB's predecessor body, the International Accounting Standards Committee (IASC) in 1999 and revised in 2000.

8   In this Basis for Conclusions, monetary amounts are denominated in 'currency units (CU)'.

Exposure draft of proposed amendments to IAS 39 published in 2002

BCZ3.4   To resolve the problems, the exposure draft published in 2002 proposed an approach to derecognition under which a transferor of a financial asset continues to recognise that asset to the extent the transferor has a continuing involvement in it. Continuing involvement could be established in two ways: (a) a reacquisition provision (such as a call option, put option or repurchase agreement) and (b) a provision to pay or receive compensation based on changes in value of the transferred asset (such as a credit guarantee or net cash-settled option).

BCZ3.5   The purpose of the approach proposed in the exposure draft was to facilitate consistent implementation and application of IAS 39 by eliminating conflicting concepts and establishing an unambiguous, more internally consistent and workable approach to derecognition. The main benefits of the proposed approach were that it would greatly clarify IAS 39 and provide transparency on the balance sheet about any continuing involvement in a transferred asset.

Comments received

BCZ3.6   Many respondents to the exposure draft agreed that there were inconsistencies in the existing derecognition requirements in IAS 39. However, there was limited support for the proposed continuing involvement approach. Respondents expressed conceptual and practical concerns, including:

(a)   any benefits of the proposed changes did not outweigh the burden of adopting a different approach that had its own set of (as yet unidentified and unsolved) problems;

(b)   the proposed approach was a fundamental change from that in the original IAS 39;

(c)   the proposal did not achieve convergence with US GAAP;

(d)   the proposal was untested; and

(e)   the proposal was not consistent with the *Framework for the Preparation and Presentation of Financial Statements*.

BCZ3.7   Many respondents expressed the view that the basic approach in the original IAS 39 should be retained and the inconsistencies removed. The reasons included: (a) the existing IAS 39 had proven to be reasonable in concept and operational in practice and (b) the approach should not be changed until the IASB developed an alternative comprehensive approach.

Revisions to IAS 39

BCZ3.8 In response to the comments received, the IASB decided to revert to the derecognition concepts in the original IAS 39 and to clarify how and in what order the concepts should be applied. In particular, the IASB decided that an evaluation of the transfer of risks and rewards should precede an evaluation of the transfer of control for all types of transactions.

BCZ3.9 Although the structure and wording of the derecognition requirements were substantially amended, the IASB concluded that the requirements in the revised IAS 39 should not be substantially different from those in the original IAS 39. In support of this conclusion, it noted that the application of the requirements in the revised IAS 39 generally resulted in answers that could have been obtained under the original IAS 39. In addition, although there would be a need to apply judgement to evaluate whether substantially all risks and rewards had been retained, this type of judgement was not new compared with the original IAS 39. However, the revised requirements clarified the application of the concepts in circumstances in which it was previously unclear how IAS 39 should be applied (this guidance is now in IFRS 9). The IASB concluded that it would be inappropriate to revert to the original IAS 39 without such clarifications.

BCZ3.10 The IASB also decided to include guidance in the Standard that clarified how to evaluate the concepts of risks and rewards and of control. The IASB regarded such guidance as important to provide a framework for applying the concepts in IAS 39 (this guidance is now in IFRS 9). Although judgement was still necessary to apply the concepts in practice, the guidance was expected to increase consistency in how the concepts were applied.

BCZ3.11 More specifically, the IASB decided that the transfer of risks and rewards should be evaluated by comparing the entity's exposure before and after the transfer to the variability in the amounts and timing of the net cash flows of the transferred asset. If the entity's exposure, on a present value basis, had not changed significantly, the entity would conclude that it had retained substantially all risks and rewards. In this case, the IASB concluded that the asset should continue to be recognised. This accounting treatment was consistent with the treatment of repurchase transactions and some assets subject to deep in-the-money options under the original IAS 39. It was also consistent with how some interpreted the original IAS 39 when an entity sells a portfolio of short-term receivables but retains all substantive risks through the issue of a guarantee to compensate for all expected credit losses (see the example in paragraph BCZ3.3).

BCZ3.12 The IASB decided that control should be evaluated by looking to whether the transferee has the practical ability to sell the asset. If the transferee could sell the asset (eg because the asset was readily obtainable in the market and the transferee could obtain a replacement asset if it needed to return the asset to the transferor), the transferor had not retained control because the transferor did not control the transferee's use of the asset. If the transferee could not sell the asset (eg because the transferor had a call option and the asset was not readily obtainable in the market, so that the transferee could not obtain a replacement asset), the transferor had retained control because the transferee was not free to use the asset as its own.

BCZ3.13 The original IAS 39 also did not contain guidance on when a part of a financial asset could be considered for derecognition. The IASB decided to include such guidance in the Standard to clarify the issue (this guidance is now in IFRS 9). It decided that an entity should apply the derecognition principles to a part of a financial asset only if that part contained no risks and rewards relating to the part not being considered for derecognition. Accordingly, a part of a financial asset would be considered for derecognition only if it comprised:

(a) only specifically identified cash flows from a financial asset (or a group of similar financial assets);

(b) only a fully proportionate (pro rata) share of the cash flows from a financial asset (or a group of similar financial assets); or

(c) only a fully proportionate (pro rata) share of specifically identified cash flows from a financial asset (or a group of similar financial assets).

In all other cases the derecognition principles would be applied to the financial asset in its entirety.

Arrangements under which an entity retains the contractual rights to receive the cash flows of a financial asset but assumes a contractual obligation to pay the cash flows to one or more recipients

BCZ3.14 The original IAS 39 did not provide explicit guidance about the extent to which derecognition is appropriate for contractual arrangements in which an entity retains its contractual right to receive the cash flows from an asset, but assumes a contractual obligation to pay those cash flows to another entity (a 'pass-through arrangement'). Questions were raised in practice about the appropriate accounting treatment and divergent interpretations evolved for more complex structures.

BCZ3.15 To illustrate the issue using a simple example, assume the following. Entity A makes a five-year interest-bearing loan (the 'original asset') of CU100 to Entity B. Entity A then enters into an agreement with Entity C in which, in exchange for a cash payment of CU90, Entity A agrees to pass to Entity C 90 per cent of all principal and interest payments collected from Entity B (as, when and if collected). Entity A accepts no obligation to make any payments to Entity C other than 90 per cent of exactly what has been received from Entity B. Entity A provides no guarantee to Entity C about the performance of the loan and has no rights to retain 90 per cent of the cash collected from Entity B nor any obligation to pay cash to Entity C if cash has not been received from Entity B. In the example above, does Entity A have a loan asset of CU100 and a liability of CU90 or does it have an asset of CU10? To make the example more complex, what if Entity A first transfers the loan to a consolidated special purpose entity (SPE), which in turn passes through to investors the cash flows from the asset? Does the accounting treatment change because Entity A first sold the asset to an SPE?[9]

BCZ3.16   To address these issues, the exposure draft of proposed amendments to IAS 39 in 2002 included guidance to clarify under which conditions pass-through arrangements could be treated as a transfer of the underlying financial asset. The IASB concluded that an entity does not have an asset and a liability, as defined in the *Framework*,[10] when it enters into an arrangement to pass through cash flows from an asset and that arrangement meets specified conditions. In these cases, the entity acts more as an agent of the eventual recipients of the cash flows than as an owner of the asset. Accordingly, to the extent that those conditions are met the arrangement is treated as a transfer and considered for derecognition even though the entity may continue to collect cash flows from the asset. Conversely, to the extent the conditions are not met, the entity acts more as an owner of the asset with the result that the asset should continue to be recognised.

BCZ3.17   Respondents to the exposure draft (2002) were generally supportive of the proposed changes. Some respondents asked for further clarification of the requirements and the interaction with the requirements for consolidation of special purpose entities (in SIC-12 *Consolidation — Special Purpose Entities*). Respondents in the securitisation industry noted that under the proposed guidance many securitisation structures would not qualify for derecognition.

BCZ3.18   Considering these and other comments, the IASB decided to proceed with its proposals to issue guidance on pass-through arrangements and to clarify that guidance in finalising the revised IAS 39 (this guidance is now in IFRS 9).

BCZ3.19   The IASB concluded that the following three conditions must be met for treating a contractual arrangement to pass through cash flows from a financial asset as a transfer of that asset:

(a)   The entity has no obligation to pay amounts to the eventual recipients unless it collects equivalent amounts from the original asset. However, the entity is allowed to make short-term advances to the eventual recipient so long as it has the right of full recovery of the amount lent plus accrued interest.

(b)   The entity is prohibited by the terms of the transfer contract from selling or pledging the original asset other than as security to the eventual recipients for the obligation to pay them cash flows.

(c)   The entity has an obligation to remit any cash flows it collects on behalf of the eventual recipients without material delay. In addition, during the short settlement period, the entity is not entitled to reinvest such cash flows except for investments in cash or cash

---

9   SIC-12 *Consolidation — Special Purpose Entities* was withdrawn and superseded by IFRS 10 *Consolidated Financial Statements* issued in May 2011. There is no longer specific accounting guidance for special purpose entities because IFRS 10 applies to all types of entities.

10   References to the *Framework* in this Basis for Conclusions are to the IASC's *Framework for the Preparation and Presentation of Financial Statements*, adopted by the IASB in 2001 and in effect when parts of the Standard were developed and revised.

equivalents and where any interest earned from such investments is remitted to the eventual recipients.

BCZ3.20   These conditions followed from the definitions of assets and liabilities in the *Framework*. Condition (a) indicates that the transferor has no liability (because there is no present obligation to pay cash), and conditions (b) and (c) indicate that the transferor has no asset (because the transferor does not control the future economic benefits associated with the transferred asset).

BCZ3.21   The IASB decided that the derecognition tests that apply to other transfers of financial assets (ie the tests of transferring substantially all the risks and rewards and control) should also apply to arrangements to pass through cash flows that meet the three conditions but do not involve a fully proportional share of all or specifically identified cash flows. Thus, if the three conditions are met and the entity passes on a fully proportional share, either of all cash flows (as in the example in paragraph BCZ3.15) or of specifically identified cash flows (eg 10 per cent of all interest cash flows), the proportion sold is derecognised, provided the entity has transferred substantially all the risks and rewards of ownership. Thus, in the example in paragraph BCZ3.15, Entity A would report a loan asset of CU10 and derecognise CU90. Similarly, if an entity enters into an arrangement that meets the three conditions above, but the arrangement is not on a fully proportionate basis, the contractual arrangement would have to meet the general derecognition conditions to qualify for derecognition. This ensures consistency in the application of the derecognition model, whether a transaction is structured as a transfer of the contractual right to receive the cash flows of a financial asset or as an arrangement to pass through cash flows.

BCZ3.22   To illustrate a disproportionate arrangement using a simple example, assume the following. Entity A originates a portfolio of five-year interest-bearing loans of CU10,000. Entity A then enters into an agreement with Entity C in which, in exchange for a cash payment of CU9,000, Entity A agrees to pay to Entity C the first CU9,000 (plus interest) of cash collected from the loan portfolio. Entity A retains rights to the last CU1,000 (plus interest), ie it retains a subordinated residual interest. If Entity A collects, say, only CU8,000 of its loans of CU10,000 because some debtors default, Entity A would pass on to Entity C all of the CU8,000 collected and Entity A keeps nothing of the CU8,000 collected. If Entity A collects CU9,500, it passes CU9,000 to Entity C and retains CU500. In this case, if Entity A retains substantially all the risks and rewards of ownership because the subordinated retained interest absorbs all of the likely variability in net cash flows, the loans continue to be recognised in their entirety even if the three pass-through conditions are met.

BCZ3.23   The IASB recognised that many securitisations might fail to qualify for derecognition either because one or more of the three conditions (now in paragraph 3.2.5 of IFRS 9) were not met or because the entity has retained substantially all the risks and rewards of ownership.

BCZ3.24 Whether a transfer of a financial asset qualifies for derecognition does not differ depending on whether the transfer is direct to investors or through a consolidated SPE or trust that obtains the financial assets and, in turn, transfers a portion of those financial assets to third-party investors.

Transfers that do not qualify for derecognition

BCZ3.25 The original IAS 39 did not provide guidance about how to account for a transfer of a financial asset that does not qualify for derecognition. The amendments included such guidance (that guidance is now in IFRS 9). To ensure that the accounting reflects the rights and obligations that the transferor has in relation to the transferred asset, there is a need to consider the accounting for the asset as well as the accounting for the associated liability.

BCZ3.26 When an entity retains substantially all the risks and rewards of the asset (eg in a repurchase transaction), there are generally no special accounting considerations because the entity retains upside and downside exposure to gains and losses resulting from the transferred asset. Consequently, the asset continues to be recognised in its entirety and the proceeds received are recognised as a liability. Similarly, the entity continues to recognise any income from the asset along with any expense incurred on the associated liability.

Continuing involvement in a transferred asset

BCZ3.27 The IASB decided that if the entity determines that it has neither retained nor transferred substantially all of the risks and rewards of an asset and that it has retained control, the entity should continue to recognise the asset to the extent of its continuing involvement. This is to reflect the transferor's continuing exposure to the risks and rewards of the asset and that this exposure is not related to the entire asset, but is limited in amount. The IASB noted that precluding derecognition to the extent of the continuing involvement is useful to users of financial statements in such cases, because it reflects the entity's retained exposure to the risks and rewards of the financial asset better than full derecognition.

BCZ3.28 When the entity transfers some significant risks and rewards and retains others and derecognition is precluded because the entity retains control of the transferred asset, the entity no longer retains all the upside and downside exposure to gains and losses resulting from the transferred asset. Consequently, the revised IAS 39 required (and IFRS 9 now requires) the asset and the associated liability to be measured in a way that ensures that any changes in value of the transferred asset that are not attributed to the entity are not recognised by the entity.

BCZ3.29 For example, special measurement and income recognition issues arise if derecognition is precluded because the transferor has retained a call option or written a put option and the asset is measured at fair value. In those situations, in the absence of additional guidance, application of the general measurement and income recognition requirements for financial assets and financial liabilities may result in accounting that does not represent the transferor's rights and obligations related to the transfer.

Improved disclosure requirements issued in October 2010

BC3.30 In March 2009 the IASB published an Exposure Draft *Derecognition* (Proposed amendments to IAS 39 and IFRS 7) (the '2009 Derecognition Exposure Draft'). In June 2009 the IASB held public round tables in North America, Asia and Europe to discuss the proposals in the 2009 Derecognition Exposure Draft. In addition to the round tables, the IASB undertook an extensive outreach programme with users, preparers, regulators, auditors, trade associations and others.

BC3.31 However, in June 2010 the IASB revised its strategy and work plan. The IASB and the US Financial Accounting Standards Board (FASB) decided that their near-term priority should be to increase the transparency and comparability of their standards by improving and aligning US GAAP and IFRS disclosure requirements for financial assets transferred to another entity. The boards also decided to conduct additional research and analysis, including a post-implementation review of the FASB's recently amended requirements, as a basis for assessing the nature and direction of any further efforts to improve or align IFRS and US GAAP. As a result, the IASB finalised the disclosure requirements that were included in the 2009 Derecognition Exposure Draft with a view to aligning the disclosure requirements in IFRS with US GAAP requirements for transfers of financial assets. Those disclosure requirements were issued in October 2010 as an amendment to IFRS 7. In October 2010 the requirements in IAS 39 for derecognition of financial assets and financial liabilities were carried forward unchanged to IFRS 9.

Exemption for repurchased financial liabilities

BC3.32 IFRS 9 sets out the requirements for the derecognition of financial liabilities. IFRS 17 *Insurance Contracts* amended those derecognition requirements in IFRS 9 by permitting an exemption when an entity repurchases its financial liability in specific circumstances. The Board's considerations in providing that exemption are set out in paragraph BC65(c) of the Basis for Conclusions on IFRS 17.

Fees in the '10 per cent' Test for Derecognition of Financial Liabilities (*Annual Improvements to IFRS Standards 2018–2020*)

BC3.33 Paragraph 3.3.2 requires an entity to derecognise the original financial liability and recognise a new financial liability when there is:

(a) an exchange between an existing borrower and lender of debt instruments with substantially different terms; or

(b) a substantial modification of the terms of an existing financial liability or a part of it.

Paragraph B3.3.6 specifies that the terms are substantially different if the discounted present value of the cash flows under the new terms using the original effective interest rate is at least 10 per cent different from the discounted present value of the remaining cash flows of the original financial liability (10 per cent test). Paragraph B3.3.6 requires an entity to include 'any fees paid net of any fees received' in the 10 per cent test.

BC3.34 The Board decided to amend paragraph B3.3.6 in response to a request to clarify which fees an entity includes in the 10 per cent test. The clarification aligns with the objective of the test, which is to quantitatively assess the significance of any difference between the old and new contractual terms on the basis of the changes in the contractual cash flows between the borrower and lender.

BC3.35 The transition requirements in paragraph 7.2.35 reflect the Board's view that the expected benefit from retrospective application of the amendment would not outweigh the cost of requiring entities to reassess all previous modifications and exchanges. In particular, retrospective application would be unlikely to provide users of financial statements with trend information because financial liabilities are generally modified or exchanged on an ad hoc basis.

BC3.36 Paragraph AG62 of IAS 39 includes the same requirements as those in paragraph B3.3.6 of IFRS 9. An entity that has not previously applied any version of IFRS 9 and whose activities are predominantly connected with insurance is permitted to apply IAS 39 for a limited period of time. In providing the temporary exemption from applying IFRS 9, the Board had not contemplated maintaining IAS 39 (other than for hedge accounting) given the temporary and limited nature of the exemption. Therefore, the Board did not amend paragraph AG62 of IAS 39.

Classification (Chapter 4)

Classification of financial assets

BC4.1 In IFRS 9 as issued in 2009 the IASB aimed to help users to understand the financial reporting of financial assets by:

(a) reducing the number of classification categories and providing a clearer rationale for measuring financial assets in a particular way that replaces the numerous categories in IAS 39, each of which has specific rules dictating how an asset can or must be classified;

(b) applying a single impairment method to all financial assets not measured at fair value, which replaces the many different impairment methods that are associated with the numerous classification categories in IAS 39; and

(c) aligning the measurement attribute of financial assets with the way the entity manages its financial assets ('business model') and their contractual cash flow characteristics, thus providing relevant and useful information to users for their assessment of the amounts, timing and uncertainty of the entity's future cash flows.

BC4.2 The IASB believes that IFRS 9 both helps users to understand and use the financial reporting of financial assets and eliminates much of the complexity in IAS 39. The IASB disagrees with the assertion made by a dissenting IASB member that IFRS 9 does not meet the objective of reducing the number of classification categories for financial assets and eliminating the specific rules associated with those categories. Unlike IAS 39, IFRS 9 provides a clear rationale for measuring a financial asset at either amortised cost or fair value, and hence helps users to understand the financial reporting of financial assets. IFRS 9 aligns the measurement attribute of financial assets with the way the entity manages its financial assets ('business model') and their contractual cash flow characteristics. In so doing, IFRS 9 significantly reduces complexity by eliminating the numerous rules associated with each classification category in IAS 39. Consistently with all other financial assets, hybrid contracts with financial asset hosts are classified and measured in their entirety, thereby eliminating the complex and rule-based requirements in IAS 39 for embedded derivatives. Furthermore, IFRS 9 requires a single impairment method, which replaces the different impairment methods associated with the many classification categories in IAS 39. The IASB believes that these changes will help users to understand the financial reporting of financial assets and to better assess the amounts, timing and uncertainty of future cash flows.

Measurement categories for financial assets

BC4.3 Some users of financial statements support a single measurement method — fair value — for all financial assets. They view fair value as more relevant than other measurements in helping them to assess the effect of current economic events on an entity. They assert that having one measurement attribute for all financial assets promotes consistency in valuation, presentation and disclosure and improves the usefulness of financial statements.

BC4.4 However, many users and others, including many preparers and auditors of financial statements and regulators, do not support the recognition in the statement of comprehensive income of changes in fair value for financial assets that are not held for trading or are not managed on a fair value basis. Some users say that they often value an entity on the basis of its business model and that in some circumstances cost-based information provides relevant information that can be used to predict likely actual cash flows.

BC4.5 Some, including some of those who generally support the broad application of fair value for financial assets, raise concerns about the use of fair value when fair value cannot be determined within a narrow range. Those views were consistent with the general concerns raised during the financial crisis. Many also believe that other issues, including financial statement presentation, need to be addressed before a comprehensive fair value measurement requirement would be feasible.

BC4.6 In response to those views, the IASB decided that measuring all financial assets at fair value is not the most appropriate approach to improving the financial reporting for financial instruments. Accordingly, the 2009 Exposure Draft *Financial Instruments: Classification and Measurement* (the '2009 Classification and Measurement Exposure Draft') proposed that entities should classify financial assets into two primary measurement categories: amortised cost and fair value (the 'mixed attribute approach'). The IASB noted that both of those measurement methods can provide useful information to users of financial statements for particular types of financial assets in particular circumstances.

BC4.7 Almost all respondents to the 2009 Classification and Measurement Exposure Draft supported the mixed attribute approach, stating that amortised cost provides relevant and useful information about particular financial assets in particular circumstances because it provides information about the entity's likely actual cash flows. Some respondents said that fair value does not provide such information because it assumes that the financial asset is sold or transferred on the measurement date.

BC4.8 Accordingly, IFRS 9 requires some financial assets to be measured at amortised cost if particular conditions are met.

Fair value information in the statements of financial position and financial performance

BC4.9 Some respondents to the 2009 Classification and Measurement Exposure Draft proposed that fair value information should be presented in the statement of financial position for financial assets measured at amortised cost. Some of those supporting such presentation said that the information provided would be more reliable and timely if it were required to be presented in the statement of financial position instead of in the notes.

BC4.10 The IASB also considered whether the total gains and losses for the period related to fair value measurements in Level 3 of the fair value measurement hierarchy (paragraph 27A of IFRS 7 describes the levels in the fair value hierarchy[11]) should be presented separately in the statement of comprehensive income. Those supporting such presentation said that its prominence would draw attention to how much of the total fair value gain or loss for the period was attributable to fair value measurements that are subject to more measurement uncertainty.

---

11 IFRS 13 *Fair Value Measurement*, issued in May 2011, defines fair value and contains requirements for measuring fair value and for disclosing information about fair value measurements. IFRS 13 contains a three-level fair value hierarchy for the inputs used in valuation techniques to measure fair value and for the related disclosures. As a consequence paragraph 27A of IFRS 7 has been deleted.

BC4.11　The IASB decided that it would reconsider both issues at a future date. The IASB noted that the Level 3 gains or losses for the period are required to be disclosed in the notes to the financial statements in accordance with IFRS 7.[12] The IASB also noted that neither proposal had been exposed for public comment and further consultation was required. The IASB decided that these two issues should form part of convergence discussions with the FASB.

Approach to classifying financial assets

BC4.12　The 2009 Classification and Measurement Exposure Draft proposed that an entity should classify its financial assets into two primary measurement categories on the basis of the financial assets' characteristics and the entity's business model for managing them. Thus, a financial asset would be measured at amortised cost if two conditions were met:

(a)　the financial asset has only basic loan features; and

(b)　the financial asset is managed on a contractual yield basis.

A financial asset that did not meet both conditions would be measured at fair value.

BC4.13　Most respondents supported classification on the basis of the contractual terms of the financial asset and how an entity manages groups of financial assets. Although they agreed with the principles proposed in the 2009 Classification and Measurement Exposure Draft, some did not agree with the way the approach was described and said that more application guidance was needed, in particular to address the following issues:

(a)　the order in which the two conditions are considered;

(b)　how the 'managed on a contractual yield basis' condition should be applied; and

(c)　how the 'basic loan features' condition should be applied.

BC4.14　Most respondents agreed that the two conditions for determining how financial assets are measured were necessary. However, many questioned the order in which the two conditions should be considered. The IASB agreed with those who commented that it would be more efficient for an entity to consider the business model condition first. Consequently, the IASB clarified that entities would consider the business model first. However, the IASB noted that the contractual cash flow characteristics of any financial asset within a business model that has the objective of collecting contractual cash flows must also be assessed to ensure that amortised cost provides relevant information to users.

12　IFRS 13, issued in May 2011, requires disclosures about fair value measurements. As a consequence paragraph 27B(c) and (d) of IFRS 7 has been deleted.

The entity's business model

BC4.15 The IASB concluded that an entity's business model affects the predictive quality of contractual cash flows—ie whether the likely actual cash flows will result primarily from the collection of contractual cash flows. Accordingly, the 2009 Classification and Measurement Exposure Draft proposed that a financial asset should be measured at amortised cost only if it is 'managed on a contractual yield basis'. This condition was intended to ensure that the measurement of a financial asset provides information that is useful to users of financial statements in predicting likely actual cash flows.

BC4.16 Almost all respondents to the exposure draft agreed that classification and measurement should reflect how an entity manages its financial assets. However, most expressed concern that the term 'managed on a contractual yield basis' would not adequately describe that principle and that more guidance was needed.

BC4.17 In August 2009 the FASB posted on its website a description of its tentative approach to classification and measurement of financial instruments. That approach also considers the entity's business model. Under that approach, financial instruments would be measured at fair value through profit or loss unless:

> ... an entity's business strategy is to hold debt instruments with principal amounts for collection or payment(s) of contractual cash flows rather than to sell or settle the financial instruments with a third party ...

The FASB also provided explanatory text:

> ... an entity's business strategy for a financial instrument would be evaluated based on how the entity manages its financial instruments rather than based on the entity's intent for an individual financial instrument. The entity also would demonstrate that it holds a high proportion of similar instruments for long periods of time relative to their contractual terms.

BC4.18 The IASB had intended 'managed on a contractual yield basis' to describe a similar condition. However, it decided not to use the FASB's proposed guidance because the additional guidance included would still necessitate significant judgement. In addition, the IASB noted that the FASB's proposed approach might be viewed as very similar to the notion of 'held to maturity' in IAS 39, which could result in 'bright line' guidance on how to apply it. Most respondents believed the IASB should avoid such bright lines and that an entity should be required to exercise judgement.

BC4.19 Therefore, in response to the concerns noted in paragraph BC4.16, the IASB clarified the condition by requiring an entity to measure a financial asset at amortised cost only if the objective of the entity's business model is to hold the financial asset to collect the contractual cash flows. The IASB also clarified in the application guidance that:

(a) it is expected that an entity may sell some financial assets that it holds with an objective of collecting the contractual cash flows. Very few business models entail holding all instruments until maturity. However, frequent buying and selling of financial assets is not consistent with a business model of holding financial assets to collect contractual cash flows.

(b) an entity needs to use judgement to determine at what level this condition should be applied. That determination is made on the basis of how an entity manages its business. It is not made at the level of an individual financial asset.

BC4.20 The IASB noted that an entity's business model does not relate to a choice (ie it is not a voluntary designation) but instead it is a matter of fact that can be observed by the way an entity is managed and information is provided to its management.

BC4.21 For example, if an investment bank uses a trading business model, it could not easily become a savings bank that uses an 'originate and hold' business model. Consequently, a business model is very different from 'management intentions', which can relate to a single instrument. The IASB concluded that sales or transfers of financial instruments before maturity would not be inconsistent with a business model with an objective of collecting contractual cash flows, as long as such transactions were consistent with that business model; instead of with a business model that has the objective of realising changes in fair values.

Contractual cash flow characteristics

BC4.22 The 2009 Classification and Measurement Exposure Draft proposed that only financial instruments with basic loan features could be measured at amortised cost. It specified that a financial instrument has basic loan features if its contractual terms give rise on specified dates to cash flows that are solely payments of principal and interest on the principal amount outstanding. For the purposes of this condition, interest is consideration for the time value of money and the credit risk associated with the principal amount outstanding during a particular period of time, which may include a premium for liquidity risk.

BC4.23 The objective of the effective interest method for financial instruments measured at amortised cost is to allocate interest revenue or expense to the relevant period. Cash flows that are interest always have a close relation to the amount advanced to the debtor (the 'funded' amount) because interest is consideration for the time value of money and the credit risk associated with the issuer of the instrument and with the instrument itself. The IASB noted that the effective interest method is not an appropriate method to allocate cash flows that are not principal or interest on the principal amount outstanding. The IASB concluded that if a financial asset contains contractual cash flows that are not principal or interest on the principal amount outstanding then a valuation overlay to contractual cash flows (fair value) is required to ensure that the reported financial information provides useful information.

BC4.24 Most respondents to the 2009 Classification and Measurement Exposure Draft agreed with the principle that classification should reflect the contractual terms of the financial asset. However, many objected to the label 'basic loan features' and requested more guidance to apply the principle to particular financial assets. Respondents were also concerned that the 2009 Classification and Measurement Exposure Draft did not discuss 'immaterial' or 'insignificant' features that they believed ought not to affect classification.

BC4.25 The IASB decided to clarify how contractual cash flow characteristics should affect classification and improve the examples that illustrate how the condition should be applied. It decided not to add application guidance clarifying that the notion of materiality applies to this condition, because that notion applies to every item in the financial statements. However, it did add application guidance that a contractual cash flow characteristic does not affect the classification of a financial asset if it is 'not genuine'.

Application of the two classification conditions to particular financial assets

Investments in contractually linked instruments (tranches)

BC4.26 A structured investment vehicle may issue different tranches to create a 'waterfall' structure that prioritises the payments by the issuer to the holders of the different tranches. In typical waterfall structures, multiple contractually linked instruments effect concentrations of credit risk in which payments to holders are prioritised. Such structures specify the order in which any losses that the issuer incurs are allocated to the tranches. The 2009 Classification and Measurement Exposure Draft concluded that tranches providing credit protection (albeit on a contingent basis) to other tranches are leveraged because they expose themselves to higher credit risk by writing credit protection to other tranches. Hence their cash flows do not represent solely payments of principal and interest on the principal amount outstanding. Thus, only the most senior tranche could have basic loan features and might qualify for measurement at amortised cost, because only the most senior tranche would receive credit protection in all situations.

BC4.27 The 2009 Classification and Measurement Exposure Draft proposed that the classification principle should be based on whether a tranche could provide credit protection to any other tranches in any possible scenario. In the IASB's view, a contract that contains credit concentration features that create ongoing subordination (not only in a liquidation scenario) would include contractual cash flows that represent a premium for providing credit protection to other tranches. Only the most senior tranche does not receive such a premium.

BC4.28 In proposing this approach, the IASB concluded that subordination in itself should not preclude amortised cost measurement. The ranking of an entity's instruments is a common form of subordination that affects almost all lending transactions. Commercial law (including bankruptcy law) typically sets out a basic ranking for creditors. This is required because not all creditors' claims are contractual (eg claims regarding damages for unlawful behaviour and for tax liabilities or social insurance contributions). Although it is often difficult to determine exactly the degree of leverage resulting from this subordination, the IASB believes that it is reasonable to assume that commercial law does not intend to create leveraged credit exposure for general creditors such as trade creditors. Thus, the IASB believes that the credit risk associated with general creditors does not preclude the contractual cash flows representing the payments of principal and interest on the principal amount outstanding. Consequently, the credit risk associated with any secured or senior liabilities ranking above general creditors should also not preclude the contractual cash flows from representing payments of principal and interest on the principal amount outstanding.

BC4.29   Almost all respondents disagreed with the approach in the 2009 Classification and Measurement Exposure Draft for investments in contractually linked instruments for the following reasons:

(a)   It focused on form and legal structure instead of the economic characteristics of the financial instruments.

(b)   It would create structuring opportunities because of the focus on the existence of a waterfall structure, without consideration of the characteristics of the underlying instruments.

(c)   It would be an exception to the overall classification model, driven by anti-abuse considerations.

BC4.30   In particular, respondents argued that the proposals in the 2009 Classification and Measurement Exposure Draft would conclude that some tranches provide credit protection and therefore were ineligible for measurement at amortised cost, even though that tranche might have a lower credit risk than the underlying pool of instruments that would themselves be eligible for measurement at amortised cost.

BC4.31   The IASB did not agree that the proposals in the 2009 Classification and Measurement Exposure Draft were an exception to the overall classification model. In the IASB's view, those proposals were consistent with many respondents' view that any financial instrument that creates contractual subordination should be subject to the proposed classification criteria and no specific guidance should be required to apply the classification approach to these instruments. However, it noted that, for contractually linked instruments that effect concentrations of credit risk, many respondents did not agree that the contractual cash flow characteristics determined by the terms and conditions of the financial asset in isolation best reflected the economic characteristics of that financial asset.

BC4.32   Respondents proposed other approaches in which an investor 'looks through' to the underlying pool of instruments of a waterfall structure and measures the instruments at fair value if looking through is not possible. They made the following points:

(a)   *Practicability*: The securitisation transactions intended to be addressed were generally over-the-counter transactions in which the parties involved had sufficient information about the assets to perform an analysis of the underlying pool of instruments.

(b)   *Complexity*: Complex accounting judgement was appropriate to reflect the complex economic characteristics of the instrument. In particular, in order to obtain an understanding of the effects of the contractual terms and conditions, an investor would have to understand the underlying pool of instruments. Also, requiring fair value measurement if it were not practicable to look through to the underlying pool of instruments would allow an entity to avoid such complexity.

(c)   *Mechanics*: Amortised cost measurement should be available only if all of the instruments in the underlying pool of instruments had contractual cash flows that represented payments of principal and interest on the principal amount outstanding. Some also suggested that instruments that change the cash flow variability of the underlying pool of instruments in a way that is consistent with representing solely payments of principal and interest on the principal amount outstanding, or aligned currency/interest rates with the issued notes, should not preclude amortised cost measurement.

(d)   *Relative exposure to credit risk*: Many favoured use of a probability-weighted approach to assess whether an instrument has a lower or higher exposure to credit risk than the average credit risk of the underlying pool of instruments.

BC4.33   The IASB was persuaded that classification solely on the basis of the contractual features of the financial asset being assessed for classification would not capture the economic characteristics of the instruments when a concentrated credit risk arises through contractual linkage. Consequently, the IASB decided that, unless it is impracticable, an entity should 'look through' to assess the underlying cash flow characteristics of the financial assets and to assess the exposure to credit risk of those financial assets relative to the underlying pool of instruments.

BC4.34   The IASB concluded that the nature of contractually linked instruments that effect concentrations of credit risk justifies this approach because the variability of cash flows from the underlying pool of instruments is a reference point, and tranching only reallocates credit risk. Thus, if the contractual cash flows of the assets in the underlying pool represent payments of principal and interest on the principal amount outstanding, any tranche that is exposed to the same or lower credit risk (as evidenced by the cash flow variability of the tranche relative to the overall cash flow variability of the underlying instrument pool) would also be deemed to represent payments of principal and interest on the principal amount outstanding. The IASB also took the view that such an approach would address many of the concerns raised in the comment letters with regard to structuring opportunities and the focus on the contractual form of the financial asset, instead of its underlying economic characteristics. The IASB also noted that in order to understand and make the judgement about whether particular types of financial assets have the required cash flow characteristics, an entity would have to understand the characteristics of the underlying issuer to ensure that the instrument's cash flows are solely payments of principal and interest on the principal amount outstanding.

BC4.35   To apply this approach, the IASB decided that an entity should:

(a)   determine whether the contractual terms of the issued instrument (the financial asset being classified) give rise to cash flows that are solely payments of principal and interest on the principal amount outstanding. The IASB concluded that the issued instrument must have contractual cash flows that are solely payments of principal and interest on the principal amount outstanding.

(b)   look through to the underlying pool of instruments until it can identify the instruments that are creating (instead of simply passing through) the cash flows.

(c)   determine whether one or more of the instruments in the underlying pool has contractual cash flows that are solely payments of principal and interest on the principal amount outstanding. The IASB concluded that the underlying pool must contain one or more instruments that have contractual cash flows that are solely payments of principal and interest on the principal amount outstanding.

(d)   assess whether any other instruments in the underlying pool only:

(i)   reduce the cash flow variability of the underlying pool of instruments in a way that is consistent with representing solely payments of principal and interest on the principal amount outstanding, or

(ii)   align the cash flows of the issued financial assets with the underlying pool of financial instruments.

The IASB concluded that the existence of such instruments does not preclude the cash flows from representing solely payments of principal and interest on the principal amount outstanding. The IASB determined that the existence of other instruments in the pool would, however, preclude the cash flows representing solely payments of principal and interest on the principal amount outstanding. For example, an underlying pool that contains government bonds and an instrument that swaps government credit risk for (riskier) corporate credit risk would not have cash flows that represent solely principal and interest on the principal amount outstanding.

(e)   measure at fair value any issued instrument in which any of the financial instruments in the underlying pool:

(i)   have cash flows that do not represent solely payments of principal and interest on the principal amount outstanding; or

(ii)   could change so that cash flows may not represent solely payments of principal and interest on the principal amount outstanding at any point in the future.

(f)   measure at fair value any issued instrument whose exposure to credit risk in the underlying pool of financial instruments is greater than the exposure to credit risk of the underlying pool of financial instruments. The IASB decided that if the range of expected losses on the issued instrument is greater than the weighted average range of expected losses on the underlying pool of financial instruments, then the issued instrument should be measured at fair value.

BC4.36   The IASB also decided that if it were not practicable to look through to the underlying pool of financial instruments, entities should measure the issued instrument at fair value.

Financial assets acquired at a discount that reflects incurred credit losses

BC4.37   The 2009 Classification and Measurement Exposure Draft proposed that if a financial asset is acquired at a discount that reflects incurred credit losses, it cannot be measured at amortised cost because:

(a)   the entity does not hold such financial assets to collect the cash flows arising from those assets' contractual terms; and

(b)   an investor acquiring a financial asset at such a discount believes that the actual losses will be less than the losses that are reflected in the purchase price. Thus, that asset creates exposure to significant variability in actual cash flows and such variability is not interest.

BC4.38   Almost all respondents disagreed with the IASB's conclusion that these assets cannot be held to collect the contractual cash flows. They regarded that conclusion as an exception to a classification approach based on the entity's business model for managing the financial assets. In particular, they noted that entities could acquire and subsequently manage such assets as part of an otherwise performing asset portfolio for which the objective of the entity's business model is to hold the assets to collect contractual cash flows.

BC4.39   Respondents also noted that an entity's expectations about actual future cash flows are not the same as the contractual cash flows of the financial asset. Those expectations are irrelevant to an assessment of the financial asset's contractual cash flow characteristics.

BC4.40   The IASB agreed that the general classification approach in IFRS 9 should apply to financial assets acquired at a discount that reflects incurred credit losses. Thus, when such assets meet the conditions in paragraph 4.1.2, they are measured at amortised cost.

Alternative approaches to classifying assets

BC4.41   In its deliberations leading to the 2009 Classification and Measurement Exposure Draft, the IASB discussed alternative approaches to classification and measurement. In particular, it considered an approach in which financial assets that have basic loan features, are managed on a contractual yield basis and meet the definition of loans and receivables in IAS 39 would be measured at amortised cost. All other financial assets would be measured at fair value. The fair value changes for each period for those financial assets with basic loan features that are managed on a contractual yield basis would be disaggregated and presented as follows:

(a) changes in recognised value determined on an amortised cost basis (including impairments determined using the incurred loss impairment requirements in IAS 39) would be presented in profit or loss; and

(b) any difference between the amortised cost measure in (a) and the fair value change for the period would be presented in other comprehensive income.

BC4.42 The IASB also considered variants in which all financial assets and financial liabilities would be measured at fair value. One variant would be to present both the amounts in paragraph BC4.41(a) and (b) in profit or loss, but separately. Another variant would be to measure all financial instruments (including financial assets that meet the two conditions specified in the 2009 Classification and Measurement Exposure Draft and meet the definition of loans and receivables in IAS 39) at fair value in the statement of financial position. All financial instruments (including financial liabilities) with basic loan features that are managed on a contractual yield basis would be disaggregated and presented as described in paragraph BC4.41(a) and (b).

BC4.43 Respondents noted that the alternative approach described in paragraph BC4.41 and both variants described in paragraph BC4.42 would result in more financial assets and financial liabilities being measured at fair value. Respondents also noted that the alternative approach would apply only to financial assets. Lastly, almost all respondents noted that splitting gains and losses between profit or loss and other comprehensive income would increase complexity and reduce understandability. The IASB concluded that those approaches would not result in more useful information than the approach in IFRS 9 and did not consider them further.

BC4.44 The IASB also considered and rejected the following approaches to classification:

(a) *Classification based on the definition of held for trading:* A few respondents suggested that all financial assets and financial liabilities that are not 'held for trading' should be eligible for measurement at amortised cost. However, in the IASB's view, the notion of 'held for trading' is too narrow and cannot appropriately reflect all situations in which amortised cost does not provide useful information.

(b) *Three-category approach:* Some respondents suggested retaining a three-category approach, ie including a third category similar to the available-for-sale category in IAS 39. However, in the IASB's view, such an approach would neither significantly improve nor reduce the complexity of the reporting for financial instruments.

(c) *Classification based only on the business model:* A small number of respondents thought the contractual terms of the instrument condition was unnecessary and that classification should depend solely on the entity's business model for managing financial instruments.

However, in the IASB's view, determining classification solely on the basis of how an entity manages its financial instruments would result in misleading information that is not useful to a user in understanding the risks associated with complex or risky instruments. The IASB concluded, as had almost all respondents, that the contractual cash flow characteristics condition is required to ensure that amortised cost is used only when it provides information that is useful in predicting the entity's future cash flows.

(d) *Amortised cost as the default option:* The IASB considered developing conditions that specified when a financial asset must be measured at fair value, with the requirement that all other financial instruments would be measured at amortised cost. The IASB rejected that approach because it believes that new conditions would have to be developed in the future to address innovative financial products. In addition, the IASB noted that such an approach would not be practical because an entity can apply amortised cost only to some types of financial instruments.

(e) *Originated loan approach:* In developing an approach to distinguish between financial assets measured at fair value and amortised cost the IASB considered a model in which only loans originated by the entity would qualify for amortised cost measurement. The IASB acknowledged that for originated instruments the entity potentially has better information about the future contractual cash flows and credit risk than for purchased loans. However, the IASB decided not to pursue that approach, mainly because some entities manage originated and purchased loans in the same portfolio. Distinguishing between originated and purchased loans, which would be done mainly for accounting purposes, would involve systems changes. In addition, the IASB noted that 'originated loans' might easily be created by placing purchased loans into an investment vehicle. The IASB also noted that the definition of loans and receivables in IAS 39 had created application problems in practice.

Tainting

BC4.45 The IASB considered whether it should prohibit an entity from classifying a financial asset as measured at amortised cost if the entity had previously sold or reclassified financial assets instead of holding them to collect the contractual cash flows. A restriction of this kind is often called 'tainting'. However, the IASB believes that classification based on the entity's business model for managing financial assets and the contractual cash flow characteristics of those financial assets provides a clear rationale for measurement. A tainting provision would increase the complexity of application, be unduly prohibitive in the context of that approach and could give rise to classification that is inconsistent with the classification approach in IFRS 9. However, in 2009 the IASB amended IAS 1 *Presentation of Financial Statements* to require an entity to present separately in the statement of comprehensive income all gains and losses arising from the derecognition of financial assets measured at amortised cost. The IASB also amended IFRS 7 in

2009 to require an entity to disclose an analysis of those gains and losses, including the reasons for derecognising those financial assets. Those requirements enable users of financial statements to understand the effects of derecognising before maturity instruments measured at amortised cost and also provides transparency in situations where an entity has measured financial assets at amortised cost on the basis of having an objective of managing those assets in order to collect the contractual cash flows but regularly sells them.

Classification of financial liabilities

BC4.46 Immediately after issuing the first chapters of IFRS 9 in November 2009, the IASB began an extensive outreach programme to gather feedback on the classification and measurement of financial liabilities, in particular how best to address the effects of changes in the fair value of a financial liability caused by changes in the risk that the issuer will fail to perform on that liability. The IASB obtained information and views from its FIWG and from users, regulators, preparers, auditors and others from a range of industries across different geographical regions. The IASB also developed a questionnaire to ask users of financial statements how they use information about the effects of changes in liabilities' credit risk (if at all) and what their preferred method of accounting is for selected financial liabilities. The IASB received over 90 responses to that questionnaire.

BC4.47 During the outreach programme, the IASB explored several approaches for classification and subsequent measurement of financial liabilities that would exclude the effects of changes in a liability's credit risk from profit or loss, including:

(a) measuring liabilities at fair value and presenting in other comprehensive income the portion of the change in fair value that is attributable to changes in the liability's credit risk. A variant of this alternative would be to present in other comprehensive income the entire change in fair value.

(b) measuring liabilities at an 'adjusted' fair value whereby the liability would be remeasured for all changes in fair value except for the effects of changes in its credit risk (ie 'the frozen credit spread method'). In other words, the effects of changes in its credit risk would be ignored in the primary financial statements.

(c) measuring liabilities at amortised cost. This would require estimating the cash flows over the life of the instrument, including those cash flows associated with any embedded derivative features.

(d) bifurcating liabilities into hosts and embedded features. The host contract would be measured at amortised cost and the embedded features (eg embedded derivatives) would be measured at fair value through profit or loss. The IASB discussed either carrying forward the bifurcation requirements in IAS 39 for financial liabilities or developing new requirements.

BC4.48 The primary message that the IASB received from users of financial statements and others during its outreach programme was that the effects of changes in a liability's credit risk ought not to affect profit or loss unless the liability is held for trading. That is because an entity generally will not realise the effects of changes in the liability's credit risk unless the liability is held for trading.

BC4.49 In addition to that view, there were several other themes in the feedback that the IASB received:

(a) Symmetry between how an entity classifies and measures its financial assets and its financial liabilities is not necessary and often does not result in useful information. Most constituents said that in its deliberations on financial liabilities the IASB should not be constrained or biased by the requirements in IFRS 9 for financial assets.

(b) Amortised cost is the most appropriate measurement attribute for many financial liabilities because it reflects the issuer's legal obligation to pay the contractual amounts in the normal course of business (ie on a going concern basis) and in many cases, the issuer will hold liabilities to maturity and pay the contractual amounts. However, if a liability has structured features (eg embedded derivatives), amortised cost is difficult to apply and understand because the cash flows can be highly variable.

(c) The bifurcation methodology in IAS 39 is generally working well and practice has developed since those requirements were issued. For many entities, bifurcation avoids the issue of own credit risk because the host is measured at amortised cost and only the derivative is measured at fair value through profit or loss. Many constituents, including users of financial statements, favoured retaining bifurcation for financial liabilities even though they supported eliminating it for financial assets. That was because bifurcation addresses the issue of own credit risk, which is only relevant for financial liabilities. Users preferred structured assets to be measured at fair value in their entirety. Many constituents were sceptical that a new bifurcation methodology could be developed that was less complex and provided more useful information than using the bifurcation methodology in IAS 39. Moreover, a new bifurcation methodology would be likely to have the same classification and measurement outcomes as the existing methodology in most cases.

(d) The IASB should not develop a new measurement attribute. The almost unanimous view was that a 'full' fair value amount is more understandable and useful than an 'adjusted' fair value amount that ignores the effects of changes in the liability's credit risk.

(e) Even for preparers with sophisticated valuation expertise, it is difficult to determine the amount of change in the fair value of a liability that is attributable to changes in its credit risk. Under existing Standards only entities that elect to designate liabilities under the fair value option are required to determine that amount. If the IASB were to extend that requirement to more entities and to more financial liabilities, many entities would have significant difficulty determining that amount and could incur significant costs in doing so.

BC4.50   Although there were common themes in the feedback received, there was no consensus on which of the alternative approaches being explored by the IASB was the best way to address the effects of changes in liabilities' credit risk. Many constituents said that none of the alternatives being discussed was less complex or would result in more useful information than the existing bifurcation requirements.

BC4.51   As a result of the feedback received, the IASB decided to retain almost all of the existing requirements for the classification and measurement of financial liabilities. The IASB decided that the benefits of changing practice at this point do not outweigh the costs of the disruption that such a change would cause. Accordingly, in October 2010 the IASB carried forward almost all of the requirements unchanged from IAS 39 to IFRS 9.[13]

BC4.52   By retaining almost all of the existing requirements, the issue of credit risk is addressed for most liabilities because they would continue to be subsequently measured at amortised cost or would be bifurcated into a host, which would be measured at amortised cost, and an embedded derivative, which would be measured at fair value. Liabilities that are held for trading (including all derivative liabilities) would continue to be subsequently measured at fair value through profit or loss, which is consistent with the widespread view that all fair value changes for those liabilities should affect profit or loss.

BC4.53   The issue of credit risk would remain only in the context of financial liabilities designated under the fair value option. Thus, in May 2010 the IASB published an Exposure Draft *Fair Value Option for Financial Liabilities* (the '2010 Own Credit Risk Exposure Draft'), which proposed that the effects of changes in the credit risk of liabilities designated under the fair value option would be presented in other comprehensive income. The IASB considered the responses to 2010 Own Credit Risk Exposure Draft and finalised amendments to IFRS 9 in October 2010 (see paragraphs BC5.35–BC5.64). Those amendments also eliminated the cost exception for particular derivative liabilities that will be settled by delivering unquoted equity instruments[14] whose fair values cannot be reliably determined (see paragraph BC5.20).

---

13   In 2017 the IASB discussed the accounting for a modification or exchange of a financial liability measured at amortised cost that does not result in derecognition of the financial liability. See paragraphs BC4.252–BC4.253.

14   IFRS 13, issued in May 2011, defines a Level 1 input as a quoted price in an active market for an identical asset or liability. Level 2 inputs include quoted prices for identical assets or liabilities in markets that are not active. As a result IFRS 9 refers to such equity instruments as 'an equity instrument that does not have a quoted price in an active market for an identical instrument (ie a Level 1 input)'.

Option to designate a financial asset or financial liability at fair value through profit or loss

Background to the fair value option in IAS 39

BCZ4.54 In 2003 the IASB concluded that it could simplify the application of IAS 39 (as revised in 2000) for some entities by permitting the use of fair value measurement for any financial instrument. With one exception, this greater use of fair value is optional. The fair value measurement option does not require entities to measure more financial instruments at fair value.

BCZ4.55 IAS 39 (as revised in 2000)[15] did not permit an entity to measure particular categories of financial instruments at fair value with changes in fair value recognised in profit or loss. Examples included:

(a) originated loans and receivables, including a debt instrument acquired directly from the issuer, unless they met the conditions for classification as held for trading (now in Appendix A of IFRS 9).

(b) financial assets classified as available for sale, unless as an accounting policy choice gains and losses on all available-for-sale financial assets were recognised in profit or loss or they met the conditions for classification as held for trading (now in Appendix A of IFRS 9).

(c) non-derivative financial liabilities, even if the entity had a policy and practice of actively repurchasing such liabilities or they formed part of an arbitrage/customer facilitation strategy or fund trading activities.

BCZ4.56 The IASB decided in IAS 39 (as revised in 2003) to permit entities to designate irrevocably on initial recognition any financial instruments as ones to be measured at fair value with gains and losses recognised in profit or loss ('fair value through profit or loss'). To impose discipline on this approach, the IASB decided that financial instruments should not be reclassified into or out of the category of fair value through profit or loss. In particular, some comments received on the exposure draft of proposed amendments to IAS 39 published in June 2002 suggested that entities could use the fair value option to recognise selectively changes in fair value in profit or loss. The IASB noted that the requirement (now in IFRS 9) to designate irrevocably on initial recognition the financial instruments for which the fair value option is to be applied results in an entity being unable to 'cherry pick' in this way. This is because it will not be known at initial recognition whether the fair value of the instrument will increase or decrease.

BCZ4.57 Following the issue of IAS 39 (as revised in 2003), as a result of continuing discussions with constituents on the fair value option, the IASB became aware that some, including prudential supervisors of banks, securities companies and insurers, were concerned that the fair value option might be used inappropriately. These constituents were concerned that:

---

15 IFRS 9 eliminated the loans and receivables and available-for-sale categories.

(a)   entities might apply the fair value option to financial assets or financial liabilities whose fair value is not verifiable. If so, because the valuation of these financial assets and financial liabilities is subjective, entities might determine their fair value in a way that inappropriately affects profit or loss.

(b)   the use of the option might increase, instead of decreasing, volatility in profit or loss, for example if an entity applied the option to only one part of a matched position.

(c)   if an entity applied the fair value option to financial liabilities, it might result in an entity recognising gains or losses in profit or loss associated with changes in its own creditworthiness.

BCZ4.58   In response to those concerns, the IASB published in April 2004 an exposure draft of proposed restrictions to the fair value option contained in IAS 39 (as revised in 2003). After discussing comments received from constituents and a series of public round-table meetings, the IASB issued an amendment to IAS 39 in June 2005 permitting entities to designate irrevocably on initial recognition financial instruments that meet one of three conditions as ones to be measured at fair value through profit or loss.

BCZ4.59   In those amendment to the fair value option, the IASB identified three situations in which permitting designation at fair value through profit or loss either results in more relevant information ((a) and (b) below) or is justified on the grounds of reducing complexity or increasing measurement reliability ((c) below). These are:

(a)   when such designation eliminates or significantly reduces a measurement or recognition inconsistency (sometimes referred to as an 'accounting mismatch') that would otherwise arise (paragraphs BCZ4.61–BCZ4.63);

(b)   when a group of financial assets, financial liabilities or both is managed and its performance is evaluated on a fair value basis, in accordance with a documented risk management or investment strategy (paragraphs BCZ4.64–BCZ4.66); and

(c)   when an instrument contains an embedded derivative that meets particular conditions (paragraphs BCZ4.67–BCZ4.70).

BCZ4.60   The ability for entities to use the fair value option simplifies the application of IAS 39 by mitigating some anomalies that result from the different measurement attributes. In particular, for financial instruments designated in this way:

(a)   it eliminates the need for hedge accounting for hedges of fair value exposures when there are natural offsets, and thereby eliminates the related burden of designating, tracking and analysing hedge effectiveness.

(b)   it eliminates the burden of separating embedded derivatives.

(c)   it eliminates problems arising from a mixed measurement model when financial assets are measured at fair value and related financial liabilities are measured at amortised cost. In particular, it eliminates volatility in profit or loss and equity that results when matched positions of financial assets and financial liabilities are not measured consistently.

(d)   the option to recognise unrealised gains and losses on available-for-sale financial assets in profit or loss is no longer necessary.

(e)   it de-emphasises interpretative issues around what constitutes trading.

Designation eliminates or significantly reduces an accounting mismatch

BCZ4.61   IAS 39, like comparable standards in some national jurisdictions, imposed (and IFRS 9 now imposes) a mixed attribute measurement model. It required some financial assets and liabilities to be measured at fair value, and others to be measured at amortised cost. It required some gains and losses to be recognised in profit or loss, and others to be recognised initially as a component of equity.[16] This combination of measurement and recognition requirements could result in inconsistencies, which some refer to as 'accounting mismatches', between the accounting for an asset (or group of assets) and a liability (or group of liabilities). The notion of an accounting mismatch necessarily involves two propositions. First, an entity has particular assets and liabilities that are measured, or on which gains and losses are recognised, inconsistently; second, there is a perceived economic relationship between those assets and liabilities. For example, a liability may be considered to be related to an asset when they share a risk that gives rise to opposite changes in fair value that tend to offset, or when the entity considers that the liability funds the asset.

BCZ4.62   Some entities could overcome measurement or recognition inconsistencies by using hedge accounting or, in the case of insurers, shadow accounting. However, the IASB recognised that those techniques are complex and do not address all situations. In developing the amendment to the fair value option in 2004, the IASB considered whether it should impose conditions to limit the situations in which an entity could use the option to eliminate an accounting mismatch. For example, it considered whether entities should be required to demonstrate that particular assets and liabilities are managed together, or that a management strategy is effective in reducing risk (as is required for hedge accounting to be used), or that hedge accounting or other ways of overcoming the inconsistency are not available.

BCZ4.63   The IASB concluded that accounting mismatches arise in a wide variety of circumstances. In the IASB's view, financial reporting is best served by providing entities with the opportunity to eliminate perceived accounting mismatches whenever that results in more relevant information. Furthermore, the IASB concluded that the fair value option may validly be used in place of hedge accounting for hedges of fair value exposures, thereby

---

16 As a consequence of the revision of IAS 1 *Presentation of Financial Statements* in 2007 these other gains and losses are recognised in other comprehensive income.

eliminating the related burden of designating, tracking and analysing hedge effectiveness. Hence, the IASB decided not to develop detailed prescriptive guidance about when the fair value option could be applied (such as requiring effectiveness tests similar to those required for hedge accounting) in the amendment on the fair value option. Instead, the IASB decided to require disclosures (now in IFRS 7) about:

- the criteria an entity uses for designating financial assets and financial liabilities as at fair value through profit or loss

- how the entity satisfies the conditions for such designation

- the nature of the assets and liabilities so designated

- the effect on the financial statement of using this designation, namely the carrying amounts and net gains and losses on assets and liabilities so designated, information about the effect of changes in a financial liability's credit quality on changes in its fair value, and information about the credit risk of loans or receivables and any related credit derivatives or similar instruments.

A group of financial assets, financial liabilities or both is managed and its performance is evaluated on a fair value basis

BCZ4.64   IAS 39 required financial instruments to be measured at fair value through profit or loss in only two situations, namely when an instrument is held for trading or when it contains an embedded derivative that the entity is unable to measure separately. However, the IASB recognised that some entities manage and evaluate the performance of financial instruments on a fair value basis in other situations. Furthermore, for instruments managed and evaluated in this way, users of financial statements may regard fair value measurement as providing more relevant information. Finally, it is established practice in some industries in some jurisdictions to recognise all financial assets at fair value through profit or loss. (This practice was permitted for many assets in IAS 39 (as revised in 2000) as an accounting policy choice in accordance with which gains and losses on all available-for-sale financial assets were reported in profit or loss.)

BCZ4.65   In the amendment to IAS 39 relating to the fair value option issued in June 2005, the IASB permitted financial instruments managed and evaluated on a fair value basis to be measured at fair value through profit or loss. The IASB also introduced two requirements to make this category operational. These requirements are that the financial instruments are managed and evaluated on a fair value basis in accordance with a documented risk management or investment strategy, and that information about the financial instruments is provided internally on that basis to the entity's key management personnel.

BCZ4.66   In looking to an entity's documented risk management or investment strategy, the IASB made no judgement on what an entity's strategy should be. However, the IASB noted that users, in making economic decisions, would find useful both a description of the chosen strategy and how designation at fair value through profit or loss is consistent with it. Such disclosures are required (now in IFRS 7). The IASB also noted that the required documentation of the entity's strategy need not be item by item, nor need it be in the level of detail required for hedge accounting. However, it should be sufficient to demonstrate that using the fair value option is consistent with the entity's risk management or investment strategy. In many cases, the entity's existing documentation, as approved by its key management personnel, should be sufficient for this purpose.

The instrument contains an embedded derivative that meets particular conditions

BCZ4.67 IAS 39 required virtually all derivative financial instruments to be measured at fair value. This requirement extended to derivatives that are embedded in an instrument that also includes a non-derivative host if the embedded derivative met particular conditions. Conversely, if the embedded derivative did not meet those conditions, separate accounting with measurement of the embedded derivative at fair value is prohibited. Consequently, to satisfy these requirements, the entity must:

(a) identify whether the instrument contains one or more embedded derivatives,

(b) determine whether each embedded derivative is one that must be separated from the host instrument or one for which separation is prohibited, and

(c) if the embedded derivative is one that must be separated, determine its fair value at initial recognition and subsequently.

BCZ4.68 For some embedded derivatives, like the prepayment option in an ordinary residential mortgage, this process is fairly simple. However, entities with more complex instruments have reported that the search for and analysis of embedded derivatives (steps (a) and (b) in paragraph BCZ4.67) significantly increase the cost of complying with the Standard. They report that this cost could be eliminated if they had the option to fair value the combined contract.

BCZ4.69 Other entities report that one of the most common uses of the fair value option is likely to be for structured products that contain several embedded derivatives. Those structured products will typically be hedged with derivatives that offset all (or nearly all) of the risks they contain, whether or not the embedded derivatives that give rise to those risks are separated for accounting purposes. Hence, the simplest way to account for such products is to apply the fair value option so that the combined contract (as well as the derivatives that hedge it) is measured at fair value through profit or loss. Furthermore, for these more complex instruments, the fair value of the combined contract may be significantly easier to measure and hence be more reliable than the fair value of only those embedded derivatives that are required to be separated.

BCZ4.70 The IASB sought to strike a balance between reducing the costs of complying with the embedded derivatives provisions and the need to respond to the concerns expressed regarding possible inappropriate use of the fair value option. The IASB determined that allowing the fair value option to be used for any instrument with an embedded derivative would make other restrictions on the use of the option ineffective, because many financial instruments include an embedded derivative. In contrast, limiting the use of the fair value option to situations in which the embedded derivative must otherwise be separated would not significantly reduce the costs of compliance and could result in less reliable measures being included in the financial statements. Consequently, the IASB decided to specify situations in which an entity cannot justify using the fair value option in place of assessing embedded derivatives — when the embedded derivative does not significantly modify the cash flows that would otherwise be required by the contract or is one for which it is clear with little or no analysis when a similar hybrid instrument is first considered that separation is prohibited.

The role of prudential supervisors

BCZ4.71 The IASB considered the circumstances of regulated financial institutions such as banks and insurers in determining the extent to which conditions should be placed on the use of the fair value option. The IASB recognised that regulated financial institutions are extensive holders and issuers of financial instruments and so are likely to be among the largest potential users of the fair value option. However, the IASB noted that some of the prudential supervisors that oversee these entities expressed concern that the fair value option might be used inappropriately.

BCZ4.72 The IASB noted that the primary objective of prudential supervisors is to maintain the financial soundness of individual financial institutions and the stability of the financial system as a whole. Prudential supervisors achieve this objective partly by assessing the risk profile of each regulated institution and imposing a risk-based capital requirement.

BCZ4.73 The IASB noted that these objectives of prudential supervision differ from the objectives of general purpose financial reporting. The latter is intended to provide information about the financial position, performance and changes in financial position of an entity that is useful to a wide range of users in making economic decisions. However, the IASB acknowledged that for the purposes of determining what level of capital an institution should maintain, prudential supervisors may wish to understand the circumstances in which a regulated financial institution has chosen to apply the fair value option and evaluate the rigour of the institution's fair value measurement practices and the robustness of its underlying risk management strategies, policies and practices. Furthermore, the IASB agreed that certain disclosures would assist both prudential supervisors in their evaluation of capital requirements and investors in making economic decisions. In particular, the IASB decided to require an entity to disclose how it has satisfied the conditions for using the fair value option, including, for instruments that are now within paragraph 4.2.2(b) of IFRS 9, a narrative description of how designation at fair value through profit or loss is consistent with the entity's documented risk management or investment strategy.

Application of the fair value option to a component or a proportion (instead of the entirety) of a financial asset or a financial liability

BCZ4.74 Some comments received on the exposure draft of proposed amendments to IAS 39 published in June 2002 argued that the fair value option should be extended so that it could also be applied to a component of a financial asset or a financial liability (eg changes in fair value attributable to one risk such as changes in a benchmark interest rate). The arguments included (a) concerns regarding inclusion of own credit risk in the measurement of financial liabilities and (b) the prohibition on using non-derivatives as hedging instruments (cash instrument hedging).

BCZ4.75 The IASB concluded that IAS 39 should not extend the fair value option to components of financial assets or financial liabilities. It was concerned (a) about difficulties in measuring the change in value of the component because of ordering issues and joint effects (ie if the component is affected by more than one risk, it may be difficult to isolate accurately and measure the component); (b) that the amounts recognised in the balance sheet would be neither fair value nor cost; and (c) that a fair value adjustment for a component might move the carrying amount of an instrument away from its fair value. In finalising the 2003 amendments to IAS 39, the IASB separately considered the issue of cash instrument hedging (see paragraphs BC144 and BC145 of the Basis for Conclusions on IAS 39).

BCZ4.76 Other comments received on the April 2004 exposure draft of proposed restrictions on the fair value option contained in IAS 39 (as revised in 2003) suggested that the fair value option should be extended so that it could be applied to a proportion (ie a percentage) of a financial asset or financial liability. The IASB was concerned that such an extension would require prescriptive guidance on how to determine a proportion. For example, if an entity were to issue a bond totalling CU100 million in the form of 100 certificates each of CU1 million, would a proportion of 10 per cent be identified as 10 per cent of each certificate, CU10 million specified certificates, the first (or last) CU10 million certificates to be redeemed, or on some other basis? The IASB was also concerned that the remaining proportion, not being subject to the fair value option, could give rise to incentives for an entity to 'cherry pick' (ie to realise financial assets or financial liabilities selectively so as to achieve a desired accounting result). For these reasons, the IASB decided not to allow the fair value option to be applied to a proportion of a single financial asset or financial liability (that restriction is now in IFRS 9). However, if an entity simultaneously issues two or more identical financial instruments, it is not precluded from designating only some of those instruments as being subject to the fair value option (for example, if doing so achieves a significant reduction in a recognition or measurement inconsistency). Thus, in the above example, the entity could designate CU10 million specified certificates if to do so would meet one of the three criteria in paragraph BCZ4.59.

Option to designate a financial asset at fair value

BC4.77   As noted above, IAS 39 allowed entities an option to designate on initial recognition any financial asset or financial liability as measured at fair value through profit or loss if one (or more) of the following three conditions is met:

(a)   Doing so eliminates or significantly reduces a measurement or recognition inconsistency (sometimes referred to as an 'accounting mismatch') that would otherwise arise from measuring assets or liabilities on different bases or recognising the gains and losses on them on different bases.

(b)   A group of financial assets, financial liabilities or both is managed and its performance is evaluated on a fair value basis, in accordance with a documented risk management or investment strategy, and information about the group is provided internally on that basis to the entity's key management personnel.

(c)   The financial asset or financial liability contains one or more embedded derivatives (and particular other conditions now described in paragraph 4.3.5 of IFRS 9 are met) and the entity elects to account for the hybrid contract in its entirety.

BC4.78   However, in contrast to IAS 39, IFRS 9 requires:

(a)   any financial asset that is not managed within a business model that has the objective of collecting contractual cash flows to be measured at fair value; and

(b)   hybrid contracts with financial asset hosts to be classified in their entirety, hence eliminating the requirement to identify and account for embedded derivatives separately.

Accordingly, the IASB concluded that the conditions described in paragraph BC4.77(b) and (c) are unnecessary for financial assets.

BC4.79   The IASB retained the eligibility condition described in paragraph BC4.77(a) because it mitigates some anomalies that result from the different measurement attributes used for financial instruments. In particular, it eliminates the need for fair value hedge accounting of fair value exposures when there are natural offsets. It also avoids problems arising from a mixed measurement model when some financial assets are measured at amortised cost and related financial liabilities are measured at fair value. A separate phase of the project is considering hedge accounting, and the fair value option will be better considered in that context. The IASB also noted that particular industry sectors believe it is important to be able to mitigate such anomalies until other IASB projects are completed (eg insurance contracts). The IASB decided to defer consideration of changes to the eligibility condition set out in paragraph BC4.77(a) as part of the future exposure draft on hedge accounting.

BC4.80   Almost all the respondents to the 2009 Classification and Measurement Exposure Draft supported the proposal to retain the fair value option if such designation eliminates or significantly reduces an accounting mismatch. Although some respondents would prefer an unrestricted fair value option, they acknowledged that an unrestricted fair value option has been opposed by many in the past and it is not appropriate to pursue it now.

Option to designate a financial liability at fair value

Eligibility conditions

BC4.81 During its discussions about subsequent classification and measurement of financial liabilities in 2010 (see paragraphs BC4.46–BC4.53), the IASB considered whether it was necessary to propose any changes to the eligibility conditions for designating financial liabilities under the fair value option. However, the IASB decided that such changes were not necessary because the IASB was not changing the underlying classification and measurement approach for financial liabilities. Consequently, the 2010 Own Credit Risk Exposure Draft proposed to carry forward the three eligibility conditions.

BC4.82 Most respondents agreed with that proposal in the 2010 Own Credit Risk Exposure Draft. The IASB confirmed the proposal and decided to carry forward to IFRS 9 the three eligibility conditions in October 2010. Some would have preferred an unrestricted fair value option. However, they acknowledged that an unrestricted fair value option had been opposed by many in the past and it was not appropriate to pursue it now.

Embedded derivatives

Hybrid contracts with a host that is an asset within the scope of IFRS 9

BC4.83 An embedded derivative is a derivative component of a hybrid contract that also includes a non-derivative host, with the effect that some of the cash flows of the combined contract vary like the cash flows of a stand-alone derivative contract. IAS 39 required an entity to assess all contracts to determine whether they contain one or more embedded derivatives that are required to be separated from the host and accounted for as stand-alone derivatives.

BC4.84 Many respondents to the Discussion Paper *Reducing Complexity in Reporting Financial Instruments* commented that the requirements and guidance in IAS 39 were complex, rule-based and internally inconsistent. Respondents, and others, also noted the many application problems that arose from requirements to assess all non-derivative contracts for embedded derivatives and, if required, to account for and measure those embedded derivatives separately as stand-alone derivatives.

BC4.85 In 2009 the IASB discussed three approaches for accounting for embedded derivatives:

(a) to maintain the requirements in IAS 39;

(b) to use 'closely related' (used in IAS 39 to determine whether an embedded derivative is required to be separated from the host) to determine the classification for the contract in its entirety; and

(c) to use the same classification approach for all financial assets (including hybrid contracts).

BC4.86   The IASB rejected the first two approaches. The IASB noted that both would rely on the assessment of whether an embedded derivative is 'closely related' to the host. The 'closely related' assessment is based on a list of examples that are inconsistent and unclear. That assessment is also a significant source of complexity. Both approaches would result in hybrid contracts being classified using conditions different from those that would be applied to all non-hybrid financial instruments. Consequently, some hybrid contracts whose contractual cash flows do not solely represent payments of principal and interest on the principal amount outstanding might be measured at amortised cost. Similarly, some hybrid contracts whose contractual cash flows do meet the conditions for measurement at amortised cost might be measured at fair value. The IASB also believes that neither approach would make it easier for users of financial statements to understand the information that financial statements present about financial instruments.

BC4.87   Therefore, the 2009 Classification and Measurement Exposure Draft proposed that entities should use the same classification approach for all financial instruments, including hybrid contracts with hosts within the scope of the proposed IFRS ('financial hosts'). The IASB concluded that a single classification approach for all financial instruments and hybrid contracts with financial hosts was the only approach that responded adequately to the criticisms described above. The IASB noted that using a single classification approach improves comparability by ensuring consistency in classification, and hence makes it easier for users to understand the information that financial statements present about financial instruments.

BC4.88   In the responses to the 2009 Classification and Measurement Exposure Draft, some respondents, mainly preparers, stated their preference for keeping or modifying the bifurcation model that was in IAS 39. They noted that:

(a)   eliminating the requirement to account for embedded derivatives as stand-alone derivatives would lead to increased volatility in profit or loss and result in accounting that did not reflect the underlying economics and risk management or business model considerations in a transaction. For example, the components of some hybrid financial instruments may be managed separately.

(b)   structuring opportunities would be created, for example if an entity entered into two transactions that have the same economic effect as entering into a single hybrid contract.

BC4.89   However, the IASB confirmed the proposals in the 2009 Classification and Measurement Exposure Draft for the following reasons:

(a)   The elimination of the embedded derivatives guidance for hybrid contracts with financial hosts reduces the complexity in financial reporting of financial assets by eliminating another classification approach and improves the reporting for financial instruments. Many constituents agreed with this conclusion.

(b) In the IASB view, the underlying rationale for separate accounting for embedded derivatives is not to reflect risk management activities, but to avoid entities circumventing the recognition and measurement requirements for derivatives. Accordingly it is an exception to the definition of the unit of account (the contract) motivated by a wish to avoid abuse. It would reduce complexity to eliminate an anti-abuse exception.

(c) The IASB noted the concerns about structuring opportunities referred to in paragraph BC4.88(b). However, two contracts represent two units of account. Reconsideration of the unit of account forms part of a far broader issue for financial reporting that is outside the scope of the IASB's considerations in IFRS 9. In addition, embedded derivative features often do not have contractual cash flows that represent payments of principal and interest on the principal amount outstanding and thus the entire hybrid contract would not be eligible to be measured at amortised cost. However, the IASB noted that this would provide more relevant information because the embedded derivative feature affects the cash flows ultimately arising from the hybrid contract. Thus, applying the classification approach to the hybrid contract in its entirety would depict more faithfully the amount, timing and uncertainty of future cash flows.

(d) In the IASB's view, accounting for the hybrid contract as one unit of account is consistent with the project's objective—to improve the usefulness for users in their assessment of the timing, amount and uncertainty of future cash flows of financial instruments and to reduce the complexity in reporting financial instruments.

This decision applies only to hybrid contracts with a host that is an asset within the scope of IFRS 9.

BC4.90 The IASB decided not to consider at this time changes to the requirements in IAS 39 for embedded derivatives in hybrid contracts with non-financial hosts. The IASB acknowledged that those requirements are also complex and have resulted in some application problems, including the question of whether particular types of non-financial contracts are within the scope of IAS 39. The IASB accepted the importance of ensuring that any proposals for hybrid contracts with non-financial hosts should also address which non-financial contracts should be within the scope of IFRS 9. The IASB also noted the importance for many non-financial entities of hedge accounting for non-financial items, and the relationship to both scope and embedded derivative requirements. Consequently, the IASB concluded that the requirements for hybrid contracts with non-financial hosts should be addressed in a later phase of the project to replace IAS 39.

Hybrid contracts with a host that is not an asset within the scope of IFRS 9

BC4.91 As discussed in paragraphs BC4.46–BC4.53, in 2010 the IASB decided to retain almost all of the requirements in IAS 39 for the classification and measurement of financial liabilities. Consequently, those requirements (including the requirements related to embedded derivatives) were carried forward unchanged to IFRS 9. Constituents told the IASB that the bifurcation methodology in IAS 39 for financial liabilities is generally working well in practice and practice has developed since those requirements were issued. Many constituents, including users of financial statements, favoured retaining bifurcation for financial liabilities even though they supported eliminating it for financial assets. That was because bifurcation addresses the issue of own credit risk, which is only relevant for financial liabilities.

Embedded foreign currency derivatives

BCZ4.92 A rationale for the embedded derivatives requirements is that an entity should not be able to circumvent the recognition and measurement requirements for derivatives merely by embedding a derivative in a non-derivative financial instrument or other contract, for example, a commodity forward in a debt instrument. To achieve consistency in accounting for such embedded derivatives, all derivatives embedded in financial instruments that are not measured at fair value with gains and losses recognised in profit or loss ought to be accounted for separately as derivatives. However, as a practical expedient, an embedded derivative need not be separated if it is regarded as closely related to its host contract. When the embedded derivative bears a close economic relationship to the host contract, such as a cap or a floor on the interest rate on a loan, it is less likely that the derivative was embedded to achieve a desired accounting result.

BCZ4.93 The original IAS 39 specified that a foreign currency derivative embedded in a non-financial host contract (such as a supply contract denominated in a foreign currency) was not separated if it required payments denominated in the currency of the primary economic environment in which any substantial party to the contract operates (their functional currencies) or the currency in which the price of the related good or service that is acquired or delivered is routinely denominated in international commerce (such as the US dollar for crude oil transactions). Such foreign currency derivatives are regarded as bearing such a close economic relationship to their host contracts that they do not have to be separated.

BCZ4.94 The requirement to separate embedded foreign currency derivatives may be burdensome for entities that operate in economies in which business contracts denominated in a foreign currency are common. For example, entities domiciled in small countries may find it convenient to denominate business contracts with entities from other small countries in an internationally liquid currency (such as the US dollar, euro or yen) instead of the local currency of any of the parties to the transaction. In addition, an entity operating in a hyperinflationary economy may use a price list in a hard currency to protect against inflation, for example, an entity that has a foreign

then a reassessment of the hybrid instrument would be required at the date of change to ensure the correct accounting treatment in future.

BCZ4.104 The IFRIC also recognised that although IAS 39 was silent on the issue of reassessment it gave relevant guidance when it stated that for the types of contracts now covered by paragraph B4.3.8(b) of IFRS 9 the assessment of whether an embedded derivative is closely related was required only at inception. Paragraph B4.3.8(b) of IFRS 9 states:

> An embedded floor or cap on the interest rate on a debt contract or insurance contract is closely related to the host contract, provided the cap is at or above the market rate of interest and the floor is at or below the market rate of interest *when the contract is issued*, and the cap or floor is not leveraged in relation to the host contract. Similarly, provisions included in a contract to purchase or sell an asset (eg a commodity) that establish a cap and a floor on the price to be paid or received for the asset are closely related to the host contract if both the cap and floor were out of the *money at inception* and are not leveraged. [Emphasis added]

BCZ4.105 The IFRIC also considered the implications of requiring subsequent reassessment. For example, assume that an entity, when it first becomes a party to a contract, separately recognises a host asset[17] and an embedded derivative liability. If the entity were required to reassess whether the embedded derivative was to be accounted for separately and if the entity concluded some time after becoming a party to the contract that the derivative was no longer required to be separated, then questions of recognition and measurement would arise. In the above circumstances, the IFRIC identified the following possibilities:

(a) The entity could remove the derivative from its balance sheet and recognise in profit or loss a corresponding gain or loss. This would lead to recognition of a gain or loss even though there had been no transaction and no change in the value of the total contract or its components.

(b) The entity could leave the derivative as a separate item in the balance sheet. The issue would then arise as to when the item was to be removed from the balance sheet. Should it be amortised (and, if so, how would the amortisation affect the effective interest rate of the asset), or should it be derecognised only when the asset is derecognised?

(c) The entity could combine the derivative (which is recognised at fair value) with the asset (which is recognised at amortised cost). This would alter both the carrying amount of the asset and its effective interest rate even though there had been no change in the economics of the whole contract. In some cases, it could also result in a negative effective interest rate.

---

17 Hybrid contracts with a host that is an asset within the scope of IFRS 9 are now classified and measured in their entirety in accordance with section 4.1 of that IFRS.

The IFRIC noted that, under its view that subsequent reassessment is appropriate only when there has been a change in the terms of the contract that significantly modifies the cash flows that otherwise would be required by the contract, the above issues do not arise.

BCZ4.106 The IFRIC noted that IAS 39 required (and now IFRS 9 requires) an entity to assess whether particular embedded derivatives need to be separated from particular host contracts and accounted for as a derivative when it first becomes a party to a contract. Consequently, if an entity purchases a contract that contains an embedded derivative it assesses whether the embedded derivative needs to be separated and accounted for as a derivative on the basis of conditions at that date.

Improvements to IFRSs issued in April 2009

BCZ4.107 In 2009 the IASB observed that the changes to the definition of a business combination in the revisions to IFRS 3 *Business Combinations* (as revised in 2008) caused the accounting for the formation of a joint venture by the venturer to be within the scope of IFRIC 9. Similarly, the Board noted that common control transactions might raise the same issue depending on which level of the group reporting entity is assessing the combination.

BCZ4.108 The IASB observed that during the development of the revised IFRS 3, it did not discuss whether it intended IFRIC 9 to apply to those types of transactions. The IASB did not intend to change existing practice by including such transactions within the scope of IFRIC 9. Accordingly, in *Improvements to IFRSs* issued in April 2009, the IASB amended paragraph 5 of IFRIC 9 (now paragraph B4.3.12 of IFRS 9) to clarify that IFRIC 9 did not apply to embedded derivatives in contracts acquired in a combination between entities or businesses under common control or the formation of a joint venture.

BCZ4.109 Some respondents to the Exposure Draft *Post-implementation Revisions to IFRIC Interpretations* published in January 2009 expressed the view that investments in associates should also be excluded from the scope of IFRIC 9. Respondents noted that paragraphs 20–23 of IAS 28 *Investments in Associates*[18] state that the concepts underlying the procedures used in accounting for the acquisition of a subsidiary are also adopted in accounting for the acquisition of an investment in an associate.

BCZ4.110 In its redeliberations, the IASB confirmed its previous decision that no scope exemption in IFRIC 9 was needed for investments in associates. However, in response to the comments received, the IASB noted that reassessment of embedded derivatives in contracts held by an associate is not required by IFRIC 9 in any event. The investment in the associate is the asset the investor controls and recognises, not the underlying assets and liabilities of the associate.

---

18 In May 2011, the IASB amended IAS 28 and changed its title to *Investments in Associates and Joint Ventures*.

Reclassification

Reclassification of financial assets

BC4.111   The 2009 Classification and Measurement Exposure Draft proposed to prohibit reclassification of financial assets between the amortised cost and fair value categories. The IASB's rationale for that proposal was as follows:

      (a)   Requiring (or permitting) reclassifications would not make it easier for users of financial statements to understand the information that financial statements provide about financial instruments.

      (b)   Requiring (or permitting) reclassifications would increase complexity because detailed guidance would be required to specify when reclassifications would be required (or permitted) and the subsequent accounting for reclassified financial instruments.

      (c)   Reclassification should not be necessary because classification is based on the entity's business model and that business model is not expected to change.

BC4.112   In their responses, some users questioned the usefulness of reclassified information, noting concerns about the consistency and rigour with which any requirements would be applied. Some were also concerned that opportunistic reclassifications would be possible.

BC4.113   However, almost all respondents (including most users) argued that prohibiting reclassification is inconsistent with a classification approach based on how an entity manages its financial assets. They noted that in an approach based on an entity's business model for managing financial assets, reclassifications would provide useful, relevant and comparable information to users because it would ensure that financial statements faithfully represent how those financial assets are managed at the reporting date. In particular, most users stated that, conceptually, reclassifications should not be prohibited when the classification no longer reflects how the instruments would be classified if the items were newly acquired. If reclassification were prohibited, the reported information would not reflect the amounts, timing and uncertainty of future cash flows.

BC4.114   The IASB was persuaded by these arguments and decided that reclassification should not be prohibited. The IASB noted that prohibiting reclassification decreases comparability for like instruments managed in the same way.

BC4.115   Some respondents contended that reclassifications should be permitted, instead of required, but did not explain their justification. However, the IASB noted that permitting reclassification would decrease comparability, both between different entities and for instruments held by a single entity, and would enable an entity to manage its profit or loss by selecting the timing of when future gains or losses are recognised. Consequently, the IASB decided that reclassification should be required when the entity's business model for managing those financial assets changes.

BC4.116   The IASB noted that, as highlighted by many respondents, such changes in business model would be very infrequent, significant and demonstrable and determined by the entity's senior management as a result of external or internal change.

BC4.117   The IASB considered arguments that reclassification should also be permitted or required when contractual cash flow characteristics of a financial asset vary (or may vary) over that asset's life based on its original contractual terms. However, the IASB noted that, unlike a change in business model, the contractual terms of a financial asset are known at initial recognition. An entity classifies the financial asset at initial recognition on the basis of the contractual terms over the life of the instrument. Consequently, the IASB decided that reclassification on the basis of a financial asset's contractual cash flows should not be permitted.

BC4.118   The IASB considered how reclassifications should be accounted for. Almost all respondents said that reclassifications should be accounted for prospectively and should be accompanied by robust disclosures. The IASB reasoned that if classification and reclassification are based on the business model within which they are managed, classification should always reflect the business model within which the financial asset was managed at the reporting date. To apply the reclassification retrospectively would not reflect how the financial assets were managed at the prior reporting dates.

BC4.119   The IASB also considered the date at which reclassifications could take effect. Some respondents stated that reclassifications should be reflected in the entity's financial statements as soon as the entity's business model for the relevant instruments changes. To do otherwise would be contradictory to the objective of reclassification—ie to reflect how the instruments are managed. However, the IASB decided that reclassifications should take effect from the beginning of the following reporting period. In the IASB's view, entities should be prevented from choosing a reclassification date to achieve an accounting result. The IASB also noted that a change in an entity's business model is a significant and demonstrable event; therefore, an entity will most likely disclose such an event in its financial statements in the reporting period in which the change in business model takes place.

BC4.120   The IASB also considered and rejected the following approaches:

(a)   *Disclosure approach:* Quantitative and qualitative disclosure (instead of reclassification) could be used to address when the classification no longer reflects how the financial assets would be classified if they were newly acquired. However, in the IASB's view, disclosure is not an adequate substitute for recognition.

(b)   *One-way reclassification:* Reclassification would be required only to fair value measurement, ie reclassification to amortised cost measurement would be prohibited. Proponents of this approach indicated that such an approach might minimise abuse of the reclassification requirements and result in more instruments being measured at fair value. However, in the IASB's view, there is no conceptual reason to require reclassification in one direction but not the other.

Reclassification of financial liabilities

BC4.121   Consistently with its decision in 2010 to retain most of the existing requirements for classifying and measuring financial liabilities (and relocate them to IFRS 9), the IASB decided to retain the requirements that prohibit reclassifying financial liabilities between amortised cost and fair value. The IASB noted that IFRS 9 requires reclassification of assets in particular circumstances. However, in line with the feedback received during the IASB's outreach programme, the classification and measurement approaches for financial assets and financial liabilities are different; therefore the IASB decided that it is unnecessary and inappropriate to have symmetrical requirements for reclassification. Moreover, although the reclassification of financial assets has been a controversial topic in recent years, the IASB is not aware of any requests or views that support reclassifying financial liabilities.

Changes in circumstances that are not reclassifications

BCZ4.122   The definition of a financial asset or financial liability at fair value through profit or loss excludes derivatives that are designated and effective hedging instruments. Paragraph 50 of IAS 39 prohibited (and unless particular conditions are met, paragraphs 4.4.1 and 4.4.2 of IFRS 9 prohibit) the reclassification of financial instruments into or out of the fair value through profit or loss category after initial recognition. The IASB noted that the prohibition on reclassification might be read as preventing a derivative financial instrument that becomes a designated and effective hedging instrument from being excluded from the fair value through profit or loss category in accordance with the definition. Similarly, it might be read as preventing a derivative that ceases to be a designated and effective hedging instrument from being accounted for at fair value through profit or loss.

BCZ4.123   The IASB decided that the prohibition on reclassification should not prevent a derivative from being accounted for at fair value through profit or loss when it does not qualify for hedge accounting and vice versa. Consequently, in *Improvements to IFRSs* issued in May 2008, the IASB addressed this point (now in paragraph 4.4.3 of IFRS 9).

Limited amendments for financial assets (July 2014)

BC4.124   When the IASB issued IFRS 9 in 2009, it acknowledged the difficulties that might be created by differences in timing between the classification and measurement phase of the project to replace IAS 39 and the Insurance Contracts project. The IASB consistently stated that the interaction between IFRS 9 and the Insurance Contracts project would be considered once the IASB's insurance contracts model had been developed sufficiently.

BC4.125   In addition, after IFRS 9 was issued in 2009, the IASB received feedback from interested parties in various jurisdictions that had chosen to apply IFRS 9 early or who had reviewed IFRS 9 in detail in preparation for application. Some asked questions or raised application issues related to the requirements for classifying and measuring financial assets.

BC4.126 Finally, when the IASB was developing the first requirements of IFRS 9, its priority was to make improvements to the accounting for financial instruments available quickly. Consequently, the IASB issued the classification and measurement requirements for financial assets in IFRS 9 in 2009 while the FASB was still developing its classification and measurement model. However, the boards remained committed to trying to achieve increased comparability internationally in the accounting for financial instruments.

BC4.127 Accordingly, in November 2011 the IASB decided to consider making limited amendments to IFRS 9 with the following objectives:

(a) consider the interaction between the classification and measurement of financial assets and the accounting for insurance contract liabilities;

(b) address specific application questions raised by interested parties since IFRS 9 was issued; and

(c) seek to reduce key differences with the FASB's tentative classification and measurement model for financial instruments.

BC4.128 In making this decision, the IASB noted that IFRS 9 was fundamentally sound and would result in useful information being provided to users of financial statements. Feedback from interested parties since IFRS 9 was issued had confirmed that it was operational. Accordingly, although some interested parties might have preferred the IASB to discuss additional issues, it decided to consider only limited amendments to IFRS 9 in line with the objectives set out in paragraph BC4.127.

BC4.129 In limiting the scope of the deliberations, the IASB was also mindful of the need to complete the entire project on financial instruments on a timely basis and minimise the cost and disruption to entities that have already applied, or have begun preparations to apply, IFRS 9. Thus, the IASB decided to focus only on the following issues:

(a) the basis for, and the scope of, a possible third measurement category for financial assets (ie fair value through other comprehensive income);

(b) the assessment of a financial asset's contractual cash flow characteristics — specifically, whether, and if so what, additional guidance is required to clarify how the assessment is to be applied and whether bifurcation of financial assets should be reintroduced; and

(c) interrelated issues arising from these topics (for example, disclosure requirements and the model for financial liabilities).

BC4.130 At the same time, the FASB had been discussing its tentative model for classifying and measuring financial instruments. Consequently, consistently with their long-standing objective to increase international comparability in the accounting for financial instruments, in January 2012, the IASB and the FASB decided to jointly deliberate these issues. However, the boards were mindful of their different starting points. Specifically, the IASB was considering limited amendments to the existing requirements in IFRS 9 whereas the FASB was considering a comprehensive new model.

BC4.131   The boards' joint deliberations led to the publication of the Exposure Draft *Classification and Measurement: Limited Amendments to IFRS 9* (Proposed amendments to IFRS 9 (2010)) (the '2012 Limited Amendments Exposure Draft') and the FASB's proposed Accounting Standards Update *Financial Instruments—Overall (Subtopic 825-10): Recognition and Measurement of Financial Assets and Financial Liabilities* in November 2012 and February 2013 respectively. While the publications had different scopes (ie to reflect the fact that the IASB was proposing limited amendments to IFRS 9 whereas the FASB was proposing a comprehensive new model) the key aspects of the boards' respective classification and measurement models were largely aligned.

BC4.132   The comment periods on the IASB's and the FASB's proposals ended on 28 March 2013 and 15 May 2013 respectively. The boards developed a plan for joint redeliberations on the basis of the feedback received. That plan reflected the fact that the feedback differed in a number of ways. Specifically, many of the FASB's respondents questioned whether a new comprehensive classification and measurement model was needed and raised concerns about the complexity of the proposals. Many of those respondents advocated that the FASB should consider making targeted improvements to current US GAAP (particularly to the current requirements for bifurcating financial instruments). Consequently, while agreeing to joint redeliberations, the FASB indicated that after those redeliberations were complete, it would consider whether it would confirm the model that the boards had been jointly discussing or pursue another approach (for example, targeted improvements to US GAAP). In contrast, overall, the IASB's respondents continued to support the classification and measurement model in IFRS 9 and supported the proposed limited amendments to that model. The boards' plan for redeliberations also reflected the fact that the boards had different scopes for their redeliberations, which reflected their different starting points. Accordingly the boards' project plan envisaged both joint and separate redeliberations.

BC4.133   At joint public meetings in September through November 2013, the boards discussed the key aspects of their respective models—specifically, the assessment of an asset's contractual cash flow characteristics and the assessment of an entity's business model for managing financial assets (including the basis for, and the scope of, the fair value through other comprehensive income measurement category). Most of the decisions were made jointly and there was general agreement on the key aspects. However, there were differences in the boards' decisions on specific details, such as the assessment of some contingent and prepayment features as well as the articulation of particular aspects of the business model assessment.

BC4.134   Subsequent to the joint discussions, the FASB continued to discuss at FASB-only public meetings the assessment of an asset's contractual cash flow characteristics and the assessment of an entity's business model for managing financial assets. The FASB tentatively decided in December 2013 and January 2014 that it would not continue to pursue the model that the boards had been jointly discussing. Instead, the FASB tentatively decided to consider targeted improvements to current US GAAP guidance for classifying and measuring financial assets.

BC4.135   At its February 2014 meeting, the IASB received and discussed an update on the FASB's tentative decisions. Although the IASB expressed disappointment that the boards had failed to achieve a more converged outcome, it decided to proceed with finalising the limited amendments to IFRS 9. The IASB noted that its stakeholders continue to support the classification and measurement model in IFRS 9 and also supported the proposed limited amendments to that model. The IASB also noted that the minor revisions to the proposed limited amendments that were made during the redeliberations of those proposals were largely to confirm and clarify the proposals in response to the feedback received on the 2012 Limited Amendments Exposure Draft.

The entity's business model

BC4.136   The requirements issued in IFRS 9 (2009) required an entity to assess its business model for managing financial assets. A financial asset was measured at amortised cost only if it was held within a business model whose objective was to hold financial assets in order to collect contractual cash flows (a 'hold to collect' business model), subject also to an assessment of the asset's contractual cash flow characteristics. All other financial assets were measured at fair value through profit or loss. Paragraph BC4.15–BC4.21 describe the IASB's rationale for that assessment.

BC4.137   Most interested parties have consistently agreed that financial assets should be classified and measured on the basis of the objective of the business model in which the assets are held, and also have consistently agreed that assets held within a hold to collect business model ought to be measured at amortised cost. However, after IFRS 9 was issued in 2009, some interested parties asked the IASB to clarify particular aspects of the hold to collect business model, including:

(a)   the level of sales activity that is consistent with a hold to collect business model;

(b)   the effect on the classification of an entity's financial assets if the entity's sales activity in a particular period appears to contradict the hold to collect business model objective—specifically, the consequences both on the classification of assets that the entity currently holds (ie those assets that the entity has already recognised) and on the classification of assets that it may hold in the future; and

(c)   how to classify some portfolios of assets—in particular, so-called 'liquidity portfolios' that banks hold to satisfy their actual or potential liquidity needs, often in response to regulatory requirements.

More generally, some interested parties said that significant judgement was needed to classify some financial assets and, as a result, there was some inconsistency in views in practice about whether the objective of particular business models was to hold to collect contractual cash flows.

BC4.138 In addition, some interested parties expressed the view that IFRS 9 should contain a third measurement category: fair value through other comprehensive income. These views mainly related to:

(a) whether measurement at fair value through profit or loss appropriately reflects the performance of financial assets that are managed both in order to collect contractual cash flows and for sale. Some believed that the requirements for the business model assessment issued in IFRS 9 (2009) resulted in classification outcomes that were too stark, ie an entity either holds financial assets to collect contractual cash flows or it is required to measure the assets at fair value through profit or loss.

(b) the potential accounting mismatch that may arise as a result of the interaction between the classification and measurement of financial assets in accordance with IFRS 9 and the accounting for insurance contract liabilities under the IASB's tentative decisions in its Insurance Contracts project. That was because the 2013 Exposure Draft *Insurance Contracts* (the '2013 Insurance Contracts Exposure Draft') proposed that insurance contract liabilities would be measured on the statement of financial position using a current value approach, but the effects of changes in the discount rate used to measure that current value would be required to be disaggregated and presented in other comprehensive income.

(c) the tentative classification and measurement model that the FASB was considering immediately prior to the start of the boards' joint deliberations, which contemplated three measurement categories: amortised cost, fair value through other comprehensive income and fair value through profit or loss.

BC4.139 Accordingly, in the 2012 Limited Amendments Exposure Draft, the IASB proposed to clarify the objective of the hold to collect business model by providing additional application guidance. The IASB also proposed to introduce a third measurement category; that is, a measurement category for particular financial assets with simple contractual cash flows that are managed both in order to collect contractual cash flows and for sale.

The hold to collect business model

BC4.140 As a result of the application questions raised by interested parties and the diversity in views expressed since IFRS 9 was issued in 2009, the IASB decided to propose clarifications to the hold to collect business model. The IASB noted that these clarifications are relevant irrespective of whether a third measurement category is ultimately introduced to IFRS 9. That is, in the IASB's view, the proposed clarifications would not change (narrow the scope of) the population of financial assets that are eligible to be measured at amortised cost on the basis of the business model in which they are held in order to accommodate an additional measurement category. Instead, the proposals reaffirmed the existing principle in IFRS 9 that financial assets are measured at amortised cost only if they are held within a hold to collect business model (subject also to the assessment of the asset's contractual cash flow characteristics). The proposals also clarified and supplemented that principle with additional application guidance on the types of business activities and the frequency and nature of sales that are consistent, and inconsistent, with a hold to collect business model.

BC4.141 The 2012 Limited Amendments Exposure Draft stated that in order to assess whether the objective of the business model is to hold financial assets to collect contractual cash flows, an entity needs to consider the frequency and significance of past sales activity and the reason for those sales, as well as expectations about future sales activity. The IASB noted that that assessment is consistent with determining whether the cash flows from the financial assets will arise from the collection of their contractual cash flows. The IASB also noted that it expects that sales out of the amortised cost measurement category will be less frequent than sales out of the other measurement categories, because holding assets to collect contractual cash flows is integral to achieving the objective of a hold to collect business model, while selling financial assets to realise cash flows (including fair value changes) is only incidental to that objective. However, the 2012 Limited Amendments Exposure Draft clarified that the credit quality of financial assets is relevant to the entity's ability to collect the assets' contractual cash flows. Consequently, selling a financial asset when its credit quality has deteriorated is consistent with an objective to collect contractual cash flows.

BC4.142 Respondents to the 2012 Limited Amendments Exposure Draft generally agreed that financial assets should be classified and measured on the basis of the objective of the business model within which the assets are held, and specifically agreed with the hold to collect business model for classifying financial assets at amortised cost. However, some respondents expressed concern about what they perceived to be an unduly narrow amortised cost measurement category and expressed the view that the application guidance seemed similar to the guidance for held-to-maturity assets in IAS 39. Specifically, the respondents said that the proposals placed too much emphasis on the frequency and volume of sales instead of focusing on the reasons for those sales and whether those sales are consistent with a hold to collect business model. In addition, while respondents agreed that selling a financial asset when its credit quality has deteriorated is consistent with an objective of collecting contractual cash flows, some asked whether such sales would be acceptable only if they occur once the entity has actually incurred a loss (or there has been significant credit deterioration and therefore lifetime expected credit losses are recognised on the financial asset in accordance with the proposals published in the Exposure Draft *Financial Instruments: Expected Credit Losses* (the '2013 Impairment Exposure Draft'). Some respondents also expressed the view that selling financial assets to manage concentrations of credit risk (for example, selling financial assets in order to limit the amount of instruments held that are issued in a particular jurisdiction) should not be inconsistent with a hold to collect business model.

BC4.143   In response to the feedback received, the IASB decided to emphasise that the business model assessment in IFRS 9 focuses on how the entity actually manages financial assets in order to generate cash flows. The IASB noted that amortised cost is a simple measurement technique that allocates interest over time using the effective interest rate, which is based on contractual cash flows. Accordingly, amortised cost provides relevant and useful information about the amounts, timing and uncertainty of cash flows only if the contractual cash flows will be collected. In order to supplement that principle and improve the clarity of the application guidance related to the hold to collect business model, the IASB also decided to expand the discussion in IFRS 9 on the activities that are commonly associated with the hold to collect business model.

BC4.144   The IASB confirmed that although the objective of an entity's business model may be to hold financial assets in order to collect contractual cash flows, the entity need not hold all of those assets until maturity. Some sales out of the hold to collect business model are expected to occur (ie some financial assets will be derecognised for accounting purposes before maturity). The IASB noted that the level of sales activity (ie the frequency and value of sales), and the reasons for those sales, play a role in assessing the objective of the business model because that assessment focuses on determining how the entity actually manages assets to generate cash flows from the financial assets.

BC4.145   The IASB decided to clarify that the value and frequency of sales do not determine the objective of the business model and therefore should not be considered in isolation. Instead, information about past sales and expectations about future sales (including the frequency, value and nature of such sales) provide evidence about the objective of the business model. Information about sales and sales patterns are useful in determining how an entity manages its financial assets and how cash flows will be realised. Information about historical sales helps an entity to support and verify its business model assessment; that is, such information provides evidence about whether cash flows have been realised in a manner that is consistent with the entity's stated objective for managing those assets. The IASB noted that while an entity should consider historical sales information, that information does not imply that newly originated or newly purchased assets should be classified differently from period to period solely on the basis of sales activity in prior periods. In other words, fluctuations in sales activity in particular periods do not necessarily mean that the entity's business model has changed. The entity will need to consider the reasons for those sales and whether they are consistent with a hold to collect business model. For example, a change in the regulatory treatment of a particular type of financial asset may cause an entity to undertake a significant rebalancing of its portfolio in a particular period. Given its nature, the selling activity in that example would likely not in itself change the entity's overall assessment of its business model if the selling activity is an isolated (ie one-time) event. The entity also needs to consider information about past sales within the context of the conditions that existed at that time as compared to existing conditions and expectations about future conditions.

BC4.146 The IASB decided to emphasise that sales due to an increase in the asset's credit risk enhance the entity's ability to collect contractual cash flows. Accordingly, the IASB noted that selling a financial asset when concerns arise about the collectability of the contractual cash flows is consistent with the objective of a hold to collect business model. The IASB noted that this guidance does not require that the entity wait to sell the financial asset until it has incurred a credit loss or until there has been a significant increase in credit risk (and lifetime expected credit losses are recognised on the asset). Instead, a sale would be consistent with the objective of a hold to collect business model if the asset's credit risk has increased based on reasonable and supportable information, including forward looking information.

BC4.147 The IASB also discussed whether sales due to managing concentrations of credit risk are consistent with a hold to collect business model. The IASB decided that such sales should be assessed in the same manner as other sales. Specifically, an entity must assess whether the assets' credit risk has increased (based on reasonable and supportable, including forward looking, information) and, if so, such sales would be consistent with a hold to collect business model. If not, the entity would need to consider the frequency, value and timing of such sales, as well as the reasons for those sales, to determine whether they are consistent with a hold to collect business model. The IASB noted that the notion of credit concentration risk is applied fairly broadly in practice and may include changes in the entity's investment policy or strategy that are not related to credit deterioration. The IASB noted that frequent sales that are significant in value and labelled as 'due to credit concentration risk' (but that are not related to an increase in the assets' credit risk) are likely to be inconsistent with the objective of collecting contractual cash flows.

Fair value through other comprehensive income

BC4.148 The requirements issued in IFRS 9 (2009) stated that financial assets were measured at either amortised cost or fair value through profit or loss.[19] However, as discussed in paragraph BC4.138, the IASB received feedback from some interested parties subsequent to IFRS 9 being issued in 2009 that the Standard should contain a third measurement category: fair value through other comprehensive income. In that feedback, some questioned whether measuring financial assets at fair value through profit or loss if those assets are not held within a hold to collect business model always results in useful information. In addition, some were concerned about the potential accounting mismatch that may arise because of the interaction between the classification and measurement of financial assets under IFRS 9 and the proposed accounting for insurance contract liabilities under the IASB's Insurance Contracts project. Others pointed out that, at the time, the FASB was considering a tentative model that included a fair value through other comprehensive income measurement category.

---

19 The requirements issued in IFRS 9 (2009) permitted an entity to make an irrevocable election at initial recognition to present fair value gains and losses on particular investments in equity instruments in other comprehensive income. That election is discussed in paragraph 5.7.5 of IFRS 9 and was outside of the scope of the 2012 Limited Amendments Exposure Draft.

BC4.149   In response to that feedback, the IASB proposed in the 2012 Limited Amendments Exposure Draft to introduce into IFRS 9 a fair value through other comprehensive income measurement category for particular financial assets. Specifically, the 2012 Limited Amendments Exposure Draft proposed that an entity would be required to measure a financial asset at fair value through other comprehensive income (unless the asset qualifies for, and the entity elects to apply, the fair value option) if the asset:

(a)   has contractual cash flow characteristics that give rise on specified dates to cash flows that are solely payments of principal and interest on the principal amount outstanding; and

(b)   is held within a business model in which assets are managed both in order to collect contractual cash flows and for sale (a 'hold to collect and sell' business model).

BC4.150   The IASB noted that the performance of a hold to collect and sell business model will be affected by both the collection of contractual cash flows and the realisation of fair values. Accordingly, the IASB decided that both amortised cost and fair value information are relevant and useful and therefore decided to propose that both sets of information are presented in the financial statements. Specifically, the 2012 Limited Amendments Exposure Draft proposed that the assets would be measured at fair value in the statement of financial position and the following amortised cost information would be presented in profit or loss:

(a)   interest revenue using the effective interest method that is applied to financial assets measured at amortised cost; and

(b)   impairment gains and losses using the same methodology that is applied to financial assets measured at amortised cost.

The difference between the total change in fair value and the amounts recognised in profit or loss would be presented in other comprehensive income.

BC4.151   The IASB noted in the 2012 Limited Amendments Exposure Draft that amortised cost information in profit or loss reflects the entity's decision to hold the assets to collect contractual cash flows unless, and until, the entity sells the assets in order to achieve the objective of the business model. Fair value information reflects the cash flows that would be realised if, and when, the assets are sold. In addition, the 2012 Limited Amendments Exposure Draft proposed that when an asset measured at fair value through other comprehensive income is derecognised, the cumulative fair value gain or loss that was recognised in other comprehensive income is reclassified ('recycled') from equity to profit or loss as a reclassification adjustment (in accordance with IAS 1). The IASB noted that amortised cost information would not be provided in profit or loss unless the gains or losses previously accumulated in other comprehensive income are recycled to profit or loss when the financial asset is derecognised—and, therefore, recycling was a key feature of the proposed fair value through other comprehensive income measurement category.

BC4.152 However, the IASB acknowledged that requiring recycling for these financial assets is different from other requirements in IFRS 9 that prohibit recycling. Specifically, in accordance with IFRS 9, an entity is prohibited from recycling the gains and losses accumulated in other comprehensive income related to the following financial instruments:

(a) investments in equity instruments for which an entity has made an irrevocable election at initial recognition to present fair value changes in other comprehensive income (see paragraphs 5.7.5 and B5.7.1 of IFRS 9); or

(b) financial liabilities designated under the fair value option for which the effects of changes in the liability's credit risk are presented in other comprehensive income (see paragraphs 5.7.7 and B5.7.9 of IFRS 9).

BC4.153 However, the IASB noted in the 2012 Limited Amendments Exposure Draft that some of the reasons for prohibiting recycling of those gains or losses do not apply to financial assets measured at fair value through other comprehensive income. Specifically:

(a) *investments in equity instruments:* paragraph BC5.25(b) discusses the reasons why these gains and losses accumulated in other comprehensive income are not recycled. One of the primary reasons is that recycling would create the need to assess these equity investments for impairment. The impairment requirements in IAS 39 for investments in equity instruments were very subjective and indeed were among the most criticised accounting requirements during the global financial crisis. In contrast, IFRS 9 does not contain impairment requirements for investments in equity instruments. For financial assets mandatorily measured in accordance with the new fair value through other comprehensive income category, the IASB proposed that the same impairment approach would apply to those financial assets as is applied to financial assets measured at amortised cost. While recycling is prohibited, the IASB observed that an entity is not prohibited from presenting information in the financial statements about realised gains or losses on investments in equity instruments; for example, as a separate line item in other comprehensive income.

(b) *financial liabilities designated under the fair value option:* paragraphs BC5.52–BC5.57 discuss the reasons why these own credit gains and losses accumulated in other comprehensive income are not recycled. One of the primary reasons is that if the entity repays the contractual amount, which will often be the case for these financial liabilities, the cumulative effect of changes in the liability's credit risk over its life will net to zero because the liability's fair value will ultimately equal the contractual amount due. In contrast, for financial assets measured at fair value through other comprehensive income, selling financial assets is integral to achieving the objective of the business model and therefore the gains and losses accumulated in other comprehensive income will not net to zero.

BC4.154　Consistently with providing amortised cost information in profit or loss, the IASB proposed that for the purposes of recognising foreign exchange gains and losses under IAS 21 *The Effects of Changes in Foreign Exchange Rates*, a financial asset measured at fair value through other comprehensive income should be treated as if it was measured at amortised cost in the foreign currency. Consequently, exchange differences on the amortised cost (ie interest revenue calculated using the effective interest method and impairment gains and losses) would be recognised in profit or loss, with all other exchange differences recognised in other comprehensive income.

BC4.155　In addition to providing relevant and useful information for financial assets that are held within a hold to collect and sell business model, the IASB noted in the 2012 Limited Amendments Exposure Draft that the introduction of the fair value through other comprehensive income measurement category may improve consistency between the classification and measurement of financial assets under IFRS 9 and the accounting for insurance contract liabilities under the IASB's tentative decisions at that time in its Insurance Contracts project. That is because the 2013 Insurance Contracts Exposure Draft proposed that insurance contract liabilities would be measured on the statement of financial position using a current value approach but the effects of changes in the discount rate used to measure that current value would be presented in other comprehensive income. Consequently, when the entity holds both insurance contract liabilities and financial assets that qualify to be measured at fair value through other comprehensive income, particular changes in both the fair value of the financial assets (ie those changes other than interest revenue and impairment gains and losses) and the current value of the insurance contract liabilities (ie those changes arising from the effects of changes in the discount rate) would be presented in other comprehensive income.

BC4.156　The majority of respondents to the 2012 Limited Amendments Exposure Draft agreed with the introduction of the fair value through other comprehensive income measurement category. Some of those respondents agreed with the measurement category as proposed by the IASB, while others agreed in principle with the proposals but made suggestions related to the conditions for that new measurement category. For example, some respondents expressed the view that a financial asset should be measured at fair value through other comprehensive income as long as it is held in a hold to collect and sell business model (ie irrespective of the asset's contractual cash flow characteristics) and others suggested that the fair value through other comprehensive income measurement category should be an option (either in addition to, or instead of, a mandatory measurement category). The suggestion that the fair value through other comprehensive income measurement category should be an option was most often made within the context of further reducing accounting mismatches between the classification and measurement of financial assets under IFRS 9 and accounting for insurance contract liabilities under the IASB's tentative decisions in its Insurance Contracts project. In addition, some respondents raised questions about the distinction between the fair value through other comprehensive income measurement category and the fair value through profit or loss measurement category. Some of these respondents asked the IASB to more clearly articulate the principle underpinning the fair value through other comprehensive income measurement category. A few respondents asked whether it would be more straightforward to define the conditions to measure a financial asset at fair value through profit or loss and therefore suggested that fair value through other comprehensive income should be the residual measurement category. They noted that this would be more aligned with the available-for-sale category in IAS 39.

BC4.157 Consistently with the proposal in the 2012 Limited Amendments Exposure Draft and the feedback received on that proposal, the IASB confirmed the introduction of a third measurement category—fair value through other comprehensive income—into IFRS 9. The IASB believes that this measurement category is appropriate for financial assets that have contractual cash flows that are solely payments of principal and interest and that are held in a hold to collect and sell business model. For those financial assets, the IASB believes that both amortised cost and fair value information are relevant and useful because such information reflects how cash flows are realised. That is, holding financial assets to collect contractual cash flows is integral to achieving the objective of the hold to collect and sell business model and therefore the amounts presented in profit or loss provide amortised cost information while the entity holds the assets. Other fair value changes are not presented in profit or loss until (and unless) they are realised through selling, which acknowledges that such changes may reverse while the entity holds the asset. However, because selling assets is also integral to achieving the objective of the hold to collect and sell business model, those other fair value changes are presented in other comprehensive income and the financial asset is presented at fair value in the statement of financial position.

BC4.158 Also, in order to be measured at fair value through other comprehensive income, a financial asset must have contractual cash flows that are solely payments of principal and interest on the principal amount outstanding. This is because amortised cost information is presented in profit or loss for assets measured at fair value through other comprehensive income and, as the IASB has consistently stated, the amortised cost measurement attribute provides relevant and useful information only for financial assets with 'simple' contractual cash flows (ie contractual cash flows that are solely principal and interest). Amortised cost is a relatively simple measurement technique that allocates interest over the relevant time period using the effective interest rate. As discussed in paragraph BC4.23, the IASB's long-held view is that the effective interest method, which underpins amortised cost measurement, is not an appropriate method for allocating 'complex' contractual cash flows (ie contractual cash flows that are not solely principal and interest).

BC4.159 The IASB also discussed during its redeliberations whether the fair value through other comprehensive income measurement category should be optional—either in addition to, or instead of, a mandatory measurement category. However, the IASB believes that such an option would be inconsistent with, and indeed would undermine, its decision to classify financial assets as measured at fair value through other comprehensive income on the basis of their contractual cash flows and the business model within which they are held. Indeed, the overall structure of IFRS 9 is based on classifying financial assets on the basis of those two conditions. Moreover, the IASB noted that users of financial statements have both consistently opposed permitting too much optionality in accounting requirements and have also advocated accounting requirements that provide comparability. However, the IASB acknowledged that accounting mismatches could arise as a result of the classification and measurement of financial assets under IFRS 9. In particular, such mismatches could arise because of the accounting for insurance contract liabilities under the IASB's tentative decisions in its Insurance Contracts project.[20] In response to those potential mismatches, the IASB noted that the introduction of the fair value through other comprehensive income measurement category, which reflects a hold to collect and sell business model, and the extension of the existing fair value option in IFRS 9 to financial assets that would otherwise be measured at fair value through other comprehensive income (see paragraphs BC4.210–BC4.211), are both relevant to many entities that have insurance contract liabilities. Consequently, the IASB believes that those requirements will assist in improving the interaction between the accounting for financial assets and the proposed accounting for insurance contract liabilities as compared to the requirements issued in IFRS 9 (2009). The IASB noted that, in a sense, these amendments to the requirements in IFRS 9 for the classification and measurement of financial assets provide a number of 'tools' that the IASB can consider when it finalises the accounting for insurance contract liabilities. Moreover, the IASB noted that it will consider the feedback related to the accounting model for insurance contract liabilities and whether that model should be modified to reflect the interaction with the classification and measurement model for financial assets in IFRS 9 as it continues to discuss its Insurance Contracts project.

BC4.160 In order to improve the clarity of the application guidance related to the hold to collect and sell business model, the IASB decided to emphasise that holding and selling are not the *objectives* of the business model, but instead are the *outcomes* of the business model. That is, collecting contractual cash flows and selling financial assets are the outcomes of the way in which an entity manages its financial assets to achieve the objective of a particular business model. For example, an entity with a long-term investment strategy that has an objective of matching the cash flows on long-term liabilities or matching the duration of liabilities with the cash flows on financial assets may have a hold to collect and sell business model. The IASB decided to clarify that measuring financial assets at fair value through other comprehensive income provides relevant and useful information to users of financial statements only when realising cash flows by collecting contractual cash flows and selling financial assets are both integral to achieving the objective of the business model.

---

20 IFRS 17 *Insurance Contracts*, issued in May 2017, replaced IFRS 4 *Insurance Contracts*.

BC4.161   The IASB acknowledges that a third measurement category adds complexity to IFRS 9 and may seem similar to the available-for-sale category in IAS 39. However, the IASB believes that measuring particular financial assets at fair value through other comprehensive income reflects the assets' performance better than measuring those assets at either amortised cost or fair value through profit or loss. The IASB also believes that the fair value through other comprehensive income measurement category in IFRS 9 is fundamentally different to the available-for-sale category in IAS 39. That is because there is a clear and logical rationale for measuring particular financial assets at fair value through other comprehensive income, which is based on the existing structure in IFRS 9 (ie financial assets are classified on the basis of their contractual cash flow characteristics and the business model in which they are held). In contrast, the available-for-sale category in IAS 39 was essentially a residual classification and, in many cases, was a free choice. Moreover, IFRS 9 requires the same interest revenue recognition and impairment approach for assets measured at amortised cost and fair value through other comprehensive income, whereas IAS 39 applied different impairment approaches to different measurement categories. Consequently, the IASB believes that the added complexity of a third measurement category (compared to the requirements issued in IFRS 9 (2009)) is justified by the usefulness of the information provided to users of financial statements.

BC4.162   The IASB noted during its redeliberations that some interested parties have expressed concerns that the introduction of the fair value through other comprehensive income measurement category would increase the use of fair value compared to the requirements issued in IFRS 9 (2009). However, as discussed in paragraph BC4.140, the introduction of the third measurement category and the clarifications to the hold to collect business model clarify, instead of change (narrow the scope of), the population of financial assets that were intended to be eligible to be measured at amortised cost. The clarifications to the guidance for the hold to collect business model address particular application questions raised by interested parties by reaffirming the existing principle in IFRS 9. The introduction of the fair value through other comprehensive income measurement category affects only assets that are not held in a hold to collect business model and thus would otherwise be measured at fair value through profit or loss under the requirements issued in IFRS 9 (2009).

Fair value through profit or loss

BC4.163   IFRS 9 (as issued in 2009) had only two measurement categories: amortised cost and fair value through profit or loss. A financial asset was measured at amortised cost only if it met particular conditions. All other financial assets were measured at fair value through profit or loss; ie fair value through profit or loss was the residual measurement category.[21]

---

21 As noted previously, IFRS 9 (as issued in 2009) permitted an entity to make an irrevocable election at initial recognition to present fair value gains and losses on particular investments in equity instruments in other comprehensive income. That election is discussed in paragraph 5.7.5 of IFRS 9 and was outside of the scope of the 2012 Limited Amendments Exposure Draft.

BC4.164   The 2012 Limited Amendments Exposure Draft proposed to introduce a third measurement category—fair value through other comprehensive income—and, during the deliberations leading to that Exposure Draft, the IASB considered whether fair value through profit or loss should remain the residual measurement category. The IASB acknowledged that there might be some benefits in making fair value through other comprehensive income the residual measurement category, because, arguably, a clearer distinction could be made between the conditions for the amortised cost measurement category and the conditions for the fair value through profit or loss measurement category. That is, it would be easier to define the two 'ends' of the classification spectrum (ie amortised cost and fair value through profit or loss) with the 'middle' (ie fair value through other comprehensive income) as the residual. As noted in paragraph BC4.156, a few respondents to the 2012 Limited Amendments Exposure Draft expressed this view.

BC4.165   However, the IASB has consistently noted that the residual measurement category must provide useful information for all of the instruments classified in that category. Amortised cost information is provided in profit or loss for both the amortised cost measurement category and the fair value through other comprehensive income measurement category, and this information is relevant only for financial assets with particular contractual cash flow characteristics that are held within particular business models. That is, amortised cost information is relevant only if the financial asset has contractual cash flows that are solely payments of principal and interest and the asset is held in a business model in which collecting contractual cash flows is integral to achieving its objective. As a result, the IASB believes that it would be inappropriate if either amortised cost or fair value through other comprehensive income was the residual measurement category. Furthermore, the IASB believes that defining the conditions for the fair value through other comprehensive income measurement category strengthens and clarifies the conditions for the amortised cost measurement category.

BC4.166   Consequently, the IASB reaffirmed the existing requirement in IFRS 9—and the proposal in the 2012 Limited Amendments Exposure Draft—that the fair value through profit or loss measurement category is the residual measurement category. In addition, to respond to feedback received, the IASB confirmed that financial assets that are held for trading purposes and financial assets that are managed and whose performance is evaluated on a fair value basis must be measured at fair value through profit or loss, because they are held neither in a hold to collect business model nor in a hold to collect and sell business model. Instead, the entity makes decisions on the basis of changes in, and with the objective of realising, the assets' fair value. Thus, the IASB believes that relevant and useful information about the amounts, timing and uncertainty of future cash flows is provided to users of financial statements only if these financial assets are measured at fair value through profit or loss.

Other considerations

BC4.167　In the deliberations leading to the publication of the 2012 Limited Amendments Exposure Draft, the IASB considered an alternative approach to assessing the business model in which financial assets are held. The approach was a 'business-activity approach' and was similar to the tentative approach that the FASB had been considering immediately prior to the start of the boards' joint deliberations. In summary, the business-activity approach would have classified financial assets on the basis of the business activity that the entity uses in acquiring and managing those financial assets, subject to an assessment of the asset's contractual cash flow characteristics. The business-activity approach focused on the strategy that resulted in an entity's initial recognition of the financial asset. Under this approach, the relevant business activities were 'customer financing' or 'lending', which would result in measurement at amortised cost; 'investing', which would result in measurement at fair value through other comprehensive income; and 'holding for sale' or 'actively managing (or monitoring) the assets at fair value', which would result in measurement at fair value through profit or loss. In order to be considered a lending (or customer financing) business activity, in addition to holding the financial assets to collect substantially all of the contractual cash flows, the entity must also have had the ability to negotiate adjustments to the contractual cash flows with the counterparty in the event of a potential credit loss.

BC4.168　The IASB noted that the business-activity approach would be different from the approach to classifying financial assets in IFRS 9 (as issued in 2009). In addition, the IASB noted that measuring financial assets at amortised cost only if the entity has the ability to negotiate the asset's terms with the counterparty might be unduly costly to implement and complex to apply and also might result in different classification of lending activities solely as a result of the different legal frameworks in different jurisdictions. The IASB also noted that, under the business-activity approach, the form of the financial asset would affect its classification; for example, widely-held bonds would typically fail to meet the criteria to be measured at amortised cost, because the holder is generally unable to renegotiate the terms with the counterparty on a bilateral basis. Accordingly, the IASB decided not to pursue the business-activity approach and instead confirmed the approach in IFRS 9, in which financial assets are measured at amortised cost if they are held with an objective to collect contractual cash flows (subject to the assessment of the asset's contractual cash flow characteristics) and reaffirmed the rationale for the business model assessment set out in paragraphs BC4.15 – BC4.21.

BC4.169　In addition, during its deliberations leading to the publication of the 2012 Limited Amendments Exposure Draft, the IASB noted that the 2009 Classification and Measurement Exposure Draft had solicited views on alternative approaches in which fair value changes for particular financial assets would be disaggregated, with the result that a portion of the fair value change would be presented in profit or loss and a portion of the fair value change would be presented in other comprehensive income. Those alternative approaches, as well as the feedback received and the IASB's rationale for ultimately rejecting the approaches, are described in more detail in paragraphs BC4.41–BC4.43. The IASB believes that the fair value through other comprehensive income measurement category that was proposed in the 2012 Limited Amendments Exposure Draft, and subsequently added to IFRS 9, is different from, and significantly less complex than, those alternative approaches. For example, the alternative approaches continued to rely on the definition of 'loans and receivables' in IAS 39 (in addition to the assessments of the entity's business model and the asset's contractual cash flows). Moreover, the alternative approaches prohibited recycling and therefore did not present both fair value and amortised cost information in the financial statements. As discussed in paragraph BC4.157, presenting both sets of information was an important factor in the IASB's decision to add the fair value through other comprehensive income measurement category to IFRS 9.

Contractual cash flow characteristics[22]

Solely payments of principal and interest

BC4.170   IFRS 9 (as issued in 2009) required an entity to assess the contractual cash flow characteristics of financial assets. A financial asset was measured at amortised cost only if its contractual terms gave rise on specified dates to cash flows that are solely payments of principal and interest on the principal amount outstanding, subject to the assessment of the business model within which the asset is held. For the purposes of assessing the contractual cash flow characteristics of a financial asset, interest was consideration for the time value of money and for the credit risk associated with the principal amount outstanding during a particular period of time. Paragraph BC4.22 noted that a premium for liquidity risk may be included.

BC4.171   The IASB's long-standing view has been that amortised cost provides relevant and useful information about particular financial assets in particular circumstances because, for those assets, it provides information about the amount, timing and uncertainty of future cash flows. Amortised cost is calculated using the effective interest method, which is a relatively simple measurement technique that allocates interest over the relevant time period using the effective interest rate.

BC4.172   The objective of the requirement in IFRS 9 to assess an asset's contractual cash flows is to identify instruments for which the effective interest method results in relevant and useful information. The IASB believes that the effective interest method is suitable only for instruments with 'simple' cash flows that represent solely principal and interest. In contrast, as set out in paragraph BC4.23, the effective interest method is not an appropriate method for allocating contractual cash flows that are not principal and interest on the principal amount outstanding. Instead those more complex cash flows require a valuation overlay to contractual cash flows (ie fair value) to ensure that the reported financial information provides useful information.

---

22   In this section, the discussion about amortised cost information is relevant to both financial assets in the amortised cost measurement category and financial assets in the fair value through other comprehensive income measurement category. That is because, for the latter, the assets are measured at fair value in the statement of financial position and amortised cost information is provided in profit or loss.

BC4.173 Most interested parties have consistently agreed that a financial asset should be classified and measured on the basis of its contractual cash flow characteristics and have found this requirement to be operational. However, subsequent to the issue of IFRS 9 in 2009, the IASB received some questions about how this assessment should be applied to particular financial assets. Specifically, the requirements in paragraph B4.1.13 of IFRS 9 (2009) set out an example of a financial asset with an interest rate tenor mismatch (that is, the variable interest rate on the financial asset is reset every month to a three-month interest rate or the variable interest rate is reset to always reflect the original maturity of the asset). The discussion of the example (Instrument B) concluded that such contractual cash flows are not payments of principal and interest, because the interest rate does not represent consideration for the time value of money for the tenor of the instrument (or the reset period). Subsequent to the issuance of IFRS 9 in 2009, many interested parties raised concerns related to that example. Specifically, those interested parties asked about the assessment of a financial asset's contractual cash flows when the consideration for the time value of money element of the interest rate is not perfect (ie it is 'modified') because of a contractual term such as an interest rate tenor mismatch feature. Generally, stakeholders expressed concerns that the application guidance issued in IFRS 9 (2009) could lead to an unduly narrow interpretation of the meaning of interest.

BC4.174 The IASB acknowledged these concerns. In the 2012 Limited Amendments Exposure Draft, it proposed a notion of a modified economic relationship between principal and the consideration for time value of money and credit risk — and also proposed corresponding clarifications to Instrument B in paragraph B4.1.13 of IFRS 9. Specifically, the IASB proposed that a financial asset does not necessarily need to be measured at fair value through profit or loss if the economic relationship between principal and the consideration for time value of money and credit risk is modified by an interest rate tenor mismatch feature. Instead, an entity would be required to assess the effect of the modified relationship on the financial asset's contractual cash flows relative to a 'perfect' benchmark instrument (ie a financial instrument with the same credit quality and with the same contractual terms except for the contractual term under evaluation). If the modification could result in contractual cash flows that are more than insignificantly different from the benchmark cash flows, the contractual terms of the financial asset would not give rise to cash flows that are solely payments of principal and interest on the principal amount outstanding. In other words, in the 2012 Limited Amendments Exposure Draft, the IASB clarified that the relationship between principal and the consideration for time value of money and credit risk does not need to be perfect, but only relatively minor modifications of that relationship are consistent with payments that are solely principal and interest.

BC4.175 While developing the 2012 Limited Amendments Exposure Draft, the IASB received feedback about interest rates in regulated environments that modify the economic relationship between principal and the consideration for the time value of money and the credit risk. Interested parties noted that in such environments the base interest rates are set by a central authority and may not be reset in a manner that reflects the reset period. In these circumstances, the effect of the interest rate tenor mismatch feature could be significant. Furthermore, in such environments, there may not be any financial instruments available that are priced on a different basis. Thus, some raised concerns about how to determine whether the cash flows on such instruments are solely payments of principal and interest and whether the proposed notion of a modified economic relationship was operational and appropriate in such environments. The IASB noted that it would gather further feedback during the comment period on whether the clarifications proposed in the 2012 Limited Amendments Exposure Draft appropriately addressed the concerns related to interest rates in regulated environments.

BC4.176 Nearly all respondents to the 2012 Limited Amendments Exposure Draft agreed that a financial asset with a modified economic relationship between principal and the consideration for the time value of money and the credit risk should be considered to have contractual cash flows that are solely payments of principal and interest. However, many respondents believed that the clarification did not go far enough in addressing common application questions and expressed concern that some financial assets that they view as 'plain vanilla' or 'normal lending' would still not have contractual cash flows that are solely payments of principal and interest. Specifically, these respondents expressed the view that the assessment of a modified economic relationship still implied an unduly narrow and strict interpretation of the time value of money element of an interest rate. They stated that amortised cost could provide useful information for a broader range of financial instruments. They asked the IASB to clarify the scope of the assessment of a modified economic relationship (for example, whether it should apply only to interest rate tenor mismatch features or more broadly to all circumstances in which the time value of money element is modified (ie imperfect)) and to reconsider the threshold used in that assessment (ie the threshold of 'not more than insignificantly different' from benchmark cash flows). Respondents also requested broader clarifications about the meaning of the time value of money as that notion is used in the description of interest in IFRS 9.

BC4.177 In its redeliberations, the IASB acknowledged respondents' questions and concerns and, as a result, decided to clarify the following items:

(a) The objective of the time value of money element is to provide consideration for *only* the passage of time, in the absence of a return for other risks (such as credit risk or liquidity risk) or costs associated with holding the financial asset. In assessing the time value of money element, the entity must consider the currency in which the financial asset is denominated, because interest rates vary by currency. In addition, as a general proposition, there must be a link between the interest rate and the period for which the interest rate is set, because the appropriate rate for an instrument varies depending on the term for which the rate is set.

(b) However, in some circumstances, the time value of money element could provide consideration for only the passage of time even if that element is modified by, for example, an interest rate tenor mismatch feature or a feature that sets the interest rate by reference to an average of particular short and long-term interest rates. In these cases, an entity must assess whether the time value of money element provides consideration for only the passage of time by performing either a quantitative or qualitative assessment. The objective of that assessment is to establish (on an undiscounted basis) how different the financial asset's contractual cash flows (ie taking into account all of the contractual cash flows) could be from the cash flows that would arise if the time value of money element were perfect (ie if there were a perfect link between the interest rate and the period for which that rate is set). The IASB decided not to prescribe when an entity must perform a quantitative versus a qualitative assessment.

(c) If the modified time value of money element could result in cash flows that are significantly different on an undiscounted basis from the 'perfect' cash flows (described as benchmark cash flows), either in a single reporting period or cumulatively over the life of the financial instrument, the financial asset does not have contractual cash flows that are solely payments of principal and interest. The IASB was persuaded by respondents' feedback that the 'not more than insignificantly different' threshold in the 2012 Limited Amendments Exposure Draft was unduly restrictive and, as a result, particular financial assets would be measured at fair value through profit or loss even though the objective of the modified time value of money element was in fact to provide consideration for only the passage of time. However, the IASB noted that the objective of a modified time value of money element is not to provide consideration for just the passage of time, and thus the contractual cash flows are not solely payments of principal and interest, if the contractual cash flows could be significantly different from the benchmark cash flows.

BC4.178 The IASB also noted that, as a general proposition, the market in which the transaction occurs is relevant to the assessment of the time value of money element. For example, in Europe it is common to reference interest rates to LIBOR and in the United States it is common to reference interest rates to the prime rate. However the IASB noted that a particular interest rate does not necessarily reflect consideration for only the time value of money merely because that rate is considered 'normal' in a particular market. For example, if an interest rate is reset every year but the reference rate is always a 15-year rate, it would be difficult for an entity to conclude that such a rate provides consideration for only the passage of time, even if such pricing is commonly used in that particular market. Accordingly the IASB believes that an entity must apply judgement to conclude whether the stated time value of money element meets the objective of providing consideration for only the passage of time.

Regulated interest rates

BC4.179   The IASB noted that in some jurisdictions the government or regulatory authority establishes interest rates and, in some cases, the objective of the time value of money element may not be to provide consideration for only the passage of time. However, the IASB decided that such a regulated interest rate is a proxy for the time value of money element if that interest rate provides consideration that is broadly consistent with the passage of time and does not provide exposure to risks or volatility in the contractual cash flows that are inconsistent with a basic lending arrangement.

BC4.180   The IASB acknowledged that this approach for regulated interest rates is broader than the approach for interest rates that are established freely by market participants. However, the IASB noted that these regulated rates are set for public policy reasons and thus are not subject to structuring to achieve a particular accounting result. For example, the IASB noted that French retail banks collect deposits on special 'Livret A' savings accounts. The interest rate is determined by the central bank and the government according to a formula that reflects protection against inflation and an adequate remuneration that incentivises entities to use these particular savings accounts. This is because legislation requires a particular portion of the amounts collected by the retail banks to be lent to a governmental agency that uses the proceeds for social programmes. The IASB noted that the time value element of interest on these accounts may not provide consideration for only the passage of time; however the IASB believes that amortised cost would provide relevant and useful information as long as the contractual cash flows do not introduce risks or volatility that are inconsistent with a basic lending arrangement.

Other clarifications

BC4.181   Respondents to the 2012 Limited Amendments Exposure Draft also asked the IASB to clarify the overall objective of the assessment of a financial asset's contractual cash flow characteristics and also raised the following specific questions and concerns related to that assessment:

(a)   the meaning of 'principal' — respondents asked the IASB to clarify the meaning of principal, in particular within the context of financial assets that are originated or purchased at a premium or discount to par;

(b)   the meaning of 'interest' — respondents asked whether elements other than the time value of money and credit risk (for example, consideration for liquidity risk, funding costs and a profit margin) could be consistent with contractual cash flows that are solely payments of principal and interest; and

(c)   de minimis features — respondents asked whether a contractual feature would affect the classification and measurement of a financial asset if, in all scenarios, that feature could impact the contractual cash flows only by a de minimis amount.

BC4.182   In response to the feedback received, the IASB decided to clarify the application guidance in IFRS 9 as follows:

(a)   for the purposes of applying the condition in paragraphs 4.1.2(b) and 4.1.2A(b) of IFRS 9, principal is the fair value of the financial asset at initial recognition. The IASB believes that this meaning reflects the economics of the financial asset from the perspective of the current holder; in other words, the entity would assess the contractual cash flow characteristics by comparing the contractual cash flows to the amount that it actually invested. However, the IASB acknowledged that the principal amount may change over the life of the financial asset (for example, if there are repayments of principal).

(b)   for the purposes of applying the condition in paragraphs 4.1.2(b) and 4.1.2A(b) of IFRS 9, the consideration for the time value of money and the credit risk are typically the most significant elements of interest; however, they may not be the only elements. In discussing the elements of interest (and indeed the overall objective of the assessment of an asset's contractual cash flows), the IASB considered the concept of a 'basic lending arrangement' (the form of which need not be that of a loan). In such an arrangement, the IASB noted that interest may include consideration for elements other than the time value of money and credit risk. Specifically, interest may include consideration for risks such as liquidity risk and costs associated with holding the asset (such as administrative costs) as well as a profit margin. But elements that introduce exposure to risks or variability in the contractual cash flows that are unrelated to lending (such as exposure to equity or commodity price risk) are not consistent with a basic lending arrangement. The IASB also noted that the assessment of interest focuses on *what* the entity is being compensated for (ie whether the entity is receiving consideration for basic lending risks, costs and a profit margin or is being compensated for something else), instead of *how much* the entity receives for a particular element. For example, the IASB acknowledged that different entities may price the credit risk element differently.

(c)   a contractual feature does not affect the classification and measurement of a financial asset if the impact of that feature on the asset's contractual cash flows could only ever be de minimis. The IASB noted that to make this determination an entity must consider the potential effect of the feature in each reporting period and cumulatively over the life of the instrument. For example, a feature would not have a de minimis effect if it could give rise to a significant increase in contractual cash flows in one reporting period and a significant decrease in contractual cash flows in another reporting period, even if these amounts offset each other on a cumulative basis.

Contractual terms that change the timing or amount of contractual cash flows, including prepayment and extension features

BC4.183   The requirements issued in IFRS 9 (2009) provided guidance for contractual terms that permit the issuer (ie the debtor) to prepay a financial instrument or that permit the holder (ie the creditor) to put the financial instrument back to the issuer before maturity (ie 'prepayment features') and contractual terms that permit the issuer or holder to extend the contractual term of the financial instrument (ie 'extension features'). In summary, that guidance stated that prepayment and extension features result in contractual cash flows that are solely payments of principal and interest only if:

(a) the prepayment or extension feature is not contingent on future events, other than to protect the holder or issuer against particular events or circumstances; and

(b) the terms of the prepayment or extension feature result in contractual cash flows that are solely payments of principal and interest.

The guidance for prepayment features stated that the prepayment amount may include reasonable additional compensation for the early termination of the contract.

BC4.184　The requirements issued in IFRS 9 (2009) also stated that a contractual term that changes the timing or amount of payments of principal or interest does not result in contractual cash flows that are solely payments of principal and interest unless the term is a variable interest rate that is consideration for the time value of money and credit risk or the term is a prepayment or extension feature (as in paragraph BC4.183). However if a contractual term is not genuine, it does not affect the classification of a financial asset. (Consistently with IAS 32, a contractual feature is not genuine if it affects the asset's contractual cash flows only on the occurrence of an event that is extremely rare, highly abnormal and very unlikely to occur.)

BC4.185　Although the 2012 Limited Amendments Exposure Draft did not propose any amendments to these requirements, some respondents asked the IASB to reconsider or clarify particular aspects of the guidance. In particular, some respondents asked why the requirements issued in IFRS 9 (2009) provided specific guidance for prepayment and extension features that are contingent on future events ('contingent prepayment and extension features'), but did not provide guidance for other types of features that are contingent on future events ('other contingent features'). Respondents also asked whether (and if so, why) the nature of the future event in itself affects whether the financial asset's contractual cash flows are solely payments of principal and interest. These respondents generally expressed the view that an entity should focus on the contractual cash flows that could arise over the life of the financial instrument (ie both before and after the future event), instead of on the nature of the future event itself.

BC4.186　In addition, some respondents expressed the view that a contingent feature should not affect the classification and measurement of a financial asset if the likelihood is remote that the future event will occur. Some of these respondents were specifically concerned about contingently convertible instruments or so-called 'bail-in' instruments. While the contractual terms of these instruments vary, generally, interested parties raised concerns about contingently convertible instruments that convert into equity instruments of the issuer on the basis of a predetermined ratio if a specified event occurs (for example, if the issuer's regulatory capital ratios decline below a specific threshold). In the case of a bail-in instrument, interested parties generally raised concerns about instruments with a contractual feature that requires (or permits) a portion or all of the unpaid amounts of principal and interest to be written off if a specified event occurs (for example, if the issuer has insufficient regulatory capital or is at a point of non-viability). These respondents expressed the view that these instruments should not be measured at fair value through profit or loss merely as a result of the contingent cash flow characteristics (ie the conversion into a predetermined number of the issuer's equity instruments or the write-off of particular unpaid amounts upon the occurrence of a particular future event) if it is unlikely that the future event will occur.

BC4.187 Other respondents asked whether a financial asset could have contractual cash flows that are solely payments of principal and interest if the asset is purchased or originated at a significant premium or discount to the contractual par amount but is prepayable at that par amount. These respondents noted that if principal is described as the fair value of the financial asset at initial recognition, then the prepayment amount (ie par) will not represent unpaid amounts of principal and interest. That is because the prepayment amount will either be *more than* unpaid amounts of principal and interest (if the asset is purchased or originated at a significant discount) or *less than* unpaid amounts of principal and interest (if the asset is purchased or originated at a significant premium). Respondents stated that discounts and premiums are generally expected to arise when the entity does not expect that the asset will be prepaid (even though prepayment is contractually possible). Many raised this issue specifically within the context of purchased credit-impaired financial assets. Many of these assets will be purchased at a significant discount to par, which reflects the credit impairment, but the contractual terms may include a prepayment feature. Respondents expressed the view that an entity should not be required to measure purchased credit-impaired financial assets at fair value through profit or loss merely as a result of the prepayment feature, particularly because it is highly unlikely that such an asset will be prepaid at its contractual par amount since it is credit impaired.

BC4.188 In its redeliberations of the 2012 Limited Amendments Exposure Draft, the IASB decided to clarify the application guidance in IFRS 9 as follows:

(a) all contingent features must be assessed in the same way. That is, there is no distinction between contingent prepayment and extension features and other types of contingent features.

(b) for all contingent features, the nature of the future event in itself does not determine whether a financial asset's contractual cash flows are solely payments of principal and interest. However, the IASB noted that there often is an important interaction between the nature of the future event and the resulting contractual cash flows. Consequently, it is often helpful (or perhaps even necessary) for the entity to consider the nature of the future event to determine whether the resulting contractual cash flows are solely payments of principal and interest. For example, if the nature of the future event is unrelated to a basic lending arrangement (for example, a particular equity or commodity index reaches or exceeds a particular level), it is unlikely that the resulting contractual cash flows are solely payments of principal and interest, because those cash flows are likely to reflect a return for equity or commodity price risk.

BC4.189 In addition, the IASB confirmed the guidance in IFRS 9 that an entity is not permitted to take into account the probability that the future event will occur, unless the contingent feature is not genuine. In other words, a financial asset must be measured at fair value through profit or loss if a remote (but genuine) contingency would result in contractual cash flows that are not solely payments of principal and interest (and those contractual cash flows are not de minimis). In reaching that conclusion, the IASB considered an alternative approach in which a contingent feature would not affect the classification and measurement of a financial asset if the likelihood is remote that the future event will occur. The IASB rejected this approach because it is inconsistent with its long-standing view that amortised cost provides relevant and useful information only for financial assets with simple contractual cash flows. As noted in paragraph BC4.23, the effective interest method is not appropriate for measuring contractual cash flows that are not solely payments of principal and interest, but instead those cash flows require a valuation overlay to contractual cash flows (ie fair value) to ensure that the reported financial information is relevant and useful.

BC4.190 In particular, the IASB noted that contingently convertible instruments and bail-in instruments could give rise to contractual cash flows that are not solely payments of principal and interest and indeed are structured for regulatory purposes such that they have contractual characteristics similar to equity instruments in particular circumstances. Consequently, the IASB believes that amortised cost does not provide relevant or useful information to users of financial statements about those financial instruments, in particular if the likelihood of that future event occurring increases. At a minimum, the IASB observed that it would be necessary to reclassify the financial asset so that it is measured at fair value through profit or loss if the future event becomes more likely than remote. Thus, the IASB observed that an approach that is based on whether the likelihood of a future event is remote would create additional complexity, because the entity would need to continuously reassess whether the likelihood of the future event has increased such that it is no longer remote, and if so, the entity would need to reclassify the financial asset so that it is measured at fair value through profit or loss at that point.

BC4.191 However, the IASB acknowledged that, as the result of legislation, some governments or other authorities have the power in particular circumstances to impose losses on the holders of some financial instruments. The IASB noted that IFRS 9 requires the holder to analyse the *contractual terms* of a financial asset to determine whether the asset gives rise to cash flows that are solely payments of principal and interest on the principal amount outstanding. In other words, the holder would not consider the payments that arise only as a result of the government's or other authority's legislative power as cash flows in its analysis. That is because that power and the related payments are not *contractual terms* of the financial instrument.

BC4.192   Moreover, the IASB decided to provide a narrow exception for particular prepayable financial assets. The exception would apply to financial assets that would otherwise have contractual cash flows that are solely payments of principal and interest but do not meet that condition only as a result of the prepayment feature. Such financial assets would be eligible to be measured at amortised cost or fair value through other comprehensive income (subject to the assessment of the business model in which they are held) if the following three conditions are met:

(a)   the financial asset is purchased or originated at a premium or discount to the contractual par amount;

(b)   the prepayment amount substantially represents the contractual par amount and accrued (but unpaid) contractual interest, which may include reasonable additional compensation for the early termination of the contract; and

(c)   the fair value of the prepayment feature on initial recognition of the financial asset is insignificant.

BC4.193   This exception would require some financial assets that otherwise do not have contractual cash flows that are solely payments of principal and interest to be measured at amortised cost or fair value through other comprehensive income (subject to the assessment of the business model in which they are held). In particular, the IASB observed that this exception will apply to many purchased credit-impaired financial assets with contractual prepayment features. If such an asset was purchased at a deep discount, apart from the exception described in paragraph BC4.192, the contractual cash flows would not be solely payments of principal and interest if, contractually, the asset could be repaid immediately at the par amount. However that contractual prepayment feature would have an insignificant fair value if it is very unlikely that prepayment will occur. The IASB was persuaded by the feedback that stated that amortised cost would provide useful and relevant information to users of financial statements about such financial assets, because the exception applies only to those financial assets that are prepayable at the contractual par amount. Consequently, the prepayment amount does not introduce variability that is inconsistent with a basic lending arrangement because that variability would result only from the time value of money and credit risk elements; ie the entity would receive more of the contractual cash flows than it previously expected, and it would receive those contractual cash flows immediately. The IASB believes that information about that variability would be appropriately captured by amortised cost via the catch-up adjustment mechanism.

BC4.194   Similarly, the IASB observed that this exception will apply to some financial assets that are originated at below-market interest rates. For example, this scenario may arise when an entity sells an item (for example, an automobile) and, as a marketing incentive, provides financing to the customer at an interest rate that is below the prevailing market rate. At initial recognition the entity would measure the financial asset at fair value[23] and, as a result of the below-market interest rate, the fair value would be at a discount to the par amount. If the customer has a contractual right to repay the par amount at any point before maturity, then without an exception, the contractual cash flows may not be solely payments of principal and interest. The IASB observed that such a contractual prepayment feature likely would have an insignificant fair value because it is unlikely that the customer will choose to prepay; in particular, because the interest rate is below-market and thus the financing is advantageous. Consistently with the discussion in paragraph BC4.193, the IASB believes that amortised cost would provide relevant and useful information to users of financial statements about this financial asset, because the prepayment amount does not introduce variability that is inconsistent with a basic lending arrangement.

BC4.195   Paragraphs BC4.193–BC4.194 discuss circumstances in which a financial asset is originated or purchased at a *discount* to the par amount. However, the IASB noted that its rationale for the exception described in paragraph BC4.192 is equally relevant for assets that are originated or purchased at a *premium* and therefore decided that the exception should apply symmetrically to both circumstances.

Bifurcation

BC4.196   The requirements issued in IFRS 9 (2009) did not bifurcate hybrid contracts with financial asset hosts. Instead, all financial assets were classified in their entirety. Since 2009, many interested parties have expressed support for that approach. However, others have expressed the view that hybrid financial assets should be bifurcated into a derivative component and a non-derivative host. Much of the feedback that was received after IFRS 9 was issued in 2009 was similar to the feedback that was received during the deliberations that led to that Standard being issued. That feedback is summarised in paragraph BC4.88. In addition, some have noted that:

(a)   components of some hybrid financial assets are managed separately and therefore bifurcation may provide more relevant information to users of financial statements about how the entity manages those instruments;

(b)   an embedded feature that has an insignificant fair value at initial recognition (for example, because it is contingent on a future event that the entity believes is unlikely to occur) could cause a hybrid financial asset to be measured at fair value through profit or loss in its entirety; and

(c)   it is important to have symmetry in the bifurcation of financial assets and financial liabilities and, consequently, hybrid financial assets should be bifurcated because the IASB retained bifurcation for hybrid financial liabilities.

---

23   Unless the financial asset is a trade receivable that does not have a significant financing component (determined in accordance with IFRS 15). Such a trade receivable is measured at initial recognition in accordance with paragraph 5.1.3 in IFRS 9.

BC4.197 During the deliberations that led to the publication of the 2012 Limited Amendments Exposure Draft, the IASB reconsidered whether bifurcation should be pursued for financial assets or financial liabilities (or both) and, if so, what the basis for that bifurcation should be. The IASB considered three approaches:

(a) 'closely-related' bifurcation (ie bifurcation using the 'closely-related' bifurcation criteria in IAS 39, which have been carried forward to IFRS 9 for financial liabilities);

(b) 'principal-and-interest' bifurcation; or

(c) no bifurcation (ie the financial instrument would be classified in its entirety).

BC4.198 In the 2012 Limited Amendments Exposure Draft, the IASB did not propose any changes to the requirements in IFRS 9 related to the bifurcation of financial instruments. As a result, hybrid financial assets are not bifurcated but are instead classified and measured in their entirety. Hybrid financial liabilities are bifurcated (unless the entity elects to apply the fair value option) on the basis of the closely-related criteria that were carried forward to IFRS 9 from IAS 39.

BC4.199 In reaching that conclusion, the IASB noted that, consistently with paragraphs BC4.46–BC4.53 and BC4.91, interested parties have consistently told the IASB that the bifurcation methodology in IAS 39 for financial liabilities is generally working well in practice and practice has developed since those requirements were issued. Specifically, many constituents, including users of financial statements, strongly supported retaining bifurcation for financial liabilities even though they supported eliminating it for financial assets. That was primarily because bifurcation addresses the issue of own credit risk, which is relevant only for financial liabilities.

BC4.200 In contrast, while the closely-related bifurcation methodology in IAS 39 works well for financial liabilities, it does not complement the guidance in IFRS 9 that requires an entity to assess the asset's contractual cash flow characteristics. For example, if IFRS 9 were to require both an assessment of the asset's contractual cash flow characteristics *and* a closely-related bifurcation assessment, the IASB would need to determine which of those assessments should have primacy. For example, the IASB discussed a scenario in which a financial asset had contractual cash flows that were not solely payments of principal and interest but did not contain an embedded derivative that required bifurcation. Specifically, the IASB considered how such a financial asset should be subsequently measured; ie either in its entirety at fair value through profit or loss because its contractual cash flows were not solely payments of principal and interest or, alternatively, in its entirety at amortised cost (or fair value through other comprehensive income, depending on the business model in which is it held) because it did not contain an embedded derivative that required bifurcation. Similar challenges would arise for a financial asset that had contractual cash flows that were solely payments of principal and interest but contained an embedded derivative that required bifurcation. As a result, the IASB concluded that combining the assessment in IFRS 9 of the asset's contractual cash flow characteristics with a closely-related bifurcation assessment would be complex and likely would give rise to contradictory outcomes — and indeed, in some cases, seemed unworkable. Consequently, the IASB decided not to pursue this approach for financial assets.

BC4.201 Under a principal-and-interest bifurcation approach, if a financial asset had cash flows that were not solely payments of principal and interest, that asset would be assessed to determine whether it should be bifurcated into a host (with cash flows that are solely payments of principal and interest) and an embedded residual feature. The host could qualify for a measurement category other than fair value through profit or loss, depending on the business model within which it was held. The embedded feature would be measured at fair value through profit or loss. The IASB also considered variations of this approach whereby bifurcation would be required only if the embedded feature met the definition of a derivative or if the components were separately managed. If these conditions were not met, the financial asset would be measured in its entirety at fair value through profit or loss.

BC4.202 The IASB noted that if principal-and-interest bifurcation is based on the separate management of the components of the instrument, such an approach would be an instrument-by-instrument assessment of the management of a financial asset. That would be inconsistent with the existing assessment in IFRS 9 of the business model, which requires the management of financial assets to be assessed at a higher level of aggregation. The IASB also noted that a principal-and-interest bifurcation approach might seem generally compatible with the existing requirements in IFRS 9, but, in fact, it would introduce new concepts into the classification and measurement of financial assets and would undoubtedly raise questions about how the host and embedded feature should be defined and measured. The IASB observed that introducing a principal-and-interest bifurcation approach into IFRS 9 would significantly increase complexity, especially because it would then contain two bifurcation approaches (ie one for hybrid financial assets and another for hybrid financial liabilities). The IASB also observed that there was significant risk of unintended consequences related to introducing a new bifurcation approach. Consequently, the IASB decided not to pursue this approach for financial assets.

BC4.203 Accordingly, during the deliberations that led to the 2012 Limited Amendments Exposure Draft, the IASB confirmed its decision that hybrid contracts with financial asset hosts should be classified and measured in their entirety. In reaching that conclusion, the IASB cited its original rationale for prohibiting bifurcation, which is set out in paragraphs BC4.83–BC4.90.

BC4.204 Some respondents to the 2012 Limited Amendments Exposure Draft from particular jurisdictions continued to express a preference for bifurcating hybrid financial assets. However, most respondents did not suggest that bifurcation should be reintroduced and some respondents specifically stated that they disagreed with reintroducing it. As a result, the IASB reconfirmed the requirements in IFRS 9 that hybrid contracts with financial asset hosts should not be bifurcated but should instead be classified and measured in their entirety.

Investments in contractually linked instruments (tranches)

BC4.205　In accordance with the requirements in paragraphs B4.1.21−B4.1.26 of IFRS 9 (issued in 2009), investments in contractually linked instruments (tranches) may have contractual cash flows that are solely payments of principal and interest if (in summary):

(a)　the contractual terms of the tranche being assessed for classification give rise to cash flows that are solely payments of principal and interest on the principal amount outstanding;

(b)　the underlying pool of instruments contains only instruments that have contractual cash flows that are solely principal and interest on the principal amount outstanding, that reduce cash flow variability on the instruments in the pool or that align the cash flows of the tranches with the cash flows of the instruments in the pool to address particular differences; and

(c)　the exposure to credit risk inherent in the tranche being assessed is equal to, or lower than, the overall exposure to credit risk of the underlying pool of financial instruments.

BC4.206　After IFRS 9 was issued in 2009, the IASB received questions about whether a tranche could have contractual cash flows that are solely payments of principal and interest if the tranche is prepayable in the event that the underlying pool of financial instruments is prepaid or if the underlying pool includes instruments that are collateralised by assets that do not meet the conditions set out in paragraphs B4.1.23–B4.1.24 of IFRS 9 (as issued in 2009). The IASB noted that a key principle underpinning the assessment of contractually linked instruments is that an entity should not be disadvantaged simply as a result of holding an investment indirectly (ie via an investment in a tranche) if the underlying pool of instruments have contractual cash flows that are solely payments of principal and interest and the tranche is not exposed to leverage or more credit risk than the credit risk of the underlying pool of financial instruments. Accordingly, in the 2012 Limited Amendments Exposure Draft, the IASB proposed to clarify that a tranche may have contractual cash flows that are solely payments of principal and interest even if:

(a)　the tranche is prepayable in the event that the underlying pool of financial instruments is prepaid. The IASB noted that because the underlying pool of assets must have contractual cash flows that are solely payments of principal and interest then, by extension, any prepayment features in those underlying financial assets must also be solely payments of principal and interest.

(b)　financial assets in the underlying pool are collateralised by assets that do not meet the conditions set out in paragraphs B4.1.23 and B4.1.24 of IFRS 9. In such cases, the entity would disregard the possibility that the pool may contain the collateral in the future unless the entity acquired the instrument with the intention of controlling the collateral. The IASB noted that this is consistent with IFRS 9; ie financial assets can themselves still have contractual cash flows that are solely payments of principal and interest if they are collateralised by assets that do not have contractual cash flows that are solely payments of principal and interest.

BC4.207 Respondents supported these proposals but asked the IASB to consider additional clarifications to the requirements for contractually linked instruments:

(a) in assessing whether the instruments in the underlying pool meet the requirements in paragraphs B4.1.23 or B4.1.24 of IFRS 9, a detailed instrument-by-instrument analysis of the pool may not be necessary; however, the entity is required to use judgement and perform sufficient analysis to determine whether those requirements are met; and

(b) an entity may assess the requirement in paragraph B4.1.21(c) of IFRS 9 by comparing the credit rating of a tranche to the weighted average credit rating of the financial assets in the underlying pool (ie comparing the credit rating of the tranche being assessed for classification to what the credit rating would be on a *single* tranche that funded the entire underlying pool of financial instruments).

BC4.208 The IASB agreed with the points in paragraph BC4.207 and indeed noted that those clarifications are consistent with the original intention of the requirements for contractually linked instruments. The IASB therefore decided to clarify the relevant paragraphs in the application guidance to IFRS 9. However, it noted that the clarification described in paragraph BC4.206(a) would be addressed as a result of the general clarifications made to the requirements for contingent prepayment features.

Other limited amendments

BC4.209 As a result of introducing the fair value through other comprehensive income measurement category into IFRS 9, the IASB considered particular interrelated issues — specifically, whether the existing requirements issued in IFRS 9 (2009) for the fair value option and for reclassifications should be extended to financial assets measured at fair value through other comprehensive income.

Fair value option for financial assets otherwise measured at fair value through other comprehensive income

BC4.210 In accordance with the requirements issued in IFRS 9 (2009), entities are permitted to designate financial assets that would otherwise be measured at amortised cost as measured at fair value through profit or loss if, and only if, such designation eliminates or significantly reduces a measurement or recognition inconsistency (sometimes referred to as an 'accounting mismatch'). Such designation is available at initial recognition and is irrevocable.

BC4.211 The IASB decided that the same fair value option that is available to financial assets that would otherwise be measured at amortised cost should be available for financial assets that would otherwise be measured at fair value through other comprehensive income. The IASB noted that the rationale set out in paragraph BC4.79 for permitting the fair value option for assets measured at amortised cost is equally applicable for financial assets measured at fair value through other comprehensive income.

Reclassifications into and out of the fair value through other comprehensive income measurement category

BC4.212 Paragraph 4.1.1 of IFRS 9 (as issued in 2009) required that an entity reclassify all affected financial assets when it changes its business model for managing financial assets. Paragraphs BC4.111–BC4.120 set out the IASB's rationale for the reclassification requirements.

BC4.213 The IASB noted that the number of measurement categories does not affect that rationale and therefore decided that the reclassification requirements issued in IFRS 9 (2009) should also apply to financial assets measured at fair value through other comprehensive income. Consequently, when an entity changes its business model for managing financial assets, it must reclassify all affected financial assets, including those in the fair value through other comprehensive income measurement category. Consistently with the requirements issued in IFRS 9 (2009), all reclassifications into and out of the fair value through other comprehensive income measurement category are applied prospectively from the reclassification date and previously recognised gains or losses (including impairment gains or losses) or interest revenue are not restated.

BC4.214 The IASB noted that because amortised cost information is provided in profit or loss for financial assets that are measured at fair value through other comprehensive income, reclassifications between the amortised cost measurement category and the fair value through other comprehensive income measurement category do not change the recognition of interest revenue or the measurement of expected credit losses. Specifically, the entity would have established the effective interest rate when the financial asset was originally recognised and would continue to use that rate if the financial asset is reclassified between the amortised cost measurement category and the fair value through other comprehensive income measurement category. Similarly, the measurement of expected credit losses does not change because both measurement categories apply the same impairment approach.

BC4.215 The IASB also decided to extend the relevant disclosure requirements in IFRS 7 and the relevant presentation requirements in IAS 1 to reclassifications into and out of the fair value through other comprehensive income measurement category.

Amendments for prepayment features with negative compensation (October 2017)[24]

BC4.216   In 2016, the IFRS Interpretations Committee (Interpretations Committee) received a submission asking how particular prepayable financial assets would be classified applying IFRS 9. Specifically, the submission asked whether a debt instrument could have contractual cash flows that are solely payments of principal and interest on the principal amount outstanding if its contractual terms permit the borrower (ie the issuer) to prepay the instrument at an amount that could be more or less than unpaid amounts of principal and interest, such as at the instrument's current fair value or an amount that reflects the instrument's remaining contractual cash flows discounted at a current market interest rate.

BC4.217   As a result of such a contractual prepayment feature, the lender (ie the holder) could be forced to accept a prepayment amount that is substantially less than unpaid amounts of principal and interest. Such a prepayment amount would, in effect, include an amount that reflects a payment *to* the borrower from the lender, instead of compensation *from* the borrower to the lender, even though the borrower chose to prepay the debt instrument. An outcome in which the party choosing to terminate the contract receives an amount, instead of pays an amount, is inconsistent with paragraph B4.1.11(b) of IFRS 9 (as issued in 2014). Specifically, it is inconsistent with the notion of reasonable additional compensation for the early termination of the contract. In this section of the Basis for Conclusions, such an outcome is referred to as negative compensation. Thus, the financial assets described in the submission would not have contractual cash flows that are solely payments of principal and interest, and those instruments would be measured at fair value through profit or loss applying IFRS 9 (as issued in 2014).

BC4.218   Nevertheless, Interpretations Committee members suggested that the IASB consider whether amortised cost measurement could provide useful information about particular financial assets with prepayment features that may result in negative compensation, and if so, whether the requirements in IFRS 9 should be changed in this respect.

BC4.219   In the light of the Interpretations Committee's recommendation and similar concerns raised by banks and their representative bodies in response to the Interpretations Committee's discussion, the IASB proposed amendments to IFRS 9 for particular financial assets that would otherwise have contractual cash flows that are solely payments of principal and interest but do not meet that condition only as a result of a prepayment feature that may result in

---

24   In this section, the discussion about amortised cost measurement is relevant to both financial assets in the amortised cost measurement category and financial assets in the fair value through other comprehensive income measurement category. That is because, for the latter, the assets are measured at fair value in the statement of financial position and amortised cost information is provided in profit or loss. A financial asset is measured at amortised cost or fair value through other comprehensive income only if both conditions in paragraph 4.1.2 or paragraph 4.1.2A of IFRS 9, respectively, are met. The amendments discussed in this section address only the condition in paragraphs 4.1.2(b) and 4.1.2A(b). Accordingly, this section does not discuss the conditions in paragraphs 4.1.2(a) and 4.1.2A(a) relating to the business model but instead assumes that the asset is held in the relevant business model.

negative compensation. The Exposure Draft *Prepayment Features with Negative Compensation* (Proposed amendments to IFRS 9) (2017 Negative Compensation Exposure Draft) proposed that such financial assets would be eligible to be measured at amortised cost or fair value through other comprehensive income, subject to an assessment of the business model in which they are held, if two eligibility conditions are met.

BC4.220 Most respondents to the 2017 Negative Compensation Exposure Draft agreed with the IASB's decision to address the classification of such prepayable financial assets, and highlighted the urgency of the issue given the proximity to the effective date of IFRS 9.

BC4.221 In October 2017, the IASB amended IFRS 9 by issuing *Prepayment Features with Negative Compensation* (Amendments to IFRS 9), which confirmed with modifications the proposals in the 2017 Negative Compensation Exposure Draft. Specifically, in the amendments issued in October 2017, the IASB amended paragraphs B4.1.11(b) and B4.1.12(b), and added paragraph B4.1.12A of IFRS 9. As a result of those amendments, particular financial assets with prepayment features that may result in reasonable negative compensation for the early termination of the contract are eligible to be measured at amortised cost or at fair value through other comprehensive income.

The prepayment amount

BC4.222 In developing the 2017 Negative Compensation Exposure Draft, the IASB noted that any proposal to measure at amortised cost financial assets with prepayment features that may result in negative compensation must be limited to those assets for which the effective interest method provides useful information to users of financial statements about the amount, timing and uncertainty of future cash flows. Accordingly, the first eligibility condition proposed in the Exposure Draft was intended to identify those prepayment features that do not introduce any contractual cash flow amounts that are different from the cash flow amounts accommodated by paragraph B4.1.11(b) of IFRS 9 (as issued in 2014).

BC4.223 In the deliberations that led to that proposal, the IASB noted that paragraph B4.1.11(b) of IFRS 9 accommodates contractual terms that permit either the borrower or the lender to choose to terminate the contract early and compensate the other party for having to accept that choice. Accordingly, that paragraph already accommodates a prepayment amount that is more or less than unpaid amounts of principal and interest, depending on which party chooses to terminate the contract early. In applying the effective interest method to measure such financial assets at amortised cost, an entity considers the contractual cash flows arising from such a prepayment feature when it estimates the future cash flows and determines the effective interest rate at initial recognition. Subsequently, consistent with the treatment of all financial instruments measured at amortised cost, the entity applies paragraph B5.4.6 of IFRS 9 and adjusts the gross carrying amount of the financial asset if it revises its estimates of contractual cash flows, including any revisions related to the exercise of the prepayment feature.

BC4.224　Similarly, for a financial asset with a prepayment feature that may result in negative compensation, the prepayment amount may be more or less than unpaid amounts of principal and interest. However, the difference is that such a prepayment feature may have the result that the party that triggers the early termination of the contract may, in effect, receive an amount *from* the other party, rather than pay compensation *to* the other party. To illustrate this difference, the IASB considered a loan with a prepayment feature that may result in negative compensation. Specifically, both the borrower and the lender have the option to terminate the loan before maturity and, if the loan is terminated early, the prepayment amount includes compensation that reflects the change in the relevant benchmark interest rate. That is, if the loan is terminated early (by either party) and the relevant benchmark interest rate has fallen since the loan was initially recognised, then the lender will effectively receive an amount representing the present value of that lost interest revenue over the loan's remaining term. Conversely, if the contract is terminated early (by either party) and the relevant benchmark interest rate has risen, then the borrower will effectively receive an amount that represents the effect of that change in that interest rate over the loan's remaining term.

BC4.225　The IASB acknowledged that the contractual terms of the loan described in paragraph BC4.224 do not introduce different contractual cash flow amounts from the contractual cash flow amounts accommodated by paragraph B4.1.11(b) of IFRS 9 (as issued in 2014). That is, the loan's prepayment amount is calculated in the same way as a prepayment amount accommodated by paragraph B4.1.11(b) of IFRS 9 (as issued in 2014). Specifically, the loan's prepayment amount reflects unpaid amounts of principal and interest plus or minus an amount that reflects the effect of the change in the relevant benchmark interest rate. The contractual terms of the loan described in paragraph BC4.224 change only the circumstances in which the compensation amounts may arise; ie the loan may result in either reasonable additional compensation or reasonable negative compensation for the early termination of the contract.

BC4.226　The IASB noted that from a computation standpoint, the effective interest method, and thus amortised cost measurement, could be applied to the contractual cash flows that arise from a prepayable financial asset like the loan described in paragraph BC4.224. As described in paragraph BC4.223, the entity would consider the prepayment feature when it estimates the future cash flows and determines the effective interest rate. Subsequently, the entity would apply paragraph B5.4.6 of IFRS 9 and make a catch-up adjustment if it revises its estimates of contractual cash flows, including any revisions related to the prepayment feature.

BC4.227　Furthermore, the IASB decided that amortised cost measurement could provide useful information to users of financial statements about financial assets whose prepayment amount is consistent with paragraph B4.1.11(b) of IFRS 9 (as issued in 2014) in all respects except that the party that chooses to terminate the contract early may receive reasonable compensation for doing so. That is because, as discussed in paragraph BC4.225, such prepayment features do not introduce different contractual cash flow amounts from the contractual cash flow amounts accommodated by paragraph B4.1.11(b) of IFRS 9 (as issued in 2014); ie the loan's prepayment amount is calculated in the same way as a prepayment amount accommodated by paragraph B4.1.11(b) of IFRS 9 (as issued in 2014). Therefore, the 2017 Negative Compensation Exposure Draft proposed an eligibility condition that was intended to capture those prepayment features that would have been accommodated by paragraph B4.1.11(b) except that a party may receive reasonable compensation for the early termination of the contract even if it is the party that chooses to terminate the contract early (or otherwise causes the early termination to occur).

BC4.228　Nearly all respondents agreed with that eligibility condition proposed in the 2017 Negative Compensation Exposure Draft. Specifically, they agreed that reasonable negative compensation for the early termination of the contract should not in itself preclude amortised cost measurement. The respondents agreed with the IASB's rationale described in paragraphs BC4.226–BC4.227 and they also agreed that the proposed eligibility condition would capture a population of financial assets for which amortised cost measurement could provide useful information to users of financial statements. The respondents said that measuring such assets at amortised cost, and including them in key metrics like net interest margin, would provide useful information to users of financial statements about the financial assets' performance. Those respondents consider information about expected credit losses and interest revenue (calculated using the effective interest method) to be more relevant than information about changes in fair value for the purpose of assessing the performance and future cash flows of those financial assets.

BC4.229　Consequently, in its redeliberations of the 2017 Negative Compensation Exposure Draft, the IASB confirmed that proposed eligibility condition. As a result, applying the amendments, a financial asset with a prepayment feature that may result in negative compensation is eligible to be measured at amortised cost or fair value through other comprehensive income if it would have been accommodated by paragraph B4.1.11(b) of IFRS 9 (as issued in 2014) except that the prepayment amount may include reasonable *negative* compensation for the early termination of the contract.

BC4.230　However, one respondent said that the IASB had not addressed the case in which the early termination of the contract is caused by an event that is outside the control of both parties to the contract, such as a change in law or regulation. That respondent asked the IASB to clarify the amendments in that regard. The IASB agreed with that observation. Consequently, the wording in paragraph B4.1.12A of the amendments refers to the *event or circumstance* that caused the early termination of the contract. Such an event or circumstance may be within the control of one of the parties to the contract (for example, the borrower may choose to prepay) or it may be beyond the control of both parties (for example, a change in law may cause the contract to automatically terminate early).

Other prepayment amounts

BC4.231   As described in paragraph BC4.229, the IASB decided to limit the scope of the amendments to those financial assets with prepayment features that would have been accommodated by paragraph B4.1.11(b) of IFRS 9 (as issued in 2014) except that the prepayment amount may include reasonable negative compensation for the early termination of the contract. The IASB observed that the effective interest method, and thus amortised cost measurement, are not appropriate when the prepayment amount is inconsistent with that paragraph for any other reason.

BC4.232   As described in the submission to the Interpretations Committee, some financial assets are prepayable at their current fair value. The IASB is also aware that some financial assets are prepayable at an amount that includes the fair value cost to terminate an associated hedging instrument (which may or may not be in a hedging relationship with the prepayable financial asset for accounting purposes). Some interested parties suggested that both of those types of prepayable financial asset should be eligible for amortised cost measurement. The IASB acknowledged that there may be some circumstances in which such a contractual prepayment feature results in contractual cash flows that are solely payments of principal and interest in accordance with IFRS 9, as amended; ie there may be circumstances in which the compensation included in such a prepayment amount is reasonable for the early termination of the contract. For example, that may be the case when the calculation of the prepayment amount is intended to approximate unpaid amounts of principal and interest plus or minus an amount that reflects the effect of the change in the relevant benchmark interest rate. However, the Board observed that it will not always be the case and therefore an entity cannot presume that all such prepayable financial assets are eligible to be measured at amortised cost. Entities must assess an instrument's specific contractual cash flow characteristics.

The probability of prepayment

BC4.233   A prepayment feature that may result in negative compensation changes the circumstances, and increases the frequency, in which the contractual compensation amounts could arise. Accordingly, in the deliberations that led to the publication of the 2017 Negative Compensation Exposure Draft, the IASB observed that if such a prepayable financial asset is measured at amortised cost, the likelihood is higher that the lender will be required to make catch-up adjustments applying paragraph B5.4.6 of IFRS 9 to reflect revisions to its estimates of contractual cash flows related to the exercise of the prepayment feature. This could include adjustments to reflect circumstances in which the lender is forced to settle the contract in a way that it would not recover its investment for reasons other than the asset's credit quality. The IASB observed that recognising frequent upward and downward adjustments in the gross carrying amount is generally inconsistent with the objective of the effective interest method, which is a relatively simple measurement technique that allocates interest using the effective interest rate over the relevant time period. Recognising more frequent adjustments in the gross carrying amount could reduce the usefulness of the interest amounts

BC4.238 The IASB also noted concerns that the fair value of the prepayment feature could be insignificant even if it is likely that negative compensation may occur. For example, that could be the case if the compensation structure of the prepayment feature is symmetrical so that the effect of reasonable negative compensation on that feature's fair value is offset by the effect of reasonable additional compensation (as accommodated by paragraph B4.1.11(b) of IFRS 9 (as issued in 2014)), or if the prepayment amount is close to the instrument's fair value at the prepayment date.

BC4.239 Consequently, during its redeliberations, the IASB concluded that, in some circumstances, the second eligibility condition proposed in the 2017 Negative Compensation Exposure Draft would not restrict the scope of the amendments in the way that the IASB intended and, in other circumstances, could restrict the scope in a way that the IASB did not intend. Therefore, on balance, the IASB decided not to confirm the second eligibility condition proposed in the 2017 Negative Compensation Exposure Draft.

BC4.240 The IASB noted that the alternatives to the second eligibility condition that were suggested by respondents were not discussed in the 2017 Negative Compensation Exposure Draft and therefore interested parties did not have the opportunity to provide feedback on them. Many respondents to that Exposure Draft highlighted the importance of finalising the amendments before the effective date of IFRS 9 and the IASB noted that prioritising such timing would preclude the Board from conducting outreach to assess those alternatives. Moreover, the IASB doubted whether those alternatives would better achieve its objective without introducing significant complexity to the amendments. Therefore, the IASB decided not to replace the second proposed eligibility condition with any of those alternatives.

Corresponding amendment to paragraph B4.1.12

BC4.241 As a consequence of its decisions to confirm the first proposed eligibility condition and remove the second proposed eligibility condition, the IASB observed that paragraph B4.1.11(b) of IFRS 9 will accommodate reasonable negative compensation for the early termination of the contract without additional restrictions; ie entities will be required to assess all amounts of reasonable compensation for the early termination of the contract in the same way.

BC4.242 Accordingly, the IASB amended paragraph B4.1.12(b) of IFRS 9 to align it with paragraph B4.1.11(b). As a result, paragraph B4.1.12(b) also accommodates reasonable negative compensation for the early termination of the contract. The IASB decided that there was no compelling reason to treat the notion of reasonable compensation for the early termination of the contract in paragraph B4.1.12(b) of IFRS 9 differently from that notion in paragraph B4.1.11(b).

Effective date

BC4.243   The 2017 Negative Compensation Exposure Draft proposed that the effective date of the amendments would be the same as the effective date of IFRS 9; that is, annual periods beginning on or after 1 January 2018, with earlier application permitted.

BC4.244   Some respondents agreed with that proposal and said there would be significant benefits if entities take into account the effect of the amendments when they initially apply IFRS 9. In contrast, others preferred a later effective date for the amendments; specifically, annual periods beginning on or after 1 January 2019 (with earlier application permitted). These respondents observed that many entities are advanced in their implementation of IFRS 9 and may not have sufficient time before the effective date of IFRS 9 to determine the effect of these amendments. Additionally, some jurisdictions will need time for translation and endorsement activities and the proposed effective date may not provide them with sufficient time for those activities.

BC4.245   In the light of the feedback received, the IASB decided to require that entities apply the amendments for annual periods beginning on or after 1 January 2019, with earlier application permitted. This alleviates the concerns about the timing of these amendments while also permitting an entity to apply the amendments and IFRS 9 at the same time if it is in a position to do so.

Transition

Entities that initially apply the amendments and IFRS 9 at the same time

BC4.246   As described in paragraph BC4.245, an entity is permitted to apply the amendments earlier than the mandatory effective date and, as a result, can take into account the effect of the amendments when it initially applies IFRS 9. In such cases, an entity would apply the transition provisions in Section 7.2 of IFRS 9 (as issued in 2014) to all financial assets and financial liabilities within the scope of that Standard. No specific transition provisions are needed for the amendments.

Entities that initially apply the amendments after previously applying IFRS 9

BC4.247   Some entities will apply the amendments after they have already applied IFRS 9. The IASB considered whether specific transition requirements are needed for those entities because, without such additional transition requirements, the transition provisions in Section 7.2 of IFRS 9 (as issued in 2014) would not be applicable. That is because, as set out in paragraph 7.2.27 of IFRS 9, an entity applies each of the transition provisions in IFRS 9 only once; ie at the relevant date of initial application of IFRS 9. This means that entities would be required to apply the amendments retrospectively applying IAS 8 *Accounting Policies, Changes in Accounting Estimates and Errors*. However, in some circumstances, an entity may not be able to apply the amendments retrospectively without the use of hindsight. When the IASB developed the transition requirements in IFRS 9, it provided requirements to address scenarios when it would be impracticable to apply particular requirements retrospectively. Accordingly, the IASB decided to provide transition requirements for entities that apply the amendments after they have already applied IFRS 9.

BC4.248   Consistent with the existing transition requirements in IFRS 9 for assessing whether the contractual terms of a financial asset give rise to cash flows that are solely payments of principal and interest, the amendments must be applied retrospectively. To do so, an entity applies the relevant transition provisions in IFRS 9 necessary for applying the amendments. For example, an entity applies the transition requirements in paragraph 7.2.11 related to the effective interest method and paragraphs 7.2.17–7.2.20 related to the impairment requirements to a financial asset that is newly measured at amortised cost or fair value through other comprehensive income as a result of applying the amendments.

BC4.249   The IASB provided specific transition provisions related to the fair value option because an entity may change the classification and measurement of some financial assets as a result of applying the amendments. Therefore, an entity is permitted to newly designate, and is required to revoke its previous designation of, a financial asset or a financial liability at the date of initial application of the amendments only to the extent that a new accounting mismatch is created, or a previous accounting mismatch no longer exists, as a result of applying the amendments.

BC4.250   Finally, the IASB decided that an entity is not required to restate prior periods to reflect the effect of the amendments, and could choose to do so only if such restatement is possible without the use of hindsight and if the restated financial statements reflect all the requirements in IFRS 9. This decision is consistent with the transition requirements in IFRS 9.

BC4.251   In addition to any disclosures required by other IFRS Standards, the IASB required disclosures that would provide information to users of financial statements about changes in the classification and measurement of financial instruments as a result of applying the amendments. These disclosures are similar to the disclosures in paragraphs 42I–42J of IFRS 7, which are required when an entity initially applies IFRS 9.

Another issue

Modification or exchange of a financial liability that does not result in derecognition

BC4.252   Concurrent with the development of the amendments to IFRS 9 for prepayment features with negative compensation, the IASB also discussed the accounting for a modification or exchange of a financial liability measured at amortised cost that does not result in the derecognition of the financial liability. More specifically, at the request of the Interpretations Committee, the Board discussed whether, applying IFRS 9, an entity recognises any adjustment to the amortised cost of the financial liability arising from such a modification or exchange in profit or loss at the date of the modification or exchange.

BC4.253　The IASB decided that standard-setting is not required because the requirements in IFRS 9 provide an adequate basis for an entity to account for modifications and exchanges of financial liabilities that do not result in derecognition. In doing so, the Board highlighted that the requirements in IFRS 9 for adjusting the amortised cost of a financial liability when a modification (or exchange) does not result in the derecognition of the financial liability are consistent with the requirements for adjusting the gross carrying amount of a financial asset when a modification does not result in the derecognition of the financial asset.

Measurement (Chapter 5)

Fair value measurement considerations[25]

BCZ5.1　The IASB decided to include in the revised IAS 39 (published in 2002) expanded guidance about how to determine fair values (the guidance is now in IFRS 9), in particular for financial instruments for which no quoted market price is available (now paragraphs B5.4.6–B5.4.13 of IFRS 9). The IASB decided that it is desirable to provide clear and reasonably detailed guidance about the objective and use of valuation techniques to achieve reliable and comparable fair value estimates when financial instruments are measured at fair value.

Use of quoted prices in active markets

BCZ5.2　The IASB considered comments received that disagreed with the proposal in the exposure draft published in 2002 that a quoted price is the appropriate measure of fair value for an instrument quoted in an active market. Some respondents argued that (a) valuation techniques are more appropriate for measuring fair value than a quoted price in an active market (eg for derivatives) and (b) valuation models are consistent with industry best practice, and are justified because of their acceptance for regulatory capital purposes.

BCZ5.3　However, the IASB confirmed that a quoted price is the appropriate measure of fair value for an instrument quoted in an active market, notably because (a) in an active market, the quoted price is the best evidence of fair value, given that fair value is defined in terms of a price agreed by a knowledgeable, willing buyer and a knowledgeable, willing seller; (b) it results in consistent measurement across entities; and (c) fair value (now defined in IFRS 9) does not depend on entity-specific factors. The IASB further clarified that a quoted price includes market-quoted rates as well as prices.

25　IFRS 13, issued in May 2011, contains the requirements for measuring fair value. As a consequence paragraphs 5.4.1–5.4.3 and B5.4.1–B5.4.13 of IFRS 9 have been deleted. *Annual Improvements to IFRSs 2010–2012 Cycle*, issued in December 2013, added paragraph BC138A to the Basis for Conclusions on IFRS 13 to clarify the IASB's reason for deleting paragraph B5.4.12.

Entities that have access to more than one active market

BCZ5.4   The IASB considered situations in which entities operate in different markets. An example is a trader that originates a derivative with a corporate in an active corporate retail market and offsets the derivative by taking out a derivative with a dealer in an active dealers' wholesale market. The IASB decided to clarify that the objective of fair value measurement is to arrive at the price at which a transaction would occur at the balance sheet date in the same instrument (ie without modification or repackaging) in the most advantageous active market[26] to which an entity has immediate access. Thus, if a dealer enters into a derivative instrument with the corporate, but has immediate access to a more advantageously priced dealers' market, the entity recognises a profit on initial recognition of the derivative instrument. However, the entity adjusts the price observed in the dealer market for any differences in counterparty credit risk between the derivative instrument with the corporate and that with the dealers' market.

Bid-ask spreads in active markets

BCZ5.5   The IASB confirmed the proposal in the exposure draft published in 2002 that the appropriate quoted market price for an asset held or liability to be issued is usually the current bid price and, for an asset to be acquired or liability held, the asking price.[27] It concluded that applying mid-market prices to an individual instrument is not appropriate because it would result in entities recognising upfront gains or losses for the difference between the bid-ask price and the mid-market price.

BCZ5.6   The IASB discussed whether the bid-ask spread should be applied to the net open position of a portfolio containing offsetting market risk positions, or to each instrument in the portfolio. It noted the concerns raised by constituents that applying the bid-ask spread to the net open position better reflects the fair value of the risk retained in the portfolio. The IASB concluded that for offsetting risk positions, entities could use mid-market prices to determine fair value, and hence may apply the bid or asking price to the net open position as appropriate. The IASB believes that when an entity has offsetting risk positions, using the mid-market price is appropriate because the entity (a) has locked in its cash flows from the asset and liability and (b) potentially could sell the matched position without incurring the bid-ask spread.[28]

BCZ5.7   Comments received on the exposure draft published in 2002 revealed that some interpret the term 'bid-ask spread' differently from others and from the IASB. Thus, the IASB clarified that the spread represents only transaction costs.

---

26   IFRS 13, issued in May 2011, states that a fair value measurement assumes that the transaction to sell an asset or to transfer a liability takes place in the principal market, or in the absence of a principal market, the most advantageous market for the asset or liability.

27   IFRS 13, issued in May 2011, states that fair value is measured using the price within the bid-ask spread that is most representative of fair value in the circumstances.

28   IFRS 13, issued in May 2011, permits an exception to the fair value measurement requirements when an entity manages its financial assets and financial liabilities on the basis of the entity's net exposure to market risks or the credit risk of a particular counterparty, allowing the entity to measure the fair value of its financial instruments on the basis of the entity's net exposure to either of those risks.

No active market

BCZ5.8   The exposure draft published in 2002 proposed a three-tier fair value measurement hierarchy as follows:

(a)   For instruments traded in active markets, use a quoted price.

(b)   For instruments for which there is not an active market, use a recent market transaction.

(c)   For instruments for which there is neither an active market nor a recent market transaction, use a valuation technique.

BCZ5.9   The IASB decided to simplify the proposed fair value measurement hierarchy[29] by requiring the fair value of financial instruments for which there is not an active market to be determined by using valuation techniques, including recent market transactions between knowledgeable, willing parties in an arm's length transaction.

BCZ5.10   The IASB also considered constituents' comments regarding whether an instrument should always be recognised on initial recognition at the transaction price or whether gains or losses may be recognised on initial recognition when an entity uses a valuation technique to estimate fair value. The IASB concluded that an entity may recognise a gain or loss at inception only if fair value is evidenced by comparison with other observable current market transactions in the same instrument (ie without modification or repackaging) or is based on a valuation technique incorporating only observable market data. The IASB concluded that those conditions were necessary and sufficient to provide reasonable assurance that fair value was other than the transaction price for the purpose of recognising upfront gains or losses. The IASB decided that in other cases, the transaction price gave the best evidence of fair value.[30] The IASB also noted that its decision achieved convergence with US GAAP.[31]

Measurement of financial liabilities with a demand feature[32]

BCZ5.11–   [Deleted]
BCZ5.12

---

29   IFRS 13, issued in May 2011, contains a three-level fair value hierarchy for the inputs used in the valuation techniques used to measure fair value.

30   IFRS 13, issued in May 2011, describes when a transaction price might not represent the fair value of an asset or a liability at initial recognition.

31   FASB Statement of Financial Accounting Standards No. 157 *Fair Value Measurements* (SFAS 157) superseded EITF Issue No. 02-3 *Issues Involved in Accounting for Derivative Contracts Held for Trading Purposes and Involved in Energy Trading and Risk Management Activities* (Topic 820 *Fair Value Measurement* in the *FASB Accounting Standards Codification®* codified SFAS 157). As a result, IFRS and US GAAP have different requirements for when an entity may recognise a gain or loss when there is a difference between fair value and the transaction price at initial recognition.

32   IFRS 13, issued in May 2011, resulted in the relocation of paragraphs BCZ5.11 and BCZ5.12 of IFRS 9 to paragraphs BCZ102 and BCZ103 of IFRS 13. As a consequence minor necessary edits have been made to that material.

Exception in IAS 39 from fair value measurement for some unquoted equity instruments[33] (and some derivative assets linked to those instruments)

BC5.13　The IASB believes that measurement at amortised cost is not applicable to equity investments because such financial assets have no contractual cash flows and hence there are no contractual cash flows to amortise. IAS 39 contained an exception from fair value measurement for investments in equity instruments (and some derivatives linked to those investments) that do not have a quoted price in an active market and whose fair value cannot be reliably measured. Those equity investments were required to be measured at cost less impairment, if any. Impairment losses are measured as the difference between the carrying amount of the financial asset and the present value of estimated future cash flows discounted at the current market rate of return for a similar financial asset.

BC5.14　The 2009 Classification and Measurement Exposure Draft proposed that all investments in equity instruments (and derivatives linked to those investments) should be measured at fair value for the following reasons:

(a)　For investments in equity instruments and derivatives, fair value provides the most relevant information. Cost provides little, if any, information with predictive value about the timing, amount and uncertainty of the future cash flows arising from the instrument. In many cases, fair value will differ significantly from historical cost (this is particularly true for derivatives measured at cost under the exception).

(b)　To ensure that a financial asset accounted for under the cost exception is not carried above its recoverable amount, IAS 39 required an entity to monitor instruments measured at cost for any impairment. Calculating any impairment loss is similar to determining fair value (ie the estimated future cash flows are discounted using the current market rate of return for a similar financial asset and compared with the carrying amount).

(c)　Removing the exception would reduce complexity because the classification model for financial assets would not have a third measurement attribute and would not require an additional impairment methodology. Although there might be an increase in the complexity of determining fair values on a recurring basis that complexity would be offset (at least partially) by the fact that all equity instruments and derivatives have one common measurement attribute; thus the impairment requirements would be eliminated.

33　IFRS 13, issued in May 2011, defines a Level 1 input as a quoted price in an active market for an identical asset or liability. Level 2 inputs include quoted prices for identical assets or liabilities in markets that are not active. As a result IFRS 9 refers to such equity instruments as 'an equity instrument that does not have a quoted price in an active market for an identical instrument (ie a Level 1 input)'.

BC5.15   Many respondents agreed that cost does not provide useful information about future cash flows arising from equity instruments and that conceptually such equity instruments should be measured using a current measurement attribute such as fair value. Some of those respondents generally agreed with the removal of the exception, but suggested that disclosures would have to include information about the uncertainties surrounding measurement.

BC5.16   However, many respondents (mainly preparers from non-financial entities and some auditors) disagreed with the proposal to eliminate the current cost exception on the grounds of the reliability and usefulness of fair value measurement and the cost and difficulty involved in determining fair value on a recurring basis. They generally preferred to keep a cost exception, similar to that in IAS 39. Some noted that the proposals would not reduce complexity, because they would increase complexity in measurement. Furthermore, a few believed that cost could provide useful information if the financial asset is held for the long term.

BC5.17   The IASB considered those arguments as follows:

(a)   *Reliability and usefulness of fair value measurement*
Respondents noted that IAS 39 included a cost exception because of the lack of reliability of fair value measurement for particular equity instruments and contended that this rationale is still valid. They believed that, given the lack of available reliable information, any fair value measurement would require significant management judgement or might be impossible. They also believed that comparability would be impaired by the requirement to measure such equity instruments at fair value. However, those respondents had considered the question of reliability of fair value for the instruments concerned in isolation. In the IASB's view, the usefulness of information must be assessed against all four of the qualitative characteristics in the *Framework*: reliability, understandability, relevance and comparability. Thus, cost is a reliable (and objective) amount, but has little, if any, relevance. In the IASB's view measuring all equity instruments at fair value, including those that are currently measured using the cost exception in IAS 39, meets the criteria in the *Framework* for information to be reliable if appropriate measurement techniques and inputs are employed. The IASB noted that its project on fair value measurement will provide guidance on how to meet that objective.[34]

(b)   *Cost and difficulty involved in determining fair value on a recurring basis*
Many respondents, particularly in emerging economies, said that they faced difficulty in obtaining information that might be relied on to use in valuation. Others said that they would inevitably rely heavily on external experts at significant cost. Many questioned whether the requirement to determine fair value on a recurring basis would involve significant costs and efforts that are not offset by the incremental benefit to usefulness from fair value. The IASB considered the costs of requiring such equity investments to be measured at fair value from

---

34   IFRS 13, issued in May 2011, contains the requirements for measuring fair value.

the perspectives of valuation methodology and expertise, as well as the ability to obtain the information required for a fair value measurement. The IASB noted that valuation methods for equity investments are well-developed and are often far less complex than those required for other financial instruments that are required to be measured at fair value, including many complex derivative products. Although some expressed concern that smaller entities applying IFRS might not have internal systems or expertise to determine easily the fair value of equity investments held, the IASB noted that basic shareholder rights generally enable an entity to obtain the necessary information to perform a valuation. The IASB acknowledged that there are circumstances in which the cost of determining fair value could outweigh the benefits from fair value measurement. In particular, the IASB noted that, in some jurisdictions, entities hold high numbers of unquoted equity instruments that are currently accounted for under the cost exception and the value of a single investment is considered low. However, the IASB concluded that if the volume of the investments individually or aggregated is material the incremental benefit of fair value generally outweighs the additional cost because of the impact of the investments on the financial performance and position of the entity.[35]

BC5.18　The IASB noted that there are some circumstances in which cost might be representative of fair value and decided to provide additional application guidance on those circumstances to alleviate some of the concerns expressed. However, the IASB also noted that those circumstances would never apply to equity investments held by particular entities such as financial institutions and investment funds.

BC5.19　The IASB considered whether a simplified approach to measurement should be provided for equity instruments when fair value measurement was impracticable. The IASB also discussed possible simplified measurement approaches, including management's best estimate of the price it would accept to sell or buy the instrument, or changes in the share of net assets. However, the IASB concluded that a simplified measurement approach would add complexity to the classification approach and reduce the usefulness of information to users of financial statements. Those disadvantages would not be offset by the benefit of reduced cost to preparers of financial statements.

Elimination of the cost exception for particular derivative liabilities

BC5.20　Consistently with the requirements in IFRS 9 for some investments in equity instruments and some derivative assets linked to those instruments (see paragraphs BC5.13 – BC5.19), the IASB decided in 2010 that the cost exception should be eliminated for derivative liabilities that will be physically settled by delivering unquoted equity instruments whose fair values cannot be reliably

---

35　IFRS 13, issued in May 2011, defines a Level 1 input as a quoted price in an active market for an identical asset or liability. Level 2 inputs include quoted prices for identical assets or liabilities in markets that are not active. As a result IFRS 9 refers to such equity instruments as 'an equity instrument that does not have a quoted price in an active market for an identical instrument (ie a Level 1 input)'.

determined. That proposal was included in the 2009 Classification and Measurement Exposure Draft.

Gains and losses

Investments in equity instruments

BC5.21 IFRS 9 permits an entity to make an irrevocable election to present in other comprehensive income changes in the value of any investment in equity instruments that is not held for trading. The term 'equity instrument' is defined in IAS 32 *Financial Instruments: Presentation*. The IASB noted that in particular circumstances a puttable instrument (or an instrument that imposes on the entity an obligation to deliver to another party a pro rata share of the net assets of the entity only on liquidation) is classified as equity. However, the IASB noted that such instruments do not meet the definition of an equity instrument.

BC5.22 In the IASB's view, fair value provides the most useful information about investments in equity instruments to users of financial statements. However, the IASB noted arguments that presenting fair value gains and losses in profit or loss for some equity investments may not be indicative of the performance of the entity, particularly if the entity holds those equity instruments for non-contractual benefits, rather than primarily for increases in the value of the investment. An example could be a requirement to hold such an investment if an entity sells its products in a particular country.

BC5.23 The IASB also noted that, in their valuation of an entity, users of financial statements often differentiate between fair value changes arising from equity investments held for purposes other than generating investment returns and equity investments held for trading. Thus, the IASB believes that separate presentation in other comprehensive income of gains and losses for some investments could provide useful information to users of financial statements because it would allow them to identify easily, and value accordingly, the associated fair value changes.

BC5.24 Almost all respondents to the 2009 Classification and Measurement Exposure Draft supported recognition of fair value gains and losses in other comprehensive income for particular equity investments. They agreed that an entity should make an irrevocable election to identify those equity instruments. However, some users did not support these proposals in the 2009 Classification and Measurement Exposure Draft.

BC5.25 The concerns expressed in the comment letters were as follows:

(a) *Dividends:* The 2009 Classification and Measurement Exposure Draft proposed that dividends on equity instruments measured at fair value with changes recognised in other comprehensive income would also be recognised in other comprehensive income. Nearly all respondents objected to that proposal. They argued that dividends are a form of income that should be presented in profit or loss in accordance with IAS 18 *Revenue* and noted that those equity investments are sometimes funded with debt instruments whose interest expense is recognised in profit or loss. As a result, presenting dividends in other comprehensive income would create a 'mismatch'. Some listed investment funds stated that without recognising dividend income in profit or loss their financial statements would become meaningless to their investors. The IASB agreed with those arguments. The IASB noted that structuring opportunities might remain because dividends could represent a return of investment, instead of a return on investment. Consequently, the IASB decided that dividends that clearly represent a recovery of part of the cost of the investment are not recognised in profit or loss. However, in the IASB's view, those structuring opportunities would be limited because an entity with the ability to control or significantly influence the dividend policy of the investment would not account for those investments in accordance with IFRS 9.[36] Furthermore, the IASB decided to require disclosures that would allow a user to compare easily the dividends recognised in profit or loss and the other fair value changes.

(b)   *Recycling*: Many respondents, including many users, did not support the proposal to prohibit subsequent transfer ('recycling') of fair value changes to profit or loss (on derecognition of the investments in an equity instrument). Those respondents supported an approach that maintains a distinction between realised and unrealised gains and losses and said that an entity's performance should include all realised gains and losses. However, the IASB concluded that a gain or loss on those investments should be recognised once only; therefore, recognising a gain or loss in other comprehensive income and subsequently transferring it to profit or loss is inappropriate. In addition, the IASB noted that recycling of gains and losses to profit or loss would create something similar to the available-for-sale category in IAS 39 and would create the requirement to assess the equity instrument for impairment, which had created application problems. That would not significantly improve or reduce the complexity of the financial reporting for financial assets. Accordingly, the IASB decided to prohibit recycling of gains and losses into profit or loss when an equity instrument is derecognised.

(c)   *Scope of exception*: Some respondents asked the IASB to identify a principle that defined the equity instruments to which the exception should apply. However, they did not specify what that principle should be. The IASB previously considered developing a principle to identify other equity investments whose fair value changes should be presented in profit or loss (or other comprehensive income), including a distinction based on whether the equity instruments represented a 'strategic investment'. However, the IASB decided that it would be difficult, and perhaps impossible, to develop a clear and robust principle that would identify investments that are different enough to

---

36 In October 2012 the IASB issued *Investment Entities* (Amendments to IFRS 10, IFRS 12 and IAS 27), which required investment entities, as defined in IFRS 10 *Consolidated Financial Statements*, to measure their investments in subsidiaries, other than those providing investment-related services or activities, at fair value through profit or loss.

justify a different presentation requirement. The IASB considered whether a list of indicators could be used to support the principle, but decided that such a list would inevitably be rule-based and could not be comprehensive enough to address all possible situations and factors. Moreover, the IASB noted that such an approach would create complexity in application without necessarily increasing the usefulness of information to users of financial statements.

(d) *Irrevocability of the exception:* A small number of respondents believed that an entity should be able to reclassify equity instruments into and out of the fair value through other comprehensive income category if an entity starts or ceases to hold the investments for trading purposes. However, the IASB decided that the option must be irrevocable to provide discipline to its application. The IASB also noted that the option to designate a financial asset as measured at fair value is also irrevocable.

BC5.26 An entity may transfer the cumulative gain or loss within equity. In the light of jurisdiction-specific restrictions on components of equity, the IASB decided not to provide specific requirements related to that transfer.

BC5.27 IFRS 9 amended IFRS 7 in 2009 to require additional disclosures about investments in equity instruments that are measured at fair value through other comprehensive income. The IASB believes those disclosures will provide useful information to users of financial statements about instruments presented in that manner and the effect of that presentation.

BC5.28 The IASB noted that permitting an option for entities to present some gains and losses in other comprehensive income is an exception to the overall classification and measurement approach and adds complexity. However, the IASB believes that the requirement that the election is irrevocable, together with the additional disclosures required, addresses many of those concerns.

Liabilities designated as at fair value through profit or loss

Previous discussions related to the effects of changes in a liability's credit risk

BCZ5.29 In 2003 the IASB discussed the issue of including changes in the credit risk of a financial liability in its fair value measurement. It considered responses to the exposure draft of proposed amendments to IAS 39 published in June 2002 that expressed concern about the effect of including this component in the fair value measurement and that suggested the fair value option should be restricted to exclude all or some financial liabilities. However, the IASB concluded that the fair value option could be applied to any financial liability, and decided not to restrict the option in IAS 39 (as revised in 2003) because to do so would negate some of the benefits of the fair value option set out in paragraph BCZ4.60.

BCZ5.30 The IASB considered comments on the exposure draft published in 2002 that disagreed with the view that, in applying the fair value option to financial liabilities, an entity should recognise income as a result of deteriorating credit quality (and expense as a result of improving credit quality). Commentators noted that it is not useful to report lower liabilities when an entity is in financial difficulty precisely because its debt levels are too high, and that it would be difficult to explain to users of financial statements the reasons why income would be recognised when a liability's creditworthiness deteriorates. These comments suggested that fair value should exclude the effects of changes in the instrument's credit risk.

BCZ5.31 However, the IASB noted that because financial statements are prepared on a going concern basis, credit risk affects the value at which liabilities could be repurchased or settled. Accordingly, the fair value of a financial liability reflects the credit risk relating to that liability. Consequently, it decided to include credit risk relating to a financial liability in the fair value measurement of that liability for the following reasons:

(a) Entities realise changes in fair value, including fair value attributable to the liability's credit risk, for example, by renegotiating or repurchasing liabilities or by using derivatives.

(b) Changes in credit risk affect the observed market price of a financial liability and hence its fair value.

(c) It is difficult from a practical standpoint to exclude changes in credit risk from an observed market price.

(d) The fair value of a financial liability (ie the price of that liability in an exchange between a knowledgeable, willing buyer and a knowledgeable, willing seller) on initial recognition reflects its credit risk. The IASB believes that it is inappropriate to include credit risk in the initial fair value measurement of financial liabilities, but not subsequently.

BCZ5.32 In 2003 the IASB also considered whether the component of the fair value of a financial liability attributable to changes in credit quality should be specifically disclosed, separately presented in the income statement, or separately presented in equity. The IASB decided that whilst separately presenting or disclosing such changes might be difficult in practice, disclosure of such information would be useful to users of financial statements and would help alleviate the concerns expressed. Consequently, it decided to require a disclosure to help identify the changes in the fair value of a financial liability that arise from changes in the liability's credit risk. The IASB believes this is a reasonable proxy for the change in fair value that is attributable to changes in the liability's credit risk, in particular when such changes are large, and will provide users with information with which to understand the profit or loss effect of such a change in credit risk.

BCZ5.33 The IASB decided to clarify that this issue relates to the credit risk of the financial liability, instead of the creditworthiness of the entity. The IASB noted that this more appropriately describes the objective of what is included in the fair value measurement of financial liabilities.

BCZ5.34 The IASB also noted that the fair value of liabilities secured by valuable collateral, guaranteed by third parties or ranking ahead of virtually all other liabilities is generally unaffected by changes in the entity's creditworthiness.

BC5.34A IFRS 13, issued in May 2011, includes requirements for measuring the fair value of a liability issued with an inseparable third-party credit enhancement from the issuer's perspective.

Requirements added to IFRS 9 in October 2010 to address the effects of changes in credit risk for liabilities designated as at fair value through profit or loss

BC5.35 As noted above, if an entity designates a financial liability under the fair value option, IAS 39 required the entire fair value change to be presented in profit or loss. However, many users and others told the IASB over a long period of time that changes in a liability's credit risk ought not to affect profit or loss unless the liability is held for trading. That is because an entity generally will not realise the effects of changes in the liability's credit risk unless the liability is held for trading.

BC5.36 To respond to that long-standing and widespread concern, in May 2010 the IASB proposed that the effects of changes in a liability's credit risk should be presented in other comprehensive income. The proposals in the 2010 Own Credit Risk Exposure Draft would have applied to all liabilities designated under the fair value option.

BC5.37 However, in its deliberations leading to the 2010 Own Credit Risk Exposure Draft, the IASB discussed whether such treatment would create or enlarge an accounting mismatch in profit or loss in some limited cases. The IASB acknowledged that this might be the case if an entity holds large portfolios of financial assets that are measured at fair value through profit or loss and there is an economic relationship between changes in the fair value of those assets and the effects of changes in the credit risk of the financial liabilities designated under the fair value option. A mismatch would arise because the entire change in the fair value of the assets would be presented in profit or loss but only a portion of the change in the fair value of the liabilities would be presented in profit or loss. The portion of the liabilities' fair value change attributable to changes in their credit risk would be presented in other comprehensive income. To address potential mismatches, the IASB set out an alternative approach in the 2010 Own Credit Risk Exposure Draft whereby the effects of changes in the liabilities' credit risk would be presented in other comprehensive income unless such treatment would create or enlarge an accounting mismatch in profit or loss (in which case, the entire fair value change would be presented in profit or loss). The 2010 Own Credit Risk Exposure Draft stated that the determination about potential mismatches would be made when the liability is initially recognised and would not be reassessed. The IASB asked respondents for feedback on the alternative approach.

BC5.38 Many respondents preferred the alternative approach. They agreed that in almost all cases the effects of changes in credit risk ought not to be presented in profit or loss. However, those respondents said that if such treatment would create or enlarge an accounting mismatch in profit or loss, the entire fair value change should be presented in profit or loss. Respondents thought such cases would be rare and asked the IASB to provide guidance on how to determine whether presenting the effects of changes in credit risk in other comprehensive income would create or enlarge an accounting mismatch in profit or loss.

BC5.39　The IASB agreed with the responses and finalised the alternative approach. Consequently, entities are required to present the effects of changes in the liabilities' credit risk in other comprehensive income unless such treatment would create or enlarge an accounting mismatch in profit or loss (in which case, the entire fair value change is required to be presented in profit or loss). The IASB acknowledged that that approach will introduce some additional complexity to financial reporting because not all liabilities designated under the fair value option will be treated the same. However, the IASB decided that it was necessary to address circumstances in which the proposals would create or enlarge a mismatch in profit or loss. Although the IASB expects those circumstances to be rare, they could be significant in some industries in some jurisdictions.

BC5.40　The IASB discussed how an entity should determine whether a mismatch would be created or enlarged. It decided that an entity has to assess whether it expects that changes in the credit risk of a liability will be offset by changes in the fair value of another financial instrument. The IASB decided that such an assessment must be based on an economic relationship between the characteristics of the liability and the characteristics of the other financial instrument. Such a relationship does not arise by coincidence.

BC5.41　The IASB believes that in many cases the relationship will be contractual (as described in paragraph B5.7.10 of IFRS 9) but decided that a contractual relationship is not required. Requiring a contractual relationship would have created a very high threshold for presenting the effects of changes in a liability's credit risk in profit or loss and the IASB decided that such a high threshold was too strict to accommodate all of the possible scenarios in which a mismatch would be created or enlarged by presenting those amounts in other comprehensive income.

BC5.42　However, to increase transparency about an entity's determination about potential mismatches, the IASB decided to require disclosures about an entity's methodology for making that determination. Also, an entity is required to apply its methodology consistently. The determination must be made at initial recognition of the liability and is not reassessed, which is consistent with the entity's overall election to use the fair value option.

BC5.43　Some respondents to the 2010 Own Credit Risk Exposure Draft asked whether the IASB intended that the proposals should apply to loan commitments and financial guarantee contracts that are designated under the fair value option. Those respondents suggested that the proposals should not apply to those items because the IASB's intention seemingly had always been to address the issue of own credit risk for non-derivative liabilities. The respondents noted that loan commitments and financial guarantee contracts either meet the definition of a derivative or are very similar to a derivative from an economic perspective and therefore changes in their fair value should always be presented in profit or loss. The IASB agreed with those respondents and decided that all changes in the fair value of loan commitments and financial guarantee contracts designated under the fair value option should be presented in profit or loss. In addition to the comments put forward by respondents, the IASB also noted that phase II of the insurance project[37] was discussing whether all financial guarantee contracts should be within the scope of that proposed Standard.

Alternative approaches to address the issue of own credit risk

BC5.44   In 2010 the IASB discussed and rejected the following approaches for addressing the issue of credit risk:

(a)   *Present the effects of changes in credit risk directly in equity:* Some believe that the effects of changes in credit risk should not affect the entity's performance; therefore they believe that those amounts should be presented directly in equity. The IASB rejected this approach in the 2010 Own Credit Risk Exposure Draft because it believes that changes in the liability's credit risk ought to affect the entity's performance if the liability is measured at fair value. If those amounts were presented directly in equity, they would never be presented in the entity's statement of comprehensive income. The IASB acknowledged that IFRS does not provide a clear objective for when an item should be presented in other comprehensive income instead of in profit or loss or whether the amounts in other comprehensive income should be reclassified to profit or loss. However, the IASB believes that presenting the effects of changes in credit risk in other comprehensive income is preferable to presenting them directly in equity because the latter would create a new problem by causing confusion or creating inconsistencies in what items are presented directly in equity. The IASB noted that remeasurements of assets and liabilities should not be presented directly in equity because remeasurements are not transactions with equity holders. The IASB asked respondents for feedback on presenting directly in equity the effects of changes in a liability's credit risk and almost all respondents, including users, did not support it. Accordingly the IASB did not pursue this alternative.

(b)   *Present the entire change in the fair value of liabilities in other comprehensive income:* Some believe that the entire change in fair value (not just the portion attributable to changes in credit risk) should be presented in other comprehensive income. They argue that this approach would avoid the difficult question of how to measure the effects of changes in credit risk. The IASB rejected this approach because it believes that at least some of the change in fair value should be presented in profit or loss. The IASB's objective was to address issues related to the effects of changes in liabilities' credit risk; therefore, presenting the entire change in fair value in other comprehensive income is not appropriate. Also, this approach would result in mismatches in profit or loss

---

37   The Board completed its insurance project with the issuance of IFRS 17. IFRS 17, issued in May 2017, replaced IFRS 4. IFRS 17 did not change the scope requirements relating to financial guarantee contracts.

because changes in the fair value of an entity's assets would be presented in profit or loss and changes in the fair value of its liabilities would be presented in other comprehensive income (see similar discussion in paragraph BC5.37). Moreover, this alternative would raise difficult questions about what (if any) amounts should be presented in profit or loss during the life of the liability (eg interest or other financing costs). The IASB has discussed the topic of disaggregating finance costs from other fair value changes on numerous occasions without reaching any conclusions.

Presenting the effects of changes in credit risk in other comprehensive income via a one-step or two-step approach

BC5.45   The 2010 Own Credit Risk Exposure Draft proposed a 'two-step approach' for presenting a liability's credit risk in the statement of comprehensive income, with the result that those changes would not affect profit or loss. In the first step, the entity would present the entire fair value change in profit or loss. In the second step, the entity would 'back out' from profit or loss the portion of the fair value change that is attributable to changes in the liability's credit risk and present that amount in other comprehensive income.

BC5.46   The 2010 Own Credit Risk Exposure Draft also set out a 'one-step approach', which would present the portion of the fair value change that is attributable to changes in the liability's credit risk directly in other comprehensive income. All other portions of the fair value change would be presented in profit or loss.

BC5.47   The IASB acknowledged that the only difference between those two approaches is how the effects of changes in the liability's credit risk are presented. The two-step approach would present those amounts first in profit or loss and then transfer them to other comprehensive income, whereas the one-step approach would present them directly in other comprehensive income.

BC5.48   The IASB proposed the two-step approach in the 2010 Own Credit Risk Exposure Draft because it thought that it would present more clearly all of the relevant information in the primary financial statements, but it decided to ask respondents which approach they supported.

BC5.49   Almost all respondents, including users, supported the one-step approach. They said that the one-step approach is more efficient and less complicated than the two-step approach. They pointed out that both approaches have the same net result in profit or loss and other comprehensive income. Respondents said that there is little (if any) added benefit of the 'gross' presentation in the two-step approach and the extra line items on the face of the performance statement result in unnecessary clutter. Furthermore, respondents noted the IASB's exposure draft published in May 2010 on the presentation of items in other comprehensive income. That exposure draft proposes that the profit or loss section and other comprehensive income should be displayed as separate components within an overall statement of profit or loss and other comprehensive income. Respondents questioned whether the two-step approach would have any added benefit if the Board finalised the proposals in that exposure draft.

BC5.50　Users told the IASB that the two-step approach would not be more helpful to their analysis than the one-step approach. Some users noted that the effects of changes in a liability's credit risk should not be presented in profit or loss, even if those effects were subsequently backed out.

BC5.51　The IASB was persuaded by respondents' arguments and decided to require the one-step approach. The IASB noted that no information is lost by using the one-step approach because IFRS 7 and IAS 1 *Presentation of Financial Statements* require entities to disclose (either on the financial statements or in the notes) all of the information required by the two-step approach.

Reclassifying amounts to profit or loss

BC5.52　The 2010 Own Credit Risk Exposure Draft proposed to prohibit reclassification of gains or losses to profit or loss (on derecognition of the liability or otherwise)—sometimes called 'recycling'. In the Basis for Conclusions on that Exposure Draft, the IASB noted that the proposal was consistent with the requirements in IFRS 9 that prohibit recycling for investments in equity instruments that are measured at fair value with changes presented in other comprehensive income.

BC5.53　Moreover, the IASB noted that if the entity repays the contractual amount, the cumulative effect over the life of the instrument of any changes in the liability's credit risk will net to zero because its fair value will equal the contractual amount. Consequently, for many liabilities, the issue of reclassification is irrelevant.

BC5.54　Most respondents to the 2010 Own Credit Risk Exposure Draft disagreed with that proposal and urged the IASB to require reclassification if the liability was derecognised and the effects of changes in its credit risk were realised. They acknowledged that there would not be any amount to reclassify if the entity repays the contractual amount. But they believe that if the entity repays an amount other than the contractual amount, the realised amounts in other comprehensive income should be reclassified. Those respondents view other comprehensive income as a 'temporary holding place' for unrealised gains and losses. They believe that unrealised and realised amounts are fundamentally different and thus should not be treated the same. The former are still uncertain and may never be crystallised. In contrast, the latter have crystallised and are backed by cash flows.

BC5.55　However, the IASB was not persuaded and confirmed the proposal to prohibit reclassification. The IASB acknowledged that it needs to address the overall objective of other comprehensive income, including when an item should be presented in other comprehensive income instead of in profit or loss and whether amounts in other comprehensive income should be reclassified to profit or loss (and if so, when). However, in the absence of such an objective, the IASB noted that its decision is consistent with the requirements in IFRS 9 that prohibit recycling for investments in equity instruments that are measured at fair value with changes presented in other comprehensive income.

BC5.56 However, to provide users with information about how much of the accumulated other comprehensive income balance has been realised during the current reporting period (ie how much would have been reclassified if the IASB had required reclassification upon derecognition), the IASB decided to require entities to disclose that amount.

BC5.57 Also, consistently with the requirements for equity investments measured at fair value with changes presented in other comprehensive income, the IASB decided that an entity may transfer the cumulative gain or loss within equity.

Determining the effects of changes in the liability's credit risk

BC5.58 IFRS 7 required an entity, when designating a financial liability under the fair value option, to disclose the amount of the change in fair value that is attributable to changes in the liability's credit risk. The application guidance in IFRS 7 provided a default method for determining that amount. If the only relevant changes in market conditions for the liability are changes in an observed (benchmark) interest rate, that method attributes all changes in fair value, other than changes in the benchmark interest rate, to changes in the credit risk of the liability. In the Basis for Conclusions on IFRS 7, the IASB acknowledged that quantifying the change in a liability's credit risk might be difficult in practice. It noted that it believes that the default method provides a reasonable proxy for changes in the liability's credit risk, in particular when such changes are large, and would provide users with information with which to understand the effect on profit or loss of such a change in credit risk. However, IFRS 7 permitted entities to use a different method if it provides a more faithful representation of the changes in the liability's credit risk.

BC5.59 During the IASB's outreach programme preceding the publication of the 2010 Own Credit Risk Exposure Draft, preparers told the IASB that the default method in IFRS 7 is appropriate in many circumstances but a more sophisticated method is sometimes needed to reflect faithfully the effects of changes in the liabilities' credit risk (eg when the volume of liabilities outstanding significantly changed during the reporting period).

BC5.60 In the user questionnaire conducted during that outreach programme, the IASB asked users whether the default method in IFRS 7 was appropriate for determining the change in a liability's credit risk. Most users said that it was an appropriate method. Many users noted the difficulty in determining that amount more precisely.

BC5.61 Therefore, for the purposes of measuring the effects of changes in the credit risk of a liability, the 2010 Own Credit Risk Exposure Draft proposed to use the guidance in IFRS 7. Under the proposals, the default method would be carried forward but entities would continue to be permitted to use a different method if it provides a more faithful representation of the amount of the change in fair value that is attributable to changes in the liability's credit risk.

BC5.62　Most respondents agreed with the proposals in the 2010 Own Credit Risk Exposure Draft. Those respondents agreed that the guidance in IFRS 7 for measuring the effects of changes in a liability's credit risk is appropriate and operational. They noted that determining the effects of changes in a liability's credit risk can be complex, and therefore it was necessary to allow some flexibility in how it is measured. They acknowledged that the default method described in IFRS 7 is imprecise but said that it is a reasonable proxy in many cases. Moreover, although some respondents acknowledged that the default method does not isolate changes in a liability's credit risk from some other changes in fair value (eg general changes in the price of credit or changes in liquidity risk), those respondents said that it is often very difficult or impossible to separate those items. However, some respondents (including those who supported the IASB's proposals in the 2010 Own Credit Risk Exposure Draft) asked for some clarification on particular aspects of the guidance in IFRS 7.

BC5.63　Consistently with the majority of responses, the IASB decided to confirm the proposals in the 2010 Own Credit Risk Exposure Draft to use the guidance in IFRS 7 related to determining the effects of changes in a liability's credit risk. Thus, that guidance was carried forward from IFRS 7 to IFRS 9. However, to respond to some of the questions raised in the comment letters, the IASB decided to clarify the difference between the creditworthiness of the entity and the credit risk of a liability. Moreover, the IASB addressed the difference between a liability's credit risk and asset-specific performance risk—and confirmed that a change in a liability's credit risk does not include changes in asset-specific performance risk. Furthermore, the IASB noted that in some cases a liability might not have credit risk. Consequently, the IASB included additional examples in the application guidance to clarify those points.

BC5.64　Also, the IASB clarified that the default method illustrated in IFRS 7 (and relocated to IFRS 9) is appropriate only if the only relevant changes in market conditions for a liability are changes in an observed (benchmark) interest rate. If that is not the case, an entity is required to use a more precise method. Moreover, an entity is always permitted to use a different method if that method more faithfully represents the effects of changes in a liability's credit risk.

Amortised cost measurement

Effective interest rate

BCZ5.65　In developing the revised IAS 39, the IASB considered whether the effective interest rate for all financial instruments should be calculated on the basis of estimated cash flows (consistently with the original IAS 39) or whether the use of estimated cash flows should be restricted to groups of financial instruments with contractual cash flows being used for individual financial instruments. The IASB agreed to reconfirm the position in the original IAS 39 because it achieves consistent application of the effective interest method throughout the Standard.

BCZ5.66 The IASB noted that future cash flows and the expected life can be reliably estimated for most financial assets and financial liabilities, in particular for a group of similar financial assets or similar financial liabilities. However, the IASB acknowledged that in some rare cases it might not be possible to estimate the timing or amount of future cash flows reliably. It therefore decided to require that if it is not possible to estimate reliably the future cash flows or the expected life of a financial instrument, the entity should use contractual cash flows over the full contractual term of the financial instrument.

BCZ5.67 The IASB also decided to clarify that expected future defaults should not be included in estimates of cash flows because this would be a departure from the incurred loss model for impairment recognition.[38] At the same time, the IASB noted that in some cases, for example, when a financial asset is acquired at a deep discount, credit losses have occurred and are reflected in the price. If an entity does not take into account such credit losses in the calculation of the effective interest rate, the entity would recognise a higher interest income than that inherent in the price paid. The IASB therefore decided to clarify that such credit losses are included in the estimated cash flows when computing the effective interest rate.

BCZ5.68 The revised IAS 39 refers to all fees 'that are an integral part of the effective interest rate'. The IASB included this reference to clarify that IAS 39 relates only to those fees that are determined to be an integral part of the effective interest rate in accordance with IAS 18.[39]

BCZ5.69 Some commentators noted that it was not always clear how to interpret the requirement in the original IAS 39 that the effective interest rate must be based on discounting cash flows through maturity or the next market-based repricing date. In particular, it was not always clear whether fees, transaction costs and other premiums or discounts included in the calculation of the effective interest rate should be amortised over the period until maturity or the period to the next market-based repricing date.

BCZ5.70 For consistency with the estimated cash flows approach, the IASB decided to clarify that the effective interest rate is calculated over the expected life of the instrument or, when applicable, a shorter period. A shorter period is used when the variable (eg interest rates) to which the fee, transaction costs, discount or premium relates is repriced to market rates before the expected maturity of the instrument. In such a case, the appropriate amortisation period is the period to the next such repricing date.

---

38 The IASB did not change this approach to determining the effective interest rate for financial instruments (other than those that are purchased or originated credit impaired) when changing from an incurred loss in IAS 39 to an expected credit loss impairment model. This was because the decoupled approach in IFRS 9 considers the recognition of interest revenue and the recognition of expected credit losses separately.

39 IFRS 15, issued in May 2014, replaced IAS 18. See paragraphs B5.4.1–B5.4.3 of IFRS 9 for the requirements for fees that are an integral part of the effective interest rate.

BCZ5.71 The IASB identified an apparent inconsistency in the guidance in the revised IAS 39. It related to whether the revised or the original effective interest rate of a debt instrument should be applied when remeasuring the instrument's carrying amount on the cessation of fair value hedge accounting. A revised effective interest rate is calculated when fair value hedge accounting ceases. The IASB removed this inconsistency as part of *Improvements to IFRSs* issued in May 2008 by clarifying that the remeasurement of an instrument in accordance with paragraph AG8 (now paragraph B5.4.6 of IFRS 9) is based on the revised effective interest rate calculated in accordance with paragraph 92 (now paragraph 6.5.10 of IFRS 9), when applicable, instead of the original effective interest rate.

Presentation of interest revenue

BC5.72 As part of its work on the Impairment project (Section 5.5 of IFRS 9), the IASB published the 2009 Exposure Draft *Financial Instruments: Amortised Cost and Impairment* (the '2009 Impairment Exposure Draft'). The 2009 Impairment Exposure Draft proposed a model in which an entity would have considered initial expectations of credit losses when determining the effective interest rate on financial assets. Consequently, interest revenue would have represented the economic yield, or the effective return, on those financial assets. In contrast, the decoupled approach in IFRS 9 considers the recognition of interest revenue and the recognition of expected credit losses separately. Under this approach, an entity recognises interest on the gross carrying amount of a financial asset without taking expected credit losses into consideration (except when financial assets become credit-impaired or are credit-impaired on initial recognition). Paragraphs BC5.88–BC5.91 discusses further the reasons why the IASB did not proceed with the proposals in the 2009 Impairment Exposure Draft in finalising IFRS 9.

BC5.73 Respondents told the IASB that calculating an effective interest rate that considers initial expected credit losses is operationally burdensome, particularly for open portfolios of financial assets. In addition, users of financial statements stressed the need for an interest revenue recognition model that allows them to continue to analyse net interest margin and credit losses separately.

BC5.74 Consequently, the IASB proposed in the 2013 Impairment Exposure Draft, consistently with the proposals in the Supplementary Document *Financial Instruments: Impairment* (the 'Supplementary Document'), that, an entity would calculate interest revenue on the gross carrying amount of a financial asset using an effective interest rate that is not adjusted for expected credit losses. However, the IASB noted that there are some financial assets for which credit risk has increased to such an extent that presenting interest revenue on the basis of the gross carrying amount of the financial asset, that reflects the contractual return, would no longer faithfully represent the economic return. The 2013 Impairment Exposure Draft therefore proposed that if a financial asset is credit-impaired at the reporting date, an entity should change the interest revenue calculation from being based on the gross carrying amount to the amortised cost of a financial asset (ie the amount net of the loss allowance) at the beginning of the following reporting period.

BC5.75 The IASB received feedback on the 2013 Impairment Exposure Draft that showed the majority of respondents agreed that the interest revenue calculation should change to a calculation on a net basis for some financial assets, because it best supported faithful representation. These requirements only affect the calculation and presentation of interest revenue and not the measurement of the loss allowance.

BC5.76 The IASB acknowledged the concerns of using 'incurred loss' criteria in a model based on expected credit losses. However, in the IASB's view, it was necessary to retain the faithful representation of interest revenue, while minimising the operational challenges of requiring entities to calculate interest revenue on the amortised cost amount for all financial assets.

BC5.77 Financial assets that are credit-impaired at the reporting date and on which interest revenue is calculated on the amortised cost of a financial asset are a subset of financial assets with a loss allowance measured at lifetime expected credit losses. IFRS preparers are already required to determine interest on the amortised cost amount of these financial assets in accordance with IAS 39 and therefore the IASB noted that this requirement would result in a minimal change in practice. Accordingly, the IASB decided to retain the scope of assets on which interest is calculated on the amortised cost amount of a financial asset that is credit-impaired as identified in by IAS 39 (but excluding the concept of 'incurred but not reported').

BC5.78 The IASB is of the view that, conceptually, an entity should assess whether financial assets have become credit-impaired on an ongoing basis, thus altering the presentation of interest revenue as the underlying economics change. However, the IASB noted that such an approach would be unduly onerous for preparers to apply. Thus, the IASB decided that an entity should be required to make the assessment of whether a financial asset is credit-impaired at the reporting date and then change the interest calculation from the beginning of the following reporting period.

BC5.79 However, a few respondents to the 2013 Impairment Exposure Draft supported presenting nil interest revenue on credit-impaired financial assets for operational reasons. In accordance with such an approach an entity would be required to offset interest revenue on a subset of financial assets with an equal amount of expected credit losses. The IASB noted that an advantage of presenting nil interest revenue is the operational simplicity. The only information that an entity would need to know to apply this approach would be the interest revenue on the subset of financial assets. That is, an entity would not be required to identify the loss allowance related to that subset of financial assets. However, the IASB noted that such an approach would blend together the effect of the unwinding of the present value of expected cash flows with other expected credit losses. In the IASB's view, a nil interest approach would not improve the calculation of interest revenue, because it would not faithfully represent the economic return in a manner that is consistent with the measurement of the gross carrying amount and expected credit losses at a present value.

BC5.80　　Consequently, the IASB decided to confirm the requirement to present interest revenue on a net basis and to do so from the beginning of the reporting period following the reporting period when the financial instrument became credit-impaired.

Write-off

BC5.81　　In the IASB's view, a definition of 'write-off' is necessary to faithfully represent the gross carrying amount of the financial assets within the scope of IFRS 9. The definition is also necessary for the newly introduced disclosure requirements about expected credit losses. The 2009 Impairment Exposure Draft proposed definitions and requirements related to the term 'write off'. Following positive comments about those definitions, the IASB decided to retain the definitions and requirements related to the term 'write-off' in IFRS 9 with minimal changes to the definition proposed in the 2009 Impairment Exposure Draft.

Impairment

Background

Objectives for depicting expected credit losses

BC5.82　　For financial assets measured at amortised cost and debt instruments measured at fair value through other comprehensive income the effect of changes in credit risk are more relevant to an investor's understanding of the likelihood of the collection of future contractual cash flows than the effects of other changes, such as changes in market interest rates. This is because an integral aspect of both business models is to collect contractual cash flows.

BC5.83　　The IASB noted that a model that faithfully represents the economic phenomenon of expected credit losses should provide users of financial statements with relevant information about the amount, timing and uncertainty of an entity's future cash flows. It should also ensure that the amounts that an entity reports are comparable, timely and understandable. Furthermore, the IASB also sought to ensure that the model address the criticisms of the incurred loss model in IAS 39. These criticisms included the concerns that the model in IAS 39 overstated interest revenue in periods before a credit loss event occurs, delayed the recognition of credit losses and was complex due to its multiple impairment approaches.

BC5.84　　In developing a model that depicts expected credit losses, the IASB observed that:

(a)　　when an entity prices a financial instrument, part of the yield, the credit risk premium, compensates the entity for the credit losses initially expected (for example, an entity will typically demand a higher yield for those instruments with higher expected credit losses at the date the instrument is issued). Consequently, no economic loss is suffered at initial recognition simply because the credit risk on a financial instrument is high at that time, because those expected credit losses are implicit in the initial pricing of the instrument.

(b)   for most financial instruments, the pricing is not adjusted for changes in expected credit losses in subsequent periods. Consequently, subsequent changes in expected credit losses are economic losses (or gains) of the entity in the period in which they occur.

BC5.85   Expected credit losses, in isolation, are not directly observable. However, because the credit risk premium is a component of the market yield for financial instruments, the indirect measurement of expected credit losses is a daily occurrence in the pricing of such instruments in the market. A number of models exist to assist market participants and regulators in the measurement of expected credit losses. But, because expected credit losses are not directly observable, their measurement is inherently based on judgement and any model that attempts to depict expected credit losses will be subject to measurement uncertainty.

BC5.86   Some interested parties would prefer an impairment model that results in a more conservative, or prudential, depiction of expected credit losses. Those interested parties argue that such a depiction would better meet the needs of both the regulators who are responsible for maintaining financial stability and investors and other users of financial statements. However, to be consistent with the *Conceptual Framework*,[40] faithful representation of expected credit losses implies that the depiction of those credit losses is neutral and free from bias. The depiction of expected credit losses in an unbiased way informs the decisions of a broad range of users of financial statements, including regulators and investors and creditors. In the IASB's view, incorporating a degree of conservatism would be arbitrary and would result in a lack of comparability. The risk of an outcome other than the probability-weighted expected outcome is only relevant for particular purposes, such as determining the extent of economic or regulatory capital requirements.

Alternative models considered to depict expected credit losses

The model proposed in the 2009 Impairment Exposure Draft

BC5.87   In November 2009 the IASB published the 2009 Impairment Exposure Draft, which proposed that an entity should measure amortised cost at the expected (credit-adjusted) cash flows discounted at the original credit-adjusted effective interest rate, ie the effective interest rate adjusted for the initial expected credit losses. The IASB was aware that these proposals were a fundamentally new approach to impairment accounting for financial reporting purposes that was much more closely linked to credit risk management concepts. In order to fully understand the consequences of this, the IASB established a panel of credit risk experts (the Expert Advisory Panel (EAP)) to provide input during the comment period.

---

40 References to the *Conceptual Framework* in this Basis for Conclusions are to the *Conceptual Framework for Financial Reporting*, issued in 2010 and in effect when parts of the Standard were developed and amended.

BC5.88   In the IASB's view, the model in the 2009 Impairment Exposure Draft most faithfully represents expected credit losses and would determine the carrying amount, interest revenue and impairment gains or losses to be recognised through a single, integrated calculation. Thus, an entity would recognise:

(a)   the initial expected credit losses over the life of the asset through the credit-adjusted effective interest rate; and

(b)   any changes in expected credit losses when those changes occurred.

BC5.89   Users of financial statements have told the IASB that they support a model that distinguishes between the effect of initial estimates of expected credit losses and subsequent changes in those estimates. They noted that such a distinction would provide useful information about changes in credit risk and the resulting economic losses. Many other respondents also supported the concepts in the 2009 Impairment Exposure Draft, but said that the proposals would present significant operational challenges. In particular, they highlighted the following:

(a)   estimating the full expected cash flows for all financial instruments;

(b)   applying a credit-adjusted effective interest rate to those cash flow estimates; and

(c)   maintaining information about the initial estimate of expected credit losses.

BC5.90   These operational challenges arose because entities typically operate separate accounting and credit risk management systems. To have applied the 2009 Impairment Exposure Draft, entities would have had to have integrated those separate systems. The IASB was told that this would have required substantial costs and lead time. Respondents noted that these operational challenges would be especially acute for open portfolios (ie portfolios to which new financial instruments are added over time).

BC5.91   The IASB initially considered different approaches to address the specific operational challenges that respondents raised while at the same time replicating the outcomes of the 2009 Impairment Exposure Draft to the maximum extent possible.

Simplifications to address operational challenges of the 2009 Impairment Exposure Draft

BC5.92   To address the operational challenges outlined in paragraph BC5.89 and as suggested by the EAP, the IASB decided to decouple the measurement and allocation of initial expected credit losses from the determination of the effective interest rate (except for purchased or originated credit-impaired financial assets). Thus, an entity would measure the financial asset and the loss allowance separately using the original effective interest rate (ie not adjusted for initial expected credit losses). The IASB considered that such an approach would address some of the operational challenges of the 2009 Impairment Exposure Draft by allowing an entity to leverage its existing accounting and credit risk management systems and reduce the extent of integration between these systems.

BC5.93   As a result of the decoupling simplification, an entity would measure the present value of expected credit losses using the original effective interest rate. This presents a dilemma, because measuring expected credit losses using such a rate double-counts the expected credit losses that were priced into the financial asset at initial recognition. The IASB therefore concluded that recognising the lifetime expected credit losses from initial recognition would be inappropriate under a model that discounts expected credit losses using the original effective interest rate. The IASB further concluded that a recognition mechanism was required that preserves, to as great an extent as possible, the objective of the 2009 Impairment Exposure Draft and reduces the effect of this double-counting. Thus, the IASB proposed to pursue a model that recognises two different amounts based on the extent of increases in credit risk since initial recognition. Such a dual-measurement model would require an entity to recognise:

(a)   a portion of the lifetime expected credit losses from initial recognition as a proxy for recognising the initial expected credit losses over the life of the financial asset; and

(b)   the lifetime expected credit losses when credit risk has increased since initial recognition (ie when the recognition of only a portion of the lifetime expected credit losses is no longer appropriate because the entity has suffered a significant economic loss).

BC5.94   The IASB considered the interaction between the timing of the recognition of the full lifetime expected credit losses, and the size of the portion of the lifetime expected credit losses that are recognised before that, to be a determinant of what would provide a more faithful representation of the economic loss. Thus, if an entity recognises a smaller portion of the lifetime expected credit losses initially, it should recognise the full lifetime expected credit losses earlier than if it had been required to recognise a larger portion of the lifetime expected credit losses initially.

BC5.95   As a result of the decoupling simplification as discussed in paragraphs BC5.92–BC5.93, the IASB acknowledges that any model that recognises different amounts of expected credit losses based on the extent of increases in credit risk since initial recognition cannot perfectly replicate the outcome of the model in the 2009 Impairment Exposure Draft. Furthermore, while there is always recognition of some expected credit losses, such a model retains a criterion for when lifetime expected credit losses are recognised. Once that criterion is met, the recognition of lifetime expected credit losses results in a loss representing the difference between the portion that was recognised previously and the lifetime expected credit losses (a 'cliff effect'). In the IASB's view, any approach that seeks to approximate the outcomes of the model in the 2009 Impairment Exposure Draft without the associated operational challenges will include a recognition threshold for lifetime expected credit losses and a resulting cliff effect.

The model proposed in the Supplementary Document

BC5.96 Based on the feedback from the 2009 Impairment Exposure Draft and the simplifications considered to address the challenges of that model, the IASB published the Supplementary Document in January 2011. The Supplementary Document proposed a two-tier loss allowance, which would be recognised as follows:

(a) the higher of, a time-proportionate allowance (TPA) or expected credit losses for the foreseeable future, for the good book. If applying a TPA, an entity would recognise the lifetime expected credit losses over the weighted average life of the portfolio of assets.

(b) the lifetime expected credit losses for the bad book. Financial assets would be moved to the bad book if the collectability of contractual cash flows on a financial asset became so uncertain that the entity's credit risk management objective changes from receiving the regular payments to recovery of all, or a portion of, the asset.

BC5.97 The Supplementary Document proposed to reflect the relationship between expected credit losses and interest revenue using the TPA. The TPA would achieve this through the allocation of expected credit losses over time, indirectly 'adjusting' the contractual interest. However, the TPA does this through a short cut and therefore it would not represent the economics as faithfully as the 2009 Impairment Exposure Draft did. Because the TPA allocates both the initial expected credit losses and the subsequent changes in lifetime expected credit losses over time, the measurement results in an understatement of changes in expected credit losses until the entity recognises lifetime expected credit losses. This effect is particularly problematic for financial assets that increase in credit risk and thus whose expected credit losses increase early in the asset's life.

BC5.98 Allocating the change in estimated expected credit losses in this way results in the deferred recognition of the full amount of the change in expected credit losses and, consequently, the TPA closely replicated the outcome of the model in the 2009 Impairment Exposure Draft only in situations in which expectations of credit losses do not change or the credit losses emerge at, or close to, maturity (extremely back-ended losses). This shortcoming was addressed by including a foreseeable future floor in the SD. However, because the calculation of the TPA relied on the weighted average age over the weighted average life of the portfolio, the outcome may not have reflected the economics of a growing or declining portfolio.

BC5.99 The TPA calculation proposed by the Supplementary Document (whereby the loss allowance was, at a minimum, equal to the expected credit losses in the foreseeable future) was unique and would not be a calculation required to be used by entities for other purposes. Some of the identified operational challenges of the proposals in the 2009 Impairment Exposure Draft would still exist, including the need to change systems to calculate the weighted average age and the weighted average life of open portfolios, as would the need to estimate the full expected cash flows for all financial assets.

BC5.100 The IASB did not receive strong support for the proposals in the Supplementary Document. Many respondents were concerned that the Supplementary Document required an entity to make two calculations to measure the loss allowance balance for the good book. They viewed the dual calculation as operationally difficult, lacking conceptual merit and providing confusing information to users of financial statements, because the basis for these loss calculations could change over time for the same financial assets and be different for different financial assets. Respondents also expressed concerns about the calculation of expected credit losses for the foreseeable future, with many expressing confusion about the conceptual basis for the time period. Many also noted that the term 'foreseeable future' had not been sufficiently defined to ensure consistent application. Furthermore, feedback on the Supplementary Document proposals were geographically split, with respondents in the US generally preferring the foreseeable future floor while respondents outside the US generally preferred the TPA approach.

BC5.101 Although the IASB did not receive strong support for the proposals in the Supplementary Document, some respondents, particularly users of financial statements and prudential regulators, supported the distinction between 'good book' and 'bad book' assets even if they were concerned that the criteria for transferring from the 'good book' to the 'bad book' were not sufficiently clear. On balance, the IASB decided not to further pursue this two-tier approach.

The model proposed in the 2013 Impairment Exposure Draft

BC5.102 The model proposed in the 2013 Impairment Exposure Draft continued to build on a tiered approach by requiring an entity to measure:

(a) the expected credit losses for a financial instrument at an amount equal to the lifetime expected credit losses, if the credit quality on that financial instrument has decreased significantly (or the credit risk increases significantly) since initial recognition; and

(b) the expected credit losses for a financial instrument at an amount equal to the 12-month expected credit losses for all other financial instruments.

BC5.103 The model proposed in the 2013 Impairment Exposure Draft eliminated the operational challenge of estimating the full expected cash flows for all financial instruments by limiting the recognition of lifetime expected credit losses to financial instruments for which credit risk has increased significantly since initial recognition.

BC5.104 To assist entities that have less sophisticated credit risk management systems, the 2013 Impairment Exposure Draft included simplifications to account for trade receivables and lease receivables. The proposed simplifications would reduce the need to track increases in credit risk by requiring (or allowing) an entity to recognise lifetime expected credit losses from the date of initial recognition.

BC5.105 The 2013 Impairment Exposure Draft proposed that interest revenue would be calculated using the effective interest method using the effective interest rate unadjusted for expected credit losses, except for purchased or originated credit-impaired financial assets, in which case the entity would use a credit-adjusted effective interest rate.

BC5.106 Overall, the majority of participants in the outreach conducted by the IASB while developing this model, including users of financial statements, supported a model that distinguishes between instruments for which credit risk has increased significantly since initial recognition and those that have not. In the IASB's view, this requirement for recognising lifetime expected credit losses strikes the best balance between the benefits of making distinctions on the basis of an increase in credit risk and the costs and complexity of making that assessment. Furthermore, the proposals aimed to limit the new information that an entity would be required to capture and maintain about the initial credit risk of financial assets by using information that preparers have said is consistent with current credit risk management systems.

BC5.107 To further reduce the cost of assessing the increases in credit risk, the proposed model included practical expedients and rebuttable presumptions (see paragraphs BC5.180–BC5.194) to assess if there have been significant increases in credit risk.

BC5.108 On the basis of the comments received about the proposals in the 2013 Impairment Exposure Draft, the IASB proceeded to refine the proposals while developing IFRS 9 and its requirements to account for impairment based on expected credit losses.

Joint deliberations with the FASB

BC5.109 In May 2010, the FASB published a proposed Accounting Standards Update *Accounting for Financial Instruments and Revisions to the Accounting for Derivative Instruments and Hedging Activities* (the '2010 proposed Update') that included proposals for impairment as part of its comprehensive approach to replacing the accounting requirements for financial instruments in US Generally Accepted Accounting Principles (US GAAP). The FASB's objective for credit impairment was to develop a single model for all financial instruments that provides more timely credit loss information for users of financial statements.

BC5.110 Many respondents to both the IASB's 2009 Impairment Exposure Draft and the FASB's 2010 proposed Update commented that achieving a common outcome for impairment accounting would be highly desirable. The boards agreed and, in January 2011, jointly published the Supplementary Document, which built on their individual original Exposure Drafts and sought to incorporate the objectives of both boards' original impairment proposals (see paragraphs BC5.96–BC5.101 for further discussions on the Supplementary Document's proposals and feedback).

BC5.111   The feedback received on the Supplementary Document, combined with the importance of achieving convergence, encouraged the IASB and the FASB to jointly develop an alternative expected credit loss model. In May 2011, the boards decided to jointly develop a model that would reflect the general pattern of increases in the credit risk of financial instruments, the so-called 'three-bucket model'. In the three-bucket model, the amount of the expected credit losses recognised as a loss allowance would depend on the extent of increases in the credit risk on financial instruments since initial recognition.

BC5.112   However, in response to feedback received from respondents in the US about that model, in July 2012 the FASB decided to develop an alternative expected credit loss model.

BC5.113   In December 2012, the FASB published the proposed Accounting Standards Update *Financial Instruments—Credit Losses* (the '2012 proposed Update'). The proposed Update would require an entity to measure the net amortised cost at the present value of cash flows that it expects to collect, discounted at the original effective interest rate. To achieve this, an entity would recognise a loss allowance for expected credit losses from initial recognition at an amount equal to the lifetime expected credit losses. The comment period on this document overlapped with the IASB's comment period on the 2013 Impairment Exposure Draft.

BC5.114   Feedback received by the IASB on the 2013 Impairment Exposure Draft and by the FASB on the 2012 proposed Update was shared at joint board meetings to enable the boards to consider the comments received and differences in the opinions of their respective stakeholders. For many respondents to the 2013 Impairment Exposure Draft convergence was still preferable; however, many noted that their preference was subject to the impairment model being similar to that proposed in the IASB's 2013 Impairment Exposure Draft. Only a limited number of the IASB's respondents preferred convergence to the 2012 proposed Update model exposed by the FASB. Furthermore, very few respondents demanded convergence at the cost of finalising the requirements in a timely manner. Many respondents urged the IASB to finalise the proposed model as soon as possible, with or without convergence, stressing the importance of improving the accounting for the impairment of financial assets in IFRS as soon as possible.

BC5.115   The FASB and the IASB reported differences in views from the users of the financial statements. The FASB reported that users of financial statements overwhelmingly supported its 2012 proposed Update model. The IASB however reported on its outreach activities that a majority of non-US users preferred an impairment model similar to what was proposed in the 2013 Impairment Exposure Draft, while the majority of US users preferred a model similar to that proposed by the FASB.

BC5.116   Because of the importance of the user perspective and the apparent inconsistency in feedback subsequent to the comment letter analysis discussed in July 2013, the IASB conducted further outreach activities to understand the reasons for the difference in the feedback received by the IASB and the FASB on their respective proposals. The IASB identified the following:

(a) the starting point of how preparers apply US GAAP for loss allowances is different from the starting point of IFRS preparers. The IASB believe that this difference in starting point has influenced users' perceptions of the two proposed models.

(b) the interaction between the role of prudential regulators and loss allowances is historically stronger in the US.

(c) many users of financial statements in the US place greater weight on the adequacy of loss allowances in the balance sheet.

BC5.117 Before and during the redeliberations the IASB was made aware of the feedback received from all respondents, including the users of financial statements. The issue of convergence was discussed at length throughout the course of the project. Having considered all the feedback and the points discussed in paragraphs BC5.114–BC5.116, the IASB decided to proceed with the model proposed in the 2013 Impairment Exposure Draft.

Scope

BC5.118 In addition to financial assets that are measured at amortised cost (including trade receivables) and at fair value through other comprehensive income, the IASB decided to include the following within the scope of the impairment requirements of IFRS 9:

(a) loan commitments and financial guarantee contracts for the issuer, that are not measured at fair value through profit or loss;

(b) lease receivables that are accounted for in accordance with IAS 17 *Leases*; and

(c) contract assets that are recognised and measured in accordance with IFRS 15.

Financial assets measured at fair value through other comprehensive income

BC5.119 The objective of the fair value through other comprehensive income measurement category is to provide users of financial statements with information on both a fair value and an amortised cost basis. To achieve that objective, paragraph 5.7.10 of IFRS 9 requires an entity to calculate interest revenue and impairment gains or losses in a manner that is consistent with the requirements that are applicable to financial assets measured at amortised cost. Thus, the IASB decided that the requirements for the recognition and measurement of expected credit losses shall apply to the fair value through other comprehensive income measurement category, in the same way as for assets measured at amortised cost. However, the loss allowance is recognised in other comprehensive income instead of reducing the carrying amount of the financial asset in the statement of financial position.

BC5.120 The IASB has noted feedback that recommended including a practical expedient that will provide relief from recognising 12-month expected credit losses on financial assets measured at fair value through other comprehensive income, when the fair value of the financial asset exceeds its amortised cost or when the loss allowance is insignificant. Interested parties noted that such a practical expedient would reduce the operational burden of assessing whether increases in credit risk since initial recognition are significant on financial assets that are already measured at fair value. They also noted that it would not be appropriate to recognise impairment gains or losses in profit or loss on financial assets that were purchased in an active market that prices the initial expectations of credit losses into the financial asset.

BC5.121 The IASB rejected these views. The IASB noted that not all debt instruments acquired in an active market are measured at fair value through other comprehensive income. In accordance with paragraph 4.1.2 of IFRS 9, such instruments can also be measured at amortised cost if the business model criteria are met (subject to the cash flow characteristics criteria). Having separate impairment models for similar financial assets that are measured differently would be inconsistent with the IASB's objective of having a single impairment model.

BC5.122 Furthermore, the IASB observed that a fair value-based practical expedient is inconsistent with the general impairment approach, which is based on an entity's assessment of the changes in the risk of a default occurring since initial recognition. Introducing a fair value-based practical expedient would represent a different impairment approach and would not result in the amounts recognised in profit or loss being the same as if the financial assets were measured at amortised cost.

BC5.123 The IASB noted that the assessment of credit risk is based on management's view of collecting contractual cash flows instead of on the perspective of a market participant as is the case with fair value measurement. It was noted that market prices are not in themselves intended to be a determinant of whether credit risk has increased significantly because, for example, market prices can be affected by factors that are not relevant to credit risk (such as changes in the level of general interest rates and the price of liquidity). However, the IASB noted that market prices are an important source of information that should be considered in assessing whether credit risk has changed. It was also noted that market information is relevant for financial instruments within the scope of the impairment model irrespective of the classification in accordance with IFRS 9. This is because the form of a financial asset (as a bond or a loan) does not determine its classification in accordance with IFRS 9 and because the accounting for expected credit losses is the same for financial assets measured at amortised cost and those measured at fair value through other comprehensive income.

BC5.124 In the IASB's view, applying a single impairment model to both financial assets at amortised cost and financial assets at fair value through other comprehensive income will facilitate comparability of amounts that are recognised in profit or loss for assets with similar economic characteristics. In addition, the IASB noted that having a single impairment model reduces a significant source of complexity for both users of financial statements and preparers compared with applying IAS 39. The IASB's view was strongly supported by respondents to the 2013 Impairment Exposure Draft. During its redeliberations on the 2013 Impairment Exposure Draft, the IASB, having noted the support from respondents, confirmed the inclusion of these financial assets within the scope of the impairment requirements.

Loan commitments and financial guarantee contracts

BC5.125　Loan commitments and financial guarantee contracts outside the scope of IAS 39 were previously accounted for in accordance with IAS 37 *Provisions, Contingent Liabilities and Contingent Assets*. The Supplementary Document asked respondents whether an entity should apply the same impairment model to loan commitments and financial guarantee contracts as for financial assets measured at amortised cost. On the basis of the support from respondents to the Supplementary Document, the 2013 Impairment Exposure Draft retained the proposal that an entity should recognise expected credit losses that result from loan commitments and financial guarantee contracts when there is a present contractual obligation to extend credit.

BC5.126　The vast majority of respondents to the 2013 Impairment Exposure Draft agreed that loan commitments and financial guarantee contracts should be within the scope of the impairment model because:

　　(a)　expected credit losses on loan commitments and financial guarantee contracts (off balance sheet exposures) are similar to those on loans and other on balance sheet exposures. The only difference is that in the latter case, the borrower has already drawn down the loan whereas in the former case it has not.

　　(b)　in practice, loan commitments and financial guarantee contracts are often managed using the same credit risk management approach and information systems as loans and other on balance sheet items.

　　(c)　a single impairment model for all credit exposures, irrespective of their type, removes the complexity previously caused by different impairment models in IFRS.

BC5.127　However, many of the respondents that supported including loan commitments and financial guarantee contracts within the scope of the impairment requirements proposed that the expected credit losses should be measured over the behavioural life of the product, instead of over the contractual life as was proposed (see paragraphs BC5.254–BC5.261).

BC5.128　The IASB therefore confirmed the inclusion within the scope of the impairment requirements of loan commitments that are not measured at fair value through profit or loss in accordance with IFRS 9 and financial guarantee contracts to which IFRS 9 is applied and that are not measured at fair value through profit or loss.

Trade receivables, contract assets and lease receivables

BC5.129　The 2009 Impairment Exposure Draft proposed that entities should apply an expected credit loss model to trade receivables. It also proposed a practical expedient by which they could use a provision matrix as the basis for measurement. Many respondents told the IASB that applying an expected credit loss model to non-interest-bearing trade receivables would not provide useful information because of their short maturity. They also noted that there would be operational challenges for non-financial institutions and less sophisticated financial institutions in applying an expected credit loss model. Consequently, the IASB conducted further outreach to gather information about current practice and the operational challenges of applying an expected credit loss model to trade receivables. That outreach indicated that the practical application of the impairment requirements in IAS 39 often results in credit losses not being recognised until trade receivables become past due.

BC5.130 In finalising IFRS 9, the IASB concluded that requiring entities to recognise a loss allowance on a more forward-looking basis before trade receivables become past due would improve financial reporting.

BC5.131 The IASB also noted in both the 2009 and 2013 Impairment Exposure Drafts, that, although the requirements in IAS 17 result in the measurement of a lease receivable in a manner that is similar to financial assets that are measured at amortised cost in accordance with IFRS 9, there are differences in the application of the effective interest method. In addition, the cash flows included in lease contracts could include features such as contingent payments that would not be present in other financial instruments. The existence of contingent and variable lease payments results in:

(a) specific requirements for identifying the cash flows that are included in the measurement of the lease receivable (such as the criteria for including contingent lease payments, the treatment of renewal options and the bifurcation of any embedded derivatives); and

(b) a consequential effect on determining the discount rate (ie given (a), the discount rate cannot always be determined in the same way as the effective interest rate for a financial asset measured at amortised cost).

BC5.132 The IASB decided that these differences do not justify applying a different impairment model and therefore included lease receivables within the scope of the impairment requirements in IFRS 9. In reaching this decision, the IASB concluded that the impairment model could be applied to lease receivables as long as:

(a) the cash flows assessed for expected credit losses are consistent with those included in the measurement of the lease receivable; and

(b) the rate used to discount the expected credit losses is consistent with the rate that is determined in accordance with IAS 17.

BC5.133 Some respondents to the 2013 Impairment Exposure Draft noted that the IASB has an active project affecting the accounting treatment of lease receivables that is yet to be finalised. They requested further clarification of the interaction between the expected credit loss requirements and the proposed accounting for lease receivables in accordance with that project. The IASB acknowledged these concerns and noted that it will further consider this interaction if needed when deliberating the accounting treatment for lease receivables as part of the leases project.

BC5.134　When finalising IFRS 15, the IASB noted that although contract assets are specifically excluded from the scope of IFRS 9 and accounted for in accordance with IFRS 15, the exposure to credit risk on contract assets is similar to that of trade receivables. The IASB therefore decided to include contract assets in the scope of the impairment requirements. The IASB also decided that if an entity applies IFRS 9 before it applies IFRS 15, an entity should apply the impairment requirements in IFRS 9 to those receivables that arise from transactions that are accounted for in accordance with IAS 18 *Revenue* and IAS 11 *Construction Contracts*.

Recognition of expected credit losses

General approach

BC5.135　On the basis of the feedback received from respondents on the proposals in the 2013 Impairment Exposure Draft about the usefulness of the information and the responsiveness of the impairment model to changes in credit risk, the IASB decided to finalise the proposed approach. In doing so, the IASB considered that this expected credit loss approach will improve financial reporting because:

(a)　financial statements will clearly distinguish between financial instruments for which credit risk has increased significantly since initial recognition and those for which it has not;

(b)　a loss allowance at an amount equal to at least 12-month expected credit losses will be recognised throughout the life of financial assets, thereby reducing the systematic overstatement of interest revenue in accordance with the requirements in IAS 39, and acting as a proxy for the recognition of initial expected credit losses over time as proposed in the 2009 Impairment Exposure Draft;

(c)　a loss allowance at an amount equal to lifetime expected credit losses will be recognised when credit risk has significantly increased since initial recognition, resulting in the timely recognition of expected credit losses; and

(d)　amounts reported about expected credit losses will better reflect the effective return and the changes in the credit risk on financial instruments compared to the requirements in IAS 39.

Collective and individual assessment of changes in credit risk

BC5.136　It was apparent in responses and comments received on the 2013 Impairment Exposure Draft that some respondents were of the view that the proposals would not require (or even allow) lifetime expected credit losses to be recognised on financial instruments unless there was evidence of significant increases in credit risk at an individual instrument level. The IASB also became aware that some understood the 2013 Impairment Exposure Draft as only requiring lifetime expected credit losses to be recognised when a financial asset became past due.

BC5.137 In considering the feedback received, the IASB confirmed that the objective of the impairment requirements is to capture lifetime expected credit losses on all financial instruments that have significant increases in credit risk, regardless of whether it is on an individual or a collective basis.

BC5.138 Consequently, the IASB considered whether the impairment requirements in Section 5.5 of IFRS 9 should specify whether an entity should evaluate financial instruments individually or collectively when deciding whether it should recognise lifetime expected credit losses. In accordance with IFRS 9, the unit of account is the individual financial instrument. The timeliness of capturing significant increases in credit risk primarily depends on whether the entity has reasonable and supportable information that is available without undue cost or effort to identify significant increases in credit risk in a timely manner before financial assets become past due. However, when credit risk management systems are heavily dependent on past due information, there may be a delay between identifying significant increases in credit risk and when the increase in credit risk has actually occurred.

BC5.139 The IASB observed that any delay is minimised when credit risk management systems capture a comprehensive range of credit risk information that is forward-looking and is updated on a timely basis at the individual instrument level. The delay is more apparent for portfolios of financial instruments that are managed on the basis of past due information.

BC5.140 The IASB noted that in some circumstances the segmentation of portfolios based on shared credit risk characteristics may assist in determining significant increases in credit risk for groups of financial instruments. The IASB considered that individual financial assets could be grouped into segments on the basis of common borrower-specific information and the effect of forward-looking information (ie changes in macroeconomic indicators) that affect the risk of a default occurring could be considered for each segment. As a result, an entity could use the change in that macroeconomic indicator to determine that the credit risk of one or more segments of financial instruments in the portfolio has increased significantly, although it is not yet possible to identify the individual financial instruments for which credit risk has increased significantly. The IASB also noted that in other cases an entity may use reasonable and supportable information to determine that the credit risk of a homogeneous portion of a portfolio should be considered to have increased significantly in order to meet the objective of recognising all significant increases in credit risk.

BC5.141 The IASB noted that measuring expected credit losses on a collective basis approximates the result of using comprehensive credit risk information that incorporates forward-looking information at an individual instrument level. However, financial instruments should not be grouped in order to measure expected credit losses on a collective basis in a way that obscures significant increases in credit risk on individual financial instruments within the group.

BC5.142 The IASB observed that, although an entity may group financial instruments in a portfolio with similar characteristics to identify significant increases in credit risk, ultimately, information will emerge that may enable an entity to distinguish between instruments that are more likely to default from instruments that are not. As the passage of time reduces the uncertainty about the eventual outcome, the risk of a default occurring on the financial instruments in the portfolio should diverge until the financial instruments either default or are collected in full. Consequently, the appropriate level of grouping is expected to change over time in order to capture all significant increases in credit risk. The IASB concluded that an entity should not group financial instruments at a higher level of aggregation if a subgroup exists for which the recognition of lifetime expected credit losses is more appropriate.

Timing of the recognition of lifetime expected credit losses

BC5.143 Some respondents to the 2009 Impairment Exposure Draft and the Supplementary Document believed that the value of a financial asset measured at amortised cost is most faithfully represented by discounting the expected cash flows (ie contractual cash flows reduced for expected credit losses) at the original effective interest rate (ie the effective interest rate that is not reduced for initial expected credit losses). In other words, an entity would be required to recognise a loss allowance for lifetime expected credit losses, discounted using the original effective interest rate, from initial recognition. Those respondents believe that because credit losses do not occur rateably throughout the life of a loan, or throughout the life of a portfolio of loans, there is a fundamental disconnect between the 'lumpy' pattern of actual credit losses and a time-based accounting approach that attempts to link the recognition of credit losses that are anticipated at initial recognition of the financial asset with the recognition of interest revenue.

BC5.144 The IASB considered and rejected this view. At initial recognition, the timing of initial expected credit losses affects the amount of the adjustment to the effective interest rate. Thus, an earlier expected credit loss would give rise to a larger credit adjustment to the effective interest rate than a later expected credit loss of an equal nominal value. Because the pattern of initially expected credit losses is priced into the asset as represented by its present value, compensation is received for the amount and timing of those initially expected credit losses. Thus, in the IASB's view, if initial credit loss expectations do not subsequently change:

(a) interest revenue should reflect the credit-adjusted effective return over time; and

(b) there is no credit loss (or gain), because no economic loss (or gain) has occurred.

BC5.145 Respondents also believe that the evaluation of the creditworthiness that influences pricing is based on historical experience for groups of similar assets. This means that, while the credit spread that is charged on the lender's overall portfolio of individual loans may be expected to compensate the entity for credit losses for a large portfolio of assets over time, the credit spread on any individual asset is not necessarily established in a way that compensates the lender for expected credit losses on that particular asset.

BC5.146 The IASB considered and rejected these views. First, expected credit losses are a probability-weighted estimate of expected cash shortfalls. Thus, the pricing of individual instruments would reflect the probability of credit losses and would be no different to the pricing of an instrument that is part of a portfolio. Market participants price individual instruments consistently, irrespective of whether they will hold that instrument in isolation or as part of a portfolio. Second, it is not necessary to measure separately the initial expected credit losses and the compensation for those credit losses, and then precisely match the amount and timing of those credit losses and the related compensation. An estimate of expected credit losses at initial recognition (which an entity could estimate in a number of different ways) would be sufficient for the purposes of determining the credit adjustment to the effective interest rate. Indeed, any models requiring the recognition of the lifetime expected credit losses at initial recognition would require an entity to make the same estimate.

BC5.147 A few respondents also argued that the amortised cost amount of a financial asset should reflect the present value of the cash flows that are expected to be collected, discounted at the original effective interest rate (ie a rate that is not adjusted for initial expected credit losses). They believe that it is misleading to investors to allow the balance sheet to reflect a greater amount.

BC5.148 The IASB considered and rejected that view. The original effective interest rate is the rate that exactly discounts the expected cash flows (before deducting expected credit losses) of the asset to the transaction price (ie the fair value or principal) at initial recognition. Thus, the original effective interest rate already takes into consideration an entity's initial estimate of expected credit losses (ie it reflects the riskiness of the contractual cash flows). One of the general principles of any present value technique is that the discount rate should reflect assumptions that are consistent with those inherent in the cash flows that are being discounted. Requiring the entity to further deduct an amount from the transaction price that represents the same amount that it has already discounted from the contractual cash flows results in the entity double-counting its initial estimate of expected credit losses. The effect of this would be most apparent at initial recognition, because the carrying amount of the asset would be below the transaction price.

BC5.149 As noted in paragraph BC5.103, the impairment model proposed in the 2013 Impairment Exposure Draft eliminated the operational challenge of having to estimate the full expected (credit-loss adjusted) cash flows for all financial instruments. It did this by limiting the measurement of lifetime expected credit losses to financial instruments for which credit risk has significantly increased since initial recognition. The majority of participants in the outreach conducted by the IASB while developing the proposals in the 2013 Impairment Exposure Draft noted that if financial instruments were to move too quickly to a lifetime expected credit loss measurement (for example, on the basis of minor increases in credit risk) the costs of implementing the model (ie one that would require lifetime expected credit losses to be measured on many financial assets in addition to requiring a distinction to be made on the basis of the extent of the change in the credit risk) might not be justified.

BC5.150 Respondents to the 2013 Impairment Exposure Draft strongly supported the proposal to recognise lifetime expected credit losses only when the credit risk of a financial instrument has increased significantly since initial recognition, because it captures the underlying economics of a transaction while easing operational complexities. They also noted that:

(a) it reflects and provides a clear indication that an economic loss occurred as a result of changes in credit risk from initial expectations.

(b) it avoids excessive front-loading of expected credit losses.

(c) measuring lifetime expected credit losses for financial instruments that have signs of significant increases in credit risk would be operationally simpler because more data is available for these financial instruments.

(d) the proposal would result in recognising lifetime expected credit losses in a timelier and more forward-looking manner compared to IAS 39. Respondents therefore believed that the proposal addresses the concerns of the G20 and others about the delayed recognition of credit losses under an incurred loss approach.

BC5.151 Consequently, in the light of the support and arguments presented, the IASB decided to require an entity to recognise lifetime expected credit losses when the credit risk of a financial instrument has increased significantly since initial recognition.

BC5.152 The IASB received requests to clarify whether a financial instrument for which the interest rate on the instrument has been repriced to reflect an increase in credit risk should continue to have a loss allowance measured at an amount equal to 12-month expected credit losses, even if the increase in credit risk since initial recognition is assessed to be significant. The IASB considered that, conceptually, the loss allowance on such an instrument should continue to be measured at 12-month expected credit losses. This is because the contractual interest rate has been repriced to reflect the entity's expectations about credit losses and is similar to the economic position on initial recognition of a similar financial instrument with a similar credit risk at origination. However, the IASB noted that requiring an entity to assess whether the increase in the interest rate appropriately compensates it for the increase in credit risk would give rise to operational complexity similar to that arising from the 2009 Impairment Exposure Draft. The IASB further noted that the objective of the impairment requirements is to recognise lifetime expected credit losses for financial instruments if there have been significant increases in credit risk since initial recognition.

BC5.153 The IASB also considered that when a financial instrument is repriced to take into account an increase in credit risk, the risk of a default occurring on the financial instrument has increased, implying that the customer is more likely to default than was expected at initial recognition. The fact that the entity is entitled to a higher yield because of the increase in credit risk does not mean that the risk of a default occurring on the financial instrument has not increased. The IASB therefore decided that, on balance, the assessment of whether lifetime expected credit losses should be recognised should be based solely on the increase in the risk of a default occurring since initial recognition.

Determining significant increases in credit risk

Use of changes in the risk of a default occurring

BC5.154   In the 2013 Impairment Exposure Draft, the IASB proposed using the risk of a default occurring on a financial instrument to determine whether there has been an increase in credit risk since initial recognition. The IASB noted that the risk of a default occurring is a measurement of the financial instrument's credit risk that does not require the full estimation of expected credit losses. The 2009 Impairment Exposure Draft required the tracking of the initial expected credit losses and the measurement of all subsequent changes in those expected credit losses. In contrast, the model proposed in the 2013 Impairment Exposure Draft required:

(a)   the tracking of the initial risk of a default occurring (a component of the expected credit losses); and

(b)   an assessment of the significance of subsequent changes in the risk of a default occurring to decide whether the recognition of lifetime expected credit losses is required.

BC5.155   Many respondents to the proposals in the 2013 Impairment Exposure Draft agreed that an assessment of when to recognise lifetime expected credit losses should take into consideration only the changes in credit risk (ie the risk of a default occurring) instead of changes in the amount of expected credit losses. These respondents noted that the risk of a default occurring was considered the most relevant factor in assessing credit risk, and that tracking only the risk of a default occurring makes the model more operational, because that generally aligns with their credit risk management practices.

BC5.156   Respondents to the 2013 Impairment Exposure Draft supported the proposed principle-based approach of assessing significant increases in credit risk instead of prescriptive rules and 'bright lines'. However, some requested clarification about the information that needs to be considered in that assessment. In particular, some thought that the 2013 Impairment Exposure Draft could be interpreted to explicitly require the use of a mechanistic approach to determine the 'probability of default' when assessing significant increases in credit risk. Respondents were concerned that this would require the explicit calculation and storage of the lifetime probability of default curve for a financial instrument to compare the expected remaining lifetime probability of default at inception with the remaining lifetime probability of default at the reporting date.

BC5.157   The IASB noted that it did not intend to prescribe a specific or mechanistic approach to assess changes in credit risk and that the appropriate approach will vary for different levels of sophistication of entities, the financial instrument and the availability of data. The IASB confirmed that the use of the term 'probability of a default' occurring was intended to capture the concept of the risk of a default occurring. A specific probability of default measure is one way in which that could be assessed, but the IASB decided that it would not be appropriate to require particular sources of information to be used to make the assessment. This is because credit analysis is a multifactor and holistic analysis, and when making that analysis entities have differences in the availability of data. Such differences include whether a specific factor is relevant, and its weight compared to other factors which will depend on the type of product, characteristics of the financial instrument and the customer as well as the geographical region. However, to reduce the risk of misinterpretation, the IASB decided to change the terminology from 'probability of a default occurring' to 'risk of a default occurring'.

BC5.158   In the IASB's view, the recognition requirements for lifetime expected credit losses in IFRS 9 strike the best balance between the benefits of making distinctions on the basis of increases in credit risk and the costs and complexity of making that assessment.

Approaches for determining significant increases in credit risk considered and rejected

BC5.159   The IASB considered a number of alternative approaches for determining when to recognise lifetime expected credit losses to make the impairment model in IFRS 9 more operational.

Absolute level of credit risk

BC5.160   The IASB considered whether lifetime expected credit losses should be recognised on the basis of an assessment of the absolute credit risk of a financial instrument at each reporting date. Under this approach, an entity would recognise lifetime expected credit losses on all financial instruments at, or above, a particular credit risk at the reporting date. An approach based on the absolute credit risk at each reporting date would be much simpler to apply, because it does not require tracking of credit risk at initial recognition. However, such an approach would provide very different information. It would not approximate the economic effect of initial credit loss expectations and subsequent changes in expectations. In addition, if the absolute credit risk threshold for recognising lifetime expected credit losses was too high, too many financial instruments would be below the threshold and expected credit losses would be understated. If the absolute threshold was too low, too many financial instruments would be above the threshold, overstating the expected credit losses (for example, financial instruments with a high credit risk that an entity prices appropriately to compensate for the higher credit risk would always have lifetime expected credit losses recognised). Furthermore, depending on which absolute credit risk threshold is selected, such an approach might be similar to the incurred loss model in IAS 39 (in which the absolute threshold is objective evidence of impairment). Consequently, the IASB rejected this approach.

BC5.161 Although the IASB rejected using an absolute level of credit risk for the recognition of lifetime expected credit losses, it noted that the assessment of significant increases in credit risk could be implemented more simply by determining the maximum initial credit risk accepted by the reporting entity for a particular portfolio of financial instruments and then comparing the credit risk of financial instruments in that portfolio at the reporting date to that maximum initial credit risk. However, the IASB noted that this would only be possible for portfolios of financial instruments with similar credit risk at initial recognition. Such an approach would enable a change in credit risk to be the basis for the recognition of lifetime expected credit losses, but does not require specific tracking of the credit risk on an individual financial instrument since initial recognition.

Change in the credit risk management objective

BC5.162 Some interested parties suggested that lifetime expected credit losses should be recognised when an entity's credit risk management objective changes; for example, when contractual cash flows are no longer received consistently with the terms of the contract, the entity changes its credit risk management objective from collecting past due amounts to recovery of the total (or part of the) contractual amount outstanding and the financial assets are being monitored on an individual basis. While recognising lifetime expected credit losses when the credit risk management objective changes would be operationally simpler (ie financial instruments that are being managed differently would be identified immediately, with no need to assess a change in credit risk since initial recognition), the approach would be likely to have a similar effect to the incurred loss model in IAS 39. Because the management of a financial instrument may change only relatively late compared with when significant increases in credit risk occur, the IASB considered this to be a less timely approach to recognising lifetime expected credit losses.

Credit underwriting policies

BC5.163 Some interested parties suggested that lifetime expected credit losses should be recognised when a financial instrument's credit risk at the reporting date is higher than the credit risk at which the entity would originate new loans for that particular class of financial instruments (ie if the level of credit risk exceeded the credit underwriting limit for that class of financial instruments at the reporting date).

BC5.164 The IASB noted a number of disadvantages to this approach. In a similar way to an approach based on the absolute level of credit risk or a change in the credit risk management objective, this approach would not require the change in credit risk since initial recognition to be assessed. It would thus be inconsistent with the IASB's objective of reflecting increases in credit risk and linking that to pricing. The objective of setting credit underwriting limits also follows a different objective compared to that of financial reporting, which could result in a misstatement of expected credit losses. For example, changes in underwriting policies may occur for business reasons, such as wishing to increase lending, resulting in changes to the recognition of expected credit losses on existing financial instruments irrespective of changes in credit risk.

BC5.165   The IASB further noted that the underwriting standards at the time that a financial instrument is initially recognised do not in themselves provide evidence of a significant increase in credit risk. This is because the new financial instruments cannot, by definition, have experienced significant increases in credit risk at initial recognition. Furthermore, the underwriting standards of new financial instruments are not relevant to the credit risk of existing financial instruments. However, the IASB notes that particular vintages may be more prone to increases in credit risk, and thus financial instruments of particular vintages may need to be monitored and assessed with increased vigilance.

Counterparty assessment

BC5.166   Some interested parties suggested that an entity should recognise lifetime expected credit losses on all financial instruments it holds with the same borrower (ie counterparty), if the credit risk of the borrower has reached a specified level at the reporting date (including on newly originated or purchased financial instruments for which the yield appropriately reflects the credit risk at the reporting date). Respondents supporting this approach noted that they manage credit risk on a counterparty level instead of an individual instrument level and that assessing significant increases in credit risk on an instrument level was in their view counterintuitive. This was because different loss allowance measurements could be recognised for similar instruments held with the same counterparty, depending on when the instruments were initially recognised.

BC5.167   The IASB noted that the objective of the impairment requirements is to reflect the economics of lending to provide users of financial statements with relevant information about the performance of financial instruments instead of the performance of a counterparty. A counterparty assessment could misstate expected credit losses if its credit risk had changed; for example, because it would not reflect that a recently recognised financial instrument of a counterparty was priced taking into consideration the current credit risk. Furthermore, like the absolute approach, this approach might be similar to the incurred loss model in IAS 39 in effect, depending on which level of credit risk is selected as the threshold for recognising lifetime expected credit losses. The IASB also noted that not all entities manage credit risk on a counterparty level and that a counterparty assessment of credit risk could produce very different information compared to the information resulting from the impairment model in IFRS 9.

BC5.168   However, the IASB acknowledged that assessing credit risk on a basis that considers a customer's credit risk (ie the risk that a customer will default on its obligations) more holistically may nevertheless be consistent with the impairment requirements. An overall assessment of a counterparty's credit risk could be undertaken, for example, to make an initial assessment of whether credit risk has increased significantly, as long as such an assessment satisfies the requirements for recognising lifetime expected credit losses and the outcome would not be different to the outcome if the financial instruments had been individually assessed.

Extent of increase in credit risk required

BC5.169   The model proposed in the 2013 Impairment Exposure Draft requires an entity to initially account for a portion of expected credit losses. However, the IASB decided that, if an entity suffers a significant economic loss, recognition of only a portion of the lifetime expected credit losses is no longer appropriate and it should recognise the full lifetime expected credit losses. The IASB considered how significant the extent of the increase in credit risk should be, from both an economic and a practical perspective, to justify the recognition of lifetime expected credit losses.

BC5.170   In the IASB's joint deliberations with the FASB, the boards had tentatively agreed that the deterioration criteria for the recognition of lifetime expected credit losses should be that the credit quality had deteriorated more than insignificantly subsequent to the initial recognition of the financial instrument. However, in the IASB's outreach undertaken while developing the model proposed in the 2013 Impairment Exposure Draft, participants expressed concern that this criterion would have the result that even a minor change in the credit quality would satisfy the test. In response to that concern, the 2013 Impairment Exposure Draft proposed that the criterion for the recognition of lifetime expected credit losses is significant increases in credit risk, expressed as an increase in the risk of a default occurring since initial recognition.

BC5.171   During outreach and as part of their responses to the 2013 Impairment Exposure Draft, some interested parties and respondents asked the IASB to specify the amount of change in the risk of a default occurring that would require the recognition of lifetime expected credit losses. Those making this request argued that this would provide clarity and improve comparability. The IASB did not pursue this approach for the following reasons:

(a)   not all entities use an explicit probability of default to measure or assess credit risk—in particular, entities other than regulated financial institutions. The IASB observed that entities manage financial instruments and credit risk in different ways, with different levels of sophistication and by using different information. If the IASB were to propose a precise definition of significant increases in credit risk, for example, a change of 5 per cent in the probability of default, then an entity would need to calculate a probability of default measure to make the assessment. Thus, the costs of assessing changes in credit risk would increase.

(b)   the measure for the risk of a default occurring (ie probability of default) selected would be arbitrary and it would be difficult to properly reflect the structure and pricing of credit that an entity should consider for different types of financial instruments, maturities and initial credit risk. Selecting a single measure could not properly reflect the assessment of credit across entities, products and geographical regions. Because of the arbitrariness of defining the extent of increases in credit risk, the IASB questioned the perceived comparability that would result.

BC5.172 Consequently, the IASB confirmed its view that the requirements for when to recognise lifetime expected credit losses should be clear but also be broadly defined and objective based.

BC5.173 The IASB noted that the assessment of the significance of the change in the risk of a default occurring for different financial instruments would depend on the credit risk at initial recognition and the time to maturity. This is because it would be consistent with the structure of credit risk and therefore with the pricing of financial instruments. In the IASB's view, an entity should consider the term structure and the initial credit risk in assessing whether it should recognise lifetime expected credit losses. Doing so will improve the comparability of the requirements for financial instruments with different maturities and different initial credit risks. For example, all other things being equal, a given increase (in absolute terms) in the risk of a default occurring reflects a greater increase in credit risk the shorter the term of the financial instrument and the lower its initial credit risk. This would also be consistent with the IASB's understanding of existing models for measuring credit risk, such as those underlying external credit ratings, option pricing models and their variants, including the models for measuring the risk of a default occurring for the purposes of prudential regulatory requirements.

BC5.174 If an entity were not required to consider both the initial credit risk and the time until maturity, the assessment would benefit shorter-term financial instruments with low credit risk and would disadvantage longer-term instruments with high credit risk. In addition, not reflecting the term structure might also result in the assessment that the risk of a default occurring has changed merely because of the passage of time. This could happen even if an entity had expected such a change at initial recognition. In the IASB's view, the assessment of the criteria should not change solely because the maturity date is closer.

BC5.175 To assist in the application of the impairment requirements, the IASB decided to provide application guidance, including guidance about the types of information that an entity should consider. The IASB reaffirmed its view that an entity should use the best information that is available without undue cost and effort when measuring expected credit losses.

Use of changes in the risk of a default occurring within the next 12 months

BC5.176 The 2013 Impairment Exposure Draft required the determination of an increase in credit risk to be based on changes in the risk of a default occurring over the life of a financial instrument but noted that a 12-month measure could be used "if the information considered did not suggest that the outcome would differ".

BC5.177 Many respondents to the 2013 Impairment Exposure Draft noted that the assessment of significant increases in credit risk could be made more operational by aligning it with credit risk management practices, including enabling the use of a 12-month instead of lifetime risk of a default occurring when assessing changes in credit risk. Many of these respondents were however concerned that the 2013 Impairment Exposure Draft would require entities to compare the outcome from a 12-month assessment and prove that it would not differ from the outcome of a lifetime assessment.

BC5.178 In response to the feedback, the IASB noted that, ideally, an entity should use changes in the lifetime risk of a default occurring to assess changes in credit risk since initial recognition. However, the IASB observed that changes in the risk of a default occurring within the next 12 months generally should be a reasonable approximation of changes in the risk of a default occurring over the remaining life of a financial instrument and thus would not be inconsistent with the requirements. The IASB also noted that some entities use a 12-month probability of default measure for prudential regulatory requirements. These entities could therefore use their existing systems and methodologies as a starting point for determining significant increases in credit risk, thus reducing the costs of implementation.

BC5.179 However, the IASB noted that there may be circumstances in which the use of the risk of a default occurring within the next 12 months will not be appropriate. For example, this may be the case for financial instruments with a payment profile in which significant payment obligations occur beyond the next 12 months or when there are changes in macroeconomic or other credit-related factors that are not adequately reflected in the risk of a default occurring in the next 12 months. Consequently, an entity may use changes in the risk of a default occurring within the next 12 months unless circumstances indicate that a lifetime assessment is necessary to meet the objective of identifying significant increases in credit risk since initial recognition.

Financial instruments that have low credit risk at the reporting date

BC5.180 The IASB proposed in the 2013 Impairment Exposure Draft that irrespective of the change in credit risk from initial recognition, an entity should not recognise lifetime expected credit losses on financial instruments with low credit risk at the reporting date. The IASB proposed this to reduce the operational costs and to make the model more cost-effective. The IASB observed that for financial instruments with low credit risk, the effect of this simplification on the timing of recognition, and the amount of expected credit losses would be minimal. This would be the case even if the recognition of lifetime expected credit losses occurred later than it otherwise would have if there had been no simplification. In the IASB's view, this would help to achieve an appropriate balance between the benefits of distinguishing between financial instruments on the basis of changes in credit risk and the costs of making that distinction. The IASB also noted that financial instruments of such a quality were not the primary focus for the recognition of lifetime expected credit losses.

BC5.181　The 2013 Impairment Exposure Draft proposed that the credit risk on a financial instrument should be considered low if the financial instrument has a low risk of default, and the borrower has a strong capacity to meet its contractual cash flow obligations in the near term. The 2013 Impairment Exposure Draft noted that this is the case even if adverse changes in economic and business conditions in the longer term may, but will not necessarily, reduce the ability to fully recover cash flows in the long term. It was noted that such credit risk is typically equivalent to the investment grade market convention, ie an entity need not assess the extent of the increase in credit risk since initial recognition for financial instruments with credit risk that is equivalent to investment grade.

BC5.182　Respondents to the 2013 Impairment Exposure Draft had mixed views on the inclusion of the low credit risk simplification. Most respondents supported a simplification based on low credit risk and noted that it reduces the costs of implementation and avoids recognising lifetime expected credit losses inappropriately. However, a number of clarifications were suggested regarding the meaning of low credit risk and its application. Some noted that the low credit risk simplification could paradoxically increase operational complexity because, in addition to assessing the change in credit risk, the absolute credit risk at the reporting date would need to be assessed.

BC5.183　In response, the IASB noted that the intention was to reduce operational complexity and therefore decided to retain the low credit risk simplification but to *allow* instead of *require* this to be used. This would allow entities to better align the assessment of increases in credit risk for the purpose of IFRS 9 with their internal credit risk systems.

BC5.184　The IASB considered whether to allow reporting entities to have an accounting policy choice on whether to apply the requirement to assess whether a financial instrument is considered to have low credit risk at the reporting date. It noted that the intention of the low credit risk concept was to provide relief from tracking changes in the credit risk of high quality financial instruments and that requiring an entity to apply it as an accounting policy choice for a class of financial instrument would be inconsistent with this intention. The assessment of low credit risk can therefore be made on an instrument-by-instrument basis.

BC5.185　Some respondents were confused about the role of the low credit risk simplification. For example, some were concerned that as soon as a financial instrument was no longer low credit risk, lifetime expected credit losses would be required to be recognised irrespective of the initial credit risk on the financial instrument.

BC5.186　The IASB therefore clarified that:

(a)　the objective of the low credit risk simplification is to provide operational relief for high quality financial instruments, in other words, those with a low risk of default.

(b)   an increase in credit risk that results in a financial instrument no longer being considered to have low credit risk at the reporting date is not an automatic trigger for the recognition of lifetime expected credit losses. Instead, if a financial instrument is not low credit risk at the reporting date, an entity should assess the extent of the increase in credit risk and recognise lifetime expected credit losses only when the increase since initial recognition is significant in accordance with the usual requirements.

BC5.187   Respondents also raised questions about the ambiguity of using 'investment grade' as an example of low credit risk. Respondents were concerned that only financial instruments that are externally rated by a credit rating agency as investment grade would be considered to have low credit risk. They also questioned whether the reference to investment grade referred to global or national rating scales.

BC5.188   The IASB noted that:

(a)   financial instruments are not required to be externally rated to meet the low credit risk requirements. Instead, the reference to investment grade serves only as an example of a financial instrument that may be considered to have low credit risk. The credit risk can be determined using alternative measures, such as internal rating grades based on commonly understood notions of credit risk.

(b)   its intention was to use a globally comparable notion of low credit risk instead of a level of risk determined, for example, by an entity or jurisdiction's view of risk based on entity-specific or jurisdictional factors.

(c)   ratings should consider or be adjusted to take into consideration the specific risks of the financial instruments being assessed.

BC5.189   Consequently, the IASB confirmed that low credit risk refers to a level of credit risk that is akin to a globally accepted definition of low credit risk. Credit risk ratings and methodologies that are consistent with these requirements and that consider the risks and the type of financial instruments that are being assessed may be used to apply the requirements in paragraph 5.5.10 of IFRS 9.

More than 30 days past due rebuttable presumption

BC5.190   In the 2013 Impairment Exposure Draft, the IASB proposed that an entity may consider information about delinquency or past due status, together with other, more forward-looking information, in its assessment of the increases in credit risk since initial recognition, if appropriate. To supplement the requirement to determine the extent of increases in credit risk since initial recognition, and to ensure that its application does not revert to an incurred loss notion, the IASB proposed a rebuttable presumption that the credit risk on a financial instrument has increased significantly, and that lifetime expected credit losses shall be recognised, when a financial asset is more than 30 days past due.

BC5.191   The majority of respondents to the 2013 Impairment Exposure Draft considered that the rebuttable presumption results in an appropriate balance between identifying significant increases in credit risk and the cost of tracking and assessing those increases in credit risk. Respondents noted that the outcome is broadly in line with existing credit risk management practices (ie looking at past due information). Field test participants observed that there was generally a correlation between financial instruments that are more than 30 days past due and significant increases in the 12-month probability of default. However, some respondents did not support having a past due measure as an indication of when there has been a significant increase in credit risk. They believe that a past due measure creates a bright line for the recognition of lifetime expected credit losses and, because past due status is a lagging indicator of increases in credit risk, it will fail to identify significant increases in credit risk on a timely basis.

BC5.192   In response, the IASB confirmed that, consistent with the forward-looking nature of expected credit losses, an entity should use forward-looking information, such as the price for credit risk, probabilities of default and internal or external credit ratings, to update the measurement of expected credit losses and when assessing whether to recognise lifetime expected credit losses. However, the IASB acknowledged the feedback that supported the view that many entities manage credit risk on the basis of information about past due status and have a limited ability to assess credit risk on an instrument-by-instrument basis in more detail on a timely basis.

BC5.193   The IASB therefore decided to retain the rebuttable presumption, but also wanted to ensure that this did not contribute to the delayed recognition of lifetime expected credit losses. The IASB clarified that the objective of the rebuttable presumption in paragraph 5.5.11 of IFRS 9 is not to be an absolute indicator of when lifetime expected credit losses should be recognised, but serves as a backstop for when there has been a significant increase in credit risk. The IASB noted that the application of the rebuttable presumption should identify significant increases in credit risk before financial assets become credit-impaired or an actual default occurs. The IASB also noted that, ideally, significant increases in credit risk should be identified before financial assets become past due.

BC5.194   The IASB decided to confirm the ability of an entity to rebut the presumption if the entity has reasonable and supportable information to support a more lagging past due measure. The IASB acknowledged that 30 days past due might not be an appropriate indicator for all types of products or jurisdictions. However, it noted that to be able to rebut the presumption, an entity would need reasonable and supportable information that indicates that the credit risk has not increased significantly. Furthermore, an entity is not required to rebut the presumption on an instrument-by-instrument basis but can rebut it if the entity has information that indicates that, for a particular product, region or customer type, more than 30 days past due is not representative of the point at which credit risk increases significantly. The IASB noted that if significant increases in credit risk were identified before a financial asset(s) was 30 days past due, the presumption does not need to be rebutted.

Recognition of 12-month expected credit losses

BC5.195 During the development of the 2013 Impairment Exposure Draft, the IASB considered what measure of expected credit losses would be both appropriate and cost-effective for financial instruments before significant increases in credit risk have occurred. The IASB accepted the concerns of interested parties about the operational complexity of the methods proposed in the 2009 Impairment Exposure Draft and the Supplementary Document. The IASB also accepted that significant judgement would be required for any estimation technique that an entity might use. Consequently, the IASB decided that an entity should measure the loss allowance at an amount equal to 12-month expected credit losses. In the IASB's view, the overall result of such a measurement, combined with the earlier recognition of the full lifetime expected credit losses compared to IAS 39, achieves an appropriate balance between the benefits of a faithful representation of expected credit losses and the operational costs and complexity. The IASB acknowledged that this is an operational simplification, and that cost-benefit is the only conceptual justification for the 12-month time horizon.

BC5.196 The majority of respondents to the 2013 Impairment Exposure Draft supported the IASB's reasoning, noting that the recognition of 12-month expected credit losses is a pragmatic solution to achieve an appropriate balance between faithfully representing the underlying economics of a transaction and the cost of implementation. Furthermore, it would allow preparers to make use of existing reporting systems that some regulated financial institutions already apply and would therefore be less costly to implement for those entities. In addition, users of financial statements considered 12 months a reliable period to estimate expected credit losses for financial instruments that have not significantly increased in credit risk.

BC5.197 However, some respondents proposed alternative measures for the loss allowance on financial instruments for which there were no significant increases in credit risk since initial recognition. These alternatives and the IASB's reasons for rejecting them are discussed in paragraphs BC5.200–BC5.209.

BC5.198 In finalising the Standard, the IASB acknowledged that the recognition of 12-month expected credit losses would result in an overstatement of expected credit losses for financial instruments, and a resulting understatement of the value of any related financial asset, immediately after initial recognition of those financial instruments. In particular, the initial carrying amount of financial assets would be below their fair value. However, isolating initial credit loss expectations for recognition over the life of financial instruments is operationally complex. Furthermore, this measurement of expected credit losses serves as a practical approximation of the adjustment of the effective interest rate for credit risk as required by the 2009 Impairment Exposure Draft. The recognition of a portion of expected credit losses for financial instruments for which there have not been significant increases in credit risk also limits the requirement to perform the more costly and complex calculation of the lifetime expected credit losses. In addition, in the IASB's view, measuring 12-month expected credit losses for some financial instruments would be less costly than always calculating the lifetime expected credit losses as proposed in the Supplementary Document.

BC5.199 The IASB decided to retain the recognition of 12-month expected credit losses for the measurement and allocation of initial expected credit losses, which was necessary as a result of the decision to decouple the measurement and allocation of initial expected credit losses from the determination of the effective interest rate as proposed in the 2009 Impairment Exposure Draft. The IASB considered such a measure of expected credit losses to be superior to the alternatives discussed below.

Approaches to recognition of 12-month expected credit losses considered and rejected

No allowance for instruments without a significant increase in credit risk

BC5.200 Some respondents did not agree with recognising any expected credit loss allowance for financial instruments that have not experienced significant increases in credit risk since initial recognition. These respondents considered initial expectations of credit losses to be included in the pricing of a financial instrument and they were conceptually opposed to the recognition of a loss allowance on initial recognition.

BC5.201 The IASB acknowledged that not recognising an allowance balance for financial instruments for which credit risk has not increased significantly would be consistent with the requirement in paragraph 5.1.1 of IFRS 9 that a financial asset should be recognised at fair value on initial recognition. However, only recognising lifetime expected credit losses when there have been significant increases in credit risk, without recognising any expected credit losses before that to reflect the changes in initial expectations of credit risk since initial recognition, would fail to appropriately reflect the economic losses experienced as a result of those (non-significant) changes. Expected credit losses are implicit in the initial pricing for the instrument, but subsequent changes in those expectations represent economic losses (or gains) in the period in which they occur. Not reflecting changes in credit risk before the change is considered significant would therefore fail to recognise those economic losses (or gains).

BC5.202 The IASB noted that not recognising any expected credit losses before there have been significant increases in credit risk would not be consistent with preserving, to as great an extent as possible, the objective of the 2009 Impairment Exposure Draft (see paragraphs BC5.87–B5.88). In the view of the IASB, this approach would fail to appropriately reflect the economic effects of over-recognition of interest revenue prior to losses being recognised and would also fail to recognise economic losses experienced as a result of non-significant changes in credit risk or significant increases not yet identified.

Recognise a portion of lifetime expected credit losses larger than 12-month expected credit losses

BC5.203 The IASB considered whether an entity should recognise a portion of lifetime expected credit losses that is greater than 12-month expected credit losses before there are significant increases in credit risk. However, it rejected requiring a larger portion of expected credit losses to be recognised because:

(a) as noted in paragraph BC5.198, the IASB acknowledges that the 12-month measure is a practical concession that initially overstates expected credit losses before there are significant increases in credit risk. Recognising a greater portion would further increase the overstatement of expected credit losses and, thus, when considered with the much earlier timing of the recognition of lifetime expected credit losses, would be a less faithful representation of the underlying economics.

(b) 12-month expected credit losses would allow preparers to make use of existing reporting systems that some regulated financial institutions already apply and would therefore be less costly to implement for those entities.

Recognise expected credit losses for the loss emergence period

BC5.204 This alternative would require entities to consider all reasonable and supportable information available, including historical information, in order to determine the average period of time over which meaningful increases in credit risk are expected to occur.

BC5.205 The IASB acknowledged that different asset classes have different loss patterns and different loss emergence periods. Consequently, estimating expected credit losses over the relevant period of time it takes for an event to happen and for the effects to be known, may have conceptual merit. However, the IASB noted that 'emergence' notions fit more naturally in an incurred loss model in which it is difficult to identify when a loss has been incurred on individual instruments.

BC5.206 The IASB also noted that emergence periods may change over the life of financial instruments and depend on the economic cycle. As a result, the IASB considered that this approach would be more operationally difficult than one that has a defined period, because an entity would have to continually assess that it was using the appropriate emergence period.

Recognise expected credit losses for the foreseeable future

BC5.207 The Supplementary Document proposed that the loss allowance for financial assets in the good book should be calculated as the greater of the time-proportionate amount and expected credit losses for the foreseeable future (see paragraphs BC5.96–BC5.101).

BC5.208 The feedback received about the foreseeable future floor for the good book was geographically split, with respondents outside the US generally opposing it. Furthermore, respondents expressed concerns about the calculation of expected credit losses for the foreseeable future, with many expressing confusion about the underlying conceptual basis for such a limitation to the time period. Many also noted that, despite the conceptual concerns, the term 'foreseeable future' was not sufficiently defined to ensure consistent application.

BC5.209 In response to the concerns raised about the foreseeable future, the IASB rejected the approach. To address these concerns about the ambiguity of the foreseeable future definition in the Supplementary Document, the IASB decided to define the measurement objective for financial instruments for which credit risk has not increased significantly as 12-month expected credit losses. The IASB did not receive any new information that caused it to change its view.

Symmetry

BC5.210 The IASB's view is that an entity should recognise favourable changes in credit risk consistently with unfavourable changes in credit risk (ie the model should be 'symmetrical'), but only to the extent that those favourable changes represent a reversal of risk that was previously recognised as unfavourable changes. In accordance with the general model, if the credit risk on financial instruments, for which lifetime expected credit losses have been recognised, subsequently improves so that the requirement for recognising lifetime expected credit losses is no longer met, the loss allowance should be measured at an amount equal to 12-month expected credit losses with a resulting gain recognised in profit or loss. Doing so would reflect the fact that the expectations of credit losses have moved back towards the initial expectations. For purchased or originated credit-impaired financial assets (to which the general model does not apply (see paragraph BC5.214–BC5.220), an entity would recognise a gain if credit risk improves after initial recognition, reflecting an increase in the expected cash flows.

BC5.211 To address concerns about potential earnings management, the IASB considered requiring a change back to a loss allowance measured at an amount equal to 12-month expected credit losses to be based on stricter criteria than is required for the recognition of lifetime expected credit losses. The IASB rejected such a requirement because it reduces the usefulness, neutrality and faithful representation of expected credit losses, and anti-abuse considerations should not override that. The IASB also noted that such arbitrary distinctions can have unintended consequences, such as creating a disincentive to recognise lifetime expected credit losses, because of the higher hurdle to change back to the recognition of 12-month expected credit losses.

BC5.212 As a result of this, the 2013 Impairment Exposure Draft proposed that the model should be symmetrical with lifetime expected credit losses being recognised, and ceasing to be recognised, depending on whether the credit risk at the reporting date has increased significantly since initial recognition. Nearly all respondents to the 2013 Impairment Exposure Draft agreed that the approach should be symmetrical. In doing so, they noted that this would be consistent with the objective of a model based on changes in credit risk and would faithfully represent the underlying economics.

BC5.213 Consequently, the IASB confirmed its reasoning in the 2013 Impairment Exposure Draft and confirmed that a loss allowance measured at an amount equal to 12-month expected credit losses shall be re-established for financial instruments for which the criteria for the recognition of lifetime expected credit losses are no longer met.

Purchased or originated credit-impaired financial assets

BC5.214 The 2013 Impairment Exposure Draft proposed to carry forward the scope and requirements in paragraph AG5 of IAS 39. That paragraph required an entity to include the initial expected credit losses in the estimated cash flows when calculating the effective interest rate for financial assets that are credit-impaired on initial recognition. In addition, it was proposed that an entity calculate interest revenue from financial assets subject to this measurement requirement by applying the credit-adjusted effective interest rate to the amortised cost of the financial asset (adjusted for any loss allowance).

BC5.215 Some users of financial statements expressed a preference for a single impairment model for all financial assets to ensure comparability. However, in the IASB's view, applying the general approach to purchased or originated credit-impaired financial assets would not achieve the desired comparability. This is because, in the IASB's view, the model proposed in the 2009 Impairment Exposure Draft more faithfully represents the underlying economics for these financial assets than the general approach proposed in the 2013 Impairment Exposure Draft, and the benefits of this better representation outweigh the costs for these financial assets.

BC5.216 The IASB noted that, while the scope of the requirements for financial assets that are credit-impaired at initial recognition usually relates to purchased financial assets, in unusual circumstances financial assets could be originated that would be within this scope. However, this does not mean that all financial assets originated at a high credit risk are within the scope—the financial assets have to be credit-impaired on initial recognition. In confirming that a financial asset could be credit-impaired on origination the IASB focussed on the potential for the modification of contractual cash flows to result in derecognition. The IASB considered an example in which a substantial modification of a distressed asset resulted in derecognition of the original financial asset. Such a case is an example of the rare situation in which a newly originated financial asset may be credit-impaired—it would be possible for the modification to constitute objective evidence that the new asset is credit-impaired at initial recognition.

BC5.217 Consistent with the 2009 Impairment Exposure Draft, for these financial assets, the 2013 Impairment Exposure Draft considered the initial credit loss expectations to be part of the effective interest rate and thus interest revenue will represent the effective yield on the asset. An entity will recognise changes in the initial expected credit losses as gains or losses. Paragraph BC5.89 sets out the operational challenges that would have arisen if the 2009 Impairment Exposure Draft had applied to all financial assets. However, in developing the proposals in the 2013 Impairment Exposure Draft, the IASB observed that this requirement in IAS 39 has not presented issues in practice and proposed to retain it, and to use a scope that is based on IAS 39 to minimise the operational challenges for preparers.

BC5.218 Respondents to the 2013 Impairment Exposure Draft almost unanimously supported the proposals for purchased or originated credit-impaired financial assets. These respondents noted that the proposals were the conceptually correct outcome, similar to the 2009 Impairment Exposure Draft, and appropriately reflect the economics of the transaction and management's objective when acquiring or originating such assets. Respondents additionally noted that the proposals were operable because they are consistent with the existing accounting treatment in accordance with IAS 39.

BC5.219 However, some respondents preferred a gross-up approach, whereby an allowance is recognised for initial expected credit losses and is used to gross-up the carrying amount of the purchased or originated credit-impaired financial asset. These respondents considered that it would be operationally simpler to have a gross presentation of expected credit losses for all financial assets, and comparability would be improved if there was an allowance balance for purchased or originated credit-impaired financial assets like there is for other financial assets.

BC5.220 The IASB noted in response that even if the loss allowance balance was calculated for purchased or originated credit-impaired financial assets at initial recognition, the carrying amounts would not be comparable. Purchased or originated credit-impaired assets are initially recognised at fair value and would be grossed-up for the loss allowance balance, resulting in a carrying amount above fair value. In contrast, other assets within the scope of IFRS 9 are carried net of the loss allowance, and so would be grossed-up to fair value. The IASB therefore rejected these arguments. Consequently, the IASB decided to confirm the proposals in the 2013 Impairment Exposure Draft.

Simplified approach for trade receivables, contract assets and lease receivables

BC5.221 The 2013 Impairment Exposure Draft proposed that trade receivables that do not have a significant financing component in accordance with IFRS 15 should be accounted for as follows:

(a) an entity would be required to measure the trade receivable at initial recognition at the transaction price as defined in IFRS 15 (ie the invoiced amount in many cases); and

(b) an entity would be required to recognise a loss allowance for lifetime expected credit losses on those trade receivables throughout their life.

BC5.222 Most respondents to the 2013 Impairment Exposure Draft supported the approach proposed for trade receivables without a significant financing component. Respondents noted that most trade receivables without a significant financing component would have a maturity that is less than one year, so the lifetime expected credit losses and the 12-month expected credit losses would be the same, or very similar. In addition, respondents supported the recognition of these trade receivables at transaction price, because it aligns the requirements in IFRS 9 with revenue recognition requirements and results in the amortised cost of these receivables at initial recognition being closer to fair value.

BC5.223 Respondents indicated that they would not have significant operational difficulty in applying an impairment model based on expected credit losses to their trade receivables without a significant financing component. While these participants acknowledge that such an impairment model would require a change in practice, they believe that they can incorporate forward-looking information within their current methodologies. In addition, the outreach participants noted that the IASB had made the application of the impairment model to current trade receivables (ie those that are not past due) more operational without the loss of useful information.

BC5.224 The IASB therefore decided to retain the proposed approach for trade receivables without a significant financing component.

BC5.225 In the 2013 Impairment Exposure Draft, the IASB noted that, in its view, a provision matrix can be an acceptable method to measure expected credit losses for trade receivables in accordance with the objectives for the measurement of expected credit losses in IFRS 9. An entity would adjust historical provision rates, which are an average of historical outcomes, to reflect relevant information about current conditions as well as reasonable and supportable forecasts and their implications for expected credit losses, including the time value of money. Such a technique would be consistent with the measurement objective of expected credit losses as set out in IFRS 9. The 2013 Impairment Exposure Draft therefore proposed that entities would have a choice of an accounting policy both for trade receivables that have a significant financing component in accordance with IFRS 15 and separately for lease receivables in accordance with IAS 17. Those accounting policy choices would allow entities to decide between fully applying the proposed model or recognising a loss allowance for lifetime expected credit losses from initial recognition until derecognition (the simplified approach). The IASB noted that allowing this option for trade receivables and lease receivables would reduce comparability. However, the IASB believed it would alleviate some of the practical concerns of tracking changes in credit risk for entities that do not have sophisticated credit risk management systems.

BC5.226 The IASB noted that feedback on the 2013 Impairment Exposure Draft indicated that many respondents agreed that the operational relief was of greater weight than concerns about comparability, and supported the simplified approach as an accounting policy choice. In addition, the IASB noted that removing the accounting policy choice would require either removing the simplified approach or making it mandatory, neither of which the IASB considered appropriate. In the IASB's view, the benefits of achieving comparability do not outweigh the costs to implement the full model in this case. The IASB therefore decided to confirm these proposals in IFRS 9. As noted in paragraph BC5.134, the IASB decided that the impairment requirements in IFRS 9 should also apply to contract assets that are recognised and measured in accordance with IFRS 15. Because the nature of contract assets and the exposure to credit risk is similar to trade receivables, the IASB decided that an entity should have the same accounting policy choice as for trade receivables with a significant financing component and for lease receivables.

Modifications of contractual cash flows

BC5.227 Some modifications of contractual cash flows result in the derecognition of a financial instrument and the recognition of a new financial instrument in accordance with IFRS 9. However, modifications frequently do not result in the derecognition of a financial instrument. The IASB considered how the proposed model will apply to these financial instruments with modified contractual cash flows.

BC5.228 In the 2013 Impairment Exposure Draft the IASB proposed that, when an entity is assessing whether it should recognise a loss allowance at an amount equal to 12-month expected credit losses or lifetime expected credit losses, it should compare the credit risk of the modified financial instrument at the reporting date to the credit risk of the (unmodified) financial instrument at initial recognition when the modification has not resulted in derecognition. The simplification for financial instruments with low credit risk would also apply to modified financial instruments.

BC5.229 This decision reflected the fact that financial instruments that are modified but not derecognised are not new financial instruments from an accounting perspective and, as a result, the amortised cost measurement would keep the same original effective interest rate. Consequently, the impairment model should apply as it does for other financial instruments, reflecting the changes in credit risk since initial recognition.

BC5.230 The IASB further noted that when the modification of a financial asset results in the derecognition of the asset and the subsequent recognition of the modified financial asset, the modified asset is considered a 'new' asset from an accounting perspective. The IASB observed that entities should consider whether a modified financial asset is originated credit-impaired at initial recognition (see paragraphs BC5.214–BC5.220). If not, subsequent recognition of a loss allowance would be determined in accordance with the requirements in Section 5.5 of IFRS 9.

BC5.231 The IASB also proposed in the 2013 Impairment Exposure Draft that the modification requirements should apply to all modifications or renegotiations of the contractual cash flows of financial instruments. Although most respondents supported the proposals, some noted that they would have preferred that the requirements be limited to modifications of credit-impaired assets or modifications undertaken for credit risk management purposes. These respondents believed that the proposed requirements do not represent the economics of modifications performed for commercial or other reasons that are unrelated to credit risk management.

BC5.232 However, the IASB has previously considered the difficulty of identifying the reason for modifications and renegotiations. Before May 2010, IFRS 7 required the disclosure of the carrying amount of financial assets that would otherwise be past due or credit-impaired but whose terms have been renegotiated. The

IASB received feedback from constituents that it is operationally difficult to determine the purpose of modifications (ie whether they are performed for commercial or credit risk management reasons). The IASB noted in paragraph BC54A of IFRS 7 the difficulty in identifying financial assets whose terms have been renegotiated for reasons other than credit reasons, especially when commercial terms of loans are often renegotiated regularly for reasons that are not related to impairment. This led the IASB to remove this requirement from IFRS 7.

BC5.233 The IASB further noted that these requirements were consistent with the previous requirements in paragraph AG8 of IAS 39, which did not differentiate between modifications based on the reason for the modification. Paragraph AG8 applied to all revisions of estimates of payments or receipts. This is because amortised cost is a measurement method whereby the carrying amount equates to the present value of the estimated future cash payments or receipts discounted at the effective interest rate. Consequently, the amortised cost amount should be updated in all cases in which those cash flows are modified (or expectations change other than in respect of impairment changes).[41]

BC5.234 The IASB also noted that even if the intention of a modification could be clearly identified to be for commercial purposes, any change in the contractual terms of a financial instrument will have a consequential effect on the credit risk of the financial instrument since initial recognition and will affect the measurement of the loss allowance. Furthermore, the difficulty involved in discerning the purpose of modifications, and to what extent a modification is related to credit risk reasons, could create opportunities for manipulation. This could happen if entities were able to select a 'preferred' treatment for modifications simply because of the purpose of the modification. Limiting the scope of the modification requirements in Section 5.5 of IFRS 9 to those undertaken for credit reasons could therefore result in different accounting treatments for the same economic event.

BC5.235 Consequently, the IASB decided to confirm the proposals in the 2013 Impairment Exposure Draft that the modification requirements should apply to all modifications or renegotiations of the contractual terms of financial instruments.

Assessment of significant increases in credit risk

BC5.236 The IASB considered whether an entity should assess the increase in credit risk by comparing it to the credit risk at the point of modification. However, the IASB noted that if the original financial instrument has not been derecognised, the modified financial instrument is not a new financial instrument. The IASB also noted that by using such an approach the financial instrument would, by definition, not have experienced an increase in credit risk that is more than insignificant since modification. As a result, if the IASB

---

41 In 2017 the IASB discussed the accounting for a modification or exchange of a financial liability measured at amortised cost that does not result in derecognition of the financial liability. See paragraphs BC4.252–BC4.253.

took this approach, an entity would recognise 12-month expected credit losses for every modified financial instrument at the point of modification.

BC5.237 Thus, the IASB decided that an entity should compare the credit risk at the reporting date with the credit risk as at initial recognition of the unmodified financial instrument in a manner that is consistent with that applied to all other financial instruments. An entity should base the risk of default occurring after a modification on the ability to meet the modified contractual cash flows. This should include an assessment of historical and forward-looking information and an assessment of the credit risk over the remaining life of the instrument, which should include the circumstances that led to the modification. Consequently, the credit risk on a financial asset will not necessarily decrease merely because of a modification.

Symmetry

BC5.238 The IASB observed that it is not unusual for distressed financial instruments to be modified more than once and, therefore, the assessment of whether lifetime expected credit losses should continue to be recognised after modification may be perceived to be based on projections that are optimistic. The IASB considered prohibiting modified financial instruments that continue to be recognised reverting to a loss allowance at an amount equal to 12-month expected credit losses or alternatively proposing more restrictive criteria than usual before allowing 12-month expected credit losses to be re-established.

BC5.239 The IASB concluded that the expected credit loss requirements should allow the loss allowance on such modified financial instruments to revert to being measured at an amount equal to 12-month expected credit losses when they no longer meet the requirements for the recognition of lifetime expected credit losses, consistent with the treatment of unmodified financial instruments. In the IASB's view, this faithfully represents the economics of the transaction and it should not override that faithful representation for anti-abuse purposes. In addition, the IASB observed that entities also modify financial instruments for reasons other than increases in credit risk and, therefore, it would be difficult from an operational standpoint to prescribe asymmetrical guidance only for financial assets that have been modified because of credit risk factors (see paragraphs BC5.227–BC5.235).

Adjustment of gross carrying amount

BC5.240 As explained in more detail in paragraphs BC5.102–BC5.108, IFRS 9 requires a decoupled approach to interest revenue and recognition of expected credit losses for financial assets. In accordance with a decoupled approach, an entity would calculate the interest revenue by multiplying the effective interest rate by the gross carrying amount (ie the amount that does not include an adjustment for the loss allowance). As a result, not adjusting the carrying amount upon a modification would result in inflating interest revenue and the loss allowance.

BC5.241 Consequently, the IASB decided that an entity should adjust the gross carrying amount of a financial asset if it modifies the contractual cash flows and recognise modification gains or losses in profit or loss. For example, if credit losses are crystallised by a modification, an entity should recognise a reduction in the gross carrying amount. There may be situations in which adjusting the gross carrying amount result in the recognition of a gain. Except for purchased or originated credit-impaired financial assets, the new gross carrying amount will represent the future contractual cash flows discounted at the original effective interest rate.

Measurement of expected credit losses

BC5.242 The 2013 Impairment Exposure Draft and 2009 Impairment Exposure Draft proposed to define expected credit losses as the expected present value of all cash shortfalls over the remaining life of the financial instrument. The IASB decided to retain the emphasis on the objective of the measurement of expected credit losses, and to keep the requirements principle-based instead of specifying techniques to measure expected credit losses. Respondents have commented that adopting such a principle-based approach would help reduce complexity and mitigate operational challenges by allowing an entity to use techniques that work best in its specific circumstances.

Loan commitments and financial guarantee contracts

BC5.243 The 2013 Impairment Exposure Draft proposed that an entity should recognise expected credit losses that result from loan commitments and financial guarantee contracts when there is a present contractual obligation to extend credit. The IASB believe that expected credit losses of obligations to extend credit (off balance sheet exposures) are similar to those of loans and other on balance sheet exposures. The only difference is that, in the latter case, the borrower has already drawn down the loan whereas in the former case it has not. The recognition of a liability for expected credit losses was limited to loan commitments and financial guarantee contracts with a present contractual obligation to extend credit. Without a present contractual obligation to extend credit, an entity may withdraw its loan commitment before it extends credit. Consequently, the IASB concluded that a liability does not exist for loan commitments or financial guarantee contracts when there is no present contractual obligation to extend credit.

BC5.244 The 2013 Impairment Exposure Draft proposed that the impairment requirements should apply to these financial instruments in the same way as for other financial instruments, including the assessment of the increase in credit risk to decide whether it should recognise 12-month or lifetime expected credit losses. When measuring expected credit losses of loan commitments and financial guarantee contracts, additional uncertainty arises in respect of one of the input factors: the exposure at default. To measure the exposure at default of the loan commitments, the issuer needs to estimate the amount that a borrower will have drawn down at the time of default. That is, the issuer needs to estimate the part of the undrawn facility that the borrower will convert into a funded amount, typically referred to as a credit conversion factor or a utilisation rate. Some financial institutions are required to make similar assessments for regulatory capital purposes.

BC5.245　Respondents to the Supplementary Document, and participants in the IASB's outreach that preceded the publication of the 2013 Impairment Exposure Draft, noted that estimating future drawdowns over the lifetime of the financial instrument will introduce additional complexities. These additional complexities arise because of the uncertainty involved in estimating the behaviour of customers over a longer period. Interested parties were concerned that the requirements would hold entities to a standard of accuracy that they would not be able to meet.

BC5.246　The IASB considered and rejected the following alternatives that were suggested for measuring future drawdowns:

(a)　limiting the estimate of future drawdowns to the next 12 months. While it would be less complex to use an estimate over a 12-month time period, such a limit would be arbitrary and inconsistent with estimating lifetime expected credit losses.

(b)　estimating future drawdowns based only on historical information. While it would be less complex to limit the estimate to historical information, it would be inconsistent with the objective of an impairment model based on expected credit losses. Historical utilisation rates might be a good indicator for future drawdowns, but an entity would also need to consider the need to make adjustments for current and future expectations when estimating expected credit losses.

(c)　using the credit conversion factor provided by prudential regulators. Regulators typically provide credit conversion factors over a 12-month period. Generally, they are not forward-looking, and are specific to product types or particular to the entity. Similarly as for the issues mentioned in (a)–(b), applying such a standardised parameter when estimating expected credit losses is inconsistent with the general approach. It also would also not address the issue for entities that are not subject to such regulations.

BC5.247　The IASB acknowledged the complexity involved in estimating future drawdowns over the life of financial instruments. Nevertheless, this estimate is necessary to have a consistent application of the impairment model. The IASB considered that not having it would defeat the purpose of removing the inconsistency between on balance sheet and off balance sheet exposures. Consequently, the IASB decided that for financial instruments that include both a loan and an undrawn commitment component and the entity's contractual ability to demand repayment and cancel the undrawn commitment does not limit the entity's exposure to credit losses to the contractual notice period, an entity shall estimate the usage behaviour over the period that the entity is exposed to credit risk and expected credit losses would not be mitigated by credit risk management actions, even if that period extends beyond the maximum contractual period (see paragraphs BC5.254–BC5.261).

Definition of default

BC5.248 The 2013 Impairment Exposure Draft did not define default. Instead, it proposed allowing entities to use different definitions of default including, when applicable, regulatory definitions of default. In making this decision, the IASB observed that expected credit losses are not expected to change as a result of differences in the definition of default that was applied, because of the counterbalancing interaction between the way an entity defines default and the credit losses that arise as a result of that definition of default.

BC5.249 Although the 2013 Impairment Exposure Draft did not ask a specific question on the definition of default, some respondents commented on the topic and most of those respondents recommended that default should be clearly described or defined. Those respondents noted that the notion of default is fundamental to the application of the model, particularly because it affects the population that is subject to the 12-month expected credit loss measure. Some of those respondents considered the term 'default event' to be ambiguous, and were unclear whether the notion of default should align more closely with indicators about significant increases in credit risk or with the indicators for credit-impaired financial assets. Those respondents also expressed concern that the absence of prescriptive guidance could result in inconsistent application. Regulators, in particular, were concerned about the delayed recognition of expected credit losses if default were interpreted solely as non-payment.

BC5.250 Other respondents supported the proposal not to define default, and noted that the point of default would be different for different instruments and across jurisdictions and legal systems. These respondents noted that any attempt to be more prescriptive or provide guidance would add confusion and could result in differing default definitions for credit risk management, regulatory and accounting purposes.

BC5.251 The IASB noted during its redeliberations on the 2013 Impairment Exposure Draft that default can be interpreted in various ways, ranging from broad judgemental definitions based on qualitative factors to narrower, non-judgemental definitions focusing only on non-payment. The appropriate definition also depends on the nature of the financial instrument in question. One of the objectives of the 2013 Impairment Exposure Draft was to allow entities to leverage existing credit risk management systems. Because of the various interpretations of default, the IASB was concerned that defining it could result in a definition for financial reporting that is inconsistent with that applied internally for credit risk management. That could result in the impairment model being applied in a way that does not provide useful information about actual credit risk management.

BC5.252 Consequently, the IASB decided not to specifically define default in IFRS 9. However, to address the feedback received and noting in particular the effect on the financial instruments captured within the scope of the 12-month expected credit losses, the IASB decided to include a rebuttable presumption that default does not occur later than 90 days past due unless an entity has reasonable and supportable information to support a more lagging default criterion. The IASB also decided to emphasise that an entity should consider qualitative indicators of default when appropriate (for example, for financial instruments that include covenants that can lead to events of default) and clarify that an entity should apply a default definition that is consistent with its credit risk management practices for the relevant financial instruments, consistently from one period to another. The IASB noted that an entity may have multiple definitions of default, for example, for different types of products.

BC5.253   The IASB noted that this rebuttable presumption serves as a 'backstop' to ensure a more consistent population of financial instruments for which significant increases in credit risk is determined when applying the model. It was also noted that the purpose of the rebuttable presumption is not to delay the default event until a financial asset becomes 90 days past due, but to ensure that entities will not define default later than that point without reasonable and supportable information to substantiate the assertion (for example, financial instruments that include covenants that can lead to events of default). The IASB acknowledges that defining the backstop as 90 days past due is arbitrary, but it considered that any number of days would be arbitrary and that 90 days past due best aligned with current practice and regulatory requirements in many jurisdictions.

Period over which to estimate expected credit losses

BC5.254   Respondents to the 2013 Impairment Exposure Draft widely supported the proposed requirements for loan commitments and financial guarantee contracts in general, and no new arguments were raised that the IASB considered would call into question its prior analysis. However, the majority of respondents that supported including loan commitments within the scope of the proposed model noted that expected credit losses on some loan commitments should be estimated over the behavioural life of the financial instrument, instead of over the contractual commitment period. Although they noted that the use of the contractual period would be conceptually appropriate, there was concern that using the contractual period:

(a)   would be contrary to how the exposures are handled for credit risk management and regulatory purposes;

(b)   could result in insufficient allowances for the exposures arising from these contracts; and

(c)   would result in outcomes for which no actual loss experience exists on which to base the estimates.

BC5.255   Respondents noted that the use of the contractual period was of particular concern for some types of loan commitments that are managed on a collective basis, and for which an entity usually has no practical ability to withdraw the commitment before a loss event occurs and to limit the exposure to credit losses to the contractual period over which it is committed to extend the credit. Respondents noted that this applies particularly to revolving credit facilities such as credit cards and overdraft facilities. For these types of facilities, estimating the expected credit losses over the behavioural life of the instruments was viewed as more faithfully representing their exposure to credit risk.

BC5.256　Respondents also noted that those revolving credit facilities lack a fixed term or repayment structure and allow borrowers flexibility in how frequently they make drawdowns on the facility. Such facilities can be viewed as a combination of an undrawn loan commitment and a drawn-down loan asset. Typically, these facilities can be contractually cancelled by a lender with little or no notice, requiring repayment of any drawn balance and cancellation of any undrawn commitment under the facility. There would be no need on a conceptual basis to recognise expected credit losses on the undrawn portion of these facilities, because the exposure period could be as little as one day under the proposals in the 2013 Impairment Exposure Draft.

BC5.257　Outreach performed during the comment period on the 2013 Impairment Exposure Draft indicated that, in practice, lenders generally continue to extend credit under these types of financial instruments for a duration longer than the contractual minimum and only withdraw the facility if observable credit risk on the facility has increased significantly. The IASB noted that, for such facilities, the contractual maturities are often set for protective reasons and are not actively enforced as part of the normal credit risk management processes. Participants also noted that it may be difficult to withdraw undrawn commitments on these facilities for commercial reasons unless there has been an increase in credit risk. Consequently, economically, the contractual ability to demand repayment and cancel the undrawn commitment does not necessarily prevent an entity from being exposed to credit losses beyond the contractual notice period.

BC5.258　The IASB noted that the expected credit losses on these type of facilities can be significant and that restricting the recognition of a loss allowance to expected credit losses in the contractual notice period would arguably be inconsistent with the notion of expected credit losses (ie it would not reflect actual expectations of loss) and would not reflect the underlying economics or the way in which those facilities are managed for credit risk purposes. The IASB also noted that the amount of expected credit losses for these facilities could be significantly lower if the exposure is restricted to the contractual period, which may be inconsistent with an economic assessment of that exposure.

BC5.259　The IASB further noted that from a credit risk management perspective, the concept of expected credit losses is as relevant to off balance sheet exposures as it is to on balance sheet exposures. These types of financial instruments include both a loan (ie financial asset) and an undrawn commitment (ie loan commitment) component and are managed, and expected credit losses are estimated, on a facility level. In other words there is only one set of cash flows from the borrower that relates to both components. Expected credit losses on the on balance sheet exposure (the financial asset) are not estimated separately from the expected credit losses on the off balance sheet exposure (the loan commitment). Consequently, the period over which the expected credit losses are estimated should reflect the period over which the entity is expected to be exposed to the credit risk on the instrument as a whole.

BC5.260   The IASB remains of the view that the contractual period over which an entity is committed to provide credit (or a shorter period considering prepayments) is the correct conceptual outcome. The IASB noted that most loan commitments will expire at a specified date, and if an entity decides to renew or extend its commitment to extend credit, it will be a new instrument for which the entity has the opportunity to revise the terms and conditions. Consequently, the IASB decided to confirm that the maximum period over which expected credit losses for loan commitments and financial guarantee contracts are estimated is the contractual period over which the entity is committed to provide credit.

BC5.261   However, to address the concerns raised about the financial instruments noted in paragraphs BC5.254–BC5.257, the IASB decided that for financial instruments that include both a loan and an undrawn commitment component and the entity's contractual ability to demand repayment and cancel the undrawn commitment does not limit the entity's exposure to credit losses to the contractual notice period, an entity shall estimate expected credit losses over the period that the entity is expected to be exposed to credit risk and expected credit losses would not be mitigated by credit risk management actions, even if that period extends beyond the maximum contractual period. When determining the period over which the entity is exposed to credit risk on the financial instrument, the entity should consider factors such as relevant historical information and experience on similar financial instruments. The measurement of expected credit losses should take into account credit risk management actions that are taken once an exposure has increased in credit risk, such as the reduction or withdrawal of undrawn limits.

Probability-weighted outcome

BC5.262   The requirement in paragraph 5.5.17 of IFRS 9 states that the estimates of cash flows are expected values. Hence, estimates of the amounts and timing of cash flows are based on probability-weighted possible outcomes.

BC5.263   The term 'expected' as used in the terms 'expected credit losses', 'expected value' and 'expected cash flow' is a technical term that refers to the probability-weighted mean of a distribution and should not be confused with a most likely outcome or an entity's best estimate of the ultimate outcome.

BC5.264   In the IASB's view, an expected value measurement is the most relevant measurement basis because it provides information about the timing, amounts and uncertainty of an entity's future cash flows. This is because an expected value measurement would:

(a)   include consideration of expected credit losses using all the available evidence, including forward-looking information. Thus, an entity will be required to consider multiple scenarios and possible outcomes and their probability of occurrence.

(b)   reflect that the pricing of financial instruments includes the consideration of expected credit losses. Although entities might not attribute specific credit loss estimates to individual financial instruments, and although competitive pressures might influence pricing, entities still consider credit loss expectations for the credit risk of similar obligors when pricing loans on origination and purchase.

(c)   not revert (at any time) to an incurred credit loss model—all financial instruments have risk of a default occurring and the measurement will therefore reflect that risk of default and not the most likely outcome.

(d)   have the same objective regardless of whether an entity performs the measurement at an individual or a portfolio level. Consequently, there is no need to specify specific conditions or criteria for grouping financial instruments for the purposes of measurement.

(e)   provide useful information to users of financial statements (ie information about the risk that the investment might not perform).

BC5.265   The IASB observed that an entity can use a variety of techniques to meet the objective of an expected value without requiring detailed statistical models. The calculation of an expected value need not be a rigorous mathematical exercise whereby an entity identifies every single possible outcome and its probability. Instead, when there are many possible outcomes, an entity can use a representative sample of the complete distribution for determining the expected value. The main objective is that at least two outcomes are considered: the risk of a default and the risk of no default. Based on the feedback received and fieldwork performed, the IASB believes that many preparers are already performing calculations for internal purposes that would provide an appropriate measure of expected values.

BC5.266   The IASB also acknowledged that an entity may use various techniques to measure expected credit losses, including, for the 12-month expected credit losses measurement, techniques that do not include an explicit 12-month probability of default as an input, such as a loss rate methodology. The requirements in Section 5.5 of IFRS 9 do not list acceptable techniques or methods for measuring the loss allowance. The IASB was concerned that listing acceptable methods might rule out other appropriate methods for measuring expected credit losses, or be interpreted as providing unconditional acceptance of a particular method even when such a measurement would result in an amount that is not consistent with the required attributes of an expected credit loss measurement. Instead, Section 5.5 of IFRS 9 sets out the objectives for the measurement of expected credit losses, allowing entities to decide the most appropriate techniques to satisfy those objectives.

Time value of money

BC5.267   Consistent with the proposals in the Supplementary Document, the 2013 Impairment Exposure Draft proposed to allow an entity to discount expected credit losses using the risk-free rate, the effective interest rate on the related financial asset or any rate in between these two rates.

BC5.268   In developing the proposals in the Supplementary Document, the IASB noted that, conceptually, the discount rate for cash flows of an asset cannot be below the risk-free rate. The IASB further noted that the discount rate used in the 2009 Impairment Exposure Draft is conceptually appropriate for calculations of amortised cost. However, if the IASB were to propose that the upper limit should be the credit-adjusted effective interest rate from the 2009 Impairment Exposure Draft, entities would need to calculate that rate to decide whether they could use a rate that is more readily determinable. Therefore, such a proposal would not avoid the operational complexity of determining that credit-adjusted effective interest rate, which would be counter-productive. Thus, the IASB proposed that an entity should use any rate between the risk-free rate and the effective interest rate, not adjusted for credit risk, as the discount rate.

BC5.269   The IASB observed that some credit risk management systems discount expected cash flows to the date of default. The proposals would require an entity to discount expected credit losses to the reporting date.

BC5.270   Most respondents to the Supplementary Document supported flexibility in an entity choosing which discount rate it should apply. These respondents agreed that this flexibility was helpful for easing the operational challenges of determining and maintaining the discount rate. They also felt that it was appropriate to allow preparers to choose a rate that is suitable for the level of sophistication of their systems and their operational capability. Those who did not support permitting flexibility in determining the appropriate rate wanted to maintain comparability between entities.

BC5.271   The IASB confirmed these proposals in the 2013 Impairment Exposure Draft, but additionally proposed that an entity should disclose the discount rate it used and any significant assumptions that it made in determining that rate. This choice of discount rates did not apply to purchased or originated credit-impaired financial assets, on which the amortised cost measurement always uses the credit-adjusted effective interest rate.

BC5.272   Given the support previously expressed for the proposals in the Supplementary Document, the 2013 Impairment Exposure Draft did not specifically ask respondents to comment on the proposals relating to the discount rate when calculating expected credit losses. However, a number of respondents commented on the proposals, the majority of which disagreed with them. The reasons for their disagreement included that:

(a)   using the effective interest rate would be consistent with the proposals for originated or purchased credit-impaired financial assets and financial assets that are credit-impaired at the reporting date (ie the rate used to recognise interest revenue should be the same as the rate used to discount expected credit losses);

(b)   discounting cash flows using a risk-free rate disregards any compensation that the entity receives to compensate it for credit risk; and

(c)   the permitted range of discount rates is too flexible and differences in the amount of the loss allowance due to different discount rates could be material.

BC5.273   Considering these views, the IASB noted that the advantages of using the effective interest rate to discount expected credit losses included:

(a)   that the effective interest rate is the conceptually correct rate and is consistent with amortised cost measurement;

(b)   it limits the range of rates that an entity can use when discounting cash shortfalls, thereby limiting the potential for manipulation;

(c)   it enhances comparability between entities; and

(d)   it avoids the adjustment that arises when financial assets become credit-impaired (interest revenue is required to be calculated on the carrying amount net of expected credit losses) if a rate other than the effective interest rate has been used up to that point.

BC5.274   The IASB acknowledged that, unlike the requirements of IAS 39, in which shortfalls on cash flows were only measured on a subset of financial instruments, the impairment requirements will result in expected credit losses being measured on all financial instruments in the scope of the requirements. Respondents have previously noted that they would have to integrate their credit risk management and accounting systems to improve the interaction between them if they have to discount cash shortfalls using the effective interest rate. However, the IASB noted that even in accordance with the requirements of IAS 39 to use the effective interest rate to discount expected cash flows, there are operational challenges with using the effective interest rate for open portfolios and that entities use approximations of the effective interest rate.

BC5.275   Consequently, on the basis of the feedback received and the advantages noted in paragraph BC5.273, the IASB decided to require the use of the effective interest rate (or an approximation of it) when discounting expected credit losses.

Loan commitments and financial guarantee contracts

BC5.276   The 2013 Impairment Exposure Draft proposed that because loan commitments and financial guarantee contracts are unfunded, the effective interest method and, hence, an effective interest rate, would not be applicable. This is because the IASB considered that those financial instruments by themselves, before they are drawn down, do not give rise to the notion of interest and that, instead, their cash flow profiles are akin to that of derivatives. The fact that interest revenue does not apply is reflected in the accounting for loan commitments and financial guarantee contracts within the scope of IFRS 9. For those loan commitments and financial guarantee contracts, revenue recognition of the related fee income does not use the effective interest method. Consequently, the IASB did not consider it appropriate to simply extend the requirements for the discount rate for measuring expected credit losses that arise from financial assets to the requirements for the discount rate for measuring expected credit losses that arise from loan commitments and financial guarantee contracts.

BC5.277 As a result, the IASB proposed in the 2013 Impairment Exposure Draft that the discount rate to be applied when discounting the expected credit losses that arise from a loan commitment or a financial guarantee contract would be the rate that reflects:

(a) current market assessments of the time value of money (ie a rate that does not provide consideration for credit risk such as a risk-free rate); and

(b) the risks that are specific to the cash flows, to the extent that the risks are taken into account by adjusting the discount rate instead of adjusting the cash flows that are being discounted.

BC5.278 Consistent with their feedback in paragraph BC5.272, respondents commented on the disconnect between the discount rate used for the financial asset component (the drawn balance) and the loan commitment component (the undrawn commitment). They noted that this was an unnecessary complication, because, in accordance with the proposals, the measurement of expected credit losses associated with the loan commitment would change when the facility is drawn, merely as a result of the difference in discount rate. Furthermore, respondents noted that for credit risk management purposes, a single discount rate is usually applied to these facilities as a whole. The loan commitment relates directly to the recognised financial asset for which the effective interest rate has already been determined. The effective interest rate applied to the financial asset therefore already reflects an assessment of the time value of money and the risks that are specific to the cash flows on the loan commitment. This rate could be considered to represent a reasonable approximation of the discount rate for loan commitments.

BC5.279 Consequently, the IASB agreed that the expected credit losses on loan commitments should be discounted using the same effective interest rate (or an approximation of it) that is used to discount the expected credit losses on the financial asset. However, for financial guarantee contracts and loan commitments for which the effective interest rate cannot be determined, the discount rate should be determined as proposed in the 2013 Impairment Exposure Draft.

Reasonable and supportable information

BC5.280 Consistent with the proposals in the 2013 Impairment Exposure Draft, the Supplementary Document and the 2009 Impairment Exposure Draft, the IASB specified that the information set required for measuring expected credit losses in accordance with Section 5.5 of IFRS 9 is the best information that is available without undue cost or effort, and that this includes reasonable and supportable forward-looking information.

BC5.281　In the IASB's view, historical information is an important foundation on which to measure expected credit losses. However, an entity should adjust the historical information using reasonable and supportable information that is available without undue cost or effort to reflect current observable data and forecasts of future conditions if such forecasts are different from past information. The IASB noted that an entity is not required to incorporate forecasts of future conditions over the entire remaining life of a financial instrument. Instead, paragraph B5.5.50 of IFRS 9 acknowledges the difficulty arising from estimating expected credit losses as the forecast horizon increases. In some cases, the best reasonable and supportable information could be the unadjusted historical information, depending on the nature of that information and when it was calculated compared to the reporting date, but it should not be assumed to be appropriate in all circumstances. The IASB notes that even if an unadjusted historical measure was not appropriate, it could still be used as a starting point from which adjustments are made to estimate expected credit losses on the basis of reasonable and supportable information that incorporates both current and forward-looking information.

Prudential information

BC5.282　Some respondents to the 2013 Impairment Exposure Draft asked the IASB to ensure that the requirements for measuring expected credit losses in accordance with Section 5.5 of IFRS 9 are aligned to the prudential capital frameworks. Certain prudential regulation and capital adequacy systems, such as the framework developed by the Basel Committee on Banking Supervision, already require financial institutions to calculate 12-month expected credit losses as part of their regulatory capital requirements. However, some of those systems only use credit loss experience based on historical events to set out 'provisioning' levels over the entire economic cycle ('through-the-cycle'). Furthermore, through-the-cycle approaches consider a range of possible economic outcomes instead of those that are actually expected at the reporting date. This would result in a loss allowance that does not reflect the economic characteristics of the financial instruments at the reporting date.

BC5.283　The IASB notes that financial reporting, including estimates of expected credit losses, are based on information, circumstances and events at the reporting date. The IASB expects entities to be able to use some regulatory measures as a basis for the calculation of expected credit losses in accordance with the requirements in IFRS 9. However, these calculations may have to be adjusted to meet the measurement requirements in Section 5.5 of IFRS 9. Only information that is available without undue cost or effort and supportable at the reporting date should be considered. This may include information about current economic conditions as well as reasonable and supportable forecasts of future economic conditions, as long as the information is supportable and available without undue cost or effort when the estimates are made.

BC5.284　Some interested parties are also of the view that loss allowance balances should be used to provide a counter-cyclical effect by building up loss allowances in good times to be used in bad times. This would, however, mask the effect of changes in credit loss expectations.

BC5.285 Some users of financial statements would prefer a representation of credit losses with a conservative or prudential bias, arguing that such a representation would better meet the needs of regulators, who are responsible for maintaining financial stability, and investors. The IASB notes that the objective of the impairment requirements is to faithfully represent the economic reality of expected credit losses in relation to the carrying amount of a financial asset. The IASB does not include in this objective the recognition of a loss allowance that will sufficiently cover unexpected credit losses, because that is not the primary objective of general purpose financial reporting.

BC5.286 The impairment requirements in IFRS 9 are based on the information available at the reporting date and are designed to reflect economic reality, instead of adjusting the assumptions and inputs applied to achieve a counter-cyclical effect. For example, when credit risk improves, the measurement of the loss allowance will faithfully represent that change. This is consistent with the objective of general purpose financial statements.

Amendments for *Interest Rate Benchmark Reform—Phase 2* (August 2020)

Background

BC5.287 In 2014, the Financial Stability Board recommended the reform of specified major interest rate benchmarks such as interbank offered rates (IBORs). Since then, public authorities in many jurisdictions have taken steps to implement interest rate benchmark reform and have increasingly encouraged market participants to ensure timely progress towards the reform of interest rate benchmarks, including the replacement of interest rate benchmarks with alternative, nearly risk-free interest rates that are based, to a greater extent, on transaction data (alternative benchmark rates). The progress towards interest rate benchmark reform follows the general expectation that some major interest rate benchmarks will cease to be published by the end of 2021. The term 'interest rate benchmark reform' refers to the market-wide reform of an interest rate benchmark as described in paragraph 6.8.2 of IFRS 9 (the reform).

BC5.288 In September 2019 the IASB amended IFRS 9, IAS 39 and IFRS 7, to address as a priority issues affecting financial reporting in the period before the reform of an interest rate benchmark, including the replacement of an interest rate benchmark with an alternative benchmark rate (Phase 1 amendments). The Phase 1 amendments provide temporary exceptions to specific hedge accounting requirements due to the uncertainty arising from the reform. Paragraphs BC6.546–BC6.603 discuss the background to the Phase 1 amendments.

BC5.289 After the issuance of the Phase 1 amendments, the IASB commenced its Phase 2 deliberations. In Phase 2 of its project on the reform, the IASB addressed issues that might affect financial reporting during the reform of an interest rate benchmark, including changes to contractual cash flows or hedging relationships arising from the replacement of an interest rate benchmark with an alternative benchmark rate (replacement issues).

BC5.290   The objective of Phase 2 is to assist entities in providing useful information to users of financial statements and to support preparers in applying IFRS Standards when changes are made to contractual cash flows or hedging relationships because of the transition to alternative benchmark rates. The IASB observed that for information about the effects of the transition to alternative benchmark rates to be useful, the information has to be relevant to users of financial statements and faithfully represent the economic effects of that transition on the entity. This objective assisted the IASB in assessing whether it should amend IFRS Standards or whether the requirements in IFRS Standards already provided an adequate basis to account for such effects.

BC5.291   In April 2020 the IASB published the Exposure Draft *Interest Rate Benchmark Reform—Phase 2* (2020 Exposure Draft), which proposed amendments to specific requirements in IFRS 9, IAS 39, IFRS 7, IFRS 4 and IFRS 16 *Leases* to address replacement issues.

BC5.292   Almost all respondents to the 2020 Exposure Draft welcomed the IASB's decision to address replacement issues and agreed that the proposed amendments would achieve the objective of Phase 2. Many respondents highlighted the urgency of these amendments, especially in some jurisdictions that have progressed towards the reform or the replacement of interest rate benchmarks with alternative benchmark rates.

BC5.293   In August 2020 the IASB amended IFRS 9, IAS 39, IFRS 7, IFRS 4 and IFRS 16 by issuing *Interest Rate Benchmark Reform—Phase 2* (Phase 2 amendments). The Phase 2 amendments, which confirmed with modifications the proposals in the 2020 Exposure Draft, added paragraphs 5.4.5–5.4.9, 6.8.13, Section 6.9 and paragraphs 7.1.10 and 7.2.43–7.2.46 to IFRS 9.

Changes in the basis for determining the contractual cash flows of financial assets and financial liabilities arising from the reform

BC5.294   The IASB was informed that changes to financial assets or financial liabilities arising from the reform could be made in different ways. Specifically, entities may change the basis for determining the contractual cash flows of a financial instrument by:

(a)   amending the contractual terms of a financial asset or a financial liability to replace the referenced interest rate benchmark with an alternative benchmark rate;

(b)   altering the method for calculating the interest rate benchmark without amending the contractual terms of the financial instrument; and/or

(c)   triggering the activation of an existing contractual term such as a fallback clause.

BC5.295   To meet the objective described in paragraph BC5.290, the IASB concluded that the scope of the Phase 2 amendments in paragraphs 5.4.5–5.4.9 of IFRS 9 should include all changes to a financial asset or financial liability as a result of the reform, regardless of the legal form triggering those changes. In each situation outlined in paragraph BC5.294 the basis for determining the contractual cash flows of a financial instrument changes as a result of the reform. Therefore, for the purpose of the Phase 2 amendments, the IASB collectively refers to these changes as 'changes in the basis for determining the contractual cash flows of a financial asset or a financial liability'.

What constitutes 'a change in the basis for determining the contractual cash flows of a financial asset or a financial liability'

BC5.296   In the IASB's view, determining whether a change in the basis for determining the contractual cash flows of a financial instrument has occurred will be straightforward in most cases, for example, when the contractual terms of a financial instrument are amended to replace the interest rate benchmark with an alternative benchmark rate. However, it may be less straightforward if the basis for determining the contractual cash flows changes after the initial recognition of the financial instrument, without an amendment to the contractual terms of that financial instrument – for example, when, to effect the reform, the method for calculating the interest rate benchmark is altered. Although the contractual terms of the financial instrument may not be amended, such a change in the method for calculating the interest rate benchmark may change the basis for determining the contractual cash flows of that financial instrument compared to the prior basis (ie the basis immediately preceding the change).

BC5.297   The IASB noted that paragraph 5.4.3 of IFRS 9 refers to the 'modification or renegotiation of the contractual cash flows' of a financial asset, while paragraph 3.3.2 of IFRS 9 refers to the 'modification of the terms' of an existing financial liability. The IASB noted that although these paragraphs use different words, both refer to a change in the contractual cash flows or contractual terms after the initial recognition of the financial instrument. In both cases, such a change was not specified or considered in the contract at initial recognition.

BC5.298   The IASB considered that if the amendments in paragraphs 5.4.6–5.4.9 of IFRS 9 applied only to cases in which the contractual terms are amended as a result of the reform, the form rather than the substance of the change would determine the appropriate accounting treatment. This could cause the economic effects of a change in the basis for determining the contractual cash flows arising as a result of the reform to be obscured by the form of the change and not reflected in the financial statements, and result in changes with equivalent economic effects being accounted for differently.

BC5.299   Consequently, the IASB highlighted that the basis for determining the contractual cash flows of a financial asset or a financial liability can change even if the contractual terms of the financial instrument are not amended. In the IASB's view, accounting consistently for a change in the basis for determining the contractual cash flows arising as a result of the reform, even if the contractual terms of the financial instrument are not amended, would reflect the economic substance of such a change and would therefore provide useful information to users of financial statements.

BC5.300   In addition, as noted in paragraph BC5.294(c), the IASB also learned that some entities may implement the reform through the activation of existing contractual terms, such as fallback provisions. For example, a fallback provision could specify the hierarchy of rates to which an interest rate benchmark would revert in case the existing benchmark rate ceases to exist. The IASB decided these situations—ie revisions to an entity's estimates of future cash payments or receipts arising from the activation of existing contractual terms that are required by the reform—should also be within the scope of the Phase 2 amendments. Doing so, avoids differences in accounting outcomes simply because the changes in the basis for determining the contractual cash flows were triggered by an existing contractual term instead of by a change in the contractual cash flows or contractual terms after the initial recognition of the financial instrument. Such diversity in accounting outcomes would reduce the usefulness of information provided to users of financial statements and would be burdensome to preparers.

Changes required by the reform

BC5.301   As set out in paragraph 5.4.7 of IFRS 9, the Phase 2 amendments provide a practical expedient that requires entities to apply paragraph B5.4.5 of IFRS 9 to account for changes in the basis for determining the contractual cash flows of a financial asset or a financial liability that are required by the reform. In reaching that decision, the IASB considered the usefulness of the information that would result from applying the requirements in IFRS 9 that would otherwise apply to these changes.

BC5.302   In the absence of the practical expedient in paragraph 5.4.7 of IFRS 9, when a financial asset or financial liability is modified, an entity applying IFRS 9 is required to determine whether the modification results in the derecognition of the financial instrument. Different accounting for the modification is specified depending on whether derecognition is required. IFRS 9 sets out separate requirements for derecognition of financial assets and derecognition of financial liabilities.

BC5.303   The IASB noted that, because alternative benchmark rates are intended to be nearly risk-free while many existing interest rate benchmarks are not, it is likely that a fixed spread will be added to compensate for a basis difference between an existing interest rate benchmark and an alternative benchmark rate to avoid a transfer of economic value between the parties to a financial instrument. If these are the only changes made, the IASB considers that it would be unlikely that the transition to an alternative benchmark rate alone would result in the derecognition of that financial instrument.

BC5.304   Paragraph 5.4.3 of IFRS 9 applies to modifications of financial assets that do not result in derecognition of those assets. Applying that paragraph, a modification gain or loss is determined by recalculating the gross carrying amount of the financial asset as the present value of the renegotiated or modified contractual cash flows that are discounted at the financial asset's original effective interest rate. Any resulting modification gain or loss is recognised in profit or loss at the date of the modification. The accounting for other revisions in estimated future contractual cash flows, including modifications of financial liabilities that do not result in the derecognition of those liabilities (see paragraph B5.4.6 of IFRS 9), is consistent with the accounting for modified financial assets that do not result in derecognition.[42]

BC5.305　Thus, in the absence of the practical expedient in paragraph 5.4.7 of IFRS 9, an entity would generally apply the requirements in paragraphs 5.4.3 or B5.4.6 of IFRS 9 to a change required by the reform, by recalculating the carrying amount of a financial instrument with any difference recognised in profit or loss. In addition, an entity would be required to use the original effective interest rate (ie the interest rate benchmark preceding the transition to the alternative benchmark rate) to recognise interest revenue or interest expense over the remaining life of the financial instrument.

BC5.306　In the IASB's view, in the context of the reform, such an outcome would not necessarily provide useful information to users of financial statements. In reaching this view, the IASB considered a situation in which a financial instrument was amended only to replace an interest rate benchmark with an alternative benchmark rate. Using the interest rate benchmark-based effective interest rate to calculate interest revenue or interest expense over the remaining life in this situation would not reflect the economic effects of the modified financial instrument. Maintaining the original effective interest rate could also be difficult, and perhaps impossible, if that rate is no longer available.

BC5.307　The IASB therefore decided that applying the practical expedient, which requires an entity to apply paragraph B5.4.5 of IFRS 9 to account for changes in the basis for determining the contractual cash flows of financial assets and financial liabilities as a result of the reform, would provide more useful information to users of financial statements in circumstances when the changes are limited to changes required by the reform and would be less burdensome for preparers for the reasons noted in paragraph BC5.306.

BC5.308　Applying the practical expedient in paragraph 5.4.7 of IFRS 9, an entity would account for a change in the basis for determining the contractual cash flows of a financial asset or a financial liability required by the reform as being akin to a 'movement in the market rates of interest' applying paragraph B5.4.5 of IFRS 9. As a result, an entity applying the practical expedient to account for a change in the basis for determining the contractual cash flows of a financial asset or a financial liability that is required by the reform would not apply the derecognition requirements to that financial instrument, and would not apply paragraphs 5.4.3 or B5.4.6 of IFRS 9 to account for the change in contractual cash flows. In other words, changes in the basis for determining the contractual cash flows of a financial asset or a financial liability that are required by the reform would not result in an adjustment to the carrying amount of the financial instrument or immediate recognition of a gain or loss. The IASB concluded that the application of the practical expedient would

---

42　Paragraph B5.4.6 does not apply to changes in estimates of expected credit losses.

provide useful information about the effect of the reform on an entity's financial instruments in the circumstances in which it applies.

BC5.309 The IASB considered the risk that the practical expedient could be applied too broadly, which could result in unintended consequences. The IASB decided to limit the scope of the practical expedient so that it applies only to changes in the basis for determining the contractual cash flows of a financial asset or a financial liability that are required by the reform. For this purpose, applying paragraph 5.4.7 of IFRS 9, a change is required by the reform if, and only if, the change is necessary as a direct consequence of the reform and the new basis for determining the contractual cash flows is economically equivalent to the previous basis (ie the basis immediately preceding the change). This is consistent with the conditions proposed in the 2020 Exposure Draft.

BC5.310 In the 2020 Exposure Draft, the IASB considered only changes in the basis for determining the contractual cash flows of a financial asset or a financial liability that are required as a direct consequence of the reform. This condition was designed to capture changes in the basis for determining the contractual cash flows that are necessary—or in other words, changes that are required—to implement the reform.

BC5.311 Furthermore, because the objective of the reform is limited to the transition to alternative benchmark rates—ie it does not encompass other changes that would lead to value transfer between the parties to a financial instrument—in the 2020 Exposure Draft, the IASB proposed economic equivalence as the second condition for applying the practical expedient. That is, to be within the scope of the practical expedient, at the date the basis is changed, the new basis for determining the contractual cash flows would be required to be economically equivalent to the previous basis.

BC5.312 In discussing the concept of economic equivalence, the IASB considered circumstances in which an entity makes changes necessary as a direct consequence of the reform in a way so that the overall contractual cash flows (including amounts relating to interest) of the financial instrument are substantially similar before and after the changes. For example, a change would be economically equivalent if it involved only replacing an interest rate benchmark with an alternative benchmark rate plus a fixed spread that compensated for the basis difference between the interest rate benchmark and the alternative benchmark rate. The IASB observed that, in this situation, applying paragraph B5.4.5 of IFRS 9 (that is, revising the effective interest rate when cash flows are re-estimated) would have an accounting outcome similar to applying paragraph 5.4.3 or B5.4.6 of IFRS 9 (that is, recognising a modification gain or loss) because it is unlikely that the resulting modification gain or loss would be significant.

BC5.313 With respect to the proposed condition described in paragraph BC5.310, some respondents to the 2020 Exposure Draft asked whether the practical expedient would apply even if the transition to alternative benchmark rates is not required by law or regulation, or if the existing interest rate benchmark is not being discontinued. For example, these respondents said that some existing interest rate benchmarks prevalent in their jurisdictions are not—at least in the near future—being discontinued. Nonetheless, entities are expected to transition to alternative benchmark rates because, for example, they anticipate reduced liquidity for the existing benchmark or want to align with global market developments. In response, the IASB noted that the practical expedient is not limited to only particular ways of effecting the reform, provided the reform is consistent with the description in paragraph 6.8.2 of IFRS 9. The IASB also noted that the Phase 2 amendments encompass changes that are required to implement the reform—or, in other words, changes that are necessary as a direct consequence of the reform—even if the reform itself is not mandatory.

BC5.314 With respect to the proposed condition described in paragraph BC5.311, some respondents to the 2020 Exposure Draft asked the IASB to specify whether an entity would need to perform detailed quantitative analysis of the cash flows of a financial instrument to demonstrate that a particular change meets the economic equivalence condition. For example, some respondents asked whether an entity would need to determine that the discounted present value of the cash flows of the affected financial instrument or its fair value are substantially similar before and after the transition to alternative benchmark rates.

BC5.315 The IASB intended 'economic equivalence' to be principle-based and therefore decided not to include detailed application guidance related to the assessment of that condition. Acknowledging that different entities in different jurisdictions would implement the reform differently, the IASB did not require a particular approach for assessing this condition. The IASB noted that because it set no 'bright lines', an entity is required to apply judgement to assess whether circumstances meet the economic equivalence condition. For example, assuming that the entity determines that replacing an interest rate benchmark with an alternative benchmark rate is necessary for the affected financial instrument as a direct consequence of the reform (ie the condition in paragraph 5.4.7(a) of IFRS 9 is met), the entity determines:

(a) what alternative benchmark rate will replace the interest rate benchmark and whether a fixed spread adjustment is necessary to compensate for a basis difference between the alternative benchmark rate and the interest rate benchmark preceding replacement. The entity would assess the overall resulting cash flows, including amounts relating to interest (ie alternative benchmark rate plus any fixed spread adjustment), to determine whether the economic equivalence condition is met. In other words, in this example, the entity would assess whether the interest rate remained substantially similar before and after the replacement—specifically, whether the interest rate after replacement (eg the alternative benchmark rate plus the fixed spread) was substantially similar to the interest rate benchmark immediately preceding the replacement; and

(b) whether the alternative benchmark rate (plus the necessary fixed spread described in paragraph BC5.315(a)) was applied to the relevant affected financial instrument(s).

BC5.316   The IASB noted that for a scenario such as the one described in the example in paragraph BC5.315, that assessment would be sufficient to determine that the economic equivalence condition had been met for those changes. As described in paragraph 5.4.8(a) of IFRS 9, an entity in such circumstances would not be required to do further analysis in order to determine that the economic equivalence condition has been satisfied (eg the entity would not be required to analyse whether the discounted present value of the cash flows of that financial instrument are substantially similar before and after the replacement).

BC5.317   The IASB acknowledged that changes in the basis for determining the contractual cash flows of a financial asset or a financial liability are likely to vary significantly across jurisdictions, product types and contracts. Developing a comprehensive list of changes required by the reform—and, hence, that qualify for the practical expedient—would not be feasible. Nonetheless, the IASB decided to include in paragraph 5.4.8 of IFRS 9 some examples of changes that give rise to a new basis for determining the contractual cash flows that is economically equivalent to the previous basis. If an entity makes only the changes specified in paragraph 5.4.8 of IFRS 9, the entity would not be required to analyse these changes further to conclude that the changes meet the condition in paragraph 5.4.7(b) of IFRS 9—ie the changes in paragraph 5.4.8 of IFRS 9 are examples of changes that satisfy that condition. The IASB concluded that adding such examples would assist entities in understanding and applying the amendments. These examples are not exhaustive.

Changes that are not required by the reform

BC5.318   The IASB noted that during negotiations with counterparties to agree on changes to the contractual cash flows required by the reform, entities could simultaneously agree to make changes to the contractual terms that are not necessary as a direct consequence of the reform or are not economically equivalent to the previous terms (eg to reflect a change in the counterparty's credit worthiness). If there are changes in addition to those required by the reform, an entity would first apply the practical expedient in paragraph 5.4.7 of IFRS 9 to account for the changes to the basis for determining the contractual cash flows of a financial asset or financial liability determined to be required by the reform (ie changes that meet the conditions in paragraph 5.4.7 of IFRS 9) by updating the effective interest rate based on the alternative benchmark rate. Then the entity would apply the relevant requirements in IFRS 9 to determine if the additional changes to that financial instrument (ie any changes to which the practical expedient does not apply) result in the derecognition of the financial instrument. If the entity determines that the additional changes do not result in derecognition of that financial asset or financial liability, the entity would account for the additional changes (ie changes not required by the reform) by applying paragraph 5.4.3 or paragraph B5.4.6 of IFRS 9. In the IASB's view, this approach would provide useful information to users of financial statements about the economic effects of any changes to financial instruments not required by the reform while consistently accounting for changes required by the reform.

Other classification and measurement issues

BC5.319 In anticipation of the potential financial reporting implications of changes to financial instruments as a result of the reform, including the potential derecognition of existing financial instruments and the recognition of new financial instruments, some stakeholders asked the IASB to consider additional matters related to applying the classification and measurement requirements in IFRS 9 to financial assets and financial liabilities. These matters included:

(a)   whether IFRS 9 provides an adequate basis to account for the derecognition of a financial instrument in the statement of financial position and the recognition of any resulting gain or loss in the statement of profit or loss when an entity determines that it is required to derecognise a financial asset or financial liability because of the reform.

(b)   determining whether derecognition of a financial asset following changes in the basis for determining the contractual cash flows resulting from the reform affects an entity's business model for managing its financial assets.

(c)   assessing the contractual cash flow characteristics of a financial asset that refers to an alternative benchmark rate. Specifically, assessing whether some alternative benchmark rates are consistent with the description of 'interest' in paragraph 4.1.3(b) of IFRS 9 including if the time value of money element of that rate is modified (ie imperfect).

(d)   assessing the effect on expected credit losses of derecognising an existing financial asset and recognising a new financial asset as a result of the reform.

(e)   determining potential effects on the accounting for embedded derivatives in the context of the reform. Specifically, following the transition to alternative benchmark rates, whether entities reassess whether an embedded derivative is required to be separated from the host contract.

(f)   determining whether the practical expedient in paragraph 5.4.7 of IFRS 9 applies to a hybrid financial liability that has been separated into a host contract (measured at amortised cost) and an embedded derivative (measured at fair value through profit or loss). Specifically, determining whether the practical expedient applies when the interest rate benchmark is not a contractual term of the host contract but instead is imputed at initial recognition.

BC5.320 The IASB discussed these matters and concluded that IFRS 9 provides an adequate basis to determine the required accounting for each of these matters. Therefore, considering the objective of Phase 2, the IASB made no amendments for these matters. Specific to paragraph BC5.319(f), the IASB observed that the practical expedient in paragraph 5.4.7 of IFRS 9 would apply to such a host contract if the conditions set out in paragraph 5.4.7 of IFRS 9 are met.

Hedge accounting (Chapter 6)

BC6.1–
BC6.75   [Relocated to paragraphs BCE.174–BCE.238]

The objective of hedge accounting

BC6.76   Hedge accounting is an exception to the normal recognition and measurement requirements in IFRS. For example, the hedge accounting guidance in IAS 39 permitted:

(a)   the recognition of items that would otherwise have not been recognised (for example, a firm commitment);

(b)   the measurement of an item on a basis that is different from the measurement basis that is normally required (for example, adjusting the measurement of a hedged item in a fair value hedge); and

(c)   the deferral of the changes in the fair value of a hedging instrument for a cash flow hedge in other comprehensive income. Such changes in fair value would otherwise have been recognised in profit or loss (for example, the hedging of a highly probable forecast transaction).

BC6.77   The IASB noted that, although hedge accounting was an exception from normal accounting requirements, in many situations the information that resulted from applying those normal requirements without using hedge accounting either did not provide useful information or omitted important information. Hence, the IASB concluded that hedge accounting should be retained.

BC6.78   In the IASB's view, a consistent hedge accounting model requires an objective that describes when and how an entity should:

(a)   override the general recognition and measurement requirements in IFRS (ie when and how an entity should apply hedge accounting); and

(b)   recognise effectiveness and/or ineffectiveness of a hedging relationship (ie when and how gains and losses should be recognised).

BC6.79   The IASB considered two possible objectives of hedge accounting – that hedge accounting should:

(a)   provide a link between an entity's risk management and its financial reporting. Hedge accounting would convey the context of hedging instruments, which would allow insights into their purpose and effect.

(b)   mitigate the recognition and measurement anomalies between the accounting for derivatives (or other hedging instruments) and the accounting for hedged items and manage the timing of the recognition of gains or losses on derivative hedging instruments used to mitigate cash flow risk.

BC6.80 However, the IASB rejected both objectives for hedge accounting. The IASB thought that an objective that linked an entity's risk management and financial reporting was too broad: it was not clear enough what risk management activity was being referred to. Conversely, the IASB thought that an objective that focused on the accounting anomalies was too narrow: it focused on the mechanics of hedge accounting instead of on why hedge accounting was being done.

BC6.81 Consequently, the IASB decided to propose in the 2010 Hedge Accounting Exposure Draft an objective that combined elements of both objectives. The IASB considered that the proposed objective of hedge accounting reflected a broad articulation of a principle-based approach with a focus on the purpose of the entity's risk management activities. In addition, the objective also provided for a focus on the statement of financial position and the statement of comprehensive income, thereby reflecting the effects of the individual assets and liabilities associated with the risk management activities on those statements. This reflected the IASB's intention: that entities should provide useful information about the purpose and effect of hedging instruments for which hedge accounting is applied.

BC6.82 The IASB also noted that, despite that an entity's risk management activities were central to the objective of hedge accounting, an entity would only achieve hedge accounting if it met all the qualifying criteria.

BC6.83 Almost all respondents to the 2010 Hedge Accounting Exposure Draft as well as participants in the IASB's outreach activities supported the objective of hedge accounting proposed in the 2010 Hedge Accounting Exposure Draft.

Open portfolios

BC6.84 Closed hedged portfolios are hedged portfolios in which items cannot be added, removed or replaced without treating each change as the transition to a new portfolio (or a new layer). The hedging relationship specifies at inception the hedged items that form that particular hedging relationship.

BC6.85 In practice, risk management often assesses risk exposures on a continuous basis and at a portfolio level. Risk management strategies tend to have a time horizon (for example, two years) over which an exposure is hedged. Consequently, as time passes new exposures are continuously added to such hedged portfolios and other exposures are removed from them. These are referred to as open portfolios.

BC6.86 Hedges of open portfolios introduce complexity to the accounting for such hedges. Changes could be addressed by treating them like a series of closed portfolios with a short life (ie by periodic discontinuations of the hedging relationships for the previous closed portfolios of items and designations of new hedging relationships for the revised closed portfolios of items). However, this gives rise to complexities related to tracking, amortisation of hedge adjustments and the reclassification of gains or losses deferred in accumulated other comprehensive income. Furthermore, it may be impractical to align such an accounting treatment with the way in which the exposures are viewed from a risk management perspective, which may update hedge portfolios more frequently (for example, daily).

BC6.87   The IASB decided not to specifically address open portfolios or 'macro' hedging (ie hedging at the level that aggregates portfolios) as part of the 2010 Hedge Accounting Exposure Draft. The IASB considered hedge accounting only in the context of groups of items that constitute a gross or net position for which the items that make up that position are included in a specified overall group of items (see paragraphs BC6.427–BC6.467).

BC6.88   Consequently, for fair value hedge accounting for a portfolio hedge of interest rate risk the 2010 Hedge Accounting Exposure Draft did not propose replacing the requirements in IAS 39.

BC6.89   The IASB received feedback from financial institutions as well as from entities outside the financial sector that addressing situations in which entities use a dynamic risk management strategy was important. Financial institutions also noted that this was important because some of their risk exposures might only qualify for hedge accounting in an open portfolio context (for example, non-interest bearing demand deposits).

BC6.90   The IASB noted that this is a complex topic that warrants thorough research and feedback from interested parties. Accordingly, the IASB decided to separately deliberate on the accounting for macro hedging as part of its active agenda with the objective of issuing a Discussion Paper. The IASB noted that this would enable IFRS 9 to be completed more quickly and would enable the new 'general' hedge accounting requirements to be available as part of IFRS 9. The IASB also noted that during the project on accounting for macro hedging the status quo of 'macro hedge accounting' under previous Standards would broadly be maintained so that entities would not be worse off in the meantime.

BC6.91   The IASB noted that broadly maintaining the status quo of 'macro hedge accounting' meant that:

(a)   an entity could continue to apply IAS 39 for fair value hedge accounting for a portfolio hedge of interest rate risk (see paragraph BC6.88), which includes the application of the specific 'macro hedge accounting' requirements in IAS 39; but

(b)   all cash flow hedges would be within the scope of the hedge accounting model of IFRS 9 — including those that are colloquially referred to as 'macro cash flow hedges' under IAS 39 today.

BC6.92   The IASB noted that this approach appropriately reflected the interaction between the IAS 39 hedge accounting requirements and the new hedge accounting model it had developed for IFRS 9 for the following reasons:

(a)   the new hedge accounting model does apply to situations in which entities manage risk in a 'macro' context, for example, for risk exposures that result from large groups of items that are managed on an aggregated level, including open portfolios. It also applies to all types of hedges and risks. But entities must use the designations that are available under the new hedge accounting model (and can only apply hedge accounting if they meet the qualifying criteria).

(b)   the new hedge accounting model does not however provide specific 'customised' solutions that would be an exception to (instead of an application of) the model designed to make the implementation of hedge accounting in those situations easier. For example, it does not provide an exception to allow a net position cash flow hedge for interest rate risk or to allow non-interest bearing demand deposits to be designated as hedged items.

(c)   the specific fair value hedge accounting for a portfolio hedge of interest rate risk is an exception to the hedge accounting model in IAS 39 and is strictly limited to that particular type of hedge. This exception does not fit into the new hedge accounting model. The IASB decided that in order to retain this exception pending the completion of the project on accounting for macro hedging, a scope exception that allows the continued application of IAS 39 for this particular type of hedge is appropriate.

(d)   in contrast, cash flow hedge accounting in a 'macro' context was an application of the (general) hedge accounting model under IAS 39. Consequently, it is consistent with that approach to include 'macro cash flow hedge accounting' as an application of the new hedge accounting model.

BC6.93   However, the IASB received feedback that some entities were unsure whether and how 'macro cash flow hedge accounting' could also be applied under the hedge accounting requirements of IFRS 9. In response, the IASB considered whether it could address those concerns by carrying forward the Implementation Guidance that accompanied IAS 39 and that illustrated 'macro cash flow hedge accounting'. The IASB noted that to do so would be inconsistent with its decision not to carry forward any of the hedge accounting Implementation Guidance that accompanied IAS 39. The IASB also noted that making an exception by carrying forward some parts of the Implementation Guidance but not others could have unintended consequences because it would inevitably create the perception that the IASB had endorsed some parts while it had rejected others.

BC6.94   The IASB also noted that carrying forward Implementation Guidance could not be justified as a means to address any concerns about whether a particular accounting practice complies with the hedge accounting requirements. Implementation Guidance only accompanies, but is not part of, a Standard, which means that it does not override the requirements of a Standard.

BC6.95   Consequently, the IASB decided to retain its original approach of not carrying forward any of the hedge accounting related Implementation Guidance that accompanied IAS 39. However, the IASB emphasised that not carrying forward the Implementation Guidance did not mean that it had rejected that guidance.

BC6.96   The IASB also received feedback that some entities were concerned that 'proxy hedging' would not be possible under the hedge accounting model in IFRS 9 — a concern that was highlighted by the 'macro cash flow hedge accounting' related Implementation Guidance that accompanied IAS 39 not being carried forward. 'Proxy hedging' is a colloquial reference to the use of designations of hedging relationships that do not exactly represent an entity's actual risk management. Examples include using a designation of a gross amount of an exposure (gross designation) when risks are actually managed on a net position basis, and using designations of variable-rate debt instruments in cash flow hedges when risk management is based on managing the interest rate risk of prepayable fixed-rate debt instruments or deposits (such as core deposits). Similarly, 'proxy hedging' can involve designating fixed-rate debt instruments in fair value hedges when risk management is based on managing the interest rate risk of variable-rate debt instruments.

BC6.97   The IASB noted that its rationale for not including a scope exception from the IFRS 9 hedge accounting requirements for 'macro cash flow hedge accounting' reflected that designations of hedging relationships that represent 'proxy hedging' are possible. The IASB was aware that many financial institutions use 'proxy hedging' as described in paragraph BC6.96.

BC6.98   The IASB considered that in those situations the designation for hedge accounting purposes was inevitably not the same as the entity's risk management view of its hedging, but that the designation reflects risk management in that it relates to the same type of risk that was being managed and the instruments used for that purpose. For example, like IAS 39, IFRS 9 also does not allow cash flow hedges of interest rate risk to be designated on a net position basis but entities must instead designate gross positions. This requires so called 'proxy hedging' because the designation for hedge accounting purposes is on a gross position basis even though risk management typically manages on a net position basis. This 'proxy hedging' also includes approaches that for risk management purposes determine the net interest rate risk position on the basis of fixed-rate items. A cash flow hedge designation can still reflect those approaches in that the net interest rate risk position can be viewed as having a dual character: the hedges bridge, for example, the economic mismatch between fixed-rate assets and variable-rate funding (existing variable-rate funding as well as funding to be obtained in the future to continue to fund the assets as existing funding matures). Such an economic mismatch can be regarded as fair value interest rate risk when looking at the assets and as cash flow interest rate risk when looking at the funding. The net position hedging combines the two aspects because both affect the net interest margin. Hence, both fair value and cash flow interest rate risk are inherent aspects of the hedged exposure. However, hedge accounting requires the designation of the hedging relationship as either a fair value hedge or as a cash flow hedge. The IASB noted that in that sense, even if a fair value hedge designation better represented a risk management perspective that considers the fixed-rate assets as the primary or leading aspect, a cash flow hedge designation would still reflect the risk management because of the dual character of the risk position. Consequently, the IASB regarded 'proxy hedging' as an eligible way of designating the hedged item under IFRS 9 as long as that still reflected risk management, which was the case in this situation.

BC6.99 The IASB noted that in such situations entities have to select some items that give rise to interest rate risk and that qualify for designation as a hedged item and designate them as a gross exposure in order to achieve hedge accounting. The IASB acknowledged that in those circumstances there is typically no obvious link between any particular designated hedged item and the designated hedging instrument, and that entities select items for designation that are most suitable for hedge accounting purposes. This means that different entities can have different ways of selecting those items depending on their situation (for example, whether designating an interest rate risk exposure related to a financial asset or a financial liability).

BC6.100 The IASB also noted that designations of hedging relationships that reflect 'proxy hedging' were not unique to hedging of interest rate risk by banks in, for example, a 'macro' context. Despite the objective of the project to represent, in the financial statements, the effect of an entity's risk management activities, the IASB considered that this would in many situations not be possible as a simple, exact '1:1 copy' of the actual risk management perspective. In the IASB's view this was already apparent from other aspects of the hedge accounting model of IFRS 9, for example:

(a) the mere fact that the IASB had limited net position cash flow hedges to foreign currency risk meant that for all other types of hedged risks an entity would have to designate gross amounts (gross designation). But this did not mean that cash flow hedge accounting was prohibited for all other risks that are managed on a net position basis.

(b) an entity that actually hedges on a risk component basis in accordance with its risk management view might not meet the criteria for designating the hedged item as a risk component. But this did not mean that the entity was prohibited from applying hedge accounting altogether. Instead, it was only prohibited from using that particular designation of a risk component. Consequently, the entity could designate the item in its entirety as the hedged item and apply hedge accounting (if it met the qualifying criteria on the basis of that designation).

(c) for many entities the actual risk management is based on a 'flow perspective' for cash flow hedges, which only considers mismatches in the variable cash flows of the hedging instrument and the hedged item as a source of hedge ineffectiveness. However, the measurement of hedge effectiveness for hedge accounting purposes does not allow an entity to assume perfect hedge effectiveness in those circumstances (or limiting the analysis to only the variable cash flows of the hedging instrument). However, this did not mean that hedge accounting was prohibited. Instead, it meant that the entity had to measure hedge ineffectiveness as required for accounting purposes.

(d) the presentation of hedges of net positions requires the use of a separate line item in the income statement instead of directly adjusting the line items affected by the hedged items (for example, grossing up revenue and cost of sales). In contrast, entities' actual risk management often considers the respective line items as hedged at the respective rates that were locked in by the hedges. This difference between the risk management and accounting views did not mean that an entity was prohibited from using hedge accounting. Instead, it meant that the entity had to follow the presentation requirements for accounting purposes if it wanted to apply hedge accounting.

BC6.101 Consequently, the IASB did not agree that designations of hedging relationships under IFRS 9 could not represent 'proxy hedging'. The IASB also decided to provide further guidance on how 'proxy hedging' is related to the discontinuation of hedge accounting (see paragraph BC6.331).

BC6.102 However, the IASB also received feedback from some entities that they did not want to have to apply the hedge accounting requirements of IFRS 9 before the IASB's project on accounting for macro hedging was completed. Those entities cited concerns about remaining uncertainty as to whether IAS 39—compliant practices of designating hedging relationships for portfolio hedging or macro hedging activities would still be available, the costs of assessing whether those practices are IFRS 9—compliant and the risk of having to change those practices twice. Some entities questioned whether it was appropriate to require entities to re-examine and potentially make changes to their hedge accounting while the project on accounting for macro hedging was ongoing.

BC6.103 The IASB considered whether it should provide a scope exception to the hedge accounting requirements of IFRS 9 to address those concerns over the interaction with macro hedging activities. This scope exception would be separate from that for fair value hedge accounting for a portfolio hedge of interest rate risk, which complements the hedge accounting requirements of IFRS 9 and which the IASB had already proposed in the 2010 Hedge Accounting Exposure Draft (see paragraph BC6.88). In this case the IASB considered whether there was a need to allow entities to continue to apply IAS 39 to cash flow hedges in the context of macro hedging activities. In the IASB's view it was not necessary from a technical perspective to make any changes in addition to the clarifications that it had already provided (see paragraphs BC6.93–BC6.101). However, the IASB acknowledged that it had not yet completed its project on accounting for macro hedging and that providing a choice to continue to apply the hedge accounting requirements in IAS 39 would allow entities to wait for the complete picture related to the accounting for hedging activities before applying a new hedge accounting model.

BC6.104 Consequently, the IASB considered whether it could provide a specific scope exception that would confine the continued application of IAS 39 to situations in which entities seek to apply 'macro cash flow hedge accounting'. However, the IASB determined that such a specific scope would be difficult to describe, resulting in added complexity and the risk that interpretation questions would arise. The IASB therefore decided to provide entities with an accounting policy choice between applying the hedge accounting requirements of IFRS 9 (including the scope exception for fair value hedge accounting for a portfolio hedge of interest rate risk) and continuing to apply the existing hedge accounting requirements in IAS 39 for all hedge accounting until its project on the accounting for macro hedging is completed. The IASB noted that an entity could subsequently decide to change its accounting policy and commence applying the hedge accounting requirements of IFRS 9 at the beginning of any reporting period (subject to the other transition requirements of IFRS 9). The IASB also emphasised that, once IFRS 9 as amended in November 2013 is applied, the new disclosure requirements related to hedge accounting are part of IFRS 7 and would consequently apply to all entities using hedge accounting under IFRS (even if electing to continue to apply IAS 39 for hedge accounting).

Hedge accounting for equity investments designated as at fair value through other comprehensive income

BC6.105 In accordance with IFRS 9 an entity may, at initial recognition, make an irrevocable election to present subsequent changes in the fair value of some investments in equity instruments in other comprehensive income. Amounts recognised in other comprehensive income for such equity instruments are not reclassified to profit or loss. However, IAS 39 defined a hedging relationship as a relationship in which the exposure to be hedged could affect profit or loss. Consequently, an entity could not apply hedge accounting if the hedged exposure affected other comprehensive income without reclassification out of other comprehensive income to profit or loss because only such a reclassification would mean that the hedged exposure could ultimately affect profit or loss.

BC6.106 For its 2010 Hedge Accounting Exposure Draft, the IASB considered whether it should amend the definition of a fair value hedge to state that the hedged exposure could affect either profit or loss or other comprehensive income, instead of only profit or loss. However, the IASB had concerns about the mechanics of matching the changes in the fair value of the hedging instrument with the changes in the value of the hedged item attributable to the hedged risk. Furthermore, the IASB was concerned about how to account for any related hedge ineffectiveness. To address these concerns, the IASB considered alternative approaches.

BC6.107 The IASB considered whether the hedge ineffectiveness should remain in other comprehensive income when the changes in the value of the hedged item attributable to the hedged risk are bigger than the changes in the fair value of the hedging instrument. This approach would:

(a) be consistent with the IASB's decision on classification and measurement (the first phase of the IFRS 9 project), whereby changes in the fair value of the equity investment designated as at fair value through other comprehensive income should not be reclassified to profit or loss; but

(b) contradict the hedge accounting principle that hedge ineffectiveness should be recognised in profit or loss.

BC6.108 Conversely, if the hedge ineffectiveness were recognised in profit or loss it would:

(a) be consistent with the hedge accounting principle that hedge ineffectiveness should be recognised in profit or loss; but

(b) contradict the prohibition of reclassifying from other comprehensive income to profit or loss gains or losses on investments in equity instruments accounted for as at fair value through other comprehensive income.

BC6.109 Consequently, in its 2010 Hedge Accounting Exposure Draft the IASB proposed prohibiting hedge accounting for investments in equity instruments designated as at fair value through other comprehensive income, because it could not be achieved within the existing framework of hedge accounting. Introducing another framework would add complexity. Furthermore, the IASB did not want to add another exception (ie contradicting the principle in IFRS 9 of not reclassifying between other comprehensive income and profit or loss, or contradicting the principle of recognising hedge ineffectiveness in profit or loss) to the existing exception of accounting for investments in equity instruments (ie the option to account for those investments at fair value through other comprehensive income).

BC6.110 However, the IASB noted that dividends from such investments in equity instruments are recognised in profit or loss. Consequently, a forecast dividend from such investments could be an eligible hedged item (if all qualifying criteria for hedge accounting are met).

BC6.111 Almost all respondents to the 2010 Hedge Accounting Exposure Draft disagreed with the IASB's proposal to prohibit hedge accounting for investments in equity instruments designated as at fair value through other comprehensive income. Those respondents argued that hedge accounting should be available for equity investments at fair value through other comprehensive income so that hedge accounting can be more closely aligned with risk management activities. In particular, respondents commented that it was a common risk management strategy for an entity to hedge the foreign exchange risk exposure of equity investments (irrespective of the accounting designation at fair value through profit or loss or other comprehensive income). In addition, an entity might also hedge the equity price risk even though it does not intend to sell the equity investment because it might still want to protect itself against equity volatility.

BC6.112 In the light of those concerns, the IASB reconsidered whether it should allow investments in equity instruments designated as at fair value through other comprehensive income to be designated as a hedged item in a fair value hedge. Some respondents argued that the inconsistencies that the IASB had discussed in its original deliberations (see paragraphs BC6.107–BC6.108) could be overcome by using a differentiating approach, whereby if fair value changes of the hedging instrument exceeded those of the hedged item hedge ineffectiveness would be presented in profit or loss and otherwise in other comprehensive income. However, the IASB noted that the cumulative ineffectiveness presented in profit or loss or other comprehensive income over the total period of the hedging relationship might still contradict the principle of not recycling to profit or loss changes in the fair value of equity investments at fair value through other comprehensive income. Hence, the IASB rejected that approach.

BC6.113   The IASB noted that recognising hedge ineffectiveness always in profit or loss would be inconsistent with the irrevocable election of presenting in other comprehensive income fair value changes of investments in equity instruments (see paragraph BC6.108). The IASB considered that that outcome would defeat its aim to reduce complexity in accounting for financial instruments.

BC6.114   The IASB considered that an approach that would recognise hedge ineffectiveness always in other comprehensive income (without recycling) could facilitate hedge accounting in situations in which an entity's risk management involves hedging risks of equity investments designated as at fair value through other comprehensive income without contradicting the classification and measurement requirements of IFRS 9. The IASB noted that, as a consequence, hedge ineffectiveness would not always be presented in profit or loss but would always follow the presentation of the value changes of the hedged item.

BC6.115   The IASB considered that, on balance, the advantages of the approach that always recognises hedge ineffectiveness in other comprehensive income (without recycling) for those investments in equity instruments would outweigh any disadvantages and, overall, that this alternative was superior to the other alternatives that the IASB had contemplated. Hence, the IASB decided to include this approach in the final requirements.

BC6.116   The IASB also considered whether hedge accounting should be more generally available for exposures that only affect other comprehensive income (but not profit or loss). However, the IASB was concerned that such a broad scope might result in items qualifying for hedge accounting that might not be suitable hedged items and hence have unintended consequences. Consequently, the IASB decided against making hedge accounting more generally available to such exposures.

Hedging instruments

Qualifying instruments

Derivatives embedded in financial assets

BC6.117   IAS 39 required the separation of derivatives embedded in hybrid financial assets and liabilities that are not closely related to the host contract (bifurcation). In accordance with IAS 39, the separated derivative was eligible for designation as a hedging instrument. In accordance with IFRS 9, hybrid financial assets are measured in their entirety (ie including any embedded derivative) at either amortised cost or fair value through profit or loss. No separation of any embedded derivative is permitted.

BC6.118　　In the light of the decision that it made on IFRS 9, the IASB considered whether derivatives embedded in financial assets should be eligible for designation as hedging instruments. The IASB considered two alternatives:

(a)　　an entity could choose to separate embedded derivatives solely for the purpose of designating the derivative component as a hedging instrument; or

(b)　　an entity could designate a risk component of the hybrid financial asset, equivalent to the embedded derivative, as the hedging instrument.

BC6.119　　The IASB rejected both alternatives. Consequently, the IASB proposed not to allow derivative features embedded in financial assets to be eligible hedging instruments (even though they can be an integral part of a hybrid financial asset that is measured at fair value through profit or loss and designated as the hedging instrument in its entirety—see paragraph BC6.129). The reasons for the IASB's decision are summarised in paragraphs BC6.120–BC6.121.

BC6.120　　Permitting an entity to separate embedded derivatives for the purpose of hedge accounting would retain the IAS 39 requirements in terms of their eligibility as hedging instruments. However, the IASB noted that the underlying rationale for separating embedded derivatives in IAS 39 was not to reflect risk management activities, but instead to prevent an entity from circumventing the requirements for the recognition and measurement of derivatives. The IASB also noted that the designation of a separated embedded derivative as a hedging instrument in accordance with IAS 39 was not very common in practice. Hence, the IASB considered that reintroducing the separation of embedded derivatives for hybrid financial assets does not target hedge accounting considerations, would consequently not be an appropriate means to address any hedge accounting concerns and in addition would reintroduce complexity for situations that are not common in practice.

BC6.121　　Alternatively, permitting an entity to designate, as the hedging instrument, a risk component of a hybrid financial asset would allow that entity to show more accurately the results of its risk management activities. However, such an approach would be a significant expansion of the scope of the Hedge Accounting project because the IASB would need to address the question of how to disaggregate a hedging instrument into components. In order to be consistent, a similar question would need to be addressed for non-financial items (for example, non-financial liabilities in IAS 37 Provisions, Contingent Liabilities and Contingent Assets with currency or commodity risk elements). The IASB did not want to expand the scope of the hedge accounting project beyond financial instruments because the outcome of exploring this alternative would be highly uncertain, could possibly necessitate a review of other Standards and could significantly delay the project.

BC6.122　　The IASB therefore retained its original decision when deliberating its 2010 Hedge Accounting Exposure Draft.

Non-derivative financial instruments

BC6.123 Hedge accounting shows how the changes in the fair value or cash flows of a hedging instrument offset the changes in the fair value or cash flows of a designated hedged item attributable to the hedged risk if it reflects an entity's risk management strategy.

BC6.124 IAS 39 permitted non-derivative financial assets and non-derivative financial liabilities (for example, monetary items denominated in a foreign currency) to be designated as hedging instruments only for a hedge of foreign currency risk. Designating a non-derivative financial asset or liability denominated in a foreign currency as a hedge of foreign currency risk in accordance with IAS 39 was equivalent to designating a risk component of a hedging instrument in a hedging relationship. This foreign currency risk component is determined in accordance with IAS 21 *The Effects of Changes in Foreign Exchange Rates*. Because the foreign currency risk component is determined in accordance with foreign currency translation requirements in IAS 21, it is already available for incorporation by reference in the financial instruments Standard. Consequently, permitting the use of a foreign currency risk component for hedge accounting purposes did not require separate, additional requirements for risk components within the hedge accounting model.

BC6.125 Not allowing the disaggregation of a non-derivative financial instrument used as a hedge into risk components, other than foreign currency risk, has implications for the likelihood of achieving hedge accounting for those instruments. This is because the effects of components of the cash instrument that are not related to the risk being hedged cannot be excluded from the hedging relationship and consequently from the effectiveness assessment. Consequently, depending on the size of the components that are not related to the risk being hedged, in most scenarios it will be difficult to demonstrate that there is an economic relationship between the hedged item and the hedging instrument that gives rise to an expectation that their values will systematically change in response to movements in either the same underlying or underlyings that are economically related in such a way that they respond in a similar way to the risk that is being hedged.

BC6.126 In the light of this consequence, the IASB considered whether it should permit non-derivative financial instruments to be eligible for designation as hedging instruments for risk components other than foreign currency risk. The IASB noted that permitting this would require developing an approach for disaggregating non-derivative hedging instruments into components. For reasons similar to those set out in paragraph BC6.121 the IASB decided not to explore such an approach.

BC6.127 The IASB also considered two alternatives to the requirements of IAS 39 (those requirements that limit the eligibility of non-derivative financial instruments as hedging instruments to hedges of foreign currency risk). The IASB considered whether for hedges of all types of risk (ie not limited to hedges of foreign currency risk) it should extend the eligibility as hedging instruments to non-derivative financial instruments:

(a) that are classified as at fair value through profit or loss; or (alternatively to those); and

(b) that are part of other categories of IFRS 9.

BC6.128 The IASB noted that extending the eligibility to non-derivative financial instruments in categories other than fair value through profit or loss would give rise to operational problems because to apply hedge accounting would require changing the measurement of non-derivative financial instruments measured at amortised cost when they are designated as hedging instruments. The IASB considered that the only way to mitigate this issue was to allow for the designation of components of the non-derivative financial instrument. This would limit the change in measurement to a component of the instrument attributable to the hedged risk. However, the IASB had already rejected that idea in its deliberations (see paragraph BC6.126).

BC6.129 However, the IASB noted that extending the eligibility to non-derivative financial instruments that are measured at fair value through profit or loss, if designated in their entirety (instead of only some risk components of them), would not give rise to the need to change the measurement or the recognition of gains and losses of the financial instrument. The IASB also noted that extending the eligibility to these financial instruments would align the new hedge accounting model more closely with the classification model of IFRS 9 and make it better able to address hedging strategies that could evolve in the future. Consequently, the IASB proposed in its 2010 Hedge Accounting Exposure Draft that non-derivative financial instruments that are measured at fair value through profit or loss should also be eligible hedging instruments if they are designated in their entirety (in addition to hedges of foreign currency risk for which the hedging instrument can be designated on a risk component basis—see paragraph BC6.124).

BC6.130 Generally, respondents to the 2010 Hedge Accounting Exposure Draft agreed that distinguishing between derivative and non-derivative financial instruments was not appropriate for the purpose of determining their eligibility as hedging instruments. Many respondents believed that extending the eligibility criteria to non-derivative financial instruments at fair value through profit or loss would allow better representation of an entity's risk management activities in the financial statements. The feedback highlighted that this was particularly relevant in countries that have legal and regulatory restrictions on the use and availability of derivative financial instruments.

BC6.131 Some respondents argued that there was no conceptual basis to restrict the eligibility of non-derivative financial instruments to those that are measured at fair value through profit or loss. In their view all non-derivative financial instruments should be eligible as hedging instruments.

BC6.132 Other respondents thought that that the proposals were not restrictive enough, particularly in relation to non-derivative financial instruments that are measured at fair value through profit or loss as a result of applying the fair value option. Those respondents thought that the IASB should specifically restrict the use of non-derivative financial instruments designated under the fair value option because these have usually been elected to be measured at fair value to eliminate an accounting mismatch and hence should not qualify for hedge accounting. Some respondents also questioned whether a financial liability that is measured at fair value, with changes in the fair value attributable to changes in the liability's credit risk presented in other comprehensive income, would be an eligible hedging instrument under the proposals in the 2010 Hedge Accounting Exposure Draft.

BC6.133 The IASB noted that in its deliberations leading to the 2010 Hedge Accounting Exposure Draft it had already considered whether non-derivative financial instruments measured at amortised cost should also be eligible for designation as hedging instruments. The IASB remained concerned that designating as hedging instruments those non-derivative financial instruments that were not already accounted for at fair value through profit or loss would result in hedge accounting that would change the measurement or recognition of gains and losses of items that would otherwise result from applying IFRS 9. For example, the IASB noted that it would have to determine how to account for the difference between the fair value and the amortised cost of the non-derivative financial instrument upon designation as a hedging instrument. Furthermore, upon discontinuation of the hedging relationship, the measurement of the non-derivative financial instrument would revert to amortised cost resulting in a difference between its carrying amount as of the date of discontinuation (the fair value as at the discontinuation date which becomes the new deemed cost) and its maturity amount. The IASB considered that addressing those aspects would inappropriately increase complexity.

BC6.134 The IASB was also concerned that allowing non-derivative financial instruments that are not already accounted for at fair value through profit or loss to be designated as hedging instruments would mean that the hedge accounting model would not only change the measurement basis of the hedged item, as the existing hedge accounting model already does, but also the measurement basis of hedging instruments. Hence, it could, for example, result in situations in which a natural hedge (ie an accounting match) is already achieved on an amortised cost basis between two non-derivative financial instruments, but hedge accounting could still be used to change the measurement basis of both those instruments to fair value (one as a hedged item and the other as the hedging instrument).

BC6.135 Consequently, the IASB decided that non-derivative financial instruments should be eligible hedging instruments only if they are already accounted for at fair value through profit or loss.

BC6.136 The IASB also discussed whether or not those non-derivative financial instruments that are accounted for at fair value through profit or loss as a result of applying the fair value option should be eligible for designation as a hedging instrument. The IASB considered that any designation as a hedging instrument should not contradict the entity's election of the fair value option (ie recreate the accounting mismatch that the election of the fair value option addressed). For example, if a non-derivative financial instrument that has previously been designated under the fair value option is included in a cash flow hedge relationship, the accounting for the non-derivative financial instrument under the fair value option would have to be overridden. This is because all (or part) of the changes in the fair value of that hedging instrument are recognised in other comprehensive income. However, recognising the changes in fair value in other comprehensive income re-introduces the accounting mismatch that the application of the fair value option eliminated in the first instance. The IASB noted that similar considerations apply to fair value hedges and hedges of net investments in foreign operations.

BC6.137 Consequently, the IASB considered whether it should introduce a general prohibition against designating, as hedging instruments, non-derivative financial instruments that are accounted for at fair value through profit or loss as a result of electing the fair value option. However, such a prohibition would not necessarily be appropriate. The IASB noted that one of the items underlying the fair value option might be sold or terminated at a later stage (ie the circumstances that made the fair value option available might be subject to change or later disappear). However, because the fair value option is irrevocable it would mean a non-derivative financial instrument for which the fair value option was initially elected could never qualify as a hedging instrument even if there was no longer a conflict between the purpose of the fair value option and the purpose of hedge accounting. A general prohibition would not allow the use of hedge accounting at a later stage even when hedge accounting might then mitigate an accounting mismatch (without recreating another one).

BC6.138 The IASB noted that when a non-derivative financial instrument is accounted for at fair value through profit or loss as a result of electing the fair value option, the appropriateness of its use as a hedging instrument depends on the relevant facts and circumstances underlying the fair value option designation. The IASB considered that if an entity designates as a hedging instrument a financial instrument for which it originally elected the fair value option, and this results in the mitigation of an accounting mismatch (without recreating another one), using hedge accounting was appropriate. However, the IASB emphasised that if applying hedge accounting recreates, in the financial statements, the accounting mismatches that electing the fair value option sought to eliminate, then designating the financial instrument for which the fair value option was elected as a hedging instrument would contradict the basis (qualifying criterion) on which the fair value option was elected. Hence, in those situations there would be a conflict between the purpose of the fair value option and the purpose of hedge accounting as they could not be achieved at the same time but instead would, overall, result in another accounting mismatch. Consequently, the IASB emphasised that designating the non-derivative financial instrument as a hedging instrument in those situations would call into question the legitimacy of electing the fair value option and would be inappropriate. The IASB considered that, to this effect, the requirements of the fair value option were sufficient and hence no additional guidance was necessary.

BC6.139   As a result, the IASB decided not to introduce a general prohibition against the eligibility of designating as hedging instruments non-derivative financial instruments accounted for at fair value through profit or loss as a result of electing the fair value option.

BC6.140   The IASB also considered whether it needed to provide more guidance on when a non-derivative financial liability designated as at fair value through profit or loss under the fair value option would qualify as a hedging instrument. The IASB noted that IFRS 9 refers to liabilities for which the fair value option is elected as "liabilities designated at fair value through profit or loss", irrespective of whether the effects of changes in the liability's credit risk are presented in other comprehensive income or (if that presentation would enlarge an accounting mismatch) in profit or loss. However, for the eligibility as a hedging instrument, the IASB considered that it would make a difference whether the effects of changes in the liability's credit risk are presented in other comprehensive income or profit or loss. The IASB noted that if a financial liability whose credit risk related fair value changes are presented in other comprehensive income was an eligible hedging instrument there would be two alternatives for what could be designated as part of the hedging relationship:

    (a)   only the part of the liability that is measured at fair value through profit or loss, in which case the hedging relationship would exclude credit risk and hence any related hedge ineffectiveness would not be recognised; or

    (b)   the entire fair value change of the liability, in which case the presentation in other comprehensive income of the changes in fair value related to changes in the credit risk of the liability would have to be overridden (ie using reclassification to profit or loss) to comply with the hedge accounting requirements.

BC6.141   Consequently, the IASB decided to clarify its proposal by adding an explicit statement that a financial liability is not eligible for designation as a hedging instrument if under the fair value option the amount of change in the fair value attributable to changes in the liability's own credit risk is presented in other comprehensive income.

Internal derivatives as hedging instruments

BC6.142   An entity may follow different risk management models depending on the structure of its operations and the nature of the hedges. Some use a centralised treasury or similar function that is responsible for identifying the exposures and managing the risks borne by various entities within the group. Others use a decentralised risk management approach and manage risks individually for entities in the group. Some also use a combination of those two approaches.

BC6.143   Internal derivatives are typically used to aggregate risk exposures of a group (often on a net basis) to allow the entity to manage the resulting consolidated exposure. However, IAS 39 was primarily designed to address one-to-one hedging relationships. Consequently, in order to explore how to align accounting with risk management, the IASB considered whether internal derivatives should be eligible for designation as hedging instruments. However, the IASB noted that the ineligibility of internal derivatives as hedging instruments was not the root cause of misalignment between risk management and hedge accounting. Instead, the challenge was how to make hedge accounting operational for groups of items and net positions.

BC6.144 The IASB noted that, for financial reporting purposes, the mitigation or transformation of risk is generally only relevant if it results in a transfer of risk to a party outside the reporting entity. Any transfer of risk within the reporting entity does not change the risk exposure from the perspective of that reporting entity as a whole. This is consistent with the principles of consolidated financial statements.

BC6.145 For example, a subsidiary might transfer cash flow interest rate risk from variable-rate funding to the group's central treasury using an interest rate swap. The central treasury might decide to retain that exposure (instead of hedging it out to a party external to the group). In that case, the cash flow interest rate risk of the stand-alone subsidiary has been transferred (the swap is an external derivative from the subsidiary's perspective). However, from the group's consolidated perspective, the cash flow interest rate risk has not changed but merely been reallocated between different parts of the group (the swap is an internal derivative from the group's perspective).

BC6.146 Consequently, in the deliberations leading to the 2010 Hedge Accounting Exposure Draft, the IASB decided that internal derivatives should not be eligible hedging instruments in the financial statements of the reporting entity (for example, intragroup derivatives in the consolidated financial statements) because they do not represent an instrument that the reporting entity uses to transfer the risk to an external party (ie outside the reporting entity). This meant that the related requirements in IAS 39 would be retained.

BC6.147 The IASB retained its original decision when redeliberating its 2010 Hedge Accounting Exposure Draft.

Intragroup monetary items as hedging instruments

BC6.148 In accordance with IAS 39, the difference arising from the translation of intragroup monetary items in the consolidated financial statements in accordance with IAS 21 was eligible as a hedged item but not as a hedging instrument. This may appear inconsistent.

BC6.149 The IASB noted that, when translating an intragroup monetary item, IAS 21 requires the recognition of a gain or loss in the consolidated statement of profit or loss and other comprehensive income. Consequently, in the IASB's view, considering intragroup monetary items for eligibility as hedging instruments would require a review of the requirements in IAS 21 at the same time as considering any hedge accounting requirements. The IASB noted that at that time there was no active project on foreign currency translation. Hence, it decided that it should not address this issue as part of its project on hedge accounting. Consequently, in the deliberations leading to the 2010 Hedge Accounting Exposure Draft, the IASB decided not to allow intragroup monetary items to be eligible hedging instruments (ie to retain the restriction in IAS 39).

BC6.150 The IASB retained its original decision when redeliberating its 2010 Hedge Accounting Exposure Draft.

Written options

BC6.151 In its 2010 Hedge Accounting Exposure Draft, the IASB retained the restriction in IAS 39 that a written option does not qualify as a hedging instrument except when it is used to hedge a purchased option or unless it is combined with a purchased option as one derivative instrument (for example, a collar) and that derivative instrument is not a net written option.

BC6.152 However, respondents to the 2010 Hedge Accounting Exposure Draft commented that a stand-alone written option should not be excluded from being eligible for designation as a hedging instrument if it is jointly designated with other instruments such that in combination they do not result in a net written option. Those respondents highlighted that entities sometimes enter into two separate option contracts because of, for example, legal or regulatory considerations, and that the two separate option contracts achieve, in effect, the same economic outcome as one contract (for example, a collar contract).

BC6.153 The IASB considered that the eligibility of an option contract to be designated as a hedging instrument should depend on its economic substance instead of its legal form. Consequently, the IASB decided to amend the requirements such that a written option and a purchased option (regardless of whether the hedging instrument arises from one or several different contracts) can be jointly designated as the hedging instrument, provided that the combination is not a net written option. The IASB also noted that by aligning the accounting for combinations of written and purchased options with that for derivative instruments that combine written and purchased options (for example, a collar contract), the assessment of what is, in effect, a net written option would be the same, ie it would follow the established practice under IAS 39. That practice considers the following cumulative factors to ascertain that an interest rate collar or other derivative instrument that includes a written option is not a net written option:

(a) no net premium is received either at inception or over the life of the combination of options. The distinguishing feature of a written option is the receipt of a premium to compensate the writer for the risk incurred.

(b) except for the strike prices, the critical terms and conditions of the written option component and the purchased option component are the same (including underlying variable or variables, currency denomination and maturity date). Also, the notional amount of the written option component is not greater than the notional amount of the purchased option component.

Hedged items

Qualifying items

Financial instruments held within a business model whose objective is to collect or pay contractual cash flows

BC6.154 Against the background of potential interaction with the classification of financial instruments in accordance with IFRS 9, the IASB, in its deliberations leading to the 2010 Hedge Accounting Exposure Draft, considered the eligibility for hedge accounting of financial instruments held within a business model whose objective is to collect or pay contractual cash flows. The IASB focused on fair value hedges of interest rate risk because other risks (for example, foreign currency risk) affect cash flows that are collected or paid and the application of hedge accounting seemed clearly appropriate. More specifically, the IASB was concerned about whether a desire to enter into a fair value hedge can be seen as calling into question whether the entity's business model is to hold the financial instrument to collect (or pay) contractual cash flows, instead of selling (or settle/transfer) the instrument before contractual maturity in order to realise the fair value changes. Consequently, some argue that, on the basis of the assertion underlying the business model assessment, the entity should be interested only in the contractual cash flows arising from those investments and not in the changes in fair value.

BC6.155 The IASB discussed several situations in which a fair value hedge of interest rate risk does not contradict the fact that a financial instrument is held with the objective to collect or pay contractual cash flows. One example is an entity that seeks to invest in a variable-rate asset of a particular credit quality, but could only obtain a fixed-rate asset of the desired credit quality. That entity could create the cash flow profile of a variable-rate asset indirectly by buying both the available fixed-rate investment and entering into an interest rate swap that transforms the fixed-interest cash flows from that asset into variable-interest cash flows. The IASB noted that this and other examples demonstrated that what is a fair value hedge for accounting purposes is, from a risk management perspective, often a choice between receiving (or paying) fixed versus variable interest cash flows, instead of a strategy to protect against fair value changes. Hence, the IASB considered that a fair value hedge of interest rate risk would not in itself contradict the assertion that a financial instrument is held with the objective to collect or pay contractual cash flows.

BC6.156 The IASB also noted that, under the classification model for financial instruments in IFRS 9, an entity may sell or transfer some financial instruments that qualify for amortised cost, even if they are held with the objective to collect or pay contractual cash flows. Consequently, the IASB decided that fair value hedge accounting should be available for financial instruments that are held with the objective to collect or pay contractual cash flows.

BC6.157 The IASB retained its original decisions when redeliberating its 2010 Hedge Accounting Exposure Draft.

Designation of derivatives

BC6.158 The guidance on implementing IAS 39 stated that derivatives could be designated as hedging instruments only, not as hedged items (either individually or as part of a group of hedged items). As the sole exception, paragraph AG94 in the application guidance in IAS 39 allowed a purchased option to be designated as a hedged item. In practice, this has generally prevented derivatives from qualifying as hedged items. Similarly, positions that are a combination of an exposure and a derivative ('aggregated exposures') failed to qualify as hedged items. The implementation guidance accompanying IAS 39 provided the rationale for not permitting derivatives (or aggregated exposures that include a derivative) to be designated as hedged items. It stated that derivative instruments were always deemed to be held for trading and measured at fair value with gains or losses recognised in profit or loss unless they are designated as hedging instruments.

BC6.159 However, this rationale is difficult to justify in the light of the exception to permit some purchased options to qualify as hedged items irrespective of whether the option is a stand-alone derivative or an embedded derivative. If a stand-alone purchased option can be a hedged item then prohibiting derivatives that are part of an aggregated exposure to be part of a hedged item is arbitrary. Many raised similar concerns in response to the Discussion Paper *Reducing Complexity in Reporting Financial Instruments* about the prohibition of designating derivatives as hedged items.

BC6.160 The IASB noted that an entity was sometimes economically required to enter into transactions that result in, for example, both interest rate risk and foreign currency risk. While those two exposures can be managed together at the same time and for the entire term, the IASB noted that entities often use different risk management strategies for the interest rate risk and foreign currency risk. For example, for 10-year fixed-rate debt denominated in a foreign currency an entity may hedge the foreign currency risk for the entire term of the debt instrument but require fixed-rate exposure in its functional currency only for the short to medium term (say, two years) and floating-rate exposure in its functional currency for the remaining term to maturity. At the end of each of the two-year intervals (ie on a two-year rolling basis) the entity fixes the next two years (if the interest level is such that the entity wants to fix interest rates). In such a situation an entity may enter into a 10-year fixed-to-floating cross-currency interest rate swap that swaps the fixed-rate foreign currency debt into a variable-rate functional currency exposure. This is then overlaid with a two-year interest rate swap that—on the basis of the functional currency—swaps variable-rate debt into fixed-rate debt. In effect, the fixed-rate foreign currency debt and the 10-year fixed-to-floating cross-currency interest rate swap in combination are viewed as a 10-year variable-rate debt functional currency exposure for risk management purposes.

BC6.161 Consequently, for the purpose of its 2010 Hedge Accounting Exposure Draft, the IASB concluded that the fact that an aggregated exposure is created by including an instrument that has the characteristics of a derivative should not, in itself, preclude the designation of that aggregated exposure as a hedged item.

BC6.162 Most respondents to the 2010 Hedge Accounting Exposure Draft supported the proposal to allow aggregated exposures to be designated as hedged items. Those respondents noted that the proposal better aligns hedge accounting with an entity's risk management by allowing hedge accounting to be used for common ways in which entities manage risks. In addition, those respondents noted that the proposal removes the arbitrary restrictions that were in IAS 39 and moves closer towards a principle-based requirement. The IASB therefore decided to retain the notion of an aggregated exposure as proposed in the 2010 Hedge Accounting Exposure Draft.

BC6.163 The main requests that respondents made to the IASB were:

(a) to provide examples that would illustrate the accounting mechanics for aggregated exposures;

(b) to clarify that accounting for aggregated exposures is not tantamount to 'synthetic accounting'; and

(c) to clarify whether an entity would, in a first step (and as a precondition), have to achieve hedge accounting for the combination of the exposure and the derivative that together constitute the aggregated exposure so that, in a second step, the aggregated exposure itself can then be eligible as the hedged item in the other hedging relationship.

BC6.164 In response to the request for examples of the accounting mechanics for aggregated exposures, the IASB decided to provide illustrative examples to accompany IFRS 9. The IASB considered that numerical examples illustrating the mechanics of the accounting for aggregated exposures would, at the same time, address other questions raised in the feedback on the proposals, such as how hedge ineffectiveness is recognised and the type of the hedging relationships involved. Moreover, the IASB noted that those examples would also demonstrate that the proposed accounting for aggregated exposures is very different from 'synthetic accounting', which would reinforce the second clarification that respondents had requested.

BC6.165 The IASB thought that the confusion about 'synthetic accounting' arose from accounting debates in the past about whether two items should be treated for accounting purposes as if they were one single item. This would have had the consequence that a derivative could have assumed the accounting treatment for a non-derivative item (for example, accounting at amortised cost). The IASB noted that, in contrast, under the 2010 Hedge Accounting Exposure Draft's proposal for aggregated exposures the accounting for derivatives would always be at fair value and hedge accounting would be applied to them. Hence, the IASB emphasised that accounting for aggregated exposures does not allow 'synthetic accounting'.

BC6.166 The IASB noted that most respondents had correctly understood the 2010 Hedge Accounting Exposure Draft (ie that it does not allow 'synthetic accounting') but the IASB was still concerned because any misconception that aggregated exposures are tantamount to 'synthetic accounting' would result in a fundamental accounting error. Hence, the IASB decided to provide, in addition to illustrative examples, an explicit statement confirming that derivatives that form part of an aggregated exposure are always recognised as separate assets or liabilities and measured at fair value.

BC6.167 The IASB also discussed the request to clarify whether an entity would have to first (as a precondition) achieve hedge accounting for the combination of the underlying exposure and the derivative that constitute the aggregated exposure (the first level relationship) so that the aggregated exposure itself can be eligible as the hedged item in the other hedging relationship (the second level relationship). The IASB noted that the effect of not achieving hedge accounting for the first level relationship depended on the circumstances (in particular, the types of hedge used). In many circumstances, it would make the accounting for the aggregated exposure more complicated and the outcome inferior compared to achieving hedge accounting for the first level relationship. However, the IASB considered that achieving hedge accounting for the first level relationship was not required to comply with the general hedge accounting requirements for the second level relationship (ie the hedging relationship in which the aggregated exposure is the hedged item). Consequently, the IASB decided not to make achieving hedge accounting for the first level relationship a prerequisite for qualifying for hedge accounting for the second level relationship.

BC6.168 The IASB also clarified two other aspects that had been raised by some respondents:

(a) that the notion of an aggregated exposure includes a highly probable forecast transaction of an aggregated exposure if that aggregated exposure, once it has occurred, is eligible as a hedged item; and

(b) how to apply the general requirements of designating a derivative as the hedging instrument in the context of aggregated exposures. The IASB noted that the way in which a derivative is included in the hedged item that is an aggregated exposure must be consistent with the designation of that derivative as the hedging instrument at the level of the aggregated exposure (ie at the level of the first level relationship—if applicable, ie if hedge accounting is applied at that level). If the derivative is not designated as the hedging instrument at the level of the aggregated exposure, it must be designated in its entirety or as a proportion of it. The IASB noted that, consistent with the general requirements of the hedge accounting model, this also ensures that including a derivative in an aggregated exposure does not allow splitting a derivative by risk, by parts of its term or by cash flows.

Designation of hedged items

Designation of a risk component

BC6.169　IAS 39 distinguished the eligibility of risk components for designation as the hedged item by the type of item that includes the component:

(a)　for financial items, an entity could designate a risk component if that risk component was separately identifiable and reliably measurable; however,

(b)　for non-financial items, an entity could only designate foreign currency risk as a risk component.

BC6.170　Risk components of non-financial items, even when they are contractually specified, were not eligible risk components in accordance with IAS 39. Consequently, other than for foreign currency risk, a non-financial item was required to be designated as the hedged item for all risks. The rationale for including this restriction in IAS 39 was that permitting risk components (portions) of non-financial assets and non-financial liabilities to be designated as the hedged item for a risk other than foreign currency risk would compromise the principles of identification of the hedged item and effectiveness testing because the portion could be designated so that no ineffectiveness would ever arise.

BC6.171　The hedge accounting model in IAS 39 used the entire item as the default unit of account and then provided rules to govern what risk components of that entire item were available for separate designation in hedging relationships. This has resulted in the hedge accounting requirements being misaligned with many risk management strategies. The outcome was that the normal approach for risk management purposes was treated as the exception by the hedge accounting requirements.

BC6.172　Many of the comment letters received on the Discussion Paper *Reducing Complexity in Reporting Financial Instruments* criticised the prohibition on designating risk components for non-financial items. This was also the most common issue raised during the IASB's outreach activities.

BC6.173　The IASB noted that the conclusion in IAS 39, that permitting, as hedged items, risk components of non-financial assets and non-financial liabilities would compromise the principles of identification of the hedged item and effectiveness testing, was not appropriate in all circumstances. As part of its deliberations, the IASB considered whether risk components should be eligible for designation as hedged items when they are:

(a)　contractually specified; and

(b)　not contractually specified.

BC6.174　Contractually specified risk components determine a currency amount for a pricing element of a contract independently of the other pricing elements and, therefore, independently of the non-financial item as a whole. Consequently, these components are separately identifiable. The IASB also noted that many pricing formulas that use a reference to, for example, benchmark commodity prices are designed in that way to ensure that there is no gap or misalignment for that risk component compared with the benchmark price. Consequently, by reference to that risk component, the exposure can be economically fully hedged using a derivative with the benchmark as the underlying. This means that the hedge effectiveness assessment on a risk components basis accurately reflects the underlying economics of the transaction (ie that there is no or very little ineffectiveness).

BC6.175　However, in many situations risk components are not an explicit part of a fair value or a cash flow. Nonetheless, many hedging strategies involve the hedging of components even if they are not contractually specified. There are different reasons for using a component approach to hedging, including:

(a)　the entire item cannot be hedged because there is a lack of appropriate hedging instruments;

(b)　it is cheaper to hedge the single components individually than the entire item (for example, because an active market exists for the risk components, but not for the entire item); and

(c)　the entity makes a conscious decision to hedge only particular parts of the fair value or cash flow risk (for example, because one of the risk components is particularly volatile and it therefore justifies the costs of hedging it).

BC6.176　The IASB learned from its outreach activities that there are circumstances in which entities are able to identify and measure many risk components (not only foreign currency risk) of non-financial items with sufficient reliability. Appropriate risk components (if they are not contractually specified) can be determined only in the context of the particular market structure related to that risk. Consequently, the determination of appropriate risk components requires an evaluation of the relevant facts and circumstances (ie careful analysis and knowledge of the relevant markets). The IASB noted that as a result there is no 'bright line' to determine eligible risk components of non-financial items.

BC6.177　Consequently, in its 2010 Hedge Accounting Exposure Draft, the IASB proposed that risk components (both those that are and those that are not contractually specified) should be eligible for designation as hedged items as long as they are separately identifiable and reliably measurable. This proposal would align the eligibility of risk components of non-financial items with that of financial items in IAS 39.

BC6.178　Most respondents to the 2010 Hedge Accounting Exposure Draft supported the IASB's proposal and its rationale for allowing risk components (both those that are and those that are not contractually specified) to be eligible for designation as hedged items. Those respondents noted that the proposal on risk components was a key aspect of the new hedge accounting model because it would allow hedge accounting to reflect that, in commercial reality, hedging risk components was the norm and hedging items in their entirety was the exception.

BC6.179   Many respondents noted that IAS 39 was biased against hedges of non-financial items such as commodity hedges. They considered the distinction between financial and non-financial items for determining which risk components would be eligible hedged items as arbitrary and without conceptual justification. The main request by respondents was for additional guidance or clarifications.

BC6.180   Only a few respondents disagreed with the IASB's proposal on risk components. Those respondents believed that, in situations in which non-contractually specified risk components of non-financial items would be designated as hedged items, no hedge ineffectiveness would be recognised.

BC6.181   The IASB noted that the debate about risk components suffered from some common misunderstandings. In the IASB's opinion, the root cause of those misunderstandings is the large number of markets and circumstances in which hedging takes place. This results in an inevitable lack of familiarity with many markets. In the light of the arguments raised and to address some of the misunderstandings, the IASB focused its discussions on non-contractually specified risk components of non-financial items and, in particular, on:

(a)   the effect of risk components; and

(b)   hedge ineffectiveness when designating a risk component.

BC6.182   The IASB noted that some believe that designating a risk component as a hedged item should not be allowed if it could result in the value of that risk component moving in an opposite direction to the value of the entire item (ie its overall price). For example, if the hedged risk component increases in value this would offset the loss on the hedging instrument, while decreases in the value of other unhedged risk components remain unrecognised.

BC6.183   The IASB noted that this was not specific to non-contractually specified risk components of non-financial items, but that it applied to risk components in general. For example, consider an entity that holds a fixed-rate bond and the benchmark interest rate decreases but the bond's spread over the benchmark increases. If the entity hedges only the benchmark interest rate using a benchmark interest rate swap, the loss on the swap is offset by a fair value hedge adjustment for the benchmark interest rate component of the bond (even though the bond's fair value is lower than its carrying amount after the fair value hedge adjustment because of the increase in the spread).

BC6.184   The IASB also noted that designating a risk component was not tantamount to 'hiding losses' or avoiding their recognition by applying hedge accounting. Instead, it would help to mitigate accounting mismatches that would otherwise result from how an entity manages its risks. If hedge accounting is not applied, only the gain or loss from the change in the fair value of the financial instrument that hedges the risk is recognised in profit or loss, whereas the gain or loss on the entire item that gives rise to the risk remains fully unrecognised (until it is realised in a later period) so that any offset is obscured. If designation on a risk component basis is not available, that initially creates an issue of whether the hedge qualifies at all for hedge accounting and is inconsistent with the economic decision of hedging done on a components basis. Consequently, the accounting assessment would be completely disconnected from the decision making of an entity, which is driven by risk management purposes. The IASB also noted that this consequence would be amplified by the fact that the hedged component is not necessarily the main or largest component (for example, in the case of a power purchase agreement with a contractual pricing formula that includes indexations to fuel oil and inflation, only the inflation risk but not the fuel oil price risk is hedged).

BC6.185 The IASB noted that even if hedge accounting can be achieved between the hedging instrument and the item (which includes the hedged risk component) in its entirety, the accounting outcome would be more akin to a fair value option for the entire item than reflecting the effect of the economic hedge. However, because hedge accounting would be disconnected from what is economically hedged, there would also be ramifications for the hedge ratio that would have to be used for designating the hedging relationship. The hedge ratio that an entity actually uses (ie for decision making purposes driven by risk management) would be based on the economic relationship between the underlyings of the hedged risk component and the hedging instrument. This is the sensible basis for hedging decisions. However, for accounting purposes, an entity would be forced to compare changes in the value of the hedging instrument to those of the entire item. This means that, in order to improve the offset for the hedging relationship that is designated for accounting purposes, an entity would have to create a deliberate mismatch compared to the economic hedging relationship, which is tantamount to distorting the economic hedge ratio for accounting purposes. The IASB noted that distorting the hedge ratio also meant that prohibiting the designation of hedged items on a risk components basis would, ultimately, not necessarily result in the financial statements reflecting the change in the value of the unhedged risk component as a gain or loss for which there is no offset. Hence, prohibiting that kind of designation would not achieve transparency about the changes in the value of unhedged components by showing a gain or loss for which there is no offset.

BC6.186 The IASB also noted that designating risk components as hedged items would reflect the fact that risk management typically operates on a 'by risk' basis instead of on a 'by item' basis (which is the unit of account for financial reporting purposes). Hence, the use of risk components as hedged items would reflect what in commercial reality is the norm instead of requiring that all hedged items are 'deemed' to be hedged in their entirety (ie for all risks).

BC6.187 The IASB also considered the effect that risk components have on the recognition of hedge ineffectiveness. A few respondents believed that if a risk component was designated as the hedged item, it would result in no hedge ineffectiveness being recognised.

BC6.188 The IASB noted that the effect of designating a risk component as the hedged item was that it became the point of reference for determining offset (ie the fair value change on the hedging instrument would be compared to the change in value of the designated risk component instead of the entire item).

This would make the comparison more focused because it would exclude the effect of changes in the value of risks that are not hedged, which would also make hedge ineffectiveness a better indicator of the success of the hedge. The IASB noted that the hedge accounting requirements would apply to the risk component in the same way as they apply to other hedged items that are not risk components. Consequently, even when a risk component was designated as the hedged item, hedge ineffectiveness could still arise and would have to be measured and recognised. For example:

(a)   a floating-rate debt instrument is hedged against the variability of cash flows using an interest rate swap. The two instruments are indexed to the same benchmark interest rate but have different reset dates for the variable payments. Even though the hedged item is designated as the benchmark interest rate related variability in cash flows (ie as a risk component), the difference in reset dates causes hedge ineffectiveness. There is no market structure that would support identifying a 'reset date' risk component in the variable payments on the floating rate debt that would mirror the reset dates of the interest rate swap. In particular, the terms and conditions of the interest rate swap cannot be simply imputed by projecting terms and conditions of the interest rate swap onto floating-rate debt.

(b)   a fixed-rate debt instrument is hedged against fair value interest rate risk using an interest rate swap. The two instruments have different day count methods for the fixed-rate payments. Even though the hedged item is designated as the benchmark interest rate related change in fair value (ie as a risk component), the difference in the day count methods causes hedge ineffectiveness. There is no market structure that would support identifying a 'day count' risk component in the payments on the debt that would mirror the day count method of the interest rate swap. In particular, the terms and conditions of the interest rate swap cannot be simply imputed by projecting terms and conditions of the interest rate swap onto the fixed-rate debt.

(c)   an entity purchases crude oil under a variable-price oil supply contract that is indexed to a light sweet crude oil benchmark. Because of the natural decline of the benchmark oil field the derivatives market for that benchmark has suffered a significant decline in liquidity. In response, the entity decides to use derivatives for a different benchmark for light sweet crude oil in a different geographical area because the derivatives market is much more liquid. The changes in the crude oil price for the more liquid benchmark and the less liquid benchmark are closely correlated but vary slightly. The variation between the two oil benchmark prices causes hedge ineffectiveness. There is no market structure that would support identifying the more liquid benchmark as a component in the variable payments under the oil supply contract. In particular, the terms and conditions of the derivatives indexed to the more liquid benchmark cannot simply be imputed by projecting terms and conditions of those derivatives onto the oil supply contract.

(d)   an entity is exposed to price risk from forecast purchases of jet fuel. The entity's jet fuel purchases are in North America and Europe. The entity determines that the relevant crude oil benchmark for jet fuel purchases at its North American locations is West Texas Intermediate (WTI) whereas it is Brent for jet fuel purchases at its European locations. Hence, the entity designates as the hedged item a WTI crude oil component for its jet fuel purchases in North America and a Brent crude oil component for its jet fuel purchases in Europe. Historically, WTI and Brent have been closely correlated and the entity's purchase volume in North America significantly exceeds its European purchase volume. Hence, the entity uses one type of hedge contract—indexed to WTI—for all its crude oil components. Changes in the price differential between WTI and Brent cause hedge ineffectiveness related to the forecast purchases of jet fuel in Europe. There is no market structure that would support identifying WTI as a component of Brent. In particular, the terms and conditions of the WTI futures cannot simply be imputed by projecting terms and conditions of those derivatives onto the forecast jet fuel purchases in Europe.

BC6.189   Consequently, the IASB noted that the designation of a risk component as a hedged item did not mean that no hedge ineffectiveness arises or that it would not be recognised.

BC6.190   The IASB noted that the concerns about hedge ineffectiveness not being recognised related particularly to non-contractually specified risk components of non-financial items. However, the IASB considered that this was not a financial versus non-financial item problem. Determining the hedge ineffectiveness, for example, for a fixed-rate debt instrument when designating the benchmark interest rate component as the hedged item is no more or less troublesome than doing so for commodity price risk. In both cases the appropriate designation of a risk component depends on an appropriate analysis of the market structure. The IASB noted that the derivative markets for commodity risk had evolved and had resulted in customs that helped improve the effectiveness of hedging. For example, very liquid commodity benchmarks have evolved, allowing for a market volume for derivatives that is far larger than the physical volume of the underlying commodity, thus facilitating benchmarks that can be widely used.

BC6.191   In the light of those considerations and the responses received on the 2010 Hedge Accounting Exposure Draft, the IASB decided to retain the notion of risk components as eligible hedged items. Because of the large variety of markets and circumstances in which hedging takes place, the IASB considered that, in order to avoid arbitrary discrimination against some markets, risks or geographies, there was no alternative to using a criteria-based approach to identifying eligible risk components. Consequently, the IASB decided that for risk components (of both financial and non-financial items) to qualify as eligible hedged items, they must be separately identifiable and reliably measureable. In response to requests from respondents, the IASB also decided to expand the examples of how to determine eligible risk components, including illustrations of the role of the market structure.

BC6.192 The IASB also discussed the proposal in the 2010 Hedge Accounting Exposure Draft to prohibit the designation of non-contractually specified inflation risk components of financial instruments. That prohibition was carried over from IAS 39. The IASB noted that an outright ban meant that the general criteria for the eligibility of risk components could not be applied and, as a result, would leave no room for the possibility that in some situations there might be circumstances that could support identifying a risk component for inflation risk. On the other hand, the IASB was concerned that the removal of the restriction would encourage the use of inflation risk components for hedge accounting when it was not necessarily appropriate to do so. This would be the case when a risk component, instead of being supported by the market structure and independently determined for the hedged item, would, for example, be determined by simply projecting the terms and conditions of the inflation derivative that was actually used as the hedge onto the hedged item. In the light of this trade-off, the IASB also considered that financial markets continuously evolve and that the requirements should be capable of addressing changes in the market over time.

BC6.193 On balance, the IASB decided to remove the prohibition. However, it was concerned that its decision could be misunderstood as simply 'rubber stamping' the use of inflation risk components for hedge accounting without proper application of the criteria for designating risk components. The IASB therefore agreed to include a caution in the final requirements that, in order to determine whether inflation risk is an eligible risk component, a careful analysis of the facts and circumstances is required so that the criteria for designating risk components are properly applied. Consequently, the IASB decided to add a rebuttable presumption related to non-contractually specified inflation risk components of financial instruments.

Designation of 'one-sided' risk components

BC6.194 IAS 39 permitted an entity to designate changes in the cash flows or fair value of a hedged item above or below a specified price or other variable (a 'one-sided' risk). So, an entity might hedge an exposure to a specific type of risk of a financial instrument (for example, interest rates) above a pre-determined level (for example, above 5 per cent) using a purchased option (for example, an interest rate cap). In this situation an entity hedged some parts of a specific type of risk (ie interest exposure above 5 per cent).

BC6.195 Furthermore, the IASB noted that hedging one-sided risk exposures is a common risk management activity. The IASB also noted that the main issue that relates to the hedging of one-sided risk is the use of options as hedging instruments. Consequently, the IASB decided to permit the designation of one-sided risk components as hedged items, as was the case in IAS 39 for some risk components. However, the IASB decided to change the accounting for the time value of options (see paragraphs BC6.386–BC6.413).

BC6.196 The IASB retained its original decisions about the eligibility of one-sided risk components as hedged items when redeliberating its 2010 Hedge Accounting Exposure Draft.

Components of a nominal amount—designation of a component that is a proportion

BC6.197　The IASB noted that components that form some quantifiable nominal part of the total cash flows of the instrument are typically separately identifiable. For example, a proportion, such as 50 per cent, of the contractual cash flows of a loan includes all the characteristics of that loan. In other words, changes in the value and cash flows for the 50 per cent component are half of those for the entire instrument.

BC6.198　The IASB noted that a proportion of an item forms the basis of many different risk management strategies and are commonly hedged in practice (often in combination with risk components). The IASB concluded that if the effectiveness of the hedging relationship can be measured, an entity should be permitted to designate a proportion of an item as a hedged item (as previously permitted by IAS 39).

BC6.199　The IASB retained its original decisions when redeliberating its 2010 Hedge Accounting Exposure Draft.

Components of a nominal amount—designation of a layer component

BC6.200　IAS 39 required an entity to identify and document anticipated (ie forecast) transactions that are designated as hedged items with sufficient specificity so that when the transaction occurs, it is clear whether the transaction is or is not the hedged transaction. As a result, IAS 39 permitted forecast transactions to be identified as a 'layer' component of a nominal amount, for example, the first 100 barrels of the total oil purchases for a specific month (ie a layer of the total oil purchase volume). Such a designation accommodates the fact that there is some uncertainty surrounding the hedged item related to the amount or timing. This uncertainty does not affect the hedging relationship to the extent that the hedged volume occurs (irrespective of which particular individual items make up that volume).

BC6.201　The IASB considered whether similar considerations should also apply to a hedge of an existing transaction or item in some situations. For example, a firm commitment or a loan might also involve some uncertainty because:

(a)　a contract might be cancelled for breach of contract (ie non-performance); or

(b)　a contract with an early termination option (for repayment at fair value) might be terminated before maturity.

BC6.202　Because there is uncertainty for both anticipated transactions and existing transactions and items, the IASB decided not to distinguish between such transactions and items for the purposes of designating a layer component.

BC6.203　The IASB noted that designating as the hedged item a component that is a proportion of an item can give rise to a different accounting outcome when compared with designating a layer component. If the designation of those components is not aligned with the risk management strategy of the entity, it might result in profit or loss providing confusing or less useful information to users of financial statements.

BC6.204   In the IASB's view there might be circumstances when it is appropriate to designate a layer component as a hedged item. Consequently, in its 2010 Hedge Accounting Exposure Draft the IASB proposed to permit the designation of a layer component as the hedged item (for anticipated and existing transactions). The IASB also proposed that a layer component of a contract that includes a prepayment option should not be eligible as a hedged item in a fair value hedge if the option's fair value is affected by changes in the hedged risk. The IASB noted that if the prepayment option's fair value changed in response to the hedged risk a layer approach would be tantamount to identifying a risk component that was not separately identifiable (because the change in the value of the prepayment option owing to the hedged risk would not be part of how the hedge effectiveness would be measured).

BC6.205   Most respondents to the 2010 Hedge Accounting Exposure Draft agreed with the proposed change for fair value hedges, which would allow an entity to designate a layer component from a defined nominal amount. They agreed that such layers would allow entities to better reflect what risk they actually hedge.

BC6.206   However, many respondents disagreed with the IASB's proposal to prohibit, in any circumstances, the designation of a layer component in a fair value hedge for all contracts that include any prepayment option whose fair value is affected by changes in the hedged risk. Those respondents' main objection was that the proposal was inconsistent with common risk management strategies and that the fair value changes of a prepayment option were irrelevant in the context of a bottom layer.

BC6.207   In the light of the comments received, the IASB discussed:

(a)   whether the prohibition to designate a layer component as the hedged item in a fair value hedge should relate to an entire item or contract containing a prepayment option or whether it should relate only to those situations in which the designated layer contains a prepayment option;

(b)   whether a layer component can be designated as the hedged item in a fair value hedge if it includes the effect of a related prepayment option; and

(c)   whether the requirement should differentiate between written and purchased prepayment options, thereby allowing a layer component to be designated for items with a purchased option, ie if the entity is the option holder (for example, a debtor's call option included in prepayable debt).

BC6.208   The IASB discussed situations in which a contract is prepayable for only a part of its entire amount, which means that the remainder is not prepayable and hence does not include a prepayment option. For example, a loan with a principal amount of CU100 and a maturity of five years that allows the debtor to repay (at par) up to CU10 at the end of each year would mean that only CU40 is prepayable (at different points in time), whereas CU60 is non-prepayable but has a five-year fixed term. Because the CU60 is fixed-term debt that is not affected by prepayments, its fair value does not include the effect of a prepayment option. Consequently, the changes in the fair value related to the CU60 are unrelated to the fair value changes of the prepayment option for other amounts. This means that if the CU60 were designated as a layer component, the hedge ineffectiveness would appropriately exclude the change in the fair value of the prepayment option. The IASB considered that this would be consistent with its rationale for proposing to prohibit a layer component of an (entire) item or contract that contains a prepayment option (see paragraph BC6.204) to be designated. However, the IASB noted that the changes in fair value of the amounts that are prepayable (ie the CU40 at inception, CU30 after one year, CU20 after two years and CU10 after three years) include a prepayment option and the designation of a layer for these amounts would therefore contradict the IASB's rationale (see paragraph BC6.204). The IASB noted that the layer of CU60 in this example should not be confused with a bottom layer of CU60 that is expected to remain at maturity from a total amount of CU100 that is prepayable in its entirety. The difference is that the expected remaining amount of a larger prepayable amount is the expected eventual outcome of a variable contractual maturity, whereas the CU60 in this example is the definite outcome of a fixed contractual maturity.

BC6.209 Consequently, the IASB decided to:

(a) confirm the proposals in the 2010 Hedge Accounting Exposure Draft to allow a layer-based designation of a hedged item (when the item does not include a prepayment option whose fair value is affected by changes in the hedged risk); and

(b) to allow a layer-based designation for those amounts that are not prepayable at the time of designation of a partially prepayable item.

BC6.210 The IASB also discussed whether a layer component should be available for designation as the hedged item in a fair value hedge if it includes the effect of a related prepayment option when determining the change in fair value of the hedged item.

BC6.211 Including the change in fair value of the prepayment option that affects a layer when determining hedge ineffectiveness has the following consequences:

(a) the designated hedged item would include the entire effect of changes in the hedged risk on the fair value of the layer, ie including those resulting from the prepayment option; and

(b) if the layer was hedged with a hedging instrument (or a combination of instruments that are designated jointly) that does not have option features that mirror the layer's prepayment option, hedge ineffectiveness would arise.

BC6.212　The IASB noted that a designation of a layer as the hedged item, if it included the effects of a related prepayment option when determining the change in fair value of the hedged item, would not conflict with its rationale for proposing the requirements related to the implication of prepayment options for layer designations (see paragraph BC6.204).

BC6.213　Consequently, the IASB decided that designating a layer as the hedged item should be allowed if it includes the effect of a related prepayment option when determining the change in fair value of the hedged item.

BC6.214　The IASB also considered whether it should differentiate between written and purchased prepayment options for the purpose of determining the eligibility of a layer-based designation of a hedged item in a fair value hedge. Some respondents had argued that if the entity was the option holder, it would control the exercise of the option and could therefore demonstrate that the option was not affected by the hedged risk.

BC6.215　However, the IASB noted that the hedged risk affects the fair value of a prepayment option irrespective of whether the particular option holder actually exercises it at that time or intends to actually exercise it in the future. The fair value of the option captures the possible outcomes and hence the risk that an amount that would be in the money might be repaid at a different amount than at fair value before taking the prepayment option into account (for example, at par). Consequently, the IASB noted that whether a prepayment option is a purchased or a written option does not affect the change in the option's absolute fair value but instead determines whether it is either a gain or a loss from the entity's perspective. In other words, the IASB considered that the aspect of who controls the exercise of the option relates to whether any intrinsic value would be realised (but not whether it exists).

BC6.216　Consequently, the IASB decided not to differentiate between written and purchased prepayment options for the purpose of the eligibility of a layer-based designation of hedged items.

Relationship between components and the total cash flows of an item

BC6.217　IAS 39 allowed an entity to designate the LIBOR component of an interest-bearing asset or liability provided that the instrument has a zero or positive spread over LIBOR. When an entity has an interest-bearing debt instrument with an interest rate that is below LIBOR (or linked to a reference rate that is demonstrably below LIBOR), it would not be able to designate a hedging relationship based on a LIBOR risk component that assumes LIBOR cash flows that would exceed the actual cash flows on that debt instrument. However, for an asset or liability with a negative spread to LIBOR, an entity could still achieve hedge accounting by designating all of the cash flows of the hedged item for LIBOR interest rate risk (which is different from designating a LIBOR component that assumes cash flows exceeding those of the hedged item).

BC6.218　When an entity (particularly a bank) has access to sub-LIBOR funding (bearing a variable-interest coupon at LIBOR minus a spread or an equivalent fixed-rate coupon), the negative spread represents a positive margin for the borrower. This is because banks on average pay LIBOR for their funding in the interbank market. Another example of when this occurs is when the reference rate is highly correlated with LIBOR and the negative spreads arise because of the better credit risk of the contributors to the reference index compared with LIBOR. When entering into hedging relationships, an entity cannot obtain (at a reasonable cost) a standardised hedging instrument for all transactions that are priced sub-LIBOR. Consequently, such an entity uses hedging instruments that have LIBOR as their underlying.

BC6.219 In the deliberations leading to the 2010 Hedge Accounting Exposure Draft, the IASB noted that it had received feedback on the sub-LIBOR issue from its outreach activities that accompanied those deliberations. That feedback showed that some participants believed that designating a risk component that assumes cash flows that would exceed the actual cash flows of the financial instrument reflected risk management in situations in which the hedged item has a negative spread to the benchmark rate. They believed that it should be possible to hedge the LIBOR risk as a benchmark component and treat the spread as a negative residual component. They argued that they were hedging their exposure to the variability of cash flows attributable to LIBOR (or a correlated index) using LIBOR swaps.

BC6.220 In the deliberations leading to the 2010 Hedge Accounting Exposure Draft, the IASB noted that, for risk management purposes, an entity normally does not try to hedge the effective interest rate of the financial instrument but instead the change in the variability of the cash flows attributable to LIBOR. By doing this, such an entity ensures that exposure to benchmark interest rate risk is managed and that the profit margin of the hedged items (ie the spread relative to the benchmark) is protected against LIBOR changes, provided that LIBOR is not below the absolute value of the negative spread. This risk management strategy provides offsetting changes related to the LIBOR-related interest rate risk in a similar way to situations in which the spread above LIBOR is zero or positive. However, if LIBOR falls below the absolute value of that negative spread it would result in 'negative' interest, or interest that is inconsistent with the movement of market interest rates (similar to a 'reverse floater'). The IASB noted that these outcomes are inconsistent with the economic phenomenon to which they relate.

BC6.221 To avoid those outcomes, the IASB proposed retaining the restriction in IAS 39 for the designation of risk components when the designated component would exceed the total cash flows of the hedged item. However, the IASB emphasised that hedge accounting would still be available on the basis of designating all the cash flows of an item for a particular risk, ie a risk component for the actual cash flows of the item (see paragraph BC6.217).

BC6.222 The IASB received mixed views on its proposal to retain this restriction. Some agreed with the restriction and the IASB's rationale for retaining it. Others were concerned that the restriction was inconsistent with common risk management practices. Those who disagreed believed that it should be possible to designate as the hedged item a benchmark risk component that is equivalent to the entire LIBOR and to treat the spread between the entire LIBOR and the contractual rate as a negative residual component. Their view reflects the fact that they are hedging their exposure to the variability of cash flows attributable to LIBOR (or a correlated index) using LIBOR swaps (see paragraph BC6.226 for an example). In their view, the IASB's proposal would not allow them to properly reflect the hedging relationship, and would force them to recognise hedge ineffectiveness that, in their view, would not reflect their risk management strategy.

BC6.223 In response to the concerns raised, the IASB considered whether it should allow the designation of risk components on a benchmark risk basis that assumes cash flows exceeding the total actual cash flows of the hedged item.

BC6.224 As part of its redeliberations, the IASB discussed how contractual terms and conditions that determine whether an instrument has a zero interest rate floor or 'negative' interest (ie no floor) might affect the designation of a full LIBOR component of a sub-LIBOR instrument.

BC6.225 The IASB discussed an example of an entity that has a liability that pays a fixed rate and grants a loan at a floating rate with both instruments being priced at sub-LIBOR interest rates. The entity enters into a LIBOR-based interest rate swap with the aim of locking in the margin that it will earn on the combined position. If the entity wants to designate the hedged item on the basis of the interest rate risk that results from its financial asset, this would be an example of a cash flow hedge of variable-rate interest cash flows from a sub-LIBOR asset.

BC6.226 The IASB noted that if the floating-rate asset had a zero interest rate floor and LIBOR decreased below the absolute value of the negative spread on the asset, the return on the asset (after taking into account the effect of the swap) would increase as a result of the interest rate swap not having a floor. This means that if designated on a full LIBOR risk component basis, the hedging relationship would have outcomes that would be inconsistent with the notion of a locked margin. In this example, the margin could become variable instead of being locked. The IASB was of the view that, in the context of hedge accounting, this would give rise to hedge ineffectiveness that must be recognised in profit or loss. The IASB noted that this hedge ineffectiveness resulted from the absence of offsetting cash flows and hence represented a genuine economic mismatch between changes in cash flows on the floating-rate asset and the swap. Hence, if a full LIBOR component was imputed for interest bearing instruments that are priced sub-LIBOR, it would inappropriately defer hedge ineffectiveness in other comprehensive income. In the IASB's view this would be tantamount to accrual accounting for the interest rate swap.

BC6.227 In contrast, the IASB noted that if the floating-rate asset had no floor, the sub-LIBOR instrument included in the hedging relationship would still have changes in their cash flows that would move with LIBOR even if LIBOR was below the absolute value of the spread. Consequently, the variability in cash flows of the hedging instrument that locks the margin would be offset by the variability of the cash flows of the sub-LIBOR instrument irrespective of the LIBOR level. In other words, the LIBOR-related cash flow variability when the asset had no floor would be equivalent to that of a full LIBOR component and therefore the proposed requirement would not prohibit designating the hedged item accordingly (ie as changes in cash flows of a full LIBOR risk component).

BC6.228　As a result, the IASB decided to confirm the proposal in the 2010 Hedge Accounting Exposure Draft that if a component of the cash flows of a financial or non-financial item is designated as the hedged item, that component must be less than or equal to the total cash flows of the entire item.

BC6.229　Furthermore, the IASB noted that the examples carried over from IAS 39 to the 2010 Hedge Accounting Exposure Draft only included financial items because under IAS 39 the issue could only apply to that type of item. But, given that under the new hedge accounting model this issue also applies to non-financial items that are traded below their respective benchmark price, the IASB decided to add an example of a hedge of commodity price risk in a situation in which the commodity is priced at a discount to the benchmark commodity price.

Qualifying criteria for hedge accounting

Effectiveness assessment

BC6.230　To qualify for hedge accounting in accordance with IAS 39, a hedge had to be highly effective, both prospectively and retrospectively. Consequently, an entity had to perform two effectiveness assessments for each hedging relationship. The prospective assessment supported the expectation that the hedging relationship would be effective in the future. The retrospective assessment determined that the hedging relationship had been effective in the reporting period. All retrospective assessments were required to be performed using quantitative methods. However, IAS 39 did not specify a particular method for testing hedge effectiveness.

BC6.231　The term 'highly effective' referred to the degree to which the hedging relationship achieved offsetting between changes in the fair value or cash flows of the hedging instrument and changes in the fair value or cash flows of the hedged item attributable to the hedged risk during the hedge period. In accordance with IAS 39, a hedge was regarded as highly effective if the offset was within the range of 80–125 per cent (often colloquially referred to as a 'bright line test').

BC6.232　In the deliberations leading to the 2010 Hedge Accounting Exposure Draft, the IASB noted that it had received feedback on the hedge effectiveness assessment under IAS 39 from its outreach activities that accompanied those deliberations. The feedback showed that:

(a)　many participants found that the hedge effectiveness assessment in IAS 39 was arbitrary, onerous and difficult to apply;

(b)　as a result, there was often little or no link between hedge accounting and the risk management strategy; and

(c) because hedge accounting was not achieved if the hedge effectiveness was outside the 80–125 per cent range, it made hedge accounting difficult to understand in the context of the risk management strategy of the entity.

BC6.233 Consequently, in its 2010 Hedge Accounting Exposure Draft the IASB proposed a more principle-based hedge effectiveness assessment. The IASB proposed that a hedging relationship meets the hedge effectiveness requirements if it:

(a) meets the objective of the hedge effectiveness assessment (ie that the hedging relationship will produce an unbiased result and minimise expected hedge ineffectiveness); and

(b) is expected to achieve other than accidental offsetting.

BC6.234 Most respondents to the 2010 Hedge Accounting Exposure Draft supported the removal of the 80–125 per cent quantitative test. Those respondents also supported the IASB in avoiding the use of bright lines in hedge accounting generally and the move towards a more principle-based effectiveness assessment.

BC6.235 Only a few respondents disagreed with the proposal, largely because they believed that the quantitative threshold in IAS 39 was appropriate. They also believed that an approach that was completely principle-based would generate operational difficulties and would have the potential to inappropriately extend the application of hedge accounting.

BC6.236 The sections below elaborate on the IASB's considerations.

The objective of the hedge effectiveness assessment

BC6.237 Traditionally, accounting standard-setters have set high thresholds for hedging relationships to qualify for hedge accounting. The IASB noted that this resulted in hedge accounting that was considered by some as arbitrary and onerous. Furthermore, the arbitrary 'bright line' of 80–125 per cent resulted in a disconnect between hedge accounting and risk management. Consequently, it made it difficult to explain the results of hedge accounting to users of financial statements. To address those concerns, the IASB decided that it would propose an objective-based model for testing hedge effectiveness instead of the 80–125 per cent 'bright line test' in IAS 39.

BC6.238 During its deliberations, the IASB initially considered an objective-based assessment to determine which hedging relationships would qualify for hedge accounting. The IASB's intention was that the assessment should not be based on a particular level of hedge effectiveness. The IASB decided that, in order to avoid the arbitrary outcomes of the assessment under IAS 39, it had to remove, instead of just move, the bright line. The IASB held the view that the objective of the hedge effectiveness assessment should reflect the fact that hedge accounting was based on the notion of offset.

BC6.239 In accordance with the approach that the IASB initially considered, the effectiveness assessment would have aimed only to identify accidental offsetting and prevent hedge accounting in those situations. This assessment would have been based on an analysis of the possible behaviour of the hedging relationship during its term to ascertain whether it could be expected to meet the risk management objective. The IASB believed that the proposed approach would therefore have strengthened the relationship between hedge accounting and risk management practice.

BC6.240 However, the IASB was concerned that this approach might not be rigorous enough. This was because, without clear guidance, an entity might designate hedging relationships that would not be appropriate because they would give rise to systematic hedge ineffectiveness that could be avoided by a more appropriate designation of the hedging relationship and hence be biased. The IASB noted that the bright line of 80–125 per cent in IAS 39 created a trade-off when an entity chose a hedge ratio that would have a biased result, because that result came at the expense of higher ineffectiveness and hence increased the risk of falling outside that range. However, the IASB noted that the 80–125 per cent range would be eliminated by its proposals and therefore decided to extend its initial objective of the effectiveness assessment so that it also included the hedge ratio. Consequently, in its 2010 Hedge Accounting Exposure Draft, the IASB proposed that the objective of assessing the effectiveness of a hedging relationship was that the entity designated the hedging relationship so that it gave an unbiased result and minimised expected ineffectiveness.

BC6.241 The IASB noted that many types of hedging relationships inevitably involve some ineffectiveness that cannot be eliminated. For example, ineffectiveness could arise because of differences in the underlyings or other differences between the hedging instrument and the hedged item that the entity accepts in order to achieve a cost-effective hedging relationship. The IASB considered that when an entity establishes a hedging relationship there should be no expectation that changes in the value of the hedging instrument will systematically either exceed or be less than the change in value of the hedged item. As a result, the IASB proposed in its 2010 Hedge Accounting Exposure Draft that hedging relationships should not be established (for accounting purposes) in such a way that they include a deliberate mismatch in the weightings of the hedged item and of the hedging instrument.

BC6.242 However, many respondents to the 2010 Hedge Accounting Exposure Draft asked the IASB to provide further guidance on the objective-based effectiveness assessment, particularly on the notions of 'unbiased result' and 'minimise expected hedge ineffectiveness'. Those respondents were concerned that the requirements, as drafted in the 2010 Hedge Accounting Exposure Draft, could be interpreted to be more restrictive and onerous than the bright line effectiveness test in IAS 39 and would be inconsistent with risk management practice. More specifically, those respondents were concerned that the objective of the hedge effectiveness assessment as drafted in the 2010 Hedge Accounting Exposure Draft could be interpreted as requiring entities to set up a hedging relationship that was 'perfectly effective'. They were concerned that this would result in an effectiveness assessment that would be based on a bright line of 100 per cent effectiveness, and that such an approach:

(a) would not take into account that, in many situations, entities do not use a hedging instrument that would make the hedging relationship 'perfectly effective'. They noted that entities use hedging instruments that do not achieve perfect hedge effectiveness because the 'perfect' hedging instrument is:

(i) not available; or

(ii) not cost-effective as a hedge (compared to a standardised instrument that is cheaper and/or more liquid, but does not provide the perfect fit).

(b) could be interpreted as a mathematical optimisation exercise. In other words, they were concerned that it would require entities to search for the perfect hedging relationship at inception (and on a continuous basis), because if they did not, the results could be considered to be biased and hedge ineffectiveness would probably not be 'minimised'.

BC6.243 In the light of the concerns about the use of hedging instruments that are not 'perfectly effective', the IASB noted that the appropriate hedge ratio was primarily a risk management decision instead of an accounting decision. When determining the appropriate hedge ratio, risk management would take into consideration, among other things, the following factors:

(a) the availability of hedging instruments and the underlyings of those hedging instruments (and, as a consequence, the level of the risk of differences in value changes involved between the hedged item and the hedging instrument);

(b) the tolerance levels in relation to expected sources of hedge ineffectiveness (which determine when the hedging relationship is adjusted for risk management purposes); and

(c) the costs of hedging (including the costs of adjusting an existing hedging relationship).

BC6.244 The IASB's intention behind its proposal in the 2010 Hedge Accounting Exposure Draft was that an entity would choose the actual hedge basing its decision on commercial considerations, designate it as the hedging instrument and use it as a starting point to determine the hedge ratio that would comply with the proposed requirements. In other words, the IASB did not intend that an entity would have to consider the hedge effectiveness and related hedge ratio that could have been achieved with a different hedging instrument that might have been a better fit for the hedged risk if it did not enter into that hedging instrument.

BC6.245 The IASB also reconsidered the proposed objective of the hedge effectiveness assessment in the light of the concerns that it might result in a mathematical optimisation exercise. In particular, the IASB considered the effect of its proposal in situations in which a derivative is designated as a hedging instrument only after its inception so that it is already in or out of the money at the time of its designation (often colloquially referred to as a 'late hedge'). The IASB considered whether the hedge ratio would have to be adjusted to take into account the (non-zero) fair value of the derivative at the time of its designation. This is because the fair value of the hedging instrument at the time of its designation is a present value. Over the remaining life of the hedging instrument this present value will accrete to the undiscounted amount (the 'unwinding of the discount'). The IASB noted that there is no offsetting fair value change in the hedged item for this effect (unless the hedged item was also in or out of the money in an equal but opposite way). Consequently, in situations in which the derivative is designated as the hedging instrument after its inception, an entity would expect that the changes in the value of the hedging instrument will systematically either exceed or be less than the changes in the value of the hedged item (ie the hedge ratio would not be 'unbiased'). To meet the proposed objective of the hedge effectiveness assessment an entity would need to explore whether it could adjust the hedge ratio to avoid the systematic difference between the value changes of the hedging instrument and the hedged item over the hedging period. However, to determine the ratio that would avoid that systematic difference, an entity would need to know what the actual price or rate of the underlying will be at the end of the hedging relationship. Hence, the IASB noted that the proposed objective of the hedge effectiveness assessment could be interpreted to the effect that, in the (quite common) situations in which an entity has a 'late hedge', the proposed hedge effectiveness requirements would not be met. This is because the entity would not be able to identify a hedge ratio for the designation of the hedging relationship that would not involve an expectation that the changes in value of the hedging instrument will systematically either exceed or be less than the changes in the value of the hedged item. The IASB did not intend this outcome when it developed its proposals in its 2010 Hedge Accounting Exposure Draft.

BC6.246   The IASB noted that the feedback about the requirement that the hedging relationship should minimise hedge ineffectiveness suggested that identifying a 'minimum' would involve considerable effort in all situations in which the terms of the hedging instrument and the hedged item are not fully matched. Hence, the requirement to minimise hedge ineffectiveness would bring back many of the operational problems of the hedge effectiveness assessment in IAS 39. Furthermore, regardless of the effort involved, it would be difficult to demonstrate that the 'minimum' had been identified.

BC6.247   The IASB noted that when it developed its 2010 Hedge Accounting Exposure Draft, it included the notions of 'unbiased' and 'minimise expected hedge ineffectiveness' to ensure that:

(a)   entities would not deliberately create a difference between the quantity actually hedged and the quantity designated as the hedged item in order to achieve a particular accounting outcome; and

(b)   an entity would not inappropriately designate a hedging relationship such that it would give rise to systematic hedge ineffectiveness, which could be avoided by a more appropriate designation.

The IASB noted that both aspects could result in undermining the 'lower of' test for cash flow hedges or achieving fair value hedge adjustments on a greater quantity of the hedged item than an entity actually hedged (ie fair value accounting would be disproportionately expanded compared to the quantity actually hedged).

BC6.248 Taking into account the responses to the 2010 Hedge Accounting Exposure Draft, the IASB decided to remove the terms 'unbiased' (ie no expectation that changes in the value of the hedging instrument will systematically either exceed or be less than the changes in the value of the hedged item such that they would produce a biased result) and 'minimising expected hedge ineffectiveness'. Instead, the IASB decided to state, more directly, that the entity's designation of the hedging relationship shall use a hedge ratio based on:

(a) the quantity of the hedged item that it actually hedges; and

(b) the quantity of the hedging instrument that it actually uses to hedge that quantity of hedged item.

BC6.249 The IASB noted that this approach has the following advantages:

(a) the use of the hedge ratio resulting from the requirement in this Standard provides information about the hedge ineffectiveness in situations in which an entity uses a hedging instrument that does not provide the best fit (for example, because of cost-efficiency considerations). The IASB noted that the hedge ratio determined for risk management purposes has the effect of showing the characteristics of the hedging relationship and the entity's expectations about hedge ineffectiveness. This includes hedge ineffectiveness that results from using a hedging instrument that does not provide the best fit.

(b) it also aligns hedge accounting with risk management and hence is consistent with the overall objective of the new hedge accounting model.

(c) it addresses the requests from respondents to the 2010 Hedge Accounting Exposure Draft for clarification that the relevant hedging instrument to be considered in the hedge effectiveness assessment is the actual hedging instrument the entity decided to use.

(d) it retains the notion proposed in the 2010 Hedge Accounting Exposure Draft that the hedge ratio is not a free choice for accounting purposes as it was in IAS 39 (subject to passing the 80–125 per cent bright line test).

BC6.250 The IASB noted that the only situation open to abuse is if the entity purposefully (for risk management purposes) used a hedge ratio that would be considered 'inappropriately loose' from an accounting perspective, for example:

(a)   if an entity uses an excess quantity of the hedging instrument it would have more costs and risks because of having more hedging instruments than needed to mitigate the risks resulting from the hedged items. However, from an accounting perspective, this would not lead to any advantage because it would create fair value changes for the hedging instrument that affect profit or loss for both fair value hedges and cash flow hedges. The result of an entity using an excess quantity of the hedging instrument would therefore solely be the presentation of fair value changes within profit or loss as hedge ineffectiveness instead of other or trading gains or losses. This would increase the hedge ineffectiveness in an entity's financial statements while having no impact on overall profit or loss.

(b)   if an entity uses a quantity of the hedging instrument that is too small it would leave, economically, a gap in its hedging. From an accounting perspective, this might create an advantage for fair value hedges if an entity wanted to achieve fair value hedge adjustments on a greater quantity of 'hedged items' than it would achieve when using an appropriate hedge ratio. In addition, for cash flow hedges, an entity could abuse the lower of test because the hedge ineffectiveness arising from the larger change in fair value on the hedged item compared to that on the hedging instrument would not be recognised. Consequently, even though using a 'deficit' quantity of the hedging instrument would not be economically advantageous, from an accounting perspective it might have the desired outcome for an entity.

BC6.251   The IASB noted that the potential for abuse, as illustrated above, was implicitly addressed in IAS 39 by the 80–125 per cent bright line of the retrospective hedge effectiveness assessment. Given its decision to remove that bright line (see paragraph BC6.237), the IASB decided to explicitly address this potential for abuse. As a consequence, this Standard requires that, for the purpose of hedge accounting, an entity shall not designate a hedging relationship in a manner that reflects an imbalance between the weightings of the hedged item and the hedging instrument that would create hedge ineffectiveness (irrespective of whether recognised or not) that could result in an accounting outcome that would be inconsistent with the purpose of hedge accounting.

Other than accidental offsetting

BC6.252   IAS 39 was based on a purely accounting-driven percentage-based bright line test (the 80–125 per cent range). This disconnected accounting from risk management (see paragraph BC6.237). Consequently, the IASB proposed replacing the bright line test with a notion that aims to reflect the way entities look at the design and monitoring of hedging relationships from a risk management perspective. Inherent in this was the notion of 'other than accidental offsetting'. This linked the risk management perspective with the hedge accounting model's general notion of offset between gains and losses on hedging instruments and hedged items. The IASB also considered that this link reflected the intention that the effectiveness assessment should not be based on a particular level of effectiveness (hence avoiding a new bright line).

BC6.253 Many respondents to the 2010 Hedge Accounting Exposure Draft asked the IASB to provide further guidance on the notion of 'other than accidental offsetting'. Many also suggested that the IASB revise the proposed guidance by introducing a direct reference to the aspect of an economic relationship between the hedged item and the hedging instrument that was included in the application guidance proposed in the 2010 Hedge Accounting Exposure Draft.

BC6.254 The IASB noted that qualifying criteria that use terminology such as 'other than accidental offsetting' can be abstract. The feedback suggested that this makes the relevant aspects or elements of the hedge effectiveness assessment more difficult to understand. The IASB considered that it could address the respondents' request and reduce the abstractness of this proposal by avoiding the use of an 'umbrella term' and instead making explicit all aspects that the requirement comprises. This would provide greater clarity and facilitate a better understanding of what aspects are relevant when assessing hedge effectiveness.

BC6.255 Consequently, the IASB decided to replace the term 'other than accidental offsetting' with requirements that better conveyed its original notion:

(a) an economic relationship between the hedged item and the hedging instrument, which gives rise to offset, must exist at inception and during the life of the hedging relationship; and

(b) the effect of credit risk does not dominate the value changes that result from that economic relationship.

A 'reasonably effective' threshold

BC6.256 A few respondents suggested that the IASB could consider using a 'qualitative threshold' instead of a principle-based hedge effectiveness assessment. Those respondents believed that, in order to meet the hedge effectiveness criteria, a hedging relationship should be required to be 'reasonably effective' in achieving offsetting changes in the fair value of the hedged item and in the fair value of the hedging instrument.

BC6.257 The IASB noted that a 'reasonably effective' criterion would retain the threshold design of the effectiveness assessment that was used in IAS 39. The IASB considered that moving, instead of removing, the threshold would not address the root cause of the problem (see paragraph BC6.237). The suggested approach would instead only change the level of the threshold. The IASB considered that, even though the threshold would be of a qualitative nature, it would still create a danger of reverting back to a quantitative measure (such as the percentage range of IAS 39) in order for it to be operational. The IASB noted that similar concerns had been raised as part of the feedback to the 2010 Hedge Accounting Exposure Draft.

BC6.258　The IASB also noted that one of the major concerns that respondents had raised about the reference in the 2010 Hedge Accounting Exposure Draft to 'unbiased result' was that it could be perceived as requiring entities to identify the 'perfect' hedging instrument or that the entity's commercial decision of which hedging instrument to actually use could be restricted or second guessed (see paragraph BC6.242).

BC6.259　The IASB considered that using a reference to 'reasonably effective' would give rise to similar concerns because it would raise the question of how much ineffectiveness that results from the choice of the actual hedging instrument is 'reasonable' (similar to the notion of 'unbiased' proposed in the 2010 Hedge Accounting Exposure Draft). The IASB was also concerned that this might have a particular impact on emerging economies because entities in those economies often have to transact hedging instruments in more liquid markets abroad, which means that it is more difficult for them to find a hedging instrument that fits their actual exposure than it is for entities in economies with those liquid markets.

BC6.260　Furthermore, the IASB was concerned that using the single term 'reasonably effective' would mingle different aspects, which would be tantamount to aggregating the different aspects of the effectiveness assessment that the IASB had considered (ie the economic relationship, the effect of credit risk and the hedge ratio). The IASB noted that it was clear from feedback received on its proposed objective of the hedge effectiveness assessment that a single term was too abstract if the notion described by that term included a number of different aspects (see also paragraph BC6.254).

BC6.261　Consequently, the IASB decided not to use a qualitative 'reasonably effective' threshold for assessing hedge effectiveness.

Frequency of assessing whether the hedge effectiveness requirements are met

BC6.262　In the deliberations leading to the 2010 Hedge Accounting Exposure Draft, as a consequence of its proposed hedge effectiveness requirements, the IASB considered how frequently an entity should assess whether the hedge effectiveness requirements were met. The IASB decided that an entity should perform this assessment at the inception of the hedging relationship.

BC6.263　Furthermore, the IASB considered that an entity should assess, on an ongoing basis, whether the hedge effectiveness requirements are still met, including any adjustment (rebalancing) that might be required in order to continue to meet those requirements (see paragraphs BC6.300–BC6.313). This was because the proposed hedge effectiveness requirements should be met throughout the term of the hedging relationship. The IASB also decided that the assessment of those requirements should be only forward-looking (ie prospective) because it related to expectations about hedge effectiveness.

BC6.264 Hence, in the deliberations leading to the 2010 Hedge Accounting Exposure Draft, the IASB concluded that the reassessment of the hedge ratio should be performed at the beginning of each reporting period or upon a significant change in the circumstances underlying the effectiveness assessment, whichever comes first.

BC6.265 Given that the changes made to the proposed hedge effectiveness requirements when redeliberating the 2010 Hedge Accounting Exposure Draft did not affect the IASB's rationale for its proposals for the frequency of the assessment, the IASB retained its original decision.

Method of assessing hedge effectiveness

BC6.266 The method used to assess the effectiveness of the hedging relationship needs to be suitable to demonstrate that the objective of the hedge effectiveness assessment has been achieved. The IASB considered whether the effectiveness of a hedging relationship should be assessed on either a qualitative or a quantitative basis.

BC6.267 Hedging relationships have one of two characteristics that affect the complexity of the hedge effectiveness assessment:

(a) the critical terms of the hedged item and hedging instrument match or are closely aligned. If there are no substantial changes in the critical terms or in the credit risk of the hedging instrument or hedged item, the hedge effectiveness can typically be determined using a qualitative assessment.

(b) the critical terms of the hedged item and hedging instrument do not match and are not closely aligned. These hedging relationships involve an increased level of uncertainty about the degree of offset and so the effectiveness of the hedge during its term is more difficult to evaluate.

BC6.268 Qualitative hedge effectiveness assessments use a comparison of the terms of the hedged item and the hedging instrument (for example, the commonly termed 'critical-terms-match' approach). The IASB considered that, in the context of an effectiveness assessment that does not use a threshold, it can be appropriate to assess the effectiveness qualitatively for a hedging relationship for which the terms of the hedging instrument and the hedged item match or are closely aligned.

BC6.269 However, assessing the hedging relationship qualitatively is less effective than a quantitative assessment in other situations. For example, when analysing the possible behaviour of hedging relationships that involve a significant degree of potential ineffectiveness resulting from terms of the hedged item that are less closely aligned with the hedging instrument, the extent of future offset has a high level of uncertainty and is difficult to determine using a qualitative approach. The IASB considered that a quantitative assessment would be more suitable in such situations.

BC6.270   Quantitative assessments or tests encompass a wide spectrum of tools and techniques. The IASB noted that selecting the appropriate tool or technique depends on the complexity of the hedge, the availability of data and the level of uncertainty of offset in the hedging relationship. The type of assessment and the method used to assess hedge effectiveness therefore depends on the relevant characteristics of the hedging relationship. Consequently, in the deliberations leading to the 2010 Hedge Accounting Exposure Draft, the IASB decided that an entity should assess the effectiveness of a hedging relationship either qualitatively or quantitatively depending on the relevant characteristics of the hedging relationship and the potential sources of ineffectiveness. However, the IASB decided not to prescribe any specific method of assessing hedge effectiveness.

BC6.271   The IASB retained its original decisions when redeliberating its 2010 Hedge Accounting Exposure Draft.

Accounting for qualifying hedging relationships

Hedge of a foreign currency risk of a firm commitment

BC6.272   IAS 39 allowed an entity to choose fair value hedge accounting or cash flow hedge accounting for hedges of the foreign currency risk of a firm commitment. When developing the 2010 Hedge Accounting Exposure Draft, the IASB considered whether it should continue to allow this choice.

BC6.273   The IASB noted that requiring an entity to apply cash flow hedge accounting for all hedges of foreign currency risk of a firm commitment could result in what some regard as 'artificial' other comprehensive income and equity volatility (see paragraphs BC6.353–BC6.354). The IASB also noted that, by requiring an entity to apply cash flow hedge accounting, the lower of test would apply to transactions that already exist (ie firm commitments).

BC6.274   However, the IASB also noted that requiring an entity to apply fair value hedge accounting for all hedges of foreign currency risk of a firm commitment would require a change in the type of hedging relationship to a fair value hedge when the foreign currency cash flow hedge of a forecast transaction becomes a hedge of a firm commitment. This results in operational complexity. For example, this would require changing the measurement of ineffectiveness from a 'lower of' test to a symmetrical test.

BC6.275   The IASB also noted that for existing hedged items (such as firm commitments) foreign currency risk affects both the cash flows and the fair value of the hedged item and hence has a dual character.

BC6.276   Consequently, the IASB proposed in its 2010 Hedge Accounting Exposure Draft to continue to permit an entity the choice of accounting for a hedge of foreign currency risk of a firm commitment as either a cash flow hedge or a fair value hedge.

BC6.277   The IASB retained its original decision when redeliberating its 2010 Hedge Accounting Exposure Draft.

Measuring the ineffectiveness of a hedging relationship

BC6.278 Because the measurement of hedge ineffectiveness is based on the actual performance of the hedging instrument and the hedged item, the IASB in its deliberations leading to the 2010 Hedge Accounting Exposure Draft decided that hedge ineffectiveness should be measured by comparing the changes in their values (on the basis of currency unit amounts).

BC6.279 The IASB retained its original decision when redeliberating its 2010 Hedge Accounting Exposure Draft.

Time value of money

BC6.280 The objective of measuring hedge ineffectiveness is to recognise, in profit or loss, the extent to which the hedging relationship did not achieve offset (subject to the restrictions that apply to the recognition of hedge ineffectiveness for cash flow hedges – often referred to as the lower of test).

BC6.281 The IASB noted that hedging instruments are subject to measurement either at fair value or amortised cost, both of which are present value measurements. Consequently, in order to be consistent, the amounts that are compared with the changes in the value of the hedging instrument must also be determined on a present value basis. The IASB noted that hedge accounting does not change the measurement of the hedging instrument, but that it might change only the location of where the change in its carrying amount is presented. As a result, the same basis (ie present value) for the hedged item must be used in order to avoid a mismatch when determining the amount to be recognised as hedge ineffectiveness.

BC6.282 Consequently, in the deliberations leading to the 2010 Hedge Accounting Exposure Draft, the IASB decided that the time value of money must be considered when measuring the ineffectiveness of a hedging relationship.

BC6.283 The IASB retained its original decision when redeliberating its 2010 Hedge Accounting Exposure Draft.

Hypothetical derivatives

BC6.284 In its deliberations leading to the 2010 Hedge Accounting Exposure Draft, the IASB considered the use of a 'hypothetical derivative', which is a derivative that would have critical terms that exactly match those of a hedged item. The IASB considered the use of a hypothetical derivative in the context of the hedge effectiveness assessment as well as for the purpose of measuring hedge ineffectiveness.

BC6.285 The IASB noted that the purpose of a hypothetical derivative is to measure the change in the value of the hedged item. Consequently, a hypothetical derivative is not a method in its own right for assessing hedge effectiveness or measuring hedge ineffectiveness. Instead, a hypothetical derivative is one possible way of determining an input for other methods (for example, statistical methods or dollar-offset) to assess the effectiveness of the hedging relationship or to measure ineffectiveness.

BC6.286 Consequently, in the deliberations leading to the 2010 Hedge Accounting Exposure Draft, the IASB decided that an entity can use the fair value of a hypothetical derivative to calculate the fair value of the hedged item. This allows determining changes in the value of the hedged item against which the changes in the fair value of the hedging instrument are compared to assess hedge effectiveness and measure ineffectiveness. The IASB noted that this notion of a hypothetical derivative means that using a hypothetical derivative is only one possible way to determine the change in the value of the hedged item and would result in the same outcome as if that change in the value was determined by a different approach (ie it is a mathematical expedient).

BC6.287 When redeliberating its 2010 Hedge Accounting Exposure Draft the IASB considered feedback that disagreed with this proposal. The main reasons cited for disagreement were:

(a) cash flow hedges and fair value hedges are different concepts. Unlike fair value hedges, cash flow hedges are not based on a valuation concept and therefore do not give rise to hedge ineffectiveness from differences in value changes between the hedging instrument and the hedged item as long as their variable cash flows match. However, some conceded that credit risk was a source of hedge ineffectiveness even if all variable cash flows were perfectly matched.

(b) the new hedge accounting model has the objective of aligning hedge accounting more closely with risk management. Risk management has a 'flow perspective' that considers cash flow hedges as (fully) effective if the variable cash flows of the actual derivative match those of the hedged item (ie if the entity uses a 'perfect derivative' to hedge the risk exposure).

(c) the accounting treatment for the effect of a foreign currency basis spread is inconsistent with that for the time value of options and the forward element of forward contracts, ie the notion of 'costs of hedging' that the new hedge accounting model introduces. The foreign currency basis spread is also a cost of hedging and should be treated consistently with the other types of costs of hedging.

BC6.288 The IASB considered whether a cash flow hedge is a different concept from a fair value hedge. The IASB noted that IFRS uses a hedge accounting model that is based on a valuation at the reporting date of both the hedging instrument and the hedged item (valuation model); hedge (in)effectiveness is then measured by comparing the changes in the value of the hedging instrument and the hedged item. Consequently, for determining the effective part of a cash flow hedge, an entity also needs to look at the change in cash flows on a present value basis, ie based on a valuation. Consequently, simply comparing the cash flow variability of the hedging instrument and the hedged item (ie a pure 'flow perspective' without involving a valuation) was not appropriate.

BC6.289 The IASB also noted that IFRS uses a hedge accounting model that does not allow perfect hedge effectiveness to be assumed, and that this applies even if for a cash flow hedge the critical terms of the hedging instrument and the hedged item perfectly match. Doing so could conceal differences in credit risk or liquidity of the hedging instrument and the hedged item, which are potential sources of hedge ineffectiveness for fair value hedges and cash flow hedges alike.

BC6.290 The IASB therefore rejected the view that cash flow hedges and fair value hedges were different concepts in that the former represented a mere comparison of cash flows whereas only the latter represented a comparison of valuations. Consequently, the IASB also rejected the view that a hypothetical derivative is meant to represent the 'perfect hedge' instead of the hedged item. Instead, the IASB confirmed its view that for fair value hedges and cash flow hedges the hedge accounting model:

(a) is a valuation model; and

(b) requires that the value of the hedged item is measured independently of the value of the hedging instrument.

BC6.291 The IASB noted that the objective of aligning hedge accounting with risk management meant that the IASB developed a new hedge accounting model that would facilitate hedge accounting in more circumstances than the previous one and would provide more useful information about the risk management associated with hedging. But this objective did not mean that an entity could override accounting requirements with its particular risk management view.

BC6.292 Consequently, the IASB rejected the view that if risk management considered cash flow hedges as fully effective when the variable cash flows of the actual derivative match those of the hedged item (ie if the entity uses a 'perfect derivative') that hedge should also be considered as fully effective for accounting purposes.

BC6.293 The IASB then considered the concern that the accounting treatment for the effect of a foreign currency basis spread was inconsistent with that for the time value of options and the forward element of forward contracts, ie the notion of 'costs of hedging' that the new hedge accounting model introduces.

BC6.294 The IASB noted that its proposals would result in hedge ineffectiveness arising from the fair value changes of the hedging instrument that are attributable to the effect of a foreign currency basis spread. Taking the example of a cross-currency interest rate swap that is a hedge of the foreign currency risk (and the interest rate risk) of a debt instrument that is denominated in a foreign currency, the IASB noted that the cross-currency interest rate swap included a pricing element that reflected that the derivative instrument resulted in the exchange of two currencies. This led to the IASB questioning whether there was a similar feature or characteristic in the hedged item that would offset the effect of the foreign currency basis spread on the fair value of the cross-currency interest rate swap. The IASB noted that the hedged debt instrument was a single-currency instrument, ie unlike the cross-currency interest rate swap, the hedged item itself did not involve the exchange of two currencies. Instead, any exchange of the debt instrument's currency of denomination for another currency was a circumstance of the holder or issuer of that debt instrument instead of a characteristic or feature of the debt instrument itself.

BC6.295   The IASB noted that whether reflecting the effect of the foreign currency basis spread within hedge ineffectiveness, as proposed in the 2010 Hedge Accounting Exposure Draft, was inconsistent with the new hedge accounting model depended on whether that spread could be regarded as a cost of hedging. Foreign currency basis spreads are an economic phenomenon that would not exist in a perfect market because the existence of such a spread creates economic arbitrage opportunities that would result in its reduction to zero. However, in the actual markets for cross-currency swaps the foreign currency basis spread is not zero because of factors that prevent perfect arbitrage. Those factors include, for example, the credit risk embedded in the underlying reference rates of the currencies as well as the demand and supply for the particular financial product (for example, cross-currency interest rate swaps), which relates to specific situations in foreign currency (product) markets. Also, the interaction between the spot and the forward foreign currency markets can sometimes have an effect.

BC6.296   The IASB considered that, overall, a foreign currency basis spread could be considered as a charge to convert one currency into another. Consequently, the IASB agreed that the foreign currency basis spread could be subsumed under the notion of 'costs of hedging' that it had developed for the accounting for the time value of options and the forward element of forward contracts. The IASB therefore decided to expand the notion of 'costs of hedging' so as to include foreign currency basis spreads. In the IASB's view, this would provide the most transparent accounting, reflect best the economics of the transaction and fit into the new hedge accounting model.

BC6.297   The IASB also considered whether it should expand the notion of 'costs of hedging' by broadening the exception it had proposed for the time value of options and the forward element of forward contracts or by replacing that exception with a broader principle. The IASB acknowledged that, conceptually, a principle would be preferable but it was concerned that using a broader principle for the costs of hedging could result in some types of hedge ineffectiveness being inappropriately deferred in accumulated other comprehensive income as costs of hedging.

BC6.298   Consequently, the IASB decided to expand the notion of 'costs of hedging' but only for foreign currency basis spreads by broadening the exception for the forward elements of forward contracts so that it also covers those spreads.

BC6.299   The IASB also decided to more closely align the structure of this exception with that used for the accounting for the time value of options. The IASB noted that for hedges of transaction related hedged items, using the forward rate method to measure the hedged item would allow entities to achieve an equivalent accounting outcome for the forward element of forward contracts (see paragraphs BC6.418–BC6.420). However, the IASB acknowledged that in order to allow a similar accounting outcome not only for the forward element of forward contracts but also for foreign currency basis spreads, entities would need to be able to apply the notion of 'costs of hedging', including for hedges of transaction related hedged items. Consequently, the IASB introduced the notion of 'costs of hedging' also for those types of cost of hedging for both hedges of time-period related hedged items and for hedges of transaction related hedged items.

Rebalancing the hedging relationship

BC6.300 IAS 39 did not allow adjustments that were not envisaged and documented at the inception of the hedge to be treated as adjustments to a continuing hedging relationship. IAS 39 treated adjustments to an existing hedging relationship that were not envisaged at the inception of the hedging relationship as a discontinuation of the original hedging relationship and the start of a new one. The IASB noted that this resulted from a hedge accounting model that did not include the notion of accounting for changes to an existing hedging relationship as a continuation of that relationship.

BC6.301 The IASB noted that this is inconsistent with risk management practices. There are instances where, although the risk management objective remains the same, adjustments to an existing hedging relationship are made because of changes in circumstances related to the hedging relationship's underlyings or risk variables. For example, such adjustments are often required to re-align the hedging relationship with risk management policies in view of changed circumstances. Hence, those adjustments to the hedged item or hedging instrument do not change the original risk management objective but instead reflect a change in how it is executed owing to the changes in circumstances. The IASB considered that in those situations the revised hedging relationship should be accounted for as a continuation of the existing hedging relationship. The IASB referred to such adjustments of hedging relationships as 'rebalancing'.

BC6.302 In its deliberations leading to the 2010 Hedge Accounting Exposure Draft, the IASB also considered the ramifications of the proposed hedge effectiveness requirements, which, for some changes in circumstances, would create the need for an adjustment to the hedging relationship to ensure that those requirements would continue to be met. An example is a change in the relationship between two variables in such a way that the hedge ratio would need to be adjusted in order to avoid a level of ineffectiveness that would fail the effectiveness requirements (which would not be met when using the original hedge ratio in the new circumstances).

BC6.303 The IASB concluded that, in such situations, if the original risk management objective remained unaltered, the adjustment to the hedging relationship should be treated as the continuation of the hedging relationship. Consequently, the IASB proposed that an adjustment to a hedging relationship is treated as a rebalancing when that adjustment changes the hedge ratio in response to changes in the economic relationship between the hedged item and the hedging instrument but risk management otherwise continues the originally designated hedging relationship.

BC6.304 However, if the adjustment represents an overhaul of the existing hedging relationship, the IASB considered that treating the adjustment as a rebalancing would not be appropriate. Instead, the IASB considered that such an adjustment should result in the discontinuation of that hedging relationship. An example is a hedging relationship with a hedging instrument that experiences a severe deterioration of its credit quality and hence is no longer used for risk management purposes.

BC6.305 Most respondents to the 2010 Hedge Accounting Exposure Draft agreed that the hedge accounting model should include a notion whereby a hedging relationship can be adjusted and accounted for as the continuation of an existing hedging relationship. Respondents thought that the inclusion of the concept of rebalancing would enhance the application of hedge accounting and would be a better representation of what entities do as part of their risk management activities. However, some respondents requested that the IASB clarify the circumstances in which rebalancing is required or permitted. They were unsure as to whether rebalancing has been designed in the narrower sense to only deal with adjustments to the hedge ratio in the context of the hedge effectiveness requirements, or whether in a wider sense it also relates to the adjustment of hedged volumes when the hedge ratio is still appropriate (ie when the entity simply wants to hedge more or less than originally).

BC6.306 Even though respondents generally supported the concept of rebalancing, some were concerned that, on the basis of how the hedge effectiveness requirement was proposed in the 2010 Hedge Accounting Exposure Draft, it would be unclear when to rebalance and that the IASB should provide more guidance to ensure consistent application. Some respondents also thought that rebalancing should be permitted but not mandatory. They argued that risk management often chose not to adjust its (economic) hedging relationships based on a mathematical optimisation exercise that was implied in the 2010 Hedge Accounting Exposure Draft (see paragraph BC6.242). This was because of cost-effectiveness considerations or simply because the hedge was still within the tolerance limits that an entity might use for adjusting the hedging relationship. There was concern that the wording, as proposed in the 2010 Hedge Accounting Exposure Draft, implied a continuous optimisation exercise (ie to always have the perfect hedge ratio) and would therefore require constant rebalancing. Consequently, almost all respondents (directly or indirectly) requested that the IASB clarify that rebalancing should only be required when done for risk management purposes. They believed that hedge accounting should follow and represent rebalancing based on what an entity actually did for risk management purposes but that rebalancing should not be triggered merely by accounting requirements.

BC6.307 In the light of the feedback, the IASB decided to retain the notion of rebalancing but to add some clarification on:

(a)   whether rebalancing should be mandatory or voluntary; and

(b)   the notion of rebalancing.

Mandatory or voluntary rebalancing

BC6.308 The IASB noted that its decision on the hedge effectiveness assessment when deliberating the 2010 Hedge Accounting Exposure Draft had ramifications for rebalancing. This decision resulted in designating hedging relationships using a hedge ratio based on the quantity of the hedged item that the entity actually hedges and the quantity of the hedging instrument that it actually uses to hedge that quantity of hedged item. However, this is provided that the hedge ratio would not reflect an imbalance that would create hedge ineffectiveness that could result in an accounting outcome that would be inconsistent with the purpose of hedge accounting (see paragraphs BC6.248–BC6.251). The IASB considered that this decision addressed the main concerns respondents had about rebalancing (ie how rebalancing for hedge accounting purposes related to rebalancing for risk management purposes).

BC6.309　The IASB's proposal in the 2010 Hedge Accounting Exposure Draft included the notion of proactive rebalancing as a complement to the proposed hedge effectiveness assessment in order to allow an entity to adjust hedging relationships on a timely basis and at the same time strengthen the link between hedge accounting and risk management. However, the IASB considered that its decision on the hedge effectiveness assessment when deliberating the 2010 Hedge Accounting Exposure Draft (see paragraph BC6.248) had an effect on rebalancing that would facilitate the adjustments to a hedging relationship that the 2010 Hedge Accounting Exposure Draft had addressed by the proposed notion of proactive rebalancing. In other words, if an entity adjusted the hedge ratio in response to changes in the economic relationship between the hedged item and the hedging instrument for risk management purposes (including adjustments that the 2010 Hedge Accounting Exposure Draft would have considered 'proactive'), the hedging relationship for hedge accounting purposes would usually be adjusted in the same way. Consequently, the IASB considered that the notion of proactive rebalancing had become obsolete.

BC6.310　The IASB also noted that the decisions that it made on the hedge effectiveness assessment when deliberating the 2010 Hedge Accounting Exposure Draft addressed respondents' concerns about the frequency of rebalancing because those decisions also clarified that rebalancing was not a mathematical optimisation exercise (see paragraphs BC6.248–BC6.249).

Clarification of the term 'rebalancing'

BC6.311　The IASB noted that it had already clarified the notion of 'rebalancing' as a result of its decision on the hedge effectiveness assessment when deliberating the 2010 Hedge Accounting Exposure Draft (see paragraphs BC6.308–BC6.310). However, the IASB considered whether it also needed to provide clarification on the scope of rebalancing—in other words, what adjustments to a hedging relationship constitute rebalancing.

BC6.312　The IASB noted that the notion of rebalancing, as proposed in its 2010 Hedge Accounting Exposure Draft, was used in the context of adjusting the designated quantities of the hedging instrument or hedged item in order to maintain a hedge ratio that complies with the hedge effectiveness requirements. Changes to designated quantities of a hedging instrument or of a hedged item for different purposes did not constitute the notion of 'rebalancing' that was proposed in the 2010 Hedge Accounting Exposure Draft.

BC6.313 Consequently, the IASB decided to clarify that rebalancing only covers adjustments to the designated quantities of the hedged item or of the hedging instrument for the purpose of maintaining a hedge ratio that complies with the requirements of the hedge effectiveness assessment (ie not when the entity simply wants to hedge more or less than it did originally).

Discontinuation of hedge accounting

Mandatory or voluntary discontinuation of hedge accounting

BC6.314 In accordance with IAS 39, an entity had to discontinue hedge accounting when the hedging relationship ceased to meet the qualifying criteria (including when the hedging instrument no longer existed or was sold). However, in accordance with IAS 39, an entity also had a free choice to voluntarily discontinue hedge accounting by simply revoking the designation of the hedging relationship (ie irrespective of any reason).

BC6.315 The IASB noted that entities voluntarily discontinued hedge accounting often because of how the effectiveness assessment in IAS 39 worked. For example, entities revoked the designation of a hedging relationship and re-designated it as a new hedging relationship in order to apply a different method of assessing hedge ineffectiveness from the method originally documented (expecting that the new method would be a better fit). Another example was entities that revoked the designation of a hedging relationship because they wanted to adjust the hedge ratio following a change in the relationship between the hedged item and the hedging instrument (typically in response to a change in the relationship between different underlyings). The hedging relationship was then re-designated, including the adjustment to the volume of the hedging instrument or the hedged item, in order to achieve the new hedge ratio. The IASB noted that in those situations the hedging relationship was discontinued and then restarted even though the risk management objective of the entity had not changed. In the IASB's view, those outcomes created a disconnect between the hedge accounting model in IAS 39 and hedging from a risk management perspective and also undermined the usefulness of the information provided.

BC6.316 In its deliberations leading to the 2010 Hedge Accounting Exposure Draft, the IASB concluded that the proposed hedge accounting model would improve the link between hedge accounting and risk management because:

(a) the new hedge effectiveness assessment requirements would not involve a percentage band or any other bright line criterion and would result in changing the method for assessing hedge effectiveness in response to changes in circumstances as part of a continuing hedging relationship; and

(b) the notion of rebalancing would allow the hedge ratio to be adjusted as part of a continuing hedging relationship.

BC6.317   The IASB also noted that sometimes a hedging relationship was discontinued because of a decrease in the hedged quantities of forecast transactions (ie the volume that remains highly probable of occurring falls or is expected to fall below the volume designated as the hedged item). Under IAS 39 this had resulted in discontinuing hedge accounting for the hedging relationship as designated, ie the volume designated as the hedged item in its entirety. The IASB considered that the quantity of forecast transactions that were still highly probable of occurring was in fact a continuation of the original hedging relationship (albeit with a lower volume). Hence, the IASB decided to propose in its 2010 Hedge Accounting Exposure Draft that hedge accounting should be discontinued only for the volume that was no longer highly probable of occurring and that the remaining volume that was still highly probable of occurring should be accounted for as a continuation of the original hedging relationship. In the IASB's view, this would more closely align hedge accounting with risk management and provide more useful information.

BC6.318   However, the IASB was concerned that this accounting might possibly undermine the requirement that forecast transactions must be highly probable in order to qualify as a hedged item. Hence, the IASB decided to also propose to clarify that a history of having designated hedges of forecast transactions and having subsequently determined that the forecast transactions are no longer expected to occur would call into question the entity's ability to predict similar forecast transactions accurately. This would affect the assessment of whether similar forecast transactions are highly probable and hence their eligibility as hedged items.

BC6.319   In view of its aim to better link hedge accounting to risk management and provide more useful hedge accounting information, the IASB also discussed whether it should retain an entity's choice to revoke the designation of a hedging relationship, taking into consideration that the designation of a hedging relationship (and hence the discontinuation of hedge accounting) at will does not result in useful information. The IASB noted that this would allow hedge accounting to be discontinued even if the entity for risk management purposes continued to hedge the exposure in accordance with its risk management objective that was part of the qualifying criteria that initially allowed the entity to achieve hedge accounting. The IASB considered that, in such situations, voluntary discontinuation of hedge accounting would be arbitrary and unjustifiable. Hence, the IASB decided to propose not to allow entities a free choice to revoke the designation of a hedging relationship in this situation. The IASB also noted that if the hedging relationship no longer reflected the risk management objective for that particular hedging relationship, discontinuation of hedge accounting was not a choice but was required because the qualifying criteria would no longer be met. The IASB considered that applying hedge accounting without a risk management objective would not provide useful information.

BC6.320   In its deliberations leading to the 2010 Hedge Accounting Exposure Draft, the IASB did not consider new designations of any hedging relationships of the acquiree in the consolidated financial statements of the acquirer following a business combination. The IASB noted that this was a requirement of IFRS 3

Business Combinations and hence not within the scope of its project on hedge accounting.

BC6.321   The responses to the proposals on the discontinuation of hedge accounting in the 2010 Hedge Accounting Exposure Draft provided mixed views. Those who agreed thought that the proposals would strengthen the reliability of financial reporting because the ability to change accounting for no valid reason would be reduced.

BC6.322   More specifically, those who agreed also thought that the model in IAS 39 provided an opportunity for structuring. They noted that allowing a hedging relationship to be arbitrarily discontinued at any point in time is not conceptually sound and does not result in useful information.

BC6.323   Even though many respondents agreed with the proposals, there were also requests that the IASB provide additional guidance on the meaning of 'risk management' and at what level it should be considered for the purpose of hedge accounting.

BC6.324   Generally, those who disagreed with the proposals argued that if starting hedge accounting was voluntary, ceasing it should also be voluntary. Some respondents who disagreed did so because they believed that voluntary discontinuation was necessary in scenarios in which an entity decided to terminate a hedging relationship on the basis that the hedge was no longer cost efficient (for example, a high administrative burden makes it is too onerous and costly to apply hedge accounting). Some of these respondents raised the concern that voluntary discontinuation was an important tool in the current hedge accounting model for financial institutions that normally run hedging programmes based on portfolios of items on a macro basis. Those portfolios were subject to constant changes and entities removed the hedge designation with the aim of adjusting the hedging relationship for new hedged items and hedging instruments.

BC6.325   Others who disagreed argued that not allowing voluntary discontinuation was inconsistent with the mechanics of cash flow hedge accounting. For example, when an entity entered into a cash flow hedge for forecast sales in a foreign currency, the risk management strategy aimed to protect the cash flows until settlement of the invoice. However, hedge accounting was only applied until the moment when the sales invoice became an on-balance-sheet item, after which the entity obtained a natural offset in the statement of profit or loss and other comprehensive income because of the translation of the hedged item in accordance with IAS 21 and the accounting for the hedging instrument at fair value through profit or loss. Those respondents thought that voluntary discontinuation of the hedging relationship was necessary at the time that the forecast transaction became an on-balance-sheet item (for example, a trade receivable).

BC6.326   Based on this feedback, the IASB, in its redeliberations, considered:

(a)   whether voluntary discontinuation should be allowed, given that hedge accounting remained optional; and

(b)   how the link of the proposed discontinuation requirements to the risk management objective and strategy would work.

BC6.327   The IASB noted that even though the application of hedge accounting remained optional, it facilitated the provision of useful information for financial reporting purposes (ie how hedging instruments are used to manage risk). The IASB considered that this purpose could not be ignored when considering the voluntary discontinuation of hedge accounting. If an entity chose to apply hedge accounting, it did so with the aim of using that particular accounting to represent in the financial statements the effect of pursuing a particular risk management objective. If the risk management objective had not changed and the other qualifying criteria for hedge accounting were still met, the ability to discontinue hedge accounting would undermine the aspect of consistency over time in accounting for, and providing information about, that hedging relationship. The IASB noted that a free choice to discontinue hedge accounting reflected a view that hedge accounting is a mere accounting exercise that does not have a particular meaning. Consequently, the IASB considered that it was not valid to argue that because hedge accounting was voluntary, the discontinuation of hedge accounting should also be voluntary.

BC6.328   In addition, the IASB noted that other optional accounting treatments of IFRS does not allow the entity to overturn its initial election:

(a)   the fair value option in IAS 39 and IFRS 9; and

(b)   the lessee's option to account for a property interest held under an operating lease as an investment property, which is available (irrevocably) on a property-by-property basis.

BC6.329   The IASB also did not think that the ability to voluntarily discontinue hedge accounting was necessary for hedge accounting to work as intended in particular situations mentioned in the feedback (see paragraphs BC6.324–BC6.325). The IASB considered that the impression of some respondents that voluntary discontinuation was necessary in those situations resulted from a lack of clarity about the distinction between the notions of risk management strategy and risk management objective. The IASB noted that that distinction was important for determining when the discontinuation of a hedging relationship was required (or not allowed). The IASB also noted that the term 'risk management strategy' was used in the 2010 Hedge Accounting Exposure Draft as a reference to the highest level at which an entity determines how it manages risk. In other words, the risk management strategy typically identified the risks to which the entity was exposed and set out how the entity responded to them. Conversely, the 2010 Hedge Accounting Exposure Draft used the term 'risk management objective' (for a hedging relationship) to refer to the objective that applies at the level of that particular hedging relationship (instead of what the entity aims to achieve with the overall strategy). In other words, it related to how the particular designated hedging instrument is used to hedge the particular exposure designated as the hedged item.

BC6.330 The IASB noted that a risk management strategy could (and often would) involve many different hedging relationships whose risk management objectives relate to executing that risk management strategy. Hence, the risk management objective for a particular hedging relationship could change even though an entity's risk management strategy remained unchanged. The IASB's intention was to prohibit voluntary discontinuation of hedge accounting when the risk management objective at the level of a particular hedging relationship (ie not only the risk management strategy) remained the same and all other qualifying criteria were still met.

BC6.331 Consequently, the IASB decided to prohibit the voluntary discontinuation of hedge accounting when the risk management objective for a particular hedging relationship remains the same and all the other qualifying criteria are still met. However, the IASB also decided to add additional guidance on how the risk management objective and the risk management strategy relate to each other using examples that contrast these two notions, including for situations in which 'proxy hedging' designations are used.

Novation of derivatives

BC6.332 When deliberating its 2010 Hedge Accounting Exposure Draft, the IASB received an urgent request to clarify whether an entity is required to discontinue hedge accounting for hedging relationships in which a derivative has been designated as a hedging instrument when that derivative is novated to a central counterparty (CCP) due to the introduction of a new law or regulation.[43] This question applied equally to the designation of hedging instruments in accordance with IAS 39 and under the new hedge accounting model for IFRS 9 that the IASB was redeliberating. Consequently, the IASB considered this question and possible solutions, both in the context of hedge accounting under IAS 39 and IFRS 9.[44]

BC6.333 The IASB considered the derecognition requirements of IFRS 9 to determine whether the novation in such a circumstance would lead to the derecognition of an existing derivative that had been designated as a hedging instrument. The IASB noted that a derivative should be derecognised only when it meets both the derecognition criteria for a financial asset and the derecognition criteria for a financial liability in circumstances in which the derivative involves two-way payments between parties (ie the payments are or could be from and to each of the parties).

BC6.334 The IASB observed that paragraph 3.2.3(a) of IFRS 9 requires that a financial asset is derecognised when the contractual rights to the cash flows from the financial asset expire. The IASB noted that through novation to a CCP, a party (Party A) to the original derivative has new contractual rights to cash flows

---

43 In this context, the term 'novation' indicates that the parties to a derivative agree that one or more clearly counterparties replace their original counterparty to each of the parties. For this purpose, a clearing counterparty is a central counterparty or an entity or entities, for example, a clearing member of a clearing organisation or a client of a clearing member of a clearing organisation, that are acting as counterparty in order to effect clearing by a central counterparty.

44 The references in the Basis for Conclusions of this Standard are to the relevant requirements of IFRS 9. The Basis for Conclusions of the equivalent amendments to IAS 39 referred to the relevant requirements in that Standard (which were equivalent).

from a (new) derivative with the CCP, and this new contract replaces the original contract with a counterparty (Party B). Thus, the original derivative with Party B has expired and, as a consequence, the original derivative through which Party A has engaged with Party B meets the derecognition criteria for a financial asset.

BC6.335 The IASB also observed that paragraph B3.3.1(b) of IFRS 9 states that a financial liability is extinguished when the debtor is legally released from primary responsibility for the liability. The IASB noted that the novation to the CCP would release Party A from the responsibility to make payments to Party B and would also oblige Party A to make payments to the CCP. Consequently, the original derivative through which Party A has transacted with Party B also meets the derecognition criteria for a financial liability.

BC6.336 Consequently, the IASB concluded that the novation of a derivative to a CCP would be accounted for as the derecognition of the original derivative and the recognition of the (new) novated derivative.

BC6.337 Taking into account the conclusion of the assessment on the derecognition requirements, the IASB considered the guidance it had proposed on the discontinuation of hedge accounting, which would require an entity to discontinue hedge accounting prospectively if the hedging instrument expires or is sold, terminated or exercised. The IASB noted that novation to a CCP would require the entity to discontinue hedge accounting because the derivative that was designated as a hedging instrument has been derecognised and consequently the hedging instrument in the existing hedging relationship no longer exists.

BC6.338 The IASB was, however, concerned about the financial reporting effects that would arise from novations that result from new laws or regulations. The IASB noted that the requirement to discontinue hedge accounting meant that although an entity could designate the new derivative as the hedging instrument in a new hedging relationship, this could result in more hedge ineffectiveness, especially for cash flow hedges, compared to a continuing hedging relationship. This is because the derivative that would be newly designated as the hedging instrument would be on terms that would be different from a new derivative, ie it was unlikely to be 'at-market' (for example, a non-option derivative such as a swap or forward might have a significant fair value) at the time of the novation.

BC6.339 The IASB, taking note of this financial reporting effect, was convinced that accounting for the hedging relationship that existed before the novation as a continuing hedging relationship, in this specific situation, would provide more useful information to users of financial statements. The IASB also considered the feedback from outreach that involved the members of the International Forum of Accounting Standard Setters (IFASS) and securities regulators and noted that this issue is not limited to a specific jurisdiction because many jurisdictions have introduced, or are expected to mandate, laws or regulations that encourage or require the novation of derivatives to a CCP.

BC6.340　The IASB noted that the widespread legislative changes across jurisdictions were prompted by a G20 commitment to improve transparency and regulatory oversight of over-the-counter (OTC) derivatives in an internationally consistent and non-discriminatory way. Specifically, the G20 agreed to improve OTC derivatives markets so that all standardised OTC derivatives contracts are cleared through a CCP.

BC6.341　Consequently, the IASB decided to publish, in January 2013, the Exposure Draft *Novation of Derivatives and Continuation of Hedge Accounting* (the '2013 Novation of Derivatives and Continuation of Hedge Accounting Exposure Draft'), which proposed amendments to IAS 39 and revisions to the IASB's hedge accounting proposals to IFRS 9. In the 2013 Novation of Derivatives and Continuation of Hedge Accounting Exposure Draft, the IASB proposed revised requirements for the discontinuation of hedge accounting to provide relief from discontinuing hedge accounting when the novation to a CCP is required by new laws or regulations and meets particular criteria.

BC6.342　When developing the 2013 Novation of Derivatives and Continuation of Hedge Accounting Exposure Draft, the IASB tentatively decided that the terms of the novated derivative should be unchanged other than the change in counterparty. However, the IASB noted that, in practice, other changes may arise as a direct consequence of the novation. For example, in order to enter into a derivative with a CCP it may be necessary to make adjustments to the collateral arrangements. Such narrow changes that are a direct consequence of, or are incidental to, the novation were acknowledged in the proposals. However, this would not include changes to, for example, the maturity of the derivatives, the payment dates or the contractual cash flows or the basis of their calculation, except for changes that may arise as a consequence of transacting with a CCP.

BC6.343　When developing the 2013 Novation of Derivatives and Continuation of Hedge Accounting Exposure Draft, the IASB also discussed whether to require an entity to disclose that it has been able to continue hedge accounting by applying the relief provided by these proposals. The IASB considered that it was not appropriate to mandate a specific disclosure in this situation because, from the perspective of a user of financial statements, hedge accounting would continue.

BC6.344　The vast majority of respondents agreed that the proposed revisions are necessary. However, a few respondents expressed disagreement with the proposal on the basis that they disagreed with the IASB's conclusion that hedge accounting would be required to be discontinued as a result of such novations. In expressing such disagreement some noted that the guidance on the discontinuation of hedge accounting expressly acknowledges that certain replacements or rollovers of hedging instruments are not expirations or terminations for the purposes of discontinuing hedge accounting. The IASB noted that this exception applies if "[a] replacement or rollover is part of, and consistent with, the entity's documented risk management objective". The IASB questioned whether replacement of a contract as a result of unforeseen legislative changes (even if documented) fits the definition of a replacement that is part of a 'documented risk management objective'.

BC6.345　Even though the vast majority of respondents agreed with the proposal, a considerable majority of respondents disagreed with the scope of the proposals. They believed that the proposed scope of 'novation required by laws or regulations' is too restrictive and that the scope should therefore be expanded by removing this criterion. In particular, they argued that voluntary novation to a CCP should be provided with the same relief as novation required by laws or regulations. A few respondents further requested that the scope should not be limited to novation to a central counterparty and that novation in other circumstances should also be considered.

BC6.346　When considering respondents' comments, the IASB noted that voluntary novation to a CCP could be prevalent in some circumstances such as novation in anticipation of regulatory changes, novation owing to operational ease, and novation induced but not actually mandated by laws or regulations as a result of the imposition of charges or penalties. The IASB also noted that many jurisdictions would not require the existing stock of outstanding historical derivatives to be moved to CCPs, although this was encouraged by the G20 commitment.

BC6.347　The IASB observed, however, that for hedge accounting to continue, voluntary novation to a CCP should be associated with laws or regulations that are relevant to central clearing of derivatives. The IASB noted that while a novation need not be required by laws or regulations for hedge accounting to be allowed to continue, allowing all novations to CCPs to be accommodated was broader than the IASB had intended. In addition, the IASB agreed that hedge accounting should continue when novations are performed as a consequence of laws or regulations or the introduction of laws or regulations but noted that the mere possibility of laws or regulations being introduced was not a sufficient basis for the continuation of hedge accounting.

BC6.348　Some respondents were concerned that restricting the relief to novation directly to a CCP was too narrow. In considering respondents' comments, the IASB noted that in some cases a CCP has a contractual relationship only with its 'clearing members', and therefore an entity must have a contractual relationship with a clearing member in order to transact with a CCP; a clearing member of a CCP provides a clearing service to its client who cannot access a CCP directly. The IASB also noted that some jurisdictions are introducing a so-called 'indirect clearing' arrangement in their laws or regulations to effect clearing with a CCP, by which a client of a clearing member of a CCP provides a (indirect) clearing service to its client in the same way as a clearing member of a CCP provides a clearing service to its client. In addition, the IASB observed that an intragroup novation can also occur in order to access a CCP; for example, if only particular group entities can transact directly with a CCP.

BC6.349　On the basis of respondents' comments, the IASB decided to expand the scope of the amendments by providing relief for novations to entities other than a CCP if such novation is undertaken with the objective of effecting the clearing with a CCP instead of limiting relief to situations in which novation is direct to a CCP. The IASB decided that in those circumstances the novation had occurred in order to effect clearing through a CCP, albeit indirectly. The IASB thus decided to also include such novations in the scope of the amendments because they are consistent with the objective of the proposed amendments — they enable hedge accounting to continue when novations occur as a consequence of laws or regulations or the introduction of laws or regulations that increase the use of CCPs. However, the IASB noted that when parties to a hedging instrument enter into novations with different counterparties (for example, with different clearing members), these amendments only apply if each of those parties ultimately effects clearing with the same central counterparty.

BC6.350 Respondents raised a concern about the phrase 'if and only if' that was used in the 2013 Novation of Derivatives and Continuation of Hedge Accounting Exposure Draft when describing that the relief is provided 'if and only if' the criteria are met. In considering respondents' comments, the IASB noted that the 2013 Novation of Derivatives and Continuation of Hedge Accounting Exposure Draft was intended to address a narrow issue — novation to CCPs — and therefore changing the phrase 'if and only if' to 'if' would target the amendment on the fact patterns that the IASB sought to address. The IASB noted that this would have the effect of requiring an analysis of whether the general conditions for the continuation of hedge accounting are satisfied in other cases (for example, as was raised by some respondents, in determining the effect of intragroup novations in consolidated financial statements).

BC6.351 The 2013 Novation of Derivatives and Continuation of Hedge Accounting Exposure Draft did not propose any additional disclosures. The vast majority of respondents agreed with this. The IASB confirmed that additional disclosures are not required. However, the IASB noted that an entity may consider disclosures in accordance with IFRS 7, which requires qualitative and quantitative disclosures about credit risk.

BC6.352 The IASB also decided to retain the transition requirements proposed in the 2013 Novation of Derivatives and Continuation of Hedge Accounting Exposure Draft so that the revised guidance should apply retrospectively and early application should be permitted. The IASB noted that even with retrospective application, if an entity had previously discontinued hedge accounting as a result of a novation, that (pre-novation) hedge accounting relationship could not be reinstated because doing so would be inconsistent with the requirements for hedge accounting (ie hedge accounting cannot be applied retrospectively).

Fair value hedges

Accounting for fair value hedges

BC6.353 In its deliberations leading to the 2010 Hedge Accounting Exposure Draft, the IASB considered reducing the complexity of hedge accounting by replacing the fair value hedge accounting mechanics with the cash flow hedge accounting mechanics. Such an approach would recognise gains or losses on the hedging instruments outside profit or loss in other comprehensive income instead of requiring the hedged item to be remeasured. The IASB considered such an approach because it would:

(a)   improve the usefulness of the reported information for users of financial statements. In accordance with such an approach, all hedging activities to which hedge accounting is applied (including hedges of fair value risk) would be reflected in other comprehensive income, resulting in greater transparency and comparability. In addition, the measurement of the hedged item would not be affected.

(b)   simplify existing requirements. Although fair value and cash flow hedge accounting are designed to address different exposures, the same mechanisms can be used to reflect how an entity manages these exposures in the financial statements. Eliminating one of two different methods (fair value hedge accounting or cash flow hedge accounting) would reduce complexity. Such an approach would align fair value hedge accounting and cash flow hedge accounting, resulting in a single method for hedge accounting.

(c)   be an expeditious approach to finalise this phase of the project to replace IAS 39. Such an approach would draw on the existing mechanics of cash flow hedge accounting in IAS 39 and, consequently, such an approach would not require much further development.

BC6.354   However, during its outreach activities conducted before publishing the 2010 Hedge Accounting Exposure Draft, the IASB received mixed views on this approach. Some supported the approach for the reasons that the IASB had considered, which was consistent with the feedback received on the Discussion Paper *Reducing Complexity in Reporting Financial Instruments*. However, others raised concerns that such an approach:

(a)   would not reflect the underlying economics. They argued that if an entity applies a fair value hedge, the hedged item exists and hence there is an actual gain or loss on the hedged item (not just an anticipated gain or loss on a forecast transaction that does not yet exist). Consequently, hedge accounting should not cause 'artificial' volatility in other comprehensive income and equity.

(b)   would make the movements in other comprehensive income less understandable.

(c)   would make it difficult to identify the type of risk management strategy that the entity employs.

(d)   could result in scenarios in which equity would be significantly reduced or even negative because of losses on the hedging instrument deferred in other comprehensive income. This could have serious implications in terms of solvency and regulatory requirements.

BC6.355   In the light of the views received, the IASB decided to propose a different approach in the 2010 Hedge Accounting Exposure Draft. The IASB proposed to continue to account for fair value hedges differently from cash flow hedges. However, the IASB proposed some changes to the presentation and mechanics of fair value hedge accounting:

(a)   in relation to the gain or loss on remeasuring the hedging instrument – IAS 39 required the gain or loss to be recognised in profit or loss. The IASB proposed to require the recognition of the gain or loss in other comprehensive income.

(b)   in relation to the gain or loss on the hedged item – IAS 39 required such a gain or loss to result in an adjustment to the carrying amount of the hedged item and to be recognised in profit or loss. The IASB proposed to require the gain or loss to be recognised as an asset or a liability that is presented in a separate line item in the statement of financial position and in other comprehensive income. That separate line item would have been presented within assets (or liabilities) for those reporting periods for which the hedged item is an asset (or a liability).

BC6.356   The IASB noted that the separate line item represented measurement adjustments to the hedged items instead of separate assets or liabilities in their own right. The IASB thought that the additional line item might be perceived to add complexity and would increase the number of line items in the statement of financial position. In addition, the IASB noted that this approach is more complex than the approach initially considered, which would have eliminated fair value hedge accounting mechanics.

BC6.357   However, the IASB decided to propose these changes because they would:

(a)   eliminate the mixed measurement for the hedged item (for example, an amount that is amortised cost with a partial fair value adjustment).

(b)   avoid volatility in other comprehensive income and equity that some consider artificial.

(c)   present in one place (ie other comprehensive income) the effects of risk management activities (for both cash flow and fair value hedges).

(d)   provide information in the statement of comprehensive income about the extent of the offsetting achieved for fair value hedges.

BC6.358   Most respondents supported providing the information proposed in the 2010 Hedge Accounting Exposure Draft, but many disagreed with providing this information on the face of the financial statements.

BC6.359   With respect to recognising gains or losses on the hedging instrument and the hedged item in other comprehensive income, many respondents thought that the use of other comprehensive income should be limited until the IASB completed a project on what 'other comprehensive income' represents. Many respondents expressed a preference for the approach in IAS 39 (ie presenting the gain or loss on the hedging instrument and the hedged item in profit or loss). As an alternative, those respondents suggested that the gain or loss on the hedging instrument and the hedged item should be disclosed in the notes to the financial statements.

BC6.360   With respect to presenting separate line items in the statement of financial position, many respondents expressed concern about the excessive number of additional line items in the statement of financial position that could result from the proposals in the 2010 Hedge Accounting Exposure Draft. Those respondents thought that the statement of financial position would appear too cluttered. As an alternative, those respondents suggested that entities disclose the accumulated adjustment made to the carrying amount of the hedged item in the notes to the financial statements.

BC6.361   In the light of this feedback, the IASB, in its redeliberations, decided to retain the fair value hedge accounting mechanics that were in IAS 39. However, the IASB also decided that it would require information to be disclosed so that users of financial statements could understand the effects of hedge accounting on the financial statements and that all hedge accounting disclosures are presented in a single note or separate section in the financial statements (those disclosure requirements were included in IFRS 7).

Linked presentation for fair value hedges

BC6.362   During its outreach activities conducted before the publication of the 2010 Hedge Accounting Exposure Draft, the IASB was alerted to the effect on financial reporting that fair value hedge accounting has on hedges of the foreign currency risk of firm commitments in a specific industry. This issue is a particular concern to that industry because of the magnitude of firm commitments that are denominated in a foreign currency because of the industry's business model. In response to that concern, the IASB considered whether applying linked presentation for fair value hedges of firm commitments might be appropriate. Linked presentation is a way of presenting information so that it shows how particular assets and liabilities are related. Linked presentation is not the same as offsetting, which presents a net asset or liability. Linked presentation displays the 'gross' amount of related items in the statement of financial position (while the net amount is included in the total for assets or liabilities).

BC6.363   The industry was concerned that the presentation resulting from fair value hedge accounting would not reflect the economic effects of hedges of foreign currency risk. For example, an entity that has a large firm commitment for a sale denominated in a foreign currency enters into currency forward contracts to hedge the foreign currency risk of that firm commitment (the forward contract and the firm commitment could be considered 'linked transactions'). The fair value of the derivative liability (asset) and the firm commitment asset (liability) could be significant depending on the volatility of the currency being hedged. That industry was concerned that, as a result, on the basis of the statement of financial position, the entity would appear to be exposed to a higher risk than it actually was. In that industry's view, confusion might arise because the statement of financial position would show large amounts for total assets and total liabilities and hence a high leverage (which typically suggests higher risk) even though the entity hedged the foreign currency risk of the firm commitment and thus sought to reduce risk.

BC6.364 That industry argued that linked presentation of the firm commitment (recognised as a result of fair value hedge accounting) and the hedging instrument could present the effect of an entity's hedging activity and the relationship of the hedged item and the hedging instrument. Linked presentation would not require changing the requirements of offsetting in IAS 32 or other requirements in IAS 39 and IFRS 9.

BC6.365 Moreover, that industry argued that a firm commitment is recognised in the statement of financial position only when fair value hedge accounting is applied. Consequently, that industry advocated that a firm commitment and the related hedging instrument should be accounted for as two parts of a single transaction. That industry also argued that totals for assets and liabilities that include only the 'net' amount (of the linked transactions) would be most appropriate for financial analysis purposes. That industry believed that the ratios, such as leverage, should be calculated on the basis of the difference between the hedged item and the hedging instrument, ie the net amount instead of the gross amount of those items.

BC6.366 The IASB noted that while linked presentation could provide some useful information about a particular relationship between an asset and a liability, it does not differentiate between the types of risk that are covered by that relationship and those that are not. Consequently, linked presentation could result in one net amount for an asset and liability that are 'linked' even though that link (ie the relationship) affects only one of several risks underlying the asset or liability (for example, only the currency risk but not the credit risk or interest rate risk). Furthermore, the IASB did not consider that linked presentation would result in more appropriate totals of assets and liabilities for the purpose of ratio analysis because the hedging affected only one risk but not all risks. Instead, the IASB believed that disclosures about hedging would be a better alternative for providing information that allows users of financial statements to assess the relevance of the information for their own analysis.

BC6.367 Consequently, the IASB decided not to propose the use of linked presentation for the purposes of hedge accounting.

BC6.368 Most respondents to the 2010 Hedge Accounting Exposure Draft agreed with the IASB's conclusion not to allow linked presentation. Some respondents also thought that linked presentation is not an appropriate topic for a project on hedge accounting, but instead that it should be considered as a separate project or as part of a project on either financial statement presentation or the *Conceptual Framework*.

BC6.369 However, those respondents that supported linked presentation argued that, without it, entities that use hedge accounting would be perceived to be riskier than those that do not, and that the true economic effects of hedges of foreign currency risk of firm commitments would not be reflected.

BC6.370 The IASB noted that in the absence of a clear principle for linked presentation, it should be considered in a broader context than just hedge accounting. Consequently, the IASB decided not to require or allow the use of linked presentation for the purpose of hedge accounting.

Cash flow hedges

The 'lower of' test

BC6.371　When a hedge accounting relationship is fully effective, the fair value changes of the hedging instrument perfectly offset the value changes of the hedged item. Hedge ineffectiveness arises when the value changes of the hedging instrument exceed those of the hedged item, or when the value changes of the hedging instrument are less than those of the hedged item.

BC6.372　For cash flow hedges, recognising in profit or loss gains and losses arising on the hedged item in excess of the gains and losses on the hedging instrument is problematic because many hedged items of cash flow hedges are highly probable forecast transactions. Those hedged items do not yet exist although they are expected to occur in the future. Hence, recognising gains and losses on those items in excess of the gains and losses on the hedging instrument is tantamount to recognising gains and losses on items that do not yet exist (instead of a deferral of the gain or loss on the hedging instrument). The IASB noted that this would be conceptually questionable as well as a counter-intuitive outcome.

BC6.373　IAS 39 required a 'lower of' test for determining the amounts that were recognised for cash flow hedges in other comprehensive income (the effective part) and profit or loss (the ineffective part). The 'lower of' test ensured that cumulative changes in the value of the hedged items that exceed cumulative fair value changes of the hedging instrument are not recognised. In contrast, the lower of test did not apply to fair value hedges because, for that type of hedge, the hedged item exists. For example, while a firm commitment might not be recognised in accordance with IFRS, the transaction already exists. Conversely, a forecast transaction does not yet exist but will occur only in the future.

BC6.374　In its deliberations leading to the 2010 Hedge Accounting Exposure Draft, the IASB discussed whether the requirements for measuring the hedge ineffectiveness that is recognised in profit or loss should be aligned for fair value hedges and cash flow hedges. The IASB noted that the requirements could be aligned by also applying the lower of test to fair value hedges or by eliminating it for cash flow hedges. In the IASB's view, aligning the requirements would reduce complexity. However, the IASB considered that, for conceptual reasons, recognising gains and losses on items that do not yet exist instead of only deferring the gain or loss on the hedging instrument was not appropriate. On the other hand, the IASB considered that the nature of fair value hedges is different from that of cash flow hedges. Also applying the lower of test to fair value hedges, even though that test was designed to address only the specific characteristics of cash flow hedges, was not justified. Consequently, the IASB decided to retain the lower of test for cash flow hedges and not to introduce it for fair value hedges.

Basis adjustments for hedges of forecast transactions that will result in the recognition of a non-financial asset or a non-financial liability

BC6.375 A forecast transaction could subsequently result in the recognition of a non-financial asset or a non-financial liability. Similarly, a forecast transaction for a non-financial asset or non-financial liability could subsequently result in the recognition of a firm commitment for which fair value hedge accounting is applied. In these cases IAS 39 permitted an entity an accounting policy choice:

(a) to reclassify the associated gains or losses that were recognised in other comprehensive income to profit or loss in the same period or periods during which the asset acquired or liability assumed affects profit or loss; or

(b) to remove the associated gains or losses that were recognised in other comprehensive income and include them in the initial cost or other carrying amount of the asset or liability. This approach was commonly referred to as a 'basis adjustment'.

BC6.376 In its deliberations leading to the 2010 Hedge Accounting Exposure Draft, the IASB considered whether to continue allowing this accounting policy choice. The IASB noted that if an entity was precluded from applying a basis adjustment, this would require the entity to track the hedging gains and losses separately (after the hedging relationship had ended) and to match them to the period or periods in which the non-financial item that had resulted from the hedged transaction affected profit or loss. The entity would also need to consider whether or not the remaining amount in other comprehensive income was recoverable in one or more future periods. In contrast, if an entity applied a basis adjustment, the hedging gain or loss was included in the carrying amount of the non-financial item and automatically recognised in profit or loss in the period in which the related non-financial item affected profit or loss (for example, through depreciation expense for items of property, plant and equipment or cost of sales for inventories). It would also be automatically considered when an entity tested a non-financial asset for impairment. The IASB noted that for a non-financial asset that is tested for impairment as part of a cash-generating unit, tracking amounts in other comprehensive income and including them in the impairment test is difficult (even more so if the composition of cash-generating units changes over time).

BC6.377 The IASB acknowledged that there were different views on whether a basis adjustment would achieve or reduce comparability. One view was that two identical assets purchased at the same time and in the same way (except for the fact that one was hedged) should have the same initial carrying amount. From this viewpoint, basis adjustments would impair comparability.

BC6.378 The other view was that basis adjustments allowed identical assets for which the acquisitions are subject to the same risk to be measured so that they had the same initial carrying amount. For example, Entity A and Entity B want to purchase the same asset from a supplier that has a different functional currency. Entity A is able to secure the purchase contract denominated in its functional currency. Conversely, while Entity B also wants to fix the purchase price in its functional currency, it has to accept a purchase contract denominated in the functional currency of the supplier (ie a foreign currency) and is therefore exposed to the variability in cash flows arising from movements in the exchange rate. Hence, Entity B hedges its exposure to foreign currency risk using a currency forward contract which, in effect, fixes the price of the purchase in its functional currency. When taking into account the currency forward contract, Entity B has, in effect, the same foreign currency risk exposure as Entity A. From this viewpoint, basis adjustments would enhance comparability.

BC6.379 The IASB also considered the interaction between basis adjustments and the choice of accounting for a hedge of foreign currency risk of a firm commitment as either a cash flow hedge or a fair value hedge (see paragraphs BC6.272–BC6.277). The IASB noted that for hedges of the foreign currency risk of a firm commitment the basis adjustment at the end of the cash flow hedge has the same effect on the presentation of the hedged item as accounting for the hedge as a fair value hedge. Thus, using fair value hedge accounting for those firm commitments was tantamount to a basis adjustment. The IASB thought that, in this context, basis adjustments would also enhance comparability.

BC6.380 Consequently, the IASB decided to eliminate the accounting policy choice in IAS 39 and require basis adjustments. The IASB decided that when the entity removes the associated gain or loss that was recognised in other comprehensive income in order to include it in the initial cost or other carrying amount of the asset or liability, that gain or loss should be directly applied against the carrying amount of the asset or liability. This means that it would not be a reclassification adjustment (see IAS 1 *Presentation of Financial Statements*) and hence would not affect other comprehensive income when removing it from equity and adding it to, or deducting it from, the asset or liability. The IASB noted that accounting for the basis adjustment as a reclassification adjustment would distort comprehensive income because the amount would affect comprehensive income twice but in different periods:

(a) first (in other comprehensive income) in the period in which the non-financial item is recognised; and

(b) again in the later periods when the non-financial item affects profit or loss (for example, through depreciation expense or cost of sales).

The IASB also noted that presenting a basis adjustment as a reclassification adjustment would create the misleading impression that the basis adjustment was a performance event.

BC6.381 The IASB acknowledged that the total comprehensive income across periods will be distorted because the gain or loss on the hedging instrument during the period of the cash flow hedge is recognised in other comprehensive income, whereas the cumulative hedging gain or loss that is removed from the cash flow hedge reserve (ie from equity) and directly applied to the subsequently recognised non-financial item does not affect other comprehensive income. The IASB considered that one type of distortion of other comprehensive income was inevitable (ie either in the period of the basis adjustment or over the total period) and hence there was a trade-off. The IASB concluded that, on balance, the effect of a reclassification adjustment in the period of the basis adjustment would be more misleading than the effect over the total period of not using a reclassification adjustment.

BC6.382　The IASB retained its original decision when deliberating its 2010 Hedge Accounting Exposure Draft.

Hedges of a net investment in a foreign operation

BC6.383　In its deliberations leading to the 2010 Hedge Accounting Exposure Draft, the IASB decided not to address a hedge of a net investment in a foreign operation as part of its hedge accounting project. The IASB noted that a net investment in a foreign operation was determined and accounted for in accordance with IAS 21. The IASB also noted that the hedge of a net investment in a foreign operation also related to IAS 21. Hence, similar to the issue of considering intragroup monetary items for eligibility as hedging instruments for hedges of foreign exchange risk (see paragraph BC6.149), the IASB considered that comprehensively addressing this type of hedge would require a review of the requirements in IAS 21 at the same time as considering the hedge accounting requirements.

BC6.384　Consequently, the IASB proposed retaining the requirements of IAS 39 for a hedge of a net investment in a foreign operation.

BC6.385　The IASB retained its original decision when redeliberating its 2010 Hedge Accounting Exposure Draft.

Accounting for the time value of options

BC6.386　IAS 39 allowed an entity a choice:

(a)　to designate an option-type derivative as a hedging instrument in its entirety; or

(b)　to separate the time value of the option and designate as the hedging instrument only the intrinsic value element.

BC6.387　The IASB noted that under the IAS 39 hedge accounting model entities typically designated option-type derivatives as hedging instruments on the basis of their intrinsic value. Consequently, the undesignated time value of the option was treated as held for trading and was accounted for as at fair value through profit or loss, which gave rise to significant volatility in profit or loss. This particular accounting treatment is disconnected from the risk management view, whereby entities typically consider the time value of an option (at inception, ie included in the premium paid) as a cost of hedging. It is a cost of obtaining protection against unfavourable changes of prices, while retaining participation in any favourable changes.

BC6.388　Against this background, the IASB, in its deliberations leading to the 2010 Hedge Accounting Exposure Draft, considered how best to portray the time value of options (in the context of hedging exposures only against changes to one side of a specified level—a 'one-sided risk'). The IASB noted that the standard-setting debate about accounting for the time value of options had historically been focused on hedge ineffectiveness. Many typical hedged transactions (such as firm commitments, forecast transactions or existing items) do not involve a time value notion because they are not options. Hence, such hedged items do not have a change in their value that offsets the fair value change related to the time value of the option that is used as a hedging instrument. The IASB concluded that, unless the time value of the option was excluded from being designated as the hedging instrument, hedge ineffectiveness would arise.

BC6.389 However, the IASB noted that the time value of an option could also be considered from a different perspective—that of a premium for protection against risk (an 'insurance premium' view).

BC6.390 The IASB noted that entities that use purchased options to hedge one-sided risks typically consider the time value that they pay as a premium to the option writer or seller as similar to an insurance premium. In order to protect themselves against the downside of an exposure (an adverse outcome) while retaining the upside, they have to compensate someone else for assuming the inverse asymmetrical position, which has only the downside but not the upside. The time value of an option is subject to 'time decay'. This means that it loses its value over time as the option approaches expiry, which occurs at an increasingly rapid rate. At expiry the option's time value reaches zero. Hence, entities that use purchased options to hedge one-sided risks know that over the life of the option they will lose the time value that they paid. This explains why entities typically view the premium paid as being similar to an insurance premium and hence as a cost of using this hedging strategy.

BC6.391 The IASB considered that by taking an insurance premium view, the accounting for the time value of options could be aligned with the risk management perspective as well as with other areas of accounting. The IASB noted that under IFRS some costs of insuring risks were treated as transaction costs that were capitalised into the costs of the insured asset (for example, freight insurance paid by the buyer in accordance with IAS 2 Inventories or IAS 16 Property, Plant and Equipment), whereas costs of insuring some other risks were recognised as expenses over the period for which the entity was insured (for example, fire insurance for a building). Hence, the IASB considered that aligning the accounting for the time value of options with such other areas would provide more comparable results that would also be more aligned with how preparers and users of financial statements think about the issue.

BC6.392 The IASB took the view that, like the distinction between the different types of costs of insuring risk, the time value of options should be distinguished by the type of hedged item that the option hedges, into time value that is:

(a) transaction related (for example, the forecast purchase of a commodity); or

(b) time-period related (for example, hedging an existing commodity inventory for commodity price changes).

BC6.393 The IASB considered that for transaction related hedged items the cumulative change in fair value of the option's time value should be accumulated in other comprehensive income and be reclassified in a way similar to that for cash flow hedges. In the IASB's view, this would best reflect the character of transaction costs (like those capitalised for inventory or property, plant and equipment).

BC6.394 In contrast, the IASB considered that for time-period related hedged items the nature of the time value of the option used as the hedging instrument is that of a cost for obtaining protection against a risk over a particular period of time. Hence, the IASB considered that the cost of obtaining the protection should be allocated as an expense over the relevant period on a systematic and rational basis. The IASB noted that this would require accumulating the cumulative change in fair value of the option's time value in other comprehensive income and amortising the original time value by transferring in each period an amount to profit or loss. The IASB considered that the amortisation pattern should be determined on a systematic and rational basis, which would best reflect principle-based standard-setting.

BC6.395 The IASB also considered situations in which the option used has critical terms (such as the nominal amount, the life and the underlying) that do not match the hedged item. This raises the following questions:

(a) which part of the time value included in the premium relates to the hedged item (and therefore should be treated as costs of hedging) and which part does not?

(b) how should any part of the time value that does not relate to the hedged item be accounted for?

BC6.396 The IASB proposed in the 2010 Hedge Accounting Exposure Draft that the part of the time value of the option that relates to the hedged item should be determined as the time value that would have been paid for an option that perfectly matches the hedged item (for example, with the same underlying, maturity and notional amount). The IASB noted that this would require an option pricing exercise using the terms of the hedged item as well as other relevant information about the hedged item (in particular, the volatility of its price or cash flow, which is a driver of an option's time value).

BC6.397 The IASB noted that the accounting for the time value of the option would need to distinguish whether the initial time value of the purchased option (actual time value) is higher or lower than the time value that would have been paid for an option that perfectly matches the hedged item (aligned time value). The IASB noted that if, at inception of the hedging relationship, the actual time value is higher than the aligned time value, the entity pays a higher premium than that which reflects the costs of hedging. Hence, the IASB considered that the amount that is recognised in accumulated other comprehensive income should be determined only on the basis of the aligned time value, whereas the remainder of the actual time value should be accounted for as a derivative.

BC6.398 Conversely, the IASB noted that if, at inception of the hedging relationship, the actual time value is lower than the aligned time value, the entity actually pays a lower premium than it would have to pay to cover the risk fully. The IASB considered that in this situation, in order to avoid accounting for a higher time value of an option than was actually paid, the amount that is recognised in accumulated other comprehensive income would have to be determined by reference to the lower of the cumulative fair value change of:

(a) the actual time value; and

(b) the aligned time value.

BC6.399 The IASB also considered whether the balances accumulated in other comprehensive income would require an impairment test. The IASB decided that because the accounting for the time value of the option was closely linked to hedge accounting, an impairment test that uses features of the hedge accounting model would be appropriate. Hence, for transaction related hedged items the impairment test would be similar to that for the cash flow hedge reserve. For time-period related hedged items the IASB considered that the part of the option's time value that remains in accumulated other comprehensive income should be immediately recognised in profit or loss when the hedging relationship is discontinued. That would reflect that the reason for amortising the amount would no longer apply after the insured risk (ie the hedged item) no longer qualifies for hedge accounting. The IASB noted that impairment of the hedged item affects the criteria for qualifying hedges and if those are no longer met it would result in an impairment loss for the remaining unamortised balance of the time value of the option.

BC6.400 Most of the respondents to the 2010 Hedge Accounting Exposure Draft agreed with the 'insurance premium' view. They thought that the proposal provided a better representation of the performance and effect of the entity's risk management strategy than under IAS 39. In their view, the proposals alleviated undue profit or loss volatility and reflected the economic substance of the transaction. They also thought that the costs of hedging should be associated with the hedged item instead of being mischaracterised as hedge ineffectiveness.

BC6.401 However, there were mixed views about the complexity of the proposals, in particular in relation to:

(a) the requirement to differentiate between transaction related and time-period related hedged items; and

(b) the requirement to measure the fair value of the aligned time value. Those concerns included the concern that the costs of implementing the proposals could outweigh the benefits, for instance, for less sophisticated (for example, smaller) entities.

BC6.402 Some respondents did not agree with the proposed accounting for transaction related hedged items. Some argued that time value should always be expensed over the option period.

BC6.403 In the light of this feedback the IASB considered in its redeliberations:

(a) whether the time value of an option should always be expensed over the life of the option instead of applying the accounting as proposed in the 2010 Hedge Accounting Exposure Draft;

(b) whether it should remove the differentiation between transaction related and time-period related hedged items and replace it with a single accounting treatment; and

(c) whether it should simplify the requirement to account for the fair value of the aligned time value.

BC6.404 The IASB discussed whether the time value of an option should always be expensed over the life of the option instead of applying the accounting as proposed in the 2010 Hedge Accounting Exposure Draft. The IASB noted that such an accounting treatment would have outcomes that would be inconsistent with the notion of the time value being regarded as costs of hedging. This is because it could result in recognising an expense in periods that are unrelated to how the hedged exposure affects profit or loss.

BC6.405 The IASB also reconsidered whether it was appropriate to defer in accumulated other comprehensive income the time value of options for transaction related hedged items. The IASB noted that the deferred time value does not represent an asset in itself, but that it is an ancillary cost that is capitalised as part of the measurement of the asset acquired or liability assumed. This is consistent with how other Standards treat ancillary costs. The IASB also noted that the 2010 Hedge Accounting Exposure Draft included an impairment test to ensure that amounts that are not expected to be recoverable are not deferred.

BC6.406 The IASB also discussed whether the proposals in the 2010 Hedge Accounting Exposure Draft could be simplified by removing the differentiation between transaction related and time-period related hedged items. However, the IASB noted that a single accounting treatment would be inconsistent with other Standards because it would not distinguish situations in a similar way (see paragraphs BC6.391–BC6.392). Hence, the IASB considered that the suggested single accounting treatment would essentially treat unlike situations as alike. The IASB noted that this would actually diminish comparability and hence not be an improvement to financial reporting.

BC6.407 The IASB also considered whether it should paraphrase the requirements as a single general principle to clarify the accounting for transaction related and time-period related hedged items, instead of having requirements that distinguish between those two types of hedged items. However, on balance the IASB decided that this approach risked creating confusion, particularly because it would still involve the two different types of accounting treatments.

BC6.408 The IASB also discussed possible ways to simplify the requirements to account for the fair value of the aligned time value. As part of those discussions the IASB considered:

(a)   applying the proposed accounting treatment for the time value of options to the entire amount of the time value paid even if it differs from the aligned time value. This means that entities would not need to perform a separate valuation for the fair value of the aligned time value. However, the IASB considered that only the time value that relates to the hedged item should be treated as a cost of hedging. Hence, any additional time value paid should be accounted for as a derivative at fair value through profit or loss.

(b)   providing entities with a choice (for each hedging relationship or alternatively as an accounting policy choice) to account for the time value of options either as proposed in the 2010 Hedge Accounting Exposure Draft or in accordance with the treatment in IAS 39. In the latter case, the amount recognised in profit or loss as a 'trading instrument' is the difference between the change in the fair value of the option in its entirety and the change in fair value of the intrinsic value. In contrast, the proposals in the 2010 Hedge Accounting Exposure Draft would require two option valuations (ie the change in fair value of the actual time value of the option and the aligned time value of the option). However, the IASB noted that the accounting treatment in accordance with IAS 39 would, in effect, present the change in fair value of the time value as a trading profit or loss. This accounting treatment would not be consistent with the character of the changes in the time value that the IASB is seeking to portray, ie that of costs of hedging. In addition, the IASB noted that providing a choice would reduce comparability between entities and it would make financial statements more difficult to understand.

BC6.409   Consequently, the IASB decided to retain the accounting requirements related to the time value of options proposed in the 2010 Hedge Accounting Exposure Draft (ie that the accounting would depend on the nature of the hedged item and that the new accounting treatment only applied to the aligned time value).

Zero-cost collars

BC6.410   The proposed accounting treatment for the time value of options in the 2010 Hedge Accounting Exposure Draft only addressed situations in which the option had a time value (other than nil) at inception. That proposed accounting would not have applied to situations in which there was a combination of a purchased and a written option (one being a put option and one being a call option) that at inception of the hedging relationship had a net time value of nil (often referred to as 'zero-cost collars' or 'zero premium collars').

BC6.411   Many respondents to the 2010 Hedge Accounting Exposure Draft commented that the proposed accounting for purchased options should also apply to all zero-cost collars. They thought that without generally aligning the accounting treatment for the time value of zero-cost collars and options, it would encourage entities to undertake particular types of transactions and replace zero-cost collars with collars with a nominal cost only to achieve a desired accounting outcome.

BC6.412 Furthermore, those respondents noted that even though the zero-cost collar had no net time value at inception, the time value of the collar would fluctuate during the life of the hedge. They noted that time value was subject to 'time decay' and that both the purchased and the written option would lose their time value over time as the collar approaches expiry. They argued that the time value of zero-cost collars should also be recognised in other comprehensive income during the life of the hedging relationship. They considered it unjustified to limit the proposed accounting to options that have an initial time value of greater than nil, given that one of the main concerns being addressed by the proposal was the volatility resulting from changes in the time value over the life of the hedge.

BC6.413 In the light of those arguments, the IASB decided to align the accounting treatment for changes in the time value of options and zero-cost collars.

Accounting for the forward element of forward contracts

BC6.414 IAS 39 allowed an entity a choice between:

(a) designating a forward contract as a hedging instrument in its entirety; or

(b) separating the forward element and designating as the hedging instrument only the spot element.

BC6.415 If not designated, the forward element was treated as held for trading and was accounted for as at fair value through profit or loss, which gave rise to significant volatility in profit or loss.

BC6.416 The IASB noted that the characteristics of forward elements depended on the underlying item, for example:

(a) for foreign exchange rate risk, the forward element represents the interest differential between the two currencies;

(b) for interest rate risk, the forward element reflects the term structure of interest rates; and

(c) for commodity risk, the forward element represents what is called the 'cost of carry' (for example, it includes costs such as storage costs).

BC6.417 Respondents to the 2010 Hedge Accounting Exposure Draft as well as participants in the IASB's outreach activities requested that the IASB consider extending the proposal on the accounting for the time value of options (see paragraphs BC6.386–BC6.413) to forward elements.

BC6.418 The IASB noted that even though under IAS 39 the hedge accounting requirements were identical for forward elements and options, the actual accounting implications were different. In contrast to many typical situations in which options were used to hedge transactions that did not involve a time value notion because they were not options (see paragraph BC6.388), in situations in which forward contracts were used the value of hedged items typically did have a forward element that corresponded to that of the hedge. The IASB noted that this meant that an entity could choose to designate the forward contract in its entirety and use the 'forward rate method' to measure the hedged item.

BC6.419 Using the forward rate method, the forward element is essentially included in the hedging relationship by measuring the change in the value of the hedged item on the basis of forward prices or rates. An entity can then recognise the forward element as costs of hedging by using the forward rate method, resulting in, for example:

(a) capitalising the forward element into the cost of the acquired asset or liability assumed; or

(b) reclassifying the forward element into profit or loss when the hedged item (for example, hedged sales denominated in a foreign currency) affects profit or loss.

BC6.420 Consequently, changes in forward elements are not recognised in profit or loss until the hedged item affects profit or loss. The IASB noted that this outcome was equivalent to what it had proposed in its 2010 Hedge Accounting Exposure Draft for accounting for the time value of options that hedge transaction related hedged items. Hence, the IASB considered that, for situations similar to hedges of transaction related hedged items using options, applying the forward rate method would, in effect, achieve an accounting outcome that treated the forward element like costs of hedging. This would be consistent with the IASB's overall approach to accounting for the costs of hedging and would therefore not require any amendments to the proposals in the 2010 Hedge Accounting Exposure Draft.

BC6.421 However, the IASB acknowledged that in situations that were equivalent to those addressed by its decision on the accounting for time-period related hedged items that were hedged using options, its proposals in the 2010 Hedge Accounting Exposure Draft (like IAS 39) would prevent an entity from achieving an equivalent accounting outcome for the forward element of a forward contract. The reason was that, like IAS 39, the proposals in the 2010 Hedge Accounting Exposure Draft did not allow the forward element to be amortised. For example, if an entity hedged the fair value changes resulting from the price changes of its existing commodity inventory (ie a time-period related hedged item) it could, under the proposals in the 2010 Hedge Accounting Exposure Draft (like IAS 39), either:

(a) use the forward rate method (ie forward elements are capitalised into the cost of inventory, instead of being accounted for as at fair value through profit or loss over the time of the hedge); or

(b) designate as the hedging instrument only changes in the spot element (ie fair value changes in the forward element of the forward contract are recognised in profit or loss).

Neither of the above accounting outcomes are aligned with the treatment for the time value of options for time-period related hedged items that requires that the time value is amortised on a systematic and rational basis.

BC6.422 The IASB also noted that the accounting for monetary financial assets and liabilities denominated in a foreign currency had an important consequence. Like IAS 39, IFRS 9 (see paragraph B5.7.2) requires an entity to apply IAS 21 to those assets and liabilities, which means that they are translated into the entity's functional currency by using the spot exchange rate. Hence, the forward rate method does not provide a solution when entities hedge monetary financial assets and liabilities denominated in a foreign currency.

BC6.423 Consequently, the IASB acknowledged that aligning the accounting for forward elements with the accounting for the time value of options was a particular concern to entities that, for example, had more funding in their functional currency than they could invest in financial assets in their functional currency. To generate an economic return on their surplus funds, such entities exchange those funds into a foreign currency and invest in assets denominated in that foreign currency. To manage their exposure to foreign exchange risk (and to stabilise their net interest margin), such entities commonly enter into foreign exchange derivatives. Such transactions usually involve the following simultaneously:

(a) swapping the functional currency surplus funds into a foreign currency;

(b) investing the funds in a foreign currency financial asset for a period of time; and

(c) entering into a foreign exchange derivative to convert the foreign currency funds back into the functional currency at the end of the investment period. This amount typically covers the principal plus the interest at maturity.

BC6.424 The difference between the forward rate and the spot rate (ie the forward element) represents the interest differential between the two currencies at inception. The net economic return (ie the interest margin) over the investment period is determined by adjusting the yield of the investment in the foreign currency by the forward points (ie the forward element of the foreign exchange derivative) and then deducting the interest expense. The combination of the three transactions described in paragraph BC6.423 allows the entity to, in effect, 'lock in' a net interest margin and generate a fixed economic return over the investment period.

BC6.425 Respondents argued that risk management viewed the forward elements as an adjustment of the investment yield on foreign currency denominated assets. They believed that, as in the case of the accounting for the time value of options, it gave rise to a similar need for adjusting profit or loss against other comprehensive income to represent the cost of achieving a fixed economic return in a way that is consistent with the accounting for that return.

BC6.426 In the light of the arguments raised by respondents, the IASB decided to permit forward points that exist at inception of the hedging relationship to be recognised in profit or loss over time on a systematic and rational basis and to accumulate subsequent fair value changes through other comprehensive income. The IASB considered that this accounting treatment would provide a better representation of the economic substance of the transaction and the performance of the net interest margin.

Hedges of a group of items

BC6.427　IAS 39 restricted the application of hedge accounting for groups of items. For example, hedged items that together constitute an overall net position of assets and liabilities could not be designated into a hedging relationship with that net position as the hedged item. Other groups were eligible if the individual items within that group had similar risk characteristics and shared the risk exposure that was designated as being hedged. Furthermore, the change in the fair value attributable to the hedged risk for each individual item in the group had to be approximately proportional to the overall change in the fair value of the group for the hedged risk. The effect of those restrictions was that a group would generally qualify as a hedged item only if all the items in that group would qualify for hedge accounting for the same hedged risk on an individual basis (ie each as an individual hedged item).

BC6.428　In response to the Discussion Paper *Reducing Complexity in Reporting Financial Instruments*, many commented that restricting the ability to achieve hedge accounting for groups of items, including net positions, had resulted in a hedge accounting model that was inconsistent with the way in which an entity actually hedges (ie for risk management purposes). Similar concerns about the restrictions of IAS 39 for applying hedge accounting to groups of items were raised as part of the IASB's outreach activities for its Hedge Accounting project.

BC6.429　In practice, most entities hedge their risk exposures using different approaches, resulting in hedges of:

(a)　individual items;

(b)　groups of items that form a gross position; or

(c)　groups of (partially) offsetting items or risks that result in a net position.

BC6.430　The group hedging approach involves identifying the risk from particular groups of items (including a net position), and then hedging some or all of that risk with one or more hedging instruments. The group hedging approach views the risk at a higher aggregated level. The reasons for taking this approach include:

(a)　items in the group have some offsetting risk positions that provide a natural hedge for some of those risks and therefore those offsetting risks do not need to be separately hedged;

(b)　hedging derivatives that hedge different risks together can be more readily available than individual derivatives that each hedge a different risk;

(c)　it is more expedient (cost, practicality, etc) to enter into fewer derivatives to hedge a group instead of hedging individual exposures;

(d) the minimisation of counterparty credit risk exposure, because offsetting risk positions are hedged on a net basis (this aspect is particularly important for an entity that has regulatory capital requirements); and

(e) the reduction of gross assets/liabilities in the statement of financial position, because offset accounting may not be achieved if multiple derivatives (with offsetting risk exposures) are entered into.

BC6.431 The restrictions in IAS 39 prevented an entity that hedges on a group or net basis from presenting its activities in a manner that is consistent with its risk management practice. For example, an entity may hedge the net (ie residual) foreign currency risk from a sequence of sales and expenses that arise over several reporting periods (say, two years) using a single foreign currency derivative. Such an entity could not designate the net position of sales and expenses as the hedged item. Instead, if it wanted to apply hedge accounting it had to designate a gross position that best matched its hedging instrument. However, the IASB noted there were a number of reasons why this could render information less useful, for example:

(a) a matching hedged item might not exist, in which case hedge accounting cannot be applied.

(b) if the entity did identify and designate a matching gross exposure from the sequence of sales and expenses, that item would be portrayed as the only hedged item and would be presented at the hedged rate. All other transactions (for instance, in earlier reporting periods) would appear unhedged and would be recognised at the prevailing spot rates, which would give rise to volatility in some reporting periods.

(c) if the designated hedged transaction did not arise, but the net position remained the same, hedge ineffectiveness would be recognised for accounting purposes even though it does not exist from an economic perspective.

BC6.432 Consequently, in its 2010 Hedge Accounting Exposure Draft, the IASB proposed that groups of items (including net positions) should be eligible for hedge accounting. However, the IASB also proposed limiting the application of cash flow hedge accounting for some types of groups of items that constitute a net position (see paragraphs BC6.442–BC6.447).

BC6.433 Respondents to the 2010 Hedge Accounting Exposure Draft supported the proposal to allow hedge accounting for groups and net positions and most supported the IASB's rationale for doing so. However, some disagreed with specific aspects of the IASB's proposals in the 2010 Hedge Accounting Exposure Draft. Their concerns focused on the proposals related to cash flow hedges of net positions.

BC6.434 The following subsections set out the IASB's considerations about the application of hedge accounting in the context of groups of items.

Criteria for the eligibility of a group of items as a hedged item

BC6.435 An individual hedge approach involves an entity entering into one or more hedging instruments to manage a risk exposure from an individual hedged item to achieve a desired outcome. This is similar for a group hedge approach. However, for a group hedge approach an entity seeks to manage the risk exposure from a group of items. Some of the risks in the group may offset (for their full term or for a partial term) and provide a hedge against each other, leaving the group residual risk to be hedged by the hedging instrument.

BC6.436 An individual hedge approach and a group hedge approach are similar in concept. Hence, the IASB decided that the requirements for qualifying for hedge accounting should also be similar. Consequently, the IASB proposed that the eligibility criteria that apply to individual hedged items should also apply to hedges of groups of items. However, some restrictions were retained for cash flow hedges of net positions.

BC6.437 The IASB retained its original decision when redeliberating its 2010 Hedge Accounting Exposure Draft.

Designation of a layer component of a nominal amount for hedges of a group of items

BC6.438 The IASB proposed in its 2010 Hedge Accounting Exposure Draft that an entity could designate a layer component of a nominal amount (a 'layer') of a single item in a hedging relationship. The IASB also considered whether it would be appropriate to extend that decision on single items to groups of items and hence allow the designation of a layer of a group in a hedging relationship.

BC6.439 The IASB noted that the benefits of identifying a layer component of a nominal amount of a group of items are similar to the benefits it had considered for layer components of single items (see paragraphs BC6.200–BC6.204). In addition, the IASB also noted other reasons that support the use of components for groups of items:

(a) uncertainties such as a breach (or cancellation) of contracts, or prepayment, can be better modelled when considering a group of items;

(b) in practice, hedging layers of groups of items (for example, a bottom layer) is a common risk management strategy; and

(c) arbitrarily identifying and designating (as hedged items) specific items from a group of items that are exposed to the same hedged risk can:

(i) give rise to arbitrary accounting results if the designated items do not behave as originally expected (while other items, sufficient to cover the hedged amount, do behave as originally expected); and

(ii) can provide opportunities for earnings management (for example, by choosing to transfer and derecognise particular items from a group of homogeneous items when only some were specifically designated into a fair value hedge and therefore have fair value hedge adjustments attached to them).

BC6.440 The IASB noted that, in practice, groups of items hedged together are not likely to be groups of identical items. Given the different types of groups that could exist in practice, in some cases it could be easy to satisfy the proposed conditions and in some cases it could be more challenging or even impossible. The IASB considered that it is not appropriate to define the cases in which the proposed conditions were satisfied because it would depend on the specific facts and circumstances. The IASB therefore considered a criteria-based approach would be more operational and appropriate. Such an approach would allow hedge accounting to be applied in situations in which the criteria are easy to meet as well as in cases in which, although the criteria are more challenging to meet, an entity is prepared to undertake the necessary efforts (for example, to invest in systems in order to achieve compliance with the hedge accounting requirements).

BC6.441 The IASB retained its original decision when redeliberating its 2010 Hedge Accounting Exposure Draft.

Cash flow hedges of a group of items that constitutes a net position that qualifies for hedge accounting

BC6.442 In a cash flow hedge, changes in the fair value of the hedging instrument are deferred in other comprehensive income to be reclassified later from accumulated other comprehensive income to profit or loss when the hedged item affects profit or loss. For hedges of net positions, items in the group have some offsetting risk positions that provide a natural hedge for some of the risks in the group (ie the gains on some items offset the losses on others). Hence, for a cash flow hedge of a net position that is a group of forecast transactions, the cumulative change in value (from the inception of the hedge) that arises on some forecast transactions (to the extent that it is effective in achieving offset) must be deferred in other comprehensive income. This is necessary because the gain or loss that arises on the forecast transactions that occur in the early phase of the hedging relationship must be reclassified to profit or loss in the later phase until the last hedged item in the net position affects profit or loss.

BC6.443 The forecast transactions that constitute a hedged net position might differ in their timing such that they affect profit or loss in different reporting periods. For example, sales and unrelated expenditure hedged for foreign currency risk might affect profit or loss in different reporting periods. When this happens, the cumulative change in value of the designated sales (to be reclassified later when the expenditure is recognised as an expense) needs to be excluded from profit or loss and instead be deferred in other comprehensive income. This is required in order to ensure that the effect of the sales on profit or loss is based on the hedged exchange rate.

BC6.444 Hence, in its deliberations leading to the 2010 Hedge Accounting Exposure Draft, the IASB noted that cash flow hedge accounting for net positions of forecast transactions would involve a deferral in accumulated other comprehensive income of cumulative gains and losses on some forecast transactions, from the time they occurred until some other forecast transactions would affect profit or loss in later reporting periods. The IASB considered that this would be tantamount to measuring the transactions that occurred first at a different amount from the transaction amount (or other amount that would be required under general IFRS requirements) in contemplation of other forecast transactions that were expected to occur in the future and that would have an offsetting gain or loss. When those other transactions occurred, their measurement would be adjusted for the amounts deferred in accumulated other comprehensive income on forecast transactions that had occurred earlier.

BC6.445 The IASB acknowledged that this approach would not result in the recognition of gains and losses on items that do not yet exist but would instead defer gains and losses on some forecast transactions as those transactions occurred. However, the IASB considered that this approach would be a significant departure from general IFRS regarding the items that resulted from the forecast transactions. The IASB noted that this departure would affect the forecast transactions:

(a) that occurred in the early phases of the hedging relationship, ie those for which gains and losses were deferred when the transaction occurred; and

(b) those that occurred in the later phases of the hedging relationship and were adjusted for the gains or losses that had been deferred on the forecast transactions as those transactions had occurred in the early phases of the hedging relationship.

BC6.446 The IASB noted that the accounting for the forecast transactions that occurred in the later phases of the hedging relationship was comparable to that of forecast transactions that were hedged items in a cash flow hedge. However, the treatment of the forecast transactions that occurred in the early phases of the hedging relationship would be more similar to that of a hedging instrument than to that of a hedged item. The IASB concluded that this would be a significant departure from general IFRS requirements and the requirements of the hedge accounting model for hedging instruments.

BC6.447 Consequently, in its 2010 Hedge Accounting Exposure Draft, the IASB proposed that a cash flow hedge of a net position should not qualify for hedge accounting when the offsetting risk positions would affect profit or loss in different periods. The IASB noted that when the offsetting risk positions affected profit or loss in the same period those concerns would not apply in the same way as no deferral in accumulated other comprehensive income of cumulative gains and losses on forecast transactions would be required. Hence, the IASB proposed that such net positions should be eligible as hedged items.

BC6.448   Some respondents to the 2010 Hedge Accounting Exposure Draft agreed with the IASB's rationale for not allowing the application of cash flow hedge accounting to net positions that consist of forecast transactions that would affect profit or loss in different reporting periods. They believed that without this restriction the potential for earnings management would arise. Despite agreeing with the proposals, some respondents asked the IASB to provide additional guidance on the treatment of the amounts deferred in accumulated other comprehensive income if, in a cash flow hedge of a net position, the offsetting risk positions that were initially expected to affect profit or loss in the same reporting period subsequently changed and, as a result, were expected to affect profit or loss in different periods.

BC6.449   Others requested the IASB to reconsider the restriction on the application of hedge accounting to cash flow hedges of a net position with offsetting risk positions that affect profit or loss in different reporting periods. Those respondents believed that this restriction would not allow entities to properly reflect their risk management activities. In addition, some respondents requested that the IASB consider the annual reporting period as the basis for this restriction (if retained) instead of any reporting period (ie including an interim reporting period), noting that the frequency of reporting would otherwise affect the eligibility for this form of hedge accounting.

BC6.450   The IASB noted that the feedback on its proposals in the 2010 Hedge Accounting Exposure Draft reflected two different perspectives:

(a)   a treasury perspective—this is a cash flow perspective. The respondents who provided comments from this perspective typically look at cash inflows and cash outflows arising from both sides of the net position. The treasury view stops at the level of the cash flows and does not take into account the time lag that might exist between the cash flow and the recognition of related income or expense in profit or loss. From this perspective, once the first forecast transaction is recognised, the natural hedge lapses and the remainder of the net position will be hedged by entering into an additional derivative (or alternatively by using, for example, the foreign currency denominated cash instrument that arises as a result of the occurrence of the first forecast transaction). Subsequently (ie at the time of settlement of the second forecast transaction), the cash flows from the financial instrument being used as a hedging instrument will be used to settle the payments resulting from the forecast transaction.

(b)   an accounting perspective—this perspective focuses on how to present the effect of the two forecast transactions in profit or loss and in which accounting period. This goes beyond the cash flow view of the treasury perspective. This is because the way in which the item affects profit or loss can be different, while the cash flow is a point-in-time event. For example, while the purchase of services and the sales of goods can be designated as part of a net position in a way that they will affect profit or loss in one reporting period, purchases of property, plant and equipment affect profit or loss over several different reporting periods through the depreciation pattern. Similarly, if inventory is sold in the period after it was purchased, the cash flow and the related effect on profit or loss occur in different periods.

BC6.451 In the light of the comments received, the IASB reconsidered the restriction on cash flow hedges of net positions with offsetting risk positions that affect profit or loss in different reporting periods, as proposed in the 2010 Hedge Accounting Exposure Draft. The IASB did not think that it was appropriate to completely remove the restriction. However, the IASB considered whether there was an alternative approach that could better reflect an entity's risk management activities but that would also address the earnings management concerns that had been raised.

BC6.452 The IASB noted that entities would only be able to reflect their risk management activities if it removed the restriction on the application of hedge accounting to cash flow hedges of a net position with offsetting risk positions that affect profit or loss in different reporting periods. However, the IASB noted that it could address the concerns about earnings management by introducing some requirements for documenting the hedging relationship instead of prohibiting the designation altogether.

BC6.453 The IASB noted that the potential for earnings management could be addressed if the recognition pattern for profit or loss arising from the hedged net position for all reporting periods affected was set at the inception of the hedge, in such a way that it was clear what amounts would affect profit or loss, when they would affect profit or loss and to which hedged volumes and types of items they related.

BC6.454 However, the IASB had concerns about applying cash flow hedges for net positions to many different types of risks because it might have unintended consequences for some risks. The IASB noted that foreign currency risk was the risk most commented on by respondents and the risk that the IASB intended to address by this type of hedge.

BC6.455 Consequently, the IASB decided that cash flow hedges of net positions would only be available for hedges of foreign currency risk (but no other risks). In addition, the IASB decided to remove the restriction that the offsetting risk positions in a net position must affect profit or loss in the same reporting period. However, the IASB was concerned that without sufficiently specific documentation of the items within the designated net position, an entity could use hindsight to allocate the hedging gains or losses to those items so as to achieve a particular result in profit or loss (selection effect). Consequently, the IASB decided that for all items within the designated net position for which there could be a selection effect, an entity must specify each period in which the transactions are expected to affect profit or loss as well as the nature and volume of each type of forecast transaction in such a way that it eliminates the selection effect. For example, depending on the circumstances, eliminating a selection effect could require that specifying the nature of a forecast purchase of items of property, plant and equipment includes aspects such as the depreciation pattern for items of the same kind, if the nature of those items is such that the depreciation pattern could vary depending on how the entity uses those items (such as different useful lives because of being used in different production processes). The IASB noted that this would also address the issue that some respondents had raised about changes in the original expectations of when the risk positions would affect profit or loss resulting in items affecting profit or loss in different reporting periods (see paragraph BC6.449).

Presentation for groups of items that are a net position

BC6.456   For cash flow hedges of groups of items with offsetting risk positions (ie net positions), the hedged items might affect different line items in the statement of profit or loss and other comprehensive income. Consequently, this raises the question of how hedging gains or losses should be presented for a cash flow hedge of such a group. In its deliberations leading to the 2010 Hedge Accounting Exposure Draft, the IASB noted that hedging gains or losses would need to be grossed up to offset each of the hedged items individually.

BC6.457   The IASB noted that if it proposed to adjust (gross up) all the affected line items in the statement of profit or loss and other comprehensive income it would result in the recognition of gross (partially offsetting) gains or losses that did not exist, and that this would not be consistent with general accounting principles. Consequently, in its 2010 Hedge Accounting Exposure Draft, the IASB decided not to propose adjusting (grossing up) all affected line items in the statement of profit or loss and other comprehensive income.

BC6.458   Instead, the IASB proposed that in the statement of profit or loss or other comprehensive income hedging gains or losses for cash flow hedges of a net position should be presented in a separate line item. This would avoid the problem of distorting gains or losses with amounts that did not exist. However, the IASB acknowledged that this results in additional disaggregation of information in the statement of profit or loss and other comprehensive income. This would also result in hedges of net positions being presented differently from hedges of gross positions.

BC6.459   In a fair value hedge, changes in the fair value of both the hedged item and the hedging instrument, for changes in the hedged risk, are recognised in the statement of profit or loss and other comprehensive income. Because the treatment of gains or losses for both the hedged item and the hedging instrument is the same, the IASB did not believe any changes to the fair value hedge accounting mechanics were necessary to accommodate net positions. However, in situations in which some hedging gains or losses are considered a modification of revenue or an expense (for example, when the net interest accrual on an interest rate swap is considered a modification of the interest revenue or expense on the hedged item), those gains or losses should be presented in a separate line when the hedged item is a net position. In the IASB's view, in those situations the same reasons applied that it had considered for cash flow hedges in relation to their presentation in the statement of profit or loss and other comprehensive income.

BC6.460   Most of the respondents to the 2010 Hedge Accounting Exposure Draft supported the IASB's proposal to require the hedging gains or losses to be presented in a separate line item for a hedging relationship that includes a group of items with offsetting risks that affect different line items in the statement of profit or loss and other comprehensive income.

BC6.461   The IASB decided to retain the proposal in the 2010 Hedge Accounting Exposure Draft, as it would make transparent that an entity is hedging on a net basis and would clearly present the effect of those hedges of net positions on the face of the statement of profit or loss and other comprehensive income.

Identifying the hedged item for hedges of a group of items that constitutes a net position

BC6.462   The IASB considered in its deliberations leading to the 2010 Hedge Accounting Exposure Draft how an entity that applies hedge accounting to net positions should identify the hedged item. The IASB concluded that an entity would need to designate a combination of gross positions if it were to apply the hedge accounting mechanics to the hedged position. Consequently, the IASB proposed that an entity could not designate a merely abstract net position (ie without specifying the items that form the gross positions from which the net position arises) as the hedged item.

BC6.463   The IASB retained its original decision when redeliberating its 2010 Hedge Accounting Exposure Draft.

Hedges of a group of items that results in a net position of nil

BC6.464   In its deliberations leading to the 2010 Hedge Accounting Exposure Draft, the IASB noted that when an entity managed and hedged risks on a net basis, the proposals would allow the entity to designate the net risk from hedged items into a hedging relationship with a hedging instrument. For an entity that hedges on such a basis, the IASB acknowledged that there might be circumstances in which, by coincidence, the net position of hedged items for a particular period was nil.

BC6.465   The IASB considered whether, when an entity hedges risk on a net basis, a nil net position should be eligible for hedge accounting. Such a hedging relationship could be, in its entirety, outside the scope of hedge accounting if it did not include any financial instruments. Furthermore, eligibility for hedge accounting would be inconsistent with the general requirement that a hedging relationship must contain both an eligible hedged item and an eligible hedging instrument.

BC6.466   However, the IASB noted that the accounting result of prohibiting the application of hedge accounting to nil net positions could distort the financial reporting of an entity that otherwise hedged (with eligible hedging instruments) and applied hedge accounting on a net basis, for example:

(a)   in periods in which hedge accounting is permitted (because a net position exists and is hedged with a hedging instrument), the transactions would affect profit or loss at an overall hedged rate or price; whereas

(b)   in periods in which hedge accounting would not be permitted (because the net position is nil), transactions would affect profit or loss at prevailing spot rates or prices.

BC6.467   Consequently, the IASB proposed that nil net positions should qualify for hedge accounting. However, the IASB noted that such situations would be coincidental and hence it expected that nil net positions would be rare in practice.

BC6.468   The IASB retained its original decision when redeliberating its 2010 Hedge Accounting Exposure Draft.

Hedging credit risk using credit derivatives

The IASB's deliberations leading to the 2010 Hedge Accounting Exposure Draft

The issue

BC6.469   Many financial institutions use credit derivatives to manage their credit risk exposures arising from their lending activities. For example, hedges of credit risk exposure allow financial institutions to transfer the risk of credit loss on a loan or a loan commitment to a third party. This might also reduce the regulatory capital requirement for the loan or loan commitment while at the same time allowing the financial institution to retain nominal ownership of the loan and to preserve the relationship with the client. Credit portfolio managers frequently use credit derivatives to hedge the credit risk of a proportion of a particular exposure (for example, a facility for a particular client) or the bank's overall lending portfolio.

BC6.470   However, the credit risk of a financial item is not a risk component that meets the eligibility criteria for hedged items. The spread between the risk-free rate and the market interest rate incorporates credit risk, liquidity risk, funding risk and any other unidentified risk component and margin elements. Although it is possible to determine that the spread includes credit risk, the credit risk cannot be isolated in a way that would allow the change in fair value that is attributable solely to credit risk to be separately identifiable (see also paragraph BC6.503).

BC6.471   As an alternative to hedge accounting, IFRS 9 permits an entity to designate, as at fair value through profit or loss, at initial recognition, financial instruments that are within the scope of that Standard if doing so eliminates or significantly reduces an accounting mismatch. However, the fair value option is only available at initial recognition, is irrevocable and an entity must designate the financial item in its entirety (ie for its full nominal amount). Because of the various optional features and the drawdown behavioural pattern of the loans and loan commitments, credit portfolio managers often engage in a flexible and active risk management strategy. Credit portfolio managers most often hedge less than 100 per cent of a loan or loan commitment. They might also hedge longer periods than the contractual maturity of the loan or the loan commitment. Furthermore, the fair value option is available only for instruments that are within the scope of IFRS 9.

Most of the loan commitments for which credit risk is managed fall within the scope of IAS 37, not IFRS 9. Consequently, most financial institutions do not (and often cannot) elect to apply the fair value option because of the associated restrictions and scope.

BC6.472 As a result, financial institutions that use credit default swaps to hedge the credit risk of their loan portfolios measure their loan portfolios at amortised cost and do not recognise most loan commitments (ie those that meet the scope exception of IFRS 9). The changes in fair value of the credit default swaps are recognised in profit or loss in every reporting period (as for a trading book). The accounting outcome is an accounting mismatch of gains and losses of the loans and loan commitments versus those of the credit default swaps, which creates volatility in profit or loss. During the IASB's outreach programme, many users of financial statements pointed out that that outcome does not reflect the economic substance of the credit risk management strategy of financial institutions.

BC6.473 In its 2010 Hedge Accounting Exposure Draft, the IASB proposed that a risk component should be separately identifiable and reliably measurable in order to qualify as a hedged item. As mentioned before, measuring the credit risk component of a loan or a loan commitment is complex. Consequently, to accommodate an equivalent to hedge accounting when entities hedge credit risk, a different accounting requirement would have to be developed specifically for this type of risk, or the proposed hedge accounting requirements would have to be significantly modified (for example, in relation to eligible hedged items and effectiveness testing).

Alternatives considered by the IASB

BC6.474 In its deliberations leading to the 2010 Hedge Accounting Exposure Draft, the IASB considered three alternative approaches to hedge accounting in order to address situations in which credit risk is hedged by credit derivatives. Those alternatives would, subject to qualification criteria, permit an entity with regard to the hedged credit exposure (for example, a bond, loan or loan commitment):

(a) Alternative 1:

   (i) to elect fair value through profit or loss only at initial recognition;

   (ii) to designate a component of nominal amounts; and

   (iii) to discontinue fair value through profit or loss accounting.

(b) Alternative 2:

   (i) to elect fair value through profit or loss at initial recognition or subsequently (if subsequently, the difference between the then carrying amount and the then fair value is recognised immediately in profit or loss);

   (ii) to designate a component of nominal amounts; and

   (iii) to discontinue fair value through profit or loss accounting.

(c)   Alternative 3:

    (i)   to elect fair value through profit or loss at initial recognition or subsequently (if subsequently, the difference between the then carrying amount and the then fair value is amortised or deferred);

    (ii)   to designate a component of nominal amounts; and

    (iii)   to discontinue fair value through profit or loss accounting.

BC6.475 The election of fair value through profit or loss would be available for a financial instrument (or a proportion of it) that is managed in such a way that an economic relationship on the basis of the same credit risk exists with credit derivatives (measured at fair value through profit or loss) that causes offset between changes in fair value of the financial instrument and the credit derivatives. This would also apply to financial instruments that fall outside the scope of IFRS 9, for example, loan commitments. Instead of the qualifying criteria for hedge accounting (see paragraphs BC6.230–BC6.271), the IASB considered the following qualifying criteria for electing fair value through profit or loss:

(a)   the name of the credit exposure matches the reference entity of the credit derivative (name matching); and

(b)   the seniority of the financial instrument matches that of the instruments that can be delivered in accordance with the credit derivative.

BC6.476 The qualification criteria in BC6.475 are set with a view to accommodating economic hedges of credit risk that would otherwise qualify for hedge accounting, but for the fact that the credit risk component within the hedged exposure cannot be separately identified and hence is not a risk component that meets the eligibility criteria for hedged items. Those qualification criteria are also consistent with regulatory requirements and the risk management strategy underlying the current business practice of financial institutions. However, using name matching as a qualifying criterion means that index-based credit default swaps would not meet that criterion.

BC6.477 For discontinuation, the IASB considered the following criteria:

(a)   the qualifying criteria are no longer met; and

(b)   retaining the measurement at fair value through profit or loss is not needed because of any other requirements.

BC6.478 Given the rationale for electing fair value through profit or loss, an entity would typically discontinue accounting at fair value through profit or loss if the discontinuation criteria in BC6.477 are met, because that would ensure that the accounting is aligned with how the exposure is managed (ie the credit risk is no longer managed using credit derivatives). The IASB noted that in circumstances when the discontinuation criteria apply, the financial instrument, if fair value through profit or loss accounting had not already been elected, would not qualify (any more) for that election. Hence, the IASB considered that it would be logical to make the discontinuation of fair value through profit or loss accounting mandatory (instead of optional) if the discontinuation criteria are fulfilled.

BC6.479 Alternative 1 permits electing fair value through profit or loss for a component of the nominal amount of the financial instrument if qualifying criteria are met. This is available only at initial recognition. Fair value through profit or loss can be discontinued if the qualification criteria are met. Loan commitments that fall outside the scope of IFRS 9 could also be eligible in accordance with this alternative if the qualification criteria are met. In accordance with Alternative 1, at the date of discontinuation of accounting for the financial instrument at fair value through profit or loss, the fair value of the financial instrument will be its deemed cost. For loan commitments outside the scope of IFRS 9 the recognition and measurement criteria of IAS 37 would apply.

BC6.480 The IASB noted that a significant disadvantage of Alternative 1 is that in many situations in practice (when a financial institution obtains credit protection for an exposure after the initial recognition of that exposure) this alternative is not aligned with the credit risk management strategy and would therefore not reflect its effect. An advantage of Alternative 1 is that it is less complex than the other alternatives that the IASB considered. By not permitting the election of fair value through profit or loss after initial recognition (or inception of a loan commitment), the difference at later points in time between the carrying amount and the fair value of the financial instrument will not arise.

BC6.481 In addition to the election of fair value through profit or loss at initial recognition in accordance with Alternative 1, Alternative 2 also permits that election after initial recognition. This means that the election is available again for an exposure for which fair value through profit or loss was elected previously (which logically cannot apply if the election is restricted to initial recognition). An example is a volatile longer-term exposure that was previously deteriorating and was then protected by credit default derivatives, then significantly improved so that the credit derivatives were sold, but then again deteriorated and was protected again. This ensures that an entity that uses a credit risk management strategy that protects exposures that drop below a certain quality or risk level could align the accounting with their risk management.

BC6.482 The IASB noted that when the financial instrument is elected for measurement as at fair value through profit or loss after initial recognition, a difference could arise between its carrying amount and its fair value. This difference is a result of the change in the measurement basis (for example, from amortised cost to fair value for a loan). The IASB considers this type of difference a measurement change adjustment. Alternative 2 proposes to recognise the measurement change adjustment in profit or loss immediately. At the date of discontinuation of fair value through profit or loss accounting, the fair value will be the deemed cost (as in Alternative 1). If the financial instrument is elected again after a previous discontinuation, the measurement change adjustment at that date is also recognised immediately in profit or loss.

BC6.483   A significant advantage of Alternative 2 is that it would eliminate the accounting mismatch and produce more consistent and relevant information. It is reflective of how credit exposures are managed. Credit exposures are actively managed by credit risk portfolio managers. Alternative 2 allows the effects of such an active and flexible risk management approach to be reflected appropriately and significantly reduces the measurement inconsistency between the credit exposures and the credit derivatives.

BC6.484   A disadvantage of Alternative 2 is that it is more complex than Alternative 1. Furthermore, it might appear susceptible to earnings management. An entity can decide at what time to elect fair value through profit or loss accounting for the financial instrument and thus when the difference between the carrying amount and the fair value at that date would be recognised in profit or loss. The accounting impact of immediately recognising the measurement change adjustment in profit or loss may also deter an entity from electing fair value through profit or loss accounting. For example, when an entity decides to take out credit protection at a time when the fair value has already moved below the carrying amount of the loan because of credit concerns in the market, it will immediately recognise a loss if it elects fair value through profit or loss accounting.

BC6.485   On the other hand, the advantage of recognising the measurement change adjustment immediately in profit or loss is that it is operationally simpler than Alternative 3. Alternative 3 provides the same eligibility of fair value through profit or loss accounting and its discontinuation as Alternative 2. Consequently, it also allows financial institutions to achieve an accounting outcome that reflects their credit risk management strategy.

BC6.486   An important difference between Alternatives 2 and 3 is the treatment of the measurement change adjustment (ie the difference that could arise between the carrying amount and the fair value of the financial instrument when fair value through profit or loss accounting is elected after initial recognition of the credit exposure). Alternative 3 proposes that the measurement change adjustment should be amortised for loans and deferred for loan commitments that fall within the scope of IAS 37.

BC6.487   As in Alternative 2, a significant advantage of Alternative 3 is that it would eliminate the accounting mismatch and produce more consistent and relevant information. It allows the effects of an active and flexible risk management approach to be reflected appropriately and significantly reduces the measurement inconsistency between the credit exposures and the credit derivatives. An advantage of Alternative 3 over Alternative 2 is that it would be less susceptible to earnings management and would not deter the election of fair value through profit or loss in scenarios after initial recognition of the exposure when the fair value of the exposure has already declined.

BC6.488   However, a disadvantage of Alternative 3 is that it is the most complex of the alternatives. The IASB noted that the measurement change adjustment in accordance with Alternative 3 would have presentation implications. The measurement change adjustment could be presented in the statement of financial position in the following ways:

(a)   as an integral part of the carrying amount of the exposure (ie it could be added to the fair value of the loan): this results in a mixed amount that is neither fair value nor amortised cost;

(b)   presentation as a separate line item next to the line item that includes the credit exposure: this results in additional line items in the statement of financial position and may easily be confused as a hedging adjustment; or

(c)   in other comprehensive income.

BC6.489   The IASB noted that disclosures could make the measurement change adjustment transparent.

BC6.490   However, in the light of the complexities that these three alternatives would introduce, the IASB decided not to propose allowing elective fair value accounting for hedged credit exposures (such as loans and loan commitments).

The feedback received on the 2010 Hedge Accounting Exposure Draft

BC6.491   Many respondents to the 2010 Hedge Accounting Exposure Draft were of the view that the IASB should consider how to accommodate hedges of credit risk using credit derivatives under IFRS. Respondents commented that hedges of credit risk using credit derivatives are becoming an increasingly significant practice issue in the application of IFRS. They noted that this issue is just as significant as other issues that had been addressed in the 2010 Hedge Accounting Exposure Draft (for example, the time value of options, hedges of aggregated exposures and risk components of non-financial items). They also noted that financial reporting under IFRS should allow entities to reflect the effects of such activities in the financial statements consistently with the overall hedge accounting objective to better reflect risk management activities.

BC6.492   Respondents also commented that IFRS today fails to represent the effect of credit risk management activities and distort the financial performance of financial institutions. They noted that, because of the accounting mismatch between loans and loan commitments on the one hand and the related credit derivatives on the other hand, the profit or loss under IFRS is significantly more volatile for financial institutions that hedge their credit risk exposures than for financial institutions that do not hedge.

BC6.493   Many respondents noted that the objective of hedge accounting would not be met if IFRS would not provide a way to account for hedges of credit risk so that financial statements can reflect the credit risk management activities of financial institutions.

BC6.494   Most users of financial statements commented that the IASB should address this issue. Many also noted that the financial statements currently reflect accounting-driven volatility when credit risk is hedged and that those financial statements do not align with those risk management activities.

BC6.495   Participants in the outreach provided the same feedback. Most of them were also of the view that this is an important practice issue that the IASB should address.

BC6.496   However, the feedback was mixed on how the IASB should address or resolve this issue. Many respondents were of the view that it was difficult to reliably measure credit risk as a risk component for the purposes of hedge accounting. However, some respondents suggested that for some types of instruments the credit risk component of financial instruments could be reliably measured on the basis of credit default swap (CDS) prices, subject to some adjustments.

BC6.497   Many agreed that the alternatives set out in the Basis for Conclusions of the 2010 Hedge Accounting Exposure Draft (see paragraph BC6.474) were too complex, although some respondents supported elective fair value through profit or loss accounting as an alternative to hedge accounting. Of the three fair value through profit or loss alternatives, most respondents supported Alternative 3.

BC6.498   Respondents who supported elective fair value through profit or loss accounting thought that it would be operational and believed that it would be no more complex than the other possible approaches, for example, identifying risk components. Most preferred Alternative 3 as it would align most closely with the dynamic credit risk management approach of many financial institutions. Some users of financial statements supported elective fair value through profit or loss accounting because they thought that the benefits of providing a better depiction of the economics of the risk management activities would outweigh the complexity.

The IASB's redeliberations of the 2010 Hedge Accounting Exposure Draft

BC6.499   In the light of the feedback received on its 2010 Hedge Accounting Exposure Draft, the IASB decided to specifically address the accounting for hedges of credit risk using credit derivatives. In its redeliberations the IASB explored various accounting alternatives.

Treating credit risk as a risk component

BC6.500   The IASB noted that for credit risk there are unique differences between how the relevant risk might affect the hedging instrument and the hedged risk exposure when compared to other risk components.

BC6.501   The IASB also noted that there is sometimes uncertainty about whether voluntary debt restructurings constitute a credit event under a standard credit default swap contract. Whether an event constitutes a credit event is determined by a committee consisting of representatives of banks and fund entities. This can (and in practice did) result in situations in which the fair value of a debt instrument has decreased, reflecting the market view of credit losses on those debt instruments while any payout on credit default swaps for those debt instruments depends on how the difficulties of the debtor will be resolved and what related measures might be considered a credit event. This is a factor that affects credit default swaps in a different way than the actual underlying debt. It is an additional factor inherent in credit default swaps that is not inherent in the debt as such. Hence, there could be scenarios in which, for example, an impairment loss on a loan might not be compensated by a payout from a credit default swap that is linked to the obligor of that debt. Also, market liquidity and the behaviour of speculators trying to close positions and taking gains affect the credit default swap and the debt market in different ways.

BC6.502 The IASB also noted that when a financial institution enters into a credit default swap to hedge the credit exposure from a loan commitment it might result in a situation in which the reference entity defaults while the loan commitment remains undrawn or partly undrawn. In such situations the financial institution receives compensation from the payout on the credit default swaps without actually incurring a credit loss.

BC6.503 Furthermore, the IASB considered the implications of the fact that, upon a credit event, the protection buyer receives the notional principal less the fair value of the reference entity's obligation. Hence, the compensation received for credit risk depends on the fair value of the reference instrument. The IASB noted that, for a fixed-rate loan, the fair value of the reference instrument is also affected by changes in market interest rates. In other words, on settlement of the credit default swap, the entity also settles the fair value changes attributable to interest rate risk—and not solely fair value changes attributable to the credit risk of the reference entity. Hence, the way credit default swaps are settled reflects that credit risk inextricably depends on interest rate risk. This in turn reflects that credit risk is an 'overlay' risk that is affected by all other value changes of the hedged exposure because those value changes determine the value of what is lost in case of a default.

BC6.504 Hence, the IASB considered that credit risk is not a separately identifiable risk component and thus does not qualify for designation as a hedged item on a risk component basis.

Exception to the general risk component criteria

BC6.505 The IASB then considered whether it should provide an exception to the general risk component criteria specifically for credit risk.

BC6.506 Some respondents suggested that, as an exception to the general risk component criteria, the IASB should consider an approach that would provide a reasonable approximation of the credit risk. This approach could be based on the guidance in IFRS 7 and IFRS 9 for the measurement of an entity's own credit risk on financial liabilities designated as at fair value through profit or loss. Those respondents noted that if this method of determining own credit risk for such liabilities is acceptable in IFRS 7 and IFRS 9, the IASB should provide the same 'relief' for measuring the credit risk component for the purposes of hedge accounting.

BC6.507 The IASB noted that, in finalising the requirement for the fair value option for financial liabilities in IFRS 9, it retained the default method in the application guidance in IFRS 7 to determine the effects of changes in the liability's credit risk. The IASB received comments on its 2010 Own Credit Risk Exposure Draft that determining the effects of changes in a liability's credit risk can be complex, and that it was therefore necessary to allow some flexibility in how a liability's credit risk could be measured. Respondents to that Exposure Draft, like the IASB, acknowledged that the default method was imprecise but considered the result a reasonable proxy in many cases. Moreover, the IASB noted that respondents to the 2010 Own Credit Risk Exposure Draft did acknowledge that the 'IFRS 7 method' did not isolate changes in a liability's credit risk from other changes in fair value (for example, general changes in the price of credit or changes in liquidity risk). Those respondents said that it was often very difficult or impossible to separate those items.

BC6.508 The IASB noted that the IFRS 7 method (which was incorporated into IFRS 9) involves the use of an observed market price at the beginning and end of the period to determine the change in the effects of credit. That method requires entities to deduct any changes in market conditions from changes in the fair value of the instrument. Any residual amount is deemed to be attributable to changes in credit. The IASB noted that the loans and loan commitments for which the credit risk is hedged very often have no observable market price and that, in order to achieve a close approximation of the credit risk, complex modelling would be involved to arrive at a 'market price'. Applying the IFRS 7 method would then require the deduction of valuations for parts of the instrument and analysing them for changes in market conditions to arrive at a credit risk component. This would also be complex when trying to achieve a close approximation of the credit risk.

BC6.509 Furthermore, the IASB noted that the loans and loan commitments for which the credit exposure is hedged often have embedded options whose fair value depends on both market and non-market conditions. For example, the exercise of prepayment options could be because of changes in general interest rates (a market condition) while loans are typically refinanced (exercise of the prepayment option) well in advance of the scheduled maturity, irrespective of movements in general interest rates. Hence, in order to achieve a close approximation of the credit risk, isolating the changes for market conditions on those embedded options could involve significant judgement and could become extremely complex.

BC6.510 The IASB also considered that applying the IFRS 7 method in a way that was operational (ie so that the approximation would provide relief) would mean using many of the same simplifications that some had suggested for applying the general risk component criteria to credit risk (for example, using a standardised haircut for prepayment and term-out options, and ignoring immaterial options).

BC6.511 The IASB considered that for exchange-traded bonds for which market prices are readily observable and that do not have embedded options, the IFRS 7 method might result in an approximation or proxy for the credit risk component in some circumstances. However, the IASB was concerned that for loans and loan commitments that are not actively traded, the IFRS 7 method could become a complicated 'circular' pricing exercise and in any case it would very likely result in only a rough approximation or imprecise measurement of the credit risk component.

BC6.512 The IASB further noted that it had acknowledged the shortcomings of the approach used for IFRS 7 and IFRS 9 and that the approach was only a proxy for measuring credit risk. Hence, the IASB had actively sought to limit the application of this approach by retaining the bifurcation requirement for hybrid financial liabilities, even though bifurcation of financial assets was eliminated. Hence, the approach was only applied to financial liabilities designated as at fair value through profit or loss.

BC6.513 The IASB acknowledged that in order to ensure that hedge ineffectiveness is recognised the qualifying criteria for risk components use a higher degree of precision than a mere proxy. Also, for the classification and measurement of financial liabilities the IASB sought to minimise the application of this proxy by retaining the separation of embedded derivatives. Consequently, the IASB decided that also using the guidance in IFRS 7 and IFRS 9 for the measurement of an entity's own credit risk on financial liabilities designated as at fair value through profit or loss for the purpose of measuring credit risk as a hedged item would be inappropriate.

BC6.514 The IASB also considered whether it should permit 'residual risks' as an eligible hedged item. Such an approach would allow an entity to designate as the hedged item those changes in cash flows or fair value of an item that are not attributable to a specific risk or risks that meet the separately identifiable and reliably measurable criteria for risk components. For example, an entity could designate as the hedged item the fair value changes of a loan that are attributable to all risks other than interest rate risk.

BC6.515 The IASB noted that that approach would have the advantage of not requiring an entity to directly measure credit risk. However, the IASB noted that this approach would entail similar complexity as the IFRS 7 method for financial instruments with multiple embedded options. Hence, determining the part of the fair value changes that is attributable to a specific risk (for example, interest rate risk) could be complex.

BC6.516 The IASB also noted that that approach would have other disadvantages:

(a) the problem that credit risk inextricably depends on interest rate risk because of the nature of credit risk as an overlay risk (see paragraphs BC6.503–BC6.504) would remain; and

(b) entities would struggle with the hedge effectiveness assessment of the new hedge accounting model as it would be difficult to establish and demonstrate a direct economic relationship between the 'residual risk' and the hedging instrument (ie the credit default swap), which gives rise to offset—a requirement to qualify for hedge accounting.

BC6.517 Consequently, the IASB decided against permitting 'residual risks' as an eligible hedged item.

Applying financial guarantee contract accounting

BC6.518   The IASB considered whether the accounting for financial guarantee contracts in IFRS 9 could be applied to credit derivatives.

BC6.519   The IASB noted that credit derivatives, such as credit default swaps, do not typically meet the definition of a financial guarantee contract in IFRS 9 because:

   (a)   the credit events that trigger payment on a standardised credit default swap (for example, bankruptcy, repudiation, moratorium or restructuring) might not directly relate to the failure to pay on the particular debt instrument held by an entity; and

   (b)   in order to meet the definition of a financial guarantee contract, it must be a precondition for payment that the holder is exposed to, and has incurred a loss on, the failure of the debtor to make payments on the guaranteed asset when due. However, it is not a precondition for entering into a credit default swap that the holder is exposed to the underlying reference financial instrument (ie an entity can hold a 'naked' position).

BC6.520   The IASB noted that it would have to broaden the definition of 'financial guarantee contract' in order to include such credit derivatives. The IASB also noted that accounting for credit default swaps as financial guarantee contracts would mean that credit default swaps would not be measured at fair value but at 'cost', ie it would result in applying accrual accounting to a derivative financial instrument.

BC6.521   The IASB therefore rejected this alternative.

Applying the accounting for the time value of options

BC6.522   Some respondents to the 2010 Hedge Accounting Exposure Draft suggested that the premium paid on credit default swaps is similar to buying protection under an insurance contract and, accordingly, the premium should be amortised to profit or loss. Those respondents supported applying to credit default swaps the accounting treatment for the time value of options that was proposed in the 2010 Hedge Accounting Exposure Draft. They argued that, from a risk management perspective, changes in the fair value of the derivative during the reporting period were irrelevant, as long as the issuer of the debt was solvent because if there was no credit event the fair value of the credit default swap on maturity would be zero. Hence, those respondents believed that 'interim' fair value changes could be recognised in other comprehensive income similarly to the accounting treatment proposed in the 2010 Hedge Accounting Exposure Draft for the time value of options.

BC6.523   The IASB noted that in contrast to 'normal' options for which the time value paid is known from the beginning (hence the amount to be amortised or deferred is known), for a credit default swap the premium is contingent on the occurrence of a credit event and hence the total premium that is ultimately paid is not known at the outset. This is because the premium for a credit default swap, or at least a large part of the premium, is paid over time—

but only until a credit event occurs. The IASB noted that in order to apply the same accounting as for the time value of options, the contingent nature of the credit default swap premium would have to be ignored so that the amortisation of the premium to profit or loss could be based on the assumption that no credit event occurs — even though that risk is reflected in the fair value of the credit default swap. The IASB also noted that in substance this would be 'as-you-go' accounting for the credit default swap premium (ie recognising it in profit or loss on an accrual basis).

BC6.524   The IASB also noted that applying to credit default swaps the same accounting treatment as for the time value of options would require splitting the fair value of the credit default swap into an intrinsic value and a time value. This raises the question of whether the credit default swap would only have time value (and hence no intrinsic value) until a credit event occurs, ie whether before a credit event occurs the entire fair value of the credit default swap should be deemed to be its time value.

BC6.525   The IASB considered that it would be inappropriate to simply attribute the entire fair value of the credit default swap before a credit event to time value. The IASB noted that hedged items such as bonds or loans have 'intrinsic' value but not an equivalent to time value. In an effective economic hedge, the changes in the intrinsic value in the hedged item would offset the changes in the intrinsic value of the hedging instrument. During times of financial difficulty, but before a credit event (for example, before an actual default), the fair value of the loan would have decreased because of credit deterioration. Also, the fair value of the related credit default swap would increase because of the higher risk of default. Hence, the IASB considered that the increase in fair value of the credit default swap includes some intrinsic value element even though it would be difficult to isolate and separately quantify it.

BC6.526   The IASB also noted that if the entire fair value on a credit default swap was treated as time value before default, there could be an accounting mismatch when an entity recognised an impairment loss on the loan or loan commitment before default. This is because all fair value changes from the credit default swap would still be recognised in other comprehensive income. One solution might be to recycle the amount recognised as an impairment loss on the loan or loan commitment from other comprehensive income to profit or loss and hence to simply deem the amount of the impairment loss to be the intrinsic value of the credit default swap. The IASB considered that this would give rise to the same problems as other approximations it had discussed when it rejected an exception to the general risk component criteria, namely that any mismatch of economic gains or losses from the hedge would not be recognised as hedge ineffectiveness. Instead, under this approach profit or loss recognition for the credit default swap would be the same as accrual accounting while assuming perfect hedge effectiveness.

BC6.527   The IASB therefore rejected this alternative.

Applying an 'insurance approach'

BC6.528 Some respondents to the 2010 Hedge Accounting Exposure Draft supported an 'insurance approach' or accrual accounting for credit derivatives. They argued that such an approach would best address the accounting mismatch between loans or loan commitments and credit derivatives and would reflect the risk management of financial institutions.

BC6.529 The IASB considered that under an insurance approach the following accounting could be applied to a credit default swap that is used to manage credit exposures:

(a) any premium paid at the inception of the credit default swap (or its fair value if an existing contract is used) would be amortised over the life of that contract;

(b) the periodic premium would be expensed as paid each period (including adjustments for premium accruals);

(c) the fair value of the credit default swap would be disclosed in the notes; and

(d) in the assessment of impairment, the cash flow that might result from the credit default swap in case of a credit event is treated in the same way as cash flows that might result from the collateral or guarantee of a collateralised or guaranteed financial asset. In other words, the loan or loan commitment for which credit risk is managed using the credit default swap is treated like a collateralised or guaranteed financial asset with the credit default swap accounted for like collateral or a guarantee.

BC6.530 The IASB noted that the insurance approach is a simple and straightforward solution if a credit default swap is used as credit protection for one particular credit exposure with a matching (remaining) maturity. Also, situations in which the maturity of the credit default swap exceeds that of the credit exposure could be addressed by using an 'aligned' credit default swap (similar to the notion of 'aligned' time value that is used for the new accounting treatment for the time value of options; see paragraphs BC6.386–BC6.409). However, the aligned credit default swap would only address maturity mismatches. It would not capture other differences between the actual credit default swap and the hedged credit exposure (for example, that a loan might be prepayable) because the insurance approach only intends to change the accounting for the credit default swap instead of adjusting the credit exposure for value changes that reflect all of its characteristics.

BC6.531 The IASB considered that the insurance approach would have a simple interaction with an impairment model as a result of treating the credit default swap like collateral or a guarantee, which means it would affect the estimate of the recoverable cash flows. Hence, this interaction would be at the most basic level of the information that any impairment model uses so that the effect would not differ by type of impairment model (assuming only credit derivatives with a remaining life equal to, or longer than, the remaining exposure period would qualify for the insurance approach).

BC6.532   However, the IASB noted that difficulties would arise when the insurance approach was discontinued before the credit exposure matures. In such a situation the consequences of using accrual (or 'as-you-go') accounting for the credit default swap would become obvious, ie it would be necessary to revert from off-balance-sheet accounting to measurement at fair value.

BC6.533   The IASB also noted that under the insurance approach neither the credit derivative nor the loan or loan commitment would be recognised in the statement of financial position at fair value. Hence, any mismatch of economic gains or losses (ie economic hedge ineffectiveness) between loans or loan commitments and the credit derivatives would not be recognised in profit or loss. In addition, it would result in omitting the fair value of the credit default swap from the statement of financial position even though fair value provides important and relevant information about derivative financial instruments.

BC6.534   The IASB therefore rejected this alternative.

Applying a 'deemed credit adjustment approach'

BC6.535   The IASB also considered an approach that would adjust the carrying amount of the hedged credit exposure against profit or loss. The adjustment would be the change in the fair value of a credit default swap that matches the maturity of the hedged credit exposure ('aligned' credit default swap value). The mechanics of this would be similar to how, in a fair value hedge, the gain or loss on the hedged item that is attributable to a risk component adjusts the carrying amount of the hedged item and is recognised in profit or loss. Essentially, the cumulative change in the fair value of the aligned credit default swap would be deemed to be the credit risk component of the exposure in a fair value hedge of credit risk (ie act as a proxy for credit risk— 'deemed credit adjustment'). When the deemed credit adjustment approach is discontinued before the credit exposure matures an accounting treatment that is similar to that used for discontinued fair value hedges could be used.

BC6.536   The IASB noted that the deemed credit adjustment approach would retain the measurement of credit default swaps at fair value through profit or loss. Hence, in contrast to the insurance approach (see paragraphs BC6.528–BC6.534), an advantage of this approach would be that the accounting for the credit default swap would not be affected by any switches between periods for which the credit derivative is used and those for which it is not used to manage a particular credit exposure.

BC6.537   However, the IASB was concerned that the interaction between the deemed credit adjustment approach and impairment accounting would be significantly more complex than under the insurance approach because the deemed credit adjustment and the impairment allowance would be 'competing mechanisms' in the accounting for impairment losses. This would also involve the danger of double counting for credit losses. The interaction would depend on the type of impairment model and would be more difficult in conjunction with an expected loss model.

BC6.538   The IASB therefore rejected this alternative.

Allowing entities to elect fair value accounting for the hedged credit exposure

BC6.539　Because the discussions of those various alternatives did not identify an appropriate solution, the IASB reconsidered the alternatives it had contemplated in its original deliberations leading to the 2010 Hedge Accounting Exposure Draft (see paragraph BC6.474).

BC6.540　The IASB considered that only Alternatives 2 and 3 of allowing an entity to elect fair value through profit or loss accounting for the hedged credit exposure would be viable. Given that Alternative 1 would be limited to an election only on initial recognition of the credit exposure (or when entering into a loan commitment), the IASB was concerned that, in many situations in practice (when an entity obtains credit protection for an exposure after the initial recognition of that exposure or entering into the loan commitment), this alternative would not be aligned with the credit risk management strategy and would therefore fail to resolve the problem (ie that no useful information is provided).

BC6.541　The IASB noted that Alternative 3 would involve amortising the measurement change adjustment (ie the difference between the carrying amount, or nil for an unrecognised loan commitment, and the fair value of the financial instrument when it is elected for measurement at fair value through profit or loss after initial recognition or after entering into a loan commitment) over the life of the financial instrument hedged for credit risk. As a consequence, to ensure that the measurement change adjustment is not inappropriately deferred but recognised immediately in profit or loss when impaired, the measurement change adjustment would require an impairment test. This would result in interaction with the impairment model.

BC6.542　The IASB was concerned that the interaction of Alternative 3 with the impairment model could create a compatibility problem and might be a potential restriction of the impairment phase of its project to replace IAS 39.

BC6.543　Hence, the IASB reconsidered Alternative 2, noting that:

(a)　the status quo under IAS 39, in which credit default swaps are accounted for at fair value through profit or loss while credit exposures are accounted for at amortised cost or are unrecognised (for example, many loan commitments), does not convey the full picture. It results in the recognition of gains on credit default swaps while the impairment is recognised on a different measurement basis and with a time lag because of the impairment models. Hence, in a situation in which the situation of a lender deteriorates but it has protected itself, gains are shown even though the protection keeps the situation neutral at best.

(b)　Alternative 2 would use fair value accounting for both the credit default swap and the credit exposure. This would best capture all economic mismatches but would come at the expense of inevitably including in the remeasurement interest rate risk in addition to credit risk. Alternative 2 would have the clearest objective of all the approaches considered (fair value measurement) and, as a result, it would require the least guidance. The IASB noted that under Alternative 2 there could be concerns about earnings management because on electing fair value accounting the difference to the previous carrying amount of the credit exposure would be immediately recognised in profit or loss. However, the IASB also noted that some would consider that outcome as relevant because it would signal a different approach to managing credit risk and this difference would often be a loss that is a reflection of any lag in the impairment model behind the 'market view'. To be consistent, this should be removed by changing the measurement basis when switching to a fair value-based credit risk management.

(c) the accounting under Alternative 2 is completely de-linked from the impairment model and consequently has the least interaction with impairment of all approaches considered.

(d) Alternative 2 is operationally the least complex of the approaches considered.

BC6.544 The IASB considered that, on balance, the advantages of Alternative 2 outweighed its disadvantages and, overall, that it was superior to all other approaches. Hence, the IASB decided to include Alternative 2 in the final requirements.

BC6.545 In response to feedback received on the 2010 Hedge Accounting Exposure Draft, the IASB also decided to align the accounting for the discontinuation of fair value through profit or loss accounting for loan commitments with that for loans (ie use amortisation unless a higher liability is required by IAS 37, instead of simply reverting to that Standard as contemplated during the IASB's initial deliberations—see paragraphs BC6.479 and BC6.482). The IASB's reasons for also using an amortisation approach for loan commitments were that:

(a) it would prevent an immediate gain from the derecognition of the loan commitment under IAS 37 if the probable threshold is not met when discontinuing fair value through profit or loss accounting. This would reduce concerns about earnings management.

(b) the amortisation of the carrying amount when discontinuing fair value through profit or loss accounting would use the effective interest method. This would require the entity to assume that a loan had been drawn under the loan commitment in order to determine an amortisation profile. The rationale for this alternative is that a credit loss only results from a loan commitment if that loan commitment gets drawn and the resulting loan is not repaid. Hence, an amortisation on an 'as if drawn' basis would be appropriate for the amortisation of the carrying amount.

(c)   this accounting also provides operational relief for loan commitments that allow repayments and redraws (for example, a revolving facility). It would avoid the need to capitalise any remaining carrying amount into individual drawings to ensure its amortisation, which would be operationally complex.

Amendments for Interest Rate Benchmark Reform (September 2019)

BC6.546   Interest rate benchmarks such as interbank offered rates (IBORs) play an important role in global financial markets. These interest rate benchmarks index trillions of dollars and other currencies in a wide variety of financial products, from derivatives to residential mortgages. However, cases of attempted market manipulation of some interest rate benchmarks, together with the post-crisis decline in liquidity in interbank unsecured funding markets, have undermined confidence in the reliability and robustness of some interest rate benchmarks. Against this background, the G20 asked the Financial Stability Board (FSB) to undertake a fundamental review of major interest rate benchmarks. Following the review, the FSB published a report setting out its recommended reforms of some major interest rate benchmarks such as IBORs. Public authorities in many jurisdictions have since taken steps to implement those recommendations. In some jurisdictions, there is already clear progress towards the reform of interest rate benchmarks, or the replacement of interest rate benchmarks with alternative, nearly risk-free interest rates that are based, to a greater extent, on transaction data (alternative benchmark rates). This has in turn led to uncertainty about the long-term viability of some interest rate benchmarks. In these amendments, the term 'interest rate benchmark reform' refers to the market-wide reform of an interest rate benchmark including its replacement with an alternative benchmark rate, such as that resulting from the FSB's recommendations set out in its July 2014 report 'Reforming Major Interest Rate Benchmarks' (the reform).[45]

BC6.547   In 2018 the IASB noted the increasing levels of uncertainty about the long-term viability of some interest rate benchmarks and decided to address as a priority the issues affecting financial reporting in the period before the reform (referred to as pre-replacement issues).

BC6.548   As part of the pre-replacement issues, the IASB considered the implications for specific hedge accounting requirements in IFRS 9 and IAS 39, which require forward-looking analysis. As a result of the reform, contractual cash flows of hedged items and hedging instruments based on an existing interest rate benchmark will likely change when that interest rate benchmark is subject to the reform—in these amendments, contractual cash flows encompass both contractually specified and non-contractually specified cash flows. The same uncertainty arising from the reform regarding the timing and the amount of future cash flows will likely affect the changes in fair value of hedged items and hedging instruments in a fair value hedge of the interest rate benchmark

---

45   The report, 'Reforming Major Interest Rate Benchmarks', is available at http://www.fsb.org/wp-content/uploads/r_140722.pdf.

exposure. Until decisions are made about what the alternative benchmark rate is, and when and how the reform will occur, including specifying its effects on particular contracts, uncertainties will exist regarding the timing and the amount of future cash flows of the hedged item and the hedging instrument.

BC6.549 The IASB noted that the hedge accounting requirements in IFRS 9 and IAS 39 provide a clear basis for accounting for such uncertainties. In applying these requirements, the uncertainties about the timing and the amount of future cash flows could affect an entity's ability to meet those specific forward-looking hedge accounting requirements in the period when uncertainty is created by the reform. In some cases, solely due to such uncertainties, entities could be required to discontinue hedge accounting for hedging relationships that would otherwise qualify for hedge accounting. Also, because of the uncertainties arising from the reform, entities may not be able to designate new hedging relationships that would otherwise qualify for hedge accounting applying IFRS 9 and IAS 39. In some cases, discontinuation of hedge accounting would require an entity to recognise gains or losses in profit or loss.

BC6.550 In the IASB's view, discontinuation of hedge accounting solely due to such uncertainties before the reform's economic effects on hedged items and hedging instruments are known would not provide useful information to users of financial statements. Therefore, the IASB decided to publish in May 2019 the Exposure Draft *Interest Rate Benchmark Reform* (2019 Exposure Draft), which proposed exceptions to IFRS 9 and IAS 39 to provide relief during this period of uncertainty.

BC6.551 The 2019 Exposure Draft proposed exceptions to specific hedge accounting requirements such that entities would apply those requirements assuming the interest rate benchmark on which the hedged risk and/or cash flows of the hedged item or of the hedging instrument are based is not altered as a result of the reform. The proposed exceptions applied only to the hedge accounting requirements specified in that Exposure Draft and were not intended to provide relief from all consequences arising from the reform.

BC6.552 Almost all respondents to the 2019 Exposure Draft agreed with the IASB's decision to address pre-replacement issues. Many highlighted the urgency of these issues, especially in some jurisdictions where there is already clear progress towards the reform or replacement of interest rate benchmarks with alternative benchmark rates.

BC6.553 In September 2019 the IASB amended IFRS 9, IAS 39 and IFRS 7 by issuing *Interest Rate Benchmark Reform*, which confirmed with modifications the proposals in the 2019 Exposure Draft. In the amendments issued in September 2019, the IASB added paragraphs 6.8.1–6.8.12 and 7.1.8 to IFRS 9 and amended paragraph 7.2.26 of IFRS 9.

BC6.554 The IASB decided to propose amendments to IAS 39 as well as IFRS 9 because when entities first apply IFRS 9, they are permitted to choose as an accounting policy to continue to apply the hedge accounting requirements of IAS 39. The IASB understands that a significant number of IFRS preparers — financial institutions in particular — have made such an accounting policy choice.

Scope of the exceptions

BC6.555   In the 2019 Exposure Draft, the IASB noted that the hedge accounting issues being addressed arise in the context of interest rate benchmark reform, and, therefore, the proposed exceptions would apply only to hedging relationships of interest rate risk that are affected by the reform. However, some respondents expressed the view that the scope of the exceptions, as set out in the 2019 Exposure Draft, would not include other types of hedging relationships that may be affected by uncertainties arising from the reform such as hedging relationships in which an entity designates cross-currency interest rate swaps to hedge its exposure to both foreign currency and interest rate risk. These respondents asked the IASB to clarify whether the scope of the exceptions was meant to include such hedging relationships.

BC6.556   In its redeliberations on the 2019 Exposure Draft, the IASB clarified that it did not intend to exclude from the scope of the amendments hedging relationships in which interest rate risk is not the only designated hedged risk. The IASB agreed with respondents that other hedging relationships could be directly affected by the reform when the reform gives rise to uncertainties about the timing or the amount of interest rate benchmark-based cash flows of the hedged item or of the hedging instrument. Therefore, the IASB confirmed that the exceptions would apply to the interest rate benchmark-based cash flows in these situations. The IASB noted that many derivatives, designated in hedging relationships in which there is no uncertainty about the timing or the amount of interest rate benchmark-based cash flows, could be indirectly affected by the reform. For example, this would be the case when the valuation of the derivatives is affected by general uncertainty in the market caused by the reform. The IASB confirmed that the exceptions do not apply to these hedging relationships, despite the indirect effect the uncertainties arising from the reform could have on the valuation of derivatives.

BC6.557   Consequently, the IASB clarified the wording in paragraph 6.8.1 of IFRS 9 to refer to all hedging relationships that are directly affected by interest rate benchmark reform. Paragraph 6.8.1 of IFRS 9 explains that a hedging relationship is directly affected by interest rate benchmark reform only if the reform gives rise to uncertainties about the interest rate benchmark (contractually or non-contractually specified) designated as a hedged risk and/or the timing or the amount of interest rate benchmark-based cash flows of the hedged item or of the hedging instrument. The scope of the exceptions does not exclude hedging relationships in which interest rate risk is not the only hedged risk.

Highly probable requirement

BC6.558   The IASB noted that, if an entity designates a forecast transaction as the hedged item in a cash flow hedge, applying paragraph 6.3.3 of IFRS 9, that transaction must be highly probable (highly probable requirement). This requirement is intended to ensure that changes in the fair value of designated hedging instruments are recognised in the cash flow hedge reserve only for those hedged forecast transactions that are highly probable to occur. This requirement is an important discipline in applying hedge accounting to forecast transactions. The IASB noted that the requirements in IFRS 9 provide a clear basis to account for the effects of the reform—that is, if the effects of the reform are such that the hedged cash flows are no longer highly probable, hedge accounting should be discontinued. As set out in paragraph BC6.550, in the IASB's view, discontinuing all affected hedging relationships solely due to such uncertainty would not provide useful information to users of financial statements.

BC6.559   Therefore, the IASB amended IFRS 9 to provide an exception to the highly probable requirement that would provide targeted relief during this period of uncertainty. More specifically, applying the exception, if the hedged future cash flows are based on an interest rate benchmark that is subject to the reform, an entity assumes that the interest rate benchmark on which the hedged cash flows are based is not altered when assessing whether the future cash flows are highly probable. If the hedged future cash flows are based on a highly probable forecast transaction, by applying the exception in paragraph 6.8.4 of IFRS 9 when performing the assessment of the highly probable requirement for that forecast transaction, the entity would assume that the interest rate benchmark on which the hedged cash flows are based will not be altered in the future contract as a result of the reform. For example, for a future issuance of a London Interbank Offered Rate (LIBOR)-referenced debt instrument, the entity would assume that the LIBOR benchmark rate on which the hedged cash flows are based will not be altered as a result of the reform.

BC6.560   The IASB noted that this exception does not necessarily result in an entity determining that the hedged cash flows are highly probable. In the example described in paragraph BC6.559, the entity assumed that the interest rate benchmark in the future contract would not be altered as a result of the reform when determining whether that forecast transaction is highly probable. However, if the entity decides not to issue the debt instrument because of uncertainty arising from the reform or for any other reason, the hedged future cash flows are no longer highly probable (and are no longer expected to occur). The exception would not permit or require the entity to assume otherwise. In this case, the entity would conclude that the LIBOR-based cash flows are no longer highly probable (and are no longer expected to occur).

BC6.561   The IASB also included an exception for discontinued hedging relationships. Applying this exception, any amount remaining in the cash flow hedge reserve when a hedging relationship is discontinued would be reclassified to profit or loss in the same period(s) during which the hedged cash flows affect profit or loss, based on the assumption that the interest rate benchmark on which the hedged cash flows are based is not altered as a result of the reform. If, however, the hedged future cash flows are no longer expected to occur for other reasons, the entity is required to immediately reclassify to profit or loss any amount remaining in the cash flow hedge reserve. In addition, the exception would not exempt entities from reclassifying the amount that is not expected to be recovered into profit or loss as required by paragraph 6.5.11(d)(iii) of IFRS 9.

Assessment of the economic relationship between the hedged item and the hedging instrument

BC6.562   Applying IFRS 9, a hedging relationship qualifies for hedge accounting only if there is an economic relationship between the hedged item and the hedging instrument.

BC6.563   Demonstrating the existence of an economic relationship requires the estimation of future cash flows because the assessment is prospective in nature. Interest rate benchmark reform could affect this assessment for hedging relationships that may extend beyond the timing of the reform. That is because entities would have to consider possible changes to the fair value or future cash flows of hedged items and hedging instruments to assess whether an economic relationship continues to exist between the hedged item and hedging instrument. Consequently, at some point in time, it is possible that entities would not be able to demonstrate the existence of an economic relationship solely because of uncertainties arising from the reform.

BC6.564   The IASB considered the usefulness of the information that would result from the potential discontinuation of hedge accounting for affected hedging relationships and decided to amend the requirements in IFRS 9 to provide an exception for assessing the economic relationship between the hedged item and the hedging instrument for the same reasons discussed in paragraph BC6.550.

BC6.565   Applying this exception, an entity shall assess whether the economic relationship as required by paragraph 6.4.1(c)(i) of IFRS 9 exists based on the assumption that the hedged risk or the interest rate benchmark on which the hedged item or the hedging instrument is based is not altered as a result of the reform. Similarly, if an entity designates a highly probable forecast transaction as the hedged item, the entity shall perform the assessment based on the assumption that the interest rate benchmark on which the hedged cash flows are based will not change as a result of the reform.

BC6.566   The IASB noted that an offset between the hedged item and the hedging instrument is a fundamental principle of the hedge accounting model in IFRS 9 and, therefore, the IASB considered it critical to maintain this principle. The exception addresses only the uncertainties arising from the reform. Therefore, if an entity is unable to demonstrate the existence of an economic relationship between the hedged item and the hedging instrument for other reasons, the entity shall discontinue hedge accounting as required by IFRS 9.

Measurement of ineffectiveness

BC6.567   The IASB noted that the exceptions were not intended to change the requirement that entities measure and recognise hedge ineffectiveness. The IASB considered that the actual results of the hedging relationships would provide useful information to users of financial statements during the period of uncertainty arising from the reform. Therefore, the IASB decided that entities should continue to measure and recognise hedge ineffectiveness as required by IFRS Standards.

BC6.568　The IASB also considered whether any exceptions should be made to the measurement of hedged items or hedging instruments because of the uncertainty arising from the reform. However, the IASB noted that such an exception would be inconsistent with the decision not to change the requirements to measure and recognise hedge ineffectiveness in the financial statements. Therefore, the IASB decided not to provide an exception from the measurement of hedging instruments and hedged items. This means that the fair value of a derivative designated as the hedging instrument should continue to be measured using the assumptions that market participants would use when pricing that derivative as required by IFRS 13 *Fair Value Measurement*.

BC6.569　For a hedged item designated in a fair value hedge, IFRS 9 requires an entity to remeasure the hedged item for changes in fair value attributable to the hedged risk and recognise the gain or loss related to that fair value hedge adjustment in profit or loss. In doing so, the entity uses the assumptions that market participants would use when pricing the hedged item for changes in fair value attributable to the hedged risk. This would include a risk premium for uncertainty inherent in the hedged risk that market participants would consider. For example, to measure changes in fair value attributable to the hedged risk such as the IBOR component of a fixed-rate loan, an entity needs to reflect the uncertainty caused by the reform. When applying a present value technique to calculate the changes in fair value attributable to the designated risk component, such measurement should reflect market participants' assumptions about the uncertainty arising from the reform.

BC6.570　When an entity designates interest rate benchmark-based cash flows as the hedged item in a cash flow hedge, to calculate the change in the value of the hedged item for the purpose of measuring hedge ineffectiveness, the entity may use a derivative that would have terms that match the critical terms of the designated cash flows and the hedged risk (this is commonly referred to as a 'hypothetical derivative'). As the IASB decided that entities should continue to measure and recognise hedge ineffectiveness as required by IFRS Standards, entities should continue to apply assumptions that are consistent with those applied to the hedged risk of the hedged item. For example, if an entity designated interest rate benchmark-based cash flows as the hedged item in a cash flow hedge, the entity would not assume for the purpose of measuring hedge ineffectiveness that the expected replacement of the interest rate benchmark with an alternative benchmark rate will result in zero cash flows after the replacement. The hedging gain or loss on the hedged item should be measured using the interest rate benchmark-based cash flows (that is, the cash flows on which the hypothetical derivative is based) when applying a present value technique, discounted at a market-based discount rate that reflects market participants' assumptions about the uncertainty arising from the reform. The IASB concluded that reflecting market participants' assumptions when measuring hedge ineffectiveness provides useful information to users of financial statements about the effects of the uncertainty arising from the reform on an entity's hedging relationships. Therefore, the IASB decided that no exceptions are needed for the measurement of actual ineffectiveness.

Hedges of risk components

BC6.571 The IASB noted that in accordance with IFRS 9 an entity may designate an item in its entirety or a component of an item as the hedged item in a hedging relationship. For example, an entity that issues a 5-year floating-rate debt instrument that bears interest at 3-month LIBOR + 1%, could designate as the hedged item either the entire debt instrument (that is, all of the cash flows) or only the 3-month LIBOR risk component of the floating-rate debt instrument. Specifically, paragraph 6.3.7(a) of IFRS 9 allows entities to designate only changes in the cash flows or fair value of an item attributable to a specific risk or risks (risk component) provided that the risk component is separately identifiable and reliably measurable.

BC6.572 The IASB observed that an entity's ability to conclude that an interest rate benchmark is a separately identifiable component in accordance with paragraph 6.3.7(a) of IFRS 9 requires a continuous assessment over the duration of the hedging relationship and could be affected by the reform. For example, if the outcome of the reform affects the market structure of an interest rate benchmark, it could affect an entity's assessment of whether a non-contractually specified LIBOR component is separately identifiable and, therefore, an eligible hedged item in a hedging relationship. The IASB considered only risk components that are implicit in the fair value or the cash flows of an item of which they are a part (referred to as non-contractually specified) because the same issue does not arise for risk components that are explicitly specified in the contract.

BC6.573 For the reasons outlined in paragraph BC6.550, the IASB noted that discontinuing hedging relationships due to uncertainty arising from the reform would not provide useful information. Consequently, the IASB decided to propose amending IFRS 9 so that entities would not discontinue hedge accounting solely because the risk component is no longer separately identifiable as a result of the reform. In the 2019 Exposure Draft, the IASB proposed that the separately identifiable requirement for hedges of the benchmark component of interest rate risk be applied only at the inception of those hedging relationships affected by the reform.

BC6.574 The IASB proposed not to extend the relief to allow entities to designate the benchmark component of interest rate risk as the hedged item in a new hedging relationship if the risk component is not separately identifiable at the inception of the hedging relationship. In the IASB's view, allowing hedge accounting for risk components that are not separately identifiable at the inception would be inconsistent with the objective of the exception. The IASB noted that such circumstances are different from allowing continued designation as the hedged item for risk components that had met the requirement at the inception of the hedging relationship.

BC6.575   Furthermore, the IASB did not propose any exception from the requirement that changes in the fair value or cash flows of the risk component must be reliably measurable. As noted in paragraph BC6.566, in the IASB's view, an offset between the hedged item and the hedging instrument is a fundamental principle of the hedge accounting model in IFRS 9 and, therefore, the IASB considered reliable measurement of the hedged item and the hedging instrument to be critical to maintain this principle.

BC6.576   Almost all respondents agreed with the exception proposed in the 2019 Exposure Draft to apply the separately identifiable requirement only at the inception of a hedging relationship. However, some respondents noted that the proposed exception did not provide equivalent relief to hedging relationships that frequently reset (ie discontinue and restart). In those hedging relationships both the hedging instrument and the hedged item frequently change (ie the entity uses a dynamic process in which both the hedged items and the hedging instruments used to manage that exposure do not remain the same for long). As hedging instruments and hedged items are being added or removed from a portfolio, entities are de-designating and redesignating hedging relationships regularly to adjust the exposure. If each redesignation of the hedging relationship is considered to be the inception of a new hedging relationship (even though it is still the same hedging strategy), then the separately identifiable requirement would need to be assessed for all hedged items at each redesignation even if they have been assessed previously. For the same reasons as those noted in paragraph BC6.572, this could affect an entity's ability to conclude that a non-contractually specified risk component remains separately identifiable and, therefore, an eligible hedged item for hedge accounting purposes.

BC6.577   The IASB noted that the exception proposed in the 2019 Exposure Draft has the effect that if a non-contractually specified risk component meets the separately identifiable requirement at the inception of a hedging relationship, then that requirement would not be reassessed subsequently. Hence, providing a similar exception for hedging relationships that frequently reset (ie discontinue and restart) would be consistent with the objective of the exception originally provided in the 2019 Exposure Draft.

BC6.578   Thus, the IASB confirmed the proposal that a risk component is only required to be separately identifiable at the inception of the hedging relationship. In addition, to respond to the feedback described in paragraph BC6.576, the IASB added the exception in paragraph 6.8.8 of IFRS 9 for hedging relationships that, consistent with an entity's hedge documentation, frequently reset (ie discontinue and restart) because both the hedging instrument and the hedged item frequently change. Applying that paragraph, an entity shall determine whether the risk component is separately identifiable only when it initially designates an item as a hedged item in the hedging relationship. The hedged item is not reassessed at any subsequent redesignation in the same hedging relationship.

BC6.579　In reaching its decision for the exception in paragraph 6.8.8 of IFRS 9 the IASB considered an example where an entity uses a dynamic process to manage interest rate risk as discussed in paragraph B6.5.24(b) of IFRS 9 and designates the LIBOR risk component of floating-rate loans as the hedged risk. At the inception of the relationship, the entity assesses whether LIBOR is a separately identifiable risk component for all loans designated within the hedging relationship. As the entity updates the risk position with the origination of new loans and the maturity or repayment of existing loans, the hedging relationship is adjusted by de-designating the 'old' hedging relationship and redesignating a 'new' hedging relationship for the updated amount of the hedged items. Applying the exception in paragraph 6.8.8 of IFRS 9 requires the entity to assess whether LIBOR is a separately identifiable risk component only for the new loans added to the hedging relationship. The entity would not reassess the separately identifiable requirement for the loans that have been redesignated.

Mandatory application

BC6.580　The IASB decided to require entities to apply the exceptions in Section 6.8 of IFRS 9 to all hedging relationships to which the exceptions are applicable. In other words, the IASB decided that an entity is required to apply the exceptions to all hedging relationships that are directly affected by the uncertainties arising from the reform and continue to apply the exceptions until required to cease their application as specified in paragraphs 6.8.9–6.8.12 of IFRS 9.

BC6.581　The IASB considered but rejected alternatives that would have allowed entities to apply the exceptions voluntarily. In the IASB's view, voluntary application of these exceptions could give rise to selective discontinuation of hedge accounting and selective reclassification of the amounts recorded in other comprehensive income related to previously discontinued hedging relationships. The IASB does not expect that requiring entities to apply the exceptions would entail significant cost for preparers and other affected parties because the exceptions require entities to assume that the interest rate benchmark, on which the hedged risk and the hedged cash flows, and cash flows of the hedging instrument are based, is not altered as a result of the reform.

BC6.582　In addition, the IASB observed that in some circumstances, the exceptions in Section 6.8 of IFRS 9 may not be applicable. For example, for a particular interest rate benchmark not subject to the reform or replacement with an alternative benchmark rate, there is no uncertainty affecting the timing or the amount of the interest rate benchmark-based cash flows arising from a hedged item or a hedging instrument. The exceptions set out in Section 6.8 of IFRS 9 would not be applicable to such a hedging relationship.

BC6.583　Furthermore, for a particular hedging relationship the exceptions may be applicable to some but not all aspects of the hedging relationship. For example, if an entity designates a hedged item that is based on LIBOR against a hedging instrument that is already referenced to an alternative benchmark rate (assuming the entity can demonstrate that hedging relationship meets the qualifying criteria for hedge accounting in IFRS 9), the exceptions in paragraphs 6.8.4 and 6.8.6 of IFRS 9 would apply for the hedged item because there is uncertainty related to its future cash flows. However, there is no uncertainty regarding how the reform would impact the cash flows of the hedging instrument and, therefore, the exception in paragraph 6.8.6 of IFRS 9 is not applicable for the hedging instrument. Similarly, the exception applicable to non-contractually specified components would not be relevant for hedging relationships that do not involve the designation of non-contractually specified risk components.

End of application

BC6.584   As described in paragraph BC6.550, the IASB decided to amend IFRS 9 to address specific aspects of hedge accounting affected by uncertainties in relation to the hedged items and hedging instruments about when the interest rate benchmarks will change to alternative benchmark rates, when any spread adjustment between the interest rate benchmark and the alternative benchmark rate will be determined (collectively, timing) and what the cash flows based on the alternative benchmark rate will be, including their frequency of reset, and any spread adjustment between the interest rate benchmark and the alternative benchmark rate (collectively, amount). Therefore, the IASB intended the exceptions set out in Section 6.8 of IFRS 9 to be available only while these uncertainties are present.

BC6.585   The IASB considered whether to provide an explicit end date for the exceptions but decided not to do so. The reform is following different timelines in different markets and jurisdictions and contracts are being modified at different times and, therefore, at this stage, it is not possible to define a period of applicability for the exceptions.

BC6.586   The IASB decided that an entity ceases applying the exceptions at the earlier of (a) when the uncertainty regarding the timing and the amount of interest rate benchmark-based cash flows is no longer present as it relates to a hedged item and/or hedging instrument (depending on the particular exception) and (b) the discontinuation of the hedging relationship.[46] The exceptions require entities to apply specific hedge accounting requirements assuming the interest rate benchmark on which the hedged risk, hedged cash flows or the cash flows of the hedging instrument are based is not altered as a result of the reform. The end of applicability of the exceptions means that entities would from that date apply all hedge accounting requirements in IFRS 9 without applying these exceptions.

BC6.587   In the IASB's view, for uncertainty regarding the timing and the amount of cash flows arising from a change in an interest rate benchmark to be eliminated, the underlying contracts are generally required to be amended to specify the timing and the amount of cash flows based on the alternative

---

46   For the purpose of applying the exception in paragraph 6.8.5 of IFRS 9 to a discontinued hedging relationship, the amendments require an entity to cease applying the exception at the earlier of (a) as described above and (b) when the entire amount accumulated in the cash flow hedge reserve with respect to the hedging relationship has been reclassified to profit or loss. See paragraph 6.8.10 of IFRS 9.

benchmark rate (and any spread adjustment between the interest rate benchmark and the alternative benchmark rate). The IASB noted that, in some cases, a contract may be amended to include reference to the alternative benchmark rate without actually altering the interest rate benchmark-based cash flows in the contract. Such an amendment may not eliminate the uncertainty regarding the timing and the amount of interest rate benchmark-based cash flows in the contract. The IASB considered the following scenarios to assess the robustness of the end of application requirements. However, these scenarios are not exhaustive and other scenarios may exist in which the uncertainties arising from the reform regarding the timing and the amount of cash flows would no longer be present.

BC6.588   Scenario A—a contract is amended to include a clause that specifies (a) the date the interest rate benchmark will be replaced by an alternative benchmark rate and (b) the alternative benchmark rate on which the cash flows will be based and the relevant spread adjustment between the interest rate benchmark and the alternative benchmark rate. In this case, the uncertainty regarding the timing and the amount of cash flows for this contract is eliminated when the contract is amended to include this clause.

BC6.589   Scenario B—a contract is amended to include a clause that states modifications of contractual cash flows will occur due to the reform but that specifies neither the date that the interest rate benchmark will be replaced nor the alternative benchmark rate on which the amended cash flows will be based. In this case, the uncertainty regarding the timing and the amount of cash flows for this contract has not been eliminated by amending the contract to include this clause.

BC6.590   Scenario C—a contract is amended to include a clause which states that conditions specifying the amount and timing of interest rate benchmark-based cash flows will be determined by a central authority at some point in the future. But the clause does not specify those conditions. In this case, the uncertainty regarding the timing and the amount of the interest rate benchmark-based cash flows for this contract has not been eliminated by including this clause in the contract. Uncertainty regarding both the timing and the amount of cash flows for this contract will be present until the central authority specifies when the replacement of the benchmark will become effective, and what the alternative benchmark rate and any related spread adjustment will be.

BC6.591   Scenario D—a contract is amended to include a clause in anticipation of the reform that specifies the date the interest rate benchmark will be replaced and any spread adjustment between the interest rate benchmark and the alternative benchmark rate will be determined. However, the amendment does not specify the alternative benchmark rate, or the spread adjustment between the interest rate benchmark and the alternative benchmark rate, on which the cash flows will be based. In this scenario, by amending the contract to include this clause, uncertainty regarding the timing has been eliminated but uncertainty about the amount remains.

BC6.592 Scenario E—a contract is amended to include a clause in anticipation of the reform that specifies the alternative benchmark rate on which the cash flows will be based and the spread adjustment between the interest rate benchmark and the alternative benchmark rate, but does not specify the date from which the amendment to the contract will become effective. In this scenario, by amending the contract to include this clause, uncertainty about the amount has been eliminated but uncertainty with respect to timing remains.

BC6.593 Scenario F—in preparation for the reform, a central authority in its capacity as the administrator of an interest rate benchmark undertakes a multi-step process to replace an interest rate benchmark with an alternative benchmark rate. The objective of the reform is to cease the publication of the current interest rate benchmark and replace it with an alternative benchmark rate. As part of the reform, the administrator introduces an interim benchmark rate and determines a fixed spread adjustment based on the difference between the interim benchmark rate and the current interest rate benchmark. Uncertainty about the timing or the amount of the alternative benchmark rate-based cash flows will not be eliminated during the interim period because the interim benchmark rate (including the fixed spread adjustment determined by the administrator) represent an interim measure in progressing towards the reform but it does not represent the alternative benchmark rate (or any related spread adjustment agreed between parties to the contract).

BC6.594 For reasons similar to those described in paragraph BC6.583, the IASB noted that there could be situations in which the uncertainty for particular elements of a single hedging relationship could end at different times. For example, assume an entity is required to apply the relevant exceptions to both the hedged item and the hedging instrument. If the hedging instrument in that hedging relationship is subsequently amended through market protocols covering all derivatives in that market, and will be based on an alternative benchmark rate such that the uncertainty about the timing and the amount of interest rate benchmark-based cash flows of the hedging instrument is eliminated, the relevant exceptions would continue to apply to the hedged item but would no longer apply to the hedging instrument.[47]

BC6.595 The IASB observed that continuing to apply the exception after the uncertainty was resolved would not faithfully represent the actual characteristics of the elements of the hedging relationship in which the uncertainty arising from the reform is eliminated. The IASB considered whether it should extend the relief provided such that the exceptions would apply at the hedging relationship level for as long as any element of that hedging relationship was affected by the uncertainties arising from the reform. The IASB agreed that doing so would be beyond the objective of addressing only those issues directly affected by the uncertainty arising from the reform. This is also because the exceptions in paragraphs 6.8.4–6.8.12 of IFRS 9 and the respective requirements in IFRS 9 apply to the same

---

47 In this scenario, the entity would first consider the accounting consequences of amending the contractual terms of the hedging instrument. The IASB will consider the accounting consequences of the actual amendment of financial instruments as a result of interest rate benchmark reform in the next phase of this project (ie the replacement phase).

elements of the hedging relationship. Therefore, applying each exception at the hedging relationship level would be inconsistent with how the underlying requirements are applied.

BC6.596 The IASB decided that the end of application requirement would also apply to hedges of a forecast transaction. The IASB noted that IFRS 9 requires an entity to identify and document a forecast transaction with sufficient specificity so that, when the transaction occurs, the entity is able to determine whether the transaction is the hedged transaction. For example, if an entity designates a future issuance of a LIBOR-based debt instrument as the hedged item, although there may be no contract at the time of designation, the hedge documentation would refer specifically to LIBOR. Consequently, the IASB concluded that entities should be able to identify when the uncertainty regarding the timing and the amount of the resulting cash flows of a forecast transaction is no longer present.

BC6.597 In addition, the IASB decided not to require end of application with respect to the exception for the separately identifiable requirements set out in paragraphs 6.8.7 and 6.8.8 of IFRS 9. Applying these exceptions, entities would continue applying hedge accounting when an interest rate benchmark meets the separately identifiable requirement at the inception of the hedging relationship (assuming all other hedge accounting requirements continue to be met). If the IASB included an end date for these exceptions, an entity may be required to immediately discontinue hedge accounting because, at some point, as the reform progresses, the component based on the interest rate benchmark may no longer be separately identifiable (for example, as the market for the alternative benchmark rate is established). Such immediate discontinuation of hedge accounting would be inconsistent with the objective of the exception. The IASB noted that linking the end of application for these exceptions to contract amendments would not achieve the IASB's intention either because, by definition, non-contractually specified risk components are not explicitly stated in a contract and, therefore, these contracts may not be amended for the reform. This is particularly relevant for fair value hedges of a fixed-rate debt instrument. Therefore, the IASB decided that an entity should cease applying the exceptions to a hedging relationship only when the hedging relationship is discontinued applying IFRS 9.

BC6.598 Some respondents to the 2019 Exposure Draft noted that the IASB had not addressed when an entity ceases applying the proposed exceptions to a group of items designated as the hedged item or a combination of financial instruments designated as the hedging instrument. Specifically, when assessing whether the uncertainty arising from the reform is no longer present, these respondents asked whether that assessment should be performed on an individual basis (that is, for each individual item within the group or financial instrument within the combination) or on a group basis (that is, for all items in the group or all financial instruments in the combination until there is no uncertainty surrounding any of the items or financial instruments).

BC6.599　Consequently, the IASB decided to add paragraph 6.8.12 of IFRS 9 to clarify that, when designating a group of items as the hedged item or a combination of financial instruments as the hedging instrument, entities assess when the uncertainty arising from the reform with respect to the hedged risk and/or the timing and amount of the interest rate benchmark-based cash flows of that item or financial instrument is no longer present on an individual basis — that is, for each individual item in the group or financial instrument in the combination.

Effective date and transition

BC6.600　The IASB decided that entities shall apply the amendments for annual periods beginning on or after 1 January 2020, with earlier application permitted.

BC6.601　The IASB decided that the amendments apply retrospectively. The IASB highlighted that retrospective application of the amendments would not allow reinstating hedge accounting that has already been discontinued. Nor would it allow designation in hindsight. If an entity had not designated a hedging relationship, the exceptions, even though applied retrospectively, would not allow the entity to apply hedge accounting in prior periods to items that were not designated for hedge accounting. Doing so would be inconsistent with the requirement that hedge accounting applies prospectively. Retrospective application of the exceptions would enable entities to continue hedge accounting for a hedging relationship that the entity had previously designated and that qualifies for hedge accounting applying IFRS 9.

BC6.602　Many respondents to the 2019 Exposure Draft commented on the clarity of the proposed retrospective application and suggested that further explanation be provided in the Standard. Consequently, the IASB amended the transition paragraph to specify that retrospective application applies only to those hedging relationships that existed at the beginning of the reporting period in which an entity first applies those requirements or were designated thereafter, and to the amount accumulated in the cash flow hedge reserve that existed at the beginning of the reporting period in which an entity first applies those requirements. The IASB used this wording to permit an entity to apply the amendments from the beginning of the reporting period in which an entity first applies these amendments even if the reporting period is not an annual period.

BC6.603　The IASB noted that these amendments would also apply to entities adopting IFRS Standards for the first time as required by IFRS 1 *First-time Adoption of International Financial Reporting Standards*. Accordingly, the IASB did not provide specific transition provisions for those entities.

Amendments for *Interest Rate Benchmark Reform—Phase 2* (August 2020)

Amendments to hedging relationships

BC6.604 The Phase 2 amendments relating to the hedge accounting requirements in IFRS 9 apply to hedging relationships directly affected by the reform as and when the requirements in paragraphs 6.8.4–6.8.8 of IFRS 9 cease to apply to a hedging relationship (see paragraphs 6.8.9–6.8.13 of IFRS 9). Therefore, an entity is required to amend the hedging relationship to reflect the changes required by the reform as and when the uncertainty arising from the reform is no longer present with respect to the hedged risk or the timing and the amount of interest rate benchmark-based cash flows of the hedged item or of the hedging instrument. The scope of the hedging relationships to which the Phase 2 amendments apply is therefore the same as the scope to which the Phase 1 amendments apply, except for the amendment to the separately identifiable requirement, which also applies to the designation of new hedging relationships (see paragraph 6.9.13 of IFRS 9).

BC6.605 As part of the Phase 1 amendments, the IASB acknowledged that, in most cases, for uncertainty regarding the timing and the amount of interest rate benchmark-based cash flows arising from the reform to be resolved, the underlying financial instruments designated in the hedging relationship would have to be changed to specify the timing and the amount of alternative benchmark rate-based cash flows.

BC6.606 The IASB noted that, applying the hedge accounting requirements in IFRS 9, changes to the basis for determining the contractual cash flows of a financial asset or a financial liability (see paragraphs 5.4.6–5.4.9 of IFRS 9) that are designated in a hedging relationship would affect the designation of such a hedging relationship in which an interest rate benchmark was designated as a hedged risk.

BC6.607 The IASB observed that amending the formal designation of a hedging relationship to reflect the changes required by the reform would result in the discontinuation of the hedging relationship. This is because, as part of the qualifying criteria for hedge accounting to be applied, IFRS 9 requires the formal designation of a hedging relationship to be documented at inception. The hedge documentation includes identification of the hedging instrument, the hedged item, the nature of the risk being hedged and how the entity will assess hedge effectiveness. IFRS 9 permits the hedge designation and documentation to be amended without causing the discontinuation of hedge accounting only in limited circumstances. In all other circumstances, amendments to the hedge designation as documented at inception of the hedging relationship, result in the discontinuation of hedge accounting.

BC6.608 The IASB therefore concluded that, in general, the hedge accounting requirements in IFRS 9 are sufficiently clear about how to account for hedging relationships directly affected by the reform after the Phase 1 exceptions set out in paragraphs 6.8.4–6.8.8 of IFRS 9 cease to apply. However, consistent with the IASB's objective for Phase 2 (see paragraph BC5.290) and its objective for Phase 1 (see paragraph BC6.550), the IASB considered that discontinuing hedge accounting solely due to the effects of the reform would not always reflect the economic effects of the changes required by the reform on a hedging relationship and therefore would not always provide useful information to users of financial statements.

BC6.609 Accordingly, the IASB decided that if the reform requires a change to a financial asset or a financial liability designated in a hedging relationship (see paragraphs 5.4.6–5.4.8 of IFRS 9), it would be consistent with the IASB's objective for Phase 2 to require the hedging relationship to be amended to reflect such a change without requiring discontinuation of that hedging relationship. For these reasons, in the 2020 Exposure Draft, the IASB proposed that an entity would be required to amend the formal designation of the hedging relationship as previously documented to make one or more of these changes:

(a) designating the alternative benchmark rate (contractually or non-contractually specified) as a hedged risk;

(b) amending the description of the hedged item so it refers to the alternative benchmark rate; or

(c) amending the description of the hedging instrument so it refers to the alternative benchmark rate.

BC6.610 Respondents to the 2020 Exposure Draft agreed with the proposed amendments because those proposals would generally result in an entity continuing to apply hedge accounting to hedging relationships directly affected by the reform. Respondents also said that changes to the hedge designation necessary to reflect changes required by the reform are not expected to represent a change in an entity's risk management strategy or risk management objective for hedging their exposure to interest rate risk. Therefore, the IASB concluded that continuing to apply hedge accounting to the affected hedging relationships when making changes required by the reform would correspond with the IASB's objective for issuing the Phase 1 amendments in September 2019.

BC6.611 However, notwithstanding their general agreement with the proposed amendments, some respondents asked the IASB to clarify the scope and timing of the required changes to the affected hedging relationships.

BC6.612 Regarding the scope of the required changes to the affected hedging relationships, the IASB acknowledged it may be necessary to amend the designated hedged portion of the cash flows or fair value being hedged when the hedging relationship is amended to reflect the changes required by the reform. The IASB also noted that the changes required by the reform described in paragraphs 5.4.6–5.4.8 of IFRS 9 were implicit in the required amendments to the hedging relationships as proposed in the 2020 Exposure Draft. In considering the timing of when entities are required to amend an affected hedging relationship, the IASB sought to balance the operational effort needed to amend the hedging relationships with maintaining the required discipline in the amendments to hedging relationships. Specifically, it sought to address the challenges associated with specifying the timing of when entities have to amend hedging relationships as required in paragraph 6.9.1 of IFRS 9 – particularly in the context of the large volume of changes that entities may need to make in a relatively short time – while also ensuring that the amendments to hedging relationships are accounted for in the applicable reporting period.

BC6.613　In response to respondents' requests, the IASB revised the proposed wording in paragraph 6.9.1 of IFRS 9 so that:

(a)　amending the description of the hedged item includes amending the description of the designated portion of the cash flows or fair value being hedged;

(b)　the changes required by the reform described in paragraphs 5.4.6–5.4.8 of IFRS 9 are relevant when amending the formal designation of a hedging relationship; and

(c)　amendments to hedging relationships are required to be made by the end of the reporting period during which the respective changes to the hedged item, hedged risk or hedging instrument are made.

BC6.614　The IASB noted that the Phase 1 amendments may cease to apply at different times to directly affected hedging relationships and to the different elements within a hedging relationship. Therefore, an entity may be required to apply the applicable Phase 2 exceptions in paragraphs 6.9.1–6.9.12 of IFRS 9 at different times, which may result in the designation of a particular hedging relationship being amended more than once. The Phase 2 amendments to the hedge accounting requirements in IFRS 9 apply only to the requirements specified in these paragraphs. All other hedge accounting requirements in IFRS 9, including the qualifying criteria in paragraph 6.4.1 of IFRS 9, apply to hedging relationships directly affected by the reform. In addition, consistent with the IASB's decision for the Phase 1 amendments (see paragraph BC6.568), the Phase 2 amendments also do not provide an exception from the measurement requirements for a hedging relationship. Therefore, entities apply the requirements in paragraphs 6.5.8 or 6.5.11 of IFRS 9 to account for any changes in the fair value of the hedged items or hedging instruments (also see paragraphs BC6.623–BC6.627).

BC6.615　As set out in paragraph BC5.318, the IASB considered that changes might be made to a financial asset or a financial liability, or to the formal designation of a hedging relationship, in addition to those changes required by the reform. The effect of such additional changes to the formal hedge designation on the application of the hedge accounting requirements would depend on whether those changes result in the derecognition of the underlying financial instrument (see paragraph 5.4.9 of IFRS 9).

BC6.616　The IASB therefore required an entity first to apply the applicable requirements in IFRS 9 to determine if those additional changes result in discontinuation of hedge accounting, for example, if the financial asset or financial liability designated as a hedged item no longer meets the qualifying criteria to be an eligible hedged item as a result of changes in addition to those required by the reform. Similarly, if an entity amends the hedge designation to make a change other than the changes described in paragraph 6.9.1 of IFRS 9 (for example, if it extends the term of the hedging relationship), the entity would first determine if those additional changes to the hedge designation result in the discontinuation of hedge accounting. If the additional changes do not result in the discontinuation of hedge accounting, the designation of the hedging relationship would be amended as required by paragraph 6.9.1 of IFRS 9.

BC6.617 Some respondents to the 2020 Exposure Draft said that entities may change a hedging relationship as a result of the reform, but such a change is not necessary as a direct consequence of the reform. This could include, for example, designating a basis swap as a new hedging instrument to mitigate ineffectiveness arising from the difference between the compounding of the alternative benchmark rates used for cash products and derivatives. These respondents asked the IASB to permit such changes to be in the scope of the required changes to the hedging relationship set out in paragraph 6.9.1 of IFRS 9. The IASB however decided not to extend the scope of paragraph 6.9.1 of IFRS 9 to other changes an entity makes as a result of the reform. The IASB considered that its objective for the Phase 2 amendments is not only to support entities in applying the IFRS requirements during the transition to alternative benchmark rates, but also to provide users of financial statements with useful information about the effect of the reform on an entity's financial statements. To balance achieving this objective with maintaining the discipline that exists in the hedge accounting requirements in IFRS 9, the IASB limited the scope of the changes required to the designation of hedging relationships to only those changes that are necessary to reflect the changes required by the reform (as described in paragraphs 5.4.6–5.4.8 of IFRS 9).

Replacement of hedging instruments in hedging relationships

BC6.618 Respondents to the 2020 Exposure Draft said that, instead of changing the contractual terms of a derivative designated as a hedging instrument, counterparties may facilitate the transition to alternative benchmark rates using approaches that result in outcomes equivalent to changing the contractual terms of the derivative. These respondents asked whether using such an approach would be within the scope of the Phase 2 amendments—ie whether paragraph 6.9.1(c) of IFRS 9 would apply—if the approach results in an economic outcome that is similar to changing the basis for determining the contractual cash flows of the derivative.

BC6.619 The IASB confirmed that, consistent with the rationale in paragraph BC5.298, it is the substance of an arrangement, rather than its form, that determines the appropriate accounting treatment. The IASB considered that the conditions in paragraph 5.4.7 of IFRS 9—ie the change is necessary as a direct consequence of the reform and is done on economically equivalent basis—are helpful in analysing the amendments to the contractual terms of derivatives described in paragraph BC6.618. In this context, the IASB noted that if these other approaches result in derivatives with substantially different terms from those of the original derivative, the change may not have been made on an economically equivalent basis. The IASB also noted that if a hedging instrument is derecognised, hedge accounting is required to be discontinued.

Therefore, the IASB decided that for hedge accounting to continue it is also necessary that the original hedging instrument would not be derecognised.

BC6.620 The IASB considered these approaches described by respondents:

(a) *close-out and replace on the same terms (ie off-market terms)* — An entity applying this approach would enter into two new derivatives with the same counterparty. These two would be, a new derivative that is equal and offsetting to the original derivative (so both contracts are based on the interest rate benchmark to be replaced), and a new alternative benchmark-based derivative with the same terms as the original derivative so its fair value at initial recognition is equivalent to the fair value — on that date — of the original derivative (ie the new derivative is off-market). Under this approach, the counterparty to the new derivatives is the same as to the original derivative, the original derivative has not been derecognised and the terms of the alternative benchmark rate derivative are not substantially different from that of the original derivative. The IASB therefore concluded that such an approach could be regarded as consistent with the changes required by the reform as required in paragraph 6.9.1 of IFRS 9.

(b) *close-out and replace on substantially different terms (eg on-market terms)* — An entity applying this approach would terminate (close-out) the existing interest rate benchmark-based derivative with a cash settlement. The entity then enters into a new on-market alternative benchmark rate derivative with substantially different terms, so that the new derivative has a fair value of zero at initial recognition. Some respondents to the 2020 Exposure Draft were of the view that since this approach does not result in any gain or loss recognised in profit or loss, it suggests the exchange was done on an economically equivalent basis. The IASB disagreed with this view because the original derivative is extinguished and replaced with an alternative benchmark rate derivative with substantially different contractual terms. Therefore, this approach is not considered consistent with the changes required by the reform as required in paragraph 6.9.1 of IFRS 9.

(c) *add a new basis swap* — An entity applying this approach would retain the original interest rate benchmark-based derivative but enter into a basis swap that swaps the existing interest rate benchmark for the alternative benchmark rate. The combination of the two derivatives is equivalent to modifying the contractual terms of the original derivative to replace the interest rate benchmark with an alternative benchmark rate. The IASB noted that, in principle, the combination of an interest rate benchmark-based derivative and an interest rate benchmark-alternative benchmark rate swap could achieve an outcome economically equivalent to amending the original interest rate benchmark-based derivative. However, the IASB observed that, in practice, basis swaps are generally entered into on an aggregated basis to economically hedge an entity's net exposure to basis risk, rather than on an individual derivative basis. The IASB, therefore, noted that for this approach to be consistent with the changes required by the reform as described in paragraph 6.9.1 of IFRS 9, the basis swap must be coupled or linked with the original derivative, ie done on an individual derivative basis. This is because a change to the basis for determining the contractual cash flows of a hedging instrument is made to an individual instrument and, to achieve the same outcome, the basis swap would need to be coupled with an individual derivative.

(d) *novating to a new counterparty* — An entity applying this approach would novate the original interest rate benchmark-based derivative to a new counterparty and subsequently change the contractual cash flows on the novated derivative to replace the interest rate benchmark with an alternative benchmark rate. The IASB noted that novation of a derivative would result in the derecognition of the original derivative and thus would require hedge accounting to be discontinued in accordance with paragraph 6.5.6 of IFRS 9 (see further paragraphs BC6.336–BC6.338). Therefore, this approach is not consistent with the changes required by the reform as set out in paragraph 6.9.1 of IFRS 9.

BC6.621 The IASB therefore added paragraph 6.9.2 of IFRS 9 so that, an entity also applies paragraph 6.9.1(c) of IFRS 9 if these three conditions are met:

(a) the entity makes a change required by the reform using an approach other than changing the basis for determining the contractual cash flows of the hedging instrument (as described in paragraph 5.4.6 of IFRS 9);

(b) the original hedging instrument is not derecognised; and

(c) the chosen approach is economically equivalent to changing the basis for determining the contractual cash flows of the original hedging instrument (as described in paragraphs 5.4.7 and 5.4.8 of IFRS 9).

BC6.622 The IASB decided not to add further amendments or provide application guidance because IFRS 9 as amended provides an adequate basis for analysing the accounting requirements in context of the approaches described in paragraph BC6.620.

Remeasurement of the hedged item and hedging instrument

BC6.623 In paragraph BC6.568, the IASB explained that no exceptions were made in Phase 1 to the measurement requirements for hedged items or hedging instruments. The IASB concluded that the most useful information would be provided to users of financial statements if requirements for recognition and measurement of hedge ineffectiveness remain unchanged (see paragraph BC6.567). This is because recognising ineffectiveness in the financial statements based on the actual results of a hedging relationship faithfully represents the economic effects of the reform, thereby providing useful information to users of financial statements.

BC6.624 Applying the hedge accounting requirements in IFRS 9, a gain or loss arising from the remeasurement of the hedged item attributable to the hedged risk or from remeasuring the hedging instrument is reflected in profit or loss when measuring and recognising hedge ineffectiveness.

BC6.625   When deliberating the Phase 2 amendments, the IASB considered that changes in the fair value of the hedged item or hedging instrument could arise when the formal designation of a hedging relationship is amended. The IASB considered whether to provide an exception from the requirement to include in hedge ineffectiveness such fair value changes when they arise. The IASB considered, but rejected, these approaches:

(a)   *recognising the measurement adjustment in profit or loss over time* — An entity applying this approach would recognise the measurement adjustment in profit or loss over time (ie amortised) as the hedged item affects profit or loss. The IASB rejected this approach because it would require an offsetting entry to be recognised either in the statement of financial position or as an adjustment to the carrying amount of the hedged item or hedging instrument. Such an offsetting entry would fail to meet the definition of an asset or a liability in the *Conceptual Framework*. Adjusting the carrying amount of the hedged item or hedging instrument would result in the recognition of a net measurement adjustment of zero and would be inconsistent with the IASB's decision that no exceptions would be made to the measurement of hedged items or hedging instruments. The IASB also noted that such an approach would likely result in increased operational complexity because an entity would need to track adjustments that occur at different times for the purpose of amortising the adjustments in the period(s) in which the hedged item affects profit or loss.

(b)   *recognising the measurement adjustment as an adjustment to retained earnings* — An entity applying this approach would recognise the measurement adjustment as an adjustment to retained earnings during the period in which the measurement difference arises. However, the IASB rejected this approach because the changes to the hedged risk might be driven by amendments to hedging relationships that may occur in different reporting periods. Therefore, recognising adjustments to retained earnings over time would be inconsistent with the IASB's previous decisions (throughout IFRS Standards) that an adjustment to retained earnings only applies on transition to new requirements in IFRS Standards. Furthermore, the IASB noted that the measurement adjustment would meet the definition of income or expense in the *Conceptual Framework* and therefore should be recognised in the statement of profit or loss. The IASB also noted that recognising measurement adjustments directly in retained earnings would be inconsistent with the decision that no exceptions should be made to the measurement of hedged items or hedging instruments.

BC6.626   Some respondents to the 2020 Exposure Draft said they would not expect any significant changes in fair value to arise from the remeasurement of a hedged item or hedging instrument based on the alternative benchmark rate. That is because these amendments would apply only when the conditions in paragraph 5.4.7 of IFRS 9 are met, which require that changes are made on an economically equivalent basis. The IASB acknowledged these comments noting that, applying paragraph 6.9.1 of IFRS 9, a significant change in fair value arising from the remeasurement of the hedged item or the hedging instrument indicates that the changes were not made on an economically equivalent basis. Furthermore, the IASB observed that the requirement in paragraph 6.9.1(b) of IFRS 9, which requires the description of the designated portion for the cash flows or fair value being hedged enables entities to amend a hedging relationship to minimise fair value changes on the remeasurement of the hedged item or the hedging instrument.

BC6.627 The IASB therefore confirmed its previous decision not to provide an exception from the requirements in IFRS 9 regarding the measurement and recognition of hedge ineffectiveness. Therefore, an entity would apply the requirements in paragraphs 6.5.8 (for a fair value hedge) and 6.5.11 (for a cash flow hedge) of IFRS 9 for the measurement and recognition of hedge ineffectiveness. The IASB considered that accounting for such fair value changes in any other way would be inconsistent with the decision to continue applying hedge accounting for such amended hedging relationships (see paragraph 6.9.1 of IFRS 9). In the IASB's view, applying the requirements in IFRS 9 for the recognition and measurement of ineffectiveness reflects the economic effects of the amendments to the formal designation of a hedging relationship and therefore, provides useful information to users of financial statements.

Accounting for qualifying hedging relationships

Assessment of the economic relationship between the hedged item and the hedging instrument

BC6.628 The Phase 1 exception in paragraph 6.8.6 of IFRS 9 requires an entity to assume that, for the purpose of assessing the economic relationship between the hedged item and the hedging instrument as required by paragraphs 6.4.1(c)(i) and B6.4.4–B6.4.6 of IFRS 9, the interest rate benchmark on which the hedged cash flows and/or the hedged risk (contractually or non-contractually specified) are based, is not altered as a result of the reform. As noted in paragraph 6.8.11 of IFRS 9, this exception ceases to apply to the hedged item and the hedging instrument, respectively, at the earlier of, when there is no longer uncertainty about the hedged risk or the timing and the amount of the interest rate benchmark-based cash flows; and when the hedging relationship that the hedged item and the hedging instrument are a part of is discontinued.

BC6.629 Consistent with the IASB's considerations on the highly probable requirement (see paragraphs BC6.630–BC6.631), the IASB considered that, when the formal designation of a hedging relationship has been amended (see paragraph 6.9.1 of IFRS 9), the assessment of the economic relationship between the hedged item and the hedging instrument should be performed based on the alternative benchmark rate on which the hedged cash flows and/or the hedged risk will be based. The IASB therefore provided no exceptions from the assessment of the economic relationship between the hedged item and the hedging instrument for the period after the Phase 1 exception in paragraph 6.8.6 of IFRS 9 ceases to apply.

Amounts accumulated in the cash flow hedge reserve

BC6.630 During the period in which a hedging relationship is affected by uncertainty arising from the reform, paragraph 6.8.4 of IFRS 9 requires an entity to assume that the interest rate benchmark on which the hedged cash flows (contractually or non-contractually specified) are based is not altered for the purpose of determining whether a forecast transaction (or a component thereof) is highly probable. An entity is required to cease applying this exception at the earlier of the date the uncertainty arising from the reform is no longer present with respect to the timing and the amount of the interest rate benchmark-based cash flows of the hedged item; and the date the hedging relationship of which the hedged item is a part of is discontinued.

BC6.631 The IASB considered that uncertainty about the timing and the amount of the hedged cash flows would no longer be present when the interest rate benchmark on which the hedged cash flows are based is altered as required by the reform. In other words, uncertainty would no longer be present when an entity amends the description of the hedged item, including the description of the designated portion of the cash flows or fair value being hedged, applying paragraph 6.9.1(b) of IFRS 9. Thereafter, applying the requirement in paragraph 6.3.3 of IFRS 9, the assessment of whether the hedged cash flows are still highly probable to occur would be based on the contractual cash flows determined by reference to the alternative benchmark rate.

BC6.632 The IASB noted that the amendment in paragraph 6.9.1(b) of IFRS 9 for amending the formal designation of a hedging relationship could lead to changes in the hedged item. Therefore, if an entity uses a hypothetical derivative — that is, a derivative that would have terms matching the critical terms of the designated cash flows and the hedged risk, commonly used in cash flow hedges to represent the forecast transaction — the entity may need to change the hypothetical derivative to calculate the change in the value of the hedged item to measure hedge ineffectiveness.

BC6.633 Consequently, as hedge accounting would not be discontinued when a hedging relationship is amended for changes required by the reform (see paragraph 6.9.1 of IFRS 9), the IASB decided that an entity would deem the amount accumulated in the cash flow hedge reserve at that point to be based on the alternative benchmark rate on which the hedged future cash flows are determined. Therefore, in applying paragraph 6.5.11(d) of IFRS 9, the amount accumulated in the cash flow hedge reserve would be reclassified to profit or loss in the same period(s) during which the hedged cash flows based on the alternative benchmark rate affect profit or loss.

BC6.634 The approach described in paragraph BC6.633 is consistent with the IASB's view that, when a hedging relationship is amended for changes required by the reform, more useful information is provided to users of financial statements if hedge accounting is not discontinued and amounts are not reclassified to profit or loss solely due to the changes required by the reform. This is because such an approach will more faithfully reflect the economic effects of changes required by the reform.

BC6.635   Consistent with the requirements in paragraphs 6.8.5 and 6.8.10 of IFRS 9, the IASB considered whether to provide similar relief for any discontinued hedging relationships in which the previously designated hedged item is subject to the reform. The IASB observed that although a hedging relationship may have been discontinued, the amount accumulated in the cash flow hedge reserve arising from that hedging relationship remains in the reserve if the hedged future cash flows are still expected to occur. The IASB noted that if the hedged future cash flows are still expected to occur, the previously designated hedged item will be subject to a change required by the reform, even if the hedging relationship has been discontinued.

BC6.636   The IASB therefore decided that, for the purpose of applying paragraph 6.5.12 of IFRS 9, an entity deems the amount accumulated in the cash flow hedge reserve for a discontinued hedging relationship to be based on the alternative benchmark rate on which the contractual cash flows will be based, which is similar to the amendment in paragraph 6.9.7 of IFRS 9. That amount is reclassified to profit or loss in the same period(s) in which the hedged future cash flows based on the alternative benchmark rate affect profit or loss.

BC6.637   Some respondents to the 2020 Exposure Draft asked the IASB to clarify whether the requirements in paragraphs 6.9.7–6.9.8 of IFRS 9 require the retrospective measurement of the hedged item based on the alternative benchmark rate-based cash flows — in other words, whether an entity would be required to recalculate what the amount accumulated in the cash flow hedge reserve would have been if the hedged item was based on the alternative benchmark rate since inception.

BC6.638   The IASB considered that the cash flow hedge reserve is adjusted as required by paragraph 6.5.11(a) of IFRS 9 (ie the cash flow hedge reserve is not subject to separate measurement requirements, but instead is derived from the cumulative changes in the fair value of the hedged item (present value) and hedging instrument). The Phase 2 amendments do not include an exception from the measurement requirements in IFRS 9. Accordingly, the fair value of the hedging instrument or of the hedged item (ie the present value of the cumulative changes in the hedged expected future cash flows) is determined at the measurement date based on the expected future cash flows and assumptions that market participants would use. In other words, the fair values are not determined retrospectively. The IASB therefore considered that the cash flow hedge reserve is not remeasured as if it had been based on the alternative benchmark rate since inception of the hedging relationship.

BC6.639   The IASB confirmed that the amendments in paragraphs 6.9.7 and 6.9.8 of IFRS 9 extend to cash flow hedges, regardless of whether the cash flow hedge is for an open or closed hedged portfolio. The general reference to cash flow hedges in these paragraphs reflects such scope, therefore the IASB considered that explicitly addressing open or closed hedged portfolios was unnecessary.

Groups of items

BC6.640   The IASB considered that for groups of items designated as hedged items in a fair value or cash flow hedge, the hedged items could consist of items still referenced to the interest rate benchmark as well as items already referenced to the alternative benchmark rate. Therefore, an entity could not amend the description of the hedged risk or the hedged item, including the designated portion of the cash flows or fair value being hedged, with reference only to an alternative benchmark rate for the whole group. The IASB also considered that it would be inconsistent with the objectives of the Phase 2 amendments to require the discontinuation of such a hedging relationship solely because of the effects of the reform. In the IASB's view, the same requirements and relief that apply to other hedging relationships should apply to groups of items designated as hedged items, including dynamic hedging relationships.

BC6.641   Paragraphs 6.9.9–6.9.10 of IFRS 9 therefore require an entity to allocate the individual hedged items to subgroups based on the benchmark rate designated as the hedged risk for each subgroup and to apply the requirements in paragraph 6.6.1 of IFRS 9 to each subgroup separately. The IASB acknowledged this approach is an exception to the hedge accounting requirements in IFRS 9 because other hedge accounting requirements, including the requirements in paragraphs 6.5.8 and 6.5.11 of IFRS 9, are applied to the hedging relationship in its entirety. However, in the IASB's view, the robustness of the hedge accounting requirements is maintained because if any subgroup fails to meet the requirements in paragraph 6.6.1 of IFRS 9, the entity is required to discontinue hedge accounting for that entire hedging relationship. The IASB concluded this accounting outcome is appropriate because the basis for designating the hedged item on a group basis is that the entity is managing the designated hedge for the group as a whole.

BC6.642   The IASB acknowledged that preparers may incur additional costs to assess each subgroup in a hedging relationship separately, and to track items moving from one subgroup to another. However, the IASB concluded that an entity is likely to have such information available because IFRS 9 already requires it to identify and document hedged items designated within a hedging relationship with sufficient specificity. Therefore, the IASB concluded that the benefits of avoiding the discontinuation of hedge accounting and the resulting accounting impacts outweigh the associated costs of this exception.

BC6.643   Respondents to the 2020 Exposure Draft asked the IASB whether the requirement for groups of items applies to dynamic hedges of interest rate benchmark-based items when the items mature and are replaced with alternative benchmark-based items. The IASB considered that although the objective of the Phase 2 amendments is to provide relief when individual items transition to an alternative benchmark rate, the replacement of items that have expired with items that reference the alternative benchmark rate is a natural consequence of a dynamic hedging relationship. Therefore, the IASB observed that new items designated as part of the group to replace interest rate benchmark-based items that have matured would be allocated to the relevant subgroup based on the benchmark rate being hedged.

BC6.644 Respondents also asked the IASB to clarify how the requirements in paragraphs 6.9.9–6.9.10 of IFRS 9 apply to the hypothetical derivative in a cash flow hedge, specifically, whether the hypothetical derivative could be amended (and therefore measured) based on the alternative benchmark rate if the actual hedged item (such as a floating rate loan) has not yet transitioned to the alternative benchmark rate. The IASB considered that IFRS 9 does not include specific requirements for the hypothetical derivative but mentions it as one possible way of calculating the change in the value of the hedged item to measure ineffectiveness (see paragraph B6.5.5 of IFRS 9). Therefore, the terms on which the hypothetical derivative is constructed replicate the hedged risk and the hedged cash flows of the hedged item an entity is hedging. The hypothetical derivative cannot include features in the value of the hedged item that exist only in the hedging instrument (but not in the hedged item). The IASB therefore decided that the identification of an appropriate hypothetical derivative is based on the requirements to measure hedge ineffectiveness and it would not be appropriate to include specific amendments for applying the requirements in paragraphs 6.9.9–6.9.10 to the hypothetical derivative.

Designation of risk components

End of application of the Phase 1 exception

BC6.645 An entity may designate an item in its entirety or a component of an item as the hedged item in a hedging relationship. Paragraphs 6.3.7(a) and B6.3.8 of IFRS 9 allow entities to designate only changes in the cash flows or fair value of an item attributable to a specific risk or risks (risk component).

BC6.646 When developing the Phase 1 amendments, the IASB decided not to set an end date for applying the exception for the separately identifiable requirement (see paragraphs 6.8.7–6.8.8 of IFRS 9). The IASB considered that including an end date for that exception could require an entity to immediately discontinue hedge accounting at a point in time because, as the reform progresses, a risk component based on the interest rate benchmark may no longer be separately identifiable (for example, as the market for the alternative benchmark rate is established). As noted in paragraph BC6.597, in the IASB's view, such an immediate discontinuation of hedge accounting would be inconsistent with the objective of this exception in Phase 1. Therefore, when issuing the Phase 1 amendments, the IASB decided that an entity should cease applying the Phase 1 exception from the separately identifiable requirement to a hedging relationship only when that hedging relationship is discontinued applying the requirements in IFRS 9.

BC6.647 Having considered the interaction between the Phase 1 exception from the separately identifiable requirement and the Phase 2 amendments to the hedge accounting requirements in IFRS 9, the IASB decided it is necessary to specify that an entity is required to cease applying the Phase 1 exception from the separately identifiable requirement when the uncertainty arising from the reform, which led to that exception, is no longer present.

BC6.648 The IASB considered that continuing to apply the Phase 1 amendments after the uncertainty arising from the reform is no longer present would not faithfully represent the actual characteristics of the elements of the hedging relationship in which the uncertainty has been eliminated nor the economic effects of the reform. The IASB therefore added paragraph 6.8.13 to IFRS 9 so the Phase 1 exception from the separately identifiable requirement ceases to apply at the earlier of:

(a) when changes required by the reform are made to the non-contractually specified risk component as set out in paragraph 6.9.1 of IFRS 9; or

(b) when the hedging relationship in which the non-contractually specified risk component was designated is discontinued.

Application of the 'separately identifiable' requirement to an alternative benchmark rate

BC6.649 In developing the Phase 2 amendments, the IASB was aware that considerations similar to those discussed in paragraphs BC6.645–BC6.648 apply to designating an alternative benchmark rate as a non-contractually specified risk component in either a cash flow hedge or a fair value hedge. This is because an entity's ability to conclude that the alternative benchmark rate meets the requirements in paragraphs 6.3.7(a) and B6.3.8 of IFRS 9 that a risk component must be separately identifiable and reliably measurable could be affected in the early stages of the reform.

BC6.650 Specific application guidance and examples on the separately identifiable requirement are already set out in paragraphs B6.3.9–B6.3.10 of IFRS 9. However, the IASB considered that an entity might expect an alternative benchmark rate to meet the separately identifiable requirement in IFRS 9 within a reasonable period of time even though the alternative benchmark rate does not meet the requirement when designated as a risk component.

BC6.651 The amendment in paragraph 6.9.11 of IFRS 9 applies to a different set of instruments from the Phase 1 exception. For items within the scope of paragraph 6.9.11 of IFRS 9, the separately identifiable requirement has never been satisfied. In contrast, the population of hedging relationships to which the Phase 1 relief applied had already satisfied the qualifying criteria for hedge accounting to be applied. The IASB therefore considered that any relief from the separately identifiable requirement in Phase 2 should be temporary.

BC6.652 Consequently, in the 2020 Exposure Draft, the IASB proposed that an alternative benchmark rate that does not meet the requirement to be separately identifiable at the date it is designated as a non-contractually specified risk component would be deemed to have met the requirement at that date if, and only if, an entity reasonably expects that the alternative benchmark rate will be separately identifiable within 24 months from the date it is designated as a risk component.

BC6.653   Respondents to the 2020 Exposure Draft agreed with this proposed amendment but asked the IASB to clarify the date from which the 24-month period applies. The IASB acknowledged respondents' concerns, and considered whether the 24-month period applies:

(a)   on a hedge-by-hedge basis—that is, to each hedging relationship individually, beginning from the date an alternative benchmark rate is designated as a risk component in that relationship; or

(b)   on a rate-by-rate basis—that is, to each alternative benchmark rate separately, beginning from the date when an entity first designates an alternative benchmark rate as a hedged risk for the first time.

BC6.654   The IASB acknowledged that applying the 24-month period to each hedging relationship individually (as proposed in the 2020 Exposure Draft)—that is, on a hedge-by-hedge basis—is consistent with the basis on which hedging relationships are designated. For each new hedge designation, an entity is required to assess whether the qualifying criteria to apply hedge accounting, including the separately identifiable requirement, have been met. However, the IASB also considered that applying the 24-month period to different hedging relationships (with the same alternative benchmark rate designated as a risk component) at different times could add an unnecessary operational burden as the period would end at different times and thus would need to be monitored over different periods, for different hedging relationships. For example, if an entity designates the alternative benchmark rate as the risk component in two hedging relationships—the first designated on 31 March 20X1 and the second on 30 June 20X1—the 24-month period for each hedge would begin and end at different dates, although the designated risk is the same in both hedging relationships.

BC6.655   Therefore, the IASB decided that the requirement in paragraph 6.9.11 would apply on a rate-by-rate basis so the 24-month period applies to each alternative benchmark rate separately and hence, starts from the date that an entity designates an alternative benchmark rate as a non-contractually specified risk component for the first time (but see also paragraph 7.2.45 of IFRS 9). The IASB considered that if an entity concludes for one hedging relationship that it no longer has a reasonable expectation that the alternative benchmark rate would meet the requirements within the 24-month period, it is likely that the entity would reach the same conclusion for all other hedging relationships in which that particular alternative benchmark rate has been designated. Applying this requirement to the example in paragraph BC6.654, the 24-month period will begin on 31 March 20X1 for that alternative benchmark rate.

BC6.656   Despite the requirement to apply the 24-month period to each alternative benchmark rate separately, the requirement to assess whether an alternative benchmark rate is separately identifiable continues to separately apply to each hedging relationship. In other words, an entity is required to assess, for each hedge designation, whether the qualifying criteria to apply hedge accounting, including the separately identifiable requirement, are met for the remainder of the 24-month period (ie until 31 March 20X3 following from the example in paragraph BC6.654).

BC6.657 Consistent with the requirement in IFRS 9 to continuously assess the separately identifiable requirement, an entity's ability to conclude that an alternative benchmark rate is a separately identifiable component requires assessment over the life of the hedging relationship including during the 24-month period discussed in paragraph BC6.655. However, the IASB decided that to avoid the complexity of detailed judgements during the 24-month period, an entity is required to cease applying the requirement during the 24-month period if, and only if, the entity reasonably expects that the alternative benchmark rate will not meet the separately identifiable requirement within that period. If an entity reasonably expects that an alternative benchmark rate will not be separately identifiable within 24 months from the date the entity designates it as a non-contractually specified risk component for the first time, the entity is required to cease applying the requirement in paragraph 6.9.11 of IFRS 9 to that alternative benchmark rate and discontinue applying hedge accounting prospectively from the date of that reassessment to all hedging relationships in which the alternative benchmark rate was designated as a non-contractually specified risk component.

BC6.658 The IASB acknowledged that 24 months is an arbitrary period. However, in the IASB's view, a clearly defined end point is necessary because of the temporary nature of the amendment. The exception described in paragraphs 6.9.11–6.9.13 is a significant relief from one of the requirements that is a basis for the robustness of the hedge accounting requirements, therefore the relief is intentionally short-lived. The IASB considered that a period of 24 months will assist entities in applying the hedge accounting requirements in IFRS 9 particularly during the early stages of the transition to alternative benchmark rates. Therefore, the IASB decided that a period of 24 months from the date an entity first designates an alternative benchmark rate as a non-contractually specified risk component is a reasonable period and would enable entities to implement the reform and comply with any regulatory requirements, while avoiding potential short-term disruption as the market for an alternative benchmark rate develops.

BC6.659 While developing the proposals in the 2020 Exposure Draft, the IASB considered proposing alternative periods for the requirement in paragraph 6.9.11 of IFRS 9, including a period of 12 months or a period longer than 24 months. However, the IASB acknowledged the diversity in the approaches to the reform or replacement of interest rate benchmarks and the timing of the expected completion across various jurisdictions. The IASB was concerned that 12 months would not provide sufficient time across all jurisdictions. At the same time, the IASB considered that entities may not be able to have a reasonable expectation that an alternative benchmark rate would satisfy the separately identifiable requirement over a period longer than 24 months.

BC6.660 The IASB emphasised that the amendments apply only for the separately identifiable requirement and not the reliably measurable requirement. Therefore, if the risk component is not reliably measurable, either when it is designated or thereafter, the alternative benchmark rate would not meet the qualifying criteria to be designated as a risk component in a hedging relationship. Similarly, if the hedging relationship fails to meet any other qualifying criteria set out in IFRS 9 to apply hedge accounting, either at the date the alternative benchmark rate is designated or during the 24-month period, the entity is required to discontinue hedge accounting prospectively from that date. The IASB decided that providing relief only for the separately identifiable requirement would achieve the objective described in paragraph BC5.290.

Effective date and transition (Chapter 7)

Effective date

Requirements issued in IFRS 9 (2009)

BC7.1 The IASB recognises that many countries require time for translation and for introducing the mandatory requirements into law. In addition, entities require time to implement new standards. The IASB usually sets an effective date of between six and eighteen months after issuing a Standard. However, the IASB has adopted a phased approach to publishing IFRS 9, so this is not possible.

BC7.2 In the response to the 2009 Classification and Measurement Exposure Draft, respondents urged that:

(a) it would be helpful to preparers if the IASB were to permit all phases of the project to replace IAS 39 to be adopted at the same time.

(b) it would be helpful to entities that issue insurance contracts if the effective date of IFRS 9 were aligned with the forthcoming Standard on accounting for insurance contracts. Most of an insurer's assets are financial assets and most of its liabilities are insurance liabilities or financial liabilities. Thus, if an insurer applies IFRS 9 before it applies any new Standard on insurance contracts, it might face two rounds of major changes in a short period. This would be disruptive for both users and preparers.

(c) because a number of countries will adopt IFRS in the next few years, it would be helpful to entities in those countries if the IASB did not require them to make two changes in a short period of time.

BC7.3 With these factors in mind, the IASB decided it should require entities to apply the requirements of IFRS 9 for annual periods beginning on or after 1 January 2013. The IASB intends that this date will allow entities to adopt at the same time the guidance from all phases of the project to replace IAS 39. (Paragraphs BC7.9A–BC7.9E, BC7.9F–BC7.9H and BC7.9J–BC7.9N describe the IASB's subsequent decisions on the effective date of IFRS 9.)

BC7.4   The IASB will consider delaying the effective date of IFRS 9 if the impairment phase of the project to replace IAS 39 makes such a delay necessary, or if the new Standard on insurance contracts has a mandatory effective date later than 2013, to avoid an insurer having to face two rounds of changes in a short period.

BC7.5   The IASB decided to permit earlier application of IFRS 9 to allow an entity to apply the new requirements on classification and measurement of financial assets. This enables entities to use IFRS 9 (as issued in November 2009) in their 2009 annual financial statements and meets one of the objectives of the phased approach, ie to have improved classification and measurement requirements for financial assets in place for 2009 year-ends. (Paragraphs BC7.7–BC7.9, BC7.9H and BC7.9O–BC7.9T describe the IASB's subsequent decisions on the early application of IFRS 9.)

BC7.6   The effect of transition will be significant for some entities. As a result, there will be less comparability between entities that apply IFRS 9 and those that do not. Accordingly, IFRS 9 includes additional disclosures about the transition to IFRS 9.

Requirements added to IFRS 9 in October 2010

BC7.7   The IASB chose to complete the project to replace IAS 39 in phases to respond to requests that the accounting for financial instruments should be improved quickly. However, the IASB is concerned that if an entity is permitted to adopt one phase early without also adopting early all of the preceding phases, there would be a period of significant incomparability among entities until all of the phases of the project are mandatorily effective. That is because there will be many possible combinations of which requirements are adopted early and which are not. Moreover, the period of incomparability would be significant because the phases will not be mandatorily effective before 1 January 2013. (Paragraphs BC7.9A–BC7.9E, BC7.9F–BC7.9H and BC7.9J–BC7.9N describe the IASB's subsequent decisions on the effective date of IFRS 9.)

BC7.8   Consequently, in the 2010 Own Credit Risk Exposure Draft the IASB proposed that if an entity elects to apply any finalised requirements early, the entity must also apply any preceding requirements in IFRS 9 that it does not already apply. Some respondents did not agree with this proposal and urged the IASB to permit an entity to adopt the proposals in the 2010 Own Credit Risk Exposure Draft early without also adopting early the requirements in IFRS 9 for financial assets. As an alternative, some respondents asked the IASB to finalise the proposals as an amendment to IAS 39, which could be applied immediately, instead of adding the proposals to IFRS 9. Those respondents thought that the proposals in the 2010 Own Credit Risk Exposure Draft are unrelated to the requirements for financial assets and would be less complex to implement. However, the IASB was not persuaded that the benefits of permitting an entity to adopt early only the proposals in the 2010 Own Credit Risk Exposure Draft exceeded the significant incomparability that would result. Moreover, the IASB noted that the transition requirements in IFRS 9 for financial assets require an entity to reassess some financial liabilities designated under the fair value option. Consequently, there is a linkage between the two phases and to permit entities to adopt early only the proposals in the 2010 Own Credit Risk Exposure Draft would be inappropriate and confusing. Moreover, the IASB decided that it would be inappropriate to amend IAS 39 while it was in the process of replacing it. For those reasons, the IASB decided to confirm the proposals in the 2010 Own Credit Risk Exposure Draft. (Paragraphs BC7.35–BC7.40 describe the IASB's subsequent decisions on the early application of the own credit risk requirements.)

BC7.9 However, if an entity chooses to adopt a phase early, the IASB does not require the entity to adopt subsequent phases early. The IASB decided that it would be unfair to require an entity to anticipate the outcomes of unfinished phases in order to make a decision about adopting a phase early. Moreover, the IASB decided that an entity is permitted to adopt early the requirements in IFRS 9 issued in 2009 without adopting early the requirements that were added to IFRS 9 in 2010. (Paragraphs BC7.9O–BC7.9T describe the IASB's subsequent decisions on the early application of IFRS 9.)

Mandatory effective date of IFRS 9—November 2011

BC7.9A IFRS 9 (2009) and IFRS 9 (2010) were issued with a mandatory effective date of 1 January 2013. At the time, the IASB noted that it would consider delaying the effective date of IFRS 9, if:

(a) the impairment phase of the project to replace IAS 39 made such a delay necessary; or

(b) the new Standard on insurance contracts had a mandatory effective date later than 2013, to avoid an insurer having to face two rounds of changes in a short period.

BC7.9B In July 2011 the IASB noted that in order to enable an appropriate period for implementation before the mandatory effective date of the new requirements, the impairment and hedge accounting phases of the project to replace IAS 39 would not be mandatory for periods beginning before 1 January 2013. In addition, any new requirements for the accounting for insurance contracts would not have a mandatory effective date as early as 1 January 2013.

BC7.9C As a result of these considerations, in August 2011 the IASB published the Exposure Draft *Mandatory Effective Date of IFRS 9* (the '2011 Mandatory Effective Date Exposure Draft'). In the 2011 Mandatory Effective Date Exposure Draft, the IASB proposed that the mandatory effective date of IFRS 9 should be deferred to annual periods beginning on or after 1 January 2015. The IASB noted that it did not want to discourage entities from applying IFRS 9 and stressed that early application would still be permitted.

BC7.9D In its redeliberations on the 2011 Mandatory Effective Date Exposure Draft, the IASB decided to confirm its proposal that IFRS 9 would be required to be applied for annual periods beginning on or after 1 January 2015. In doing so, the IASB noted that there are compelling reasons for all project phases to be implemented at the same time and that, based on current circumstances, it is still appropriate to pursue an approach of requiring the same effective date for all phases of this project. (Paragraphs BC7.9F–BC7.9H and BC7.9J–BC7.9N describe the IASB's subsequent decisions on the effective date of IFRS 9.)

BC7.9E However, the IASB noted that it is difficult to assess the amount of lead time that will be necessary to implement all phases of the project because the entire project to replace IAS 39 is not yet complete. Ultimately this may affect the IASB's conclusion on the appropriateness of requiring the same mandatory effective date for all phases of this project.

Requirements added to, and amendments of, IFRS 9 in November 2013

Mandatory effective date of IFRS 9—November 2013

BC7.9F The 2012 Limited Amendments Exposure Draft did not propose to change the mandatory effective date of IFRS 9 and the IASB did not ask a question on that topic. However, as part of the 2013 Impairment Exposure Draft, the IASB noted that all phases of IFRS 9 would have the same effective date and asked respondents for feedback on the lead time that would be needed to implement the proposals on expected credit losses and what the resulting mandatory effective date for IFRS 9 should be.

BC7.9G Many respondents to the 2012 Limited Amendments Exposure Draft urged the IASB to confirm as soon as possible that the mandatory effective date of IFRS 9 of 1 January 2015 would be deferred. Respondents noted that the IASB has a practice of allowing a minimum of 18 months between the finalisation of a Standard and the mandatory effective date. They noted that even if the remaining phases of IFRS 9 were completed by the end of 2013, there would not be 18 months remaining until 1 January 2015. The feedback received in response to the 2013 Impairment Exposure Draft indicated that entities believed that they would need around three years to implement the proposed impairment model.

BC7.9H In the light of the feedback received, the IASB decided to defer the mandatory effective date of IFRS 9. The IASB decided that it will be able to determine the appropriate mandatory effective date only after it finalises the requirements for impairment and classification and measurement and has considered the lead time that is necessary to implement those new requirements. Consequently, the IASB decided that the mandatory effective date should not be specified in IFRS 9 but will be determined when the outstanding phases are finalised. However, the IASB confirmed that in the meantime application of IFRS 9 is still permitted. (Paragraphs BC7.9J–BC7.9N describe the IASB's subsequent decisions on the effective date of IFRS 9. Paragraphs BC7.35–BC7.40 describe the IASB's decisions in November 2013 on the early application of the own credit risk requirements.)

Hedge accounting

BC7.9I The IASB decided that the effective date of the hedge accounting requirements should be aligned with the effective date for the other requirements of IFRS 9 (see paragraph BC7.9H) and confirmed that the hedge accounting requirements cannot be applied prior to the application of the classification and measurement requirements in IFRS 9.

Requirements added to IFRS 9 in July 2014

Mandatory effective date of IFRS 9

BC7.9J The IASB concluded that the mandatory effective date for IFRS 9 would largely depend on the time and effort required to implement the impairment requirements. Accordingly, the 2013 Impairment Exposure Draft requested feedback on how much time entities would require to implement those requirements.

BC7.9K Some respondents noted that the impairment model that would be incorporated into IFRS 9 is arguably the most important part of the IASB's response to the global financial crisis. Consequently, although they believe that sufficient time should be allowed for the implementation of IFRS 9, they expressed concern about any delay that is not strictly necessary. These respondents recommended that the IASB should allow no more than two years for the implementation of IFRS 9.

BC7.9L However, most respondents noted that they would require approximately three years, noting the following reasons:

(a) entities would need to make system and model changes, in particular credit risk management systems, to monitor significant increases in credit risk and to modify credit risk models to incorporate appropriate forward-looking data;

(b) entities may have limited availability of historical and trend information. Such information is needed to build relevant models and incorporate forward-looking data in measuring expected credit losses;

(c) entities would need to undertake parallel testing and running of new systems before final implementation; and

(d) entities would need to consider the interaction of the expected credit loss requirements with various other regulatory reforms and regulatory capital requirements. Respondents noted that resource constraints would hamper their efforts for a quicker implementation.

BC7.9M In addition, the IASB noted that most respondents to the IASB's 2013 Insurance Contracts Exposure Draft commented that it would be ideal if the requirements of the new Standard on insurance contracts could have the same mandatory effective date as IFRS 9. Those respondents were concerned that the designations and assessments that an entity would make on initial application of IFRS 9 might not be the same as those that the entity would have made if it had been applying the new Standard on insurance contracts at the same time. Although the IASB had not concluded deliberations on the

Standard on insurance contracts, it had tentatively decided that it would allow approximately three years between finalising that Standard and its mandatory effective date.

BC7.9N   The IASB noted that IFRS 9 is relevant to a broad range of entities. Accordingly, it concluded that it may not be appropriate to delay the application of IFRS 9 solely to mitigate the concerns of insurers since it would delay the benefits of improved financial reporting for a broad range of entities. However, in balancing the competing objectives of timely implementation of IFRS 9 and allowing entities sufficient time to implement IFRS 9 and, at the same time, considering the concerns raised in response to the 2013 Insurance Contracts Exposure Draft, the IASB concluded that a mandatory effective date of 1 January 2018 would be appropriate. In the IASB's view, that date would allow sufficient time for entities to implement IFRS 9 and give it the opportunity to progress its project on insurance contracts so that affected entities would be able to understand the direction of the insurance contracts requirements prior to implementing IFRS 9.

Early application of IFRS 9

BC7.9O   Prior to IFRS 9 being issued in July 2014, three versions of IFRS 9 existed— IFRS 9 (2009), IFRS 9 (2010) and IFRS 9 (2013)—and each of these previous versions of IFRS 9 permitted early application. The relevant rationale is set out in paragraphs BC7.5, BC7.7–BC7.9 and BC7.9H–BC7.9I. In addition, an entity is permitted to early apply only the requirements in IFRS 9 related to the presentation of 'own credit' gains and losses on financial liabilities designated under the fair value option; ie without applying the other requirements in IFRS 9. The relevant rationale is set out in paragraphs BC7.35–BC7.40.

BC7.9P   In the 2012 Limited Amendments Exposure Draft, the IASB proposed to limit the versions of IFRS 9 available for early application. Specifically, entities:

(a)   would be permitted to early apply the completed version of IFRS 9; but

(b)   entities would not be permitted to newly early apply a previous version of IFRS 9 if the entity's relevant date of initial application is six months or more after the completed version of IFRS 9 is issued. However, if the entity's relevant date of initial application is less than six months after the completed version of IFRS 9 is issued, an entity would be permitted to continue to apply that version until the completed version of IFRS 9 becomes mandatorily effective.

These proposals did not affect the provision in IFRS 9 that permits an entity to early apply only the requirements related to the presentation of 'own credit' gains and losses on financial liabilities designated under the fair value option. Moreover, the proposals did not affect those entities that chose to early apply a previous version of IFRS 9 before the completed version of IFRS 9 was issued. Those entities would be permitted to continue to apply that previous version of IFRS 9 until the completed version of IFRS 9 is mandatorily effective.

BC7.9Q In considering those proposals, the IASB noted that having multiple versions of IFRS 9 available for early application (in addition to IAS 39) is complex and significantly reduces the comparability of information that is provided to users of financial statements.

BC7.9R The IASB acknowledged in the 2012 Limited Amendments Exposure Draft that the phased approach to replacing IAS 39 (including the phased approach to the application of, and transition to, IFRS 9) was originally developed in response to requests from the G20, the Financial Stability Board and others that improvements to the accounting for financial instruments should be available quickly. For this reason, the classification and measurement requirements in IFRS 9 were issued before the phases for impairment and hedge accounting were completed. However, the IASB noted that when the completed version of IFRS 9 is issued (ie when all of the phases of the project to replace IAS 39 are completed), the lack of comparability, as well as the complexity, that results from permitting entities to early apply more than one version of IFRS 9 is no longer justified.

BC7.9S Despite the conclusion in paragraph BC7.9R, the IASB decided to propose that an entity would be permitted to early apply a previous version of IFRS 9 for six months after the completed version of IFRS 9 is issued. This was a practical accommodation to minimise the cost and disruption to entities that are preparing to apply a previous version of IFRS 9 at the time that the completed version is issued.

BC7.9T Of those respondents who commented on these proposals in the 2012 Limited Amendments Exposure Draft, nearly all agreed. Many agreed with the IASB's rationale that this would increase comparability compared to the phased early application that is currently permitted. Consequently, the IASB confirmed the proposals set out in paragraph BC7.9P.

Transition related to IFRS 9 as issued in November 2009

BC7.10 IAS 8 *Accounting Policies, Changes in Accounting Estimates and Errors* states that retrospective application results in the most useful information to users because the information presented for all periods is comparable. Consequently, the 2009 Classification and Measurement Exposure Draft proposed retrospective application subject to some transition relief in particular circumstances. The IASB considered the difficulties and associated costs of full retrospective application of the proposals in the 2009 Classification and Measurement Exposure Draft.

BC7.11 Most respondents agreed, in principle, with requiring retrospective application, but many questioned the practicability of the approach. In particular, many noted that the extensive exceptions to retrospective application that would be required to make such transition practicable significantly reduced (and possibly eliminated) any benefit that users might obtain from requiring comparative information to be restated.

BC7.12   The IASB considered whether to require prospective application, but noted that such an approach does not provide comparable information for users of financial statements. In addition, the IASB noted that any transition approach (such as prospective application) that requires resetting the effective interest rate for financial assets measured at amortised cost reduces the usefulness of information about interest income.

BC7.13   The IASB decided to require retrospective application but provide transition relief to address particular difficulties that might arise from retrospective application. The IASB also noted that IAS 8 sets out transition requirements that apply if retrospective application is impracticable and prohibits the use of hindsight when applying a new accounting policy to a prior period.

Transition relief

Impracticability exceptions

BC7.14   The IASB acknowledged that it may be impracticable for an entity to apply the effective interest method or impairment requirements in IAS 39 retrospectively in some situations. The process would be cumbersome, in particular for an entity with a large number of financial assets that were previously measured at fair value but are measured at amortised cost in accordance with the approach in IFRS 9. Several loss events and reversals might have occurred between the date when the asset was initially recognised and the date of initial application of the Standard. IFRS 9 requires that if applying the impairment requirements is impracticable or requires the use of hindsight, an entity should use previously determined fair value information to determine whether a financial asset was impaired in comparative periods. IFRS 9 also requires that the fair value at the date of initial application of the new requirements should be treated as the new amortised cost carrying amount of that financial asset in that case. The IASB rejected proposals that entities should be permitted, but not required, to treat the fair value at the date of initial application as amortised cost because it would impair comparability and require significant guidance about when such an option should be permitted. (Paragraphs BC7.72–BC7.81 describe the IASB's subsequent decisions on transition to the new impairment requirements.)

BC7.15   The IASB noted that an entity would not have determined the fair value of an investment in an unquoted equity instrument[48] (or a derivative on such an investment) that was previously accounted for in accordance with paragraphs 46(c) and 66 of IAS 39. Moreover, an entity will not have the necessary information to determine fair value retrospectively without using hindsight. Accordingly, IFRS 9 requires such instruments to be measured at fair value at the date of initial application.

---

48 IFRS 13, issued in May 2011, defines a Level 1 input as a quoted price in an active market for an identical asset or liability. Level 2 inputs include quoted prices for identical assets or liabilities in markets that are not active. As a result, IFRS 9 refers to such equity instruments as 'an equity instrument that does not have a quoted price in an active market for an identical instrument (ie a Level 1 input)'.

Hybrid contracts

BC7.16   An entity may not have previously determined the fair value of a hybrid contract in its entirety. Moreover, an entity will not have the necessary information to determine fair value retrospectively without using hindsight. However, an entity would have been required to measure both the embedded derivative and host separately at fair value to apply the disclosure requirements in IFRS 7. Consequently, in comparative periods, IFRS 9 requires the sum of the fair value of the embedded derivative and the host to be used as an approximation of the fair value of the entire hybrid contract.

BC7.17   The proposals in the 2009 Classification and Measurement Exposure Draft would have resulted in fair value measurement for many hybrid contracts for which the embedded derivative was accounted for separately in accordance with IAS 39. Some respondents asked for such treatment under IAS 39 to be 'grandfathered'. The IASB noted that many such requests had been related to the proposed treatment of hybrid contracts with financial liability hosts, which were not included in IFRS 9 (2009). Consequently, the IASB decided not to permit an option to grandfather hybrid contracts with financial asset hosts that were bifurcated in accordance with IAS 39 as an accounting policy choice because it would impair comparability, and because some such contracts may still have a significant remaining maturity.

Assessment of the objective of the entity's business model for managing financial assets

BC7.18   IFRS 9 requires an entity to assess whether the objective of an entity's business model is to manage financial assets to collect the contractual cash flows on the basis of circumstances at the date of initial application. The IASB believes it would be difficult, and perhaps impossible, to assess that condition on the basis of circumstances when the instrument first satisfied the recognition criterion in IAS 39.

Assessment of qualifying criteria for the fair value option

BC7.19   The IASB decided that the assessment of whether a financial asset or financial liability meets the eligibility criterion for designation under the fair value option should be based on the circumstances at the date of initial application. IFRS 9 changes the classification of some financial assets, including eliminating two of the three eligibility criteria in IAS 39 for the fair value option for financial assets. Consequently, the IASB believes that an entity should reconsider at transition its original assessment of whether to designate a financial asset or financial liability as at fair value through profit or loss.

Comparative information

BC7.20   As noted above, many respondents were concerned that the inevitable exceptions to full retrospective application would result in restated information that is incomplete. They proposed an approach similar to that used on first-time adoption of IFRS and when entities adopted IAS 39 in 2005, in which the requirement to provide comparative information was waived. Some respondents believe that such an approach would address the concerns that, although IAS 1 requires only one year of comparative information, the legal and regulatory frameworks in many jurisdictions require further comparative periods to be presented. In those situations, the restatement of comparatives would be virtually impossible for an entity wishing to adopt IFRS 9 early.

BC7.21 In the IASB's view, waiving the requirement to restate comparatives strikes a balance between the conceptually preferable method of full retrospective application (as stated in IAS 8) and the practicability of adopting the new classification model within a short time frame. Accordingly, the IASB decided that it would permit, but not require, restatement of comparative periods by entities that implement IFRS 9 for reporting periods beginning before 1 January 2012. However, those considerations would be less applicable for entities that adopted outside a short time frame. Consequently, restated comparative information is required if an entity adopts IFRS 9 for reporting periods beginning after 1 January 2012. (Paragraphs BC7.34A–BC7.34M and BC7.82–BC7.84 describe the IASB's subsequent decisions on restating comparative information.)

Date of initial application

BC7.22 The 2009 Classification and Measurement Exposure Draft stated that the date of initial application would be the date when an entity first applies the requirements in the Standard. Many respondents questioned whether the date of initial application could be an arbitrary date between the date of issue of the Standard (or even earlier) and the mandatory effective date, resulting in a loss of comparability over a long period of time. The IASB agreed that a free choice would impair comparability, but noted it intended that entities should be able to apply the Standard in 2009 or 2010 financial statements. Accordingly, the Standard requires the date of initial application to be the beginning of a reporting period, but provides relief from this requirement for entities applying the Standard for reporting periods beginning on or before 1 January 2011.

Hedge accounting

BC7.23 The IASB decided not to carry forward the specific transition provisions on hedge accounting proposed in the 2009 Classification and Measurement Exposure Draft because they are not necessary.

Transitional disclosures

BC7.24 The 2009 Classification and Measurement Exposure Draft proposed disclosures for entities that apply the new IFRS 9 early. However, many noted that such disclosures would be useful for all entities applying IFRS 9 for the first time, and not only early adopters. The IASB noted that the information necessary to make those disclosures would be readily available to the entity to make the necessary journal entries on transition and to account for the financial assets in the future. Accordingly, IFRS 9 requires all entities to supply additional disclosures on transition. (Paragraphs BC7.34A–BC7.34M and BC7.63–BC7.68 describe the IASB's subsequent decisions on disclosures at transition to IFRS 9.)

BC7.25 The IASB rejected a proposal in the comment letters that entities should apply disclosures similar to those based on IFRS 1 *First-time Adoption of International Financial Reporting Standards* explaining the transition to the new Standard. The IASB noted that the disclosures in IFRS 1 relate to first-time adoption and not to changes in accounting policies. Disclosures about changes in an accounting policy are required by IAS 8.

Transition related to the requirements added to IFRS 9 in October 2010

BC7.26 As noted above, IAS 8 states that retrospective application results in the most useful information to users because the information presented for all periods is comparable. The IASB noted that IFRS 7 already requires disclosure of the amount of the change in fair value that is attributable to changes in the credit risk of the liability. Consequently, entities are already calculating the information necessary to present the effects of changes in liabilities' credit risk in other comprehensive income. Thus, the 2010 Own Credit Risk Exposure Draft proposed retrospective application and almost all respondents agreed. The IASB confirmed that proposal.

BC7.27 The IASB did not change the classification and measurement approach for financial liabilities, including the eligibility conditions for the fair value option for financial liabilities. Consequently, the proposals in the 2010 Own Credit Risk Exposure Draft did not permit entities to make new designations or revoke its previous designations as a result of the proposals. Some respondents believed that the IASB should permit entities to reassess their designations in the light of the new requirements related to own credit risk.

BC7.28 However, the IASB was not persuaded that there is a compelling reason to permit entities to reassess their elections, especially because the underlying classification and measurement approach has not changed. As noted in paragraph BC7.19, when an entity initially applies IFRS 9 to assets, it is required to reassess particular liabilities designated under the fair value option. That was necessary because the requirements issued in IFRS 9 (2009) introduced a new classification and measurement approach for financial assets, which would change the classification of some (and perhaps many) financial assets. Those changes require an entity to reassess liabilities designated under the fair value option to the extent that designation was originally elected to address an accounting mismatch. However, the IASB believed that a similar case could not be made for the requirements added to IFRS 9 in 2010. And because the requirements issued in IFRS 9 (2009) already require reassessment of particular liabilities, the IASB believes that a second reassessment would make transition unnecessarily complex. Consequently, the IASB decided to confirm the proposal in the 2010 Own Credit Risk Exposure Draft.

Transition relief

BC7.29 When the IASB issued the new requirements for financial assets in November 2009, it granted some transition relief from full retrospective transition. To be consistent with the transition requirements for assets, the IASB decided to grant similar transition relief for the requirements added to IFRS 9 in October 2010:

(a) The requirements are not applied to liabilities that have been derecognised at the date of initial application. The IASB concluded that applying the requirements in IFRS 9 to some derecognised items but not others would be confusing and unnecessarily complex.

(b) An entity is required to assess whether presenting the effects of changes in a liability's credit risk in other comprehensive income would create or enlarge an accounting mismatch in profit or loss on the basis of facts and circumstances that exist at the date of initial application. This is consistent with the other transition requirements in IFRS 9 related to the fair value option. Moreover, the IASB noted that the conclusion will most likely be the same regardless of whether it is made on the basis of facts and circumstances that existed at initial recognition of the liability or at the date of initial application.

(c) Derivative liabilities that were previously accounted for at cost are measured at fair value at the date of initial application. Consistently with the requirements for financial assets, an entity will not have the necessary information to determine fair value retrospectively without using hindsight.

(d) An entity is not required to restate prior periods if the requirements are adopted for reporting periods beginning before 1 January 2012. The IASB decided that it would be inappropriate and confusing to require an entity to restate prior periods for some of the requirements in IFRS 9 but not others. However, the IASB decided that if the entity elects to restate prior periods to reflect the requirements added to IFRS 9 in October 2010, it must also restate prior periods to reflect the other requirements in IFRS 9. That conclusion is consistent with the IASB's decision that if an entity elects to adopt the requirements early, it must at the same time adopt early all of the requirements in IFRS 9 that it does not already apply. (Paragraphs BC7.34A–BC7.34M and BC7.82–BC7.84 describe the IASB's subsequent decision on restating comparative information.)

Transitional insurance issues[49]

BC7.30 The IASB noted that insurers may face particular problems if they apply IFRS 9 before they apply the new Standard on insurance contracts (the new IFRS 4). To avoid accounting mismatches in profit or loss, many insurers classify many of their financial assets as available-for-sale. If those insurers apply IFRS 9 before the new IFRS 4, they might decide to classify many of their financial

---

49 IFRS 17 *Insurance Contracts*, issued in May 2017, replaced IFRS 4 *Insurance Contracts*.

assets at amortised cost (assuming they meet the relevant conditions in IFRS 9). When those insurers later apply the new IFRS 4, they may wish to reclassify those assets from amortised cost to fair value through profit or loss, but that may not generally be possible in accordance with IFRS 9. Thus, those insurers might have either to classify those assets at fair value through profit or loss during the intervening period or to continue to classify them at amortised cost when they apply the new IFRS 4. Either choice might lead to an accounting mismatch.

BC7.31   The IASB considered whether it could reduce such mismatches by maintaining the available-for-sale category for insurers until they can apply the new IFRS 4. However, if the IASB did so, it would have to create detailed and arbitrary descriptions of the entities and instruments to which that approach would apply. The IASB concluded that permitting the continuation of that category would not provide more useful information for users.

BC7.32   The IASB will consider in developing the new IFRS 4 whether to provide an option for insurers to reclassify some or all financial assets when they first apply the new IFRS 4. This would be similar to the option in paragraph 45 of IFRS 4 and paragraph D4 of IFRS 1. The IASB included such an option in IFRS 4 for reasons that may be equally valid for phase II.

Shadow accounting for participating contracts

BC7.33   Some insurers expressed concerns that an accounting mismatch will arise if the assets backing participating insurance liabilities include equity investments and the insurer elects to present gains and losses on those investments in other comprehensive income. That accounting mismatch would arise because paragraph 30 of IFRS 4 does not give explicit authority to apply 'shadow accounting' in such cases.

BC7.34   The IASB acknowledges that this accounting mismatch is undesirable. However, for the following reasons, the IASB did not amend paragraph 30 of IFRS 4:

(a)   This accounting mismatch will arise only if an insurer elects to present gains and losses on equity investments in other comprehensive income.

(b)   As described in paragraph BC5.23, in creating the option to present gains and losses on equity investments in other comprehensive income, the IASB's intention was to provide a presentation alternative for some equity investments in which presenting fair value gains and losses in profit or loss may not be indicative of the performance of the entity, particularly if the entity holds those equity instruments for non-contractual benefits, rather than primarily to generate increases in the value of the investment. The IASB did not intend to provide an alternative for investments in any other circumstances, including if an entity intends to hold an equity investment over a long time frame. In the IASB's view, if an insurer holds investments with the primary objective of realising a profit from increases in their value, for the benefit of either the insurer itself or its policyholders, the most transparent place to present those value changes is in profit or loss.

Disclosures on transition from IAS 39 to IFRS 9— November 2011

BC7.34A   When IFRS 9 (2009) and IFRS 9 (2010) were issued, they provided limited relief from restating comparative financial statements. Entities that adopted the Standard for reporting periods beginning before 1 January 2012 were not required to restate prior periods. At the time, the IASB's view was that waiving the requirement to restate comparative financial statements struck a balance between the conceptually preferable method of full retrospective application (as stated in IAS 8) and the practicability of adopting the new classification model within a short time frame.

BC7.34B   In August 2011 the IASB published the 2011 Mandatory Effective Date Exposure Draft. At the time, the IASB noted that these practicability considerations would be less relevant for entities that adopted outside a short time frame, and therefore proposed that restated comparative financial statements would continue to be required if an entity adopts IFRS 9 for reporting periods beginning on or after 1 January 2012.

BC7.34C   Some respondents to the 2011 Mandatory Effective Date Exposure Draft believed that comparative financial statements should be required to be restated for the following reasons:

(a)   The presentation of restated comparative financial statements is consistent with IAS 8.

(b)   A delay in the mandatory effective date of IFRS 9 would allow a sufficient time frame for entities to prepare restated comparative financial statements.

(c)   IAS 39 and IFRS 9 are sufficiently different from each other, so restatement will be necessary to provide meaningful information to users of financial statements.

BC7.34D   In contrast, those who did not believe that comparative financial statements should be required to be restated argued that:

(a)   Comparative relief was granted for IAS 32 and IAS 39 upon first-time adoption of IFRS for European reporting entities.

(b)   Comparability is impaired by the transition requirements, which are complex and inconsistent across various phases of the project, reducing the usefulness of the comparative information (for example, the classification and measurement phase requires retrospective application with some transition reliefs, whereas the hedge accounting phase requires prospective application).

(c)   Time pressures similar to those existing when IFRS 9 (2009) and IFRS 9 (2010) were initially issued will nonetheless exist when the last phase of the project to replace IAS 39 is issued.

BC7.34E   Respondents to the 2011 Mandatory Effective Date Exposure Draft also raised specific implementation issues that increased the cost of applying the classification and measurement requirements of IFRS 9 in periods prior to their date of initial application. These reasons were the interaction between the date of initial application and:

    (a)   the fact that IFRS 9 is not applied to items that have already been derecognised as of the date of initial application;

    (b)   the initial business model determination; and

    (c)   the elections for the fair value option and the fair value through other comprehensive income presentation alternative at the date of initial application.

BC7.34F   In providing views on their preferred transition approach for the project to replace IAS 39, investors consistently emphasised a need for comparable period-to-period information—that is, information that enabled them to understand the effect of the transition from IAS 39 to IFRS 9. Investors, irrespective of their preferred approach, noted that the mix of transition requirements between phases, and the modifications to retrospective application in the classification and measurement phase, would diminish the usefulness of comparative financial statements. Many also noted that the partial restatement of comparative financial statements could create either confusion or a misleading impression of period-to-period comparability.

BC7.34G   Some investor respondents, despite sharing the views in the preceding paragraph, favoured the presentation of comparative financial statements with full retrospective application of all project phases (ie including hedge accounting) as the preferred way of achieving comparability. Some of the respondents who favoured full retrospective application agreed that the modifications to retrospective application would diminish the usefulness of comparative financial statements but believed that the effect of the modifications would not be significant.

BC7.34H   Due to the variation in transition requirements of the phases in the project to replace IAS 39, other investors did not favour the presentation of restated comparative financial statements. Their primary concern was having information that enabled them to understand the effect of the transition from IAS 39 to IFRS 9. They did not believe that restating comparative financial statements on the basis of the transition requirements across the phases of IFRS 9 would necessarily provide that information.

BC7.34I   In addition to feedback on their preferred approach to understanding the effect of the transition to IFRS 9, investors also provided information about what they focus on when analysing financial instruments in financial statements. They noted that the statement of profit or loss and other comprehensive income (and restatement of it in comparative periods) is less important to their analysis than the statement of financial position, aside from situations where it allows for a link to the statement of financial position (for example net interest income). Similarly, where restatement means primarily the presentation of historical fair value changes, comparative information is less useful as extrapolation is not possible in the same way as it is for amortised cost information.

BC7.34J   Investors also provided feedback on those disclosures that would be useful in understanding the transition from IAS 39 to IFRS 9. They cited examples that they found useful on the transition from other GAAPs to IFRS in Europe in 2005. It was also noted that disclosures similar to those required by IFRS 7 for transfers of financial assets between classification categories would be useful —ie disclosures about reclassifications are also useful when the reclassifications result from applying a new accounting standard.

BC7.34K   In the light of this feedback received, the IASB considered whether modified transition disclosures could provide the information necessary for investors to understand the effect of the transition from IAS 39 to IFRS 9, while reducing the burden on preparers that would result from the restatement of comparative financial statements. The IASB also considered whether this approach would address concerns about the diminished usefulness and period-to-period comparability of comparative financial statements due to the different transition requirements of the phases of the project to replace IAS 39. The IASB believes that modified disclosures can achieve these objectives and decided to require modified transition disclosures instead of the restatement of comparative financial statements.

BC7.34L   The IASB noted that much of the information requested by investors was already required by IAS 8 and IFRS 7 on transition from IAS 39 to IFRS 9. The IASB also noted that it was not modifying the requirements of IAS 8. The IASB, however, decided that the reclassification disclosures in IFRS 7 (as amended by IFRS 9 (2009)) should be required on transition from IAS 39 to IFRS 9, irrespective of whether they would normally be required due to a change in business model. The IASB also specified that the reclassification disclosures, and other disclosures required when initially applying IFRS 9, should allow reconciliations between the measurement categories in accordance with IAS 39 and IFRS 9 and individual line items in the financial statements or classes of financial instruments. This would provide useful information that would enable users to understand the transition from IAS 39 to IFRS 9.

BC7.34M   The IASB also considered whether the transition disclosures should be required if the entity presents restated comparative financial statements, or only if they are not provided. The IASB noted that the disclosures provide useful information to investors on transition from IAS 39 to IFRS 9, irrespective of whether comparative financial statements are restated. The IASB also believed that the burden of these comparative transition disclosures for preparers would not be unreasonable because it was based largely on existing disclosure requirements and should require disclosure of information available as a result of preparing for transition. Consequently, the IASB decided to require these disclosures even if restated comparative financial statements are provided. However, the IASB did not want to unduly burden those who were in the process of applying IFRS 9 early by requiring disclosures that the entity was not previously required to provide. Consequently, for entities that initially apply the classification and measurement requirements from 1 January 2012 until 31 December 2012, the

IASB decided to permit, but not require, the presentation of the additional disclosures. If an entity elects to provide these disclosures when initially applying IFRS 9 between 1 January 2012 and 31 December 2012, it would not be required to restate comparative periods. (Paragraphs BC7.63–BC7.68 describe the IASB's subsequent decisions on disclosures at transition to IFRS 9.)

Transition related to the requirements added to IFRS 9 in November 2013

Presentation of 'own credit' gains and losses on financial liabilities

BC7.35   After requirements were added to IFRS 9 in October 2010 to address the effects of changes in own credit risk for liabilities designated under the fair value option, many interested parties requested that the IASB permit an entity to apply those requirements without also applying the other requirements in IFRS 9. That is because markets continued to be volatile and own credit gains or losses remained significant, which accentuated the concerns about the usefulness of presenting gains in profit or loss when an entity is experiencing deterioration in its own credit quality.

BC7.36   In the 2012 Limited Amendments Exposure Draft, the IASB proposed that six months after the completed version of IFRS 9 is issued, entities would no longer be permitted to newly early apply previous versions of IFRS 9. Consequently, entities wishing to apply the classification and measurement requirements after the completed version of IFRS 9 was issued would have to develop and implement the necessary systems changes for applying the new impairment requirements before they would be able to apply the classification and measurement requirements. In effect, that would have made the availability of the own credit requirements for early application dependent on the implementation of an expected credit loss impairment model.

BC7.37   Consequently, in order to make the own credit requirements in IFRS 9 available more quickly, the 2012 Limited Amendments Exposure Draft proposed that once the completed version of IFRS 9 was issued, an entity would be permitted to early apply the requirements for presenting in other comprehensive income the 'own credit' gains or losses on financial liabilities designated under the fair value option without early applying the other requirements of IFRS 9. However, at the time, the IASB noted that its decision to incorporate the possibility to apply early only the own credit requirements into the final version of IFRS 9 instead of IFRS 9 (2010) and later versions, was based on the expectation that there would not be a significant delay in the completion of IFRS 9. In other words, the IASB believed that the own credit requirements would be available for early application at roughly the same time under both approaches. However, the IASB noted that by exposing the proposals as part of the 2012 Limited Amendments Exposure Draft, it would be possible to change this approach if necessary.

BC7.38　Nearly all respondents to the 2012 Limited Amendments Exposure Draft supported the proposal that an entity would be permitted to early apply only the own credit requirements in IFRS 9 without applying any other requirements of IFRS 9 at the same time. However, most of these respondents also asked the IASB to make these requirements available for early application before the IFRS 9 project is completed and the final Standard is issued. Many of these respondents suggested that this could be accomplished by incorporating the own credit requirements into IAS 39, whereas others suggested incorporating the requirements into IFRS 9 (2010) and later versions.

BC7.39　During the redeliberations the IASB confirmed the proposal in the 2012 Limited Amendments Exposure Draft that the own credit requirements should be made available for early application without early applying the other requirements of IFRS 9. However, in order to respond to the feedback that the own credit requirements should be made available as soon as possible, the IASB decided to incorporate those requirements into IFRS 9 (2010) and later versions. The IASB also confirmed its previous decision not to incorporate the own credit requirements into IAS 39 because that Standard is being replaced by IFRS 9.

BC7.40　Although the topic was not within the scope of the 2012 Limited Amendments Exposure Draft, some respondents asked the IASB to reconsider the requirements in IFRS 9 that prohibit an entity from reclassifying (recycling) own credit gains or losses to profit or loss when the financial liability is derecognised. The IASB noted that it is currently discussing the objective of other comprehensive income, including whether amounts should be recycled to profit or loss (and if so, when), in its project on the *Conceptual Framework* and therefore the IASB noted that it would be inappropriate to reconsider those requirements in IFRS 9 before it completes that work.[50]

Transition related to the hedge accounting requirements

BC7.41　IAS 8 states that retrospective application results in the most useful information to users of the financial statements. IAS 8 also states that retrospective application is the preferred approach to transition, unless such retrospective application is impracticable. In such a scenario the entity adjusts the comparative information from the earliest date practicable. In conformity with these requirements, the classification and measurement chapters of IFRS 9 require retrospective application (with some relief in particular circumstances).

BC7.42　The proposals in the 2010 Hedge Accounting Exposure Draft were a significant change from the requirements in IAS 39. However, in accordance with the proposals, a hedge accounting relationship could be designated only prospectively. Consequently, retrospective application was not applicable. This reflects that retrospective application gives rise to similar concerns about using hindsight as retrospective designation of hedging relationships, which is prohibited.

50　In 2018 the IASB issued a revised *Conceptual Framework for Financial Reporting*.

BC7.43   In developing the transition requirements proposed in the 2010 Hedge Accounting Exposure Draft, the IASB considered two alternative approaches:

(a)   prospective application only for new hedging relationships; or

(b)   prospective application for all hedging relationships.

BC7.44   The IASB rejected the approach using prospective application of hedge accounting only for new hedging relationships. This approach would have required the current hedge accounting model in IAS 39 to be maintained until hedge accounting is discontinued for the hedging relationships established in accordance with IAS 39. Also, the proposed disclosures would be provided only for the hedging relationships accounted for in accordance with the proposed model. This approach entails the complexity of applying the two models simultaneously and also involves a set of disclosures that would be inconsistent and difficult to interpret. Because some hedging relationships are long-term, two hedge accounting models would co-exist for a potentially long period. This would make it difficult for users to compare the financial statements of different entities. Comparability would also be difficult when entities apply the old and the new model in the same financial statements, as well as for information provided over time.

BC7.45   Consequently, the IASB proposed prospective application of the proposed hedge accounting requirements for all hedging relationships, while ensuring that 'qualifying' hedging relationships could be moved from the existing model to the proposed model on the adoption date.

BC7.46   Almost all respondents agreed with prospective application of the new hedge accounting requirements to all hedging relationships because that would avoid the administrative burden of maintaining both the IAS 39 model and the new hedge accounting model and would also mitigate the risk of hindsight arising from retrospective designation of hedging relationships. Respondents also noted that prospective application is consistent with hedge accounting transition requirements that were used for previous amendments to IAS 39.

BC7.47   The IASB also received feedback that suggested a general provision, whereby hedging relationships designated under IAS 39 would be automatically 'grandfathered', ie entities could continue applying the requirements of IAS 39 to these hedging relationships. However, consistent with its proposal in the 2010 Hedge Accounting Exposure Draft (see paragraph BC7.44), the IASB decided not to allow the grandfathering of the application of IAS 39. Instead, the IASB retained its original decision that the new hedge accounting requirements are applied to hedging relationships that qualify for hedge accounting in accordance with IAS 39 and this Standard and that those are treated as continuing hedging relationships.

BC7.48   Some respondents supported varying forms of retrospective application. However, consistent with previous hedge accounting transition requirements in IAS 39 and the 2010 Hedge Accounting Exposure Draft, the IASB decided not to allow retrospective application in situations that would require retrospective designation because that would involve hindsight.

BC7.49   Some responses to the 2010 Hedge Accounting Exposure Draft suggested using retrospective application in two particular situations in which the outcomes under IAS 39 and the new hedge accounting model significantly differ but retrospective designation would not be necessary. The particular situations are when an entity under IAS 39 designated as the hedging instrument only changes in the intrinsic value (but not the time value) of an option or changes in the spot element (but not the forward element) of a forward contract. The IASB noted that in both circumstances applying the new requirements for accounting for the time value of options or the forward element of forward contracts would not involve hindsight from retrospective designation but instead use the designation that was previously made under IAS 39. The IASB also noted that in situations in which mismatches between the terms of the hedging instrument and the hedged item exist there might still be some risk of hindsight related to Level 3 fair value measurements when calculating the 'aligned' time value of an option and the 'aligned' forward element of a forward contract. However, the IASB concluded that such hindsight would be limited because hedge accounting was applied to these hedging relationships under IAS 39, meaning that the changes in the intrinsic value of an option or the changes in the value of the spot element of a forward contract had to have a high degree of offset with the changes in value of the hedged risks. Hence, the valuation inputs used for the calculation of the aligned values could not significantly differ from the valuation inputs for the overall fair value of the hedging instruments, which were known from previously applying IAS 39. The IASB also noted that retrospective application in these cases would significantly improve the usefulness of the information for the reasons that underpinned the IASB's decisions on accounting for the time value of options and the forward element of forward contracts (see paragraphs BC6.386–BC6.426). Consequently, the IASB decided to provide for those two particular situations an exception to prospective application of the hedge accounting requirements of this Standard but only for those hedging relationships that existed at the beginning of the earliest comparative period or were designated thereafter. For the forward element of forward contracts retrospective application is permitted but not required because unlike the new treatment for time value of options the new treatment for the forward element of forward contracts is an election. However, in order to address the risk of using hindsight, the IASB decided that on transition this election is only available on an 'all-or-nothing' basis (ie not a hedge-by-hedge basis). IAS 39 did not allow excluding foreign currency basis spreads from the designation of a financial instrument as the hedging instrument. Consequently, the requirement for the time value of options and the forward element of forward contracts, that an entity excluded the part of the financial instrument that represents costs of hedging from the designation as the hedging instrument under IAS 39, does not apply to foreign currency basis spreads. The restriction that retrospective application is available only on an 'all-or-nothing' basis does not apply to foreign currency basis spreads because of the variety of hedging instruments that involve those spreads.

BC7.50   Some respondents asked the IASB to consider allowing discontinuing at the date of initial application of the new hedge accounting requirements hedging relationships designated under IAS 39 and then designating new hedging relationships in a way that is better aligned with the new hedge accounting requirements.

BC7.51   The IASB noted that an entity could revoke designations of hedging relationships without any restriction until the last day of applying IAS 39 in accordance with the requirements in that Standard. Hence, the IASB considered that any specific transition requirements to address this request were unnecessary. However, in order to address some concerns over potential practical transition issues in the context of prospective application, the IASB decided:

(a)   to allow an entity to consider the moment it initially applies the new hedge accounting requirements and the moment it ceases to apply the hedge accounting requirements of IAS 39 as the same point in time. The IASB noted that this would avoid any time lag between starting the use of the new hedge accounting model and discontinuing the old hedge accounting model (because the end of the last business day of the previous reporting period often does not coincide with the beginning of the first business day of the next reporting period), which otherwise might involve significant changes in fair values between those points in time and as a result could cause difficulties in applying hedge accounting under the new hedge accounting model for hedging relationships that would otherwise qualify.

(b)   to require that an entity uses the hedge ratio in accordance with IAS 39 as the starting point for rebalancing the hedge ratio of a continuing hedging relationship (if applicable) and to recognise any related gain or loss in profit or loss. The IASB considered that any change to the hedge ratio that might be required on transition so that a hedging relationship designated under IAS 39 continues to qualify for hedge accounting should not result in an entity having to discontinue that hedging relationship on transition and then newly designating it. The IASB decided to require the recognition of any gain or loss on rebalancing in profit or loss in a broadly similar manner for ongoing hedge accounting under the new model to address any concerns that hedge ineffectiveness might otherwise be recognised as a direct adjustment to retained earnings on transition. The accounting is broadly similar to that for ongoing hedge accounting under the new model in that the hedge ineffectiveness in the context of rebalancing is recognised in profit or loss. However, in contrast to ongoing hedge accounting under the new model, rebalancing on transition applies because a different hedge ratio has already been used for risk management purposes (but did not coincide with the designation of the hedging relationship under IAS 39). In other words, rebalancing does not reflect a concurrent adjustment for risk management purposes but results in aligning the hedge ratio for accounting purposes with a hedge ratio that was already in place for risk management purposes.

BC7.52 The IASB decided not to change the requirements of IFRS 1 for hedge accounting. The IASB noted that a first-time adopter would need to look at the entire population of possible hedging relationships and assess which ones would meet the qualifying criteria of the new hedge accounting model. To the extent that an entity wants to apply hedge accounting, those hedging relationships should be documented on or before the transition date. This is consistent with the transition requirements for existing users of IFRS and the existing transition requirements of IFRS 1, which state that an entity shall discontinue hedge accounting if it had designated a hedging relationship but that hedging relationship does not meet the qualifying criteria in IAS 39.

Transition related to the requirements added to IFRS 9 in July 2014

Transition related to the limited amendments to the requirements for classifying and measuring financial assets

Assessment of an asset's contractual cash flow characteristics

BC7.53 In accordance with the existing transition provisions in IFRS 9, when IFRS 9 is initially applied, the assessment of an asset's contractual cash flow characteristics is based on the facts and circumstances that existed at the initial recognition of the financial asset, and the resulting classification is applied retrospectively.

BC7.54 The 2012 Limited Amendments Exposure Draft introduced a notion of a modified economic relationship between principal and the consideration for time value of money and credit risk. In that Exposure Draft, the IASB noted that assessing the contractual cash flow characteristics in accordance with the requirements issued in IFRS 9 (2009) requires judgement, but acknowledged that the proposed clarification introduces a greater degree of judgement and presents a greater risk that hindsight will be necessary to make the assessment. Accordingly, the IASB proposed specific transition requirements for situations in which it is impracticable (for example, because of the risk of using hindsight) to assess a modified economic relationship on the basis of the facts and circumstances that existed at initial recognition of the financial asset.

BC7.55 Specifically, the IASB proposed that in cases in which it is impracticable for an entity to apply the assessment of an asset's contractual cash flow characteristics based on the new requirements, an entity would be required to make that assessment without taking into account the specific requirements related to the modified economic relationship. In other words, the IASB proposed that, in those cases, the entity would apply the assessment of the asset's contractual cash flows characteristics as that assessment was set out in the requirements issued in IFRS 9 (2009); ie without the notion of a modified economic relationship.

BC7.56　During its redeliberations of the 2012 Limited Amendments Exposure Draft, the IASB confirmed the notion of a modified time value of money element in the assessment of an asset's contractual cash flows and therefore also confirmed the transition provision described in paragraph BC7.55. The IASB also noted that a similar transition provision is needed for the exception for particular prepayment features described in paragraph B4.1.12 of IFRS 9. That is because an entity will need to determine whether a prepayable financial asset meets the conditions set out in that paragraph on the basis of the facts and circumstances that existed at the initial recognition of the financial asset, including whether the fair value of the prepayment feature was insignificant. The IASB noted that, in some cases, it may be impracticable for an entity to determine whether the fair value of the prepayment feature was insignificant at the date of initial recognition. For example, this determination might be impracticable if the entity did not account for that embedded prepayment feature separately at fair value through profit or loss as an embedded derivative under IAS 39. Consequently, the IASB decided that in cases in which it is impracticable for an entity to assess whether the fair value of a prepayment feature was insignificant based on the facts and circumstances that existed at the initial recognition of the asset, the entity must assess the contractual cash flow characteristics of the financial asset without taking into account the specific exception for prepayment features.

Fair value option

BC7.57　In accordance with paragraph 7.2.9–7.2.10 of IFRS 9, when an entity initially applies the classification and measurement requirements for financial assets, it is:

(a)　permitted to reconsider its fair value option elections for both financial assets and financial liabilities; that is, to elect to apply the fair value option even if an accounting mismatch already existed before the date of initial application and/or revoke the fair value option even if an accounting mismatch continues to exist; and

(b)　required to revoke its fair value option elections for both financial assets and financial liabilities if an accounting mismatch no longer exists at the date of initial application.

BC7.58　In accordance with paragraph 7.2.27 of IFRS 9, the transition provisions described in paragraph BC7.57 are available only when the entity initially applies the classification and measurement requirements for financial assets; ie an entity applies those provisions only once. The relevant rationale is set out in paragraphs BC7.19 and BC7.27–BC7.28.

BC7.59　In the deliberations that led to the publication of the 2012 Limited Amendments Exposure Draft, the IASB noted that if an entity had already applied an earlier version of IFRS 9 (ie IFRS 9 (2009), IFRS 9 (2010) or IFRS 9 (2013)), it would have already applied the transition provisions described in paragraph BC7.57. However, the application of the proposals in the 2012 Limited Amendments Exposure Draft could cause some financial assets to be measured differently as compared to a previous version of IFRS 9 and, as a result, new accounting mismatches could arise.

BC7.60 Accordingly, the IASB proposed that an entity that has already applied a previous version of IFRS 9 should, when it applies the proposals in the 2012 Limited Amendments Exposure Draft, be:

(a) permitted to apply the fair value option to new accounting mismatches created by the initial application of the proposed amendments to the classification and measurement requirements; and

(b) required to revoke previous fair value option elections if an accounting mismatch no longer exists as a result of the initial application of the proposed amendments to the classification and measurement requirements.

BC7.61 In other words, an entity would be permitted or required to reconsider its designations under the fair value option only to the extent that previous accounting mismatches no longer exist, or new accounting mismatches are created, as a result of applying the limited amendments to the classification and measurement requirements for financial assets.

BC7.62 During its redeliberations of the 2012 Limited Amendments Exposure Draft, the IASB confirmed the transition provision described above.

Transition disclosures

BC7.63 The IASB decided to clarify the disclosure requirements in IFRS 7 that are relevant to an entity's transition to IFRS 9. That is, the IASB clarified that on transition to IFRS 9, an entity is required to comply with the quantitative disclosures set out in IFRS 7 instead of applying the general quantitative disclosure requirements in other Standards.

BC7.64 Specifically, the IASB amended paragraph 42Q of IFRS 7 to state that an entity need not disclose the line item amounts that would have been reported:

(a) in prior reporting periods in accordance with IFRS 9; or

(b) in the current reporting period in accordance with IAS 39.

BC7.65 The IASB noted that requiring disclosure of the line item amounts that would have been reported in prior reporting periods in accordance with IFRS 9 would contradict paragraph 7.2.15 of IFRS 9, which states that an entity need not restate prior periods.

BC7.66 The IASB considered three primary factors in evaluating whether an entity should be required to disclose line item amounts in the current reporting period in accordance with IAS 39:

(a) the usefulness of the disclosures;

(b) the cost of providing such disclosures; and

(c) whether the existing transition disclosure requirements are sufficient and enable users of financial statements to assess the effect of transition to IFRS 9.

BC7.67 In assessing the usefulness of this disclosure, the IASB considered the interaction at transition to IFRS 9 between the requirements for classification and measurement and hedge accounting. The IASB observed that the concept of hedge accounting does not lend itself to making assumptions about what hedge accounting (under IAS 39) might have been. That is because hedge accounting is an elective accounting treatment that allows the resolution of accounting mismatches. In order to apply hedge accounting, an entity must make that election and then, if the hedging relationship meets the qualifying criteria, the entity prospectively applies hedge accounting. In accordance with IAS 39, an entity can also discontinue hedge accounting at any time and for any reason (or for no reason). This means that any IAS 39-based hedge accounting information 'as if applied in the current period' would be based on highly speculative assumptions. Consequently, the IASB noted that it would be inappropriate to disclose hedge accounting in accordance with IAS 39 in the period during which hedge accounting is first applied in accordance with IFRS 9. Given that conclusion, providing line-item disclosures for classification and measurement in the current period in accordance with IAS 39 would be incomplete, because it would not fully or accurately reflect IFRS 9 relative to IAS 39. The IASB also noted that requiring disclosure of IAS 39 amounts in the current period would require entities to incur the costs of running parallel systems, which could be onerous.

BC7.68 In addition, the IASB noted that IFRS 7 already includes modified transition disclosure requirements that focus on changes in the statement of financial position at the date of initial application of IFRS 9 and also focus on the effect on the key financial statement line items for the current period. The IASB believes that these disclosures will allow users of financial statements to assess the effect of transition to IFRS 9. The IASB noted that users of financial statements expressed support for these disclosures because they provide the necessary information to explain the transition.

Transition for first-time adopters of IFRS

BC7.69 The 2012 Limited Amendments Exposure Draft did not propose amendments to IFRS 1. However it specifically requested feedback on transition to IFRS 9 by first-time adopters of IFRS, including whether there are any unique considerations. The IASB stated that the transition to IFRS 9 by first-time adopters would be considered in the redeliberations of the 2012 Limited Amendments Exposure Draft to ensure that they are given adequate lead time to apply IFRS 9 and are not at a disadvantage in comparison to existing IFRS preparers.

BC7.70 Most respondents who provided feedback on this question stated that they were not aware of any unique considerations for first-time adopters. Some specifically stated that the IASB should provide relief to first-time adopters from presenting comparative information that complies with IFRS 9. Generally, this request was made in order to give first-time adopters adequate lead time to prepare for the transition to IFRS 9 and ensure that they are not at a disadvantage compared to existing IFRS preparers.

BC7.71 Consequently, to ensure that first-time adopters are given adequate lead time to apply IFRS 9 and are not at a disadvantage in comparison to existing IFRS preparers, the IASB decided the following:

(a) first-time adopters are not required to present comparative information that complies with the completed version of IFRS 9 (issued in 2014) if the beginning of their first IFRS reporting period is earlier than the mandatory effective date of IFRS 9 plus one year (ie 1 January 2019). This ensures that a first-time adopter is not required to start applying IFRS 9 before an existing IFRS preparer.

(b) if a first-time adopter chooses to present comparative information that does not comply with the completed version of IFRS 9 (issued in 2014), it will be required to provide the same disclosures that were required by IFRS 1 for a first-time adopter that transitioned to IFRS 9 (2009) or IFRS 9 (2010) and that chose not to present comparative information that complied with those new Standards. Those disclosures are set out in paragraph E2 of IFRS 1.

Impairment

BC7.72 The 2013 Impairment Exposure Draft proposed that the expected credit loss requirements should be applied retrospectively on initial application, except when it is not possible to determine, without undue cost and effort, whether the credit risk of a financial instrument has increased significantly since initial recognition. If determining the credit risk on a financial instrument when the instrument was initially recognised would require undue cost or effort, the measurement of the loss allowance should always be determined only on the basis of whether the credit risk is low at the reporting date. However, this requirement did not apply to financial instruments whose past due status is used to assess changes in credit risk, because it is assumed that the information will be available to make the assessment.

BC7.73 In addition, the 2013 Impairment Exposure Draft did not require comparative information to be restated. Entities were, however, permitted to provide restated comparative information if it is possible to do so without the use of hindsight.

BC7.74 IAS 8 provides the principles and framework for changes in accounting policies in the absence of specific transition provisions in a Standard. IAS 8 states that, as a general rule, retrospective application results in the most useful information to users of financial statements, and that it is the preferred approach unless it is impracticable to calculate the period-specific effect or the cumulative effect of the change. The definition of impracticability is relevant to situations in which it is not possible to objectively distinguish the historical information that is relevant for estimating expected credit losses from the information that would not have been available at that earlier date (IAS 8 refers to this situation as 'hindsight').

BC7.75 During development of the proposals in the 2013 Impairment Exposure Draft the IASB identified two main issues about retrospective application for the proposed impairment model:

(a)   availability of initial credit risk data—the model relies on entities assessing whether there has been a significant increase in credit risk since the initial recognition of a financial instrument to decide whether they should establish a loss allowance balance at an amount equal to lifetime expected credit losses. Entities told the IASB that they typically do not currently retain information about initial credit risk, so making this assessment on transition is likely to be difficult.

(b)   risk of hindsight—entities have not previously been required to recognise or disclose expected credit losses for accounting purposes. Accordingly, there was a risk that hindsight would be needed to recognise and measure the amount of expected credit losses in prior periods.

Alternatives previously considered and rejected

BC7.76   During the deliberations that resulted in the publication of the 2013 Impairment Exposure Draft, the IASB considered and rejected the following alternatives:

(a)   grandfathering existing requirements—one approach to transition that would have addressed both of the issues set out in paragraph BC7.75 would have been for the IASB to 'grandfather' the existing impairment requirements for existing financial instruments at the date of initial application. That is, entities would continue to apply the IAS 39 impairment requirements to all financial instruments that exist on transition to the proposed requirements. This would have been a form of prospective application of the proposed requirements. This grandfathering approach would have removed the need to measure expected credit losses for periods prior to the application of the proposed requirements, and would also have eliminated the problem of applying the proposed requirements to financial instruments for which information about the credit risk at initial recognition is not available or would have been very burdensome to obtain on transition to the proposed requirements. It would also have allowed the IASB to specify an earlier mandatory effective date than would otherwise be possible if full retrospective application was required (ie retrospective application that also includes a restatement of comparative periods). Although those who are concerned about the potentially significant effect on equity when making the transition to the new model (which may have regulatory consequences for some) may view this approach positively, it would delay the improvements to accounting for expected credit losses and would reduce comparability. In addition, entities would need to prepare information in accordance with both the IAS 39 impairment model and the new impairment model until they derecognised all grandfathered financial instruments, which would be burdensome, at least for some entities. For these reasons, the IASB rejected the grandfathering approach to transition.

(b)   resetting the credit risk at initial recognition of the financial instrument so that it reflects the credit risk at the date that the proposed model is initially applied—this would have been the least burdensome of the three alternatives to apply, because entities would ignore credit history for all financial instruments. An entity would consider deteriorations or improvements in credit risk from the date of initial application of the proposed model, instead of relative to the credit risk at initial recognition. The IASB rejected this approach because it would have ignored changes in credit risk that had occurred since initial recognition and would not have faithfully represented expected credit losses.

(c)   recognising a loss allowance at an amount equal to lifetime expected credit losses on transition until derecognition for financial instruments for which an entity does not use initial credit risk information—this alternative would have been relatively simple to apply because there would have been no requirement for an entity to analyse changes in credit risk either at transition or over the life of the relevant instruments. However, this alternative is inconsistent with the objective of the overall model, which is designed to reflect changes in credit risk. This approach would also have resulted in an entity recognising lifetime expected credit losses for financial instruments whose credit risk is actually better than that on initial recognition.

Availability of initial credit risk data

BC7.77   The 2013 Impairment Exposure Draft proposed that an entity should use available information about credit risk at initial recognition for existing financial instruments when it applies the impairment requirements for the first time, unless obtaining such information requires undue cost or effort. For financial instruments for which an entity has not used information about the initial credit risk on transition, an entity would recognise lifetime expected credit losses, except if the credit risk was low, at each reporting date until the financial instrument was derecognised.

BC7.78   The IASB considered that such an approach should be relatively simple to apply, because it would not require any assessment of changes in credit risk for these financial instruments relative to the initial credit risk. In addition, it corresponds with credit risk management systems that assess credit risk as at the reporting date. However, the IASB decided that this relief would not be appropriate when an entity uses the past due status of payments to apply the model, because in these cases an entity would have the necessary information to decide whether a financial instrument has deteriorated since initial recognition.

BC7.79   The IASB acknowledged that if an entity uses an approach that is based solely on credit risk at the reporting date, then, when the entity is deciding the amount of expected credit losses to recognise, that approach will not allow the entity to consider the increases in credit risk that have occurred since initial recognition. Thus, entities would be required to recognise lifetime expected credit losses for a financial instrument for which the credit risk is not considered low, even if the instrument had been priced to reflect that risk and there has not been a significant increase in credit risk since initial recognition. It would also have a more negative impact for entities whose business model focuses on originating or purchasing financial instruments with credit risk that is not low (for example, their credit risk is not equivalent to investment grade). Requiring an assessment of the credit risk alone might encourage the use of information about the initial credit risk on transition to the proposed requirements, which will enhance comparability and the quality of the information provided. However, under some circumstances, such an approach may discourage the use of information about initial credit risk, particularly if an entity is able to absorb lifetime expected credit losses on those financial instruments on transition to the proposed requirements. While acknowledging the inconsistency with the overall model, the IASB decided that such an approach was the best way to balance the provision of useful information with the associated cost of providing it.

BC7.80 The majority of respondents to the 2013 Impairment Exposure Draft supported the proposed transition requirements. Respondents noted that these proposals achieve a balance between the cost to implement the proposals and presenting relevant information. However, respondents asked the IASB to consider practical ways in which to assess whether, at the date of initial application, there have been significant increases in credit risk since initial recognition. Respondents noted that the proposed requirements could effectively result in the loss allowance for all financial instruments that are not considered to have low credit risk to be measured at lifetime expected credit losses if the entity could not obtain information about the credit risk at initial recognition. They argued that if financial instruments were inappropriately measured at lifetime expected credit losses, it might result in large releases of loss allowance balances when the instruments are derecognised.

BC7.81 The IASB considered that the intention was not to penalise entities that could not obtain information about the initial credit risk without undue cost or effort. It also noted that an entity need not have specific information about the initial credit risk of a financial instrument and clarified this in IFRS 9. For example, the IASB noted that if an entity is able to assess the change in credit risk of a financial instrument on the basis of a portfolio analysis, such an approach could similarly be applied on transition to assess the change in credit risk since initial recognition.

Restatement of comparative periods, including the use of hindsight

BC7.82 At the date of initial application of the requirements in IFRS 9, the transition requirements permit, but do not require, the restatement of comparative periods if the necessary information is available without the use of hindsight (see paragraphs BC7.34A–BC7.34M). This was also proposed in the 2013 Impairment Exposure Draft to address the risk of hindsight being used to decide whether lifetime expected credit losses would be required to be recognised in prior periods and, more generally, in measuring expected credit losses in prior periods. This would prevent entities 'looking back' to make those determinations. Instead, at the beginning of the period in which the proposed model were to be initially applied, an entity would adjust the loss allowance to be in accordance with the proposed model at that date, with an adjustment to an opening component of equity. An entity would still apply the proposed model on a (modified) retrospective basis, because the loss allowance balances would be determined on the basis of information about initial credit risk, subject to the transition relief. As a result, an entity would still assess the changes in credit risk since the initial recognition of financial instruments to decide whether, on transition to the new requirements, it should measure the loss allowance at an amount equal to lifetime or 12-month expected credit losses. A prohibition on restating comparatives would mean that an entity could only reflect the loss allowance balances that result from applying the new model in the financial statements from the beginning of the current period in which the entity applies the proposals for the first time.

BC7.83 The IASB noted that another way to address the risk of hindsight might be to allow a long lead time between issuing the new requirements and the mandatory effective date, so that an entity could calculate expected credit losses contemporaneously for comparative periods to provide restated comparative information. However, in considering a longer lead time, the IASB noted the urgency of this project. Establishing a lead time that would allow an entity to apply the proposed model on a retrospective basis, including the provision of restated comparative information, in a way that addresses the risk of hindsight would result in a significant delay between issuing the final requirements and their mandatory application.

BC7.84 The vast majority of respondents agreed with the transition proposals not to require, but to allow, the restatement of comparative information if the necessary information is available without the use of hindsight. Consequently, the IASB confirmed those proposals during redeliberations.

Transition for first-time adopters of IFRS

BC7.85 The 2013 Impairment Exposure Draft did not propose amendments to IFRS 1. However it specifically requested feedback on transition to IFRS 9 by first-time adopters of IFRS, including whether there are any unique considerations. In the redeliberations on the proposals in the 2013 Impairment Exposure Draft, the IASB confirmed that the same transition relief available on the initial application of the requirements in Section 5.5 of IFRS 9 should be available to first-time adopters of IFRS (see also paragraphs BC7.72–BC7.75).

Amendments for *Interest Rate Benchmark Reform—Phase 2* (August 2020)

Mandatory application

BC7.86 The IASB decided to require application of the Phase 2 amendments. The IASB considered that allowing voluntary application of these amendments could lead to selective application to achieve specific accounting results. The IASB also noted that the amendments are, to a large extent, interlinked and need to be applied consistently. Voluntary application, even if only possible by area or type of financial instruments, would reduce comparability of information provided in the financial statements between entities. The IASB also does not expect that mandatory application of these amendments would result in significant additional costs for preparers and other affected parties because these amendments are designed to ease the operational burden on preparers, while providing useful information to users of financial statements, and would not require significantly more effort by preparers in addition to what is already required to implement the changes required by the reform.

End of application

BC7.87　The IASB did not add specific end of application requirements for the Phase 2 amendments because the application of these amendments is associated with the point at which changes to financial instruments or hedging relationships occur as a result of the reform. Therefore, by design, the application of these amendments has a natural end.

BC7.88　The IASB noted that, in a simple scenario, the Phase 2 amendments will be applied only once to each financial instrument or element of a hedging relationship. However, the IASB acknowledged that because of differences in the approach to the reform applied in different jurisdictions, and differences in timing, implementing the reform could require more than one change to the basis for determining the contractual cash flows of a financial asset or a financial liability. This could be the case, for example, when a central authority, as the administrator of an interest rate benchmark, undertakes a multi-step process to replace an interest rate benchmark with an alternative benchmark rate. As each change to the basis for determining the contractual cash flows of the instrument is made as required by the reform, an entity would be required to apply the Phase 2 amendments to account for that change.

BC7.89　As noted in paragraph 6.9.3 of IFRS 9, the IASB considered that an entity may be required to amend the formal designation of its hedging relationships at different times, or to amend the formal designation of a hedging relationship more than once. For example, an entity may first make changes required by the reform to a derivative designated as a hedging instrument, while only making changes required by the reform to the financial instrument designated as the hedged item later. In applying the amendments, the entity would be required to amend the hedge documentation to amend the description of the hedging instrument. The hedge documentation of the hedging relationship would then have to be amended again to change the description of the hedged item and/or hedged risk as required in paragraph 6.9.1 of IFRS 9.

BC7.90　The amendment for hedges of risk components in paragraph 6.9.11 of IFRS 9 applies only at the date an entity first designates a particular alternative benchmark rate as a non-contractually specified risk component for the first time if an entity's ability to conclude that an alternative benchmark rate is separately identifiable is directly affected by the reform. Thus, an entity could not apply this amendment in other circumstances in which the entity is not able to conclude that an alternative benchmark rate is a separately identifiable risk component.

Effective date and transition

BC7.91 Acknowledging the urgency of the amendments, the IASB decided that entities must apply the Phase 2 amendments for annual periods beginning on or after 1 January 2021, with earlier application permitted.

BC7.92 The IASB decided that the amendments apply retrospectively in accordance with IAS 8 (except as discussed in paragraphs BC7.94–BC7.98) because prospective application would have resulted in entities applying the amendments only if the transition to alternative benchmark rates occurred after the effective date of the amendments.

BC7.93 The IASB acknowledged that there could be situations in which an entity amended a hedging relationship as specified in paragraph 6.9.1 of IFRS 9 in a period before the entity first applied the Phase 2 amendments; and in the absence of the Phase 2 amendments, IFRS 9 would require the entity to discontinue hedge accounting. The IASB noted that the reasons for the amendment in paragraph 6.9.1 of IFRS 9 (see paragraphs BC6.608–BC6.609), apply equally in such situations. The IASB therefore considered that discontinuation of hedge accounting solely because of amendments an entity made in hedge documentation to reflect appropriately the changes required by the reform, regardless of when those changes occurred, would not provide useful information to users of financial statements.

BC7.94 The IASB acknowledged that the reinstatement of discontinued hedging relationships is inconsistent with the IASB's previous decisions about hedge accounting in IFRS 9. This is because hedge accounting is applied prospectively and applying it retrospectively to discontinued hedging relationships usually requires the use of hindsight. However, the IASB considered that in the specific circumstances of the reform, an entity would typically be able to reinstate a discontinued hedging relationship without the use of hindsight. The IASB noted that this reinstatement of discontinued hedging relationships would apply to a very targeted population for a short period – that is, for hedging relationships which would not have been discontinued if the Phase 2 amendments relating to hedge accounting had been applied at the point of discontinuation. The IASB therefore proposed in the 2020 Exposure Draft that an entity would be required to reinstate hedging relationships that were discontinued solely due to changes required by the reform before an entity first applies the proposed amendments.

BC7.95 Respondents to the 2020 Exposure Draft generally supported and welcomed the transition proposals but asked the IASB to reconsider a specific aspect of the proposal that would require entities to reinstate particular discontinued hedging relationships. Specifically, these respondents highlighted circumstances in which reinstating discontinued hedging relationships would be challenging or have limited benefit – for example, when:

(a) the hedging instruments or the hedged items in the discontinued hedging relationships have been subsequently designated into new hedging relationships;

(b) the hedging instruments in the discontinued hedging relationships no longer exist at the date of initial application of the amendments—eg they have been terminated or sold; or

(c) the hedging instruments in the discontinued hedging relationships are now being managed within a trading mandate with other trading positions and reported as trading instruments.

BC7.96   The IASB noted that the transition requirements as proposed in the 2020 Exposure Draft to apply the amendments retrospectively in accordance with IAS 8—including the requirement to reinstate particular discontinued hedging relationships—would be subject to impracticability applying IAS 8. However, the IASB agreed with respondents' concerns that there could be other circumstances in which it would not be impracticable to reinstate the hedging relationship, but such reinstatement would be challenging or would have limited benefit. For example, if the hedging instrument or hedged item has been designated in a new hedging relationship, it appears inappropriate to require entities to reinstate the 'old' (original) hedging relationship and discontinue or unwind the 'new' (valid) hedging relationship. Consequently, the IASB added paragraph 7.2.44(b) to IFRS 9 to address these concerns.

BC7.97   In addition, the IASB concluded that if an entity reinstates a discontinued hedging relationship applying paragraph 7.2.44 of IFRS 9, for the purpose of applying paragraphs 6.9.11–6.9.12 of IFRS 9, the 24-month period for the alternative benchmark rate designated as a non-contractually specified risk component begins from the date of initial application of the Phase 2 amendments (ie it does not begin from the date the entity designated the alternative benchmark rate as a non-contractually specified risk component for the first time in the original hedging relationship).

BC7.98   Consistent with the transition requirements for Phase 1, the IASB decided that an entity is not required to restate comparative information. However, an entity may choose to restate prior periods if, and only if, it is possible without the use of hindsight.

BC7.99   The IASB decided that it did not need to amend IFRS 1. Entities adopting IFRS Standards for the first time as required by IFRS 1 would apply IFRS Standards, including the Phase 2 amendments, and the transition requirements in IFRS 1 as applicable.

Analysis of the effects of IFRS 9

Introduction

BCE.1   Before the IASB issues new requirements, or makes amendments to existing Standards, it considers the costs and benefits of the new pronouncements. This includes assessing the effects on the costs for both preparers and users of financial statements. The IASB also considers the comparative advantage that preparers have in developing information that would otherwise cost users of financial statements to develop. One of the main objectives of developing a single set of high quality global accounting Standards is to improve the allocation of capital. The IASB therefore takes into account the benefits of economic decision-making resulting from improved financial reporting. The IASB gains insight on the likely effects of the proposals for new or revised Standards through its formal exposure of proposals and through its analysis and consultations with relevant parties through outreach activities.

BCE.2   The IASB conducted extensive outreach activities with interested parties for each phase of IFRS 9. This included extensive discussions with regulators, users of financial statements, preparers and audit firms worldwide. In addition, as part of the Impairment project, the IASB formed the Expert Advisory Panel (EAP) to address some of the operational challenges of an expected cash flow approach and conducted fieldwork to assess the proposals of the 2013 Exposure Draft *Financial Instruments: Expected Credit Losses* (the '2013 Impairment Exposure Draft'). This Effects Analysis is based on the feedback received through this process.

BCE.3   The evaluation of costs and benefits are necessarily qualitative, instead of quantitative. This is because quantifying costs and, particularly, benefits, is inherently difficult. Although other standard-setters undertake similar types of analyses, there is a lack of sufficiently well-established and reliable techniques for quantifying this analysis. Consequently, the IASB sees this Effects Analysis as being part of an evolving process. In addition, the assessment undertaken is that of the likely effects of the new requirements, because the actual effects will not be known until after the new requirements have been applied. These are subsequently analysed through the Post-implementation Review process.

BCE.4   The IASB is committed to assessing and sharing knowledge about the likely costs of implementing proposed new requirements and the likely associated ongoing costs and benefits of each new Standard – these costs and benefits are collectively referred to as 'effects'.

BCE.5   In evaluating the likely effects of the proposals, the IASB has considered how:

(a)   activities would be reported in the financial statements of those applying IFRS;

(b)   comparability of financial information would be improved both between different reporting periods for the same entity and between different entities in a particular reporting period;

(c)   more useful financial reporting would result in better economic decision-making;

(d)   better economic decision-making as a result of improved financial reporting could be achieved;

(e)   the compliance costs for preparers would likely be affected; and

(f)   the costs of analysis for users of financial statements would likely be affected.

BCE.6   Paragraphs BCE.7–BCE.238 describe the IASB's analysis of the likely effects that will result from IFRS 9. It reflects the three phases of IFRS 9, with the analysis of the classification and measurement requirements described in paragraphs BCE.7–BCE.89, the impairment requirements described in paragraphs BCE.90–BCE.173 and the hedge accounting requirements described in paragraphs BCE.174–BCE.238.

Analysis of the effects: classification and measurement

Overview

BCE.7   Many users of financial statements and other interested parties have told the IASB that the requirements in IAS 39 are difficult to understand, apply and interpret. They have urged the IASB to develop a new Standard for the financial reporting for financial instruments that is principle-based and less complex. The need to enhance the relevance and understandability of information about financial instruments was also raised by respondents to the Discussion Paper *Reducing Complexity in Reporting Financial Instruments* (published in 2008). That need became more urgent in the light of the global financial crisis, so the IASB decided to replace IAS 39 in its entirety as expeditiously as possible.

BCE.8   IFRS 9 is the IASB's response to the need to improve and simplify the financial reporting for financial instruments. The IASB believes that the new classification and measurement requirements address the issue that IAS 39 has many classification categories for financial assets, each with its own rules for determining which financial asset must, or can be, included and how impairment is identified and measured.

BCE.9   Overall, the IASB's assessment is that the classification and measurement requirements in IFRS 9 will bring significant and sustained improvements to the reporting of financial instruments because they:

   (a)   introduce a logical and clear rationale for the classification and measurement of financial assets. It is a principle-based approach, in contrast to the complex rules in IAS 39, which often result in financial assets being measured on the basis of free choice.

   (b)   eliminate the complex requirements for bifurcating hybrid financial assets because financial assets will be classified in their entirety.

   (c)   require reclassification between measurement categories when, and only when, the entity's business model for managing them changes. This eliminates the complex rules for reclassification in IAS 39 and ensures that users of financial statements are always provided with information that reflects how the cash flows on financial assets are expected to be realised.

   (d)   accommodate known business models with objectives to hold financial assets to collect contractual cash flows or that result in both collecting contractual cash flows and selling financial assets.

(e)   respond to the long-standing concerns about the volatility that occurs in profit or loss due to changes in own credit risk when an entity elects to measure non-derivative financial liabilities at fair value. But otherwise the existing accounting for financial liabilities has been retained because it has worked well in practice.

BCE.10   The classification and measurement requirements included in IFRS 9 change many aspects of IAS 39 and these changes will affect a variety of preparers. However, it is difficult to generalise the likely impact on these entities, because it depends on their individual circumstances. In particular, the overall change in the classification of financial assets will depend on the choices previously made by preparers in applying IAS 39, their business models for managing the financial assets and the contractual cash flow characteristics of their financial assets.

BCE.11   It was not the IASB's objective to increase or decrease the application of fair value measurement, instead the IASB wanted to ensure that financial assets are measured in a way that provides useful information to investors and other users of financial statements to predict likely future cash flows. Whether an entity will have more or fewer financial assets measured at fair value through profit or loss as a result of applying IFRS 9 will depend on the way in which the financial assets are being managed (ie the entity's business model) and the characteristics of the instrument's contractual cash flows. For example, a financial asset with contractual cash flows that are solely payments of principal and interest on the principal amount outstanding will be measured at amortised cost, fair value through other comprehensive income or fair value through profit or loss, depending on the entity's business model (ie amortised cost if the financial assets are held to collect the contractual cash flows or fair value through other comprehensive income if the financial assets are held within a business model whose objective is achieved by collecting contractual cash flows and selling the financial assets and otherwise at fair value through profit or loss).

BCE.12   The requirements for the classification of financial liabilities are largely unchanged from IAS 39. This reflects feedback received that the accounting for financial liabilities has worked well in practice, except for the issue of own credit. However, IFRS 9 addresses the own credit issue by requiring the changes in fair value attributable to changes in the liability's credit risk to be recognised in other comprehensive income for financial liabilities that an entity elects to measure at fair value.

BCE.13   The IASB expects that most costs for preparers will be incurred on transition. The ongoing costs will be mitigated primarily by the fact that:

(a)   the business model assessment for the classification of a financial asset is determined on an aggregate basis and is a matter of fact (ie consistent with the entity's actual business model rather being simply an accounting concept);

(b)   the contractual cash flow assessment for financial assets need not be analysed in all business models; and

(c) the requirements for the classification of financial liabilities are largely unchanged or should not create incremental costs (such as for the new own credit requirements given that entities are already required to disclose the gains or losses recognised for changes in own credit risk).

The IASB's assessment is that the significant improvements in terms of comparability and transparency will outweigh those costs.

How activities would be reported in the financial statements of those applying IFRS

BCE.14 The following analysis focuses on the key differences between the existing classification model in IAS 39 and the new classification and measurement model in IFRS 9 and how the new model will affect financial reporting.

Objective of the classification and measurement requirements of IFRS 9

BCE.15 The classification and measurement requirements are part of the IASB's response to a long recognised need to improve the accounting for financial instruments.

BCE.16 In view of the criticisms of IAS 39, the IASB introduced a single classification approach for all financial assets in IFRS 9 that is principle-based. Its objective is to faithfully represent, in the financial statements, how the cash flows on financial assets are expected to be realised.

BCE.17 The classification approach is based on the entity's business model and thereby focuses on the matter of fact instead of on management's intention or free choice as is often the case in IAS 39. Most interested parties have agreed that information is improved by a single classification approach as introduced by IFRS 9.

BCE.18 The requirements for the classification and measurement of financial liabilities are largely unchanged from IAS 39, except for the own credit requirements, which was a response to long-standing concerns about the volatility that occurs in profit or loss because of changes in an issuer's own credit risk.

Approach to classifying financial assets

BCE.19 IAS 39 requires financial assets to be classified into one of four categories, each having its own eligibility criteria and different measurement requirements. The eligibility criteria are a combination of the nature of the instrument, its manner of use and management choice.

BCE.20 The IASB believed that the best way to address the complexity arising from the different classification categories in IAS 39 was to replace them with a single classification approach based on a logical structure and clear rationale. IFRS 9 requires entities to classify financial assets on the basis of the entity's business model for managing the financial assets and the characteristics of the financial asset's contractual cash flows.

BCE.21   The business model is relevant to the classification because it determines whether an entity's future cash flows will arise from contractual amounts or by realising the fair value. The nature of the contractual cash flows is relevant to ensure that the cash flows on a financial asset can be properly and adequately reflected by amortised cost measurement, which is a simple technique for allocating interest over the life of a financial instrument. In IFRS 9 such simple cash flows are described as being 'solely payments of principal and interest'.

BCE.22   The requirements issued in IFRS 9 (2009) included only two categories for financial assets—amortised cost and fair value through profit or loss. Financial instruments were classified and measured at amortised cost only if:

(a)   they are held in a business model whose objective is to hold financial assets in order to collect contractual cash flows ('held to collect' business model); and

(b)   their contractual cash flow terms represented solely payments of principal and interest.

In accordance with the requirements issued in IFRS 9 (2009), all other financial assets were measured at fair value through profit or loss.

BCE.23   The completed version of IFRS 9, issued in 2014, introduces a fair value through other comprehensive income measurement category for debt instruments but retains the classification structure that always existed in IFRS 9. Accordingly, a financial asset shall be measured at fair value through other comprehensive income if:

(a)   it is held in a business model whose objective is achieved by both collecting contractual cash flows and selling financial instruments; and

(b)   its contractual cash flows represent solely payments of principal and interest.[51]

In this measurement category the statement of financial position will reflect the fair value carrying amount while amortised cost information will be presented in profit or loss. The difference between the fair value information and amortised cost information will be recognised in other comprehensive income.

BCE.24   The fair value through other comprehensive income measurement category was added to IFRS 9 in response to feedback requesting accommodation of known business models whose objective results in both collecting contractual cash flows and selling financial assets. This means that both amortised cost (ie information about contractual cash flows) and fair value information are relevant. In addition to providing relevant and useful information for financial assets that are held within a 'hold to collect and sell' business model,

---

51   The fair value through other comprehensive income measurement category is available only for debt instruments. It is different from the presentation election set out in paragraph 5.7.5 of IFRS 9 that permits an entity to present in other comprehensive income subsequent changes in the fair value of particular investments in equity instruments.

the introduction of the fair value through other comprehensive income measurement category also addresses potential accounting mismatches that could arise because of the interaction between the accounting for financial assets and the accounting for insurance contract liabilities.

BCE.25   Although the fair value through other comprehensive income measurement category has been introduced, the existing structure of IFRS 9 has been retained. Thus, IFRS 9 still eliminates the specific rules (which dictate how an asset can or must be classified) and accounting choice in IAS 39. For example, the fair value through other comprehensive income measurement category in IFRS 9 is fundamentally different to the available-for-sale measurement category in IAS 39. That is because financial assets are classified on the basis of their contractual cash flow characteristics and of the business model in which they are held. In contrast, the available-for-sale measurement category in IAS 39 is essentially a residual classification and, in many cases, is a free choice.

Bifurcation of embedded features in financial assets

BCE.26   Another key change is that IFRS 9 eliminates the application of the complex, internally inconsistent and rule-based requirements in IAS 39 for the bifurcation of hybrid financial assets.

BCE.27   In accordance with IFRS 9, a financial asset is accounted for in its entirety on the basis of its contractual cash flow features and the business model within which it is held. Thus, under IFRS 9, a hybrid financial asset is classified as a whole using the same classification approach as all other financial assets. That is in contrast to IAS 39, in which components of a financial asset could have been classified and measured separately—resulting in a component of a financial asset being measured at amortised cost or classified as available-for-sale, while some or all of the embedded features were measured at fair value through profit or loss, even though the financial asset was a single instrument that was settled as a whole on the basis of all of its features.

BCE.28   Consequently, IFRS 9 simplifies the classification of hybrid financial instruments. Consistently with all other financial assets, hybrid contracts with financial asset hosts are classified and measured in their entirety, thereby eliminating the complexity of bifurcation for financial assets.

Effect of classification on impairment

BCE.29   IAS 39 requires different impairment assessments and methods for financial assets depending on their classification. Some of those impairments could not be reversed.

BCE.30   During the global financial crisis some users of financial statements were confused, because the same financial assets were impaired differently simply because they were classified differently for accounting purposes.

BCE.31   As a result of the classification requirements issued in IFRS 9 (2009), only financial assets measured at amortised cost were subject to impairment accounting. IFRS 9 (2014) extends the impairment model to financial assets measured at fair value through other comprehensive income. Consequently, the same impairment model is applied for all financial assets that are not measured at fair value through profit or loss (ie financial assets measured at amortised cost and financial assets measured at fair value through other comprehensive income). This replaces the many different impairment methods that are associated with the numerous classification categories in IAS 39 and thereby addresses the criticism that the impairment models in IAS 39 were not aligned and were therefore confusing. In addition, by using the same impairment model, amortised cost information is provided in profit or loss for financial assets measured at fair value through other comprehensive income.

Reclassification

BCE.32 IAS 39 includes complex rules for the reclassification of financial assets, and different entities could choose to reclassify financial assets in different circumstances. In contrast, IFRS 9 requires the reclassification of financial assets when, and only when, the business model for managing those financial assets changes. IFRS 9 states that changes in a business model are demonstrable events and are expected to be very infrequent. For example, a change in a business model can arise from a business combination or if a reporting entity changes the way it manages its financial assets following the acquisition of a new business. By requiring financial assets to be reclassified when the business model changes, IFRS 9 ensures that relevant information is always provided about the cash flows that an entity expects to realise from managing its financial assets.

The cost exception for unquoted equity investments

BCE.33 IAS 39 has an exception to the measurement requirements for investments in unquoted equity instruments that do not have a quoted market price in an active market (and derivatives on such an instrument) and for which fair value cannot therefore be measured reliably. Such financial instruments are measured at cost. IFRS 9 removes this exception, requiring all equity investments (and derivatives on them) to be measured at fair value. However, IFRS 9 provides guidance on when cost may be an appropriate estimate of fair value.

Gains and losses—equity investments

BCE.34 IFRS 9 provides a presentation option for investments in equity instruments that are not held for trading. Otherwise, equity investments are measured at fair value through profit or loss.

BCE.35 IFRS 9 permits an entity to make an irrevocable election on an instrument-by-instrument basis to present in other comprehensive income changes in the fair value of an investment in an equity instrument that is not held for trading. Dividends received from those investments are presented in profit or loss. Gains and losses presented in other comprehensive income cannot be subsequently transferred to profit or loss (ie there is no recycling). However, the entity may transfer the cumulative gain or loss within equity.

BCE.36   Although the IASB believes that fair value provides the most useful information about investments in equity instruments to users of financial statements, the IASB provided this presentation option because it notes that changes in the value of particular investments in equity instruments may not be indicative of the performance of the entity. This would be the case, for example, if the entity holds those equity instruments primarily for non-contractual benefits. Another reason was because users of financial statements often differentiate between fair value changes arising from equity investments held for purposes other than generating investment returns and equity investments held for trading.

BCE.37   The IASB decided to prohibit recycling of gains and losses into profit or loss when an equity investment is derecognised, even though many respondents said that subsequent transfers of fair value changes to profit or loss should be required. These respondents view the sale of an investment as the realisation of the changes in its fair value. However, such recycling of gains and losses would have made it necessary to introduce an impairment test to ensure that impairments were presented on a consistent basis. Impairment accounting for equity investments has been a significant source of complexity in IAS 39. The IASB thus decided that introducing recycling and associated impairment accounting would create application problems in practice and would not significantly improve or reduce the complexity of the financial reporting for financial assets. Accordingly, the IASB decided to prohibit recycling.

BCE.38   Although IFRS 9 prohibits recycling of gains and losses into profit or loss when an equity investment is derecognised, entities are able to transfer the cumulative gain or loss within equity at any time; for example, to provide information on realisation. The IASB considered specific requirements relating to that transfer, such as requiring the accumulated gain or loss to be transferred to retained earnings upon derecognition of the equity investment, but did not adopt such an approach because of jurisdiction-specific restrictions on components of equity. For example, a transfer to retained earnings may give rise to tax consequences in some jurisdictions. However, additional disclosures are required about investments in equity instruments with fair value changes presented in other comprehensive income to provide useful information to users of financial statements about the effect of that presentation for instruments presented in that manner. For example, paragraph 11B of IFRS 7 requires an entity to disclose the cumulative gain or loss on disposal if the entity derecognised investments in equity instruments with fair value changes presented in other comprehensive income during the reporting period.

Main changes to the approach to classifying and measuring financial liabilities

BCE.39   IFRS 9 carries forward almost all of the requirements in IAS 39 for the classification and measurement of financial liabilities, including the bifurcation of particular embedded derivatives. As a result, most financial liabilities, apart from derivatives or financial liabilities that an entity designates under the fair value option, will continue to be measured at amortised cost.

BCE.40 The main concern that the IASB was asked to address in relation to financial liabilities was the so-called 'own credit' issue, whereby changes in the credit risk of a financial liability give rise to gains or losses in profit or loss. For financial liabilities designated under the fair value option, the requirements issued in IFRS 9 (2010) required an entity to present in other comprehensive income changes in the fair value of a financial liability that are attributable to changes in credit risk.[52]

BCE.41 Users of financial statements continued to support the measurement of financial liabilities on the balance sheet at fair value in accordance with the fair value option noting that this provided a useful source of information on a timely basis about changes in an entity's credit quality. However, the requirement to present these fair value changes in other comprehensive income addressed the concern raised by many, including users of financial statements, that reflecting these fair value changes in profit or loss is counterintuitive and does not result in useful information. In particular, the requirement addresses the concern that a gain is recognised in profit or loss as the credit risk on a financial liability increases (ie its credit quality deteriorates).

BCE.42 The requirements issued in IFRS 9 (2010) enabled entities to apply the change to the presentation of such fair value gains and losses only if all the requirements in that Standard for the classification and measurement of financial assets and liabilities were applied. However, the requirements issued in IFRS 9 (2013) changed this requirement. Consequently, prior to the mandatory effective date of IFRS 9 an entity is permitted to apply the requirements for the presentation of own credit in isolation; ie earlier than the other requirements in IFRS 9.

BCE.43 This allows entities to present the effects of own credit in other comprehensive income, thus improving their financial reporting, without also needing to make other changes to their accounting for financial instruments. It makes the own credit requirements available on a more timely basis, particularly because an entity will be able to make this change before undertaking the changes that would be required in order to implement the expected credit loss impairment model.

Early application

BCE.44 In order to address critical issues during the global financial crisis and to make improvements to financial reporting available more quickly, the IASB decided to replace IAS 39 in phases and to allow entities to early apply only some phases of IFRS 9 (although if a later phase was applied, earlier phases were also required to be applied). Consequently, entities had the option to apply only the requirements for financial assets (IFRS 9 (2009)), the requirements for financial assets and financial liabilities (IFRS 9 (2010)) or the requirements for financial assets, financial liabilities and hedge accounting (IFRS 9 (2013)). In contrast, six months from the issue in 2014 of the completed version of IFRS 9, an entity that newly elects to apply IFRS 9 must

---

52 This applies unless that treatment would create or enlarge an accounting mismatch in profit or loss, in which case all changes in fair value are presented in profit or loss.

either apply the entire Standard (ie all of the classification and measurement, impairment and hedge accounting requirements in the completed version of IFRS 9) or apply only the own credit requirements.[53]

BCE.45 This means that before the mandatory effective date of the completed version of IFRS 9, fewer combinations of the accounting for financial instruments will be available than was previously the case. Having multiple versions of IFRS 9 available for early application (in addition to IAS 39) is complex and would significantly reduce the comparability of information that is provided to users of financial statements.

Comparability of financial information

BCE.46 At a high level, classification and measurement, in accordance with both IAS 39 and IFRS 9, requires consideration of similar aspects of financial instruments – their contractual cash flow characteristics and how they are managed. However, IAS 39 and IFRS 9 approach these aspects of financial instruments in very different ways. IAS 39 is complex and rule-based and the classification of financial assets places emphasis on an entity's intentions in respect of individual financial assets and also considers aspects such as the liquidity of the market for a financial asset. IAS 39 also involves an element of free choice. As discussed in the following paragraphs, IFRS 9 provides a logical structure and a clearer rationale for the classification and measurement of financial assets, with less accounting choice. Consequently, differences in financial reporting between reporting periods for an individual entity, and between different entities in a particular reporting period, will more often reflect the differences in underlying economics instead of resulting from differences in accounting choices. Or, put another way, similar financial assets managed in the same way should be classified in the same way for accounting purposes.

The business model assessment

BCE.47 In contrast to IAS 39, the business model assessment in IFRS 9 is determined by how financial assets are actually managed. This is not a question of intention for an individual instrument but is instead based on an assessment of objective evidence at a higher level of aggregation. As a result, the assessment is a matter of fact, which results in less accounting choice than is available in IAS 39.

BCE.48 The IASB was made aware of differences in the interpretation of these requirements as they were issued in IFRS 9 (2009) so the completed version of IFRS 9 (issued in 2014) reaffirms and supplements the business model principle. It emphasises that the business model assessment focuses on how the entity actually manages financial assets to generate cash flows. In addition, IFRS 9 (2014) enhances the application guidance for the 'hold to collect' business model, addressing particular application questions raised by interested parties since the issue of IFRS 9 in 2009. It expands the discussion about the activities that are commonly associated with the hold to collect

---

53 However, entities have an accounting policy choice between applying the new hedge accounting requirements of IFRS 9 and retaining the existing requirements in IAS 39.

business model, clarifying, for example, that entities do not need to hold all assets until maturity and that sales in themselves do not determine the objective of the business model (although information about sales can be useful in determining an entity's business model). The clarifications are expected to improve comparability by enhancing the consistency in how different entities apply the hold to collect business model and classify their financial assets.

BCE.49 As discussed in paragraph BCE.23, a fair value through other comprehensive income measurement category was introduced to IFRS 9 in 2014. The fair value through other comprehensive income measurement category will allow some business models to be better reflected in the financial statements, improving comparability between entities with economically similar instruments that are managed in a similar way.

Reclassifications

BCE.50 A further improvement to the comparability of financial information is that, compared to the complex rules for reclassification in IAS 39, IFRS 9 makes reclassifications between measurement categories mandatory when, and only when, there has been a change in the entity's business model.

BCE.51 The reclassification requirements will enhance comparability because an entity will generally account for its financial instruments consistently over time. The exception will be in the rare circumstance that an entity's business model changes, in which case the required reclassification strengthens comparability because financial assets will be accounted for consistently with how they are managed.

Usefulness of financial information in assessing the future cash flows of an entity

Financial assets

BCE.52 In the Basis for Conclusions on IFRS 9, the IASB acknowledges that some users of financial statements support a single measurement method – fair value – for all financial assets. However, the IASB continues to believe that both amortised cost and fair value can provide useful information to users of financial statements for particular types of financial assets in particular circumstances. In issuing IFRS 9, the IASB did not seek to increase or reduce the use of fair value measurement. Instead, it sought to ensure that information based on a specific measurement attribute is provided when it is relevant. The IASB decided that if the measurement attribute for financial assets and the assets' effect on profit or loss are aligned with both the business model for managing financial assets and their contractual cash flow characteristics, financial reporting will provide relevant information about the timing, amounts and uncertainty of an entity's future cash flows.

The business model

BCE.53   The business model for managing financial assets determines whether their cash flows are realised through the collection of contractual cash flows, the sale of financial assets or both. Consequently, the business model provides information that is useful in assessing the amounts, timing and uncertainty of the entity's future cash flows.

BCE.54   If the objective of an entity's business model is to collect contractual cash flows then, depending on the characteristics of the contractual cash flows, amortised cost measurement in both the statement of financial position and in profit or loss provides information about future cash flows. However, in contrast, if the objective of the business model is achieved by realising cash flows by selling financial assets, fair value measurement provides more relevant information about future cash flows in both the statement of financial position and in profit or loss.

BCE.55   IFRS 9 (2014) clarifies the application guidance for a hold to collect business model that results in financial assets being measured at amortised cost (depending on their contractual cash flow characteristics). The clarification will improve the quality of the financial information and its usefulness in assessing the amounts, timing and uncertainty of an entity's future cash flows by resulting in amortised cost measurement only for financial assets that are held with the objective of collecting contractual cash flows.

BCE.56   Usefulness of financial information will be further improved by the introduction of the fair value through other comprehensive income measurement category to IFRS 9. The fair value through other comprehensive income measurement category results in a fair value carrying amount in the statement of financial position, while the effect on profit or loss would be the same as if the financial assets were measured at amortised cost. This is considered appropriate for such a business model because, by design, both holding and selling activities are taking place, making both amortised cost and fair value information relevant to users of the financial statements. Due to the addition of the fair value through other comprehensive income measurement category, some question whether the classification and measurement approach will still be an improvement over IAS 39. However, in contrast to the available-for-sale measurement category in IAS 39, there is a clear business model in IFRS 9 that results in measurement at fair value through other comprehensive income. This will allow entities to better reflect the way in which financial assets are managed and improves the usefulness of the information provided for those business models in assessing the timing, amounts and uncertainty of an entity's future cash flows. Also, unlike the available-for-sale category in IAS 39, this measurement category has information content—it provides information about the entity's business model.

Contractual cash flow characteristics

BCE.57   Because the effective interest method is not an appropriate method for allocating 'complex' contractual cash flows, the contractual cash flow test in IFRS 9 ensures that amortised cost information is presented only for assets with simple contractual cash flows.

BCE.58   IFRS 9 (2014) makes a number of enhancements to the application guidance on the contractual cash flow characteristics. For example, it provides additional guidance about the attributes of cash flows that provide returns consistent with principal and interest and clarifies that interest is typically represented by a return for the time value of money and credit risk, but also can include other elements, such as a return for liquidity risk. In addition, it clarifies that a financial asset does not have cash flows that are solely payments of principal and interest if the effect of an interest rate tenor mismatch is significant, compared with the cash flows of an instrument that does not contain such a feature but is otherwise identical. In addition, IFRS 9 (2014) relaxes the original requirements in respect to contingencies. It eliminates the distinction between contingent prepayment and extension features and other types of contingent features, clarifying that all contingent features must be assessed in the same way and irrespective of the nature of the contingent event itself. As a result of these clarifications, the IASB expects that financial instruments considered to pay solely principal and interest will be better aligned with the economic concept of principal and interest.

BCE.59   The IASB was also made aware of regulated interest rates in some jurisdictions that are created with an objective of providing a return that is economically consistent with principal and interest, and that do not introduce volatility that is inconsistent with a basic lending arrangement. However, there is a mismatch between the interest rate set and the duration of the interest rate period. IFRS 9 (2014) provides explicit guidance for such financial instruments so that they are, in specific circumstances, considered to have payments that are solely principal and interest cash flows despite their structure. This will allow financial instruments that are considered 'simple' in the relevant jurisdiction to be measured other than at fair value through profit or loss, depending on an entity's business model. This is expected to provide relevant information for the entities that hold such financial assets.

BCE.60   In addition to these questions of clarity, after the publication of IFRS 9 in 2009 some interested parties suggested that bifurcation for financial assets should be reintroduced, partly because of a concern that some financial assets will be measured at fair value through profit or loss in their entirety, whereas under IAS 39 only the derivative component would have been measured at fair value through profit or loss. The IASB believes that the concern is addressed for some financial assets by the clarifications to the principal and interest criterion outlined above. This is because, despite the presence of embedded features, these financial assets may economically have principal and interest cash flows. This is expected to be the case, for example, for many financial instruments with regulated interest rates and financial instruments with interest rate tenor mismatches. However, for other financial assets, for example, when the contractual cash flows are linked to an underlying that is unrelated to principal or interest, such as a commodity price, IFRS 9 (2014) will not change the requirements issued in IFRS 9 (2009). For the reasons discussed in detail in paragraphs BC4.88–BC4.89 and BC4.196–BC4.204, the IASB believes that classifying financial assets in their entirety instead of bifurcating them will result in financial information that is more useful in assessing the amounts, timing and uncertainty of future cash flows.

BCE.61   In addition to providing information that is more useful in assessing future cash flows, the elimination of bifurcation also simplifies the information about financial assets that is provided to users of financial statements. When a financial asset was bifurcated, the components of that financial asset were measured in different ways, and could also have been presented in different places in the financial statements. Consequently, although the settlement of the financial asset takes into consideration all of its contractual terms, it was difficult to understand that financial asset as a whole until settlement took place.

Financial liabilities

BCE.62   In IFRS 9, the IASB made fewer changes to the classification and measurement of financial liabilities than to financial assets. Views received from users of financial statements, and others, indicated that amortised cost is the most appropriate measurement attribute for many financial liabilities, because it reflects the issuer's legal obligation to pay the contractual amounts in the normal course of business (ie on a going concern basis) and, in many cases, the issuer plans to hold liabilities to maturity and pay the contractual amounts.

BCE.63   However, if a liability has structured features (for example, embedded derivatives), amortised cost is difficult to apply and understand because the cash flows can be highly variable. Consequently, the IASB decided to retain the bifurcation requirements in IAS 39 for financial liabilities. The views received by the IASB indicated that the bifurcation approach in IAS 39 is generally working well for financial liabilities and that a new bifurcation approach would most likely have the same classification and measurement outcomes as the approach in IAS 39. The bifurcation approach also reduces the incidence of fair value changes caused by the issuer's own credit risk.

BCE.64   Views received indicated, and the IASB agreed, that the effects of changes in a liability's credit risk ought not to affect profit or loss unless the liability is held for trading, because an entity will generally not realise the effects of changes in the liability's credit risk unless the liability is held for trading. However, many users of financial statements confirmed that fair value information on the balance sheet does provide useful information because, for example, it can provide early information about an entity's credit problems. The IASB thus decided that entities should continue to have the ability to measure their non-derivative liabilities at fair value (subject to the relevant criteria that are unchanged from IAS 39), but that the portion of the fair value change that is a consequence of changes in the financial instrument's credit risk should be recognised in other comprehensive income. The result of the IASB's decisions, including the own credit requirements for financial liabilities described in paragraphs BC5.35–BC5.64, result in information being reported for financial liabilities that is more useful in assessing the amounts, timing and uncertainty of the entity's future cash flows.

BCE.65 The IASB noted that *prima facie* it would seem preferable to eliminate bifurcation for financial liabilities if it was eliminated for financial assets. However, in discussions with users of financial statements they did not raise concerns regarding this apparent asymmetry in treatment.

Equity instruments

BCE.66 IFRS 9 removes the measurement exception for investments in unquoted equity instruments (and derivatives on them). Measuring those instruments at fair value provides the most relevant information to users of financial statements, because, although cost is a reliable and objective amount, it provides little, if any, information with predictive value about the timing, amount and uncertainty of future cash flows arising from the instrument.

BCE.67 The classification model for financial assets in IFRS 9 results in cost-based information when amortised cost is a relevant measure. Because equity instruments do not have cash flows that represent solely payments of principal and interest, the IASB believes that fair value information is always relevant, irrespective of the business model in which the asset is held. In addition, the IASB believes that changes in the fair value of equity investments usually provide relevant information about an entity's performance and should therefore be included in profit or loss. However, the IASB acknowledges that for some equity investments information about fair value may not be considered relevant to profit or loss, such as when an investment is held for strategic purposes. IFRS 9 therefore allows an entity to elect to present fair value changes on equity investments in other comprehensive income as long as the investment is not held for trading. Because this presentation choice was designed for circumstances in which these fair value changes were not relevant to profit or loss, even though the category is not expressly limited to these circumstances, the IASB decided that gains or losses would not be recycled to profit or loss. This decision was also made so that impairment accounting need not be reintroduced for investments in equity instruments to ensure that this complexity was not introduced in IFRS 9.

BCE.68 Accounting for impairment on equity investments, including assessing whether fair value changes are 'significant or prolonged', has been one of the most difficult application areas of IAS 39. Without an impairment model, recycling could not be allowed because of the risk of asymmetry caused by recognising gains in profit or loss with the risk that losses would be retained in other comprehensive income by avoiding derecognition. This would risk reducing the usefulness and representational faithfulness of the information provided.

BCE.69 Some have expressed concerns that this approach may create a disincentive for entities to invest in equity instruments. However, if an entity is of the view that the users of its financial statements need to see the effects in profit or loss of holding equity investments, they need not elect the other comprehensive income presentation. If the other comprehensive income presentation is elected, entities can choose to present the effects of realising fair value changes by, for example, transferring accumulated gains or losses from other comprehensive income to retained earnings.

Reclassifications

BCE.70 IAS 39 permits reclassifications at the entity's discretion in rare circumstances. Users of financial statements consistently commented that these reclassifications decreased the comparability and usefulness of financial reporting. In contrast, IFRS 9 makes reclassifications mandatory when, and only when, there has been a change in business model. The reclassification requirements will enhance useful and relevant information, because reclassification is based on changes in the entity's business model for managing financial assets. This ensures that financial statements always faithfully represent how those financial assets are managed at the reporting date, reflecting the amounts, timing and uncertainty of future cash flows.

Better economic decision-making as a result of improved financial reporting

BCE.71 The IASB believes that the requirements in IFRS 9 satisfy the fundamental qualitative characteristics of useful financial information as stated in Chapter 3 of the IASB's *Conceptual Framework*. That is, they would:

(a) provide information that is more useful in assessing the amounts, timing and uncertainty of an entity's future cash flows than the information reported in accordance with IAS 39 and is therefore more relevant and timely; and

(b) reduce accounting choice and instead require classifications that are consistent with economic substance. Consequently, the financial reporting is a more faithful representation than the financial reporting in accordance with IAS 39. It is also more complete and neutral and is supported by economic substance, which will help it to be free from error and verifiable.

In addition, the IASB notes that IFRS 9 enhances the comparability and understandability of the financial information relative to IAS 39.

BCE.72 In assessing whether IFRS 9 would improve financial reporting, the IASB considered the concerns voiced by some interested parties regarding the changes in accounting for financial assets. Some believe that IFRS 9 will result in more financial assets being reported at fair value compared to the requirements in IAS 39, and this concerns them for one or more of the following reasons:

(a) while fair value might be relevant during times of relative market stability, they considered that it lacks relevance and reliability during times of market instability.

(b) fair value reporting leads to procyclicality, meaning that it reflects or even magnifies economic or financial fluctuations. For example, in response to changes in fair value, entities may need, or choose, to sell different amounts of financial assets than they normally would, and the entity may have a different estimate of the present value of the future cash flows than is indicated by the fair value or market price; fair value amounts that are lower than the entity's estimate of future cash flows are of particular concern. (Such as when an entity intends to hold an asset to collect its contractual cash flows.)

(c) fair value reporting may impact the activities of regulated entities. Regulatory reporting uses some of the amounts reported in general purpose financial statements. Consequently, IFRS reporting may have effects for regulated entities. For example, regulated entities (especially banks) are often required to maintain a minimum level of capital reserves. Decreases in the fair value of some financial assets may impact the level of those capital reserves. As a consequence, some expressed concern that regulated entities may decrease lending during an economic downturn, which can further exacerbate the downturn.

BCE.73 Some are of the view that fair value information is less relevant for all financial instruments in times of relative market instability. Others, including the IASB, agree that fair value is not equally relevant for all financial instruments, but believe that fair value is relevant in all market conditions for some financial instruments. Consequently, the IASB believes that the new approach to classifying and measuring financial instruments will provide relevant information that will lead to better economic decision-making throughout economic cycles.

BCE.74 The IASB did not seek to increase or reduce the number of financial instruments that would be measured at fair value. For financial liabilities, the use of fair value is essentially unchanged in IFRS 9 relative to IAS 39 (and in fact, a portion of the fair value changes will now be recognised in other comprehensive income instead of profit or loss). In addition, financial assets are measured at fair value only when it is relevant because of the contractual cash flow characteristics of the asset and/or the entity's business model. Depending on the entity, its particular financial assets and how it manages them, IFRS 9 may actually result in fewer financial assets being measured at fair value than under IAS 39. For example, because of the rule-based criteria for amortised cost measurement under IAS 39, debt securities that are quoted in active markets are typically measured at fair value in accordance with IAS 39, even if they are held within a business model in which assets are managed to collect contractual cash flows. Such financial assets may be measured at amortised cost in accordance with IFRS 9.

BCE.75 The effect on the classification of an entity's financial assets will depend on the choices it made when applying IAS 39, its business models for managing its financial assets and the contractual cash flow characteristics of those financial assets. It is thus not possible to determine the overall changes in the classification of financial assets that will occur. However, the drivers of possible changes can be considered.

BCE.76 The following examples illustrate how the measurement of the financial assets may or may not change when IFRS 9 is first applied:

Example 1

Entity X invests in a portfolio of bonds that are quoted in an active market. The entity generally holds the investments in order to collect their contractual cash flows but would sell them if the instrument no longer meets the credit criteria specified in the entity's documented investment policy (for example, if a bond's credit risk increases so that it is higher than the credit limit as defined by the investment policy for that class of financial instruments at the reporting date).

Instrument A is a bond that pays principal and interest on the principal amount outstanding. In accordance with IAS 39, the entity classified Instrument A as available-for-sale because of the restrictions and tainting rules associated with the held-to-maturity category. At transition to IFRS 9, the entity reclassifies Instrument A to be measured at amortised cost because:

(a)   the financial assets are held within a business model whose objective is to hold assets in order to collect contractual cash flows;[54] and

(b)   the contractual cash flows are solely payments of principal and interest on the principal amount outstanding. The contractual cash flows reflect a return that is consistent with a basic lending arrangement.

Example 2

In contrast, consider the same fact pattern except that the entity invests in the bonds to achieve the business model's objective by both collecting contractual cash flows and selling bonds. Accordingly, upon transition to IFRS 9 the entity reclassifies Instrument A from available-for-sale to the fair value through other comprehensive income measurement category. This is because:

(a)   the financial assets are managed to achieve the business model's objective by both collecting contractual cash flows and selling financial assets; and

(b)   the contractual cash flows are solely payments of principal and interest on the principal amount outstanding. The contractual cash flows reflect a return that is consistent with a basic lending arrangement.

Example 3

Entity Y invests in bonds that are quoted in an active market. The bonds' contractual cash flows are linked to an equity index. The entity holds the bonds to collect the contractual cash flows. In accordance with IAS 39, Entity Y separated the embedded derivative from the financial asset host and measured the embedded derivative at fair value through profit or loss. The host financial asset was classified as available-for-sale. At transition to IFRS 9, Entity Y applies the classification approach to the hybrid financial instrument as a whole. Consequently, it measures the hybrid financial instrument in its

---

54 Sales do not contradict the hold to collect business model if they are in response to the increase in the instrument's credit risk.

entirety at fair value though profit or loss despite a business model that is a 'hold to collect' model. This is because the contractual cash flows introduce exposure to changes in equity prices that do not give rise to contractual cash flows that are solely payments of principal and interest on the principal amount outstanding. Thus, the contractual cash flows are inconsistent with a basic lending arrangement and the instrument must be measured at fair value through profit or loss.

Example 4

Entity Z invests in senior tranches of securitised bonds that are collateralised by mortgage loans. The underlying mortgage loans have payments that are solely payments of principal and interest. Entity Z invests in these senior tranches in order to collect contractual cash flows. The credit risk of the tranches is lower than that of the overall mortgage pool. In accordance with IAS 39, Entity Z determined that there is not an embedded derivative and classified its investment in these senior tranches as available-for-sale. At transition to IFRS 9, if the contractual terms of the senior tranches give rise to payments that are solely payments of principal and interest on the principal amount outstanding, Entity Z measures its investments at amortised cost. However, if the contractual payments are not solely payments of principal and interest on the principal amount outstanding (that is, they are inconsistent with a basic lending arrangement), the senior tranche must be measured at fair value through profit or loss.

BCE.77   The IASB acknowledges that the fair value through other comprehensive income measurement category may affect some regulated banks, because the Basel III regulatory framework removes the 'regulatory filter' for fair value gains or losses recognised in other comprehensive income.[55] Consequently, if this regulatory change remains in place, for those affected the fair value changes of financial assets that are measured at fair value through other comprehensive income will have a direct effect on regulatory capital. However, the addition of the fair value through other comprehensive income measurement category will only have this potential adverse effect on regulatory capital if those financial assets would otherwise have been measured at amortised cost. The objective of the hold to collect business model in IFRS 9 (as issued in 2009) has not been changed. Some financial assets held in business models that would have been measured at fair value through profit or loss can now be measured at fair value through other comprehensive income. In that case, the value changes in other comprehensive income could still affect regulatory capital but the effect on regulatory capital would be a neutral one relative to the requirements issued in IFRS 9 (2009).

---

55 Footnote 10 of Basel III: A global regulatory framework for more resilient banks and banking systems ('Basel III'), published by the Basel Committee on Banking Supervision, states 'that '[t]here is no adjustment applied to remove from Common Equity Tier 1 unrealised gains or losses recognised on the balance sheet [the 'regulatory filter'] ... The Committee will continue to review the appropriate treatment of unrealised gains, taking into account the evolution of the accounting framework.' In contrast, Basel II did contain a regulatory filter.

BCE.78   The objective of financial reporting should be to provide transparent information that is useful for economic decision-making. The IASB notes that the objective of providing useful information does not contradict the objective of economic stability. Instead, the IASB believes that transparency is essential to maintain stability in the long term.

The likely effect on compliance costs for preparers, both on initial application and on an ongoing basis

BCE.79   As with all new requirements, the IASB acknowledges that different areas of the requirements will have different effects and hence different types of costs and benefits will arise when considering both preparers and users of financial statements. Given that the new classification model for financial assets is based on the entity's business model for managing its financial assets and those assets' contractual cash flow characteristics, it is reasonable to conclude that the costs incurred and the benefits obtained in complying with the new requirements will depend on the entity's business model and the contractual cash flow characteristics of its financial assets.

BCE.80   Entities will incur a one-time cost on initial application such as costs for:

    (a)   developing new processes, systems and controls;

    (b)   undertaking the initial analysis of business models and contractual cash flows on transition;

    (c)   creating capabilities for new eligible presentations, if intended to be used (for example, the presentation of the change in the fair value of equity investments in other comprehensive income);

    (d)   educating accounting functions and obtaining expert advice for compliance; and

    (e)   explaining to users of financial statements the differences between the information produced under IAS 39 and IFRS 9.

BCE.81   The IASB believes that the transition to IFRS 9 and the associated costs (as well as the ongoing costs of applying IFRS 9) will depend on the individual circumstances of the entity, ie the type (and diversity of) business models for its financial assets as well as the contractual cash flow characteristics of the instruments. It is therefore difficult to generalise the likely impact on transition on preparers and on their costs.

BCE.82   However, the IASB does not expect preparers to incur significant incremental costs on an ongoing basis in comparison to applying IAS 39. The IASB notes the following initial and ongoing costs and factors that mitigate the ongoing costs of applying IFRS 9 in comparison to IAS 39:

    (a)   the need to assess the business model. The entity's business model is determined on a more aggregated basis than an individual financial instrument level that was the basis for classification under IAS 39. An entity's business model is a matter of fact that can be observed by the way in which an entity is managed and information is provided to its management. The assessment is based on, for example, business plans and internal reporting, which should be available. Thus, the reporting is in a manner consistent with the entity's actual business model and entities need not maintain dual reporting models for internal and external reporting.

(b) the need to assess the contractual cash flows of a financial asset. However:

(i) the contractual cash flows need not be analysed in all business models. They only need to be analysed to assess cash flows for the held to collect and the held to collect or sell business models.

(ii) financial assets with more complex cash flows are expected to already have an analysis in place to assess the need to bifurcate and to measure the fair value of the asset in its entirety (under the fair value option) or in part in accordance with IAS 39; and

(iii) in other cases an entity is expected to already analyse contractual cash flows in order to determine the fair value for disclosure purposes in accordance with IFRS 7, particularly for assets below Level 1 of the fair value hierarchy.

BCE.83 In addition, the IASB notes that eliminating bifurcation and tainting for financial assets measured at amortised cost, as well as introducing a single impairment method, will simplify compliance with the classification and measurement requirements for financial assets.

BCE.84 Furthermore, for financial liabilities, the classification and measurement model is largely unchanged from IAS 39, except for the own credit requirements for financial liabilities designated as at fair value through profit or loss under the fair value option. Entities are already required to disclose the gains or losses recognised for changes in own credit risk and therefore there should not be any incremental costs to preparers from this change.

BCE.85 Finally, IFRS 9 provides a number of illustrative examples and detailed application guidance that illustrate various aspects of the new Standard. In addition, the IASB has responded to the requests for clarifications and to the application questions raised since the issue of IFRS 9 in 2009. The IASB believes that this will help to reduce the initial and ongoing costs of compliance with the classification and measurement requirements.

BCE.86 For the reasons described in the preceding paragraphs, the IASB believes that the benefits of the improvements to financial reporting will justify the costs to implement and apply the classification and measurement requirements of IFRS 9.

The likely effect on costs of analysis for users of financial statements

BCE.87 The likely benefits of improved reporting are expected to outweigh the costs of analysis for users of financial statements. However, the extent of the benefit will depend on existing practices.

BCE.88　Some of the complexity in IAS 39 is eliminated and it is therefore easier for users of financial statements to understand and use information about financial instruments. In addition, although some users of financial statements favour fair value as a primary measurement attribute for all financial assets, users of financial statements as a group have consistently said that both amortised cost information and fair value information are useful in particular circumstances. The IASB has developed IFRS 9 to provide information that is useful in predicting an entity's future cash flows. In addition, accompanying disclosures provide information that will enable users of financial statements to understand how financial instruments have been classified and measured, and supplementary information from disclosures is available to be used in their financial modelling (for example, the fair value of financial instruments measured at amortised cost).

Conclusion

BCE.89　The requirements result in more relevant and transparent information because they introduce a single classification approach for all financial assets, which always provides users of financial statements with information that reflects how the cash flows on financial assets are expected to be realised given the entity's business model and the nature of the contractual cash flows. In addition, they respond to long standing concerns about the volatility that occurs in profit or loss due to changes in an issuer's own credit risk that was not considered to provide useful information, when an entity elects to measure non-derivative financial liabilities at fair value.

Analysis of the effects: Impairment

Overview

BCE.90　During the global financial crisis, the delayed recognition of credit losses on loans and other financial instruments was identified as a weakness in the existing accounting standards. Specifically, concerns were raised about the timeliness of recognising credit losses because the existing 'incurred loss' model in IAS 39 delays the recognition of credit losses until there is evidence of a credit loss event. The Financial Crisis Advisory Group (FCAG) and others recommended exploring alternatives to the incurred loss model that would use more forward-looking information.

BCE.91　The complexity of having multiple impairment models for financial instruments was also identified as a major concern.

BCE.92　The impairment requirements in IFRS 9 are the IASB's response to the need to improve the accounting for impairment for financial instruments and to remove the complexity of multiple impairment models. The IASB believes that the new impairment requirements address the issue of delayed recognition of credit losses and the complexity of multiple impairment models for financial instruments.

BCE.93　Overall, the IASB's assessment is that the impairment requirements will bring significant and sustained improvements to the reporting of financial instruments because:

(a)   the same impairment model applies to all financial instruments within the scope of IFRS 9 that are subject to impairment accounting. This removes a major source of current complexity.

(b)   entities will be required to recognise a loss allowance at an amount equal to at least 12-month expected credit losses throughout the life of their financial instruments that are subject to impairment accounting. This reduces the systematic overstatement of interest revenue in IAS 39 and acts as a proxy for the recognition of initial expected credit losses over time.

(c)   more timely information will be provided about expected credit losses. The requirements eliminate the threshold for recognising credit losses so that it would no longer be necessary for a credit event to have occurred before credit losses are recognised. Instead, expected credit losses and changes in expected credit losses are always recognised. In particular, IFRS 9 will require:

    (i)   earlier recognition of lifetime expected credit losses for financial instruments relative to IAS 39 (ie instruments with a significant increase in credit risk since initial recognition); and

    (ii)   in addition, 12-month expected credit losses for all other instruments. The amount of expected credit losses will be updated at each reporting date to reflect changes in credit risk since initial recognition. Consequently, the impairment model in IFRS 9 will be more responsive to changes in economic circumstances that affect credit risk.

(d)   the requirements broaden the information that an entity is required to consider when accounting for credit losses. An entity is required to base its measurement of expected credit losses on relevant information about past events, including historical credit loss information for similar financial instruments, current conditions and reasonable and supportable forecasts. Thus, the effects of future credit loss expectations need to be considered. As a result of the broadening of the information that is required to be considered, the impairment model will be more forward looking.

BCE.94   Some interested parties would prefer an impairment model that results in a 'conservative', or prudential, depiction of expected credit losses. Those parties are concerned about higher or lower loss allowances or the 'adequacy' of the loss allowance. They argue that such a depiction would better meet the needs of both the regulators who are responsible for maintaining financial stability and of investors. However, the debate about higher or lower loss allowances or the adequacy of the loss allowance in isolation is primarily a debate for prudential regulators instead of accounting standard-setters. The IASB's objective is not to require higher or lower loss allowances; instead it is to present information to users of financial statements that is neutral and portrays the economic characteristics of the financial instrument at the reporting date. This is consistent with the objectives of financial reporting and the qualitative characteristics in the *Conceptual Framework*. While the IASB does not have an objective to increase allowance balances, loss allowances may quite naturally be higher under IFRS 9 relative to IAS 39. This is because IFRS 9 requires earlier recognition of lifetime expected credit losses as significant increases in credit risk are expected to occur before there is objective evidence of impairment in accordance with IAS 39 and, in addition, 12-month expected credit losses are required to be recognised for all other instruments.[56]

BCE.95   The IASB expects that most costs for preparers will be incurred preparing to transition to the new impairment model. In particular, investments will be required in substantial system changes. The ongoing costs will be mitigated by the fact that several simplifications and clarifications have been put in place that reduce the operational burden of the impairment model in IFRS 9 (see paragraphs BCE.151–BCE.164). The IASB's assessment is that the significant improvements in terms of timeliness of information about expected credit losses and transparency will outweigh those costs.

Objective of the impairment requirements of IFRS 9

BCE.96   The IASB's main objective in developing the impairment model was to provide users of financial statements with more useful information about an entity's expected credit losses on its financial assets and its commitments to extend credit to facilitate their assessment of the amount, timing and uncertainty of future cash flows.

BCE.97   Conceptually, when an entity prices a financial instrument, the credit risk premium in the yield compensates the entity for the initial expected credit losses. For example, at the time of lending, the margin on a financial instrument compensates the lender for the credit risk of the borrower. This means that loss expectations do not give rise to an economic loss at initial recognition. In contrast, subsequent increases in the credit risk of the borrower represent an economic loss. These changes represent an economic loss because they are not priced into the financial instrument. Ideally, to reflect this an entity would include the initial estimate of the expected credit losses in determining the effective interest rate used to recognise interest revenue. Thus, the initial expected credit losses would adjust the interest revenue over the life of the financial asset. The entity would then recognise impairment gains or losses only when changes in the expected credit losses occur. This is what the IASB proposed in the 2009 Impairment Exposure Draft.

BCE.98   In the IASB's view, expected credit losses are most faithfully represented by the proposals in the 2009 Impairment Exposure Draft. Users of financial statements have told the IASB that they support an impairment model that distinguishes between the effect of initial estimates of expected credit losses and subsequent changes in those loss expectations. Many respondents,

---

56   Purchased credit-impaired assets will not have a 12-month allowance at inception. Instead, the effective interest rate will be adjusted to reflect initial loss expectations and then a loss allowance will be established for all changes in lifetime expected credit losses. Also lifetime expected credit losses are always recognised on trade receivables that do not have a significant financing element and instead of measuring 12-month expected credit losses on assets that have not significantly increased in credit risk, lifetime expected credit losses may be recognised at all times on other trade receivables, lease receivables and contract assets.

including the EAP, also supported the concepts in the 2009 Impairment Exposure Draft but said that the proposals would present significant operational challenges.

BCE.99　To overcome the operational challenges of the 2009 Impairment Exposure Draft, the IASB simplified the approach for the recognition of expected credit losses. The impairment model in IFRS 9 seeks to achieve a balance between the benefits of the faithful representation of expected credit losses and the operational cost and complexity. In other words, IFRS 9 seeks to approximate the 2009 Impairment Exposure Draft to the maximum extent possible in a way that is less operationally burdensome and more cost-effective.

BCE.100　IFRS 9 reflects the link between the pricing of financial instruments and the initial recognition of a loss allowance, generally separating the calculation of interest revenue and expected credit losses, by recognising a portion of expected credit losses from initial recognition as a proxy for the yield adjustment and lifetime expected credit losses after there has been a significant increase in the credit risk of a financial instrument. At each reporting date, expected credit losses are measured using updated information.

How activities would be reported in the financial statements of those applying IFRS 9

BCE.101　The analysis in paragraphs BCE.102–BCE.110 focuses on the key differences between the existing impairment model in IAS 39 and the new impairment model in IFRS 9 and how the new impairment model will affect financial reporting.

Single impairment model

BCE.102　IAS 39 requires different impairment assessments and methods for financial assets depending on their classification. Some of those financial asset impairments cannot be reversed. During the global financial crisis, some users of financial statements were confused because the same financial assets were impaired differently simply because they were classified differently for accounting purposes. In contrast, under IFRS 9 the same impairment model is applied to *all* financial instruments subject to impairment accounting. This addresses the criticism that having multiple impairment models in IAS 39 is confusing.

BCE.103　The impairment of debt instruments that are classified as available-for-sale financial assets under IAS 39 was criticised by some users of financial statements, because it is based on fair value fluctuations and is not aligned with the impairment model that is applied to similar financial assets measured at amortised cost. Some questioned the relevance of fair value-based impairment if a financial asset would not be realised through sale.

BCE.104　Similar to financial assets that are measured at amortised cost, in accordance with IFRS 9, the contractual cash flow characteristics of financial assets measured at fair value through other comprehensive income would solely represent payments of principal and interest. In addition, holding financial assets to collect contractual cash flows is an integral feature of the business model. The IASB therefore believes that an impairment model that is based on shortfalls in contractual cash flows and changes in credit risk, instead of changes in fair value, more faithfully reflects the economic reality of expected credit losses that are associated with these financial assets. It is also consistent with both amortised cost and fair value information about these financial assets being provided to the users of financial statements, which was the IASB's objective in introducing the fair value through other comprehensive income measurement category.

BCE.105 Previously, an entity that provided a loan commitment that was not accounted for at fair value through profit or loss and financial guarantee contracts to which IFRS 9 applies but that are not accounted for at fair value through profit or loss, accounted for in accordance with IAS 37. This was the case even though exposure to credit risk on these instruments is similar to that on loans or other financial instruments and the credit risk is managed in the same way. The IASB therefore concluded that an entity shall apply the same impairment model to those loan commitments and financial guarantee contracts. Aligning the impairment requirements for all credit exposures irrespective of their type reduces operational complexity because, in practice, loan commitments and financial guarantee contracts are often managed using the same credit risk management approach and information systems.

Measurement of expected credit losses

BCE.106 In accordance with IFRS 9, expected credit losses are the present value of expected cash shortfalls over the remaining life of a financial instrument. It requires that the estimates of cash flows are expected values. Consequently, estimates of the amounts and timing of cash flows are the probability-weighted possible outcomes. In the IASB's view, an expected value measurement provides relevant information about the timing, amounts and uncertainty of an entity's future cash flows. It provides information about the risk that the investment might not perform. The amount of expected credit losses will reflect both the risk of a default occurring and the loss amount that would arise if a default were to occur. This is because all financial instruments have a risk of a default occurring. The measurement will therefore reflect that risk of default and not the most likely outcome, as is often the case in practice in accordance with IAS 39.

Timely recognition of expected credit losses

BCE.107 The impairment models in IAS 39 require the recognition of credit losses only once there is objective evidence of impairment or when a credit loss is incurred (thus the impairment model includes a 'recognition threshold'). As a result, the effect of future events, even when expected, cannot be considered. This recognition threshold is perceived to have caused a delay in the recognition of credit losses and was identified during the global financial crisis as a weakness in accounting standards. It also resulted in differences in application because the recognition threshold was applied differently between entities.

BCE.108   IFRS 9 eliminates this threshold. Instead, expected credit losses would always be recognised and updated for changes in credit loss expectations using the best available information at the reporting date. This enables economic credit losses to be better reflected in the financial statements.

BCE.109   Consistent with the recommendations by the G20 Leaders, the FCAG and others, IFRS 9 is more forward-looking and considers a broader range of information than the existing incurred loss model. Such information includes reasonable and supportable forecast information that is available without undue cost or effort.

BCE.110   Consequently, the impairment model in IFRS 9 is expected to be more responsive to changing economic conditions than the existing IAS 39 incurred loss model and requires earlier recognition of expected credit losses.

Comparability of financial information

BCE.111   The IASB acknowledges that the more judgement that is required in the application of an expected credit loss approach, the more subjective the estimates will be, and that this subjectivity will affect the comparability of reported amounts between different entities. Despite the concerns about the application of judgement, in the IASB's view, the new impairment model will improve the comparability of reported amounts. This is because under the incurred loss model in accordance with IAS 39, increases in credit risk are not reported in the absence of a loss event, which limited the comparability of the reported amounts and the effective return on the financial assets. In addition, in practice, the point at which losses were considered to be incurred varied between entities.

BCE.112   In the IASB's view, considering the term structure and initial credit risk when assessing whether lifetime expected credit losses should be recognised will better reflect existing models for measuring credit risk and improve the comparability of the requirements for financial instruments with different maturities and different initial credit risk.

BCE.113   However, any approach that attempts to reflect expected credit losses will be subject to measurement uncertainty and will rely on management's judgement and the quality of the information used. Both qualitative and quantitative disclosures are necessary to assist users of financial statements in understanding and comparing different measures of expected credit losses. Consequently, disclosures are required by IFRS 7 to enable users of the financial statements to identify and understand the inputs, assumptions and techniques applied to identify significant increases in credit risk and measure expected credit losses, the amounts arising from the expected credit losses and the effect of changes in credit risk since initial recognition. The IASB believes that this will lead to greater comparability between different reporting periods of the same entity and assist in enabling comparisons to be made between entities.

Usefulness of financial information in assessing future cash flows of an entity

BCE.114   The IASB noted that the impairment model in IFRS 9 should reflect how an entity approaches credit risk management for different classes of financial instruments and provides information on the effect of the changes in the credit risk of financial instruments since initial recognition.

BCE.115   In assessing the usefulness of the information provided by this approach, the IASB has compared it to the information provided by a general provisioning approach and a fair value approach. In the IASB's view, a general provisioning approach, whereby entities build up reserves to absorb both expected and unexpected credit losses (without any reference to an increase in credit risk) lacks any measurement objective and fails to provide a link between the loss allowance that is recognised and the change in credit risk. Furthermore, a full fair value model does not provide explicit information on expected credit losses. Changes in the fair value of a financial instrument include changes in risks other than credit risk, such as interest rate risk, liquidity risk and market risk. The IASB believes that such an approach does not provide useful information for impairment purposes, because measuring expected credit losses using fair value information is inconsistent with a cost-based measurement that focuses on contractual cash flows.

BCE.116   In the IASB's view, the criterion that determines when lifetime expected credit losses shall be recognised, together with the related disclosure requirements, achieves the best balance between the benefits of distinguishing financial instruments for which there has been a significant increase in credit risk since initial recognition and the costs and complexity of making that assessment.

BCE.117   The IASB is aware that some interested parties favour a lifetime expected credit loss approach, whereby an entity recognises a loss allowance at an amount equal to lifetime expected credit losses from initial recognition, regardless of the credit risk and relative credit pricing of the financial instrument. Under such an approach, the recognition of initial lifetime expected credit losses is triggered by the initial recognition of a financial asset instead of by the increase in credit risk since initial recognition. The IASB believes that this is not appropriate because it would result in financial assets being recognised at a carrying amount that is significantly below fair value on initial recognition and would therefore be inconsistent with the economics of the asset. However, the IASB acknowledges that some users of financial statements find this information useful.

BCE.118   The IASB believes that the impairment requirements in Section 5.5 in IFRS 9 provide useful information by distinguishing between financial instruments for which the credit risk has increased significantly since initial recognition and those financial instruments for which this has not occurred. The feedback to the IASB from the majority of users of financial statements has been that this distinction provides useful information.

Modified financial instruments

BCE.119   As noted in paragraphs BC5.238–BC5.239, the IASB concluded that financial instruments with modified contractual cash flows should be permitted to revert to 12-month expected credit losses in the same way as unmodified financial instruments, if there is no longer a significant increase in credit risk since initial recognition. The IASB believes that such a symmetrical approach faithfully represents the economics of the transaction and that faithful representation should not be sacrificed for anti-abuse purposes.

BCE.120   Some users of financial statements were concerned that such a symmetrical approach would be more permissive than the current IAS 39 requirements. This is because currently in IAS 39 forbearance, as generally used in the regulatory sense, is regarded as an event that indicates objective evidence of impairment. The IASB however notes that because a significant increase in credit risk is determined by reference to the initial credit risk (on the original contractual terms), financial instruments will not necessarily revert to 12-month expected credit losses as a result of a modification of contractual cash flows. IFRS 9 requires an entity to base its assessment of significant increases in credit risk on the credit risk at initial recognition of the original financial instrument (assuming derecognition has not occurred), based on all reasonable and supportable information that is available without undue cost or effort. This includes historical, current and forward-looking information and an assessment of the credit risk over the remaining life of the instrument, which should include the circumstances that led to the modification.

BCE.121   Furthermore, while forbearance may provide objective evidence for the recognition of an incurred loss in accordance with IAS 39, the effect of the modification of contractual cash flows is reflected in the measurement of the impairment loss under that Standard. Consequently, if a modified financial instrument is not considered to have increased significantly in credit risk, it is likely that only a small incurred loss would currently be recognised under IAS 39. As a result, the IASB believes that even if, subsequent to a modification, a loss allowance at an amount equal to 12-month expected credit losses is recognised, it should not result in a smaller loss allowance than would be recognised under IAS 39. The IASB notes that entities are required to disclose the gross carrying amount for modified financial assets for which the loss allowance has reverted back to 12-month expected credit losses during the reporting period.

Better economic decision-making as a result of improved financial reporting

BCE.122   The IASB believes that the new impairment model provides information that is relevant for economic decision-making by depicting changes in the credit risk of financial instruments through the use of a broad range of information, including forward-looking information and the recognition of expected credit losses on a timelier basis. Users of financial statements will also be provided with more information to understand entities' credit risk management processes and the credit risk inherent in their financial instruments. The IASB is of the view that loss allowances should reflect credit loss expectations for financial instruments as at the reporting date.

BCE.123   The IASB acknowledges that the new impairment model would result in an overstatement of expected credit losses for financial assets, and a resulting understatement of the value of the related financial assets, through the recognition of a loss allowance for 12-month expected credit losses. However, the IASB has sought to provide a proxy for the 2009 Impairment Exposure Draft that is less operationally burdensome and more cost-effective. The IASB determined that the impairment requirements in IFRS 9 provides the best balance of the benefits of providing useful information and the costs of providing it. In addition, the overstatement will not be of the same magnitude as if full lifetime expected credit losses were to be recognised on initial recognition. For long-term financial assets and those with a high risk of default occurring as at initial recognition, the difference between a 12-month and lifetime expected credit loss measure can be significant.

BCE.124   Furthermore, relevant information is provided by updating expected credit loss estimates for changes in expectations, by updating the measurement of the loss allowance at each reporting date, and in particular through the recognition of lifetime expected credit losses when there has been a significant increase in credit risk since initial recognition. In addition, information is provided by requiring the calculation of interest revenue on the amortised cost amount (ie net of the loss allowance) of a financial asset when it becomes credit-impaired subsequent to initial recognition.

Regulatory concept of expected credit losses

BCE.125   Some users of financial statements asked the IASB to ensure that the impairment model is both aligned to the prudential capital frameworks and is counter-cyclical, resulting in a loss allowance that is sufficient to absorb all credit losses.

BCE.126   Some prudential regulation and capital adequacy systems, such as the framework developed by the Basel Committee on Banking Supervision, already require financial institutions to calculate 12-month expected credit losses as part of their regulatory capital provisions. However, these estimates only use credit loss experience based on historical events to set out 'provisioning' levels over the entire economic cycle ('through-the-cycle'). Furthermore, through-the-cycle approaches consider a range of possible economic outcomes instead of those that are actually expected at the reporting date. This would result in a loss allowance that is not designed to reflect the economic characteristics of the financial instruments at the reporting date. In addition, the default measures used may be adjusted to reflect a more 'conservative' outlook instead of actual expectations.

BCE.127   The IASB notes that financial reporting, including estimates of expected credit losses, are based on information, circumstances and events at the reporting date. The IASB expects entities to be able to use the systems and processes in place to determine amounts for regulatory purposes as a basis for the application of the impairment requirements in IFRS 9. However, these calculations would have to be adjusted to meet the measurement requirements of IFRS 9.

BCE.128   The IASB acknowledges that any transition adjustments arising on the initial application of IFRS 9 will affect retained earnings, which potentially could have a negative impact on regulatory capital. However, the IASB believes that the objective of financial reporting should be to provide transparent information that is useful to a broad range of users of financial statements and that prudential regulators are best placed to consider how to address the interaction between IFRS and the regulatory requirements. The IASB has discussed the new impairment model and shared information with the Basel Committee on Banking Supervision—through its Accounting Experts Group— throughout the course of the project in order to enable the interaction of the new impairment model with relevant regulatory requirements to be considered. The actual effect on regulatory capital will depend on the decisions made by relevant regulators about the interaction between the IFRS impairment requirements and the prudential requirements.

BCE.129   Some are of the view that loss allowance balances should be used to provide a counter-cyclical effect by building up loss allowances in the good times, to be used in the bad times. This would, however, mask the effect of changes in credit loss expectations. The impairment model in IFRS 9 is based on reasonable and supportable information that is available without undue cost or effort at the reporting date and is designed to reflect economic reality, instead of adjusting the assumptions and inputs applied to achieve a counter-cyclical effect. When credit risk changes, the impairment model will faithfully represent that change. This is consistent with the objective of general purpose financial statements.

BCE.130   Also, because the objective of the new impairment model is to faithfully represent changes in credit risk since initial recognition, the IASB does not believe it would be consistent to also have an objective of ensuring that the recognition of a loss allowance will be sufficient to cover unexpected credit losses. Some users of financial statements would however prefer a representation of credit losses with a conservative or prudential bias, arguing that such a representation would better meet both the needs of regulators who are responsible for maintaining financial stability and those of investors. The majority of users of financial statements that the IASB discussed the impairment requirements with, however supported an impairment model that focuses on expected credit losses and the changes in credit risk since initial recognition.

Fieldwork

BCE.131   The IASB undertook detailed fieldwork during the comment period for the 2013 Impairment Exposure Draft. A key objective of the fieldwork was to understand how responsive the proposed impairment model was expected to be to changes in credit risk expectations over time. It was also designed to provide an understanding of the operational impact of the implementation of the proposals and to provide some directional information about the magnitude of the allowance balance on transition from IAS 39.

BCE.132 In order to understand the responsiveness of the proposed impairment model, the IASB asked participants to use real portfolio information and simulate changes in the credit risk of those portfolios based on a time series of macroeconomic information. To undertake this analysis properly was a very intensive exercise, because it required not only an understanding of existing data but also that entities analyse how they would expect the macroeconomic changes described to affect credit risk over time for their chosen portfolios.[57] Given the intensiveness of the exercise, the sample size was necessarily limited and only 15 participants took part in the fieldwork. However, in order to make the exercise as representative as possible, participants included both financial and non-financial (lessor) entities, multinational and regional (or country)-based businesses, Basel-regulated and non-Basel-regulated entities and entities with various levels of sophistication in credit risk management systems. There was also a mixture of the type of portfolios that participants selected, which in aggregate had a total carrying amount in excess of US $500 billion and included:[58]

    (a)   retail mortgages, including:

        (i)   amortising loans;

        (ii)   interest only loans; and

        (iii)   equity-line loans.

    (b)   corporate (wholesale) loans;

    (c)   revolving credit products (for example, credit cards);

    (d)   lease receivables (for example, vehicle finance); and

    (e)   other unsecured lending, for example, personal loans/payday loans.

BCE.133 To meet the objective of the fieldwork, participants were asked to measure the loss allowance over a period of five years and apply different impairment requirements for their respective portfolios, including the requirements in IAS 39, the proposals in the 2013 Impairment Exposure Draft and full lifetime expected credit losses for all financial instruments.

BCE.134 While participants were generally able to operationalise the proposals of the 2013 Impairment Exposure Draft, it was not without obstacles. One of the reasons was that there was only a very limited time frame for the fieldwork to be completed in. In addition, by necessity participants could only use information provided as part of the fieldwork or that existed in their credit risk management systems. This meant that the approaches taken could not fully represent those which may ultimately be undertaken. So for retail portfolios, participants were often only able to identify significant increases in credit risk based on past due information plus some adjustments (for example,

---

57 The man-hours invested during fieldwork were between 200–250 for smaller businesses, 400–450 for larger businesses and 500–550 for a few participants. The IASB staff invested approximately 400 man-hours, which involved the development of the fieldwork, meetings with participants and portfolio analysis.

58 The portfolios excluded derivatives and financial guarantee contracts to make the calculations easier and to help participants meet the short deadline of the fieldwork.

including restructurings). They found it difficult to incorporate more forward-looking data (for example, macroeconomic data) at a level that enabled them to identify specific financial assets for which there have been significant increases in credit risk since initial recognition.

BCE.135 As a result of this feedback, additional work was undertaken with participants to consider how to ensure that lifetime expected credit losses are recognised for *all* financial instruments for which there have been significant increases in credit risk, even if the significant increase in credit risk is not yet evident on an individual financial instrument level. This has led the IASB to emphasise the need for a portfolio perspective when significant increases in credit risk cannot be identified on an individual financial instrument level to ensure that IFRS 9 is applied on an appropriately forward-looking basis. The work with participants showed that statistical methods and techniques could be used to analyse subportfolios to capture significant increases in credit risk even when that is not evident based on customer-specific information at the level of individual financial instruments.

BCE.136 Nevertheless, participants in the fieldwork found that the impairment model proposed in the 2013 Impairment Exposure Draft was more responsive to changing economic circumstances in both downturn and upturn macroeconomic environments compared to the IAS 39 model.[59] During a downturn, the loss allowances increased quickly and reached their peak around a year before the lowest point in the economy (reflecting that the data provided was used as forecast data for a 12-month period). During an upturn, the loss allowances recovered faster than those under IAS 39, which often still had a lagging effect from the downturn in the economic cycle. Participants noted that the better an entity is able to incorporate forward-looking and macroeconomic data into its credit risk management models, the more responsive the loss allowance would be to changes in credit risk.

BCE.137 In addition, almost all the participants observed a noticeable increase in the loss allowance on the hypothetical transition date and throughout the economic cycle as compared to IAS 39. For example, on transition, the loss allowance for portfolios other than mortgage portfolios was between 25 per cent and 60 per cent higher compared to the IAS 39 balance and the loss allowance for mortgage portfolios was between 30 per cent and 250 per cent higher compared to the IAS 39 balance. In addition, at the point in the economic cycle when the economic forecast was worst (ie when loss allowances were the highest), the loss allowance measured in accordance with the 2013 Impairment Exposure Draft was between 50 per cent and 150 per cent higher compared to the IAS 39 balance for portfolios other than

---

59 Participants were provided a series of economic information so their proxy forecasting was more accurate than it would be in reality. Although this assessment has imperfections, it nevertheless provided an estimate of the responsiveness of the impairment model.

mortgage portfolios and between 80 per cent and 400 per cent higher compared to the IAS 39 balance for mortgage portfolios.[60, 61]

BCE.138   In performing these calculations, participants that had higher 'incurred but not reported' allowances in accordance with IAS 39 because of longer emergence periods tended to see less of an impact when applying the 2013 Impairment Exposure Draft. In addition, participants that identified and recognised impairment losses on an individual level in a timelier manner under IAS 39 also saw a smaller impact. Finally, participants noted jurisdictional differences because of different macroeconomic factors that affect expected credit losses and therefore the loss allowance.

BCE.139   The IASB notes that it cannot quantify the magnitude of the impact of moving to the new impairment model on an entity's financial reporting. The magnitude of the impact from the requirements in IFRS 9 depends on the financial instruments that an entity holds, when the financial instruments were originally recognised, how the entity has applied the IAS 39 requirements, the sophistication of the entity's credit risk management systems and the availability of information about, for example, the probabilities of a default occurring, past due statuses and estimates of lifetime expected credit losses for all financial instruments (for example, products, geographical areas and vintages). While all entities will be required to meet the objective of the impairment requirements in Section 5.5 of IFRS 9, in practice, the loss allowance will depend in part on how entities operationalise IFRS 9. The IASB is aware that entities across different jurisdictions have applied the existing impairment requirements in IAS 39 differently, in part as a result of the interaction with local or jurisdictional regulatory definitions and requirements.

BCE.140   Finally, the magnitude of the impact will also depend on the prevalent economic conditions at the time of transitioning to the new requirements. The loss allowance always reflects expectations at the reporting date, so economic conditions at the date of initial application (including forecasts of economic conditions) will affect the loss allowance. The effect on transition will also depend on the information that an entity has available on transition. For example, if an entity is unable to determine the change in credit risk of a financial instrument since initial recognition and will not use past due information to apply the model to that instrument, if it is a low credit risk financial asset, it will have an allowance balance equal to 12-month expected credit losses; otherwise it will have a loss allowance equal to lifetime expected credit losses.

---

60   The difference in percentages reflect the extreme effects of differences in expected lives between jurisdictions.

61   This is reflective of the results of the majority of participants in the fieldwork. Excluded from the results, were the responses from participants based on:

(a) qualitative feedback due to timing requirements of the fieldwork; or

(b) the simplified approach (ie measured lifetime expected credit losses on all financial assets) or an absolute approach (for example, when lifetime expected credit losses were recognised on all financial assets of higher credit risk irrespective of whether the credit risk had increased significantly since initial recognition).

The likely effect on compliance costs for preparers, both at initial application and on an ongoing basis

BCE.141 IFRS 9 seeks to address the cost of identifying deteriorated financial instruments by using significant increases in credit risk as a basis for the distinction. This is intended to ensure that only meaningful changes in credit risk are captured that should align with changes that would be monitored for credit risk management.

BCE.142 The IASB acknowledges that the implementation and ongoing application of an impairment model based on expected credit losses is complex and costly. The costs resulting from the impairment model in IFRS 9 include:

(a) monitoring changes in credit risk of financial instruments since initial recognition and implementing processes to make that assessment; and

(b) calculating expected credit losses including lifetime expected credit losses.

Cost of initial application

BCE.143 The IASB acknowledges that the impairment model in IFRS 9 is different from a credit risk management perspective, because an entity needs to assess the change in credit risk since initial recognition, whereas credit risk managers assess credit risk at a particular date. For example, entities have raised concerns that two loans to the same entity could have different loss allowances when they are originated at different times. Although such a difference in perspective is likely to add cost and complexity to the impairment model, the IASB believes that it is justified because of the underlying concept that a loss only arises when the credit loss expectations on a financial instrument exceed those that are considered when pricing the instrument. Thus, this approach provides information that is useful for users of financial statements.

BCE.144 The implementation of the impairment model will require system changes that may be substantial, and time and resource commitments, resulting in significant costs for most entities with substantial amounts of financial instruments subject to impairment accounting including financial institutions that are already calculating expected credit losses for regulatory purposes. Entities will need to develop new systems and controls to integrate information produced for credit risk management purposes, or elsewhere in their business, into their accounting process. In addition, entities will incur one-time implementation costs to educate personnel in accounting functions to enable them to assess whether the information prepared for credit risk management would suffice to comply with the new impairment requirements. Finally, entities will need to explain to users of financial statements the new impairment model and how it differs from IAS 39 and from the information produced for credit risk management and regulatory purposes. However, these costs are mitigated because the impairment model is based upon changes in credit risk that should be monitored for credit risk management purposes and enables a variety of approaches to be taken to identify such changes, enabling entities to use credit risk information as a basis for implementation.

BCE.145 Participants in outreach activities, preparers responding to the 2013 Impairment Exposure Draft and participants in the fieldwork noted that the cost of implementing the proposed impairment model would depend on how entities segment their portfolios. An entity may, for example, in cases in which the credit risk at origination is similar for particular portfolios, segment its portfolios by credit risk at origination and assess increases in credit risk by comparing the credit risk at the reporting date with the initial credit risk for the relevant portfolio. Thus, the costs of applying the criteria to determine whether lifetime expected credit losses must be recognised would vary depending on the diversity of initial credit risk and the sophistication of credit risk management systems.

BCE.146 The IASB also clarified that a specific or mechanistic assessment is not required. This means that entities need not have explicit probability of default information to assess changes in credit risk, which will enhance the operability of the model and reduce the implementation and ongoing costs.

BCE.147 In addition, the IASB clarified that on initial application of the impairment requirements, entities are permitted to use reasonable and supportable information that is available without undue cost or effort to approximate the credit risk at initial recognition of a financial instrument. Participants in outreach activities and in the fieldwork noted that they would often not have the original credit risk information at transition, which could result in financial instruments being measured inappropriately at lifetime expected credit losses (ie when there have not been in fact a significant increase in credit risk). The IASB clarified the transition requirements because its intention is not to penalise those entities that could not obtain information about the initial credit risk without undue cost or effort. This clarification will enhance the operability of the impairment model and reduce preparers' costs on transition.

BCE.148 For the calculation of expected credit losses (and in particular for the calculation of lifetime expected credit losses), systems need to be updated or newly developed. Field participants used different methods to calculate expected credit losses and noted, for example, that current systems do not discount cash flows used to determine expected credit losses or may discount only to the date of expected default. As a result, systems would need to be modified to discount expected cash flows to the reporting date and to capture the expected timing of credit losses better.

BCE.149 The new disclosure requirements will result in the need to capture more data than under the current disclosure requirements in IFRS 7. Those costs arise on transition to establish the capability to provide those disclosures but will also include ongoing costs. However, if entities embed this in their systems that they use for preparing their financial statements, the ongoing costs can be reduced.

BCE.150   The IASB notes that significant implementation costs are not limited to the impairment model in IFRS 9 and that, regardless of which expected credit loss approach an entity implements, the cost and effort of implementation will be significant. The IASB believes that IFRS 9 appropriately balances the complex requirements of an impairment model based on expected credit losses, with simplifications designed to make the approach more operational, thereby reducing the cost of implementation.

Cost of ongoing application

Interest revenue recognition

BCE.151   The requirement to change the recognition of interest revenue from a gross basis to a net basis at a different level of increase in credit risk compared to when lifetime expected credit losses are recognised (ie when credit losses are incurred) adds a further level of complexity. However, the financial assets that are credit-impaired will be a subset of the financial assets for which lifetime expected credit losses are recognised in accordance with IFRS 9. In addition, because the criteria listed for an instrument to be credit-impaired are the same as the existing incurred loss criteria in IAS 39 (except for the exclusion of 'incurred but not reported'), the IASB believes that the application of these concepts should result in minimal change in practice and will therefore have no significant cost implications for existing IFRS preparers.[62]

Allowance for 12-month expected credit losses

BCE.152   The measurement of a loss allowance at an amount equal to 12-month expected credit losses adds costs and complexity to the impairment model. These costs will be less for financial institutions that are already required to calculate 12-month expected credit losses for prudential purposes; however, that measure would have to be adjusted to meet the measurement requirements of IFRS 9. In some cases, entities can use information such as loss rates to calculate 12-month expected credit losses, thus building on information that they already use for risk management purposes. However, the cost of measuring a loss allowance at an amount equal to 12-month expected credit losses will be higher for non-Basel II financial institutions and entities that are not financial institutions, because 12-month expected credit losses are a unique calculation that would not normally be required for other purposes. Participants in the fieldwork considered the 12-month allowance to be operational, because information on the 12-month risk of a default occurring is often readily available and already often used (albeit sometimes requiring adjustments) for internal credit risk or regulatory purposes. When information was not readily available internally, participants indicated that information is obtainable in the market to enable this to be determined. However, because of the uniqueness of the calculation, IFRS 9 also provides some relief; for example, the calculation of 12-month expected credit losses is not required for trade receivables, contract assets or lease receivables. In addition, as a result of the 12-month calculation, the lifetime expected credit

---

62   Almost all participants in the fieldwork considered the proposal to measure interest revenue on the net basis for financial assets that are credit-impaired operable, because it is consistent with the current requirements in IAS 39.

losses are required to be recognised on fewer financial instruments. As this can be a complex exercise, (see further below in paragraph BCE.155) in effect the 12-month measure also is a source of cost mitigation.

Assessment of significant increases in credit risk

BCE.153   Respondents to the 2009 Impairment Exposure Draft highlighted that the proposals would have required entities to track the initial estimate of lifetime expected credit losses through the credit-adjusted effective interest rate and recognise subsequent changes in the lifetime expected credit losses. This would have led to significant operational challenges and substantial costs, because the effective interest rate information is not contained in the same systems as the credit risk information. To address this, IFRS 9 requires an assessment of the changes in credit risk that have occurred since initial recognition separately from the determination of the effective interest rate. It only requires the effective interest rate to be adjusted for a limited population of financial assets – those that are purchased or originated credit impaired. This reduces the cost of implementation and, in addition, this does not result in an incremental cost for IFRS preparers as this population is unchanged from IAS 39.

BCE.154   Some preparers, particularly credit risk managers, indicated that the tracking of credit risk, in most circumstances, is simpler and more closely aligned to credit risk management practices than the tracking of expected credit losses. To enable the model to be implemented more easily based on existing credit risk management systems, IFRS 9 therefore requires entities to measure and track the initial credit risk instead of changes in expected credit losses to determine whether there has been a significant increase in credit risk since initial recognition.

BCE.155   Some interested parties are concerned that the distinction between financial instruments whose credit risk has increased significantly since initial recognition and financial instruments for which this has not occurred will be operationally challenging. They would prefer lifetime expected credit losses to be measured for all financial instruments (ie also for those financial instruments that have a loss allowance measured at an amount equal to 12-month expected credit losses in accordance with IFRS 9). However, any impairment model that is based on expected credit losses will require monitoring of changes in credit risk to update the expected credit loss amounts. Consequently, differentiating significant changes in credit risk from those that are not, is only an incremental cost to any other impairment model based on expected credit losses. Participants in the fieldwork and respondents to the 2013 Impairment Exposure Draft supported the operability of the impairment proposals for a model in which the measurement of the loss allowance changes when there is a significant increase in credit risk since initial recognition. They stated that this is similar to their credit risk management actions. In addition, it is also expected to be less costly compared to measuring lifetime expected credit losses for all financial instruments. This is because lifetime expected credit losses are most difficult to calculate for long-dated financial assets that are fully performing (ie the 'good' loans, which are measured at 12-month expected credit losses in accordance with

IFRS 9), as noted by fieldwork participants. In addition, they observed that lifetime expected credit losses were more sensitive to the underlying assumptions. Their results from the fieldwork showed that updated macroeconomic forecasts led to more volatility in an impairment model based on lifetime expected credit losses for all financial instruments because of the extrapolation effects. They also observed that if lifetime expected credit losses were recognised for all financial instruments the allowance balances increased by at least 100 per cent compared to the 2013 Impairment Exposure Draft for both their mortgages and other portfolios. Finally, they stated that recognising lifetime expected credit losses for financial instruments that have not increased significantly in credit risk is not reflective of the economics of their business.

BCE.156 Some respondents to the 2013 Impairment Exposure Draft were concerned that the assessment of significant increases in credit risk as drafted in that Exposure Draft would require the explicit calculation and storage of the lifetime probability of default curve for a financial instrument to compare the expected remaining lifetime probability of default at inception with the remaining lifetime probability of default at the reporting date. However, the IASB had no intention to prescribe a specific or mechanistic approach to assess whether there has been a significant increase in credit risk. In fact, prescribing a specific method would be contrary to the approach taken by the IASB throughout the development of the new impairment requirements in IFRS 9, whereby the IASB took into account different levels of sophistication of entities and different data availability. Consequently, the IASB has clarified in IFRS 9 that an entity may apply different approaches when assessing whether the credit risk of a financial instrument has increased significantly since initial recognition for different financial instruments. This addresses different levels of sophistication and reduces the operational burden to assess whether a financial instrument shall be measured at lifetime expected credit losses.

BCE.157 In order to further reduce the operational burden of tracking the risk of a default occurring for all financial instruments since initial recognition, IFRS 9 does not require an entity to recognise lifetime expected credit losses on financial instruments with low credit risk at a reporting date, irrespective of the change in credit risk since initial recognition. Consequently, if an entity applies this simplification, it will not need to assess the change in credit risk from initial recognition for financial instruments that have low credit risk on a reporting date (for example, financial instruments whose credit risk is equivalent to investment grade).

BCE.158 The IASB acknowledges that not all entities have advanced credit risk management systems that will enable them to track the changes in credit risk over time. To further reduce the operational burden on such entities, IFRS 9 allows entities to use past due information to determine whether credit risk has increased significantly if information (either on an individual or a portfolio level) that is more forward-looking is not available without undue cost or effort, instead of requiring the implementation of more sophisticated credit risk management systems.

BCE.159   Some preparers were concerned that lifetime expected credit losses would need to be determined for each individual financial instrument, which would add to the operational burden of tracking. However, the IASB clarified that IFRS 9 does not require individual financial instruments to be identifiable as having significantly increased in credit risk in order to recognise lifetime expected credit losses. Financial instruments that share common risk characteristics can be assessed on a collective basis. In particular, IFRS 9 clarifies that the assessment of significant increases in credit risk could be implemented by establishing the maximum credit risk accepted for a particular portfolio on initial recognition (by product type and/or region; the 'origination' credit risk), and then comparing the credit risk of financial instruments in that portfolio at the reporting date with that origination credit risk.[63] In addition, it clarifies that in some cases the assessment of significant increases in credit risk can be implemented through a counterparty assessment instead of an assessment of each individual facility provided to the counterparty as long as such an assessment achieves the objectives of the impairment model and the outcome would not be different to what it would have been if financial instruments had been individually assessed.[64] Both of these clarifications are expected to reduce the operational burden of tracking.

Loan commitments and financial guarantee contracts

BCE.160   IFRS 9 requires the application of the impairment requirements to loan commitments and financial guarantee contracts that are not measured at fair value through profit or loss. While respondents to the 2013 Impairment Exposure Draft widely supported the proposal to recognise a loss allowance for expected credit losses that result from these loan commitments and financial guarantee contracts when there is a present contractual obligation to extend credit, the majority of those respondents noted that expected credit losses on some loan commitments should not be estimated over the contractual commitment period. This is because it would be contrary to credit risk management and regulatory reporting, which could result in loss allowances that do not represent the credit losses expected on the off-balance sheet exposures resulting in outcomes for which no actual loss experience exists on which to base the estimates. Participants in the fieldwork who applied the proposed impairment model to credit cards also raised these concerns and suggested that the expected credit loss on these types of loan commitments should be estimated over the behavioural life instead of the contractual life of the instrument. IFRS 9 addresses these concerns and requires expected credit losses for revolving credit facilities, such as credit cards and overdraft facilities, to be measured over the period that the entity expects to be exposed to credit risk and not over the contractual commitment period. This change should enable the measurement of expected credit losses to be more closely

---

63   Some of the participants in the fieldwork confirmed that this is a more practical way to implement the assessment of significant increases in credit risk for financial instruments, thus making the impairment model more operational.

64   During the fieldwork, some participants were initially concerned that the assessment of significant increases in credit risk is not based on changes in the counterparty's credit risk. However, over the course of the fieldwork, a number of those participants found ways to deal with the difference between the change in the counterparty credit risk and the change in the credit risk of the instrument since origination and stated this to be no longer an area of concern.

aligned to credit risk management systems and enable the loss allowance to more faithfully represent expected credit losses on those exposures.

Simplified approach for trade receivables, contract assets and lease receivables

BCE.161 IFRS 9 addresses the costs and complexities for non-financial institutions and other entities through the simplified approach that removes the need to calculate 12-month expected credit losses and track the increase in credit risk for trade receivables, contract assets and lease receivables.[65]

The effect on entities with less sophisticated credit risk management systems

BCE.162 While a few interested parties have expressed concern that it would be costlier to implement the proposals in some jurisdictions, and for entities that have less sophisticated credit risk management systems, it is the IASB's view that systems and processes that would be required to apply IFRS 9 generally also would be required to manage the entity's business effectively.

BCE.163 However, in order to reduce the operational burden and cost of application for entities, IFRS 9:

   (a)   does not require lifetime expected credit losses to be determined for all financial instruments;

   (b)   has a 'low credit risk' simplification (see paragraph 5.5.10 of IFRS 9);

   (c)   allows entities to use past due information to implement the model (in conjunction with more forward-looking information that is reasonably available without undue cost or effort);

   (d)   does not require a specific approach for assessing whether there has been a significant increase in credit risk, thus enabling entities to build upon their credit risk management information;

   (e)   clarifies that significant increases in credit risk can be assessed on an individual instrument or a portfolio basis; and

   (f)   allows entities to use practical expedients when measuring expected credit losses (such as a provision matrix for trade receivables) if doing so is consistent with the principles of IFRS 9.

BCE.164 In addition, IFRS 9 emphasises that an exhaustive search for information is not required. For example, when assessing significant increases in credit risk, entities shall consider all internal and external information that is reasonably available without undue cost or effort. This may mean that entities with little

---

65 The non-financial institutions that participated in the fieldwork supported the accounting policy election for lease receivables. They applied the simplified approach because:

(a) the assets in the portfolio were short term in nature; and

(b) the simplified approach fitted better into their current credit risk systems, which were not sophisticated systems.

The majority of the respondents to the 2013 Impairment Exposure Draft also supported the accounting policy election for lease and trade receivables.

historical information would draw their estimates from internal reports and statistics (which may, for example, have been generated when deciding whether to launch a new product), information that they have about similar products or from peer group experience for comparable financial instruments.

Disclosures

BCE.165   Disclosures are a major contributor to the overall benefits of the model. As mentioned in paragraph BCE.172, the IASB decided to include requirements that provide users of financial statements with information about how an entity manages its credit risk and estimates and measures expected credit losses. The IASB received feedback that a number of the disclosure requirements in the 2013 Impairment Exposure Draft were operationally challenging. With this in mind, the IASB decided on a number of changes and clarifications to reduce the burden of compliance while still providing the information needed by the users of the financial statements.

BCE.166   The IASB considers the requirement in the 2013 Impairment Exposure Draft to provide a reconciliation between the opening balance and the closing balance of the loss allowance and the gross carrying amount of financial assets as a core disclosure. Respondents to the 2013 Impairment Exposure Draft were concerned that this disclosure would be operationally too challenging. Given the feedback raised on operational concerns, the IASB made the disclosure less prescriptive and more principle-based by clarifying that its objective is to provide information about the significant changes in the gross carrying amount that contributed to changes in the loss allowance during the period. In particular, the disclosures are intended to enable users of the financial statements to differentiate between the effects of changes in the amount of exposure (for example, those due to increased lending) and the effect of changes in credit risk. The IASB considers that the requirement, as clarified, is less operationally burdensome but still provides useful information to users of financial statements.

BCE.167   Another important disclosure is the disclosure about modified financial assets. The requirement in the 2013 Impairment Exposure Draft to disclose the gross carrying amount of financial assets that have been modified resulted from a request from users of financial statements to understand the amount of assets that have been modified and subsequently improved in credit risk. The IASB addressed preparers' concerns that the disclosure of the gross carrying amount of modified financial assets for which the measurement objective has changed from lifetime to 12-month expected credit losses during the entire remaining lifetime of the asset (ie until derecognition) would be too onerous, because it would require the tracking of individual assets even after they have returned to a performing status and are no longer closely monitored for credit risk management purposes. Instead, entities shall now only disclose financial assets modified during the reporting period. This still provides an important source of information about the amount of restructuring activity being undertaken while being less burdensome.

The likely effect on costs of analysis for users of financial statements

BCE.168 The IASB believes that users of financial statements will benefit from the timelier information provided about credit risk and the changes in credit risk. The impairment model in IFRS 9 is in strong contrast to the incurred loss model in IAS 39, in which credit losses were only recognised once there was objective evidence that a loss event had occurred. In accordance with IFRS 9, a loss allowance at an amount equal to 12-month expected credit losses will be recognised for all financial instruments unless there has been a significant increase in credit risk since initial recognition, in which case a loss allowance at an amount equal to lifetime expected credit losses should be recognised. Lifetime expected credit losses are therefore recognised earlier than under the incurred loss model in IAS 39, because the credit risk will generally increase significantly before one or more credit loss events occur, particularly given the use of forward-looking information.

BCE.169 The IASB acknowledges that some users of financial statements might have preferred lifetime expected credit losses to be recognised for high credit risk financial instruments that are not purchased or originated credit impaired at initial recognition, whereas only 12-month expected credit losses will be recognised until there has been a significant increase in the credit risk since initial recognition. However, the IASB did not want to create an 'artificial' disincentive for entities to lend to customers with higher credit risk. Furthermore, the IASB believes that full lifetime expected credit losses should not be recognised on initial recognition irrespective of the initial credit risk because financial instruments are priced reflecting initial credit risk expectations. In particular, the IASB was concerned about the effect on the balance sheet carrying amount at initial recognition that would result if lifetime expected credit losses were recognised from inception.

BCE.170 The IASB noted that by reducing the effect on initial recognition by limiting the loss allowance to 12-month expected credit losses the risk of unintended consequences (such as reducing lending to higher risk customers even when correctly priced or reducing lending as the economic environment weakens in order to enable loss allowances to run down creating a gain in profit or loss) would be reduced.

BCE.171 The IASB acknowledges that it would be preferable for users of financial statements if the accounting for expected credit losses was aligned between IFRS and US GAAP. At the time of completing IFRS 9 it appeared likely that accounting for impairment would not be converged despite the efforts of the IASB and the FASB. However, the IASB noted that it was important to improve impairment accounting in accordance with IFRS.

BCE.172 The IASB acknowledges that the assessment of changes in credit risk since initial recognition inherently involves a significant amount of subjectivity and therefore reduces the verifiability and comparability of reported amounts. This inevitably results in costs of analysis to users of financial statements. However, decisions about when credit losses are incurred and the measurement of impairment losses currently in accordance with IAS 39 also involve subjectivity and there is a lack of comparability because of the differences in the application of the incurred loss criteria. IFRS 9 mitigates these issues to some extent by expanding the disclosure requirements to provide users of financial statements with information about the inputs, assumptions and techniques that entities use when assessing the criteria for the recognition of lifetime expected credit losses and the measurement of expected credit losses. For example, a reconciliation is required between the opening balance and the closing balance of the loss allowance and the gross carrying amount of financial assets, which the IASB considers provides useful information about the development and evolution of expected credit losses. Disclosure is also required of information about financial assets with a loss allowance at an amount equal to lifetime expected credit losses that have been modified, including the gross carrying amount of the financial assets and the gain or loss resulting from the modification. Information on modifications is responsive to requests for enhanced information in this area from users of financial statements, because this information was found to be inadequate during the global financial crisis.

Conclusion

BCE.173   The IASB expects that the requirements will provide timelier and more representationally faithful information about an entity's current estimates of expected credit losses and the changes in those estimates over time for all financial instruments subject to impairment accounting. In addition, the requirements include a comprehensive package of disclosures that will help investors to understand the judgements, assumptions and information used by an entity in developing its estimates of expected credit losses. As a result, more relevant and transparent information will be provided to users of financial statements.

Analysis of the effects: Hedge Accounting

Introduction

BCE.174   Throughout the Hedge Accounting project, the IASB performed outreach and consulted with interested parties, with the largest outreach meeting being attended by over 200 participants. The IASB also had extensive discussions with regulators and audit firms worldwide. The analysis in paragraphs BCE.175–BCE.238 is based on the feedback received through this process. Overall, the IASB held over 145 outreach meetings in all the major jurisdictions and also evaluated 247 comment letters received in response to the Exposure Draft *Hedge Accounting*, which was published in 2010 ('2010 Hedge Accounting Exposure Draft'). The IASB also considered comments received on the draft Standard posted on its website in September 2012.

Overview

BCE.175   Financial reporting should provide transparent information to enable better economic decision-making. Hedge accounting relates to the reporting of risk management activities that entities enter into, to manage their exposures to the risks identified as relevant, from a business perspective.

BCE.176   Over the last decades, the extent and complexity of hedging activities have increased substantially. This has been caused not only by entities' increasing willingness and ability to manage their exposures, but also by the increased availability of financial instruments to manage those exposures.

BCE.177   The hedge accounting requirements in IAS 39 *Financial Instruments: Recognition and Measurement* were complex and rule-based. They involved trying to fit transactions that were originated for risk management purposes into an accounting framework that was largely divorced from the purpose of the transactions. This was pointed out by respondents to the Discussion Paper *Reducing Complexity in Reporting Financial Instruments* (published in 2008) and the sentiment has been confirmed in the outreach and feedback received by the IASB while developing the new hedge accounting requirements.

BCE.178   This also caused difficulties for users of financial statements when trying to understand the information reported in financial statements. Some users of financial statements regarded hedge accounting as being incomprehensible and often removed its effects from their various analyses. Users frequently argued that they had to request additional information (often on a non-GAAP basis) to be able to perform their analyses (for example, making forecasts), because the way in which the hedging activities were accounted for and the disclosures that were provided were often considered not to portray risk management in a useful way. The disclosures under IAS 39 were perceived as too accounting-centric and lacking transparency. This led to entities presenting non-GAAP information in various ways, with various levels of detail across different documents that range from the Management Discussion and Analysis to investor presentations.

BCE.179   The complexity of the hedge accounting model in IAS 39 and the resulting increased importance of non-GAAP information led preparers and users of financial statements to ask the IASB to develop a model that, instead of reporting the results of an accounting-centric exercise, would report the performance of an entity's hedging activities in the financial statements on a basis that was consistent with that entity's risk management activities.

BCE.180   The IASB believes that the new hedge accounting requirements address this issue. Under the new model, it is possible for the financial statements of an entity to reflect its risk management activities instead of simply complying with a rule-based approach, such as the approach in IAS 39.

BCE.181   Overall, the IASB's assessment is that these new requirements will bring significant and sustained improvements to the reporting of hedging activities. In addition, entities will be able to use information that they have prepared for the purpose of undertaking their hedging activities as the basis for demonstrating compliance with the hedge accounting requirements.

BCE.182   The hedge accounting requirements included in IFRS 9 reflect a substantial change from many aspects of hedge accounting in IAS 39. These amendments to hedge accounting will affect a variety of entities, including both financial and non-financial institutions. The new model will benefit from a more principle-based approach, including the revised eligibility criteria both for hedged items and hedging instruments, and a new objective-based hedge effectiveness assessment. In addition a targeted solution has been introduced for hedges of credit risk using credit derivatives. Entities dealing with hedging of non-financial items are likely to have significant benefits, albeit with some costs to be incurred when implementing the new model. Banks and other financial institutions will also benefit from the general hedge accounting model.

BCE.183 Areas in which it is expected that the new requirements will produce the greatest impact include: hedge effectiveness testing; eligibility of risk components of non-financial instruments; disclosures; accounting for the costs of hedging; aggregated exposures; groups and net positions; the rebalancing and discontinuation of hedging relationships; and hedges of credit risk using credit derivatives.

BCE.184 The IASB expects that most costs for preparers will be incurred at the transition date and will relate to the links that need to be created between the accounting and the risk management functions. Under the current model for hedge accounting such links have generally been weak or non-existent, reflecting the accounting-centric character of that model. Additional costs will be incurred in explaining to the users of financial statements the impact of the hedging activities. This cost will, however, be mitigated by the fact that, given the greater alignment with risk management, some of the information, although not used for accounting purposes, is already being produced for risk management purposes or is being produced for the reporting of alternative performance measures (the latter often being presented on a non-GAAP basis). In particular, the costs for the hedge effectiveness test for many hedging relationships, especially simple ones, should be reduced on an ongoing basis. The IASB's assessment is that the significant improvements in terms of comparability and transparency will outweigh those costs.

How activities would be reported in the financial statements of those applying IFRS 9

BCE.185 The analysis in paragraphs BCE.186–BCE.238 focuses on the key differences between the existing model in IAS 39 and the new hedge accounting model in this Standard and how the new model will impact financial reporting. In particular, an analysis of some of the key changes introduced by the IFRS 9 hedge accounting model that will change entities' ability to apply hedge accounting is included in paragraphs BCE.190–BCE.205.

Objective of the Standard

BCE.186 During its outreach activities the IASB learnt that both preparers and users of financial statements were frustrated about the lack of connection between actual risk management and the hedge accounting requirements. In particular, preparers found it difficult to reflect their risk management and users of financial statements found it difficult to understand the reflection of risk management on the basis of the hedge accounting requirements in IAS 39. In view of the criticisms received, the IASB, instead of merely considering improvements to the existing model, decided to rethink the entire paradigm of hedge accounting.

BCE.187   The IASB decided that the "objective of hedge accounting is to represent, in the financial statements, the effect of an entity's risk management activities that use financial instruments".[66] This is a principle-based instead of a rule-based approach that focuses on an entity's risk management. Almost all respondents to the 2010 Hedge Accounting Exposure Draft as well as participants in the IASB's outreach activities supported the objective of improving information about risk management through hedge accounting as proposed by the IASB.

BCE.188   Consequently, subject to qualifying criteria, the model developed by the IASB uses the risk management activities of an entity as the foundation for deciding what qualifies (or what does not qualify) for hedge accounting. The aim of the model is to faithfully represent, in the financial statements, the impact of the risk management activities of an entity.

Qualifying hedging instruments

BCE.189   IAS 39 imposed restrictions on what could and what could not be considered as hedging instruments. Respondents to the 2010 Hedge Accounting Exposure Draft questioned the logic behind the arbitrary disallowance of certain types of financial instruments as hedging instruments in IAS 39 even when such financial instruments provided an effective offset for risks managed under common risk management strategies. The key restriction in IAS 39 was the disallowance of designating non-derivative instruments as hedging instruments for hedges of risks other than foreign currency risk.

BCE.190   The IASB decided to expand the types of eligible financial instruments under the new hedge accounting model, to allow non-derivative financial assets and liabilities at fair value through profit or loss to be designated as hedging instruments, ie to acknowledge their effect also for accounting purposes.

BCE.191   The other key change brought in by the new hedge accounting model is the removal of the distinction between combinations of stand-alone written and purchased options and those combined in one contract. The IASB decided that the eligibility of an option contract to be designated as a hedging instrument should depend on its economic substance and risk management objectives instead of its legal form alone. Consequently, the IASB decided that a stand-alone written option would be eligible for designation as a hedging instrument if it is jointly designated with other hedging instruments so that, in combination, they do not result in a net written option.

Qualifying hedged items

BCE.192   A key change brought about by the Standard is the ability to hedge a risk component of a non-financial item. The IASB decided to align the treatment of financial and non-financial items to also allow the hedging of risk components in non-financial items, when they are separately identifiable and reliably measurable. This, as noted by many respondents, represents a key aspect of the new hedge accounting model as it allows the accounting to reflect the commercial reality in hedges of non-financial items because, in practice,

---

66   See paragraph 6.1.1 of IFRS 9.

components of non-financial items are often hedged because hedging the entire item is commercially not viable (because of, for example, a lack of availability of cost effective hedging instruments) or not desired (because, for example, the entity regards accepting the risk as more economical than transferring it to others using hedges). This change will enable such hedges to be reflected in the designation used for hedge accounting, thereby enabling preparers to better reflect, and users of financial statements to better understand, the actual risk management activity and the effectiveness of hedging strategies.

BCE.193   Under IAS 39 hedged items that together constitute an overall net position of assets and liabilities could only be designated in a hedging relationship with the gross position (a group) being the hedged item if certain restrictive criteria were met. These restrictions made achieving hedge accounting for items managed as part of a net position under IAS 39 difficult in practice and made it necessary to designate gross positions instead of the net position that is being economically hedged. This created a disconnect between the accounting and the actual risk management activity.

BCE.194   Consequently, the IASB decided that groups of items (including net positions) would be eligible for hedge accounting. In the case of foreign currency exposures this would mean that all of the actual cash flows included within the group of cash flows being hedged could be designated in line with actual risk management. However, the IASB also decided that for cash flow hedges such net position hedging would not be available for risks other than foreign currency exposures. However, the IASB noted that this did not prevent entities from getting hedge accounting through gross designations that are determined by the net exposure that is monitored for risk management purposes.

BCE.195   In the area of 'risk components', respondents believed that it should be possible to designate a risk component that assumes cash flows that would exceed the actual cash flows of the hedged item, as it reflects risk management in situations in which the hedged item has a negative spread to the benchmark rate. For example, being able to designate a full LIBOR component in a financial instrument that yields LIBOR less a spread (colloquially referred to as 'sub-LIBOR'). Such respondents believed that it should be possible to hedge the LIBOR risk as a benchmark component and treat the spread as a negative residual component, as they hedged their exposure to the variability of cash flows attributable to LIBOR (or a correlated index) using LIBOR swaps.

BCE.196   In its deliberations, the focus was primarily on the sub-LIBOR scenario although the issue is not unique to that situation (see paragraphs BC6.217–BC6.229). In that context, the IASB noted that, for risk management purposes, an entity normally does not try to hedge the entire interest rate of a financial instrument but instead the change in the variability of the cash flows attributable to LIBOR. Such a strategy protects an entity's exposure to benchmark interest rate risk and, importantly, the profit margin of the hedged items (ie the spread relative to the benchmark) is protected against LIBOR changes. This is, of course, only feasible if LIBOR does not fall below the absolute value of the negative spread. However, if LIBOR does fall below the absolute value of that negative spread it would result in 'negative' interest, or interest that is inconsistent with the movement of market interest rates. Consequently, in contrast to exposures with full LIBOR variability, hedging sub-LIBOR exposures means that the entity remains exposed to cash flow variability in some situations. The IASB noted that allowing a designation that ignores this fact would not faithfully represent the economic phenomenon.

BCE.197 Consequently, in the Standard the IASB retained the restriction in IAS 39 for the designation of risk components when the designated risk component exceeds the total cash flows of the hedged item. However, hedge accounting would still be available in such situations if all the cash flows hedged for a particular risk are designated as the hedged item.

Qualifying criteria for hedge accounting

BCE.198 As with the other aspects of the current hedge accounting model in IAS 39, the IASB received information during outreach and comments from respondents to the 2010 Hedge Accounting Exposure Draft about the hedge effectiveness requirements in IAS 39. The feedback received clearly showed that participants believed that the hedge effectiveness assessment in IAS 39 was formulaic, onerous and difficult to apply. As a consequence, there was often little or no link between the analysis undertaken by risk managers who hedge the risk and the analysis required to apply hedge accounting, and as a result between the hedge accounting and risk management operations. This was reflected, for example, in the fact that hedge accounting could be required to be discontinued in situations in which the hedging relationship was regarded as satisfactory and could be continued from a risk management perspective and for which the entity could achieve hedge accounting again — but only as a new hedging relationship. Also, given the specified bright lines for effectiveness and the accounting consequences of deviating from the same, it made hedge accounting difficult to understand and apply.

BCE.199 To address these concerns, the IASB decided to require an objective-based model for testing hedge effectiveness instead of the bright line test (80–125 per cent) in IAS 39. Instead of setting quantitative thresholds or bright lines, this approach focuses on the achievement of economic offset, a concept used by risk managers when designing and implementing hedging strategies. It also has the benefit of removing the burden of working out hedge effectiveness purely for accounting purposes and instead leverages the assessment done by risk management to ensure compliance with the hedge effectiveness requirements in the Standard. The principles and the concepts behind this change received widespread support.

BCE.200 In addition, IAS 39 did not allow adjustments in the hedging relationship subsequent to designation, except for rollover strategies documented at contract inception, to be treated as adjustments to a continuing hedging relationship. Consequently, IAS 39 treated such adjustments to an existing hedging relationship as a discontinuation of the original hedging relationship and the start of a new one. The IASB, in its deliberations, noted that this was inconsistent with risk management practices and did not represent the economic phenomenon in practice. There are instances when, although the risk management objective remains the same, adjustments to an existing hedging relationship are made because of changes in circumstances related to the hedging relationship's underlyings or risk variables. The IASB concluded that, in situations in which the original risk management objective remained unaltered, the adjustment to the hedging relationship should be treated as the continuation of the hedging relationship. This will have the effect of enabling changes in risk management to be properly portrayed in hedge accounting.

BCE.201 Under IAS 39 an entity had to discontinue hedge accounting when the hedging relationship ceased to meet the qualifying criteria. Also, the entity had a free choice to discontinue hedge accounting by simply revoking the designation of the hedging relationship, irrespective of the reason behind it. The IASB noted that entities often voluntarily discontinued hedge accounting because of how the effectiveness assessment in IAS 39 worked. The IASB noted that, in some situations, the hedging relationship was discontinued and then restarted even though the risk management objective of the entity had not changed. In the IASB's view, this created a disconnect between the hedge accounting model in IAS 39 and hedging from a risk management perspective. In the light of this, the IASB decided that the ability of an entity to voluntarily revoke a hedge designation, even when all qualifying criteria are met, would no longer be available. However, if the risk management objective for the hedging relationship changes then hedge accounting needs to be discontinued. This will improve the link with risk management by ensuring that once hedge accounting commences it will continue as long as the hedge still qualifies for hedge accounting.

Mechanics of hedge accounting

BCE.202 The IASB considered the fact that the mechanics for hedge accounting in IAS 39 were well established and understood by most interested parties, and therefore decided to retain those hedge accounting mechanics in the new model. The IASB did, however, note that many users of financial statements were confused by the accounting distinction made between cash flow hedges and fair value hedges and how that distinction related to risk and the strategies for managing such risks. Consequently, the IASB decided to include new disclosure requirements in IFRS 7, whereby all disclosures for hedge accounting are presented in a single section in the financial statements with the objective of alleviating this confusion.

BCE.203 Under IAS 39 entities typically designated option-type derivatives as hedging instruments on the basis of their intrinsic value. This meant that the time value that was not designated was required to be presented similarly to financial instruments held for trading. This created a disconnect between the accounting treatment and the risk management view, whereby entities typically consider the time value of an option at contract inception (the premium paid) as a cost of hedging akin to a cost of buying protection (like insurance).

BCE.204　The IASB agreed that the time value of an option could be viewed as a premium paid for protection against risk and, consequently, decided to align the accounting for the time value with the risk management perspective. The IASB took the view that, like the distinction between the different types of costs related to insuring risk, the time value of options should be similarly distinguished. For transaction related hedged items the cumulative change in the fair value of the option's time value should be accumulated in other comprehensive income and should be reclassified in a similar way to that for cash flow hedges. In contrast, for time-period related hedged items the nature of the time value of the option used as the hedging instrument is that of a cost for obtaining protection against a risk over a particular period of time. Hence, the IASB considered that the cost of obtaining the protection should be allocated as an expense over the relevant period on a systematic and rational basis.

BCE.205　The effect of this change is that the time value paid is treated like a cost of hedging instead of as held for trading with the resulting volatility recognised in profit or loss. This enables the costs of such a hedging strategy to be presented in a manner that reflects the inter-relation with the hedging relationship in which the option's intrinsic value is designated, and is consistent with risk management. It also removes a potential disincentive against the use of options as hedging instruments and improves transparency of the costs of hedging.

BCE.206　The IASB made similar changes to the accounting for the forward element of forward contracts and the foreign currency basis spread of hedging instruments.

Accounting for macro hedging

BCE.207　In practice, risk management often considers exposures on an aggregated basis over time. Over time, exposures are either added or removed from the hedged portfolio resulting in what are generally called hedges of 'open positions'. Hedges of open positions introduce significant complexity in the accounting model as the continuous changes in the hedged item need to be monitored and tracked for accounting purposes. The continuous changes in the hedged item also mean there is no direct one-to-one relationship with particular hedges.

BCE.208　The IASB decided not to specifically address open portfolios or the accounting for 'macro hedging' as part of the new hedge accounting model. The IASB noted that under IAS 39 entities often already account for 'macro' activities by applying the general hedge accounting model. The IASB received feedback from financial institutions, as well as from entities outside the financial sector, that addressing situations in which entities use a dynamic risk management strategy was important. Given the nature and complexity of the topic, the IASB has decided to separately deliberate the accounting for macro hedging with the objective of issuing a Discussion Paper.

BCE.209   IFRS 9 (like IAS 39) does not allow cash flow hedges of interest rate risk to be designated on a net position basis but instead on the basis of gross designations. However, so called 'proxy hedging' (when, for example, the designation for hedge accounting purposes is on a gross position basis even though actual risk management typically manages on a net position basis) is still an eligible way to designate a hedged item as long as the designation reflects risk management in that it is related to the same type of risk that is being managed and the financial instruments used for that purpose. Thus, while the separate project continues to explore a more comprehensive model to address the accounting for macro hedging activities, the ability to apply hedge accounting is not expected to change as a result of applying IFRS 9.

BCE.210   In addition, entities can elect to continue to apply the IAS 39 hedge accounting requirements until completion of the project on accounting for macro hedging.

Hedges of credit risk

BCE.211   Financial institutions use credit derivatives to manage their credit risk exposures arising from their lending activities and also, on occasion, to reduce their regulatory capital requirements. However, the credit risk of a financial item is not a risk component that meets the eligibility criteria for hedged items. This is currently a significant issue, particularly for financial institutions because, by using derivatives to manage credit risk, an activity designed to reduce risk, volatility in profit or loss is increased, thereby creating the perception of increased risk.

BCE.212   Many respondents were of the view that the IASB should address the accounting for hedges of credit risk using credit derivatives. Most of them also believed that this is an important issue in practice that the IASB should address.

BCE.213   The IASB decided to use a targeted fair value option to reflect the management of credit risk. The IASB decided to allow the designation of financial instruments, both recognised and unrecognised, to be at fair value through profit or loss if the credit risk of those financial instruments is managed using a credit derivative that is also measured at fair value through profit or loss. This eliminates the accounting mismatch that would otherwise arise from measuring credit derivatives at fair value and hedged items (such as loans) at amortised cost. It also enables entities to appropriately reflect this risk management activity in their financial statements. By allowing entities to make this election also for a proportion of a financial instrument and after its initial recognition, and to subsequently discontinue the fair value measurement for the hedged credit exposure, this approach enables entities to reflect their risk management activity more effectively than using the fair value option (which is available only on initial recognition for the financial instrument in its entirety, and is irrevocable). This becomes important because entities often do not hedge items for their entire life. This targeted fair value option is also available for credit exposures that are outside the scope of this Standard, such as most loan commitments.

Comparability of financial information

BCE.214   The IASB decided that by its very essence, hedge accounting should continue to be voluntary. As a result, there will never be full comparability because, for example, despite identical risk management activity one entity may choose to apply hedge accounting whereas the other may not. However, by improving the link to risk management, which in itself makes hedge accounting less burdensome to apply and facilitates a more useful reflection of risk management activities, increased use of hedge accounting should occur thus improving comparability.

BCE.215   With this in mind the IASB discussed whether it should retain an entity's choice to revoke the designation of a hedging relationship. The IASB decided not to allow the discontinuation of hedge accounting when an entity's risk management objective is unchanged. This will assist in improving comparability.

BCE.216   One of the key contributors to comparability is disclosure. The IASB decided to retain the scope of the hedge accounting disclosures because it provides, to users of financial statements, information on exposures that an entity hedges and for which hedge accounting is applied. For this population of hedging relationships, disclosure is required that will enable users of financial statements to better understand risk management (its effects on cash flows) and the effect of hedge accounting on financial statements. In addition, the IASB decided that all hedge accounting disclosures (ie irrespective of the type of hedge and the type of information required) should be presented in one location within an entity's financial statements. Hedge accounting has been difficult for users of financial statements to understand, which in turn has made risk management difficult to understand. These enhanced disclosures will assist in improving the ability of users of financial statements to compare entities' risk management activities.

Better economic decision making as a result of improved financial reporting

BCE.217   One of the fundamental changes introduced by the Standard is that the entire paradigm of hedge accounting has been changed to align more closely with the risk management activities of an entity. The IASB is of the view that this fundamental shift in focus—whereby the accounting and risk management objectives are brought in congruence—will result in better economic decision making through improved financial reporting. One such example is the accounting for options.

BCE.218   In the IASB's outreach some entities said that the accounting consequences of using options (non-linear instruments) were a consideration in their risk management activities. This was because the undesignated time value of the option was accounted for as at fair value through profit or loss, thereby resulting in significant profit or loss volatility. The IASB has addressed this issue and has better aligned the reported results with the risk management perspective. Time value is now considered to be a cost of hedging instead of a trading position. Similarly, the IASB addressed the accounting for the forward element of forward contracts and the foreign currency basis spread in instruments that hedge foreign currency risk and decided on a treatment similar to that of the time value of options. The latter issue was, for example, of particular concern to entities that raised funds in a currency other than their functional currency.

BCE.219 The IASB expects that these amendments will significantly reduce the accounting considerations affecting risk management decisions and also provide users of financial statements with more useful information about hedging activities, including the cost of such activities, resulting in better economic decision making.

BCE.220 As discussed previously (see paragraphs BCE.189–BCE.190) the IASB decided to expand the types of eligible financial instruments under the new hedge accounting model to allow non-derivative financial assets and liabilities at fair value through profit or loss as eligible hedging instruments. The IASB noted the comments received from respondents that such a treatment enables an entity to better capture its risk management activities in its financial statements. In the IASB's view this will significantly contribute to better economic decision making by capturing established risk management strategies in reported results through hedge accounting. It is particularly relevant for jurisdictions in which the use of derivatives is restricted.

BCE.221 Aligning the treatment of risk components for financial and non-financial items represents a fundamental change in the hedge accounting model, as this will allow entities to better represent their hedging and risk management activities for non-financial items in their financial statements. Entities will be able to more readily designate hedges in a manner that is consistent with risk management and to recognise hedge effectiveness on this basis. The IASB believes that this will significantly improve the usefulness of reported information for entities hedging non-financial items, which will enable preparers to better reflect their performance and result in better economic decision making.

BCE.222 The removal of the bright-line hedge effectiveness requirements will avoid discontinuation of hedging relationships in the financial statements under circumstances in which the hedge is still economically effective. Instead of a percentage-based test that does not meaningfully capture the characteristics of a hedging relationship in all situations, the effectiveness of hedging relationships will be evaluated on the basis of the features that drive their economic success. The new model will ensure that when the economics of a transaction demand that a hedge be rebalanced, such rebalancing does not lead to the hedging relationship being portrayed as discontinued. The IASB believes that such amendments will enable the economic success of an entity's hedging programme to be reflected in the financial statements, thereby leading to better decision making by both management and users of financial statements, because they will be in a better position to make informed judgements about an entity's hedging operations.

BCE.223   The IASB's decision to require the continuation of hedge accounting when a derivative is novated to effect clearing with a central clearing party also improves the usefulness of information for users of financial statements. This is achieved by preventing the discontinuation of hedge accounting and the ineffectiveness that would arise from a new hedging relationship being designated as a replacement.

BCE.224   Risk management also takes into consideration the risk positions that have been created by aggregating exposures that include derivative financial instruments. IAS 39 only allowed derivatives to be designated as hedging instruments, but not to be part of hedged items. Consequently, positions that are a combination of an exposure and a derivative (aggregated exposures) failed to qualify as hedged items. Under the new model an aggregated exposure (comprising a derivative and non-derivative) is an eligible hedged item. Similarly, by modifying the requirements for hedges of groups of items, the accounting for such hedges can now be better represented in the financial statements. Again, the IASB believes that, aligning the accounting model with risk management will result in better information for economic decision making.

BCE.225   This Standard also makes changes to aspects of the accounting for financial instruments outside hedge accounting that allow risk management to be more faithfully represented in the financial statements. One area is the accounting for contracts to buy or sell non-financial items, so called 'own use contracts'. Currently, those contracts are not treated as derivatives in particular circumstances (they are executory contracts that are off the statement of financial position). This can create an artificial perspective when they are measured as part of a portfolio that includes other items that are recognised in the statement of financial position and measured at fair value through profit or loss. By allowing entities to elect to measure own use contracts at fair value through profit or loss, entities are better able to provide information about their risk management activities in the financial statements. The IASB believes that these changes, along with those concerning the management of credit risk, will provide better information for economic decision making.

Compliance costs for preparers

BCE.226   As with all new requirements, the IASB acknowledges that different areas of the requirements will have different effects and hence different types of costs and benefits will arise when considering both preparers and users of financial statements. Given that the new model is based on an entity's risk management practices, it is reasonable to conclude that one of the key drivers of the costs incurred and the benefits obtained, in complying with the new requirements, will be the level of development and the sophistication of the entities' risk management functions.

BCE.227   Entities will incur a one-time cost on initial application to address:

(a)   development of new processes, systems and controls to integrate information produced for risk management purposes into their accounting processes;

(b)　　creating accounting capabilities for some new eligible accounting treatments (if they are intended to be used—for example, the new accounting for costs of hedging);

(c)　　updating of the documentation for existing hedging relationships on transition to the new requirements;

(d)　　education of accounting functions to enable them to assess whether the information prepared for risk management purposes would suffice to comply with the new hedge accounting requirements; and

(e)　　the need to explain to users of financial statements the difference between the information produced for risk management purposes and the hedge accounting disclosures.

BCE.228　The IASB believes that the costs of the transition, as well as the ongoing costs of applying the new hedge accounting requirements, will very much depend on the individual circumstances of each entity—for example, what type of hedging instruments and hedged items it has, what types of hedges it uses, and how it has implemented hedge accounting in terms of processes and systems. It is therefore difficult to generalise the likely impact of costs on preparers. Broadly, the IASB expects:

(a)　　entities with more sophisticated risk management functions, that produce reliable information for the entity's own management, will have costs of initial application in establishing better links between those functions and their accounting function, but the ongoing costs of application should then be lower because of the new hedge effectiveness test.

(b)　　entities that have embedded hedge accounting in their accounting systems may have to adjust their systems, depending on the particular implementation of IAS 39 and what additional new accounting treatments the entity wants to use. Entities using bespoke or self-developed solutions are affected differently from those using standard software. In all cases, the costs are one-off transition costs.

(c)　　entities that use a master documentation approach, whereby the documentation of individual hedging relationships includes references to master documents that set out risk management strategies or effectiveness testing methods, will have lower costs of making the transition than entities that include that information in full in the documentation of each individual hedging relationship. Those costs are also one-off transition costs.

(d)　　the new disclosure requirements will result in the need to capture more data than under the current hedge accounting disclosures in IAS 39. Costs arise on transition when the capability to provide those disclosures is created but will also include ongoing costs. However, if entities embed this in their systems that they use for preparing their financial statements the ongoing costs can be significantly reduced.

BCE.229 Overall, given the fact that the new model developed by the IASB is more aligned with the day-to-day risk management activities of an entity, the IASB believes that the following benefits will outweigh the costs of initial implementation and on-going application:

(a) better consistency between accounting and risk management;

(b) better operational efficiency;

(c) less need for non-GAAP information to explain to users of financial statements the impact of hedging for which hedge accounting was not achieved;

(d) reduction in the costs of workarounds to deal with the restrictions in IAS 39; and

(e) standardised and more transparent information, resulting in a better understanding of the company's hedging performance.

BCE.230 In addition to those costs set out in paragraph BCE.228, the IASB notes that one of the key costs of compliance with the hedge accounting requirements of IAS 39 is the infrastructure and resources required to maintain the hedge documentation and effectiveness testing. Under the new model, linking the hedge documentation requirements with that of risk management systems will, in the IASB's view, bring in efficiencies and cost savings as entities integrate such systems. In addition, the new model includes an objective-based effectiveness assessment, which is linked to the way that the hedging relationship is designed and monitored for risk management purposes. This will substantially reduce the costs of ongoing compliance compared with IAS 39.

BCE.231 This will be further reinforced by the fact that the IASB, after due consideration, decided to keep the mechanics of hedge accounting for fair value, cash flow and net investment hedges the same. This will avoid any major costs involved with changing accounting systems both on initial application and on an ongoing basis.

BCE.232 One of the costs involved with the application of any new Standard is the cost of developing ways to implement it. One of the main requests that respondents made to the IASB was to provide examples that would illustrate the various aspects of the new proposals. In response, the IASB has provided detailed guidance whenever possible (for example, detail about the accounting mechanics for aggregated exposures). The IASB believes that this will help in reducing both the initial and ongoing cost of compliance.

BCE.233 The IASB always intended to retain the 'macro fair value hedge accounting model' in IAS 39 pending completion of the project on the accounting for macro hedging. In addition, as noted in paragraphs BCE.208–BCE.209, the IASB is of the view that those using the general requirements in IAS 39 to achieve hedge accounting for their macro hedging activities should be able to continue to do so under the IFRS 9 model. Thus, the ability to apply hedge accounting to macro hedging activities should not be adversely affected by the introduction of IFRS 9. However, the IASB acknowledged that some entities may want to migrate from accounting for their macro hedging activities using IAS 39 directly to any new model for accounting for macro hedging. Consequently, the IASB decided to provide an option to preparers to continue to apply hedge accounting under IAS 39 without requiring them to move to the new hedge accounting model in IFRS 9. This means that those who do not want to change their accounting for macro hedging need not do so until completion of the project on the accounting for macro hedging. This will, however, mean that all of their hedge accounting will continue to be in accordance with IAS 39 (ie the election is made for hedge accounting as a whole).

BCE.234 However, the IASB is of the view that the migration from the accounting for macro hedging using the cash flow hedge accounting requirements in IAS 39 to the accounting using IFRS 9 will not be unduly burdensome for preparers. This is because the new hedge accounting model does not change how risk components of financial items can be designated as hedged items. In addition, while there are changes to the hedge effectiveness requirements, these have introduced simplifications compared with IAS 39. Entities would need to update their documentation of their hedging relationships to reflect the new effectiveness assessment. However, if hedge accounting was applied under IAS 39, the sources of ineffectiveness should be known, and it should be possible to update documentation efficiently by using a master document approach for similar hedges. This can be achieved by one central document being included by a cross reference in the documentation of specific hedging relationships that includes the identification of the specific hedging instruments and hedged items.

Costs of analysis for users of financial statements

BCE.235 Given that the mechanics for hedge accounting were well established and understood by most interested parties, the IASB decided to retain the mechanics of hedge accounting that were in IAS 39 for fair value, cash flow and net investment hedges. Consequently, from the perspective of users of financial statements, the costs in educating themselves about these proposals will be reduced.

BCE.236 The IASB also decided that it would require comprehensive information to be disclosed so that users of financial statements could understand the effects of hedge accounting on the financial statements and so that all hedge accounting disclosures are presented in a single note in the financial statements. This will enable users to access a set of information that is more relevant to their needs and will therefore reduce the need to rely on information prepared on a non-GAAP basis. In addition, they will also benefit from more meaningful information that is more closely linked to the decision making for risk management purposes.

BCE.237 Finally, the IASB expects that users of financial statements will obtain a higher level of transparency from the financial statements of entities applying hedge accounting. This will allow them to better form their own view of the entity's risk management and its effect on reported results. The opportunity for more extensive analyses would, of course, entail costs of performing those analyses, as with any use of financial reporting information.

Conclusion

BCE.238 The IASB expects that preparers will be able to better reflect their risk management activities using hedge accounting under the new model. This should facilitate an increased use of hedge accounting by preparers. In addition, because risk management can be better reflected, and as a result of enhanced disclosures, more relevant and transparent information will be provided to users of financial statements.

General

Summary of main changes from the Exposure Draft
Financial Instruments: Classification and Measurement

BCG.1 The main changes made by IFRS 9 issued in 2009 from the 2009 Exposure Draft *Financial Instruments: Classification and Measurement* (the '2009 Classification and Measurement Exposure Draft') were:

(a) IFRS 9 dealt with the classification and measurement of financial assets only, instead of financial assets and financial liabilities as proposed in the 2009 Classification and Measurement Exposure Draft.

(b) IFRS 9 requires entities to classify financial assets on the basis of the objective of the entity's business model for managing the financial assets and the characteristics of the contractual cash flows. It points out that the entity's business model should be considered first, and that the contractual cash flow characteristics should be considered only for financial assets that are eligible to be measured at amortised cost because of the business model. It states that both classification conditions are essential to ensure that amortised cost provides useful information.

(c) Additional application guidance was added on how to apply the conditions necessary for amortised cost measurement.

(d) IFRS 9 requires a 'look through' approach for investments in contractually linked instruments that effect concentrations of credit risk. The 2009 Classification and Measurement Exposure Draft had proposed that only the most senior tranche could have cash flows that represented payments of principal and interest on the principal amount outstanding.

(e) IFRS 9 requires (unless the fair value option is elected) financial assets purchased in the secondary market to be recognised at amortised cost if the instruments are managed within a business model that has an objective of collecting contractual cash flows and the financial asset has only contractual cash flows representing principal and interest on the principal amount outstanding even if such assets were acquired at a discount that reflects incurred credit losses.

(f) IFRS 9 requires that when an entity elects to present gains and losses on equity instruments measured at fair value in other comprehensive income, dividends are to be recognised in profit or loss. The 2009 Classification and Measurement Exposure Draft had proposed that those dividends would be recognised in other comprehensive income.

(g) IFRS 9 requires reclassifications between amortised cost and fair value classifications when the entity's business model changes. The 2009 Classification and Measurement Exposure Draft had proposed prohibiting reclassification.

(h) For entities that adopt IFRS 9 for reporting periods before 1 January 2012, IFRS 9 provides transition relief from restating comparative information.

(i) IFRS 9 requires additional disclosures for all entities when they first apply the Standard.

Summary of main changes from the Exposure Draft *Fair Value Option for Financial Liabilities*

BCG.2 The main changes from the 2010 Exposure Draft *Fair Value Option for Financial Liabilities* (the '2010 Own Credit Risk Exposure Draft') are:

(a) For liabilities designated under the fair value option, IFRS 9 requires an entity to present the effects of changes in the liability's credit risk in other comprehensive income unless that treatment would create or enlarge an accounting mismatch in profit or loss. If that treatment would create or enlarge an accounting mismatch in profit or loss, the entire fair value change is presented in profit or loss. That was the alternative approach set out in the 2010 Own Credit Risk Exposure Draft. The proposed approach in the 2010 Own Credit Risk Exposure Draft had treated all liabilities designated under the fair value option in the same way and had not addressed cases in which the proposed treatment would create or enlarge an accounting mismatch in profit or loss.

(b) IFRS 9 requires a 'one-step' approach for presenting the effects of changes in a liability's credit risk in the performance statement. That approach requires the effects of changes in a liability's credit risk to be presented directly in other comprehensive income, with the remaining amount of fair value change presented in profit or loss. The 2010 Own Credit Risk Exposure Draft had proposed a 'two-step' approach, which would have required the total fair value change to be presented in profit or loss. The effects of changes in a liability's credit risk would have been backed out and presented in other comprehensive income.

Dissenting opinions

Dissent of James J Leisenring from IFRS 9 *Financial Instruments* (issued 2009)

DO1 Mr Leisenring supports efforts to reduce the complexity of accounting for financial instruments. In that regard, he supports requiring all financial instruments to be measured at fair value, with that measurement being recognised in profit or loss. He finds no compelling reason related to improving financial reporting to reject that approach. It is an approach that maximises comparability and minimises complexity.

DO2 It maximises comparability because all financial instruments would be measured at one attribute within an entity and across entities. No measurement or presentation would change to reflect either arbitrary distinctions or management behaviour or intentions. IFRS 9 emphasises management intentions and behaviour, which substantially undermines comparability.

DO3 Complexity of accounting would be drastically reduced if all financial instruments were measured at fair value. The approach favoured by Mr Leisenring provides at least the following simplifications:

(a) no impairment model is necessary.

(b) criteria for when a given instrument must or can be measured with a given attribute are unnecessary.

(c) there is no need to bifurcate embedded derivatives or to identify financial derivatives.

(d) it eliminates the need for fair value hedge accounting for financial instruments.

(e) it eliminates the disparity in the measurement of derivatives within and outside the scope of IAS 39.

(f) it minimises the incentives for structuring transactions to achieve a particular accounting outcome.

(g) no fair value option would be needed to eliminate accounting mismatches.

(h) it provides a superior foundation for developing a comprehensive standard for the derecognition of financial instruments that is not present in a mixed attribute model.

DO4 Mr Leisenring accepts that measuring more instruments at fair value increases measurement complexity, but this increase is minimal compared with the reductions in complexity that would be otherwise achieved. There is no disagreement that derivatives must be measured at fair value. Those instruments raise the most difficult measurement issues, as cash instruments have many fewer problems. Indeed, some suggestions for an impairment model would measure at fair value the credit loss component of cash instruments. If that were to be the conclusion on impairment (an expected loss approach), it would minimise the incremental fair value measurement complexity of recording at fair value instruments now at amortised cost.

DO5   Mr Leisenring recognises that measuring all instruments at fair value through profit or loss raises presentation issues about disaggregation of fair value changes. However, he does not believe that these issues are insurmountable.

DO6   Investors have often told both the IASB and the FASB that fair value of financial instruments recognised in profit or loss provides the most useful information for their purposes. There is a worldwide demand for an improved and common solution to the accounting for financial instruments. Investors are disappointed that the Board will not take this opportunity to make, with other standard-setters, truly substantive changes rather than these minimal changes that perpetuate all the legitimate concerns that have been expressed about the mixed attribute model.

DO7   IFRS 9 does to some extent reduce complexity but that reduction is minimal. Certain measurement classifications are eliminated but others have been added. Mr Leisenring does not think that, on balance, this is an improvement over IAS 39.

DO8   Fundamental to IFRS 9 is the distinction between financial instruments measured at amortised cost and those at fair value. Mr Leisenring is concerned that neither of the two conditions necessary for that determination is operational. Paragraph BC4.86 criticises IAS 39 because the embedded derivative requirement of that Standard is based on a list of examples. However, the basic classification model of IFRS 9 is based on lists of examples in paragraphs B4.1.4, B4.1.13 and B4.1.14. The examples are helpful but are far from exhaustive of the issues that will be problematic in applying the two criteria for classification at amortised cost.

DO9   Mr Leisenring also thinks that the two criteria are inconsistently applied. When the objective of the entity's business model is to hold the assets to collect the contracted cash flows of an instrument there is no requirement that the entity must actually do so. The cash flow characteristics of the instrument are also ignored when the guidance is applied to investments in contractually linked instruments (tranches). In those circumstances the contractual cash flows of the instrument are ignored and one is required to look through to the composition of assets and liabilities of the issuing entity. This 'look through' requirement is also potentially complex and in Mr Leisenring's opinion is likely to be not very operational. Mr Leisenring also objects to eliminating the requirement to bifurcate derivatives embedded in cash instruments. This objection is primarily because of concern that the two criteria to qualify for amortised cost will not be operational. The pressure on those two conditions will be enormous because there will be an incentive to embed derivatives in a cash instrument in anticipation that the instrument might qualify for amortised cost. Derivatives should be at fair value whether embedded or standing alone and a bifurcation requirement would achieve that accounting. If Mr Leisenring were confident that the criteria for amortised cost could be applied as intended he would not be as concerned because instruments with embedded derivatives would be at fair value in their entirety.

DO10   Mr Leisenring is concerned that, in the current crisis, instruments that have provided some of the most significant losses when measured at fair value would be eligible for amortised cost. That conclusion is not responsive to the present environment. The approach also allows actively traded debt instruments, including treasury securities, to be at amortised cost. These results are unacceptable and reduce the usefulness of reported information for investors.

DO11   The Board is required by its *Framework*[67] to be neutral in its decision-making and to strive to produce neutral information to maximise the usefulness of financial information. IFRS 9 fails in that regard because it produces information based on free choice, management intention and management behaviour. Reporting that will result from this approach will not produce neutral information and diminishes the usefulness of financial reporting.

DO12   The Board is insistent in paragraph BC4.20 that accounting based on a business model is not free choice but never explains why selection of a business model is not a management choice. The existence of a trading account, a fair value option and the objective of a business model are all free choices.

DO13   The classification of selected equity instruments at fair value with the result of the remeasurement reported outside profit or loss is also a free choice. The Board concludes that reporting fair value changes in profit or loss may not reflect the operating performance of an entity. Mr Leisenring could accept accounting for changes in fair value of some instruments outside profit or loss in other comprehensive income. That accounting, however, should not be a free choice and why that presentation is superior in defined circumstances should be developed. In addition, when these securities are sold any realised gains and losses are not 'recycled' to profit or loss. That conclusion is inconsistent with the Board's conclusion that dividends received on these instruments should be reported in profit or loss. Such dividends would represent a return on investment or a form of 'recycling' of changes in the value of the instruments.

DO14   Mr Leisenring believes that a business model is rarely relevant in writing accounting standards. Identical transactions, rights and obligations should be accounted for in the same way if comparability of financial information is to be achieved. The result of applying IFRS 9 ignores any concern for comparability of financial information.

DO15   The credit crisis has provided confirmation that a drastic change in accounting for financial instruments is desirable. However, many have said that while they agree that the approach suggested by Mr Leisenring would be superior, and a significant improvement, the world is not ready to embrace such change. It is unclear to Mr Leisenring what factors need to be present for

---

67 The reference to the *Framework* is to the IASC's *Framework for the Preparation and Presentation of Financial Statements*, adopted by the Board in 2001 and in effect when the Standard was developed.

the optimal solution to be acceptable. He has concluded that it is hard to envisage circumstances that would make the case any more compelling for fundamental change and improvement than the present circumstances. Therefore, IFRS 9 will inevitably preserve a mixed attribute model and the resulting complexity for a significant period of time.

DO16 An objective of replacing IAS 39 was to provide a basis for convergence with accounting standards issued by the FASB. Mr Leisenring is concerned that IFRS 9 does not provide such a basis. As a consequence, allowing early adoption of the IFRS is undesirable. For convergence to be achieved significant changes in the IFRS are inevitable. Early adoption of the IFRS will therefore necessitate another costly accounting change when convergence is achieved. Permitting early adoption of this IFRS is also undesirable as it permits a lack of comparability in accounting for many years due to the deferred required effective date.

DO17 Mr Leisenring would accept that if, for reasons other than the desire to provide useful information to investors, his approach is politically unattainable, an alternative could be developed that would be operational. That approach would require all financial assets and financial liabilities to be recorded at fair value through profit or loss except originated loans retained by the originator, trade receivables and accounts payable. If certain derivatives were embedded in an instrument to be accounted for at amortised cost the derivative would be either bifurcated and accounted for at fair value or the entire instrument would be measured at fair value. Either approach would be acceptable.

Dissent of Patricia McConnell from IFRS 9 *Financial Instruments* (2009)

DO1 Ms McConnell believes that fair value is the most relevant and useful measurement attribute for financial assets. However, she acknowledges that many investors prefer not to measure all financial assets at fair value. Those investors believe that both amortised cost and fair value can provide useful information for particular kinds of financial assets in particular circumstances. Therefore, in order to meet the objective of developing high quality, global accounting standards that serve the interests of all investors, Ms McConnell believes that no single measurement attribute should have primacy over another. Thus any new IFRS setting classification and measurement principles for financial assets should require disclosure of sufficient information in the primary financial statements to permit determination of profit or loss and financial position using both amortised cost and fair value. For example, when a measurement attribute other than fair value is used for financial assets, information about fair value should be displayed prominently in the statement of financial position. The Board did not adopt such disclosure in IFRS 9, as discussed in paragraphs BC4.9–BC4.11 of the Board's Basis for Conclusions.

DO2   As stated in paragraph BC4.1, an objective of the Board in developing IFRS 9 was to reduce the number of classification categories for financial instruments. However, Ms McConnell believes that IFRS 9 has not accomplished that objective. IFRS 9 would permit or require the following categories: (1) amortised cost, (2) a fair value option through profit or loss for financial assets that qualify for amortised cost but for which amortised cost would create an accounting mismatch, (3) fair value through profit or loss for debt instruments that fail to qualify for amortised cost, (4) fair value though profit or loss for trading securities, (5) fair value through profit or loss for equity securities not held for trading and (6) fair value through other comprehensive income for equity investments not held for trading. Ms McConnell does not view those six categories as a significant improvement over the six categories in IAS 39; like the categories in IAS 39, they will hinder investors' understanding of an already complex area of financial reporting.

DO3   IFRS 9 sets out two criteria for measuring financial assets at amortised cost: (1) the way the entity manages its financial assets ('business model') and (2) the contractual cash flow characteristics of its financial assets. On the surface, this appears to be an improvement over IAS 39's criterion that was based on management's intention to trade, hold available for sale, hold to maturity, or hold for the foreseeable future. However, Ms McConnell finds it difficult to see how IFRS 9's criterion based on the objective of the entity's business model differs significantly from management's intention. In her opinion selection of a business model is a management choice, as is the decision to have a trading account, use the fair value option for debt instruments or the fair value option for equity instruments with gains and losses reported in other comprehensive income. In paragraphs BC4.20 and BC4.21 the Board argues that selection of a measurement method based on an entity's business model is not a free choice. Ms McConnell does not find the arguments persuasive.

DO4   IFRS 9 permits an entity to make an irrevocable election to present in other comprehensive income changes in the value of any investment in equity instruments that is not held for trading. Ms McConnell could accept accounting for changes in fair value of some instruments outside profit or loss in other comprehensive income. However, that treatment should not be a free choice; criteria for that presentation should be developed. In addition, the Board decided that when those securities are sold any realised gains and losses are not 'reclassified' to profit or loss. That conclusion is inconsistent with the Board's decision to report dividends received on these investments in profit or loss. Such dividends represent a return on investment or a form of 'reclassifying' changes in the value of the instruments.

DO5   In addition, Ms McConnell believes the 'look through' guidance for contractually linked investments (tranches) is an exception to one of the criteria necessary for applying amortised cost, namely the contractual cash flow characteristics of the instrument. In those circumstances the contractual cash flows of the instrument are ignored. Instead an entity is required to 'look through' to the underlying pool of instruments and assess their cash flow characteristics and credit risk relative to a direct investment in the underlying instruments. Ms McConnell believes that this provision adds complexity to the IFRS and reduces the usefulness of the reporting for financial assets. Moreover, since an entity is required to 'look through' only upon initial recognition of the financial asset, subsequent changes in the relative exposure to credit risk over the life of a structured investment vehicle would be ignored. Consequently, Ms McConnell believes it is possible that highly volatile investments, such as those owning sub-prime residential mortgage loans, would be reported at amortised cost.

Dissent of Patricia McConnell from *Mandatory Effective Date of IFRS 9 and Transition Disclosures* (Amendments to IFRS 9 (2009), IFRS 9 (2010) and IFRS 7)

DO1   Ms McConnell concurs with the Board's decision to defer the mandatory effective date of IFRS 9 (2009) and IFRS 9 (2010), but not with its decision to set a mandatory effective date of 1 January 2015. She agrees with the Board that there are compelling reasons for all project phases to be implemented at the same time and, therefore, that the mandatory application of all phases of the project to replace IAS 39 should occur concurrently. However, Ms McConnell does not believe that a mandatory effective date for IFRS 9 (2009) and IFRS 9 (2010) should be established until there is more clarity on the requirements and completion dates of the remaining phases of the project to replace IAS 39, including possible improvements to existing IFRS 9.

DO2   Ms McConnell commends the Board for requiring modified transition disclosures and acknowledges that the modified disclosures will provide useful information that will enable users of financial statements to better understand the transition from IAS 39 to IFRS 9, just as they would provide useful information when financial assets are reclassified in accordance with IFRS 9.

DO3   Although Ms McConnell believes that the modified disclosures are useful, she does not believe that they are an adequate substitute for restated comparative financial statements. Ms McConnell believes that comparative statements are vitally important to users of financial statements. To the extent that the accounting policies applied in comparative financial statements are comparable period-to-period, comparative financial statements enable users to more fully understand the effect of the accounting change on a company's statements of comprehensive income, financial position and cash flows.

DO4   Ms McConnell agrees with the Board that the date of initial application should be defined as a fixed date. In the absence of a fixed date, entities would have to go back to the initial recognition of each individual instrument for classification and measurement. This would be very burdensome, if not impossible. Moreover, particularly because reclassifications in accordance with IFRS 9 only occur (and are required) upon a change in business model for the related group of instruments, reclassifications should be very rare. Consequently, the expected benefit of not naming a fixed date of initial application would not exceed the costs.

DO5　　However, Ms McConnell disagrees with defining the date of initial application as the date that an entity first applies this IFRS. She believes that the date of initial application should be defined as the beginning of the earliest period presented in accordance with IFRS 9. This date of initial application would enable entities to compile information in accordance with IFRS 9 while still preparing their external financial reports in accordance with IAS 39. Ms McConnell does not consider that there is a significant risk that entities would use hindsight when applying IFRS 9 to comparative periods prior to those financial statements being reported publicly in accordance with IFRS 9. She also notes that, although it would be costly for entities to prepare financial reporting information in accordance with an extra set of requirements during the comparative period (or periods), this would address concerns on the part of preparers that it is overly burdensome for them to compile information in accordance with IFRS 9 before the date of initial application has passed.

DO6　　Ms McConnell acknowledges that defining the date of initial application as the beginning of the earliest date presented would delay the release of financial statements prepared in accordance with IFRS 9 for at least one year, or longer, if the date of initial application were set as she believes it should be. Delays would also result if the mandatory effective date of IFRS 9 was set so that entities could prepare more than one comparative period under IFRS 9 on the basis of requirements in many jurisdictions. Ms McConnell has also considered that it is costly for entities to prepare financial reporting information in accordance with an extra set of requirements during the comparative period (or periods). However, Ms McConnell believes that the benefits to users of financial statements of restated comparative financial statements justify the costs.

Dissent of Patrick Finnegan from the issue in November 2013 of IFRS 9 *Financial Instruments* ('IFRS 9 (2013)')

DO1　　Mr Finnegan dissents from the issue of the amendments to IFRS 9 (2013) due to the addition of the requirements related to hedge accounting (Chapter 6 of IFRS 9).

DO2　　Mr Finnegan dissents because he disagrees with the decision to provide entities with an accounting policy choice between applying the new hedge accounting requirements of IFRS 9 and retaining the existing hedge accounting requirements in IAS 39 until the completion of the project on the accounting for macro hedging. He believes that such an accounting policy choice combined with the existing approach of replacing IAS 39 in phases creates an unacceptable level of complexity and cost for both preparers and users of financial statements when accounting for financial instruments.

DO3　　Mr Finnegan believes that a principal reason for the Board creating an option was to address the concerns of entities who believe that 'proxy hedging' (the use of designations of hedging relationships that do not exactly represent an entity's risk management) would be prohibited under IFRS 9. The Board has made it clear that this is not the case and, therefore, an option to continue to apply the hedge accounting requirements of IAS 39 creates the potential for the misunderstanding and misapplication of the new requirements in IFRS 9.

DO4   Mr Finnegan is concerned that the duration of the option to apply the new hedge accounting requirements is open-ended because it depends on the Board's ability to complete its project on the accounting for macro hedging. Consequently, the length of time that preparers and users of financial statements would be dealing with a variety of complex alternatives related to the accounting for financial instruments is also open-ended. Mr Finnegan believes that this outcome conflicts with the Board's stated goal of making timely improvements to simplify such accounting.

DO5   Mr Finnegan believes that the original goal of the Board to replace IAS 39 in phases was sound, given the initial expectation that a new comprehensive Standard would be completed expeditiously. However, the process of completing the three phases dealing with classification and measurement, impairment, and hedge accounting has proved to be thorny because of many complex and interrelated issues as well as its interaction with the project to create a new Standard for insurance contracts. In the light of that experience, Mr Finnegan believes that preparers and users of financial statements are better served by adopting a new IFRS dealing with all three phases simultaneously because it would involve substantially less cost and complexity and provide more useful information for users of financial statements.

DO6   Mr Finnegan believes that a principal reason for undertaking a fresh examination of the accounting for financial instruments was to achieve converged accounting with US GAAP. The IASB and the FASB are still examining ways of achieving convergence of the accounting for classification and measurement as well as impairment. Mr Finnegan believes that when a classification and measurement model is completed, a reporting entity may need to modify its application of the new requirements for hedge accounting, which would create unnecessary costs for such entities and additional complexity for users of financial statements in their analysis and use of financial statements.

Dissent of Stephen Cooper and Jan Engström from the issue in July 2014 of IFRS 9 *Financial Instruments* ('IFRS 9 (2014)')

DO1   Messrs Cooper and Engström dissent from the issue of IFRS 9 (2014) because of the limited amendments to the classification and measurement requirements for financial assets. They disagree with the introduction of the fair value through other comprehensive income measurement category. They believe that:

(a)   this additional measurement category unnecessarily increases the complexity for the reporting of financial instruments;

(b)   the distinction between the supposed different business models that justify measurement at fair value through other comprehensive income versus measurement at fair value through profit or loss is unclear and does not justify a difference in accounting treatment; and

(c)   faithful representation of insurance contracts in the financial statements does not need the fair value through other comprehensive income measurement category for (some) assets that back insurance liabilities.

DO2   Messrs Cooper and Engström believe that the requirements in IFRS 9 (issued in 2009), which classified financial assets at either amortised cost or fair value through profit or loss, are preferable and should have been retained. However, they support the clarifications to the hold to collect business model and the amendments to the contractual cash flow assessment in IFRS 9 (2014).

Increased complexity that is undesirable and unnecessary

DO3   One of IASB's main objectives for replacing IAS 39 with IFRS 9 is to reduce the complexity of accounting for financial instruments. An important component of that is to reduce the number of categories of financial instruments and the even larger number of different measurement and presentation methods in IAS 39. Interested parties widely supported this objective and Messrs Cooper and Engström believe that it had been achieved in the classification and measurement requirements that were issued in IFRS 9 in 2009. They consider that the introduction of a fair value through other comprehensive income measurement category reverses a significant part of this improvement in reporting.

DO4   Messrs Cooper and Engström believe that, when amortised cost is judged to be the most appropriate basis for reporting, this measurement attribute should be applied consistently throughout the financial statements. Likewise, if fair value provides more relevant information, it should be applied consistently. In their view the fair value through other comprehensive income measurement category provides a confusing mixture of amortised cost and fair value information that will make financial statements more complex and harder to understand. While they accept that in many cases fair value is an important additional piece of information for assets that are appropriately measured and reported at amortised cost, they believe that this fair value information should be provided as supplementary information in the notes, albeit with prominent and clear disclosure.

'A business model whose objective is achieved by both collecting contractual cash flows and selling financial assets' is not a distinct business model

DO5   The amendments are based on the assertion that there are distinct business models that justify accounting for qualifying debt instruments at either fair value through other comprehensive income or fair value through profit or loss. Messrs Cooper and Engström believe that, while the reasons for holding debt instruments outside a hold to collect business model can vary significantly, it is not possible to identify distinct business models or that these reasons justify different accounting. For example, managing assets with the objective of maximising the return on the portfolio through collecting contractual cash flows and opportunistic selling and reinvestment is given as an illustration of a business model whose objective is achieved by both collecting contractual cash flows and selling financial assets (see Example 5 in paragraph B4.1.4C of IFRS 9). However, measurement at fair value through profit or loss is required when assets are managed, and their performance is evaluated, on a 'fair value basis' with collection of contractual cash flows being incidental (see paragraph B4.1.6 of IFRS 9). Messrs Cooper and Engström believe that managing to maximise the return on the portfolio and managing on a fair value basis is a distinction without a difference and is not a valid justification for a very different accounting treatment.

DO6   Messrs Cooper and Engström believe that if fair value is indeed the most appropriate measurement basis then the full fair value change is relevant in assessing overall performance and should be presented within profit or loss. If a portfolio of debt instruments is, for example, managed with the objective of maximising return, then showing in profit or loss only amortised cost-based interest revenue, expected credit losses and realised value changes fails to provide a faithful representation of this economic activity. Furthermore, the use of fair value through other comprehensive income provides an entity with significant freedom to manage profit or loss simply through the selective sale of assets. While Messrs Cooper and Engström believe that all fair value changes should be reported in profit or loss if assets are measured at fair value, they observe that an entity is able to disaggregate fair value gains and losses to highlight particular components (such as the interest yield) if this helps to provide relevant information about performance.

The fair value through other comprehensive income measurement category does not achieve improvements to insurance contracts accounting

DO7   The IASB's decision to introduce the fair value through other comprehensive income measurement category is related to its tentative decision in the Insurance Contracts project that some changes in insurance contract liabilities (ie those arising from changes in the discount rate) would be recognised in other comprehensive income. Messrs Cooper and Engström believe that the use of other comprehensive income for insurance contracts combined with measurement at fair value through other comprehensive income for (some) financial assets that back insurance contract liabilities would lead to unnecessary complexity, a lack of transparency in insurance accounting, and would create opportunities for earnings management through selective realisation of gains or losses on the sale of financial assets and would not faithfully represent the performance of entities engaged in this activity. Accordingly, they believe that the introduction of the fair value through other comprehensive income measurement category in IFRS 9, combined with the use of other comprehensive income for some changes in insurance contract liabilities, will undermine the potential improvements in the quality of financial reporting by entities engaged in issuing insurance contracts that would otherwise result from the introduction of a new insurance contracts Standard.

Appendix A
Previous dissenting opinions

In 2003 and later some IASB members dissented from the issue of IAS 39 and subsequent amendments, and portions of their dissenting opinions relate to requirements that have been carried forward to IFRS 9. Those dissenting opinions are set out below.

Cross references that relate to the requirements that have been carried forward to IFRS 9 have been updated.

Dissent of Anthony T Cope, James J Leisenring and Warren J McGregor from the issue of IAS 39 in December 2003

DO1   Messrs Cope, Leisenring and McGregor dissent from the issue of this Standard.

DO2   Mr Leisenring dissents because he disagrees with the conclusions concerning derecognition, impairment of certain assets and the adoption of basis adjustment hedge accounting in certain circumstances.

DO3   The Standard requires in paragraphs 30 and 31 (now paragraphs 3.2.16 and 3.2.17 of IFRS 9) that to the extent of an entity's continuing involvement in an asset, a liability should be recognised for the consideration received. Mr Leisenring believes that the result of that accounting is to recognise assets that fail to meet the definition of assets and to record liabilities that fail to meet the definition of liabilities. Furthermore, the Standard fails to recognise forward contracts, puts or call options and guarantees that are created, but instead records a fictitious 'borrowing' as a result of rights and obligations created by those contracts. There are other consequences of the continuing involvement approach that has been adopted. For transferors, it results in very different accounting by two entities when they have identical contractual rights and obligations only because one entity once owned the transferred financial asset. Furthermore, the 'borrowing' that is recognised is not accounted for like other loans, so no interest expense may be recorded. Indeed, implementing the proposed approach requires the specific override of measurement and presentation standards applicable to other similar financial instruments that do not arise from derecognition transactions. For example, derivatives created by derecognition transactions are not accounted for at fair value. For transferees, the approach also requires the override of the recognition and measurement requirements applicable to other similar financial instruments. If an instrument is acquired in a transfer transaction that fails the derecognition criteria, the transferee recognises and measures it differently from an instrument that is acquired from the same counterparty separately.

DO4   Mr Leisenring also disagrees with the requirement in paragraph 64 to include an asset that has been individually judged not to be impaired in a portfolio of similar assets for an additional portfolio assessment of impairment. Once an asset is judged not to be impaired, it is irrelevant whether the entity owns one or more similar assets as those assets have no implications for whether the asset that was individually considered for impairment is or is not impaired. The result of this accounting is that two entities could each own 50 per cent of a single loan. Both entities could conclude the loan is not impaired. However, if one of the two entities happens to have other loans that are similar, it would be allowed to recognise an impairment with respect to the loan where the other entity is not. Accounting for identical exposures differently is unacceptable. Mr Leisenring believes that the arguments in paragraph BC115 are compelling.

DO5   Mr Leisenring also dissents from paragraph 98 which allows but does not require basis adjustment for hedges of forecast transactions that result in the recognition of non-financial assets or liabilities. This accounting results in always adjusting the recorded asset or liability at the date of initial recognition away from its fair value. It also records an asset, if the basis adjustment alternative is selected, at an amount other than its cost as defined in IAS 16 *Property, Plant and Equipment* and further described in paragraph 16 of that Standard. If a derivative were to be considered a part of the cost of acquiring an asset, hedge accounting in these circumstances should not be elective to be consistent with IAS 16. Mr Leisenring also objects to creating this alternative as a result of an improvement project that ostensibly had as an objective the reduction of alternatives. The non-comparability that results from this alternative is both undesirable and unnecessary.

DO6   Mr Leisenring also dissents from the application guidance in paragraph AG71[68] and in particular the conclusion contained in paragraph BC98. He does not believe that an entity that originates a contract in one market should measure the fair value of the contract by reference to a different market in which the transaction did not take place. If prices change in the transacting market, that price change should be recognised when subsequently measuring the fair value of the contract. However, there are many implications of switching between markets when measuring fair value that the Board has not yet addressed. Mr Leisenring believes a gain or loss should not be recognised based on the fact a transaction could occur in a different market.

DO7   Mr Cope dissents from paragraph 64 and agrees with Mr Leisenring's analysis and conclusions on loan impairment as set out above in paragraph DO4. He finds it counter-intuitive that a loan that has been determined not to be impaired following careful analysis should be subsequently accounted for as if it were impaired when included in a portfolio.

DO8   Mr Cope also dissents from paragraph 98, and, in particular, the Board's decision to allow a free choice over whether basis adjustment is used when accounting for hedges of forecast transactions that result in the recognition of non-financial assets or non-financial liabilities. In his view, of the three courses of action open to the Board—retaining IAS 39's requirement to use basis adjustment, prohibiting basis adjustment as proposed in the June 2002 Exposure Draft,[69] or providing a choice—the Board has selected the worst

---

68 IFRS 13 *Fair Value Measurement*, issued in May 2011, now contains the requirements for measuring fair value.

69 Exposure Draft *Proposed Amendments to IAS 32, Financial Instruments: Disclosure and Presentation, and IAS 39, Financial Instruments: Recognition and Measurement*.

course. Mr Cope believes that the best approach would have been to prohibit basis adjustment, as proposed in the Exposure Draft, because, in his opinion, basis adjustments result in the recognition of assets and liabilities at inappropriate amounts.

DO9　Mr Cope believes that increasing the number of choices in international standards is bad policy. The Board's decision potentially creates major differences between entities choosing one option and those choosing the other. This lack of comparability will adversely affect users' ability to make sound economic decisions.

DO10　In addition, Mr Cope notes that entities that are US registrants may choose not to adopt basis adjustment in order to avoid a large reconciling difference to US GAAP. Mr Cope believes that increasing differences between IFRS-compliant entities that are US registrants and those that are not is undesirable.

DO11　Mr McGregor dissents from paragraph 98 and agrees with Mr Cope's and Mr Leisenring's analyses and conclusions as set out above in paragraphs DO5 and DO8–DO10.

DO12　Mr McGregor also dissents from this Standard because he disagrees with the conclusions about impairment of certain assets.

DO13　Mr McGregor disagrees with paragraphs 67 and 69, which deal with the impairment of equity investments classified as available for sale. These paragraphs require impairment losses on such assets to be recognised in profit or loss when there is objective evidence that the asset is impaired. Previously recognised impairment losses are not to be reversed through profit and loss when the assets' fair value increases. Mr McGregor notes that the Board's reasoning for prohibiting reversals through profit or loss of previously impaired available-for-sale equity investments, set out in paragraph BC130 of the Basis for Conclusions, is that it ' ... could not find an acceptable way to distinguish reversals of impairment losses from other increases in fair value'. He agrees with this reasoning but believes that it applies equally to the recognition of impairment losses in the first place. Mr McGregor believes that the significant subjectivity involved in assessing whether a reduction in fair value represents an impairment (and thus should be recognised in profit or loss) or another decrease in value (and should be recognised directly in equity) will at best lead to a lack of comparability within an entity over time and between entities, and at worst provide an opportunity for entities to manage reported profit or loss.

DO14　Mr McGregor believes that all changes in the fair value of assets classified as available for sale should be recognised in profit or loss. However, such a major change to the Standard would need to be subject to the Board's full due process. At this time, to overcome the concerns expressed in paragraph DO13, he believes that for equity investments classified as available for sale, the Standard should require all changes in fair value below cost to be recognised in profit or loss as impairments and reversals of impairments and all changes in value above cost to be recognised in equity. This approach treats all changes in value the same way, no matter what their cause. The problem of how to distinguish an impairment loss from another decline in value (and of deciding whether there is an impairment in the first place) is eliminated because there is no longer any subjectivity involved. In addition, the approach is consistent with IAS 16 *Property, Plant and Equipment* and IAS 38 *Intangible Assets*.

DO15   Mr McGregor disagrees with paragraph 106 of the Standard and with the consequential amendments to paragraph 27[70] of IFRS 1 *First-time Adoption of International Financial Reporting Standards*. Paragraph 106 requires entities to apply the derecognition provisions prospectively to financial assets. Paragraph 27 of IFRS 1 requires first-time adopters to apply the derecognition provisions of IAS 39 (as revised in 2003) prospectively to non-derivative financial assets and financial liabilities. Mr McGregor believes that existing IAS 39 appliers should apply the derecognition provisions retrospectively to financial assets, and that first-time adopters should apply the derecognition provisions of IAS 39 retrospectively to all financial assets and financial liabilities. He is concerned that financial assets may have been derecognised under the original IAS 39 by entities that were subject to it, which might not have been derecognised under the revised IAS 39. He is also concerned that non-derivative financial assets and financial liabilities may have been derecognised by first-time adopters under previous GAAP that would not have been derecognised under the revised IAS 39. These amounts may be significant in many cases. Not requiring recognition of such amounts will result in the loss of relevant information and will impair the ability of users of financial statements to make sound economic decisions.

Dissent of Mary E Barth, Robert P Garnett and Geoffrey Whittington from the issue in June 2005 of *The Fair Value Option* (Amendment to IAS 39)

DO1   Professor Barth, Mr Garnett and Professor Whittington dissent from the amendment to IAS 39 *Financial Instruments: Recognition and Measurement—The Fair Value Option*. Their dissenting opinions are set out below.

DO2   These Board members note that the Board considered the concerns expressed by the prudential supervisors on the fair value option as set out in the December 2003 version of IAS 39 when it finalised IAS 39. At that time the Board concluded that these concerns were outweighed by the benefits, in terms of simplifying the practical application of IAS 39 and providing relevant information to users of financial statements, that result from allowing the fair value option to be used for any financial asset or financial liability. In the view of these Board members, no substantive new arguments have been raised that would cause them to revisit this conclusion. Furthermore, the majority of constituents have clearly expressed a preference for the fair value option as set out in the December 2003 version of IAS 39 over the fair value option as contained in the amendment.

---

70   As a result of the revision of IFRS 1 in November 2008, paragraph 27 became paragraph B2.

DO3   Those Board members note that the amendment introduces a series of complex rules, including those governing transition which would be entirely unnecessary in the absence of the amendment. There will be consequential costs to preparers of financial statements, in order to obtain, in many circumstances, substantially the same result as the much simpler and more easily understood fair value option that was included in the December 2003 version of IAS 39. They believe that the complex rules will also inevitably lead to differing interpretations of the eligibility criteria for the fair value option contained in the amendment.

DO4   These Board members also note that, for paragraph 9(b)(i) (now paragraphs 4.1.5 and 4.2.2(a) of IFRS 9), application of the amendment may not mitigate, on an ongoing basis, the anomaly of volatility in profit or loss that results from the different measurement attributes in IAS 39 any more than would the option in the December 2003 version of IAS 39. This is because the fair value designation is required to be continued even if one of the offsetting instruments is derecognised. Furthermore, for paragraphs 9(b)(i), 9(b)(ii) and 11A (now paragraphs 4.1.5, 4.2.2 and 4.3.5 of IFRS 9), the fair value designation continues to apply in subsequent periods, irrespective of whether the initial conditions that permitted the use of the option still hold. Therefore, these Board members question the purpose of and need for requiring the criteria to be met at initial designation.

Appendix B
Amendments to the Basis for Conclusions on other Standards

The amendments in this appendix to the Basis for Conclusions on other Standards are necessary in order to ensure consistency with IFRS 9 and the related amendments to other Standards.

* * * * *

The amendments contained in this appendix when IFRS 9 was issued in 2014 have been incorporated into the Basis for Conclusions on the relevant Standards included in this volume.

IASB documents published to accompany

IFRS 10

Consolidated Financial Statements

The text of the unaccompanied standard, IFRS 10, is contained in Part A of this edition. Its effective date when issued was 1 January 2013. The text of the Accompanying Guidance on IFRS 10 is contained in Part B of this edition. This part presents the following documents:

BASIS FOR CONCLUSIONS

APPENDICES TO THE BASIS FOR CONCLUSIONS

Previous Board approvals and dissenting opinions

Amendments to the Basis for Conclusions on other IFRSs

CONTENTS

...continued

Basis for Conclusions on
IFRS 10 *Consolidated Financial Statements*

This Basis for Conclusions accompanies, but is not part of, IFRS 10.

Introduction

BC1 This Basis for Conclusions summarises the International Accounting Standards Board's considerations in developing IFRS 10 *Consolidated Financial Statements*. Individual Board members gave greater weight to some factors than to others. Unless otherwise stated, any reference below to IAS 27 is to IAS 27 *Consolidated and Separate Financial Statements*, and to IAS 28 is to IAS 28 *Investments in Associates*.

BC2 The Board added a project on consolidation to its agenda to deal with divergence in practice in applying IAS 27 and SIC-12 *Consolidation—Special Purpose Entities*. For example, entities varied in their application of the control concept:

(a) in circumstances in which an investor controls an investee but the investor has less than a majority of the voting rights of the investee (and voting rights are clearly the basis for control).

(b) in circumstances involving special purpose entities (to which the notion of 'economic substance' in SIC-12 applied).

(c) in circumstances involving agency relationships.

(d) in circumstances involving protective rights.

BC3 IAS 27 required the consolidation of entities that are controlled by a reporting entity, and it defined control as the power to govern the financial and operating policies of an entity so as to obtain benefits from its activities. SIC-12, which interpreted the requirements of IAS 27 in the context of special purpose entities,[1] placed greater emphasis on risks and rewards. This perceived conflict of emphasis had led to inconsistent application of the concept of control. This was aggravated by a lack of clear guidance on which investees were within the scope of IAS 27 and which were within the scope of SIC-12. As a result, assessing control sometimes resulted in a quantitative assessment of whether the investor had a majority of the risks. Such tests based on sharp 'bright line' distinctions created structuring opportunities to achieve particular accounting outcomes.

---

1 To maintain consistency with the terminology used in the original documents this Basis for Conclusions refers to 'special purpose entities (SPEs)' when discussing SIC-12 and 'structured entities' when discussing the exposure draft ED 10 *Consolidated Financial Statements* and the related deliberations and redeliberations. SIC-12 described an SPE as an entity that may be created to accomplish a narrow and well-defined objective, often created with legal arrangements that impose strict and sometimes permanent limits on the decision-making powers of its governing board, trustee or management over the SPE's operations. ED 10 defined a structured entity as an entity whose activities are restricted to the extent that those activities are, in essence, not directed by voting or similar rights.

BC4   The global financial crisis that started in 2007 highlighted a lack of transparency about the risks to which investors were exposed from their involvement with 'off balance sheet vehicles' (such as securitisation vehicles), including those that they had set up or sponsored. As a result, the G20 leaders, the Financial Stability Board and others asked the Board to review the accounting and disclosure requirements for such 'off balance sheet vehicles'.

BC5   In developing IFRS 10, the Board considered the responses to ED 10 *Consolidated Financial Statements*, published in December 2008. Respondents to ED 10 pointed out that the Board and the US Financial Accounting Standards Board (FASB), in their Memorandum of Understanding, had agreed to work towards developing common standards on consolidation by 2011. Therefore, they asked the boards to discuss the consolidation project jointly to ensure that the ensuing standards contained identical, not only similar, requirements. As a result, the Board's deliberations in developing IFRS 10 were conducted jointly with the FASB from October 2009.

BC6   The FASB decided in January 2011 that it would not change the consolidation requirements in US generally accepted accounting principles (GAAP) at this time with one exception. The FASB tentatively decided that it would propose changes to the consolidation requirements relating to both variable interest entities and voting interest entities in the context of assessing whether a decision maker is a principal or an agent. Those proposals would be similar to the requirements developed jointly by the IASB and the FASB regarding the principal/agent assessment, which are included in IFRS 10.

BC7   ED 10 proposed disclosure requirements for consolidated and unconsolidated investees. In its deliberation of the responses to those proposals, the Board decided to combine the disclosure requirements for interests in subsidiaries, joint arrangements, associates and unconsolidated structured entities within a single comprehensive standard, IFRS 12 *Disclosure of Interests in Other Entities*. The Basis for Conclusions accompanying IFRS 12 summarises the Board's considerations in developing that IFRS, including its consideration of responses to the disclosure proposals in ED 10. Accordingly, IFRS 10 does not include disclosure requirements and this Basis for Conclusions does not describe the Board's consideration of responses to the proposed disclosure requirements in ED 10.

The structure of IFRS 10 and the Board's decisions

BC8   IFRS 10 replaces the requirements and guidance in IAS 27 relating to consolidated financial statements. It also replaces SIC-12. As part of its consolidation project, the Board is examining how an investment entity accounts for its interests in subsidiaries, joint ventures and associates and what, if any, additional disclosures might be made about those interests. The

Board expects to publish an exposure draft on investment entities later in 2011.[2]

BC9 In developing IFRS 10, the Board did not reconsider all the requirements that are included in the IFRS. The scope in paragraph 4 and the accounting requirements for consolidated financial statements in paragraphs 19–25 and B86–B99 were carried forward from IAS 27 or SIC-12 to IFRS 10 without being reconsidered by the Board because their reconsideration was not part of the Board's consolidation project.

BC10 When revised in 2003, IAS 27 was accompanied by a Basis for Conclusions summarising the considerations of the Board, as constituted at the time, in reaching some of its conclusions in that Standard. That Basis for Conclusions was subsequently updated to reflect amendments to the Standard. The Board has incorporated into this Basis for Conclusions material from the Basis for Conclusions on IAS 27 that discusses matters that the Board has not reconsidered. That material is contained in paragraphs denoted by numbers with the prefix BCZ. In those paragraphs cross-references to the IFRS have been updated accordingly and minor necessary editorial changes have been made.

BC11 In order to portray the historical background of IFRS 10, the documents recording the Board's approval of the revision of IAS 27 in 2003 and the subsequent amendments are set out after this Basis for Conclusions. In addition, in 2003 and later, some Board members dissented from the revision of IAS 27 and subsequent amendments, and portions of their dissenting opinions relate to requirements that have been carried forward to IFRS 10. Those dissenting opinions are set out after the Basis for Conclusions.

Presentation of consolidated financial statements (2003 revision)

Exemption from preparing consolidated financial statements

BCZ12 Paragraph 7 of IAS 27 (as revised in 2000) required consolidated financial statements to be presented. However, paragraph 8 permitted a parent that was a wholly-owned or virtually wholly-owned subsidiary not to prepare consolidated financial statements. In 2003 the Board considered whether to withdraw or amend this exemption from the general requirement.

BCZ13 The Board decided to retain an exemption, so that entities in a group that are required by law to produce financial statements available for public use in accordance with International Financial Reporting Standards, in addition to consolidated financial statements, would not be unduly burdened.

---

2 *Investment Entities* (Amendments to IFRS 10, IFRS 12 and IAS 27), issued in October 2012, introduced an exception to the principle that all subsidiaries shall be consolidated. The amendments define an investment entity and require a parent that is an investment entity to measure its investments in particular subsidiaries at fair value through profit or loss instead of consolidating those subsidiaries. These amendments are discussed in paragraphs BC215–BC317.

BCZ14　The Board noted that in some circumstances users can find sufficient information for their purposes about a subsidiary from either its separate financial statements or the consolidated financial statements. In addition, the users of financial statements of a subsidiary often have, or can get access to, more information.

BCZ15　Having concluded that it should retain an exemption, the Board decided to modify the circumstances in which an entity would be exempt and considered the following criteria.

Unanimous agreement of the owners of the minority interests[3]

BCZ16　The 2002 exposure draft proposed to extend the exemption to a parent that is not wholly-owned if the owners of the minority interests, including those not otherwise entitled to vote, unanimously agree.

BCZ17　Some respondents disagreed with this proposal, largely because of the practical difficulties in obtaining responses from all the minority shareholders. Acknowledging this argument, the Board decided that the exemption should be available to a parent that is not wholly-owned when the owners of the minority interests have been informed about, and do not object to, consolidated financial statements not being presented.

Exemption available only to non-public entities

BCZ18　The Board believed that the information needs of users of financial statements of entities whose debt or equity instruments are traded in a public market were best served when investments in subsidiaries, jointly controlled entities and associates were accounted for in accordance with IAS 27, IAS 28 and IAS 31 *Interests in Joint Ventures*.[4] It therefore decided that the exemption from preparing consolidated financial statements should not be available to such entities or to entities in the process of issuing instruments in a public market.

Scope of consolidated financial statements (2003 revision)

Scope exclusions

BCZ19　Paragraph 13 of IAS 27 (as revised in 2000) required a subsidiary to be excluded from consolidation when control is intended to be temporary or when the subsidiary operates under severe long-term restrictions.

Temporary control

BCZ20　In 2003 the Board considered whether to remove this scope exclusion and thereby converge with other standard-setters that had recently eliminated a similar exclusion. It decided to consider this question as part of a comprehensive standard dealing with asset disposals. It decided to retain an

---

3　IAS 27 (as amended in 2008) changed the term 'minority interest' to 'non-controlling interest'.

4　IAS 31 was superseded by IFRS 11 *Joint Arrangements* issued in May 2011.

exemption from consolidating a subsidiary when there is evidence that the subsidiary is acquired with the intention of disposing of it within twelve months and that management is actively seeking a buyer. The Board's exposure draft ED 4 *Disposal of Non-current Assets and Presentation of Discontinued Operations* proposed to measure and present assets held for sale in a consistent manner irrespective of whether they are held by an investor or in a subsidiary. Therefore, ED 4 proposed to eliminate the exemption from consolidation when control is intended to be temporary and it contained a draft consequential amendment to IAS 27 to achieve this.[5]

Severe long-term restrictions impairing ability to transfer funds to the parent

BCZ21   The Board decided to remove the exclusion of a subsidiary from consolidation when there are severe long-term restrictions that impair a subsidiary's ability to transfer funds to the parent. It did so because such circumstances may not preclude control. The Board decided that a parent, when assessing its ability to control a subsidiary, should consider restrictions on the transfer of funds from the subsidiary to the parent. In themselves, such restrictions do not preclude control.

BCZ22–   [Deleted]
BCZ28

Exemption from preparing consolidated financial statements for an intermediate parent of an investment entity

BC28A   In December 2014, the Board amended IFRS 10 to confirm that the exemption from preparing consolidated financial statements set out in paragraph 4(a) of IFRS 10 is available to a parent entity that is a subsidiary of an investment entity. This question came about because an investment entity may measure all of its subsidiaries at fair value through profit or loss in accordance with paragraph 31 of IFRS 10. This decision was consistent with the proposal in the Exposure Draft *Investment Entities: Applying the Consolidation Exception* (Proposed amendments to IFRS 10 and IAS 28), which was published in June 2014.

BC28B   Paragraph 4(a)(iv) of IFRS 10, which is one of the criteria for the exemption from preparing consolidated financial statements, previously specified the requirement that the entity's ultimate or any intermediate parent 'produces consolidated financial statements that are available for public use and comply with IFRSs.' The IFRS Interpretations Committee was asked whether the exemption set out in paragraph 4(a) was available to a parent entity that is a subsidiary of an ultimate, or any intermediate, investment entity parent, if the conditions set out in paragraph 4(a)(i)–(iii) are met, but the investment entity parent does not consolidate any of its subsidiaries. Instead, the investment entity parent prepares financial statements in which all of its subsidiaries are

---

5   In March 2004 the Board issued IFRS 5 *Non-current Assets Held for Sale and Discontinued Operations*. IFRS 5 removed this scope exclusion and eliminated the exemption from consolidation when control is intended to be temporary. For further discussion see the Basis for Conclusions on IFRS 5.

measured at fair value through profit or loss in accordance with paragraph 31 of IFRS 10.

BC28C   The Board observed that the exemption for intermediate parent entities was provided because the cost of requiring each intermediate parent entity within a group to prepare consolidated financial statements would outweigh the benefits in cases in which the conditions in paragraph 4(a) of IFRS 10 are met. The Board had previously decided that the conditions in paragraph 4(a) provide safeguards for the users of the intermediate parent's financial statements. In addition, the Board noted that the combination of information available in the consolidated financial statements of the higher level parent and the separate financial statements of the intermediate parent entity provide useful information to users.

BC28D   The Board additionally observed that, when an investment entity measures its interest in a subsidiary at fair value, the disclosures required by IFRS 12 are supplemented by those required in IFRS 7 *Financial Instruments: Disclosures* and IFRS 13 *Fair Value Measurement*. Accordingly, the Board decided that this combination of information is sufficient to support the decision to retain the existing exemption from presenting consolidated financial statements for a subsidiary of an investment entity that is itself a parent entity. The Board noted that requiring an intermediate parent that is a subsidiary of an investment entity to prepare consolidated financial statements could result in significant additional costs, without commensurate benefit. The Board noted that this would be contrary to its intention in requiring investment entities to measure investments at fair value, which was to provide more relevant information at a reduced cost, as described in paragraphs BC309 and BC314 of IFRS 10.

BC28E   The Board also decided to amend paragraph 17 of IAS 28 *Investments in Associates and Joint Ventures* for the same reasons. Paragraph 17 of IAS 28 uses the same criteria as paragraph 4(a) of IFRS 10 to provide an exemption from applying the equity method for entities that are subsidiaries and that hold interests in associates and joint ventures.

BC28F   Furthermore, the Board decided to amend paragraph 6(b) of IFRS 12 to clarify that the relevant disclosure requirements in IFRS 12 apply to an investment entity. Paragraph 6 of IFRS 12 previously stated that IFRS 12 did not apply to an entity's separate financial statements without stating the applicability of IFRS 12 to investment entities. The Board decided to clarify that this scope exclusion does not apply to the financial statements of a parent that is an investment entity and has measured all of its subsidiaries at fair value through profit or loss in accordance with paragraph 31 of IFRS 10. In such cases, the investment entity shall present the disclosures relating to investment entities required by IFRS 12.

Control as the basis for consolidation

BC29   The Board's objective in issuing IFRS 10 is to improve the usefulness of consolidated financial statements by developing a single basis for consolidation and robust guidance for applying that basis to situations where it has proved difficult to assess control in practice and divergence has evolved (see paragraphs BC2–BC4). The basis for consolidation is control and it is applied irrespective of the nature of the investee.

BC30   Almost all respondents to ED 10 supported control as the basis for consolidation. However, some noted that it can be difficult to identify an investor that has power over investees that do not require substantive continuous decision-making. They suggested that exposure to risks and rewards should be used as a proxy for control when power is not evident. Some respondents were also concerned that applying the proposed control definition to all investees could lead to more structuring opportunities than was the case when applying the requirements in IAS 27 and SIC-12. Others did not think that ED 10 expressed with sufficient clarity the importance of risks and rewards when assessing control.

BC31   The Board confirmed its view that control should be the only basis for consolidation—an investor should consolidate an investee and present in its consolidated financial statements the investee's assets, liabilities, equity, income, expenses and cash flows, if the investor has the current ability to direct those activities of the investee that significantly affect the investee's returns and can benefit by using that ability. An investor that is exposed, or has rights, to variable returns from its involvement with an investee but does not have power over the investee so as to affect the amount of the investor's return from its involvement does not control the investee.

BC32   Control as the basis for consolidation does not mean that the consideration of risks and rewards is unimportant when assessing control of an investee. The more an investor is exposed to risks and rewards from its involvement with an investee, the greater the incentive for the investor to obtain decision-making rights that give it power. However, risks and rewards and power are not necessarily perfectly correlated. Therefore, the Board confirmed that exposure to risks and rewards (referred to in IFRS 10 as variable returns) is an *indicator of control* and an important factor to consider when assessing control, but an investor's exposure to risks and rewards alone does not determine that the investor has control over an investee.

BC33   The Board observed that to conclude that exposure to risks and rewards is anything more than an indicator of control would be inconsistent with a control model that contains both a power element and a returns element.

BC34   The Board confirmed that an investor must have exposure to risks and rewards in order to control an investee—without any exposure to risks and rewards (ie variable returns) an investor is unable to benefit from any power that it might have and therefore cannot control an investee.

BC35   In reaching its conclusions regarding control as the basis for consolidation, the Board also noted the following:

(a)   One of the main objectives of the consolidation project is to develop a consistent basis for determining when an investor should consolidate an investee, irrespective of the nature of the investee. Some respondents to ED 10 suggested including a particular level of exposure to risks and rewards as a presumption of, or proxy for, control, in the context of investees that are not directed through voting or similar rights. The Board concluded that introducing such a presumption for a particular set of investees would contradict the objective of developing a single consistent basis for consolidation that applies to all investees.

(b)   Having a different consolidation model for some investees necessitates defining precisely those investees to which that model applies. There have been difficulties, in practice, in identifying which investees are special purpose entities to which SIC-12 applied. A number of respondents to ED 10 noted that any attempt to split the continuum of investee types into distinct populations and to subject the different populations of entities to different consolidation models would lead to divergence in practice for investees that are not clearly in the specified population sets. For that reason, the Board decided not to carry forward the distinction proposed in ED 10 between different types of investees when assessing control (see paragraphs BC71–BC75).

(c)   Including exposure to risks and rewards as a presumption of, or proxy for, control in particular situations puts more pressure on the measurement of that exposure. The Board was particularly concerned that the need to measure risks and rewards might result in the adoption of a consolidation model based on quantitative criteria (for example, a model focused on the majority of risks and rewards). Any quantitative analysis of risks and rewards would inevitably be complex and, as a consequence, difficult to understand, apply and audit. The Board noted that, depending on the specific facts and circumstances, a quantitative model might identify a controlling party that is different from the party that a qualitative analysis of the power over, and returns from, an investee would identify as the controlling party. The Board's analysis is consistent with concerns raised by the FASB's constituents on the quantitative consolidation model in Interpretation 46 (Revised) *Consolidation of Variable Interest Entities*. The FASB has since issued Statement of Financial Accounting Standard No. 167 *Amendments to FIN 46 (Revised)* to amend Interpretation 46 to require a qualitative analysis focusing on the power over and returns from an investee to determine control.[6]

---

6   SFAS 167 was subsequently nullified by Accounting Standards Update No. 2009-17. The requirements of SFAS 167 have been included in Accounting Standards Update No. 2009-17.

(d)   The Board believes that having a control model that applies to all investees is likely to reduce the opportunities for achieving a particular accounting outcome that is inconsistent with the economics of an investor's relationship with an investee—ie it will reduce structuring opportunities.

BC36   The Board does not regard control and risks and rewards as competing models. The exposure to risks and rewards, or variable returns as it is expressed in IFRS 10, is an essential element of control. In the great majority of cases the approaches would lead to the same accounting conclusions. However, a control-based model forces an investor to consider all its rights in relation to the investee rather than relying on arbitrary bright lines that are associated with risks and rewards approaches, such as paragraph 10(c) and (d) of SIC-12, which referred to control if the investor has rights to obtain the majority of the benefits of the investee or if the investor retains the majority of the risks related to the investee. The Board believes that an investor will, generally, want to control an investee when it has significant economic exposure. This should reduce the likelihood of structuring simply to achieve a particular accounting outcome.

Reputational risk

BC37   During the financial crisis, some financial institutions provided funding or other support to securitisation or investment vehicles because they established or promoted those vehicles. Rather than allowing them to fail and facing a loss of reputation, the financial institutions stepped in, and in some cases took control of the vehicles. ED 10 did not make any explicit reference to reputational risk in relation to control because the Board decided that having reputational risk in isolation is not an appropriate basis for consolidation. The term 'reputational risk' relates to the risk that failure of an investee would damage an investee's reputation and, therefore, that of an investor or sponsor, compelling the investor or sponsor to provide support to an investee in order to protect its reputation, even though the investor or sponsor has no legal or contractual requirement to do so.

BC38   Respondents to ED 10 agreed with the Board, almost unanimously, that reputational risk is not an appropriate basis for consolidation. Some, however, were of the view that reputational risk is part of an investor's exposure to risks and rewards and should be considered when determining control of an investee.

BC39   The Board believes that reputational risk is part of an investor's exposure to risks and rewards, albeit a risk that arises from non-contractual sources. For that reason, the Board concluded that when assessing control, reputational risk is a factor to consider along with other facts and circumstances. It is not an indicator of power in its own right, but may increase an investor's incentive to secure rights that give the investor power over an investee.

Definition of control

BC40   IFRS 10 states that an investor controls an investee when the investor is exposed, or has rights, to variable returns from its involvement with the investee and has the current ability to affect those returns through its power over the investee.

BC41   The definition of control includes three elements, namely an investor's:

(a)   power over the investee;

(b)   exposure, or rights, to variable returns from its involvement with the investee; and

(c)   ability to use its power over the investee to affect the amount of the investor's returns.

Power

BC42   ED 10 proposed that in order to control an investee, an investor must have the power to direct the activities of that investee. IAS 27 defines control as the power to govern the financial and operating policies of an entity. The Board decided to change the definition of control because even though power is often obtained by governing the strategic operating and financing policies of an investee, that is only one of the ways in which power to direct the activities of an investee can be achieved. An investor can have the power to direct the activities of an investee through decision-making rights that relate to particular activities of an investee. Indeed, referring to the power to govern the financial and operating policies of an investee would not necessarily apply to investees that are not directed through voting or similar rights.

BC43   Respondents to ED 10 did not object to changing the definition of control to power to direct the activities of an investee. Many were confused, however, about what the Board meant by 'power to direct' and which 'activities' the Board had in mind. They asked for a clear articulation of the principle behind the term 'power to direct'. They also expressed the view that power should relate to significant activities of an investee, and not those activities that have little effect on the investee's returns.

BC44   ED 10 described various characteristics of power—power need not be absolute; power need not have been exercised; power precludes others from controlling an investee. ED 10 also implied that power could arise from rights that appeared to be exercisable only at some point in the future when particular circumstances arise or events happen. Respondents to ED 10 were confused about whether power referred to the legal or contractual power to direct, or to the ability to direct, which does not necessarily require the investor to have the legal or contractual right to direct the activities. Some respondents to ED 10 also commented that the statement that power precludes others from controlling an investee was confusing because it implied that an investor with less than a majority of the voting rights in an investee could never have power.

BC45   In response to the comments from respondents, the Board considered whether power should refer to having the *legal* or *contractual right* to direct the activities, or the *ability* to direct the activities.

BC46   According to a legal or contractual right approach, some would suggest that an investor has power only when it has an unassailable legal or contractual right to direct. This means having the right to make decisions about the activities of an investee that could potentially be contrary to the wishes of others in every possible scenario, within the boundaries of protective rights. Therefore, for example, an investor with less than half the voting rights of an investee could not have power unless it had additional legal or contractual rights (see paragraph BC101). Also, potential voting rights would not affect the assessment of control until exercised or converted because in and of themselves they do not give the holder the contractual right to direct. A consistent application of this view to 'kick-out' (removal) or similar rights would suggest that a decision maker could never have power when such rights are held by others because those rights could be exercised to remove the decision maker.

BC47   Supporters of the legal or contractual right approach point out that this approach requires less judgement than other approaches and, accordingly, is likely to result in more consistent application of the control definition. They are also concerned that other approaches might result in an investor frequently changing its assessment of control because of changes in circumstances. These changes could be outside the control of the investor (for example, changes in the shareholdings of others or market changes that affect the terms and conditions of potential voting rights).

BC48   The Board acknowledged that defining power as the legal or contractual right to direct the activities of an investee would require less judgement than some other approaches. Nonetheless, the Board rejected that approach because it would create opportunities for an investor to ignore those circumstances in which the Board believes that an investor controls an investee without having the unassailable legal or contractual right to direct the activities of the investee.

BC49   In addition, the Board concluded that preparers and others should be able to apply the judgement required by an 'ability' approach, as long as the principles underlying that approach were articulated clearly and the IFRS included application guidance, illustrating how control should be assessed.

BC50   Consequently, the Board concluded that power should refer to having the *current ability* to direct the activities of an investee. The Board observed that the current ability to direct the activities of an investee would, in all cases, arise from rights (such as voting rights, potential voting rights, rights within other arrangements, or a combination of these).

BC51   In addition, an investor would have the current ability to direct the relevant activities if that investor were able to make decisions at the time that those decisions need to be taken.

BC52   The Board also noted that an investor can have the current ability to direct the activities of an investee even if it does not actively direct the activities of the investee. Conversely, an investor is not assumed to have the current ability to direct simply because it is actively directing the activities of an investee. For example, an investor that holds a 70 per cent voting interest in an investee (when no other relevant factors are present) has the current ability to direct the activities of the investee even if it has not exercised its right to vote. Even if the remaining 30 per cent of voting rights were held by a single party actively exercising its voting rights, that minority shareholder would not have power.

BC53   The Board also noted that having the current ability to direct the activities of an investee is not limited to being able to act today. There may be steps to be taken in order to act—for example, an investor may need to initiate a meeting before it can exercise its voting or other rights that give it power. However, such a delay would not prevent the investor from having power, assuming that there are no other barriers that would prevent the investor from exercising its rights when it chooses to do so.

BC54   In addition, the Board observed that for some investees, particularly those with most of their operating and financing decisions predetermined, decisions that significantly affect the returns of the investee are not made continuously. Such decisions may be made only if particular events occur or circumstances arise. For such investees, having the ability to make those decisions if and when they arise is a source of a current ability to direct the relevant activities.

BC55   When discussing the principles underlying power, the Board rejected the assertion that an 'ability' approach could result in an investee moving *frequently* in and out of consolidation because of changes that are outside the control of the investor (see paragraph BC47). Changes as to which party controls an investee could occur according to any control model, including a 'contractual rights' model, when relevant facts and circumstances change. For a discussion of concerns in respect to changes in market conditions and the assessment of potential voting rights see paragraphs BC124 and BC152.

Relevant activities

BC56   ED 10 did not propose explicit guidance explaining the activities of an investee to which the definition of control referred. In response to comments received from respondents, the Board decided to clarify that in order to control an investee an investor must have the current ability to direct the activities of the investee that *significantly affect the investee's returns* (ie the relevant activities).

BC57   The comments on ED 10 suggested that such a clarification would be particularly helpful when assessing control of investees that are not directed through voting or similar rights and for which there may be multiple parties with decision-making rights over different activities.

BC58   If an investor controls such an investee, its power should relate to the activities of the investee that significantly affect the investee's returns, rather than administrative activities that have little or no effect on the investee's returns. For an investee that is not directed through voting or similar rights it can be difficult to determine which investor, if any, meets the power element of the control definition. There is also a risk that, without adding the modifier 'significant', an investor with very little ability to affect the returns could be considered to have power over that investee (for example, if the investor has the ability to direct the most significant of a number of insignificant activities that have little effect on the investee's returns).

BC59 Although the guidance included in IFRS 10 in this respect would be particularly helpful in the context of investees that are not directed through voting or similar rights, the Board concluded that the amended wording would work well for all investees. For an investee that is directed through voting or similar rights, it is generally the case that a range of operating and financing activities are those that significantly affect the investee's returns— for example, selling goods or services, purchasing inventory, making capital expenditures or obtaining finance. In that case, an investor that is able to determine the strategic operating and financing policies of the investee would usually have power.

Returns

BC60 The definition of control in IFRS 10 uses the concept of returns in two ways.

BC61 In order to have power over an investee an investor must have the current ability to direct the relevant activities, ie the activities that significantly affect the investee's returns. The link to returns was included in the first element of control in order to clarify that having the current ability to direct inconsequential activities is not relevant to the assessment of power and control (see paragraph BC58).

BC62 The second element of control requires the investor's involvement with the investee to provide the investor with rights, or exposure, to variable returns. This retains the concept that control conveys the rights to returns from an investee. To have control an investor must have power over the investee, exposure or rights to returns from its involvement with the investee and the ability to use its power to affect its own returns. Control is not a synonym of power, because equating power and control would result in incorrect conclusions in situations when an agent acts on behalf of others. ED 10 used the term 'returns' rather than 'benefits' because 'benefits' are often interpreted as implying only positive returns.

BC63 The Board confirmed its intention to have a broad definition of 'returns' that would include synergistic returns as well as more direct returns, for example, dividends or changes in the value of an investment. In practice, an investor can benefit from controlling an investee in a variety of ways. The Board concluded that to narrow the definition of returns would artificially restrict those ways of benefiting.

BC64 Although some respondents to ED 10 commented that 'returns' could be interpreted narrowly to refer only to financial returns such as dividends, the Board believed that the broad description of returns included in the IFRS should ensure that the Board's intention to have a broad definition is clear.

The Board also confirmed that an investor's returns could have the potential to be wholly positive, wholly negative or both positive and negative.

BC65 When assessing control of an investee, an investor determines whether it is exposed, or has rights, to variable returns from its involvement with the investee. The Board considered whether this criterion should refer to involvement through instruments that must absorb variability, in the sense that those instruments reduce the exposure of the investee to risks that cause variability.

BC66 Some instruments are designed to transfer risk from a reporting entity to another entity. During its deliberations, the Board concluded that such instruments create variability of returns for the other entity but do not typically expose the reporting entity to variability of returns from the performance of the other entity. For example, assume an entity (entity A) is established to provide investment opportunities for investors who wish to have exposure to entity Z's credit risk (entity Z is unrelated to any other party involved in the arrangement). Entity A obtains funding by issuing to those investors notes that are linked to entity Z's credit risk (credit-linked notes) and uses the proceeds to invest in a portfolio of risk-free financial assets. Entity A obtains exposure to entity Z's credit risk by entering into a credit default swap (CDS) with a swap counterparty. The CDS passes entity Z's credit risk to entity A, in return for a fee paid by the swap counterparty. The investors in entity A receive a higher return that reflects both entity A's return from its asset portfolio and the CDS fee. The swap counterparty does not have involvement with entity A that exposes it to variability of returns from the performance of entity A because the CDS transfers variability to entity A, rather than absorbing variability of returns of entity A.

BC67 Consequently, the Board decided that it was not necessary to refer specifically to instruments that absorb variability, although it expects that an investor will typically have rights, or be exposed, to variability of returns through such instruments.

Link between power and returns

BC68 To have control, an investor must have power and exposure or rights to variable returns and be able to use that power to affect its own returns from its involvement with the investee. Thus, power and the returns to which an investor is exposed, or has rights to, must be linked. The link between power and returns does not mean that the proportion of returns accruing to an investor needs to be perfectly correlated with the amount of power that the investor has. The Board noted that many parties can have the right to receive variable returns from an investee (eg shareholders, debt providers and agents), but only one party can control an investee.

Control is not shared

BC69 ED 10 proposed that only one party, if any, can control an investee. The Board confirmed this in deliberating IFRS 10. (See further comments regarding joint arrangements in paragraph BC83.)

BC70   ED 10 proposed that an investor need not have absolute power to control an investee. Other parties can have protective rights relating to the activities of an investee. For example, limits on power are often imposed by law or regulations. Similarly, other parties — such as non-controlling interests — may hold protective rights that limit the power of the investor. During its redeliberations the Board confirmed that an investor can control an investee even if other entities have protective rights relating to the activities of the investee. Paragraphs BC93–BC124 discuss rights that give an investor power over an investee.

Assessing control

BC71   In developing IFRS 10 the Board, while acknowledging that the factors to be considered in assessing control will vary, had the objective of developing a control model that applies the same concept of control as the basis for consolidation to all investees, irrespective of their nature.

BC72   In ED 10, the Board set out specific factors to consider when assessing control of a structured entity. ED 10 defined a structured entity as an entity whose activities are restricted to the extent that those activities are, in essence, not directed by voting or similar rights.

BC73   The Board's intention when including the subsection specifically for structured entities was as a convenience for those assessing control of traditional operating entities that are typically controlled through voting rights — the Board did not want to force those assessing control of traditional operating entities to read, and assess whether to apply, all the guidance relating to structured entities if that guidance was not relevant.

BC74   However, the vast majority of respondents to ED 10 were opposed to creating a subset of investees for which different guidance would apply when assessing control. In their view, such an approach would perpetuate problems faced in applying the guidance in IAS 27 and SIC-12 — two control models leading to inconsistent application and, therefore, potential arbitrage by varying investee-specific characteristics. Respondents also noted that the guidance provided for structured entities should apply generally to all investees. Therefore, they suggested that there should be a single section that combines guidance on assessing control of all investees.

BC75   The Board was persuaded by this reasoning and decided to combine the guidance for assessing control of an investee within a single section, noting that its intention is to have a single basis for consolidation that could be applied to all investees and that that basis is control. However, the Board acknowledged that the way in which control would need to be assessed would vary depending on the nature of investees.

Understanding the purpose and design of an investee

BC76 Some respondents to ED 10 expressed the view that involvement in the design of an investee (with restricted activities) is a strong indicator of control and, indeed, in some situations, they would conclude that involvement in the design alone is sufficient to meet the power element of the control definition. SIC-12 included this notion as one of its indicators of control and the accompanying Basis for Conclusions explained that:

> SPEs [special purpose entities] frequently operate in a predetermined way so that no entity has explicit decision-making authority over the SPE's ongoing activities after its formation (ie they operate on 'autopilot'). Virtually all rights, obligations, and aspects of activities that could be controlled are predefined and limited by contractual provisions specified or scheduled at inception. In these circumstances, control may exist for the sponsoring party or others with a beneficial interest, even though it may be particularly difficult to assess, because virtually all activities are predetermined. However, the predetermination of the activities of the SPE through an 'autopilot' mechanism often provides evidence that the ability to control has been exercised by the party making the predetermination for its own benefit at the formation of the SPE and is being perpetuated.

BC77 When developing IFRS 10 the Board confirmed the position in ED 10 that being involved in setting up an investee was not, in and of itself, sufficient to conclude that an investor has control. Being involved in the design does not necessarily mean that an investor has decision-making rights to direct the relevant activities. Often several parties are involved in the design of an investee and the final structure of the investee includes whatever is agreed to by all those parties (including investors, the sponsor of the investee, the transferor(s) of the assets held by the investee and other parties involved in the transaction).

BC78 Although the success of, for example, a securitisation will depend on the assets that are transferred to the securitisation vehicle, the transferor might not have any further involvement with the vehicle and thereby may not have any decision-making rights to direct the relevant activities. The benefits from being involved in setting up a vehicle could cease as soon as the vehicle is established. The Board concluded that, in isolation, being involved in setting up an investee would not be an appropriate basis for consolidation.

BC79 The Board confirmed, however, that considering the purpose and design of an investee is important when assessing control. Understanding the purpose and design of an investee is the means by which an investor identifies the relevant activities, the rights from which power arises and who holds those rights. It can also assist in identifying investors that may have sought to secure control and whose position should be understood and analysed when assessing control.

BC80 The Board noted that understanding the purpose and design of an investee also involves consideration of all activities and returns that are closely related to the investee, even though they might occur outside the legal boundaries of the investee. For example, assume that the purpose of a securitisation vehicle is to allocate risks (mainly credit risk) and benefits (cash flows received) of a portfolio of receivables to the parties involved with the vehicle. The vehicle is designed in such a way that the only activity that can be directed, and can significantly affect the returns from the transaction, is managing those receivables when they default. An investor might have the current ability to direct those activities that significantly affect the returns of the transaction by, for example, writing a put option on the receivables that is triggered when the receivables default. The design of the vehicle ensures that the investor has decision-making authority over the relevant activities at the only time that such decision-making authority is required. In this situation, the terms of the put agreement are integral to the overall transaction and the establishment of the investee. Therefore, the terms of the put agreement would be considered together with the founding documents of the investee to conclude whether the investor has the current ability to direct the activities of the securitisation vehicle that significantly affect the returns of the transaction (even before the default of the receivables).

Different activities significantly affect the returns

BC81   IAS 27, SIC-12 and ED 10 did not specifically address situations in which multiple parties have decision-making authority over the activities of an investee. Some respondents to ED 10 questioned how the control model would be applied in such situations. Respondents were concerned that the absence of specific guidance would create structuring opportunities to avoid the consolidation of structured entities—they asserted that, without any guidance, power could easily be disguised and divided among different parties so that it could be argued that no one would have power over the investee.

BC82   The Board identified the following situations in which multiple parties may have decision-making authority over the activities of an investee:

(a)   joint control

(b)   shared decision-making that is not joint control

(c)   multiple parties that each have unilateral decision-making rights to direct different activities of an investee that significantly affect the investee's returns.

Joint control

BC83   IFRS 11 *Joint Arrangements* defines joint control as the contractually agreed sharing of control of an arrangement. Joint control exists only when decisions about the relevant activities require the unanimous consent of the parties sharing control. When two or more parties have joint control of an investee, no single party controls that investee and, accordingly, the investee is not consolidated. IFRS 11 is applicable to all investees for which two or more parties have joint control. The Board confirmed that IFRS 10 does not change or amend the arrangements that are now within the scope of IFRS 11.

Shared decision-making that is not joint control

BC84   The power to direct the relevant activities can be shared by multiple parties but those rights may not meet the definition of joint control. For example, five parties each own 20 per cent of entity Z, and each has one seat on entity Z's board of directors. All strategic operating and financing decisions (ie decisions in respect of the activities that significantly affect the returns of entity Z) require the consent of any four of the five directors. The five parties do not jointly control entity Z because unanimous consent is not required for decisions relating to the activities of entity Z that significantly affect its returns. Nevertheless, it is clear that the power to direct the activities of entity Z is shared and no single party controls entity Z. Again, the Board confirmed that the requirements of IFRS 10 do not change or amend the application of IFRSs to such situations.

Multiple parties with decision-making rights

BC85   When discussing the sharing of power, the Board noted that for most investees it will be clear that one party or body has decision-making authority to direct the activities of an investee that significantly affect the investee's returns. For example, for an investee that is directed by voting or similar rights, the governing body or board of directors would typically be responsible for strategic decision-making. Thus, the current ability to direct that body would be the basis for power.

BC86   Nonetheless, it is possible that more than one party has decision-making authority over different activities of an investee and that each such activity may significantly affect the investee's returns—respondents to ED 10 noted the following as examples: multi-seller conduits, multi-seller securitisations, and investees for which the assets are managed by one party and the funding is managed by another. The Board was persuaded by the comments from respondents that IFRS 10 should specifically address situations for which multiple parties each have unilateral decision-making rights to direct different activities of the investee.

BC87   The Board considered whether, for such investees, none of the parties controls the investee because the ability to direct the activities is shared. If those different activities, in fact, significantly affect the returns of the investee, some would reason that it would be artificial to force the parties involved to conclude that one activity is more important than the others. An investor might be required to consolidate an investee when the investor would not have the power to direct all the activities of the investee that significantly affect the investee's returns.

BC88   Nonetheless, the Board decided that when two or more unrelated investors each have unilateral decision-making rights over different activities of an investee that significantly affect the investee's returns, the investor that has the current ability to direct the activities of the investee that *most* significantly affect the investee's returns meets the power element of the control definition. The expectation is that one investor will have that ability to direct the activities that *most* significantly affect the investee's returns and consequently would be deemed to have power. In effect, power is attributed to the party that looks most like the party that controls the investee. However, the Board decided not to prescribe a specific mechanism for assessing which activities of an investee *most* significantly affect the investee's returns.

BC89 The Board was concerned about creating the potential to avoid consolidation if an investor were to conclude that it has power only when it has the current ability to direct *all* the relevant activities. Such a requirement would be open to abuse because an investor could avoid consolidation by involving other parties in an investee's decision-making.

BC90 The Board's conclusions result in greater potential for an investee to be consolidated because one party would be deemed to have power when multiple parties have unilateral decision-making authority over different activities of an investee.

BC91 In reaching its conclusions, the Board noted that the situation in which two or more investors (individually or as a group) have decision-making rights over different activities of an investee that significantly affect the investee's returns is not expected to arise frequently. This is because one party or body usually has overall decision-making responsibility for an investee (see paragraph BC85). The Board believes that its conclusions in this respect will ensure that it does not create an incentive to structure investees to achieve an accounting outcome by involving multiple parties in decision-making when there is no business rationale to do so.

BC92 The Board noted that in situations where two or more parties have the current ability to direct the activities that most significantly affect the investee's returns and if unanimous consent is required for those decisions IFRS 11 applies.

Rights that give an investor power

BC93 IAS 27 and SIC-12 do not include guidance on rights that give an investor power, other than voting rights and potential voting rights. In addition, neither discusses the effect that such rights held by other parties have on the rights of an investor.

BC94 The Board addressed this issue to some extent in ED 10 by including guidance on protective rights. However, comments from respondents to ED 10 suggested that the guidance was not sufficient.

BC95 The Board decided to address the insufficiency by providing additional guidance about the activities that an investor must be able to direct in order to have power (ie those activities that significantly affect the investee's returns) and by providing guidance on when those rights are substantive. The Board believes that including such guidance should help an investor to determine whether it controls an investee, or whether the rights held by other parties are sufficient to prevent an investor from controlling an investee.

Voting rights

BC96　As with IAS 27 and ED 10, the Board decided to include guidance in IFRS 10 that addresses the assessment of control of investees that are controlled by voting rights.

Majority of voting rights

BC97　The Board carried forward the concept from IAS 27, with a modification to the words, that an investor that holds more than half the voting rights of an investee has power over the investee when those voting rights give the investor the current ability to direct the relevant activities (either directly or by appointing the members of the governing body). The Board concluded that such an investor's voting rights are sufficient to give it power over the investee regardless of whether it has exercised its voting power, unless those rights are not substantive or there are separate arrangements providing another entity with power over the investee (such as through a contractual arrangement over decision-making or substantive potential voting rights).

Less than a majority of voting rights

BC98　In October 2005[7] the Board stated that IAS 27 contemplates that there are circumstances in which an investor can control an investee without owning more than half the voting rights of that investee. The Board accepted that at that time IAS 27 did not provide clear guidance about the particular circumstances in which this will occur and that, as a consequence, there was likely to be diversity in practice.

BC99　The Board decided that in ED 10 it would explain clearly that an investor can control an investee even if the investor does not have more than half the voting rights, as long as the investor's voting rights are sufficient to give the investor the current ability to direct the relevant activities. ED 10 included an example of when a dominant shareholder holds voting rights and all other shareholdings are widely dispersed, and those other shareholders do not actively co-operate when they exercise their votes, so as to have more voting power than the dominant shareholder.

BC100　Respondents to ED 10 expressed mixed views about whether an investor could ever control an investee with less than half the voting rights and without other contractual rights relating to the activities of the investee.

BC101　Some who supported a 'contractual rights' control model believe that an investor with less than half the voting rights of an investee (and without other contractual rights) cannot control that investee. They reasoned that this is because the investor contractually does not have the unassailable right to direct the activities of the other investee in every possible scenario and cannot necessarily block the actions of others.

7　The October 2005 edition of *IASB Update* included a statement from the Board outlining its views on control with less than a majority of voting rights.

BC102   Supporters of the 'contractual rights' model believe that power should not be defined in a way that relies on the inactivity of other shareholders, as would be the case in an 'ability' model. In addition, they believe that if an investor wishes to control an investee, that investor would need to have a majority of the voting rights, or further contractual rights (in addition to its voting rights if necessary) that guarantee its power over the investee.

BC103   Other respondents supported the 'ability' model proposed in ED 10. They agreed with the Board that there are situations in which an investor with less than half the voting rights of an investee can control that investee, even when the investor does not have other contractual rights relating to the activities of the investee. However, they asked the Board to clarify when that would be the case. In particular, they questioned the following:

(a)   The proposals in the exposure draft implied that an investor might have to consolidate an investee simply because the remaining shareholdings are widely dispersed or attendance at shareholder meetings is low, even though the investor might hold only a low percentage of voting rights in that investee (eg 10 per cent or 15 per cent).

(b)   The proposals implied that an investor might be forced to obtain information about the shareholder structure, the degree of organisation and the other shareholders' future intentions. This would be particularly difficult to obtain if the investor owned a low percentage of the voting rights of an investee.

BC104   The Board noted the concerns raised by respondents but concluded that it would be inappropriate to limit power to situations in which an investor would have the contractual right to direct the activities of an investee, for the reasons noted in paragraphs BC45–BC50. Specifically in the context of voting rights, the Board believes that there are situations in which an investor can control an investee even though it does not own more than half the voting rights of an investee and does not have other contractual rights relating to the activities of the investee.

BC105   In reaching that conclusion, the Board noted that jurisdictions have differing legal and regulatory requirements relating to the protection of shareholders and investors. Those requirements often determine or influence the rights held by shareholders and consequently have an influence on the ability of an investor to have power over an investee with less than half the voting rights. For that reason, the Board concluded that drawing a line at 50 per cent in terms of voting power could lead to inappropriate consolidation conclusions in some jurisdictions.

BC106   The Board also concluded that an 'ability' model would result in more appropriate consolidation conclusions not only when applied in different jurisdictions, but also when applied to all investees. This is because the 'ability' model would be applied consistently to all investees by considering the rights held by the investor, as well as the rights held by other parties, when assessing control. For example, in the context of voting rights, an investor would assess whether its voting and any other contractual rights would be sufficient to give it the current ability to direct the relevant activities, or whether the voting and other rights held by other shareholders could prevent it from directing the relevant activities if those shareholders chose to act. The model would be applied in a similar way when other parties hold potential voting rights, kick-out rights or similar rights.

BC107   In response to the concerns raised by respondents to ED 10, the Board clarified that its intentions were neither to require the consolidation of all investees, nor to require an investor that owns a low percentage of voting rights of an investee (such as 10 per cent or 15 per cent) to consolidate that investee. An investor should always assess whether its rights, including any voting rights that it owns, are sufficient to give it the current ability to direct the relevant activities. That assessment requires judgement, considering all available evidence.

BC108   The Board decided to add application requirements setting out some of the factors to consider when applying that judgement to situations in which no single party holds more than half the voting rights of an investee. In particular, the Board decided to clarify that it expects that:

(a)   the more voting rights an investor holds (ie the larger its absolute holding), the more likely it will have power over an investee;

(b)   the more voting rights an investor holds relative to other vote holders (ie the larger its relative holding), the more likely the investor will have power over an investee; and

(c)   the more parties that would need to act together to outvote the investor, the more likely the investor will have power over an investee.

BC109   The Board also noted that, in some cases, considering the voting rights and potential voting rights that an investor and others hold, together with contractual rights, will be sufficient to determine whether the investor has power. However, in other cases these factors may not be sufficient to enable a determination to be made and additional evidence would need to be considered for an investor to determine whether it has power. IFRS 10 sets out additional factors to be considered in these circumstances. In particular, the Board noted that the fewer voting rights an investor holds and the fewer parties that would need to act together to outvote the investor, the more reliance would need to be placed on additional evidence to determine whether the investor has power.

BC110   The Board also decided to clarify that if, after all available evidence has been considered, the evidence is not sufficient to conclude that the investor has power, the investor should not consolidate the investee. If an investor controls an investee, that conclusion is reached on the basis of evidence that is sufficient to conclude that the investor's rights give it the current ability to direct the relevant activities. The Board's intention was not to create a presumption that in the absence of evidence to the contrary the shareholder with the largest proportion of voting rights controls an investee.

BC111   It might be the case that when an investor initially acquires voting rights in an investee and assesses control solely by considering the size of that holding and the voting rights held by others, sufficient evidence is not available to conclude that the investor has power. If that is the case, the investor would not consolidate the investee. However, the assessment should be reconsidered as additional evidence becomes available. For example, the voting rights held by an investor and others may be unchanged but over time the investor may have been able to appoint a majority of the investee's board of directors and may have entered into significant transactions with the investee, thereby enabling the overall assessment to be made that the investor now has control and should consolidate the investee.

Potential voting rights

BC112   An investor might own options, convertible instruments or other instruments that, if exercised, would give the investor voting rights.

BC113   IAS 27 referred to those instruments as potential voting rights. According to that standard, the existence and effect of potential voting rights that are currently exercisable or convertible were considered when assessing control. If the options or convertible instruments that give an investor potential voting rights are currently exercisable, IAS 27 required the investor to treat those potential voting rights as if they were current voting rights. According to IAS 27, the investor had to consider all facts and circumstances except the intentions of management and the financial ability to exercise or convert such rights.

BC114   Because of the revised definition of control, the Board reconsidered potential voting rights in developing the guidance in IFRS 10.

BC115   The questions that the Board considered with respect to potential voting rights were:

   (a)   Can potential voting rights give the holder the current ability to direct the relevant activities of an investee to which those potential voting rights relate?

   (b)   If so, in what situations do potential voting rights give the holder the current ability to direct the relevant activities of that investee?

BC116   The Board proposed in ED 10 that an investor should assess whether its power from holding potential voting rights, considered together with other facts and circumstances, gives it power over the investee. Such an investor would have power if the governing body acts in accordance with the wishes of the investor, the counterparty to the instrument acts as an agent for the investor or the investor has particular contractual rights that give it power.

BC117   Most respondents to ED 10 agreed that unexercised potential voting rights, taken in conjunction with other facts and circumstances, could give an investor power. However, many were confused by the application guidance— how would one know whether the decisions of the governing body were in accordance with the wishes of the investor? The respondents suggested that the other situations described in the discussion of power through potential voting rights could lead to power for reasons other than the potential voting rights instrument.

BC118　The Board concluded that the guidance in IFRS 10 that addresses control should apply to potential voting rights, ie when assessing control, an investor should consider all rights that it and other parties hold, including potential voting rights, to determine whether its rights are sufficient to give it control.

BC119　The Board observed that concluding that such instruments always or never give the holder control would cause inappropriate consolidation decisions in some cases.

BC120　Accordingly, the Board concluded that potential voting rights can give the holder the current ability to direct the relevant activities. This will be the case if those rights are substantive and on exercise or conversion (when considered together with any other existing rights the holder has) they give the holder the current ability to direct the relevant activities. The holder of such potential voting rights has the contractual right to 'step in', obtain voting rights and subsequently exercise its voting power to direct the relevant activities — thus the holder has the current ability to direct the activities of an investee at the time that decisions need to be taken if those rights are substantive.

BC121　The Board noted that the holder of such potential voting rights is, in effect, in the same position as a passive majority shareholder or the holder of substantive kick-out rights. The control model would provide that, in the absence of other factors, a majority shareholder controls an investee even though it can take time for the shareholder to organise a meeting and exercise its voting rights. In a similar manner, it can take time for a principal to remove or 'kick out' an agent. The holder of potential voting rights must also take steps to obtain its voting rights. In each case, the question is whether those steps are so significant that they prevent the investor from having the current ability to direct the relevant activities of an investee.

BC122　The Board observed that if power was characterised as requiring either the contractual right to direct the activities or active direction of the activities, the holder of unexercised potential voting rights would never have power without other contractual rights. However, power is the current ability to direct the activities of an investee. As such, the Board concluded that there are situations in which substantive potential voting rights can give the holder power before exercise or conversion to obtain those rights.

BC123　In response to comments from respondents to add clarity about when the holder of potential voting rights has power and to ensure that the control model is applied consistently, the Board added guidance and application examples to help assess when potential voting rights are substantive. Although that assessment requires judgement, the Board believes that an investor should be able to apply the judgement required. This is because potential voting rights exist for a reason — the terms and conditions of the instruments reflect that reason. Therefore, an assessment of the terms and conditions of the instrument (ie the purpose and design of the instrument) should provide information about whether the instrument was designed to give the holder power before exercise or conversion.

BC124 Some constituents were concerned about whether the proposed model would lead to frequent changes in the control assessment solely because of changes in market conditions—would an investor consolidate and deconsolidate an investee if potential voting rights moved in and out of the money? In response to those comments, the Board noted that determining whether a potential voting right is substantive is not based solely on a comparison of the strike or conversion price of the instrument and the then current market price of its underlying share. Although the strike or conversion price is one factor to consider, determining whether potential voting rights are substantive requires a holistic approach, considering a variety of factors. This includes assessing the purpose and design of the instrument, considering whether the investor can benefit for other reasons such as by realising synergies between the investor and the investee, and determining whether there are any barriers (financial or otherwise) that would prevent the holder of potential voting rights from exercising or converting those rights. Accordingly, the Board believes that a change in market conditions (ie the market price of the underlying shares) alone would not typically result in a change in the consolidation conclusion.

Delegated power (agency relationships)

BC125 IAS 27 and SIC-12 did not contain requirements or guidance to assess whether a decision maker is an agent or principal. The absence of guidance has allowed divergence to develop in practice. The Board decided to introduce principles that address agency relationships to reduce this divergence.

BC126 ED 10 proposed criteria to identify an agency relationship on the basis of the following assumptions:

(a) Both the principal and the agent seek to maximise their own benefits. Therefore, the principal is likely to introduce additional measures that are intended to ensure that the agent does not act against the interest of the principal. For example, the principal may have rights to remove the agent with or without cause.

(b) A principal has no incentive to remunerate an agent more than what is commensurate with the services provided. Accordingly, remuneration that is not commensurate with the services provided is an indicator that a decision maker is not an agent.

BC127 ED 10 included guidance on dual roles and addressed situations in which an investor holds voting rights, both directly and on behalf of other parties as an agent. The exposure draft proposed that when assessing whether an investor acts as an agent or a principal, the investor would exclude the voting rights that it holds as an agent only if it could demonstrate that it is obliged to act in the best interests of other parties or has implemented policies and procedures that ensure the independence of the decision maker in its role as an agent from that as a holder of voting rights directly.

BC128   Most respondents to ED 10 agreed with the Board that the consolidation standard should provide application guidance to identify an agency relationship. However, some respondents believed that the exposure draft was not clear on whether the Board intended the proposed application guidance to be limited to legal or contractual agency relationships. Most respondents agreed that the form of remuneration can be an indicator of an agency relationship. However, many found the application guidance, in this respect, confusing. They did not agree with the dual role guidance that required an investor to assess in aggregate its rights as an agent and a principal. Nor did they believe that such an investor should automatically exclude its rights as an agent from the control assessment.

BC129   In response to those comments, the Board decided to base its principal/agent guidance on the thinking developed in agency theory. Jensen and Meckling (1976) define an agency relationship as 'a contractual relationship in which one or more persons (the principal) engage another person (the agent) to perform some service on their behalf which involves delegating some decision-making authority to the agent.'[8]

BC130   The Board clarified that, as defined, an agent is obliged to act in the best interests of the parties that delegated the power (ie the principal or principals) and not other parties by way of a wider fiduciary responsibility. The Board did not think it would be appropriate to conclude that every party that is obliged, by law or contract, to act in the best interests of other parties is an agent for the purposes of assessing control. This conclusion, in effect, assumes that a decision maker that is legally or contractually obliged to act in the best interests of other parties will always do so, even if that decision maker receives the vast majority of the returns that are influenced by its decision-making. Although this assumption might be appropriate for some decision makers, the Board observed that it would not be appropriate for all, in particular many investees that are not directed through voting or similar rights. Almost every investment or asset manager could contend that it is contractually obliged to act in the best interests of others. This conclusion could result in virtually every investee that is not directed through voting or similar rights being unconsolidated.

BC131   The Board observed that the difficulty in developing guidance that addresses agency relationships is that the link between power and returns is often missing. To have control, an investor must have power and be able to use that power for its own benefit.

BC132   If a decision maker receives a return that is relatively insignificant or varies insignificantly, most would be comfortable concluding that the decision maker uses any decision-making authority delegated to it to affect the returns received by others—this is because the decision maker would not have power for its own benefit. Similarly, if the decision maker held a substantial investment in the investee (say, a 95 per cent investment), most would conclude that the decision maker uses any decision-making authority

---

8   M C Jensen and W H Meckling, *Theory of the Firm: Managerial Behavior Agency Costs and Ownership Structure*, Journal of Financial Economics 1976, pp. 305–360.

delegated to it primarily to affect the returns it receives—the decision maker would have power for its own benefit. But at what point, between insignificant and very significant, does the decision maker change from using any decision-making authority primarily for others to using its authority primarily for itself?

BC133　The Board concluded that the guidance in IFRS 10 that addresses control should apply to agency relationships, ie when assessing control, a decision maker should consider whether it has the current ability to direct the relevant activities of an investee that it manages to affect the returns it receives, or whether it uses the decision-making authority delegated to it primarily for the benefit of other parties.

BC134　The Board observed that a decision maker always acts as an agent of another party when that other party holds a unilateral substantive right to remove the decision maker. Therefore, a substantive removal right that is held by a single party is a conclusive indicator of an agency relationship.

BC135　At the FASB's round-table meeting on consolidation in November 2010, participants asked whether a board of directors (or other governing body) can be evaluated as one party when considering whether a single party holds substantive removal rights. The IASB observed that the function of such governing bodies is to act as a fiduciary for the investors and therefore any rights given to an investee's board of directors (or other governing body) is a pass-through mechanism for the exercise of the investors' rights. Thus, the governing body itself cannot be considered to have or restrict decision-making authority over the investee. Rather it is the rights given to such a governing body by the investors and their effect on the decision-making authority that should be considered. Consequently, a governing body is not generally viewed as a single party.

BC136　In the absence of a substantive removal right that is held by a single party, judgement must be applied when assessing whether a decision maker acts as a principal or an agent. That assessment includes considering the overall relationship between the decision maker, the entity being managed and the other interest holders, taking into account all available evidence.

BC137　With the exception of substantive removal rights that are held by one party, no single factor would provide conclusive evidence of an agency relationship. The Board observed that, depending on the facts and circumstances, a particular factor may be a strong indicator of an agency relationship and would receive a greater weighting than other factors when assessing control. However, the weighting would depend on the relevant facts and circumstances in each case and it would be inappropriate to specify that any factor would always be more important than the others.

Scope of decision-making authority

BC138　One of the factors to consider when assessing whether a decision maker is an agent or principal is the scope of its decision-making authority. The Board considered whether a decision maker would always be considered an agent if the breadth of its decision-making authority were restricted by contractual arrangements. The Board rejected such a conclusion for two reasons. First, it noted that it is rare for a parent to have unrestricted power over a subsidiary because debt providers or non-controlling interests often have protective rights that restrict the decision-making powers of a parent to some extent. Consequently, it would be difficult to set a particular threshold of restriction on decision-making that would automatically lead to a conclusion that the decision maker is an agent. The second reason was that it would inappropriately lead to many investees, such as securitisation vehicles, not being classified as a controlled entity by a decision maker even though it might have significant economic interests in the investee as well as discretion in making decisions about the relevant activities of the investee. The Board observed that a decision maker can have power over an investee if it has discretion in directing the relevant activities, even if those activities are restricted when the investee is established.

Rights held by other parties

BC139 When considering rights held by other parties in the context of a principal/agent analysis, the Board noted that an entity would assess whether those rights are substantive in the same way as any other rights held by other parties, such as voting rights. An entity would assess whether those rights give their holders the practical ability to prevent the decision maker from directing the activities of the investee if the holders choose to exercise those rights.

BC140 Some constituents said that it would be beneficial to address liquidation rights held by other parties. The Board observed that removal rights are defined as 'rights to deprive the decision maker of its decision-making authority' and that some other rights (such as some liquidation rights) may have the same effect on the decision-making authority as removal rights. If those other rights meet the definition of removal rights, they should be treated as such regardless of their label. Therefore, the Board concluded that there was no need to add further guidance in this respect in the IFRS.

Exposure to variability of returns

BC141 The Board considered whether to specify that in the absence of other parties having substantive removal rights, a decision maker that receives a particular level of returns or exposure to variability of returns would be deemed to control an investee (for example, exposure to more than half of the variability of returns of an investee). However, the Board rejected developing a model that would specify a particular level of returns that would result in the determination of an agency relationship. Rather, the Board concluded that the more a decision maker is exposed to the variability of returns from its involvement with an investee, the more likely it is that the decision maker is a principal.

BC142 Although prescribing a quantitative approach for assessing returns, and specifying a particular level of returns, might lead to more consistent application of the requirements by removing some of the judgement required, the Board observed that such an approach was likely to lead to inappropriate consolidation conclusions in some situations. It would create a bright line that might encourage structuring to achieve a particular accounting outcome. The Board also noted that when assessing agency relationships, a decision maker's exposure to variability of returns is not necessarily correlated with the amount of power that it has, unlike the general assumption when investees are controlled by voting rights. Therefore, a decision maker does not necessarily have any more power over an investee when it is exposed, for example, to more than half of the variability of an investee's returns than when it is not.

Relationship with other parties

BC143   The Board decided that an investor should, when assessing control, consider the nature of its relationships with other parties. An investor may conclude that the nature of its relationship with other parties is such that those other parties are acting on the investor's behalf (they are 'de facto agents'). Such a relationship need not involve a contractual arrangement, thereby creating a non-contractual agency relationship. The Board concluded that a party is a de facto agent when the investor has, or those that direct the activities of the investor have, the ability to direct that party to act on the investor's behalf.

BC144   ED 10 included a list of examples of parties that often act for the investor. The Board's intention was that an investor would look closely at its relationships with such parties and assess whether the party is acting on behalf of the investor.

BC145   Some respondents said that the list of examples of parties that often act on behalf of an investor was not helpful because they could think of circumstances in which it would be appropriate to regard each of the parties as agents of the investor and other circumstances when it would not. Respondents were unclear about the consequences of concluding that a party acts for an investor.

BC146   The Board clarified its intentions by stating that, when assessing control, an investor would consider its de facto agent's decision-making rights and exposure (or rights) to variable returns together with its own as if the rights were held by the investor directly. In reaching this decision, the Board noted that it would be inappropriate to assume that all other parties listed in paragraph B75 would *always* or *never* act for the investor. It acknowledged that the assessment of whether the nature of the relationship between the investor and the other party is such that the other party is a de facto agent requires judgement, including consideration of the nature of the relationship and the way that the parties interact with each other.

Control of specified assets

BC147   ED 10 introduced the term 'silo'—an investee within a legal structure—without defining it, noting that an investee can comprise more than one entity. This would be the case when the legal and contractual arrangements relating to an investee give one party control of a particular set of assets and liabilities, whereas another party might have control over another set of assets and liabilities within the investee. Respondents to ED 10 requested more guidance in order to apply the concept in practice.

BC148   In response to those requests, IFRS 10 includes application requirements regarding interests in specified assets. This guidance is consistent with the current guidance in US GAAP in that it sets out when a portion of an investee is treated as a separate entity for the purposes of consolidation. The Board noted that this situation arises most often in the context of investees that are not directed through voting or similar rights. However, the Board decided that to restrict the application requirements to investees that are not directed through voting or similar rights would be contrary to the objective of developing a control model that is applied consistently to all investees. In addition, the Board was not aware of any reason for such a restriction. Therefore, the guidance regarding interests in specified assets is applicable to all investees. This is in contrast with US GAAP, which applies this guidance only to portions of variable interest entities.

Continuous assessment

BC149   ED 10 proposed that an investor should assess control continuously. This is because the Board believes that the assessment of control requires consideration of all facts and circumstances and it would be impossible to develop reconsideration criteria that would apply to every situation in which an investor obtains or loses control of an investee. Therefore, the reassessment of control only when particular reconsideration criteria are met would lead to inappropriate consolidation decisions in some cases.

BC150   Most respondents to ED 10 did not comment on the requirement to assess control continuously. Some questioned whether the continuous assessment of control could be interpreted as requiring preparers to reassess control at the end of each reporting period.

BC151   The Board confirmed the proposal in ED 10 to require an investor to assess control continuously, and clarified that this would mean reassessing control when there is a change in relevant facts and circumstances that suggest that there is a change to one or more of the three elements of control. Such reassessment would not be restricted to each reporting date, nor would the requirement necessarily demand the reassessment of all control or potential control relationships at each reporting date.

BC152   Participants in the FASB's round-table meeting on consolidation held in November 2010 expressed concern about the reassessment of control (including a decision maker's status as principal or agent) when there are changes in market conditions, in particular the reassessment of control in the context of potential voting rights. In response to those concerns, the IASB decided to add guidance to address the reassessment of control (including a decision maker's status as principal or agent) when there are changes in market conditions (for the reassessment of control in the context of potential voting rights see paragraph BC124). The Board observed that a change in market conditions alone would not generally affect the consolidation conclusion, or the status as a principal or an agent, for two reasons. The first is that power arises from substantive rights, and assessing whether those rights are substantive includes the consideration of many factors, not only those that are affected by a change in market conditions. The second is that an investor is not required to have a particular specified level of exposure to variable returns in order to control an investee. If that were the case, fluctuations in an investor's expected returns might result in changes in the consolidation conclusion.

BC153 Nonetheless, the Board confirmed that control should be reassessed when relevant facts and circumstances change to such an extent that there is a change in one or more of the three elements of control or in the overall relationship between a principal and an agent.

Accounting requirements

Consolidation procedures

BC154 The application requirements in IFRS 10 explain how potential voting rights should be accounted for in the consolidated financial statements. Paragraphs B89–B91 replace the guidance previously included in the implementation guidance accompanying IAS 27, but are not intended to change consolidation procedures.

Non-controlling interests (2003 revision and 2008 amendments)

BCZ155 The 2008 amendments to IAS 27 changed the term 'minority interest' to 'non-controlling interest'. The change in terminology reflects the fact that the owner of a minority interest in an entity might control that entity and, conversely, that the owners of a majority interest in an entity might not control the entity. 'Non-controlling interest' is a more accurate description than 'minority interest' of the interest of those owners who do not have a controlling interest in an entity.

BCZ156 Non-controlling interest was defined in IAS 27 as the equity in a subsidiary not attributable, directly or indirectly, to a parent (this definition is now in IFRS 10). Paragraph 26 of IAS 27 (as revised in 2000) required minority (non-controlling) interests to be presented in the consolidated balance sheet (statement of financial position) separately from liabilities and the equity of the shareholders of the parent.

BCZ157 As part of its revision of IAS 27 in 2003, the Board amended this requirement to require minority (non-controlling) interests to be presented in the consolidated statement of financial position within equity, separately from the equity of the shareholders of the parent. The Board concluded that a minority (non-controlling) interest is not a liability because it did not meet the definition of a liability in the *Framework for the Preparation and Presentation of Financial Statements*.[9]

---

9 References to the *Framework* in this Basis for Conclusions are to the IASC's *Framework for the Preparation and Presentation of Financial Statements*, adopted by the Board in 2001 and in effect when the Standard was revised and amended.

BCZ158   Paragraph 49(b) of the *Framework* stated that a liability is a present obligation of the entity arising from past events, the settlement of which is expected to result in an outflow from the entity of resources embodying economic benefits. Paragraph 60 of the *Framework* explained that an essential characteristic of a liability is that the entity has a present obligation and that an obligation is a duty or responsibility to act or perform in a particular way. The Board noted that the existence of a minority (non-controlling) interest in the net assets of a subsidiary does not give rise to a present obligation, the settlement of which is expected to result in an outflow of economic benefits from the group.

BCZ159   Instead, the Board noted that minority (non-controlling) interests represent the residual interest in the net assets of those subsidiaries held by some of the shareholders of the subsidiaries within the group, and therefore met the *Framework*'s definition of equity. Paragraph 49(c) of the *Framework* stated that equity is the residual interest in the assets of the entity after deducting all its liabilities.

Attribution of losses (2008 amendments)

BCZ160   IAS 27 (as revised in 2003) stated that when losses attributed to the minority (non-controlling) interests exceed the minority's interests in the subsidiary's equity, the excess, and any further losses applicable to the minority, is allocated against the majority interest except to the extent that the minority has a binding obligation and is able to make an additional investment to cover the losses.

BCZ161   In 2005 the Board decided that this treatment was inconsistent with its conclusion that non-controlling interests are part of the equity of the group, and proposed that an entity should attribute total comprehensive income applicable to non-controlling interests to those interests, even if this results in the non-controlling interests having a deficit balance.

BCZ162   If the parent enters into an arrangement that places it under an obligation to the subsidiary or to the non-controlling interests, the Board believes that the entity should account for that arrangement separately and the arrangement should not affect how the entity attributes comprehensive income to the controlling and non-controlling interests.

BCZ163   Some respondents to the 2005 exposure draft agreed with the proposal, noting that non-controlling interests share proportionately in the risks and rewards of the subsidiary and that the proposal was consistent with the classification of non-controlling interests as equity.

BCZ164   Other respondents disagreed, often on the grounds that controlling and non-controlling interests have different characteristics and should not be treated the same way. They argued that there was no need to change the guidance in IAS 27 (as revised in 2003) (ie that an entity should allocate excess losses to the controlling interest unless the non-controlling interests have a binding obligation and are able to make an additional investment to cover the losses). The reasons given by those respondents were:

(a)   The non-controlling interests are not compelled to cover the deficit (unless they have specifically agreed to do so) and it is reasonable to assume that, if the subsidiary requires additional capital in order to continue operations, the non-controlling interests would abandon their investments. In contrast, respondents asserted that in practice the controlling interest often has an implicit obligation to maintain the subsidiary as a going concern.

(b)   Often guarantees or other support arrangements by the parent protect the non-controlling interests from losses of the subsidiary in excess of equity and do not affect the way losses are attributed to the controlling and non-controlling interests. Respondents argued that allocating those losses to the parent and non-controlling interests and recognising separately a guarantee would not reflect the underlying economics, which are that only the parent absorbs the losses of the subsidiary. In their view, it would be misleading for financial statements to imply that the non-controlling interests have an obligation to make additional investments.

(c)   Recognising guarantees separately is contrary to the principle of the non-recognition of transactions between owners.

(d)   Loss allocation should take into account legal, regulatory or contractual constraints, some of which may prevent entities from recognising negative non-controlling interests, especially for regulated businesses (eg banks and insurers).

BCZ165   The Board considered these reasons but observed that, although it is true that non-controlling interests have no further obligation to contribute assets to the subsidiary, neither does the parent. Non-controlling interests participate proportionally in the risks and rewards of an investment in the subsidiary.

BCZ166   Some respondents asked the Board to provide guidance on the accounting for guarantees and similar arrangements between the parent and the subsidiary or the non-controlling interests. They also suggested that the Board should require additional disclosures about inter-company guarantees and the extent of deficits, if any, of non-controlling interests.

BCZ167   The Board considered these requests but observed that this was an issue wider than negative non-controlling interests. For example, the parent is not necessarily responsible for the liabilities of a subsidiary, and often there are factors that restrict the ability of a parent to move assets in a group, which means that the assets of the group are not necessarily freely available to the parent. The Board decided that it would be more appropriate to address comprehensively disclosures about non-controlling interests (disclosures about non-controlling interests are included in IFRS 12).

Changes in ownership interests in subsidiaries (2008 amendments)

BCZ168   The Board decided that after control of an entity is obtained, changes in a parent's ownership interest that do not result in a loss of control are accounted for as equity transactions (ie transactions with owners in their capacity as owners). This means that no gain or loss from these changes should be recognised in profit or loss. It also means that no change in the carrying amounts of the subsidiary's assets (including goodwill) or liabilities should be recognised as a result of such transactions.

BCZ169   The Board reached this conclusion because it believed that the approach adopted in the amendments was consistent with its previous decision that non-controlling interests are a separate component of equity (see paragraphs BCZ156–BCZ159).

BCZ170   Some respondents agreed that non-controlling interests are equity but said that they should be treated as a special class of equity. Others disagreed with the requirement because in their view recognising transactions with non-controlling interests as equity transactions would mean that the Board had adopted an entity approach whereas they preferred a proprietary approach. The Board disagreed with this characterisation of the accounting treatment, noting that the accounting proposed was a consequence of classifying non-controlling interests as equity. The Board did not consider comprehensively the entity and proprietary approaches as part of the amendments to IAS 27 in 2008.

BCZ171   Many respondents to the 2005 exposure draft suggested alternative approaches for the accounting for changes in controlling ownership interests. The most commonly suggested alternative would result in increases in controlling ownership interests giving rise to the recognition of additional goodwill, measured as the excess of the purchase consideration over the carrying amount of the separately identified assets in the subsidiary attributable to the additional interest acquired.

BCZ172   Some respondents suggested that when an entity reduces its ownership interest in a subsidiary, without losing control, it should recognise a gain or loss attributable to the controlling interest. They would measure that gain or loss as the difference between the consideration received and the proportion of the carrying amount of the subsidiary's assets (including recognised goodwill) attributable to the ownership interest being disposed of. Respondents supporting this alternative said that it would provide relevant information about the gains and losses attributable to the controlling interest arising on the partial disposal of ownership interests in subsidiaries.

BCZ173   The Board rejected this alternative. Recognising a change in any of the assets of the business, including goodwill, was inconsistent with the Board's decision in IFRS 3 *Business Combinations* (as revised in 2008) that obtaining control in a business combination is a significant economic event. That event causes the initial recognition and measurement of all the assets acquired and liabilities assumed in the business combination. Subsequent transactions with owners should not affect the measurement of those assets and liabilities.

BCZ174　The parent already controls the assets of the business, although it must share the income from those assets with the non-controlling interests. By acquiring the non-controlling interests the parent is obtaining the rights to some, or all, of the income to which the non-controlling interests previously had rights. Generally, the wealth-generating ability of those assets is unaffected by the acquisition of the non-controlling interests. That is to say, the parent is not investing in more or new assets. It is acquiring more rights to the income from the assets it already controls.

BCZ175　By acquiring some, or all, of the non-controlling interests the parent will be allocated a greater proportion of the profits or losses of the subsidiary in periods after the additional interests are acquired. The adjustment to the controlling interest will be equal to the unrecognised share of the value changes that the parent will be allocated when those value changes are recognised by the subsidiary. Failure to make that adjustment will cause the controlling interest to be overstated.

BCZ176　The Board noted that accounting for changes in controlling ownership interests as equity transactions, as well as ensuring that the income of the group and the reported controlling interests are faithfully represented, is less complex than the other alternatives considered.

BCZ177　Some respondents disagreed with the proposal because they were concerned about the effect on reported equity of the subsequent acquisition of non-controlling interests by the parent. They seemed to be particularly concerned about the effect on the reported leverage of an entity that acquires non-controlling interests and whether this might, for example, cause those entities to have to renegotiate loan agreements.

BCZ178　The Board observed that all acquisitions of an entity's equity reduce the entity's equity, regardless of whether it is an acquisition of the parent's ordinary or preference shares or non-controlling interests. Hence, the treatment of a subsequent acquisition of non-controlling interests is consistent with the general accounting for the acquisition by an entity of instruments classified as equity.

BCZ179　The Board understands the importance of providing owners of the parent with information about the total changes in their reported equity. Therefore, the Board decided to require entities to present in a separate schedule the effects of any changes in a parent's ownership interest in a subsidiary that do not result in a loss of control on the equity attributable to owners of the parent (this disclosure requirement is now in IFRS 12).

Loss of control (2008 amendments)

BCZ180　A parent loses control of a subsidiary when it loses the power to govern the financial and operating policies of an investee so as to obtain benefit from its activities. Loss of control can result from the sale of an ownership interest or by other means, such as when a subsidiary issues new ownership interests to third parties. Loss of control can also occur in the absence of a transaction. It may, for example, occur on the expiry of an agreement that previously allowed an entity to control a subsidiary.

BCZ181 On loss of control, the parent-subsidiary relationship ceases to exist. The parent no longer controls the subsidiary's individual assets and liabilities. Therefore, the parent derecognises the individual assets, liabilities and equity related to that subsidiary. Equity includes any non-controlling interests as well as amounts previously recognised in other comprehensive income in relation to, for example, foreign currency translation.

BCZ182 The Board decided that any investment the parent has in the former subsidiary after control is lost should be measured at fair value at the date that control is lost and that any resulting gain or loss should be recognised in profit or loss. Some respondents disagreed with that decision. They asserted that the principles for revenue and gain recognition in the *Framework* would not be satisfied for the retained interest. The Board disagreed with those respondents. Measuring the investment at fair value reflected the Board's view that the loss of control of a subsidiary is a significant economic event. The parent-subsidiary relationship ceases to exist and an investor-investee relationship begins that differs significantly from the former parent-subsidiary relationship. Therefore, the new investor-investee relationship is recognised and measured initially at the date when control is lost.

BCZ183 The Board decided that the loss of control of a subsidiary is, from the group's perspective, the loss of control over some of the group's individual assets and liabilities. Accordingly, the general requirements in IFRSs should be applied in accounting for the derecognition from the group's financial statements of the subsidiary's assets and liabilities. If a gain or loss previously recognised in other comprehensive income would be reclassified to profit or loss on the separate disposal of those assets and liabilities, the parent reclassifies the gain or loss from equity to profit or loss on the indirect disposal of those assets and liabilities through loss of control of a subsidiary.

BCZ184 The Board also discussed the accounting when an entity transfers its shares in a subsidiary to its own shareholders with the result that the entity loses control of the subsidiary (commonly referred to as a spin-off). The International Financial Reporting Interpretations Committee had previously discussed this matter, but decided not to add the matter to its agenda while the business combinations project was in progress. The Board observed that the issue was outside the scope of the business combinations project. Therefore, the Board decided not to address the measurement basis of distributions to owners in the amendments to IAS 27.

Multiple arrangements

BCZ185 The Board considered whether its decision that a gain or loss on the disposal of a subsidiary should be recognised only when that disposal results in a loss of control could give rise to opportunities to structure transactions to achieve a particular accounting outcome. For example, would an entity be motivated to structure a transaction or arrangement as multiple steps to maximise gains or minimise losses if an entity were planning to dispose of its controlling interest in a subsidiary? Consider the following example. Entity P controls 70 per cent of entity S. Entity P intends to sell all of its 70 per cent controlling interest in entity S. Entity P could initially sell 19 per cent of its ownership interest in entity S without loss of control and then, soon afterwards, sell the remaining 51 per cent and lose control. Alternatively, entity P could sell all of its 70 per cent interest in entity S in one transaction. In the first case, any difference between the amount by which the non-controlling interests are adjusted and the fair value of the consideration received on the sale of the 19 per cent interest would be recognised directly in equity, whereas the gain or loss from the sale of the remaining 51 per cent interest would be recognised in profit or loss. In the second case, a gain or loss on the sale of the whole 70 per cent interest would be recognised in profit or loss.

BCZ186   The Board noted that the opportunity to conceal losses through structuring would be reduced by the requirements of IAS 36 *Impairment of Assets* and IFRS 5 *Non-current Assets Held for Sale and Discontinued Operations.* Paragraph 12 of IAS 36 includes significant changes to how an entity uses or expects to use an asset as one of the indicators that the asset might be impaired.

BCZ187   Once an asset meets the criteria to be classified as held for sale (or is included in a disposal group that is classified as held for sale), it is excluded from the scope of IAS 36 and is accounted for in accordance with IFRS 5. In accordance with paragraph 20 of IFRS 5 'an entity shall recognise an impairment loss for any initial or subsequent write-down of the asset (or disposal group) to fair value less costs to sell...'. Therefore, if appropriate, an impairment loss would be recognised for the goodwill and non-current assets of a subsidiary that will be sold or otherwise disposed of before control of the subsidiary is lost. Accordingly, the Board concluded that the principal risk is the minimising of gains, which entities are unlikely to strive to do.

BCZ188   The Board decided that the possibility of such structuring could be overcome by requiring entities to consider whether multiple arrangements should be accounted for as a single transaction to ensure that the principle of faithful representation is adhered to. The Board believes that all the terms and conditions of the arrangements and their economic effects should be considered in determining whether multiple arrangements should be accounted for as a single arrangement. Accordingly, the Board included indicators in paragraph 33 of IAS 27 (as revised in 2008) to assist in identifying when multiple arrangements that result in the loss of control of a subsidiary should be treated as a single arrangement (those indicators are now in paragraph B97 of IFRS 10).

BCZ189   Some respondents disagreed with the indicators that were provided in the exposure draft. They said that the need for guidance on when multiple arrangements should be accounted for as a single arrangement indicates a conceptual weakness in the accounting model developed in the exposure draft. Moreover, such guidance would be unnecessary under other alternatives for accounting for decreases in ownership interests. The Board acknowledges that guidance on multiple arrangements would be unnecessary under some other accounting alternatives. However, the Board does not accept that this means that those models are conceptually superior.

BCZ190 Some respondents suggested that IAS 27 should include examples rather than indicators for when multiple transactions should be treated as a single transaction or arrangement, but that those examples should not be regarded as a complete list. The Board considered that suggestion, but decided to confirm the indicators that were proposed in the exposure draft. The Board believed that the indicators could be applied to a variety of situations and were preferable to providing what could be an endless list of examples to try to capture every possible arrangement.

Sale or contribution of assets between an investor and its associate or joint venture—amendments to IFRS 10 and IAS 28 (issued in September 2014)

BC190A The IFRS Interpretations Committee received a request to clarify whether a business meets the definition of a 'non-monetary asset'. The question was asked within the context of identifying whether the requirements of SIC-13 *Jointly Controlled Entities—Non-Monetary Contributions by Venturers*[10] and IAS 28 (as amended in 2011) apply when a business is contributed to a jointly controlled entity (as defined in IAS 31[11]), a joint venture (as defined in IFRS 11) or an associate, in exchange for an equity interest in that jointly controlled entity, joint venture or associate. The business may be contributed either when the jointly controlled entity, joint venture or associate is established or thereafter.

BC190B The Board noted that this matter is related to the issues arising from the acknowledged inconsistency between the requirements in IAS 27 (as revised in 2008) and SIC-13, when accounting for the contribution of a subsidiary to a jointly controlled entity, joint venture or associate (resulting in the loss of control of the subsidiary). In accordance with SIC-13, the amount of the gain or loss recognised resulting from the contribution of a non-monetary asset to a jointly controlled entity in exchange for an equity interest in that jointly controlled entity is restricted to the extent of the interests attributable to the unrelated investors in the jointly controlled entity. However, IAS 27 (as revised in 2008) requires full profit or loss recognition on the loss of control of a subsidiary.

BC190C This inconsistency between IAS 27 (as revised in 2008) and SIC-13 remained after IFRS 10 replaced IAS 27 (as revised in 2008) and SIC-13 was withdrawn. The requirements in IFRS 10 on the accounting for the loss of control of a subsidiary are similar to the requirements in IAS 27 (as revised in 2008). The requirements in SIC-13 are incorporated into paragraphs 28 and 30 of IAS 28 (as amended in 2011) and apply to the sale or contribution of assets between an investor and its associate or joint venture. Because IAS 27 (as revised in 2008) and SIC-13 have been superseded at the time when the amendments become effective, the Board decided to amend only IFRS 10 and IAS 28 (as amended in 2011).

---

10 SIC-13 has been withdrawn. The requirements in SIC-13 are incorporated into IAS 28 (as amended in 2011).

11 IAS 31 was superseded by IFRS 11 *Joint Arrangements* issued in May 2011.

BC190D   In dealing with the conflict between the requirements in IFRS 10 and IAS 28 (as amended in 2011), the Board was concerned that the existing requirements could result in the accounting for a transaction being driven by its form rather than by its substance. For example, different accounting might be applied to a transaction involving the same underlying assets depending on whether those assets were:

(a)   transferred in a transaction that is structured as a sale of assets or as a sale of the entity that holds the assets; or

(b)   sold in exchange for cash or contributed in exchange for an equity interest.

BC190E   The Board concluded that:

(a)   the accounting for the loss of control of a business, as defined in IFRS 3, should be consistent with the conclusions in IFRS 3; and

(b)   a full gain or loss should therefore be recognised on the loss of control of a business, regardless of whether that business is housed in a subsidiary or not.

BC190F   Because assets that do not constitute a business were not part of the Business Combinations project, the Board concluded that:

(a)   the current requirements in IAS 28 (as amended in 2011) for the partial gain or loss recognition for transactions between an investor and its associate or joint venture should only apply to the gain or loss resulting from the sale or contribution of assets that do not constitute a business; and

(b)   IFRS 10 should be amended so that a partial gain or loss is recognised in accounting for the loss of control of a subsidiary that does not constitute a business as a result of a transaction between an investor and its associate or joint venture.

BC190G   The Board discussed whether all sales and contributions (including the sale or contribution of assets that do not constitute a business) should be consistent with IFRS 3. Although it considered this alternative to be the most robust from a conceptual point of view, it noted that this would require addressing multiple cross-cutting issues. Because of concerns that the cross-cutting issues could not be addressed on a timely basis, the conclusions described in paragraphs BC190E–BC190F were considered the best way to address this issue.

BC190H   The Board decided that both 'upstream' and 'downstream' transactions should be affected by the amendments to IFRS 10 and IAS 28 (as amended in 2011). The Board noted that if assets that constitute a business were sold by an associate or a joint venture to the investor (in an upstream transaction), with the result that the investor takes control of that business, the investor would account for this transaction as a business combination in accordance with IFRS 3.

BC190I   In response to concerns expressed by some interested parties, the Board clarified that paragraph B99A of IFRS 10 applies to all transactions between an investor and its associate or joint venture (that is accounted for using the equity method) that result in the loss of control of a subsidiary that does not constitute a business. Consequently, paragraph B99A of IFRS 10 does not apply:

(a)   to transactions with third parties, even if the parent retains an investment in the former subsidiary that becomes an associate or a joint venture accounted for using the equity method; or

(b)   when the investor elects to measure its investments in associates or joint ventures at fair value in accordance with IFRS 9.

BC190J   During the finalisation of the amendments, the Board also clarified that the gain or loss resulting from a transaction within the scope of paragraph B99A of IFRS 10 includes:

(a)   the amounts previously recognised in other comprehensive income that would be reclassified to profit or loss in accordance with paragraph B99 of IFRS 10. This is because those amounts are part of the gain or loss recognised on the disposal of the subsidiary.

(b)   the part of the gain or loss resulting from the remeasurement of the investment retained in a former subsidiary. The Board noted that if the former subsidiary is now an associate or a joint venture that is accounted for using the equity method, the parent will recognise this part of the gain or loss in its profit or loss only to the extent of the unrelated investors' interests in the new associate or joint venture. This is because the Board had previously decided that when a subsidiary is not a business the requirements of IAS 28 for the partial gain or loss recognition should be applied. If the parent retains an investment in the former subsidiary that is now accounted for in accordance with IFRS 9, the part of the gain or loss resulting from the remeasurement at fair value of the investment retained in the former subsidiary is recognised in full in the parent's profit or loss. This is because, in this case, the requirements of IFRS 9, rather than the requirements of IAS 28, apply for the partial gain or loss recognition.

BC190K   The Board decided that the amendments to IFRS 10 and IAS 28 (as amended in 2011) should apply prospectively to transactions that occur in annual periods beginning on or after the date that the amendments become effective. The Board observed that the requirements in IAS 27 (as revised in 2008) for the loss of control of a subsidiary were applied prospectively (see paragraph 45(c) of IAS 27 as revised in 2008). The Board also noted that transactions dealing with the loss of control of a subsidiary or a business between an investor and its associate or joint venture are discrete non-recurring transactions. Consequently, the Board concluded that the benefits of comparative information would not exceed the cost of providing it. The Board also decided to allow entities to early apply the amendments to IFRS 10 and IAS 28 (as amended in 2011).

Deferral of the *Effective Date of Amendments to IFRS 10 and IAS 28* (issued in September 2014)

BC190L   In September 2014, the Board amended IFRS 10 and IAS 28, for reasons described in paragraphs BC190A–BC190K ('the September 2014 Amendment'). Subsequently, the IFRS Interpretations Committee and the Board considered a number of other issues with respect to the sale or contribution of assets between an investor and its associate.

BC190M   In June 2015, the Board decided:

(a)   that these further issues should be addressed as part of its research project on equity accounting; and

(b)   to defer the effective date of the September 2014 Amendment so that entities need not change how they apply IAS 28 twice in a short period. The Board published for public comment a proposal for that deferral in August 2015 in an Exposure Draft *Effective Date of Amendments to IFRS 10 and IAS 28*. The majority of respondents agreed with that proposal and with the rationale provided by the Board. In the light of that feedback, the Board finalised the deferral of the September 2014 Amendment in December 2015.

BC190N   In the December 2015 amendment, the Board deferred the effective date of the September 2014 Amendment. This was done by removing the original effective date of 1 January 2016 and indicating that a new effective date will be determined at a future date when the Board finalises the revisions, if any, that result from the research project. Any future proposal to insert an effective date will be exposed for public comment.

BC190O   In deferring the effective date of the September 2014 Amendment, the Board continued to allow early application of that amendment. The Board did not wish to prohibit the application of better financial reporting.

Effective date and transition

Effective date

BC191   The Board decided to align the effective date for the IFRS with the effective date for IFRS 11, IFRS 12, IAS 27 *Separate Financial Statements* and IAS 28. When making this decision, the Board noted that the five IFRSs all deal with the assessment of, and related accounting and disclosure requirements about, a reporting entity's special relationships with other entities (ie when the reporting entity has control or joint control of, or significant influence over, another entity). As a result, the Board concluded that applying IFRS 10 without also applying the other four IFRSs could cause unwarranted confusion.

BC192   The Board usually sets an effective date of between twelve and eighteen months after issuing an IFRS. When deciding the effective date for those IFRSs, the Board considered the following factors:

(a)   the time that many countries require for translation and for introducing the mandatory requirements into law.

(b)   the consolidation project was related to the global financial crisis that started in 2007 and was accelerated by the Board in response to urgent requests from the leaders of the G20, the Financial Stability Board, users of financial statements, regulators and others to improve the accounting and disclosure of an entity's 'off balance sheet' activities.

(c)   the comments received from respondents to the Request for Views *Effective Date and Transition Methods* that was published in October 2010 regarding implementation costs, effective date and transition requirements of the IFRSs to be issued in 2011. Most respondents did not identify the consolidation and joint arrangements IFRSs as having a high impact in terms of the time and resources that their implementation would require. In addition, only a few respondents commented that the effective dates of those IFRSs should be aligned with those of the other IFRSs to be issued in 2011.

BC193   With these factors in mind, the Board decided to require entities to apply the five IFRSs for annual periods beginning on or after 1 January 2013.

BC194   The majority of the respondents to the Request for Views supported early application of the IFRSs to be issued in 2011. Respondents stressed that early application was especially important for first-time adopters in 2011 and 2012. The Board was persuaded by these arguments and decided to permit early application of IFRS 10 but only if an entity applies it in conjunction with the other IFRSs (ie IFRS 11, IFRS 12, IAS 27 (as amended in 2011) and IAS 28 (as amended in 2011)) to avoid a lack of comparability among financial statements, and for the reasons noted in paragraph BC191 that triggered the Board's decision to set the same effective date for all five IFRSs. Even though an entity should apply the five IFRSs at the same time, the Board noted that an entity should not be prevented from applying any of the disclosure requirements of IFRS 12 early if by doing so users gained a better understanding of the entity's relationships with other entities.

Transition

BC195   IAS 8 *Accounting Policies, Changes in Accounting Estimates and Errors* states that retrospective application results in the most useful information to users because the information presented for all periods is comparable.

BC196   In reaching its conclusions, the Board observed that IFRS 10 might result in an investor consolidating investees that were not previously consolidated or not consolidating investees that were previously consolidated. If an investor is required to consolidate a previously unconsolidated investee and has been accounting for its investment in that investee using proportionate consolidation or the equity method, the Board noted that the investor would often have the information available to consolidate the investee retrospectively as if IFRS 10 had always been in place. This is also likely to be the case if an investor no longer consolidates an investee that it previously consolidated but would now have to account for its investment in the investee using the equity method.

BC196A IFRS 3 *Business Combinations* was initially issued in 2004 and was then substantially revised in 2008. Those revisions apply prospectively. The Board noted that, when developing the transition guidance in paragraphs C4–C4A, it had not specified which version of IFRS 3 should be used when an investor concludes that it shall consolidate an investee that was not previously consolidated and over which control was obtained before the effective date of IFRS 3 (revised in 2008). Applying the current version of IFRS 3 in such cases may provide more comparable information.

BC196B However, as noted in BC196, if an investor has been accounting for its investment in such an investee using proportionate consolidation or the equity method, it will have already identified the fair values, goodwill and other amounts required to apply IFRS 3 (issued in 2004). Allowing investors to use existing information in such cases reduces the risk of using hindsight and may provide a more reliable basis for consolidation. Consequently, if control was obtained before the effective date of IFRS 3 (2008), the Board decided to allow entities to use either IFRS 3 (2008) or IFRS 3 (2004) in applying the transition requirements.

BC196C Similarly, IAS 27 *Consolidated and Separate Financial Statements*, as issued in 2003, was substantially revised in 2008. Those revisions apply prospectively. The requirements of IAS 27 (revised in 2008) have been carried forward into IFRS 10. For the same reasons as those described in BC196A–BC196B relating to IFRS 3, if control was obtained before the effective date of IAS 27 (2008), the Board also decided to allow entities to use either IAS 27 (2008) or IAS 27 (2003) in applying the transition requirements.

BC197 In addition, the Board acknowledged that retrospective application of IFRS 10 may not be practicable in some circumstances. If an investor on initial application of IFRS 10 consolidates an investee it previously did not consolidate and it is impracticable to apply the provisions of IFRS 10 retrospectively, the reporting entity would apply the acquisition method in IFRS 3 with the acquisition date being the beginning of the earliest period for which application of those requirements is practicable (goodwill would not be recognised for an investee that is not a business).

BC198 If an investor on initial application of IFRS 10 ceases to consolidate an investee that was previously consolidated, the investor measures its retained interest in the investee on the date of initial application, at the amount at which the interest would have been measured if the requirements of IFRS 10 had been effective when the investor first became involved with (but did not obtain control in accordance with this IFRS), or lost control of, the investee. If, in accordance with IFRS 10, the investor never obtained control, then it would eliminate the previous consolidation from the date that it first became involved with the investee and account for that interest in accordance with other IFRSs as applicable. Alternatively, the investor may have obtained control in accordance with both IAS 27 and IFRS 10, but then later lost control in accordance with IFRS 10 but not IAS 27. In this case, the investor would cease to consolidate from the date control was lost as defined by IFRS 10. If measurement of the retained interest at the date the investor first became involved with (but did not obtain control in accordance with this IFRS), or lost control of, the investee is impracticable, the investor would apply the requirements in IFRS 10 for accounting for a loss of control at the beginning of the earliest period for which application of those requirements is practicable. The earliest period may be the current period.

BC199   As stated in paragraph BC192, respondents to the Request for Views also commented on the transition requirements of the IFRSs to be issued in 2011. In relation to the transition requirements relating to consolidation, the Board noted that the majority of the respondents to the Request for Views had agreed with limited retrospective application for IFRS 10.

BC199A   The Board identified a need to clarify the transition guidance that was intended to achieve limited retrospective application of IFRS 10. The Board noted that the main intention when issuing IFRS 10 was to ensure consistent accounting for transactions when IFRS 10 was applied for the first time (ie 1 January 2013 for a calendar-year entity, assuming no early application). In other words, the intention was to use the date of initial application as the point at which to determine the interests that should be accounted for in accordance with IFRS 10. The Board also noted that the intention was to provide transition relief if the consolidation conclusion would be the same whether applying IAS 27/SIC-12 or IFRS 10 at the date that IFRS 10 was applied for the first time. The Board concluded that, in those situations, the incremental benefit to users of applying IFRS 10 retrospectively would not outweigh the costs.

BC199B   Consequently, the Board confirmed that the 'date of initial application' means the beginning of the annual reporting period for which IFRS 10 is applied for the first time. The Board amended the transition guidance to confirm that an entity is not required to make adjustments to the previous accounting for its involvement with entities if the consolidation conclusion reached at the date of initial application is the same whether applying IAS 27/SIC-12 or IFRS 10. In making this clarification, the Board confirmed that the transition relief in paragraph C3(b) would also apply to interests in investees that were disposed of before the date of initial application of IFRS 10, (ie 1 January 2013 for a calendar-year entity, assuming no early application).

BC199C   In clarifying how an entity should retrospectively adjust its comparative information on initial application of IFRS 10, the Board acknowledged that presenting all adjusted comparatives would be burdensome for preparers in jurisdictions where several years of comparatives are required. Without changing the requirement to apply the recognition and measurement requirements of IFRS 10 retrospectively, the Board decided to limit the requirement to present adjusted comparatives to the annual period immediately preceding the date of initial application. This is consistent with the minimum comparative disclosure requirements contained in IAS 1 *Presentation of Financial Statements* as amended by *Annual Improvements to IFRSs 2009–2011 Cycle* (issued May 2012). Those amendments confirmed that when an entity applies a changed accounting policy retrospectively, it shall present, as a minimum, three statements of financial position (ie 1 January 2012, 31 December 2012 and 31 December 2013 for a calendar-year entity, assuming no early application of this IFRS) and two of each of the other statements (IAS 1 paragraphs 40A–40B). Notwithstanding this requirement, the Board confirmed that an entity is not prohibited from presenting adjusted comparative information for earlier periods. The Board noted that if all comparative periods are not adjusted then entities should be required to state that fact, clearly identify the information that has not been adjusted, and explain the basis on which it has been prepared.

BC199D The Board also considered the disclosure requirements of IAS 8 *Accounting Policies, Changes in Accounting Estimates and Errors*. On the initial application of an IFRS, paragraph 28(f) of IAS 8 requires an entity to disclose, for the current period and for each prior period presented, the amount of any adjustment for each financial statement line item affected. Changes in the consolidation conclusion on transition to IFRS 10 are likely to affect many line items throughout the financial statements. The Board agreed that this requirement would be burdensome for preparers and so agreed to limit the disclosure of the quantitative impact of any changes in the consolidation conclusion to only the annual period immediately preceding the date of initial application. An entity may also present this information for the current period or for earlier comparative periods, but is not required to do so.

BC199E The Board considered whether IFRS 1 *First-time Adoption of Financial Reporting Standards* should be amended to allow first-time adopters to use the transition guidance of IFRS 10. It was noted that some respondents to the exposure draft had commented that, particularly when an investee is disposed of or control is lost during the comparative period, the cost of providing temporary consolidation information is not justified. The Board noted that this raised broader issues with the application of IFRS 1 and, rather than address this issue in the context of clarifying IFRS 10 transition relief, it would be more appropriately addressed in the context of IFRS 1 itself.

Transitional provisions (2008 amendments)

BCZ200 To improve the comparability of financial information across entities, amendments to IFRSs are usually applied retrospectively. Therefore, the Board proposed in its 2005 exposure draft to require retrospective application of the amendments to IAS 27, on the basis that the benefits of retrospective application outweigh the costs. However, in that exposure draft the Board identified two circumstances in which it concluded that retrospective application would be impracticable:

(a) accounting for increases in a parent's ownership interest in a subsidiary that occurred before the effective date of the amendments. Therefore, the accounting for any previous increase in a parent's ownership interest in a subsidiary before the effective date of the amendments should not be adjusted.

(b) accounting for a parent's investment in a former subsidiary for which control was lost before the effective date of the amendments. Therefore, the carrying amount of any investment in a former subsidiary should not be adjusted to its fair value on the date when control was lost. In addition, an entity should not recalculate any gain or loss on loss of control of a subsidiary if the loss of control occurred before the effective date of the amendments.

BCZ201 The Board concluded that the implementation difficulties and costs associated with applying the amendments retrospectively in these circumstances outweigh the benefits of improved comparability of financial information. Therefore, the Board decided to require prospective application. In addition, the Board concluded that identifying those provisions for which retrospective application of the amendments would be impracticable, and thus prospective application would be required, would reduce implementation costs and result in greater comparability between entities.

BCZ202 Some respondents were concerned that the transitional provisions were different for increases and decreases in ownership interests. They argued that accounting for decreases in non-controlling interests retrospectively imposes compliance costs that are not justifiable, mainly because the requirement to account for increases prospectively reduces comparability anyway. The Board accepted those arguments and decided that prospective application would be required for all changes in ownership interests (those transitional provisions are now in Appendix C of IFRS 10). The revised transitional provisions will lead to increases and decreases in ownership interests being treated symmetrically and the recasting of financial statements being limited to disclosure and presentation. The recognition and measurement of previous transactions will not be changed upon transition.

BCZ203 In response to practical concerns raised by respondents, the Board also decided to require prospective application of the requirement to allocate losses in excess of the non-controlling interests in the equity of a subsidiary to the non-controlling interests, even if that would result in the non-controlling interests being reported as a deficit balance (this transitional provision is now in Appendix C of IFRS 10).

Withdrawal of IAS 27 (2008) and SIC-12

BC204 IFRS 10 identifies the principle of control and determines how to identify whether an investor controls an investee and therefore should consolidate the investee. IFRS 10 also identifies the principles for preparation of consolidated financial statements. IFRS 10 supersedes the requirements related to consolidated financial statements in IAS 27 (as amended in 2008) and SIC-12.

BC205 IFRS 10 does not address the accounting for investments in subsidiaries, jointly controlled entities and associates in separate financial statements as specified in IAS 27. The parts of IAS 27 that relate to separate financial statements have been included in the amended IAS 27.

Summary of main changes from ED 10

BC206   The main changes made by IFRS 10 from the exposure draft ED 10 published in 2008 are:

    (a)   IFRS 10 includes application guidance on all the following topics:

        (i)   the meaning of 'power', 'activities' and 'returns' within the definition of control.

        (ii)   when assessing control of an investee:

- understanding the purpose and design of an investee.

- different activities of an investee that significantly affect the investee's returns.

- a discussion of rights that give an investor power and protective rights.

- power to direct the activities of an investee without a majority of the voting rights, including potential voting rights.

- contractual and non-contractual agency relationships.

    (b)   IFRS 10 requires retrospective application of its requirements subject to the practicability exemption in IAS 8. The exposure draft had proposed prospective application using the requirements of IFRS 3 or the requirements relating to the loss of control on the date of first applying the IFRS.[12]

Cost-benefit considerations

BC207   The objective of general purpose financial reporting is to provide information about the financial position, performance and changes in financial position of a reporting entity that is useful to a wide range of users in making economic decisions. To attain this objective, the Board seeks to ensure that an IFRS will meet a significant need and that the overall benefits of the resulting information justify the costs of providing it. Although the costs of implementing a new IFRS might not be borne evenly, users of financial statements benefit from improvements in financial reporting, thereby facilitating the functioning of markets for capital and credit and the efficient allocation of resources in the economy.

BC208   The evaluation of costs and benefits is necessarily subjective. In making its judgement, the Board considered the following:

    (a)   the costs incurred by preparers of financial statements;

---

12 *Investment Entities* (Amendments to IFRS 10, IFRS 12 and IAS 27), issued in October 2012, introduced an exception to the principle that all subsidiaries shall be consolidated. The amendments define an investment entity and require a parent that is an investment entity to measure its investments in particular subsidiaries at fair value through profit or loss instead of consolidating those subsidiaries. These amendments are discussed in paragraphs BC215–BC317.

(b)   the costs incurred by users of financial statements when information is not available;

(c)   the comparative advantage that preparers have in developing information, compared with the costs that users would incur to develop surrogate information;

(d)   the benefit of better economic decision-making as a result of improved financial reporting; and

(e)   the costs of transition for users, preparers and others.

BC209   The Board observed that IFRS 10 will improve the usefulness of consolidated financial statements by developing a single basis for consolidation (control) and robust guidance for applying that basis to situations in which it has proved difficult to assess control in practice and divergence has evolved. IFRS 10 introduces a definition of control of an investee that is applied consistently when assessing whether an investor should consolidate an investee, irrespective of the nature of the investee. IFRS 10 also requires retrospective application of the requirements subject to the practicability exemptions in IAS 8 that will result in comparable information for all periods presented.

BC210   Users prefer information that is comparable from reporting period to reporting period for an individual entity and between different entities in a particular reporting period. The Board concluded that IFRS 10 provides much clearer principles that underlie the definition of control of an investee and provides more application guidance when assessing control than the requirements it replaces. As a consequence, users should have more comparable and verifiable information about the activities controlled by the reporting entity.

BC211   If the requirements in an IFRS are not clear, or there is no guidance, the preparer will often have to seek independent advice and engage with its auditors to resolve uncertainty about how to account for a particular type of transaction. These costs should decrease if the requirements in the revised IFRS are clearer. Accordingly, because IFRS 10 addresses the concerns conveyed to the Board about the absence of guidance in IAS 27 and SIC-12, the Board concluded that preparers will benefit from the new requirements. The Board accepts that any new IFRS will cause preparers to incur one--off costs associated with learning the new requirements and reassessing their accounting. However, the Board's assessment is that the benefits from providing clearer principles and more application guidance outweigh those costs.

BC212   The changes to the definition of control will inevitably lead to some reporting entities consolidating some entities that were previously not consolidated and ceasing consolidation of some entities, or both. The Board does not think it is appropriate to consider whether there will be 'more or less consolidation' by applying the new proposals. However, the clarifications in relation to less than a majority of the voting rights will lead to more consolidation. In the case of what SIC-12 referred to as special purpose entities, the Board believes that the new requirements will result in more appropriate consolidation.

BC213 Given the benefits for users and preparers noted in paragraphs BC209–BC211 the Board believes that the benefits of IFRS 10 outweigh the costs.

BC214 This project also considered disclosure requirements in relation to consolidation. Those requirements, and the related costs and benefits, are assessed in the Basis for Conclusions on IFRS 12.

Exception to consolidation for investment entities (2012 amendments)

Background

BC215 In October 2012, the Board issued *Investment Entities* (Amendments to IFRS 10, IFRS 12 and IAS 27), which provides an exception to consolidation for a class of entities that are defined as 'investment entities'. The Board added the Investment Entities project to its agenda in the course of its deliberations on IFRS 10 as a response to the comments received on ED 10.

BC216 The Board had considered this issue previously. In 2002, the respondents to the Exposure Draft of IAS 27 asked the Board to provide an exception to consolidation for the subsidiaries of venture capital organisations, private equity entities and similar organisations. At that time, the Board decided not to introduce such an exception because it did not think that it should differentiate between the types of entity, or the types of investment, when applying a control model of consolidation. It also did not agree that management's reasons for holding an investment should determine whether or not that investment is consolidated. The Board concluded that for investments under the control of venture capital organisations, private equity entities and similar organisations, users' information needs are best served by financial statements in which those investments are consolidated, thus revealing the extent of the operations of the entities they control.

BC217 The scope of the proposals in ED 10 was the same as the scope of the proposals in IAS 27. IAS 27 required reporting entities to consolidate all controlled entities, regardless of the nature of the reporting entity. Respondents to ED 10 questioned the usefulness of financial statements of investment entities that consolidate investees that the investment entity controls. They pointed out that some national accounting requirements, including United States Generally Accepted Accounting Principles (US GAAP), have historically provided industry-specific guidance that requires investment entities to measure all of their investments, including those that they control, at fair value. The respondents argued that an investment entity holds investments for the sole purpose of capital appreciation, investment income (such as dividends or interest), or both. Users of the financial statements of these investment entities told the Board that the fair value of the investments and an understanding of how the investment entity measures the fair value of its investments is the most useful information.

BC218 Furthermore, respondents to ED 10 argued that consolidated financial statements of an investment entity may hinder users' ability to assess an investment entity's financial position and results, because it emphasises the financial position, operations and cash flows of the investee, rather than those of the investment entity. Often, an investment entity holds non-controlling interests in some entities that are reported at fair value, as well as controlling interests in other entities that are consolidated in accordance with current principles in IFRSs. Reporting investments on more than one basis hinders comparability within the financial statements, because all investments are held by an investment entity for a similar purpose—returns from capital appreciation, investment income, or both. In addition, some of the items consolidated may be measured at historical cost, which distorts the performance assessment of the investment entity and does not reflect the way in which the business of the entity is managed.

BC219 Respondents to ED 10 also argued that when an investment entity consolidates entities that it controls, it is not required to provide the disclosures related to fair value measurements that would be required if the subsidiaries were measured at fair value. For example, IFRS 7 relates only to recognised financial assets and liabilities. There is no requirement to provide disclosures related to fair value for investments in consolidated subsidiaries. Information about fair value and the methodology and inputs used for determining fair value is vital for users to make investment decisions about investment entities. Investors in an investment entity are interested in the fair value of their interest in that entity and often transact with it on a fair value basis (ie their investment in the investment entity is based on a share of the net assets of that entity). Reporting the fair value of substantially all of the net assets of an investment entity allows the investors in that entity to more easily identify the value of their share of those net assets.

BC220 In response to this feedback, the Board published an Exposure Draft *Investment Entities* (*Investment Entities* ED) in August 2011. The *Investment Entities* ED proposed that investment entities would be required to measure their investments in subsidiaries (except those subsidiaries that provide investment–related services) at fair value through profit or loss in accordance with IFRS 9 *Financial Instruments* (or IAS 39,[13] if IFRS 9 has not yet been adopted).[14] The majority of respondents to the *Investment Entities* ED broadly supported the proposed exception to consolidation for the reasons outlined in paragraphs BC217–BC219.

BC221 The Board conducted its deliberations leading to the publication of the *Investment Entities* ED and the final investment entities requirements jointly with the FASB. The similarities and differences between the investment entities guidance in IFRS and US GAAP are discussed further in paragraphs BC289–BC291.

---

13 IFRS 9 *Financial Instruments* replaced IAS 39. IFRS 9 applies to all items that were previously within the scope of IAS 39.

14 In December 2014, the Board issued *Investment Entities: Applying the Consolidation Exception* (Amendments to IFRS 10, IFRS 12 and IAS 28). These amendments clarified which subsidiaries of an investment entity are consolidated in accordance with paragraph 32 of IFRS 10, instead of being measured at fair value through profit or loss (see paragraphs BC240A–BC240I).

Scope of the project

BC222 The *Investment Entities* ED proposed a limited-scope exception to consolidation for investment entities. A number of respondents to the *Investment Entities* ED asked the Board to expand the scope of its proposals.

BC223 Some respondents asked the Board to expand the scope of the project to require an investment entity to measure all of its investments at fair value. However, the Board noted that, in most cases, existing IFRSs require or permit investments held by an investment entity to be measured at fair value. For example an entity:

(a) may elect the fair value option in IAS 40 *Investment Property*; and

(b) would be required to measure its financial assets at fair value through profit or loss in accordance with IFRS 9 (or IAS 39[15]) when those assets are managed on a fair value basis.

Consequently, the Board decided to limit the scope of the project to only providing an exception to consolidation for investment entities.

BC224 Other respondents requested an extension of the proposed exception to consolidation. In particular, respondents from the insurance industry requested an exception to consolidating their interests in insurance investment funds. They argued that presenting the fair value of their interests in insurance investment funds as a single line item, along with a single line item for the current value of their liability to policyholders who receive the returns from those investment funds, would provide more useful information to users than consolidation. The Board noted that providing an exception to consolidation for insurers' interests in insurance investment funds is outside the scope of the Investment Entities project, which was meant to provide an exception to consolidation for investment entities. In addition, any additional exceptions to consolidation would require the Board to do further work to define the entities that could apply those exceptions. The Board noted that this additional exception to consolidation was not contemplated in the scope of the project nor was it exposed for comment. Consequently, the Board decided not to extend the proposed exception to consolidation.

BC225 Other respondents asked the Board to provide guidance permitting an investor in an investment entity to use the reported net asset value (NAV) per share of that investment entity as a practical expedient for measuring the fair value of its investment in that investment entity. Similar guidance exists in US GAAP. The Board considered providing such a practical expedient in their deliberations on IFRS 13 but decided against it because, at the time, there was no specific accounting guidance for investment entities in IFRS and because there are different practices for calculating NAVs in jurisdictions around the world. The Board decided that it is outside the scope of the Investment Entities project to provide fair value measurement guidance for investments in investment entities. The Board developed the definition of an investment entity to identify which entities should qualify for an exception to

---

15 IFRS 9 *Financial Instruments* replaced IAS 39. IFRS 9 applies to all items that were previously within the scope of IAS 39.

consolidation. The definition was not designed to decide which entities should qualify for a fair value measurement practical expedient. Moreover, the Board still has concerns that NAV could be calculated differently in different jurisdictions. Consequently, the Board decided not to provide an NAV practical expedient for fair value measurement as part of the Investment Entities project.

BC226 The Board has decided to adopt an entity-based approach to the exception to consolidation. That is, the exception to consolidation is based on the type of entity that owns the subsidiary. The Board considered providing an asset-based approach to the exception to consolidation. Under an asset-based approach, an entity would consider its relationship with, and the characteristics of, each of its subsidiaries (that is, each individual asset) to decide whether fair value measurement is more appropriate than consolidation. However, the Board decided to retain the entity-based exception to consolidation that was proposed in the Investment Entities ED. The Board was concerned that an asset-based approach would significantly broaden the exception to consolidation by making the exception available to any entity holding relevant assets. This would represent a significant conceptual change to the consolidation model that the Board has developed in this IFRS. In addition, the Board believes that investment entities have a unique business model that makes reporting subsidiaries at fair value more appropriate than consolidation. An entity-based approach captures the unique business model of investment entities.

BC227 The Board also considered providing an option to allow investment entities to either consolidate subsidiaries or measure them at fair value through profit or loss. However, the Board believes that providing this option would be inconsistent with their view that fair value information is the most relevant information for all investment entities. Moreover, providing an option would reduce comparability between different investment entities. Consequently, the Board decided that an investment entity should be required to measure its subsidiaries at fair value through profit or loss.

Approach to assessing investment entity status

BC228 In the Investment Entities ED, the Board proposed six criteria that must be met in order for an entity to qualify as an investment entity. These criteria were based on guidance in US GAAP (Topic 946 Financial Services—Investment Companies in the FASB Accounting Standards Codification®).

BC229 Many respondents expressed concern that requiring an entity to meet all six criteria proposed in the Investment Entities ED would be too prescriptive. They thought that the proposed criteria inappropriately focused on the structure of an investment entity rather than on its business model and did not allow for the use of judgement in determining whether an entity is an investment entity. These respondents stated that a less prescriptive approach to assessing the criteria would result in more consistent reporting by entities with similar business models.

BC230   In addition, many respondents argued that the six proposed criteria in the *Investment Entities* ED did not provide a general description of an investment entity and an explanation of why fair value measurement is more relevant for the subsidiaries of an investment entity. Because the concept of an investment entity is new to IFRS, those respondents argued that the guidance should include a more general definition of an investment entity (rather than merely criteria to be an investment entity) and a justification for the exception to consolidation.

BC231   In response to the comments from respondents, the Board decided to provide a definition of an investment entity based on some of the criteria originally proposed in the *Investment Entities* ED. An entity that meets the definition of an investment entity would not consolidate its controlled subsidiaries (other than those subsidiaries that provide investment-related services or activities).[16]

BC232   The Board agreed with respondents who stated that some of the proposed criteria were too strict and would inappropriately exclude some structures from qualifying as investment entities. The Board believes that there are structures in practice in which an entity does not meet one or more of the criteria that were described in the *Investment Entities* ED, but should still qualify as an investment entity. For example, the *Investment Entities* ED required an investment entity to have more than one investor; the Board thinks that some pension funds, sovereign wealth funds, and other investment funds with a single investor should qualify as investment entities. Moreover, respondents commented that the application guidance in the *Investment Entities* ED provided too many exceptions to the strict criteria.

BC233   Consequently, the Board decided that an entity would not be required to satisfy the remaining criteria to meet the definition of an investment entity and qualify for the exception to consolidation. However, the Board noted that the remaining criteria represent typical characteristics of an investment entity and decided to include these typical characteristics in the investment entities guidance to help entities determine whether they qualify as an investment entity. If an entity does not display one or more of the typical characteristics, it indicates that additional judgement is required in determining whether the entity meets the definition of an investment entity. Consequently, the Board also decided that an investment entity that does not have one or more of the typical characteristics would be required to disclose how it still meets the definition of an investment entity.

BC234   The Board thinks that it is very unlikely that an entity that displays none of the typical characteristics of an investment entity would meet the definition of one. However, it may be possible in rare circumstances. For example, a pension fund that has a single investor and does not issue equity ownership interests could qualify as an investment entity even if it only holds a single investment temporarily (eg at commencement or wind-down of the entity).

---

16 In December 2014, the Board issued *Investment Entities: Applying the Consolidation Exception* (Amendments to IFRS 10, IFRS 12 and IAS 28). These amendments clarified which subsidiaries of an investment entity are consolidated in accordance with paragraph 32 of IFRS 10, instead of being measured at fair value through profit or loss (see paragraphs BC240A–BC240I).

BC235   The Board believes that defining an investment entity and describing its typical characteristics achieves a balance between clearly defining those entities that qualify for the exception to consolidation and avoiding the use of bright lines. In addition, this approach allows the definition to stand on its own, with application guidance providing clarification rather than exceptions.

Definition of an investment entity

BC236   The definition of an investment entity has three essential elements that differentiate investment entities from other types of entities.

Investment management services

BC237   The Board noted that one of the essential activities of an investment entity is that it obtains funds from investors in order to provide those investors with investment management services. The Board believes that this provision of investment management services differentiates investment entities from other entities. Consequently, the Board decided that the definition of an investment entity should state that an investment entity obtains funds from an investor or investors and provides the investor(s) with investment management services.

Business purpose

BC238   The Board believes that an entity's activities and business purpose are critical to determining whether it is an investment entity. An investment entity collects funds from investors and invests those funds to obtain returns solely from capital appreciation, investment income, or both. Consequently, the Board decided that the definition of an investment entity should state that an investment entity commits to its investor(s) that its business purpose is to provide investment management services and invest funds solely for returns from capital appreciation, investment income, or both.

BC239   The *Investment Entities* ED did not allow an entity to qualify as an investment entity if it provided substantive investment-related services to third parties. While some respondents agreed with this, others argued that an investment entity should be allowed to provide such services to third parties. They argued that the provision of these investment-related services to third parties is simply an extension of the investment entity's investing activities and should not prohibit an entity from qualifying as an investment entity. The Board agreed with these arguments, concluding that the provision of such services is within the business model of an investment entity. Although such an entity may earn fee income from the provision of investment-related services, its sole business purpose is still investing for capital appreciation, investment income, or both (whether that is for itself, for its investors or for external parties).

BC240   The Board noted that an investment entity may sometimes hold an interest in a subsidiary that provides investment-related services for its investment activities. The Board did not think that the existence of such a subsidiary should prohibit an entity from qualifying as an investment entity, even if those services were substantial or were provided to third parties in addition to the entity. The Board views such services as an extension of the operations of the investment entity and therefore concluded that subsidiaries that provide those services should be consolidated.

BC240A   In December 2014, the Board issued *Investment Entities: Applying the Consolidation Exception* (Amendments to IFRS 10, IFRS 12 and IAS 28). This amended paragraphs 32, BC85C and B85E of IFRS 10 to clarify which subsidiaries of an investment entity should be consolidated instead of being measured at fair value. The amendments were made in response to a request for the Board to clarify how to apply paragraph 32 when the subsidiary of an investment entity itself meets the definition of an investment entity and provides services that relate to the parent's investment activities.

BC240B   The Board decided to clarify that an investment entity shall measure at fair value through profit or loss all of its subsidiaries that are themselves investment entities. This is consistent with its decision not to distinguish between investment entity subsidiaries established for different purposes (see paragraph BC272). This was supported by the majority of respondents to both the *Investment Entities* ED and the Exposure Draft *Investment Entities: Applying the Consolidation Exception* (Proposed amendments to IFRS 10 and IAS 28), published in June 2014 (the 'Consolidation Exception ED').

BC240C   Some respondents to the *Consolidation Exception* ED suggested that requiring an investment entity to measure each investment entity subsidiary at fair value as a single item results in a loss of information about each subsidiary's underlying investments and the activities of that subsidiary. They suggested that an investment entity parent should be able to apply a 'dual-model' of consolidation, which would allow an investment entity parent to show its directly and indirectly held investments at fair value while consolidating other activities. This is similar to the asset-based approach previously rejected by the Board (see paragraph BC226).

BC240D   The Board acknowledged some of the potential benefits of an asset-based approach. In particular, this approach may better avoid some structuring issues, particularly in multi-layer groups in which different types of subsidiaries are held at different levels within the group. However, the Board decided that developing a broader principle-based approach, together with guidance to enable consistent application, would be too difficult to achieve within the limited scope of the consolidation exception clarification project. In addition, the Board decided that such an approach and related guidance could not be developed within the short time frame that was needed to provide the necessary clarification before the end of 2014. These decisions were, in part, based on the variety of suggestions provided by respondents to the *Consolidation Exception* ED about which activities should be consolidated and which should be measured at fair value.

BC240E   The Board noted that the requirement in paragraph 32 of IFRS 10 to consolidate particular subsidiaries of an investment entity was intended to be a limited exception, capturing only operating subsidiaries that support the investment entity parent's investing activities as an extension of the operations of the investment entity parent. It was not intended to capture subsidiaries that are themselves investment entities. The definition of an investment entity requires that the investment entity's business purpose and, therefore, its core activity is providing investment management services to its investors and investing the funds obtained from its investors solely for returns from capital appreciation, investment income, or both. When the Board decided that providing investment-related services to third parties would not prevent an entity from qualifying as an investment entity, it recognised that investment entities could benefit from synergies between the core investing activities and the provision of investment-related services to third parties.

BC240F   The Board noted that, therefore, when an entity assesses whether it qualifies as an investment entity, it considers whether providing services to third parties is ancillary to its core investing activities. However, the definition of an investment entity requires that the purpose of the entity is to invest solely for capital appreciation, investment income (such as dividends, interest and rental income) or both (see paragraph B85B of IFRS 10). Consequently, an entity whose main purpose is to provide investment-related services in exchange for consideration from third parties has a business purpose that is different from the business purpose of an investment entity. This is because the entity's main activity is earning fee income in exchange for its services. In contrast, for an entity that qualifies as an investment entity, such fee income, which could be substantial in amount, will be derived from its core investment activities, which are designed for earning capital appreciation, investment income or both.

BC240G   The Board decided that requiring an investment entity to measure all of its subsidiaries that are themselves investment entities at fair value through profit or loss is consistent with the entity-based approach and decided to confirm its proposal in the *Consolidation Exception* ED. Consequently, when an investment entity parent assesses whether a subsidiary should be measured at fair value in accordance with paragraph 31 of IFRS 10 or, instead, should be consolidated in accordance with paragraph 32 of IFRS 10, the parent assesses whether the subsidiary meets the definition of an investment entity. If so, the investment entity parent measures its investment entity subsidiary at fair value through profit or loss in accordance with paragraph 31.

BC240H   If the subsidiary is not an investment entity, the investment entity parent assesses whether the main activities undertaken by the subsidiary support the core investment activities of the parent. If so, the subsidiary's activities are considered to be an extension of the parent's core investing activities and the subsidiary would be consolidated in accordance with paragraph 32 of IFRS 10. The Board noted that a subsidiary of an investment entity that provides support services to its parent and other members of the group, such as administration, treasury, payroll and accounting services, is considered to be providing those services as an extension of the operations of the parent. Such a non-investment entity subsidiary would be consolidated in accordance with paragraph 32 of IFRS 10.

BC240I   The Board concluded that these outcomes are consistent with its basic decision that measuring all investments of investment entities at fair value through profit or loss provides the most relevant information, except for operating subsidiaries that act as an extension of the investment entity parent.

BC241   The Board considered prohibiting investment entities from engaging in some activities, such as providing financial support to its investees or actively managing its investees. However, the Board understands that an investment entity may engage in these activities in order to maximise the overall value of the investee (ie to maximise capital appreciation), rather than to obtain other benefits. Consequently, the Board believes that these activities can be consistent with the overall activities of an investment entity and should not be prohibited as long as they do not represent a separate substantial business activity or source of income other than capital appreciation.

BC242   The Board was concerned that an entity that meets the definition of an investment entity could be inserted into a larger corporate structure to achieve a particular accounting outcome. For example, a parent entity could use an 'internal' investment entity subsidiary to invest in subsidiaries that may be making losses (eg research and development activities on behalf of the overall group) and would record its investments at fair value, rather than reflecting the underlying activities of the investee. To address these concerns and to emphasise the business purpose of an investment entity, the Board decided to include a requirement that an investment entity, or other members of the group containing the entity, should not obtain benefits from its investees that would be unavailable to other parties that are not related to the investee. In the Board's view, this is one of the factors that differentiate an investment entity from a non-investment entity holding company. If an entity or another member of the group containing the entity obtains benefits from its investees that are unavailable to other investors, then the investment will benefit that entity or the group in some operating or strategic capacity and the entity will therefore not qualify as an investment entity.

BC243   However, the Board also clarified that an investment entity may have more than one investment in the same industry, market or geographical area in order to benefit from synergies that increase the capital appreciation of those investments. It noted that such a fact pattern may be common in the private equity industry. Some Board members expressed concern that allowing transactions or synergies between investments may artificially increase the fair value of each investment and, consequently, inappropriately increase the assets reported by the investment entity. However, the Board decided that trading transactions or synergies that arise between the investments of an investment entity should not be prohibited because their existence does not necessarily mean that the investment entity is receiving any returns beyond solely capital appreciation, investment income, or both.

Exit strategy

BC244 The Board believes that a parent with operating subsidiaries often plans to own and operate its subsidiaries indefinitely to realise returns from those operations. However, the Board does not think that an entity that holds its investments indefinitely, especially its subsidiaries, should qualify as an investment entity. Accordingly, the Board considered requiring an exit strategy for substantially all investments held by an investment entity, including debt investments.

BC245 However, respondents to the *Investment Entities* ED noted that some investment funds that would otherwise qualify as investment entities may hold a significant amount of debt investments to maturity and therefore would not have an exit strategy for those debt investments. For example, the Board understands that, in some cases, private equity funds may make both debt and equity investments in their investees. The debt investments may have shorter maturities than the anticipated term of the fund's equity investment and may be held to maturity. Moreover, an investment entity may hold debt instruments to maturity to manage liquidity risk or to mitigate the risk from holding other types of more volatile investments. Although the entity does not have an exit strategy for these debt investments, it does not plan to hold them indefinitely—even if the entity does not plan to sell these investments before maturity, the vast majority of debt investments have a limited life.

BC246 The Board decided that such an entity should not be prohibited from qualifying as an investment entity, provided that substantially all of its investments (including debt investments) are measured at fair value. The Board noted that debt investments may be measured at fair value in accordance with IFRS 9 or IAS 39[17] even in the absence of an exit strategy.

BC247 However, the Board decided that an investment entity must have an exit strategy for substantially all of its investments that can be held indefinitely (typically equity investments and non-financial assets). The Board does not think it is appropriate for an entity to qualify for an exception to consolidation if that entity is holding equity investments indefinitely and is not planning to realise capital appreciation from those investments. Although the exit strategy may vary depending on circumstances, potential exit strategies that include a substantive time frame for exiting from the investment should still be identified and documented for equity and non-financial investments in order to meet the definition of an investment entity.

BC248 The Board noted that an entity may fail to meet this component of the definition of an investment entity if it is formed in connection with an investment entity investee for legal, regulatory, tax or similar business reasons (eg a 'blocker' entity or a 'master-feeder' structure), and that that investee holds investments on behalf of the entity. The Board decided that the entity should not be prohibited from qualifying as an investment entity merely because it does not have an exit strategy for the investee, if that

---

17 IFRS 9 *Financial Instruments* replaced IAS 39. IFRS 9 applies to all items that were previously within the scope of IAS 39.

investee qualifies as an investment entity and has appropriate exit strategies for its own investments.

Fair value measurement

BC249   In the development of IFRS 10 and the *Investment Entities* ED, the Board heard that fair value information is the primary driver of the decision-making processes both of the management of, and the investors in, investment entities. Many respondents stated that both management and investors evaluate the performance of an investment entity by reference to the fair value of its investments. The Board heard that some investors in investment entities disregard the consolidated financial statements of investment entities and instead rely on non-GAAP fair value reports.

BC250   The basis for the exception to consolidation that is provided to investment entities is that fair value information is the most relevant for an investment entity's investments, including its investments in subsidiaries. The Board therefore decided that an essential feature of the definition of an investment entity is that the entity would use existing IFRS requirements or accounting policy options to measure substantially all of its investments at fair value. The Board does not think that an entity that fails to elect the fair value measurement options available in IAS 28 *Investments in Associates and Joint Ventures* or IAS 40, or that accounts for more than an insignificant amount of its financial assets at amortised cost under IFRS 9 or IAS 39,[18] should qualify as an investment entity.

BC251   The Board noted that some investments may be measured at fair value in the statement of financial position, with fair value changes recognised in other comprehensive income rather than through profit or loss, and agreed that this would satisfy the fair value measurement element of the definition of an investment entity.

BC252   The Board considers that a significant distinguishing characteristic of an investment entity is that investors in an investment entity are primarily interested in fair value and make their investing decisions based on the fair value of the investment entity's underlying investments. The Board notes that this is partly because, in many cases, investors in an investment entity transact with it on a fair value basis (for example, on the basis of a net asset value per share, which is calculated using the fair value of the entity's underlying investments). Similarly, the Board believes that fair value should also be used by an investment entity's key management personnel to assess the entity's performance and to make investing decisions. Consequently, the Board decided that, in order to meet the definition of an investment entity, an entity should demonstrate that fair value is the primary measurement attribute used to evaluate the performance of its investments, both internally and externally.

---

18   IFRS 9 *Financial Instruments* replaced IAS 39. IFRS 9 applies to all items that were previously within the scope of IAS 39.

Regulatory requirements

BC253 The Board considered whether to include a reference to regulatory requirements in the definition of an investment entity. The Board noted that the FASB proposed, in their own Exposure Draft, that any entity that was regulated as an investment company under the US Securities and Exchange Commission's Investment Company Act of 1940 would automatically be considered to be an investment company for US GAAP financial reporting purposes. Some respondents to the Board's *Investment Entities* ED also asked the Board to include a reference to regulatory requirements in the definition of an investment entity, which would allow any entity regulated as an investment entity to fall within the scope of the investment entity requirements.

BC254 However, the Board was concerned that:

(a) the regulatory requirements in different jurisdictions may result in similar entities qualifying as an investment entity in one jurisdiction but not in another;

(b) regulatory requirements may change over time, resulting in an ever-changing population of entities that would be eligible for an exception to consolidation; and

(c) it would have no control over which entities would qualify for the exception to consolidation.

Consequently, the Board decided not to reference regulatory requirements in the definition of an investment entity.

Typical characteristics of investment entities

BC255 The Board identified several 'typical characteristics' of an investment entity. The Board decided that these typical characteristics could be used to help an entity decide if it meets the definition of an investment entity. The absence of any of these typical characteristics may indicate that an entity does not meet the definition of an investment entity. However, an entity that does not display all of these typical characteristics could, nevertheless, meet the definition of an investment entity.

BC256 The Board identified the following typical characteristics of an investment entity:

(a) more than one investment (paragraphs BC257–BC258);

(b) more than one investor (paragraphs BC259–BC260);

(c) unrelated investors (paragraphs BC261–BC262); and

(d) ownership interests (paragraphs BC263–BC267).

More than one investment

BC257 The *Investment Entities* ED proposed that an investment entity should hold more than one investment. However, respondents provided examples of entities that they believed should qualify as investment entities, but that only hold a single investment. These included single investment funds set up because the required minimum investment is too high for individual investors, or investment funds that hold a single investment temporarily.

BC258   The Board agreed with these arguments and therefore decided that an investment entity would not be required to hold more than one investment. However, the Board understands that investment entities typically invest in more than one investment as a means of diversifying their portfolio and maximising their returns. Consequently, investing in more than one investment is described as a typical characteristic of an investment entity in this IFRS.

More than one investor

BC259   The presence of more than one investor was originally proposed as a requirement in the *Investment Entities* ED. However, respondents provided many examples of investment funds with a single investor. These included funds that temporarily have a single investor, government-owned investment funds, funds wholly-owned by pension plans and endowments, and funds set up by an investment manager for an unrelated single investor with a unique investment strategy.

BC260   The Board does not think that there is a conceptual reason why an investment fund with a single investor should be disqualified from being an investment entity. However, the Board thinks that having more than one investor would make it less likely that the entity, or other members of the group that contains the entity, would obtain benefits other than capital appreciation or investment income from its investment. Consequently, the Board decided to include the presence of more than one investor as a typical characteristic of an investment entity rather than as part of the definition of an investment entity.

Unrelated investors

BC261   The *Investment Entities* ED proposed that an investment entity be required to have investors that are unrelated to the entity or its parent (if any), partly to prevent entities from structuring around the requirement to have more than one investor. However, respondents provided examples of entities with related investors that they believed should qualify as investment entities. For example, a separate 'parallel' entity may be formed to allow the employees of an investment entity to invest in a fund that mirrors the investments in the main fund. The Board agreed with the respondents' arguments and decided that an investment entity would not be required to have investors that are unrelated to the investment entity or to other members of the group that contains the investment entity.

BC262   However, the Board understands that investment entities typically have unrelated investors. Again, having unrelated investors is one way to help ensure that the entity, or another member of the group that contains the entity, does not receive returns from investments that are other than capital appreciation or investment income. Having investors that are unrelated to the entity or its parent (if any), is therefore described as a typical characteristic of an investment entity in this IFRS.

Ownership interests

BC263 An investment entity would typically have ownership interests in the form of equity or similar (eg partnership) interests that entitle investors to a proportionate share of the net assets of the investment entity. This characteristic explains in part why fair value is more relevant to investment entity investors: each unit of ownership in the investment entity entitles an investor to a proportionate share of the net assets of that investment entity. The value of each ownership interest is linked directly to the fair value of the investment entity's investments.

BC264 However, the Board believes that this form of ownership interests in an entity should not be the deciding factor as to whether it is an investment entity. Respondents provided examples of entities that do not have units of ownership in the form of equity or similar interests but provide investors with a proportionate share of their net assets. For example, a pension fund or sovereign wealth fund with a single direct investor may have beneficiaries that are entitled to the net assets of the investment fund, but do not have ownership units. In addition, respondents noted that funds with different share classes or funds in which investors have discretion to invest in individual assets would be disqualified from investment entity status because they did not provide each investor with a proportionate share of net assets.

BC265 The Board does not believe that an entity that provides its investors only a return of their investment plus interest should qualify as an investment entity. Fair value information is more relevant to investors that are entitled to a specifically identifiable portion of the investment entity's net assets and are, therefore, exposed to the upside and downside of the investment entity's performance.

BC266 However, the Board agreed that the requirement proposed in the *Investment Entities* ED (that an investment entity's ownership interests entitle investors to a proportionate share of its net assets) would have inappropriately excluded certain structures from investment entity status. As an alternative, the Board considered requiring that an investment entity's ownership interests be in the form of equity or similar interests. However, the Board was concerned that this would put too much emphasis on the debt/equity classification in IAS 32 *Financial Instruments: Presentation* and would inappropriately exclude some structures whose ownership interests were classified as debt. Moreover, the Board was also concerned that including the 'ownership interest' concept as part of the definition of an investment entity would put too much emphasis on the form of the entity, rather than emphasising its business model.

BC267 Consequently, the Board decided not to include ownership interests as part of the definition of an investment entity but that it should instead be regarded as a typical characteristic of an investment entity.

Reassessment and change of status

BC268 The Board included guidance in the *Investment Entities* ED on reassessing investment entity status. A few respondents asked the Board to clarify this guidance.

BC269   In the *Investment Entities* ED, the Board proposed that an entity would reassess its investment entity status whenever facts or circumstances changed. The Board decided to retain this requirement unchanged because it is consistent with the requirements for reassessment elsewhere in IFRS, including the general reassessment requirements in IFRS 10. The Board noted that they do not believe that the reassessment of facts and circumstances in other situations is considered unduly onerous for preparers or their auditors.

BC270   The Board decided that, when an entity loses investment entity status, it should account for that change as a 'deemed acquisition'. That is, the investment entity would use the fair value of the investment at the date of the change of status as the 'deemed' consideration transferred to obtain control of the investee. This recognises the change in status in the same way as a business combination achieved in stages, as described in IFRS 3. This would result in the recognition of goodwill or a gain on a bargain purchase.

BC271   The Board also decided that, when an entity becomes an investment entity, the entity should account for the change in status as a 'deemed disposal' or 'loss of control' of its subsidiaries. The fair value of the investment at the date of the change of status should be used as the consideration received when applying the guidance in IFRS 10. The Board considered how to account for the gain or loss on the 'deemed disposal' and decided to recognise it as a gain or loss in profit or loss. This treats the change in the business purpose of the investor as a significant economic event and is consistent with the rationale for gains and losses being recognised in profit or loss in IFRS 10 when control is lost.

Parent of an investment entity

Investment entity parent of an investment entity subsidiary

BC272   The *Investment Entities* ED proposed that an investment entity would measure all of its subsidiaries at fair value (except for those subsidiaries providing investment-related services), even those investees who were themselves investment entities. Some respondents questioned this proposal and suggested that at least some investment entity subsidiaries should be consolidated (for example, wholly-owned investment entity subsidiaries that are created for legal, tax or regulatory purposes). However, the Board thinks that fair value measurement of all an investment entity's subsidiaries (except for those subsidiaries providing investment-related services or activities) would provide the most useful information and therefore decided to retain this proposal. The Board considered requiring an investment entity to consolidate only those investment entity subsidiaries that are formed for legal, tax or regulatory purposes, but decided against this because there is no conceptual basis for distinguishing between different investment entity subsidiaries. Moreover, the Board thinks that it would be very difficult to distinguish between an investment entity subsidiary formed for a specific legal, tax or regulatory purpose and those that are set up only for other business reasons.

BC273　The Board considered whether it should require certain investment entity parents to attach the financial statements of their investment entity subsidiaries to the parent's financial statements. Some respondents argued that it would be essential for users of the financial statements of an investment entity parent to have information about the underlying investments of its investment entity subsidiary, particularly when the investment entity parent has only one investment entity subsidiary (eg 'master-feeder funds').

BC274　However, the Board decided against requiring financial statements of an investment entity subsidiary to be attached to the financial statements of an investment entity parent. The Board believed that it would be difficult to define which types of structures should be covered by such a requirement. Moreover, the Board thought that such a requirement would be inconsistent with the proposal that fair value information is always the most relevant information for investment entities.

Non-investment entity parent of an investment entity subsidiary

BC275　The Board also considered whether to retain investment entity accounting in the financial statements of a non-investment entity parent. In the *Investment Entities* ED, the Board proposed that a non-investment entity parent of an investment entity subsidiary would be required to consolidate all of its subsidiaries; that is, the exception to consolidation available to an investment entity would not be available to its non-investment entity parent.

BC276　The Board noted that the majority of respondents disagreed with the proposal, arguing that if fair value information is more relevant than consolidation at an investment entity subsidiary level, it is also more relevant information at the non-investment entity parent level.

BC277　The Board acknowledged the comments received but decided to retain the proposal to require all non-investment entity parents to consolidate all of their subsidiaries.

BC278　The Board has decided to provide an exception to consolidation because of the unique business model of investment entities. Non-investment entities do not have this unique business model; they have other substantial activities besides investing, or do not manage substantially all of their assets on a fair value basis. Consequently, the argument for a fair value measurement requirement is weakened at a non-investment entity level.

BC279　The Board also noted that the decision to define an investment entity and describe its typical characteristics rather than requiring an investment entity to meet a number of criteria has increased the population of entities that could qualify as investment entities, and has also increased the amount of judgement needed to determine whether an entity is an investment entity. For example, an entity with a single investor, or an entity that provides day-to-day management services or strategic advice to its subsidiary, can qualify as an investment entity under this IFRS, when such entities would have been excluded under the *Investment Entities* ED.

BC280   The Board was concerned that some of these changes would increase the likelihood that a non-investment entity parent could achieve different accounting outcomes by holding subsidiaries directly or indirectly through an investment entity. The Board noted that, for example, a non-investment entity parent may elect to hold subsidiaries through an investment entity subsidiary in order to hide leverage or loss-making activities.

BC281   In addition, the Board considered the practical difficulties in retaining the exception to consolidation when a non-investment entity parent and an investment entity subsidiary invest in the same investment or when an investment entity subsidiary holds a subsidiary that invests in the equity of a non-investment entity parent.

BC282   The Board noted that the retention of the specialised accounting used by an investment company subsidiary at a non-investment company level is a long-standing requirement in US GAAP. However, US GAAP has industry-specific guidance for a number of industries, and the application of that industry-specific guidance by a subsidiary is retained by a parent entity, regardless of whether the parent entity is part of that industry. IFRSs generally do not contain such industry-specific guidance.

BC283   Some respondents to the *Investment Entities* ED noted that not retaining the fair value accounting of an investment entity subsidiary in its non-investment entity parent's financial statements seems inconsistent with IAS 28 *Investments in Associates and Joint Ventures*. IAS 28 allows a parent that indirectly holds an investment in an associate through a venture capital organisation, mutual fund, unit trust or similar entity to measure that portion of the investment at fair value through profit or loss in accordance with IFRS 9 or IAS 39.[19] The Board acknowledged the inconsistency but thought it was important to keep the retention of fair value accounting that is currently allowed for venture capital organisations, mutual funds, unit trusts and similar entities. The Board also noted that the difference between using the equity method and fair value measurement for investments in associates and joint ventures is smaller than that between consolidation and fair value measurement for investments in subsidiaries.

Transition

BC284   The Board proposed in the *Investment Entities* ED that the exception to consolidation should be applied prospectively. Some respondents disagreed with the proposal, arguing that retrospective application would result in more useful information. In addition, they noted that retrospective application should not be onerous because investment entities would be expected to have information about the fair value of their investments. Those respondents also argued that retrospective application would be consistent with the other transition requirements in IFRS 10.

---

19   IFRS 9 *Financial Instruments* replaced IAS 39. IFRS 9 applies to all items that were previously within the scope of IAS 39.

BC285   The Board agreed with these arguments and decided to require retrospective application of the exception to consolidation, subject to specific transition reliefs, such as:

    (a)   a relief for when it is impracticable to identify the fair value of investments;

    (b)   a relief for when an investment entity disposes of investments prior to the date of initial application; and

    (c)   a relief from providing comparative information for more than one period preceding the date of initial application.

BC286   The Board also noted that entities that adopt these amendments early may not have adopted IFRS 13, which has an effective date of 1 January 2013. Consequently, the Board decided that when an investment entity has not yet adopted IFRS 13, it may use the fair value amounts previously reported to investors or to management, as long as those amounts represent the amount for which the investment could have been exchanged between knowledgeable, willing parties in an arm's length transaction at the date of the valuation. The Board noted that if previously used fair value measurements are not available, it may be impracticable to measure fair value without using hindsight. In such cases, transition relief is available.

BC287   The Board also decided to require first-time adopters to apply the requirements retrospectively, subject to specific transition reliefs.[20]

BC287A   The Board decided that no specific transition guidance was needed and, therefore, an entity should apply *Investment Entities: Applying the Consolidation Exception* (Amendments to IFRS 10, IFRS 12 and IAS 28) retrospectively in accordance with IAS 8. However, the Board decided that an entity need only present the quantitative information required by paragraph 28(f) of IAS 8 for the annual period immediately preceding the date of initial application of this IFRS (the 'immediately preceding period') when the amendments are first applied.

Effective date and early application

BC288   The Board decided on a 1 January 2014 effective date for the requirements for investment entities. The Board noted that because these requirements provide an exception to consolidation, they should have the same effective date as the revised consolidation requirements in IFRS 10 (annual periods beginning on or after 1 January 2013). However, given that the investment entities requirements were published in October 2012, the Board did not believe that a 1 January 2013 effective date would give adequate time for implementation between the publication and effective dates. However, the Board decided to permit early application of the investment entity requirements. The Board noted that it expects many entities to apply the requirements early. Some

---

20   *Annual Improvements to IFRS Standards 2014–2016 Cycle*, issued in December 2016, amended IFRS 1 *First-time Adoption of International Financial Reporting Standards* by deleting the short-term exemption for first-time adopters (see paragraph BC99 of IFRS 1), because it was no longer applicable.

investments in subsidiaries may not have been consolidated in accordance with IAS 27 and SIC-12 but, without the exception to consolidation, would need to be consolidated in accordance with IFRS 10. The Board noted that it would be potentially confusing to users of financial statements and time-consuming for the investment entity to consolidate a subsidiary in one accounting period and then carry the same investee at fair value in the following period. In addition, investment entities should already have the fair value information needed for implementation. Finally, the exception to consolidation has been a long-standing request from the investment entity industry. Consequently, the Board believes that many investment entities will want to adopt the requirements early.

Joint deliberations with the FASB

BC289   The Board deliberated this project jointly with the FASB. US GAAP has had comprehensive accounting guidance for investment companies for many years (contained in Topic 946 *Investment Companies*). By deliberating this project jointly, the boards hoped to achieve as similar guidance as possible. To that end, they came up with similar definitions of investment entities and guidance on how to assess investment entity status.

BC290   However, the scope of the project was different for the IASB and the FASB. The IASB's Investment Entities project started during the deliberations on the Consolidations project and was only intended to provide an exception to consolidation for investment entities. The FASB was seeking to improve and converge the definition of an investment company with that of the IASB because it already has comprehensive accounting and reporting guidance for investment companies.

BC291   While the boards reached many common decisions, as a result of this scope difference, and other jurisdictional differences, the IASB and the FASB came to different decisions in a number of areas. These include:

(a)   whether there should be a requirement that an investment entity measure and evaluate substantially all of its investments on a fair value basis rather than identifying such an activity as a typical characteristic of an investment entity;

(b)   whether there should be a reference to existing regulatory requirements in the definition of an investment entity;

(c)   whether an investment entity is permitted to provide investment-related services to third parties other than its own investors;

(d)   the accounting by an investment entity parent for an investment entity subsidiary; and

(e)   the accounting by a non-investment entity parent for an investment entity subsidiary.

Effects analysis for investment entities

BC292   The Board is committed to assessing and sharing knowledge about the likely costs of implementing proposed new requirements and the likely ongoing costs and benefits of each new IFRS—the costs and benefits are collectively referred to as 'effects'. The Board gains insight on the likely effects of the proposals for new or revised IFRSs through its formal exposure of proposals, analysis and consultations with relevant parties.

BC293   In evaluating the likely effects of introducing an exception to consolidation for investment entities to IFRS 10, the Board has considered the following factors:

(a)   how the changes to IFRS 10 affect the financial statements of an investment entity;

(b)   how those changes improve the comparability of financial information between different reporting periods for an investment entity and between different investment entities in a particular reporting period;

(c)   how the changes will improve the quality of the financial information available to investors and its usefulness in assessing the future cash flows of an investment entity;

(d)   how users will benefit from better economic decision-making as a result of improved financial reporting;

(e)   the likely effect on compliance costs for preparers, both on initial application and on an ongoing basis; and

(f)   whether the likely costs of analysis for users are affected.

Financial statements of investment entities

BC294   Before the exception to consolidation for investment entities was issued, IFRS 10 (and its predecessor, IAS 27) required reporting entities to consolidate all controlled entities, regardless of the nature of the reporting entity. Consequently, the assets, liabilities and non-controlling interests of each subsidiary were aggregated with those of the parent to represent the group of entities as a single reporting entity.

BC295   Respondents to ED 10 argued that an investment entity often holds non-controlling investments in some entities that are reported at fair value, as well as subsidiaries that are consolidated in accordance with current principles in IFRS. Reporting investments on more than one basis hinders comparability within the financial statements, because all investments are held by an investment entity for a similar purpose—capital appreciation, investment income, or both. In addition, some of the items consolidated would be measured at historical cost, which distorts the performance assessment of the investment entity and does not reflect the way in which the business of the entity is managed.

BC296   The exception to consolidation will change the way in which an investment entity parent reports its interest in an entity that it controls. Rather than consolidating its subsidiaries, an investment entity is now required to recognise a subsidiary as a single-line investment measured at fair value through profit or loss in accordance with IFRS 9 (or IAS 39,[21] if IFRS 9 has not yet been adopted).

BC297   Accordingly, the exception to consolidation will affect investment entities that hold, as investments, controlling interests in other entities. However, although the changes are important to those entities affected, the changes are only expected to affect a narrow range of entities. Only those entities that meet the definition of an investment entity and hold controlling interests in other entities will be affected by these changes.

BC298   The entities most likely to be affected are:

(a)   private equity or venture capital funds; these have business models in which it is more likely that it would be beneficial to take a larger interest in a company, or control investees through debt and equity investment.

(b)   master-feeder or fund-of-funds structures where an investment entity parent has controlling interests in investment entity subsidiaries.

BC299   Some pension funds and sovereign wealth funds may also be affected; these may meet the definition of an investment entity and may also hold controlling investments in other entities.

BC300   Other types of entities may meet the definition of an investment entity, such as mutual funds and other regulated investment funds, but are less likely to hold controlling investments in other entities. Instead, they tend to hold lower levels of investments in a wider range of entities. Consequently, the exception to consolidation is less likely to affect these entities.

Comparability

BC301   An investment entity's control of an investee may change from one reporting period to the next. Without the exception to consolidation, an investment entity could be required to consolidate an investment in one period and present it as an investment measured at fair value through profit or loss in the following period (or vice versa). This would reduce comparability between reporting periods. With the introduction of the exception to consolidation, an investment entity can report all investments at fair value, regardless of whether those investments are controlled. This will improve the comparability between reporting periods.

BC302   Many respondents to ED 10 and the *Investment Entities* ED pointed out that some national accounting requirements, including US GAAP, have historically had industry-specific guidance that requires investment entities to measure investments that they control at fair value. Some of these respondents argued

---

21 IFRS 9 *Financial Instruments* replaced IAS 39. IFRS 9 applies to all items that were previously within the scope of IAS 39.

          © IFRS Foundation

that investment entities were actively choosing to adopt those national accounting requirements rather than IFRS so that they could measure all of their investments at fair value. Respondents also pointed out that some investment entities that followed IFRS provided non-GAAP information about the fair value of all of their investments. Consequently, comparability of the financial statements of different investment entities was hindered. The Board expects the introduction of the exception to consolidation to encourage adoption of IFRS among investment entities and to eliminate the need to provide non-GAAP information about fair value. This should improve the comparability of financial statements of different investment entities.

Usefulness of financial statements in assessing the future cash flows of an entity

BC303   Consolidated financial statements of an investment entity emphasise the financial position, operations and cash flows of the investee, rather than merely those of the investment entity. The exception to consolidation will reduce the information about the cash flows of those subsidiaries. However, the main business purpose of an investment entity is to invest funds solely for capital appreciation, investment income, or both. The relevant cash flows relating to these activities are those of the investment entity itself. Consolidating the cash flows of a subsidiary may hinder users' ability to predict the cash flows that may be passed on to investors. The Board therefore believes that these amendments will improve the quality of the financial information reported by an investment entity and will make that information more useful in assessing the future cash flows of the investment entity.

Better economic decision-making

BC304   One of the essential features of an investment entity is that, in order to make better investment decisions, it measures and evaluates substantially all of its investments on a fair value basis. Presenting consolidated financial statements does not reflect this method of management. Requiring an investment entity to account for its investments in subsidiaries at fair value provides a better insight into the information that management uses to evaluate the performance of its investments.

BC305   In addition, investors in an investment entity are typically entitled to a proportionate share of the net assets of the entity when they withdraw their investment. Reporting the fair value of substantially all of the net assets of the investment entity allows the investors to more easily identify the value of their share of those net assets. As a result, the Board expect significant benefits for most users of investment entity financial statements arising from the provision of more fair value information.

BC306   However, some respondents in some jurisdictions objected to the exception to consolidation because it undermines the control-based approach to consolidation used in IFRS 10. These respondents noted that an exception to consolidation would deprive financial statement users of information about the activities of subsidiaries and the economic effects of the relationships between an investment entity and its subsidiaries. In addition, some respondents expressed concern that an exception to consolidation may encourage structuring to avoid consolidation, which would result in a loss of such information to users.

BC307   The Board acknowledges these arguments, but notes that the exception to consolidation has been introduced in response to comments from users that the most useful information for an investment entity is the fair value of its investments. Users also commented that consolidated financial statements of an investment entity may hinder users' ability to assess an investment entity's financial position and results, because it emphasises the financial position, operations and cash flows of the investee, rather than those of the investment entity.

BC308   In developing these amendments, the Board deliberately restricted the population of entities that would qualify for the exception to consolidation. In particular, the Board prohibited the use of the exception to consolidation by non-investment entity parents of investment entities, in order to address respondents' concerns about structuring and to restrict the use of the exception to situations where fair value information would be more relevant than information arising from the consolidation of subsidiaries.

Effect on compliance costs for preparers

BC309   The Board expects that the introduction of the exception to consolidation will result in significant compliance cost savings for preparers, particularly on an ongoing basis. This expectation is based on the feedback the Board has received from respondents to the *Investment Entities* ED and conversations with entities that are expected to qualify as investment entities.

BC310   On initial application, there may be some costs involved in identifying and documenting some of the additional disclosures introduced. In particular, investment entities will need to collect information to comply with the general disclosure requirements of IFRS 7, IFRS 13 and the amended requirements of IFRS 12. However, the Board has been told that the majority of investment entities will already have much of the fair value information that they need in order to comply with the new requirements, because they already measure substantially all of their investments on a fair value basis and many elect to provide this information to their investors already. The Board expects this to mitigate the initial and ongoing costs of applying the exception to consolidation.

BC311   In arriving at its decisions, the Board has considered those costs and believes that the benefits of the information produced as a result of its decisions would outweigh the costs of providing that information. In addition, the initial application costs will be more than offset by the cost savings resulting from the removal of the need to gather information from subsidiaries in order to consolidate details of their financial performance, position and cash flows on a line-by-line basis.

BC312　　As described in paragraphs BC275–BC283, the Board decided not to expand the scope of the project to allow a non-investment entity parent to retain the fair value accounting of its investment entity subsidiary. Consequently, the compliance cost savings described above will not be available to non-investment entity parents. Because these entities are not within the scope of these amendments, they may incur ongoing costs because they will have two different bases of accounting within the group. At the investment entity subsidiary level, subsidiaries held by the investment entity will be measured at fair value, but at the non-investment entity parent level, those subsidiaries will be consolidated.

How the costs of analysis for users are affected

BC313　　The likely effect of these amendments on the costs of analysis for users of financial statements is expected to be outweighed by the benefits of improved reporting, given that these amendments have been developed on request from users. However, the extent of the benefit will depend on existing practice.

BC314　　In general, these amendments will provide improved information about the fair values of investments and the way in which the fair value is measured. Such information could reduce the cost of analysis by providing information more directly to users of financial statements. However, in many cases, investment entities already provide investors with fair value information, although this is often done in an alternative report rather than in the financial statements. This serves to emphasise that the main benefit of the changes is a reduction in costs to preparers because it eliminates what they see as a cumbersome reporting requirement that has little value.

BC315　　For analysts or potential investors that use financial statements to analyse investment entities from different countries, the existing problems of diversity in accounting models creates costs that would be reduced by standardised accounting requirements.

BC316　　In addition, the Board expects that the requirement to apply the exception to consolidation retrospectively will mitigate some of the transition costs for users. However, some of the transition reliefs will mean that users may receive less information on transition. In particular, the fact that investment entities will be required to provide only one period of comparative information may affect users who might otherwise receive more than one period of comparative information. However, again, the Board expects the benefits to outweigh the costs incurred as a result of the implementation of these amendments.

Summary

BC317　　In summary, the cost savings resulting from implementing these amendments are expected to be significant for investment entities and the users of their financial statements. Additionally, the implementation of the investment entities amendments should result in the benefits of increased comparability between entities and across jurisdictions, and more relevant reporting of information used by investors in making economic decisions.

Appendix
Previous Board approvals and dissenting opinions

Approval by the Board of IAS 27 issued in December 2003

International Accounting Standard 27 *Consolidated and Separate Financial Statements* (as revised in 2003) was approved for issue by thirteen of the fourteen members of the International Accounting Standards Board. Mr Yamada dissented. His dissenting opinion is set out after the previous Board approvals.

Sir David Tweedie	Chairman
Thomas E Jones	Vice-Chairman
Mary E Barth	
Hans-Georg Bruns	
Anthony T Cope	
Robert P Garnett	
Gilbert Gélard	
James J Leisenring	
Warren J McGregor	
Patricia L O'Malley	
Harry K Schmid	
John T Smith	
Geoffrey Whittington	
Tatsumi Yamada	

Approval by the Board of amendments to IAS 27 issued in January 2008

The amendments to International Accounting Standard 27 *Consolidated and Separate Financial Statements* in 2008 were approved for issue by nine of the fourteen members of the International Accounting Standards Board. Messrs Danjou, Engström, Garnett, Gélard and Yamada dissented. Their dissenting opinions are set out after the previous Board approvals.

Sir David Tweedie	Chairman
Thomas E Jones	Vice-Chairman
Mary E Barth	
Hans-Georg Bruns	
Anthony T Cope	
Philippe Danjou	
Jan Engström	
Robert P Garnett	
Gilbert Gélard	
James J Leisenring	
Warren J McGregor	
Patricia L O'Malley	
John T Smith	
Tatsumi Yamada	

Dissenting opinions

Dissent of Tatsumi Yamada from IAS 27 (as revised in 2003)

Cross-references have been updated.

DO1   Mr Yamada dissents from this Standard because he believes that the change in classification of minority interests in the consolidated balance sheet, that is to say, the requirement that it be shown as equity, should not be made as part of the Improvements project. He agrees that minority interests do not meet the definition of a liability under the *Framework for the Preparation and Presentation of Financial Statements*,[22] as stated in paragraph BCZ158 of the Basis for Conclusions, and that the current requirement, for minority interests to be presented separately from liabilities and the parent shareholders' equity, is not desirable. However, he does not believe that this requirement should be altered at this stage. He believes that before making the change in classification, which will have a wide variety of impacts on current consolidation practices, various issues related to this change need to be considered comprehensively by the Board. These include consideration of the objectives of consolidated financial statements and the accounting procedures that should flow from those objectives. Even though the Board concluded as noted in paragraph BC27, he believes that the decision related to the classification of minority interests should not be made until such a comprehensive consideration of recognition and measurement is completed.[23]

DO2   Traditionally, there are two views of the objectives of consolidated financial statements; they are implicit in the parent company view and the economic entity view. Mr Yamada believes that the objectives, that is to say, what information should be provided and to whom, should be considered by the Board before it makes its decision on the classification of minority interests in IAS 27. He is of the view that the Board is taking the economic entity view without giving enough consideration to this fundamental issue.

DO3   Step acquisitions are being discussed in the second phase of the Business Combinations project, which is not yet finalised at the time of finalising IAS 27 under the Improvements project. When the ownership interest of the parent increases, the Board has tentatively decided that the difference between the consideration paid by the parent to minority interests and the carrying value of the ownership interests acquired by the parent is recognised as part of equity, which is different from the current practice of recognising a change in the amount of goodwill. If the parent retains control of a subsidiary

---

22   The reference is to the IASC's *Framework for the Preparation and Presentation of Financial Statements*, adopted by the Board in 2001 and in effect when the Standard was revised.

23   Paragraph BC27 of the Basis for Conclusions on IAS 27 (as revised in 2003) was deleted as part of the amendments to IAS 27 in 2008. The paragraph stated: The Board acknowledged that this decision gives rise to questions about the recognition and measurement of minority interests but it concluded that the proposed presentation is consistent with current standards and the *Framework* and would provide better comparability than presentation in the consolidated balance sheet with either liabilities or parent shareholders' equity. It decided that the recognition and measurement questions should be addressed as part of its project on business combinations.

but its ownership interest decreases, the difference between the consideration received by the parent and the carrying value of the ownership interests transferred is also recognised as part of equity, which is different from the current practice of recognising a gain or a loss. Mr Yamada believes that the results of this discussion are predetermined by the decision related to the classification of minority interests as equity. The changes in accounting treatments are fundamental and he believes that the decision on which of the two views should govern the consolidated financial statements should be taken only after careful consideration of the ramifications. He believes that the amendment of IAS 27 relating to the classification of minority interests should not be made before completion of the second phase of the Business Combinations project.

Dissent of Philippe Danjou, Jan Engström, Robert P Garnett, Gilbert Gélard and Tatsumi Yamada from the amendments to IAS 27 issued in January 2008 on the accounting for non-controlling interests and the loss of control of a subsidiary

Cross-references have been updated.

DO1　Messrs Danjou, Engström, Garnett, Gélard and Yamada dissent from the 2008 amendments to IAS 27.

Accounting for changes in ownership interests in a subsidiary

DO2　Messrs Danjou, Engström, Gélard and Yamada do not agree that acquisitions of non-controlling interests in a subsidiary by the parent should be accounted for in full as equity transactions.

DO3　Those Board members observe that the consideration paid for an additional interest in a subsidiary will reflect the additional interest's share in:

(a)　the carrying amount of the subsidiary's net assets at that date;

(b)　additionally acquired goodwill; and

(c)　unrecognised increases in the fair value of the subsidiary's net assets (including goodwill) since the date when control was obtained.

DO4　Paragraphs 23 and B96 of IFRS 10 require such a transaction to be accounted for as an equity transaction, by adjusting the relative interests of the parent and the non-controlling interests. As a consequence, the additionally acquired goodwill and any unrecognised increases in the fair value of the subsidiary's net assets would be deducted from equity. Those Board members disagree that such accounting faithfully represents the economics of such a transaction.

DO5　Those Board members believe that an increase in ownership interests in a subsidiary is likely to provide additional benefits to the parent. Although control has already been obtained, a higher ownership interest might increase synergies accruing to the parent, for example, by meeting legal thresholds provided in company law, which would give the parent an additional level of discretion over the subsidiary. If the additional ownership interest has been acquired in an arm's length exchange transaction in which knowledgeable, willing parties exchange equal values, these additional benefits are reflected in the purchase price of the additional ownership interest. Those Board members believe that the acquisition of non-controlling interests by the parent should give rise to the recognition of goodwill, measured as the excess of the consideration transferred over the carrying amount of the subsidiary's net assets attributable to the additional interest acquired. Those Board members acknowledge that this amount also includes unrecognised increases in the fair value of the subsidiary's net assets since the date when control was obtained. However, on the basis of cost-benefit considerations, they believe that it is a reasonable approximation of the additionally acquired goodwill.

DO6 Messrs Danjou, Gélard and Yamada agree that, in conformity with the *Framework for the Preparation and Presentation of Financial Statements*,[24] non-controlling interests should be presented within the group's equity, because they are not liabilities. However, they believe that until the debates over the objectives of consolidated financial statements (ie what information should be provided and to whom) and the definition of the reporting entity have been settled at the conceptual level, transactions between the parent and non-controlling interests should not be accounted for in the same manner as transactions in which the parent entity acquires its own shares and reduces its equity. In their view, non-controlling interests cannot be considered equivalent to the ordinary ownership interests of the owners of the parent. The owners of the parent and the holders of non-controlling interests in a subsidiary do not share the same risks and rewards in relation to the group's operations and net assets because ownership interests in a subsidiary share only the risks and rewards associated with that subsidiary.

DO7 In addition, Messrs Danjou and Gélard observe that IFRS 3 *Business Combinations* (as revised in 2008) provides an option to measure non-controlling interests in a business combination as their proportionate share of the acquiree's net identifiable assets rather than at their fair value. However, paragraph BC207 of the Basis for Conclusions on IFRS 3 (as revised in 2008) states that accounting for the non-controlling interests at fair value is conceptually superior to this alternative measurement. This view implies that the subsidiary's portion of goodwill attributable to the non-controlling interests at the date when control was obtained is an asset at that date and there is no conceptual reason for it no longer to be an asset at the time of any subsequent acquisitions of non-controlling interests.

DO8 Mr Garnett disagrees with the treatment of changes in controlling interests in subsidiaries after control is established (paragraphs BCZ168–BCZ179 of the Basis for Conclusions). He believes that it is important that the consequences of such changes for the owners of the parent entity are reported clearly in the financial statements.

DO9 Mr Garnett believes that the amendments to IAS 27 adopt the economic entity approach that treats all equity interests in the group as being homogeneous. Transactions between controlling and non-controlling interests are regarded as mere transfers within the total equity interest and no gain or loss is recognised on such transactions. Mr Garnett observes that the non-controlling interests represent equity claims that are restricted to particular subsidiaries, whereas the controlling interests are affected by the performance of the entire group. The consolidated financial statements should therefore report performance from the perspective of the controlling interest (a parent entity perspective) in addition to the wider perspective provided by the economic entity approach. This implies the recognition of additional goodwill on purchases, and gains or losses on disposals of the parent entity's interest in a subsidiary.

---

24 The reference is to the IASC's *Framework for the Preparation and Presentation of Financial Statements*, adopted by the Board in 2001 and in effect when the Standard was amended.

DO10   If, as Mr Garnett would prefer, the full goodwill method were not used (see paragraphs DO7–DO10 of the dissenting views on IFRS 3), the acquisition of an additional interest in a subsidiary would give rise to the recognition of additional purchased goodwill, measured as the excess of the consideration transferred over the carrying amount of the subsidiary's net assets attributable to the additional interest acquired.

DO11   Mr Garnett does not agree with the requirement in paragraph B96 of this IFRS that, in respect of a partial disposal of the parent's ownership interest in a subsidiary that does not result in a loss of control, the carrying amount of the non-controlling interests should be adjusted to reflect the change in the parent's interest in the subsidiary's net assets. On the contrary, he believes that the carrying amount of the non-controlling interests should be adjusted by the fair value of the consideration paid by the non-controlling interests to acquire that additional interest.

DO12   Mr Garnett also believes that it is important to provide the owners of the parent entity with information about the effects of a partial disposal of holdings in subsidiaries, including the difference between the fair value of the consideration received and the proportion of the carrying amount of the subsidiary's assets (including purchased goodwill) attributable to the disposal.

Loss of control

DO13   Mr Garnett disagrees with the requirement in paragraph B98 of this IFRS that if a parent loses control of a subsidiary, it measures any retained investment in the former subsidiary at fair value and any difference between the carrying amount of the retained investment and its fair value is recognised in profit or loss, because the retained investment was not part of the exchange. The loss of control of a subsidiary is a significant economic event that warrants deconsolidation. However, the retained investment has not been sold. Under current IFRSs, gains and losses on cost method, available-for-sale and equity method investments are recognised in profit or loss only when the investment is sold (other than impairment). Mr Garnett would have recognised the effect of measuring the retained investment at fair value as a separate component of other comprehensive income instead of profit or loss.

Accounting for losses attributable to non-controlling interests

DO14   Mr Danjou disagrees with paragraph B94 of this IFRS according to which losses can be attributed without limitation to the non-controlling interests even if this results in the non-controlling interests having a deficit balance.

DO15   In many circumstances, in the absence of any commitment or binding obligation of the non-controlling interests to make an additional investment to cover the excess losses of the subsidiary, the continuation of the operations of a subsidiary will be funded through the contribution of additional capital by the parent and with the non-controlling interests being diluted. In those circumstances, the deficit balance attributable to the non-controlling interests that would result from the amendment in paragraph B94 does not present faithfully the equity of the consolidating entity.

DO16   Mr Danjou believes that the Standard should therefore not preclude the allocation against the parent equity of losses that exceed the non-controlling interests in a consolidated subsidiary when the facts and circumstances are as outlined in paragraph DO15.

Dissenting Opinions from *Sale or Contribution of Assets between an Investor and its Associate or Joint Venture* (Amendments to IFRS 10 and IAS 28) as issued in September 2014

DO1   Mr Kabureck, Ms Lloyd and Mr Ochi voted against the publication of *Sale or Contribution of Assets between an Investor and its Associate or Joint Venture* (Amendments to IFRS 10 and IAS 28). The reasons for their dissents are set out below.

Dissent of Mr Kabureck

DO2   Mr Kabureck dissents from the amendments to IFRS 10 and IAS 28, which require full gain or loss recognition in the accounting for the loss of control when a parent (investor) sells or contributes a business, as defined in IFRS 3 *Business Combinations*, to an investee (ie an associate or a joint venture) that is accounted for using the equity method.

DO3   He agrees that the control of a business can be lost regardless of whether the acquirer is a related or an unrelated party. However, he believes that the accounting for the gain or loss should be different if the sale or contribution is to an investee that is accounted for using the equity method. He observes that the investor's interest in the gain or loss will eventually affect the future investee's profit or loss recognised in the investor's profit or loss.

DO4   His concern can be illustrated by a simple example:

An investor sells a business to a 40 per cent-owned associate accounted for using the equity method. The full gain is CU100.[25] This gain of CU100 is reflected in the associate's financial statements through the higher value of the net assets acquired. Over time, assuming that no goodwill or indefinite lived intangible assets are involved, the associate's future profits or losses will be lower by CU100 as the assets are consumed and, therefore, the investor's share of the associate's profits or losses will be lower by CU40. Consequently, the net gain of the investor over time is CU60, not CU100.

DO5   Accordingly, he believes that a more faithful representation of the transaction would be to recognise an immediate gain of CU60 and a deferred gain of CU40, which would be amortised into income, making it consistent with the consumption of the sold assets in the investee's operations. He believes that it would be inappropriate to immediately recognise the full gain knowing that over time there would be lower profits to the extent of the equity interest in the investee.

DO6   Mr Kabureck observes that his preferred partial gain or loss accounting is consistent with the accounting for the sales of assets that do not constitute a business, as described in paragraphs BC190F of IFRS 10 and BC37F of IAS 28. Whether or not the assets sold or contributed do, or do not, constitute a business, seems to him to provide little rationale for different gain or loss treatment. He further observes that the line between what constitutes a business versus a collection of assets is frequently unclear, often based on

---

25   In this document, monetary items are denominated by 'currency units' (CU).

judgement and represents an interpretation challenge in practice. He disagrees with introducing another accounting difference that is dependent on the interpretation of the definition of a business.

Dissent of Ms Lloyd and Mr Ochi

DO7 Ms Lloyd and Mr Ochi agree that the sale of assets that constitute a business and the sale of assets that do not constitute a business should be treated differently for the reasons given in paragraphs BC190G of IFRS 10 and BC37G of IAS 28. However, they also believe that the accounting result should not differ depending on whether assets that do not constitute a business are transferred in a transaction that is structured as a sale of assets or as a sale of the entity that holds those assets. Ms Lloyd and Mr Ochi believe that these amendments do not achieve that result.

DO8 The stated objective of these amendments is to address the conflict between the requirements of IFRS 10 and IAS 28. Prior to these amendments, IFRS 10 required full gain or loss recognition on the loss of control of a subsidiary, whereas IAS 28 restricted the gain or loss resulting from the sale or contribution of assets to an associate or a joint venture to the extent of the interests that were attributable to unrelated investors in that associate or joint venture (downstream transactions).

DO9 As a result of these amendments, there will continue to be a full gain or loss recognition on the loss of control of a subsidiary that constitutes a business under IFRS 10, as well as a full gain or loss recognition resulting from the sale or contribution of assets that constitute a business between an investor and its associate or joint venture under IAS 28. The gain or loss recognised on the sale of the business will be the same whether it is structured as a sale of assets that constitute a business or as a sale of the entity that contains a business. As stated above, Ms Lloyd and Mr Ochi agree with this result.

DO10 Even after the amendments, IAS 28 will continue to restrict the gain or loss resulting from the sale or contribution of assets that do not constitute a business to an associate or a joint venture to the extent of the interests that are attributable to unrelated investors in that associate or joint venture. However, as a result of these amendments, under IFRS 10, when an entity sells an interest in a subsidiary that does not contain a business to an associate or a joint venture and as a result loses control of that subsidiary but retains joint control or significant influence over it, the gain or loss recognised is also limited to the unrelated investor's interests in the associate or joint venture to which the interest in the subsidiary was sold. In addition, the entity will remeasure its retained interest in the former subsidiary to fair value at the date it loses control, even though that retained interest is not in an entity that constitutes a business. Ms Lloyd and Mr Ochi acknowledge that under the amendments, recognition of the gain or loss on remeasurement will be limited to the unrelated investor's interests in the associate or joint venture to which the interest in the subsidiary was sold. However, because Ms Lloyd and Mr Ochi believe the sale of a subsidiary that does not constitute a business, and the sale of the assets held in that subsidiary, is substantially the same transaction, they do not find any justification for the recognition of any additional gain on the remeasurement of the retained portion.

DO11   Furthermore, Ms Lloyd and Mr Ochi note that if the retained interest in the former subsidiary is an investment accounted for in accordance with IFRS 9 *Financial Instruments* or IAS 39 *Financial Instruments: Recognition and Measurement*, the amount of gain or loss recognised on remeasurement will not be restricted. A full gain or loss will be recognised on remeasurement of the retained interest even though that interest is not in an entity that constitutes a business. As a result of the remeasurement of the retained interest in the former subsidiary, the amount of gain or loss recognised in a transaction involving the same underlying assets will still be different depending on whether those assets are transferred in a transaction that is structured as a sale of assets or as a sale of the entity that holds the assets. Ms Lloyd and Mr Ochi disagree with this result. They believe that the remeasurement of a retained interest in a former subsidiary to fair value when control is lost is a fundamental principle of IFRS 10. They also believe that accounting for equity interests that do not represent control, joint control or significant influence at fair value is a fundamental principle of IFRS 9 and IAS 39. Ms Lloyd and Mr Ochi do not believe that these principles can be reconciled in a limited-scope amendment to the treatment in IAS 28 of downstream transactions that involve the sale of assets that do not constitute a business.

DO12   Consequently, Ms Lloyd and Mr Ochi dissent from these amendments because they do not fully address the concerns of the Board and the IFRS Interpretations Committee as set out in paragraphs BC190D of IFRS 10 and BC37D of IAS 28.

Appendix
Amendments to the Basis for Conclusions on other IFRSs

This appendix contains amendments to the Basis for Conclusions on other IFRSs that are necessary in order to ensure consistency with IFRS 10 and the related amendments to other IFRSs. Amended footnotes are shown with new text underlined and deleted text struck through.

* * * * *

The amendments contained in this appendix when IFRS 10 was issued in 2011 have been incorporated into the Basis for Conclusions on the relevant IFRSs published in this volume.

IASB documents published to accompany

IFRS 11

Joint Arrangements

The text of the unaccompanied standard, IFRS 11, is contained in Part A of this edition. Its effective date when issued was 1 January 2013. The text of the Accompanying Guidance on IFRS 11 is contained in Part B of this edition. This part presents the following documents:

BASIS FOR CONCLUSIONS

APPENDIX TO THE BASIS FOR CONCLUSIONS

Amendments to the Basis for Conclusions on other IFRSs

CONTENTS

Basis for Conclusions on
IFRS 11 *Joint Arrangements*

This Basis for Conclusions accompanies, but is not part of, IFRS 11.

Introduction

BC1   This Basis for Conclusions summarises the International Accounting Standards Board's considerations in reaching the conclusions in IFRS 11 *Joint Arrangements*. Individual Board members gave greater weight to some factors than to others.

BC2   The Board added the joint ventures project to its agenda as part of the project to reduce differences between International Financial Reporting Standards (IFRSs) and US generally accepted accounting principles (GAAP). The requirements of IFRS 11 were not deliberated by the US Financial Accounting Standards Board (FASB).

BC3   The Board focused its deliberations on enhancing the faithful representation of joint arrangements that an entity provides in its financial statements, by establishing a principle-based approach to accounting for joint arrangements, and by requiring enhanced disclosures. Even though the Board focused its efforts on improving the reporting of joint arrangements, the result is that the requirements of the IFRS achieve closer convergence with US GAAP than did IAS 31 *Interests in Joint Ventures*, which IFRS 11 supersedes.

Objective

BC4   IFRS 11 sets out requirements for the recognition and measurement of an entity's interest in joint arrangements. The requirements for the disclosure of an entity's interest in joint arrangements have been included in IFRS 12 *Disclosure of Interests in Other Entities* (see paragraphs BC52–BC55). IFRS 11 is concerned principally with addressing two aspects of IAS 31 that the Board regarded as impediments to high quality reporting of joint arrangements: first, that the structure of the arrangement was the only determinant of the accounting, and second, that an entity had a choice of accounting treatment for interests in jointly controlled entities.

BC5   The Board did not reconsider all the requirements in IAS 31. For example, the Board did not reconsider the equity method. Accordingly, this Basis for Conclusions does not discuss requirements of IAS 31 that the Board did not reconsider.

BC6   The Board published its proposals in an exposure draft, ED 9 *Joint Arrangements*, in September 2007 with a comment deadline of 11 January 2008. The Board received over 110 comment letters on the exposure draft.

The problems with IAS 31

BC7   IAS 31 established different accounting requirements depending on whether the arrangements were structured through an entity. Jointly controlled operations and jointly controlled assets were arrangements that did not require the establishment of an entity or financial structure that is separate from the parties. IAS 31 required parties to these arrangements to recognise assets, liabilities, revenues and expenses arising from the arrangements. When arrangements were structured through an entity, IAS 31 classified them as jointly controlled entities. Parties with interests in jointly controlled entities accounted for them using proportionate consolidation or, as an alternative, the equity method.

BC8   The problem with basing different accounting requirements solely on the existence of an entity, combined with the choice of accounting treatment for jointly controlled entities, was that some arrangements that gave the parties similar rights and obligations were accounted for differently and, conversely, arrangements that gave the parties different rights and obligations were accounted for similarly. The Board's policy is to exclude options in accounting treatment from accounting standards whenever possible. Such options can lead to similar transactions being accounted for in different ways and, therefore, can impair comparability.

Improving IAS 31 with the principles of IFRS 11

BC9   In the Board's view, the accounting for joint arrangements should reflect the rights and obligations that the parties have as a result of their interests in the arrangements, regardless of those arrangements' structure or legal form. This is the principle that IFRS 11 establishes for parties to a joint arrangement when accounting for their interests in the arrangements. However, the Board acknowledges that sometimes the structure or the legal form of the joint arrangements is decisive in determining the parties' rights and obligations arising from the arrangements and, consequently, in determining the classification of the joint arrangements (see paragraphs BC26 and BC31).

BC10   Entities applying IAS 31 were required to choose the same accounting treatment (ie proportionate consolidation or equity method) when accounting for all of their interests in jointly controlled entities. Applying the same accounting treatment to all the interests that an entity has in different jointly controlled entities might not always lead to the faithful representation of each of those interests. For example, an entity whose policy was to account for all of its interests in jointly controlled entities using proportionate consolidation might have recognised assets and liabilities proportionately even though this did not faithfully represent the entity's rights and obligations in the assets and liabilities of particular joint arrangements. Conversely, an entity might have accounted for all of its interests in jointly controlled entities using the equity method, when the recognition of the entity's rights and obligations in particular joint arrangements would instead have led to the recognition of assets and liabilities.

BC11   The accounting for joint arrangements required by the IFRS is not a function of an entity's accounting policy choice but is, instead, determined by an entity applying the principles of the IFRS to each of its joint arrangements and recognising, as a result, the rights and obligations arising from each of them. The Board concluded that proportionate consolidation is not an appropriate method to account for interests in joint arrangements when the parties have neither rights to the assets, nor obligations for the liabilities, relating to the arrangement. The Board also concluded that the equity method is not an appropriate method to account for interests in joint arrangements when parties have rights to the assets, and obligations for the liabilities, relating to the arrangement. The Board believes that it is misleading for users of financial statements if an entity recognises assets and liabilities for which it does not have rights or obligations, or does not recognise assets and liabilities for which it does have rights and obligations.

BC12   The Board also reconsidered the disclosure requirements in IAS 31 for interests in joint arrangements. The Board believes that the disclosure requirements in IFRS 12 will enable users to gain a better understanding of the nature and extent of an entity's operations undertaken through joint arrangements.

Scope

BC13   The IFRS should be applied by all entities that are a party to a joint arrangement. The IFRS does not change the two essential characteristics that IAS 31 required arrangements to have in order to be deemed 'joint ventures', ie that a contractual arrangement that binds the parties to the arrangement exists, and that the contractual arrangement establishes that two or more of those parties have joint control of the arrangement.

BC14   The Board believes that the new definition of control and the application requirements to assess control in IFRS 10 *Consolidated Financial Statements* will assist entities in determining whether an arrangement is controlled or jointly controlled, and in that respect it might cause entities to reconsider their previous assessment of their relationship with the investee. Despite the changes that these reassessments might cause, the Board believes that arrangements that were within the scope of IAS 31 would generally also be within the scope of IFRS 11.

Scope exception

BC15   The Board reconsidered the scope exception of IAS 31 that had also been proposed in ED 9. The Board concluded that the scope exception in ED 9 for interests in joint ventures held by venture capital organisations, or mutual funds, unit trusts and similar entities, including investment-linked insurance funds, that are measured at fair value through profit or loss in accordance with IFRS 9 *Financial Instruments*, is more appropriately characterised as a measurement exemption, not as a scope exception.

BC16   The Board observed that when venture capital organisations, or mutual funds, unit trusts and similar entities, including investment-linked insurance funds, conclude that they have an interest in a joint arrangement, this is because the arrangement has the characteristics of a joint arrangement as specified in IFRS 11 (ie a contractual arrangement exists that establishes that two or more parties have joint control of the arrangement).

BC17   The Board also observed that the scope exception in ED 9 did not relate to the fact that these arrangements do not have the characteristics of joint arrangements, but to the fact that for investments held by venture capital organisations, or mutual funds, unit trusts and similar entities, including investment-linked insurance funds, fair value measurement provides more useful information for users of the financial statements than would application of the equity method.

BC18   Accordingly, the Board decided to maintain the option that permits such entities to measure their interests in joint ventures at fair value through profit or loss in accordance with IFRS 9, but clarified that this is an exemption from the requirement to measure interests in joint ventures using the equity method, rather than an exception to the scope of IFRS 11 for joint ventures in which these entities have interests.

Joint arrangements

BC19   The Board decided to use the term 'joint arrangement', rather than 'joint venture', to describe arrangements that are subject to the requirements of the IFRS. As noted in paragraph BC13, the IFRS does not change the two essential characteristics that IAS 31 required for arrangements to be 'joint ventures': a contractual arrangement that binds the parties to the arrangement exists, and the contractual arrangement establishes that two or more of those parties have joint control of the arrangement.

Joint control

BC20   In ED 9, the proposed definition of 'joint arrangement' required 'shared decision-making' by all the parties to the arrangement. Some respondents questioned how 'shared decision-making' was intended to operate and how it differed from 'joint control'. The Board introduced the term 'shared decision-making' in the exposure draft instead of 'joint control' because control was defined in IAS 27 *Consolidated and Separate Financial Statements* in the context of having power over the financial and operating policies of an entity.[1] During its redeliberation of ED 9, the Board concluded that in joint arrangements, it is the activity undertaken by the parties that is the matter over which the parties share control or share decision-making, regardless of whether the activity is conducted in a separate entity. Consequently, the Board concluded that 'joint control' is a term that expresses better than 'shared decision-making' that the control of the activity that is the subject matter of the

---

1   The consolidation requirements in IAS 27 were replaced by IFRS 10 *Consolidated Financial Statements* issued in 2011 and the definition of control was revised.

arrangement is shared among the parties with joint control of the arrangement.

BC21   The Board did not reconsider the concept of 'joint control' as defined in IAS 31 or in ED 9 (ie the requirement of unanimous consent for the decisions that give the parties control of an arrangement). However, the definition of 'joint control' in the IFRS is different from those in IAS 31 and ED 9. The reason for the change is to align the definition of 'joint control' with the definition of 'control' in IFRS 10. IFRS 11 directs parties to an arrangement to assess first whether all the parties, or a group of the parties, control the arrangement collectively, on the basis of the definition of control and corresponding guidance in IFRS 10. Once an entity has concluded that the arrangement is collectively controlled by all the parties, or by a group of the parties, joint control exists only when decisions about the activities that significantly affect the returns of the arrangement (ie the relevant activities) require the unanimous consent of those parties.

BC22   In response to concerns expressed by some respondents who pointed out that, unlike IAS 31, ED 9 did not include the term 'investors in a joint arrangement', the Board clarified during its redeliberation of ED 9 that not all the parties to a joint arrangement need to have joint control for the arrangement to be a joint arrangement. Indeed, some of the parties to a joint arrangement can have joint control whereas others, although able to participate, do not have joint control of the arrangement. The Board decided to use the terms 'joint operators' to designate parties with joint control of a 'joint operation' and 'joint venturers' to designate parties with joint control of a 'joint venture' (see paragraph BC24).

BC23   The Board observed that the parties to a joint arrangement might agree to change or modify the governance and decision-making process of the arrangement at any time. As a result of such a change, a party might gain or lose joint control of the arrangement. Consequently, the Board concluded that if facts and circumstances change, the parties to a joint arrangement should reassess whether they are parties with joint control of the arrangement.

Types of joint arrangement

BC24   The IFRS classifies joint arrangements into two types—'joint operations' and 'joint ventures'. Parties with joint control of a joint operation have rights to the assets, and obligations for the liabilities, relating to the arrangement ('joint operators'), whereas parties with joint control of a joint venture ('joint venturers') have rights to the net assets of the arrangement.

BC25   The classification of joint arrangements into two types was considered by the Board in its redeliberation of the exposure draft. ED 9 proposed to classify joint arrangements into three types—'joint operations', 'joint assets' and 'joint ventures'. The Board observed that in some instances it might be difficult to assess whether an arrangement is a 'joint operation' or a 'joint asset'. This is because elements from both types of joint arrangement are sometimes present (in many arrangements joint assets are also jointly operated, and therefore such arrangements could be viewed as a 'joint asset' or as a 'joint operation').

Additionally, both types of joint arrangement result in the same accounting outcome (ie recognition of assets and liabilities and corresponding revenues and expenses). For these reasons, the Board decided to merge 'joint operations' and 'joint assets' into a single type of joint arrangement called 'joint operation'. This decision simplifies the IFRS by aligning the two types of joint arrangement presented by the IFRS (ie 'joint operations' and 'joint ventures') with the two possible accounting outcomes (ie recognition of assets, liabilities, revenues and expenses, or recognition of an investment accounted for using the equity method).

BC26 The Board observed that when the parties do not structure their joint arrangement through a separate vehicle (ie arrangements that were formerly 'jointly controlled operations' and 'jointly controlled assets' in IAS 31), the parties determine in the contractual arrangements their rights to the assets, and their obligations for the liabilities, relating to the arrangement. Such arrangements are joint operations.

BC27 In reaching this conclusion, the Board acknowledged the possibility that parties to a joint arrangement that is not structured through a separate vehicle might establish terms in the contractual arrangement under which the parties have rights only to the net assets of the arrangement. The Board thought that this possibility was likely to be rare and that the benefits of introducing an additional assessment in the classification of joint arrangements when these are not structured through separate vehicles would not outweigh the costs of increasing the complexity of the IFRS. This is because in the vast majority of cases, accounting for joint arrangements that are not structured through separate vehicles on a gross basis leads to the faithful representation of the parties' rights and obligations arising from those arrangements.

BC28 The Board acknowledged that classifying jointly controlled entities in IAS 31 into joint operations or joint ventures in the IFRS requires an entity to assess its rights and obligations arising from these arrangements, which will require the entity to exercise judgement.

BC29 The Board considered whether the definition of a 'business', as defined in IFRS 3 *Business Combinations*, would be helpful in distinguishing between a joint venture and a joint operation. Because a 'business' can be found in all types of joint arrangement, the Board decided not to pursue this approach.

BC30 The Board also concluded that there should not be a rebuttable presumption that the arrangement is a joint venture when it has been structured through a separate vehicle. The Board decided that parties to a joint arrangement that is structured through a separate vehicle should assess the classification of the arrangement by taking into consideration all facts and circumstances. The Board noted that an entity should take into consideration the legal form of the separate vehicle, the terms agreed in the contractual arrangement and, when relevant, any other facts and circumstances.

BC31   In taking this approach, the Board observed that the legal form of the separate vehicle in which the joint arrangement is structured provides an initial indicator of the parties' rights to the assets, and obligations for the liabilities, relating to the arrangement. The exception is when the legal form of the separate vehicle does not confer separation between the parties and the vehicle. In such a case, the Board concluded that the assessment of the rights and obligations conferred upon the parties by the legal form of that separate vehicle would be sufficient to conclude that the arrangement is a joint operation.

BC32   The Board believes that the selection of a particular legal form is in many cases driven by the intended economic substance that the particular legal form delivers. However, the Board observed that in some cases the choice of a particular legal form responds to tax, regulatory requirements or other reasons that can alter the intended economic substance initially sought by the parties to the arrangement. In those instances, the parties might use their contractual arrangements to modify the effects that the legal form of the arrangement would otherwise have on their rights and obligations.

BC33   The Board noted that other facts and circumstances might also affect the rights and obligations of the parties to a joint arrangement and, ultimately, affect the classification of the arrangement. Therefore, the parties should recognise the assets and liabilities relating to an arrangement if the parties designed the arrangement so that its activities primarily aimed to provide the parties with an output (ie the parties are entitled to substantially all the economic benefits of the assets relating to the arrangement) and they are, as a result of the design of the arrangement, obliged to settle the liabilities relating to the arrangement.

BC34   The IFRS defines 'joint ventures' as arrangements whereby the parties that have joint control of the arrangement (ie the joint venturers) have rights to the net assets of the arrangement. The Board observed that the term 'net assets' in the definition of joint ventures aimed to portray that the joint venturers have rights to an investment in the arrangement. However, such a definition (ie 'rights to the net assets of the arrangement') would not prevent a joint venturer from having a net liability position arising from its involvement in the joint venture. This could happen, for example, if the joint venture had incurred losses that had reduced the joint venturer's investment to zero, and as a result of the joint venturer having provided a guarantee to cover any losses that the joint venture might incur, the joint venturer has an obligation for those losses. The Board observed that neither the provision of the guarantee by the joint venturer, nor the liability assumed by the joint venturer as a result of the joint venture incurring losses, determines that the arrangement is a joint operation.

BC35   Many respondents to ED 9 were concerned that joint ventures could be merely 'residuals'. This is because these respondents interpreted joint ventures to mean that after parties had identified rights to individual assets or obligations for expenses or financing, joint ventures would be merely any remaining assets and liabilities of the arrangement. As a result of these concerns, the Board clarified that the unit of account of a joint arrangement is the activity that two or more parties have agreed to control jointly, and that a party should assess its rights to the assets, and obligations for the liabilities, relating to that activity. Consequently, the term 'joint venture' refers to a jointly controlled activity in which the parties have an investment.

BC36 During its redeliberation of ED 9, the Board made it clear that different joint arrangements or different types of joint arrangement can be established beneath the umbrella of a single arrangement or framework agreement to deal with, for example, different activities that are interrelated. The Board also observed the possibility that within the same separate vehicle the parties may undertake different activities in which they have different rights to the assets, and obligations for the liabilities, relating to these different activities resulting in different types of joint arrangement conducted within the same separate vehicle. However, the Board acknowledged that even though this situation is conceptually possible, it would be rare in practice.

BC37 The Board observed that the rights and obligations of parties to joint arrangements might change over time. This might happen, for example, as a result of a change in the purpose of the arrangement that might trigger a reconsideration of the terms of the contractual arrangements. Consequently, the Board concluded that the assessment of the type of joint arrangement needs to be a continuous process, to the extent that facts and circumstances change.

Financial statements of parties to a joint arrangement

Joint operation

BC38 In relation to the accounting for a party's interest in a joint operation, some respondents to ED 9 enquired how proportionate consolidation differed from the recognition of (or recognition of shares of) assets, liabilities, revenues and expenses arising from a joint operation. The Board noted that there are two main differences between recognising assets, liabilities, revenues and expenses relating to the activity of the joint operation and proportionate consolidation. The first difference relates to the fact that the rights and obligations, as specified in the contractual arrangement, that an entity has with respect to the assets, liabilities, revenues and expenses relating to a joint operation might differ from its ownership interest in the joint operation. The IFRS requires an entity with an interest in a joint operation to recognise assets, liabilities, revenues and expenses according to the entity's shares in the assets, liabilities, revenues and expenses of the joint operation as determined and specified in the contractual arrangement, rather than basing the recognition of assets, liabilities, revenues and expenses on the ownership interest that the entity has in the joint operation. The second difference from proportionate consolidation is that the parties' interests in a joint operation are recognised in their separate financial statements. Consequently, there is no difference in what is recognised in the parties' separate financial statements and the parties' consolidated financial statements or the parties' financial statements in which investments are accounted for using the equity method.

BC39 Respondents also suggested that the IFRS should provide more clarity in stating the requirements for the accounting for shares of assets in joint operations. Many respondents to ED 9 were not clear whether parties to a joint operation that had rights to the assets should recognise a 'right to use' or a 'right to a share' or whether they should instead directly recognise 'their share of the joint assets, classified according to the nature of the asset'. The concern raised by this uncertainty was the different accounting implications of these interpretations – ie accounting for rights or accounting for shares of assets. The Board concluded that a party to a joint operation should recognise its assets or its share of any assets in accordance with the IFRSs applicable to the particular assets.

BC40 An additional concern raised by some respondents to ED 9 was how the unit of account relating to the share of assets and liabilities to be accounted for by the parties to a joint operation should be delineated. The Board observed that ED 9 had not been intended to change this aspect of IAS 31, where the 'share' is determined in accordance with the contractual arrangement. The Board concluded that the contractual arrangement generally delineates the 'share' or 'part' not only of the assets or liabilities of the parties to joint operations, but also of their 'share' of any revenues and expenses arising from the joint operation.

Joint venture

BC41 In relation to the accounting for interests in joint ventures, the Board decided that entities should recognise their interests using the equity method in accordance with IAS 28 *Investments in Associates and Joint Ventures*, unless the entity is exempted from applying the equity method as stated in that standard. In reaching that conclusion, the Board considered the views of some respondents to ED 9 who pointed out that joint control and significant influence are different. Proponents of this view argue that it is not appropriate to account for an associate and a joint venture in the same way using the equity method. Although the Board acknowledged that significant influence and joint control are different, the Board concluded that, except for specific circumstances that are addressed in IAS 28 (as amended in 2011), the equity method is the most appropriate method to account for joint ventures because it is a method that accounts for an entity's interest in the net assets of an investee. Reconsideration of the equity method was outside the scope of the joint ventures project.

BC42 Other respondents expressed concerns about the elimination of proportionate consolidation. Those respondents believe that proportionate consolidation more faithfully represents the economic substance of the arrangements, and better meets the information needs of users of financial statements. The Board acknowledged these concerns, but observed that the approach in the IFRS is consistent with its view of what constitutes the economic substance of an entity's interests in joint arrangements, a view that it concedes may differ from that of those respondents. This seems inevitable given that, the evidence suggests that in accounting for interests in jointly controlled entities approximately half of the entities applying IFRSs use proportionate consolidation and half use the equity method. The variation in practice, which is facilitated by the option in IAS 31, is a prime motivation for developing IFRS 11 (see paragraphs BC7 and BC8). That variation will, inevitably, be a source of disagreement.

BC43   The Board believes that the accounting for joint arrangements should faithfully reflect the rights and obligations that the parties have in respect of the assets and liabilities relating to the arrangement. In that respect, the Board observes that the activities that are the subject of different joint arrangements might be operationally very similar, but that the contractual terms agreed by the parties to these joint arrangements might confer on the parties very different rights to the assets, and obligations for the liabilities, relating to such activities. Consequently, the Board believes that the economic substance of the arrangements does not depend exclusively on whether the activities undertaken through joint arrangements are closely related to the activities undertaken by the parties on their own, or on whether the parties are closely involved in the operations of the arrangements. Instead, the economic substance of the arrangements depends on the rights and obligations assumed by the parties when carrying out such activities. It is those rights and obligations that the accounting for joint arrangements should reflect.

BC44   The Board observes that the IFRS requires parties to account for assets and liabilities when the contractual arrangement specifies that they have rights to the assets and obligations for the liabilities. The Board believes that accounting for joint arrangements that is based on the principles of the IFRS will contribute not only to improving the faithful representation of an entity's interests in joint arrangements, but also to enhancing comparability. This is because arrangements in which the parties have rights to the assets and obligations for the liabilities will require the same accounting treatment. In the same way, arrangements in which the parties have rights to the net assets of the arrangement will also require the same accounting treatment.

BC45   The Board does not believe that the elimination of proportionate consolidation will cause a loss of information for users of financial statements. This is because the disclosure requirements in IFRS 12, when compared with IAS 31, will improve the quality of the information provided to users relating to an entity's interest in joint ventures. The disclosure requirements in IFRS 12 will provide users with information about individual joint ventures when those joint ventures are material to the reporting entity. In addition, the Board notes that the summarised financial information required in IFRS 12 results in a higher degree of detail than did IAS 31, which gives users a better basis for assessing the effect on the reporting entity of the activities carried out through joint ventures.

Accounting for acquisitions of interests in joint operations

BC45A   The IFRS Interpretations Committee (the Interpretations Committee) reported to the IASB that practice differed in accounting for the acquisition of interests in jointly controlled operations or jointly controlled assets, as specified in IAS 31.[2] In particular, the Interpretations Committee noted diversity in practice if the activity of the jointly controlled operations or jointly controlled assets constitutes a business, as defined in IFRS 3.

BC45B   The principal approaches observed in practice were:

(a)   **IFRS 3 approach:** some preparers of IFRS financial statements, when accounting for the acquisition of interests in jointly controlled operations or jointly controlled assets in which the activity constitutes a business, applied IFRS 3 and the guidance on business combinations in other IFRSs. Identifiable assets and liabilities were measured, subject to the exceptions in IFRS 3, at fair value and the residual was recognised as goodwill. Furthermore, transaction costs were not capitalised and deferred taxes were recognised on initial recognition of assets and liabilities. Only guidance on business combinations in IFRS 3 and other IFRSs that was not appropriate for the acquisition of an interest in jointly controlled operations or jointly controlled assets was not applied, for example, the guidance on non-controlling interests.

(b)   **cost approach:** others allocated the total cost of acquiring the interest in the joint operation to the individual identifiable assets on the basis of their relative fair values. Accordingly, any premium paid was allocated to the identifiable assets rather than being recognised as goodwill. Transaction costs were capitalised and deferred taxes were not recognised, because of the initial recognition exceptions in paragraphs 15 and 24 of IAS 12 *Income Taxes*.

(c)   **hybrid approach:** a third group of preparers of IFRS financial statements only applied the principles on business combinations accounting in IFRS 3 and other IFRSs to issues that were not addressed elsewhere in IFRS. Identifiable assets and liabilities were measured at fair value, with exceptions, and the residual was recognised as a separate asset, ie goodwill. Transaction costs, however, were capitalised and contingent liabilities and deferred taxes were not recognised because these issues were considered as being addressed elsewhere in IFRS. Deferred taxes were not recognised, because of the initial recognition exceptions in paragraphs 15 and 24 of IAS 12.

BC45C   The different approaches have led to different accounting outcomes, in particular:

(a)   in accounting for premiums paid in excess of the value of the identifiable net assets;

---

2   IFRS 11 *Joint Arrangements* shall be applied for annual periods beginning on or after 1 January 2013. It replaces IAS 31 *Interests in Joint Ventures*.

(b) in capitalising or expensing acquisition-related costs; and

(c) in accounting for deferred tax assets and deferred tax liabilities that arise from the initial recognition of assets and liabilities.

BC45D The IASB noted that the diversity in practice resulted from the fact that IAS 31 did not give specific guidance on the accounting for acquisitions of interests in jointly controlled operations or jointly controlled assets, the activity of which constitutes a business, as defined in IFRS 3. The IASB was concerned that this diversity in practice may continue in the accounting for acquisitions of interests in joint operations, as defined in IFRS 11, when the activities of those joint operations constitute businesses. Arrangements that were formerly 'jointly controlled operations' and 'jointly controlled assets' in IAS 31 are joint operations in IFRS 11 (see paragraph BC26). As was the case in IAS 31, a joint operator recognises its (share in the) assets, liabilities, revenue and expenses relating to such arrangements.

BC45E The IASB considered the guidance in current IFRS on the acquisition of an interest in a business. The IASB recognised that the acquisition of an interest in a joint operation does not meet the definition of a business combination in IFRS 3. Nonetheless, the IASB concluded that the most appropriate approach to account for an acquisition of an interest in a joint operation in which the activity of the joint operation constitutes a business, as defined in IFRS 3, is to apply all of the principles on business combinations accounting in IFRS 3 and other IFRSs that do not conflict with the guidance in this IFRS.

BC45F The IASB reached this conclusion because:

(a) it considers that separate recognition of goodwill, when present, is preferable to allocating premiums to identifiable assets acquired on the basis of relative fair values;

(b) it thinks that an approach that limits the application of business combinations accounting only to issues that are not addressed elsewhere in IFRS lacks a strong conceptual basis; and

(c) the guidance in IFRS 3 and other IFRSs on business combinations give a comprehensive and consistent set of accounting principles for the different components of such complex transactions as acquisitions of interests in businesses.

BC45G The IASB also concluded that an entity that is acquiring an interest in a joint operation in which the activity of the joint operation constitutes a business, as defined in IFRS 3, shall disclose the relevant information that is specified in IFRS 3 and other IFRSs on business combinations. This is because these requirements are an integral part of the financial reporting about the acquisition of interests in businesses.

BC45H Consequently, the IASB amended IFRS 11 to address the accounting for both the acquisition of an interest in a joint operation in which the activity of the joint operation constitutes a business, as defined in IFRS 3, and the related disclosure requirements, as a means to resolve the diversity in practice.

BC45I   The IASB noted that the fact patterns raised with the Interpretations Committee were limited to circumstances involving a business, as defined in IFRS 3. The IASB noted that IFRS already provides guidance for the acquisition of an interest in an asset or a group of assets that is not a business, as defined in IFRS 3. Consequently, the amendments apply only when an entity acquires an interest in a joint operation in which the activity constitutes a business, as defined in IFRS 3, either on formation of that joint operation or when acquiring an interest in an existing joint operation.

BC45J   The Exposure Draft *Acquisition of an Interest in a Joint Operation* (Proposed amendment to IFRS 11), which was published in December 2012, used the term 'relevant principles on business combinations accounting in IFRS 3 and other IFRSs' to describe the principles that have to be applied in accounting for the acquisition of an interest in a joint operation in which the activity constitutes a business. In analysing the comment letters on the Exposure Draft, the IASB noted divergent understanding of what the 'relevant principles on business combinations accounting in IFRS 3 and other IFRSs' are, within the context of the proposed amendment.

BC45K   In order to avoid diversity in practice from the application of the term 'relevant principles on business combinations accounting in IFRS 3 and other IFRSs', the IASB decided to replace this term with 'all of the principles on business combinations accounting in IFRS 3 and other IFRSs that do not conflict with the guidance in this IFRS'. In addition, to aid understanding the application guidance includes a non-exhaustive list of five principles related to business combinations accounting in IFRS 3 and other IFRSs that do not conflict with the principles in this IFRS. Four of them relate to the areas in which the Interpretations Committee observed different accounting outcomes from the application of different approaches to the accounting for acquisitions of interests in jointly controlled operations or jointly controlled assets in which the activity constitutes a business (see paragraphs BC45B–BC45C).

BC45L   The IASB also noted that the reference to 'all of the principles on business combinations accounting in IFRS 3 and other IFRSs' is ambiguous for acquisitions of additional interests in joint operations that result in the joint operator retaining joint control of the joint operation. It might be understood as a reference to either:

      (a)   paragraph 42 of IFRS 3 with the result of remeasuring a previously held interest in a joint operation on the acquisition of an additional interest while retaining joint control; or

      (b)   paragraph 23 of IFRS 10 with the result of not remeasuring a previously held interest in a joint operation on the acquisition of an additional interest while retaining joint control.

BC45M   In order to resolve this ambiguity, the IASB decided to clarify that previously held interests in a joint operation are not remeasured if the joint operator retains joint control. Paragraph 23 of IFRS 10 addresses the accounting for the acquisition of an additional interest in a business that is already controlled by the acquirer. This is the analogous transaction to the acquisition of an interest in a business that is already jointly controlled by the acquirer and will continue to be jointly controlled by it. Paragraph 42 of IFRS 3 instead addresses the acquisition of an interest that results in the acquirer obtaining control over the business. This is the analogous transaction to the acquisition of an interest in a business that results in the acquirer obtaining joint control of the business.

BC45N   The IASB decided to add a scope exclusion for joint operations under common control to the amendments to IFRS 11. The IASB concluded that the amendments to IFRS 11 should not require the application of all of the principles on business combinations accounting for transactions that would be outside the scope of IFRS 3 if control, rather than joint control, would be obtained or retained by the acquirer.

Previously held interest in a joint operation (amendments issued in December 2017)

BC45O   The Board was informed that entities, on obtaining joint control of a business that is a joint operation, accounted for their previously held interest in the joint operation differently. In particular, there were different views on whether an entity applied the principles for accounting for a business combination achieved in stages to its previously held interest when it obtained joint control.

BC45P   The Board observed that although such a transaction changes the nature of an entity's interest in a joint operation, it does not result in a change in the group boundaries. In this respect, the transaction is similar to an investment in an associate becoming an investment in a joint venture and vice versa. The Board noted that paragraph 24 of IAS 28 prohibits an entity from remeasuring its previously held interest in those circumstances. The Board also observed that remeasuring a previously held interest in a joint operation could conflict with the requirement in IFRS 11 for an entity to account for its assets and liabilities relating to its interest in a joint operation applying the applicable IFRSs.

BC45Q   Consequently, the Board added paragraph B33CA to clarify that when an entity obtains joint control of a business that is a joint operation, it does not remeasure its previously held interests.

Transactions between an entity and a joint operation in which that entity is a joint operator and incorporation of SIC-13 into the IFRS

BC46   In its redeliberation of ED 9, the Board noted that the exposure draft was silent on the accounting for transactions between an entity and a joint operation in which that entity is a joint operator. The Board observed that the IFRS did not aim to change the accounting procedures that entities applied when accounting for such transactions in accordance with IAS 31, but it did acknowledge that the IFRS should state what those requirements were.

BC47 The Board also decided to include the requirements for the accounting for transactions entered into between a joint venturer and a joint venture, including the consensus of SIC-13 *Jointly Controlled Entities – Non-Monetary Contributions by Venturers*, in IAS 28 (as amended in 2011).

Reporting interests in joint arrangements in the financial statements of parties that participate in, but do not have joint control of, a joint arrangement

BC48 The Board decided to clarify in the IFRS that an arrangement can be a joint arrangement even though not all of its parties have joint control of the arrangement. This was consistent with IAS 31, which defined an 'investor in a joint venture' as a party to a joint venture that does not have joint control of that joint venture. The Board noted, however, that relating the term 'investor' exclusively to parties with no joint control of the arrangement can be confusing because the parties with joint control of the arrangement are also investors in those arrangements. Accordingly, the Board modified the language in the IFRS to avoid that confusion. However, even though in its redeliberation of ED 9 the Board highlighted that the IFRS establishes recognition and measurement requirements for the parties with joint control of a joint arrangement, the Board decided to address the accounting requirements for parties that participate in, but do not have joint control of, a joint arrangement, to reduce divergence in practice.

BC49 In relation to parties that participate in, but do not have joint control of, a joint arrangement that is a joint operation, the Board focused its discussions on those parties for which the contractual arrangements specify that they have rights to the assets, and obligations for the liabilities, relating to the joint operation. The Board concluded that, even though those parties are not joint operators, they do have rights and obligations for the assets, liabilities, revenues and expenses relating to the joint operation, which they should recognise in accordance with the terms of the contractual arrangement.

BC50 The Board considered that the requirements in IAS 31 for parties that participate in, but do not have joint control of, joint ventures were appropriate and therefore decided to carry them forward to the IFRS. Consequently, such a party should account for its investment in accordance with IFRS 9 or, if that party has significant influence over the joint venture, in accordance with IAS 28 (as amended in 2011).

Joint operation held for sale

BC51 ED 9 was silent on how an entity should account for an interest in a joint operation that is classified as held for sale. The Board decided that a joint operator should account for an interest in a joint operation that is classified as held for sale in accordance with IFRS 5 *Non-current Assets Held for Sale and Discontinued Operations*. The Board also confirmed that the guidance in IFRS 5 for the classification of a disposal group as held for sale would apply to interests in joint operations held for sale.

Disclosure

BC52   As part of its redeliberation of ED 9 and ED 10 *Consolidated Financial Statements*, the Board identified an opportunity to integrate and make consistent the disclosure requirements for subsidiaries, joint arrangements, associates and unconsolidated structured entities, and to present those requirements in a single IFRS.

BC53   The Board observed that IAS 27 (as revised in 2003), IAS 28 (as revised in 2003) and IAS 31 contained many similar disclosure requirements. ED 9 had already proposed amendments to the disclosure requirements for joint ventures and associates to align the disclosure requirements for those two types of investments more closely. The Board noted that the majority of respondents agreed with the proposals in ED 9 to align the disclosures for joint ventures with the disclosures in IAS 28 for associates.

BC54   As a result, the Board combined the disclosure requirements for interest with subsidiaries, joint arrangements, associates and unconsolidated structured entities within a single comprehensive standard, IFRS 12.

BC55   The Basis for Conclusions accompanying IFRS 12 summarises the Board's considerations in developing that IFRS, including its review of responses to the disclosure proposals in ED 9. Accordingly, IFRS 11 does not include disclosure requirements and this Basis for Conclusions does not incorporate the Board's considerations of responses to the proposed disclosure requirements in ED 9.

Effective date

BC56   The Board decided to align the effective date for the IFRS with the effective date for IFRS 10, IFRS 12, IAS 27 *Separate Financial Statements* and IAS 28 (as amended in 2011). When making this decision, the Board noted that the five IFRSs all deal with the assessment of, and related accounting and disclosure requirements about, a reporting entity's special relationships with other entities (ie when the reporting entity has control or joint control of, or significant influence over, another entity). As a result, the Board concluded that applying IFRS 11 without also applying the other four IFRSs could cause unwarranted confusion.

BC57   The Board usually sets an effective date of between twelve and eighteen months after issuing an IFRS. When deciding the effective date for those IFRSs, the Board considered the following factors:

(a)   the time that many countries require for translation and for introducing the mandatory requirements into law.

(b)   the consolidation project was related to the global financial crisis that started in 2007 and was accelerated by the Board in response to urgent requests from the leaders of the G20, the Financial Stability Board, users of financial statements, regulators and others to improve the accounting and disclosure of an entity's 'off balance sheet' activities.

(c)   the comments received from respondents to the Request for Views *Effective Date and Transition Methods* that was published in October 2010 regarding implementation costs, effective date and transition requirements of the IFRSs to be issued in 2011. Most respondents did not identify the consolidation and joint arrangements IFRSs as having a high impact in terms of the time and resources that their implementation would require. In addition, only a few respondents commented that the effective dates of those IFRSs should be aligned with those of the other IFRSs to be issued in 2011.

BC58   With those factors in mind, the Board decided to require entities to apply the five IFRSs for annual periods beginning on or after 1 January 2013.

BC59   Most respondents to the Request for Views supported early application of the IFRSs to be issued in 2011. Respondents stressed that early application was especially important for first-time adopters in 2011 and 2012. The Board was persuaded by these arguments and decided to permit early application of IFRS 11 but only if an entity applies it in conjunction with the other IFRSs (ie IFRS 10, IFRS 12, IAS 27 (as amended in 2011) and IAS 28 (as amended in 2011)) to avoid a lack of comparability among financial statements, and for the reasons noted in paragraph BC56 that triggered the Board's decision to set the same effective date for all five IFRSs. Even though an entity should apply the five IFRSs at the same time, the Board noted that an entity should not be prevented from providing any information required by IFRS 12 early if by doing so users gained a better understanding of the entity's relationships with other entities.

Transition

BC60   The exposure draft proposed retrospective application of the requirements. In its redeliberation of ED 9, the Board observed that entities affected by the changes introduced by the IFRS would have enough time to prepare to apply the new requirements retrospectively. The Board was informed of a few cases in which entities, on the basis of their analysis of the proposals in ED 9, had already changed their accounting for interests in joint arrangements retrospectively, taking advantage of the accounting option that IAS 31 offered to jointly controlled entities.

BC61   However, in its discussions, the Board considered the views of some respondents to ED 9 who had expressed their concern about applying the requirements retrospectively, because of undue cost and effort. In response to these concerns, the Board decided that in the case of changing from proportionate consolidation to the equity method, an entity should not adjust retrospectively any differences between the accounting methods of proportionate consolidation and equity method, but should instead aggregate the carrying amounts of the assets and liabilities, including any goodwill arising from acquisition, that the entity had previously proportionately consolidated into a single line investment as at the beginning of the earliest period presented.

BC62   The Board also decided that the opening balance of the investment should be tested for impairment in accordance with paragraphs 40–43 of IAS 28 (as amended in 2011), with any resulting impairment loss being adjusted against retained earnings at the beginning of the earliest period presented.

BC63   The Board also considered the case when an arrangement that was previously proportionately consolidated has a negative net asset position on transition. In such a case, an entity should assess whether it has legal or constructive obligations in relation to those negative net assets. The Board concluded that if the entity does not have legal or constructive obligations in relation to the negative net assets, it should not recognise the corresponding liability but it should adjust retained earnings at the beginning of the earliest period presented. The entity should also be required to disclose this fact along with its cumulative unrecognised share of losses of the joint venture as at the beginning of the earliest period presented and at the date at which the IFRS is first applied.

BC64   The Board also considered requiring disclosures to help users of financial statements to understand the consequences of the accounting change for those joint arrangements that would be changing from proportionate consolidation to the equity method. To address this need, the Board decided that an entity should disclose a breakdown of the assets and liabilities that have been aggregated into the single line investment as at the beginning of the earliest period presented.

BC65   The Board redeliberated the transition requirements for entities changing from the equity method to accounting for assets and liabilities in respect of their interest in a joint operation. The Board decided to require an entity to recognise each of the assets, including any goodwill arising from acquisition, and the liabilities relating to its interest in the joint operation at its carrying amount on the basis of the information used by the entity in applying the equity method, instead of requiring the entity to remeasure its share of each of those assets and liabilities at the date of transition. The Board did not believe that the costs of requiring entities to remeasure the assets and liabilities relating to the joint operation as a result of the accounting change would outweigh the benefits.

BC66   The Board observed that changing from the equity method to accounting for assets and liabilities in respect of an entity's interest in a joint operation could result in the net amount of the assets and liabilities recognised being either higher or lower than the investment (and any other items that formed part of the entity's net investment in the arrangement) derecognised. In the first case, the Board noted that assets and liabilities recognised could be higher than the investment derecognised when the entity had previously impaired the carrying amount of the investment. The Board observed that, in accordance with IAS 28 (as amended in 2011), such an impairment loss would not have been allocated to any asset, including goodwill, that formed part of the carrying amount of the investment and that as a result, the net amount of the underlying assets and liabilities could be higher than the carrying amount of the investment. To address this, the Board concluded that in such a case, an entity should first adjust the difference against any goodwill related to the investment, with any remaining difference adjusted against retained earnings at the beginning of the earliest period presented. In the second case, the Board noted that the net amount of the assets and liabilities recognised could be lower than the investment derecognised when, for example, an entity applied the same percentage interest to all the underlying assets and liabilities of its investee when determining the carrying amount of its investment using the equity method. However, for some of those underlying assets the entity could have a lower interest when accounting for it as a joint operation. The Board concluded that in such a case, an entity should adjust any difference between the net amount of the assets and liabilities recognised and the investment (and any other items that formed part of the entity's net investment in the arrangement) derecognised against retained earnings at the beginning of the earliest period presented.

BC67 The Board also redeliberated the transition requirements for entities accounting for an interest in a joint operation in its separate financial statements when the entity had previously accounted for this interest at cost or in accordance with IFRS 9. As stated in paragraph BC38, the Board observed that the parties' interests in a joint operation are recognised in their separate financial statements, resulting in no difference between what is recognised in the parties' separate financial statements and in the parties' consolidated financial statements. The Board decided that an entity should adjust any difference between the investment derecognised and the assets and liabilities recognised in respect of the entity's interest in a joint operation against retained earnings at the beginning of the earliest period presented.

BC68 The Board also considered requiring disclosures to help users of financial statements to understand the consequences of the accounting change from the equity method to accounting for assets and liabilities, and when accounting for an interest in a joint operation in the separate financial statements of an entity when the entity had previously accounted for this interest at cost or in accordance with IFRS 9. The Board decided that in both cases, an entity should provide a reconciliation between the investment derecognised and the breakdown of the assets and liabilities recognised, together with any remaining difference adjusted against retained earnings, at the beginning of the earliest period presented.

BC69 As stated in paragraph BC57, respondents to the Request for Views also commented on the transition requirements of the IFRSs to be issued in 2011. In relation to the transition requirements relating to the consolidation and joint arrangements IFRSs, the Board noted that the majority of the respondents to the Request for Views had agreed with the tentative decisions that the Board had previously made at the time of the consultation on the transition requirements for those IFRSs.

BC69A In June 2012, the Board amended the transition guidance in Appendix C to IFRS 10 Consolidated Financial Statements. When making those amendments, the Board decided to limit the requirement to present adjusted comparatives to the annual period immediately preceding the date of initial application of IFRS 10. This is consistent with the minimum comparative disclosure requirements contained in IAS 1 Presentation of Financial Statements as amended by *Annual Improvements to IFRSs 2009–2011 Cycle* (issued May 2012). Those amendments confirmed that when an entity applies a changed accounting policy retrospectively, it shall present, as a minimum, three statements of financial position (ie 1 January 2012, 31 December 2012 and 31 December 2013 for a calendar-year entity, assuming no early application of this IFRS) and two of each of the other statements (IAS 1 paragraphs 40A–40B). Notwithstanding this requirement, the Board confirmed that an entity is not prohibited from presenting adjusted comparative information for earlier periods. The Board also decided to make similar amendments to the transition guidance in Appendix C to this IFRS and Appendix C to IFRS 12 *Disclosure of Interests in Other Entities* to be consistent with this decision. The Board noted that if all comparative periods are not adjusted then entities should be required to state that fact, clearly identify the information that has not been adjusted, and explain the basis on which it has been prepared.

BC69B   The Board also considered the disclosure requirements of IAS 8 *Accounting Policies, Changes in Accounting Estimates and Errors*. On the initial application of an IFRS, paragraph 28(f) of IAS 8 requires an entity to disclose, for the current period and for each prior period presented, the amount of any adjustment for each financial statement line item affected. Changes in the accounting for a joint arrangement on transition to IFRS 11 are likely to affect many line items throughout the financial statements. The Board agreed that this requirement would be burdensome for preparers and so agreed to limit the disclosure of the quantitative impact of any changes in the accounting for a joint arrangement to only the annual period immediately preceding the first annual period for which IFRS 11 is applied. An entity may also present this information for the current period or for earlier comparative periods, but is not required to do so.

Accounting for acquisitions of interests in joint operations

BC69C   The IASB considered the transition provisions and effective date of the amendments to IFRS 11. The IASB noted that applying all of the principles of business combinations accounting in IFRS 3 and other IFRSs that do not conflict with the guidance in this IFRS to transactions that have previously been accounted for by applying one of the divergent approaches presented in paragraph BC45B might involve the use of hindsight in determining the acquisition-date fair values of the identifiable assets and liabilities that are to be recognised as part of the transaction and in performing the impairment test for goodwill. Consequently, the IASB decided that an entity would apply the amendments to IFRS 11 prospectively for transactions occurring in annual periods beginning on or after 1 January 2016 with early application permitted.

Previously held interest in a joint operation (amendments issued in December 2017)

BC69D   The Board decided that an entity applies paragraph B33CA to transactions in which joint control is obtained on or after the date it first applies the amendments. The Board concluded that the benefits of applying the amendments retrospectively were unlikely to exceed the costs of doing so because:

(a)   the nature of such transactions varies and restatement might not provide useful trend information to users of financial statements; and

(b)   applying a retrospective approach could result in significant costs for some entities because doing so could require an entity to analyse earlier acquisitions of interests in joint operations.

Summary of main changes from ED 9

BC70   The main changes from the exposure draft ED 9 are:

(a)   IFRS 11 applies to all entities that have an interest in a joint arrangement. The scope exception in the exposure draft for venture capital organisations, or mutual funds, unit trusts and similar entities, including investment-linked insurance funds, has been removed and has been recharacterised as an exemption from the requirement to measure investments in joint ventures in accordance with the equity method.

(b)   IFRS 11 replaces the term 'shared decisions' introduced by ED 9 with the term 'joint control'. As in IAS 31, 'joint control' is one of the features that, along with the existence of a contractual arrangement, defines 'joint arrangements'.

(c)   IFRS 11 classifies joint arrangements into two types—'joint operations' and 'joint ventures'. Each type of joint arrangement is aligned with a specific accounting requirement. ED 9 had classified joint arrangements into three types—'joint operations', 'joint assets' and 'joint ventures'.

(d)   IFRS 11 provides application requirements to assist entities in the classification of their joint arrangements. The IFRS requires an entity to determine the type of joint arrangement in which it is involved by considering its rights and obligations. In particular, the IFRS requires an entity to give consideration to the structure and legal form of the arrangement, to the terms agreed by the parties in the contractual arrangement and, when relevant, it should also consider other facts and circumstances.

(e)   IFRS 11 clarifies that not all the parties to a joint arrangement need to have joint control for the arrangement to be a joint arrangement. As a result, some of the parties to a joint arrangement might participate in the joint arrangement, but might not have joint control of it.

(f)   The consensus of SIC-13 has been incorporated into IAS 28 (as amended in 2011), and SIC-13 is accordingly withdrawn. ED 9 had proposed to incorporate the consensus of SIC-13 into the standard on joint arrangements.

(g)   The disclosure requirements have been placed in IFRS 12. ED 9 had proposed to incorporate the disclosure requirements for joint arrangements into the standard on joint arrangements.

(h)   IFRS 11 does not require an entity to adjust the differences between the proportionate consolidation method and the equity method retrospectively when an entity changes from proportionate consolidation to the equity method when accounting for its joint ventures. Instead, it requires an entity to recognise its investment in a joint venture as at the beginning of the earliest period presented, by measuring it as the aggregate of the carrying amounts of the assets and liabilities that the entity had previously proportionately consolidated, including any goodwill arising from acquisition. ED 9 had proposed retrospective application of the requirements.

Cost-benefit considerations

BC71   The objective of general purpose financial reporting is to provide financial information about the reporting entity that is useful to existing and potential investors, lenders and other creditors in making decisions about providing resources to the entity. To attain this objective, the Board seeks to ensure that an IFRS will meet a significant need and that the overall benefits of the resulting information justify the costs of providing it. Although the costs to implement a new IFRS might not be borne evenly, users of financial statements benefit from improvements in financial reporting, thereby facilitating the functioning of markets for capital and credit and the efficient allocation of resources in the economy.

BC72   The evaluation of costs and benefits is necessarily subjective. In making its judgement, the Board considered the following:

(a)   the costs incurred by preparers of financial statements;

(b)   the costs incurred by users of financial statements when information is not available;

(c)   the comparative advantage that preparers have in developing information, compared with the costs that users would incur to develop surrogate information;

(d)   the benefit of better economic decision-making as result of improved financial reporting; and

(e)   the costs of transition for users, preparers and others.

BC73   The Board concluded that the IFRS benefits preparers and users of financial statements. This is because the accounting for joint arrangements in the IFRS follows a principle-based approach. This approach has allowed the Board to remove the accounting option in IAS 31 so that each type of joint arrangement (ie 'joint operations' and 'joint ventures') is accounted for on a consistent basis. This contributes to enhancing the verifiability, comparability and understandability of these arrangements in entities' financial statements.

BC74   In the IFRS, the accounting for joint arrangements depends on the rights and obligations arising from the arrangement (not exclusively on whether the parties have chosen a particular structure or legal form to carry out their arrangements, or on the consistent application of an accounting policy— proportionate consolidation or equity method). Thus, the IFRS promotes greater comparability by applying the same approach to different joint arrangements.

BC75   The Board believes that basing the accounting on the principles in the IFRS results in enhanced verifiability, comparability and understandability, to the benefit of both preparers and users. First, verifiability and understandability are enhanced because the accounting reflects more faithfully the economic phenomena that it purports to represent (ie an entity's rights and obligations arising from its arrangements), which allows them to be better understood. Second, requiring the same accounting for each type of arrangement will enable entities to account for joint arrangements consistently: arrangements that confer on the parties rights to the assets and obligations for the liabilities are joint operations and arrangements that confer on the parties rights to the net assets are joint ventures. Consistency in the accounting for joint arrangements will help to achieve comparability among financial statements, which will enable users to identify and understand similarities in, and differences between, different arrangements.

BC76   The Board noted that the costs that preparers will have to bear when applying the IFRS to their arrangements are concentrated in the assessment of the type of joint arrangement rather than in the accounting for the arrangements. This is because entities accounting for joint arrangements in accordance with IAS 31 were not required to classify their arrangements on the basis of their rights and obligations arising from the arrangement, but instead on whether the arrangement was structured in an entity. The IFRS will require entities to assess the type of joint arrangement in which they are involved when those arrangements have been structured through a separate vehicle. Even though the classification of the joint arrangements represents an additional assessment that was not required in IAS 31, the application requirements in the IFRS that should assist preparers in the classification of their arrangements are not unduly complex. The Board does not think that the additional assessment that the IFRS will require for the classification of arrangements will result in an undue cost to preparers.

BC77   The Board noted that the IFRS, by comparison with the exposure draft, simplifies the proposals by aligning the types of joint arrangement with the accounting methods. The Board concluded that once an entity has determined the classification of the arrangement, the accounting for the arrangement will follow accounting procedures that have not been modified by the IFRS (ie entities will either account for assets and liabilities or they will account for an investment using the equity method). However, the Board acknowledged that the requirement for joint operations to be accounted for in the same way in the entity's consolidated financial statements as in the entity's separate financial statements might lead to additional costs to entities in jurisdictions in which separate financial statements are required to be reported in accordance with IFRSs. This is because those requirements might cause entities to perform additional manual procedures such as reconciliations between the statutory accounts and the tax returns, and might require an entity to provide additional explanations of the impact of the changes to, for example, its creditors. Except for these costs and any other costs required on transition, the costs of accounting for joint arrangements once the entities have determined their classification will remain unchanged as a result of the IFRS.

BC78   The Board concluded that enhanced verifiability, comparability and understandability result in a more faithful representation of joint arrangements in the financial statements of the entities that are involved in such arrangements, and that those benefits outweigh the costs that preparers might incur when implementing the IFRS.

Appendix
Amendments to the Basis for Conclusions on other IFRSs

This appendix contains amendments to the Basis for Conclusions on other IFRSs that are necessary in order to ensure consistency with IFRS 11 and the related amendments to other IFRSs. Amended paragraphs are shown with new text underlined and deleted text struck through.

* * * * *

The amendments contained in this appendix when IFRS 11 was issued in 2011 have been incorporated into the Basis for Conclusions on the relevant IFRSs published in this volume.

IASB documents published to accompany

IFRS 12

Disclosure of Interests in Other Entities

The text of the unaccompanied standard, IFRS 12, is contained in Part A of this edition. Its effective date when issued was 1 January 2013. This part presents the following document:

BASIS FOR CONCLUSIONS

Contents

Basis for Conclusions on
IFRS 12 *Disclosure of Interests in Other Entities*

This Basis for Conclusions accompanies, but is not part of, IFRS 12.

Introduction

BC1   This Basis for Conclusions summarises the International Accounting Standards Board's considerations in developing IFRS 12 *Disclosure of Interests in Other Entities*. Individual Board members gave greater weight to some factors than to others.

BC2   Users of financial statements have consistently requested improvements to the disclosure of a reporting entity's interests in other entities to help identify the profit or loss and cash flows available to the reporting entity and determine the value of a current or future investment in the reporting entity.

BC3   They highlighted the need for better information about the subsidiaries that are consolidated, as well as an entity's interests in joint arrangements and associates that are not consolidated but with which the entity has a special relationship.

BC4   The global financial crisis that started in 2007 also highlighted a lack of transparency about the risks to which a reporting entity was exposed from its involvement with structured entities, including those that it had sponsored.

BC5   IFRS 12 addresses the disclosure of a reporting entity's interests in other entities when the reporting entity has a special relationship with those other entities, ie it controls another entity, has joint control of or significant influence over another entity or has an interest in an unconsolidated structured entity.

BC6   In developing IFRS 12, the Board considered the responses to its exposure drafts, ED 9 *Joint Arrangements* and ED 10 *Consolidated Financial Statements*. ED 9 proposed amendments to the disclosure requirements for joint ventures and associates to align more closely the disclosure requirements for those two types of investments. ED 10 proposed amendments to the disclosure requirements for subsidiaries and new disclosure requirements for unconsolidated structured entities.

BC7   During its consideration of the responses to ED 9 and ED 10, the Board identified an opportunity to integrate and make consistent the disclosure requirements for subsidiaries, joint arrangements, associates and unconsolidated structured entities and present those requirements in a single IFRS. The Board observed that the disclosure requirements of IAS 27 *Consolidated and Separate Financial Statements*, IAS 28 *Investments in Associates* and IAS 31 *Interests in Joint Ventures* overlapped in many areas. In addition, many respondents to ED 10 commented that the disclosure requirements for interests in unconsolidated structured entities should not be located in a consolidation standard. Therefore, the Board concluded that a combined disclosure standard for interests in other entities would make it easier to understand and apply the disclosure requirements for subsidiaries, joint ventures, associates and unconsolidated structured entities.

BC8   The Board decided to extend the scope of IFRS 12 to interests in joint operations. A joint operation is a joint arrangement that is not necessarily structured through an entity that is separate from the parties to the joint arrangement. Therefore, an interest in a joint operation does not necessarily represent an interest in another entity. The Board decided to include disclosure requirements for joint operations in IFRS 12 because it believes that the benefits of having all disclosure requirements for joint arrangements in one place outweighs the disadvantages of including disclosure requirements about interests in joint operations in a standard that otherwise deals with an entity's interests in other entities.

Clarification of the scope of the Standard (amendments issued in December 2016)

BC8A   The Board was asked to clarify the scope of IFRS 12 with respect to interests in entities within the scope of IFRS 5 *Non-current Assets Held for Sale and Discontinued Operations*. Paragraph B17 states that an entity is not required to disclose summarised financial information in accordance with paragraphs B10–B16 for interests classified as held for sale. However, the requirements in paragraph 5B of IFRS 5 made it unclear whether all other requirements in IFRS 12 apply to interests in entities classified as held for sale or discontinued operations in accordance with IFRS 5.

BC8B   The Board noted that it had not intended to exempt an entity from all of the disclosure requirements in IFRS 12 with respect to interests in entities classified as held for sale or discontinued operations. The objective of IFRS 12 (ie to disclose information that enables users of financial statements to evaluate the nature of, and risks associated with, interests in other entities, and the effects of those interests on financial statements) is relevant to interests in other entities, regardless of whether they are within the scope of IFRS 5.

BC8C   Accordingly, in *Annual Improvements to IFRS Standards 2014–2016 Cycle*, the Board added paragraph 5A to clarify that, except as described in paragraph B17, the requirements in IFRS 12 apply to interests in entities within the scope of IFRS 5—ie interests that are classified (or included in a disposal group that is classified) as held for sale, held for distribution to owners in their capacity as owners, or discontinued operations. Paragraph 5A refers only to interests that are classified as held for sale or discontinued operations because the clarification was needed only for interests referred to in paragraph 5B of IFRS 5.

BC8D   A few respondents to the Board's proposals suggested that the Board consider which requirements in IFRS 12 are particularly relevant for interests in entities within the scope of IFRS 5, and specify that an entity applies only those relevant requirements.

BC8E   The Board decided not to change the proposals in this respect. Although acknowledging that some requirements in IFRS 12 might be more relevant to interests within the scope of IFRS 5 than others, the Board noted that this is also true for interests not within the scope of IFRS 5. This is because the relevance of each disclosure requirement for particular interests depends on the specific facts and circumstances relating to such interests. This is implicit in the requirements in paragraph 4, which require an entity to apply judgement in determining the amount of information to disclose about its interests in other entities to satisfy the disclosure objective.

BC8F   In response to the Board's proposal to apply the amendments retrospectively, a few respondents asked the Board to consider whether to provide transition relief for interests in entities disposed of before or during the first year of application.

BC8G   The Board decided not to provide such transition relief because: (a) the incremental costs of collecting data and preparing information are not expected to be significant—this is because such information is needed for disclosure before the interests are classified as held for sale or discontinued operations; and (b) it would be inconsistent with IFRS 12, which requires disclosure even when an entity no longer has any contractual involvement with another entity.

BC8H   The Board decided on an effective date of 1 January 2017 for the amendments. Because the requirements in IFRS 12 generally apply only to annual financial statements, an effective date of 1 January 2017 would typically mean that the earliest an entity would be required to apply the amendments would be within financial statements for the year ended 31 December 2017. Accordingly, an effective date of 1 January 2017 provides an entity with more than a year to prepare to implement the amendments. In addition, the Board noted that the amendments are clarifying in nature.

BC8I   The Board decided that an option to apply the amendments early is not necessary. This is because an entity is not prohibited from disclosing additional information.

The structure of IFRS 12 and the Board's deliberations

BC9   IFRS 12 replaces the disclosure requirements in IAS 27, IAS 28 and IAS 31, except for the disclosure requirements that apply only when preparing separate financial statements, which are included in IAS 27 *Separate Financial Statements*.

BC10   Unless otherwise stated, any references in this Basis for Conclusions to:

(a)   IAS 27 are to IAS 27 *Consolidated and Separate Financial Statements*.

(b)   IAS 28 are to IAS 28 *Investments in Associates*.

(c)   IAS 31 are to IAS 31 *Interests in Joint Ventures*.

BC11   In developing IFRS 12, the Board did not reconsider all the requirements that are included in the IFRS. The requirements in paragraphs 11, 18 and 19 relate to disclosures about some of the accounting requirements in IFRS 10 *Consolidated Financial Statements*, which were carried forward from IAS 27 to IFRS 10 without being reconsidered by the Board. Consequently, the Board did not reconsider the requirements in those paragraphs. In addition, the requirements in paragraph 22 relate to disclosures about the application of the equity method and restrictions on the ability of joint ventures and associates to transfer funds to the reporting entity. The Board did not reconsider the equity method as part of its joint ventures project. Consequently, and with the exception of its decision to align the requirements for joint ventures and associates as stated in paragraph BC6, the requirements in paragraph 22 were carried forward from IAS 28 without being reconsidered by the Board. Accordingly, when the Board approved IFRS 12 for issue, it brought forward from IAS 27 and IAS 28 without reconsideration the requirements now in paragraphs 11, 18, 19 and 22 of IFRS 12.

BC12   When revised in 2003, IAS 27 was accompanied by a Basis for Conclusions summarising the considerations of the Board, as constituted at the time, in reaching some of its conclusions in that standard. The Basis for Conclusions was subsequently updated to reflect amendments to the standard. For convenience, the Board has incorporated into its Basis for Conclusions on IFRS 12 material from the Basis for Conclusions on IAS 27 that discusses the requirements in paragraphs 18 and 19 that the Board has not reconsidered. That material is contained in paragraphs BC37–BC41. In those paragraphs cross-references to the IFRS have been updated accordingly and minor necessary editorial changes have been made.

BC13   As part of its consolidation project, the Board is examining how an investment entity accounts for its interests in subsidiaries, joint ventures and associates and what, if any, additional disclosures might be made about those interests. The Board expects to publish later in 2011 an exposure draft on investment entities.[1]

Significant judgements and assumptions

BC14   The assessment of whether an entity controls another entity sometimes requires judgement. Paragraph 122 of IAS 1 *Presentation of Financial Statements* requires an entity to disclose the judgements that management has made in the process of applying the entity's accounting policies and that have the most significant effect on the amounts recognised in the financial statements.

---

1 *Investment Entities* (Amendments to IFRS 10, IFRS 12 and IAS 27), issued in October 2012, introduced an exception to the principle that all subsidiaries shall be consolidated. The amendments define an investment entity and require a parent that is an investment entity to measure its investments in particular subsidiaries at fair value through profit or loss instead of consolidating those subsidiaries. In addition, the amendments introduce new disclosure requirements related to investment entities in IFRS 12 *Disclosure of Interests in Other Entities* and IAS 27 *Separate Financial Statements*. The amendments are discussed in paragraphs BC215–BC317 of IFRS 10 *Consolidated Financial Statements*, and the disclosure requirements are discussed in paragraphs BC61A–BC61H of this IFRS.

BC15   IAS 27 and IAS 28 supplemented the general disclosure requirement in IAS 1 with more specific requirements relating to an entity's decision about whether it controls or has significant influence over another entity. Those standards required disclosure of information when an entity's control or significant influence assessment was different from the presumptions of control or significant influence in IAS 27 and IAS 28 (ie more than 50 per cent voting power for control and 20 per cent or more voting power for significant influence).

BC16   The Board decided to replace the specific disclosure requirements in IAS 27 and IAS 28 with a principle that an entity must disclose all significant judgements and assumptions made in determining the nature of its interest in another entity or arrangement, and in determining the type of joint arrangement in which it has an interest. Moreover, the requirement for such disclosures should not be limited to particular scenarios. Instead, disclosure should be required for all situations in which an entity applies significant judgement in assessing the nature of its interest in another entity. The disclosure requirements formerly in IAS 27 and IAS 28 in this respect were included as examples of situations for which significant judgement might need to be applied.

BC17   ED 10 proposed that, for two particular scenarios for which the control assessment was different, an entity should provide information, in aggregate, that would help users evaluate the accounting consequences of the decision to consolidate another entity.

BC18   Most users supported the proposal. However, other respondents to ED 10 expressed the view that disclosing such quantitative information about the accounting consequences was a step too far. They were concerned that such a disclosure would encourage 'second-guessing' by users of financial statements and, therefore, replace the judgement made by management with that made by users of financial statements.

BC19   The Board acknowledged those concerns, but observed that consideration of different scenarios is common practice when analysing financial statements and does not necessarily mean that the judgement of management is replaced with that of other parties. However, the Board noted that IFRS 3 *Business Combinations* requires an entity to disclose information that enables users of financial statements to evaluate the nature and financial effect of a business combination—ie when an entity obtains control of another business or businesses. Furthermore, if an entity's assessment that it does not control another entity requires significant judgement, the entity will often conclude that it has either joint control of or significant influence over that other entity. The Board observed that IFRS 12 will require an entity to disclose quantitative information about its interests in joint ventures and associates, and information about its exposure to risk from its interests in unconsolidated structured entities. Therefore, the Board concluded that there was no need for a separate requirement to disclose quantitative information to help assess the accounting consequences of an entity's decision to consolidate (or not to consolidate) another entity.

Interests in subsidiaries

BC20   IFRS 12 requires an entity to disclose information that enables users of financial statements

  (a)   to understand:

    (i)   the composition of the group; and

    (ii)   the interest that non-controlling interests have in the group's activities and cash flows; and

  (b)   to evaluate:

    (i)   the nature and the effect of significant restrictions on its ability to access and use assets of the group, and settle liabilities of the group;

    (ii)   the nature of, and changes in, the risks associated with its interests in consolidated structured entities;

    (iii)   the consequences of changes in the parent's ownership interest in a subsidiary that do not result in a loss of control; and

    (iv)   the consequences of losing control of a subsidiary during the reporting period.

Composition of the group and non-controlling interests

BC21   Consolidated financial statements present the financial position, comprehensive income and cash flows of the group as a single entity. They ignore the legal boundaries of the parent and its subsidiaries. However, those legal boundaries could affect the parent's access to and use of assets and other resources of its subsidiaries and, therefore, affect the cash flows that can be distributed to the shareholders of the parent.

BC22   When the Board was developing IFRS 12, users informed the Board that, as part of their analysis of financial statements, they need to identify profit or loss and cash flows attributable to the shareholders of the parent and those attributable to non-controlling interests.

BC23   IAS 1 provides some of the information necessary to perform the valuations by requiring an entity to present:

  (a)   in the statement of financial position, the non-controlling interest within equity;

  (b)   in the statement of comprehensive income, profit or loss and total comprehensive income for the period attributable to the non-controlling interest; and

  (c)   in the statement of changes in equity, a reconciliation between the non-controlling interest at the beginning of the period and the end of the period.

BC24   Although confirming that the presentation requirements in IAS 1 provide important information, users of financial statements requested additional information to enable them to make better estimates of future profit or loss and cash flows attributable to the shareholders of the parent. The Board was advised that, in particular, an analyst requires information about the non-controlling interests' share of the profit or loss, cash flows and net assets of subsidiaries with material non-controlling interests.

BC25   Those users of financial statements also requested specific disclosure requirements in this respect, rather than simply a disclosure objective as was proposed in ED 10. In their view, only specific disclosure requirements would enhance their ability to estimate the profit or loss and cash flows attributable to the ordinary shareholders of the parent and provide comparable information for different entities. Users specifically requested additional financial information about consolidated entities.

BC26   The Board was convinced by those comments and decided to require an entity to provide the following information for each subsidiary that has non-controlling interests that are material to the group:

    (a)   *the name of the subsidiary*, because naming subsidiaries that have non-controlling interests that are material to the group helps users search for other information that might be useful for their analysis of the subsidiary.

    (b)   *the principal place of business (and country of incorporation, if different)*, because this helps users understand the political, economic and currency risks associated with those subsidiaries and the laws with which those subsidiaries must comply.

    (c)   *the proportion of ownership interests held by non-controlling interests; if different, the proportion of voting rights held by non-controlling interests; profit or loss allocated to non-controlling interests and accumulated non-controlling interests at the end of the reporting period*, because this information helps users understand the profit or loss and cash flows attributable to the shareholders of the parent and the amount attributable to non-controlling interests.

    (d)   *summarised financial information for the subsidiary*, because this information helps users understand the profit or loss and cash flows attributable to the shareholders of the parent and the amount attributable to non-controlling interests.

BC27   The Board believes that the disclosures required will help users when estimating future profit or loss and cash flows by identifying, for example:

    (a)   the assets and liabilities that are held by subsidiaries;

    (b)   risk exposures of particular group entities (eg by identifying which subsidiaries hold debt); and

    (c)   those subsidiaries that generate significant cash flows.

BC28   In reaching its decision, the Board noted that users have consistently requested additional financial information about consolidated entities for many years. Although users have requested financial information about all subsidiaries that are material to the group, the Board decided to require financial information only for those subsidiaries with material non-controlling interests. A requirement to disclose information about subsidiaries with immaterial or no non-controlling interests might prove to be onerous to prepare without any significant benefit for users, who are expected to benefit most from having financial information about subsidiaries with material non-controlling interests. Summarised financial information about subsidiaries with material non-controlling interests helps users predict how future cash flows will be distributed among those with claims against the entity including the non-controlling interests.

BC29   In addition, the Board does not think that this requirement to provide information about subsidiaries with material non-controlling interests will be particularly onerous to prepare. This is because an entity should have the information available in preparing its consolidated financial statements.

Restrictions on assets and liabilities

BC30   IAS 27 required disclosures about the nature and extent of significant restrictions on the ability of subsidiaries to transfer funds to the parent. Users of financial statements noted that, in addition to legal requirements, the existence of non-controlling interests in a subsidiary might restrict the subsidiary's ability to transfer funds to the parent or any of its other subsidiaries. However, the disclosure requirement in IAS 27 regarding significant restrictions did not refer explicitly to non-controlling interests.

BC31   Accordingly, the Board decided to amend the requirement in IAS 27 to disclose restrictions in order to clarify that the information disclosed should include the nature and extent to which protective rights of non-controlling interests can restrict the entity's ability to access and use the assets and settle the liabilities of a subsidiary.

BC32   In response to concerns raised by respondents to ED 10 about the extent of the disclosure requirement, the Board decided to limit the disclosures to information about the nature and effect of *significant* restrictions on an entity's ability to access and use assets or settle liabilities of the group. In reaching that decision, the Board confirmed that the proposal was never intended to require an entity to disclose, for example, a list of all the protective rights held by non-controlling interests that are embedded in law and regulation.

BC33   The Board also confirmed that the restrictions required to be disclosed by IFRS 12 are those that exist because of the legal boundaries within the group, such as restrictions on transferring cash between group entities. The requirement in IFRS 12 is not intended to replicate those in other IFRSs relating to restrictions, such as those in IAS 16 *Property, Plant and Equipment* or IAS 40 *Investment Property*.

Risks associated with an entity's interests in consolidated structured entities

BC34   An entity can be exposed to risks from both consolidated and unconsolidated structured entities. The Board concluded that it would help users of financial statements in understanding an entity's exposure to risks if the entity disclosed the terms of contractual arrangements that could require it to provide financial support to a consolidated structured entity, including events or circumstances that could expose the entity to a loss.

BC35   The Board concluded for the same reason that an entity should disclose its risk exposure from non-contractual obligations to provide support to both consolidated and unconsolidated structured entities (see paragraphs BC102–BC106).

BC36   The Board noted that US generally accepted accounting principles (GAAP) require similar disclosures, which have been well received by users of financial statements in the US.

Changes in ownership interests in subsidiaries

BC37   In its deliberations in the second phase of the business combinations project, the US Financial Accounting Standards Board (FASB) decided to require entities with one or more partially-owned subsidiaries to disclose in the notes to the consolidated financial statements a schedule showing the effects on the controlling interest's equity of changes in a parent's ownership interest in a subsidiary that do not result in a loss of control.

BC38   In the exposure draft proposing amendments to IAS 27 published in 2005, the Board did not propose to require this disclosure. The Board noted that IFRSs require this information to be provided in the statement of changes in equity or in the notes to the financial statements. This is because IAS 1 requires an entity to present, within the statement of changes in equity, a reconciliation between the carrying amount of each component of equity at the beginning and end of the period, disclosing separately each change.

BC39   Many respondents to the 2005 exposure draft requested more prominent disclosure of the effects of transactions with non-controlling interests on the equity of the owners of the parent. Therefore, the Board decided to converge with the FASB's disclosure requirement and to require that if a parent has equity transactions with non-controlling interests, it should disclose in a separate schedule the effects of those transactions on the equity of the owners of the parent.

BC40   The Board understands that some users will be interested in information pertaining only to the owners of the parent. The Board expected that the presentation and disclosure requirements of IAS 27, as amended in 2008, would meet their information needs. (These presentation and disclosure requirements are now included in IFRS 12.)

Loss of control

BC41   The Board decided that the amount of any gain or loss arising on the loss of control of a subsidiary, including the portion of the gain or loss attributable to recognising any investment retained in the former subsidiary at its fair value at the date when control is lost, and the line item in the statement of comprehensive income in which the gains or losses are recognised should be disclosed. This disclosure requirement, which took effect from 1 July 2009, provides information about the effect of the loss of control of a subsidiary on the financial position at the end of, and performance for, the reporting period.

Interests in joint arrangements and associates

BC42   The Board proposed in ED 9 to align the disclosure requirements for joint ventures and associates by proposing consequential amendments to IAS 28 and by extending the application of some disclosure requirements in IAS 28 to investments in joint ventures.

BC43   During its consideration of responses to ED 9, the Board questioned whether it was possible to achieve further alignment between the disclosure requirements for joint ventures and associates, to the extent that the nature of the particular type of interest does not justify different disclosure requirements. Although joint control is different from significant influence, the Board concluded that the disclosure requirements for joint arrangements and associates could share a common disclosure objective – to disclose information that enables users of financial statements to evaluate the nature, extent and financial effects of an entity's interests in joint arrangements and associates, and the nature of the risks associated with those interests.

Nature, extent and financial effects of interests in joint arrangements and associates

BC44   In response to requests from users of financial statements, the Board proposed in ED 9 that an entity should disclose a list and description of investments in significant joint ventures and associates. Respondents to ED 9 generally welcomed the proposal. The Board decided to carry the proposals forward into IFRS 12 with some modifications as described in paragraphs BC45 and BC46.

BC45   The Board decided to require the information for joint arrangements and associates that are material to the reporting entity rather than for significant joint arrangements and associates. The *Conceptual Framework for Financial Reporting (Conceptual Framework)*[2] defines materiality whereas the term 'significant' is undefined and can be interpreted differently. Consequently, the Board decided to replace 'significant' with 'material', which is also used in IFRS 3. The Board noted that materiality should be assessed in relation to an entity's consolidated financial statements or other primary financial statements in which joint ventures and associates are accounted for using the equity method.

---

2   References to the *Conceptual Framework* in this Basis for Conclusions are to the *Conceptual Framework for Financial Reporting*, issued in 2010 and in effect when the Standard was developed.

BC46   In addition, the Board noted that ED 9 unintentionally changed the application of the requirement in IAS 31 to provide a description of interests in all joint arrangements to interests in joint ventures only. As such, the Board modified the requirement so that it would continue to be required for all joint arrangements that are material to an entity.

Summarised financial information

BC47   IAS 28 and IAS 31 required disclosure of aggregated summarised financial information relating to joint ventures and associates. In response to requests from users of financial statements, ED 9 proposed to expand the requirements so that summarised financial information would be provided for each joint venture that is material to an entity.

BC48   Respondents to ED 9 generally agreed that summarised financial information should be provided. Some had concerns about confidentiality when providing summarised financial information on an individual basis for some joint ventures that were established to implement a single project. Others, including users of financial statements, were concerned that the elimination of proportionate consolidation would result in a loss of information. They therefore requested more detailed disclosures so that the effect of joint ventures on the activities of an entity could be better understood. They stated that there was a need for a detailed breakdown of current assets and current and non-current liabilities (in particular, cash and financial liabilities excluding trade payables and provisions), which would help users understand the net debt position of joint ventures. These users also highlighted the need for a more detailed breakdown of amounts presented in the statement of comprehensive income (such as depreciation and amortisation) that would help when valuing an entity's investment in a joint venture.

BC49   ED 9 proposed that an entity should present summarised financial information for each material joint venture on the basis of its proportionate interest in the joint venture. The Board reconsidered the proposal, noting that it would be confusing to present the entity's share of the assets, liabilities and revenue of a joint venture or associate when the entity has neither rights to, nor obligations for, the assets and liabilities of the joint venture or associate. Rather, the entity has an interest in the net assets of the joint ventures or associates. Consequently, the Board concluded that an entity should present the summarised financial information for each material joint venture on a '100 per cent' basis, and reconcile that to the carrying amount of its investment in the joint venture or associate.

BC50   The Board observed that the requirement to present the amounts on a '100 per cent' basis would be appropriate only when the information is disclosed for individual joint ventures and associates. This is because presenting the financial information on a '100 per cent' basis when aggregating that information for all joint ventures or associates would not result in useful information when the entity holds different percentage ownership interests in its joint ventures or associates. In addition, some users and respondents to ED 9 recommended that the disclosures for associates should be aligned with those for joint ventures because investments in associates can be material and are often strategic to an investor with significant influence. Accordingly, the Board decided that summarised financial information should also be provided for each material associate.

BC51 Nonetheless, the minimum line item disclosures required for each material associate would be less than those required for each material joint venture. The Board noted that an entity is generally more involved with joint ventures than with associates because joint control means that the entity has a right of veto over decisions relating to the relevant activities of the joint venture. Accordingly, the different nature of the relationship between a joint venturer and its joint ventures from that between an investor and its associates warrants a different level of detail in the disclosures of summarised financial information.

BC52 The Board also considered the views of some users who suggested that summarised financial information should be required for joint operations. Assets and liabilities arising from joint operations are an entity's assets and liabilities and consequently are recognised in the entity's financial statements. Those assets and liabilities would be accounted for in accordance with the requirements of applicable IFRSs, and would be subject to the relevant disclosure requirements of those IFRSs. Therefore the Board concluded that entities should not be required to provide summarised financial information separately for joint operations.

Commitments

BC53 ED 9 proposed that an entity should disclose any capital commitments that it has relating to its interests in joint arrangements. IAS 31 had similar requirements.

BC54 When discussing responses to ED 9, the Board examined two aspects of the proposals. The first was whether an entity should separately disclose commitments relating to all types of joint arrangements. The second was the need to maintain the adjective 'capital' when referring to commitments.

BC55 In response to concerns raised by respondents to ED 9, the Board reconsidered the proposals to disclose commitments for all types of joint arrangements. Respondents said that disclosure of commitments relating to joint operations would be of limited value because such commitments would be included within the disclosures of the entity itself. The Board was convinced by those reasons and decided not to require separate disclosure of commitments relating to an entity's interests in joint operations.

BC56 Regarding the nature of the commitments to be disclosed, the Board noted that 'capital commitment' is not a defined term in IFRSs. Consequently, 'capital' could potentially be interpreted to restrict the disclosures only to those commitments that would result in the capitalisation of assets. Instead, the Board concluded that the objective of the disclosure requirement was to provide information about all unrecognised commitments that could result in future operating, investing or financing cash outflows, or in any other type of outflow of resources from the entity in relation to its interests in joint ventures. Consequently, the Board decided to remove 'capital' from the requirement to disclose commitments.

Contingent liabilities

BC57 ED 9 carried forward the requirement in IAS 31 regarding contingent liabilities and proposed that an entity should separately disclose contingent liabilities relating to its interests in joint arrangements. The Board reconsidered that proposal in response to concerns raised by respondents to ED 9 who stated that separate disclosure of contingent liabilities relating to joint operations would be of limited value for the reasons noted in paragraph BC55.

BC58 The Board was again convinced by those reasons and, accordingly, decided not to require separate disclosure of contingent liabilities relating to an entity's interests in joint operations.

Disclosure requirements for venture capital organisations, mutual funds, unit trusts or similar entities that have an interest in a joint venture or associate

BC59 IAS 28 and IAS 31 established specific disclosure requirements for an entity that had investments in joint ventures or associates when the entity is a venture capital organisation, mutual fund, unit trust or similar entity, including investment-linked insurance funds. The Board discussed whether IFRS 12 should retain the specific disclosure requirements for those types of entities, or whether the disclosure requirements should be the same for all types of entities with interests in joint ventures or associates.

BC60 With the exception of those disclosures that are required only when using the equity method, the Board concluded that the disclosure requirements for interests in joint ventures and associates should be the same for all entities, regardless of whether those entities are venture capital organisations, mutual funds, unit trusts or similar entities. This decision is consistent with the Board's decision to remove the scope exclusion in IAS 28 and IAS 31 for those entities. The Board decided that such entities that hold interests in joint ventures and associates should not be excluded from the relevant standards. Rather, they are simply permitted to use a different measurement basis (ie fair value) for their investments.

Fair value of investments in joint ventures for which there are published price quotations

BC61 IAS 28 required an entity to disclose the fair value of investments in associates for which published price quotations were available. Such quotations might also be available for joint ventures. Consequently, the Board decided to align this disclosure requirement by requiring an entity to disclose the fair value of investments in joint ventures for which there are published price quotations.

Investment entities

BC61A   *Investment Entities* (Amendments to IFRS 10, IFRS 12 and IAS 27) introduced a requirement for investment entities to measure their investments in particular subsidiaries at fair value through profit or loss instead of consolidating them. The Board also decided on specific disclosure requirements for investment entities.

BC61B   In deciding on the appropriate disclosure requirements for investment entities, the Board noted that investment entities would be required to make the disclosures already contained in other Standards. In particular, the disclosure requirements in IFRS 7 *Financial Instruments: Disclosures*, IFRS 13 *Fair Value Measurement* and IAS 24 *Related Party Disclosures* are likely to be relevant for users of investment entity financial statements.

BC61C   Users told the Board that disclosures relating to the valuation methodology used for measuring fair value and the underlying inputs are essential to their analyses. This information is already required by IFRS 7 and by IFRS 13 when reporting investments at fair value through profit or loss or other comprehensive income in accordance with IFRS 9 *Financial Instruments* or IAS 39 *Financial Instruments: Recognition and Measurement*.[3] Accordingly, the Board decided that it was not necessary to propose any additional disclosure requirements relating to the fair value measurements made by investment entities.

BC61D   In the Exposure Draft *Investment Entities* (the *Investment Entities* ED), the Board proposed that an investment entity would be required to meet a disclosure objective that addressed all of an investment entity's investing activities. The *Investment Entities* ED also gave a number of examples of ways in which an investment entity could meet that disclosure objective. Respondents generally supported the disclosure guidance. However, the Board noted that it was outside the scope of the Investment Entities project to require all investment entities to provide disclosures about their investing activities. Consequently, the Board decided to remove the disclosure objective and the examples on how to meet the objective from the final requirements. Because the Investment Entities project focuses on providing an exception to consolidation, the Board decided to limit additional disclosures to information about unconsolidated subsidiaries.

BC61E   The Board also decided to require an investment entity to disclose the fact that it has applied the exception to consolidation, noting that such a disclosure would represent useful information. Moreover, the Board decided to require an investment entity to disclose when it does not display one or more of the typical characteristics of an investment entity, along with a justification of why it still meets the definition of an investment entity.

---

3   IFRS 9 *Financial Instruments* replaced IAS 39. IFRS 9 applies to all items that were previously within the scope of IAS 39.

BC61F   The Board considered whether all of the disclosures in this IFRS should apply to the investments in unconsolidated subsidiaries, associates and joint ventures of investment entities. The Board decided that some (eg summarised financial information and information about non-controlling interests) are not applicable to investment entities and are inconsistent with the assertion that fair value information is the most relevant information for investment entities. Consequently, the Board decided to specify the IFRS 12 requirements applicable to the unconsolidated subsidiaries, associates and joint ventures held by investment entities.

BC61G   Consistently with the principles in this IFRS, the Board decided to require an investment entity to disclose when any explicit or implicit financial support has been provided to entities that it controls. The Board concluded that it would help users of financial statements to understand an investment entity's exposure to risk.

BC61H   The Board decided that an investment entity should disclose the nature and extent of any significant restrictions (eg resulting from borrowing arrangements or regulatory requirements) on the ability of investees to transfer funds to the investment entity in the form of cash dividends, or repayment of loans or advances. The Board considered this requirement to be useful for investors because such restrictions could potentially affect distributions to investors of the investment entity's returns from investments.

BC61I   In December 2014, the Board issued *Investment Entities: Applying the Consolidation Exception* (Amendments to IFRS 10, IFRS 12 and IAS 28). This amended paragraph 6(b) of IFRS 12 to clarify the applicability of IFRS 12 to the financial statements of an investment entity. In June 2014, the Board published the Exposure Draft *Investment Entities: Applying the Consolidation Exception* (Proposed amendments to IFRS 10 and IAS 28) (the 'Consolidation Exception ED'). The comments received in response to the *Consolidation Exception* ED highlighted a lack of clarity about the applicability of IFRS 12 to the financial statements of an investment entity. In particular, the respondents to the *Consolidation Exception* ED pointed out that paragraph 6 of IFRS 12 stated that the Standard did not apply to an entity's separate financial statements without stating the applicability of IFRS 12 to an investment entity. The Board noted that, in contrast, paragraph 16A of IAS 27 *Separate Financial Statements* requires that an investment entity shall present the disclosures relating to investment entities required by IFRS 12. Accordingly, in response to the feedback received, the Board decided to clarify that the scope exclusion in paragraph 6(b) does not apply to the financial statements of a parent that is an investment entity and has measured all of its subsidiaries at fair value through profit or loss in accordance with paragraph 31 of IFRS 10. In such a case, the investment entity shall present the disclosures relating to investment entities required by IFRS 12. The Board also noted that if an investment entity has a subsidiary that it consolidates in accordance with paragraph 32 of IFRS 10, the disclosure requirements in IFRS 12 apply to the financial statements in which the investment entity consolidates that subsidiary.

Interests in unconsolidated structured entities

The need for the disclosure requirements

BC62   IAS 27 did not require disclosures relating to interests in unconsolidated entities. The Board was asked by users of financial statements, regulators and others (such as the G20 leaders and the Financial Stability Board) to improve the disclosure requirements for what are often described as 'off balance sheet' activities. Unconsolidated structured entities, particularly securitisation vehicles and asset-backed financings, were identified as forming part of such activities.

BC63   The Board concluded that when an entity has an interest in an unconsolidated structured entity, users of financial statements would benefit from information about the risks to which the entity is exposed from that interest. Such information is relevant in assessing the amount, timing and uncertainty of the entity's future cash flows.

BC64   As proposed in ED 10, IFRS 12 requires an entity to disclose information that enables users of financial statements to evaluate the nature of, and risks associated with, the entity's interest in unconsolidated structured entities.

BC65   Virtually all respondents to ED 10 agreed that there is a need for improved disclosures about an entity's exposure to risk from 'off balance sheet' activities. However, respondents expressed differing views on the nature and amount of information that should be disclosed. Some, including users of financial statements, supported the approach proposed in ED 10 to require disclosure of risks arising from interests in unconsolidated structured entities.

BC66   Other respondents pointed out that an entity can be exposed to the same risks from having interests in all types of entities. Therefore, they questioned why an entity should be required to provide particular information about its exposure to risk from its interests in unconsolidated structured entities, but not with other unconsolidated entities.

BC67   Some respondents were also concerned that the proposals would duplicate the risk disclosures in IFRS 7 *Financial Instruments: Disclosures*. IFRS 7 requires an entity to disclose qualitative and quantitative information about risks arising from financial instruments that the entity holds. Those respondents expressed the view that ED 10 proposed disclosures about the counterparties of financial instruments to which the disclosure requirements in IFRS 7 already apply.

BC68   In addition, some respondents disagreed with the proposals because they suspected that the Board had included the proposed disclosures as a 'safety net' because it was concerned that some structured entities might fail the consolidation criteria in ED 10, even though, in their view, consolidation would be appropriate.

BC69   When deliberating the responses to ED 10, the Board agreed with those respondents who emphasised that disclosures about unconsolidated structured entities cannot replace robust consolidation requirements. The disclosures proposed were never intended to compensate for weaknesses in the control definition. IFRS 10 documents the Board's determination to develop appropriate and robust consolidation criteria. Rather, the disclosure proposals were intended to complement the consolidation criteria, focusing on an entity's exposure to risk from interests in structured entities that the entity rightly does not consolidate because it does not control them.

BC70 The Board acknowledged that the same types of risks that the disclosure proposals in ED 10 were intended to capture can arise from an entity's interests in other types of entities and that it may be appropriate to develop risk disclosures that apply to an entity's interests in all types of unconsolidated entities. However, the Board noted that when it proposed the disclosure requirements in ED 10, it intended to provide a timely response to particular information needs identified during the global financial crisis that started in 2007. More specifically, users and regulators had expressed concerns about the lack of disclosure relating to investment and securitisation activities that an entity conducts through structured entities. They asked the Board to introduce specific risk disclosures for an entity's interests in unconsolidated structured entities because those particular interests had exposed entities to significant risks in the past. The proposed disclosure requirements in ED 10 were intended to meet those requests. To go beyond structured entities would delay addressing the concerns raised, which would not be beneficial to users.

BC71 The Board also noted that addressing disclosures for interests in unconsolidated structured entities would be an opportunity to align the disclosure requirements in IFRSs and US GAAP in this respect.

BC72 Regarding IFRS 7, the Board agreed with respondents that both requirements will often result in disclosure of the same underlying risks. What is different is how the disclosure requirements describe an entity's risk exposure. IFRS 7 requires qualitative and quantitative disclosures about the credit, liquidity, market and other risks associated with financial instruments. IFRS 12 adopts a different perspective and requires an entity to disclose its exposure to risk from its interest in a structured entity.

BC73 The Board believes that information from both perspectives assists users of financial statements in their analysis of an entity's exposure to risk – the disclosures in IFRS 7 by identifying those financial instruments that create risk, and the disclosures in IFRS 12 by providing, when relevant, information about:

(a) the extent of an entity's transactions with structured entities;

(b) concentrations of risk that arise from the nature of the entities with which the entity has transactions; and

(c) particular transactions that expose the entity to risk.

BC74 Accordingly, the Board concluded that although the disclosures in IFRS 7 and IFRS 12 regarding unconsolidated structured entities might overlap to some extent, they complement each other.

BC75   The Board was also persuaded by information received from users of financial statements in the US, who had been using the disclosures required by US GAAP for variable interest entities in their analysis. Those users confirmed that the new disclosures provided them with information that was not previously available to them, but which they regarded as important for a thorough understanding of an entity's exposure to risk.

BC76   Many of those users referred also to the global financial crisis and emphasised that a better understanding of an entity's interests in unconsolidated structured entities might have helped to identify earlier the extent of risks to which entities were exposed. Accordingly, those users stated that the new disclosures had significantly improved the quality of financial reporting and strongly encouraged the Board to require similar disclosures for IFRS preparers.

BC77   The Board considered whether an entity should be required to disclose the information for interests in unconsolidated structured entities as well as for interests in joint ventures or associates if a joint venture or an associate meets the definition of a structured entity. The Board concluded that an entity should provide information that meets both sets of disclosure requirements if it has interests in joint ventures or associates that are structured entities. In reaching this conclusion, the Board noted that an entity should capture most, and in some cases all, of the disclosures required for interests in unconsolidated structured entities by providing the disclosures for interests in joint ventures and associates. Accordingly, the Board does not think that this conclusion should significantly increase the amount of information that an entity would be required to provide.

The scope of the risk disclosures

Interests in unconsolidated structured entities

BC78   In response to concerns raised by respondents to ED 10 about the scope of the risk disclosures, the Board considered whether it should try to define 'interests in' more narrowly, for example, by stating that an entity would be required to disclose information only about interests that give rise to exposure to loss beyond amounts recognised in its financial statements. However, the Board concluded that any such attempt to narrow the definition of 'interests in' would complicate the guidance and would probably exclude disclosure of information that users would find useful.

BC79   The Board also considered whether to require disclosure of significant interests in structured entities — some respondents to ED 10 had suggested clarifying that an entity would not be required to disclose information about insignificant interests with structured entities. The Board decided against adding 'significant' for a number of reasons. First, the Board noted that because the concept of materiality underpins the disclosure requirements in IFRS 12 as it does in all other IFRSs, an entity would be required to disclose only information that is material as defined and described in the *Conceptual Framework*. The Board also noted that the term 'significant' is not defined in IFRSs. Comments received on other projects suggest that 'significant' is interpreted in different ways. The Board concluded that, without defining the term, adding 'significant' would be of no benefit to those using IFRS 12 to prepare or audit financial statements.

BC80 The Board decided to retain the wider definition of 'interest in' (ie an entity's involvement with another entity, whether contractual or non-contractual, that exposes the entity to variability of returns from the performance of the other entity). The Board was convinced by comments received from US preparers, auditors and users about their experience with the US GAAP requirements to disclose information about involvement with variable interest entities. Involvement is not defined by US GAAP but is interpreted in a way similar to how 'interest in' is defined in IFRS 12. US preparers and users generally agreed with the scope of the disclosure requirements—US users of financial statements thought that the revised disclosure requirements provided them with an appropriate degree of detail; US preparers and accountants thought that the disclosure requirements allow entities to focus on presenting information that is considered relevant for users of financial statements. US preparers and accountants also noted that both the aggregation guidance and the requirement that an entity should determine, in the light of facts and circumstances, how much detail it must give to satisfy the disclosure requirements provide sufficient flexibility for preparers.

BC81 Consequently, the Board decided to include in IFRS 12 the requirement to consider the level of detail necessary to meet the disclosure objectives and to include aggregation principles and guidance to assist preparers when determining what level of detail is appropriate.

The definition of a structured entity

BC82 IFRS 12 introduces the term 'structured entity'. The type of entity the Board envisages being characterised as a structured entity is unlikely to differ significantly from an entity that SIC-12 *Consolidation—Special Purpose Entities* described as a special purpose entity (SPE). SIC-12 described an SPE as an entity created to accomplish a narrow and well-defined objective, listing as examples entities established to effect a lease, research and development activities or a securitisation of financial assets.

BC83 The Board considered whether to define a structured entity in a way similar to a variable interest entity (VIE) in US GAAP. US GAAP defines a VIE, in essence, as an entity whose activities are not directed through voting or similar rights. In addition, the total equity at risk in a VIE is not sufficient to permit the entity to finance its activities without additional subordinated financial support. US GAAP contains extensive application guidance to help determine the sufficiency of the equity, including a 10 per cent equity threshold that is generally used to determine whether an entity's equity is sufficient. The Board decided against this approach because it would introduce complicated guidance solely for disclosure purposes that was not previously in IFRSs.

BC84 The Board therefore decided to define a structured entity as an entity that has been designed so that voting rights are not the dominant factor in deciding who controls the entity. The Board also decided to include guidance similar to that included in SIC-12 to reflect the Board's intention that the term 'structured entity' should capture a set of entities similar to SPEs in SIC-12. The Board also decided to incorporate some of the attributes of a VIE included in US GAAP. In particular, a structured entity is an entity whose equity is often not sufficient to permit the entity to finance its activities without additional subordinated financial support. The Board reasoned that users had requested risk disclosures relating to structured entities because being involved with such entities inherently exposes an entity to more risk than being involved with traditional operating entities. The increased risk exposure arises because, for example, the entity has restricted activities, is created to pass risks and returns arising from specified assets to investors, or there is insufficient equity to fund losses on the assets, if they arise.

BC85   The definition does not state that if an entity has insufficient equity at risk, it would always be deemed to be a structured entity. There are two reasons for this. The first is that such a definition would require extensive application guidance to help determine the sufficiency of the equity, similar to US GAAP, to which the Board was opposed for the reasons noted in paragraph BC83. The second is that the Board feared that some traditional operating entities might be caught by such a definition when it had no intention of doing so. For example, a traditional operating entity whose financing had been restructured following a downturn in activities might be deemed to be a structured entity, which was not what the Board intended.

Nature of interest

BC86   IFRS 12 requires an entity to disclose information that enables users of financial statements to understand the nature of, and changes in, the risks associated with its interests in structured entities (see paragraphs BC92–BC114). As a consequence, an entity would be required to provide disclosures about its exposure to risk when it has sponsored an unconsolidated structured entity and has retained an interest in the structured entity, for example by holding debt or equity instruments of the structured entity.

BC87   However, that decision would not require an entity to provide disclosures if the entity does not retain any interest in the structured entity through explicit or implicit involvement. The Board received views from many constituents who reasoned that sponsoring a structured entity can create risks for an entity, even though the entity might not retain any interest in the structured entity. If the structured entity encounters difficulties, it is possible that the sponsor could be challenged on its advice or actions, or might choose to act to protect its reputation.

BC88   IFRS 12 also requires disclosure regarding the provision of financial and other support to a structured entity when there is no contractual obligation to do so and about any current intentions to provide financial support or other assistance in the future (see paragraphs BC102–BC106). Although helpful, the disclosure provides an incomplete picture of an entity's exposure to risk from its sponsoring activities because:

(a)   the disclosure requirement applies only when the entity has provided, or intends to provide, financial support to a structured entity.

(b)   an entity's exposure to risk from its sponsoring activities is broader than the risk to provide implicit support to the structured entity. For example, an entity that does not intend to provide any implicit support might be exposed to litigation risk from sponsoring a failed structured entity.

(c)   there is currently no other disclosure requirement that would inform users of financial statements about an entity's risk exposure from its sponsoring activities. For example, the disclosure requirements in IFRS 7 do not result in such information because there is usually no financial instrument associated with the sponsorship that would trigger the disclosures. The disclosure requirements relating to transfers of financial assets apply only if an entity has transferred its own financial assets to the structured entities that it sponsors. In addition, an unconsolidated structured entity is unlikely to meet the definition of a related party in IAS 24 *Related Party Disclosures*.

BC89   Users said that it would be useful to have information about the scale of an entity's operations that is derived from transactions with unconsolidated structured entities, ie to have more information about an entity's business model and the risks associated with that business model. This would be particularly useful to help understand the likely effect on the performance of an entity attributable to either a loss of income or a restriction on the entity's ability to carry out its usual business activities if there were a significant decrease in the use of structured entities for investing or financing purposes. They noted that during the global financial crisis that started in 2007 investors became concerned about the extent to which entities had been involved with structured investment vehicles. However, few entities disclosed information about the extent of their involvement in establishing such vehicles. It was, therefore, difficult to assess the potential exposure an entity might have. Those users also confirmed that their request for such information precedes the global financial crisis, and is not simply a reaction to it.

BC90   In response to requests from users and others, the Board decided to require an entity to disclose income derived from, and asset information about, structured entities that the entity has sponsored. The Board noted that the requirements are not intended to help assess the actual risk of failure or recourse to an entity. Rather, they would give a sense of the scale of the operations an entity had managed with these types of transactions and the extent of the entity's reliance on such entities to facilitate its business. For this reason, the Board concluded that the asset information disclosed should refer not only to assets transferred by the sponsor but to all assets transferred to the structured entity during the reporting period. The information provided would be a signpost that would enable users to identify when to ask for further information.

BC91   Because an entity is required to disclose information about its exposure to risk when it retains an interest in an unconsolidated structured entity, the Board decided that the requirement to disclose income and asset information when acting as a sponsor should be required only when an entity has not provided disclosures about the nature of its risks from that interest in the unconsolidated structured entity.

Nature of risks

BC92   ED 10 proposed that an entity should disclose information to help users of financial statements evaluate the nature and extent of the entity's risk from its interests in unconsolidated structured entities. To support that objective, the exposure draft proposed that an entity should disclose the carrying amounts of its assets and liabilities relating to its interests in structured entities, its maximum exposure to loss and the reported amount of assets of structured entities. ED 10 also listed other information (such as information about the assets and funding of structured entities) that might be useful to an assessment of the risks to which an entity is exposed.

BC93   Users generally supported the disclosures proposed. However, other respondents to ED 10, although agreeing that risk disclosures were required, thought that the proposed disclosure requirements were too prescriptive. In their view, an entity should be allowed to disclose its risk exposure on the basis of the information generated by its internal risk reporting system rather than on the basis of the information proposed in ED 10.

BC94   Although agreeing with respondents that an entity should generally be allowed to tailor its disclosures to meet the specific information needs of its users, the Board decided that the disclosure requirements should contain a minimum set of requirements that should be applied by all entities. The Board was convinced by comments from users who pointed out that without any specific disclosure requirements, comparability would be impaired and an entity might not disclose information that users find important.

BC95   Users of financial statements confirmed that information about an entity's exposure to loss from its interests in unconsolidated structured entities and supplementary information about the financial position of both the entity and the structured entity is relevant to their analysis of financial statements.

The assets of structured entities

BC96   The Board was persuaded by the views of respondents who argued that disclosure of assets held by structured entities without information about the funding of the assets is of limited use, and could be difficult to interpret. Therefore, the Board decided to require an entity to disclose information about the nature, purpose, size and activities of a structured entity and how the structured entity is financed. The Board concluded that this requirement should provide users with sufficient information about the assets held by structured entities and the funding of those assets, without requiring specific disclosure of the assets of unconsolidated structured entities in which the entity has an interest in all circumstances. If relevant to an assessment of its exposure to risk, an entity would be required to provide additional information about the assets and funding of structured entities.

Exposure to loss

BC97 The Board acknowledged that, sometimes, information about an entity's expected losses might be more relevant than information about its maximum exposure to loss and that the disclosure of either amount would require the application of judgement. However, if IFRS 12 required the disclosure of expected losses only, the Board was concerned that an entity might often identify a positive expected value of returns from its interests in unconsolidated structured entities and, as a consequence, would not disclose any loss exposure. Accordingly, the Board retained the requirement to disclose an entity's maximum exposure to loss from interests in unconsolidated structured entities.

BC98 The Board decided not to provide a definition of what represents a loss but to leave it to an entity to identify what constitutes a loss in the particular context of that reporting entity. The entity should then disclose how it has determined its maximum loss exposure.

BC99 The Board acknowledged that it may not always be possible to calculate the maximum exposure to loss, such as when a financial instrument exposes an entity to theoretically unlimited losses. The Board decided that when this is the case an entity should disclose the reasons why it is not possible to calculate its maximum exposure to loss.

BC100 Lastly, the Board decided to require an entity to disclose a comparison of the carrying amounts of the assets and liabilities in its statement of financial position and its maximum exposure to loss. This is because the information will provide users with a better understanding of the differences between the maximum loss exposure and the expectation of whether it is likely that an entity will bear all or only some of those losses. In the past, maximum exposure to loss information (when it was provided) was often accompanied by a statement that the information did not in any way represent the losses to be incurred. The Board reasoned that this disclosure requirement should help an entity explain why the maximum exposure to loss is unrepresentative of its actual exposure if that is the case.

BC101 The Board also noted that the disclosures required regarding an entity's exposure to loss mirror those required by US GAAP, which have been well received by users of financial statements in the US.

Providing financial support without having an obligation to do so

BC102 ED 10 proposed requiring the disclosure of support that an entity has provided to unconsolidated structured entities without having a contractual obligation to do so.

BC103   Most respondents to ED 10 agreed with the proposed disclosures, noting that an entity's past actions may be an important factor in considering the substance of its relationship with structured entities. Some, however, questioned the proposal to disclose any current intentions to provide support to a structured entity and questioned how to interpret 'support'.

BC104   The Board agreed with those respondents who thought that it would be unreasonable to expect an entity to include forward-looking disclosures about a decision that might be made in the future. However, the Board concluded that IFRS 12 should retain the requirement to disclose any current intentions to provide non-contractual financial or other support because if an entity has decided that it will provide support (ie it has current intentions to do so), this should be disclosed.

BC105   The Board decided not to define 'support' because a definition of support would either be so broad that it would be an ineffective definition or invite structuring so as to avoid the disclosure. The Board believes that financial support is widely understood as a provision of resources to another entity, either directly or indirectly. In the case of implicit arrangements, the support is provided without having the contractual obligation to do so. Nonetheless, the Board decided to include some examples of financial support in IFRS 12. In order to address respondents' concerns about distinguishing this provision of financial support from any other commercial transaction, the Board clarified that the disclosure is required when an entity has provided non-contractual support to an unconsolidated structured entity in which it previously had or currently has an interest.

BC106   The Board also decided to extend the requirement to support provided to both consolidated and unconsolidated structured entities. US GAAP includes this requirement and users confirmed that they find the disclosure of such information useful.

Risks arising from previous involvement with unconsolidated structured entities

BC107   The actions of some entities during the global financial crisis that started in 2007 demonstrated that an entity can have exposure to risk from involvement with a structured entity, even though it may not control or have any contractual involvement with that entity at the reporting date. For example, failure of a structured entity might damage an entity's reputation, compelling the entity to provide support to the structured entity in order to protect its reputation, even though the entity has no legal or contractual requirement to do so.

BC108   The Board considered how best to address requests to improve the disclosure requirements in this area. The difficulty faced by the Board was to determine which disclosures might help assess an entity's exposure to reputational risk in advance of a financial crisis happening.

BC109　　The Board considered asking for five-year historical information about the assets transferred to unconsolidated structured entities that the reporting entity had sponsored. However, the Board concluded that historical information beyond that required by paragraph 27 of the IFRS would not necessarily provide any useful information about the risks to which a sponsor is currently exposed. Information at the reporting date about total assets of unconsolidated structured entities that an entity had sponsored might be useful. However, this information would be difficult, if not impossible, for entities to provide because the entity does not control, or have an interest in, the structured entity at the reporting date. The Board also considered whether to ask for additional information when a particular triggering event occurred (for example, when a structured entity holds troubled assets). However, again, the Board rejected such an approach. Requiring additional disclosures only when the triggering event happens would probably yield information that was too late to be useful.

BC110　　The Board decided that the objective in this respect is that an entity should provide information about its exposure to risk associated with its interests in structured entities, regardless of whether that risk arises from having an existing interest in the entity or from being involved with the entity in previous periods. Therefore the Board decided to define 'an interest in an entity' as contractual or non-contractual involvement that exposes the entity to variability of returns. In addition, the Board decided to state explicitly that the disclosures about an entity's exposure to risk should include risk that arises from previous involvement with a structured entity even if an entity no longer has any contractual involvement with the structured entity at the end of the reporting period.

Additional information that might be relevant to an assessment of risk

BC111　　When the Board included a list of other information that might be relevant to an assessment of risk in ED 10, it did not intend each item in the list of proposed supplemental disclosures to apply in all circumstances, ie no item was intended to be mandatory. Rather, the Board thought that all the proposed disclosures had the potential to provide important information. Depending on a particular set of facts and circumstances, some of the proposed disclosures would be very relevant whereas others would not. Therefore, an entity might be expected to provide some, but not all, of the disclosures included in the list.

BC112　　The difficulty facing the Board was that preparers and users generally have differing views about the level of prescriptive detail to include in disclosure requirements. Preparers generally propose having clear disclosure principles but with a limited number of prescriptive disclosure requirements. They believe that each reporting entity should be able to determine what information meets the disclosure principles on the basis of the particular facts and circumstances surrounding the entity. Users, on the other hand, prefer to have prescriptive disclosure requirements so that the information provided by preparers is comparable.

BC113   The Board's intentions regarding the disclosure of exposure to risk is for an entity to disclose information that is important when assessing that exposure, but not to cloud the information with unnecessary detail that would be considered irrelevant. If an entity has a large exposure to risk because of transactions with a particular unconsolidated structured entity, then the Board would expect extensive disclosure about that exposure. In contrast, if the entity has very limited exposure to risk, little disclosure would be required.

BC114   The Board decided to retain a list of examples of disclosures that might be relevant to emphasise the level of detail that would be required when an entity has a large exposure to risk from its interests in unconsolidated structured entities. However, the Board decided to make clear that the list of additional information that, depending on the circumstances, might be relevant is a list of examples of information that might be relevant and not a list of requirements that should be applied regardless of the circumstances.

Effective date and transition

BC115   The Board decided to align the effective date for the IFRS with the effective date for IFRS 10, IFRS 11 *Joint Arrangements*, IAS 27 *Separate Financial Statements* and IAS 28 *Investments in Associates and Joint Ventures*. When making this decision, the Board noted that the five IFRSs all deal with the assessment of, and related accounting and disclosure requirements about, a reporting entity's special relationships with other entities (ie when the reporting entity has control or joint control of, or significant influence over, another entity). As a result, the Board concluded that applying IFRS 12 without also applying the other four IFRSs could cause unwarranted confusion.

BC116   The Board usually sets an effective date of between twelve and eighteen months after issuing an IFRS. When deciding the effective date for those IFRSs, the Board considered the following factors:

(a)   the time that many countries require for translation and for introducing the mandatory requirements into law.

(b)   the consolidation project was related to the global financial crisis that started in 2007 and was accelerated by the Board in response to urgent requests from the leaders of the G20, the Financial Stability Board, users of financial statements, regulators and others to improve the accounting and disclosure of an entity's 'off balance sheet' activities.

(c)   the comments received from respondents to the Request for Views *Effective Date and Transition Methods* that was published in October 2010 regarding implementation costs, effective date and transition requirements of the IFRSs to be issued in 2011. Most respondents did not identify the consolidation and joint arrangements IFRSs as having a high impact in terms of the time and resources that their implementation would require. In addition, only a few respondents commented that the effective dates of those IFRSs should be aligned with those of the other IFRSs to be issued in 2011.

BC117   With those factors in mind, the Board decided to require entities to apply the five IFRSs for annual periods beginning on or after 1 January 2013.

BC118   Most respondents to the Request for Views supported early application of the IFRSs to be issued in 2011. Respondents stressed that early application was especially important for first-time adopters in 2011 and 2012. The Board was persuaded by these arguments and decided to permit early application of the five IFRSs (ie IFRS 10, IFRS 11, IFRS 12, IAS 27 (as amended in 2011) and IAS 28 (as amended in 2011)) but only if an entity applies all those IFRSs.

BC119   Notwithstanding that decision, the Board noted that an entity should not be prevented from providing any information required by IFRS 12 early if by doing so users gained a better understanding of the entity's relationships with other entities. In reaching that decision, the Board observed that if an entity chooses to apply some, but not all, of the requirements of IFRS 12 early, the entity would be required to continue to apply the disclosure requirements of IAS 27, IAS 28 and IAS 31 until such time that it applies all the requirements of IFRS 12.

BC119A   In June 2012, the Board amended the transition guidance in Appendix C to IFRS 10 *Consolidated Financial Statements*. When making those amendments, the Board decided to limit the requirement to present adjusted comparatives to the annual period immediately preceding the date of initial application of IFRS 10. This is consistent with the minimum comparative disclosure requirements contained in IAS 1 *Presentation of Financial Statements* as amended by *Annual Improvements to IFRSs 2009–2011 Cycle* (issued May 2012). Those amendments confirmed that when an entity applies a changed accounting policy retrospectively, it shall present, as a minimum, three statements of financial position (ie 1 January 2012, 31 December 2012 and 31 December 2013 for a calendar-year entity, assuming no early application of this IFRS) and two of each of the other statements (IAS 1 paragraphs 40A–40B). The Board also decided to make similar amendments to the transition guidance in Appendix C to IFRS 11 *Joint Arrangements* and Appendix C to this IFRS to be consistent with this decision.

BC119B   IFRS 12 introduces new disclosures relating to unconsolidated structured entities. Feedback from interested parties informed the Board that the changes to their accounting and reporting systems that are needed to capture this information were more onerous than originally envisaged, particularly in respect of comparative periods prior to the effective date of IFRS 12. Consequently, the Board decided to provide additional transition relief by eliminating the requirement to present comparatives for this information for periods beginning before the first year that IFRS 12 is applied.

BC119C   The Board decided that no specific transition guidance was needed and, therefore, an entity should apply *Investment Entities: Applying the Consolidation Exception* (Amendments to IFRS 10, IFRS 12 and IAS 28) retrospectively in accordance with IAS 8 *Accounting Policies, Changes in Accounting Estimates and Errors*.

Summary of main changes from ED 9 and ED 10

BC120   The main changes from the exposure drafts ED 9 and ED 10 are:

(a)   The disclosure requirements for subsidiaries, joint arrangements, associates and unconsolidated structured entities are included in IFRS 12, separately from the accounting requirements relating to an entity's interests in those entities. ED 9 and ED 10 had proposed that the disclosure requirements would be located with the accounting requirements in IAS 28, IFRS 10 and IFRS 11. (paragraphs BC7 and BC8)

(b)   IFRS 12 includes application guidance dealing with the aggregation of information disclosed in accordance with the requirements of the IFRS.

(c)   IFRS 12 requires the disclosure of significant judgements and assumptions made in determining whether an entity has a special relationship (ie control, joint control or significant influence) with another entity. ED 10 had proposed disclosure of the basis of an entity's assessment of whether it controls another entity in particular scenarios. (paragraphs BC14–BC19)

(d)   IFRS 12 requires the disclosure of summarised financial information for subsidiaries that have non-controlling interests that are material to the entity. ED 9 had proposed disclosing a list of significant subsidiaries. (paragraphs BC21–BC29)

(e)   IFRS 12 requires disclosure of the nature of, and risks associated with, an entity's interests in consolidated structured entities. (paragraphs BC34–BC36)

(f)   IFRS 12 requires the disclosure of summarised financial information for each material joint venture and associate, and requires more detailed information for joint ventures than for associates. ED 9 had proposed less detailed summarised financial information for each material joint venture and summarised financial information in aggregate for associates. (paragraphs BC47–BC52)

(g)   IFRS 12 requires entities that are venture capital organisations, mutual funds, unit trusts and similar entities to provide all the disclosures relating to interests in joint ventures and associates. ED 9 proposed that such entities would be required to provide only some of the disclosures relating to interests in joint ventures and associates. (paragraphs BC59 and BC60)

(h)   IFRS 12 does not require the disclosure of the reported amount of assets held by structured entities in which an entity has an interest. ED 10 had proposed disclosing such information. (paragraph BC96)

Convergence with US GAAP

BC121 Most of the disclosure requirements for consolidated and unconsolidated structured entities are similar to those for variable interest entities in Subtopic 810-10 in the *FASB Accounting Standards Codification*®. The Board developed many of those disclosure requirements in conjunction with the FASB, following the Financial Stability Board's recommendation to work with other accounting standard-setters to achieve international convergence in this area. However, IFRS 12 goes further than the disclosure requirements in Subtopic 810-10 because it requires an entity to disclose information about:

(a) the interest that non-controlling interests have in the activities of a consolidated structured entity; and

(b) the risks from sponsoring an unconsolidated structured entity for which the entity does not provide other risk disclosures.

BC122 IFRS 12 also includes more detailed disclosure requirements than US GAAP for subsidiaries, joint arrangements and associates (eg summarised financial information for subsidiaries with material non-controlling interests, and material joint ventures and associates).

Cost-benefit considerations

BC123 The objective of financial statements is to provide information about the financial position, performance and changes in financial position of an entity that is useful to a wide range of users in making economic decisions. To attain this objective, the Board seeks to ensure that an IFRS will meet a significant need and that the overall benefits of the resulting information justify the costs of providing it. Although the costs to implement a new IFRS might not be borne evenly, users of financial statements benefit from improvements in financial reporting, thereby facilitating the functioning of markets for capital and credit and the efficient allocation of resources in the economy.

BC124 The evaluation of costs and benefits is necessarily subjective. In making its judgement, the Board considers the following:

(a) the costs incurred by preparers of financial statements;

(b) the costs incurred by users of financial statements when information is not available;

(c) the comparative advantage that preparers have in developing information, compared with the costs that users would incur to develop surrogate information;

(d) the benefit of better economic decision-making as a result of improved financial reporting; and

(e) the costs of transition for users, preparers and others.

BC125　The Board observed that IFRS 12 will improve the ability of users to understand consolidated financial statements by requiring disclosure of information about the interests that non-controlling interests have in the group's activities. IFRS 12 will also improve users' understanding of the special relationships that a reporting entity has with entities that are not consolidated (ie the relationships with joint arrangements, associates and unconsolidated structured entities).

BC126　In particular, an entity was not previously required to provide information specifically about its exposure to risk from interests in structured entities. The requirements in IFRS 12 relating to interests in unconsolidated structured entities respond to the conclusions of the G20 leaders and the recommendations of international bodies such as the Financial Stability Board following the global financial crisis that started in 2007. The G20 leaders and the Financial Stability Board recommended that the IASB should accelerate its work on enhancing disclosure requirements for 'off balance sheet' vehicles (such as structured investment vehicles), in particular to ensure that entities are required to disclose their exposure to risk and potential losses associated with their involvement with such vehicles.

BC127　During the development of IFRS 12, the Board consulted users of financial statements, who confirmed the benefit of having more information about:

(a)　an entity's exposure to risk from interests in structured entities;

(b)　non-controlling interests within the group; and

(c)　joint arrangements and associates.

BC128　There are costs involved in the adoption and ongoing application of IFRS 12. Those costs will depend on the nature and complexity of the relationships that a reporting entity has with other entities. However, given the benefits for users noted in paragraphs BC125–BC127, the Board believes that the benefits of IFRS 12 outweigh the costs.

IASB documents published to accompany

IFRS 13

Fair Value Measurement

The text of the unaccompanied standard, IFRS 13, is contained in Part A of this edition. Its effective date when issued was 1 January 2013. The text of the Accompanying Guidance on IFRS 13 is contained in Part B of this edition.

BASIS FOR CONCLUSIONS

APPENDIX TO THE BASIS FOR CONCLUSIONS

Amendments to the Basis for Conclusions on other IFRSs

Contents

...continued

SUMMARY OF MAIN CHANGES FROM THE EXPOSURE DRAFT   **BC244**

APPENDIX

Amendments to the Basis for Conclusions on other IFRSs

Basis for Conclusions on
IFRS 13 *Fair Value Measurement*

This Basis for Conclusions accompanies, but is not part of, IFRS 13.

Introduction

BC1 This Basis for Conclusions summarises the considerations of the International Accounting Standards Board (IASB) in reaching the conclusions in IFRS 13 *Fair Value Measurement*. It includes the reasons for accepting particular views and rejecting others. Individual IASB members gave greater weight to some factors than to others.

BC2 IFRS 13 is the result of the IASB's discussions about measuring fair value and disclosing information about fair value measurements in accordance with International Financial Reporting Standards (IFRSs), including those held with the US national standard-setter, the Financial Accounting Standards Board (FASB), in their joint project on fair value measurement.

BC3 As a result of those discussions, the FASB amended particular aspects of Topic 820 *Fair Value Measurement* in the *FASB Accounting Standards Codification®* (which codified FASB Statement of Financial Accounting Standards No. 157 *Fair Value Measurements* (SFAS 157)). The FASB separately developed a Basis for Conclusions summarising its considerations in reaching the conclusions resulting in those amendments.

Overview

BC4 Some IFRSs require or permit entities to measure or disclose the fair value of assets, liabilities or their own equity instruments. Because those IFRSs were developed over many years, the requirements for measuring fair value and for disclosing information about fair value measurements were dispersed and in many cases did not articulate a clear measurement or disclosure objective.

BC5 As a result, some of those IFRSs contained limited guidance about how to measure fair value, whereas others contained extensive guidance and that guidance was not always consistent across those IFRSs that refer to fair value. Inconsistencies in the requirements for measuring fair value and for disclosing information about fair value measurements have contributed to diversity in practice and have reduced the comparability of information reported in financial statements.

BC6 To remedy that situation, the IASB added a project to its agenda with the following objectives:

    (a) to establish a single set of requirements for all fair value measurements required or permitted by IFRSs to reduce complexity and improve consistency in their application, thereby enhancing the comparability of information reported in financial statements;

    (b) to clarify the definition of fair value and related guidance to communicate the measurement objective more clearly;

(c)   to enhance disclosures about fair value measurements that will help users of financial statements assess the valuation techniques and inputs used to develop fair value measurements; and

(d)   to increase the convergence of IFRSs and US generally accepted accounting principles (GAAP).

BC7   IFRS 13 is the result of that project. IFRS 13 is a single source of fair value measurement guidance that clarifies the definition of fair value, provides a clear framework for measuring fair value and enhances the disclosures about fair value measurements. It is also the result of the efforts of the IASB and the FASB to ensure that fair value has the same meaning in IFRSs and in US GAAP and that their respective fair value measurement and disclosure requirements are the same (except for minor differences in wording and style; see paragraphs BC237 and BC238 for the differences between IFRS 13 and Topic 820).

BC8   IFRS 13 applies to IFRSs that require or permit fair value measurements or disclosures. It does not introduce new fair value measurements, nor does it eliminate practicability exceptions to fair value measurements (eg the exception in IAS 41 *Agriculture* when an entity is unable to measure reliably the fair value of a biological asset on initial recognition). In other words, IFRS 13 specifies *how* an entity should measure fair value and disclose information about fair value measurements. It does not specify *when* an entity should measure an asset, a liability or its own equity instrument at fair value.

Background

BC9   The IASB and the FASB began developing their fair value measurement standards separately.

BC10   The FASB began working on its fair value measurement project in June 2003. In September 2005, during the FASB's redeliberations on the project, the IASB added to its agenda a project to clarify the meaning of fair value and to provide guidance for its application in IFRSs.

BC11   In September 2006 the FASB issued SFAS 157 (now in Topic 820). Topic 820 defines fair value, establishes a framework for measuring fair value and requires disclosures about fair value measurements.

BC12   In November 2006 as a first step in developing a fair value measurement standard, the IASB published a discussion paper *Fair Value Measurements*. In that discussion paper, the IASB used SFAS 157 as a basis for its preliminary views because of the consistency of SFAS 157 with the existing fair value measurement guidance in IFRSs and the need for increased convergence of IFRSs and US GAAP. The IASB received 136 comment letters in response to that discussion paper. In November 2007 the IASB began its deliberations for the development of the exposure draft *Fair Value Measurement*.

BC13   In May 2009 the IASB published that exposure draft, which proposed a definition of fair value, a framework for measuring fair value and disclosures about fair value measurements. Because the proposals in the exposure draft were developed using the requirements of SFAS 157, there were many similarities between them. However, some of those proposals were different from the requirements of SFAS 157 and many of them used wording that was similar, but not identical, to the wording in SFAS 157. The IASB received 160 comment letters in response to the proposals in the exposure draft. One of the most prevalent comments received was a request for the IASB and the FASB to work together to develop common fair value measurement and disclosure requirements in IFRSs and US GAAP.

BC14 In response to that request, the IASB and the FASB agreed at their joint meeting in October 2009 to work together to develop common requirements. The boards concluded that having common requirements for fair value measurement and disclosure would improve the comparability of financial statements prepared in accordance with IFRSs and US GAAP. In addition, they concluded that having common requirements would reduce diversity in the application of fair value measurement requirements and would simplify financial reporting. To achieve those goals, the boards needed to ensure that fair value had the same meaning in IFRSs and US GAAP and that IFRSs and US GAAP had the same fair value measurement and disclosure requirements (except for minor differences in wording and style). Consequently, the FASB agreed to consider the comments received on the IASB's exposure draft and to propose amendments to US GAAP if necessary.

BC15 The boards began their joint discussions in January 2010. They discussed nearly all the issues together so that each board would benefit from hearing the rationale for the other board's decisions on each issue. They initially focused on the following:

(a) differences between the requirements in Topic 820 and the proposals in the IASB's exposure draft;

(b) comments received on the IASB's exposure draft (including comments received from participants at the IASB's round-table meetings held in November and December 2009); and

(c) feedback received on the implementation of Topic 820 (eg issues discussed by the FASB's Valuation Resource Group).

BC16 In March 2010 the boards completed their initial discussions. As a result of those discussions, in June 2010 the FASB issued a proposed Accounting Standards Update (ASU) *Fair Value Measurements and Disclosures (Topic 820): Amendments for Common Fair Value Measurement and Disclosure Requirements in U.S GAAP and IFRSs* and the IASB re-exposed a proposed disclosure of the unobservable inputs used in a fair value measurement (*Measurement Uncertainty Analysis Disclosure for Fair Value Measurements*). The IASB concluded that it was necessary to re-expose that proposal because in their discussions the boards agreed to require a measurement uncertainty analysis disclosure that included the effect of any interrelationships between unobservable inputs (a requirement that was not proposed in the May 2009 exposure draft and was not already required by IFRSs). The IASB received 92 comment letters on the re-exposure document.

BC17   In September 2010, after the end of the comment periods on the IASB's re-exposure document and the FASB's proposed ASU, the boards jointly considered the comments received on those exposure drafts. The boards completed their discussions in March 2011.

BC18   Throughout the process, the IASB considered information from the IFRS Advisory Council, the Analysts' Representative Group and the IASB's Fair Value Expert Advisory Panel (see paragraph BC177) and from other interested parties.

Scope

BC19   The boards separately discussed the scope of their respective fair value measurement standards because of the differences between IFRSs and US GAAP in the measurement bases specified in other standards for both initial recognition and subsequent measurement.

BC20   IFRS 13 applies when another IFRS requires or permits fair value measurements or disclosures about fair value measurements (and measurements, such as fair value less costs to sell, based on fair value or disclosures about those measurements), except in the following circumstances:

(a)   The measurement and disclosure requirements of IFRS 13 do not apply to the following:

(i)   share-based payment transactions within the scope of IFRS 2 *Share-based Payment*;

(ii)   leasing transactions within the scope of IAS 17 *Leases*; and

(iii)   measurements that have some similarities to fair value but are not fair value, such as net realisable value in accordance with IAS 2 *Inventories* and value in use in accordance with IAS 36 *Impairment of Assets*.

(b)   The disclosures required by IFRS 13 are not required for the following:

(i)   plan assets measured at fair value in accordance with IAS 19 *Employee Benefits*;

(ii)   retirement benefit plan investments measured at fair value in accordance with IAS 26 *Accounting and Reporting by Retirement Benefit Plans*; and

(iii)   assets for which recoverable amount is fair value less costs of disposal in accordance with IAS 36.

BC21   The exposure draft proposed introducing a new measurement basis for IFRS 2, a market-based value. The definition of *market-based value* would have been similar to the exit price definition of fair value except that it would specify that the measurement does not take into account market participant assumptions for vesting conditions and reload features. Respondents pointed out that some items measured at fair value in IFRS 2 were consistent with the proposed definition of fair value, not with the proposed definition of market-based value, and were concerned that there could be unintended consequences of moving forward with a market-based value measurement basis in IFRS 2. The IASB agreed with those comments and concluded that amending IFRS 2 to distinguish between measures that are fair value and those based on fair value would require new measurement guidance for measures based on fair value. The IASB concluded that such guidance might result in unintended changes in practice with regard to measuring share-based payment transactions and decided to exclude IFRS 2 from the scope of IFRS 13.

BC22   The IASB concluded that applying the requirements in IFRS 13 might significantly change the classification of leases and the timing of recognising gains or losses for sale and leaseback transactions. Because there is a project under way to replace IAS 17, the IASB concluded that requiring entities to make potentially significant changes to their accounting systems for the IFRS on fair value measurement and then for the IFRS on lease accounting could be burdensome.

BC23   The exposure draft proposed that the disclosures about fair value measurements would be required for the fair value of plan assets in IAS 19 and the fair value of retirement benefit plan investments in IAS 26. In its project to amend IAS 19 the IASB decided to require an entity to disaggregate the fair value of the plan assets into classes that distinguish the risk and liquidity characteristics of those assets, subdividing each class of debt and equity instruments into those that have a quoted market price in an active market and those that do not. As a result, the IASB decided that an entity does not need to provide the disclosures required by IFRS 13 for the fair value of plan assets or retirement benefit plan investments.

BC24   The exposure draft was not explicit about whether the measurement and disclosure requirements in the exposure draft applied to measurements based on fair value, such as fair value less costs to sell in IFRS 5 *Non-current Assets Held for Sale and Discontinued Operations* or IAS 41. In the boards' discussions, they concluded that the measurement and disclosure requirements should apply to all measurements for which fair value is the underlying measurement basis (except that the disclosure requirements would not apply to assets with a recoverable amount that is fair value less costs of disposal in IAS 36; see paragraphs BC218–BC221). Consequently, the boards decided to clarify that the measurement and disclosure requirements apply to both fair value measurements and measurements based on fair value. The boards also decided to clarify that the measurement and disclosure requirements do not apply to measurements that have similarities to fair value but are not fair value, such as net realisable value in accordance with IAS 2 or value in use in accordance with IAS 36.

BC25   The boards decided to clarify that the measurement requirements apply when measuring the fair value of an asset or a liability that is not measured at fair value in the statement of financial position but for which the fair value is disclosed (eg for financial instruments subsequently measured at amortised cost in accordance with IFRS 9 *Financial Instruments* or IAS 39 *Financial*

Instruments: Recognition and Measurement[1] and for investment property subsequently measured using the cost model in accordance with IAS 40 *Investment Property*).

BC26   The IASB decided that two of the proposals about scope in the exposure draft were not necessary:

(a)   The exposure draft proposed excluding financial liabilities with a demand feature in IAS 39[2] from the scope of an IFRS on fair value measurement. In the light of the comments received, the IASB confirmed its decision when developing IAS 39 that the fair value of financial liabilities with a demand feature cannot be less than the present value of the demand amount (see paragraphs BC101–BCZ103) and decided to retain the term *fair value* for such financial liabilities.

(b)   The exposure draft proposed replacing the term *fair value* with another term that reflects the measurement objective for reacquired rights in a business combination in IFRS 3 *Business Combinations*. In the redeliberations, the IASB concluded that because IFRS 3 already describes the measurement of reacquired rights as an exception to fair value, it was not necessary to change that wording.

Measurement

Definition of fair value

Clarifying the measurement objective

BC27   IFRS 13 defines fair value as:

> The price that would be received to sell an asset or paid to transfer a liability in an orderly transaction between market participants at the measurement date.

BC28   IFRS 13 also provides a framework that is based on an objective to estimate the price at which an orderly transaction to sell the asset or to transfer the liability would take place between market participants at the measurement date under current market conditions (ie an exit price from the perspective of a market participant that holds the asset or owes the liability at the measurement date).

BC29   That definition of fair value retains the exchange notion contained in the previous definition of fair value in IFRSs:

> The amount for which an asset could be exchanged, or a liability settled, between knowledgeable, willing parties in an arm's length transaction.

BC30   Like the previous definition of fair value, the revised definition assumes a hypothetical and orderly exchange transaction (ie it is not an actual sale or a forced transaction or distress sale). However, the previous definition of fair value:

---

1   IFRS 9 *Financial Instruments* replaced IAS 39. IFRS 9 applies to all items that were previously within the scope of IAS 39.
2   IFRS 9 *Financial Instruments* replaced IAS 39. IFRS 9 applies to all items that were previously within the scope of IAS 39.

(a)   did not specify whether an entity is buying or selling the asset;

(b)   was unclear about what is meant by settling a liability because it did not refer to the creditor, but to knowledgeable, willing parties; and

(c)   did not state explicitly whether the exchange or settlement takes place at the measurement date or at some other date.

BC31   The IASB concluded that the revised definition of fair value remedies those deficiencies. It also conveys more clearly that fair value is a market-based measurement, and not an entity-specific measurement, and that fair value reflects current market conditions (which reflect market participants', not the entity's, current expectations about future market conditions).

BC32   In determining how to define fair value in IFRSs, the IASB considered work done in its project to revise IFRS 3. In that project, the IASB considered whether differences between the definitions of fair value in US GAAP (an explicit exit price) and IFRSs (an exchange amount, which might be interpreted in some situations as an entry price) would result in different measurements of assets acquired and liabilities assumed in a business combination. That was a particularly important issue because in many business combinations the assets and liabilities are non-financial.

BC33   The IASB asked valuation experts to take part in a case study involving the valuation of the identifiable assets acquired and liabilities assumed in a sample business combination. The IASB learned that differences between an exit price and an exchange amount (which might be interpreted as an entry price in a business combination) were unlikely to arise, mainly because transaction costs are not a component of fair value in either definition. The IASB observed that although the definitions used different words, they articulated essentially the same concepts.

BC34   However, the valuation experts identified potential differences in particular areas. The valuation experts told the IASB that an exit price for an asset acquired or a liability assumed in a business combination might differ from an exchange amount if:

(a)   an entity's intended use for an acquired asset is different from its highest and best use by market participants (ie when the acquired asset provides defensive value); or

(b)   a liability is measured on the basis of settling it with the creditor rather than transferring it to a third party and the entity determines that there is a difference between those measurements. Paragraphs BC80–BC82 discuss perceived differences between the settlement and transfer notions.

BC35   With respect to highest and best use, the IASB understood that the ways of measuring assets on the basis of their defensive value (ie the value associated with improving the prospects of the entity's other assets by preventing the acquired asset from being used by competitors) in accordance with US GAAP at the time IFRS 3 was issued were still developing. As a consequence, the IASB thought it was too early to assess the significance of any differences that might result. With respect to liabilities, it was also not clear at that time whether entities would use different valuation techniques to measure the fair value of liabilities assumed in a business combination. In the development of IFRS 13, the IASB observed the discussions of the FASB's Valuation Resource Group to learn from the implementation of SFAS 157 and Topic 820 in US GAAP.

Fair value as a current exit price

BC36   The definition of fair value in IFRS 13 is a current exit price. That definition in and of itself is not a controversial issue. Many respondents thought the proposal to define fair value as a current, market-based exit price was appropriate because that definition retains the notion of an exchange between unrelated, knowledgeable and willing parties in the previous definition of fair value in IFRSs, but provides a clearer measurement objective. Other respondents thought an entry price would be more appropriate in some situations (eg at initial recognition, such as in a business combination).

BC37   However, the issue of *when* fair value should be used as a measurement basis in IFRSs is controversial. There is disagreement about the following:

(a)   which assets and liabilities should be measured at fair value (eg whether fair value should be restricted to assets and liabilities with quoted prices in active markets that the entity intends to sell or transfer in the near term);

(b)   when those assets and liabilities should be measured at fair value (eg whether the measurement basis should change when markets have become less active); and

(c)   where any changes in fair value should be recognised.

BC38   Although IFRS 13 does not address when fair value should be used as a measurement basis for a particular asset or liability or revisit when fair value has been used in IFRSs, the IASB did consider whether each use of the term *fair value* in IFRSs was consistent with an exit price definition (see paragraphs BC41–BC45). Furthermore, IFRS 13 will inform the IASB in the future as it considers whether to require fair value as a measurement basis for a particular type of asset or liability.

BC39   The IASB concluded that an exit price of an asset or a liability embodies expectations about the future cash inflows and outflows associated with the asset or liability from the perspective of a market participant that holds the asset or owes the liability at the measurement date. An entity generates cash inflows from an asset by using the asset or by selling it. Even if an entity intends to generate cash inflows from an asset by using it rather than by selling it, an exit price embodies expectations of cash flows arising from the use of the asset by selling it to a market participant that would use it in the same way. That is because a market participant buyer will pay only for the benefits it expects to generate from the use (or sale) of the asset. Thus, the IASB concluded that an exit price is always a relevant definition of fair value for assets, regardless of whether an entity intends to use an asset or sell it.

BC40　Similarly, a liability gives rise to outflows of cash (or other economic resources) as an entity fulfils the obligation over time or when it transfers the obligation to another party. Even if an entity intends to fulfil the obligation over time, an exit price embodies expectations of related cash outflows because a market participant transferee would ultimately be required to fulfil the obligation. Thus, the IASB concluded that an exit price is always a relevant definition of fair value for liabilities, regardless of whether an entity intends to fulfil the liability or transfer it to another party that will fulfil it.

BC41　In developing the revised definition of fair value, the IASB completed a standard-by-standard review of fair value measurements required or permitted in IFRSs to assess whether the IASB or its predecessor intended each use of fair value to be a current exit price measurement basis. If it became evident that a current exit price was not the intention in a particular situation, the IASB would use another measurement basis to describe the objective. The other likely measurement basis candidate was a current entry price. For the standard-by-standard review, the IASB defined current entry price as follows:

> The price that would be paid to buy an asset or received to incur a liability in an orderly transaction between market participants (including the amount imposed on an entity for incurring a liability) at the measurement date.

BC42　That definition of current entry price, like fair value, assumes a hypothetical orderly transaction between market participants at the measurement date. It is not necessarily the same as the price an entity paid to acquire an asset or received to incur a liability, eg if that transaction was not at arm's length. In discussions with interested parties, the IASB found that most people who assert that an asset or a liability should be measured using an entry price measurement basis, rather than an exit price measurement basis, would actually prefer to use the entity's actual transaction price (or cost), not the market-based current entry price defined above. The IASB observed that in some cases there is not an actual transaction price (eg when a group of assets is acquired but the unit of account is an individual asset, or when a biological asset regenerates) and, as a result, an assumed, or hypothetical, price must be used.

BC43　During the standard-by-standard review, the IASB asked various parties to provide information on whether, in practice, they interpreted fair value in a particular context in IFRSs as a current entry price or a current exit price. The IASB used that information in determining whether to define fair value as a current exit price, or to remove the term *fair value* and use the terms *current exit price* and *current entry price* depending on the measurement objective in each IFRS that used the term *fair value*.

BC44　As a result of the standard-by-standard review, the IASB concluded that a current entry price and a current exit price will be equal when they relate to the same asset or liability on the same date in the same form in the same market. Therefore, the IASB considered it unnecessary to make a distinction between a current entry price and a current exit price in IFRSs with a market-based measurement objective (ie fair value), and the IASB decided to retain the term fair value and define it as a current exit price.

BC45　The IASB concluded that some fair value measurement requirements in IFRSs were inconsistent with a current exit price or the requirements for measuring fair value. For those fair value measurements, IFRS 13 excludes the measurement from its scope (see paragraphs BC19–BC26).

The asset or liability

BC46　IFRS 13 states that a fair value measurement takes into account the characteristics of the asset or liability, eg the condition and location of the asset and restrictions, if any, on its sale or use. Restrictions on the sale or use of an asset affect its fair value if market participants would take the restrictions into account when pricing the asset at the measurement date. That is consistent with the fair value measurement guidance already in IFRSs. For example:

(a)　IAS 40 stated that an entity should identify any differences between the property being measured at fair value and similar properties for which observable market prices are available and make the appropriate adjustments; and

(b)　IAS 41 referred to measuring the fair value of a biological asset or agricultural produce in its present location and condition.

BC47　The IASB concluded that IFRS 13 should describe how to measure fair value, not what is being measured at fair value. Other IFRSs specify whether a fair value measurement considers an individual asset or liability or a group of assets or liabilities (ie the unit of account). For example:

(a)　IAS 36 states that an entity should measure the fair value less costs of disposal for a cash-generating unit when assessing its recoverable amount.

(b)　In IAS 39[3] and IFRS 9 the unit of account is generally an individual financial instrument.

The transaction

BC48　The exposure draft proposed that the transaction to sell an asset or transfer a liability takes place in the most advantageous market to which the entity has access. That was different from the approach in Topic 820, which refers to the principal market for the asset or liability or, in the absence of a principal market, the most advantageous market for the asset or liability. The IASB concluded that in most cases the principal market for an asset or a liability will be the most advantageous market and that an entity need not continuously monitor different markets in order to determine which market is most advantageous at the measurement date. That proposal contained a presumption that the market in which the entity normally enters into transactions for the asset or liability is the most advantageous market and that an entity may assume that the principal market for the asset or liability is the most advantageous market.

3　IFRS 9 *Financial Instruments* replaced IAS 39. IFRS 9 applies to all items that were previously within the scope of IAS 39.

BC49   Many respondents agreed with the most advantageous market notion because most entities enter into transactions that maximise the price received to sell an asset or minimise the price paid to transfer a liability. Furthermore, they thought that a most advantageous market notion works best for all assets and liabilities, regardless of the level of activity in a market or whether the market for an asset or a liability is observable.

BC50   However, some respondents were concerned about the difficulty with identifying and selecting the most advantageous market when an asset or a liability is exchanged in multiple markets throughout the world. Other respondents found the guidance confusing because it was not clear whether the most advantageous market must be used or how the market in which the entity normally enters into transactions relates to the principal market or to the most advantageous market. In general, respondents preferred the approach in Topic 820.

BC51   Although the boards think that in most cases the principal market and the most advantageous market would be the same, they concluded that the focus should be on the principal market for the asset or liability and decided to clarify the definition of the principal market.

BC52   Some respondents to the exposure draft stated that the language in US GAAP was unclear about whether the principal market should be determined on the basis of the volume or level of activity *for the asset or liability* or on the volume or level of activity *of the reporting entity's transactions in a particular market*. Consequently, the boards decided to clarify that the principal market is the market for the asset or liability that has the greatest volume or level of activity *for the asset or liability*. Because the principal market is the most liquid market for the asset or liability, that market will provide the most representative input for a fair value measurement. As a result, the boards also decided to specify that a transaction to sell an asset or to transfer a liability takes place in the principal (or most advantageous) market, provided that the entity can access that market on the measurement date.

BC53   In addition, the boards concluded that an entity normally enters into transactions in the principal market for the asset or liability (ie the most liquid market, assuming that the entity can access that market). As a result, the boards decided to specify that an entity can use the price in the market in which it normally enters into transactions, unless there is evidence that the principal market and that market are not the same. Consequently, an entity does not need to perform an exhaustive search for markets that might have more activity for the asset or liability than the market in which that entity normally enters into transactions. Thus, IFRS 13 addresses practical concerns about the costs of searching for the market with the greatest volume or level of activity for the asset or liability.

BC54   The boards also concluded that the determination of the most advantageous market (which is used in the absence of a principal market) for an asset or a liability takes into account both transaction costs and transport costs. However, regardless of whether an entity measures fair value on the basis of the price in the principal market or in the most advantageous market, the fair value measurement takes into account transport costs, but not transaction costs (see paragraphs BC60–BC62 for a discussion on transport and transaction costs). That is consistent with the proposal in the exposure draft.

Market participants

BC55   IFRS 13 states that a fair value measurement is a market-based measurement, not an entity-specific measurement. Therefore, a fair value measurement uses the assumptions that market participants would use when pricing the asset or liability.

BC56   The previous definition of fair value in IFRSs referred to 'knowledgeable, willing parties in an arm's length transaction'. The IASB concluded that the previous definition expressed the same notion as the definition of fair value in IFRS 13, but that the previous definition was less clear. Thus, IFRS 13 defines market participants as buyers and sellers in the principal (or most advantageous) market for the asset or liability who are independent of each other (ie they are not related parties), knowledgeable about the asset or liability, and able and willing to enter into a transaction for the asset or liability.

Independence

BC57   IFRS 13 states that market participants are independent of each other (ie they are not related parties). That is consistent with the proposal in the exposure draft. Given that proposal, some respondents noted that in some jurisdictions entities often have common ownership (eg state-owned enterprises or entities with cross ownership) and questioned whether transactions observed in those jurisdictions would be permitted as an input into a fair value measurement. The boards decided to clarify that the price in a related party transaction may be used as an input into a fair value measurement if the entity has evidence that the transaction was entered into at market terms. The boards concluded that this is consistent with IAS 24 *Related Party Disclosures*.

Knowledge

BC58   The exposure draft stated that market participants were presumed to be as knowledgeable as the entity about the asset or liability. Some respondents questioned that conclusion because they thought the entity might have access to information that is not available to other market participants (information asymmetry).

BC59   In the IASB's view, if a market participant is willing to enter into a transaction for an asset or a liability, it would undertake efforts, including usual and customary due diligence efforts, necessary to become knowledgeable about the asset or liability and would factor any related risk into the measurement.

The price

BC60   IFRS 13 states that the price used to measure fair value should not be reduced (for an asset) or increased (for a liability) by the costs an entity would incur when selling the asset or transferring the liability (ie transaction costs).

BC61　Some respondents stated that transaction costs are unavoidable when entering into a transaction for an asset or a liability. However, the IASB noted that the costs may differ depending on how a particular entity enters into a transaction. Therefore, the IASB concluded that transaction costs are not a characteristic of an asset or a liability, but a characteristic of the transaction. That decision is consistent with the requirements for measuring fair value already in IFRSs. An entity accounts for those costs in accordance with relevant IFRSs.

BC62　Transaction costs are different from transport costs, which are the costs that would be incurred to transport the asset from its current location to its principal (or most advantageous) market. Unlike transaction costs, which arise from a transaction and do not change the characteristics of the asset or liability, transport costs arise from an event (transport) that does change a characteristic of an asset (its location). IFRS 13 states that if location is a characteristic of an asset, the price in the principal (or most advantageous) market should be adjusted for the costs that would be incurred to transport the asset from its current location to that market. That is consistent with the fair value measurement guidance already in IFRSs. For example, IAS 41 required an entity to deduct transport costs when measuring the fair value of a biological asset or agricultural produce.

Application to non-financial assets

Distinguishing between financial assets, non-financial assets and liabilities

BC63　The exposure draft stated that the concepts of highest and best use and valuation premise would not apply to financial assets or to liabilities.

The IASB reached that conclusion for the following reasons:

(a)　Financial assets do not have alternative uses because a financial asset has specific contractual terms and can have a different use only if the characteristics of the financial asset (ie the contractual terms) are changed. However, a change in characteristics causes that particular asset to become a different asset. The objective of a fair value measurement is to measure the asset that exists at the measurement date.

(b)　Even though an entity may be able to change the cash flows associated with a liability by relieving itself of the obligation in different ways, the different ways of doing so are not alternative uses. Moreover, although an entity might have entity-specific advantages or disadvantages that enable it to fulfil a liability more or less efficiently than other market participants, those entity-specific factors do not affect fair value.

(c)　Those concepts were originally developed within the valuation profession to value non-financial assets, such as land.

BC64 Before the amendments to Topic 820, US GAAP specified that the concepts of highest and best use and valuation premise applied when measuring the fair value of assets, but it did not distinguish between financial assets and non-financial assets.

BC65 The FASB agreed with the IASB that the concepts of highest and best use and valuation premise are relevant when measuring the fair value of non-financial assets, and are not relevant when measuring the fair value of financial assets or the fair value of liabilities. The boards also concluded that those concepts do not apply to an entity's own equity instruments because those arrangements, similar to financial instruments, typically have specific contractual terms. Paragraphs BC108–BC131 describe the boards' rationale in developing the requirements for measuring the fair value of financial assets and financial liabilities with offsetting positions in market risks and counterparty credit risk.

BC66 Some respondents to the FASB's proposed ASU were concerned that limiting the highest and best use concept to non-financial assets removed the concept of value maximisation by market participants, which they considered fundamental to a fair value measurement for financial assets and financial liabilities.

BC67 The boards decided to clarify that although there are no excess returns available from holding financial assets and financial liabilities within a portfolio (because in an efficient market, the price reflects the benefits that market participants would derive from holding the asset or liability in a diversified portfolio), a fair value measurement assumes that market participants seek to maximise the fair value of a financial or non-financial asset or to minimise the fair value of a financial or non-financial liability by acting in their economic best interest in a transaction to sell the asset or to transfer the liability in the principal (or most advantageous) market for the asset or liability. Such a transaction might involve grouping assets and liabilities in a way in which market participants would enter into a transaction, if the unit of account in other IFRSs does not prohibit that grouping.

Highest and best use

BC68 Highest and best use is a valuation concept used to value many non-financial assets (eg real estate). The highest and best use of a non-financial asset must be physically possible, legally permissible and financially feasible. In developing the proposals in the exposure draft, the IASB concluded that it was necessary to describe those three criteria, noting that US GAAP at the time did not.

BC69 Some respondents asked for further guidance about whether a use that is legally permissible must be legal at the measurement date, or if, for example, future changes in legislation can be taken into account. The IASB concluded that a use of an asset does not need to be legal at the measurement date, but must not be legally prohibited in the jurisdiction (eg if the government of a particular country has prohibited building or development in a protected area, the highest and best use of the land in that area could not be to develop it for industrial use). The illustrative examples that accompany IFRS 13 show how an asset can be zoned for a particular use at the measurement date, but how a fair value measurement can assume a different zoning if market participants would do so (incorporating the cost to convert the asset and obtain that different zoning permission, including the risk that such permission would not be granted).

BC70   IFRS 13 states that fair value takes into account the highest and best use of an asset from the perspective of market participants. That is the case even if an entity acquires an asset but, to protect its competitive position or for other reasons, the entity does not intend to use it actively or does not intend to use the asset in the same way as other market participants (eg if an intangible asset provides defensive value because the acquirer holds the asset to keep it from being used by competitors). When revising IFRS 3 in 2008, the IASB decided that an entity must recognise such an asset at fair value because the intention of IFRS 3 was that assets, both tangible and intangible, should be measured at their fair values regardless of how or whether the acquirer intends to use them (see paragraph BC262 of IFRS 3). IFRS 13 sets out requirements for measuring the fair value of those assets.

BC71   IFRS 13 does not require an entity to perform an exhaustive search for other potential uses of a non-financial asset if there is no evidence to suggest that the current use of an asset is not its highest and best use. The IASB concluded that an entity that seeks to maximise the value of its assets would use those assets at their highest and best use and that it would be necessary for an entity to consider alternative uses of those assets only if there was evidence that the current use of the assets is not their highest and best use (ie an alternative use would maximise their fair value). Furthermore, after discussions with valuation professionals, the IASB concluded that in many cases it would be unlikely for an asset's current use not to be its highest and best use after taking into account the costs to convert the asset to the alternative use.

BC72   When the IASB was developing the proposals in the exposure draft, users of financial statements asked the IASB to consider how to account for assets when their highest and best use within a group of assets is different from their current use by the entity (ie when there is evidence that the current use of the assets is not their highest and best use, and an alternative use would maximise their fair value). For example, the fair value of a factory is linked to the value of the land on which it is situated. The fair value of the factory would be nil if the land has an alternative use that assumes the factory is demolished. The IASB concluded when developing the exposure draft that measuring the factory at nil would not provide useful information when an entity is using that factory in its operations. In particular, users would want to see depreciation on that factory so that they could assess the economic resources consumed in generating cash flows from its operation. Therefore, the exposure draft proposed requiring an entity to separate the fair value of the asset group into its current use and fair value components.

BC73 Respondents found that proposal confusing and thought that calculating two values for a non-financial asset would be costly. As a result, the boards decided that when an entity uses a non-financial asset in a way that differs from its highest and best use (and that asset is measured at fair value), the entity must simply disclose that fact and why the asset is being used in a manner that differs from its highest and best use (see paragraphs BC213 and BC214).

Valuation premise

Terminology

BC74 As an application of the highest and best use concept, the exposure draft identified two valuation premises that may be relevant when measuring the fair value of an asset:

(a) The *in-use valuation premise*, which applies when the highest and best use of an asset is to use it with other assets or with other assets and liabilities as a group. The in-use valuation premise assumes that the exit price would be the price for a sale to a market participant that has, or can obtain, the other assets and liabilities needed to generate cash inflows by using the asset (complementary assets and the associated liabilities).

(b) The *in-exchange valuation premise*, which applies when the highest and best use of an asset is to use it on a stand-alone basis. It assumes that the sale would be to a market participant that uses the asset on a stand-alone basis.

BC75 Many respondents found the terms *in use* and *in exchange* confusing because they thought that the terminology did not accurately reflect the objective of the valuation premise (ie in both cases the asset is being exchanged, and both cases involve an assessment of how the asset will be used by market participants). In addition, some respondents stated that the in-use valuation premise could be confused with the term *value in use*, as defined in IAS 36.

BC76 In response, the boards decided to remove the terms *in use* and *in exchange* and instead describe the objective of the valuation premise: the valuation premise assumes that an asset would be used either (a) in combination with other assets or with other assets and liabilities (formerly referred to as *in use*) or (b) on a stand-alone basis (formerly referred to as *in exchange*). Respondents to the FASB's proposed ASU generally supported that proposal. The boards concluded that the change improves the understandability of the valuation premise concept.

Valuation premise for a single non-financial asset

BC77 IFRS 13 states that the valuation premise assumes that the non-financial asset being measured at fair value is sold on its own (at the unit of account level) and should be measured accordingly, even if transactions in the asset are typically the result of sales of the asset as part of a group of assets or a business. Even when an asset is used in combination with other assets, the exit price for the asset is a price for that asset individually because a fair value measurement assumes that a market participant (buyer) of the asset already holds the complementary assets and the associated liabilities. Because the buyer is assumed to hold the other assets (and liabilities) necessary for the asset to function, that buyer would not be willing to pay more for the asset solely because it was sold as part of a group. That conclusion is consistent with the conclusion reached in IFRS 3 for measuring the fair value of the identifiable assets acquired in a business combination.

Valuation premise for specialised non-financial assets

BC78   Some respondents to the exposure draft expressed concerns about using an exit price notion for specialised non-financial assets that have a significant value when used together with other non-financial assets, for example in a production process, but have little value if sold for scrap to another market participant that does not have the complementary assets. They were concerned that an exit price would be based on that scrap value (particularly given the requirement to maximise the use of observable inputs, such as market prices) and would not reflect the value that an entity expects to generate by using the asset in its operations. However, IFRS 13 clarifies that this is not the case. In such situations, the scrap value for an individual asset would be irrelevant because the valuation premise assumes that the asset would be used in combination with other assets or with other assets and liabilities. Therefore, an exit price reflects the sale of the asset to a market participant that has, or can obtain, the complementary assets and the associated liabilities needed to use the specialised asset in its own operations. In effect, the market participant buyer steps into the shoes of the entity that holds that specialised asset.

BC79   It is unlikely in such a situation that a market price, if available, would capture the value that the specialised asset contributes to the business because the market price would be for an unmodified asset. When a market price does not capture the characteristics of the asset (eg if that price represents the use of the asset on a stand-alone basis, not installed or otherwise configured for use, rather than in combination with other assets, installed and configured for use), that price will not represent fair value. In such a situation, an entity will need to measure fair value using another valuation technique (such as an income approach) or the cost to replace or recreate the asset (such as a cost approach) depending on the circumstances and the information available.

Application to liabilities

General principles

BC80   The exposure draft proposed that a fair value measurement assumes that a liability is transferred to a market participant at the measurement date because the liability that is the subject of the fair value measurement remains outstanding (ie it is owed by the entity and is not settled with the counterparty or otherwise extinguished at the measurement date). Because the liability is assumed to be transferred to a market participant, the liability remains outstanding and the market participant transferee, like the entity, would be required to fulfil it. The same concept applies to an entity's own equity instrument, as discussed in paragraphs BC104–BC107.

BC81   In many cases, an entity might not intend (or be able) to transfer its liability to a third party. For example, an entity might have advantages relative to the market that would make it more beneficial for the entity to fulfil the liability using its own internal resources or the counterparty might not permit the liability to be transferred to another party. However, the IASB concluded that a fair value measurement provides a market benchmark to use as a basis for assessing an entity's advantages or disadvantages in performance or settlement relative to the market (for both assets and liabilities). Therefore, when a liability is measured at fair value, the relative efficiency of an entity in settling the liability using its own internal resources appears in profit or loss over the course of its settlement, and not before.

BC82   Furthermore, even if an entity is unable to transfer its liability to a third party, the IASB concluded that the transfer notion was necessary in a fair value measurement because that notion captures market participants' expectations about the liquidity, uncertainty and other factors associated with the liability, whereas a settlement notion may not because it may incorporate entity-specific factors. In the IASB's view, the fair value of a liability from the perspective of a market participant that owes the liability is the same regardless of whether it is settled or transferred. That is because:

(a)   both a settlement and a transfer of a liability reflect all costs that would be incurred to fulfil the obligation, including the market-based profit an entity and a market participant transferee desire to earn on all their activities.

(b)   an entity faces the same risks when fulfilling an obligation that a market participant transferee faces when fulfilling that obligation. Neither the entity nor the market participant transferee has perfect knowledge about the timing and amount of the cash outflows, even for financial liabilities.

(c)   a settlement in a fair value measurement does not assume a settlement with the counterparty over time (eg as principal and interest payments become due), but a settlement at the measurement date. Accordingly, the settlement amount in a fair value measurement reflects the present value of the economic benefits (eg payments) the counterparty would have received over time.

As a result, the IASB concluded that similar thought processes are needed to estimate both the amount to settle a liability and the amount to transfer that liability.

BC83   The exposure draft proposed that an entity could estimate the amount at which a liability could be transferred in a transaction between market participants by using the same methodology that would be used to measure the fair value of the liability held by another entity as an asset (ie the fair value of the corresponding asset). If the liability was traded as an asset, the observed price would also represent the fair value of the issuer's liability. If there was no corresponding asset (eg as would be the case with a decommissioning liability), the fair value of the liability could be measured using a valuation technique, such as the present value of the future cash outflows that market participants would expect to incur in fulfilling the obligation.

BC84   That proposal was consistent with the approach in Topic 820 in US GAAP (in August 2009, after the IASB's exposure draft was published, the FASB amended Topic 820 to provide additional guidance about measuring the fair value of liabilities). However, Topic 820 provided more guidance than the IASB's exposure draft, including additional examples for applying that guidance. Because the guidance in Topic 820 was consistent with but not identical to the proposals in the IASB's exposure draft, the boards worked together to develop a combination of the two.

BC85   The boards concluded that the objective of a fair value measurement of a liability when using a valuation technique (ie when there is not an observable market to provide pricing information about the transfer of the liability) is to estimate the price that would be paid to transfer the liability in an orderly transaction between market participants at the measurement date under current market conditions.

BC86   Therefore, the boards decided to describe how an entity should measure the fair value of a liability when there is no observable market to provide pricing information about the transfer of a liability. For example, IFRS 13 states that an entity may measure the fair value of a liability by using a quoted price for an identical or a similar liability held by another party as an asset or by using another valuation technique (such as an income approach).

BC87   The boards clarified that regardless of the approach used, when there is no observable market price for the transfer of a liability and the identical liability is held by another party as an asset, an entity measures the fair value of the liability from the perspective of a market participant that holds the identical liability as an asset at the measurement date. That approach is consistent with the exposure draft and US GAAP.

BC88   Thus, in the boards' view, the fair value of a liability equals the fair value of a properly defined corresponding asset (ie an asset whose features mirror those of the liability), assuming an exit from both positions in the same market. In reaching their decision, the boards considered whether the effects of illiquidity could create a difference between those values. The boards noted that the effects of illiquidity are difficult to differentiate from credit-related effects. The boards concluded that there was no conceptual reason why the liability value would diverge from the corresponding asset value in the same market because the contractual terms are the same, unless the unit of account for the liability is different from the unit of account for the asset or the quoted price for the asset relates to a similar (but not identical) liability held as an asset.

BC89   Furthermore, the boards concluded that in an efficient market, the price of a liability held by another party as an asset must equal the price for the corresponding asset. If those prices differed, the market participant transferee (ie the party taking on the obligation) would be able to earn a profit by financing the purchase of the asset with the proceeds received by taking on the liability. In such cases the price for the liability and the price for the asset would adjust until the arbitrage opportunity was eliminated.

BC90   The exposure draft stated that when using a present value technique to measure the fair value of a liability that is not held by another party as an asset, an entity should include the compensation that a market participant would require for taking on the obligation. Topic 820 contained such a requirement. Respondents asked for clarification on the meaning of compensation that a market participant would require for taking on the obligation. Therefore, the boards decided to provide additional guidance about the compensation that market participants would require, such as the compensation for taking on the responsibility of fulfilling an obligation and for assuming the risk associated with an uncertain obligation (ie the risk that the actual cash outflows might differ from the expected cash outflows). The boards concluded that including this description will improve the application of the requirements for measuring the fair value of liabilities that are not held as assets.

BC91   Some respondents to the FASB's proposed ASU requested clarification about applying risk premiums when measuring the fair value of a liability that is not held by another party as an asset (eg a decommissioning liability assumed in a business combination) when using a present value technique. They noted that the description of present value techniques described adjustments for risk as *additions* to the discount rate, which they agreed was consistent with asset valuation, but not necessarily consistent with liability valuation in the absence of a corresponding asset. The boards reasoned that from a market participant's perspective, compensation for the uncertainty related to a liability results in an increase to the amount that the market participant would expect to receive for assuming the obligation. If that compensation was accounted for in the discount rate, rather than in the cash flows, it would result in a reduction of the discount rate used in the fair value measurement of the liability. Therefore, the boards concluded that, all else being equal, the risk associated with an asset decreases the fair value of that asset, whereas the risk associated with a liability increases the fair value of that liability. However, the boards decided not to prescribe how an entity would adjust for the risk inherent in an asset or a liability, but to state that the objective is to ensure that the fair value measurement takes that risk into account. That can be done by adjusting the cash flows or the discount rate or by adding a risk adjustment to the present value of the expected cash flows (which is another way of adjusting the cash flows).

Non-performance risk

BC92   IFRS 13 states that a fair value measurement assumes that the fair value of a liability reflects the effect of non-performance risk, which is the risk that an entity will not fulfil an obligation. Non-performance risk includes, but is not limited to, an entity's own credit risk (credit standing). That is consistent with the fair value measurement guidance already in IFRSs. For example, IAS 39[4]

---

4   IFRS 9 *Financial Instruments* replaced IAS 39. IFRS 9 applies to all items that were previously within the scope of IAS 39.

and IFRS 9 referred to making adjustments for credit risk if market participants would reflect that risk when pricing a financial instrument. However, there was inconsistent application of that principle because:

(a) IAS 39 and IFRS 9 refer to credit risk generally and do not specifically refer to the reporting entity's *own* credit risk; and

(b) there were different interpretations about how an entity's own credit risk should be reflected in the fair value of a liability using the settlement notion in the previous definition of fair value because it is unlikely that the counterparty would accept a different amount as settlement of the obligation if the entity's credit standing changed.

BC93 As a result, some entities took into account changes in their own credit risk when measuring the fair value of their liabilities, whereas other entities did not. Consequently, the IASB decided to clarify in IFRS 13 that the fair value of a liability includes an entity's own credit risk.

BC94 In a fair value measurement, the non-performance risk related to a liability is the same before and after its transfer. Although the IASB acknowledges that such an assumption is unlikely to be realistic for an actual transaction (because in most cases the reporting entity transferor and the market participant transferee are unlikely to have the same credit standing), the IASB concluded that such an assumption was necessary when measuring fair value for the following reasons:

(a) A market participant taking on the obligation would not enter into a transaction that changes the non-performance risk associated with the liability without reflecting that change in the price (eg a creditor would not generally permit a debtor to transfer its obligation to another party of lower credit standing, nor would a transferee of higher credit standing be willing to assume the obligation using the same terms negotiated by the transferor if those terms reflect the transferor's lower credit standing).

(b) Without specifying the credit standing of the entity taking on the obligation, there could be fundamentally different fair values for a liability depending on an entity's assumptions about the characteristics of the market participant transferee.

(c) Those who might hold the entity's obligations as assets would consider the effect of the entity's credit risk and other risk factors when pricing those assets (see paragraphs BC83–BC89).

The FASB reached the same conclusions when developing SFAS 157 and ASU No. 2009-05 *Fair Value Measurements and Disclosures (Topic 820): Measuring Liabilities at Fair Value.*

BC95 Few respondents questioned the usefulness of reflecting non-performance risk in the fair value measurement of a liability at initial recognition. However, many questioned the usefulness of doing so after initial recognition, because they reasoned that it would lead to counter-intuitive and potentially confusing reporting (ie gains for credit deterioration and losses for credit improvements).

The IASB understands that these concerns are strongly held, but concluded that addressing them was beyond the scope of the fair value measurement project. The purpose of that project was to define fair value, not to determine when to use fair value or how to present changes in fair value. A measurement that does not consider the effect of an entity's non-performance risk is not a fair value measurement. The IASB addressed those concerns in developing IFRS 9 (issued in October 2010).

Liabilities issued with third-party credit enhancements

BC96   IFRS 13 includes requirements for measuring the fair value of a liability issued with an inseparable third-party credit enhancement from the issuer's perspective. Those requirements are consistent with Topic 820.

BC97   A credit enhancement (also referred to as a guarantee) may be purchased by an issuer that combines it with a liability, such as debt, and then issues the combined security to an investor. For example, debt may be issued with a financial guarantee from a third party that guarantees the issuer's payment obligations. Generally, if the issuer of the liability fails to meet its payment obligations to the investor, the guarantor has an obligation to make the payments on the issuer's behalf and the issuer has an obligation to the guarantor. By issuing debt combined with a credit enhancement, the issuer is able to market its debt more easily and can either reduce the interest rate paid to the investor or receive higher proceeds when the debt is issued.

BC98   The boards concluded that the measurement of a liability should follow the unit of account of the liability for financial reporting purposes. When the unit of account for such liabilities is the obligation without the credit enhancement, the fair value of the liability from the issuer's perspective will not equal its fair value as a guaranteed liability held by another party as an asset. Therefore, the fair value of the guaranteed liability held by another party as an asset would need to be adjusted because any payments made by the guarantor in accordance with the guarantee result in a transfer of the issuer's debt obligation from the investor to the guarantor. The issuer's resulting debt obligation to the guarantor has not been guaranteed. Consequently, the boards decided that if the third-party credit enhancement is accounted for separately from the liability, the fair value of that obligation takes into account the credit standing of the issuer and not the credit standing of the guarantor.

Restrictions preventing transfer

BC99   A restriction on an entity's ability to transfer its liability to another party is a function of the requirement to fulfil the obligation and the effect of such a restriction normally is already reflected in the price. As a result, IFRS 13 states that the fair value of a liability should not be adjusted further for the effect of a restriction on its transfer if that restriction is already included in the other inputs to the fair value measurement. However, if an entity is aware that a restriction on transfer is not already reflected in the price (or in the other inputs used in the measurement), the entity would adjust those inputs to reflect the existence of the restriction.

BC100   The boards concluded that there are two fundamental differences between the fair value measurement of an asset and the fair value measurement of a liability that justify different treatments for asset restrictions and liability restrictions. First, restrictions on the transfer of a liability relate to the performance of the obligation (ie the entity is legally obliged to satisfy the obligation and needs to do something to be relieved of the obligation), whereas restrictions on the transfer of an asset relate to the marketability of the asset. Second, nearly all liabilities include a restriction preventing the transfer of the liability, whereas most assets do not include a similar restriction. As a result, the effect of a restriction preventing the transfer of a liability, theoretically, would be consistent for all liabilities and, therefore, would require no additional adjustment beyond the factors considered in determining the original transaction price. The inclusion of a restriction preventing the sale of an asset typically results in a lower fair value for the restricted asset than for the non-restricted asset, all other factors being equal.

Measurement of financial liabilities with a demand feature[5]

BC101   In developing IFRS 13, the IASB confirmed its decision in developing IAS 39 that the fair value of a financial liability with a demand feature cannot be less than the amount payable on demand, discounted from the first date that the amount could be required to be repaid.

BCZ102   Some comments received on the exposure draft published in 2002 preceding IAS 39 requested clarification of how to measure the fair value of financial liabilities with a demand feature (eg demand deposits) when the fair value measurement option is applied or the liability is otherwise measured at fair value. In other words, could the fair value be less than the amount payable on demand, discounted from the first date that an amount could be required to be paid (the demand amount), such as the amount of the deposit discounted for the period that the entity expects the deposit to be outstanding? Some commentators believed that the fair value of financial liabilities with a demand feature is less than the demand amount, for reasons that include the consistency of such measurement with how those financial liabilities are treated for risk management purposes.

BCZ103   In developing IAS 39 the IASB agreed that this issue should be clarified. It confirmed that the fair value of a financial liability with a demand feature is not less than the amount payable on demand, discounted from the first date that the amount could be required to be paid (this is now in paragraph 47 of IFRS 13). That conclusion is the same as in the original IAS 32 *Financial Instruments: Disclosure and Presentation* (issued by the IASB's predecessor body, IASC, in 1995), which is now IAS 32 *Financial Instruments: Presentation*. The IASB noted that in many cases, the market price observed for such financial liabilities is the price at which they are originated between the customer and the deposit-taker—ie the demand amount. It also noted that recognising a financial liability with a demand feature at less than the demand amount

---

5   IFRS 9 *Financial Instruments* replaced IAS 39. IFRS 9 applies to all items that were previously within the scope of IAS 39.

would give rise to an immediate gain on the origination of such a deposit, which the IASB believes is inappropriate.

Application to an entity's own equity instruments[6]

BC104   The exposure draft and Topic 820 stated that although the definition of fair value refers to assets and liabilities, it also should be applied to an instrument measured at fair value that is classified in an entity's own shareholders' equity. Respondents to the discussion paper asked for explicit guidance for measuring the fair value of such instruments because Topic 820 did not contain explicit guidance. Consequently, the boards decided to describe how an entity should measure the fair value of its own equity instruments (eg when an acquirer issues equity in consideration for an acquiree in a business combination).

BC105   The exposure draft proposed requiring an entity to measure the fair value of its own equity instruments from the perspective of a market participant that holds the instrument as an asset. That was because the issuer of an equity instrument can exit from that instrument only if the instrument ceases to exist or if the entity repurchases the instrument from the holder. The FASB agreed with that conclusion.

BC106   The boards also noted that some instruments may be classified as liabilities or equity, depending on the characteristics of the transaction and the characteristics of the instrument. Examples of such instruments include contingent consideration issued in a business combination in accordance with IFRS 3 and equity warrants issued by an entity in accordance with IAS 39[7] or IFRS 9. The boards concluded that the requirements for measuring the fair value of an entity's own equity instruments should be consistent with the requirements for measuring the fair value of liabilities. Consequently, the boards decided to clarify that the accounting classification of an instrument should not affect that instrument's fair value measurement.

BC107   The boards decided to clarify that the objective of a fair value measurement for liabilities and an entity's own equity instruments should be an exit price from the perspective of a market participant that holds the instrument as an asset at the measurement date if there is a corresponding asset, regardless of whether there is an observable market for the instrument as an asset. That decision is consistent with the boards' decisions about the requirements for measuring the fair value of a liability.

---

6   IFRS 9 *Financial Instruments* replaced IAS 39. IFRS 9 applies to all items that were previously within the scope of IAS 39.

7   IFRS 9 *Financial Instruments* replaced IAS 39. IFRS 9 applies to all items that were previously within the scope of IAS 39.

Application to financial assets and financial liabilities with offsetting positions in market risks or counterparty credit risk[8]

BC108   An entity that holds a group of financial assets and financial liabilities is exposed to market risks (ie interest rate risk, currency risk or other price risk) and to the credit risk of each of the counterparties. Financial institutions and similar entities that hold financial assets and financial liabilities often manage those instruments on the basis of the entity's net exposure to a particular market risk (or risks) or to the credit risk of a particular counterparty.

BC109   The previous requirements in IFRSs and US GAAP for measuring the fair value of financial assets and financial liabilities that are managed in this way were expressed differently. Therefore, the boards concluded that it is important that IFRSs and US GAAP express the requirements for measuring the fair value of those financial instruments in the same way.

BC110   When applying IFRSs, entities applied IFRS 9 or IAS 39, which permitted an entity to take into account the effects of offsetting positions in the same market risk (or risks) when measuring the fair value of a financial asset or financial liability. Many entities were using the same approach for offsetting positions in the credit risk of a particular counterparty by analogy.

BC111   When applying US GAAP, many entities applied the in-use valuation premise when measuring the fair value of such financial assets and financial liabilities. In other words, an entity would take into account how the fair value of each financial asset or financial liability might be affected by the combination of that asset or liability with other financial assets or financial liabilities held by the entity. Other entities applied the in-exchange valuation premise to the entity's net risk exposure and assumed that the transaction took place for the net position, not for the individual assets and liabilities making up that position. Those differing applications of the valuation premise arose because Topic 820 did not specify the valuation premise for financial assets.

BC112   In developing the exposure draft, the IASB concluded that the fair value of a financial asset reflects any benefits that market participants would derive from holding that asset within a diversified portfolio. An entity derives no incremental value from holding a financial asset within a portfolio. Furthermore, the IASB noted that the valuation premise related only to assets, not to liabilities, and as such could not be applied to portfolios of financial instruments that include financial liabilities. Therefore, the exposure draft proposed that the in-exchange valuation premise must be used to measure the fair value of a financial asset. The IASB also proposed an amendment to IAS 39 making it explicit that the unit of account for financial instruments is the individual financial instrument at all levels of the fair value hierarchy (Level 1, 2 or 3).

---

8   IFRS 9 *Financial Instruments* replaced IAS 39. IFRS 9 applies to all items that were previously within the scope of IAS 39.

BC113   The boards understand that although the approaches used to measure the fair value of financial assets and financial liabilities were expressed differently in IFRSs and US GAAP, they resulted in similar fair value measurement conclusions in many cases. However, the FASB was aware that before the amendments Topic 820 was sometimes interpreted more broadly than the FASB intended, such as when an entity used the in-use valuation premise to measure the fair value of a group of financial assets when the entity did not have offsetting positions in a particular market risk (or risks) or counterparty credit risk. That interpretation led the IASB to propose requiring the in-exchange valuation premise for financial assets in its exposure draft.

BC114   The IASB's proposal to require the fair value of a financial asset to be measured using the in-exchange valuation premise was one of the more controversial proposals in the exposure draft. That proposal, combined with a proposed amendment to IAS 39 about the unit of account for financial instruments, led respondents to believe that the fair value of financial assets cannot reflect the fact that those assets are held within a portfolio, even when an entity manages its financial instruments on the basis of the entity's net exposure, rather than its gross exposure, to market risks and credit risk.

BC115   Respondents were concerned that the proposal in the exposure draft would separate the valuation of financial instruments for financial reporting from the entity's internal risk management practices. In addition, they were concerned about the systems changes that would be necessary to effect a change in practice. To preserve the relationship between financial reporting and risk management, some respondents asked whether they would be able to apply the bid-ask spread guidance to each of the individual instruments so that the sum of the fair values of the individual instruments equals the value of the net position.

BC116   Other respondents suggested that the IASB should continue to allow the practice that has developed using paragraph AG72 of IAS 39, which stated:

> When an entity has assets and liabilities with offsetting market risks, it may use mid-market prices as a basis for establishing fair values for the offsetting risk positions and apply the bid or asking price to the net open position as appropriate.

BC117   The previous requirements in IFRSs and US GAAP did not clearly specify the relationship between the fair value measurement of financial instruments and how an entity manages its net risk exposure. For example, Topic 820, IAS 39 and IFRS 9 did not explicitly address how the following meet the objective of a fair value measurement for financial instruments:

(a)   Entities typically do not manage their exposure to market risks and credit risk by *selling* a financial asset or transferring a financial liability (eg by unwinding a transaction). Instead, they manage their risk exposure by entering into a transaction for another financial instrument (or instruments) that would result in an offsetting position in the same risk. The resulting measurement represents the fair value of the net risk exposure, not the fair value of an individual financial instrument. The sum of the fair values of the individual instruments is not equal to the fair value of the net risk exposure.

(b) An entity's net risk exposure is a function of the other financial instruments held by the entity and of the entity's risk preferences (both of which are entity-specific decisions and, thus, do not form part of a fair value measurement). Market participants may hold different groups of financial instruments or may have different risk preferences, and it is those factors that are taken into account when measuring fair value. However, the boards understand that market participants holding that particular group of financial instruments and with those particular risk preferences would be likely to price those financial instruments similarly (ie using similar valuation techniques and similar market data). As a result, the market participants' measurement of those financial instruments within that particular group is a market-based measurement, and a measurement using an entity's risk preferences would not be a fair value measurement, but an entity-specific measurement.

BC118 Consequently, the boards decided to permit an exception to the requirements in IFRS 13 and Topic 820 for measuring fair value when an entity manages its financial assets and financial liabilities on the basis of the entity's net exposure to market risks or to the credit risk of a particular counterparty. Respondents to the FASB's proposed ASU generally supported that proposal and stated that it was consistent with current practice for measuring the fair value of such financial assets and financial liabilities.

BC119 That exception permits an entity to measure the fair value of a group of financial assets and financial liabilities on the basis of the price that would be received to sell a net long position (ie asset) for a particular risk exposure or to transfer a net short position (ie liability) for a particular risk exposure in an orderly transaction between market participants at the measurement date under current market conditions, subject to specific requirements.

Scope of paragraph 52

BC119A After issuing IFRS 13, the IASB was made aware that it was not clear whether the scope of the exception for measuring the fair value of a group of financial assets and financial liabilities on a net basis (the 'portfolio exception') includes all contracts that are within the scope of IAS 39 or IFRS 9. The exception is set out in paragraph 48 and the scope of the exception is set out in paragraph 52. In particular, the IASB was asked whether the scope of the portfolio exception included contracts that are accounted for as if they were financial instruments, but that do not meet the definitions of financial assets or financial liabilities in IAS 32. Examples of such a situation would be some contracts to buy or sell a non-financial item that can be settled net in cash by another financial instrument or by exchanging financial instruments as if the contracts were financial instruments within the scope of, and accounted for in accordance with, IAS 39 or IFRS 9.

BC119B   The IASB did not intend to exclude from the scope of the portfolio exception any contracts that are within the scope of IAS 39 or IFRS 9. Consequently, the IASB amended paragraph 52 of this Standard to clarify that the portfolio exception applies to all contracts within the scope of, and accounted for in accordance with, IAS 39 or IFRS 9, regardless of whether they meet the definitions of financial assets or financial liabilities as defined in IAS 32.

Evidence of managing financial instruments on the basis of the net risk exposure

BC120   IFRS 13 states that to use the exception, an entity must provide evidence that it consistently manages its financial instruments on the basis of its net exposure to market risks or credit risk. In addition, the entity must be required (or must have elected, for example, in accordance with the fair value option) to measure the financial instruments at fair value on a recurring basis. The boards concluded that if an entity does not manage its risk exposure on a net basis and does not manage its financial instruments on a fair value basis, the entity should not be permitted to measure the fair value of its financial instruments on the basis of the entity's net risk exposure.

BC121   The boards decided to require an entity to provide evidence that it manages its net risk exposure consistently from period to period. The boards decided this because an entity that can provide evidence that it manages its financial instruments on the basis of its net risk exposure would do so consistently for a particular portfolio from period to period, and not on a net basis for that portfolio in some periods and on a gross basis in other periods. Some respondents to the FASB's proposed ASU found that requirement limiting because they noted that the composition of a portfolio changes continually as the entity rebalances the portfolio and changes its risk exposure preferences over time. Although the entity does not need to maintain a static portfolio, the boards decided to clarify that the entity must make an accounting policy decision (in accordance with IAS 8 *Accounting Policies, Changes in Accounting Estimates and Errors*) to use the exception described in paragraphs BC118 and BC119. The boards also decided that the accounting policy decision could be changed if the entity's risk exposure preferences change. In that case the entity can decide not to use the exception but instead to measure the fair value of its financial instruments on an individual instrument basis. However, if the entity continues to value a portfolio using the exception, it must do so consistently from period to period.

Exposure to market risks

BC122   The boards decided that an entity could apply the bid-ask spread guidance to the entity's net position in a particular market risk (rather than to each individual financial instrument included in that position) only if the market risks that are being offset are substantially the same. Some respondents to the FASB's proposed ASU asked for additional guidance on what is meant by *substantially the same* given the different instruments and types of instruments that might make up a portfolio. In addition, they were concerned that the proposed requirement that the market risks be substantially the same meant that there could be no basis risk in the portfolio or, conversely, that the basis risk would not be reflected in the fair value measurement.

BC123 Consequently, the boards decided to include additional guidance for determining whether market risks are substantially the same. The boards held discussions with several financial institutions that manage their financial assets and financial liabilities on the basis of their net exposure to market risks. From those discussions, the boards concluded that when measuring fair value on the basis of an entity's net exposure to market risks, the entity should not combine a financial asset that exposes it to a particular market risk with a financial liability that exposes it to a different market risk that does not mitigate either of the market risk exposures that the entity faces. The boards also concluded that it is not necessary that the grouping of particular financial assets and financial liabilities results in an entity having no basis risk because the fair value measurement would take into account any basis risk. Furthermore, on the basis of their discussions with financial institutions, the boards concluded that an entity should not combine a financial asset that exposes it to a particular market risk over a particular duration with a financial liability that exposes it to substantially the same market risk over a different duration without taking into account the fact that the entity is fully exposed to that market risk over the time period for which the market risks are not offset. If there is a time period in which a market risk is not offset, the entity may measure its net exposure to that market risk over the time period in which the market risk is offset and must measure its gross exposure to that market risk for the remaining time period (ie the time period in which the market risk is not offset).

Exposure to the credit risk of a particular counterparty

BC124 Because the bid-ask spread (which is the basis for making adjustments for an entity's exposure to market risk to arrive at the fair value of the net position) does not include adjustments for counterparty credit risk (see paragraph BC164), the boards decided to specify that an entity may take into account its net exposure to the credit risk of a particular counterparty when applying the exception.

BC125 The boards decided that when measuring fair value, an entity may consider its net exposure to credit risk when it has entered into an arrangement with a counterparty that mitigates its credit risk exposure in the event of default (eg a master netting agreement). On the basis of their discussions with financial institutions the boards concluded that a fair value measurement reflects market participants' expectations about the likelihood that such an arrangement would be legally enforceable.

BC126 Some respondents to the FASB's proposed ASU asked whether the existence of a master netting agreement was necessary or whether other credit mitigating arrangements could be taken into account in the fair value measurement. The boards decided to clarify that in a fair value measurement, an entity must take into account other arrangements that mitigate credit risk, such as an agreement that requires the exchange of collateral on the basis of each party's net exposure to the credit risk of the other party, if market participants would expect such arrangements to be legally enforceable in the event of default.

BC127 The boards acknowledged that the group of financial assets and financial liabilities for which an entity manages its net exposure to a particular market risk (or risks) could differ from the group of financial assets and financial liabilities for which an entity manages its net exposure to the credit risk of a particular counterparty because it is unlikely that all contracts would be with the same counterparty.

Relationship between measurement and presentation

BC128 In some cases the basis for the presentation of financial instruments in the statement of financial position differs from the basis for the measurement of those financial instruments. For example, that would be the case if an IFRS does not require or permit financial instruments to be presented on a net basis. The FASB's proposed ASU stated that the exception would not apply to financial statement presentation (ie an entity must comply with the financial statement presentation requirements specified in other standards).

BC129 The boards discussed the different approaches to measurement and presentation, particularly in the light of their currently differing requirements for offsetting financial assets and financial liabilities. In IAS 32 an entity may not use net presentation unless specific criteria are met, whereas in US GAAP many entities are able to use net presentation in their financial statements. However, the criteria for net presentation in US GAAP relate to credit risk, not to market risks. As a result, the presentation and measurement bases are different when an entity applies bid-ask adjustments on a net basis but is required to present fair value information on a gross basis (although generally the financial instruments with bid-ask adjustments would qualify for net presentation in US GAAP because of the existence of master netting agreements and other credit risk mitigating arrangements).

BC130 The boards concluded that a relationship between presentation and measurement is not necessary and that adjustments for market risks or credit risk (ie portfolio-level adjustments) are a matter of measurement rather than presentation. They reasoned that fair value measurements are meant to reflect (a) the risk exposure faced by the entity and (b) how that risk exposure would be priced by market participants (which is one reason the boards decided to permit the exception; see paragraph BC117). When pricing financial instruments, a market participant would take into account the other instruments it holds to the extent that those instruments reduce or enhance its overall risk exposure. That is a consequence of requiring or permitting financial instruments to be measured at fair value. The boards' considerations for requiring net or gross presentation of financial instruments are different from those for requiring net or gross measurement.

BC131 Some respondents asked for additional guidance for allocating the bid-ask and credit adjustments to the individual assets and liabilities that make up the group of financial assets and financial liabilities. Although any allocation method is inherently subjective, the boards concluded that a quantitative allocation would be appropriate if it was reasonable and consistently applied. Therefore, the boards decided not to require a particular method of allocation.

Fair value at initial recognition[9]

BC132　The exposure draft proposed guidance for measuring fair value at initial recognition, using both observable and unobservable inputs (as appropriate). The exposure draft also proposed a list of indicators specifying when the transaction price might not be the best evidence of the fair value of an asset or a liability at initial recognition.

BC133　Respondents generally agreed with the list of indicators, but thought that the wording used implied that those were the only indicators, rather than examples of indicators. They suggested that the IFRS on fair value measurement should use the wording in US GAAP. The boards agreed with respondents that the list of indicators was not exhaustive and decided to use the wording in Topic 820.

BC134　Some respondents suggested that market inactivity should be included in the list of indicators. The boards concluded that market inactivity is not an indicator that the transaction price may not represent fair value, but an indicator that the entity should do further work to determine whether the transaction price represents fair value.

BC135　The exposure draft did not address the recognition of a day 1 gain or loss but stated that an entity would recognise such gains or losses unless another IFRS specifies otherwise. For example, IAS 39 and IFRS 9 state that an entity cannot recognise a day 1 gain or loss for a financial instrument unless its fair value is evidenced by a quoted price in an active market for an identical asset or liability or based on a valuation technique that uses only data from observable markets. In contrast, IFRS 3 and IAS 41 require the recognition of day 1 gains or losses even when fair value is measured using unobservable inputs.

BC136　The IASB concluded that fair value should be measured at initial recognition without regard to whether it would result in a gain or loss at initial recognition of the asset or liability. Respondents' views ranged from the view that the transaction price is the best evidence of fair value at initial recognition unless the fair value is measured using only observable inputs (the approach in IAS 39 and IFRS 9) to the view that the transaction price might sometimes, but not always, represent fair value at initial recognition, and that the degree of observability of inputs is not always the best indicator of whether this is the case (the approach in US GAAP).

BC137　Many respondents suggested that IFRSs and US GAAP should have the same requirements for recognising gains or losses at initial recognition. The boards concluded that determining whether to recognise a day 1 gain or loss was beyond the scope of the fair value measurement project. The boards noted that the measurement basis at initial recognition of financial instruments in IFRSs and US GAAP is not always the same, and so the boards could not

---

9　IFRS 9 *Financial Instruments* replaced IAS 39. IFRS 9 applies to all items that were previously within the scope of IAS 39.

address comparability at this time. As a result, the boards decided that an entity would refer to relevant IFRSs for the asset or liability when determining whether to recognise those amounts. The boards concluded that if the relevant IFRS does not specify whether and, if so, where to recognise those amounts, the entity should recognise them in profit or loss.

BC138 Although the IASB did not change the recognition threshold, it amended IAS 39[10] and IFRS 9 to clarify that the fair value of financial instruments at initial recognition should be measured in accordance with IFRS 13 and that any deferred amounts arising from the application of the recognition threshold in IAS 39 and IFRS 9 are separate from the fair value measurement. In other words, the recognition threshold in IAS 39 and IFRS 9 is not a constraint when measuring fair value. Rather, it determines whether (and when) the resulting difference (if any) between fair value at initial recognition and the transaction price is recognised.

Short-term receivables and payables

BC138A After issuing IFRS 13, the IASB was made aware that an amendment to IFRS 9 and IAS 39, which resulted in the deletion of paragraphs B5.4.12 and AG79 respectively, might be perceived as removing the ability to measure short-term receivables and payables with no stated interest rate at invoice amounts without discounting, when the effect of not discounting is immaterial. The IASB did not intend to change the measurement requirements for those short-term receivables and payables, noting that paragraph 8 of IAS 8 already permits entities not to apply accounting policies set out in accordance with IFRSs when the effect of applying them is immaterial.

Valuation techniques

BC139 When measuring fair value, the objective of using a valuation technique is to estimate the price at which an orderly transaction would take place between market participants at the measurement date under current market conditions.

BC140 To meet that objective, the exposure draft proposed that valuation techniques used to measure fair value should be consistent with the market approach, income approach or cost approach. Such valuation techniques are consistent with those already described in IFRSs and with valuation practice.

BC141 Respondents generally agreed with the descriptions of the three valuation techniques. Some respondents questioned whether a cost approach is consistent with an exit price definition of fair value because they think that the cost to replace an asset is more consistent with an entry price than an exit price. The IASB noted that an entity's cost to replace an asset would equal the amount that a market participant buyer of that asset (that would use it similarly) would pay to acquire it (ie the entry price and the exit price would be equal in the same market). Thus, the IASB concluded that the cost approach is consistent with an exit price definition of fair value.

---

10 IFRS 9 *Financial Instruments* replaced IAS 39. IFRS 9 applies to all items that were previously within the scope of IAS 39.

Single versus multiple valuation techniques

BC142　IFRS 13 does not contain a hierarchy of valuation techniques because particular valuation techniques might be more appropriate in some circumstances than in others. The IASB concluded that determining the appropriateness of valuation techniques in the circumstances requires judgement and noted that Topic 820 and the fair value measurement guidance already in IFRSs do not contain a hierarchy of valuation techniques. For example, IAS 41 acknowledged that in some cases the various approaches used by an entity might suggest different fair value conclusions for a biological asset or agricultural produce, but that the entity should consider the reasons for the differences to arrive at a fair value within a reasonable range.

Valuation adjustments

BC143　Some respondents asked for more explicit requirements about applying valuation adjustments (including risk adjustments related to the uncertainty inherent in the inputs used in a fair value measurement; see paragraphs BC149 and BC150). They found the descriptions of valuation adjustments in the IASB's Fair Value Expert Advisory Panel's October 2008 report *Measuring and disclosing the fair value of financial instruments in markets that are no longer active* helpful (see paragraph BC177). In addition, regulators asked the IASB to address measurement uncertainty to ensure that fair value measurements are not overstated or understated in the statement of financial position, thus improving the quality of information available to users of financial statements.

BC144　Although the exposure draft was not explicit with respect to valuation adjustments, it stated that an entity must use the assumptions that market participants would use in pricing the asset or liability, including assumptions about the risk inherent in a particular valuation technique or in the inputs to the valuation technique. That implicitly included measurement uncertainty.

BC145　The boards noted that entities found the IASB's Fair Value Expert Advisory Panel's report helpful when measuring the fair value of financial instruments during a period of market inactivity. As a result, the boards decided to describe the valuation adjustments that entities might need to make when using a valuation technique because market participants would make those adjustments when pricing a financial asset or financial liability under the market conditions at the measurement date, including adjustments for measurement uncertainty. Those valuation adjustments include the following:

(a)　an adjustment to a valuation technique to take into account a characteristic of an asset or a liability that is not captured by the valuation technique (the need for such an adjustment is typically identified during calibration of the value calculated using the valuation technique with observable market information).

(b)　applying the point within the bid-ask spread that is most representative of fair value in the circumstances.

(c)   an adjustment to take into account non-performance risk (eg an entity's own credit risk or the credit risk of the counterparty to a transaction).

(d)   an adjustment to take into account measurement uncertainty (eg when there has been a significant decrease in the volume or level of activity when compared with normal market activity for the asset or liability, or similar assets or liabilities, and the entity has determined that the transaction price or quoted price does not represent fair value).

BC146   The boards decided that it would be appropriate to apply such valuation adjustments if those adjustments are consistent with the objective of a fair value measurement. Valuation adjustments may help avoid an understatement or overstatement of a fair value measurement and should be applied when a valuation technique or the inputs to a valuation technique do not capture factors that market participants would take into account when pricing an asset or a liability at the measurement date, including assumptions about risk.

Consistency constraint

BC147   IFRS 13 emphasises the need for consistency in the valuation technique or techniques used to measure fair value. It does not preclude a change in valuation technique, provided that the change results in a measurement that is equally or more representative of fair value in the circumstances. The exposure draft proposed requiring an entity to disclose the effect of a change in valuation technique on a fair value measurement (similar to the disclosures required by IAS 8 for a change in valuation technique). Respondents did not support that proposal because they thought it would be difficult to determine whether a change in fair value was attributable to a change in the valuation technique used or attributable to changes in other factors (such as changes in the observability of the inputs used in the measurement).

BC148   The IASB agreed with those respondents and decided that in the absence of an error (eg in the selection or application of a particular valuation technique), revisions resulting from a change in the valuation technique or its application should be accounted for as a change in accounting estimate in accordance with IAS 8. The IASB concluded that disclosing the effect of a change in valuation technique on the fair value measurement or requiring the disclosures in IAS 8 for a change in accounting estimate would not be cost-beneficial.

Inputs to valuation techniques

Assumptions about risk

BC149   In IFRS 13 inputs refer broadly to the assumptions that market participants would use when pricing the asset or liability, including assumptions about risk. The IASB decided that a necessary input to a valuation technique is an adjustment for risk because market participants would make such an adjustment when pricing an asset or a liability. Therefore, including an adjustment for risk ensures that the measurement reflects an exit price for the asset or liability, ie the price that would be received in an orderly transaction to sell an asset or paid in an orderly transaction to transfer the liability at the measurement date under current market conditions.

BC150   The IASB accepted that it might be difficult for an entity to quantify a risk adjustment in some cases, but concluded that this difficulty does not justify the exclusion of this input if market participants would take it into account. The exposure draft focused on the need to adjust for the risk inherent in a particular valuation technique used to measure fair value, such as a pricing model (model risk) and the risk inherent in the inputs to the valuation technique (input risk). That proposal was consistent with US GAAP.

Observable and unobservable inputs

BC151   IFRS 13 distinguishes between observable inputs and unobservable inputs, and requires an entity to maximise the use of relevant observable inputs and minimise the use of unobservable inputs (consistently with the fair value measurement guidance that was already in IFRSs). Respondents to the exposure draft expressed concerns about being required to use observable inputs during the global financial crisis that started in 2007 when the available observable inputs were not representative of the asset or liability being measured at fair value. Given that feedback, the IASB wanted to ensure that observability was not the only criterion applied when selecting the inputs to a valuation technique. Consequently, IFRS 13 focuses on *relevant* observable inputs because the IASB noted that in some cases the available observable inputs will require an entity to make significant adjustments to them given the characteristics of the asset or liability and the circumstances at the measurement date (eg market conditions).

Application of premiums and discounts in a fair value measurement

BC152   The exposure draft proposed an amendment to IAS 39[11] making it explicit that the unit of account for a financial instrument is the individual financial instrument at all levels of the fair value hierarchy. That proposal in effect would have prohibited the application of premiums and discounts related to the size of an entity's holding in a fair value measurement categorised within any level of the fair value hierarchy for financial instruments within the scope of IAS 39. The IASB proposed that amendment for the following reasons:

(a)   The unit of account for a financial instrument should not depend on an instrument's categorisation within the fair value hierarchy.

(b)   Market participants will enter into a transaction to sell a financial instrument that maximises the fair value of an asset or minimises the fair value of a liability. An entity's decision to sell at a less advantageous price because it sells an entire holding rather than each instrument individually is a factor specific to that reporting entity.

---

11   IFRS 9 *Financial Instruments* replaced IAS 39. IFRS 9 applies to all items that were previously within the scope of IAS 39.

            © IFRS Foundation

BC153   Before the amendments to Topic 820, US GAAP generally prohibited any adjustment to a quoted price in an active market for an identical asset or liability for a fair value measurement categorised within Level 1 of the fair value hierarchy (including either a blockage factor, which was described as an adjustment to a quoted price for an asset or a liability when the normal daily trading volume for the asset or liability is not sufficient to absorb the quantity held and therefore placing orders to sell the asset or liability in a single transaction might affect the quoted price, or any other premium or discount). However, Topic 820 did not specify whether a blockage factor (or another premium or discount, such as a control premium or a non-controlling interest discount) should be applied in a fair value measurement categorised within Level 2 or Level 3 of the fair value hierarchy if market participants would take it into account when pricing the asset or liability.

BC154   Respondents interpreted the proposal in the exposure draft as being consistent with Topic 820 for fair value measurements categorised within Level 1 of the fair value hierarchy, but they thought it was inconsistent with Topic 820 for fair value measurements categorised within Level 2 and Level 3. For example, some respondents thought that the IASB intended to prohibit the application of any premiums or discounts (such as a control premium) for fair value measurements categorised within Level 2 and Level 3 of the fair value hierarchy even when market participants would take into account a premium or discount when pricing the asset or liability for a particular unit of account.

BC155   Some respondents supported the proposal for fair value measurements categorised within Level 1 of the fair value hierarchy even though, in their view, entities do not typically exit a position on an individual instrument basis (eg by entering into a transaction to sell a single share of equity). Those respondents understood the boards' concerns about verifiability within Level 1. Other respondents stated that the fair value measurement should reflect the fair value of the entity's *holding*, not of each individual instrument within that holding (ie they did not agree that the unit of account for a financial instrument should be a single instrument). Those respondents maintained that the principle should be that the unit of account reflects how market participants would enter into a transaction for the asset or liability. They asserted that market participants would not (and often cannot) sell individual items. The FASB received similar comments when developing SFAS 157. The boards concluded that such concerns were outside the scope of the fair value measurement project because the project addressed *how* to measure fair value and not *what* is measured at fair value.

BC156   In addition, the comments received on the exposure draft indicated that respondents had different interpretations of the term *blockage factor*. Many respondents interpreted a blockage factor as any adjustment made because of the size of an asset or a liability. In the boards' view, there is a difference between size being a characteristic of the asset or liability and size being a characteristic of the entity's holding. Accordingly, the boards clarified that a blockage factor encompasses the latter and is not relevant in a fair value measurement because a fair value measurement reflects the value of the asset or liability to a market participant for a particular unit of account and is not necessarily representative of the value of the entity's entire holding.

BC157 Given the description of a blockage factor, the boards concluded that an entity's decision to realise a blockage factor is specific to that entity, not to the asset or liability. In many cases the unit of account for a financial instrument for financial reporting is the individual financial instrument. In such cases the size of an entity's holding is not relevant in a fair value measurement. An entity would realise a blockage factor when that entity decides to enter into a transaction to sell a block consisting of a large number of identical assets or liabilities. Therefore, blockage factors are conceptually similar to transaction costs in that they will differ depending on how an entity enters into a transaction for an asset or a liability. The boards concluded that if an entity decides to enter into a transaction to sell a block, the consequences of that decision should be recognised when the decision is carried out regardless of the level of the fair value hierarchy in which the fair value measurement is categorised.

BC158 Therefore, the boards decided to clarify that the application of premiums and discounts in a fair value measurement is related to the characteristics of the asset or liability being measured at fair value and its unit of account. IFRS 13 specifies that when a Level 1 input is not available, a fair value measurement should incorporate premiums or discounts if market participants would take them into account in a transaction for the asset or liability. Paragraph BC168 describes the IASB's rationale for requiring an entity to use Level 1 inputs without adjustment whenever available. However, the boards decided to clarify that the application of premiums or discounts must be consistent with the unit of account in the IFRS that requires or permits the fair value measurement.

BC159 The boards decided not to provide detailed descriptions of premiums and discounts or to provide detailed guidance about their application in a fair value measurement. They reasoned that such descriptions and guidance would be too prescriptive because the application of premiums and discounts in a fair value measurement depends on the facts and circumstances at the measurement date. In the boards' view, different facts and circumstances might lead to particular premiums or discounts being relevant for some assets and liabilities but not for others (eg in different jurisdictions). Furthermore, the boards did not intend to preclude the use of particular premiums or discounts, except for blockage factors.

Inputs based on bid and ask prices

BC160 In some situations, inputs might be determined on the basis of bid and ask prices, eg an input from a dealer market, in which the bid price represents the price the dealer is willing to pay and the ask price represents the price at which the dealer is willing to sell. IAS 39 required the use of bid prices for asset positions and ask prices for liability positions. IAS 36 and IAS 38 *Intangible Assets* had similar requirements.

BC161   The exposure draft proposed that a fair value measurement should use the price within the bid-ask spread that is most representative of fair value in the circumstances. Furthermore, the exposure draft stated that the bid-ask spread guidance applied at all levels of the fair value hierarchy, when bid and ask prices are relevant (see paragraph BC165), and did not preclude the use of mid-market pricing or other pricing conventions that are used by market participants as a practical expedient.

BC162   Many respondents supported the proposal because in their experience different market participants enter into transactions at different prices within a bid-ask spread. Some respondents preferred a single bid-ask spread pricing method, as described in IAS 39, because it would maximise the consistency and comparability of fair value measurements using bid and ask prices.

BC163   The IASB observed that, in many situations, bid and ask prices establish the boundaries within which market participants would negotiate the price in the exchange for the asset or liability. Having clarified the fair value measurement objective, the IASB concluded that an entity should use judgement in meeting that objective. Accordingly, IFRS 13 states that a fair value measurement should use the price within the bid-ask spread that is most representative of fair value in the circumstances, and that the use of bid prices for asset positions and ask prices for liability positions is permitted but is not required.

BC164   IAS 39 stated that the *bid-ask spread* includes only transaction costs. In IAS 39 other adjustments to arrive at fair value (eg for counterparty credit risk) were not included in the term *bid-ask spread*. Some respondents asked whether the proposed bid-ask guidance reflected that view. Although the boards decided not to specify what, if anything, is in a bid-ask spread besides transaction costs, in the boards' view the bid-ask spread does not include adjustments for counterparty credit risk (see paragraphs BC124–BC127 for a discussion on adjustments for counterparty credit risk when measuring fair value). Therefore, an entity will need to make an assessment of what is in the bid-ask spread for an asset or a liability when determining the point within the bid-ask spread that is most representative of fair value in the circumstances.

BC165   Some respondents noted that there could be a difference between entry prices and exit prices when entities enter into transactions at different points within the bid-ask spread. For example, an entity might buy an asset at the ask price (entry price) and measure fair value using the bid price (exit price). The boards concluded that bid-ask spreads are only relevant for financial instruments and in markets in which an intermediary (eg a broker) is necessary to bring together a buyer and a seller to engage in a transaction (ie when the buyer and seller need an intermediary to find one another). When measuring the fair value of a non-financial asset or non-financial liability, the notion of a bid-ask spread will not be relevant because the buyers and sellers in the principal (or most advantageous) market have already found one another and are assumed to have negotiated the transaction price (ie fair value).

Fair value hierarchy

BC166   IFRS 13 uses a three-level fair value hierarchy, as follows:

(a)   Level 1 comprises unadjusted quoted prices in active markets for identical assets and liabilities.

(b)   Level 2 comprises other observable inputs not included within Level 1 of the fair value hierarchy.

(c)   Level 3 comprises unobservable inputs (including the entity's own data, which are adjusted if necessary to reflect the assumptions market participants would use in the circumstances).

BC167   The IASB noted that many IFRSs already contained an implicit fair value hierarchy by referring to observable market transactions or measuring fair value using a valuation technique. For example, the following three-level measurement hierarchy was implicit in IAS 39 and IFRS 9:

(a)   financial instruments quoted in an active market;

(b)   financial instruments whose fair value is evidenced by comparison with other observable current market transactions in the same instrument (ie without modification or repackaging) or based on a valuation technique whose variables include only data from observable markets; and

(c)   financial instruments whose fair value is determined in whole or in part using a valuation technique based on assumptions that are not supported by prices from observable current market transactions in the same instrument (ie without modification or repackaging) and not based on available observable market data.

Level 1 inputs

BC168   Level 1 inputs are unadjusted quoted prices in active markets for identical assets and liabilities. The IASB concluded that those prices generally provide the most reliable evidence of fair value and should be used to measure fair value whenever available.

BC169   IFRS 13 defines an active market as a market in which transactions for the asset or liability take place with sufficient frequency and volume to provide pricing information on an ongoing basis. The IASB concluded that although different words are used, that definition is consistent with the definitions of an active market already in IFRSs:

(a)   IASs 36, 38 and 41 stated that an active market is one in which '(i) the items traded in the market are homogeneous; (ii) willing buyers and sellers can normally be found at any time; and (iii) prices are available to the public.'

(b)   IAS 39 and IFRS 9 stated that an active market is one in which 'quoted prices are readily and regularly available from an exchange, dealer, broker, industry group, pricing service or regulatory agency, and those prices represent actual and regularly occurring market transactions on an arm's length basis.'

BC170   IFRS 13 states that when an entity holds a large number of similar assets and liabilities that are required to be measured at fair value and a quoted price in an active market is not readily accessible for each of those assets and liabilities, the entity can use an alternative pricing method that does not rely exclusively on quoted prices as a practical expedient (although the resulting fair value measurement is a lower level measurement). For example, an entity might hold a large number of similar debt instruments (such as sovereign debt securities) and use matrix pricing, which does not rely exclusively on quoted prices, to measure the fair value of those instruments. In such a situation, although a Level 1 input is used to measure fair value, the fair value measurement would not be categorised within Level 1 of the fair value hierarchy. That is a departure from the principle that a fair value measurement should maximise the use of relevant observable inputs. However, the IASB regards this particular practical expedient as justified on cost-benefit grounds.

Level 2 inputs

BC171   Level 2 inputs are all inputs other than quoted prices included in Level 1 that are observable (either directly or indirectly) for the asset or liability. The IASB concluded that it is appropriate to include in Level 2 market-corroborated inputs that might not be directly observable, but are based on or supported by observable market data, because such inputs are less subjective than unobservable inputs classified within Level 3.

Level 3 inputs

BC172   Level 3 inputs are unobservable inputs for the asset or liability.

BC173   Some respondents stated that it would be misleading to describe a measurement using significant unobservable inputs as a fair value measurement. They also expressed concerns that unobservable inputs may include entity-specific factors that market participants would not consider. Therefore, they suggested that the IASB should use a different label for measurements that use significant unobservable inputs. However, the IASB concluded that it would be more helpful to users of financial statements to use the label *fair value* for all three levels of the hierarchy described in the exposure draft, for the following reasons:

(a)   The proposed definition of fair value identifies a clear objective for valuation techniques and the inputs to them: consider all factors that market participants would consider and exclude all factors that market participants would exclude. An alternative label for Level 3 measurements would be unlikely to identify such a clear objective.

(b)   The distinction between Levels 2 and 3 is inevitably subjective. It is undesirable to adopt different measurement objectives on either side of such a subjective boundary.

Rather than requiring a different label for measurements derived using significant unobservable inputs, the IASB concluded that concerns about the subjectivity of those measurements are best addressed by requiring enhanced disclosure for those measurements (see paragraphs BC187–BC210).

BC174   The IASB accepts that the starting point for Level 3 inputs might be estimates developed by the entity. However, the entity must adjust those inputs if reasonably available information indicates that other market participants would use different data when pricing the asset or liability or there is something particular to the entity that is not available to other market participants (eg an entity-specific synergy).

BC175   Some respondents expressed concerns that an entity would be compelled by its auditors or regulators to undertake exhaustive efforts to obtain information about the assumptions that market participants would use when pricing the asset or liability. Furthermore, they were concerned that their judgement would be questioned when asserting the absence of contrary data. IFRS 13 states that such exhaustive efforts would not be necessary. However, when information about market participant assumptions is reasonably available, an entity cannot ignore it.

Measuring fair value when the volume or level of activity for an asset or a liability has significantly decreased

BC176   The global financial crisis that started in 2007 emphasised the importance of having common fair value measurement requirements in IFRSs and US GAAP, particularly for measuring fair value when the market activity for an asset or a liability declines. As a result, and consistently with the recommendations of the Group of Twenty (G20) Leaders, the Financial Stability Board and the IASB's and FASB's Financial Crisis Advisory Group, the IASB and the FASB worked together to develop common requirements for measuring the fair value of assets and liabilities when markets are no longer active.

BC177   In May 2008 the IASB set up a Fair Value Expert Advisory Panel in response to recommendations made by the Financial Stability Forum (now the Financial Stability Board) to address the measurement and disclosure of financial instruments when markets are no longer active. The Panel's discussions were observed by FASB staff. In October 2008 the IASB staff published a staff report on the Panel's discussions.

BC178   Also in response to the global financial crisis, in April 2009 the FASB issued FASB Staff Position (FSP) No. FAS 157-4 *Determining Fair Value When the Volume and Level of Activity for the Asset or Liability Have Significantly Decreased and Identifying Transactions That Are Not Orderly*. That FSP was codified in Topic 820 and provides guidance for:

(a)   measuring fair value when the volume or level of activity for the asset or liability has significantly decreased; and (b)　identifying circumstances that indicate a transaction is not orderly.

BC179　IASB published a Request for Views that asked respondents whether they believed that the guidance in that FSP was consistent with the Panel's report. The IASB also asked members of the Fair Value Expert Advisory Panel the same question. The IASB received 69 responses to the Request for Views. The respondents to the Request for Views and the members of the Fair Value Expert Advisory Panel indicated that the FSP was consistent with the Panel's report. As a result, the IASB included the guidance from FSP FAS 157-4 in the exposure draft.

BC180　Respondents to the exposure draft generally agreed with the proposed guidance and found it consistent with the concepts in the IASB's Fair Value Expert Advisory Panel's report and in US GAAP. However, some respondents noted that the words used in the exposure draft were different from those used in US GAAP and wondered whether the requirements were meant to be different. The boards acknowledged those concerns and decided to align the wording. In addition, the boards decided to clarify that the requirements pertain to when there has been a significant decline in the volume or level of activity for the asset or liability, not to assets and liabilities for which there is typically no observable market.

BC181　Furthermore, the boards concluded that when applying IFRS 13 and Topic 820 an entity should focus on whether an observed transaction price is the result of an orderly transaction, not only on the level of activity in a market, because even in a market with little activity, transactions can be orderly. Accordingly, the boards concluded that an entity should consider observable transaction prices unless there is evidence that the transaction is not orderly. If an entity does not have sufficient information to determine whether a transaction is orderly, it performs further analysis to measure fair value.

BC182　Also as a result of the global financial crisis, there was a particularly urgent need to improve transparency of fair value measurements for financial instruments. To address that need, the IASB amended IFRS 7 *Financial Instruments: Disclosures* in March 2009. The amended disclosures about fair value measurements have been relocated to IFRS 13.

Disclosure

BC183　The disclosures about fair value measurements in IFRSs vary, although many require, at a minimum, information about the methods and significant assumptions used in the measurement, and whether fair value was measured using observable prices from recent market transactions for the same or a similar asset or liability.

BC184　The IASB decided that having established a framework for measuring fair value, it should also enhance and harmonise the disclosures about fair value measurements. The IASB decided to limit the disclosures to fair values measured in the statement of financial position after initial recognition, whether those measurements are made on a recurring or non-recurring basis, because other IFRSs address the disclosure of fair values at initial recognition (eg IFRS 3 requires disclosure of the measurement of assets acquired and liabilities assumed in a business combination).

BC185 The objective of the disclosures in IFRS 13 is to provide users of financial statements with information about the valuation techniques and inputs used to develop fair value measurements and how fair value measurements using significant unobservable inputs affected profit or loss or other comprehensive income for the period. To meet those objectives, the disclosure framework (a) combines the disclosures currently required by IFRSs and US GAAP and (b) provides additional disclosures that users of financial statements suggested would be helpful in their analyses. In developing the disclosures, the IASB used information received from users and preparers of financial statements and the IASB's Fair Value Expert Advisory Panel.

Distinguishing between recurring and non-recurring fair value measurements

BC186 The disclosures in US GAAP differentiate fair value measurements that are recurring from those that are non-recurring. The exposure draft did not propose differentiating recurring from non-recurring fair value measurements and required the same information about all fair value measurements. However, users of financial statements asked the IASB to include the same principles for disclosing information about fair value measurements in IFRSs that are in US GAAP. As a result, the boards decided to differentiate the two types of fair value measurements and to describe their differences.

Information about fair value measurements categorised within Level 3 of the fair value hierarchy

BC187 The boards received requests from users of financial statements for more information about fair value measurements categorised within Level 3 of the fair value hierarchy. The following sections describe the boards' response to those requests.

Quantitative information

BC188 The exposure draft proposed requiring an entity to disclose the methods and inputs used in a fair value measurement, including the information used to develop those inputs. That proposal was developed using feedback from users of financial statements and the IASB's Fair Value Expert Advisory Panel. Although the proposal was not explicit, the IASB intended that the information about the inputs used in the measurement would be quantitative.

BC189 Before the amendments to Topic 820, US GAAP required an entity to provide a description of the inputs used when measuring the fair value of an asset or a liability that is categorised within Level 2 or Level 3 of the fair value hierarchy. Topic 820 was not explicit about whether that description needed to include quantitative information.

BC190   Users of financial statements asked the boards to clarify that entities must provide quantitative information about the inputs used in a fair value measurement, particularly information about unobservable inputs used in a measurement categorised within Level 3 of the fair value hierarchy. When limited or no information is publicly available, disclosures about such information help users to understand the measurement uncertainty inherent in the fair value measurement.

BC191   Therefore, the boards decided to clarify that an entity should disclose *quantitative* information about the significant unobservable inputs used in a fair value measurement categorised within Level 3 of the fair value hierarchy.

BC192   Some respondents to the FASB's proposed ASU questioned the usefulness of quantitative information about the unobservable inputs used in a fair value measurement because of the level of aggregation required in those disclosures. The boards noted that the objective of the disclosure is not to enable users of financial statements to replicate the entity's pricing models, but to provide enough information for users to assess whether the entity's views about individual inputs differed from their own and, if so, to decide how to incorporate the entity's fair value measurement in their decisions. The boards concluded that the information required by the disclosure will facilitate comparison of the inputs used over time, providing users with information about changes in management's views about particular unobservable inputs and about changes in the market for the assets and liabilities within a particular class. In addition, that disclosure might facilitate comparison between entities with similar assets and liabilities categorised within Level 3 of the fair value hierarchy.

BC193   IFRS 13 and Topic 820 state that an entity should determine appropriate classes of assets and liabilities on the basis of the nature, characteristics and risks of the assets and liabilities, noting that further disaggregation might be required for fair value measurements categorised within Level 3 of the fair value hierarchy. Consequently, the boards concluded that the meaningfulness of the disclosure of quantitative information used in Level 3 fair value measurements will depend on an entity's determination of its asset and liability classes.

BC194   Some respondents to the IASB's re-exposure document and the FASB's proposed ASU suggested requiring quantitative information about the unobservable inputs used in fair value measurements categorised within Level 2 of the fair value hierarchy because determining whether to categorise fair value measurements within Level 2 or Level 3 can be subjective. The boards concluded that for a fair value measurement to be categorised within Level 2 of the fair value hierarchy, the unobservable inputs used, if any, must not be significant to the measurement in its entirety. As a result, the boards decided that quantitative information about unobservable inputs would be of limited use for those measurements.

BC195　　In addition, the boards understand that fair value is sometimes measured on the basis of prices in prior transactions (eg adjustments to the last round of financing for a venture capital investment) or third-party pricing information (eg broker quotes). Such measurements might be categorised within Level 3 of the fair value hierarchy. In such cases, the boards concluded that an entity should be required to disclose how it has measured the fair value of the asset or liability, but that it should not need to create quantitative information (eg an implied market multiple or future cash flows) to comply with the disclosure requirement if quantitative information other than the prior transaction price or third-party pricing information is not used when measuring fair value. However, the boards concluded that when using a prior transaction price or third-party pricing information, an entity cannot ignore other quantitative information that is reasonably available. If there was an adjustment to the price in a prior transaction or third-party pricing information that is significant to the fair value measurement in its entirety, that adjustment would be an unobservable input about which the entity would disclose quantitative information even if the entity does not disclose the unobservable information used when pricing the prior transaction or developing the third-party pricing information.

Level 3 reconciliation for recurring fair value measurements

BC196　　The exposure draft proposed requiring an entity to provide a reconciliation from the opening balances to the closing balances of fair value measurements categorised within Level 3 of the fair value hierarchy. IFRS 7 required such a disclosure for financial instruments after it was amended in March 2009 to introduce a three-level fair value hierarchy, and to require more detailed information about fair value measurements categorised within Level 3 of the fair value hierarchy. In addition, many IFRSs already required a similar reconciliation for all fair value measurements, not only for those that are categorised within Level 3 of the fair value hierarchy.

BC197　　Some respondents agreed with the proposed reconciliation disclosure because they thought it would help meet the objective to provide meaningful information to users of financial statements about the relative subjectivity of fair value measurements. Other respondents thought that the disclosure requirement would be onerous and did not believe that the benefits would outweigh the costs, particularly for non-financial assets and liabilities. The IASB received similar feedback on the proposed amendments to IFRS 7. However, users of financial statements told the IASB that the disclosures made in accordance with US GAAP and IFRS 7 were helpful, particularly in the light of the global financial crisis that started in 2007. They indicated that the disclosures allowed them to make more informed judgements and to segregate the effects of fair value measurements that are inherently subjective, thereby enhancing their ability to assess the quality of an entity's reported earnings. Consequently, the IASB decided to require an entity to provide such a reconciliation.

BC198   The exposure draft and IFRS 7 did not distinguish between *realised* and *unrealised* gains or losses. That was because those documents referred to *gains or losses attributable to assets and liabilities held at the end of the reporting period*, which the IASB meant to be equivalent to unrealised gains or losses (ie realised gains or losses result from the sale, disposal or settlement of an asset or a liability, and therefore the asset or liability is no longer held by the entity at the reporting date, whereas unrealised gains or losses relate to changes in the fair value of an asset or a liability that is held by the entity at the reporting date). Respondents to the exposure draft wondered whether the different terminology used in the exposure draft and in Topic 820 meant that the disclosure proposed for IFRSs would be different from the disclosure required by US GAAP. To ensure that there would be no differences in interpretation of the requirements in IFRSs and US GAAP, the IASB decided to use the terms *realised* and *unrealised* in the reconciliation disclosure.

BC199   The IASB concluded that the disclosure should focus on recurring fair value measurements because it would be difficult to reconcile the opening balances to the closing balances for non-recurring fair value measurements when the carrying amount of an asset or a liability is not determined on the basis of fair value at each reporting period. For example, it would be difficult to reconcile changes in fair value when an asset held for sale is recognised at its carrying amount in accordance with IFRS 5 in one period and at fair value less costs to sell in the next period. The information gained from requiring a reconciliation of changes in fair value from one period to the next is not available when requiring changes resulting from the use of different measurement bases from one period to the next.

Valuation processes

BC200   The boards decided to require an entity to disclose the valuation processes used for fair value measurements categorised within Level 3 of the fair value hierarchy (including, for example, how an entity decides its valuation policies and procedures and analyses changes in fair value measurements from period to period). They made that decision because users of financial statements told the boards that information about an entity's valuation processes helps them assess the relative subjectivity of the entity's fair value measurements, particularly for those categorised within Level 3 of the fair value hierarchy.

BC201   In addition, the requirements in IFRS 13 are consistent with the conclusions of the IASB's Fair Value Expert Advisory Panel as described in its report in October 2008.

Sensitivity to changes in unobservable inputs

BC202   The exposure draft proposed requiring a quantitative sensitivity analysis for fair value measurements categorised within Level 3 of the fair value hierarchy. That proposal was taken from the requirement in IFRS 7 to disclose a sensitivity analysis if changing any of the unobservable inputs used in the measurement to reasonably possible alternative assumptions would change the fair value significantly. Although in IFRS 7 that disclosure was required for financial assets and financial liabilities measured at fair value, under the proposal it would have been required for all assets and liabilities measured at fair value.

BC203   In August 2009 the FASB proposed a similar disclosure requirement in its proposed ASU *Fair Value Measurements and Disclosures (Topic 820): Improving Disclosures about Fair Value Measurements*, although that proposal would have required an entity to take into account the effect of interrelationships between inputs. Very few respondents to that proposed ASU supported the proposed disclosure, stating that it would not provide useful information and would be costly and operationally challenging. However, users were supportive of the proposed disclosure. The FASB decided to defer the consideration of a sensitivity analysis disclosure requirement to the joint fair value measurement project.

BC204   In the boards' discussions about that sensitivity analysis disclosure, they considered whether the IASB's proposed disclosure and that in IFRS 7 would be improved if the boards required an entity to include the effect of interrelationships between unobservable inputs, thereby showing a range of fair values (exit prices) that reasonably could have been measured in the circumstances as of the measurement date. Because that refinement of the disclosure was not included in the IASB's May 2009 exposure draft and was not required by IFRS 7, the IASB needed to expose the proposal to require the sensitivity analysis including the effect of interrelationships between unobservable inputs. That disclosure was referred to in the IASB's re-exposure document and the FASB's proposed ASU in June 2010 as a *measurement uncertainty analysis disclosure*.

BC205   Respondents to the FASB's proposed ASU and the IASB's re-exposure document were concerned about whether the proposal would be operational (those comments were consistent with those received on the FASB's proposed ASU in August 2009). Although that proposal was in response to requests from users of financial statements to require additional information about the measurement uncertainty inherent in fair value measurements (particularly those categorised within Level 3 of the fair value hierarchy), the responses from preparers of financial statements indicated that the costs associated with preparing such a disclosure would outweigh the benefits to users once the information had been aggregated by class of asset or liability. As an alternative to the proposal, those respondents suggested that the boards should require a qualitative assessment of the subjectivity of fair value measurements categorised within Level 3 of the fair value hierarchy, as well as an alternative quantitative approach that would be less costly to prepare (see paragraphs BC188–BC195).

BC206   Therefore, the boards decided to require an entity to provide a narrative description, by class of asset or liability, of the sensitivity of a recurring fair value measurement categorised within Level 3 of the fair value hierarchy to changes in the unobservable inputs used in the measurement if a change in those inputs to a different amount would result in a significantly higher or lower fair value measurement. If there are interrelationships between those inputs and other unobservable inputs, the boards decided to require an entity to provide a description of those interrelationships and of how they might magnify or mitigate the effect of changes in the unobservable inputs on the fair value measurement. The boards concluded that such information would provide users of financial statements with information about how the selection of unobservable inputs affects the valuation of a particular class of assets or liabilities. The boards expect that the narrative description will focus on the unobservable inputs for which quantitative information is disclosed because those are the unobservable inputs that the entity has determined are most significant to the fair value measurement. They will continue to assess whether a quantitative measurement uncertainty analysis disclosure would be practical after issuing IFRS 13, with the aim of reaching a conclusion about whether to require such a disclosure at a later date.

BC207   The boards concluded that a narrative description about sensitivity provides users of financial statements with information about the directional effect of a change in a significant unobservable input on a fair value measurement. That disclosure, coupled with quantitative information about the inputs used in fair value measurements categorised within Level 3 of the fair value hierarchy, provides information for users to assess whether the entity's views about individual inputs differed from their own and, if so, to decide how to incorporate the entity's fair value measurement in their decisions. In addition, that disclosure provides information about the pricing model for those users who are not familiar with the valuation of a particular class of assets or liabilities (eg complex financial instruments).

BC208   In addition to the narrative sensitivity analysis disclosure, IFRS 13 requires a quantitative sensitivity analysis for financial instruments that are measured at fair value and categorised within Level 3 of the fair value hierarchy (ie the disclosure that was previously in IFRS 7). The IASB decided to move that requirement from IFRS 7 to IFRS 13 so that all the fair value measurement disclosure requirements in IFRSs are in a single location. When developing IFRS 7, the IASB concluded that information about the sensitivities of fair value measurements to the main valuation assumptions would provide users of financial statements with a sense of the potential variability of the measurement. In forming that conclusion, the IASB considered the view that disclosure of sensitivities could be difficult, particularly when there are many assumptions to which the disclosure would apply and those assumptions are interdependent. However, the IASB noted that a detailed quantitative disclosure of sensitivity to all assumptions is not required (only those that could result in a significantly different estimate of fair value are required) and that the disclosure does not require the entity to reflect interdependencies between assumptions when making the disclosure.

BC209   The boards concluded that the objective of the narrative and quantitative sensitivity analysis disclosures about fair value are different from the objectives of other disclosures that an entity may be required to make in IFRSs and US GAAP, such as the market risk sensitivity analysis disclosure required by IFRS 7 (see paragraph 40 of IFRS 7). The IASB concluded that even though there is some overlap in those disclosures, the objective of each disclosure is different: the market risk sensitivity analysis disclosure in IFRS 7 provides information about an entity's exposure to future changes in market risks (ie currency risk, interest rate risk and other price risk), whereas the fair value measurement disclosures provide information about the sensitivity of the fair value measurement at the measurement date to changes in unobservable inputs for those fair value measurements with the greatest level of subjectivity (ie fair value measurements categorised within Level 3 of the fair value hierarchy). In addition, the market risk sensitivity analysis disclosure in IFRS 7 relates only to financial instruments (as does the quantitative sensitivity analysis disclosure in IFRS 13), whereas the narrative sensitivity analysis disclosure in IFRS 13 relates to all assets and liabilities measured at fair value.

BC210　The IASB identified the following differences between the market risk and fair value sensitivity analysis disclosures:

    (a)　The market risk disclosure is not specific to financial instruments measured at fair value, but also relates to financial instruments measured at amortised cost.

    (b)　The market risk disclosure focuses on the effect on profit or loss and equity, not specifically on the change in value.

    (c)　The market risk disclosure focuses only on the entity's exposure to market risks (ie interest rate risk, currency risk or other price risk), whereas the fair value disclosures take into account the effect on a fair value measurement of changes in significant unobservable inputs.

    (d)　The market risk disclosure does not distinguish between observable and unobservable inputs (or level in the fair value hierarchy, ie Level 1, 2 or 3), whereas the fair value disclosures relate only to the unobservable inputs used in fair value measurements categorised within Level 3 of the fair value hierarchy.

Transfers between Levels 1 and 2 of the fair value hierarchy

BC211　The exposure draft proposed requiring an entity to disclose the amounts of *significant* transfers into or out of Level 1 and Level 2 of the fair value hierarchy and the reasons for those transfers. That disclosure was also required in Topic 820. In their discussions, the boards decided instead to require a disclosure of *any* transfers into or out of Levels 1 and 2. Respondents to the FASB's proposed ASU generally did not support that proposal because it would require an entity to monitor all transfers on a daily basis, regardless of whether those transfers were significant. In addition, respondents were concerned about the accuracy of information about all transfers because there can be an unclear distinction between less active Level 1 fair value measurements and more active Level 2 fair value measurements.

BC212　The boards concluded that the objective of the disclosure is to provide information that will help users of financial statements assess changes in market and trading activity (the entity's or others') so that users can (a) incorporate into their analyses the entity's future liquidity risk and (b) analyse the entity's exposure to the relative subjectivity of its fair value measurements. In the boards' view, the only way to provide that information, and to reduce the subjectivity involved in preparing the information, is to require information about *all* transfers between Level 1 and Level 2 of the fair value hierarchy.

When an entity uses a non-financial asset in a way that differs from its highest and best use

BC213   The boards decided to require an entity to disclose information about when it uses a non-financial asset in a way that differs from its highest and best use (when that asset is measured at fair value in the statement of financial position or when its fair value is disclosed). The boards concluded that such a disclosure provides useful information for users of financial statements that rely on fair value information when forecasting future cash flows, whether that fair value information is presented in the statement of financial position or is disclosed in the notes. Users told the boards that they would need to know how non-financial assets are being used and how that use fits with an entity's strategic and operating plans.

BC214   The boards considered whether to limit the disclosure to some non-financial assets and not others. The boards concluded that because the measurement and disclosure requirements are principle-based, those requirements should not need to be amended in the future if the boards should decide to use fair value as the measurement basis for particular assets or liabilities. Therefore, the disclosure is required for any non-financial asset measured at fair value that an entity uses in a way that differs from its highest and best use.

The categorisation within the level of the fair value hierarchy for items that are not measured at fair value in the statement of financial position

BC215   IFRS 7 requires an entity to disclose the fair value of financial instruments even if they are not measured at fair value in the statement of financial position. An example is a financial instrument that is measured at amortised cost in the statement of financial position.

BC216   The boards decided to require an entity to disclose the level of the fair value hierarchy in which an asset or a liability (financial or non-financial) would be categorised if that asset or liability had been measured at fair value in the statement of financial position. The boards concluded that such a disclosure would provide meaningful information about the relative subjectivity of that fair value measurement.

BC217   Respondents to the IASB's exposure draft and the FASB's proposed ASU were concerned about the cost associated with preparing that disclosure because it is not always clear in which level a fair value measurement would be categorised. The boards concluded that even if determining the level in which to categorise a fair value measurement requires judgement, the benefits of doing so outweigh the costs. Therefore, the boards decided to require an entity to disclose the level of the fair value hierarchy in which an asset or a liability would be categorised if that asset or liability had been measured at fair value in the statement of financial position.

Assets with a recoverable amount that is fair value less costs of disposal

BC218 Because IAS 36 requires disclosures that are specific to impaired assets, the exposure draft did not propose requiring the disclosures about fair value measurements for assets with a recoverable amount that is fair value less costs of disposal in IAS 36. Some respondents (mainly users of financial statements) noted that the disclosures about impaired assets are different in IFRSs and in US GAAP (which requires assets to be tested for impairment by comparing their carrying amounts with their fair values) and asked the IASB to minimise those differences to ensure that users have access to similar information for their analyses of impaired assets.

BC219 The IASB noted that the disclosure requirements in IAS 36 were developed specifically to ensure consistency in the disclosure of information about impaired assets so that the same type of information is provided whether the recoverable amount was determined on the basis of value in use or fair value less costs of disposal. Consequently, the IASB did not think it would be appropriate to require an entity to provide information when the recoverable amount is determined on the basis of fair value less costs of disposal (ie as required by IFRS 13) that is significantly different from what the entity would provide when the recoverable amount is determined on the basis of value in use.

BC220 Although IFRSs and US GAAP have different impairment models, the IASB concluded that requiring the following information (in addition to what IAS 36 currently requires) about impaired assets measured at fair value less costs of disposal would improve comparability between entities applying IFRSs and those applying US GAAP as well as increase the convergence of IFRSs and US GAAP:

(a) the fair value less costs of disposal;

(b) the level of the fair value hierarchy within which the fair value less costs of disposal is categorised in its entirety (Level 1, 2 or 3);

(c) if applicable, changes to valuation techniques and reasons for those changes; and

(d) quantitative information about significant inputs used when measuring fair value less costs of disposal (along with a conforming amendment to the disclosures about value in use).

BC221 In addition, those disclosures are consistent with the disclosures required for non-recurring fair value measurements in IFRS 13 and in US GAAP.

Interim financial reporting

BC222   For financial instruments, the exposure draft proposed that particular fair value disclosures required in annual financial statements would also be required for interim financial reports. That differed from the approach proposed for non-financial assets and non-financial liabilities, for which there is no specific fair value disclosure requirement beyond the existing requirements in IAS 34 *Interim Financial Reporting*.

BC223   Respondents generally thought that the principle underlying IAS 34 addresses when disclosures should be updated in interim financial reports. Some respondents thought the costs of providing updated information outweighed the benefits to users of financial statements of having that information.

BC224   The IASB decided to include in IAS 34 an explicit requirement to provide updated disclosures because it concluded that the benefit of having incremental disclosures for financial instruments outweighed the associated costs given the increased interest in those instruments during the global financial crisis that started in 2007.

Effective date and transition

BC225   When deciding the effective date for IFRS 13, the IASB considered the comments received on the Request for Views *Effective Date and Transition Methods*. Many respondents said that the effective date should allow enough time for them to put the necessary systems in place to ensure that their accounting policies and models meet the requirements of IFRS 13. Some of those respondents, particularly those with many assets and liabilities measured at fair value, requested a later effective date. Other respondents requested an earlier effective date, mainly for comparability reasons and because in their view many entities might have inadvertently already started applying the revised concepts.

BC226   The IASB concluded that although IFRS 13 is a major new standard, it does not require any new fair value measurements and it does not fundamentally change many of the requirements for measuring fair value or for disclosing information about those measurements. The IASB concluded that in many respects, IFRS 13 uses different words to articulate the concepts already present in IFRSs. However, the IASB also considered the time that a particular country might require for translation and for introducing the mandatory requirements into law.

BC227   Consequently, the IASB decided that IFRS 13 should be effective for annual periods beginning on or after 1 January 2013. Because IFRS 13 applies when other IFRSs require or permit fair value measurements (and does not introduce any new fair value measurements), the IASB believes that the extended transition period for IFRS 13 provides enough time for entities, their auditors and users of financial statements to prepare for implementation of its requirements.

BC228   The IASB decided to permit early application of IFRS 13 because that would allow entities to apply the measurement and disclosure requirements as soon as practicable, thereby improving comparability in measurement and transparency in disclosures. That would also improve comparability with entities applying US GAAP.

BC229   The exposure draft proposed prospective application because the IASB concluded that a change in the methods used to measure fair value would be inseparable from a change in the fair value measurements (ie as new events occur or as new information is obtained, eg through better insight or improved judgement). Respondents to the exposure draft and the Request for Views supported that proposal. Therefore, the IASB concluded that IFRS 13 should be applied prospectively (in the same way as a change in accounting estimate).

BC230   To achieve comparability in future periods, the IASB decided to require the disclosures in IFRS 13 for the first interim period in which the IFRS is initially applied. However, those disclosures need not be presented in periods before initial application of the IFRS because it would be difficult to apply some of the requirements in IFRS 13 without the use of hindsight in selecting the inputs that would have been appropriate in prior periods.

BC230A   *Annual Improvements Cycle 2011–2013* issued in December 2013 amended paragraph 52 and added paragraph C4 to clarify the scope of the portfolio exception. It considered the transition provisions and effective date of the amendments to IFRS 13. It decided that an entity should apply that amendment for annual periods beginning on or after 1 July 2014. In order to be consistent with the prospective initial application of IFRS 13, the IASB decided that an entity would apply the amendment to IFRS 13 prospectively from the beginning of the annual period in which IFRS 13 was initially applied.

Application in emerging and transition economies

BC231   During the development of IFRS 13, the IASB received information from entities in emerging and transition economies that had concerns about applying the fair value measurement principles in IFRS 13 in their jurisdictions. Common concerns included the following:

(a)   The fair value measurement guidance is not detailed enough to allow them to measure fair value on a consistent basis.

(b)   There is limited availability of practitioners in their jurisdictions who have the skills to apply the guidance (and as a result entities might be unfamiliar with applying the necessary judgements).

(c)   There is limited access to market data to develop fair value measurements because there are few deep and liquid markets, there are often few willing buyers and sellers and prices often fluctuate considerably within short periods of time.

(d) Models, inputs and assumptions may be new and may not be comparable across entities because of rapidly developing socio-economic changes.

(e) Measuring fair value (and preparing the resulting disclosures) could be expensive.

BC232 The IASB noted that because fair value is used in many IFRSs, knowledge about its application is necessary for applying IFRSs generally and noted that the concerns raised are not specific to entities in emerging and transition economies. Entities in developed economies faced similar challenges during the global financial crisis that started in 2007 and asked the IASB for guidance for measuring the fair value of equity instruments without active markets given the requirement to recognise them at fair value in IFRS 9. Furthermore, the IASB concluded that there should not be a different threshold for measuring fair value depending on jurisdiction. Only by performing fair value measurements will entities applying IFRSs learn how to do those measurements appropriately and robustly.

BC233 Therefore, the IASB concluded that entities applying IFRSs would benefit from educational material to accompany IFRS 13. The IFRS Foundation sometimes publishes educational material that is leveraged from the standard-setting process to reinforce the goal of promoting the adoption and consistent application of a single set of high quality international accounting standards. The IASB asked the staff to develop educational material on fair value measurement that describes at a high level the thought process for measuring assets, liabilities and an entity's own equity instruments at fair value consistent with the objective of a fair value measurement.

BC234 The IASB concluded that any educational material developed must benefit all entities equally. Thus, the educational material cannot benefit entities in emerging and transition economies without being made available to entities in developed economies.

BC235 The IASB staff and the FASB staff will liaise during the development of the educational material.

Convergence with US GAAP

BC236 As noted above, the fair value measurement project was a joint project with the FASB. The boards worked together to ensure that fair value has the same meaning in IFRSs and in US GAAP and that their respective fair value measurement and disclosure requirements are the same (except for minor differences in wording and style).

BC237 The boards worked together to ensure that, to the extent possible, IFRS 13 and Topic 820 are identical. The following style differences remain:

(a) There are differences in references to other IFRSs and US GAAP—For example, regarding related party transactions, IFRS 13 refers to IAS 24 *Related Party Disclosures* and Topic 820 refers to Topic 850 *Related Party Disclosures*.

(b)   There are differences in style—For example, IFRS 13 refers to *an entity* and Topic 820 refers to *a reporting entity*.

(c)   There are differences in spelling—For example, IFRS 13 refers to *labour costs* and Topic 820 refers to *labor costs*.

(d)   There are differences in whether references are to a particular jurisdiction or are generic—For example, IFRS 13 refers to *risk-free government securities* and Topic 820 refers to *US Treasury securities*.

The boards concluded that those differences will not result in inconsistent interpretations in practice by entities applying IFRSs or US GAAP.

BC238   In addition, IFRS 13 and Topic 820 have the following differences:

(a)   There are different accounting requirements in IFRSs and US GAAP for measuring the fair value of investments in investment companies. Topic 946 *Financial Services—Investment Companies* in US GAAP requires an investment company to recognise its underlying investments at fair value at each reporting period. Topic 820 provides a practical expedient that permits an entity with an investment in an investment company to use as a measure of fair value in specific circumstances the reported net asset value without adjustment. IFRS 10 *Consolidated Financial Statements* requires an investment company to consolidate its controlled underlying investments. Because IFRSs do not have accounting requirements that are specific to investment companies, the IASB decided that it would be difficult to identify when such a practical expedient could be applied given the different practices for calculating net asset values in jurisdictions around the world. For example, investment companies may report in accordance with national GAAP, which may have recognition and measurement requirements that differ from those in IFRSs (ie the underlying investments might not be measured at fair value, or they might be measured at fair value in accordance with national GAAP, not IFRSs). The boards are reviewing the accounting for investment companies as part of a separate project.[12]

(b)   There are different requirements for measuring the fair value of a financial liability with a demand feature. In US GAAP, Topic 825 *Financial Instruments* and Topic 942 *Financial Services—Depository and Lending* describe the fair value measurement of a deposit liability as the amount payable on demand at the reporting date. In IFRSs, IFRS 13 states that the fair value measurement of a financial liability with a demand feature (eg demand deposits) cannot be less than the present value of the amount payable on demand. That requirement in IFRS 13

---

12 In October 2012 the Board issued *Investment Entities* (Amendments to IFRS 10, IFRS 12 and IAS 27), which required investment entities, as defined in IFRS 10 *Consolidated Financial Statements*, to measure their investments in subsidiaries, other than those providing investment-related services or activities, at fair value through profit or loss. In their redeliberations on the Investment Entities project, the Board considered providing a net asset value practical expedient. However, the Board decided against this because there are different calculation methods in different jurisdictions and it is outside the scope of the Investment Entities project to provide fair value measurement guidance for investments in investment entities.

        © IFRS Foundation

was relocated unchanged from IAS 39 and IFRS 9 as a consequence of the IASB's fair value measurement project.

(c)   There are different disclosure requirements in IFRSs and US GAAP. For example:

(i)   Because IFRSs generally do not allow net presentation for derivatives, the amounts disclosed for fair value measurements categorised within Level 3 of the fair value hierarchy might differ. The boards are reviewing the presentation requirements for offsetting financial assets and financial liabilities in their joint project on the accounting for financial instruments.

(ii)   IFRSs require a quantitative sensitivity analysis for financial instruments that are measured at fair value and categorised within Level 3 of the fair value hierarchy (that disclosure was previously in IFRS 7). The boards will analyse the feasibility of incorporating information about interrelationships between unobservable inputs into a quantitative measurement uncertainty analysis disclosure. After completing that analysis, the boards will decide whether to require such a disclosure.

(iii)   Topic 820 has different disclosure requirements for non-public entities. The FASB concluded that some of the disclosures should not be required for non-public entities because of the characteristics of the users of the financial statements of those entities. The FASB considered the ability of those users to access information about the financial position of the entity and the relevance to those users of the information that would be provided by the requirements in the disclosure amendments. In contrast, the IASB recently completed a project on the accounting for small and medium-sized entities. As a result, the *IFRS for Small and Medium-Sized Entities* addresses the accounting for entities that do not have public accountability, and the disclosures about their fair value measurements.

Cost-benefit considerations

BC239   The objective of general purpose financial reporting is to provide financial information about the reporting entity that is useful to existing and potential investors, lenders and other creditors in making decisions about providing resources to the entity. To meet that objective, the IASB seeks to ensure that an IFRS will meet a significant need and that the overall benefits of the resulting information justify the costs of providing it. Although the costs to implement a new standard might not be borne evenly, users of financial statements benefit from improvements in financial reporting, thereby facilitating the functioning of markets for capital and credit and the efficient allocation of resources in the economy.

BC240　The evaluation of costs and benefits is necessarily subjective. In making its judgement, the IASB considers the following:

(a)　the costs incurred by preparers of financial statements;

(b)　the costs incurred by users of financial statements when information is not available;

(c)　the comparative advantage that preparers have in developing information, compared with the costs that users would incur to develop surrogate information; and

(d)　the benefit of better economic decision-making as a result of improved financial reporting.

BC241　IFRS 13 defines fair value, provides a framework for measuring fair value and requires disclosures about fair value measurements. A clear definition of fair value, together with a framework for measuring fair value that eliminates inconsistencies across IFRSs that have contributed to diversity in practice, should improve consistency in application, thereby enhancing the comparability of information reported in financial statements.

BC242　The disclosures about fair value measurements would increase transparency and improve the quality of information provided to users of financial statements. In developing the disclosure requirements in IFRS 13, the IASB obtained input from users and preparers of financial statements and other interested parties to enable the IASB to assess whether the disclosures could be provided within reasonable cost-benefit constraints.

BC243　Although the framework for measuring fair value builds on current practice and requirements, some methods in IFRS 13 may result in a change to practice for some entities. Furthermore, some entities will need to make systems and operational changes, thereby incurring incremental costs. Other entities also might incur incremental costs in applying the measurement and disclosure requirements. However, the IASB concluded that the benefits resulting from increased consistency in application of fair value measurement requirements and enhanced comparability of fair value information and improved communication of that information to users of financial statements will continue. On balance, the IASB concluded that improvements in financial reporting resulting from the application of the requirements in IFRS 13 will exceed the increased costs of applying the requirements.

Summary of main changes from the exposure draft

BC244　The main changes from the proposals in the exposure draft published in May 2009 are as follows:

(a)　IFRS 13 excludes from its scope share-based payment transactions in IFRS 2 and leasing transactions in IAS 17. The exposure draft proposed the following:

        (i)   replacing the term *fair value* with another term that reflects the measurement objective for share-based payment transactions in IFRS 2 and for reacquired rights in a business combination in IFRS 3.

        (ii)   excluding financial liabilities with a demand feature in IAS 39[13] from the scope of an IFRS on fair value measurement.

        The exposure draft did not propose excluding leasing transactions from the scope of an IFRS on fair value measurement.

(b)   IFRS 13 requires fair value to be measured using the price in the principal market for the asset or liability, or in the absence of a principal market, the most advantageous market for the asset or liability. The exposure draft proposed that fair value should be measured using the price in the most advantageous market.

(c)   IFRS 13 states that market participants have a reasonable understanding about the asset or liability and the transaction using all available information, including information that might be obtained through due diligence efforts that are usual and customary. The exposure draft stated that market participants are presumed to be as knowledgeable as the entity about the asset or liability (ie there was no information asymmetry between market participants and the entity).

(d)   IFRS 13 contains detailed guidance for measuring the fair value of liabilities, including the compensation market participants would require to assume the liability and how a third-party credit enhancement affects the fair value of a liability. The exposure draft provided high level guidance.

(e)   IFRS 13 contains detailed guidance for measuring the fair value of an entity's own equity instruments. That guidance is consistent with the guidance for measuring the fair value of a liability. The exposure draft proposed requiring an entity to measure the fair value of its own equity instruments by reference to the fair value of the instrument held by a market participant as an asset (ie the corresponding asset) without providing information about when the fair value of the equity instrument might differ from the fair value of the corresponding asset.

(f)   IFRS 13 provides guidance for measuring the fair value of financial assets and financial liabilities with offsetting positions in market risks or counterparty credit risk. The exposure draft proposed requiring financial assets to be measured using an in-exchange valuation premise.

(g)   IFRS 13 states that classes of asset or liability for disclosure purposes should be determined on the basis of the nature, characteristics and risks of the asset or liability and the level of the fair value hierarchy within which the fair value measurement is categorised. The exposure

---

13   IFRS 9 *Financial Instruments* replaced IAS 39. IFRS 9 applies to all items that were previously within the scope of IAS 39.

draft did not provide guidance for determining the appropriate class of asset or liability for disclosures about fair value measurements.

(h)   IFRS 13 provides examples of policies for when to recognise transfers between levels of the fair value hierarchy, such as the date of the transfer, the beginning of the reporting period or the end of the reporting period. IFRS 13 also states that the policy about the timing of recognising transfers must be the same for transfers into a level as that for transfers out of a level. The exposure draft did not provide guidance for determining when transfers are deemed to have occurred or propose to require an entity to disclose its policy for determining when transfers between levels are recognised.

(i)   IFRS 13 requires a narrative discussion of the sensitivity of a fair value measurement categorised within Level 3 of the fair value hierarchy to changes in significant unobservable inputs and any interrelationships between those inputs that might magnify or mitigate the effect on the measurement. It also requires a quantitative sensitivity analysis for financial instruments categorised within Level 3 of the fair value hierarchy (that disclosure was relocated from IFRS 7). The exposure draft proposed a quantitative sensitivity analysis for assets and liabilities categorised within Level 3 of the fair value hierarchy. The IASB re-exposed that proposal, including a requirement to take into account the interrelationships between unobservable inputs in the analysis (referred to as a measurement uncertainty analysis disclosure). Respondents were concerned about whether the proposal would be operational. The boards will continue to assess whether a quantitative measurement uncertainty analysis disclosure would be practical after the IFRS is issued, with the aim of reaching a conclusion about whether to require such a disclosure at a later date.

(j)   IFRS 13 requires an entity to disclose information about its valuation processes (eg valuation policies and procedures) for fair value measurements categorised within Level 3 of the fair value hierarchy. The disclosure is similar to the description of valuation processes in the IASB's Fair Value Expert Advisory Panel's October 2008 report.

(k)   If the highest and best use of a non-financial asset differs from its current use, IFRS 13 requires an entity to disclose that fact and why the asset is being used in a manner that differs from its highest and best use. The exposure draft proposed requiring an entity to disclose the value of the asset assuming its current use, the amount by which the fair value of the asset differs from its fair value in its current use (ie the incremental value of the asset group) and the reasons the asset is being used in a manner that differs from its highest and best use.

Appendix
Amendments to the Basis for Conclusions on other IFRSs

This appendix contains amendments to the Basis for Conclusions on other IFRSs that are necessary in order to ensure consistency with IFRS 13 and the related amendments to other IFRSs. Amended paragraphs are shown with new text underlined and deleted text struck through.

* * * * *

The amendments contained in this appendix when IFRS 13 was issued in 2011 have been incorporated into the Basis for Conclusions on the relevant IFRSs published in this volume.

IASB documents published to accompany

IFRS 14

Regulatory Deferral Accounts

The text of the unaccompanied standard, IFRS 14, is contained in Part A of this edition. Its effective date when issued was 1 January 2016. The text of the Accompanying Guidance on IFRS 14 is contained in Part B of this edition. This part presents the following documents:

BASIS FOR CONCLUSIONS

DISSENTING OPINIONS

CONTENTS

© IFRS Foundation

Basis for Conclusions on
IFRS 14 *Regulatory Deferral Accounts*

This Basis for Conclusions accompanies, but is not part of, IFRS 14.

Introduction

BC1　This Basis for Conclusions summarises the considerations of the International Accounting Standards Board (IASB) in reaching the conclusions in IFRS 14 *Regulatory Deferral Accounts*. Individual IASB members gave greater weight to some factors than to others.

BC2　The IASB and the IFRS Interpretations Committee (the 'Interpretations Committee') received several requests for guidance on whether rate-regulated entities can or should recognise, in their IFRS financial statements, a regulatory deferral or variance account debit or credit balance as a result of price or rate regulation by regulatory bodies or governments. Some national accounting standard-setting bodies permit or require such balances to be recognised as assets and liabilities under some circumstances, depending on the type of rate regulation in force. In such cases, these regulatory deferral account balances are often referred to as 'regulatory assets' and 'regulatory liabilities'. However, as explained in this Basis for Conclusions (see paragraphs BC11–BC12 and BC21), the term 'regulatory deferral account balances' has been chosen as a neutral descriptor for these items for the purpose of this Standard.

BC3　US generally accepted accounting principles (US GAAP) have recognised the economic effect of certain types of rate regulation since at least 1962. In 1982, the US national standard-setter, the Financial Accounting Standards Board (FASB) issued SFAS 71 *Accounting for the Effects of Certain Types of Regulation*.[1] SFAS 71 formalised many of those principles. In the absence of specific national guidance, practice in many other jurisdictions followed SFAS 71. In the financial statements of rate-regulated entities that apply such guidance, regulatory deferral account balances are often incorporated into the carrying amount of items such as property, plant and equipment and intangible assets, or are recognised as separate items in the financial statements.

BC4　In June 2005, the Interpretations Committee received a request about SFAS 71. The request asked whether an entity could apply SFAS 71 in accordance with the hierarchy in paragraphs 10–12 of IAS 8 *Accounting Policies, Changes in Accounting Estimates and Errors* when selecting an accounting policy in the absence of specific guidance in IFRS.

BC5　The Interpretations Committee previously discussed the possible recognition of regulatory deferral account debit balances as part of its project on service concessions. As a result of its consideration at that time, the Interpretations Committee concluded that "entities applying IFRS should recognise only assets that qualified for recognition in accordance with the IASB's *Framework for the*

1　The guidance in SFAS 71, together with subsequent amendments and related guidance, has now been incorporated into Topic 980 *Regulated Operations* in the FASB *Accounting Standards Codification*.

Preparation and Presentation of Financial Statements[2] ... and relevant accounting standards, such as IAS 11 *Construction Contracts*, IAS 18 *Revenue*, IAS 16 *Property, Plant and Equipment* and IAS 38 *Intangible Assets*." In other words, the Interpretations Committee thought that an entity should recognise 'regulatory assets' only to the extent that they meet the criteria to be recognised as assets in accordance with existing IFRS.

BC6   The Interpretations Committee concluded that the recognition criteria in SFAS 71 were not fully consistent with the recognition criteria in IFRS. Applying the guidance in SFAS 71 would result in the recognition of regulatory deferral account balances under certain circumstances that would not meet the recognition criteria of relevant Standards. Consequently, the requirements of SFAS 71 were not indicative of the requirements of IFRS. The Interpretations Committee decided not to add a project on regulatory assets to its agenda.

BC7   In January 2008, the Interpretations Committee received a second request to consider whether rate-regulated entities could or should recognise a regulatory liability (or a regulatory asset) as a result of rate regulation by regulatory bodies or governments. The Interpretations Committee again decided not to add the issue to its agenda for several reasons. Importantly, it concluded that divergence did not seem to be significant in practice for entities that were applying IFRS. The established practice of almost all entities is to eliminate regulatory deferral account balances when IFRS is adopted and not to recognise such balances in IFRS financial statements. However, the Interpretations Committee also noted that rate regulation is widespread and significantly affects the economic environment of many entities.

BC8   The IASB noted the ongoing requests for guidance on this issue. It also considered the comments that had been received on the Interpretations Committee's tentative agenda decisions. Those comments pointed out that although divergence in IFRS practice did not exist, several jurisdictions whose local accounting principles permitted or required the recognition of regulatory deferral account balances would be adopting IFRS in the near future. This would increase pressure for definitive guidance on the recognition of regulatory deferral account balances as assets or liabilities.

BC9   Consequently, in December 2008, the IASB added a project on rate-regulated activities to its agenda and subsequently, in July 2009, published an Exposure Draft Rate-regulated Activities (the '2009 ED'). The responses to the 2009 ED raised complex and fundamental issues at a conceptual level. In September 2010, the IASB decided that the complex technical issues could not be resolved quickly, and suspended the project until it had considered whether to include rate-regulated activities in its future agenda. The 2011 Agenda Consultation asked stakeholders to provide their views as to which projects the IASB should give priority.[3] The responses to this consultation, received through comment

---

2   The reference is to the IASC's *Framework for the Preparation and Presentation of Financial Statements*, adopted by the IASB in 2001 and in effect when the Interpretations Committee discussed this matter.

3   In July 2011, the IASB published a formal Request for Views document to provide a channel for formal public input on the broad aspects of our agenda-setting process.

letters and other outreach activities, persuaded the IASB to prioritise addressing the unresolved issues related to rate-regulated activities.

BC10   As a result of its agenda-setting process, in September 2012 the IASB decided to add to its agenda a comprehensive project on rate-regulated activities to investigate these complex issues. In addition, the *Conceptual Framework for Financial Reporting* (the '*Conceptual Framework*')[4] is currently being reviewed and updated. The outcome of the Rate-regulated Activities project will be influenced by the outcome of the *Conceptual Framework* project. The initial objective is to develop a Discussion Paper for each of these projects, which the IASB hopes will provide a basis for developing guidance in the long term. It also decided, in December 2012, to develop an interim Standard on the accounting for regulatory deferral accounts that would apply until the completion of the comprehensive project. This Standard is the result of that decision.

Reasons for issuing this Standard

BC11   Many rate-regulated entities think that recognising regulatory deferral account balances as assets and liabilities would provide more relevant information and would provide a more faithful representation of their rate-regulated activities than the established practice in IFRS currently. They suggest that rate regulation creates special conditions that support the recognition of regulatory deferral account balances, even when those balances consist of deferred costs that other Standards require to be recognised as an expense in the period in which they are incurred. The 2009 ED, which proposed that regulatory deferral account balances should be recognised when arising from activities that are subject to a specific type of rate regulation (referred to in the 2009 ED as "cost-of-service rate regulation"), raised expectations that the IASB had agreed that there was merit to the arguments used to support recognition of such balances as assets and liabilities.

BC12   Consequently, some respondents have noted that, although the case has not been made conclusively for amending IFRS to permit or require the recognition of regulatory deferral account balances as assets and liabilities, neither has it been made conclusively for an approach that eliminates such balances and changes existing accounting policies. These policies are being widely applied in accordance with some national GAAPs, and are familiar to many users of financial statements in jurisdictions that currently permit or require the recognition of rate-regulated items.

BC13   The IASB recognises that discontinuing the recognition of regulatory deferral account balances in advance of the conclusion of the comprehensive Rate-regulated Activities project could be a significant barrier to the adoption of IFRS for entities for which regulatory deferral account balances represent a significant proportion of net assets. This has led to an industry-specific 'carve-out' from the application of IFRS in at least one jurisdiction that has otherwise adopted IFRS, to allow rate-regulated entities to continue to use local GAAP

---

4   References to the *Conceptual Framework* in this Basis for Conclusions are to the *Conceptual Framework for Financial Reporting*, issued in 2010 and in effect when the Standard was developed.

(or, in some cases, US GAAP). In addition, there are examples of 'carve-ins' being created that introduce specific guidance for rate-regulated activities that overlies IFRS requirements as issued by the IASB. However, the interaction of such guidance when it is in conflict with the requirements of IFRS can create diversity of application in practice.

BC14   During outreach, some respondents told the IASB that, in many jurisdictions, the accounting policies developed for regulatory deferral account balances are based on US GAAP or local GAAP that provides similar guidance. This is understood to provide a reasonable level of comparability for regulatory deferral account balances across jurisdictions. However, different approaches to accommodating existing practice for such balances have reduced comparability for users of financial statements in these jurisdictions, because the rest of the items in the financial statements are now accounted for using different accounting frameworks (for example, IFRS, US GAAP or local GAAP), depending on which approach has been adopted. In some cases, the development of these carve-in or carve-out options has been in direct response to the publication of the 2009 ED.

BC15   The IASB acknowledges the difficult practice problems related to this issue. The IASB has, therefore, decided to issue this Standard, which allows entities that currently recognise regulatory deferral account balances in accordance with their previous GAAP to continue to do so when making the transition to IFRS. In accordance with paragraph 5, an entity is only eligible to apply this Standard if it:

(a)   is subject to oversight and/or approval from an authorised body (the rate regulator);

(b)   recognised regulatory deferral account balances in its financial statements in accordance with its previous GAAP; and

(c)   elected to apply the requirements of this Standard in its first IFRS financial statements.

BC16   Consequently, an entity that does not recognise regulatory deferral account balances in accordance with its previous GAAP in the period immediately preceding its first IFRS financial statements is not eligible to apply this Standard in order to start recognising such balances. An entity would not, therefore, be eligible if, for example:

(a)   the entity did not have any relevant rate-regulated activities in the period before it made the transition to IFRS but then acquires or commences rate-regulated activities after the date that it adopts IFRS; or

(b)   the entity is a newly formed business and adopts IFRS in its first IFRS financial statements.

BC17   The IASB thinks that this restriction balances the needs of preparers and users in jurisdictions that currently recognise regulatory deferral account balances in accordance with previous GAAP, and those that already prepare IFRS financial statements and do not recognise such balances.

BC18　A Standard that permits first-time adopters of IFRS to continue to apply their existing policies for the recognition, measurement, impairment and derecognition of regulatory deferral account balances will help those entities avoid having to make a major change to their accounting policies for regulatory deferral account balances until the comprehensive Rate-regulated Activities project is completed. The related presentation and disclosure requirements should help to reduce the disruption to information available for trend analyses for these entities on transition to IFRS, until the IASB can consider these issues in its comprehensive project. This would enable rate-regulated entities to overcome the barrier noted in paragraph BC13 and, consequently, to make the transition to IFRS.

BC19　Although comparability will be improved overall by having more entities applying IFRS, the IASB acknowledges that permitting only a limited population of entities to recognise regulatory deferral account balances will introduce some inconsistency and diversity into IFRS practice for the treatment of regulatory deferral account balances, when it does not currently exist. In order to improve comparability between IFRS preparers that are subject to rate regulation but that do not recognise regulatory deferral account balances and entities that are permitted to recognise such balances in accordance with this Standard, the IASB decided to require segregated presentation of these balances. The IASB thinks that the resulting presentation and disclosure requirements in this Standard will help to minimise the impact of introducing this inconsistency, and that the benefits to users and preparers of financial statements outweigh the costs.

BC20　The IASB thinks that the following benefits of this Standard justify introducing this diversity:

(a)　it is likely to remove a major barrier to the adoption of IFRS for entities for which regulatory deferral account balances represent a significant proportion of net assets;

(b)　it should reduce the risk of entities adopting locally developed carve-ins or carve-outs that would otherwise create greater diversity of accounting treatment and greater confusion for users of financial statements. Having more entities applying IFRS would ensure that their other activities are reported in accordance with IFRS, thereby increasing comparability for those other assets and liabilities; and

(c)　it is likely to improve transparency and consistency in the way that regulatory deferral account balances and movements in those balances are presented, thereby highlighting the impact of recognising such items and improving comparability between those entities that recognise such balances in accordance with the Standard.

BC21　However, the IASB noted that, by issuing this Standard, it is not anticipating the outcome of the comprehensive Rate-regulated Activities project referred to in paragraph BC10. Consequently, regulatory deferral account balances are not described as regulatory assets or regulatory liabilities in this Standard because the IASB has yet to decide whether they meet the definitions of assets or liabilities in the *Conceptual Framework*. The separation of these balances from the amounts that are recognised as assets and liabilities in accordance with other Standards is designed to maintain the integrity of the application of existing Standards.

Scope

BC22   This Standard does not allow entities to recognise regulatory deferral account balances if those entities have a dominant position in a market and decide to self-regulate to avoid the potential government intervention that might occur if it were perceived to be abusing its dominant position. Instead, it requires there to be a formal rate regulator involved to ensure that the rate-regulatory mechanism in place is supported by statute or regulation and that the regulatory mechanism binds the entity.

BC23   However, the IASB does not intend to exclude entities that are regulated by their own governing body in cases in which:

(a)   the governing body sets prices both in the interests of the customers and to ensure the financial viability of the entity within a specified framework; and

(b)   the framework is subject to oversight and/or approval by an authorised body that is empowered by statute or regulation.

BC24   This situation could arise, for example, when the entity conducts previously state-run activities and the government delegates regulatory powers to an entity (that may be state-controlled) within a statutory framework that is overseen by an authorised body of the government. Another example is a co-operative that may be subject to some form of regulatory oversight in order to obtain preferential loans, tax relief or other incentives to maintain the supply of goods or services that the government consider to be essential or near essential.

BC25   This Standard does not address an entity's accounting for reporting to rate regulators (regulatory accounting). Rate regulators may require a regulated entity to maintain its accounts in a form that permits the rate regulator to obtain the information that is needed for regulatory purposes. Rate regulators' actions are based on many considerations. This Standard neither limits nor endorses a rate regulator's actions.

BC26   Although rate regulators can affect the timing of the recovery of the costs or the reversal of over-recoveries through future increases and decreases in rates, they cannot change the characteristics of assets and liabilities that exist and that are accounted for in accordance with IFRS. The IASB has not, therefore, introduced any changes to the accounting for assets or liabilities that are already addressed in other Standards. Those items should be accounted for in accordance with those Standards, irrespective of whether the entity is subject to rate regulation or not.

BC27   Consequently, the IASB decided that the scope of the Standard should be limited to specifying how an entity reports the differences that arise between the regulatory accounting requirements of rate regulators and the accounting that would otherwise be required in financial statements that are prepared in accordance with IFRS, in the absence of this Standard.

Recognition, measurement, impairment and derecognition

Temporary exemption from paragraph 11 of IAS 8

BC28   As noted in paragraph BC7, the established practice in IFRS has been that rate-regulated entities do not recognise regulatory deferral accounts in IFRS financial statements. Some IASB members are concerned that entities that will recognise regulatory deferral account balances in accordance with this Standard could give the appearance of being compliant with IFRS while being inconsistent with the stated objectives of the IASB, ie to provide users of financial statements with financial information that is transparent, comparable and of high quality. The IASB did not consider the exemption from parts of IAS 8 lightly, but introduced this interim step to lower a significant barrier to adopting IFRS for some jurisdictions, pending the completion of the comprehensive Rate-regulated Activities project. This step is also intended to minimise disruption, both for users (for example, a lack of continuity of information available for trend analyses) and preparers (for example, extensive system changes) when entities in these jurisdictions make the transition to IFRS.

BC29   The IASB has been told that the majority of the national standard-setting bodies that permit or require the recognition of regulatory deferral account balances in accordance with local GAAP do so using the requirements of US GAAP (Topic 980 *Regulated Operations* in the FASB *Accounting Standards Codification*®) or local requirements that are based on US GAAP. Consequently, the IASB does not expect there to be significant diversity in the accounting for regulatory deferral account balances in jurisdictions that currently apply regulatory accounting in financial statements.

BC30   Paragraph 12 of IAS 8 could permit Topic 980 or similar local GAAP requirements to be applied in IFRS financial statements, but only to the extent that those national GAAPs do not conflict with the sources of guidance listed in paragraph 11 of IAS 8 (ie other Standards and the *Conceptual Framework*). As noted in paragraph BC6, the Interpretations Committee concluded that the recognition criteria in SFAS 71 (now incorporated into Topic 980) were not fully consistent with the recognition criteria in IFRS. This is because some regulatory deferral account balances are specifically prohibited from being recognised as assets and liabilities by other Standards. It is this conflict with the sources listed in paragraph 11 of IAS 8 that has prevented almost all existing IFRS preparers from recognising regulatory deferral account balances. Consequently, the IASB has decided that entities within the scope of this Standard should be granted a temporary exemption from paragraph 11 of IAS 8 in order to overcome the restriction on the use of the sources of accounting guidance referred to in paragraph 12 of IAS 8.

BC31 When developing IFRS 4 *Insurance Contracts*[5] and IFRS 6 *Exploration for and Evaluation of Mineral Resources*, the IASB considered whether they should require an entity to follow its national accounting requirements (ie national GAAP) when accounting for insurance contracts or the exploration for and evaluation of mineral resources respectively to prevent the selection of accounting policies that do not form a comprehensive basis of accounting. Consistent with its conclusions in those Standards, the IASB concluded that defining national GAAP would have posed problems. Further definitional problems could have arisen because some entities do not apply the national GAAP of their own country. For example, some non-US entities with rate-regulated activities apply US GAAP (Topic 980). Moreover, it is unusual and, arguably, beyond the IASB's mandate to impose requirements set by another body.

BC32 Consequently, the IASB decided that an entity could continue to follow the accounting policies that it was using when it first applied the IFRS requirements, provided that they satisfy the requirements of paragraphs 10 and 12 of IAS 8. This should help to ensure that those policies are generally accepted in the local jurisdiction, either because the local GAAP allows the use of another standard-setter's pronouncement or because of accepted industry practice. The IASB decided to adopt the same approach in this Standard that it adopted with IFRSs 4 and 6, for the same reasons.

Changes in accounting policies

BC33 IAS 8 prohibits a change in accounting policies that is not required by a Standard, unless the change will result in information that is reliable and more relevant. Paragraph 15 of IAS 8 explains that this is because users of financial statements need to be able to compare the financial statements of an entity over time to identify trends in financial position, financial performance and cash flows. Consistent with its conclusions in IFRSs 4 and 6, the IASB decided to permit changes in accounting policies for regulatory deferral account balances if they make the financial statements more relevant and no less reliable, or more reliable and no less relevant, judged in accordance with the criteria in IAS 8.

BC34 As previously noted, the IASB has started the research phase of a comprehensive project to investigate how IFRS financial statements might reflect the effects of rate regulation (see paragraph BC10). Until that project is completed, the IASB wishes to minimise disruption to information used for trend analyses of IFRS financial statements and thus the limitation on changes in accounting policy is intended to be restrictive. The established practice in IFRS has been that almost all rate-regulated entities do not recognise regulatory deferral account balances in IFRS financial statements. Consequently, the IASB thinks that changing an accounting policy to start to recognise such balances, or to recognise a wider range of such balances by modifying a previous GAAP policy, when that changed policy might need to change again following the completion of the Rate-regulated Activities project, would not make the financial statements more reliable. The scope of this

---

5 IFRS 17 *Insurance Contracts*, issued in May 2017, replaced IFRS 4.

Standard and the restriction on changes in accounting policies in paragraphs 13–15, therefore, prohibit entities that currently do not recognise regulatory deferral account balances from starting to do so.

BC35   The IASB wished to avoid imposing unnecessary changes of accounting policy as a result of applying this Standard. However, it did not want to prevent entities that currently recognise regulatory deferral account balances from ceasing to recognise them when adopting IFRS because this would be consistent with the established IFRS practice. The IASB thinks that this would result in an entity presenting more comparable information with existing IFRS preparers, which would bring the financial statements closer to the criteria in IAS 8. The IASB has, therefore, decided that the continued recognition of regulatory deferral account balances in accordance with this Standard should be optional. An entity that is eligible to apply this Standard but that elects not to apply it and, consequently, ceases to recognise its regulatory deferral account balances, is not required to apply any of the disclosure requirements of this Standard. However, such entities, and other entities that are not eligible to apply this Standard, are not prohibited from providing supplementary disclosures, such as those set out in paragraphs 30–36.

BC36   In addition, this Standard contains some specific accounting requirements for presentation that may require entities to change the presentation of regulatory deferral account balances that they recognise in accordance with their previous GAAP accounting policies. The IASB thinks that these changes, together with the specific disclosure requirements set out in this Standard, will improve comparability and understandability, and provide relevant information to users.

Interaction with other Standards

BC37   Any specific exception, exemption or additional requirements related to the interaction of this Standard with other Standards is contained within this Standard. The IASB thinks that, except for IFRS 1, other Standards should not be subject to consequential amendments relating only to this Standard because its application is restricted to a limited population of entities. In addition, it is intended to be applicable only as a short-term interim solution until the comprehensive Rate-regulated Activities project is completed.

BC38   As previously noted, in order to apply this Standard an eligible entity must elect to apply it in the entity's first IFRS financial statements. Consequently, a first-time adopter will initially apply this Standard at the same time as it applies IFRS 1. Paragraph D8B of IFRS 1 provides an exemption to allow first-time adopters to use, as the deemed cost at the date of transition to IFRS, the previous GAAP carrying amount of items of property, plant and equipment or intangible assets that are used, or were previously used, in operations subject to rate regulation. For the purposes of that exemption, paragraph D8B defined operations that are subject to rate regulation in the context of a cost-plus or cost-of-service type of rate regulation. The IASB has decided to make a consequential amendment to paragraph D8B of IFRS 1 to make the definition of rate regulation used in that paragraph consistent with the definition used in this Standard. This will ensure that a first-time adopter that applies this

Standard is not prohibited from using the exemptions available to other first-time adopters in IFRS 1.

Recoverability

BC39   Although the approval by the rate regulator may not guarantee that a regulatory deferral account balance will be recovered (or reversed) through future sales, it does provide a high degree of assurance that the anticipated economic benefits will flow to or from the entity. In some cases, an entity may incur costs several months or even years before the rate regulator formally approves them. The IASB concluded that, in such cases, judgement is required to determine whether the costs can be considered recoverable. Consequently, the IASB decided not to develop specific recognition or impairment requirements for these circumstances, but instead decided that an entity should continue to apply its previous GAAP accounting policies for the recognition and measurement of such amounts.

Presentation

Cost of self-constructed or internally generated assets

BC40   The IASB noted that in some cases, a rate regulator requires, for rate-setting purposes, an entity to include, as part of the cost of property, plant and equipment or other assets, amounts that would not be included by non-rate-regulated entities. For example, a rate regulator might specify how to calculate the carrying value of an item of property, plant and equipment for rate-setting purposes (the rate-base or regulatory value), which might differ from the method required by IAS 16.

BC41   The IASB acknowledges that at least two alternatives exist for accounting for these amounts: present them separately or include them within the amounts presented for property, plant and equipment or other assets. Proponents of the first alternative think that regulatory deferral account balances that would be recognised as a result of this Standard do not have the same characteristics as assets and liabilities that would be recognised in accordance with other Standards. Consequently, proponents of this alternative think that all amounts that qualify for recognition as regulatory deferral account balances should be presented separately from the assets and liabilities that are recognised in accordance with other Standards, instead of being included within the carrying amount of the item of property, plant and equipment or other asset.

BC42   Proponents of the second alternative think that some regulatory deferral account balances that would be recognised as a result of this Standard are so closely related to other assets of the entity that accounting for them separately does not provide additional information to users. Proponents of this alternative think that when regulatory assets are complementary to other assets and have similar useful lives, there is no need to incur the costs of separate accounting. Instead, they think that the other assets should be measured at the amount allowed for rate-regulatory purposes. In accordance with this alternative, an entity includes the regulatory deferral account balances in the cost of the asset that is recognised in accordance with other Standards as a single asset. This approach is consistent with that applied in US GAAP (Topic 980).

BC43   The IASB will consider this issue as part of the comprehensive Rate-regulated Activities project. For the purpose of this Standard, the IASB has decided to require the first alternative. This decision does not change the relief available to first-time adopters using the deemed cost exemption provided by paragraph D8B of IFRS 1 (see paragraph BC38). This is consistent with the IASB's decision not to introduce any changes to the accounting for assets and liabilities that are already addressed in other Standards (see paragraph BC26). Some IASB members think that this separate presentation is essential until the consideration of the more fundamental issues about accounting for rate-regulated activities is completed through the comprehensive project.

Separate presentation in the primary financial statements

BC44   Many of the items included in regulatory deferral account balances would not otherwise be capitalised as assets (or liabilities) in the absence of the temporary exemption from paragraph 11 of IAS 8 that is contained in this Standard (see paragraph BC30). Consequently, and consistent with the IASB's decision discussed in paragraph BC43, the Standard requires the total of all regulatory deferral account debit balances and the total of all regulatory deferral account credit balances to be presented as separate line items in the statement of financial position. Similarly, the net movement between the opening and closing balances is presented separately within the statement(s) of profit or loss and other comprehensive income, split between amounts related to other comprehensive income and amounts related to profit or loss. Any movements not related to profit or loss or other comprehensive income, such as amounts acquired or disposed of, are disclosed in the reconciliation of opening and closing balances required by paragraph 33.

BC45   In addition, the IASB concluded that presenting the regulatory impact separately would provide more useful information about the regulatory environment and would be consistent with the enhancing qualitative characteristic of comparability in paragraphs QC20–QC25 of the *Conceptual Framework*. In particular, it would enable users to more directly compare the property, plant and equipment or intangible assets of comparable rate-regulated entities (in addition to comparing them to those of non-rate-regulated entities), regardless of whether they recognise regulatory deferral account balances in their financial statements. This would also result in more consistent application of IFRS for all other transactions or activities, irrespective of whether an entity has rate-regulated activities and the type of rate-regulatory environment that the entity is subject to.

BC46   The IASB concluded that the separate presentation of regulatory deferral account balances, especially those amounts that are often permitted by national GAAP practices to be included within the carrying amounts of property, plant and equipment and other assets, is an important improvement because it contributes to increased transparency in financial reporting. The

IASB noted that a first-time adopter of IFRS may apply the deemed cost exemption in paragraph D8B of IFRS 1, which allows adopters to use their previous GAAP carrying amounts at the date of transition to IFRS. This exemption provides relief for first-time adopters that would otherwise be required to separate out the regulatory component of the carrying amount of sometimes very large and old items of property, plant and equipment or intangible assets at the date of transition to IFRS, which may be impracticable. The IASB has made a consequential amendment to the scope of the IFRS 1 exemption to make it consistent with the scope of this Standard. Consequently, entities that apply this Standard will only need to isolate the regulatory deferral account amounts for those items on a prospective basis from the date of transition to IFRS. The IASB also noted that the information required for separate presentation on an ongoing basis is normally available in any case, due to the information requirements of rate regulators.

Current/non-current allocation and offset

BC47   Regulatory deferral account balances arise from specific individual costs (income) that the rate regulator requires or permits to be deferred to future periods. The rates charged for goods or services in the current period may be intended to recover a combination of past costs, current costs and, in some cases, anticipated future costs. Although the rate regulator may specify the period over which the recovery of the regulatory deferral account balances is intended, judgement may be needed to identify the costs that the revenue billed in a period recovers. This means that detailed scheduling of the timing of recovery or reversal of each regulatory deferral account debit or credit balance may be needed for the purpose of identifying which amounts should be classed as current or for determining which amounts would be recovered or reversed in the same period for the purposes of offsetting. Consequently, the IASB has decided that regulatory deferral account balances should not be presented as current or non-current and that debit and credit balances should not be offset in the statement of financial position. Instead, this Standard requires information about the period(s) over which regulatory deferral account balances are expected to be recovered or reversed to be disclosed. An entity is not, however, prohibited from identifying current and non-current amounts within the information disclosed if the relevant information is available.

Disclosure

BC48   In December 2012, the IASB launched a survey on disclosures, which was directed at preparers, users and others interested in or affected by disclosure requirements. The results were discussed in a public discussion forum on *Disclosures in Financial Reporting* in January 2013. The survey and the discussion forum were aimed at assisting the IASB to gain a clearer picture on the perceived "disclosure problem" (ie identifying disclosure requirements that create a burden for preparers but do not provide users with sufficient relevant information). The views of most financial statement preparers that took part in these events identified the primary problem as the disclosure requirements being too extensive, with not enough being done to exclude immaterial information, which has been referred to as "disclosure overload". Similarly, many users of financial statements felt that preparers could do more to improve the communication of relevant information within the financial statements, rather than leaving users to sift through large amounts of data.

BC49   With this in mind, this Standard sets out a general objective for disclosure as well as a list of detailed items that might be useful in achieving that objective. The IASB has previously concluded that it is unnecessary, in general, to state explicitly that specified disclosures relate only to material items because all Standards are governed by the concept of materiality as described in IAS 1 *Presentation of Financial Statements* and in IAS 8. The IASB has decided, consistent with its previous conclusions, not to specifically refer to materiality in this Standard. However, this Standard contains other explicit guidance to clarify that preparers should use their judgement to decide which of the detailed items are necessary to achieve the objective and what level of detail to provide.

BC50   The IASB thinks that an understanding of an entity's different types of rate-regulated activities is important for understanding the entity as a whole. In addition, an understanding of each class of regulatory deferral account is considered important because that can provide information about the nature of the rate regulation and the potential timing of related cash flows. Consequently, this Standard requires the disclosure of qualitative and quantitative information for each type of an entity's rate-regulated activities and each class of regulatory deferral account balance, because this will provide information that is more useful in assessing the impact of different rate-regulatory environments.

BC51   The IASB thinks that most entities that already recognise regulatory deferral account balances in accordance with US GAAP, or similar requirements or practices in other jurisdictions, currently provide most of the information required to be disclosed by paragraph 33 of this Standard. However, the IASB observed that the information is often disclosed in various places throughout the financial statements in a way that can make it difficult for a user to appreciate the overall effect that rate regulation has had on the amounts recognised in the financial statements. Consequently, this Standard requires that entities meet the disclosure requirements by providing a table, containing aggregated information, and showing a reconciliation of the movements in the carrying amounts in the statement of financial position of the various categories of regulatory items. This table will be required unless another format is more appropriate. The IASB noted that such a table, presenting information in a structured manner, would assist financial statement users in understanding how the entity's reported financial position and comprehensive income have been affected by rate regulation.

Location of qualitative disclosures

BC52   The IASB observed that many entities provide, often in the management commentary reports that accompany the financial statements, a qualitative description of the nature and extent of the effect of rate regulation on its activities. The IASB acknowledges that the nature and extent of rate regulation can have a significant impact on the amount and timing of revenue and cash flows of a rate-regulated entity. Hence, the IASB concluded that such disclosures should be part of the financial statements and they could be given either in the financial statements or incorporated by cross-reference from the financial statements to some other statement that is available to users of the financial statements on the same terms as the financial statements and at the same time. This approach is intended to reduce duplication of information and is consistent with some types of risk disclosure required by IFRS 7 *Financial Instruments: Disclosures*.

Effective date and transition

BC53   This Standard will only be available to first-time adopters of IFRS and will need to be applied retrospectively at the date of transition to IFRS. The IASB usually intends to allow a minimum of one year between the date when wholly new Standards or major amendments to Standards are issued and the date when implementation is required. Consequently, the IASB has set 1 January 2016 as the effective date for this Standard. Earlier application is permitted to make the benefits outlined in paragraph BC20 available at the earliest opportunity.

BC54   The IASB concluded that no explicit relief from full retrospective application of the Standard is needed because existing recognition, measurement, impairment and derecognition policies are continued when this Standard is applied. First-time adopters of IFRS can use the deemed cost exemption for property, plant and equipment and intangible assets that is already available in IFRS 1 that allows first-time adopters to use their previous GAAP carrying amounts at the date of transition to IFRS. Consequently, they will only need to change their presentation policies for these items to isolate the regulatory deferral account amounts on a prospective basis from the date of transition to IFRS.

Summary of main changes from the Exposure Draft *Regulatory Deferral Accounts*

BC55   The proposed definition of the rate regulator included the term "or contract" when establishing the authority of the rate regulator. Some respondents to the Exposure Draft *Regulatory Deferral Accounts*, which was published in April 2013 (the '2013 ED'), were concerned that this term resulted in the definition being too broad. Those respondents assumed that the intention of including the entity's own governing body was to (appropriately) capture those cases in which an entity conducts previously state-run monopolistic activities and is consequently delegated regulatory powers by the government. However, the respondents were concerned that the scope could be applied, by analogy, to other commercial entities having monopolistic features. This concern was raised within the context of entities that, in the absence of an external regulator, self-regulate (for example, by formally agreeing this with investors through the articles of association or other contractual arrangement). Entities may do this to avoid potential government intervention if they might otherwise be perceived to be abusing their strong market position.

BC56   Consequently, the IASB decided to refine the definition of the rate regulator to exclude self-regulation and instead require the rate regulator to be supported by statute or other formal regulations.

BC57   In addition, the definitions of rate regulation and the rate regulator were further refined to clarify that the regulation can permit some flexibility in the prices to be charged, within a range of prices established or approved by the rate regulator.

BC58   The scope criterion in paragraph 7(b) of the 2013 ED, which proposed that the price established by regulation (the rate) should be designed to recover the entity's allowable costs of providing the regulated goods or services, has been removed. The IASB was persuaded by arguments from some respondents that this criterion was inconsistent with the underlying objective of the IASB to reduce barriers to the adoption of IFRS. In addition, retaining this criterion may be perceived as prejudging the outcome of the comprehensive project.

BC59   The other main changes from the proposals in the 2013 ED are as follows:

   (a)   application guidance has been added to:

         (i)   clarify some group accounting issues. Paragraph 19 of IFRS 10 *Consolidated Financial Statements* requires that a "parent shall prepare consolidated financial statements using uniform accounting policies for like transactions and other events in similar circumstances". Consequently, if a parent recognises regulatory deferral account balances in accordance with this Standard, it shall apply the same accounting policies for the recognition, measurement, impairment and derecognition of regulatory deferral account balances arising from the rate-regulated activities of all of its subsidiaries, even if some of those subsidiaries do not recognise such balances in their own financial statements. A similar requirement applies to an investor applying the equity method to investments in associates and joint ventures.

         (ii)   introduce a limited exception to IFRS 3 *Business Combinations* to require the continuation of the acquirer's previous GAAP accounting policies for the recognition and measurement of regulatory deferral account balances acquired or assumed in a business combination. The IASB noted that, if an acquirer does not recognise regulatory deferral account balances in accordance with this Standard, but subsequently acquires a subsidiary that does recognise such balances, the acquirer is not eligible to apply this Standard. Consequently, the acquirer is not eligible to recognise the acquiree's regulatory deferral account balances within the consolidated financial statements.

         (iii)   clarify that an entity is not prohibited from recognising new regulatory deferral account balances for timing differences that are created as a consequence of a change in an accounting policy for other items required by IFRS. The IASB noted that the recognition of timing differences between its applied accounting policies and rate-regulatory requirements is a key element of what regulatory deferral account balances represent. When an entity adopts IFRS, the accounting policies that it uses in its opening IFRS statement of financial position may differ from those that it used at the same date when it used its previous GAAP. Such changes in accounting policies may create new timing differences that will be recorded by the entity in regulatory deferral accounts. For example, the rate regulator might allow pension costs to be reflected in rates when benefits or other costs are paid. The previous GAAP accounting policy for pension costs may have been consistent with this 'as paid' policy and thus no regulatory deferral account balance would have existed for those costs. However, IAS 19 *Employee Benefits* requires pension costs to be attributed to periods of service in accordance with the plan's benefit formula, or in some cases on a straight-line basis. For defined benefit pension costs, this would create a new timing difference for which a regulatory deferral account balance would be created. Some respondents were concerned that the prohibition to change accounting policies would prevent such newly created regulatory deferral account balances from being recognised. However, this was not the IASB's intention, because the recognition of such timing differences would be consistent with the recognition of other timing differences already recognised as regulatory deferral account balances.

(b)   the requirement to continue previous GAAP accounting policies for the recognition, measurement and impairment of regulatory deferral account balances has been extended to include derecognition.

(c)   the requirement to present the net movement in regulatory deferral account balances in the statement of profit or loss and other comprehensive income has been modified to require the net movement to be split between amounts related to items reported in profit or loss and those reported in other comprehensive income. The IASB was persuaded by those respondents that stated that the proposal to recognise all net movements in regulatory deferral account balances in a single line item in the profit or loss section of the statement of profit or loss and other comprehensive income could be confusing or misleading when a material portion of the movement related to items that are recognised in other comprehensive income.

(d)   the references to materiality as a factor to consider in deciding the level of detail to disclose has been deleted. The IASB noted that the consideration of materiality is already dealt with in IAS 1 and IAS 8. The IASB is currently assessing the adequacy of the guidance contained in those Standards as part of its Disclosure Initiative project.

BC60 A few respondents to the 2013 ED asked for additional guidance for the application of IAS 34 *Interim Financial Reporting*. In particular, they requested that it should be made clear that separate line items for regulatory deferral account balances and movements therein should also be included in a condensed set of financial statements. However, the IASB did not agree that additional guidance is necessary. Paragraph 10 of IAS 34 requires that condensed financial statements "shall include, at a minimum, each of the headings and subtotals that were included in its most recent annual financial statements and the selected explanatory notes as required by this Standard." In addition, paragraphs 15–15A of IAS 34 require that an entity shall include an explanation of events and transactions that are significant to an understanding of the changes in the financial position and performance of the entity.

BC61 The IASB concluded that the existing requirements, together with the detailed year-end information required in this Standard, are sufficient to provide users with the relevant information to understand the regulatory deferral account balances that are recognised.

BC62 The Illustrative examples and the Basis for Conclusions on the 2013 ED contained some educational background information about rate regulation, which was not related specifically to the contents of the proposed requirements. This background information has been deleted from this Standard.

Effects analysis

BC63 The IASB is committed to assessing and sharing knowledge about the likely costs of implementing new requirements and the likely ongoing costs and benefits of each new Standard. The costs and benefits are collectively referred to as 'effects'. The IASB gains insight on the likely effects of the proposals for new or revised Standards through its formal exposure of proposals, analysis and consultations with relevant parties.

BC64 In evaluating the likely effects of permitting rate-regulated entities that are first-time adopters of IFRS to continue to recognise regulatory deferral account balances, the IASB has considered the following factors:

(a) how the changes to the presentation of regulatory deferral account balances affect the financial statements of a rate-regulated entity;

(b) whether the changes improve the comparability of financial information between different reporting periods for a rate-regulated entity and between different rate-regulated entities in a particular reporting period;

(c) whether the changes improve the quality of financial information that is available to investors and its usefulness in assessing the future cash flows of a rate-regulated entity;

(d) whether users will benefit from better economic decision-making as a result of improved financial reporting;

(e)   the likely effect on compliance costs for preparers, both on initial application and on an ongoing basis; and

(f)   whether the likely costs of analysis for users are affected.

Financial statements of rate-regulated entities

BC65   The scope of this Standard is limited to first-time adopters of IFRS that already recognise regulatory deferral account balances in their financial statements in accordance with their previous GAAP. Consequently, the financial statements of rate-regulated entities that already apply IFRS, or that do not otherwise recognise such balances, will not be affected by this Standard.

BC66   This Standard permits rate-regulated entities within its scope to continue to apply their existing recognition, measurement, impairment and derecognition policies for regulatory deferral account balances. Consequently, the application of this Standard should have little or no impact on the net assets or the net profit reported in the financial statements.

BC67   However, the presentation of some regulatory deferral account balances will be changed to isolate the impact of their recognition and present this impact as separate line items within the statement of financial position and the statement of profit or loss and other comprehensive income. In particular, some regulatory deferral account balances that would be presented within the carrying amount of items of property, plant and equipment, intangible assets and inventories in accordance with previous GAAP will, in future, be presented separately from those classes of asset in accordance with this Standard.

Comparability

BC68   The IASB acknowledges that the requirements of this Standard will reduce comparability in some ways, but thinks that this reduction will be outweighed by other improvements in comparability that will result from applying the requirements in this Standard.

BC69   As noted in paragraph BC19, permitting only a limited population of entities to recognise regulatory deferral account balances will introduce some inconsistency and diversity into IFRS practice, when it does not currently exist. However, this is mitigated by the requirements to isolate the regulatory deferral account balances, and the movements in those balances, into separate line items in the financial statements.

BC70   The IASB is aware that many rate-regulated entities view the inability to recognise regulatory deferral account balances in IFRS financial statements as a major barrier to the adoption of IFRS. Although many of these entities are understood to use similar policies for the recognition and measurement of these balances, they use different frameworks of accounting for the preparation and presentation of the financial statements as a whole. The IASB thinks that reducing the barriers for these entities to adopt IFRS will improve the comparability of the financial statements of rate-regulated entities across jurisdictions.

BC71   In addition, the IASB thinks that the requirements to isolate the regulatory deferral account balances, and the movements in those balances, from other items in the financial statements will increase the transparency of these items. This will provide greater comparability across those entities within the scope of this Standard. This will, as a result, assist users of financial statements to understand more clearly the impact of recognising regulatory deferral account balances, and will allow direct comparisons not only against those entities that will be permitted to recognise these balances, but also against entities that do not recognise them.

Usefulness in assessing the future cash flows of an entity

BC72   Rate regulation imposes a framework for establishing prices that can be charged to customers for goods or services. Consequently, a rate-regulated entity is usually unable to react quickly in order to change its selling price in response to changes in its operating or other costs. Many of those who support the recognition of regulatory deferral account balances in financial statements argue that these balances provide some indication of the impact of these time delays on the cash flows that will be generated through future sales that will be made at a higher or lower price. The disclosures required by this Standard should provide more information about the amount and expected timing of the recovery or reversal of the regulatory deferral account balances recognised.

Better economic decision-making

BC73   The IASB has been told by many users in jurisdictions that currently permit or require regulatory deferral account balances to be recognised in financial statements that the information about those balances is useful in making economic decisions. At the same time, many other users of IFRS financial statements have noted that the inclusion of such balances could be confusing because it is not clear whether they meet the definitions of assets and liabilities. As a result, these users think that it is unclear what these balances represent.

BC74   The IASB thinks that this Standard will allow entities within its scope to continue to provide information that some users find useful, but that the presentation requirements will provide clarity to avoid confusion for those who are not familiar with the recognition of regulatory deferral account balances.

BC75   In particular, the IASB thinks that the improvements in comparability noted in paragraphs BC69–BC71 will provide users of financial statements with more information to help them better understand the impact of rate regulation on those rate-regulated entities that will be able to continue to recognise regulatory deferral account balances in accordance with this Standard.

Effect on compliance costs for preparers

BC76   This Standard will not change the recognition or measurement policies of entities within its scope, and thus will not result in any cost change in this respect. However, the IASB acknowledges that the separate presentation of regulatory deferral account balances is likely to result in changes to most existing presentation policies. Existing policies of entities within the scope of this Standard usually require or permit certain regulatory deferral account balances to be included within the carrying amount of items of property, plant and equipment and other assets. The separate presentation required by this Standard may add some cost on an ongoing basis, because preparers would need to track some of the differences between the regulatory amounts and those reported in the financial statements in more detail than is currently required.

BC77   However, the cost on the initial application of this Standard would largely be mitigated by the exemption that is already contained in paragraph D8B of IFRS 1. This exemption applies to first-time adopters of IFRS that hold items of property, plant and equipment or intangible assets that are, or were previously, used in operations subject to rate regulation. It allows those first-time adopters to use the previous GAAP carrying amount of such an item at the date of transition to IFRS as deemed cost. Consequently, the additional administrative burden of tracking changes need only apply on a prospective basis for differences arising after the date of transition.

BC78   In addition, the IASB understands that in many regulatory regimes, the regulatory accounting requirements require that regulatory deferral account balances are recorded in separate accounts within the entity's financial record-keeping system, at least until such time that the regulator issues a formal rate decision. Consequently, the IASB thinks that the incremental costs of retaining this separation beyond the time normally required by the regulator should not be significant.

How the costs of analysis for users are affected

BC79   The likely effect of these requirements on the costs of analysis for users of financial statements is expected to be outweighed by the benefits of improved reporting. Some users have commented that information related to the impact that rate regulation has on the amount, timing and certainty of returns and cash flows is important. The IASB think that the segregated presentation and related disclosures required by this Standard will highlight more clearly this impact. As noted in paragraph BC66, the requirements should have little or no impact on the net assets or the net profit reported in the financial statements of those entities within the scope of this Standard. Consequently, there is expected to be little disruption to the information available for trend analyses. Although the changes to the presentation of the amounts may cause some initial costs to be incurred, the IASB thinks that the added transparency introduced by this Standard will provide users with clearer and more comparable information.

Dissenting opinions

Dissent of Messrs Edelmann, Gomes and Zhang

DO1   Messrs Edelmann, Gomes and Zhang voted against the publication of IFRS 14.

Reduced comparability and inconsistency with existing IFRS practice

DO2   The established practice in IFRS has been that rate-regulated entities do not recognise regulatory deferral account balances in IFRS financial statements. Consequently, almost all rate-regulated entities around the world that previously recognised regulatory deferral account balances in their financial statements in accordance with their previous GAAP did not continue to recognise such balances but instead, derecognised them when they first adopted IFRS. In the view of Messrs Edelmann, Gomes and Zhang, to now permit an unknown population of rate-regulated entities to recognise these balances when adopting IFRS will introduce inconsistent accounting treatment into IFRS reporting and will reduce existing comparability.

DO3   In addition, Messrs Edelmann, Gomes and Zhang disagree with permitting first-time adopters of IFRS to continue to measure the regulatory deferral account balances that are recognised in the statement of financial position using their previous GAAP accounting policies. They believe that further inconsistency might be introduced by entities continuing to apply existing practices that might not be comparable with other entities that have different existing practices. In their view, isolating the impact of recognising regulatory deferral account balances by presenting them separately is not sufficient to eliminate the effect of this inconsistency. Messrs Edelmann, Gomes and Zhang are also concerned that entities might encounter operational difficulties in applying other general Standards to regulatory deferral account balances because there is uncertainty as to whether these balances are assets and liabilities, and there is no single clear and consistent recognition and measurement policy for them. This in turn might create additional diversity and further reduce comparability in practice.

Creating uncertainty for potential future adopters of IFRS

DO4   Messrs Edelmann, Gomes and Zhang acknowledge that this Standard is intended to be a practical and short-term interim solution to address a significant barrier to the adoption of IFRS in some jurisdictions. They note that a major argument for this Standard is to avoid rate-regulated entities having to make a major change to their accounting policies when making the transition to IFRS (ie derecognise their regulatory deferral account balances in accordance with the current established practice in IFRS of almost all rate-regulated entities) until guidance can be developed through the comprehensive project on rate-regulated activities (see paragraph BC18). However, they also note that this argument is not new, and nor is it specific to this particular subject. Despite this argument, when developing major projects, the IASB does not usually introduce interim Standards to be applied only by first-time adopters of IFRS. In particular, the IASB did not decide to introduce an interim Standard when it worked on the Exposure Draft *Rate-regulated Activities*, published in July 2009 (the '2009 ED'), which, at that time, would have equally avoided the issue for many entities in jurisdictions that have since adopted IFRS.

DO5   In addition, Messrs Edelmann, Gomes and Zhang note that the majority of IFRS Advisory Council members, at their meeting in October 2012, did not support the development of an interim Standard that would permit the continuation of existing previous GAAP policies. Many of those members warned against setting a precedent of implementing a policy of adopting an interim solution whenever a major standard-setting project is activated. Messrs Edelmann, Gomes and Zhang are concerned that developing an interim solution in this situation might create uncertainty as to what the IASB's approach might be when major projects are being researched in the future.

Recognition is contrary to the *Conceptual Framework for Financial Reporting*

DO6   Messrs Gomes and Zhang also disagree with permitting regulatory deferral account balances to be recognised in the statement of financial position because they do not think that all such balances meet the definitions of assets and liabilities in the IASB's *Conceptual Framework*.[6] This is one of the issues that the comprehensive Rate-regulated Activities project is looking to resolve. Consequently, the IASB has stated that IFRS 14 does not anticipate the outcome of the comprehensive project, and uses the neutral term 'regulatory deferral account balances' instead of 'regulatory assets' and 'regulatory liabilities' (see paragraph BC21). However, Messrs Gomes and Zhang believe that permitting them to be included in the statement of financial position is equivalent to recognising them as assets and liabilities, which, in their view, is contrary to the current accounting principles in the *Conceptual Framework* and the application of existing Standards.

DO7   In addition, Messrs Gomes and Zhang are concerned that allowing regulatory deferral account balances to be recognised in the financial statements is contrary to the IASB's objectives of requiring high-quality, transparent and comparable information in financial statements by requiring similar transactions and events to be accounted for and reported in a similar way. The IASB acknowledges that rate regulators have different objectives for regulatory reporting than the IASB has for financial reporting. In the view of Messrs Gomes and Zhang, allowing regulatory deferral account balances to be recognised will effectively allow the objectives of the rate regulator(s) to take precedence over the objectives of general purpose financial reporting, as expressed in the *Conceptual Framework*. In particular, they believe that allowing regulatory deferral account balances to be recognised effectively allows the objectives of the rate regulator(s) for setting rates and smoothing out the volatility, which results from real economic events, to be reflected in the financial statements. Messrs Gomes and Zhang think that this is inconsistent with paragraph OB17 of the *Conceptual Framework*, which notes the importance

---

6   References to the *Conceptual Framework* in this Dissent are to the *Conceptual Framework for Financial Reporting*, issued in 2010 and in effect when the Standard was developed.

of depicting the effects of transactions and other events and circumstances on a reporting entity's economic resources and claims in the periods in which those effects occur, even if the resulting cash receipts and payments occur in a different period.

IASB documents published to accompany

IFRS 15

Revenue from Contracts with Customers

The text of the unaccompanied standard, IFRS 15, is contained in Part A of this edition. Its effective date when issued was 1 January 2017. In September 2015 the Board issued *Effective Date of IFRS 15* which deferred the effective date to 1 January 2018. The text of the Accompanying Guidance on IFRS 15 is contained in Part B of this edition. This part presents the following documents:

BASIS FOR CONCLUSIONS

DISSENTING OPINION

APPENDICES TO THE BASIS FOR CONCLUSIONS

A Comparison of IFRS 15 and Topic 606

B Amendments to the Basis for Conclusions on other Standards

Contents

...continued

continued...

...continued

Basis for Conclusions on
IFRS 15 *Revenue from Contracts with Customers*

This Basis for Conclusions accompanies, but is not part of, IFRS 15.

Introduction

BC1 This Basis for Conclusions summarises the joint considerations of the International Accounting Standards Board (IASB) and the US national standard-setter, the Financial Accounting Standards Board (FASB), in reaching the conclusions in their standards, IFRS 15 *Revenue from Contracts with Customers* and Topic 606, which is introduced into the FASB *Accounting Standards Codification®* by the Accounting Standards Update 2014-09 *Revenue from Contracts with Customers*. It includes the reasons for accepting particular views and rejecting others. Individual Board members gave greater weight to some factors than to others.

BC1A In April 2016, the IASB issued *Clarifications to IFRS 15* Revenue from Contracts with Customers. The objective of these amendments is to clarify the IASB's intentions when developing the requirements in IFRS 15 but not to change the underlying principles of IFRS 15. Further details are contained in paragraphs BC27A–BC27H. In some cases, the boards made the same amendments to IFRS 15 and Topic 606. In other cases, the boards did not make the same amendments to the standards. The FASB also amended Topic 606 for issues for which the IASB concluded that it was not necessary to amend IFRS 15. The IASB added a further practical expedient to the transition requirements, which the FASB decided not to provide. Accordingly, Appendix A *Comparison of IFRS 15 and Topic 606* to this Basis for Conclusions has been updated to reflect the differences between the amendments to IFRS 15 and the amendments to Topic 606.

Overview

BC2 IFRS 15 and Topic 606 are the result of the IASB's and the FASB's joint project to improve the financial reporting of revenue under International Financial Reporting Standards (IFRS) and US Generally Accepted Accounting Principles (US GAAP). The boards undertook this project because their requirements for revenue needed improvement for the following reasons:

(a) US GAAP comprised broad revenue recognition concepts and detailed guidance for particular industries or transactions, which often resulted in different accounting for economically similar transactions.

(b) the previous revenue Standards in IFRS had different principles and were sometimes difficult to understand and apply to transactions other than simple ones. In addition, IFRS had limited guidance on important topics such as revenue recognition for multiple-element arrangements. Consequently, some entities that were applying IFRS referred to parts of US GAAP to develop an appropriate revenue recognition accounting policy.

(c)   the disclosures required under both IFRS and US GAAP were inadequate and often did not provide users of financial statements with information to sufficiently understand revenue arising from contracts with customers.

BC3   IFRS 15 and Topic 606[1] eliminate those inconsistencies and weaknesses by providing a comprehensive revenue recognition model that applies to a wide range of transactions and industries. The comprehensive model also improves previous IFRS and US GAAP by:

(a)   providing a more robust framework for addressing revenue recognition issues;

(b)   improving comparability of revenue recognition practices across entities, industries, jurisdictions and capital markets;

(c)   simplifying the preparation of financial statements by reducing the amount of guidance to which entities must refer; and

(d)   requiring enhanced disclosures to help users of financial statements better understand the nature, amount, timing and uncertainty of revenue that is recognised.

Background

BC4   In December 2008, the boards published for public comment the Discussion Paper *Preliminary Views on Revenue Recognition in Contracts with Customers* and received more than 200 comment letters in response. In the Discussion Paper, the boards proposed the general principles of a contract-based revenue recognition model with a measurement approach that was based on an allocation of the transaction price. That revenue recognition model was developed after extensive discussions by the boards on alternative models for recognising and measuring revenue (see paragraphs BC16–BC27).

BC5   Respondents to the Discussion Paper generally supported the objective of developing a comprehensive revenue recognition model for both IFRS and US GAAP. Most respondents also generally supported the recognition and measurement principles proposed in the Discussion Paper, which are the basic building blocks of the revenue recognition model. In particular, the Discussion Paper introduced the concepts that a contract contains performance obligations for the entity to transfer goods or services to a customer and that revenue is recognised when the entity satisfies its performance obligations as a result of the customer obtaining control of those goods or services.

---

1   Unless indicated otherwise, all references to IFRS 15 in this Basis for Conclusions can be read as also referring to Topic 606.

BC6   Respondents to the Discussion Paper were mainly concerned about the following proposals:

   (a)   identifying performance obligations only on the basis of the timing of the transfer of the good or service to the customer. Respondents commented that this would be impractical, especially when many goods or services are transferred over time to the customer (for example, in construction contracts).

   (b)   using the concept of control to determine when a good or service is transferred. Respondents asked the boards to clarify the application of the concept of control to avoid the implication that the proposals would require completed contract accounting for all construction contracts (ie revenue is recognised only when the customer obtains legal title or physical possession of the completed asset).

BC7   The boards considered those comments when developing the Exposure Draft *Revenue from Contracts with Customers* (the FASB's Exposure Draft was a proposed Accounting Standards Update), which was published in June 2010 (the '2010 Exposure Draft'). Nearly 1,000 comment letters were received from respondents representing a wide range of industries, including construction, manufacturing, telecommunications, technology, pharmaceutical, biotechnology, financial services, consulting, media and entertainment, energy and utilities, freight and logistics, and industries with significant franchising operations, such as hospitality and quick-service restaurant chains. The boards and their staffs also consulted extensively on the proposals in the 2010 Exposure Draft by participating in round-table discussions, conferences, working group sessions, discussion forums and one-to-one discussions that were held across all major geographical regions.

BC8   The boards also received a substantial number of comment letters in response to a question asked by the FASB on whether the proposals should apply to non-public entities. Almost all of those comment letters were from respondents associated with sections of the US construction industry (for example, private construction contractors, accounting firms that serve those contractors and surety providers who use the financial statements of construction contractors when deciding whether to guarantee that those contractors will meet their obligations under a contract). Those respondents also raised concerns about the application of the proposed model to non-public entities. Those issues were considered and discussed separately by the FASB.

BC9   With the exception of many of the responses from non-public entities in the construction industry, most of the feedback from the comment letters and from the consultation activities generally supported the boards' proposal for a comprehensive revenue recognition model for both IFRS and US GAAP. Moreover, most respondents supported the core principle of that model, which was that an entity should recognise revenue to depict the transfer of goods or services to a customer in an amount that reflects the amount of consideration that the entity expects to receive for those goods or services.

BC10　　Almost all respondents to the 2010 Exposure Draft indicated that the boards should clarify further the operation of the core principle. In particular, respondents were concerned about the application of the following:

　　　　(a)　　the concept of control and, in particular, the application of the indicators of the transfer of control to service contracts and to contracts for the transfer of an asset over time to a customer as it is being constructed (for example, a work-in-progress asset).

　　　　(b)　　the principle of distinct goods or services for identifying performance obligations in a contract. Many respondents were concerned that the proposed principle would lead to inappropriate disaggregation of the contract.

BC11　　The boards addressed those concerns during the redeliberations of the proposals in the 2010 Exposure Draft. As the redeliberations of those proposals drew to a close, the boards decided to issue a revised Exposure Draft for public comment to provide interested parties with an opportunity to comment on the revisions that the boards had made since the 2010 Exposure Draft was published. The boards decided unanimously that it was appropriate to go beyond their established due process and re-expose their revised revenue proposals, because of the importance of revenue to all entities and to avoid unintended consequences in the recognition of revenue for specific contracts or industries. The revised Exposure Draft *Revenue from Contracts with Customers* was published in November 2011 (the '2011 Exposure Draft') and approximately 350 comment letters were received from respondents representing a wide range of industries. As in the case of the 2010 Exposure Draft, the boards and their staffs consulted extensively on the proposals in the 2011 Exposure Draft. This consultation also included all major geographical regions and occurred in a number of formats. Many of the discussions focused on detailed analyses related to the application of the revenue recognition model and the principles in the 2011 Exposure Draft.

BC12　　Almost all respondents continued to support the core principle of the revenue recognition model, which is that an entity should recognise revenue to depict the transfer of promised goods or services to customers in an amount that reflects the consideration to which the entity expects to be entitled in exchange for those goods or services. Moreover, most of the feedback from the comment letters and from the consultation activities generally supported the revisions to the boards' proposed revenue recognition model in the 2011 Exposure Draft. However, respondents raised issues or questions on some of the proposals in the 2011 Exposure Draft. That feedback could be broadly divided into three categories:

　　　　(a)　　requests for clarifications and further refinements—such as on the criteria for identifying performance obligations, determining when a performance obligation is satisfied over time and constraining estimates of variable consideration;

　　　　　　　　© IFRS Foundation

(b) difficulties in the practical application of the requirements—such as on the time value of money (referred to as a significant financing component in IFRS 15) and the retrospective application of the proposed Standard; and

(c) disagreement with some of the proposed requirements for the following topics:

(i) identifying onerous performance obligations;

(ii) disclosing information about revenue;

(iii) applying the requirements for licences; and

(iv) applying the allocation principles to contracts that are prevalent in the telecommunications industry.

BC13   The boards addressed those concerns during the redeliberations of the proposals in the 2011 Exposure Draft. The boards' discussion of those concerns and their conclusions are included in the relevant sections of this Basis for Conclusions.

Why make the change?

BC14   Throughout the project, some respondents questioned the need to replace the requirements for revenue recognition, particularly because those requirements seemed to work reasonably well in practice and provided useful information about the different types of contracts for which they were intended.

(a) For US GAAP, some questioned whether a new revenue recognition model was necessary, because Accounting Standards Update No. 2009-13 *Revenue Recognition (Topic 605): Multiple-Deliverable Revenue Arrangements* resolved some of the issues that the Revenue Recognition project had originally intended to resolve. Furthermore, the *FASB Accounting Standards Codification®* (the Codification) had simplified the process of accessing and researching previous requirements for revenue.

(b) For IFRS, some indicated that the IASB could have improved, rather than replace, its previous revenue Standards by developing additional requirements for critical issues (for example, multiple-element arrangements).

BC15   The boards acknowledged that it would have been possible to improve many of the previous revenue recognition requirements without replacing them. However, even after the changes to US GAAP mentioned in paragraph BC14(a), the requirements in US GAAP would have continued to result in inconsistent accounting for revenue and, consequently, would not have provided a robust framework for addressing revenue recognition issues in the future. Furthermore, amending the requirements would have failed to achieve one of the goals of the Revenue Recognition project, which was to develop a common revenue standard for IFRS and US GAAP that entities could apply consistently across industries, jurisdictions and capital markets. Because revenue is a crucial number to users of financial statements, the boards decided that a common standard on revenue for IFRS and US GAAP is an important step toward achieving the goal of a single set of high-quality global accounting standards. To be consistent with that goal, the boards noted that previous revenue recognition requirements in IFRS and US GAAP should not be used to supplement the principles in IFRS 15.

Alternative revenue recognition models

BC16   During the early stages of their Revenue Recognition project, the boards considered various alternative revenue recognition models, including the following:

(a)   the basis for recognising revenue—specifically, whether an entity should recognise revenue only when it transfers a promised good or service to a customer (a contract-based revenue recognition principle) or when (or as) the entity undertakes a productive activity (which could be an activity that is undertaken regardless of whether a contract exists); and

(b)   the basis for measuring revenue—specifically, whether revenue should be measured at an allocated customer consideration amount (ie the transaction price) or at a current exit price.

Basis for recognising revenue

BC17   In the Discussion Paper, the boards proposed a principle to recognise revenue on the basis of the accounting for the asset or the liability arising from a contract with a customer. The boards had two reasons for developing a standard on revenue that applies only to contracts with customers. First, contracts to provide goods or services to customers are important economic phenomena and are crucial to most entities. Second, most previous revenue recognition requirements in IFRS and US GAAP focused on contracts with customers. The boards decided that focusing on the recognition and measurement of the asset or liability arising from a contract with a customer and the changes in that asset or liability over the life of the contract would bring discipline to the earnings process approach. Consequently, it would result in entities recognising revenue more consistently than they did under previous revenue recognition requirements.

BC18   Upon entering into a contract with a customer, an entity obtains rights to receive consideration from the customer and assumes obligations to transfer goods or services to the customer (performance obligations). The combination of those rights and performance obligations gives rise to a (net) asset or a (net) liability depending on the relationship between the remaining rights and the performance obligations. The contract is an asset (a contract asset) if the measure of the remaining rights exceeds the measure of the remaining performance obligations. Conversely, the contract is a liability (a contract liability) if the measure of the remaining performance obligations exceeds the measure of the remaining rights.

BC19   By definition, revenue from a contract with a customer cannot be recognised until a contract exists. Conceptually, revenue recognition could occur at the point at which an entity enters into a contract with a customer. For an entity to recognise revenue at contract inception (before either party has performed), the measure of the entity's rights must exceed the measure of the entity's performance obligations. This could occur if the rights and obligations were measured at current exit prices and would lead to revenue recognition because of an increase in a contract asset. However, as described in paragraph BC25, the boards proposed in the Discussion Paper that performance obligations should be measured at the same amount as the rights in the contract at contract inception, thereby precluding the recognition of a contract asset and revenue at contract inception.

BC20   Therefore, the boards decided that revenue should be recognised only when an entity transfers a promised good or service to a customer, thereby satisfying a performance obligation in the contract. That transfer results in revenue recognition, because upon satisfying a performance obligation an entity no longer has that obligation to provide the good or service. Consequently, its position in the contract increases—either its contract asset increases or its contract liability decreases—and that increase leads to revenue recognition.

BC21   Although, conceptually, revenue arises from an increase in a contract asset or a decrease in a contract liability, the boards articulated the requirements in terms of the recognition and measurement of revenue rather than the recognition and measurement of the contract. The boards noted that focusing on the timing and amount of revenue from a contract with a customer would simplify the requirements. Feedback from respondents to the Discussion Paper and the 2010 and 2011 Exposure Drafts confirmed that view.

BC22   Nearly all respondents to the Discussion Paper agreed with the boards' view that an entity generally should not recognise revenue if there is no contract with a customer. However, some respondents requested that the boards instead develop an activities model in which revenue would be recognised as the entity undertakes activities in producing or providing goods or services, regardless of whether those activities result in the transfer of goods or services to the customer. Those respondents reasoned that recognising revenue over time, for example, throughout long-term construction or other service contracts, regardless of whether goods or services are transferred to the customer, would provide users of financial statements with more useful information.

BC23   However, the boards noted the following concerns about an activities model:

    (a)   revenue recognition would not have been based on accounting for the contract. In an activities model, revenue arises from increases in the entity's assets, such as inventory or work-in-progress, rather than only from rights under a contract. Consequently, conceptually, an activities model does not require a contract with a customer for revenue recognition, although revenue recognition could be precluded until a contract exists. However, that would have resulted in revenue being recognised at contract inception for any activities completed to that point.

(b)   it would have been counterintuitive to many users of financial statements. An entity would have recognised consideration as revenue when the customer had not received any promised goods or services in exchange.

(c)   there would have been potential for abuse. An entity could have accelerated revenue recognition by increasing its activities (for example, production of inventory) at the end of a reporting period.

(d)   it would have resulted in a significant change to previous revenue recognition requirements and practices. In many of those requirements, revenue was recognised only when goods or services were transferred to the customer. For example, previous requirements in IFRS required revenue from the sale of a good to be recognised when the entity transferred ownership of the good to the customer. The boards also observed that the basis for percentage-of-completion accounting in previous revenue recognition requirements could be viewed as similar to the core principle in IFRS 15.

BC24   Accordingly, the boards did not develop an activities model and they maintained their view that a contract-based revenue recognition principle is the most appropriate principle for a general revenue recognition standard for contracts with customers.

Basis for measuring revenue

BC25   The boards decided that an allocated transaction price approach should be applied to measure performance obligations. Using that approach, an entity would allocate the transaction price to each performance obligation in the contract (see paragraphs BC181 and BC266). In the Discussion Paper, the boards considered an alternative approach to measure performance obligations directly at current exit prices. However, the boards rejected that approach for the following reasons:

(a)   an entity would have recognised revenue before transferring goods or services to the customer at contract inception if the measure of rights to consideration exceeded the measure of the remaining performance obligations. That would have been a typical occurrence at contract inception, because the transaction price often includes amounts that enable an entity to recover its costs to obtain a contract.

(b)   any errors in identifying or measuring performance obligations could have affected revenue recognised at contract inception.

(c)   a current exit price (ie the price that would be received to sell an asset or paid to transfer a liability) for the remaining performance obligations is typically not observable and an estimated current exit price could be complex and costly to prepare and difficult to verify.

BC26   Almost all respondents supported the boards' proposal to measure performance obligations using an allocated transaction price approach.

BC27   In the Discussion Paper, the boards also considered whether it would be appropriate to require an alternative measurement approach for some types of performance obligations (for example, performance obligations with highly variable outcomes, for which an allocated transaction price approach may not result in useful information). However, the boards decided that the benefits of accounting for all performance obligations within the scope of the requirements using the same measurement approach outweighed any concerns about using that approach for some types of performance obligations. The boards also noted that a common type of contract with customers that has highly variable outcomes would be an insurance contract, which is excluded from the scope of IFRS 15.

Clarifications to IFRS 15 (amendments issued in April 2016)

BC27A   After issuing IFRS 15 and Topic 606 in May 2014, the boards formed the Transition Resource Group (TRG) for Revenue Recognition to support implementation of these standards. One of the objectives of the TRG is to inform the boards about implementation issues to help the boards determine what, if any, action should be undertaken to address those issues. The substantial majority of the submissions from stakeholders regarding the implementation of IFRS 15, as discussed by the TRG, were determined to be sufficiently addressed by the requirements in IFRS 15. However, the TRG's discussions on five topics indicated potential differences of views on how to implement the requirements and, therefore, were considered by the boards. Those topics were:

(a)   identifying performance obligations;

(b)   principal versus agent considerations;

(c)   licensing;

(d)   collectability; and

(e)   measuring non-cash consideration.

BC27B   The boards also received requests from some stakeholders for practical expedients in respect of the following:

(a)   accounting for contract modifications that occurred before transition to IFRS 15;

(b)   for entities electing to use the full retrospective transition method, accounting for a contract completed under previous revenue Standards before transition to IFRS 15; and

(c)   assessing whether a sales tax (or a similar tax) is collected on behalf of a third party.

BC27C   The boards discussed the five topics and the possible practical expedients, and each board decided to make amendments to clarify the requirements in IFRS 15 and Topic 606 respectively. As a result, the IASB issued *Clarifications to IFRS 15* in April 2016 making targeted amendments to IFRS 15 with respect to three of the five topics considered – identifying performance obligations, principal versus agent considerations and licensing. The IASB concluded that it was not necessary to amend IFRS 15 with respect to the other two topics – collectability and measuring non-cash consideration. In respect of the practical expedients, the IASB provided transition relief for modified contracts and completed contracts.

BC27D In reaching its conclusions to make clarifying amendments and provide transition relief to IFRS 15, the IASB considered the need to balance being responsive to issues raised to help entities implement IFRS 15 but, at the same time, not creating a level of uncertainty about IFRS 15 to the extent that the IASB's actions might be disruptive to the implementation process. The IASB noted that, when new Standards are issued, there are always initial questions that arise. Those questions are generally resolved as entities, auditors and others work through them over time, and gain a better understanding of the new requirements. The IASB also considered the effect of any differences between its decisions and those made by the FASB.

BC27E With these wider considerations in mind, the IASB decided to apply a high hurdle when considering whether to amend IFRS 15 and, thus, to minimise changes to the extent possible. On this basis, the IASB made clarifying amendments to IFRS 15 only when (a) it considered those amendments to be essential to clarifying the IASB's intentions when developing the requirements in IFRS 15; or (b) it viewed the benefits of retaining converged requirements as greater than any potential costs of amending the requirements.

BC27F The FASB decided to make more extensive amendments to Topic 606, as explained in paragraph BC27G. The FASB issued amendments to the application guidance in Topic 606 on principal versus agent considerations, Accounting Standards Update (ASU) *2016-08, Revenue from Contracts with Customers (Topic 606): Principal versus Agent Considerations (Reporting Revenue Gross versus Net)*, in March 2016. The FASB is expected to issue two further ASUs:

(a) one ASU for its amendments to the requirements with respect to identifying performance obligations and the application guidance on licensing; and

(b) another ASU for its amendments to the requirements in Topic 606 with respect to the other topics and the practical expedients.

BC27G The FASB's amendments to Topic 606 are the same as the IASB's amendments to IFRS 15 with respect to (a) the requirements on identifying performance obligations relating to the determination of whether an entity's promise to transfer a good or service to a customer is distinct within the context of the contract; and (b) the application guidance on principal versus agent considerations. The FASB made further amendments regarding some other requirements on identifying performance obligations. In relation to licensing, the boards made the same clarifying amendments for sales-based and usage-based royalties. The boards decided to make different amendments to the application guidance relating to identifying the nature of an entity's promise in granting a licence. The FASB also decided to amend Topic 606 for other issues relating to licensing for which the IASB decided not to make any amendments to IFRS 15. The FASB has also decided (a) to amend Topic 606 with respect to collectability and measuring non-cash consideration and (b) to provide an accounting policy election to present all sales taxes on a net basis. The FASB decided to provide similar transition relief to that provided in IFRS 15 for contract modifications. However, with respect to completed contracts, the FASB decided to (a) amend the definition of a completed contract; and (b) provide transition relief, similar to the relief provided by the IASB, only for entities that apply Topic 606 in accordance with paragraph 606-10-65-1(d)(2) (equivalent to paragraph C3(b) of IFRS 15).

BC27H Because of the different decisions of the boards, Appendix A *Comparison of IFRS 15 and Topic 606* to this Basis for Conclusions has been updated. The IASB's considerations together with an overview of the FASB's considerations (based on both the amendments to Topic 606 issued and decisions made by the FASB until March 2016) in reaching their respective decisions are explained in the following paragraphs.

Topics for which both the IASB and FASB decided to amend IFRS 15 and Topic 606

Topic	Reference
Identifying performance obligations	paragraphs BC116A–BC116U
Principal versus agent considerations	paragraphs BC385A–BC385Z
Licensing	paragraphs BC414A–BC414Y paragraphs BC421A–BC421J
Practical expedients on transition	paragraphs BC445A–BC445B paragraphs BC445J–BC445R

Topics for which the IASB decided not to amend IFRS 15 but the FASB decided to amend Topic 606

Topic	Reference
Collectability	paragraphs BC46A–BC46H
Presentation of sales taxes (determining the transaction price)	paragraphs BC188A–BC188D
Non-cash consideration	paragraphs BC254A–BC254H
Definition of a completed contract	paragraphs BC445C–BC445I

Scope

BC28 The boards decided that IFRS 15 should apply only to a subset of revenue as defined in each of the boards' conceptual frameworks (ie revenue from contracts with customers). Revenue from transactions or events that does not arise from a contract with a customer is not within the scope of IFRS 15 and, therefore, those transactions or events will continue to be recognised in accordance with other Standards, for example:

    (a)   dividends received (although these requirements existed in previous revenue Standards in IFRS, the IASB has moved them unchanged, and without changing their effect, into IFRS 9 *Financial Instruments*);

    (b)   non-exchange transactions (for example, donations or contributions received);

    (c)   for IFRS, changes in the value of biological assets, investment properties and the inventory of commodity broker-traders; and

    (d)   for US GAAP, changes in regulatory assets and liabilities arising from alternative revenue programmes for rate-regulated entities in the scope of Topic 980 on regulated operations. (The FASB decided that the revenue arising from those assets or liabilities should be presented separately from revenue arising from contracts with customers. Therefore, the FASB made amendments to Subtopic 980-605 *Regulated Operations – Revenue Recognition*.)

BC29   The boards decided not to amend the existing definitions of revenue in each of their conceptual frameworks. The boards decided that they will consider the definition of revenue when they revise their respective conceptual frameworks. However, the IASB decided to carry forward into IFRS 15 the description of revenue from the IASB's *Conceptual Framework for Financial Reporting*[2] rather than the definition of revenue from a previous revenue Standard. The IASB noted that the definition in a previous revenue Standard referred to 'gross inflow of economic benefits' and it had concerns that some might have misread that reference as implying that an entity should recognise as revenue a prepayment from a customer for goods or services. As described in paragraphs BC17–BC24, the principle is that revenue is recognised in accordance with IFRS 15 as a result of an entity satisfying a performance obligation in a contract with a customer. In addition, the FASB decided to carry forward a definition of revenue that is based on the definition in FASB Concepts Statement No. 6 *Elements of Financial Statements*.

BC30   The converged definitions of a contract and a customer establish the scope of IFRS 15.

Definition of a contract (Appendix A)

BC31   The boards' definition of contract is based on common legal definitions of a contract in the United States and is similar to the definition of a contract used in IAS 32 *Financial Instruments: Presentation*. The IASB decided not to adopt a single definition of a contract for both IAS 32 and IFRS 15, because the IAS 32 definition implies that contracts can include agreements that are not enforceable by law. Including such agreements would have been inconsistent with the boards' decision that a contract with a customer must be enforceable by law for an entity to recognise the rights and obligations arising from that contract. The IASB also noted that amending the IAS 32 definition would have

---

2   References to the *Conceptual Framework* in this Basis for Conclusions are to the *Conceptual Framework for Financial Reporting*, issued in 2010 and in effect when the Standard was developed.

posed the risk of unintended consequences in accounting for financial instruments.

BC32   The definition of a contract emphasises that a contract exists when an agreement between two or more parties creates enforceable rights and obligations between those parties. The boards noted that the agreement does not need to be in writing to be a contract. Whether the agreed-upon terms are written, oral or evidenced otherwise (for example, by electronic assent), a contract exists if the agreement creates rights and obligations that are enforceable against the parties. Determining whether a contractual right or obligation is enforceable is a question to be considered within the context of the relevant legal framework (or equivalent framework) that exists to ensure that the parties' rights and obligations are upheld. The boards observed that the factors that determine enforceability may differ between jurisdictions. Although there must be enforceable rights and obligations between parties for a contract to exist, the boards decided that the performance obligations within the contract could include promises that result in the customer having a valid expectation that the entity will transfer goods or services to the customer even though those promises are not enforceable (see paragraph BC87).

BC33   The boards decided to complement the definition of a contract by specifying criteria that must be met before an entity can apply the revenue recognition model to that contract (see paragraph 9 of IFRS 15). Those criteria are derived mainly from previous revenue recognition requirements and other existing standards. The boards decided that when some or all of those criteria are not met, it is questionable whether the contract establishes enforceable rights and obligations. The boards' rationale for including those criteria is discussed in paragraphs BC35–BC46.

BC34   The boards also decided that those criteria would be assessed at contract inception and would not be reassessed unless there is an indication that there has been a significant change in facts and circumstances (see paragraph 13 of IFRS 15). The boards decided that it was important to reassess the criteria in those cases, because that change might clearly indicate that the remaining contractual rights and obligations are no longer enforceable. The word 'remaining' in paragraph 13 of IFRS 15 indicates that the criteria would be applied only to those rights and obligations that have not yet transferred. That is, an entity would not include in the reassessment (and therefore would not reverse) any receivables, revenue or contract assets already recognised.

The parties have approved the contract and are committed to perform their respective obligations (paragraph 9(a))

BC35   The boards decided to include this criterion because if the parties to a contract have not approved the contract, it is questionable whether that contract is enforceable. Some respondents questioned whether oral and implied contracts could meet this criterion, especially if it is difficult to verify an entity's approval of that contract. The boards noted that the form of the contract does not, in and of itself, determine whether the parties have approved the contract. Instead, an entity should consider all relevant facts and circumstances in assessing whether the parties intend to be bound by the terms and conditions of the contract. Consequently, in some cases, the parties to an oral or an implied contract (in accordance with customary business practices) may have agreed to fulfil their respective obligations. In other cases, a written contract may be required to determine that the parties to the contract have approved it.

BC36   In addition, the boards decided that the parties should be committed to performing their respective obligations under the contract. However, the boards decided that an entity and a customer would not always need to be committed to fulfilling all of their respective rights and obligations for a contract to meet the requirements in paragraph 9(a) of IFRS 15. For example, a contract might include a requirement for the customer to purchase a minimum quantity of goods from the entity each month, but the customer's past practice indicates that the customer is not committed to always purchasing the minimum quantity each month and the entity does not enforce the requirement to purchase the minimum quantity. In that example, the criterion in paragraph 9(a) of IFRS 15 could still be satisfied if there is evidence that demonstrates that the customer and the entity are substantially committed to the contract. The boards noted that requiring all of the rights and obligations to be fulfilled would have inappropriately resulted in no recognition of revenue for some contracts in which the parties are substantially committed to the contract.

The entity can identify each party's rights regarding the goods or services to be transferred (paragraph 9(b))

BC37   The boards decided to include this criterion because an entity would not be able to assess the transfer of goods or services if it could not identify each party's rights regarding those goods or services.

The entity can identify the payment terms for the goods or services to be transferred (paragraph 9(c))

BC38   The boards decided to include this criterion because an entity would not be able to determine the transaction price if it could not identify the payment terms in exchange for the promised goods or services.

BC39   Respondents from the construction industry questioned whether an entity can identify the payment terms for orders for which the scope of work may already have been defined even though the specific amount of consideration for that work has not yet been determined and may not be finally determined for a period of time (sometimes referred to as unpriced change orders or claims). The boards clarified that their intention is not to preclude revenue recognition for unpriced change orders if the scope of the work has been approved and the entity expects that the price will be approved. The boards noted that, in those cases, the entity would consider the requirements for contract modifications (see paragraphs BC76–BC83).

The contract has commercial substance (paragraph 9(d))

BC40   The boards decided to include 'commercial substance' as a criterion when they discussed whether revenue should be recognised in contracts with customers that include non-monetary exchanges. Without that requirement, entities might transfer goods or services back and forth to each other (often for little or no cash consideration) to artificially inflate their revenue. Consequently, the boards decided that an entity should not recognise revenue from a non-monetary exchange if the exchange has no commercial substance.

BC41   The boards decided to describe commercial substance in paragraph 9(d) of IFRS 15 in a manner that is consistent with its existing meaning in other financial reporting contexts, such as existing requirements for non-monetary exchange transactions. The boards also observed that this criterion is important in all contracts (not only non-monetary exchanges) because without commercial substance it is questionable whether an entity has entered into a transaction that has economic consequences. Consequently, the boards decided that all contracts should have commercial substance before an entity can apply the other requirements in the revenue recognition model.

It is probable that the entity will collect the consideration to which it will be entitled (paragraph 9(e))

BC42   The boards included the criterion in paragraph 9(e) of IFRS 15 (which acts like a collectability threshold) because they concluded that the assessment of a customer's credit risk was an important part of determining whether a contract is valid. Furthermore, the boards decided to include this criterion as a consequence of their decision that customer credit risk should not affect the measurement or presentation of revenue (see paragraphs BC259–BC265).

BC43   The boards decided that a collectability threshold is an extension of the other requirements in paragraph 9 of IFRS 15 on identifying the contract. In essence, the other criteria in paragraph 9 require an entity to assess whether the contract is valid and represents a genuine transaction. The collectability threshold is related to that assessment because a key part of assessing whether a transaction is valid is determining the extent to which the customer has the ability and the intention to pay the promised consideration. In addition, entities generally only enter into contracts in which it is probable that the entity will collect the amount to which it will be entitled.

BC44   The boards noted that the term 'probable' has different meanings under US GAAP and IFRS. Under US GAAP, the term was initially defined in Topic 450 *Contingencies* as 'likely to occur' whereas under IFRS, probable is defined as 'more likely than not'. The boards noted that using the same term which has different meanings in US GAAP and IFRS could result in accounting that is not converged when determining whether the criterion in paragraph 9(e) of IFRS 15 is met. However, the boards noted that the term 'probable' was used in some of the collectability thresholds in their previous revenue recognition requirements and both boards wanted to maintain consistency with those requirements. (The term 'reasonably assured' was also used in collectability thresholds in some parts of US GAAP. However, in this context, the FASB understood that in practice, probable and reasonably assured had similar meanings.) In addition, the boards observed that in most transactions, an entity would not enter into a contract with a customer in which there was significant credit risk associated with that customer without also having adequate economic protection to ensure that it would collect the consideration. Consequently, the boards decided that there would not be a significant practical effect of the different meaning of the same term because the population of transactions that would fail to meet the criterion in paragraph 9(e) of IFRS 15 would be small.

BC45   In determining whether it is probable that an entity will collect the amount of consideration to which the entity will be entitled, an entity might first need to determine the amount of consideration to which the entity will be entitled. This is because, in some circumstances, the amount of consideration to which an entity will be entitled may be less than the price stated in the contract. This could be because the entity might offer the customer a price concession (see paragraph 52 of IFRS 15) or because the amount of consideration to which an entity will be entitled varies for other reasons, such as the promise of a bonus. In either of those circumstances, an entity considers whether it is probable that the entity will collect the amount of consideration to which it will be entitled when the uncertainty relating to that consideration is resolved. The entity assesses whether it is probable of collecting that amount by considering both of the following:

(a)   the ability (ie the financial capacity) of the customer to pay the amount of consideration to which the entity will be entitled in exchange for the goods or services transferred.

(b)   the customer's intention to pay that amount. The boards observed that an assessment of the customer's intention would require an entity to consider all of the facts and circumstances, including the past practice of that customer or customer class. The boards noted that this assessment should be made on the assumption that the amount will be due (ie the corresponding performance obligation will be satisfied and the consideration is not subject to further variability that might affect the entity's entitlement to that consideration).

BC46   In addition, the boards specified in paragraph 9(e) of IFRS 15 that an entity should assess only the consideration to which it will be entitled in exchange for the goods or services that will be transferred to a customer. Therefore, if the customer were to fail to perform as promised and consequently the entity would respond to the customer's actions by not transferring any further goods or services to the customer, the entity would not consider the likelihood of payment for those goods or services that would not be transferred.

Clarifications to IFRS 15 (amendments issued in April 2016)—topics for which the IASB decided not to amend IFRS 15

BC46A   The TRG discussed an implementation question raised by stakeholders about how to apply the collectability criterion in paragraph 9(e) of IFRS 15 in instances in which the entity has received non-refundable consideration from a customer assessed as having poor credit quality. The discussion informed the boards that there are potentially different interpretations of:

(a)   how to apply the collectability criterion in paragraph 9(e) when it is not probable that the total consideration promised in the contract is collectable; and

(b)   when to recognise the non-refundable consideration received from the customer as revenue in accordance with paragraph 15 of IFRS 15 when the contract does not meet the criteria in paragraph 9 of IFRS 15.

Assessing collectability

BC46B   Paragraph 9(e) requires an entity to assess whether it is probable that it will collect the consideration to which it will be entitled in exchange for the goods or services that will be transferred to the customer. This assessment forms part of Step 1 of IFRS 15 *Identify the contract(s) with a customer*. The TRG's discussions informed the boards that some stakeholders interpreted this requirement to mean that an entity should assess the probability of collecting all of the consideration promised in the contract. Under this interpretation, some contracts with customers that are assessed as having poor credit quality would not meet the criteria in paragraph 9(e), even though they are otherwise valid contracts. Other stakeholders asserted that those contracts would be valid if the entity has the ability to protect itself from credit risk.

BC46C   The boards noted that the assessment in paragraph 9(e) requires an entity to consider how the entity's contractual rights to the consideration relate to its performance obligations. That assessment considers the entity's exposure to the customer's credit risk and the business practices available to the entity to manage its exposure to credit risk throughout the contract. For example, an entity may be able to stop providing goods or services to the customer or require advance payments. This is consistent with the explanation of the boards' considerations as described in paragraph BC46.

BC46D   The FASB decided to amend the implementation guidance and illustrations in Topic 606 to clarify that an entity should assess the collectability of the consideration promised in a contract for the goods or services that will be transferred to the customer rather than assessing the collectability of the consideration promised in the contract for all of the promised goods or services.

BC46E   Having considered the wider implications of amending IFRS 15 before its effective date, the IASB concluded that the existing requirements in IFRS 15 and the explanations in paragraphs BC42–BC46 are sufficient. The IASB noted that it expects practice to develop consistently with the boards' intentions in developing the collectability criterion in paragraph 9(e). The IASB does not expect the FASB's anticipated clarifications to the paragraph equivalent to paragraph 9(e) in Topic 606 to result in any additional differences in outcomes. In reaching its decision, the IASB observed that an entity will generally not enter into a contract with a customer if the entity does not consider it to be probable that the entity will collect the consideration to which it will be entitled in exchange for the goods or services that will be transferred to the customer. This is consistent with the boards' reasoning in paragraph BC43. It was not the boards' intention that many contracts should fail the condition in paragraph 9(e). On this basis, the IASB thinks that the population of contracts to which any clarification to paragraph 9(e) might apply is small.

Contract termination

BC46F   Paragraph 15 specifies when an entity should recognise any consideration received from a customer as revenue when the contract does not meet Step 1 of the revenue recognition model. Paragraph 15(b) states that an entity should recognise revenue when the contract has been terminated and the consideration received from the customer is non-refundable. The TRG's discussions informed the boards about potential diversity in stakeholders' understanding of when a contract is terminated. The assessment of when a contract is terminated affects when an entity recognises revenue in a contract that does not meet Step 1 of the revenue recognition model. Some stakeholders asserted that a contract is terminated when an entity stops transferring promised goods or services to the customer. Other stakeholders asserted that a contract is terminated only when the entity stops pursuing collection from the customer. Stakeholders noted that those two events often occur at different points in time. For example, entities sometimes pursue collection for a significant period of time after they have stopped transferring promised goods or services to the customer. As a result, non-refundable consideration received from the customer might be recognised as a liability for a significant period of time during which an entity pursues collection, even though the entity may have stopped transferring promised goods or services to the customer and has no further obligations to transfer goods or services to the customer.

BC46G   The FASB decided to amend paragraph 606-10-25-7 of Topic 606 (equivalent to paragraph 15 of IFRS 15) to add an additional event in which an entity should recognise any consideration received as revenue. This amendment is expected to allow an entity to recognise any consideration received as revenue when (a) the entity has transferred control of the goods or services to which the consideration received relates; (b) the entity has stopped transferring additional goods or services and has no obligation to transfer additional goods or services; and (c) the consideration received from the customer is non-refundable.

BC46H   The IASB noted that contracts often specify that an entity has the right to terminate the contract in the event of non-payment by the customer and that this would not generally affect the entity's rights to recover any amounts owed by the customer. The IASB also noted that an entity's decision to stop pursuing collection would not typically affect the entity's rights and the customer's obligations under the contract with respect to the consideration owed by the customer. On this basis, the IASB concluded that the existing requirements in IFRS 15 are sufficient for an entity to conclude, without any additional clarification, that a contract is terminated when it stops providing goods or services to the customer. Some IASB members also expressed concerns about the potential for unintended consequences relating to other areas of IFRS if contract termination were to be defined in IFRS 15. Consequently, the IASB decided not to amend paragraph 15.

Accounting for contracts that do not meet the criteria in paragraph 9

BC47 The boards decided to include the requirements in paragraphs 14–16 of IFRS 15 in response to questions from some respondents about how an entity should account for its rights and obligations when a contract does not meet the criteria in paragraph 9 of IFRS 15. Those respondents were concerned that if a contract did not meet the criteria in paragraph 9 of IFRS 15, in the absence of specific requirements, an entity would seek alternative guidance and potentially apply the revenue recognition model by analogy, which might not result in appropriate accounting. Consequently, the boards specified that in cases in which the contract does not meet the criteria in paragraph 9 of IFRS 15, an entity should recognise the consideration received as revenue only when one of the events in paragraph 15 of IFRS 15 has occurred or the entity reassesses the criteria in paragraph 9 of IFRS 15 and the contract subsequently meets those criteria.

BC48 The requirements in paragraph 15 are consistent with the boards' rationale for paragraph 9 of IFRS 15, which is to filter out contracts that may not be valid and that do not represent genuine transactions, and therefore recognising revenue for those contracts would not provide a faithful representation of such transactions. The requirements therefore preclude an entity from recognising any revenue until the contract is either complete or cancelled or until a subsequent reassessment indicates that the contract meets all of the criteria in paragraph 9 of IFRS 15. The boards noted that this approach is similar to the 'deposit method' that was previously included in US GAAP and that was applied when there was no consummation of a sale.

BC49 The boards considered whether to include asset derecognition requirements (and therefore cost recognition requirements) for assets related to a contract that does not meet the criteria in paragraph 9 of IFRS 15. However, the boards decided not to include requirements for asset derecognition for these types of transactions, because including those requirements would be outside the scope of this project. (However, the FASB added some asset derecognition guidance to other Standards for transactions outside the scope of the requirements—that is, for the transfer of non-financial assets. See paragraphs BC494–BC503.) The boards noted that entities should apply existing IFRS and US GAAP to assets related to contracts that do not meet the criteria in paragraph 9 of IFRS 15.

Wholly unperformed contracts

BC50 The boards decided that IFRS 15 should not apply to wholly unperformed contracts if each party to the contract has the unilateral enforceable right to terminate the contract without penalty. Those contracts would not affect an entity's financial position or performance until either party performs. In contrast, there could be an effect on an entity's financial position and performance if only one party could terminate a wholly unperformed contract without penalty. For instance, if only the customer could terminate the wholly unperformed contract without penalty, the entity is obliged to stand ready to perform at the discretion of the customer. Similarly, if only the entity could terminate the wholly unperformed contract without penalty, it has an enforceable right to payment from the customer if it chooses to perform.

BC51   In accordance with IFRS 15, an entity's rights and obligations in wholly unperformed non-cancellable contracts are measured at the same amount and, therefore, would offset each other at inception. However, by including those contracts within the scope of IFRS 15, an entity would provide additional information about a change in its financial position that resulted from entering into those contracts, that is, disclosing the amount of transaction price allocated to the remaining performance obligations in that wholly unperformed contract (see paragraph 120 of IFRS 15).

Definition of a customer (paragraph 6 and Appendix A)

BC52   The boards decided to define the term 'customer' to enable an entity to distinguish contracts that should be accounted for under IFRS 15 (ie contracts with customers) from contracts that should be accounted for under other requirements.

BC53   The definition of a customer in IFRS 15 refers to an entity's ordinary activities. Some respondents asked the boards to clarify the meaning of ordinary activities; however, the boards decided not to provide additional requirements, because the notion of ordinary activities is derived from the definitions of revenue in the boards' respective conceptual frameworks. In particular, the IASB's *Conceptual Framework* description of revenue refers specifically to the 'ordinary activities of an entity' and the definition of revenue in FASB Concepts Statement No. 6 refers to the notion of an entity's 'ongoing major or central operations'. As noted in paragraph BC29, the boards did not reconsider those definitions as part of the Revenue Recognition project.

BC54   Some respondents asked the boards to clarify whether the parties to some common types of contracts (for example, contracts with collaborators or partners) would meet the definition of a customer. However, the boards decided that it would not be feasible to develop application guidance that would apply uniformly to various industries because the nature of the relationship (ie supplier-customer versus collaboration or partnership) would depend on specific terms and conditions in those contracts. The boards observed that in many arrangements highlighted by respondents, an entity would need to consider all relevant facts and circumstances, such as the purpose of the activities undertaken by the counterparty, to determine whether the counterparty is a customer. Examples of arrangements in which an entity would need to make that assessment are as follows:

(a)   collaborative research and development efforts between biotechnology and pharmaceutical entities or similar arrangements in the aerospace and defence, technology and healthcare industries or in higher education;

(b)   arrangements in the oil and gas industry in which partners in an offshore oil and gas field may make payments to each other to settle any differences between their proportionate entitlements to production volumes from the field during a reporting period; and

(c)   arrangements in the not-for-profit industry in which an entity receives grants and sponsorship for research activity and the grantor or sponsor may specify how any output from the research activity will be used.

BC55   The boards noted that a contract with a collaborator or a partner (for example, a joint arrangement as defined in IFRS 11 *Joint Arrangements* or a collaborative arrangement within the scope of Topic 808 *Collaborative Arrangements*) could also be within the scope of IFRS 15 if that collaborator or partner meets the definition of a customer for some or all of the terms of the arrangement.

BC56   The boards also noted that in some cases it might be appropriate for an entity to apply the principles of IFRS 15 to some transactions with collaborators or partners. For example, an entity might consider applying IFRS 15 to a collaborative arrangement or partnership, provided such application is appropriate in accordance with IAS 8 *Accounting Policies, Changes in Accounting Estimates and Errors* or, for an entity applying US GAAP, provided there are not more relevant authoritative requirements in US GAAP.

BC57   Notwithstanding the boards' decision that only contracts with customers should be accounted for under IFRS 15, the boards also decided that some of the requirements in IFRS 15 should apply to the transfer of non-financial assets that are not an output of an entity's ordinary activities (see paragraphs BC494–BC503).

Exchanges of products to facilitate a sale to another party (paragraph 5(d))

BC58   In industries with homogeneous products, it is common for entities in the same line of business to exchange products to facilitate sales to customers or potential customers other than the parties to the exchange. For example, an oil supplier may swap inventory with another oil supplier to reduce transport costs, meet immediate inventory needs, or otherwise facilitate the sale of oil to the end customer. The boards noted that the party exchanging inventory with the entity meets the definition of a customer, because it has contracted with the entity to obtain an output of the entity's ordinary activities. Consequently, in the absence of specific requirements, an entity might recognise revenue once for the exchange of inventory and then again for the sale of the inventory to the end customer. The boards decided that this outcome would be inappropriate for the following reasons:

(a)   it would have grossed up revenues and expenses and made it difficult for users of financial statements to assess the entity's performance and gross margins during the reporting period; and

(b)   some view the counterparty in those arrangements as also acting as a supplier and not as a customer.

BC59   The boards considered modifying the definition of a customer. However, they rejected that alternative because of concerns about unintended consequences. Consequently, the boards decided to exclude from the scope of IFRS 15 transactions involving non-monetary exchanges between entities in the same line of business to facilitate sales to customers or to potential customers. The

FASB noted such exchanges should remain within the scope of Topic 845 on non-monetary transactions.

Contracts with customers outside the scope of the requirements (paragraph 5)

BC60   The boards also excluded from the scope of IFRS 15 three types of contracts with customers that they are addressing in other Standards:

(a)   leases;

(b)   insurance contracts;[3] and

(c)   financial instruments and other contractual rights or obligations within the scope of the boards' other Standards.

BC61   Some respondents asked the FASB to clarify what is meant by 'contractual rights or obligations' in paragraph 5 of the requirements, because those respondents stated that it is unclear whether financial instrument arrangements that are addressed elsewhere in the Codification, such as letters of credit and loan commitments (addressed in Topic 440 *Commitments*), would be included within the scope of Topic 606. The FASB noted that its intention is that if specific requirements in other Topics of the Codification deal with a transaction, the more detailed requirements from those other Topics should be applied rather than the requirements in Topic 606. For example, the FASB decided to exclude from the scope of Topic 606 guarantees (other than product warranties) that are within the scope of Topic 460 *Guarantees*, because the focus of the existing accounting requirements for those guarantee arrangements relates primarily to recognising and measuring a guarantee liability.

BC62   Some respondents reasoned that excluding some contracts with customers from the scope of IFRS 15 (such as those identified in paragraph BC60) could perpetuate the development of industry-specific or transaction-specific revenue recognition guidance, which would be inconsistent with the Revenue Recognition project's stated objective. The boards disagreed with that view. In the boards' view, IFRS 15 provides them with a framework for considering revenue issues in other standard-setting projects. The boards decided that, within the context of those other projects, a different basis of accounting for those contracts with customers might provide users of financial statements with more relevant information.

BC63   Other respondents identified what they perceived to be a contradiction within the scope requirements in IFRS 15 and IFRS 9. Those respondents stated that some of the requirements for accounting for contract assets (which would meet the definition of a financial asset) are inconsistent with the requirements in financial instruments Standards for accounting for financial assets. For example, in some cases a contract asset is not required to be

---

3   IFRS 17 *Insurance Contracts*, issued in May 2017, permits an entity to choose whether to apply IFRS 17 or IFRS 15 to fixed-fee service contracts that meet the definition of an insurance contract. The Board's considerations for permitting this choice are set out in paragraphs BC95–BC97 of the Basis for Conclusions on IFRS 17.

adjusted for the time value of money (see paragraph BC236), and in other cases the contract asset might initially be measured at an amount that excludes some of the expected cash flows if the transaction price includes variable consideration (see paragraphs BC189–BC223). However, the IASB disagreed with those respondents. The IASB noted that the requirements in paragraph 5 of IFRS 15 (together with paragraph 2(k) of IAS 39 *Financial Instruments: Recognition and Measurement*, which is a consequential amendment to IAS 39 added by IFRS 15) are clear that when a contract asset is within the scope of IFRS 15, it is not within the scope of IFRS 9.

Contracts partially within the scope of other Standards (paragraph 7)

BC64   Some contracts with customers are partially within the scope of IFRS 15 and partially within the scope of other Standards (for example, a lease with a service contract). The boards decided that it would be inappropriate in those cases for an entity to account for the entire contract in accordance with one standard or another. This is because it could result in different accounting outcomes depending on whether the goods or services were sold on a stand-alone basis or together with other goods or services.

BC65   The boards considered whether the requirements in IFRS 15 should be the default approach for separating a contract and allocating consideration to each part. However, specific issues could arise in separating contracts that are not within the scope of IFRS 15. For example, a financial instrument or an insurance contract might require an entity to provide services that are best accounted for in accordance with IFRS 9, Subtopic 942-605 *Financial Services— Depository and Lending—Revenue Recognition*, IFRS 4 *Insurance Contracts*,[4] or Subtopic 944-605 *Financial Services—Insurance—Revenue Recognition*.

BC66   Consequently, the boards decided that if other Standards specify how to separate and/or initially measure parts of a contract, an entity should first apply those Standards. In other words, the more specific Standard would take precedence in accounting for a part of a contract and any residual consideration should be allocated to the part(s) of the contract within the scope of IFRS 15. This rationale is consistent with the principle in IFRS 15 related to scope, which is that another Standard should be applied to a portion of the contract or arrangement if that Standard provides specific requirements for that portion of the contract or arrangement. The boards' decision is also consistent with the requirements for multiple-element arrangements in US GAAP that were replaced by Topic 606. The boards noted that this decision results in any discount in the overall arrangement being allocated to the portion of the arrangement within the scope of IFRS 15.

Identifying the contract (paragraphs 9–16)

BC67   The boards decided that the revenue recognition model would apply to a contract with a customer only when the criteria in paragraph 9 of IFRS 15 are met. The rationale for those criteria is described in paragraphs BC33–BC46.

---

4   IFRS 17 *Insurance Contracts*, issued in May 2017, replaced IFRS 4.

BC68 IFRS 15 applies to a single contract with a customer. In many cases, the contract that is accounted for separately will be the individual contract negotiated with the customer. However, the structure and scope of a contract can vary depending on how the parties to the contract decide to record their agreement. For instance, there may be legal or commercial reasons for the parties to use more than one contract to document the sale of related goods or services or to use a single contract to document the sale of unrelated goods or services. One of the boards' objectives in developing IFRS 15 is that the accounting for a contract should depend on an entity's present rights and obligations rather than on how the entity structures the contract.

Applying IFRS 15 at a portfolio level

BC69 IFRS 15 specifies the accounting required for an individual contract. Many entities have a large number of contracts and as a result some respondents noted practical challenges in applying the model on a contract-by-contract basis. These respondents questioned whether it would always be necessary to apply IFRS 15 on a contract-by-contract basis. The boards observed that the way in which an entity applies the model to its contracts is not a matter for which the boards should specify requirements. Nonetheless, in the light of the feedback, the boards decided to include a practical expedient in paragraph 4 of IFRS 15 to acknowledge that a practical way to apply IFRS 15 to some contracts may be to use a 'portfolio approach'. The boards acknowledged that an entity would need to apply judgement in selecting the size and composition of the portfolio in such a way that the entity reasonably expects that application of the revenue recognition model to the portfolio would not differ materially from the application of the revenue recognition model to the individual contracts or performance obligations in that portfolio. In their discussions, the boards indicated that they did not intend for an entity to quantitatively evaluate each outcome and, instead, the entity should be able to take a reasonable approach to determine the portfolios that would be appropriate for its types of contracts.

BC70 The boards observed that because it is a practical way to apply IFRS 15, the portfolio approach may be particularly useful in some industries in which an entity has a large number of similar contracts and applying the model separately for each contract may be impractical. For example, entities in the telecommunications industry explained that implementing accounting systems to determine the stand-alone selling price for the promised goods or services in each contract and, in turn, allocating the transaction price to the performance obligations identified in that contract would be complex and costly (see paragraphs BC287–BC293).

Combination of contracts (paragraph 17)

BC71 The boards decided to include requirements in paragraph 17 of IFRS 15 for when an entity should combine two or more contracts and account for them as a single contract. This is because, in some cases, the amount and timing of revenue might differ depending on whether an entity accounts for two or more contracts separately or accounts for them as one contract.

BC72   The boards decided that entering into contracts at or near the same time is a necessary condition for the contracts to be combined. That decision is consistent with the objective of identifying the contract that is to be accounted for as the unit of account because that assessment is also performed at contract inception.

BC73   The boards decided that in addition to entering into contracts at or near the same time, the contracts should satisfy one or more of the criteria in paragraph 17 of IFRS 15 for the contracts to be combined. The boards observed that when either criterion (a) or (b) in paragraph 17 of IFRS 15 is met, the relationship between the consideration in the contracts (ie the price interdependence) is such that if those contracts were not combined, the amount of consideration allocated to the performance obligations in each contract might not faithfully depict the value of the goods or services transferred to the customer. The boards decided to include the criterion in paragraph 17(c) of IFRS 15 to avoid the possibility that an entity could effectively bypass the requirements for identifying performance obligations depending on how the entity structures its contracts.

BC74   The boards clarified that for two or more contracts to be combined, they should be with the same customer. However, the boards acknowledged that in some situations, contracts with related parties (as defined in IAS 24 *Related Party Disclosures* and Topic 850 *Related Party Disclosures*) should be combined if there are interdependencies between the separate contracts with those related parties. Thus, in those situations, combining the contracts with related parties results in a more appropriate depiction of the amount and timing of revenue recognition.

BC75   The boards also considered whether to specify that all contracts should be combined if they were negotiated as a package to achieve a single commercial objective, regardless of whether those contracts were entered into at or near the same time with the same customer. However, the boards decided not to do this, primarily because they were concerned that doing so could have had the unintended consequence of an entity combining too many contracts and not faithfully depicting the entity's performance. Furthermore, the boards decided that an entity should apply judgement to determine whether a contract is entered into 'at or near the same time'. However, the boards noted that the longer the period between the commitments of the parties to the contracts, the more likely it is that the economic circumstances affecting the negotiations have changed.

Contract modifications (paragraphs 18–21)

BC76   The boards observed that previous revenue recognition requirements did not include a general framework for accounting for contract modifications. Therefore, the boards decided to include requirements regarding contract modifications in IFRS 15 to improve consistency in the accounting for contract modifications. As the revenue recognition model developed, the boards proposed different approaches to account for contract modifications. However, each approach was developed with the overall objective of faithfully depicting an entity's rights and obligations in the modified contract. The boards concluded that to faithfully depict the rights and obligations arising from a modified contract, an entity should account for some modifications prospectively and for other modifications on a cumulative catch-up basis.

BC77   The boards decided that a contract modification should be accounted for prospectively if the additional promised goods or services are distinct and the pricing for those goods or services reflects their stand-alone selling price (see paragraph 20 of IFRS 15). The boards decided that when those criteria are met, there is no economic difference between an entity entering into a separate contract for the additional goods or services and an entity modifying an existing contract.

BC78   The boards also decided that a contract modification should be accounted for prospectively when the goods or services to be provided after the modification are distinct from the goods or services already provided (see paragraph 21(a) of IFRS 15). The boards decided that this should be the case regardless of whether the pricing of the additional promised goods or services reflected their stand-alone selling prices. This is because accounting for those types of modifications on a cumulative catch-up basis could be complex and may not necessarily faithfully depict the economics of the modification, because the modification is negotiated after the original contract and is based on new facts and circumstances. Therefore, this approach avoids opening up the accounting for previously satisfied performance obligations and, thus, avoids any adjustments to revenue for satisfied performance obligations.

BC79   Some respondents were concerned that an entity would also be required to use a cumulative catch-up basis to account for modifications to a contract with a single performance obligation that is made up of a series of distinct goods or services. Those contracts typically include repetitive services, such as energy contracts or mobile phone airtime services. The boards considered those concerns and clarified in paragraph 21(a) of IFRS 15 that the determination of whether a modification is accounted for prospectively depends on whether the remaining promises in the contract are for distinct goods or services. This is the case even if an entity determines that it has a single performance obligation, provided that the performance obligation represents a series of distinct goods or services (see paragraphs BC113–BC116).

BC80   The boards decided that if the remaining goods or services are not distinct and are part of a single performance obligation that is partially satisfied (ie a performance obligation satisfied over time), an entity should recognise the effect of the modification on a cumulative catch-up basis. This requires an entity to update the transaction price and the measure of progress towards complete satisfaction of a performance obligation, both of which may change as a result of the contract modification. That approach is particularly relevant to, and generally accepted in, the construction industry because a modification to those types of contracts would typically not result in the transfer of additional goods or services that are distinct from those promised in the existing contract.

BC81 Respondents also asked how the requirements for contract modifications would apply to unpriced change orders (see paragraph BC39) and contract claims (ie specific modifications in which the changes in scope and price are unapproved or in dispute). IFRS and US GAAP previously included specific guidance for unpriced change orders and contract claims within construction-type and production-type contracts. The boards decided that it was unnecessary to provide specific requirements for the accounting for these types of modifications because IFRS 15 includes the relevant requirements, specifically:

(a) paragraphs 18 and 19 of IFRS 15 require an entity to determine whether the rights and obligations of the parties to the contract that are created or changed by the unpriced change order or contract claim are enforceable;

(b) paragraph 19 of IFRS 15 requires an entity to estimate the change to the transaction price for the unpriced change order or contract claim; and

(c) paragraph 21 of IFRS 15 requires an entity to determine whether the unpriced change order or contract claim should be accounted for on a prospective basis or a cumulative catch-up basis.

Interaction between changes in the transaction price and contract modifications

BC82 The 2011 Exposure Draft proposed that an entity would account for contract modifications that result only in a change in the contract price on a cumulative catch-up basis because this would be consistent with the requirements for changes in the transaction price (as a result of changes in the estimate of variable consideration). In their redeliberations, the boards noted that the proposal would result in very different accounting outcomes depending on whether a distinct good or service was included in the modification. This is because modifications that change only the price would be accounted for on a cumulative catch-up basis, whereas modifications in which a distinct good or service (no matter how small) is added to the contract at the same time as a price change would be accounted for on a prospective basis. Furthermore, the boards noted that changes in the transaction price arising from a contract modification and changes in the expectations of variable consideration are the result of different economic events – a change in the expectation of variable consideration arises from a change in a variable that was identified and agreed upon at contract inception, whereas a change in price arising from a contract modification arises from a separate and subsequent negotiation between the parties to the contract. Consequently, the boards decided that a contract modification resulting only in a change in the contract price should be accounted for in a manner that is consistent with other contract modifications.

BC83 Some respondents requested that the boards clarify how an entity should allocate a change in the transaction price that occurs after a modification of the contract (that is accounted for in accordance with paragraph 21(a) of IFRS 15) but the change in the transaction price is attributable to an amount of variable consideration promised before the modification. This may occur because the estimate of the amount of variable consideration in the initial contract has changed or is no longer constrained. Specifically, those respondents asked whether, in those circumstances, an entity should allocate the corresponding change in the transaction price to the performance obligations in the modified contract, or to the performance obligations identified in the contract before the modification (ie the initial contract), including to performance obligations that were satisfied before the modification. In response to that feedback, the boards clarified in paragraph 90 of IFRS 15 that the allocation of the change in transaction price in those circumstances depends on whether, and the extent to which, the change in the transaction price is attributable to an amount of variable consideration promised before the modification. In providing that clarification, the boards noted that it would be appropriate in those circumstances to allocate a change in the transaction price to the performance obligations identified in the initial contract, if the promised variable consideration and the resolution of the uncertainty associated with that amount of variable consideration are not affected by the contract modification.

Identifying performance obligations

Definition of a performance obligation (Appendix A)

BC84   IFRS 15 distinguishes between obligations to provide goods or services to a customer and other obligations by defining those obligations to provide goods or services as performance obligations. The notion of a performance obligation is similar to the notions of deliverables, components or elements of a contract in previous revenue Standards. Although the notion of a performance obligation is implicit in previous revenue Standards, the term 'performance obligation' has not been defined previously.

BC85   The boards' objective in developing the definition of a performance obligation was to ensure that entities appropriately identify the unit of account for the goods and services promised in a contract with a customer. The boards decided that because the revenue recognition model is an allocated transaction price model, identifying a meaningful unit of account that depicts the goods and services in the contract is fundamental for the purpose of recognising revenue on a basis that faithfully depicts the entity's performance in transferring the promised goods or services to the customer.

BC86   The boards decided that a performance obligation could be either of the following:

(a)   a good or service (or a bundle of goods or services) that is distinct (see paragraphs BC94–BC112); or

(b)   a series of distinct goods or services that are substantially the same and have the same pattern of transfer (see paragraphs BC113–BC116).

Identifying the promised goods or services (paragraphs 24–25)

BC87   Before an entity can identify its performance obligations in a contract with a customer, the entity would first need to identify all of the promised goods or services in that contract. The boards noted that in many cases, all of the promised goods or services in a contract might be identified explicitly in that contract. However, in other cases, promises to provide goods or services might be implied by the entity's customary business practices. The boards decided that such implied promises should be considered when determining the entity's performance obligations, if those practices create a valid expectation of the customer that the entity will transfer a good or service (for example, some when-and-if-available software upgrades). The boards also noted that the implied promises in the contract do not need to be enforceable by law. If the customer has a valid expectation, then the customer would view those promises as part of the negotiated exchange (ie goods or services that the customer expects to receive and for which it has paid). The boards noted that in the absence of these requirements developed by the boards, an entity might recognise all of the consideration in a contract as revenue even though the entity continues to have remaining (implicit) promises related to the contract with the customer.

BC88   Some respondents suggested that some promised goods or services should be excluded from the scope of IFRS 15 and accounted for as marketing expenses or incidental obligations, even though those promises would meet the definition of a performance obligation. Examples of such promised goods or services may include 'free' handsets provided by telecommunication entities, 'free' maintenance provided by automotive manufacturers and customer loyalty points awarded by supermarkets, airlines and hotels. Those respondents stated that revenue should be recognised only for the main goods or services for which the customer has contracted and not for what they consider to be marketing incentives and other incidental obligations.

BC89   The boards observed that when a customer contracts with an entity for a bundle of goods or services, it can be difficult and subjective for the entity to identify the main goods or services for which the customer has contracted. In addition, the outcome of that assessment could vary significantly depending on whether the entity performs the assessment from the perspective of its business model or from the perspective of the customer. Consequently, the boards decided that all goods or services promised to a customer as a result of a contract give rise to performance obligations because those promises were made as part of the negotiated exchange between the entity and its customer. Although the entity might consider those goods or services to be marketing incentives or incidental goods or services, they are goods or services for which the customer pays and to which the entity should allocate consideration for purposes of revenue recognition. However, the boards observed that in some cases, an entity might provide incentives to a customer that would not represent a performance obligation if those incentives are provided independently of the contract that they are designed to secure. (See paragraphs BC386–BC395 for additional discussion on marketing incentives and the accounting for customer options to acquire additional goods or services.)

BC90 For similar reasons, the boards decided not to exempt an entity from accounting for performance obligations that the entity might regard as being perfunctory or inconsequential.[5] Instead, an entity should assess whether those performance obligations are immaterial to its financial statements as described in IAS 8 and FASB Concepts Statement No. 8 *Conceptual Framework for Financial Reporting*.

BC91 To help an entity identify the promised goods or services, IFRS 15 provides examples of the types of promises that can represent goods or services to the customer. In response to feedback received, the boards clarified that the following can also represent promised goods or services:

(a) providing a service of standing ready or making goods or services available (see paragraph BC160); and

(b) granting rights to goods or services to be provided in the future (see paragraph BC92).

BC92 The boards observed that it was important to clarify that granting a right to goods or services to be provided in the future, such as when an entity makes a promise to provide goods or services to its customer's customer, would give rise to performance obligations for the entity. Those types of promises exist in distribution networks in various industries but are particularly common in the automotive industry. For example, when a manufacturer sells a motor vehicle to its customer (a dealer), the manufacturer may also promise to provide additional goods or services (such as maintenance) to the dealer's customer. IFRS 15 requires an entity to identify all of the promises—both explicit and implicit—that are made to the customer as part of the contract with that customer. Consequently, a promise of a good or service (such as maintenance) that the customer can pass on to its customer would be a performance obligation if the promise could be identified (explicitly or implicitly) in the contract with the customer. However, the boards noted that some promised goods or services might not represent performance obligations if those promises did not exist (explicitly or implicitly) at the time that the parties agreed to the contract.

BC93 The boards also clarified that an entity should not account for activities it may perform that do not transfer goods or services to the customer. This may occur in many contracts in which an entity undertakes separate activities that do not directly transfer goods or services to the customer (for example, service contracts that require significant setup costs), even though those activities are required to successfully transfer the goods or services for which the customer has contracted. The boards decided that including those activities as performance obligations would have been inconsistent with the core revenue

---

5 The FASB subsequently decided to amend Topic 606 to state that an entity is not required to assess whether promised goods or services are performance obligations if they are immaterial within the context of the contract with the customer. The IASB's considerations for deciding not to make similar amendments to IFRS 15 are explained in paragraphs BC116A–BC116E.

recognition principle because those activities do not result in a transfer of goods or services to the customer.

Identifying when promises represent performance obligations (paragraphs 22–30)

BC94   Contracts with customers can include many promises to transfer goods or services. In the Discussion Paper, the boards proposed that an entity should review the timing of the transfer of the promised goods or services to identify the performance obligations that it should account for separately. Respondents to the Discussion Paper were concerned that this proposal would have required an entity to account separately for every promised good or service in a contract that is transferred at a different time, which would not be practical for many contracts, especially for long-term service and construction contracts. Consequently, the boards decided to provide clearer requirements that result in an entity identifying performance obligations in a way that is practical and results in a pattern of revenue recognition that faithfully depicts the transfer of goods or services to the customer.

BC95   In developing those requirements, the boards observed that in many contracts, identifying the promised goods or services that an entity should account for separately is straightforward. Consequently, the boards developed a principle for identifying performance obligations that separates promised goods or services in a relevant way when applied across the various industries and transactions within the scope of IFRS 15. That principle is the notion of a distinct good or service. The term 'distinct', in an ordinary sense, suggests something that is different, separate or dissimilar. A majority of respondents agreed with using the principle of distinct goods or services to identify the performance obligations in a contract. However, many asked the boards to refine and further clarify the requirements for determining when a good or service is distinct.

BC96   Consequently, the boards decided that for a good or service to be distinct, the criteria in paragraph 27 of IFRS 15 must be met. The boards' deliberations of those criteria are discussed in the following sections.

Capable of being distinct

BC97   The boards decided that a good or service must possess some specified minimum characteristics to be accounted for separately. Specifically, the good or service must be capable of being distinct — that is, the good or service is capable of providing a benefit to the customer either on its own or together with other resources that are readily available to the customer. The boards were concerned that requiring an entity to account separately (and estimate a stand-alone selling price) for a good or service that is not capable of providing a benefit to the customer might result in information that would not be relevant to users of financial statements. For example, if an entity transferred a machine to the customer, but the machine is only capable of providing a benefit to the customer after an installation process that only the entity can provide, the machine would not be distinct.

BC98　　The 2010 Exposure Draft addressed this notion of a minimum characteristic by proposing that a good or service should have a distinct function – that is, the good or service should have utility either on its own or together with other goods or services that the customer has acquired from the entity or that are sold separately by the entity or another entity. Respondents requested additional guidance on the meaning of 'distinct function' because they considered that almost any element of a contract could have utility in combination with other goods or services.

BC99　　Consequently, the boards refined the notion of distinct function and developed the criterion in paragraph 27(a) of IFRS 15. In addition, the boards included the requirements in paragraph 28 of IFRS 15 (which were derived from the Basis for Conclusions on the 2011 Exposure Draft) to help an entity apply that criterion and assess whether a customer can benefit from the good or service on its own or together with other resources. Those requirements focus on the notion of economic benefits, which many respondents explained was helpful in assessing whether the customer can benefit from the good or service on its own or together with other resources. The boards noted that, conceptually, any good or service that is regularly sold separately should be able to be used on its own or with other resources. Otherwise, there would be no market for an entity to provide that good or service on a stand-alone basis.

BC100　The boards observed that the assessment of whether the 'customer can benefit from the goods or services on its own' should be based on the characteristics of the goods or services themselves instead of the way in which the customer may use the goods or services. Consequently, an entity would disregard any contractual limitations that might preclude the customer from obtaining readily available resources from a source other than the entity.

BC101　The attributes of a distinct good or service are comparable to previous revenue recognition requirements for identifying separate deliverables in a multiple-element arrangement, which specified that a delivered item must have 'value to the customer on a stand-alone basis' for an entity to account for that item separately. However, the boards decided against using that terminology to avoid the implication that an entity must assess the customer's intended use for the promised goods or services in identifying the performance obligations in a contract. The boards observed that it would be difficult, if not impossible, for an entity to know the customer's intentions in a given contract.

Distinct within the context of the contract[6]

BC102   In some cases, even though the individual goods or services promised as a bundle of goods or services might be capable of being distinct, those goods or services should not be accounted for separately because it would not result in a faithful depiction of the entity's performance in that contract. As an example, many construction-type and production-type contracts involve transferring to the customer many goods and services that are capable of being distinct (such as various building materials, labour and project management services). However, identifying all of those individual goods and services as separate performance obligations would be impractical and, more importantly, it would neither faithfully represent the nature of the entity's promise to the customer nor result in a useful depiction of the entity's performance. This is because it would result in an entity recognising and measuring revenue when the materials and other inputs to the construction or production process are provided, instead of recognising and measuring revenue when the entity performs (and uses those inputs) in the construction or production of the item (or items) for which the customer has contracted. Consequently, the boards decided that, when identifying whether goods or services are distinct, an entity should not only consider the characteristics of an individual good or service (see paragraph 27(a) of IFRS 15) but should also consider whether the promise to transfer the good or service is separately identifiable (ie distinct within the context of the contract, see paragraph 27(b) of IFRS 15).

BC103   During the development of IFRS 15, the existence of 'separable risks' was identified as a basis for assessing whether a good or service is distinct within the context of the contract. In that assessment, the individual goods or services in a bundle would not be distinct if the risk that an entity assumes to fulfil its obligation to transfer one of those promised goods or services to the customer is a risk that is inseparable from the risk relating to the transfer of the other promised goods or services in that bundle. The boards considered whether to specify 'separable risks' as a necessary attribute of a distinct good or service. However, the boards decided that the concept of 'separable risks' may not be a practical criterion for determining whether a good or service is distinct.

BC104   To make the notion of separable risks more operable, the boards considered other approaches for articulating the notion. However, the boards rejected those approaches for the following reasons:

---

6   *Clarifications to IFRS 15* issued in April 2016 amended paragraphs 27 and 29 of IFRS 15 to clarify that the objective of assessing whether an entity's promises to transfer goods or services to the customer are separately identifiable is to determine whether the entity's promise is to transfer (a) each of those goods or services; or (b) a combined item or items to which the promised goods or services are inputs. Amendments were also made to the factors in paragraph 29 to more clearly align them with the revised 'separately identifiable' principle. Paragraphs BC102–BC112 should therefore be read together with paragraphs BC116F–BC116Q, which explain the boards' considerations in making these amendments.

(a)   distinct profit margin — in some cases, entities may decide to assign the same margin to various goods or services, even though those goods or services use different resources and are subject to different risks. In addition, for some goods or services, especially software and other types of intellectual property, cost is not a significant factor in determining price and, therefore, margins could be highly variable because they may be determined by the customer's ability to pay or to obtain substitute goods or services from another entity.

(b)   criteria based on the notions of goods or services that are significantly modified or customised, and highly interrelated goods or services that require an entity to provide a significant service of integrating those goods or services — respondents explained that while these are relevant factors to consider to determine whether a good or service is distinct, expressing those factors as criteria could be too restrictive because they could force bundling or unbundling that did not reflect the economics of the arrangement.

BC105   Consequently, the boards decided to specify in paragraph 27(b) of IFRS 15 that the objective in identifying whether a promised good or service is distinct within the context of the contract is to determine whether an entity's promise to transfer that good or service is separately identifiable from other promises in the contract. The notion of 'separately identifiable' is based on the notion of separable risks in paragraph BC103 (ie whether the risk that an entity assumes to fulfil its obligation to transfer one of those promised goods or services to the customer is a risk that is inseparable from the risk relating to the transfer of the other promised goods or services). The boards observed that determining whether the entity's promise to transfer a good or service is separately identifiable requires judgement, taking into account all of the facts and circumstances. The boards decided to assist entities in making that judgement by including the factors in paragraph 29 of IFRS 15.

BC106   The boards observed that the factors in paragraph 29 of IFRS 15 are not mutually exclusive. On the contrary, because the factors are based on the same underlying principle of inseparable risks, the boards noted that in many cases more than one of the factors might apply to a contract with a customer. However, each factor was developed because it may be more applicable for particular contracts or industries. The rationale for each factor is discussed in paragraphs BC107–BC112.

Significant integration service (paragraph 29(a))

BC107   In circumstances in which an entity provides an integration service, the risk of transferring individual goods or services is inseparable, because a substantial part of the entity's promise to a customer is to ensure the individual goods or services are incorporated into the combined output. Thus, the individual goods or services are inputs to produce a single output. The boards observed that this factor may be relevant in many construction contracts in which the contractor provides an integration (or contract management) service to manage and co-ordinate the various construction tasks and to assume the risks associated with the integration of those tasks.

Moreover, the integration service will require a contractor to co-ordinate the tasks performed by any subcontractors and ensure that those tasks are performed in accordance with the contract specifications, thus ensuring the individual goods or services are appropriately incorporated into the combined item for which the customer has contracted.

BC108   The boards observed that this factor could apply to industries other than the construction industry. For example, some software development contracts with significant integration services will similarly have promised goods and services that meet the criterion in paragraph 27(b) of IFRS 15. However, the boards did not intend for this factor to be applied too broadly to software integration services for which the risk that the entity assumes in integrating the promised goods or services is negligible (for example, a simple installation of software that does not require significant modification). Therefore, to provide some additional clarification for many software-type contracts, the boards included the factor in paragraph 29(b) of IFRS 15.

Significant modification or customisation (paragraph 29(b))

BC109   In some industries, such as the software industry, the notion of inseparable risks is more clearly illustrated by assessing whether one good or service significantly modifies or customises another good or service. This is because if a good or service modifies or customises another good or service in the contract, each good or service is being assembled together (ie as inputs) to produce a combined output for which the customer has contracted.

BC110   For example, an entity may promise to provide a customer with existing software and also promise to customise that software so that it will function with the customer's existing infrastructure such that the entity is providing the customer with a fully integrated system. In this case, if the customisation service requires the entity to significantly modify the existing software in such a way that the risks of providing the software and the customisation service are inseparable, the entity may conclude that the promises to transfer the software and the customisation service would not be separately identifiable and, therefore, those goods or services would not be distinct within the context of the contract.

Highly dependent or highly interrelated (paragraph 29(c))

BC111   The boards decided to include the factor in paragraph 29(c) of IFRS 15 because, in some cases, it might be unclear whether the entity is providing an integration service (see paragraph 29(a)) or whether the goods or services are significantly modified or customised (see paragraph 29(b)). However, the individual goods and services in the contract may still not be separately identifiable from the other goods or services promised in the contract. This may be because the goods or services are highly dependent on, or highly interrelated with, other promised goods or services in the contract in such a way that the customer could not choose to purchase one good or service without significantly affecting the other promised goods or services in the contract.

BC112 Consider the following example – an entity agrees to design an experimental new product for a customer and to manufacture 10 prototype units of that product. The specifications for the product include functionality that has yet to be proved. Consequently, the entity will be required to continue to revise the design of the product during the construction and testing of the prototypes and make any necessary modifications to in-progress or completed prototypes. The entity expects that most or all of the units to be produced may require some rework because of design changes made during the production process. In that case, the customer may not be able to choose whether to purchase only the design service or the manufacturing service without significantly affecting one or the other. This is because the risk of providing the design service is inseparable from the manufacturing service. Thus, although each promise may have benefit on its own, within the context of the contract, they are not separately identifiable. This is because the entity determines that each promise is highly dependent on, and highly interrelated with, the other promises in the contract.

A series of distinct goods or services that are substantially the same and have the same pattern of transfer (paragraph 22(b))

BC113 The boards decided to specify that a promise to transfer a series of distinct goods or services that are substantially the same and that have the same pattern of transfer to the customer would be a single performance obligation if two criteria are met. The boards decided to include this notion as part of the definition of a performance obligation to simplify the application of the model and to promote consistency in the identification of performance obligations in circumstances in which the entity provides the same good or service consecutively over a period of time (for example, a repetitive service arrangement). To be accounted for as a single performance obligation, each of those promised goods or services must be performance obligations satisfied over time in accordance with paragraph 35 of IFRS 15.

BC114 The boards observed that without this part of the definition, applying the model might present some operational challenges when an entity provides a series of distinct goods or services that are substantially the same. Otherwise, the entity would be required to identify multiple distinct goods or services, allocate the transaction price to each of the resulting performance obligations on a stand-alone selling price basis and then recognise revenue when those performance obligations are satisfied. For example, in a repetitive service contract such as a cleaning contract, transaction processing or a contract to deliver electricity, an entity would be required to allocate the overall consideration to each increment of service (for example, each hour of cleaning) to be provided in the contract. The boards decided that it would not be cost-effective to apply the model in this manner and determined that including paragraph 22(b) of IFRS 15 as part of the definition of a performance obligation would alleviate costs. This is because when paragraph 22(b) of IFRS 15 applies (ie the contract includes a promise to transfer a series of distinct goods or services that are substantially the same and have the same pattern of transfer to the customer), an entity will identify a single performance obligation and allocate the transaction price to the performance obligation. The entity will then recognise revenue by applying a single measure of progress to that performance obligation.

BC115   The boards noted that if an entity determines it has a performance obligation that meets the criterion in paragraph 22(b) of IFRS 15, an entity should consider the distinct goods or services in the contract, rather than the performance obligation, for the purposes of contract modifications and the allocation of variable consideration.

BC116   In their redeliberations, the boards observed that paragraph 22(b) of IFRS 15 applies to goods or services that are delivered consecutively, rather than concurrently. The boards noted that IFRS 15 would not need to specify the accounting for concurrently delivered distinct goods or services that have the same pattern of transfer. This is because, in those cases, an entity is not precluded from accounting for the goods or services as if they were a single performance obligation, if the outcome is the same as accounting for the goods and services as individual performance obligations.

Clarifications to IFRS 15 (amendments issued in April 2016)

Promised goods or services that are immaterial within the context of the contract

BC116A The TRG discussed an implementation question about whether an entity should identify items or activities as promised goods or services that were not identified as deliverables or components under previous revenue Standards. A specific concern was raised about the boards' decision (see paragraph BC90) not to exempt an entity from accounting for performance obligations that the entity might regard as being perfunctory or inconsequential. Some stakeholders held the view that IFRS 15 might require an entity to identify significantly more performance obligations than would have been the case under previous revenue Standards.

BC116B In response to stakeholders' concerns, the FASB decided to amend Topic 606 to state that an entity is not required to assess whether promised goods or services are performance obligations if they are immaterial within the context of the contract with the customer. The FASB decided to specify that an entity is required to consider whether a promised good or service is material only at the contract level because it would be unduly burdensome to require an entity to aggregate and determine the effect on its financial statements of those items or activities determined to be immaterial at the contract level. In addition, the FASB decided to specify that an entity is required to accrue the costs, if any, to transfer immaterial goods or services to the customer in instances in which the costs will be incurred after the satisfaction of the performance obligation (and recognition of revenue) to which those immaterial goods or services relate.

BC116C   Having considered the wider implications of amending IFRS 15, the IASB decided that it was not necessary to incorporate similar wording into IFRS 15. The TRG's discussion highlighted that the concerns raised primarily related to potential changes to practice under US GAAP. Previous revenue Standards under IFRS did not contain similar language to the guidance issued by the staff of the US Securities and Exchange Commission on inconsequential or perfunctory performance obligations. The TRG's discussion also indicated that IFRS stakeholders can understand and apply the requirements of IFRS 15 in this area.

BC116D   In its deliberations, the IASB expressed the view that the concerns raised relate to the application of materiality concepts rather than the application of the requirements in IFRS 15. As described in paragraph BC84, the boards intended the notion of a performance obligation to be similar to the notions of deliverables, components or elements of a contract in previous revenue Standards. The IASB noted that IFRS 15 requires an entity to identify performance obligations rather than promised goods or services. Accordingly, although an entity makes an assessment of the goods or services promised in a contract in order to identify material performance obligations, the boards did not intend to require an entity to individually identify every possible promised good or service.

BC116E   In reaching its decision, the IASB also observed that the explanation in paragraph BC90 should be read within the context of the boards' explanation of the development of IFRS 15 rather than as implying that an entity is required to identify perfunctory or inconsequential goods or services promised in a contract. One of the reasons that the IASB decided not to introduce an exemption for perfunctory or inconsequential performance obligations is that it was not considered necessary, both because of how the concept of 'distinct' is applied and also because of the application of materiality. In assessing promised goods or services and identifying performance obligations, entities should consider not only materiality considerations but also the overall objective of IFRS 15. The IASB further noted that materiality is an overarching concept that applies throughout IFRS and not just when it is mentioned explicitly.

Identifying performance obligations (paragraphs 27–30)

BC116F   The TRG discussed issues relating to the principle in paragraph 27(b) regarding when a promised good or service is separately identifiable (ie distinct within the context of a contract) and the supporting factors in paragraph 29. The discussion informed the boards about potential diversity in stakeholders' understanding and indicated that there was a risk of paragraph 29(c) being applied more broadly than intended, resulting in promised goods or services being inappropriately combined and accounted for as a single performance obligation. Stakeholders asked about the application of this factor to scenarios in which one of the promised goods or services is dependent on the transfer of the other, such as a contract for equipment and related consumables that are required for the equipment to function. Some stakeholders suggested that, although the promised goods or services may be capable of being distinct, if one of the goods or services was dependent on the other, the promised goods or services would not be distinct within the context of the contract.

BC116G   In the light of the TRG discussions, the IASB was initially of the view that the discussions highlighted educational needs and that, given the nature of the issues raised, amendments to IFRS 15 were not required and that the examples accompanying IFRS 15 could be clarified to illustrate the application of the requirements. Consequently, in its Exposure Draft *Clarifications to IFRS 15*, the IASB proposed to add some new examples, and to amend some of the existing examples that accompany IFRS 15. The FASB decided to propose amendments to Topic 606 to clarify the guidance relating to the identification of performance obligations. In particular, their proposed amendments included expanding the articulation of the 'separately identifiable' principle and reframing the existing factors in paragraph 606-10-25-21 (paragraph 29 of IFRS 15) to align them with the amended principle.

BC116H   Some respondents to the IASB's Exposure Draft asked for the amendments proposed by the FASB to be incorporated into paragraph 29 of IFRS 15. They expressed concerns about differences in wording between IFRS and US GAAP and also indicated that the FASB's proposed amendments would improve the understanding of the separately identifiable principle and the operability of the requirements. Step 2 is a fundamental part of IFRS 15 that affects accounting in subsequent steps of the revenue recognition model. Consequently, in its redeliberations of the amendments the IASB concluded that the benefits of retaining converged requirements on this topic outweigh the potential costs of amending the requirements. Accordingly, the IASB decided to amend IFRS 15 to clarify the principle and the factors that indicate when two or more promises to transfer goods or services are not separately identifiable. Those amendments are the same as the FASB's related amendments to Topic 606.

BC116I   Although the wording describing the separately identifiable principle in paragraph 29 has been amended, the amendments clarify the boards' intentions and are not a change to the underlying principle. The boards observed that applying the principle in paragraph 27(b) requires judgement, taking into account facts and circumstances (see paragraph BC105). Even after amending the factors in paragraph 29 of IFRS 15, the boards recognise that judgement will be needed to determine whether promised goods or services are distinct within the context of the contract.

BC116J   The amendments are intended to convey that an entity should evaluate whether its promise, within the context of the contract, is to transfer each good or service individually or a combined item (or items) that comprises the individual goods or services promised in the contract. Therefore, entities should evaluate whether the promised goods or services in the contract are outputs or, instead, are inputs to a combined item (or items). In many cases, the inputs to a combined item concept might be further explained as a situation in which an entity's promise to transfer goods or services results in a combined item that is more than (or substantively different from) the sum of those individual promised goods and services. For example, in a contract to build a wall, the promise to provide bricks and the promise to provide labour are not separately identifiable from each other within the context of the contract because those promises together comprise the promise to the customer to build the wall.

BC116K The boards previously considered the concept of 'separable risks' (see paragraph BC103) as an alternative basis for assessing whether an entity's promise to transfer a good or service is separately identifiable from other promises in the contract. Although the boards decided not to use this terminology in IFRS 15, the notion of separable risks continues to influence the separately identifiable principle. The evaluation of whether an entity's promise is separately identifiable considers the relationship between the various goods or services within the contract in the context of the process of fulfilling the contract. Therefore, an entity should consider the level of integration, interrelation or interdependence among the promises to transfer goods or services. The boards observed that rather than considering whether one item, by its nature, depends on the other (ie whether two items have a functional relationship), an entity evaluates whether there is a transformative relationship between the two items in the process of fulfilling the contract.

BC116L The boards decided to reframe the factors in paragraph 29 of IFRS 15 to more clearly align them with the revised wording of the separately identifiable principle. This clarification emphasises that the separately identifiable principle is applied within the context of the bundle of promised goods or services in the contract rather than within the context of each individual promised good or service. The separately identifiable principle is intended to identify when an entity's performance in transferring a bundle of goods or services in a contract is fulfilling a single promise to a customer. Accordingly, the boards revised the wording to emphasise that an entity should evaluate whether two or more promised goods or services each significantly affect the other (and, therefore, are highly interdependent or highly interrelated) in the contract. Furthermore, the boards concluded that it may be clearer to structure those factors to identify when the promises in a bundle of promised goods or services are *not* separately identifiable and, therefore, constitute a single performance obligation.

BC116M In addition to reframing the factors in the context of a bundle of goods or services, the boards amended the factor relating to a significant integration service in paragraph 29(a) of IFRS 15 to clarify two related issues—that application of this factor is not limited to circumstances that result in a single output, and that a combined output may include more than one phase, element or unit. This concept is illustrated by the example in paragraph BC112, in which an entity agrees to design an experimental product for a customer and to manufacture 10 prototype units of that product. In the example, the design and production of the units is an iterative process and the significant integration service provided by the entity relates to all 10 prototype units.

BC116N The TRG's discussions also highlighted that some stakeholders may have been interpreting the factors supporting paragraph 27(b) as a series of criteria. Paragraph 29, where the factors are set out, provides a non-exhaustive list of factors to consider; not all of those factors need to exist (or not exist) to conclude that the entity's promises to transfer goods or services are not (are) separately identifiable. Similarly, the boards also noted that the factors are not intended to be criteria that are evaluated independently of the separately identifiable principle. Given the wide variety of revenue arrangements that are within the scope of IFRS 15, the boards expect that there will be some instances for which the factors will be less relevant to the evaluation of the separately identifiable principle. Consequently, entities should consider the objective of the principle, not just the factors provided in paragraph 29 of IFRS 15.

BC116O Stakeholders also asked about the effect of contractual restrictions on the identification of performance obligations. Accordingly, one of the examples added (Case D of Example 11) illustrates the boards' observation in paragraph BC100 of IFRS 15 that an entity should focus on the characteristics of the promised goods or services themselves instead of on the way in which the customer might be required to use the goods or services.

BC116P The IASB decided that it was not necessary to add some of the examples that the FASB included in its amendments to Topic 606. In particular, the IASB concluded that an example relating to whether an anti-virus software licence is distinct from when-and-if-available updates to the software during the licence period (Example 10, Case C in Topic 606) was unnecessary. The IASB thought that this additional example was not required because Example 55 that accompanies IFRS 15 illustrates the application of the requirements on identifying performance obligations to a similar fact pattern.

BC116Q Respondents to the Exposure Draft expressed concern that the proposed Example 10, Case B may imply that any contract manufacturing or similar arrangement would be a single performance obligation comprising goods that are not distinct. There are some similarities between the fact pattern in the example and other contracts with customers that involve project management, the production of customised goods or the manufacture of a series of identical goods. However, an entity should evaluate the nature of its promise(s) to a customer within the context of the contract. Example 10, Case B illustrates a scenario in which the entity is contractually required to undertake a significant effort to establish a customised production process specifically in order to produce the highly complex, specialised devices for which the customer has contracted. As a result, the entity's promise is to establish and provide a service of producing the contracted devices based on the customer's specifications. In contrast, other manufacturing scenarios may involve the development of a production process that can be used to produce goods for multiple contracts with the same or additional customers. In that case, the contract may not include a promise to establish a customised production process.

Shipping and handling activities

BC116R Some stakeholders in the United States expressed differing views about when shipping and handling activities that occur after the transfer of control to the customer should be accounted for as a promised service or as a fulfilment activity. Under previous revenue Standards, entities often did not account for shipping provided in conjunction with the sale of their goods as an additional service. As a result, some stakeholders raised cost-benefit concerns and asked whether relief should be provided in respect of shipping and handling activities from the general requirement to assess the goods or services promised in a contract with a customer in order to identify performance obligations.

BC116S   When the boards discussed these concerns, board members noted that shipping and handling activities that occur before the customer obtains control of the related good are fulfilment activities. However, if control of a good has been transferred to a customer, shipping and handling services are provided in relation to the customer's good, which may indicate that the entity is providing a service to the customer.

BC116T   In response to the cost-benefit concerns raised by stakeholders, the FASB decided to amend Topic 606 to:

(a)   permit an entity, as an accounting policy election, to account for shipping and handling activities that occur after the customer has obtained control of a good as fulfilment activities; and

(b)   explicitly state that shipping and handling activities that occur before the customer obtains control of the related good are fulfilment activities.

BC116U   Having considered the wider implications of amending IFRS 15, the IASB decided not to make a similar amendment, for the following reasons:

(a)   An accounting policy choice for shipping and handling activities after control of goods has been transferred to the customer would create an exception to the revenue recognition model and potentially reduce comparability between entities. Paragraph 22 of IFRS 15 requires an entity to assess the goods or services promised in a contract with a customer in order to identify performance obligations. The introduction of a policy choice would override this requirement.

(b)   In addition, a policy choice is applicable to all entities. Consequently, it is possible that entities with significant shipping operations would make different policy elections. This would make it more difficult for users of financial statements to understand and compare the revenue reported by different entities, including those within the same industry.

The IASB acknowledged that, because the policy choice is not available in IFRS 15, this gives rise to a difference between IFRS 15 and Topic 606.

Satisfaction of performance obligations (paragraphs 31–45)

BC117   Revenue is recognised when (or as) goods or services are transferred to a customer. This is because an entity satisfies its performance obligation by transferring control of the promised good or service underlying that performance obligation to the customer. Consequently, assessing when control of a good or service is transferred is a critical step in applying IFRS 15.

Control

BC118   Most previous revenue Standards required an entity to assess the transfer of a good or service by considering the transfer of risks and rewards of ownership. However, the boards decided that an entity should assess the transfer of a good or service by considering when the customer obtains control of that good or service, for the following reasons:

(a)   Both goods and services are assets that a customer acquires (even if many services are not recognised as an asset because those services are simultaneously received and consumed by the customer), and the boards' existing definitions of an asset use control to determine when an asset is recognised or derecognised.

(b)   Assessing the transfer of goods or services using control should result in more consistent decisions about when goods or services are transferred, because it can be difficult for an entity to judge whether an appropriate level of the risks and rewards of ownership of a good or service has been transferred to the customer if the entity retains some risks and rewards.

(c)   A risks-and-rewards approach could conflict with identifying performance obligations. For example, if an entity transfers a product to a customer but retains some risks associated with that product, an assessment based on risks and rewards might result in the entity identifying a single performance obligation that could be satisfied (and therefore revenue would be recognised) only after all the risks are eliminated. However, an assessment based on control might appropriately identify two performance obligations—one for the product and another for a remaining service, such as a fixed price maintenance agreement. Those performance obligations would be satisfied at different times.

BC119   Many respondents to both the 2010 and the 2011 Exposure Drafts agreed with using control to determine when a good or service is transferred to a customer. However, some respondents indicated that the transfer of the risks and rewards of ownership is sometimes a helpful indicator that control has transferred (see paragraph BC154).

Developing the notion of control

BC120   The boards' description of control is based on the meaning of control in the definitions of an asset in the boards' respective conceptual frameworks. Thus, the boards determined that control of a promised good or service (ie an asset) is the customer's ability to direct the use of, and obtain substantially all of the remaining benefits from, the asset. The components that make up the description of control are explained as follows:

(a)   ability—a customer must have the present right to direct the use of, and obtain substantially all of the remaining benefits from, an asset for an entity to recognise revenue. For example, in a contract that requires a manufacturer to produce an asset for a particular customer, it might be clear that the customer will ultimately have the right to direct the use of, and obtain substantially all of the remaining benefits from, the asset. However, the entity should not recognise revenue until the customer has actually obtained that right (which, depending on the contract, might occur during production or afterwards).

(b)   direct the use of—a customer's ability to direct the use of an asset refers to the customer's right to deploy that asset in its activities, to allow another entity to deploy that asset in its activities, or to restrict another entity from deploying that asset.

(c)   obtain the benefits from—the customer must have the ability to obtain substantially all of the remaining benefits from an asset for the customer to obtain control of it. Conceptually, the benefits from a good or service are potential cash flows (either an increase in cash inflows or a decrease in cash outflows). A customer can obtain the benefits directly or indirectly in many ways, such as by using, consuming, disposing of, selling, exchanging, pledging or holding an asset.

BC121   The boards observed that the assessment of when control has transferred could be applied from the perspective of either the entity selling the good or service or the customer purchasing the good or service. Consequently, revenue could be recognised when the seller surrenders control of a good or service or when the customer obtains control of that good or service. Although in many cases both perspectives lead to the same result, the boards decided that control should be assessed primarily from the perspective of the customer. That perspective minimises the risk of an entity recognising revenue from undertaking activities that do not coincide with the transfer of goods or services to the customer.

Applying the notion of control

BC122   As described in paragraph BC119, many respondents agreed with using control as the basis for assessing when the transfer of a promised good or service (ie an asset) occurs. However, most respondents to the 2010 Exposure Draft explained that the definition was most helpful when applied to performance obligations for the transfer of goods. They commented that applying the concept of control is straightforward in those cases because, typically, it is clear that an asset has transferred from the entity to its customer. They noted, however, that the requirements were more difficult to apply to performance obligations for services and construction-type contracts, because it could be difficult to determine when a customer obtains control of a service. This is because in many service contracts the service asset is simultaneously created and consumed and, therefore, is never recognised as an asset by the customer. Even in the case of a construction contract in which there is a recognisable asset, it can be difficult to assess whether a customer has the ability to direct the use of, and obtain substantially all of the remaining benefits from, a partially completed asset that the seller is creating. Consequently, many respondents in the construction industry were concerned that they would be required to change their revenue recognition policy from using a percentage-of-completion method to a completed contract method (ie on the basis that the transfer of assets occurs only upon transfer of legal title or physical possession of the finished asset, which typically occurs upon contract completion). Those respondents explained that the outcome of applying the completed contract method to their contracts with customers would not be a faithful depiction of the economics of those contracts.

BC123   As a result, some respondents suggested that the boards provide guidance for the transfer of control of services separately from the guidance for goods. However, the boards observed that it would be difficult to clearly define a service and not all contracts that are commonly regarded as services result in a transfer of resources to customers over time. Furthermore, the boards decided that the notion of control should apply equally to both goods and services. Consequently, to address respondents' concerns, the boards decided to specify requirements that focus on the attribute of the timing of when a performance obligation is satisfied (ie when a good or service is transferred to a customer). Accordingly, IFRS 15 includes criteria for determining whether a performance obligation is satisfied over time. Those criteria are explained in the following paragraphs.

Performance obligations satisfied over time (paragraphs 35–37)

BC124   The boards developed the criteria in paragraph 35 of IFRS 15 to provide an objective basis for assessing when control transfers over time and, thus, when a performance obligation is satisfied over time.

Customer simultaneously receives and consumes benefits as entity performs (paragraph 35(a))

BC125   In many typical service contracts, the entity's performance creates an asset only momentarily, because that asset is simultaneously received and consumed by the customer. In those cases, the simultaneous receipt and consumption of the asset that has been created means that the customer obtains control of the entity's output as the entity performs and, thus, the entity's performance obligation is satisfied over time. For example, consider an entity that promises to process transactions on behalf of a customer. The customer simultaneously receives and consumes a benefit as each transaction is processed.

BC126   The boards observed that there may be service-type contracts in which it is unclear whether the customer receives and consumes the benefit of the entity's performance over time. This is because the notion of 'benefit' can be subjective. Consider, for example, a freight logistics contract in which the entity has agreed to transport goods from Vancouver to New York City. Many respondents suggested that the customer receives no benefit from the entity's performance until the goods are delivered to New York City. However, the boards observed that the customer does benefit from the entity's performance as it occurs because if the goods were delivered only part way (for example, to Chicago), another entity would not need to substantially re-perform the entity's performance to date – that is, another entity would not need to take the goods back to Vancouver to deliver them to New York City. The boards observed that, in those cases, the assessment of whether another entity would need to substantially re-perform the performance completed to date can be used as an objective basis for determining whether the customer receives benefit from the entity's performance as it is provided.

BC127 The boards decided that an entity should disregard any contractual or practical limitations when it assesses the 'simultaneously receives and consumes' criterion and whether another entity would need to substantially re-perform the performance completed to date. This is because the objective of this criterion is to determine whether control of the goods or services has already been transferred to the customer. This is done by using a hypothetical assessment of what another entity would need to do if it were to take over the remaining performance. Thus, actual practical or contractual limitations on the remaining performance would have no bearing on the assessment of whether the entity has transferred control of the goods or services provided to date.

BC128 The boards also observed that this criterion is not intended to apply to contracts in which the entity's performance is not immediately consumed by the customer, which would be typical in cases in which the entity's performance results in an asset (such as work-in-progress). Consequently, an entity that applies IFRS 15 to contracts in which the entity's performance results in an asset (which could be intangible) being created or enhanced should consider the criteria in paragraph 35(b) and (c) of IFRS 15.

Performance creates or enhances an asset that the customer controls as it is created (paragraph 35(b))

BC129 The boards included this criterion to address situations in which an entity's performance creates or enhances an asset that a customer clearly controls as the asset is created or enhanced. In those cases, because the customer controls any work in progress, the customer is obtaining the benefits of the goods or services that the entity is providing and, thus, the performance obligation is satisfied over time. For example, in the case of a construction contract in which the entity is building on the customer's land, the customer generally controls any work in progress arising from the entity's performance.

BC130 The boards observed that the basis for this criterion is consistent with the rationale for using the 'percentage-of-completion' revenue recognition approach in previous revenue guidance in US GAAP. That guidance acknowledged that in many construction contracts the entity has, in effect, agreed to sell its rights to the asset (ie work-in-progress) as the entity performs. Accordingly, the parties have agreed, in effect, to a continuous sale (ie the customer controls the work-in-progress) that occurs as the work progresses.

BC131 Many respondents explained that this criterion would be straightforward and helpful in cases in which the customer clearly controls the asset that is being constructed or enhanced. However, the boards observed that for some performance obligations, it may be unclear whether the asset that is created or enhanced is controlled by the customer. Consequently, it may be more challenging to determine when control transfers in those cases and, therefore, the boards developed a third criterion in paragraph 35(c) of IFRS 15.

Performance does not create an asset with an alternative use to the entity and the entity has an enforceable right to payment for performance completed to date (paragraph 35(c))

BC132   The boards observed that, in some cases, applying the criteria in paragraph 35(a) and (b) of IFRS 15 could be challenging. Consequently, the boards developed a third criterion to help with the assessment of control. The boards observed that this criterion may be necessary for services that may be specific to a customer (for example, consulting services that ultimately result in a professional opinion for the customer) but also for the creation of tangible (or intangible) goods.

BC133   The notions of 'alternative use' and 'right to payment' are described in the following paragraphs.

Performance does not create an asset with an alternative use

BC134   The boards developed the notion of alternative use to exclude the circumstances in which the entity's performance would not result in the transfer of control of goods or services to the customer over time. This is because when the entity's performance creates an asset with an alternative use to the entity, the entity could readily direct the asset to another customer and, therefore, the customer would not control the asset as it is being created. This may occur in the creation of many standard inventory-type items for which the entity has the discretion to substitute across different contracts with customers. In those cases, the customer cannot control the asset because the customer does not have the ability to restrict the entity from directing that asset to another customer.

BC135   Conversely, when an entity creates an asset that is highly customised for a particular customer, the asset would be less likely to have an alternative use. This is because the entity would incur significant costs to reconfigure the asset for sale to another customer (or would need to sell the asset for a significantly reduced price). In that case, the customer could be regarded as receiving the benefit of that performance and, consequently, as having control of the goods or services (ie the asset being created) as the performance occurs. (However, an entity would also need to consider whether a right to payment exists to conclude that control transfers over time, see paragraphs BC142–BC148.)

BC136   In assessing whether the asset has an alternative use, the entity would need to consider practical limitations and contractual restrictions on directing the asset for another use. In determining whether the entity is limited practically from directing the asset for another use, the boards decided that an entity should consider the characteristics of the asset that will ultimately be transferred to the customer. This is because, for some assets, it is not the period of time for which the asset has no alternative use that is the critical factor in making the assessment but, instead, whether the asset that is ultimately transferred could be redirected without a significant cost of rework. This may occur in some manufacturing contracts in which the basic design of the asset is the same across all contracts, but the customisation is substantial. Consequently, redirecting the asset in its completed state to another customer would require significant rework.

BC137 Although the level of customisation might be a helpful factor to consider when assessing whether an asset has an alternative use, the boards decided that it should not be a determinative factor. This is because in some cases (for example, some real estate contracts), an asset may be standardised but may still not have an alternative use to an entity, as a result of substantive contractual restrictions that preclude the entity from readily directing the asset to another customer. If a contract precludes an entity from transferring an asset to another customer and that restriction is substantive, the entity does not have an alternative use for that asset because it is legally obliged to direct the asset to the customer. Consequently, this indicates that the customer controls the asset as it is created, because the customer has the present ability to restrict the entity from directing that asset to another customer (an entity would also need to consider whether a right to payment exists to conclude that control of the asset transfers over time as it is created, see paragraphs BC142–BC148). The boards observed that contractual restrictions are often relevant in real estate contracts, but might also be relevant in other types of contracts.

BC138 The boards also noted that contractual restrictions that provide a protective right to the customer would not be sufficient to establish that an asset has no alternative use to the entity. The boards observed that a protective right typically results in the entity having the practical ability to physically substitute or redirect the asset without the customer being aware of or objecting to the change. For example, a contract might state that an entity cannot transfer a good because a customer has legal title to the goods in the contract. However, the customer's legal title to the goods is intended to protect the customer in the event of the entity's liquidation and the entity can physically substitute and redirect the goods to another customer for little cost. In this example, the contractual restriction is merely a protective right and does not indicate that control of the goods have transferred to the customer.

BC139 Some respondents observed that requiring an entity to consider contractual and practical restrictions in paragraph 35(c) of IFRS 15 seems to contradict the requirements in paragraph B4 of IFRS 15 to ignore contractual and practical limitations when applying the criterion in paragraph 35(a) of IFRS 15. The boards noted that this difference is appropriate. Although the objective of both criteria is to assess when control transfers over time, each criterion provides a different method for assessing when that control transfers, because the criteria were designed to apply to different scenarios.

BC140 The boards decided that the assessment of alternative use should be completed only at contract inception and should not be updated. Otherwise, an entity would need to continually reassess whether the asset has an alternative use, which could lead to a pattern of performance (and, therefore, revenue recognition) that is not useful.

BC141 The boards also decided that while the notion of alternative use is a necessary part of the criterion in paragraph 35(c), it is not enough to conclude that a customer controls an asset. Consequently, the boards decided that to demonstrate that a customer controls an asset that has no alternative use as it is being created, an entity must also have an enforceable right to payment for performance completed to date.

The entity has an enforceable right to payment for performance completed to date

BC142 The boards decided that there is a link between the assessment of control and the factors of no alternative use and a 'right to payment'. This is because if an asset that an entity is creating has no alternative use to the entity, the entity is effectively constructing an asset at the direction of the customer. Consequently, the entity will want to be economically protected from the risk of the customer terminating the contract and leaving the entity with no asset or an asset that has little value to the entity. That protection will be established by requiring that if the contract is terminated, the customer must pay for the entity's performance completed to date. This is consistent with other exchange contracts in which a customer would typically be obliged to pay only if it has received control of goods or services in the exchange. Consequently, the fact that the customer is obliged to pay for the entity's performance (or, in other words, is unable to avoid paying for that performance) suggests that the customer has obtained the benefits from the entity's performance.

BC143 The boards intended the term 'right to payment' to refer to a payment that compensates an entity for its performance completed to date rather than, for example, a payment of a deposit or a payment to compensate the entity for inconvenience or loss of profit. This is because the underlying objective of the criterion is to determine whether the entity is transferring control of goods or services to the customer as an asset is being created for that customer. Consequently, assuming there is rational behaviour and that there are no broader perceived economic benefits that might exist outside the scope of the contract with the customer, the entity would only agree to transfer control of the goods or services to the customer if the entity is compensated for the costs associated with fulfilling the contract and it receives a profit margin that includes a return on those costs.

BC144 The boards noted that the compensation to which the entity would be entitled upon termination by the customer might not always be the contract margin, because the value transferred to a customer in a prematurely terminated contract may not be proportional to the value if the contract was completed. However, the boards decided that to demonstrate compensation for performance completed to date, the compensation should be based on a reasonable proportion of the entity's expected profit margin or be a reasonable return on the entity's cost of capital. Furthermore, the boards noted that the focus should be on the amount to which the entity would be entitled upon termination rather than the amount to which the entity might ultimately be willing to settle for in a negotiation. Consequently, the boards clarified their intention about what a 'reasonable profit margin' is intended to represent in paragraph B9 of IFRS 15.

BC145   In addition, the boards clarified that an entity need not have a present unconditional right to payment but, instead, it must have an enforceable right to demand and/or retain payment for performance completed to date if the customer were to terminate the contract without cause before completion. For example, consider a consulting contract in which the consulting entity agrees to provide a report at the end of the contract for a fixed amount that is conditional on providing that report. If the entity were performing under that contract, it would have a right to payment for performance completed to date if the terms of the contract (or other law) require the customer to compensate the entity for its work completed to date if the customer terminates the contract without cause before completion. The boards clarified this notion because the contractual payment terms in the contract might not always align with the entity's enforceable rights to payment for performance completed to date.

BC146   A few respondents asked whether a 100 per cent non-refundable upfront payment would meet the 'right to payment for performance completed to date' criterion (ie because a 100 per cent payment would at least compensate the entity for work completed to date throughout the contract). The boards decided that that type of payment would meet that criterion if the entity's right to retain (and not refund) that payment would be enforceable if the customer terminated the contract. Furthermore, the boards noted that the right to payment should be enforceable; otherwise, it is questionable whether the entity actually has a right to payment. Consequently, the boards included the factors in paragraph B12 of IFRS 15 to help an entity determine whether the right to payment would be enforceable.

BC147   The boards also decided to clarify that an entity could have an enforceable right to payment in some cases in which a customer might not have a right to terminate the contract or might have a right to terminate the contract only at specified times. This would be the case if the contract or other laws in the jurisdiction require the entity and the customer to complete their respective obligations (often referred to as specific performance).

Right to payment as a separate revenue recognition criterion

BC148   The boards considered but rejected specifying a right to payment as a more overarching criterion in determining when revenue is recognised, for the following reasons:

(a)   an entity must have a contract to recognise revenue in accordance with IFRS 15 and a component of a contract is a right to payment.

(b)   the core revenue recognition principle is about determining whether goods or services have been transferred to a customer, not whether the entity has a right to payment (although it is an important part of determining whether a contract exists—see paragraphs BC31–BC46). Including a right to payment as an overarching criterion for determining when a performance obligation is satisfied could have potentially overridden that revenue recognition principle.

(c) a right to payment does not necessarily indicate a transfer of goods or services (for example, in some contracts, customers are required to make non-refundable upfront payments and do not receive any goods or services in exchange). In cases in which the customer clearly receives benefits as the entity performs, as in many service contracts, the possibility that the entity will ultimately not retain the payment for its performance is addressed in the measurement of revenue. For example, in some service contracts in which the customer simultaneously receives and consumes benefits as the entity performs, the customer may be able to terminate the contract and receive a full refund of any consideration paid. The boards decided that in those cases, because the entity is transferring services to the customer, it should recognise revenue subject to an assessment of whether it should constrain the amount of the transaction price to which it is entitled (see paragraphs BC203–BC223).

Agreements for the construction of real estate

BC149 In developing the requirements for assessing when goods or services transfer to the customer, the boards considered the diversity in practice from applying previous revenue recognition requirements in IFRS that were specific to the construction of real estate. That diversity in practice resulted from the difficulty in determining when control of real estate transferred to the customer over time by applying the previous IFRS revenue recognition criteria to complex contracts with different facts and circumstances.

BC150 The boards envisage that the diversity in practice should be reduced by the requirements in paragraphs 35–37 of IFRS 15, which provide specific requirements for determining when goods or services transfer over time. However, the boards observe that the pattern of transfer may be different for different real estate contracts because it will depend on the relevant facts and circumstances of each contract. For example, some real estate contracts may result in an asset that cannot (under the terms of the contract) be readily directed to another customer (ie the entity's performance does not create an asset with an alternative use to the entity), and the contracts require the customer to pay for performance completed to date (thus meeting the criterion in paragraph 35(c) of IFRS 15). However, other real estate contracts that create an asset with no alternative use to the entity may not require the customer to pay for performance completed to date. Therefore, an entity would reach a different conclusion on the pattern of transfer for those contracts.

BC151 Some respondents applying IFRS in the residential real estate industry supported the addition of the criteria for determining whether a performance obligation is satisfied over time, because they reasoned it would assist them in assessing whether revenue could be recognised over time as construction of residential units in a multi-unit real estate development occurs. Other respondents in this industry explained that although they were able to conclude that their performance does not create an asset with an alternative use, they were unable to meet the 'right to payment for performance completed to date' criterion. This would mean that they would be able to recognise revenue only at the point in time when each unit transfers to the customer (often only after construction is complete and the customer has physical possession), which they stated would be an inappropriate depiction of their performance.

BC152   However, the boards concluded that if either of the criteria in paragraph 35(c) of IFRS 15 is not met, recognising revenue over time would not faithfully depict the entity's performance and the entity's and the customer's respective rights and obligations in the contract. Furthermore, the boards decided that clarifying the 'no alternative use and right to payment for performance completed to date' criterion would ensure greater certainty and consistency in recognising revenue for multi-unit residential real estate developments.

Performance obligations satisfied at a point in time (paragraph 38)

BC153   The boards decided that all performance obligations that do not meet the criteria for being satisfied over time should be accounted for as performance obligations satisfied at a point in time. For performance obligations satisfied at a point in time, the performance obligation is satisfied at the point in time when control of the goods or services transfers to the customer. The boards included indicators of the transfer of control in paragraph 38 of IFRS 15.

BC154   Many respondents commented that the indicators were useful for contracts for the sales of goods to assist an entity in determining when it has transferred control of an asset (whether tangible or intangible). The boards included the indicator 'the customer has the significant risks and rewards of ownership of the asset' because of comments from respondents who disagreed with the boards' initial proposal to eliminate considerations of the 'risks and rewards of ownership' from the recognition of revenue. Respondents observed that risks and rewards can be a helpful factor to consider when determining the transfer of control, as highlighted by the IASB in IFRS 10 *Consolidated Financial Statements*, and can often be a consequence of controlling an asset. The boards decided that adding risks and rewards as an indicator provides additional guidance, but does not change the principle of determining the transfer of goods or services on the basis of the transfer of control.

BC155   Some respondents questioned whether all of the indicators would need to be present for an entity to conclude that it had transferred control of a good or service. Some respondents also questioned what an entity should do if some but not all of the indicators were present. In their redeliberations, the boards emphasised that the indicators in paragraph 38 of IFRS 15 are not a list of conditions that must be met before an entity can conclude that control of a good or service has transferred to a customer. Instead, the indicators are a list of factors that are often present if a customer has control of an asset and that list is provided to assist entities in applying the principle of control in paragraph 31 of IFRS 15.

BC156　The boards considered including an indicator that the 'design or function of the good or service is customer-specific'. However, the boards decided not to include this indicator in IFRS 15, because it would apply mainly to service contracts (for example, construction-type contracts) and it would be unnecessary in the light of the requirements for determining when performance obligations are satisfied over time. As described in paragraphs BC134–BC141, the notion of customer-specific design or function has been developed into the criterion of 'an asset with no alternative use to the entity'.

BC157　Respondents also suggested additional indicators such as the entity's lack of continuing involvement in the good or service (for example, a call option on a delivered good). The boards included application guidance to help an entity assess the transfer of control in circumstances in which put or call options exist in a contract with a customer (see paragraphs BC422–BC433).

Measuring progress towards complete satisfaction of a performance obligation (paragraphs 39–45 and B14–B19)

BC158　The boards decided that when an entity determines that a performance obligation is satisfied over time, it should determine how much revenue to recognise in each reporting period by measuring its progress towards complete satisfaction of the performance obligation.

BC159　There are various methods that an entity might use to measure its progress towards complete satisfaction of a performance obligation. Because of the breadth of the scope of IFRS 15, the boards decided that it would not be feasible to consider all possible methods and prescribe when an entity should use each method. Accordingly, an entity should use judgement when selecting an appropriate method of measuring progress towards complete satisfaction of a performance obligation. That does not mean that an entity has a 'free choice'. The requirements state that an entity should select a method of measuring progress that is consistent with the clearly stated objective of depicting the entity's performance – that is, the satisfaction of an entity's performance obligation – in transferring control of goods or services to the customer.

BC160　To meet that objective of depicting the entity's performance, an entity would need to consider the nature of the promised goods or services and the nature of the entity's performance. For example, in a typical health club contract, the entity's promise is to stand ready for a period of time (ie by making the health club available), rather than providing a service only when the customer requires it. In this case, the customer benefits from the entity's service of making the health club available. This is evidenced by the fact that the extent to which the customer uses the health club does not, in itself, affect the amount of the remaining goods or services to which the customer is entitled. In addition, the customer is obliged to pay the consideration regardless of whether it uses the health club. Consequently, in those cases, the entity would need to select a measure of progress based on its service of making goods or services available, instead of when the customer uses the goods or services made available to them.

BC161   The boards decided that an entity should apply the selected method for measuring progress consistently for a particular performance obligation and also across contracts that have performance obligations with similar characteristics. An entity should not use different methods to measure its performance in satisfying the same or similar performance obligations, otherwise that entity's revenue would not be comparable in different reporting periods. The boards also noted that if an entity were permitted to apply more than one method to measure its performance in fulfilling a performance obligation, it would effectively bypass the requirements for identifying performance obligations.

BC162   Although the boards did not consider all possible methods and prescribe when an entity should use each method, they observed that there are broadly two methods that the entity might consider when determining the method of measuring progress towards complete satisfaction of the performance obligation—that is, output and input methods. Requirements for the application of those methods are included in the application guidance (see paragraphs B14–B19 of IFRS 15).

Output methods

BC163   Output methods recognise revenue on the basis of direct measurements of the value to the customer of the goods or services transferred to date (for example, surveys of performance completed to date, appraisals of results achieved, milestones reached, time elapsed and units delivered or units produced). When applying an output method, 'value to the customer' refers to an objective measure of the entity's performance in the contract. However, value to the customer is not intended to be assessed by reference to the market prices or stand-alone selling prices of the individual goods or services promised in the contract, nor is it intended to refer to the value that the customer perceives to be embodied in the goods or services.

BC164   The boards decided that, conceptually, an output measure is the most faithful depiction of an entity's performance because it directly measures the value of the goods or services transferred to the customer. However, the boards observed that it would be appropriate for an entity to use an input method if that method would be less costly and would provide a reasonable proxy for measuring progress.

BC165   In the redeliberations, some respondents, particularly those in the contract manufacturing industry, requested the boards to provide more guidance on when units-of-delivery or units-of-production methods would be appropriate. Those respondents observed that such methods appear to be output methods and, therefore, questioned whether they would always provide the most appropriate depiction of an entity's performance. The boards observed that such methods may be appropriate in some cases; however, they may not always result in the best depiction of an entity's performance if the performance obligation is satisfied over time. This is because a units-of-delivery or a units-of-production method ignores the work in progress that belongs to the customer. When that work in progress is material to either the contract or the financial statements as a whole, the boards observed that using a units-of-delivery or a units-of-production method would distort the entity's performance because it would not recognise revenue for the assets that are created before delivery or before production is complete but are controlled by the customer.

BC166   The boards also observed that a units-of-delivery or a units-of-production method may not be appropriate if the contract provides both design and production services because, in this case, each item produced or delivered may not transfer an equal amount of value to the customer. However, a units-of-delivery method may be an appropriate method for measuring progress for a long-term manufacturing contract of standard items that individually transfer an equal amount of value to the customer on delivery. Thus, the boards clarified that in selecting an output method for measuring progress and determining whether a units-of-delivery or a units-of-production method is appropriate, an entity should consider its facts and circumstances and select the method that depicts the entity's performance and the transfer of control of the goods or services to the customer.

BC167   The boards also decided that, in some circumstances, as a practical expedient, another appropriate output method is to recognise revenue at the amount of consideration to which an entity has a right to invoice. This method is appropriate if the amount of consideration that the entity has a right to invoice corresponds directly with the value to the customer of each incremental good or service that the entity transfers to the customer (ie the entity's performance completed to date). This may occur, for example, in a services contract in which an entity invoices a fixed amount for each hour of service provided.

Input methods

BC168   Input methods recognise revenue on the basis of an entity's efforts or inputs towards satisfying a performance obligation (for example, resources consumed, labour hours expended, costs incurred, time elapsed or machine hours used) relative to the total expected inputs to satisfy the performance obligation.

BC169   In some contracts, an entity promises to transfer both goods and services to a customer, but the customer takes control of the goods, which represent a significant part of the performance obligation, at a different time from that of the services (for example, the customer obtains control of the goods before they are installed). If those goods and services are not distinct, then the entity would have a single performance obligation. Because there is diversity in practice about how to apply an input method to measure progress in such situations, the boards decided to provide additional guidance related to uninstalled materials.

Uninstalled materials

BC170   The boards decided to clarify that the adjustment to the input method for uninstalled materials is intended to ensure that the input method meets the objective of measuring progress towards complete satisfaction of a performance obligation, as described in paragraph 39 of IFRS 15 — that is, to depict an entity's performance.

BC171   The boards observed that if a customer obtains control of the goods before they are installed by an entity, then it would be inappropriate for the entity to continue to recognise the goods as inventory. Instead, the entity should recognise revenue for the transferred goods in accordance with the core principle of IFRS 15. The boards also observed that if the entity applies a cost-to-cost method of measuring progress (ie costs incurred compared with total expected costs), the entity might (in the absence of clear requirements) include the cost of the goods in the cost-to-cost calculation and, therefore, recognise a contract-wide profit margin for the transfer of the goods. The boards noted that recognising a contract-wide profit margin before the goods are installed could overstate the measure of the entity's performance and, therefore, revenue would be overstated. Alternatively, requiring an entity to estimate a profit margin that is different from the contract-wide profit margin could be complex and could effectively create a performance obligation for goods that are not distinct (thus bypassing the requirements for identifying performance obligations). Therefore, the boards decided that, in specified circumstances, an entity should recognise revenue for the transfer of the goods but only in an amount equal to the cost of those goods. In those circumstances, an entity should also exclude the costs of the goods from the cost-to-cost calculation to be consistent with the cost-to-cost methodology.

BC172   The boards noted that the adjustment to the cost-to-cost measure of progress for uninstalled materials is generally intended to apply to a subset of goods in a construction-type contract — that is, only to those goods that have a significant cost relative to the contract and only if the entity is essentially providing a simple procurement service to the customer. For goods that meet the conditions in paragraph B19(b) of IFRS 15, recognising revenue to the extent of the costs of those goods ensures that the depiction of the entity's profit (or margin) in the contract is similar to the profit (or margin) that the entity would recognise if the customer had supplied those goods themselves for the entity to install or use in the construction activity.

BC173   Some respondents disagreed with the requirements that an entity recognise a profit margin of zero on the transfer of the uninstalled materials to the customer. In their view, recognising different profit margins for different parts of a single performance obligation is inconsistent with the principle of identifying performance obligations. Other respondents disagreed with recognising revenue for uninstalled materials at a zero profit margin because it might not properly depict an entity's rights under the contract (for example, if the entity was entitled on termination of the contract to a payment at an amount that reflects the contract-wide margin for all work performed, including the transfer of uninstalled materials to the customer).

BC174   The boards considered those arguments but decided that the adjustment to the input method specified in paragraph B19(b) of IFRS 15 will ensure that the input method meets the objective of measuring progress to depict an entity's performance. The boards disagreed with the concern raised by some respondents that paragraph B19(b) of IFRS 15 is inconsistent with the principle of identifying performance obligations. Although the outcome of applying paragraph B19(b) of IFRS 15 is that some goods or services that are part of a single performance obligation attract a margin, while any uninstalled materials attract only a zero margin, that difference arises only as a consequence of the need to adjust the cost-to-cost calculation so that the input method faithfully depicts the entity's performance in the contract.

BC175   To be consistent with their decision on uninstalled materials, the boards also clarified that if an entity selects an input method such as cost-to-cost to measure its progress, the entity should adjust the measure of progress if including some of those costs incurred (for example, inefficiencies and wasted materials) would distort the entity's performance in the contract.

Inefficiencies and wasted materials

BC176   Paragraph B19 of IFRS 15 acknowledges that a shortcoming of input methods is that there may not be a direct relationship between an entity's inputs and the transfer of control of goods or services to a customer. This would be the case if the cost-to-cost method includes costs attributable to wasted materials or other inefficiencies that do not contribute to the satisfaction of a performance obligation. Consequently, an entity should exclude the effects of any inputs that do not depict the transfer of control of goods or services to the customer (for example, the costs of wasted materials, labour or other resources to fulfil the contract that were not reflected in the price of the contract). In that regard, the requirements in paragraph B19 of IFRS 15 can be viewed as a reminder that a mechanical application of the cost-to-cost method might not always provide a faithful depiction of the entity's performance.

BC177   As part of their redeliberations, the boards considered whether more guidance should be provided on the notions of inefficiency and wasted materials. For instance, some respondents asked if the assessment should focus on entity-specific inefficiencies or market-driven inefficiencies, and some requested a clear distinction between the accounting for normal expected wasted materials and the accounting for abnormal wasted materials.

BC178   The boards acknowledged the concerns but decided that it would not be feasible to develop additional guidance that would clearly and consistently identify the costs of inefficiencies and wasted materials that should be excluded from a cost-to-cost measure of progress. Instead, the boards decided to emphasise that the objective of measuring progress towards complete satisfaction of the performance obligation is to depict an entity's performance in the contract and therefore a cost-to-cost calculation may require adjustment if some of the costs incurred do not contribute to the progress in the contract.

Reasonable measures of progress

BC179　The boards clarified that when selecting a method to measure progress and, thus, determining when to recognise revenue, an entity should recognise revenue for its performance only if it can reasonably measure its progress towards complete satisfaction of the performance obligation. Some asked whether an entity's inability to measure progress would mean that costs would also be deferred. However, the boards observed that unless the entity can recognise an asset from the costs to fulfil a contract in accordance with paragraph 95 of IFRS 15, those costs would not represent an asset of the entity and, therefore, should be recognised as expenses as they are incurred.

BC180　The boards also concluded that in cases in which an entity cannot reasonably measure its progress towards complete satisfaction of a performance obligation, but nevertheless expects eventually to recover the costs incurred in satisfying the performance obligation, the entity should recognise at least some amount of revenue to reflect the fact that it is making progress in satisfying the performance obligation. Consequently, the boards decided that in those cases, an entity should recognise revenue for the satisfaction of the performance obligation only to the extent of the costs incurred. (That method is consistent with previous revenue recognition requirements in both IFRS and US GAAP for measuring progress.) However, the boards also decided that an entity should stop using that method when it can reasonably measure its progress towards complete satisfaction of the performance obligation.

Measurement of revenue (paragraphs 46–90)

BC181　The boards decided that an entity should measure revenue based on an allocated transaction price approach. Using that approach, an entity allocates the transaction price to each performance obligation at an amount that depicts the amount of consideration to which the entity expects to be entitled in exchange for satisfying each performance obligation. That allocation determines the amount of revenue that an entity recognises when (or as) it satisfies each performance obligation. Most respondents supported the allocated transaction price approach.

BC182　The boards considered, but rejected, an alternative measurement approach, which would have been to measure the remaining performance obligations directly at the end of each reporting period. The boards observed that this alternative would have made accounting for the contract more complex. In addition, the boards expected that in many cases it would have provided users of financial statements with little additional information, either because the values of goods or services promised are not inherently volatile or because the effect of any volatility that might exist is limited when an entity transfers the goods or services to the customer over a relatively short time. Paragraphs BC25–BC27 include additional discussion on rejected measurement approaches.

BC183　The allocated transaction price approach generally requires an entity to follow three main steps to determine the amount of revenue that can be recognised for satisfied performance obligations. Those steps are as follows:

(a)   determine the transaction price for the contract;

(b)   allocate the transaction price to performance obligations; and

(c)   recognise revenue at the amount allocated to the satisfied performance obligation.

Determining the transaction price (paragraphs 47–72)

BC184   Determining the transaction price is an important step in the revenue recognition model because the transaction price is the amount that an entity allocates to the performance obligations in a contract and ultimately recognises as revenue.

BC185   The boards decided to define the transaction price as the amount of consideration to which an entity expects to be entitled in exchange for transferring goods or services. Consequently, the objective in determining the transaction price at the end of each reporting period is to predict the total amount of consideration to which the entity will be entitled from the contract. In developing IFRS 15, the boards decided that the transaction price should not be adjusted for the effects of the customer's credit risk (see paragraphs BC259–BC265) unless the contract includes a significant financing component (see paragraphs BC229–BC247).

BC186   The boards clarified that the transaction price should include only amounts (including variable amounts) to which the entity has rights under the present contract. For example, the transaction price does not include estimates of consideration from the future exercise of options for additional goods or services or from future change orders. Until the customer exercises the option or agrees to the change order, the entity does not have a right to consideration.

BC187   The boards also clarified that the amounts to which the entity has rights under the present contract can be paid by any party (ie not only by the customer). For example, in the healthcare industry, an entity may determine the transaction price based on amounts to which it will be entitled to payment from the patient, insurance companies and/or governmental organisations. This may also occur in other industries in which an entity receives a payment from a manufacturer as a result of the manufacturer issuing coupons or rebates directly to the entity's customer. However, it would not include amounts collected on behalf of another party such as some sales taxes and value added taxes in some jurisdictions.

BC188   Determining the transaction price when a customer promises to pay a fixed amount of cash consideration (ie an amount that will not vary) will be simple. However, determining the transaction price may be more difficult in the following cases:

(a)   the promised amount of consideration is variable (see paragraphs BC189–BC202), which will also require an entity to consider whether it should constrain the estimated amount of consideration to be included in the transaction price (see paragraphs BC203–BC223);

(b)   the contract has a significant financing component (see paragraphs BC229–BC247);

(c)   the promised amount of consideration is in a form other than cash (see paragraphs BC248–BC254); and

(d)   there is consideration payable to the customer by the entity (see paragraphs BC255–BC258).

Clarifications to IFRS 15 (amendments issued in April 2016)—topics for which the IASB decided not to amend IFRS 15 (presentation of sales taxes)

BC188A   Paragraph 47 of IFRS 15 specifies that amounts collected on behalf of third parties, such as some sales taxes, are excluded from the determination of the transaction price. Entities are therefore required to identify and assess sales taxes to determine whether to include or exclude those taxes from the transaction price.

BC188B   After the issuance of Topic 606 and IFRS 15, some US stakeholders expressed concerns about the cost and complexity of assessing tax laws in each jurisdiction, because many entities operate in numerous jurisdictions, and the laws in some jurisdictions are unclear about which party to the transaction is primarily obligated for payment of the taxes. These stakeholders also stated that the variety of, and changes in, tax laws among jurisdictions contributes to that complexity. Consequently, some preparers and auditors asked the boards to amend the Standard to add a practical expedient to reduce the complexity and practical difficulties in assessing whether a sales tax is collected on behalf of a third party. An accounting policy choice to either include or exclude all sales taxes in or from revenue was available in the previous revenue standards under US GAAP.

BC188C   The FASB decided to amend Topic 606 to provide an accounting policy election that permits an entity to exclude from the measurement of the transaction price all taxes assessed by a governmental authority that are both imposed on, and concurrent with, a specific revenue-producing transaction and collected from customers (for example, sales taxes, use taxes, value added taxes, and some excise taxes). Taxes assessed on an entity's total gross receipts or imposed during the inventory procurement process are excluded from the scope of the election.

BC188D   The IASB decided not to provide a similar accounting policy choice, for the following reasons:

(a)   It would reduce the comparability of revenue between entities operating under different tax regimes in different jurisdictions, as well as between entities operating in the same jurisdictions to the extent that they choose different approaches.

(b)   The previous revenue Standards under IFRS contained requirements applicable to sales tax similar to those in IFRS 15. Consequently, assessing whether sales taxes are collected on behalf of a third party is not a new requirement for IFRS preparers.

(c)   It would create an exception to the revenue recognition model that does not reflect the economics of the arrangement in cases for which a sales (or similar) tax is a tax on the entity rather than a tax collected by the entity from the customer on behalf of a tax authority.

The IASB acknowledged that, because the policy choice is not available in IFRS 15, this gives rise to a difference between IFRS 15 and Topic 606.

Variable consideration (paragraphs 50–59)

BC189   The boards noted that in contracts with customers in which the promised consideration is variable, an entity needs to estimate the amount of consideration to which the entity expects to be entitled. Consequently, the boards decided to provide requirements that address:

(a)   identifying when variable consideration is present in a contract with a customer (see paragraphs BC190–BC194);

(b)   the methods for estimating variable consideration (see paragraphs BC195–BC202);

(c)   when those estimates of variable consideration should be constrained and, thus, not included in the transaction price (see paragraphs BC203–BC223); and

(d)   how to account for subsequent changes in the transaction price (see paragraphs BC224–BC228).

Identifying variable consideration

BC190   The boards noted that variable consideration can arise in any circumstance in which the consideration to which the entity will be entitled under the contract may vary. The examples in paragraph 51 of IFRS 15 include common types of variable consideration that may occur in a contract with a customer.

BC191   The boards observed that consideration can be variable even in cases in which the stated price in the contract is fixed. This is because the entity may be entitled to the consideration only upon the occurrence or non-occurrence of a future event. Consider, for example, a fixed-price service contract in which the customer pays upfront and the terms of the contract provide the customer with a full refund of the amount paid if the customer is dissatisfied with the service at any time. In those cases, the consideration is variable because the entity might be entitled to all of the consideration or none of the consideration if the customer exercises its right to a refund.

BC192   The contract will often specify the terms that result in the consideration being classified as variable. However, in some cases the promised consideration may be variable because the facts and circumstances indicate that the entity may accept a lower price than that stated in the contract (ie the contract contains an implicit price concession). The boards observed that an entity's customary business practices, published policies or specific statements may provide evidence that the entity is willing to accept a lower price in exchange for the promised goods and services. For example, an entity might grant a price concession to a customer for goods that were previously sold to that customer to enable the customer to discount the goods and, therefore, more easily sell them to a third party. The boards noted that in many cases, price concessions are likely to be granted to enhance a customer relationship to encourage future sales to that customer.

BC193 The boards decided that an entity should also consider all facts and circumstances to determine whether the entity will accept a lower amount of consideration than the price stated in the contract. For example, an entity might enter into a contract with a new customer with a strategy to develop the customer relationship. In that case, although there may not be past evidence that the entity will provide a price concession, there may be other factors present that result in the entity concluding that it will accept a lower price than that stated in the contract.

BC194 The boards observed that in some cases it may be difficult to determine whether the entity has implicitly offered a price concession or whether the entity has chosen to accept the risk of default by the customer of the contractually agreed-upon consideration (ie customer credit risk). The boards noted that an entity should use judgement and consider all relevant facts and circumstances in making that determination. The boards observed that this judgement was being applied under previous revenue recognition requirements. Consequently, the boards decided not to develop detailed requirements for differentiating between a price concession and impairment losses.

The method for estimating the variable consideration

BC195 The boards decided to specify that an entity should estimate variable consideration using either the expected value or the most likely amount, depending on which method the entity expects will better predict the amount of consideration to which the entity will be entitled (see paragraph 53 of IFRS 15). The boards noted that this is not intended to be a 'free choice'; an entity needs to consider which method it expects to better predict the amount of consideration to which it will be entitled and apply that method consistently for similar types of contracts.

BC196 The boards concluded on the methods to estimate the transaction price in response to the feedback on the 2010 Exposure Draft. That exposure draft proposed that when the consideration in a contract is variable, an entity should measure the transaction price (at its expected value) using only a probability-weighted method. A probability-weighted method reflects the full range of possible consideration amounts, weighted by their respective probabilities. Many respondents to the 2010 Exposure Draft disagreed with measuring the transaction price using a probability-weighted method because they reasoned it would:

(a) add complexity and be costly to apply; and

(b) impede the reporting of meaningful results in all circumstances because, for example, it could result in an entity determining the transaction price at an amount of consideration that the entity could never obtain under the contract.

BC197   Some respondents suggested that the boards not specify a measurement model and, instead, require that the transaction price be determined using management's best estimate. Many noted that this would provide management with the flexibility to estimate on the basis of its experience and available information, without the documentation that would be required when a measurement model is specified.

BC198   In their redeliberations, the boards reaffirmed their decision to specify an objective and an appropriate measurement method for estimating the transaction price. This is because specifying an objective and an appropriate measurement method would provide the necessary framework to ensure rigour in the process of estimation. Furthermore, without such a framework, the measurement of revenue might not be understandable to users of financial statements and might lack comparability between entities.

BC199   However, in their redeliberations, the boards reconsidered what the appropriate measurement method(s) should be. They noted that a probability-weighted method reflects all of the uncertainties existing in the transaction price at the end of the reporting period. Therefore, it best reflects the conditions that are present at the end of each reporting period. For instance, it reflects the possibility of receiving a greater amount of consideration as well as the risk of receiving a lesser amount. However, the boards observed that users of financial statements are most interested in knowing the total amount of consideration that will ultimately be realised from the contract. Consequently, the boards decided that for the estimate of the transaction price to be meaningful at the end of each reporting period, it should be an amount that the entity expects to better predict the amount of consideration to which it will be entitled (the boards decided to address the issue of credit risk separately—see paragraphs BC259–BC265).

BC200   The boards observed that in some cases, a probability-weighted estimate (ie an expected value) predicts the amount of consideration to which an entity will be entitled. For example, that is likely to be the case if the entity has a large number of contracts with similar characteristics. However, the boards agreed with respondents that an expected value may not always faithfully predict the consideration to which an entity will be entitled. For example, if the entity is certain to receive one of only two possible consideration amounts in a single contract, the expected value would not be a possible outcome in accordance with the contract and, therefore, might not be relevant in predicting the amount of consideration to which the entity will be entitled. The boards decided that in those cases, another method—the most likely amount method—is necessary to estimate the transaction price. This is because the most likely amount method identifies the individual amount of consideration in the range of possible consideration amounts that is more likely to occur than any other individual outcome.

BC201   Theoretically, although an entity using the most likely amount method must consider all possible outcomes to identify the most likely one, in practice, there is no need to quantify the less probable outcomes. Similarly, in practice, estimating the expected value using a probability-weighted method does not require an entity to consider all possible outcomes using complex models and techniques, even if an entity has extensive data and can identify many outcomes. In many cases, a limited number of discrete outcomes and probabilities can often provide a reasonable estimate of the distribution of possible outcomes. Therefore, the boards decided that neither of the two approaches should be too costly or complex to apply.

BC202 The boards also decided that, to provide better information to users, an entity should apply one method consistently throughout the contract when estimating the effect of an uncertainty on the amount of variable consideration to which the entity expects to be entitled. However, the boards observed that this would not mean an entity would need to use one method to measure each uncertainty in a single contract. Instead, an entity may use different methods for different uncertainties.

Constraining estimates of variable consideration

BC203 The boards decided that to provide useful information to users of financial statements, some estimates of variable consideration should not be included in the transaction price. This would be the case if the estimate of variable consideration (and consequently the amount of revenue recognised) is too uncertain and, therefore, may not faithfully depict the consideration to which the entity will be entitled in exchange for the goods or services transferred to the customer. In that case, the boards decided that an entity should constrain the estimate of variable consideration to be included in the transaction price.

BC204 Many respondents agreed that it was necessary to include some form of constraint on the recognition of revenue that results from variable consideration because a significant portion of errors in financial statements under previous revenue recognition requirements have related to the overstatement or premature recognition of revenue. However, the boards noted that their intention was not to eliminate the use of estimates, which are commonplace and necessary in financial reporting, but instead to ensure that those estimates are robust and result in useful information. This is because revenue is an important metric and users of financial statements explained that it is critical that those estimates of variable consideration be included in revenue only when there is a high degree of confidence that revenue will not be reversed in a subsequent reporting period.

BC205 In developing the requirements for constraining estimates of variable consideration, the boards considered the following:

(a) the objective of constraining estimates of variable consideration and specifying a level of confidence (see paragraphs BC206–BC213);

(b) application of the requirements for constraining estimates of variable consideration and sales-based and usage-based royalties on licences of intellectual property (see paragraphs BC214–BC219); and

(c) whether the requirements for constraining estimates of variable consideration should be included in the determination of the transaction price (Step 3 of the revenue recognition model) or the determination of the cumulative amount of revenue recognised when a performance obligation is satisfied (Step 5 of the revenue recognition model) (see paragraphs BC220–BC223).

The objective of constraining estimates of variable consideration and specifying a level of confidence

BC206 In their redeliberations, the boards decided that it would be helpful to clarify the objective for constraining estimates of variable consideration. In making their decision, the boards considered the feedback received from users of financial statements. The majority of users of financial statements that were consulted indicated that the most relevant measure for revenue in a reporting period would be one that will not result in a significant reversal in a subsequent period. This is because an amount that would not reverse in the future would help users of financial statements better predict future revenues of an entity. Therefore, the boards decided that the focus for constraining revenue should be on possible downward adjustments (ie revenue reversals), rather than on all revenue adjustments (ie both downward and upward adjustments). Specifically, the boards decided that an entity should include some or all of an estimate of variable consideration in the transaction price only to the extent it is highly probable that a significant revenue reversal will not occur.

BC207 The boards acknowledge that the requirement to constrain estimates of variable consideration and the objective they have defined creates a tension with the notion of neutrality in the boards' respective conceptual frameworks. This is because the boards' decision introduces a downward bias into estimates that will be included in the transaction price. However, the boards decided that this bias was reasonable because users of financial statements indicated that revenue is more relevant if it is not expected to be subject to significant future reversals.

BC208 In the redeliberations, preparers and auditors indicated that meeting the objective of constraining estimates of variable consideration would be difficult if no level of confidence was specified, for instance, if the boards merely specified that an entity should include variable consideration to the extent that it expects that doing so would not result in a significant revenue reversal. Many also observed that omitting a level of confidence from the objective could result in diversity in practice if entities interpreted the implicit confidence level in different ways (for example, some might interpret the implicit confidence level as virtually certain while others might presume it to mean more likely than not).

BC209 Consequently, the boards decided that specifying a level of confidence would provide clarity and thus ensure more consistent application of the requirements to constrain estimates of variable consideration. In determining the appropriate level of confidence, the boards considered whether they could use the proposal in the 2011 Exposure Draft that constrained revenue to the amount to which an entity would be reasonably assured to be entitled. However, many respondents to the 2011 Exposure Draft were unsure about what the boards intended by using the term 'reasonably assured'. Those respondents observed that the term is used elsewhere in IFRS, US GAAP and auditing requirements and further noted that its meaning is often interpreted differently in those contexts.

BC210　The boards also considered using terminology that has not previously been used in IFRS and US GAAP. However, the boards decided that any new term that was used might result in diversity in practice, because entities might interpret the new term in different ways. Consequently, the boards decided that the most appropriate level of confidence would be 'highly probable' for IFRS and 'probable' for US GAAP as a result of the usage of those terms in existing requirements.

BC211　The boards observed that the term 'probable' is widely used and understood in practice in the United States and is defined in US GAAP as 'the future event or events are likely to occur' (Topic 450). In contrast, the term 'probable' is defined in IFRS as 'more likely than not' (IFRS 5 *Non-current Assets Held for Sale and Discontinued Operations* and IAS 37 *Provisions, Contingent Liabilities and Contingent Assets*). Therefore, to achieve the same meaning in IFRS as US GAAP, the boards decided to use the term 'highly probable' for IFRS purposes and 'probable' for US GAAP purposes. The boards noted that this is consistent with the approach that the IASB adopted in developing IFRS 5, for which the IASB used the term 'highly probable' to achieve the same meaning as 'probable' in US GAAP (see paragraph BC81 of IFRS 5).

BC212　The boards observed that the analysis an entity would undertake to determine if its estimate met the required level of confidence would still be largely qualitative. Specifically, that analysis would require the entity to use judgement and consider the factors in paragraph 57 of IFRS 15 to assess whether it was highly probable that a significant revenue reversal would not occur. In other words, the boards did not expect that an entity would need to prepare a quantitative analysis each time it assessed the likelihood of whether a significant revenue reversal could occur. Therefore, the boards concluded that including a confidence level would not result in application of the requirements that is too costly or complex.

BC213　The factors in paragraph 57 of IFRS 15 were derived in part from previous requirements in US GAAP on estimating sales returns. Those indicators were also proposed in the 2010 and the 2011 Exposure Drafts and respondents generally agreed that the indicators were relevant and helpful. In their redeliberations, the boards also decided to add an indicator in paragraph 57(d) of IFRS 15 to address the circumstances in which there is no explicit requirement to adjust the price stated in the contract, but the entity has a past practice of offering a broad range of price concessions (or similar types of price adjustments). This is because the boards observed that a practice of offering a broad range of price concessions would increase the probability that a significant revenue reversal would occur if the entity included the contractual amount of consideration in the transaction price.

Application of the requirements to constrain estimates of variable consideration

BC214 The requirements for constraining estimates of variable consideration first require an entity to estimate the consideration to which the entity will be entitled (see paragraph 53 of IFRS 15). The entity then assesses whether the objective of the requirements for constraining estimates of variable consideration can be met—that is by determining whether it is highly probable that a significant revenue reversal will not occur when the uncertainty associated with the variable consideration is subsequently resolved. If the entity determines that it is highly probable that the inclusion of its estimate will not result in a significant revenue reversal, that amount is included in the transaction price.

BC215 Although some respondents explained that they reasoned that these requirements would inappropriately require a two-step process, the boards observed that an entity would not be required to strictly follow those two steps if the entity's process for estimating variable consideration already incorporates the principles on which the requirements for constraining estimates of variable consideration are based. For example, an entity might estimate revenue from sales of goods with a right of return. In that case, the entity might not practically need to estimate the expected revenue and then apply the constraint requirements to that estimate, if the entity's calculation of the estimated revenue incorporates the entity's expectations of returns at a level at which it is highly probable that the cumulative amount of revenue recognised would not result in a significant revenue reversal.

BC216 The requirements for constraining estimates of variable consideration require an entity to assess whether a significant revenue reversal would not occur for the amount of cumulative revenue recognised for a satisfied (or partially satisfied) performance obligation. This is because the boards did not intend for an entity to inappropriately recognise revenue by offsetting the risk of a future revenue reversal for a satisfied (or partially satisfied) performance obligation against expected revenue from future performance.

BC217 The requirements for constraining estimates of variable consideration also require an entity to assess the magnitude of a significant revenue reversal for both variable consideration and fixed consideration. For example, if the consideration for a single performance obligation included a fixed amount and a variable amount, the entity would assess the magnitude of a possible revenue reversal of the variable amount relative to the total consideration (ie variable and fixed consideration). This is because the objective of constraining estimates of variable consideration is focused on a possible revenue reversal of the amount of cumulative revenue recognised for a performance obligation, rather than on a reversal of only the variable consideration allocated to that performance obligation.

BC218 The boards noted that in some cases, when an entity applies the requirements for constraining estimates of variable consideration, the entity might determine that it should not include the entire estimate of the variable consideration in the transaction price when it is not highly probable that doing so would not result in a significant revenue reversal. However, the entity might determine that it is highly probable that including some of the estimate of the variable consideration in the transaction price would not result in a significant revenue reversal. The boards decided that, in such cases, the entity should include that amount in the estimate of the transaction price. Respondents to both the 2010 and the 2011 Exposure Drafts supported including some of the variable consideration in the transaction price (and therefore recognising that portion as revenue when the entity satisfies the related performance obligation) if including that amount would meet the objective of the requirements for constraining estimates of variable consideration.

BC219 However, the boards decided that for a licence of intellectual property for which the consideration is based on the customer's subsequent sales or usage, an entity should not recognise any revenue for the uncertain amounts until the uncertainty is resolved (ie when the customer's subsequent sales or usage occurs). The boards included these requirements because both users and preparers of financial statements generally indicated that if an entity recognised a minimum amount of revenue for those contracts it would not provide relevant information (see paragraphs BC419–BC421).

Constraining the estimate of the transaction price (Step 3) or constraining the cumulative amount of revenue that is recognised (Step 5)

BC220 During the development of the requirements for constraining estimates of variable consideration, the boards considered where in the revenue recognition model it would be most appropriate to apply those requirements.

BC221 Some respondents suggested that if the objective is to constrain the measurement of revenue, it might be more appropriate to constrain the transaction price (ie include a constraint at Step 3). In contrast, if the objective is to limit the amount of revenue recognised, it might be more appropriate to constrain the cumulative amount of revenue recognised (ie include a constraint at Step 5). However, the boards observed that those are not truly independent objectives because the measurement of revenue determines the amount of revenue recognised. In other words, the requirements for constraining estimates of variable consideration restrict revenue recognition and use measurement uncertainty as the basis for determining if (or how much) revenue should be recognised. The boards noted that applying the requirements for constraining estimates of variable consideration to the transaction price or to the cumulative amount of revenue recognised should have an equal effect on the amount of revenue recognised in a contract.

BC222 Consequently, the boards decided that the requirements for constraining estimates of variable consideration should be incorporated into the determination of the transaction price because feedback from respondents indicated that this would be consistent with the way in which management often considers variable consideration.

BC223   Respondents in the asset management and hotel management industries questioned whether constraining the transaction price would result in a pattern of revenue recognition that would faithfully depict their performance under the contract. In many of the contracts in those industries, when a portion of the variable consideration becomes fixed, it relates only to the performance for the period. The boards observed that the requirements for allocating variable consideration (see paragraphs BC284–BC293) would ensure that the revenue recognised would faithfully depict the performance in such a contract.

Subsequent changes in the transaction price

BC224   After contract inception, an entity will revise its expectations about the amount of consideration to which it expects to be entitled as uncertainties are resolved or as new information about remaining uncertainties becomes available. To depict conditions that exist at the end of each reporting period (and changes in conditions during the reporting period), the boards decided that an entity should update its estimate of the transaction price throughout the contract. The boards concluded that reflecting current assessments of the amount of consideration to which the entity expects to be entitled will provide more useful information to users of financial statements than retaining the initial estimates, especially for long-term contracts that are subject to significant changes in conditions during the life of the contract.

BC225   The boards considered whether an entity should do either of the following if the transaction price changes during a contract:

(a)   recognise those changes in profit or loss when the changes occur; or

(b)   allocate those changes to performance obligations.

BC226   The boards rejected the alternative of recognising the entire amount of a change in the estimate of the transaction price in profit or loss when that change occurs. In the boards' view, that alternative could have resulted in a pattern of revenue recognition that would not faithfully depict the pattern of the transfer of goods or services. Moreover, recognising revenue immediately (and entirely) for a change in the estimate of the transaction price would have been prone to abuse in practice. The boards considered whether changes in the estimate of the transaction price could be presented as a gain or loss separately from revenue, thus preserving the pattern of revenue recognition. However, the boards rejected that alternative because the total amount of revenue recognised for the contract would not have equalled the amount of consideration to which the entity was entitled under the contract.

BC227   Instead, the boards decided that an entity should allocate a change in the transaction price to all the performance obligations in the contract, subject to the conditions in paragraphs 87–90 of IFRS 15 (see paragraph BC286). This is because the cumulative revenue recognised will then depict the revenue that the entity would have recognised at the end of the subsequent reporting period, if the entity had the information at contract inception. Consequently, the transaction price that is allocated to performance obligations that have already been satisfied should be recognised as revenue (or as a reduction of revenue) immediately.

BC228   The boards noted that in some cases, an entity might make an estimate of the amount of variable consideration to include in the transaction price at the end of a reporting period. However, information relating to the variable consideration might arise between the end of the reporting period and the date when the financial statements are authorised for issue. The boards decided not to provide guidance on the accounting in these situations because they noted that the accounting for subsequent events is already addressed in IAS 10 *Events after the Reporting Period* and Topic 855 *Subsequent Events*.

The existence of a significant financing component in the contract (paragraphs 60–65)

BC229   Some contracts with customers include a financing component. The financing component may be explicitly identified in the contract or may be implied by the contractual payment terms of the contract. A contract that has a financing component includes, conceptually, two transactions—one for the sale and one for the financing. The boards decided to require an entity to adjust the promised amount of consideration for the effects of financing components if those financing components are significant, for the following reasons:

(a)   not recognising a financing component could misrepresent the revenue of a contract. For example, if a customer pays in arrears, ignoring the financing component of the contract would result in full revenue recognition on the transfer of the good or service, despite the fact that the entity is providing a service of financing to the customer.

(b)   in some contracts, entities (or customers) consider the timing of the cash flows in a contract. Consequently, identifying a significant financing component acknowledges an important economic feature of the contract, which is that the contract includes a financing arrangement as well as the transfer of goods or services. A contract in which the customer pays for a good or service when that good or service is transferred to the customer may be significantly different from a contract in which the customer pays before or after the good or service is transferred in order to provide or receive a financing benefit.

BC230   The objective of adjusting the promised amount of consideration for the effects of a significant financing component is to reflect, in the amount of revenue recognised, the 'cash selling price' of the underlying good or service at the time that the good or service is transferred. The boards observed that adjusting the promised consideration to obtain the cash selling price may only be required when the timing of payments specified in the contract provides the customer or the entity with a significant benefit of financing the transfer of goods or services to the customer. This is because, in other cases, the timing of payments may be for a purpose other than financing, such as protection for non-performance. This is described further in the following paragraphs.

Determining whether a contract includes a significant financing component

BC231   The boards considered whether the requirements for identifying a financing component should be based only on whether payment is due either significantly before, or significantly after, the transfer of goods or services to the customer. However, a number of respondents explained that this might have required an entity to adjust for the time value of money when the parties did not contemplate a financing arrangement as part of the negotiated terms of the contract. Those respondents explained that, in some cases, although there is a significant period of time between the transfer of the goods or services and the payment, the reason for that timing difference is not related to a financing arrangement between the entity and the customer. The boards agreed with those respondents and clarified their intention by specifying in paragraph 60 of IFRS 15 that an entity should adjust for financing only if the timing of payments specified in the contract provides the customer or the entity with a significant benefit of financing.

BC232   The boards also decided to remove the term 'time value of money' from the discussion about adjustments for financing components, to reflect their decision that the focus is on whether the payment terms provide the customer or the entity with a significant benefit of financing. This is because the term 'time value of money' is a broader economic term that may suggest that it is necessary to adjust the promised amount of consideration in circumstances other than when the cash sales price may differ from the contractual payments. In addition, the boards decided to refine the factors in paragraph 61 of IFRS 15 that an entity should consider when deciding whether a contract includes a significant financing component. Those factors require evaluation of:

(a)   the difference, if any, between the amount of promised consideration and the cash selling price of the promised goods or services. If the entity (or another entity) sells the same good or service for a different amount of consideration depending on the timing of the payment terms, this generally provides observable data that the parties are aware that there is a financing component in the contract. This factor is presented as an indicator because in some cases the difference between the cash selling price and the consideration promised by the customer is due to factors other than financing (see paragraph BC233).

(b)   the combined effect of (1) the expected length of time between when the entity transfers the promised goods or services to the customer and when the customer pays for those goods or services and (2) the prevailing interest rates in the relevant market. Although the boards decided that the difference in timing between the transfer of goods and services and payment for those goods and services is not determinative, the combined effect of timing and the prevailing interest rates may provide a strong indication that a significant benefit of financing is being provided.

BC233   In addition, the boards included criteria in paragraph 62 of IFRS 15 to clarify the circumstances in which a contract does *not* provide the customer or the entity with a significant benefit of financing:

(a)   the customer has paid for the goods or services in advance and, the timing of the transfer of those goods or services is at the discretion of the customer. The boards noted that for some types of goods or services, such as prepaid phone cards and customer loyalty points, the customer will pay for those goods or services in advance and the transfer of those goods or services to the customer is at the customer's discretion. The boards expected that, in those cases, the purpose of the payment terms is not related to a financing arrangement between the parties. In addition, the boards decided that the costs of requiring an entity to account for the time value of money in these cases would outweigh any perceived benefit because the entity would need to continually estimate when the goods or services will transfer to the customer.

(b)   a substantial amount of the consideration promised by the customer is variable and that consideration varies on the basis of factors that are outside the control of the customer or the entity. The boards observed that for some arrangements, the primary purpose of the specified timing or amount of the payment terms might not be to provide the customer or the entity with a significant benefit of financing but, instead, to resolve uncertainties that relate to the consideration for the goods or services. For example, in a royalty arrangement, the entity and the customer might not be willing to fix the price and timing of payment because there are significant uncertainties about the goods or services. The primary purpose of those payment terms may be to provide the parties with assurance of the value of the goods or services rather than to provide significant financing to the customer.

(c)   the difference between the promised consideration and the cash selling price of the good or service arises for reasons other than the provision of financing to either the customer or the entity. In some circumstances, a payment in advance or in arrears in accordance with the typical payment terms of an industry or jurisdiction may have a primary purpose other than financing. For example, a customer may retain or withhold some consideration that is payable only on successful completion of the contract or on achievement of a specified milestone. Alternatively, the customer might be required to pay some consideration upfront to secure a future supply of limited goods or services. The primary purpose of those payment terms may be to provide the customer with assurance that the entity will complete its obligations satisfactorily under the contract, rather than to provide financing to the customer or the entity respectively.

BC234   The boards also observed that for many contracts, an entity will not need to adjust the promised amount of customer consideration because the effects of the financing component will not materially change the amount of revenue that should be recognised in relation to a contract with a customer. In other words, for those contracts, the financing component will not be significant. During their redeliberations, the boards clarified that an entity should consider only the *significance* of a financing component at a contract level rather than consider whether the financing is *material* at a portfolio level. The boards decided that it would have been unduly burdensome to require an entity to account for a financing component if the effects of the financing component were not material to the individual contract, but the combined effects for a portfolio of similar contracts were material to the entity as a whole.

Practical reliefs from the significant financing component requirements

BC235   Some previous requirements required an entity to recognise the effects of a significant financing component with a customer only if the time period exceeded a specified period, often one year. For example, Subtopic 835-30 *Interest — Imputation of Interest*, excluded 'transactions with customers or suppliers in the normal course of business that are due in customary trade terms not exceeding approximately one year'. The boards decided to include similar relief in IFRS 15 from the requirements to account for a significant financing component in circumstances in which the period between when the entity transfers the promised goods or services to the customer, and when the customer pays for those goods or services, is one year or less (see paragraph 63 of IFRS 15). The boards observed that, as with the other practical expedients in IFRS 15, an entity should apply the practical expedient consistently to similar contracts in similar circumstances.

BC236   The boards acknowledged that the relief could produce arbitrary outcomes in some cases because the financing component could be material for short-term contracts with high implicit interest rates and, conversely, could be immaterial for long-term contracts with low implicit interest rates. However, the boards decided to exempt an entity from accounting for the effects of any significant financing component on contracts with an expected duration of one year or less for the following reasons:

(a)   application of IFRS 15 would be simplified. This is because an entity would not be required to:

(i)   conclude whether those contracts contain the attributes of a financing component that are significant to those contracts (see paragraph BC232); and

(ii)   determine the interest rate that is implicit within those contracts.

(b)   the effect on the pattern of profit recognition should be limited because the exemption would apply only to financing arrangements that are expected to expire within 12 months (ie when either the customer pays or the entity performs).

BC237   Some respondents also suggested that the boards should exempt an entity from reflecting in the measurement of the transaction price the effect of a significant financing component associated with advance payments from customers. Those respondents commented that accounting for any effects of a significant financing component arising from advance payments would result in the following:

    (a)   change previous practices in which entities typically did not recognise the effects of the financing implicit in advance payments;

    (b)   revenue that is higher than the cash received (for example, if the discount rate implicit in the contract resulted in the accretion of interest of CU21[7] over two years, revenue would be recognised in the amount of the CU121 rather than the CU100 in cash that was paid in advance); and

    (c)   not reflect the economics of the arrangement when the customer pays in advance for reasons other than financing (for example, the customer has significant credit risk or is compensating the entity for incurring upfront contract costs).

BC238   The boards decided not to exempt an entity from accounting for the effects of a significant financing component for advance payments. This is because ignoring the effects of advance payments could substantially skew the amount and pattern of profit recognition if the advance payment is significant and the primary purpose of that payment is to provide financing to the entity. Consider the example in which an entity requires a customer to pay in advance for a long-term construction contract, because the entity requires financing to obtain materials for the contract. If the entity did not require the customer to pay in advance, the entity would need to obtain the financing from a third party and, consequently, would charge the customer a relatively higher amount to cover the finance costs incurred. However, in either scenario the goods or services transferred to the customer are the same; it is only the party providing the financing to the entity that changes. Consequently, the entity's revenue should be consistent regardless of whether it receives the significant financing benefit from the customer or from a third party.

Discount rate

BC239   The boards considered whether the discount rate used to adjust the promised amount of consideration for the effects of a significant financing component should be a risk-free rate or a risk-adjusted rate. A risk-free rate would have been observable and simple to apply in many jurisdictions and it would have avoided the costs of determining a rate specific to each contract. However, the boards decided that using a risk-free rate would not result in useful information, because the resulting interest rate would not have reflected the characteristics of the parties to the contract. In addition, the boards noted that it would not necessarily have been appropriate to use any rate explicitly specified in the contract because the entity might offer 'cheap' financing as a

---

7   Monetary items in the Basis for Conclusions are denominated as 'currency units' (CU).

marketing incentive and, therefore, using that rate would not have resulted in an appropriate recognition of profit over the life of the contract. Consequently, the boards decided that an entity should apply the rate used in a financing transaction between the entity and its customer that does not involve the provision of goods or services because that rate reflects the characteristics of the party receiving financing in the contract. That rate also reflects the customer's creditworthiness, among other risks.

BC240 Some respondents mentioned that determining the discount rate that would be used in a separate financing transaction between an entity and a customer would be difficult and costly because most entities within the scope of IFRS 15 do not enter into separate financing transactions with their customers. In addition, it would have been impractical for entities with large volumes of customer contracts to determine a discount rate specifically for each individual customer.

BC241 The boards addressed many of those concerns by providing both the exemption for contracts with a term of up to one year from being considered to have a significant financing component and the factors in paragraph 62 of IFRS 15, which describe when there is no significant financing component that needs to be accounted for. The boards expect that in those remaining contracts in which an entity is required to account separately for the financing component, the entity and its customer will typically negotiate the contractual payment terms separately after considering factors such as inflation rates and the customer's credit risk. Therefore, an entity should have access to sufficient information to determine the discount rate that would be used in a separate financing between the entity and the customer.

Re-evaluating the discount rate used for a significant financing component

BC242 Some respondents asked whether an entity would be required to revise the discount rate used in determining the amount of a significant financing component if there was a change in circumstances.

BC243 The boards clarified that an entity should not update the discount rate for a change in circumstances because an entity should reflect in the measurement of the transaction price only the discount rate that is determined at contract inception. They also observed that it would be impractical for an entity to update the transaction price for changes in the assessment of the discount rate.

Presentation of the effect of a significant financing component

BC244 As a result of the boards' decision on the existence of a significant financing component (see paragraphs BC229–BC243), a contract with a customer that has a significant financing component would be separated into a revenue component (for the notional cash sales price) and a loan component (for the effect of the deferred or advance payment terms). Consequently, the accounting for a trade receivable arising from a contract that has a significant financing component should be comparable to the accounting for a loan with the same features. Consider the following example: Customer A purchases a good on credit and promises to pay CU1,000 in three years. The present value of this trade receivable is CU751. Now consider Customer B who borrows CU751 from a bank with a promise to pay CU1,000 in three years. Customer B uses the loan to purchase the same good as Customer A. Economically, those transactions are the same, but, in the absence of the requirements in IFRS 15 to account for a significant financing component, the form of the transaction would determine whether an entity would recognise revenue of CU751 or CU1,000 (ie on a discounted or an undiscounted basis). For this reason, paragraphs 60–65 of IFRS 15 require a contract with a financing component that is significant to the contract to be separated, which results in the same revenue recognition for both transactions.

BC245 The boards observed that the presentation, in the statement of comprehensive income, of any impairment losses from long-term trade receivables (ie receivables arising from the financing components of contracts with customers) would be consistent with the presentation of impairment losses for other types of financial assets within the scope of the boards' respective financial instruments Standards. The boards decided that impairment losses on short-term trade receivables (ie receivables arising from contracts with customers that do not have separately identified financing components) should be presented in the statement of comprehensive income in a consistent manner with impairment losses on long-term trade receivables (see paragraphs BC259–BC265).

BC246 The boards decided that an entity should present the effect of the financing (ie the unwinding of the discount) separately from revenue from contracts with customers, as interest revenue or interest expense, rather than as a change to the measurement of revenue. This is because contracts with financing components that are significant have distinct economic characteristics—one relating to the transfer of goods or services to the customer and one relating to a financing arrangement—and those characteristics should be accounted for and presented separately.

BC247 The boards noted that some entities (for example, banks and other entities with similar types of operations) regularly enter into financing transactions and, therefore, interest represents income arising from ordinary activities for those entities. The boards noted that the requirements in paragraph 65 of IFRS 15 do not preclude an entity from presenting interest as a type of revenue in circumstances in which the interest represents income from the entity's ordinary activities.

Non-cash consideration (paragraphs 66–69)

BC248 When an entity receives cash from a customer in exchange for a good or service, the transaction price and, therefore, the amount of revenue, should be the amount of cash received (ie the value of the inbound asset). To be consistent with that approach, the boards decided that an entity should measure non-cash consideration at fair value. The non-cash consideration could be in the form of goods or services, but it may also be in the form of a financial instrument or property, plant and equipment. For example, an entity might receive an electrical substation in exchange for connecting houses in a new residential development to the electricity network.

BC249　The boards decided that if an entity cannot reasonably estimate the fair value of the non-cash consideration, it should measure the promised consideration indirectly by reference to the stand-alone selling price of the goods or services promised in exchange for the consideration. That approach is consistent both with requirements in previous revenue Standards in IFRS and with requirements for other situations in which the fair value of the assets surrendered in exchange for assets received may be estimated more reliably. (For instance, IFRS 2 *Share-based Payment* and Subtopic 505-50 *Equity-Based Payments to Non-Employees* state that if the fair value of the goods or services received cannot be estimated reliably, then the entity measures them indirectly by reference to the fair value of the granted equity instrument.)

BC250　Some respondents observed that estimates of fair value of non-cash consideration may vary like other types of variable consideration that the entity will receive in cash. For example, an entity's entitlement to a bonus that will be received in non-cash consideration may also depend on the occurrence or non-occurrence of a future event. Consequently, those respondents asked the boards to clarify whether the requirements for constraining estimates of variable consideration (see paragraphs 56–58 of IFRS 15) should be applied to estimates of the fair value of non-cash consideration.

BC251　The boards observed that while the fair value of the non-cash consideration could change because of the occurrence or non-occurrence of a future event, it could also vary because of the form of the consideration. That is, the fair value could vary because of changes in the price or value of the non-cash consideration, such as a change in the price per share.

BC252　The boards decided that it would be most appropriate to apply the requirements for constraining estimates of variable consideration to the same types of variability regardless of whether the amount that will be received will be in the form of cash or non-cash consideration. Consequently, the boards decided to constrain variability in the estimate of the fair value of the non-cash consideration if that variability relates to changes in the fair value for reasons other than the form of the consideration (ie for reasons other than changes in the price of the non-cash consideration). For example, if an entity is entitled to a performance bonus that is payable in the form of non-cash consideration, the entity would apply the requirements for constraining estimates of variable consideration to the uncertainty of whether the entity will receive the bonus, because that uncertainty is related to something other than the form of the consideration (ie the entity's performance). The boards observed that this principle is not that different from previous revenue recognition requirements under US GAAP for changes in the fair value of equity instruments that are granted as consideration in exchange for goods or services, although those requirements differentiated between the variability on the basis of performance conditions and market conditions (which were defined terms in those requirements).

BC253   The boards also observed that once recognised, any asset arising from the non-cash consideration would be measured and accounted for in accordance with other relevant requirements (for example, IFRS 9 or Topic 320 *Investments— Debt and Equity Securities* or Topic 323 *Equity Method And Joint Ventures*).

BC254   The FASB noted that the requirements in Topic 606 will result in the removal of previous requirements for the accounting for share-based payments received by an entity in exchange for goods or services. Those previous requirements provided detailed guidance for the measurement and recognition of revenue when the consideration was in the form of shares or share options. However, the FASB decided to remove those requirements because equity instruments are merely another form of non-cash consideration. Therefore, equity instruments received as promised consideration in a contract with a customer would be accounted for consistently with other forms of non-cash consideration.

Clarifications to IFRS 15 (amendments issued in April 2016)—topics for which the IASB decided not to amend IFRS 15

BC254A   The TRG discussed the following implementation questions raised by stakeholders in connection with applying IFRS 15 to contracts that involve non-cash consideration:

(a)   At which date should the fair value of non-cash consideration be measured in determining the transaction price?

(b)   How should the constraint on variable consideration be applied to transactions for which the fair value of non-cash consideration might vary due to both the form of the consideration and for other reasons?

Date of measurement of non-cash consideration

BC254B   Paragraph 66 of IFRS 15 requires non-cash consideration to be measured at fair value (or by reference to the stand-alone selling price of the goods or services promised to the customer if an entity cannot reasonably estimate fair value of the non-cash consideration). The TRG's discussion informed the boards that the measurement date for non-cash consideration is unclear and could be interpreted as one of several dates: (a) at contract inception; (b) when the non-cash consideration is received; or (c) at the earlier of when the non-cash consideration is received and when the related performance obligation is satisfied.

BC254C   In its discussions, the IASB observed that this issue has important interactions with other Standards (including IFRS 2 *Share-based Payment* and IAS 21 *The Effects of Changes in Foreign Exchange Rates*) and, thus, any decisions made would create a risk of potential unintended consequences. Accordingly, the IASB decided that, if needed, issues relating to the measurement of non-cash consideration should be considered more comprehensively in a separate project.

BC254D   The FASB decided to amend the guidance in Topic 606 to require non-cash consideration to be measured at its fair value at contract inception. In the FASB's view, measuring non-cash consideration at contract inception is most consistent with the requirements in Topic 606 on determining the transaction price and on allocating the transaction price to performance obligations. The FASB also expects this approach to be typically less costly and less complex to apply in practice than other alternatives.

BC254E   The IASB acknowledged that, because it has concluded that a change equivalent to that decided by the FASB is not needed, the use of a measurement date other than contract inception would not be precluded under IFRS. Consequently, it is possible that diversity between IFRS and US GAAP entities could arise in practice. The IASB observed that, unlike US GAAP, existing IFRS does not contain any specific requirements about the measurement date for non-cash consideration for revenue transactions. In addition, discussions with some stakeholders highlighted that any practical effect of different measurement dates would arise in only limited circumstances. The IASB also noted that paragraph 126 of IFRS 15 requires an entity to disclose information about the methods, inputs and assumptions used for measuring non-cash consideration.

Application of the variable consideration constraint to changes in fair value of non-cash consideration

BC254F   The TRG discussed the concerns raised by some stakeholders that it is not clear whether the variable consideration requirements in paragraphs 56–58 of IFRS 15 apply in circumstances in which the fair value of non-cash consideration varies due to both the form of the consideration and for other reasons. In particular, some stakeholders are concerned that bifurcating the effects of variability might be challenging in some circumstances.

BC254G   The FASB decided to amend Topic 606 to specify that the constraint on variable consideration applies only to variability that arises for reasons other than the form of the consideration. Paragraph 68 of IFRS 15 indicates that the requirements for constraining estimates of variable consideration are applied if the fair value of the non-cash consideration promised by a customer varies for reasons other than only the form of the consideration (for example, a change in the exercise price of a share option because of the entity's performance). The FASB observed that applying the variable consideration requirements to both types of variability might not provide users of financial statements with useful information, because the timing of revenue recognition might differ for similar transactions settled in different forms of consideration (for example, cash and shares). Additionally, the inclusion of a minor performance condition could significantly affect the amount of non-cash consideration that would be subject to the constraint on variable consideration.

BC254H   The IASB noted that paragraph BC252 explains that the boards decided to constrain variability in the estimate of the fair value of the non-cash consideration if that variability relates to changes in the fair value for reasons other than the form of the consideration (ie for reasons other than changes in the price of the non-cash consideration). The IASB also noted the view of some TRG members that in practice it might be difficult to distinguish between variability in the fair value due to the form of the consideration and other reasons, in which case applying the variable consideration constraint to the whole of the estimate of the non-cash consideration might be more practical. However, for reasons similar to those discussed in paragraph BC254E, the IASB decided not to amend IFRS 15 for this issue. Consequently, the IASB acknowledged that differences may arise between an entity reporting under IFRS and an entity reporting under US GAAP.

Consideration payable to a customer (paragraphs 70–72)

BC255 In some cases, an entity pays consideration to one of its customers or to its customer's customer (for example, an entity may sell a product to a dealer or distributor and subsequently pay a customer of that dealer or distributor). That consideration might be in the form of a payment in exchange for goods or services received from the customer, a discount or refund for goods or services provided to the customer, or a combination of both.

BC256 To help an entity distinguish between those types of payments, the boards decided that the only circumstance in which an entity should account for any good or service received in the same way as for other purchases from suppliers is if the good or service is distinct. Previous requirements in US GAAP on the consideration that a vendor gives to a customer used the term 'identifiable benefit', which was described as a good or service that is 'sufficiently separable from the recipient's purchase of the vendor's products such that the vendor could have entered into an exchange transaction with a party other than a purchaser of its products or services in order to receive that benefit'. The boards concluded that the principle in IFRS 15 for assessing whether a good or service is distinct is similar to the previous requirements in US GAAP.

BC257 The amount of consideration received from a customer for goods or services, and the amount of any consideration paid to that customer for goods or services, could be linked even if they are separate events. For instance, a customer may pay more for goods or services from an entity than it would otherwise have paid if it was not receiving a payment from the entity. Consequently, the boards decided that to depict revenue faithfully in those cases, any amount accounted for as a payment to the customer for goods or services received should be limited to the fair value of those goods or services, with any amount in excess of the fair value being recognised as a reduction of the transaction price.

BC258 If the payment of consideration is accounted for as a reduction of the transaction price, an entity would recognise less revenue when it satisfies the related performance obligation(s). However, in some cases, an entity promises to pay consideration to a customer only after it has satisfied its performance obligations and, therefore, after it has recognised revenue. When this is the case, a reduction in revenue should be recognised immediately. Accordingly, the boards clarified that the reduction of revenue is recognised at the later of when the entity transfers the goods or services to the customer and when the entity promises to pay the consideration. By using the phrase 'promises to pay', the boards clarified that an entity should reflect in the transaction price payments to customers that are conditional on future events (for example, a promise to pay a customer that is conditional on the customer making a specified number of purchases would be reflected in the transaction price when the entity makes the promise).

Customer credit risk

BC259　The 2010 Exposure Draft proposed that an entity would recognise revenue at the amount that the entity expects to *receive* from the customer. In other words, the customer's credit risk would be reflected in the measurement of the transaction price allocated to the performance obligations in the contract.

BC260　Many respondents to the 2010 Exposure Draft commented specifically about the proposed requirements for customer credit risk. Although some respondents agreed with the proposal that the transaction price should reflect the customer's credit risk, nearly all respondents (including preparers, users of financial statements and securities regulators) expressed concerns about applying that concept in practice. In particular, many users of financial statements commented that they would prefer revenue to be measured at the 'gross' amount so that revenue growth and receivables management (or bad debts) could be analysed separately. Those users of financial statements indicated that they were interested in assessing the performance of an entity's sales function and receivables collection function separately because those functions are often managed separately. However, that information would not be available if an entity's assessment of sales and collectability were reflected only on a 'net' basis in the revenue line.

BC261　After considering that feedback, the boards decided not to adopt that proposal. Instead, in the 2011 Exposure Draft, the boards proposed that revenue should be recognised at the amount to which the entity expects to be entitled, which would not reflect any adjustments for amounts that the entity might not be able to collect from the customer. However, to provide transparency to all users of financial statements for the portion of the entity's gross revenue that is expected to be uncollectable, the boards proposed to link the presentation of the revenue line and the impairment loss line. Consequently, the 2011 Exposure Draft proposed that initial and subsequent impairment losses (and reversals) on transactions that did not include a significant financing component should be presented as a separate line item adjacent to the revenue line item.

BC262　In redeliberating the 2011 Exposure Draft, the boards considered the following challenges arising from the proposed linked presentation of revenue and impairment losses:

(a)　different interpretations might have emerged about whether the reported revenue amount of the entity is the gross revenue before the impairment losses that are presented adjacent to revenue or the net revenue after those impairment losses.

(b)   the impairment losses that would have been presented as a separate line item adjacent to the revenue line item might have related to uncollectable consideration that had been recognised as revenue in previous reporting periods. Consequently, there would not necessarily be a connection between the revenue recognised in a particular reporting period and the impairment losses that would have been presented adjacent to the revenue line item in that period.

(c)   the impairment losses on short-term trade receivables (ie receivables arising from contracts with customers that do not have separately identified financing components) would have been presented differently from all other financial assets that are subject to impairment. This is because the impairment losses for short-term trade receivables would have been presented adjacent to revenue, whereas for all other financial assets, impairment losses would have been presented together with other expense items in the statement of comprehensive income. For the reasons described in paragraphs BC244–BC247, those other financial assets would have included receivables arising from contracts with customers that include a financing component that is significant to the contract.

BC263   The boards considered addressing some of those challenges by requiring that initial impairment losses be presented adjacent to the revenue line item and subsequent impairment losses be presented as a separate expense. The boards observed that this approach would have provided a clearer link between revenue and the impairment losses related to the revenue recognised in that period. However, many respondents noted that it would have been challenging to distinguish between initial and subsequent impairment losses without incurring significant costs to obtain the information.

BC264   Consequently, the boards decided to modify the presentation requirements for impairment losses and to require disclosure of impairment losses on short-term trade receivables arising from a contract with a customer separate from other impairment losses (if not otherwise presented and subject to the usual materiality considerations). The boards decided that this approach is the most appropriate because it addresses the challenges identified in the 2011 Exposure Draft and still provides users of financial statements with the information that they had said would be most useful, which is gross revenue to provide revenue trend information and the impairment loss to provide information on receivables management (or bad debts). Furthermore, the boards noted that this would provide greater consistency with the accounting for impairment losses on contracts with customers that include a significant financing component.

BC265   However, the boards were concerned that for some transactions in which there is significant credit risk at contract inception, an entity might recognise revenue for the transfer of goods or services and, at the same time, recognise a significant bad debt expense. The boards decided that in those cases, 'grossing up' revenue and recognising a significant impairment loss would not faithfully represent the transaction and would not provide useful information.

Consequently, the boards included the criterion in paragraph 9(e) of IFRS 15 (see paragraphs BC42–BC46).

Allocating the transaction price to performance obligations (paragraphs 73–86)

BC266　The boards decided that an entity should generally allocate the transaction price to all performance obligations in proportion to the stand-alone selling prices of the goods or services underlying each of those performance obligations at contract inception (ie on a relative stand-alone selling price basis). They decided that in most cases an allocation based on stand-alone selling prices faithfully depicts the different margins that may apply to promised goods or services.

BC267　Most respondents agreed with the requirement to allocate the transaction price on a relative stand-alone selling price basis. Some of those respondents observed that the requirements were broadly consistent with previous changes to US GAAP for multiple-element arrangements. However, respondents expressed concerns about the following topics:

(a)　estimating the stand-alone selling price; and

(b)　allocating discounts and contingent consideration.

Estimating stand-alone selling prices (paragraphs 76–80)

BC268　IFRS 15 specifies that if an entity does not have an observable price from selling a good or service separately, the entity should instead estimate the stand-alone selling price. Paragraph 79 of IFRS 15 includes examples of suitable estimation methods for estimating the stand-alone selling price. However, the boards decided not to preclude or prescribe any particular method for estimating a stand-alone selling price so long as the estimate is a faithful representation of the price at which the entity would sell the distinct good or service if it were sold separately to the customer. The boards clarified that the method used by the entity to estimate a stand-alone selling price should maximise the use of observable inputs and should be applied consistently to estimate the stand-alone selling price of other goods or services with similar characteristics.

BC269　The boards observed that many entities may already have robust processes for determining stand-alone selling prices on the basis of reasonably available data points and the effects of market considerations and entity-specific factors. However, other entities may need to develop processes for estimating selling prices of goods or services that are typically not sold separately. The boards decided that when developing those processes, an entity should consider all reasonably available information on the basis of the specific facts and circumstances. That information might include the following:

(a)   reasonably available data points (for example, a stand-alone selling price of the good or service, the costs incurred to manufacture or provide the good or service, related profit margins, published price listings, third-party or industry pricing and the pricing of other goods or services in the same contract);

(b)   market conditions (for example, supply and demand for the good or service in the market, competition, restrictions and trends);

(c)   entity-specific factors (for example, business pricing strategies and practices); and

(d)   information about the customer or class of customer (for example, type of customer, geographical region and distribution channel).

Residual approach

BC270   In response to questions from respondents, the boards decided to specify that a residual approach might be a suitable technique for estimating the stand-alone selling price of a good or service. Using a residual approach, an entity would estimate a stand-alone selling price of a good or service on the basis of the difference between the total transaction price and the (observable) stand-alone selling prices of other goods or services in the contract.

BC271   The boards also decided to specify how and when an entity can use the residual approach as an estimation method in paragraph 79(c) of IFRS 15. Specifically, in situations in which one or more promised goods or services have a stand-alone selling price that is highly variable or uncertain. In specifying those circumstances, the boards were particularly mindful of the challenges in determining stand-alone selling prices in contracts for intellectual property and other intangible products. In those arrangements, the pricing can be highly variable because there is little or no incremental cost to the entity in providing those goods or services to a customer. In those circumstances, the most reliable way of determining the stand-alone selling price in the contract will often be to use a residual approach. For the same reason, the boards noted that the residual approach might be appropriate in situations in which an entity has not yet established the selling price for a good or service that previously has not been sold on a stand-alone basis.

BC272   Most respondents agreed with the boards' proposals on the residual approach. However, some respondents, particularly those in the software industry, asked the boards to clarify whether they could use a residual approach if there is more than one good or service in the contract with highly variable or uncertain stand-alone selling prices. Those respondents observed that this may occur in contracts that include three or more performance obligations, in which at least one of the performance obligations has an observable stand-alone selling price. The boards decided that even if a contract includes more than one good or service with a highly variable or uncertain stand-alone selling price, an entity should not be prevented from applying the residual approach because it may still be a reliable method for determining the stand-alone selling price. However, the boards observed that using the residual approach when there are two or more goods or services with highly variable or uncertain stand-alone selling prices may require an entity to use a combination of techniques to estimate the stand-alone selling prices as follows:

(a)　apply the residual approach to estimate the aggregate of the stand-alone selling prices for all the promised goods or services with highly variable or uncertain stand-alone selling prices; and

(b)　then use another technique to estimate the stand-alone selling prices of each of those promised goods or services with highly variable or uncertain stand-alone selling prices.

BC273　In determining whether the estimate is reasonable, the boards observed that it was important to understand that the residual approach for estimating the stand-alone selling price of a promised good or service is different from the residual method permitted under previous revenue Standards. This is because in IFRS 15 the residual approach is used to determine the stand-alone selling price of a distinct good or service. By definition, the outcome of this approach cannot realistically result in a stand-alone selling price of zero if the good or service is in fact distinct because to be distinct that good or service must have value on a stand-alone basis. In contrast, the residual method in previous revenue Standards could have resulted in an outcome of zero because the residual method was an allocation method. Thus, under previous revenue recognition requirements, zero could be the only amount of consideration that remained to be allocated to a performance obligation. Consequently, the boards noted that if the residual approach in paragraph 79(c) of IFRS 15 results in no, or very little, consideration being allocated to a good or service or a bundle of goods or services, the entity should consider whether that estimate is appropriate in those circumstances.

Specifying a hierarchy of evidence

BC274　The boards decided not to specify a hierarchy of evidence to determine the stand-alone selling price of a good or service. Instead, they decided to emphasise that an entity should maximise the use of observable inputs when developing estimates of stand-alone selling prices.

BC275　Most respondents agreed with the boards' decision not to prescribe a hierarchy of evidence for estimating a stand-alone selling price. However, some respondents recommended that the boards should specify a hierarchy of evidence, because specifying a hierarchy of evidence for determining stand-alone selling prices (and requiring disclosures using that hierarchy) would enhance the quality and reliability of an entity's reported revenues. The hierarchy suggested by those respondents was similar to that in previous revenue Standards:

(a)　if vendor-specific objective evidence of a selling price is available, an entity would use this price to determine the selling price of a promised good or service;

(b)　if vendor-specific objective evidence is not available, an entity would determine the selling price using third-party evidence, if available; and

(c)   if third-party evidence is not available, an entity would use its best estimate of the selling price.

BC276   The boards observed that IFRS 15 requires an entity to use observable prices when a good or service is sold separately by the entity (which is similar to a vendor-specific objective evidence notion). It is only when a good or service is not sold separately that an entity is required to estimate the stand-alone selling price. In that estimation process, an entity is still required to maximise the use of observable inputs. The boards noted that in the hierarchy in paragraph BC275 there is little distinction between third-party evidence and a best estimate of a selling price. For instance, third-party evidence of a selling price might require adjustments to reflect differences in either (a) the good or service (because the third-party price could be for a similar, rather than an identical, good or service) or (b) pricing strategies between the third party and the entity. Therefore, the boards affirmed their decision not to specify a hierarchy in IFRS 15. Instead, the boards decided that it was important to emphasise that an entity should maximise the use of observable inputs when developing estimates of stand-alone selling prices.

Allocating discounts and variable consideration (paragraphs 81–86)

BC277   A consequence of allocating the transaction price on a relative stand-alone selling price basis is that any discount in the contract is allocated proportionately to each of the performance obligations in the contract. Some respondents noted that this would not always faithfully depict the amount of consideration to which an entity is entitled for satisfying a particular performance obligation. For example, those respondents noted that the allocation of the discount could result in a loss on one part of the contract although the contract as a whole may be profitable (for example, the contract contains both a high-margin item and a low-margin item). They suggested that the boards should permit an entity to allocate the discount in a contract using one of the following alternatives:

(a)   a management approach, in which an entity would assess which promised good or service is priced at a discount to its stand-alone selling price.

(b)   a residual approach, in which any discount in the contract would be allocated entirely to the satisfied performance obligations.

(c)   a profit margin approach, in which an entity would allocate the discount in a contract in proportion to the individual profit margin on each performance obligation. The individual profit margin for each performance obligation is the difference between the stand-alone selling price and the direct costs of the good or service underlying each performance obligation.

BC278   Another consequence of allocating the transaction price on a relative stand-alone selling price basis is that any amount of consideration that is variable will be allocated to each of the performance obligations in the contract. Some respondents noted that this allocation will not always faithfully depict the amount of consideration to which an entity is entitled upon satisfying a particular performance obligation, if the variable consideration does not relate to all of the performance obligations in the contract. Many suggested that any adjustment in the transaction price as a result of variable amounts should be allocated only to the performance obligation(s) to which the variable amounts relate.

BC279 The boards noted that the objective of the revenue recognition model is for an entity to recognise revenue in the amount of consideration to which it expects to be entitled from the customer in exchange for transferring goods or services. The relative stand-alone selling price basis allocation is simply a method to achieve that objective rather than being the allocation principle.

BC280 However, the boards also noted that allocating the transaction price on a relative stand-alone selling price basis brings rigour and discipline to the process of allocating the transaction price and, therefore, enhances comparability both within an entity and across entities. Consequently, the boards decided that it should be the default method for allocating the transaction price. However, they agreed with respondents that it might not always result in a faithful depiction of the amount of consideration to which the entity expects to be entitled from the customer. Accordingly, in paragraphs 81–86 of IFRS 15, the boards specified the circumstances in which other methods should be used.

Allocating discounts (paragraphs 81–83)

BC281 IFRS 15 requires an entity to allocate a discount entirely to one or more, but not all, performance obligations in the contract if the entity has observable selling prices for each performance obligation in the contract and those observable stand-alone selling prices provide evidence that the entire discount in the contract is specifically attributable to one or more of those performance obligations. Those requirements are largely based on the 'contract segmentation' principle that was included in the 2010 Exposure Draft, which only allowed a discount to be allocated entirely to one or more performance obligations on the basis of goods or services that are priced independently.

BC282 Some respondents questioned whether the requirements in paragraph 82 of IFRS 15 for allocating a discount are too restrictive and, therefore, might yield outcomes that are inconsistent with the economics of some transactions. However, the boards noted that the requirements are included to maintain the rigour and discipline of a stand-alone selling price allocation and, thus, appropriately restrict the situations in which a discount should not be allocated pro rata to all performance obligations in the contract.

BC283 The boards also noted that paragraph 82 of IFRS 15 would typically apply to contracts for which there are at least three performance obligations. This is because an entity could demonstrate that a discount relates to two or more performance obligations when it has observable information supporting the stand-alone selling price of a group of those promised goods or services when they are sold together. The boards noted that it may be possible for an entity to have sufficient evidence to be able to allocate a discount to only one performance obligation in accordance with the criteria in paragraph 82, but the boards expected that this could only occur in rare cases.

Allocating variable consideration (paragraphs 84–86)

BC284   The boards agreed with respondents that it would not always be appropriate for an entity to allocate the variable consideration in a transaction price to all of the performance obligations in a contract. For example, an entity may contract to provide two products at different times with a bonus that is contingent on the timely delivery of only the second product. In that example, it might be inappropriate to attribute variable consideration included in the transaction price to both products. Similarly, an entity may contract to provide two products at different times with a fixed amount for the first product that represents that product's stand-alone selling price, and a variable amount that is contingent on the delivery of the second product. That variable amount might be excluded from the estimate of the transaction price (ie because of the requirements for constraining estimates of the transaction price). In that case, it might be inappropriate to attribute the fixed consideration included in the transaction price to both products. Consequently, the boards specified the criteria in paragraphs 84–86 of IFRS 15 to identify the circumstances in which an entity should allocate the variable consideration entirely to a performance obligation or to a distinct good or service (that forms part of a single performance obligation) rather than to the contract as a whole. The boards decided that those criteria are necessary to ensure an appropriate allocation of the transaction price when there is variable consideration in the transaction price.

BC285   The boards clarified in paragraph 84(b) of IFRS 15 that variable consideration can be allocated to distinct goods or services even if those goods or services form a single performance obligation. The boards made this clarification to ensure that an entity can, in some cases, attribute the reassessment of variable consideration to only the satisfied portion of a performance obligation when that performance obligation meets the criterion in paragraph 22(b) of IFRS 15. Consider the example of a contract to provide hotel management services for one year (ie a single performance obligation in accordance with paragraph 22(b) of IFRS 15) in which the consideration is variable and determined based on two per cent of occupancy rates. The entity provides a daily service of management that is distinct and the uncertainty related to the consideration is also resolved on a daily basis when the occupancy occurs. In those circumstances, the boards did not intend for an entity to allocate the variable consideration determined on a daily basis to the entire performance obligation (ie the promise to provide management services over a one-year period). Instead, the variable consideration should be allocated to the distinct service to which the variable consideration relates, which is the daily management service.

Changes in transaction price

BC286   The boards also decided to specify that any subsequent changes in the transaction price should be allocated in a manner that is consistent with the allocation methodology at contract inception. This ensures that changes in the estimate of the variable consideration that are included in (or excluded from) the transaction price are allocated to the performance obligation(s) to which the variable consideration relates. Consequently, the boards specified in paragraph 89 of IFRS 15 that an entity should allocate a change in the transaction price entirely to one or more distinct goods or services if the criteria in paragraph 85 of IFRS 15 are met.

Contingent revenue cap and the portfolio approach to allocation

BC287   Some respondents disagreed with the boards' proposal that the transaction price should be allocated on a relative stand-alone selling price basis. Those respondents (primarily from the telecommunications and cable television industries) disagreed because allocating the transaction price using relative stand-alone selling prices on a contract-by-contract basis could be complex and costly for their industries. This is because entities in those industries:

(a)   have a high volume of contracts with various potential configurations;

(b)   provide multiple goods and services in those contracts;

(c)   include a discount in the contracts; and

(d)   provide the goods or services at different times.

BC288   Those respondents also disagreed with allocating the transaction price on the basis of relative stand-alone selling prices because it would provide a revenue recognition pattern that they considered would not be useful to users of their financial statements.

BC289   Those respondents requested that the boards should carry forward previous revenue recognition requirements in US GAAP (previously referred to as 'the contingent revenue cap'). Those requirements were previously used by many telecommunications entities applying US GAAP and IFRS. In the respondents' view, carrying forward those requirements would have simplified the application of the revenue recognition model by limiting the amount of consideration that a telecommunications entity could allocate to a handset that is bundled with network services to the amount that is not contingent on the delivery of network services in the future. Consequently, revenue would have been recognised at the amount that the customer paid for the handset at contract inception when the handset was transferred to the customer. The remaining contractual payments would have been recognised subsequently as revenue as the entity provided network services to the customer. Many users of financial statements of entities in the telecommunications industry agreed that this revenue recognition pattern would have been useful because it closely relates to the timing of cash received.

BC290   Respondents from the telecommunications industry commented that without a contingent revenue cap, not only will the application of the revenue recognition model be complex, but revenue will also be recognised for delivering a handset in an amount that exceeds the amount of consideration paid for the handset. In their view, this is inappropriate because it will not be useful to users of their financial statements and, in a separate objection, because they will be entitled to collect the excess only when they provide the network services. Consequently, they reasoned that the contract asset that will result from recognising revenue for delivery of the handset will not meet the definition of an asset. In addition, they suggested that without a contingent revenue cap, the model will be complex and costly to apply because of the high volume of contracts that they will have to manage and the various potential configurations of handsets and network service plans.

BC291   However, the boards decided not to carry forward the contingent revenue cap for the following reasons:

     (a)   limiting the amount of consideration that can be allocated to a satisfied performance obligation is tantamount to cash-basis accounting and does not meet the core principle of IFRS 15. This is because revenue recognised would not depict the amount of consideration to which an entity expects to be entitled for the delivered good or service. Consequently, the contingent revenue cap could result in economically similar contracts being accounted for differently.

     (b)   the contingent revenue cap can result in the recognition of losses if the contract is profitable. That would occur if the amount allocated to a satisfied performance obligation is limited to an amount (potentially to zero) that is less than the expenses recognised for the costs of providing the good or service (unless those costs are deferred). However, costs relating to a good or service already transferred to a customer would not give rise to an asset.

     (c)   recognising a contract asset in the situation described in paragraph BC290 is appropriate because the entity has a valuable contractual right as a result of satisfying a performance obligation and that right meets the definition of an asset. That right exists even if the entity does not have the unconditional right to collect consideration from the customer. This is because if the entity were to transfer the remaining rights and performance obligations in the contract to a third party after it had delivered a handset, it would expect to be compensated for that past performance.

     (d)   applying the contingent cap more broadly than it was applied in previous revenue Standards could have had far-reaching consequences. For example, in many service contracts (including construction contracts), it is appropriate to recognise revenue when services are provided even though the amount of consideration is contingent on the entity's future performance. Otherwise, the entity would not recognise any revenue until reaching a contract milestone or potentially until completion of the contract (which would not depict the transfer of goods or services to the customer).

(e) although the consequences for construction and other service contracts could have been reduced by limiting the amount allocated to satisfied performance obligations (rather than limiting the amount allocated to a satisfied portion of a single performance obligation), the boards decided that this would have created an arbitrary distinction and would have put additional pressure on the criteria for identifying performance obligations.

(f) for many contracts that were previously accounted for under the contingent revenue cap, the amount of consideration allocated to delivered items was not contingent because, even if the customer cancelled the contract, the customer would have been obliged to pay for the delivered item(s). For example, in some contracts for the sale of a handset and network services, either the contract was not cancellable or, if it was, the customer was obliged to pay a termination fee that corresponded with the value of the handset that was delivered upfront (even if the entity might choose not to enforce payment of that fee).

BC292 In addition, the boards decided not to introduce an exception to the revenue recognition model for telecommunications and similar contracts because they do not view those contracts as being different from other contracts in which an entity transfers a bundle of goods or services. Furthermore, the boards decided that IFRS 15 provides a more consistent basis for recognising revenue and produces results in accounting that more closely match the underlying economics of transactions.

BC293 The boards also observed that entities in the telecommunications industry may be able to simplify the application of the model by using portfolio techniques (as envisioned by the practical expedient specified in paragraph 4 of IFRS 15) to allocate the transaction price for a group of similar contracts (see paragraphs BC69–BC70). The boards considered whether they should provide more specific guidance as to when an entity could use a portfolio approach for allocating the transaction price. However, the boards decided not to do so because they were concerned that any further guidance (for example, by including criteria that an entity would need to meet to apply a portfolio approach) might make the practical expedient less useful across entities or jurisdictions.

Onerous performance obligations

BC294 In the 2010 and the 2011 Exposure Drafts, the boards proposed including requirements for identifying and measuring onerous performance obligations in contracts with customers (ie an 'onerous test'). In those proposals, the boards concluded that an onerous test was needed because the initial measurements of performance obligations are not routinely updated. In addition, the boards noted that including an onerous test would achieve greater convergence of IFRS and US GAAP.

BC295   However, many respondents to the 2010 and the 2011 Exposure Drafts disagreed with the onerous test and highlighted a number of practical application difficulties. Furthermore, many explained that strict application of the onerous test would have resulted in recognition of liabilities in cases in which the outcome of fulfilling a single performance obligation was onerous but the outcome of fulfilling the entire contract would be profitable. A number of respondents suggested removing the onerous test from the revenue proposals because, in addition to being complex and difficult to apply, the requirements for recognition of onerous losses are already sufficiently addressed in other Standards. Those respondents commented that:

(a)   for IFRS, the onerous test in IAS 37 and the requirements in IAS 2 *Inventories* already provide sufficient guidance for determining when to recognise losses arising from contracts with customers.

(b)   for US GAAP, existing requirements for recognition of losses from contracts are adequate and if a change to those requirements is necessary, that change could instead be handled in a separate project that addresses liabilities in Topic 450.

BC296   The boards agreed that existing requirements in both IFRS and US GAAP could adequately identify onerous contracts. Furthermore, the boards noted that although their existing requirements for onerous contracts are not identical, they are not aware of any pressing practice issues resulting from the application of those existing requirements. Consequently, the boards decided that IFRS 15 should not include an onerous test. Instead, entities applying IFRS or US GAAP will use their respective existing requirements for the identification and measurement of onerous contracts.

Contract costs (paragraphs 91–104)

Incremental costs of obtaining a contract (paragraphs 91–94)

BC297   The boards decided that an entity should recognise as an asset the incremental costs of obtaining a contract with a customer if the entity expects to recover those costs. The boards defined the incremental costs of obtaining a contract as the costs that an entity incurs in its efforts to obtain a contract that would not have been incurred if the contract had not been obtained. The boards acknowledged that, in some cases, an entity's efforts to recognise an asset from incremental acquisition costs might exceed the financial reporting benefits. Consequently, as a practical expedient, the boards decided to allow an entity to recognise those costs as expenses when incurred for contracts in which the amortisation period for the asset that the entity otherwise would have recognised is one year or less.

BC298   The boards considered requiring an entity to recognise all of the costs of obtaining a contract as expenses when those costs are incurred. The boards observed that, conceptually, an entity may obtain a contract asset as a result of its efforts to obtain a contract (because the measure of the remaining rights might exceed the measure of the remaining obligations). However, because the principle in IFRS 15 requires an entity to recognise a contract asset and revenue only as a result of satisfying a performance obligation in the contract, the boards observed that on the basis of that reasoning, the contract asset would be measured at zero at contract inception and any costs of obtaining a contract would therefore be recognised as expenses when incurred.

BC299　Many respondents disagreed with recognising all costs to obtain a contract as expenses when incurred because those costs meet the definition of an asset in some cases. In addition, they noted the following:

(a)　other Standards require some of the costs of obtaining a contract to be included in the carrying amount of an asset on initial recognition; and

(b)　the recognition of the costs of obtaining a contract as expenses would be inconsistent with the tentative decisions in the boards' projects on leases and insurance contracts.

BC300　During the redeliberations, the boards decided that, in some cases, it might be misleading for an entity to recognise all the costs of obtaining a contract as expenses, when incurred. For example, the boards observed that recognising the full amount of a sales commission as an expense at inception of a long-term service contract (when that sales commission is reflected in the pricing of that contract and is expected to be recovered) would fail to acknowledge the existence of an asset.

BC301　Consequently, the boards decided that an entity would recognise an asset from the costs of obtaining a contract and would present the asset separately from the contract asset or the contract liability. To limit the acquisition costs to those that can be clearly identified as relating specifically to a contract, the boards decided that only the incremental costs of obtaining a contract should be included in the measurement of the asset, if the entity expects to recover those costs. The boards decided that determining whether other costs relate to a contract is too subjective.

BC302　The boards noted that it might be difficult for some entities to determine whether a commission payment is incremental to obtaining a new contract (for example, payment of a commission might depend on the entity successfully acquiring several contracts). The boards considered whether to allow an accounting policy election for contract costs, under which an entity would have been able to choose to recognise an asset from the acquisition costs or recognise those costs as an expense (with disclosure of the accounting policy election). The boards noted that this would have been consistent with previous revenue recognition requirements in US GAAP for public entities. However, the boards noted that introducing accounting policy elections into IFRS 15 would have reduced comparability and therefore would not have met one of the key objectives of the Revenue Recognition project to improve comparability in accounting among entities and industries. Consequently, the boards decided not to allow entities an accounting policy election with respect to contract acquisition costs.

BC303   The FASB noted that depending on the specific facts and circumstances of the arrangement between an asset manager and the other parties in the relationship, the application of the requirements for incremental costs of obtaining a contract might have resulted in different accounting for sales commissions paid to third-party brokers (ie in some cases the commission would have been recognised as an asset while in others it would have been recognised as an expense). The FASB observed that it had not intended the application of the cost requirements to result in an outcome for these specific types of sales commissions that would be different from applying existing US GAAP. Consequently, the FASB decided to retain the specific cost requirements for investment companies in paragraph 946-605-25-8 of the Codification which has been moved to Subtopic 946-720 *Financial Services— Investment Companies—Other Expenses*.

Costs to fulfil a contract (paragraphs 95–98)

BC304   The boards developed requirements for accounting for some costs to fulfil a contract. Those requirements were developed in response to concerns that the proposals in the Discussion Paper focused on how an entity should recognise revenue in a contract without considering how the entity should account for the costs to fulfil a contract. Some respondents, particularly those from the construction industry, said that requirements for profit margin recognition are as important as requirements for revenue recognition. Other respondents, mainly preparers who apply US GAAP, were concerned about the withdrawal of requirements for costs that were developed specifically for their own industries.

BC305   The cost requirements in IFRS 15 are intended to achieve the following:

(a)   fill the gap arising from the withdrawal of previous revenue Standards — IFRS 15 will result in the withdrawal of some requirements for contract costs, in particular, the previous requirements for accounting for construction contracts.

(b)   improve current practice—the cost requirements provide clearer requirements for accounting for some costs to fulfil a contract (for example, setup costs for services) and result in an entity no longer having to rely on, or analogise to, requirements that were not developed specifically for contracts with customers. For instance, in accounting for setup costs, an entity applying US GAAP may previously have needed to analogise to the guidance on the deferral of direct loan origination costs in paragraph 310-20-25-2 of the Codification. An entity applying IFRS may have evaluated those costs in accordance with IAS 38 *Intangible Assets*. Specifying clear requirements will also result in greater consistency in practice.

(c)   promote convergence in accounting for contract costs—more costs will be accounted for similarly under IFRS and US GAAP (although total consistency in accounting for costs to fulfil a contract will not be achieved unless the boards align their respective Standards on inventories; property, plant and equipment; intangible assets and impairment of assets).

BC306 Most respondents supported the boards' inclusion of requirements that address some of the costs to fulfil a contract. Some respondents recommended that the boards address cost requirements comprehensively in a separate project. However, because cost requirements are included in many Standards (such as the ones described in paragraph BC305(c)), the boards noted that this would require reconsideration of those Standards and, therefore, decided against broadening the scope of the cost requirements.

BC307 Because the boards decided not to reconsider all cost requirements comprehensively, paragraphs 91–98 of IFRS 15 specify the accounting for contract costs that are not within the scope of other Standards. Consequently, if the other Standards preclude the recognition of any asset arising from a particular cost, an asset cannot then be recognised under IFRS 15 (for example, in IFRS, initial operating losses, such as those incurred while demand for an item builds, will continue to be accounted for in accordance with paragraph 20(b) of IAS 16 and, in US GAAP, pre-production costs under long-term supply arrangements will continue to be accounted for in accordance with paragraphs 340-10-25-5 through 25-8 of the Codification).

BC308 IFRS 15 clarifies that only costs that give rise to resources that will be used in satisfying performance obligations in the future and that are expected to be recovered are eligible for recognition as assets. Those requirements ensure that only costs that meet the definition of an asset are recognised as such and that an entity is precluded from deferring costs merely to normalise profit margins throughout a contract by allocating revenue and costs evenly over the life of the contract. To provide a clear objective for recognising and measuring an asset arising from the costs to fulfil a contract, the boards decided that only costs that relate directly to a contract should be included in the cost of the asset.

Amortisation and impairment (paragraphs 99–104)

BC309 The boards decided that an entity should amortise the asset recognised from the costs of obtaining and fulfilling a contract in accordance with the pattern of transfer of goods or services to which the asset relates. Respondents broadly agreed; however, some asked the boards to clarify whether those goods or services could relate to future contracts. Consequently, the boards clarified that in amortising the asset in accordance with the transfer of goods or services to which the asset relates, those goods or services could be provided under a specifically anticipated (ie future) contract. That conclusion is consistent with the notion of amortising an asset over its useful life and with other Standards. However, amortising the asset over a longer period than the initial contract would not be appropriate in situations in which an entity pays a commission on a contract renewal that is commensurate with the commission paid on the initial contract. In that case, the acquisition costs from the initial contract do not relate to the subsequent contract.

BC310   The boards considered testing a recognised asset arising from fulfilment costs for impairment using one of the existing impairment tests in their respective requirements (for example, IAS 2 and IAS 36 *Impairment of Assets* or Topic 330 *Inventory*, Topic 360 *Property, Plant and Equipment* and Subtopic 985-20 *Software — Costs of Software to Be Sold, Leased, or Marketed*). However, the boards decided that an entity should consider only the economic benefits in the contract with the customer and, consequently, the impairment test should be based on comparing the carrying amount of the asset with the remaining amount of promised consideration in exchange for the goods or services to which the asset relates, less the remaining costs of providing those goods or services. The boards decided that for purposes of impairment testing, the entity should consider future cash flows that may be too uncertain to include in the recognition of revenue (see paragraphs BC203–BC223). The boards decided this because their objective for measuring and recognising impairments of contract acquisition and fulfilment costs is different from the measurement objective for revenue. The impairment objective is to determine whether the carrying amount of the contract acquisition and fulfilment costs asset is recoverable. Consequently, the measurement objective is consistent with other impairment methods in IFRS and US GAAP that include an assessment of customer credit risk and expectations of whether amounts of variable consideration will be received.

BC311   The FASB decided that an entity should not reverse an impairment charge when the reasons for the impairment no longer exist. Conversely, the IASB decided that the impairment charge should be reversed in those circumstances under IFRS. The boards acknowledged that this would result in entities accounting differently for those contract costs using IFRS and US GAAP. However, the boards decided that it is important for the requirements to be consistent with their respective impairment models for other types of assets and those impairment models differ in their accounting for reversals of impairments.

Learning curve

BC312   A 'learning curve' is the effect of efficiencies realised over time when an entity's costs of performing a task (or producing a unit) decline in relation to how many times the entity performs that task (or produces that unit). The phenomenon of a learning curve can exist independently of a contract with a customer. For example, a typical manufacturer that produces units of inventory would become more efficient in its production process over time. Some respondents asked how to apply the proposals to account for the effects of learning costs in a contract with a customer.

BC313   The boards noted that IFRS 15 addresses the accounting for the effects of learning costs if both of the following conditions are satisfied:

(a)   an entity has a single performance obligation to deliver a specified number of units; and

(b)   the performance obligation is satisfied over time.

BC314   In that situation, an entity recognises revenue by selecting a method of measuring progress that depicts the transfer over time of the good or service to the customer. An entity would probably select a method (for example, cost-to-cost) that results in the entity recognising more revenue and expense for the early units produced relative to the later units. That effect is appropriate because of the greater value of the entity's performance in the early part of the contract because, if an entity were to sell only one unit, it would charge the customer a higher price for that unit than the average unit price the customer pays when the customer purchases more than one unit.

BC315   In other situations, an entity may promise to deliver a specified number of units in a contract, but that promise does not give rise to a single performance obligation that is satisfied over time. The boards decided that, in those situations, an entity should apply the requirements of other Standards (for example, IAS 2) for the following reasons:

(a)   if an entity incurs costs to fulfil a contract without also satisfying a performance obligation over time, the entity probably would be creating an asset included within the scope of other Standards (for example, the costs of producing tangible units would accumulate as inventory, and the entity would select an appropriate method of measuring that inventory). In those cases, the boards decided that an entity should not account for the learning curve differently depending on whether or not a contract exists.

(b)   the type of contract described in this paragraph is not the type of contract typically entered into by respondents who asked how the requirements of IFRS 15 would apply to learning curve effects (in most cases, those respondents enter into contracts that would be accounted for as a performance obligation satisfied over time).

BC316   The boards, however, acknowledged the diversity in practice when accounting (in accordance with other Standards) for the costs of products produced under long-term production programmes, but agreed that they could not address these matters as part of the Revenue Recognition project.

Presentation (paragraphs 105–109)

BC317   The boards decided that the remaining rights and performance obligations in a contract should be accounted for and presented on a net basis, as either a contract asset or a contract liability. The boards noted that the rights and obligations in a contract with a customer are interdependent—the right to receive consideration from a customer depends on the entity's performance and, similarly, the entity performs only as long as the customer continues to pay. The boards decided that those interdependencies are best reflected by accounting and presenting on a net basis the remaining rights and obligations in the statement of financial position.

BC318   The boards considered whether the rights and performance obligations in contracts that are subject to the legal remedy of specific performance should be presented on a gross basis, that is, as separate assets and liabilities. The boards observed that in the event of a breach of contract, some contracts require the entity and the customer to perform as specified in the contract. Consequently, unlike most contracts that can be settled net, specific performance contracts generally result in a two-way flow of resources between the customer and the entity. Specific performance contracts are akin to financial contracts that are settled by physical delivery rather than by a net cash payment and for which the units of account are the individual assets and liabilities arising from the contractual rights and obligations.

BC319   However, the boards decided against making an exception for specific performance contracts. This is because the remedy of specific performance is relatively rare and is not available in all jurisdictions. In addition, it is only one of a number of possible remedies that could be awarded by a court if legal action were taken for breach of contract.

BC320   The boards decided that IFRS 15 should not specify whether an entity is required to present its contract assets and contract liabilities as separate line items in the statement of financial position. Instead, an entity should apply the general principles for the presentation of financial statements to determine whether to present contract assets and contract liabilities separately in the statement of financial position. For example, IAS 1 *Presentation of Financial Statements* requires an entity to present separately each class of similar items and items of a dissimilar nature or function unless they are immaterial.

BC321   The boards also observed that some industries have historically used different labels to describe contract assets and contract liabilities or may recognise them in more than one line item either in the financial statements or in the notes. Because that additional detail is often useful to users of those financial statements, the boards decided that an entity could use different descriptions of contract assets, contract liabilities and receivables, and could use additional line items to present those assets and liabilities if the entity also provides sufficient information for users of financial statements to be able to distinguish them.

Relationship between contract assets and receivables

BC322   When an entity performs first by satisfying a performance obligation before a customer performs by paying the consideration, the entity has a contract asset —a right to consideration from the customer in exchange for goods or services transferred to the customer.

BC323   In many cases, that contract asset is an unconditional right to consideration— a receivable—because only the passage of time is required before payment of that consideration is due. However, in other cases, an entity satisfies a performance obligation but does not have an unconditional right to consideration, for example, because it first needs to satisfy another performance obligation in the contract. The boards decided that when an entity satisfies a performance obligation but does not have an unconditional right to consideration, an entity should recognise a contract asset in accordance with IFRS 15. The boards noted that making the distinction between a contract asset and a receivable is important because doing so provides users of financial statements with relevant information about the risks associated with the entity's rights in a contract. That is because although both would be subject to credit risk, a contract asset is also subject to other risks, for example, performance risk.

BC324   Once an entity has an unconditional right to consideration, it should present that right as a receivable separately from the contract asset and account for it in accordance with other requirements (for example, IFRS 9 or Topic 310). The boards decided that IFRS 15 need not address the accounting for receivables in addition to revenue recognition. Issues such as the measurement (or impairment) of receivables and disclosures relating to those assets are already addressed in IFRS and US GAAP.

BC325   In many cases, an unconditional right to consideration arises when the entity satisfies the performance obligation and invoices the customer. For example, a payment for goods or services is typically due and an invoice is issued when the entity has transferred the goods or services to the customer. However, the act of invoicing the customer for payment does not indicate whether the entity has an unconditional right to consideration. For instance, the entity may have an unconditional right to consideration before it invoices (unbilled receivable) if only the passage of time is required before payment of that consideration is due. In other cases, an entity can have an unconditional right to consideration before it has satisfied a performance obligation. For example, an entity may enter into a non-cancellable contract that requires the customer to pay the consideration a month before the entity provides goods or services. In those cases, on the date when payment is due, the entity has an unconditional right to consideration. (However, in those cases, the entity should recognise revenue only after it transfers the goods or services.)

BC326   The boards observed that in some cases, an entity will have an unconditional right to consideration, even though the entity may be required to refund some or all of that consideration in the future. In those cases, the possible obligation to refund consideration in the future will not affect the entity's present right to be entitled to the gross amount of consideration. In those cases, the boards observed that an entity may recognise a receivable and a refund liability (for example, when a right of return exists).

Disclosure (paragraphs 110–129)

BC327   Some of the main criticisms from regulators and users of financial statements about prior revenue Standards in IFRS and US GAAP related to the disclosure requirements. Broadly, regulators and users of financial statements found the disclosure requirements to be inadequate and lacking cohesion with the disclosure of other items in the financial statements. This lack of cohesion made it difficult to understand an entity's revenues, as well as the judgements and estimates made by the entity in recognising those revenues. For example, many users of financial statements observed that entities presented revenue in isolation, with the result that users of financial statements could not relate revenue to the entity's financial position. Consequently, one of the boards' goals in undertaking the Revenue Recognition project was to provide users of financial statements with more useful information through improved disclosure requirements. Many respondents broadly supported that goal. However, respondents' views about the proposed disclosure requirements in the 2011 Exposure Draft were polarised—users of financial statements supported the proposed disclosure requirements because those requirements would have been a significant improvement over previous requirements. In contrast, other respondents (primarily preparers) noted that, when viewed as a whole, the proposed disclosure requirements would have resulted in voluminous disclosures and they questioned whether the proposed disclosures were justifiable on a cost-benefit basis.

BC328　Because of those polarised views, the boards held workshops with users of financial statements and preparers between September and December 2012 in London (United Kingdom), Tokyo (Japan), and Norwalk and New York City (United States). The objective of those workshops was to discuss issues on disclosure and transition and to identify potential solutions to address both users' needs for useful information and preparers' concerns about the costs of providing that information. As a result of the feedback provided through workshops, other outreach efforts and the comment letters, the boards refined the disclosure requirements proposed in the 2011 Exposure Draft. Those refinements and the reasons for the boards' decisions are explained in paragraphs BC330–BC361.

BC329　The boards noted that the disclosure requirements in paragraphs 110–129 of IFRS 15 are comprehensive and represent a significant improvement from previous requirements. Some may observe that the overall volume of disclosure has increased compared with previous revenue disclosure requirements. However, the boards observed that, to some extent, concerns about the increased volume were the inevitable consequence of addressing the shortcoming in the previous disclosure requirements. In addition, the boards noted that many entities provide voluntary revenue disclosures outside the financial statements and the boards concluded that the increase in disclosure is necessary to improve previous disclosure practices and the usefulness of financial reporting.

Disclosure objective and materiality (paragraphs 110–112)

BC330　The boards decided that, consistently with other recent Standards, IFRS 15 should specify an objective for the revenue disclosures. In the boards' view, a clear objective improves the interpretation and implementation of the disclosure requirements. This is because a preparer can assess whether the overall quality and informational value of its revenue disclosures are sufficient to meet the stated objectives. The boards also observed that specifying an overall disclosure objective avoids the need for detailed and prescriptive disclosure requirements to accommodate the many and varied types of contracts with customers that are within the scope of IFRS 15.

BC331　The boards also decided to include disclosure requirements to help an entity meet the disclosure objective. However, those disclosures should not be viewed as a checklist of minimum disclosures, because some disclosures may be relevant for some entities or industries but may be irrelevant for others. The boards also observed that it is important for an entity to consider the disclosures together with the disclosure objective and materiality. Consequently, paragraph 111 of IFRS 15 clarifies that an entity need not disclose information that is immaterial.

Contracts with customers

BC332　To provide context for the disclosures, the boards decided to require an entity to disclose the amount of revenue recognised from contracts with customers. The FASB noted that in the absence of a general financial statement presentation standard, it would require an entity to present or disclose the amount of revenue recognised from contracts with customers. However, the IASB noted that the general principles of IAS 1 would apply and, therefore, an entity would need to disclose the amount of revenue recognised from contracts with customers in the notes to the financial statements only if it was not otherwise presented.

BC333　In addition to the amount of revenue recognised, the boards also decided to require an entity to disclose impairment losses from contracts with customers (if not presented in the statement of comprehensive income). The boards made this decision as a consequence of their previous decisions not to reflect customer credit risk in the measurement of the transaction price and, therefore, the amount of revenue recognised for transactions that do not include a significant financing component (see paragraphs BC259–BC265). This is reflected in the core principle of IFRS 15 that specifies that an entity recognise revenue at an amount that reflects the consideration to which the entity expects to be entitled.

BC334　In the light of those decisions, the boards decided that separately disclosing (or presenting) the impairment losses on contracts with customers provides the most relevant information to users of financial statements.

Disaggregation of revenue (paragraphs 114–115)

BC335　Revenue recognised in the statement of comprehensive income is a composite amount arising from many contracts with customers. This is because revenue can arise from the transfer of different goods or services and from contracts that involve different types of customers or markets. Users of financial statements explained that understanding those differences was critical to their analyses. Consequently, the boards decided to require an entity to provide disaggregated revenue information to help users of financial statements understand the composition of the revenue from contracts with customers recognised in the current period.

BC336   In developing the requirements for disclosing disaggregated revenue, the boards observed that some previous revenue recognition requirements required revenue to be disaggregated into its significant categories, including revenue arising from goods or services. However, because the most useful disaggregation of revenue depends on various entity-specific or industry-specific factors, the boards decided that IFRS 15 should not prescribe any specific factor to be used as the basis for disaggregating revenue from contracts with customers. Instead, the boards decided to specify in paragraph 114 of IFRS 15 an objective for providing disaggregated information. The boards noted that specifying an objective will result in the most useful information for users of financial statements, because it enables an entity to disaggregate revenue into categories that are meaningful for its business. In addition, specifying an objective should result in disaggregation that is neither too aggregated nor too detailed.

BC337   The boards also decided to provide application guidance because of requests for additional guidance about how to implement the objective and, in particular, how to determine the appropriate categories that an entity may use to disaggregate revenue from contracts with customers. The application guidance explains that the most appropriate categories depend on facts and circumstances; however, an entity should consider how revenue is disaggregated in other communications or for the purposes of evaluating financial performance. This is because entities often already disaggregate revenue in those communications and the categories used may be those that are most useful for users of financial statements and that meet the objective in paragraph 114 of IFRS 15. The application guidance also includes a list of examples of categories (for example, geographical region or product type) by which an entity might disaggregate its revenue. The boards noted that the list of categories was compiled as examples that could be applied to many different entities, industries and contracts. As a result, the list should not be viewed either as a checklist or as an exhaustive list. However, the boards observed that an entity may need to disaggregate by more than one category to meet the objective.

BC338   The boards also decided to require that an entity explain the relationship between the disaggregated revenue information required by paragraph 114 of IFRS 15 and the segment information required by IFRS 8 *Operating Segments* and Topic 280 *Segment Reporting*. The boards decided this because users of financial statements explained that it is critical to their analyses to understand not only the composition of revenue, but also how that revenue relates to other information provided in segment disclosures such as costs of goods sold, expenses and assets used.

BC339   In developing the requirements, the boards also considered whether the current segment reporting requirements in IFRS 8 and Topic 280 provided adequate information for users of financial statements in understanding the composition of revenue. Those requirements require an entity to disaggregate and disclose revenue for each operating segment (reconciled to total revenue). In addition, those requirements also require an entity to disaggregate total revenue by products or services (or by groups of similar products or services) and geographical areas – if the entity's operating segments are not based on those factors.

BC340 However, despite some similarity to segment reporting, the boards decided to require disaggregated revenue information for revenue from contracts with customers in IFRS 15 because some entities are exempt from providing segment disclosures (for example, entities that are not listed on a public stock exchange). Furthermore, the boards observed that segment information might be based on non-GAAP information (ie the revenue that is reported to the chief operating decision maker may be recognised and measured on a basis that is not in accordance with IFRS 15). The boards also observed that the objective of providing segment information in accordance with IFRS 8 or Topic 280 is different from the objective for the disaggregation disclosure in IFRS 15 and, therefore, segment revenue disclosures may not always provide users of financial statements with enough information to help them understand the composition of revenue recognised in the period. Nonetheless, the boards clarified in paragraph 112 of IFRS 15 that an entity does not need to provide disaggregated revenue disclosures if the information about revenue provided in accordance with IFRS 8 or Topic 280 meets the requirements specified in paragraph 114 of IFRS 15 and those revenue disclosures are based on the recognition and measurement requirements in IFRS 15.

Contract balances (paragraphs 116–118)

BC341 Users of financial statements explained that they need to understand the relationship between the revenue recognised in a reporting period and the changes in the balances of the entity's contract assets and contract liabilities (ie contract balances) to assess the nature, amount, timing and uncertainty of revenue and cash flows arising from an entity's contracts with customers. Those users of financial statements noted that even though many entities currently recognise working capital balances such as unbilled receivables and deferred revenue, previous revenue recognition requirements did not require adequate disclosure about the relationship between those balances and the amount of revenue recognised. Consequently, the 2010 and the 2011 Exposure Drafts proposed that an entity disclose a reconciliation of the contract asset and the contract liability balances in a tabular format.

BC342 However, many preparers strongly opposed any requirements to reconcile the contract asset and the contract liability balances in a tabular format. Those preparers noted that it would be costly to compile and present the information because it was not tracked. Preparers also questioned the usefulness of this reconciliation to users of financial statements, because the information was not used by management. In contrast, users of financial statements reiterated that some of the information in the reconciliation would be useful, including the information about contract liabilities, which would provide greater transparency about future revenues, which is critical to their analyses. However, users of financial statements also acknowledged that the rigid format of the proposed reconciliation had limitations that would have reduced its usefulness. This is because, for example, changes in contract assets and contract liabilities would have been disclosed on an aggregate basis (ie changes in contract assets would have been offset by changes in contract liabilities) and, therefore, the extent of the changes in contract balances (and the reasons for those changes) would have been obscured.

BC343 In the discussion at the disclosure and transition workshops in 2012 (see paragraph BC328), preparers agreed that they could provide further information about contract balances that would be useful to users of financial statements. However, to limit the costs of providing that information, those preparers explained that they need greater flexibility in the format of this disclosure. Users of financial statements emphasised that it was critical to them to have information on the movements in the contract balances presented separately because it would help them understand information about the following:

(a) the amount of the opening balance of the contract liability balance that will be recognised as revenue during the period; and

(b) the amount of the opening balance of the contract asset that will be transferred to accounts receivable or collected in cash during the period.

BC344 Before addressing concerns about format, the boards considered whether they could address the cost concerns of preparers by limiting the scope of the reconciliation requirements to only contract balances for specific types of contracts (for example, long-term contracts). They did this because many users of financial statements observed that information about contract balances would be particularly important for entities that enter into long-term contracts with customers or that carry significant contract liability balances for other reasons (for example, prepaid service contracts). However, the boards rejected this alternative for the following reasons:

(a) it would have been difficult to clearly identify the types of contracts or industries for which a reconciliation would (or would not) provide useful information.

(b) limiting the scope of the reconciliation would have added complexity. This is because limiting the scope could have resulted in excluding some of an entity's contract assets and contract liabilities from the reconciliation and, therefore, additional information would have been required to relate the reconciled amounts of contract assets or contract liabilities to those recognised in the statement of financial position.

(c) information on contract balances is useful for other contracts, in addition to long-term contracts, because, for example, there may be a number of contracts or businesses that have significant timing differences between payment and performance.

BC345 In the light of their decision not to limit the scope of the disclosure, the boards considered whether they could instead modify the format of the disclosure to address the concerns of preparers and users of financial statements. The boards observed that neither users of financial statements nor preparers supported the format proposed in the 2010 and the 2011 Exposure Drafts because users of financial statements were concerned that the information about the movements in the contract balances was too aggregated to be useful and because preparers were concerned about the cost of compliance with such a rigid format. The boards acknowledged that a previously rejected alternative format of a gross reconciliation of contract balances (ie to show the remaining contractual rights and performance obligations in separate columns) would have been inappropriate because it would not respond to preparers' concerns about costs. This is because the cost of preparing and auditing the gross reconciliation would have been high, and possibly higher than the 'net' reconciliation proposed in the 2011 Exposure Draft, because an entity would have been required to measure all unperformed contracts which would have required a high level of judgement.

BC346   Consequently, the boards decided that, instead of requiring a tabular reconciliation of the aggregate contract balances, they would require an entity to disclose qualitative and quantitative information about the entity's contract balances (see paragraphs 116–118 of IFRS 15). This approach balances the needs of users of financial statements with preparers' concerns because the qualitative and quantitative disclosures provide users of financial statements with the information they requested (ie information on when contract assets are typically transferred to accounts receivable or collected as cash and when contract liabilities are recognised as revenue). In addition, the boards decided that those disclosures would be more cost-effective than a reconciliation. The boards also observed that this approach would not result in a significant change for many entities that are already disclosing similar information. For example, the boards observed that some long-term construction entities already disclosed information relating to balances similar to contract assets and contract liabilities – often referred to as 'due from customers' or 'unbilled accounts receivable' and 'due to customers' or 'deferred revenue'.

BC347   The boards also decided to require that an entity disclose the amount of revenue recognised in the period that relates to amounts allocated to performance obligations that were satisfied (or partially satisfied) in previous periods (for example, as a result of a change in transaction price or estimates related to the constraint on revenue recognised). Disclosing those amounts provides relevant information about the timing of revenue recognition that was not a result of performance in the current period and thus provides useful information about the current period operating results and on predicting future revenues. In addition, the boards noted that this information is not provided elsewhere in the financial statements. Finally, the boards noted that, consistent with general materiality requirements, they did not expect this disclosure to be provided if the amounts are immaterial.

Disclosure of the transaction price allocated to the remaining performance obligations (paragraphs 120–122)

BC348   Many users of financial statements explained that information about the amount and timing of revenue that the entity expects to recognise from its existing contracts would be useful in their analyses of revenue. They also explained that the information would be most useful for long-term contracts, because those contracts typically have the most significant amounts of unrecognised revenue.

BC349   The boards observed that a number of entities often voluntarily disclose information about their long-term contracts, which is commonly referred to as 'backlog' information. (Some entities are also required to produce this information outside the financial statements in regulatory filings.) However, this information is typically presented outside the financial statements and may not be comparable across entities because there is not a common definition of backlog.

BC350   In the light of those factors, the boards decided to specify disclosure requirements to capture information about the amount and timing of revenue that an entity expects to recognise from the remaining performance obligations in the entity's existing contracts. The boards observed that by disclosing that information, an entity would provide users of the entity's financial statements with additional information about the following:

     (a)   the amount and expected timing of revenue to be recognised from the remaining performance obligations in existing contracts;

     (b)   trends relating to the amount and expected timing of revenue to be recognised from the remaining performance obligations in existing contracts;

     (c)   risks associated with expected future revenue (for example, some observe that revenue is more uncertain if an entity does not expect to satisfy a performance obligation until a much later date); and

     (d)   the effect of changes in judgements or circumstances on an entity's revenue.

BC351   Many respondents (including most preparers) disagreed with the boards' decision to require such information to be disclosed in the financial statements. Those respondents highlighted different reasons for their disagreement, as follows:

     (a)   the disclosure would be difficult and costly to prepare and audit because existing accounting systems are not designed to track and capture the required information, including the information on scheduling the timing of the satisfaction of those remaining performance obligations.

     (b)   the information provided by the disclosure could be misinterpreted because, depending on the nature of the entity's business(es), the disclosure may give prominence to only a relatively small subset of the entity's potential future revenues. In addition, the disclosure may include less information than the entity previously included in its backlog disclosure because future and cancellable executory contracts are excluded from the scope of the disclosure.

     (c)   the information appeared to be forward-looking in nature and thus should not be presented in the notes to the financial statements.

     © IFRS Foundation

BC352 In redeliberating the disclosure requirements, taking into consideration the feedback received at the disclosure workshops, the boards observed that the requirement to disclose information about remaining performance obligations should not impose significant incremental costs on an entity because the entity is already required by the revenue recognition requirements to determine and allocate the transaction price to the remaining performance obligations. Nonetheless, the boards decided to address preparers' concerns about costs of preparation as follows:

(a) providing practical expedients to limit the scope of the disclosure (see paragraph 121 of IFRS 15). The boards decided that including the practical expedient in paragraph 121(a) of IFRS 15 would ease the burden for the preparation of the disclosure and yet would not significantly decrease the usefulness of the information for users of financial statements. This is because users indicated that information for remaining performance obligations is most critical to their analyses when the contracts are long-term. In addition, including the practical expedient in paragraph 121(b) of IFRS 15 would maintain the relief provided to an entity in paragraph B16 of IFRS 15 on measuring progress for those performance obligations (ie performance obligations for which the entity has a right to consideration that corresponds directly with its performance completed to date). The boards provided practical expedients rather than specifically limiting the scope because some preparers commented that it would be easier for them to comply with the requirement from an accounting systems and processes perspective if they could choose to include all of their remaining performance obligations in the disclosure.

(b) eliminating the prescriptive approach to disclosing when the entity expects to satisfy its remaining performance obligations (see paragraph 120 of IFRS 15). Initially, the boards proposed that an entity should follow a prescriptive approach in determining when the entity expects to satisfy its remaining performance obligations (ie by requiring a quantitative disclosure of the remaining performance obligations, scheduled into one-year time bands). However, many respondents disagreed with that proposal on the basis that the rigid nature of the prescribed time bands would imply a degree of precision in the timing of revenue recognition that may not exist and, furthermore, would increase the costs of preparation. In response to that feedback, the boards decided to permit an entity to estimate and present such information either on a quantitative basis, with time bands that are most appropriate for the duration of the remaining performance obligations (ie not necessarily one-year time bands) or by using qualitative information (or both).

BC353 Some users of financial statements also asked for more information to be provided about the relationship between the amounts disclosed as an entity's remaining performance obligations and the entity's contract liabilities. (A contract liability arises if an entity receives consideration from a customer before the entity satisfies its performance obligations to the customer.) This is because the amount of the remaining performance obligations for which cash has been received is useful information. However, the boards noted that contract liabilities are a subset of the amounts disclosed as the transaction price allocated to the remaining performance obligations and paragraph 116(a) of IFRS 15 already requires the contract liability balance to be disclosed. Consequently, the boards decided that no further disclosures should be required.

Performance obligations (paragraph 119)

BC354   Previous requirements in IFRS and US GAAP require entities to disclose their accounting policies for recognising revenue (see paragraph 10(e) of IAS 1 and the requirements in Topic 235 *Notes to Financial Statements*). However, users of financial statements suggested that in many cases, an entity provides a 'boilerplate' description of the accounting policy adopted without explaining how the accounting policy relates to the contracts that the entity enters into with customers. To address this criticism, paragraph 119 of IFRS 15 requires that an entity disclose information about its performance obligations in contracts with customers. This disclosure complements the accounting policy disclosure requirements in existing Standards by requiring an entity to provide more descriptive information about its performance obligations.

Significant judgements (paragraphs 123–126)

BC355   IFRS and US GAAP have general requirements for disclosing significant accounting estimates and judgements made by an entity. Because of the importance placed on revenue by users of financial statements, the boards decided to require specific disclosures about the estimates used and the judgements made in determining the amount and timing of revenue recognition.

Assets recognised from the costs to obtain or fulfil a contract with a customer (paragraphs 127–128)

BC356   The boards decided to require that an entity disclose information about assets that it recognises from the costs to obtain or fulfil a contract, because information about those assets is useful to users. That information will help users of financial statements understand the types of costs that the entity has recognised as assets and how those assets are subsequently amortised or impaired. The boards also decided that this disclosure was necessary to replace some of the previous disclosure requirements that were superseded by IFRS 15.

BC357   The boards decided not to require that information to be provided as a reconciliation because the cost of providing such a rigid disclosure would outweigh the benefit to users. In addition, most users agreed that the disclosure about the assets recognised from the costs to obtain or fulfil a contract did not need to be provided as a reconciliation to provide relevant information. Consequently, the boards decided to require disclosure of only the most critical information about assets recognised from the costs to obtain or fulfil a contract.

Disclosures required for interim financial reports

BC358　The boards observed that in the absence of more specific disclosure requirements for interim financial reports, an entity should apply IAS 34 *Interim Financial Reporting* or Topic 270 *Interim Reporting* to determine the information about revenue from contracts with customers that the entity should disclose in its interim financial reports. Those requirements require, as a general principle, an entity to disclose information about significant changes in its financial position and performance since the end of the last annual reporting period. The boards considered whether to amend IAS 34 and Topic 270 to specify that the entity provide the same quantitative disclosures about revenue in its interim financial reports as those in its annual financial statements.

BC359　Many preparers and other respondents broadly disagreed with the boards' proposals to make amendments to IAS 34 and Topic 270. They explained that requiring all of the quantitative disclosures in interim financial reports would be too burdensome and difficult to achieve in the short time frames required for interim reporting. In contrast, users of financial statements had mixed views. Some users (including nearly all US-based users) suggested that IAS 34 and Topic 270 should be amended to require the quantitative disclosures because of the importance of revenue and the need to have timely disclosures provided regularly in the interim financial reports. However, other users of financial statements explained that only the information about the disaggregation of revenue was critical to their interim analyses. Those users of financial statements also explained that timeliness in interim reporting was critical and that a requirement to provide other interim disclosures might unnecessarily delay the issuance of interim financial reports.

BC360　The IASB and the FASB reached different decisions on the amendments to IAS 34 and Topic 270. The IASB decided to amend IAS 34 to only add specific requirements that an entity should disclose disaggregated revenue information in interim financial reports. For all other disclosures related to revenue from contracts with customers, the IASB decided that the general principles of IAS 34 should apply. The IASB decided to add to IAS 34 a requirement to disclose disaggregated revenue information because users of financial statements explained that disaggregation was critical to their analyses and because the information is typically already provided in interim financial statements; therefore, the requirement should not result in an entity incurring significant incremental costs. Furthermore, the general principle of IAS 34 to disclose information about an entity's significant changes in financial position and performance should provide users of financial statements with the other information they need about revenue at an interim reporting period. The IASB decided not to make further changes to IAS 34 without a more comprehensive review of the role of disclosure in interim financial reporting.

BC361　The FASB decided to amend Topic 270 to require the same quantitative disclosures about revenue in its interim financial reports as those in its annual financial statements (excluding the cost disclosures). The FASB noted that it is helpful to provide entities with certainty about the information that should be provided in interim financial reports. In addition, the FASB observed that an entity would be compiling most of the information required for the disclosures on an interim basis for the purposes of revenue recognition, and therefore disclosing that information might not result in a significant amount of incremental costs. The FASB also observed that this information is useful to users of financial statements in assessing an entity's current and future financial performance.

Application guidance (paragraphs B2–B89)

BC362   The boards decided to include application guidance to clarify how the principles in IFRS 15 should be applied, including how those principles should be applied to features found in a number of typical contracts with customers. Some of that application guidance has been included based on previous requirements in IFRS or US GAAP that arose as a result of entities requesting clarification in more complex areas of revenue recognition. However, to be consistent with the objective of developing a single revenue recognition model, the boards did not provide requirements that would have applied only to specific industries (see paragraphs BC2–BC3).

Sale with a right of return (paragraphs B20–B27)

BC363   In some contracts, an entity transfers a good to a customer and also grants the customer the right to return it. The boards decided that, conceptually, a contract with a right of return includes at least two performance obligations —a performance obligation to provide the good to the customer and a performance obligation for the return right service, which is a stand-ready obligation to accept the goods returned by the customer during the return period.

BC364   In relation to performance obligations to provide customers with goods, the boards decided that, in effect, an entity has made an uncertain number of sales. This is because it is only after the return right expires that the entity will know with certainty how many sales it has made (ie how many sales did not fail). Consequently, the boards decided that an entity should not recognise revenue for the sales that are expected to fail as a result of customers exercising their return rights. Instead, the entity should recognise a liability for its obligation to refund amounts to customers.

BC365   The boards decided that in determining the amount of revenue to recognise (ie the amount of the refund obligation), an entity should use the principles for recognising and measuring variable consideration. Using those principles, an entity would recognise revenue only to the extent that it is highly probable that a significant reversal in the amount of cumulative revenue recognised will not occur when the uncertainty associated with the right of return is subsequently resolved. When the entity determines that it cannot recognise all of the consideration received as revenue for the sale of goods with a right of return, the entity would recognise some of the consideration received as a refund liability.

BC366   The boards considered whether to account for the return right service as a performance obligation, in addition to any refund liability that is recognised. If an entity does not recognise a performance obligation for the return right service, it should recognise all of the revenue and margin in the contract once the customer obtains control of the good. That outcome might not faithfully depict the entity's performance under the contract. However, the boards noted that accounting for the return right service as a performance obligation, in addition to the refund liability, would typically require the entity to estimate the stand-alone selling price of that service. Because, in many cases, the number of returns is expected to be only a small percentage of the total sales and the return period is often short (such as 30 days), the boards decided that the incremental information provided to users of financial statements by accounting for the return right service as a performance obligation would not have justified the complexities and costs of doing so. Consequently, the boards decided that the return right service should not be accounted for as a performance obligation.

BC367   A return right gives an entity a contractual right to recover the good from a customer if the customer exercises its option to return the good and obtain a refund. The boards decided that the right to recover the good should be recognised as an asset rather than offset against the refund liability. The boards observed that recognising the asset separately from the refund liability provides greater transparency and ensures that the asset is considered for impairment testing.

Warranties (paragraphs B28–B33)

BC368   When an entity sells a product (whether that product is a good or service) to a customer, the entity may also provide the customer with a warranty on that product. The warranty might be described as, for example, a manufacturer's warranty, a standard warranty or an extended warranty. The boards decided to provide specific requirements for applying the revenue recognition model to warranties, because many contracts with customers for the sale of products include a warranty and the nature of that warranty may vary across products, entities and jurisdictions.

BC369   In the Discussion Paper, the boards proposed accounting for all warranties consistently because a unifying feature of all warranties is that an entity promises to stand ready to replace or repair the product in accordance with the terms and conditions of the warranty. The Discussion Paper proposed that a promise to stand ready would provide a customer with a service of warranty coverage, which would have been a performance obligation to which revenue would be attributed. However, most respondents to the Discussion Paper stated that the accounting for warranties should reflect the fact that some product warranties are different from others. Some warranties protect the customer from defects that exist when the product is transferred to the customer and other warranties protect the customer from faults that arise after the product has been transferred to the customer. Those respondents commented that the customer does not receive a separate service if the warranty only protects the customer from the product defects that were present at the time of sale. Consequently, any subsequent repairs or replacements to remedy those defects are additional costs of providing the product and, therefore, relate to an entity's past performance.

BC370 In the light of that feedback, the boards decided to account for some warranties differently from others. The boards considered distinguishing warranties on the basis of when the fault in the products arises; however, respondents explained that such a distinction was not operational. Therefore, the boards decided to distinguish warranties on the basis of whether the warranty provides the customer with a service in addition to the assurance that the related product complies with the agreed-upon specifications. Specifically, the boards decided that when the warranty provides a service (ie a service-type warranty), the warranty should be accounted for as a performance obligation.

Warranties that are performance obligations (service-type warranties)

BC371 For some types of warranties, an entity either sells separately or negotiates separately with a customer so that the customer can choose whether to purchase the warranty coverage. That fact provides objective evidence that the promised warranty provides a service to the customer in addition to the promised product. Consequently, the boards decided that this type of promised warranty is a performance obligation in accordance with paragraphs 22–30 of IFRS 15.

BC372 The boards decided that warranties that are not sold separately by the entity, or negotiated separately with the customer, should also be identified as performance obligations if the facts and circumstances suggest that the warranty (or a part of the warranty) provides a service to the customer, in addition to the assurance that the entity's past performance was as specified in the contract. The boards noted the following about this decision:

(a) it provides a clear principle that allows an entity to account for economically similar warranties in a similar manner, regardless of whether the warranties are separately priced or negotiated;

(b) it is consistent with the general principles for identifying performance obligations; and

(c) it removes the bright line in previous US GAAP that distinguishes between different types of warranties based solely on whether the warranty is separately priced.

BC373 A warranty that meets the requirements in paragraphs B28–B33 of IFRS 15 to be accounted for as a performance obligation might also meet the criteria for classification as an insurance contract. However, only warranties issued directly by a third party would be accounted for as insurance contracts[8] according to the proposals in the boards' respective projects on the accounting for insurance contracts.

---

8   The Board completed its insurance project with the issuance of IFRS 17 *Insurance Contracts*. IFRS 17, issued in May 2017, replaced IFRS 4.

Warranties that are not performance obligations (assurance-type warranties)

BC374　The boards considered whether an assurance-type warranty should be accounted for as either of the following:

(a)　a separate liability to replace or repair a defective product; or

(b)　an unsatisfied performance obligation, because the entity has not provided the customer with a product that is free from defects at the time of sale.

BC375　The proposals in the 2010 Exposure Draft would have required an entity that provides an assurance-type warranty to a customer to assess whether it had satisfied its performance obligation to transfer the product specified in the contract. The entity would have been required to determine the likelihood of the existence of defective products that it had sold to customers and their quantity and, as a consequence, not recognise revenue to the extent that those performance obligations were not satisfied. An advantage of that proposal would have been that an entity would not have recognised the entire transaction price as revenue when the product transferred to the customer, because a portion of the transaction price would not have been recognised as revenue until the entity had repaired or replaced the products that were expected to be defective. However, the boards decided not to retain that proposal, mainly for the following practical reasons:

(a)　there would have been complexities associated with the requirements for an entity to continue to recognise as 'inventory' products that had been delivered to customers and that were expected to be defective; and

(b)　any margin attributable to the repair or replacement of a product in an assurance-type warranty would have been unlikely to significantly distort the pattern of recognition of the overall contract margin.

BC376　Accordingly, the boards decided that an entity should recognise an assurance-type warranty as a separate liability to replace or repair a defective product. Consequently, an entity should recognise a warranty liability and corresponding expense when it transfers the product to the customer and the liability should be measured in accordance with IAS 37 or Topic 460 *Guarantees*. In contrast to the accounting for service-type warranties, an entity should not attribute any of the transaction price (and therefore revenue) to an assurance-type warranty. Some warranties may include both assurance features and service features. The boards decided that if an entity cannot reasonably account for those assurance features of the warranty separately from the service features, the entity should be allowed to account for the warranties together as a single performance obligation. That accounting ensures that the entity does not overstate the recognition of revenue at the time that the product transfers to the customer and also relieves the entity from identifying and accounting separately for the two components of the warranty coverage.

Statutory warranties

BC377　In some jurisdictions, the law requires an entity to provide warranties with the sale of its products. The law might state that an entity is required to repair or replace products that develop faults within a specified period from the time of sale. Consequently, those statutory warranties may appear to be service-type warranties because they cover faults arising after the time of sale, not merely defects existing at the time of sale. However, the boards decided that the law can be viewed as simply operationalising an assurance-type warranty. In other words, the objective of those statutory warranties is to protect the customer against the risk of purchasing a defective product. But rather than requiring the entity to determine whether the product was defective at the time of sale, the law presumes that if a fault arises within a specified period (which can vary depending on the nature of the product), the product was defective at the time of sale. Consequently, these statutory warranties should be accounted for as assurance-type warranties.

Product liability laws

BC378　The boards clarified that product liability laws do not give rise to performance obligations. Those laws typically require an entity to pay compensation if one of its products causes harm or damage. The boards noted that an entity should not recognise a performance obligation arising from those laws because the performance obligation in a contract is to transfer the product to the customer. To the extent that an entity expects the product(s) to be defective, the entity should recognise a liability for the expected costs to repair or replace the product (see paragraph B33 of IFRS 15). Any obligation of the entity to pay compensation for the damage or harm that its product causes is separate from the performance obligation. The boards noted that an entity should account for this obligation separately from the contract with the customer and in accordance with the requirements for loss contingencies in IAS 37 or Topic 450.

Principal versus agent considerations (paragraphs B34–B38)[9]

BC379　Previous revenue Standards required an entity to assess whether it was acting as a principal or an agent when goods or services were transferred to a customer. That assessment was necessary to determine whether an entity should recognise revenue for the gross amount of customer consideration (if the entity was determined to be a principal) or for a net amount after the supplier was compensated for its goods or services (if the entity was determined to be an agent).

9　*Clarifications to IFRS 15* issued in April 2016 amended the application guidance in paragraphs B34–B38 and, as a consequence, amended paragraph BC383. The objective of amending the application guidance in paragraphs B34–B38 is to (a) provide a better framework to be applied when assessing whether an entity is a principal or an agent; (b) clarify the application of the control principle to intangible goods and services; and (c) clarify the role of the indicators in paragraph B37 when applying the control principle. Paragraphs BC379–BC385 should therefore be read together with paragraphs BC385A–BC385Z, which explain the boards' considerations for amending the application guidance.

BC380   IFRS 15 also requires an entity to determine whether it is a principal or an agent. This is because the performance obligations of principals and agents are different. A principal controls the goods or services before they are transferred to a customer. Consequently, the principal's performance obligation is to transfer those goods or services to the customer. Therefore, recognising revenue at the gross amount of the customer consideration faithfully depicts the consideration to which the entity is entitled for the transfer of the goods and services. In contrast, an agent does not control the goods or services before they are transferred to a customer. The agent merely facilitates the sale of goods or services between a principal and the customer. Consequently, an agent's performance obligation is to arrange for another party to provide the goods or services to the customer. Therefore, the transaction price attributable to an agent's performance obligation is the fee or commission that the agent receives for providing those services.

BC381   The boards observed that identifying an entity's promise (ie the performance obligation) in a contract is fundamental to the determination of whether the entity is acting as a principal or an agent. This is because identifying the nature of the entity's performance obligation is necessary for the entity to determine whether it controls the goods or services that have been promised before they are transferred to a customer. For example, a travel agent could be the principal in some contracts with customers if the travel agent determines that its promise is to provide a right to a flight (ie a ticket), instead of a promise to provide the flight. However, to conclude whether they are a principal or an agent, the travel agent would need to also consider whether it controlled that right before transferring it to the customer, which may occur when the travel agent purchases the tickets in advance for sales to future customers.

BC382   The nature of the entity's promise may not always be readily apparent. For that reason, the boards included indicators in paragraph B37 of IFRS 15 to help an entity determine whether the entity controls the goods or services before transferring them and thus whether the entity is a principal or an agent. Those indicators are based on indicators that were included in previous revenue recognition requirements in IFRS and US GAAP. However, as noted in paragraph BC380, the indicators in IFRS 15 have a different purpose than previous revenue recognition requirements in that they are based on the concepts of identifying performance obligations and the transfer of control of goods or services.

BC383   After an entity identifies its promise and determines whether it is the principal or the agent, the entity would recognise revenue when it satisfies its performance obligation. This would, for an entity that is a principal, occur when control of the promised goods or services transfers to the customer. The boards observed that in some contracts in which the entity is the agent, control of the goods or services promised to the customer might transfer before the customer receives the goods or services from the principal. For example, an entity that issues loyalty points to its customers when they purchase goods or services from the entity might satisfy its performance obligation with respect to the loyalty points on issuing those points to the customers if:

(a) the points entitle the customers to future discounted purchases with another party (ie the points represent a material right to a future discount); and

(b) the entity determines that it is an agent (ie its promise is to arrange for the customers to be provided with points) and the entity does not control those points before they are transferred to the customer.

BC384 In contrast, the boards observed that if the points entitle the customers to future goods or services to be provided by the entity, the entity may conclude it is not an agent. This is because the entity's promise is to provide those future goods or services and thus the entity controls both the points and the future goods or services before they are transferred to the customer. In these cases, the entity's performance obligation may only be satisfied when the future goods or services are provided.

BC385 In other cases, the points may entitle customers to choose between future goods or services provided by either the entity or another party. The boards observed that in those cases, to determine when the performance obligation is satisfied, the entity would need to consider the nature of its performance obligation. This is because until the customer has chosen the goods or services to be provided (and thus whether the entity or the third party will provide those goods or services), the entity is obliged to stand ready to deliver goods or services. Thus, the entity may not satisfy its performance obligation until such time as it either delivers the goods or services or is no longer obliged to stand ready. The boards also observed that if the customer subsequently chooses the goods or services from another party, the entity would need to consider whether it was acting as an agent and thus should recognise revenue for only a fee or commission that the entity received from providing the services to the customer and the third party. The boards noted that this is consistent with previous revenue recognition requirements in IFRS for customer loyalty programmes.

Clarifications to IFRS 15 (amendments issued in April 2016)

BC385A The TRG discussed a number of issues in relation to paragraphs B34–B38 of IFRS 15. Some stakeholders asked whether control is always the basis for determining whether an entity is a principal or an agent, and how the control principle and the indicators in paragraph B37 work together. Other stakeholders asked how to apply the control principle to contracts involving intangible goods or services. In the light of those discussions and the feedback received, the boards discussed, and decided to clarify, the principal versus agent guidance by making the same targeted amendments to the application guidance and the related Illustrative Examples in IFRS 15 and Topic 606.

BC385B When another party is involved in providing goods or services to a customer, the amendments to the application guidance clarify how an entity determines whether it is a principal or an agent. These amendments focus on (a) the need for appropriately identifying the good or service that is transferred to the customer (the 'specified good or service'); and (b) determining whether the entity has promised to provide the specified good or service itself (ie the entity is a principal) or to arrange for the specified good or service to be provided to the customer by the other party (ie the entity is an agent). The entity determines the nature of its promise on the basis of whether the entity controls the specified good or service before that good or service is transferred to the customer. Throughout the guidance on principal versus agent considerations, the boards decided to refer to the *specified good or service* transferred to the customer (as in paragraph B34), rather than the *performance obligation*. This is because use of the term 'performance obligation' would have been confusing if the entity is an agent. An agent's performance obligation is to arrange for the other party to provide its goods or services to the customer; it does not promise to provide the goods or services itself to the end customer. Accordingly, the specified good or service to be provided to the end customer is not the performance obligation of the agent.

Principle for determining whether an entity is a principal or an agent

BC385C   Paragraph B34 requires an entity to determine whether it is a principal or an agent on the basis of whether the nature of the entity's promise is a performance obligation to provide the specified goods or services itself (ie the entity is a principal) or to arrange for those goods or services to be provided by another party (ie the entity is an agent). Assessing whether the entity controls the specified good or service before it is transferred to the customer is the basis for determining the nature of the entity's promise.

BC385D   The boards observed that in order for an entity to conclude that it is providing the specified good or service to the customer, it must first control that good or service (as defined in paragraph 33). The entity cannot provide the specified good or service to a customer if the entity does not first control the good or service to be provided. If an entity controls the specified good or service before that good or service is transferred to the customer, the entity is the principal in the transaction with the customer. If the entity does not control the specified good or service before that good or service is transferred to a customer, the entity is not a principal in the transaction with the customer. The boards noted that their considerations in this respect are explained in paragraph BC380.

BC385E   In addition, the boards noted that an entity that itself manufactures a good or performs a service is always a principal if the entity transfers control of that good or service to another party. Such an entity does not need to evaluate whether it is a principal or an agent using the guidance in paragraphs B34–B38 because the entity transfers the good or provides the service directly to its customer, without the involvement of another party. If the entity transfers a good or provides a service to an intermediary that is a principal in providing that good or service to an end customer (whether individually or as part of a distinct bundle of goods or services), the entity's customer is the intermediary.

BC385F   Because of the concerns highlighted in the TRG's discussions, the boards decided to clarify the following aspects of the application guidance on principal versus agent considerations:

        (a)   the relationship between the control principle and the indicators in paragraph B37; and

        (b)   the application of the control principle to intangible goods and services.

The relationship between control and the indicators in paragraph B37

BC385G   The boards observed that the questions about the relationship between the assessment of control and the indicators of control in paragraph B37 arose, at least in part, because the indicators in that paragraph were carried forward from IAS 18 *Revenue* and Topic 605 *Revenue Recognition*. IAS 18 had a principle for this assessment (based on risks and rewards) that was different from the control principle in IFRS 15 and, although Topic 605 did not explicitly include a principle, the indicators in Topic 605 were understood to be indicators of risks and rewards. In addition, the structure of the analysis in Examples 45–48 accompanying IFRS 15 added to the confusion.

BC385H   The boards' considerations (explained in paragraph BC382) highlight that the indicators in paragraph B37 were included to support an entity's assessment of whether it controls a specified good or service before transfer in scenarios for which that assessment might be difficult. The indicators (a) do not override the assessment of control; (b) should not be viewed in isolation; (c) do not constitute a separate or additional evaluation; and (d) should not be considered a checklist of criteria to be met, or factors to be considered, in all scenarios. Considering one or more of the indicators will often be helpful and, depending on the facts and circumstances, individual indicators will be more or less relevant or persuasive to the assessment of control.

BC385I   The boards acknowledged that the indicators are similar to those in IAS 18 and Topic 605, but also noted their considerations in this respect, explained in paragraph BC382. Paragraph BC382 explains that the boards decided to carry over some of the indicators in previous revenue recognition Standards even though those indicators have a different purpose in IFRS 15. In IFRS 15, the indicators support the concepts of identifying performance obligations and the transfer of control of goods or services. Accordingly, the boards had expected that the conclusions about principal versus agent under IFRS 15 could be different in some scenarios from those reached under the previous revenue recognition Standards. Furthermore, the boards observed that, although exposure to risks and rewards alone does not give an entity control, exposure to risks and rewards can be a helpful factor to consider in determining whether an entity has obtained control (see paragraph 38).

BC385J   The boards decided to amend the indicators in paragraph B37 to more clearly establish a link between the control principle and the indicators by:

        (a)   reframing the indicators as indicators of when an entity controls a specified good or service before transfer, rather than as indicators that an entity does not control the specified good or service before transfer.

(b) adding guidance to explain how each indicator supports the assessment of control as defined in paragraph 33 of IFRS 15. This should help entities apply indicators that are similar to those in the previous revenue recognition Standards but within the context of the control principle in IFRS 15.

(c) removing the indicator relating to the form of the consideration. Although that indicator might sometimes be helpful in assessing whether an entity is an agent, the boards concluded that it would not be helpful in assessing whether an entity is a principal.

(d) removing the indicator relating to exposure to credit risk. The feedback on the Exposure Draft *Clarifications to IFRS 15* highlighted that exposure to credit risk is generally not a helpful indicator when assessing whether an entity controls the specified good or service. Stakeholders observed that the credit risk indicator in the previous revenue guidance has been problematic from the perspective of entities trying to use exposure to credit risk to override stronger evidence of agency. The boards concluded that removing the credit risk indicator should reduce some of the complexity in the principal versus agent evaluation because the credit risk indicator will typically be less relevant, or not relevant, to the evaluation for contracts within the scope of IFRS 15.

(e) clarifying that the indicators are not an exhaustive list and merely support the assessment of control—they do not replace or override that assessment. The boards decided to explicitly state that one or more of the indicators might provide more persuasive evidence to support the assessment of control in different scenarios.

BC385K   In the light of the IASB's decision to generally apply a high hurdle when considering whether to amend IFRS 15, the IASB initially thought that it would not be necessary to add explanatory text to each indicator in paragraph B37 to establish a link to the concept of control. In the IASB's view, clarity about the interaction between the control principle and the indicators could have been achieved by amending only the Illustrative Examples. The IASB noted concerns about adding explanatory text to the indicators in paragraph B37 because of (a) the risk of new questions arising with respect to those additional explanations; and (b) the risk that some of those additional explanations might be used inappropriately to reach a conclusion that an entity is a principal when the entity is an agent. Nonetheless, despite those concerns, the IASB decided to amend the indicators in paragraph B37 of IFRS 15 in order to align the wording of the amendments with the wording of those made by the FASB. The IASB concluded that the benefits of retaining converged requirements on this topic outweigh the potential costs of amending the requirements.

The use of the indicators in paragraph B37 rather than the indicators in paragraph 38

BC385L   Some stakeholders asked why the indicators in paragraph B37 are different from the indicators on the satisfaction of performance obligations (paragraph 38), noting that both sets of indicators relate to control. The boards observed that the indicators in paragraph 38 are indicators of the point in time at which the customer obtains control of the promised good or service. Accordingly, the indicators in paragraph 38 serve a different purpose than the indicators in paragraph B37. The indicators in paragraph 38 are not intended to indicate whether the customer obtains control of a promised asset—within the context of IFRS 15 as a whole, it is assumed that the customer will obtain control of the promised asset at some point—instead, they are intended to indicate when the customer has obtained control. In contrast, the indicators in paragraph B37 are intended to indicate whether the entity controls a specified good or service before that good or service is transferred to the customer.

Application of the control principle to intangible goods and services

BC385M   The boards observed that at least some of the difficulty that stakeholders had in applying the control principle, in particular to intangible goods and services, was linked to challenges in identifying the specified good or service to be provided to the customer. The boards observed that this also had frequently been a challenge for entities under previous revenue recognition Standards.

BC385N   The principal versus agent considerations relate to the application of Step 2 of the revenue recognition model. Appropriately identifying the good or service to be provided is a critical step in appropriately identifying whether the nature of an entity's promise is to act as a principal or an agent. When the appropriate specified good or service is identified, the assessment of control is often relatively straightforward, even when the specified good or service is an intangible good or a service. For example, the specified good or service to be provided to the customer could be:

(a)   a right to goods or services (see paragraph 26). For example, the airline ticket (a right to fly) in Example 47 and the meal voucher (a right to a meal) in Example 48 accompanying IFRS 15; or

(b)   a bundle of goods or services that are not distinct from each other (for example, the specialised equipment in Example 46 accompanying IFRS 15).

BC385O   The boards observed that when the specified good or service to be provided to the customer is a right to goods or services to be provided in the future by another party, the entity would determine whether its performance obligation is a promise to provide a right to goods or services or whether it is arranging for the other party to provide that right. The fact that the entity will not provide the goods or services itself is not determinative. Instead, the entity evaluates whether it controls the right to goods or services before that right is transferred to the customer. In doing so, it is often relevant to assess whether the right is created only when it is obtained by the customer, or whether the right to goods or services exists before the customer obtains the right. If the right does not exist before the customer obtains it, an entity would be unable to control that right before it is transferred to the customer.

BC385P   Some respondents to the Exposure Draft stated that it could be difficult in some cases to determine whether the specified good or service is the right to a good or service to be provided by another party or the underlying good or service itself (for example, in the case of Example 47, whether the specified good or service is the right to the flight (the ticket) or the flight itself). The boards observed that a careful consideration of the facts and circumstances, and exercise of judgement may be required in identifying the specified good or service (just as identifying an entity's performance obligations outside the context of a principal versus agent evaluation will often require judgement). The boards also observed that assessing whether an entity controls a right to a good or service to be provided by another party is important to the principal versus agent evaluation. The boards noted that the Illustrative Examples accompanying IFRS 15 on principal versus agent considerations have been designed to address and explain scenarios in which the specified good or service is a right to a good or service to be provided by another party (as in Example 47 accompanying IFRS 15) and scenarios in which the specified good or service is the underlying service itself (as in Example 46A accompanying IFRS 15).

BC385Q   The boards also observed that the specified good or service to which the control principle is applied should be a distinct good or service, or a distinct bundle of goods or services. If individual goods or services are not distinct from each other, then they may be, for example, merely inputs to a combined item and are each only part of a single promise to the customer. Accordingly, an entity should evaluate the nature of its promise (ie to act as a principal or an agent) within the context of the promise to the customer, rather than for part of that promise. Consequently, for contracts in which goods or services provided by another party are inputs to a combined item (or items) for which the customer has contracted, the entity assesses whether it controls the combined item before that item is transferred to the customer.

BC385R   When a specified good or service is a distinct bundle of goods or services, the principal versus agent analysis may, in some cases, be straightforward. The boards concluded (in paragraph B35A(c)) that when an entity provides a significant service of integrating two or more goods or services into the combined output that is the specified good or service for which the customer contracted, it controls that specified good or service before it is transferred to the customer. When the entity provides a significant integration service it controls the inputs to the combined item that is the specified good or service (including goods or services provided by another party that are inputs to the specified good or service). The entity controls the inputs by directing their use to create the combined item. In that case, the inputs provided by the other party would be a fulfilment cost to the entity. In contrast, if a third party provides the significant integration service, then the entity's customer for its goods or services (which would be inputs to the specified good or service) is likely to be the other party.

BC385S   Consequently, the boards decided to clarify the thought process to be applied when assessing whether an entity is a principal or an agent by specifically requiring an entity to identify the specified good or service before applying the control principle to each specified good or service. The amended paragraph B34 and the additional paragraph B34A should:

(a)   provide a better framework for assessing whether an entity is a principal or an agent.

(b)   emphasise the importance of appropriately identifying the specified good or service (which could be a right to a good or service to be provided by another party) that will be transferred to the customer.

(c)   clarify that the specified good or service (ie the unit of account for the principal versus agent evaluation) is each distinct good or service (or distinct bundle of goods or services). Accordingly, those paragraphs also clarify that, because a contract with a customer could include more than one specified good or service, an entity could be a principal for one or more specified goods or services in a contract and an agent for others.

(d)   emphasise that control (as defined in paragraph 33 of IFRS 15) is the determining factor when assessing whether an entity is a principal or an agent.

BC385T   The IASB noted that, in many respects, paragraph B34A simply points to other relevant parts of the requirements in IFRS 15. Accordingly, the IASB did not view the inclusion of that additional paragraph as essential to clarifying the requirements in IFRS 15. In its view, clarity about the thought process to be applied could have been achieved by amending only the Illustrative Examples. Nonetheless, given the concerns raised by stakeholders, the IASB concluded that including paragraph B34A would be helpful to the principal versus agent evaluation, and would align the wording of the amendments with the wording of those made by the FASB. Therefore, the IASB concluded that the benefits of adding the paragraph outweigh the potential costs of amending the requirements.

Assessment of control of a service

BC385U   The TRG's discussions highlighted concerns about the application of the control principle to services to be provided to a customer. Questions discussed included how an entity (other than the service provider) could control a service before that service is transferred to the customer, because a service comes into existence only at the moment that it is delivered. The boards observed that an entity can control a service to be provided by another party when it controls the right to the specified service from the other party that will be provided to the customer. The entity then either transfers the right to the service to the customer (for example, the airline ticket in Example 47) or uses its right to direct the other party to provide the service to the customer on the entity's behalf (ie to satisfy the entity's performance obligation in the contract with the customer), such as in Example 46A. Determining whether the entity controls a right to a specified service requires consideration of the facts and circumstances. The boards noted that contracts involving services provided by another party in which the entity is a principal can be broadly categorised as follows:

(a) Contracts in which an entity provides the customer with a right to a future service to be provided by another party, such as the right to a specified flight (in the form of a ticket) to be provided by an airline (as discussed in paragraph BC385O).

(b) Contracts in which the service provided by the other party is not distinct from other goods or services promised to the customer, and the entity directs the use of that service to create the combined item that is the specified good or service for which the customer has contracted (as discussed in paragraphs BC385Q–BC385R). Paragraph B35A(c) states that this scenario would exist whenever the entity provides a significant service of integrating the service provided by another party into the specified good or service for which the customer has contracted. Example 46 accompanying IFRS 15 illustrates this scenario.

(c) Contracts in which an entity directs another party to provide the service to the customer on the entity's behalf in satisfying the entity's performance obligation. Example 46A accompanying IFRS 15 illustrates this scenario.

BC385V The boards observed that determining whether an entity is a principal or an agent may be more difficult in the third category of contracts listed above in which the entity has entered into a contract with a customer and has engaged another party (a subcontractor) to satisfy a performance obligation within that contract on its behalf. In these contracts, the entity assesses whether it controls a right to the specified services. An entity could control the right to the specified services by entering into a contract with the subcontractor and defining the services to be performed by the subcontractor on the entity's behalf. In that scenario, which is illustrated in Example 46A, the entity obtains the right to the services of the subcontractor and then directs the subcontractor to provide the services to the customer on the entity's behalf. This scenario is equivalent to the entity fulfilling the contract using its own resources rather than engaging another party to do so. The entity would remain responsible for the satisfactory provision of services in accordance with the contract with the customer. In other scenarios in which the specified services provided to the customer are provided by another party and the entity did not have the ability to direct those services, the entity would typically be an agent. In those scenarios, the entity is likely to be facilitating (and arranging for) the provision of services by the other party rather than controlling the rights to the services that the entity then directs to the customer.

BC385W The boards noted that paragraph B35 explains that an entity that is a principal in a contract may satisfy a performance obligation by itself or it may engage another party to satisfy some or all of a performance obligation on its behalf. The boards decided to add further explanation (paragraph B35A) to clarify the assessment of control of a service by explaining the scenarios in which a principal can control a service to be provided by another party. The boards also decided to add Example 46A to the Illustrative Examples accompanying IFRS 15 to illustrate the application of control to services.

Estimating revenue as a principal

BC385X   Some TRG participants asked how an entity that is a principal would estimate the amount of revenue to recognise if it were not aware of the amounts being charged to end customers by an intermediary that is an agent. The IASB observed that this question is largely unrelated to the application guidance on principal versus agent considerations in paragraph B34–B38 of IFRS 15, but rather relates to applying the requirements in paragraphs 46–90 on determining the consideration to which an entity is entitled. The IASB noted that the situations in which an entity that is a principal may be unaware of the amount charged to end customers by an intermediary that is an agent are generally limited to situations in which the intermediary (a) has some flexibility in setting prices; or (b) is procuring the good or service on behalf of the end customer. The IASB concluded that the issue does not require any clarifications or additional guidance because the issue is expected to affect a limited number of entities and contracts.

BC385Y   The FASB has also decided not to amend Topic 606 to address this issue. This is mainly because the FASB had observed that the situations in which an entity that is a principal is (and expects to remain) unaware of the amount charged by an intermediary that is an agent to the end customer are not pervasive and the issue affects only a limited number of entities and contracts. For those limited situations, the FASB is of the view that the determination of whether revenue may be estimated is based on an assessment of the requirements for determining the transaction price and estimating variable consideration.

BC385Z   The IASB did not specifically consider how the transaction price requirements would be applied in those situations but concluded that an entity that is a principal would generally be expected to be able to apply judgement and determine the consideration to which it is entitled using all relevant facts and circumstances available to it.

Customer options for additional goods or services (paragraphs B39–B43)

BC386   In some contracts, customers are given an option to purchase additional goods or services. The boards considered when those options should be accounted for as a performance obligation. During those discussions, the boards observed that it can be difficult to distinguish between the following:

(a)   an option that the customer pays for (often implicitly) as part of an existing contract, which would be a performance obligation to which part of the transaction price is allocated; and

(b)   a marketing or promotional offer that the customer did not pay for and, although made at the time of entering into a contract, is not part of the contract and that would not be a performance obligation in that contract.

BC387   Similar difficulties in distinguishing between an option and an offer have arisen in US GAAP for the software industry. Previous US GAAP revenue recognition requirements for the software industry specified that an offer of a discount on future purchases of goods or services was presumed to be a separate option in the contract, if that discount was significant and also incremental both to the range of discounts reflected in the pricing of other elements in that contract and to the range of discounts typically given in comparable transactions. Those notions of 'significant' and 'incremental' form the basis for the principle of a material right that is used to differentiate between an option and a marketing or promotional offer. However, the boards observed that even if the offered discount is not incremental to other discounts in the contract, it nonetheless could, in some cases, give rise to a material right to the customer. Consequently, the boards decided not to carry forward that part of the previous revenue recognition requirements from US GAAP into IFRS 15.

BC388   Some respondents asked the boards to clarify whether specific options, such as customer loyalty points, should be accounted for as a performance obligation when the arrangement involves more than two parties. This often occurs in a credit card arrangement in which an entity provides the credit card holder with points based on the amount of purchases made at other entities (often referred to as 'merchants'). The boards determined that the assessment of whether any loyalty points represent a performance obligation requires an analysis of the facts and circumstances in each arrangement. The boards decided not to provide any further guidance because the issue was specific to the credit card industry and the boards observed that these arrangements are often complex and can vary significantly. Furthermore, the boards noted that IFRS 15 includes all the requirements to enable entities to account for the various arrangements.

Allocating the transaction price

BC389   In accordance with IFRS 15, an entity is required to determine the stand-alone selling price of the option so that it can allocate part of the transaction price to that performance obligation. In some cases, the stand-alone selling price of the option may be directly observable. In many cases though, the stand-alone selling price of the option will need to be estimated.

BC390   Option pricing models can be used to estimate the stand-alone selling price of an option. The price of an option includes the intrinsic value of the option (ie the value of the option if it were exercised today) and its time value (ie the value of the option that depends on the time until the expiry and the volatility of the price of the underlying goods or services). The boards decided that the benefits to users of financial statements of allocating some of the transaction price to the price and availability guarantees inherent in the time value component of the option price would not have justified the costs and difficulties to do so. However, the boards decided that an entity should be able to readily obtain the inputs necessary to measure the intrinsic value of the option in accordance with paragraph B42 of IFRS 15 and that those calculations should be relatively straightforward and intuitive. This measurement approach is consistent with the application guidance that was provided for measuring customer loyalty points in previous revenue recognition requirements in IFRS.

Renewal options

BC391   A renewal option gives a customer the right to acquire additional goods or services of the same type as those supplied under an existing contract. This type of option could be described as a renewal option within a relatively short contract (for example, a one-year contract with an option to renew that contract for a further year at the end of the first and second years) or a cancellation option within a longer contract (for example, a three-year contract that allows the customer to discontinue the contract at the end of each year). A renewal option could be viewed similarly to other options to provide additional goods or services. In other words, the renewal option could be a performance obligation in the contract if it provides the customer with a material right that it otherwise could not obtain without entering into that contract.

BC392   However, there are typically a series of options in cases in which a renewal option provides a customer with a material right. In other words, to exercise any option in the contract, the customer must have exercised all the previous options in the contract. The boards decided that determining the stand-alone selling price of a series of options would have been complex because doing so would have required an entity to identify various inputs, such as the stand-alone selling prices for the goods or services for each renewal period and the likelihood that the customers will renew for the subsequent period. In other words, the entity would have had to consider the entire potential term of the contract to determine the amount of the transaction price from the initial period that should be deferred until later periods.

BC393   For that reason, the boards decided to provide an entity with a practical alternative to estimating the stand-alone selling price of the option. The practical alternative requires an entity to include the optional goods or services that it expects to provide (and corresponding expected customer consideration) in the initial measurement of the transaction price. In the boards' view, it is simpler for an entity to view a contract with renewal options as a contract for its expected term (ie including the expected renewal periods) rather than as a contract with a series of options.

BC394   The boards developed two criteria to distinguish renewal options from other options to acquire additional goods or services. The first criterion specifies that the additional goods or services underlying the renewal options must be similar to those provided under the initial contract—that is, an entity continues to provide what it was already providing. Consequently, it is more intuitive to view the goods or services underlying such options as part of the initial contract. In contrast, customer loyalty points and many discount vouchers should be considered to be separate deliverables in the contract, because the underlying goods or services may be of a different nature.

BC395　The second criterion specifies that the additional goods or services in the subsequent contracts must be provided in accordance with the terms of the original contract. Consequently, the entity's position is restricted because it cannot change those terms and conditions and, in particular, it cannot change the pricing of the additional goods or services beyond the parameters specified in the original contract. That too is different from examples such as customer loyalty points and discount vouchers. For example, if an airline offers flights to customers in exchange for points from its frequent flyer programme, the airline is not restricted, because it can subsequently determine the number of points that are required to be redeemed for any particular flight. Similarly, when an entity grants discount vouchers, it has typically not restricted itself with respect to the price of the subsequent goods or services against which the discount vouchers will be redeemed.

Customers' unexercised rights (breakage) (paragraphs B44–B47)

BC396　Some respondents asked the boards to provide guidance on how to account for a customer's non-refundable prepayment for the right to receive goods or services in the future. Common examples include the purchase of gift cards and non-refundable tickets.

BC397　The boards noted that the requirements for the allocation of the transaction price to customer options implicitly explains how to account for situations in which the customer does not exercise all of its contractual rights to those goods or services (ie breakage). However, the boards decided to clarify how to account for breakage in situations in which there is only one performance obligation in the contract (ie how to account for breakage in customer options when there is no need to allocate the transaction price and, therefore, no need to determine a stand-alone selling price).

BC398　Consequently, the boards included application guidance on the accounting for breakage. Those requirements require the same pattern of revenue recognition as the requirements for customer options. Thus, an entity should recognise revenue from breakage as it performs under the contract on the basis of the transfer of the goods or services promised in the contract. This effectively increases the transaction price allocated to the individual goods or services transferred to the customer to include the revenue from the entity's estimate of unexercised rights. The boards decided that this approach represents the most appropriate pattern of revenue recognition for breakage, because if an entity expected that customers would exercise all of their rights (ie if the entity did not expect any breakage), it might increase the price of its goods or services. For example, an airline that sells non-refundable tickets would presumably charge a higher price per ticket if there was no expectation of breakage.

BC399　The boards also decided that an entity should recognise revenue for breakage only if it is highly probable that doing so would not result in a subsequent significant revenue reversal (see paragraphs 56–58 of IFRS 15). Otherwise, the entity's performance obligation to stand ready to provide future goods or services could be understated.

BC400　The boards considered but rejected an approach that would have required an entity to recognise estimated breakage as revenue immediately on the receipt of prepayment from a customer. The boards decided that because the entity has not performed under the contract, recognising revenue would not have been a faithful depiction of the entity's performance and could also have understated its obligation to stand ready to provide future goods or services.

BC401　Some respondents questioned whether the accounting for breakage is consistent with that for customer options in IFRS 15. Those respondents explained that for customer options, breakage is taken into account when determining the stand-alone selling price of the option as required by paragraph B42 of IFRS 15. Therefore, those respondents were concerned that when the consideration is allocated between the option and another performance obligation, some of the breakage on the option would be recognised when the other performance obligation is satisfied, which could occur before any rights under the options are exercised by the customer. However, the boards observed that when there are two (or more) performance obligations, IFRS 15 requires an entity to allocate the overall consideration between the performance obligations based on their relative stand-alone selling prices and, therefore, any discount on the combined bundle of goods or services is allocated on that basis (unless the entity meets the requirements in paragraph 82 or 85 of IFRS 15 to allocate on another basis). In other words, any difference between the sum of the stand-alone selling prices of the option and the other promised goods or services compared with the overall consideration would be recognised when (or as) the entity transfers the goods or services promised in the contract, which is consistent with the pattern of revenue recognition for breakage when there is only one performance obligation.

Licensing (paragraphs B52–B63B)[10]

BC402　In the 2011 Exposure Draft, the boards proposed that a licence grants a customer a right to use, but not own, intellectual property of the entity. Consequently, the 2011 Exposure Draft viewed the nature of the promised asset in a licence as a right to use an intangible asset that is transferred at a point in time. This is because the boards' view at that time was that there is a point at which the customer obtains the ability to direct the use of, and obtain substantially all of the benefits from, the right to use the intellectual property. However, the 2011 Exposure Draft also explained that revenue may be recognised over time for some contracts that include a licence if that

---

10　*Clarifications to IFRS 15* issued in April 2016 deleted paragraph B57 and added paragraph B59A of IFRS 15 to clarify the application guidance on determining the nature of the entity's promise in granting a licence of intellectual property. Paragraphs BC402–BC414 should therefore be read together with paragraphs BC414A–BC414Y, which explain the IASB's considerations in amending the application guidance.

licence is not distinct from other promises in the contract that may transfer to the customer over time.

BC403 In the light of the feedback received on the 2011 Exposure Draft, the boards reconsidered whether the nature of the promised asset in a licence is always a right that transfers at a point in time. In the examples they considered, the boards observed that licences vary significantly and include a wide array of different features and economic characteristics, which lead to significant differences in the rights provided by a licence. In some of the examples, the boards observed that the customer might be viewed as not obtaining control of the licence at a point in time. This is because the intellectual property to which the customer has obtained rights is dynamic and will change as a result of the entity's continuing involvement in its intellectual property, including activities that affect that intellectual property. In those cases, the customer may not be able to direct the use of, and obtain substantially all of the remaining benefits from, the licence at the time of transfer. In other words, what the licence provides to the customer is access to the intellectual property in the form in which it exists at any given moment. (Those notions were supported by some respondents who opposed the proposal in the 2011 Exposure Draft that all distinct licences represent the transfer of a right to use an intangible asset.)

BC404 Consequently, the boards decided to specify criteria for determining whether the nature of the entity's promise in granting a licence is to provide a customer with a right to access the entity's intellectual property as it exists throughout the licence period, or a right to use the entity's intellectual property as it exists at a point in time when the licence is granted. The boards noted that these criteria were necessary to distinguish between the two types of licences, rather than strictly relying on the control requirements, because it is difficult to assess when the customer obtains control of assets in a licence without first identifying the nature of the entity's performance obligation.

BC405 However, the boards observed that before applying the criteria, an entity should assess the goods or services promised in the contract and identify, as performance obligations, the promises that transfer the goods or services to the customer.

Identifying the performance obligations

BC406 The boards observed that, as is the case with other contracts, contracts that include a licence require an assessment of the promises in the contract and the criteria for identifying performance obligations (see paragraphs 27–30 of IFRS 15). This would include an assessment of whether the customer can benefit from the licence on its own or together with other resources that are readily available (see paragraph 27(a) of IFRS 15) and whether the licence is separately identifiable from other goods or services in the contract (see paragraph 27(b) of IFRS 15). The boards observed that this assessment may sometimes be challenging because the customer can often obtain benefit from the licence on its own (ie the licence is capable of being distinct). However, in many cases, the customer can benefit from the licence only with another good or service that is also promised (explicitly or implicitly) in the contract;

therefore, the licence is not separately identifiable from other goods or services in the contract. This may occur when:

(a) a licence forms a component of a tangible good and is integral to the good's functionality—software (ie a licence) is often included in tangible goods (for example, a car) and in most cases, significantly affects how that good functions. In those cases, the customer cannot benefit from the licence on its own (see paragraph 27(a) of IFRS 15) because the licence is integrated into the good (see paragraph 29(a) of IFRS 15); that is, the licence is an input to produce that good, which is an output.

(b) a licence that the customer can benefit from only in conjunction with a related service—this may occur when an entity provides a service, such as in some hosting or storage services, that enables the customer to use a licence, such as software, only by accessing the entity's infrastructure. In those cases, the customer does not take control of the licence and, therefore, cannot benefit from (or use) the licence on its own (see paragraph 27(a) of IFRS 15) without the hosting service. In addition, the use of the licence is highly dependent on, or highly interrelated with, the hosting service (see paragraph 29(c) of IFRS 15).

BC407 If the customer cannot benefit from the licence on its own, and/or the licence cannot be separated from other promises in the contract, the licence would not be distinct and thus would be combined with those other promises (see paragraph 30 of IFRS 15). The entity would then determine when the single performance obligation is satisfied on the basis of when the good or service (ie the output) is transferred to the customer. The boards noted that in some cases the combined good or service transferred to the customer may have a licence as its primary or dominant component. When the output that is transferred is a licence or when the licence is distinct, the entity would apply the criteria in paragraph B58 of IFRS 15 to determine whether the promised licence provides the customer with access to the entity's intellectual property or a right to use the entity's intellectual property.

Developing the criteria for licences that provide a right to access

BC408 As noted in paragraph BC404, the boards decided to specify criteria in paragraph B58 of IFRS 15 for determining if the intellectual property will change and, thus, if a licence provides a customer with a right to access the entity's intellectual property. If those criteria are not met, the licence provides the customer with a right to use an entity's intellectual property as that intellectual property exists (in the form and with the functionality) at the point in time when the licence transfers to the customer. To ensure that all licences are accounted for as either a right of access or a right to use, the boards decided to specify criteria for only one type of licence. In determining for which type of licence they should develop criteria, the boards observed that it was easier to determine when the intellectual property to which the customer has rights was changing (ie was dynamic), rather than when it was static.

BC409　In developing the criteria, the boards observed that the main factor that results in the intellectual property changing is when the contract requires, or the customer reasonably expects, that the entity undertakes activities that do not directly transfer goods or services to a customer (ie they do not meet the definition of a performance obligation). The activities may be part of an entity's ongoing and ordinary activities and customary business practices. However, the boards noted that it was not enough that the entity undertook activities, but also that those activities affected the intellectual property to which the customer has rights and, thus, exposes the customer to positive or negative effects. In those cases, the customer will essentially be using the most recent form of the intellectual property throughout the licence period. The boards observed that when the activities do not affect the customer, the entity is merely changing its own asset, which, although it may affect the entity's ability to provide future licences, would not affect the determination of what the licence provides or what the customer controls.

BC410　The boards noted that the assessment of the criteria would not be affected by other promises in the contract to transfer goods or services (ie performance obligations) that are separate from the licence. This is because the nature and pattern of transfer of each (separate) performance obligation in a contract would not affect the timing of other promised goods or services in the contract and, thus, would not affect the identification of the rights provided by the licence. This is because, by definition, a performance obligation is separate from the other promises in the contract. Consider a contract to provide a car and ongoing maintenance services—that is, two distinct goods or services (and thus two separate performance obligations). In this case, it seems counterintuitive to include the promise to provide a (separate) maintenance service when determining the nature and timing of the entity's performance related to the transfer of the car. A similar example can be drawn from a contract that includes a software licence and a promise to provide a service of updating the customer's software (sometimes included in a contract as post-contract support), in which the post-contract support is identified as a distinct good or service. This is because the entity would not consider the post-contract support when determining when control of the software transfers to the customer. In other words, a promise to transfer separate updates to the licence would not be considered in the assessment of the criteria in paragraph B58 of IFRS 15 and, furthermore, would be specifically excluded by criterion (c) in that paragraph.

BC411　The boards also noted that an entity would exclude the factors specified in paragraph B62 of IFRS 15 for the following reasons:

(a)　restrictions of time, geographical region or use that define the attributes of the asset conveyed in a licence—an entity would not consider restrictions of time, geographical region or use, because they define attributes of the rights transferred rather than the nature of the underlying intellectual property and the rights provided by the licence. Consider, for example, a term licence that permits the customer to show a movie in its theatre six times over the next two years. The restrictions in that example determine the nature of the asset that the entity has obtained (ie six showings of the movie), rather than the nature of the underlying intellectual property (ie the underlying movie).

(b)   guarantees provided by the entity that it has a valid patent to intellectual property and that it will defend and maintain that patent —guarantees that the entity has a valid patent would not be included in the assessment of the criteria for determining the rights provided in a licence, because those promises are part of the entity's representation that the intellectual property is legal and valid (this notion was previously included in the 2011 Exposure Draft).

BC412   In developing the criteria, the boards considered, but rejected, differentiating licences based on the following factors:

(a)   term of the licence—the length of a licence term is a restriction that represents an attribute of the asset transferred and does not provide information on the nature of the underlying intellectual property or on the nature of the entity's promise. For those reasons, the licence term does not depict when a customer obtains control of the promised licence.

(b)   exclusivity—the 2010 Exposure Draft proposed to distinguish between licences (ie whether they were a performance obligation satisfied over time or at a point in time) on the basis of whether the licence was exclusive. Many respondents to the 2010 Exposure Draft explained that a distinction based on exclusivity was inconsistent with the control principle, because exclusivity does not affect the determination of the entity's performance. In addition, respondents stated that a distinction based on exclusivity would not be operational, because it would require the boards to provide more clarity on how the term 'exclusive' would be interpreted. The boards observed that exclusivity is another restriction that represents an attribute of the asset transferred, rather than the nature of the underlying intellectual property or the entity's promise in granting a licence.

(c)   consumption of the underlying intellectual property—the boards also considered but rejected an approach that would differentiate between licences on the basis of the amount of the underlying intellectual property that was used up, or consumed by, a licence. This is because the intellectual property can be divided in many ways such as by time, geographical region or other restriction on use, and the rights can be provided to more than one customer at the same time through different licences. Consequently, it would be difficult for an entity to determine how much of the intellectual property was consumed by a particular licence.

(d)   payment terms—the boards decided not to use payment terms to differentiate between licences. This is because payment terms are not indicative of whether the licence provides the customer with a right to access or right to use the intellectual property of the entity and thus when the performance obligation is satisfied. Instead, payment terms will be agreed by the customer and the entity and will reflect other economic factors such as credit risk and potential cash flows of the asset.

BC413   The boards also considered whether to include a criterion that differentiated the nature of an entity's promise when the promised consideration is dependent on the customer's sales from, or usage of, the licence (often referred to as a sales-based or a usage-based royalty). As a criterion for differentiating licences, this would have resulted in *all* of the promised consideration being recognised over time for such licences, including any fixed amount. The boards decided not to include royalties as a criterion for differentiating licences, because the existence of a sales-based or a usage-based royalty does not solely define performance over time. However, the boards observed that, in some cases, the existence of a sales-based or a usage-based royalty can indicate a 'shared economic interest' between the entity and the customer in the intellectual property being licensed and therefore the customer could reasonably expect that the entity will undertake activities that affect the intellectual property to which the licence relates. The boards also decided, however, to include an exception for the revenue recognition pattern of sales-based or usage-based royalties (see paragraphs BC415–BC421).

When is the performance obligation satisfied?

BC414   The boards observed that when the licence provides the customer with a right to access the entity's intellectual property, the promised licence represents a performance obligation satisfied over time because the customer will simultaneously receive and benefit from the entity's performance as the performance occurs—that is, the criterion in paragraph 35(a) of IFRS 15 will be met. However, when the licence provides the customer with a right to use the entity's intellectual property, the boards decided that the performance obligation will be satisfied at a point in time. In those cases, an entity would need to assess the point in time at which the performance obligation is satisfied (ie when the customer obtains control of the licence) by applying paragraph 38 of IFRS 15. The boards also decided to specify that control of a licence could not transfer before the beginning of the period during which the customer can use and benefit from the licenced property. If the customer cannot use and benefit from the licenced property then, by definition, it does not control the licence. The boards noted that when viewed from the entity's perspective, performance may appear to be complete when a licence has been provided to the customer, even if the customer cannot yet use that licence. However, the boards observed that the definition of control in paragraph 33 of IFRS 15 focuses on the customer's perspective, as explained in paragraph BC121.

Clarifications to IFRS 15 (amendments issued in April 2016)

BC414A   The TRG discussed issues relating to the application of the licensing guidance in IFRS 15. The main issues discussed related to:

(a)   determining the nature of the entity's promise in granting a licence of intellectual property;

      (b)   the scope and applicability of the sales-based and usage-based royalties exception;

      (c)   the effect of contractual restrictions in a licence on identifying the performance obligations in the contract; and

      (d)   when the guidance on determining the nature of the entity's promise in granting a licence applies.

BC414B   In the light of those discussions and the feedback received, the IASB decided to clarify the application guidance on licensing and the accompanying Illustrative Examples to improve its operability and understandability. In some cases, the IASB concluded that a clarification is not necessary because there is adequate guidance in IFRS 15 with sufficient explanation of the boards' considerations in the Basis for Conclusions. Except for the scope and applicability of the sales-based and usage-based royalties exception, the FASB reached different conclusions about whether and how to address stakeholder concerns.

Determining the nature of the entity's promise in granting a licence of intellectual property

BC414C   IFRS 15 specifies criteria in paragraph B58 for determining whether the nature of the entity's promise in granting a licence is to provide a customer with a right to access the entity's intellectual property as it exists throughout the licence period, or a right to use the entity's intellectual property as it exists at a point in time when the licence is granted. In developing IFRS 15, the boards noted that these criteria were necessary because it is difficult to assess when the customer obtains control of assets in a licence without first identifying the nature of the entity's performance obligation.

BC414D   Paragraph B57 of IFRS 15 (now deleted, see paragraph BC414J) explained that the determination of whether an entity's promise to grant a licence provides a customer with a right to access or a right to use an entity's intellectual property is based on whether the customer can direct the use of, and obtain substantially all of the remaining benefits from, a licence at the point in time at which the licence is granted. A customer can direct the use of, and obtain substantially all the benefits from, the intellectual property, if the intellectual property to which the customer has rights is not significantly affected by activities of the entity. In contrast, a customer cannot direct the use of, and obtain substantially all of the remaining benefits from, a licence at the point in time at which the licence is granted if the intellectual property to which the customer has rights changes throughout the licence period. The intellectual property will change when the entity continues to be involved with its intellectual property and undertakes activities that significantly affect the intellectual property to which the customer has rights. Paragraph B58 provides criteria to help an entity assess whether its activities 'change' the intellectual property to which the customer has rights, including whether the expected activities of the entity significantly affect the intellectual property to which the customer has rights.

BC414E   Stakeholders agree that activities that change the form or functionality of the intellectual property would represent activities that affect the intellectual property to which the customer has rights. However, stakeholders have indicated that it was unclear whether the reference in IFRS 15 to changes in the intellectual property solely refers to changes in the form or functionality of the intellectual property, or also includes changes in the value of the intellectual property. This had resulted in different interpretations about how to apply the criteria in paragraph B58(a). Some stakeholders held the view that, for activities to significantly affect the intellectual property to which the customer has rights, those activities must be expected to change the form or functionality of that intellectual property. They thought that changes that solely affect the value of the intellectual property do not significantly affect the intellectual property to which the customer has rights. Others thought that activities that significantly affect the value of the intellectual property are sufficient to conclude that the licence provides a right to access the intellectual property.

BC414F   The IASB decided to clarify the requirements of paragraph B58(a) by providing additional application guidance on when activities change the intellectual property to which the customer has rights in such a way that the ability of the customer to obtain benefit from the intellectual property is significantly affected. The IASB noted that the reference to form or functionality in paragraph B61 (and the Illustrative Examples and the Basis for Conclusions) was not intended to suggest that the nature of a licence is a right to access intellectual property only if the entity's activities significantly affect the form or functionality of the intellectual property to which the customer has rights. Determining the nature of a licence is defined by the criteria in paragraph B58, which do not refer to form or functionality.

BC414G   Paragraph B59A clarifies that the assessment of whether the entity's activities significantly change the intellectual property to which the customer has rights is based on whether those activities affect the intellectual property's ability to provide benefit to the customer. In some cases, the ability of the intellectual property to provide benefit to the customer is derived from the form or functionality of the intellectual property to which the customer has rights and, in other cases, from the value of that intellectual property. If the activities are expected to significantly change the form or functionality of the intellectual property, those activities are considered to significantly affect the customer's ability to obtain benefit from the intellectual property. If the activities do not significantly change the form or functionality, but the ability of the customer to obtain benefit from the intellectual property is substantially derived from, or dependent upon, the entity's activities after the licence is granted, then the activities are also considered to significantly affect the intellectual property (as long as those activities do not result in the transfer of a good or service to the customer). In these cases, it is not necessary for those activities to change the form or functionality of the intellectual property to significantly affect the ability of the customer to obtain benefit from the intellectual property. For example, in some circumstances (eg many licences of brands), the benefit of the intellectual property is derived from its value and the entity's activities to support or maintain that value.

BC414H   The IASB observed that intellectual property that has significant stand-alone functionality derives a substantial portion of its benefit from that functionality. Consequently, if the entity's activities do not significantly change the form or functionality of such intellectual property, then the entity's activities will not significantly affect the customer's ability to derive benefit from that intellectual property. Therefore, the IASB clarified that in these cases the criterion in paragraph B58(a) would not be met and the licence would be a right to use the intellectual property as it existed at the time that it was transferred.

BC414I   The IASB has not defined the term 'significant stand-alone functionality' but has made clarifications to the Illustrative Examples to illustrate when the intellectual property to which the customer has rights might have significant stand-alone functionality. In many cases, it will be clear when intellectual property has significant stand-alone functionality. If there is no significant stand-alone functionality, the benefit to the customer might be derived substantially from the value of the intellectual property and the entity's activities to support or maintain that value. The IASB noted, however, that an entity may need to apply judgement to determine whether the intellectual property to which the customer has rights has significant stand-alone functionality.

BC414J   The IASB has deleted paragraph B57. This is in response to stakeholder concerns that paragraph B57 has contributed to the confusion about whether the reference to change solely refers to changes in the form or functionality of intellectual property or also includes changes in the value of intellectual property. The IASB is of the view that the addition of paragraph B59A provides clarity about the intended meaning of change in intellectual property, which makes the discussion in paragraph B57 redundant within the context of the application guidance. The discussion in paragraph B57 explained the IASB's logic for the requirements for determining whether an entity's promise to grant a licence provides a customer with either a right to access or a right to use an entity's intellectual property. Accordingly, the IASB has incorporated the content of paragraph B57 into this Basis for Conclusions.

BC414K   Having considered the wider implications of amending IFRS 15 before its effective date, the IASB decided to clarify the approach to determining the nature of an entity's promise in providing a licence, rather than change that approach. The IASB is of the view that stakeholder concerns have been addressed adequately by providing greater clarity about how to apply the requirements within the Standard. The IASB acknowledge that, in some cases, the outcome of using its clarified approach may differ from the outcome achieved using the alternative approach contained in the amendments issued by the FASB (see paragraphs BC414L–BC414N).

Alternative approach developed by the FASB

BC414L   The FASB developed an alternative approach to determine whether a licence constitutes a right to access or a right to use, based on the nature of the intellectual property. The FASB explained that the basis for this approach is whether an entity's promise to a customer includes supporting or maintaining the intellectual property to which the customer has rights, which in turn largely depends on whether the intellectual property has significant stand-alone functionality.

BC414M   The FASB decided that intellectual property is either:

(a)   functional intellectual property, which is intellectual property that has significant stand-alone functionality and derives a substantial portion of its utility (ie its ability to provide benefit or value) from its significant stand-alone functionality. In this case, a customer generally obtains a licence for the right to use intellectual property unless the functionality of the intellectual property is expected to substantively change during the licence period as a result of activities of the entity that do not transfer a good or service to the customer and the customer is contractually or practically required to use the updated intellectual property; or

(b)   symbolic intellectual property, which is intellectual property that does not have significant stand-alone functionality. Substantially all of the utility of symbolic intellectual property is derived from its association with the entity's past or ongoing activities, including its ordinary business activities. In this case, a customer obtains a licence for the right to access intellectual property.

BC414N   The FASB's approach looks to the nature of the intellectual property to determine whether the entity's activities significantly affect the intellectual property to which the customer has rights. The FASB's approach has the potential to result in some licences of symbolic intellectual property being classified as a right to access intellectual property, even though there is no expectation that the entity will undertake activities after making the intellectual property available to the customer. For example, the entity may own a brand that it does not support or maintain, but still grants licences to customers to use the brand in television or movie productions that are set in a time period during which the brand was active. Nonetheless, the FASB decided to adopt this alternative approach on the basis of feedback that the approach would be more operable than the approach contained in Topic 606 when it was issued in May 2014, particularly for entities with a significant number of licensing arrangements and those with diversified operations.

Contractual restrictions in a licence and the identification of performance obligations

BC414O   Some stakeholders suggested that it was unclear whether particular types of contractual restrictions would affect the identification of the promised goods or services in the contract. For example, an arrangement might grant a customer a licence of a well-known television programme or movie for a period of time (for example, three years), but the customer might be restricted to showing that licensed content only once per year during each of those three years. Those stakeholders acknowledged that paragraph B62 is clear that restrictions of time, geographical region or use do not affect the licensor's determination about whether the licence is satisfied over time or at a point in time. However, in their view, it was unclear whether contractual restrictions affect the entity's identification of its promises in the contract (ie whether the airing restrictions affect whether the entity has granted one licence or three licences). Subsequent to the publication, in July 2015, of the Exposure Draft *Clarifications to IFRS 15*, the TRG discussed some further examples considering whether particular contractual restrictions create separate promises or, instead, merely define attributes of a promise. The TRG also discussed time attributes within the context of applying paragraph B61 of IFRS 15 to renewals of, or extensions to, existing licences (see paragraphs BC414S–BC414U).

BC414P   Having considered the wider implications of amending IFRS 15 before its effective date, the IASB decided that no clarification on the identification of performance obligations in a contract containing one or more licences was necessary. This is because, in its view, the clarifications made to IFRS 15 by the amendments issued in April 2016 will assist all entities in applying the requirements for identifying performance obligations contained in paragraphs 22–30 of IFRS 15. Paragraphs BC405–BC406 of IFRS 15 explain that, as is the case with other contracts, contracts that include a promise to grant a licence to a customer require an assessment of the promises in the contract using the criteria for identifying performance obligations (see paragraphs 27–30 of IFRS 15). This assessment is done before applying the criteria to determine the nature of an entity's promise in granting a licence. Consequently, the entity considers all of the contractual terms to determine whether the promised rights result in the transfer to the customer of one or more licences. In making this determination, judgement is needed to distinguish contractual provisions that create promises to transfer rights to use the entity's intellectual property from contractual provisions that establish when, where and how those rights may be used.

BC414Q   The IASB considered Example 59 in the Illustrative Examples accompanying IFRS 15. The entity concludes that its only performance obligation is to grant the customer a right to use the music recording. When, where and how the right can be used is defined by the attributes of time (two years), geographical scope (Country A) and permitted use (in commercials). If, instead, the entity had granted the customer rights to use the recording for two different time periods in two geographical locations, for example, years X1–X3 in Country A and years X2–X4 in Country B, the entity would need to use the criteria for identifying performance obligations in paragraphs 27–30 of IFRS 15 to determine whether the contract included one licence covering both countries or separate licences for each country.

BC414R   The FASB decided to amend Topic 606 to confirm that the requirements about contractual restrictions of the nature described in paragraph B62 do not replace the requirement for the entity to identify the number of licences promised in the contract. Similarly to the IASB, the FASB also observed that judgement is often required in distinguishing a contract that contains a single licence with multiple attributes from a contract that contains multiple licences to the customer that represent separate performance obligations.

Renewals of licences of intellectual property

BC414S   As noted in paragraph BC414O, the TRG discussed the application of paragraph B61 of IFRS 15 within the context of licence renewals. Paragraph B61 states that '... revenue cannot be recognised for a licence that provides a right to use the entity's intellectual property before the beginning of the period during which the customer is able to use and benefit from the licence'. Some stakeholders asked whether paragraph B61 applies to the renewal of an existing licence or whether the entity could recognise revenue for the renewal when the parties agree to the renewal.

BC414T   The discussion at the TRG indicated that this is an area in which judgement is needed. This is because when the entity and the customer enter into a contract to renew (or extend the period of) an existing licence, the entity will evaluate whether the renewal or extension should be treated as a new licence or, alternatively, as a modification of the existing contract. A modification would be accounted for in accordance with the contract modifications requirements in paragraphs 18–21 of IFRS 15. The IASB noted that, although some diversity may arise, IFRS 15 provides a more extensive framework for applying judgement than its predecessor, IAS 18. Again, having considered the wider implications of amending IFRS 15 before its effective date, the IASB decided that a clarification about the application of the contract modification requirements specifically for renewals of licensing arrangements was not necessary.

BC414U   The FASB decided to amend Topic 606 and provide an additional example to specify that the entity would generally not recognise revenue relating to the renewal until the beginning of the licence renewal period. Consequently, in some cases, this may result in the recognition of revenue with respect to the renewal or extension at a later date using Topic 606 than using IFRS 15.

When to consider the nature of the entity's promise in granting a licence

BC414V   Paragraph B55 requires an entity to apply the general revenue recognition model (paragraphs 31–38) to determine whether a performance obligation that contains a licence that is not distinct (in accordance with paragraph 27) is satisfied at a point in time or over time. Since IFRS 15 was issued, some stakeholders have asked when the licensing guidance on determining the nature of an entity's promise applies to a performance obligation that contains a licence and other goods or services. Some held the view that paragraph B55 suggests that an entity would consider the nature of its promise in granting a licence only when the licence is distinct. Others noted that an entity would have to consider the nature of its promise in granting a licence, even when the licence is not distinct, to (a) determine whether a single performance obligation that includes a licence of intellectual property is satisfied over time or at a point in time; and (b) measure progress towards complete satisfaction of that single performance obligation if it is satisfied over time.

BC414W Again, having considered the wider implications of amending IFRS 15 before its effective date, the IASB decided that a clarification in this respect is not necessary. IFRS 15 and the explanatory material in the Basis for Conclusions provide adequate guidance to account for a licence that is combined with another good or service in a single performance obligation. An entity will, however, need to apply judgement to determine the nature of the performance obligation, and to select a method of measuring progress that is consistent with the objective of depicting the entity's performance.

BC414X In making this judgement, the IASB noted that it did not intend for an entity to disregard the guidance on determining the nature of its promise in granting a licence when applying the general revenue recognition model. In some cases, it might be necessary for an entity to consider the nature of its promise in granting a licence even when the licence is not distinct. The IASB discussed an example in which an entity grants a 10-year licence that is not distinct from a one-year service arrangement. The IASB noted that a distinct licence that provides access to an entity's intellectual property over a 10-year period could not be considered completely satisfied before the end of the access period. The IASB observed that it would, therefore, be inappropriate to conclude that a single performance obligation that includes that licence is satisfied over the one-year period of the service arrangement. Paragraph BC407 further highlights that an entity considers the nature of its promise in granting the licence if the licence is the primary or dominant component (ie the predominant item) of a single performance obligation.

BC414Y The FASB decided to make amendments that explicitly state that an entity considers the nature of its promise in granting a licence when applying the general revenue recognition model to a single performance obligation that includes a licence and other goods or services (ie when applying the requirements in Topic 606 equivalent to those set out in paragraphs 31–45 of IFRS 15). Consequently, when the licence is not the predominant item of a single performance obligation, this may result in an entity that applies Topic 606 considering the nature of its promise in granting a licence in a greater number of circumstances than an entity applying IFRS 15.

Consideration in the form of sales-based or usage-based royalties[11]

BC415 The boards decided that for a licence of intellectual property for which the consideration is based on the customer's subsequent sales or usage, an entity should not recognise any revenue for the variable amounts until the uncertainty is resolved (ie when a customer's subsequent sales or usage occurs). The boards had proposed a similar requirement in the 2011 Exposure Draft because both users and preparers of financial statements indicated that it would not be useful for an entity to recognise a minimum amount of revenue for those contracts. This is because that approach would inevitably

---

11 *Clarifications to IFRS 15* issued in April 2016 added paragraphs B63A–B63B of IFRS 15 to clarify when an entity should recognise revenue for a sales-based or usage-based royalty using the requirement in paragraph B63 of IFRS 15. Paragraphs BC415–BC421 should therefore be read together with paragraphs BC421A–BC421J, which explain the boards' considerations in amending the application guidance.

have required the entity to report, throughout the life of the contract, significant adjustments to the amount of revenue recognised at inception of the contract as a result of changes in circumstances, even though those changes in circumstances are not related to the entity's performance. The boards observed that this would not result in relevant information, particularly in contracts in which the sales-based or usage-based royalty is paid over a long period of time.

BC416   In redeliberating the 2011 Exposure Draft, the boards observed that because the restriction for a sales-based or usage-based royalty on a licence of intellectual property was structured to apply to only a particular type of transaction, other economically similar types of transactions might be accounted for differently. For example, the restriction would not apply to tangible goods that include a significant amount of intellectual property and, instead, any variable consideration to which the entity is entitled in exchange for those tangible goods would be considered under the general requirements for constraining estimates of variable consideration. Some respondents questioned the conceptual rationale for including a restriction that could in some cases result in an outcome that was not consistent with the requirement to recognise some or all of an estimate of variable consideration. Others asked whether they could apply the restriction by analogy if the promised good or service had characteristics similar to a licence of intellectual property and the consideration depended on the customer's future actions. Consequently, the boards considered whether they should do either of the following:

(a)   expand the scope of paragraph B63 of IFRS 15 to constrain all estimates of variable consideration when that consideration depends on the customer's future actions; or

(b)   develop a general principle that could be applied to all contracts that would achieve broadly the same outcomes.

Expand the scope

BC417   The boards considered whether to expand the restriction for a sales-based or usage-based royalty on a licence of intellectual property, whereby revenue recognition would be constrained to zero for any performance obligation when the amount that an entity is entitled to is based on a customer's future actions. However, the boards decided not to introduce this principle into IFRS 15. This is because it would have prevented an entity from recognising any revenue when the goods and services were transferred in cases in which the entity could estimate the variable consideration and meet the objective of constraining estimates of variable consideration.

BC418   The boards also observed that expanding the scope to constrain revenue when consideration is based on the customer's future actions would also have increased complexity. It would have required the boards to create another exception to maintain the requirements for accounting for customer rights of return, which also results in consideration that is dependent on the customer's future actions.

Develop a general principle

BC419   The boards also considered whether the restriction for a sales-based or usage-based royalty on a licence of intellectual property could be incorporated into a general principle. The boards considered various ways of articulating this principle, including doing so on the basis of the timing of satisfaction of a performance obligation—that is, whether the performance obligation is satisfied over time or at a point in time. Specifically, if the performance obligation to which the variable consideration related was satisfied at a point in time, an entity would include an estimate of variable consideration in the transaction price only to the extent that it is highly probable that a significant reversal in the amount of cumulative revenue recognised will not occur when the uncertainty associated with the variable consideration is subsequently resolved. Conversely, if the performance obligation to which the variable consideration related was satisfied over time, an entity could include any estimate in the transaction price (even a minimum amount) provided that the objective of constraining estimates of variable consideration could be met.

BC420   This approach was based on the rationale that, for a performance obligation satisfied at a point in time, recognition of revenue that could be adjusted up or down would not be a meaningful depiction of the consideration for the related goods or services and, furthermore, any future adjustments to the transaction price (and therefore revenue) would have little correlation with the entity's performance in that period. Conversely, when a performance obligation is satisfied over time, the initial recognition of some but not all of the estimate of variable consideration would be affected by the entity's future performance, so future adjustments to the transaction price would provide useful information because they explain whether the entity's subsequent performance was beneficial (ie the minimum amount is increased) or detrimental (ie the minimum amount is subject to an unexpected reversal). However, the boards rejected this approach because it would have added complexity to the model that would outweigh the benefit.

BC421   Consequently, the boards decided against applying the restriction for sales-based or usage-based royalties on intellectual property more broadly. Although the boards acknowledge that the requirements in paragraph B63 of IFRS 15 constitute an exception that might not be consistent with the principle of recognising some or all of the estimate of variable consideration, they decided that this disadvantage was outweighed by the simplicity of these requirements, as well as by the relevance of the resulting information for this type of transaction. The boards also noted that because this is a specific requirement intended for only limited circumstances, entities should not apply it by analogy to other types of promised goods or services or other types of variable consideration.

Clarifications to IFRS 15 (amendments issued in April 2016)

BC421A Paragraph B63 requires an entity to recognise revenue for a sales-based or usage-based royalty promised in exchange for a licence of intellectual property when the later of the following events occurs: (a) the customer's subsequent sales or usage; and (b) the performance obligation to which some or all of the sales-based or usage-based royalty has been allocated has been satisfied (or partially satisfied). This guidance in paragraph B63 is referred to as the 'royalties constraint'.

BC421B Stakeholders had indicated that it was unclear when a sales-based or usage-based royalty is 'promised in exchange for a licence'. Some stakeholders held the view that the royalties constraint applies whenever the royalty relates to a licence of intellectual property, regardless of whether the royalty is also consideration for other goods or services in the contract. Other stakeholders had suggested that the royalties constraint applies only when the royalty relates solely to a licence that is distinct in accordance with paragraph 27 of IFRS 15 or only when the licence is the predominant item to which the royalty relates. Stakeholders had also indicated that it was unclear whether a single sales-based or usage-based royalty should be split into a portion to which the royalties constraint would apply and a portion to which it would not, for example, when the royalty relates to a licence and another good or service that is not a licence.

BC421C In response to stakeholder concerns, the boards decided to clarify the application of the royalties constraint as follows:

(a) the royalties constraint applies whenever a licence of intellectual property is the sole or predominant item to which the royalty relates; and

(b) an entity should not split a single royalty into a portion subject to the royalties constraint and a portion that is subject to the general constraint on variable consideration contained in paragraphs 50–59 of IFRS 15.

Applying the royalties constraint

BC421D The boards decided to clarify in paragraph B63A that the royalties constraint applies to those arrangements for which the licence is the predominant item to which the royalty relates. This is because users of financial statements are likely to view those arrangements as licensing arrangements. The boards had previously observed in paragraph BC415 that it would not be useful for an entity to recognise a minimum amount of revenue for licences of intellectual property for which the consideration is based on the customer's sales or usage. Applying the royalties constraint only when the royalty relates solely to a licence that is distinct in accordance with paragraph 27 of IFRS 15 might unduly restrict its application.

BC421E The boards observed that judgement is required to determine when a licence is the predominant item to which a sales-based or usage-based royalty relates. However, the judgement needed for that determination is likely to be less than the judgement needed to apply the general requirements on variable consideration to those arrangements that would fall outside the scope of the royalties constraint if that scope were to be more restrictive.

BC421F The boards decided against changing the scope of the royalties constraint, including expanding it beyond those situations for which a licence is the predominant item to which a royalty relates. This is because doing so would capture arrangements for which the boards previously concluded that the royalties constraint should not apply (for example, sales of intellectual property or sales of tangible goods that include intellectual property). As noted in paragraphs BC416 and BC421, the royalties constraint is intended to apply only to limited circumstances involving licences of intellectual property and, therefore, entities cannot apply it by analogy to other types of transactions.

BC421G The boards observed that an entity might conclude that a licence is the predominant item to which a sales-based or usage-based royalty relates when there is more than one performance obligation. This conclusion might be reached regardless of whether the entity concludes that the royalty can be allocated entirely to one performance obligation in accordance with the requirements for allocating variable consideration in paragraphs 84–85 of IFRS 15. The boards also observed that the royalties constraint would also apply when the royalty predominantly relates to two or more licences promised in a contract, rather than a single licence.

BC421H The boards made consistent clarifying amendments to the Illustrative Examples to more clearly support the conclusions reached about when a sales-based royalty would be recognised. However, the boards decided not to amend paragraph B63 or provide further Illustrative Examples for more complex fact patterns.

BC421I In reaching this decision, the IASB considered a similar example to Example 60 accompanying IFRS 15 and concluded that when a time-based measure of progress appropriately depicts an entity's performance under the licence, recognising the sales-based royalty as and when the customer's sales occur would generally be appropriate. This is because, as noted in paragraph BC219, the objective of the royalties constraint is to prevent an entity from recognising revenue for uncertain amounts until the uncertainty is resolved (ie when the customer's subsequent sales or usage occurs). In effect, the requirement in paragraph B63 constrains the amount of revenue that can be recognised when or as a performance obligation is satisfied, rather than constraining the total amount of the transaction price to be allocated. Paragraph B63(b) reflects one of the key principles of IFRS 15, which is to recognise revenue only when (or as) an entity satisfies a performance obligation. If the entity has satisfied (or partially satisfied) the performance obligation to which the royalty relates, paragraph B63(a) further constrains the recognition of revenue until the uncertainty about the amount of revenue is resolved. Consequently, an entity recognises revenue from a sales-based or usage-based royalty when (or as) the customer's subsequent sales or usage occur, unless recognition in that manner would accelerate the recognition of revenue for the performance obligation to which the royalty solely or partially relates ahead of the entity's performance towards complete satisfaction of the performance obligation based on an appropriate measure of progress.

Splitting a royalty

BC421J   Paragraph B63B of IFRS 15 clarifies that an entity should recognise revenue from a sales-based or usage-based royalty wholly in accordance with either the requirement in paragraph B63 (if paragraph B63 applies) or the requirements on variable consideration contained in paragraphs 50–59 of IFRS 15 (if paragraph B63 does not apply). The boards made this clarification in paragraph B63B because the boards concluded that (a) it would be more complex to account for part of a royalty under the royalties constraint and another part under the general requirements for variable consideration; and (b) doing so would not provide any additional useful information to users of financial statements. This is because splitting a royalty would result in an entity recognising an amount at contract inception that would reflect neither the amount to which the entity expects to be entitled based on its performance, nor the amount to which the entity has become legally entitled during the period.

Repurchase agreements (paragraphs B64–B76)

BC422   When developing the requirements for control, the boards considered how an entity should apply the requirements to contracts in which the entity sells an asset and also enters into a repurchase agreement (either in the same contract or in another contract).

BC423   The boards observed that repurchase agreements generally come in three forms – forwards, call options and put options. However, the boards decided that an arrangement in which an entity subsequently decides to repurchase a good after transferring control of that good to a customer would not constitute a repurchase agreement as described in paragraph B64 of IFRS 15. This is because the entity's subsequent decision to repurchase a good without reference to any pre-existing contractual right does not affect the customer's ability to direct the use of, and obtain substantially all of the remaining benefits from, the good upon initial transfer. In other words, the customer is not obliged to resell that good to the entity as a result of the initial contract. The boards observed that in those cases, the entity should, however, consider whether the customer obtained control of the good initially and may need to consider the requirements for principal versus agent in paragraphs B34–B38 of IFRS 15.

A forward or a call option

BC424   If an entity has an obligation or a right to repurchase an asset (ie a forward or a call option, respectively), the boards decided that the customer does not obtain control of the asset and, therefore, no revenue should be recognised. This is because the customer is constrained in its ability to direct the use of, and obtain substantially all of the remaining benefits from, the asset. Because the customer is obliged to return, or to stand ready to return, the asset to the entity, the customer cannot use up or consume the entire asset. Moreover, the customer cannot sell the asset to another party (unless that sale is subject to a repurchase agreement, in which case the customer's benefit from the sale is constrained).

BC425   Theoretically, a customer is not constrained in its ability to direct the use of, and obtain substantially all the benefits from, the asset if an entity agrees to repurchase, at the prevailing market price, an asset from the customer that is substantially the same and is readily available in the marketplace. However, the boards noted that an entity would be unlikely to enter into such a transaction.

BC426   The boards decided that an entity would account for a forward or a call option as a lease or a financing arrangement, depending on the relationship between the repurchase amount and the original selling price. The FASB also decided to specify that when the forward or call option accounted for as a lease is part of a sale-leaseback transaction, the contract should be accounted for as a financing transaction. Otherwise, the FASB observed that an entity would have been required to account for the transaction as a lease and then as a leaseback, which would not have been appropriate.

BC427   The boards noted that an entity would not need to consider the likelihood that a call option can be exercised, because the existence of the call option effectively limits the customer's ability to control the asset. However, the boards observed that if the call option is non-substantive, that option should be ignored in assessing whether and when the customer obtains control of a good or service (to be consistent with the general requirement for any non-substantive term in a contract).

A put option

BC428   The boards decided that if the sale and repurchase agreement resulted in an entity's obligation to repurchase the asset at a customer's request (ie a put option), the customer would obtain control of the asset because the customer is neither obliged to return the asset nor obliged to stand ready to do so. Consequently, the customer has the ability to direct the use of, and obtain substantially all of the remaining benefits from, the asset (ie the customer can sell, use up or consume the entire asset and choose not to exercise the put option). The boards decided that the entity should account for its obligation to stand ready to repurchase the asset, to be consistent with the accounting for the sale of a product with a right of return (see paragraphs BC363–BC367). That results in the entity recognising the following:

    (a)   a liability for its obligation to repurchase the asset, measured at the amount of the consideration expected to be paid to the customer;

    (b)   an asset for the entity's right to receive that asset upon settling that liability, measured at an amount that may or may not equal the entity's previous carrying value of the asset; and

    (c)   revenue on transfer of the asset for the difference between the sales price of the asset and the liability recognised for the obligation to repurchase the asset.

BC429   Some respondents questioned whether that accounting would be appropriate in all cases in which a customer has a put option. For instance, some noted that the contract appears to be economically similar to a lease with a purchase option rather than to a right of return. That might be the case if the entity is required to repurchase the asset at a price that is lower than the original sales price and the surrounding facts and circumstances indicate that the customer will exercise its put option. In those cases, the difference between the original sales price and the repurchase price can be viewed as the amount that the customer pays for a right to use the asset, thereby compensating the entity for the decline in the value of the asset. Some respondents noted that, in other cases, the contract is, in effect, a financing arrangement.

BC430   The boards agreed with those respondents and decided that if a customer has a right to require an entity to repurchase the asset at a price that is lower than the original sales price and the customer has a significant economic incentive to exercise that right, then the customer does not obtain control of the asset. Although the customer is not obliged to exercise its put option, the fact that it has a significant economic incentive to exercise that right means that it would probably incur a loss if it did not do so. (For example, the repurchase price may be set significantly above the expected market value of the asset at the date of the repurchase. However, the boards observed that an entity should consider factors other than the price when determining that it has a significant economic incentive to exercise its right.) The boards decided that in those cases, the existence of the option effectively restricts the customer's ability to direct the use of, and obtain substantially all of the remaining benefits from, the asset. For similar reasons, the boards decided that if the customer has the unconditional right to require the entity to repurchase the asset at a price that is greater than the original sales price, and higher than the expected market value of the asset, the customer does not obtain control of the asset.

BC431   The boards also considered whether other arrangements should be accounted for as a lease, such as when an entity provides its customer with a guaranteed amount to be paid on resale (ie a guaranteed minimum resale value). Accounting for those transactions as leases would be consistent with previous US GAAP, and a number of respondents, primarily from the automotive industry, explained that they viewed the transactions to be economically similar. However, the boards observed that while the cash flows may be similar, the customer's ability to control the asset in each case is different. If the customer has a put option that it has significant economic incentive to exercise, the customer is restricted in its ability to consume, modify or sell the asset. However, when the entity guarantees that the customer will receive a minimum amount of sales proceeds, the customer is not constrained in its ability to direct the use of, and obtain substantially all of the benefits from, the asset. Thus, the boards decided that it was not necessary to expand the requirements for repurchase agreements to consider guaranteed amounts of resale.

Accounting for repurchase agreements in which the customer does not obtain control of the asset

BC432   If an entity enters into a contract with a repurchase agreement and the customer does not obtain control of the asset, the boards decided the following:

(a)   the contract should be accounted for as a lease in accordance with IAS 17 *Leases* or Topic 840 *Leases* if the customer is paying for a right to use the asset; and

(b)   the contract is a financing arrangement if the net consideration that the entity receives is equal to or less than zero (ie the entity is paying interest).

BC433   To ensure consistent accounting in IFRS and US GAAP for a financing arrangement that arises from a contract with a customer, the boards decided to provide guidance consistent with Subtopic 470-40 *Debt—Product Financing Arrangements*. Consequently, the FASB decided to amend the guidance in Subtopic 470-40 that discusses arrangements in which an entity sells a product to another entity and, in a related transaction, agrees to repurchase the product. However, the FASB decided not to amend Subtopic 470-40 for transactions in which an entity arranges for another party to purchase products on its behalf and agrees to purchase those products from the other party. In those cases, the entity is required to recognise the products as an asset and to recognise a related liability when the other party purchases the product. The FASB noted that although IFRS 15 results in similar accounting when the other party acts as an agent of the entity (ie the other party does not obtain control of the products), Subtopic 470-40 provides explicit requirements for transactions in which no sale has occurred.

Transition, effective date and early application (paragraphs C1–C9)

Transition (paragraphs C2–C8A)

BC434   The boards decided that an entity should apply IFRS 15 using either of the following methods:

(a)   retrospectively to each prior reporting period presented in accordance with IAS 8 or Topic 250 *Accounting Changes and Error Corrections*, subject to some optional practical expedients (see paragraphs BC435–BC438); or

(b)   retrospectively with the cumulative effect of initially applying IFRS 15 recognised as an adjustment to the opening balance of retained earnings   at   the   date   of   initial   application   (see paragraphs BC439–BC444).

Retrospective application

BC435   The 2010 and 2011 Exposure Drafts proposed that an entity should apply the requirements retrospectively in accordance with IAS 8 or Topic 250. Retrospective application ensures that all contracts with customers are recognised and measured consistently both in the current period and in the comparative periods presented, regardless of whether those contracts were entered into before or after the requirements became effective. Furthermore, retrospective application provides users of financial statements with useful trend information across the current period and comparative periods.

Feedback received from users of financial statements confirmed that retrospective application would be the most useful transition approach for them to be able to understand trends in revenue.

BC436　In contrast to the feedback received from users of financial statements, many respondents commented that applying the requirements retrospectively would be burdensome, especially for entities with long-term contracts or large and complex multiple-element arrangements. The main concerns raised by those respondents were as follows:

(a)　it may not be possible to obtain historical information for contracts that were completed under previous revenue Standards in IFRS or US GAAP because the relevant information is no longer retained by the entity.

(b)　applying IFRS 15 retrospectively (particularly to completed contracts) may not result in a materially different pattern of revenue recognition, and the significant costs incurred to confirm this fact would not provide much benefit to users of financial statements. For example, for contracts that were considered to be completed (as assessed under previous revenue Standards) several years before the date of initial application, an entity would, theoretically, need to obtain the relevant information to ensure that there was no effect on the pattern of revenue recognition in the financial statements in the year of initial application.

(c)　presenting the effect of IFRS 15 in the comparative years would incur significant preparation and audit costs, because a change in revenue could affect many other line items in the financial statements (such as deferred tax, receivables, interest and foreign currency gains/losses) as well as items that reference an entity's revenue in the financial statements (such as taxes, statutory reporting and financing arrangements).

(d)　the historical information needed to estimate stand-alone selling prices of goods or services in a contract with many performance obligations may not exist.

(e)　entities make assumptions and estimates throughout a contract's life, and it may not be possible to recreate the circumstances that apply historically without the use of hindsight.

Retrospective application with practical expedients (paragraphs C4–C6)

BC437　The boards decided that although retrospective application would generally impose increased preparation costs, those costs would be outweighed by the increased benefits to users of financial statements. Consequently, the boards considered how the burden of retrospective application could be eased while, at the same time, retaining the benefits of comparability and consistency that retrospective application would provide. To ease the burden of transition without sacrificing comparability, the boards decided to allow an entity to elect to use one or more of the following practical expedients when applying IFRS 15 retrospectively.

Practical expedient	Rationale
Reducing the number of contracts that require restatement[a]	
For contracts completed before the date of initial application of IFRS 15, an entity need not restate contracts that begin and end within the same annual reporting period.	In considering whether an entity should be required to review and restate all contracts completed before the date of initial application, the boards decided that trend information should be preserved for completed contracts that span annual reporting periods. Consequently, the boards decided to limit the relief to only those contracts that begin and end within the same annual reporting period, because the amount and timing of revenue recognition relating to those contracts would not change between annual reporting periods. The boards noted that this relief would significantly reduce the transition burden on entities that have a large number of short-term contracts. A consequence of this relief is that revenue reported in interim periods before and after the effective date would not necessarily be accounted for on a comparable basis. The boards expect that an entity would not elect to use this relief if it operates in an industry in which comparability across interim reporting periods is particularly important to users of financial statements.
Simplifying how an entity restates contracts with customers[b]	
For contracts completed before the date of initial application of IFRS 15 and that have variable consideration, an entity may use the transaction price at the date that the contract was completed rather than estimating variable consideration amounts in the comparative reporting periods.	Full retrospective application of IFRS 15 in accordance with IAS 8 or Topic 250 would require an entity to determine the estimates that it would have made at each of the reporting dates in the comparative periods. The boards considered that making those estimates in the comparative years would increase the complexity and costs of retrospective application. By allowing an entity to use hindsight in estimating variable consideration, the boards decided that transition would be simplified for the following reasons: (a) it would reduce the amount of information that an entity would need to collect throughout the transition period; and (b) the entity would not need to determine the transaction price at the end of each period.

continued...

...continued

Practical expedient	Rationale
Simplifying retrospective application of other aspects of the requirements	
For all reporting periods presented before the date of initial application of IFRS 15, an entity need not disclose the amount of the transaction price allocated to the remaining perform- ance obligations and an explanation of when the entity expects to recognise that amount as revenue (as specified in paragraph 120 of IFRS 15).	The boards decided that the disclosure of the amount of the transaction price allocated to the remaining performance obligations (as would be required by paragraph 120 of IFRS 15) should not be required for periods presented before the date of initial applica- tion of IFRS 15 for the following reasons:
	(a) the disclosure would be most useful for the current period; and
	(b) the disclosure could be burdensome to prepare for comparative years, especially when trying to avoid the use of hindsight to estimate the transaction price and the expected timing of satisfaction of those performance obligations.

(a) *Clarifications to IFRS 15* issued in April 2016 amended paragraph C5 of IFRS 15 to add a further practical expedient to permit an entity not to restate contracts that are completed contracts at the beginning of the earliest period presented. This practical expedient, if applied, would further reduce the number of contracts that require restatement. The IASB's considerations in adding the practical expedient are explained in paragraphs BC445M–BC445N.

(b) *Clarifications to IFRS 15* issued in April 2016 amended paragraph C5 and added paragraph C7A to add a further practical expedient to simplify how an entity restates contracts with customers that are modified before transition to IFRS 15. The boards' considerations in adding the practical expedient are explained in paragraphs BC445O–BC445R.

BC438   As a result of the practical expedients providing some relief from applying IFRS 15 retrospectively, the boards also decided to supplement the transitional disclosure requirements of IAS 8 or Topic 250 to require an entity to provide additional disclosure if it elects to use one or more of the practical expedients. Accordingly, paragraph C6 of IFRS 15 requires an entity to provide an explanation to users of financial statements about which practical expedients were used and, to the extent reasonably possible, a qualitative assessment of the estimated effect of applying those practical expedients.

Retrospective application with the cumulative effect recognised in the current period (paragraphs C7–C8)

BC439   The boards decided to develop an alternative transition method to ease the burden of retrospectively applying IFRS 15 because feedback from preparers and auditors indicated that, although helpful, the practical expedients (see paragraph BC437) would not mitigate much of the implementation challenge of a retrospective transition approach. In contrast, users of financial statements generally supported the requirements for retrospective application with practical expedients because it would provide them with useful information on transition and assist their financial statement analyses.

BC440　As a result of those differing views, transition was one of the topics discussed at four disclosure and transition workshops that were held in late 2012 with both users and preparers of financial statements (see paragraph BC328). During those workshops, users of financial statements acknowledged that another transition method might be appropriate to ease the burden of transition; however, they emphasised their need for trend information, regardless of which method is used.

BC441　After considering this feedback, the boards decided that as an alternative to retrospective application with practical expedients, an entity could apply IFRS 15 (including the requirements for costs) retrospectively, with the cumulative effect of initially applying IFRS 15 recognised in the current year (referred to as the 'cumulative catch-up' transition method). Specifically, the cumulative effect would be an adjustment to the appropriate opening balance of equity in the year of initial application (ie comparative years would not be restated) for contracts that are not completed at the date of initial application.[12] (The boards clarified that a completed contract is a contract in which the entity has fully performed in accordance with revenue recognition requirements in effect before the date of initial application. Thus, a completed contract would include a contract for which the entity's performance was complete but there was a change in the transaction price after the date of initial application.)[13] The boards observed that the cumulative catch-up transition method responds to feedback from auditors and preparers by eliminating the need to restate prior periods and thus reducing costs.

BC442　The boards noted that applying the cumulative catch-up transition method results in consistent presentation of contracts under previous IFRS or US GAAP during the comparative years and in consistent presentation of any contracts not yet completed at the date of initial application under IFRS 15 in the current year. However, because the comparative information will not be restated under the cumulative catch-up transition method, the boards decided to require additional disclosures to help users of financial statements understand the effect on trend information. Consequently, when an entity uses the cumulative catch-up transition method, it is required to disclose the following information for reporting periods that include the date of initial application:

12　*Clarifications to IFRS 15* issued in April 2016 amended paragraph C7 of IFRS 15 to permit an entity using the transition method described in paragraph C3(b) to apply IFRS 15 (a) only to contracts that are not completed contracts at the date of initial application (as originally required in paragraph C7 when IFRS 15 was issued); or (b) to all contracts including completed contracts at the date of initial application. The boards' considerations in amending paragraph C7 are explained in paragraphs BC445J–BC445L.

13　The FASB subsequently decided to amend the definition of a completed contract as a contract for which all or substantially all of the revenue was recognised in accordance with the revenue guidance that was in effect before the date of initial application of Topic 606. The IASB's considerations for deciding not to amend the definition, together with an overview of the FASB's considerations for amending the definition, are explained in paragraphs BC445C–BC445I.

(a)   the amount by which each financial statement line item is affected in the current year as a result of the entity applying IFRS 15 rather than previous revenue Standards in IFRS; and

(b)   an explanation of the reasons for the significant changes in those financial statement line items.

BC443   In other words, to provide the required disclosures, an entity would apply both IFRS 15 and the previous revenue Standards in the year of initial application. Despite requiring an entity to account for revenue transactions in the year of initial application using two different sets of accounting requirements, the boards decided that this method would reduce the overall cost of applying IFRS 15 while still providing information about trends that was requested by users of financial statements.

BC444   The boards also considered other transition methods as alternatives to the cumulative catch-up method to try to ease the burden of retrospective application. For example, the boards considered requiring a prospective approach that would require entities to apply IFRS 15 only to new contracts or those that are materially modified on or after the date of initial application. However, the boards rejected this approach because prospective application would not result in consistent presentation of existing contracts and new contracts and thus would reduce comparability. In addition, this approach would not provide useful trend information for users of financial statements until existing contracts have been fully satisfied after the date of initial application. Furthermore, the boards observed that this approach would require some entities to incur significant costs of maintaining two accounting systems for contracts that are accounted for in accordance with IFRS 15 and previous revenue Standards in IFRS, until all existing contracts have been completed, which could take many years for entities with long-term contracts.

Other relief

BC445   If an entity applies IFRS 15 retrospectively in accordance with paragraph C3(a) of IFRS 15 (ie without electing to use the cumulative catch-up transition method), comparative information *would* be restated. Consequently, the IASB clarified that if an entity applies IFRS 15 retrospectively in accordance with paragraph C3(a), it is not required to provide the current year transition disclosure in paragraph 28(f) of IAS 8.

Clarifications to IFRS 15 (amendments issued in April 2016)

BC445A   The boards discussed requests from some stakeholders for further transition relief in respect of (a) accounting for a completed contract (as defined in paragraph C2(b)) on transition to IFRS 15; and (b) accounting for modifications to a contract that occurred before transition to IFRS 15. The IASB decided (a) to expand the application of the transition method described in paragraph C3(b) by allowing an entity a choice to apply IFRS 15 to all contracts including completed contracts; and (b) to provide transition relief for contract modifications. The FASB decided to make similar amendments to Topic 606. The IASB additionally decided to allow an entity using the transition method described in paragraph C3(a) not to restate completed contracts at the beginning of the earliest period presented. The following paragraphs explain the boards' considerations in providing the additional practical expedients.

Completed contracts

BC445B   The boards considered the following questions about the transition requirements in IFRS 15 with respect to a completed contract:

(a)   definition of and accounting for a completed contract.

(b)   providing an entity applying paragraph C3(b) of IFRS 15 with the choice of applying IFRS 15 to all contracts including completed contracts at the date of initial application.

(c)   permitting an entity applying paragraph C3(a) of IFRS 15 not to restate completed contracts at the beginning of the earliest period presented.

Definition of and accounting for a completed contract

BC445C   Some stakeholders, mainly in the US, highlighted potential difficulties with respect to the definition of a completed contract in paragraph C2(b) and the accounting for a completed contract once IFRS 15 becomes effective. They were unclear whether the boards intended that any previously unrecognised revenue from a completed contract that is not transitioned to IFRS 15 would continue to be accounted for in accordance with the previous revenue Standards. In addition, referring to the words 'transferred all of the goods or services' in the definition of a completed contract, they commented that:

(a)   *transfer* of goods or services is a notion that is introduced in IFRS 15 and does not exist in previous revenue Standards.

(b)   it is unclear how an entity would continue to account for a completed contract in accordance with the previous revenue Standards, which would be withdrawn once IFRS 15 becomes effective.

(c)   the boards' considerations explained in paragraph BC444 for rejecting a prospective transition method do not support the use of the previous revenue Standards once IFRS 15 becomes effective. As explained in paragraph BC444, one of the reasons for rejecting prospective transition methods was the 'significant costs of maintaining two accounting systems...until all existing contracts have been completed, which could take many years for entities with long-term contracts'.

BC445D   The IASB concluded that it was not necessary to change the definition of a completed contract to address the issues raised. In relation to the words 'transferred all of the goods or services' in the definition of a completed contract, the IASB noted that it did not intend that an entity would apply the 'transfer of control' notion in IFRS 15 to goods or services identified in accordance with previous revenue Standards. The IASB noted that paragraph BC441 refers to performance in accordance with previous revenue Standards. Consequently, in many situations the term 'transferred' would mean 'delivered' within the context of contracts for the sale of goods and 'performed' within the context of contracts for rendering services and construction contracts. In some situations, the entity would use judgement when determining whether it has transferred goods or services to the customer. For example, an entity may need to use judgement to determine when it has transferred rights to use its assets (for example, rights granted within a licence agreement), because there is no specific guidance on the transfer or delivery of such rights in IAS 18.

BC445E   The IASB observed that if an entity chooses not to apply IFRS 15 to completed contracts in accordance with paragraph C5(a)(ii) or the amended paragraph C7, only contracts that are not completed contracts are included in the transition to IFRS 15. The entity would continue to account for the completed contracts in accordance with its accounting policies based on the previous revenue Standards. The IASB's decision, when it issued IFRS 15 in May 2014, was not to require such an entity to apply IFRS 15 either prospectively or retrospectively to completed contracts.

BC445F   Furthermore, the IASB also observed that its rationale for rejecting a prospective transition method because of the costs of maintaining two systems is less relevant to completed contracts for two reasons. First, the IASB expects the volume of completed contracts with unrecognised revenue at the date of transition to IFRS 15 to be significantly less than the volume of all ongoing contracts that would be included in the transition to IFRS 15. Second, for many completed contracts, the IASB does not expect the accounting under previous revenue Standards to continue for many years after transition, because the goods or services have been transferred before the transition to IFRS 15.

BC445G   Some stakeholders expressed a view that accounting for completed contracts using the previous revenue Standards after IFRS 15 becomes effective would not provide useful financial information to users of financial statements. When developing the transition method described in paragraph C3(b), the boards considered feedback from users of financial statements and decided to require an entity to provide additional disclosures to help users understand the effect of that transition method on trend information (see paragraphs BC442–BC443). The IASB observed that as part of the disclosures required by paragraph C8 an entity could provide additional information about the amount of revenue recognised using previous revenue Standards, if the entity concludes that such information would be helpful to users. In addition, when selecting a transition method, the IASB expects that an entity would consider whether the selected transition method provides useful information to users of its financial statements. If the entity were to conclude that excluding completed contracts from the transition to IFRS 15 would not provide useful information to users, and if that is an important consideration for the entity, then the entity could decide to include completed contracts in its transition to IFRS 15.

BC445H   The FASB decided to amend Topic 606 to define a completed contract as a contract for which all (or substantially all) of the revenue was recognised in accordance with the previous revenue Standards. The FASB believes that the objective of the transition guidance in Topic 606 should be to ensure that all (or substantially all) of the revenue from contracts with customers that is recognised after transition to Topic 606 should be recognised in accordance with Topic 606. Accordingly, the FASB decided to amend the definition of a completed contract so that an entity would apply Topic 606 to all contracts for which all (or substantially all) of the revenue was not recognised under the previous revenue Standards. The FASB acknowledged that an entity would need to apply judgement in some cases to determine whether a contract is completed.

BC445I   The IASB observed that the boards' different decisions regarding amendments to the definition of a completed contract give rise to a difference between IFRS 15 and Topic 606. However, the IASB noted that an entity could avoid the consequences of the different definitions by choosing to apply IFRS 15 retrospectively to all contracts including completed contracts (see paragraph BC445K).

Providing an entity applying IFRS 15 in accordance with paragraph C3(b) with the choice of applying IFRS 15 to all contracts including completed contracts at the date of initial application

BC445J   The boards decided to amend paragraph C7 to provide an entity with a choice of applying IFRS 15 in accordance with paragraph C3(b) either (a) only to contracts that are not completed contracts at the date of initial application (which was the original requirement in paragraph C7 when IFRS 15 was issued); or (b) to all contracts including completed contracts at the date of initial application. The boards acknowledged that this choice might result in a decrease in comparability between entities. However, the boards observed that applying the transition method described in paragraph C3(b) to all contracts, including completed contracts, at the date of initial application could result in financial information that is more comparable with financial information provided by entities using the transition method described in paragraph C3(a). Furthermore, the IASB observed that any decrease in comparability between entities because of the choice will be transitory.

BC445K   The IASB also observed that:

(a)   an entity that wishes to use the transition method described in paragraph C3(b) and also avoid the consequences of the different definitions of a completed contract in IFRS 15 and Topic 606 could choose to apply IFRS 15 in accordance with paragraph C3(b) to all contracts including contracts that are completed contracts at the date of initial application; and

(b)   some entities will find applying the transition method described in paragraph C3(b) to all contracts less complex operationally than continuing to account for completed contracts under previous revenue Standards and all other contracts under IFRS 15, or using the method described in paragraph C3(a).

BC445L   The FASB observed that allowing the choice may help mitigate some of the unanticipated financial reporting consequences that some entities may experience as a result of its amendments to the definition of a completed contract.

Permitting an entity applying IFRS 15 in accordance with paragraph C3(a) not to restate completed contracts at the beginning of the earliest period presented

BC445M The IASB decided to provide an additional practical expedient to permit an entity applying IFRS 15 in accordance with paragraph C3(a) not to restate contracts that are completed contracts at the beginning of the earliest period presented. The IASB noted that reducing the population of contracts to which IFRS 15 applies (the consequence of applying this practical expedient) could reduce the effort and cost of initial application of IFRS 15. In addition, the IASB observed that a similar expedient is currently given to first-time adopters in paragraph D35 of IFRS 1 *First-time Adoption of International Financial Reporting Standards*.

BC445N The FASB decided not to provide a similar expedient to the transition guidance because it concluded that application of such an expedient would not faithfully depict a full retrospective application of Topic 606. The IASB acknowledged that the expedient could affect the comparability of financial information under the full retrospective method, but concluded that this would be outweighed by the benefit provided by the reduced transition costs.

Modified contracts

BC445O Some stakeholders highlighted that applying the requirements in paragraphs 20–21 of IFRS 15 to past contract modifications could be complex, especially if the entity has long-term contracts that are modified frequently. To simplify how an entity retrospectively applies IFRS 15 to its contracts with customers, the boards decided to provide an additional practical expedient that would permit an entity to use hindsight when evaluating contract modifications when making the transition to IFRS 15. Consequently, when restating contracts on transition to IFRS 15, an entity could either (a) follow the requirements in paragraphs 20–21; or (b) use the new practical expedient in paragraph C5(c) of IFRS 15. The new practical expedient allows the entity to reflect the aggregate effect of all past contract modifications when identifying the performance obligations, and determining and allocating the transaction price, instead of accounting for the effects of each contract modification separately. The boards observed that the practical expedient would provide some cost relief and yet would result in financial information that closely aligns with the financial information that would be available under IFRS 15 without the expedient.

BC445P The boards' conclusions on the date at which this practical expedient should be applied are not fully aligned. Both boards decided that an entity applying IFRS 15 in accordance with paragraph C3(a) should apply the practical expedient at the beginning of the earliest period presented. For an entity applying Topic 606 in accordance with paragraph 606-10-65-1(d)(2) (equivalent to paragraph C3(b) of IFRS 15), the FASB decided that the entity should apply the practical expedient at the date of initial application. However, the IASB decided that an entity applying IFRS 15 in accordance with paragraph C3(b) may apply the practical expedient either (a) at the beginning of the earliest period presented; or (b) at the date of initial application.

BC445Q   The IASB observed that without the choice of the date at which the practical expedient is applied, entities that apply IFRS 15 in accordance with paragraph C3(b), especially entities with a large number of contracts subject to frequent modifications (for example, some telecommunication companies), might have practical difficulties if they are required to wait until the date of initial application for finalising the cumulative effect of past contract modifications. This is because of the large number of contracts that would have to be evaluated in a relatively short time. Those entities highlighted that the benefit of the practical expedient would be considerably constrained if they cannot finalise the cumulative effect of past contract modifications ahead of the date of initial application of IFRS 15. The IASB observed that this decision creates a difference between IFRS 15 and Topic 606. However, an entity applying IFRS 15 in accordance with paragraph C3(b) could avoid the different reporting outcomes between IFRS 15 and Topic 606 by choosing to apply the practical expedient at the date of initial application.

BC445R   The boards considered, but rejected, permitting an entity to account for the unsatisfied performance obligations in a modified contract at transition as if the original contract were terminated and a new contract created as of the transition date. This would be computationally simpler because it eliminates the need to evaluate the effects of modifications before transition to IFRS 15. Under this approach, the amount of consideration allocated to the unsatisfied performance obligations would be the total consideration promised by the customer (including amounts already received) less any amounts already recognised as revenue under previous revenue Standards. Although this might significantly reduce the cost and complexity of applying the transition requirements to contract modifications, the approach was rejected by the boards because it could result in financial information that differed significantly from that under IFRS 15 without the expedient.

Transition to Clarifications to IFRS 15

BC445S   The IASB decided to require an entity to apply the amendments to IFRS 15 retrospectively in accordance with IAS 8. In reaching its decision to require retrospective application, the IASB observed that the amendments were intended to clarify the IASB's intentions when developing the requirements in IFRS 15 rather than to change the underlying principles of IFRS 15. The IASB decided not to allow prospective application of the amendments because that would reduce comparability in the limited cases that the amendments may have resulted in significant changes to an entity's application of IFRS 15. This is consistent with feedback received from users of financial statements during the development of IFRS 15 highlighting that retrospective application would be the most useful transition method for them to understand trends in revenue.

BC445T   By requiring an entity to apply the amendments as if those amendments had been included in IFRS 15 at the date of initial application, the IASB observed that:

(a)　if the entity applies both IFRS 15 and *Clarifications to IFRS 15* at the same time, any effect of applying the amendments would be reflected in the effects of initially applying IFRS 15.

(b)　if the entity applies *Clarifications to IFRS 15* after the date of initial application of IFRS 15, the effects of initially applying IFRS 15 would be restated for the effects, if any, of initially applying the amendments.

BC445U　The outcome of retrospective application of *Clarifications to IFRS 15* will depend on which transition method an entity chooses when it first applies IFRS 15. The choice of the transition method will determine, for example, whether periods before the date of initial application of IFRS 15 are restated as well as the amount and date of the adjustment to retained earnings. Retrospective application of *Clarifications to IFRS 15* will affect only those reporting periods and those contracts to which IFRS 15 is applied. For example, consider an entity that applies IFRS 15 in accordance with paragraph C3(b) on 1 January 2017 and *Clarifications to IFRS 15* on 1 January 2018. Retrospective application of *Clarifications to IFRS 15* would not require the restatement of financial information before 1 January 2017 for the effects of the amendments. Any effect of applying the amendments would be included in a restated cumulative effect adjustment as of 1 January 2017.

Effective date and early application (paragraphs C1–C1B)

Effective date[14]

BC446　In the 2011 Exposure Draft, the boards indicated that the effective date of IFRS 15 would be set to ensure that the start of the earliest comparative period for an entity that is required to present two comparative annual periods (in addition to the current annual period) would be after the final requirements are issued. The boards developed this approach in response to feedback obtained from interested parties through a number of activities, including:

(a)　the IASB's Request for Views on *Effective Dates and Transition Methods* and the FASB's Discussion Paper *Effective Dates and Transition Methods* (October 2010);

(b)　the boards' joint investor outreach questionnaire (April 2011); and

(c)　consultation with systems providers and preparers in 2010 and 2011.

BC447　On the basis of that proposed formula for setting an effective date and of the estimated issue date of IFRS 15 at the time of their decision, the boards would have set the effective date as 1 January 2016. However, many respondents, including respondents in industries for which there could be significant process and system changes required to comply with IFRS 15 (for example, in the telecommunications and software industries), indicated that the proposed formula would not provide them with adequate time. Specifically, those respondents explained that providing only a short time before the earliest comparative period would not be sufficient to ensure that processes and

---

14　The boards subsequently deferred the effective date of IFRS 15 and Topic 606 by one year. See paragraphs BC453A–BC453H.

systems were in place to capture the information that would be required to apply IFRS 15 retrospectively. Some respondents further explained that because of the large volume of contracts in their businesses, it would be far more cost-effective to process the information on a real-time basis to ensure that the adjustments to the financial statements were being calculated during the transition period, rather than attempting to retrospectively calculate the adjustments at the date of initial application.

BC448 The boards considered whether their decision to permit an alternative transition method (see paragraphs BC439–BC444) would provide sufficient relief that an effective date of 1 January 2016, would be appropriate. However, the boards noted that if a contract is not completed at the date of initial application, the entity would need to apply IFRS 15 to that entire contract to calculate any cumulative effect that would be recognised in the opening retained earnings in the year of initial application. The boards noted that the industries that would be most affected generally have contracts with durations that would result in those industries still having only a few months to prepare their processes and systems to capture the required information on a real-time basis.

BC449 Consequently, the FASB decided to require that a public entity apply Topic 606 for annual reporting periods beginning after 15 December 2016, and the IASB decided to require that an entity apply IFRS 15 for annual reporting periods beginning on or after 1 January 2017. Although the effective dates are not identical, the boards noted that this difference has resulted from precedents in IFRS and US GAAP. Furthermore, the difference is not significant and the boards did not expect that it would result in a difference in the way that an entity considers the effective date.

BC450 The boards acknowledged that the period of time from which IFRS 15 is issued until its effective date is longer than usual. However, in this case, the boards decided that a delayed effective date is appropriate because of the unique attributes of IFRS 15, including the wide range of entities that will be affected and the potentially significant effect that a change in revenue recognition has on other financial statement line items.

BC451 To ensure consistency with the IASB's requirements in IAS 34, the FASB clarified that the first set of interim financial reports in which Topic 606 will apply is the first set of interim financial reports after the effective date (ie 31 March 2017 for a calendar year-end entity). The FASB also decided that this is appropriate because of the relatively long lead time that has been provided to entities.

Early application

BC452 The FASB decided not to allow entities to apply Topic 606 early, because doing so would have reduced the comparability of financial reporting in the period up to the date of initial application.[15] Although the IASB agreed that allowing early application would reduce the comparability of financial reporting in the

---

15 The FASB subsequently amended Topic 606 to allow all entities to apply the Standard early for annual periods beginning after 15 December 2016. See paragraph BC453H.

period up to the date of initial application, the IASB noted that IFRS 15 improves accounting for revenue in areas in which there was little guidance under previous revenue Standards in IFRS and, thus, entities should not be precluded from applying IFRS 15 before its effective date. Furthermore, the IASB noted that IFRS 15 should resolve some pressing issues in practice arising from previous revenue recognition requirements. For example, the requirements for determining whether a performance obligation is satisfied over time should address the current diversity in practice associated with the application of the interpretation of IFRS on the construction of real estate.

BC453　　The boards observed that the IASB-only decision to permit early application should not result in differences after the date of initial application in the accounting for revenue between entities applying US GAAP and those applying IFRS that apply IFRS 15 early, even for contracts that straddle the date of initial application.

Deferral of effective date (amendment issued in September 2015)

BC453A　　After issuing IFRS 15 and Topic 606, the IASB and the FASB formed a joint Transition Resource Group (TRG) for Revenue Recognition to support the implementation of the Standard. The TRG discussed submissions from stakeholders and its discussions on five topics indicated potential differences of views on how to implement the requirements in IFRS 15. Consequently, those topics were discussed by the boards and each board decided to propose targeted amendments to IFRS 15 and Topic 606. The IASB published an Exposure Draft *Clarifications to IFRS 15* in July 2015. In the light of those proposed amendments, the IASB and the FASB each discussed whether to defer the effective date of the Standard.

BC453B　　The IASB observed that changing the effective date of a Standard shortly after its issuance creates uncertainty for stakeholders and has the potential to set a bad precedent. The effective date is set after consideration of information obtained in the exposure process about the time needed to implement the requirements. Accordingly, the IASB would consider changing the effective date only in exceptional circumstances. The IASB noted that it had already provided a considerable amount of time between issuing IFRS 15 and the effective date, anticipating that some entities would be required to change information technology systems and processes when applying the Standard. The IASB has also provided substantive relief on transition to IFRS 15 by giving entities a choice of transition methods, one of which does not involve the restatement of comparative financial information. In addition, the IASB observed that the proposed amendments noted in paragraph BC453A are expected to clarify, rather than change, the requirements of the Standard.

BC453C　　Nonetheless, the IASB decided to propose a deferral of the effective date of IFRS 15 by one year to 1 January 2018 because of the combination of the following factors that result in the circumstances surrounding the implementation of IFRS 15 being exceptional:

(a) The IASB acknowledged that, although intended to provide clarity, the proposed amendments to IFRS 15 noted in paragraph BC453A may affect some entities that would wish to apply any amendments at the same time as they first apply IFRS 15. Those entities are likely to wish to avoid reporting changes to revenue when first implementing the Standard and then, within a year or two, potentially reporting further changes to revenue as a result of applying any amendments to the Standard. For those entities, a deferral of the effective date by one year would provide additional time to implement any amendments to the Standard.

(b) IFRS 15 was issued later than had been anticipated when the IASB set the effective date of the Standard, which absorbed some of the implementation time that entities were expecting to have.

(c) IFRS 15 is a converged Standard with Topic 606 — although this was not the only consideration, the IASB observed that there are benefits for a broad range of stakeholders of retaining an effective date that is aligned with the effective date of Topic 606.

BC453D Accordingly, the IASB published the Exposure Draft *Effective Date of IFRS 15* in May 2015 proposing to defer the effective date of IFRS 15 by one year.

BC453E The IASB concluded that a one-year deferral would be sufficient in terms of providing additional time to implement IFRS 15. IASB members observed that the issuance of IFRS 15 in May 2014 had been later than anticipated by some months, not years. Accordingly, a deferral of the effective date of IFRS 15 for anything longer than one year would unnecessarily delay transition by many entities to a new Standard that the IASB views as a substantial improvement to financial reporting.

BC453F Almost all respondents to the Exposure Draft agreed with the proposal to defer the effective date of IFRS 15 for one or more of the reasons noted by the IASB, some noting the exceptional nature of the circumstances surrounding the implementation of IFRS 15. Most also agreed that a one-year deferral should be sufficient and would improve the quality of implementation.

BC453G In the light of the feedback received, the IASB confirmed its decision to defer the effective date of the Standard. The IASB did not change its previous decision to permit early application of IFRS 15.

BC453H For factors similar to those considered by the IASB, the FASB issued an Accounting Standards Update 2015-14 *Revenue from Contracts with Customers (Topic 606): Deferral of the Effective Date* in August 2015 also deferring the effective date of Topic 606 for all entities by one year. Consequently, a public entity would be required to apply Topic 606 to annual reporting periods beginning after 15 December 2017. The FASB decided to permit early application of Topic 606 by all entities, but not before the original effective date of Topic 606 for a public entity (ie annual reporting periods beginning after 15 December 2016).

Clarifications to IFRS 15 (amendments issued in April 2016)

BC453I   As explained in paragraph BC453C, one of the considerations of the IASB in deferring the effective date of IFRS 15 from 1 January 2017 to 1 January 2018 was that the deferral would provide additional time to entities that wish to implement *Clarifications to IFRS 15* along with IFRS 15. Consequently, the IASB set an effective date for *Clarifications to IFRS 15* that aligns with the revised effective date of IFRS 15.

BC453J   Furthermore, the IASB decided that an entity should be permitted to apply *Clarifications to IFRS 15* earlier than its effective date. This would allow an entity the choice of either:

(a)   applying *Clarifications to IFRS 15* on the same date as it first applies IFRS 15; or

(b)   applying *Clarifications to IFRS 15* at a date later than when it early applies IFRS 15.

In other words, an entity that has decided to early apply IFRS 15 would have the flexibility to apply *Clarifications to IFRS 15* either together with the Standard or at a subsequent date.

Analysis of the effects of IFRS 15

BC454   The objective of financial statements is to provide information about the financial position, financial performance and cash flows of an entity that is useful to a wide range of users of financial statements in making economic decisions. To attain that objective, the boards try to ensure that new requirements meet a significant need and that the overall benefits to economic decision-making that would result from improved financial reporting justify the costs of providing such information. For example, the boards consider the comparative advantage that preparers have in developing information, compared with the costs that users of financial statements would incur to develop surrogate information. In this evaluation, the boards recognise that the costs of implementing a new standard might not be borne evenly by participants in the financial reporting system. However, both the users of financial statements and the entities that prepare those financial statements benefit from improvements in financial reporting that facilitate the functioning of markets for capital, including credit and the efficient allocation of resources in the economy.

BC455   The IASB is committed to assessing and sharing knowledge about the likely costs of implementing new requirements and the likely, associated ongoing costs and benefits of each new Standard—these costs and benefits are collectively referred to as 'effects'. The evaluation of these effects is necessarily subjective and qualitative. This is because quantifying costs and, particularly, benefits, is inherently difficult. Although other standard-setters undertake similar types of analyses, there is a lack of sufficiently well-established and reliable techniques for quantifying this analysis. Consequently, the IASB sees this analysis of the effects as being part of an evolving process. In addition, the assessment undertaken is that of the likely effects of the new requirements because the actual effects would not be known until after the new requirements had been applied. These are subsequently analysed through the Post-implementation Review process.

Overview

BC456   As explained in paragraphs BC2–BC3, the boards developed IFRS 15 to eliminate the inconsistencies and weaknesses in previous revenue recognition requirements and to improve disclosure requirements related to revenue. However, throughout the project, many preparers and some users of financial statements explained that they did not perceive significant weaknesses in previous revenue recognition requirements. Therefore, those preparers and users questioned whether the benefits of applying a new revenue standard would justify the costs of implementing that standard.

BC457   To gain insight on the likely effects of IFRS 15, the boards conducted extensive consultation with interested parties through the formal exposure of the proposals and outreach activities. This consultation included three formal exposure documents—a Discussion Paper and two Exposure Drafts—in response to which the boards received and assessed more than 1,500 comment letters. Over the course of the project, the boards and staff also held more than 650 meetings with users of financial statements, preparers, auditors, regulators and other interested parties in a wide range of industries and a number of jurisdictions. Those meetings included general educational sessions about the proposals and in-depth discussions in relation to particular topics. Some meetings also focused on gaining an understanding of the effects of the proposals in specific industries or on particular transactions. In some cases, the boards undertook additional outreach in those specific industries or on those particular topics for which there were significant operational or other concerns about the effects of the boards' proposals. For example, because of the disparate views of preparers and users of financial statements on the topic of disclosure requirements, the boards sought further feedback in four workshops that brought user and preparer groups together to discuss how to balance the requirements to be more useful for users of financial statements and less burdensome for preparers (see paragraph BC328). In addition, because of the effect of the principles for allocating the transaction price on a typical mobile phone contract, the boards also held a number of meetings with representatives from the telecommunications industry to better understand their concerns and so that those concerns could be considered during redeliberations. The boards' consideration of the feedback received from this industry and their conclusions is included in paragraphs BC287–BC293 and BC473–BC476.

BC458   The boards considered in their redeliberations all of the feedback received and, as a result, decided to modify or clarify many aspects of the revenue recognition model to reduce the burden of implementing and applying the proposed requirements. Discussion of this feedback and the resulting changes in different aspects of the model are included throughout the Basis for Conclusions and are summarised in this analysis of the effects.

BC459   Overall, the boards concluded that the improvements to financial reporting would justify the costs of implementing IFRS 15. In making this assessment, the boards considered:

(a)   how revenue from contracts with customers would be reported in the financial statements;

(b)   how the comparability of financial information would be improved and the benefit of better economic decision-making as a result of improved financial reporting;

(c)   the likely compliance costs for preparers of financial statements; and

(d)   the likely costs of analysis for users of financial statements.

Reporting revenue from contracts with customers in the financial statements

BC460   IFRS 15 replaces the previous limited revenue recognition requirements in IFRS and the broad revenue recognition concepts and industry-specific requirements in US GAAP with a robust and comprehensive framework that is applied to all revenue contracts with customers (except for lease, insurance and financial instruments contracts which fall within the scope of other Standards). This framework provides a basis that should be more easily applied to complex transactions and that provides timely guidance for evolving revenue transactions.

BC461   The framework in IFRS 15 also fills a gap by providing requirements for revenue transactions that had not previously been addressed comprehensively, such as transactions for revenue for the provision of services and for revenue resulting from licences of intellectual property. In addition, IFRS 15 provides requirements for issues such as contract modifications that were previously addressed only for a particular industry. IFRS 15 also provides improved requirements for some transactions such as multiple-element arrangements (see paragraphs BC470–BC472).

BC462   By providing a comprehensive framework, one of the most significant effects of IFRS 15 in reporting revenue from contracts with customers is greater consistency in the accounting for economically similar transactions. This is because the diversity in practice that developed as a result of weaknesses in previous revenue recognition requirements in IFRS and US GAAP would be eliminated. However, the previous inconsistencies in the accounting and the diversity in practice that existed before the issuance of IFRS 15 may mean that the nature and extent of the changes would likely vary between entities and industries. For example, some industries, such as the telecommunications and software industries, may have significant changes. This is because those industries had narrow and transaction-specific industry revenue recognition requirements in US GAAP (which were often referred to by entities applying IFRS). However, other industries, such as the construction industry, may see minimal changes overall but significant changes for particular entities or jurisdictions that may have interpreted previous requirements differently to apply to their specific transactions. For other contracts, such as straightforward retail transactions, IFRS 15 would have little, if any, effect. The boards were aware of those varying effects when developing IFRS 15 and took them into account in their decision-making. In many cases, the boards observed that the requirements in IFRS 15 may be broadly consistent with previous revenue recognition requirements or practices, thus limiting the effects of IFRS 15 for many entities.

BC463 In making their assessment of the nature of the changes in the reporting of revenue from contracts with customers (ie the recognition and measurement of revenue), the boards observed that the following parts of the revenue recognition model are expected to result in the most significant changes for some entities:

(a) transfer of control: basis for the timing of revenue recognition;

(b) identification of performance obligations in a contract;

(c) allocating the transaction price to performance obligations based on relative stand-alone selling prices; and

(d) measurement of revenue.

Transfer of control: basis for the timing of revenue recognition

BC464 Previous revenue recognition requirements typically determined the timing of revenue recognition depending on whether the asset transferred was a good or a service. Both IFRS and US GAAP required revenue to be recognised for goods when risks and rewards transferred and, for services, as the service was performed. However, both approaches presented challenges in determining when to recognise revenue and often resulted in accounting for economically similar transactions differently. For example, when determining when to recognise revenue for the transfer of a good, it was often difficult for an entity to judge whether a preponderance (or some other balance) of the risks and rewards had been transferred to the customer. In some contracts, there could be significant difficulty in interpreting whether the asset to be transferred was a good or a service, therefore, making it difficult to rationalise why for one asset, revenue should be recognised only when the asset was complete (ie a good), whereas for another asset, revenue should be recognised continuously as that asset is created (ie a service). Some of this difficulty was due to the vague and narrow definition of services in US GAAP and the lack of clear rationale (ie a Basis for Conclusions) in IFRS for why, in some cases, revenue should be recognised for a service over time. In some cases, entities that applied IFRS consulted the rationale in US GAAP for why revenue would be recognised over time for a service. That rationale explained that this was because the entity was transferring a service continuously. However, that rationale did not address many specific application questions in IFRS about determining whether specific items met the definition of a service. In response, the IASB developed an Interpretation to help clarify whether the construction of real estate would be accounted for as a good or a service (ie a performance obligation satisfied at a point in time or over time). However, many observed that the principle in that Interpretation was difficult to understand and apply.

BC465   In the light of the challenges with previous revenue recognition requirements, the boards observed that applying the single framework in IFRS 15 to determine the timing of revenue recognition for both goods *and* services would improve the consistency in accounting for revenue. This is because the framework would be applied to the attributes of the goods and services transferred, together with the terms of the contract, rather than only to the type of contract. In addition, the boards determined that the core principle in IFRS 15, based on the notion of transferring control, would further improve the consistency of reporting because it would provide a more objective assessment for determining the timing of revenue recognition.

BC466   The boards noted that the application of the core principle may not result in changes for all contracts. For example, the boards acknowledge that for construction contracts, the application of the criteria for when a good or service transfers over time (and thus, is a performance obligation satisfied over time) in IFRS 15 would likely broadly result in the same accounting as required by previous revenue recognition requirements for contracts that met the definition of 'services'. However, the boards observed that the application of IFRS 15 could result in changes for those contracts for which, under previous revenue recognition requirements, it may have been difficult to conclude that the contracted activities were services. This may occur in some manufacturing service contracts and contracts for the construction of residential real estate.

Application guidance: licensing

BC467   Previous revenue recognition requirements did not determine the timing of revenue recognition for licences based on an assessment of whether the licence was a good or a service. However, those previous requirements were limited and industry-specific. For example, in US GAAP, revenue recognition for licences differed depending on the industry (for example, franchisors, media and entertainment and software) and often was based on features of the licence (for example, licence period or payment terms). Therefore, the previous revenue recognition requirements did not coalesce into a single principle or rule. In IFRS, previous revenue recognition requirements for licences required revenue to be recognised 'in accordance with the substance of the agreement'. However, because those requirements provided minimal guidance on how an entity should assess the 'substance of the agreement', there was significant diversity in practice for the accounting for licences.

BC468   The boards included in IFRS 15 application guidance on how an entity should assess and account for its licence arrangements. That guidance is anchored in applying key steps of the revenue recognition model—specifically, identifying the performance obligations in a contract and assessing the transfer of control, which the boards operationalised by differentiating between two types of licences. The boards also decided to include in the application guidance the rationale for the guidance and additional illustrative examples to explain the intention, objective and application of those steps and the differentiation between licences.

BC469   The detailed application guidance for licences in IFRS 15 is intended to help entities determine when a licence is transferred to a customer and thus when revenue can be recognised. Because of the previous diversity in practice in revenue recognition for licences, the addition of the application guidance in IFRS 15 may change practice for some entities. However, the boards observed that the diversity and inconsistencies that previously existed meant that some changes in practice would have occurred regardless of how the boards decided to apply the revenue recognition model to licences.

Identification of performance obligations in a contract

BC470   The boards cited deficiencies in previous IFRS and US GAAP in the accounting for arrangements with multiple elements as one of the reasons for adding the Revenue Recognition project to its agenda. Although US GAAP was improved after the Revenue Recognition project began, deficiencies still existed. For example, there was no definition of a 'deliverable' in previous US GAAP, even though the term was used to determine the unit of account for revenue transactions. IFRS had even fewer requirements because it only acknowledged that revenue could be recognised for 'separately identifiable components of a single transaction', without providing guidance on how to determine what constituted a 'separately identifiable component'.

BC471   IFRS 15 addresses those weaknesses by defining promised goods or services that should be accounted for separately as performance obligations. IFRS 15 defines a performance obligation and provides criteria and factors for identifying performance obligations, which are based on the notion of distinct goods or services. These requirements were developed on the basis of extensive consultation and attempts to separate contracts in a meaningful and cost-effective way with intuitive outcomes.

BC472   The boards observed that the requirements in IFRS 15 for identifying performance obligations may not result in significant changes for many entities. This is because many entities have developed practices to separate contracts with customers in a manner that was similar to the requirements in IFRS 15. However, the boards observed that because there were specific requirements in previous US GAAP, there would be a change in the accounting for incidental obligations and marketing incentives (see paragraphs BC87–BC93). This is because the requirements in IFRS 15 would require an entity to identify and recognise revenue for those goods or services, when previously they may have been recognised as an expense or ignored for the purposes of revenue recognition. The boards observed that two industries that would be particularly affected by this change are the automotive industry (which previously recognised as an expense the promise of maintenance with the purchase of an automobile) and the telecommunications industry (which sometimes did not attribute any revenue to the handsets provided as part of a bundled offering).

Allocating the transaction price to performance obligations based on relative stand-alone selling prices

BC473 Previous revenue recognition requirements in IFRS and US GAAP for the allocation of consideration in multiple-element arrangements were different. Before IFRS 15, there were no general requirements in IFRS for allocation of consideration (there were some specific requirements in an Interpretation for one type of transaction—that is, customer loyalty points). This was due in part to the lack of guidance on defining an element or unit of account for revenue. In contrast, US GAAP specified that an allocation of the consideration to multiple-elements should be made on a relative selling price basis for some industries. US GAAP also included explicit requirements for some industries on determining the selling price of an item, which required an entity to use vendor-specific objective evidence, but it also permitted the use of estimation techniques in some cases. However, the allocation requirements in the software industry strictly prohibited allocation to individual elements unless the entity obtained vendor-specific objective evidence for all elements of the contract. Because there was often no vendor-specific objective evidence available for one or more undelivered elements, revenue recognition was delayed until all elements had been delivered.

BC474 Although the principle for allocating the transaction price in IFRS 15 is broadly consistent with previous US GAAP for some industries—that is, allocating the transaction price on a relative stand-alone selling price basis— there may be a change in some outcomes, in particular in the software industry. This is because the boards decided to eliminate the restrictive, industry-specific requirements in US GAAP for allocating consideration in software arrangements (ie the requirement to have vendor-specific objective evidence for all elements in the arrangements before consideration can be allocated). Instead, IFRS 15 requires an entity to estimate the stand-alone selling price of a good or service, if the stand-alone selling price is not directly observable. The boards observed that this change would permit an entity in the software industry to better depict performance by recognising revenue for performance obligations when they are satisfied, instead of when all performance in a contract is complete. In some instances, the boards observed that this may permit entities to eliminate the disclosure of non-GAAP measures that were created because the outcomes from applying previous revenue recognition requirements did not faithfully depict an entity's performance.

BC475 The boards observed that the requirements for allocating the transaction price in IFRS 15, in conjunction with the requirements for identifying performance obligations, may also result in a significant change in the accounting for bundled arrangements in the automotive and telecommunications industries. As explained in paragraph BC457, the boards' consideration of the feedback received from the telecommunications industry and their conclusions are included in paragraphs BC287–BC293.

BC476   The boards observed that even though IFRS 15 may result in significant differences in the allocation of the transaction price to performance obligations (and consequently in the amount and timing of the recognition of revenue) in some industries, the change was necessary to provide greater consistency in the recognition of revenue across industries. In addition, the boards observed that the effects were a consequence of the boards' objectives of eliminating industry-specific requirements and defining a common framework that could be applied to all revenue transactions. Furthermore, the boards observed that the allocation requirements in IFRS 15 would result in accounting for a transaction in a manner that more closely reflects the underlying economics.

Measurement of revenue

BC477   Previous requirements for the measurement of revenue in US GAAP were limited and differed for goods and for services. US GAAP did not provide specific requirements for how to measure revenue for goods, but it nevertheless restricted the amount of revenue that could be recognised for goods to the amount that was fixed or determinable. IFRS required revenue to be recognised for the transfer of goods and services at the fair value of the consideration received/receivable; but, there was no guidance on how to apply that principle because IFRS 13 *Fair Value Measurement* was not effective until 1 January 2013. Consequently, that principle was not consistently applied. In addition, IFRS contained little guidance on how to measure variable consideration. However, both IFRS and US GAAP indicated that the amount of revenue to be recognised for services should be limited to an amount that could be 'estimated reliably'.

BC478   Thus, IFRS 15 appears to be a significant change from previous revenue recognition requirements because it introduces a customer consideration model and measures revenue using the transaction price, which is defined as the amount to which the entity expects to be entitled in exchange for transferring goods or services. However, previous practices were broadly consistent with this approach and many entities determined the amount of revenue on the basis of the amounts the customer promised to pay. Where IFRS 15 differs from previous revenue recognition requirements is in the additional guidance it provides for estimating consideration when it is variable and in constraining those estimates to ensure revenue is not overstated. In addition, IFRS 15 provides requirements related to other aspects of measuring revenue such as accounting for significant financing components, non-cash consideration and consideration payable to a customer.

BC479   The additional guidance includes two methods for estimating variable consideration, which may not substantially change the amount of revenue recognised in many industries in which robust estimation methods have been developed over time. However, it may result in changes in the timing of revenue recognised in other cases, for which estimation of variable consideration was either prohibited or not used in the recognition of revenue. For example, in some distribution channels, entities may not have estimated the price of a good or service when that price depended on the eventual sale to an end customer. In those cases, revenue was not recognised until that final sale occurred. The boards concluded that the additional guidance for estimation methods should ensure that performance is better reflected in the financial statements in those cases and should provide greater consistency in estimating variable consideration. The additional guidance would also provide users of financial statements with more transparency on the estimation process, which was often masked with undefined terms such as 'best estimates'.

BC480   In addition, the requirements for constraining estimates of variable consideration provide entities with a more specific approach for assessing the likelihood of an entity being entitled to variable consideration and, therefore, whether or not to include an estimate of that variable consideration in the amount of revenue recognised. It would also give users of financial statements more confidence in the amount of revenue recognised in the financial statements by requiring a consistent approach to estimating the amount of variable consideration to which an entity is entitled. The boards included the requirements for constraining estimates of variable consideration in part because of feedback from users of financial statements who demanded that estimates should be of high quality, but also because a significant portion of errors in financial statements have related to the overstatement of revenue.

Improved comparability of financial information and better economic decision-making

BC481   Before the issuance of IFRS 15, there were significant differences in accounting for economically similar revenue transactions, both within and across industries for entities applying US GAAP. There was also significant diversity in practice in accounting for revenue transactions for entities applying IFRS. Those differences made it difficult for users of financial statements to understand and compare revenue numbers. As explained in paragraphs BC460–BC480, some of this diversity arose because there were limited revenue recognition requirements in IFRS in general and on particular topics. Furthermore, the requirements that were provided were difficult to apply to complex transactions, in part because there was no rationale for those requirements (ie there was no Basis for Conclusions). Those differences also arose because previous revenue recognition requirements in US GAAP were voluminous and often industry-specific or transaction-specific, which also created difficulty for users of financial statements in interpreting the information about revenue. The boards noted that the diversity in practice and challenges to users were often amplified for entities applying IFRS because some preparers selectively referenced US GAAP.

BC482   Analysis of revenue by users of financial statements was made even more difficult because previous disclosure requirements for revenue were inadequate. Consequently, users of financial statements found it difficult to understand an entity's revenues, as well as the judgements and estimates made by that entity in recognising those revenues. However, many entities acknowledged a need to provide investors with additional information about revenue and therefore provided this information in other reports outside the financial statements (for example, in earnings releases and shareholder reports).

BC483 By providing a robust, comprehensive framework that would be applied by entities applying both IFRS and US GAAP, IFRS 15 would eliminate the previous diversity in practice and create greater comparability across entities, industries and reporting periods. In addition, the boards observed that a common revenue Standard should make the financial reporting of revenue comparable between entities that prepare financial statements in accordance with IFRS or US GAAP, resulting in a significant benefit to users. Furthermore, by providing a rationale for the requirements (ie a Basis for Conclusions), the framework should be more easily applied to a broad range of transactions and contracts.

BC484 In addition, IFRS 15 provides comprehensive disclosure requirements that should greatly improve the information about revenue reported in the financial statements (see paragraphs BC327–BC361). Specifically, the information about revenue would enable users of financial statements to better understand an entity's contracts with customers and revenue from those contracts and to better predict cash flows. This information should also help users of financial statements to make more informed economic decisions. The boards acknowledged that these improvements may increase the costs of the application of IFRS 15 for preparers. However, the boards concluded that these costs were necessary to improve the usefulness of financial reporting in an area that is critical for users of financial statements to the analysis and understanding of an entity's performance and prospects.

BC485 During outreach, the boards learned that the disclosures required by IFRS 15 may help some entities to eliminate various alternative reporting measures that were created because previous revenue recognition requirements did not adequately depict their performance. Conversely, the boards noted that other industries in which changes may be more significant may be required to create alternative performance measures to help users understand the difference between previous accounting requirements and the requirements under IFRS 15. However, because the requirements adequately depict performance, the boards do not expect that these performance measures would be necessary in the longer term.

Compliance costs for preparers

BC486 As with any new requirements, there will be costs to implement IFRS 15. The breadth of industries and entities that will be required to apply IFRS 15, and the diversity in practice that existed under previous revenue recognition requirements, make it difficult to generalise the costs to preparers. However, because of the breadth of industries and entities that will be affected, most entities will incur at least some costs. Broadly, the boards expect that a majority of preparers may incur the following costs:

(a) costs to implement changes in or develop new systems, processes and controls used to gather and archive contract data, make required estimates and provide required disclosures, possibly including fees paid to external consultants;

(b) costs to hire additional employees that may be needed to comply with IFRS 15 and modify processes and internal controls accordingly;

(c) incremental fees paid to external auditors to audit the financial statements in the period of initial application of IFRS 15;

(d) costs required to educate management, finance and other personnel about the effects of IFRS 15; and

(e) costs required to educate users of financial statements about the effects on the financial statements.

BC487 Many of the costs listed in paragraph BC486 will be non-recurring, because they will be incurred only upon initial application of IFRS 15. However, some entities that expect significant changes as a result of applying IFRS 15 expect that the continued application of IFRS 15 will likely cause the following long-term increases in costs:

(a) increase in audit fees because of the increased volume of disclosures and the difficulty of auditing some of the required estimates (for example, estimates of stand-alone selling price and variable consideration);

(b) costs to maintain improved systems and make modifications for transactions; and

(c) higher personnel costs.

BC488 The boards considered those costs in their analysis of the effects for the Standard as a whole and in relation to specific provisions in IFRS 15 when making their decisions. Board members and staff consulted extensively across a wide range of industries and jurisdictions to better understand some of the operational issues arising from the proposals in the Discussion Paper and both Exposure Drafts. The boards took that feedback into consideration in their redeliberations and, as a result, modified or clarified many aspects of the revenue recognition model to reduce the burden of implementing and applying the requirements. Those decisions and their rationale are documented throughout the Basis for Conclusions in relation to specific aspects of the model such as variable consideration and significant financing components. Those clarifications and modifications included:

(a) clarifying the use of portfolios — the boards clarified that many entities would not need to develop systems to account for each contract individually, especially entities that have a large volume of similar contracts with similar classes of customer. In those cases, the boards noted that entities may apply the requirements to a portfolio of similar contracts.

(b)   practical expedients—the boards added some practical expedients (for example, in the requirements for adjusting the transaction price for significant financing components) to simplify compliance with the requirements in circumstances in which the boards determined that applying the practical expedient would have a limited effect on the amount or timing of revenue recognition.

(c)   disclosure requirements—the boards eliminated the rigidity in the disclosure requirements proposed in the 2011 Exposure Draft that required entities to provide a detailed reconciliation of their contract balances. Instead, the boards decided to require only the opening and closing balances as well as some information on the changes in those balances. The boards also provided similar relief for the reconciliation proposed in the 2011 Exposure Draft for the costs to obtain or fulfil a contract.

(d)   transition requirements—the boards expected that the costs of the systems and operational changes would be incurred primarily during the transition from previous revenue recognition requirements to IFRS 15. Therefore, to ease implementation costs and complexities associated with transition to IFRS 15, the boards decided to provide practical expedients that an entity may elect to use when applying the requirements retrospectively. In addition, the boards introduced an alternative transition method (ie the cumulative catch-up transition method) that would alleviate the costs of transition for many entities because it would not require restatement of prior periods.

(e)   additional illustrations—the boards responded to requests from respondents to provide examples that would illustrate the various aspects of IFRS 15 by providing educational guidance designed to help with implementation and understandability wherever possible. The boards concluded that this would help to reduce both the initial and ongoing cost of compliance, as well as enhancing the consistency of application and therefore comparability of financial statements.

Costs of analysis for users of financial statements

BC489   The boards note that, as with all new requirements, there will be an educational and adjustment period for users of financial statements, during which they may incur costs. Those costs may include costs to modify their processes and analyses. However, the costs are likely to be non-recurring and are likely to be offset by a longer-term reduction in costs from the additional information that would be provided by the improved disclosure requirements. Users of financial statements may also observe a longer-term reduction in education costs, because of the common framework created by IFRS 15, which applies across jurisdictions, industries and transactions.

BC490   In the boards' view, the significant benefits to users of financial statements from IFRS 15 will justify the costs that the users may incur. Those benefits include:

(a) greater comparability and consistency of reporting revenue from contracts with customers;

(b) a better depiction of entities' performance; and

(c) improved understanding of entities' contracts and revenue-generating activities.

Conclusion

BC491 The boards concluded that the issuance of IFRS 15[16] achieves their objectives as outlined in paragraph BC3. This is because IFRS 15 provides a robust and comprehensive framework that:

(a) will apply to a broad range of transactions and industries and will improve the comparability of the recognition of revenue across industries and jurisdictions;

(b) can be applied to complex transactions and evolving transactions, resulting in greater consistency in the recognition of revenue; and

(c) will require enhanced disclosures that will improve the understandability of revenue, which is a critical part of the analysis of an entity's performance and prospects.

BC492 In the light of these achievements, the boards determined that the issuance of IFRS 15 would result in an overall improvement to financial reporting. The boards also concluded that these benefits would be ongoing and would justify the costs of implementing IFRS 15 (for example, systems and operational changes) that would be incurred primarily during the transition from previous revenue recognition requirements.

BC493 However, because of differences in their previous revenue recognition requirements, the boards noted that their rationale for the conclusion that IFRS 15 results in 'an improvement to financial reporting' was slightly different. The differences in their rationale are as follows:

(a) Previous revenue recognition requirements in US GAAP were rules-based and provided specific requirements for particular transactions and industries. In addition, there were transactions that were not directly in the scope of specific guidance. Consequently, economically similar transactions were often accounted for differently. Overall, the robust and comprehensive framework in Topic 606 should improve comparability in the accounting for economically similar transactions and should result in accounting that better reflects the economics of those transactions.

---

16 As indicated in footnote 1, unless indicated otherwise, all references to IFRS 15 in this Basis for Conclusions can be read as also referring to Topic 606 in the FASB's Accounting Standards Codification.

(b)   As described in paragraph BC460, the previous revenue recognition requirements in IFRS were limited. In particular, IFRS did not include general requirements related to many key issues in revenue recognition such as multiple-element arrangements and how to allocate consideration to those elements. In addition, the lack of a Basis for Conclusions in those previous revenue recognition requirements in IFRS created challenges in assessing how to apply the principles in those requirements. In combination, these factors contributed to diversity in practice across jurisdictions and industries. By providing a comprehensive framework and a Basis for Conclusions, IFRS 15 should be a significant improvement to the previous revenue recognition requirements. Consequently, IFRS 15 should eliminate that previous diversity in practice and thus improve financial reporting.

Consequential amendments

Sales of assets that are not an output of an entity's ordinary activities

BC494   For the transfer of non-financial assets that are not an output of an entity's ordinary activities, the boards decided to amend their respective Standards to require that an entity apply the requirements from IFRS 15 for the following topics:

(a)   control—to determine when to derecognise the asset.

(b)   measurement—to determine the amount of the gain or loss to recognise when the asset is derecognised (including any constraints on the transaction price because it is variable).

BC495   The FASB also decided to apply the requirements from Topic 606 for the existence of a contract to transfer a non-financial asset. Those requirements require an entity to determine whether the parties are committed to perform under the contract, which can be difficult in sales of real estate in which the seller has provided significant financing to the purchaser.

BC496   Those amendments will result in changes to IAS 16 *Property, Plant and Equipment*, IAS 38 and IAS 40 *Investment Property* and to Topic 360 and Topic 350 *Intangibles—Goodwill and Other*. The changes to those Standards will result in the same accounting requirements under IFRS and US GAAP for the transfer of non-financial assets that are not an output of an entity's ordinary activities. However, because the requirements in those Standards were previously different under IFRS and US GAAP, the boards have different reasons for making those changes.

Consequential amendments to US GAAP

BC497   A contract for the sale of real estate that is an output of an entity's ordinary activities meets the definition of a contract with a customer and, therefore, is within the scope of Topic 606. Because Subtopic 360-20 *Real Estate Sales* provided requirements for recognising profit on *all* real estate sales, regardless of whether real estate is an output of an entity's ordinary activities, the FASB considered the implications of retaining the requirements in Subtopic 360-20 for contracts that are not within the scope of Topic 606. The FASB noted that retaining those requirements could result in an entity recognising the profit or loss on a real estate sale differently, depending on whether the transaction is a contract with a customer. However, there is economically little difference between the sale of real estate that is an output of the entity's ordinary activities and the sale of real estate that is not. Consequently, the difference in accounting should relate only to the presentation of the profit or loss in the statement of comprehensive income—revenue and expense or gain or loss.

BC498 Consequently, the FASB decided to amend Topic 360 and create Subtopic 610-20 *Gains and Losses from the Derecognition of Nonfinancial Assets* to require that an entity apply the requirements in Topic 606 for the existence of a contract, for control, and for measurement of a contract for the transfer of real estate (including in-substance real estate) that is not an output of the entity's ordinary activities. If the real estate is a business (and not an in-substance non-financial asset), the requirements in Subtopic 810-10 for consolidation apply.

BC499 The FASB also decided to specify that an entity apply the requirements in Topic 606 for the existence of a contract, for control and for measurement to contracts for the transfer of all non-financial assets in non-revenue transactions, such as tangible assets within the scope of Topic 360 and intangible assets within the scope of Topic 350. The primary reason for that decision was the lack of clear requirements in US GAAP for accounting for the transfer of non-financial assets when those assets are not an output of an entity's ordinary activities and do not constitute a business or non-profit activity. In addition, the FASB decided, due to the lack of guidance in Topics 350 and 360, to add guidance for how to account for a contract that fails to meet the criteria in paragraph 606-10-25-1.

Consequential amendments to IFRS

BC500 In IFRS, an entity selling an asset within the scope of IAS 16, IAS 38 or IAS 40 would have applied the recognition principles of the previous revenue Standards in IFRS to determine when to derecognise the asset and, in determining the gain or loss on the transfer, would have measured the consideration at fair value. However, the IASB noted that there is diversity in practice in the recognition of the gain or loss when the transfer of those assets involves variable consideration, because the previous revenue Standard in IFRS did not provide specific requirements for variable consideration. The IASB decided that requiring application of the requirements in IFRS 15 for control and for measurement (including constraining the amount of variable consideration used in determining the gain or loss) would eliminate the diversity in practice because the requirements in IFRS 15 provide a clear principle for accounting for variable consideration.

BC501 The IASB considered whether it should retain fair value as the measurement basis for transfers of non-financial assets within the scope of IAS 16, IAS 38 and IAS 40. However, the IASB rejected this proposal and, as explained in paragraph BC500, decided to require that an entity apply the measurement requirements in IFRS 15 to transfers of non-financial assets that are not an output of the entity's ordinary activities, for the following reasons:

(a) measuring the gain on the transfers of non-financial assets that are not an output of the entity's ordinary activities by using the same requirements as for measuring revenue provides users of financial statements with useful information. The IASB decided that it would provide useful information if entities apply the requirements for constraining estimates of variable consideration to any gain that will be recognised on the transfer of the non-financial asset. The IASB acknowledged that in some cases this may result in a loss on the transfer when the transferred asset has a cost basis that is greater than the constrained consideration, which may occur when the asset has a cost basis that is determined using fair value. However, the IASB noted that this outcome is appropriate and useful to users, because of the significant uncertainty about the variable consideration. The IASB also noted that this outcome is consistent with the outcome in a transaction with a customer in which the variable consideration is constrained, but the entity has transferred control of the good or service to the customer.

(b) it is not necessary to measure the gains on the transfers of non-financial assets to be consistent with other asset disposals, such as disposals of an entity, that are accounted for at fair value in accordance with other Standards (for example, IFRS 10). This is because transfers of non-financial assets that are not an output of an entity's ordinary activities are more like transfers of assets to customers, rather than other asset disposals.

(c) applying the measurement requirements in IFRS 15 achieves consistency with US GAAP.

A separate project

BC502 The boards also considered whether they should consider the changes to the guidance on transfers of non-financial assets in a separate project. The boards noted that undertaking a separate project would mean that changes to existing Standards would not be made until that project had been completed and became effective. Because of the boards' other standard-setting priorities, and the time required to complete all relevant due process steps for issuing a standard, it might be several years before the existing requirements were replaced. The boards observed that the implications of not proceeding with the proposed consequential amendments would have been as follows:

(a) for IFRS reporters, the IASB would have needed to amend IAS 16, IAS 38 and IAS 40 to include the revenue recognition criteria from previous revenue Standards in IFRS. This would have resulted in different recognition and measurement requirements for transfers of non-financial assets as compared to contracts with customers.

(b) for US GAAP reporters, there would have been two sets of recognition and measurement requirements for real estate sales, depending on whether the transfer was with a customer. In addition, no specific requirements would have been provided in US GAAP for transfers of non-financial assets (other than real estate) within the scope of Subtopic 360-10 (for example, equipment) or Topic 350 (for example, intangible assets).

BC503 Consequently, the boards reaffirmed their decision in the 2011 Exposure Draft that consequential amendments should be made, because this results in consistency in the accounting for the transfers of non-financial assets between IFRS and US GAAP, addresses the lack of requirements for the accounting for transfers of non-financial assets in US GAAP and eliminates possible complexities that might result from retaining separate recognition criteria for transfers of non-financial assets in IFRS.

Transition for first-time adopters of IFRS

BC504 During redeliberations of the transition requirements, the IASB considered whether to amend IFRS 1 *First-time Adoption of International Financial Reporting Standards* to allow a first-time adopter of IFRS to use the same transition methods for adopting IFRS 15 as specified in paragraph C3 of IFRS 15 as follows:

(a) retrospectively to each prior period presented in accordance with IAS 8, subject to the practical expedients in paragraph C5 of IFRS 15; and

(b) retrospectively with the cumulative effect of initially applying IFRS 15 recognised at the date of initial application (for a first-time adopter of IFRS, this would be the entity's first IFRS reporting period) in accordance with paragraphs C7–C8 of IFRS 15.

BC505 The IASB decided that the practical expedients in paragraph C5 of IFRS 15 should also apply to a first-time adopter, because both first-time adopters and entities that already apply IFRS would face similar challenges. The IASB observed that IFRS 1 requires that the accounting policies effective at the end of the first IFRS reporting period are applied to all reporting periods from the date of transition to IFRS onwards. This is identical to retrospective application for entities already applying IFRS. Some IASB members also noted that in many jurisdictions that have not yet adopted IFRS, revenue standards are similar to current IFRS. In those jurisdictions, the starting point for transition for a first-time adopter will be similar to entities already applying IFRS.

BC506 The IASB also clarified that, for any of the practical expedients in paragraph C5 of IFRS 15 that the entity uses, the entity should apply that expedient consistently to all reporting periods presented and disclose which expedients have been used, together with the estimated effect of applying those expedients (see paragraph C6 of IFRS 15).

recognise revenue for estimates of variable consideration when an entity was 'reasonably assured' that it would be entitled to that amount.

(c) IFRS 15 provides additional guidance on the allocation of the transaction price to performance obligations:

    (i) the residual approach may be used for two or more goods or services with highly variable or uncertain stand-alone selling prices if at least one good or service has a stand-alone selling price that is not highly variable or uncertain; and

    (ii) allocation of a discount among performance obligations should be done before using the residual approach to estimate the stand-alone selling price for a good or service with a highly variable or uncertain stand-alone selling price.

(d) IFRS 15 carries forward from the 2011 Exposure Draft the principles related to identifying performance obligations in a contract and determining whether a performance obligation is satisfied over time. However, IFRS 15 clarifies those principles and provides additional guidance for entities in applying those principles.

(e) IFRS 15 provides additional guidance for determining when a customer obtains control of a licence, by distinguishing between licences that provide a right to access the entity's intellectual property as it exists throughout the licence period and licences that provide a right to use the entity's intellectual property as it exists at the point in time at which the licence is granted. This determination will affect whether the entity satisfies its performance obligation to transfer a licence at a point in time or over time. This represents a change from the 2011 Exposure Draft, which specified that all licences were transferred to the customer at the point in time at which the customer obtained control of the rights. IFRS 15 also clarifies that before determining when the licence transfers to the customer, an entity considers the promises in the contract and applies the requirements for identifying performance obligations.

(f) IFRS 15 does not include the requirements proposed in the 2011 Exposure Draft to test a performance obligation to determine whether it is onerous.

(g) IFRS 15 clarifies the disclosures required for revenue from contracts with customers. Specifically, it requires an entity to provide a combination of qualitative and quantitative information about contract balances. The 2011 Exposure Draft required this disclosure to be provided as a reconciliation of contract balances.

(h) IFRS 15 provides entities with an additional transition method that does not require a restatement of prior periods. The 2011 Exposure Draft proposed only one transition method (ie a retrospective transition method with practical expedients) that requires a restatement of all previous periods presented.

Dissenting Opinion

Dissenting Opinion from *Clarifications to IFRS 15* Revenue from Contracts with Customers as issued in April 2016

DO1   Mr Ochi voted against the publication of *Clarifications to IFRS 15* Revenue from Contracts with Customers. He agrees with all of the clarifying amendments to IFRS 15 and the additional transition reliefs. However, he disagrees with the IASB's decision to require entities to apply *Clarifications to IFRS 15* retrospectively as if those amendments had been included in IFRS 15 at the date of initial application.

DO2   Referring to the IASB's considerations explained in paragraph BC445T, he thinks that requiring an entity that has applied IFRS 15 before applying these amendments to restate the effects of initially applying IFRS 15 for the effects, if any, of initially applying the amendments is inconsistent with allowing early application of IFRS 15. That entity might be required to restate some contracts twice, first on initially applying IFRS 15 and again on initial application of these amendments. Furthermore, that entity is deprived of the benefit of the new practical expedients added by the IASB.

DO3   Mr Ochi does not disagree with issuing clarifications, if absolutely necessary, to a Standard before its effective date. However, the IASB's actions in issuing any such clarifying amendments should not be perceived as penalising those entities that begin their implementation process early and rewarding those that delay. Such perceptions could discourage entities from starting the implementation of any new Standard on a timely basis.

DO4   Mr Ochi noted that the effective date of the new leases Standard has been set so as to provide a long initial implementation period. In that regard, he believes that allowing early application of a Standard supports the smooth application of new Standards.

DO5   To encourage early application of Standards, he thinks that the IASB should, when deciding the transition requirements for amendments such as *Clarifications to IFRS 15*, give due consideration to those entities that have already early applied the Standard or are in advanced stages of preparing to do so. When deciding the transition requirements, he thinks it is not just a question of considering the extent or potential effect of any clarifications to a Standard; rather it is a matter of principle.

Appendix A
Comparison of IFRS 15 and Topic 606[17]

A1   IFRS 15, together with the FASB's Topic 606, issued in May 2014 completes a joint effort by the IASB and the FASB to improve financial reporting by creating a common revenue standard for IFRS and US GAAP that can be applied consistently across various transactions, industries and capital markets. In IFRS 15 and Topic 606, the boards achieved their goal of reaching the same conclusions on all requirements for the accounting for revenue from contracts with customers. However, there are some minor differences in the standards as issued in May 2014, which are as follows:

(a)   **Collectability threshold** – the boards included an explicit collectability threshold as one of the criteria that a contract must meet before an entity can recognise revenue. For a contract to meet that criterion, an entity must conclude that it is probable that it will collect the consideration to which it will be entitled in exchange for the goods or services that will be transferred to the customer. In setting the threshold, the boards acknowledged that the term 'probable' has different meanings in IFRS and in US GAAP. However, the boards decided to set the threshold at a level that is consistent with previous revenue recognition practices and requirements in IFRS and in US GAAP. (See paragraphs BC42–BC46.)

(b)   **Interim disclosure requirements** – the boards noted that the general principles in their respective interim reporting requirements (IAS 34 *Interim Financial Reporting* and Topic 270 *Interim Reporting*) would apply to revenue from contracts with customers. However, the IASB decided to also amend IAS 34 to specifically require the disclosure of disaggregated information of revenue from contracts with customers in interim financial reports. The FASB similarly decided to amend Topic 270, to require a public entity to disclose disaggregated revenue information in interim financial reports, but also made amendments to require information about both contract balances and remaining performance obligations to be disclosed on an interim basis. (See paragraphs BC358–BC361.)

(c)   **Early application and effective date** – paragraph C1 of IFRS 15 allows entities to apply the requirements early, whereas Topic 606 prohibits a public entity from applying the requirements earlier than the effective date.[18] In addition, the effective date for IFRS 15 is for annual reporting periods beginning on or after 1 January 2017, whereas Topic 606 has

---

17   This Appendix reflects the differences between IFRS 15 and Topic 606 when those standards were issued in May 2014 updated to reflect the issue of *Clarifications to IFRS 15* in April 2016.

18   The FASB subsequently amended Topic 606 in August 2015 to allow all entities to apply the standard early for annual periods beginning after 15 December 2016. See paragraph BC453H.

an effective date for public entities for annual reporting periods beginning after 15 December 2016.[19] (See paragraphs BC452–BC453.)

(d) **Impairment loss reversal** — paragraph 104 of IFRS 15 requires an entity to reverse impairment losses, which is consistent with the requirements for the impairment of assets within the scope of IAS 36 *Impairment of Assets*. In contrast, consistent with other areas of US GAAP, Topic 606 does not allow an entity to reverse an impairment loss on an asset that is recognised in accordance with the guidance on costs to obtain or fulfil a contract. (See paragraphs BC309–BC311.)

(e) **Non-public entity requirements** — there are no specific requirements included in IFRS 15 for non-public entities. Entities that do not have public accountability may apply *IFRS for Small and Medium-sized Entities*. Topic 606 applies to non-public entities, although some specific reliefs relating to disclosure, transition and effective date have been included in Topic 606 for non-public entities.

A1A As explained in paragraph BC1A, the IASB issued *Clarifications to IFRS 15* in April 2016, which differed in some respects from the amendments to Topic 606 issued by the FASB, and those expected to be issued by the FASB based on its decisions, until March 2016. The differences are as follows:

(a) **Collectability criterion** — The FASB decided to amend paragraph 606-10-25-1(e) of Topic 606 (equivalent to paragraph 9(e) of IFRS 15), and add implementation guidance and illustrations to clarify that an entity should assess the collectability of the consideration promised in a contract for the goods or services that will be transferred to the customer rather than assessing the collectability of the consideration promised in the contract for all of the promised goods or services. The IASB did not make similar amendments to IFRS 15. (See paragraphs BC46B–BC46E.)

(b) **Revenue recognition for contracts with customers that do not meet the Step 1 criteria** — The FASB decided to amend paragraph 606-10-25-7 of Topic 606 (equivalent to paragraph 15 of IFRS 15) to add an event in which an entity recognises any consideration received as revenue when (a) the entity has transferred control of the goods or services to which the consideration received relates; (b) the entity has stopped transferring additional goods or services and has no obligation to transfer additional goods or services; and (c) the consideration received from the customer is non-refundable. The IASB did not make similar amendments to IFRS 15. (See paragraphs BC46F–BC46H.)

(c) **Promised goods or services that are immaterial within the context of the contract** — The FASB decided to amend Topic 606 to state that an entity is not required to assess whether promised goods or services are performance obligations if they are immaterial within the context of

---

19 The IASB issued *Effective Date of IFRS 15* in September 2015 deferring the effective date of IFRS 15 by one year. Similarly, the FASB amended Topic 606 in August 2015 deferring the effective date of Topic 606 by one year. See paragraphs BC453A–BC453H.

the contract with the customer. The IASB did not make similar amendments to IFRS 15. (See paragraphs BC116A–BC116E.)

(d) **Shipping and handling activities** – The FASB decided to amend Topic 606 to permit an entity, as an accounting policy election, to account for shipping and handling activities that occur after the customer has obtained control of a good as fulfilment activities. The IASB decided not to make a similar amendment to IFRS 15. (See paragraphs BC116R–BC116U.)

(e) **Presentation of sales taxes** – The FASB decided to amend Topic 606 to provide an accounting policy election that permits an entity to exclude from the measurement of the transaction price all taxes assessed by a governmental authority that are both imposed on and concurrent with a specific revenue-producing transaction and collected from customers (for example, sales taxes, use taxes, value added taxes and some excise taxes). The IASB decided not to provide a similar accounting policy choice in IFRS 15. (See paragraphs BC188A–BC188D.)

(f) **Non-cash consideration** – The FASB decided to amend Topic 606 to require non-cash consideration to be measured at its fair value at contract inception. The FASB also decided to specify that the constraint on variable consideration applies only to variability in the fair value of the non-cash consideration that arises for reasons other than the form of the consideration. The IASB did not make similar amendments to IFRS 15. (See paragraphs BC254A–BC254H.)

(g) **Licensing**

(i) **Determining the nature of the entity's promise in granting a licence of intellectual property** – IFRS 15 and Topic 606 require entities to determine whether the nature of an entity's promise in granting a licence is a right to use or a right to access the entity's intellectual property. The IASB did not amend the criteria in IFRS 15 to determine the nature of the licence but clarified that the assessment of whether the entity's activities significantly change the intellectual property to which the customer has rights is based on whether those activities affect the intellectual property's ability to provide benefit to the customer. The FASB decided to amend the criteria to determine the nature of the licence by requiring an entity to classify the intellectual property underlying the licence as functional or symbolic based on whether the intellectual property has significant stand-alone functionality. A licence to functional intellectual property is considered a right to use, while a licence to symbolic intellectual property is considered a right to access the underlying intellectual property. (See paragraphs BC414C–BC414N.)

    (ii)   **Contractual restrictions in a licence and the identification of performance obligations** – The FASB decided to amend Topic 606 to clarify that the requirements about contractual restrictions of the nature described in paragraph B62 do not replace the requirement for the entity to identify the number of licences promised in the contract. The IASB did not make similar amendments to IFRS 15. (See paragraphs BC414O–BC414R.)

    (iii)   **Renewals of licences of intellectual property** – The FASB decided to amend Topic 606 and provide an additional example to specify that the entity would generally not recognise revenue from the transfer of the renewal licence until the beginning of the licence renewal period. The IASB did not make similar amendments. (See paragraphs BC414S–BC414U.)

    (iv)   **When to consider the nature of an entity's promise in granting a licence** – The FASB decided to make amendments that explicitly state that an entity considers the nature of its promise in granting a licence when applying the general revenue recognition model to a single performance obligation that includes a licence and other goods or services. The IASB did not make similar amendments to IFRS 15. (See paragraphs BC414V–BC414Y.)

  (h)   **Completed contracts** – The FASB decided to amend the definition of a completed contract to be a contract for which all (or substantially all) of the revenue was recognised in accordance with the previous revenue Standards. The IASB did not make a similar amendment to IFRS 15. (See paragraphs BC445C–BC445I.) Furthermore, the IASB added a practical expedient to allow an entity applying IFRS 15 in accordance with paragraph C3(a) not to restate contracts that are completed contracts at the beginning of the earliest period presented. The FASB decided not to provide the practical expedient. (See paragraphs BC445M–BC445N.)

  (i)   **Date of application of the contract modifications practical expedient** – For an entity applying Topic 606 in accordance with paragraph 606-10-65-1(d)(2) (equivalent to paragraph C3(b) of IFRS 15), the FASB decided that the entity should apply the practical expedient at the date of initial application. However, the IASB decided that an entity applying IFRS 15 in accordance with paragraph C3(b) may apply the practical expedient either (a) at the beginning of the earliest period presented; or (b) at the date of initial application. (See paragraphs BC445O–BC445R.)

A2   IFRS 15 and Topic 606 have been structured to be consistent with the style of other Standards in IFRS and US GAAP (respectively). As a result, the paragraph numbers of IFRS 15 and Topic 606 are not the same. The wording in most of the paragraphs is consistent because IFRS 15 and Topic 606 were issued in May 2014 as a common revenue standard for IFRS and US GAAP. However, the wording in some paragraphs differs because of the different amendments to IFRS 15 and Topic 606 (see paragraph A1A). The following table illustrates how the paragraphs of IFRS 15 and Topic 606, and the related illustrative examples, correspond. Paragraphs in which the wording differs are marked with '*'. The table reflects amendments issued by the FASB, and those expected to be issued by the FASB based on its decisions, until March 2016.

IASB	FASB
MAIN FEATURES	**OVERVIEW AND BACKGROUND**
N/A	606-10-05-1
IN7	606-10-05-2
IN8	606-10-05-3
	606-10-05-4
IN9	606-10-05-5
N/A	606-10-05-6

OBJECTIVE	
1	606-10-10-1
Meeting the Objective	
2	606-10-10-2
3	606-10-10-3
4	606-10-10-4

SCOPE	
Entities	
N/A	606-10-15-1
Transactions	
5	606-10-15-2
6	606-10-15-3
7	606-10-15-4
8	606-10-15-5

RECOGNITION	
Identifying the Contract	
9	606-10-25-1*
10	606-10-25-2
11	606-10-25-3*
12	606-10-25-4
13	606-10-25-5
14	606-10-25-6
15	606-10-25-7*
16	606-10-25-8
Combination of Contracts	
17	606-10-25-9
Contract Modifications	
18	606-10-25-10
19	606-10-25-11
20	606-10-25-12
21	606-10-25-13
Identifying Performance Obligations	
22	606-10-25-14
23	606-10-25-15
Promises in Contracts with Customers	
24	606-10-25-16*
N/A	606-10-25-16A through 25-16B*
25	606-10-25-17*
Distinct Goods or Services	
26	606-10-25-18
N/A	606-10-25-18A through 25-18B*
27	606-10-25-19
28	606-10-25-20
29	606-10-25-21
30	606-10-25-22

continued...

...continued

RECOGNITION	
Satisfaction of Performance Obligations	
31	606-10-25-23
32	606-10-25-24
33	606-10-25-25
34	606-10-25-26
Performance Obligations Satisfied Over Time	
35	606-10-25-27
36	606-10-25-28
37	606-10-25-29
Performance Obligations Satisfied at a Point in Time	
38	606-10-25-30
Measuring Progress towards Complete Satisfaction of a Performance Obligation	
39	606-10-25-31
40	606-10-25-32
Methods for Measuring Progress	
41	606-10-25-33
42	606-10-25-34
43	606-10-25-35
Reasonable Measures of Progress	
44	606-10-25-36
45	606-10-25-37

MEASUREMENT	
46	606-10-32-1
Determining the Transaction Price	
47	606-10-32-2
N/A	606-10-32-2A*
48	606-10-32-3
49	606-10-32-4

continued...

...continued

MEASUREMENT	
Variable Consideration	
50	606-10-32-5
51	606-10-32-6
52	606-10-32-7
53	606-10-32-8
54	606-10-32-9
Refund Liabilities	
55	606-10-32-10
Constraining Estimates of Variable Consideration	
56	606-10-32-11
57	606-10-32-12
58	606-10-32-13
Reassessment of Variable Consideration	
59	606-10-32-14
The Existence of a Significant Financing Component in the Contract	
60	606-10-32-15
61	606-10-32-16
62	606-10-32-17
63	606-10-32-18
64	606-10-32-19
65	606-10-32-20
Non-cash Consideration	
66	606-10-32-21*
67	606-10-32-22
68	606-10-32-23*
69	606-10-32-24
Consideration Payable to a Customer	
70	606-10-32-25
71	606-10-32-26
72	606-10-32-27

continued...

...continued

MEASUREMENT	
Allocating the Transaction Price to Performance Obligations	
73	606-10-32-28
74	606-10-32-29
75	606-10-32-30
Allocation Based on Stand-alone Selling Prices	
76	606-10-32-31
77	606-10-32-32
78	606-10-32-33
79	606-10-32-34
80	606-10-32-35
Allocation of a Discount	
81	606-10-32-36
82	606-10-32-37
83	606-10-32-38
Allocation of Variable Consideration	
84	606-10-32-39
85	606-10-32-40
86	606-10-32-41
Changes in the Transaction Price	
87	606-10-32-42
88	606-10-32-43
89	606-10-32-44
90	606-10-32-45

CONTRACT COSTS	
Overview and Background	
N/A	340-40-05-1
N/A	340-40-05-2
Scope and Scope Exceptions	
N/A	340-40-15-1
N/A	340-40-15-2
N/A	340-40-15-3

continued...

...continued

CONTRACT COSTS	
Incremental Costs of Obtaining a Contract	
91	340-40-25-1
92	340-40-25-2
93	340-40-25-3
94	340-40-25-4
Costs to Fulfil a Contract	
95	340-40-25-5
96	340-40-25-6
97	340-40-25-7
98	340-40-25-8
Amortisation and Impairment	
99	340-40-35-1
100	340-40-35-2
101	340-40-35-3
102	340-40-35-4
103	340-40-35-5
104	340-40-35-6

PRESENTATION	
105	606-10-45-1
106	606-10-45-2
107	606-10-45-3
108	606-10-45-4
109	606-10-45-5

DISCLOSURE	
110	606-10-50-1
111	606-10-50-2
112	606-10-50-3
Contracts with Customers	
113	606-10-50-4

continued...

...continued

DISCLOSURE	
Disaggregation of Revenue	
114	606-10-50-5
115	606-10-50-6
N/A	606-10-50-7
Contract Balances	
116	606-10-50-8
117	606-10-50-9
118	606-10-50-10
N/A	606-10-50-11
Performance Obligations	
119	606-10-50-12
Transaction Price Allocated to the Remaining Performance Obligations	
120	606-10-50-13
121	606-10-50-14
122	606-10-50-15
N/A	606-10-50-16
Significant Judgements in the Application of this Standard	
123	606-10-50-17
Determining the Timing of Satisfaction of Performance Obligations	
124	606-10-50-18
125	606-10-50-19
Determining the Transaction Price and the Amounts Allocated to Performance Obligations	
126	606-10-50-20
N/A	606-10-50-21
Assets Recognised from the Costs to Obtain or Fulfil a Contract with a Customer	
N/A	340-40-50-1
127	340-40-50-2
128	340-40-50-3
N/A	340-40-50-4
129	340-40-50-5
N/A	340-40-50-6

continued...

...continued

DISCLOSURE	
Practical Expedients	
129	606-10-50-22
N/A	606-10-50-23

TRANSITION AND EFFECTIVE DATE	
Appendix C	606-10-65-1*

APPLICATION GUIDANCE	
B1	606-10-55-3*
Assessing Collectability	
N/A	606-10-55-3A through 55-3C*
Performance Obligations Satisfied Over Time	
B2	606-10-55-4
Simultaneous Receipt and Consumption of the Benefits of the Entity's Performance	
B3	606-10-55-5
B4	606-10-55-6
Customer Controls the Asset as it is Created or Enhanced	
B5	606-10-55-7
Entity's Performance Does Not Create an Asset with an Alternative Use	
B6	606-10-55-8
B7	606-10-55-9
B8	606-10-55-10
Right to Payment for Performance Completed to Date	
B9	606-10-55-11
B10	606-10-55-12
B11	606-10-55-13
B12	606-10-55-14
B13	606-10-55-15
Methods for Measuring Progress Towards Complete Satisfaction of a Performance Obligation	
B14	606-10-55-16

continued...

...continued

APPLICATION GUIDANCE	
Output Methods	
B15	606-10-55-17
B16	606-10-55-18
B17	606-10-55-19
Input Methods	
B18	606-10-55-20
B19	606-10-55-21
Sale with a Right of Return	
B20	606-10-55-22
B21	606-10-55-23
B22	606-10-55-24
B23	606-10-55-25
B24	606-10-55-26
B25	606-10-55-27
B26	606-10-55-28
B27	606-10-55-29
Warranties	
B28	606-10-55-30
B29	606-10-55-31
B30	606-10-55-32
B31	606-10-55-33
B32	606-10-55-34
B33	606-10-55-35
Principal Versus Agent Considerations	
B34	606-10-55-36
B34A	606-10-55-36A
B35	606-10-55-37
B35A	606-10-55-37A
B35B	606-10-55-37B
B36	606-10-55-38
B37	606-10-55-39
B37A	606-10-55-39A
B38	606-10-55-40

continued...

...continued

APPLICATION GUIDANCE	
Customer Options for Additional Goods or Services	
B39	606-10-55-41
B40	606-10-55-42
B41	606-10-55-43
B42	606-10-55-44
B43	606-10-55-45
Customers' Unexercised Rights	
B44	606-10-55-46
B45	606-10-55-47
B46	606-10-55-48
B47	606-10-55-49
Non-refundable Upfront Fees (and Some Related Costs)	
B48	606-10-55-50
B49	606-10-55-51
B50	606-10-55-52
B51	606-10-55-53
Licensing	
B52	606-10-55-54*
B53	606-10-55-55
B54	606-10-55-56
B55	606-10-55-57*
B56	606-10-55-58*
Determining the Nature of the Entity's Promise	
B57 [Deleted]	N/A*
N/A	606-10-55-59*
B58 and B59A	606-10-55-60, 55-62 through 55-63A*
B59	606-10-55-61 [Superseded]*
B60	606-10-55-58A*
B61	606-10-55-58B through 55-58C*
B62	606-10-55-64 through 55-64A*
Sales-Based or Usage-Based Royalties	
B63	606-10-55-65
B63A–B63B	606-10-55-65A through 55-65B

continued...

...continued

APPLICATION GUIDANCE	
Repurchase Agreements	
B64	606-10-55-66
B65	606-10-55-67
A Forward or a Call Option	
B66	606-10-55-68
B67	606-10-55-69
B68	606-10-55-70
B69	606-10-55-71
A Put Option	
B70	606-10-55-72
B71	606-10-55-73
B72	606-10-55-74
B73	606-10-55-75
B74	606-10-55-76
B75	606-10-55-77
B76	606-10-55-78
Consignment Arrangements	
B77	606-10-55-79
B78	606-10-55-80
Bill-and-Hold Arrangements	
B79	606-10-55-81
B80	606-10-55-82
B81	606-10-55-83
B82	606-10-55-84
Customer Acceptance	
B83	606-10-55-85
B84	606-10-55-86
B85	606-10-55-87
B86	606-10-55-88
Disclosure of Disaggregated Revenue	
B87	606-10-55-89
B88	606-10-55-90
B89	606-10-55-91

ILLUSTRATIONS	
IE1	606-10-55-92
N/A	606-10-55-93

IDENTIFYING THE CONTRACT	
IE2	606-10-55-94*
Example 1—Collectability of the Consideration	
IE3	606-10-55-95
IE4	606-10-55-96*
IE5	606-10-55-97*
IE6	606-10-55-98*
N/A	606-10-55-98A through 55-98L*
Example 2—Consideration Is Not the Stated Price—Implicit Price Concession	
IE7	606-10-55-99
IE8	606-10-55-100
IE9	606-10-55-101
Example 3—Implicit Price Concession	
IE10	606-10-55-102
IE11	606-10-55-103
IE12	606-10-55-104
IE13	606-10-55-105
Example 4—Reassessing the Criteria for Identifying a Contract	
IE14	606-10-55-106
IE15	606-10-55-107
IE16	606-10-55-108
IE17	606-10-55-109

CONTRACT MODIFICATIONS	
IE18	606-10-55-110
Example 5—Modification of a Contract for Goods	
IE19	606-10-55-111
IE20	606-10-55-112
IE21	606-10-55-113
IE22	606-10-55-114
IE23	606-10-55-115
IE24	606-10-55-116
Example 6—Change in the Transaction Price after a Contract Modification	
IE25	606-10-55-117
IE26	606-10-55-118
IE27	606-10-55-119
IE28	606-10-55-120
IE29	606-10-55-121
IE30	606-10-55-122
IE31	606-10-55-123
IE32	606-10-55-124
Example 7—Modification of a Services Contract	
IE33	606-10-55-125
IE34	606-10-55-126
IE35	606-10-55-127
IE36	606-10-55-128
Example 8—Modification Resulting in a Cumulative Catch-Up Adjustment to Revenue	
IE37	606-10-55-129
IE38	606-10-55-130
IE39	606-10-55-131
IE40	606-10-55-132
IE41	606-10-55-133
Example 9—Unapproved Change in Scope and Price	
IE42	606-10-55-134
IE43	606-10-55-135

IDENTIFYING PERFORMANCE OBLIGATIONS	
IE44	606-10-55-136*
Example 10—Goods and Services Not Distinct	
IE45	606-10-55-137
IE46	606-10-55-138
IE47	606-10-55-139
IE48	606-10-55-140
IE48A–IE48C	606-10-55-140A through 55-140C
N/A	606-10-55-140D through 55-140F*
Example 11—Determining Whether Goods or Services Are Distinct	
IE49	606-10-55-141
IE50	606-10-55-142
IE51	606-10-55-143*
IE52	606-10-55-144
IE53	606-10-55-145
IE54	606-10-55-146
IE55	606-10-55-147
IE56	606-10-55-148
IE57	606-10-55-149
IE58	606-10-55-150*
IE58A–IE58K	606-10-55-150A through 55-150K
Example 12—Explicit and Implicit Promises in a Contract	
IE59	606-10-55-151
IE60	606-10-55-152
IE61	606-10-55-153
IE61A	606-10-55-153A
IE62	606-10-55-154
IE63	606-10-55-155*
IE64	606-10-55-156
IE65	606-10-55-157
IE65A	606-10-55-157A
Example 12A—Series of Distinct Goods or Services	
N/A	606-10-55-157B through 55-157E*

PERFORMANCE OBLIGATIONS SATISFIED OVER TIME	
IE66	606-10-55-158
Example 13—Customer Simultaneously Receives and Consumes the Benefits	
IE67	606-10-55-159
IE68	606-10-55-160
Example 14—Assessing Alternative Use and Right to Payment	
IE69	606-10-55-161
IE70	606-10-55-162
IE71	606-10-55-163
IE72	606-10-55-164
Example 15—Asset Has No Alternative Use to the Entity	
IE73	606-10-55-165
IE74	606-10-55-166
IE75	606-10-55-167
IE76	606-10-55-168
Example 16—Enforceable Right to Payment for Performance Completed to Date	
IE77	606-10-55-169
IE78	606-10-55-170
IE79	606-10-55-171
IE80	606-10-55-172
Example 17—Assessing Whether a Performance Obligation Is Satisfied at a Point in Time or Over Time	
IE81	606-10-55-173
IE82	606-10-55-174
IE83	606-10-55-175
IE84	606-10-55-176
IE85	606-10-55-177
IE86	606-10-55-178
IE87	606-10-55-179
IE88	606-10-55-180
IE89	606-10-55-181
IE90	606-10-55-182

MEASURING PROGRESS TOWARDS COMPLETE SATISFACTION OF A PERFORMANCE OBLIGATION	
IE91	606-10-55-183

Example 18—Measuring Progress When Making Goods or Services Available	
IE92	606-10-55-184
IE93	606-10-55-185
IE94	606-10-55-186

Example 19—Uninstalled Materials	
IE95	606-10-55-187
IE96	606-10-55-188
IE97	606-10-55-189
IE98	606-10-55-190
IE99	606-10-55-191
IE100	606-10-55-192

VARIABLE CONSIDERATION	
IE101	606-10-55-193

Example 20—Penalty Gives Rise to Variable Consideration	
IE102	606-10-55-194
IE103	606-10-55-195
IE104	606-10-55-196

Example 21—Estimating Variable Consideration	
IE105	606-10-55-197
IE106	606-10-55-198
IE107	606-10-55-199
IE108	606-10-55-200

CONSTRAINING ESTIMATES OF VARIABLE CONSIDERATION	
IE109	606-10-55-201
Example 22—Right of Return	
IE110	606-10-55-202
IE111	606-10-55-203
IE112	606-10-55-204
IE113	606-10-55-205
IE114	606-10-55-206
IE115	606-10-55-207
Example 23—Price Concessions	
IE116	606-10-55-208
IE117	606-10-55-209
IE118	606-10-55-210
IE119	606-10-55-211
IE120	606-10-55-212
IE121	606-10-55-213
IE122	606-10-55-214
IE123	606-10-55-215
Example 24—Volume Discount Incentive	
IE124	606-10-55-216
IE125	606-10-55-217
IE126	606-10-55-218
IE127	606-10-55-219
IE128	606-10-55-220
Example 25—Management Fees Subject to the Constraint	
IE129	606-10-55-221
IE130	606-10-55-222
IE131	606-10-55-223
IE132	606-10-55-224
IE133	606-10-55-225

THE EXISTENCE OF A SIGNIFICANT FINANCING COMPONENT IN THE CONTRACT	
IE134	606-10-55-226

Example 26—Significant Financing Component and Right of Return	
IE135	606-10-55-227
IE136	606-10-55-228
IE137	606-10-55-229
IE138	606-10-55-230
IE139	606-10-55-231
IE140	606-10-55-232

Example 27—Withheld Payments on a Long-Term Contract	
IE141	606-10-55-233
IE142	606-10-55-234

Example 28—Determining the Discount Rate	
IE143	606-10-55-235
IE144	606-10-55-236
IE145	606-10-55-237
IE146	606-10-55-238
IE147	606-10-55-239

Example 29—Advance Payment and Assessment of the Discount Rate	
IE148	606-10-55-240
IE149	606-10-55-241
IE150	606-10-55-242
IE151	606-10-55-243

Example 30—Advance Payment	
IE152	606-10-55-244
IE153	606-10-55-245
IE154	606-10-55-246

NON-CASH CONSIDERATION	
IE155	606-10-55-247

Example 31—Entitlement to Non-cash Consideration	
IE156	606-10-55-248
IE157	606-10-55-249
IE158	606-10-55-250*

BC507   Paragraphs BC439–BC444 explain the boards' rationale for including an additional transition method in IFRS 15. That method requires an entity (that is not a first-time adopter of IFRS) to apply IFRS 15 retrospectively with the cumulative effect of initially applying IFRS 15 recognised in the current year (referred to as the 'cumulative catch-up' transition method). Using the cumulative catch-up transition method, an entity would apply the requirements retrospectively only to contracts that are not completed at the beginning of the date of initial application (which, if applied to a first-time adopter would be the entity's first IFRS reporting period).

BC508   However, the IASB decided not to amend IFRS 1 to permit first-time adopters of IFRS to use the cumulative catch-up transition method because it is not consistent with the principles of IFRS 1. This is because it would eliminate comparability within a first-time adopter's first IFRS financial statements by providing relief from restating comparative years. The IASB also observed that the cumulative catch-up transition method may not reduce the burden of retrospective application because it would potentially require two separate reconciliations of equity—one for the transition to IFRS, which would be recognised in the earliest comparative period, and one for the transition to IFRS 15, which would be recognised at the beginning of the entity's first IFRS reporting period. This would not only be challenging for preparers, but might also be confusing for users of financial statements.

BC509   Despite deciding not to amend IFRS 1 to allow first-time adopters to use the cumulative catch-up transition method, the IASB decided to amend IFRS 1 to provide an optional exemption for first-time adopters from the requirements of IFRS 15 in accounting for contracts completed before the earliest period presented. Under this exemption, a first-time adopter would not be required to restate all of its contracts for which it has recognised all of its revenue in accordance with its previous GAAP before the earliest period presented.

Summary of main changes from the 2011 Exposure Draft

BC510   The main changes from the proposals in the 2011 Exposure Draft are as follows:

(a)   IFRS 15 includes additional requirements related to identifying a contract with a customer. Specifically, IFRS 15 includes an additional criterion that must be met before an entity can apply the requirements in IFRS 15 to a contract. This criterion in paragraph 9(e) of IFRS 15 requires an entity to conclude that it is probable that a customer will pay the consideration to which the entity will be entitled by assessing the customer's ability and intention to pay. In addition, IFRS 15 provides guidance for accounting for contracts that do not meet the specified criteria and thus cannot apply IFRS 15.

(b)   IFRS 15 clarifies the objective of the requirements for constraining estimates of variable consideration and provides a level of confidence of 'highly probable' for determining when to include those estimates in the transaction price. This represents a change from the 2011 Exposure Draft, which specified that an entity could only

CONTRACT COSTS	
IE188	340-40-55-1
Example 36—Incremental Costs of Obtaining a Contract	
IE189	340-40-55-2
IE190	340-40-55-3
IE191	340-40-55-4
Example 37—Costs That Give Rise to an Asset	
IE192	340-40-55-5
IE193	340-40-55-6
IE194	340-40-55-7
IE195	340-40-55-8
IE196	340-40-55-9

PRESENTATION	
IE197	606-10-55-283
Example 38—Contract Liability and Receivable	
IE198	606-10-55-284
IE199	606-10-55-285
IE200	606-10-55-286
Example 39—Contract Asset Recognised for the Entity's Performance	
IE201	606-10-55-287
IE202	606-10-55-288
IE203	606-10-55-289
IE204	606-10-55-290
Example 40—Receivable Recognised for the Entity's Performance	
IE205	606-10-55-291
IE206	606-10-55-292
IE207	606-10-55-293
IE208	606-10-55-294

DISCLOSURE	
IE209	606-10-55-295
Example 41—Disaggregation of Revenue—Quantitative Disclosure	
IE210	606-10-55-296
IE211	606-10-55-297

continued...

...continued

DISCLOSURE	
Example 42—Disclosure of the Transaction Price Allocated to the Remaining Performance Obligations	
IE212	606-10-55-298
IE213	606-10-55-299
IE214	606-10-55-300
IE215	606-10-55-301
IE216	606-10-55-302
IE217	606-10-55-303
IE218	606-10-55-304
IE219	606-10-55-305
Example 43—Disclosure of the Transaction Price Allocated to the Remaining Performance Obligations—Qualitative Disclosure	
IE220	606-10-55-306
IE221	606-10-55-307

WARRANTIES	
IE222	606-10-55-308
Example 44—Warranties	
IE223	606-10-55-309*
IE224	606-10-55-310
IE225	606-10-55-311
IE226	606-10-55-312
IE227	606-10-55-313
IE228	606-10-55-314
IE229	606-10-55-315

PRINCIPAL VERSUS AGENT CONSIDERATIONS	
IE230	606-10-55-316
Example 45—Arranging for the Provision of Goods or Services (Entity is an Agent)	
IE231	606-10-55-317
IE232	606-10-55-318
IE232A–IE232C	606-10-55-318A through 55-318C
IE233	606-10-55-319

continued...

...continued

PRINCIPAL VERSUS AGENT CONSIDERATIONS	
Example 46—Promise to Provide Goods or Services (Entity is a Principal)	
IE234	606-10-55-320
IE235	606-10-55-321
IE236	606-10-55-322
IE237	606-10-55-323
IE237A–IE237B	606-10-55-323A through 55-323B
IE238	606-10-55-324
Example 46A—Promise to Provide Goods or Services (Entity Is a Principal)	
IE238A–IE238G	606-10-55-324A through 55-324G
Example 47—Promise to Provide Goods or Services (Entity is a Principal)	
IE239	606-10-55-325
IE240	606-10-55-326
IE241	606-10-55-327
IE242	606-10-55-328
IE242A–IE242C	606-10-55-328A through 55-328C
IE243	606-10-55-329
Example 48—Arranging for the Provision of Goods or Services (Entity is an Agent)	
IE244	606-10-55-330
IE245	606-10-55-331
IE246	606-10-55-332
IE247	606-10-55-333
IE247A–IE247B	606-10-55-333A through 55-333B
IE248	606-10-55-334
Example 48A—Entity Is a Principal and an Agent in the Same Contract	
IE248A–IE248F	606-10-55-334A through 55-334F

CUSTOMER OPTIONS FOR ADDITIONAL GOODS OR SERVICES	
IE249	606-10-55-335
Example 49—Option That Provides the Customer with a Material Right (Discount Voucher)	
IE250	606-10-55-336
IE251	606-10-55-337
IE252	606-10-55-338
IE253	606-10-55-339
Example 50—Option That Does Not Provide the Customer with a Material Right (Additional Goods or Services)	
IE254	606-10-55-340
IE255	606-10-55-341
IE256	606-10-55-342
Example 51—Option That Provides the Customer with a Material Right (Renewal Option)	
IE257	606-10-55-343
IE258	606-10-55-344
IE259	606-10-55-345
IE260	606-10-55-346
IE261	606-10-55-347
IE262	606-10-55-348
IE263	606-10-55-349
IE264	606-10-55-350
IE265	606-10-55-351
IE266	606-10-55-352
Example 52—Customer Loyalty Programme	
IE267	606-10-55-353
IE268	606-10-55-354
IE269	606-10-55-355
IE270	606-10-55-356

NON-REFUNDABLE UPFRONT FEES	
IE271	606-10-55-357
Example 53—Non-refundable Upfront Fee	
IE272	606-10-55-358
IE273	606-10-55-359
IE274	606-10-55-360

LICENSING	
IE275	606-10-55-361*
Example 54—Right to Use Intellectual Property	
IE276	606-10-55-362
IE277	606-10-55-363 through 55-363B*
Example 55—Licence of Intellectual Property	
IE278	606-10-55-364
IE279	606-10-55-365
IE279A	606-10-55-365A
IE280	606-10-55-366*
Example 56—Identifying a Distinct Licence	
IE281	606-10-55-367*
IE282	606-10-55-368*
IE283	606-10-55-369
IE284	606-10-55-370*
IE285	606-10-55-371
IE286	606-10-55-372
IE286A	606-10-55-372A
IE287	606-10-55-373*
IE288	606-10-55-374*

continued...

...continued

LICENSING	
Example 57—Franchise Rights	
IE289	606-10-55-375*
IE290	606-10-55-376*
IE291	606-10-55-377
IE292	606-10-55-378*
IE293	606-10-55-379*
IE294	606-10-55-380*
IE295	606-10-55-381*
IE296	606-10-55-382*
Example 58—Access to Intellectual Property	
IE297	606-10-55-383*
IE298	606-10-55-384
IE299	606-10-55-385*
IE300	606-10-55-386*
IE301	606-10-55-387*
IE302	606-10-55-388*
Example 59—Right to Use Intellectual Property	
IE303	606-10-55-389
IE304	606-10-55-390
IE305	606-10-55-391*
IE306	606-10-55-392*
N/A	606-10-55-392A through 55-392D*
Example 60—Sales-based royalty for a licence of intellectual property	
IE307	606-10-55-393
IE308	606-10-55-394
Example 61—Access to Intellectual Property	
IE309	606-10-55-395
IE310	606-10-55-396*
IE311	606-10-55-397*
IE312	606-10-55-398*
IE313	606-10-55-399*
Example 61A—Right to Use Intellectual Property	
N/A	606-10-55-399A through 55-399J*

continued...

...continued

LICENSING	
Example 61B—Distinguishing Multiple Licences from Attributes of a Single Licence	
N/A	606-10-55-399K through 55-399O*

REPURCHASE AGREEMENTS	
IE314	606-10-55-400
Example 62—Repurchase Agreements	
IE315	606-10-55-401
IE316	606-10-55-402
IE317	606-10-55-403
IE318	606-10-55-404
IE319	606-10-55-405
IE320	606-10-55-406
IE321	606-10-55-407

BILL-AND-HOLD ARRANGEMENTS	
IE322	606-10-55-408
Example 63—Bill-and-Hold Arrangement	
IE323	606-10-55-409
IE324	606-10-55-410
IE325	606-10-55-411
IE326	606-10-55-412
IE327	606-10-55-413

Appendix B
Amendments to the Basis for Conclusions on other Standards

The amendments in this appendix to the Basis for Conclusions on other Standards are necessary in order to ensure consistency with IFRS 15 and the related amendments to other Standards.

* * * * *

The amendments contained in this appendix when IFRS 15 was issued in 2014 have been incorporated into the Basis for Conclusions on the relevant Standards included in this volume.

IASB documents published to accompany

IFRS 16

Leases

The text of the unaccompanied standard, IFRS 16, is contained in Part A of this edition. Its effective date when issued was 1 January 2019. The text of the Accompanying Guidance on IFRS 16 is contained in Part B of this edition. This part presents the following documents:

BASIS FOR CONCLUSIONS

DISSENTING OPINION

Contents

...continued

continued...

...continued

Basis for Conclusions on
IFRS 16 *Leases*

This Basis for Conclusions accompanies, but is not part of, IFRS 16.

Introduction

BC1   This Basis for Conclusions summarises the IASB's considerations in developing IFRS 16 *Leases*. It includes the reasons for accepting particular views and rejecting others. Individual Board members gave greater weight to some factors than to others.

BC2   IFRS 16 is also accompanied by an Effects Analysis. The Effects Analysis describes the likely costs and benefits of IFRS 16, which the IASB has prepared based on insight gained through the exposure of proposals and feedback on these proposals, and through the IASB's analysis and consultation with stakeholders.

Overview

Why the need to change previous accounting?

BC3   The previous accounting model for leases required lessees and lessors to classify their leases as either finance leases or operating leases and to account for those two types of leases differently. It did not require lessees to recognise assets and liabilities arising from operating leases, but it did require lessees to recognise assets and liabilities arising from finance leases. The IASB, together with the US national standard-setter, the Financial Accounting Standards Board (FASB) (together 'the Boards'), initiated a joint project to improve the financial reporting of leasing activities under IFRS and US Generally Accepted Accounting Principles (US GAAP) in the light of criticisms that the previous accounting model for leases failed to meet the needs of users of financial statements. In particular:

(a)   information reported about operating leases lacked transparency and did not meet the needs of users of financial statements. Many users adjusted a lessee's financial statements to capitalise operating leases because, in their view, the financing and assets provided by leases should be reflected on the statement of financial position ('balance sheet'). Some tried to estimate the present value of future lease payments. However, because of the limited information that was available, many used techniques such as multiplying the annual lease expense by eight to estimate, for example, total leverage and the capital employed in operations. Other users were unable to make adjustments — they relied on data sources such as data aggregators when screening potential investments or making investment decisions. These different approaches created information asymmetry in the market.

(b)   the existence of two different accounting models for leases, in which assets and liabilities associated with leases were not recognised for operating leases but were recognised for finance leases, meant that transactions that were economically similar could be accounted for very differently. The differences reduced comparability for users of financial statements and provided opportunities to structure transactions to achieve a particular accounting outcome.

(c)   the previous requirements for lessors did not provide adequate information about a lessor's exposure to credit risk (arising from a lease) and exposure to asset risk (arising from the lessor's retained interest in the underlying asset), particularly for leases of equipment and vehicles that were classified as operating leases.

BC4   The Boards decided to address the first two criticisms by developing a new approach to lessee accounting that requires a lessee to recognise assets and liabilities for the rights and obligations created by leases. IFRS 16 requires a lessee to recognise assets and liabilities for all leases with a term of more than 12 months and for which the underlying asset is not of low value. The IASB concluded that such an approach will result in a more faithful representation of a lessee's assets and liabilities and, together with enhanced disclosures, greater transparency of a lessee's financial leverage and capital employed. To address the third criticism, IFRS 16 requires enhanced disclosure by lessors of information about their risk exposure.

Background

BC5   In March 2009 the Boards published a joint Discussion Paper *Leases: Preliminary Views*. The Discussion Paper set out the Boards' preliminary views on lessee accounting, proposing a 'right-of-use' accounting model. Feedback on the Discussion Paper generally supported the 'right-of-use' model for lessees, by which a lessee would recognise a right-of-use asset and a lease liability at the commencement date of the lease. The Discussion Paper did not discuss lessor accounting in any detail.

BC6   In August 2010 the Boards published a joint Exposure Draft *Leases* (the '2010 Exposure Draft'). The Boards developed the 2010 Exposure Draft after considering the comment letters received on the Discussion Paper, as well as input obtained from their Lease Accounting Working Group and from others who were interested in the financial reporting of leases. The 2010 Exposure Draft:

(a)   further developed the 'right-of-use' accounting model for lessees that had been proposed in the Discussion Paper, and that respondents had generally supported.

(b)   added proposals for changes to lessor accounting. The Boards decided to include lessor accounting in the proposals in response to comments from respondents to the Discussion Paper. Some respondents had recommended that the Boards develop accounting models for lessees and lessors on the basis of a consistent rationale. The Boards also saw merit in developing lessor accounting proposals at the same time as they were developing proposals for recognising revenue (which the IASB subsequently finalised in IFRS 15 *Revenue from Contracts with Customers*).

BC7   For lessors, the 2010 Exposure Draft proposed a dual accounting model:

(a)   for some leases, a lessor would apply a 'performance obligation' approach. Applying this approach, a lessor would recognise a lease receivable and a liability at the commencement date, and would also continue to recognise the underlying asset.

(b)   for other leases, a lessor would apply a 'derecognition' approach. Applying this approach, a lessor would derecognise the underlying asset, and recognise a lease receivable and any retained interest in the underlying asset (a 'residual asset') at the commencement date.

BC8   The 2010 Exposure Draft also included detailed proposals on the measurement of the lessee's lease liability and the lessor's lease receivable. Of particular note was its proposal that in estimating the lease payments, a lessee should:

(a)   assume the longest possible term that was more likely than not to occur, taking into account any options to extend or terminate the lease; and

(b)   include an estimate of variable lease payments, if those payments could be measured reliably.

BC9   The Boards received 786 comment letters in response to the 2010 Exposure Draft. The Boards also conducted extensive outreach on the proposals in the 2010 Exposure Draft. Round table discussions were held in Hong Kong, the United Kingdom and the United States. Workshops were organised in Australia, Brazil, Canada, Japan, South Korea, the UK and the US. Members of the Boards also participated in conferences, working group meetings, discussion forums, and one-to-one discussions that were held across all major geographical regions. In 2011 and 2012, while redeliberating the proposals in the 2010 Exposure Draft, the Boards conducted additional targeted outreach with more than 100 organisations. The purpose of the targeted outreach was to obtain additional feedback to assist the Boards in developing particular aspects of the revised proposals. The targeted outreach meetings involved international working group members, representatives from accounting firms, local standard-setters, users and preparers of financial statements, particularly those from industries most affected by the lease accounting proposals.

BC10   Responses to the 2010 Exposure Draft indicated that:

(a)   there was general support for lessees recognising assets and liabilities arising from a lease. That support was consistent with comments received on the Discussion Paper.

(b)   there were mixed views on the effects of the proposed right-of-use model on a lessee's profit or loss. The effect was that a lessee would recognise two separate expenses in its statement of profit or loss and other comprehensive income ('income statement')—depreciation of the right-of-use asset and interest on the lease liability. Some respondents supported the identification of two separate expenses, on the grounds that leases are a source of finance for a lessee and should be accounted for accordingly. However, others did not support these effects because they thought that they would not properly reflect the economics of all lease transactions. In particular, some respondents referred to shorter-term property leases as examples of leases that, in their view, were not financing transactions from either the lessee's or lessor's perspective.

(c)   many respondents disagreed with the proposals for lessor accounting:

    (i)   some respondents were concerned that the dual accounting model proposed for lessors was not consistent with the single accounting model proposed for lessees.

    (ii)   many respondents opposed the performance obligation approach. In the view of those respondents, the approach would artificially inflate a lessor's assets and liabilities.

    (iii)   some respondents recommended applying the derecognition approach to all leases. However, many disagreed with the proposal to prevent a lessor from accounting for the effects of the time value of money on the residual asset.

    (iv)   some respondents thought that the lessor accounting requirements in IAS 17 *Leases* and FASB Topic 840 *Leases* work well in practice and supported retaining those requirements.

(d)   almost all respondents were concerned about the cost and complexity of the proposals, in particular the proposals regarding the measurement of the lessee's lease liability and the lessor's lease receivable. Some questioned whether lease payments to be made during optional extension periods would meet the definition of an asset (for the lessor) or a liability (for the lessee). Others suggested that it would be extremely difficult in many cases to estimate variable lease payments if the amounts depended on future sales or use of the underlying asset and that such estimates would be subject to a high level of measurement uncertainty. Many expressed a view that, because of the amount of judgement involved, the cost of including variable lease payments and payments to be made during optional periods in the measurement of lease assets and lease liabilities would outweigh the benefit for users of financial statements.

(e)   many respondents also were concerned about the breadth of the scope of the proposals, indicating that the proposed definition of a lease had the potential to capture some contracts that they considered to be for services.

BC11   The Boards considered the feedback received on the 2010 Exposure Draft and observed that it would not be possible to reflect the views of all stakeholders because stakeholders did not have a united view of the economics of leases. However, in response to views that the economics of leases can be different the Boards decided to develop a revised model that identified two classes of leases and specified different requirements for each type. The classification depended on the extent to which the lessee was expected to consume the economic benefits embedded in the underlying asset.

BC12 Consequently, in May 2013 the Boards published a second joint Exposure Draft *Leases* (the '2013 Exposure Draft'). The 2013 Exposure Draft proposed:

(a) for lessees, simpler measurement requirements and a dual approach for the recognition and measurement of expenses related to a lease:

    (i) for leases for which the lessee was expected to consume more than an insignificant amount of the economic benefits embedded in the underlying asset, a lessee would apply an approach similar to that proposed in the 2010 Exposure Draft, ie recognise depreciation of the right-of-use asset and interest on the lease liability separately in the income statement.

    (ii) for leases for which the lessee was expected to consume only an insignificant amount of the economic benefits embedded in the underlying asset, a lessee would recognise a single lease expense in the income statement. This approach was based on the view that a single lease expense would provide better information about leases for which the lessee in essence is paying mainly for the use of the underlying asset and is expected to consume only an insignificant amount of the economic benefits embedded in the underlying asset itself.

(b) for lessors, a dual approach for the recognition and measurement of lease assets:

    (i) for leases for which the lessee was expected to consume more than an insignificant portion of the economic benefits embedded in the underlying asset, a lessor would recognise its residual interest in the underlying asset separately from its receivable from the lessee.

    (ii) for other leases, a lessor would recognise the underlying asset, ie apply requirements similar to those in IAS 17 for operating leases.

BC13 The Boards received 641 comment letters in response to the 2013 Exposure Draft. In addition, the Boards conducted extensive outreach on the proposals in the 2013 Exposure Draft, including:

(a) consultations with over 270 users of financial statements based in Australia, Belgium, Canada, France, Hong Kong, Japan, the Netherlands, New Zealand, Sweden, Switzerland, the UK and the US;

(b) fieldwork meetings with individual preparers of financial statements from various industries including consumer goods, retail, aviation, oil and gas, telecommunications and automotive industries. These meetings were held in Brazil, France, Germany, Japan, Spain, the UK and the US and included detailed discussions about the costs of implementation for those entities.

(c)   round table discussion held in London, Los Angeles, Norwalk, São Paulo and Singapore. These discussions were attended by approximately 100 stakeholder representatives.

(d)   meetings with the IASB's advisory bodies—the Capital Markets Advisory Committee, the Global Preparers Forum, the IFRS Advisory Council and the Accounting Standards Advisory Forum.

(e)   outreach meetings with various other individual preparers and groups of preparers, standard-setters and regulators. These meetings included presentations during accounting conferences and at industry forums, and meetings with individual organisations or groups.

(f)   project webcasts that attracted over 2,000 participants.

BC14   The feedback received on the proposals in the 2013 Exposure Draft indicated that:

(a)   consistently with the views they had expressed on the 2010 Exposure Draft, many stakeholders supported the recognition of a right-of-use asset and a lease liability by a lessee for all leases of more than 12 months in duration. These stakeholders included the majority of users of financial statements consulted, who were of the view that the proposed recognition of assets and liabilities by a lessee would provide them with a better starting point for their analyses.

(b)   nonetheless, many stakeholders had significant concerns about the proposed lessee accounting model. Some were of the view that the previous lessee accounting model in IAS 17 did not need to be changed, or that deficiencies in that model could be rectified by improving the disclosure requirements, instead of changing the recognition and measurement requirements. Others disagreed with one or more specific aspects of the proposed lessee accounting model, such as the proposed dual approach or the proposal to periodically reassess the measurement of lease assets and lease liabilities.

(c)   many stakeholders thought that the measurement proposals in the 2013 Exposure Draft represented a significant improvement over the proposals in the 2010 Exposure Draft, especially relating to simplifications in respect of variable lease payments and payments under renewal and purchase options. Nonetheless, the majority of stakeholders still had concerns about the cost and complexity of the proposals in the 2013 Exposure Draft. Specific areas of the proposals that stakeholders highlighted as being particularly costly or complex included the dual lessee and lessor accounting models (both the lease classification proposals and the accounting requirements), the reassessment proposals, the disclosure proposals and the scope of the transactions subject to the proposals.

(d)   the majority of stakeholders disagreed with the proposed lessor accounting model. Most of these stakeholders were of the view that the previous lessor accounting model in IAS 17 was not fundamentally flawed and should not be changed.

BC15   The Boards considered the feedback they had received in response to the different models proposed in the 2010 and 2013 Exposure Drafts. The Boards confirmed their previous decision that a lessee should be required to recognise right-of-use assets and lease liabilities for all leases (with limited exceptions). However, the Boards reached different decisions with respect to the expense recognition model. For the reasons described in paragraphs BC41–BC56, the IASB decided to adopt a single lessee accounting model in which a lessee would account for all leases as providing finance. In the light of all of the feedback received, the IASB is of the view that this model provides the most useful information to the broadest range of users of financial statements. The IASB thinks that the model also addresses many of the concerns raised by stakeholders about cost and complexity, and the concerns raised about the conceptual basis of the dual model proposed in the 2013 Exposure Draft (see paragraph BC45). In contrast, the FASB decided to adopt a dual lessee expense recognition model, classifying leases in a similar manner to the previous US GAAP requirements for distinguishing between operating leases and capital leases. In making these decisions, the Boards observed that, for lessees with a portfolio of leases starting and ending at different times, any difference in reported profit or loss between IFRS and US GAAP is not expected to be significant for many lessees.

BC16   There are a number of other differences between IFRS 16 and the decisions made by the FASB, mainly because of the different decisions reached on the lessee accounting model. This Basis for Conclusions summarises only the reasons for decisions made by the IASB and reflected in IFRS 16. Paragraphs BC303–BC310 summarise the differences between IFRS 16 and the decisions made by the FASB.

BC17   In response to feedback received, the IASB and the FASB also decided to substantially carry forward the lessor accounting requirements in IAS 17 and Topic 840 respectively.

BC18   IFRS 16 addresses many of the concerns raised by stakeholders about the cost and complexity of the proposals in the 2010 and 2013 Exposure Drafts. In addition to the single lessee accounting model, which removes the need for lessees to classify leases, and the decision to substantially carry forward the lessor accounting requirements in IAS 17, the IASB decided to:

   (a)   permit a lessee not to recognise assets and liabilities for short-term leases and leases of low-value assets;

   (b)   confirm that an entity may apply the Standard at a portfolio level for leases with similar characteristics;

   (c)   further simplify the measurement requirements for lease liabilities, in particular the requirements for variable lease payments, payments during optional periods and the reassessment of lease liabilities;

   (d)   simplify the requirements for separating lease and non-lease components of a contract;

(e)   change the lessee disclosure requirements to enable lessees to more effectively focus disclosures on the most significant features of their lease portfolios; and

(f)   simplify the lessee transition requirements.

The approach to lease accounting

BC19   All contracts create rights and obligations for the parties to the contract. Lessee accounting in IFRS 16 considers the rights and obligations created by a lease from the perspective of the lessee. As discussed further in paragraphs BC105–BC126, a lease is defined as a 'contract, or part of a contract, that conveys the right to use an asset (the underlying asset) for a period of time in exchange for consideration'. The lessee accounting model in IFRS 16 reflects the economics of a lease because, at the commencement date, a lessee obtains the right to use an underlying asset for a period of time, and the lessor has delivered that right by making the asset available for use by the lessee.

BC20   A lessee has the right to use an underlying asset during the lease term and an obligation to make payments to the lessor for providing the right to use that asset. The lessee also has an obligation to return the underlying asset in a specified condition to the lessor at the end of the lease term. The lessor has a right to receive payments from the lessee for providing the right to use the underlying asset. The lessor also retains rights associated with ownership of the underlying asset.

BC21   Having identified the rights and obligations that arise from a lease, the IASB considered which of those rights and obligations create assets and liabilities for the lessee and lessor.

Rights and obligations arising from a lease that create assets and liabilities for the lessee

Right to use an underlying asset

BC22   The IASB's *Conceptual Framework for Financial Reporting* (*Conceptual Framework*)[1] defines an asset as 'a resource controlled by the entity as a result of past events and from which future economic benefits are expected to flow to the entity'. The IASB concluded that a lessee's right to use an underlying asset meets the definition of an asset for the following reasons:

(a)   the lessee controls the right to use the underlying asset throughout the lease term. Once the asset is made available for use by the lessee, the lessor is unable to retrieve or otherwise use the underlying asset for its own purposes during the lease term, despite being the legal owner of the underlying asset.

---

1   References to the *Conceptual Framework* in this Basis for Conclusions are to the *Conceptual Framework for Financial Reporting*, issued in 2010 and in effect when the Standard was developed.

(b)   the lessee has the ability to determine how to use the underlying asset and, thus, how it generates future economic benefits from that right of use. This ability demonstrates the lessee's control of the right of use. For example, suppose a lessee leases a truck for four years, for up to a maximum of 160,000 miles over the lease term. Embedded in the right to use the truck is a particular volume of economic benefits or service potential that is used up over the period that the truck is driven by the lessee. After the truck is made available for use by the lessee, the lessee can decide how it wishes to use up or consume the economic benefits embedded in its right of use within the parameters defined in the contract. The lessee could decide to drive the truck constantly during the first three years of the lease, consuming all of the economic benefits in those first three years. Alternatively, it could use the truck only during particular months in each year or decide to use it evenly over the four-year lease term.

(c)   the right to control and use the asset exists even when a lessee's right to use an asset includes some restrictions on its use. Although restrictions may affect the value and scope of a lessee's right to use an asset (and thus the payments made for the right of use), they do not affect the existence of the right-of-use asset. It is not unusual for restrictions to be placed on the use of owned assets as well as leased assets. For example, assets acquired from a competitor may be subject to restrictions on where they can be used, how they can be used or to whom they can be sold; assets that are used as security for particular borrowings may have restrictions placed on their use by the lender; or a government may place restrictions on the use or transfer of assets in a particular region for environmental or security reasons. Those restrictions do not necessarily result in the owner of such assets failing to control those assets—the restrictions may simply affect the economic benefits that will flow to the entity from the asset and that will be reflected in the price that the entity is willing to pay for the asset. Similarly, such restrictions do not prevent a lessee from controlling a right-of-use asset.

(d)   the lessee's control of the right of use arises from past events—not only the commitment to the lease contract but also the underlying asset being made available for use by the lessee for the duration of the non-cancellable period of the lease. Some have noted that the lessee's right to use an asset is conditional on the lessee making payments during the lease term, ie that the lessee may forfeit its right to use the asset if it does not make payments. However, unless the lessee breaches the contract, the lessee has an unconditional right to use the underlying asset. Its position is similar to that of an entity that had made an instalment purchase and has not yet made the instalment payments.

BC23   The IASB also considered the proposed definition of an asset in the May 2015 Exposure Draft *The Conceptual Framework for Financial Reporting* (the '*Conceptual Framework* Exposure Draft'). That exposure draft proposes to define an asset as 'a present economic resource controlled by the entity as a result of past events' and defines an economic resource as 'a right that has the potential to produce economic benefits'. In the IASB's view, a lessee's right to use an underlying asset would meet this proposed definition of an asset, for the reasons described in paragraph BC22.

BC24   Consequently, the IASB concluded that the lessee's right to use an underlying asset meets both the existing and proposed definitions of an asset.

Obligation to make lease payments

BC25   The *Conceptual Framework* defines a liability as 'a present obligation of the entity arising from past events, the settlement of which is expected to result in an outflow from the entity of resources embodying economic benefits'. The IASB concluded that the lessee's obligation to make lease payments meets the definition of a liability for the following reasons:

   (a)   the lessee has a present obligation to make lease payments once the underlying asset has been made available to the lessee. That obligation arises from past events—not only the commitment to the lease contract but also the underlying asset being made available for use by the lessee. Unless the lessee renegotiates the lease, the lessee has no right to cancel the lease and avoid the contractual lease payments (or termination penalties) before the end of the lease term.

   (b)   the obligation results in a future outflow of economic benefits from the lessee—typically contractual cash payments in accordance with the terms and conditions of the lease.

BC26   The IASB also considered the *Conceptual Framework* Exposure Draft, which proposes to define a liability as 'a present obligation of the entity to transfer an economic resource as a result of past events'. In the IASB's view, a lessee's obligation to make lease payments would also meet this definition of a liability for the reasons described in paragraph BC25.

BC27   Consequently, the IASB concluded that a lessee's obligation to make lease payments meets both the existing and proposed definitions of a liability.

Obligation to return the underlying asset to the lessor

BC28   The lessee controls the use of the underlying asset during the lease term, and has an obligation to return the underlying asset to the lessor at the end of the lease term. That obligation is a present obligation that arises from past events (the underlying asset being made available for use by the lessee under the terms of the lease contract).

BC29   Some are of the view that there is an outflow of economic benefits at the end of the lease term because the lessee must surrender the underlying asset, which will frequently still have some potential to generate economic benefits. However, in the IASB's view, there is no outflow of economic benefits (other than incidental costs) from the lessee when it returns the leased item, because the lessee does not control the economic benefits associated with the asset that it returns to the lessor. Even if the lessee has physical possession of the underlying asset, it has no right to obtain the remaining economic benefits associated with the underlying asset once the lease term expires (ignoring any options to extend the lease or purchase the underlying asset). Once it reaches the end of the lease term, the position of the lessee is like that of an asset custodian. The lessee is holding an asset on behalf of a third party, the lessor, but has no right to the economic benefits embodied in that asset at the end of the lease term.

BC30　Consequently, the IASB concluded that the lessee's obligation to return the underlying asset does not meet the definition of a liability in the *Conceptual Framework*. The IASB is of the view that the changes proposed to the definition of a liability in the *Conceptual Framework* Exposure Draft would not affect this conclusion.

BC31　Having considered whether the lessee's right to use an underlying asset, obligation to make lease payments and obligation to return the underlying asset meet the definition of an asset or a liability, the IASB considered the lessee accounting model. This is discussed in paragraphs BC41–BC56.

Why leases are different from service contracts for the lessee

BC32　The IASB concluded that leases create rights and obligations that are different from those that arise from service contracts. This is because, as described in paragraph BC22, the lessee obtains and controls the right-of-use asset at the time that the underlying asset is made available for use by the lessee.

BC33　When the lessor makes the underlying asset available for use by the lessee, the lessor has fulfilled its obligation to transfer the right to use that asset to the lessee—the lessee now controls that right of use. Consequently, the lessee has an unconditional obligation to pay for that right of use.

BC34　In contrast, in a typical service contract, the customer does not obtain an asset that it controls at commencement of the contract. Instead, the customer obtains the service only at the time that the service is performed. Consequently, the customer typically has an unconditional obligation to pay only for the services provided to date. In addition, although fulfilment of a service contract will often require the use of assets, fulfilment typically does not require making those assets available for use by the customer throughout the contractual term.

Rights and obligations arising from a lease that create assets and liabilities for the lessor

Lease receivable

BC35　When the lessor makes the underlying asset available for use by the lessee, the lessor has fulfilled its obligation to transfer the right to use that asset to the lessee—the lessee controls the right of use. Accordingly, the lessor has an unconditional right to receive lease payments (the lease receivable). The lessor controls that right—for example, it can decide to sell or securitise that right. The right arises from past events (not only the commitment to the lease contract but also the underlying asset being made available for use by the lessee) and is expected to result in future economic benefits (typically cash from the lessee) flowing to the lessor.

BC36 Consequently, the IASB concluded that the lessor's lease receivable meets the definition of an asset in the *Conceptual Framework*. The IASB is of the view that the changes proposed to the definition of an asset in the *Conceptual Framework* Exposure Draft would not affect this conclusion.

Rights retained in the underlying asset

BC37 Although the lessor transfers the right to use the underlying asset to the lessee at the commencement date, the lessor has the right to the underlying asset at the end of the lease term (and retains some rights to the underlying asset during the lease term; for example, the lessor retains title to the asset). Consequently, the lessor retains some of the potential economic benefits embedded in the underlying asset.

BC38 The lessor controls the rights that it retains in the underlying asset. A lessor can often, for example, sell the underlying asset (with the lease attached) or agree at any time during the initial lease term to sell or re-lease the underlying asset at the end of the lease term. The lessor's rights to the underlying asset arise from a past event—the purchase of the underlying asset or commitment to a head lease, if the lessor subleases the asset. Future economic benefits from the lessor's retained rights in the underlying asset are expected to flow to the lessor, assuming that the lease is for anything other than the full economic life of the underlying asset. The lessor would expect to obtain economic benefits either from the sale, re-lease or use of the underlying asset at the end of the lease term.

BC39 Consequently, the IASB concluded that the lessor's rights retained in the underlying asset meet the definition of an asset in the *Conceptual Framework*. The IASB is of the view that the changes proposed to the definition of an asset in the *Conceptual Framework* Exposure Draft would not affect this conclusion.

BC40 Having considered whether the lessor's lease receivable and rights retained in the underlying asset meet the definition of an asset, the IASB considered the lessor accounting model. This is discussed in paragraphs BC57–BC66.

The lessee accounting model

BC41 Having concluded that the lessee's right to use the underlying asset meets the definition of an asset and the lessee's obligation to make lease payments meets the definition of a liability (as described in paragraphs BC22–BC40), the IASB then considered whether requiring a lessee to recognise that asset and liability for all leases would improve financial reporting to the extent that the benefits from the improvements would outweigh the costs associated with such a change.

BC42　　The IASB considered comments from respondents to the Discussion Paper and the 2010 and 2013 Exposure Drafts, and from participants at consultation meetings (including meetings with users of financial statements) as described in paragraphs BC9 and BC13. In the light of these comments, the IASB concluded that there would be significant benefits from requiring a lessee to recognise right-of-use assets and lease liabilities for all leases (except short-term leases and leases of low-value assets as described in paragraphs BC87–BC104), particularly for users of financial statements and others who have raised concerns about the extent of off balance sheet financing provided through operating leases.

BC43　　The IASB considered the costs associated with requiring a lessee to recognise right-of-use assets and lease liabilities for all leases throughout its redeliberations. In the light of comments from respondents to the 2010 and 2013 Exposure Drafts, IFRS 16 contains a number of simplifications and practical expedients to address concerns about costs. The costs and benefits of the lessee accounting model are discussed extensively in the Effects Analysis.

BC44　　The IASB also consulted extensively on the approach to the recognition of lease expenses. The feedback from that consultation emphasised that different stakeholders have different views about the economics of lease transactions. Some view all leases as providing finance. Some view almost no leases as providing finance. Others think that the economics are different for different leases.

BC45　　The 2010 Exposure Draft proposed a single lessee expense recognition model that was based on the premise that all leases provide finance to the lessee. The IASB received a significant amount of feedback in response to the 2010 Exposure Draft with stakeholders expressing differing views. In the light of this feedback, the IASB decided to expose for comment an alternative lessee expense recognition model—a dual model—that was responsive to those stakeholders who thought that a dual model would provide more useful information than a single model. Applying the dual model proposed in the 2013 Exposure Draft, leases would have been classified based upon the extent to which the lessee was expected to consume the economic benefits embedded in the underlying asset. Although some stakeholders supported that model, the feedback received in response to the proposals reiterated the mixed views that had been received throughout the project regarding lessee accounting. In particular:

(a)　　some stakeholders, including most users of financial statements, were of the view that all leases provide finance to lessees and, thus, create assets and 'debt-like' liabilities. Consequently, they supported a single lessee expense recognition model according to which a lessee would recognise interest on those debt-like liabilities separately from depreciation of lease assets for all leases.

(b)　　some were of the view that a lessee receives equal benefits from use of the underlying asset in each period and pays equal amounts for that benefit. Consequently, they supported a single lessee expense recognition model in which a lessee would allocate the total cost of the lease to each period on a straight-line basis to reflect the pattern in which the lessee consumes benefits from use of the underlying asset. These stakeholders also noted that a decision to lease assets rather than purchase them is sometimes made in order to obtain operational flexibility (rather than to obtain finance). Consequently, they were of the view that a single straight-line lease expense would be a more faithful representation of the transaction in the income statement.

(c) some supported a single lessee expense recognition model because they had concerns about the cost and complexity of a dual expense recognition model. They noted the administrative benefits of removing the need for a lease classification test and having only one method of accounting for all leases. They also questioned whether more than one expense recognition pattern would provide useful information to users of financial statements.

(d) some supported a single lessee expense recognition model for conceptual reasons. They thought that, if all leases are recognised on a lessee's balance sheet, any attempt to differentiate between those leases in the income statement would be arbitrary and result in inconsistencies with the accounting for a non-financial asset and a financial liability in the balance sheet. Many also criticised the accounting that would result from a dual model that required the recognition of assets and liabilities together with a single, straight-line lease expense (as was proposed for some leases in the 2013 Exposure Draft). This is because, under that model, the right-of-use asset would have been measured as a balancing figure.

(e) some stakeholders noted that any dual model perpetuates the risk of structuring to gain a particular accounting outcome.

(f) some stakeholders thought that there are real economic differences between different leases, particularly between property leases and leases of assets other than property. These stakeholders recommended a dual lessee expense recognition model in which a lessee would recognise a single, straight-line lease expense for most property leases. They recommended such a model because they view property lease expenses as an important part of operating expenses, particularly for entities such as retailers, hoteliers and restaurateurs.

(g) some stakeholders recommended retaining a dual model that classified leases using the classification principle in IAS 17. They thought that recognition of a single, straight-line lease expense for all leases previously classified as operating leases would appropriately reflect the benefit that the lessee receives evenly over the lease term. This accounting would also align the lease expense more closely with lease payments, which some stakeholders viewed as preferable.

BC46 The IASB also consulted many users of financial statements (see paragraphs BC9 and BC13). Most users consulted (including almost all of those who analyse industrial, airline, transport and telecommunications sectors) were of the view that leases create assets and 'debt-like' liabilities. Consequently, they thought that recognising interest on lease liabilities separately from depreciation of right-of-use assets would be beneficial to their analyses, particularly in assessing the operating performance of an entity. The separate recognition of those expenses would be particularly beneficial for those users of financial statements who use reported information for their analyses without making further adjustments—it would create greater comparability in the income statement between entities that borrow to buy assets and those that lease similar assets. Separating interest and depreciation would also provide coherency between the lessee's balance sheet and income statement (ie the interest expense would correspond to the lease liabilities presented as financial liabilities, and depreciation would correspond to the right-of-use assets presented as non-financial assets). This coherency is important for some analyses, such as calculating return on capital employed and some leverage ratios.

BC47 Credit analysts consulted were generally of the view that all leases create assets and 'debt-like' liabilities for lessees. Consequently, they saw benefit in recognising interest on lease liabilities separately from depreciation of right-of-use assets. Many of those credit analysts already adjust a lessee's income statement for operating leases to estimate an allocation of operating lease expense between depreciation and interest.

BC48 Most users of the financial statements of retailers, hoteliers and restaurateurs (ie those entities that typically have significant amounts of leased property) expressed support for a model that would recognise a single lease expense for property leases. Some of those users view leases of property as executory contracts. For them, a single lease expense recognised within operating expenses would have best satisfied their needs. However, other users of the financial statements of retailers, hoteliers and restaurateurs had estimated an allocation of operating lease expense between depreciation and interest in their analyses based on previous lessee accounting requirements. Consequently, those users thought that requiring a lessee to recognise interest on lease liabilities separately from depreciation of right-of-use assets would provide them with information that is useful for their analyses.

BC49 The IASB also considered the adjustments made by those lessees that, in applying the previous lessee accounting requirements, reported lease-adjusted 'non-GAAP' information alongside their financial statements. These lessees often reported ratios based on amounts in the balance sheet, income statement and statement of cash flows that were adjusted to reflect the amounts that would have been reported if operating leases were accounted for as financing transactions (as is required by IFRS 16). For example, a commonly reported amount was lease-adjusted return on capital employed which was often calculated as (a) operating profit adjusted for the estimated interest on operating leases; divided by (b) reported equity plus financial liabilities adjusted to include liabilities for operating leases.

BC50 The IASB also observed that the consequence of any model that requires both the recognition of right-of-use assets and lease liabilities in the balance sheet together with a single, straight-line lease expense in the income statement (as was proposed for some leases in the 2013 Exposure Draft) would be a lack of coherency between the primary financial statements. In particular, any such model:

(a)   would result in a lessee recognising a financial liability in the balance sheet without presenting a commensurate interest expense in the income statement. Similarly, a lessee would recognise a non-financial asset without any commensurate depreciation in the income statement. These inconsistencies could distort ratio analyses performed on the basis of the amounts reported in the primary financial statements.

(b)   would require either the right-of-use asset or the lease liability to be measured as a balancing figure. This is because measuring (i) the right-of-use asset on the basis of cost less accumulated depreciation and impairment; and (ii) the lease liability using an effective interest method would generally not result in a straight-line lease expense.

BC51   Consequently, the IASB concluded that:

(a)   a lessee model that separately presents depreciation and interest for all leases recognised in the balance sheet provides information that is useful to the broadest range of users of financial statements. The IASB reached this conclusion for three main reasons:

(i)   most users of financial statements consulted think that leases create assets and 'debt-like' liabilities for a lessee. Consequently, they benefit from lessees recognising interest on those liabilities in a similar way to interest on other financial liabilities, because that enables them to perform meaningful ratio analyses. The same is true regarding the recognition of depreciation of right-of-use assets in a similar way to depreciation of other non-financial assets such as property, plant and equipment. The model is particularly beneficial for those users that rely on reported information without making adjustments.

(ii)   the model is easy to understand — a lessee recognises assets and financial liabilities, and corresponding amounts of depreciation and interest.

(iii)   the model addresses the concern of some users of financial statements that a dual model would perpetuate the risk of structuring to create a particular accounting outcome.

(b)   accounting for all leases recognised in the balance sheet in the same way appropriately reflects the fact that all leases result in a lessee obtaining the right to use an asset, regardless of the nature or remaining life of the underlying asset.

(c)   a single model reduces cost and complexity by removing the need to classify leases and the need for systems that can deal with two lessee accounting approaches.

BC52　In reaching its decisions relating to the lessee expense recognition model, the IASB observed that much of the negative feedback received in response to the single model proposed in the 2010 Exposure Draft related to the proposed measurement of lease assets and lease liabilities—in particular, the requirements for a lessee to estimate future variable lease payments and to determine the lease term based on the longest possible term that was more likely than not to occur. The measurement proposals for variable lease payments and optional lease periods were simplified in the 2013 Exposure Draft, and these simplifications have been retained in IFRS 16. As described in paragraph BC18, the IASB also introduced a number of further simplifications and exemptions after considering feedback on the 2013 Exposure Draft. The IASB expects the simpler measurement requirements and exemptions in IFRS 16 to alleviate many of the concerns that were received in response to the single model proposed in the 2010 Exposure Draft.

BC53　Consequently, the IASB decided to require a single lessee accounting model for all leases recognised in a lessee's balance sheet. This model requires a lessee to depreciate the right-of-use asset similarly to other non-financial assets and to account for the lease liability similarly to other financial liabilities.

Other approaches considered for the lessee accounting model

BC54　The IASB also considered an approach similar to the lessee accounting requirements that have been decided upon by the FASB. Applying that approach, a lessee would generally recognise a single, straight-line lease expense for leases that would have been classified as operating leases applying IAS 17.

BC55　Most lessees that predominantly lease property supported such an approach, as did some users of financial statements that analyse entities that predominantly lease property. In the view of those lessees and users, recognising lease expenses for property leases on a straight-line basis reflects the nature of the transaction. For example, some noted that, when a lessee enters into a typical five-year lease of retail space, the lessee is simply paying to use the retail space rather than consuming any of the value of the underlying asset. In their view, a lessee should recognise these rentals on a straight-line basis.

BC56　The IASB did not adopt the approach decided upon by the FASB because, in its view:

　　(a)　information reported under the single lessee accounting model specified in IFRS 16 would provide the most useful information to the broadest range of users of financial statements as described in paragraphs BC46–BC52; and

　　(b)　the costs for preparers under the approach decided upon by the FASB would be broadly similar to the costs of the single lessee accounting model specified in IFRS 16. For both approaches, the most significant cost associated with a new lessee accounting model would be the cost associated with recognising and measuring right-of-use assets and lease liabilities for all leases. Although the approach decided upon by the

FASB would have retained the classification requirements of IAS 17 (which are familiar to lessees), it would still have required a lessee to recognise right-of-use assets and lease liabilities on a discounted basis for all leases (with some exceptions).

The lessor accounting model

BC57 Having concluded that the lessor's lease receivable and rights retained in the underlying asset both meet the definition of an asset (as described in paragraphs BC35–BC40), the IASB considered whether requiring a lessor to recognise those assets for all leases would improve financial reporting to the extent that the benefits from the improvements would outweigh the costs associated with such a change.

BC58 The IASB considered the feedback received throughout the project regarding lessor accounting and concluded that the costs associated with making changes to lessor accounting would be difficult to justify at this time because most stakeholders (including users of financial statements) were of the view that lessor accounting in IAS 17 is not 'broken'. Consequently, the IASB decided to substantially carry forward the lessor accounting model in IAS 17.

BC59 In reaching this decision, the IASB noted that criticisms of the accounting model for leases under IAS 17 were primarily focused on lessee accounting. Consequently, when the IASB initially added the Leases project to its agenda, the project was intended to address only lessee accounting and not lessor accounting.

BC60 The IASB had earlier proposed to address lessor accounting in response to feedback received from some respondents to the Discussion Paper (as described in paragraph BC6). Those respondents had asked the IASB to address both lessee and lessor accounting at the same time because they thought that developing consistent and symmetrical accounting for lessees and lessors would be beneficial. In addition, some users of financial statements had argued that the lessor accounting model in IAS 17 did not provide sufficient information about a lessor's exposure to residual asset risk (ie the risks retained as a result of its remaining interest in the underlying asset). Accordingly, the IASB proposed changes to lessor accounting in the 2010 and 2013 Exposure Drafts that were more symmetrical with the lessee accounting model ultimately included in IFRS 16, because these proposals would have required a lessor to recognise a lease receivable for all (or many) leases.

BC61 The feedback received in response to the proposals in the 2010 and 2013 Exposure Drafts highlighted that the majority of stakeholders did not support changing the lessor accounting model in IAS 17. In particular, stakeholders observed that:

(a) the lessor accounting model in IAS 17 is well understood.

(b) most users of financial statements do not currently adjust lessors' financial statements for the effects of leases—indicating that the lessor accounting model in IAS 17 already provides users of financial statements with the information that they need. In addition, investors generally analyse the financial statements of individual entities (and not a lessee and lessor of the same underlying asset). Accordingly, it is not essential that the lessee and lessor accounting models are symmetrical.

(c)   in contrast to lessee accounting, lessor accounting in IAS 17 is not fundamentally flawed and should not be changed solely because lessee accounting is changing.

BC62   Some stakeholders also acknowledged that their views on lessor accounting had changed over the life of the Leases project. These stakeholders noted that they had originally suggested that the IASB should address lessor accounting at the same time as lessee accounting. However, in response to the 2013 Exposure Draft, they suggested that no changes should be made to lessor accounting. These stakeholders had changed their views primarily for cost-benefit reasons.

BC63   In the light of this feedback, the IASB concluded that requiring a lessor to recognise a lease receivable for all leases would not improve financial reporting to the extent that the benefits from the improvements would outweigh the costs associated with such a change.

BC64   Nonetheless, the IASB decided to change selected elements of the lessor accounting model in IAS 17 in the light of the decisions made about the lessee accounting model. In particular, the IASB made changes to the accounting for subleases, the definition of a lease, initial direct costs and lessor disclosures.

BC65   Accordingly, IFRS 16 substantially carries forward the lessor accounting requirements in IAS 17, with the exception of the definition of a lease (see paragraphs BC105–BC126), initial direct costs (see paragraph BC237) and lessor disclosures (see paragraphs BC251–BC259). IFRS 16 also includes requirements and examples on subleases (see paragraphs BC232–BC236) in the light of the new lessee accounting requirements, and includes requirements on lease modifications (see paragraphs BC238–BC240). The IASB has also incorporated into this Basis for Conclusions material from the Basis for Conclusions on IAS 17 that discusses matters relating to the lessor accounting requirements that are carried forward in IFRS 16 (see paragraphs BCZ241–BCZ250). That material is contained in paragraphs denoted by numbers with the prefix BCZ. In those paragraphs cross-references to IFRS 16 have been updated accordingly and necessary editorial changes have been made.

BC66   The IASB also decided to carry forward substantially all of the wording in IAS 17 with respect to lessor accounting. This is because any changes to the words in the Standard would have a risk of unintended consequences for lessors applying IFRS 16 and may imply that changes in application of the lessor accounting requirements were intended when that was not the case.

Scope (paragraphs 3–4)

BC67   The IASB decided that the scope of IFRS 16 should be based on the scope of the leases requirements in IAS 17. IAS 17 applies to all leases, with specified exceptions.

BC68   Accordingly, IFRS 16 contains scope exceptions for:

    (a)   leases to explore for or use minerals, oil, natural gas and similar non-regenerative resources. IFRS 6 *Exploration for and Evaluation of Mineral Resources* specifies the accounting for rights to explore for and evaluate mineral resources.

    (b)   leases of biological assets within the scope of IAS 41 *Agriculture* held by a lessee. IAS 41 specifies the accounting for biological assets, other than bearer plants, which are within the scope of IAS 16. Consequently, leases of bearer plants such as orchards and vineyards held by a lessee are within the scope of IFRS 16.

    (c)   service concession arrangements within the scope of IFRIC 12 *Service Concession Arrangements* (see paragraph BC69).

    (d)   licences of intellectual property granted by a lessor within the scope of IFRS 15. There are specific requirements relating to those licences within IFRS 15.

    (e)   leases of intangible assets held by a lessee (see paragraphs BC70–BC71).

Service concession arrangements

BC69   The IASB decided to exclude from the scope of IFRS 16 service concession arrangements within the scope of IFRIC 12. Consistently with the conclusions in IFRIC 12, any arrangement within its scope (ie that meets the conditions in paragraph 5 of the Interpretation) does not meet the definition of a lease. This is because the operator in a service concession arrangement does not have the right to control the use of the underlying asset. For this reason, the IASB considered whether it was necessary to explicitly exclude from the scope of IFRS 16 service concession arrangements within the scope of IFRIC 12. However, such a scope exclusion had been included in IFRIC 4 *Determining whether an Arrangement contains a Lease*, and stakeholders informed the IASB that including a scope exclusion for service concession arrangements in IFRS 16 would provide clarity in this respect.

Intangible assets

BC70   IFRS 16 excludes from its scope rights held by a lessee under licensing agreements within the scope of IAS 38 *Intangible Assets* for such items as motion picture films, video recordings, plays, manuscripts, patents and copyrights. This is because these licensing agreements are accounted for applying IAS 38.

BC71   IFRS 16 also states that a lessee may, but is not required to, apply IFRS 16 to leases of other intangible assets. The IASB did not want to prevent a lessee from applying IFRS 16 to leases of intangible assets for which there are no specific requirements in other Standards. The IASB acknowledged that there is no conceptual basis for excluding leases of intangible assets from the scope of IFRS 16 for lessees. However, the IASB concluded that a separate and comprehensive review of the accounting for intangible assets should be performed before requiring leases of intangible assets to be accounted for applying the requirements of IFRS 16. Many stakeholders agreed with this approach.

Onerous contracts

BC72   The IASB decided not to specify any particular requirements in IFRS 16 for onerous contracts. The IASB made this decision because:

(a)   for leases that have already commenced, no requirements are necessary. After the commencement date, an entity will appropriately reflect an onerous lease contract by applying the requirements of IFRS 16. For example, a lessee will determine and recognise any impairment of right-of-use assets applying IAS 36 *Impairment of Assets*.

(b)   for leases that have not already commenced, the requirements for onerous contracts in IAS 37 *Provisions, Contingent Liabilities and Contingent Assets* are sufficient. The requirements in IAS 37 apply to any contract (and hence any lease contract) that meets the definition of an onerous contract in that Standard.

Subleases

BC73   The IASB decided that an entity should account for leases of right-of-use assets (ie subleases) in the same way as other leases. Accordingly, subleases are within the scope of IFRS 16 (see paragraphs BC232–BC236).

Inventory

BC74   IFRS 16 does not specifically exclude leases of inventory from its scope. The term 'leased inventory' is sometimes used to describe purchases of non-depreciating spare parts, operating materials, and supplies that are associated with leasing another underlying asset. The IASB noted that few of these transactions, if any, would meet the definition of a lease because a lessee is unlikely to be able to hold an asset that it leases (and that is owned by another party) for sale in the ordinary course of business, or for consumption in the process of production for sale in the ordinary course of business. Accordingly, the IASB decided that a scope exclusion was not necessary.

Non-core assets

BC75   Information about assets that are not essential to the operations of an entity is sometimes of less interest to users of financial statements, because those assets are often less significant to the entity. Accordingly, some think that the costs associated with recognising and measuring the assets and liabilities arising from leases of non-core assets could outweigh the benefits to users. For example, information about assets and liabilities arising from leases of delivery vans is important to assess the operations of a delivery company, but it may not be important for materiality reasons in assessing the operations of a bank that uses vans to deliver supplies to its retail banking locations. Consequently, the IASB considered whether to exclude leases of non-core assets from IFRS 16.

BC76   Although some Board members favoured such an approach, the IASB noted that:

(a)   defining 'core' and 'non-core' would be extremely difficult. For example, would office buildings used by a bank be a core asset, and would the conclusion be different if the bank has retail banking operations? Would an entity consider some offices or cars to be core assets and others non-core? If core assets were defined as those essential to the operations of an entity, it could be argued that every lease would be a lease of a core asset. Otherwise, why would an entity enter into the lease?

(b)   different entities might interpret the meaning of non-core assets differently, thereby reducing comparability for users of financial statements.

(c)   other Standards do not distinguish between core and non-core purchased assets. Because of this, it would be difficult to justify distinguishing a right-of-use asset relating to a core asset from one that relates to a non-core asset.

BC77   Consequently, IFRS 16 does not make any distinction in accounting on the basis of whether the underlying asset is core to an entity's operations.

Long-term leases of land

BC78   A long-term lease of land is sometimes regarded as being economically similar to the purchase of the land. Consequently, some stakeholders suggested that long-term leases of land should be excluded from the scope of IFRS 16. However, the IASB decided not to specifically exclude such leases from the scope of IFRS 16 because:

(a)   there is no conceptual basis for differentiating long-term leases of land from other leases. If the contract does not transfer control of the land to the lessee, but gives the lessee the right to control the use of the land throughout the lease term, the contract is a lease and should be accounted for as such.

(b)   for a long-term lease of land (for example, a 99-year lease), the present value of the lease payments is likely to represent substantially all of the fair value of the land. In this case, the accounting applied by the lessee will be similar to accounting for the purchase of the land. If the lessee obtains control of the land, it will account for the contract as the purchase of the land by applying IAS 16 *Property, Plant and Equipment*, rather than by applying IFRS 16.

BC79   The IASB also noted that the IFRS Interpretations Committee had received questions about distinguishing between a lease and a sale or purchase when legal title to the underlying asset is not transferred. This is discussed in paragraphs BC138–BC140.

Leases of investment property at fair value

BC80   The IASB considered whether leases of investment property measured at fair value should be excluded from the scope of IFRS 16. It considered such an exclusion because many users of the financial statements of investment property lessors informed the IASB that the requirements of IAS 40 *Investment Property* provide useful information about the leasing activities of a lessor, especially when the fair value model is used. However, the IASB concluded that a lessor of investment property should apply IAS 40 when accounting for its investment property and apply IFRS 16 when accounting for the lease. That is similar to how IAS 17 and IAS 40 interacted. Accordingly, a user of financial statements would obtain fair value information about investment property subject to operating leases, which is required by IAS 40, and information about rental income earned by the lessor, which is required by IFRS 16.

Embedded derivatives

BC81   The IASB decided to require an entity to separate from a lease any derivatives embedded in the lease (as defined in IFRS 9 *Financial Instruments*), and account for the derivatives applying IFRS 9. Nonetheless, IFRS 16 includes specific requirements for features of a lease such as options and residual value guarantees that may meet the definition of a derivative. The IASB noted that the lease accounting model in IFRS 16 was not developed with derivatives in mind and, thus, IFRS 16 would not provide an appropriate basis on which to account for derivatives. Accordingly, if derivatives embedded in leases were not accounted for separately, unrelated derivative contracts could be bundled with leases to avoid measuring the derivatives at fair value.

Portfolio application (paragraph B1)

BC82   The 2010 and 2013 Exposure Drafts would not have precluded an entity from applying the leases requirements at a portfolio level. However, many entities noted that the 2011 Exposure Draft *Revenue from Contracts with Customers* proposed guidance on applying its requirements at a portfolio level (which has subsequently been confirmed in IFRS 15). These stakeholders asked whether the absence of guidance on this subject meant that an entity would not be permitted to apply IFRS 16 at a portfolio level.

BC83   In response to these concerns, the IASB decided to add application guidance on portfolios to IFRS 16. The guidance clarifies that an entity is permitted to apply the requirements in IFRS 16 to a portfolio of leases with similar characteristics, if the entity reasonably expects that the effects on the financial statements of applying IFRS 16 to the portfolio would not differ materially from applying IFRS 16 to the individual leases within that portfolio. This approach may be particularly useful for lessees with a large number of similar leases.

Materiality

BC84 Many lessees expressed concerns about the costs of applying the requirements in IFRS 16 to leases that are large in number but low in value, particularly when the aggregate value of those leases would have little effect on the financial statements as a whole. These lessees thought that applying the requirements of IFRS 16 to those leases would involve a significant amount of time and effort without a corresponding benefit in terms of the effect on reported information.

BC85 In the light of these concerns, the IASB considered including explicit guidance on materiality within IFRS 16—either an explicit reminder that immaterial leases are excluded from the scope of IFRS 16 or by providing clarity about how the concept of materiality in the *Conceptual Framework* and in IAS 1 *Presentation of Financial Statements* applies to leases. The IASB observed that the concept of materiality applies to leases, however, other Standards do not provide materiality guidance about particular transactions and events. The IASB also noted that applying materiality considerations to the requirements in IFRS 16 is no different from applying those considerations to the requirements of other Standards. Accordingly, the IASB decided not to provide specific guidance on materiality within IFRS 16. The IASB concluded that it would be appropriate, and consistent with other Standards, to rely on the materiality guidance in the *Conceptual Framework* and in IAS 1. Nonetheless, IFRS 16 includes some recognition exemptions as described in paragraphs BC87–BC104.

BC86 In making this decision not to include materiality guidance in IFRS 16, the IASB noted that a lessee would not be required to apply the recognition and measurement requirements in IFRS 16 if the effect of doing so would not be material to its financial statements. Similarly, if a lessee's leasing activities are material to its financial statements, but the effect of measuring lease liabilities on a discounted basis is not material, the lessee would not be required to measure its lease liabilities on a discounted basis and could instead, for example, measure them on an undiscounted basis.

Recognition exemptions (paragraphs 5–8)

Short-term leases

BC87 The IASB concluded that the benefits of requiring a lessee to apply all of the requirements in IFRS 16 to short-term leases do not outweigh the associated costs. In considering how to reduce the costs for lessees, the IASB considered both the nature and the scope of a possible exemption.

Nature of the exemption

BC88 The IASB considered simplifying the measurement requirements for short-term leases. Specifically, it considered exempting lessees from the requirement to discount the payments used to measure the assets and liabilities arising from short-term leases. Many stakeholders, however, thought that this exemption would provide insufficient cost relief for lessees because it would still require an entity to track a possibly large volume of leases of a low value.

BC89 The IASB concluded that, even with simplified measurement requirements, the benefits of requiring a lessee to recognise right-of-use assets and lease liabilities for short-term leases would not outweigh the associated costs. Consequently, paragraph 5(a) of IFRS 16 permits a lessee to elect not to apply the recognition requirements to short-term leases. Instead, a lessee can recognise the lease payments associated with short-term leases as an expense over the lease term, typically on a straight-line basis. The IASB decided that this choice should be made by class of underlying asset.

BC90 In the light of the feedback that an exemption for short-term leases did not provide sufficient relief for leases of low-value assets, the IASB also developed a separate exemption for those leases (see paragraphs BC98–BC104).

Definition of 'short-term'

BC91 The IASB first considered defining a short-term lease as a lease that, at the commencement date, has a maximum possible term of 12 months or less. However, many stakeholders thought that a short-term lease exemption defined in this way would provide limited cost relief for lessees. These stakeholders noted that, in their experience, a lease rarely has a maximum possible term of 12 months or less. For example, stakeholders suggested that many leases that run month-to-month would not qualify for the exemption.

BC92 In the light of these comments, the IASB considered expanding the short-term lease exemption to leases of more than 12 months. Some stakeholders had suggested that 'short-term' should be up to five years. The IASB, however, did not adopt this approach because, for example, three-year leases are more likely to give rise to material assets and liabilities than 12 month leases, and the objective of the project was to ensure greater transparency about an entity's leasing activities.

BC93 Instead, the IASB decided to expand the short-term lease exemption by making the determination of duration of short-term leases consistent with the determination of lease term, thus considering the likelihood of extension options being exercised or termination options not being exercised (see paragraphs BC152–BC159). Accordingly, IFRS 16 defines a short-term lease as a lease that, at the commencement date, has a lease term of 12 months or less.

BC94 In reaching this decision, the IASB considered the risk that leases could be structured to meet the short-term lease exemption. The IASB concluded that this risk is mitigated by the economic consequences of a short-term lease for a lessor. There would often be an economic disincentive for lessors to grant shorter term leases, because shortening the lease term would increase the risk associated with a lessor's residual interest in the underlying asset. Consequently, the IASB is of the view that a lessor would often either demand increased lease payments from the lessee to compensate for this change in risk or refuse to shorten the non-cancellable period of the lease. In addition, the IASB noted the rigour that lessees are expected to apply when determining the lease term, as described in paragraphs B37–B40 of IFRS 16. This should reduce the risk of non-substantive break clauses being inserted within contracts solely for accounting purposes. The IASB also decided that a lessee should reassess the lease term of a short-term lease by treating it as a new lease if that lease term changes.

BC95 The IASB observed that little incremental information would be lost by defining short-term leases by reference to the IFRS 16 determination of lease term, instead of the maximum possible term. That is because a lessee would include only lease payments for the duration of the lease term as an asset and a liability, irrespective of the maximum possible term. For example, for a lease with an extension option after six months which the lessee is not reasonably certain to exercise, the lease term is six months. If that lease were not captured by the short-term lease exemption (because the maximum term is longer than the lease term), the lessee would include only lease payments for the six-month lease term in measuring the asset and liability. Consequently, by aligning the determination of short-term with the determination of lease term, the only incremental change in information would be that the lessee would no longer reflect the six months of lease payments on its balance sheet.

BC96 The IASB also considered whether identifying short-term leases using the IFRS 16 determination of lease term would be more complex to apply, because more judgement would be needed to identify that lease term than the maximum term. However, on the basis of feedback received, the IASB concluded that any additional complexity in determining the lease term would be more than compensated for by the additional cost relief provided overall as a result of:

(a) applying the exemption to a wider group of leases; and

(b) requiring lessees to perform only one assessment of lease term for the purposes of both identifying whether the lease is a short-term lease and measuring the assets and liabilities for leases that are not short-term.

BC97 The IASB also decided to require a lessee to disclose the expense related to short-term leases for which the lessee has elected to apply the short-term lease exemption (see paragraph 53(c) of IFRS 16 and paragraph BC217(c)). In the IASB's view, this disclosure provides useful information to users of financial statements about the lease payments that are excluded from lease liabilities as a consequence of the short-term lease exemption.

Leases of low-value assets

BC98 As noted in paragraph BC84, many lessees expressed concerns about the costs of applying the requirements of IFRS 16 to leases that are large in number but low in value. They suggested that such an exercise would require a significant amount of effort with potentially little effect on reported information.

BC99   In the light of these concerns, the IASB decided to provide a recognition exemption for leases of low-value assets. Consequently, IFRS 16 permits a lessee to elect, on a lease-by-lease basis, not to apply the recognition requirements of IFRS 16 to leases for which the underlying asset is of low value.

BC100   In developing the exemption, the IASB attempted to provide substantive relief to preparers while retaining the benefits of the requirements in IFRS 16 for users of financial statements. The IASB intended the exemption to apply to leases for which the underlying asset, when new, is of low value (such as leases of tablet and personal computers, small items of office furniture and telephones). At the time of reaching decisions about the exemption in 2015, the IASB had in mind leases of underlying assets with a value, when new, in the order of magnitude of US$5,000 or less. A lease will not qualify for the exemption if the nature of the underlying asset is such that, when new, its value is typically not low. The IASB also decided that the outcome of the assessment of whether an underlying asset is of low value should not be affected by the size, nature, or circumstances of the lessee – ie the exemption is based on the value, when new, of the asset being leased; it is not based on the size or nature of the entity that leases the asset.

BC101   The IASB conducted fieldwork to assess the effect that low-value asset leases would have if the right-of-use assets and lease liabilities were recognised in the financial statements of lessees. On the basis of this fieldwork, the IASB observed that, in most cases, assets and liabilities arising from leases within the scope of the exemption would not be material, even in aggregate. The IASB considered whether these findings demonstrated that the exemption would be of limited benefit to lessees because most leases that would be within its scope might instead be excluded from the recognition requirements of IFRS 16 by applying the concept of materiality in the *Conceptual Framework* and in IAS 1. However, in the light of feedback received from preparers of financial statements, the IASB concluded that the exemption would provide substantial cost relief to many lessees (and, in particular, smaller entities) by removing the burden of justifying that such leases would not be material in the aggregate.

BC102   The IASB acknowledged the risk that the aggregate value of leases captured by the exemption might be material in some cases. The IASB's fieldwork suggested that the aggregate value is most likely to be material for large assets made up of a number of individual leases of low-value assets (such as IT equipment made up of individually low-value component parts). Consequently, the IASB decided that if an underlying asset is highly dependent on, or highly interrelated with, other underlying assets, a lessee should not apply the recognition exemption to the lease of that individual asset. Similarly, the IASB decided that a lessee should not apply the recognition exemption to a lease of an underlying asset if the lessee cannot benefit from that underlying asset on its own or together with other readily available resources, irrespective of the value of that underlying asset.

BC103 The IASB decided that the recognition exemption for leases of low-value assets should be applied on a lease-by-lease basis. A requirement to apply the exemption by class of underlying asset, instead of lease-by-lease, would have introduced a burden on lessees to assess every individual asset within a class. Consequently, in the IASB's view, the recognition exemption for leases of low-value assets will be easier to apply, and of more benefit to lessees, if applied on a lease-by-lease basis.

BC104 The IASB also decided to require a lessee to disclose the amount of the expense recognised related to leases of low-value assets for which the lessee has elected to apply the recognition exemption (see paragraph 53(d) of IFRS 16 and paragraph BC217(c)). In the IASB's view, this disclosure provides useful information to users of financial statements about the amount of lease payments that are excluded from lease liabilities as a consequence of a lessee applying the exemption relating to leases of low-value assets.

Identifying a lease (paragraphs 9–17)

Definition of a lease (paragraphs 9–11)

BC105 IFRS 16 defines a lease on the basis of whether a customer controls the use of an identified asset for a period of time, which may be determined by a defined amount of use. If the customer controls the use of an identified asset for a period of time, then the contract contains a lease. This will be the case if the customer can make the important decisions about the use of the asset in a similar way to that in which it makes decisions about owned assets that it uses. In such cases, the customer (the lessee) has obtained the right to use an asset (the right-of-use asset) that it should recognise in its balance sheet (subject to the recognition exemptions in paragraph 5 of IFRS 16). In contrast, in a service contract, the supplier controls the use of any assets used to deliver the service.

BC106 The 2010 Exposure Draft essentially retained the definition of a lease in IAS 17 and the accompanying requirements in IFRIC 4. Many respondents expressed concerns about the population of contracts that would be captured by the proposed requirements (and in particular that some contracts that they viewed as service contracts would be captured). Respondents also identified practice issues with IFRIC 4, such as difficulties in assessing the pricing structure of a contract, and questioned why the control criteria used in IFRIC 4 to define a lease were different from the control proposals that were then being developed within the context of revenue recognition and the control principle in IFRS 10 *Consolidated Financial Statements*.

BC107 Accordingly, in the 2013 Exposure Draft, the IASB proposed changes to the guidance on the definition of a lease to address those concerns. The 2013 Exposure Draft proposed using a control principle as the means of distinguishing between a service and a lease, and to align the principle with that in other Standards. Respondents generally supported these changes. However, many respondents stressed the increased importance of the definition of a lease, noting that the assessment of whether a contract contains a lease would generally determine whether a customer would recognise lease assets and lease liabilities. Some of these respondents thought that the IASB had not provided adequate guidance to support consistent application of the proposed definition to more complicated scenarios.

BC108   Accordingly, IFRS 16 generally retains the approach to the definition of a lease that was proposed in the 2013 Exposure Draft, but makes a number of changes to clarify the IASB's intentions and reduce the risk of inconsistent application.

BC109   The IASB is of the view that, in most cases, the assessment of whether a contract contains a lease should be straightforward. A contract will either fail to meet the definition of a lease by failing to meet many of the requirements or will clearly meet the requirements to be a lease without requiring a significant amount of judgement. However, application guidance has been added to make it easier for entities to make the lease assessment for more complicated scenarios.

BC110   inception of the contract, ~~~~~ ~~~~ an entity to assess whether a contract contains a lease at inception of the contract, ~~~~~ ~~~~ than at commencement. This is because a lessor is required to classify a lease as either finance lease or an operating lease at the inception date; this is consistent with the previous lessor lease classification requirements in IAS 17, which the IASB decided not to change. In addition, a lessee is required to disclose information about leases not yet commenced to which the lessee is committed if that information is relevant to users of financial statements.

Identified asset

BC111   The first requirement for a contract to meet the definition of a lease in IFRS 16 is that a customer should control the use of an identified asset. The requirement for an identified asset is substantially the same as the requirement in IFRIC 4 for the contract to depend on the use of a specified asset. It is important to know what the asset is in order to assess whether the customer has the right to control the use of that asset and, for example, to determine which asset finance lessors should derecognise. Nonetheless, when assessing at the inception date whether there is an identified asset, an entity does not need to be able to identify the particular asset (for example, a specific serial number) that will be used to fulfil the contract to conclude that there is an identified asset. Instead, the entity simply needs to know whether an identified asset is needed to fulfil the contract from commencement. If that is the case, then an asset is implicitly specified. IFRS 16 clarifies that an asset can be implicitly specified at the time that the asset is made available for use by the customer.

BC112   IFRS 16 includes requirements on asset substitution. If a supplier has a substantive right to substitute the asset throughout the period of use, then there is no identified asset and the contract does not contain a lease. This is because the supplier (and not the customer) controls the use of an asset if it can substitute the asset throughout the period of use.

BC113   The IASB has included application guidance to help determine the circumstances in which substitution rights are substantive. This guidance focuses on whether the supplier has the practical ability to substitute the asset and would benefit economically from doing so. The IASB's intention in including this guidance is to differentiate between:

(a)   substitution rights that result in there being no identified asset because the supplier, rather than the customer, controls the use of an asset; and

(b)   substitution rights that do not change the substance or character of the contract because it is not likely, or practically or economically feasible, for the supplier to exercise those rights.

If a substitution clause is not substantive because it does not change the substance of the contract, then that substitution clause should not affect an entity's assessment of whether a contract contains a lease. The IASB thinks that, in many cases, it will be clear that the supplier would not benefit from the exercise of a substitution right because of the costs associated substituting an asset.

BC114   Substitution rights may not be substantive for a number of reasons. Some substitution rights are not substantive because the contract restricts when a supplier can substitute the asset. For example, if a contract states that a supplier can substitute the asset only on a specified future date or after the occurrence of a specified event, that substitution right is not substantive because it does not give the supplier the practical ability to substitute the asset throughout the period of use. Other substitution rights are not substantive even if the supplier contractually has the right to substitute the asset at any time. For example, if a supplier substitutes an asset for purposes of repair and maintenance, or if a supplier would benefit from substitution only in circumstances that are not considered likely to arise, those substitution rights are not substantive, regardless of whether those circumstances are specified in the contract.

BC115   Stakeholders raised concerns that in some cases it would be difficult, if not impossible, for a customer to determine whether a supplier's substitution right is substantive. Difficulties may arise because the customer often does not have information about the costs of substitution that would be incurred by the supplier. On the basis of this feedback, the IASB decided to state in IFRS 16 that, if a customer cannot readily determine whether a supplier has a substantive substitution right, then the customer should presume that any substitution right is not substantive. It is intended that a customer should assess whether substitution rights are substantive if it is reasonably able to do so—if substitution rights are substantive, then the IASB thinks that this would be relatively clear from the facts and circumstances. However, the requirement is also intended to clarify that a customer is not expected to exert undue effort in order to provide evidence that a substitution right is not substantive.

BC116   IFRS 16 also clarifies that an asset must be physically distinct to be an identified asset. The IASB concluded that a customer is unlikely to have the right to control the use of a capacity portion of a larger asset if that portion is not physically distinct (for example, if it is a 20 per cent capacity portion of a pipeline). The customer is unlikely to have the right to control the use of its portion because decisions about the use of the asset are typically made at the larger asset level. Widening the notion of an identified asset to possibly capture portions of a larger asset that are not physically distinct might have forced entities to consider whether they lease assets used to fulfil any contract for services, only to conclude that they do not. Consequently, the IASB concluded that widening the definition to include capacity portions of a larger asset would increase complexity for little benefit.

The right to control the use of an identified asset

BC117   IFRS 16 contains application guidance regarding what it means to have the right to control the use of an asset. The IASB decided that, to control the use of an asset, a customer is required to have not only the right to obtain substantially all of the economic benefits from use of an asset throughout the period of use (a 'benefits' element) but also the ability to direct the use of that asset (a 'power' element), ie a customer must have decision-making rights over the use of the asset that give it the ability to influence the economic benefits derived from use of the asset throughout the period of use. Without any such decision-making rights, the customer would have no more control over the use of the asset than any customer purchasing supplies or services. If this were the case, the customer would not control the use of the asset. This guidance is consistent with the concept of control in IFRS 10 and IFRS 15, and with the IASB's proposals regarding control in the *Conceptual Framework* Exposure Draft. IFRS 10 and IFRS 15 define control to require both a 'benefits' element and a 'power' element.

Right to obtain substantially all of the economic benefits from use of the identified asset

BC118   IFRS 16 clarifies that only the economic benefits arising from use of an asset, rather than the economic benefits arising from ownership of that asset, should be considered when assessing whether a customer has the right to obtain the benefits from use of an asset. A lease does not convey ownership of an underlying asset; it conveys only the right to use that underlying asset. Accordingly, the IASB concluded that, when considering whether a contract contains a lease, a customer should not consider economic benefits relating to ownership of an asset (for example, tax benefits as a result of owning an asset). However, a customer should consider benefits relating to the use of the asset (for example, renewable energy credits received from the use of an asset or by-products resulting from the use of an asset).

Right to direct the use of the identified asset

BC119   IFRS 16 clarifies that a customer has the right to direct the use of an asset if it has the right to direct how and for what purpose the asset is used throughout the period of use (ie the right to make relevant decisions about how and for what purpose the asset is used throughout the period of use). If the supplier has that right, the supplier directs the use of the asset and, thus, no lease exists.

BC120   In the IASB's view, the decisions about how and for what purpose an asset is used are more important in determining control of the use of an asset than other decisions to be made about use, including decisions about operating and maintaining the asset. This is because decisions about how and for what purpose an asset is used determine how, and what, economic benefits are derived from use. How and for what purpose an asset is used is a single concept, ie 'how' an asset is used is not assessed separately from 'for what purpose' an asset is used. Decisions regarding operating an asset are generally about implementing the decisions about how and for what purpose an asset is used and are dependent upon (and subordinate to) those decisions. For example, a supplier's operational decisions would have no effect on the economic benefits derived from use of an asset if the customer decides that the asset should not be used. In addition, if the supplier makes decisions about operating or maintaining an underlying asset, it often does so to protect its interest in that asset. The IASB observed that considering decisions about how and for what purpose an asset is used can be viewed as similar to considering the decisions made by a board of directors when assessing control of the entity. Decisions made by a board of directors about the operating and financing activities of an entity are generally the decisions that matter in that control assessment, rather than the actions of individuals in implementing those decisions.

BC121   The IASB noted that, in some cases, decisions about how and for what purpose an asset is used are predetermined and cannot be made by either the customer or the supplier during the period of use. This could happen if, for example, all decisions about how and for what purpose an asset is used are agreed between the customer and supplier in negotiating the contract and cannot be changed after the commencement date, or are, in effect, predetermined by the design of the asset. The IASB noted that it would expect decisions about how and for what purpose an asset is used to be predetermined in relatively few cases.

BC122   The approach to determining whether a customer has the right to direct the use of an identified asset changes if the decisions about how and for what purpose an asset is used are predetermined. IFRS 16 clarifies that, if decisions about how and for what purpose an asset is used are predetermined, a customer can still direct the use of an asset if it has the right to operate the asset, or if it designed the asset in a way that predetermines how and for what purpose the asset will be used. In either of these cases the customer controls rights of use that extend beyond the rights of a customer in a typical supply or service contract (ie the customer has rights that extend beyond solely ordering and receiving output from the asset). In these cases, the customer has the right to make (or has made in the case of design) decisions that affect the economic benefits to be derived from use of the asset throughout the period of use. Although the IASB thinks that each of these cases represents a scenario in which the customer directs the use of an asset, it expects that, for most leases, the assessment of whether a customer directs the use of an asset will be based on identifying the party that decides how and for what purpose an asset is used.

BC123 IFRS 16 also clarifies that only decisions made during the period of use (and not before the period of use) should be considered in the control assessment, unless the customer designed the asset in a way that predetermines how and for what purpose the asset will be used. In the IASB's view, if a customer specifies the output from an asset at or before the beginning of the period of use (for example, within the terms of the contract), and cannot change that specification during the period of use, it generally does not control the use of an asset. In that case, it would have no more decision-making rights than any customer in a typical supply or service contract.

BC124 In addition, IFRS 16 provides application guidance about protective rights—for example, terms and conditions included in the contract to protect the supplier's interest in the underlying asset or other assets, to protect its personnel or to ensure the supplier's compliance with applicable laws and regulations. In the IASB's view, such protective rights define the scope of the rights obtained by a customer without preventing a customer from having the right to direct the use of that asset. Accordingly, protective rights may affect the price paid for the lease (ie a lessee may pay less for the use of the asset if it is more restricted in its use of that asset). However, protective rights generally would not affect the existence of the customer's right to direct the use of the asset.

Other approaches considered for the definition of a lease

BC125 In developing IFRS 16, the IASB considered alternatives suggested by stakeholders regarding the definition of a lease. The main alternatives considered are described below:

(a) *Financing component*: the IASB considered requiring a lease to be a financing arrangement for the right to use an asset. In other words, there would have to be a clearly identifiable financing component for a contract to contain a lease. However, the IASB did not adopt this approach because:

(i) in the IASB's view, it is appropriate to focus on whether the customer has obtained control of a right-of-use asset to determine whether a contract contains a lease. The right-of-use asset gives rise to a corresponding lease liability if payments are made over time, but exists even if there is no lease liability (for example, when lease payments are fully prepaid). If an entity obtains the right to use an asset for a period of time, the contract contains a lease, regardless of the timing of payments for that right of use. The focus on the asset obtained in a lease also distinguishes leases from other contracts, such as service or supply arrangements.

(ii)   many of the suggested indicators of 'financing arrangements' focus on the form of the payments, and on those payments being similar to payments within a loan agreement. The IASB was concerned that if it focused on the form of an arrangement, rather than its substance:

    (A)   many existing leases, including many existing finance leases and property leases, would no longer meet the definition of a lease, even when it is clear that the customer has obtained a right of use at contract commencement.

    (B)   it would be relatively easy to structure a contract to fail to meet the definition of a lease by, for example, changing the payment structure, while not changing the customer's right to use an asset.

(b)   *IFRS 15*: the IASB considered whether to link the requirements on the definition of a lease more closely to the requirements in IFRS 15, in particular the requirements on whether a good or service is 'distinct'. Applying such an approach, the concept of 'distinct' could have been used to distinguish between contracts that contain distinct lease and service components (that an entity should unbundle and account for separately) and those that do not contain distinct lease and service components (and therefore would be accounted for entirely as a contract for services). The IASB did not adopt this approach because:

    (i)   the 'distinct' requirements in IFRS 15 were developed to address a different objective from that of identifying a lease. They were developed to identify the nature of an entity's promises in a contract with a customer to ensure the most appropriate allocation and recognition of revenue. In contrast, the lease definition requirements aim to identify whether a customer has obtained the right to use an asset and, therefore, should recognise the assets and liabilities associated with that transaction. Because the 'distinct' requirements in IFRS 15 were developed for a different purpose, applying those requirements might have resulted in customers failing to recognise items that meet the conceptual definition of assets and liabilities (see paragraphs BC22–BC27). The IASB thinks that control is a more appropriate basis on which to make this determination.

    (ii)   the IASB was concerned that a requirement to determine whether lease and service components were distinct would add unnecessary complexity to the guidance. This is because such an approach was expected to result in little difference in outcomes and yet would have included an additional requirement that could have been complicated to interpret and apply within the context of leases.

(c) *Stand-alone utility*: the IASB considered whether to specify that a customer controls the use of an asset only if that asset has stand-alone utility to the customer, ie only if the customer has the ability to derive the economic benefits from use of an asset, either on its own or together with other resources that could be sourced in a reasonable period of time. The IASB decided not to add this criterion because:

(i) the additional criterion is not necessary to appropriately determine if a customer controls the use of an asset. Such an approach is not used elsewhere in IFRS when assessing control of an asset, such as the purchase of an item of property, plant and equipment.

(ii) entities might reach different conclusions for contracts that contain the same rights of use, depending on differences in customers' resources or suppliers' business models.

(iii) assessing whether the criterion had been met would have been subjective and required judgement beyond that required to apply the definition of a lease in IFRS 16. It may also have had unintended consequences. In addition, the IASB did not identify any existing scenarios for which the inclusion of such a criterion would have been expected to change the lease conclusion. Consequently, the IASB concluded that the costs of including such a criterion would outweigh any possible benefits.

(d) *Substantial services*: the IASB considered whether to require an entity to account for a contract with lease and service components entirely as a service if the service components are substantial and are the predominant portion of the overall contract. The IASB decided not to include this requirement. Again, in the IASB's view, if a contract conveys to the customer the right to use an asset, the contract contains a lease. The presence of services, no matter how substantial, does not change the rights of use that a lessee obtains. The IASB was concerned that similar rights of use could be accounted for differently because services of a more significant value had been bundled together with some right-of-use assets and not with others.

Assessing whether a contract contains a lease when the customer is a joint arrangement

BC126 When two or more parties form a joint arrangement of which they have joint control as defined in IFRS 11 *Joint Arrangements*, those parties can decide to lease assets to be used in the joint arrangement's operations. The joint arrangement might be a joint venture or a joint operation. The contract might be signed by the joint arrangement itself if the joint arrangement has its own legal identity, or it might be signed by one or more of the parties to the joint arrangement on behalf of the joint arrangement. In these cases, the IASB decided to clarify that an entity should consider the joint arrangement to be the customer when assessing whether the contract contains a lease applying paragraphs 9–11 of IFRS 16—ie the parties to the joint arrangement should not each be considered to be a customer. Accordingly, if the parties to the joint arrangement collectively have the right to control the use of an identified asset throughout the period of use through their joint control of the arrangement, the contract contains a lease. In that scenario, it would be inappropriate to conclude that a contract does not contain a lease on the grounds that each of the parties to the joint arrangement either obtains only a portion of the economic benefits from use of the underlying asset or does not unilaterally direct the use of the underlying asset.

Cancellable leases

BC127   For the purposes of defining the scope of IFRS 16, the IASB decided that a contract would be considered to exist only when it creates rights and obligations that are enforceable. Any non-cancellable period or notice period in a lease would meet the definition of a contract and, thus, would be included as part of the lease term. To be part of a contract, any options to extend or terminate the lease that are included in the lease term must also be enforceable; for example the lessee must be able to enforce its right to extend the lease beyond the non-cancellable period. If optional periods are not enforceable, for example, if the lessee cannot enforce the extension of the lease without the agreement of the lessor, the lessee does not have the right to use the asset beyond the non-cancellable period. Consequently, by definition, there is no contract beyond the non-cancellable period (plus any notice period) if there are no enforceable rights and obligations existing between the lessee and lessor beyond that term. In assessing the enforceability of a contract, an entity should consider whether the lessor can refuse to agree to a request from the lessee to extend the lease.

BC128   Accordingly, if the lessee has the right to extend or terminate the lease, there are enforceable rights and obligations beyond the initial non-cancellable period and the parties to the lease would be required to consider those optional periods in their assessment of the lease term. In contrast, a lessor's right to terminate a lease is ignored when determining the lease term because, in that case, the lessee has an unconditional obligation to pay for the right to use the asset for the period of the lease, unless and until the lessor decides to terminate the lease.

BC129   The IASB considered whether applying enforceability to leases in this way might encourage entities to add a clause to a lease that does not have economic substance, for example, stating that the lease could be cancelled at any point, knowing that, in practice, it would not be cancelled. However, the IASB is of the view that such clauses are unlikely to be added because there often is an economic disincentive for either the lessor or lessee to agree to their inclusion. For example, if a lessor has priced a contract assuming that the lessee will not cancel the contract, including such a clause would put the lessor at risk of being exposed to higher residual asset risk than had been anticipated when pricing the contract, which would be an economic disincentive for the lessor. Conversely, if the lessor has priced the contract assuming that the lessee will or may cancel the contract, the lessee would be likely to have to pay higher rentals to compensate the lessor for taking on more residual asset risk. Those higher rentals would be an economic disincentive for the lessee, if it does not intend to cancel the contract.

Combination of contracts (paragraph B2)

BC130   The IASB noted that, although it is usually appropriate to account for contracts individually, it is also necessary to assess the combined effect of contracts that are interdependent. An entity may enter into a number of contracts in contemplation of one another such that the transactions, in substance, form a single arrangement that achieves an overall commercial objective that cannot be understood without considering the contracts together. For example, assume that a lessee enters into a one-year lease of an asset with particular characteristics. The lessee also enters into a one-year lease for an asset with those same characteristics starting in one year's time and a similar forward contract starting in two years' time and in three years' time. The terms and conditions of all four contracts are negotiated in contemplation of each other such that the overall economic effect cannot be understood without reference to the series of transactions as a whole. In effect, the lessee has entered into a four-year lease. In such situations, accounting for the contracts independently of each other might not result in a faithful representation of the combined transaction.

BC131   The IASB noted that some view the concept of faithful representation in the *Conceptual Framework* as sufficient to identify the circumstances in which contracts should be combined. However, in the IASB's view, it is beneficial to add more clarity as to when to combine contracts within the context of leases, particularly with respect to sale and leaseback transactions, short-term leases and leases of low-value assets.

BC132   Consequently, the IASB decided to specify in IFRS 16 circumstances in which contracts should be combined and accounted for as a single contract. The requirements are similar to those in IFRS 15 and consistent with the concepts proposed in the *Conceptual Framework* Exposure Draft.

Separating components of a contract (paragraphs 12–17 and B32–B33)

BC133   Some contracts contain both lease and non-lease (service) components. For example, a contract for a car may combine a lease with maintenance services. In addition, many contracts contain two or more lease components. For example, a single contract may include leases of land, buildings and equipment.

Separating lease components

BC134   IFRS 16 contains requirements for determining whether a contract that contains a lease has only one lease component or a number of lease components. The IASB noted that the identification of separate lease components in a lease contract is similar to the identification of performance obligations in a revenue contract – in both circumstances, an entity is trying to identify whether a customer or a lessee is contracting for a number of separate deliverables or contracting for one deliverable that may incorporate a number of different assets. Accordingly, rather than developing new requirements addressing how to identify separate lease components, the IASB decided to include in IFRS 16 requirements similar to those in IFRS 15 on the identification of performance obligations. The IASB intends that those requirements in IFRS 16 are applied in a similar way to their application within the context of a revenue contract in IFRS 15.

Separating lease and non-lease components

BC135 The objective of the Leases project is to change the accounting for leases — not the accounting for services. The IASB, therefore, took the view that IFRS 16 should apply only to the lease components of any contract. The accounting for services (or the service components of a contract) should not be affected, regardless of whether the contract is only for services or includes the purchase, or lease, of an asset as well as services. Accordingly, IFRS 16 requires:

(a) a lessor to separate lease components and non-lease components of a contract. On the basis of feedback received from lessors, the IASB concluded that a lessor should be able to separate payments made for lease and non-lease components. This is because the lessor would need to have information about the value of each component, or a reasonable estimate of it, when pricing the contract.

(b) a lessee to separate lease components and non-lease components of a contract, unless it applies a practical expedient whereby it is not required to separate a lease component from any associated non-lease components and can instead elect to treat these as a single lease component. The IASB decided to permit this practical expedient for cost benefit reasons and in response to requests from preparers not to require separation in all scenarios. In the IASB's view, the practical expedient will reduce cost and complexity for some lessees, while not creating significant issues of comparability. This is because, in general, a lessee is not expected to adopt the practical expedient for contracts with significant service components because that would significantly increase the lessee's lease liabilities for those contracts. The IASB expects that lessees are likely to adopt this practical expedient only when the non-lease components of a contract are relatively small.

BC136 IFRS 16 requires a lessor to allocate the consideration in a contract to lease components and non-lease components applying the requirements in IFRS 15 on allocating the transaction price to performance obligations. This approach will ensure consistency for entities that are both a lessor and a seller of goods or services in the same contract. The IASB concluded that the approach applied by a lessor should not be different from the approach applied by a seller to allocate consideration in a revenue contract with more than one performance obligation.

BC137 If a lessee separates lease and non-lease components of a contract, IFRS 16 requires the lessee to allocate the consideration to those components on the basis of the relative stand-alone price of each lease component and the aggregate stand-alone price of the non-lease components. The IASB acknowledged that the stand-alone price of lease and non-lease components might not be readily available and, consequently, decided to permit the use of estimates, maximising the use of observable information. In the IASB's view, the use of estimated stand-alone prices by a lessee, if observable prices are not readily available, addresses some of the most significant concerns raised by both lessors and lessees with respect to the separation of lease and non-lease components: lessors had expressed concerns about providing pricing information to lessees and lessees had expressed concerns that obtaining observable stand-alone pricing information that is not readily available could be onerous and costly. The IASB also observed that applying the previous requirements in IAS 17, a lessee had been required to allocate the consideration in a contract between lease and non-lease components using estimates of the relative fair value of those components. The IASB was not aware of any significant practical difficulties in applying those requirements.

Distinguishing between a lease and a sale or purchase

BC138   The IASB considered whether to include requirements in IFRS 16 to distinguish a lease from the sale or purchase of an asset. The IFRS Interpretations Committee had received questions about whether particular contracts that do not transfer legal title of land should be considered to be a lease or a purchase of the land.

BC139   The IASB decided not to provide requirements in IFRS 16 to distinguish a lease from a sale or purchase of an asset. There was little support from stakeholders for including such requirements. In addition, the IASB observed that:

(a)   the accounting for leases that are similar to the sale or purchase of the underlying asset would be similar to that for sales and purchases applying the respective requirements of IFRS 15 and IAS 16; and

(b)   accounting for a transaction depends on the substance of that transaction and not its legal form. Consequently, if a contract grants rights that represent the in-substance purchase of an item of property, plant and equipment, those rights meet the definition of property, plant and equipment in IAS 16 and would be accounted for applying that Standard, regardless of whether legal title transfers. If the contract grants rights that do not represent the in-substance purchase of an item of property, plant and equipment but that meet the definition of a lease, the contract would be accounted for applying IFRS 16.

BC140   IFRS 16 applies to contracts that convey the right to use an underlying asset for a period of time and does not apply to transactions that transfer control of the underlying asset to an entity – such transactions are sales or purchases within the scope of other Standards (for example, IFRS 15 or IAS 16).

Recognition and the date of initial measurement: lessee (paragraphs 22–23 and 26)

Inception versus commencement of a lease

BC141 IFRS 16 requires a lessee to initially recognise and measure right-of-use assets and lease liabilities at the commencement date (ie the date on which the lessor makes the underlying asset available for use by the lessee).

BC142 Recognising assets and liabilities arising from a lease at the commencement date is consistent with the lessee accounting model, in which a lessee recognises an asset representing its right to use an underlying asset for the period of the lease and a liability representing its obligation to make lease payments. A lessee does not obtain and control its right to use the underlying asset until the commencement date. Before that date, the lessor has not yet performed under the contract. Although a lessee may have a right and an obligation to exchange lease payments for a right-of-use asset from the date of inception, the lessee is unlikely to have an obligation to make lease payments before the asset is made available for its use. The IASB noted that an obligation to exchange payments for a right-of-use asset could be onerous if the terms of the exchange are unfavourable. In such circumstances, a lessee could have an onerous contract liability before the commencement date. That liability would be accounted for consistently with other onerous contracts applying IAS 37.

BC143 The IASB noted that its intentions with respect to initial measurement of right-of-use assets and lease liabilities were that the measurement would reflect the nature of the transaction and the terms and conditions of the lease. That would require a lessee to look to the terms and conditions agreed to in the contract at the inception date (which could be before the commencement date). However, if the inception date was considered to be the date of initial measurement, that could result in a lessee recognising a gain or loss relating to changes between the dates of inception and commencement when recognising lease assets and lease liabilities at the commencement date. Therefore, the IASB decided to align the date of recognition with the date of initial measurement of right-of-use assets and lease liabilities.

BC144 The IASB noted that this approach has the following benefits:

(a) it clarifies that a gain or loss should not arise on initial recognition of right-of-use assets and lease liabilities by a lessee.

(b) it removes the need to add requirements (and thus potentially increase complexity) on how to account for changes to the terms and conditions of a lease, or assumptions used in measuring right-of-use assets and lease liabilities, between the inception date and the commencement date. Any changes to a lease that occur after the inception date and before the commencement date are taken into account when initially measuring the right-of-use asset and lease liability at the commencement date.

(c) it is more consistent with the measurement date for other transactions, such as the acquisition of property, plant and equipment.

Measurement: lessee (paragraphs 23–46B)

Measurement bases of the right-of-use asset and the lease liability

BC145 The IASB decided to require a cost measurement basis for the right-of-use asset and lease liability, with cost measured by reference to the present value of the lease payments. The IASB concluded that this approach will provide useful information to users of financial statements. This is because it is consistent with the approach used to measure other similar assets and liabilities and thus is expected to result in more comparable information than other approaches. The IASB also concluded that using a cost measurement basis will be less costly for preparers than other approaches.

BC146 The IASB considered whether to refer to other Standards rather than specify in IFRS 16 the initial and subsequent measurement of the right-of-use asset and lease liability. The IASB did not adopt an approach that would refer to other Standards because:

(a) the approach would have been inconsistent with the IASB's decision not to apply a components approach to lease accounting (see paragraph BC153). For example, if a lessee were to account for all of the features of a lease applying other Standards, the requirements on financial instruments may have routinely required options in a lease to be accounted for separately.

(b) the approach could have been complex to apply, particularly when a lease contains relatively common features such as extension options, variable lease payments and residual value guarantees.

Initial measurement of the right-of-use asset (paragraphs 23–25)

BC147 The IASB decided that a lessee should measure the right-of-use asset at cost, defined as:

(a) the present value of the lease payments;

(b) any initial direct costs incurred by the lessee (see paragraphs BC149–BC151); and

(c) an estimate of costs to be incurred by the lessee in dismantling and removing the underlying asset, restoring the site on which it is located or restoring the underlying asset to the condition required by the terms and conditions of the lease, unless those costs are incurred to produce inventories.

BC148   The IASB considered whether a lessee should initially measure the right-of-use asset at fair value, which may provide more relevant information about the economic benefits to be derived from use of the underlying asset. However, initial measurement of a right-of-use asset at cost is consistent with the measurement of many other non-financial assets, such as assets within the scope of IAS 16 and IAS 38. Measuring right-of-use assets on a basis similar to that used to measure the underlying asset maintains the comparability of amounts reported for leased and owned assets, which contributes to the usefulness of the information provided to users of financial statements. Furthermore, measuring the right-of-use asset at cost is less complex and less costly for entities than measuring that asset at fair value, because there often is not an active market for right-of-use assets. The IASB thinks that, for many leases, a cost measurement basis will also provide a reasonable approximation of the fair value of the right-of-use asset at the commencement date.

Initial direct costs (paragraph 24(c))

BC149   IFRS 16 requires a lessee to include initial direct costs in the initial measurement of the right-of-use asset and depreciate those costs over the lease term. Including initial direct costs in the measurement of the right-of-use asset is consistent with the treatment of costs associated with acquiring other non-financial assets (for example, property, plant and equipment and intangible assets).

BC150   The IASB decided that lessees and lessors should apply the same definition of initial direct costs. This decision was made primarily to reduce complexity in applying IFRS 16. As described in paragraph BC237, the IASB also decided that the definition of initial direct costs for lessors should be consistent with the definition of 'incremental costs' in IFRS 15. Consequently, IFRS 16 defines initial direct costs as incremental costs of obtaining a lease that would not have been incurred if the lease had not been obtained.

BC151   The IASB considered whether initial direct costs incurred by lessees should be allocated between the right-of-use asset and the lease liability at the commencement date. However, the IASB concluded that such an approach could be costly for entities to apply, with little incremental benefit for users of financial statements.

Initial measurement of the lease liability

Lease term: options to extend or terminate a lease (paragraphs 18–19)

BC152   Leases often grant the lessee a right to extend a lease beyond the non-cancellable period, or to terminate a lease before the end of the lease period. Depending on the terms and conditions of the option, a three-year lease with an option to extend for two years could be economically similar to a three-year non-cancellable lease or a five-year non-cancellable lease. However, a lease with options would never be exactly the same as a lease without any options.

BC153   There are a number of different ways that an entity could reflect duration-related options that exist in leases:

(a)   *a components approach*, in which options in a lease are recognised and measured as separate components of the lease. The IASB did not adopt a components approach because it would have created a complex lease accounting model, would have been difficult to apply because options may be difficult to measure, and would have ignored the interrelationship between the term of a lease and the exercise of options.

(b)   *a disclosure approach*, in which an entity recognises a lease liability or a lease receivable for the non-cancellable period and discloses the existence of any options to extend the term. Although simple to apply, the IASB did not adopt this approach because the measurement of lease assets and lease liabilities would ignore the existence of options, including those that are virtually certain to be exercised. Consequently, this approach would potentially misrepresent the assets and liabilities arising from a lease.

(c)   *a measurement approach*, in which options in a lease are included in the measurement of lease assets and lease liabilities using a particular method. That method could be, for example:

(i)   a probability-weighted measurement method (in which the measurement of lease assets and lease liabilities reflects the probability of each possible lease term);

(ii)   a probability threshold method (in which an entity includes optional periods in the lease term if the exercise of the options meets a specified threshold, for example reasonably certain, virtually certain or more likely than not); or

(iii)   an economic incentive method (in which an entity includes optional periods in the lease term if an entity has an economic incentive to exercise the option).

BC154   Different views were expressed on whether optional periods should be included within an entity's determination of the lease term. Some stakeholders were of the view that payments to be made during future optional periods do not meet the definition of a liability for the lessee (or an asset for the lessor) until those options are exercised. This is because, before the exercise date, a lessee can avoid those payments by choosing to exercise a termination option or not to exercise an extension option. These stakeholders suggested limiting the lease term to the contractually committed period, ie the non-cancellable period. In addition, some stakeholders expressed concerns that including future optional periods within the lease term would not distinguish between, for example, a five-year non-cancellable lease and a three-year lease with an option to extend for two years. In their view, an entity with a five-year non-cancellable lease is in a different economic position from an entity with a three-year lease with an option to extend for two years that may or may not be exercised.

BC155   Conversely, many stakeholders thought that because options to extend or terminate leases affect the economics of those leases, there is a need to include some options when determining the lease term. If a lessee expects to exercise an option to extend the lease term, some think that including that longer lease term in the measurement of the right-of-use asset and lease liability would provide a more faithful representation of the economics of the lease. Inclusion of some renewal options is also needed to mitigate the risk of lessees inappropriately excluding lease liabilities from the balance sheet (for example, by excluding lease payments in optional periods for which the lessee has a clear economic incentive to exercise those options).

BC156   In the IASB's view, the lease term should reflect an entity's reasonable expectation of the period during which the underlying asset will be used because that approach provides the most useful information. Over the course of the Leases project, the IASB considered a number of ways of determining that reasonable expectation of what the term will be. These included:

(a)   requiring an entity to determine the lease term as the longest possible term that is more likely than not to occur. Many stakeholders disagreed with this approach because, in their view, it would have been complex to apply to thousands of leases (which some entities have), and it would include payments in optional periods, which many stakeholders did not view as liabilities.

(b)   requiring an entity to include in the lease term optional periods for which the lessee has a significant economic incentive to exercise an option. Under this approach, an expectation of exercise alone (and without any economic incentive to do so) would not be sufficient. The IASB noted that requiring an economic incentive provides a threshold that is more objective than a threshold based solely on management's estimates or intention, and consequently would help to address concerns that other approaches would be complex to apply. However, stakeholders were concerned about the costs of implementing any new concept regarding the lease term, particularly for entities with decentralised leasing operations and large volumes of leases with diverse individual lease term clauses. These stakeholders also asked whether a significant economic incentive threshold was similar to the 'reasonably certain' threshold that existed in IAS 17. They suggested that, if the IASB viewed the 'significant economic incentive' threshold as similar to the 'reasonably certain' threshold in IAS 17, the IASB should retain the terminology in IAS 17. They argued that the IAS 17 terminology was well understood, which would help to achieve consistent application between entities.

BC157   In the light of the feedback received, the IASB decided to retain the concept in IAS 17 that the lease term used to measure a lease liability should include optional periods to the extent that it is reasonably certain that the lessee will exercise its option to extend (or not to terminate) the lease. The IASB observed that applying the concept of 'reasonably certain' requires judgement and, therefore, also decided to provide application guidance in IFRS 16 to help entities to apply this concept. Accordingly, when initially determining the lease term, an entity should consider all relevant facts and circumstances that create an economic incentive for the lessee to exercise that option. The IASB decided to include guidance on the types of facts and circumstances that an entity should consider for two reasons:

(a) to help entities identify the relevant factors, which are not confined to the contractual payments during the optional periods. For example, within the context of property leases, the IASB noted the relevance of considering the costs of finding a new location at the end of the non-cancellable period and of relocating to that new location, or the importance of the location (for example, a head office or a flagship store) to the lessee.

(b) to reduce the risk of non-substantive break clauses being inserted within contracts solely to reduce the lease term beyond what is economically reasonable for the lessee.

BC158 The IASB observed that a lessee is sometimes obliged to choose between one or more options in a lease contract, each of which will result in an outflow of economic benefits for the lessee. In such cases, a lessee considers how the arrangement is most faithfully represented in the financial statements. For example, a lease contract might contain a set of options that results in:

(a) a choice for the lessee that represents an in-substance fixed payment. This might be the case, for example, if a lessee has the choice of either exercising an option to extend a lease or purchasing the underlying asset. The set of payments that aggregate to the lowest amount (on a discounted basis) from the available realistic options is the minimum amount that the lessee is obliged to pay. In the IASB's view, this minimum amount is an in-substance fixed payment that should be recognised as part of the cost of the right-of-use asset and as a liability by the lessee (see paragraph B42(c) of IFRS 16).

(b) a choice for the lessee that represents a guarantee provided to the lessor under which the lessee guarantees the lessor a minimum or fixed cash return regardless of whether an option is exercised. Such a situation might occur, for example, if an extension option is associated with a residual value guarantee or a termination penalty under which the lessor is guaranteed to receive an economic inflow at least equivalent to the payments that would be made by the lessee during the optional period. In the IASB's view, such an arrangement creates an economic incentive for the lessee to exercise the option to extend (or not to terminate) the lease (see paragraph B38 of IFRS 16).

BC159 Subsequent measurement of options to extend or terminate a lease is discussed in paragraphs BC184–BC187.

Discount rate (paragraph 26)

BC160 The IASB's objective in specifying the discount rate to apply to a lease is to specify a rate that reflects how the contract is priced. With this in mind, the IASB decided that, if readily determinable by the lessee, a lessee should use the interest rate implicit in the lease.

BC161   The interest rate implicit in the lease is likely to be similar to the lessee's incremental borrowing rate in many cases. This is because both rates, as they have been defined in IFRS 16, take into account the credit standing of the lessee, the length of the lease, the nature and quality of the collateral provided and the economic environment in which the transaction occurs. However, the interest rate implicit in the lease is generally also affected by a lessor's estimate of the residual value of the underlying asset at the end of the lease, and may be affected by taxes and other factors known only to the lessor, such as any initial direct costs of the lessor. Consequently, the IASB noted that it is likely to be difficult for lessees to determine the interest rate implicit in the lease for many leases, particularly those for which the underlying asset has a significant residual value at the end of the lease.

BC162   Accordingly, IFRS 16 requires a lessee to discount the lease liability using the interest rate implicit in the lease if that rate can be readily determined. If the interest rate implicit in the lease cannot be readily determined, then the lessee should use its incremental borrowing rate. In reaching this decision, the IASB decided to define the lessee's incremental borrowing rate to take into account the terms and conditions of the lease. The IASB noted that, depending on the nature of the underlying asset and the terms and conditions of the lease, a lessee may be able to refer to a rate that is readily observable as a starting point when determining its incremental borrowing rate for a lease (for example, the rate that a lessee has paid, or would pay, to borrow money to purchase the type of asset being leased, or the property yield when determining the discount rate to apply to property leases). Nonetheless, a lessee should adjust such observable rates as is needed to determine its incremental borrowing rate as defined in IFRS 16.

Lease payments

Variable lease payments (paragraph 27(a)–(b))

BC163   Some or all of the lease payments for the right to use an asset during the lease term can be variable. That variability arises if lease payments are linked to:

(a)   price changes due to changes in a market rate or the value of an index. For example, lease payments might be adjusted for changes in a benchmark interest rate or a consumer price index.

(b)   the lessee's performance derived from the underlying asset. For example, a lease of retail property may specify that lease payments are based on a specified percentage of sales made from that property.

(c)   the use of the underlying asset. For example, a vehicle lease may require the lessee to make additional lease payments if the lessee exceeds a specified mileage.

Variable lease payments that are in-substance fixed lease payments

BC164   In-substance fixed lease payments are payments that may, in form, contain variability but that in substance are unavoidable. IFRS 16 requires a lessee to include in-substance fixed lease payments in the measurement of lease liabilities because those payments are unavoidable and, thus, are economically indistinguishable from fixed lease payments. The IASB understands that this approach is similar to the way in which entities applied IAS 17, even though IAS 17 did not include explicit requirements in this respect. In response to requests from stakeholders, IFRS 16 also includes examples in the application guidance of the types of payments that are considered to be in-substance fixed payments to help in applying the requirement.

Variable lease payments that depend on an index or a rate

BC165   For similar reasons, the IASB decided to include variable lease payments that depend on an index or a rate in the measurement of lease liabilities. Those payments meet the definition of liabilities for the lessee because they are unavoidable and do not depend on any future activity of the lessee. Any uncertainty, therefore, relates to the measurement of the liability that arises from those payments and not to the existence of that liability.

BC166   In the IASB's view, forecasting techniques could be used to determine the expected effect of changes in an index or a rate on the measurement of lease liabilities. However, forecasting changes in an index or a rate requires macroeconomic information that may not be readily available to all entities, and may result in measurement uncertainty. The IASB noted that the usefulness of the enhanced information obtained using such a forecast often might not justify the costs of obtaining it, particularly for those lessees with a high volume of leases. The IASB considered requiring a lessee to use forward rates when measuring lease liabilities if those rates are readily available. However, it decided not to do so because this would reduce comparability between those using forward rates and those not doing so. Consequently, at initial recognition, IFRS 16 requires a lessee to measure payments that depend on an index or a rate using the index or rate at the commencement date (ie a lessee does not estimate future inflation but, instead, measures lease liabilities using lease payments that assume no inflation over the remainder of the lease term).

BC167   Subsequent measurement of variable lease payments that depend on an index or a rate is discussed in paragraphs BC188–BC190.

Variable lease payments linked to future performance or use of an underlying asset

BC168   There are differing views about whether variable payments linked to future performance or use of an underlying asset meet the definition of a liability. Some think that a lessee's liability to make variable lease payments does not exist until the future event requiring the payment occurs (for example, when the underlying asset is used, or a sale is made). Others think that a lessee's obligation to make variable lease payments exists at the commencement date by virtue of the lease contract and receipt of the right-of-use asset. Consequently, they think that all variable lease payments meet the definition of a liability for the lessee because it is the amount of the liability that is uncertain, rather than the existence of that liability.

BC169　The IASB decided to exclude variable lease payments linked to future performance or use of an underlying asset from the measurement of lease liabilities. For some Board members, this decision was made solely for cost-benefit reasons. Those Board members were of the view that all variable lease payments meet the definition of a liability for the lessee. However, they were persuaded by the feedback received from stakeholders that the costs of including variable lease payments linked to future performance or use would outweigh the benefits, particularly because of the concerns expressed about the high level of measurement uncertainty that would result from including them and the high volume of leases held by some lessees. Other Board members did not think that variable lease payments linked to future performance or use meet the definition of a liability for the lessee until the performance or use occurs. They regarded those payments to be avoidable by the lessee and, accordingly, concluded that the lessee does not have a present obligation to make those payments at the commencement date. In addition, variable lease payments linked to future performance or use could be viewed as a means by which the lessee and lessor can share future economic benefits to be derived from use of the asset.

Residual value guarantees (paragraph 27(c))

BC170　The IASB decided that a lessee should account for a residual value guarantee that it provides to the lessor as part of the lease liability (and as part of the cost of the right-of-use asset). In reaching this decision, the IASB noted that payments resulting from a residual value guarantee cannot be avoided by the lessee—the lessee has an unconditional obligation to pay the lessor if the value of the underlying asset moves in a particular way. Accordingly, any uncertainty relating to the payment of a residual value guarantee does not relate to whether the lessee has an obligation. Instead, it relates to the amount that the lessee may have to pay, which can vary in response to movements in the value of the underlying asset. In that respect, residual value guarantees are similar to variable lease payments that depend on an index or a rate for the lessee.

BC171　Therefore, the IASB decided that a lessee should estimate the amount expected to be payable to the lessor under residual value guarantees and include that amount in the measurement of the lease liability. In the IASB's view, the measurement of a residual value guarantee should reflect an entity's reasonable expectation of the amount that will be paid.

BC172　The IASB considered whether a lessee should recognise and measure residual value guarantees as separate components of a lease, because such guarantees are linked to the value of the underlying asset and may meet the definition of a derivative. However, the IASB noted that residual value guarantees are often interlinked with other terms and conditions in a lease so that accounting for the guarantees as separate components could diminish the relevance and faithful representation of the information provided. Recognising such guarantees separately could also be costly to apply.

Options to purchase the underlying asset (paragraph 27(d))

BC173   The IASB decided that purchase options should be included in the measurement of the lease liability in the same way as options to extend the term of a lease (ie the exercise price of a purchase option would be included in the measurement of a lease liability if the lessee is reasonably certain to exercise that option). This is because the IASB views a purchase option as effectively the ultimate option to extend the lease term. A lessee that has an option to extend a lease for all of the remaining economic life of the underlying asset is, economically, in a similar position to a lessee that has an option to purchase the underlying asset. Accordingly, the IASB concluded that, for the same reasons underlying the decision to include extension options, including the exercise price within the measurement of a lease liability if the lessee is reasonably certain to exercise the option provides the most useful information to users of financial statements.

Lease Incentives (Annual Improvements to IFRS Standards 2018–2020)

BC173A   The Board was informed about the potential for confusion in applying IFRS 16 because of the way Illustrative Example 13 accompanying IFRS 16 had illustrated the requirements for lease incentives. Before the amendment, Illustrative Example 13 had included as part of the fact pattern a reimbursement relating to leasehold improvements; the example had not explained clearly enough the conclusion as to whether the reimbursement would meet the definition of a lease incentive in IFRS 16.

BC173B   The Board decided to remove the potential for confusion by deleting from Illustrative Example 13 the reimbursement relating to leasehold improvements. The Board concluded that little would be lost by deleting it.

Subsequent measurement of the right-of-use asset (paragraphs 29–35)

BC174   The IASB decided that, after the commencement date, a lessee should measure the right-of-use asset at cost less accumulated depreciation and accumulated impairment losses, adjusted for remeasurements of the lease liability (see paragraph BC192). Paragraphs BC41–BC56 include a detailed discussion of the feedback received on the lessee accounting model and the basis for the IASB's decisions regarding the subsequent measurement of a lessee's right-of-use asset.

BC175   The IASB did not adopt an alternative approach whereby a lessee would be required to measure the right-of-use asset at fair value after initial measurement, because this approach would be:

(a)   inconsistent with the subsequent measurement of many other non-financial assets; and

(b)   more complex and costly for entities to apply than a cost-based approach, because it requires the use of both current expected cash flows and current interest rates.

Impairment of the right-of-use asset (paragraph 33)

BC176　The IASB decided that a lessee should apply the impairment requirements of IAS 36 to the right-of-use asset. In the IASB's view, this requirement enables users of financial statements to better compare assets that a lessee owns with those that it leases. In addition, it could be difficult for a lessee to implement an impairment model for right-of-use assets that is different from the model applied to other non-financial assets, particularly if a lessee is required to assess a group of assets (comprising both leased and owned assets) for impairment together.

Other measurement models for the right-of-use asset (paragraphs 34–35)

BC177　IFRS permits the revaluation of non-financial assets, such as property, plant and equipment. Accordingly, the IASB saw no reason not to allow a lessee to revalue right-of-use assets, albeit only if the lessee revalues similar classes of owned assets.

BC178　IFRS also permits investment properties to be measured at fair value. IAS 40 requires an entity to measure all investment property using the same measurement basis (either the cost model or the fair value model). This is because measuring all investment property on the same basis provides more useful information than allowing an entity to choose the measurement basis for each property. IFRS 16 has amended the scope of IAS 40 by defining investment property to include both owned investment property and investment property held by a lessee as a right-of-use asset. This results in lessees using either the cost model and disclosing fair value, or using the fair value model, depending on whether the lessee accounts for the remainder of its investment property under the cost model or the fair value model. In the IASB's view, this approach will provide useful information to users of financial statements about the fair value of investment property held by a lessee as a right-of-use asset, which is consistent with information provided about owned investment property.

BC179　Some stakeholders expressed concerns about the costs of determining the fair value of right-of-use assets (whether for disclosure or measurement purposes). The IASB acknowledged that there might be costs involved with determining the fair value of right-of-use assets, particularly for entities that are not in the property industry but sublease property, for example, because that property is not needed for use within their business. However, the IASB noted that there are two factors that will lessen the likelihood that entities that are not in the property industry will hold investment property as a right-of-use asset:

(a)　IFRS 16 requires an entity to classify a sublease by reference to the right-of-use asset arising from the head lease (see paragraphs BC233–BC234). Consequently, an intermediate lessor would classify a sublease as a finance lease if it subleases the asset for all or most of the remaining term of the head lease. In those cases, the intermediate lessor would apply finance lease accounting (ie recognise a net investment in the sublease rather than the underlying right-of-use asset) and, thus, would not be required to apply the requirements of

IAS 40. The IASB observed that entities that are not in the property industry that wish to reduce property costs would generally aim to secure a sublease for the entire remaining period of the head lease, which (if successful) would result in finance lease accounting.

(b) entities that are not in the property industry may not be within the scope of IAS 40 if they sublease a property under an operating lease with the intention of subsequently using the property within their own business. Such a property would not meet the definition of an investment property in IAS 40 because it would not be held solely for rentals, capital appreciation or both.

BC180 In the IASB's view it should be relatively straightforward to determine the fair value of right-of-use assets if the sublease does not contain any options or variable lease payments. Determining the fair value would involve projecting the cash flows that the entity expects to receive from subleasing the asset. The IASB concluded that, for an entity that is not in the property industry, determining these cash flows would normally be relatively straightforward because it is likely that a sublease would already be in place.

BC181 Some stakeholders asked that IAS 40 provide additional requirements on measuring the fair value of right-of-use assets if leases have variable and optional payments, or if there is no active market for the right-of-use asset. In the IASB's view, the principles in IFRS 13 *Fair Value Measurement* and IAS 40 are sufficient to help lessees to measure the fair value of those right-of-use assets. In particular, the IASB noted that paragraph 50(d) of IAS 40 explains when to include in the measurement of the right-of-use asset options and variable lease payments that are not included in the measurement of the lease liability.

Subsequent measurement of the lease liability (paragraphs 20–21 and 36–43)

BC182 The IASB decided that a lessee should measure lease liabilities similarly to other financial liabilities using an effective interest method, so that the carrying amount of the lease liability is measured on an amortised cost basis and the interest expense is allocated over the lease term.

BC183 IFRS 16 does not require or permit a lessee to measure lease liabilities at fair value after initial measurement. In the IASB's view, this approach would have been:

(a) inconsistent with the subsequent measurement of many other non-derivative financial liabilities, thus decreasing comparability for users of financial statements; and

(b) more complex and costly for entities to apply than a cost-based approach, because it requires the use of both current expected cash flows and current interest rates.

Reassessment of options (paragraph 20)

BC184   In principle, the IASB is of the view that users of financial statements receive more relevant information if lessees reassess extension, termination and purchase options on a regular basis. The resulting information is more relevant because reassessment reflects current economic conditions, and using a lease term established at the commencement date throughout the lease could be misleading.

BC185   However, requiring reassessment at each reporting date would be costly for an entity with many leases that include options. The IASB considered ways in which IFRS 16 could address that concern while still providing useful information to users of financial statements. It decided that an appropriate balance would be achieved by:

(a)   requiring reassessment only upon the occurrence of a significant event or a significant change in circumstances that affects whether the lessee is reasonably certain to exercise, or not to exercise, an option to extend a lease, to terminate a lease or to purchase an underlying asset. The IASB noted that this requirement is similar in some respects to the approach taken for the impairment of long-lived assets (other than goodwill and indefinite-lived intangible assets) in IAS 36. IAS 36 does not require impairment testing at each reporting date. Instead, an entity tests for impairment when there has been an indication that the asset may be impaired.

(b)   requiring reassessment only if the significant event or significant change in circumstances is within the control of the lessee. Limiting the reassessment requirement in this way means that a lessee is not required to reassess options in response to purely market-based events or changes in circumstances.

BC186   The IASB noted that an entity will need to apply judgement in identifying significant events or significant changes in circumstances that trigger reassessment and that it would be impossible to provide a list of all possible triggering events. Nonetheless, the IASB decided to provide some examples of possible triggering events to help entities apply that judgement.

BC187   The IASB considered but did not adopt the following approaches:

(a)   *requiring a lessee to reassess options when there has been a change in facts or circumstances that would indicate that there is a significant change in the right-of-use asset or lease liability.* Many stakeholders thought that it could be difficult to interpret when a change in the right-of-use asset or lease liability is significant. In addition, stakeholders were concerned about both the costs of performing reassessment and, if relevant, the costs associated with demonstrating that reassessment was not required, which might be as costly as reassessing options at each reporting date.

(b)   *requiring a lessee to reassess options when the lessee has, or no longer has, a significant economic incentive that would make exercise of an option reasonably certain.* Many stakeholders thought that the cost of applying this approach would exceed any benefit, because an entity might incur significant costs in continuously assessing and monitoring relevant factors that give rise to a significant economic incentive even though the lease term conclusion might not change.

Reassessment of variable lease payments that depend on an index or a rate (paragraph 42(b))

BC188   In principle the IASB is of the view that users of financial statements receive more relevant information about a lessee's lease liabilities if the lessee updates the measurement of its liabilities to reflect a change in an index or a rate used to determine lease payments (including, for example, a change to reflect changes in market rental rates following a market rent review). For example, without such remeasurement, the measurement of the lease liability for a 20-year property lease, for which lease payments are linked to an inflation index, is unlikely to provide users of financial statements with useful information about the entity's future cash outflows relating to that lease throughout the lease term.

BC189   Some stakeholders expressed concerns about the cost of performing reassessments each time a rate or an index changes, and questioned whether the benefits for users of financial statements would outweigh the costs for lessees. For example, some stakeholders noted that the total expenses related to leases recognised in profit or loss by a lessee would be substantially the same, regardless of whether the lessee remeasures the lease liability for changes in an index or a rate.

BC190   In the light of this feedback, the IASB decided that a lessee should reassess variable lease payments that are determined by reference to an index or a rate only when there is a change in the cash flows resulting from a change in the reference index or rate (ie when the adjustment to the lease payments takes effect). The IASB noted that this approach is less complex and costly to apply than requiring a lessee to reassess variable lease payments at each reporting date. This is because a lessee would typically be expected to report its financial results more frequently than the occurrence of a contractual change in the cash flows of a lease with payments that depend on an index or a rate.

Reassessment of residual value guarantees (paragraph 42(a))

BC191   The IASB decided that lessees should reassess the amounts expected to be payable under residual value guarantees, because that provides more relevant information to users of financial statements, by reflecting current economic conditions.

Accounting for the effects of reassessing lease payments (paragraph 39)

BC192   The IASB decided that, if a lessee remeasures its lease liability to reflect changes in future lease payments, the lessee should recognise the amount of the remeasurement as an adjustment to the cost of the right-of-use asset. The IASB considered whether some changes to the measurement of the lease liability should be recognised in profit or loss because, for example, the reassessment of an option or a change in an index or a rate could be viewed as an event relating to the current period. However, the IASB decided that a lessee should recognise the remeasurement as an adjustment to the right-of-use assets for the following reasons:

(a)   a change in the assessment of extension, termination or purchase options reflects the lessee's determination that it has acquired more or less of the right to use the underlying asset. Consequently, that change is appropriately reflected as an adjustment to the cost of the right-of-use asset.

(b)   a change in the estimate of the future lease payments is a revision to the initial estimate of the cost of the right-of-use asset, which should be accounted for in the same manner as the initial estimated cost.

(c)   the requirement to update the cost of the right-of-use asset is similar to the requirements in IFRIC 1 *Changes in Existing Decommissioning, Restoration and Similar Liabilities*. IFRIC 1 requires an entity to adjust the cost of the related asset for a change in the estimated timing or amount of the outflow of resources associated with a change in the measurement of an existing decommissioning, restoration or similar liability.

Reassessment of the discount rate (paragraphs 41 and 43)

BC193   The IASB decided that, in most cases, an entity should not reassess the discount rate during the lease term. This approach is generally consistent with the approach applied to financial instruments accounted for using the effective interest method. The IASB noted that in other Standards in which the discount rate is required to be reassessed, it is typically because the liability to which the discount rate relates is measured on a current value measurement basis.

BC194   Nonetheless, in the IASB's view, there are some circumstances in which an entity should reassess the discount rate. Consequently, IFRS 16 requires a lessee to remeasure the lease liability using revised payments and a revised discount rate when there is a change in the lease term or a change in the assessment of whether the lessee is reasonably certain to exercise an option to purchase the underlying asset. In the IASB's view, in those circumstances, the economics of the lease have changed and it is appropriate to reassess the discount rate to be consistent with the change in the lease payments included in the measurement of the lease liability (and right-of-use asset).

BC195   The IASB also decided that, in a floating interest rate lease, a lessee should use a revised discount rate to remeasure the lease liability when there is a change in lease payments resulting from changes in the floating interest rate. This approach is consistent with the requirements in IFRS 9 for the measurement of floating-rate financial liabilities subsequently measured at amortised cost.

Foreign currency exchange

BC196   IFRS 16 does not provide specific requirements on how a lessee should account for the effects of foreign currency exchange differences relating to lease liabilities that are denominated in a foreign currency. Consistently with other financial liabilities, a lessee's lease liability is a monetary item and consequently, if denominated in a foreign currency, is required to be remeasured using closing exchange rates at the end of each reporting period applying IAS 21 *The Effects of Changes in Foreign Exchange Rates*.

BC197   Some stakeholders suggested that a lessee should recognise any foreign currency exchange differences as an adjustment to the carrying amount of the right-of-use asset. This approach would treat translation adjustments as an update to the cost of the right-of-use asset, which is initially measured on the basis of the initial measurement of the lease liability. These stakeholders are of the view that lease payments denominated in a foreign currency are in effect another form of variable lease payment, and should be accounted for similarly to variable lease payments that depend on an index or a rate. These stakeholders also questioned whether useful information will be obscured as a result of the profit or loss volatility that might arise as a result of recognising foreign currency exchange differences on a lessee's lease liability in profit or loss.

BC198   The IASB decided that any foreign currency exchange differences relating to lease liabilities denominated in a foreign currency should be recognised in profit or loss, for the following reasons:

(a)   this approach is consistent with the requirements for foreign exchange differences arising from other financial liabilities (for example, loans and previous finance lease liabilities accounted for applying IAS 17).

(b)   a lessee with a liability denominated in a foreign currency is exposed to foreign currency risk. Consequently, foreign currency exchange gains or losses recognised in profit or loss faithfully represent the economic effect of the lessee's currency exposure to the foreign exchange risk.

(c)   if a lessee enters into derivatives to hedge its economic exposure to foreign currency risk, the recognition of foreign currency exchange differences relating to lease liabilities as an adjustment to the cost of right-of-use assets would prevent a natural offset of the economic exposure in profit or loss. This is because an entity would recognise any change in the foreign currency risk for the derivatives in profit or loss, whereas it would recognise the corresponding change in lease liabilities in the balance sheet—thus introducing volatility as a result of reducing exposure to foreign currency risk. This mismatch could distort the reported economic position of the lessee.

(d)   in the IASB's view, subsequent changes to a foreign exchange rate should not have any effect on the cost of a non-monetary item. Consequently, it would be inappropriate to include such changes in the remeasurement of the right-of-use asset.

BC199   Although this approach could result in volatility in profit or loss from the recognition of foreign currency exchange differences, an entity would disclose those changes separately as foreign currency exchange gains or losses. Accordingly, it would be clear to users of financial statements that the gain or loss results solely from movements in foreign exchange rates. Because this approach is consistent with the requirements for foreign currency exchange differences in IAS 21, the IASB concluded that it was not necessary to include any specific requirements in IFRS 16.

Lease modifications (paragraphs 44–46B)

BC200   IAS 17 did not address the accounting for lease modifications. The IASB decided that it would be useful to include a general framework for accounting for lease modifications in IFRS 16 because modifications occur frequently for many types of leases.

BC201   The IASB decided to define a lease modification as a change in the scope of a lease (for example, adding or terminating the right to use one or more underlying assets, or extending or shortening the contractual lease term), or the consideration for a lease, that was not part of the original terms and conditions of the lease. In defining lease modifications, the IASB differentiated between scenarios resulting in the remeasurement of existing lease assets and lease liabilities that are not lease modifications (for example, a change in lease term resulting from the exercise of an option to extend the lease when that option was not included in the original lease term) and those resulting in a lease modification (for example, a change in the lease term resulting from changes to the terms and conditions of the original lease).

BC202   The IASB decided that an entity should further distinguish between those lease modifications that, in substance, represent the creation of a new lease that is separate from the original lease and those that, in substance, represent a change in the scope of, or the consideration paid for, the existing lease. Consequently, IFRS 16 requires a lessee to account for a lease modification as a separate lease if the modification increases the scope of the lease by adding the right to use one or more underlying assets and the consideration paid for the lease increases by an amount commensurate with the stand-alone price for the increase in scope.

BC203   For those lease modifications that do not result in a separate lease, the IASB decided that a lessee should remeasure the existing lease liability using a discount rate determined at the effective date of the modification. The IASB decided that:

(a)   for lease modifications that decrease the scope of a lease, a lessee should decrease the carrying amount of the right-of-use asset to reflect the partial or full termination of the lease and recognise a corresponding gain or loss. In the IASB's view, this gain or loss appropriately reflects the economic effect of the partial or full termination of the existing lease resulting from the decrease in scope.

(b)　for all other lease modifications, a lessee should make a corresponding adjustment to the carrying amount of the right-of-use asset. In these cases, the original lease is not terminated because there is no decrease in scope. The lessee continues to have the right to use the underlying asset identified in the original lease. For lease modifications that increase the scope of a lease, the adjustment to the carrying amount of the right-of-use asset effectively represents the cost of the additional right of use acquired as a result of the modification. For lease modifications that change the consideration paid for a lease, the adjustment to the carrying amount of the right-of-use asset effectively represents a change in the cost of the right-of-use asset as a result of the modification. The use of a revised discount rate in remeasuring the lease liability reflects that, in modifying the lease, there is a change in the interest rate implicit in the lease (which the discount rate is intended to approximate).

BC204　The IASB concluded that this approach results in accounting outcomes that faithfully represent the substance of a lease modification and will closely align gain or loss recognition with a corresponding change in the lessee's rights and obligations under the lease. This is because a lease gives rise to both a right-of-use asset and a lease liability. Accordingly, a lease modification can result in a change to the lessee's rights (ie a change to the right-of-use asset), a change to the lease liability, or both.

BC205　The IASB considered requiring a lessee to distinguish between changes to a lease that are substantial and those that are not substantial, in a manner similar to that required for contract modifications relating to financial liabilities within the scope of IFRS 9. This approach would require a lessee to account for the lease modification as (a) a new lease, when the change represents a substantial modification; or (b) a continuation of the original lease, when the change does not represent a substantial modification. However, the IASB did not adopt this approach because, as a result of the link to the right-of-use asset, it could result in outcomes that would not faithfully represent the differing nature of each of those changes. For example, there are scenarios in which this approach would result in the extinguishment of the original lease (and the recognition of a corresponding gain or loss in profit or loss) when the lessee continues to have all of the rights it had in the original lease after the modification.

Covid-19-related rent concessions

BC205A　In May 2020 the Board provided a practical expedient that permits lessees not to assess whether rent concessions that occur as a direct consequence of the covid-19 pandemic and meet specified conditions are lease modifications and, instead, to account for those rent concessions as if they were not lease modifications. The Board provided the practical expedient in response to information about the effects of the covid-19 pandemic.

BC205B   The Board was informed that many lessors are providing rent concessions to lessees as a result of the pandemic. The Board learned that lessees could find it challenging to assess whether a potentially large volume of covid-19-related rent concessions are lease modifications and, for those that are, to apply the required accounting in IFRS 16, especially in the light of the many challenges lessees face during the pandemic. Further, those challenges arising during the pandemic add to the work undertaken by lessees in implementing the new lessee accounting model in IFRS 16. The Board concluded that the practical expedient would provide relief to lessees, while enabling lessees to continue providing useful information about their leases to users of financial statements (see paragraph BC205F). To provide the relief when needed most, the Board enabled immediate application of the amendment in any financial statements—interim or annual—not authorised for issue at the date the amendment was issued.

BC205C   The Board decided to permit, but not require, a lessee to apply the practical expedient. Some lessees (for example, those with systems to address changes in lease payments) may prefer to apply, or have already applied, the requirements in paragraphs 36–46 of IFRS 16 to all changes in lease contracts. A lessee that chooses to apply the practical expedient would be required by paragraph 2 of IFRS 16 to apply it consistently to all lease contracts with similar characteristics and in similar circumstances.

BC205D   The Board considered the risk of the practical expedient being applied too broadly, which could result in unintended consequences. The Board therefore limited the scope of the practical expedient so that it applies only to rent concessions that occur as a direct consequence of the covid-19 pandemic and:

    (a)   result in revised consideration for the lease that is substantially the same as, or less than, the consideration for the lease immediately preceding the change. The Board was of the view that a rent concession that increases total payments for the lease should not be considered a direct consequence of the covid-19 pandemic, except to the extent the increase reflects only the time value of money.

    (b)   reduce only lease payments originally due on or before 30 June 2021. The Board noted that a related increase in lease payments that extends beyond 30 June 2021 would not prevent a rent concession from meeting this condition. In contrast, if reductions in lease payments extend beyond 30 June 2021, the rent concession in its entirety would not be within the scope of the practical expedient. In developing this condition, the Board observed that the economic effects of the covid-19 pandemic could continue for some time. If the practical expedient were not limited to a particular time frame, a lessee could conclude that many future changes in lease payments would be a consequence of the covid-19 pandemic. Limiting the practical expedient to rent concessions that reduce only lease payments originally due on or before 30 June 2021 provides relief to lessees when they are expected to need it most, while being responsive to concerns from users of financial statements about comparability if lessees were to apply the practical expedient beyond when it is needed. The Board also expected the condition in paragraph 46B(b) to be easy to apply, and to help lessees in identifying rent concessions occurring as a direct consequence of the covid-19 pandemic.

(c)   introduce no substantive change to other terms and conditions of the lease, considering both qualitative and quantitative factors. Consequently, if a modification to a lease incorporates other substantive changes—beyond a rent concession occurring as a direct consequence of the covid-19 pandemic—the modification in its entirety does not qualify for the practical expedient. The Board noted that, for example, a three-month rent holiday before 30 June 2021 followed by three additional months of substantially equivalent payments at the end of the lease would not constitute a substantive change to other terms and conditions of the lease.

BC205E   The Board developed the practical expedient to relieve lessees from assessing whether rent concessions occurring as a direct consequence of the covid-19 pandemic are lease modifications and from applying the lease modification requirements to those concessions. The practical expedient does not otherwise interpret or change any requirements in IFRS 16. The Board observed therefore that a lessee would account for the lease liability and right-of-use asset applying the requirements in IFRS 16, which, for example, incorporate requirements in IAS 16 *Property, Plant and Equipment*. With this in mind, the Board considered how a lessee applying the practical expedient would account for three types of change in lease payments:

(a)   a lessee applying the practical expedient would generally account for a forgiveness or waiver of lease payments as a variable lease payment applying paragraph 38 of IFRS 16. The lessee would also make a corresponding adjustment to the lease liability—in effect, derecognising the part of the lease liability that has been forgiven or waived.

(b)   a change in lease payments that reduces payments in one period but proportionally increases payments in another does not extinguish the lessee's lease liability or change the consideration for the lease—instead, it changes only the timing of individual payments. In this case, applying paragraph 36 of IFRS 16, a lessee would continue to both recognise interest on the lease liability and reduce that liability to reflect lease payments made to the lessor.

(c)   some covid-19-related rent concessions reduce lease payments, incorporating both a forgiveness or waiver of payments and a change in the timing of payments.

BC205F   The Board was of the view that the information provided by a lessee that applies the practical expedient would be useful to users of financial statements, noting that the lease liability recognised would reflect the present value of future lease payments owed to the lessor. Users of financial statements supported a lessee recognising in profit or loss at the time of the covid-19 pandemic the effects of a rent concession occurring as a direct consequence of the pandemic. Nonetheless, the Board acknowledged concerns from users of financial statements that the practical expedient, because it is optional, could affect comparability between lessees that apply the practical expedient and those that do not—disclosure of the effects of applying the practical expedient is therefore important to meet users' information needs. Consequently, the Board decided to require a lessee applying the practical expedient to some or all eligible contracts to disclose that fact, as well as the amount recognised in profit or loss to reflect changes in lease payments that arise from rent concessions to which the practical expedient is applied (paragraph 60A of IFRS 16).

BC205G Users of financial statements also highlighted the importance of cash flow information about covid-19-related rent concessions. The main effect on cash flows would be the reduction or absence of cash outflows for leases during the period of the rent concession. For a concession that adjusts the carrying amount of the lease liability, a lessee would disclose this effect as a non-cash change in lease liabilities applying paragraph 44A of IAS 7 *Statement of Cash Flows*. The Board noted that cash flow effects, and other information about, for example, the nature of rent concessions, would be relevant regardless of whether a lessee applies the practical expedient. The Board expected paragraphs 51 and 59 of IFRS 16 to require a lessee to disclose such information, if material.

Presentation: lessee (paragraphs 47–50)

Statement of financial position (paragraph 47–48)

BC206 The IASB decided that, if not presented separately in the balance sheet, right-of-use assets should be included within the same line item as similar owned assets. The IASB concluded that, if right-of-use assets are not presented as a line item, presenting similar leased and owned assets together would provide more useful information to users of financial statements than other approaches. This is because a lessee often uses owned assets and leased assets for the same purpose and derives similar economic benefits from the use of owned assets and leased assets.

BC207 However, the IASB noted that there are differences between a right-of-use asset and an owned asset, and that users of financial statements may want to know the carrying amount of each separately. For example, right-of-use assets may be viewed as being (a) less risky than owned assets, because a right-of-use asset may not embed residual asset risk; or (b) more risky than owned assets, because the lessee may need to replace the right-of-use asset at the end of the lease term, but may not be able to secure a similar rate for the replacement lease. Accordingly, IFRS 16 requires a lessee to provide information about the carrying amount of right-of-use assets separately from assets that are owned, either in the balance sheet or in the notes.

BC208 Similarly, the IASB decided that a lessee should present lease liabilities separately from other liabilities, either in the balance sheet or in the notes. In reaching this decision, the IASB noted that leasing is an important activity for many lessees. Although a lease liability shares many common characteristics with other financial liabilities, a lease liability is contractually related to a corresponding asset and often has features, such as options and variable lease payments, that differ from those typically found in other liabilities. Thus, presenting lease liabilities separately from other financial liabilities (along with the disclosure requirements discussed in paragraphs BC212–BC230) provides users of financial statements with information that is useful in understanding an entity's obligations arising from lease arrangements. The IASB also noted that paragraph 55 of IAS 1 requires a lessee to further disaggregate line items in the balance sheet if such presentation is relevant to an understanding of the lessee's financial position.

Statement of profit or loss and other comprehensive income (paragraph 49)

BC209   The IASB decided that a lessee should present interest expense on the lease liability separately from the depreciation charge for the right-of-use asset in the income statement. The IASB concluded that a lessee would provide more useful information to users of financial statements by presenting interest on the lease liability together with interest on other financial liabilities and depreciation of the right-of-use asset together with other similar expenses (for example, depreciation of property, plant and equipment). Paragraphs BC41–BC56 include a discussion of the basis for the IASB's decisions relating to amounts recognised in profit or loss by a lessee.

Statement of cash flows (paragraph 50)

BC210   The IASB's decisions on the presentation of lease cash outflows are linked to the nature of the right-of-use asset and lease liability, and the presentation of expenses arising from a lease in the income statement. In the IASB's view, it would be misleading to portray payments in one manner in the income statement and in another in the statement of cash flows.

BC211   Consequently, the IASB decided that a lessee should classify the principal portion of cash repayments of the lease liability as financing activities in the statement of cash flows and classify cash payments relating to interest consistently with other interest payments. This approach is consistent with the requirements in IAS 7 *Statement of Cash Flows* for cash flows relating to financial liabilities and provides comparability between interest paid on leases and interest paid on other financial liabilities. This approach also results in a lessee accounting for a lease consistently in the balance sheet, income statement and statement of cash flows. For example, a lessee (a) measures and presents the lease liability similarly to other financial liabilities; (b) recognises and presents interest relating to that liability in a similar manner to interest on other financial liabilities; and (c) presents cash paid relating to interest on lease liabilities similarly to interest on other financial liabilities.

Disclosure: lessee (paragraphs 51–60)

BC212   In determining the disclosures for leases, the IASB considered the following:

(a)   the disclosure requirements of IAS 17;

(b) the disclosure requirements for financial liabilities in IFRS 7 *Financial Instruments: Disclosures*;

(c) the disclosure requirements for non-current assets such as property, plant and equipment;

(d) work on other related projects such as the Disclosure Initiative (a broad-based initiative to explore how disclosures in IFRS financial reporting can be improved); and

(e) feedback received on the disclosure proposals in the 2010 and 2013 Exposure Drafts.

BC213 The IASB received significant feedback regarding lessee disclosures. In particular:

(a) many lessees had significant concerns about the costs of complying with the disclosures proposed in the 2010 and 2013 Exposure Drafts. This was a particular concern for lessees with a high volume of leases with unique terms and conditions. These lessees suggested that there should be no need to expand the disclosure requirements beyond those in IAS 17 if the lessee accounting model in IFRS 16 provides the information that investors need. These lessees also argued that the proposed lessee disclosure requirements did not seem to be consistent with the IASB's efforts to address 'disclosure overload' in other projects (ie increases in the volume of disclosures and a perceived reduction in the quality and usefulness of those disclosures).

(b) in contrast, many users of financial statements thought that the detailed disclosure requirements proposed in the 2010 and 2013 Exposure Drafts would provide useful information. Over the course of the project, the IASB held meetings with investors and analysts to discuss how particular disclosures would be used in their analysis and which disclosures would be the most useful.

(c) both preparers and users of financial statements had concerns that lengthy detailed disclosure requirements could lead to the use of 'boilerplate' statements rather than the provision of useful information. These stakeholders were particularly concerned about the risk of material information being 'lost' within lengthy and complex financial statement notes. Similarly, many stakeholders suggested that IFRS 16 should explicitly state that entities should apply materiality in determining the extent to which disclosures are required.

(d) some users of financial statements noted that the most useful information would be different for different lease portfolios. These users noted that, for leases with complex terms and conditions (which, for some entities, are the leases in which users are most interested), compliance with standardised disclosure requirements often does not meet their information needs.

BC214　In response to this feedback, the IASB decided to:

(a)　include an overall disclosure objective in IFRS 16 (paragraphs BC215–BC216);

(b)　require a lessee to disclose quantitative information about its right-of-use assets, and expenses and cash flows related to leases (paragraphs BC217–BC223); and

(c)　require a lessee to disclose any additional information that is necessary to satisfy the overall disclosure objective, and to supplement this requirement with a list of user information needs that any additional disclosures should address (paragraphs BC224–BC227).

Overall disclosure objective (paragraph 51)

BC215　Consistently with other recently issued Standards, the IASB decided that IFRS 16 should specify an overall objective for lessee disclosures. In the IASB's view, a clear objective should improve the interpretation and implementation of the disclosure requirements. This is because a lessee is required to assess whether the overall quality and informational value of its lease disclosures are sufficient to meet the stated objective.

BC216　The IASB considered stakeholder suggestions that an explicit statement about materiality would be useful in applying the lessee disclosure requirements. However, such statements are not included in other Standards. The concept of materiality in the *Conceptual Framework* and in IAS 1 is pervasive across IFRS and applies to the requirements in IFRS 16 in the same way that it applies to the requirements in all other Standards. The IASB thought that including a statement about materiality within the disclosure requirements in IFRS 16 might be interpreted as implying that materiality does not apply to the disclosure requirements in other Standards, because materiality is not explicitly mentioned in those Standards. The IASB is of the view that implicit in the overall disclosure objective is the notion that the level of detail provided in disclosures should reflect the significance of a lessee's leasing activities to its financial statements. The IASB concluded that guidance on applying the overall disclosure objective would be helpful to lessees but noted that such guidance is already provided in paragraphs 30A and 31 of IAS 1.

Disclosures about right-of-use assets, and expenses and cash flows related to leases (paragraph 53)

BC217　The IASB decided that there are particular items of information that, if material, should be disclosed by lessees to meet the information needs of users of financial statements. The IASB noted the importance of comparable information being provided by different lessees and that comparability could be achieved by including some specific disclosure requirements in IFRS 16. These disclosure requirements relate to the information that users of financial statements have identified as being most useful to their analyses and, consequently, that they would like to have for all lease portfolios that are material to an entity. Consequently, IFRS 16 requires a lessee to disclose:

(a)   the carrying amount of right-of-use assets, and depreciation charge for those assets, split by class of underlying asset. This information is useful in understanding the nature of a lessee's leasing activities and in comparing entities that lease their assets with those that purchase them.

(b)   interest expense on lease liabilities. Together with the disclosure of the carrying amount of lease liabilities separately from other liabilities (see paragraph BC208), this disclosure provides information about a lessee's lease obligations and finance costs.

(c)   the expenses related to short-term leases and leases of low-value assets accounted for applying paragraph 6 of IFRS 16, and the expense related to variable lease payments not included in the measurement of lease liabilities. These disclosures provide information about lease payments for which assets and liabilities are not recognised in the balance sheet.

(d)   total cash outflow for leases. This disclosure was identified by users of financial statements as providing the most useful information about lease cash flows and is expected to help in forecasting future lease payments.

(e)   additions to right-of-use assets. This disclosure provides comparable information about capital expenditure on leased and owned assets.

(f)   gains and losses arising from sale and leaseback transactions. This disclosure helps to better understand the unique characteristics of sale and leaseback transactions and the effect that such transactions have on a lessee's financial performance.

(g)   income from subleasing right-of-use assets. This disclosure is useful because, along with the information about expenses related to leases discussed above, it provides a complete depiction of the overall income statement effect of an entity's leasing activities.

Maturity analysis (paragraph 58)

BC218   IFRS 16 requires a lessee to disclose a maturity analysis for lease liabilities applying paragraphs 39 and B11 of IFRS 7.

BC219   Users of financial statements identified the main objective of a maturity analysis as being to help them understand liquidity risk and estimate future cash flows. The IASB's view is that the requirements of IFRS 7 achieve this objective, and also provide a lessee with the flexibility to present the maturity analysis that is most relevant to its particular lease portfolio.

BC220   The IASB considered whether IFRS 16 should instead include more prescriptive requirements for a maturity analysis similar to that required by IAS 17 (for example, by requiring a lessee to disclose undiscounted lease payments in each of the first five years and a total for the periods thereafter). Feedback from users of financial statements relating to the maturity analysis requirements of IAS 17 was generally positive. In particular, the prescriptive nature of the requirement ensured that different lessees provided information that was comparable.

BC221   Applying IFRS 7 to lease liabilities requires lessees to apply judgement in selecting time bands for the maturity analysis. The IASB thinks that, in a scenario in which disclosing undiscounted cash flows for each of the first five years and a total for the periods thereafter provides the most useful information to users of financial statements, the requirements of IFRS 7 should lead a lessee to disclose this level of detail. In contrast, in a scenario in which an alternative (and possibly more detailed) set of time bands provides the most useful information to users of financial statements, the requirements of IFRS 7 should lead a lessee to disclose that alternative and more useful set of time bands. For example, for a portfolio of 15–20 year leases, the requirements of IFRS 7 should lead a lessee to provide a more detailed maturity analysis than a single amount for the years beyond the fifth year.

BC222   In addition, the IASB is of the view that it is appropriate to apply the same maturity analysis disclosure requirements to lease liabilities as those applied to other financial liabilities. This is because the lessee accounting model in IFRS 16 is based on the premise that a lease liability is a financial liability (for the reasons described in paragraphs BC46–BC51).

BC223   The IASB decided not to require the disclosure of a maturity analysis of non-lease components. The IASB thinks that users of financial statements would find information about the maturities of any contractual commitments of an entity useful, regardless of the nature of the entity's rights under the contract. However, the IASB noted that it could be misleading to require the disclosure of contractual commitments for services that are embedded within a lease without also requiring the disclosure of contractual commitments for services that are provided as part of other contracts. The IASB decided that adding such a disclosure requirement would be beyond the scope of the Leases project.

Additional disclosures (paragraph 59)

BC224   Many leases contain more complex features, which can include variable payments, termination and extension options and residual value guarantees. These features of a lease are often determined on the basis of the individual circumstances of the parties to the contract and, in some cases, are particularly complex or are unique to the particular contract. The feedback received from stakeholders demonstrated that, for these features of a lessee's lease portfolio, a standard disclosure requirement for all entities is unlikely to meet the needs of users of financial statements.

BC225   With respect to these more complex features, IFRS 16 requires a lessee to disclose any material entity-specific information that is necessary in order to meet the disclosure objective and is not covered elsewhere in the financial statements. IFRS 16 supplements this requirement with a list of user information needs that any additional disclosures should address, and with illustrative examples of disclosures that a lessee might provide in complying with the additional disclosure requirements. The IASB noted that these examples are not exhaustive. Nonetheless, the IASB thinks that the illustrative examples are useful in demonstrating that judgement should be applied in determining the most useful and relevant disclosures, which will depend on a lessee's individual circumstances. In the IASB's view, this approach facilitates the provision of more relevant and useful disclosures by (a) discouraging the use of generic or 'boilerplate' statements; and (b) enabling a lessee to apply judgement to identify the information that is relevant to users of financial statements and focus its efforts on providing that information.

BC226 The IASB acknowledged that, for lessees with many complex, unique or otherwise significant lease arrangements, there are likely to be incremental costs associated with the additional disclosure requirements in paragraph 59 of IFRS 16. However, the IASB thinks that:

(a) the measurement requirements in IFRS 16 are simplified in several ways that are expected to reduce the cost of applying IFRS 16 for a lessee, but also mean that users of financial statements need additional information to understand any significant features that are excluded from the measurement of lease liabilities. For example, a lessee is not required to include payments during optional periods unless those payments are reasonably certain to occur (see paragraphs BC152–BC159). Similarly, a lessee is not required to reassess variable lease payments unless they depend on an index or a rate and there is a change in future lease payments resulting from a change in the reference index or rate (see paragraphs BC188–BC190).

(b) many lessees will not need to provide any additional disclosures as a result of these requirements. This is because the disclosures required by paragraphs 53 and 58 of IFRS 16 are expected to provide sufficient information for those leases that do not have complex or unique features. In the IASB's view, it is appropriate that greater cost will be required in preparing lease disclosures for entities whose leasing activity is particularly complex or unique.

BC227 The IASB considered requiring disclosure of specific information about these more complex features. Such information could have included, for example, the basis and terms and conditions on which variable lease payments and options are determined. However, lessees informed the IASB that this information would be difficult to capture in a meaningful way, particularly for large or diverse lease portfolios. Some users of financial statements also expressed concerns that such an approach could lead to 'boilerplate' compliance statements, which generally do not provide useful information. The approach taken enables lessees to determine the best way to provide information while considering both the costs of providing that information and the information needs of users of financial statements.

Presentation of lessee disclosures in the notes to the financial statements (paragraphs 52 and 54)

BC228 IFRS 16 requires a lessee to disclose information about its leases in a single note or separate section in its financial statements, and to present quantitative information in a tabular format, unless another format is more appropriate. On the basis of feedback from users of financial statements, the IASB thinks that this presentation best conveys an overall understanding of a lessee's lease portfolio and improves the transparency of the information. In the IASB's view, presenting all lessee disclosures in a single note or separate section will often be the most effective way to present information about leases in the systematic manner required by paragraph 113 of IAS 1.

Other approaches considered for lessee disclosure

BC229 Rather than creating specific lease disclosure requirements, the IASB considered an alternative approach whereby a lessee would be required to disclose information about its right-of-use assets applying the disclosure requirements for property, plant and equipment in IAS 16, and information about its lease liabilities applying the disclosure requirements for financial liabilities in IFRS 7. Those supporting this approach thought that it would be consistent with the lessee accounting model in IFRS 16.

BC230 Although noting that there are significant similarities between right-of-use assets and other assets and between lease liabilities and other financial liabilities, the IASB did not adopt this approach because:

(a) it would not provide specific information to users of financial statements about some features of a lessee's lease portfolio that are common in lease arrangements (such as variable payments, options to extend or terminate leases and residual value guarantees). Similarly, it would not provide information about some right-of-use assets and lease liabilities that are not recognised in the balance sheet (such as those arising from short-term leases and leases of low-value assets) as a consequence of some of the simplifications that have been introduced in IFRS 16.

(b) information about a lessee's lease portfolio might be obscured by being included within different disclosures about different types of assets and liabilities. Consequently, this approach might compromise the transparency and usefulness of lease information for users of financial statements.

Lessor: accounting (paragraphs 61–97)

BC231 Paragraphs BC57–BC66 discuss the basis for the IASB's decision to substantially carry forward the IAS 17 lessor accounting requirements. The IASB also decided to carry forward substantially all of the language used in the IAS 17 lessor accounting requirements (with the exception of editorial amendments). Consequently, the significant differences between the lessor accounting requirements in IFRS 16 and those in IAS 17 are primarily a direct consequence of the lessee accounting model in IFRS 16.

Subleases

BC232   IFRS 16 requires an intermediate lessor to account for a head lease and a sublease as two separate contracts, applying both the lessee and lessor accounting requirements. The IASB concluded that this approach is appropriate because in general each contract is negotiated separately, with the counterparty to the sublease being a different entity from the counterparty to the head lease. Accordingly, for an intermediate lessor, the obligations that arise from the head lease are generally not extinguished by the terms and conditions of the sublease.

Classification (paragraph B58)

BC233   The IASB decided that, when classifying a sublease, an intermediate lessor should evaluate the lease by reference to the right-of-use asset arising from the head lease and not by reference to the underlying asset. This is because:

(a)   an intermediate lessor (ie the lessor in a sublease) does not own the underlying asset and does not recognise that underlying asset in its balance sheet. In the IASB's view, the intermediate lessor's accounting should be based on the asset that the intermediate lessor controls (ie the right-of-use asset) and not the underlying asset that is controlled by the head lessor.

(b)   an intermediate lessor's risks associated with a right-of-use asset can be converted into credit risk by entering into a sublease, the term of which covers most or all of the term of the head lease. Accounting for such a sublease as a finance lease (by classifying it by reference to the right-of-use asset) would reflect that risk, because the intermediate lessor would recognise the net investment in the sublease (a receivable) rather than a right-of-use asset.

(c)   if a sublease is for all of the remaining term of the corresponding head lease, the intermediate lessor no longer has the right to use the underlying asset. In the IASB's view, it is appropriate for an intermediate lessor in such a case to derecognise the right-of-use asset and recognise the net investment in the sublease.

BC234   The IASB observed that, in classifying a sublease by reference to the right-of-use asset arising from the head lease, an intermediate lessor will classify more subleases as finance leases than it would have done if those same subleases were classified by reference to the underlying asset. Accordingly, a lessor may classify similar leases (for example, those with a similar lease term for a similar underlying asset) differently depending on whether the lessor owns or leases the underlying asset. However, the IASB concluded that any difference in classification reflects real economic differences. The intermediate lessor only has a right to use the underlying asset for a period of time. If the sublease is for all of the remaining term of the head lease, the intermediate lessor has in effect transferred that right to another party. In contrast, in an operating lease of an owned asset, the lessor would expect to derive economic benefits from the underlying asset at the end of the lease term.

Presentation

BC235 IFRS 16 does not include requirements relating to the presentation of subleases. This is because the IASB decided that specific requirements were not warranted because there is sufficient guidance elsewhere in IFRS. In particular, applying the requirements for offsetting in IAS 1, an intermediate lessor should not offset assets and liabilities arising from a head lease and a sublease of the same underlying asset, unless the financial instruments requirements for offsetting are met. The IASB considered whether to create an exception that would permit or require an intermediate lessor to offset assets and liabilities arising from a head lease and a sublease of the same underlying asset. However, the IASB noted that the exposures arising from those assets and liabilities are different from the exposures arising from a single net lease receivable or lease liability, and concluded that presenting these on a net basis could provide misleading information about an intermediate lessor's financial position, because it could obscure the existence of some transactions.

BC236 For the same reasons, the IASB also decided that an intermediate lessor should not offset lease income and lease expenses relating to a head lease and a sublease of the same underlying asset, unless the requirements for offsetting in IAS 1 are met.

Initial direct costs (paragraphs 69 and 83)

BC237 IFRS 16 defines initial direct costs consistently with the definition of incremental costs of obtaining a contract in IFRS 15. Defining initial direct costs in this way means that the costs incurred by a lessor to obtain a lease are accounted for consistently with costs incurred to obtain other contracts with customers.

Lease modifications (paragraphs 79–80 and 87)

BC238 IFRS 16 requires a lessor—like a lessee—to account for a modification to a finance lease as a separate lease if:

(a) the modification increases the scope of the lease by adding the right for the lessee to use one or more underlying assets; and

(b) the consideration received for the lease increases by an amount commensurate with the stand-alone price for the increase in scope.

This is because, in the IASB's view, such a modification in substance represents the creation of a new lease that is separate from the original lease. This requirement is substantially aligned with equivalent requirements in IFRS 15 that require a seller to account for modifications that add distinct goods or services as separate contracts if those additional goods or services are priced commensurately with their stand-alone selling price.

BC239   For modifications to a finance lease that are not accounted for as a separate lease, IFRS 16 requires a lessor to account for the modification applying IFRS 9 (unless the lease modification would have been classified as an operating lease if the modification had been in effect at the inception date). The IASB expects that this approach will not result in any substantive change to previous lessor accounting for modifications of finance leases. This is because, although IAS 17 did not include requirements relating to lease modifications, the IASB understands that a lessor generally applied an approach that was consistent with the requirements in IFRS 9 (or the equivalent requirements in IAS 39 *Financial Instruments: Recognition and Measurement*) to the net investment in a finance lease.

BC240   IFRS 16 requires a lessor to account for a modification to an operating lease as a new lease from the effective date of the modification, considering any prepaid or accrued lease payments relating to the original lease as part of the lease payments for the new lease. This approach is consistent with the approach required by IFRS 15 if, at the time of a contract modification (that is accounted for as a separate contract), the remaining goods or services to be transferred are distinct from the goods or services already transferred. It is also expected that this approach will not result in any substantive change to previous lessor accounting.

Covid-19-related rent concessions

BC240A   In 2020, when the Board provided lessees with a practical expedient for rent concessions occurring as a direct consequence of the covid-19 pandemic (see paragraphs BC205A–BC205G), the Board considered whether to provide similar practical relief for lessors. Lessors informed the Board that, like lessees, they face many practical challenges associated with large volumes of covid-19-related rent concessions. Having considered the feedback, the Board decided not to provide a practical expedient for lessors for the following reasons:

(a)   IFRS 16 does not specify how a lessor accounts for a change in lease payments that is not a lease modification—this is a consequence of the Board's decision to substantially carry forward the lessor accounting requirements in IAS 17 when it developed IFRS 16 (see paragraphs BC57–BC66). Consequently, to ensure consistency in financial reporting, a practical expedient for lessors would have to include new recognition and measurement requirements. Such requirements might not effectively address all of the practical challenges identified by lessors, and might have unintended consequences. Such requirements would also take time to develop, preventing a practical expedient from being provided in time to be useful.

(b)   Any practical expedient would adversely affect the comparability of, and interaction between, the lessor accounting requirements in IFRS 16 and related requirements in other Standards, thus impairing the quality of information provided to users of financial statements. For example, the lessor accounting requirements in IFRS 16 interact with:

(i) IFRS 9 for finance leases. A lessor applies IFRS 9 in accounting for particular finance lease modifications and, therefore, the accounting for those modifications is aligned with the accounting for modifications to similar financial assets within the scope of IFRS 9.

(ii) IFRS 15 for operating leases. The application of IFRS 16 to operating lease modifications results in outcomes similar to those that result from the application of IFRS 15 to particular service contracts, and the definitions of a modification in IFRS 16 and IFRS 15 are similar.

(c) Although acknowledging the practical challenges lessors face during the pandemic, the Board noted that, unlike lessees, lessors have not recently implemented a new accounting model for their leases.

(d) The Board was of the view that accounting for covid-19-related rent concessions using the existing lessor accounting requirements provides useful information to users of financial statements.

Lessor: classification of leases—leases of land and buildings (2003 and 2009 amendments to IAS 17) (paragraphs B55–B57)

Land element in long-term leases

BCZ241 In 2009, the IASB amended the IAS 17 requirements for classification of the land element in long-term leases. IAS 17 had previously stated that a lease of land with an indefinite economic life would normally be classified as an operating lease. However, in 2009, the IASB removed that statement from IAS 17, having concluded that it might lead to a classification of land that does not reflect the substance of the transaction.

BCZ242 In reaching this conclusion the IASB had considered the example of a 999-year lease of land and buildings. It had noted that, for such a lease, significant risks and rewards associated with the land during the lease term would have been transferred by the lessor despite there being no transfer of title.

BCZ243 The IASB had also noted that the lessor in leases of this type will typically be in a position economically similar to an entity that sold the land and buildings. The present value of the residual value of the property in a lease with a term of several decades would be negligible. The IASB had concluded that the accounting for the land element as a finance lease in such circumstances would be consistent with the economic position of the lessor.

BCZ244 The IASB replaced the previous guidance with a statement (now in paragraph B55 of IFRS 16) that, in determining whether the land element is an operating lease or a finance lease, an important consideration is that land normally has an indefinite economic life.

Allocation of lease payments between land and buildings

BCZ245　In 2003, the IASB introduced into IAS 17 the requirement for a lessor to assess the classification of the land element of a lease separately from the buildings element. The Exposure Draft of the 2003 amendments had further proposed that, whenever necessary for the purposes of classification, the lease payments should be allocated between the land and building elements in proportion to their relative fair values at the inception of the lease. However, respondents to that Exposure Draft had questioned whether the relevant fair values were the fair values of the underlying land and buildings or the fair values of the leasehold interests in the land and buildings.

BCZ246　In redeliberating that Exposure Draft, the IASB noted that an allocation of the lease payments by reference to the relative fair values of the underlying land and buildings would not reflect the fact that land often has an indefinite economic life, and therefore would be expected to maintain its value beyond the lease term. In contrast, the future economic benefits of a building are likely to be used up, at the least to some extent, over the lease term. Therefore, it would be reasonable to expect that the lease payments relating to the building would be set at a level that enabled the lessor not only to make a return on initial investment, but also to recoup the value of the building used up over the term of the lease. In the case of land, the lessor would not normally need compensation for using up the land.

BCZ247　Therefore, the IASB decided to clarify in the 2003 amendments that the allocation of the lease payments is weighted to reflect their role in compensating the lessor, and not by reference to the relative fair values of the underlying land and buildings. In other words, the weighting should reflect the leasehold interest in the land element and the buildings element of the lease at the inception date. In the extreme case that a building is fully depreciated over the lease term, the lease payments would need to be weighted to provide a return plus the full depreciation of the building's value at the inception of the lease. The leasehold interest in the land would, assuming a residual value that equals its value at the inception of the lease, have a weighting that reflects only a return on the initial investment. These clarifications are now in paragraph B56 of IFRS 16.

Impracticability of split between land and buildings

BCZ248　When amending IAS 17 in 2003, the IASB considered how to treat leases for which it is not possible to measure the two elements reliably (for example, because similar land and buildings are not sold or leased separately). One possibility would be to classify the entire lease as a finance lease. However, the IASB noted that it may be apparent from the circumstances that classifying the entire lease as a finance lease is not representationally faithful. In view of this, the IASB decided that when it is not possible to measure the two elements reliably, the entire lease should be classified as a finance lease unless it is clear that both elements should be classified as an operating lease. This requirement is now in paragraph B56 of IFRS 16.

Exception to the requirement to separate the land and buildings elements

BCZ249　When amending IAS 17 in 2003, the IASB discussed whether to allow or require an exception from the requirement to separate the land and buildings elements in cases in which the present value of the land element at the inception of the lease is small in relation to the value of the entire lease. In such cases the benefits of separating the lease into two elements and accounting for each separately may not outweigh the costs. The IASB noted that generally accepted accounting principles in Australia, Canada and the US allow or require such leases to be classified and accounted for as a single unit, with finance lease treatment being used when the relevant criteria are met. The IASB decided to allow land and buildings to be treated as a single unit when the land element is immaterial. This exception is now in paragraph B57 of IFRS 16.

BCZ250　Some stakeholders requested guidance on how small the relative value of the land element needs to be in relation to the total value of the lease. The IASB decided not to introduce a bright line such as a specific percentage threshold. The IASB decided that the normal concepts of materiality should apply.

Lessor: disclosure (paragraphs 89–97)

BC251　IFRS 16 enhances the previous lessor disclosure requirements in IAS 17 to enable users of financial statements to better evaluate the amount, timing and uncertainty of cash flows arising from a lessor's leasing activities. The enhancements are in response to views expressed by some stakeholders that the lessor accounting model in IAS 17 did not provide sufficient information relating to all elements of a lessor's leasing activities. In particular, some investors and analysts requested additional information about a lessor's exposure to residual asset risk.

Table of income (paragraphs 90–91)

BC252　IFRS 16 requires a lessor to disclose information about the different components of lease income recognised during the reporting period. This requirement is similar to the requirement in IFRS 15 for an entity to disclose a disaggregation of revenue recognised during the reporting period into categories.

Information about residual asset risk (paragraph 92(b))

BC253　Academic research, outreach performed and feedback received throughout the project highlighted that the main concern associated with lessor disclosure in IAS 17 was the lack of information about a lessor's exposure to credit risk (associated with the lease payments receivable from the lessee) and asset risk (associated with the lessor's residual interest in the underlying asset). Particularly for leases classified as operating leases, lessors could retain significant residual asset risk and little, if any, information was generally available about that exposure to risk in the financial statements.

BC254　A decline in the market value of, for example, leased equipment and vehicles at a rate greater than the rate the lessor projected when pricing the lease would adversely affect the profitability of the lease. Uncertainty about the residual value of the underlying asset at the end of the lease is often a lessor's primary risk. Accordingly, IFRS 16 requires a lessor to disclose information about how it manages its risk associated with any rights it retains in the underlying asset. The IASB also noted that disclosing information about residual asset risk will also provide users of financial statements with useful information about the distribution of risk for a lessor between credit risk relating to lease payments receivable and residual asset risk related to the interest in the underlying asset.

BC255　The IASB considered requiring a lessor to disclose the fair value of residual assets at each reporting date. However, the IASB concluded that such a requirement could be onerous for lessors. Although it is fundamental to a lessor's business that the lessor manage its exposure to residual asset risk, the IASB thought that the costs associated with having to disclose, and have audited, fair value information about residual assets would outweigh the benefit for users of financial statements.

Information about assets subject to operating leases (paragraphs 95–96)

BC256　The IASB observed that a lessor accounts for assets leased under operating leases similarly to owned assets that are held and used (for example, in the lessor's operations). However, leased and owned assets are typically used for different purposes—ie leased assets generate rental income rather than contributing towards any other revenue-generating activity of the lessor. For that reason, the IASB concluded that users of financial statements would benefit from obtaining information about leased assets that generate rental income separately from owned assets held and used by the lessor. Consequently, IFRS 16 requires a lessor to disaggregate each class of property, plant and equipment into assets subject to operating leases and assets not subject to operating leases.

Maturity analyses (paragraphs 94 and 97)

BC257　IFRS 16 requires a lessor to disclose a maturity analysis of the undiscounted lease payments to be received on an annual basis for a minimum of each of the first five years following the reporting date and a total of the amounts for the remaining years.

BC258　The IASB noted that this requirement would provide more information about a lessor's liquidity risk than previous requirements in IAS 17 (which had, instead, required a maturity analysis showing lease payments due in three bands: within one year, in the second to fifth years and after five years). In the IASB's view, a more detailed maturity analysis will enable users of financial statements to more accurately forecast future lease cash flows and estimate liquidity risk. The IASB does not expect the incremental cost (compared to the IAS 17 requirements) to be significant because lessors typically needed the same information to provide the disclosures required by IAS 17. The IASB also noted that some lessors had already disclosed a maturity analysis relating to lease payments to be received in more detail than was required by IAS 17.

Changes in net investment in finance leases (paragraph 93)

BC259   IFRS 16 requires a lessor to provide a qualitative and quantitative explanation of the significant changes in the net investment in finance leases during the reporting period to allow users of financial statements to understand these significant changes. On the basis of the feedback received, the IASB concluded that this information is useful to users of financial statements and is not otherwise available.

Sale and leaseback transactions (paragraphs 98–103)

BC260   In a sale and leaseback transaction, one entity (the seller-lessee) transfers an asset to another party (the buyer-lessor) and leases back that same asset. IAS 17 included specific requirements on sale and leaseback transactions and the IASB decided that it would be helpful to continue to include specific requirements for sale and leaseback transactions in IFRS 16.

When a sale occurs

BC261   The IASB decided that, within the context of a sale and leaseback transaction, the transfer of an asset is accounted for as a sale only if the transfer meets the requirements in IFRS 15 for the transfer of an asset. In the IASB's view, applying the recognition requirements of IFRS 15 to sale and leaseback transactions will be beneficial for both preparers and users of financial statements because it will increase comparability between sales entered into as part of sale and leaseback transactions and all other sales. The IASB observed that, in considering whether a transaction should be accounted for as a sale and leaseback transaction, an entity should consider not only those transactions structured in the form of a legal sale and leaseback, but should also consider other forms of transactions for which the economic effect is the same as a legal sale and leaseback (for example, a sale and leaseback transaction may be structured in the form of a lease and leaseback).

BC262   In reaching its decisions on sale and leaseback transactions, the IASB noted that:

(a)   the presence of a leaseback (ie the seller-lessee obtaining the right to use the underlying asset for a period of time) does not, in isolation, preclude the seller-lessee from concluding that it has transferred the underlying asset to the buyer-lessor. This is because a lease is different from the purchase or sale of the underlying asset, in that a lease does not transfer control of the underlying asset to the lessee; instead, it transfers the right to control the use of the underlying asset for the period of the lease. Consequently, if there are no features in a sale and leaseback transaction that prevent sale accounting, the buyer-lessor is considered to obtain control of the underlying asset, and immediately transfer the right to control the use of that asset to the seller-lessee for the lease term. The fact that the buyer-lessor purchases the underlying asset from the entity that is the lessee in the subsequent leaseback does not change the buyer-lessor's ability to obtain control of the underlying asset.

(b) many lessors purchase from a third party an asset that will be the subject of a lease only when the terms and conditions of the lease have already been negotiated. The lessor may not receive physical possession of the asset until the end of the lease term (for example, a vehicle could be delivered directly by a manufacturer to the lessee, even though the lessor purchases the vehicle from the manufacturer). Similarly, the buyer-lessor may not receive physical possession of the underlying asset in a sale and leaseback transaction until the end of the lease term. In the IASB's view, these circumstances do not, in isolation, preclude the seller-lessee from concluding that it has transferred the underlying asset to the buyer-lessor. In both cases, the IASB concluded that it is appropriate for the lessor to be deemed to control the asset immediately before the commencement date (if the sale of the underlying asset otherwise meets the requirements in IFRS 15 for the transfer of an asset).

(c) IFRS 15 states that if an entity has a right to repurchase an asset (a call option), the customer does not obtain control of the asset, because the customer is limited in its ability to direct the use of, and obtain substantially all of the remaining benefits from the asset, even though the customer may have physical possession of the asset. Consequently, if the seller-lessee has a substantive repurchase option with respect to the underlying asset, then no sale has occurred.

BC263 The IASB considered, but did not adopt, an alternative approach whereby IFRS 16 would require a higher threshold than the IFRS 15 threshold for recognising a sale within the context of a sale and leaseback transaction because many stakeholders expressed concerns about such an approach. In particular, they questioned the rationale for having a higher threshold for sale accounting in a sale and leaseback transaction than for any other sale. Some were also of the view that different thresholds for achieving sale accounting in IFRS 15 and IFRS 16 would not be operational. The IASB also noted that some of the structuring concerns relating to sale and operating leaseback transactions that had existed under IAS 17 would be substantially reduced by the lessee accounting model in IFRS 16, which requires the recognition of lease assets and lease liabilities by the seller-lessee.

BC264 The IASB considered whether to include additional application guidance in IFRS 16 regarding the determination of whether there is a sale in a sale and leaseback transaction. Such guidance would be intended to help entities to apply the IFRS 15 requirements relating to the satisfaction of performance obligations to sale and leaseback transactions. However, the IASB concluded that this was not necessary because, in its view, the principles in IFRS 15 can be applied appropriately and consistently to sale and leaseback transactions without any further guidance.

BC265   The IASB also decided that, if the transfer of the asset does not meet the requirements for a transfer in IFRS 15, then no sale is recognised by the seller-lessee and no purchase is recognised by the buyer-lessor. Instead, the seller-lessee and buyer-lessor will account for any amounts received or paid relating to the leaseback as a financial asset or a financial liability applying IFRS 9. This is because such a transaction represents, in substance, a financing arrangement.

Gain or loss on a sale and leaseback

BC266   The IASB decided that the gain or loss recognised by a seller-lessee on a completed sale in a sale and leaseback transaction should reflect the amount that relates to the rights transferred to the buyer-lessor. In reaching this decision, the IASB considered requiring the sale element of the transaction (ie the sale of the underlying asset) to be accounted for applying IFRS 15 because, from a legal standpoint, the seller-lessee will often have sold the entire underlying asset to the buyer-lessor. However, from an economic standpoint, the seller-lessee has sold only its interest in the value of the underlying asset at the end of the leaseback—it has retained its right to use the asset for the duration of the leaseback. The seller-lessee had already obtained that right to use the asset at the time that it purchased the asset—the right of use is an embedded part of the rights that an entity obtains when it purchases, for example, an item of property, plant and equipment. Accordingly, in the IASB's view, recognising the gain that relates to the rights transferred to the buyer-lessor appropriately reflects the economics of the transaction.

BC267   The lease payments and the sale price in a sale and leaseback transaction are typically interdependent because they are negotiated as a package. For example, the sale price might be more than the fair value of the asset because the leaseback rentals are above a market rate; conversely the sale price might be less than the fair value because the leaseback rentals are below a market rate. Accounting for the transaction using those amounts could result in the misstatement of gains or losses on disposal of the asset for the seller-lessee and the misstatement of the carrying amount of the asset for the buyer-lessor. Consequently, IFRS 16 requires that if the sale consideration or leaseback rentals are not at market rates, any below-market terms should be accounted for as a prepayment of lease payments and any above-market terms should be accounted for as additional financing provided by the buyer-lessor to the seller-lessee. Similarly, IFRS 16 requires the seller-lessee to measure the right-of-use asset as a proportion of the asset retained as a result of the leaseback—consequently any off-market terms are effectively accounted for in measuring the gain or loss on sale.

Temporary exception arising from interest rate benchmark reform

BC267A In April 2020 the Board published the Exposure Draft *Interest Rate Benchmark Reform—Phase 2* (2020 Exposure Draft), which proposed amendments to specific requirements in IFRS 9, IAS 39, IFRS 7, IFRS 4 and IFRS 16 to address issues that might affect financial reporting during the reform of an interest rate benchmark, including the replacement of an interest rate benchmark with an alternative benchmark rate. The term 'interest rate benchmark reform' refers to the market-wide reform of an interest rate benchmark as described in paragraph 6.8.2 of IFRS 9 (the reform). The Board issued the final amendments to IFRS 9, IAS 39, IFRS 7, IFRS 4 and IFRS 16 in August 2020 (Phase 2 amendments). Paragraphs BC5.287–BC5.293 of the Basis for Conclusions on IFRS 9 and paragraphs BC289–BC295 of the Basis for Conclusions on IAS 39 discuss the background to these amendments.

BC267B   In developing the Phase 2 amendments, the Board also considered the potential effects of the reform on the financial statements of an entity applying the requirements of IFRS Standards, other than IFRS 9 and IAS 39. The Board specifically considered the potential effects arising in the context of IFRS 16.

BC267C   Some leases include lease payments that are referenced to an interest rate benchmark that is subject to the reform as described in paragraph 6.8.2 of IFRS 9. IFRS 16 requires a lessee to include variable lease payments referenced to an interest rate benchmark in the measurement of the lease liability.

BC267D   Applying IFRS 16, modifying a lease contract to change the basis for determining the variable lease payments meets the definition of a lease modification because a change in the calculation of the lease payments would change the original terms and conditions determining the consideration for the lease.

BC267E   IFRS 16 requires that an entity accounts for a lease modification by remeasuring the lease liability by discounting the revised lease payments using a revised discount rate. That revised discount rate would be determined as the interest rate implicit in the lease for the remainder of the lease term, if that rate can be readily determined, or the lessee's incremental borrowing rate at the effective date of the modification, if the interest rate implicit in the lease cannot be readily determined.

BC267F   However, in the Board's view, reassessing the lessee's entire incremental borrowing rate when the modification is limited to what is required by the reform (ie when the conditions in paragraph 105 of IFRS 16 are met) would not reflect the economic effects of the modified lease. Such a requirement might also impose additional cost on preparers, particularly when leases that are referenced to a benchmark rate that is subject to the reform are expected to be amended at different times. This is because preparers would have to determine a new incremental borrowing rate at the effective date of each such lease modification.

BC267G   For the reasons set out in paragraph BC5.306 of the Basis for Conclusions to IFRS 9, the Board provided a practical expedient to account for a lease modification required by the reform applying paragraph 42 of IFRS 16. This practical expedient requires remeasurement of the lease liability using a discount rate that reflects the change to the basis for determining the variable lease payments as required by the reform. This practical expedient would apply to all lease modifications that change the basis for determining future lease payments that are required as a result of the reform (see paragraphs

5.4.6 and 5.4.8 of IFRS 9). For this purpose, consistent with the amendments to IFRS 9, a lease modification required by the reform is a lease modification that satisfies two conditions — the modification is necessary as a direct consequence of the reform and the new basis for determining the lease payments is economically equivalent to the previous basis (ie the basis immediately preceding the modification).

BC267H   The practical expedient provided for lease modifications applies only to the lease modifications required by the reform. If lease modifications in addition to those required by the reform are made, an entity is required to apply the requirements in IFRS 16 to account for all modifications made at the same time, including those required by the reform.

BC267I   In contrast to the amendments for financial assets and financial liabilities in IFRS 9 (see paragraph 5.4.9 of IFRS 9), the Board decided not to specify the order of accounting for lease modifications required by the reform and other lease modifications. This is because the accounting outcome would not differ regardless of the order in which an entity accounts for lease modifications required by the reform and other lease modifications.

BC267J   The Board also considered that, from the perspective of a lessor, lease payments included in the measurement of the net investment in a finance lease may include variable lease payments that are referenced to an interest rate benchmark. The Board decided not to amend the requirements for accounting for modifications to lease contracts from the lessor's perspective. The Board did not make such amendments because, for finance leases, a lessor is required to apply the requirements in IFRS 9 to a lease modification, so the amendments in paragraphs 5.4.5–5.4.9 of IFRS 9 would apply when those modifications are required by the reform. For operating leases, the Board decided that applying the requirements in IFRS 16 for lessors will provide useful information about the modification in terms and conditions required by the reform in the light of the mechanics of the operating lease accounting model.

Effective date and early application (paragraph C1)

BC268   In determining the effective date of IFRS 16, the IASB considered feedback received from preparers about the amount of time they would need to implement the requirements of IFRS 16 in the light of the transition requirements. The IASB also considered feedback received from both users and preparers of financial statements about the interaction of IFRS 16 with the implementation of other recently issued Standards (most notably IFRS 9 and IFRS 15).

BC269   The IASB acknowledged that users of financial statements would generally prefer the effective date of IFRS 16 to be 1 January 2018. This is because users would prefer IFRS 16 to have the same effective date as IFRS 9 and IFRS 15 — this would avoid accounting uncertainty arising from entities implementing new Standards over a number of years. Users of financial statements also noted that, in their view, the effective date of IFRS 16 should be as soon as possible in the light of the significant improvements in financial reporting that will result from the implementation of IFRS 16. Consequently, they did not support a period of three years between publication of IFRS 16 and the effective date.

BC270 However, almost all preparers that provided feedback indicated that an effective date of 1 January 2018 would not give them adequate time to implement IFRS 16, IFRS 9 and IFRS 15. The majority of preparers reported that they would need approximately three years to implement the requirements of IFRS 16 between publication and the effective date.

BC271 The IASB concluded that implementation of IFRS 16 by 1 January 2018 would not be achievable for all preparers taking into consideration that entities are also required to implement IFRS 9 and IFRS 15 in that period of time. Consequently, the IASB decided that an entity is required to apply IFRS 16 for annual reporting periods beginning on or after 1 January 2019.

BC272 The IASB also decided to permit early application of IFRS 16 for entities that apply IFRS 15 on or before the date of initial application of IFRS 16. In reaching this decision, the IASB noted that early application would allow any entity that wishes to apply IFRS 16 at the same time as IFRS 9 and IFRS 15 to do so. The IASB also noted that early application might be beneficial to an entity that adopts IFRS for the first time between the publication of IFRS 16 and its effective date. However, the IASB decided to limit early application of IFRS 16 to entities that also apply IFRS 15. This is because some of the requirements of IFRS 16 depend on an entity also applying the requirements of IFRS 15 (and not the Standards that were superseded by IFRS 15).

Transition (paragraphs C2–C20)

Definition of a lease (paragraphs C3–C4)

BC273 The IASB decided that an entity is not required to reassess whether contracts are, or contain, leases on transition to IFRS 16. Consequently, an entity can choose to apply the requirements of IFRS 16 to all existing contracts that met the definition of a lease applying the requirements of IAS 17 and IFRIC 4. Similarly, an entity does not need to apply IFRS 16 to existing contracts that did not meet the definition of a lease applying the requirements of IAS 17 and IFRIC 4.

BC274 Preparers provided feedback that it could be costly for them to reassess all of their existing contracts using the definition of a lease requirements in IFRS 16. The IASB observed that it envisages only a limited number of scenarios in which application of the lease definition requirements in IFRIC 4 would result in a different outcome from the application of the lease definition guidance in IFRS 16. The IASB identified a small population of contracts that would be classified as leases applying IFRIC 4 but as service contracts applying IFRS 16, and none for which the converse is expected to be true. The IASB expects that the consequence of an entity not reassessing its existing contracts applying the lease definition requirements in IFRS 16 would be the recognition of slightly more leases on transition to IFRS 16 than would otherwise be the case. On this basis, the IASB concluded that the costs of requiring entities to reassess existing contracts applying the lease definition guidance in IFRS 16 would not be justified.

Lessees (paragraphs C5–C13)

BC275 The IASB decided that, on transition, a lessee should apply IFRS 16 using either of the following methods:

(a) retrospectively to each prior reporting period presented applying IAS 8 *Accounting Policies, Changes in Accounting Estimates and Errors*; or

(b) retrospectively with the cumulative effect of initially applying IFRS 16 recognised as an adjustment to the opening balance of retained earnings (or other component of equity, as appropriate) of the annual reporting period that includes the date of initial application. The IASB decided that, applying this approach, a lessee is permitted to apply some optional practical expedients on a lease-by-lease basis (see paragraphs BC282–BC287).

BC276 The IASB decided not to require a full retrospective approach for all lessees because the costs of such an approach could be significant and would be likely to outweigh the benefits. A full retrospective approach would require entities to determine the carrying amounts of all leases in existence at the earliest comparative period as if those leases had always been accounted for applying IFRS 16 and to restate comparative information. That could be impracticable for entities that have thousands of leases. Nonetheless, the IASB did not wish to prohibit entities from applying a full retrospective approach, because that approach would provide better information to users of financial statements than other approaches. Consequently, the IASB decided to permit entities to choose to apply IFRS 16 fully retrospectively with restatement of comparative information.

BC277 The IASB also rejected a prospective approach (ie applying IFRS 16 only to leases that commence after the date of transition). Although such an approach would be the least costly for preparers to apply, the information provided would not be beneficial for users of financial statements, particularly for entities that enter into long-term operating leases. For example, some entities enter into operating leases with lease terms of 20 to 30 years. For such entities, a user would not obtain the full benefits of IFRS 16 or full comparability of lease accounting for up to 30 years after implementing the new requirements, because the accounting for leases during that period would not be consistent. This is because right-of-use assets and lease liabilities would not be recognised for leases that were previously classified as operating leases applying IAS 17.

Retrospective application with the cumulative effect recognised at the date of initial application

BC278 In the 2010 and 2013 Exposure Drafts, the IASB had proposed simplifying the full retrospective approach by introducing a number of practical expedients on transition (some of which are included in IFRS 16). However, feedback from preparers indicated that, although helpful, the practical expedients proposed in the 2010 and 2013 Exposure Drafts would mitigate little of the implementation challenge of a retrospective transition approach. Furthermore, although users of financial statements find the trend information from restated comparative periods useful, many also acknowledged that the costs of full retrospective application with restatement of comparative information would be significant for many lessees and might not be justified.

BC279 In the light of this feedback, the IASB decided to allow an entity to apply IFRS 16 retrospectively (with some practical expedients), with the cumulative effect of initially applying IFRS 16 recognised at the date of initial application (referred to as the 'cumulative catch-up' transition method). The IASB observed that the cumulative catch-up transition method responds to feedback from stakeholders by eliminating the need to restate financial information in comparative periods on transition and thereby reducing costs. The cost of restating comparative data could be significant because the implementation of IFRS 16 affects a number of elements of the financial statements.

BC280 Because comparative information will not be restated under the cumulative catch-up transition method, the IASB decided to require additional disclosures to help users of financial statements to understand the effect of applying IFRS 16 for the first time. Consequently, IFRS 16 requires an entity using the cumulative catch-up transition method to disclose information on transition about leases that were previously classified as operating leases. This disclosure requirement replaces the requirements of paragraph 28(f) of IAS 8—ie a lessee applying the cumulative catch-up transition method is not required to disclose the amount of the adjustment to each financial statement line item that is normally required by IAS 8 on initial application of a new Standard.

BC281 The IASB observed that the cumulative catch-up transition method and the required disclosures mean that a lessee does not need to operate two different sets of accounting requirements at any point. Consequently, the IASB concluded that this approach would substantially reduce the overall cost of implementing IFRS 16 while enabling information to be provided to users of financial statements to explain the effect of the change in accounting for leases previously classified as operating leases.

Leases previously classified as operating leases

BC282 To reduce the costs of implementing IFRS 16, the IASB decided to introduce a number of additional practical expedients relating to leases previously classified as operating leases for a lessee that adopts the cumulative catch-up transition method.

Right-of-use assets (paragraph C8(b))

BC283 Determining the measurement of the right-of-use asset under a retrospective approach could be onerous, because it would require a lessee to determine the initial measurement of the lease liability for leases that may have commenced many years before transition to IFRS 16. Consequently, the 2010 Exposure Draft proposed that the right-of-use asset should be measured at an amount equal to the lease liability on transition, adjusted for any impairment. However, many stakeholders noted that this approach would increase lease-related costs artificially in the years immediately following transition to IFRS 16 (because the depreciation charge would typically be higher than if IFRS 16 had always been applied). These stakeholders thought that the artificial increase in the depreciation charge immediately after transition would distort the financial information provided to users of financial statements.

BC284   In response to this feedback, the 2013 Exposure Draft proposed that a lessee calculate right-of-use assets in a similar manner to a full retrospective approach, but using information available at the date of transition. However, many preparers thought that the cost of capturing historical information, such as lease start dates and historical payment schedules, would still be significant—particularly for entities with a high volume of leases.

BC285   On the basis of the feedback received, the IASB concluded that it is not possible to provide one method of measuring the right-of-use asset on transition that would (a) avoid an artificial higher expense related to leases following initial application of IFRS 16; and (b) address the cost concerns of preparers. Consequently, the IASB decided to permit lessees to choose, on a lease-by-lease basis, how to measure the right-of-use asset on transition to IFRS 16. Paragraph C8(b) permits a lessee either to measure the right-of-use asset as if IFRS 16 had always been applied or to measure the right-of-use asset at an amount equal to the lease liability (adjusted by the amount of any previously recognised prepaid or accrued lease payments).

BC286   Although acknowledging that a choice of approach could result in reduced comparability, the IASB concluded that permitting a choice of measurement approaches for the right-of-use asset on transition to IFRS 16 should be largely 'self-policing' in terms of application. This is because the effect of the less costly option (measuring the right-of-use asset equal to the lease liability, adjusted by the amount of any previously recognised prepaid or accrued lease payments) is an increase in operating expense (ie higher depreciation) for the remainder of the term of the lease. The IASB concluded that a lessee is expected to select the less costly option only for leases for which the costs of applying a more accurate transition approach outweigh the benefit of achieving a 'correct' post-transition income statement. The IASB expects this to apply to leases that are high in volume but low in value but not to leases such as long-term leases of property or large equipment.

Other practical expedients

BC287　To further ease the costs on transition, the IASB also decided to allow a lessee to elect to use one or more of the following practical expedients.

Practical expedient	Rationale
Portfolio approach	
A lessee may apply a single discount rate to a portfolio of leases with reasonably similar characteristics.	The IASB expects that permitting a lessee to apply a single discount rate to a portfolio of similar leases on transition will provide cost savings to lessees and will not have a significant effect on reported information. For leases for which the right-of-use asset is measured at an amount equal to the lease liability (adjusted by the amount of any previously recognised prepaid or accrued lease payments) on the date of initial application (see paragraph BC285), this practical expedient will enable a lessee to apply the transition requirements collectively to portfolios of leases of similar assets in similar economic environments with the same end date.
Previously recognised onerous lease provisions	
A lessee may rely on its assessment of whether leases are onerous applying IAS 37 immediately before the date of initial application and adjust the right-of-use asset at the date of initial application by the amount of any provision for onerous leases recognised immediately before the date of initial application. This approach is an alternative to performing an impairment review.	It could be costly for a lessee to perform an impairment review of each of its right-of-use assets on transition to IFRS 16. In addition, any onerous operating lease liability identified applying IAS 37 is likely to reflect impairment of the right-of-use asset. Accordingly, the IASB concluded that this practical expedient will provide a cost saving to lessees on initial application of IFRS 16 without any significant effect on reported information.

continued...

...continued

Practical expedient	Rationale
Leases for which the lease term ends within 12 months	
A lessee may elect not to apply the requirements of IFRS 16 to leases for which the term ends within 12 months of the date of initial application.	For a lessee that does not restate its comparative information, leases for which the term ends within 12 months of the date of initial application are very similar in effect to those captured by the short-term lease exemption and thus similar considerations apply (see paragraphs BC87–BC97). In addition, feedback from lessees indicated that this practical expedient will provide a significant cost saving on initial application of IFRS 16.
Initial direct costs	
A lessee may exclude initial direct costs from the measurement of the right-of-use asset at the date of initial application.	The IASB expects that including initial direct costs in the measurement of right-of-use assets would not have a significant effect on reported information. Consequently, the IASB decided that the cost for lessees of requiring initial direct costs to be identified and included in the measurement of right-of-use assets would outweigh the benefits in terms of reported information.
Use of hindsight	
A lessee may use hindsight in applying IFRS 16, for example, in determining the lease term if the contract contains options to extend or terminate the lease.	Permitting lessees to apply hindsight on transition to IFRS 16 will result in useful information, particularly with respect to areas of judgement such as the determination of lease term for contracts that contain options to extend or terminate a lease. Feedback from stakeholders also indicated that permitting the use of hindsight will make initial application of IFRS 16 somewhat simpler for lessees.

Leases previously classified as finance leases (paragraph C11)

BC288   The lessee accounting model in IFRS 16 is similar to the accounting requirements for finance leases in IAS 17. Consequently, IFRS 16 does not contain detailed transition requirements for leases previously classified as finance leases if a lessee elects to apply the cumulative catch-up transition approach. For these leases, IFRS 16 requires a lessee to measure the carrying amount of the right-of-use asset and the lease liability at the date of initial application of IFRS 16 as the carrying amount of the lease asset and lease liability immediately before that date applying the finance lease accounting requirements in IAS 17.

Lessors (paragraphs C14–C15)

BC289   The lessor accounting requirements in IFRS 16 are substantially unchanged from those in IAS 17. Consequently, the IASB decided that a lessor is not required to make any adjustments on transition and should account for its leases applying IFRS 16 from the date of initial application (except for intermediate lessors in a sublease—see paragraphs BC290–BC291).

BC290   Subleases that were classified by an intermediate lessor as operating leases applying IAS 17 may be classified as finance leases applying IFRS 16. This is because IFRS 16 requires an intermediate lessor to evaluate the classification of a sublease by reference to the right-of-use asset arising from the head lease and not by reference to the underlying asset as was required by IAS 17. If an intermediate lessor were to continue to apply previous operating lease accounting to these subleases, it would recognise the right-of-use asset arising from the head lease, despite the fact that, in effect, it no longer has a right to use the underlying asset. The IASB thought that this could be misleading for users of financial statements.

BC291   Consequently, IFRS 16 requires an intermediate lessor to reassess a sublease that was classified as an operating lease applying IAS 17 at the date of initial application to determine whether the sublease should be classified as an operating lease or a finance lease applying IFRS 16, and to account for it accordingly.

Sale and leaseback transactions before the date of initial application (paragraphs C16–C18)

BC292   In response to feedback from stakeholders, the IASB decided to provide transition requirements for sale and leaseback transactions that are consistent with the general transition requirements for all leases. Consequently, a seller-lessee should not perform any retrospective accounting specific to the sale element of a sale and leaseback transaction on transition to IFRS 16. A seller-lessee is required to account for the leaseback on transition to IFRS 16 in the same way as it accounts for any other lease that is in existence at the date of initial application.

BC293   The IASB considered requiring a lessee to reassess historic sale and leaseback transactions to determine whether the transfer would have been accounted for as a sale applying IFRS 15. However, the IASB concluded that the costs of performing the reassessment would not be justified.

BC294   The IASB also decided that a seller-lessee should apply the approach to gain or loss recognition on sale and leaseback transactions in IFRS 16 (described in paragraph BC266) only to sale and leaseback transactions entered into after the date of initial application of IFRS 16. The IASB concluded that the costs of applying a retrospective approach would outweigh the benefits in terms of reported information.

Consequential amendments

Investment property

BC295   IFRS 16 amends the scope of IAS 40 by defining investment property to include both owned investment property and investment property held by a lessee as a right-of-use asset. A summary of the IASB's considerations in developing the amendments to the scope of IAS 40 is described in paragraphs BC178–BC181.

Business combinations

BC296   The IASB decided that when the acquiree in a business combination is a lessee, the acquirer should measure the acquiree's lease liability at the present value of the remaining lease payments as if the acquired lease were a new lease at the date of acquisition. The acquiree's right-of-use asset should be measured at an amount equal to the lease liability, with an adjustment for any off-market terms present in the lease.

BC297   The IASB considered whether an acquirer should be required to follow the general principle in IFRS 3 *Business Combinations* and measure the acquiree's right-of-use assets and lease liabilities at fair value on the date of acquisition. However, in the IASB's view, the costs associated with measuring lease assets and lease liabilities at fair value would outweigh the benefits because obtaining fair value information might be difficult and, thus, costly. The IASB also noted that, when the acquiree is a lessee, the requirements of IFRS 3 (as amended by IFRS 16) for the measurement of lease assets and lease liabilities would result in the recognition of a net carrying amount for the lease at the date of acquisition that approximates the fair value of the lease at that date.

BC298   The IASB also considered whether to require an acquirer to recognise assets and liabilities relating to any off-market terms if an acquiree is the lessee in a lease for which either the short-term lease or low-value asset lease exemptions described in paragraph 5 of IFRS 16 are applied. Such a requirement would be consistent with the general principles of IFRS 3, under which assets and liabilities relating to contracts with off-market terms are recognised separately in the balance sheet and not subsumed within goodwill on acquisition. However, the IASB observed that the effect of any such off-market terms would rarely be material for short-term leases and leases of low-value assets. Consequently, it decided not to include this requirement in IFRS 3.

Transition for first-time adopters of IFRS

BC299   The IASB considered whether the transition relief for lessees in paragraphs C2–C19 of IFRS 16 should also apply to lessees applying IFRS 1 *First-time Adoption of International Financial Reporting Standards*.

BC300   The IASB decided that a first-time adopter of IFRS should be permitted to apply some of the transition reliefs available to an existing IFRS preparer. This is because first-time adopters will face issues similar to those faced by existing IFRS preparers, and the transition requirements provide relief when first applying the requirements of IFRS 16. However, the IASB decided that a first-time adopter is not permitted to apply those transition reliefs that depend upon the lease having previously been accounted for applying IAS 17. This is because the IASB is not aware of, nor is it possible to consider, the accounting for leases required by every other GAAP. The amounts recognised in accordance with other GAAPs could be significantly different from the amounts recognised applying IAS 17 and IFRS 16.

BC301 The IASB also decided that a first-time adopter should apply IFRS 16 at the date of transition to IFRSs as defined in IFRS 1. Accordingly, a first-time adopter is not able to apply the transition relief provided in IFRS 16, which permits a lessee not to restate comparative information. A first-time adopter is required to restate comparative information applying IFRS 1 for all elements of its financial statements. For this reason, the IASB concluded that it would be inconsistent and impractical for a first-time adopter to not restate comparative information about leases in its first IFRS financial statements.

BC302 The IASB also decided not to permit a first-time adopter of IFRS to apply the transition relief in IFRS 16 for leases classified as finance leases applying IAS 17. The transition relief in IFRS 16 requires an IFRS preparer to measure the carrying amount of the right-of-use asset and the lease liability at the date of initial application of IFRS 16 as the carrying amount immediately before that date applying IAS 17. The rationale for this requirement is that the requirements of IAS 17 for leases classified as finance leases were similar to the requirements of IFRS 16. However, as described in paragraph BC300 above, the IASB cannot consider the accounting required by every other GAAP for leases that would have been classified as finance leases applying IAS 17. Consequently, the IASB concluded that carrying forward a first-time adopter's previous accounting could be misleading to users of financial statements, and could result in a lack of comparability with other IFRS preparers, perhaps for many years after first implementing IFRS.

Comparison with FASB decisions

BC303 The IASB and the FASB reached different decisions about the lessee accounting model. The differences largely affect leases that were previously classified as operating leases. There are a number of other differences between IFRS 16 and the decisions made by the FASB, primarily because of the different decisions reached on the lessee accounting model. The following paragraphs set out the main differences between IFRS 16 and the decisions made by the FASB.

Lessee accounting model

BC304 IFRS 16 applies a single lessee accounting model, which views all leases recognised in the balance sheet as providing finance. The IASB's reasons are explained in paragraphs BC41–BC56. The FASB decided upon a dual lessee accounting model that requires a lessee to classify leases in a similar manner to the previous US GAAP requirements for distinguishing between operating leases and capital leases. Under the FASB lessee accounting model, a lessee:

(a) accounts for finance leases (ie leases previously classified as capital leases) similarly to the IASB model; and

(b) accounts for operating leases by:

  (i) recognising right-of-use assets and lease liabilities;

  (ii) measuring lease liabilities in the same way as they would be measured applying IFRS 16, but without a requirement to reassess variable lease payments;

  (iii) recognising a single lease expense typically on a straight-line basis over the lease term; and

  (iv) presenting total cash paid within operating activities in the statement of cash flows.

Subleases

BC305 IFRS 16 requires an intermediate lessor to classify a sublease as either an operating lease or a finance lease by reference to the right-of-use asset arising from the head lease and not by reference to the underlying asset. The IASB's reasons are explained in paragraphs BC233–BC234. The FASB decided to require an intermediate lessor to determine the classification of the sublease by reference to the underlying asset.

Sale and leaseback transactions

BC306 In a sale and leaseback transaction, IFRS 16 requires a seller-lessee to recognise only the amount of any gain or loss on sale that relates to the rights transferred to the buyer-lessor. The IASB's reasons are explained in paragraph BC266. The FASB decided to require a seller-lessee to account for any gain or loss on sale consistently with the guidance that would apply to any other sale of an asset.

Presentation, disclosure and transition

BC307 There are a number of differences between the presentation, disclosure and transition requirements of IFRS 16 and the decisions made by the FASB. These differences are primarily a consequence of either the differences between the lessee accounting models or differences between other requirements of IFRS and US GAAP that are relevant to leases (for example, differences in the general disclosure requirements applicable to financial liabilities).

Recognition exemption for leases of low-value assets

BC308 IFRS 16 permits a lessee not to apply the recognition requirements to leases for which the underlying asset is of low value. The IASB's reasons are explained in paragraphs BC98–BC104. The FASB decided not to include such an exemption.

Reassessment of variable lease payments

BC309   IFRS 16 requires a lessee to reassess variable lease payments that depend on an index or a rate when there is a change in the future lease payments resulting from a change in the reference index or rate. The IASB's reasons are explained in paragraphs BC188–BC190. The FASB decided not to include any requirements to reassess variable lease payments.

Lessor accounting

BC310   Both the IASB and the FASB decided to substantially carry forward the previous lessor accounting requirements in IAS 17 and Topic 840 respectively. Consequently, there are a number of differences between the lessor accounting requirements in IFRS 16 and the decisions made by the FASB that are effectively carried forward from previous lessor accounting requirements.

Dissenting Opinion

Dissent of Wei-Guo Zhang

DO1   Mr Zhang supports the lessee accounting requirements in IFRS 16. However, Mr Zhang voted against publication of IFRS 16 for the following reasons:

(a)   firstly, Mr Zhang does not support retaining a dual accounting model for lessors while requiring a single accounting model for lessees; and

(b)   secondly, Mr Zhang disagrees with the recognition exemption for leases of low-value assets.

Lessor accounting

DO2   Mr Zhang agrees with the right-of-use lessee accounting model and believes that it should be applied symmetrically to lessor accounting. Mr Zhang is of the view that a lessor should recognise a lease receivable and a residual asset for all leases for which a lessee recognises a lease liability and a right-of-use asset. He believes that it is conceptually inconsistent to require a single accounting model for lessees while retaining a dual accounting model for lessors.

DO3   Mr Zhang agrees with the IASB's view set out in paragraphs BC35–BC36 that a lessor's right to receive lease payments arising from a lease is a financial asset. Mr Zhang believes that this financial asset should be reflected as such in a lessor's financial statements, and thus Mr Zhang disagrees with the conclusions reached in paragraphs BC57–BC66 regarding the costs and benefits of changing the lessor accounting model in IAS 17. This is because the nature of the risks associated with a financial asset are different from those of the underlying asset, and information about those different risks is of great importance to users of a lessor's financial statements.

DO4   Additionally, Mr Zhang is concerned about the complexity and potential for misapplication of the dual lessor accounting model. Mr Zhang acknowledges that this dual model is consistent with the requirements in IAS 17. However, Mr Zhang notes that one of the biggest criticisms of IAS 17 was the potential for complexity and structuring inherent in a dual model. Mr Zhang believes that two transactions that are economically the same could be structured in a way that results in those transactions being accounted for differently under the dual lessor accounting model.

Leases of low-value assets

DO5   Mr Zhang also disagrees with the recognition exemption for leases of low-value assets of a lessee because he does not believe that these leases should be treated differently from a lessee's other leases.

DO6   Mr Zhang believes that the recognition exemption for leases of low-value assets is unnecessary. This is because, in his view, the materiality guidance in IFRS and the recognition exemption for short-term leases in IFRS 16 should be sufficient to identify those leases for which the costs of recognising assets and liabilities would outweigh the benefits. When leases of low-value assets are material in the aggregate, Mr Zhang believes that recognising assets and liabilities has significant benefit. Mr Zhang also thinks that the costs of recognising assets and liabilities would be mitigated because an entity would have a record of leases of low-value assets for internal control purposes. The only incremental cost might be the cost associated with applying a discount rate to the lease payments.

DO7   Mr Zhang believes that the recognition exemption has the potential to set an inappropriate precedent by implying that the materiality guidance in IFRS is insufficient to capture contracts for which the costs of applying IFRS outweigh the benefits. Mr Zhang believes that a similar argument could be used to justify many other exemptions from applying the requirements in IFRS.

DO8   Mr Zhang also notes that the recognition exemption for leases of low-value assets could create the same tension between leasing and buying low-value assets that existed applying the requirements of IAS 17. Mr Zhang is concerned that entities that require material amounts of low-value assets would be incentivised to lease those assets rather than buy them in order to achieve off balance sheet accounting.

DO9   Finally, Mr Zhang is concerned about the operationality of determining whether an asset is of 'low value'. Mr Zhang notes that paragraph BC100 states that 'at the time of reaching decisions about the exemption in 2015, the IASB had in mind leases of underlying assets with a value, when new, in the order of magnitude of US$5,000 or less.' Mr Zhang does not think that this reference to US$5,000 is appropriate. He notes that the same asset, when new, can have a different value in different markets, and that the value of a particular asset, when new, can change over time. Moreover, many countries or regions use different currencies, and exchange rates for those currencies change over time. Mr Zhang acknowledges that the exemption is optional and, thus, that entities are not required to apply the exemption. Nonetheless, Mr Zhang is of the view that stating a quantitative amount based on a particular currency may cause difficulties in applying the exemption among entities in different jurisdictions over time.

Appendix
Amendments to the Basis for Conclusions on other Standards

This appendix describes the amendments to the Basis for Conclusions on other Standards that the IASB made when it finalised IFRS 16.

* * * * *

The amendments contained in this appendix when this Standard was issued in 2016 have been incorporated into the Basis for Conclusions of IAS 40 included in this volume.

IASB documents published to accompany

IFRS 17

Insurance Contracts

The text of the unaccompanied standard, IFRS 17, is contained in Part A of this edition. Its effective date when issued was 1 January 2021. In June 2020 the Board issued *Amendments to IFRS 17* which deferred the effective date to 1 January 2023. The text of the Accompanying Guidance on IFRS 17 is contained in Part B of this edition. This part presents the following documents:

BASIS FOR CONCLUSIONS

APPENDICES TO THE BASIS FOR CONCLUSIONS

A Summary of changes since the 2013 Exposure draft

B Amendments to the Basis for Conclusions on other IFRS Standards

C List of amendments issued in 2020

Contents

...continued

continued...

...continued

APPENDIX A

Summary of changes since the 2013 Exposure Draft

APPENDIX B

Amendments to the Basis for Conclusions on other IFRS Standards

APPENDIX C

List of amendments issued in 2020

Basis for Conclusions on
IFRS 17 *Insurance Contracts*

This Basis for Conclusions accompanies, but is not part of, IFRS 17. It summarises the considerations of the International Accounting Standards Board (the Board) in developing IFRS 17. Individual Board members gave greater weight to some factors than to others. The Board also published an Effects Analysis which describes the likely costs and benefits of IFRS 17.

The need to change previous accounting and history of the project

BC1   The previous IFRS Standard on insurance contracts, IFRS 4 *Insurance Contracts*, allowed entities to use a wide variety of accounting practices for insurance contracts, reflecting national accounting requirements and variations in those requirements. The differences in accounting treatment across jurisdictions and products made it difficult for investors and analysts to understand and compare insurers' results. Most stakeholders, including insurers, agreed on the need for a common global insurance accounting standard even though opinions varied as to what it should be. Long-duration and complex insurance risks are difficult to reflect in the measurement of insurance contracts. In addition, insurance contracts are not typically traded in markets and may include a significant investment component, posing further measurement challenges. Some previous insurance accounting practices permitted under IFRS 4 did not adequately reflect the true underlying financial positions or performance arising from these insurance contracts. To address these issues, the Board undertook a project to make insurers' financial statements more useful and insurance accounting practices consistent across jurisdictions. IFRS 17 completes this project.

History of the project

BC2   The Board's predecessor organisation, the International Accounting Standards Committee, began a project on insurance contracts in 1997. The Board was created in 2001 and included an insurance project in its initial work plan. Because it was not feasible to complete the project in time for the many entities that would adopt IFRS Standards in 2005, the Board split the project into two phases.

BC3   The Board completed Phase I in 2004 by issuing IFRS 4, which:

(a)   made limited improvements to then existing accounting practices for insurance contracts; and

(b)   required an entity to disclose information about insurance contracts.

BC4   However, the Board had always intended to replace IFRS 4 because it permits a wide range of practices. In particular, IFRS 4 included a 'temporary exemption' that explicitly stated that an entity need not ensure that its accounting policies are relevant to the economic decision-making needs of users of financial statements or that such accounting policies are reliable. As a result, there was wide diversity in the financial reporting of insurance contracts across entities applying IFRS Standards, and within some entities' financial statements. In addition, some of that financial reporting did not provide useful information about those contracts to users of financial statements.

BC5   IFRS 17 is the outcome of the second phase of the Board's project. It is a comprehensive Standard for accounting for insurance contracts. It is the result of the proposals set out in the following consultation documents previously published by the Board:

(a)   the 2007 Discussion Paper, which set out the Board's preliminary views on the main components of an accounting model for an entity's rights and obligations (assets and liabilities) arising from an insurance contract. The Board received 162 comment letters about those preliminary views.

(b)   the 2010 Exposure Draft of proposals for a Standard on insurance contracts. The Board received 251 comment letters about the proposals.

(c)   the 2013 Exposure Draft of revised proposals on targeted aspects of the proposed Standard. The Board received 194 comment letters about the proposals.

BC6   When developing IFRS 17, the Board consulted with multiple stakeholders over many years. In addition to considering comment letters on the 2007 Discussion Paper, the 2010 Exposure Draft and the 2013 Exposure Draft, the Board developed IFRS 17 after considering:

(a)   input from the Insurance Working Group, a group of senior financial executives of insurers, analysts, actuaries, auditors and regulators established in 2004;

(b)   four rounds of field work conducted in 2009, 2011, 2013 and 2016, which helped the Board to better understand some of the practical challenges of applying the proposed insurance model; and

(c)   more than 900 meetings with individuals and with groups of users and preparers of financial statements, actuaries, auditors, regulators and others to test proposals and to understand affected parties' concerns about the 2010 and 2013 Exposure Drafts.

Amendments to IFRS 17

BC6A   After IFRS 17 was issued in May 2017, the Board undertook activities to support entities and monitor their progress in implementing the Standard. These activities included establishing a Transition Resource Group for IFRS 17 to discuss implementation questions, and meeting with stakeholders affected by the changes introduced by IFRS 17, including preparers and users of financial statements, auditors and regulators. These activities helped the Board to understand the concerns and challenges that arose for some entities while implementing the Standard. In the light of these activities, the Board concluded that the costs of proposing targeted amendments to IFRS 17 to address concerns and challenges could be justified if those amendments would not change the fundamental principles of the Standard. The Board considered suggestions to amend the Standard in relation to 25 topics.

BC6B To maintain the benefits of IFRS 17, the Board decided that any amendments to IFRS 17 must not:

(a) result in a significant loss of useful information for users of financial statements compared with the information that would have resulted from applying IFRS 17 as issued in May 2017; or

(b) unduly disrupt implementation already under way.

BC6C The 2019 Exposure Draft *Amendments to IFRS 17* set out the targeted amendments that the Board proposed, considering the criteria described in paragraph BC6B. The Board received 123 comment letters about the proposed amendments. Having considered the feedback on the 2019 Exposure Draft, the Board issued *Amendments to IFRS 17* in June 2020.

The need for a new approach

BC7 The Board considered whether the following approaches could be used to account for insurance contracts:

(a) applying generally applicable IFRS Standards (see paragraphs BC9–BC12); and

(b) selecting an existing model for accounting for insurance contracts (see paragraphs BC13–BC15).

BC8 The paragraphs that follow explain why the Board rejected these approaches and developed a new Standard for insurance contracts.

Applying generally applicable IFRS Standards

BC9 Insurance contracts are excluded from the scope of many existing IFRS Standards that might otherwise apply to such contracts, including Standards on:

(a) revenue (see IFRS 15 *Revenue from Contracts with Customers*);

(b) liabilities (see IAS 37 *Provisions, Contingent Liabilities and Contingent Assets*); and

(c) financial instruments (see IFRS 9 *Financial Instruments* and IAS 32 *Financial Instruments: Presentation*).

BC10 If the Board extended the scope of existing IFRS Standards to include insurance contracts, an entity would need to:

(a) identify service components and investment components within each premium that it receives. The Board decided that it would be difficult for an entity to routinely separate components of an insurance contract, and setting requirements to do so would result in complexity. Such separation would also ignore interdependencies between components, with the result that the sum of the values of the components may not always equal the value of the contract as a whole, even on initial recognition.

(b) account for the service component in applying IFRS 15. As noted in paragraph BC26(a), the Board decided that the results of IFRS 17 are broadly consistent with those of IFRS 15, subject to requiring additional remeasurement. But the Board also decided that:

    (i) the specific requirements of IFRS 17 are necessary to determine how to account for particular aspects of insurance contracts.

    (ii) the additional remeasurement is necessary to give relevant information; for example, information about the financial aspects of insurance contracts that are more significant for many insurance contracts than for contracts in the scope of IFRS 15. In particular, when applying IFRS 17, changes in financial assumptions will be recognised earlier for some insurance contracts than they would be when applying IFRS 15.

(c) account for its liability for incurred claims in applying IAS 37. IAS 37 would require the measurement of the liability to reflect current estimates of cash flows and a current market-based discount rate, which would reflect risks specific to the liability. This measurement would be broadly consistent with the requirements in IFRS 17 for the measurement of the liability for incurred claims.

(d) apply the financial instruments Standards to the investment component. If an entity accounted for the investment components of an insurance contract in the same way it accounts for other financial liabilities, it would, consistent with IFRS 17, not recognise principal deposited as revenue and would account separately for embedded options and guarantees when so required by IFRS 9. However, it would also:

    (i) measure the investment components at fair value through profit or loss or at amortised cost, as applicable. The Board decided that measuring all interrelated cash flows using the same current value measurement required by IFRS 17 provides more useful information.

    (ii) measure the investment components so that the fair value of the investment component would be no less than the amount payable on demand, discounted from the first date the payment could be required (the deposit floor). This is discussed in paragraphs BC165–BC166.

    (iii) recognise, for investment components measured at fair value through profit or loss, the costs of originating contracts as an expense when incurred, with no corresponding gain at inception. For investment components measured at amortised cost, incremental transaction costs relating to the investment component would reduce the initial carrying amount of that liability. The treatment of insurance acquisition cash flows applying IFRS 17 is discussed in paragraphs BC175–BC184K.

BC11 Overall, applying generally applicable IFRS Standards would provide useful information for users of financial statements and would be relatively easy to apply to insurance contracts for which there is no significant variability in outcomes and no significant investment component. This is because, in those cases, the issues arising with IFRS 15 and IFRS 9 discussed above would not occur. However, simply applying generally applicable Standards would be difficult and would produce information of limited relevance for other types of insurance contracts. In contrast, the model required by IFRS 17 can be applied to all types of insurance contracts.

BC12 Although the Board has rejected an approach that requires routine separation of components of an insurance contract, IFRS 17 requires some components of an insurance contract to be separated if the cash flows attributable to the individual components are distinct. In those cases, the problems created by interdependencies are less significant. The requirements for separating and measuring non-insurance components of an insurance contract are discussed in paragraphs BC98–BC114.

Selecting an existing model

BC13 Some stakeholders, mainly from the United States (US), suggested that the Board develop an approach based on existing US generally accepted accounting principles (US GAAP) for insurance contracts. The Board rejected this suggestion because such an approach would be based on the type of entity issuing the contract and on numerous standards developed at different times. In addition, although US GAAP is widely used as a basis for accounting for insurance contracts, it was developed in the context of US insurance products and the US regulatory environment. Further, when IFRS 17 was developed, the US Financial Accounting Standards Board was working on a project to improve, simplify and enhance the financial reporting requirements for long-term insurance contracts issued by entities applying US GAAP.

BC14 The Board also decided that it would be inappropriate to account for insurance contracts using other national insurance accounting models because many such models:

(a) do not use current estimates of all cash flows;

(b) require no explicit risk measurement, even though risk is the essence of insurance;

(c) fail to reflect the time value or the intrinsic value of some or all embedded options and guarantees, or else they measure time value or intrinsic value in a way that is inconsistent with current market prices;

(d) lack global acceptance; and

(e) present an entity's financial performance, particularly for life insurance, in a manner difficult for users of financial statements to understand.

BC15   The Board considered whether regulatory requirements already being used by insurers could form the basis of the requirements in IFRS 17 for financial reporting purposes. However, the Board noted that:

(a)   although some regulatory requirements require current market-consistent measurement of future cash flows, their focus is on solvency, and they do not consider reporting of financial performance. Hence, for example, the measurement required by Solvency II, a regulation adopted by the European Union, is broadly consistent with the measurement of the fulfilment cash flows required by IFRS 17. However, Solvency II does not consider the determination or reporting of an entity's financial performance over time, which under IFRS 17 is achieved through the contractual service margin.

(b)   regulatory requirements may include simplifications and practical expedients that are appropriate in the context of the regulatory regime in which they were developed, but which may not be appropriate in an international financial reporting environment.

(c)   regulatory reporting frequently includes jurisdiction-specific requirements, which accommodate issues specific to that jurisdiction, including policy objectives.

Overview of the approach taken in the Standard

BC16   IFRS 17 reflects the Board's view that an insurance contract combines features of both a financial instrument and a service contract. In addition, many insurance contracts generate cash flows with substantial variability over a long period. To provide useful information about these features, the Board developed an approach that:

(a)   combines current measurement of the future cash flows with the recognition of profit over the period that services are provided under the contract (see paragraphs BC18–BC26);

(b)   presents insurance service results (including presentation of insurance revenue) separately from insurance finance income or expenses (see paragraphs BC27–BC37); and

(c)   requires an entity to make an accounting policy choice at a portfolio level of whether to recognise all insurance finance income or expenses in profit or loss or to recognise some of that income or expenses in other comprehensive income (see paragraphs BC38–BC49).

BC17   The Board developed this approach rather than a fair value model. Fair value is the price that would be received to sell an asset or paid to transfer a liability in an orderly transaction between market participants at the measurement date (see IFRS 13 *Fair Value Measurement*). However, many stakeholders suggested that such an approach places too much emphasis on hypothetical transactions that rarely happen. Therefore, IFRS 17 requires an entity to measure insurance contracts in a way that reflects the fact that entities generally fulfil insurance contracts directly over time by providing services to policyholders, rather than by transferring the contracts to a third party.

Measurement of insurance contracts and recognition of profit

BC18   An insurance contract typically combines features of a financial instrument and a service contract in such a way that those components are interrelated. Hence, the Board concluded that entities should not unbundle the components and account for them separately, except as discussed in paragraphs BC98–BC114. Instead, the Board developed requirements to account for both the financial and service components without unbundling them. Measurement at current value is consistent with the requirements for comparable financial instruments. Recognising profit at the same time services are provided is consistent with IFRS 15. Therefore, IFRS 17 requires an entity to measure insurance contracts at:

(a)   a current risk-adjusted present value that incorporates all reasonable and supportable information available without undue cost or effort about the future cash flows, in a way that is consistent with observable market information (the fulfilment cash flows (see paragraphs BC19–BC20)); and

(b)   an amount representing the unearned profit in the contracts relating to services still to be provided (the contractual service margin (see paragraphs BC21–BC26)).

Fulfilment cash flows (paragraphs 33–37 of IFRS 17)

BC19   The current value of the fulfilment cash flows allocated to a group of insurance contracts includes:

(a)   a current, unbiased estimate of the future cash flows expected to fulfil the insurance contracts. The estimate of future cash flows reflects the perspective of the entity, provided that the estimates of any relevant market variables are consistent with the observable market prices for those variables (see paragraphs BC147–BC184N).

(b)   an adjustment for the time value of money and the financial risks associated with the future cash flows, to the extent that the financial risks are not included in the estimate of the future cash flows. For example, if the cash flows being discounted are an estimate of the probability-weighted average (the mean), that mean itself does not include an adjustment for risk, and any financial risk (ie uncertainty relating to financial risk on whether the ultimate cash flows will equal the mean) will be included in the discount rate (a risk-adjusted rate). If, in contrast, the cash flows being discounted are an estimate of the mean with an adjustment to reflect uncertainty related to financial risk, the discount rate will be a rate that reflects only the time value of money (ie not adjusted for risk). The discount rates are consistent with observable current market prices for instruments whose cash flow characteristics are consistent with the estimates of the cash flows of the insurance contracts. The discount rates also exclude the effects of any factors that influence observable market prices but are not relevant to the estimates of the cash flows of the insurance contracts (see paragraphs BC185–BC205B).

(c)   an adjustment for the effects of non-financial risk, referred to as a risk adjustment for non-financial risk. The risk adjustment for non-financial risk is defined as the compensation that the entity requires for bearing the uncertainty about the amount and timing of the cash flows that arises from non-financial risk (see paragraphs BC206–BC217).

BC20   The underlying objective of the Board's approach to the measurement of the fulfilment cash flows is to achieve consistent measurement with current market information when possible. That market-consistent measurement includes any options and guarantees embedded in the insurance contracts. The Board decided that the use of a market-consistent current value measurement model for the fulfilment cash flows is desirable because it provides the most relevant information about:

(a)   fulfilment cash flows, by incorporating all reasonable and supportable information available without undue cost or effort on a timely basis; and, hence,

(b)   changes in the fulfilment cash flows, including changes in the economic value of options and guarantees embedded in insurance contracts. This means that there is no need for a separate liability adequacy test.

Contractual service margin on initial recognition (paragraphs 38 and 47 of IFRS 17)

BC21   On initial recognition, the contractual service margin is an amount that reflects the excess of the consideration charged for a group of insurance contracts over the risk-adjusted expected present value of the cash outflows expected to fulfil the group of contracts and any insurance acquisition cash flows incurred before the recognition of the group of contracts. It depicts the profit that the entity expects to earn by providing the services promised under the contracts in the group over the duration of the coverage of the group.[1] Accordingly, IFRS 17 does not permit the entity to recognise that excess as a gain on initial recognition, but instead requires the entity to recognise that gain as the entity satisfies its obligation to provide services over the coverage period. However, if a group of contracts is onerous on initial recognition, IFRS 17 requires an entity to recognise a loss immediately (see paragraph BC284). Accordingly, if a group of contracts is onerous on initial recognition, no contractual service margin would be recognised. This reflects the Board's view that the carrying amount of a group of insurance contracts should reflect the obligation of the entity to provide future service, and that

---

1   In June 2020, the Board amended IFRS 17 to require an entity to recognise an amount of the contractual service margin in profit or loss in each period to reflect the insurance contract services provided in that period (see paragraphs BC283A–BC283J).

amount should be at least equal to the fulfilment cash flows. This is consistent with the approach to the recognition of profits and losses on contracts with customers required in IFRS 15.

Subsequent measurement and recognition of profit (paragraphs 40–46 of IFRS 17)

BC22   After initial recognition, IFRS 17 requires the measurement of the fulfilment cash flows to reflect estimates based on current assumptions, for the reasons set out in paragraphs BC20 and BC155.

BC23   After initial recognition, IFRS 17 also requires an entity to recognise specified changes in the contractual service margin for a group of insurance contracts. These changes depict changes in the future profit to be earned from providing services under the contracts, and include:

(a)   changes in the estimates of the fulfilment cash flows that relate to future service (see paragraphs BC222–BC269C);

(b)   the effect of the time value of money on the contractual service margin (see paragraphs BC270–BC276E) and, for insurance contracts with direct participation features, changes in the entity's share of the underlying items (see paragraphs BC238–BC263);

(c)   the effect of changes in foreign currency exchange rates on the contractual service margin (see paragraphs BC277–BC278); and

(d)   the profit earned in the period from providing services (see paragraphs BC279–BC283J).

BC24   Although the service and financial components of an insurance contract are not separated for measurement on initial recognition, the Board decided that changes in the carrying amount of the insurance contract have different information value, depending on the nature of the change. As a result of the combined treatment of the changes in the fulfilment cash flows and the changes in the contractual service margin:

(a)   changes in estimates that relate to future service only affect the measurement of the total liability[2] to the extent they make a group of insurance contracts onerous (except as described in paragraph BC275);

(b)   changes in estimates relating to current period and past period service are recognised in profit or loss (see paragraphs BC224(c) and BC232–BC236); and

(c)   changes in estimates arising from assumptions that relate to financial risks, including the effects of changes in discount rates, are recognised in profit or loss, or profit or loss and other comprehensive income, in the period in which the change occurs (except for some such changes for insurance contracts with direct participation features (see paragraphs BC238–BC247)).

---

2   Insurance contracts can be assets or liabilities depending on the timing of their cash flows. For simplicity, this Basis generally describes the carrying amount as a liability.

BC25   The total carrying amount of a group of insurance contracts (ie the fulfilment cash flows plus the contractual service margin) can be regarded as having the following components:

(a)   a liability for remaining coverage, being the portion of the fulfilment cash flows that relates to coverage that will be provided under the contracts in future periods, plus the remaining contractual service margin, if any;[3] and

(b)   a liability for incurred claims, being the fulfilment cash flows for claims and expenses already incurred but not yet paid.

BC26   Overall, the measurement required by IFRS 17 results in:

(a)   the measurement of the liability for remaining coverage and the resulting profit and revenue recognition being broadly consistent with IFRS 15, except that:

(i)   for insurance contracts without direct participation features — the measurement is updated for changes in financial assumptions; and

(ii)   for insurance contracts with direct participation features — the measurement is updated for changes in the fair value of the items in which the entity and the policyholder participate; and

(b)   the component relating to incurred claims being measured broadly consistently with IAS 37.

Presentation of insurance revenue (paragraphs 83, 85 and B120–B127 of IFRS 17)

BC27   The determination of revenue under previous insurance accounting practices varied across jurisdictions and often resulted in the presentation of revenue amounts that could not be easily compared with the information reported by other entities, either in the insurance industry or in other industries. Two common factors that resulted in this lack of comparability were:

(a)   the accounting of deposits as revenue; and

(b)   the recognition of revenue on a cash basis.

BC28   In contrast, IFRS 17 requires entities to present revenue for insurance contracts determined in a way that is broadly consistent with the general principles in IFRS 15. Consistent with that Standard, an entity depicts revenue for the transfer of promised coverage and other services at an amount that reflects the consideration to which the entity expects to be entitled in exchange for the services. This means that the entity:

(a)   excludes from insurance revenue any investment components; and

---

3   In June 2020, the Board amended the definition of a liability for remaining coverage to include amounts for which an entity will provide investment-return service or investment-related service (see paragraphs BC283A–BC283J).

(b)   recognises insurance revenue in each period as it satisfies the performance obligations in the insurance contracts.

BC29   IFRS 17, consistent with IFRS 15, requires that the statement of financial position reports the asset or liability for a group of insurance contracts, and the statement(s) of financial performance reports the progress towards satisfaction of the performance obligations in the contracts:

(a)   IFRS 15 establishes the amount of revenue to be recognised each period and adjusts the contract asset or contract liability at the start of the period by the amount of revenue recognised to measure the contract asset or contract liability at the end of the period; and

(b)   IFRS 17 requires a measurement model that establishes the carrying amount of the asset or liability for the group of insurance contracts at the start and end of the reporting period. The amount of insurance revenue presented is determined by reference to these two measurements.

BC30   The Board decided that determining insurance revenue in this way makes the financial statements of entities that issue insurance contracts more understandable and more comparable with other entities. It also increases comparability among entities that issue insurance contracts. Both this approach and the simpler premium allocation approach (see paragraphs BC288–BC295) allocate customer consideration in a way that reflects the transfer of services provided under the contract. As a result, the insurance revenue presented for contracts accounted for using the general requirements in IFRS 17 can be meaningfully combined with the insurance revenue for contracts accounted for using the premium allocation approach. Many users of financial statements use measures of revenue to provide information about the volume of business and gross performance.

BC31   The Board considered the view that lack of comparability between the presentation of insurance results and revenue amounts reported by entities in other sectors would not be a significant disadvantage to users of financial statements of entities that issue insurance contracts. In the view of some, users of financial statements do not typically compare the results of entities that issue insurance contracts with those of other entities. Instead, they argue that many users of financial statements that specialise in the insurance sector rely on the disaggregated information in the notes to the financial statements. Therefore, those who held this view expected users of financial statements to derive little value from the information reported in the statement(s) of financial performance because:

(a)   the accounting models for life insurance contracts, unlike those for other transactions, typically measure the profit from insurance contracts directly through the changes in the insurance contract liability. In contrast, the profit from other transactions is measured as the difference between revenue and expenses.

(b)   measures of total premiums that include both revenue and investment components are considered by some to be the most meaningful measure of gross performance and growth for insurance contracts. Such measures give information about the total increase in assets under management. However, those with this view accept that this measure is inconsistent with usual concepts of revenue and therefore accept that this information should not be presented in the statement(s) of financial performance. Applying IFRS 17, this would instead be reported in the notes to the financial statements and elsewhere.

BC32   The Board rejected this view. The Board hopes that the changes brought in by IFRS 17 will enable a wider range of users to understand financial statements of entities that issue insurance contracts and compare them with financial statements of other entities. Alternative approaches to the presentation of revenue considered but also rejected by the Board are discussed in paragraphs BC332–BC339.

Excluding investment components from insurance revenue and incurred claims (paragraph 85 of IFRS 17)

BC33   An investment component is an amount that the insurance contract requires the entity to repay to the policyholder even if an insured event does not occur.[4] Such obligations, if not included within an insurance contract, would be measured and presented in accordance with IFRS 9. The Board decided that when an investment component is interrelated with the insurance components in an insurance contract, it is appropriate to measure both the investment component and the insurance component in accordance with IFRS 17, for the reasons set out in paragraphs BC10(a) and BC108. However, the Board decided that it would not faithfully represent the similarities between financial instruments within the scope of IFRS 9 and investment components embedded in insurance contracts within the scope of IFRS 17 if an entity were to present the receipts and repayments of such investment components as insurance revenue and incurred claims. To do so would be equivalent to a bank recognising a deposit as revenue and its repayment as an expense. Accordingly, the requirements of the Standard exclude such investment components from insurance revenue and incurred claims.[5]

BC34   To achieve this without separating the investment component for measurement purposes, the Board decided to identify the investment components only at the time revenue and incurred claims are recognised, and to exclude the amounts so identified. In doing this, the Board considered defining the investment component as (a) the amount that the contract requires to be repaid when no insured event occurs, rather than (b) the

---

4   In June 2020, the Board amended the definition of an investment component to clarify that an investment component is the amounts that an insurance contract requires the entity to repay to a policyholder in all circumstances, regardless of whether an insured event occurs (see paragraph BC34A).

5   In June 2020, the Board amended paragraph B123 of IFRS 17 to clarify that changes caused by cash flows from loans to policyholders do not give rise to insurance revenue. This treatment is similar to the treatment of investment components.

amount that would be repaid even if an insured event does not occur. For example, if the entity pays the higher of an account balance and a fixed amount in the event of a policyholder's death, using the definition in (a) the whole of the payment that results from the policyholder's death would be regarded as relating to the insurance component rather than to the investment component. Using the definition in (a) has the practical advantage that an entity would need to identify cash flows relating to an investment component only if it made a payment in the absence of an insured event. However, the Board decided that defining an investment component in this way does not faithfully represent the fact that the amount accumulated in the account balance through deposits by the policyholder is paid to the policyholder in all circumstances, including in the event of the policyholder's death. In the Board's view, the insurance benefit is the additional amount that the entity would be required to pay if an insured event occurs.

Amendments to IFRS 17—definition of an investment component

BC34A   In June 2020, the Board amended the definition of an investment component to clarify that an investment component is the amounts that an insurance contract requires the entity to repay to a policyholder in all circumstances, regardless of whether an insured event occurs (see paragraph BC34). A discussion at a meeting of the Transition Resource Group for IFRS 17 suggested that the wording of the definition before the amendment did not capture fully the explanation in paragraph BC34.

Recognising revenue as the entity satisfies its performance obligations (paragraphs 83 and B120–B127 of IFRS 17)

BC35   The Board noted the inherent challenges for some insurance contracts in identifying and measuring progress in satisfying the performance obligations during the period; for example, for stop-loss contracts and for contracts that include financial guarantees. However, the liability for remaining coverage represents the obligation to provide coverage for a future period and other services needed to fulfil the contract. As a result, recognising insurance revenue to the extent of a reduction in the liability for remaining coverage, adjusted to eliminate changes that do not relate to the satisfaction of the performance obligation, would faithfully represent the entity's performance in providing services. The adjustments to the liability for remaining coverage exclude from total insurance revenue the part of the change in the liability for remaining coverage that does not relate to cash flows expected to generate revenue; for example, insurance finance income or expenses, and losses on groups of onerous contracts. These adjustments ensure that the total insurance revenue presented over the duration of the group of insurance contracts is the same as the premiums received for services, adjusted for a financing component.

BC36   The Board considered whether each period's coverage should be treated as a separate performance obligation or whether the coverage for the entire contract should be regarded as a single performance obligation that would be satisfied over time. When considering the principle from IFRS 15, the Board concluded that the obligation to provide coverage in any particular part of the entire coverage period would generally not be a separate performance obligation, and the coverage and services provided over the whole duration of the contract would generally be treated as a single performance obligation that is satisfied over time. Hence, a change in the pattern of expected cash flows results in the entity updating its measure of progress and adjusting the amount of revenue recognised accordingly. That approach is also consistent with the requirements in IFRS 17 to adjust the contractual service margin for changes in estimates of cash flows relating to future service (see paragraphs BC222–BC226).

BC37   A consequence of the decision to measure the satisfaction of the entity's performance obligations in each period using the change in the measurement of the liability for remaining coverage during each period is that insurance revenue will be recognised partly on the basis of the expected claims and benefits. Some expressed concern about this and hence questioned whether the service provided by an insurance contract was adequately represented by the change in the measurement of an entity's obligation. Rather, they thought that revenue (the gross amount) ought to be determined independently of changes in the obligation (the net amount). One way of doing this would be to use time-based methods for measuring progress, such as those typically used for other contracts. However, the Board concluded that time-based methods of allocating premiums would not reflect the fact that the value of the services provided in each period may differ. Instead, the Board noted that the amount reported as the liability for remaining coverage represents the value of the obligation to provide services. The Board therefore concluded that the reduction in the liability for remaining coverage is a reasonable representation of the value of the performance obligation to provide services that was satisfied in the period. The reduction in the liability for remaining coverage includes an allocation of the contractual service margin to reflect the services provided in the period. That allocation reflects the quantity of benefits provided and duration of contracts in a group. The other changes in the liability for remaining coverage that represent revenue for the period are measured using current assumptions. The total change in the liability for remaining coverage that represents revenue therefore faithfully represents the amount of insurance revenue that the entity is entitled to.

Presentation of insurance finance income or expenses (paragraphs 87–92 and B128–B136 of IFRS 17)

BC38   Insurance finance income or expenses comprise the changes in the carrying amount of the asset or liability for a group of insurance contracts arising from:

(a)   the effect of the time value of money and changes in the time value of money; and

(b)   the effect of financial risks and changes in financial risks; but

© IFRS Foundation

(c) excluding any such effects for groups of insurance contracts with direct participation features that would normally adjust the contractual service margin but do not do so because the group of insurance contracts is onerous. These effects are recognised as part of the insurance service result, for the reasons given in paragraph BC247.

BC39 The definition of financial risk in IFRS 17 is unchanged from that in IFRS 4. To provide clarity on the treatment of assumptions about inflation when applying IFRS 17, the Board decided to specify that for the purposes of IFRS 17:

(a) assumptions about inflation based on an index of prices or rates or on prices of assets with inflation-linked returns are financial assumptions; and

(b) assumptions about inflation based on an entity's expectation of specific price changes are non-financial assumptions.

BC40 The Board has not considered whether this specification would be appropriate outside the context of IFRS 17.

BC41 Consistent with the requirement in IAS 1 *Presentation of Financial Statements* to present finance costs separately, an entity is required to present insurance finance income or expenses separately from the insurance service result. Doing so provides useful information about different aspects of the entity's performance.

BC42 IFRS 17 requires entities to make an accounting policy choice for each portfolio on how to present insurance finance income or expenses. Such income or expenses for a portfolio of insurance contracts is either all included in profit or loss or is disaggregated between profit or loss and other comprehensive income. If disaggregated, the amount in profit or loss is based on a systematic allocation of the expected total finance income or expenses over the duration of the groups of insurance contracts in the portfolio. The systematic allocation is based on the characteristics of the insurance contracts, without reference to factors that do not affect the cash flows expected to arise under the contracts. For example, the allocation of the insurance finance income or expenses should be based on expected recognised returns on assets only if those expected recognised returns affect the cash flows of the contracts. (In specific circumstances, an amount that eliminates accounting mismatches is included in profit or loss rather than an amount based on a systematic allocation (see paragraph BC48)).

BC43 The Board decided to allow entities to choose an accounting policy for the presentation of insurance finance income or expenses to balance the sometimes competing demands of understandability and comparability. By allowing an accounting policy choice, the Board:

(a) acknowledges that it could be appropriate for an entity to disaggregate the effect of changes in assumptions that relate to financial risks between profit or loss and other comprehensive income by presenting the insurance finance income or expenses in profit or loss using a systematic allocation based on the characteristics of the insurance contract;

(b) but also:

(i) acknowledges that an inherent feature of such a systematic allocation in profit or loss is that accounting mismatches are likely to arise; hence, an accounting policy choice allows entities to avoid such mismatches by permitting them to present the insurance finance income or expenses using a current measurement basis; and

(ii) allows entities to avoid the costs and complexity of using other comprehensive income when the benefits of doing so do not outweigh those costs (because permitting entities to present the total insurance finance income or expenses in a period in profit or loss allows entities to avoid additional calculations to derive separate amounts to be presented in profit or loss and other comprehensive income).

BC44 The Board noted that, in selecting an accounting policy, entities would need to apply judgement regarding the policy's relative benefits and costs. The Board decided to require entities to make the accounting policy choice for each portfolio because a key factor in making the choice will be what assets the entity regards as backing the insurance contracts. The Board received feedback that many entities regard the choice of strategies for assets backing insurance contracts to be driven by the differences between portfolios of insurance contracts. Hence, an entity might hold financial assets measured at fair value through other comprehensive income for one portfolio, and for another portfolio, hold financial assets measured at fair value through profit or loss. Accordingly, an option applied to portfolios of insurance contracts would allow entities to reduce accounting mismatches. The Board concluded that even if it were to allow an accounting policy choice, entities within the same jurisdiction are likely to remain comparable because they are likely to issue similar products and adopt similar asset strategies for those products. Thus, the entities are likely to make similar accounting policy choices.

BC45 Alternative approaches to the presentation of insurance finance income or expenses considered but rejected by the Board are discussed in paragraphs BC340–BC342C.

Basis of disaggregation (paragraphs B129–B136 of IFRS 17)

BC46 Allowing an accounting policy choice on whether to present in profit or loss insurance finance income or expenses using a systematic allocation raises the question of what constitutes a systematic allocation.

BC47 The Board considered a cost-based presentation approach and discussed various practical methods of determining a cost measurement basis for the insurance finance income or expenses. However, the Board concluded that some potentially appropriate approaches, such as some projected crediting methods, could not be described as cost measurements. Instead, the Board decided to set an objective for disaggregating the insurance finance income or expenses of a systematic allocation based on the characteristics of the insurance contracts. The Board considered whether this disaggregation objective alone would be sufficient, given the variety of contracts and the need to tailor more specific requirements to the features of different contracts. However, the Board concluded that a lack of prescribed methods might result in a lack of comparable information. Therefore the Board set out constraints on how a systematic allocation should be determined in paragraphs B130–B133 of IFRS 17.

BC48 An inherent feature of any systematic allocation of insurance finance income or expenses based on the characteristics of a group of insurance contracts is potential accounting mismatches between the insurance contracts and the finance income or expenses on assets held by the entity. The only way of completely eliminating such accounting mismatches for all insurance contracts would be to measure both the insurance contracts and the assets using the same measure of current value and to include all finance income or expenses in profit or loss. The Board rejected such an approach for the reasons set out in paragraph BC340. However, for insurance contracts for which there can be no economic mismatch with the assets held, it is possible to eliminate accounting mismatches between the insurance contracts and the assets in a different way, by using the current period book yield. The current period book yield is the change in the carrying amount of assets regarded as backing the insurance contracts, recognised in profit or loss for the period. The Board concluded that this approach is appropriate only for groups of insurance contracts for which there can be no economic mismatch with the assets held; ie groups of insurance contracts with direct participation features as defined in IFRS 17 if the entity holds the underlying items. The Board concluded this approach is inappropriate for other insurance contracts for the reasons set out in paragraph BC342.

BC49 If an entity fulfils its obligations under the contracts in the group, the systematic allocation required by IFRS 17 means that the cumulative amount recognised in other comprehensive income over the duration of the group equals zero. To achieve this outcome if an entity transfers a group of insurance contracts before the fulfilment of all the contracts in the group, IFRS 17 requires that the cumulative amount recognised in other comprehensive income by the date of the transfer should be reclassified to profit or loss at the date of the transfer. The Board considered whether the same requirement should apply to groups of insurance contracts to which the current period book yield applies. However, the Board noted that the cumulative amount recognised in other comprehensive income over the duration of a group that is not transferred will not necessarily equal zero under the current period book yield. The Board concluded that to achieve the objective of the current period book yield, which is to eliminate accounting mismatches between the insurance contracts and the assets held, no amounts should be reclassified from other comprehensive income to profit or loss on a transfer of a group beyond any such amounts arising because of the change in carrying amount of the assets recognised in profit or loss in the period of the transfer.

Pervasive issues

BC50   In developing the approach outlined in paragraph BC16, the Board considered the following pervasive issues:

(a)   the level of aggregation;

(b)   accounting mismatches; and

(c)   the complexity of the Standard.

The level of aggregation

BC51   An entity's rights and obligations arise from individual contracts with policyholders. However, a fundamental aspect of much insurance activity is that the entity issues a large number of similar contracts knowing that some will result in claims and others will not. The large number of contracts reduces the risk that the outcome across all the contracts will differ from that expected by the entity. This aspect of insurance activity, combined with the requirements of IFRS 17 that require different timing of recognition of gains and losses (for example losses on onerous contracts are recognised earlier than gains on profitable contracts), means that the level of aggregation at which contracts are recognised and measured is an important factor in the representation of an entity's financial performance.

BC52   In reaching a decision on the level of aggregation, the Board balanced the loss of information inevitably caused by the aggregation of contracts with the usefulness of the resulting information in depicting the financial performance of an entity's insurance activities and with the operational burden of collecting the information (see paragraphs BC115–BC139T).

Accounting mismatches

BC53   The Board decided to set the scope of IFRS 17 as insurance contracts rather than insurance entities for the reasons set out in paragraphs BC63–BC64. The Board was aware that the development of an accounting model for insurance contracts would inevitably result in possible accounting mismatches because of the different basis of accounting for assets and liabilities in other Standards. Nonetheless the Board has minimised the extent of accounting mismatch, when possible, while recognising this limitation. Particular consideration was given to potential or perceived accounting mismatches arising from:

(a)   the presentation of insurance finance income or expenses (see paragraphs BC38–BC49);

(b)   risk mitigation activities (see paragraphs BC54–BC55);

(c)   the measurement of underlying items for insurance contracts with direct participation features (see paragraph BC56); and

(d)   reinsurance (see paragraph BC298).

BC54   Some stakeholders noted that the approach to accounting for risk mitigation activities in IFRS 17 does not fully eliminate accounting mismatches. In particular:

(a)   some requested that the Board create a hedge accounting solution for insurance contracts without direct participation features;

(b)   some noted that the Board is researching a model for dynamic risk management, and suggested aligning the projects; and

(c)   some noted that the application of the risk mitigation requirements on a prospective basis would not eliminate accounting mismatches for relationships that started before the date of initial application.

BC55   The Board's decisions on risk mitigation techniques related to insurance contracts with direct participation features reduce the accounting mismatches that were introduced by the variable fee approach by providing an option to align the overall effect of the variable fee approach more closely to the model for other insurance contracts (see paragraphs BC250–BC256H). However, the Board concluded that it would not be appropriate to develop a bespoke solution for all hedging activities for insurance contracts, noting that such a solution should form part of a broader project. The Board did not want to delay the publication of IFRS 17 pending finalisation of that broader project. The Board also concluded that a prospective basis was necessary for the application of the risk mitigation requirements on transition, for the reasons set out in paragraph BC393.

BC56   Insurance contracts with direct participation features are measured by reference to the fair value of the underlying items (see paragraphs BC238–BC249D). This measurement reflects the investment-related nature of the contracts. Applying IFRS Standards, many underlying items will also be measured at fair value. The Board also decided to amend some IFRS Standards to enable additional underlying items to be measured at fair value (see paragraph BC65(c)). However, there could still be underlying items that cannot be measured at fair value applying IFRS Standards; for example, other insurance contracts or net assets of a subsidiary. The Board noted that all such mismatches would be eliminated only if all assets and liabilities were recognised and measured at fair value.

Complexity of the Standard

BC57   The Board acknowledges that the following important aspects of IFRS 17 add complexity to the Standard, compared with the original proposals in the 2007 Discussion Paper:

(a)   the existence and treatment of the contractual service margin, including:

(i)   recognising it as profit over the coverage period of the contracts (see paragraph BC59);

(ii)   adjusting it for changes in estimates of cash flows relating to future service, with different requirements for different types of insurance contracts (see paragraph BC60); and

      (iii)   the consequent need for a specified level of aggregation (see paragraphs BC51–BC52).

  (b)   the statement(s) of financial performance presentation, including:

      (i)   the presentation of revenue on a basis consistent with IFRS 15 (see paragraph BC61); and

      (ii)   the option to disaggregate insurance finance income or expenses between profit or loss and other comprehensive income (see paragraph BC62).

BC58   For each aspect, the Board was persuaded by stakeholder feedback that the requirements in IFRS 17 are necessary to provide useful information about insurance contracts issued by an entity.

BC59   The recognition of the contractual service margin as profit over the coverage period, rather than as a gain immediately on initial recognition of the group of insurance contracts, adds complexity for preparers because they will need to track and allocate the contractual service margin. This method of recognising the contractual service margin also may add complexity for users of financial statements because of the need to understand the amounts recognised in the statement of financial position and in the statement(s) of financial performance. However, the Board concluded that recognition of the profit in the group of insurance contracts over the coverage period is necessary to represent faithfully an entity's financial performance over the coverage period.

BC60   The requirement to adjust the contractual service margin for changes in estimates relating to future service increases complexity for both users and preparers of financial statements. For users of financial statements, complexity may arise from the need to understand how gains and losses arising from events of previous years affect current-year profit or loss. For preparers of financial statements, complexity arises from the need to identify the changes in estimates of future cash flows that adjust the contractual service margin separately from changes in estimates that do not adjust the contractual service margin. For both, a particular source of complexity arises from the distinction between changes in estimates relating to future service and changes relating to past service. That distinction may be subjective and may vary according to when the entity makes the change in estimate. An entity adjusts the contractual service margin for a change in estimates of cash flows that is made before the cash flows occur. In contrast, the entity recognises an experience adjustment in profit or loss and does not adjust the contractual service margin if there is no change in estimate before the cash flows occur. However, in the light of the feedback received, the Board concluded that adjusting the contractual service margin for changes in future service provides relevant information about the unearned profit in the group of insurance contracts and is consistent with the approach in IFRS 15 (see paragraphs BC222–BC224).

BC61   The requirement to present insurance revenue in the financial statements increases complexity for preparers because entities must identify investment components and exclude them from insurance revenue and from incurred claims presented in the statement of profit or loss. Some preparers expressed concern about the operational challenges of compliance. However, the Board decided that these potential challenges are outweighed by the following benefits of the requirements:

(a)   distinguishing insurance revenue from investment components provides significant benefits for users of financial statements. For example, many users have indicated that if entities reported investment components as revenue, they would overstate revenue and could distort performance measures such as combined ratios. Such reporting would also hamper comparability between insurers and entities in other industries.

(b)   measuring insurance revenue to depict the consideration the entity expects to receive in exchange for providing services would increase consistency between the measurement and presentation of insurance revenue and the revenue from other types of contracts with customers within the scope of IFRS 15. Such a measurement would reduce the complexity of financial statements overall.

BC62   Requiring an entity to make an accounting policy choice on how to present insurance finance income or expenses introduces complexity for both preparers of financial statements, who have to assess what choice to make, and for users of financial statements who have to understand what choice has been made and its implications on the amounts presented. The Board had proposed requiring insurance finance income or expenses to be disaggregated between profit or loss and other comprehensive income. However, the Board was persuaded that the balance between the costs and benefits of such disaggregation will vary significantly across entities depending on the type of insurance contracts that they issue and the information that the users of their financial statements find most useful. The Board therefore concluded that it should leave the assessment of that balance to be made by the entity.

Scope of the Standard and definition of insurance contracts (paragraphs 3–8A and B2–B30 of IFRS 17)

BC63   Some argued that IFRS 17 should deal with all aspects of financial reporting by entities that issue insurance contracts to ensure that the financial reporting is internally consistent. They noted that regulatory requirements often cover all aspects of an entity's insurance business, as do some national accounting requirements. However, the Board decided that IFRS 17 should apply only to insurance contracts and should be applicable to all entities holding those contracts. The Board decided to base its approach on the type of activity rather than on the type of the entity because:

(a)   a robust definition of an insurer that could be applied consistently from country to country would be difficult to create;

(b)   entities that might meet the definition frequently have major activities in other areas as well as in insurance, and would need to determine how and to what extent these non-insurance activities would be accounted for in a manner similar to insurance activities or in a manner similar to how other entities account for their non-insurance activities;

(c)   if an entity that issues insurance contracts accounted for a transaction in one way and an entity that does not issue insurance contracts accounted for the same transaction in a different way, comparability across entities would be reduced.

BC64   Accordingly, IFRS 17 applies to all insurance contracts (as defined in IFRS 17) throughout the duration of those contracts, regardless of the type of entity issuing the contracts.

BC65   IFRS 17 generally does not set requirements for the other assets and liabilities of entities that issue insurance contracts, because those assets and liabilities fall within the scope of other IFRS Standards. However, IFRS 17 provides the following exceptions:

(a)   it applies to investment contracts with discretionary participation features, provided that the issuer also issues insurance contracts. In the Board's view, applying the requirements in IFRS 17 provides more relevant information about such contracts than would be provided by applying other Standards. The Board also noted that investment contracts with discretionary participation features are almost exclusively issued by entities that issue insurance contracts (see paragraphs BC82–BC86).

(b)   it applies to financial guarantee contracts provided they meet the definition of insurance contracts in IFRS 17, the entity has previously asserted that it regards such contracts as insurance contracts and the entity has used accounting that is applicable to insurance contracts for such financial guarantee contracts. The Board noted that it has previously heard incompatible views on the appropriate accounting model for financial guarantee contracts and does not view work in this area as a high priority (see paragraphs BC91–BC94).

(c)   it amends other IFRS Standards (see Appendix D of IFRS 17) to permit an entity to recognise its own shares as assets and to measure such assets, own debt and owner-occupied property at fair value when held in an investment fund that provides investors with benefits determined by units in the fund or when an entity holds the investment as an underlying item for insurance contracts with direct participation features. The Board decided that for many contracts that specify a link to returns on underlying items, those underlying items include a mix of assets that are almost all measured at fair value through profit or loss. Measurement of own shares, own debt and owner-occupied property at fair value through profit or loss would be consistent with the measurement of the majority of the underlying assets and would prevent accounting mismatches.

BC66　IFRS 17 does not set requirements for insurance contracts held by policyholders, other than reinsurance contracts held. Other IFRS Standards include requirements that may apply to some aspects of such contracts. For example, IAS 37 sets requirements for reimbursements from insurance contracts held that provide cover for expenditure required to settle a provision and IAS 16 *Property, Plant and Equipment* sets requirements for some aspects of reimbursement under an insurance contract held that provides coverage for the impairment or loss of property, plant and equipment. Furthermore, IAS 8 *Accounting Policies, Changes in Accounting Estimates and Errors* specifies a hierarchy that an entity should use when developing an accounting policy if no IFRS Standard applies specifically to an item. Accordingly, the Board did not view work on policyholder accounting as a high priority.

Definition of an insurance contract (paragraph 6, Appendix A and paragraphs B2–B30 of IFRS 17)

BC67　The definition of an insurance contract determines which contracts are within the scope of IFRS 17 and outside the scope of other IFRS Standards. The definition of an insurance contract in IFRS 17 is the same as the definition in IFRS 4, with clarifications to the related guidance in Appendix B of IFRS 4 to require that:

(a)　an insurer should consider the time value of money in assessing whether the additional benefits payable in any scenario are significant (see paragraph B20 of IFRS 17 and paragraph BC78); and

(b)　a contract does not transfer significant insurance risk if there is no scenario with commercial substance in which the insurer can suffer a loss on a present value basis (see paragraph B19 of IFRS 17 and paragraph BC78).

BC68　The following aspects of the definition of an insurance contract are discussed below:

(a)　the definition of a contract (see paragraphs BC69–BC70);

(b)　the insurance risk (see paragraphs BC71–BC72);

(c)　the insurable interest (see paragraphs BC73–BC75);

(d)　the quantity of insurance risk (see paragraphs BC76–BC80); and

(e)　the expiry of insurance-contingent rights and obligations (see paragraph BC81).

Definition of a contract (paragraph 2 of IFRS 17)

BC69　IFRS 17 defines a contract as an agreement between two or more parties that creates enforceable rights and obligations, and explains that contracts can be written, oral or implied by an entity's business practices. IFRS 17 also requires an entity to consider all its substantive rights and obligations, whether they arise from contract, law or regulation. Thus, when referring to contractual terms the effects of law and regulation are also considered. These requirements are consistent with IFRS 15. They apply when an entity considers how to classify a contract and when assessing the substantive rights and obligations for determining the boundary of a contract. However, in measuring a group of insurance contracts, IFRS 17 requires an entity to include estimates of future cash flows that are at the discretion of the entity and hence may not be enforceable. The Board's reasons for requiring such cash flows to be included in the measurement are set out in paragraphs BC167–BC169.

BC70   IFRS 17 is consistent with the Board's principle set out in the 2015 Exposure Draft of *The Conceptual Framework* that contracts should be combined as necessary to report their substance.

Insurance risk (Appendix A and paragraphs B7–B25 of IFRS 17)

BC71   The definition of an insurance contract in IFRS 17 focuses on the feature unique to insurance contracts—insurance risk.

BC72   Some contracts have the legal form of insurance contracts but do not transfer significant insurance risk to the issuer. IFRS 17 does not treat such contracts as insurance contracts even though the contracts are traditionally described as insurance contracts and may be subject to regulation by insurance supervisors. Similarly, some contracts may contain significant insurance risk and therefore may meet the definition of insurance contracts in IFRS 17, even though they do not have the legal form of insurance contracts. Thus, IFRS 17 adopts a definition of an insurance contract that reflects the contract's economic substance and not merely its legal form.

Insurable interest (paragraphs B7–B16 of IFRS 17)

BC73   The definition of an insurance contract reflects the risk the entity accepts from the policyholders by agreeing to compensate the policyholders if they are adversely affected by an uncertain event (paragraph B12 of IFRS 17). The notion that the uncertain event must have an adverse effect on the policyholder is known as 'insurable interest'.

BC74   The Board considered whether it should eliminate the notion of insurable interest and replace it with the notion that insurance involves assembling risks into a pool in which they can be managed together. Some argued that doing so would appropriately include the following within the scope of the Standard:

(a)   contracts that require payment if a specified uncertain future event occurs, causing economic exposure similar to insurance contracts, whether the other party has an insurable interest or not; and

(b)   some contracts used as insurance that do not include a notion of insurable interest, for example, weather derivatives.

BC75   However, the Board decided to retain the notion of insurable interest because without the reference to 'adverse effect', the definition might have captured any prepaid contract to provide services with uncertain costs. Such a definition would have extended the meaning of the term 'insurance contract' beyond its traditional meaning, which the Board did not want to do. The notion of insurable interest is also needed to avoid including gambling in the definition of insurance. Furthermore, it is a principle-based distinction, particularly between insurance contracts and contracts used for hedging.

Quantity of insurance risk (paragraphs B17–B25 of IFRS 17)

BC76   Paragraphs B17–B25 of IFRS 17 discuss how much insurance risk must be present before a contract qualifies as an insurance contract.

BC77   In developing this material, the Board considered the criteria in US GAAP for a contract to be treated as an insurance contract, which includes the notion that there should be a 'reasonable possibility' of a 'significant loss'. The Board observed that some practitioners use the following guideline when applying US GAAP: a reasonable possibility of a significant loss is at least a 10 per cent probability of a loss of at least 10 per cent of premium.

BC78   However, quantitative guidance risks creating an arbitrary dividing line that results in different accounting treatments for similar transactions that fall marginally on different sides of the line. Quantitative guidance also creates opportunities for accounting arbitrage by encouraging transactions that fall marginally on one side of the line or the other. For these reasons, IFRS 17 does not include quantitative guidance. Instead, noting the criteria applied in US GAAP, the Board decided to add the requirement that a contract transfers insurance risk only if there is a scenario with commercial substance in which the issuer has a possibility of a loss on a present value basis.

BC79
The Board also considered whether it should define the significance of insurance risk by referring to materiality, which the *Conceptual Framework for Financial Reporting*[6] describes as follows:

> Information is material if omitting it or misstating it could influence decisions that users make on the basis of financial information about a specific reporting entity.[7]

However, a single contract, or even a single book of similar contracts, would rarely generate a material loss in relation to the financial statements as a whole. Although entities manage contracts by portfolios, the contractual rights and obligations arise from individual contracts. Consequently, IFRS 17 defines the significance of insurance risk in relation to individual contracts (see paragraph B22 of IFRS 17).

BC80   The Board also rejected the notion of defining the significance of insurance risk by expressing the expected (ie probability-weighted) average of the present values of the adverse outcomes as a proportion of the expected present value of all outcomes, or as a proportion of the premium. This notion had some intuitive appeal because it would include both amount and probability. However, such a definition would have meant that a contract could start as a financial liability and become an insurance contract as time

---

6   References to the *Conceptual Framework for Financial Reporting* (*Conceptual Framework*) in this Basis for Conclusions are to the *Conceptual Framework for Financial Reporting*, issued in 2010 and in effect when the Standard was developed.

7   Amendments to the definition of material in the *Conceptual Framework for Financial Reporting* were issued in October 2018.

passes or probabilities are reassessed. In the Board's view, it would be too burdensome to require an entity to continuously monitor whether a contract meets the definition of an insurance contract over its duration. Instead, the Board adopted an approach that requires the decision about whether a contract is an insurance contract to be made once only, at contract inception (unless the terms of the contract are modified). The requirements in paragraphs B18–B24 of IFRS 17 focus on whether insured events could cause an entity to pay additional amounts, judged on a contract-by-contract basis. Further, paragraph B25 of IFRS 17 states that an insurance contract remains an insurance contract until all rights and obligations expire.

Expiry of insurance-contingent rights and obligations

BC81 Some stakeholders suggested that a contract should not be accounted for as an insurance contract if the insurance-contingent rights and obligations expire after a very short time. IFRS 17 addresses aspects of this issue: paragraph B18 of IFRS 17 explains the need to ignore scenarios that lack commercial substance and paragraph B21(b) of IFRS 17 notes that there is no significant transfer of pre-existing risk in some contracts that waive surrender penalties on death.

Investment contracts with discretionary participation features (paragraphs 4(b) and 71 of IFRS 17)

BC82 The Board decided that issuers of investment contracts with discretionary participation features should apply IFRS 17 to those contracts provided that the issuer also issues insurance contracts. Because investment contracts with discretionary participation features do not transfer insurance risk, the requirements of IFRS 17 are modified for such contracts.

BC83 Although investment contracts with discretionary participation features do not meet the definition of insurance contracts, the advantages of treating them the same as insurance contracts rather than as financial instruments when they are issued by entities that issue insurance contracts are that:

(a) investment contracts with discretionary participation features and insurance contracts that specify a link to returns on underlying items are sometimes linked to the same underlying pool of assets. Sometimes investment contracts with discretionary participation features share in the performance of insurance contracts. Using the same accounting for both types of contracts will produce more useful information for users of financial statements because it enhances comparability within an entity. It also simplifies the accounting for those contracts. For example, some cash flow distributions to participating policyholders are made in aggregate both for insurance contracts that specify a link to returns on underlying items and for investment contracts with discretionary participation features. This makes it challenging to apply different accounting models to different parts of that aggregate participation.

(b)   both of these types of contract often have characteristics, such as long maturities, recurring premiums and high acquisition cash flows that are more commonly found in insurance contracts than in most other financial instruments. The Board developed the model for insurance contracts specifically to generate useful information about contracts containing such features.

(c)   if investment contracts with discretionary participation features were not accounted for by applying IFRS 17, some of the discretionary participation features might be separated into an equity component in accordance with the Board's existing requirements for financial instruments. Splitting these contracts into components with different accounting treatments would cause the same problems that would arise if insurance contracts were separated (see paragraph BC10(a)). Also, in the Board's view, the accounting model it has developed for insurance contracts, including the treatment of discretionary cash flows (see paragraphs BC167–BC170), is more appropriate than using any other model for these types of contracts.

BC84   Accordingly, the Board decided that entities that issue insurance contracts should apply IFRS 17 to account for investment contracts with discretionary participation features.

BC85   The Board considered whether IFRS 17 should be applied to all investment contracts with discretionary participation features regardless of whether they are issued by an entity that also issues insurance contracts. However, the Board was concerned that for the few entities that did not issue insurance contracts the costs of implementing IFRS 17 would outweigh the benefits.

BC86   Because investment contracts with discretionary participation features transfer no significant insurance risk, IFRS 17 made the following modifications to the general requirements for insurance contracts (see paragraph 71 of IFRS 17) for these contracts:

(a)   the date of initial recognition is the date the entity becomes party to the contract, because there is no pre-coverage period and hence the practical concerns noted in paragraph BC141 do not arise;

(b)   the contract boundary principle builds on the defining characteristic, namely the presence of the discretionary participation features, rather than on the existence of insurance risk; and

(c)   the requirement for the recognition of the contractual service margin in profit or loss refers to the pattern of the provision of investment related services.

Scope exclusions (paragraphs 7–8A of IFRS 17)

BC87   The scope of IFRS 17 excludes various items that may meet the definition of insurance contracts, such as:

   (a)   warranties provided by a manufacturer, dealer or retailer in connection with the sale of its goods or services to a customer (see paragraphs BC89–BC90).

   (b)   employers' assets and liabilities that arise from employee benefit plans, and retirement benefit obligations reported by defined benefit retirement plans (see IAS 19 *Employee Benefits*, IFRS 2 *Share-based Payment* and IAS 26 *Accounting and Reporting by Retirement Benefit Plans*).

   (c)   contractual rights or contractual obligations contingent on the future use of, or right to use, a non-financial item (see IFRS 15, IFRS 16 *Leases* and IAS 38 *Intangible Assets*).

   (d)   residual value guarantees provided by the manufacturer, dealer or retailer and lessees' residual value guarantees embedded in a lease (see IFRS 15 and IFRS 16). However, stand-alone residual value guarantees that transfer insurance risk are not addressed by other IFRS Standards and are within the scope of IFRS 17.

   (e)   some financial guarantee contracts (see paragraphs BC91–BC94).

   (f)   contingent consideration payable or receivable in a business combination (see IFRS 3 *Business Combinations*).

   (g)   insurance contracts in which the entity is the policyholder, unless those contracts are reinsurance contracts (see paragraph BC66).

   (h)   some credit card contracts and similar contracts that provide credit or payment arrangements (see paragraphs BC94A–BC94C).

BC88   IFRS 17 also allows an entity a choice of applying IFRS 17 or another IFRS Standard to some contracts, specifically:

   (a)   applying IFRS 17 or IFRS 15 to some fixed-fee service contracts (see paragraphs BC95–BC97); and

   (b)   applying IFRS 17 or IFRS 9 to specified contracts such as loan contracts with death waivers (see paragraphs BC94D–BC94F).

Product warranties (paragraphs 7(a) and B26(g) of IFRS 17)

BC89   IFRS 17 includes the scope exclusion previously included in IFRS 4 for warranties provided by the manufacturer, dealer or retailer in connection with the sale of its goods or services to a customer. Such warranties might provide a customer with assurance that the related product will function as the parties intended because it complies with agreed-upon specifications, or they might provide the customer with a service in addition to the assurance that the product complies with agreed-upon specifications.

BC90 Such warranties meet the definition of an insurance contract. However, the Board decided to exclude them from the scope of IFRS 17. The Board noted that, if IFRS 17 were to apply, entities would generally apply the premium allocation approach to such contracts, which would result in accounting similar to that which would result from applying IFRS 15. Further, in the Board's view, accounting for such contracts in the same way as other contracts with customers would provide comparable information for the users of financial statements for the entities that issue such contracts. Hence, the Board concluded that changing the existing accounting for these contracts would impose costs and disruption for no significant benefit.

Financial guarantee contracts (paragraph 7(e) of IFRS 17)

BC91 IFRS Standards define a financial guarantee contract as a contract that requires the issuer to make specified payments to reimburse the holder for a loss it incurs because a specified debtor fails to make payment when due in accordance with the original or modified terms of a debt instrument. These contracts transfer credit risk and may have various legal forms, such as a guarantee, some types of letters of credit, a credit default contract or an insurance contract.

BC92 Some view all contracts that transfer credit risk as financial instruments. However, a precondition for a payment in the contracts described in paragraph BC91 is that the holder has suffered a loss—a distinguishing feature of insurance contracts. The Board heard two incompatible views on the appropriate accounting model for financial guarantee contracts:

(a) financial guarantee contracts meet the definition of an insurance contract because the issuer of the contract agrees to compensate the holder when an uncertain future event (ie default) occurs that would adversely affect the holder. Consequently, an entity should account for financial guarantee contracts in the same way as other insurance contracts.

(b) financial guarantee contracts are economically similar to other credit-related contracts within the scope of IFRS 9. Similar accounting should apply to similar contracts. As a result, an entity should account for financial guarantee contracts in the same way as other financial instruments.

BC93 IFRS 4 included an option that permitted an issuer of a financial guarantee contract to account for it as if it were an insurance contract, if the issuer had previously asserted that it regards the contract as an insurance contract. This option had been intended as a temporary solution, pending the publication of IFRS 17. However, although the terms of the option may appear to be imprecise, in the vast majority of cases the accounting choice for financial guarantee contracts is clear and no implementation problems appear to have been identified in practice. Therefore, the Board decided to carry forward to IFRS 17 the option to account for a financial guarantee contract as if it were an insurance contract, without any substantive changes, because the option has worked in practice and results in consistent accounting for economically similar contracts issued by the same entity. The Board did not view it as a high priority to address the inconsistency that results from accounting for financial guarantee contracts differently depending on the issuer.

BC94   Some credit-related contracts lack the precondition for payment that the holder has suffered a loss. An example of such a contract is one that requires payments in response to changes in a specified credit rating or credit index. The Board concluded that those contracts are derivatives and do not meet the definition of an insurance contract. Therefore, such contracts will continue to be accounted for as derivatives. The Board noted that these contracts were outside the scope of the policy choice in IFRS 4 carried forward in IFRS 17, so continuing to account for them as derivatives would not create further diversity.

Amendments to IFRS 17—scope exclusions

Credit card contracts and similar contracts that provide credit or payment arrangements (paragraph 7(h) of IFRS 17)

BC94A   Some contracts that provide credit or payment arrangements meet the definition of an insurance contract – for example, some credit card contracts, charge card contracts, consumer financing contracts or bank account contracts. In June 2020, the Board amended IFRS 17 to exclude from the scope of the Standard such contracts if, and only if, an entity does not reflect an assessment of the insurance risk associated with an individual customer in setting the price of the contract with that customer. When the entity does not reflect such an assessment in the price of the contract, the Board concluded that IFRS 9 would provide more useful information about those contracts than would IFRS 17.

BC94B   The Board was aware that, applying IFRS 4, most entities separated the components of such contracts. For example, an entity applying IFRS 4 might have accounted for the credit card component applying IFRS 9, the insurance component applying IFRS 4 and any other service components applying IFRS 15. IFRS 17 has different criteria from IFRS 4 for separating components of an insurance contract. However, the Board acknowledged that entities had already identified methods to separate the components of the contracts described in paragraph BC94A, and concluded that prohibiting such separation would impose costs and disruption for no significant benefit.

BC94C   The Board instead decided to specify that an entity's rights and obligations that are financial instruments arising under such contracts are within the scope of IFRS 9. However, an entity is required to separate and apply IFRS 17 to an insurance coverage component if, and only if, that component is a contractual term of that financial instrument. In the Board's view, applying IFRS 17 to those insurance coverage components will result in the most useful information for users of financial statements. Applying IFRS 17 to those components will also increase comparability between insurance coverage provided as part of the contractual terms of a credit card contract and insurance coverage provided as a separate stand-alone contract. Other IFRS Standards, such as IFRS 15 or IAS 37, might apply to other components of the contract, such as other service components or insurance components required by law or regulation.

Specified contracts such as loan contracts with death waivers (paragraph 8A of IFRS 17)

BC94D   In June 2020, the Board amended IFRS 17 to allow entities to apply either IFRS 17 or IFRS 9 to contracts that meet the definition of an insurance contract but limit the compensation for insured events to the amount otherwise required to settle the policyholder's obligation created by the contract (for example, loan contracts with death waivers).

BC94E   The Board noted that an entity would provide useful information about such contracts whether it applied IFRS 17 or IFRS 9. Hence, the Board concluded that requiring an entity to apply IFRS 17 to those contracts when the entity had previously been applying an accounting policy consistent with IFRS 9 or IAS 39 could impose costs and disruption for no significant benefit.

BC94F   An entity is required to choose whether to apply IFRS 17 or IFRS 9 for each portfolio of insurance contracts described in paragraph BC94D, and this choice is irrevocable. The Board concluded that such restrictions would mitigate the lack of comparability that might otherwise arise between similar contracts issued by the same entity.

Fixed-fee service contracts (paragraphs 8 and B6 of IFRS 17)

BC95   A fixed-fee service contract is a contract in which the level of service depends on an uncertain event. Examples include roadside assistance programmes and maintenance contracts in which the service provider agrees to repair specified equipment after a malfunction. Such contracts meet the definition of an insurance contract because:

   (a)   it is uncertain whether, or when, assistance or a repair will be needed;

   (b)   the owner is adversely affected by the occurrence; and

   (c)   the service provider compensates the owner if assistance or repair is needed.

BC96   Fixed-fee service contracts meet the definition of an insurance contract. However, the Board originally proposed to exclude from the scope of IFRS 17 fixed-fee service contracts whose primary purpose is the provision of service. Instead, entities would have been required to apply IFRS 15 to those contracts. The Board noted that, if IFRS 17 were to apply, entities would generally apply the premium allocation approach to such contracts, which would result in accounting similar to that which would result from applying IFRS 15. Further, the Board decided the practice of accounting for these contracts in the same way as other contracts with customers would provide useful information for the users of financial statements for the entities that issue such contracts. Hence, the Board thought that changing the accounting for these contracts would impose costs and disruption for no significant benefit.

BC97   However, some stakeholders noted some entities issue both fixed-fee service contracts and other insurance contracts. For example, some entities issue both roadside assistance contracts and insurance contracts for damage arising from accidents. The Board decided to allow entities a choice of whether to apply

IFRS 17 or IFRS 15 to fixed-fee service contracts to enable such entities to account for both types of contract in the same way.

Separating components from an insurance contract (paragraphs 10–13 and B31–B35 of IFRS 17)

BC98   Insurance contracts create rights and obligations that work together to generate cash inflows and cash outflows. Some insurance contracts may:

(a)   contain embedded derivatives that, if bifurcated, would be within the scope of IFRS 9;

(b)   contain investment components that, if they were provided under separate contracts, would be within the scope of IFRS 9; or

(c)   provide goods and non-insurance services that, if they were provided under separate contracts, would be within the scope of IFRS 15.

BC99   Separating such non-insurance components from an insurance contract can improve comparability. Accounting for such components using other applicable IFRS Standards makes them more comparable to similar contracts that are issued as separate contracts, and allows users of financial statements to better compare the risks undertaken by entities in different businesses or industries.

BC100   However, separating components also has limitations. Separating a single contract into components could result in complex accounting that does not provide useful information for interdependent cash flows attributable to the components. Furthermore, when cash flows are interdependent, separating the cash flows for each component can be arbitrary, particularly if the contract includes cross-subsidies between components or discounts. Also, as noted in paragraph BC10(a), when separation ignores interdependencies between components, the sum of the values of the components may not always equal the value of the contract as a whole, even on initial recognition.

BC101   The Board originally proposed that an entity separate a component not closely related to the insurance coverage specified in the contract and identified some common examples of such components. The term 'closely related' is used in IFRS 9 in the criteria that determine whether embedded derivatives must be bifurcated. However, stakeholders indicated that some were unsure how to interpret the term closely related for non-insurance components embedded in insurance contracts. The Board noted that the principles for separating embedded derivatives were long-established in IFRS 9 (and previously in IAS 39 *Financial Instruments: Recognition and Measurement*). However, IFRS 17 clarifies the principles for the separation of other non-insurance components from an insurance contract based on the principles developed in IFRS 15.

BC102   Hence, IFRS 17 includes requirements for the separation of the following non-insurance components:

(a)   embedded derivatives (see paragraphs BC104–BC107);

(b)   investment components (see paragraphs BC108–BC109); and

(c) goods and non-insurance services (see paragraphs BC110–BC113).[8]

BC103 The criteria for separating such non-insurance components from insurance components differ to reflect the different characteristics of the non-insurance components. This is consistent with applying different accounting models to the equivalent contracts accounted for on a stand-alone basis.

Embedded derivatives (paragraph 11(a) of IFRS 17)

BC104 When applying IFRS 9 (and previously IAS 39) entities are required to account separately for some derivatives embedded in hybrid contracts. The Board noted that accounting separately for some embedded derivatives in hybrid contracts:

(a) ensures that contractual rights and obligations that create similar risk exposures are treated alike whether or not they are embedded in a non-derivative host contract.

(b) counters the possibility that entities might seek to avoid the requirement to measure derivatives at fair value through profit or loss by embedding a derivative in a non-derivative host contract. In the Board's view, fair value through profit or loss is the only measurement basis that provides relevant information about derivatives. If derivatives were measured at cost or at fair value through other comprehensive income, their role in reducing or increasing risk would not be visible. In addition, the value of derivatives often changes disproportionately in response to market movements and fair value is the measurement basis that best captures such non-linear responses to changes in risk. That information is essential to communicate the nature of the rights and obligations inherent in derivatives to users of financial statements.

BC105 IFRS 4 confirmed that the requirements of IAS 39 for embedded derivatives apply to derivatives embedded in insurance contracts. The Board has updated this requirement in IFRS 17 so that an entity applies IFRS 9 to determine whether a contract includes an embedded derivative to be separated and, if so, how entities account for that derivative. The Board's approach is consistent with the approach it has taken with hybrid contracts other than hybrid financial assets. This results in the following changes from the requirements of IFRS 4:

(a) IFRS 4 did not require the separation of an embedded derivative from the host contract if the contract and the embedded derivative are so interdependent that an entity cannot measure the derivative separately. By applying IFRS 9 to determine whether a contract includes an embedded derivative to be separated, the Board replaced this option with a prohibition from separating such closely related embedded derivatives from the host contract. The Board concluded that when embedded derivatives are closely related to the host

---

8 In June 2020, the Board amended IFRS 17 and replaced 'non-insurance services' with 'services other than insurance contract services' (see paragraphs BC283A–BC283J).

insurance contract, the benefits of separating those embedded derivatives fail to outweigh the costs. Applying the measurement requirements of IFRS 17, such embedded derivatives are measured using current market-consistent information; and

(b)   IFRS 17 removes the statement in IFRS 4 that an entity is not required to separate specified surrender options in an insurance contract. Instead, the entity applies the requirements in IFRS 9 to decide whether it needs to separate a surrender option.

BC106   Some respondents suggested that separating embedded derivatives from insurance contracts introduces excessive complexity with little additional benefit.

BC107   The Board agreed that when embedded derivatives are closely related to the host insurance contract, the benefits of separating those embedded derivatives do not outweigh the costs. However, the Board decided that those benefits would exceed the costs when the embedded derivatives are not closely related to the host insurance contract. Previous practice indicates that the costs of separating such embedded derivatives from host insurance contracts would not be excessive.

Investment components (paragraphs 11(b) and B31–B32 of IFRS 17)

BC108   An investment component is the amount an insurance contract requires the entity to repay to the policyholder even if an insured event does not occur.[9] Many insurance contracts have an implicit or explicit investment component that would, if it were a separate financial instrument, be within the scope of IFRS 9. As explained in paragraph BC10(a), the Board decided that it would be difficult to routinely separate such investment components from insurance contracts. Accordingly, IFRS 17 requires an entity to:

(a)   separate only any distinct investment components from insurance contracts. An investment component is distinct if the cash flows of the insurance contract are not highly interrelated with the cash flows from the investment component. Separating such components does not create the problems noted in paragraph BC10(a).

(b)   account for all investment components with cash flows that are highly interrelated with the insurance contract by applying IFRS 17, but, as explained in paragraphs BC33–BC34, eliminate any investment components from insurance revenue and insurance service expenses reported in accordance with paragraph 85 of IFRS 17.

9   In June 2020, the Board amended the definition of an investment component to clarify that an investment component is the amounts that an insurance contract requires the entity to repay to a policyholder in all circumstances, regardless of whether an insured event occurs (see paragraph BC34A).

BC109   IFRS 17 requires the cash flows allocated to a separated investment component to be measured on a stand-alone basis as if the entity had issued that investment contract separately. This requirement is consistent with the objective of separation, which is to account for a separated component the way stand-alone contracts with similar characteristics are accounted for. The Board concluded that, in all cases, entities would be able to measure the stand-alone value for an investment component by applying IFRS 9.[10]

Goods and non-insurance services (paragraphs 12 and B33–B35 of IFRS 17)[11]

BC110   In principle, an entity should use similar principles to those in IFRS 15 to separate performance obligations to provide goods and non-insurance services[12] from the host contract, regardless of whether the host contract is within the scope of IFRS 17 or of IFRS 15. Accordingly, IFRS 17 requires entities to separate only the goods and services that are distinct from the provision of insurance coverage,[13] consistent with the separation criteria in IFRS 15.

BC111   Consistent with IFRS 15, IFRS 17 requires an entity to allocate the cash inflows of an insurance contract between the host insurance contract and the distinct good or non-insurance service,[14] based on the stand-alone selling price of the components. In the Board's view, in most cases, entities would be able to determine an observable stand-alone selling price for the goods or services bundled in an insurance contract if those components meet the separation criteria.

BC112   However, if the stand-alone selling price were not directly observable, an entity would need to estimate the stand-alone selling prices of each component to allocate the transaction price. This might be the case if the entity does not sell the insurance and the goods or services components separately, or if the consideration charged for the two components together differs from the stand-alone selling prices because the entity charges more or less for the bundled contract than the sum of the prices for each component. Applying IFRS 15, any discounts and cross-subsidies are allocated to components proportionately or on the basis of observable evidence. In the Board's view, this approach ensures that the allocation of cross-subsidies and discounts/supplements reflects the economics of the separated components.

---

10 In June 2020, the Board amended paragraph 11(b) of IFRS 17 to clarify that an entity applies IFRS 17 to a separated investment component if that component meets the definition of an investment contract with discretionary participation features within the scope of IFRS 17.

11 In June 2020, the Board amended IFRS 17 and replaced 'non-insurance services' with 'services other than insurance contract services' (see paragraphs BC283A–BC283J).

12 In June 2020, the Board amended IFRS 17 and replaced 'non-insurance services' with 'services other than insurance contract services' (see paragraphs BC283A–BC283J).

13 In June 2020, the Board amended IFRS 17 to require entities to separate only goods and services that are distinct from the provision of insurance contract services (see paragraphs BC283A–BC283J).

14 In June 2020, the Board amended IFRS 17 and replaced 'non-insurance services' with 'services other than insurance contract services' (see paragraphs BC283A–BC283J).

BC113   IFRS 17 requires that cash outflows should be allocated to their related component, and that cash outflows not clearly related to one of the components should be systematically and rationally allocated between components. Insurance acquisition cash flows and some fulfilment cash flows relating to overhead costs do not clearly relate to one of the components. A systematic and rational allocation of such cash flows is consistent with the requirements in IFRS 17 for allocating acquisition and fulfilment cash flows that cover more than one group of insurance contracts to the individual groups of contracts, and is also consistent with the requirements in other IFRS Standards for allocating the costs of production — the requirements in IFRS 15 and IAS 2 *Inventories*, for example.

Prohibition on separating non-insurance components when not required (paragraph 13 of IFRS 17)

BC114   The Board considered whether to permit an entity to separate a non-insurance component when not required to do so by IFRS 17; for example, some investment components with interrelated cash flows, such as policy loans. Such components may have been separated when applying previous accounting practices. However, the Board concluded that it would not be possible to separate in a non-arbitrary way a component that is not distinct from the insurance contract nor would such a result be desirable. Permitting an entity to separate such components would mean that the entity measures the components in the contract on an arbitrary basis. The Board also noted that when separation ignores interdependencies between insurance and non-insurance components, the sum of the values of the components may not always equal the value of the contract as a whole, even on initial recognition. That would reduce the comparability of the financial statements across entities.

Level of aggregation of insurance contracts (paragraphs 14–24 of IFRS 17)

Background

BC115   A key issue in developing the measurement requirements for the contractual service margin in IFRS 17 was the level of aggregation of insurance contracts to which the requirements should be applied. Some aspects of the adjustments to the carrying amount of the contractual service margin result in gains being treated differently from losses or changes in estimates relating to current and past service being treated differently from changes in estimates relating to future service (see paragraphs BC21–BC24). These different treatments mean that the accounting result depends on the level of aggregation at which the adjustments are made, because amounts that would offset each other within the measurement of a group of insurance contracts would be treated differently (and hence not offset each other) if contracts were measured individually.

BC116 For example, suppose an entity issued a group of identical contracts expecting that there would be more claims from some of the contracts than others, but not knowing which contracts would be the ones with more claims. Subsequently it becomes apparent which contracts are likely to give rise to claims and which are not, and the number of contracts in each category is as expected. If the contracts were measured individually, the expected claims may cause the contracts for which they are likely to arise to become onerous, with an equal and opposite reduction in the fulfilment cash flows of the other contracts. The entity would recognise a loss for the onerous contracts immediately in profit or loss and an increase in the contractual service margin for the other contracts. That increase in the contractual service margin would not be recognised immediately in profit or loss but instead would be recognised over the current and future coverage period. In contrast, if the contracts were measured as one group, there would be no loss for a group of onerous contracts or increase in the contractual service margin to be recognised.

BC117 This issue does not arise in the measurement of the fulfilment cash flows. The fulfilment cash flows include all changes in estimates, regardless of whether they are gains or losses or they relate to past, current or future service. Hence, IFRS 17 allows an entity to estimate the fulfilment cash flows at whatever level of aggregation is most appropriate from a practical perspective. All that is necessary is that the entity is able to allocate such estimates to groups of insurance contracts so that the resulting fulfilment cash flows of the group comply with requirements of IFRS 17.

BC118 For the contractual service margin, the Board considered whether contracts should be measured individually despite the resulting lack of offsetting. Doing so would be consistent with the general requirements in IFRS 9 and IFRS 15 and would reflect the fact that the entity's rights and obligations arise from individual contracts with policyholders. Measuring contracts individually would also provide a clear measurement objective. However, the Board decided that such an approach would not provide useful information about insurance activities, which often rely on an entity issuing a number of similar contracts to reduce risk. The Board concluded, therefore, that the contractual service margin should be measured at a group level.

Characteristics of a group

BC119 Once the Board had decided that the contractual service margin should be measured for a group, the Board considered what that group level should be. The Board considered whether it could draw on requirements for groups set by insurance regulators. However, as noted in paragraph BC15, regulatory requirements focus on solvency not on reporting financial performance. The decisions about grouping in IFRS 17 were driven by considerations about reporting profits and losses in appropriate reporting periods. For example, in some cases the entity issues two groups of insurance contracts expecting that, on average, the contracts in one group will be more profitable than the contracts in the other group. In such cases, the Board decided, in principle, there should be no offsetting between the two groups of insurance contracts because that offsetting could result in a loss of useful information. In particular, the Board noted that the less profitable group of contracts would have a lesser ability to withstand unfavourable changes in estimates and might become onerous before the more profitable group would do so. The Board regards information about onerous contracts as useful information about an entity's decisions on pricing contracts and about future cash flows, and wanted this information to be reported on a timely basis. The Board did not want this information to be obscured by offsetting onerous contracts in one group with profitable contracts in another.

BC120   The level of aggregation is also relevant to the recognition of the contractual service margin in profit or loss. Paragraph BC279 explains that, following the Board's principle for the allocation of the contractual service margin, an entity should systematically recognise the remaining contractual service margin in profit or loss over the current and remaining coverage period to reflect the remaining transfer of services to be provided by the insurance contracts.

BC121   In many cases, the coverage period of individual contracts in a group will differ from the average coverage period for the group. When this is the case, measuring the contracts on:

      (a)   an individual basis would mean that the contractual service margin associated with contracts with a shorter than average coverage period would be fully recognised in profit or loss over that shorter period;

      (b)   a group basis would mean that the contractual service margin associated with contracts with a shorter than average coverage period would not be fully recognised in profit or loss over that shorter period.

BC122   Thus, measuring the contracts as a group creates the risk that the contractual service margin for a group might fail to reflect the profit relating to the coverage[15] remaining in the group, unless the entity tracked the allocation of the contractual service margin separately for groups of insurance contracts:

      (a)   that have similar expected profitability, on initial recognition, and for which the amount and timing of cash flows are expected to respond in similar ways to key drivers of risk. In principle, this condition would ensure the contractual service margin of a particularly profitable individual contract within a group is not carried forward after the individual contract has expired.

      (b)   that have coverage periods that were expected to end at a similar time. In principle, this condition would ensure the contractual service margin of an individual contract that expired was not carried forward after the contract had expired.

---

15   In June 2020, the Board amended IFRS 17 to require an entity to recognise an amount of the contractual service margin in profit or loss in each period to reflect insurance contract services provided in that period (see paragraphs BC283A–BC283J).

BC123   The Board concluded that it was necessary to strike a balance between the loss of information discussed in paragraphs BC119 and BC121–BC122, and the need for useful information about the insurance activity as discussed in paragraphs BC118 and BC120. The Board:

     (a)   did not want entities to depict one type of contract as cross-subsidised by a different type of contract, but also did not want to recognise losses for claims developing as expected within a group of similar contracts; and

     (b)   did not want the contractual service margin of an expired contract to exist as part of the average contractual service margin of a group long after the coverage provided by the contract ended, but also did not want to recognise a disproportionate amount of contractual service margin for contracts lapsing as expected within a group of similar contracts.

BC124   The Board concluded that the balance described above could be achieved in principle by:

     (a)   requiring contracts in a group to have future cash flows the entity expects will respond similarly in amount and timing to changes in key assumptions—meaning that losses on insurance contracts for one type of insurance risk would not be offset by gains on insurance contracts for a different type of risk, and would provide useful information about the performance of contracts insuring different types of risk.

     (b)   requiring contracts in a group to have similar expected profitability—meaning that loss-making contracts could not be grouped with profitable contracts, whether at initial recognition or if changes in conditions make a previously profitable group loss-making. Hence, such a requirement would provide information about loss-making groups of insurance contracts.

     (c)   requiring groups not be reassessed after initial recognition.

BC125   The Board also noted that, in principle, it would be possible to meet the objective of the recognition of the contractual service margin in profit or loss discussed in paragraph BC120 either by grouping only contracts with a similar size of contractual service margin and the same remaining coverage period, or by reflecting the different duration and profitability of the contracts within the group in the allocation of the contractual service margin.

Practical considerations

BC126   The Board noted that entities could interpret the approach described in paragraphs BC124–BC125 as requiring an excessively large number of groups that may provide insufficiently useful information to justify the operational burden that would be imposed by extensive disaggregation of portfolios. Accordingly, the Board sought a balance to reflect profit and potential losses in the statement of financial performance in appropriate periods and the operational burden.

BC127   To achieve that balance, the Board concluded that an entity should be required to identify portfolios of contracts subject to similar risks and managed together, and to divide a portfolio into, at a minimum, groups of:

    (a)   contracts that are onerous at initial recognition, if any;

    (b)   contracts that are not onerous at initial recognition and that have no significant possibility of becoming onerous subsequently, if any; and

    (c)   all other contracts, if any.

BC128   The same principle of grouping applies to insurance contracts to which the premium allocation approach applies and to reinsurance contracts held, but the wording is adapted to reflect their specific characteristics.

BC129   The objective of the requirement to identify contracts that are onerous at initial recognition is to identify contracts that are onerous measured as individual contracts. An entity typically issues individual contracts and it is the characteristics of the individual contracts that determine how they should be grouped. However, the Board concluded this does not mean that the contracts must be measured individually. If an entity can determine using reasonable and supportable information that a set of contracts will all be in the same group, then the entity can measure that set to determine whether the contracts are onerous or not, because there will be no offsetting effects in the measurement of the set. The same principle applies to the identification of contracts that are not onerous at initial recognition and that have no significant possibility of becoming onerous subsequently—the objective is to identify such contracts at an individual contract level, but this objective can be achieved by assessing a set of contracts if the entity can conclude using reasonable and supportable information that the contracts in the set will all be in the same group.

BC130   To identify whether contracts (or sets of contracts) are onerous at initial recognition, an entity measures the contracts (or sets of contracts) applying the measurement requirements of IFRS 17. The Board decided that to assess whether contracts that are not onerous at initial recognition have no significant possibility of becoming onerous subsequently, an entity should use the information provided by its internal reporting system but need not gather additional information. The Board concluded that such information would provide a sufficient basis for making this assessment and that it would not be necessary to impose costs of gathering additional information. Some stakeholders nonetheless expressed the view that separating contracts that have no significant possibility of becoming onerous from other contracts that are not onerous was burdensome and unnecessary. The Board, however, concluded that in the absence of such a requirement, should the likelihood of losses increase, IFRS 17 would fail to require timely recognition of contracts that become onerous.

BC131   In some jurisdictions, law or regulation specifically constrains the entity's practical ability to set a different price or level of benefits for contracts or policyholders with different characteristics. The Board considered whether to give an exemption from dividing contracts into separate groups if the only reason that they would fall into different groups specified in paragraph BC127 is because of such constraints. In general, the Board seeks to minimise exemptions because they increase complexity for both users of financial statements and preparers and may have unintended consequences for future standard-setting activities. Further, providing an exemption for accounting for economic differences caused by the effect of law or regulation on pricing may create an undesirable precedent, given that such effects are not restricted to insurance contracts. However, the notion of grouping contracts to determine the profit or losses recognised is a specific feature of the requirements in IFRS 17. In deciding the appropriate grouping of contracts, the Board sought to balance the need to group contracts to reflect the economics of issuing insurance contracts against grouping at too high a level, which would reduce the usefulness of information produced (see paragraph BC123).

BC132   The Board concluded it would not provide useful information to group separately contracts that an entity is required by specific law or regulation to group together for determining the pricing or level of benefits. All market participants in that jurisdiction will be constrained in the same way, particularly if such entities are unable to refuse to provide insurance coverage solely on the basis of differences in that characteristic.

BC133   The Board considered whether to extend further any exemption from including contracts in separate groups, because it can be difficult to define when an entity's action is constrained by law or regulation and any distinction drawn by the Board could be considered arbitrary. The following situations could be considered economically similar to the situation in which an entity chooses to issue contracts in a jurisdiction where the law or regulation explicitly prohibits (or limits) the consideration of a specific characteristic in pricing the contract:

(a)   the entity sets the price for contracts without considering differences in a specific characteristic because it thinks using that characteristic in pricing may result in a law or regulation prohibiting the use of that specified characteristic in the future or because doing so is likely to fulfil a public policy objective. These practices are sometimes termed 'self-regulatory practices'.

(b)   the entity sets the price for contracts without considering differences in a specific characteristic because the law or regulation in a neighbouring jurisdiction explicitly prohibits consideration of differences in that specific characteristic.

(c)   the entity sets the price for contracts without considering differences in a specific characteristic because using differences in that specific characteristic may have a negative effect on the entity's brand and reputation.

BC134   However, the Board decided that in these circumstances a difference in the likelihood of a contract being or becoming onerous is an important economic difference between groups of insurance contracts. Grouping contracts that have different likelihoods of becoming onerous reduces the information provided to users of financial statements. Hence, the exemption in IFRS 17 applies only when law or regulation specifically constrains the entity's practical ability to set a different price or level of benefits for policyholders with different characteristics.

BC135   Despite the development of an approach designed to respond to the practical concerns raised by stakeholders, some continued to argue that the level of aggregation set out in paragraph BC127 might lead to excessive granularity that is, in their view, contrary to the essence of the insurance business. These stakeholders do not think that contracts that have been priced on the same basis by the entity should be in different groups. The Board noted that applying IFRS 17, an entity would not be expected under normal circumstances to group separately contracts priced on the same basis by the entity. This is because:

(a)   groups are determined on the basis of information available to the entity at initial recognition of the contracts, which will be at their inception if they are onerous at inception. In that case, the information that is used to determine the groups will be the same information that is available to the entity for pricing purposes. If contracts are onerous at inception, that will generally be the result of an intentional pricing strategy (and is likely to be relatively infrequent). If contracts are not onerous at inception, the date of initial recognition may be later than inception (see paragraphs BC140–BC144). Hence, the information used for determining the groups may differ from the information that had been available for pricing purposes. However, the difference between the information available at inception and initial recognition will often not be significant and stakeholders had indicated that always determining groups at inception (ie measuring the contracts at inception) would be unduly costly for little benefit (see paragraph BC141).

(b)   IFRS 17 provides an exception for circumstances in which law or regulation specifically constrains the entity's practical ability to set a different price or level of benefits for contracts or policyholders with different characteristics.

BC136   The Board noted that the decisions outlined in paragraph BC127 could lead to perpetual open portfolios. The Board was concerned that this could lead to a loss of information about the development of profitability over time, could result in the contractual service margin persisting beyond the duration of contacts in the group, and consequently could result in profits not being recognised in the correct periods. Consequently, in addition to dividing contracts into the groups specified in paragraph BC127, the Board decided to prohibit entities from including contracts issued more than one year apart in the same group. The Board observed that such grouping was important to ensure that trends in the profitability of a portfolio of contracts were reflected in the financial statements on a timely basis.

BC137   The Board considered whether there were any alternatives to using a one-year issuing period to constrain the duration of groups. However, the Board considered that any principle-based approach that satisfied the Board's objective would require the reintroduction of a test for similar profitability, which as set out in paragraph BC126, was rejected as being operationally burdensome. The Board acknowledged that using a one-year issuing period was an operational simplification given for cost-benefit reasons.

BC138   The Board considered whether prohibiting groups from including contracts issued more than one year apart would create an artificial divide for contracts with cash flows that affect or are affected by cash flows to policyholders of contracts in another group. Some stakeholders asserted that such a division would distort the reported result of those contracts and would be operationally burdensome. However, the Board concluded that applying the requirements of IFRS 17 to determine the fulfilment cash flows for groups of such contracts provides an appropriate depiction of the results of such contracts (see paragraphs BC171–BC174). The Board acknowledged that, for contracts that fully share risks, the groups together will give the same results as a single combined risk-sharing portfolio, and therefore considered whether IFRS 17 should give an exception to the requirement to restrict groups to include only contracts issued within one year. However, the Board concluded that setting the boundary for such an exception would add complexity to IFRS 17 and create the risk that the boundary would not be robust or appropriate in all circumstances. Hence, IFRS 17 does not include such an exception. Nonetheless, the Board noted that the requirements specify the amounts to be reported, not the methodology to be used to arrive at those amounts. Therefore it may not be necessary for an entity to restrict groups in this way to achieve the same accounting outcome in some circumstances.

BC139   Once an entity has established a group of insurance contracts, it becomes the unit of account to which the entity applies the requirements of IFRS 17. However, as noted above, an entity will typically enter into transactions for individual contracts. IFRS 17 therefore includes requirements that specify how to recognise groups that include contracts issued in more than one reporting period, and how to derecognise contracts from within a group.

Amendments to IFRS 17—feedback on the level of aggregation

BC139A   Entities implementing IFRS 17 raised concerns relating to the level of aggregation requirements. The Board therefore considered whether to amend the requirements, and if so, how (see paragraph BC139B). Having considered a number of possible amendments, the Board reaffirmed its view that the benefits of the level of aggregation requirements significantly outweigh the costs. The Board therefore decided to retain the requirements unchanged.

BC139B   The Board considered suggestions to:

    (a)   replace all level of aggregation requirements in paragraphs 14–24 of IFRS 17 with approaches that reflect an entity's internal management (see paragraph BC139C);

(b)   reduce the minimum number of groups required by paragraph 16 of IFRS 17 (profitability groups) from three to two—contracts that are onerous at initial recognition and contracts that are not onerous at initial recognition (see paragraph BC139D); and

(c)   remove or exempt some groups of insurance contracts from the annual cohort requirement in paragraph 22 of IFRS 17 (see paragraph BC139E).

BC139C   The Board considered but rejected suggestions to replace all level of aggregation requirements with approaches that reflect an entity's internal management, for example approaches based on an entity's asset and liability management strategy or risk management strategy. The objective of the level of aggregation requirements in IFRS 17 is to provide useful information for users of financial statements. Aspects of internal management such as asset and liability management strategy or risk management strategy have different objectives. Hence an approach based on those aspects would not necessarily achieve the Board's objective.

BC139D   The Board considered but rejected the suggestion to reduce the minimum number of profitability groups from three to two (see paragraph BC127) for the reason set out in paragraph BC130. This suggestion would have removed the requirement to group separately insurance contracts that at initial recognition have no significant possibility of becoming onerous from other insurance contracts that are not onerous at initial recognition. The Board noted that an entity will generally issue contracts expecting them to be profitable, and losses will arise subsequently as a result of changes in expectations. Including all contracts that are profitable at initial recognition in a single group could significantly delay loss recognition or increase the risk of losses for onerous contracts never being recognised.

BC139E   Some suggestions to remove or exempt some groups of insurance contracts from the annual cohort requirement related to all insurance contracts issued (see paragraphs BC139F–BC139H). Other suggestions related to specific types of insurance contracts—those with intergenerational sharing of risks between policyholders (see paragraphs BC139I–BC139S).

Annual cohort requirement—all insurance contracts

BC139F   The Board considered but rejected a suggestion to exempt contracts from the annual cohort requirement if an entity has reasonable and supportable information to conclude that contracts issued more than one year apart would be classified in the same profitability group. Such an exemption could result in a portfolio consisting of only the three groups of contracts described in paragraph BC127, that would each last for the entire life of the portfolio, which may be indefinite. The contractual service margin of each group would average the profitability of all contracts in the group over the life of the portfolio, resulting in the loss of useful information about trends in profitability. The contracts placed in any of the three profitability groups could be significantly more or less profitable than other contracts in the group. The effect of averaging profits of the contracts in the group could therefore be substantially increased, leading to a greater likelihood that:

(a)   the contractual service margin of a contract would outlast the coverage period of that contract; and

(b)   the continuing profitability of some contracts would absorb the subsequent adverse changes in expectations that make some contracts onerous.

BC139G   Some stakeholders said that in some circumstances they could achieve at much less cost the same or a similar outcome without applying the annual cohort requirement as would be achieved applying that requirement. The Board concluded that it is unnecessary to amend IFRS 17 to reflect such circumstances. The Board reaffirmed its view that the requirements specify the amounts to be reported, not the methodology to be used to arrive at those amounts (see paragraph BC138). An entity is required to apply judgement and to consider all possible scenarios for future changes in expectations to conclude whether it could achieve the same accounting outcome without applying the annual cohort requirement.

BC139H   The Board recognised that entities will incur costs to identify the contractual service margin for each group of insurance contracts that is an annual cohort. However, the Board concluded that information about higher or lower profits earned by an entity from different generations of contracts is sufficiently useful to justify such costs.

Annual cohort requirement—insurance contracts with intergenerational sharing of risks between policyholders

BC139I   The Board considered but rejected a suggestion to exempt from the annual cohort requirement insurance contracts with intergenerational sharing of risks between policyholders. Some stakeholders commented that:

(a)   applying the requirement to such contracts requires arbitrary allocations, and the resulting information is therefore not useful; and

(b)   implementing the requirement is particularly costly and complex for such contracts, and the cost exceeds the resulting benefit.

BC139J   Intergenerational sharing of risks between policyholders is reflected in the fulfilment cash flows and therefore in the contractual service margin of each generation of contracts applying paragraphs B67–B71 of IFRS 17 (see paragraph BC171). However, each generation of contracts may be more or less profitable for an entity than other generations. Applying the variable fee approach (see paragraphs BC238–BC249) the profit for a group of insurance contracts reflects the entity's share in the fair value returns on underlying items. The entity's share in the fair value returns on underlying items is unaffected by the way the policyholders' share is distributed among generations of policyholders. For example, even if all generations of policyholders share equally in the fair value returns on the same pool of underlying items, the amount of the entity's share in those fair value returns created by each generation may differ. The entity's share in the fair value returns depends on the contractual terms of each annual cohort and the economic conditions during the coverage period of each annual cohort. For example, a 20 per cent share in fair value returns created by an annual cohort for which the fair value returns during the coverage period are 5 per cent is more profitable for an entity than a 20 per cent share in fair value returns created by an annual cohort for which the fair value returns during the coverage period are 1 per cent. Removing the annual cohort requirement for groups of insurance contracts with intergenerational sharing of risks between policyholders would average higher or lower profits from each generation of contracts, resulting in a loss of information about changes in profitability over time.

BC139K   Nonetheless, the Board identified two aspects of applying the annual cohort requirement to some contracts with intergenerational sharing of risks between policyholders that could increase the costs of applying the requirement and reduce the benefits of the resulting information:

(a)   distinguishing between the effect of risk sharing and the effect of discretion (paragraph BC139L); and

(b)   allocating changes in the amount of the entity's share of the fair value of underlying items between annual cohorts that share in the same pool of underlying items (paragraph BC139M).

BC139L   The aspect set out in paragraph BC139K(a) relates to circumstances in which an entity has discretion over the portion of the fair value returns on underlying items that the entity pays to policyholders and the portion that the entity retains. For example, an entity may be required under the terms of the insurance contracts to pay policyholders a minimum of 90 per cent of the total fair value returns on a specified pool of underlying items, but have discretion to pay more. The Board acknowledged that an entity with such discretion is required to apply additional judgement compared to an entity without such discretion to allocate changes in fulfilment cash flows between groups in a way that appropriately reflects the effect of risk sharing and the effect of the discretion. However, that judgement is required to measure new contracts recognised in a period, so would be needed even without the annual cohort requirement.

BC139M   The aspect set out in paragraph BC139K(b) relates to insurance contracts with direct participation features. For such contracts, an entity adjusts the contractual service margin for changes in the amount of the entity's share of the fair value of underlying items. IFRS 17 does not include specific requirements for allocating those changes between annual cohorts that share in the same pool of underlying items. The Board acknowledged that an entity needs to apply judgement to choose an allocation approach that provides useful information about the participation of each annual cohort in the underlying items.

BC139N   Nonetheless, in the Board's view, the information that results from the judgements an entity makes in determining the allocation approaches discussed in paragraphs BC139L–BC139M will provide users of financial statements with useful information about how management expects the performance of insurance contracts to develop.

BC139O   Further, the Board identified specific insurance contracts with intergenerational sharing of risks for which the information provided by the annual cohort requirement is particularly useful. Those contracts:

(a)   include features such as financial guarantees on the returns on underlying items or other cash flows that do not vary with returns on underlying items (for example, insurance claims); and

(b)   do not share the changes in the effect of the features in (a) between the entity and policyholders, or share the changes in the effect between the entity and policyholders in a way that results in the entity bearing more than a small share.

BC139P   The Board acknowledged that for some insurance contracts with substantial intergenerational sharing of risks, the effect of financial guarantees and other cash flows that do not vary with returns on underlying items would rarely cause an annual cohort to become onerous. However, the Board disagreed with stakeholders who said that the rarity of such an event makes less useful the information that results from applying the annual cohort requirement to such insurance contracts. The Board instead observed the rarity makes the information particularly useful to users of financial statements when such an event occurs. The Board identified such information about the effect of financial guarantees as being particularly important when interest rates are low.

BC139Q   Consequently, the Board concluded the costs of the annual cohort requirement might exceed the benefits of the resulting information for only a very limited population of contracts. The population is much smaller than some stakeholders had suggested.

BC139R   Nonetheless, the Board considered whether it could create an exemption from the annual cohort requirement that would capture only that very limited population of contracts, without the risk of capturing a wider population. However:

(a)   any focused exemption would be complex because of the interaction between contract features that increase the costs and reduce the benefits. An exemption would therefore result in difficulties for entities and auditors in identifying which contracts would be exempted, and for users of financial statements in understanding which contracts had been exempted. A significant difference in outcomes could arise in some circumstances depending on whether the annual cohort requirement has been applied, and thus it would be essential that the scope of an exemption from that requirement is clear to understand.

(b)   the purpose of any exemption would be to balance the costs and benefits. However, there is no way to specify the scope of the exemption other than by using arbitrary thresholds because the balance of costs and benefits for different contracts vary across a range and there is no clearly identifiable point at which the costs exceed the benefits. Entities would be able to avoid applying the annual cohort requirement by structuring contracts to meet those thresholds. The Board concluded there was a high risk that contracts for which the benefits of the annual cohort requirement heavily outweigh the costs would be included in the exemption, resulting in a loss of information critical for users of financial statements.

BC139S   The Board concluded that for all but a very limited population of contracts there is no question that the benefits of the annual cohort requirement significantly outweigh the costs. For a very limited population of contracts the costs and benefits of the requirement are more finely balanced. However, it is not possible to define that population in a way that does not risk it becoming too broad. The Board therefore decided to retain the annual cohort requirement unchanged.

Annual cohort requirement—group based on issue date

BC139T   In June 2020, the Board amended paragraph 28 of IFRS 17 to clarify that an entity is required to add an insurance contract to a group of insurance contracts at the date the contract is recognised, instead of the date the contract is issued (see paragraph BC145A). The Board considered but rejected a suggestion to also amend the annual cohort requirement in paragraph 22 of IFRS 17 to base it on the date contracts are recognised, instead of the date they are issued. The objective of the annual cohort requirement is to facilitate timely recognition of profits, losses and trends in profitability. The profitability of a contract is initially set when the contract is issued, based on facts and circumstances at that date—for example, interest rates, underwriting expectations and pricing. Hence, the Board concluded that determining annual cohorts based on the date that contracts are issued is necessary to provide useful information about trends in profitability.

Recognition (paragraphs 25–28F of IFRS 17)

BC140   The Board considered whether an entity should recognise the obligations and associated benefits arising from a group of insurance contracts from the time at which it accepts risk. Doing so would be consistent with the aspects of IFRS 17 that focus on measuring the obligations accepted by the entity. However, such an approach would differ from that required for revenue contracts within the scope of IFRS 15, which focuses on measuring performance. Under IFRS 15, an entity recognises no rights or obligations until one party has performed under the contract. That model would be consistent with the aspects of IFRS 17 that focus on measuring performance.

BC141   Further, some stakeholders were concerned that a requirement to recognise the group of insurance contracts from the time the entity accepts risk would mean that the entity would need to track and account for the group even before the coverage period begins. Those expressing that view stated that accounting for the group of insurance contracts before the coverage period begins would require system changes whose high costs outweigh the benefits of doing so, particularly because the amount recognised before the coverage period begins might be immaterial, or even nil. In the view of these respondents, even if amounts recognised before the coverage period begins are insignificant, requiring an entity to account for groups of insurance contracts in the pre-coverage period would impose on the entity the requirement to track groups to demonstrate that the amounts are insignificant.

BC142 The Board was sympathetic to those concerns. Accordingly, the Board adopted an approach that combines aspects of both approaches set out in paragraph BC140 by requiring that an entity recognise a group of insurance contracts from the earliest of:

(a) the beginning of the coverage period of the group of contracts;

(b) the date on which the first payment from a policyholder in the group becomes due; or

(c) for a group of onerous contracts, when the group becomes onerous.

BC143 Typically, the first premium is due at the start of the coverage period and the entity recognises the group of insurance contracts at that point. In the Board's view:

(a) the rationale described in paragraph BC141 for not recognising a group of insurance contracts in the pre-coverage period—ie tracking information before the coverage period begins does not generate benefits that outweigh costs—applies only to contracts before payments are due; and

(b) the benefits of reporting insurance contracts that are onerous in the pre-coverage period outweigh the costs of recognising the contracts.

BC144 In some cases, changes in circumstances make a group of insurance contracts onerous before coverage begins.[16] The Board decided that entities should recognise such onerous groups in the pre-coverage period. However, IFRS 17 requires onerous groups to be recognised only when facts and circumstances indicate that a group of insurance contracts is onerous. That approach ensures that entities recognise adverse changes in circumstances without the need to track groups before the coverage period begins.

BC145 The costs of originating insurance contracts are often incurred before the coverage period begins. As discussed in paragraph BC176, the Board concluded that an entity should not recognise such costs as separate assets. Instead, IFRS 17 requires such costs to be recognised as part of the cash flows of the group of insurance contracts once it qualifies for initial recognition. The Board observed that, in effect, entities will recognise groups from the date that the insurance acquisition cash flows are incurred. However, although an asset or liability is recognised from that date, entities do not need to update assumptions until the date the group qualifies for initial recognition and they are required only to determine the contractual service margin at that later date.[17]

---

16 In June 2020, the Board amended the definition of a coverage period to be the period during which the entity provides insurance contract services (see paragraphs BC283A–BC283I).

17 In June 2020, the Board amended the requirements relating to assets for insurance acquisition cash flows (see paragraphs BC184A–BC184K). The Board also specified that an entity recognises an asset for insurance acquisition cash flows paid (or for which a liability has been recognised applying another IFRS Standard) (see paragraphs BC184L–BC184N).

Amendments to IFRS 17—recognition

BC145A   In June 2020, the Board amended paragraph 28 of IFRS 17 to clarify that an entity is required to add an insurance contract to a group of insurance contracts (that is, to recognise an insurance contract) at the date the insurance contract meets any one of the recognition criteria in paragraph 25 of IFRS 17 (see paragraph BC142). That date may differ from the date on which the insurance contract is issued—for example, it may be the date that premiums become due.

Measurement of fulfilment cash flows (paragraphs 29–37 and B36–B92 of IFRS 17)

BC146   As explained in paragraphs BC19–BC20, IFRS 17 requires an entity to measure the fulfilment cash flows at a risk-adjusted present value. The sections below discuss the measurement of the fulfilment cash flows, in particular:

(a)   how an entity estimates the expected value of cash flows (see paragraphs BC147–BC157);

(b)   which cash flows should be included in the expected value of cash flows (see paragraphs BC158–BC184N);

(c)   how the cash flows are adjusted to reflect the time value of money and the financial risks, to the extent that the financial risks are not included in the estimates of future cash flows (see paragraphs BC185–BC205B); and

(d)   how the cash flows are adjusted to depict the effects of non-financial risk (see paragraphs BC206–BC217).

Estimates of future cash flows (paragraphs 33–35 and B36–B71 of IFRS 17)

BC147   This section discusses the requirements of IFRS 17 relating to how an entity estimates the future cash flows, including:

(a)   the unbiased use of all reasonable and supportable information available without undue cost or effort (see paragraphs BC148–BC152);

(b)   estimates that are consistent with available market information (see paragraphs BC153–BC154);

(c)   current estimates at the reporting date (see paragraphs BC155–BC156); and

(d)   explicit estimates (see paragraph BC157).

Unbiased use of all reasonable and supportable information available without undue cost or effort (paragraphs 33(a) and B37–B41 of IFRS 17)

BC148   Because insurance contracts transfer risk, the cash flows generated by insurance contracts are uncertain. Some argue that the measurement of insurance contracts should use a single estimate of the cash flows, for example, the most likely outcome or an outcome that is likely to prove 'sufficient' at an implicit or explicit level of confidence. However, the Board decided that a measure of insurance contracts is most useful if it captures information about the full range of possible outcomes and their probabilities.

BC149   Consequently, the Board concluded that the measurement of insurance contracts should start with an estimate of the expected present value of the cash flows generated by the contracts. The expected present value is the probability-weighted mean of the present value of the possible cash flows. The Board also noted that, because IFRS 17 sets the measurement requirement as the probability-weighted mean of the present value of the possible cash flows, when an entity determines that amount, estimates of the probabilities associated with each cash flow scenario should be unbiased. In other words, the estimates should not be biased by the intention of attaining a predetermined result or inducing particular behaviour. A lack of bias is important because biased financial reporting information cannot faithfully represent economic phenomena. A lack of bias requires that estimates of cash flows and the associated probabilities should be neither conservative nor optimistic.

BC150   In principle, determining an expected present value involves the following steps:

(a)   identifying each possible scenario;

(b)   measuring the present value of the cash flows in that scenario— paragraphs BC185–BC205B discuss the discount rate; and

(c)   estimating the probability of that scenario occurring.

Consistent with the approach taken in IFRS 9, the Board decided to specify that an entity should use reasonable and supportable information available without undue cost or effort in determining an expected present value.

BC151   An expected present value is not a forecast of a particular outcome. Consequently, differences between the ultimate outcome and the previous estimate of expected value are not 'errors' or 'failures'. The expected value is a summary that incorporates all foreseeable outcomes. When one or more of those outcomes do not occur, that does not invalidate the previous estimate of the expected value.

BC152   Many insurance contracts contain significant embedded options and guarantees. Many previous insurance accounting models attributed no value to embedded options or guarantees that lack 'intrinsic value' (ie when they were 'out of the money'). However, such embedded options and guarantees also have a time value because they could be 'in the money' at expiry. To the extent that those options and guarantees remain embedded in the insurance contract (see paragraphs BC104–BC107), the expected present value of future cash flows is an estimate based on all possible outcomes about cash flows. IFRS 17 also requires the measurement to include the effect of financial risk, either in the estimates of future cash flows or in the discount rate. The measurement approach in IFRS 17, therefore, incorporates both the intrinsic value and the time value of embedded options and guarantees. The use of the IFRS 17 approach will mean that the measurement of any options and guarantees included in the insurance contracts is consistent with observable market variables (see paragraph B48 of IFRS 17). The Board concluded that this measurement approach provides the most relevant information about embedded options and guarantees.

Estimates that are consistent with available market information (paragraphs 33(b) and B42–B53 of IFRS 17)

BC153   The Board decided that measurements are more relevant, have less measurement uncertainty, and are more understandable if they are consistent with observed market prices, because such measurements:

(a)   involve less subjectivity than measurements that use entity-specific expectations that differ from market consensus;

(b)   reflect all evidence available to market participants; and

(c)   are developed using a common and publicly accessible benchmark that users of financial statements can understand more easily than information developed using a private, internal benchmark.

BC154   This view has the following consequences:

(a)   an entity is required to use observable current market variables, such as interest rates, as direct inputs without adjustment when possible; and

(b)   when variables cannot be observed in, or derived directly from, market prices, the estimates should not contradict current market variables. For example, estimated probabilities for inflation scenarios should not contradict probabilities implied by market interest rates.

Current estimates at the reporting date (paragraphs 33(c) and B54–B60 of IFRS 17)

BC155   The Board concluded that estimates of cash flows should be based on current information, updated at the end of every reporting period. Insurance measurement models before IFRS 17 often required entities to make estimates at initial recognition and to use the same estimates throughout the duration of the contract, without updating to include information that became available later in the duration of the contract. However, the Board concluded that using current estimates:

(a)   gives more relevant information about the entity's contractual obligations and rights by better reflecting information about the amounts, timing and uncertainty of the cash flows generated by those obligations and rights. Because of the uncertainty associated with insurance contract liabilities and the long duration of many insurance contracts, current information reflecting the amount, timing and uncertainty of cash flows is particularly relevant for users of financial statements.

(b) incorporates all reasonable and supportable information available without undue cost or effort in the measurement, thus avoiding the need for a separate test to ensure that the liability is not understated (sometimes known as a 'liability adequacy test'). Any liability adequacy test is likely to involve some arbitrary components. For example, any specified timing for such a test would inevitably be arbitrary, unless current information were required at each reporting date.

(c) is broadly consistent with other IFRS Standards for provisions (IAS 37) and financial liabilities (IFRS 9). That is, for liabilities with characteristics similar to insurance contract liabilities, both IAS 37 and IFRS 9 would require measurements based on current estimates of future cash flows.

BC156 The Board noted that IAS 37 includes in the measurement of liabilities the effect of possible new legislation only when the legislation is virtually certain to be enacted, and that IAS 12 *Income Taxes* includes in the measurement of income taxes only changes in legislation that are substantively enacted. Consistent with these Standards, the Board concluded that an entity should include the effect of possible changes in legislation on future cash flows only when the change in legislation is substantively enacted.

Explicit estimates (paragraphs 33(d) and B46 of IFRS 17)

BC157 The Board concluded that explicit estimates of cash flows, which require an entity to consider actively whether circumstances have changed, result in more useful information about the entity's obligations to policyholders than estimates that combine cash flows with either the risk adjustment for non-financial risk or the adjustment to reflect the time value of money and financial risks. Explicit estimates also reduce the possibility that the entity does not identify some changes in circumstances. However, IFRS 17 allows an exception to the requirement to use explicit estimates of cash flows separate from the adjustment to reflect the time value of money and financial risks. This exception applies if the entity uses the fair value of a replicating portfolio of assets to measure some of the cash flows that arise from insurance contracts, which will combine the cash flows and the adjustment to reflect the time value of money and financial risks. The fair value of a replicating portfolio of assets reflects both the expected present value of the cash flows from the portfolio of assets and the risk associated with those cash flows (see paragraph B46 of IFRS 17).

The cash flows used to measure insurance contracts (paragraphs 34–35 and B61–B71 of IFRS 17)

BC158 This section discusses which cash flows should be included in the expected value of cash flows, including:

(a)   cash flows that arise from future premiums (see paragraphs BC159–BC164);

(b)   deposit floors (see paragraphs BC165–BC166);

(c)   cash flows over which the entity has discretion (see paragraphs BC167–BC170);

(ca)   cash flows relating to policyholder taxes (see paragraph BC170A);

(d)   cash flows that affect or are affected by cash flows to policyholders of other contracts (see paragraphs BC171–BC174);

(e)   insurance acquisition cash flows (see paragraphs BC175–BC184K); and

(f)   pre-recognition cash flows other than insurance acquisition cash flows (see paragraphs BC184L–BC184N).

Cash flows that arise from future premiums (paragraphs 34–35 and B61–B66 of IFRS 17)

BC159   The measurement of a group of insurance contracts includes all the cash flows expected to result from the contracts in the group, reflecting estimates of policyholder behaviour. Thus, to identify the future cash flows that will arise as the entity fulfils its obligations, it is necessary to draw a contract boundary that distinguishes whether future premiums, and the resulting benefits and claims, arise from:

(a)   existing insurance contracts. If so, those future premiums, and the resulting benefits and claims, are included in the measurement of the group of insurance contracts; or

(b)   future insurance contracts. If so, those future premiums, and the resulting benefits and claims, are not included in the measurement of the group of existing insurance contracts.

BC160   The essence of a contract is that it binds one or both of the parties. If both parties are bound equally, the boundary of the contract is generally clear. Similarly, if neither party is bound, it is clear that no genuine contract exists. Thus:

(a)   the outer limit of the existing contract is the point at which the entity is no longer required to provide coverage and the policyholder has no right of renewal. Beyond that outer limit, neither party is bound.[18]

(b)   the entity is no longer bound by the existing contract at the point at which the contract confers on the entity the practical ability to reassess the risk presented by a policyholder and, as a result, the right to set a price that fully reflects that risk. Thus, any cash flows arising beyond that point occur beyond the boundary of the existing contract and relate to a future contract, not to the existing contract.

---

18 In June 2020, the Board amended the definition of a coverage period to be the period during which the entity provides insurance contract services (see paragraphs BC283A–BC283J).

BC161   However, if an entity has the practical ability to reassess the risk presented by a policyholder, but does not have the right to set a price that fully reflects the reassessed risk, the contract still binds the entity. Thus, that point would lie within the boundary of the existing contract, unless the restriction on the entity's ability to reprice the contract is so minimal that it is expected to have no commercial substance (ie the restriction has no discernible effect on the economics of the transaction). In the Board's view, a restriction with no commercial substance does not bind the entity.

BC162   However, it may be more difficult to decide the contract boundary if the contract binds one party more tightly than the other. For example:

(a)   an entity may price a contract so that the premiums charged in early periods subsidise the premiums charged in later periods, even if the contract states that each premium relates to an equivalent period of coverage. This would be the case if the contract charges level premiums and the risks covered by the contract increase with time. The Board concluded that the premiums charged in later periods would be within the boundary of the contract because, after the first period of coverage, the policyholder has obtained something of value, namely the ability to continue coverage at a level price despite increasing risk.[19]

(b)   an insurance contract might bind the entity, but not the policyholder, by requiring the entity to continue to accept premiums and provide coverage but permitting the policyholder to stop paying premiums, although possibly incurring a penalty. In the Board's view, the premiums the entity is required to accept and the resulting coverage it is required to provide fall within the boundary of the contract.[20]

(c)   an insurance contract may permit an entity to reprice the contract on the basis of general market experience (for example, mortality experience), without permitting the entity to reassess the individual policyholder's risk profile (for example, the policyholder's health). In this case, the insurance contract binds the entity by requiring it to provide the policyholder with something of value: continuing insurance coverage without the need to undergo underwriting again. Although the terms of the contract are such that the policyholder has a benefit in renewing the contract, and thus the entity expects that renewals will occur, the contract does not require the policyholder to renew the contract. The Board originally decided that ignoring the entity's expectation of renewals would not reflect the economic circumstances created by the contract for the entity. Consequently, the Board originally proposed that if the entity can reprice an existing contract for general but not individual-specific changes in policyholders' risk profiles, the cash flows resulting from the renewals repriced in this way lie within the boundaries of the existing contract.

---

19 In June 2020, the Board amended the definition of a coverage period to be the period during which the entity provides insurance contract services (see paragraphs BC283A–BC283J).

20 In June 2020, the Board amended the definition of a coverage period to be the period during which the entity provides insurance contract services (see paragraphs BC283A–BC283J).

BC163   Many stakeholders suggested that the original proposal in paragraph BC162(c) resulted in some cash flows for which the entity was not bound being included within the boundary of some contracts. Even when an entity is prevented from repricing an existing contract using an individual policyholder's risk assessment, the entity may nonetheless be able to reprice a portfolio to which the contract belongs with the result that the price charged for the portfolio as a whole fully reflects the risk of the portfolio. As a result, these stakeholders argued that in such cases the entity is no longer bound by the existing portfolio of contracts and that any cash flows that arise beyond that repricing point should be considered to be beyond the boundary of the existing contract. To the extent that an entity would not be able to charge a price that fully reflects the risks of the portfolio as a whole, it would be bound by the existing contract. The Board was persuaded by this view and modified the contract boundary so that such cash flows are considered to be outside the contract boundary, provided the pricing of the premiums for coverage up to the date when the risks are reassessed does not take into account the risks that relate to periods subsequent to the reassessment date.[21]

BC164   Because the entity updates the measurement of the group of insurance contracts to which the individual contract belongs and, hence, the portfolio of contracts in each reporting period, the assessment of the contract boundary is made in each reporting period. For example, in one reporting period an entity may decide that a renewal premium for a portfolio of contracts is outside the contract boundary because the restriction on the entity's ability to reprice the contract has no commercial substance. However, if circumstances change so that the same restrictions on the entity's ability to reprice the portfolio take on commercial substance, the entity may conclude that future renewal premiums for that portfolio of contracts are within the boundary of the contract.

Deposit floors

BC165   The Board also addressed how deposit floors are considered when measuring insurance contracts. The 'deposit floor' is a term used to describe the following requirement in paragraph 47 of IFRS 13:

> The fair value of a financial liability with a demand feature (eg a demand deposit) is not less than the amount payable on demand, discounted from the first date that the amount could be required to be paid.

BC166   If a deposit floor were to be applied when measuring insurance contracts, the resulting measurement would ignore all scenarios other than those involving the exercise of policyholder options in the way that is least favourable to the entity. Such a requirement would contradict the principle that an entity should incorporate in the measurement of an insurance contract future cash flows on a probability-weighted basis. Consequently, IFRS 17 does not require or allow the application of a deposit floor when measuring insurance contracts. This applies both to the general measurement requirements of IFRS 17 and when IFRS 17 requires the use of fair value (see paragraphs BC327

---

21 In June 2020, the Board amended the definition of a coverage period to be the period during which the entity provides insurance contract services (see paragraphs BC283A–BC283J).

and BC385). However, paragraph 132(c) of IFRS 17 requires entities to disclose the amount payable on demand in a way that highlights the relationship between such amounts and the carrying amount of the related contracts.

Cash flows over which the entity has discretion (paragraph B65 of IFRS 17)

BC167 Some insurance contracts give policyholders the right to share in the returns on specified underlying items. In some cases, the contract gives the entity discretion over the resulting payments to the policyholders, either in their timing or in their amount. Such discretion is usually subject to some constraint, including constraints in law or regulation and market competition.

BC168 IFRS 17 requires the measurement of a group of insurance contracts to include an unbiased estimate of the expected cash outflows from the contracts. The expected cash outflows include outflows over which the entity has discretion. The Board decided to require this because:

(a) it can be difficult to determine whether an entity is making payments because it believes that it is obliged to do so, rather than for some other reason that does not justify the recognition of a stand-alone liability. Those reasons could be to maintain the entity's competitive position or because the entity believes it is under some moral pressure. Thus, it could be difficult to make a reasonable estimate of the level of distribution that would ultimately be enforceable in the unlikely event that an entity asserts that its discretion to pay or withhold amounts to policyholders is unfettered.

(b) even if it were possible to make a reasonable estimate of non-discretionary cash flows, users of financial statements would not benefit from knowing how much might be enforceable in the highly unlikely event that an entity tried to avoid paying amounts to policyholders of insurance contracts when the entity and its policyholders currently expect that such benefits will be paid. That amount does not provide relevant information about the amount, timing and uncertainty of future cash flows. On the other hand, users of financial statements would want to know:

(i) how much of the cash flows will be unavailable to investors because the entity expects to pay them to policyholders. The requirements in IFRS 17 convey that information by including those cash flows in the measurement of the liability.

(ii) how much of the risk in the contracts is borne by the policyholders through the participation mechanism and how much by the shareholders. This information is conveyed by the required disclosures about risk.

BC169 The Board considered whether payments that are subject to the entity's discretion meet the definition of a liability in the Conceptual Framework for Financial Reporting (the *Conceptual Framework*). The contract, when considered as a whole, clearly meets the *Conceptual Framework*'s definition of a liability. Some components, if viewed in isolation, may not meet the definition of a liability. However, in the Board's view, including such components in the measurement of insurance contracts would generate more useful information for users of financial statements.

BC170 The Board considered whether to provide specific guidance on amounts that have accumulated over many decades in participating funds and whose 'ownership' may not be attributable definitively between shareholders and policyholders. It concluded that it would not. In principle, IFRS 17 requires an entity to estimate the cash flows in each scenario. If that requires difficult judgements or involves unusual levels of uncertainty, an entity would consider those matters in deciding what disclosures it must provide to satisfy the disclosure objective in IFRS 17.

Amendments to IFRS 17—cash flows relating to policyholder taxes (paragraphs B65–B66 of IFRS 17)

BC170A In June 2020, the Board amended IFRS 17 to resolve an inconsistency between the description of cash flows within the boundary of an insurance contract in paragraph B65(m) of IFRS 17 and the description of cash flows outside the boundary of an insurance contract in paragraph B66(f) of IFRS 17. Before the amendment, paragraph B66(f) of IFRS 17 required an entity to exclude income tax payments and receipts not paid or received in a fiduciary capacity from the estimate of the cash flows that will arise as the entity fulfils an insurance contract. Some stakeholders said that some income tax payments and receipts, although not paid or received in a fiduciary capacity, are costs specifically chargeable to the policyholder under the terms of the contract. Accordingly, those costs should be included in the boundary of an insurance contract applying paragraph B65(m) of IFRS 17. The Board agreed that any costs specifically chargeable to the policyholder are cash flows that will arise as the entity fulfils an insurance contract. Therefore, the Board amended paragraph B66(f) of IFRS 17 to avoid excluding from the fulfilment cash flows income tax payments or receipts specifically chargeable to the policyholder under the terms of the contract. An entity recognises insurance revenue for the consideration paid by the policyholder for such income tax amounts when the entity recognises in profit or loss the income tax amounts. This treatment is consistent with the recognition of insurance revenue for other incurred expenses applying IFRS 17 (see paragraph BC37).

Cash flows that affect or are affected by cash flows to policyholders of other contracts (paragraphs B67–B71 in IFRS 17)

BC171 Sometimes insurance contracts in one group affect the cash flows to policyholders of contracts in a different group. This effect is sometimes called 'mutualisation'. However, that term is used in practice to refer to a variety of effects, ranging from the effects of specific contractual terms to general risk diversification. Consequently, the Board decided not to use the term but instead to include in IFRS 17 requirements that ensure the fulfilment cash flows of any group are determined in a way that does not distort the contractual service margin, taking into account the extent to which the cash flows of different groups affect each other. Hence the fulfilment cash flows for a group:

(a) include payments arising from the terms of existing contracts to policyholders of contracts in other groups, regardless of whether those payments are expected to be made to current or future policyholders; and

(b) exclude payments to policyholders in the group that, applying (a), have been included in the fulfilment cash flows of another group.

BC172 The reference to future policyholders is necessary because sometimes the terms of an existing contract are such that the entity is obliged to pay to policyholders amounts based on underlying items, but with discretion over the timing of the payments. That means that some of the amounts based on underlying items may be paid to policyholders of contracts that will be issued in the future that share in the returns on the same underlying items, rather than to existing policyholders. From the entity's perspective, the terms of the existing contract require it to pay the amounts, even though it does not yet know when or to whom it will make the payments.

BC173 The Board considered whether it was necessary to amend the requirements in IFRS 17 relating to the determination of the contractual service margin for insurance contracts with cash flows that affect or are affected by cash flows to policyholders of contracts in another group. The Board concluded that it was not necessary because the fulfilment cash flows allocated to a group described in paragraph BC171 result in the contractual service margin of a group appropriately reflecting the future profit expected to be earned from the contracts in the group, including any expected effect on that future profit caused by other contracts.

BC174 The Board also considered whether it was necessary to amend the requirements in IFRS 17 restricting contracts in a group to those issued not more than one year apart, but concluded that it was not necessary (see paragraph BC138).[22]

Insurance acquisition cash flows (paragraphs B65(e) and B125 of IFRS 17)

BC175 Entities often incur significant costs to sell, underwrite and start new insurance contracts. These costs are commonly referred to as 'insurance acquisition cash flows'. Insurance contracts are generally priced to recover those costs through premiums or through surrender charges, or both.

Measurement approach

BC176 The measurement approach required in IFRS 17 represents a change from many previous accounting models that measure insurance contract liabilities initially at the amount of the premiums received, with deferral of insurance acquisition cash flows. Such models treat insurance acquisition cash flows as a representation of the cost of a recognisable asset, which, depending on the model, might be described as a contract asset or a customer relationship

---

22 When developing the June 2020 amendments to IFRS 17, the Board considered but rejected suggestions to exempt from the annual cohort requirement insurance contracts with intergenerational sharing of risks (see paragraphs BC139I–BC139S). These considerations were similar to those in developing the Standard as described in paragraph BC174.

intangible asset. The Board concluded that such an asset either does not exist, if the entity recovers insurance acquisition cash flows from premiums already received, or relates to future cash flows that are included in the measurement of the contract.[23] The Board noted that an entity typically charges the policyholder a price the entity regards as sufficient to compensate it for undertaking the obligation to pay for insured losses and for the cost of originating the contracts. Thus, a faithful representation of the remaining obligation to pay for insured losses should not include the part of the premium intended to compensate for the cost of originating the contracts.

BC177   Consequently, the Board concluded that an entity should recognise insurance acquisition cash flows as an expense, and should recognise an amount of revenue equal to the portion of the premium that relates to recovering its insurance acquisition cash flows. IFRS 17 achieves this by requiring that the cash flows for a group of insurance contracts include the insurance acquisition cash outflows or inflows associated with the group of contracts (including amounts received or to be received by the entity to acquire new insurance contracts).[24] This approach reduces the contractual service margin on initial recognition of the group of insurance contracts and has the advantage that the insurance acquisition cash flows are treated the same as other cash flows incurred in fulfilling contracts.

BC178   In many cases, insurance acquisition cash flows occur at the beginning of the coverage period of a group of insurance contracts, before any coverage or other service has been provided. Because insurance revenue is recognised in the same pattern as changes in the liability for remaining coverage, this would mean that some of the insurance revenue would be recognised when the insurance acquisition cash flows are paid, often at the beginning of the coverage period.

BC179   The Board was concerned that recognising insurance revenue at the beginning of the coverage period would be inconsistent with the principles in IFRS 15 because, at the beginning of the coverage period, the entity has not satisfied any of the obligations to the policyholder under the contract. In contrast, IFRS 15 requires an entity to recognise as revenue the consideration received from the customer as it satisfies its performance obligations under the contract. Accordingly, the Board decided to include an exception in IFRS 17 for the treatment of insurance acquisition cash flows so that the premium related to insurance acquisition cash flows is not recognised as revenue when the insurance acquisition cash flows occur, but is separately identified and recognised over the coverage period. IFRS 17 also requires the insurance acquisition cash flows to be recognised as an expense over the same period.

---

23 An asset for insurance acquisition cash flows is derecognised when those insurance acquisition cash flows are included in the measurement of the group of insurance contracts to which they have been allocated. In June 2020, the Board amended IFRS 17 so that allocation reflects an entity's expectations about future contract renewals (see paragraphs BC184A–BC184K).

24 In June 2020, the Board amended IFRS 17 to clarify that insurance acquisition cash flows paid before a group of insurance contracts is recognised cannot be a liability.

BC180   The requirement to recognise insurance acquisition cash flows as an expense over the coverage period differs from recognising an asset or an explicit or implicit reduction in the carrying amount of the group of insurance contracts. At all times, the liability for the group is measured as the sum of the fulfilment cash flows, including any expected future insurance acquisition cash flows, and the contractual service margin. Because the contractual service margin cannot be less than zero, the entity need not test separately whether it will recover the insurance acquisition cash flows that have occurred but have not yet been recognised as an expense. The measurement model captures any lack of recoverability automatically by remeasuring the fulfilment cash flows.[25]

Insurance acquisition cash flows included in measurement

BC181   The Board considered whether only insurance acquisition cash flows that are incremental at a contract level should be included in the measurement of an insurance contract. Those cash flows can be clearly identified as relating specifically to the contract. Including cash flows that relate to more than one contract requires a more subjective judgement to identify which cash flows to include.

BC182   However, the Board noted that:

(a)   including only insurance acquisition cash flows that are incremental at a contract level would mean that entities would recognise different contractual service margins and expenses depending on the way they structure their acquisition activities. For example, there would be different liabilities reported if the entity had an internal sales department rather than outsourcing sales to external agents. In the Board's view, differences in the structure of insurance acquisition activities would not necessarily reflect economic differences between insurance contracts issued by the entities.

(b)   an entity typically prices insurance contracts to recover not only incremental costs, but also other direct costs and a proportion of indirect costs incurred in originating insurance contracts—such as costs of underwriting, medical tests and inspection, and issuing the policy. The entity measures and manages these costs for the portfolio, rather than for the individual contract. Accordingly, including insurance acquisition cash flows that are incremental at the portfolio level in the fulfilment cash flows of the insurance contracts would be consistent with identification of other cash flows that are included in the measurement of the contracts.

BC183   The Board also considered whether to restrict insurance acquisition cash flows to be included in the measurement of a group of insurance contracts to those cash flows related directly to the successful acquisition of new or renewed insurance contracts. The approach in IFRS 17 to the measurement of a group

---

25   In June 2020, the Board amended IFRS 17 to include specific requirements relating to an asset for insurance acquisition cash flows recognised before a group of insurance contracts is recognised (see paragraphs BC184A–BC184K).

of insurance contracts is to estimate the profit expected to be generated over the duration of the group. In this context, excluding some insurance acquisition cash flows that relate to issuing a portfolio of contracts would result in an understatement of the fulfilment cash flows and an overstatement of the contractual service margins of groups in the portfolio. In addition, the Board wanted to avoid measuring liabilities and expenses at different amounts depending on how an entity structures its insurance acquisition activities, as described in paragraph BC182(a).

BC184 The Board also noted that the measurement approach in IFRS 17 automatically recognises as an immediate expense any insurance acquisition cash flows that cannot be recovered from the cash flows of the portfolio of contracts, because such cash flows reduce the contractual service margin below zero and must therefore be recognised as an expense. Hence, no amount can be recognised in the statement of financial position for insurance acquisition cash flows that are not recoverable.[26]

Amendments to IFRS 17—insurance acquisition cash flows (paragraphs 28A–28F and B35A–B35D of IFRS 17)

BC184A In June 2020, the Board amended IFRS 17 to require an entity to use a systematic and rational method to allocate insurance acquisition cash flows that are directly attributable to a group of insurance contracts:

(a) to that group; and

(b) to groups that will include insurance contracts that are expected to arise from renewals of insurance contracts in that group (see paragraph B35A of IFRS 17).

BC184B Before the amendment, an entity was required to allocate insurance acquisition cash flows directly attributable to a group to only that group. In contrast, insurance acquisition cash flows directly attributable to a portfolio of insurance contracts but not directly attributable to a group of insurance contracts are systematically and rationally allocated to groups of insurance contracts in the portfolio.

BC184C Stakeholders said an entity that issues an insurance contract with a short coverage period, such as one year, might incur high up-front costs, such as commissions to sales agents, relative to the premium the entity will charge for the contract. The entity agrees to those costs because it expects that some policyholders will renew their contracts. Often, those costs are fully directly attributable to the initial insurance contract issued because those costs are non-refundable and are not contingent on the policyholder renewing the contracts.

---

26 In June 2020, the Board amended IFRS 17 to include specific requirements relating to an asset for insurance acquisition cash flows recognised before a group of insurance contracts is recognised (see paragraphs BC184A–BC184K).

BC184D   In some circumstances, such commissions are higher than the premium charged and applying IFRS 17 before it was amended would have resulted in the initial insurance contract being identified as onerous. In the Board's view, an entity recognising a loss in that circumstance would provide useful information to users of financial statements. The information would reflect that the entity does not have a right to either oblige policyholders to renew the contracts, or to reclaim the commissions from sales agents if policyholders choose not to renew the contracts.

BC184E   However, the Board was persuaded that an amendment to IFRS 17 requiring an entity to allocate insurance acquisition cash flows to expected renewal contracts (expected renewals) would also provide useful information to users of financial statements. Such a requirement depicts the payment of up-front costs such as commissions as an asset that an entity expects to recover through both initial insurance contracts issued and expected renewals. The asset reflects the right of an entity to not pay again costs it had already paid to obtain renewals. The Board noted that the information resulting from the amendment is comparable to the information provided by IFRS 15 for the incremental costs of obtaining a contract.

BC184F   The Board concluded it did not need to develop requirements to specify how to allocate insurance acquisition cash flows to expected renewals. It concluded that requiring a systematic and rational method of allocation, consistent with paragraph B65(l) of IFRS 17, is sufficient.

BC184G   The Board noted that if an entity allocates assets for insurance acquisition cash flows to groups expected to be recognised across more than one reporting period in the future, an entity would need to update its allocation at the end of each reporting period to reflect any changes in assumptions about expected renewals. The Board also decided to clarify that an entity must apply a consistent method across reporting periods by referring in the requirements to a systematic and rational method (rather than a systematic and rational basis).

BC184H   Amending IFRS 17 to require an entity to allocate insurance acquisition cash flows to expected renewals creates assets for insurance acquisition cash flows that will be recognised for longer than assets would have been recognised applying the requirements before the amendment. The amendment will therefore increase the carrying amount of assets for insurance acquisition cash flows. Accordingly, the Board considered whether it should specify requirements for:

(a)   accretion of interest on assets for insurance acquisition cash flows. The Board decided against specifying such requirements because doing so would be inconsistent with IFRS 15.

(b)   assessments of the recoverability of assets for insurance acquisition cash flows. The Board decided to specify such requirements for the reasons set out in paragraphs BC184I–BC184K.

BC184I When the Board issued IFRS 17 in May 2017, it concluded that requiring an entity to assess the recoverability of an asset for insurance acquisition cash flows would be unnecessary. The asset was typically of relatively short duration and any lack of recoverability would be reflected on a timely basis when the asset was derecognised and the insurance acquisition cash flows were included in the measurement of a group of insurance contracts (see paragraph BC180). As a result of the June 2020 amendment set out in paragraph BC184A, the Board concluded that it needed to require an entity to assess the recoverability of an asset for insurance acquisition cash flows at the end of each reporting period if facts and circumstances indicate the asset may be impaired.

BC184J Consistent with the impairment test in paragraph 101 of IFRS 15, an entity recognises an impairment loss in profit or loss and reduces the carrying amount of an asset for insurance acquisition cash flows so that the carrying amount does not exceed the expected net cash inflow for the related group.

BC184K The Board noted that an entity measures an asset for insurance acquisition cash flows at the level of a group of insurance contracts. An impairment test at a group level compares the carrying amount of an asset for insurance acquisition cash flows allocated to a group with the expected net cash inflow of the group. That net cash inflow includes cash flows for contracts unrelated to any expected renewals but expected to be in that group. The Board therefore decided to require an additional impairment test specific to cash flows for expected renewals. This additional impairment test results in the recognition of any impairment losses when the entity no longer expects the renewals supporting the asset to occur, or expects the net cash inflows to be lower than the amount of the asset. Without the additional impairment test, cash flows from contracts unrelated to any expected renewals might prevent the recognition of such an impairment loss.

Amendments to IFRS 17—pre-recognition cash flows other than insurance acquisition cash flows (paragraphs 38, B66A and B123A of IFRS 17)

BC184L In June 2020, the Board amended IFRS 17 to address the treatment of assets or liabilities for cash flows related to a group of insurance contracts that have been recognised before the group of insurance contracts is recognised. Such assets and liabilities might have been recognised before the group of insurance contracts is recognised because the cash flows occur or because a liability is recognised applying another IFRS Standard. Cash flows are related to a group of insurance contracts if they would have been included in the fulfilment cash flows at the date of initial recognition of the group had they been paid or received after that date.

BC184M The Board agreed with feedback that such cash flows should be included in the determination of the contractual service margin and insurance revenue for the group of insurance contracts. These cash flows should affect profit and revenue in the same way as the fulfilment cash flows regardless of their timing (or of the timing of their recognition as a liability).

BC184N   The amendment requires an entity to derecognise any asset or liability for such cash flows when the entity recognises the related group of insurance contracts to the extent that the asset or liability would not have been recognised separately from the group of insurance contracts if the cash flows (or the event that triggered their recognition as a liability) had occurred at the date of initial recognition of the group of insurance contracts. In addition the Board concluded that, to be consistent with the recognition of insurance revenue and incurred expenses required by IFRS 17, to the extent that an asset is derecognised when the entity recognises the related group of insurance contracts, insurance revenue and expenses should be recognised. In contrast, no insurance revenue or expenses arise on the derecognition of a liability at that date. The derecognition of a liability results either in the amounts expected to settle the liability being included in the fulfilment cash flows or the performance obligation depicted by the liability being subsumed within the recognition of the group of insurance contracts. For example, an entity that recognised a liability for premiums received in advance of the recognition of a group of insurance contracts would derecognise that liability when the entity recognises a group of insurance contracts to the extent the premiums relate to the contracts in the group. The performance obligation that was depicted by the liability would not be recognised separately from the group of insurance contracts had the premiums been received on the date of the initial recognition of the group. No insurance revenue arises on the derecognition of the liability.

Discount rates (paragraphs 36 and B72–B85 of IFRS 17)

BC185   This section discusses:

(a)   whether the measurement of all insurance contracts should be discounted (see paragraphs BC186–BC191);

(b)   current, market-consistent estimates of the time value of money and financial risks, to the extent not included in the estimates of future cash flows (see paragraph BC192);

(c)   the approach taken in respect of liquidity and own credit risk factors in determining the discount rate for a group of insurance contracts (see paragraphs BC193–BC197);

(d)   disclosure of the yield curve (see paragraph BC198);

(e)   reflecting dependence on underlying items in the discount rate (see paragraphs BC199–BC205); and

(f)   subjectivity in determining discount rates (see paragraphs BC205A–BC205B).

Discounting for all insurance contracts (paragraphs 36 and B72 of IFRS 17)

BC186   An amount payable tomorrow has a value different from that of the same amount payable in 10 years' time. In other words, money has a time value. The Board concluded that the measurement of all insurance contracts should reflect the effect of the timing of cash flows, because such a measure gives more relevant information about the entity's financial position.

BC187   When applying some previous accounting practices, entities did not discount their non-life (property and casualty) insurance contract liabilities. Some suggested that measuring non-life insurance contracts at a discounted amount would produce information that is less reliable (ie has more measurement uncertainty) than measuring it at its undiscounted amount because non-life insurance contracts are more uncertain than life insurance contracts with respect to:

(a)   whether the insured event will occur, whereas the insured event in some life insurance contracts is certain to occur unless the policy lapses;

(b)   the amount of the future payment that would be required if an insured event occurs, whereas the future payment obligation is generally specified in, or readily determinable from, a life insurance contract; and

(c)   the timing of any future payments required when the insured event occurs, whereas the timing of future payments in a life insurance contract is typically more predictable.

BC188   These uncertainties mean that the cash flows for many non-life insurance contracts have greater variability than do the cash flows for many life insurance contracts. Some stakeholders argued that estimating the timing of payments and calculating a discount rate would introduce additional subjectivity into the measurement of insurance contracts and that this could reduce comparability and permit earnings management. Furthermore, these stakeholders stated that the benefits of presenting a discounted measure of non-life insurance contracts might not justify the costs of preparing that measure. These stakeholders stated that the timing of cash flows and the resulting interest is an essential component of the pricing and profitability of life insurance contracts, but is less relevant for non-life insurance contracts for which the stakeholders viewed underwriting results as the most critical component of pricing and profitability.

BC189   These arguments did not persuade the Board. Measuring a group of insurance contracts using undiscounted cash flows would fail to represent faithfully the entity's financial position and would be less relevant to users of financial statements than a measurement that includes the discounted amounts. The Board also concluded that discount rates and the amount and timing of future cash flows can generally be estimated without excessive measurement uncertainty at a reasonable cost. Absolute precision is unattainable, but it is also unnecessary. The Board is of the view that the measurement uncertainty caused by discounting does not outweigh the additional relevance of the resulting measurement of the entity's obligations. Furthermore, many entities have experience in discounting, both to support investment decisions and to measure items for which other IFRS Standards require discounting, such as financial instruments, employee benefit obligations and long-term non-financial liabilities. Additionally, the Board has learned that, for internal managerial purposes, some insurance entities discount some of their non-life insurance portfolios or groups of insurance contracts.

BC190　Some stakeholders suggested that measuring non-life insurance contracts at undiscounted amounts that ignore future inflation could provide a reasonable approximation of the value of the liability, especially for short-tail liabilities, at less cost and with less complexity than measuring such contracts at explicitly discounted amounts. However, this approach of implicitly discounting the liability makes the unrealistic assumption that two variables (claim inflation and the effect of timing) will more or less offset each other in every case. As this is unlikely, the Board concluded that financial reporting will be improved if entities estimate those effects separately.

BC191　As discussed in paragraphs BC292(a) and BC294, for contracts to which the entity applies the simpler premium allocation approach, the Board decided that an entity need not reflect the effects of discounting in some cases in which those effects would be generally expected to be insignificant.

Current, market-consistent discount rates (paragraphs 36 and B74–B85 of IFRS 17)

BC192　Paragraphs BC20 and BC146–BC156 describe the Board's reasoning for using current, market-consistent estimates of cash flows. That reasoning also applies to the discount rate for those cash flows. Accordingly, IFRS 17 requires entities to discount cash flows using current, market-consistent discount rates that reflect the time value of money, the characteristics of the cash flows and the liquidity characteristics of the insurance contracts.

Factors to include in the discount rate (paragraphs B78–B85 of IFRS 17)

Liquidity

BC193　Discussions of the time value of money often use the notion of risk-free rates. Many entities use highly liquid, high-quality bonds as a proxy for risk-free rates. However, the holder can often sell such bonds in the market at short notice without incurring significant costs or affecting the market price. This means that the holder of such bonds effectively holds two things:

(a)　a holding in an underlying non-tradable investment, paying a higher return than the observed return on the traded bond; and

(b)　an embedded option to sell the investment to a market participant, for which the holder pays an implicit premium through a reduction in the overall return.

In contrast, for many insurance contracts, the entity cannot be forced to make payments earlier than the occurrence of insured events, or dates specified in the contract.

BC194   The Board concluded that, in principle, the discount rate for a group of insurance contracts should reflect the liquidity characteristics of the items being measured. Thus, the discount rate should equal the return on the underlying non-tradable investment (see paragraph BC193(a)), because the entity cannot sell or put the contract liability without significant cost. There should be no deduction in the rate for the implicit premium for the embedded put option, because no such put option is present in the liability.

BC195   The Board concluded that it is not appropriate in a principle-based approach:

(a)   to ignore the liquidity characteristics of the item being measured, or to use an arbitrary benchmark (for example, high-quality corporate bonds) as an attempt to develop a practical proxy for measuring the specific liquidity characteristics of the item being measured; or

(b)   to provide detailed guidance on how to estimate liquidity adjustments.

BC196   However, in response to feedback suggesting that it may be difficult to determine a liquidity premium in isolation, the Board observed that in estimating liquidity adjustments, an entity could apply either of the following:

(a)   a 'bottom-up' approach based on highly liquid, high-quality bonds, adjusted to include a premium for the illiquidity.

(b)   a 'top-down' approach based on the expected returns of a reference portfolio, adjusted to eliminate factors that are not relevant to the liability, for example market and credit risk. The Board expects a reference portfolio will typically have liquidity characteristics closer to the liquidity characteristics of the group of insurance contracts than highly liquid, high-quality bonds. Because of the difficulty in assessing liquidity premiums, the Board decided that in applying a top-down approach an entity need not make an adjustment for any remaining differences in liquidity characteristics between the reference portfolio and the insurance contracts.

Own credit risk (paragraph 31 of IFRS 17)

BC197   IFRS 17 requires an entity to disregard its own credit risk when measuring the fulfilment cash flows. Some stakeholders expressed the view that information about own credit risk relating to a liability that must be fulfilled by the issuer, and about gains and losses arising from changes in the issuer's own credit risk, is not relevant for users of financial statements. The Board concluded that including the effect of a change in the entity's own non-performance risk in the measurement of an insurance contract liability would not provide useful information. The Board considered concerns that excluding own credit risk could lead to accounting mismatches, because the fair value of the assets viewed as backing insurance contracts includes changes in credit risk on those assets, while the measurement of a group of insurance contracts would exclude changes in the credit risk of the group of contracts. In the Board's view, such mismatches will often be economic in nature, because the credit risk associated with the insurance contracts differs from the credit risk of the assets held by the entity.

Disclosure of yield curve (paragraph 120 of IFRS 17)

BC198   Paragraphs B80 and B81 of IFRS 17 note that the different approaches the Board allows for determining the discount rate could give rise to different rates. Accordingly, the Board decided that an entity should disclose the yield curve or range of yield curves used to discount cash flows that do not vary based on returns on underlying items to supplement the requirement in paragraph 117 of IFRS 17 that an entity disclose the methods and inputs that are used to estimate the discount rates. The Board decided that disclosure of the yield curves used will allow users of financial statements to understand how those yield curves might differ from entity to entity.

Reflecting dependence on assets in the discount rate (see paragraphs 36 and B74–B85 of IFRS 17)

BC199   Some previous accounting approaches applied discount rates to insurance contract liabilities derived from the expected return on assets viewed as backing the liabilities, even when the cash flows arising from the liability do not vary based on the cash flows of the underlying items. Proponents of such approaches stated that doing so:

(a)   prevents losses arising at initial recognition for groups of insurance contracts that are expected to be profitable overall and so reflects the most likely outcome of the insurance activity as a whole, taking into consideration the underwriting and investment functions together.

(b)   prevents the volatility that would arise if short-term fluctuations in asset spreads affect the measurement of the assets, but not the measurement of the liabilities. Because an entity holds those assets for the long term to fulfil its obligations under the insurance contracts it has issued, some say that those fluctuations make it more difficult for users of financial statements to assess an entity's long-term performance.

BC200   However, the Board did not agree with these views. The Board decided that recognising a loss at contract inception is appropriate if the amount paid by the policyholder is insufficient to cover the expected present value of the policyholder's benefits and claims as well as to compensate the entity for bearing the risk that the benefits might ultimately exceed the expected premiums. Further, the Board noted that, to the extent that market spreads affect assets and insurance contracts differently, useful information is provided about economic mismatches, particularly about duration mismatches.

BC201   The Board rejected the application of an asset-based discount rate when the cash flows from the group of insurance contracts do not vary based on returns on assets, because those rates are unrelated to the cash flows. The objective of the discount rate is to adjust estimated future cash flows for the time value of money and for financial risks (for example, the liquidity risk), to the extent that they are not included in the estimated cash flows, in a way that captures the characteristics of the contract. To capture the characteristics of the contract:

(a) to the extent that the cash flows from assets (or other underlying items) affect the cash flows that arise from the liability, the appropriate discount rate should reflect the dependence on the underlying items; and

(b) to the extent that the cash flows that arise from the contracts are expected not to vary with returns on underlying items, the appropriate discount rate should exclude any factors that influence the underlying items that are irrelevant to the contracts. Such factors include risks that are not present in the contracts but are present in the financial instrument for which the market prices are observed. Thus, the discount rate should not capture all of the characteristics of those assets, even if the entity views those assets as backing those contracts.

BC202 Some view the cash flows that result from a guarantee embedded in an insurance contract as:

(a) variable in scenarios in which the guarantee amount is lower than the proportion of returns on underlying items promised to the policyholder; and

(b) fixed in scenarios in which the guaranteed amount is higher than the proportion of returns on underlying items promised to the policyholder.

BC203 However, the cash flows resulting from the guarantees do not vary directly with returns on underlying items because they are not expected to vary directly with such returns in all scenarios. Accordingly, an asset-based discount rate (from assets with variable returns) would be inappropriate for such cash flows.

BC204 The Board noted that a link between cash flows and underlying items could be captured by using replicating portfolio techniques, or portfolio techniques that have similar outcomes (see paragraphs B46–B48 of IFRS 17). A replicating portfolio is a theoretical portfolio of assets providing cash flows that exactly match the cash flows from the liability in all scenarios. If such a portfolio exists, the appropriate discount rate(s) for the replicating portfolio would also be the appropriate discount rate(s) for the liability. If a replicating portfolio existed and could be measured directly, there would be no need to determine separately the cash flows and the discount rate for the part of the liability replicated by that portfolio. The measurements of the replicating portfolio and the replicated cash flows arising from the contracts would be identical.

BC205 However, the Board also noted that using a replicating portfolio technique might require splitting the cash flows of the insurance contracts into those that match the cash flows from the asset portfolio and those that do not. As discussed in paragraph BC261, many stakeholders argued that it is impossible to split the cash flows in this way. Hence, IFRS 17 permits, but does not require, the use of a replicating portfolio technique and allows other approaches, such as risk-neutral modelling.

Amendments to IFRS 17—feedback on the subjectivity in determining discount rates

BC205A   When the Board considered feedback from entities implementing IFRS 17, it also considered feedback from users of financial statements that the principle-based requirements for determining discount rates could limit comparability between entities.

BC205B   The Board made no amendments to IFRS 17 in response to that feedback. In the Board's view, requiring an entity to determine discount rates using a rule-based approach would result in outcomes that are appropriate only in some circumstances. IFRS 17 requires entities to apply judgement when determining the inputs most applicable in the circumstances. To enable users of financial statements to understand the discount rates used, and to facilitate comparability between entities, IFRS 17 requires entities to disclose information about the methods used and judgements applied.

Risk adjustment for non-financial risk (paragraphs 37 and B86–B92 of IFRS 17)

BC206   IFRS 17 requires entities to depict the risk that is inherent in insurance contracts by including a risk adjustment for non-financial risk in the measurement of those contracts. The risk adjustment for non-financial risk directly measures the non-financial risk in the contract.

BC207   This section discusses:

(a)   the reasons for including a risk adjustment for non-financial risk in the measurement of a group of insurance contracts (see paragraphs BC208–BC212);

(b)   the techniques for estimating the risk adjustment for non-financial risk (see paragraphs BC213–BC214C); and

(c)   the reason to disclose a confidence level equivalent (see paragraphs BC215–BC217).

Reasons for including a risk adjustment for non-financial risk in the measurement of insurance contracts (paragraphs 37 and B86–B89 of IFRS 17)

BC208   IFRS 17 requires the risk adjustment for non-financial risk to reflect the compensation that the entity requires for bearing the uncertainty about the amount and timing of the cash flows that arises from non-financial risk.

BC209   In developing the objective of the risk adjustment for non-financial risk, the Board concluded that a risk adjustment for non-financial risk should not represent:

(a)   the compensation that a market participant would require for bearing the non-financial risk that is associated with the contract. As noted in paragraph BC17, the measurement model is not intended to measure the current exit value or fair value, which reflects the transfer of the liability to a market participant. Consequently, the risk adjustment for non-financial risk should be determined as the amount of compensation that the entity—not a market participant—would require.

(b)   an amount that would provide a high degree of certainty that the entity would be able to fulfil the contract. Although such an amount might be appropriate for some regulatory purposes, it is not compatible with the Board's objective of providing information that will help users of financial statements make decisions about providing resources to the entity.

BC210   The Board considered arguments that it not include a risk adjustment for non-financial risk in the fulfilment cash flows because:

(a)   no single well-defined approach exists for developing risk adjustments for non-financial risks that would meet the objective described in paragraph BC208 and provide consistency and comparability of results.

(b)   some techniques are difficult to explain to users of financial statements and, for some techniques, it may be difficult to provide clear disclosures that would give users of financial statements an insight into the measure of the risk adjustment for non-financial risk that results from the technique.

(c)   it is impossible to assess retrospectively whether a particular adjustment was reasonable, although preparers of financial statements may, in time, develop tools that help them to assess whether the amount of a risk adjustment for non-financial risk is appropriate for a given fact pattern. Over time, an entity may be able to assess whether subsequent outcomes are in line with its previous estimates of probability distributions. However, it would be difficult for the entity to assess whether, for example, a decision to set a confidence level at a particular percentile was appropriate.

(d)   developing systems to determine risk adjustments for non-financial risk will involve cost, and some stakeholders doubt whether the benefits of such systems will be sufficient to justify that cost for the

(e)   the inclusion of an explicitly measured risk adjustment for non-financial risk in identifying a loss on initial recognition is inconsistent with IFRS 15.

(f)   if the remeasurement of the risk adjustment for non-financial risk for an existing group of insurance contracts results in a loss, that loss will reverse in later periods as the entity is released from that risk. Reporting a loss followed by an expected reversal of that loss may confuse some users of financial statements.

(g)   the risk adjustment for non-financial risk could be used to introduce bias into the measurement of an insurance contract.

BC211   However, even given some of the limitations noted above, IFRS 17 requires a separate risk adjustment for non-financial risk because the Board decided that such an adjustment:

(a)   will result in an explicit measurement of the non-financial risk that will provide a clearer insight into the insurance contracts. In particular, it distinguishes risk-generating liabilities from risk-free liabilities. It will convey useful information to users of financial statements about the entity's view of the economic burden imposed by the non-financial risk associated with the entity's insurance contracts.

(b)   will result in a profit recognition pattern that reflects both the profit recognised by bearing risk and the profit recognised by providing services. As a result, the profit recognition pattern is more sensitive to the economic drivers of the contract.

(c)   will faithfully represent circumstances in which the entity has charged insufficient premiums for bearing the risk that the claims might ultimately exceed expected premiums.

(d)   will report changes in estimates of risk promptly and in an understandable way.

BC212   IFRS 17 requires entities to consider the risk adjustment for non-financial risk separately from the adjustment for the time value of money and financial risks. The Board observed that some previous accounting models combined these two adjustments by using discount rates adjusted for non-financial risk. However, the Board concluded that combining the two adjustments is inappropriate unless the risk is directly proportional to both the amount of the liability and the remaining time to maturity. Insurance contract liabilities often do not have these characteristics. For example, the average risk in a group of claims liabilities may rise over time because more complex claims incurred may take longer to resolve. Similarly, lapse risk may affect cash inflows more than it affects cash outflows. A single risk-adjusted discount rate is unlikely to capture such differences in risk. The Board therefore decided to require a separate risk adjustment for non-financial risk.

Techniques for measuring risk adjustments for non-financial risk (paragraphs B90–B92 of IFRS 17)

BC213   The Board decided a principle-based approach for measuring the risk adjustment for non-financial risk, rather than identifying specific techniques, would be consistent with the Board's approach on how to determine a similar risk adjustment for non-financial risk in IFRS 13. Furthermore, the Board concluded that:

(a)   limiting the number of risk adjustment techniques would conflict with the Board's desire to set principle-based IFRS Standards. In particular situations, some techniques may be more applicable, or may be easier to implement, and it would not be practicable for an IFRS Standard to specify in detail every situation in which particular techniques would be appropriate. Furthermore, techniques may evolve over time. Specifying particular techniques might prevent an entity from improving its techniques.

(b)   the objective of the risk adjustment for non-financial risk is to reflect the entity's perception of the economic burden of its non-financial risks. Specifying a level of aggregation for determining the risk adjustment for non-financial risk that was inconsistent with the entity's view of the burden of non-financial risk would contradict the objective of reflecting the entity's perception in the risk adjustment for non-financial risk.

BC214   As a result, IFRS 17 states only the principle that the risk adjustment for non-financial risk should be the compensation the entity requires for bearing the uncertainty arising from non-financial risk that is inherent in the cash flows that arise as the entity fulfils the group of insurance contracts. Accordingly, the risk adjustment for non-financial risk reflects any diversification benefit the entity considers when determining the amount of compensation it requires for bearing that uncertainty.

Amendments to IFRS 17—feedback on the subjectivity in determining the risk adjustment for non-financial risk

BC214A   When the Board considered feedback from entities implementing IFRS 17, it also considered feedback from users of financial statements that the principle-based requirements for determining the risk adjustment for non-financial risk could limit comparability between entities. The Board made no amendments to IFRS 17 in response to that feedback, for the same reason it made no amendments in response to similar feedback on discount rates (see paragraph BC205B).

Amendments to IFRS 17—feedback on the risk adjustment for non-financial risk in consolidated financial statements

BC214B   The Transition Resource Group for IFRS 17 discussed an implementation question on determining the risk adjustment for non-financial risk in the consolidated financial statements of a group of entities. Transition Resource Group members held different views. Some members thought the risk adjustment for non-financial risk for a group of insurance contracts must be the same in the issuing subsidiary's stand-alone financial statements as in the consolidated financial statements of the group of entities. Other members thought the risk adjustment for non-financial risk may be measured differently in the issuing subsidiary's stand-alone financial statements from how it is measured in the consolidated financial statements of the group of entities.

BC214C   The Board considered whether it should clarify its intention for determining the risk adjustment for non-financial risk in the consolidated financial statements of a group of entities in response to those different views. The Board concluded that doing so would address only some differences that could arise in the application of the requirements for determining the risk adjustment for non-financial risk, given the judgement required to apply those requirements. The Board concluded that practice needs to develop in this area. If necessary, the Board will seek to understand how the requirements are being applied as part of the Post-implementation Review of IFRS 17.

Confidence level disclosure (paragraph 119 of IFRS 17)

BC215   An important difference between IFRS 17 and IFRS 13 is that the risk adjustment for non-financial risk in IFRS 17 relies on an entity's own perception of its degree of risk aversion, rather than on a market participant's perception. This could result in entities determining different risk adjustments for non-financial risk for similar groups of insurance contracts. Accordingly, to allow users of financial statements to understand how the entity-specific assessment of risk aversion might differ from entity to entity, IFRS 17 requires entities to disclose the confidence level to which the risk adjustment for non-financial risk corresponds.

BC216   The Board acknowledges concerns that disclosure of the confidence level would be burdensome to prepare and may not provide information that is directly comparable. However, the Board did not identify any other approaches that would provide quantitative disclosure that would allow users of financial statements to compare the risk adjustments for non-financial risk using a consistent methodology across entities. In particular, the Board noted that this objective would not be achieved by:

(a)   disclosing the range of values of key inputs used to measure the risk adjustment for non-financial risk from a market participant's perspective; or

(b)   providing information about the relative magnitude of the risk adjustment for non-financial risk compared to total insurance contract liabilities.

BC217   The Board also considered whether a different technique, such as the cost of capital approach, should be used as the basis for comparison. Although the usefulness of the confidence level technique diminishes when the probability distribution is not statistically normal, which is often the case for insurance contracts, the cost of capital approach would be more complicated to calculate than would the confidence level disclosure. Also, the confidence level technique has the benefit of being relatively easy to communicate to users of financial statements and relatively easy to understand. The Board expects that many entities will have the information necessary to apply the cost of capital technique because that information will be required to comply with local regulatory requirements. However, the Board decided not to impose the more onerous requirements on entities when a simpler approach would be sufficient.

Measurement of the contractual service margin (paragraphs 38, 43–46 and B96–B119B of IFRS 17)

BC218   The contractual service margin depicts the unearned profit the entity expects to generate from a group of insurance contracts (see paragraph BC21). The contractual service margin is determined on initial recognition of a group as the amount that eliminates any gains arising at that time. Subsequent adjustments to the carrying amount of the contractual service margin and its recognition in profit or loss determine how profit and revenue are recognised over the coverage period of the group.

BC219   The contractual service margin cannot depict unearned losses. Instead, IFRS 17 requires an entity to recognise a loss in profit or loss for any excess of the expected present value of the future cash outflows above the expected present value of the future cash inflows, adjusted for risk (see paragraphs BC284–BC287 on losses on onerous contracts).

BC220   IFRS 17 requires the carrying amount of the contractual service margin to be adjusted for (see paragraphs 44 and 45 of IFRS 17):

      (a)   changes in estimates of the future unearned profit (see paragraphs BC222–BC269);

      (b)   insurance finance income or expenses (see paragraphs BC270–BC276E); and

      (c)   currency exchange differences (see paragraphs BC277–BC278).

BC221   The resulting carrying amount at the end of the reporting period is allocated over the current and future periods, and the amount relating to the current period is recognised in profit or loss (see paragraphs BC279–BC283J).

Changes in estimates of the future unearned profit (paragraphs 44, 45 and B96–B118 of IFRS 17)

BC222   The key service provided by insurance contracts is insurance coverage, but contracts may also provide investment-related or other services. The measurement of a group of insurance contracts at initial recognition includes a contractual service margin, which represents the margin the entity has charged for the services it provides in addition to bearing risk. The expected margin charged for bearing risk is represented by the risk adjustment for non-financial risk (see paragraphs BC206–BC214C).

BC223   IFRS 17 requires an entity to measure the contractual service margin, on initial recognition of the group of insurance contracts, as the difference between the expected present value of cash inflows and the expected present value of cash outflows, after adjusting for uncertainty and any cash flows received or paid before or on initial recognition. IFRS 17 also requires an entity to update the measurement of the contractual service margin for changes in estimates of the fulfilment cash flows relating to future service, for the following reasons:

(a) changes in estimates of the fulfilment cash flows relating to future service affect the future profitability of the group of insurance contracts. Thus, adjusting the contractual service margin to reflect these changes provides more relevant information about the remaining unearned profit in the group of insurance contracts after initial recognition than not adjusting the contractual service margin. Paragraphs BC227–BC237 discuss which changes in estimates relate to future service for insurance contracts without direct participation features, and paragraphs BC238–BC256H discuss which changes relate to future service for insurance contracts with direct participation features.

(b) increased consistency between measurement at initial recognition and subsequent measurement. If the contractual service margin were not adjusted for changes in estimates relating to future service, the estimates made at initial recognition would determine the contractual service margin, but changes in those estimates thereafter would not.

BC224 Having concluded that changes in estimates of the fulfilment cash flows relating to future service should adjust the contractual service margin, the Board further decided that:

(a) it would not limit the amount by which the contractual service margin could be increased. Favourable changes in estimates—whether lower than expected cash outflows, higher than expected cash inflows or reductions in the risk adjustment for non-financial risk—increase the profit that the entity will recognise from the group.

(b) the contractual service margin cannot be negative for a group of insurance contracts issued. Therefore, once the contractual service margin is reduced to zero, expected losses arising from the group will be recognised immediately in profit or loss. Any excess of the increase in the fulfilment cash flows over the contractual service margin means the group is expected to be onerous (ie loss-making) rather than profit-making in the future. Such losses are recognised as an increase in the liability and corresponding expense in the period.

(c) only changes in estimates of fulfilment cash flows relating to future service result in an adjustment to the contractual service margin. Consistent with viewing the contractual service margin as unearned future profit, changes that relate to current or past periods do not affect the contractual service margin. Paragraphs BC227–BC247 discuss which changes in estimates relate to future service.

(d) changes in estimates of fulfilment cash flows relating to future service include changes in the risk adjustment for non-financial risk that relate to future service.[27]

---

27 In June 2020, the Board amended paragraph B96(d) of IFRS 17 to clarify that if an entity chooses to disaggregate changes in the risk adjustment for non-financial risk between the insurance service result and insurance finance income or expenses, the entity should adjust the contractual service margin only for the changes related to non-financial risk (and not for changes in the risk adjustment for non-financial risk that result from the effects of the time value of money).

(e)   adjustments to the contractual service margin are recognised prospectively using the latest estimates of the fulfilment cash flows. Except in the case of onerous groups of insurance contracts as explained in (b), any changes are recognised in profit or loss when the contractual service margin is recognised over the current period and the coverage period remaining after the adjustments are made. Revisions in estimates that adjust the contractual service margin result in a transfer between the components of the insurance contract liability, with no change in the total carrying amount of the liability. Therefore, the total insurance contract liability is remeasured for changes in estimates of expected cash flows only if there is an unfavourable change relating to future service that exceeds the remaining balance of the contractual service margin, ie if the group of insurance contracts becomes onerous. This remeasurement requirement is consistent with the measurement of contract liabilities under IFRS 15, which also does not remeasure performance obligations based on changes in estimates of future cash flows unless a contract is onerous.

Other approaches considered but rejected

Not adjusting the contractual service margin for subsequent changes in the future cash flows and risk adjustment for non-financial risk

BC225   The Board originally proposed that the contractual service margin recognised at initial recognition should not be adjusted subsequently to reflect the effects of changes in the estimates of the fulfilment cash flows. The reasons underlying that view were that:

(a)   changes in estimates during a reporting period are economic changes in the cost of fulfilling a group of insurance contracts in that period, even when they relate to future service. Recognising changes in estimates immediately in profit or loss would provide relevant information about changes in circumstances for insurance contracts.

(b)   the contractual service margin represents an obligation to provide services that is separate from the obligation to make the payments required to fulfil the contracts. Changes in the estimates of the payments required to fulfil the contracts do not increase or decrease the obligation to provide services and consequently do not adjust the measurement of that obligation.

(c)   there would be accounting mismatches for changes in the estimates of financial market variables, such as discount rates and equity prices, if the assets that back insurance contract liabilities were measured at fair value through profit or loss and the contractual service margin was adjusted for those changes rather than being recognised in profit or loss.

BC226   However, many stakeholders stated that the measurement of the insurance contract liability would not provide relevant information about the unearned profit that would be recognised over the remaining coverage period if the contractual service margin were not adjusted to reflect changes in estimates made after initial recognition. Those with this view argued that it would be inconsistent to prohibit the recognition of gains on initial recognition, but then to require the subsequent recognition of gains on the basis of changes in estimates made immediately after initial recognition. The Board, persuaded by these views, accordingly decided to adjust the contractual service margin for changes in estimates of fulfilment cash flows that relate to future service.

Insurance contracts without direct participation features (paragraphs 44 and B96–B100 of IFRS 17)

BC227   In determining which changes in estimates relate to future service, IFRS 17 distinguishes two types of insurance contracts: those without direct participation features and those with direct participation features. Insurance contracts with direct participation features are discussed in paragraphs BC238–BC269C.

Time value of money and changes in assumptions relating to financial risk (paragraph B97(a) of IFRS 17)

BC228   For insurance contracts without direct participation features, the Board concluded that changes in the effects of the time value of money and financial risk do not affect the amount of unearned profit. This is the case even if the payments to policyholders vary with returns on underlying items through a participation mechanism, for the reasons set out in paragraphs BC229–BC231. Accordingly, the entity does not adjust the contractual service margin to reflect the effects of changes in these assumptions.

BC229   For insurance contracts without direct participation features, the underwriting result is regarded as the difference between the amount of premiums the entity charges (less any investment component) and the payments the entity makes because of the occurrence of the insured event. The insurance finance result reflects the interest arising on the group of insurance contracts because of the passage of time and the effect of changes in assumptions relating to financial risk. The statement(s) of financial performance also reflect gains and losses from the investments in which the premiums are invested. Such gains and losses would be recognised in profit or loss according to other applicable IFRS Standards.

BC230   Thus, for insurance contracts without direct participation features, the entity's profit from financing activities arises from the difference between:

(a)   the gains (or losses) from the investments; and

(b)   the change in the insurance contract liability depicted by the insurance finance income or expenses including the gains (or losses) the entity passes to the policyholder through any indirect participation mechanism.

BC231　This approach to determining profit from financing activities reflects the separate accounting for the investment portfolio and the group of insurance contracts, regardless of any participation mechanism in the insurance contracts, consistent with the following:

(a)　the entity controls the cash flows of the investments, even when the entity is required to act in a fiduciary capacity for the policyholder.

(b)　in most cases, an entity would be unlikely to have a legally enforceable right to set off the insurance contract liability with the investment portfolio, even if the investment portfolio were to be invested in assets that exactly match the entity's obligation, because the entity retains the obligation to pay the policyholders the amounts that are determined on the basis of the investments in the portfolio, irrespective of the entity's investment strategy.

Experience adjustments and changes in assumptions that do not relate to financial risk (Appendix A and paragraphs B96–B97 of IFRS 17)

BC232　The Board decided that all changes in estimates of the liability for incurred claims relate to current or past service because they relate to coverage in previous periods.

BC233　The Board defined experience adjustments as (a) differences between the premium receipts (and related cash flows) that were expected to happen in the period and the actual cash flows or (b) differences between incurred claims and expenses that were expected to happen in the period and the actual amounts incurred. The Board decided that for the liability for remaining coverage, in general, it was reasonable to assume that experience adjustments relate to current or past service. In contrast, changes in estimates of future cash flows in general can be assumed to relate to future service. The Board noted that experience adjustments relating to premiums received for future coverage relate to future service and are an exception to this general rule.

BC234　The Board considered whether to establish a further exception to the general rule, for situations in which an experience adjustment directly causes a change in the estimates of the future cash flows. In some such cases, the experience adjustment and the change in the estimates of the future cash flows largely offset and adjusting the contractual service margin for only one effect might not seem an appropriate depiction of the single event. However, in other cases, the experience adjustment and the change in the estimates of the future cash flows do not offset each other and recognising the experience adjustment in profit or loss in the current period while adjusting the contractual service margin for the change in the estimates of the future cash flows appropriately depicts both effects. The Board concluded that not establishing any further exceptions to the general rule described in paragraph BC233 gave an appropriate result in most cases and avoided excessively complex requirements.

BC235   The Board also considered the treatment of investment components. The Board did not regard as useful information, for example, the recognition of a gain for a delay in repaying an investment component accompanied by a loss that adjusts the contractual service margin for the expected later repayment. Acceleration or delay in repayments of investment components only gives rise to a gain or loss for the entity to the extent that the amount of the repayment is affected by its timing. Also, IFRS 17 does not require an entity to determine the amount of an investment component until a claim is incurred (see paragraph BC34). Accordingly, when a claim is incurred, IFRS 17 requires an entity to determine how much of that claim is an investment component, and whether it was expected to become payable that period. IFRS 17 requires any unexpected repayment of an investment component to adjust the contractual service margin. The contractual service margin will also be adjusted for changes in future estimates of cash flows which will include (but not separately identify) the reduction in future repayments of investment components. This achieves the desired result of the net effect on the contractual service margin being the effect of the change in timing of the repayment of the investment component.[28]

BC236   Requiring the contractual service margin to be adjusted for changes in estimates of the fulfilment cash flows but not for experience adjustments has the consequence that the accounting depends on the timing of a reporting date. To avoid IAS 34 *Interim Financial Reporting* being interpreted as requiring the recalculation of previously reported amounts, the Board decided that IFRS 17 should specifically prohibit entities from changing the treatment of accounting estimates made in previous interim financial statements when applying IFRS 17 in subsequent interim financial statements or in the annual reporting period.[29]

Amendments to IFRS 17—the effect of accounting estimates made in interim financial statements

BC236A   In June 2020, the Board amended IFRS 17 to require an entity to choose whether to change the treatment of accounting estimates made in previous interim financial statements when applying IFRS 17 in subsequent interim financial statements and in the annual reporting period.

BC236B   The requirement relating to accounting estimates made in interim financial statements as described in paragraph BC236 was developed in response to feedback during the development of IFRS 17 that recalculating the carrying amount of the contractual service margin from the beginning to the end of an annual reporting period, when an entity has prepared interim financial statements during that period, would be a significant practical burden.

---

28   Paragraph B96(c) of IFRS 17 requires changes in fulfilment cash flows that arise from differences between any investment component expected to become payable in the period and the actual investment component that becomes payable in the period to adjust the contractual service margin. In June 2020, the Board amended IFRS 17 to specify that paragraph B96(c) of IFRS 17 does not apply to insurance finance income or expenses that depict the effect on the investment component of the time value of money and financial risk between the beginning of the period and the unexpected payment or non-payment of the investment component.

29   In June 2020, the Board amended the requirements relating to the effect of accounting estimates made in interim financial statements (see paragraphs BC236A–BC236D).

However, some entities implementing IFRS 17 as issued in May 2017 said that the requirement described in paragraph BC236 would result in a practical burden that would be more significant than the burden the Board had intended to alleviate. Some of those entities said that the requirement was a burden particularly for entities in a consolidated group that report at different frequencies from each other, because there would be a need to maintain two sets of records to reflect the different treatments of the accounting estimates.

BC236C   The Board concluded that permitting an accounting policy choice as described in paragraph BC236A would ease IFRS 17 implementation by enabling an entity to assess which accounting policy would be less burdensome. To avoid a significant loss of useful information for users of financial statements, an entity is required to consistently apply its choice to all groups of insurance contracts it issues and groups of reinsurance contracts it holds (that is, the accounting policy choice is at the reporting entity level).

BC236D   The Board added a relief, related to the amendment, to the transition requirements for entities applying IFRS 17 for the first time (see paragraphs C14A and C19A of IFRS 17).

Discretionary cash flows (paragraphs B98–B100 of IFRS 17)

BC237   Insurance contracts without direct participation features often give rise to cash flows to policyholders over which the entity has some discretion regarding the amount or timing (see paragraphs BC167–BC170). IFRS 17 requires an entity to distinguish between the effect of changes in assumptions that relate to financial risks (which do not adjust the contractual service margin) and the effect of changes in discretion (which do adjust the contractual service margin). The Board noted that there are potentially many ways in which an entity could make that distinction. To ensure a consistent approach, the Board decided to require an entity to specify at the inception of a contract the basis on which it expects to determine its commitment under the contract, for example, based on a fixed interest rate, or on returns that vary based on specified asset returns.

Insurance contracts with direct participation features (the variable fee approach) (paragraphs 45 and B101–B118 of IFRS 17)

BC238   Insurance contracts with direct participation features are insurance contracts for which, on inception:

(a)   the contractual terms specify that the policyholder participates in a share of a clearly identified pool of underlying items;

(b)   the entity expects to pay to the policyholder an amount equal to a substantial share of the fair value returns from the underlying items; and

(c)   the entity expects a substantial proportion of any change in the amounts to be paid to the policyholder to vary with the change in fair value of the underlying items.

BC239   The Board views these contracts as creating an obligation to pay policyholders an amount equal in value to specified underlying items, minus a variable fee for service. That fee is an amount equal to the entity's share of the fair value of the underlying items minus any expected cash flows that do not vary directly with the underlying items.

BC240   IFRS 17 requires the contractual service margin for insurance contracts with direct participation features to be updated for more changes than those affecting the contractual service margin for other insurance contracts. In addition to the adjustments made for other insurance contracts, the contractual service margin for insurance contracts with direct participation features is also adjusted for the effect of changes in:

(a)   the entity's share of the underlying items; and

(b)   financial risks other than those arising from the underlying items, for example the effect of financial guarantees.

BC241   The Board decided that these differences are necessary to give a faithful representation of the different nature of the fee in these contracts. As explained in paragraphs BC228–BC231, the Board concluded that for many insurance contracts it is appropriate to depict the gains and losses on any investment portfolio related to the contracts in the same way as gains and losses on an investment portfolio unrelated to insurance contracts. However, the Board also considered a contrasting view that, for some contracts, the returns to the entity from a pool of underlying items should be viewed as the compensation that the entity charges the policyholder for service provided by the insurance contract, rather than as a share of returns from an unrelated investment. Under this contrasting view, changes in the estimate of the entity's share of returns are regarded as a change in the entity's compensation for the contract. Such changes in the entity's compensation should be recognised over the periods in which the entity provides the service promised in the contract, in the same way that changes in the estimates of the costs of providing the contract are recognised.

BC242   In support of this view, the Board also noted that any benefit the entity receives from its share of the pool of underlying items can be regarded as a consequence of the entity holding those items to provide benefits to the policyholder. In addition, the Board also observed that the entity is often constrained when exercising its control over the underlying items because:

(a)   the quantum of underlying items is determined entirely by the premiums paid by the policyholder;

(b)   the entity is usually expected to manage the policyholder's invested premiums for the benefit of the policyholders, acting for them in a fiduciary capacity; and

(c)   some aspects of the entity's management of the underlying items might be specified in the contract.

BC243   Because of these features, some believe that, in some cases, the entity's interest in the underlying items is not, in substance, the equivalent of a direct holding in assets, but is equivalent to a variable fee the entity charges the policyholder, expressed as a share of the fair value of the underlying items. When applying this view:

    (a)   the entity's obligation to the policyholder is considered to be the net of:

        (i)   the obligation to pay the policyholder an amount equal to the fair value of the underlying items; and

        (ii)   a variable fee that the entity deducts in exchange for the services provided by the insurance contract.

    (b)   changes in the estimate of the obligation to pay the policyholder an amount equal to the fair value of the underlying items would be recognised in profit or loss or other comprehensive income, just as would changes in the fair value of most underlying items.

    (c)   changes in the estimate of the variable fee for future service and changes in estimates of the cash flows relating to future service would be accounted for consistently. Accordingly, changes in the entity's share of the underlying items would adjust the contractual service margin so that the changes would be recognised in profit or loss over the coverage period.

    (d)   the financial statements of the entity report a net investment return only to the extent that the return on the assets the entity holds (if measured at fair value through profit or loss) do not match the returns on the promised underlying items.

BC244   The Board concluded that returns to the entity from underlying items should be viewed as part of the compensation the entity charges the policyholder for service provided by the insurance contract, rather than as a share of returns from an unrelated investment, in a narrow set of circumstances in which the policyholders directly participate in a share of the returns on the underlying items. In such cases, the fact that the fee for the contract is determined by reference to a share of the returns on the underlying items is incidental to its nature as a fee. The Board concluded, therefore, that depicting the gains and losses on the entity's share of the underlying items as part of a variable fee for service faithfully represents the nature of the contractual arrangement.

BC245   The Board then considered how to specify when the entity's share of underlying items is viewed as part of the variable fee for service. The Board decided the underlying items do not need to be a portfolio of financial assets. They can comprise items such as the net assets of the entity or a subsidiary within the group that is the reporting entity. The Board also decided that all the following conditions need to be met:

(a) the contract specifies a determinable fee. For this to be the case, the contract needs to specify that the policyholder participates in a share of a clearly identified pool of underlying items. Without a determinable fee, which can be expressed as a percentage of portfolio returns or portfolio asset values rather than only as a monetary amount, the share of returns on the underlying items the entity retains would be entirely at the discretion of the entity, and, in the Board's view, this would not be consistent with that amount being equivalent to a fee.

(b) the entity's primary obligation is to pay to the policyholder an amount equal to the fair value of the underlying items. For this to be the case:

(i) the entity should expect to pay to the policyholder an amount equal to a substantial share of the fair value returns on the underlying items. It would not be a faithful representation to depict an obligation to pay an amount equal to the fair value of the underlying items if the policyholder does not expect to receive a substantial part of the fair value returns on the underlying items.

(ii) the entity should expect a substantial proportion of any change in the amounts to be paid to the policyholder to vary with the change in fair value of the underlying items. It would not be a faithful representation to depict an obligation to pay an amount equal to the fair value of the underlying items if the entity were not to expect changes in the amount to be paid to vary with the change in fair value of the underlying items.

BC246 The Board used these conditions to define insurance contracts with direct participation features as described in paragraph BC238. The Board also decided that the entity need not hold the underlying items, because the measurement of insurance contracts should not depend on what assets the entity holds. The Board extended the adjustments to the contractual service margin as described in paragraphs BC239–BC240 to reflect the view that the entity's share of underlying items is part of the variable fee for service. In such cases, variability in the fee is driven by changes in assumptions relating to financial risk. Therefore, the Board decided that it is also appropriate to regard as part of the fee the effect of changes in assumptions relating to financial risk on the fulfilment cash flows that do not vary based on returns on the underlying items.

BC247 Hence, the additional adjustments to the contractual service margin described in paragraph BC246 are caused by changes in assumptions related to financial risk. However, the contractual service margin is adjusted only to the extent that it does not become negative. Beyond that, the changes in assumptions cause a gain or loss to be recognised in the statement(s) of financial performance. The Board considered whether such gains and losses should be included as losses on groups of onerous contracts in insurance service result or as insurance finance income or expenses. The Board concluded that the former provided information that was consistent with the treatment of such changes as being part of the variable fee for service.

BC248　For reinsurance contracts an entity holds, the entity and the reinsurer do not share in the returns on underlying items, and so the criteria in paragraph BC238 are not met, even if the underlying insurance contracts issued are insurance contracts with direct participation features. The Board considered whether it should modify the scope of the variable fee approach to include reinsurance contracts held, if the underlying insurance contracts issued are insurance contracts with direct participation features. But such an approach would be inconsistent with the Board's view that a reinsurance contract held should be accounted for separately from the underlying contracts issued.

BC249　Although some types of reinsurance contracts issued might meet the criteria in paragraph BC238, the Board decided that reinsurance contracts issued are not eligible for the variable fee approach. This is because the view that the returns to the entity from a pool of underlying items should be viewed as part of the compensation that the entity charges the policyholder for the service provided by the insurance contract (see paragraph BC241) does not apply to reinsurance contracts issued.[30]

Amendments to IFRS 17—scope of the variable fee approach (paragraphs B101 and B107 of IFRS 17)

BC249A　The requirements of IFRS 17 with the additional adjustments to the contractual service margin described in paragraph BC246 are referred to as the variable fee approach. Some entities implementing IFRS 17 suggested the Board expand the scope of the variable fee approach to include:

(a)　insurance contracts that some stakeholders view as economically similar to insurance contracts with direct participation features, except that these contracts do not meet the criterion in paragraph B101(a) of IFRS 17; and

(b)　reinsurance contracts issued and reinsurance contracts held, which are explicitly excluded from the scope of the variable fee approach applying paragraph B109 of IFRS 17.

BC249B　The Board considered but rejected the suggestions described in paragraph BC249A(a). The additional adjustments to the contractual service margin in the variable fee approach were designed specifically to faithfully represent the profit from insurance contracts within the scope of the variable fee approach. Therefore, if the Board were to amend the scope of the variable fee approach, it would need to consider amending those adjustments. The Board also observed that whatever the scope of the variable fee approach, differences would arise between the accounting for contracts within the scope and contracts outside the scope.

---

30 The Board subsequently reaffirmed this view when it considered similar feedback from entities implementing IFRS 17 (see paragraph BC249C).

BC249C The Board considered but rejected suggestions described in paragraph BC249A(b). The Board concluded that reinsurance contracts are not substantially investment-related service contracts. The variable fee approach was designed specifically so an entity issuing insurance contracts that are substantially investment-related service contracts would account for profit similarly to an entity issuing asset management contracts. Some stakeholders said that excluding reinsurance contracts held from the scope of the variable fee approach creates an accounting mismatch when a reinsurance contract held covers underlying insurance contracts that are within the scope of the variable fee approach. The Board responded to that concern by amending the risk mitigation option (see paragraphs BC256A–BC256B).

BC249D In June 2020, the Board amended paragraph B107 of IFRS 17 to replace a reference to 'the group of insurance contracts' with 'the insurance contract'. Applying paragraph B101 of IFRS 17, an entity assesses whether an insurance contract (rather than a group of insurance contracts) is within the scope of the variable fee approach. The reference to a group of insurance contracts in paragraph B107 of IFRS 17 was a drafting error and was inconsistent with the requirements in paragraph B101 of IFRS 17. Some stakeholders said this amendment would be a major change and disruptive to IFRS 17 implementation. Those stakeholders had assumed that an entity was required to apply the criteria for the scope of the variable fee approach at a group level. The Board concluded that it needed to fix the drafting error in paragraph B107 of IFRS 17 to enable consistent application of the requirements. The Board noted that some stakeholders had interpreted a contract-level assessment as being more burdensome than it is because they thought an individual assessment was required for every contract. However, the Board observed that one assessment should be sufficient for an entity to determine whether the criteria are met for each contract in a set of homogenous contracts issued in the same market conditions and priced on the same basis.

Effect of risk mitigation (paragraphs B115–B118 of IFRS 17)

BC250 Amounts payable to policyholders create risks for an entity, particularly if the amounts payable are independent of the amounts that the entity receives from investments; for example, if the insurance contract includes guarantees. An entity is also at risk from possible changes in its share of the fair value returns on underlying items. An entity may purchase derivatives to mitigate such risks. When applying IFRS 9, such derivatives are measured at fair value.

BC251 For contracts without direct participation features, the contractual service margin is not adjusted for the changes in fulfilment cash flows the derivatives are intended to mitigate. Hence, both the change in the carrying amount of fulfilment cash flows and the change in the value of the derivative will be recognised in the statement(s) of financial performance. If the entity chooses to recognise all insurance finance income or expenses in profit or loss, there will be no accounting mismatch between the recognition of the change in the value of the derivative and the recognition of the change in the carrying amount of the insurance contract.

BC252   However, for contracts with direct participation features the contractual service margin would be adjusted for the changes in the fulfilment cash flows, including changes that the derivatives are intended to mitigate. Consequently, the change in the value of the derivative would be recognised in profit or loss, but, unless the group of insurance contracts was onerous, there would be no equivalent change in the carrying amount to recognise, creating an accounting mismatch.

BC253   A similar accounting mismatch arises if the entity uses derivatives to mitigate risk arising from its share of the fair value return on underlying items.

BC254   The Board concluded that, to avoid such accounting mismatches created by the variable fee approach, an entity should be allowed not to adjust the contractual service margin for the changes in the fulfilment cash flows and the entity's share in the fair value return on the underlying items that the derivatives are intended to mitigate.

BC255   Such an option reduces the comparability of the measurement of insurance contracts because the contractual service margin will be adjusted by a different amount depending on whether, and the extent to which, an entity chooses to apply this approach. To limit the reduction in comparability, the Board decided that an entity may make this choice only to the extent that, in accordance with a previously documented risk management objective and strategy for using derivatives to mitigate financial market risk arising from those fulfilment cash flows:[31]

   (a)   the entity uses a derivative to mitigate the financial risk arising from the group of insurance contracts.[32]

   (b)   an economic offset exists between the group of insurance contracts and the derivative, ie the values of the group of insurance contracts and the derivative generally move in opposite directions because they respond in a similar way to the changes in the risk being mitigated. An entity does not consider accounting measurement differences in assessing the economic offset.

   (c)   credit risk does not dominate the economic offset.

BC256   The Board considered an alternative approach to reducing accounting mismatches arising from such derivatives. This approach would have allowed an entity to recognise in profit or loss the change in fair value of a hypothetical derivative that matches the critical terms of the specified fulfilment cash flows or the entity's share of the fair value return on the underlying items. This might have resulted in a greater reduction in accounting mismatches, because a fair value measurement would have been used in profit or loss for both the 'hedged' fulfilment cash flows and the 'hedging' derivative, relative to the measurement being used for the

---

31 In June 2020, the Board amended IFRS 17 to clarify that an entity ceases to apply the risk mitigation option if, and only if, the conditions described in paragraph BC255 cease to be met.

32 In June 2020, the Board amended IFRS 17 so that the risk mitigation option also applies in specified circumstances when an entity mitigates financial risk using reinsurance contracts held or non-derivative financial instruments measured at fair value through profit or loss (see paragraphs BC256A–BC256F).

fulfilment cash flows under IFRS 17. However, the Board concluded that such an approach would involve too much additional complexity.

Amendments to IFRS 17—risk mitigation using instruments other than derivatives

BC256A   In June 2020, the Board amended IFRS 17 to extend the risk mitigation option in paragraphs B115–B116 of IFRS 17 to apply when an entity uses:

(a)   reinsurance contracts held to mitigate the effect of financial risk on the amount of the entity's share of the underlying items or the fulfilment cash flows set out in paragraph B113(b) of IFRS 17 (see paragraph BC256B); or

(b)   non-derivative financial instruments measured at fair value through profit or loss to mitigate the effect of financial risk on the fulfilment cash flows set out in paragraph B113(b) of IFRS 17 (see paragraph BC256C).

BC256B   Some stakeholders said that applying the requirements in IFRS 17 results in an accounting mismatch when an entity holds a reinsurance contract that covers insurance contracts with direct participation features. The entity accounts for the underlying insurance contracts issued, but not the reinsurance contract held, applying the variable fee approach. Reinsurance contracts that cover insurance contracts with direct participation features transfer both non-financial and financial risk to the reinsurer. The Board considered but rejected a suggestion to permit an entity to apply the variable fee approach to such reinsurance contracts held (see paragraph BC249C). However, the Board acknowledged that when an entity mitigates the effect of financial risk using a reinsurance contract held, an accounting mismatch could arise that is similar to the mismatch that could arise when an entity mitigates the effect of financial risk using derivatives (see paragraph BC252). Accordingly, the Board amended IFRS 17 so that the risk mitigation option applies in the same way when an entity uses reinsurance contracts held as when an entity uses derivatives.

BC256C   Some stakeholders said that some entities mitigate the effect of some financial risk on fulfilment cash flows that do not vary with returns on underlying items (the cash flows set out in paragraph B113(b) of IFRS 17) using non-derivative financial instruments. The Board was persuaded that if such non-derivative financial instruments are measured at fair value through profit or loss, an accounting mismatch could arise, which is similar to the accounting mismatch for derivatives (see paragraph BC252). Accordingly, the Board extended the risk mitigation option to apply in such circumstances. The Board decided to limit the extension to only non-derivative financial instruments measured at fair value through profit or loss. For such non-derivative financial instruments, the extension resolves the accounting mismatch in the same way it resolves the accounting mismatch for derivatives (which are also measured at fair value through profit or loss).

BC256D   The Board considered but rejected a suggestion that an entity should be permitted to apply the risk mitigation option when it uses non-derivative financial instruments measured at fair value through other comprehensive income. The Board observed that in most circumstances the risk mitigation option would not resolve perceived mismatches between amounts recognised in profit or loss relating to:

(a)   insurance contracts with direct participation features using the other comprehensive income option in IFRS 17; and

(b)   assets measured at fair value through other comprehensive income.

BC256E   The amounts described in paragraph BC256D will differ depending on when the financial assets and the insurance liabilities are acquired or issued and depending on their duration. Further, the suggestion in paragraph BC256D would have resulted in any ineffectiveness of the risk mitigation strategy being recognised in other comprehensive income. That would be inconsistent with the hedge accounting requirements in IFRS 9 which result in the ineffectiveness of hedging strategies having a transparent effect on profit or loss. The Board observed that an entity could avoid mismatches by applying together the fair value option in IFRS 9 (to designate financial assets at fair value through profit or loss) and the risk mitigation option in IFRS 17.

BC256F   The Board also considered but rejected a suggestion that an entity should be permitted to apply the risk mitigation option when it uses non-derivative financial instruments to mitigate the effect of financial risk on the entity's share of the fair value of the underlying items (see paragraph B112 of IFRS 17). Some stakeholders said that an entity may mitigate such financial risk by investing premiums in assets other than the underlying items—for example, fixed rate bonds. The Board concluded that permitting an entity to apply the risk mitigation option in that circumstance would contradict the principle that an entity need not hold the underlying items for the variable fee approach to apply (see paragraph BC246).

Amendments to IFRS 17—applying the risk mitigation option and the other comprehensive income option (paragraphs 87A–89 and B117A of IFRS 17)

BC256G   In June 2020, the Board amended IFRS 17 to specify that paragraphs 88 and 89 of IFRS 17 do not apply to the insurance finance income or expenses that arise from the application of the risk mitigation option. Instead, the Board specified that such insurance finance income or expenses are presented in:

(a)   profit or loss if the entity mitigates financial risk using financial instruments measured at fair value through profit or loss; and

(b)   profit or loss or other comprehensive income applying the same accounting policy the entity applies to a reinsurance contract held if the entity mitigates financial risk using that reinsurance contract held.

BC256H The amendment described in paragraph BC256G resolves a mismatch that would otherwise have arisen between amounts recognised in profit or loss for a group of insurance contracts with direct participation features and amounts recognised in profit or loss on the items used to mitigate financial risk arising from the insurance contracts. The mismatch would have arisen if an entity determined the amounts recognised in profit or loss on the group of insurance contracts by applying both paragraph 89 of IFRS 17 (to include some insurance finance income or expenses in other comprehensive income) and paragraph B115 of IFRS 17 (the risk mitigation option).

Complexity

BC257 Treating insurance contracts with direct participation features differently from insurance contracts without direct participation features adds complexity for preparers and users of financial statements. Preparers have to determine the category in which their insurance contracts belong, and users need to understand the implications of the different accounting requirements. The Board noted that the measurement of the fulfilment cash flows is the same for both types of contract, and the differences are limited to the treatment of the contractual service margin. The Board was persuaded that those differences are necessary to provide a faithful representation of the different nature of the types of contract.

Other approaches considered but rejected

Adjusting the contractual service margin by changes in the carrying amount of underlying items for all contracts

BC258 Some stakeholders advocated adjusting the contractual service margin for changes in the carrying amount of underlying items whenever the insurance contracts require the amounts paid to policyholders to vary with returns on underlying items. However, the Board rejected that broad application of the variable fee concept, after deciding that it is useful only for insurance contracts that are substantially investment-related service contracts.

A 'mirroring' approach

BC259 In the 2013 Exposure Draft, the Board proposed a 'mirroring approach' for the measurement and presentation of contracts that require an entity to hold underlying items and that specify a link to returns on those underlying items. The essence of the mirroring approach was that, to the extent that an entity expects to settle fulfilment cash flows payable to policyholders with assets or other underlying items it holds, the entity would measure those fulfilment cash flows just as it measures the underlying items. Similarly, an entity would recognise changes in fulfilment cash flows subject to the mirroring approach (those that are expected to vary directly with returns on underlying items) in profit or loss or other comprehensive income on the same basis as the recognition of changes in the value of the underlying items. All other cash flows would be measured using the general requirements.

BC260 Mirroring would have eliminated accounting, but not economic, mismatches between the cash flows from an insurance contract and underlying items when the terms of the contract mean that the entity will not suffer any economic mismatches. However, not all cash flows in an insurance contract will vary directly with returns on underlying items.

BC261 Many stakeholders endorsed the Board's intention to eliminate accounting mismatches for some participating contracts. However, many criticised the Board's approach as being unduly complex and questioned whether the proposals could be made workable. In particular, many stakeholders stated that it would be difficult for entities to separate and measure separately the different components of the insurance contract. Some suggested that any decomposition of interrelated cash flows would be arbitrary and that separate measurement would lead to different valuations of an insurance contract depending on arbitrary decisions.

BC262 Many stakeholders were also concerned because the mirroring proposals would mean that the measurement outcome for some participating contracts would differ markedly from the measurement outcome for other insurance contracts based on only subtle differences in the characteristics of the contracts. In addition, some preparers and regulators were concerned that when the underlying items are measured at cost, the carrying value of the insurance contract would not be a current value. As a result, mirroring would widen the difference between the liability measured for financial reporting purposes and the liability recognised for regulatory purposes.

BC263 Given this feedback, the Board rejected the mirroring approach and developed the variable fee approach instead.

Insurers that are mutual entities

BC264 Some stakeholders supported the mirroring approach particularly for insurers that are mutual entities. They argued that mirroring was necessary for such insurers because the effect of accounting mismatches between assets that cannot be measured at fair value and fulfilment cash flows measured at current value can have a particularly significant effect on their reported financial position and financial performance.

BC265 A defining feature of an insurer that is a mutual entity is that the most residual interest of the entity is due to a policyholder and not a shareholder. When applying IFRS 17, payments to policyholders form part of the fulfilment cash flows regardless of whether those payments are expected to be made to current or future policyholders. Thus, the fulfilment cash flows of an insurer that is a mutual entity generally include the rights of policyholders to the whole of any surplus of assets over liabilities. This means that, for an insurer that is a mutual entity, there should, in principle, normally be no equity remaining and no net comprehensive income reported in any accounting period.[33]

BC266　However, there may be accounting mismatches between the measurement of insurance contracts and the measurement of the other net assets of an insurer that is a mutual entity. Insurance contracts are measured at current value, which, for an insurer that is a mutual entity, incorporates information about the fair value of the other assets and liabilities of the entity. Many of these other assets and liabilities are not required to be measured at fair value in applying IFRS Standards; for example, amortised cost financial assets, deferred tax balances, goodwill in subsidiaries and pension scheme surpluses and deficits. Furthermore, the carrying amounts of assets that are not measured at fair value are more likely to be measured at a value lower rather than higher than fair value because of requirements to recognise impairments.[34]

BC267　Hence, when liabilities are measured in applying IFRS 17, insurers that are mutual entities might report liabilities greater than recognised assets in their financial statements, even though those entities are solvent for regulatory purposes and economically have no equity (rather than negative equity). To prevent insurers that are mutual entities from reporting negative equity, some stakeholders suggested that the mirroring approach be retained for such entities to eliminate or reduce the effect of accounting mismatches.[35]

BC268　However, the Board noted that one consequence of retaining the mirroring approach for insurers that are mutual entities would be that an identical insurance contract would be measured on a different basis only because it was issued by an insurer that is a mutual entity. Comparability across entities is enhanced if economically similar products are accounted for in a similar way regardless of the legal form of the entity holding or issuing the product. In addition, the Board noted that applying the mirroring approach would mean that part of the fulfilment cash flows of an insurer that is a mutual entity would not be measured at current value, which was a major concern about the mirroring approach for some regulators (see paragraph BC262). Hence, the

---

33　When developing the June 2020 amendments to IFRS 17, the Board noted that some entities described in practice as mutual entities do not have the feature that the most residual interest of the entity is due to a policyholder (see paragraphs BC269A–BC269C). Paragraphs BC265–BC269 describe the outcome of applying IFRS 17 for entities for which the most residual interest of the entity is due to a policyholder.

34　When developing the June 2020 amendments to IFRS 17, the Board noted that some entities described in practice as mutual entities do not have the feature that the most residual interest of the entity is due to a policyholder (see paragraphs BC269A–BC269C). Paragraphs BC265–BC269 describe the outcome of applying IFRS 17 for entities for which the most residual interest of the entity is due to a policyholder.

35　When developing the June 2020 amendments to IFRS 17, the Board noted that some entities described in practice as mutual entities do not have the feature that the most residual interest of the entity is due to a policyholder (see paragraphs BC269A–BC269C). Paragraphs BC265–BC269 describe the outcome of applying IFRS 17 for entities for which the most residual interest of the entity is due to a policyholder.

Board concluded that it should not retain the mirroring approach for insurers that are mutual entities.[36]

BC269 The Board noted that to provide useful information about its financial position and financial performance, an insurer that is a mutual entity can distinguish:

(a) in the statement of financial position, the liability attributable to policyholders in their capacity as policyholders from the liability attributable to policyholders with the most residual interest in the entity; and

(b) in the statement(s) of financial performance, the income or expenses attributable to policyholders in their capacity as policyholders before determination of the amounts attributable to policyholders with the most residual interest in the entity.[37]

Amendments to IFRS 17—feedback on insurers that are mutual entities

BC269A Entities implementing IFRS 17 expressed the following concerns about mutual entities:

(a) applying IFRS 17 as described in paragraph BC265 would result in a misleading depiction of the financial position and financial performance of an entity with the feature that the most residual interest of the entity is due to a policyholder; and

(b) some entities described in practice as mutual entities do not have the feature that the most residual interest of the entity is due to a policyholder.

BC269B The Board reaffirmed its decision that IFRS 17 should not include any specific requirements or exceptions to requirements in IFRS 17 for entities that issue insurance contracts under which the most residual interest of the entity is due to a policyholder because:

(a) a core principle of IFRS 17 applicable to all entities is the requirement to include in the fulfilment cash flows all the expected future cash flows that arise within the boundary of insurance contracts, including discretionary cash flows and those due to future policyholders;

(b) if entities were required to account for the same insurance contract differently depending on the type of entity issuing the contract, comparability among entities would be reduced; and

---

36 When developing the June 2020 amendments to IFRS 17, the Board noted that some entities described in practice as mutual entities do not have the feature that the most residual interest of the entity is due to a policyholder (see paragraphs BC269A–BC269C). Paragraphs BC265–BC269 describe the outcome of applying IFRS 17 for entities for which the most residual interest of the entity is due to a policyholder.

37 When developing the June 2020 amendments to IFRS 17, the Board noted that some entities described in practice as mutual entities do not have the feature that the most residual interest of the entity is due to a policyholder (see paragraphs BC269A–BC269C). Paragraphs BC265–BC269 describe the outcome of applying IFRS 17 for entities for which the most residual interest of the entity is due to a policyholder.

(c)   a robust definition of entities to which different requirements would apply would be difficult to create.

BC269C   In response to the concern described in paragraph BC269A(b), the Board added the footnote to paragraphs BC265–BC269.

Insurance finance income or expenses on the contractual service margin (paragraphs 44(b) and 45(b) of IFRS 17)

BC270   IFRS 17 requires an entity to adjust the contractual service margin for a financing effect. The contractual service margin is one part of an overall measure of insurance contracts, and including in it a financing effect is consistent with the measurement of the other part (the fulfilment cash flows), which is adjusted for the time value of money and the effect of financial risks. Some argued that the contractual service margin should not be adjusted for a financing effect on the grounds of simplicity and because they view the contractual service margin as being a deferred credit rather than a representation of a component of an obligation. However, adjusting the contractual service margin for a financing effect is consistent with IFRS 15.

BC271   The way in which a financing effect is included in the contractual service margin differs between insurance contracts without direct participation features and insurance contracts with direct participation features.

BC272   For insurance contracts without direct participation features, IFRS 17 requires an entity to calculate interest on the contractual service margin. In the Board's view, on initial recognition the contractual service margin can be viewed as an allocation of part of the transaction price, which is the consideration paid or payable by the policyholder. Calculating interest on the contractual service margin is consistent with IFRS 15, which requires an entity to adjust the promised consideration to reflect the time value of money if the contract has a significant financing component. As a result of that adjustment, the transaction price would reflect the amount the customer would pay in cash for the promised good or service when they receive the good or service. Consequently, an entity would recognise revenue at an amount that corresponds to the cash selling price of the good or service, with the effects of the financing presented separately from revenue (as interest expense or interest income).

BC273   Because the contractual service margin is measured at initial recognition of the group of insurance contracts, the Board decided that the interest rate used to accrete interest on the contractual service margin for insurance contracts without direct participation features should be locked in at initial recognition and not adjusted subsequently. The Board also decided, for the sake of simplicity, that the rate should be a rate applicable to nominal cash flows that do not vary based on asset returns. Locking in the rate is consistent with the determination of the contractual service margin on initial recognition and making no adjustments for changes in assumptions relating to financial risk.

BC274　Some stakeholders argued that interest should be accreted at a current rate on the grounds that the current rate would be consistent with the measurement of the fulfilment cash flows. Also, a locked-in rate requires information about historical rates that would not otherwise be needed for entities not using the option to include insurance finance income or expenses in profit or loss using a systematic allocation (see paragraphs BC42–BC44). However, the Board noted that accreting interest on the contractual service margin for an accounting period at a current rate differs from measuring cash flows at a current rate. The contractual service margin does not represent future cash flows; it represents the unearned profit in the contract, measured at the point of initial recognition and adjusted only for specified amounts. For insurance contracts without direct participation features, the contractual service margin is not adjusted (remeasured) for changes in interest rates for the reasons set out in paragraphs BC228–BC231. Accreting interest for a period at a current rate without also remeasuring the contractual service margin at the start of the period would create an internally inconsistent measurement of the contractual service margin.

BC275　For insurance contracts without direct participation features, IFRS 17 requires the contractual service margin to be adjusted for changes in estimates of future cash flows that relate to future service. When measuring the fulfilment cash flows, these changes in estimates are measured consistently with all other aspects of the fulfilment cash flows using a current discount rate. However, the contractual service margin is determined using the discount rate that applies on initial recognition. To make the contractual service margin internally consistent, the Board decided that the adjustments for changes in estimates of future cash flows also need to be measured at the rate that applied on initial recognition. This leads to a difference between the change in the fulfilment cash flows and the adjustment to the contractual service margin—the difference between the change in the future cash flows measured at a current rate and the change in the future cash flows measured at the rate that had applied on initial recognition. That difference gives rise to a gain or loss that is included in profit or loss or other comprehensive income, depending on the accounting policy choice an entity makes for the presentation of insurance finance income or expenses.

BC276　For insurance contracts with direct participation features, IFRS 17 requires an entity to remeasure the contractual service margin for the entity's share in the change in the fair value of the underlying items. The remeasurement of the contractual service margin reflects current rates and changes in the value of the consideration received. Remeasuring the contractual service margin in this way is consistent with the view that the entity is earning a variable fee from the contract—the amount it deducts from its obligation to return the value of underlying items to the policyholder (see paragraphs BC238–BC247). A consequence of this is that insurance revenue includes changes in the entity's share in the change in the fair value of the underlying items. As set out in paragraphs B121–B124 of IFRS 17, insurance revenue includes the amount of contractual service margin allocated to the period for services provided in the period. The allocation of the contractual service margin amount is based on the remeasured contractual service margin. Insurance revenue for the period is therefore also based on that remeasured amount. The Board decided this appropriately reflects the variable nature of the fee for such contracts.

Amendments to IFRS 17—feedback on discount rates used to determine adjustments to the contractual service margin

BC276A For insurance contracts without direct participation features, differences arise between a change in the fulfilment cash flows measured using current discount rates, and the resulting adjustment to the contractual service margin measured using discount rates locked in at initial recognition (see paragraph BC275). Consistent with the feedback set out in paragraph BC274, entities implementing IFRS 17 continued to express concerns about such differences.

BC276B Some stakeholders suggested that an amendment to require an entity to measure adjustments to the contractual service margin using the current discount rates used for the measurement of the fulfilment cash flows would reduce the operational burden of applying the Standard. Others said such an amendment would be conceptually appropriate.

BC276C The fulfilment cash flows and the contractual service margin are the two components of the measurement of insurance contracts. The fulfilment cash flows are a current risk-adjusted estimate of future cash flows expected to arise from a group of insurance contracts. In contrast, the contractual service margin is the profit expected to arise from future service that an entity will provide for a group of insurance contracts. The contractual service margin on initial recognition of a group is the difference between the estimated cash inflows and estimated cash outflows (adjusted for the effect of the time value of money, non-financial risk and financial risk). The contractual service margin is not a future cash flow. When changes in fulfilment cash flows relate to future service, the expected profit relating to that future service changes. Accordingly, those changes in estimates adjust the contractual service margin.

BC276D The Board considered but rejected the suggestions to amend IFRS 17 described in paragraph BC276B for the reasons that led it to conclude, while developing IFRS 17, that an entity should determine adjustments to the contractual service margin using locked-in discount rates (see paragraphs BC273–BC275). An entity would measure profit inconsistently if it were to measure the effect of future cash flows on the contractual service margin at discount rates that differed depending on when such future cash flows become part of the expected cash flows. The Board concluded that measuring the contractual service margin at the discount rates determined at the date of initial recognition (that is, locked-in discount rates) provides a faithful representation of the revenue earned as the entity provides services, reflecting the price set at the contract issue date for that service. In contrast, measuring changes in the contractual service margin using current rates would result in arbitrary amounts relating to the effects of changes in discount rates being reflected in the insurance service result rather than in insurance finance income or expenses. A core benefit introduced by IFRS 17 is the presentation of insurance finance income or expenses separately from the insurance service result.

BC276E   The Board disagreed with stakeholders who said that entities would have difficulty explaining to users of financial statements a gain or loss arising from the differences between a change in fulfilment cash flows and a change in the adjustment to the contractual service margin. The Board observed that the gain or loss provides information about the cumulative amount of insurance finance income or expenses that had been previously recognised and should be reversed, or the amount that was not previously recognised and now is.

Foreign currency (paragraph 30 of IFRS 17)

BC277   When applying IAS 21 *The Effects of Changes in Foreign Exchange Rates*, the fulfilment cash flows are clearly monetary items. However, the contractual service margin component might be classified as non-monetary because it is similar to prepayments for goods and services. The Board decided that it would be simpler to treat all components of the measurement of an insurance contract denominated in a single currency as either monetary or non-monetary. Because the measurement in IFRS 17 is largely based on estimates of future cash flows, the Board concluded that it is more appropriate to view an insurance contract as a whole as a monetary item.

BC278   Accordingly, IFRS 17 requires an insurance contract to be treated as a monetary item for foreign currency translation in applying IAS 21. This applies for both the fulfilment cash flows and the contractual service margin. The Board's conclusion that the insurance contract is a monetary item does not change if an entity measures a group of insurance contracts using the simplified approach for the measurement of the liability for remaining coverage.

Recognition in profit or loss (paragraphs 44(e), 45(e) and B119–B119B of IFRS 17)

BC279   As discussed in paragraph BC21, the Board views the contractual service margin as depicting the unearned profit for coverage and other services provided over the coverage period. Insurance coverage is the defining service provided by insurance contracts. The Board noted that an entity provides this service over the whole of the coverage period, and not just when it incurs a claim. Consequently, IFRS 17 requires the contractual service margin to be recognised over the coverage period in a pattern that reflects the provision of coverage as required by the contract. To achieve this, the contractual service margin for a group of insurance contracts remaining (before any allocation) at the end of the reporting period is allocated over the coverage provided in the current period and expected remaining future coverage, on the basis of coverage units, reflecting the expected duration and quantity of benefits provided by contracts in the group. The Board considered whether:

(a) the contractual service margin should be allocated based on the pattern of expected cash flows or on the change in the risk adjustment for non-financial risk caused by the release of risk. However, the Board decided the pattern of expected cash flows and the release of the risk adjustment for non-financial risk are not relevant factors in determining the satisfaction of the performance obligation of the entity. They are already included in the measurement of the fulfilment cash flows and do not need to be considered in the allocation of the contractual service margin. Hence, the Board concluded that coverage units better reflect the provision of insurance coverage.

(b) the contractual service margin should be allocated before any adjustments made because of changes in fulfilment cash flows that relate to future service. However, the Board concluded that allocating the amount of the contractual service margin adjusted for the most up-to-date assumptions provides the most relevant information about the profit earned from service provided in the period and the profit to be earned in the future from future service.[38]

BC280 The Board considered whether the allocation of the contractual service margin based on coverage units would result in profit being recognised too early for insurance contracts with fees determined based on the returns on underlying items. For such contracts, IFRS 17 requires the contractual service margin to be determined based on the total expected fee over the duration of the contracts, including expectations of an increase in the fee because of an increase in underlying items arising from investment returns and additional policyholder contributions over time. The Board rejected the view that the allocation based on coverage units results in premature profit recognition. The Board noted that the investment component of such contracts is accounted for as part of the insurance contract only when the cash flows from the investment component and from insurance and other services are highly interrelated and hence cannot be accounted for as distinct components. In such circumstances, the entity provides multiple services in return for an expected fee based on the expected duration of contracts, and the Board concluded the entity should recognise that fee over the coverage period as the insurance services are provided, not when the returns on the underlying items occur.[39]

BC281 The Board also considered a proposal to constrain the amount of contractual service margin recognised in an accounting period just as IFRS 15 constrains the recognition of revenue. The approach would have constrained the cumulative amount of the contractual service margin that the entity recognised in profit or loss to the amount to which the entity is reasonably assured to be entitled. However, in the Board's view, it would be inconsistent with other aspects of IFRS 17 to constrain the amount of contractual service margin on a 'reasonably assured' basis. IFRS 17 requires a current

---

38 In June 2020, the Board amended the definition of a coverage period to be the period during which the entity provides insurance contract services (see paragraphs BC283A–BC283J).

39 In June 2020, the Board amended the definition of a coverage period to be the period during which the entity provides insurance contract services (see paragraphs BC283A–BC283J).

measurement model based on a probability-weighted average of all possible scenarios and the contractual service margin depicts a current view of the unearned profit relating to services consistent with that measurement model.

BC282 IFRS 17 requires the contractual service margin remaining at the end of the reporting period to be allocated equally to the coverage units provided in the period and the expected remaining coverage units. IFRS 17 does not specify whether an entity should consider the time value of money in determining that equal allocation and consequently does not specify whether that equal allocation should reflect the timing of the expected provision of the coverage units. The Board concluded that should be a matter of judgement by an entity.

BC283 Consistent with the requirements in IFRS 15, the settlement of a liability is not considered to be a service provided by the entity. Thus, the recognition period for the contractual service margin is the coverage period over which the entity provides the coverage promised in the insurance contract, rather than the period over which the liability is expected to be settled. The margin the entity recognises for bearing risk is recognised in profit or loss as the entity is released from risk in both the coverage period and the settlement period.[40]

Amendments to IFRS 17—contractual service margin attributable to investment-return service and investment-related service

BC283A In June 2020, the Board amended IFRS 17 to:

(a) require an entity to identify coverage units for insurance contracts without direct participation features considering the quantity of benefits and expected period of investment-return service, if any, in addition to insurance coverage. Paragraph B119B of IFRS 17 specifies criteria for when such contracts may provide an investment-return service.

(b) clarify that an entity is required to identify coverage units for insurance contracts with direct participation features considering the quantity of benefits and expected period of both insurance coverage and investment-related service.

(c) require an entity to include investment activity costs in the fulfilment cash flows, to the extent that the entity performs those activities to:

   (i) enhance benefits from insurance coverage for policyholders (see paragraph B65(ka)(i) of IFRS 17);

   (ii) provide investment-return service to policyholders of insurance contracts without direct participation features (see paragraph B119B of IFRS 17); or

   (iii) provide investment-related service to policyholders of insurance contracts with direct participation features.

---

40 In June 2020, the Board amended the definition of a coverage period to be the period during which the entity provides insurance contract services (see paragraphs BC283A–BC283J).

(d) define 'insurance contract services' as comprising insurance coverage, investment-return service and investment-related service.

(e) expand the definitions of a liability for remaining coverage and a liability for incurred claims to reflect an entity's obligation to provide insurance contract services and any other obligations arising from insurance contracts.

BC283B The Board was persuaded that some insurance contracts without direct participation features provide an investment-return service (see paragraph BC283A(a)). Recognising the contractual service margin considering both insurance coverage and an investment-return service will provide useful information to users of financial statements, particularly for contracts that have an insurance coverage period that differs from the period in which the policyholder benefits from an investment-return service.

BC283C The Board concluded that an investment-return service exists only if the contract includes an investment component or the policyholder has a right to withdraw an amount from the entity. Further, those amounts must be expected to include an investment return that the entity generates by performing investment activity. The Board concluded that if those conditions are not met, the policyholder has no right to benefit from investment returns. In this context, a 'right to withdraw an amount from the entity' includes a policyholder's right to:

(a) receive a surrender value or refund of premiums on cancellation of a policy; or

(b) transfer an amount to another insurance provider.

BC283D Without the Standard specifying conditions for the existence of an investment-return service, entities issuing the same type of contracts might make different decisions from each other about whether those contracts provide an investment-return service. Entities might also conclude that an investment-return service exists in circumstances in which the Board would conclude otherwise (for example, when an entity provides only custodial services relating to an investment component). On the other hand, specifying conditions creates the risk of an inappropriate outcome in some scenarios.

BC283E Balancing the potential risks described in paragraph BC283D, the Board decided to specify conditions that are necessary to identify, but are not determinative of, the existence of an investment-return service (see paragraph B119B of IFRS 17). An entity is required to apply judgement, considering the facts and circumstances, to determine whether an insurance contract that meets the conditions provides an investment-return service.

BC283F Including an investment-return service in addition to insurance coverage in determining coverage units for insurance contracts without direct participation features adds subjectivity and complexity to that determination. However, the Board noted that entities are required to make similar assessments for insurance contracts with direct participation features and for contracts that provide more than one type of insurance coverage. Furthermore, any additional subjectivity and complexity would be mitigated by the related disclosure required by paragraph 109 of IFRS 17, which provides users of financial statements with useful information about the pattern of service provision.

BC283G   Applying IFRS 17 as amended in June 2020, an entity recognises the contractual service margin in profit or loss over the period the entity provides insurance contract services. Therefore, as part of the June 2020 amendments, the Board added 'insurance contract services' to the defined terms of IFRS 17 (see paragraph BC283A(d)) and inserted the defined term into the requirements in IFRS 17 for the recognition of the contractual service margin. Insurance contract services are the only services that an entity considers when determining coverage units and hence the recognition of the contractual service margin in profit or loss.

BC283H   The Board decided against inserting that defined term into the requirements in IFRS 17 relating to the recognition of insurance revenue (for example, paragraph 83 of IFRS 17). This is not because other services are considered in determining insurance revenue, but rather because inserting that defined term there might be interpreted as prohibiting an entity from recognising insurance revenue unrelated to the contractual service margin before the coverage period begins. Insurance revenue can be analysed as consisting of the amount of the contractual service margin allocated to the period, the release of the risk adjustment for non-financial risk in the period and the expenses the entity expected to incur in the period. Some insurance contracts include a pre-coverage period, between the date the contract is recognised and the date the entity first provides insurance contract services. In contracts with a pre-coverage period, an entity may be released from non-financial risk, or may incur expenses before the coverage period begins—in other words, before the entity starts providing insurance contract services. The Board did not want to preclude an entity from recognising the related insurance revenue in that pre-coverage period.

BC283I   Investment activity costs that an entity incurs are included in the fulfilment cash flows to the extent that the entity incurs those costs to provide investment-return service or investment-related service. The Board acknowledged that an entity may also incur investment activity costs to enhance benefits from insurance coverage for policyholders. Therefore, the Board amended IFRS 17 to specify that an entity is required to include investment activity costs in the fulfilment cash flows to the extent that the entity performs those activities to enhance benefits from insurance coverage for policyholders. The Board also specified when investment activities enhance benefits from insurance coverage. The Board noted that in determining whether investment activity costs enhance benefits from insurance coverage for policyholders, an entity needs to apply judgement in a similar manner to when an entity determines whether an investment-return service exists.

Other approaches considered but rejected

BC283J   Some stakeholders said the Board should replace the requirements for the recognition of the contractual service margin in profit or loss with a less specific requirement based on all services provided by the contract. Applying this suggestion, an entity would decide what services are provided by the contract, potentially including services other than insurance coverage or services related to investment returns. The Board concluded that specifying that an entity recognises the contractual service margin by considering all services would result in more subjectivity and complexity than entities already face when determining the pattern of service provision. Feedback the Board received when developing IFRS 17 supports that view. Furthermore, the Board noted that the concerns leading to this suggestion were generally about services related to investment returns. The Board concluded that the amendment described in paragraph BC283A(a) responds to feedback that some insurance contracts without direct participation features have two defining services—insurance coverage and investment-return service. Thus, the amendment balances the need for relevant information about the way in which profit from the contract is earned and the need for comparable information, as well as the costs of applying the coverage units requirement.

Onerous contracts (paragraphs 47–52 of IFRS 17)

BC284   The contractual service margin represents the unearned profit arising from a group of insurance contracts. IFRS 17 prohibits the contractual service margin from becoming negative (except in relation to reinsurance contracts held) because the Board decided that expected losses on groups of insurance contracts should be recognised immediately in profit or loss.[41] Doing so provides timely information about loss-making groups of insurance contracts, and is consistent with the recognition of losses for onerous contracts in accordance with IFRS 15 and IAS 37.

BC285   After an entity recognises a loss for a group of onerous contracts, there may subsequently be favourable changes in the estimates of the fulfilment cash flows relating to future service. The Board considered whether such changes should be recognised in profit or loss to the extent that they reverse previously recognised losses or whether the changes should adjust, or rebuild, the contractual service margin. In the 2013 Exposure Draft, the Board proposed that the changes adjust the contractual service margin, rather than being recognised in profit or loss, because of the complexity in assessing the extent to which the favourable changes reverse previous losses. However, some stakeholders stated that it would be counterintuitive to rebuild a contractual service margin for future profit from contracts that were considered loss-making overall.

---

41   In June 2020, the Board amended paragraphs 48(a) and 50(b) of IFRS 17 for measuring onerous insurance contracts to clarify that those paragraphs relate to both changes in estimates of future cash flows and changes in the risk adjustment for non-financial risk.

BC286   The Board noted that, under the proposals in the 2013 Exposure Draft, the determination of insurance revenue required entities to exclude losses for groups of onerous contracts (see paragraph BC35). Subsequent changes in the fulfilment cash flows that relate to the losses for groups of onerous contracts would also need to be excluded from insurance revenue, otherwise insurance revenue would be understated or overstated. Hence, the Board decided that some tracking of the loss component of the liability for remaining coverage would be needed. Further, the Board concluded that the complexity added by requiring this tracking was outweighed by the benefits of the more faithful representation of performance that would be provided to users of financial statements if the effect of favourable changes were recognised in profit or loss to the extent that they reverse losses previously recognised in profit or loss. Accordingly, IFRS 17 requires that, to the extent that favourable changes in the estimates of the fulfilment cash flows relating to future service reverse losses previously recognised in profit or loss, the changes should also be recognised in profit or loss.

BC287   The Board considered whether to require specific methods to track the loss component, but concluded that any such methods would be inherently arbitrary. The Board therefore decided to require an entity to make a systematic allocation of changes in the fulfilment cash flows for the liability for remaining coverage that could be regarded as affecting either the loss component or the rest of the liability.

Premium allocation approach (paragraphs 53–59 of IFRS 17)

BC288   IFRS 17 allows an entity to simplify the measurement of some groups of insurance contracts by applying a premium allocation approach.

BC289   The premium allocation approach permitted in IFRS 17 is similar to the customer consideration approach in IFRS 15. In the premium allocation approach, the initial measurement of the liability equals the premium received, and unless the group of insurance contracts is onerous, the entity does not identify explicitly the components otherwise used in IFRS 17 to build the measurement of the insurance contract, ie the estimate of future cash flows, the time value of money and the effects of risk. Nevertheless, that initial measurement can be described as containing the components that build the measurement of the group of insurance contracts implicitly, as follows:

(a)   an estimate of the future cash flows, made at initial recognition;

(b)   the effect of the time value of money and of financial risks, measured at initial recognition;

(c)   the effect of non-financial risk, measured at initial recognition; and

(d)   a contractual service margin, if any, measured at initial recognition.

BC290   Subsequently, the liability for remaining coverage is recognised over the coverage period on the basis of the passage of time unless the expected pattern of release from risk differs significantly from the passage of time, in which case it is recognised based on the expected timing of incurred claims and benefits.

BC291   The Board decided that an entity should be permitted, but not required, to apply the premium allocation approach when that approach provides a reasonable approximation to the general requirements of IFRS 17. The Board views the premium allocation approach as a simplification of those general requirements. To simplify its application, the Board also decided to provide guidance that an entity could assume, without further investigation, that the approach provides a reasonable approximation of the general requirements of IFRS 17 if the coverage period of each contract in the group is one year or less.

BC292   To keep the approach simple, the Board decided that entities:

(a)   should accrete interest on the liability for remaining coverage only for groups of insurance contracts that have a significant financing component. When the period between premiums being due and the provision of coverage is one year or less, the group is deemed not to have a significant financing component.[42]

(b)   need to assess whether groups of insurance contracts are onerous only when facts and circumstances indicate that a group of insurance contracts has become onerous.

(c)   are permitted to recognise all insurance acquisition cash flows as an expense when incurred for groups of insurance contracts each with a coverage period of one year or less.

BC293   The premium allocation approach measures the group of insurance contracts using estimates made at initial recognition and does not update those estimates in the measurement of the liability for remaining coverage unless the group is or becomes onerous. Accordingly, IFRS 17 requires that entities, when accreting interest on the liability for remaining coverage, set the discount rate when the group is initially recognised.

BC294   IFRS 17 also allows a simplification for the measurement of the liability for incurred claims—an entity need not discount claims that are expected to be paid within one year. The Board concluded that no other simplifications were needed for the measurement of the liability for incurred claims because it comprises only the fulfilment cash flows for settling the incurred claims and expenses, with no contractual service margin. However, in considering how to disaggregate insurance finance income or expenses between profit or loss and other comprehensive income (see paragraphs BC42–BC44), the Board considered requiring the interest expense for the liability for incurred claims to be measured using either:

(a)   the discount rate at initial recognition of the contract; or

---

42 In June 2020, the Board amended the definition of a coverage period to be the period during which the entity provides insurance contract services (see paragraphs BC283A–BC283J).

(b)   the discount rate at the date the claims included in the liability for incurred claims occur.

BC295   In the 2013 Exposure Draft, the Board proposed using the discount rate at initial recognition to achieve consistency with the measurement of the liability for remaining coverage. However, both preparers and users of financial statements expressed the view that using the discount rate at the date the claim was incurred would be less complex than using the rate at the inception of the contract. The liability for incurred claims is zero when the group of insurance contracts is initially recognised and the entity may not have determined a discount rate at that time. The Board concluded that the premium allocation approach, which was developed as a simplification, should not burden entities by creating high costs and operational complexity. Consequently, IFRS 17 requires that entities measure the interest expense for the liability for incurred claims using the rate that applied when the liability for incurred claims was initially recognised, rather than when the group of insurance contracts was initially recognised.

Reinsurance contracts (paragraphs 60–70A of IFRS 17)

BC296   A reinsurance contract is a type of insurance contract. The Board identified no reason to apply different requirements to reinsurance contracts from those applied to other insurance contracts an entity issues. Consequently, IFRS 17 requires entities that issue reinsurance contracts to use the same recognition and measurement approach as they use for other insurance contracts.

BC297   Although both an issuer of direct insurance contracts and a reinsurer of those contracts will measure their contractual rights and obligations on the same basis, in practice they will not necessarily arrive at the same amount. Differences between the estimates for the reinsurance contract and the underlying contracts may arise because the issuer of the underlying insurance contracts and the reinsurer may base estimates on access to different information; they may also make different adjustments for diversification effects.

BC298   IFRS 17 also applies to reinsurance contracts held by an entity (ie in which the entity is the policyholder). IFRS 17 requires a reinsurance contract held to be accounted for separately from the underlying insurance contracts to which it relates. This is because an entity that holds a reinsurance contract does not normally have a right to reduce the amounts it owes to the underlying policyholder by amounts it expects to receive from the reinsurer. The Board acknowledged that separate accounting for the reinsurance contracts and their underlying insurance contracts might create mismatches that some regard as purely accounting, for example on the timing of recognition (see paragraphs BC304–BC305), the measurement of the reinsurance contracts (see paragraphs BC310–BC312) and the recognition of profit (see paragraph BC313). However, the Board concluded that accounting for a reinsurance contract held separately from the underlying insurance contracts gives a faithful representation of the entity's rights and obligations and the related income and expenses from both contracts.

BC299   The amount an entity pays for reinsurance coverage consists of premiums the entity pays minus any amounts paid by the reinsurer to the entity to compensate the entity for expenses it incurs, such as underwriting or acquisition expenses (often referred to as 'ceding commissions'). The amount paid for reinsurance coverage by the entity can be viewed as payment for the following:

(a)   the reinsurer's share of the expected present value of the cash flows generated by the underlying insurance contract(s). That amount includes an adjustment for the risk that the reinsurer may dispute coverage or fail to satisfy its obligations under the reinsurance contract held.

(b)   a contractual service margin that makes the initial measurement of the reinsurance asset equal to the premium paid. This margin depends on the pricing of the reinsurance contract held and, consequently, may differ from the contractual service margin arising for the underlying insurance contract(s).

BC300   When estimating cash flows and the associated adjustments for the financial risk and the time value of money arising from reinsurance contracts held, the entity would use assumptions consistent with those it uses for the underlying contracts. As a result, the cash flows used to measure the reinsurance contracts held would reflect the extent to which those cash flows depend on the cash flows of the contracts they cover.

BC301   Consistent with the requirements for the measurement of insurance contracts an entity issues, the entity also may apply the premium allocation approach to simplify the measurement of reinsurance contracts held, provided that the resulting measurement is a reasonable approximation of the results that would be obtained by applying the general requirements of IFRS 17. The entity may also apply the premium allocation approach if the coverage period of each reinsurance contract held in the group is one year or less. Because groups of reinsurance contracts are separate from the groups of underlying insurance contracts, the assessment of whether a group of reinsurance contracts meets conditions for applying the premium allocation approach may differ from the assessment of whether the group(s) of underlying insurance contracts meet(s) those conditions.

BC302   IFRS 17 modifies the requirements for reinsurance contracts held to reflect the fact that:

(a)   groups of reinsurance contracts held are generally assets, rather than liabilities; and

(b)   entities holding reinsurance contracts generally pay a margin to the reinsurer as an implicit part of the premium, rather than making profits from the reinsurance contracts.

BC303   The following paragraphs discuss aspects of the general principles in IFRS 17 in relation to groups of reinsurance contracts held:

   (a)   recognition for groups of reinsurance contracts held (see paragraphs BC304–BC305);

   (b)   derecognition (see paragraph BC306);

   (c)   cash flows (see paragraphs BC307–BC309F); and

   (d)   contractual service margin (see paragraphs BC310–BC315L).

Recognition for groups of reinsurance contracts held (paragraphs 62–62A of IFRS 17)

BC304   Many reinsurance arrangements are designed to cover the claims incurred under underlying insurance contracts written during a specified period. In some cases, the reinsurance contract held covers the losses of separate contracts on a proportionate basis. In other cases, the reinsurance contract held covers aggregate losses from a group of underlying contracts that exceed a specified amount.

BC305   The Board decided to simplify the application of the principle that a contract should be recognised from the date the entity is exposed to risk for reinsurance contracts as follows:

   (a)   when the group of reinsurance contracts held covers the loss of a group of insurance contracts on a proportionate basis, the group of reinsurance contracts held is recognised at the later of the beginning of the coverage period of the group of reinsurance contracts held or the initial recognition of any underlying contracts. This means that the entity will not recognise the group of reinsurance contracts until it has recognised at least one of the underlying contracts.

   (b)   when the group of reinsurance contracts held covers aggregate losses arising from a group of insurance contracts over a specified amount, the group of reinsurance contracts held is recognised when the coverage period of the group of reinsurance contracts begins. In these contracts the entity benefits from coverage—in case the underlying losses exceed the threshold—from the beginning of the group of reinsurance contracts held because such losses accumulate throughout the coverage period.

BC305A   In June 2020, the Board amended IFRS 17 for reinsurance contracts held when underlying insurance contracts are onerous at initial recognition (see paragraphs BC315A–BC315L). As a consequence of that amendment, the Board also amended the requirement in paragraph 62 of IFRS 17 (for recognising a group of reinsurance contracts held) to require an entity to recognise a group of reinsurance contracts held when the entity recognises onerous underlying insurance contracts, if it does so earlier than when the entity would otherwise recognise the group of reinsurance contracts held. The Board concluded such an amendment was necessary for income to be recognised on a group of reinsurance contracts held at the same time that losses are recognised on initial recognition of onerous underlying insurance contracts.

Derecognition of underlying contracts (paragraphs 74–75 of IFRS 17)

BC306 An entity does not derecognise an insurance contract until the contractual obligations are extinguished by discharge, cancellation or expiry (or on specified modifications of the contract). A reinsurance contract held typically protects the entity from the effects of some defined losses on the underlying group of insurance contracts, but does not eliminate the entity's responsibility for fulfilling its obligations under those contracts. It follows that the entity typically would not derecognise the related underlying insurance contracts upon entering into a reinsurance contract.

Cash flows in reinsurance contracts held (paragraph 63 of IFRS 17)

Expected credit losses

BC307 As required by paragraph 63 of IFRS 17, cash flows for a group of reinsurance contracts held should be estimated using assumptions that are consistent with those used for the group(s) of underlying insurance contracts. In addition, IFRS 17 requires entities to reflect expected credit losses in the measurement of the fulfilment cash flows. This is discussed in paragraphs BC308–BC309.

BC308 An entity holding reinsurance contracts faces the risk that the reinsurer may default, or may dispute whether a valid claim exists for an insured event. IFRS 17 requires the estimates of expected credit losses to be based on expected values. Hence, estimates of the amounts and timing of cash flows are probability-weighted outcomes after calculating the effect of credit losses.

BC309 IFRS 17 prohibits changes in expected credit losses adjusting the contractual service margin. In the Board's view, differences in expected credit losses do not relate to future service. Accordingly, any changes in expected credit losses are economic events that the Board decided should be reflected as gains and losses in profit or loss when they occur. This would result in consistent accounting for expected credit losses between reinsurance contracts held and purchased, and originated credit-impaired financial assets accounted for in accordance with IFRS 9.

Amendments to IFRS 17—feedback on the cash flows in the boundary of a reinsurance contract held

BC309A Estimates of future cash flows included in the measurement of a group of reinsurance contracts held include future cash flows that relate to insurance contracts an entity expects to be covered by the reinsurance contracts held in the group. Such cash flows include cash flows related to insurance contracts the entity expects to issue in the future if the entity has a substantive right to receive reinsurance coverage for those insurance contracts. The Board considered a suggestion from entities implementing IFRS 17 to amend IFRS 17 to exclude from the measurement of the group of reinsurance contracts held cash flows that relate to underlying insurance contracts that are yet to be issued.

BC309B   The Board noted that the suggestion in paragraph BC309A, which is consistent with feedback during the development of IFRS 17, would achieve an outcome similar to the practice often used applying IFRS 4 whereby an entity measured reinsurance contracts held based on the measurement of existing underlying insurance contracts.

BC309C   The Board reaffirmed its view that the accounting for a reinsurance contract held should be consistent with the accounting for insurance contracts issued (see paragraph BC298). Consistent accounting includes measuring the expected value of all the entity's rights and obligations arising from a contract. When an entity holds a reinsurance contract that provides the entity with a substantive right to receive reinsurance coverage for insurance contracts it expects to issue, cash flows arising from that substantive right are included in the measurement of the reinsurance contract held (that is, those cash flows are within the boundary of the reinsurance contract held applying paragraph 34 of IFRS 17). In contrast, if a reinsurance contract held provides an entity with neither substantive rights nor substantive obligations relating to insurance contracts it expects to issue, those insurance contracts would be outside the boundary of the reinsurance contract held. The requirements for expected future cash flows in paragraphs 33–35 of IFRS 17 form a core aspect of the Standard. The Board identified no reason for these requirements to be applied inconsistently—they should be applied both to insurance contracts issued and reinsurance contracts held.

BC309D   The Board noted that including all expected future cash flows in the measurement of the contractual service margin at initial recognition of the group of reinsurance contracts held reflects the conditions under which the entity agreed, under specified terms, to receive services from the reinsurer for future insurance contracts it expects to issue.

BC309E   Some stakeholders said that the requirements in IFRS 17 create an accounting mismatch when an entity has a substantive right to receive reinsurance coverage relating to insurance contracts it expects to issue. They said such a mismatch arises because expected future cash flows that relate to the reinsurance of those insurance contracts will be included in the measurement of the reinsurance contract held before those underlying insurance contracts are issued. The Board disagreed that differences between the carrying amount of the reinsurance contract held and the underlying insurance contracts are accounting mismatches. The carrying amount of a reinsurance contract held is nil before any cash flows occur or any service is received. Thereafter any differences that arise between the carrying amount of the reinsurance contract held and the underlying insurance contracts are not accounting mismatches. Rather they are differences caused by:

(a)   the provision of coverage—for example, because the reinsurer provides coverage for less than 100 per cent of the risks the entity covers;

(b)   the timing of cash flows; and

(c) interest accreted on the contractual service margin of the reinsurance contract held from an earlier period than, and at a different discount rate from, the interest accreted on the contractual service margin of the underlying insurance contracts, reflecting the different effects of the time value of money on the contractual service margin and fulfilment cash flows.

BC309F The Board acknowledged that some entities will incur costs implementing IFRS 17 for reinsurance contracts held because doing so would be a change from previous practice. However, the Board concluded that the benefits of appropriately reflecting an entity's rights and obligations as the holder of a reinsurance contract outweigh those costs. Accordingly, the Board rejected the suggestion to amend the contract boundary requirements in IFRS 17 for reinsurance contracts held.

Gains and losses on buying reinsurance (paragraphs 65–65A, 66A–66B and B119D–B119F of IFRS 17)

BC310 The amount paid by the entity to buy reinsurance contracts would typically exceed the expected present value of cash flows generated by the reinsurance contracts held, plus the risk adjustment for non-financial risk. Thus, a debit contractual service margin, which represents the net expense of purchasing reinsurance, would typically be recognised on the initial recognition of a group of reinsurance contracts held. The Board considered whether the contractual service margin of the group of reinsurance contracts held could be a credit if, as happens in rare cases, the amount paid by the entity is less than the expected present value of cash flows plus the risk adjustment for non-financial risk. Such a credit contractual service margin would represent a net gain on purchasing reinsurance. The most likely causes of such a net gain would be either of the following:

(a) an overstatement of the underlying insurance contract(s). An entity would evaluate this by reviewing the measurement of the underlying insurance contract(s).

(b) favourable pricing by the reinsurer; for example, as a result of diversification benefits that are not available to the entity.

BC311 The Board originally proposed that entities should recognise a gain when such a negative difference arose. The Board proposed this for symmetry with the model for the underlying group of insurance contracts and for consistency with the Board's conclusion that the contractual service margin for the underlying group of insurance contracts should not be negative. However, IFRS 17 requires entities to instead recognise the negative difference over the coverage period of the group of reinsurance contracts held. The Board was persuaded by the view that the apparent gain at initial recognition represents a reduction in the cost of purchasing reinsurance, and that it would be appropriate for an entity to recognise that reduction in cost over the coverage period as services are received.

BC312　The Board also decided that the net expense of purchasing reinsurance should be recognised over the coverage period as services are received unless the reinsurance covers events that have already occurred. For such reinsurance contracts held, the Board concluded that entities should recognise the whole of the net expense at initial recognition, to be consistent with the treatment of the net expense of purchasing reinsurance before an insured event has occurred. The Board acknowledged that this approach does not treat the coverage period of the reinsurance contract consistently with the view that for some insurance contracts the insured event is the discovery of a loss during the term of the contract, if that loss arises from an event that had occurred before the inception of the contract. However, the Board concluded that consistency of the treatment of the net expense across all reinsurance contracts held would result in more relevant information.

BC313　The Board considered the view that the amount of the contractual service margin included in the measurement of the group of reinsurance contracts held should be proportional to the contractual service margin on the group of underlying contracts instead of being measured separately by reference to the reinsurance premium. Under this approach, any difference between the amount recognised for the group of underlying insurance contracts and the reinsurance premium would be recognised in profit or loss when the group of reinsurance contracts held is initially recognised. This approach would depict a gain or loss equal to the shortfall or excess of the reinsurance premium the entity pays to the reinsurer above or below the premium that the entity receives from the policyholder. Thereafter, unearned profit from the group of underlying contracts would be offset by an equal and opposite expense for the reinsurance premium. However, in the Board's view, measuring the group of reinsurance contracts held on the basis of the premium the entity receives for the underlying contracts when that premium does not directly affect the cash flows arising from the group of reinsurance contracts held would be contrary to viewing the group of reinsurance contracts held and the underlying contracts as separate contracts. Such a measurement approach would also not reflect the economics of the group of reinsurance contracts the entity holds — that the expense of purchasing the group of reinsurance contracts (that should be recognised over the coverage period) equals the whole of the consideration paid for the group of reinsurance contracts.

BC314　For the measurement of the group of insurance contracts the entity issues, IFRS 17 specifies that the contractual service margin can never be negative. IFRS 17 does not include a limit on the amount by which the contractual service margin of a group of reinsurance contracts held could be adjusted as a result of changes in estimates of cash flows. In the Board's view, the contractual service margin for a group of reinsurance contracts held is different from that for a group of insurance contracts issued — the contractual service margin for the group of reinsurance contracts held depicts the expense the entity incurs when purchasing reinsurance coverage rather than the profit it will make by providing services under the insurance contract. Accordingly, the Board placed no limit on the amount of the adjustment to the contractual service margin for the group of reinsurance contracts held, subject to the amount of premium paid to the reinsurer.

BC315 The Board considered the situation that arises when the underlying group of insurance contracts becomes onerous after initial recognition because of adverse changes in estimates of fulfilment cash flows relating to future service. In such a situation, the entity recognises a loss on the group of underlying insurance contracts. The Board concluded that corresponding changes in cash inflows from a group of reinsurance contracts held should not adjust the contractual service margin of the group of reinsurance contracts held, with the result that the entity recognises no net effect of the loss and gain in the profit or loss for the period. This means that, to the extent that the change in the fulfilment cash flows of the group of underlying contracts is matched with a change in fulfilment cash flows on the group of reinsurance contracts held, there is no net effect on profit or loss.

Amendments to IFRS 17—recovery of losses on underlying insurance contracts (paragraphs 66A–66B and B119D–B119F of IFRS 17)

BC315A In June 2020, the Board amended IFRS 17 to require an entity to adjust the contractual service margin of a group of reinsurance contracts held, and as a result recognise income, when the entity recognises a loss on initial recognition of an onerous group of underlying insurance contracts or on addition of onerous contracts to a group. An entity determines the income on the reinsurance contract held (ie the amount of loss recovered) by multiplying:

(a) the loss recognised on the underlying insurance contracts; and

(b) the percentage of claims on underlying insurance contracts the entity expects to recover from the reinsurance contracts held.

BC315B As a practical assumption, the amendment treats:

(a) a loss recognised on an underlying insurance contract as the early recognition of a portion of expected claims; and

(b) a loss recovery recognised on the reinsurance contract held as the early recognition of a portion of expected claim recoveries.

BC315C For the amendment described in paragraph BC315A to apply, an entity must enter into the reinsurance contract held before or at the same time as the entity recognises the onerous underlying insurance contracts. The Board concluded it would not be appropriate for an entity to recognise a recovery of loss when the entity does not hold a reinsurance contract.

BC315D As a consequence of the amendment described in paragraph BC315A, the Board also:

(a) amended IFRS 17 to require an entity that has entered into a reinsurance contract held to recognise the related group of reinsurance contracts held when the entity recognises onerous underlying insurance contracts, if that is earlier than the date the entity would otherwise recognise the group of reinsurance contracts held (see paragraphs 62–62A of IFRS 17).

(b)   added requirements to IFRS 17 relating to recovery of losses from a reinsurance contract held:

   (i)   in a transfer of insurance contracts that do not form a business and in a business combination within the scope of IFRS 3 (see paragraphs B95B–B95D of IFRS 17); and

   (ii)   in applying IFRS 17 for the first time (see paragraphs C16A–C16C and C20A–C20B of IFRS 17).

BC315E The amendment responds to concerns that, applying IFRS 17 before the amendment, an entity would have recognised a loss on initial recognition of an onerous group of insurance contracts (or on addition of onerous contracts to a group), without recognising corresponding income on a reinsurance contract held that covers that onerous group of insurance contracts. Some stakeholders said this is an accounting mismatch and suggested the Board amend IFRS 17 so that income is recognised on the reinsurance contract held at the same time losses are recognised on initial recognition of onerous underlying insurance contracts. That income would reflect the entity's right to recover those losses.

BC315F The Board was persuaded that such an amendment was justified because:

(a)   paragraph 66(c) of IFRS 17 provides a similar exception from the general measurement requirements for changes in the measurement of a group of reinsurance contracts held that arise from changes in the measurement of underlying insurance contracts (see paragraph BC315).

(b)   the amendment provides users of financial statements with useful information about expected loss recoveries on reinsurance contracts held that complements the information about expected losses on underlying insurance contracts. The information provided about onerous underlying contracts is unchanged. Losses and loss recoveries are presented in separate line items in the statement(s) of financial performance and are disclosed separately in the notes to the financial statements.

BC315G The Board acknowledged, however, that the amendment adds complexity to IFRS 17 because it requires an entity to track a loss-recovery component. On balance, the Board concluded that the added complexity is justified given the strong stakeholder support for the information that will result from entities applying the amendment. The Board also noted that, applying the amendment, the loss-recovery component of a reinsurance contract held is treated similarly to the loss component of insurance contracts issued. That similarity will help entities to understand how to apply the amendment, reducing the complexity caused.

BC315H An entity might group together onerous insurance contracts covered by a reinsurance contract held and onerous insurance contracts not covered by a reinsurance contract held. To apply the amendment described in paragraph BC315A in that circumstance, an entity needs to determine amounts at a level that is lower than the level of the group of insurance contracts. IFRS 17 does not require an entity to track insurance contracts at a level lower than the level of the group of insurance contracts. Accordingly, the Board specified that, in that circumstance, an entity applies a systematic and rational method of allocation to determine the portion of losses on a group of insurance contracts that relates to underlying insurance contracts covered by a reinsurance contract held. Requiring a systematic and rational method of allocation is consistent with other requirements in IFRS 17.

BC315I   The Board noted that specifying that an entity use a systematic and rational method of allocation in a specified circumstance, such as the one described in paragraph BC315H, does not prohibit an entity from using a systematic and rational method of allocation as part of other estimation processes required in applying IFRS 17 if doing so meets the objective set by IFRS 17 for those estimation processes. The Board's decision to specify that an entity use a systematic and rational method of allocation in the specific circumstance described in paragraph BC315H was driven by the need to avoid the potential misinterpretation described in that paragraph. The need for such specification in this case does not imply that an entity cannot use a systematic and rational method of allocation in circumstances when it is not specified in the requirements of IFRS 17.

Other approaches considered but rejected

BC315J   In the 2019 Exposure Draft, the Board had proposed limiting the amendment to a defined population of reinsurance contracts held—those that provide proportionate coverage. For such contracts, an entity can easily identify the portion of losses on underlying insurance contracts that the entity has a right to recover. For other reinsurance contracts held, the Board was concerned that entities would have difficulty identifying that portion and thus may need to make arbitrary allocations. However, in the light of feedback on the Exposure Draft, the Board concluded that it should not impose that limitation. Respondents to the Exposure Draft reported that if the Board had limited the amendment in that way, the amendment would apply to few reinsurance contracts held in practice. Further, respondents said that an entity could identify the portion of losses the entity has a right to recover for any reinsurance contract held in a non-arbitrary way based on the expected claim recovery cash flows included in the measurement of the reinsurance contract held. For example, consider a reinsurance contract held that provides cover over an aggregate amount of claims on 100 underlying insurance contracts— some of which are in a profitable group and the others in an onerous group. The entity could determine the portion of losses on the onerous contracts that the entity has a right to recover by comparing:

(a)   total expected claim recoveries from the reinsurance contract held; and

(b)   total expected claims for all underlying insurance contracts.

BC315K   The Board considered a view that the amendment described in paragraph BC315A should apply only when a reinsurance contract held is in a net gain position—in other words, when an entity expects to receive from the reinsurer claim recoveries that are higher than the premium the entity pays to the reinsurer (see paragraph BC310). The Board disagreed with this view because an entity has a right to recover claims from the reinsurance contract held regardless of whether claim recoveries are expected to be higher or lower than the premiums the entity pays to the reinsurer.

BC315L   The Board also considered an alternative suggestion to require a loss on a group of insurance contracts to be treated as a negative contractual service margin to the extent that the contracts in the group are covered by a reinsurance contract held on a proportionate basis. The Board disagreed with this suggestion because it is inconsistent with the Board's objective to recognise losses on insurance contracts when expected.

Modification and derecognition (paragraphs 72–77 of IFRS 17)

BC316   Paragraph B25 of IFRS 17 states that a contract that qualifies as an insurance contract remains an insurance contract until all rights and obligations are extinguished. An obligation is extinguished when it has expired or has been discharged or cancelled. However, in some cases, an entity may modify the terms of an existing contract in a way that would have significantly changed the accounting of the contract if the new terms had always existed. IFRS 17 specifies different requirements for these and other modifications. In some cases, insurance contract modifications will result in derecognising the insurance contract.

Modifications that would have resulted in significantly different accounting for the contract (paragraphs 72, 76 and 77 of IFRS 17)

BC317   A modification of an insurance contract amends the original terms and conditions of the contract (for example, extending or shortening the coverage period or increasing the benefits in return for higher premiums). It differs from a change arising from either party to the contract exercising a right that is part of the original terms and conditions of the contract. If an insurance contract modification meets specific criteria (see paragraph 72 of IFRS 17), the contract is modified in a way that would have significantly changed the accounting of the contract had the new terms always existed. IFRS 17 therefore requires the original contract to be derecognised and a new contract based on the modified terms to be recognised. The consideration for the new contract (ie the implicit premium) is deemed to be the price the entity would have charged the policyholder had it entered into a contract with equivalent terms at the date of the modification. That deemed consideration determines:

(a)   the adjustment to the contractual service margin of the group to which the existing contract belonged on derecognition of the existing contract; and

(b)   the contractual service margin for the new contract.

BC318　The Board concluded that modifications to contracts that trigger derecognition should be measured using the premium the entity would have charged had it entered into a contract with equivalent terms as the modified contract at the date of the contract modification. Such an approach measures the modified contract consistently with the measurement of other insurance contract liabilities.

BC319　The Board considered whether the contractual service margin of the group to which the existing contract belonged should be adjusted for the gain or loss arising on the derecognition of the existing contract and recognition of the modified contract (paragraph BC317(a)). The alternative (not adjusting the contractual service margin) would result in a gain or loss in profit or loss. However, the Board concluded that: (a) not adjusting the contractual service margin of the group from which the existing contract is derecognised; and (b) establishing the contractual service margin for the group that includes the new modified contract based on the premiums that would have been charged for that new contract would result in the contractual service margin of the two groups double-counting the future profit to be earned from the contract. Hence, the Board decided that the contractual service margin of the group from which the existing contract has been derecognised should be adjusted.

Modifications that would not have resulted in significantly different accounting for the contract (paragraph 73 of IFRS 17)

BC320　The Board decided that all modifications that would not have resulted in significantly different accounting for the contract should be accounted for in the same way as changes in estimates of fulfilment cash flows. Doing so results in symmetrical accounting for contract modifications that eliminate rights and obligations and for contract modifications that add rights and obligations. This reduces the potential for accounting arbitrage through contract modification.

Derecognition (paragraphs 74–75 of IFRS 17)

BC321　IFRS 17 requires an entity to derecognise an insurance contract liability from its statement of financial position only when it is extinguished or modified in the way discussed in paragraph BC317. An insurance contract is extinguished when the obligation specified in the insurance contract expires or is discharged or cancelled. This requirement is consistent with requirements in other IFRS Standards, including the derecognition requirements for financial liabilities in IFRS 9. The requirement also provides symmetrical treatment for the recognition and derecognition of insurance contracts.

BC322　The Board considered concerns that an entity might not know whether a liability has been extinguished because claims are sometimes reported years after the end of the coverage period. It also considered concerns that an entity might be unable to derecognise those liabilities. Some argued that, in some cases, the delayed derecognition would result in unreasonable and unduly burdensome accounting. In the Board's view, ignoring contractual obligations that remain in existence and that can generate valid claims would not give a faithful representation of an entity's financial position. However, the Board expects that when the entity has no information to suggest there are unasserted claims on a contract with an expired coverage period, the entity would measure the insurance contract liability at a very low amount. Accordingly, there may be little practical difference between recognising an insurance liability measured at a very low amount and derecognising the liability.

Transfers of insurance contracts and business combinations (paragraphs 39 and B93–B95F of IFRS 17)

BC323   IFRS 17 requires an entity to treat the consideration for insurance contracts acquired in a transfer of insurance contracts or a business combination, including contracts in their settlement period, as a proxy for premiums received. This means that the entity determines the contractual service margin, in accordance with the general requirements of IFRS 17, in a way that reflects the consideration paid for the contracts.

BC324   Thus, when applying paragraph B95 of IFRS 17, the entity determines the contractual service margin or loss component of the liability for remaining coverage at initial recognition for a group of insurance contracts acquired in a transfer of insurance contracts or a business combination using the consideration received or paid for the contracts as a proxy for premiums received.[43] There is no contractual service margin if a group of insurance contracts issued is onerous. In those cases, the amount by which the group is onerous is recognised:

(a)   immediately as an expense in profit or loss for a transfer of insurance contracts, in the same way as for insurance contracts that the entity issues.

(b)   as an adjustment to the initial measurement of goodwill or gain from a bargain purchase, for a business combination. Although this requires a new measurement exception to the principle of fair value measurement in IFRS 3, similar exceptions are contained in that Standard for other cases in which liabilities, such as pension liabilities, are measured on a current value basis that is not fair value.

BC325   The requirements described in paragraphs BC323–BC324 mean that an entity will recognise insurance contracts it acquires in a transfer of insurance contracts or a business combination at the amount of the fulfilment cash flows rather than at the amount of the consideration (which equals the fair value in a business combination) when:

(a)   the insurance contracts are in a liability position at the date of the transfer or business combination and the fulfilment cash flows are higher than the fair value; or

---

43   In June 2020, the Board amended IFRS 17 to replace references to 'a business combination' in paragraphs 39 and B93–B95 of IFRS 17 with 'a business combination within the scope of IFRS 3' (see paragraph BC327A).

(b)   the insurance contracts are in an asset position at the date of the transfer or business combination and the fulfilment cash flows are lower than the fair value.[44]

BC326   The Board considered how the amount of the fulfilment cash flows could differ as described in paragraph BC325 from the amount of the consideration received, ie the fair value. For transfers of insurance contracts, the most likely cause of the difference is that the fair value would include the risk of non-performance by the entity. The Board concluded that, for contracts in a liability position acquired in a transfer, the immediate recognition of a loss faithfully represents the entity's assumption of an obligation it expects to fulfil but for which it received a lower price because of the risk that it might not be able to fulfil the obligation.

BC327   For a business combination, the Board concluded that the most likely reason that fulfilment cash flows differ from the fair value is that the acquirer may have been willing to pay more for the contracts because of other synergies that might arise as the contracts are fulfilled. Consequently, the recognition of that difference as an adjustment to the gain on the business combination or goodwill is consistent with the accounting for similar effects in a business combination. The Board decided to clarify that in determining fair value of a group of insurance contracts, an entity should not apply the concept of a deposit floor set out in IFRS 13 (see paragraphs BC165–BC166).

Amendments to IFRS 17—business combinations outside the scope of IFRS 3

BC327A   In June 2020, the Board amended IFRS 17 to specify that an entity is required to apply paragraph 38 of IFRS 17 in accordance with paragraphs B93–B95F of IFRS 17 to insurance contracts acquired in a business combination within the scope of IFRS 3. An entity is not required to apply the measurement requirements in those paragraphs to insurance contracts acquired in a business combination outside the scope of IFRS 3 (that is, a business combination under common control). The Board did not intend to set requirements for business combinations outside the scope of IFRS 3. Such business combinations are the subject of a separate Board project.

Amendments to IFRS 17—feedback on insurance contracts acquired in a transfer of insurance contracts or in a business combination within the scope of IFRS 3

Classification as an insurance contract

BC327B   Applying IFRS 4, an entity acquiring a contract in a business combination determined whether that contract met the definition of an insurance contract based on facts and circumstances at the date the contract was issued, instead of the date of the business combination transaction (the acquisition date). This requirement was an exception to the general principles in IFRS 3. In contrast,

---

44 In June 2020, the Board amended IFRS 17 to replace references to 'a business combination' in paragraphs 39 and B93–B95 of IFRS 17 with 'a business combination within the scope of IFRS 3' (see paragraph BC327A).

entities applying IFRS 17 assess the classification of contracts using the general principles in IFRS 3.

BC327C   When considering feedback from entities implementing IFRS 17, the Board considered but rejected a suggestion to reinstate that exception in IFRS 3 to continue to apply when an entity applies IFRS 17 instead of IFRS 4.

BC327D   By removing the exception described in paragraph BC327B, IFRS 17 makes the accounting for the acquisition of insurance contracts consistent with the accounting for acquisitions of other contracts acquired in a business combination. Differences in accounting between an acquirer's financial statements and an acquiree's financial statements can arise because of the requirements in IFRS 3. Such differences reflect changes in facts and circumstances at the acquisition date compared to facts and circumstances at the date the acquiree recognised the contracts. Such differences depict the economics of the acquisition, are not unique to insurance contracts and are not unusual when applying IFRS Standards.

Contracts acquired in their settlement period

BC327E   The Board also considered but rejected a suggestion to create an exception to the general classification and measurement requirements in IFRS 17 for contracts acquired in their settlement period. The Board concluded that an entity that acquires a contract should, at the acquisition date, apply the requirements for identifying whether a contract has an insured event and meets the definition of an insurance contract—just as an entity that issues a contract applies the requirements at the issue date.

BC327F   An acquirer identifies assets and liabilities acquired based on the contractual terms, rights and obligations and economic conditions at the acquisition date, including the consideration to which the acquirer agreed at that date. The Board noted that for a contract to meet the definition of an insurance contract from the perspective of the acquirer at the acquisition date, the acquirer must compensate the policyholder for the adverse effect of an uncertain future event (that is, the acquirer must provide insurance coverage). If the acquirer provides insurance coverage, the contract is an insurance contract accounted for applying the requirements of IFRS 17. Contracts acquired in their settlement period with claim amounts that are uncertain in timing or amount could meet the definition of an insurance contract at the acquisition date.

BC327G   The Board observed that some contracts acquired in their settlement period will not meet the definition of an insurance contract at the acquisition date. In some circumstances, all claim amounts are known at the acquisition date but remain unpaid. In such circumstances, the acquirer is not providing insurance coverage, the contract does not meet the definition of an insurance contract and the acquirer would account for the contract as a financial liability applying IFRS 3 and subsequently IFRS 9. The Board also observed that for contracts that meet the definition of an insurance contract at the acquisition date, an entity would need to consider whether any amounts payable to the policyholder meet the definition of an investment component (and are therefore excluded from insurance revenue).

Amendments to IFRS 17—assets for insurance acquisition cash flows in a transfer of insurance contracts and in a business combination within the scope of IFRS 3 (paragraphs B95E–B95F of IFRS 17)

BC327H   In June 2020, the Board amended IFRS 17 to require an entity that acquires insurance contracts in a transfer of insurance contracts that do not form a business or in a business combination within the scope of IFRS 3 to recognise an asset measured at fair value at the acquisition date for the rights to obtain:

(a)   future insurance contracts that are renewals of insurance contracts recognised at that date; and

(b)   future insurance contracts, other than those in (a), after the acquisition date without paying again insurance acquisition cash flows the acquiree has already paid.

BC327I   Requiring an entity to recognise such assets at the acquisition date is consistent with the requirements in IFRS 17 for recognising an asset for insurance acquisition cash flows (paragraph 28B of IFRS 17). As a result, the contractual service margin for a group of insurance contracts recognised after the acquisition date will appropriately reflect the rights relating to that future group which the entity paid for as part of the consideration for the acquisition. The Board decided that to achieve consistency between the requirements at the acquisition date and after the acquisition date, an entity should determine the rights described in paragraph BC327H(b) by reference to insurance acquisition cash flows the acquiree has already paid. Otherwise, broader rights to obtain future contracts from intangible assets such as customer relationships, unconnected to any previously paid insurance acquisition cash flows, could be included in the assets for insurance acquisition cash flows and therefore subsequently included in the contractual service margin of future groups of insurance contracts. In contrast, the Board decided that such reference is unnecessary to determine the rights described in paragraph BC327H(a)—these rights relate only to renewals, so they are sufficiently constrained.

Presentation in the statement of financial position and statement(s) of financial performance (paragraphs 78–92 and B120–B136 of IFRS 17)

BC328   IFRS 17 requires an entity to present the combination of rights and obligations arising from a group of insurance contracts as a single insurance contract asset or liability in the statement of financial position. This requirement is consistent with the measurement of a group of insurance contracts as a package of cash inflows and cash outflows. Consistent with the requirement in IAS 1 that an entity not offset assets and liabilities, IFRS 17 prohibits entities from offsetting groups of insurance contracts in an asset position with groups of insurance contracts in a liability position.[45]

BC329　IFRS 17 amended IAS 1, which specifies the line items that are required to be presented in the statement of financial position, to require an entity to present separately groups of insurance contracts issued and groups of reinsurance contracts held. The Board concluded that such contracts are sufficiently distinct to warrant separate presentation in the statement of financial position.[46]

BC330　Paragraphs BC27–BC37 discuss the presentation of insurance revenue and paragraphs BC38–BC49 discuss the presentation of insurance finance income and expenses. The Board considered and rejected:

(a)　other approaches to the presentation of insurance revenue, including:

(i)　the summarised-margin approach; and

(ii)　premium approaches; and

(b)　other approaches to the presentation of insurance finance income and expenses:

(i)　include all insurance finance income or expenses in profit or loss; and

(ii)　use the current period book yield for all contracts.

Amendments to IFRS 17—presentation in the statement of financial position

BC330A　In June 2020, the Board amended IFRS 17 to require an entity to present separately in the statement of financial position the carrying amount of portfolios of insurance contracts issued that are assets and portfolios of insurance contracts issued that are liabilities. Before the amendment, IFRS 17 required an entity to present separately groups of insurance contracts issued that are assets and groups of insurance contracts issued that are liabilities (see paragraph BC328). The amendment also applies to portfolios of reinsurance contracts held.

BC330B　The presentation requirement prior to the amendment was consistent with the requirements for recognising and measuring groups of insurance contracts. However, entities implementing IFRS 17 told the Board that they would need to allocate some fulfilment cash flows to groups only for the purpose of presentation (for example, fulfilment cash flows for incurred claims). These entities said that an amendment to require an entity to present insurance contracts at a portfolio level would provide significant operational relief. Feedback on the 2019 Exposure Draft, including from users of financial

---

45　In June 2020, the Board amended IFRS 17 to require an entity to present separately portfolios of insurance contracts that are assets and portfolios of insurance contracts that are liabilities (see paragraphs BC330A–BC330B).

46　In June 2020, the Board amended IFRS 17 to require an entity to present separately portfolios of insurance contracts that are assets and portfolios of insurance contracts that are liabilities (see paragraphs BC330A–BC330B).

statements, suggested that the amendment would not significantly diminish the usefulness of information compared to that which would have been provided without the amendment.

Other approaches considered but rejected

BC330C   Some stakeholders suggested the Board require an entity to present one insurance contract asset or liability for all insurance contracts issued by the entity (that is, present insurance contracts at an entity level). The Board rejected that suggestion because such presentation would risk an unacceptable loss of useful information for users of financial statements.

BC330D   Some stakeholders suggested a different, more disaggregated approach to presentation in the statement of financial position. Applying IFRS 4, some entities presented separately in the statement of financial position different amounts arising from an insurance contract, as if those different amounts were separate assets or liabilities. For example, some entities presented an insurance contract liability and line items labelled as premiums receivable, claims payable and deferred acquisition costs. Entities differed in what line items they presented and in the definitions of those line items. For example, some entities presented amounts that were not yet billed as premiums receivable whereas other entities presented only billed amounts that remain outstanding. Some stakeholders said they would like to continue further disaggregation because they view such disaggregated line items as providing meaningful information to users of financial statements. The Board disagreed with suggestions to permit an entity to continue such disaggregation because it could result in the presentation of amounts that are not separable assets or liabilities. For example, premiums receivable for future insurance coverage is not a gross asset separable from the related liability for the future insurance coverage.

Presentation of insurance revenue

BC331   As noted in paragraph BC61, some complexity in the requirements of IFRS 17 arises from the need to eliminate investment components from insurance revenue. Investment components may be more significant in some contracts than in others. For example, significant investment components exist in many long-term life insurance contracts and in some large long-term or bespoke non-life insurance or reinsurance contracts. Some argued that any attempt to distinguish between investment components that have not been separated and the premium charged for insurance and other services would be arbitrary and complex to apply.

BC332   The Board considered an approach that avoided this issue: a 'summarised-margin approach' in profit or loss. This approach would have applied to most insurance contracts with a coverage period of more than one year. The summarised-margin approach would have been operationally less complex than any presentation that provides a gross performance measure in profit or loss. This is because the summarised-margin approach would not have distinguished between investment components and premiums for services provided. Further, the Board would not have needed an exception for the treatment of insurance acquisition cash flows (see paragraphs BC175–BC180) to avoid a situation in which an entity recognises insurance revenue before the coverage has been provided.[47]

BC333   Nonetheless, the summarised-margin approach would have been a significant change from previous practice because it would have precluded presenting revenue-type line items in profit or loss. Furthermore:

(a)   the summarised-margin approach would not have provided relevant information about the extent to which an entity provides services under an insurance contract because it would not have presented any amounts as revenue or expenses in profit or loss.

(b)   the summarised-margin approach, as with other substitutes for revenue that are unique to insurance contracts, would have reduced the comparability between the financial reporting for insurance contracts and the financial reporting for other contracts.

(c)   many of those who report, use and quote financial measures expect such financial measures to include a measure of gross performance. If IFRS 17 did not require the presentation of an amount that is measured using principles that are applicable to revenue from contracts with customers, preparers and users of financial statements might substitute other inconsistently calculated measures for them.

BC334   Accordingly, the Board rejected the summarised-margin approach.

BC335   The Board also considered two approaches for the presentation of insurance revenue that were often used in previous practice:

(a)   a written-premium approach, which allocates the total expected insurance revenue to the period in which the contracts are initially recognised (written). At the same time, an expense is presented for the total expected claims and expenses relating to those contracts.

(b)   a premiums-due approach, which allocates the total expected insurance revenue to the periods in which the premiums become unconditionally due to the entity, whether or not the premiums are collected in that period. At the same time, the entity recognises expenses which must be reconciled to the incurred claims (see paragraphs BC343–BC344).

BC336   A written-premium approach would have provided information about new business during the period, including the expected present value of the amounts to be received and the obligations assumed. The Board rejected this approach because the premiums, claims and expenses presented in profit or loss are not measured by applying commonly understood notions of revenue and expenses. In particular, the revenue is recognised before the entity has performed a service and the claims and expenses are recognised before they have been incurred.

---

47   In June 2020, the Board amended IFRS 17 to require an entity to recognise an amount of the contractual service margin in profit or loss in each period to reflect the insurance contract services provided in that period (see paragraph BC283H).

BC337   Many entities that issue long-duration insurance contracts previously applied a premiums-due approach in profit or loss. A premiums-due approach would have:

(a)   provided information about the additional premiums for services to which the entity has an unconditional right; and

(b)   provided a measure of growth and a denominator for claims and expenses ratios that is objective, sufficient for that purpose and simpler to provide than insurance revenue.

BC338   However, the Board rejected this approach because:

(a)   the gross performance measure presented using a premiums-due approach would be inconsistent with commonly understood concepts of revenue and would be likely to mislead non-specialist users of financial statements. In particular, in a premiums-due approach:

(i)   revenue would typically be recognised before the entity has performed the corresponding service.

(ii)   the amounts presented as revenue and claims, benefits and expenses would vary depending on when a contract requires payment of the premium. For example, if a premium is due at the start of the contract, then all revenue and expenses are presented in the period the contract is issued. If the premium is instead due annually, the revenue and expenses would be presented at that point in each year. Thus, revenue and expenses may not indicate when the entity performs the service.

(b)   the premiums-due approach typically reports amounts billed in the period and includes in expenses an amount representing the premiums expected to relate to claims in the future. The Board decided that reporting claims and expenses when incurred would provide useful information to users of financial statements, as discussed in paragraphs BC343–BC344. As noted in paragraph BC344, when revenue is measured using a premium approach, the incurred claims must be reconciled to the amount of expenses presented in the period and a balancing figure must be presented in profit or loss. Feedback from users of financial statements suggested that this balancing figure is difficult for users to interpret when analysing insurers' performance in the period.

BC339   Although the Board rejected a premiums-due approach for the reasons given above, it noted that some of the information provided by a premiums-due approach could be useful. Hence IFRS 17 requires disclosure of other measures of gross performance (see paragraphs BC358–BC362).

Presentation of insurance finance income or expenses

BC340   The Board considered requiring entities to include all insurance finance income or expenses in profit or loss. This would prevent accounting mismatches with finance income from assets measured at fair value through profit or loss, and could also reduce the complexity inherent in disaggregating changes in the liability. However, many stakeholders expressed concern that gains and losses from underwriting and investing activities would be obscured by more volatile gains and losses arising from changes in the current discount rate applied to the cash flows in insurance contracts. In addition, many preparers of financial statements expressed concern that they would be forced to measure their financial assets at fair value through profit or loss to avoid accounting mismatches. These preparers noted that the Board has indicated that amortised cost and fair value through other comprehensive income are appropriate measures for financial assets in some circumstances and that IFRS 9 would generally require an entity to measure financial liabilities at amortised cost. Accordingly, these preparers say that the volatility in profit or loss that would result from a current value measurement of insurance contracts would impair the faithful representation of their financial performance and users of financial statements would face difficulties in comparing insurers with entities that have no significant insurance contracts. The Board was not persuaded that entities that issue insurance contracts would be disadvantaged if insurance contracts were to be measured at current value. However, the Board was persuaded that users of financial statements may find that, for some contracts, the presentation of insurance finance income or expenses based on a systematic allocation in profit or loss would be more useful than the presentation of total insurance finance income or expenses in profit or loss.

BC341   The Board also considered requiring all insurance finance income or expenses to be included in profit or loss with separate presentation of some or all such income or expenses. Such presentation would provide disaggregated information about the effects of changes in insurance contract assets and liabilities in profit or loss. However, the Board rejected this approach for the same reasons given in paragraph BC340 and also because it would introduce operational complexity similar to that discussed in paragraph BC43(b)(ii).

BC342   The Board also considered requiring a current period book yield for all insurance contracts. The current period book yield is the change in the carrying amount of assets regarded as backing the insurance contracts that is recognised in profit or loss for the period. The Board rejected this approach, except as discussed in paragraph BC48, because recognising insurance finance income or expenses in profit or loss measured using a discount rate that has no relationship to the rate that is used to measure the group of insurance contracts does not provide useful information. In addition, it may be difficult in some circumstances to identify the assets that are held by the entities to back insurance contract liabilities.

Amendments to IFRS 17—insurance finance income or expenses

BC342A   In June 2020, the Board amended paragraph B128 of IFRS 17 to clarify that changes in the measurement of a group of insurance contracts resulting from changes in underlying items are changes arising from the effect of the time value of money and assumptions that relate to financial risk for the purposes of IFRS 17. Otherwise, changes in underlying items could adjust the contractual service margin of insurance contracts without direct participation features. The Board considered a view that the effects of changes in cash flows resulting from the participation in underlying items that are not solely financial in nature (for example, insurance contracts) should be presented within the insurance service result, instead of within insurance finance income or expenses. The Board disagreed with this view because the requirement to reflect changes from participation in underlying items in insurance finance income or expenses appropriately depicts the nature of the participation—as an investment. The Board concluded that policyholder participation in underlying items, including underlying items that are not solely financial in nature such as insurance contracts, should have no effect on the depiction of the entity's insurance service result. Further, splitting the effect of changes in cash flows resulting from the participation in underlying items that are not solely financial in nature into an amount that should be included in the insurance service result and an amount that should be included in insurance finance income or expenses would be complex and could disrupt implementation for some entities.

BC342B   Some users of financial statements were concerned that the requirements in paragraphs 88–89 of IFRS 17 for disaggregating insurance finance income or expenses allow an accounting policy choice. They would rather IFRS 17 required one consistent presentation. The Board acknowledged that requiring entities to report insurance finance income or expenses entirely in profit or loss instead of permitting the choice in paragraphs 88–89 of IFRS 17 would improve comparability between entities. However, consistent with the Board's previous conclusion explained in paragraph BC340, the Board concluded that the presentation of insurance finance income or expenses as a systematic allocation in profit or loss may provide more useful information than total insurance finance income or expenses in profit or loss for some contracts and less useful information for other contracts.

BC342C   Some stakeholders said that accounting mismatches might arise between financial assets the entity holds and insurance contract liabilities if an entity were to apply the option in paragraph 88 of IFRS 17 to recognise some insurance finance income or expenses in other comprehensive income. That feedback led to no amendment because the Board noted that an entity can avoid such mismatches by not applying the option. The Board received similar feedback about accounting mismatches before IFRS 17 was issued (see paragraphs BC53–BC56).

Recognition of incurred claims (paragraph 84 of IFRS 17)

BC343   Reporting claims and expenses (other than insurance acquisition expenses) when incurred is consistent with the reporting of expenses for other types of contracts and, the Board decided, provides useful information to users of financial statements.

BC344   Reporting claims and expenses in this way is only possible when insurance revenue is measured using changes in the liability for remaining coverage as a measure of progress towards satisfying an obligation. When insurance revenue is measured in any other way, the incurred claims must be reconciled to the amount of expenses that is presented in the period. This is because both insurance revenue and incurred claims and benefits are measures of changes in the liability for the group of insurance contracts relating to coverage in the period.

Reinsurance contracts held (paragraphs 78, 82 and 86 of IFRS 17)

BC345   The Board noted that assets for reinsurance contracts held and liabilities for the underlying insurance contracts would rarely meet the criteria established by IAS 32 for offsetting financial assets against financial liabilities. Rather than incorporating those criteria in IFRS 17, the Board decided that it was simpler to prohibit an entity from offsetting reinsurance contract assets held against related insurance contract liabilities.

BC346   Consistent with the prohibition on offsetting reinsurance contracts assets against insurance contract liabilities, IFRS 17 requires an entity to present income or expenses from reinsurance contracts held separately from expenses or income from insurance contracts issued. However, IFRS 17 allows an entity to present income or expenses from reinsurance contracts held either as a single net amount or as separate amounts recovered from the reinsurer and an allocation of the premiums paid. If it presents separate amounts, IFRS 17 requires the entity to treat:

(a)   cash flows contingent on the claims or benefits in the underlying contracts, including ceding commissions, as part of the claims that are expected to be reimbursed under the reinsurance contracts held, unless those cash flows need to be accounted for as investment components. In the Board's view, the economic effect of changes in those cash flows is equivalent to the effect of reimbursing a different amount of claims than expected.

(b)   ceding commissions that are not contingent on claims of the underlying contracts as a reduction of the premiums to be paid to the reinsurer. The economic effect of such ceding commissions is equivalent to the effect of charging a lower premium with no ceding commission.

Disclosure (paragraphs 93–132 of IFRS 17)

BC347   The Board decided that an entity should disclose information that gives a basis for users of financial statements to assess the effect that contracts within the scope of IFRS 17 have on the entity's financial position, financial performance and cash flows. To achieve this disclosure objective, information is needed about the amounts recognised in the financial statements, the significant judgements and changes in judgements made when applying IFRS 17, and the nature and extent of risks that arise from contracts within the scope of IFRS 17. The disclosure objective is supplemented with some specific disclosure requirements designed to help the entity satisfy this objective. By specifying the objective of the disclosures, the Board aims to ensure that entities provide the information that is most relevant for their circumstances and to emphasise the importance of communication to users of financial statements rather than compliance with detailed and prescriptive disclosure requirements. In situations in which the information provided to meet the specific disclosure requirements is not sufficient to meet the disclosure objective, paragraph 94 of IFRS 17 requires the entity to disclose additional information necessary to achieve that objective.

BC348   The Board used the disclosure requirements in IFRS 4, including the disclosure requirements in IFRS 7 *Financial Instruments: Disclosures* that are incorporated in IFRS 4 by cross-reference, as a basis for the requirements in IFRS 17. This is because stakeholders have indicated that such disclosures provide useful information to users of financial statements for understanding the amount, timing and uncertainty of future cash flows from insurance contracts. The disclosure requirements brought forward from IFRS 4 include information about:

(a)   significant judgements in applying the Standard, including an explanation of methods used to measure contracts within the scope of the Standard, the processes for estimating the inputs to those methods, and any changes in those methods and processes (see paragraph 117 of IFRS 17); and

(b)   the nature and extent of risks that arise from insurance contracts, including:

(i)   the exposures to insurance risk and each type of financial risk and how they arise, and the entity's objectives, policies and processes for managing the risk and the methods used to measure those risks (see paragraphs 121–125 of IFRS 17);

(ii)   concentrations of risk (see paragraph 127 of IFRS 17);

(iii)   sensitivities to insurance risk and each type of market risk (see paragraphs 128–129 of IFRS 17);[48]

(iv)   information about claims development (see paragraph 130 of IFRS 17);

---

48   In June 2020, the Board amended IFRS 17 to correct the terminology used in paragraphs 128–129 of IFRS 17 by replacing 'risk exposures' with 'risk variables'.

        (v)   information about credit risk arising from insurance contracts, including the credit quality of reinsurance contracts held (see paragraph 131 of IFRS 17); and

        (vi)   information about liquidity risk arising from insurance contracts (see paragraph 132 of IFRS 17).

BC349   In addition, when developing IFRS 17 the Board identified key items it views as critical to understanding the financial statements of entities issuing insurance contracts, in the light of the requirement to update the measurement of insurance contracts at each reporting date. The Board therefore decided that entities should disclose the following items:

    (a)   reconciliations from the opening to closing balances for each of:

        (i)   changes in insurance contract liabilities (or assets), analysed to provide information about the determination of insurance revenue and the linkage between amounts in the statements of financial position and financial performance (see paragraph 100 of IFRS 17); and

        (ii)   changes in insurance contract liabilities (or assets), analysed to provide information about the measurement model (see paragraph 101 of IFRS 17).

      These reconciliations are discussed in paragraphs BC350–BC356.

    (b)   an analysis of insurance revenue (see paragraph 106 of IFRS 17 and paragraphs BC352–BC353).

    (c)   information about the initial recognition of insurance contracts in the statement of financial position (see paragraphs 107–108 of IFRS 17 and paragraphs BC358–BC362).

    (d)   an explanation of when the entity expects to recognise the contractual service margin remaining at the end of the reporting period in profit or loss (see paragraph 109 of IFRS 17 and paragraph BC363).

    (e)   an explanation of the total amount of insurance finance income or expenses in the reporting period (see paragraph 110 of IFRS 17 and paragraphs BC364–BC366) and the composition and fair value of underlying items for contracts with direct participation features (see paragraph 111 of IFRS 17 and paragraphs BC238–BC247).

    (f)   to the extent not already included in meeting the requirements in paragraph 117(a) of IFRS 17, information about the entity's approach to determine (see paragraph 117(c) of IFRS 17):

        (i)   how to distinguish changes in estimates of future cash flows arising from the exercise of discretion from other changes in estimates of future cash flows (see paragraph BC237);

        (ii)   the risk adjustment for non-financial risk (see paragraphs BC213–BC217);

        (iii)   discount rates (see paragraphs BC193–BC205); and

(iv)   investment components (see paragraphs BC33–BC34A).

(g)   the confidence level used to determine the risk adjustment for non-financial risk (see paragraph 119 of IFRS 17 and paragraphs BC215–BC217).

(h)   information about the yield curves used to discount cash flows that do not vary based on the returns on underlying items (see paragraph 120 of IFRS 17 and paragraph BC198).

(i)   information about the effect of the regulatory framework in which the entity operates (see paragraph 126 of IFRS 17 and paragraphs BC369–BC371).

Explanation of recognised amounts (paragraphs 97–116 of IFRS 17)

Reconciliation of components of the insurance contract liability (paragraphs 98–105 of IFRS 17)

BC350   IFRS 17 requires an entity to disaggregate the insurance contract liability into components as follows (see paragraph 40 of IFRS 17):

(a)   the liability for remaining coverage, excluding the amounts in (b) below. For liabilities measured using the premium allocation approach, this is the unearned premium, less any unamortised insurance acquisition cash flows.

(b)   the loss component of the liability for remaining coverage (see paragraph 49 of IFRS 17). For liabilities measured using the premium allocation approach, this is the additional liability for onerous contracts (see paragraph 58 of IFRS 17).

(c)   the liability for incurred claims.

BC351   IFRS 17 requires entities to disclose a reconciliation from the opening to the closing balance separately for each of the components listed in paragraph BC350 and separately for insurance contracts issued and reinsurance contracts held, to explain how insurance revenue is determined, and to show how the amounts in the statements of financial position and financial performance are linked.

BC352   The Board noted that insurance revenue can also be analysed as the total of the changes in the liability for remaining coverage in the period that relate to coverage or other services for which the entity expects to receive consideration. Those changes include insurance service expenses incurred in the period, the change in the risk adjustment for non-financial risk and the amount of the contractual service margin allocated to the period.

BC353   The Board concluded that requiring such an analysis of insurance revenue recognised in the period provides useful information about the drivers of insurance revenue and assists users of financial statements to understand how insurance revenue relates to more familiar metrics.

BC354   In addition, the Board decided that, except for insurance contracts to which an entity applies the premium allocation approach described in paragraphs 53–59 or 69–70 of IFRS 17, the entity must disclose a reconciliation as set out in paragraph 101 of IFRS 17 that shows the sources of profit for the period, by separately reconciling from the opening to the closing balances:

    (a)   the estimates of the present value of the future cash flows;

    (b)   the risk adjustment for non-financial risk; and

    (c)   the contractual service margin.

BC355   The Board concluded that a reconciliation showing sources of profit would provide useful information for users of financial statements. Furthermore, in the Board's view, information about changes in the components used in the measurement of insurance contracts will be important in the light of the Board's decision to adjust the contractual service margin for the effects of changes in estimates of fulfilment cash flows relating to future service (see paragraphs 44(c) and 45(c) of IFRS 17). That decision means that those effects do not appear directly in the statement(s) of financial performance.

BC356   As noted in paragraphs BC350 and BC354, entities are required to disclose two reconciliations from the opening to the closing carrying amounts in the statement of financial position, except for insurance contracts to which the premium allocation approach described in paragraphs 53–59 or 69–70 of IFRS 17 has been applied. The Board decided to require both reconciliations because feedback received from stakeholders generally indicated that the information required in each reconciliation will be useful. The Board considered the costs and benefits of requiring both reconciliations and concluded that the benefits of providing such information outweigh the costs of preparing two reconciliations. The Board noted that, in some cases, it may be possible to combine the information required into one reconciliation.

Insurance revenue (paragraph 85 of IFRS 17)

BC357   IAS 1 requires an entity to present additional line items in the statement(s) of financial performance when such a presentation is relevant to an understanding of the entity's financial performance. However, IFRS 17 prohibits an entity from presenting information about premiums in profit or loss if that information is inconsistent with insurance revenue determined applying IFRS 17. Given the varied amounts presented under previous insurance accounting practices (see paragraphs BC335–BC339), the Board decided to prohibit entities from presenting information about premiums that is inconsistent with insurance revenue in additional line items in the statement(s) of financial performance.

The effect of new contracts initially recognised in the period (paragraphs 107 and 108 of IFRS 17)

BC358   The Board considered arguments that it would be useful for entities to disclose information about the effect of new contracts initially recognised in the period. Such information differs from revenue. A measure of insurance revenue by itself provides only part of the information users of financial statements seek, and is not intended to measure an entity's insurance contracts business growth or shrinkage. In particular, many users of financial statements find information about the amount, and profitability, of new business written in each period to be important when assessing an entity's future prospects.

BC359　As noted in paragraphs BC28–BC29, the purpose of insurance revenue is to measure the consideration to which an entity expects to be entitled in exchange for services provided in the period. This consideration may differ from premiums from new contracts generated or cash collected. The Board noted, therefore, that the use of accruals-based accounting for any contract initiated in advance of services provided (ie any contract for which the performance obligation is not satisfied in the period in which the contract is written) can result in revenue increasing even if the volume of new contracts issued decreased. The Board noted that this effect is not unique to insurance contracts and sought to identify other ways to provide useful information regarding an entity's growth.

BC360　The Board agreed that information about the effect of new contracts initially recognised in the period would provide useful information for users of financial statements. In particular, information about the contractual service margin, and the risk adjustment for non-financial risk initially recognised in the period, would provide useful information about the profitability of new contracts issued in the period. Accordingly, unless the entity applies the premium allocation approach described in paragraphs 53–59 or 69–70 of IFRS 17, paragraph 107 of IFRS 17 requires an entity to disclose the effect of new contracts initially recognised in the period, showing separately their effect on:

(a)　the estimates of the present value of future cash flows;

(b)　the risk adjustment for non-financial risk; and

(c)　the contractual service margin.

BC361　The estimates of the present value of future cash flows are further disaggregated into estimates of the present value of future cash outflows, showing separately the amount of insurance acquisition cash flows, and estimates of the present value of future cash inflows. The separate disclosure of the estimates of the present value of future cash inflows, including any investment components:

(a)　provides useful information about the volume of sales that supplements the insurance revenue presented in the statement(s) of financial performance; and

(b)　allows users of financial statements to compare the volume of business written in prior years with the volume of contracts written in the current year.

BC362 New contracts initially recognised in the period might include contracts issued by the entity and contracts acquired from other entities in transfers of insurance contracts or business combinations. IFRS 17 requires an entity to disclose separately the effects of new contracts initially recognised in the period that are acquired from other entities in transfers of insurance contracts or business combinations, so that the separate effects on future profitability and insurance revenue from contracts issued and acquired in the period is provided to users of financial statements. IFRS 17 also requires an entity to disclose separately the effect of new contracts initially recognised in the period that are onerous.

Recognition of the contractual service margin (paragraph 109 of IFRS 17)

BC363 Many stakeholders suggested they would like to know when the contractual margin is expected to be recognised in profit or loss in future periods, because this information would be helpful in assessing future profitability. The Board agreed this information would be useful to users of financial statements. IFRS 17 requires entities to disclose when they expect to recognise the contractual service margin remaining at the end of the reporting period in profit or loss, either quantitatively, in appropriate time bands, or by providing qualitative information.[49]

Insurance finance income or expenses (paragraphs 110–113 and 118 of IFRS 17)

BC364 Insurance finance income or expenses are expected to have a significant effect on the performance of an insurer, particularly if it issues long-duration contracts. IFRS 17 allows an entity to choose how to present insurance finance income or expenses; therefore, the Board concluded it is important for an entity to disclose or explain:

(a) the total amount of its insurance finance income or expenses in each period;

(b) the basis for any disaggregation of the total between amounts recognised in profit or loss and other comprehensive income; and

(c) the relationship between insurance finance income or expenses and investment income on the related assets the entity holds.

BC365 For contracts with direct participation features, IFRS 17 allows an entity to choose how to recognise changes in the effect of financial risk (for example, the value of financial guarantees embedded in a group of insurance contracts or the entity's share of the underlying items), if the entity uses a derivative to mitigate the financial risk, and the criteria in paragraph B116 of IFRS 17 are met.[50] Such changes may be recognised either in profit or loss, or by adjusting

---

49 In June 2020, the Board amended IFRS 17 to require an entity to disclose when it expects to recognise the contractual service margin remaining at the end of the reporting period in profit or loss quantitatively, in appropriate time bands (see paragraph BC366B).

50 In June 2020, the Board extended the risk mitigation option to be applicable when an entity uses reinsurance contracts held or non-derivative financial instruments measured at fair value through profit or loss to mitigate financial risk (see paragraphs BC256A–BC256F).

the contractual service margin. Recognising the lack of comparability that this accounting policy choice creates, the Board decided to require an entity that chooses to recognise such changes in profit or loss to disclose the effect of that choice on the adjustment to the contractual service margin in the current period.

BC366   For contracts with direct participation features, an entity choosing to disaggregate insurance finance income or expenses between profit or loss and other comprehensive income might change the basis on which it determines the amounts to be included in profit or loss from a systematic allocation to the current period book yield (see paragraph BC48), or vice versa. A change of basis is required if the entity becomes eligible, or ceases to be eligible, to apply the current period book yield because it starts to hold, or ceases to hold, the underlying items for a group of insurance contracts. In such cases, IFRS 17 requires an entity to include in a specified way in profit or loss the accumulated amount previously recognised in other comprehensive income. The Board requires the specified method to prevent an entity from including or excluding gains and losses permanently in profit or loss simply by choosing to buy or sell underlying items. The Board also decided to require entities to disclose, in the period the change in basis occurs:

(a)   the reason why the entity changed the basis of disaggregation;

(b)   the amount of any adjustment for each financial statement line item affected; and

(c)   the carrying amount of the groups of insurance contracts to which the change applied.

Amendments to IFRS 17—disclosure of amounts recognised

Insurance acquisition cash flows (paragraphs 105A–105B and 109A of IFRS 17)

BC366A   In June 2020, the Board amended IFRS 17 to require an entity to allocate insurance acquisition cash flows to future groups of insurance contracts that are expected to include contracts that are renewals of other contracts (see paragraphs BC184A–BC184K). That amendment extends the period for which an asset for insurance acquisition cash flows exists, and therefore increases the total amount of such assets at the end of each reporting period. In the light of the amendment, the Board amended the disclosure requirements in IFRS 17 to require an entity to disclose a reconciliation from the opening to the closing balance of any asset for insurance acquisition cash flows recognised applying paragraph 28B of IFRS 17. An entity is also required to provide quantitative disclosure, in appropriate time bands, of the expected inclusion of insurance acquisition cash flows recognised as an asset in the measurement of the group of insurance contracts to which they are allocated (see paragraph 105A of IFRS 17).

Recognition of the contractual service margin (paragraphs 109 and 117 of IFRS 17)

BC366B   In June 2020, the Board amended IFRS 17 to require an entity to determine the quantity of benefits provided by an insurance contract considering either investment-return service or investment-related service in addition to insurance coverage (see paragraphs BC283A–BC283J). That amendment adds complexity and judgement to the determination of the quantity of benefits provided by an insurance contract for the purpose of recognising the contractual service margin in profit or loss. Accordingly, the Board decided to require an entity to disclose:

(a)   quantitative information, in appropriate time bands, about when the entity expects to recognise in profit or loss the contractual service margin remaining at the end of the reporting period (instead of permitting an entity to provide only qualitative information); and

(b)   the approach used to assess the relative weighting of the benefits from insurance coverage and either investment-return service or investment-related service.

Other additional disclosures

BC366C   In June 2020, the Board also amended the disclosure requirements in IFRS 17 to clarify that an entity:

(a)   is not required to disclose refunds of premiums separately from investment components in the reconciliation required by paragraph 100 of IFRS 17; and

(b)   cannot present separately amounts relating to the risk adjustment for non-financial risk that are experience adjustments applying paragraph 104(b)(iii) of IFRS 17 if the entity already discloses those amounts applying paragraph 104(b)(ii) of IFRS 17 (to prevent double counting those amounts).

Disclosures that the Board considered but did not include in IFRS 17

Reconciliation of premium receipts to insurance revenue

BC367   The Board originally proposed that an entity reconcile the insurance revenue to the premium receipts in each period because it wanted entities to explain how insurance revenue differs from previously familiar metrics. However, the Board found that such information will be provided in the reconciliation of the insurance contract balance required by paragraph 100 of IFRS 17. Hence, a separate reconciliation, while permissible, is not required. Paragraphs BC27–BC37 and BC337–BC339 explain why IFRS 17 prohibits the use of premiums-due as a measure of insurance revenue.

Measurement uncertainty analysis

BC368   The Board originally proposed the disclosure of an analysis of the measurement uncertainty in the inputs that have a material effect on the measurement. This would have been similar to the disclosure for unobservable inputs in fair value measurement considered by the Board when developing IFRS 13 (as described in paragraphs BC202–BC210 of the Basis for Conclusions on IFRS 13). When finalising IFRS 13, the Board decided not to require such a disclosure for unobservable inputs in IFRS 13 because of concerns about costs relative to benefits, but instead required more quantitative information about the inputs as well as narrative information about how those inputs influence the measurement (as described in paragraphs BC188–BC195 and BC206–BC208 of the Basis for Conclusions on IFRS 13). Accordingly, consistent with its decision for IFRS 13, the Board did not include such a disclosure requirement in IFRS 17.

Regulatory capital

BC369   IFRS 17 requires an entity to disclose information about the effect of the regulatory frameworks in which it operates; for example, minimum capital requirements or required interest rate guarantees (see paragraph 126 of IFRS 17). Many users of financial statements indicated a desire for additional disclosures that would help them to understand and analyse those effects; in particular:

(a)   information about how much regulatory capital an entity needs to hold for the new contracts written in the period, and when that capital will cease to be required; and

(b)   information about the amount of equity generated in a reporting period that is not needed to service the regulatory capital requirements. That amount is sometimes referred to as 'free cash flow'.

BC370   Disclosure of the regulatory capital required could provide users of financial statements with information about:

(a)   the entity's profitability, ongoing capital needs and, thus, financial flexibility;

(b)   an entity's capacity to write new business in future periods, because the excess over regulatory capital held is available to support future new business; and

(c)   improved understanding of the financial position, financial performance and cash flows during the reporting period.

BC371   However, entities that issue insurance contracts are not the only entities that operate in a regulated environment. Such disclosures might be useful for all entities operating in a regulated environment. The Board was concerned about developing such disclosures in isolation in a project on accounting for insurance contracts that would go beyond the existing requirements in paragraphs 134–136 of IAS 1. Accordingly, the Board decided to limit the disclosures about regulation to those set out in paragraph 126 of IFRS 17.

Applying the Standard for the first time (Appendix C of IFRS 17)

BC372 IFRS 17 includes specific requirements for applying the Standard for the first time. An entity is therefore required to apply the IFRS 17 transition requirements instead of the general requirements of IAS 8 *Accounting Policies, Changes in Accounting Estimates and Errors*. In the light of the diversity in previous insurance accounting practices and the long duration of many types of insurance contracts, the Board decided that retrospective application of IFRS 17 provides the most useful information to users of financial statements by allowing comparisons between contracts written before and after the date of initial application of the Standard. Consistent with IAS 8, which requires retrospective application of a new accounting policy except when it would be impracticable, the Board concluded that entities should apply IFRS 17 retrospectively (see paragraphs BC374–BC378) and should be allowed to use alternatives only when retrospective application of IFRS 17 is impracticable.[51]

BC373 The Board developed two alternative transition methods that may be used when retrospective application is impracticable (see paragraphs BC379–BC384B for the alternative transition method referred to as the 'modified retrospective approach' and paragraphs BC385–BC386 for the alternative transition method referred to as the 'fair value approach'). The Board decided to permit an entity to choose between the modified retrospective approach and the fair value approach if the entity cannot apply IFRS 17 retrospectively. The Board acknowledged a choice of transition methods results in a lack of comparability of transition amounts but concluded it was appropriate for the following reasons. The objective of the modified retrospective approach is to achieve the closest outcome to a retrospective application of the Standard. The Board noted that the similarity between a modified retrospective approach and a full retrospective application would depend on the amount of reasonable and supportable information available to an entity. If an entity has relatively little reasonable and supportable information available, and, therefore, would need to use many of the permitted modifications, the cost of the modified retrospective approach might exceed the benefits.

Amendments to IFRS 17—feedback on transition approaches

BC373A When the Board considered feedback from entities implementing IFRS 17, the Board also considered feedback from users of financial statements that the optionality in the transition requirements reduces comparability between entities—in particular, the option to apply the modified retrospective approach or the fair value approach. The Board concluded that the choices provided are appropriate, for the reasons set out in paragraph BC373.

---

51 In June 2020, the Board amended IFRS 17 to permit an entity that has the information to apply a fully retrospective approach to instead apply the fair value approach for transition for a group of insurance contracts with direct participation features when specified conditions relating to risk mitigation are met (see paragraph BC393A).

BC373B   In the Board's view, providing practical one-off reliefs to help entities with their transition to IFRS 17 is worth a limited loss of comparability for a limited period. The Board therefore decided not to reduce the options available in the transition requirements, because doing so would be likely to cause undue disruption to implementation already under way. The Board noted the reduced comparability that the transition options cause has no effect on the current value measurement of the fulfilment cash flows. The Board also noted that entities are required to provide disclosures on the transition approaches used. Such disclosures assist users of financial statements in making comparisons between entities, and in understanding the transition reliefs used and how those reliefs affect reported information.

Retrospective application (paragraphs C3–C5B of IFRS 17)

BC374   To apply IFRS 17 retrospectively, at the transition date an entity is required to:

(a)   recognise and measure each group of insurance contracts as if IFRS 17 had always applied;[52]

(b)   derecognise any existing balances that would not exist had IFRS 17 always applied; and

(c)   recognise any resulting net difference in equity.

Consistent with retrospective application, the Board noted that an entity would need not only to adjust the measurement of its insurance contracts when first applying the Standard but also to eliminate any items such as deferred acquisition costs and some intangible assets that relate solely to existing contracts. The requirement to recognise any resulting net differences in equity means that no adjustment is made to the carrying amount of goodwill from any previous business combinations.

BC375   The measurement model in IFRS 17 comprises two components:

(a)   a direct measurement, which is based on estimates of the present value of future cash flows and an explicit risk adjustment for non-financial risk; and

(b)   a contractual service margin, which is measured on initial recognition of the group of insurance contracts, then adjusted for subsequent changes in estimates relating to future service and adjusted for subsequent changes in estimates relating to future services and a financing component and recognised in profit or loss over the coverage period.

---

52   In June 2020, the Board amended IFRS 17 to clarify that an entity recognises and measures any assets for insurance acquisition cash flows as if IFRS 17 had always applied, except that an entity is not required to assess the recoverability of any such assets before the transition date (see paragraphs BC184A–BC184K).

BC376   The Board identified no specific transition problems for the introduction of the direct measurement component of the insurance contracts, other than in the assessments made on initial recognition described in paragraphs BC381–BC382. That measurement reflects only circumstances at the measurement date. Consequently, provided an entity has sufficient lead time to set up the necessary systems, performing that direct measurement at the transition date will be no more difficult than performing it at a later date.

BC377   Measuring the remaining amount of the contractual service margin at the transition date, and the information needed for presentation in the statement(s) of financial performance in subsequent periods, is more challenging. These amounts reflect a revision of estimates for all periods after the initial recognition of the group of insurance contracts.

BC378   The Board concluded that measuring the following amounts needed for retrospective application would often be impracticable:

   (a)   the estimates of cash flows at the date of initial recognition;

   (b)   the risk adjustment for non-financial risk at the date of initial recognition;

   (c)   the changes in estimates that would have been recognised in profit or loss for each accounting period because they did not relate to future service, and the extent to which changes in the fulfilment cash flows would have been allocated to the loss component;

   (d)   the discount rates at the date of initial recognition; and

   (e)   the effect of changes in discount rates on estimates of future cash flows for contracts for which changes in financial assumptions have a substantial effect on the amounts paid to policyholders.

   The Board therefore developed two transition methods entities are allowed to use for groups of insurance contracts for which retrospective application of IFRS 17 would be impracticable.

Modified retrospective approach (paragraphs C6–C19A of IFRS 17)

BC379   Although many entities may not have sufficient information for retrospective application of IFRS 17, the Board was told that, in many cases, entities may have much of the information needed, and that some entities may face only a small number of limitations on retrospective application. In such situations, the Board concluded that more comparable information about insurance contracts could result if an entity were permitted to modify retrospective application only when needed because it lacked information to apply a fully retrospective approach. Furthermore, the Board concluded that an entity should:

   (a)   use the minimum modifications necessary for achieving the closest outcome to retrospective application that is possible using reasonable and supportable information; and

(b)   be prohibited from disregarding any reasonable and supportable information that could be used in the retrospective application of IFRS 17 if that information is available without undue cost or effort.

BC380   The Board decided to specify some modifications that could be applied if retrospective application as defined in IAS 8 is impracticable, to address the issues noted in paragraph BC378. Those modifications are permitted only to the extent necessary because an entity does not have reasonable and supportable information to apply the retrospective approach. Those modifications:

(a)   simplify the information necessary for an entity to make assessments about insurance contracts or groups of insurance contracts that would be made at the date of inception or initial recognition (see paragraphs BC381–BC382B).

(b)   simplify how an entity determines amounts related to the contractual service margin (see paragraphs BC383–BC383B).

(c)   simplify how an entity determines the information necessary to determine insurance revenue (see paragraphs BC383–BC383B).

(d)   permit an entity to determine insurance finance income and expenses included in profit or loss using the discount rates at the transition date if an entity chooses to disaggregate insurance finance income or expenses into an amount included in profit or loss and an amount included in other comprehensive income. In addition, the modification provides an expedient for determining the amount of the accumulated balance in equity relating to insurance finance income and expenses (see paragraphs BC384–BC384B).

Amendments to IFRS 17—feedback on using reasonable and supportable information and making estimates

BC380A   Some entities implementing IFRS 17 suggested that to provide operational relief, the Board should remove from the modified retrospective approach the requirements to:

(a)   maximise the use of reasonable and supportable information available without undue cost or effort that would have been used to apply a fully retrospective approach.

(b)   use reasonable and supportable information to apply the modifications.

BC380B   The Board considered but rejected the suggestions in paragraph BC380A because:

(a)   with regards to the suggestion in paragraph BC380A(a), permitting an entity to ignore reasonable and supportable information available without undue cost or effort that the entity would have used to apply a fully retrospective approach would be contrary to the objective of the modified retrospective approach. The objective is to achieve the closest outcome to retrospective application possible using reasonable and supportable information available without undue cost or effort. The suggestion would also reduce comparability between contracts issued before and after the transition date.

(b)   with regards to the suggestion in paragraph BC380A(b), permitting an entity to apply a modification when it does not have reasonable and supportable information to do so would undermine the credibility of information that results from applying IFRS 17. In the Board's view, applying a fair value approach would result in more useful information for users of financial statements than would applying a modified retrospective approach without the reasonable and supportable information necessary to do so.

BC380C   Some entities implementing IFRS 17 suggested that the inclusion of specified modifications implies that an entity cannot make estimates in applying IFRS 17 retrospectively. The Board noted that paragraph 51 of IAS 8 acknowledges the need for estimates in retrospective application. This paragraph applies to entities applying IFRS 17 for the first time just as it does to entities applying other IFRS Standards for the first time. The Board expects that entities will often need to make estimates when applying a specified modification in the modified retrospective approach.

BC380D   Some stakeholders suggested that the Board could reduce the burden of applying the transition requirements by specifying methods that could be used—for example, methods using information from embedded value reporting or information prepared for regulatory reporting. The Board rejected this suggestion. The Board concluded that specifying methods would conflict with the approach in IFRS 17 of establishing measurement objectives that can be satisfied using various methods. The appropriateness of a method depends on facts and circumstances. Furthermore, if the Board were to specify methods, it could risk incorrectly implying that entities cannot use other methods that would satisfy the requirements of IFRS 17.

Assessments made at inception or initial recognition of insurance contracts (paragraphs C9–C10 of IFRS 17)

BC381   IFRS 17 requires some assessments to be made at the inception or initial recognition of a contract, in particular:

(a)   whether a contract is eligible for the variable fee approach;

(b)   how to group contracts; and

(c)   how to determine the effect of discretion on estimated cash flows for contracts subject to the general model.

BC382   The Board concluded that often it would be impracticable for entities to make such assessments using assumptions at the date of inception or initial recognition. Such assessments might be impossible without the use of hindsight (ie making an assumption of what an entity would have expected in the past). The need for hindsight could be avoided if the assessments were made at the transition date instead of at the date of inception or initial recognition of the contract. However, the Board noted that assessing contracts only at the transition date could impose grouping for entities that is significantly different from an assessment as at the date of the inception or initial recognition of the contract. Accordingly, the Board decided that entities should be allowed to make the assessments either:

(a)   at the date of inception or initial recognition of a contract, if such assessments could be made based on reasonable and supportable evidence for what the entity would have determined given the terms of the contract and the market conditions at that time; or

(b)   at the transition date.[53]

Amendments to IFRS 17—classification of contracts acquired in their settlement period (paragraphs C9A and C22A of IFRS 17)

BC382A   In June 2020, the Board considered but rejected a suggestion to create an exception to the general classification and measurement requirements in IFRS 17 for contracts acquired in their settlement period (see paragraphs BC327E–BC327G). However, the Board amended IFRS 17 to provide reliefs on transition in response to feedback that to apply IFRS 17 retrospectively to contracts acquired before the transition date (that is, to classify and measure those contracts as a liability for remaining coverage) would often be impracticable. Those reliefs permit an entity applying the modified retrospective approach or the fair value approach to classify as a liability for incurred claims a liability for the settlement of claims when:

(a)   that liability relates to an insurance contract that was acquired in a transfer of insurance contracts that do not form a business or in a business combination within the scope of IFRS 3; and

(b)   the acquisition date was before the transition date.

BC382B   An entity applying the modified retrospective approach applies the relief in paragraph BC382A only to the extent permitted by paragraph C8 of IFRS 17.

Determining amounts relating to the contractual service margin and insurance revenue (paragraphs C11–C17 of IFRS 17)

BC383   In many cases, the estimates described in paragraph BC378 can be determined only using hindsight, which would mean that the entity would not be able to apply IFRS 17 retrospectively. Accordingly, the Board decided that it would specify modifications that could be used for making those estimates. Those modifications:

(a)   avoid the need for entities to measure the changes in estimates that would have been recognised in profit or loss because they did not relate to future service, or to assess the extent to which such changes in estimates had been reversed as claims were incurred;

---

53   In June 2020, the Board amended IFRS 17 to permit an entity to assess whether a contract meets the definition of an investment contract with discretionary participation features either at the date of initial recognition of the contract or at the transition date. This assessment is consistent with other assessments described in paragraph BC382.

(b) provide an objective way for entities to estimate what the risk adjustment for non-financial risk would have been at the date of initial recognition;

(c) provide a way for entities to estimate the discount rates at the date of initial recognition; and

(d) provide guidance on how an entity should determine how much of the estimated contractual service margin on initial recognition should remain at the date of transition.

Amendments to IFRS 17—modifications considered but rejected

BC383A The Board considered a suggestion from entities implementing IFRS 17 to permit an entity to develop the modifications that it thinks would achieve the closest possible outcome to retrospective application. The Board disagreed with this suggestion, because if such modifications were permitted:

(a) an entity could use modifications that would result in an outcome that the Board would consider insufficiently close to retrospective application; and

(b) each entity could use different modifications, reducing comparability and increasing complexity for users of financial statements.

BC383B Paragraph C17 of IFRS 17 provides a modification for determining the contractual service margin at the transition date for insurance contracts with direct participation features. An entity applying that modification determines the carrying amount of the contractual service margin at the transition date in a more direct way than the entity would by applying the modifications in paragraphs C11–C16 of IFRS 17 for determining the contractual service margin at the transition date for insurance contracts without direct participation features. An entity can determine the contractual service margin in this more direct way because of the extent to which the contractual service margin is remeasured for insurance contracts with direct participation features. Some stakeholders suggested that an entity should be able to apply the modifications in paragraphs C11–C16 of IFRS 17 to insurance contracts with direct participation features. The Board disagreed with this suggestion because applying those modifications to such contracts would be unlikely to achieve an outcome as close to retrospective application as would applying paragraph C17 of IFRS 17.

Determining insurance finance income and expenses (paragraphs C18 and C19 of IFRS 17)

BC384 If an entity chooses to include some insurance finance income or expenses in other comprehensive income, applying IFRS 17 retrospectively, the entity would need to track historical information and make assessments about the allocation of amounts from other comprehensive income to profit or loss in each period to determine the accumulated balance recognised in other comprehensive income. This information would be particularly difficult to determine if, consistent with paragraph C10 of IFRS 17, the entity included within a group insurance contracts issued more than one year apart.

Accordingly, the Board decided to provide modifications that would enable an entity to determine those amounts at the transition date.

Amendments to IFRS 17—feedback relating to the accumulated balance recognised in other comprehensive income

BC384A   Some entities implementing IFRS 17 said they would prefer alternative modifications to the modifications set out in paragraphs C18–C19 of IFRS 17 for determining the amount of insurance finance income or expenses accumulated in other comprehensive income at the transition date. These entities suggested that for all insurance contracts (insurance contracts with and without direct participation features), an entity should be required to:

(a)   deem as nil the accumulated amount in other comprehensive income for financial assets accounted for applying IFRS 9 that are related to insurance contracts; or

(b)   deem the accumulated amount of insurance finance income or expenses in other comprehensive income as equal to the accumulated amount in other comprehensive income arising on financial assets accounted for applying IFRS 9 that are related to insurance contracts.

BC384B   The Board considered but rejected the suggestions in paragraph BC384A because:

(a)   both suggested amendments involve significant subjectivity in determining which assets relate to insurance contracts.

(b)   both suggested amendments could result in an outcome that the Board would consider to be insufficiently close to retrospective application of IFRS 17 requirements.

(c)   the suggested amendment to IFRS 9 described in BC384A(a) would reduce comparability of entities first applying IFRS 9 and IFRS 17 at the same time choosing this approach with other entities that have already applied IFRS 9. The Board noted that the amount accumulated in other comprehensive income relating to financial assets measured at fair value through other comprehensive income includes amounts that relate to expected credit losses. Hence, setting the cumulative amount to nil on transition would affect the accounting for expected credit losses in future periods.

(d)   the suggested amendment to IFRS 17 described in BC384A(b) would mean that insurance finance income or expenses recognised in profit or loss in future periods would reflect the historical discount rate for assets held at the transition date that an entity determines are related to insurance contracts. The Board concluded that using that historical discount rate could result in a significant loss of useful information, because of the subjectivity in determining which assets relate to insurance contracts and because comparability for insurance contracts would be reduced between entities that hold different assets.

Fair value approach (paragraphs C20–C24B of IFRS 17)

BC385 The Board noted that in some cases an entity might not have reasonable and supportable information available without undue cost or effort to apply the modified retrospective approach. Accordingly, the Board specified that in such cases, an entity must apply a fair value approach in which the contractual service margin at the transition date is determined as the difference between the fulfilment cash flows and the fair value of the group of insurance contracts, determined in accordance with IFRS 13. The Board also decided to allow the use of the fair value approach whenever retrospective application is impracticable (see paragraph BC373). The Board decided to clarify that in determining fair value of a group of insurance contracts, an entity should not apply the concept of a deposit floor (see paragraphs BC165–BC166).

BC386 The fair value approach also permits the same modifications as the modified retrospective approach relating to:

(a) assessments about insurance contracts or groups of insurance contracts that would be made at the date of inception or initial recognition;[54] and

(b) determining the discount rates and the effect of changes in discount rates necessary to determine insurance finance income and expenses.

Comparative information (paragraphs C25–C28 of IFRS 17)

BC387 IFRS 17 requires entities to present comparative information, applying the requirements of IFRS 17 for the period immediately before the date of initial application of IFRS 17, to provide the most useful information to users of financial statements by allowing comparisons among entities and using trend information. However, if an entity presents comparative information for earlier periods, that comparative information need not be restated applying the requirements of IFRS 17.

BC388 The Board concluded that providing restated comparative information for at least one reporting period was necessary because of the diversity of previous accounting and the extent of the changes introduced by IFRS 17. Because IFRS 17 only requires retrospective application on transition if practicable, and specifies simplified approaches when retrospective application is impracticable, the Board expects that determining the comparative amounts will not require significant incremental time and resources beyond those required to first apply IFRS 17. The Board set the effective date for IFRS 17 based on information given about the necessary time to prepare, in the knowledge that restated comparative information for one reporting period would be required.

---

54 An entity applying the fair value approach is permitted to classify as a liability for incurred claims a liability for the settlement of claims incurred before an insurance contract was acquired in a transfer of insurance contracts that do not form a business or in a business combination within the scope of IFRS 3 (see paragraph BC382A).

BC389   The requirement to restate comparative information for one reporting period is different from the transition requirements of IFRS 9, which did not require restatement of comparative amounts at transition to that Standard, including the fair value of financial instruments (and which did not allow restatement if doing so required the use of hindsight). However, the Board noted that different circumstances applied when it developed the transition requirements for IFRS 9, which were developed with the intention of minimising obstacles to voluntary application of IFRS 9 before its effective date. In addition, entities applying those transition requirements of IFRS 9 had all previously applied the same requirements, ie those in IAS 39. In contrast, the Board expects that most entities will apply IFRS 17 no earlier than the effective date and believes that the restatement of comparative amounts is particularly important, for the reasons given in paragraph BC388. Therefore, the Board decided not to provide relief from the restatement of comparative information to facilitate early application of IFRS 17.

BC389A   In June 2020, the Board deferred the effective date of IFRS 17 from 1 January 2021 to 1 January 2023 (see paragraphs BC404A–BC404F). The Board considered but rejected a suggestion to provide relief from the restatement of comparative information, because the Board concluded that restatement of comparative information is particularly important given the diversity in previous accounting practices and the extent of change introduced by IFRS 17.

Other transition issues

Contracts derecognised before the transition date

BC390   The Board decided that it would not provide a simplification for contracts that have been derecognised before the transition date. The Board noted that reflecting the effect of contracts derecognised before the transition date on the remaining contractual service margin was necessary to provide a faithful representation of the remaining profit of the group of insurance contracts. Furthermore, although entities may have difficulty obtaining details of cash flows for all contracts that have been derecognised, the Board concluded that an entity would be able to make estimates and extrapolations using reasonable and supportable information to enable the effect of derecognised contracts to be determined. Finally, the Board observed that when an entity is not able to make such estimates and extrapolations, the fair value approach would be available.

Level of aggregation (paragraphs C9(a) and C10 of IFRS 17)

BC391   To apply the Standard retrospectively, an entity needs to determine the group of insurance contracts to which individual contracts would have belonged on initial recognition. The Standard requires entities to group only contracts written within one year.

BC392   The Board noted that it may not always be practicable for entities to group contracts written in the same one-year period retrospectively. Accordingly, the Board decided to provide a transition relief so that entities would not need to divide contracts into groups of contracts that were written within one year. In addition, entities are allowed to accrete and adjust the resulting contractual service margin after transition using the discount rates at the transition date. Furthermore, the Board decided that entities that choose to disaggregate insurance finance income or expenses between profit or loss and other comprehensive income in accordance with paragraphs 88(b) and 89(b) of IFRS 17 should be permitted to determine insurance finance income or expenses included in profit or loss using the discount rates at the transition date. Although this results in a different accumulated balance in equity compared with the amount that would result from a full retrospective approach, and hence different insurance finance income or expenses in profit or loss in the future, the Board concluded that users of financial statements could be alerted to these differences through disclosures.

Amendments to IFRS 17—feedback on applying the level of aggregation requirements on transition

BC392A In the modified retrospective approach, an entity is permitted to group together contracts that were issued more than one year apart, to the extent that the entity does not have reasonable and supportable information to separately group those contracts—in other words, the entity is permitted not to apply the annual cohort requirement in paragraph 22 of IFRS 17. In the fair value approach, an entity is permitted a choice to group together contracts that were issued more than one year apart. Some stakeholders suggested the Board provide further relief by permitting an entity a choice to group together contracts issued more than one year apart in a fully retrospective approach and in the modified retrospective approach, regardless of whether the entity has reasonable and supportable information to apply the annual cohort requirement. The Board disagreed with the suggestion for such transition relief because permitting an entity not to apply the annual cohort requirement:

(a) when the entity has the information available to apply a fully retrospective approach would have the effect that the entity would not be applying a fully retrospective approach; and

(b) when the entity has reasonable and supportable information to apply that requirement in the modified retrospective approach would be inconsistent with the objective of the modified retrospective approach.

Derivatives used to mitigate financial risk (paragraph C3(b) of IFRS 17)[55]

BC393 Paragraph B115 of IFRS 17 permits entities not to recognise a change in the contractual service margin for changes in fulfilment cash flows and the entity's share in the fair value returns on underlying items for which an entity uses derivatives to mitigate their financial risk.[56] However, an entity

---

55 In June 2020, the Board extended the risk mitigation option to be applicable when an entity uses reinsurance contracts held and non-derivative financial instruments measured at fair value through profit or loss to mitigate financial risk (see paragraphs BC256A–BC256F).

56 In June 2020, the Board extended the risk mitigation option to be applicable when an entity uses reinsurance contracts held and non-derivative financial instruments measured at fair value through profit or loss to mitigate financial risk (see paragraphs BC256A–BC256F).

applying this option is required to document its risk management objective and the strategy for mitigating the risk before doing so. This documentation requirement is analogous to the documentation requirements for hedge accounting in IFRS 9. Consistent with the transition requirements for hedge accounting in IFRS 9, the Board concluded that retrospective application of the risk mitigation treatment would give rise to the risk of hindsight. In particular, the Board was concerned that documentation after the event could enable entities to choose the risk mitigation relationships to which it would apply this option, particularly because the application of this approach is optional. Consequently, IFRS 17, consistent with the transition requirements for hedge accounting in IFRS 9, requires prospective application of the risk mitigation option from the date of initial application of the Standard.[57]

Amendments to IFRS 17—the prohibition from applying the risk mitigation option retrospectively (paragraphs C3(b) and C5A of IFRS 17)

BC393A   In June 2020, the Board amended the transition requirements relating to the risk mitigation option to:

(a)   permit an entity to apply the risk mitigation option in paragraph B115 of IFRS 17 prospectively from the transition date instead of the date of initial application; and

(b)   permit an entity that can apply IFRS 17 retrospectively to a group of insurance contracts to instead apply the fair value approach if, and only if:

(i)   the entity chooses to apply the risk mitigation option to the group prospectively from the transition date; and

(ii)   before the transition date, the entity had been using derivatives, reinsurance contracts held or non-derivative financial instruments measured at fair value through profit or loss to mitigate financial risk arising from the group of insurance contracts.

BC393B   The amendments described in paragraph BC393A respond to concerns that prohibiting retrospective application of the risk mitigation option reduces comparability between risk mitigation activities that took place before the date of initial application and those that take place after that date. Most stakeholders agreed with the Board that the amendments described in paragraph BC393A resolve these concerns.

BC393C   Nonetheless, some stakeholders suggested the Board amend IFRS 17 to permit retrospective application of the risk mitigation option, and so the Board considered whether it should make such an amendment. The Board observed that if an entity were permitted to apply the option retrospectively, it could decide the extent to which it reflects risk mitigation activities in the contractual service margin based on known accounting outcomes. The entity could apply the option in a way that differs from how the entity would have

---

57   In June 2020, the Board amended IFRS 17 to require prospective application of the risk mitigation option from the transition date instead of the date of initial application (see paragraph BC393A).

applied the option in previous periods without hindsight, had it always applied IFRS 17. Permitting retrospective application of the option would therefore affect the credibility of information presented on transition to IFRS 17 and in subsequent periods in which those groups of insurance contracts exist. The Board therefore reaffirmed its decision to prohibit retrospective application of the option because of the risk of the use of hindsight.

BC393D Some stakeholders suggested the Board amend IFRS 17 to permit an entity to apply the risk mitigation option retrospectively if, and only if, the entity applies the option for all risk mitigation relationships that would meet the conditions in paragraphs B115–B116 of IFRS 17 (an 'all or nothing' approach). These stakeholders thought such an amendment would avoid the risk of hindsight. The Board considered what an 'all or nothing' approach would be and whether the Board should add such an approach to the IFRS 17 transition requirements. The Board noted that an 'all or nothing' approach would require:

(a) 'all' to mean all insurance contracts issued by the entity that exist at the transition date (that is, all would be at a reporting entity level);

(b) 'all' to mean all past and current risk mitigation relationships that meet the criteria in paragraph B116 of IFRS 17 at any point between initial recognition of a group of insurance contracts and the transition date;

(c) an entity to hold historical documentation of each of those risk mitigation relationships described in (b), and that documentation to have existed at the beginning of the first reporting period that the entity would have met the criteria in paragraph B116 of IFRS 17; and

(d) an entity to retrospectively determine the effect of applying the risk mitigation option for all relationships described in (b) at each reporting date between initial recognition of a group of insurance contracts and the transition date.

BC393E The Board noted that any approach other than the one described in paragraph BC393D would involve the risk of hindsight. The approach described in paragraph BC393D would not involve the risk of hindsight. However, the Board concluded that applying that approach would be impracticable in almost all cases. Meeting the conditions necessary for an 'all or nothing' approach would be a high hurdle that entities would overcome in only a narrow set of circumstances. Accordingly, the Board decided not to add those requirements to IFRS 17.

Redesignation of financial assets (paragraphs C29–C33 of IFRS 17)

BC394 When first applying IFRS 17, an entity will either:

(a) have already applied IFRS 9; or

(b) also be applying IFRS 9 for the first time.

BC395   IFRS 9 includes requirements for the classification of financial assets. IFRS 9 also includes an option on the date of initial application of IFRS 9 for entities to designate financial assets as measured at fair value through profit or loss when doing so mitigates an accounting mismatch (the fair value option). An entity applying both IFRS 9 and IFRS 17 for the first time will be able to assess financial asset classifications, elections and designations while, at the same time, assessing the implications of the requirements of IFRS 17.

BC396   The Board considered whether an entity that has previously applied IFRS 9 when it first applies IFRS 17 should be permitted to revisit its IFRS 9 financial asset classifications, elections and designations. IFRS 9 determines classification based on the contractual cash flow characteristics of a financial asset and the business model in which it is held. After IFRS 9 is applied, changes in classification can only occur when an entity's business model changes; the Board expects such changes to be infrequent. In addition, IFRS 9 does not usually permit either subsequent redesignation under the fair value option or subsequent redesignation of equity instruments into, or out of, the category of equity instruments at fair value through other comprehensive income after initial recognition.

BC397   The interaction between the classification of financial assets and the presentation of changes in the insurance contract liability could create accounting mismatches in profit or loss. New accounting mismatches could arise on first applying IFRS 17 if an entity were unable to reconsider the classification of financial assets that were classified at an earlier date in accordance with IFRS 9. The Board concluded that entities should be able to designate financial assets using the fair value option on first applying IFRS 17 to the same extent that they would have been able to do so when first applying IFRS 9. In addition, the Board decided that, following earlier application of IFRS 9, an entity should be permitted to newly elect to use other comprehensive income to recognise changes in the fair value of some or all equity investments that are not held for trading, or to revoke such an election. The criterion for this classification option does not refer to accounting mismatches, so the Board decided that entities should be able to reconsider this election regardless of whether there is an effect on accounting mismatches when IFRS 17 is applied. Even though accounting mismatches do not determine the availability of this classification option, the Board noted that in practice entities may consider accounting mismatches when deciding whether to apply the option.

BC398   A major factor in the classification of financial assets in accordance with IFRS 9 is an entity's business model. The application of IFRS 17 would not of itself have been likely to have resulted in a change in an entity's business model in accordance with IFRS 9. However, the Board acknowledged that there is a relationship between how entities manage their financial assets and their insurance contract liabilities. Therefore, to reduce the risk of accounting mismatches arising, the Board decided to allow an entity to reassess its business models on the initial application of IFRS 17 if they have previously applied IFRS 9.

Amendments to IFRS 17—feedback on redesignation of financial assets

BC398A The Board considered but rejected a suggestion from entities implementing IFRS 17 that on initial application of IFRS 17 an entity that:

(a) first applied IFRS 9 before IFRS 17 be permitted to apply the transition relief in paragraph C29 of IFRS 17 to redesignate financial assets that were derecognised during the IFRS 17 comparative period; and

(b) first applied IFRS 9 at the same time it first applied IFRS 17 be permitted to apply IFRS 9 to financial assets that were derecognised during the IFRS 17 comparative period.

BC398B The Board extensively discussed and consulted on the requirements in IFRS 9 relating to transition when IFRS 9 was being developed. Such requirements include prohibiting an entity from applying IFRS 9 to derecognised items, and permitting but not requiring an entity to restate comparative periods in some circumstances.

Amendments to IFRS 17—transition requirements when an entity chooses to apply IFRS 9 to contracts specified in paragraph 8A of IFRS 17 (paragraphs 7.2.36–7.2.42 of IFRS 9)

BC398C Some entities will first apply IFRS 17 after they first apply IFRS 9. In June 2020, the Board amended IFRS 9 to provide transition requirements for such entities that apply paragraph 8A of IFRS 17 and choose to apply IFRS 9 to insurance contracts that limit the compensation for insured events to the amount otherwise required to settle the policyholder's obligation created by the contract (see paragraphs BC94D–BC94F). The amendment enables those entities to use the transition requirements in Section 7.2 of IFRS 9 (as issued in 2014) when first applying IFRS 9 to those contracts.

BC398D The Board also considered transition requirements related to the fair value option in IFRS 9. An entity's decision to apply IFRS 9 to insurance contracts that limit the compensation for insured events to the amount otherwise required to settle the policyholder's obligation created by the contract could change, either partially or in full, the classification and measurement of such contracts. Such changes may create or eliminate accounting mismatches between the contracts and financial liabilities an entity might consider to be related to the contracts. Therefore, the Board amended the IFRS 9 transition requirements to permit an entity to designate, or require an entity to revoke its previous designation of, a financial liability at the date of initial application of these amendments to the extent that a new accounting mismatch is created, or a previous accounting mismatch no longer exists, as a result of the application of these amendments.

BC398E Consistent with the transition requirements in IFRS 9 and IFRS 17, the Board decided to specify that when an entity applies the amendment described in paragraph BC398C and chooses to apply IFRS 9 to such contracts, the entity:

(a) can choose to restate prior periods to reflect the effect of applying these amendments only if the entity can do so without the use of hindsight and if the restated financial statements reflect all the requirements in IFRS 9 for the affected financial instruments;

(b)   will be required to disclose information about the changes in the classification and measurement of contracts as a result of applying these amendments in addition to any disclosures required by other IFRS Standards; and

(c)   can choose to not disclose the quantitative information otherwise required by paragraph 28(f) of IAS 8 for the current period or any prior period presented.

BC398F   The Board added these transition requirements as a consequence of adding paragraph 8A to the requirements of IFRS 17 (see paragraph BC398C). In June 2020, the Board also added a scope exclusion in paragraph 7(h) of IFRS 17 for some contracts that provide credit or payment arrangements such as particular credit card contracts (see paragraphs BC94A–BC94C). Stakeholders said that, for such contracts, many entities already apply IFRS 9 to the credit or payment arrangement component applying the separation requirements in IFRS 4. However, some may not have. Accordingly, the transition requirements discussed in paragraphs BC398A–BC398E will apply if an entity has already applied IFRS 9 but has not applied IFRS 9 to those components.

Transition disclosures (paragraphs 114–116 of IFRS 17)

BC399   The Board expects that there will be some differences in the measurement of insurance contracts when applying the different transition approaches permitted in IFRS 17. Accordingly, the Board decided to require that an entity provides disclosures that enable users of financial statements to identify the effect of groups of insurance contracts measured at the transition date applying the modified retrospective approach or the fair value approach on the contractual service margin and revenue in subsequent periods. Furthermore, the Board decided that entities should explain how they determined the measurement of insurance contracts that existed at the transition date for all periods in which these disclosures are required, for users of financial statements to understand the nature and significance of the methods used and judgements applied.

Disclosure of the amount of adjustment for each financial statement line item affected (paragraph 28(f) of IAS 8)

BC400   An entity is required to apply the disclosure requirements of IAS 8 unless another Standard specifies otherwise. The Board decided that entities should not be required to disclose, for the current period and for each prior period presented, the amount of the adjustment for each financial statement line item affected, as required by paragraph 28(f) of IAS 8. In the Board's view, the cost of providing this disclosure, which would include the running of parallel systems, would exceed the benefits, particularly because IFRS 4 permitted an entity to use a wide range of practices.

Disclosure of claims development (paragraph 130 of IFRS 17)

BC401 Paragraph 44 of IFRS 4 exempted an entity from disclosing some information about claims development in prior periods on first application of that Standard. The Board decided to carry forward in IFRS 17 a similar exemption for cost-benefit reasons.

Effective date (paragraphs C1 and C2 of IFRS 17)

BC402 The Board generally allows at least 12 to 18 months between the publication of a new Standard and its mandatory effective date. However, in the case of major Standards, such as IFRS 17, that have a pervasive effect on entities, the Board has allowed longer implementation periods to allow entities time to resolve the operational challenges in implementing those Standards. At the same time, the Board needs to balance the advantage of a longer implementation period for preparers against the disadvantages of allowing inferior accounting practices, arising from IFRS 4, to continue.

BC403 The Board noted that IFRS 17 will be complex for entities to apply. Accordingly, the Board decided that IFRS 17 should be applied by all entities for annual periods beginning on or after 1 January 2021, a period of approximately three and a half years from publication of the Standard. This allows entities a period of two and a half years to prepare, taking into account the need to restate comparative information.[58]

BC404 While the Board noted that this long implementation period may assist entities in meeting any increased regulatory capital requirements that follow the reporting of the higher liabilities that are expected in some jurisdictions, regulatory capital requirements and IFRS Standards have different objectives. The Board decided that the possible effects of regulatory capital requirements should not delay the implementation of a Standard intended to provide transparency about an entity's financial position.

Amendments to IFRS 17—deferral of the effective date

BC404A In June 2020, the Board deferred the effective date of IFRS 17 by two years to require entities to apply IFRS 17 for annual reporting periods beginning on or after 1 January 2023.

BC404B In the 2019 Exposure Draft, the Board proposed a one-year deferral of the effective date to balance:

(a) providing certainty about the effective date considering the uncertainty caused by the Board's decision in October 2018 to explore possible amendments to IFRS 17 (see paragraphs BC6A–BC6C); and

(b) requiring IFRS 17 implementation as soon as possible because:

---

58 In June 2020, the Board deferred the effective date of IFRS 17 by two years to require entities to apply IFRS 17 for annual reporting periods beginning on or after 1 January 2023 (see paragraphs BC404A–BC404F).

(i) IFRS 17 is a Standard urgently needed to address many inadequacies in previous accounting practices for insurance contracts; and

(ii) undue delay in the effective date of the Standard may increase workload and costs, particularly for entities that are advanced in their implementation projects.

BC404C Feedback on the 2019 Exposure Draft generally supported the proposed deferral of the effective date. Some stakeholders, particularly users of financial statements and regulators, expressed concern about any deferral of the effective date beyond one year, but other stakeholders suggested a longer deferral was necessary.

BC404D Some stakeholders said a longer deferral was necessary because some entities required more time to implement IFRS 17, for example because of challenges in developing systems and determining appropriate accounting policies, and because of the effect on implementation projects already under way of the amendments proposed in the 2019 Exposure Draft. The Board acknowledged that implementing IFRS 17 is a major undertaking. However, it noted that it had allowed an implementation period of three and a half years when it issued IFRS 17. Furthermore, given that IFRS 17 is urgently needed, the Board thought that a year's deferral of the effective date as proposed in the 2019 Exposure Draft ought to be sufficient to allow for the effects of any disruption caused by amending the Standard before its effective date. The Board was careful to propose only targeted amendments and not to reopen fundamental aspects of the Standard. The Board acknowledged, however, that implementing the Standard by 2022, as proposed in the 2019 Exposure Draft, would be demanding, in particular for smaller insurers.

BC404E Some stakeholders suggested a longer deferral was necessary to ensure that the initial application of IFRS 17 would be aligned in major markets around the world. These stakeholders were uncertain whether such an alignment would occur if the Board confirmed a one-year deferral. They commented on uncertainties and delays in jurisdictional endorsement and adoption processes and the consequential uncertainty about the effective dates that might be set in some jurisdictions. The Board noted that it had set the effective date of IFRS 17 so that jurisdictions would have sufficient time to adopt the new Standard. However, the Board acknowledged that considering amendments to the Standard before its effective date inevitably caused some disruption to those processes. The Board noted that the initial application of IFRS 17 will significantly affect insurers' financial statements and acknowledged that users of financial statements would benefit if the initial application of IFRS 17 were aligned around the world.

BC404F Accordingly, although the Board was aware of the costs of delaying the implementation of IFRS 17, particularly for users of financial statements, the Board decided to defer the effective date by two years to annual reporting periods beginning on or after 1 January 2023. The Board concluded that a two-year deferral should allow time for an orderly adoption of the amended IFRS 17 by jurisdictions. It should therefore enable more entities to initially apply IFRS 17 around the same time for the benefit of users of financial statements. The additional year's deferral compared to that proposed in the 2019 Exposure Draft should also assist those entities for whom implementing IFRS 17 by 2022 would have been challenging, including those entities for whom implementation projects were affected by the covid-19 pandemic in 2020. The deferral should thereby help to improve the quality of the initial application of the Standard.

Early application (paragraphs C1 and C2 of IFRS 17)

BC405   IFRS 4 permitted an entity to change its accounting policies for insurance contracts if it showed that the change resulted in more relevant or reliable information. As a result, IFRS 4 would have permitted an entity to apply the requirements in IFRS 17, except for the requirements relating to other comprehensive income and transition relief. Accordingly, the Board concluded that it would be inappropriate to prohibit early application of IFRS 17.

BC406   However, because IFRS 17 was developed in the context of IFRS 15 and IFRS 9, and given the extent of changes the Board expects will be needed to apply IFRS 17, the Board concluded that an entity should be permitted to apply IFRS 17 only when it also applies IFRS 15 and IFRS 9.[59]

First-time adopters of IFRS Standards (Appendix D of IFRS 17)

BC407   The Board sees no reason to give different transition approaches to first-time adopters of IFRS Standards from other entities. Consequently, the Board has amended IFRS 1 *First-time Adoption of International Financial Reporting Standards* to require the modified retrospective approach or the fair value approach in IFRS 17 when retrospective application of IFRS 17 is impracticable, as defined by IAS 8. The Board decided not to give any additional relief on the restatement of comparative amounts from that already in IFRS 1.

---

59 In June 2020, the Board amended IFRS 17. The reference to IFRS 15 in paragraph C1 of IFRS 17 was deleted, because IFRS 15 was effective at the time the June 2020 amendments were issued.

Appendix A
Summary of changes since the 2013 Exposure Draft

The following table summarises the main differences between the 2013 Exposure Draft and IFRS 17 *Insurance Contracts*.[60]

Area of change	Description of change
Scope	
Fixed-fee service contracts	• Removed the requirement that an entity must apply IFRS 15 *Revenue from Contracts with Customers* to fixed-fee service contracts that meet the definition of an insurance contract. An entity is permitted, but not required, to apply IFRS 15 to those contracts.
Combination of contracts	• Revised the requirements on combining contracts so that insurance contracts should be combined only when a set of insurance contracts with the same or a related counterparty may achieve, or is designed to achieve, an overall commercial effect and combining those contracts is necessary to report the substance of those contracts.
Measurement	
Level of aggregation	• Revised the requirements to require disaggregation of a portfolio of insurance contracts at initial recognition into groups of insurance contracts that are onerous, profitable with no significant possibility of becoming onerous and other profitable contracts, with a narrow exemption for the effects of law or regulatory constraints on pricing. Groups cannot contain contracts that are written more than one year apart. A portfolio of insurance contracts is defined as insurance contracts subject to similar risks and managed together.
Discount rate	• Clarified the guidance when there is no, or little, observable market data.

continued...

---

60 This appendix compares IFRS 17 as issued in May 2017 with the 2013 Exposure Draft. In June 2020, the Board amended IFRS 17. A list summarising the June 2020 amendments, including references to the relevant paragraphs of this Basis for Conclusions, is included in Appendix C.

...continued

Area of change	Description of change
Contractual service margin	• Clarified the principle for the recognition pattern of the contractual service margin by providing guidance that, for contracts other than investment contracts with discretionary participation features, an entity should recognise the contractual service margin in profit or loss on the basis of coverage units.
	• Revised the requirements so that an entity adjusts the contractual service margin for the changes in risk relating to future service, consistent with the changes in estimates of cash flows.
	• Revised the requirements so that favourable changes in estimates that arise after losses were previously recognised in profit or loss are recognised in profit or loss, to the extent that they reverse previously recognised losses.
	• Clarified what adjusts the contractual service margin. For example, changes in discretionary cash flows, as specified by the entity, are regarded as relating to future service.

continued...

...continued

Area of change	Description of change
Insurance contracts with participation features	• Eliminated the mirroring approach proposed in the 2013 Exposure Draft for insurance contracts that require an entity to hold underlying items and specify a link to returns on those underlying items. • Introduced a definition of an insurance contract with direct participation features—ie a contract for which: (a) the contractual terms specify that the policyholder participates in a share of a clearly identified pool of underlying items; (b) the entity expects to pay the policyholder an amount equal to a substantial share of the returns from the underlying items; and (c) the entity expects a substantial proportion of any change in the amounts to be paid to the policyholder to vary with the change in fair value of the underlying items. • Introduced a requirement that, for insurance contracts with direct participation features, changes in the estimate of the fee (equal to the entity's expected share of the returns on underlying items minus any expected cash flows that do not vary directly with the underlying items) that the entity expects to earn from a group of insurance contracts adjust the contractual service margin. • Introduced an option for an entity not to adjust the contractual service margin for changes in fulfilment cash flows or the entity's share of underlying items for which an entity uses derivatives to mitigate their financial risk in specified circumstances.

continued...

...continued

Area of change	Description of change
Premium allocation approach	
Measurement	• Revised the recognition of revenue over the coverage period to be according to the passage of time or, when the expected pattern of release of risk differs significantly from the passage of time, the expected timing of incurred insurance service expenses.
	• Revised to require an entity to determine the insurance finance income or expenses in profit or loss for the liability for incurred claims using the discount rates determined at the date the liability for incurred claims is recognised. This occurs when the entity applies the premium allocation approach to contracts for which the entity discounts the liability for incurred claims and chooses to present the effect of changes in discount rates in other comprehensive income.
Reinsurance contracts held	
Measurement	• Revised to require an entity that holds a group of reinsurance contracts to recognise immediately in profit or loss any changes in estimates of fulfilment cash flows that arise from changes in estimates of fulfilment cash flows for a group of underlying insurance contracts that are recognised immediately in profit or loss.
Presentation and disclosure	
Presentation of insurance revenue	• Amended to prohibit an entity from presenting premium information in profit or loss if that information is not consistent with insurance revenue determined by applying IFRS 17.

continued...

...continued

Area of change	Description of change
Presentation of insurance finance income or expenses	• Introduced an accounting policy choice for an entity to: (a) include insurance finance income or expenses for the period in profit or loss; or (b) disaggregate insurance finance income or expenses for the period into an amount recognised in profit or loss and an amount recognised in other comprehensive income.
	• Specified that if the entity disaggregates insurance finance income or expenses into an amount recognised in profit or loss and an amount recognised in other comprehensive income:
	• in most circumstances, the amount included in profit or loss is determined by a systematic allocation of the total expected insurance finance income or expenses over the duration of the group of insurance contracts.
	• when the contracts are insurance contracts with direct participation features and the entity holds the underlying items (ie there is no economic mismatch between the group of insurance contracts and the related underlying items), the amount included in profit or loss is determined to eliminate accounting mismatches with the finance income or expenses arising on the underlying items held.
Transition	
When retrospective application is impracticable	• Revised to provide further simplifications for groups of insurance contracts for which retrospective application is impracticable, including allowing entities to choose between a modified retrospective approach and a fair value approach. The modified retrospective approach allows an entity to use specified simplifications to retrospective application, to the extent necessary because the entity lacks reasonable and supportable information to apply IFRS 17 retrospectively. The fair value approach requires an entity to determine the contractual service margin by reference to the fair value of the group of insurance contracts at the transition date.

continued...

...continued

Area of change	Description of change
Designation of financial instruments using IFRS 9 *Financial Instruments*	• Revised to permit an entity, when first applying IFRS 17 after having applied IFRS 9, to newly assess the business model for eligible financial assets based on facts and circumstances applicable at the date of initial application. • Revised to require an entity to provide additional disclosures to assist users of financial statements in understanding those changes when the classification and measurement of financial assets change as a result of applying any of the transition reliefs in IFRS 17.
Comparative information	• Revised to require only one comparative period to be restated, applying IFRS 17 on transition.

Appendix B
Amendments to the Basis for Conclusions on other IFRS Standards

This appendix sets out the amendments to the Basis for Conclusions on other IFRS Standards that are a consequence of the International Accounting Standards Board issuing IFRS 17 Insurance Contracts.

* * * * *

The amendments contained in this appendix when this Standard was issued in 2017 have been incorporated into the Basis for Conclusions on the relevant Standards included in this volume.

Appendix C
List of amendments issued in 2020

Table C lists the main amendments to IFRS 17 issued in June 2020 with a reference to the rationale for those amendments included in this Basis for Conclusions (see paragraphs BC6A–BC6C).

The Board also:

(a)   made minor amendments to correct cases in which the drafting of IFRS 17 did not achieve the Board's intended outcome; and

(b)   considered but rejected other amendments suggested by stakeholders—for example, suggestions to amend the annual cohort requirement (see paragraphs BC139A–BC139T).

Table C Main amendments to IFRS 17 issued in June 2020	
Area of amendment	**Paragraphs in Basis for Conclusions on IFRS 17**
Scope exclusions—credit card contracts and similar contracts that provide credit or payment arrangements	BC94A–BC94C
Scope exclusions—specified contracts such as loan contracts with death waivers	BC94D–BC94F
Insurance acquisition cash flows	BC184A–BC184K BC327H–BC327I
The effect of accounting estimates made in interim financial statements	BC236A–BC236D
Risk mitigation option using instruments other than derivatives	BC256A–BC256F
Contractual service margin attributable to investment-return service and investment-related service	BC283A–BC283J
Reinsurance contracts—recovery of losses on underlying insurance contracts	BC315A–BC315L
Presentation in the statement of financial position	BC330A–BC330D
Applying the Standard for the first time—classification of contracts acquired in their settlement period	BC382A–BC382B
Applying the Standard for the first time—the prohibition from applying the risk mitigation option retrospectively	BC393A–BC393E
Applying the Standard for the first time—deferral of the effective date	BC404A–BC404F

IASB documents published to accompany

IAS 1

Presentation of Financial Statements

The text of the unaccompanied standard, IAS 1, is contained in Part A of this edition. Its effective date when issued was 1 January 2009. The text of the Accompanying Guidance on IAS 1 is contained in Part B of this edition. This part presents the following documents:

BASIS FOR CONCLUSIONS

APPENDIX TO THE BASIS FOR CONCLUSIONS

Amendments to the Basis for Conclusions on other IFRSs

DISSENTING OPINIONS

CONTENTS

© IFRS Foundation

...continued

Basis for Conclusions on
IAS 1 *Presentation of Financial Statements*

This Basis for Conclusions accompanies, but is not part of, IAS 1.

The International Accounting Standards Board revised IAS 1 Presentation of Financial Statements in 2007 as part of its project on financial statement presentation. It was not the Board's intention to reconsider as part of that project all the requirements in IAS 1.

For convenience, the Board has incorporated into this Basis for Conclusions relevant material from the Basis for Conclusions on the revision of IAS 1 in 2003 and its amendment in 2005. Paragraphs have been renumbered and reorganised as necessary to reflect the new structure of the Standard.

Introduction

BC1   The International Accounting Standards Committee (IASC) issued the first version of IAS 1 *Disclosure of Accounting Policies* in 1975. It was reformatted in 1994 and superseded in 1997 by IAS 1 *Presentation of Financial Statements.*[1] In 2003 the International Accounting Standards Board revised IAS 1 as part of the Improvements project and in 2005 the Board amended it as a consequence of issuing IFRS 7 *Financial Instruments: Disclosures*. In 2007 the Board revised IAS 1 again as part of its project on financial statement presentation. This Basis for Conclusions summarises the Board's considerations in reaching its conclusions on revising IAS 1 in 2003, on amending it in 2005 and revising it in 2007. It includes reasons for accepting some approaches and rejecting others. Individual Board members gave greater weight to some factors than to others.

The Improvements project—revision of IAS 1 (2003)

BC2   In July 2001 the Board announced that, as part of its initial agenda of technical projects, it would undertake a project to improve a number of standards, including IAS 1. The project was undertaken in the light of queries and criticisms raised in relation to the standards by securities regulators, professional accountants and other interested parties. The objectives of the Improvements project were to reduce or eliminate alternatives, redundancies and conflicts within standards, to deal with some convergence issues and to make other improvements. The Board's intention was not to reconsider the fundamental approach to the presentation of financial statements established by IAS 1 in 1997.

BC3   In May 2002 the Board published an exposure draft of proposed *Improvements to International Accounting Standards*, which contained proposals to revise IAS 1. The Board received more than 160 comment letters. After considering the responses the Board issued in 2003 a revised version of IAS 1. In its revision the Board's main objectives were:

---

1   IASC did not publish a Basis for Conclusions.

(a) to provide a framework within which an entity assesses how to present fairly the effects of transactions and other events, and assesses whether the result of complying with a requirement in an IFRS would be so misleading that it would not give a fair presentation;

(b) to base the criteria for classifying liabilities as current or non-current solely on the conditions existing at the balance sheet date;

(c) to prohibit the presentation of items of income and expense as 'extraordinary items';

(d) to specify disclosures about the judgements that management has made in the process of applying the entity's accounting policies, apart from those involving estimations, and that have the most significant effect on the amounts recognised in the financial statements; and

(e) to specify disclosures about sources of estimation uncertainty at the balance sheet date that have a significant risk of causing a material adjustment to the carrying amounts of assets and liabilities within the next financial year.

BC4 The following sections summarise the Board's considerations in reaching its conclusions as part of its Improvements project in 2003:

(a) departures from IFRSs (paragraphs BC23–BC30)

(b) criterion for exemption from requirements (paragraphs BC34–BC36)

(c) effect of events after the reporting period on the classification of liabilities (paragraphs BC39–BC48)

(d) results of operating activities (paragraphs BC55 and BC56)

(e) minority interest (paragraph BC59)[2]

(f) extraordinary items (paragraphs BC60–BC64)

(g) disclosure of the judgements management has made in the process of applying the entity's accounting policies (paragraphs BC77 and BC78)

(h) disclosure of major sources of estimation uncertainty (paragraphs BC79–BC84).

Amendment to IAS 1—*Capital Disclosures* (2005)

BC5 In August 2005 the Board issued an Amendment to IAS 1—*Capital Disclosures*. The amendment added to IAS 1 requirements for disclosure of:

(a) the entity's objectives, policies and processes for managing capital.

(b) quantitative data about what the entity regards as capital.

---

2 In January 2008 the IASB issued an amended IAS 27 *Consolidated and Separate Financial Statements*, which amended 'minority interest' to 'non-controlling interests'. The consolidation requirements in IAS 27 were superseded by IFRS 10 *Consolidated Financial Statements* issued in May 2011. The term 'non-controlling interests' and the requirements for non-controlling interests were not changed.

(c)   whether the entity has complied with any capital requirements; and if it has not complied, the consequences of such non-compliance.

BC6   The following sections summarise the Board's considerations in reaching its conclusions as part of its amendment to IAS 1 in 2005:

(a)   disclosures about capital (paragraphs BC85–BC89)

(b)   objectives, policies and processes for managing capital (paragraphs BC90 and BC91)

(c)   externally imposed capital requirements (paragraphs BC92–BC97)

(d)   internal capital targets (paragraphs BC98–BC100).

Amendments to IAS 32 and IAS 1—*Puttable Financial Instruments and Obligations Arising on Liquidation* (2008)

BC6A   In July 2006 the Board published an exposure draft of proposed amendments to IAS 32 and IAS 1 relating to the classification of puttable instruments and instruments with obligations arising only on liquidation. The Board subsequently confirmed the proposals and in February 2008 issued an amendment that now forms part of IAS 1.

Presentation of Items of Other Comprehensive Income (Amendments to IAS 1)

BC6B   In May 2010 the Board published an exposure draft of proposed amendments to IAS 1 relating to the presentation of items of other comprehensive income (OCI). The Board subsequently modified and confirmed the proposals and in June 2011 issued *Presentation of Items of Other Comprehensive Income* (Amendments to IAS 1). The amendments were developed in a joint project with the US national standard-setter, the Financial Accounting Standards Board (FASB), with the aim of aligning the presentation of OCI so that information in financial statements prepared by entities using IFRSs and entities using US generally accepted accounting principles (GAAP) can be more easily compared.

Financial statement presentation—Joint project

BC7   In September 2001 the Board added to its agenda the performance reporting project (in March 2006 renamed the 'financial statement presentation project'). The objective of the project was to enhance the usefulness of information presented in the income statement. The Board developed a possible new model for reporting income and expenses and conducted preliminary testing. Similarly, in the United States, the Financial Accounting Standards Board (FASB) added a project on performance reporting to its agenda in October 2001, developed its model and conducted preliminary testing. Constituents raised concerns about both models and about the fact that they were different.

BC8   In April 2004 the Board and the FASB decided to work on financial statement presentation as a joint project. They agreed that the project should address presentation and display not only in the income statement, but also in the other statements that, together with the income statement, would constitute a complete set of financial statements – the balance sheet, the statement of changes in equity, and the cash flow statement. The Board decided to approach the project in two phases. Phase A would address the statements that constitute a complete set of financial statements and the periods for which they are required to be presented. Phase B would be undertaken jointly with the FASB and would address more fundamental issues relating to presentation and display of information in the financial statements, including:

(a)   consistent principles for aggregating information in each financial statement.

(b)   the totals and subtotals that should be reported in each financial statement.

(c)   whether components of other comprehensive income should be reclassified to profit or loss and, if so, the characteristics of the transactions and events that should be reclassified and when reclassification should be made.

(d)   whether the direct or the indirect method of presenting operating cash flows provides more useful information.

BC9   In March 2006, as a result of its work in phase A, the Board published an exposure draft of proposed amendments to IAS 1 – *A Revised Presentation*. The Board received more than 130 comment letters. The exposure draft proposed amendments that affected the presentation of owner changes in equity and the presentation of comprehensive income, but did not propose to change the recognition, measurement or disclosure of specific transactions and other events required by other IFRSs. It also proposed to bring IAS 1 largely into line with the US standard – SFAS 130 *Reporting Comprehensive Income*. After considering the responses to the exposure draft the Board issued a revised version of IAS 1. The FASB decided to consider phases A and B issues together, and therefore did not publish an exposure draft on phase A.

BC10   The following sections summarise the Board's considerations in reaching its conclusions as part of its revision in 2007:

(a)   general purpose financial statements (paragraphs BC11–BC13)

(b)   titles of financial statements (paragraphs BC14–BC21)

(c)   equal prominence (paragraph BC22)

(d)   a statement of financial position as at the beginning of the earliest comparative period (paragraphs BC31 and BC32)

(e)   IAS 34 *Interim Financial Reporting* (paragraph BC33)

(f)   reporting owner and non-owner changes in equity (paragraphs BC37 and BC38)

(g)   reporting comprehensive income (paragraphs BC49–BC54)

(h)   subtotal for profit or loss (paragraphs BC57 and BC58)

(i)   other comprehensive income-related tax effects (paragraphs BC65–BC68)

(j)   reclassification adjustments (paragraphs BC69–BC73)

(k)   effects of retrospective application or retrospective restatement (paragraph BC74)

(l)   presentation of dividends (paragraph BC75)

(m)   IAS 7 *Cash Flow Statements* (paragraph BC76)

(n)   presentation of measures per share (paragraphs BC101–BC104)

(o)   effective date and transition (paragraph BC105)

(p)   differences from SFAS 130 (paragraph BC106).

Definitions

General purpose financial statements (paragraph 7)

BC11   The exposure draft of 2006 proposed a change to the explanatory paragraph of what 'general purpose financial statements' include, in order to produce a more generic definition of a set of financial statements. Paragraph 7 of the exposure draft stated:

> General purpose financial statements include those that are presented separately or within other *public* documents such as a *regulatory filing* or report to shareholders. [emphasis added]

BC12   Respondents expressed concern about the proposed change. They argued that it could be understood as defining as general purpose financial statements any financial statement or set of financial statements filed with a regulator and could capture documents other than annual reports and prospectuses. They saw this change as expanding the scope of IAS 1 to documents that previously would not have contained all of the disclosures required by IAS 1. Respondents pointed out that the change would particularly affect some entities (such as small private companies and subsidiaries of public companies with no external users of financial reports) that are required by law to place their financial statements on a public file.

BC13   The Board acknowledged that in some countries the law requires entities, whether public or private, to report to regulatory authorities and include information in those reports that could be beyond the scope of IAS 1. Because the Board did not intend to extend the definition of general purpose financial statements, it decided to eliminate the explanatory paragraph of what 'general purpose financial statements' include, while retaining the definition of 'general purpose financial statements'.

Definition of Material (paragraph 7)

Background

BC13A   The Board was informed at the *Discussion Forum on Financial Reporting Disclosure* it hosted in January 2013,[3] through feedback on the amendments to IAS 1 in the 2014 Exposure Draft *Disclosure Initiative*, the 2017 Discussion Paper *Disclosure Initiative—Principles of Disclosure*, and from other sources, that entities experience difficulties in making materiality judgements when preparing financial statements.

BC13B   The feedback indicated that difficulties in making materiality judgements are generally behavioural rather than related to the definition of material. That feedback indicated that some entities apply the disclosure requirements in IFRS Standards mechanically, using them as a checklist for disclosures in their financial statements, rather than applying their judgement to determine what information is material. Some entities have said that it is easier to use a checklist approach than to apply judgement because of management resource constraints, and because following a mechanical approach means that their judgement is less likely to be challenged by auditors, regulators or users of their financial statements. Similarly, some entities say that they prefer to be cautious when deciding whether to omit disclosures to avoid the risk of being challenged by these parties.

BC13C   The Board concluded that these behavioural difficulties could best be addressed by providing guidance to help entities make materiality judgements, rather than by making substantive changes to the definition of material. Consequently, in September 2017 the Board issued IFRS Practice Statement 2 *Making Materiality Judgements* (Materiality Practice Statement).

BC13D   Although many stakeholders agreed that substantive changes to the definition of material were unnecessary, the Board received some feedback that the definition of material might encourage entities to disclose immaterial information in their financial statements. Feedback suggested that the Board should address the following points:

(a)   the phrase 'could influence decisions of users', to describe the threshold for deciding whether information is material, may be understood as requiring too much information to be provided, because almost anything 'could' influence the decisions of some users of the financial statements, even if such a possibility were remote;

(b)   the phrase 'information is material if omitting it or misstating it' focuses only on information that cannot be omitted (material information) and does not also consider the effect of including immaterial information; and

---

3   A Feedback Statement summarising the feedback from that forum and from the Board's related survey on financial reporting disclosure is available on the IFRS Foundation website at http://www.ifrs.org/-/media/project/disclosure-initative/feedback-statement-discussion-forum-financial-reporting-disclosure-may-2013.pdf.

(c)   the definition refers to 'users' but does not specify their characteristics, which is interpreted by some as implying that an entity is required to consider all possible users of its financial statements when deciding what information to disclose.

BC13E   The Board also observed that the wording of the definition of material in the *Conceptual Framework for Financial Reporting* (*Conceptual Framework*) differed from the wording used in IAS 1 *Presentation of Financial Statements* and IAS 8 *Accounting Policies, Changes in Accounting Estimates and Errors*. The Board believes that the substance of the definitions is the same because these definitions all cover the omission or misstatement of information that could influence the decisions of users of financial statements. Nevertheless, the existence of more than one definition of material could be confusing and could imply that the Board intended these definitions to have different meanings and be applied differently in practice.

BC13F   Consequently, the Board decided to propose refinements to the definition of material and to align the definition across IFRS Standards and other publications. The Board observed that these refinements were intended to make the definition easier to understand and were not intended to alter the concept of materiality in IFRS Standards.

Refinements to the definition of material

BC13G   In September 2017 the Board published the Exposure Draft *Definition of Material* (Proposed amendments to IAS 1 and IAS 8) which proposed a revised definition.

BC13H   The Board developed this definition by:

(a)   replacing the description of the threshold 'could influence' with 'could reasonably be expected to influence' to incorporate the existing clarification in paragraph 7 of IAS 1 which states: 'Therefore, the assessment needs to take into account how users with such attributes *could reasonably be expected to be influenced* in making economic decisions' [emphasis added]. This wording helps to address concerns raised by some parties that the threshold 'could influence' in the existing definition of material is too low and might be applied too broadly (see paragraph BC13D(a)).

(b)   using the wording of the definition of material in the *Conceptual Framework*.[4] The Board concluded that this wording was clearer than the definition in IAS 1 and IAS 8. However, the Board decided to refer to 'financial statements' rather than 'financial reports' in the amendments to IAS 1 to be consistent with the scope of that Standard.[5] The *Conceptual Framework* definition also clarifies that the users to whom the definition refers are the primary users of an entity's

---

4   The wording in paragraph 2.11 of the *Conceptual Framework* is: 'Information is material if omitting it or misstating it could influence decisions that the primary users of general purpose financial reports make on the basis of those reports, which provide financial information about a specific reporting entity'.

5   Financial statements are a type of financial report.

financial reports or statements. Referring to the primary users in the definition of material in IAS 1 helps to respond to concerns that the term 'users' may be interpreted too widely (see paragraph BC13D(c)).

(c) including 'obscuring' in the definition of material to incorporate the existing concept in paragraph 30A of IAS 1 which states: 'An entity shall not reduce the understandability of its financial statements by obscuring material information with immaterial information or by aggregating items that have different natures or functions.' Referring to 'obscuring' in the definition of material is intended to respond to concerns that the effect of including immaterial information should also be considered in addition to 'misstating' and 'omitting' (see paragraphs BC13D(a) and (b)).

(d) relocating wording that explains rather than defines material from the definition itself to its explanatory paragraphs. This reorganisation clarifies which requirements are part of the definition and which paragraphs explain the definition.

BC13I Some parties said that the Board should raise the threshold at which information becomes material by replacing 'could' with 'would' in the definition. However, the Board did not do this because it concluded that using 'would' would be a substantive change that might have unintended consequences. For example, 'would influence decisions' might be interpreted as a presumption that information is not material unless it can be proved otherwise, ie for information to be seen as material it would be necessary to prove that the information would influence the decisions of users of the financial statements.

Obscuring information

BC13J Responses to the Exposure Draft *Definition of Material* (Proposed amendments to IAS 1 and IAS 8) indicated strong support for the definition of material to be aligned across the *Conceptual Framework* and IFRS Standards. However, many respondents had some concerns—in particular about including the existing concept of 'obscuring' (as set out in paragraph 30A of IAS 1) in the definition of material in the way proposed in the Exposure Draft. Many respondents thought that if the Board were to include this concept in the definition, then 'obscuring information' would need to be more precisely defined or explained than it was in the Exposure Draft.

BC13K The Board agreed with respondents that the concept of 'obscuring information' is inherently more judgemental than 'omitting' or 'misstating' information and considered removing the concept from the definition of material and its explanatory paragraphs altogether. However, the Board decided that the benefit of including 'obscuring' in the definition of material outweighed these concerns. Including this concept emphasises that obscuring information can affect the decisions of primary users just as omitting or misstating that information can. In particular, including 'obscuring' in the definition of material addresses concerns that the former definition could be perceived by stakeholders as focusing only on information that cannot be omitted (material information) and not also on why it may be unhelpful to include immaterial information.

BC13L   The Board did not intend to be prescriptive by including the word 'obscuring' in the definition of material and by further clarifying it—the Board is not prohibiting entities from disclosing immaterial information or introducing a required quality of explanations and information included in the financial statements. For example, the Board did not intend the addition of the word 'obscure' to prevent entities from providing information required by local regulators or prescribe how an entity organises and communicates information in the financial statements. Rather, the Board's intention is to:

(a)   support the existing requirements in paragraph 30A of IAS 1 which state that 'An entity shall not reduce the understandability of its financial statements by obscuring material information with immaterial information or by aggregating material items that have different natures or functions'; and

(b)   help entities and other stakeholders avoid instances in which material information may be obscured by immaterial information to the extent that it has a similar effect on the primary users of financial statements to omitting or misstating that information.

Other amendments

BC13M   While the revised definition of material in IAS 1 has been based on the definition of material in the *Conceptual Framework*, some adjustments were made to the *Conceptual Framework* definition to improve clarity and consistency between the *Conceptual Framework* and the IFRS Standards. The definition in the *Conceptual Framework*, however, continues to refer to 'financial reports' rather than 'financial statements'.

BC13N   The Board also made amendments to the Materiality Practice Statement to align it with the revised definition of material. The Materiality Practice Statement continues to refer to both 'immaterial' and 'not material' as the Board concluded that these terms have the same meaning.

BC13O   As explained in paragraph BC13H, the amendments incorporate existing guidance from the *Conceptual Framework* and IAS 1 and are not substantive changes to the existing requirements in IFRS Standards. For this reason, the Board concluded that the guidance in the Materiality Practice Statement and the *Conceptual Framework* would not be affected by these amendments.

BC13P   Because the amendments are based on existing guidance, they are not considered to be substantive changes. The Board consequently concluded that amendments to other requirements in IFRS Standards are unnecessary, other than to update the definition of material where it is quoted or referred to directly.

BC13Q   The Board also decided that it was unnecessary to change all instances of 'economic decisions' to 'decisions', and all instances of 'users' to 'the primary users of financial statements' in IFRS Standards. In its Conceptual Framework project, the Board clarified that:

(a) the terms 'primary users' and 'users' are intended to be interpreted the same way and both refer to existing and potential investors, lenders and other creditors who must rely on general purpose financial reports for much of the financial information they need (see the footnote to paragraph 1.5 of the *Conceptual Framework*); and

(b) the terms 'decisions' and 'economic decisions' are intended to be interpreted the same way.

Likely effects of the amendments to IFRS Standards

BC13R In the Board's view, the amendments will improve understanding of the definition of material by:

(a) aligning the wording of the definition in IFRS Standards and the *Conceptual Framework* to avoid the potential for confusion arising from different definitions;

(b) incorporating supporting requirements in IAS 1 into the definition to give them more prominence and clarify their applicability; and

(c) providing existing guidance on the definition of material in one place, together with the definition.

BC13S The Board concluded that the amendments do not change existing requirements substantively because:

(a) the refinements to the definition of material:

(i) are based on wording in the *Conceptual Framework* that is similar to but clearer than the existing definition in IAS 1 and IAS 8 (see paragraphs BC13E and BC13H(b)); and

(ii) incorporate wording that already exists in IAS 1 (see paragraphs BC13H(a), (c) and (d)).

(b) the clarification that 'users' are the primary users and the description of their characteristics have been taken from the *Conceptual Framework*.

(c) the inclusion of 'obscuring information' reflects the existing requirement, as set out in paragraph 30A of IAS 1, that an entity shall not reduce the understandability of its financial statements by obscuring material information. This amendment is not expected to substantively change an entity's decisions about whether information is material—in no circumstances would obscuring information influence the decisions of users, if omitting or misstating the same information would have no influence on those decisions.

Consequently, the Board expects that the effect of the revised definition will be to help entities to make better materiality judgements.

Effective date of the amendments

BC13T Because the amendments do not substantively change existing requirements, the Board decided that:

 (a) prospective application is appropriate;

 (b) a long implementation period is unnecessary; and

 (c) early adoption of the amendments should be permitted.

Financial statements

Complete set of financial statements

Titles of financial statements (paragraph 10)

BC14 The exposure draft of 2006 proposed changes to the titles of some of the financial statements – from 'balance sheet' to 'statement of financial position', from 'income statement' to 'statement of profit or loss' and from 'cash flow statement' to 'statement of cash flows'. In addition, the exposure draft proposed a 'statement of recognised income and expense' and that all owner changes in equity should be included in a 'statement of changes in equity'. The Board did not propose to make any of these changes of nomenclature mandatory.

BC15 Many respondents opposed the proposed changes, pointing out that the existing titles had a long tradition and were well understood. However, the Board reaffirmed its view that the proposed new titles better reflect the function of each financial statement, and pointed out that an entity could choose to use other titles in its financial report.

BC16 The Board reaffirmed its conclusion that the title 'statement of financial position' not only better reflects the function of the statement but is consistent with the *Framework for the Preparation and Presentation of Financial Statements*, which contains several references to 'financial position'. Paragraph 12 of the *Framework*[6] states that the objective of financial statements is to provide information about the financial position, performance and changes in financial position of an entity; paragraph 19 of the *Framework* states that information about financial position is primarily provided in a balance sheet. In the Board's view, the title 'balance sheet' simply reflects that double entry bookkeeping requires debits to equal credits. It does not identify the content or purpose of the statement. The Board also noted that 'financial position' is a well-known and accepted term, as it has been used in auditors' opinions internationally for more than 20 years to describe what the 'balance sheet' presents. The Board decided that aligning the statement's title with its content and the opinion rendered by the auditor would help the users of financial statements.

---

6 References to the *Framework* in this Basis for Conclusions are to the IASC's *Framework for the Preparation and Presentation of Financial Statements*, adopted by the Board in 2001 and in effect when the Standard was revised and amended.

BC17   As to the other statements, respondents suggested that renaming the balance sheet the 'statement of financial position' implied that the 'cash flow statement' and the 'statement of recognised income and expense' do not also reflect an entity's financial position. The Board observed that although the latter statements reflect changes in an entity's financial position, neither can be called a 'statement of changes in financial position', as this would not depict their true function and objective (ie to present cash flows and performance, respectively). The Board acknowledged that the titles 'income statement' and 'statement of profit or loss' are similar in meaning and could be used interchangeably, and decided to retain the title 'income statement' as this is more commonly used.

BC18   The title of the proposed new statement, the 'statement of recognised income and expense', reflects a broader content than the former 'income statement'. The statement encompasses both income and expenses recognised in profit or loss and income and expenses recognised outside profit or loss.

BC19   Many respondents opposed the title 'statement of recognised income and expense', objecting particularly to the use of the term 'recognised'. The Board acknowledged that the term 'recognised' could also be used to describe the content of other primary statements as 'recognition', explained in paragraph 82 of the *Framework*, is 'the process of incorporating in the balance sheet or income statement an item that meets the definition of an element and satisfies the criteria for recognition set out in paragraph 83.' Many respondents suggested the term 'statement of comprehensive income' instead.

BC20   In response to respondents' concerns and to converge with SFAS 130, the Board decided to rename the new statement a 'statement of comprehensive income'. The term 'comprehensive income' is not defined in the *Framework* but is used in IAS 1 to describe the change in equity of an entity during a period from transactions, events and circumstances other than those resulting from transactions with owners in their capacity as owners. Although the term 'comprehensive income' is used to describe the aggregate of all components of comprehensive income, including profit or loss, the term 'other comprehensive income' refers to income and expenses that under IFRSs are included in comprehensive income but excluded from profit or loss.

BC20A   In May 2010 the Board published the exposure draft *Presentation of Items of Other Comprehensive Income* (proposed amendments to IAS 1) relating to the presentation of items of other comprehensive income (OCI). One of the proposals in the exposure draft related to the title of the statement containing profit or loss and other comprehensive income. The Board proposed this change so that it would be clear that the statement had two components: profit or loss and other comprehensive income. A majority of the respondents to the exposure draft supported the change and therefore the Board confirmed the proposal in June 2011. IAS 1 allows preparers to use other titles for the statement that reflect the nature of their activities.

BC20B   Several other IFRSs refer to the 'statement of comprehensive income'. The Board considered whether it should change all such references to 'statement of profit or loss and other comprehensive income'. The Board noted that the terminology used in IAS 1 is not mandatory and that 'statement of comprehensive income' is one of the examples used in the standard. The Board decided that there was little benefit in replacing the title 'statement of comprehensive income' in other IFRSs or 'income statement' with the 'statement of profit or loss'. However, the Board did change the terminology when an IFRS made reference to the two-statement option.

BC21   In finalising its revision, the Board confirmed that the titles of financial statements used in this Standard would not be mandatory. The titles will be used in future IFRSs but are not required to be used by entities in their financial statements. Some respondents to the exposure draft expressed concern that non-mandatory titles will result in confusion. However, the Board believes that making use of the titles non-mandatory will allow time for entities to implement changes gradually as the new titles become more familiar.

Equal prominence (paragraphs 11 and 12)

BC22   The Board noted that the financial performance of an entity is not assessed by reference to a single financial statement or a single measure within a financial statement. The Board believes that the financial performance of an entity can be assessed only after all aspects of the financial statements are taken into account and understood in their entirety. Accordingly, the Board decided that in order to help users of the financial statements to understand the financial performance of an entity comprehensively, all financial statements within the complete set of financial statements should be presented with equal prominence.

Departures from IFRSs (paragraphs 19–24)

BC23   IAS 1 (as issued in 1997) permitted an entity to depart from a requirement in a Standard 'in the extremely rare circumstances when management concludes that compliance with a requirement in a Standard would be misleading, and therefore that departure from a requirement is necessary to achieve a fair presentation' (paragraph 17, now paragraph 19). When such a departure occurred, paragraph 18 (now paragraph 20) required extensive disclosure of the facts and circumstances surrounding the departure and the treatment adopted.

BC24   The Board decided to clarify in paragraph 15 of the Standard that for financial statements to present fairly the financial position, financial performance and cash flows of an entity, they must represent faithfully the effects of transactions and other events in accordance with the definitions and recognition criteria for assets, liabilities, income and expenses set out in the *Framework*.

BC25　　The Board decided to limit the occasions on which an entity should depart from a requirement in an IFRS to the extremely rare circumstances in which management concludes that compliance with the requirement would be so misleading that it would conflict with the objective of financial statements set out in the *Framework*. Guidance on this criterion states that an item of information would conflict with the objective of financial statements when it does not represent faithfully the transactions, other events or conditions that it either purports to represent or could reasonably be expected to represent and, consequently, it would be likely to influence economic decisions made by users of financial statements.

BC26　　These amendments provide a framework within which an entity assesses how to present fairly the effects of transactions, other events and conditions, and whether the result of complying with a requirement in an IFRS would be so misleading that it would not give a fair presentation.

BC27　　The Board considered whether IAS 1 should be silent on departures from IFRSs. The Board decided against making that change, because it would remove the Board's capability to specify the criteria under which departures from IFRSs should occur.

BC28　　Departing from a requirement in an IFRS when considered necessary to achieve a fair presentation would conflict with the regulatory framework in some jurisdictions. The revised IAS 1 takes into account the existence of different regulatory requirements. It requires that when an entity's circumstances satisfy the criterion described in paragraph BC25 for departure from a requirement in an IFRS, the entity should proceed as follows:

(a)　　When the relevant regulatory framework requires — or otherwise does not prohibit — a departure from the requirement, the entity should make that departure and the disclosures set out in paragraph 20.

(b)　　When the relevant regulatory framework prohibits departure from the requirement, the entity should, to the maximum extent possible, reduce the perceived misleading aspects of compliance by making the disclosures set out in paragraph 23.

This amendment enables entities to comply with the requirements of IAS 1 when the relevant regulatory framework prohibits departures from accounting standards, while retaining the principle that entities should, to the maximum extent possible, ensure that financial statements provide a fair presentation.

BC29　　After considering the comments received on the exposure draft of 2002, the Board added to IAS 1 a requirement in paragraph 21 to disclose the effect of a departure from a requirement of an IFRS in a prior period on the current period's financial statements. Without this disclosure, users of the entity's financial statements could be unaware of the continuing effects of prior period departures.

BC30   In view of the strict criteria for departure from a requirement in an IFRS, IAS 1 includes a rebuttable presumption that if other entities in similar circumstances comply with the requirement, the entity's compliance with the requirement would not be so misleading that it would conflict with the objective of financial statements set out in the *Framework*.

Materiality and aggregation (paragraphs 29–31)

BC30A   The Board was informed at the Discussion Forum *Financial Reporting Disclosure* in January 2013, in its related survey and by other sources, that there are difficulties applying the concept of materiality in practice. Some are of the view that these difficulties contribute to a disclosure problem, namely, that there is both too much irrelevant information and not enough relevant information in financial statements. A number of factors have been identified for why materiality may not be applied well in practice. One of these is that the guidance on materiality in IFRS is not clear.

BC30B   Some think that the statement in IAS 1 that an entity need not provide a specific disclosure if the information is not material means that an entity does not need to present an item in the statement(s) of profit or loss and other comprehensive income, the statement of financial position, the statement of cash flows and the statement of changes in equity, but must instead disclose it in the notes. However, the Board noted that the concept of materiality is applicable to financial statements, which include the notes, and not only to those statements.

BC30C   Some are of the view that when IFRS states that a specific disclosure is required, the concept of materiality does not apply to those disclosure requirements, ie disclosures specifically identified in IFRS are required irrespective of whether they result in material information. In addition, some people think that when a line item is presented, or a material item is otherwise recognised, in the statement(s) of profit or loss and other comprehensive income and the statement of financial position, all the disclosures in IFRS specified for that item must be disclosed. The Board observed that paragraph 31 of IAS 1 is clear that the concept of materiality applies to specific disclosures required by an IFRS and therefore an entity does not have to disclose information required by an IFRS if that information would not be material.

BC30D   The Board understands that these misconceptions may have arisen because of the wording that is used when specifying presentation or disclosure requirements in IFRS; for example, the use of the words 'as a minimum'. For this reason, the Board removed the phrase 'as a minimum' in paragraph 54 of IAS 1, which lists line items for presentation in the statement of financial position. This also makes the requirement broadly consistent with the corresponding requirement in paragraph 82 of IAS 1 for the profit or loss section of the statement of comprehensive income or the statement of profit or loss.

BC30E   On the basis of its observations and conclusions set out in paragraphs BC30A–BC30D, the Board added a new paragraph, paragraph 30A, and amended paragraph 31 of IAS 1.

BC30F   Paragraph 30A was added to IAS 1 to highlight that when an entity decides how it aggregates information in the financial statements, it should take into consideration all relevant facts and circumstances. Paragraph 30A emphasises that an entity should not reduce the understandability of its financial statements by providing immaterial information that obscures the material information in financial statements or by aggregating material items that have different natures or functions. Obscuring material information with immaterial information in financial statements makes the material information less visible and therefore makes the financial statements less understandable. The amendments do not actually prohibit entities from disclosing immaterial information, because the Board thinks that such a requirement would not be operational; however, the amendments emphasise that disclosure should not result in material information being obscured.

BC30G   The Exposure Draft *Disclosure Initiative* (Proposed amendments to IAS 1) (the 'March 2014 Exposure Draft'), which was published in March 2014, also proposed that an entity should not 'disaggregate' information in a manner that obscures useful information. Disaggregation is often used to describe the process of expanding totals, subtotals and line items into further items that themselves may reflect the aggregated results of transactions or other events. Because the process of expanding totals, subtotals and line items is more likely to increase the transparency of information rather than obscuring it, the Board decided not to include the term disaggregation in paragraph 30A of IAS 1. In addition, the Board was of the view that items resulting from the process of disaggregation that themselves reflect the aggregated results of transactions would be covered by paragraphs 29–31 of IAS 1.

BC30H   The Board amended paragraph 31 of IAS 1 to highlight that materiality also applies to disclosures specifically required by IFRS. In addition, to highlight that materiality not only involves decisions about excluding information from the financial statements, the Board amended paragraph 31 to reiterate the notion already stated in paragraph 17(c) of IAS 1 that materiality also involves decisions about whether to include additional information in the financial statements. Consequently, an entity should make additional disclosures when compliance with the specific requirements in IFRS is insufficient to enable users of financial statements to understand the impact of particular transactions, other events and conditions on the entity's financial position and financial performance.

BC30I   The Board noted that the definition of 'material' in paragraph 7 of IAS 1 discusses omissions or misstatements of items being material if they could individually or collectively influence economic decisions. The Board considered making amendments to paragraph 31 of IAS 1 to say that an entity need not provide a specific disclosure if the information provided by that disclosure is not material, either individually or collectively. However, the Board decided not to make that change since the definition of material already incorporates the notions of individual and collective assessment and, therefore, reference to the term material in paragraph 31 is sufficient to incorporate this concept.

BC30J   In the March 2014 Exposure Draft the Board proposed to use the term 'present' to refer to line items, subtotals and totals on the statement(s) of profit or loss and other comprehensive income, the statement of financial position, the statement of cash flows and the statement of changes in equity, and the term 'disclose' to mean information in the notes. However, respondents to the March 2014 Exposure Draft did not support the distinction between present and disclose because they considered that the terminology has not been used consistently throughout IAS 1 and that any changes in how these terms are used should be done as part of a comprehensive review of IAS 1. Because of this, and because making such comprehensive changes to IAS 1 would be outside the scope of these amendments, the Board did not finalise the proposed changes regarding use of the terms present and disclose.

Comparative information

A statement of financial position as at the beginning of the earliest comparative period (paragraph 39)

BC31   The exposure draft of 2006 proposed that a statement of financial position as at the beginning of the earliest comparative period should be presented as part of a complete set of financial statements. This statement would provide a basis for investors and creditors to evaluate information about the entity's performance during the period. However, many respondents expressed concern that the requirement would unnecessarily increase disclosures in financial statements, or would be impracticable, excessive and costly.

BC32   By adding a statement of financial position as at the beginning of the earliest comparative period, the exposure draft proposed that an entity should present three statements of financial position and two of each of the other statements. Considering that financial statements from prior years are readily available for financial analysis, the Board decided to require only two statements of financial position, except when the financial statements have been affected by retrospective application or retrospective restatement, as defined in IAS 8 *Accounting Policies, Changes in Accounting Estimates and Errors*, or when a reclassification has been made. In those circumstances three statements of financial position are required.

Clarification of requirements for comparative information

BC32A   In *Annual Improvements 2009–2011 Cycle* (issued in May 2012) the Board addressed a request to clarify the requirements for providing comparative information for:

(a)   the comparative requirements for the opening statement of financial position when an entity changes accounting policies, or makes retrospective restatements or reclassifications, in accordance with IAS 8 *Accounting Policies, Changes in Accounting Estimates and Errors*; and

(b)   the requirements for providing comparative information when an entity provides financial statements beyond the minimum comparative information requirements.

Opening statement of financial position

BC32B   In *Annual Improvements 2009–2011 Cycle* (issued in May 2012) the Board addressed a request to clarify the appropriate date for the opening statement of financial position. The Board decided to amend the current requirements in IAS 1 that relate to the presentation of a statement of financial position for the beginning of the earliest comparative period presented in cases of changes in accounting policies, retrospective restatements or reclassifications to clarify that the appropriate date for the opening statement of financial position is the beginning of the preceding period.

BC32C   The Board also decided to change the previous requirements so that related notes to this opening statement of financial position are no longer required to be presented. The Board's decision to give this relief was based on the fact that circumstances in which an entity changes an accounting policy, or makes a retrospective restatement or a reclassification in accordance with IAS 8, are considered narrow, specific and limited. However, the circumstances in which an entity chooses to provide additional financial statements (ie on a voluntary basis) can be viewed as more generic and may arise for different reasons. Accordingly, this relief is not available when additional financial statements are provided on a voluntary basis.

BC32D   The Board added the guidance in paragraph 40A(a) to clarify when an opening statement of financial position provides useful information and, should therefore be required. Paragraph 40A(b) is a reminder that the concept of materiality should be considered in applying the guidance in paragraph 40A(a). The Board noted that the entity would still be required to disclose the information required by IAS 8 for changes in accounting policies and retrospective restatements.

Comparative information beyond minimum requirements

BC32E   In *Annual Improvements 2009–2011 Cycle* (issued in May 2012) the Board addressed a request to clarify the requirements for providing comparative information. Specifically, the Board was asked to consider whether an entity should be required to present a complete set of financial statements when it provides financial statements beyond the minimum comparative information requirements (ie additional comparative information). In response to this request, the Board decided to clarify that additional financial statement information need not be presented in the form of a complete set of financial statements for periods beyond the minimum requirements. The Board also noted that additional comparative information might include:

(a)   information that is presented voluntarily, beyond the information that is included within a complete set of financial statements; or

(b)   comparative information that is required by law or other regulations but that is not required by IFRSs.

BC32F   The Board also decided to amend paragraphs 38–41 of IAS 1 to clarify that, when additional comparative information (that is not required by IFRSs) is provided by an entity, this information should be presented in accordance with IFRSs and the entity should present comparative information in the related notes for that additional information. The Board determined that requiring full notes for additional information in accordance with paragraph 38C is necessary to ensure that the additional information that the entity provides is balanced and results in financial statements that achieve a fair presentation.

BC32G   In the light of the concerns raised by interested parties, the Board decided that the amendments should be introduced through the Annual Improvements process instead of through the Financial Statement Presentation project, so that the changes could be made more quickly.

IAS 34 *Interim Financial Reporting*

BC33   The Board decided not to reflect in paragraph 8 of IAS 34 (ie the minimum components of an interim financial report) its decision to require the inclusion of a statement of financial position as at the beginning of the earliest comparative period in a complete set of financial statements. IAS 34 has a year-to-date approach to interim reporting and does not replicate the requirements of IAS 1 in terms of comparative information.

Criterion for exemption from requirements (paragraphs 41–44)

BC34   IAS 1 as issued in 1997 specified that when the presentation or classification of items in the financial statements is amended, comparative amounts should be reclassified unless it is impracticable to do so. Applying a requirement is impracticable when the entity cannot apply it after making every reasonable effort to do so.

BC35   The exposure draft of 2002 proposed a different criterion for exemption from particular requirements. For the reclassification of comparative amounts, and its proposed new requirement to disclose key assumptions and other sources of estimation uncertainty at the end of the reporting period (discussed in paragraphs BC79–BC84), the exposure draft proposed that the criterion for exemption should be that applying the requirements would require undue cost or effort.

BC36   In the light of respondents' comments on the exposure draft, the Board decided that an exemption based on management's assessment of undue cost or effort was too subjective to be applied consistently by different entities. Moreover, balancing costs and benefits was a task for the Board when it sets accounting requirements rather than for entities when they apply them. Therefore, the Board retained the 'impracticability' criterion for exemption. This affects the exemptions now set out in paragraphs 41–43 and 131 of IAS 1. Impracticability is the only basis on which IFRSs allow specific exemptions from applying particular requirements when the effect of applying them is material.[7]

Reporting owner and non-owner changes in equity

BC37   The exposure draft of 2006 proposed to separate changes in equity of an entity during a period arising from transactions with owners in their capacity as owners (ie all owner changes in equity) from other changes in equity (ie non-owner changes in equity). All owner changes in equity would be presented in the statement of changes in equity, separately from non-owner changes in equity.

BC38   Most respondents welcomed this proposal and saw this change as an improvement of financial reporting, by increasing the transparency of those items recognised in equity that are not reported as part of profit or loss. However, some respondents pointed out that the terms 'owner' and 'non-owner' were not defined in the exposure draft, the *Framework* or elsewhere in IFRSs, although they are extensively used in national accounting standards. They also noted that the terms 'owner' and 'equity holder' were used interchangeably in the exposure draft. The Board decided to adopt the term 'owner' and use it throughout IAS 1 to converge with SFAS 130, which uses the term in the definition of 'comprehensive income'.

Statement of financial position

Information to be presented in the statement of financial position (paragraphs 54–55A)

BC38A   Paragraph 54 of IAS 1 lists line items that are required to be presented in the statement of financial position. The Board has been informed that some have interpreted that list as prescriptive and that those line items cannot be disaggregated. There is also a perception by some that IFRS prevents them from presenting subtotals in addition to those specifically required by IFRS.

BC38B   Paragraph 55 of IAS 1 requires an entity to present additional line items, headings and subtotals when their presentation is relevant to an understanding of the entity's financial position. This highlights that the line items listed for presentation in paragraph 54 of IAS 1 should be disaggregated and that subtotals should be presented, when relevant. Paragraphs 78 and 98 of IAS 1 give examples of potential disaggregations of line items in the statement of financial position and the statement(s) of profit or loss and other comprehensive income.

---

7   In 2006 the IASB issued IFRS 8 *Operating Segments*. As explained in paragraphs BC46 and BC47 of the Basis for Conclusions on IFRS 8, that IFRS includes an exemption from some requirements if the necessary information is not available and the cost to develop it would be excessive.

BC38C   Consequently, the Board:

      (a)   removed the wording 'as a minimum' from paragraph 54 of IAS 1 (see paragraph BC30D) to address the possible misconception that this wording prevents entities from aggregating the line items specified in paragraph 54 if those specified line items are immaterial; and

      (b)   clarified that the presentation requirements in paragraphs 54–55 may be fulfilled by disaggregating a specified line item.

BC38D   The Board noted that there are similar presentation requirements in paragraph 85 of IAS 1 for the statement(s) of profit or loss and other comprehensive income. The Board therefore amended those requirements to make them consistent.

BC38E   Some respondents to the proposals suggested that the Board should make clear that the line items listed in paragraph 54 of IAS 1 are required 'when material'. The Board decided not to state that the line items are only required when material, because materiality is generally not referenced specifically in disclosure requirements in IFRS and so including a specific reference in this case could make it less clear that materiality applies to other disclosure requirements.

BC38F   The Board understands that some are concerned about the presentation of subtotals, in addition to those specified in IFRS, in the statement of financial position and the statement(s) of profit or loss and other comprehensive income. Those with this concern think that some subtotals can be misleading, for example, because they are given undue prominence. The Board noted that paragraphs 55 and 85 of IAS 1 require the presentation of subtotals when such presentation is relevant to an understanding of the entity's financial position or financial performance.

BC38G   The Board therefore included additional requirements in IAS 1 to help entities apply paragraphs 55 and 85. These additional requirements supplement the existing guidance on fair presentation in paragraphs 15 and 17 of IAS 1. They are designed to clarify the factors that should be considered when fairly presenting subtotals in the statement of financial position and the statement(s) of profit or loss and other comprehensive income. Specifically, the subtotal should:

      (a)   be comprised of line items made up of amounts recognised and measured in accordance with IFRS.

      (b)   be understandable. It should be clear what line items are included in the subtotal by the way that the subtotal is presented and labelled. For example, if an entity presents a commonly reported subtotal, but excludes items that would normally be considered as part of that subtotal, the label should reflect what has been excluded.

      (c)   be consistent from period to period. The subtotal should be consistently presented and calculated from period to period (in accordance with paragraph 45 of IAS 1), subject to possible changes in accounting policy or estimates assessed in accordance with IAS 8.

(d)   not be displayed with more prominence than those subtotals and totals required in IFRS for either the statement(s) of profit or loss and other comprehensive income or the statement of financial position.

Current assets and current liabilities (paragraphs 68 and 71)

BC38H   As part of its improvements project in 2007, the Board identified inconsistent guidance regarding the current/non-current classification of derivatives. Some might read the guidance included in paragraph 71 as implying that financial liabilities classified as held for trading in accordance with IAS 39 *Financial Instruments: Recognition and Measurement*[8] are always required to be presented as current.

BC38I   The Board expects the criteria set out in paragraph 69 to be used to assess whether a financial liability should be presented as current or non-current. The 'held for trading' category in paragraph 9 of IAS 39[9] is for measurement purposes and includes financial assets and liabilities that may not be held primarily for trading purposes.

BC38J   The Board reaffirmed that if a financial liability is held primarily for trading purposes it should be presented as current regardless of its maturity date. However, a financial liability that is not held for trading purposes, such as a derivative that is not a financial guarantee contract or a designated hedging instrument, should be presented as current or non-current on the basis of its settlement date. For example, derivatives that have a maturity of more than twelve months and are expected to be held for more than twelve months after the reporting period should be presented as non-current assets or liabilities.

BC38K   Therefore, the Board decided to remove the identified inconsistency by amending the examples of current liabilities in paragraph 71. The Board also amended paragraph 68 in respect of current assets to remove a similar inconsistency.

BC38L–   [Deleted]
BC38P

Current liabilities (paragraphs 69–76B)

Effect of events after the reporting period (paragraphs 69–76)

BC39   Paragraph 63 of IAS 1 (as issued in 1997) included the following:

> An enterprise should continue to classify its long-term interest-bearing liabilities as non-current, even when they are due to be settled within twelve months of the balance sheet date if:
>
> (a)   the original term was for a period of more than twelve months;
>
> (b)   the enterprise intends to refinance the obligation on a long-term basis; and

---

8   IFRS 9 *Financial Instruments* replaced IAS 39. IFRS 9 applies to all items that were previously within the scope of IAS 39. This paragraph refers to matters relevant when IAS 1 was issued.

9   IFRS 9 *Financial Instruments* replaced IAS 39. IFRS 9 applies to all items that were previously within the scope of IAS 39. This paragraph refers to matters relevant when IAS 1 was issued.

(c)   that intention is supported by an agreement to refinance, or to reschedule payments, which is completed before the financial statements are authorised for issue.

BC40   Paragraph 65 stated:

> Some borrowing agreements incorporate undertakings by the borrower (covenants) which have the effect that the liability becomes payable on demand if certain conditions related to the borrower's financial position are breached. In these circumstances, the liability is classified as non-current only when:
>
> (a)   the lender has agreed, prior to the authorisation of the financial statements for issue, not to demand payment as a consequence of the breach; and
>
> (b)   it is not probable that further breaches will occur within twelve months of the balance sheet date.

BC41   The Board considered these requirements and concluded that refinancing, or the receipt of a waiver of the lender's right to demand payment, that occurs after the reporting period should not be taken into account in the classification of a liability.

BC42   Therefore, the exposure draft of 2002 proposed:

(a)   to amend paragraph 63 to specify that a long-term financial liability due to be settled within twelve months of the balance sheet date should not be classified as a non-current liability because an agreement to refinance, or to reschedule payments, on a long-term basis is completed after the balance sheet date and before the financial statements are authorised for issue. This amendment would not affect the classification of a liability as non-current when the entity has, under the terms of an existing loan facility, the discretion to refinance or roll over its obligations for at least twelve months after the balance sheet date.

(b)   to amend paragraph 65 to specify that a long-term financial liability that is payable on demand because the entity breached a condition of its loan agreement should be classified as current at the balance sheet date even if the lender has agreed after the balance sheet date, and before the financial statements are authorised for issue, not to demand payment as a consequence of the breach. However, if the lender has agreed by the balance sheet date to provide a period of grace within which the entity can rectify the breach and during which the lender cannot demand immediate repayment, the liability is classified as non-current if it is due for settlement, without that breach of the loan agreement, at least twelve months after the balance sheet date and:

(i)   the entity rectifies the breach within the period of grace; or

(ii)   when the financial statements are authorised for issue, the period of grace is incomplete and it is probable that the breach will be rectified.

BC43   Some respondents disagreed with these proposals. They advocated classifying a liability as current or non-current according to whether it is expected to use current assets of the entity, rather than strictly on the basis of its date of maturity and whether it is callable at the end of the reporting period. In their view, this would provide more relevant information about the liability's future effect on the timing of the entity's resource flows.

BC44   However, the Board decided that the following arguments for changing paragraphs 63 and 65 were more persuasive:

(a)   refinancing a liability after the balance sheet date does not affect the entity's liquidity and solvency *at the balance sheet date*, the reporting of which should reflect contractual arrangements in force on that date. Therefore, it is a non-adjusting event in accordance with IAS 10 *Events after the Balance Sheet Date* and should not affect the presentation of the entity's balance sheet.

(b)   it is illogical to adopt a criterion that 'non-current' classification of short-term obligations expected to be rolled over for at least twelve months after the balance sheet date depends on whether the roll-over is at the discretion of the entity, and then to provide an exception based on refinancing occurring after the balance sheet date.

(c)   in the circumstances set out in paragraph 65, unless the lender has waived its right to demand immediate repayment or granted a period of grace within which the entity may rectify the breach of the loan agreement, the financial condition of the entity at the balance sheet date was that the entity did not hold an absolute right to defer repayment, based on the terms of the loan agreement. The granting of a waiver or a period of grace changes the terms of the loan agreement. Therefore, an entity's receipt from the lender, after the balance sheet date, of a waiver or a period of grace of at least twelve months does not change the nature of the liability to non-current until it occurs.

BC45   IAS 1 now includes the amendments proposed in 2002, with one change. The change relates to the classification of a long-term loan when, at the end of the reporting period, the lender has provided a period of grace within which a breach of the loan agreement can be rectified, and during which period the lender cannot demand immediate repayment of the loan.

BC46   The exposure draft proposed that such a loan should be classified as non-current if it is due for settlement, without the breach, at least twelve months after the balance sheet date and:

(a)   the entity rectifies the breach within the period of grace; or

(b)   when the financial statements are authorised for issue, the period of grace is incomplete and it is probable that the breach will be rectified.

BC47   After considering respondents' comments, the Board decided that the occurrence or probability of a rectification of a breach after the reporting period is irrelevant to the conditions existing at the end of the reporting period. The revised IAS 1 requires that, for the loan to be classified as non-current, the period of grace must end at least twelve months after the reporting period (see paragraph 75). Therefore, the conditions (a) and (b) in paragraph BC46 are redundant.

BC48　The Board considered arguments that if a period of grace to remedy a breach of a long-term loan agreement is provided before the end of the reporting period, the loan should be classified as non-current regardless of the length of the period of grace. These arguments are based on the view that, at the end of the reporting period, the lender does not have an unconditional legal right to demand repayment before the original maturity date (ie if the entity remedies the breach during the period of grace, it is entitled to repay the loan on the original maturity date). However, the Board concluded that an entity should classify a loan as non-current only if it has an unconditional right to defer settlement of the loan for at least twelve months after the reporting period. This criterion focuses on the legal rights of the entity, rather than those of the lender.

Right to defer settlement for at least twelve months (paragraphs 69(d) and 72A–76)

BC48A　Paragraph 69(d) specifies that, to classify a liability as non-current, an entity must have the right to defer settlement of the liability for at least twelve months after the reporting period. In January 2020, the Board amended aspects of this classification principle and related application requirements in paragraphs 73–76. The Board made the amendments in response to a request to reconcile apparent contradictions between paragraph 69(d)—which required an 'unconditional right' to defer settlement—and paragraph 73— which referred to an entity that 'expects, and has the discretion, to' refinance or roll over an obligation.

BC48B　The Board added to the classification principle in paragraph 69(d) and the example in paragraph 73 clarification that an entity's right to defer settlement must exist 'at the end of the reporting period'. The need for the right to exist at the end of the reporting period was already illustrated in the examples in paragraphs 74 and 75 but was not stated explicitly in the classification principle.

BC48C　The Board also observed that the classification principle requires an assessment of whether an entity has the right to defer settlement of a liability and not whether the entity will exercise that right. Accordingly:

(a)　the Board amended paragraph 73, which discusses liabilities an entity has a right to roll over for at least twelve months after the reporting period. The Board deleted from paragraph 73 a suggestion that to classify such a liability as non-current, an entity must not only have the right to roll over the liability but also expect to exercise that right. The Board also aligned the terminology by replacing 'discretion' with 'right' in paragraph 73.

(b)   the Board added paragraph 75A, which explicitly clarifies that classification is unaffected by management intentions or expectations, or by settlement of the liability within twelve months after the reporting period.

BC48D   The Board considered whether an entity's right to defer settlement needs to be unconditional. The Board noted that rights to defer settlement of a loan are rarely unconditional—they are often conditional on compliance with covenants. The Board decided that if an entity's right to defer settlement of a liability is subject to the entity complying with specified conditions, the entity has a right to defer settlement of the liability at the end of the reporting period if it complies with those conditions at that date. Accordingly, the Board:

(a)   deleted the word 'unconditional' from the classification principle in paragraph 69(d); and

(b)   added paragraph 72A to clarify that if an entity's right to defer settlement is subject to compliance with specified conditions:

(i)   the right exists at the end of the reporting period only if the entity complies with those conditions at the end of the reporting period; and

(ii)   the entity must comply with the conditions at the end of the reporting period even if the lender does not test compliance until a later date.

BC48E   The Board considered whether to specify how management assesses an entity's compliance with a condition relating to the entity's cumulative financial performance (for example, profit) for a period extending beyond the reporting period. The Board concluded that comparing the entity's actual performance up to the end of the reporting period with the performance required over a longer period would not provide useful information—one of these measures would have to be adjusted to make the two comparable. However, the Board decided not to specify a method of adjustment because any single method could be inappropriate in some situations.

Settlement (paragraphs 76A–76B)

BC48F   While developing the amendments discussed in paragraphs BC48A–BC48E, the Board considered whether a liability is 'settled' when it is rolled over under an existing loan facility. The Board concluded that rolling over a liability does not constitute settlement because it is the extension of an existing liability, which does not involve any transfer of economic resources. The Board also observed that a liability is defined as an obligation 'to transfer an economic resource' and that some types of liabilities are settled by transferring economic resources other than cash. For example, performance obligations within the scope of IFRS 15 *Revenue from Contracts with Customers* are settled by transferring promised goods or services. The Board decided it would be helpful to clarify those aspects of the meaning of the term 'settlement' and so added paragraph 76A.

BC48G   While considering the meaning of the term settlement, the Board also considered liabilities an entity will or may settle by issuing its own equity instruments or, in other words, by converting the liability to equity. In *Improvements to IFRSs* issued in 2009, the Board had added to paragraph 69(d) a statement that 'terms of a liability that could, at the option of the counterparty, result in its settlement by the issue of equity instruments do not affect its classification'. The effect of this statement is that a bond that the holder may convert to equity before maturity is classified as current or non-current according to the terms of the bond, without considering the possibility of earlier settlement by conversion to equity.

BC48H   The Board concluded that, when it had added the statement about counterparty conversion options in 2009, it had intended the statement to apply only to liabilities that include a counterparty conversion option that meets the definition of an equity instrument and, applying IAS 32 *Financial Instruments: Presentation*, is recognised separately from the host liability as the equity component of a compound financial instrument. The Board further concluded that, in other cases—that is, if an obligation to transfer equity instruments is classified applying IAS 32 as a liability or part of a liability—the transfer of equity instruments would constitute settlement of the liability for the purpose of classifying it as current or non-current. To reflect those conclusions, the Board moved the statement about counterparty conversion options from paragraph 69(d) to new paragraph 76B and clarified its scope.

Statement of comprehensive income

Reporting comprehensive income (paragraph 81)

BC49   The exposure draft of 2006 proposed that all non-owner changes in equity should be presented in a single statement or in two statements. In a single-statement presentation, all items of income and expense are presented together. In a two-statement presentation, the first statement ('income statement') presents income and expenses recognised in profit or loss and the second statement ('statement of comprehensive income') begins with profit or loss and presents, in addition, items of income and expense that IFRSs require or permit to be recognised outside profit or loss. Such items include, for example, translation differences related to foreign operations and gains or losses on available-for-sale financial assets.[10] The statement of comprehensive income does not include transactions with owners in their capacity as owners. Such transactions are presented in the statement of changes in equity.

BC50   Respondents to the exposure draft had mixed views about whether the Board should permit a choice of displaying non-owner changes in equity in one statement or two statements. Many respondents agreed with the Board's proposal to maintain the two-statement approach and the single-statement approach as alternatives and a few urged the Board to mandate one of them. However, most respondents preferred the two-statement approach because it

---

10   IFRS 9 *Financial Instruments* eliminated the category of available-for-sale financial assets. This paragraph refers to matters relevant when IAS 1 was issued.

distinguishes profit or loss and total comprehensive income; they believe that with the two-statement approach, the 'income statement' remains a primary financial statement. Respondents supported the presentation of two separate statements as a transition measure until the Board develops principles to determine the criteria for inclusion of items in profit or loss or in other comprehensive income.

BC51 The exposure draft of 2006 expressed the Board's preference for a single statement of all non-owner changes in equity. The Board provided several reasons for this preference. All items of non-owner changes in equity meet the definitions of income and expenses in the *Framework*. The *Framework* does not define profit or loss, nor does it provide criteria for distinguishing the characteristics of items that should be included in profit or loss from those items that should be excluded from profit or loss. Therefore, the Board decided that it was conceptually correct for an entity to present all non-owner changes in equity (ie all income and expenses recognised in a period) in a single statement because there are no clear principles or common characteristics that can be used to separate income and expenses into two statements.

BC52 However, in the Board's discussions with interested parties, it was clear that many were strongly opposed to the concept of a single statement. They argued that there would be undue focus on the bottom line of the single statement. In addition, many argued that it was premature for the Board to conclude that presentation of income and expense in a single statement was an improvement in financial reporting without also addressing the other aspects of presentation and display, namely deciding what categories and line items should be presented in a statement of recognised income and expense.

BC53 In the light of these views, although it preferred a single statement, the Board decided that an entity should have the choice of presenting all income and expenses recognised in a period in one statement or in two statements. An entity is prohibited from presenting components of income and expense (ie non-owner changes in equity) in the statement of changes in equity.

BC54 Many respondents disagreed with the Board's preference and thought that a decision at this stage would be premature. In their view the decision about a single-statement or two-statement approach should be subject to further consideration. They urged the Board to address other aspects of presentation and display, namely deciding which categories and line items should be presented in a 'statement of comprehensive income'. The Board reaffirmed its reasons for preferring a single-statement approach and agreed to address other aspects of display and presentation in the next stage of the project.

BC54A In *Presentation of Items of Other Comprehensive Income* published in May 2010 the Board proposed to eliminate the option to present all items of income and expense recognised in a period in two statements, thereby requiring presentation in a continuous statement displaying two sections: *profit or loss* and *other comprehensive income*. The Board also proposed to require items of OCI to be classified into items that might be reclassified (recycled) to profit or loss in subsequent periods and items that would not be reclassified subsequently.

BC54B   In its deliberations on financial instruments and pensions the Board discussed the increasing importance of consistent presentation of items of OCI. Both projects will increase the number of items presented in OCI, particularly items that will not be reclassified subsequently to profit or loss. Therefore the Board thought it important that all income and expenses that are components of the total non-owner changes in equity should be presented transparently.

BC54C   The Board has no plans to eliminate profit or loss as a measure of performance. Profit or loss will be presented separately and will remain the required starting point for the calculation of earnings per share.

BC54D   The Board had previously received responses to similar proposals for a single statement of comprehensive income. In October 2008 the Board and the FASB jointly published a discussion paper, *Preliminary Views on Financial Statement Presentation*. In that paper, the boards proposed eliminating the alternative presentation formats for comprehensive income and to require an entity to present comprehensive income and its components in a single statement. The boards asked for views on that proposal. The responses were split on whether an entity should present comprehensive income and its components in a single statement or in two separate statements. In general, respondents supporting a single statement of comprehensive income said that it would lead to greater transparency, consistency and comparability. Furthermore, the process of calculating financial ratios would be made easier.

BC54E   Respondents disagreeing with the proposal for a single statement of comprehensive income urged the boards to defer any changes to the guidance on the statement of comprehensive income until the boards had completed a project to revise the guidance on what items should be presented in OCI. Those respondents also said that a single statement would undermine the importance of profit or loss by making it a subtotal and that presenting total comprehensive income as the last number in the statement would confuse users. They also feared that requiring all items of income and expense to be presented in a single statement was the first step by the boards towards eliminating the notion of profit or loss. In addition, they argued that the items that are presented in OCI are different from items presented in profit or loss. Therefore they preferred either to keep the presentation of profit or loss separate from the presentation of OCI or to allow management to choose to present them either in a single statement or in two statements.

BC54F   In the responses to the exposure draft of May 2010 many of the respondents objected to the proposals to remove the option to present all items of income and expense in two statements. The arguments used by those objecting were much the same as those received on the discussion paper. However, many respondents, regardless of their views on the proposed amendments, said that the Board should establish a conceptual basis for what should be presented in OCI. Those opposed to a continuous statement cited OCI's lack of a conceptual definition and therefore believed that OCI should not be presented in close proximity to profit or loss because this would confuse users. However, users generally said that the lack of a conceptual framework made it difficult to distinguish the underlying economics of items reported in profit or loss (net income) from items reported in other comprehensive income. Although users also asked for a conceptual framework for OCI, most supported the notion of a single statement of comprehensive income.

BC54G   Another issue on which many respondents commented was the reclassification (recycling) of OCI items. Those respondents said that in addition to addressing the conceptual basis for the split between profit or loss and OCI the Board should set principles for which OCI items should be reclassified (recycled) to profit or loss and when they should be reclassified. The Board acknowledges that it has not set out a conceptual basis for how it determines whether an item should be presented in OCI or in profit or loss. It also agrees that it has not set out principles to determine whether items should be reclassified to profit or loss. Those matters were not within the scope of this project, which focused on presentation, and therefore the Board has not addressed them at this time. However, the Board is consulting on its future agenda, which could lead to those matters becoming part of the work programme.

BC54H   In the light of the response the Board confirmed in June 2011 the requirement for items of OCI to be classified into items that will not be reclassified (recycled) to profit or loss in subsequent periods and items that might be reclassified.

BC54I   The Board also decided not to mandate the presentation of profit or loss in a continuous statement of profit or loss and other comprehensive income but to maintain an option to present two statements. The Board did this in the light of the negative response to its proposal for a continuous statement and the resistance to this change signified by a majority of respondents.

BC54J   The FASB also proposed in its exposure draft to mandate a continuous statement of comprehensive income but decided in the light of the responses not to go as far as mandating a single statement and instead to allow the two-statement option. Nevertheless, the changes made by the FASB are a significant improvement for US GAAP, which previously allowed an option to present OCI items in stockholders' equity or in the notes to the financial statements.

BC54K   In 2013 the IFRS Interpretations Committee reported to the Board that there was uncertainty about the requirements in paragraph 82A of IAS 1 for presenting an entity's share of items of other comprehensive income of associates and joint ventures accounted for using the equity method. The Board agreed that paragraph 82A allowed for diverse interpretations, and therefore decided to amend IAS 1 as follows:

(a)   to clarify that paragraph 82A requires entities to present the share of other comprehensive income of associates and joint ventures accounted for using the equity method, separated into the share of items that:

(i)   will not be reclassified subsequently to profit or loss; and

(ii)   will be reclassified subsequently to profit or loss when specific conditions are met.

(b)   to amend the Guidance on Implementing IAS 1 to reflect the clarification of paragraph 82A.

The Board noted that whether an amount is reclassified to profit or loss is determined by the nature of the underlying item. It also noted that the timing of reclassification is usually determined by the actions of the investee. It may however also be triggered by the investor, which would be the case on the disposal of the investee by the investor.

BC54L   The feedback received on the March 2014 Exposure Draft included requests for the Board to clarify whether the investor's share of the other comprehensive income of its associate or joint venture should be presented net or gross of tax and the applicability of the guidance in paragraphs 90–91 of IAS 1 in this regard. The Board noted that an investor's share of other comprehensive income of associates or joint ventures is after tax and non-controlling interests of the associate or joint venture, as illustrated in the Guidance on Implementing IAS 1. It also noted that the disclosure requirements in paragraphs 90–91 do not apply to the tax of the associate or joint venture that is already reflected in the investor's share of other comprehensive income of the associate or joint venture. However, the Board noted that if the investor itself is liable for tax in respect of its share of other comprehensive income of the associate or joint venture, then paragraphs 90–91 would apply to this tax. Therefore, the Board decided not to add additional guidance to IAS 1 on this topic.

Results of operating activities

BC55   IAS 1 omits the requirement in the 1997 version to disclose the results of operating activities as a line item in the income statement. 'Operating activities' are not defined in IAS 1, and the Board decided not to require disclosure of an undefined item.

BC56   The Board recognises that an entity may elect to disclose the results of operating activities, or a similar line item, even though this term is not defined. In such cases, the Board notes that the entity should ensure that the amount disclosed is representative of activities that would normally be regarded as 'operating'. In the Board's view, it would be misleading and would impair the comparability of financial statements if items of an operating nature were excluded from the results of operating activities, even if that had been industry practice. For example, it would be inappropriate to exclude items clearly related to operations (such as inventory write-downs and restructuring and relocation expenses) because they occur irregularly or infrequently or are unusual in amount. Similarly, it would be inappropriate to exclude items on the grounds that they do not involve cash flows, such as depreciation and amortisation expenses.

Subtotal for profit or loss (paragraph 82)

BC57 As revised, IAS 1 requires a subtotal for profit or loss in the statement of comprehensive income. If an entity chooses to present comprehensive income by using two statements, it should begin the second statement with profit or loss—the bottom line of the first statement (the 'income statement')—and display the components of other comprehensive income immediately after that. The Board concluded that this is the best way to achieve the objective of equal prominence (see paragraph BC22) for the presentation of income and expenses. An entity that chooses to display comprehensive income in one statement should include profit or loss as a subtotal within that statement.

BC58 The Board acknowledged that the items included in profit or loss do not possess any unique characteristics that allow them to be distinguished from items that are included in other comprehensive income. However, the Board and its predecessor have required some items to be recognised outside profit or loss. The Board will deliberate in the next stage of the project how items of income and expense should be presented in the statement of comprehensive income.

Information to be presented in the profit or loss section or the statement of profit or loss (paragraphs 85–85B)

BC58A In December 2014 the Board issued *Disclosure Initiative* (Amendments to IAS 1). Those amendments included amendments to paragraph 85 of IAS 1 and the addition of paragraph 85A. These amendments are consistent with similar amendments to the requirements for the statement of financial position and therefore the Basis for Conclusions for these amendments has been included in the section dealing with that statement (see paragraphs BC38A–BC38G).

BC58B In addition to those amendments, the Board decided to require entities to present line items in the statement(s) of profit or loss and other comprehensive income that reconcile any subtotals presented in accordance with paragraphs 85–85A of IAS 1 with those that are required in IFRS for the statement(s) of profit or loss and other comprehensive income. Consequently, it added paragraph 85B to IAS 1. The purpose of this requirement is to help users of financial statements understand the relationship between the subtotals presented in accordance with paragraph 85 and the specific totals and subtotals required in IFRS to address concerns that that relationship would not be clear. The Board noted that such a requirement is already implicit in existing IFRS requirements. IFRS requires entities to present aggregated information as line items when such presentation provides material information. Consequently, because all recognised items of income and expense must be included in the statement(s) of profit or loss and other comprehensive income totals, any intervening line items and subtotals necessarily reconcile. However, the Board decided to make the requirement more explicit for the statement(s) of profit or loss and other comprehensive income to help users of financial statements understand the relationship between subtotals and totals presented in the statement(s) of profit or loss and other comprehensive income.

Minority interest (paragraph 83)[11]

BC59   IAS 1 requires the 'profit or loss attributable to minority interest' and 'profit or loss attributable to owners of the parent' each to be presented in the income statement in accordance with paragraph 83. These amounts are to be presented as allocations of profit or loss, not as items of income or expense. A similar requirement has been added for the statement of changes in equity, in paragraph 106(a). These changes are consistent with IAS 27 *Consolidated and Separate Financial Statements*, which requires that in a consolidated balance sheet (now called 'statement of financial position'), minority interest is presented within equity because it does not meet the definition of a liability in the *Framework*.

Extraordinary items (paragraph 87)

BC60   IAS 8 *Net Profit or Loss for the Period, Fundamental Errors and Changes in Accounting Policies* (issued in 1993) required extraordinary items to be disclosed in the income statement separately from the profit or loss from ordinary activities. That standard defined 'extraordinary items' as 'income or expenses that arise from events or transactions that are clearly distinct from the ordinary activities of the enterprise and therefore are not expected to recur frequently or regularly'.

BC61   In 2002, the Board decided to eliminate the concept of extraordinary items from IAS 8 and to prohibit the presentation of items of income and expense as 'extraordinary items' in the income statement and the notes. Therefore, in accordance with IAS 1, no items of income and expense are to be presented as arising from outside the entity's ordinary activities.

BC62   Some respondents to the exposure draft of 2002 argued that extraordinary items should be presented in a separate component of the income statement because they are clearly distinct from all of the other items of income and expense, and because such presentation highlights to users of financial statements the items of income and expense to which the least attention should be given when predicting an entity's future performance.

BC63   The Board decided that items treated as extraordinary result from the normal business risks faced by an entity and do not warrant presentation in a separate component of the income statement. The nature or function of a transaction or other event, rather than its frequency, should determine its presentation within the income statement. Items currently classified as 'extraordinary' are only a subset of the items of income and expense that may warrant disclosure to assist users in predicting an entity's future performance.

---

11   In January 2008 the IASB issued an amended IAS 27 *Consolidated and Separate Financial Statements*, which amended 'minority interest' to 'non-controlling interests'. The consolidation requirements in IAS 27 were superseded by IFRS 10 *Consolidated Financial Statements* issued in May 2011. The term 'non-controlling interests' and the requirements for non-controlling interests were not changed.

BC64 Eliminating the category of extraordinary items eliminates the need for arbitrary segregation of the effects of related external events – some recurring and others not – on the profit or loss of an entity for a period. For example, arbitrary allocations would have been necessary to estimate the financial effect of an earthquake on an entity's profit or loss if it occurs during a major cyclical downturn in economic activity. In addition, paragraph 97 of IAS 1 requires disclosure of the nature and amount of material items of income and expense.

Other comprehensive income—related tax effects (paragraphs 90 and 91)

BC65 The exposure draft of 2006 proposed to allow components of 'other recognised income and expense' (now 'other comprehensive income') to be presented before tax effects ('gross presentation') or after their related tax effects ('net presentation'). The 'gross presentation' facilitated the traceability of other comprehensive income items to profit or loss, because items of profit or loss are generally displayed before tax. The 'net presentation' facilitated the identification of other comprehensive income items in the equity section of the statement of financial position. A majority of respondents supported allowing both approaches. The Board reaffirmed its conclusion that components of other comprehensive income could be displayed either (a) net of related tax effects or (b) before related tax effects.

BC66 Regardless of whether a pre-tax or post-tax display was used, the exposure draft proposed to require disclosure of the amount of income tax expense or benefit allocated separately to individual components of other comprehensive income, in line with SFAS 130. Many respondents agreed in principle with this disclosure, because they agreed that it helped to improve the clarity and transparency of such information, particularly when components of other comprehensive income are taxed at rates different from those applied to profit or loss.

BC67 However, most respondents expressed concern about having to trace the tax effect for each one of the components of other comprehensive income. Several observed that the tax allocation process is arbitrary (eg it may involve the application of subjectively determined tax rates) and some pointed out that this information is not readily available for some industries (eg the insurance sector), where components of other comprehensive income are multiple and tax allocation involves a high degree of subjectivity. Others commented that they did not understand why tax should be attributed to components of comprehensive income line by line, when this is not a requirement for items in profit or loss.

BC68 The Board decided to maintain the disclosure of income tax expense or benefit allocated to each component of other comprehensive income. Users of financial statements often requested further information on tax amounts relating to components of other comprehensive income, because tax rates often differed from those applied to profit or loss. The Board also observed that an entity should have such tax information available and that a disclosure requirement would therefore not involve additional cost for preparers of financial statements.

BC68A   In its exposure draft *Presentation of Items of Other Comprehensive Income* published in May 2010 the Board proposed requiring that income tax on items presented in OCI should be allocated between items that will not be subsequently reclassified to profit or loss and those that might be reclassified, if the items in OCI are presented before tax. Most respondents agreed with this proposal as this would be in line with the existing options in IAS 1 regarding presentation of income tax on OCI items. Therefore the Board confirmed the proposal in June 2011.

Reclassification adjustments (paragraphs 92–96)

BC69   In the exposure draft of 2006, the Board proposed that an entity should separately present reclassification adjustments. These adjustments are the amounts reclassified to profit or loss in the current period that were previously recognised in other comprehensive income. The Board decided that adjustments necessary to avoid double-counting items in total comprehensive income when those items are reclassified to profit or loss in accordance with IFRSs. The Board's view was that separate presentation of reclassification adjustments is essential to inform users of those amounts that are included as income and expenses in different periods – as income or expenses in other comprehensive income in previous periods and as income or expenses in profit or loss in the current period. Without such information, users may find it difficult to assess the effect of reclassifications on profit or loss and to calculate the overall gain or loss associated with available-for-sale financial assets,[12] cash flow hedges and on translation or disposal of foreign operations.

BC70   Most respondents agreed with the Board's decision and believe that the disclosure of reclassification adjustments is important to understanding how components recognised in profit or loss are related to other items recognised in equity in two different periods. However, some respondents suggested that the Board should use the term 'recycling', rather than 'reclassification' as the former term is more common. The Board concluded that both terms are similar in meaning, but decided to use the term 'reclassification adjustment' to converge with the terminology used in SFAS 130.

BC71   The exposure draft proposed to allow the presentation of reclassification adjustments in the statement of recognised income and expense (now 'statement of comprehensive income') or in the notes. Most respondents supported this approach.

BC72   Some respondents noted some inconsistencies in the definition of 'reclassification adjustments' in the exposure draft (now paragraphs 7 and 93 of IAS 1). Respondents suggested that the Board should expand the definition in paragraph 7 to include gains and losses recognised in current periods in addition to those recognised in earlier periods, to make the definition consistent with paragraph 93. They commented that, without

---

12 IFRS 9 *Financial Instruments* eliminated the category of available-for-sale financial assets. This paragraph refers to matters relevant when IAS 1 was issued.

clarification, there could be differences between interim and annual reporting, for reclassifications of items that arise in one interim period and reverse out in a different interim period within the same annual period.

BC73 The Board decided to align the definition of reclassification adjustments with SFAS 130 and include an additional reference to 'current periods' in paragraph 7.

Statement of changes in equity

Effects of retrospective application or retrospective restatement (paragraph 106(b))

BC74 Some respondents to the exposure draft of 2006 asked the Board to clarify whether the effects of retrospective application or retrospective restatement, as defined in IAS 8, should be regarded as non-owner changes in equity. The Board noted that IAS 1 specifies that these effects are included in the statement of changes in equity. However, the Board decided to clarify that the effects of retrospective application or retrospective restatement are not changes in equity in the period, but provide a reconciliation between the previous period's closing balance and the opening balance in the statement of changes in equity.

Reconciliation for each component of other comprehensive income (paragraphs 106(d)(ii) and 106A)

BC74A Paragraph 106(d) requires an entity to provide a reconciliation of changes in each component of equity. In *Improvements to IFRSs* issued in May 2010, the Board clarified that entities may present the required reconciliations for each component of other comprehensive income either in the statement of changes in equity or in the notes to the financial statements.

Presentation of dividends (paragraph 107)

BC75 The Board reaffirmed its conclusion to require the presentation of dividends in the statement of changes in equity or in the notes, because dividends are distributions to owners in their capacity as owners and the statement of changes in equity presents all owner changes in equity. The Board concluded that an entity should not present dividends in the statement of comprehensive income because that statement presents non-owner changes in equity.

Statement of cash flows

IAS 7 *Cash Flow Statements* (paragraph 111)

BC76 The Board considered whether the operating section of an indirect method statement of cash flows should begin with total comprehensive income instead of profit or loss as is required by IAS 7 *Cash Flow Statements*. When components of other comprehensive income are non-cash items, they would become reconciling items in arriving at cash flows from operating activities and would add items to the statement of cash flows without adding information content. The Board concluded that an amendment to IAS 7 is not required; however, as mentioned in paragraph BC14 the Board decided to relabel this financial statement as 'statement of cash flows'.

Notes

Structure (paragraphs 112–116)

BC76A   The Board is aware that some had interpreted paragraph 114 of IAS 1 as requiring a specific order for the notes. Paragraph 114 stated that 'an entity normally presents notes in the [following] order' and then listed a particular order for the notes. Some think that the use of 'normally' makes it difficult for an entity to vary the order of the notes from the one that is listed in paragraph 114; for example, by disclosing the notes in order of importance or disclosing related information together in sections.

BC76B   Investors' feedback indicates that some investors prefer an entity to vary the order of the notes from the one that is listed in paragraph 114 of IAS 1. Other investors would prefer entities to use that order because they think it will increase comparability between periods and across entities.

BC76C   The Board considered the use of the word normally in paragraph 114 of IAS 1 and concluded that it was not intended that entities be required to disclose their notes in that order. Instead, it thinks that the order listed was intended to provide an example of how an entity could order the notes and that the term normal was not meant to imply that alternative ordering of the notes is 'abnormal'. The Board therefore amended IAS 1 to clarify that the order listed in paragraph 114 is an example of how an entity could order or group its notes in a systematic manner. The Board also made amendments to clarify that significant accounting policies do not need to be disclosed in one note, but instead can be included with related information in other notes.

BC76D   The Board also noted the requirement in paragraph 113 of IAS 1 for entities to, as far as practicable, present the notes in a systematic manner. In the Board's view, this means that there must be a system or reason behind the ordering and grouping of the notes. For example, notes could be ordered by importance to the entity, in the order line items are presented in the financial statements or a combination of both. The Board amended paragraph 113 to clarify that an entity should consider the effect on the understandability and comparability of its financial statements when determining the order of the notes. The Board acknowledged that there is a trade-off between understandability and comparability; for example, ordering notes to increase understandability could mean that comparability, including consistency, between entities and periods is reduced. In particular, the Board acknowledged that consistency in the order of the notes for a specific entity from period to period is important. The Board noted that it would generally be helpful for users of financial statements if the ordering of notes by an entity is consistent and noted that it does not expect the order of an entity's notes to change frequently. A change in the order of the notes previously determined to be an optimal mix of understandability and comparability should generally result from a specific event or transaction, such as a change in business. The Board also noted that the existing requirements in paragraph 45 of IAS 1 for consistency of presentation still apply.

BC76E   The Board also observed that electronic versions of financial statements can make it easier to search for, locate and compare information within the financial statements, between periods and between entities.

Disclosure of accounting policies (paragraphs 117–121)

BC76F   Paragraph 117 of IAS 1 requires significant accounting policies to be disclosed and gives guidance, along with paragraphs 118–124 of IAS 1, about what a significant accounting policy could be. That guidance includes, as examples of significant accounting policies, the income taxes accounting policy and the foreign currency accounting policy.

BC76G   Some suggested that it is not helpful to provide the income taxes accounting policy as an example of a policy that users of financial statements would expect to be disclosed. Being liable to income taxes is typical for many entities and it was not clear, from the example, what aspect of the entity's operations would make a user of financial statements expect an accounting policy on income taxes to be disclosed. Consequently, the example does not illustrate why an accounting policy on income taxes is significant. The Board also thought that the foreign currency accounting policy example in paragraph 120 of IAS 1 was unhelpful for the same reasons and therefore deleted the income taxes and foreign currency examples.

Disclosure of the judgements that management has made in the process of applying the entity's accounting policies (paragraphs 122–124)

BC77   The revised IAS 1 requires disclosure of the judgements, apart from those involving estimations, that management has made in the process of applying the entity's accounting policies and that have the most significant effect on the amounts recognised in the financial statements (see paragraph 122). An example of these judgements is how management determines whether financial assets are held-to-maturity investments.[13] The Board decided that disclosure of the most important of these judgements would enable users of financial statements to understand better how the accounting policies are applied and to make comparisons between entities regarding the basis on which managements make these judgements.

BC78   Comments received on the exposure draft of 2002 indicated that the purpose of the proposed disclosure was unclear. Accordingly, the Board amended the disclosure explicitly to exclude judgements involving estimations (which are the subject of the disclosure in paragraph 125) and added another four examples of the types of judgements disclosed (see paragraphs 123 and 124).

---

13 IFRS 9 *Financial Instruments* eliminated the category of held-to-maturity financial assets. This paragraph refers to matters relevant when IAS 1 was issued.

Disclosure of major sources of estimation uncertainty (paragraphs 125–133)

BC79   IAS 1 requires disclosure of the assumptions concerning the future, and other major sources of estimation uncertainty at the end of the reporting period, that have a significant risk of causing a material adjustment to the carrying amounts of assets and liabilities within the next financial year. For those assets and liabilities, the proposed disclosures include details of:

    (a)   their nature; and

    (b)   their carrying amount as at the end of the reporting period (see paragraph 125).

BC80   Determining the carrying amounts of some assets and liabilities requires estimation of the effects of uncertain future events on those assets and liabilities at the end of the reporting period. For example, in the absence of recently observed market prices used to measure the following assets and liabilities, future-oriented estimates are necessary to measure the recoverable amount of classes of property, plant and equipment, the effect of technological obsolescence of inventories, provisions subject to the future outcome of litigation in progress, and long-term employee benefit liabilities such as pension obligations. These estimates involve assumptions about items such as the risk adjustment to cash flows or discount rates used, future changes in salaries and future changes in prices affecting other costs. No matter how diligently an entity estimates the carrying amounts of assets and liabilities subject to significant estimation uncertainty at the end of the reporting period, the reporting of point estimates in the statement of financial position cannot provide information about the estimation uncertainties involved in measuring those assets and liabilities and the implications of those uncertainties for the period's profit or loss.

BC81   The *Framework* states that 'The economic decisions that are made by users of financial statements require an evaluation of the ability of an entity to generate cash and cash equivalents and of the timing and certainty of their generation.' The Board decided that disclosure of information about assumptions and other major sources of estimation uncertainty at the end of the reporting period enhances the relevance, reliability and understandability of the information reported in financial statements. These assumptions and other sources of estimation uncertainty relate to estimates that require management's most difficult, subjective or complex judgements. Therefore, disclosure in accordance with paragraph 125 of the revised IAS 1 would be made in respect of relatively few assets or liabilities (or classes of them).

BC82   The exposure draft of 2002 proposed the disclosure of some 'sources of measurement uncertainty'. In the light of comments received that the purpose of this disclosure was unclear, the Board decided:

    (a)   to amend the subject of that disclosure to 'sources of estimation uncertainty at the end of the reporting period'; and

                                                © IFRS Foundation

(b)   to clarify in the revised Standard that the disclosure does not apply to assets and liabilities measured at fair value based on recently observed market prices (see paragraph 128 of IAS 1).

BC83   When assets and liabilities are measured at fair value on the basis of recently observed market prices, future changes in carrying amounts would not result from using estimates to measure the assets and liabilities at the end of the reporting period. Using observed market prices to measure assets or liabilities obviates the need for estimates at the end of the reporting period. The market prices properly reflect the fair values at the end of the reporting period, even though future market prices could be different. The objective of fair value measurement is to reflect fair value at the measurement date, not to predict a future value.[14]

BC84   IAS 1 does not prescribe the particular form or detail of the disclosures. Circumstances differ from entity to entity, and the nature of estimation uncertainty at the end of the reporting period has many facets. IAS 1 limits the scope of the disclosures to items that have a significant risk of causing a material adjustment to the carrying amounts of assets and liabilities within the next financial year. The longer the future period to which the disclosures relate, the greater the range of items that would qualify for disclosure, and the less specific are the disclosures that could be made about particular assets or liabilities. A period longer than the next financial year might obscure the most relevant information with other disclosures.

Disclosures about capital (paragraphs 134 and 135)

BC85   In July 2004 the Board published an exposure draft—ED 7 *Financial Instruments: Disclosures*. As part of that project, the Board considered whether it should require disclosures about capital.

BC86   The level of an entity's capital and how it manages capital are important factors for users to consider in assessing the risk profile of an entity and its ability to withstand unexpected adverse events. The level of capital might also affect the entity's ability to pay dividends. Consequently, ED 7 proposed disclosures about capital.

BC87   In ED 7 the Board decided that it should not limit the requirements for disclosures about capital to entities that are subject to external capital requirements (eg regulatory capital requirements established by legislation or other regulation). The Board believes that information about capital is useful for all entities, as is evidenced by the fact that some entities set internal capital requirements and norms have been established for some industries. The Board noted that the capital disclosures are not intended to replace disclosures required by regulators. The Board also noted that the financial statements should not be regarded as a substitute for disclosures to regulators (which may not be available to all users) because the function of disclosures made to regulators may differ from the function of those to other users. Therefore, the Board decided that information about capital should be

---

14   IFRS 13 *Fair Value Measurement*, issued in May 2011, defines fair value and contains the requirements for measuring fair value.

required of all entities because it is useful to users of general purpose financial statements. Accordingly, the Board did not distinguish between the requirements for regulated and non-regulated entities.

BC88   Some respondents to ED 7 questioned the relevance of the capital disclosures in an IFRS dealing with disclosures relating to financial instruments. The Board noted that an entity's capital does not relate solely to financial instruments and, thus, capital disclosures have more general relevance. Accordingly, the Board included these disclosures in IAS 1, rather than IFRS 7 *Financial Instruments: Disclosures*, the IFRS resulting from ED 7.

BC89   The Board also decided that an entity's decision to adopt the amendments to IAS 1 should be independent of the entity's decision to adopt IFRS 7. The Board noted that issuing a separate amendment facilitates separate adoption decisions.

Objectives, policies and processes for managing capital (paragraph 136)

BC90   The Board decided that disclosure about capital should be placed in the context of a discussion of the entity's objectives, policies and processes for managing capital. This is because the Board believes that such a discussion both communicates important information about the entity's capital strategy and provides the context for other disclosures.

BC91   The Board considered whether an entity can have a view of capital that differs from what IFRSs define as equity. The Board noted that, although for the purposes of this disclosure capital would often equate with equity as defined in IFRSs, it might also include or exclude some components. The Board also noted that this disclosure is intended to give entities the opportunity to describe how they view the components of capital they manage, if this is different from what IFRSs define as equity.

Externally imposed capital requirements (paragraph 136)

BC92   The Board considered whether it should require disclosure of any externally imposed capital requirements. Such a capital requirement could be:

(a)   an industry-wide requirement with which all entities in the industry must comply; or

(b)   an entity-specific requirement imposed on a particular entity by its prudential supervisor or other regulator.

BC93   The Board noted that some industries and countries have industry-wide capital requirements, and others do not. Thus, the Board concluded that it should not require disclosure of industry-wide requirements, or compliance with such requirements, because such disclosure would not lead to comparability between different entities or between similar entities in different countries.

BC94   The Board concluded that disclosure of the existence and level of entity-specific capital requirements is important information for users, because it informs them about the risk assessment of the regulator. Such disclosure improves transparency and market discipline.

BC95   However, the Board noted the following arguments against requiring disclosure of externally imposed entity-specific capital requirements.

(a)   Users of financial statements might rely primarily on the regulator's assessment of solvency risk without making their own risk assessment.

(b)   The focus of a regulator's risk assessment is for those whose interests the regulations are intended to protect (eg depositors or policyholders). This emphasis is different from that of a shareholder. Thus, it could be misleading to suggest that the regulator's risk assessment could, or should, be a substitute for independent analysis by investors.

(c)   The disclosure of entity-specific capital requirements imposed by a regulator might undermine that regulator's ability to impose such requirements. For example, the information could cause depositors to withdraw funds, a prospect that might discourage regulators from imposing requirements. Furthermore, an entity's regulatory dialogue would become public, which might not be appropriate in all circumstances.

(d)   Because different regulators have different tools available, for example formal requirements and moral suasion, a requirement to disclose entity-specific capital requirements could not be framed in a way that would lead to the provision of information that is comparable across entities.

(e)   Disclosure of capital requirements (and hence, regulatory judgements) could hamper clear communication to the entity of the regulator's assessment by creating incentives to use moral suasion and other informal mechanisms.

(f)   Disclosure requirements should not focus on entity-specific capital requirements in isolation, but should focus on how entity-specific capital requirements affect how an entity manages and determines the adequacy of its capital resources.

(g)   A requirement to disclose entity-specific capital requirements imposed by a regulator is not part of Pillar 3 of the Basel II Framework developed by the Basel Committee on Banking Supervision.

BC96   Taking into account all of the above arguments, the Board decided not to require quantitative disclosure of externally imposed capital requirements. Rather, it decided to require disclosures about whether the entity complied with any externally imposed capital requirements during the period and, if not, the consequences of non-compliance. This retains confidentiality between regulators and the entity, but alerts users to breaches of capital requirements and their consequences.

BC97   Some respondents to ED 7 did not agree that breaches of externally imposed capital requirements should be disclosed. They argued that disclosure about breaches of externally imposed capital requirements and the associated regulatory measures subsequently imposed could be disproportionately damaging to entities. The Board was not persuaded by these arguments because it believes that such concerns indicate that information about breaches of externally imposed capital requirements may often be material by its nature. The *Framework* states that 'Information is material if its omission or misstatement could influence the economic decisions of users taken on the basis of the financial statements.' Similarly, the Board decided not to provide an exemption for temporary non-compliance with regulatory requirements during the year. Information that an entity is sufficiently close to its limits to breach them, even on a temporary basis, is useful for users.

Internal capital targets

BC98   The Board proposed in ED 7 that the requirement to disclose information about breaches of capital requirements should apply equally to breaches of internally imposed requirements, because it believed the information is also useful to a user of the financial statements.

BC99   However, this proposal was criticised by respondents to ED 7 for the following reasons:

(a)   The information is subjective and, thus, not comparable between entities. In particular, different entities will set internal targets for different reasons, so a breach of a requirement might signify different things for different entities. In contrast, a breach of an external requirement has similar implications for all entities required to comply with similar requirements.

(b)   Capital targets are not more important than other internally set financial targets, and to require disclosure only of capital targets would provide users with incomplete, and perhaps misleading, information.

(c)   Internal targets are estimates that are subject to change by the entity. It is not appropriate to require the entity's performance against this benchmark to be disclosed.

(d)   An internally set capital target can be manipulated by management. The disclosure requirement could cause management to set the target so that it would always be achieved, providing little useful information to users and potentially reducing the effectiveness of the entity's capital management.

BC100   As a result, the Board decided not to require disclosure of the capital targets set by management, whether the entity has complied with those targets, or the consequences of any non-compliance. However, the Board confirmed its view that when an entity has policies and processes for managing capital, qualitative disclosures about these policies and processes are useful. The Board also concluded that these disclosures, together with disclosure of the components of equity and their changes during the year (required by paragraphs 106–110), would give sufficient information about entities that are not regulated or subject to externally imposed capital requirements.

Puttable financial instruments and obligations arising on liquidation

BC100A The Board decided to require disclosure of information about puttable instruments and instruments that impose on the entity an obligation to deliver to another party a pro rata share of the net assets of the entity only on liquidation that are reclassified in accordance with paragraphs 16E and 16F of IAS 32. This is because the Board concluded that this disclosure allows users of financial statements to understand the effects of any reclassifications.

BC100B The Board also concluded that entities with puttable financial instruments classified as equity should be required to disclose additional information to allow users to assess any effect on the entity's liquidity arising from the ability of the holder to put the instruments to the issuer. Financial instruments classified as equity usually do not include any obligation for the entity to deliver a financial asset to another party. Therefore, the Board concluded that additional disclosures are needed in these circumstances. In particular, the Board concluded that entities should disclose the expected cash outflow on redemption or repurchase of those financial instruments that are classified as equity and information about how that amount was determined. That information allows liquidity risk associated with the put obligation and future cash flows to be evaluated.

Presentation of measures per share

BC101 The exposure draft of 2006 did not propose to change the requirements of IAS 33 *Earnings per Share* on the presentation of basic and diluted earnings per share. A majority of respondents agreed with this decision. In their opinion, earnings per share should be the only measure per share permitted or required in the statement of comprehensive income and changing those requirements was beyond the scope of this stage of the financial statement presentation project.

BC102 However, some respondents would like to see alternative measures per share whenever earnings per share is not viewed as the most relevant measure for financial analysts (ie credit rating agencies that focus on other measures). A few respondents proposed that an entity should also display an amount per share for total comprehensive income, because this was considered a useful measure. The Board did not support including alternative measures per share in the financial statements, until totals and subtotals, and principles for aggregating and disaggregating items, are addressed and discussed as part of the next stage of the financial statement presentation project.

BC103 Some respondents also interpreted the current provisions in IAS 33 as allowing de facto a display of alternative measures in the income statement. In its deliberations, the Board was clear that paragraph 73 of IAS 33 did not leave room for confusion. However, it decided that the wording in paragraph 73 could be improved to clarify that alternative measures should be shown 'only in the notes'. This will be done when IAS 33 is revisited or as part of the annual improvements process.

BC104   One respondent commented that the use of the word 'earnings' was inappropriate in the light of changes proposed in the exposure draft and that the measure should be denominated 'profit or loss per share', instead. The Board considered that this particular change in terminology was beyond the scope of IAS 1.

Transition and effective date

BC105   The Board is committed to maintaining a 'stable platform' of substantially unchanged standards for annual periods beginning between 1 January 2006 and 31 December 2008. In addition, some preparers will need time to make the system changes necessary to comply with the revisions to IAS 1. Therefore, the Board decided that the effective date of IAS 1 should be annual periods beginning on or after 1 January 2009, with earlier application permitted.

BC105A   The exposure draft *Presentation of Items of Other Comprehensive Income* published in May 2010 proposed changes to presentation of items of OCI. The Board finalised these changes in June 2011 and decided that the effective dates for these changes should be for annual periods beginning on or after 1 July 2012, with earlier application permitted. The Board did not think that a long transition period was needed as the changes to presentation are small and the presentation required by the amendments is already allowed under IAS 1.

BC105B   The Board had consulted on the effective date and transition requirements for this amendment in its *Request for Views on Effective Dates and Transition Requirements* in October 2010 and the responses to that document did not give the Board any reason to reconsider the effective date and the transition requirements.

Disclosure Initiative (Amendments to IAS 1)

BC105C   The Board decided that *Disclosure Initiative* (Amendments to IAS 1) should be applied for annual periods beginning on or after 1 January 2016 with early application permitted.

BC105D   The Board noted that these amendments clarify existing requirements in IAS 1. They provide additional guidance to assist entities to apply judgement when meeting the presentation and disclosure requirements in IFRS. These amendments do not affect recognition and measurement. They should not result in the reassessment of the judgements about presentation and disclosure made in periods prior to the application of these amendments.

BC105E   Paragraph 38 of IAS 1 requires an entity to present comparative information for all amounts reported in the current period financial statements and for narrative or descriptive information 'if it is relevant to understanding the current period's financial statements'. If an entity alters the order of the notes or the information presented or disclosed compared to the previous year, it also adjusts the comparative information to align with the current period presentation and disclosure. For that reason, IAS 1 already provides relief from having to disclose comparative information that is not considered relevant in the current period and requires comparative information for new amounts presented or disclosed in the current period.

BC105F   The March 2014 Exposure Draft proposed that if an entity applies these amendments early that it should disclose that fact. However, the Board removed this requirement and stated in the transition provisions that an entity need not disclose the fact that it has applied these amendments (regardless of whether the amendments have been applied for annual periods beginning on or after 1 January 2016 or if they have been applied early). This is because the Board considers that these amendments are clarifying amendments that do not directly affect an entity's accounting policies or accounting estimates. Similarly, an entity does not need to disclose the information required by paragraphs 28–30 of IAS 8 in relation to these amendments. The Board noted that if an entity decides to change its accounting policies as a result of applying these amendments then it would be required to follow the existing requirements in IAS 8 in relation to those accounting policy changes.

Classification of Liabilities as Current or Non-current (Amendments to IAS 1)

BC105FA   In January 2020 the Board issued *Classification of Liabilities as Current or Non-current* for the reasons described in paragraphs BC48A–BC48H. When issued, those amendments had an effective date of annual reporting periods beginning on or after 1 January 2022. Subsequently, the Board noted that the covid-19 pandemic has created pressures that could make it more challenging to implement any changes in classification of liabilities as current or non-current resulting from the application of these amendments. The pressures caused by the covid-19 pandemic could also delay the start and extend the duration of any renegotiation of loan covenants resulting from those changes. Consequently, the Board decided to provide entities with operational relief by deferring the effective date of the amendments by one year to annual reporting periods beginning on or after 1 January 2023. Earlier application of the amendments continues to be permitted.

BC105FB   The Board noted that deferring the effective date would delay the implementation of the improvements to the classification of liabilities that the amendments intend to bring about. However, the amendments clarify the requirements for presentation of liabilities instead of fundamentally changing the required accounting; recognition and measurement requirements are unaffected by the amendments. Consequently, the Board concluded that the advantages of a deferral during a time of significant disruption would outweigh the disadvantages.

BC105FC   The Board considered whether to introduce disclosure requirements as part of the amendment but concluded that this was unnecessary because an entity is required to comply with paragraph 30 of IAS 8. Application of that paragraph requires disclosure of known or reasonably estimable information relevant to assessing the possible impact of the application of the amendments issued in January 2020 on an entity's financial statements.

Amended references to the *Conceptual Framework*

BC105G   Following the issue of the revised *Conceptual Framework for Financial Reporting* in 2018 (2018 *Conceptual Framework*), the Board issued *Amendments to References to the Conceptual Framework in IFRS Standards*. In IAS 1, that document replaced references in paragraphs 15, 19–20, 23–24, 28 and 89 to the *Framework* with references to the 2018 *Conceptual Framework*.

BC105H   The Board does not expect the replacement of the references to the *Framework* to have a significant effect on the application of the Standard for the following reasons:

(a)   In paragraph 15, replacing the reference to the *Framework* should not change the assessment of whether the financial statements present fairly the financial position, financial performance and cash flows of an entity. Paragraph 15 explains that the application of IFRS Standards, with additional disclosure when necessary, is presumed to result in financial statements that achieve fair presentation. Revisions of the *Conceptual Framework* will not automatically lead to changes in IFRS Standards. Hence, entities are expected to continue applying IFRS Standards in preparing their financial statements even in cases in which the requirements of a particular Standard depart from aspects of the *Conceptual Framework*.

(b)   In paragraphs 19–20 and 23–24, replacing the reference to the *Framework* means referring to the revised description of the objective of financial statements in the 2018 *Conceptual Framework* instead of the description provided by the *Framework*. The objective did not change substantively—it is an adapted and updated version of the objective of financial statements from the *Framework* and paragraph 9 of IAS 1. Hence, applying the revised objective is not expected to lead to changes in the application of the requirements in paragraphs 19–20 and 23–24.

(c)   In paragraph 28, replacing the reference to the *Framework* in the discussion of the accrual basis of accounting is not expected to result in any changes because no changes were made to the discussion of the accrual basis of accounting in the 2018 *Conceptual Framework*.

(d)   In paragraph 89, replacing the reference to the *Framework* means referring to the revised definitions of income and expenses in the 2018 *Conceptual Framework*. The Board concluded that this is unlikely to lead to changes in applying the requirements of IAS 1 because the definitions of income and expenses in the 2018 *Conceptual Framework* were updated only to align them with the revised definitions of an asset and a liability. Moreover, the main purpose of paragraph 89 is to indicate that particular items of income or expenses can be recognised outside profit or loss only if required by other IFRS Standards.

BC105I   IAS 1 referred to the *Framework* in paragraph 7 and quoted the description of users of financial statements from the *Framework*. To retain the requirements of this paragraph, the Board decided to embed that description in the Standard itself instead of updating the reference and the related quotation.

BC105J   In developing the 2018 *Conceptual Framework* the Board retained the term 'faithful representation' as a label for the qualitative characteristic previously called 'reliability' (see paragraphs BC2.22–BC2.31 of the Basis for Conclusions on the 2018 *Conceptual Framework*). In order to avoid possible unintended consequences, the Board decided against replacing the term 'reliability' with the term 'faithful representation' in the Standards at this time.

Differences from SFAS 130

BC106   In developing IAS 1, the Board identified the following differences from SFAS 130:

(a)   **Reporting and display of comprehensive income** Paragraph 22 of SFAS 130 permits a choice of displaying comprehensive income and its components, in one or two statements of financial performance or in a statement of changes in equity. IAS 1 (as revised in 2007) does not permit display in a statement of changes in equity.

(b)   **Reporting other comprehensive income in the equity section of a statement of financial position** Paragraph 26 of SFAS 130 specifically states that the *total of other comprehensive income* is reported separately from retained earnings and additional paid-in capital in a statement of financial position at the end of the period. A descriptive title such as *accumulated other comprehensive income* is used for that component of equity. An entity discloses accumulated balances for each classification in that separate component of equity in a statement of financial position, in a statement of changes in equity, or in notes to the financial statements. IAS 1 (as revised in 2007) does not specifically require the display of a total of accumulated other comprehensive income in the statement of financial position.

(c)   **Display of the share of other comprehensive income items of associates and joint ventures accounted for using the equity method** Paragraph 82 of IAS 1 (as revised in 2007) requires the display in the statement of comprehensive income of the investor's share of the investee's other comprehensive income. Paragraph 122 of SFAS 130 does not specify how that information should be displayed. An investor is permitted to combine its proportionate share of other comprehensive income amounts with its own other comprehensive income items and display the aggregate of those amounts in an income statement type format or in a statement of changes in equity.

Appendix
Amendments to the Basis for Conclusions on other IFRSs

This appendix contains amendments to the Basis for Conclusions on other IFRSs that are necessary in order to ensure consistency with the revised IAS 1. Amended paragraphs are shown with the new text underlined and deleted text struck through.

* * * * *

The amendments contained in this appendix when this Standard was revised in 2007 have been incorporated into the relevant IFRSs published in this volume.

© IFRS Foundation

Dissenting opinions

Dissent of Mary E Barth, Anthony T Cope, Robert P Garnett and James J Leisenring from IAS 1 (as revised in September 2007)

DO1   Professor Barth and Messrs Cope, Garnett and Leisenring voted against the issue of IAS 1 *Presentation of Financial Statements* in 2007. The reasons for their dissent are set out below.

DO2   Those Board members agree with the requirement to report all items of income and expense separately from changes in net assets that arise from transactions with owners in their capacity as owners. Making that distinction clearly is a significant improvement in financial reporting.

DO3   However, they believe that the decision to permit entities to divide the statement of comprehensive income into two separate statements is both conceptually unsound and unwise.

DO4   As noted in paragraph BC51, the *Framework*[15] does not define profit or loss, or net income. It also does not indicate what criteria should be used to distinguish between those items of recognised income and expense that should be included in profit or loss and those items that should not. In some cases, it is even possible for identical transactions to be reported inside or outside profit or loss. Indeed, in that same paragraph, the Board acknowledges these facts, and indicates that it had a preference for reporting all items of income and expense in a single statement, believing that a single statement is the conceptually correct approach. Those Board members believe that some items of income and expense that will potentially bypass the statement of profit and loss can be as significant to the assessment of an entity's performance as items that will be included. Until a conceptual distinction can be developed to determine whether any items should be reported in profit or loss or elsewhere, financial statements will lack neutrality and comparability unless all items are reported in a single statement. In such a statement, profit or loss can be shown as a subtotal, reflecting current conventions.

DO5   In the light of those considerations, it is puzzling that most respondents to the exposure draft that proposed these amendments favoured permitting a two-statement approach, reasoning that it 'distinguishes between profit and loss and total comprehensive income' (paragraph BC50). Distinguishing between those items reported in profit or loss and those reported elsewhere is accomplished by the requirement for relevant subtotals to be included in a statement of comprehensive income. Respondents also stated that a two-statement approach gives primacy to the 'income statement'; that conflicts with the Board's requirement in paragraph 11 of IAS 1 to give equal prominence to all financial statements within a set of financial statements.

---

15   The reference to the *Framework* is to the IASC's *Framework for the Preparation and Presentation of Financial Statements*, adopted by the Board in 2001 and in effect when the Standard was revised.

DO6　Those Board members also believe that the amendments are flawed by offering entities a choice of presentation methods. The Board has expressed a desire to reduce alternatives in IFRSs. The *Preface to International Financial Reporting Standards*, in paragraph 13,[16] states: 'the IASB intends not to permit choices in accounting treatment ... and will continue to reconsider ... those transactions and events for which IASs permit a choice of accounting treatment, with the objective of reducing the number of those choices.' The *Preface* extends this objective to both accounting and reporting. The same paragraph states: 'The IASB's objective is to require like transactions and events to be accounted for *and reported* in a like way and unlike transactions and events to be accounted for *and reported* differently' (emphasis added). By permitting a choice in this instance, the IASB has abandoned that principle.

DO7　Finally, the four Board members believe that allowing a choice of presentation at this time will ingrain practice, and make achievement of the conceptually correct presentation more difficult as the long-term project on financial statement presentation proceeds.

16　Amended to paragraph 11 when the *Preface to IFRS Standards* was revised and renamed in December 2018.

　　　　　© IFRS Foundation

Dissent of Paul Pacter from *Presentation of Items of Other Comprehensive Income* (Amendments to IAS 1)

DO1 Mr Pacter voted against issuing the amendments to IAS 1 *Presentation of Financial Statements* set out in *Presentation of Items of Other Comprehensive Income* in June 2011. Mr Pacter believes that the Board has missed a golden opportunity to align the performance statement with the Board's *Conceptual Framework*[17] and, thereby, improve information for users of IFRS financial statements.

DO2 Mr Pacter believes that ideally this project should have provided guidance, to the Board and to those who use IFRSs, on which items of income and expense (if any) should be presented as items of other comprehensive income (OCI) and which of those (if any) should subsequently be recycled through profit or loss. Mr Pacter acknowledges and accepts that this project has a more short-term goal – 'to improve the consistency and clarity of the presentation of items of OCI'. He believes that this project fails to deliver on that objective, for the following reasons:

(a) Consistency is not achieved because the standard allows choice between presenting performance in a single performance statement or two performance statements. Users of financial statements – and the Board itself – have often said that accounting options are not helpful for understandability and comparability of financial statements.

(b) Clarity is not achieved because allowing two performance statements is inconsistent with the *Conceptual Framework*. The *Conceptual Framework* defines two types of items that measure an entity's performance – income and expenses. Mr Pacter believes that all items of income and expense should be presented in a single performance statement with appropriate subtotals (including profit or loss, if that can be defined) and supporting disclosures. This is consistent with reporting all assets and liabilities in a single statement of financial position, rather than multiple statements. Unfortunately, neither IAS 1 nor any other IFRS addresses criteria for which items are presented in OCI. And the recent history of which items are presented in OCI suggests that the decisions are based more on expediency than conceptual merit. In Mr Pacter's judgement, that is all the more reason to have all items of income and expense reported in a single performance statement.

DO3 Mr Pacter believes that the Board should breathe new life into its former project on performance reporting as a matter of urgency.

---

17 References to the *Conceptual Framework* in this Dissent are to the *Conceptual Framework for Financial Reporting*, issued in 2010 and in effect when the Standard was amended.

IASB documents published to accompany

IAS 2

Inventories

The text of the unaccompanied standard, IAS 2, is contained in Part A of this edition. Its effective date when issued was 1 January 2005. This part presents the following document:

BASIS FOR CONCLUSIONS

Basis for Conclusions on
IAS 2 *Inventories*

This Basis for Conclusions accompanies, but is not part of, IAS 2.

Introduction

BC1 This Basis for Conclusions summarises the International Accounting Standards Board's considerations in reaching its conclusions on revising IAS 2 *Inventories* in 2003. Individual Board members gave greater weight to some factors than to others.

BC2 In July 2001 the Board announced that, as part of its initial agenda of technical projects, it would undertake a project to improve a number of Standards, including IAS 2. The project was undertaken in the light of queries and criticisms raised in relation to the Standards by securities regulators, professional accountants and other interested parties. The objectives of the Improvements project were to reduce or eliminate alternatives, redundancies and conflicts within Standards, to deal with some convergence issues and to make other improvements. In May 2002 the Board published its proposals in an Exposure Draft of *Improvements to International Accounting Standards*, with a comment deadline of 16 September 2002. The Board received over 160 comment letters on the Exposure Draft.

BC3 Because the Board's intention was not to reconsider the fundamental approach to the accounting for inventories established by IAS 2, this Basis for Conclusions does not discuss requirements in IAS 2 that the Board has not reconsidered.

Scope

Reference to historical cost system

BC4 Both the objective and the scope of the previous version of IAS 2 referred to 'the accounting treatment for inventories under the historical cost system.' Some had interpreted those words as meaning that the Standard applied only under a historical cost system and permitted entities the choice of applying other measurement bases, for example fair value.

BC5 The Board agreed that those words could be seen as permitting a choice, resulting in inconsistent application of the Standard. Accordingly, it deleted the words 'in the context of the historical cost system in accounting for inventories' to clarify that the Standard applies to all inventories that are not specifically exempted from its scope.

Inventories of broker-traders

BC6   The Exposure Draft proposed excluding from the scope of the Standard inventories of non-producers of agricultural and forest products and mineral ores to the extent that these inventories are measured at net realisable value in accordance with well-established industry practices. However, some respondents disagreed with this scope exemption for the following reasons:

   (a)   the scope exemption should apply to all types of inventories of broker-traders;

   (b)   established practice is for broker-traders to follow a mark-to-market approach rather than to value these inventories at net realisable value;

   (c)   the guidance on net realisable value in IAS 2 is not appropriate for the valuation of inventories of broker-traders.

BC7   The Board found these comments persuasive. Therefore it decided that the Standard should not apply to the measurement of inventories of:

   (a)   producers of agricultural and forest products, agricultural produce after harvest, and minerals and mineral products, to the extent that they are measured at net realisable value (as in the previous version of IAS 2), or

   (b)   commodity broker-traders when their inventories are measured at fair value less costs to sell.

BC8   The Board further decided that the measurement of the effect of inventories on profit or loss for the period needed to be consistent with the measurement attribute of inventories for which such exemption is allowed. Accordingly, to qualify under (a) or (b), the Standard requires changes in the recognised amount of inventories to be included in profit or loss for the period. The Board believes this is particularly appropriate in the case of commodity broker-traders because they seek to profit from fluctuations in prices and trade margins.

Cost formulas

BC9   The combination of the previous version of IAS 2 and SIC-1 *Consistency— Different Cost Formulas for Inventories* allowed some choice between first-in, first-out (FIFO) or weighted average cost formulas (benchmark treatment) and the last-in, first-out (LIFO) method (allowed alternative treatment). The Board decided to eliminate the allowed alternative of using the LIFO method.

BC10   The LIFO method treats the newest items of inventory as being sold first, and consequently the items remaining in inventory are recognised as if they were the oldest. This is generally not a reliable representation of actual inventory flows.

BC11   The LIFO method is an attempt to meet a perceived deficiency of the conventional accounting model (the measurement of cost of goods sold expense by reference to outdated prices for the inventories sold, whereas sales revenue is measured at current prices). It does so by imposing an unrealistic cost flow assumption.

BC12   The use of LIFO in financial reporting is often tax-driven, because it results in cost of goods sold expense calculated using the most recent prices being deducted from revenue in the determination of the gross margin. The LIFO method reduces (increases) profits in a manner that tends to reflect the effect that increased (decreased) prices would have on the cost of replacing inventories sold. However, this effect depends on the relationship between the prices of the most recent inventory acquisitions and the replacement cost at the end of the period. Thus, it is not a truly systematic method for determining the effect of changing prices on profits.

BC13   The use of LIFO results in inventories being recognised in the balance sheet at amounts that bear little relationship to recent cost levels of inventories. However, LIFO can distort profit or loss, especially when 'preserved' older 'layers' of inventory are presumed to have been used when inventories are substantially reduced. It is more likely in these circumstances that relatively new inventories will have been used to meet the increased demands on inventory.

BC14   Some respondents argued that the use of LIFO has merit in certain circumstances because it partially adjusts profit or loss for the effects of price changes. The Board concluded that it is not appropriate to allow an approach that results in a measurement of profit or loss for the period that is inconsistent with the measurement of inventories for balance sheet purposes.

BC15   Other respondents argued that in some industries, such as the oil and gas industry, inventory levels are driven by security considerations and often represent a minimum of 90 days of sales. They argue that, in these industries, the use of LIFO better reflects an entity's performance because inventories held as security stocks are closer to long-term assets than to working capital.

BC16   The Board was not convinced by these arguments because these security stocks do not match historical layers under a LIFO computation.

BC17   Other respondents argued that in some cases, for example, when measuring coal dumps, piles of iron or metal scraps (when stock bins are replenished by 'topping up'), the LIFO method reflects the actual physical flow of inventories.

BC18   The Board concluded that valuation of these inventories follows a direct costing approach where actual physical flows are matched with direct costs, which is a method different from LIFO.

BC19   The Board decided to eliminate the LIFO method because of its lack of representational faithfulness of inventory flows. This decision does not rule out specific cost methods that reflect inventory flows that are similar to LIFO.

BC20   The Board recognised that, in some jurisdictions, use of the LIFO method for tax purposes is possible only if that method is also used for accounting purposes. It concluded, however, that tax considerations do not provide an adequate conceptual basis for selecting an appropriate accounting treatment and that it is not acceptable to allow an inferior accounting treatment purely because of tax regulations and advantages in particular jurisdictions. This may be an issue for local taxation authorities.

BC21   IAS 2 continues to allow the use of both the FIFO and the weighted average methods for interchangeable inventories.

Cost of inventories recognised as an expense in the period

BC22   The Exposure Draft proposed deleting paragraphs in the previous version of IAS 2 that required disclosure of the cost of inventories recognised as an expense in the period, because this disclosure is required in IAS 1 *Presentation of Financial Statements*.

BC23   Some respondents observed that IAS 1 does not specifically require disclosure of the cost of inventories recognised as an expense in the period when presenting an analysis of expenses using a classification based on their function. They argued that this information is important to understand the financial statements. Therefore the Board decided to require this disclosure specifically in IAS 2.

IASB documents published to accompany

IAS 7

Statement of Cash Flows

The text of the unaccompanied standard, IAS 7, is contained in Part A of this edition. Its effective date when issued was 1 January 1994. The text of the Accompanying Guidance on IAS 7 is contained in Part B of this edition. This part presents the following documents:

BASIS FOR CONCLUSIONS

DISSENTING OPINION

Basis for Conclusions on
IAS 7 *Statement of Cash Flows*

This Basis for Conclusions accompanies, but is not part of, IAS 7.

BC1   This Basis for Conclusions summarises the considerations of the International
        Accounting Standards Board in reaching its conclusions on amending IAS 7
        Statement of Cash Flows as part of *Improvements to IFRSs* issued in April 2009.
        Individual Board members gave greater weight to some factors than to others.

BC2   IAS 7 was developed by the International Accounting Standards Committee in
        1992 and was not accompanied by a Basis for Conclusions. This Basis refers to
        clarification of guidance on classification of cash flows from investing
        activities.

Classification of expenditures on unrecognised assets

BC3   In 2008 the International Financial Reporting Interpretations Committee
        (IFRIC) reported to the Board that practice differed for the classification of
        cash flows for expenditures incurred with the objective of generating future
        cash flows when those expenditures are not recognised as assets in accordance
        with IFRSs. Some entities classified such expenditures as cash flows from
        operating activities and others classified them as investing activities. Examples
        of such expenditures are those for exploration and evaluation activities, which
        IFRS 6 *Exploration for and Evaluation of Mineral Resources* permits to be recognised
        as either an asset or an expense depending on the entity's previous accounting
        policies for those expenditures. Expenditures on advertising and promotional
        activities, staff training, and research and development could also raise the
        same issue.

BC4   The IFRIC decided not to add this issue to its agenda but recommended that
        the Board should amend IAS 7 to state explicitly that only an expenditure that
        results in a recognised asset can be classified as a cash flow from investing
        activity.

BC5   In 2008, as part of its annual improvements project, the Board considered the
        principles in IAS 7, specifically guidance on the treatment of such
        expenditures in the statement of cash flows. The Board noted that even
        though paragraphs 14 and 16 of IAS 7 appear to be clear that only expenditure
        that results in the recognition of an asset should be classified as cash flows
        from investing activities, the wording is not definitive in this respect. Some
        might have misinterpreted the reference in paragraph 11 of IAS 7 for an entity
        to assess classification by activity that is most appropriate to its business to
        imply that the assessment is an accounting policy choice.

BC6   Consequently, in *Improvements to IFRSs* issued in April 2009, the Board removed
        the potential misinterpretation by amending paragraph 16 of IAS 7 to state
        explicitly that only an expenditure that results in a recognised asset can be
        classified as a cash flow from investing activities.

BC7   The Board concluded that this amendment better aligns the classification of cash flows from investing activities in the statement of cash flows and the presentation of recognised assets in the statement of financial position, reduces divergence in practice and, therefore, results in financial statements that are easier for users to understand.

BC8   The Board also amended the Basis for Conclusions on IFRS 6 to clarify the Board's view that the exemption in IFRS 6 applies only to recognition and measurement of exploration and evaluation assets, not to the classification of related expenditures in the statement of cash flows, for the same reasons set out in paragraph BC7.

Changes in liabilities arising from financing activities (paragraphs 44A–44E)

Background to the January 2016 Amendments

BC9   In January 2016 the Board amended IAS 7 to require entities to provide disclosures that enable users of financial statements to evaluate changes in liabilities arising from financing activities. The amendments were in response to requests from users, including those received at the Board's *Financial Reporting Disclosure Discussion Forum* in January 2013 and reflected in the resulting Feedback Statement ('the Feedback Statement'), which was issued in May 2013. Users highlighted that understanding an entity's cash flows is critical to their analysis and that there is a need for improved disclosures about an entity's debt, including changes in debt during the reporting period. The Feedback Statement noted that users had been consistently asking for the Board to introduce a requirement for entities to disclose and explain a net debt reconciliation.

BC10   In early 2014, to understand the reasons for their requests for more disclosure about net debt, the Board undertook a survey of investors. The survey sought information about why investors seek to understand the changes in debt between the beginning and the end of a reporting period. The survey also sought input on disclosures about cash and cash equivalents. On the basis of the survey, the Board identified that investors use a net debt reconciliation in their analysis of the entity:

(a)   to check their understanding of the entity's cash flows, because it provides a reconciliation between the statement of financial position and the statement of cash flows;

(b)   to improve their confidence in forecasting the entity's future cash flows when they can use a reconciliation to check their understanding of the entity's cash flows;

(c)   to provide information about the entity's sources of finance and how those sources have been used over time; and

(d)   to help them understand the entity's exposure to risks associated with financing.

BC11   The survey helped the Board to understand why investors were calling for improved disclosures about changes in debt during the reporting period. The Board noted that one challenge in responding to this need was that debt is not defined or required to be disclosed in current IFRS Standards. The Board noted that finding a commonly agreed definition of debt would be difficult. However, the Board decided that it could use the definition of financing activities in IAS 7. It therefore decided to propose a requirement to disclose a reconciliation between the amounts in the opening and the amounts in the closing statements of financial position for liabilities for which cash flows were, or future cash flows will be, classified as financing activities in the statement of cash flows.

BC12   IAS 7 defines financing activities as activities that result in changes in the size and composition of the contributed equity and borrowings of the entity. The Board proposed that a reconciliation of liabilities arising from financing activities would provide the information about debt that users of financial statements were requesting.

BC13   In December 2014 the Board published an Exposure Draft *Disclosure Initiative* (Proposed amendments to IAS 7) ('the 2014 Exposure Draft') seeking views on the proposals for a reconciliation of liabilities arising from financing activities.

Feedback on the proposals set out in the Exposure Draft

BC14   The feedback received on the 2014 Exposure Draft provided evidence that the disclosure would provide users of financial statements with the information they were seeking in order to analyse an entity's cash flows. The Board decided to finalise the amendments to IAS 7 ('the 2016 Amendments'); paragraphs BC15–BC24 set out how the Board responded to the feedback received on the 2014 Exposure Draft.

The objective of the disclosure

BC15   Feedback on the 2014 Exposure Draft noted that the proposal did not set out a disclosure objective, and consequently it was not sufficiently clear how entities would determine the most appropriate way to provide the required disclosure. The Board agreed with this feedback and included an objective within the requirement set out in paragraph 44A of the 2016 Amendments.

BC16   In setting the disclosure objective the Board decided the objective should reflect the needs of the users of financial statements, including those summarised in paragraph BC10.

Application of the 2016 Amendments to financial institutions

BC17   Some respondents to the 2014 Exposure Draft from financial institutions stated that the proposals would provide little or no relevant information to users of their financial statements because:

       (a)   only some of the sources of finance for a financial institution are classified as 'financing activities' (for example, deposits from customers provide finance but in practice the resulting cash flows are typically classified as operating cash flows). A reconciliation may therefore provide an incomplete picture of the changes in the financing structure of a financial institution; and

(b)   other disclosure requirements (for example, comprehensive regulatory disclosure requirements) may already result in sufficient disclosure about an entity's financing structure.

BC18   After taking into consideration the feedback from respondents from financial institutions, the Board decided that the disclosure requirement could be satisfied in various ways, and not only by providing a reconciliation. The Board noted that when an entity is considering whether it has fulfilled the disclosure requirement, it should take into consideration:

(a)   the extent to which information about changes in liabilities arising from financing activities provides relevant information to its users, considering the needs of users summarised in paragraph BC10; and

(b)   whether the entity is satisfying the disclosure requirement through other disclosures included in the financial statements.

BC19   The Board therefore decided that a reconciliation between the opening and closing balances in the statement of financial position for liabilities arising from financing activities is one way to fulfil the disclosure requirement but should not be a mandatory format.

Information that supplements the disclosures

BC20   Some respondents to the 2014 Exposure Draft expressed a concern that the proposals in the Exposure Draft were too restrictive because, in their view:

(a)   the proposed disclosure would not include liabilities that an entity considers to be sources of finance although the entity does not classify them as financing activities (for example, pension liabilities); and

(b)   entities that already provided a net debt reconciliation (a reconciliation of movements in a net balance comprising debt less cash and cash equivalents) would be prevented from providing such a reconciliation, even if users would find it useful.

BC21   The Board did not intend to prevent entities from providing information required by paragraph 44A in a format that combines it with information about changes in other assets and liabilities. For example, an entity could provide that information as part of a net debt reconciliation, as described in paragraph BC20(b). To ensure users can identify the information required by paragraph 44A, the format selected needs to distinguish that information from information about changes in other assets and liabilities. In finalising the 2016 Amendments, the Board clarified these points in paragraph 44E.

Financial assets

BC22   Some respondents to the 2014 Exposure Draft asked the Board to clarify whether changes in financial assets held to hedge financial liabilities could also be included in the disclosure required by the 2016 Amendments. The Board noted that paragraph G.2 of the Guidance on implementing IFRS 9

Financial Instruments states that cash flows arising from a hedging instrument are classified as operating, investing or financing activities, on the basis of the classification of the cash flows arising from the hedged item. Consequently, the Board clarified in paragraph 44C that changes in financial assets held to hedge financial liabilities are included in the disclosure required by paragraph 44A.

Cost-benefit considerations

BC23   The Board considered the feedback received on perceived costs and benefits in finalising the 2016 Amendments. The Board noted that there will be initial costs for preparers to update information technology systems to enable changes in liabilities arising from financing activities to be tracked and collated. The Board also acknowledged that disclosing additional information could result in costs relating to extending the existing internal controls and audit processes of the entity. However, the Board noted that much of the information is already available to preparers. It also noted that the 2016 Amendments do not change the recognition or measurement for liabilities arising from financing activities; instead, they track changes in those items. Consequently, the Board concluded that it does not foresee any significant ongoing cost related to providing this information, and that the informational benefits to users of financial statements would outweigh the costs.

Illustrative example

BC24   Some respondents to the 2014 Exposure Draft stated that the example proposed within the Exposure Draft was too simplistic and might not help preparers in disclosing relevant information, because in practice the reconciliation would be more detailed. To address this feedback, the Board inserted a further example in the illustrative examples accompanying IAS 7.

Other disclosures

BC25   To supplement the current disclosure requirements in paragraph 48 of IAS 7 the 2014 Exposure Draft proposed additional disclosure requirements about an entity's liquidity such as restrictions that affect an entity's decision to use cash and cash equivalent balances. However, in the light of the responses, the Board decided that further work is needed before it can determine whether and how to finalise requirements arising from that proposal. The Board decided to continue that work without delaying the improvements to financial reporting that it expects will result from adding paragraphs 44A–44E to IAS 7. The Board may also, in due course, consider adding to its technical work programme a project that would look at liquidity disclosures more broadly.

Transition and effective date

Amendments to IAS 7

BC26   The Board concluded that timely application of the 2016 Amendments would respond to a long-standing request from users of financial statements. Thus, the Board decided that the 2016 Amendments should be applied for annual reporting periods beginning on or after 1 January 2017, with early application permitted.

BC27   Because the 2016 Amendments were issued in January 2016, which is less than one year before the beginning of the period when some entities could be required to apply them, the Board exempted entities from providing comparative information when they first apply the amendments.

Dissenting opinion

Dissent of Mr Takatsugu Ochi from *Disclosure Initiative* (Amendments to IAS 7)

DO1   Mr Ochi voted against the publication of *Disclosure Initiative* (Amendments to IAS 7) (the 2016 Amendments). The reasons for his dissent are set out below.

DO2   Mr Ochi believes that financial statements that reflect the 2016 Amendments may provide incomplete information about an entity's management of liquidity. The objective of the 2016 Amendments is to require disclosures that enable users to evaluate changes in liabilities arising from financing activities, including both changes arising from cash flows and non-cash changes. However, Mr Ochi thinks that users of financial statements are seeking clearer information about entities' management of liquidity risk. Consequently, he thinks that the information provided by the 2016 Amendments will not meet users' needs. Mr Ochi thinks that the Board has issued these amendments without setting a clear vision of overall improvements to the disclosure about an entity's liquidity risk management. He thinks that this could confuse and mislead users of financial statements.

DO3   The objective mentioned in paragraph DO2 refers to liabilities arising from financing activities. Paragraph 44C specifies that those liabilities are liabilities for which cash flows were, or future cash flows will be, classified in the statement of cash flows as cash flows from financing activities. However, Mr Ochi thinks that specifying the scope of the disclosure requirement in this way does not capture the information that users need. This is because changes in liabilities arising from financing activities are different from the information used to assess liquidity risk management. Because IAS 7 permits an entity to classify some cash flows (such as interest payments) as either operating or financing, the understanding of what constitutes changes in liabilities arising from financing activities may vary among preparers. In Mr Ochi's view, preparers may have a more precise understanding about what constitutes information on liquidity risk than simply understanding changes in liabilities arising from financing activities.

DO4   Mr Ochi also thinks that if an entity provides the disclosures required by paragraph 44A in combination with disclosure of changes in the amount of cash and cash equivalents and does not disclose information about the location and availability of the cash and cash equivalents, the disclosure is sometimes irrelevant to how an entity manages liquidity. If users expect to obtain a full picture of an entity's liquidity risk management as a result of the 2016 Amendments, they may be confused and misled.

DO5   Mr Ochi thinks that providing the disclosure may require excessive work and hence may be inefficient from a preparer's point of view. He notes that the Board may conduct research regarding the effectiveness of IAS 7. Because he regards IAS 7 as having some significant shortcomings, he believes that issuing amendments based on the existing statement of cash flows is not a worthwhile endeavour. He also thinks that it could reduce the clarity of the statement of cash flows.

DO6   Mr Ochi also has a significant concern regarding the costs required to prepare the disclosure. Although the 2016 Amendments are disclosure-only amendments, all reporting entities will need to consider providing this disclosure. For this disclosure, an entity may be required to adjust items already presented as operating and financing activities in a statement of cash flows (for example, interest payments that are classified as operating activities), which may require system changes. Concurrently, an entity may also have to initiate system changes to prepare for applying IFRS 9 *Financial Instruments* and IFRS 15 *Revenue from Contracts with Customers* (both effective on 1 January 2018) as well as IFRS 16 *Leases* (effective on 1 January 2019). Mr Ochi believes that the costs that will be incurred by entities as a consequence of those other changes will be considerable and he thinks that this fact is not reflected in the conclusion the Board had reached as a consequence of its assessment of costs pertaining to this disclosure. Taking these matters into consideration, Mr Ochi believes that the costs of the 2016 Amendments will outweigh the benefits.

IASB documents published to accompany

IAS 8

Accounting Policies, Changes in Accounting Estimates and Errors

The text of the unaccompanied standard, IAS 8, is contained in Part A of this edition. Its effective date when issued was 1 January 2005. The text of the Accompanying Guidance on IAS 8 is contained in Part B of this edition. This part presents the following document:

BASIS FOR CONCLUSIONS

Basis for Conclusions on
IAS 8 *Accounting Policies, Changes in Accounting Estimates and Errors*

This Basis for Conclusions accompanies, but is not part of, IAS 8.

Introduction

BC1   This Basis for Conclusions summarises the International Accounting Standards Board's considerations in reaching its conclusions on revising IAS 8 *Net Profit or Loss for the Period, Fundamental Errors and Changes in Accounting Policies* in 2003. Individual Board members gave greater weight to some factors than to others.

BC2   In July 2001 the Board announced that, as part of its initial agenda of technical projects, it would undertake a project to improve a number of Standards, including IAS 8. The project was undertaken in the light of queries and criticisms raised in relation to the Standards by securities regulators, professional accountants and other interested parties. The objectives of the Improvements project were to reduce or eliminate alternatives, redundancies and conflicts within Standards, to deal with some convergence issues and to make other improvements. In May 2002 the Board published its proposals in an Exposure Draft of *Improvements to International Accounting Standards*, with a comment deadline of 16 September 2002. The Board received over 160 comment letters on the Exposure Draft.

BC3   The Standard includes extensive changes to the previous version of IAS 8. The Board's intention was not to reconsider all of the previous Standard's requirements for selecting and applying accounting policies, and accounting for changes in accounting policies, changes in accounting estimates and corrections of errors. Accordingly, this Basis for Conclusions does not discuss requirements in IAS 8 that the Board did not reconsider.

Removing allowed alternative treatments

BC4   The previous version of IAS 8 included allowed alternative treatments of voluntary changes in accounting policies (paragraphs 54–57) and corrections of fundamental errors (paragraphs 38–40). Under those allowed alternatives:

(a)   the adjustment resulting from retrospective application of a change in an accounting policy was included in profit or loss for the current period; and

(b)   the amount of the correction of a fundamental error was included in profit or loss for the current period.

BC5   In both circumstances, comparative information was presented as it was presented in the financial statements of prior periods.

BC6   The Board identified the removal of optional treatments for changes in accounting policies and corrections of errors as an important improvement to the previous version of IAS 8. The Standard removes the allowed alternative treatments and requires changes in accounting policies and corrections of prior period errors to be accounted for retrospectively.

BC7   The Board concluded that retrospective application made by amending the comparative information presented for prior periods is preferable to the previously allowed alternative treatments because, under the now required method of retrospective application:

(a)   profit or loss for the period of the change does not include the effects of changes in accounting policies or errors relating to prior periods.

(b)   information presented about prior periods is prepared on the same basis as information about the current period, and is therefore comparable. This information possesses a qualitative characteristic identified in the *Framework for the Preparation and Presentation of Financial Statements (Framework)*,[1] and provides the most useful information for trend analysis of income and expenses.

(c)   prior period errors are not repeated in comparative information presented for prior periods.

BC8   Some respondents to the Exposure Draft argued that the previously allowed alternative treatments are preferable because:

(a)   correcting prior period errors by restating prior period information involves an unjustifiable use of hindsight;

(b)   recognising the effects of changes in accounting policies and corrections of errors in current period profit or loss makes them more prominent to users of financial statements; and

(c)   each amount credited or debited to retained earnings as a result of an entity's activities has been recognised in profit or loss in some period.

BC9   The Board concluded that restating prior period information to correct a prior period error does not involve an unjustifiable use of hindsight because prior period errors are defined in terms of a failure to use, or misuse of, reliable information that was available when the prior period financial statements were authorised for issue and could reasonably be expected to have been obtained and taken into account in the preparation and presentation of those financial statements.

BC10   The Board also concluded that the disclosures about changes in accounting policies and corrections of prior period errors in paragraphs 28, 29 and 49 of the Standard should ensure that their effects are sufficiently prominent to users of financial statements.

---

1   References to the *Framework* in this Basis for Conclusions are to the IASC's *Framework for the Preparation and Presentation of Financial Statements*, adopted by the Board in 2001 and in effect when the Standard was revised.

BC11   The Board further concluded that it is less important for each amount credited or debited to retained earnings as a result of an entity's activities to be recognised in profit or loss in some period than for the profit or loss for each period presented to represent faithfully the effects of transactions and other events occurring in that period.

Eliminating the distinction between fundamental errors and other material prior period errors

BC12   The Standard eliminates the distinction between fundamental errors and other material prior period errors. As a result, all material prior period errors are accounted for in the same way as a fundamental error was accounted for under the retrospective treatment in the previous version of IAS 8. The Board concluded that the definition of 'fundamental errors' in the previous version was difficult to interpret consistently because the main feature of the definition — that the error causes the financial statements of one or more prior periods no longer to be considered to have been reliable — was also a feature of all material prior period errors.

Applying a Standard or an Interpretation that specifically applies to an item

BC13   The Exposure Draft proposed that when a Standard or an Interpretation applies to an item in the financial statements, the accounting policy (or policies) applied to that item is (are) determined by considering the following in descending order:

(a)   the Standard (including any Appendices that form part of the Standard);

(b)   the Interpretation;

(c)   Appendices to the Standard that do not form a part of the Standard; and

(d)   Implementation Guidance issued in respect of the Standard.

BC14   The Board decided not to set out a hierarchy of requirements for these circumstances. The Standard requires only applicable IFRSs to be applied. In addition, it does not mention Appendices.

BC15   The Board decided not to rank Standards above Interpretations because the definition of International Financial Reporting Standards (IFRSs) includes Interpretations, which are equal in status to Standards. The rubric to each Standard clarifies what material constitutes the requirements of an IFRS and what is Implementation Guidance.[2] The term 'Appendix' is retained only for material that is part of an IFRS.

---

2   In 2007 the Board was advised that paragraphs 7 and 9 may appear to conflict, and may be misinterpreted to require mandatory consideration of Implementation Guidance. The Board amended paragraphs 7, 9 and 11 by *Improvements to IFRSs* issued in May 2008 to state that only guidance that is identified as an integral part of IFRSs is mandatory.

Pronouncements of other standard-setting bodies

BC16   The Exposure Draft proposed that in the absence of a Standard or an Interpretation specifically applying to an item, management should develop and apply an accounting policy by considering, among other guidance, pronouncements of other standard-setting bodies that use a similar conceptual framework to develop accounting standards. Respondents to the Exposure Draft commented that this could *require* entities to consider the pronouncements of various other standard-setting bodies when IASB guidance does not exist. Some commentators argued that, for example, it could require consideration of all components of US GAAP on some topics. After considering these comments, the Board decided that the Standard should indicate that considering such pronouncements is voluntary (see paragraph 12 of the Standard).

BC17   As proposed in the Exposure Draft, the Standard states that pronouncements of other standard-setting bodies are used only if they do not conflict with:

(a)   the requirements and guidance in IFRSs dealing with similar and related issues; and

(b)   the definitions, recognition criteria and measurement concepts for assets, liabilities, income and expenses in the *Framework*.[3]

BC18   The Standard refers to the most recent pronouncements of other standard-setting bodies because if pronouncements are withdrawn or superseded, the relevant standard-setting body no longer thinks they include the best accounting policies to apply.

BC19   Comments received indicated that it was unclear from the Exposure Draft whether a change in accounting policy following a change in a pronouncement of another standard-setting body should be accounted for under the transitional provisions in that pronouncement. As noted above, the Standard does not mandate using pronouncements of other standard-setting bodies in any circumstances. Accordingly, the Board decided to clarify that such a change in accounting policy is accounted for and disclosed as a voluntary change in accounting policy (see paragraph 21 of the Standard). Thus, an entity is precluded from applying transitional provisions specified by the other standard-setting body if they are inconsistent with the treatment of voluntary changes in accounting policies specified by the Standard.

Materiality

BC20   The Standard states that accounting policies specified by IFRSs need not be applied when the effect of applying them is immaterial. It also states that financial statements do not comply with IFRSs if they contain material errors, and that material prior period errors are to be corrected in the first set of

---

3   In 2018 the Board issued a revised *Conceptual Framework for Financial Reporting* (*Conceptual Framework*). The Board also issued *Amendments to References to the Conceptual Framework in IFRS Standards*. That document replaced the reference to the *Framework* in paragraph 11(b) of IAS 8 with a reference to the *Conceptual Framework*, except in the case of some regulatory account balances, as explained in paragraphs 54G of IAS 8 and BC38–BC40.

financial statements authorised for issue after their discovery. The Standard includes a definition of material omissions or misstatements, which is based on the description of materiality in IAS 1 *Presentation of Financial Statements* (as issued in 1997) and in the *Framework*.

BC21   The former *Preface to Statements of International Accounting Standards* stated that International Accounting Standards were not intended to apply to immaterial items. There is no equivalent statement in the *Preface to International Financial Reporting Standards*.[4] The Board received comments that the absence of such a statement from the *Preface* could be interpreted as requiring an entity to apply accounting policies (including measurement requirements) specified by IFRSs to immaterial items. However, the Board decided that the application of the concept of materiality should be in Standards rather than in the *Preface*.

BC21A   As a consequence of the *Definition of Material* (Amendments to IAS 1 and IAS 8), issued in October 2018, the definition of material and the accompanying explanatory paragraphs have been replaced with a reference to the definition of material and explanatory paragraphs in IAS 1.[5] The Board made this change to avoid the duplication of the definition of material in the Standards.

BC22   The application of the concept of materiality is set out in two Standards. IAS 1 (as revised in 2007) continues to specify its application to disclosures. IAS 8 specifies the application of materiality in applying accounting policies and correcting errors (including errors in measuring items).

Criterion for exemption from requirements

BC23   The previous version of IAS 8 included an impracticability criterion for exemption from retrospective application of voluntary changes in accounting policies and retrospective restatement for fundamental errors, and from making related disclosures, when the allowed alternative treatment of those items was not applied. The Exposure Draft proposed instead an exemption from retrospective application and retrospective restatement when it gives rise to undue cost or effort.

BC24   In the light of comments received on the Exposure Draft, the Board decided that an exemption based on management's assessment of undue cost or effort is too subjective to be applied consistently by different entities. Moreover, the Board decided that balancing costs and benefits is a task for the Board when it sets accounting requirements rather than for entities when they apply those requirements. Therefore, the Board decided to retain the impracticability criterion for exemption in the previous version of IAS 8. This affects the exemptions in paragraphs 23–25, 39 and 43–45 of the Standard. Impracticability is the only basis on which specific exemptions are provided in

---

4   *Preface to International Financial Reporting Standards* renamed *Preface to IFRS Standards*, December 2018.

5   Refer to paragraphs BC13A–BC13T of the Basis for Conclusions on IAS 1.

IFRSs from applying particular requirements when the effect of applying them is material.[6]

Definition of 'impracticable'

BC25   The Board decided to clarify the meaning of 'impracticable' in relation to retrospective application of a change in accounting policy and retrospective restatement to correct a prior period error.

BC26   Some commentators suggested that retrospective application of a change in accounting policy and retrospective restatement to correct a prior period error are impracticable for a particular prior period whenever significant estimates are required as of a date in that period. However, the Board decided to specify a narrower definition of impracticable because the fact that significant estimates are frequently required when amending comparative information presented for prior periods does not prevent reliable adjustment or correction of the comparative information. Thus, the Board decided that an inability to distinguish objectively information that both provides evidence of circumstances that existed on the date(s) as at which those amounts are to be recognised, measured or disclosed and would have been available when the financial statements for that prior period were authorised for issue from other information is the factor that prevents reliable adjustment or correction of comparative information for prior periods (see part (c) of the definition of 'impracticable' and paragraphs 51 and 52 of the Standard).

BC27   The Standard specifies that hindsight should not be used when applying a new accounting policy to, or correcting amounts for, a prior period, either in making assumptions about what management's intentions would have been in a prior period or estimating the amounts in a prior period. This is because management's intentions in a prior period cannot be objectively established in a later period, and using information that would have been unavailable when the financial statements for the prior period(s) affected were authorised for issue is inconsistent with the definitions of retrospective application and retrospective restatement.

Applying the impracticability exemption

BC28   The Standard specifies that when it is impracticable to determine the cumulative effect of applying a new accounting policy to all prior periods, or the cumulative effect of an error on all prior periods, the entity changes the comparative information as if the new accounting policy had been applied, or the error had been corrected, prospectively from the earliest date practicable (see paragraphs 25 and 45 of the Standard). This is similar to paragraph 52 of the previous version of IAS 8, but it is no longer restricted to changes in accounting policies. The Board decided to include such provisions in the Standard because it agrees with comments received that it is preferable to require prospective application from the start of the earliest period practicable

---

6   In 2006 the IASB issued IFRS 8 *Operating Segments*. As explained in paragraphs BC46 and BC47 of the Basis for Conclusions on IFRS 8, that IFRS includes an exemption from some requirements if the necessary information is not available and the cost to develop it would be excessive.

than to permit a change in accounting policy only when the entity can determine the cumulative effect of the change for all prior periods at the beginning of the current period.

BC29 Consistently with the Exposure Draft's proposals, the Standard provides an impracticability exemption from retrospective application of changes in accounting policies, including retrospective application of changes made in accordance with the transitional provisions in an IFRS. The previous version of IAS 8 specified the impracticability exemption for retrospective application of only *voluntary* changes in accounting policies. Thus, the applicability of the exemption to changes made in accordance with the transitional provisions in an IFRS depended on the text of that IFRS. The Board extended the applicability of the exemption because it decided that the need for the exemption applies equally to all changes in accounting policies applied retrospectively.

Disclosures about impending application of newly issued IFRSs

BC30 The Standard requires an entity to provide disclosures when it has not yet applied a new IFRS that has been issued but is not yet effective. The entity is required to disclose that it has not yet applied the IFRS, and known or reasonably estimable information relevant to assessing the possible impact that initial application of the new IFRS will have on the entity's financial statements in the period of initial application (paragraph 30). The Standard also includes guidance on specific disclosures the entity should consider when applying this requirement (paragraph 31).

BC31 Paragraphs 30 and 31 of the Standard differ from the proposals in the Exposure Draft in the following respects:

(a) they specify that an entity needs to disclose information only if it is known or reasonably estimable. This clarification responds to comments on the Exposure Draft that the proposed disclosures would sometimes be impracticable.

(b) whereas the Exposure Draft proposed to mandate the disclosures now in paragraph 31, the Standard sets out these disclosures as items an entity should consider disclosing to meet the general requirement in paragraph 30. This amendment focuses the requirement on the objective of the disclosure, and, in response to comments on the Exposure Draft that the proposed disclosures were more onerous than the disclosures in US GAAP, clarifies that the Board's intention was to converge with US requirements, rather than to be more onerous.

Recognising the effects of changes in accounting estimates

BC32 The Exposure Draft proposed to retain without exception the requirement in the previous version of IAS 8 that the effect of a change in accounting estimate is *recognised in profit or loss* in:

(a) the period of the change, if the change affects that period only; or

(b)   the period of the change and future periods, if the change affects both.

BC33   Some respondents to the Exposure Draft disagreed with requiring the effects of all changes in accounting estimates to be recognised in profit or loss. They argued that this is inappropriate to the extent that a change in an accounting estimate gives rise to changes in assets and liabilities, because the entity's equity does not change as a result. These commentators also argued that it is inappropriate to preclude recognising the effects of changes in accounting estimates directly in equity when that is required or permitted by a Standard or an Interpretation. The Board concurs, and decided to provide an exception to the requirement described in paragraph BC32 for these circumstances.

Amended references to the *Conceptual Framework*

BC34   Following the issue of the revised *Conceptual Framework for Financial Reporting* in 2018 (2018 *Conceptual Framework*), the Board issued *Amendments to References to Conceptual Framework in IFRS Standards*. In IAS 8, that document amended paragraphs 6 and 11(b).

BC35   Paragraph 6 of IAS 8 quoted the description of users of financial statements from the *Framework*. To retain the requirements of this paragraph, the Board decided to embed that description of users in the Standard itself instead of updating the reference and the related quotation.

BC36   *Amendments to References to the Conceptual Framework in IFRS Standards* replaced the reference in paragraph 11(b) to the *Framework* with a reference to the 2018 *Conceptual Framework*. Following this replacement, if management developed accounting policies in accordance with paragraph 11(b), management will need to review whether those policies are still consistent with the 2018 *Conceptual Framework*.

BC37   The Board analysed the effects on preparers of financial statements of replacing the reference to the *Framework* in paragraph 11(b) of IAS 8 and discussed the results of the analysis at the November 2016 Board meeting (see November 2016 AP10G *Effects of the proposed changes to the Conceptual Framework on preparers*). The analysis suggested that the scope of any changes to preparers' accounting policies is likely to be limited because:

(a)   most preparers of financial statements do not develop accounting policies by reference to the *Framework* because most transactions are:

(i)   covered by IFRS Standards;

(ii)   accounted for by applying accounting policies developed using other sources referred to in paragraphs 11–12 of IAS 8; or

(iii) exempt from the requirement to apply paragraph 11 of IAS 8; for example, IFRS 6 *Exploration for and Evaluation of Mineral Resources* exempts entities from applying paragraph 11 of IAS 8 to the recognition and measurement of exploration and evaluation assets; and

(b)   in most of the few remaining areas, application of the revised concepts in the 2018 *Conceptual Framework* would be expected to result in similar accounting outcomes to application of the concepts in the *Framework*.

Application by rate-regulated entities

BC38   While assessing possible effects of updating the reference to the *Framework* in IAS 8, the Board identified a potential disadvantage for entities that conduct rate-regulated activities and develop their accounting policies for regulatory account balances by reference to the *Framework* rather than by applying IFRS 14 *Regulatory Deferral Accounts*. If the reference to the *Framework* had been updated, such entities might have needed to revise those accounting policies twice within a short period of time—first, when the 2018 *Conceptual Framework* comes into effect; and, later, when a new IFRS Standard on rate-regulated activities is issued. In the absence of specific guidance, there might have been uncertainty about what would be acceptable if the 2018 *Conceptual Framework* was applied. Establishing what would be acceptable might have been costly and the outcome might have been diversity in practice and a loss of trend information for users.

BC39   To prevent unhelpful and unnecessary disruption for users of the financial statements of entities that conduct rate-regulated activities and for the entities themselves, the Board provided a temporary exception: paragraph 54G prohibits entities from applying the 2018 *Conceptual Framework* to accounting policies relating to regulatory account balances. Instead, entities are required to continue to apply the *Framework* when developing or revising those accounting policies. Once the Board issues a new IFRS Standard on rate-regulated activities, that prohibition is likely to become unnecessary.

BC40   The Board based the definition of 'a regulatory account balance' on the definition of 'a regulatory deferral account balance' in IFRS 14, with one difference: the definition of a regulatory account balance does not mention qualifying for deferral. The reference to deferral in IFRS 14 reflects the fact that IFRS 14 permits continued recognition of some regulatory deferral account balances that an entity previously recognised as assets or liabilities immediately before it adopted IFRS Standards for the first time. In contrast, paragraph 54G of IAS 8 applies only when an entity is not applying IFRS 14 but is instead developing an accounting policy after considering paragraph 11 of IAS 8. Paragraph 54G applies regardless of whether that accounting policy results in recognition of any assets or liabilities, and regardless of whether such recognition could be viewed as deferral.

Transition relief

BC41   The Board concluded that the retrospective application of revised accounting policies in accordance with IAS 8 would provide the most useful information to users of financial statements. However, in order to keep disruption for users and preparers of financial statements to a minimum, the Board decided not to require retrospective application of any amendment in *Amendments to References to the Conceptual Framework in IFRS Standards* if doing so would either be impracticable or involve undue cost or effort.

IASB documents published to accompany

IAS 10

Events after the Reporting Period

The text of the unaccompanied standard, IAS 10, is contained in Part A of this edition. Its effective date when issued was 1 January 2005. This part presents the following document:

BASIS FOR CONCLUSIONS

Basis for Conclusions on
IAS 10 *Events after the Reporting Period*[1]

This Basis for Conclusions accompanies, but is not part of, IAS 10.

Introduction

BC1   This Basis for Conclusions summarises the International Accounting Standards Board's considerations in reaching its conclusions on revising IAS 10 *Events After the Balance Sheet Date* in 2003. Individual Board members gave greater weight to some factors than to others.

BC2   In July 2001 the Board announced that, as part of its initial agenda of technical projects, it would undertake a project to improve a number of Standards, including IAS 10. The project was undertaken in the light of queries and criticisms raised in relation to the Standards by securities regulators, professional accountants and other interested parties. The objectives of the Improvements project were to reduce or eliminate alternatives, redundancies and conflicts within Standards, to deal with some convergence issues and to make other improvements. In May 2002 the Board published its proposals in an Exposure Draft of *Improvements to International Accounting Standards*, with a comment deadline of 16 September 2002. The Board received over 160 comment letters on the Exposure Draft.

BC3   Because the Board's intention was not to reconsider the fundamental approach to the accounting for events after the balance sheet date established by IAS 10, this Basis for Conclusions does not discuss requirements in IAS 10 that the Board has not reconsidered.

Limited clarification

BC4   For this limited clarification of IAS 10 the main change made is in paragraphs 12 and 13 (paragraphs 11 and 12 of the previous version of IAS 10). As revised, those paragraphs state that if dividends are declared after the balance sheet date,[2] an entity shall not recognise those dividends as a liability at the balance sheet date. This is because undeclared dividends do not meet the criteria of a present obligation in IAS 37 *Provisions, Contingent Liabilities and Contingent Assets*. The Board discussed whether or not an entity's past practice of paying dividends could be considered a constructive obligation. The Board concluded that such practices do not give rise to a liability to pay dividends.[3]

---

1   In September 2007 the IASB amended the title of IAS 10 from *Events after the Balance Sheet Date* to *Events after the Reporting Period* as a consequence of the amendments in IAS 1 *Presentation of Financial Statements* (as revised in 2007).

2   IAS 1 *Presentation of Financial Statements* (as revised in 2007) replaced the term 'balance sheet date' with 'end of the reporting period'.

3   In 2007 the Board was advised that paragraph 13, taken in isolation, could be read to imply that a liability should be recognised in some circumstances on the basis that a constructive obligation exists, such as when there is an established pattern of paying a dividend. Therefore, the Board amended paragraph 13 by *Improvements to IFRSs* issued in May 2008 to state that no such obligation exists.

IASB documents published to accompany

IAS 12

Income Taxes

The text of the unaccompanied standard, IAS 12, is contained in Part A of this edition. Its effective date when issued was 1 January 1998. The text of the Accompanying Guidance on IAS 12 is contained in Part B of this edition. This part presents the following document:

BASIS FOR CONCLUSIONS

Basis for Conclusions on
IAS 12 *Income Taxes*

This Basis for Conclusions accompanies, but is not part of, IAS 12.

Introduction

BC1   When IAS 12 *Income Taxes* was issued by the International Accounting Standards Committee in 1996 to replace the previous IAS 12 *Accounting for Taxes on Income* (issued in July 1979), the Standard was not accompanied by a Basis for Conclusions. This Basis for Conclusions is not comprehensive. It summarises only the International Accounting Standards Board's considerations in making the amendments to IAS 12 contained in *Deferred Tax: Recovery of Underlying Assets* issued in December 2010. Individual Board members gave greater weight to some factors than to others.

BC1A   In August 2014 the Board published an Exposure Draft of proposed amendments to IAS 12 to clarify the requirements on recognition of deferred tax assets for unrealised losses on debt instruments measured at fair value. The Board subsequently modified and confirmed the proposals and in January 2016 issued *Recognition of Deferred Tax Assets for Unrealised Losses* (Amendments to IAS 12). The Board's considerations and reasons for its conclusions are discussed in paragraphs BC37–BC62.

BC2   The Board amended IAS 12 to address an issue that arises when entities apply the measurement principle in IAS 12 to temporary differences relating to investment properties that are measured using the fair value model in IAS 40 *Investment Property*.

BC3   In March 2009 the Board published an exposure draft, *Income Tax* (the 2009 exposure draft), proposing a new IFRS to replace IAS 12. In the 2009 exposure draft, the Board addressed this issue as part of a broad proposal relating to the determination of tax basis. In October 2009 the Board decided not to proceed with the proposals in the 2009 exposure draft and announced that, together with the US Financial Accounting Standards Board, it aimed to conduct a fundamental review of the accounting for income tax in the future. In the meantime, the Board would address specific significant current practice issues.

BC4   In September 2010 the Board published proposals for addressing one of those practice issues in an exposure draft *Deferred Tax: Recovery of Underlying Assets* with a 60-day comment period. Although that is shorter than the Board's normal 120-day comment period, the Board concluded that this was justified because the amendments were straightforward and the exposure draft was short. In addition, the amendments were addressing a problem that existed in practice and needed to be solved as soon as possible. The Board considered the comments it received on the exposure draft and in December 2010 issued the amendments to IAS 12. The Board intends to address other practice issues arising from IAS 12 in due course, when other priorities on its agenda permit this.

Recovery of revalued non-depreciable assets

BC5   In December 2010, the Board incorporated in paragraph 51B of IAS 12 the consensus previously contained in SIC Interpretation 21 *Income Taxes—Recovery of Revalued Non-Depreciable Assets*. However, because paragraph 51C addresses investment property carried at fair value, the Board excluded such assets from the scope of paragraph 51B. Paragraphs BC6 and BC7 set out the basis that the Standing Interpretations Committee (SIC) gave for the conclusions it reached in developing the consensus expressed in SIC-21.

BC6   The SIC noted that the *Framework for the Preparation and Presentation of Financial Statements*[1] stated that an entity recognises an asset if it is probable that the future economic benefits associated with the asset will flow to the entity. Generally, those future economic benefits will be derived (and therefore the carrying amount of an asset will be recovered) through sale, through use, or through use and subsequent sale. Recognition of depreciation implies that the carrying amount of a depreciable asset is expected to be recovered through use to the extent of its depreciable amount, and through sale at its residual value. Consistently with this, the carrying amount of a non-depreciable asset, such as land having an unlimited life, will be recovered only through sale. In other words, because the asset is not depreciated, no part of its carrying amount is expected to be recovered (ie consumed) through use. Deferred taxes associated with the non-depreciable asset reflect the tax consequences of selling the asset.

BC7   The SIC noted that the expected manner of recovery is not predicated on the basis of measuring the carrying amount of the asset. For example, if the carrying amount of a non-depreciable asset is measured at its value in use, the basis of measurement does not imply that the carrying amount of the asset is expected to be recovered through use, but through its residual value upon ultimate disposal.

Recovery of investment properties

Reason for the exception

BC8   IAS 12 applies the principle that the measurement of deferred tax liabilities and deferred tax assets should reflect the tax consequences that would follow from the manner in which the entity expects to recover or settle the carrying amount of its assets and liabilities. In many cases, however, an entity expects to rent out investment property to earn rental income and then sell it to gain from capital appreciation at some point in the future. Without specific plans for disposal of the investment property, it is difficult and subjective to estimate how much of the carrying amount of the investment property will be recovered through cash flows from rental income and how much of it will be recovered through cash flows from selling the asset.

---

1   The reference is to the IASC's *Framework for the Preparation and Presentation of Financial Statements*, adopted by the Board in 2001 and in effect when the SIC discussed this matter.

BC9   It is particularly difficult and subjective to determine the entity's expected manner of recovery for investment property that is measured using the fair value model in IAS 40. In contrast, for investment property that is measured using the cost model in IAS 40, the Board believes that the estimates required for depreciation establish the expected manner of recovery because there is a general presumption that an asset's carrying amount is recovered through use to the extent of the amount subject to depreciation and through sale to the extent of the residual value.

BC10   To address this issue, the Board introduced an exception to the principle in IAS 12 that applies when an entity adopts an accounting policy of remeasuring investment property at fair value. The purpose of the exception is to reflect the entity's expectation of recovery of the investment property in a practical manner that involves little subjectivity.

BC11   Many respondents to the exposure draft of September 2010 commented that the Board should develop application guidance rather than creating an exception. The Board could have achieved a similar result in some cases by providing application guidance on how to apply the underlying principle to investment property. However, the Board chose an exception because it is simple, straightforward and can avoid unintended consequences by a strict definition of its scope. In fact, this exception is very similar to application guidance. However, it is technically an exception because, in some cases, the asset's carrying amount is assumed to be recovered entirely through sale even though an entity expects it to be recovered partly through sale and partly through use.

BC12   The Board also noted that application guidance would not resolve a practice issue that arises when the future income generated from an asset is expected to exceed the carrying amount of that asset and that future income will be subject to two or more different tax regimes. In those situations, IAS 12 provides no basis for determining which tax rate and tax base apply to the recovery of the carrying amount. The Board concluded that the practical way to resolve this issue was to create an exception that determines the manner of recovery of an asset within the scope of that exception.

Scope of the exception

BC13   The Board understands that the concerns raised in practice relate primarily to investment property measured using the fair value model in IAS 40. The Board proposed in the exposure draft that the exception should also apply to property, plant and equipment or intangible assets measured using the revaluation model in IAS 16 *Property, Plant and Equipment* or IAS 38 *Intangible Assets*. That was because in assessing the difficulty and subjectivity involved in determining the expected manner of recovering the carrying amount of the underlying asset, there is no underlying difference between regularly fair valuing assets through a revaluation accounting policy and applying a fair value measurement model.

BC14   Many respondents disagreed with the proposal to include property, plant and equipment or intangible assets measured using the revaluation model in IAS 16 or IAS 38 in the scope of the exception. They stated that many items of property, plant and equipment are recovered through use rather than through sale, and that this is consistent with the definition of property, plant and equipment in IAS 16. In addition, many respondents disagreed with the presumption of recovery through sale when the underlying assets are intangible assets for similar reasons. They also warned of unintended consequences that could arise because of the varying nature of intangible assets. Many respondents suggested limiting the scope of the exception to investment properties measured using the fair value model in IAS 40. Having considered those comments, the Board adopted that suggestion.

BC15   Some respondents supported inclusion of property, plant and equipment in the scope of the exception, including property, plant and equipment measured on a cost basis, because of their concerns about the lack of discounting deferred tax assets and deferred tax liabilities and about a possible double-counting of tax effects (see paragraph BC19). However, the Board concluded that considering concerns about the lack of discounting and about the possible double-counting was outside the limited scope of the amendments.

BC16   The Board made it clear that the exception also applies on initial measurement of investment property acquired in a business combination if the investment property will subsequently be measured using the fair value model in IAS 40. If the exception did not apply in these circumstances, deferred taxes might reflect the tax consequences of use at the acquisition date, but at a later date reflect the tax consequences of sale. The Board believes that measurement of deferred taxes at the acquisition date should be consistent with the subsequent measurement of the same deferred taxes. For the same reason, the Board concluded that the exception should not apply to investment property initially measured at fair value in a business combination if the entity subsequently uses the cost model.

BC17   Having considered the responses to the exposure draft, the Board decided not to extend the exception to other underlying assets and liabilities that are measured at fair value, including financial instruments or biological assets. This is because the Board understands that the most significant current practice issues relate to investment property. In addition, the Board wished to avoid unintended consequences of expanding the scope to other assets and liabilities that are measured on a fair value basis.

BC18   The Board concluded that the amendments should apply to all temporary differences that arise relating to underlying assets within the scope of the exception, not just those separate temporary differences created by the remeasurement of the underlying asset. This is because the unit of account applied in determining the manner of recovery in the Standard is the underlying asset as a whole, not the individual temporary differences.

Measurement basis

BC19   The Board decided that when the exception applies, there should be a presumption that deferred taxes should be measured to reflect the tax consequences of recovering the carrying amount of the investment property entirely through sale. In making that decision, the Board considered various views expressed by interested parties, which included, but were not limited to the following:

(a)   the tax effect would be double-counted in some situations if deferred taxes are measured on the basis of the tax consequences of use, because the investment property is measured at fair value, which reflects some of these tax consequences; and

(b)   presuming sale is consistent with a fair value measurement basis that reflects the price that would be received if the investment property is sold.

BC20   Many respondents to the exposure draft said that choosing a measurement basis of fair value is an accounting policy choice that does not imply or predict recovery of the investment property through sale. Many also said that the proposed exception would solve the double-counting problem partially but not completely. The Board noted that the aim of the exception was neither to link the accounting policy with measurement of deferred taxes (see paragraph BC7), nor to remove completely the double-counting of tax effects (see paragraph BC15). The aim of this exception is to provide a practical approach when determination of the expected manner of recovery is difficult and subjective.

BC21   In many cases when an entity chooses the fair value model for investment property, investment properties are recovered through sale. Even if an investment property earns income through rental use in a given period, the value of the future earnings capacity of the investment property will often not decrease and that value will ultimately be realised through sale. Therefore, the Board retained its proposal to introduce a presumption of recovery through sale.

BC22   The Board made that presumption rebuttable because the Board believes that it is not always appropriate to assume the recovery of investment property through sale. The Board initially proposed in the exposure draft that the presumption of recovery through sale is not appropriate when the entity has clear evidence that it will consume the asset's economic benefits throughout its economic life. The Board set a criterion that refers to consumption of the asset's economic benefits, rather than to the recovery of the carrying amount, because the Board understands that there is diverse practice regarding the meaning of the recovery of the carrying amount through use or through sale.

BC23   After considering the responses to the exposure draft, the Board reworded the rebuttable presumption so that clear evidence would not be required to rebut it. Instead, the presumption is rebutted if an asset is held within a business model whose objective is to consume substantially all of the economic benefits embodied in the investment property over time, rather than through sale.

Many respondents were concerned that, because clear evidence is an ambiguous term, the requirement to gather clear evidence would have been onerous for entities that have no problem applying the existing principle in IAS 12, and could have led to abuse by entities that choose whether to gather clear evidence to achieve a favourable result. The Board chose to use the term 'business model' because it is already used in IFRS 9 *Financial Instruments* and would not depend on management's intentions for an individual asset. Many respondents were concerned that the presumption would lead to inappropriate results in some cases because it would not be rebutted if a minor scrap value would be recovered through sale. The Board also reworded the rebuttable presumption in order to respond to those concerns. The Board also made it clear that the presumption of recovery through sale cannot be rebutted if the asset is non-depreciable because that fact implies that no part of the carrying amount of the asset would be consumed through use (see paragraph BC6).

BC24   The Board also considered other approaches to the measurement of deferred tax liabilities and deferred tax assets when the exception applies, specifically whether deferred taxes should be measured on the basis of the lower of the tax consequences of recovery through use and through sale. However, the Board rejected such an approach, noting that it would have created:

(a)   conceptual and practical concerns about whether deferred tax assets should be measured to reflect the lower of, or higher of, the tax consequences of use and of sale;

(b)   a measurement basis that some believe would be arbitrary; and

(c)   concerns that entities might be required to measure deferred taxes on a basis that is inconsistent with their expectations of recovery of the carrying amount of the underlying asset.

BC25   Some respondents to the exposure draft drew the mistaken conclusion that the exposure draft required presumption of *immediate* sale at the end of the reporting period when assessing the presumption of recovery through sale. The Board observed that paragraph 47 of IAS 12 requires deferred tax assets and liabilities to be measured at the tax rates that are expected to apply to the period when the asset is realised or the liability is settled on the basis of tax rates (and tax laws) that have been enacted or substantively enacted by the end of the reporting period. This requirement applies even when the presumption of recovery through sale is used. For clarification, the Board adjusted the illustrative example following paragraph 51C to reflect the requirement in paragraph 47.

BC26   In the exposure draft, the Board proposed to withdraw SIC-21. However, many respondents commented that SIC-21 should be retained in order to avoid unintended consequences. Having considered the responses to the exposure draft, the Board decided to incorporate SIC-21 into IAS 12 in its entirety after excluding from the scope of SIC-21 the investment property subject to the requirement in paragraph 51C.

Assessment of deferred tax assets

BC27 The Board inserted paragraph 51E to confirm that the requirements in paragraphs 24–33 (deductible temporary differences) and paragraphs 34–36 (unused tax losses and unused tax credits) relating to assessment of deferred tax assets continue to apply even when the presumption of recovery through sale arises. The Board did not think that additional guidance would be necessary.

Disclosure requirement

BC28 The Board proposed in the exposure draft disclosure of the fact of, and reasons for, the rebuttal of the presumption of recovery through sale if the entity has rebutted the presumption. However, many respondents said that this disclosure would add little or no value to the financial statements. IAS 1 *Presentation of Financial Statements* already requires disclosures regarding material judgements. Thus, there is no need to disclose a particular judgement on specific types of assets. The Board was convinced by those arguments and did not proceed with the proposed disclosure requirement.

The costs and benefits of the amendments to IAS 12

BC29 Computation of the tax consequences of selling assets is complex in some tax jurisdictions and there are concerns that the amendments to IAS 12 will increase the administrative burden for some entities in those tax jurisdictions.

BC30 However, the Board believes that the benefit of providing the exception outweighs this potential increase in administrative burden for some entities. This is because the purpose of the exception is to enable preparers to measure deferred taxes in these circumstances in the least subjective manner and in so doing enhance the comparability of financial information about deferred taxes for the benefit of users of financial statements. It is also expected to result in an overall reduction of the administrative burden for entities that have previously had to consider the tax consequence of both use and sale of an investment property when measuring deferred taxes.

BC31 Many respondents to the exposure draft said that entities would not benefit from the amendments in jurisdictions in which this practice issue did not exist but would suffer from an increased administrative burden as a result of the amendments. Their criticism mainly focused on the rebuttable presumption, as discussed in paragraphs BC22 and BC23. They also said that the disclosure requirement proposed in the exposure draft would be onerous.

BC32 After considering the responses to the exposure draft, the Board narrowed the scope of the exception to apply only to investment property carried at fair value. It reworded the rebuttable presumption so that clear evidence would no longer be required to rebut the presumption. The Board also did not pursue the proposed disclosure requirement regarding the fact of, and reason for, the rebuttal. After those changes, the Board believes that the amendments will not be onerous for entities that have previously been able to establish without difficulty how they expect to recover investment property carried at fair value.

Transition and effective date

BC33   IAS 8 *Accounting Policies, Changes in Accounting Estimates and Errors* requires an entity to apply retrospectively a change in accounting policy resulting from the initial application of an IFRS that does not have a transition provision. The Board did not include any transition provision in the amendments because, in the Board's view, it would not be unduly burdensome for entities to apply the changes to IAS 12 retrospectively.

BC34   The Board acknowledges that the amendments may add some administrative burden if they apply to investment property acquired in a business combination that occurred in a previous reporting period. For example, it could be difficult to restate goodwill and recalculate previous impairment reassessments if some information is not available and an entity is unable to separate the effects of hindsight. However, the Board reasoned that the amendments apply only to specific circumstances. Moreover, IAS 8 provides sufficient guidance to deal with cases when it might be impracticable to reassess impairment of goodwill or recoverability of deferred tax assets.

BC35   Consequently, the Board concluded that the cost of requiring retrospective application is outweighed by the benefit of consistent application of the amendments by entities to all periods presented in the financial statements. Accordingly, the Board decided that entities should apply the amendments to IAS 12 retrospectively in accordance with IAS 8.

First-time adoption of IFRSs

BC36   The Board identified no reason to adjust the exception for application by a first-time adopter at its date of transition to IFRSs.

Recognition of Deferred Tax Assets for Unrealised Losses (2016 amendments)

BC37   The IFRS Interpretations Committee (the 'Interpretations Committee') was asked to provide guidance on how an entity determines, in accordance with IAS 12, whether to recognise a deferred tax asset when:

(a)   the entity has a debt instrument that is classified as an available-for-sale financial asset in accordance with IAS 39 *Financial Instruments: Recognition and Measurement*.[2] Changes in the market interest rate result in a decrease in the fair value of the debt instrument to below its cost (ie it has an 'unrealised loss');

(b)   it is probable that the issuer of the debt instrument will make all the contractual payments;

(c)   the tax base of the debt instrument is cost;

---

2   IFRS 9 *Financial Instruments* replaced IAS 39. IFRS 9 applies to all items that were previously within the scope of IAS 39. Under IFRS 9, the same question arises for debt instruments measured at fair value.

(d)   tax law does not allow a loss to be deducted on a debt instrument until the loss is realised for tax purposes;

(e)   the entity has the ability and intention to hold the debt instrument until the unrealised loss reverses (which may be at its maturity);

(f)   tax law distinguishes between capital gains and losses and ordinary income and losses. While capital losses can only be offset against capital gains, ordinary losses can be offset against both capital gains and ordinary income; and

(g)   the entity has insufficient taxable temporary differences and no other probable taxable profits against which the entity can utilise deductible temporary differences.

BC38   The Interpretations Committee reported to the Board that practice differed because of divergent views on the following questions:

(a)   Do decreases in the carrying amount of a fixed-rate debt instrument for which the principal is paid on maturity always give rise to a deductible temporary difference if this debt instrument is measured at fair value and if its tax base remains at cost? In particular, do they give rise to a deductible temporary difference if the debt instrument's holder expects to recover the carrying amount of the asset by use, ie continuing to hold it, and if it is probable that the issuer will pay all the contractual cash flows? (see paragraphs BC39–BC45)

(b)   Does an entity assume that it will recover an asset for more than its carrying amount when estimating probable future taxable profit against which deductible temporary differences are assessed for utilisation if such recovery is probable? This question is relevant when taxable profit from other sources is insufficient for the utilisation of the deductible temporary differences related to debt instruments measured at fair value. In this case, an entity may only be able to recognise deferred tax assets for its deductible temporary differences if it is probable that it will collect the entire cash flows from the debt instrument and therefore recover it for more than its carrying amount. (see paragraphs BC46–BC54)

(c)   When an entity assesses whether it can utilise deductible temporary differences against probable future taxable profit, does that probable future taxable profit include the effects of reversing deductible temporary differences? (see paragraphs BC55–BC56)

(d)   Does an entity assess whether a deferred tax asset is recognised for each deductible temporary difference separately or in combination with other deductible temporary differences? This question is relevant, for example, when tax law distinguishes capital gains and losses from other taxable gains and losses and capital losses can only be offset against capital gains. (see paragraphs BC57–BC59)

Existence of a deductible temporary difference

BC39   In the case of many debt instruments, the collection of the principal on maturity does not increase or decrease taxable profit that is reported for tax purposes. This is the case in the example illustrating paragraph 26(d) of IAS 12. Interest is paid at the contractual rate each year, and on maturity of the debt instrument the issuer pays the principal of CU1,000. In this example, if the investor continues to hold the debt instrument, the investor only pays taxes on the interest income. The collection of the principal does not trigger any tax payments.

BC40   Because the collection of the principal does not increase or decrease the taxable profit that is reported for tax purposes, some thought that the collection of the principal is a non-taxable event. Sometimes, tax law does not explicitly address whether the collection of the principal has tax consequences. Consequently, proponents of this view thought that a difference between the carrying amount of the debt instrument in the statement of financial position and its higher tax base does not give rise to a deductible temporary difference, if this difference results from a loss that they expect will not be realised for tax purposes.

BC41   Those who held this view thought that the loss would not be realised for tax purposes if the entity has the ability and intention to hold the debt instrument over the period until the loss reverses, which might be until maturity, and it is probable that the entity will receive all the contractual cash flows. In this case, differences between the carrying amount of the debt instrument in the statement of financial position and its tax base reverse over the period to maturity, as a result of continuing to hold the debt instrument.

BC42   The Board considered the guidance in IAS 12 on the identification of temporary differences and rejected the reasoning presented in paragraphs BC40 and BC41. Paragraphs 20 and 26(d) of IAS 12 specify that a difference between the carrying amount of an asset measured at fair value and its higher tax base gives rise to a deductible temporary difference. This is because the calculation of a temporary difference in IAS 12 is based on the premise that the entity will recover the carrying amount of an asset, and hence economic benefits will flow to the entity in future periods to the extent of the asset's carrying amount at the end of the reporting period. In contrast, the view presented in paragraphs BC40 and BC41 is based on the assessment of the economic benefits that are expected at maturity. The Board noted that the existence of a deductible temporary difference depends solely on a comparison of the carrying amount of an asset and its tax base at the end of the reporting period, and is not affected by possible future changes in the carrying amount.

BC43   Consequently, the Board concluded that decreases below cost in the carrying amount of a fixed-rate debt instrument measured at fair value for which the tax base remains at cost give rise to a deductible temporary difference. This applies irrespective of whether the debt instrument's holder expects to recover the carrying amount of the debt instrument by sale or by use, ie continuing to hold it, or whether it is probable that the issuer will pay all the contractual cash flows. Normally, the collection of the entire principal does not increase or decrease taxable profit that is reported for tax purposes, because the tax base equals the inflow of taxable economic benefits when the principal is paid. Typically, the tax base of the debt instrument is deducted either on sale or on maturity.

BC44 The economic benefit embodied in the related deferred tax asset arises from the ability of the holder of the debt instrument to achieve future taxable gains in the amount of the deductible temporary difference without paying taxes on those gains. In contrast, an entity that acquires the debt instrument described in the example illustrating paragraph 26(d) of IAS 12 for its fair value at the end of Year 2 (in the example, CU918) and continues to hold it, has to pay taxes on a gain of CU82, whereas the entity in that example will not pay any taxes on the collection of the CU1,000 of principal. The Board concluded that it was appropriate for the different tax consequences for these two holders of the same instrument to be reflected in the deferred tax accounting for the debt instrument.

BC45 The Board has added an example after paragraph 26 of IAS 12 to illustrate the identification of a deductible temporary difference in the case of a fixed-rate debt instrument measured at fair value for which the principal is paid on maturity.

Recovering an asset for more than its carrying amount

BC46 The Board noted that paragraph 29 of IAS 12 identifies taxable profit in future periods as one source of taxable profits against which an entity can utilise deductible temporary differences. Future taxable profit has to be probable to justify the recognition of deferred tax assets.

BC47 The guidance in paragraph 29 of IAS 12 does not refer to the carrying amount of assets within the context of estimating probable future taxable profit. Some thought, however, that the carrying amount of an asset to which a temporary difference is related limits the estimate of future taxable profit. They argued that accounting for deferred taxes should be based on consistent assumptions, which implies that an entity cannot assume that, for one and the same asset, the entity will recover it:

(a) for its carrying amount when determining deductible temporary differences and taxable temporary differences; as well as

(b) for more than its carrying amount when estimating probable future taxable profit against which deductible temporary differences are assessed for utilisation.

BC48 Consequently, proponents of this view thought that an entity cannot assume that it will collect the entire principal of CU1,000 in the example illustrating paragraph 26(d) of IAS 12 when determining probable future taxable profit. Instead, they thought that an entity must assume that it will collect only the carrying amount of the asset.

BC49 The Board noted however that determining temporary differences and estimating probable future taxable profit against which deductible temporary differences are assessed for utilisation are two separate steps and the carrying amount of an asset is relevant only to determining temporary differences. The carrying amount of an asset does not limit the estimation of probable future taxable profit. In its estimate of probable future taxable profit, an entity includes the probable inflow of taxable economic benefits that results from recovering an asset. This probable inflow of taxable economic benefits may exceed the carrying amount of the asset.

BC50 Moreover, a limitation on the estimate of probable future taxable profit by the carrying amount of assets can lead to inappropriate results in other scenarios. For example, a significant part of the assets of a profitable manufacturing entity is property, plant and equipment and inventories. Property, plant and equipment may be measured using the cost model (paragraph 30 of IAS 16 *Property, Plant and Equipment)* and inventories are measured at the lower of cost and net realisable value (paragraph 9 of IAS 2 *Inventories*). If such an entity expects to generate future taxable profit, it may be inconsistent to assume that it will only recover these assets for their carrying amount. This is because a significant part of the manufacturing entity's probable future taxable profit results from using those assets to generate taxable profit in excess of their carrying amount.

BC51 If a limitation such as the one described in paragraph BC50 was made, then, for the purpose of consistency, the entity would need to assume that it will not recover any of its assets for more than their carrying amount. The Board decided that it would not be appropriate to limit the estimate of probable future taxable profit to the carrying amount of related assets only for assets to which temporary differences are related, because there is no basis for a different assessment that would depend on whether a deductible temporary difference is related to an asset or not.

BC52 Some respondents to the Exposure Draft expressed concern that the guidance might be applied more broadly, and in their view, inappropriately, to other assets, and not merely to debt instruments measured at fair value. Some other respondents were concerned that any guidance would give the false impression that future taxable profit should be estimated on an individual asset basis. The Board noted that the principle that the estimate of probable future taxable profit includes an expected recovery of assets for more than their carrying amounts is not limited to any specific type or class of assets.

BC53 However, the Board also noted that there are cases in which it may not be probable that an asset will be recovered for more than its carrying amount. An entity should not inappropriately assume that an asset will be recovered for more than its carrying amount. The Board thought that this is particularly important when the asset is measured at fair value. In response to that concern, the Board noted that entities will need to have sufficient evidence on which to base their estimate of probable future taxable profit, including when that estimate involves the recovery of an asset for more than its carrying amount. For example, in the case of a fixed-rate debt instrument measured at fair value, the entity may judge that the contractual nature of future cash flows, as well as the assessment of the likelihood that those contractual cash flows will be received, adequately supports the conclusion that it is probable that it will recover the fixed-rate debt instrument for more than its carrying amount, if the expected cash flows exceed the debt instrument's carrying amount. The Board thought that such an example could enhance understanding and reduce the risk of arbitrary estimates of future taxable profit.

BC54   The Board has added paragraph 29A to IAS 12 to clarify to what extent an entity's estimate of future taxable profit (paragraph 29) includes amounts from recovering assets for more than their carrying amounts.

Probable future taxable profit against which deductible temporary differences are assessed for utilisation

BC55   The Interpretations Committee observed that there is uncertainty about how to determine probable future taxable profit against which deductible temporary differences are assessed for utilisation when this profit is being assessed to determine the recognition of all deferred tax assets. The uncertainty relates to whether the probable future taxable profit should include or exclude deductions that will arise when those deductible temporary differences reverse.

BC56   The Board noted that deductible temporary differences are utilised by deduction against taxable profit, excluding deductions arising from reversal of those deductible temporary differences. Consequently, taxable profit used for assessing the utilisation of deductible temporary differences is different from taxable profit on which income taxes are payable, as defined in paragraph 5 of IAS 12. If those deductions were not excluded, then they would be counted twice. The Board has amended paragraph 29(a) to clarify this.

Combined versus separate assessment

BC57   The Board considered the guidance in IAS 12 on the recognition of deferred tax assets. Paragraph 24 of IAS 12 requires deferred tax assets to be recognised only to the extent of probable future taxable profit against which the deductible temporary differences can be utilised. Paragraph 27 explains that:

(a)   the deductible temporary differences are utilised when their reversal results in deductions that are offset against taxable profits of future periods; and

(b)   economic benefits in the form of reductions in tax payments will flow to the entity only if it earns sufficient taxable profits against which the deductions can be offset.

BC58   The Board noted that:

(a)   tax law determines which deductions are offset against taxable income in determining taxable profits. The Board also noted that paragraph 5 of IAS 12 defines taxable profit as the profit of a period, determined in accordance with the rules established by the taxation authorities, upon which income taxes are payable.

(b)   no deferred tax asset is recognised if the reversal of the deductible temporary difference will not lead to tax deductions.

BC59   Consequently, if tax law offsets a deduction against taxable income on an entity basis, without segregating deductions from different sources, an entity carries out a combined assessment of all its deductible temporary differences relating to the same taxation authority and the same taxable entity. However, if tax law offsets specific types of losses only against a particular type, or types, of income (for example, if tax law limits the offset of capital losses to capital gains), an entity assesses a deductible temporary difference in combination with other deductible temporary differences of that type(s), but separately from other deductible temporary differences. Segregating deductible temporary differences in accordance with tax law and assessing them on such a basis is necessary to determine whether taxable profits are sufficient to utilise deductible temporary differences. The Board has added paragraph 27A to IAS 12 to clarify this.

Transition

BC60   The Board decided to require the adjustment of comparative information for any earlier periods presented. However, this amendment allows the change in opening equity of the earliest comparative period presented that arises upon the first application of the amendment to be recognised in opening retained earnings (or in another component of equity, as appropriate), without the need to allocate the change between opening retained earnings and other components of equity. This is to avoid undue cost and effort.

BC61   The Board noted that, with the exception of the amounts that would have to be adjusted within equity, the accounting required by these amendments is based on amounts and estimates at the end of the reporting periods. The changes to the accounting are mechanical in nature and so the Board expects that the cost of adjusting comparatives should not exceed the benefits of greater comparability.

BC62   The Board has not added additional transition relief for first-time adopters. This is consistent with the fact that IFRS 1 *First-time Adoption of International Financial Reporting Standards* does not include an exception to, or exemption from, the retrospective application of the requirements in IAS 12.

Income tax consequences of payments on financial instruments classified as equity (amendments issued in December 2017)

BC63   The Board was asked about the income tax consequences of payments on financial instruments classified as equity; should an entity recognise them in profit or loss, or in equity? In particular, the Board was asked whether the requirements in paragraph 57A (paragraph 52B before the amendments were made) apply only in the circumstances described in paragraph 52A (for example, when there are different tax rates for distributed and undistributed profits), or whether those requirements apply as long as payments on financial instruments classified as equity are distributions of profit.

BC64   The Board observed that:

    (a)   paragraph 57A describes how an entity accounts for income tax consequences of dividends paid. Dividends are defined in IFRS 9 as 'distributions of profits to holders of equity instruments in proportion to their holdings of a particular class of capital'.

    (b)   paragraph 57A first requires an entity to link the income tax consequences of dividends to past transactions or events that generated distributable profits. An entity then applies the requirements in paragraph 58 to determine where to recognise those income tax consequences. Applying paragraph 57A, the entity recognises the income tax consequences of dividends according to where it has recognised the past transactions or events that generated distributable profits.

    (c)   the reason for the income tax consequences of dividends should not affect where those income tax consequences are recognised. It does not matter whether such consequences arise, for example, because of different tax rates for distributed and undistributed profits or because of the deductibility of dividends for tax purposes. This is because, in both cases, the income tax consequences arise from the distribution of profits.

    (d)   linking the recognition of the income tax consequences of dividends to how the tax consequences arise (for example, because of different tax rates, rather than because of different tax-deductibility rules) would lead to arbitrary results and a lack of comparability across entities in different tax jurisdictions. Tax jurisdictions choose different methods of imposing tax or providing tax relief. What matters is the resulting tax effect, not the mechanism.

BC65   Accordingly, the Board concluded that an entity should recognise all income tax consequences of dividends applying the requirements in paragraph 57A. However, the Board also observed that, before those requirements were amended, the requirements in paragraph 57A could be misread to imply that paragraph 57A applied only in the circumstances described in paragraph 52A.

BC66   Consequently, the Board clarified that the requirements in paragraph 57A apply to all income tax consequences of dividends.

BC67   The Board noted that the amendments do not suggest that an entity applies paragraph 57A to the income tax consequences of all payments on financial instruments classified as equity. Rather, paragraph 57A applies only when an entity determines payments on such instruments are distributions of profits (ie dividends). An entity may need to apply judgement in making this determination.

BC68   The Board considered whether to include requirements on how to determine if payments on financial instruments classified as equity are distributions of profits. It decided not to do so for the following reasons:

(a)   including indicators or requirements that distinguish distributions of profits from other distributions goes beyond the scope of the amendments to IAS 12. Any attempt by the Board to define or describe distributions of profits could affect other IFRS Standards and IFRIC Interpretations, and risks unintended consequences.

(b)   the amendments do not change what is and is not a distribution of profits. They simply clarify that the requirements in paragraph 57A apply to all income tax consequences of dividends.

BC69   The Board concluded that finalising the amendments without adding the possible requirements mentioned in paragraph BC68 would nonetheless be beneficial to preparers and users of financial statements. In particular, the amendments would eliminate the potential for inconsistent accounting that resulted from the ambiguity of the scope of the requirements in paragraph 57A that existed before those requirements were amended.

Transition

BC70   The Board decided that an entity applies the amendments to income tax consequences of dividends recognised on or after the beginning of the earliest comparative period when it first applies the amendments. This is because application of the amendments before that date could affect only components of equity as at the beginning of the earliest comparative period. The Board concluded that entities would have sufficient information to apply the amendments to the income tax consequences of dividends that occur in comparative reporting periods and that applying the amendments in this way will enhance comparability of reporting periods.

IASB documents published to accompany

IAS 16

Property, Plant and Equipment

The text of the unaccompanied standard, IAS 16, is contained in Part A of this edition. Its effective date when issued was 1 January 2005. This part presents the following documents:

BASIS FOR CONCLUSIONS

DISSENTING OPINION

CONTENTS

continued...

...continued

Basis for Conclusions on
IAS 16 *Property, Plant and Equipment*

This Basis for Conclusions accompanies, but is not part of, IAS 16.

Introduction

BC1   This Basis for Conclusions summarises the International Accounting Standards Board's considerations in reaching its conclusions on revising IAS 16 *Property, Plant and Equipment* in 2003. Individual Board members gave greater weight to some factors than to others.

BC2   In July 2001 the Board announced that, as part of its initial agenda of technical projects, it would undertake a project to improve a number of Standards, including IAS 16. The project was undertaken in the light of queries and criticisms raised in relation to the Standards by securities regulators, professional accountants and other interested parties. The objectives of the Improvements project were to reduce or eliminate alternatives, redundancies and conflicts within Standards, to deal with some convergence issues and to make other improvements. In May 2002 the Board published its proposals in an Exposure Draft of *Improvements to International Accounting Standards*, with a comment deadline of 16 September 2002. The Board received over 160 comment letters on the Exposure Draft.

BC2A   *Agriculture: Bearer Plants* (Amendments to IAS 16 and IAS 41), issued in June 2014, amended the scope of IAS 16 to include bearer plants. IAS 41 *Agriculture* applies to the produce growing on those bearer plants. The amendments define a bearer plant and require bearer plants to be accounted for as property, plant and equipment in accordance with IAS 16. These amendments are discussed in paragraphs BC38–BC117.

BC3   Because the Board's intention was not to reconsider the fundamental approach to the accounting for property, plant and equipment that was established by IAS 16, this Basis for Conclusions does not discuss requirements in IAS 16 that the Board has not reconsidered.

Scope

BC4   The Board clarified that the requirements of IAS 16 apply to items of property, plant and equipment that an entity uses to develop or maintain (a) biological assets and (b) mineral rights and mineral reserves such as oil, natural gas and similar non-regenerative resources. The Board noted that items of property, plant and equipment that an entity uses for these purposes possess the same characteristics as other items of property, plant and equipment.

Recognition

BC5   In considering potential improvements to the previous version of IAS 16, the Board reviewed its subsequent expenditure recognition principle for two reasons. First, the existing subsequent expenditure recognition principle did not align with the asset recognition principle in the *Framework*.[1] Second, the Board noted difficulties in practice in making the distinction it required between expenditures that maintain, and those that enhance, an item of property, plant and equipment. Some expenditures seem to do both.

BC6   The Board ultimately decided that the separate recognition principle for subsequent expenditure was not needed. As a result, an entity will evaluate all its property, plant and equipment costs under IAS 16's general recognition principle. Also, if the cost of a replacement for part of an item of property, plant and equipment is recognised in the carrying amount of an asset, then an entity will derecognise the carrying amount of what was replaced to avoid carrying both the replacement and the replaced portion as assets. This derecognition occurs whether or not what is replaced is a part of an item that the entity depreciates separately.

BC7   The Board's decision on how to handle the recognition principles was not reached easily. In the Exposure Draft (ED), the Board proposed to include within IAS 16's general recognition principle only the recognition of subsequent expenditures that are replacements of a part of an item of property, plant and equipment. Also in the ED, the Board proposed to modify the subsequent expenditure recognition principle to distinguish more clearly the expenditures to which it would continue to apply.

BC8   Respondents to the ED agreed that it was appropriate for subsequent expenditures that were replacements of a part of an item of property, plant and equipment that an entity depreciated separately to be covered by the general recognition principle. However, the respondents argued, and the Board agreed, that the modified second principle was not clearer because it would result in an entity recognising in the carrying amount of an asset and then depreciating subsequent expenditures that were for the day-to-day servicing of items of property, plant and equipment, those that might commonly be regarded as for 'repairs and maintenance'. That result was not the Board's intention.

BC9   In its redeliberation of the ED, the Board concluded it could not retain the proposed modified subsequent expenditure recognition principle. It also concluded that it could not revert to the subsequent expenditure principle in the previous version of IAS 16 because, if it did, nothing was improved; the *Framework* conflict was not resolved and the practice issues were not addressed.

---

1   References to the *Framework* in this Basis for Conclusions are to the IASC's *Framework for the Preparation and Presentation of Financial Statements*, adopted by the Board in 2001 and in effect when the Standard was revised.

BC10   The Board concluded that it was best for all subsequent expenditures to be covered by IAS 16's general recognition principle. This solution had the following advantages:

   (a)   use of IAS 16's general recognition principle fits the *Framework*.

   (b)   use of a single recognition principle is a straightforward approach.

   (c)   retaining IAS 16's general recognition principle and combining it with the derecognition principle will result in financial statements that reflect what is occurring, ie both the flow of property, plant and equipment through an entity and the economics of the acquisition and disposal process.

   (d)   use of one recognition principle fosters consistency. With two principles, consistency is not achieved unless it is clear when each should apply. Because IAS 16 does not address what constitutes an 'item' of property, plant and equipment, this clarity was not assured because some might characterise a particular cost as the initial cost of a new item of property, plant and equipment and others might regard it as a subsequent cost of an existing item of property, plant and equipment.

BC11   As a consequence of placing all subsequent expenditures under IAS 16's general recognition principle, the Board also included those expenditures under IAS 16's derecognition principle. In the ED, the Board proposed the derecognition of the carrying amount of a part of an item that was depreciated separately and was replaced by a subsequent expenditure that an entity recognised in the carrying amount of the asset under the general recognition principle. With this change, replacements of a part of an item that are not depreciated separately are subject to the same approach.

BC12   The Board noted that some subsequent expenditures on property, plant and equipment, although arguably incurred in the pursuit of future economic benefits, are not sufficiently certain to be recognised in the carrying amount of an asset under the general recognition principle. Thus, the Board decided to state in the Standard that an entity recognises in profit or loss as incurred the costs of the day-to-day servicing of property, plant and equipment.

Classification of servicing equipment

BC12A   In *Annual Improvements 2009–2011 Cycle* (issued in May 2012) the Board responded to a request to address a perceived inconsistency in the classification requirements for servicing equipment. Paragraph 8 of IAS 16 was unclear on the classification of servicing equipment as inventory or property, plant and equipment and led some to think that servicing equipment used during more than one period would be classified as part of inventory. The Board decided to clarify that items such as spare parts, stand-by equipment and servicing equipment shall be recognised as property, plant and equipment when they meet the definition of property, plant and equipment. If they do not meet this definition they are classified as inventory. In the light of respondents' comments to the June 2011 exposure draft, the

Board did not make explicit reference to the classification of particular types of equipment, because the definition of property, plant and equipment already provides sufficient guidance. The Board also deleted from paragraph 8 the requirement to account for spare parts and servicing equipment as property, plant and equipment only if they were used in connection with an item of property, plant and equipment because this requirement was too restrictive when compared with the definition of property, plant and equipment.

Measurement at recognition

Asset dismantlement, removal and restoration costs

BC13   The previous version of IAS 16 provided that in initially measuring an item of property, plant and equipment at its cost, an entity would include the cost of dismantling and removing that item and restoring the site on which it is located to the extent it had recognised an obligation for that cost. As part of its deliberations, the Board evaluated whether it could improve this guidance by addressing associated issues that have arisen in practice.

BC14   The Board concluded that the relatively limited scope of the Improvements project warranted addressing only one matter. That matter was whether the cost of an item of property, plant and equipment should include the initial estimate of the cost of dismantlement, removal and restoration that an entity incurs as a consequence of using the item (instead of as a consequence of acquiring it). Therefore, the Board did not address how an entity should account for (a) changes in the amount of the initial estimate of a recognised obligation, (b) the effects of accretion of, or changes in interest rates on, a recognised obligation or (c) the cost of obligations an entity did not face when it acquired the item, such as an obligation triggered by a law change enacted after the asset was acquired.

BC15   The Board observed that whether the obligation is incurred upon acquisition of the item or while it is being used, its underlying nature and its association with the asset are the same. Therefore, the Board decided that the cost of an item should include the costs of dismantlement, removal or restoration, the obligation for which an entity has incurred as a consequence of having used the item during a particular period other than to produce inventories during that period. An entity applies IAS 2 *Inventories* to the costs of these obligations that are incurred as a consequence of having used the item during a particular period to produce inventories during that period. The Board observed that accounting for these costs initially in accordance with IAS 2 acknowledges their nature. Furthermore, doing so achieves the same result as including these costs as an element of the cost of an item of property, plant and equipment, depreciating them over the production period just completed and identifying the depreciation charge as a cost to produce another asset (inventory), in which case the depreciation charge constitutes part of the cost of that other asset.

BC16　The Board noted that because IAS 16's initial measurement provisions are not affected by an entity's subsequent decision to carry an item under the cost model or the revaluation model, the Board's decision applies to assets that an entity carries under either treatment.

Property, Plant and Equipment—Proceeds before Intended Use (2020 amendments)

Background

BC16A　Before the 2020 amendments, paragraph 17(e) specified that directly attributable costs included the costs of testing whether an asset was functioning properly, after deducting the net proceeds from selling items produced while bringing the asset to the location and condition necessary for it to be capable of operating in the manner intended by management. The Board received a request asking whether:

(a)　the proceeds specified in paragraph 17(e) related only to items produced while testing; and

(b)　an entity was required to deduct from the cost of an item of property, plant and equipment any such proceeds that exceeded the costs of testing.

BC16B　The Board's research indicated that different entities had applied the requirements in paragraph 17(e) differently. Some entities deducted only proceeds from selling items produced while testing; others deducted the proceeds of all sales until an asset was in the location and condition necessary for it to be capable of operating in the manner intended by management (ie available for use). For some entities, the proceeds deducted from the cost of an item of property, plant and equipment could be significant and could exceed the costs of testing.

Recognising proceeds and related cost in profit or loss

BC16C　After considering the findings in paragraph BC16B, the Board decided to amend paragraph 17 to prohibit an entity from deducting from the cost of an item of property, plant and equipment the proceeds from selling items produced before that asset is available for use (proceeds before intended use).

BC16D　In the Board's view, the amendments will improve financial reporting. Proceeds before intended use and related cost meet the definition of income and expenses in the *Conceptual Framework for Financial Reporting*. Those items of income and expenses reflect an entity's performance for the period and they should, therefore, be included in the statement of profit or loss.

BC16E　The previous requirement to offset proceeds against the cost of an item of property, plant and equipment reduced the usefulness of financial statements to users of financial statements. This is because the previous requirement resulted in an entity including amounts that did not faithfully represent:

(a)   its performance. Offsetting proceeds against the cost of an asset understates an entity's revenue (or income) in the period. Moreover, doing so could also have a pervasive and long-term effect on an entity's performance when the asset has a long useful life. Offsetting proceeds decreased the depreciable amount of such an asset and, consequently, reduced the depreciation charge recognised as an expense over the asset's useful life.

(b)   the cost of an item of property, plant and equipment. Offsetting proceeds could result in the carrying amount of the asset understating its cost. This, in turn, could reduce the usefulness of financial metrics, such as return on assets, that use the asset's carrying amount.

BC16F   The Board considered suggestions that recognising proceeds before intended use and related cost in profit or loss might not provide useful information to users of financial statements. Those holding this view suggested that such sales proceeds — and the related margin — may have little predictive value because:

(a)   the sales proceeds are generally non-recurring and are not necessarily an output of an entity's ordinary activities; and

(b)   the cost of items produced would not include depreciation of the item of property, plant and equipment — because depreciation of that asset begins when it is available for use.

BC16G   In the Board's view, however, the fact that the proceeds may have little predictive value was not a compelling argument for excluding them from profit or loss — the statement of profit or loss includes other items of income or expenses that may have little predictive value but the inclusion of which nonetheless provides useful information to users of financial statements. Recognising proceeds before intended use and related cost in profit or loss will result in entities reporting amounts that more faithfully represent their performance and financial position. It will also have confirmatory value about an entity's performance. The disclosure requirements in paragraph 74A(b) will highlight such proceeds and cost for users of financial statements (see paragraphs BC16L–BC16M).

Measuring the cost of items produced

BC16H   When it exposed draft amendments for comment, the Board proposed no requirements on measuring the cost of items produced before an item of property, plant and equipment is available for use. A number of respondents to the Board's draft amendments suggested that the Board develop such requirements. They said measuring the cost of items produced could require extensive judgement, which in turn could result in differences in how entities measure that cost. Respondents' views differed on how prescriptive any requirements should be — some suggested the Board develop only high-level principles while others suggested providing detailed application guidance.

BC16I   After considering this feedback, the Board decided to require an entity to apply IAS 2 *Inventories* in measuring the cost of items produced. The Board made this decision because:

(a)   IAS 2 sets out a framework for measuring cost without being overly prescriptive; and

(b)   an entity would already be required to apply IAS 2 in measuring cost if the entity were to determine that the sale of items produced is an output of its ordinary activities – in this case, the items produced would meet IAS 2's definition of inventories. It would be useful to apply the same requirements to the cost of items produced irrespective of whether the sale of those items is an output of an entity's ordinary activities.

BC16J   In addition, the Board concluded that the judgement involved in measuring the cost of items produced is not substantially different from judgements already required when applying IAS 2 and other IFRS Standards in measuring cost, in particular for assets that take a substantial period of time to get ready for their intended use (for example, measuring the cost of abnormal amounts of wasted materials and labour, allocating costs to joint products or measuring the cost of operations incidental to the construction or development of an item of property, plant and equipment).

BC16K   The Board acknowledged the amendments might result in implementation costs for some entities. However, the Board concluded that a requirement to measure the cost of items produced applying IAS 2 would not impose costs that outweigh the usefulness of the information provided.

Presentation and disclosure

BC16L   The Board developed the requirements in paragraph 74A(b) to provide users of financial statements with information about the sale of items that are not an output of an entity's ordinary activities. Users of financial statements said information that enables them to identify proceeds before intended use, and to understand how those proceeds and related cost affect an entity's performance, would be useful.

BC16M   The Board decided not to develop similar requirements for sales of items that are an output of an entity's ordinary activities because the requirements of IFRS 15 *Revenue from Contracts with Customers* and IAS 2 would apply to the proceeds from such sales and related cost.

BC16N   Measuring the cost of items produced could necessitate the use of estimates and judgement. However, the Board decided not to add disclosure requirements in this respect because other IFRS Standards such as IAS 1 *Presentation of Financial Statements* already require the disclosure of information about estimates and judgements.

BC16O   The Board also decided not to develop specific presentation requirements for proceeds before intended use and related cost because IAS 1 already includes relevant requirements, for example on:

(a)   the offsetting of income and expenses; and

(b)   the presentation of income and expenses as separate line items in the statement of profit or loss.

Available for use and the meaning of 'testing'

BC16P Paragraph 20 requires an entity to determine when an item of property, plant and equipment is available for use. The Board was informed of differences in how entities make that determination, and considered suggestions to clarify when an asset is available for use. Some of those making this suggestion said the existence of significant proceeds before intended use might indicate that an asset is already available for use before it is determined to be so. In their view, such a clarification would reduce the amount of proceeds being deducted from the cost of an asset than had previously been the case and, thus, would address the matter identified in paragraph BC16B without changing how those proceeds are recognised.

BC16Q The Board decided not to amend IAS 16 to clarify when an asset is available for use. Such an amendment would not be narrow in scope—it might affect the measurement of many items of property, plant and equipment, and additional research would be required to assess potential unintended consequences. Furthermore, the Board had obtained no evidence that differences in how entities determine when an asset is available for use could lead to material differences in the entities' financial statements.

BC16R Nonetheless, the Board decided to clarify the meaning of 'testing' in paragraph 17, noting that such a clarification might help an entity in determining when an asset is available for use. The Board concluded that when testing whether an asset is functioning properly, an entity assesses the technical and physical performance of the asset. The assessment of functioning properly is not an assessment of the financial performance of an asset, such as assessing whether the asset has achieved the level of operating margin initially anticipated by management.

Asset exchange transactions

BC17 Paragraph 22 of the previous version of IAS 16 indicated that if (a) an item of property, plant and equipment is acquired in exchange for a similar asset that has a similar use in the same line of business and has a similar fair value or (b) an item of property, plant and equipment is sold in exchange for an equity interest in a similar asset, then no gain or loss is recognised on the transaction. The cost of the new asset is the carrying amount of the asset given up (rather than the fair value of the purchase consideration given for the new asset).

BC18 This requirement in the previous version of IAS 16 was consistent with views that:

(a) gains should not be recognised on exchanges of assets unless the exchanges represent the culmination of an earning process;

(b) exchanges of assets of a similar nature and value are not a substantive event warranting the recognition of gains; and

    (c)   requiring or permitting the recognition of gains from such exchanges enables entities to 'manufacture' gains by attributing inflated values to the assets exchanged, if the assets do not have observable market prices in active markets.

BC19   The approach described above raised issues about how to identify whether assets exchanged are similar in nature and value. The Board reviewed this topic, and noted views that:

    (a)   under the *Framework*, the recognition of income from an exchange of assets does not depend on whether the assets exchanged are dissimilar;

    (b)   income is not necessarily earned only at the culmination of an earning process, and in some cases it is arbitrary to determine when an earning process culminates;

    (c)   generally, under both measurement bases after recognition that are permitted under IAS 16, gain recognition is not deferred beyond the date at which assets are exchanged; and

    (d)   removing 'existing carrying amount' measurement of property, plant and equipment acquired in exchange for similar assets would increase the consistency of measurement of acquisitions of assets.

BC20   The Board decided to require in IAS 16 that all items of property, plant and equipment acquired in exchange for non-monetary assets or a combination of monetary and non-monetary assets should be measured at fair value, except that, if the exchange transaction lacks commercial substance or the fair value of neither of the assets exchanged can be determined reliably, then the cost of the asset acquired in the exchange should be measured at the carrying amount of the asset given up.

BC21   The Board added the 'commercial substance' test in response to a concern raised in the comments it received on the ED. This concern was that, under the Board's proposal, an entity would measure at fair value an asset acquired in a transaction that did not have commercial substance, ie the transaction did not have a discernible effect on an entity's economics. The Board agreed that requiring an evaluation of commercial substance would help to give users of the financial statements assurance that the substance of a transaction in which the acquired asset is measured at fair value (and often, consequentially, a gain on the disposal of the transferred asset is recognised in income) is the same as its legal form.

BC22   The Board concluded that in evaluating whether a transaction has commercial substance, an entity should calculate the present value of the post-tax cash flows that it can reasonably expect to derive from the portion of its operations affected by the transaction. The discount rate should reflect the entity's current assessment of the time value of money and the risks specific to those operations rather than those that marketplace participants would make.

BC23   The Board included the 'reliable measurement' test for using fair value to measure these exchanges to minimise the risk that entities could 'manufacture' gains by attributing inflated values to the assets exchanged. Taking into consideration its project for the convergence of IFRSs and US GAAP, the Board discussed whether to change the manner in which its 'reliable measurement' test is described. The Board observed this was unnecessary because it believes that its guidance and that contained in US GAAP are intended to have the same meaning.

BC24   The Board decided to retain, in IAS 18 *Revenue*,[2] its prohibition on recognising revenue from exchanges or swaps of goods or services of a similar nature and value. The Board has on its agenda a project on revenue recognition and does not propose to make any significant amendments to IAS 18 until that project is completed.

Measurement after recognition

Revaluation model

BC25   The Board is taking part in research activities with national standard-setters on revaluations of property, plant and equipment. This research is intended to promote international convergence of standards. One of the most important issues is identifying the preferred measurement attribute for revaluations. This research could lead to proposals to amend IAS 16.

Revaluation method–proportionate restatement of accumulated depreciation when an item of property, plant and equipment is revalued

BC25A   The IFRS Interpretations Committee reported to the Board that practice differed in calculating the accumulated depreciation for an item of property, plant and equipment that is measured using the revaluation method in cases in which the residual value, the useful life or the depreciation method has been re-estimated before a revaluation.

BC25B   Paragraph 35(a) required that, in instances in which the gross carrying amount is revalued, the revalued accumulated depreciation is restated proportionately with the change in the gross carrying amount.

BC25C   The submission noted that applying the same proportionate factor to restate the accumulated depreciation as for the change in the gross carrying amount has caused problems in practice if the residual value, the useful life or the depreciation method has been re-estimated before the revaluation. The submission used an example in which both the gross carrying amount and the carrying amount were revalued.

---

2   IFRS 15 *Revenue from Contracts with Customers*, issued in May 2014, replaced IAS 18 *Revenue*. IFRS 15 also excludes from its scope non-monetary exchanges between entities in the same line of business to facilitate sales to customers, or to potential customers, other than the parties to the exchange.

BC25D   In such cases, divergent views existed as to how to calculate the accumulated depreciation when the item of property, plant and equipment is revalued:

    (a)   some think that the restatement of the accumulated depreciation is not always proportionate to the change in the gross carrying amount and that paragraph 35(a) should be amended accordingly.

    (b)   others are of the opinion that the accumulated depreciation and the gross carrying amount should always be restated proportionately when applying paragraph 35(a). The difference between the amount required for a proportionate restatement of the depreciation and the actual restatement of the depreciation required for the gross carrying amount to result in a carrying amount equal to the revalued amount being treated as an accounting error in accordance with IAS 8 *Accounting Policies, Changes in Accounting Estimates and Errors*.

BC25E   The definition of 'carrying amount' in paragraph 6 is "the amount at which an asset is recognised after deducting any accumulated depreciation and accumulated impairment loss". The Board noted that, when revaluing an item of property, plant and equipment, the definition implies that the accumulated depreciation is calculated as the difference between the gross carrying amount and the carrying amount, after taking into account accumulated impairment losses.

BC25F   The Board agrees with the proponents of the view presented in paragraph BC25D(a) that the restatement of the accumulated depreciation is not always proportionate to the change in the gross carrying amount. The Board noted that the accumulated depreciation would not be able to be restated proportionately to the gross carrying amount in situations in which both the gross carrying amount and the carrying amount are revalued non-proportionately to each other. It was noted that this was the case regardless of whether there had been a re-estimation of residual value, the useful life or the depreciation method in a prior period.

BC25G   For example, when the revalued amounts for the gross carrying amount and the carrying amount both reflect non-proportionate observable data, it is demonstrated that accumulated depreciation cannot be proportionately restated to the gross carrying amount in order for the carrying amount to equal the gross carrying amount less any accumulated depreciation and accumulated impairment losses. In that respect, the Board thinks that the requirements in paragraph 35(a) may be perceived as being inconsistent with the definition of carrying amount.

BC25H   In addition, the Board noted that the second sentence in paragraph 35(a) reinforced that inconsistency because it states that proportionate restatement is often used when an asset is revalued by means of applying an index to determine its replacement cost. It reinforced the inconsistency because the determination of the accumulated depreciation does not depend on the selection of the valuation technique used for the revaluation under the revaluation model for property, plant and equipment.

BC25I   Consequently, the Board decided to:

(a)   amend paragraph 35(a) to state that the gross carrying amount is adjusted in a manner that is consistent with the revaluation of the carrying amount;

(b)   amend paragraph 35(a) to state that the accumulated depreciation is calculated as the difference between the gross carrying amount and the carrying amount after taking into account accumulated impairment losses; and

(c)   delete the references to valuation methods in paragraph 35(a)–(b).

The Board also decided to amend paragraph 35(b) to be consistent with the wording used in those amendments.

BC25J   The Board decided to include wording in paragraph 35(a) to require an entity to take into account accumulated impairment losses when adjusting the depreciation on revaluation. This was to ensure that when future revaluation increases occur, the correct split, in accordance with paragraph 39 of IAS 16 and paragraph 119 of IAS 36 *Impairment of Assets*, is made between profit or loss and other comprehensive income when reversing prior accumulated impairment losses.

Depreciation: unit of measure

BC26   The Board's discussions about the potential improvements to the depreciation principle in the previous version of IAS 16 included consideration of the unit of measure an entity uses to depreciate its items of property, plant and equipment. Of particular concern to the Board were situations in which the unit of measure is the 'item as a whole' even though that item may be composed of significant parts with individually varying useful lives or consumption patterns. The Board did not believe that, in these situations, an entity's use of approximation techniques, such as a weighted average useful life for the item as a whole, resulted in depreciation that faithfully represents an entity's varying expectations for the significant parts.

BC27   The Board sought to improve the previous version of IAS 16 by proposing in the ED revisions to existing guidance on separating an item into its parts and then further clarifying in the Standard the need for an entity to depreciate separately any significant parts of an item of property, plant and equipment. By doing so an entity will also separately depreciate the item's remainder.

Depreciation: depreciable amount

BC28   During its discussion of depreciation principles, the Board noted the concern that, under the cost model, the previous version of IAS 16 does not state clearly why an entity deducts an asset's residual value from its cost to determine the asset's depreciable amount. Some argue that the objective is one of precision, ie reducing the amount of depreciation so that it reflects the item's net cost. Others argue that the objective is one of economics, ie stopping depreciation if, because of inflation or otherwise, an entity expects that during its useful life an asset will increase in value by an amount greater than it will diminish.

BC29 The Board decided to improve the previous version of IAS 16 by making clear the objective of deducting a residual value in determining an asset's depreciable amount. In doing so, the Board did not adopt completely either the 'net cost' or the 'economics' objective. Given the concept of depreciation as a cost allocation technique, the Board concluded that an entity's expectation of increases in an asset's value, because of inflation or otherwise, does not override the need to depreciate it. Thus, the Board changed the definition of residual value to the amount an entity could receive for the asset currently (at the financial reporting date) if the asset were already as old and worn as it will be when the entity expects to dispose of it. Thus, an increase in the expected residual value of an asset because of past events will affect the depreciable amount; expectations of future changes in residual value other than the effects of expected wear and tear will not.

Depreciation: depreciation period

BC30 The Board decided that the useful life of an asset should encompass the entire time it is available for use, regardless of whether during that time it is in use or is idle. Idle periods most commonly occur just after an asset is acquired and just before it is disposed of, the latter while the asset is held either for sale or for another form of disposal.

BC31 The Board concluded that, whether idle or not, it is appropriate to depreciate an asset with a limited useful life so that the financial statements reflect the consumption of the asset's service potential that occurs while the asset is held. The Board also discussed but decided not to address the measurement of assets held for sale. The Board concluded that whether to apply a different measurement model to assets held for sale—which may or may not be idle—was a different question and was beyond the scope of the Improvements project.

BC32 In July 2003 the Board published ED 4 *Disposal of Non-current Assets and Presentation of Discontinued Operations*. ED 4 was published as part of the Board's short-term convergence project, the scope of which was broader than that of the Improvements project. In ED 4, the Board proposed that an entity should classify some of its assets as 'assets held for sale' if specified criteria are met. Among other things, the Board proposed that an entity should cease depreciating an asset classified in this manner, irrespective of whether the asset is idle. The basis for this proposal was that the carrying amount of an asset held for sale will be recovered principally through sale rather than future operations, and therefore accounting for the asset should be a process of valuation rather than allocation. The Board will amend IAS 16 accordingly when ED 4 is finalised.

Depreciation: depreciation method

BC33　The Board considered how an entity should account for a change in a depreciation method. The Board concluded that a change in a depreciation method is a change in the technique used to apply the entity's accounting policy to recognise depreciation as an asset's future economic benefits are consumed. Therefore, it is a change in an accounting estimate.

BC33A　The IASB decided to amend IAS 16 to address the concerns regarding the use of a revenue-based method for depreciating an asset. The IASB's decision was in response to a request to clarify the meaning of the term 'consumption of the expected future economic benefits embodied in the asset' when determining the appropriate amortisation method for intangible assets of service concession arrangements (SCA) that are within the scope of IFRIC 12 *Service Concession Arrangements*. The issue raised is related to the application of paragraphs 97–98 of IAS 38 *Intangible Assets* although the IASB decided to address the issue broadly, rather than limit it only to intangible assets arising in an SCA.

BC33B　The IASB observed that a revenue-based depreciation method is one that allocates an asset's depreciable amount based on revenues generated in an accounting period as a proportion of the total revenues expected to be generated over the asset's useful economic life. The total revenue amount is affected by the interaction between units (ie quantity) and price and takes into account any expected changes in price.

BC33C　The IASB observed that paragraph 60 of IAS 16 states that the depreciation method used shall reflect the pattern in which the asset's future economic benefits are expected to be consumed by the entity. The IASB noted that even though revenue could sometimes be considered to be a measurement of the output generated by the asset, revenue does not, as a matter of principle, reflect the way in which an item of property, plant and equipment is used or consumed. The IASB observed that the price component of revenue may be affected by inflation and noted that inflation has no bearing upon the way in which an asset is consumed.

BC33D　On the basis of the guidance in IAS 16, the IASB proposed to clarify in the Exposure Draft *Clarification of Acceptable Methods of Depreciation and Amortisation* (Proposed amendments to IAS 16 and IAS 38) (the 'ED') that a method of depreciation that is based on revenue generated from an activity that includes the use of an asset is not appropriate, because it reflects a pattern of economic benefits being generated from operating the business (of which the asset is part) rather than the economic benefits being consumed through the use of the asset.

BC33E　During its redeliberations of the ED the IASB decided to reaffirm its conclusion that the use of a revenue-based method is not appropriate, because the principle in paragraph 60 of IAS 16 is that the "depreciation method shall reflect the pattern in which the asset's future economic benefits are expected to be consumed by the entity". A method that is based on revenue generated from an activity that includes the use of an asset would be, in contrast, a method based on the generation of future economic benefits from the use of the asset. As a result of the feedback received on the ED, the IASB also decided not to retain the comments that it had included in the Basis for Conclusions on the ED on the limited circumstances in which a revenue-based method gives the same result as a units of production method. Many respondents to the ED found these comments contradictory to the guidance proposed in the Standard.

BC33F   In the ED the IASB proposed to provide guidance to clarify the role of obsolescence in the application of the diminishing balance method. In response to the comments received about the proposed guidance the IASB decided to change the focus of this guidance. The IASB decided to explain that expected future reductions in the selling price of an item could indicate the expectation of technical or commercial obsolescence of the asset, which, in turn, might reflect a reduction of the future economic benefits embodied in the asset. The IASB noted that the expectation of technical or commercial obsolescence is relevant for estimating both the pattern of consumption of future economic benefits and the useful life of an asset. The IASB noted that the diminishing balance method is an accepted depreciation methodology in paragraph 62 of IAS 16, which is capable of reflecting an accelerated consumption of the future economic benefits embodied in the asset.

BC33G   Some respondents to the ED suggested that the IASB should define the notion of 'consumption of economic benefits' and provide guidance in this respect. During its redeliberations the IASB decided against doing so, noting that explaining the notion of consumption of economic benefits would require a broader project.

Exemption for owner-occupied property

BC33H   IFRS 17 *Insurance Contracts* amended the subsequent measurement requirements in IAS 16 by permitting entities to elect to measure owner-occupied properties in specified circumstances as if they were investment properties measured at fair value through profit or loss in accordance with IAS 40 *Investment Property*. The Board's considerations in providing that exemption are set out in paragraph BC65(c) of the Basis for Conclusions on IFRS 17.

Derecognition

Derecognition date

BC34   The Board decided that an entity should apply the revenue recognition principle in IAS 18[3] for sales of goods to its gains from the sales of items of property, plant and equipment. The requirements in that principle ensure the representational faithfulness of an entity's recognised revenue. Representational faithfulness is also the appropriate objective for an entity's recognised gains. However, in IAS 16, the revenue recognition principle's criteria drive derecognition of the asset disposed of rather than recognition of

---

3   IFRS 15 *Revenue from Contracts with Customers*, issued in May 2014, replaced IAS 18 *Revenue* and amended paragraph 69 of IAS 16 for consistency with the requirements in IFRS 15.

the proceeds received. Applying the principle instead to the recognition of the proceeds might lead to the conclusion that an entity will recognise a deferred gain. Deferred gains do not meet the definition of a liability under the *Framework*. Thus, the Board decided that an entity does not derecognise an item of property, plant and equipment until the requirements in IAS 18 to recognise revenue on the sale of goods are met.

Gain classification

BC35 Although the Board concluded that an entity should apply the recognition principle for revenue from sales of goods to its recognition of gains on disposals of items of property, plant and equipment, the Board concluded that the respective approaches to income statement display should differ. The Board concluded that users of financial statements would consider these gains and the proceeds from an entity's sale of goods in the course of its ordinary activities differently in their evaluation of an entity's past results and their projections of future cash flows. This is because revenue from the sale of goods is typically more likely to recur in comparable amounts than are gains from sales of items of property, plant and equipment. Accordingly, the Board concluded that an entity should not classify as revenue gains on disposals of items of property, plant and equipment.

Assets held for rental to others[4]

BC35A The Board identified that, in some industries, entities are in the business of renting and subsequently selling the same assets.

BC35B The Board noted that the Standard prohibits classification as revenue of gains arising from derecognition of items of property, plant and equipment. The Board also noted that paragraph BC35 states the reason for this is 'users of financial statements would consider these gains and the proceeds from an entity's sale of goods in the course of its ordinary activities differently in their evaluation of an entity's past results and their projections of future cash flows.'

BC35C Consistently with that reason, the Board concluded that entities whose ordinary activities include renting and subsequently selling the same assets should recognise revenue from both renting and selling the assets. In the Board's view, the presentation of gross selling revenue, rather than a net gain or loss on the sale of the assets, would better reflect the ordinary activities of such entities.

BC35D The Board concluded that the disclosure requirements of IAS 16, IAS 2 and IAS 18[5] would lead an entity to disclose relevant information for users.

---

4   Paragraphs BC35A–BC35F were added as a consequence of amendments to IAS 16 by *Improvements to IFRSs* issued in May 2008. At the same time, the Board also amended paragraph 6 by replacing the term 'net selling price' in the definition of 'recoverable amount' with 'fair value less costs to sell' for consistency with the wording used in IFRS 5 *Non-current Assets Held for Sale and Discontinued Operations* and IAS 36.

5   IFRS 15 *Revenue from Contracts with Customers*, issued in May 2014, replaced IAS 18 *Revenue*.

BC35E   The Board also concluded that paragraph 14 of IAS 7 *Statement of Cash Flows* should be amended to present within operating activities cash payments to manufacture or acquire such assets and cash receipts from rents and sales of such assets.

BC35F   The Board discussed the comments received in response to its exposure draft of proposed *Improvements to International Financial Reporting Standards* published in 2007 and noted that a few respondents would prefer the issue to be included in one of the Board's major projects such as the revenue recognition project or the financial statement presentation project. However, the Board noted that the proposed amendment would improve financial statement presentation before those projects could be completed and decided to add paragraph 68A as previously exposed. A few respondents raised the concern that the term 'held for sale' in the amendment could be confused with the notion of held for sale in accordance with IFRS 5 *Non-current Assets Held for Sale and Discontinued Operations.* Consequently, the Board clarified in the amendment that IFRS 5 should not be applied in those circumstances.

Transitional provisions

BC36   The Board concluded that it would be impracticable for an entity to determine retrospectively whether a previous transaction involving an exchange of non-monetary assets had commercial substance. This is because it would not be possible for management to avoid using hindsight in making the necessary estimates as of earlier dates. Accordingly, the Board decided that in accordance with the provisions of IAS 8 an entity should consider commercial substance only in evaluating the initial measurement of future transactions involving an exchange of non-monetary assets.

BC36A   *Annual Improvements to IFRSs 2010–2012 Cycle,* issued in December 2013, amended paragraph 35. The Board also decided that the amendment should be required to be applied to all revaluations occurring in annual periods beginning on or after the date of initial application of the amendments and in the immediately preceding annual period. The Board was concerned that the costs of full retrospective application might outweigh the benefits.

Property, Plant and Equipment—Proceeds before Intended Use (2020 amendments)

BC36B   The 2020 amendments are expected mainly to affect only a few industries, such as mining and petrochemicals. The Board therefore considered the need, if any, for transition requirements beyond those in IAS 8 *Accounting Policies, Changes in Accounting Estimates and Errors.*

BC36C   The Board concluded that the expected benefits of retrospectively applying the amendments in accordance with IAS 8 might be outweighed by the costs of doing so—in particular, an affected entity might find it difficult and costly to apply the amendments retrospectively to assets made available for use many years ago. In the Board's view, the transition requirements in paragraph 80D promote consistency in application of the amendments for all periods presented, but limit the number of assets an entity is required to reassess on first applying the amendments.

BC36D The Board decided not to provide transition requirements for first-time adopters of IFRS Standards because:

(a) IFRS 1 *First-time Adoption of International Financial Reporting Standards* provides deemed cost exemptions for items of property, plant and equipment. These exemptions allow a first-time adopter to measure such assets without reference to IAS 16.

(b) if a first-time adopter does not apply those deemed cost exemptions, it would apply all the requirements in IAS 16 retrospectively. The Board concluded that there would be little benefit in providing first-time adopters with an exception or exemption relating to only one aspect of the requirements in IAS 16.

Summary of changes from the Exposure Draft

BC37 The main changes from the ED proposals to the revised Standard are as follows:

(a) The ED contained two recognition principles, one applying to subsequent expenditures on existing items of property, plant and equipment. The Standard contains a single recognition principle that applies to costs incurred initially to acquire an item and costs incurred subsequently to add to, replace part of or service an item. An entity applies the recognition principle to the latter costs at the time it incurs them.

(b) Under the approach proposed in the ED, an entity measured an item of property, plant and equipment acquired in exchange for a non-monetary asset at fair value irrespective of whether the exchange transaction in which it was acquired had commercial substance. Under the Standard, a lack of commercial substance is cause for an entity to measure the acquired asset at the carrying amount of the asset given up.

(c) Compared with the Standard, the ED did not as clearly set out the principle that an entity separately depreciates at least the parts of an item of property, plant and equipment that are of significant cost.

(d) Under the approach proposed in the ED, an entity derecognised the carrying amount of a replaced part of an item of property, plant and equipment if it recognised in the carrying amount of the asset the cost of the replacement under the general recognition principle. In the Standard, an entity also applies this approach to a replacement of a part of an item that is not depreciated separately.

(e) In finalising the Standard, the Board identified further necessary consequential amendments to IFRS 1, IAS 14, IAS 34, IAS 36, IAS 37, IAS 38, IAS 40, SIC-13, SIC-21, SIC-22 and SIC-32.

Accounting for bearer plants (2014 amendments)

Overview

BC38   The Board observed that there is a class of biological assets, bearer plants, that are held by an entity solely to grow produce over their productive life. The Board's principal decision underlying the 2014 amendments is that bearer plants should be treated as property, plant and equipment, for which the accounting is prescribed in IAS 16. IAS 16 permits the use of either a cost model or a revaluation model.

Background

BC39   Prior to the 2014 amendments, IAS 41 required all biological assets related to agricultural activity to be measured at fair value less costs to sell based on the principle that their biological transformation is best reflected by fair value measurement. IAS 41 defines 'biological transformation' as follows:

> Biological transformation comprises the processes of growth, degeneration, production, and procreation that cause qualitative or quantitative changes in a biological asset.

BC40   IAS 41 has a single accounting treatment for all bearer and consumable biological assets within its scope. IAS 41 only distinguishes between bearer and consumable biological assets for disclosure purposes (see paragraphs 43–44 of IAS 41).

BC41   Stakeholders told the Board that they think that fair value measurement is not appropriate for mature bearer biological assets such as oil palms and rubber trees because they are no longer undergoing significant biological transformation. The use of mature bearer biological assets such as these is seen by many as similar to that of manufacturing. Consequently, they said that a cost model should be permitted for those bearer biological assets, because it is permitted for property, plant and equipment. They also said that they had concerns about the cost, complexity and practical difficulties of fair value measurements of bearer biological assets in the absence of markets for those assets, and about the volatility from recognising changes in the fair value less costs to sell in profit or loss. Furthermore, they asserted that investors, analysts and other users of financial statements adjust the reported profit or loss to eliminate the effects of changes in the fair values of these bearer biological assets.

BC42   Most respondents who cited agriculture in their responses to the Board's 2011 Agenda Consultation raised concerns in relation to fair value measurement of plantations, for example oil palm and rubber trees plantations, and favoured a limited-scope project for these bearer biological assets to address the concerns in paragraph BC41. Only a small number of respondents favoured a broader consideration of IAS 41 or a Post-implementation Review, or said that there is no need to amend IAS 41.

BC43   Before the limited-scope project for bearer biological assets was added to its work programme, the Board was monitoring the work undertaken by the Asian-Oceanian Standard-Setters Group (AOSSG), primarily by the Malaysian Accounting Standards Board (MASB), on a proposal to remove some bearer biological assets from the scope of IAS 41 and account for them in accordance with IAS 16. Those proposals were discussed several times by national standard-setters, the Board's Emerging Economies Group (EEG) and the IFRS Advisory Council. Feedback from these meetings indicated strong support for the AOSSG/MASB proposals and for the Board to start a limited-scope project for bearer biological assets.

BC44   In September 2012 the Board decided to add to its agenda a limited-scope project for bearer biological assets, with the aim of considering whether to account for some or all of them as property, plant and equipment, thereby permitting use of a cost model. The limited-scope project was supported by the following reasons:

   (a)   it addressed the accounting treatment for those biological assets for which respondents to the 2011 Agenda Consultation had concerns. It also had significant support among national standard-setters and other interested parties. Furthermore, on the basis of feedback from the 2011 Agenda Consultation and other outreach, the expected changes under the project would be likely to reduce compliance costs for preparers and would not adversely affect users of financial statements.

   (b)   it had the advantage of timeliness compared to a more comprehensive project. The Board was able to use the research performed by the MASB and address the main issues relatively quickly. A more comprehensive project would have had to wait for space on the Board's agenda and, once started, might have taken several years.

BC45   The Board decided that it had received sufficient information to develop an Exposure Draft (ED) from work performed by the MASB, meetings of national standard-setters, feedback from preparers on the 2011 Agenda Consultation and user outreach performed by staff. Furthermore, the project was expected to result in limited changes that were sought by both users and preparers of financial statements, as explained in more detail in the analysis of the likely effects of the amendments in paragraphs BC99–BC117. Consequently, the Board decided that the project could proceed without a Discussion Paper and developed an ED that was issued in June 2013.

Changes to the proposals in the ED

BC46   The Board received 72 comment letters on the ED. The vast majority of respondents supported the proposal in the ED to account for bearer plants in accordance with IAS 16. Three additional issues raised by respondents were:

   (a)   extend the scope of the amendments to other biological assets (see paragraphs BC54–BC58);

   (b)   do not require fair value measurement of growing produce (see paragraphs BC75–BC78); and

(c)   provide guidance on when a bearer plant is in the 'location and condition necessary for it to be capable of operating in the manner intended by management' in accordance with paragraph 16(b) of IAS 16—ie when it reaches maturity (see paragraph BC82).

BC47   As a result of the Board's redeliberations of the issues raised on the ED, three changes were made to the proposed amendments in the ED, other than drafting changes. Those three changes were:

(a)   modifying criterion (c) of the definition of a bearer plant (see paragraph BC62);

(b)   clarifying the transition provisions (see paragraph BC96); and

(c)   exempting entities from the disclosure requirements in paragraph 28(f) of IAS 8 for the current period in both the amendments to IAS 16 and the amendments to IAS 41 (see paragraph BC97).

Paragraphs BC48–BC117 summarise the Board's considerations in developing the amendments and its reasons for only making limited changes to the amendments proposed in the ED.

Scope of the amendments

BC48   The Board decided that, before it could consider whether some or all bearer biological assets should be accounted for in accordance with IAS 16 instead of IAS 41, it first needed to define bearer biological assets for the purposes of the amendments. The Board initially discussed four options when deciding on the scope:

(a)   Option 1: no-alternative-use model. Limit the scope of the amendments to IAS 41 to biological assets that are solely used in the production or supply of agricultural produce (ie only used as bearer biological assets) and that are expected to be used for more than one period.

(b)   Option 2: predominant-use model. Limit the scope of the amendments to IAS 41 to biological assets that are used predominantly in the production or supply of agricultural produce (ie used primarily as bearer biological assets) and that are expected to be used for more than one period.

(c)   Option 3: no-alternative-use model—plants only. This is the same as Option 1 except that it would only include plants, not livestock.

(d)   Option 4: predominant-use model—plants only. This is the same as Option 2 except that it would only include plants, not livestock.

BC49   The Board's first consideration when setting the scope of the amendments to IAS 41 was whether to follow a 'no-alternative-use' model or a 'predominant-use' model. The Board observed that many types of livestock that are used as bearer biological assets by an entity also have a common alternative use as a consumable biological asset. For example, an entity may choose to rear a sheep for its wool (bearer attribute) and/or for its meat (consumable attribute). It was also observed that some trees are cultivated both for their lumber, for example, for furniture production (consumable attribute) and for their fruit (bearer attribute).

BC50   The Board observed that a predominant-use model would be more difficult to apply than a no-alternative-use model because it would require additional judgement to be applied in order to determine the predominant use, and would need to address the consequences of reclassifications between IAS 16 and IAS 41 if the predominant use changes. In contrast, if the scope is restricted to biological assets that are solely used as bearer biological assets, the need to apply judgement and make reclassifications would be expected to be rare.

BC51   The Board further noted that, if an entity intends to sell a biological asset as agricultural produce after it has been used as a bearer biological asset for a period of time, fair value measurement would provide useful information about the future economic benefits from the future sale of the asset. Furthermore, if a biological asset is commonly sold as agricultural produce, there will often be an active market for sale of that biological asset separately from land, meaning that fair value information is likely to be readily available and easier to apply than cost measurement. The Board also noted that the concerns raised by respondents to the 2011 Agenda Consultation generally relate to plants that do not have an alternative use to the entity and that do not have a market value separate from the land component. Consequently, any sales transactions that take place in the market are likely to be of bearer plants plus land, and possibly whole plantations. For these reasons, the Board decided to limit the scope to biological assets that are solely used as bearer biological assets.

BC52   The Board's second consideration when setting the scope was whether livestock should be included within the amendments to IAS 41. The Board observed that including livestock would make the use of a cost model more complex. Unlike plants, livestock is not attached to land and there is usually an active market for it, meaning that fair value information is likely to be readily available and easier to apply than cost measurement. As noted in paragraph BC51, concerns raised by respondents to the 2011 Agenda Consultation mainly relate to plants, not livestock. Consequently, the Board decided to restrict the scope to plants.

BC53   On the basis of the considerations in paragraphs BC49–BC52, the Board decided on Option 3.

BC54   Many respondents to the ED said that the concerns outlined by interested parties in paragraph BC41 about fair value measurement and the Board's reasoning in the ED for accounting for bearer plants in accordance with IAS 16 (repeated in paragraphs BC63–BC68) apply equally to other biological assets, such as bearer livestock and plants predominantly used to produce agricultural produce. These respondents said that there was no conceptual basis for singling out bearer plants and that all biological assets used in the production or supply of agricultural produce should be accounted for in the same way.

BC55   During redeliberations of the proposals in the ED, the Board noted that the limited-scope project was added to the Board's agenda to respond to concerns raised by respondents to the 2011 Agenda Consultation, which were raised primarily about plants used solely to bear agricultural produce, for example, oil palm and rubber tree plantations. When the limited-scope project was added to the Board's agenda, the Board had noted that it did not have the resources at that time to perform a comprehensive review of IAS 41. However, the Board had observed that a limited-scope project could be addressed quickly.

BC56   Most respondents to the ED who suggested expanding the scope to livestock did not acknowledge that a key reason the Board limited the scope to bearer plants was the complexities of measuring the initial cost of bearer livestock. A few respondents disagreed with the Board's observation in paragraph BC52 that a cost model would be complex to implement for bearer livestock and noted that cost-based models are used for livestock in some jurisdictions. However, they did not provide any further information on how a cost model like the one in IAS 16 can be applied to livestock.

BC57   The Board observed that before and during development of the amendments it had received significant information from interested parties about the consequences of including bearer plants in IAS 16. However, the Board noted that it had only received limited information about these issues within the context of other biological assets. The Board agreed that the scope of the project should not be expanded without understanding whether IAS 16 is appropriate and can be applied consistently to those biological assets. The Board observed that obtaining this understanding would take time and delay completion of the ED. The Board also noted that such requests for an expanded scope would increase the complexity of the project and raise conceptual issues that did not belong in a limited-scope project but instead in a comprehensive review of IAS 41.

BC58   The Board agreed that the amendments address an immediate need for plantation businesses and are generally perceived by respondents to result in a significant improvement in financial reporting. Consequently, the Board decided not to expand the limited scope of the amendments with the aim of finalising the amendments quickly.

BC59   The ED defined a bearer plant as a plant that is:

(a)   used in the production or supply of agricultural produce;

(b)   expected to bear produce for more than one period; and

(c)   not intended to be sold as a living plant or harvested as agricultural produce, except for incidental scrap sales.

BC60   The Board noted that some crops are perennial plants because their roots remain in the ground to sprout for the next period's crop. An example would be sugarcane if its roots are retained for a second harvest. The Board agreed that if an entity retains the roots to bear produce for more than one period and the roots are not later sold, the roots would meet the definition of a bearer plant. The Board decided that this did not need to be clarified in the amendments and most respondents to the ED agreed.

BC61 Some respondents to the ED asked for guidance on applying the definition of a bearer plant to a range of plants. Because of the diversity of bearer plants, the Board decided not to add guidance on specific types of plants.

BC62 The Board decided to amend criterion (c) of the definition to state 'has a remote likelihood of being sold as agricultural produce, except for incidental scrap sales' to ensure that the amendment captures only those plants used solely in the production or supply of agricultural produce. The Board also clarified in the definition that a bearer plant is a living plant. No other changes were made to the proposed definition.

Basis for accounting for bearer plants in IAS 16

BC63 The Board considered whether the current requirements in IAS 16 for property, plant and equipment are appropriate for bearer plants and also considered the concerns raised by interested parties in paragraph BC41. The Board concluded that applying IAS 16 to bearer plants is appropriate. Paragraphs BC64–BC68 explain the reasons supporting the Board's conclusion.

Support for the use of IAS 16

BC64 Prior to the 2014 amendments, IAS 41 required all biological assets related to agricultural activity to be measured at fair value less costs to sell, based on the principle that their biological transformation is best reflected by fair value measurement. However, mature bearer plants are fully grown and so, apart from bearing produce, biological transformation is no longer significant in generating future economic benefits. Bearer plants are used solely to grow produce over several periods. After this time they are usually scrapped. Consequently, the only significant future economic benefits from bearer plants arise from selling the agricultural produce that they create.

BC65 The Board noted that while fair value measurement may provide an indication of the quality and productive capacity of the bearer plants at a point in time, it is less important to users of financial statements than it is for biological assets whose value may be realised through sale as agricultural produce.

BC66 Bearer plants meet the definition of property, plant and equipment. The use of mature bearer plants to produce agricultural produce is similar to the use of machinery to manufacture goods. The manner in which an entity derives economic benefits from bearer plants and a production plant is similar and that manner differs from biological assets that are harvested for sale. The progressive decline in the future earning potential of a bearer plant over its life is also similar to other depreciable assets, for example, plant and machinery.

BC67   There is an assumption inherent in the *Conceptual Framework*[6] that accounting for similar assets in similar ways enhances the decision-usefulness of the reported information. The land upon which bearer plants are growing, the structures used to support their growth and the agricultural machinery are measured in accordance with IAS 16. Although bearer plants are dissimilar in form to plant and machinery, similarities in how they are used supports accounting for them in the same way.

Cost-benefit considerations

BC68   The Board noted that, on the basis of the responses to the 2011 Agenda Consultation and the outreach performed by the staff, the costs of measuring bearer plants at fair value are perceived by many preparers to exceed the benefits to users of financial statements. The Board also observed that nearly all investors and analysts consulted during the outreach performed by the staff said that the IAS 41 fair value information about bearer plants has limited use to them. The main reasons given by the investors and analysts were:

(a)   information about operating performance and cash flows is more relevant to their forecasting and analysis. Consequently, they eliminate changes in the fair value less costs to sell of bearer plants from the figures used for their analysis.

(b)   there are concerns about relying on the fair value measurements because valuations involve significant management judgement, have the potential for manipulation, and assumptions vary significantly between companies.

(c)   fair value information about bearer plants is not very useful without fair value information about the related land, land improvements, agricultural machinery, etc.

Biological transformation

BC69   The IAS 41 fair value model is based on the principle that biological transformation is best reflected by fair value measurement. Once bearer plants mature, they are held by an entity solely to grow produce and so, apart from bearing produce, their biological transformation is no longer significant in generating future economic benefits. Consequently, the Board decided bearer plants should be accounted for under IAS 16 instead of IAS 41 (see paragraphs BC63–BC68). However, the Board noted that the same argument is not true for bearer plants before they reach maturity and bear produce. Until they reach maturity, bearer plants are in a growth phase and so undergo significant biological transformation. Furthermore, the Board noted that the produce growing on the bearer plants is undergoing biological transformation until it is harvested (for example, grapes growing on a grape vine). Paragraphs BC70–BC79 explain the reasons supporting the Board's

---

6   References to the *Conceptual Framework* in this Basis for Conclusions are to the *Conceptual Framework for Financial Reporting*, issued in 2010 and in effect when the Standard was amended.

conclusions regarding bearer plants before they reach maturity and the produce growing on the bearer plants.

Accounting for bearer plants before they mature

BC70 The Board considered whether a fair value approach or a cost accumulation approach should be applied to bearer plants before they reach maturity.

BC71 The Board noted that, before they mature, bearer plants undergo biological transformation and this distinguishes them from self-constructed property, plant and equipment. Such biological transformation would not be reflected by a cost accumulation approach. The Board further noted that a fair value approach would be consistent with the principle in IAS 41 that biological transformation is best reflected by fair value measurement.

BC72 However, the Board noted that IAS 16 does not incorporate internal profit in the measurement of a self-constructed item of machinery. By analogy, biological transformation should not be included either. The Board further noted that most of the investors and analysts consulted during the outreach performed by the staff said that the IAS 41 fair value information about bearer plants is of limited use to them and that the measurement of the fair values of bearer plants is particularly subjective during the early years of the life cycle of those bearer plants. For these reasons the Board decided that bearer plants should be measured at accumulated cost before they reach maturity. The Board also observed that it would be simpler to keep bearer plants in IAS 16 throughout their life. Virtually all respondents to the ED supported measuring bearer plants using a cost accumulation approach before they mature.

Accounting for produce growing on a bearer plant

BC73 The Board considered whether produce should be recognised at fair value less costs to sell only at the point of harvest or from the date that it starts to grow.

BC74 The Board observed that the produce is a consumable biological asset growing on the bearer plant and the growth of the produce directly increases the expected revenue from the sale of the produce. Consequently, fair value measurement of the growing produce provides useful information to users of financial statements about future cash flows that an entity will actually realise. In contrast the bearer plants themselves are not sold and the changes in the fair value of the bearer plants do not directly influence the entity's future cash flows. The Board also observed that produce will ultimately be detached from the bearer plants and is normally sold separately, meaning it has a market value on its own. This is in contrast to many bearer plants that are unlikely to have an observable market value on their own because they can only be sold while attached to the land.

BC75 Many respondents to the ED acknowledged the conceptual reasons for accounting for produce at fair value less costs to sell, but expressed concern with the likely practical challenges. Some respondents suggested only requiring fair value less costs to sell to be measured at the point of harvest, or providing additional relief from fair value measurement on the basis of cost-benefit considerations. Other respondents suggested accounting for produce using a cost model before harvest, similarly to inventories or work in progress. Several respondents said further guidance should be provided on how to measure the produce at fair value.

BC76 The Board acknowledged that measuring produce growing on bearer plants at fair value less costs to sell might sometimes be difficult to apply in practice. However, it was noted that similar difficulties are encountered when measuring the fair value less costs to sell of produce growing in the ground. Consequently, the Board decided that it would be inconsistent to provide additional relief from fair value measurement for produce growing on a bearer plant and not also for other biological assets within the scope of IAS 41.

BC77 The Board observed that if preparers encounter significant practical difficulties on initial measurement of produce, they should consider whether they meet the requirements of the exemptions in paragraphs 10(c) and 30 of IAS 41. Paragraph 10(c) of IAS 41 states that an entity shall recognise a biological asset only when the fair value or cost of the asset can be measured reliably. Paragraph 30 of IAS 41 requires a biological asset to be measured using a cost model if fair value measurement is determined to be clearly unreliable. The Board noted that this limited-scope project was not intended to address the fair value model in IAS 41. Consequently, the Board agreed not to further discuss the exemptions in IAS 41 as part of this project.

BC78 On the basis of the considerations above, the Board decided to reaffirm that produce is a biological asset within the scope of IAS 41 and consequently should be measured at fair value less costs to sell with changes recognised in profit and loss as the produce grows. This would maintain the consistency of accounting for produce growing in the ground and produce growing on a bearer plant. Consequently, the Board decided to keep the produce within the scope of IAS 41.

BC79 The Board noted that most of the areas for which respondents to the ED asked for additional guidance were specific to a particular type of bearer plant or produce. The Board decided that because of the specialised nature and diversity of bearer plants and produce it would be too difficult for the Board to develop additional guidance on measuring the fair value of produce.

Application of the IAS 16 requirements to bearer plants

Unit of measure

BC80 Agricultural activity is often a continuous process, meaning that older plants are continuously removed from service and replaced. The Board noted that, if bearer plants are accounted for using a cost model, this continuous process needs to be made discrete. Consequently, the question arises as to what the unit of measure is—for example, is it the individual plant or some larger aggregation, such as a field or a planting cycle?

BC81　The Board noted that IAS 16 does not prescribe the unit of measure, or the extent to which items can be aggregated and treated as a single item of property, plant and equipment. Consequently, applying the recognition criteria in IAS 16 to bearer plants will require judgement. This would give an entity flexibility, depending on its circumstances, to decide how to aggregate individual plants for the purpose of determining a measurable unit of bearer plants. The Board noted that accounting for an aggregation of plants would be similar to accounting for a large quantity of equipment that is acquired or constructed in batches. For example a company may construct a large number of moulds for use within its business. Some aggregation of the moulds would usually be necessary for determining an item of property, plant and equipment. Consequently, the Board decided that the requirements for the unit of measure in IAS 16 would provide sufficient guidance for bearer plants without modification.

Point of maturity

BC82　Most respondents to the ED requested additional guidance on when a bearer plant is in the 'location and condition necessary for it to be capable of operating in the manner intended by management' in accordance with paragraph 16(b) of IAS 16 – ie when it is deemed to have reached maturity. For example, an oil palm may start to grow produce after two years, but only reach its maximum yield after seven years. Respondents suggested either defining the date of maturity to be 'the date of the first harvest of commercial value' or 'the date commercial quantities of produce are produced'. The Board noted that without further clarification these terms would not assist entities in applying judgement in this area and would be likely to lead to interpretation requests in the future. The Board also noted that a similar scenario arises for a factory or retail outlet that is not yet capable of operating at full capacity and did not think that this was a major issue in practice. Consequently, the Board decided not to add guidance in this area.

Other recognition and measurement requirements of the cost model

BC83　The Board considered whether the other recognition and measurement requirements of the cost model in IAS 16 were sufficient to address the unique costs of growing bearer plants both before and after they reach maturity. The following were the main requests for guidance raised by respondents to the ED:

(a)　how to assess what is an abnormal amount of wastage/mortality during the growth phase of the bearer plants. The Board noted that there is a similar issue when an entity constructs a large number of fragile items of machinery for use within the business.

(b)　the nature of costs that can be capitalised before maturity. The Board noted that although the examples in IAS 16 are about non-living items, paragraph 17(a)–(b) and (e) of IAS 16 adequately covers the types of costs incurred to cultivate and grow bearer plants.

(c)   allocation of costs after maturity between the growing fruit and the bearer plant. The Board noted that an entity may recognise all costs as an expense after maturity unless they meet the criteria for capitalisation as part of bearer plants in accordance with paragraph 7 of IAS 16. Consequently, such guidance would not be necessary.

(d)   transfers between IAS 16 and IAS 41 if the entity changes its intention for a bearer plant or if scrap sales are no longer considered incidental. The Board noted that it would be rare for transfers to take place between IAS 16 and IAS 41 for bearer plants, particularly in the light of the Board's decision to change criterion (c) of the definition of a bearer plant to 'has a remote likelihood of being sold as agricultural produce, except for incidental scrap sales' (see paragraph BC62).

BC84   The Board decided that the current principles in IAS 16 are sufficient to cater for bearer plants without modification or supplement.

BC85   Some respondents to the ED requested guidance on the application of other Standards to bearer plants, for example, IAS 17 *Leases*, IAS 20 *Accounting for Government Grants and Disclosure of Government Assistance*, IAS 23 *Borrowing Costs* and IAS 36 *Impairment of Assets*. However, when commenting on those Standards, respondents did not highlight issues unique to bearer plants. The Board noted that bearer plants meet the definition of property, plant and equipment in IAS 16 and are accounted for as property, plant and equipment. Consequently, bearer plants are items of property, plant and equipment when applying other Standards.

Disclosure requirements of the cost model

BC86   The Board considered the disclosure requirements in IAS 16 and decided that they could be applied to bearer plants without modification. The Board also considered whether any additional disclosures should be required for bearer plants.

BC87   Some Board members were concerned that if entities move from a fair value model to a cost model for bearer plants, decision-useful information about the fair values of bearer plants and the assumptions used to determine those fair value measurements would be lost. However, the Board noted that most of the investors and analysts consulted during the user outreach performed by the staff said that fair value information about bearer plants has limited use to them without fair value information about the related land, agricultural machinery, etc. Furthermore, virtually all respondents to the ED said that disclosure of fair value information about bearer plants and/or information about the significant inputs used in valuation techniques should not be required.

BC88   The Board noted that there is no clear basis for requiring fair value disclosures for bearer plants when such disclosures are not required for the rest of the property, plant and machinery involved in the process of growing the produce. It also noted that there is also no clear basis for requiring entities with bearer plants to provide fair value disclosures for their land when these disclosures are not required for land used for other purposes. The Board further acknowledged that the limited-scope project was not intended to address fair value disclosure requirements for other assets in IAS 16. Consequently, the Board decided not to require additional fair value disclosures for entities with bearer plants.

BC89 During user outreach, many investors and analysts told the staff that instead of using fair value information they use other information, for example, about yield, acreage and age of bearer plants. This information is usually obtained via the presentations made to analysts, the front of annual reports (for example, in the Management Commentary) or is otherwise received directly from companies. Many respondents to the ED acknowledged that disclosures about productivity and future cash flows are useful to users of financial statements, but most said that such disclosures should not be mandatory and belonged outside the financial statements.

BC90 Some respondents to the ED noted that disclosure of non-financial measures of physical quantities of biological assets and output of agricultural produce is currently required for all biological assets in paragraph 46 of IAS 41. They said that including bearer plants in IAS 16 would mean that this disclosure requirement would no longer apply to them. The Board observed that this is likely to have a limited effect in practice because the disclosures in paragraph 46 of IAS 41 will continue to apply to the produce in IAS 41 as follows:

(a) paragraph 46(a) and (b)(ii) of IAS 41—the Board noted that the disclosures made by entities in accordance with paragraphs 46(a) and (b)(ii) would be the same regardless of whether those paragraphs refer to the entire plant or only the produce.

(b) paragraph 46(b)(i) of IAS 41—the Board noted that paragraph 46(b)(i) now applies to physical quantities of produce instead of physical quantities of entire plants. The Board noted that paragraph 46(b)(i) does not stipulate the type of non-financial measures or estimates that an entity needs to provide. The Board also noted that plantation companies generally provide more information about productivity of bearer plants outside the financial statements than is required by paragraph 46 of IAS 41 and would be likely to continue to disclose their chosen non-financial measures of bearer plants even if this paragraph only refers to produce.

Consequently, the Board decided not to add the disclosures in paragraph 46 of IAS 41 to IAS 16.

BC91 The Board observed that agricultural activity is diverse and it would be difficult to identify specific productivity disclosures that would provide useful information for users of financial statements and cover all types of bearer plants. The Board also observed that if additional productivity disclosures were included in IAS 16 for bearer plants (other than those in paragraph 46 of IAS 41), it would be difficult to justify requiring them in IAS 16 for bearer plants and not in IAS 41 for other biological assets. The Board noted that reconsidering the disclosure requirements of IAS 41 was outside the scope of this project. Consequently, the Board decided not to add any additional disclosures in IAS 16 for bearer plants.

Revaluation model

BC92 IAS 16 permits entities to choose either the cost model or the revaluation model for each class of property, plant and equipment. The Board decided that the same accounting policy options should be permitted for bearer plants. Consequently, the Board decided that the revaluation model in IAS 16 should be permitted for bearer plants.

BC93 Most respondents to the ED supported allowing entities an option to use the revaluation model. However, some respondents asked for guidance on applying the revaluation model to bearer plants. The Board decided that the requirements of the revaluation model are clear without additional guidance and it noted its expectation that the vast majority of entities with bearer plants will use the cost model for the reasons set out in paragraph BC103. Consequently, the Board confirmed that the revaluation model would be permitted for bearer plants and decided not to add additional guidance.

Positioning of requirements

BC94 The Board observed that there was some benefit to keeping all of the requirements for agricultural activity together. However, the Board noted that the requirements in IAS 16 would be applied to bearer plants with virtually no modification. Furthermore, bearer plants meet the definition of property, plant and equipment and are used like property, plant and equipment within the business. Virtually all respondents to the ED supported including bearer plants within the scope of IAS 16. The Board thus confirmed that it would include bearer plants within the scope of IAS 16.

Transition requirements

Current IFRS preparers

BC95 The Board noted that if an entity currently measures its bearer plants at fair value less costs to sell and has not previously collected cost information, collecting this information to measure the cost of those bearer plants may be costly. If bearer plants have long life cycles, entities could be required to look back several decades in order to obtain the necessary information. Consequently, for cost-benefit reasons, the Board decided that the amendments to IAS 16 should permit the use of fair value as deemed cost for items of bearer plants at the beginning of the earliest comparative period presented in the financial statements. The Board also noted that the amendments address an immediate need for entities with bearer plants. Consequently, the Board decided that the amendments should be available for early application.

BC96   Virtually all respondents to the ED supported the transition requirements without change. However, some respondents said that the Board should clarify how to account for differences between fair value and the carrying value determined in accordance with IAS 41 (fair value less costs to sell) at the transition date. The Board agreed.

BC97   The Board noted that on the initial application of the amendments, paragraph 28(f) of IAS 8 would require an entity to disclose, for the current period and for each prior period presented, the amount of any adjustment for each financial statement line item affected. The Board observed that requiring this disclosure requirement for the current year would be burdensome because it would require an entity to maintain dual systems in the year of initial application. The Board noted that not requiring this disclosure for the current year would be consistent with its other decisions during the project. Consequently for both the amendments to IAS 16 and the amendments to IAS 41, the Board decided to exempt entities from providing the disclosure required by paragraph 28(f) for the current period. Entities would still be required to provide those disclosures for each prior period presented in the financial statements.

First-time adoption of IFRS

BC98   Consistent with the reasoning for accounting for bearer plants as property, plant and equipment (see paragraphs BC63–BC68), the Board decided that the same deemed cost exemptions provided for property, plant and equipment in IFRS 1 *First-time Adoption of International Financial Reporting Standards* should be available for bearer plants. Virtually all respondents to the ED supported this requirement for first-time adopters of IFRSs. The Board thus confirmed the proposals for first-time adopters. The Board noted that no consequential amendments to IFRS 1 were required because bearer plants are accounted for as items of property, plant and equipment. Consequently, exemptions already provided in IFRS 1 would address first-time application issues related to bearer plants.

Analysis of the likely effects of the amendments

BC99   The following paragraphs describe the Board's analysis of the likely effects that will result from the amendments to the requirements for the accounting for bearer plants.

BC100   The Board is committed to assessing and sharing knowledge about the likely costs of implementing new requirements, and the likely ongoing application costs and benefits of each new or revised Standard—the costs and benefits are collectively referred to as 'effects'.

BC101   The Board gains insight on the likely effects of the proposals for new or revised Standards through its formal exposure of proposals and through its fieldwork, analysis and consultations with relevant parties through outreach activities. The likely effects are assessed:

      (a)   in the light of the Board's objective of financial reporting transparency; and

      (b)   in comparison to the existing financial reporting requirements.

BC102   In evaluating the likely effects of the amendments, the Board has considered the following issues (see paragraphs BC106–BC117):

      (a)   how the changes are likely to affect how bearer plants are reported in the financial statements of those applying IFRS;

      (b)   whether those changes improve the comparability of financial statements between different reporting periods for an individual entity and between different entities in a particular reporting period;

      (c)   whether the changes will improve the ability of users of financial statements to assess the future cash flows of an entity;

      (d)   whether the improvements to financial reporting will result in better economic decision-making;

      (e)   the likely effect on compliance costs for preparers, both on initial application and on an ongoing basis; and

      (f)   whether the likely costs of analysis for users of financial statements, including the costs of extracting data, identifying how it has been measured and adjusting it for the purposes of including that data in, for example, a valuation model, are affected.

BC103   The amendments will permit entities to apply either the cost model or the revaluation model, in accordance with IAS 16, for bearer plants. The Board expects that most entities will choose the cost model instead of the revaluation model, because:

      (a)   the revaluation model would not eliminate the main concerns raised by preparers, in particular the cost and complexity of regularly measuring the fair value of bearer plants.

      (b)   most entities apply a cost model to agricultural land and machinery and the Board expects that those entities would favour using a consistent approach for all assets used in the production of income, including bearer plants.

      (c)   IAS 16 only permits the revaluation model to be used if the fair value of bearer plants can be measured reliably. Many entities with bearer plants told the Board that fair value estimations are often complex and subjective. If fair value cannot be measured reliably, use of the revaluation model would be precluded.

BC104   Consequently, the analysis of the likely effects in paragraphs BC106–BC117 only considers the likely effects of applying the IAS 16 cost model in comparison to the IAS 41 fair value model.

BC105   If entities choose to account for bearer plants using the revaluation model in IAS 16, the most significant effect would be to require changes in the revalued amount, which approximates fair value, to be recognised in other comprehensive income. Currently, changes in fair value less costs to sell are recognised in profit or loss under IAS 41.

How the amendments are likely to affect how activities are reported

BC106   The amendments will only affect specific types of agricultural activity, namely those entities with bearer plants.

BC107   Assuming that current IFRS adopters choose to apply the cost model in IAS 16 to bearer plants the main changes will be as follows:

Effect	Fair value model in IAS 41	Cost model in IAS 16	Effect
Financial position	Measured at fair value less costs to sell (together with the produce).	Measured at cost less any accumulated depreciation and any accumulated impairment losses. (Produce measured separately at fair value less costs to sell.)	Net asset amounts are likely to be lower for the cost model than the fair value model during the earlier part of the productive life of a bearer plant. This is because the future cash flows that can be generated by the bearer plant, and reflected in a fair value measurement, will likely be higher than the cost on initial recognition. Over time, the carrying amounts measured in accordance with the two models are expected to converge as the asset approaches the end of its productive life.
Profit or loss	Changes in fair value less costs to sell are recognised in profit or loss. Costs may be recognised as an expense immediately or capitalised. If they are capitalised there is an equal reduction in the change in the fair value less costs to sell.	The depreciation charge for each period, and any impairment loss, will be recognised in profit or loss.	Over the life of the bearer plants the net amount recognised in profit or loss will likely be the same whether applying the fair value model or the cost model. However, if an entity applies the fair value model the effect on profit or loss will be variable (changes in fair value). If an entity applies the cost model the effect on profit or loss is likely to be more systematic (depreciation, with possible impairment).

How the amendments affect the comparability of financial statements

Comparability between entities

BC108　The Board does not expect the amendments to significantly reduce the comparability between entities because:

(a)　IAS 41 requires biological assets to be accounted for using the fair value model. The Board does not expect the choice of accounting policy in IAS 16 to reduce comparability between entities with bearer plants because most entities are expected to choose the cost model for the reasons explained in paragraph BC103.

(b)　The primary benefits of using fair value for biological assets are that fair value captures biological development (ie the growth of the produce) and is closely aligned with how the entity expects to convert the asset to cash (ie through sale). The Board has retained fair value for the produce of a bearer plant (for which these primary benefits are applicable) while aligning the accounting for the bearer plant with the accounting for property, plant and equipment. The Board considers that this change will improve comparability by distinguishing between types of biological asset.

(c)　The Board observed that some entities may elect to measure bearer plants at fair value on initial application of the amendments and use that fair value as its deemed cost at that date, while others may elect to apply the amendments retrospectively (eg if they currently use a cost model in accordance with IAS 16 for management purposes). However, the Board noted that if there is any lack of comparability between entities on initial application, it is just as likely to arise from the aggregation of costs incurred at different dates as from the use of fair value as deemed cost by some but not all entities. Furthermore, the use of fair value as the deemed cost for bearer plants means that an entity will report the same cost data as if it had acquired bearer plants with the same remaining service potential at the date of transition to IFRS, eg if it had purchased an area of plantation on that date.

Comparability between reporting periods for an individual entity

BC109　The Board does not expect the amendments to significantly reduce the comparability between reporting periods for an individual entity choosing the cost model. This is because under IAS 41 the change in the fair value less costs to sell of bearer plants can fluctuate significantly between reporting periods as a result of small changes in assumptions. Furthermore, most investors and analysts consulted during the user outreach performed by staff said that they eliminate the change in the fair value less costs to sell of bearer plants when comparing an entity's operating performance between reporting periods.

BC110   Currently, bearer plants are accounted for in a different way from the land, land improvements and agricultural machinery used in the production process. In most cases entities account for these assets at cost under IAS 16. Consequently, accounting for the bearer plants under IAS 16 will improve comparability between the producing assets of the entity by accounting for similar assets in similar ways.

How the amendments will improve a user's ability to assess future cash flows

BC111   IAS 41 currently requires bearer plants to be measured at fair value less costs to sell. Consequently, the requirement to measure fair value applies to both the bearer plant and the produce growing on the bearer plant. As a result of the amendments, only the produce growing on bearer plants will be measured at fair value less costs to sell.

BC112   The produce of bearer plants is usually grown for sale. Consequently, fair value changes in the produce have a direct relationship to the expectations of future cash flows that the entity will receive on sale. In contrast, bearer plants are normally held by an entity for the whole of their useful life and then scrapped, so changes in fair value are not directly recognised as cash flows on sale of the bearer plants. Consequently, the Board thinks that providing separate fair value information for the produce is likely to improve the ability of users of the financial statements to assess future cash flows.

BC113   During the project the staff sought the views of investors and analysts that use the financial statements of companies with bearer plants. Many of these investors and analysts told the staff that they focus on cash flows that an entity is expected to realise. These investors and analysts said that the fair value of bearer plants is not considered in their analysis because the bearer plants themselves are not sold and the changes in the fair value of the bearer plants do not directly influence the entity's future cash flows. Furthermore, some of these investors and analysts said that they would prefer a cost model for bearer plants because it provides a better basis to forecast future capital expenditure than a fair value model.

How the amendments will affect economic decision-making and the costs of analysis for users of financial statements

BC114   There is an assumption inherent in the *Conceptual Framework* that accounting for similar assets in similar ways enhances the usefulness of the reported information. Although bearer plants are dissimilar in form to plant and machinery, similarities in how they are used provides support for accounting for them in the same way.

BC115   As a result of the amendments, users of financial statements will generally receive cost information about bearer plants instead of fair value information. This is not expected to result in less relevant information for users of financial statements because nearly all investors and analysts consulted during the user outreach performed by staff said that the IAS 41 fair value information about bearer plants is of limited use to them for the reasons set out in paragraph BC68.

Effect on the compliance costs for preparers

BC116   Preparers of financial statements have expressed concern that, in the absence of active markets for bearer plants, fair value measurements are complex, time-consuming and costly, especially for entities that hold large plantations with varying maturities, yield profiles and locations. The amendments respond to this concern and are expected to significantly reduce costs for preparers of financial statements by permitting a cost model for bearer plants. However, entities will still be required to perform the following fair value measurements:

(a)   the produce growing on the bearer plants will still be measured at fair value less costs to sell. The Board's reasoning for requiring the produce to be measured at fair value less costs to sell is set out in paragraphs BC73–BC79.

(b)   as is the case for all items of property, plant and equipment, bearer plants will be subject to an impairment test under IAS 36. Consequently, if there is an indication that bearer plants are impaired at the reporting date, the entity would be required to estimate the recoverable amount of the asset (or its cash-generating unit). The recoverable amount of an asset or a cash-generating unit is the higher of its fair value less costs of disposal and its value in use.

BC117   Nevertheless, the amendments will reduce compliance costs for the majority of entities because:

(a)   the Board thinks that measuring the produce at fair value less costs to sell would be less complex than measuring the bearer plants and produce together at fair value less costs to sell. This is because the produce is growing on the bearer plants only for a short period and so the valuation of produce will not involve forecasting over long time periods. Furthermore, there is usually an active market for the harvested produce, whereas there is rarely an active market for bearer plants and observable market prices generally exist only for many bearer plants together with the land.

(b)   IAS 41 currently requires entities to determine the fair value less costs to sell of bearer plants at each reporting date. As a result of the amendments, an entity applying the cost model in accordance with IAS 16 would be required to estimate the recoverable amount of an item of bearer plants (or the relevant cash-generating unit) only if there are indicators of impairment at the reporting date. In general, bearer plants do not generate cash flows independently of the land. Consequently, the impairment test would take place at the cash-generating unit level. If the fair value of the land is greater than the carrying amount of the cash-generating unit containing the land and bearer plants, the cash-generating unit would not be impaired.

Consequently, as a result of the amendments, fair value measurements are expected to be less frequent.

Dissenting opinions

Dissent of Mary Tokar from *Clarification of Acceptable Methods of Depreciation and Amortisation* (Amendments to IAS 16 and IAS 38) as issued in May 2014

DO1   Ms Tokar is dissenting from the publication of this amendment. She does not object to the IASB's objective of clarifying acceptable methods of depreciation and amortisation, nor to its conclusions to preclude revenue-based depreciation and nor to the introduction of a rebuttable presumption that revenue cannot be used as a basis for amortisation of intangibles. She also agrees that expectations of obsolescence should be considered when determining the useful life of an asset and selecting an amortisation or depreciation method that reflects the pattern of consumption of the asset. However, she is concerned that the amendments will not fully resolve the practice issue that was originally raised with the IFRS Interpretations Committee. She believes that the amendments are not sufficiently clear regarding what evidence is required to overcome the presumption and instead support the use of revenue as the basis for amortisation of an intangible asset. She believes that further guidance should be included to explain when the pattern of consumption of economic benefits is the same as the pattern in which revenue is generated.

Dissent of Patrick Finnegan and Patricia McConnell from *Agriculture: Bearer Plants* (Amendments to IAS 16 and IAS 41) June 2014

DO1   Mr Finnegan and Ms McConnell voted against the publication of *Agriculture: Bearer Plants* (Amendments to IAS 16 and IAS 41) issued in June 2014 (the 'June 2014 Amendment') because they believe that including bearer plants within the scope of IAS 16 *Property, Plant and Equipment* instead of IAS 41 *Agriculture* will eliminate information about the fair value changes in bearer plants and the underlying assumptions used to estimate those changes. Information about the fair values of all biological assets including bearer plants is critical both to managing agricultural activities and to investing in entities that engage in those activities. Without such information, investors are unable to assess changes in expectations of future net cash inflows for an entity engaged in agricultural activity. The fact that published price quotations have developed throughout the world for orchards and plantations that include bearer plants demonstrates the importance of fair value information to those who invest in agricultural activities.

DO2   IAS 41 prescribes the accounting for agricultural activity, that is, the management by an entity of the biological transformation of living animals or plants (biological assets) for sale, into agricultural produce or into additional biological assets. The underlying principle of IAS 41 is that fair value measurement best reflects the biological transformation of biological assets. It requires measurement at fair value less costs to sell (referred to hereafter as fair value) from initial recognition of biological assets up to and including the point of harvest, other than when fair value cannot be measured reliably on initial recognition.

DO3   The June 2014 Amendment changes the measurement for one subset of biological assets, bearer plants, from fair value to a cost-based measure. Bearer plants are plants that are used only in the production or supply of agricultural produce and are expected to bear produce for more than one period. The June 2014 Amendment includes bearer plants within the scope of IAS 16. Consequently, entities would be permitted to choose either the cost model or the revaluation model for bearer plants. All other biological assets related to agricultural activity will remain under the fair value model in IAS 41, including bearer animals.

The importance of fair value information for biological assets

DO4   Fundamentally, IAS 41 is a Standard on accounting for biological transformation. Biological transformation of bearer assets occurs both prior to maturity and after maturity. A cost model ignores biological transformation when it occurs. That is why IAS 41 requires fair value measurement. The Basis for Conclusions of IAS 41 states:

> "Those who support fair value measurement argue that the effects of changes brought about by biological transformation are best reflected by reference to the fair value changes in biological assets. They believe that fair value changes in biological assets have a direct relationship to changes in expectations of future economic benefits to the entity."

Mr Finnegan and Ms McConnell see no reason to abandon that principle with respect to bearer plants. Consequently, they do not agree that prior to maturity, bearer plants should be measured at accumulated cost. They do not believe that accounting for bearer plants in the same way as for self-constructed items of property, plant and equipment will provide users of financial statements with information that is useful to an understanding of the agricultural entity's performance for the period or of its productive capacity at a point in time.

DO5   While maturing, bearer plants are undergoing biological transformation. Mr Finnegan and Ms McConnell continue to believe that fair value measurement for the biological transformation process provides the best information about bearer assets' quality and quantitative changes during their growth period. They also believe that the fair value of bearer plants at maturity provides the best measure of an entity's resources being placed into the production of produce at maturity. Investors need that information to assess management's stewardship of the resources invested in the production process and the performance of the entity using those resources. Consequently, they believe that bearer plants must be measured at fair value while maturing because fair value provides users of financial statements with the best information about an important aspect of an agricultural entity's performance and management stewardship.

DO6   They also reject the view that biological transformation of bearer assets is no longer a key element for understanding the future net cash flows to an entity once such assets reach maturity. By definition, biological transformation is not limited to merely the growth process to maturity, but also includes the cycles of production and degeneration, which are critical phases in the life cycle of bearer assets. Fair value measurements of bearer assets throughout their lives provide information about the effectiveness and efficiency of the production process, and about the capability of such assets to generate net cash inflows into the future. In contrast, depreciation of the cost of a mature bearer asset only approximates the biological transformation of a bearer asset throughout its productive life and has only an indirect relationship, at best, to changes in future net cash inflows.

Effects of the use of fair value measurement

DO7   Mr Finnegan and Ms McConnell acknowledge that measuring bearer plants at fair value may sometimes be difficult. In particular, the Board has been told that the fair value of bearer plants is particularly subjective during the early years of their life cycle. However, Mr Finnegan and Ms McConnell note that IAS 41 contains an exception from fair value for biological assets for which quoted market prices are not available and for which alternative fair value measurements are determined to be clearly unreliable on initial recognition. They believe that this exception is sufficient to deal with the concerns about the reliability of fair value measures of bearer plants during the early years of their life cycle. They also note that entities throughout the world have been applying IAS 41 in a wide variety of agricultural activities since 2003. In fact, some national accounting standards required or recommended measurement of bearer assets at fair values even before IAS 41 was issued. They do not believe that measuring fair value of bearer plants, in general, is any more difficult than measuring fair value for other biological assets such as bearer animals. Furthermore, they believe that applying a cost measure to bearer plants may be equally as difficult in some situations. Fair value measurements are required in assessing bearer plants for impairment, and surely those who are urging a reversion to a cost model for bearer assets would not suggest that impairment should be ignored because fair value measurement may sometimes be difficult. Moreover, the June 2014 Amendment would permit fair value measurements as a pure accounting policy choice. Mr Finnegan and Ms McConnell believe that accounting should reflect underlying economic circumstances and should not merely be left to choice. The existing fair value exception in IAS 41 is based on circumstances (measurement reliability), and is not an accounting policy choice.

DO8 In addition to concerns about the reliability of fair value measures, entities with bearer assets expressed concern about the volatility that arises from recognising changes in the fair value of the bearer plants in profit or loss and said that users of financial statements adjust reported profit or loss to eliminate the effects of changes in fair values of bearer biological assets. Mr Finnegan and Ms McConnell accept the view that the use of fair value for bearer assets makes the analysis of profit or loss and financial position more difficult. At the same time, they note that price volatility is an indicator of risk, and risk assessment is part of an analyst's job. Mr Finnegan and Ms McConnell note that sound financial statement analysis will always adjust reported profit or loss and financial position for the effects of unusual or non-recurring changes in reported information. However, if critical information about changes in the economic benefits arising in an agricultural operation is not reported, such analysis is impaired or not possible at all.

DO9 Mr Finnegan and Ms McConnell believe that instead of ignoring the fair value volatility, which a cost model does, volatility should be addressed as a matter of financial statement presentation—such as by putting the fair value changes in other comprehensive income. They note that under the June 2014 Amendment, the bearer assets will be within the scope of IAS 16 and revaluation will be permitted. If an entity were to choose revaluation, the change in the revaluation amount (which approximates fair value) would be reported in other comprehensive income. Consequently, they believe that requiring fair value measurement during the entirety of the bearer plant's life cycle with the fair value changes reported in other comprehensive income would be consistent with permitting revaluation of the bearer asset. Furthermore, Mr Finnegan and Ms McConnell believe that such a change would preserve relevant information for investors through prominent display in the primary financial statements, while addressing the concerns of those who believe that fair value changes distort profit or loss.

Current proposals are not improvements to IFRS

DO10 Mr Finnegan and Ms McConnell believe that if bearer assets are measured at accumulated cost, then at a minimum, the fair value of the bearer plants should be a required disclosure, including information about the valuation techniques and key inputs/assumptions used. However, the 2014 Amendment is not requiring disclosure of fair value. Consequently, critical information is being eliminated from the financial statements of entities engaged in agricultural activities using bearer assets. Mr Finnegan and Ms McConnell do not believe that this is an improvement to financial reporting. In January 2013, the Trustees of the IFRS Foundation approved a new *Due Process Handbook* that specifies, among other things, the criteria for new Standards or major improvements. The main criteria (in addition to pervasiveness of the issue) are (a) whether there is a deficiency in the way particular types of transactions or activities are reported in financial reports, and (b) the importance of the matter to those who use financial reports. Mr Finnegan and Ms McConnell believe that, from a user perspective, there is no deficiency in the accounting for, and disclosures about, bearer assets in IAS 41 and that fair value information is important (indeed essential) to those who use the financial reports of entities engaged in agricultural activity.

DO11   In the user outreach performed by the staff, most investors and analysts said that fair value information about bearer plants is of either limited or no use to them *without* fair value information about the related land, agricultural machinery, etc. Instead of meeting the needs of users by providing this additional fair value information to make the fair value of bearer plants more useful, the Board has chosen to withdraw the requirement to provide the fair value of bearer plants. In the view of Mr Finnegan and Ms McConnell this solution does not adequately address the needs of users of financial statements.

DO12   A better solution would have been for the Board to require the fair value of bearer plants in combination with the fair value of the land to which such plants are attached. One of the weaknesses in IAS 41 is that it does not require the use of fair value to measure land to which bearer plants are attached. This is a weakness because the value of bearer plants is inextricably tied to the value of the land. By understanding the value of the bearer plants and the land, investors know the true potential of an entity's future net cash inflows. A historical cost model for either or both is incapable of providing such information.

DO13   As just discussed, Mr Finnegan and Ms McConnell do not believe the June 2014 Amendment represents an improvement to IFRS and, in fact, represents a step towards lowering the quality of the information available in the financial statements of entities engaged in agricultural activities. The June 2014 Amendment therefore fails to meet the Board's own criteria for a new or amended Standard.

IASB documents published to accompany

IAS 19

Employee Benefits

The text of the unaccompanied standard, IAS 19, is contained in Part A of this edition. Its effective date when issued was 1 January 1999. The text of the Accompanying Guidance on IAS 19 is contained in Part B of this edition. This part presents the following documents:

BASIS FOR CONCLUSIONS

APPENDIX TO THE BASIS FOR CONCLUSIONS

Amendments to the Basis for Conclusions on other IFRSs

DISSENTING OPINIONS

Contents

continued...

...continued

Basis for Conclusions on
IAS 19 *Employee Benefits*

Introduction

BC1 This Basis for Conclusions summarises the International Accounting Standards Board's considerations in reaching its conclusions on IAS 19 *Employee Benefits*. Individual Board members gave greater weight to some factors than to others.

BC2 The Board's predecessor, the International Accounting Standards Committee (IASC), approved IAS 19 *Employee Benefits* in 1998, replacing a previous version of the standard. IASC developed the revision of IAS 19 in 1998 following its consideration of the responses to its exposure draft E54 *Employee Benefits* published in 1996. Since that date, IASC and the Board have made the following amendments that are still relevant:

(a) In October 2000 IASC extended the definition of plan assets (see paragraphs BC178–BC190) and introduced recognition and measurement requirements for reimbursements (see paragraphs BC195–BC199).

(b) In December 2004 the Board amended the accounting for multi-employer plans and group plans (see paragraphs BC35–BC38 and BC40–BC50).

(c) In June 2011 the Board eliminated previous options for deferred recognition of changes in the net defined benefit liability (asset), amended where those changes should be recognised, amended the disclosure requirements for defined benefit plans and multi-employer plans, and made a number of other amendments (see paragraphs BC3–BC13).

Amendments made in 2011

BC3 Accounting for post-employment benefit promises is an important financial reporting issue. Anecdotal evidence and academic research suggested that many users of financial statements did not fully understand the information that entities provided about post-employment benefits under the requirements of IAS 19 before the amendments made in 2011. Both users and preparers of financial statements criticised those accounting requirements for failing to provide high quality, transparent information about post-employment benefits. For example, delays in the recognition of gains and losses give rise to misleading amounts in the statement of financial position and the existence of various options for recognising gains and losses and a lack of clarity in the definitions lead to poor comparability.

BC4 In July 2006 the Board added to its agenda a project on the accounting for post-employment benefit promises in response to calls for a comprehensive review of the accounting for post-employment benefit promises to improve the quality and transparency of financial statements. However, a comprehensive project to address all areas of post-employment benefit accounting could take many years to complete. Nevertheless, the Board recognised a short-term need to provide users of financial statements with better information about post-employment benefit promises.

BC5 Accordingly, the Board undertook a limited scope project, and in March 2008 the Board published a discussion paper *Preliminary Views on Amendments to IAS 19* Employee Benefits that included the Board's preliminary views on the following areas of IAS 19:

(a) the deferred recognition of some gains and losses arising from defined benefit plans.

(b) presentation of the changes in the net defined benefit liability or asset.

(c) accounting for employee benefits that are based on contributions and a promised return and employee benefits with a 'higher of' option (contribution-based promises).

BC6 The discussion paper also asked respondents to identify:

(a) any additional issues that should be addressed in this project given that its objective was to address specific issues in a limited time frame.

(b) what disclosures the Board should consider as part of its review of disclosures.

BC7 The IASB received 150 comment letters in response to that discussion paper. In the light of those responses, the Board deferred its review of contribution-based promises to a possible future project. The Board considered the additional issues raised in those responses and extended the scope of the project to include:

(a) a review of the disclosures for defined benefit plans and multi-employer plans; and

(b) additional issues raised in the responses to the discussion paper and matters that had been submitted to the International Financial Reporting Interpretations Committee (IFRIC) for interpretation that the Board considered could be addressed expeditiously, would not require a fundamental review of defined benefit obligation measurement and would lead to an improvement in the reporting of defined benefit plans.

BC8 In April 2010 the Board published an exposure draft *Defined Benefit Plans* (the 2010 ED). The Board received 227 comment letters in response. In addition to the formal consultation provided by the 2010 ED, the Board undertook an extensive programme of outreach activities during the exposure period with a wide range of users and preparers of financial statements, regulators and others interested in the financial reporting of employee benefits from a wide variety of geographical areas.

BC9   Some respondents to the 2010 ED and the discussion paper requested a comprehensive review of the accounting for employee benefits, preferably as a joint project with the US national standard-setter, the Financial Accounting Standards Board (FASB), and questioned why the Board was addressing employee benefits in a limited scope project, expressing concern that successive changes could be disruptive. The Board reiterated its previous concern that a comprehensive review of the accounting for employee benefits would take many years to complete and that there was an urgent need to improve the financial reporting of employee benefits in the short term, so that users of financial statements receive more useful and understandable information.

BC10   In June 2011 the Board issued amendments to IAS 19 that targeted improvements in the following areas:

(a)   recognition of changes in the net defined benefit liability (asset) (see paragraphs BC65–BC100), including:

    (i)   immediate recognition of defined benefit cost (see paragraphs BC70–BC72).

    (ii)   disaggregation of defined benefit cost into components (see paragraphs BC73–BC87).

    (iii)   recognition of remeasurements in other comprehensive income (see paragraphs BC88–BC100).

(b)   plan amendments, curtailments and settlements (see paragraphs BC152–BC173).

(c)   disclosures about defined benefit plans (see paragraphs BC203–BC252).

(d)   accounting for termination benefits (see paragraphs BC11 and BC254–BC268).

(e)   miscellaneous issues, including:

    (i)   the classification of employee benefits (see paragraphs BC16–BC24).

    (ii)   current estimates of mortality rates (see paragraph BC142).

    (iii)   tax and administration costs (see paragraphs BC121–BC128).

    (iv)   risk-sharing and conditional indexation features (see paragraphs BC143–BC150).

(f)   some matters that had been submitted to the IFRIC for interpretation, including:

    (i)   IFRIC rejection March 2007 – Special wage tax (see paragraphs BC121–BC124).

    (ii)   IFRIC rejection November 2007 – Treatment of employee contributions (see paragraphs BC143–BC150).

(iii)   IFRIC rejection January 2008—Pension promises based on performance hurdles (see paragraphs BC143–BC150).

(iv)   IFRIC rejection May 2008—Settlements (see paragraph BC163).

BC11   The Board issued the amendments resulting from the 2010 ED together with amendments relating to termination benefits resulting from the exposure draft *Proposed Amendments to IAS 37* Provisions, Contingent Liabilities and Contingent Assets *and IAS 19* Employee Benefits (the 2005 ED), published in June 2005. The Board concluded that it would be better to issue both sets of amendments together rather than delay the completion of the amendments for termination benefits until it completed its work on IAS 37 *Provisions, Contingent Liabilities and Contingent Assets*.

Matters not addressed as part of the limited scope project

BC12   Respondents to the 2010 ED and the discussion paper raised matters that were outside the scope of this project (such as measurement of the defined benefit obligation). The Board did not consider these matters in detail. Any project addressing issues beyond the scope of the targeted improvements would be subject to the Board's agenda-setting process.

BC13   In selecting issues to address, the Board discussed the following issues, but took no action in the amendments made in 2011.

(a)   *Contribution-based promises*—The discussion paper included proposals on contribution-based promises. The Board will consider whether to develop those proposals further if it undertakes a comprehensive review of employee benefit accounting.

(b)   *Discount rate for employee benefits*—The Board did not proceed with the proposals in its exposure draft *Discount Rate for Employee Benefits*, published in August 2009. The Board decided it would address issues relating to the discount rate only in the context of a fundamental review (see paragraphs BC138 and BC139).

(c)   *The effect of expected future salary increases on the attribution of benefits*—The 2010 ED proposed that expected future salary increases should be included in determining whether a benefit formula expressed in terms of current salary allocates a materially higher level of benefit to later years. The Board did not proceed with that proposal because it is closely related to a fundamental review of the accounting for contribution-based promises (see paragraphs BC117–BC120).

(d)   *Exemption for entities participating in multi-employer defined benefit plans*—The Board rejected a proposal to permit all entities participating in a multi-employer defined benefit plan to account for these plans as defined contribution plans. The Board concluded that extending that exemption would be contrary to its general approach of limiting exceptions. The Board also believes that such an exemption would not be appropriate for all multi-employer plans, such as when an entity becomes a dominant participant in a multi-employer plan, perhaps because other participants leave the plan (see paragraph BC39).

(e)   *IFRIC-related matters*—The Board did not incorporate into IAS 19 the requirements of IFRIC 14 *IAS 19—The Limit on a Defined Benefit Asset, Minimum Funding Requirements and their Interaction.* Incorporating IFRIC 14 would require changes to the drafting, which could have unintended consequences. The Board also considered other questions received by the IFRIC but concluded that it would not amend IAS 19 at this time.

Employee Benefits Working Group

BC14   The Board established an Employee Benefits Working Group in 2007 to help by providing a variety of expert perspectives, including those of auditors, preparers and users of financial statements, actuaries and regulators. The group consisted of senior professionals with extensive practical experience in the operation, management, valuation, financial reporting, auditing or regulation of a variety of post-employment benefit arrangements.

BC15   Members of the group assisted the Board by reviewing early drafts of the amendments made in 2011, and the preceding discussion paper and exposure draft. The Board greatly appreciates the time and energy that group members have devoted to this process and the quality of their contributions.

Classification of benefits

Short-term employee benefits: amendments issued in 2011

BC16   The amendments made in 2011 clarify that the classification of benefits as short-term employee benefits depends on the period between the end of the annual reporting period in which the employee renders the service that gives rise to the benefit and the date when the benefit is expected to be settled.

BC17   The Board's objective in defining the scope of the short-term employee benefits classification was to identify the set of employee benefits for which a simplified measurement approach would not result in measuring those benefits at an amount different from the general measurement requirements of IAS 19.

BC18   The Board concluded that the classification of a short-term employee benefit on the basis of the timing of expected settlement would best meet this objective and would be most consistent with the measurement basis in IAS 19.

BC19   Other alternatives that the Board considered for the basis for classification of short-term employee benefits included:

(a)   *The earliest possible settlement date (ie entitlement)*—The Board rejected this alternative because it would have the result that a benefit classified as a short-term employee benefit could be measured at an amount materially different from its present value. For example, this could occur if an employee is entitled to a benefit within twelve months, but the benefit is not expected to be settled until many years later.

(b) *The latest possible settlement date* — The Board rejected this alternative because, although the latest possible settlement date would be consistent with the Board's objective of minimising differences between the measurement of short-term employee benefits and the measurement of the same benefits using the model for post-employment benefits, this would result in the smallest set of benefits that would meet the definition.

BC20 However, classifying short-term employee benefits on the basis of expected settlement raises the following additional concerns:

(a) *Unit of account* — the expected settlement date is determined on the basis of a combination of the characteristics of the benefits and the characteristics of the employees, and would reflect the actuarial assumptions for a particular year rather than the characteristics of the benefits promised. The Board concluded that the classification of the benefits should reflect the characteristics of the benefits, rather than the demographic or financial assumptions at a point in time.

(b) *Splitting benefits into components* — some benefits are expected to be settled over a period of time. The Board concluded that an entity should classify a benefit as a short-term employee benefit if the whole of the benefit is expected to be settled before twelve months after the end of the annual reporting period in which the related service was provided. This will ensure that the benefit is measured on the same basis throughout its life and is consistent with the measurement requirements of paragraph 69.

(c) *Reclassification* — if the expected settlement date of a benefit classified initially as a short-term employee benefit changes subsequently to a date more than twelve months after the end of the reporting period, then the undiscounted amount of that benefit could differ materially from its present value. The Board concluded that the classification of a short-term employee benefit should be revisited if it no longer meets the definition. This maintains the objective that the benefits should not be measured at an amount that would differ materially from their present value. However, the Board concluded that a temporary change in expectation should not trigger reclassification because such a change would not be indicative of a change in the underlying characteristics of the benefit. The Board noted that reclassification of a benefit from other long-term employee benefits to short-term employee benefits is less of a concern because in that case measuring the benefit at its undiscounted amount should not differ materially from measuring the benefit at its present value.

BC21 Other approaches that the Board considered for addressing the concerns above included:

(a) *Unit of account* — by requiring an entity to classify benefits on an employee-by-employee basis. The Board concluded that this would not be practical and would not meet the objectives of the classification.

(b) *Reclassification* — prohibiting the entity from revising the classification of a short-term employee benefit after initial classification. This approach would maintain continuity of measurement throughout the life of the benefit, but the Board rejected it because measuring the benefit at the undiscounted amount could result in an amount that differs from its present value if the entity no longer expects to settle the benefit before twelve months after the end of the annual reporting period.

Long-term employee benefits: exposure draft published in 2010

BC22 The Board considered combining post-employment benefits and other long-term employee benefits into a single category. The main differences between accounting for other long-term benefits and accounting for post-employment benefits were:

(a) the previous option to defer recognition of actuarial gains and losses ('the corridor'); and

(b) the previous requirement to recognise unvested past service cost over the vesting period.

BC23 As proposed in the 2010 ED, the Board removed these differences in 2011. In the light of that proposal, the 2010 ED also proposed the removal of the distinction between post-employment benefits and other long-term employee benefits. However, many respondents to the 2010 ED did not support this removal of that distinction. They did not think that the recognition and disclosure requirements for post-employment benefits were appropriate for other long-term employee benefits, because in their view:

(a) the costs of applying the recognition and disclosure requirements for post-employment benefits to other long-term employee benefits outweigh the benefits.

(b) accounting for other long-term employee benefits was not originally within the scope of the project. Accounting for other long-term employee benefits was not an area they viewed as requiring improvement.

BC24 After reviewing the responses to the 2010 ED, the Board decided not to combine post-employment and other long-term employee benefits into a single category for the reasons expressed by respondents.

Short-term employee benefits

Paid absences

BC25 Some argue that an employee's entitlement to future paid absences does not create an obligation if that entitlement is conditional on future events other than future service. However, IASC concluded in 1998 that an obligation arises as an employee renders service that increases the employee's entitlement (conditional or unconditional) to future paid absences; for example, accumulating paid sick leave creates an obligation because any unused entitlement increases the employee's entitlement to sick leave in future periods. The probability that the employee will be sick in those future periods affects the measurement of that obligation, but does not determine whether that obligation exists.

BC26   IASC considered three alternative approaches to measuring the obligation that results from unused entitlement to accumulating paid absences:

(a)   recognise the entire unused entitlement as a liability, on the basis that any future payments are made first out of unused entitlement and only subsequently out of entitlement that will accumulate in future periods (a FIFO approach);

(b)   recognise a liability to the extent that future payments for the employee group as a whole are expected to exceed the future payments that would have been expected in the absence of the accumulation feature (a group LIFO approach); or

(c)   recognise a liability to the extent that future payments for individual employees are expected to exceed the future payments that would have been expected in the absence of the accumulation feature (an individual LIFO approach).

These methods are illustrated by the following example.

BC Example 1

An entity has 100 employees, who are each entitled to five working days of paid sick leave for each year. Unused sick leave may be carried forward for one year. Such leave is taken first out of the current year's entitlement and then out of any balance brought forward from the previous year (a LIFO basis).

At 31 December 20X1 the average unused entitlement is two days per employee. The entity expects, on the basis of past experience that is expected to continue, that 92 employees will take no more than four days of paid sick leave in 20X2 and that the remaining 8 employees will take an average of six and a half days each.

Method (a):	*The entity recognises a liability equal to the undiscounted amount of 200 days of sick pay (two days each, for 100 employees). It is assumed that the first 200 days of paid sick leave result from the unused entitlement.*
Method (b):	*The entity recognises no liability because paid sick leave for the employee group as a whole is not expected to exceed the entitlement of five days each in 20X2.*
Method (c):	*The entity recognises a liability equal to the undiscounted amount of 12 days of sick pay (one and a half days each, for 8 employees).*

BC27　　IASC selected method (c), the individual LIFO approach, because that method measures the obligation at the present value of the additional future payments that are expected to arise solely from the accumulation feature. IAS 19 notes that, in many cases, the resulting liability will not be material.

Post-employment benefits

Distinction between defined contribution plans and defined benefit plans

Defined contribution plans

BC28　　IAS 19 before its revision in 1998 defined:

(a)　**defined contribution plans** as retirement benefit plans under which amounts to be paid as retirement benefits are determined by reference to contributions to a fund together with investment earnings thereon; and

(b)　**defined benefit plans** as retirement benefit plans under which amounts to be paid as retirement benefits are determined by reference to a formula usually based on employees' remuneration and/or years of service.

BC29　　IASC considered these definitions unsatisfactory because they focused on the benefit receivable by the employee, rather than on the cost to the entity. The definitions introduced in 1998 focused on the downside risk that the cost to the entity may increase. The definition of defined contribution plans does not exclude the upside potential that the cost to the entity may be less than expected.

Defined benefit plans: amendments issued in 2011

BC30　　The amendments made in 2011 clarify that the existence of a benefit formula does not, by itself, create a defined benefit plan, but rather that there needs to be a link between the benefit formula and contributions that creates a legal or constructive obligation to contribute further amounts to meet the benefits specified by the benefit formula. This amendment to paragraph 29 addressed a concern that can arise when a plan has a benefit formula determining the benefits to be paid if there are sufficient plan assets, but not requiring the employer to pay additional contributions if there are insufficient plan assets to pay those benefits. In effect, the benefit payments are based on the lower of the benefit formula and the plan assets available. The amendments clarify that such a plan is a defined contribution plan.

Multi-employer plans and state plans

BC31　　An entity may not always be able to obtain sufficient information from multi-employer plans to use defined benefit accounting. IASC considered three approaches to this problem:

(a)   use defined contribution accounting for some and defined benefit accounting for others;

(b)   use defined contribution accounting for all multi-employer plans, with additional disclosure where the multi-employer plan is a defined benefit plan; or

(c)   use defined benefit accounting for those multi-employer plans that are defined benefit plans. However, where sufficient information is not available to use defined benefit accounting, an entity should disclose that fact and use defined contribution accounting.

BC32   IASC believed that there was no conceptually sound, workable and objective way to draw a distinction so that an entity could use defined contribution accounting for some multi-employer defined benefit plans and defined benefit accounting for others. In addition, IASC believed that it was misleading to use defined contribution accounting for multi-employer plans that are defined benefit plans. This is illustrated by the case of French banks that used defined contribution accounting for defined benefit pension plans operated under industry-wide collective agreements on a pay-as-you-go basis. Demographic trends made these plans unsustainable and a major reform in 1993 replaced them by defined contribution arrangements for future service. At that point, the banks were compelled to quantify their obligations. Those obligations had previously existed, but had not been recognised as liabilities.

BC33   IASC concluded that an entity should use defined benefit accounting for those multi-employer plans that are defined benefit plans. However, where sufficient information is not available to use defined benefit accounting, an entity should disclose that fact and use defined contribution accounting. IASC applied the same principle to state plans, observing that most state plans are defined contribution plans.

BC34   In response to comments on E54, IASC considered a proposal to exempt wholly-owned subsidiaries (and their parents) participating in group defined benefit plans from the recognition and measurement requirements in their individual non-consolidated financial statements, on cost-benefit grounds. IASC concluded that such an exemption would not be appropriate.

Multi-employer plans: amendments issued in 2004

BC35   In April 2004 the IFRIC published a draft Interpretation, D6 *Multi-employer Plans*, which proposed the following guidance on how multi-employer plans should apply defined benefit accounting, if possible:

(a)   The plan should be measured in accordance with IAS 19 using assumptions appropriate for the plan as a whole.

(b)   The plan should be allocated to plan participants so that they recognise an asset or liability that reflects the impact of the surplus or deficit on the future contributions from the participant.

BC36   The concerns raised by respondents to D6 about the availability of the information about the plan as a whole, the difficulties in making an allocation as proposed and the resulting lack of usefulness of the information provided by defined benefit accounting were such that the IFRIC decided not to proceed with the proposals.

BC37   When discussing group plans (see paragraphs BC40–BC50) in 2004 the Board noted that, if there were a contractual agreement between a multi-employer plan and its participants on how a surplus would be distributed or a deficit funded, the same principle that applied to group plans should apply to multi-employer plans, ie the participants should recognise an asset or liability. In relation to the funding of a deficit, the Board regarded this principle as consistent with the recognition of a provision in accordance with IAS 37.

BC38   The Board therefore clarified that a participant in a multi-employer defined benefit plan must recognise the asset or liability arising from that contractual agreement if the participant:

(a)   accounts for that participation on a defined contribution basis in accordance with paragraph 34 because it has insufficient information to apply defined benefit accounting, but

(b)   has a contractual agreement that determines how a surplus would be distributed or a deficit funded.

Multi-employer plans: exposure draft published in 2010

BC39   The Board considered and rejected a proposal to permit all entities participating in multi-employer defined benefit plans to account for those plans as defined contribution plans. The Board concluded that extending that exemption would be contrary to its general approach of limiting exceptions. In the Board's view such an exemption would not be appropriate for all multi-employer plans, such as when an entity becomes a dominant participant in a multi-employer plan, perhaps because other participants leave the plan.

Group plans: amendments issued in 2004

BC40   Some constituents asked the Board to consider whether entities participating in a group defined benefit plan should, in their separate or individual financial statements, either have an unqualified exemption from defined benefit accounting or be able to treat the plan as a multi-employer plan.

BC41   In developing the exposure draft *Actuarial Gains and Losses, Group Plans and Disclosures* published in April 2004 (the 2004 ED), the Board did not agree that an unqualified exemption from defined benefit accounting for group defined benefit plans in the separate or individual financial statements of group entities was appropriate. In principle, the requirements of International Financial Reporting Standards (IFRSs) should apply to separate or individual financial statements in the same way as they apply to any other financial statements. Following that principle would mean amending IAS 19 to allow group entities that participate in a plan that meets the definition of a multi-employer plan, except that the participants are under common control, to be treated as participants in a multi-employer plan in their separate or individual financial statements.

BC42 However, in the 2004 ED the Board concluded that entities within a group should always be presumed to be able to obtain the necessary information about the plan as a whole. This implies that, in accordance with the requirements for multi-employer plans, defined benefit accounting should be applied if there is a consistent and reliable basis for allocating the assets and obligations of the plan.

BC43 In the 2004 ED the Board acknowledged that entities within a group might not be able to identify a consistent and reliable basis for allocating the plan that results in the entity recognising an asset or liability that reflects the extent to which a surplus or deficit in the plan would affect its future contributions. This is because there may be uncertainty in the terms of the plan about how surpluses will be used or deficits funded across the consolidated group. However, the Board concluded that entities within a group should always be able to make at least a consistent and *reasonable* allocation, for example on the basis of a percentage of pensionable pay.

BC44 The Board then considered whether, for some group entities, the benefits of defined benefit accounting using a consistent and reasonable basis of allocation were worth the costs involved in obtaining the information. The Board decided that this was not the case for entities that meet criteria similar to those in IAS 27 *Consolidated and Separate Financial Statements*[1] for the exemption from preparing consolidated financial statements.

BC45 The 2004 ED therefore proposed the following for entities that participate in a plan that would meet the definition of a multi-employer plan except that the participants are under common control:

(a) If the entities meet the criteria as proposed in the 2004 ED, they should be treated as if they were participants in a multi-employer plan. This means that if there is no consistent and reliable basis for allocating the assets and liabilities of the plan, the entity should use defined contribution accounting and provide additional disclosures.

(b) In all other cases, the entities should be required to apply defined benefit accounting by making a consistent and reasonable allocation of the assets and liabilities of the plan.

BC46 Respondents to the 2004 ED generally supported the proposal to extend the requirements on multi-employer plans to group entities. However, many disagreed with the criteria proposed in the 2004 ED, for the following reasons:

(a) The proposed amendments and the interaction with D6 (see paragraphs BC35–BC38) were unclear.

(b) The provisions for multi-employer accounting should be extended to a listed parent company.

---

1   The consolidation requirements in IAS 27 were superseded by IFRS 10 *Consolidated Financial Statements* issued in May 2011. The criteria for the exemption from preparing consolidated financial statements were not changed.

(c)   The provisions for multi-employer accounting should be extended to group entities with listed debt.

(d)   The provisions for multi-employer plan accounting should be extended to all group entities, including partly-owned subsidiaries.

(e)   There should be a blanket exemption from defined benefit accounting for all group entities.

BC47   The Board agreed that the proposed requirements for group plans were unnecessarily complex. The Board also concluded that it would be better to treat group plans separately from multi-employer plans because of the difference in information available to the participants: in a group plan, information about the plan as a whole should generally be available. The Board further noted that, if the parent wishes to comply with IFRSs in its separate financial statements or wishes its subsidiaries to comply with IFRSs in their individual financial statements, then it must obtain and provide the necessary information at least for the purposes of disclosure.

BC48   The Board noted that, if there were a contractual agreement or stated policy on charging the net defined benefit cost to group entities, that agreement or policy would determine the cost for each entity. If there is no such contractual agreement or stated policy, the entity that is the sponsoring employer bears the risk relating to the plan by default. The Board therefore concluded that a group plan should be allocated to the individual entities within a group in accordance with any contractual agreement or stated policy. If there is no such agreement or policy, the net defined benefit cost is allocated to the sponsoring employer. The other group entities recognise a cost equal to any contribution collected by the sponsoring employer.

BC49   This approach has the advantages of (a) all group entities recognising the cost they have to bear for the defined benefit promise and (b) being simple to apply.

BC50   The Board also noted that participation in a group plan is a related party transaction. As such, disclosures are required to comply with IAS 24 *Related Party Disclosures*. IAS 24 requires an entity to disclose the nature of the related party relationship as well as information about the transactions and outstanding balances necessary for an understanding of the potential effect of the relationship on the financial statements. The Board noted that information about each of (a) the policy on charging the defined benefit cost, (b) the policy on charging current contributions and (c) the status of the plan as a whole was required to give an understanding of the potential effect of the participation in the group plan on the entity's separate or individual financial statements.

State plan and group plan disclosures: amendments issued in 2011

BC51   The amendments made in 2011 updated, without reconsideration, the disclosure requirements for entities that participate in state plans or defined benefit plans that share risks between various entities under common control, to be consistent with the disclosure requirements for multi-employer plans and defined benefit plans. However, those amendments permit an entity to include those disclosures by cross-reference to the required disclosures in another group entity's financial statements, if specified conditions are met.

Defined benefit plans: recognition and measurement

BC52 Although IAS 19 before its revision in 1998 did not deal explicitly with the recognition of retirement benefit obligations as a liability, it is likely that most entities recognised a liability for retirement benefit obligations at the same time under the requirements in IAS 19 before and after its revision in 1998. However, the requirements in IAS 19 before and after its revision in 1998 differed in the measurement of the resulting liability.

BC53 Paragraph 63 of IAS 19 is based on the definition of, and recognition criteria for, a liability in the IASC's *Framework for the Preparation and Presentation of Financial Statements (Framework)*.[2] The *Framework* defined a liability as 'a present obligation of the entity arising from past events, the settlement of which is expected to result in an outflow from the entity of resources embodying economic benefits'. The *Framework* stated that an item which meets the definition of a liability should be recognised if:

(a) it is probable that any future economic benefit associated with the item will flow from the entity; and

(b) the item has a cost or value that can be measured with reliability.

BC54 IASC believed that:

(a) an entity has an obligation under a defined benefit plan when an employee has rendered service in return for the benefits promised under the plan. Paragraphs 70–74 deal with the attribution of benefit to individual periods of service in order to determine whether an obligation exists.

(b) an entity should use actuarial assumptions to determine whether the entity will pay those benefits in future reporting periods (see paragraphs 75–98).

(c) actuarial techniques allow an entity to measure the obligation with sufficient reliability to justify recognition of a liability.

BC55 IASC believed that an obligation exists even if a benefit is not vested, in other words if the employee's right to receive the benefit is conditional on future employment. For example, consider an entity that provides a benefit of CU100[3] to employees who remain in service for two years. At the end of the first year, the employee and the entity are not in the same position as at the beginning of the first year, because the employee will need to work for only one more year, instead of two, before becoming entitled to the benefit. Although there is a possibility that the benefit may not vest, that difference is

---

2 References to the *Framework* in this Basis for Conclusions are to the IASC's *Framework for the Preparation and Presentation of Financial Statements*, adopted by the Board in 2001 and in effect when the Standard was revised.

3 In this Basis for Conclusions monetary amounts are denominated in 'currency units (CU)'.

an obligation and, in IASC's view, should result in the recognition of a liability at the end of the first year. The measurement of that obligation at its present value reflects the entity's best estimate of the probability that the benefit may not vest.

Measurement date

BC56 Some national standards permit entities to measure the present value of defined benefit obligations at a date up to three months before the end of the reporting period. However, IASC decided that entities should measure the present value of defined benefit obligations, and the fair value of any plan assets, at the end of the reporting period. Consequently, if an entity carries out a detailed valuation of the obligation at an earlier date, the results of that valuation should be updated to take account of any significant transactions and other significant changes in circumstances up to the balance sheet date (end of the reporting period).

BC57 In response to comments on E54, IASC clarified that full actuarial valuation was not required at the end of the reporting period, provided that an entity determined the present value of defined benefit obligations and the fair value of any plan assets with sufficient regularity that the amounts recognised in the financial statements did not differ materially from the amounts that would be determined at the balance sheet date.

Interim reporting: effects of the amendments issued in 2011

BC58 The 2010 ED did not propose any substantial amendments to the requirements in IAS 34 *Interim Financial Reporting*. Respondents to the 2010 ED were concerned that the requirements for the immediate recognition of changes in the net defined benefit liability (asset) would imply that entities should remeasure the net defined benefit liability (asset) at each interim reporting date.

BC59 The Board noted that an entity is not always required to remeasure a net defined benefit liability (asset) for interim reporting purposes under IAS 19 and IAS 34. Both indicate that the entity needs to exercise judgement in determining whether it needs to remeasure the net defined benefit liability (asset) at the end of the (interim or annual) reporting period.

BC60 The amendments made in 2011 require an entity to recognise remeasurements in the period in which they arise. Thus, remeasurements are now more likely to have a material effect on the amount recognised in the financial statements than would have been the case before those amendments if an entity elected to defer recognition of actuarial gains and losses. It follows that entities previously deferring recognition of some gains and losses are now more likely to judge that remeasurement is required for interim reporting.

BC61 The Board considered setting out explicitly whether an entity should remeasure a net defined benefit liability (asset) at interim dates. However, in the Board's view, such a change would be an exemption from the general requirements of IAS 34 and consequently it decided against such an amendment. The Board is not aware of concerns with the application of these interim reporting requirements for entities that applied the immediate recognition option under the previous version of IAS 19.

BC62   Some respondents to the 2010 ED asked the Board to clarify whether the assumptions used to determine defined benefit cost for subsequent interim periods should reflect the assumptions used at the end of the prior financial year or for the most recent measurement of the defined benefit obligation (for example, in an earlier interim period or in determining the effect of a plan amendment or settlement).

BC63   The Board noted that if assumptions for each interim reporting period were updated to the most recent interim date, the measurement of the entity's annual amounts would be affected by how frequently the entity reports, ie whether the entity reports quarterly, half-yearly or with no interim period. In the Board's view this would not be consistent with the requirements of paragraphs 28 and 29 of IAS 34.

BC64   [Deleted][4]

Recognition: amendments issued in 2011

BC65   The amendments made in 2011 require entities to recognise all changes in the net defined benefit liability (asset) in the period in which those changes occur, and to disaggregate and recognise defined benefit cost as follows:

(a)   service cost, relating to the cost of the services received, in profit or loss.

(b)   net interest on the net defined benefit liability (asset), representing the financing effect of paying for the benefits in advance or in arrears, in profit or loss.

(c)   remeasurements, representing the period-to-period fluctuations in the amounts of defined benefit obligations and plan assets, in other comprehensive income.

BC66   Before those amendments, IAS 19 permitted three options for the recognition of actuarial gains and losses:

(a)   leaving actuarial gains and losses unrecognised if they were within a 'corridor' and deferred recognition of actuarial gains and losses outside the corridor in profit or loss;

(b)   immediate recognition in profit or loss; or

---

4   *Plan Amendment, Curtailment or Settlement* (Amendments to IAS 19), issued in February 2018, requires an entity to use updated actuarial assumptions to determine current service cost and net interest for the remainder of the annual reporting period after the plan amendment, curtailment or settlement when the entity remeasures its net defined benefit liability (asset) in accordance with paragraph 99. Paragraphs BC173A–BC173F explain the Board's rationale for the amendments. Before the amendments, IAS 19 did not require an entity to use updated assumptions to determine current service cost and net interest for the period after the plan amendment, curtailment or settlement. Paragraph BC64 explained the Board's rationale for those previous requirements. Because the previous requirements no longer apply, the Board deleted paragraph BC64.

(c)   immediate recognition in other comprehensive income. Actuarial gains and losses recognised in other comprehensive income are transferred directly to retained earnings.

BC67   The amendments in 2011 made the following changes to the recognition requirements:

(a)   immediate recognition—elimination of the corridor (paragraphs BC70–BC72).

(b)   redefining the components of defined benefit cost (paragraphs BC73–BC87).

(c)   recognition of the remeasurements component in other comprehensive income (paragraphs BC88–BC100).

BC68   Many respondents to the 2010 ED agreed that the Board should address within the project the disaggregation of defined benefit cost and where the components of defined benefit cost should be recognised. However, some respondents said that the determination of an appropriate disaggregation method was intrinsically linked to the accounting model and should not be considered until there is a fundamental review of IAS 19. The Board considered the components of defined benefit cost in the context of the accounting model of IAS 19. In the Board's view, the disaggregation requirements are consistent with that model and provide useful information.

BC69   Others said that the Board should not address those matters until it completes its project on financial statement presentation, including the conceptual basis for deciding whether items should ultimately be reclassified to profit or loss from other comprehensive income. However, the Board concluded that improving the understandability and comparability of the changes in the net defined benefit liability or asset would be necessary if changes are to be recognised immediately, and that improving the understandability of those changes should not be delayed until it completes its project on financial statement presentation.

Immediate recognition: elimination of the corridor

BC70   In the Board's view, immediate recognition provides information that is more relevant to users of financial statements than the information provided by deferred recognition. It also provides a more faithful representation of the financial effect of defined benefit plans on the entity and is easier for users to understand. In contrast, deferred recognition can produce misleading information: for example,

(a)   an asset may be recognised in the statement of financial position, even when a plan is in deficit; or

(b)   the statement of comprehensive income may include gains and losses that arise from economic events that occurred in past periods.

BC71   In addition, eliminating accounting options makes it easier for users to compare entities.

BC72 Most respondents supported the proposal to recognise all changes in the present value of the defined benefit obligation and in the fair value of plan assets when they occur. However, some respondents expressed concerns about immediate recognition:

(a) *Measurement model requires further work* — some respondents expressed the view that the measurement model needs a comprehensive review and that it would be disruptive to move to immediate recognition of changes arising from the measurement model in IAS 19. However, in the Board's view, deferred recognition makes accounting for defined benefit plans obscure and difficult for users to understand. Consequently, the Board decided not to delay the introduction of the requirement for immediate recognition.

(b) *Relevance of information* — some respondents expressed the view that some changes to the net defined benefit liability (asset) occurring in a period are not relevant to the measurement of a long-term liability. This is because past gains or losses may be offset by future losses or gains. However, in the Board's view it is not inevitable that future gains or losses will occur and offset past losses or gains.

(c) *Volatility* — many respondents were concerned that volatility might result if an entity reported all changes in the net defined benefit liability (asset) in each period and that this volatility would impede year-on-year comparability, and would obscure the profitability of the entity's core business. However, the Board believes that a measure should be volatile if it faithfully represents transactions and other events that are themselves volatile, and that financial statements should not omit such information. In the Board's view, that information should be presented in a way that is most useful to users of financial statements. Therefore, the Board introduced a presentation that allows users of financial statements to isolate remeasurements of the entity's net defined benefit liability (asset) (see paragraphs BC88–BC100).

(d) *Behavioural and social consequences* — some respondents expressed concerns that immediate recognition might have adverse behavioural and social consequences. For example, they were concerned that entities might try to eliminate short-term volatility by making long-term economically inefficient decisions about the allocation of plan assets, or by making socially undesirable amendments to plan terms. However, in the Board's view, it is not the responsibility of accounting standard-setters to encourage or discourage particular behaviour. Their responsibility is to set standards that result in the provision of relevant information that faithfully represents an entity's financial position, financial performance and cash flows so that users of that information can make well-informed decisions.

(e) *Potential effect on debt covenants* — some respondents were concerned that immediate recognition could lead to difficulties with debt covenants based on earnings or net assets, and impair entities' ability to pay dividends because of legal restrictions based on amounts in financial statements. In the Board's view, it is up to the entity and the holder of a covenant to determine whether to insulate a debt covenant from the effects of a new or amended accounting standard or to determine how they might renegotiate any existing covenant.

Components of defined benefit cost: service cost

BC73　The service cost component includes current service cost, past service cost and any gain or loss on settlement, but excludes changes in the defined benefit obligation that result from changes in demographic assumptions that are included in the remeasurements component together with other actuarial gains and losses. In the Board's view, including the effect of changes in demographic assumptions in the service cost component would combine amounts with different predictive values and, consequently, the service cost component is more relevant for assessing an entity's continuous operational costs if it does not include changes in past estimates of service cost. Most respondents agreed with the proposals in the 2010 ED that service cost should exclude changes in demographic assumptions.

Components of defined benefit cost: net interest

BC74　The amendments made in 2011 require an entity to calculate net interest on the net defined benefit liability (asset) using the same discount rate used to measure the defined benefit obligation (the net interest approach).

BC75　The amendments are consistent with the view that a net defined benefit liability is equivalent to a financing amount owed by the entity to the plan or to the employees. The economic cost of that financing is interest cost, calculated using the rate specified in paragraph 83. Similarly, a net defined benefit asset is an amount owed by the plan or by the employees to the entity. The entity accounts for the present value of economic benefits that it expects to receive from the plan or from the employees in the form of reductions in future contributions or as refunds. The entity discounts those economic benefits using the rate specified in paragraph 83.

BC76　In the Board's view, a net interest approach provides more understandable information than would be the case if finance income and expenses were to be determined separately on the plan assets and defined benefit obligation that combine to make a net defined benefit liability (asset). The net interest approach results in an entity recognising interest income when the plan has a surplus, and interest cost when the plan has a deficit.

BC77　The Board concluded that, in principle, the change in value of any asset can be divided into an amount that arises from the passage of time and amounts that arise from other changes. The interest cost on the defined benefit obligation arises from the passage of time. Consequently, the 2010 ED proposed that the net interest component of defined benefit cost should include not only the interest cost on the defined benefit obligation, but also the part of the return on plan assets that arises from the passage of time. In addition, the Board concluded that, to be consistent with the principle of separating components of defined benefit cost with different predictive implications, the net interest component should not include the part of the return on plan assets that does not arise from the passage of time.

BC78　　The Board found it difficult to identify a practical method for identifying the change in the fair value of plan assets that arises from the passage of time, particularly for assets that do not bear explicit interest. The Board rejected approximations to this amount using:

(a)　　the expected return on plan assets (as required by IAS 19 before the amendments made in 2011) because it could not be determined in an objective way, and because it might include a return that is not simply attributable to the passage of time; and

(b)　　dividends (but not capital gains) received on equity plan assets and interest earned on debt plan assets. In the Board's view, dividends are not a faithful representation of the time value of money.

BC79　　Consequently, the 2010 ED proposed that entities should calculate interest income on plan assets using the rate used to discount the defined benefit obligation. This approach produces interest income that is equivalent to determining a net interest on the net defined benefit liability (asset). The difference between the actual return on assets and the interest income on plan assets is included in the remeasurements component (see paragraph BC86).

BC80　　Respondents generally agreed with the principle that the net interest component should include changes both in the defined benefit obligation and in plan assets that arise from the passage of time. However, some supported the approach proposed in the 2010 ED and others supported the expected return approach used in IAS 19 before the amendments made in 2011 (ie based on the expected return on plan assets).

BC81　　The Board agreed with the views of respondents who reasoned that the net interest approach is a simple and pragmatic solution that is consistent with the presentation in the statement of financial position and, by reflecting the underlying economics of the net defined benefit liability (asset), provides more relevant and understandable information than the expected return approach. The net interest approach represents the economics of the entity's decision on how to finance the plan by reporting net interest income when the plan is in surplus and net interest expense when the plan is in deficit.

BC82　　Respondents to the 2010 ED expressed concerns that:

(a)　　plan assets may be made up of many different types of investments. The return on high quality corporate bonds would be arbitrary and would not be a faithful representation of the return that investors require or expect from each type of asset. However, in the Board's view, using the same rate as the rate used to discount the liability is a practical approach that:

(i)   would not require an entity to make a subjective judgement on how to divide the return on plan assets into an interest component and a remeasurement.

(ii)   results in amounts recognised in profit or loss that reflect the effect of the time value of money on both the defined benefit obligation and on plan assets. Consequently, the amounts recognised in profit or loss reflect the differences between funded and unfunded plans.

(b)   the requirements in paragraph 83 for determining the discount rate can result in economically similar defined benefit obligations being reported at different amounts, depending on whether there is a deep market in high quality corporate bonds. As noted in paragraph BC13, the Board considered improving the discount rate requirements of IAS 19, but decided to defer consideration of the discount rate until it decides whether to review measurement of the defined benefit obligation as a whole.

BC83   The Board considered the expected return approach, but noted that:

(a)   although the expected return approach is consistent with the discount rate used in the measurement of the plan assets at fair value, the net interest approach better represents the economics of the net defined benefit liability (asset) and consequently provides more comparable information on the changes in that net amount presented in the statement of financial position.

(b)   although the expected return approach is not theoretically more subjective than the net interest approach, in practice it is more likely that observable information will not be available to determine the expected return than is the case for the discount rate used for the net interest approach.

(c)   the expected return approach results in the reporting of the expected performance of the plan assets, regardless of their actual performance during the period. For a high risk investment, this has the effect of recognising the anticipated higher return in profit or loss, and the effect of higher risk in other comprehensive income. In contrast, the net interest approach recognises in other comprehensive income both the higher return and the effects of higher risk.

BC84   Supporters of both the net interest approach and the expected return approach reasoned that their favoured approach produces more relevant, comparable and understandable information. These contrasting views may reflect how different respondents consider the net defined benefit liability (asset) recognised in the statement of financial position as either comprising two components (the plan assets and the defined benefit obligation), which are measured separately but presented together (the gross view), or representing a single amount owed to, or from, the plan (the net view). These differences in views may also reflect differences in plan design, such as the degree of an entity's control over the plan assets. The expected return approach is more consistent with the gross view and the net interest approach is more consistent with the net view. The Board concluded that the net view is more consistent with the presentation of the net defined benefit liability (asset) in the statement of financial position, and therefore the disaggregation of the defined benefit cost in the statement of comprehensive income should also be based on the net view.

BC85　Supporters of both the net interest approach and the expected return approach reasoned that their approach does not provide an uneconomic incentive to invest assets in a particular way. In coming to its conclusion, the Board did not aim to encourage or discourage any particular behaviour, but considered which approach would provide the most relevant information that faithfully represents the changes in the plan assets and defined benefit obligation.

Components of defined benefit cost: remeasurements

BC86　As a result of the Board's decisions on the service cost and net interest components, the amendments made in 2011 define the remeasurement component as comprising:

(a)　actuarial gains and losses on the defined benefit obligation;

(b)　the return on plan assets, excluding amounts included in net interest on the net defined benefit liability (asset); and

(c)　any changes in the effect of the asset ceiling, excluding the amount included in net interest on the net defined benefit liability (asset).

BC87　The definition of remeasurements differs from the definition of actuarial gains and losses in IAS 19 before the amendments made in 2011 because the introduction of the net interest approach changed the disaggregation of the return on plan assets and the effect of the asset ceiling.

Components of defined benefit cost: recognition of the remeasurements component

BC88　As described in paragraphs BC70–BC72, the amendments made in 2011 eliminated deferred recognition. To distinguish the remeasurement component from service cost and net interest in an informative way, the 2010 ED proposed that entities should recognise the remeasurements component as an item of other comprehensive income, thus removing the previous option to recognise in profit or loss all changes in the net defined benefit liability (asset). The Board noted that although changes included in the remeasurements component may provide more information about the uncertainty and risk of future cash flows, they provide less information about the likely amount and timing of those cash flows.

BC89　Most respondents agreed with the proposal in the 2010 ED to recognise remeasurements in other comprehensive income. But some respondents expressed the following concerns:

(a)　*Remeasurements in profit or loss* — some respondents did not support the proposal in the 2010 ED because, in their view:

(i)   there is no conceptual basis for recognising amounts in other comprehensive income, thus recognition in profit or loss would be more appropriate.

(ii)   the fact that the remeasurements component's predictive value is different from that of other components should not lead to the conclusion that this component should be recognised in other comprehensive income, but instead should indicate that there is a need to present this component as a separate line item in profit or loss.

(iii)   if changes in assumptions are not recognised in profit or loss in the same way as service costs, this might encourage mis-estimation of service costs to achieve an accounting result.

(b)   *Remeasurements option*—some respondents expressed the view that the Board should maintain the option to recognise remeasurements in profit or loss:

(i)   because the Board should not eliminate this option until it develops a principle for determining which items should be recognised in profit or loss and which items should be recognised in other comprehensive income;

(ii)   because recognising remeasurements in profit or loss is the conceptually best method;

(iii)   to keep the accounting simple for entities with small plans; and

(iv)   because recognising remeasurements in other comprehensive income may lead to an accounting mismatch (eg for an unfunded plan, if the entity holds assets to fund the obligation, and gains and losses on the assets are recognised in profit or loss).

(c)   *Reclassification to profit or loss*—some respondents were concerned that amounts recognised in other comprehensive income are not reclassified to profit or loss in subsequent periods because:

(i)   the amounts in other comprehensive income would never be recognised in profit or loss.

(ii)   this change diverges from US generally accepted accounting principles (GAAP), because amounts in other comprehensive income under US GAAP are subsequently reclassified to profit or loss.

BC90   In finalising the amendments made in 2011, the Board confirmed the proposal made in the 2010 ED that an entity should recognise remeasurements in other comprehensive income. The Board acknowledged that the *Conceptual Framework*[5] and IAS 1 do not describe a principle that would identify the items an entity should recognise in other comprehensive income rather than in

---

5   The reference to the *Conceptual Framework* is to the *Conceptual Framework for Financial Reporting*, issued in 2010 and in effect when the Standard was amended.

profit or loss. However, the Board concluded that the most informative way to disaggregate the components of defined benefit cost with different predictive values is to recognise the remeasurements component in other comprehensive income.

BC91   The Board considered and rejected alternative approaches that would address some of the concerns expressed in paragraph BC89(a) and (b) for the reasons discussed in paragraphs BC92–BC98. Subsequent reclassification of amounts recognised in other comprehensive income to profit or loss is discussed in paragraph BC99.

Components of defined benefit cost: other approaches to recognising remeasurements

BC92   The Board considered the following alternatives for recognising the remeasurements component:

(a)   previous options in IAS 19 for immediate recognition (paragraph BC93).

(b)   recognition of all components in profit or loss (paragraphs BC94–BC96).

(c)   a hybrid approach requiring recognition of the remeasurements component in other comprehensive income or profit or loss in different circumstances (paragraphs BC97 and BC98).

BC93   Before its amendment in 2011, IAS 19 permitted two methods for recognising actuarial gains and losses immediately: in profit or loss or in other comprehensive income. Many respondents to the 2010 ED suggested that the Board should permit an entity to recognise remeasurements either in profit or loss or in other comprehensive income. Retaining those options would have allowed entities with small plans to keep the accounting simple and would have allowed entities to eliminate the accounting mismatches noted in paragraph BC89(b). However, the Board concluded that eliminating options would improve financial reporting.

BC94   Some respondents to the 2010 ED expressed the view that entities should recognise all components of defined benefit cost within profit or loss, rather than using other comprehensive income for some items. They offered the following reasons for their position:

(a)   Some indicated that the *Framework* and IAS 1 do not describe a principle that would identify the items an entity should recognise in other comprehensive income rather than in profit or loss.

(b)   Some believe that an entity should show amounts relating to defined benefit plans in aggregate, as a single net amount arising from personnel or employment expense, in conformity with the presentation of a single net amount in the statement of financial position.

BC95   However, most respondents to the 2010 ED expressed the view that it would be inappropriate to recognise in profit or loss short-term fluctuations in an item that is long-term in nature. The Board concluded that in the light of the improved presentation of items of other comprehensive income in its amendment to IAS 1 issued in June 2011, the most informative way to disaggregate the components of defined benefit cost with different predictive values is to recognise the remeasurement component in other comprehensive income.

BC96   Many respondents urged the Board to carry out a project to identify what items of income and expense an entity should recognise in other comprehensive income, and whether an entity should subsequently reclassify items recognised in other comprehensive income to profit or loss. If the Board carries out such a project, the Board may need in due course to revisit its decisions on the recognition of the remeasurements component.

BC97   The Board noted that an accounting mismatch could arise for entities that hold assets to fund the obligation that do not qualify as plan assets because an entity would recognise changes in the defined benefit obligation in other comprehensive income, but changes in the carrying amount of those assets in profit or loss. The Board considered whether to permit (or perhaps require) entities to recognise the remeasurement component in profit or loss if that would reduce or eliminate an accounting mismatch from profit or loss.

BC98   However, the Board did not pursue such a hybrid approach because doing so would have required the Board to add significant complexity to the requirements in IAS 19 to address matters such as the following:

(a)   introducing criteria to identify an accounting mismatch.

(b)   determining whether to make such an election irrevocable, and whether an entity could revisit its election if there are changes in facts (such as in the case of a plan amendment, merger or plans switching between funded and unfunded status).

Components of defined benefit cost: reclassification to profit or loss

BC99   Both before and after the amendments made in 2011, IAS 19 prohibits subsequent reclassification of remeasurements from other comprehensive income to profit or loss. The Board prohibited such reclassification because:

(a)   there is no consistent policy on reclassification to profit or loss in IFRSs, and it would have been premature to address this matter in the context of the amendments made to IAS 19 in 2011.

(b)   it is difficult to identify a suitable basis to determine the timing and amount of such reclassifications.

Components of defined benefit cost: cumulative remeasurements

BC100   The 2010 ED proposed to carry forward the requirement that an entity should transfer amounts recognised in other comprehensive income directly to retained earnings. However, IFRSs do not define the phrase 'retained earnings' and the Board has not discussed what it should mean. Moreover, there exist jurisdiction-specific restrictions on components of equity. The amendments made in 2011 permit an entity to transfer the cumulative remeasurements within equity, and do not impose specific requirements on that transfer.

The asset ceiling

BC101   In some cases, paragraph 63 of IAS 19 requires an entity to recognise an asset. E54 proposed that the amount of the asset recognised should not exceed the aggregate of the present values of:

(a)   any refunds expected from the plan; and

(b)   any expected reduction in future contributions arising from the surplus.

In approving E54, IASC took the view that an entity should not recognise an asset at an amount that exceeds the present value of the future benefits that are expected to flow to the entity from that asset. This view was consistent with IASC's proposal in its exposure draft E55 *Impairment of Assets* that assets should not be carried at more than their recoverable amount. IAS 19 before its revision in 1998 contained no such restriction.

BC102   Some commentators argued that the limit in E54 was not operable because it would require an entity to make extremely subjective forecasts of expected refunds or reductions in contributions. In response to those comments, IASC agreed that the limit should reflect the available refunds or reductions in contributions.

An additional minimum liability

BC103   IASC considered whether it should require an entity to recognise an additional minimum liability where:

(a)   an entity's immediate obligation if it discontinued a plan at the balance sheet date would be greater than the present value of the liability that would otherwise be recognised on the statement of financial position.

(b)   vested post-employment benefits are payable at the date when an employee leaves the entity. Consequently, because of the effect of discounting, the present value of the vested benefit would be greater if an employee left immediately after the balance sheet date than if the employee completed the expected period of service.

(c)   the present value of vested benefits exceeds the amount of the liability that would otherwise be recognised in the balance sheet. Before the amendments made to IAS 19 in 2011 this could have occurred where a large proportion of the benefits were fully vested and an entity had not recognised actuarial losses or past service cost.

BC104   One example of a requirement for an entity to recognise an additional minimum liability was in the US standard SFAS 87 *Employers' Accounting for Pensions*: the minimum liability was based on current salaries and excluded the effect of deferring some past service cost and actuarial gains and losses. If the minimum liability exceeded the obligation measured on the normal projected salary basis (with deferred recognition of some types of income and expense), the excess was recognised as an intangible asset (not exceeding the amount of any unamortised past service cost, with any further excess deducted directly from equity) and as an additional minimum liability.

BC105 IASC believed that such additional measures of the liability were potentially confusing and did not provide relevant information. They would also conflict with the *Framework*'s assumption that the entity is a going concern and with its definition of a liability. IAS 19 does not require the recognition of an additional minimum liability. Some of the circumstances discussed in the preceding two paragraphs might have given rise to contingent liabilities requiring disclosure under IAS 37.

Recognition of defined benefit cost as part of an asset: amendments issued in 2011

BC106 IAS 19 requires an entity to recognise defined benefit costs as income or expense unless another IFRS requires or permits their inclusion in the cost of an asset. Some respondents to the 2010 ED asked the Board to clarify whether remeasurements recognised in other comprehensive income result in income or expense that is eligible for inclusion in the cost of an asset. Some respondents said that recognising remeasurements as part of an asset and then recognising that asset as an expense in profit or loss would be inconsistent with the Board's conclusion that reclassification from other comprehensive income to profit or loss should be prohibited.

BC107 In relation to determining the cost of an asset, IFRSs include no principle distinguishing between income and expense presented in profit or loss and income and expense recognised in other comprehensive income. In the Board's view, whether an item is included in the cost of an asset depends on its nature and whether it meets the definition of cost in the relevant IFRS for that asset. Furthermore, in the Board's view this would be consistent with its conclusions on the reclassification of amounts recognised in other comprehensive income because amounts recognised as part of an asset would not be recognised in other comprehensive income first. Accordingly, the Board added no further guidance on this matter.

Actuarial valuation method

BC108 IAS 19 before its revision in 1998 permitted both accrued benefit valuation methods (benchmark treatment) and projected benefit valuation methods (allowed alternative treatment). The two groups of methods were based on fundamentally different, and incompatible, views of the objectives of accounting for employee benefits:

(a) **accrued benefit methods** (sometimes known as 'benefit', 'unit credit' or 'single premium' methods) determine the present value of employee benefits attributable to service to date; but

(b)   **projected benefit methods** (sometimes described as 'cost', 'level contribution' or 'level premium' methods) project the estimated total obligation at retirement and then calculate a level funding cost, taking into account investment earnings, that will provide the total benefit at retirement.

BC109   The two methods may have similar effects on the income statement, but only by chance or if the number and age distribution of participating employees remain relatively stable over time. There can be significant differences in the measurement of liabilities under the two groups of methods. For these reasons, IASC believed that a requirement to use a single group of methods would significantly enhance comparability.

BC110   IASC considered whether it should continue to permit projected benefit methods as an allowed alternative treatment while introducing a new requirement to disclose information equivalent to the use of an accrued benefit method. However, IASC believed that disclosure cannot rectify inappropriate accounting in the balance sheet and income statement. IASC concluded that projected benefit methods were not appropriate, and should be eliminated, because such methods:

(a)   focus on future events (future service) as well as past events, whereas accrued benefit methods focus only on past events;

(b)   generate a liability that does not represent a measure of any real amount and can be described only as the result of cost allocations; and

(c)   do not attempt to measure fair value and cannot, therefore, be used in a business combination, as required by IAS 22 *Business Combinations*.[6] If an entity used an accrued benefit method in a business combination, it would not be feasible for the entity to use a projected benefit method to account for the same obligation in subsequent periods.

BC111   IAS 19 before its revision in 1998 did not specify which forms of accrued benefit valuation method should be permitted under the benchmark treatment. IAS 19 as revised in 1998 required a single accrued benefit method: the most widely used accrued benefit method, which is known as the projected unit credit method (sometimes known as the 'accrued benefit method pro-rated on service' or as the 'benefit/years of service method').

BC112   IASC acknowledged that the elimination of projected benefit methods, and of accrued benefit methods other than the projected unit credit method, had cost implications. However, with modern computing power, it would be only marginally more expensive to run a valuation on two different bases and the advantages of improved comparability would outweigh the additional cost.

BC113   An actuary may sometimes recommend, for example in the case of a closed fund, a method other than the projected unit credit method for funding purposes. Nevertheless, IASC agreed to require the use of the projected unit credit method in all cases because that method was more consistent with the accounting objectives laid down in IAS 19 as revised in 1998.

---

6   IAS 22 was withdrawn in 2004 and replaced by IFRS 3 *Business Combinations*.

Attributing benefit to periods of service

BC114　As explained in paragraph BC54, IASC believed that an entity has an obligation under a defined benefit plan when an employee has rendered service in return for the benefits promised under the plan. IASC considered three alternative methods of accounting for a defined benefit plan that attributes different amounts of benefit to different periods:

(a)　apportion the entire benefit on a straight-line basis over the entire period to the date when further service by the employee will lead to no material amount of further benefits under the plan, other than from further salary increases.

(b)　apportion benefit under the plan's benefit formula. However, a straight-line basis should be used if the plan's benefit formula attributes a materially higher benefit to later years.

(c)　apportion the benefit that vests at each interim date on a straight-line basis over the period between that date and the previous interim vesting date.

The three methods are illustrated by the following two examples.

BC Example 2

A plan provides a benefit of CU400 if an employee retires after more than ten and less than twenty years of service and a further benefit of CU100 (CU500 in total) if an employee retires after twenty or more years of service.

The amounts attributed to each year are as follows:

	Years 1–10	Years 11–20
Method (a)	25	25
Method (b)	40	10
Method (c)	40	10

BC Example 3

A plan provides a benefit of CU100 if an employee retires after more than ten and less than twenty years of service and a further benefit of CU400 (CU500 in total) if an employee retires after twenty or more years of service.

The amounts attributed to each year are as follows:

	Years 1–10	Years 11–20
Method (a)	25	25
Method (b)	25	25
Method (c)	10	40

Note: this plan attributes a higher benefit to later years, whereas the plan in BC Example 2 attributes a higher benefit to earlier years.

BC115   In approving E54, IASC adopted method (a) on the grounds that this method was the most straightforward and that there were no compelling reasons to attribute different amounts of benefit to different years, as would occur under either of the other methods.

BC116   A significant minority of commentators on E54 favoured following the benefit formula (or alternatively, if the standard were to retain straight-line attribution, the recognition of a minimum liability based on the benefit formula). IASC agreed with these comments and decided to require the method described in paragraph BC114(b).

Attributing benefit to periods of service: exposure draft published in 2010

BC117   Paragraph 70 requires an entity to attribute benefits on a straight-line basis if an employee's service in later years will lead to a materially higher level of benefit than in earlier years. If a benefit formula is expressed as a constant proportion of current salary, some believe that expected future salary increases are not included in determining whether the benefit formula allocates a higher level of benefit in later years.

BC118   However, if that view is taken, the attribution for career average salary benefits (benefits described as a percentage of the average salary multiplied by the number of years of service) would differ from the attribution for current salary benefits (benefits described as a percentage of current salary), even though such benefits could be the same economically. In the Board's view, benefits that are economically the same should be measured similarly regardless of how the benefit formula describes them. Consequently, the 2010 ED proposed that expected future salary increases should be included in determining whether a benefit formula expressed in terms of current salary allocates a materially higher level of benefit in later years.

BC119   Some respondents to the 2010 ED disagreed with that proposal for the reason that:

(a)   service in previous or subsequent periods does not change the benefit increment earned in a particular year; and

(b)   the fact that the entity remunerates later periods of service at higher levels is an intrinsic part of the plans and there is no reason for smoothing costs over all periods of service – they are not intended to remunerate for overall services on a straight-line basis.

BC120   The Board concluded that it should not address this issue at this stage because the issue is closely related to a fundamental review of the accounting for contribution-based promises that the Board decided was beyond the scope of the project (see paragraph BC13).

Actuarial assumptions—tax payable by the plan: amendments issued in 2011

BC121 The amendments made in 2011 clarify that:

(a) the estimate of the defined benefit obligation includes the present value of taxes payable by the plan if they relate to service before the reporting date or are imposed on benefits resulting from that service, and

(b) other taxes should be included as a reduction to the return on plan assets.

BC122 The Board noted that IAS 19 requires an entity to estimate the ultimate cost of providing long-term employee benefits. Thus, if the plan is required to pay taxes when it ultimately provides benefits, the taxes payable will be part of the ultimate cost. Similarly, the ultimate cost would include any taxes payable by the plan when the contribution relates to service before the period (such as in the case of contributions to reduce a deficit).

BC123 Some respondents to the 2010 ED asked the Board to address:

(a) country-specific tax regimes;

(b) taxes paid by the employer; and

(c) taxes on the return on plan assets.

BC124 However, the Board noted that a wide variety of taxes on pension costs exists worldwide and it is a matter of judgement whether they are income taxes within the scope of IAS 12 *Income Taxes*, costs of liabilities within the scope of IAS 37, or costs of employee benefits within the scope of IAS 19. Given the variety of tax arrangements, the Board decided that it could not address issues beyond those relating to taxes payable by the plan itself in a reasonable period of time and therefore did not address them in the amendment made in 2011.

Actuarial assumptions—administration costs: amendments issued in 2011

BC125 The amendments made in 2011 require administration costs to be recognised when the administration services are provided, with costs relating to the management of plan assets deducted from the return on plan assets. Before those amendments, IAS 19 required that costs of administering the plan, other than those included in the actuarial assumptions used to measure the defined benefit obligation, should be deducted from the return on plan assets. But IAS 19 did not specify which costs should be included in those actuarial assumptions.

BC126 In the Board's view, the treatment of plan administration costs should depend on the nature of those costs. Therefore, the 2010 ED proposed that:

(a)   costs of managing plan assets should be the only administration costs that are deducted in determining the return on plan assets (that is part of the remeasurements component). Other administration costs, eg the cost of administering benefit payments, are unrelated to the plan assets.

(b)   the present value of the defined benefit obligation should include the present value of costs relating to the administration of benefits attributable to current or past service. This is consistent with the measurement objective that the defined benefit obligation should be determined on the basis of the ultimate cost of the benefits.

BC127   Respondents to the 2010 ED raised practical concerns, including how entities should identify and estimate costs of managing plan assets and other administration services, and how the other administration services costs should be allocated to current, past and future service. In response to those concerns, the Board decided that an entity should recognise administration costs when the administration services are provided. This practical expedient avoids the need to attribute costs between current and past service and future service.

BC128   In some cases, a total fee is charged for both managing plan assets and other administration services, but in the Board's view the cost of managing plan assets would not be excessively costly or difficult to estimate under these circumstances. An entity could estimate such costs by estimating the administration costs if there were no plan assets, or by observing the prices for such services in the market.

Actuarial assumptions—discount rate

BC129   One of the most important issues in measuring defined benefit obligations is the selection of the criteria used to determine the discount rate. According to IAS 19 before its revision in 1998, the discount rate that was assumed in determining the actuarial present value of promised retirement benefits reflected the long-term rates, or an approximation thereto, at which such obligations were expected to be settled. IASC rejected the use of such a rate because it was not relevant for an entity that does not contemplate settlement and it was an artificial construct, because there may be no market for settlement of such obligations.

BC130   Some believe that, for funded benefits, the discount rate should be the expected rate of return on the plan assets actually held by a plan, because the return on plan assets represents faithfully the expected ultimate cash outflow (ie future contributions). IASC rejected this approach because the fact that a fund has chosen to invest in particular kinds of asset does not affect the nature or amount of the obligation. In particular, assets with a higher expected return carry more risk and an entity should not recognise a smaller liability merely because the plan has chosen to invest in riskier assets with a higher expected return. Consequently, the measurement of the obligation should be independent of the measurement of any plan assets actually held by a plan.

BC131　The most significant decision was whether the discount rate should be a risk-adjusted rate (one that attempts to capture the risks associated with the obligation). Some expressed the view that the most appropriate risk-adjusted rate is given by the expected return on an appropriate portfolio of plan assets that would, over the long term, provide an effective hedge against such an obligation. An appropriate portfolio might include:

(a)　fixed interest securities for obligations to former employees to the extent that the obligations are not linked, in form or in substance, to inflation;

(b)　index-linked securities for index-linked obligations to former employees; and

(c)　equity securities for benefit obligations towards current employees that are linked to final pay. This is based on the view that the long-term performance of equity securities is correlated with general salary progression in the economy as a whole and hence with the final-pay element of a benefit obligation.

It is important to note that the portfolio actually held need not necessarily be an appropriate portfolio in this sense. Indeed, in some countries, regulatory constraints may prevent plans from holding an appropriate portfolio. For example, in some countries, plans are required to hold a specified proportion of their assets in the form of fixed interest securities. Furthermore, if an appropriate portfolio is a valid reference point, it is equally valid for both funded and unfunded plans.

BC132　Those who support using the interest rate on an appropriate portfolio as a risk-adjusted discount rate argue that:

(a)　portfolio theory suggests that the expected return on an asset (or the interest rate inherent in a liability) is related to the undiversifiable risk associated with that asset (or liability). Undiversifiable risk reflects not the variability of the returns (payments) in absolute terms but the correlation of the returns (or payments) with the returns on other assets. If cash inflows from a portfolio of assets react to changing economic conditions over the long term in the same way as the cash outflows of a defined benefit obligation, the undiversifiable risk of the obligation (and hence the appropriate discount rate) must be the same as that of the portfolio of assets.

(b)　an important aspect of the economic reality underlying final salary plans is the correlation between final salary and equity returns that arises because they both reflect the same long-term economic forces. Although the correlation is not perfect, it is sufficiently strong that ignoring it will lead to systematic overstatement of the liability. In addition, ignoring this correlation will result in misleading volatility due to short-term fluctuations between the rate used to discount the obligation and the discount rate that is implicit in the fair value of the plan assets. These factors will deter entities from operating defined benefit plans and lead to switches from equities to fixed-interest investments. Where defined benefit plans are largely funded by equities, this could have a serious impact on share prices. This switch will also increase the cost of pensions. There will be pressure on companies to remove the apparent (but non-existent) shortfall.

(c) if an entity settled its obligation by purchasing an annuity, the insurance company would determine the annuity rates by looking to a portfolio of assets that provides cash inflows that substantially offset all the cash flows from the benefit obligation as those cash flows fall due. Consequently, the expected return on an appropriate portfolio measures the obligation at an amount that is close to its market value. In practice, it is not possible to settle a final pay obligation by buying annuities because no insurance company would insure a final pay decision that remained at the discretion of the person insured. However, evidence can be derived from the purchase or sale of businesses that include a final salary pension scheme. In this situation the vendor and purchaser would negotiate a price for the pension obligation by reference to its present value, discounted at the rate of return on an appropriate portfolio.

(d) although investment risk is present even in a well-diversified portfolio of equity securities, any general decline in securities would, in the long term, be reflected in declining salaries. Because employees accepted that risk by agreeing to a final salary plan, the exclusion of that risk from the measurement of the obligation would introduce a systematic bias into the measurement.

(e) time-honoured funding practices in some countries use the expected return on an appropriate portfolio as the discount rate. Although funding considerations are distinct from accounting issues, the long history of this approach calls for careful scrutiny of any other proposed approach.

BC133 Those who oppose a risk-adjusted rate argue that:

(a) it is incorrect to look at returns on assets in determining the discount rate for liabilities.

(b) if a sufficiently strong correlation between asset returns and final pay actually existed, a market for final salary obligations would develop, yet this has not happened. Furthermore, where any such apparent correlation does exist, it is not clear whether the correlation results from shared characteristics of the portfolio and the obligations or from changes in the contractual pension promise.

(c) the return on equity securities does not correlate with other risks associated with defined benefit plans, such as variability in mortality, timing of retirement, disability and adverse selection.

(d) in order to evaluate a liability with uncertain cash flows, an entity would normally use a discount rate lower than the risk-free rate, but the expected return on an appropriate portfolio is higher than the risk-free rate.

(e)   the assertion that final salary is strongly correlated with asset returns implies that final salary will tend to decrease if asset prices fall, yet experience shows that salaries tend not to decline.

(f)   the notion that equities are not risky in the long term, and the associated notion of long-term value, are based on the fallacious view that the market always bounces back after a crash. Shareholders do not get credit in the market for any additional long-term value if they sell their shares today. Even if some correlation exists over long periods, benefits must be paid as they become due. An entity that funds its obligations with equity securities runs the risk that equity prices may be down when benefits must be paid. In addition, the hypothesis that the real return on equities is uncorrelated with inflation does not mean that equities offer a risk-free return, even in the long term.

(g)   the expected long-term rate of return on an appropriate portfolio cannot be determined sufficiently objectively in practice to provide an adequate basis for an accounting standard. The practical difficulties include specifying the characteristics of the appropriate portfolio, selecting the time horizon for estimating returns on the portfolio and estimating those returns.

BC134   IASC had not identified clear evidence that the expected return on an appropriate portfolio of assets provides a relevant and reliable indication of the risks associated with a defined benefit obligation, or that such a rate can be determined with reasonable objectivity. Consequently, IASC decided that the discount rate should reflect the time value of money, but should not attempt to capture those risks. Furthermore, the discount rate should not reflect the entity's own credit rating, because otherwise an entity with a lower credit rating would recognise a smaller liability. IASC decided that the rate that best achieves these objectives is the yield on high quality corporate bonds. In countries where there is no deep market in such bonds, the yield on government bonds should be used.

BC135   Another issue was whether the discount rate should be the long-term average rate, based on past experience over a number of years, or the current market yield at the balance sheet date for an obligation of the appropriate term. Those who supported a long-term average rate expressed the view that:

(a)   a long-term approach is consistent with the transaction-based historical cost approach that was either required or permitted by other International Accounting Standards.

(b)   point in time estimates aim at a level of precision that is not attainable in practice and lead to volatility in reported profit that may not be a faithful representation of changes in the obligation, but may simply reflect an unavoidable inability to predict accurately the future events that are anticipated in making period-to-period measurements.

(c) for an obligation based on final salary, neither market annuity prices nor simulation by discounting expected future cash flows can determine an unambiguous annuity price.

(d) over the long term, a suitable portfolio of plan assets may provide a reasonably effective hedge against an employee benefit obligation that increases in line with salary growth. However, there is much less assurance that, at a given measurement date, market interest rates will match the salary growth built into the obligation.

BC136 IASC decided that the discount rate should be determined by reference to market yields at the balance sheet date, because:

(a) there is no rational basis for expecting efficient market prices to drift towards any assumed long-term average, because prices in a market of sufficient liquidity and depth incorporate all publicly available information and are more relevant and reliable than an estimate of long-term trends by any individual market participant.

(b) the cost of benefits attributed to service during the current period should reflect prices of that period.

(c) if expected future benefits are defined in terms of projected future salaries that reflect current estimates of future inflation rates, the discount rate should be based on current market interest rates (in nominal terms), because these also reflect current market expectations of inflation rates.

(d) if plan assets are measured at a current value (ie fair value), the related obligation should be discounted at a current discount rate in order to avoid introducing irrelevant volatility through a difference in the measurement basis.

BC137 The reference to market yields at the balance sheet date did not mean that short-term discount rates should be used to discount long-term obligations. IAS 19 requires that the discount rate should reflect market yields (at the balance sheet date) on bonds with an expected term that is consistent with the expected term of the obligations.

Actuarial assumptions—discount rate: exposure draft published in 2009

BC138 The discount rate requirements in IAS 19 may result in an entity reporting a significantly higher defined benefit obligation in a jurisdiction that does not have a deep market in high quality corporate bonds than it would in a similar jurisdiction that does have a deep market in such bonds, even when the underlying obligations are very similar.

BC139 To address this issue, in August 2009 the Board published an exposure draft *Discount Rate for Employee Benefits*, that proposed eliminating the requirement to use a government bond rate if there is no deep market in high quality corporate bonds. However, responses to that exposure draft indicated that the proposed amendment raised more complex issues than had been expected. After considering those responses, the Board decided not to proceed with the proposals but to address issues relating to the discount rate only in the context of a fundamental review (see paragraph BC13(b)).

Actuarial assumptions—salaries, benefits and medical costs

BC140 Some argue that estimates of future increases in salaries, benefits and medical costs should not affect the measurement of assets and liabilities until they are granted, on the grounds that:

(a) future increases are future events; and

(b) such estimates are too subjective.

BC141 IASC believed that the assumptions were used not to determine whether an obligation exists, but to measure an existing obligation on a basis that provides the most relevant measure of the estimated outflow of resources. If no increase was assumed, this was an implicit assumption that no change will occur and it would be misleading to assume no change if an entity did expect a change. IAS 19 maintains the requirement in IAS 19 before its revision in 1998 that measurement should take account of estimated future salary increases. IASC also believed that increases in future medical costs can be estimated with sufficient reliability to justify incorporation of those estimated increases in the measurement of the obligation.

Actuarial assumptions—mortality: amendments issued in 2011

BC142 The amendments made in 2011 make explicit that the mortality assumptions used to determine the defined benefit obligation are current estimates of the expected mortality rates of plan members, both during and after employment. In the Board's view, current mortality tables might need to be adjusted for expected changes in mortality (such as expected mortality improvement) to provide the best estimate of the amount that reflects the ultimate cost of settling the defined benefit obligation.

Actuarial assumptions—risk-sharing: amendments issued in 2011

BC143 The amendments made in 2011 clarify that:

(a) the effect of employee and third-party contributions should be considered in determining the defined benefit cost, the present value of the defined benefit obligation and the measurement of any reimbursement rights.

(b) the benefit to be attributed to periods of service in accordance with paragraph 70 of IAS 19 is net of the effect of any employee contributions in respect of service.[7]

---

7 *Defined Benefit Plans: Employee Contributions*, issued in November 2013, clarified the requirements that relate to how contributions from employees or third parties that are linked to service should be attributed to periods of service. In addition, it permits a practical expedient if the amount of the contributions is independent of the number of years of service. See paragraphs BC150G–BC150Q.

(c)   any conditional indexation should be reflected in the measurement of the defined benefit obligation, whether the indexation or changes in benefits are automatic or are subject to a decision by the employer, the employee or a third party, such as trustees or administrators of the plan.

(d)   if any limits exist on the legal and constructive obligation to pay additional contributions, the present value of the defined benefit obligation should reflect those limits.

BC144   Some defined benefit plans include features that share the benefits of a surplus or the cost of a deficit between the employer and the plan participants. Similarly, some defined benefit plans provide benefits that are conditional to some extent on whether there are sufficient assets in the plan to fund them. Such features share risk between the entity and the plan participants and affect the ultimate cost of the benefits. Hence, the 2010 ED proposed to clarify that the present value of the defined benefit obligation should reflect the best estimate of the effect of risk-sharing and conditional indexation features. Many respondents agreed with that proposal.

BC145   However, some respondents expressed doubts about whether the proposals could adequately address risk-sharing features because of the existing defined benefit and defined contribution distinction and because of the existing measurement model for defined benefit plans. They suggested that the Board should not address risk-sharing features until it conducted a fundamental review of classification and measurement in order to address the whole spectrum of plans from defined contribution to defined benefit (including contribution-based promises). However, the Board observed that the current model is based on the ultimate cost of the benefit, and thus should be able to take into account risk-sharing features that reduce the ultimate cost of the benefit to the entity.

BC146   Many respondents requested further clarification on:

(a)   conditional indexation (paragraphs BC147–BC149); and

(b)   other points (paragraph BC150).

Conditional indexation

BC147   Some defined benefit plans provide conditional indexation (such as additional benefits contingent on returns on plan assets). In general, according to paragraph 88, the measurement of the benefit obligation must reflect the best estimate of any future effect of such conditional indexation. However, some respondents noted that the strict separation of the measurement of plan assets and liabilities under IAS 19 results in a mismatch: the conditional indexation is included in the present value of the defined benefit obligation, but not in the measurement of the plan assets. Some argue that the effect of conditional indexation should not be included in the measurement of the liability until the underlying returns are included in the measurement of the plan assets.

BC148   In the Board's view, projecting the benefit on the basis of current assumptions of future investment performance (or other criteria to which the benefits are indexed) is consistent with estimating the ultimate cost of the benefit, which is the objective of the measurement of the defined benefit obligation, as stated in paragraph 76. The Board also considered other changes to the measurement approach, such as using option pricing techniques to capture the effect of the conditional indexation in a manner consistent with the fair value of the plan assets. However, the Board rejected those alternatives because they would require changing the fundamental measurement of the defined benefit obligation. The Board noted that concerns regarding measurement of benefits with conditional indexation are similar to concerns regarding the measurement of contribution-based promises discussed in its 2008 discussion paper. Addressing these concerns was beyond the scope of the amendments made in 2011.

BC149   Some respondents interpreted the 2010 ED as proposing that in determining the effect of conditional indexation, an entity would be required to project the future funding position (on the basis used to set contribution rates) and then establish the effect that the funding level might have on future benefits and contribution requirements. These respondents believe that projecting the funding position would involve a significant amount of additional work and that in most regions it would be very difficult to establish a suitable adjustment to the liabilities to reflect the effect of conditional indexation based on the funding position. In the Board's view, an entity should estimate the likely conditional indexation of benefits based on the current funding status of the plan, consistently with how financial assumptions are determined in accordance with paragraph 80. Paragraph 80 requires financial assumptions to be based on market expectations at the end of the reporting period for the period over which the obligations are to be settled.

Other clarifications

BC150   The Board clarified the following points in the light of responses to the 2010 ED:

(a)   Contributions from employees in respect of service should be attributed to periods of service in accordance with paragraph 70 using the benefit formula, or on a straight-line basis (ie the back-end loading test and attribution in paragraph 70 should be based on the net benefit).[8] This reflects the Board's view that contributions from employees can be viewed as a negative benefit. In addition, the Board noted that a portion of future employee contributions may be connected with salary increases included in the defined benefit obligation. Applying the same method of attribution to that portion of the contribution and the salary increases avoids an inconsistency.

---

8   *Defined Benefit Plans: Employee Contributions*, issued in November 2013, clarified the requirements that relate to how contributions from employees or third parties that are linked to service should be attributed to periods of service. In addition, it permits a practical expedient if the amount of the contributions is independent of the number of years of service. See paragraphs BC150G–BC150Q.

(b)   An entity would apply judgement in determining whether a change in an input is a change in the terms of the benefit (resulting in past service cost) or a change in an assumption (resulting in an actuarial gain or loss). This clarification is consistent with guidance that existed in IAS 19 before 2011, describing how to address employee contributions for medical costs.

(c)   The best estimate of the ultimate cost of the benefits reflects the best estimate of the effect of terms of the plan that require or allow a change to the level of benefit, or that provide other benefit options, regardless of whether the benefits are adjustable by the entity, by the managers of the plan, or by the employees.

(d)   The measurement of the defined benefit obligation takes account of the effect of any limit on contributions by the employer (see paragraph 91). In the Board's view, this is consistent with the objective of determining the ultimate cost of the benefits. The Board concluded that the effect of such a limit should be determined over the shorter of the expected life of the plan and the expected life of the entity. Determining the limit over a period longer than the current period is necessary to identify whether the effect of the limit is temporary or permanent. For example, the service cost may be higher than the maximum contribution amount in the current period, but if in subsequent years the service cost is lower than the contribution amount, then the effect of the limit is more of a deferral of current period contributions than a limit on the total contributions required.

(e)   The amendments relating to risk-sharing are not intended to be limited to particular relationships. Some respondents noted that some plans' risks are shared not only with employees, but also with other parties (such as the government). In the Board's view, an entity should consider such arrangements in determining the defined benefit obligation. Nevertheless, entities need to consider whether those contributions are reimbursements as described in paragraphs 116–119 (and therefore must be recognised as reimbursement rights) or reductions in the defined benefit obligation.

Actuarial assumptions—discount rate: regional market issue

BC150A   The Board was asked to clarify the requirements of IAS 19 to determine the discount rate in a regional market sharing the same currency (for example, the Eurozone). The issue arose because some think that the basket of high quality corporate bonds should be determined at a country level, and not at a currency level, because paragraph 83 of IAS 19 states that in countries in which there is no deep market in such bonds, the market yields at the end of the reporting period on government bonds shall be used.

BC150B   The Board noted that paragraph 83 of IAS 19 states that the currency and term of the corporate bonds or government bonds shall be consistent with the currency and estimated term of the post-employment benefit obligations.

BC150C   The Board decided to amend paragraph 83 of IAS 19 in order to clarify that the depth of the market for high quality corporate bonds should be assessed at a currency level.

BC150D   Some respondents to the Exposure Draft *Annual Improvements to IFRSs 2012–2014 Cycle* (the '2013 Annual Improvements Exposure Draft'), published in December 2013, suggested to the Board that it should clarify the objectives and the rationale underlying the selection and use of the discount rate for post-employment benefit obligations. The Board noted that the IFRS Interpretations Committee (the 'Interpretations Committee') had already discussed a potential broader amendment relating to the discount rate and, after several meetings, recommended that the determination of the discount rate for post-employment benefit obligations should be addressed in the Board's research project on discount rates.

BC150E   Some respondents to the 2013 Annual Improvements Exposure Draft suggested to the Board that it should clarify whether the proposed amendment prohibits an entity that operates in a country/regional market in which there is a deep market for high quality corporate bonds from using only the high quality corporate bonds issued in its own country/regional market. The Board noted that the amendment only clarifies that the depth of the market for high quality corporate bonds should be assessed at a currency level and not a country/regional market level. It does not require that the basket of high quality corporate bonds used to determine the discount rate for post-employment obligations must include all the high quality corporate bonds issued in a currency.

BC150F   Some respondents to the 2013 Annual Improvements Exposure Draft expressed concerns about the potential effects of the amendment on countries that have adopted a currency as their official or legal currency without being members of a regional market or part of one with a common currency. They think that the proposed amendment could result in anomalous outcomes in these countries, because a discount rate determined from high quality corporate bonds denominated in a stronger currency could be inconsistent with the inflation rate (and the other assumptions) used in these countries to determine the cost of providing post-employment benefits. The Board noted that this anomaly is not unique to the fact pattern raised. Instead, inflation rates in one location may be different to those in another, even if they are in the same country, state or regional market with a shared currency. In the Board's view, an analysis of the potential effect of the amendment would not provide useful additional information. The Board concluded that the amendment is an improvement that should not be delayed for a narrow range of situations that the Board had already considered in proposing the amendment.

Contributions from employees or third parties: amendments issued in 2013

BC150G   In 2012, the Interpretations Committee received two submissions that requested clarification of the accounting requirements set out in paragraph 93 of IAS 19 for contributions from employees or third parties.

BC150H   The Interpretations Committee considered whether some types of contributions from employees or third parties to a defined benefit plan should reduce the cost of short-term employee benefits instead of reducing the cost of post-employment benefits. The Interpretations Committee observed that the wording in paragraph 93 of IAS 19 appeared to suggest that all employee contributions that are linked to service should be attributed to periods of service as a reduction of service cost (ie as a negative benefit). However, employee contributions that are linked solely to the employee's service rendered in the same period in which those contributions are payable (for example, contributions that are a fixed percentage of salary throughout the period of the employment) might also be considered to be a reduction of the cost of short-term employee benefits (ie a reduction in salary). Consequently, the Interpretations Committee recommended to the IASB that it should amend IAS 19 regarding the accounting for such contributions.

BC150I   In the IASB's view, contributions from employees or third parties that are required by the terms of a defined benefit plan should form part of the post-employment benefit rather than the short-term employee benefit. Consequently, such contributions should be attributed to periods of service as a reduction of service cost (ie as a negative benefit). However, the IASB acknowledged the general concern about the complexity of the required calculations that could result from the requirement to attribute the net benefit to periods of service. The IASB thus concluded that the costs of applying the attribution requirements to some simple types of contributory plans outweighed the benefits and so the IASB decided to add a practical expedient to paragraph 93.

BC150J   Consequently, in March 2013, the IASB published the Exposure Draft ED/2013/4 Defined Benefit Plans: Employee Contributions ('ED/2013/4'), which proposed amendments to paragraph 93 of IAS 19. In ED/2013/4 the IASB proposed that some contributions from employees or third parties may be excluded from being attributed to periods of service as a negative benefit. Instead, those contributions could be recognised as a reduction in the service cost in the period in which they are payable if, and only if, they are linked solely to the employee's service rendered in that period. An example of such a situation would be contributions based on an employee's salary at a fixed percentage that does not depend on the number of years of service by the employee to the employer. On the other hand, if an employee is required to contribute a higher percentage of salary in later years of service, then the contributions are not linked solely to the employee's service that is rendered in the period in which the contributions are payable.

BC150K   When developing ED/2013/4, the IASB observed that paragraph 93 first states that contributions from employees or third parties in respect of service are attributed to periods of service as a negative benefit in accordance with paragraph 70, and then states that the net benefit is attributed in accordance with paragraph 70. The references to both the negative benefit and net benefit might cause confusion as to whether the back-end loading test in paragraph 70 is required to be performed on the net benefit, or on the gross benefit and the negative benefit separately. The IASB observed that performing the test on the net benefit would add complexity and that the outcome of that test would differ from the outcome of performing the test on the gross benefit and the negative benefit separately. Consequently, the IASB proposed to specify in paragraph 93 that the contributions from employees or third parties that are not solely linked to current-year service should be attributed to periods of service using the same method of attribution as the gross benefit in accordance with paragraph 70.

BC150L A total of 63 respondents commented on ED/2013/4. The majority of respondents supported the proposed amendments, but about half of them requested either further clarification of the scope of the practical expedient or the addition of application guidance or examples.

BC150M Some respondents requested clarification of whether they could apply the proposed practical expedient if the amount of the contributions depended on the employee's age instead of the number of years of service (age-based contributions). The IASB observed that examples illustrating the proposed practical expedient in ED/2013/4 implied two criteria—one is whether contributions are a fixed percentage of salary and the other is whether the contributions are independent of the number of years of service.

BC150N The IASB considered whether contributions should have to meet either or both of the criteria to qualify for the practical expedient. In some circumstances, age-based contributions could approximate contributions that depend on the number of years of service, because both of the contribution formulas depend on time. However, age-based contributions are independent of the number of years of service. For example, the terms of a plan require employee contributions of four per cent of salary for the first ten years and then six per cent thereafter. The increase to six per cent is not only related to the service in the current year, but is also related to the first ten years of service, which is a prerequisite for the change in the contribution percentage. If the terms of the plan required employee contributions of four per cent of salary if the employee was 30 years old or younger and six per cent if the employee was more than 30 years old, then an employee would be required to contribute either four per cent or six per cent regardless of the length of their service. In other words, the contributions paid for each year are not dependent on prior service.

BC150O Consequently, the IASB decided that the practical expedient should be permitted if the amount of the contributions is independent of the number of years of service. This principle would also help to clarify whether the practical expedient would apply to other types of contribution arrangements, including contributions that are a fixed amount (as opposed to a fixed percentage) regardless of the number of years of service.

BC150P One respondent to ED/2013/4 was concerned that some might interpret the requirements to attribute contributions from employees or third parties to periods of service to mean that the accumulated value of contributions should be deducted from both the defined benefit obligation and the plan assets. The IASB noted that the plan assets and the defined benefit obligation would increase by the amount of the contributions paid. This is because the contributions that are paid increase the employer's obligation to the employees even if those contributions are attributed to other periods of service to reflect the net cost to the employer.

BC150Q   When developing the amendments, the IASB observed that paragraph 94 sets out requirements for the accounting for changes in employee or third-party contributions. The IASB noted that the requirements in that paragraph apply to contributions that are attributed to periods of service using the same attribution method that is required by paragraph 70 for the gross benefit. Consequently, the IASB decided to amend paragraph 94 to clarify the scope of the requirements in that paragraph.

Curtailments and settlements

BC151   Under IAS 19 before its revision in 1998, curtailment and settlement gains were recognised when the curtailment or settlement occurred, but losses were recognised when it was probable that the curtailment or settlement would occur. IASC concluded that management's intention to curtail or settle a defined benefit plan was not a sufficient basis to recognise a loss. IAS 19 revised in 1998 required that curtailment and settlement losses, as well as gains, should be recognised when the curtailment or settlement occurs. The guidance on the recognition of curtailments and settlements conformed to the proposals in E59 *Provisions, Contingent Liabilities and Contingent Assets*.

Plan amendments, curtailments and settlements: amendments issued in 2011

BC152   The amendments made in 2011:

    (a)   require immediate recognition of all past service cost (paragraphs BC154–BC159); and

    (b)   amend the definitions of past service cost, curtailments and settlements (paragraphs BC160–BC163).

BC153   The Board also considered other approaches to account for plan amendments and settlements (paragraphs BC164–BC173).

Immediate recognition—past service cost

BC154   The amendments made in 2011 require an entity to recognise both vested and unvested past service cost in the period of the plan amendment that gives rise to the past service cost. Before that amendment, IAS 19 required immediate recognition for *vested* past service cost and recognition over the vesting period for *unvested* past service cost.

BC155   Many respondents to the 2010 ED supported the proposal for immediate recognition of unvested past service cost. Other respondents objected to the proposal for the reasons set out below:

    (a)   Most plan amendments are initiated with the intention of benefiting the entity in future periods. Moreover, the principle in IAS 19 is that employee benefit expense is recognised in the period when the employee must provide the service needed to qualify for the benefit. It would be more consistent with that principle to require recognition of unvested past service cost over the remaining service periods until vesting.

(b)   Recognising unvested past service cost over the vesting period would be consistent with what the Board thought were the best conceptual answers that it adopted in IFRS 2 *Share-based Payment*.

(c)   The proposal may provide potential for arbitrage. If unvested past service cost were recognised immediately, an entity could change how much of the total expense is recognised by changing the past service period without changing the amount and timing of benefits.

BC156   For the following reasons, the Board confirmed the requirement to recognise both vested and unvested past service cost immediately:

(a)   IAS 19 requires an entity to attribute benefits to periods of service in accordance with the benefit formula, even if the benefits are conditional on future employment. Therefore, recognising unvested past service cost immediately is consistent with the recognition of unvested current service cost that IAS 19 treats as an obligation in paragraph 72. The Board noted that recognising unvested past service cost immediately would not be consistent with IFRS 2. However, in the Board's view, internal consistency within IAS 19 is more desirable than consistency with IFRS 2.

(b)   The Board acknowledged that recognising unvested past service cost immediately may introduce an opportunity for accounting arbitrage by selection of the benefit formula, but recognising unvested past service cost over the vesting period may also be open to accounting arbitrage. If an entity recognised unvested past service cost over the vesting period, an entity could change how much of the total expense is recognised by changing the amount subject to vesting conditions and the vesting period. Any approach to attributing unvested benefits to periods of service is arbitrary. However, recognising unvested past service cost immediately is more consistent with paragraph 72 and the recognition of unvested current service cost.

BC157   Before the amendments made in 2011, an entity recognised curtailments resulting from a significant reduction in the number of employees covered by the plan when the entity was demonstrably committed to making the reduction. The amendments made in 2011 require an entity to recognise a plan amendment and a curtailment when they occur.

BC158   Some respondents to the 2010 ED asked the Board to clarify whether, in the context of a plan amendment or curtailment, 'occurs' means when the change is announced, when it is executed or when the change is effective. If a plan amendment or curtailment occurs in isolation (ie it is not triggered by a settlement, termination benefit or restructuring), determining when the plan amendment occurs requires the exercise of judgement. The timing of recognition would depend on the individual facts and circumstances and how they interact with the constructive obligation requirements in paragraphs 61 and 62. The Board concluded that providing further guidance on when a plan amendment 'occurs' is beyond the scope of the amendments made in 2011.

BC159   The amendments made in 2011 also:

(a)   remove the 'demonstrably committed' recognition criterion for termination benefits (paragraphs BC258–BC260); and

(b)   align the recognition of related plan amendments, curtailments, termination benefits and restructuring costs (paragraphs BC262–BC268).

Definitions of past service cost, curtailments and settlements

BC160   The Board noted that recognising unvested past service cost immediately results in the same accounting for past service cost and curtailments. As a result, the amendments made in 2011 revised the definitions of plan amendments and curtailments. Before those amendments, IAS 19 defined the curtailment of a plan as follows:

A curtailment occurs when an entity either:

(a)   is demonstrably committed to make a significant reduction in the number of employees covered by a plan; or

(b)   amends the terms of a defined benefit plan so that a significant element of future service by current employees will no longer qualify for benefits, or will qualify only for reduced benefits.

BC161   The distinction between past service cost and curtailments was necessary in IAS 19 before the amendments made in 2011 because curtailments were ~~recognised~~ immediately, but unvested past service cost was recognised over the vesting period. However, because the amendments made in 2011 require immediate recognition of unvested past service costs, there is no longer any reason for the distinction between past service cost and the second part of the definition of curtailments. Accordingly, the Board removed the second part of that definition. Consequently, past service cost will include amounts attributed to past service resulting from any plan amendment and would be recognised immediately.

BC162   The Board retained the first part of the definition of curtailments. This distinguishes the closure of a plan to a significant number of employees (which is closer to a plan amendment) and an increase in estimated employee turnover (which is closer to a change in actuarial assumption). Thus, if a reduction in the number of employees is judged significant, then an entity accounts for it in the same way as for a plan amendment, and if not significant an entity will have to determine whether it is a change in actuarial assumption or a plan amendment. Because IAS 19 now treats plan amendments and curtailments in the same way, it now treats gains or losses on a curtailment as one form of past service cost.

BC163   The amendment made in 2011 clarifies that a settlement is a payment of benefits that is not set out in the terms of the plan. The payment of benefits that are set out in the terms of the plan, including terms that provide members with options on the nature of benefit payment such as an option to take a lump sum instead of an annuity, would be included in the actuarial assumptions. Therefore, any difference between an estimated benefit payment and the actual benefit payment is an actuarial gain or loss.

Other alternatives considered for accounting for plan amendments and settlements

BC164   The Board considered two other alternatives:

(a)   *Confirming the proposals in the 2010 ED* — the 2010 ED proposed that past service cost and a gain or loss on curtailment should be included in the service cost component and a gain or loss on settlement should be included in the remeasurements component (see paragraphs BC165–BC170).

(b)   *Remeasurements approach* — requiring past service cost and a gain or loss on curtailment or settlement to be included in the remeasurements component (see paragraphs BC171–BC173).

Other alternatives considered: confirming the proposals in the 2010 ED

BC165   The Board's view in developing the 2010 ED was that gains and losses arise on settlements because of a difference between the defined benefit obligation, as remeasured at the transaction date, and the settlement amount. Therefore, the 2010 ED proposed that:

(a)   gains and losses on settlements should be treated in the same way as actuarial gains and losses, by being included in the remeasurements component; and

(b)   the effect of plan amendments and curtailments should be included in the service cost component.

BC166   Many respondents to the 2010 ED supported the proposals for the recognition of past service cost and gains and losses on curtailments in profit or loss and the recognition of gains and losses on routine settlements in other comprehensive income. But many respondents disagreed with the proposal to recognise the effects of settlements in other comprehensive income, for the following reasons:

(a)   There is overlap between the definitions of settlements, curtailments and plan amendments and the transactions usually happen at the same time, so it can be difficult to allocate the gains and losses between them. Requiring different accounting treatments for settlements, curtailments and plan amendments would introduce practical difficulties, diversity in practice and structuring opportunities.

(b)   Settlements with third parties typically involve additional cost (such as a profit margin for the third party) and the effect of management's decision to incur this additional cost should be reflected in profit or loss when that transaction occurs.

(c)   Recognising a gain or loss on derecognition of a liability in other comprehensive income seems inconsistent with other IFRSs that require a gain or loss on derecognition of a liability to be recognised in profit or loss.

(d)   If settlements are the result of an event accounted for separately in profit or loss, then the gain or loss on settlement should be recognised in the same place as that event.

(e)   A settlement can be interpreted as an 'action' of the plan sponsor, so the argument that past service cost should be recognised in profit or loss 'because [the plan amendment] occurs [when] an entity takes an action that reduces the benefits provided by the plan to employees' (Basis for Conclusions on 2010 ED, paragraph BC48) is applicable for the treatment of settlements as well.

BC167   Some interpret the definition of settlements as overlapping with the definitions of plan amendments, curtailments and changes in actuarial assumptions. If a transaction closes a plan and eliminates all further legal or constructive obligations, the transaction may have elements of plan amendments, curtailments and changes in actuarial assumptions because the definitions are not mutually exclusive. For example, if an entity negotiates a lump sum to be paid in connection with the closure of a defined benefit plan, one view is that the entire change in the defined benefit obligation is a settlement, because the lump sum eliminates all further legal and constructive obligations. The other view is that the effect of eliminating future pay growth, earlier payment than expected and the conversion of the benefits to a lump sum is a plan amendment and curtailment, with the settlement occurring when the payment is made.

BC168   In the Board's view, it is not clear whether the definitions overlap (because the definitions are not mutually exclusive) or whether it is merely difficult to distinguish the effects of a plan amendment, curtailment and settlement when they occur together. However, entities would need to distinguish these items if entities were required to include the amount relating to each in a different component of defined benefit cost.

BC169   The Board decided to treat past service cost and gains and losses arising from settlements (defined as non-routine settlements in the 2010 ED) as part of the service cost component. This does not require entities to make a distinction between those items if they occur at the same time. It is also consistent with the requirements in IAS 19 before the amendments made in 2011, and with the recognition in profit or loss of amounts from other related transactions, such as termination benefits and restructuring costs.

BC170   Such an approach requires a distinction between routine benefit payments and settlements (ie routine and non-routine settlements as defined in the 2010 ED), because a gain or loss on a settlement is included in the service cost component, and a gain or loss on a routine benefit payment is included in remeasurements. However, respondents appeared less concerned about making this distinction than about making one between plan amendments and settlements.

Other alternatives considered: remeasurements approach

BC171 Some respondents suggested that the effect of past service cost and gains or losses on settlement should be included in the remeasurements component. Such an approach would not require a distinction between past service cost, gains and losses on settlements and actuarial gains and losses. The gains and losses arising from all of these transactions would be included in the remeasurements component.

BC172 These respondents justified including the effects of plan amendments in the remeasurements component on the basis that past service cost provides less information about the amount and timing of future cash flows than does current service cost. Respondents noted that this would have the effect of limiting the service cost component to current service cost, and would maintain the Board's conclusion that amounts with different predictive value should be presented separately. Furthermore, such an approach would eliminate the requirement to distinguish between past service cost, the effects of settlements, and actuarial gains and losses for the purpose of presentation.

BC173 However, the Board concluded that past service cost and gains and losses on settlements arise as a result of a new transaction, as opposed to the remeasurement of a prior period transaction, and therefore should be differentiated from remeasurements of the defined benefit obligation. In addition, a plan amendment or settlement might occur as part of a related restructuring or termination benefit, for which the resulting gain or loss is recognised in profit or loss.

Plan Amendment, Curtailment or Settlement—amendments issued in 2018

BC173A Paragraph 99 requires an entity to remeasure the net defined benefit liability (asset) when there is a plan amendment, curtailment or settlement, to determine past service cost or a gain or loss on settlement. The amendments specify that when an entity remeasures the net defined benefit liability (asset) in accordance with paragraph 99, the entity determines:

(a) current service cost and net interest for the remainder of the annual reporting period using the assumptions used for the remeasurement; and

(b) net interest for the remainder of the annual reporting period on the basis of the remeasured net defined benefit liability (asset).

BC173B The Board concluded that it is inappropriate to ignore the updated assumptions when determining current service cost and net interest for the remainder of the annual reporting period. In the Board's view, using updated assumptions to determine current service cost and net interest for the remainder of the annual reporting period provides more useful information to users of financial statements and enhances the understandability of financial statements.

BC173C The Board considered whether the amendments could change whether and when an entity remeasures the net defined benefit liability (asset) in accordance with paragraph 99. An entity applies paragraph 99 when the effect of a plan amendment, curtailment or settlement on past service cost, or a gain or loss on a settlement, is material. In accordance with IAS 8 *Accounting Policies, Changes in Accounting Estimates and Errors*, an entity need not apply the requirements in paragraph 99 when the effect of applying those requirements is immaterial. The amendments require an entity to use updated assumptions to determine current service cost and net interest for the period after a plan amendment, curtailment or settlement. Accordingly, when an entity assesses whether remeasuring its net defined benefit liability (asset) in accordance with paragraph 99 has a material effect, the entity considers not only the effect on past service cost, or a gain or loss on settlement, but also the effects of using updated assumptions for determining current service cost and net interest for the remainder of the annual reporting period after the plan amendment, curtailment or settlement.

BC173D The Board concluded that the amendments could change whether and when an entity remeasures the net defined benefit liability (asset) in accordance with paragraph 99. The Board decided that this is appropriate because in situations in which the application of paragraph 99 would have a material effect on financial statements, the amendments would result in providing more relevant information for users of financial statements, in keeping with the objective of the amendments (see paragraph BC173B).

BC173E During its deliberations, the Board considered specifying that an entity applies the requirements in paragraph 99 on a plan-by-plan basis (and not, for example, on a country-by-country basis or an entity-by-entity basis). The Board decided against this approach because paragraph 57 already states that an entity accounts separately for each material defined benefit plan.

BC173F The Board also considered whether it should address the accounting for 'significant market fluctuations', which are discussed in paragraph B9 of IAS 34. Plan amendments, curtailments or settlements generally result from management decisions and thus differ from significant market fluctuations, which occur independently of management decisions. The Board decided that the accounting for 'significant market fluctuations' is outside the scope of these amendments. Consequently, the amendments address only the measurement of current service cost and net interest for the period after a plan amendment, curtailment or settlement.

Effect on the asset ceiling requirements

BC173G The accounting for a plan amendment, curtailment or settlement may reduce or eliminate a surplus, which may cause the effect of the asset ceiling to change. The Board added paragraph 101A to clarify how the requirements on accounting for a plan amendment, curtailment or settlement affect the asset ceiling requirements.

BC173H In the Board's view, the amendments are consistent with and clarify the requirements in IAS 19. The amendments:

(a)   do not reclassify amounts recognised in other comprehensive income. This is because recognising past service cost, or a gain or loss on settlement, is distinct from determining the effect of the asset ceiling.

(b)   could result in entities recognising past service cost, or a gain or loss on settlement, that reduces a surplus that was not previously recognised. In the Board's view, recognising past service cost, or a gain or loss on settlement, in this situation faithfully represents the transaction because the surplus has in effect been made available to, and recovered by, the entity either through a change in the defined benefit obligation or through a settlement.

(c)   result in similar outcomes, regardless of whether an entity makes a payment to a plan just before a settlement or makes payments directly to employees as part of a settlement.

Plan assets

BC174   IAS 19 requires explicitly that the defined benefit liability or asset should be recognised as the defined benefit obligation after deducting plan assets (if any) out of which the obligations are to be settled directly (see paragraph 8). IASC noted that this was already widespread, and probably universal, practice. IASC believed that plan assets reduce (but do not extinguish) an entity's own obligation and result in a single, net liability. Although the presentation of that net liability as a single amount in the balance sheet differs conceptually from the offsetting of separate assets and liabilities, IASC decided that the definition of plan assets should be consistent with the offsetting criteria in IAS 32 *Financial Instruments: Disclosure and Presentation*.[9] IAS 32 states that a financial asset and a financial liability should be offset and the net amount reported in the balance sheet when an entity:

(a)   has a legally enforceable right to set off the recognised amounts; and

(b)   intends either to settle on a net basis, or to realise the asset and settle the liability simultaneously.

BC175   IAS 19 as revised in 1998 defined plan assets as assets (other than non-transferable financial instruments issued by the reporting entity) held by an entity (a fund) that satisfies all of the following conditions:

(a)   The entity is legally separate from the reporting entity.

(b)   The assets of the fund are to be used only to settle the employee benefit obligations, are not available to the entity's own creditors and cannot be returned to the entity (or can be returned to the entity only if the remaining assets of the fund are sufficient to meet the plan's obligations).

(c)   To the extent that sufficient assets are in the fund, the entity will have no legal or constructive obligation to pay the related employee benefits directly.

---

9   In 2005 the IASB amended IAS 32 as *Financial Instruments: Presentation*.

BC176   In issuing IAS 19 in 1998, IASC considered whether the definition of plan assets should include a fourth condition: that the entity does not control the fund. IASC concluded that control is not relevant in determining whether the assets in a fund reduce an entity's own obligation.

BC177   In response to comments on E54, IASC modified the definition of plan assets to exclude non-transferable financial instruments issued by the reporting entity. If this had not been done, an entity could reduce its liabilities, and increase its equity, by issuing non-transferable equity instruments to a defined benefit plan.

Plan assets: amendments issued in 2000

BC178   In 1999 IASC began a limited scope project to consider the accounting for assets held by a fund that satisfies parts (a) and (b) of the definition set out in paragraph BC175, but does not satisfy condition (c) because the entity retains a legal or constructive obligation to pay the benefits directly. IAS 19 before the amendments made in 2000 did not address assets held by such funds.

BC179   IASC considered two main approaches to such funds:

(a)   a **net** approach—the entity recognises its entire obligation as a liability after deducting the fair value of the assets held by the fund; and

(b)   a **gross** approach—the entity recognises its entire obligation as a liability and recognises its rights to a refund from the fund as a separate asset.

BC180   Supporters of a net approach made one or more of the following arguments:

(a)   A gross presentation would be misleading, because:

(i)   where conditions (a) and (b) of the definition in paragraph BC175 are met, the entity does not control the assets held by the fund; and

(ii)   even if the entity retains a legal obligation to pay the entire amount of the benefits directly, this legal obligation is a matter of form rather than substance.

(b)   A gross presentation would be an unnecessary change from current practice, which generally permits a net presentation. It would introduce excessive complexity into the standard, for limited benefit to users, given that paragraph 140(a) already requires disclosure of the gross amounts.

(c)   A gross approach may lead to measurement difficulties because of the interaction with the 10 per cent corridor that existed for the obligation before the amendments made to IAS 19 in 2011.

(d)   A net approach might be viewed as analogous to the treatment of joint and several liabilities under paragraph 29 of IAS 37. An entity recognises a provision for the part of the obligation for which an outflow of resources embodying economic benefits is probable. The part of the obligation that is expected to be met by other parties is treated as a contingent liability.

BC181 Supporters of a gross approach advocated that approach for one or more of the following reasons:

(a) Paragraph BC174 gives a justification for presenting defined benefit obligations net of plan assets. The explanation focuses on whether offsetting is appropriate. Part (c) of the 1998 definition focuses on offsetting. This suggests that assets that satisfy parts (a) and (b) of the definition, but fail part (c), should be treated in the same way as plan assets for recognition and measurement purposes, but should be shown gross in the balance sheet without offsetting.

(b) If offsetting is allowed when condition (c) is not met, this would seem to be equivalent to permitting a net presentation for 'in-substance defeasance' and other analogous cases where IAS 32 indicates explicitly that offsetting is inappropriate. IASC rejected 'in-substance defeasance' for financial instruments (see IAS 39 *Financial Instruments: Recognition and Measurement*[10] paragraph AG59) and there was no obvious reason to permit it in accounting for defined benefit plans. In these cases the entity retains an obligation that should be recognised as a liability and the entity's right to reimbursement from the plan is a source of economic benefits that should be recognised as an asset. Offsetting would be permitted if the conditions in paragraph 42 of IAS 32 are satisfied.

(c) IASC decided in IAS 37 to require a gross presentation for reimbursements related to provisions, even though this was not previously general practice. There is no conceptual reason to require a different treatment for employee benefits.

(d) Although some consider that a gross approach requires an entity to recognise assets that it does not control, others believe that this view is incorrect. A gross approach requires the entity to recognise an asset representing its right to receive reimbursement from the fund that holds those assets. It does not require the entity to recognise the underlying assets of the fund.

(e) In a plan with plan assets that meet the definition adopted in 1998, the employees' first claim is against the fund—they have no claim against the entity if sufficient assets are in the fund. In the view of some, the fact that employees must first claim against the fund is more than just a difference in form—it changes the substance of the obligation.

---

10 IFRS 9 *Financial Instruments* replaced IAS 39. IFRS 9 applies to all items that were previously within the scope of IAS 39. The requirements in paragraph AG59 of IAS 39 were relocated to paragraph B3.3.3 of IFRS 9.

(f)   Defined benefit plans might be regarded under SIC-12 *Consolidation— Special Purpose Entities*[11] as special purpose entities that the entity controls—and that it should consolidate. Because the offsetting criterion in IAS 19 was consistent with offsetting criteria in other International Accounting Standards, it was relatively unimportant whether the pension plan is consolidated in cases where the obligation and the plan assets qualify for offset. If the assets are presented as a deduction from the related benefit obligations in cases where condition (c) is not met, it could become important to assess whether the entity should consolidate the plan.

BC182   Some argued that a net approach should be permitted when an entity retains an obligation to pay the entire amount of the benefits directly, but the obligation was considered unlikely to have any substantive effect in practice. IASC concluded that it would not be practicable to establish guidance of this kind that could be applied in a consistent manner.

BC183   IASC also considered the possibility of adopting a 'linked presentation' that UK Financial Reporting Standard FRS 5 *Reporting the Substance of Transactions* required for non-recourse finance. Under FRS 5, the balance sheet presents both the gross amount of the asset and, as a direct deduction, the related non-recourse debt. Supporters of this approach argued that it portrays the close link between related assets and liabilities without compromising general offsetting requirements. Opponents of the linked presentation argued that it creates a form of balance sheet presentation that IASC had not previously used and might cause confusion. IASC decided not to adopt the linked presentation.

BC184   IASC concluded that a net presentation is justified where there are restrictions (including restrictions that apply on bankruptcy of the reporting entity) on the use of the assets so that the assets can be used only to pay or fund employee benefits. Accordingly, it modified the definition of plan assets set out in paragraph BC175 by:

(a)   emphasising that the creditors of the entity should not have access to the assets held by the fund, even on bankruptcy of the reporting entity; and

(b)   deleting condition (c), so that the existence of a legal or constructive obligation to pay the employee benefits directly does not preclude a net presentation, and modifying condition (b) to explicitly permit the fund to reimburse the entity for paying the long-term employee benefits.

BC185   When an entity retains a direct obligation to the employees, IASC acknowledged that the net presentation was inconsistent with the derecognition requirements for financial instruments in IAS 39[12] and with the offsetting requirements in IAS 32. However, in IASC's view, the restrictions on

---

11 SIC-12 *Consolidation—Special Purpose Entities* was withdrawn and superseded by IFRS 10 *Consolidated Financial Statements* issued in May 2011. There is no longer specific accounting guidance for special purpose entities because IFRS 10 applies to all types of entities.

12 IFRS 9 *Financial Instruments* replaced IAS 39. IFRS 9 applies to all items that were previously within the scope of IAS 39. This paragraph refers to matters relevant when IAS 19 was issued.

the use of the assets created a sufficiently strong link with the employee benefit obligations that a net presentation was more relevant than a gross presentation, even if the entity retained a direct obligation to the employees.

BC186   IASC believed that such restrictions were unique to employee benefit plans and did not intend to permit this net presentation for other liabilities if the conditions then in IAS 32 and IAS 39 were not met. Accordingly, condition (a) in the new definition refers to the reason for the existence of the fund. IASC believed that an arbitrary restriction of this kind was the only practical way to permit a pragmatic exception to IASC's general offsetting criteria without permitting an unacceptable extension of this exception to other cases.

BC187   In some plans in some countries, an entity is entitled to receive a reimbursement of employee benefits from a separate fund, but the entity has discretion to delay receipt of the reimbursement or to claim less than the full reimbursement. Some argue that this element of discretion weakens the link between the benefits and the reimbursement so much that a net presentation is not justifiable. They believe that the definition of plan assets should exclude assets held by such funds and that a gross approach should be used in such cases. IASC concluded that the link between the benefits and the reimbursement was strong enough in such cases that a net approach was still appropriate.

BC188   IASC's proposal for extending the definition of plan assets was set out in exposure draft E67 *Pension Plan Assets*, published in July 2000. The vast majority of the 39 respondents to E67 supported the proposal.

BC189   A number of respondents to E67 proposed a further extension of the definition to include particular insurance policies that have similar economic effects to funds whose assets qualify as plan assets under the revised definition proposed in E67. Accordingly, IASC extended the definition of plan assets to include some insurance policies (described in IAS 19 as qualifying insurance policies) that satisfy the same conditions as other plan assets. These decisions were implemented in amendments to IAS 19 approved by IASC in October 2000.

BC190   A qualifying insurance policy is not necessarily an insurance contract as defined in IFRS 4 *Insurance Contracts*.[13]

Plan assets—measurement

BC191   IAS 19 before its revision in 1998 stated that plan assets are valued at fair value, but did not define fair value. However, other International Accounting Standards defined fair value as 'the amount for which an asset could be exchanged or a liability settled between knowledgeable, willing parties in an arm's length transaction'.[14] This might be taken to imply that no deduction is made for the estimated costs that would be necessary to sell the asset (in other words, it is a mid-market value, with no adjustment for transaction costs).

---

13 IFRS 17 *Insurance Contracts*, issued in May 2017, replaced IFRS 4.

14 IFRS 13 *Fair Value Measurement*, issued in May 2011, defines fair value, describes the effect transaction costs have on a fair value measurement and addresses the application of bid and ask prices when measuring fair value.

However, some argue that a plan will eventually have to dispose of its assets in order to pay benefits. Consequently, IASC concluded in E54 that plan assets should be measured at market value. Market value was defined, as in IAS 25 *Accounting for Investments*,[15] as the amount obtainable from the sale of an asset, in an active market.

BC192　Some commentators on E54 felt that the proposal to measure plan assets at market value would not be consistent with IAS 22 *Business Combinations*[16] and with the measurement of financial assets as proposed in the discussion paper *Accounting for Financial Assets and Financial Liabilities* published by IASC's Financial Instruments Steering Committee in March 1997. Consequently, IASC decided that plan assets should be measured at fair value.

BC193　Some argue that concerns about volatility in reported profit should be countered by permitting or requiring entities to measure plan assets at a market-related value that reflects changes in fair value over an arbitrary period, such as five years. IASC believed that the use of market-related values would add excessive and unnecessary complexity and that the combination of the 'corridor' approach to actuarial gains and losses with deferred recognition outside the 'corridor' was sufficient to deal with concerns about volatility.[17]

BC194　IASC decided that there should not be a different basis for measuring investments that have a fixed redemption value and those that match the obligations of the plan, or specific parts thereof. IAS 26 *Accounting and Reporting by Retirement Benefit Plans* permits such investments to be measured on an amortised cost basis.

Reimbursements: amendments issued in 2000

BC195　Paragraph 48 states that an entity recognises its rights under an insurance policy as an asset if the policy is held by the entity itself. IAS 19 before the amendments made in 2000 did not address the measurement of these insurance policies. The entity's rights under the insurance policy might be regarded as a financial asset. However, rights and obligations arising under insurance contracts are excluded from the scope of IAS 39.[18] In addition, IAS 39 does not apply to 'employers' rights and obligations under employee benefit plans, to which IAS 19 *Employee Benefits* applies'. Paragraphs 46–49 discuss insured benefits in distinguishing defined contribution plans and defined benefit plans, but this discussion does not deal with measurement.

15　IAS 25 was superseded by IAS 39 *Financial Instruments: Recognition and Measurement* and IAS 40 *Investment Property*. IFRS 9 *Financial Instruments* replaced IAS 39. IFRS 9 applies to all items that were previously within the scope of IAS 39. This paragraph refers to matters relevant when IAS 19 was issued.

16　IAS 22 was withdrawn in 2004 and replaced by IFRS 3 *Business Combinations*.

17　The amendments made in 2011 eliminated the 10 per cent corridor from IAS 19.

18　IFRS 9 *Financial Instruments* replaced IAS 39. IFRS 9 applies to all items that were previously within the scope of IAS 39. This paragraph refers to matters relevant when IAS 19 was issued.

BC196   In reviewing the definition of plan assets (see paragraphs BC178–BC190), IASC reviewed the treatment of insurance policies that an entity holds in order to fund employee benefits. Even under the revised definition adopted in 2000, the entity's rights under an insurance policy that is not a qualifying insurance policy (as defined in the 2000 revision of IAS 19) are not plan assets.

BC197   In 2000 IASC introduced recognition and measurement requirements for reimbursements under such insurance policies (see paragraphs 116–119). IASC based those requirements on the treatment of reimbursements under paragraphs 53–58 of IAS 37. In particular, IAS 19 requires an entity to recognise a right to reimbursement of post-employment benefits as a separate asset, rather than as a deduction from the related obligations. In all other respects (for example, the treatment of actuarial gains and losses), the standard requires an entity to treat such reimbursement rights in the same way as plan assets. This requirement reflects the close link between the reimbursement right and the related obligation.

BC198   Paragraph 115 states that where plan assets include insurance policies that exactly match the amount and timing of some or all of the benefits payable under the plan, the plan's rights under those insurance policies are measured at the same amount as the related obligations. Paragraph 119 extends that conclusion to insurance policies that are assets of the entity itself.

BC199   IAS 37 states that the amount recognised for the reimbursement should not exceed the amount of the provision. Paragraph 116 contains no similar restriction, because the limit in paragraph 64 already applies to prevent the recognition of a net defined benefit asset that exceeds the asset ceiling.

Defined benefit plans—presentation of assets and liabilities

BC200   IASC decided not to specify whether an entity should distinguish current and non-current portions of assets and liabilities arising from post-employment benefits, because such a distinction may sometimes be arbitrary.

Defined benefit plans—presentation of defined benefit cost: amendments issued in 2011

BC201   The amendments made in 2011 do not specify how an entity should present the service cost and net interest components in profit or loss. Instead, an entity is required to present them in accordance with the requirements of IAS 1 *Presentation of Financial Statements*, consistently with IAS 19 before the amendments made in 2011.

BC202   The Board also considered:

        (a)   requiring the net interest component to be included in the finance cost line item of IAS 1, as proposed in the 2010 ED. However, if the Board had adopted this approach, it would have needed to consider whether the requirement would apply when the net interest component represents income because IAS 1 requires only finance cost and not finance income to be presented separately. The Board would also have needed to consider in due course whether it should apply similar treatment to amounts related to the passage of time in other projects, such as revenue recognition, insurance contracts and leases. The Board concluded that this would be beyond the scope of the project and that it should consider this aspect of presentation in the statement of profit or loss and other comprehensive income more broadly as part of the financial statement presentation project.

(b)   amending IAS 1 to require a separate line item for the net interest component or to require presentation of a line item that would combine service cost and net interest. The Board concluded that although these amounts would be material to many entities, there is no reason to single out post-employment benefits for special treatment in the statement of profit or loss and other comprehensive income. If an entity thinks that information about pensions is sufficiently important to the users of its financial statements, IAS 1 already permits that entity to provide disaggregated information in the performance statements. The Board would also have had to consider the implications of adding mandatory line items to IAS 1 if the entity presented its expenses by function. The Board concluded that this was beyond the scope of the project.

Defined benefit plans—disclosures: amendments issued in 2011

BC203   The amendments made in 2011 updated the disclosure requirements, because of concerns:

(a)   that the disclosures required by the previous version of IAS 19 did not enable users of financial statements to understand the financial effect of liabilities and assets arising from defined benefit plans on the financial statements as a whole.

(b)   that the volume of disclosures about defined benefit plans in many financial statements risked reducing understandability and usefulness by obscuring important information. This concern was particularly pronounced for multinational entities that have many varied plans in many jurisdictions.

BC204   The disclosure amendments made in 2011 related to:

(a)   disclosure objectives (paragraphs BC212–BC214).

(b)   the characteristics of the defined benefit plan and amounts in the financial statements (paragraphs BC215–BC228).

(c)   the amount, timing and uncertainty of the entity's future cash flows (paragraphs BC229–BC243).

(d)   multi-employer defined benefit plans (paragraphs BC245–BC252).

BC205   Paragraph BC244 discusses disclosures considered but rejected by the Board.

BC206   In reviewing the disclosure requirements, the Board considered:

   (a)   the comment letters on the discussion paper and the 2010 ED.

   (b)   publications from other bodies interested in financial reporting, including the Pro-active Accounting Activities in Europe (PAAinE) discussion paper *The Financial Reporting of Pensions*; the UK Accounting Standards Board (ASB) Reporting Statement *Retirement Benefits– Disclosures*; and FASB Staff Position No.132(R) *Employers' Disclosures about Postretirement Benefit Plan Assets* (FSP FAS 132(R)–1).

   (c)   proposals from the Investors Technical Advisory Committee (ITAC) of the FASB for a 'principle-based' disclosure framework, and a draft discussion paper on the disclosure of information in financial statements, prepared by the staff of the Canadian Accounting Standards Board (AcSB).

   (d)   advice received from the Global Preparers' Forum and the Board's Analyst Representative Group and Employee Benefits Working Group.

   (e)   the need to update the disclosure requirements in IAS 19 to reflect developments in IFRSs on disclosures, in particular IFRS 7 *Financial Instruments: Disclosures* and IFRS 13 *Fair Value Measurement*.

The Board's approach to disclosures about defined benefit plans

BC207   The Board sought an approach that:

   (a)   provides sufficient disclosures about defined benefit plans when those plans are material to the entity's operations.

   (b)   provides users of financial statements with relevant information that is not obscured by excessive detail.

BC208   Accordingly, the amendments made in 2011 introduced explicit objectives for disclosures about defined benefit plans.

BC209   In developing the proposals in the 2010 ED, the Board noted that entities must comply with the general materiality requirements in paragraphs 17(c) and 31 of IAS 1, including the requirement to disclose additional information if necessary, and that the financial statements need not contain disclosures that are not material.

BC210   However, some respondents were concerned that entities might have difficulty in exercising judgement when assessing the materiality of disclosures because:

   (a)   there is no universal quantitative criterion for defined benefit plans for separating material disclosure items from immaterial ones; and

   (b)   the notion of materiality seems best suited to a binary decision (whether to provide or omit a particular disclosure) and is not well suited to determining the extent of disclosure required to meet a disclosure requirement or to determining the overall balance with other disclosure requirements.

BC211 Although many respondents supported the inclusion of disclosure objectives, they believed that supplementing the objectives with an extensive list of disclosure requirements would not achieve the result that the Board intended. Many supported a principle-based approach to disclosure that would put more emphasis on meeting the disclosure objectives. Some suggested that it would be better if the Board supported the disclosure objectives through the use of 'encouraged but not required' disclosures or by including examples illustrating the application of the disclosure objectives in different circumstances. In response to these concerns the Board included a requirement that an entity should consider the level of disclosure necessary to satisfy the disclosure objectives and how much emphasis to place on each requirement.

Selecting disclosure objectives

BC212 The Board considered whether it should require the same disclosure objectives for defined benefit plans as for long-term financial instruments and insurance contracts. All three expose the entity to similar risks, including risks that the ultimate cost of settling the liability may vary from the amount estimated and risks arising from the complexity of measuring the liability. Many respondents stated that the disclosures in IAS 19 do not provide users of financial statements with the information about risk that is provided for other assets and liabilities. However, the Board concluded that much of the information required by IFRS 7 and IFRS 4 *Insurance Contracts*[19] for assets would be unnecessary in depicting an entity's involvement with a defined benefit plan because:

(a) the entity may not manage plan assets directly and may not have an unrestricted ability to access the economic benefits from those assets. Thus, plan assets differ from assets held directly by the entity. Consequently, disclosures about market risk and credit risk of plan assets are less relevant than for assets an entity holds directly. Moreover, an entity may have limited information about them.

(b) liquidity risk arises from the timing and amount of contributions that the entity is required to make to the plan and not from the need to meet directly the payments required by the defined benefit obligation.

BC213 Accordingly, the Board focused the disclosure objectives in IAS 19 on the matters most relevant to users of the employer's financial statements, ie information that:

(a) explains the characteristics of the defined benefit plans.

(b) identifies and explains the amounts in the financial statements arising from the defined benefit plans.

(c) describes how involvement in defined benefit plans affects the amount, timing and uncertainty of the entity's future cash flows.

---

19 IFRS 17 *Insurance Contracts*, issued in May 2017, replaced IFRS 4.

BC214   In response to suggestions by respondents, the Board included a requirement for entities to disclose additional information if required to meet the disclosure objectives.

Characteristics of the defined benefit plan and amounts in the financial statements

BC215   The disclosures about the characteristics of defined benefit plans and the amounts in the financial statements arising from defined benefit plans are based on those in IAS 19 before the amendments made in 2011 with the following changes:

(a)   additional information about exposure to risk (paragraphs BC216–BC218);

(b)   distinguishing between actuarial gains and losses arising from demographic and financial assumptions (paragraph BC219);

(c)   not requiring an entity to distinguish between plan amendments, curtailments and settlements if they occur together (paragraph BC220);

(d)   stating a principle for the disaggregation of plan assets rather than listing the categories required (paragraphs BC221–BC226); and

(e)   stating a principle for the disclosure of significant actuarial assumptions rather than listing the assumptions required to be disclosed (paragraphs BC227 and BC228).

Exposure to risk

BC216   The amendments in 2011 require entities to provide a narrative description of exposure to risk arising from their involvement with the plan. The 2010 ED proposal for additional disclosure regarding risk was in response to requests from users.

BC217   Some respondents to the 2010 ED suggested limiting the narrative disclosure about risk to any risks that are specific to the entity, or that are unusual, so that it does not result in boilerplate disclosure regarding generic risks to which all entities with defined benefit plans are exposed.

BC218   The Board agreed with respondents that requiring disclosure of all material risks would result in extensive generic disclosures that would not be particularly useful. However, in the Board's view it would not be practical to limit the disclosure to risks that are specific or unusual without providing a clear definition of those terms. Instead, the amendments in 2011 require an entity to focus the disclosure on risks that the entity judges to be significant or unusual.

Actuarial gains and losses arising from demographic and financial assumptions

BC219   The amendments made to IAS 19 in 2011 require entities to disclose the effect of changes in demographic assumptions separately from the effect of changes in financial assumptions. Some respondents to the 2010 ED stated that this separation would be arbitrary because of the interrelationships between some actuarial assumptions, particularly between financial assumptions. For example, discount rates may be correlated with inflation rates. However, the Board observed that, in general, financial assumptions are less intertwined with demographic assumptions than with other financial assumptions. Thus, the Board concluded that it would not be unduly difficult to distinguish the effects of changes in financial assumptions from the effects of changes in demographic assumptions.

Plan amendments, curtailments and settlements

BC220 The amendments made in 2011 retain similar disclosure for plan amendments, curtailments and settlements. However, the Board agreed with the views of respondents to the 2010 ED that when plan amendments, curtailments and settlements occur together, requiring entities to distinguish them for disclosure would be excessive. Therefore, the amendments do not require an entity to distinguish them when they occur together.

Plan assets

BC221 The amendments made in 2011 replace the minimum list of categories for the disaggregation of plan assets with a requirement to disaggregate the fair value of the plan assets:

 (a) into assets that have a quoted price in an active market and assets that do not; and

 (b) into classes that distinguish the risk and liquidity characteristics of those assets.

BC222 In addition to stating the principle for the disaggregation, the 2010 ED proposals would have required an entity to distinguish, at a minimum, debt instruments and equity instruments that have a quoted market price in an active market from those that do not. The proposals also specified a list of minimum categories into which an entity should disaggregate plan assets (based on the categories in IAS 19 at that time).

BC223 Respondents to the 2010 ED agreed with the principle of the disaggregation, but noted that the proposed minimum categories may not always meet that principle. The Board agreed with respondents that entities should focus on the principle of the disclosure: to disaggregate plan assets into classes that distinguish the risk and liquidity characteristics of those assets. In support of that principle, the amendments provide a list of example categories that would allow entities to adapt their disclosures to the nature and risks of the assets in their plans.

BC224 Some respondents also had concerns about the requirement to distinguish assets that have a quoted market price from those that do not. They indicated that disaggregating debt and equity instruments into those that have a quoted market price and those that do not would result in extensive disclosures that would be unlikely to add much to the understandability of the financial statements. However, users have requested information about the level of measurement uncertainty in items measured at fair value, such as the fair value hierarchy in IFRS 13. Therefore, the Board retained the proposal to disaggregate debt and equity instruments into those that have a quoted market price and those that do not.

BC225 In coming to this conclusion, the Board noted that this disaggregation requirement would be less onerous than the requirement in IFRS 13 to disaggregate on the basis of a three-level hierarchy.

BC226 Some hold the view that entities should disclose disaggregated information about how they invest plan assets. However, the Board concluded that extensive disaggregated information about plan assets is not necessary for users of the employer entity's financial statements because the entity does not hold those assets directly. Similarly, the Board concluded that for plan assets the disclosures about fair value required by IFRS 13 would not be relevant.

Actuarial assumptions

BC227 The amendments made in 2011 replace the previous mandatory list of actuarial assumptions with a requirement to disclose the significant actuarial assumptions used to determine the present value of the defined benefit obligation.

BC228 The Board did not specify particular assumptions for which disclosure is required, because particular disclosures may not be needed in every case to meet the disclosure objectives. Indeed, such disclosures may obscure important information with excessive detail. Accordingly, the 2010 ED proposed an approach in which entities would use judgement to determine which actuarial assumptions require disclosure. Respondents to the 2010 ED generally supported this proposal.

Amount, timing and uncertainty of future cash flows

BC229 The amendments made in 2011 improve the required disclosures about the amount, timing and uncertainty of future cash flows in the following respects:

(a) information about asset-liability matching strategies (paragraphs BC230–BC234);

(b) sensitivity analysis (paragraphs BC235–BC239); and

(c) information about the funding and duration of the liability (paragraphs BC240–BC243).

Asset-liability matching strategies

BC230 The amendments made in 2011 require an entity to disclose information about its asset-liability matching strategy.

BC231 In developing the proposals in the 2010 ED, the Board considered requiring entities to discuss their strategies for mitigating risks arising from defined benefit plans. However, the Board concluded that such a requirement would result in generic disclosure that would not provide enough specific information to be useful to users of financial statements. Nonetheless, in the Board's view, information about an entity's use of asset-liability matching strategies, or about the use of techniques such as annuities or longevity swaps to manage longevity risk, would provide additional information on how the entity manages the risk inherent in its defined benefit plan. Accordingly, the 2010 ED proposed a requirement to disclose information about these items.

BC232   Respondents' views on the proposals regarding asset-liability matching strategies were mixed. Some respondents to the 2010 ED supported the disclosure, whereas others expressed the view that it should be part of a broader disclosure regarding risk management and investment strategy or that it should be removed altogether. Those who believed that it should be part of a broader discussion about risks suggested linking the disclosure with the requirement to describe the nature of risks to which the plan exposes the entity, by requiring the entity to describe how it manages those risks. Respondents also noted that the disclosure could be better integrated with the disclosures on plan assets. Respondents that did not support the asset-liability matching disclosure were concerned that:

(a)   any disclosure of strategy would be generic and boilerplate;

(b)   a user would be able to perform a better assessment using the disclosures on plan assets and on defined benefit obligations (ie the results of such a strategy are more relevant than a narrative discussion); and

(c)   the requirement might be interpreted as implying that all entities should be performing asset-liability matching.

BC233   In the Board's view, disclosure about the asset-liability matching strategy may be more useful than disclosure about the general investment strategy because an asset-liability matching strategy aims to match the amount and timing of cash inflow from plan assets with those of cash outflow from the defined benefit obligation.

BC234   The amendments require the entity to disclose details of asset-liability matching strategies used by the plan or the entity, if any, and do not intend to imply that all plans or entities should be performing asset-liability matching.

Sensitivity analysis

BC235   The amendments made in 2011 require an entity to disclose how the effect of reasonably possible changes to significant actuarial assumptions affect the defined benefit obligation.

BC236   Users of financial statements have consistently emphasised the fundamental importance of sensitivity analyses to their understanding of the risks underlying the amounts recognised in the financial statements.

BC237   In the Board's view, a sensitivity analysis on the net defined benefit liability (asset) would be more useful than a sensitivity analysis on the defined benefit obligation only. However, the Board concluded that a sensitivity analysis on the net defined benefit liability (asset) should not be required because, for example, showing how the fair value of equities would respond to changes in the assumptions used to measure the present value of the defined benefit obligation would be complex and difficult to perform.

BC238   The Board proposed in the 2010 ED a sensitivity analysis for service cost showing how the service cost would have varied in response to changes in assumptions that were reasonably possible at the beginning of the period. Many respondents did not see the relevance of disclosing how the effect of a change to an assumption at the beginning of the reporting period would have affected current service cost. The Board agreed with this view and consequently withdrew that proposal.

BC239   Respondents expressed the following concerns about the sensitivity analysis on the defined benefit obligation:

     (a)   The sensitivity disclosure would not take into account the correlations between various actuarial assumptions. Some respondents suggested that a scenario analysis would be more useful. The Board concluded that, although a scenario analysis could provide more useful information, the complexity and cost of producing the information would outweigh the benefits.

     (b)   Some respondents were concerned that carrying out a series of sensitivity analyses on several actuarial assumptions would be onerous. Some requested that the sensitivity analysis should be limited to the assumptions that have a significant effect on the financial statements, such as the discount rate. The Board agreed with these respondents that in many cases the discount rate would be one of the most significant assumptions. However, depending on the plan and other facts and circumstances, other assumptions might be significant. The 2010 ED proposed that the sensitivity analysis should apply only to 'significant actuarial assumptions'. Consequently, the Board confirmed that proposal.

     (c)   Some respondents raised a concern that a 'reasonably possible' change is open to subjectivity and suggested that IAS 19 should specify a quantitative range. However, although setting the range to a particular percentage might improve comparability, the Board was concerned that a quantitative range might not reflect the reasonably possible ranges in different circumstances. The Board noted that requiring sensitivity on the basis of changes in the relevant actuarial assumption that were 'reasonably possible' at that date is consistent with the sensitivity disclosure requirements of other standards, such as IFRS 7.

Information about the funding and duration of the liability

BC240   The amendments made in 2011 require an entity to disclose:

     (a)   a narrative description of any funding arrangement and funding policy;

     (b)   the amount of expected contribution in the next year (carried forward from the previous version of IAS 19); and

     (c)   information about the maturity profile of the obligation, including the weighted average duration.

BC241 To provide users with information about the effect of a defined benefit plan on an entity's future cash flow, the 2010 ED proposed that an entity should discuss the factors that may cause contributions to differ from service cost. However, many respondents suggested that a disclosure about the effect of a defined benefit plan on an entity's future cash flows should instead focus on:

(a) the funding arrangement and funding policy; and

(b) the amount and timing of expected contributions and benefit payments.

BC242 In the Board's view, the disclosures suggested by respondents will be more relevant to users in assessing the risk related to changes in contribution and forecasting how much cash outflow will be incurred to cover the employee benefits than the proposal in the 2010 ED, discussed further in paragraph BC244(d).

BC243 Accordingly, the Board concluded that disclosing when, on average, the liabilities of a defined benefit plan mature would help users to understand the profile of cash flows required to meet the obligation. The Board considered requiring entities to disclose a maturity analysis of the obligation but, because the cost of such a disclosure might be onerous, the Board concluded that an entity should be required to disclose only the weighted average duration of the obligation. However, the amendments include a maturity analysis as an example of additional disclosures that could meet the disclosure objectives. The disclosure of the average duration provides information similar to the maturity analysis and will enhance the usefulness of other disclosures, such as the disclosure of actuarial assumptions dependent on the duration.

Other disclosures considered but rejected by the Board

BC244 The Board also considered, but rejected, requiring disclosure of:

(a) *actuarial assumptions and the process used to determine them* — the 2010 ED proposed that if the disclosure of demographic assumptions (such as mortality) would be difficult to interpret without additional demographic information, the entity should explain how it made those actuarial assumptions. Few respondents supported that proposal. Respondents commented that the disclosure would lead to boilerplate descriptions that would not be particularly helpful and that users rely on the entity, its actuaries and auditors to ensure that the demographic assumptions are reasonable. The Board agreed with these views and withdrew the proposal.

(b) *an alternative measure of the long-term employee benefit liability* — the 2010 ED proposed that entities should disclose the defined benefit obligation, excluding projected growth in salaries (sometimes referred to as the accumulated benefit obligation). Many respondents said that the relevance of such a disclosure would vary by country and by plan and that it would be inappropriate to require a disclosure simply because it would be relevant to some users in limited circumstances. The Board agreed with those respondents and withdrew the proposal.

(c) *disaggregation of the defined benefit obligation*—some respondents suggested that instead of the proposed disclosure as described in paragraph BC244(b), a more relevant disclosure would be a disaggregation of the defined benefit obligation showing, for example, vested benefits, accrued but unvested benefits, future salary increases, other constructive obligations and amounts owing to active members, deferred members and pensioners. The Board concluded that disaggregating the defined benefit obligation to distinguish components with different risk characteristics, as suggested by some respondents, would better meet the disclosure objectives, but requiring any particular disaggregation would be costly for preparers. However, disaggregation of the defined benefit obligation is included as an example of additional information that an entity may provide in order to meet the disclosure objectives.

(d) *factors that may cause contributions to differ from service cost*—in the Board's view, information about the effect of a surplus or deficit on the timing and amount of an entity's contributions is useful. Consequently, the 2010 ED proposed disclosure of factors that could cause contributions over the next five years to differ from current service cost. Many respondents did not support that proposal, observing that an entity's cash flows would be determined by funding requirements and not by the service cost as determined in accordance with IAS 19. Consequently, a discussion of those factors would not be relevant to a user's understanding of the entity's cash flows. The Board agreed with those respondents and withdrew the proposal.

(e) *historical information*—the amendments made in 2011 deleted the previous requirement to disclose historical information over five years about amounts in the statement of financial position and experience adjustments. The Board concluded that this requirement provided information about the defined benefit plan that was already available in previous financial statements and therefore was redundant.

Multi-employer plans

BC245 The amendments made in 2011 require disclosures for multi-employer defined benefit plans based on those in the previous version of IAS 19 with the following additional disclosure:

(a) qualitative information about any agreed deficit or surplus allocation on wind-up of the plan, or the amount that is required to be paid on withdrawal of the entity from the plan (paragraphs BC247–BC249).

(b) the expected contribution for the next annual period (paragraph BC250).

(c) the level of participation in a multi-employer plan (paragraphs BC251 and BC252).

BC246   In the Board's view, entities participating in a defined benefit multi-employer plan face greater risks than other entities: for example, risks that result from actions by other participants in the plan. Respondents to the discussion paper expressed the view that the disclosures in IAS 19 were insufficient to inform users about the potential effect on the amount, timing and uncertainty of future cash flows associated with an entity's participation in multi-employer defined benefit plans. Accordingly, the 2010 ED proposed additional disclosures about participation in a multi-employer plan and respondents generally welcomed those proposals.

Withdrawal obligations

BC247   IAS 37 requires an entity to disclose information about contingent liabilities and IAS 19 notes that contingent liabilities may arise from an entity's participation in a multi-employer plan. The Board identified two cases in which such information may be relevant, namely withdrawal from the plan and the wind-up of a plan. In the Board's view, disclosure of the withdrawal liability should be limited to qualitative information, for the following reasons:

(a)   If an entity is not committed to withdrawing from the plan, the plan is not committed to being wound up or a withdrawal liability has not been agreed between the entity and the plan, determining the withdrawal liability would be difficult. Furthermore, additional measurement requirements would have to be developed as well as further disclosure about the assumptions used.

(b)   Withdrawal is not always an option for an entity. However, the Board decided that an entity should disclose whether it is unable to withdraw from a plan because that would be useful information for a user of the financial statements.

(c)   The cost of obtaining the information would make the disclosure onerous if it were required for all entities in all circumstances. Moreover, an entity may be unable to obtain the information.

BC248   Some respondents stated that disclosure of a withdrawal liability should not be required because different plans or jurisdictions use different assumptions to determine the withdrawal amount, and therefore the amounts are not comparable. The Board did not agree with that view. The amount required to withdraw from a plan faithfully represents the obligation, whether that amount is determined on the same basis as for another plan or on a different basis. If the amounts are determined on the basis of different underlying requirements, the actual amounts required to withdraw will differ.

BC249   The Board noted that if it is probable that the entity will withdraw from the plan, any additional liability should be recognised and measured under IAS 37. This requirement was implicit in IAS 19, but the Board made it explicit in the amendments made in 2011. Requiring entities to recognise an additional liability when it is probable that the entity will withdraw from the plan also converges with similar requirements in US GAAP.

Future contributions

BC250   The Board agreed with respondents' views that the proposal in the 2010 ED for an entity to disclose the contributions for the next five years would require estimates that may be difficult to determine and very subjective. Thus the Board aligned this disclosure with the general requirement for defined benefit plans, which requires an entity to disclose the expected contribution for a defined benefit plan for the next annual period. The Board confirmed the proposal in the ED for a narrative description of any funding arrangement and funding policy. That requirement is consistent with the requirement for single employer defined benefit plans.

Level of participation

BC251   The amendments made in 2011 require an entity that accounts for its participation in a multi-employer defined benefit plan as a defined contribution plan to disclose an indication of the level of its participation in the plan compared with other plan participants. Together with information about the whole plan, that disclosure provides information about the effect of any surplus or deficit on the amount, timing and uncertainty of an entity's future cash flows.

BC252   The Board provided examples of measures that might indicate the entity's level of participation, but did not specify a particular measure because a single measure may not be relevant in all cases.

Other long-term employee benefits

Death-in-service benefits

BC253   E54 proposed guidance on cases where death-in-service benefits are not insured externally and are not provided through a post-employment benefit plan. IASC concluded that such cases will be rare. Accordingly, IASC deleted the guidance on death-in-service benefits.

Termination benefits: amendments issued in 2011

BC254   The proposals in the 2005 ED proposed to align the accounting for termination benefits with the requirements in FASB Accounting Standards Codification (ASC) Topic 420 *Exit or Disposal Cost Obligations* (FASB ASC Topic 420), relating to 'one-time termination benefits' and FASB ASC Topic 712 *Compensation—Nonretirement Postemployment Benefits*, relating to 'special termination benefits'. The Board acknowledged that differences with US GAAP would remain following the introduction of these amendments. Nonetheless, the Board believed that the proposed amendments would converge with some US GAAP requirements and would improve the accounting for termination benefits. The proposals for termination benefits complemented proposed amendments to the requirements on restructurings in IAS 37 in the 2005 ED. The Board received 123 comment letters in response to the proposals in the 2005 ED.

BC255　　The Board considered the following:

　　　　(a)　　benefits payable in exchange for future service (see paragraphs BC256 and BC257);

　　　　(b)　　recognition of termination benefits (see paragraphs BC258–BC260);

　　　　(c)　　measurement of termination benefits (see paragraph BC261); and

　　　　(d)　　interaction with restructuring costs, plan amendments, curtailments and settlements (see paragraphs BC262–BC268).

Benefits payable in exchange for services

BC256　　IAS 19 requires an entity to account for termination benefits separately from other employee benefits, because the event that gives rise to a present obligation is the termination of employment rather than employee service. In contrast, FASB ASC Topic 420 regards some involuntary termination benefits as being provided in exchange for employees' future services (or, expressed another way, a 'stay bonus'). In such cases under US GAAP, an entity recognises the cost of those benefits over the period of the employees' service, consistently with the accounting for other employee benefits.

BC257　　In the 2005 ED, the Board proposed that IAS 19 should specify recognition requirements for an entity providing termination benefits in exchange for future service, consistent with Topic 420. However, when finalising the amendments made in 2011, the Board noted the potential for confusion caused by accounting for some benefits provided in exchange for future service as termination benefits. The Board concluded that treating benefits provided in exchange for future service as short-term or other long-term employee benefits or post-employment benefits would result in the same recognition as is required under Topic 420 (ie the cost of those benefits would be recognised over the period of service), and would maintain the existing distinction between benefits provided in exchange for termination of employment and benefits provided in exchange for services.

Recognition

BC258　　IAS 19 before the amendments made in 2011 specified that an entity should recognise termination benefits when the entity was demonstrably committed to providing those benefits. In revisiting that conclusion, the Board considered the following circumstances:

　　　　(a)　　an offer of termination benefits that an entity can withdraw at its own discretion before acceptance by the employee.

　　　　(b)　　an offer of termination benefits that an entity cannot withdraw, including benefits provided as a result of an entity's decision to terminate an employee's employment (ie if the employee has no choice but to accept what is given).

BC259   The Board decided that the factor determining the timing of recognition is the entity's inability to withdraw the offer of termination benefits. In the circumstances in (a) this would be when the employee accepts the offer and in the circumstances in (b) this would be when the entity communicates a termination plan to the affected employees. The Board concluded that until these events occur the employer has discretion to avoid paying termination benefits and, therefore, a liability does not exist.

BC260   The criteria in Topic 420 relating to the termination plan are similar to the criteria in IAS 19 before the amendments made in 2011 for establishing whether an entity is demonstrably committed to a termination plan and, therefore, should recognise termination benefits. However, there was no requirement in that version of IAS 19 to communicate the plan of termination to employees. The Board added a requirement specifying that an entity does not have a present obligation to provide termination benefits until it has communicated its plan of termination to each of the affected employees. The Board also replaced the criteria in IAS 19 relating to the plan of termination with those in Topic 420. Although those criteria were very similar, the Board concluded that it would be better if they were identical.

Measurement

BC261   IAS 19 before the amendments made in 2011 required termination benefits that become due more than twelve months after the reporting date to be discounted, but provided no further measurement guidance. The Board amended the standard to state explicitly that the measurement of termination benefits should be consistent with the measurement requirements for the nature of the underlying benefits.

Interaction between plan amendments, curtailments, settlements, termination benefits and restructuring costs

BC262   In finalising the amendments made in 2011, the Board decided that an entity should:

(a)   recognise a plan amendment or curtailment when it occurs (paragraphs BC154–BC159); and

(b)   recognise termination benefits when the entity can no longer withdraw the offer of those benefits (paragraphs BC258–BC260).

BC263   Respondents to the 2010 ED were concerned about the accounting interactions between plan amendments, curtailments, settlements, termination benefits and restructurings because they often occur together, and it could be difficult to distinguish the gain or loss that arises from each transaction if they have different recognition requirements or are included in different components of defined benefit cost. Some respondents to the 2010 ED suggested aligning the timing of recognition of amounts resulting from plan amendments, curtailments, settlements, termination benefits and restructuring if they are related.

BC264   The requirements of IAS 19 before the amendments made in 2011 aligned the timing of recognition for a curtailment with the timing of recognition of a related restructuring, and suggested that when an entity recognises termination benefits the entity may also have to account for a curtailment. The objective of these requirements was to ensure that any gain or loss on curtailment is recognised at the same time as an expense resulting from a related termination benefit, from a restructuring provision or from both. In IAS 19 before the amendments made in 2011 and IAS 37, the recognition criteria for termination benefits and restructuring provisions were very similar and would have resulted in related termination benefits and restructuring being recognised together because both required recognition when an entity was demonstrably committed to the transaction.

BC265   The 2005 ED proposed to amend the timing of recognition of curtailments from being aligned with a related restructuring to being aligned with a related termination benefit. The 2010 ED did not include this amendment because the Board was in the process of finalising the amendments for termination benefits at the time.

BC266   To avoid an inconsistency in the timing of recognition for related transactions, the Board decided that:

(a)   past service cost should be recognised at the earlier of:

(i)   when the plan amendment occurs; and

(ii)   when any related restructuring costs or termination benefits are recognised.

(b)   termination benefits should be recognised at the earlier of:

(i)   when the entity can no longer withdraw the offer of those benefits; and

(ii)   when any related restructuring costs are recognised.

BC267   The Board also considered other approaches, including the proposal in the 2010 ED to align the timing of recognition for a plan amendment or curtailment with a related termination benefit but not with a related restructuring. In the Board's view the amendments made in 2011 have the following benefits over other approaches:

(a)   They align the timing of recognition for related transactions for all combinations of curtailments, termination benefits and restructurings (which is consistent with the current requirements).

(b)   They include the stand-alone recognition criteria developed for plan amendments and curtailments (ie that the plan amendment will be recognised when it occurs).

BC268   The 2005 ED proposed that the specific recognition criterion for restructuring costs should be withdrawn from IAS 37. If the Board confirms this proposal as part of its future discussion, then the references to the timing of recognition for restructuring costs will become redundant and the timing of recognition for plan amendments and curtailments will be aligned only with the timing of recognition for termination benefits. The Board will review the timing of recognition for restructuring costs when it finalises the amendments to IAS 37 resulting from the 2005 ED.

Transition

BC269   The amendments made in 2011 are to be applied retrospectively in accordance with the general requirements of IAS 8 *Accounting Policies, Changes in Accounting Estimates and Errors*, with two exceptions:

(a)   The carrying amount of assets outside the scope of IAS 19 need not be adjusted for changes in employee benefit costs that were included in the carrying amount before the beginning of the financial year in which the amendments are first applied. Thus entities may recognise previously unrecognised actuarial gains and losses and past service cost by adjusting equity, instead of by allocating part of those adjustments against the carrying amount of assets such as inventories. In the Board's view, such an allocation could have been costly and would have provided little or no benefit to users.

(b)   In financial statements for periods beginning before 1 January 2014, an entity need not provide comparatives for the disclosures about the sensitivity of the defined benefit obligation. The Board provided this exemption to provide sufficient lead time for entities to implement the necessary systems.

First-time adopters

BC270   For entities adopting IFRSs for the first time, the amendments made in 2011 are to be applied retrospectively as required by IFRS 1 *First-time Adoption of International Financial Reporting Standards*. The Board included a temporary exemption for entities adopting IFRSs to use paragraph 173(b) for the same reasons as given in paragraph BC269(b).[20]

Early application

BC271   The amendments made in 2011 will improve the accounting and, in particular, the disclosures provided by a reporting entity in relation to its participation in defined benefit plans. In addition, some of the amendments address existing problems in applying IAS 19 in practice. The Board noted that the majority of the amendments made in 2011 are permitted by the previous version of IAS 19. Consequently, the Board permitted early application of all the amendments made in 2011.

---

20   *Annual Improvements to IFRS Standards 2014–2016 Cycle*, issued in December 2016, amended IFRS 1 *First-time Adoption of International Financial Reporting Standards* by deleting the short-term exemption for first-time adopters (see paragraph BC99 of IFRS 1), because it was no longer applicable.

Transition provisions for *Defined Benefit Plans: Employee Contributions*

BC271A In ED/2013/4, the IASB proposed retrospective application and to permit earlier application of the amendments. The majority of the respondents supported those proposals. Some respondents questioned whether retrospective application was practicable because some calculations might require information that is not readily available. The IASB observed that in current practice, contributions from employees or third parties are generally reduced from service cost without being attributed to periods of service. The proposed amendments are intended to provide relief so that entities can deduct contributions from service cost in the period in which the service is rendered, which was common practice prior to the 2011 amendments to IAS 19. The impact of retrospective application would therefore be minimal in those cases. Consequently, the IASB decided to retain the requirement for retrospective application.

BC271B The amendments to IAS 19 published in 2011 are effective for annual periods beginning on or after 1 January 2013. In the IASB's view, the objective of the amendments published in 2013 is to provide relief in the accounting for contributions from employees or third parties and, therefore, the effective date should be set as early as possible, while allowing jurisdictions to have sufficient time to prepare for the new requirements. Consequently, the IASB decided that the effective date of the amendments should be 1 July 2014, with earlier application permitted.

Annual Improvements to IFRSs 2012–2014 Cycle

BC271C *Annual Improvements to IFRSs 2012–2014 Cycle*, issued in September 2014, amended paragraph 83. The Board noted that for some entities a full retrospective application of the amendment could be burdensome. Consequently, the Board decided that the amendment should be applied from the beginning of the earliest comparative period presented in the first financial statements in which an entity applies the amendment. Any initial adjustment arising from the application of the amendment should be recognised in opening retained earnings of the earliest comparative period presented.

Plan Amendment, Curtailment or Settlement— amendments issued in 2018

BC271D The Board decided that an entity would not apply *Plan Amendment, Curtailment or Settlement* (Amendments to IAS 19) retrospectively. The Board concluded that the benefits of applying the amendments retrospectively were unlikely to exceed the cost of doing so because retrospective application:

(a) might result in significant cost for some entities that choose to present, as a separate component of equity, the cumulative amount of remeasurements recognised in other comprehensive income. As explained in paragraphs BC173C–BC173D, the amendments could change whether and when an entity remeasures the net defined benefit liability (asset) in accordance with paragraph 99. Accordingly, such entities might have had to revisit plan amendments, curtailments and settlements that occurred several years previously and remeasure the net defined benefit liability (asset) as of those dates.

(b) would not provide useful trend information to users of financial statements because plan amendments, curtailments and settlements are discrete one-off events.

(c) would affect only amounts recognised in profit or loss or in other comprehensive income for prior periods presented—it would affect neither total comprehensive income nor the amounts recognised in the statement of financial position for those periods.

BC271E   The Board did not provide an exemption for first-time adopters. This is because IFRS 1 does not exempt a first-time adopter from applying the requirements in IAS 19 retrospectively. The Board concluded there would be little benefit in providing a first-time adopter with relief from applying these amendments retrospectively when it would have to retrospectively apply all the other requirements in IAS 19.

Summary of changes from the 2010 ED and 2005 ED: amendments issued in 2011

BC272   The main changes from the 2010 ED are:

(a) The amendments do not specify where in profit or loss an entity should present the net interest component. The 2010 ED proposed that an entity should include the net interest component as part of finance cost in profit or loss.

(b) The amendments require gains and losses on settlement to be included in service cost. The 2010 ED proposed that gains and losses on settlement should be included in remeasurements.

(c) The amendments do not require the following disclosures proposed in the 2010 ED:

(i) the defined benefit obligation, excluding projected growth in salaries;

(ii) sensitivity of current service cost to changes in actuarial assumptions; and

(iii) a description of the process used to determine the demographic actuarial assumptions.

(d) The amendments align the timing of recognition for plan amendments, termination benefits and restructuring costs. The 2010 ED proposed aligning the timing of recognition for plan amendments and termination benefits only.

(e) The amendments do not:

    (i) combine the post-employment and other long-term employee benefit categories, as had been proposed in the 2010 ED.

    (ii) state whether expected future salary increases should be included in determining whether a benefit formula allocates a materially higher level of benefit to later years, as had been proposed in the 2010 ED.

    (iii) incorporate IFRIC 14 *IAS 19 — The Limit on a Defined Benefit Asset, Minimum Funding Requirements and their Interaction* as had been proposed in the 2010 ED.

BC273 The main changes from the 2005 ED are:

(a) The amendment requires entities to recognise termination benefits when the entity can no longer withdraw an offer of those benefits. The 2005 ED proposed that voluntary termination benefits should be recognised when accepted by the employee, and that involuntary termination benefits should be recognised when the entity has a plan that meets specified criteria.

(b) The amendment clarifies the measurement requirements for termination benefits.

Convergence with US GAAP: amendments issued in 2011

Multi-employer plan disclosures

BC274 In March 2010 the FASB announced a new project to review disclosures about an employer's participation in a multi-employer plan and to develop disclosure requirements that would give better information about the risks that an entity faces by participating in a multi-employer plan. The FASB published a proposed Accounting Standards Update in the second quarter of 2010 with disclosure requirements similar to those relating to multi-employer defined benefit plans. The FASB expects to issue a final Accounting Standards Update in 2011.

Recognition of defined benefit cost

BC275 The amendments made in 2011 result in the measurement of an entity's surplus or deficit in a defined benefit plan in the statement of financial position, consistently with the requirements in US GAAP. Although both US GAAP and IAS 19 require the immediate recognition of changes in the net defined benefit liability (asset), there are differences in where those changes are recognised.

BC276   US GAAP defines net periodic pension cost[21] as comprising current service cost, interest cost on the defined benefit obligation, expected return on plan assets, amortisation of unrecognised prior service cost (if any), gains or losses recognised and amortised after exceeding a specified corridor (if any), amortisation of unrecognised initial net obligation and/or initial net asset. The IAS 19 requirements for the disaggregation of defined benefit cost and recognition of the components of defined benefit cost differ from the requirements in US GAAP as follows:

(a)   *Disaggregation of the return on plan assets* — US GAAP distinguishes the expected return on plan assets and the difference between the expected and actual returns. The net interest approach in IAS 19 distinguishes an implied interest income on plan assets and the difference between the implied interest income and actual returns.

(b)   *Past service cost* — US GAAP recognises past service cost in other comprehensive income initially, and then reclassifies past service cost from other comprehensive income to profit or loss in subsequent periods. IAS 19 requires past service cost to be included together with current service cost in profit or loss.

(c)   *Reclassification* — US GAAP requires the reclassification of amounts recognised in other comprehensive income to profit or loss in subsequent periods. IAS 19 prohibits subsequent reclassification.

Termination benefits

BC277   FASB ASC Topic 420 specifies the accounting for a class of termination benefits known as 'one-time termination benefits'. Topic 420 requires an entity to recognise a 'stay bonus' over the period of the employees' service and to recognise other termination benefits when the entity has a plan of termination that meets specified criteria. The amendments made in 2011 distinguish benefits provided in exchange for service and benefits provided in exchange for the termination of employment. A 'stay bonus' would not be classified as a termination benefit under IAS 19 because it is provided in exchange for service and, therefore, would be attributed to periods of service in accordance with paragraph 70 of IAS 19.

BC278   FASB ASC Topic 712 specifies the accounting for a class of termination benefits known as 'special termination benefits'. Topic 712 requires an entity to recognise these special termination benefits when the employees accept the employer's offer of termination benefits. The amendments made to IAS 19 in 2011 are consistent with those requirements. Topic 712 also specifies the accounting for a class of termination benefits known as 'contractual termination benefits'. Topic 712 requires an entity to recognise contractual termination benefits when it is probable that employees will be entitled to benefits and the amount can be reasonably estimated. The amendments made in 2011 do not converge with those requirements; instead, IAS 19 requires

---

21   FASB ASC Section 715-30-20 *Defined Benefit Plans — Pension Glossary*

those benefits to be recognised when an entity can no longer withdraw an offer of those benefits.

BC279 FASB ASC Topic 420 specifies that an entity should measure 'one-time' termination benefits at fair value (or at an amount based on fair value for benefits provided in exchange for future service). The Board did not align the measurement requirements of IAS 19 for termination benefits with those of Topic 420. When an entity provides termination benefits through a post-employment defined benefit plan (for example, by enhancing retirement benefits) the Board concluded that it would be unduly complex to specify that an entity should measure the benefits at fair value. To do so would require the effect of the changes to the plan arising from the termination of employment to be isolated, on a continuous basis, from the remainder of the plan.

Cost-benefit considerations: amendments issued in 2011

BC280 The objective of financial statements is to provide information about the financial position, performance and changes in financial position of an entity that is useful to a wide range of users in making economic decisions. To attain this objective, the Board seeks to ensure that an IFRS will meet a significant need and that the overall benefits of the resulting information justify the costs of providing it. Although the costs to implement changes to existing requirements might not be borne evenly, users of financial statements benefit from improvements in financial reporting, thereby facilitating the functioning of markets for capital and credit and the efficient allocation of resources in the economy.

BC281 The evaluation of costs and benefits is necessarily subjective. In making its judgement, the Board considered the following:

(a)   the costs incurred by preparers of financial statements.

(b)   the costs incurred by users of financial statements when information is not available.

(c)   the comparative advantage that preparers have in developing information, compared with the costs that users would incur to develop surrogate information.

(d)   the benefit of better economic decision-making as a result of improved financial reporting.

(e)   the costs of transition for users, preparers and others.

BC282 The objective of the amendments made in 2011 is to improve the usefulness of information available to users for their assessment of the amounts, timing and uncertainty of future cash flows arising from defined benefit plans of the entity. However, the Board also considered the cost of implementing the proposed amendments and applying them on a continuous basis. In evaluating the relative costs and benefits of the proposed amendments, the Board was assisted by the information received in meetings with its Employee Benefits Working Group.

BC283   The amendments should improve the ability of users to understand the financial reporting for post-employment benefits by:

（a）   reporting changes in the carrying amounts of defined benefit obligations and changes in the fair value of plan assets in a more understandable way;

（b）   eliminating some recognition options that were allowed by IAS 19, thus improving comparability;

（c）   clarifying requirements that have resulted in diverse practices; and

（d）   improving information about the risks arising from an entity's involvement in defined benefit plans.

BC284   Costs will be involved in the adoption and continuing application of the amendments. Those costs will depend on the complexity of an entity's defined benefit arrangements and the options in IAS 19 that the entity currently elects to apply. However, those costs should be minimal because in order to apply the previous version of IAS 19 entities need to obtain much of the information that the amendments require. Consequently, the Board believes that the benefits of the amendments outweigh the costs.

Appendix
Amendments to the Basis for Conclusions on other IFRSs

This appendix contains amendments to the Basis for Conclusions (and related appendices) on other IFRSs that are necessary in order to ensure consistency with IAS 19 and the related amendments to other IFRSs. Amended paragraphs are shown with new text underlined and deleted text struck through.

* * * * *

The amendments contained in this appendix when IAS 19, as amended in 2011, was issued have been incorporated into the Basis for Conclusions on the relevant IFRSs published in this volume.

Dissenting opinions

Dissent of James J Leisenring and Tatsumi Yamada from the issue in December 2004 of *Actuarial Gains and Losses, Group Plans and Disclosures* (Amendment to IAS 19)[22]

Mr Leisenring

DO1   Mr Leisenring dissents from the issue of the Amendment to IAS 19 Employee Benefits — *Actuarial Gains and Losses, Group Plans and Disclosures*.

DO2   Mr Leisenring dissents because he disagrees with the deletion of the last sentence in paragraph 40 and the addition of paragraphs 41 and 42. He believes that group entities that give a defined benefit promise to their employees should account for that defined benefit promise in their separate or individual financial statements. He further believes that separate or individual financial statements that purport to be prepared in accordance with IFRSs should comply with the same requirements as other financial statements that are prepared in accordance with IFRSs. He therefore disagrees with the removal of the requirement for group entities to treat defined benefit plans that share risks between entities under common control as defined benefit plans and the introduction instead of the requirements of paragraph 41.

DO3   Mr Leisenring notes that group entities are required to give disclosures about the plan as a whole but does not believe that disclosures are an adequate substitute for recognition and measurement in accordance with the requirements of IAS 19.

Mr Yamada

DO4   Mr Yamada dissents from the issue of the Amendment to IAS 19 Employee Benefits — *Actuarial Gains and Losses, Group Plans and Disclosures*.

DO5   Mr Yamada agrees that an option should be added to IAS 19 that allows entities that recognise actuarial gains and losses in full in the period in which they occur to recognise them outside profit or loss in a statement of recognised income and expense, even though under the previous IAS 19 they can be recognised in profit or loss in full in the period in which they occur. He agrees that the option provides more transparent information than the deferred recognition options commonly chosen under IAS 19. However, he also believes that all items of income and expense should be recognised in profit or loss in some period. Until they have been so recognised, they should be included in a component of equity separate from retained earnings. They should be transferred from that separate component of equity into retained earnings when they are recognised in profit or loss. Mr Yamada does not, therefore, agree with the requirements of paragraph 93D.[23]

---

22   Cross-references have been updated.

23   The amendments to IAS 19 made in 2011 deleted paragraph 93D.

DO6   Mr Yamada acknowledges the difficulty in finding a rational basis for recognising actuarial gains and losses in profit or loss in periods after their initial recognition in a statement of recognised income and expense when the plan is ongoing. He also acknowledges that, under IFRSs, some gains and losses are recognised directly in a separate component of equity and are not subsequently recognised in profit or loss. However, Mr Yamada does not believe that this justifies expanding this treatment to actuarial gains and losses.

DO7   The cumulative actuarial gains and losses could be recognised in profit or loss when a plan is wound up or transferred outside the entity. The cumulative amount recognised in a separate component of equity would be transferred to retained earnings at the same time. This would be consistent with the treatment of exchange gains and losses on subsidiaries that have a measurement currency different from the presentation currency of the group.

DO8   Therefore, Mr Yamada believes that the requirements of paragraph 93D mean that the option is not an improvement to financial reporting because it allows gains and losses to be excluded permanently from profit or loss and yet be recognised immediately in retained earnings.

Dissent of Jan Engström and Tatsumi Yamada from the issue in June 2011 of IAS 19 as amended

Mr Engström

DO1　Mr Engström voted against the amendments made to IAS 19 in 2011. The project was a limited scope project focused on bringing the full post-employment benefit onto the statement of financial position and on eliminating the corridor approach.

DO2　In Mr Engström's view, during the project it has become increasingly clear that a review of the measurement principles is much needed— something not included in the limited scope of the project. During the recent financial crisis the defined benefit obligation could be as much as 50 per cent higher in one company compared with an identical defined benefit obligation in another company operating in an adjacent country, with basically equal macroeconomic parameters, due to the imperfections in measurement requirements of IAS 19.

DO3　In Mr Engström's view, the amendments to IAS 19 made in 2011 introduce some radical changes from a principle point of view by not requiring some income and expenses truly related to a company's activities ever to be presented in profit or loss, indeed actually prohibiting such presentation. The adjustments of the defined benefit obligation, and of the plan assets, have for many companies been a very significant amount and by presenting income and expenses resulting from these adjustments only in other comprehensive income this project continues the gradual erosion of the concept of profit or loss.

DO4　Mr Engström sees no reason why the remeasurements component could not be subsequently reclassified to profit or loss on a reasonable basis consistently with the assumptions used to measure the defined benefit obligation.

DO5　Mr Engström would favour a comprehensive review of IAS 19, including a review of measurement, and he would prefer presentation to be decided only after the IASB has taken a stance on what profit or loss is, what other comprehensive income is and what should be subsequently reclassified into profit or loss.

DO6　As a consequence of these amendments made to IAS 19, and of the option introduced in IFRS 9 *Financial Instruments*, some material amounts may never be presented in profit or loss. IFRS 9 introduced an option to present some gains and losses on equity instruments not held for trading in other comprehensive income, without subsequent reclassification to profit or loss. In Mr Engström's view, these recent ad hoc decisions push financial reporting de facto towards a single income statement as some matters truly related to a company's activities are never to be presented in profit or loss.

Mr Yamada

DO7   Mr Yamada voted against the amendments made to IAS 19 in 2011.

DO8   Mr Yamada agrees with the Board's view in paragraph BC70 that immediate recognition of all changes in the fair values of plan assets and in the defined benefit obligation in the period in which those changes occur provides information that is more relevant to users of financial statements than the information provided by deferred recognition. Mr Yamada also agrees that immediate recognition provides a more faithful representation of defined benefit plans and is easier for a user to understand.

DO9   However, Mr Yamada does not agree with:

(a)   the disaggregation of defined benefit cost (see paragraph DO10);

(b)   the definition of net interest and remeasurements of the net defined benefit liability (asset) (see paragraphs DO11–DO14); and

(c)   the presentation of remeasurements of the net defined benefit liability (asset) in other comprehensive income (see paragraphs DO15–DO17).

Disaggregation of defined benefit cost

DO10   In Mr Yamada's view the disaggregation of defined benefit cost into components (ie service cost, net interest and remeasurements) in profit or loss and other comprehensive income in paragraph 120 is not consistent with the presentation of plan assets and the defined benefit obligation in the statement of financial position. In his view, to be consistent with the presentation of a single net defined benefit liability (asset) in the statement of financial position, the presentation of changes in the net defined benefit liability (asset) should be a single net amount presented in profit or loss. Therefore, he does not agree with paragraph 134 not to specify how to present service cost and net interest on the net defined benefit liability (asset). He understands the usefulness of disaggregated information, but believes that an appropriate way of providing information on the components of defined benefit cost is to show them in the notes to the financial statements.

Definition of net interest and remeasurements on the net defined benefit liability (asset)

DO11   Mr Yamada sees no principle behind the disaggregation described in paragraph 120 (ie service cost, net interest and remeasurements). In particular, in his view the approach for calculating net interest on the net defined benefit liability (asset) is not an improvement in financial reporting.

DO12   In Mr Yamada's view there is no reason for requiring the component of the return on plan assets presented in profit or loss to be determined using the rate used to discount the defined benefit obligation as is in paragraph 125. He agrees with the respondents' concerns summarised in paragraph BC82 that plan assets may be made up of many different types of investments, and that 'the return on high quality corporate bonds would be arbitrary and would not be a faithful representation of the return that investors require or expect from each type of asset.' Therefore, in his view, it does not provide more useful information to use the rate used to discount the defined benefit obligation in place of the previous requirement to use expected return on plan assets.

DO13 Mr Yamada does not agree that the Board should require 'using the same rate [for plan assets] as the rate used to discount the liability [as] a practical approach that ... would not require an entity to make a subjective judgement on how to divide the return on plan assets into an interest component and a remeasurement' (paragraph BC82). He agrees that determining the 'expected return on plan assets' that is used by the previous version of IAS 19 requires judgement by management, but this does not mean that the 'expected return on plan assets' is unreliable. In his view, estimating the 'expected return on plan assets' requires the same degree of judgement as do other accounting estimates.

DO14 In Mr Yamada's view, there is no clear explanation about the nature of the remeasurements component, nor why disaggregation of this amount is appropriate. In the previous version of IAS 19, actuarial gains and losses on plan assets were defined as experience adjustments, ie the effects of differences between the previous actuarial assumptions (the expected return on assets) and what actually occurred. However, paragraph BC86 explains the nature of the remeasurements component as being a residual after determining the service cost and net interest components, and simply restates the definition of remeasurements in paragraph 7.

Presentation of remeasurements in other comprehensive income

DO15 Paragraph BC88 sets out the Board's reasoning that the remeasurement component should be presented in other comprehensive income because 'although changes included in the remeasurements component may provide more information about the uncertainty and risk of future cash flows, they provide less information about the likely amount and timing of those cash flows'. Mr Yamada does not agree with that reasoning because, in his view, the actual return on plan assets provides information about the performance of plan assets during the period, but the disaggregation of the actual return into interest income and a remeasurements component does not provide information about the likely timing and amount of future cash flows. Therefore, in his view, it does not represent faithfully the performance of plan assets if the actual returns on plan assets in excess of the interest income on plan assets are presented in other comprehensive income and not presented in profit or loss when they occur. Instead, all the components should be presented in profit or loss when they occur. Therefore, he does not agree with paragraph 120(c). In his view the amount representing remeasurements does not have a clearly defined characteristic that justifies its presentation in other comprehensive income.

DO16 Mr Yamada notes that the definition of net interest on the net defined benefit liability (asset) results in the difference between the rate used to discount the defined benefit obligation applied to plan assets and the actual return on plan assets being presented in other comprehensive income. To do so eliminates from profit or loss the effects of differences between the actual return on plan assets and the rate applied to the defined benefit obligation. In his view the elimination of these differences introduces a type of smoothing mechanism. Thus, in his view the proposal is not an improvement on the previous version of IAS 19.

DO17   Given that the Board decided to present part of the defined benefit cost (ie remeasurements) in other comprehensive income, he is of the view that the Board should have retained the notion of actuarial gains and losses in the previous version of IAS 19 (paragraphs 93A–93D) rather than introduce a similar but not clearly better new notion of 'remeasurements'. This would mean that the expected return on plan assets is recognised in profit or loss and the difference between the expected return on plan assets and the actual return on plan assets is recognised in other comprehensive income. As stated in paragraph DO15, in Mr Yamada's view, this difference gives better information than the revised remeasurement component.

IASB documents published to accompany

IAS 20

Accounting for Government Grants and Disclosure of Government Assistance

The text of the unaccompanied standard, IAS 20, is contained in Part A of this edition. Its effective date when issued was 1 January 1984. This part presents the following document:

BASIS FOR CONCLUSIONS

Basis for Conclusions on
IAS 20 *Accounting for Government Grants and Disclosure of Government Assistance*

This Basis for Conclusions accompanies, but is not part of, IAS 20.

BC1 This Basis for Conclusions summarises the International Accounting Standards Board's considerations in amending IAS 20 *Accounting for Government Grants and Disclosure of Government Assistance* as part of *Improvements to IFRSs* issued in May 2008.

BC2 IAS 20 was developed by the International Accounting Standards Committee in 1983 and did not include a Basis for Conclusions. This Basis refers to the insertion of paragraphs 10A and 43 and the deletion of paragraph 37. Those changes require government loans with below-market rates of interest to be recognised and measured in accordance with IAS 39 *Financial Instruments: Recognition and Measurement*[1] and the benefit of the reduced interest to be accounted for using IAS 20.

Accounting for loans from government with a below-market rate of interest

BC3 The Board identified an apparent inconsistency between the guidance in IAS 20 and IAS 39.[2] It related to the accounting for loans with a below-market rate of interest received from a government. IAS 20 stated that no interest should be imputed for such a loan, whereas IAS 39 required all loans to be recognised at fair value, thus requiring interest to be imputed to loans with a below-market rate of interest.

BC4 The Board decided to remove this inconsistency. It believed that the imputation of interest provides more relevant information to a user of the financial statements. Accordingly the Board amended IAS 20 to require that loans received from a government that have a below-market rate of interest should be recognised and measured in accordance with IAS 39. The benefit of the government loan is measured at the inception of the loan as the difference between the cash received and the amount at which the loan is initially recognised in the statement of financial position. This benefit is accounted for in accordance with IAS 20.

BC5 Noting that applying IAS 39 to loans retrospectively may require entities to measure the fair value of loans at a past date, the Board decided that the amendment should be applied prospectively to new loans.

---

1 IFRS 9 *Financial Instruments* replaced IAS 39. IFRS 9 applies to all items that were previously within the scope of IAS 39. This paragraph refers to matters relevant when IAS 20 was amended in 2008.

2 IFRS 9 *Financial Instruments* replaced IAS 39. IFRS 9 applies to all items that were previously within the scope of IAS 39. This paragraph refers to matters relevant when IAS 20 was amended in 2008.

IASB documents published to accompany

IAS 21

The Effects of Changes in Foreign Exchange Rates

The text of the unaccompanied standard, IAS 21, is contained in Part A of this edition. Its effective date when issued was 1 January 2005. This part presents the following document:

BASIS FOR CONCLUSIONS

Basis for Conclusions on
IAS 21 *The Effects of Changes in Foreign Exchange Rates*

This Basis for Conclusions accompanies, but is not part of, IAS 21.

Paragraph BC1 was amended and paragraphs BC25A–BC25F were added in relation to the amendment to IAS 21 issued in December 2005.

In this Basis for Conclusions the terminology has not been amended to reflect the changes made by IAS 1 Presentation of Financial Statements *(as revised in 2007).*

Introduction

BC1   This Basis for Conclusions summarises the International Accounting Standards Board's considerations in reaching its conclusions on revising IAS 21 *The Effects of Changes in Foreign Exchange Rates* in 2003, and on the amendment to IAS 21 *Net Investment in a Foreign Operation* in December 2005. Individual Board members gave greater weight to some factors than to others.

BC2   In July 2001 the Board announced that, as part of its initial agenda of technical projects, it would undertake a project to improve a number of Standards, including IAS 21. The project was undertaken in the light of queries and criticisms raised in relation to the Standards by securities regulators, professional accountants and other interested parties. The objectives of the Improvements project were to reduce or eliminate alternatives, redundancies and conflicts within Standards, to deal with some convergence issues and to make other improvements. In May 2002 the Board published its proposals in an Exposure Draft of *Improvements to International Accounting Standards*, with a comment deadline of 16 September 2002. The Board received over 160 comment letters on the Exposure Draft.

BC3   Because the Board's intention was not to reconsider the fundamental approach to accounting for the effects of changes in foreign exchange rates established by IAS 21, this Basis for Conclusions does not discuss requirements in IAS 21 that the Board has not reconsidered.

Functional currency

BC4   The term 'reporting currency' was previously defined as 'the currency used in presenting the financial statements'. This definition comprises two separate notions (which were identified in SIC-19 *Reporting Currency—Measurement and Presentation of Financial Statements under IAS 21 and IAS 29*):

- the measurement currency (the currency in which the entity measures the items in the financial statements); and

- the presentation currency (the currency in which the entity presents its financial statements).

The Board decided to revise the previous version of IAS 21 to incorporate the SIC-19 approach of separating these two notions. The Board also noted that the term 'functional currency' is more commonly used than 'measurement currency' and decided to adopt the more common term.

BC5 The Board noted a concern that the guidance in SIC-19 on determining a measurement currency could permit entities to choose one of several currencies, or to select an inappropriate currency. In particular, some believed that SIC-19 placed too much emphasis on the currency in which transactions are denominated and too little emphasis on the underlying economy that determines the pricing of those transactions. To meet these concerns, the Board defined functional currency as 'the currency of the primary economic environment in which the entity operates'. The Board also provided guidance on how to determine the functional currency (see paragraphs 9–14 of the Standard). This guidance draws heavily on SIC-19 and equivalent guidance in US and other national standards, but also reflects the Board's decision that some factors merit greater emphasis than others.

BC6 The Board also discussed whether a foreign operation that is integral to the reporting entity (as described in the previous version of IAS 21) could have a functional currency that is different from that of its 'parent'.[1] The Board decided that the functional currencies will always be the same, because it would be contradictory for an integral foreign operation that 'carries on business as if it were an extension of the reporting enterprise's operations'[2] to operate in a primary economic environment different from its parent.

BC7 It follows that it is not necessary to translate the results and financial position of an integral foreign operation when incorporating them into the financial statements of the parent — they will already be measured in the parent's functional currency. Furthermore, it is not necessary to distinguish between an integral foreign operation and a foreign entity. When a foreign operation's functional currency is different from that of its parent, it is a foreign entity, and the translation method in paragraphs 38–49 of the Standard applies.

BC8 The Board also decided that the principles in the previous version of IAS 21 for distinguishing an integral foreign operation from a foreign entity are relevant in determining an operation's functional currency. Hence it incorporated these principles into the Standard in that context.

BC9 The Board agreed that the indicators in paragraph 9 are the primary indicators for determining the functional currency and that paragraphs 10 and 11 are secondary. This is because the indicators in paragraphs 10 and 11 are not linked to the primary economic environment in which the entity operates but provide additional supporting evidence to determine an entity's functional currency.

---

1 The term 'parent' is used broadly in this context to mean an entity that has a branch, associate or joint venture, as well as one with a subsidiary.
2 IAS 21 (revised 1993), paragraph 24

Presentation currency

BC10   A further issue is whether an entity should be permitted to present its financial statements in a currency (or currencies) other than its functional currency. Some believe it should not. They believe that the functional currency, being the currency of the primary economic environment in which the entity operates, most usefully portrays the economic effect of transactions and events on the entity. For a group that comprises operations with a number of functional currencies, they believe that the consolidated financial statements should be presented in the functional currency that management uses when controlling and monitoring the performance and financial position of the group. They also believe that allowing an entity to present its financial statements in more than one currency may confuse, rather than help, users of those financial statements. Supporters of this view believe that any presentation in a currency other than that described above should be regarded as a 'convenience translation' that is outside the scope of IFRSs.

BC11   Others believe that the choice of presentation currency should be limited, for example, to the functional currency of one of the substantive entities within a group. However, such a restriction might be easily overcome—an entity that wished to present its financial statements in a different currency might establish a substantive, but relatively small operation with that functional currency.

BC12   Still others believe that, given the rising trend towards globalisation, entities should be permitted to present their financial statements in any currency. They note that most large groups do not have a single functional currency, but rather comprise operations with a number of functional currencies. For such entities, they believe it is not clear which currency should be the presentation currency, or why one currency is preferable to another. They also point out that management may not use a single currency when controlling and monitoring the performance and financial position of such a group. In addition, they note that in some jurisdictions, entities are required to present their financial statements in the local currency, even when this is not the functional currency.[3] Hence, if IFRSs required the financial statements to be presented in the functional currency, some entities would have to present two sets of financial statements: financial statements that comply with IFRSs presented in the functional currency and financial statements that comply with local regulations presented in a different currency.

BC13   The Board was persuaded by the arguments in the previous paragraph. Accordingly, it decided that entities should be permitted to present their financial statements in any currency (or currencies).

BC14   The Board also clarified that the Standard does not prohibit the entity from providing, as supplementary information, a 'convenience translation'. Such a 'convenience translation' may display financial statements (or selected portions of financial statements) in a currency other than the presentation

---

3   This includes entities operating in another country and, for example, publishing financial statements to comply with a listing requirement of that country.

       © IFRS Foundation

currency, as a convenience to some users. The 'convenience translation' may be prepared using a translation method other than that required by the Standard. These types of 'convenience translations' should be clearly identified as supplementary information to distinguish them from information required by IFRSs and translated in accordance with the Standard.

Translation method

BC15   The Board debated which method should be used to translate financial statements from an entity's functional currency into a different presentation currency.

BC16   The Board agreed that the translation method should not have the effect of substituting another currency for the functional currency. Put another way, presenting the financial statements in a different currency should not change the way in which the underlying items are measured. Rather, the translation method should merely express the underlying amounts, as measured in the functional currency, in a different currency.

BC17   Given this, the Board considered two possible translation methods. The first is to translate all amounts (including comparatives) at the most recent closing rate. This method has several advantages: it is simple to apply; it does not generate any new gains and losses; and it does not change ratios such as return on assets. This method is supported by those who believe that the process of merely expressing amounts in a different currency should preserve the relationships among amounts as measured in the functional currency and, as such, should not lead to any new gains or losses.

BC18   The second method considered by the Board is the one that the previous version of IAS 21 required for translating the financial statements of a foreign operation.[4] This method results in the same amounts in the presentation currency regardless of whether the financial statements of a foreign operation are:

(a)   first translated into the functional currency of another group entity (eg the parent) and then into the presentation currency, or

(b)   translated directly into the presentation currency.

BC19   This method avoids the need to decide the currency in which to express the financial statements of a multinational group before they are translated into the presentation currency. As noted above, many large groups do not have a single functional currency, but comprise operations with a number of functional currencies. For such entities it is not clear which functional currency should be chosen in which to express amounts before they are translated into the presentation currency, or why one currency is preferable to another. In addition, this method produces the same amounts in the

---

4   This is to translate balance sheet items at the closing rate and income and expense items at actual (or average) rates, except for an entity whose functional currency is that of a hyperinflationary economy.

presentation currency for a stand-alone entity as for an identical subsidiary of a parent whose functional currency is the presentation currency.

BC20   The Board decided to require the second method, ie that the financial statements of any entity (whether a stand-alone entity, a parent or an operation within a group) whose functional currency differs from the presentation currency used by the reporting entity are translated using the method set out in paragraphs 38–49 of the Standard.

BC21   With respect to translation of comparative amounts, the Board adopted the approach required by SIC-30 for:

(a)   an entity whose functional currency is not the currency of the hyperinflationary economy (assets and liabilities in the comparative balance sheet are translated at the closing rate at the date of that balance sheet and income and expenses in the comparative income statement are translated at exchange rates at the dates of the transactions); and

(b)   an entity whose functional currency is the currency of a hyperinflationary economy, and for which the comparative amounts are being translated into the currency of a hyperinflationary economy (both balance sheet and income statement items are translated at the closing rate of the most recent balance sheet presented).

BC22   However, the Board decided not to adopt the SIC-30 approach for the translation of comparatives for an entity whose functional currency is the currency of a hyperinflationary economy, and for which the comparative amounts are being translated into a presentation currency of a non-hyperinflationary economy. The Board noted that in such a case, the SIC-30 approach requires restating the comparative amounts from those shown in last year's financial statements for both the effects of inflation and for changes in exchange rates. If exchange rates fully reflect differing price levels between the two economies to which they relate, the SIC-30 approach will result in the same amounts for the comparatives as were reported as current year amounts in the prior year financial statements. Furthermore, the Board noted that in the prior year, the relevant amounts had been already expressed in the non-hyperinflationary presentation currency, and there was no reason to change them. For these reasons the Board decided to require that all comparative amounts are those presented in the prior year financial statements (ie there is no adjustment for either subsequent changes in the price level or subsequent changes in exchange rates).

BC23   The Board decided to incorporate into the Standard most of the disclosure requirements of SIC-30 *Reporting Currency—Translation from Measurement Currency to Presentation Currency* that apply when a different translation method is used or other supplementary information, such as an extract from the full financial statements, is displayed in a currency other than the functional currency (see paragraph 57 of the Standard). These disclosures enable users to distinguish information prepared in accordance with IFRSs from information that may be useful to users but is not the subject of IFRSs, and also tell users how the latter information has been prepared.

Capitalisation of exchange differences

BC24   The previous version of IAS 21 allowed a limited choice of accounting for exchange differences that arise 'from a severe devaluation or depreciation of a currency against which there is no practical means of hedging and that affects liabilities which cannot be settled and which arise directly on the recent acquisition of an asset'.[5] The benchmark treatment was to recognise such exchange differences in profit or loss. The allowed alternative was to recognise them as an asset.

BC25   The Board noted that the allowed alternative (of recognition as an asset) was not in accordance with the *Framework for the Preparation and Presentation of Financial Statements*[6] because exchange losses do not meet the definition of an asset. Moreover, recognition of exchange losses as an asset is neither allowed nor required by any liaison standard-setter, so its deletion would improve convergence. Finally, in many cases when the conditions for recognition as an asset are met, the asset would be restated in accordance with IAS 29 *Financial Reporting in Hyperinflationary Economies*. Thus, to the extent that an exchange loss reflects hyperinflation, this effect is taken into account by IAS 29. For all of these reasons, the Board removed the allowed alternative treatment and the related SIC Interpretation is superseded.

Net investment in a foreign operation

BC25A   The principle in paragraph 32 is that exchange differences arising on a monetary item that is, in substance, part of the reporting entity's net investment in a foreign operation are initially recognised in a separate component of equity[7] in the consolidated financial statements of the reporting entity. Among the revisions to IAS 21 made in 2003 was the provision of guidance on this principle that required the monetary item to be denominated in the functional currency of either the reporting entity or the foreign operation. The previous version of IAS 21 did not include such guidance.

BC25B   The requirements can be illustrated by the following example. Parent P owns 100 per cent of Subsidiary S. Parent P has a functional currency of UK sterling. Subsidiary S has a functional currency of Mexican pesos. Parent P grants a loan of 100 US dollars to Subsidiary S, for which settlement is neither planned nor likely to occur in the foreseeable future. IAS 21 (as revised in 2003) requires the exchange differences arising on the loan to be recognised in profit or loss in the consolidated financial statements of Parent P, whereas those differences would be recognised initially in equity in the consolidated financial statements of Parent P, if the loan were to be denominated in sterling or Mexican pesos.

---

5   IAS 21 (revised 1993), paragraph 21.

6   The reference is to the IASC's *Framework for the Preparation and Presentation of Financial Statements*, adopted by the Board in 2001 and in effect when the Standard was revised.

7   As a consequence of the revision of IAS 1 *Presentation of Financial Statements* in 2007 such differences are recognised in other comprehensive income.

BC25C   After the revised IAS 21 was issued in 2003, constituents raised the following concerns:

(a)   It is common practice for a monetary item that forms part of an entity's investment in a foreign operation to be denominated in a currency that is not the functional currency of either the reporting entity or the foreign operation. An example is a monetary item denominated in a currency that is more readily convertible than the local domestic currency of the foreign operation.

(b)   An investment in a foreign operation denominated in a currency that is not the functional currency of the reporting entity or the foreign operation does not expose the group to a greater foreign currency exchange difference than arises when the investment is denominated in the functional currency of the reporting entity or the foreign operation. It simply results in exchange differences arising in the foreign operation's individual financial statements and the reporting entity's separate financial statements.

(c)   It is not clear whether the term 'reporting entity' in paragraph 32 should be interpreted as the single entity or the group comprising a parent and all its subsidiaries. As a result, constituents questioned whether the monetary item must be transacted between the foreign operation and the reporting entity, or whether it could be transacted between the foreign operation and any member of the consolidated group, ie the reporting entity or any of its subsidiaries.

BC25D   The Board noted that the nature of the monetary item referred to in paragraph 15 is similar to an equity investment in a foreign operation, ie settlement of the monetary item is neither planned nor likely to occur in the foreseeable future. Therefore, the principle in paragraph 32 to recognise exchange differences arising on a monetary item initially in a separate component of equity effectively results in the monetary item being accounted for in the same way as an equity investment in the foreign operation when consolidated financial statements are prepared. The Board concluded that the accounting treatment in the consolidated financial statements should not be dependent on the currency in which the monetary item is denominated, nor on which entity within the group conducts the transaction with the foreign operation.

BC25E   Accordingly, in 2005 the Board decided to amend IAS 21. The amendment requires exchange differences arising on a monetary item that forms part of a reporting entity's net investment in a foreign operation to be recognised initially in a separate component of equity in the consolidated financial statements. This requirement applies irrespective of the currency of the monetary item and of whether the monetary item results from a transaction with the reporting entity or any of its subsidiaries.

BC25F   The Board also proposed amending IAS 21 to clarify that an investment in a foreign operation made by an associate of the reporting entity is not part of the reporting entity's net investment in that foreign operation. Respondents to the exposure draft disagreed with this proposal. Many respondents said that the proposed amendment added a detailed rule that was not required because the principle in paragraph 15 was clear. In redeliberations, the Board agreed with those comments and decided not to proceed with that proposed amendment.

Goodwill and fair value adjustments

BC26   The previous version of IAS 21 allowed a choice of translating goodwill and fair value adjustments to assets and liabilities that arise on the acquisition of a foreign entity at (a) the closing rate or (b) the historical transaction rate.

BC27   The Board agreed that, conceptually, the correct treatment depends on whether goodwill and fair value adjustments are part of:

(a)   the assets and liabilities of the acquired entity (which would imply translating them at the closing rate); or

(b)   the assets and liabilities of the parent (which would imply translating them at the historical rate).

BC28   The Board agreed that fair value adjustments clearly relate to the identifiable assets and liabilities of the acquired entity and should therefore be translated at the closing rate.

BC29   Goodwill is more complex, partly because it is measured as a residual. In addition, the Board noted that difficult issues can arise when the acquired entity comprises businesses that have different functional currencies (eg if the acquired entity is a multinational group). The Board discussed how to assess any resulting goodwill for impairment and, in particular, whether the goodwill would need to be 'pushed down' to the level of each different functional currency or could be accounted for and assessed at a higher level.

BC30   One view is that when the parent acquires a multinational operation comprising businesses with many different functional currencies, any goodwill may be treated as an asset of the parent/acquirer and tested for impairment at a consolidated level. Those who support this view believe that, in economic terms, the goodwill is an asset of the parent because it is part of the acquisition price paid by the parent. Thus, they believe, it would be incorrect to allocate the goodwill to the many acquired businesses and translate it into their various functional currencies. Rather, the goodwill, being treated as an asset of the parent, is not exposed to foreign currency risks, and translation differences associated with it should not be recognised. In addition, they believe that such goodwill should be tested for impairment at a consolidated level. Under this view, allocating or 'pushing down' the goodwill to a lower level, such as each different functional currency within the acquired foreign operation, would not serve any purpose.

BC31   Others take a different view. They believe that the goodwill is part of the parent's net investment in the acquired entity. In their view, goodwill should be treated no differently from other assets of the acquired entity, in particular intangible assets, because a significant part of the goodwill is likely to comprise intangible assets that do not qualify for separate recognition. They also note that goodwill arises only because of the investment in the foreign entity and has no existence apart from that entity. Lastly, they point out that when the acquired entity comprises a number of businesses with different functional currencies, the cash flows that support the continued recognition of goodwill are generated in those different functional currencies.

BC32 The Board was persuaded by the reasons set out in the preceding paragraph and decided that goodwill is treated as an asset of the foreign operation and translated at the closing rate. Consequently, goodwill should be allocated to the level of each functional currency of the acquired foreign operation. This means that the level to which goodwill is allocated for foreign currency translation purposes may be different from the level at which the goodwill is tested for impairment. Entities follow the requirements in IAS 36 *Impairment of Assets* to determine the level at which goodwill is tested for impairment.

Disposal or partial disposal of a foreign operation[8]

BC33 In the second phase of the business combinations project the Board decided that the loss of control, significant influence or joint control of an entity is accounted for as a disposal for the purposes of IAS 21. Accordingly, a former parent accounts for the loss of control over a subsidiary as a disposal of the subsidiary, even if the former subsidiary becomes an associate or jointly controlled entity[9] of the former parent. Similarly an investor accounts for the loss of significant influence over an associate or the loss of joint control over a jointly controlled entity as a disposal. The Board decided that the change in the nature of the investment is a significant economic event.

BC34 The Board also decided in the second phase of the business combinations project that:

(a) changes in the parent's ownership interest in a subsidiary that do not result in a loss of control are accounted for as equity transactions (ie transactions with owners in their capacity as owners);

(b) if a parent loses control of a subsidiary, the parent reclassifies from equity to profit or loss (as a reclassification adjustment) the parent's share of the exchange differences recognised in other comprehensive income relating to a foreign operation in that subsidiary; and

(c) if an investor loses significant influence over an associate or loses joint control over a jointly controlled entity, the investor reclassifies from equity to profit or loss (as a reclassification adjustment) the exchange differences recognised in other comprehensive income relating to a foreign operation in that associate or jointly controlled entity.

---

8 This heading and paragraphs BC33 and BC34 were added as a consequence of amendments to IAS 27 *Consolidated and Separate Financial Statements* made as part of the second phase of the business combinations project in 2008. The consolidation requirements in IAS 27 were superseded by IFRS 10 *Consolidated Financial Statements* issued in May 2011. The accounting requirements did not change.

9 'Jointly controlled entities' were defined in IAS 31 *Interests in Joint Ventures*. IFRS 11 *Joint Arrangements*, issued in May 2011, replaced IAS 31 and changed the terminology.

The amendments in paragraphs 48A–49 of the Standard reflect those decisions for the disposal or partial disposal of a foreign operation.

BC35   As part of *Cost of an Investment in a Subsidiary, Jointly Controlled Entity or Associate* (Amendments to IFRS 1 *First-time Adoption of International Financial Reporting Standards* and IAS 27 *Consolidated and Separate Financial Statements*), issued in May 2008 the Board amended IAS 27 to remove the definition of the 'cost method'. The cost method required an entity to recognise distributions as income only if they came from post-acquisition retained earnings. Distributions received in excess of such profits were regarded as a recovery of the investment and were recognised as a reduction of its cost. Consequently, the Board amended paragraph 49 to remove the reference to pre-acquisition profits and to clarify that a dividend accounted for in accordance with paragraph 38A of IAS 27 cannot be a disposal or partial disposal of a net investment in IAS 21.[10]

Disposal or partial disposal of a foreign operation (amendment 2011)

BC36   During its redeliberation of the exposure draft ED 9 *Joint Arrangements*, the Board reconsidered whether its decision in the second phase of the business combinations project to characterise loss of joint control or loss of significant influence as a significant economic event (ie in the same way that loss of control is characterised as a significant economic event) was appropriate. If it were, the Board thought that the entity should be required to recalibrate the accounting as required by IFRS 10 *Consolidated Financial Statements*. However, the Board concluded that, although significant, the events are fundamentally different. In the case of loss of control, the cessation of the parent-subsidiary relationship results in the derecognition of assets and liabilities because the composition of the group changes. If joint control or significant influence is lost the composition of the group is unaffected.

BC37   The Board also noted that retaining the characterisation of significant economic event in the case of loss of joint control or significant influence when the retained interest is a financial asset is unnecessary. IFRS 9 already requires that in such cases the retained interest (ie a financial asset) must be measured at fair value.

BC38   In the case of loss of joint control when significant influence is maintained, the Board acknowledged that the investor-investee relationship changes and, consequently, so does the nature of the investment. However, in this instance, both investments (ie the joint venture and the associate) continue to be measured using the equity method. Considering that there is neither a change in the group boundaries nor a change in the measurement requirements, the Board concluded that losing joint control and retaining significant influence is not an event that warrants remeasurement of the retained interest at fair value.

---

10 The consolidation guidance was removed from IAS 27 and the Standard was renamed *Separate Financial Statements* by IFRS 10 *Consolidated Financial Statements* issued in May 2011. The accounting requirements for dividends were not changed.

BC39   Consequently, the Board removed all descriptions that characterise loss of joint control or significant influence as a significant economic event as introduced in the second phase of the Board's project on business combinations.

BC40   The Board also decided to align the conclusions reached on the loss of joint control when significant influence is maintained with the requirements in IAS 21 so that the change from joint control to significant influence is treated as a 'partial' disposal rather than deemed to be an 'entire' disposal. As a consequence, the Board concluded that when an entity loses joint control of a joint arrangement that includes a foreign operation but retains significant influence, an entity reclassifies to profit or loss only the proportionate share of the cumulative amount of the exchange differences recognised in other comprehensive income relating to a foreign operation in that joint arrangement.

IASB documents published to accompany

IAS 23

Borrowing Costs

The text of the unaccompanied standard, IAS 23, is contained in Part A of this edition. Its effective date when issued was 1 January 2009. The text of the Accompanying Guidance on IAS 23 is contained in Part B of this edition. This part presents the following documents:

BASIS FOR CONCLUSIONS

APPENDIX TO THE BASIS FOR CONCLUSIONS

Amendments to Basis for Conclusions on other pronouncements

DISSENTING OPINIONS

Basis for Conclusions on IAS 23 *Borrowing Costs*

This Basis for Conclusions accompanies, but is not part of, IAS 23.

Introduction

BC1   This Basis for Conclusions summarises the International Accounting Standards Board's considerations in reaching its conclusions on revising IAS 23 *Borrowing Costs* in 2007. Individual Board members gave greater weight to some factors than to others.

BC2   The revisions to IAS 23 result from the Board's Short-term Convergence project. The project is being conducted jointly with the United States standard-setter, the Financial Accounting Standards Board (FASB). The objective of the project is to reduce differences between IFRSs and US generally accepted accounting principles (GAAP) that are capable of resolution in a relatively short time and can be addressed outside major projects. The revisions to IAS 23 are principally concerned with the elimination of one of the two treatments that exist for borrowing costs directly attributable to the acquisition, construction or production of a qualifying asset. The application of only one method will enhance comparability. For the reasons set out below, the Board decided to eliminate the option of immediate recognition of such borrowing costs as an expense. It believes this will result in an improvement in financial reporting as well as achieving convergence in principle with US GAAP.

BC3   The Board considered whether to seek convergence on the detailed requirements for the capitalisation of borrowing costs directly attributable to the acquisition, construction or production of a qualifying asset. However, the Board noted statements by the US Securities and Exchange Commission (SEC) and the European Commission that the IASB and FASB should focus their short-term convergence effort on eliminating major differences of principle between IFRSs and US GAAP. For their purposes, convergence on the detailed aspects of accounting treatments is not necessary. The Board further noted that both IAS 23 and SFAS 34 *Capitalization of Interest Cost* were developed some years ago. Consequently, neither set of specific provisions may be regarded as being of a clearly higher quality than the other. Therefore, the Board concluded that it should not spend time and resources considering aspects of IAS 23 beyond the choice between capitalisation and immediate recognition as an expense. This Basis for Conclusions does not, therefore, discuss aspects of IAS 23 that the Board did not reconsider. Paragraphs BC19–BC26 analyse the differences between IAS 23 and SFAS 34.

Amendments to the scope

Assets measured at fair value

BC4   The exposure draft of proposed amendments to IAS 23 proposed excluding from the scope of IAS 23 assets measured at fair value. Some respondents objected to the proposal, interpreting the scope exclusion as limiting capitalisation of borrowing costs to qualifying assets measured at cost. The Board confirmed its decision not to require capitalisation of borrowing costs relating to assets that are measured at fair value. The measurement of such assets will not be affected by the amount of borrowing costs incurred during their construction or production period. Therefore, requirements on how to account for borrowing costs are unnecessary, as paragraphs B61 and B62 of the Basis for Conclusions on IAS 41 *Agriculture* explain. But the Board noted that the exclusion of assets measured at fair value from the requirements of IAS 23 does not prohibit an entity from presenting items in profit or loss as if borrowing costs had been capitalised on such assets before measuring them at fair value.

Inventories that are manufactured, or otherwise produced, in large quantities on a repetitive basis

BC5   The US standard, SFAS 34, requires an entity to recognise as an expense interest costs for inventories that are routinely manufactured or otherwise produced in large quantities on a repetitive basis because, in the FASB's view, the informational benefit from capitalising interest costs does not justify the cost. The exposure draft did not make an exception for borrowing costs relating to such inventories. The exposure draft, therefore, proposed to require an entity to capitalise borrowing costs relating to inventories that are manufactured in large quantities on a repetitive basis and take a substantial period of time to get ready for sale. Respondents argued that capitalising those borrowing costs would create a significant administrative burden, would not be informative to users and would create a reconciling item between IFRSs and US GAAP.

BC6   The Board decided to exclude from the scope of IAS 23 inventories that are manufactured, or otherwise produced, in large quantities on a repetitive basis, even if they take a substantial period of time to get ready for sale. The Board acknowledges the difficulty in both allocating borrowing costs to inventories that are manufactured in large quantities on a repetitive basis and monitoring those borrowing costs until the inventory is sold. It concluded that it should not require an entity to capitalise borrowing costs on such inventories because the costs of capitalisation are likely to exceed the potential benefits.

Elimination of the option of immediate recognition as an expense of borrowing costs directly attributable to the acquisition, construction or production of a qualifying asset

BC7 The previous version of IAS 23 permitted two treatments for accounting for borrowing costs that are directly attributable to the acquisition, construction or production of a qualifying asset. They could be capitalised or, alternatively, recognised immediately as an expense. SFAS 34 requires the capitalisation of such borrowing costs.

BC8 The Board proposed in the exposure draft to eliminate the option of immediate recognition as an expense. Many respondents disagreed with the Board's proposal in the exposure draft, arguing that:

 (a) borrowing costs should not be the subject of a short-term convergence project.

 (b) the Board had not explored in sufficient detail the merits of both accounting options.

 (c) the proposal did not result in benefits for users of financial statements because:

  (i) it addressed only one of the differences between IAS 23 and SFAS 34.

  (ii) comparability would not be enhanced because the capital structure of an entity could affect the cost of an asset.

  (iii) credit analysts reverse capitalised borrowing costs when calculating coverage ratios.

 (d) the costs of implementing the capitalisation model in IAS 23 would be burdensome.

 (e) the proposal was not consistent with the Board's approach on other projects (in particular, the second phase of the Business Combinations project).

BC9 The Board concluded that borrowing costs that are directly attributable to the acquisition, construction or production of a qualifying asset are part of the cost of that asset. During the period when an asset is under development, the expenditures for the resources used must be financed. Financing has a cost. The cost of the asset should include all costs necessarily incurred to get the asset ready for its intended use or sale, including the cost incurred in financing the expenditures as a part of the asset's acquisition cost. The Board reasoned that recognising immediately as an expense borrowing costs relating to qualifying assets does not give a faithful representation of the cost of the asset.

BC10 The Board confirmed that the objective of the project is not to achieve full convergence on all aspects of accounting for borrowing costs. Rather, it is to reduce differences between IFRSs and US GAAP that are capable of resolution in a relatively short time. The removal of a choice of accounting treatment and convergence in principle with US GAAP will enhance comparability. The Board acknowledges that capitalising borrowing costs does not achieve comparability between assets that are financed with borrowings and those financed with equity. However, it achieves comparability among all non-equity financed assets, which is an improvement.

BC11 A requirement to recognise immediately as an expense borrowing costs relating to qualifying assets would not enhance comparability. Rather, comparability between assets that are internally developed and those acquired from third parties would be impaired. The purchase price of a completed asset purchased from a third party would include financing costs incurred by the third party during the development phase.

BC12 Respondents to the exposure draft argued that requiring the capitalisation of borrowing costs is not consistent with the Board's proposal in the second phase of the Business Combinations project to require an entity to treat as an expense acquisition costs relating to a business combination. The Board disagrees with those respondents. Acquisition costs as defined in the context of a business combination are different from borrowing costs incurred in constructing or producing a qualifying asset. Borrowing costs are part of the cost necessarily incurred to get the asset ready for its intended use or sale. Acquisition costs relating to a business combination are costs incurred for services performed to help with the acquisition, such as due diligence and professional fees. They are not costs of assets acquired in a business combination.

BC13 The Board concluded that the additional benefits in terms of higher comparability, improvements in financial reporting and achieving convergence in principle with US GAAP exceed any additional costs of implementation. Achieving convergence in principle with US GAAP on this topic is a milestone in the Memorandum of Understanding published by the FASB and IASB in February 2006, which is a step towards removal of the requirement imposed on foreign registrants with the SEC to reconcile their financial statements to US GAAP.

BC14 The Board observes that there is an unavoidable cost of complying with any new financial reporting standard. Accordingly, the Board carefully considers the costs and benefits of any new pronouncement. In this case, the Board has not been told that preparers who elected to capitalise borrowing costs under the previous version of IAS 23 found doing so unnecessarily burdensome. In the Board's judgement, any additional costs of capitalising an item of cost of an asset are offset by the advantage of having all entities account for that item in the same way.

Borrowing costs eligible for capitalisation (amendments issued in December 2017)

BC14A When determining the funds that an entity borrows generally, paragraph 14 of IAS 23 required an entity to exclude borrowings made specifically for the purpose of obtaining a qualifying asset. The Board was asked whether an entity includes borrowings made specifically to obtain a qualifying asset in general borrowings when that qualifying asset is ready for its intended use or sale.

BC14B   The Board concluded that the reference to 'borrowings made specifically for the purpose of obtaining a qualifying asset' in paragraph 14 should not apply to a borrowing originally made specifically to obtain a qualifying asset if that qualifying asset is now ready for its intended use or sale.

BC14C   The Board observed that paragraph 8 requires an entity to capitalise borrowing costs directly attributable to the acquisition, construction or production of a qualifying asset as part of the cost of that asset. Paragraph 10 states that borrowing costs are directly attributable to a qualifying asset if those borrowing costs would have been avoided had the expenditure on the qualifying asset not been made. In other words, an entity could have repaid that borrowing if the expenditure on the qualifying asset had not been made. Accordingly, paragraph 14 requires an entity to use all outstanding borrowings in determining the capitalisation rate, except those made specifically to obtain a qualifying asset not yet ready for its intended use or sale.

BC14D   The Board concluded that if a specific borrowing remains outstanding after the related qualifying asset is ready for its intended use or sale, it becomes part of the funds an entity borrows generally. Accordingly, the Board amended paragraph 14 to clarify this requirement.

BC14E   Some respondents to the exposure draft of the proposed amendments to IAS 23 asked the Board to clarify that an entity includes funds borrowed specifically to obtain an asset other than a qualifying asset as part of general borrowings. The amendments to paragraph 14 referring to 'all' borrowings clarify the requirements in this respect.

Effective date and transition

BC15   Development of a qualifying asset may take a long time. Additionally, some assets currently in use may have undergone and completed their production or construction process many years ago. If the entity has been following the accounting policy of immediately recognising borrowing costs as an expense, the costs of gathering the information required to capitalise them retrospectively and to adjust the carrying amount of the asset may exceed the potential benefits. Hence, the Board decided to require prospective application, which was supported by respondents to the exposure draft.

BC16   The Board noted that the revisions would result in information that is more comparable between entities. On that basis, if an entity wished to apply the revised Standard from any date before the effective date, users of the entity's financial statements would receive more useful and comparable information than previously.

BC17   Therefore, an entity is permitted to apply the revised Standard from any designated date before the effective date. However, if an entity applies the Standard from such an earlier date, it should apply the Standard to all qualifying assets for which the commencement date for capitalisation is on or after that designated date.

BC18   The Board recognises that the Standard may require an entity that reconciles its IFRS financial statements to US GAAP to maintain two sets of capitalisation information—one set that complies with the requirements of IAS 23 and one that complies with the requirements of SFAS 34. The Board wishes to avoid imposing on such entities the need to maintain two sets of capitalisation information. Therefore, before the effective date, the Board will consider what actions it might take to avoid this outcome.

Borrowing costs eligible for capitalisation (amendments issued in December 2017)

BC18A   Developing a qualifying asset may take a long time. Moreover, the development of some assets currently in use may have been completed many years ago. The costs of gathering the information required to capitalise borrowing costs retrospectively may therefore be significant. In addition, the nature of each development generally varies and therefore retrospective application might not provide useful trend information to users of financial statements. The Board concluded that the costs of applying the amendments retrospectively might exceed the potential benefits of doing so. Consequently, an entity applies the amendments only to borrowing costs incurred on or after the date it first applies the amendments.

Differences between IAS 23 and SFAS 34

BC19   The following paragraphs summarise the main differences between IAS 23 and SFAS 34.

Definition of borrowing costs

BC20   IAS 23 uses the term 'borrowing costs' whereas SFAS 34 uses the term 'interest costs'. 'Borrowing costs' reflects the broader definition in IAS 23, which encompasses interest and other costs, such as:

(a)   exchange differences arising from foreign currency borrowings to the extent that they are regarded as an adjustment to interest costs;. [1]and

(b)   amortisation of ancillary costs incurred in connection with the arrangement of borrowings.

---

1   In 2007 the Board was advised that some of the components of borrowing costs in paragraph 6 are broadly equivalent to the components of interest expense calculated using the effective interest method in accordance with IAS 39 *Financial Instruments: Recognition and Measurement*. Consequently, the Board amended paragraph 6 to refer to the relevant guidance in IAS 39 when describing the components of borrowing costs. Subsequently, IFRS 9 *Financial Instruments* replaced IAS 39. IFRS 9 applies to all items that were previously within the scope of IAS 39.

BC21   EITF Issue No. 99–9 concludes that derivative gains and losses (arising from the effective portion of a derivative instrument that qualifies as a fair value hedge) are part of the capitalised interest cost. IAS 23 does not address such derivative gains and losses.

Definition of a qualifying asset

BC22   The main differences are as follows:

(a)   IAS 23 defines a qualifying asset as one that takes a substantial period of time to get ready for its intended use or sale. The SFAS 34 definition does not include the term *substantial*.

(b)   IAS 23 excludes from its scope qualifying assets that are measured at fair value. SFAS 34 does not address assets measured at fair value.

(c)   SFAS 34 includes as qualifying assets investments in investees accounted for using the equity method, in some circumstances.[2] Such investments are not qualifying assets according to IAS 23.

(d)   SFAS 34 does not permit the capitalisation of interest costs on assets acquired with gifts or grants that are restricted by the donor or grantor in some situations. IAS 23 does not address such assets.

Measurement

BC23   When an entity borrows funds specifically for the purpose of obtaining a qualifying asset:

(a)   IAS 23 requires an entity to capitalise the actual borrowing costs incurred on that borrowing. SFAS 34 states that an entity may use the rate of that borrowing.

(b)   IAS 23 requires an entity to deduct any income earned on the temporary investment of actual borrowings from the amount of borrowing costs to be capitalised. SFAS 34 does not generally permit this deduction, unless particular tax-exempt borrowings are involved.

BC24   SFAS 34 requires an entity to use judgement in determining the capitalisation rate to apply to the expenditures on the asset—an entity selects the borrowings that it considers appropriate to meet the objective of capitalising the interest costs incurred that otherwise could have been avoided. When an entity borrows funds generally and uses them to obtain a qualifying asset, IAS 23 permits some flexibility in determining the capitalisation rate, but requires an entity to use all outstanding borrowings other than those made specifically to obtain a qualifying asset.

---

2   While the investee has activities in progress necessary to commence its planned principal operations provided that the investee's activities include the use of funds to acquire qualifying assets for its operations.

         © IFRS Foundation

Disclosure requirements

BC25   IAS 23 requires disclosure of the capitalisation rate used to determine the amount of borrowing costs eligible for capitalisation. SFAS 34 does not require this disclosure.

BC26   SFAS 34 requires disclosure of the total amount of interest cost incurred during the period, including the amount capitalised and the amount recognised as an expense. IAS 23 requires disclosure only of the amount of borrowing costs capitalised during the period. IAS 1 *Presentation of Financial Statements* requires the disclosure of finance costs for the period.

BC27   [Deleted]

Appendix
Amendments to Basis for Conclusions on other pronouncements

This appendix contains amendments to the Basis for Conclusions on other pronouncements that are necessary in order to ensure consistency with the revised IAS 23.

* * * * *

The amendments contained in this appendix when IAS 23 was issued in 2007 have been incorporated into the text of the Basis for Conclusions on IFRS 1 and IFRICs 1 and 12.

Dissenting opinions

Dissent of Anthony T Cope, Philippe Danjou and Robert P Garnett

DO1   The Board's decision to require the capitalisation of borrowing costs relating to qualifying assets will cause a significant change in accounting for the many preparers that currently apply the benchmark treatment of recognising borrowing costs as an expense. Messrs Cope, Danjou and Garnett believe that such a change will require the establishment of cumbersome measurement processes and monitoring of capitalised costs over a long period. This is likely to involve considerable accounting work and incremental auditing costs.

DO2   Users of financial statements responding to the exposure draft did not support the change because they saw no informational benefit in a model that capitalises costs, other than the capitalisation of the actual economic cost of capital of the investment. In addition, Messrs Cope, Danjou and Garnett believe that a standard requiring the capitalisation of borrowing costs should discuss more extensively which assets qualify for the purpose of capitalising which borrowing costs.

DO3   As a consequence, Messrs Cope, Danjou and Garnett dissent because, in their view, the costs of this particular change will far outweigh the benefits to users.

DO4   In addition, this requirement to capitalise borrowing costs will achieve only limited convergence with US GAAP—differences will remain that could lead to materially different capitalised amounts. Furthermore, entities that are required to reconcile net income and shareholders' equity to US GAAP already have the option to capitalise borrowing costs and, thus, may recognise amounts that are more comparable to, albeit still potentially materially different from, those recognised in accordance with US GAAP.

DO5   The Memorandum of Understanding published by the FASB and the IASB states that trying to eliminate differences between standards that are both in need of significant improvement is not the best use of resources. Messrs Cope, Danjou and Garnett support the convergence work programme, but only if it results in higher quality standards and improved financial reporting. They are of the opinion that IAS 23 and SFAS 34 are both in need of significant improvement and should not have been addressed as part of short-term convergence.

IASB documents published to accompany

IAS 24

Related Party Disclosures

The text of the unaccompanied standard, IAS 24, is contained in Part A of this edition. Its effective date when issued was 1 January 2011. The text of the Accompanying Guidance on IAS 24 is contained in Part B of this edition. This part presents the following documents:

BASIS FOR CONCLUSIONS

APPENDIX TO THE BASIS FOR CONCLUSIONS

Amendment to the Basis for Conclusions on IAS 19 *Employee Benefits*

DISSENTING OPINION

Basis for Conclusions on
IAS 24 *Related Party Disclosures*

This Basis for Conclusions accompanies, but is not part of, IAS 24.

Introduction

BC1   This Basis for Conclusions summarises the International Accounting Standards Board's considerations in reaching its conclusions on revising IAS 24 *Related Party Disclosures* in 2003 and 2009. Individual Board members gave greater weight to some factors than to others.

BC2   In July 2001 the Board announced that, as part of its initial agenda of technical projects, it would undertake a project to improve a number of standards, including IAS 24. The project was undertaken in the light of queries and criticisms raised in relation to the standards by securities regulators, professional accountants and other interested parties. The objectives of the Improvements project were to reduce or eliminate alternatives, redundancies and conflicts within existing standards, to deal with some convergence issues and to make other improvements. In May 2002 the Board published its proposals in an exposure draft of *Improvements to International Accounting Standards* (the 2002 ED), with a comment deadline of 16 September 2002. The Board received over 160 comment letters on the exposure draft. After reviewing the responses, the Board issued a revised version of IAS 24 in December 2003.

BC3   In February 2007 the Board published an exposure draft *State-controlled Entities and the Definition of a Related Party* (the 2007 ED), proposing:

(a)   an exemption from the disclosure requirements in IAS 24 for transactions between entities that are controlled, jointly controlled or significantly influenced by a state ('state-controlled entities'[1]); and

(b)   amendments to the definition of a related party.

BC4   The Board received 72 comment letters on the 2007 ED. After considering those comments, in December 2008 the Board published revised proposals in an exposure draft *Relationships with the State* (the 2008 ED). The 2008 ED:

(a)   presented revised proposals for state-controlled entities; and

(b)   proposed one further amendment to the definition of a related party.

BC5   The Board received 75 comment letters on the 2008 ED. After reviewing the responses, the Board issued a revised version of IAS 24 in November 2009.

BC6   Because the Board's intention was not to reconsider the fundamental approach to related party disclosures established by IAS 24, this Basis for Conclusions discusses only the following requirements in IAS 24:

(a)   management compensation (paragraphs BC7–BC10);

---

1   In finalising the revised version of IAS 24 in 2009, the Board replaced the term 'state' with 'government'.

(b)   related party disclosures in separate financial statements (paragraphs BC11–BC17);

(c)   definition of a related party (paragraphs BC18–BC32);

(d)   government-related entities (paragraphs BC33–BC48); and

(e)   other minor changes made in 2009 (paragraph BC49).

Management compensation

BC7   The version of IAS 24 issued by the Board's predecessor in 1984 had no exemption for the disclosure of key management personnel compensation. In developing the 2002 ED, the Board proposed that the disclosure of management compensation, expense allowances and similar items paid in the ordinary course of business should not be required because:

(a)   the approval processes for key management personnel compensation in some jurisdictions remove the rationale for related party disclosures;

(b)   privacy issues arise in some jurisdictions where accountability mechanisms other than disclosure in financial statements exist; and

(c)   requiring these disclosures placed weight on the determination of 'key management personnel' and 'compensation', which was likely to prove contentious. In addition, comparability of these disclosures would be unlikely until measurement requirements are developed for all forms of compensation.

BC8   However, some respondents to the 2002 ED objected to the proposed exemption because they were concerned that information relating to management compensation is relevant to users' information needs and that an exemption based on 'items paid in the ordinary course of business' could lead to abuse. Establishing a disclosure exemption on such a criterion without a definition of the terms could lead to exempting other transactions with management from being disclosed, because they could all be structured as 'compensation paid in the ordinary course of an entity's operations'. Respondents argued that such an exemption could lead to abuse because it could potentially apply to any transactions with management.

BC9   The Board was persuaded by the respondents' views on the 2002 ED and decided that the Standard should require disclosure of key management personnel compensation because:

(a)   the principle underpinning the requirements in IAS 24 is that transactions with related parties should be disclosed, and key management personnel are related parties of an entity.

(b)   key management personnel compensation is relevant to decisions made by users of financial statements when it represents a material amount. The structure and amount of compensation are major drivers in the implementation of the business strategy.

(c)   the benefit of this information to users of financial statements largely outweighs the potential lack of comparability arising from the absence of recognition and measurement requirements for all forms of compensation.

BC10   The Board believes that although some jurisdictions have processes for approving compensation for key management personnel in an attempt to ensure an arm's length result, it is clear that some jurisdictions do not. Furthermore, although approval processes for management compensation may involve other parties such as shareholders or investors, key management personnel may still have a significant input. In addition, the Board noted that disclosing key management personnel compensation would improve transparency and comparability, thereby enabling users of financial statements to make a better assessment of the impact of such compensation on the entity's financial position and profit or loss. The Board also noted that the definition of key management personnel and the guidance on compensation in IAS 19 *Employee Benefits* are sufficient to enable entities to disclose the relevant information.

Related party disclosures in separate financial statements

BC11   The version of IAS 24 issued by the Board's predecessor in 1984 exempted disclosures about related party transactions in:

(a)   parents' financial statements when they are made available or published with the consolidated statements; and

(b)   financial statements of a wholly-owned subsidiary if its parent is incorporated in the same country and provides consolidated financial statements in that country.

BC12   In the 2002 ED the Board proposed to continue exempting separate financial statements of parents and financial statements of wholly-owned subsidiaries from disclosures about any related parties in specified circumstances. It proposed that disclosure of related party transactions and outstanding balances in the separate financial statements of a parent or the financial statements of a wholly-owned subsidiary would not be required, but only if those statements were made available or published with consolidated financial statements for the group.

BC13   The Board proposed to retain this exemption so that entities that are required by law to produce financial statements available for public use in accordance with International Financial Reporting Standards (IFRSs) in addition to the group's consolidated financial statements would not be unduly burdened. The Board noted that in some circumstances, users can find sufficient information for their purposes regarding a subsidiary from either its financial statements or the group's consolidated financial statements. In addition, the users of financial statements of a subsidiary often have, or can obtain access to, more information. The Board also noted that users should be aware that amounts recognised in the financial statements of a wholly-owned subsidiary can be affected significantly by the subsidiary's relationship with its parent.

BC14   However, respondents to the 2002 ED objected to this exemption, on the grounds that disclosure of related party transactions and outstanding balances is essential information for external users, who need to be aware of the level of support provided by related parties. The respondents also argued that financial statements prepared in accordance with IFRSs could be presented on a stand-alone basis. Therefore, financial statements prepared on the basis of this proposed exemption would not achieve a fair presentation without related party disclosures.

BC15   The Board was persuaded by those arguments and decided to require the disclosure of related party transactions and outstanding balances in separate financial statements of a parent, investor or venturer in addition to the disclosure requirements in IAS 27 *Consolidated and Separate Financial Statements*,[2] IAS 28 *Investments in Associates*[3] and IAS 31 *Interests in Joint Ventures*.[4]

BC16   The Board noted that the financial statements of an entity that is part of a consolidated group may include the effects of extensive intragroup transactions. Indeed, potentially all of the revenues and expenses for such an entity may derive from related party transactions. The Board concluded that the disclosures required by IAS 24 are essential to understanding the financial position and financial performance of such an entity and therefore should be required for separate financial statements presented in accordance with IAS 27.

BC17   The Board also believed that disclosure of such transactions is essential because the external users need to be aware of the interrelationships between related parties, including the level of support provided by related parties, to assist external users in their economic decisions.

Definition of a related party

BC18   The definition of a related party in IAS 24 was widely considered to be too complex and difficult to apply in practice. The Board noted that the existing definition of a related party had weaknesses: it was cumbersome and included several cross-references that made it difficult to read (and to translate). Therefore, the 2007 and 2008 EDs proposed revised definitions.

BC19   In revising the definition, the Board adopted the following approach:

   (a)   When an entity assesses whether two parties are related, it would treat significant influence as equivalent to the relationship that exists between an entity and a member of its key management personnel. However, those relationships are not as close as a relationship of control or joint control.

---

2   The consolidation guidance was removed from IAS 27 and the Standard was renamed *Separate Financial Statements* by IFRS 10 *Consolidated Financial Statements* issued in May 2011. The accounting requirements for separate financial statements were not changed.

3   In May 2011, the Board amended IAS 28 and changed its title to *Investments in Associates and Joint Ventures*.

4   IFRS 11 *Joint Arrangements*, issued in May 2011, replaced IAS 31.

(b)   If two entities are both subject to control (or joint control) by the same entity or person, the two entities are related to each other.

(c)   If one entity (or person) controls (or jointly controls) a second entity and the first entity (or person) has significant influence over a third entity, the second and third entities are related to each other.

(d)   Conversely, if two entities are both subject to significant influence by the same entity (or person), the two entities are not related to each other.

(e)   If the revised definition treats one party as related to a second party, the definition should also treat the second party as related to the first party, by symmetry.

BC20   The new definition was not intended to change the meaning of a related party except in the three respects detailed in paragraphs BC21–BC26. The 2008 ED proposed other amendments to the definition for one additional case that had been inadvertently omitted from the 2007 ED and the elimination of further inconsistencies (paragraphs BC27–BC29). In finalising the amendments in 2009, the Board also removed the term 'significant voting power' from the definition of a related party (paragraphs BC30 and BC31).

An associate of a subsidiary's controlling investor

BC21   First, the Board considered the relationship between an associate and a subsidiary of an investor that has significant influence over the associate. The Board observed that when an associate prepares individual or separate financial statements, its investor is a related party. If the investor has a subsidiary, that subsidiary is also related to the associate, because the subsidiary is part of the group that has significant influence over the associate. Although the definition in the 2003 version of IAS 24 incorporated such relationships, the Board concluded that the revised definition should state this more clearly.

BC22   In contrast, when a subsidiary prepares individual or separate financial statements, an associate of the subsidiary's controlling investor was not a related party as defined in the 2003 version of IAS 24. The subsidiary does not have significant influence over the associate, nor is it significantly influenced by the associate.

BC23   However, the Board decided that, for the same reasons that the parties described in paragraph BC21 are related, the parties described in paragraph BC22 are also related. Thus, the Board amended the definition of a related party to include the relationship discussed in paragraph BC22.

BC24   Furthermore, the Board decided that in the situations described in paragraphs BC21 and BC22, if the investor is a person who has significant influence over one entity and control or joint control over another entity, sufficient influence exists to warrant concluding that the two entities are related.

Two associates of a person

BC25 Secondly, the Board considered the relationship between associates of the investor. IAS 24 does not define associates as related to each other if the investor is an entity. This is because there is insufficient influence through the common investment in two associates. However, the Board noted a discrepancy in that if a person significantly influences one entity and a close member of that person's family significantly influences another entity, those entities were treated as related parties of each other. The Board amended the definition to exclude the entities described in the latter scenario, thereby ensuring a consistent treatment of associates.

Investments of members of key management personnel

BC26 Thirdly, IAS 24 treats some investees of the key management personnel of a reporting entity as related to that entity. However, the definition in the 2003 version of IAS 24 did not include the reciprocal of this—ie for the financial statements of the investee, the other entity managed by the key management personnel was not a related party. To eliminate this inconsistency, the Board amended the definition so that for both sets of financial statements the entities are related parties.

Joint control

BC27 Respondents to the 2007 ED pointed out that one case had been excluded from the restructured definition without being explicitly stated as a change to IAS 24. When a person has joint control over a reporting entity and a close member of that person's family has joint control or significant influence over the other entity, the 2003 version of IAS 24 defined the other entity as related to the reporting entity.

BC28 The Board noted that joint control is generally regarded as influence that is stronger than significant influence. Therefore, the Board concluded that the relationship described in paragraph BC27 should continue to be treated as a related party relationship.

BC29 The definition in the 2003 version of IAS 24 did not include the reciprocal of the case described in paragraph BC27, nor did it deal with cases when a person or a third entity has joint control or significant influence over the two entities. The definition proposed in the 2007 ED would not have rectified these omissions. The Board decided to include these cases in the definition, to treat similar relationships in a consistent manner. In summary, whenever a person or entity has both joint control over a second entity and joint control or significant influence over a third entity, the amendments described in this paragraph and paragraph BC27 treat the second and third entities as related to each other.

Removal of 'significant voting power'

BC30 Respondents to the 2007 and 2008 EDs raised concerns about the term 'significant voting power' in the definition of a related party. They identified anomalies in its use such as when significant voting power created a related party relationship only when that power is held by individuals, not when that power is held by an entity. A further anomaly arose because two entities were classified as related to each other when a third person was a member of the key management personnel of one and had significant voting power in the other; however, they were not treated as related when a third person had significant voting power in both entities.

BC31 In response to these comments, the Board deleted the reference to 'significant voting power' because it was undefined, used inconsistently and created unnecessary complexity. The Board concluded that if the effect of 'significant voting power' was considered to be the same as 'significant influence', its deletion would have no effect because 'significant influence' is in the definition. On the other hand, if the effect of 'significant voting power' was considered to be different from that of 'significant influence', IAS 24 did not explain what that difference was.

Other minor changes to the definition of a related party

BC32 The revisions to IAS 24 in 2009 included the following other minor changes:

(a) The definition of a **related party** is amended:

(i) to replace references to 'individual' with 'person';

(ii) to clarify that an associate includes subsidiaries of an associate and a joint venture includes subsidiaries of the joint venture; and

(iii) to clarify that two entities are not related parties simply because a member of key management personnel of one entity has significant influence over the other entity.

(b) The definition of a **close member of the family** is amended:

(i) to replace references to 'individual' with 'person'; and

(ii) to delete 'may' from the list of examples to state that close members of a person's family include (rather than 'may include') that person's spouse or domestic partner and children.

Government-related entities

Exemption (paragraph 25)

BC33 The version of IAS 24 that preceded its revision in 2003 did not require 'state-controlled' entities to disclose transactions with other such entities. The revised version of IAS 24 issued in 2003 omitted this exemption because at the time the Board concluded that the disclosure requirements would not be a burden for those entities.

BC34   Subsequently concerns were raised that in environments where government control is pervasive, compliance with IAS 24 was problematic. To address those concerns, the 2007 ED proposed an exemption from the disclosure requirements now in paragraph 18 of IAS 24 for government-related entities. In developing that proposal, the Board noted the following:

    (a)   It can be difficult to identify other government-related entities, particularly in jurisdictions with a large number of such entities. Such entities might not even be aware that an entity with which they have transactions is a related party.

    (b)   For these transactions, the cost of meeting the requirements in IAS 24 was not always offset by the benefit of increased information for users of financial statements. More specifically:

        (i)   extensive disclosures were required for transactions that are unaffected by the relationship;

        (ii)   if some entities are not aware that their transactions are with other government-related entities, the disclosures provided would be incomplete; and

        (iii)   transactions that are affected by the relationship might well be obscured by excessive disclosures about unaffected transactions.

    (c)   Some governments establish subsidiaries, joint ventures and associates to compete with each other. In this case, transactions between such entities are likely to be conducted as if they are unrelated parties.

BC35   Respondents to the 2007 ED generally supported an exemption for government-related entities. However, they expressed concerns about the complexity of the specific proposal and asked the Board to clarify various aspects of it. After considering all comments received, the Board proposed a revised exemption for those entities in the 2008 ED.

BC36   Respondents to the 2008 ED generally supported the revised proposal, but some argued that the exemption should not apply to transactions:

    (a)   between members of a group that is controlled by a government (paragraph BC37); and

    (b)   between government-related entities that are related for a reason in addition to their relationship with the same government (paragraph BC38).

BC37   Some respondents reasoned that the exemption should not apply to transactions between members of a group that is controlled by a government, for example between a government-related entity and its parent or its fellow subsidiaries. Those respondents noted that the relationship within such a group might sometimes be closer and more influential than between government-related entities in an environment where government control is pervasive. However, for the following reasons the Board concluded that the exemption should also apply within such groups:

(a)   Sometimes, requiring disclosure in such cases would negate the purpose of the exemption and could lead to significant differences in the level of disclosure when the substance of the relationships and transactions could be very similar. For example, suppose one government controls all entities directly but another government has similar entities and controls them all through a single holding company. The entities controlled by the first government would all qualify for the exemption but those controlled by the second government would not.

(b)   Requiring disclosure in such cases would place considerable pressure on the definition of the boundary between government and entities controlled by the government. For example, suppose a government controls entities through an intermediate institution. It would be necessary to determine whether that institution is an entity controlled by the government (in which case the exemption would not apply) or part of the government (in which case the exemption would apply). This may be answered easily if the institution is a company incorporated under normal company law that simply happens to have the government as a controlling shareholder. It may be less clear if the institution is, for example, a government agency or department.

BC38   The Board identified only one case when government-related entities might be related to each other for reasons other than their relationships with the same government: a government might control both a post-employment benefit plan and the sponsoring employer. However, the main transactions between such a plan and the sponsoring employer are (a) employer contributions and (b) investments by the plan in the employer or in assets used by the employer. IAS 19 already requires a sponsoring employer to disclose most, if not all, of the information that IAS 24 would require if the exemption did not apply. Thus the Board concluded that no significant loss of disclosure would arise from applying the exemption in these cases.

BC39   Paragraph BC34 explains why the Board provided an exemption from the disclosure requirements in paragraph 18 of IAS 24 for government-related entities. It was beyond the scope of the project to consider whether similar exemptions would be appropriate in other circumstances.

BC40   Some respondents to the 2008 ED noted that many financial institutions had recently become government-related entities when governments took significant and sometimes controlling equity interests in them during the global financial crisis. They queried whether the exemption was appropriate in such cases. In finalising the amendments in 2009, the Board identified no reason to treat such entities differently from other government-related entities. The Board noted that in addition to the disclosure requirements in IAS 24, IAS 20 *Accounting for Government Grants and Disclosure of Government Assistance* requires the reporting entity to disclose information about the receipt of government grants or assistance.

BC41   Respondents to the 2008 ED noted that the proposed definition of 'state' was similar to the definition of 'government' in IAS 20. To avoid confusion and provide consistency, the Board adopted the latter definition when finalising the amendments to IAS 24 in 2009. The Board decided that it need not provide a more comprehensive definition or additional guidance on how to determine what is meant by 'government'. In the Board's view, a more detailed definition could not capture every conceivable government structure across every jurisdiction. In addition, judgement is required by the reporting entity when applying the definition because every jurisdiction has its own way of organising government-related activities.

Disclosure requirements when the exemption applies (paragraph 26)

BC42   The Board considered whether the disclosure requirements in paragraph 26:

(a)   met the objective of IAS 24 (paragraphs BC43–BC46); and

(b)   were operational (paragraphs BC47 and BC48).

BC43   The objective of IAS 24 is to provide 'disclosures necessary to draw attention to the possibility that [the entity's] financial position and profit or loss may have been affected by the existence of related parties and by transactions and outstanding balances, including commitments, with such parties.' To meet that objective, paragraph 26 requires some disclosure when the exemption applies. Those disclosures are intended to put users on notice that related party transactions have occurred and to give an indication of their extent. The Board did not intend to require the reporting entity to identify **every** government-related entity, or to quantify in detail **every** transaction with such entities, because such a requirement would negate the exemption.

BC44   Some respondents to the 2008 ED were concerned that qualitative disclosure of individually significant related party transactions alone would not meet the objective of IAS 24 and that combining individually significant transactions with collectively significant transactions would not provide sufficient transparency. The Board concluded that it should require an entity to disclose:

(a)   the nature and amount of each individually significant transaction; and

(b)   quantitative or qualitative information about other types of transactions that are collectively, but not individually, significant.

BC45   The Board noted that this requirement should not be too onerous for the reporting entity because:

(a)   individually significant transactions should be a small subset, by number, of total related party transactions;

(b)   the reporting entity should know what those transactions are; and

(c)   reporting such items on an exceptional basis takes into account cost-benefit considerations.

BC46   The Board also noted that more disclosure of individually significant transactions would better meet the objective of IAS 24 because this approach focuses on transactions that, through their nature or size, are of more interest to users and are more likely to be affected by the related party relationship.

BC47   Some respondents raised concerns about whether the reporting entity would be able to identify whether the counterparty to individually significant or collectively significant transactions is a related party because it is controlled, jointly controlled or significantly influenced by the same government. The problem of identifying all such counterparties was one of the primary reasons for the exemption.

BC48   However, as discussed in paragraph BC43, it was not the Board's intention to require the reporting entity to identify every government-related entity, or to quantify every transaction with such entities. Moreover, individually significant transactions are likely to attract more scrutiny by management. The Board concluded that management will know, or will apply more effort in establishing, who the counterparty to an individually significant transaction is and will have, or be able to obtain, background information on the counterparty.

Other minor changes made in 2009

BC49   The revisions to IAS 24 in 2009 included the following other changes:

(a)   The list of examples of **related party transactions** is amended to include in paragraph 21(i) commitments to do something if a particular event occurs or does not occur in the future, including executory contracts. The Board concluded that commitments were one type of transaction, but to avoid doubt decided to make explicit reference to them.

(b)   Paragraph 3 relating to the **scope** of IAS 24 is amended to clarify that the Standard applies to individual, as well as separate and consolidated, financial statements because individual financial statements relate to something different from the defined term in IAS 27.[5]

(c)   Paragraph 34 of IFRS 8 *Operating Segments* is amended. The Board recognised that in applying the requirements in IFRS 8 it may not be practicable or meaningful to regard all government-related entities as a single customer, especially for environments in which government control is pervasive.

(d)   A consequential amendment to the Basis for Conclusions on IAS 19 draws attention to the new definition of a related party. The definition of a qualifying insurance policy in IAS 19 refers to this definition.

---

5   The consolidation guidance was removed from IAS 27 and the Standard was renamed *Separate Financial Statements* by IFRS 10 *Consolidated Financial Statements* issued in May 2011. The definition of separate financial statements was not changed.

Key management personnel

BC50   The Board was asked to address the identification and disclosure of related party transactions that arise when a management entity provides key management personnel services to a reporting entity. The Board understood that divergence existed because some reporting entities do not identify this as a related party transaction. Of those who do identify this as a related party transaction, some reporting entities would disclose the compensation paid by the management entity to those employees or directors of the management entity that act as key management personnel of the reporting entity. Other reporting entities would disclose the service fee that is paid or payable to the management entity, which is incurred by the reporting entity.

BC51   The Board noted that IAS 24 is unclear as to what information to disclose for key management personnel when those persons are not employees of the reporting entity. To address the diversity in disclosures that has arisen from IAS 24 being unclear, the Board decided to amend the definition of 'related party'. The amendment clarified that a management entity that provides key management services to a reporting entity is deemed to be a related party of the reporting entity. In discussing these proposals, the Board acknowledged that the relationship between the management entity and the reporting entity is not symmetrical. The reporting entity is not a related party of the management entity solely as a consequence of being a customer of the management entity. The reporting entity cannot affect the management entity's activities, financial position or profit except through some other relationship. Consequently, the reporting entity is required to disclose the amount incurred for the service fee paid or payable to the management entity that employs, or has as directors, the persons that provide the key management personnel services. As a result of identifying the management entity as a related party of the reporting entity, the Board noted that the reporting entity is also required to disclose other transactions with the management entity, for example, loans, under the existing disclosure requirements of IAS 24 with respect to related parties.

BC52   The Board was informed of concerns that it is impracticable to access the detailed information that is required in paragraph 17 when compensation is paid to a separate management entity as fees. The Board therefore decided to provide relief so that the reporting entity is not required to disclose the components of compensation to key management personnel that is paid through another entity. Instead, amounts incurred in respect of key management personnel compensation or key management personnel services, paid or payable to another entity, shall be disclosed in accordance with paragraph 18A.

Appendix
Amendment to the Basis for Conclusions on IAS 19 *Employee Benefits*

This Appendix contains an amendment to the Basis for Conclusions on IAS 19 that is necessary in order to ensure consistency with IAS 24.

* * * * *

The amendment contained in this appendix when IAS 24 (as revised) was issued in 2009 has been incorporated into the Basis for Conclusions on IAS 19 published in this volume.

Dissenting opinion

Dissent of Robert P Garnett

DO1   Mr Garnett disagrees with the Board's decision to exempt only government-related entities from the requirements of paragraph 18 to disclose information about all transactions with related parties. He also disagrees with the decision not to require all entities to provide information about each individually significant transaction with a related party as set out in paragraph 26(b)(i).

DO2   The Basis for Conclusions sets out clearly the need to remove the unnecessary burden of collecting data for all transactions, entered into and priced on normal business terms, because the counterparty was identified as a related party. It also explains the need to inform investors of individually significant transactions with related parties. Mr Garnett agrees with the explanations in paragraphs BC33–BC48.

DO3   Paragraph 25, however, restricts these changes to entities that are controlled, jointly controlled or significantly influenced by the same government. Mr Garnett sees no reason to make such a distinction, other than to provide limited relief to certain entities.

IASB documents published to accompany

IAS 27

Separate Financial Statements

The text of the unaccompanied standard, IAS 27, is contained in Part A of this edition. Its effective date when issued was 1 January 2013. The text of the Accompanying Guidance on IAS 27 is contained in Part B of this edition. This part presents the following documents:

BASIS FOR CONCLUSIONS

DISSENTING OPINION

Basis for Conclusions on
IAS 27 *Separate Financial Statements*

This Basis for Conclusions accompanies, but is not part of, IAS 27.

Introduction

BC1　This Basis for Conclusions summarises the International Accounting Standards Board's considerations in reaching its conclusions on issuing IAS 27 *Consolidated and Separate Financial Statements* in 2003, and amending IAS 27 in 2008 and again in 2011. Individual Board members gave greater weight to some factors than to others. Unless otherwise noted, references below to IAS 27 are to previous versions of the Standard.

BC2　The amendment of IAS 27 in 2011 resulted from the Board's project on consolidation. A new IFRS, IFRS 10 *Consolidated Financial Statements*, addresses the principle of control and requirements relating to the preparation of consolidated financial statements. As a result, IAS 27 now contains requirements relating only to separate financial statements. This change is reflected in the Standard's amended title, *Separate Financial Statements*.

BC3　In approving the publication of IFRS 10 in 2011, the Board also approved consequential amendments to IAS 27 that removed from the Standard all requirements relating to consolidated financial statements.

BC4　At the same time, the Board relocated to IAS 27 requirements from IAS 28 *Investments in Associates* and IAS 31 *Interests in Joint Ventures* regarding separate financial statements. Those requirements are in paragraphs 6–8 of the Standard. Given the extent of the material that has been removed or relocated, the Board decided, for clarity, to renumber the paragraphs in the amended IAS 27. The definitions and wording in the Standard were also updated to be consistent with the requirements in IFRS 10, IFRS 11 *Joint Arrangements*, IFRS 12 *Disclosure of Interests in Other Entities*, and IAS 28 *Investments in Associates and Joint Ventures*.

BC5　When issued in 2003, IAS 27 was accompanied by a Basis for Conclusions summarising the considerations of the Board, as constituted at the time, in reaching its conclusions. The Basis for Conclusions was subsequently updated to reflect amendments to the Standard.

BC6　This Basis for Conclusions now includes only the Board's considerations on separate financial statements. Cross-references have been updated accordingly and minor necessary editorial changes have been made. The paragraphs discussing consolidated financial statements have been relocated to the Basis for Conclusions on IFRS 10 as appropriate.

Consolidation exemption available for non-public entities

BC7   The Board decided that a parent that meets the criteria in paragraph 4(a) of IFRS 10 for exemption from the requirement to prepare consolidated financial statements should, in its separate financial statements, account for those subsidiaries in the same way as other parents, joint venturers with interests in joint ventures or investors in associates account for investments in their separate financial statements. The Board draws a distinction between accounting for such investments as equity investments and accounting for the economic entity that the parent controls. In relation to the former, the Board decided that each category of investment should be accounted for consistently.

BC8   The Board decided that the same approach to accounting for investments in separate financial statements should apply irrespective of the circumstances for which they are prepared. Thus, a parent that presents consolidated financial statements, and a parent that does not because it is exempted, should present the same form of separate financial statements.

Investment entities

BC8A   *Investment Entities* (Amendments to IFRS 10, IFRS 12 and IAS 27), issued in October 2012, introduced an exception to the principle in IFRS 10 that all subsidiaries shall be consolidated. The amendments define an investment entity and require a parent that is an investment entity to measure its investments in particular subsidiaries at fair value through profit or loss in accordance with IFRS 9 *Financial Instruments* (or IAS 39 *Financial Instruments: Recognition and Measurement*,[1] if IFRS 9 has not yet been adopted) instead of consolidating those subsidiaries. Consequently, the Board decided to amend IAS 27 to require an investment entity to also measure its investments in subsidiaries at fair value through profit or loss in its separate financial statements. The Board also made corresponding amendments to the disclosure requirements for an investment entity's separate financial statements, noting that if an investment entity prepares separate financial statements as its only financial statements, it is still appropriate for the investment entity to make the disclosures otherwise required in IFRS 12 about its interests in subsidiaries.

---

1   IFRS 9 *Financial Instruments* replaced IAS 39. IFRS 9 applies to all items that were previously within the scope of IAS 39.

Measurement of investments in subsidiaries, joint ventures and associates in separate financial statements

2003 revision

BC9   IAS 27 (as revised by the Board's predecessor body in 2000) permitted entities to measure investments in subsidiaries in any one of three ways in the parent's separate financial statements. These were at cost, using the equity method, or as available-for-sale[2] financial assets in accordance with IAS 39 *Financial Instruments: Recognition and Measurement*.[3] IAS 28 *Investments in Associates* permitted the same choices for investments in associates in separate financial statements, and IAS 31 *Interests in Joint Ventures* stated that IAS 31 did not indicate a preference for any particular treatment for accounting for interests in joint ventures in a joint venturer's separate financial statements. However, in 2003 the Board decided to require the use of cost or IAS 39 for all investments included in separate financial statements and to remove the equity method as one of the measurement options.

BC10   Although the equity method would provide users with some profit or loss information similar to that obtained from consolidation, the Board noted that such information is reflected in the investor's consolidated or individual financial statements and does not need to be provided to the users of its separate financial statements. For separate financial statements, the focus is upon the performance of the assets as investments. The Board concluded that separate financial statements prepared using either the fair value method in accordance with IAS 39[4] or the cost method would be relevant. Using the fair value method in accordance with IAS 39 would provide a measure of the economic value of the investments. Using the cost method can result in relevant information, depending on the purpose of preparing the separate financial statements. For example, they may be needed only by particular parties to determine the dividend income from subsidiaries.

Equity method in separate financial statements (amendments issued in 2014)

BC10A   In their responses to the Board's 2011 Agenda Consultation, some respondents said that:

(a)   the laws of some countries require listed companies to present separate financial statements prepared in accordance with local regulations, and those local regulations require the use of the equity method to account for investments in subsidiaries, joint ventures and associates; and

---

2   IFRS 9 *Financial Instruments* eliminated the category of available-for-sale financial assets.

3   IFRS 9 *Financial Instruments* replaced IAS 39. IFRS 9 applies to all items that were previously within the scope of IAS 39.

4   In May 2011 the Board issued IFRS 13 *Fair Value Measurement*, which contains requirements for measuring fair value.

(b) in most cases, the use of the equity method would be the only difference between the separate financial statements prepared in accordance with IFRS and those prepared in accordance with local regulations.

BC10B Those respondents strongly supported the inclusion of the equity method as one of the options for measuring investments in subsidiaries, joint ventures and associates in the separate financial statements of an entity. In May 2012, the Board decided to consider restoring the option to use the equity method in separate financial statements through a narrow-scope project. Consequently, the Board issued an Exposure Draft in December 2013, the proposals in which would facilitate convergence of local GAAP in those jurisdictions with IFRS for separate financial statements, and that would help to reduce compliance costs for some entities without the loss of information.

Definition of separate financial statements

BC10C Some respondents to the Exposure Draft commented that the proposed amendments to paragraphs 4 and 6 of IAS 27 create an inconsistency in the definition of 'separate financial statements', especially for an investor that has investments in associates or joint ventures and no investments in subsidiaries. The financial statements of such an investor in which the investments in joint ventures and associates are accounted for using the equity method would be the investor's primary financial statements as well as its separate financial statements. Consequently, they assert that there could be confusion about the applicability of the disclosure requirements in IAS 27 and IFRS 12. IFRS 12 does not apply to an entity's separate financial statements.

BC10D The Board noted that the financial statements of an investor that has no investments in subsidiaries, and has investments in associates or joint ventures that are required by IAS 28 to be accounted for using the equity method, are not separate financial statements. Consequently, in those financial statements, such an investor is required to comply with the disclosure requirements in IFRS 12. As a logical consequence, such an investor is less likely to prepare separate financial statements in which investments in associates or joint ventures are accounted for using the equity method. If such an investor presents separate financial statements, the Board expects that the investor is likely to account for its investments in associates or joint ventures either at cost or in accordance with IFRS 9.

BC10E The Board also noted that an investor that is exempted in accordance with paragraph 17 of IAS 28 from applying the equity method to its investments in joint ventures and associates may elect to present separate financial statements in which the investor elects to account for those investments using the equity method. In those separate financial statements, the investor is not required to present the information required by IFRS 12 for its investments in joint ventures and associates (see paragraph 6(b) of IFRS 12).

Application of the equity method

BC10F   IAS 28 contains guidance on the application of the equity method. IAS 28 notes that many of the procedures that are appropriate for the application of the equity method are similar to the consolidation procedures described in IFRS 10 (see paragraph 26 of IAS 28).

BC10G   In general, the application of the equity method to investments in subsidiaries, joint ventures and associates in the separate financial statements of an entity is expected to result in the same net assets and profit or loss attributable to the owners as in the entity's consolidated financial statements. However, there could be situations in which applying the equity method in separate financial statements to investments in subsidiaries would give a different result compared to the consolidated financial statements. Some of those situations are:

(a)   *impairment testing requirements in IAS 28.* For an investment in a subsidiary accounted for in separate financial statements using the equity method, goodwill that forms part of the carrying amount of the investment in the subsidiary is not tested for impairment separately. Instead, the entire carrying amount of the investment in the subsidiary is tested for impairment in accordance with IAS 36 *Impairment of Assets* as a single asset. However, in the consolidated financial statements of the entity, because goodwill is recognised separately, it is tested for impairment by applying the requirements in IAS 36 for testing goodwill for impairment.

(b)   *subsidiary that has a net liability position.* IAS 28 requires an investor to discontinue recognising its share of further losses when its cumulative share of losses of the investee equals or exceeds its interest in the investee, unless the investor has incurred legal or constructive obligations or made payments on behalf of the investee, in which case a liability is recognised, whereas there is no such requirement in relation to the consolidated financial statements.

(c)   *capitalisation of borrowing costs incurred by a parent in relation to the assets of a subsidiary.* IAS 23 *Borrowing Costs* notes that, in some circumstances, it may be appropriate to include all borrowings of the parent and its subsidiaries when computing a weighted average of the borrowing costs. When a parent borrows funds and its subsidiary uses them for the purpose of obtaining a qualifying asset, in the consolidated financial statements of the parent the borrowing costs incurred by the parent are considered to be directly attributable to the acquisition of the subsidiary's qualifying asset. However, this would not be appropriate in the separate financial statements of the parent if the parent's investment in the subsidiary is a financial asset, which is not a qualifying asset.

Some respondents to the Exposure Draft asked the Board to consider providing additional guidance to align the carrying amount of a subsidiary in the parent's separate financial statements with the net assets of the subsidiary that are attributable to the parent in the parent's consolidated financial statements. The Board concluded that creating any additional guidance within IAS 28 to eliminate such differences was outside the scope of this project. The Board was concerned that the development of such guidance would not be possible without adequate research and analysis, which would delay the amendments. Consequently, the Board decided not to consider these requests.

BC10H   Some respondents to the Exposure Draft commented that IAS 28 should be amended to provide guidance on the application of the equity method to a subsidiary in the separate financial statements of the parent. The Board concluded that amending IAS 28 to provide such guidance was outside the scope of the project, and a parent that has elected to apply the equity method to account for its subsidiaries in its separate financial statements should follow the methodology in IAS 28 as applicable to an associate or a joint venture.

2008 amendments

BC11   As part of its annual improvements project begun in 2007, the Board identified an apparent inconsistency with IFRS 5 *Non-current Assets Held For Sale and Discontinued Operations*. The inconsistency related to the accounting by a parent in its separate financial statements when investments it accounts for in accordance with IAS 39 are classified as held for sale in accordance with IFRS 5. Paragraph 10 requires an entity that prepares separate financial statements to account for such investments that are classified as held for sale (or included in a disposal group that is classified as held for sale) in accordance with IFRS 5 if they are measured at cost. However, financial assets that an entity accounts for in accordance with IAS 39 are excluded from IFRS 5's measurement requirements.

BC12   Paragraph BC13 of the Basis for Conclusions on IFRS 5 explains that the Board decided that non-current assets should be excluded from the measurement scope of IFRS 5 only 'if (i) they are already carried at fair value with changes in fair value recognised in profit or loss or (ii) there would be difficulties in determining their fair value less costs to sell.'[5] The Board acknowledged in the Basis for Conclusions on IFRS 5 that not all financial assets within the scope of IAS 39 are recognised at fair value with changes in fair value recognised in profit or loss, but it did not want to make any further changes to the accounting for financial assets at that time.

BC13   Therefore, the Board amended paragraph 10 by *Improvements to IFRSs* issued in May 2008 to align the accounting in separate financial statements for those investments that are accounted for in accordance with IAS 39 with the measurement exclusion that IFRS 5 provides for other assets that are accounted for in accordance with IAS 39 before classification as held for sale. Thus, an entity should continue to account for such investments in accordance with IAS 39 when they meet the held for sale criteria in IFRS 5.

---

5   In May 2011 the Board issued IFRS 13 *Fair Value Measurement*, which contains requirements for measuring fair value.

Dividend received from a subsidiary, a joint venture or an associate

BC14   Before *Cost of an Investment in a Subsidiary, Jointly Controlled Entity or Associate* was issued in May 2008, IAS 27 described a 'cost method'. This required an entity to recognise distributions as income only if they came from post-acquisition retained earnings. Distributions received in excess of such retained earnings were regarded as a recovery of investment and were recognised as a reduction in the cost of the investment. To apply that method retrospectively upon first-time adoption of IFRSs in its separate financial statements, an investor would need to know the subsidiary's pre-acquisition retained earnings in accordance with IFRSs.

BC15   Restating pre-acquisition retained earnings would be a task tantamount to restating the business combination (for which IFRS 1 *First-time Adoption of International Financial Reporting Standards* provides an exemption in Appendix C). It might involve subjective use of hindsight, which would diminish the relevance and reliability of the information. In some cases, the restatement would be time-consuming and difficult. In other cases, it would be impossible (because it would involve making judgements about the fair values of the assets and liabilities of a subsidiary at the acquisition date).

BC16   Therefore, in *Cost of an Investment in a Subsidiary*, an exposure draft of proposed amendments to IFRS 1 (published in January 2007), the Board proposed to give first-time adopters an exemption from restating the retained earnings of the subsidiary at the date of acquisition for the purpose of applying the cost method.

BC17   In considering the responses to that exposure draft, the Board observed that the principle underpinning the cost method is that a return of an investment should be deducted from the carrying amount of the investment. However, the wording in the previous version of IAS 27 created a problem in some jurisdictions because it made specific reference to retained earnings as the means of making that assessment. The Board decided that the best way to resolve this issue was to delete the definition of the cost method.

BC18   In removing the definition of the cost method, the Board concluded that an investor should recognise a dividend from a subsidiary, a joint venture or an associate as income in its separate financial statements. Consequently, the requirement to separate the retained earnings of an entity into pre-acquisition and post-acquisition components as a method for assessing whether a dividend is a recovery of its associated investment has been removed from IFRSs.

BC19   To reduce the risk that removing the definition of the cost method would lead to investments in subsidiaries, joint ventures and associates being overstated in the separate financial statements of the investor, the Board proposed that the related investment should be tested for impairment in accordance with IAS 36.

BC20   The Board published its revised proposals in *Cost of an Investment in a Subsidiary, Jointly Controlled Entity or Associate*, an exposure draft of proposed amendments to IFRS 1 and IAS 27, in December 2007. Respondents generally supported the proposed amendments to IAS 27, except for the proposal to require impairment testing of the related investment when an investor recognises a dividend. In the light of the comments received, the Board revised its proposal and identified specific indicators of impairment. This was done to narrow the circumstances in which impairment testing of the related investment would be required when an investor recognises a dividend (see paragraph 12(h) of IAS 36). The Board included the amendments in *Cost of an Investment in a Subsidiary, Jointly Controlled Entity or Associate* issued in May 2008.

Measurement of cost in the separate financial statements of a new parent

BC21   In 2007 the Board received enquiries about the application of paragraph 10(a) when a parent reorganises the structure of its group by establishing a new entity as its parent. The new parent obtains control of the original parent by issuing equity instruments in exchange for existing equity instruments of the original parent.

BC22   In this type of reorganisation, the assets and liabilities of the new group and the original group are the same immediately before and after the reorganisation. In addition, the owners of the original parent have the same relative and absolute interests in the net assets of the new group immediately after the reorganisation as they had in the net assets of the original group before the reorganisation. Finally, this type of reorganisation involves an existing entity and its shareholders agreeing to create a new parent between them. In contrast, many transactions or events that result in a parent-subsidiary relationship are initiated by a parent over an entity that will be positioned below it in the structure of the group.

BC23   Therefore, the Board decided that in applying paragraph 10(a) *in the limited circumstances in which a parent establishes a new parent in this particular manner*, the new parent should measure the cost of its investment in the original parent at the carrying amount of its share of the equity items shown in the separate financial statements of the original parent at the date of the reorganisation. In December 2007 the Board published an exposure draft proposing to amend IAS 27 to add a paragraph with that requirement.

BC24   In response to comments received from respondents to that exposure draft, the Board modified the drafting of the amendment (paragraphs 13 and 14) to clarify that it applies to the following types of reorganisations when they satisfy the criteria specified in the amendment:

(a)   reorganisations in which the new parent does not acquire all the equity instruments of the original parent. For example, a new parent might issue equity instruments in exchange for ordinary shares of the original parent, but not acquire the preference shares of the original parent. In addition, a new parent might obtain control of the original parent, but not acquire all the ordinary shares of the original parent.

(b)   the establishment of an intermediate parent within a group, as well as the establishment of a new ultimate parent of a group.

(c)   reorganisations in which an entity that is not a parent establishes a new entity as its parent.

BC25   In addition, the Board clarified that the amendment focuses on the measurement of one asset—the new parent's investment in the original parent in the new parent's separate financial statements. The amendment does not apply to the measurement of any other assets or liabilities in the separate financial statements of either the original parent or the new parent or in the consolidated financial statements.

BC26   The Board included the amendment in *Cost of an Investment in a Subsidiary, Jointly Controlled Entity or Associate* issued in May 2008.

BC27   The Board did not consider the accounting for other types of reorganisations or for common control transactions more broadly. Accordingly, paragraphs 13 and 14 apply only when the criteria in those paragraphs are satisfied. Therefore, the Board expects that entities would continue to account for transactions that do not satisfy the criteria in paragraphs 13 and 14 in accordance with their accounting policies for such transactions. The Board plans to consider the definition of common control and the accounting for business combinations under common control in a future project on common control transactions.

Disclosure (2011 amendments)

BC28   When IAS 27 was amended in 2011, the Board clarified the disclosures required by an entity preparing separate financial statements so that the entity would be required to disclose the principal place of business (and country of incorporation, if different) of significant investments in subsidiaries, joint ventures and associates and, if applicable, of the parent that prepares consolidated financial statements that comply with IFRSs. IAS 27 (as amended in 2008) had previously required the disclosure of the country of incorporation or residence of such entities. The clarification of the disclosure requirement is more consistent with those requirements in other IFRSs (eg IFRS 12 and IAS 1 *Presentation of Financial Statements*) that also require disclosure of the principal place of business and country of incorporation.

Effective date (2011 amendments)

BC29   The Board decided to align the effective date for the Standard with the effective date for IFRS 10, IFRS 11, IFRS 12 and IAS 28 (as amended in 2011). When making this decision, the Board noted that the five IFRSs all deal with the assessment of, and related accounting and disclosure requirements about, a reporting entity's special relationships with other entities (ie when the reporting entity has control or joint control of, or significant influence over, another entity). As a result, the Board concluded that applying IAS 27 without also applying the other four IFRSs could cause unwarranted confusion.

BC30   The Board usually sets an effective date of between twelve and eighteen months after issuing an IFRS. When deciding the effective date for the five IFRSs, the Board considered the following factors:

    (a)   the time that many countries require for translation and for introducing the mandatory requirements into law.

    (b)   the consolidation project was related to the global financial crisis that started in 2007 and was accelerated by the Board in response to urgent requests from the leaders of the G20, the Financial Stability Board, users of financial statements, regulators and others to improve the accounting and disclosure of an entity's 'off balance sheet' activities.

    (c)   the comments received from respondents to the Request for Views *Effective Date and Transition Methods* that was published in October 2010 regarding implementation costs, effective date and transition requirements of the IFRSs to be issued in 2011. Most respondents did not identify the consolidation and joint arrangements IFRSs as having a high impact in terms of the time and resources that their implementation would require. In addition, only a few respondents commented that the effective dates of those IFRSs should be aligned with those of the other IFRSs to be issued in 2011.

BC31   With these factors in mind, the Board decided to require entities to apply the five IFRSs for annual periods beginning on or after 1 January 2013.

BC32   Most respondents to the Request for Views supported early application of the IFRSs to be issued in 2011. Respondents stressed that early application was especially important for first-time adopters in 2011 and 2012. The Board was persuaded by these arguments and decided to permit early application of IAS 27 but only if an entity applies it in conjunction with the other IFRSs (ie IFRS 10, IFRS 11, IFRS 12 and IAS 28 (as amended in 2011)) to avoid a lack of comparability among financial statements, and for the reasons noted in paragraph BC29 that triggered the Board's decision to set the same effective date for all five IFRSs. Even though an entity should apply the five IFRSs at the same time, the Board noted that an entity should not be prevented from providing any information required by IFRS 12 early if by doing so users gained a better understanding of the entity's relationships with other entities.

Transition requirements (2014 amendments)

BC33   Some respondents to the Exposure Draft suggested that the Board should consider providing some form of relief to make the transition to accounting for investments in subsidiaries, joint ventures and associates using the equity method easier. However, the Board noted that an entity should be able to use the information that is used for consolidation of the subsidiary in its consolidated financial statements for applying the equity method to the investment in the subsidiary in its separate financial statements. Investments in associates and joint ventures (after applying the transition provisions of IFRS 11) are accounted for using the equity method in the consolidated financial statements, which means that an entity need not perform any additional procedures and can use the same information in its separate financial statements. The Board also noted that many entities would be able to draw on the information in the financial statements of its ultimate, or any intermediate, parent in order to calculate the carrying amount of its investment in a subsidiary, joint venture and associate on the initial application of these amendments. Furthermore, the application of the equity method in separate financial statements is optional and not mandatory. Consequently, the Board concluded that additional transition relief was not needed and that an entity that elects to use the equity method should be required to apply the amendments retrospectively in accordance with IAS 8.

Dissenting Opinion

Dissent of Mary E Barth and Philippe Danjou from *Cost of an Investment in a Subsidiary, Jointly Controlled Entity or Associate* (Amendments to IFRS 1 and IAS 27) issued in May 2008

Cross-references have been updated.

DO1 Professor Barth and Mr Danjou voted against the publication of *Cost of an Investment in a Subsidiary, Jointly Controlled Entity or Associate* (Amendments to IFRS 1 *First-time Adoption of International Financial Reporting Standards* and IAS 27 *Consolidated and Separate Financial Statements*). The reasons for their dissent are set out below.

DO2 These Board members disagree with the **requirement** in paragraphs 13 and 14 of IAS 27 that when a reorganisation satisfies the criteria specified in those paragraphs and the resulting new parent accounts for its investment in the original parent at cost in accordance with paragraph 10(a) of IAS 27, the new parent must measure the cost at the carrying amount of its share of the equity items shown in the separate financial statements of the original parent at the date of the reorganisation.

DO3 These Board members acknowledge that a new parent could choose to apply paragraph 10(b) of IAS 27 and account for its investment in the original parent in accordance with IAS 39 *Financial Instruments: Recognition and Measurement*.[6] However, the new parent then would be required to account for the investment in accordance with IAS 39 in subsequent periods and to account for all other investments in the same category in accordance with IAS 39.

DO4 These Board members also acknowledge, as outlined in paragraph BC23 of the Basis for Conclusions on IAS 27, that this type of reorganisation is different from other types of reorganisations in that the assets and liabilities of the new group and the original group are the same immediately before and after the reorganisation, as are the interests of the owners of the original parent in the net assets of those groups. Therefore, using the previous carrying amount to measure the cost of the new parent's investment in the original parent might be appropriate on the basis that the separate financial statements of the new parent would reflect its position as part of a pre-existing group.

DO5 However, these Board members believe that it is inappropriate to preclude a new parent from measuring the cost of its investment in the original parent at the fair value of the shares that it issues as part of the reorganisation. Separate financial statements are prepared to reflect the parent as a separate legal entity (ie not considering that the entity might be part of a group). Although such a reorganisation does not change the assets and liabilities of the group and therefore should have no accounting effect at the consolidated level, from the perspective of the new parent as a separate legal entity, its position has

---

6   IFRS 9 *Financial Instruments* replaced IAS 39. IFRS 9 applies to all items that previously were within the scope of IAS 39.

changed—it has issued shares and acquired an investment that it did not have previously. Also, in many jurisdictions, commercial law or corporate governance regulations require entities to measure new shares that they issue at the fair value of the consideration received for the shares.

DO6   These Board members believe that the appropriate measurement basis for the new parent's cost of its investment in the original parent depends on the Board's view of separate financial statements. The Board is or will be discussing related issues in the reporting entity phase of its *Conceptual Framework* project and in its project on common control transactions. Accordingly, these Board members believe that the Board should have permitted a new parent to measure the cost of its investment in the original parent either at the carrying amount of its share of the equity items shown in the separate financial statements of the original parent or at the fair value of the equity instruments that it issues until the Board discusses the related issues in its projects on reporting entity and common control transactions.

IASB documents published to accompany

IAS 28

Investments in Associates and Joint Ventures

The text of the unaccompanied standard, IAS 28, is contained in Part A of this edition. Its effective date when issued was 1 January 2013. The text of the Accompanying Guidance on IAS 28 is contained in Part B of this edition. This part presents the following documents:

BASIS FOR CONCLUSIONS

DISSENTING OPINIONS

CONTENTS

Basis for Conclusions on
IAS 28 *Investments in Associates and Joint Ventures*

This Basis for Conclusions accompanies, but is not part of, IAS 28.

Introduction

BC1 This Basis for Conclusions summarises the International Accounting Standards Board's considerations in reaching its conclusions on amending IAS 28 *Investments in Associates* in 2011. Individual Board members gave greater weight to some factors than to others.

BC2 The amendment of IAS 28 resulted from the Board's project on joint ventures. When discussing that project, the Board decided to incorporate the accounting for joint ventures into IAS 28 because the equity method is applicable to both joint ventures and associates.

BC3 As a result, the title of IAS 28 was changed to *Investments in Associates and Joint Ventures*. Because the Board's intention was not to reconsider the fundamental approach to the accounting for investments in associates established by IAS 28, the Board has incorporated into its Basis for Conclusions on IAS 28 material from the Basis for Conclusions on IAS 28 (as revised in 2003) that the Board has not reconsidered.

The structure of IAS 28 and the Board's deliberations

BC4 IAS 28 as amended in 2011 superseded IAS 28 (as revised in 2003 and amended in 2010). As stated in paragraph BC3, in amending IAS 28, the Board did not reconsider all the Standard's requirements. The requirements in paragraphs 5–11, 15, 22–23, 25–28 and 32–43 relate to the assessment of significant influence and to the equity method and its application, and paragraphs 12–14 relate to the accounting for potential voting rights. With the exception of the Board's decision to incorporate the accounting for joint ventures into IAS 28, those paragraphs were carried forward from IAS 28 and from the Guidance on Implementing IAS 27 *Consolidated and Separate Financial Statements*, IAS 28 *Investments in Associates* and IAS 31 *Interests in Joint Ventures* that was withdrawn when IFRS 10 *Consolidated Financial Statements*, IFRS 11 *Joint Arrangements* and IAS 28 (as amended in 2011) were issued. As a result, those paragraphs were not reconsidered by the Board.

BC5 When revised in 2003 IAS 28 was accompanied by a Basis for Conclusions summarising the considerations of the Board, as constituted at the time, in reaching its conclusions. That Basis for Conclusions was subsequently updated to reflect amendments to the Standard.

BC6 The Board has incorporated into its Basis for Conclusions on IAS 28 (as amended in 2011) material from the previous Basis for Conclusions because it discusses matters that the Board has not reconsidered. That material is contained in paragraphs denoted by numbers with the prefix BCZ. In those paragraphs cross-references have been updated accordingly and minor necessary editorial changes have been made.

BC7　　One Board member dissented from an amendment to IAS 28 issued in May 2008, which has been carried forward to IAS 28 (as amended in 2011). His dissenting opinion is also set out after this Basis for Conclusions.

BC8　　The requirements in paragraphs 2, 16–21, 24 and 29–31 relate to matters addressed within the joint ventures project that led to amendments to IAS 28. Paragraphs describing the Board's considerations in reaching its conclusions on IAS 28 are numbered with the prefix BC.

BC9　　As part of its project on consolidation, the Board is examining how an investment entity accounts for its interests in subsidiaries, joint ventures and associates. The outcome might affect how organisations such as venture capital organisations, or mutual funds, unit trusts and similar entities account for their interests in joint ventures and associates. The Board expects to publish later in 2011 an exposure draft on investment entities.[1,2]

Scope

BC10　　During its redeliberation of the exposure draft ED 9 *Joint Arrangements*, the Board reconsidered the scope exception of IAS 31 that had also been proposed in ED 9. The Board concluded that the scope exception in ED 9 for interests in joint ventures held by venture capital organisations, or mutual funds, unit trusts and similar entities, including investment-linked insurance funds, that are measured at fair value through profit or loss in accordance with IFRS 9 *Financial Instruments* is more appropriately characterised as a measurement exemption, and not as a scope exception.

BC11　　The Board observed that IAS 28 had a similar scope exception for investments in associates held by venture capital organisations, or mutual funds, unit trusts and similar entities, including investment-linked insurance funds, that are measured at fair value through profit or loss in accordance with IFRS 9.

BC12　　The Board observed that the scope exception in ED 9 and IAS 28 related not to the fact that these arrangements do not have the characteristics of joint arrangements or those investments are not associates, but to the fact that for investments held by venture capital organisations, or mutual funds, unit trusts and similar entities including investment-linked insurance funds, fair value measurement provides more useful information for users of the financial statements than would application of the equity method.

1　In October 2012 the Board issued *Investment Entities* (Amendments to IFRS 10, IFRS 12 and IAS 27), which required investment entities, as defined in IFRS 10 *Consolidated Financial Statements*, to measure their investments in subsidiaries, other than those providing investment-related services or activities, at fair value through profit or loss. The amendments did not introduce any new accounting requirements for investments in associates or joint ventures.

2　In December 2014, the IASB issued *Investment Entities: Applying the Consolidation Exception* (Amendments to IFRS 10, IFRS 12 and IAS 28). The amendments introduced relief to permit a non-investment entity investor in an associate or joint venture that is an investment entity to retain the fair value through profit or loss measurement applied by the associate or joint venture to its subsidiaries (see paragraphs BC46A–BC46G).

BC13   Accordingly, the Board decided to maintain the option that permits venture capital organisations, or mutual funds, unit trusts and similar entities including investment-linked insurance funds to measure their interests in joint ventures and associates at fair value through profit or loss in accordance with IFRS 9, but clarified that this is an exemption from the requirement to measure interests in joint ventures and associates using the equity method, rather than an exception to the scope of IAS 28 for the accounting for joint ventures and associates held by those entities.

BC14   As a result of that decision and of the decision to incorporate the accounting for joint ventures into IAS 28, the Board decided that IAS 28 should be applied to the accounting for investments held by all entities that have joint control of, or significant influence over, an investee.

Significant influence

Potential voting rights

BC15   In its deliberation of the amendments to IAS 28, the Board considered whether the requirements now in paragraphs 7–9 of IAS 28 regarding potential voting rights when assessing significant influence should be changed to be consistent with the requirements developed in the consolidation project.

BC16   The Board observed that the definition of significant influence in IAS 28 (ie 'the power to participate in the financial and operating policy decisions of the investee but is not control or joint control of those policies') was related to the definition of control as it was defined in IAS 27. The Board had not considered the definition of significant influence when it amended IAS 28 and concluded that it would not be appropriate to change one element of significant influence in isolation. Any such consideration should be done as part of a wider review of the accounting for associates.

Equity method

Long-term interests in associates and joint ventures

BC16A   The Board received a submission relating to long-term interests in an associate or joint venture that, in substance, form part of the net investment in the associate or joint venture (long-term interests). The submission asked whether long-term interests are within the scope of IFRS 9 and, if so, whether the impairment requirements in IFRS 9 apply to such long-term interests.

BC16B   In considering the submission, the Board and the IFRS Interpretations Committee discussed the accounting for long-term interests applying the requirements in IFRS 9 and IAS 28, without reconsidering those requirements. The submission was narrowly and clearly defined, and both bodies concluded they could respond to the submission most efficiently by considering only the submission received. Any reconsideration of the accounting for long-term interests could not be undertaken as a narrow-scope project and would be likely to involve reconsideration of the equity method, a topic included in the Board's pipeline of future research projects. Consequently, the Board limited the amendments to clarifying its intentions when it issued the requirements in IFRS 9 and IAS 28.

BC16C   The Board concluded that with respect to interests in an associate or joint venture, paragraph 2.1(a) of IFRS 9 excludes from the scope of IFRS 9 only interests to which the equity method is applied. Accordingly, the scope exclusion in that paragraph does not include long-term interests (as described in paragraph 38 of IAS 28). In reaching this conclusion, the Board noted that IAS 28 mentions long-term interests and the net investment, which includes long-term interests, only in the context of recognising losses of an associate or joint venture and impairment of the net investment in the associate or joint venture. IAS 28 does not specify requirements for other aspects of recognising or measuring long-term interests. Thus, long-term interests are not accounted for in accordance with IAS 28, as envisaged in paragraph 2.1(a) of IFRS 9. The Board also noted that paragraph 14 of IAS 28 states that 'IFRS 9 *Financial Instruments* does not apply to interests in associates and joint ventures that are accounted for using the equity method'.

BC16D   The Board clarified in paragraph 14A of IAS 28 that IFRS 9, including its impairment requirements, applies to long-term interests. The Board also deleted paragraph 41 as part of the amendments. That paragraph had merely reiterated requirements in IFRS 9, and had created confusion about the accounting for long-term interests.

BC16E   Respondents to the Board's Exposure Draft on long-term interests suggested that it further clarify how the requirements in IAS 28 and IFRS 9 apply to long-term interests because, in the respondents' view, the benefits of the amendments would be limited without such clarifications. Respondents also suggested including an illustrative example.

BC16F   In response, the Board clarified that an entity applies IFRS 9, rather than IAS 28, in accounting for long-term interests. Thus, when applying IFRS 9, it does not take account of any losses of the associate or joint venture, or any impairment losses on the net investment, recognised as adjustments to the net investment in the associate or joint venture applying IAS 28.

BC16G   In addition, at the same time it issued the amendments, the Board published an example that illustrates how entities apply the requirements in IAS 28 and IFRS 9 with respect to long-term interests.

Effective date and transition

BC16H   The Board proposed to align the effective date of the amendments with the effective date of IFRS 9—annual reporting periods beginning on or after 1 January 2018. Some respondents said an effective date of 1 January 2018 would not allow sufficient time to implement the amendments. In particular, the respondents mentioned entities in jurisdictions that have a translation or endorsement process for IFRS Standards.

BC16I   In the light of these concerns, the Board set an effective date of annual reporting periods beginning on or after 1 January 2019, with earlier application permitted. The Board noted that if an entity elects to apply the amendments when it first applies IFRS 9, then it would benefit from applying the transition requirements in IFRS 9 to long-term interests.

BC16J   Considering the effective date of 1 January 2019 and the requirement to apply the amendments retrospectively, the Board also provided transition requirements similar to those in IFRS 9 for entities that apply the amendments after they first apply IFRS 9. This is because retrospective application may not have been possible without the use of hindsight. When the Board developed IFRS 9, it provided transition requirements for scenarios in which it would have been impracticable for an entity to apply particular requirements retrospectively. Consequently, the Board provided similar transition requirements in the amendments to IAS 28 for long-term interests because the effect of the amendments might be that an entity applies IFRS 9 for the first time to those interests. Accordingly, for example, such an entity would assess its business model for such long-term interests based on the facts and circumstances that exist on the date it first applies the amendments (for example, 1 January 2019 for an entity applying the amendments from that date).

BC16K   The Board noted that at the date of initial application of the amendments an entity would be able to use these transition requirements only for long-term interests and not for other financial instruments to which the entity has already applied IFRS 9. Accordingly, for example, an entity is not permitted (or required) to reconsider any of its fair value option elections for financial instruments to which the entity has already applied IFRS 9.

BC16L   The Board also decided to provide relief from restating prior periods for entities electing, in accordance with IFRS 4 *Insurance Contracts*, to apply the temporary exemption from IFRS 9. The Board observed that the effect of the amendments for such entities might be that they apply IAS 39 for the first time to long-term interests.

Application of the equity method

Temporary joint control and significant influence (2003 revision)

BCZ17   In IFRS 5 *Non-current Assets Held for Sale and Discontinued Operations* the Board decided not to exempt an entity from applying the equity method for accounting for its investments in joint ventures and associates when joint control of, or significant influence over, an investee is intended to be temporary.

Severe long-term restrictions impairing ability to transfer funds to the investor (2003 revision)

BCZ18   The Board decided not to exempt an entity from applying the equity method for accounting for its investments in joint ventures or associates when severe long-term restrictions impaired a joint venture or an associate's ability to transfer funds to the investor. It did so because such circumstances may not preclude the entity's joint control of, or significant influence over, the joint venture or the associate. The Board decided that an entity should, when assessing its ability to exercise joint control of, or significant influence over, an investee, consider restrictions on the transfer of funds from the joint venture or from the associate to the entity. In themselves, such restrictions do not preclude the existence of joint control or significant influence.

Non-coterminous year-ends (2003 revision)

BCZ19   The exposure draft that preceded the revision of IAS 28 in 2003 proposed to limit to three months any difference between the reporting dates of an entity and its associate or its joint venture when applying the equity method. Some respondents to that exposure draft believed that it could be impracticable for the entity to prepare financial statements as of the same date when the date of the entity's financial statements and those of the associate or joint venture differ by more than three months. The Board noted that a three-month limit operates in several jurisdictions and it was concerned that a longer period, such as six months, would lead to the recognition of stale information. Therefore, it decided to retain the three-month limit.

Exemption from applying the equity method: subsidiary of an investment entity

BC19A   In December 2014, the Board amended IFRS 10 to confirm that the exemption from preparing consolidated financial statements set out in paragraph 4(a) of IFRS 10 is available to a parent entity that is a subsidiary of an investment entity. The Board also decided to amend paragraph 17 of IAS 28 for the same reasons. Paragraph 17 of IAS 28 uses the same criteria as paragraph 4(a) of IFRS 10 to provide an exemption from applying the equity method for entities that are subsidiaries and that hold interests in associates and joint ventures.

Exemption from applying the equity method: measuring an associate or joint venture at fair value (amendments issued in December 2016)

BC19B   When an investment in an associate or joint venture is held by, or is held indirectly through, a venture capital organisation, or a mutual fund, unit trust and similar entities including investment-linked insurance funds, the entity may elect, in accordance with paragraph 18 of IAS 28, to measure that investment at fair value through profit or loss. The Board received a request to clarify whether the entity is able to choose between applying the equity method or measuring the investment at fair value for each investment, or whether instead the entity applies the same accounting to all of its investments in associates and joint ventures.

BC19C   The Board noted that, before it was revised in 2011, IAS 28 *Investments in Associates* permitted a venture capital organisation, or a mutual fund, unit trust and similar entities to elect to measure investments in an associate at fair value through profit or loss separately for each associate. However, after the revision, it had become less clear whether such an election was still available to those entities. The Board noted that it did not consider changing these requirements when revising IAS 28 in 2011, and any lack of clarity that arose as a consequence of the amendments in 2011 was unintentional.

BC19D   Accordingly, in *Annual Improvements to IFRS Standards 2014–2016 Cycle*, the Board amended paragraph 18 of IAS 28 to clarify that a venture capital organisation, or a mutual fund, unit trust and similar entities may elect, at initial recognition, to measure investments in an associate or joint venture at fair value through profit or loss separately for each associate or joint venture.

BC19E   In addition, paragraph 36A of IAS 28 permits an entity that is not an investment entity to retain the fair value measurement applied by its associates and joint ventures (that are investment entities) when applying the equity method. The Board also decided to amend that paragraph to clarify that this choice is available, at initial recognition, for each investment entity associate or joint venture.

BC19F   Some respondents to the Board's proposals said that it was not clear whether, in its separate financial statements, a venture capital organisation or a mutual fund, unit trust and similar entities:

(a)   could choose to measure investments in an associate or joint venture at fair value through profit or loss for each associate or joint venture; or

(b)   would be required to measure all such investments at fair value through profit or loss, on the grounds that paragraph 10 of IAS 27 *Separate Financial Statements* requires the same accounting for each category of investments and paragraph 11 of IAS 27 requires investments measured at fair value in accordance with IAS 28 to be measured at fair value in separate financial statements. If this were to be the case, those respondents note that such an outcome would appear to be inconsistent with the objective of the amendments to IAS 28.

BC19G   The Board noted that 'category' is not defined in IFRS Standards, but is used in a number of Standards. For example, IFRS 7 *Financial Instruments: Disclosures* uses 'category' to refer to groupings of financial assets and financial liabilities that are measured in different ways—for example, financial assets measured at fair value through profit or loss is one category of financial asset and financial assets measured at amortised cost is another category of financial asset. The Board observed that paragraph 10 of IAS 27 should not be read to mean that, in all circumstances, all investments in associates are one 'category' of investment and all investments in joint ventures are one 'category' of investment. The issue raised by respondents arises only if the requirement in paragraph 10 of IAS 27 were to be interpreted in that way. An entity that elects to measure some associates or joint ventures at fair value through profit or loss in accordance with paragraph 18 of IAS 28 would retain that measurement basis for those associates and joint ventures in its separate financial statements, as required by paragraph 11 of IAS 27. The entity could then choose to measure its remaining associates and joint ventures either at cost, in accordance with IFRS 9 or using the equity method in accordance with paragraph 10 of IAS 27.

BC19H   In response to the Board's proposal to apply the amendments retrospectively, some respondents questioned whether the information needed would be available without the use of hindsight. Others suggested providing transition relief for entities that previously interpreted IAS 28 as requiring the same accounting for all investments in associates and joint ventures. They suggested that, when first applying the amendments, such entities should be allowed to elect to measure each existing investment either at fair value through profit or loss or using the equity method.

BC19I   The Board decided to retain retrospective application of the amendments because the amendments are expected to affect only a narrow population of entities, and such entities (being venture capital organisations, or mutual funds, unit trusts and similar entities) would typically be expected to have fair value information for their investments for management purposes. In addition, if the costs of applying the amendments retrospectively are considered excessive, an entity can choose not to change any of its previous decisions regarding measurement. This is because retrospective application of a choice of measurement for each associate or joint venture, in effect, means that an entity is not required to reassess its previous decisions. The Board also noted that retrospective application in accordance with IAS 8 *Accounting Policies, Changes in Accounting Estimates and Errors* means that an entity will not use hindsight when first applying the amendments—paragraph 53 of IAS 8 states that hindsight should not be used when applying a new accounting policy to a prior period, either in making assumptions about what management's intentions would have been in a prior period or in estimating the amounts recognised, measured and disclosed in a prior period.

Exemptions from applying the equity method: partial use of fair value measurement of associates

BC20   The Board received a request to clarify whether different measurement bases can be applied to portions of an investment in an associate when part of the investment is not accounted for using the equity method in accordance with paragraph 18 of IAS 28, but it is instead measured at fair value through profit or loss in accordance with IFRS 9. The Board initially deliberated this amendment to IAS 28 as part of the *Improvements to IFRSs* issued in April 2010; however, at its meeting in February 2010 the Board decided to address this issue within the joint ventures project.

BC21   The Board noted that two views exist with respect to measurement. The first view identifies all direct and indirect interests held in the associate either by the parent or through any of its subsidiaries, and then applies IAS 28 to the entire investment in the associate. In accordance with this view, there is only one investment in the associate and it should be accounted for as a single unit.

The second view identifies all direct and indirect interests held in an associate, but then allows the use of the measurement exemption to portions of an investment in an associate if the portion is held by a venture capital organisation, or a mutual fund, unit trust and similar entities including investment-linked insurance funds, regardless of whether those entities have significant influence over their portion of the investment in the associate. The Board agreed with the second view and therefore amended IAS 28. The Board decided that equivalent guidance on the partial use of fair value for the measurement of investments in joint ventures should not be provided because the Board thought that such events would be unlikely in practice.

BC22 The Board also discussed whether the partial use of fair value should be allowed only in the case of venture capital organisations, or mutual funds, unit trusts and similar entities including investment-linked insurance funds, that have designated their portion of the investment in the associate at fair value through profit or loss in their own financial statements. The Board noted that several situations might arise in which those entities do not measure their portion of the investment in the associate at fair value through profit or loss. In those situations, however, from the group's perspective, the appropriate determination of the business purpose would lead to the measurement of this portion of the investment in the associate at fair value through profit or loss in the consolidated financial statements. Consequently, the Board decided that an entity should be able to measure a portion of an investment in an associate held by a venture capital organisation, or a mutual fund, unit trust and similar entities including investment-linked insurance funds, at fair value through profit or loss regardless of whether this portion of the investment is measured at fair value through profit or loss in those entities' financial statements.

Classification as held for sale

BC23 ED 9 proposed that an entity should account for an interest in a joint venture that is classified as held for sale in accordance with IFRS 5.

BC24 During its redeliberation of ED 9 the Board noted that the exposure draft *Improvements to IFRSs* published in August 2009 had proposed to amend IFRS 5 so as to require an entity to classify as held for sale its interest in an associate, or in a jointly controlled entity, when it is committed to a sale plan involving loss of significant influence or loss of joint control. Those proposals aimed to clarify that all the interest ('the whole interest') an entity had in an associate or a joint venture had to be classified as held for sale if the entity was committed to a sale plan involving loss of, significant influence over, or joint control of that interest.

BC25 The Board observed that those proposals were not aligned with the decisions made during the Board's redeliberation of ED 9 to remove all descriptions that associated the loss of joint control and the loss of significant influence with the term 'significant economic event' as introduced in the second phase of the Board's project on business combinations (see paragraphs BC28–BC31).

BC26   The Board decided that classifying an interest as held for sale should be on the basis of whether the intended disposal meets the criteria for classification as held for sale in accordance with IFRS 5, rather than on whether the entity had lost joint control of, or significant influence over, that interest. As a result, the Board concluded that when the disposal of an interest, or a portion of an interest, in a joint venture or an associate fulfilled the criteria for classification as held for sale in accordance with IFRS 5, an entity should classify the whole interest, or a portion of the interest, as held for sale.

BC27   The Board decided that, in the case of a partial disposal, an entity should maintain the use of the equity method for the retained interest in the joint venture or associate until the portion classified as held for sale is finally disposed of. The Board reasoned that even if the entity has the intention of selling a portion of an interest in an associate or a joint venture, until it does so it still has significant influence over, or joint control of, that investee. After the disposal, an entity should measure the retained interest in the joint venture or associate in accordance with IFRS 9 or in accordance with IAS 28 if the entity still has significant influence over, or joint control of, the retained interest.

Discontinuing the use of the equity method

BC28   During its redeliberation of ED 9, the Board reconsidered whether its decision in the second phase of the business combinations project to characterise loss of joint control or loss of significant influence as a significant economic event (ie in the same way that loss of control is characterised as a significant economic event) was appropriate. If it were, the Board thought that the entity should be required to recalibrate the accounting as required by IFRS 10. However, the Board concluded that, although significant, the events are fundamentally different. In the case of loss of control, the cessation of the parent-subsidiary relationship results in the derecognition of assets and liabilities because the composition of the group changes. If joint control or significant influence is lost the composition of the group is unaffected.

BC29   The Board also noted that retaining the characterisation of significant economic event in the case of loss of joint control or significant influence when the retained interest is a financial asset is unnecessary. IFRS 9 already requires that in such cases the retained interest (ie a financial asset) must be measured at fair value.

BC30   In the case of loss of joint control when significant influence is maintained, the Board acknowledged that the investor-investee relationship changes and, consequently, so does the nature of the investment. However, in this instance, both investments (ie the joint venture and the associate) continue to be measured using the equity method. Considering that there is neither a change in the group boundaries nor a change in the measurement requirements, the Board concluded that losing joint control and retaining significant influence is not an event that warrants remeasurement of the retained interest at fair value.

BC31   Consequently, the Board removed all descriptions that characterise loss of joint control or significant influence as a significant economic event as introduced in the second phase of the Board's project on business combinations.

Incorporation of SIC-13

BC32   In the joint ventures project, the Board decided to extend the requirements and guidance in IAS 28 for the accounting for 'downstream' and 'upstream' transactions between an entity and its associate to the accounting for transactions between an entity and its joint venture.

BC33   In ED 9, the Board proposed to incorporate into the standard on joint arrangements the consensus of SIC-13 *Jointly Controlled Entities—Non-Monetary Contributions by Venturers*. Because the Board relocated all the requirements for the accounting for joint ventures into IAS 28, the Board incorporated the consensus of SIC-13 into IAS 28 and extended it to associates.

BC34   The Board noted that the consensus of SIC-13 regarding non-monetary contributions made by a venturer[3] to a joint venture is consistent with IAS 28, except for the following aspect. SIC-13 established three exceptions for the recognition of gains or losses attributable to the equity interests of the other parties. In response to comments raised by some respondents to ED 9, the Board redeliberated the need to incorporate into IAS 28 the exceptions included in SIC-13 for the recognition by an entity of the portion of a gain or loss attributable to the interests of other unrelated investors in the investee.

BC35   The Board concluded that only when the transaction lacks commercial substance should there be an exception for the recognition of gains or losses to be carried forward from the consensus of SIC-13 into IAS 28, because the other two exceptions in SIC-13 (ie 'the significant risks and rewards of ownership of the contributed non-monetary asset(s) have not been transferred to the jointly controlled entity' and 'the gain or loss on the non-monetary contribution cannot be measured reliably') either relate to requirements that are not aligned with the principles and requirements of IFRS 11 or relate to a criterion for the recognition of gain or losses (ie 'reliability of measurement') that is already included in the *Conceptual Framework for Financial Reporting*.[4]

BCZ36   To the extent that the entity also receives monetary or non-monetary assets dissimilar to the assets contributed in addition to equity interests in the investee, the realisation of which is not dependent on the future cash flows of the investee, the earnings process is complete. Accordingly, an entity should recognise in full in profit or loss the portion of the gain or loss on the non-monetary contribution relating to the monetary or non-monetary assets received.

---

3   IFRS 11 *Joint Arrangements*, issued in May 2011, uses the term 'joint venturers' to designate parties that have joint control of a joint venture.

4   The reference is to the *Conceptual Framework for Financial Reporting*, issued in 2010 and in effect when the Standard was amended.

BC37   Additionally, the Board considered whether the requirements in IAS 31 for recognition of losses when downstream or upstream transactions provide evidence of a reduction in the net realisable value or impairment loss of the assets transacted or contributed were still relevant and decided to bring them forward to IAS 28.

Sale or contribution of assets between an investor and its associate or joint venture—amendments to IFRS 10 and IAS 28 (issued in September 2014)

BC37A   The IFRS Interpretations Committee received a request to clarify whether a business meets the definition of a 'non-monetary asset'. The question was asked within the context of identifying whether the requirements of SIC-13[5] and IAS 28 (as revised in 2011) apply when a business is contributed to a jointly controlled entity (as defined in IAS 31[6]), a joint venture (as defined in IFRS 11) or an associate, in exchange for an equity interest in that jointly controlled entity, joint venture or associate. The business may be contributed either when the jointly controlled entity, joint venture or associate is established or thereafter.

BC37B   The Board noted that this matter is related to the issues arising from the acknowledged inconsistency between the requirements in IAS 27 (as revised in 2008) and SIC-13, when accounting for the contribution of a subsidiary to a jointly controlled entity, joint venture or associate (resulting in the loss of control of the subsidiary). In accordance with SIC-13, the amount of the gain or loss recognised resulting from the contribution of a non-monetary asset to a jointly controlled entity in exchange for an equity interest in that jointly controlled entity is restricted to the extent of the interests attributable to the unrelated investors in the jointly controlled entity. However, IAS 27 (as revised in 2008) requires full profit or loss recognition on the loss of control of a subsidiary.

BC37C   This inconsistency between IAS 27 (as revised in 2008) and SIC-13remained after IFRS 10 replaced IAS 27 (as revised in 2008) and SIC-13was withdrawn. The requirements in IFRS 10 on the accounting for the loss of control of a subsidiary are similar to the requirements in IAS 27 (as revised in 2008). The requirements in SIC-13are incorporated into paragraphs 28 and 30 of IAS 28 (as amended in 2011) and apply to the sale or contribution of assets between an investor and its associate or joint venture. Because IAS 27 (as revised in 2008) and SIC-13have been superseded at the time when the amendments become effective, the Board decided to amend only IFRS 10 and IAS 28 (as amended in 2011).

BC37D   In dealing with the conflict between the requirements in IFRS 10 and IAS 28 (as amended in 2011), the Board was concerned that the existing requirements could result in the accounting for a transaction being driven by its form rather than by its substance. For example, different accounting might be

---

5   SIC-13 has been withdrawn. The requirements in SIC-13are incorporated into IAS 28 (as amended in 2011).

6   IAS 31 was superseded by IFRS 11 *Joint Arrangements* issued in May 2011.

applied to a transaction involving the same underlying assets depending on whether those assets were:

(a)   transferred in a transaction that is structured as a sale of assets or as a sale of the entity that holds the assets; or

(b)   sold in exchange for cash or contributed in exchange for an equity interest.

BC37E   The Board concluded that:

(a)   the accounting for the loss of control of a business, as defined in IFRS 3, should be consistent with the conclusions in IFRS 3; and

(b)   a full gain or loss should therefore be recognised on the loss of control of a business, regardless of whether that business is housed in a subsidiary or not.

BC37F   Because assets that do not constitute a business were not part of the Business Combinations project, the Board concluded that:

(a)   the current requirements in IAS 28 (as amended in 2011) for the partial gain or loss recognition for transactions between an investor and its associate or joint venture should only apply to the gain or loss resulting from the sale or contribution of assets that do not constitute a business; and

(b)   IFRS 10 should be amended so that a partial gain or loss is recognised in accounting for the loss of control of a subsidiary that does not constitute a business as a result of a transaction between an investor and its associate or joint venture.

BC37G   The Board discussed whether all sales and contributions (including the sale or contribution of assets that do not constitute a business) should be consistent with IFRS 3. Although it considered this alternative to be the most robust from a conceptual point of view, it noted that this would require addressing multiple cross-cutting issues. Because of concerns that the cross-cutting issues could not be addressed on a timely basis the conclusions described in paragraphs BC37E–BC37F were considered the best way to address this issue.

BC37H   The Board decided that both 'upstream' and 'downstream' transactions should be affected by the amendments to IFRS 10 and IAS 28 (as amended in 2011). The Board noted that if assets that constitute a business were sold by an associate or a joint venture to the investor (in an upstream transaction), with the result that the investor takes control of that business, the investor would account for this transaction as a business combination in accordance with IFRS 3.

BC37I   The Board decided that the amendments to IFRS 10 and IAS 28 (as amended in 2011) should apply prospectively to transactions that occur in annual periods beginning on or after the date that the amendments become effective. The Board observed that the requirements in IAS 27 (as revised in 2008) for the loss of control of a subsidiary (see paragraph 45(c) of IAS 27 as revised in 2008) were applied prospectively. The Board also noted that transactions dealing with the loss of control of a subsidiary or a business between an investor and its associate or joint venture are discrete non-recurring transactions. Consequently, the Board concluded that the benefits of comparative information would not exceed the cost of providing it. The Board also decided to allow entities to early apply the amendments to IFRS 10 and IAS 28 (as amended in 2011).

Deferral of the *Effective Date of Amendments to IFRS 10 and IAS 28* (issued in September 2014)

BC37J   In December 2015, the Board decided to defer indefinitely the effective date of the amendments made to IFRS 10 and IAS 28 in September 2014. See paragraphs BC190L–BC190O of the Basis for Conclusions on IFRS 10 *Consolidated Financial Statements*.

Recognition of losses (2003 revision)

BCZ38   The 2000 version of IAS 28 and SIC-20 *Equity Accounting Method — Recognition of Losses* restricted application of the equity method when, in accounting for the entity's share of losses, the carrying amount of the investment is reduced to zero.

BCZ39   The Board decided that the base to be reduced to zero should be broader than residual equity interests and should also include other non-equity interests that are in substance part of the net investment in the associate or joint venture, such as long-term receivables. Therefore, the Board decided to withdraw SIC-20.

BCZ40   The Board also noted that if non-equity investments are not included in the base to be reduced to zero, an entity could restructure its investment to fund the majority in non-equity investments to avoid recognising the losses of the associate or joint venture under the equity method.

BCZ41   In widening the base against which losses are to be recognised, the Board also clarified the application of the impairment provisions of IAS 39 *Financial Instruments: Recognition and Measurement*[7] to the financial assets that form part of the net investment.

Impairment losses (2008 amendment)

BCZ42   In 2008 the Board identified unclear guidance in IAS 28 regarding the extent to which an impairment reversal should be recognised as an adjustment to the carrying amount of an investment in an associate or in a joint venture.

BCZ43   The Board noted that applying the equity method involves adjusting the entity's share of the impairment loss recognised by the associate or joint venture on assets such as goodwill or property, plant and equipment to take account of the acquisition date fair values of those assets. The Board proposed in the exposure draft *Improvements to International Financial Reporting Standards* published in October 2007 that an additional impairment recognised by the

---

7   IFRS 9 *Financial Instruments* replaced IAS 39. IFRS 9 applies to all items that previously were within the scope of IAS 39.

entity, after applying the equity method, should not be allocated to any asset, including goodwill, that forms part of the carrying amount of the investment. Therefore, such an impairment should be reversed in a subsequent period to the extent that the recoverable amount of the investment increases.

BCZ44   Some respondents to the exposure draft expressed the view that the proposed amendment was not consistent with IAS 39 (regarding reversal of an impairment loss on an available-for-sale equity instrument[8]), or with IAS 36 *Impairment of Assets* (regarding the allocation of an impairment loss to goodwill and any reversal of an impairment loss relating to goodwill).

BCZ45   In its redeliberations, the Board affirmed its previous decisions but, in response to the comments made, decided to clarify the reasons for the amendments. The Board decided that an entity should not allocate an impairment loss to any asset that forms part of the carrying amount of the investment in the associate or joint venture because the investment is the only asset that the entity controls and recognises.

BCZ46   The Board also decided that any reversal of this impairment loss should be recognised as an adjustment to the investment in the associate or joint venture to the extent that the recoverable amount of the investment increases. This requirement is consistent with IAS 36, which permits the reversal of impairment losses for assets other than goodwill. The Board did not propose to align the requirements for the reversal of an impairment loss with those in IAS 39[9] relating to equity instruments, because an entity recognises an impairment loss on an investment in an associate or joint venture in accordance with IAS 36, rather than in accordance with IAS 39.

Retaining the fair value measurement applied by an associate or joint venture that is an investment entity

BC46A   In October 2012, the Board issued *Investment Entities* (Amendments to IFRS 10, IFRS 12 and IAS 27), which required investment entities, as defined in IFRS 10, to measure most investments in subsidiaries at fair value through profit or loss. The amendments did not introduce any new accounting requirements for investments in associates or joint ventures. This is because paragraphs 18–19 of IAS 28 already allowed an investment entity to measure its investments in associates and joint ventures at fair value through profit or loss in accordance with IFRS 9. A wider range of entities, including venture capital organisations, or mutual funds, unit trusts and similar entities including investment-linked insurance funds, may also elect to measure their investments in associates and joint ventures in the same way.

BC46B   Paragraph 33 of IFRS 10 requires a non-investment entity parent of an investment entity to consolidate all entities that it controls, including those controlled through an investment entity subsidiary. This is consistent with the proposal contained in the Exposure Draft *Investment Entities* (the 'Investment Entities ED'), which was published in August 2011. Some respondents to the

---

8   IFRS 9 *Financial Instruments* eliminated the category of available-for-sale financial assets.

9   IFRS 9 *Financial Instruments* replaced IAS 39. IFRS 9 applies to all items that previously were within the scope of IAS 39.

Investment Entities ED noted that this seemed inconsistent with paragraphs 18–19 of IAS 28, which allow a wider group of entities than only investment entities to measure their investments in associates and joint ventures at fair value through profit or loss. The Board acknowledged this inconsistency, and explained its reasons for not amending IAS 28 in line with IFRS 10, in paragraph BC283 of IFRS 10.

BC46C Subsequently, the IFRS Interpretations Committee (the 'Interpretations Committee') received a request to clarify whether an entity that is not an investment entity should, when applying the equity method of accounting for its investment in an associate or joint venture that is an investment entity, retain the fair value measurement that is applied by that associate or joint venture to its subsidiaries or, instead, 'unwind' that treatment and apply consolidation procedures. Members of the Interpretations Committee had mixed views on the matter and, because of the need to provide clarity before the end of 2014, the matter was passed to the Board.

BC46D The Board noted that the scope of the amendment in the *Investment Entities* ED was restricted to providing an exception to the consolidation requirements for investment entity parents. This exception reflects the unique business model of an investment entity, for which fair value information is more relevant than consolidation. This unique business model is not applicable to a non-investment entity parent. Consequently, paragraph 33 of IFRS 10 requires a non-investment entity parent of an investment entity to consolidate all entities that it controls, both directly and indirectly through an investment entity. This requires the non-investment entity parent to unwind the fair value through profit or loss measurement used by its investment entity subsidiaries for indirectly held subsidiaries.

BC46E The Board also noted that paragraphs 35–36 of IAS 28, which require the use of uniform accounting policies, would apply for a non-investment entity investor and its investment entity associates or joint ventures. This would mean that the subsidiaries of those investment entity associates and joint ventures should be consolidated into the financial statements of those associates and joint ventures prior to the equity method being applied. The Board noted that this is conceptually consistent with the requirement in IFRS 10 for a non-investment entity parent to consolidate subsidiaries held through an investment entity subsidiary.

BC46F However, some Board members raised concerns about the potentially significant practical difficulties or additional costs that may arise for an entity in unwinding the fair value through profit or loss measurement applied by an investment entity associate or joint venture for their interests in subsidiaries. Some Board members noted that the degree of practical difficulty is different depending on whether the investee is an associate or joint venture. In addition, some Board members noted the structuring risks highlighted in paragraph BC280 of IFRS 10 and noted that an investor's ability to achieve different accounting outcomes by holding investments through an investment entity investee is different depending on whether the investee is an associate or a joint venture. Consequently, in the Exposure Draft *Investment Entities: Applying the Consolidation Exception* (Proposed amendments to IFRS 10 and

IAS 28) (the 'Consolidation Exception ED'), which was published in June 2014, the Board proposed to provide relief to non-investment entity investors for their interests in investment entity associates, but not for their interests in investment entity joint ventures.

BC46G The practicality and cost concerns were noted by the majority of respondents to the *Consolidation Exception* ED. However, the majority of respondents disagreed with the proposal to limit the relief to interests in investment entity associates, noting that the practicality and cost issues also applied to interests in joint ventures. In addition, some respondents disagreed with the concerns about the risk of structuring, noting that the difference between significant influence and joint control is much smaller than the difference between control and joint control. Consequently, the Board decided to provide relief to non-investment entity investors in both investment entity associates and joint ventures and to retain the consistency in treatment in applying the equity method to both associates and joint ventures. This relief permits, but does not require, a non-investment entity investor to retain the fair value through profit or loss measurement applied by an investment entity associate or joint venture for their subsidiaries when applying the equity method.

Effective date and transition

BC47 The Board decided to align the effective date for the Standard with the effective date for IFRS 10, IFRS 11, IFRS 12 *Disclosure of Interests in Other Entities* and IAS 27 *Separate Financial Statements*. When making this decision, the Board noted that the five IFRSs all deal with the assessment of, and related accounting and disclosure requirements about, a reporting entity's special relationships with other entities (ie when the reporting entity has control or joint control of, or significant influence over, another entity). As a result, the Board concluded that applying IAS 28 without also applying the other four IFRSs could cause unwarranted confusion.

BC48 The Board usually sets an effective date of between twelve and eighteen months after issuing an IFRS. When deciding the effective date for those IFRSs, the Board considered the following factors:

(a) the time that many countries require for translation and for introducing the mandatory requirements into law.

(b) the consolidation project was related to the global financial crisis that started in 2007 and was accelerated by the Board in response to urgent requests from the leaders of the G20, the Financial Stability Board, users of financial statements, regulators and others to improve the accounting and disclosure of an entity's 'off balance sheet' activities.

(c) the comments received from respondents to the Request for Views *Effective Date and Transition Methods* that was published in October 2010 regarding implementation costs, effective date and transition requirements of the IFRSs to be issued in 2011. Most respondents did not identify the consolidation and joint arrangements IFRSs as having a high impact in terms of the time and resources that their implementation would require. In addition, only a few respondents commented that the effective dates of those IFRSs should be aligned with those of the other IFRSs to be issued in 2011.

BC49   With those factors in mind, the Board decided to require entities to apply the five IFRSs for annual periods beginning on or after 1 January 2013.

BC50   Most respondents to the Request for Views supported early application of the IFRSs to be issued in 2011. Respondents stressed that early application was especially important for first-time adopters in 2011 and 2012. The Board was persuaded by these arguments and decided to permit early application of IAS 28 but only if an entity applies it in conjunction with the other IFRSs (ie IFRS 10, IFRS 11, IFRS 12 and IAS 27 (as amended in 2011)) to avoid a lack of comparability among financial statements, and for the reasons noted in paragraph BC47 that triggered the Board's decision to set the same effective date for all five IFRSs. Even though an entity should apply the five IFRSs at the same time, the Board noted that an entity should not be prevented from providing any information required by IFRS 12 early if by doing so users gained a better understanding of the entity's relationships with other entities.

BC50A   The Board decided that no specific transition guidance was needed and, therefore, an entity should apply *Investment Entities: Applying the Consolidation Exception* (Amendments to IFRS 10, IFRS 12 and IAS 28) retrospectively in accordance with IAS 8 *Accounting Policies, Changes in Accounting Estimates and Errors*.

General

Withdrawal of IAS 28 (2003 revision)

BC51   IAS 28 *Investments in Associates and Joint Ventures* replaces IAS 28 *Investments in Associates* (as revised in 2003 and amended in 2010). IAS 28 (as amended in 2011) incorporates the accounting for joint ventures and includes some amendments discussed by the Board during its redeliberation of the exposure draft ED 9.

Disclosure

BC52   IAS 28 does not address the disclosure requirements for entities with joint control of, or significant influence over, an investee. As part of its redeliberation of ED 9 and ED 10 *Consolidated Financial Statements*, the Board identified an opportunity to integrate and make consistent the disclosure requirements for subsidiaries, joint arrangements, associates and unconsolidated structured entities, and to present those requirements in a single IFRS.

BC53   The Board observed that IAS 27, IAS 28 and IAS 31 contained many similar disclosure requirements. ED 9 had already proposed amendments to the disclosure requirements for joint ventures and associates to align the disclosure requirements for those two types of investments more closely. The Board noted that the majority of respondents agreed with the proposals in

ED 9 to align the disclosures for joint ventures with the disclosures in IAS 28 for associates.

BC54   As a result, the Board combined the disclosure requirements for interest with subsidiaries, joint arrangements, associates and unconsolidated structured entities within a single comprehensive standard, IFRS 12.

BC55   The Basis for Conclusions accompanying IFRS 12 summarises the Board's considerations in developing that IFRS, including its review of responses to the disclosure proposals in ED 9. Accordingly, IAS 28 does not include disclosure requirements and this Basis for Conclusions does not incorporate the Board's considerations of responses to the proposed disclosure requirements in ED 9.

Summary of main changes from IAS 28 (2003 revision)

BC56   The main changes from the previous version of IAS 28 are as follows:

(a)   The accounting for joint ventures has been incorporated into the Standard.

(b)   The scope exception for venture capital organisations, or mutual funds, unit trusts and similar entities, including investment-linked insurance funds has been eliminated and has been characterised as a measurement exemption from the requirement to measure investments in associates and joint ventures in using the equity method.

(c)   IAS 28 now permits an entity that has an investment in an associate, a portion of which is held indirectly through venture capital organisations, or mutual funds, unit trusts and similar entities including investment-linked insurance funds, to elect to measure that portion of the investment in the associate at fair value through profit or loss in accordance with IFRS 9 regardless of whether these entities have significant influence over that portion of the investment.

(d)   IAS 28 requires a portion of an investment in an associate or a joint venture to be classified as held for sale if the disposal of that portion of the interest would fulfil the criteria to be classified as held for sale in accordance with IFRS 5.

(e)   The consensus of SIC-13 has been incorporated into IAS 28. As a result, gains and losses resulting from a contribution of a non-monetary asset to an associate or a joint venture in exchange for an equity interest in an associate or a joint venture are recognised only to the extent of unrelated investors' interests in the associate or joint venture, except when the contribution lacks commercial substance, as that term is described in IAS 16 *Property, Plant and Equipment*.

(f)   The disclosure requirements have been placed in IFRS 12.

Dissenting opinion on amendment issued in May 2008

Dissent of Tatsumi Yamada

DO1 Mr Yamada voted against one of the amendments to IAS 28 *Investments in Associates* issued in *Improvements to IFRSs* in May 2008.

DO2 Mr Yamada believes it is inappropriate not to allocate any additional impairment losses to the goodwill and other assets that form part of the carrying amount of the investment in the associate. In his view, because he believes that an investor can identify attributable goodwill when it makes an investment, all impairment losses recognised with respect to the investor's investment in an associate should be allocated to the goodwill and other assets that form part of the carrying amount of the investment.

DO3 Mr Yamada also believes that all impairment losses allocated to goodwill should not be subsequently reversed. In his view the non-allocation of impairment losses to goodwill as required by the amendment and the subsequent reversal of such impairment losses in substance leads to the recognition of internally generated goodwill. He believes that the amendment to IAS 28 is not consistent with paragraphs 124 and 125 of IAS 36 *Impairment of Assets*, which prohibit the reversal of impairment losses related to goodwill.

Dissenting Opinions from *Sale or Contribution of Assets between an Investor and its Associate or Joint Venture* (Amendments to IFRS 10 and IAS 28) as issued in September 2014

DO1   Mr Kabureck, Ms Lloyd and Mr Ochi voted against the publication of *Sale or Contribution of Assets between an Investor and its Associate or Joint Venture* (Amendments to IFRS 10 and IAS 28). The reasons for their dissents are set out below.

Dissent of Mr Kabureck

DO2   Mr Kabureck dissents from the amendments to IFRS 10 and IAS 28, which require full gain or loss recognition in the accounting for the loss of control when a parent (investor) sells or contributes a business, as defined in IFRS 3 *Business Combinations*, to an investee (ie an associate or a joint venture) that is accounted for using the equity method.

DO3   He agrees that the control of a business can be lost regardless of whether the acquirer is a related or an unrelated party. However, he believes that the accounting for the gain or loss should be different if the sale or contribution is to an investee that is accounted for using the equity method. He observes that the investor's interest in the gain or loss will eventually affect the future investee's profit or loss recognised in the investor's profit or loss.

DO4   His concern can be illustrated by a simple example:

An investor sells a business to a 40 per cent-owned associate accounted for using the equity method. The full gain is CU100.[10] This gain of CU100 is reflected in the associate's financial statements through the higher value of the net assets acquired. Over time, assuming that no goodwill or indefinite lived intangible assets are involved, the associate's future profits or losses will be lower by CU100 as the assets are consumed and, therefore, the investor's share of the associate's profits or losses will be lower by CU40. Consequently, the net gain of the investor over time is CU60, not CU100.

DO5   Accordingly, he believes that a more faithful representation of the transaction would be to recognise an immediate gain of CU60 and a deferred gain of CU40, which would be amortised into income, making it consistent with the consumption of the sold assets in the investee's operations. He believes that it would be inappropriate to immediately recognise the full gain knowing that over time there would be lower profits to the extent of the equity interest in the investee.

DO6   Mr Kabureck observes that his preferred partial gain or loss accounting is consistent with the accounting for the sales of assets that do not constitute a business, as described in paragraphs BC190F of IFRS 10 and BC37F of IAS 28. Whether or not the assets sold or contributed do, or do not, constitute a business, seems to him to provide little rationale for different gain or loss treatment. He further observes that the line between what constitutes a business versus a collection of assets is frequently unclear, often based on

---

10   In this document, monetary items are denominated by 'currency units' (CU).

judgement and represents an interpretation challenge in practice. He disagrees with introducing another accounting difference that is dependent on the interpretation of the definition of a business.

Dissent of Ms Lloyd and Mr Ochi

DO7   Ms Lloyd and Mr Ochi agree that the sale of assets that constitute a business and the sale of assets that do not constitute a business should be treated differently for the reasons given in paragraphs BC190G of IFRS 10 and BC37G of IAS 28. However, they also believe that the accounting result should not differ depending on whether assets that do not constitute a business are transferred in a transaction that is structured as a sale of assets or as a sale of the entity that holds those assets. Ms Lloyd and Mr Ochi believe that these amendments do not achieve that result.

DO8   The stated objective of these amendments is to address the conflict between the requirements of IFRS 10 and IAS 28. Prior to these amendments, IFRS 10 required full gain or loss recognition on the loss of control of a subsidiary, whereas IAS 28 restricted the gain or loss resulting from the sale or contribution of assets to an associate or a joint venture to the extent of the interests that were attributable to unrelated investors in that associate or joint venture (downstream transactions).

DO9   As a result of these amendments, there will continue to be a full gain or loss recognition on the loss of control of a subsidiary that constitutes a business under IFRS 10, as well as a full gain or loss recognition resulting from the sale or contribution of assets that constitute a business between an investor and its associate or joint venture under IAS 28. The gain or loss recognised on the sale of the business will be the same whether it is structured as a sale of assets that constitute a business or as a sale of the entity that contains a business. As stated above, Ms Lloyd and Mr Ochi agree with this result.

DO10   Even after the amendments, IAS 28 will continue to restrict the gain or loss resulting from the sale or contribution of assets that do not constitute a business to an associate or a joint venture to the extent of the interests that are attributable to unrelated investors in that associate or joint venture. However, as a result of these amendments, under IFRS 10, when an entity sells an interest in a subsidiary that does not contain a business to an associate or a joint venture and as a result loses control of that subsidiary but retains joint control or significant influence over it, the gain or loss recognised is also limited to the unrelated investor's interests in the associate or joint venture to which the interest in the subsidiary was sold. In addition, the entity will remeasure its retained interest in the former subsidiary to fair value at the date it loses control, even though that retained interest is not in an entity that constitutes a business. Ms Lloyd and Mr Ochi acknowledge that under the amendments, recognition of the gain or loss on remeasurement will be limited to the unrelated investor's interests in the associate or joint venture to which the interest in the subsidiary was sold. However, because Ms Lloyd and Mr Ochi believe the sale of a subsidiary that does not constitute a business, and the sale of the assets held in that subsidiary, is substantially the same transaction, they do not find any justification for the recognition of any additional gain on the remeasurement of the retained portion.

DO11   Furthermore, Ms Lloyd and Mr Ochi note that if the retained interest in the former subsidiary is an investment accounted for in accordance with IFRS 9 *Financial Instruments* or IAS 39 *Financial Instruments: Recognition and Measurement*, the amount of gain or loss recognised on remeasurement will not be restricted. A full gain or loss will be recognised on remeasurement of the retained interest even though that interest is not in an entity that constitutes a business. As a result of the remeasurement of the retained interest in the former subsidiary, the amount of gain or loss recognised in a transaction involving the same underlying assets will still be different depending on whether those assets are transferred in a transaction that is structured as a sale of assets or as a sale of the entity that holds the assets. Ms Lloyd and Mr Ochi disagree with this result. They believe that the remeasurement of a retained interest in a former subsidiary to fair value when control is lost is a fundamental principle of IFRS 10. They also believe that accounting for equity interests that do not represent control, joint control or significant influence at fair value is a fundamental principle of IFRS 9 and IAS 39. Ms Lloyd and Mr Ochi do not believe that these principles can be reconciled in a limited-scope amendment to the treatment in IAS 28 of downstream transactions that involve the sale of assets that do not constitute a business.

DO12   Consequently, Ms Lloyd and Mr Ochi dissent from these amendments because they do not fully address the concerns of the Board and the IFRS Interpretations Committee as set out in paragraphs BC190D of IFRS 10 and BC37D of IAS 28.

Dissent of Mr Takatsugu Ochi from *Long-term Interests in Associates and Joint Ventures* (Amendments to IAS 28)

DO1 Mr Ochi voted against the publication of *Long-term Interests in Associates and Joint Ventures* (Amendments to IAS 28). The reasons for his dissent are set out below.

DO2 Mr Ochi believes that interests in an associate or joint venture should be subject to either the requirements in IFRS 9 or the requirements in IAS 28, but not both. Accordingly, he disagrees with amending IAS 28 without also specifying the types of interests in an associate or joint venture that an entity accounts for using the equity method, and the types of interests in such entities that an entity accounts for applying IFRS 9.

DO3 Mr Ochi notes that the amendments would result in 'dual application' of accounting requirements to the same asset, which he thinks is contrary to basic principles of accounting standards. He believes that such dual application of accounting requirements might result in double counting and, therefore, could undermine the quality of financial statements.

IASB documents published to accompany

IAS 29

Financial Reporting in Hyperinflationary Economies

The text of the unaccompanied standard, IAS 29, is contained in Part A of this edition. Its effective date when issued was 1 January 1990. This part presents the following document:

BASIS FOR CONCLUSIONS

Basis for Conclusions on
IAS 29 *Financial Reporting in Hyperinflationary Economies*

This Basis for Conclusions accompanies, but is not part of, IAS 29.

BC1   This Basis for Conclusions summarises the International Accounting Standards Board's considerations in reaching its conclusions on amending IAS 29 *Financial Reporting in Hyperinflationary Economies* in 2008. Individual Board members gave greater weight to some factors than to others.

BC2   Paragraph 6 of the previous version of the Standard did not reflect the fact that a number of assets and liabilities may or must be measured on the basis of a current value rather than a historical value. Therefore, the Board included examples rather than a definitive list of such items by *Improvements to IFRSs* issued in May 2008.

IASB documents published to accompany

IAS 32

Financial Instruments: Presentation

The text of the unaccompanied standard, IAS 32, is contained in Part A of this edition. Its effective date when issued was 1 January 2005. The text of the Accompanying Guidance on IAS 32 is contained in Part B of this edition. This part presents the following documents:

BASIS FOR CONCLUSIONS

DISSENTING OPINIONS

Contents

Basis for Conclusions on
IAS 32 *Financial Instruments: Presentation*

This Basis for Conclusions accompanies, but is not part of, IAS 32.

BC1   This Basis for Conclusions summarises the International Accounting Standards Board's considerations in reaching its conclusions on revising IAS 32 *Financial Instruments: Disclosure and Presentation*[1] in 2003. Individual Board members gave greater weight to some factors than to others.

BC2   In July 2001 the Board announced that, as part of its initial agenda of technical projects, it would undertake a project to improve a number of Standards, including IAS 32 and IAS 39 *Financial Instruments: Recognition and Measurement*.[2] The objectives of the Improvements project were to reduce the complexity in the Standards by clarifying and adding guidance, eliminating internal inconsistencies, and incorporating into the Standards elements of Standing Interpretations Committee (SIC) Interpretations and IAS 39 implementation guidance. In June 2002 the Board published its proposals in an Exposure Draft of proposed amendments to IAS 32 *Financial Instruments: Disclosure and Presentation* and IAS 39 *Financial Instruments: Recognition and Measurement*, with a comment deadline of 14 October 2002. The Board received over 170 comment letters on the Exposure Draft.

BC3   Because the Board did not reconsider the fundamental approach to the accounting for financial instruments established by IAS 32 and IAS 39, this Basis for Conclusions does not discuss requirements in IAS 32 that the Board has not reconsidered.

BC3A   In July 2006 the Board published an exposure draft of proposed amendments to IAS 32 relating to the classification of puttable instruments and instruments with obligations arising on liquidation. The Board subsequently confirmed the proposals and in 2008 issued an amendment that now forms part of IAS 32. A summary of the Board's considerations and reasons for its conclusions is in paragraphs BC50–BC74.

Scope

BC3B   In November 2013 the Board amended the scope of IAS 32 so that it conformed to the scope of IAS 39 as amended in November 2013 regarding the accounting for some executory contracts (which was changed as a result of replacing the hedge accounting requirements in IAS 39).

BC3C   IFRS 9 replaced IAS 39 and consequentially in July 2014 the scope of IAS 39 was relocated to IFRS 9.

---

1   In August 2005, the IASB relocated all disclosures relating to financial instruments to IFRS 7 *Financial Instruments: Disclosures*. The paragraphs relating to disclosures that were originally published in this Basis for Conclusions were relocated, if still relevant, to the Basis for Conclusions on IFRS 7.

2   IFRS 9 *Financial Instruments* replaced IAS 39. IFRS 9 applies to all items that were previously within the scope of IAS 39.

Definitions (paragraphs 11–14 and AG3–AG24)

Financial asset, financial liability and equity instrument (paragraphs 11 and AG3–AG14)

BC4   The revised IAS 32 addresses the classification as financial assets, financial liabilities or equity instruments of financial instruments that are indexed to, or settled in, an entity's own equity instruments. As discussed further in paragraphs BC6–BC15, the Board decided to preclude equity classification for such contracts when they (a) involve an obligation to deliver cash or another financial asset or to exchange financial assets or financial liabilities under conditions that are potentially unfavourable to the entity, (b) in the case of a non-derivative, are not for the receipt or delivery of a fixed number of shares or (c) in the case of a derivative, are not for the exchange of a fixed number of shares for a fixed amount of cash or another financial asset. The Board also decided to preclude equity classification for contracts that are derivatives on derivatives on an entity's own equity. Consistently with this decision, the Board also decided to amend the definitions of financial asset, financial liability and equity instrument in IAS 32 to make them consistent with the guidance about contracts on an entity's own equity instruments. The Board did not reconsider other aspects of the definitions as part of this project to revise IAS 32, for example the other changes to the definitions proposed by the Joint Working Group in its Draft Standard *Financial Instruments and Similar Items* published by the Board's predecessor body, IASC, in 2000.

Foreign currency denominated pro rata rights issues

BC4A   In 2005 the International Financial Reporting Interpretations Committee (IFRIC) was asked whether the equity conversion option embedded in a convertible bond denominated in a foreign currency met IAS 32's requirements to be classified as an equity instrument. IAS 32 states that a derivative instrument relating to the purchase or issue of an entity's own equity instruments is classified as equity only if it results in the exchange of a fixed number of equity instruments for a fixed amount of cash or other assets. At that time, the IFRIC concluded that if the conversion option was denominated in a currency other than the issuing entity's functional currency, the amount of cash to be received in the functional currency would be variable. Consequently, the instrument was a derivative liability that should be measured at its fair value with changes in fair value included in profit or loss.

BC4B   However, the IFRIC also concluded that this outcome was not consistent with the Board's approach when it introduced the 'fixed for fixed' notion in IAS 32. Therefore, the IFRIC decided to recommend that the Board amend IAS 32 to permit a conversion or stand-alone option to be classified as equity if the exercise price was fixed in any currency. In September 2005 the Board decided not to proceed with the proposed amendment.

BC4C   In 2009 the Board was asked by the IFRIC to consider a similar issue. This issue was whether a right entitling the holder to receive a fixed number of the issuing entity's own equity instruments for a fixed amount of a currency other than the issuing entity's functional currency (foreign currency) should be accounted for as a derivative liability.

BC4D   These rights are commonly described as 'rights issues' and include rights, options and warrants. Laws or regulations in many jurisdictions throughout the world require the use of rights issues when raising capital. The entity issues one or more rights to acquire a fixed number of additional shares pro rata to all existing shareholders of a class of non-derivative equity instruments. The exercise price is normally below the current market price of the shares. Consequently, a shareholder must exercise its rights if it does not wish its proportionate interest in the entity to be diluted. Issues with those characteristics are discussed in IFRS 2 *Share-based Payment* and IAS 33 *Earnings per Share*.

BC4E   The Board was advised that rights with the characteristics discussed above were being issued frequently in the current economic environment. The Board was also advised that many issuing entities fixed the exercise price of the rights in currencies other than their functional currency because the entities were listed in more than one jurisdiction and might be required to do so by law or regulation. Therefore, the accounting conclusions affected a significant number of entities in many jurisdictions. In addition, because these are usually relatively large transactions, they can have a substantial effect on entities' financial statement amounts.

BC4F   The Board agreed with the IFRIC's 2005 conclusion that a contract with an exercise price denominated in a foreign currency would not result in the entity receiving a fixed amount of cash. However, the Board also agreed with the IFRIC that classifying rights as derivative liabilities was not consistent with the substance of the transaction. Rights issues are issued only to existing shareholders on the basis of the number of shares they already own. In this respect they partially resemble dividends paid in shares.

BC4G   The Board decided that a financial instrument that gives the holder the right to acquire a fixed number of the entity's own equity instruments for a fixed amount of any currency is an equity instrument if, and only if, the entity offers the financial instrument pro rata to all of its existing owners of the same class of its own non-derivative equity instruments.

BC4H   In excluding grants of rights with these features from the scope of IFRS 2, the Board explicitly recognised that the holder of the right receives it as a holder of equity instruments, ie as an owner. The Board noted that IAS 1 *Presentation of Financial Statements* requires transactions with owners in their capacity as owners to be recognised in the statement of changes in equity rather than in the statement of comprehensive income.

BC4I   Consistently with its conclusion in IFRS 2, the Board decided that a pro rata issue of rights to all existing shareholders to acquire additional shares is a transaction with an entity's owners in their capacity as owners. Consequently, those transactions should be recognised in equity, not comprehensive income.

Because the Board concluded that the rights were equity instruments, it decided to amend the definition of a financial liability to exclude them.

BC4J   Some respondents to the exposure draft expressed concerns that the wording of the amendment was too open-ended and could lead to structuring risks. The Board rejected this argument because of the extremely narrow amendment that requires the entity to treat all of its existing owners of the same class of its own non-derivative equity instruments equally. The Board also noted that a change in the capital structure of an entity to create a new class of non-derivative equity instruments would be transparent because of the presentation and disclosure requirements in IFRSs.

BC4K   The Board decided not to extend this conclusion to other instruments that grant the holder the right to purchase the entity's own equity instruments such as the conversion feature in convertible bonds. The Board also noted that long-dated foreign currency rights issues are not primarily transactions with owners in their capacity as owners. The equal treatment of all owners of the same class of equity instruments was also the basis on which, in IFRIC 17 *Distributions of Non-cash Assets to Owners*, the IFRIC distinguished non-reciprocal distributions to owners from exchange transactions. The fact that the rights are distributed pro rata to existing shareholders is critical to the Board's conclusion to provide an exception to the 'fixed for fixed' concept in IAS 32 as this is a narrow targeted transaction with owners in their capacity as owners.

Presentation (paragraphs 15–50 and AG25–AG39)

Liabilities and equity (paragraphs 15–27 and AG25–AG29)

BC5   The revised IAS 32 addresses whether derivative and non-derivative contracts indexed to, or settled in, an entity's own equity instruments are financial assets, financial liabilities or equity instruments. The original IAS 32 dealt with aspects of this issue piecemeal and it was not clear how various transactions (eg net share settled contracts and contracts with settlement options) should be treated under the Standard. The Board concluded that it needed to clarify the accounting treatment for such transactions.

BC6   The approach agreed by the Board can be summarised as follows:

A contract on an entity's own equity is an equity instrument if, and only if:

(a)   it contains no contractual obligation to transfer cash or another financial asset, or to exchange financial assets or financial liabilities with another entity under conditions that are potentially unfavourable to the entity; and

(b)   if the instrument will or may be settled in the entity's own equity instruments, it is either (i) a non-derivative that includes no contractual obligation for the entity to deliver a variable number of its own equity instruments, or (ii) a derivative that will be settled by the entity exchanging a fixed amount of cash or another financial asset for a fixed number of its own equity instruments.

No contractual obligation to deliver cash or another financial asset (paragraphs 17–20, AG25 and AG26)

Puttable instruments (paragraph 18(b))

BC7   The Board decided that a financial instrument that gives the holder the right to put the instrument back to the entity for cash or another financial asset is a financial liability of the entity. Such financial instruments are commonly issued by mutual funds, unit trusts, co-operative and similar entities, often with the redemption amount being equal to a proportionate share in the net assets of the entity. Although the legal form of such financial instruments often includes a right to the residual interest in the assets of an entity available to holders of such instruments, the inclusion of an option for the holder to put the instrument back to the entity for cash or another financial asset means that the instrument meets the definition of a financial liability. The classification as a financial liability is independent of considerations such as when the right is exercisable, how the amount payable or receivable upon exercise of the right is determined, and whether the puttable instrument has a fixed maturity.

BC7A   The Board reconsidered its conclusions with regards to some puttable instruments and amended IAS 32 in February 2008 (see paragraphs BC50–BC74).

BC8   The Board noted that the classification of a puttable instrument as a financial liability does not preclude the use of descriptors such as 'net assets attributable to unitholders' and 'change in net assets attributable to unitholders' on the face of the financial statements of an entity that has no equity (such as some mutual funds and unit trusts) or whose share capital is a financial liability under IAS 32 (such as some co-operatives). The Board also agreed that it should provide examples of how such entities might present their income statement[3] and balance sheet[4] (see Illustrative Examples 7 and 8).

Implicit obligations (paragraph 20)

BC9   The Board did not debate whether an obligation can be established implicitly rather than explicitly because this is not within the scope of an improvements project. This question will be considered by the Board in its project on revenue, liabilities and equity. Consequently, the Board retained the existing notion that an instrument may establish an obligation indirectly through its terms and conditions (see paragraph 20). However, it decided that the example of a preference share with a contractually accelerating dividend which, within the foreseeable future, is scheduled to yield a dividend so high that the entity will be economically compelled to redeem the instrument, was insufficiently clear. The example was therefore removed and replaced with others that are clearer and deal with situations that have proved problematic in practice.

---

3   IAS 1 *Presentation of Financial Statements* (as revised in 2007) requires an entity to present all income and expense items in one statement of comprehensive income or in two statements (a separate income statement and a statement of comprehensive income).

4   IAS 1 (revised 2007) replaced the term 'balance sheet' with 'statement of financial position'.

Settlement in the entity's own equity instruments (paragraphs 21–24 and AG27)

BC10 The approach taken in the revised IAS 32 includes two main conclusions:

(a) When an entity has an obligation to purchase its own shares for cash (such as under a forward contract to purchase its own shares), there is a financial liability for the amount of cash that the entity has an obligation to pay.

(b) When an entity uses its own equity instruments 'as currency' in a contract to receive or deliver a variable number of shares whose value equals a fixed amount or an amount based on changes in an underlying variable (eg a commodity price), the contract is not an equity instrument, but is a financial asset or a financial liability. In other words, when a contract is settled in a variable number of the entity's own equity instruments, or by the entity exchanging a fixed number of its own equity instruments for a variable amount of cash or another financial asset, the contract is not an equity instrument but is a financial asset or a financial liability.

When an entity has an obligation to purchase its own shares for cash, there is a financial liability for the amount of cash that the entity has an obligation to pay.

BC11 An entity's obligation to purchase its own shares establishes a maturity date for the shares that are subject to the contract. Therefore, to the extent of the obligation, those shares cease to be equity instruments when the entity assumes the obligation. This treatment under IAS 32 is consistent with the treatment of shares that provide for mandatory redemption by the entity. Without a requirement to recognise a financial liability for the present value of the share redemption amount, entities with identical obligations to deliver cash in exchange for their own equity instruments could report different information in their financial statements depending on whether the redemption clause is embedded in the equity instrument or is a free-standing derivative contract.

BC12 Some respondents to the Exposure Draft suggested that when an entity writes an option that, if exercised, will result in the entity paying cash in return for receiving its own shares, it is incorrect to treat the full amount of the exercise price as a financial liability because the obligation is conditional upon the option being exercised. The Board rejected this argument because the entity has an obligation to pay the full redemption amount and cannot avoid settlement in cash or another financial asset for the full redemption amount unless the counterparty decides not to exercise its redemption right or specified future events or circumstances beyond the control of the entity occur or do not occur. The Board also noted that a change would require a reconsideration of other provisions in IAS 32 that require liability treatment for obligations that are conditional on events or choices that are beyond the entity's control. These include, for example, (a) the treatment of financial instruments with contingent settlement provisions as financial liabilities for the full amount of the conditional obligation, (b) the treatment of preference shares that are redeemable at the option of the holder as financial liabilities for the full amount of the conditional obligation, and (c) the treatment of financial instruments (puttable instruments) that give the holder the right to put the instrument back to the issuer for cash or another financial asset, the amount of which is determined by reference to an index, and which therefore has the potential to increase and decrease, as financial liabilities for the full amount of the conditional obligation.

When an entity uses its own equity instruments as currency in a contract to receive or deliver a variable number of shares, the contract is not an equity instrument, but is a financial asset or a financial liability.

BC13   The Board agreed that it would be inappropriate to account for a contract as an equity instrument when an entity's own equity instruments are used as currency in a contract to receive or deliver a variable number of shares whose value equals a fixed amount or an amount based on changes in an underlying variable (eg a net share-settled derivative contract on gold or an obligation to deliver as many shares as are equal in value to CU10,000). Such a contract represents a right or obligation of a specified amount rather than a specified equity interest. A contract to pay or receive a specified amount (rather than a specified equity interest) is not an equity instrument. For such a contract, the entity does not know, before the transaction is settled, how many of its own shares (or how much cash) it will receive or deliver and the entity may not even know whether it will receive or deliver its own shares.

BC14   In addition, the Board noted that precluding equity treatment for such a contract limits incentives for structuring potentially favourable or unfavourable transactions to obtain equity treatment. For example, the Board believes that an entity should not be able to obtain equity treatment for a transaction simply by including a share settlement clause when the contract is for a specified value, rather than a specified equity interest.

BC15   The Board rejected the argument that a contract that is settled in the entity's own shares must be an equity instrument because no change in assets or liabilities, and thus no gain or loss, arises on settlement of the contract. The Board noted that any gain or loss arises before settlement of the transaction, not when it is settled.

Contingent settlement provisions (paragraphs 25 and AG28)

BC16   The revised Standard incorporates the conclusion previously in SIC-5 *Classification of Financial Instruments—Contingent Settlement Provisions* that a financial instrument for which the manner of settlement depends on the occurrence or non-occurrence of uncertain future events, or on the outcome of uncertain circumstances that are beyond the control of both the issuer and the holder (ie a 'contingent settlement provision'), is a financial liability.

BC17   The amendments do not include the exception previously provided in paragraph 6 of SIC-5 for circumstances in which the possibility of the entity being required to settle in cash or another financial asset is remote at the time the financial instrument is issued. The Board concluded that it is not consistent with the definitions of financial liabilities and equity instruments to classify an obligation to deliver cash or another financial asset as a financial liability only when settlement in cash is probable. There is a contractual obligation to transfer economic benefits as a result of past events because the entity is unable to avoid a settlement in cash or another financial asset unless an event occurs or does not occur in the future.

BC18 However, the Board also concluded that contingent settlement provisions that would apply only in the event of liquidation of an entity should not influence the classification of the instrument because to do so would be inconsistent with a going concern assumption. A contingent settlement provision that provides for payment in cash or another financial asset only on the liquidation of the entity is similar to an equity instrument that has priority in liquidation and therefore should be ignored in classifying the instrument.

BC19 Additionally, the Board decided that if the part of a contingent settlement provision that could require settlement in cash or a variable number of own shares is not genuine, it should be ignored for the purposes of classifying the instrument. The Board also agreed to provide guidance on the meaning of 'genuine' in this context (see paragraph AG28).

Settlement options (paragraphs 26 and 27)

BC20 The revised Standard requires that if one of the parties to a contract has one or more options as to how it is settled (eg net in cash or by exchanging shares for cash), the contract is a financial asset or a financial liability unless all of the settlement alternatives would result in equity classification. The Board concluded that entities should not be able to circumvent the accounting requirements for financial assets and financial liabilities simply by including an option to settle a contract through the exchange of a fixed number of shares for a fixed amount. The Board had proposed in the Exposure Draft that past practice and management intentions should be considered in determining the classification of such instruments. However, respondents to the Exposure Draft noted that such requirements can be difficult to apply because some entities do not have any history of similar transactions and the assessment of whether an established practice exists and of what is management's intention can be subjective. The Board agreed with these comments and accordingly concluded that past practice and management intentions should not be determining factors.

Alternative approaches considered

BC21 In finalising the revisions to IAS 32 the Board considered, but rejected, a number of alternative approaches:

(a) To classify as an equity instrument any contract that will be settled in the entity's own shares. The Board rejected this approach because it does not deal adequately with transactions in which an entity is using its own shares as currency, eg when an entity has an obligation to pay a fixed or determinable amount that is settled in a variable number of its own shares.

(b)   To classify a contract as an equity instrument only if (i) the contract will be settled in the entity's own shares, and (ii) the changes in the fair value of the contract move in the same direction as the changes in the fair value of the shares from the perspective of the counterparty. Under this approach, contracts that will be settled in the entity's own shares would be financial assets or financial liabilities if, from the perspective of the counterparty, their value moves inversely with the price of the entity's own shares. An example is an entity's obligation to buy back its own shares. The Board rejected this approach because its adoption would represent a fundamental shift in the concept of equity. The Board also noted that it would result in a change to the classification of some transactions, compared with the existing *Framework*[5] and IAS 32, that had not been exposed for comment.

(c)   To classify as an equity instrument a contract that will be settled in the entity's own shares unless its value changes in response to something other than the price of the entity's own shares. The Board rejected this approach to avoid an exception to the principle that non-derivative contracts that are settled in a variable number of an entity's own shares should be treated as financial assets or financial liabilities.

(d)   To limit classification as equity instruments to outstanding ordinary shares, and classify as financial assets or financial liabilities all contracts that involve future receipt or delivery of the entity's own shares. The Board rejected this approach because its adoption would represent a fundamental shift in the concept of equity. The Board also noted that it would result in a change to the classification of some transactions compared with the existing IAS 32 that had not been exposed for comment.

Compound financial instruments (paragraphs 28–32 and AG30–AG35)

BC22   The Standard requires the separate presentation in an entity's balance sheet[6] of liability and equity components of a single financial instrument. It is more a matter of form than a matter of substance that both liabilities and equity interests are created by a single financial instrument rather than two or more separate instruments. The Board believes that an entity's financial position is more faithfully represented by separate presentation of liability and equity components contained in a single instrument.

---

5   References to the *Framework* in this Basis for Conclusions are to the IASC's *Framework for the Preparation and Presentation of Financial Statements*, adopted by the Board in 2001 and in effect when the Standard was revised and amended.

6   IAS 1 (as revised in 2007) replaced the term 'balance sheet' with 'statement of financial position'.

Allocation of the initial carrying amount to the liability and equity components (paragraphs 31, 32 and AG36–AG38 and Illustrative Examples 9–12)

BC23   The previous version of IAS 32 did not prescribe a particular method for assigning the initial carrying amount of a compound financial instrument to its separated liability and equity components. Rather, it suggested approaches that might be considered, such as:

(a)   assigning to the less easily measurable component (often the equity component) the residual amount after deducting from the instrument as a whole the amount separately determined for the component that is more easily determinable (a 'with-and-without' method); and

(b)   measuring the liability and equity components separately and, to the extent necessary, adjusting these amounts pro rata so that the sum of the components equals the amount of the instrument as a whole (a 'relative fair value' method).

BC24   This choice was originally justified on the grounds that IAS 32 did not deal with the measurement of financial assets, financial liabilities and equity instruments.

BC25   However, since the issue of IAS 39,[7] IFRSs contain requirements for the measurement of financial assets and financial liabilities. Therefore, the view that IAS 32 should not prescribe a particular method for separating compound financial instruments because of the absence of measurement requirements for financial instruments is no longer valid. IAS 39, paragraph 43, requires a financial liability to be measured on initial recognition at its fair value. Therefore, a relative fair value method could result in an initial measurement of the liability component that is not in compliance with IAS 39.

BC26   After initial recognition, a financial liability that is classified as at fair value through profit or loss is measured at fair value under IAS 39,[8] and other financial liabilities are measured at amortised cost. If the liability component of a compound financial instrument is classified as at fair value through profit or loss, an entity could recognise an immediate gain or loss after initial recognition if it applies a relative fair value method. This is contrary to IAS 32, paragraph 31, which states that no gain or loss arises from recognising the components of the instrument separately.

BC27   Under the *Framework*, and IASs 32 and 39, an equity instrument is defined as any contract that evidences a residual interest in the assets of an entity after deducting all of its liabilities. Paragraph 67 of the *Framework* further states that the amount at which equity is recognised in the balance sheet is dependent on the measurement of assets and liabilities.

---

7   IFRS 9 *Financial Instruments* replaced IAS 39. The requirements of paragraph 43 of IAS 39 relating to the initial measurement of financial assets were relocated to paragraph 5.1.1 of IFRS 9.

8   IFRS 9 *Financial Instruments* replaced IAS 39. IFRS 9 applies to all items that were previously within the scope of IAS 39.

BC28   The Board concluded that the alternatives in IAS 32 to measure on initial recognition the liability component of a compound financial instrument as a residual amount after separating the equity component or on the basis of a relative fair value method should be eliminated. Instead the liability component should be measured first (including the value of any embedded non-equity derivative features, such as an embedded call feature), and the residual amount assigned to the equity component.

BC29   The objective of this amendment is to make the requirements about the entity's separation of the liability and equity components of a single compound financial instrument consistent with the requirements about the initial measurement of a financial liability in IAS 39 and the definitions in IAS 32 and the *Framework* of an equity instrument as a residual interest.

BC30   This approach removes the need to estimate inputs to, and apply, complex option pricing models to measure the equity component of some compound financial instruments. The Board also noted that the absence of a prescribed approach led to a lack of comparability among entities applying IAS 32 and that it therefore was desirable to specify a single approach.

BC31   The Board noted that a requirement to use the with-and-without method, under which the liability component is determined first, is consistent with the proposals of the Joint Working Group of Standard Setters in its Draft Standard and Basis for Conclusions in *Financial Instruments and Similar Items*, published by IASC in December 2000 (see Draft Standard, paragraphs 74 and 75 and Application Supplement, paragraph 318).

Treasury shares (paragraphs 33–34 and AG36)

BC32   The revised Standard incorporates the guidance in SIC-16 *Share Capital—Reacquired Own Equity Instruments (Treasury Shares)*. The acquisition and subsequent resale by an entity of its own equity instruments represents a transfer between those holders of equity instruments who have given up their equity interest and those who continue to hold an equity instrument, rather than a gain or loss to the entity.

BC32A   IFRS 17 *Insurance Contracts* amended IAS 32 by permitting an exemption to the requirements for treasury shares in paragraph 33 of IAS 32 in specified circumstances. The Board's considerations in providing that exemption are set out in paragraph BC65(c) of the Basis for Conclusions on IFRS 17.

Interest, dividends, losses and gains (paragraphs 35–41 and AG37)

Costs of an equity transaction (paragraphs 35 and 37–39)

BC33   The revised Standard incorporates the guidance in SIC-17 *Equity—Costs of an Equity Transaction*. Transaction costs incurred as a necessary part of completing an equity transaction are accounted for as part of the transaction to which they relate. Linking the equity transaction and costs of the transaction reflects in equity the total cost of the transaction.

Income tax consequences of distributions to holders of an equity instrument and of transaction costs of an equity transaction

BC33A   In *Annual Improvements 2009–2011 Cycle* (issued in May 2012) the Board addressed perceived inconsistencies between IAS 12 *Income Taxes* and IAS 32 *Financial Instruments: Presentation* with regards to recognising the consequences of income tax relating to distributions to holders of an equity instrument and to transaction costs of an equity transaction. Paragraph 52B of IAS 12 requires the recognition of the income tax consequences of dividends in profit or loss except when the circumstances described in paragraph 58(a) and (b) of IAS 12 arise. However, paragraph 35 of IAS 32 required the recognition of income tax relating to distributions to holders of an equity instrument in equity (prior to the amendment).[9]

BC33B   The Board noted that the intention of IAS 32 was to follow the requirements in IAS 12 for accounting for income tax relating to distributions to holders of an equity instrument and to transaction costs of an equity transaction. Consequently, the Board decided to add paragraph 35A to IAS 32 to clarify this intention.

BC33C   The Board noted that this amendment is not intended to address the distinction between income tax consequences of dividends in accordance with paragraph 52B, and withholding tax for dividends in accordance with paragraph 65A, of IAS 12. In this respect, the Board observed that the income tax consequences of distributions to holders of an equity instrument are recognised in profit or loss in accordance with paragraph 52B of IAS 12. Consequently, to the extent that the distribution relates to income arising from a transaction that was originally recognised in profit or loss, the income tax on the distribution should be recognised in profit or loss. However, if the distribution relates to income or to a transaction that was originally recognised in other comprehensive income or equity, the entity should apply the exception in paragraph 58(a) of IAS 12, and recognise the income tax consequences of the distribution outside of profit or loss. The Board also observed that, in accordance with paragraph 65A, when an entity pays dividends to its shareholders the portion of the dividends paid or payable to taxation authorities as withholding tax is charged to equity as part of the dividends.[10]

BC34–   [Deleted]
BC48

---

9 *Annual Improvements to IFRS Standards 2015–2017 Cycle*, issued in December 2017, deleted paragraph 52B of IAS 12. The requirements previously specified in that paragraph were moved to paragraph 57A of IAS 12.

10 *Annual Improvements to IFRS Standards 2015–2017 Cycle*, issued in December 2017, deleted paragraph 52B of IAS 12. The requirements previously specified in that paragraph were moved to paragraph 57A of IAS 12.

Summary of changes from the Exposure Draft

BC49   The main changes from the Exposure Draft's proposals are as follows:

(a)   The Exposure Draft proposed to define a financial liability as a contractual obligation to deliver cash or another financial asset to another entity or to exchange financial instruments with another entity under conditions that are potentially unfavourable. The definition in the Standard has been expanded to include some contracts that will or may be settled in the entity's own equity instruments. The Standard's definition of a financial asset has been similarly expanded.

(b)   The Exposure Draft proposed that a financial instrument that gives the holder the right to put it back to the entity for cash or another financial asset is a financial liability. The Standard retains this conclusion, but provides additional guidance and illustrative examples to assist entities that, as a result of this requirement, either have no equity as defined in IAS 32 or whose share capital is not equity as defined in IAS 32.

(c)   The Standard retains and clarifies the proposal in the Exposure Draft that terms and conditions of a financial instrument may indirectly create an obligation.

(d)   The Exposure Draft proposed to incorporate in IAS 32 the conclusion previously in SIC-5. This is that a financial instrument for which the manner of settlement depends on the occurrence or non-occurrence of uncertain future events or on the outcome of uncertain circumstances that are beyond the control of both the issuer and the holder is a financial liability. The Standard clarifies this conclusion by requiring contingent settlement provisions that apply only in the event of liquidation of an entity or are not genuine to be ignored.

(e)   The Exposure Draft proposed that a derivative contract that contains an option as to how it is settled meets the definition of an equity instrument if the entity had all of the following: (i) an unconditional right and ability to settle the contract gross; (ii) an established practice of such settlement; and (iii) the intention to settle the contract gross. These conditions have not been carried forward into the Standard. Rather, a derivative with settlement options is classified as a financial asset or a financial liability unless all the settlement alternatives would result in equity classification.

(f)   The Standard provides explicit guidance on accounting for the repurchase of a convertible instrument.

(g)   The Standard provides explicit guidance on accounting for the amendment of the terms of a convertible instrument to induce early conversion.

(ii) when the entity performs poorly, the present value of the settlement amount of the liability decreases, and a gain is recognised.

(c) It is possible, again depending on the basis for which the redemption value is calculated, that the entity will report negative net assets because of unrecognised intangible assets and goodwill, and because the measurement of recognised assets and liabilities may not be at fair value.

(d) The issuing entity's statement of financial position portrays the entity as wholly, or mostly, debt funded.

(e) Distributions of profits to shareholders are recognised as expenses. Hence, it may appear that profit or loss is a function of the distribution policy, not performance.

Furthermore, constituents contended that additional disclosures and adapting the format of the statement of comprehensive income and statement of financial position did not resolve these concerns.

BC51 The Board agreed with constituents that many puttable instruments, despite meeting the definition of a financial liability, represent a residual interest in the net assets of the entity. The Board also agreed with constituents that additional disclosures and adapting the format of the entity's financial statements did not resolve the problem of the lack of relevance and understandability of that current accounting treatment. Therefore, the Board decided to amend IAS 32 to improve the financial reporting of these instruments.

BC52 The Board considered the following ways to improve the financial reporting of instruments that represent a residual interest in the net assets of the entity:

(a) to continue to classify these instruments as financial liabilities, but amend their measurement so that changes in their fair value would not be recognised;

(b) to amend IAS 32 to require separation of all puttable instruments into a put option and a host instrument; or

(c) to amend IAS 32 to provide a limited scope exception so that financial instruments puttable at fair value would be classified as equity, if specified conditions were met.

Amend the measurement of some puttable financial instruments so that changes in their fair value would not be recognised

BC53 The Board decided against this approach because:

(a) it is inconsistent with the principle in IAS 32 and IAS 39[12] that only equity instruments are not remeasured after their initial recognition;

---

12 IFRS 9 *Financial Instruments* replaced IAS 39. IFRS 9 applies to all items that were previously within the scope of IAS 39.

(b)   it retains the disadvantage that entities whose instruments are all puttable would have no equity instruments; and

(c)   it introduces a new category of financial liabilities to IAS 39, and thus increases complexity.

Separate all puttable instruments into a put option and a host instrument

BC54   The Board concluded that conducting further research into an approach that splits a puttable share into an equity component and a written put option component (financial liability) would duplicate efforts of the Board's longer-term project on liabilities and equity. Consequently, the Board decided not to proceed with a project at this stage to determine whether a puttable share should be split into an equity component and a written put option component.

Classify as equity instruments puttable instruments that represent a residual interest in the entity

BC55   The Board decided to proceed with proposals to amend IAS 32 to require puttable financial instruments that represent a residual interest in the net assets of the entity to be classified as equity provided that specified conditions are met. The proposals represented a limited scope exception to the definition of a financial liability and a short-term solution, pending the outcome of the longer-term project on liabilities and equity. In June 2006 the Board published an exposure draft proposing that financial instruments puttable at fair value that meet specific criteria should be classified as equity.

BC56   In response to comments received from respondents to that exposure draft, the Board amended the criteria for identifying puttable instruments that represent a residual interest in the entity, to those included in paragraphs 16A and 16B. The Board decided on those conditions for the following reasons:

(a)   to ensure that the puttable instruments, as a class, represent the residual interest in the net assets of the entity;

(b)   to ensure that the proposed amendments are consistent with a limited scope exception to the definition of a financial liability; and

(c)   to reduce structuring opportunities that might arise as a result of the amendments.

BC57   The Board decided that the instrument must entitle the holder to a pro rata share of the net assets on liquidation because the net assets on liquidation represent the ultimate residual interest of the entity.

BC58   The Board decided that the instrument must be in the class of instruments that is subordinate to all other classes of instruments on liquidation in order to represent the residual interest in the entity.

BC59   The Board decided that all instruments in the class that is subordinate to all other classes of instruments must have identical contractual terms and conditions. In order to ensure that the class of instruments as a whole is the *residual class*, the Board decided that no instrument holder in that class can have preferential terms or conditions in its position as an owner of the entity.

BC60   The Board decided that the puttable instruments should contain no contractual obligation to deliver a financial asset to another entity other than the put. That is because the amendments represent a limited scope exception to the definition of a financial liability and extending that exception to instruments that also contain other contractual obligations is not appropriate. Moreover, the Board concluded that if the puttable instrument contains another contractual obligation, that instrument may not represent the residual interest because the holder of the puttable instrument may have a claim to some of the net assets of the entity in preference to other instruments.

BC61   As well as requiring a direct link between the puttable instrument and the performance of the entity, the Board also decided that there should be no financial instrument or contract with a return that is more residual. The Board decided to require that there must be no other financial instrument or contract that has total cash flows based substantially on the performance of the entity and has the effect of significantly restricting or fixing the return to the puttable instrument holders. This criterion was included to ensure that the holders of the puttable instruments represent the residual interest in the net assets of the entity.

BC62   An instrument holder may enter into transactions with the issuing entity in a role other than that of an owner. The Board concluded that it is inappropriate to consider cash flows and contractual features related to the instrument holder in a non-owner role when evaluating whether a financial instrument has the features set out in paragraph 16A or paragraph 16C. That is because those cash flows and contractual features are separate and distinct from the cash flows and contractual features of the puttable financial instrument.

BC63   The Board also decided that contracts (such as warrants and other derivatives) to be settled by the issue of puttable financial instruments should be precluded from equity classification. That is because the Board noted that the amendments represent a limited scope exception to the definition of a financial liability and extending that exception to such contracts is not appropriate.

Amendment for obligations to deliver to another party a pro rata share of the net assets of the entity only on liquidation

BC64   Issues similar to those raised by constituents relating to classification of puttable financial instruments apply to some financial instruments that create an obligation only on liquidation of the entity.

BC65   In the exposure draft published in June 2006, the Board proposed to exclude from the definition of a financial liability a contractual obligation that entitles the holder to a pro rata share of the net assets of the entity only on liquidation of the entity. The liquidation of the entity may be:

(a)   certain to occur and outside the control of the entity (limited life entities); or

(b) uncertain to occur but at the option of the holder (for example, some partnership interests).

BC66 Respondents to that exposure draft were generally supportive of the proposed amendment.

BC67 The Board decided that an exception to the definition of a financial liability should be made for instruments that entitle the holder to a pro rata share of the net assets of an entity only on liquidation if particular requirements are met. Many of those requirements, and the reasons for them, are similar to those for puttable financial instruments. The differences between the requirements are as follows:

(a) there is no requirement that there be no other contractual obligations;

(b) there is no requirement to consider the expected total cash flows throughout the life of the instrument;

(c) the only feature that must be identical among the instruments in the class is the obligation for the issuing entity to deliver to the holder a pro rata share of its net assets on liquidation.

The reason for the differences is the timing of settlement of the obligation. The life of the financial instrument is the same as the life of the issuing entity; the extinguishment of the obligation can occur only at liquidation. Therefore, the Board concluded that it was appropriate to focus only on the obligations that exist at liquidation. The instrument must be subordinate to all other classes of instruments and represent the residual interests only at that point in time. However, if the instrument contains other contractual obligations, those obligations may need to be accounted for separately in accordance with the requirements of IAS 32.

Non-controlling interests

BC68 The Board decided that puttable financial instruments or instruments that impose on the entity an obligation to deliver to another party a pro rata share of the net assets of the entity only on liquidation should be classified as equity in the separate financial statements of the issuer if they represent the residual class of instruments (and all the relevant requirements are met). The Board decided that such instruments were not the residual interest in the consolidated financial statements and therefore that non-controlling interests that contain an obligation to transfer a financial asset to another entity should be classified as a financial liability in the consolidated financial statements.

Analysis of costs and benefits

BC69 The Board acknowledged that the amendments made in February 2008 are not consistent with the definition of a liability in the *Framework*, or with the underlying principle of IAS 32, which is based on that definition. Consequently, those amendments added complexity to IAS 32 and introduced the need for detailed rules. However, the Board also noted that IAS 32 contains other exceptions to its principle (and the definition of a liability in the *Framework*) that require instruments to be classified as liabilities that otherwise would be treated as equity. Those exceptions highlight the need for a comprehensive reconsideration of the distinctions between liabilities and equity, which the Board is undertaking in its long-term project.

BC70   In the interim, the Board concluded that classifying as equity the instruments that have all the features and meet the conditions in paragraphs 16A and 16B or paragraphs 16C and 16D would improve the comparability of information provided to the users of financial statements. That is because financial instruments that are largely equivalent to ordinary shares would be consistently classified across different entity structures (eg some partnerships, limited life entities and co-operatives). The specified instruments differ from ordinary shares in one respect; that difference is the obligation to deliver cash (or another financial asset). However, the Board concluded that the other characteristics of the specified instruments are sufficiently similar to ordinary shares for the instruments to be classified as equity. Consequently, the Board concluded that the amendments will result in financial reporting that is more understandable and relevant to the users of financial statements.

BC71   Furthermore, in developing the amendments, the Board considered the costs to entities of obtaining information necessary to determine the required classification. The Board believes that the costs of obtaining any new information would be slight because all of the necessary information should be readily available.

BC72   The Board also acknowledged that one of the costs and risks of introducing exceptions to the definition of a financial liability is the structuring opportunities that may result. The Board concluded that financial structuring opportunities are minimised by the detailed criteria required for equity classification and the related disclosures.

BC73   Consequently, the Board believed that the benefits of the amendments outweigh the costs.

BC74   The Board took the view that, in most cases, entities should be able to apply the amendments retrospectively. The Board noted that IAS 8 *Accounting Policies, Changes in Accounting Estimates and Errors* provides relief when it is impracticable to apply a change in accounting policy retrospectively as a result of a new requirement. Furthermore, the Board took the view that the costs outweighed the benefits of separating a compound financial instrument with an obligation to deliver a pro rata share of the net assets of the entity only on liquidation when the liability component is no longer outstanding on the date of initial application. Hence, there is no requirement on transition to separate such compound instruments.

Amendments to the application guidance for offsetting financial assets and financial liabilities

Background

BC75 Following requests from users of financial statements and recommendations from the Financial Stability Board, in June 2010 the IASB and the US national standard-setter, the Financial Accounting Standards Board (FASB), added a project to their respective agendas to improve, and potentially achieve convergence of, the requirements for offsetting financial assets and financial liabilities. The boards made this decision because the differences in their requirements for offsetting financial assets and financial liabilities cause significant differences between amounts presented in statements of financial position prepared in accordance with IFRSs and amounts presented in statements of financial position prepared in accordance with US GAAP. This is particularly so for entities that have large amounts of derivative activities.

BC76 Consequently, in January 2011 the Board published the exposure draft *Offsetting Financial Assets and Financial Liabilities*. The proposals in the exposure draft would have established a common approach with the FASB. The exposure draft also proposed disclosures about financial assets and financial liabilities that are subject to set-off rights and related arrangements (such as collateral agreements), and the effect of those rights and arrangements on an entity's financial position.

BC77 As a result of the feedback received on the exposure draft, the IASB and the FASB decided to maintain their current offsetting models. However, the boards noted that requiring common disclosures of gross and net information would be helpful for users of financial statements. Accordingly, the boards agreed on common disclosure requirements by amending and finalising the disclosures that were initially proposed in the exposure draft. The amendments *Disclosures—Offsetting Financial Assets and Financial Liabilities* (Amendments to IFRS 7) were issued in December 2011.

BC78 In addition, the IASB decided to add application guidance to IAS 32 to address inconsistencies identified in applying some of the offsetting criteria. This included clarifying the meaning of 'currently has a legally enforceable right of set-off' and that some gross settlement systems may be considered equivalent to net settlement.

Requirements for offsetting financial assets and financial liabilities

Criterion that an entity 'currently has a legally enforceable right to set off the recognised amounts' (paragraph 42(a))

BC79 To meet the criterion in paragraph 42(a) of IAS 32, an entity must currently have a legally enforceable right to set off the recognised amounts. However, IAS 32 did not previously provide guidance on what was meant by 'currently has a legally enforceable right to set off'. Feedback from the exposure draft revealed inconsistencies in the application of this criterion by IFRS preparers.

Consequently, the Board decided to include application guidance in IAS 32 (paragraphs AG38A–AG38D) to clarify the meaning of this criterion.

BC80 The Board believes that the net amounts of financial assets and financial liabilities presented in the statement of financial position should represent an entity's exposure in the normal course of business and its exposure if one of the parties will not or cannot perform under the terms of the contract. The Board therefore clarified in paragraph AG38B that to meet the criterion in paragraph 42(a) of IAS 32 a right of set-off is required to be legally enforceable in the normal course of business, the event of default and the event of insolvency or bankruptcy of the entity and all of the counterparties. The right must exist for all counterparties so that if an event occurs for one of the counterparties, including the entity, the other counterparty or parties will be able to enforce the right of set-off against the party that has defaulted or gone insolvent or bankrupt.

BC81 If a right of set-off cannot be enforced in the event of default and in the event of insolvency or bankruptcy, then offsetting would not reflect the economic substance of the entity's rights and obligations and would therefore not meet the objective of offsetting in paragraph 43 of IAS 32. The Board uses the term 'in the event of default and in the event of insolvency or bankruptcy' to describe scenarios where an entity will not or cannot perform under the contract.

BC82 The use of the word 'currently' in paragraph 42(a) of IAS 32 means that the right of set-off cannot be contingent on a future event. If a right of set-off were contingent or conditional on a future event an entity would not currently have a (legally enforceable) right of set-off. The right of set-off would not exist until the contingency occurred, if at all.

BC83 In addition, the Board believes that the passage of time or uncertainties in amounts to be paid do not preclude an entity from currently having a (legally enforceable) right of set-off. The fact that the payments subject to a right of set-off will only arise at a future date is not in itself a condition or a form of contingency that prevents offsetting in accordance with paragraph 42(a) of IAS 32.

BC84 However, if the right of set-off is not exercisable during a period when amounts are due and payable, then the entity does not meet the offsetting criterion as it has no right to set off those payments. Similarly, a right of set-off that could disappear or that would no longer be enforceable after a future event that could take place in the normal course of business or in the event of default, or in the event of insolvency or bankruptcy, such as a ratings downgrade, would not meet the currently (legally enforceable) criterion in paragraph 42(a) of IAS 32.

BC85 The application of the word 'currently' in paragraph 42(a) of IAS 32 was not a source of inconsistency in practice but rather a question that arose as a result of the wording in the exposure draft. Consequently, the Board decided that further application guidance was only required for the legal enforceability part of the criterion.

BC86   In developing the proposals in the exposure draft, the Board concluded that the net amount represents the entity's right or obligation if (a) the entity has the ability to insist on net settlement or to enforce net settlement in all situations (ie the exercise of that right is not contingent on a future event), (b) that ability is assured, and (c) the entity intends to receive or pay a single net amount, or to realise the asset and settle the liability simultaneously.

BC87   Some respondents were concerned that the terms 'in all situations' and 'the ability is assured' as referred to in paragraph BC86 create a higher hurdle than IAS 32 today. The Board however believes that the conclusions in the exposure draft are consistent with the offsetting criteria and principle in IAS 32, specifically paragraphs 42, 43, 46 and 47. In addition, the application guidance in paragraph AG38B of IAS 32 addresses respondents' concerns by clarifying the circumstances in which an entity should be able to net (ie what 'in all situations' means), and by requiring legal enforceability in such circumstances, a term commonly used in applying IAS 32 today.

Applicability to all counterparties

BC88   The proposals in the exposure draft required that the right of set-off be legally enforceable in the event of default and in the event of insolvency or bankruptcy of 'one of the counterparties' (including the entity itself). There were differing views as to whether the requirement that the right of set-off must be enforceable in the event of the entity's default and/or insolvency or bankruptcy changed the criteria in IAS 32 today.

BC89   Some respondents disagreed that the right of set-off must be enforceable in the events of default and insolvency or bankruptcy of the entity. Although consideration is given to enforceability today to achieve offsetting in accordance with IAS 32, some have only focused on the effects of the insolvency or bankruptcy of the counterparty. These respondents questioned whether legal opinions as to enforceability in the event of their own insolvency or bankruptcy could be obtained and considered this to be a change in practice from IAS 32 that could increase costs and the burden for preparers. They also believed that such a requirement would be inconsistent with the going concern basis of preparation for financial statements.

BC90   Other respondents, however, agreed that, to represent the entity's net exposure at all times, the right of set-off must be enforceable in the insolvency or bankruptcy of all of the counterparties to the contract.

BC91   The Board believes that limiting the enforcement of the right of set-off to the event of default and the event of insolvency or bankruptcy of the counterparty (and not the entity itself) is not consistent with the principle and objective of offsetting in IAS 32.

BC92   If a right of set-off cannot also be enforced in the event of default and in the event of insolvency or bankruptcy of the entity, then offsetting would not reflect the economic substance of the entity's rights and obligations or the financial position of the entity (ie offsetting would not reflect an entity's expected future cash flows from settling two or more separate financial instruments in accordance with paragraph 43 of IAS 32) and would therefore not meet the objective of offsetting in IAS 32.

BC93   Consequently, the Board decided to clarify that, to meet the offsetting criterion in paragraph 42(a) of IAS 32, a right of set-off must be enforceable in the event of default and in the event of insolvency or bankruptcy of both the entity and its counterparties (paragraphs AG38A and AG38B of IAS 32).

Criterion that an entity 'intends either to settle on a net basis, or to realise the asset and settle the liability simultaneously' (paragraph 42(b))

BC94   In the exposure draft the boards noted that offsetting financial assets and financial liabilities is appropriate and reflects the financial position of an entity only if the entity has, in effect, a right to, or an obligation for, only the net amount (ie the entity has, in effect, a single net financial asset or net financial liability). The amount resulting from offsetting must also reflect the entity's expected future cash flows from settling two or more separate financial instruments. This is consistent with the principle in paragraph 43 of IAS 32.

BC95   When developing that principle the boards understood that entities may currently have a legally enforceable right and desire to settle net, but may not have the operational capabilities to effect net settlement. The gross positions would be settled at the same moment such that the outcome would not be distinguishable from net settlement. As a result the boards included simultaneous settlement as a practical exception to net settlement. Simultaneous settlement was intended to capture payments that are essentially equivalent to actual net settlement. The proposals in the exposure draft also defined simultaneous settlement as settlement 'at the same moment'.

BC96   Simultaneous settlement as 'at the same moment' is already a concept in paragraph 48 of IAS 32 that enables an entity to meet the criterion in paragraph 42(b) of IAS 32. However, feedback received during outreach indicated that there was diversity in practice related to the interpretation of 'simultaneous settlement' in IAS 32. Many preparers and accounting firms have interpreted paragraph 48 of IAS 32 to mean that settlement through a clearing house always meets the simultaneous settlement criterion even if not occurring at the same moment.

BC97   Respondents also noted that settlement of two positions by exchange of gross cash flows at exactly the same moment (simultaneously) rarely occurs in practice today. They argued that 'simultaneous' is not operational and ignores settlement systems that are established to achieve what is economically considered to be net exposure.

BC98   Some preparers also indicated that settlement through some gross settlement mechanisms, though not simultaneous, effectively results in the same exposure as in net settlement or settlement at the same moment and are currently considered to meet the requirements in IAS 32, without actually taking place 'at the same moment'. For particular settlement mechanisms, once the settlement process commences, the entity is not exposed to credit or liquidity risk over and above the net amount and therefore the process is equivalent to net settlement.

BC99   Paragraph 48 of IAS 32 states that simultaneous settlement results in 'no exposure to credit or liquidity risk'. In its redeliberations the Board considered gross settlement mechanisms with features that both (i) eliminate credit and liquidity risk; and (ii) process receivables and payables in a single settlement process. The Board agreed that gross settlement systems with such features are effectively equivalent to net settlement.

BC100   To clarify the application of the IAS 32 offsetting criteria and to reduce diversity in practice, the Board therefore clarified the principle behind net settlement and included an example of a gross settlement system with characteristics that would satisfy the IAS 32 criterion for net settlement in paragraph AG38F of IAS 32.

BC101   However, the Board decided not to refer specifically to clearing houses or central counterparties when describing systems that may be treated as equivalent to net settlement for the purposes of the set-off criterion. Systems that meet the principle in paragraph AG38F of IAS 32 may be referred to by different names in different jurisdictions. Referring to specific types of settlement systems may exclude other systems that are also considered equivalent to net settlement. In addition, the Board did not want to imply that settlement through specific systems would always meet the net settlement criterion. Entities must determine whether a system meets the principle in paragraph AG38F of IAS 32 by determining whether or not the system eliminates or results in insignificant credit and liquidity risk and processes receivables and payables in the same settlement process or cycle.

Offsetting collateral amounts

BC102   The proposals in the exposure draft specifically prohibited offsetting assets pledged as collateral (or the right to reclaim the collateral pledged) or the obligation to return collateral sold with the associated financial assets and financial liabilities. A number of respondents disagreed with the proposed treatment of collateral and noted that the proposed prohibition was more restrictive than the offsetting criteria in paragraph 42 of IAS 32.

BC103   The offsetting criteria in IAS 32 do not give special consideration to items referred to as 'collateral'. The Board confirmed that a recognised financial instrument referred to as collateral should be set off against the related financial asset or financial liability in the statement of financial position if, and only if, it meets the offsetting criteria in paragraph 42 of IAS 32. The Board also noted that if an entity can be required to return or receive back collateral, the entity would not currently have a legally enforceable right of set-off in all of the following circumstances: in the normal course of business, the event of default and the event of insolvency or bankruptcy of one of the counterparties.

BC104 Because no particular practice concerns or inconsistencies were brought to the Board's attention related to the treatment of collateral in accordance with the offsetting criteria in IAS 32, and as the concerns that arose originated from the proposals in the exposure draft, the Board did not consider it necessary to add application guidance for the treatment of collateral.

Unit of account

BC105 Neither IAS 32 nor the exposure draft specifies the unit of account to which the offsetting requirements should be applied. During the outreach performed on the exposure draft, it became apparent that there was diversity in practice regarding the unit of account that was used for offsetting in accordance with IAS 32.

BC106 Entities in some industries (for example, energy producers and traders) apply the offsetting criteria to identifiable cash flows. Other entities apply the offsetting criteria to entire financial assets and financial liabilities. For those entities (for example, financial institutions), applying the offsetting criteria to individual identifiable cash flows (portions of financial assets and financial liabilities) within contracts would be impractical and burdensome, even though requiring application of the offsetting criteria to entire financial instruments results in less offsetting in the statement of financial position.

BC107 The Board acknowledged that the focus of the offsetting model is the entity's net exposure and expected future cash flows from settling the related financial instruments.

BC108 The Board also noted that some of the entities for whom the offsetting requirements are most relevant are those that would have the most significant operational challenges with applying the model to individual cash flows (such as financial institutions with large derivative activities). This is important to consider because IAS 32 requires offsetting if the offsetting criteria are met.

BC109 On the other hand, if the application of the offsetting criteria to individual cash flows was prohibited, entities in some industries (for example, energy producers and traders) that apply the criteria in IAS 32 to individual cash flows of financial instruments, and achieve set-off on that basis today, would no longer be permitted to do so.

BC110 The Board considered clarifying the application guidance in IAS 32 to indicate that offsetting should apply to individual cash flows of financial instruments. However, if it made such clarification, the Board felt that it would be necessary to consider an exemption from this requirement on the basis of operational complexity. This would result in the offsetting requirements still being applied differently between entities.

BC111 Although different interpretations of the unit of account are applied today, the Board concluded that this does not result in inappropriate application of the offsetting criteria. The benefits of amending IAS 32 would not outweigh the costs for preparers and therefore the Board decided not to amend the application guidance to IAS 32 on this subject.

Cost-benefit considerations

BC112   Before issuing an IFRS or an amendment to an IFRS, the Board seeks to ensure that it will meet a significant need and that the overall benefits of the resulting information will justify the costs of providing it. The Board issued *Offsetting Financial Assets and Financial Liabilities* (Amendments to IAS 32) to eliminate inconsistencies in the application of the offsetting criteria in paragraph 42 of IAS 32 by clarifying the meaning of 'currently has a legally enforceable right of set-off' and that some gross settlement systems may be considered equivalent to net settlement.

BC113   Some respondents were concerned that requiring a right of set-off to be enforceable in the event of default and in the event of insolvency or bankruptcy of the entity would increase the cost of applying the offsetting criteria in IAS 32, if, for example, they needed to obtain additional legal opinions on enforceability. However, the Board noted that without this clarification the offsetting criteria would continue to be applied inconsistently, and the resulting offsetting would be inconsistent with the offsetting objective in IAS 32. This would also reduce comparability for users of financial statements. Consequently, the Board concluded that the benefit of clarifying this criterion outweighed the cost to preparers of applying these amendments.

BC114   During redeliberations the Board also considered feedback received on the proposals in the exposure draft related to the treatment of collateral and unit of account. However, as described in greater detail in other sections of this Basis for Conclusions, the Board did not consider it necessary to add application guidance for the treatment of these items.

BC115   The amendments to the IAS 32 application guidance (paragraphs AG38A–AG38F of IAS 32) are intended to clarify the Board's objective for the offsetting criteria and therefore eliminate inconsistencies noted in applying paragraph 42 of IAS 32.

BC116   Based on the considerations described in the Basis for Conclusions of these amendments, and summarised in paragraphs BC112–BC115, the Board concluded that the benefits of *Offsetting Financial Assets and Financial Liabilities* (Amendments to IAS 32) outweigh the costs to preparers of applying those amendments.

Transition and effective date

BC117   During redeliberations, the Board originally decided to require retrospective application of the application guidance in paragraphs AG38A–AG38F of IAS 32 for annual periods beginning on or after 1 January 2013. The Board did not expect significant changes in practice as a result of the clarifications made to the application guidance and hence aligned the effective date and transition of these amendments with that of *Disclosures—Offsetting Financial Assets and Financial Liabilities* (Amendments to IFRS 7), issued in December 2011.

BC118   However, the Board received additional feedback from some preparers that the clarifications to the application guidance could change their practice. These preparers indicated that they needed more time to evaluate the effects of the amendments. They indicated that it would be difficult for them to make this assessment in time to allow application of the amendments to the application guidance for the first comparative reporting period.

BC119   Preparers therefore requested that the Board consider aligning the effective date of the amendments with the then revised effective date of IFRS 9 *Financial Instruments* (1 January 2015),[13] with earlier application permitted. This would give them sufficient time to determine if there would be any changes to their financial statements.

BC120   The Board believed that the amendments to the IAS 32 application guidance should be effective as soon as possible to ensure comparability of financial statements prepared in accordance with IFRSs. In addition, the Board did not consider that the effective date needed to be aligned with that of IFRS 9. However, the Board also understood the concerns of preparers. The Board therefore decided to require the amendments to the IAS 32 application guidance to be effective for periods beginning 1 January 2014 with earlier application permitted. This would provide a balance between the time needed to implement the amendments with the need for consistent application of the IAS 32 offsetting requirements.

---

13 In the completed version of IFRS 9, issued in July 2014, the Board specified that entities must adopt the completed version of IFRS 9 for annual periods beginning on or after 1 January 2018.

Dissenting opinions

Dissent of James J Leisenring from the issue of IAS 32 in December 2003

DO1   Mr Leisenring dissents from IAS 32 because, in his view, the conclusions about the accounting for forward purchase contracts and written put options on an issuer's equity instruments that require physical settlement in exchange for cash are inappropriate. IAS 32 requires a forward purchase contract to be recognised as though the future transaction had already occurred. Similarly it requires a written put option to be accounted for as though the option had already been exercised. Both of these contracts result in combining the separate forward contract and the written put option with outstanding shares to create a synthetic liability.

DO2   Recording a liability for the present value of the fixed forward price as a result of a forward contract is inconsistent with the accounting for other forward contracts. Recording a liability for the present value of the strike price of an option results in recording a liability that is inconsistent with the *Framework*[14] as there is no present obligation for the strike price. In both instances the shares considered to be subject to the contracts are outstanding, have the same rights as any other shares and should be accounted for as outstanding. The forward and option contracts meet the definition of a derivative and should be accounted for as derivatives rather than create an exception to the accounting required by IAS 39.[15] Similarly, if the redemption feature is embedded in the equity instrument (for example, a redeemable preference share) rather than being a free-standing derivative contract, the redemption feature should be accounted for as a derivative.

DO3   Mr Leisenring also objects to the conclusion that a purchased put or call option on a fixed number of an issuer's equity instruments is not an asset. The rights created by these contracts meet the definition of an asset and should be accounted for as assets and not as a reduction in equity. These contracts also meet the definition of derivatives that should be accounted for as such consistently with IAS 39.

---

14 The reference to the *Framework* is to the IASC's *Framework for the Preparation and Presentation of Financial Statements*, adopted by the Board in 2001 and in effect when the Standard was revised.

15 IFRS 9 *Financial Instruments* replaced IAS 39. IFRS 9 applies to all items that were previously within the scope of IAS 39.

Dissent of Mary E Barth and Robert P Garnett from the issue of *Puttable Financial Instruments and Obligations Arising on Liquidation* (Amendments to IAS 32 and IAS 1) in February 2008

DO1 Professor Barth and Mr Garnett voted against the publication of *Puttable Financial Instruments and Obligations Arising on Liquidation* (Amendments to IAS 32 and IAS 1 *Presentation of Financial Statements*). The reasons for their dissent are set out below.

DO2 These Board members believe that the decision to permit entities to classify as equity some puttable financial instruments and some financial instruments that entitle the holder to a pro rata share of the net assets of the entity only on liquidation is inconsistent with the *Framework*.[16] The contractual provisions attached to those instruments give the holders the right to put the instruments to the entity and demand cash. The *Framework*'s definition of a liability is that it is a present obligation of the entity arising from a past event, the settlement of which is expected to result in an outflow of resources of the entity. Thus, financial instruments within the scope of the amendments clearly meet the definition of a liability in the *Framework*.

DO3 These Board members do not agree with the Board that an exception to the *Framework* is justified in this situation. First, the Board has an active project on the *Framework*, which will revisit the definition of a liability. Although these Board members agree that standards projects can precede decisions in the *Framework* project, the discussions to date in the *Framework* project do not make it clear that the Board will modify the existing elements definitions in such a way that these instruments would be equity. Second, the amendments would require disclosure of the expected cash outflow on redemption or repurchase of puttable instruments classified as equity. These disclosures are similar to those for financial liabilities; existing standards do not require similar disclosure for equity instruments. The Board's decision to require these disclosures reveals its implicit view these instruments are, in fact, liabilities. Yet, the *Framework* is clear that disclosure is not a substitute for recognition. Third, these Board members see no cost-benefit or practical reasons for making this exception. The amendments require the same or similar information to be obtained and disclosed as would be the case if these obligations were classified as liabilities. Existing standards offer presentation alternatives for entities that have no equity under the *Framework*'s definitions.

DO4 These Board members also do not agree with the Board that there are benefits to issuing these amendments. First, paragraph BC70 in the Basis for Conclusions states that the amendments will result in more relevant and understandable financial reporting. However, as noted above, these Board members do not believe that presenting as equity items that meet the *Framework*'s definition of a liability results in relevant information. Also as

---

16 References to the *Framework* in this Dissent are to the IASC's *Framework for the Preparation and Presentation of Financial Statements*, adopted by the Board in 2001 and in effect when the Standard was amended.

noted above, existing standards offer presentation alternatives that result in understandable financial reporting.

DO5 Second, paragraph BC70 states that the amendments would increase comparability by requiring more consistent classification of financial instruments that are largely equivalent to ordinary shares. These Board members believe that the amendments decrease comparability. These instruments are not comparable to ordinary shares because these instruments oblige the entity to transfer its economic resources; ordinary shares do not. Also, puttable instruments and instruments that entitle the holder to a pro rata share of the net assets of the entity only on liquidation will be classified as equity by some entities and as liabilities by other entities, depending on whether the other criteria specified in the amendments are met. Thus, these amendments account similarly for economically different instruments, which decreases comparability.

DO6 Finally, these Board members do not believe that the amendments are based on a clear principle. Rather, they comprise several paragraphs of detailed rules crafted to achieve a desired accounting result. Although the Board attempted to craft these rules to minimise structuring opportunities, the lack of a clear principle leaves open the possibility that economically similar situations will be accounted for differently and economically different situations will be accounted for similarly. Both of these outcomes also result in lack of comparability.

Dissent of James J Leisenring and John T Smith from the issue of *Classification of Rights Issues* in October 2009

DO1   Messrs Leisenring and Smith dissent from the amendment *Classification of Rights Issues* for the reasons set out below.

DO2   Mr Smith agrees with the concept of accounting for a rights issue as equity in specified circumstances and supports both the IFRIC recommendation and staff recommendation in July 2009 that the Board make 'an extremely narrow amendment' to IAS 32 to deal with this issue. However, he dissents because he believes the change is not extremely narrow and will provide a means for an entity to use its equity instruments as a way to engage in speculative foreign currency transactions and structure them as equity transactions, a concern identified by the Board in the Basis for Conclusions on IAS 32.

DO3   In their comment letters on the exposure draft, some respondents expressed concerns that the wording of the amendment was too open-ended and could lead to structuring risks. Mr Smith believes that these concerns are well-founded because there is no limitation on what qualifies as a class of equity. Without some limitation, an entity could, for example, establish a foreign currency trading subsidiary, issue shares to a non-controlling interest and deem the shares to be a class of equity in the consolidated group.

DO4   The staff acknowledged the concerns expressed in comment letters that a new class of equity could be created for the purpose of obtaining a desired accounting treatment. However, the Board decided not to attempt to limit such structuring opportunities. The Board was concerned that a requirement that a pro rata offer of rights must be made to all existing owners (rather than only all existing owners of a particular class) of equity instruments would mean that the amendment would not be applicable to most of the transactions to which the Board intended the amendment to apply.

DO5   Instead of trying to narrow the amendment, the Board simply acknowledged that under the amendment, 'You could set up a new class of shares today and one minute later issue shares to that class and ... speculate in foreign currency without it going through the income statement.' Mr Smith believes the Board should have explored other alternatives. Mr Smith believes that the Board should have sought solutions that could in fact provide a means of narrowing the amendment to limit structuring while accommodating appropriate transactions.

DO6   Mr Smith believes that structuring opportunities could be curtailed significantly if some limitations were placed on the type of class of equity instruments that qualify for the exemption. There are a number of factors or indicators that could have been incorporated into the amendment that would limit the exception. For example, the amendment could have specified that non-controlling interests do not constitute a class. The amendment could have further required that qualification for the exemption is limited to those classes of equity instruments in which (a) ownership in the class is diverse or (b) the class is registered on an exchange and shares are exchanged in the marketplace or (c) shares in that class when issued were offered to the public at large and sold in more than one jurisdiction and there was no agreement to subsequently offer rights to shares of the entity; and the amount of capital provided by the class is substantial relative to the other classes of equity. Clearly, some combination of these and other alternatives could have been used to limit structuring opportunities. Mr Smith believes that a better solution could have been found and without introducing some limits around the type of class of equity instruments that qualify, the Board did not produce an extremely narrow amendment.

DO7   Mr Leisenring agrees that when an entity issues rights to acquire its own equity instruments those rights should be classified as equity. However, he does not accept that the issue must be pro rata to all existing shareholders of a class of non-derivative equity instruments. He does not accept that whether or not the offer is pro rata is relevant to determining if the transaction meets the definition of a liability.

DO8   Paragraph BC4J suggests that the Board limited its conclusion to those transactions issued on a pro rata basis because of concerns about structuring risks. If that is of concern the suggestions contained in Mr Smith's dissent would be much more effective and desirable than introducing a precedent that transactions such as this rights offering must simply be pro rata to be considered a transaction with owners as owners.

DO9   Mr Leisenring would have preferred to conclude that a right granted for a fixed amount of a currency was a 'fixed for fixed' exchange rather than create additional conditions to the determination of a liability.

IASB documents published to accompany

IAS 33

Earnings per Share

The text of the unaccompanied standard, IAS 33, is contained in Part A of this edition. Its effective date when issued was 1 January 2005. The text of the Accompanying Guidance on IAS 33 is contained in Part B of this edition. This part presents the following document:

BASIS FOR CONCLUSIONS

Basis for Conclusions on
IAS 33 *Earnings per Share*

This Basis for Conclusions accompanies, but is not part of, IAS 33.

Introduction

BC1 This Basis for Conclusions summarises the International Accounting Standards Board's considerations in reaching its conclusions on revising IAS 33 *Earnings Per Share* in 2003. Individual Board members gave greater weight to some factors than to others.

BC2 In July 2001 the Board announced that, as part of its initial agenda of technical projects, it would undertake a project to improve a number of Standards, including IAS 33. The project was undertaken in the light of queries and criticisms raised in relation to the Standards by securities regulators, professional accountants and other interested parties. The objectives of the Improvements project were to reduce or eliminate alternatives, redundancies and conflicts within Standards, to deal with some convergence issues and to make other improvements. In May 2002 the Board published its proposals in an Exposure Draft of *Improvements to International Accounting Standards*, with a comment deadline of 16 September 2002. The Board received over 160 comment letters on the Exposure Draft.

BC3 Because the Board's intention was not to reconsider the fundamental approach to the determination and presentation of earnings per share established by IAS 33, this Basis for Conclusions does not discuss requirements in IAS 33 that the Board has not reconsidered.

Presentation of parent's separate earnings per share

BC4 The Exposure Draft published in May 2002 proposed deleting paragraphs 2 and 3 of the previous version of IAS 33, which stated that when the parent's separate financial statements and consolidated financial statements are presented, earnings per share need be presented only on the basis of consolidated information.

BC5 Some respondents expressed concern that the presentation of two earnings per share figures (one for the parent's separate financial statements and one for the consolidated financial statements) might be misleading.

BC6 The Board noted that disclosing the parent's separate earnings per share amount is useful in limited situations, and therefore decided to retain the option. However, the Board decided that the Standard should prohibit presentation of the parent's separate earnings per share amounts in the consolidated financial statements (either on the face of the financial statements or in the notes).

Contracts that may be settled in ordinary shares or cash

BC7   The Exposure Draft proposed that an entity should include in the calculation of the number of potential ordinary shares in the diluted earnings per share calculation contracts that may be settled in ordinary shares or cash, at the issuer's option, based on a rebuttable presumption that the contracts will be settled in shares. This proposed presumption could be rebutted if the issuer had acted through an established pattern of past practice, published policies, or by having made a sufficiently specific current statement indicating to other parties the manner in which it expected to settle, and, as a result, the issuer had created a valid expectation on the part of those other parties that it would settle in a manner other than by issuing shares.

BC8   The majority of the respondents on the Exposure Draft agreed with the proposed treatment of contracts that may be settled in ordinary shares or cash at the issuer's option. However, the Board decided to withdraw the notion of a rebuttable presumption and to incorporate into the Standard the requirements of SIC-24 *Earnings Per Share—Financial Instruments and Other Contracts that May Be Settled in Shares*. SIC-24 requires financial instruments or other contracts that may result in the issue of ordinary shares of the entity to be considered potential ordinary shares of the entity.

BC9   Although the proposed treatment would have converged with that required by several liaison standard-setters, for example, in US SFAS 128 *Earnings per Share*, the Board concluded that the notion of a rebuttable presumption is inconsistent with the stated objective of diluted earnings per share. The US Financial Accounting Standards Board has agreed to consider this difference as part of the joint short-term convergence project with the IASB.

Calculation of year-to-date diluted earnings per share

BC10   The Exposure Draft proposed the following approach to the year-to-date calculation of diluted earnings per share:

(a)   The number of potential ordinary shares is a year-to-date weighted average of the number of potential ordinary shares included in each interim diluted earnings per share calculation, rather than a year-to-date weighted average of the number of potential ordinary shares weighted for the period they were outstanding (ie without regard for the diluted earnings per share information reported during the interim periods).

(b)   The number of potential ordinary shares is computed using the average market price during the interim periods, rather than using the average market price during the year-to-date period.

(c)   Contingently issuable shares are weighted for the interim periods in which they were included in the computation of diluted earnings per share, rather than being included in the computation of diluted earnings per share (if the conditions are satisfied) from the beginning of the year-to-date reporting period (or from the date of the contingent share agreement, if later).

BC11   The majority of the respondents on the Exposure Draft disagreed with the proposed approach to the year-to-date calculation of diluted earnings per share. The most significant argument against the proposed approach was that the proposed calculation of diluted earnings per share could result in an amount for year-to-date diluted earnings per share that was different for entities that report more frequently, for example, on a quarterly or half-yearly basis, and for entities that report only annually. It was also noted that this problem would be exacerbated for entities with seasonal businesses.

BC12   The Board considered whether to accept that differences in the frequency of interim reporting would result in different earnings per share amounts being reported. However, IAS 34 *Interim Financial Reporting* states 'the frequency of an entity's reporting (annual, half-yearly, or quarterly) should not affect the measurement of its annual results. To achieve that objective, measurements for interim reporting purposes should be made on a year-to-date basis.'

BC13   The Board also considered whether it could mandate the frequency of interim reporting to ensure consistency between all entities preparing financial statements in accordance with IFRSs, ie those that are brought within the scope of IAS 33 by virtue of issuing publicly traded instruments or because they elect to present earnings per share. However, IAS 34 states that, 'This Standard does not mandate which entities should be required to publish interim financial reports, how frequently, or how soon after the end of an interim period.' The frequency of interim reporting is mandated by securities regulators, stock exchanges, governments, and accountancy bodies, and varies by jurisdiction.

BC14   Although the proposed approach for the calculation of year-to-date diluted earnings per share would have converged with US SFAS 128, the Board concluded that the approach was inconsistent with IAS 34 and that it could not mandate the frequency of interim reporting. The US Financial Accounting Standards Board has agreed to consider this difference as part of the joint short-term convergence project with the IASB as well as the issue noted in paragraph BC9.

Other changes

BC15   Implementation questions have arisen since the previous version of IAS 33 was issued, typically concerning the application of the Standard to complex capital structures and arrangements. In response, the Board decided to provide additional application guidance in the Appendix as well as illustrative examples on more complex matters that were not addressed in the previous version of IAS 33. These matters include the effects of contingently issuable shares, potential ordinary shares of subsidiaries, joint ventures or associates, participating equity instruments, written put options, and purchased put and call options.

IASB documents published to accompany

IAS 34

Interim Financial Reporting

The text of the unaccompanied standard, IAS 34, is contained in Part A of this edition. Its effective date when issued was 1 January 1999. The text of the Accompanying Guidance on IAS 34 is contained in Part B of this edition. This part presents the following document:

BASIS FOR CONCLUSIONS

Basis for Conclusions on
IAS 34 *Interim Financial Reporting*

This Basis for Conclusions accompanies, but is not part of, IAS 34.

BC1   This Basis for Conclusions summarises the International Accounting Standards Board's considerations in amending paragraphs 15–18 of IAS 34 *Interim Financial Reporting* as part of *Improvements to IFRSs* issued in May 2010. Those changes aim to emphasise the disclosures principles in IAS 34 and to add further guidance to illustrate how to apply these principles.

BC2   IAS 34 was developed by the International Accounting Standards Committee (IASC) in 1998 and did not include a Basis for Conclusions.

Significant events and transactions

BC3   In *Improvements to IFRSs* issued in May 2010, the Board addressed requests for clarification of the disclosures required by IAS 34 when considered against changes in the disclosure requirements of other IFRSs. IAS 34 was issued by the Board's predecessor body, IASC, in 1998. In the light of recent improvements to disclosure requirements, many users of financial statements asked the Board to consider whether particular disclosures required by IFRS 7 *Financial Instruments: Disclosures* for annual financial statements should also be required in interim financial statements. IAS 34 sets out disclosure principles to determine what information should be disclosed in an interim financial report. The Board concluded that amending IAS 34 to place greater emphasis on those principles and the inclusion of additional examples relating to more recent disclosure requirements, ie fair value measurements, would improve interim financial reporting.

BC4   As part of *Improvements to IFRSs* issued in May 2010, the Board deleted paragraph 18 of IAS 34 because it repeats paragraph 10 of IAS 34 and because the Board's intention is to emphasise those disclosures that are required rather than those that are not required.

Content of an interim financial report

BC5   As part of *Annual Improvements 2009–2011 Cycle* (issued in May 2012) the Board amended paragraph 5 to achieve consistency with paragraphs 10(ea) and 10(f) of IAS 1 *Presentation of Financial Statements*.

Selected explanatory notes

BC6   In *Annual Improvements 2009–2011 Cycle* (issued in May 2012) the Board decided to clarify the requirements on segment information for total assets and liabilities for each reportable segment to enhance consistency with the requirements in paragraph 23 of IFRS 8 *Operating Segments*. The amendment clarifies that the total assets and liabilities for a particular reportable segment are required to be disclosed if, and only if:

(a)   a measure of total assets or of total liabilities (or both) is regularly provided to the chief operating decision maker; and

(b)   there has been a material change from those measures disclosed in the last annual financial statements for that reportable segment.

Other disclosures incorporated by cross-reference to information outside the interim financial statements

BC7   The Board received a request to clarify the meaning of disclosure of information 'elsewhere in the interim financial report' as used in IAS 34. The submitter noted that the definition of 'interim financial report' in paragraph 4 of IAS 34 was not sufficiently clear with respect to whether the interim financial report covers only the information reported under IFRS (meaning the IFRS interim financial statements) or whether it also includes management reports or other elements in addition to IFRS interim financial statements.

BC8   The Board observed that presenting information 'elsewhere in the interim financial report' in accordance with paragraph 16A of IAS 34 is unclear. In the Exposure Draft *Annual Improvements to IFRSs 2012–2014 Cycle* (the '2013 Annual Improvements Exposure Draft'), published in December 2013, the Board proposed to clarify that an entity discloses information elsewhere in the interim financial report when it incorporates disclosures by cross-reference to information in another statement. This information should be available to users of the interim financial statements on the same terms as the interim financial statements and at the same time.

BC9   Some respondents to the 2013 Annual Improvements Exposure Draft observed that the proposed amendment seemed to suggest that the interim financial report was not a single report and that, instead, it included multiple documents. In response to these comments, the Board observed that in accordance with paragraphs 4 and 8 of IAS 34, an interim financial report is a single report that includes a set of condensed financial statements and selected explanatory notes. The Board further clarified that the amendment is not extending the scope of the interim financial report, because the disclosures required in paragraph 16A(a)–(k) of IAS 34 are part of the selected explanatory notes (and therefore part of the interim financial report), even if they are presented in another statement, such as a management commentary or risk report. If they are not presented, the interim financial report would be incomplete.

BC10   In response to the comments received on the 2013 Annual Improvements Exposure Draft the Board decided to clarify what was meant by the requirement that disclosures incorporated by cross-reference should be made available 'on the same terms' as the financial statements. This means that users of the financial statements should have access to the referenced material on the same basis as they have for accessing the financial statements from where the reference is made.

Amended references to the *Conceptual Framework*

BC11   Following the issue of the revised *Conceptual Framework for Financial Reporting* in 2018 (2018 *Conceptual Framework*), the Board issued *Amendments to References to the Conceptual Framework in IFRS Standards*. In IAS 34, that document replaced references in paragraphs 31 and 33 to the *Framework for the Preparation and Presentation of Financial Statements* adopted by the Board in 2001 (*Framework*) with references to the 2018 *Conceptual Framework*, and updated a related quotation. The Board does not expect that replacement to have a significant effect on the application of the Standard because the Board made no significant changes to the aspects of recognition that those paragraphs refer to — that is, the importance of definitions for recognition.

BC12   *Amendments to References to the Conceptual Framework in IFRS Standards* also replaced the term 'balance sheet' with the term 'statement of financial position' in paragraphs 31 and 33 of IAS 34. The term 'balance sheet' had been replaced in IFRS Standards following the revision of IAS 1 *Presentation of Financial Statements* in 2007. However, paragraphs 31 and 33 of IAS 34 had not been amended then because the term was part of direct quotations from the *Framework*. Upon issuing the 2018 *Conceptual Framework*, the Board replaced the term 'balance sheet' in those paragraphs so that the terminology used in the 2018 *Conceptual Framework* and in IFRS Standards is consistent.

IASB documents published to accompany

IAS 36

Impairment of Assets

The text of the unaccompanied IAS 36 is contained in Part A of this edition. Its effective date when issued was 31 March 2004. The text of the Accompanying Guidance on IAS 36 is contained in Part B of this edition. This part presents the following accompanying documents:

BASIS FOR CONCLUSIONS

DISSENTING OPINIONS

CONTENTS

continued...

...continued

Basis for Conclusions on
IAS 36 *Impairment of Assets*

The International Accounting Standards Board revised IAS 36 as part of its project on business combinations. It was not the Board's intention to reconsider as part of that project all of the requirements in IAS 36.

The previous version of IAS 36 was accompanied by a Basis for Conclusions summarising the former International Accounting Standards Committee's considerations in reaching some of its conclusions in that Standard. For convenience the Board has incorporated into its own Basis for Conclusions material from the previous Basis for Conclusions that discusses (a) matters the Board did not reconsider and (b) the history of the development of a standard on impairment of assets. That material is contained in paragraphs denoted by numbers with the prefix BCZ. Paragraphs describing the Board's considerations in reaching its own conclusions are numbered with the prefix BC.

In this Basis for Conclusions the terminology has not been amended to reflect the changes made by IAS 1 Presentation of Financial Statements (as revised in 2007).

In developing IFRS 13 Fair Value Measurement, issued in May 2011, the Board changed the definition of fair value less costs to sell. As a consequence all references to 'fair value less costs to sell' in IAS 36 were replaced with 'fair value less costs of disposal'. This Basis for Conclusions has not been amended to reflect that change.

Introduction

BC1 This Basis for Conclusions summarises the International Accounting Standards Board's considerations in reaching the conclusions in IAS 36 *Impairment of Assets*. Individual Board members gave greater weight to some factors than to others.

BC2 The International Accounting Standards Committee (IASC) issued the previous version of IAS 36 in 1998. It has been revised by the Board as part of its project on business combinations. That project had two phases. The first resulted in the Board issuing simultaneously in 2004 IFRS 3 *Business Combinations* and revised versions of IAS 36 and IAS 38 *Intangible Assets*. The Board's intention in revising IAS 36 as part of the first phase of the project was not to reconsider all of the requirements in IAS 36. The changes to IAS 36 were primarily concerned with the impairment tests for intangible assets with indefinite useful lives (hereafter referred to as 'indefinite-lived intangibles') and goodwill. The second phase of the project on business combinations resulted in the Board issuing simultaneously in 2008 a revised IFRS 3 and an amended version of IAS 27 *Consolidated and Separate Financial Statements*.[1] The Board amended IAS 36 to reflect its decisions on the measurement of a non-controlling interest in an acquiree (see paragraph BC170A). The Board has not deliberated the other requirements in IAS 36. Those other requirements will be considered by the Board as part of a future project on impairment of assets.

---

1 The consolidation requirements in IAS 27 were superseded by IFRS 10 *Consolidated Financial Statements* issued in May 2011.

BC3   The previous version of IAS 36 was accompanied by a Basis for Conclusions summarising IASC's considerations in reaching some of its conclusions in that Standard. For convenience, the Board has incorporated into this Basis for Conclusions material from the previous Basis for Conclusions that discusses matters the Board did not consider. That material is contained in paragraphs denoted by numbers with the prefix BCZ. The views expressed in paragraphs denoted by numbers with the prefix BCZ are those of IASC.

Scope (paragraph 2)

BCZ4   IAS 2 *Inventories* requires an enterprise to measure the recoverable amount of inventory at its net realisable value. IASC believed that there was no need to revise this requirement because it was well accepted as an appropriate test for recoverability of inventories. No major difference exists between IAS 2 and the requirements included in IAS 36 (see paragraphs BCZ37–BCZ39).

BCZ5   IAS 11 *Construction Contracts*[2] and IAS 12 *Income Taxes* already deal with the impairment of assets arising from construction contracts and deferred tax assets respectively. Under both IAS 11 and IAS 12, recoverable amount is, in effect, determined on an undiscounted basis. IASC acknowledged that this was inconsistent with the requirements of IAS 36. However, IASC believed that it was not possible to eliminate that inconsistency without fundamental changes to IAS 11 and IAS 12. IASC had no plans to revise IAS 11 or IAS 12.

BCZ6   IAS 19 *Employee Benefits* contains an upper limit on the amount at which an enterprise should recognise an asset arising from employee benefits. Therefore, IAS 36 does not deal with such assets. The limit in IAS 19 is determined on a discounted basis that is broadly compatible with the requirements of IAS 36.[3]

BCZ7   IAS 39 *Financial Instruments: Recognition and Measurement*[4] sets out the requirements for impairment of financial assets.

BCZ8   IAS 36 is applicable to all assets, unless specifically excluded, regardless of their classification as current or non-current. Before IAS 36 was issued, there was no International Accounting Standard on accounting for the impairment of current assets other than inventories.

Measuring recoverable amount (paragraphs 18–57)

BCZ9   In determining the principles that should govern the measurement of recoverable amount, IASC considered, as a first step, what an enterprise will do if it discovers that an asset is impaired. IASC concluded that, in such cases, an enterprise will either keep the asset or dispose of it. For example, if an enterprise discovers that the service potential of an asset has decreased:

2   IFRS 15 *Revenue from Contracts with Customers*, issued in May 2014, replaced IAS 11 *Construction Contracts*. IFRS 15 includes requirements for the impairment of some assets arising from contracts with customers and amended paragraph 2 of IAS 36 for consistency with the requirements of IFRS 15.

3   sentence deleted when IAS 19 *Employee Benefits* was amended in 2011.

4   IFRS 9 *Financial Instruments* replaced IAS 39. IFRS 9 applies to all items that were previously within the scope of IAS 39.

(a)   the enterprise may decide to sell the asset if the net proceeds from the sale would provide a higher return on investment than continuing use in operations; or

(b)   the enterprise may decide to keep the asset and use it, even if its service potential is lower than originally expected. Some reasons may be that:

    (i)   the asset cannot be sold or disposed of immediately;

    (ii)   the asset can be sold only at a low price;

    (iii)   the asset's service potential can still be recovered but only with additional efforts or expenditure; or

    (iv)   the asset could still be profitable although not to the same extent as expected originally.

IASC concluded that the resulting decision from a rational enterprise is, in substance, an investment decision based on estimated net future cash flows expected from the asset.

BCZ10   IASC then considered which of the following four alternatives for determining the recoverable amount of an asset would best reflect this conclusion:

(a)   recoverable amount should be the sum of undiscounted future cash flows.

(b)   recoverable amount should be the asset's fair value: more specifically, recoverable amount should be derived primarily from the asset's market value. If market value cannot be determined, then recoverable amount should be based on the asset's value in use as a proxy for market value.[5]

(c)   recoverable amount should be the asset's value in use.

(d)   recoverable amount should be the higher of the asset's net selling price and value in use.[6]

Each of these alternatives is discussed below.

BCZ11   It should be noted that fair value, net selling price and value in use all reflect a present value calculation (implicit or explicit) of estimated net future cash flows expected from an asset:

(a)   fair value[7] reflects the market's expectation of the present value of the future cash flows to be derived from the asset;

---

5   IFRS 13 *Fair Value Measurement*, issued in May 2011, defines fair value and contains the requirements for measuring fair value. As a result the term 'market value' has been changed to 'fair value'.

6   In IFRS 5 *Non-current Assets Held for Sale and Discontinued Operations*, issued by the IASB in 2004, the term 'net selling price' was replaced in IAS 36 by 'fair value less costs to sell'.

7   IFRS 13, issued in May 2011, defines fair value and contains the requirements for measuring fair value.

(b)   net selling price reflects the market's expectation of the present value of the future cash flows to be derived from the asset, less the direct incremental costs to dispose of the asset; and

(c)   value in use is the enterprise's estimate of the present value of the future cash flows to be derived from continuing use and disposal of the asset.

These bases all consider the time value of money and the risks that the amount and timing of the actual cash flows to be received from an asset might differ from estimates. Fair value and net selling price may differ from value in use because the market may not use the same assumptions as an individual enterprise.

Recoverable amount based on the sum of undiscounted cash flows

BCZ12   Some argue that recoverable amount should be measured as the sum of undiscounted future cash flows from an asset. They argue that:

(a)   historical cost accounting is not concerned with measuring the economic value of assets. Therefore, the time value of money should not be considered in estimating the amount that will be recovered from an asset.

(b)   it is premature to use discounting techniques without further research and debates on:

(i)   the role of discounting in the financial statements; and

(ii)   how assets should be measured generally.

If financial statements include assets that are carried on a variety of different bases (historical cost, discounted amounts or other bases), this will be confusing for users.

(c)   identifying an appropriate discount rate will often be difficult and subjective.

(d)   discounting will increase the number of impairment losses recognised. This, coupled with the requirement for reversals of impairment losses, introduces a volatile element into the income statement. It will make it harder for users to understand the performance of an enterprise.

A minority of commentators on E55 *Impairment of Assets* supported this view.

BCZ13   IASC rejected measurement of recoverable amount based on the sum of undiscounted cash flows because:

(a)   the objective of the measurement of recoverable amount is to reflect an investment decision. Money has a time value, even when prices are stable. If future cash flows were not discounted, two assets giving rise to cash flows of the same amount but with different timings would show the same recoverable amount. However, their current market values would be different because all rational economic transactions take account of the time value of money.

(b) measurements that take into consideration the time value of money are more relevant to investors, other external users of financial statements and management for resource allocation decisions, regardless of the general measurement basis adopted in the financial statements.

(c) many enterprises were already familiar with the use of discounting techniques, particularly for supporting investment decisions.

(d) discounting was already required for other areas of financial statements that are based on expectations of future cash flows, such as long-term provisions and employee benefit obligations.

(e) users are better served if they are aware on a timely basis of assets that will not generate sufficient returns to cover, at least, the time value of money.

Recoverable amount based on fair value

BCZ14 IAS 32 *Financial Instruments: Disclosure and Presentation*[8] and a number of other International Accounting Standards define fair value[9] as:

'... the amount for which an asset could be exchanged, or a liability settled, between knowledgeable, willing parties in an arm's length transaction ...'

BCZ15 International Accounting Standards include the following requirements or guidance for measuring fair value:[10]

(a) for the purpose of revaluation of an item of property, plant or equipment to its fair value, IAS 16 *Property, Plant and Equipment* indicates that fair value is usually an asset's market value, normally determined by appraisal undertaken by professionally qualified valuers and, if no market exists, fair value is based on the asset's depreciated replacement cost.

(b) for the purpose of revaluation of an intangible asset to its fair value, IASC proposed in E60 *Intangible Assets* that fair value be determined by reference to market values obtained from an active market. E60 proposed a definition of an active market.[11]

(c) IASC proposed revisions to IAS 22 (see E61 *Business Combinations*) so that fair value would be determined without consideration of the acquirer's intentions for the future use of an asset.[12]

---

8 In 2005 the IASB amended IAS 32 as *Financial Instruments: Presentation*.

9 IFRS 13, issued in May 2011, defines fair value as an exit price.

10 IFRS 13, issued in May 2011, defines fair value and contains the requirements for measuring fair value. As a consequence the relevant requirements in IAS 16 and IAS 39 have been deleted from those Standards.

11 IASC approved an International Accounting Standard on intangible assets in 1998.

12 IASC approved revisions to IAS 22 *Business Combinations* in 1998.

(d)   IAS 39[13] indicates that if an active market exists, the fair value of a financial instrument is based on a quoted market price. If there is no active market, fair value is determined by using estimation techniques such as market values of similar types of financial instruments, discounted cash flow analysis and option pricing models.

BCZ16   Some argue that the only appropriate measurement for the recoverable amount of an asset is fair value (based on observable market prices or, if no observable market prices exist, estimated considering prices for similar assets and the results of discounted future cash flow calculations).[14] Proponents of fair value argue that:

(a)   the purpose of measuring recoverable amount is to estimate a market value, not an enterprise-specific value. An enterprise's estimate of the present value of future cash flows is subjective and in some cases may be abused. Observable market prices that reflect the judgement of the marketplace are a more reliable measurement of the amounts that will be recovered from an asset. They reduce the use of management's judgement.

(b)   if an asset is expected to generate greater net cash inflows for the enterprise than for other participants, the superior returns are almost always generated by internally generated goodwill stemming from the synergy of the business and its management team. For consistency with IASC's proposals in E60 that internally generated goodwill should not be recognised as an asset, these above-market cash flows should be excluded from assessments of an asset's recoverable amount.

(c)   determining recoverable amount as the higher of net selling price and value in use is tantamount to determining two diverging measures whilst there should be only one measure to estimate recoverable amount.

A minority of commentators on E55 supported measuring recoverable amount at fair value (based on observable market prices or, if no observable market prices exist, estimated considering prices for similar assets and the results of discounted future cash flow calculations).

BCZ17   IASC rejected the proposal that an asset's recoverable amount should be determined by reference to its fair value (based on observable market prices or, if no observable market prices exist, estimated considering prices for similar assets and the results of discounted future cash flow calculations). The reasons are the following:

---

13 The Board's project to revise IAS 32 and IAS 39 in 2003 resulted in the relocation of the requirements on fair value measurement from IAS 32 to IAS 39. Subsequently to that, IFRS 9 *Financial Instruments* replaced IAS 39. IFRS 9 applies to all items that were previously within the scope of IAS 39. In 2011 the Board's project on fair value measurement resulted in the relocation of the requirements for measuring fair value to IFRS 13.

14 IFRS 13, issued in May 2011, describes valuation techniques for measuring the fair value of an asset that is being used (and would not be sold) by an entity, eg a current replacement cost valuation technique.

(a) IASC believed that no preference should be given to the market's expectation of the recoverable amount of an asset (basis for fair value when market values are available and for net selling price) over a reasonable estimate performed by the individual enterprise that owns the asset (basis for fair value when market values are not available and for value in use). For example, an enterprise may have information about future cash flows that is superior to the information available in the marketplace. Also, an enterprise may plan to use an asset in a manner different from the market's view of the best use.

(b) market values are a way to estimate fair value but only if they reflect the fact that both parties, the acquirer and the seller, are willing to enter a transaction. If an enterprise can generate greater cash flows by using an asset than by selling it, it would be misleading to base recoverable amount on the market price of the asset because a rational enterprise would not be willing to sell the asset. Therefore, recoverable amount should not refer only to a transaction between two parties (which is unlikely to happen) but should also consider an asset's service potential from its use by the enterprise.

(c) IASC believed that in assessing the recoverable amount of an asset, it is the amount that an enterprise can expect to recover from that asset, including the effect of synergy with other assets, that is relevant.

The following two examples illustrate the proposal (rejected by IASC) that an enterprise should measure an asset's recoverable amount at its fair value (primarily based on observable market values if these values are available).

Example 1

10 years ago, an enterprise bought its headquarters building for 2,000. Since then, the real estate market has collapsed and the building's market value at balance sheet date is estimated to be 1,000. Disposal costs of the building would be negligible. The building's carrying amount at the balance sheet date is 1,500 and its remaining useful life is 30 years. The building meets all the enterprise's expectations and it is likely that these expectations will be met for the foreseeable future. As a consequence, the enterprise has no plans to move from its current headquarters. The value in use of the building cannot be determined because the building does not generate independent cash inflows. Therefore, the enterprise assesses the recoverable amount of the building's cash-generating unit, that is, the enterprise as a whole. That calculation shows that the building's cash-generating unit is not impaired.

Proponents of fair value (primarily based on observable market values if these values are available) would measure the recoverable amount of the building at its market value (1,000) and, hence, would recognise an impairment loss of 500 (1,500 less 1,000), even though calculations show that the building's cash-generating unit is not impaired.

IASC did not support this approach and believed that the building was not impaired. IASC believed that, in the situation described, the enterprise would not be willing to sell the building for 1,000 and that the assumption of a sale was not relevant.

Example 2

At the end of 20X0, an enterprise purchased a computer for 100 for general use in its operations. The computer is depreciated over 4 years on a straight-line basis. Residual value is estimated to be nil. At the end of 20X2, the carrying amount of the computer is 50. There is an active market for second-hand computers of this type. The market value of the computer is 30. The enterprise does not intend to replace the computer before the end of its useful life. The computer's cash-generating unit is not impaired.

Proponents of fair value (primarily based on observable market values if these values are available) would measure the recoverable amount of the computer at its market value (30) and, therefore, would recognise an impairment loss of 20 (50 less 30) even though the computer's cash-generating unit is not impaired.

IASC did not support this approach and believed that the computer was not impaired as long as:

(a) the enterprise was not committed to dispose of the computer before the end of its expected useful life; and

(b) the computer's cash-generating unit was not impaired.

BCZ18   If no deep and liquid market exists for an asset, IASC considered that value in use would be a reasonable estimate of fair value. This is likely to happen for many assets within the scope of IAS 36: observable market prices are unlikely to exist for goodwill, most intangible assets and many items of property, plant and equipment. Therefore, it is likely that the recoverable amount of these assets, determined in accordance with IAS 36, will be similar to the recoverable amount based on the fair value of these assets.

BCZ19   For some assets within the scope of IAS 36, observable market prices exist or consideration of prices for similar assets is possible. In such cases, the asset's net selling price will differ from the asset's fair value only by the direct incremental costs of disposal. IASC acknowledged that recoverable amount as the higher of net selling price and value in use would sometimes differ from fair value primarily based on market prices (even if the disposal costs are negligible). This is because, as explained in paragraph BCZ17(a), the market may not use the same assumptions about future cash flows as an individual enterprise.[15]

BCZ20   IASC believed that IAS 36 included sufficient requirements to prevent an enterprise from using assumptions different from the marketplace that are unjustified. For example, an enterprise is required to determine value in use using:

(a)   cash flow projections based on reasonable and supportable assumptions and giving greater weight to external evidence; and

(b)   a discount rate that reflects current market assessments of the time value of money and the risks specific to the asset.

---

15 IFRS 13, issued in May 2011, describes the objective of a fair value measurement and the use of market participant assumptions.

Recoverable amount based on value in use

BCZ21   Some argue that value in use is the only appropriate measurement for the recoverable amount of an asset because:

(a)   financial statements are prepared under a going concern assumption. Therefore, no consideration should be given to an alternative measurement that reflects a disposal, unless this reflects the enterprise's intentions.

(b)   assets should not be carried at amounts higher than their service potential from use by the enterprise. Unlike value in use, a market value does not necessarily reflect the service potential of an asset.

Few commentators on E55 supported this view.

BCZ22   IASC rejected this proposal because:

(a)   if an asset's net selling price is higher than its value in use, a rational enterprise will dispose of the asset. In this situation, it is logical to base recoverable amount on the asset's net selling price to avoid recognising an impairment loss that is unrelated to economic reality.

(b)   if an asset's net selling price is greater than its value in use, but management decides to keep the asset, the extra loss (the difference between net selling price and value in use) properly falls in later periods because it results from management's decision in these later periods to keep the asset.

Recoverable amount based on the higher of net selling price and value in use[16]

BCZ23   The requirement that recoverable amount should be the higher of net selling price and value in use stems from the decision that measurement of the recoverable amount of an asset should reflect the likely behaviour of a rational management. Furthermore, no preference should be given to the market's expectation of the recoverable amount of an asset (basis for net selling price) over a reasonable estimate performed by the individual enterprise which owns the asset (basis for value in use) or vice versa (see paragraphs BCZ17–BCZ20 and BCZ22). It is uncertain whether the assumptions of the market or the enterprise are more likely to be true. Currently, perfect markets do not exist for many of the assets within the scope of IAS 36 and it is unlikely that predictions of the future will be entirely accurate, regardless of who makes them.

BCZ24   IASC acknowledged that an enterprise would use judgement in determining whether an impairment loss needed to be recognised. For this reason, IAS 36 included some safeguards to limit the risk that an enterprise may make an over-optimistic (pessimistic) estimate of recoverable amount:

---

16   In IFRS 5 *Non-current Assets Held for Sale and Discontinued Operations*, issued by the IASB in 2004, the term 'net selling price' was replaced in IAS 36 by 'fair value less costs to sell'.

(a) IAS 36 requires a formal estimate of recoverable amount whenever there is an indication that:

   (i) an asset may be impaired; or

   (ii) an impairment loss may no longer exist or may have decreased.

   For this purpose, IAS 36 includes a relatively detailed (although not exhaustive) list of indicators that an asset may be impaired (see paragraphs 12 and 111 of IAS 36).

(b) IAS 36 provides guidelines for the basis of management's projections of future cash flows to be used to estimate value in use (see paragraph 33 of IAS 36).

BCZ25   IASC considered the cost of requiring an enterprise to determine both net selling price and value in use, if the amount determined first is below an asset's carrying amount. IASC concluded that the benefits of such a requirement outweigh the costs.

BCZ26   The majority of the commentators on E55 supported IASC's view that recoverable amount should be measured at the higher of net selling price and value in use.

Assets held for disposal

BCZ27   IASC considered whether the recoverable amount of an asset held for disposal should be measured only at the asset's net selling price. When an enterprise expects to dispose of an asset within the near future, the net selling price of the asset is normally close to its value in use. Indeed, the value in use usually consists mostly of the net proceeds to be received for the asset, since future cash flows from continuing use are usually close to nil. Therefore, IASC believed that the definition of recoverable amount as included in IAS 36 is appropriate for assets held for disposal without a need for further requirements or guidance.

Other refinements to the measurement of recoverable amount

Replacement cost as a ceiling

BCZ28   Some argue that the replacement cost of an asset should be adopted as a ceiling for its recoverable amount. They argue that the value of an asset to the business would not exceed the amount that the enterprise would be willing to pay for the asset at the balance sheet date.

BCZ29   IASC believed that replacement cost techniques are not appropriate to measuring the recoverable amount of an asset. This is because replacement cost measures the cost of an asset and not the future economic benefits recoverable from its use and/or disposal.

Appraisal values

BCZ30   In some cases, an enterprise might seek external appraisal of recoverable amount. External appraisal is not a separate technique in its own right. IASC believed that if appraisal values are used, an enterprise should verify that the external appraisal follows the requirements of IAS 36.

Net selling price (paragraphs 25–29)[17]

BCZ31   IAS 36 defines net selling price as the amount obtainable from the sale of an asset in an arm's length transaction between knowledgeable, willing parties, less the incremental costs directly attributable to the disposal of the asset.

BCZ32   In other words, net selling price reflects the market's expectations of the future cash flows for an asset after the market's consideration of the time value of money and the risks inherent in receiving those cash flows, less the disposal costs.

BCZ33   Some argue that direct incremental costs of disposal should not be deducted from the amount obtainable from the sale of an asset because, unless management has decided to dispose of the asset, the going concern assumption should apply.

BCZ34   IASC believed that it is appropriate to deduct direct incremental costs of disposal in determining net selling price because the purpose of the exercise is to determine the net amount that an enterprise could recover from the sale of an asset at the date of the measurement and to compare it with the alternative of keeping the asset and using it.

BCZ35   IAS 36 indicates that termination benefits (as defined in IAS 19 *Employee Benefits*) and costs associated with reducing or reorganising a business following the disposal of an asset are not direct incremental costs to dispose of the asset. IASC considered these costs as incidental to (rather than a direct consequence of) the disposal of an asset. In addition, this guidance is consistent with the direction of the project on provisions.[18]

BCZ36   Although the definition of 'net selling price' would be similar to a definition of 'net fair value', IASC decided to use the term 'net selling price' instead of 'net fair value'. IASC believed that the term 'net selling price' better describes the amount that an enterprise should determine and that will be compared with an asset's value in use.

Net realisable value

BCZ37   IAS 2 *Inventories* defines net realisable value as:

'... the estimated selling price in the ordinary course of business ... less the estimated costs necessary to make the sale ...'

---

17   In IFRS 5 *Non-current Assets Held for Sale and Discontinued Operations*, issued by the IASB in 2004, the term 'net selling price' was replaced in IAS 36 by 'fair value less costs to sell'.

18   IASC approved an International Accounting Standard on provisions, contingent liabilities and contingent assets in 1998.

BCZ38   For the purpose of determining recoverable amount, IASC decided not to use the term 'net realisable value' as defined in IAS 2 because:

(a)   IAS 2's definition of net realisable value does not refer explicitly to transactions carried out on an arm's length basis.

(b)   net realisable value refers to an estimated selling price in the ordinary course of business. In certain cases, net selling price will reflect a forced sale, if management is compelled to sell immediately.

(c)   it is important that net selling price uses, as a starting point, a selling price agreed between knowledgeable, willing buyers and sellers. This is not explicitly mentioned in the definition of net realisable value.

BCZ39   In most cases, net selling price and net realisable value will be similar. However, IASC did not believe that it was necessary to change the definition of net realisable value used in IAS 2 because, for inventories, the definition of net realisable value is well understood and seems to work satisfactorily.

Value in use (paragraphs 30–57 and Appendix A)

BCZ40   IAS 36 defines value in use as the present value of the future cash flows expected to be derived from an asset.

Expected value approach

BCZ41   Some argue that, to better reflect uncertainties in timing and amounts inherent in estimated future cash flows, expected future cash flows should be used in determining value in use. An expected value approach considers all expectations about possible future cash flows instead of the single, most likely, future cash flows.

Example
An enterprise estimates that there are two scenarios for future cash flows: a first possibility of future cash flows amounts to 120 with a 40 per cent probability and a second possibility amounts to 80 with a 60 per cent probability.
The most likely future cash flows would be 80 and the expected future cash flows would be 96 (80 × 60% + 120 × 40%).

BCZ42   In most cases, it is likely that budgets/forecasts that are the basis for cash flow projections will reflect a single estimate of future cash flows only. For this reason, IASC decided that an expected value approach should be permitted but not required.

Future cash flows from internally generated goodwill and synergy with other assets

BCZ43   IASC rejected a proposal that estimates of future cash inflows should reflect only future cash inflows relating to the asset that was initially recognised (or the remaining portion of that asset if part of it has already been consumed or sold). The purpose of such a requirement would be to avoid including in an asset's value in use future cash inflows from internally generated goodwill or from synergy with other assets. This would be consistent with IASC's proposal in E60 *Intangible Assets* to prohibit the recognition of internally generated goodwill as an asset.[19]

BCZ44   In many cases, it will not be possible in practice to distinguish future cash inflows from the asset initially recognised from the future cash inflows from internally generated goodwill or a modification of the asset. This is particularly true when businesses are merged or once an asset has been enhanced by subsequent expenditure. IASC concluded that it is more important to focus on whether the carrying amount of an asset will be recovered rather than on whether the recovery stems partly from internally generated goodwill.

BCZ45   The proposal—that future cash inflows should reflect only future cash inflows relating to the asset that was initially recognised—would also conflict with the requirement under IAS 36 that cash flow projections should reflect reasonable and supportable assumptions that represent management's best estimate of the set of economic conditions that will exist over the remaining useful life of the asset (see paragraph 33 of IAS 36). Therefore, the Standard requires that future cash inflows should be estimated for an asset in its current condition, whether or not these future cash inflows are from the asset that was initially recognised or from its subsequent enhancement or modification.

Example
Several years ago, an enterprise purchased a customer list with 10,000 addresses that it recognised as an intangible asset. The enterprise uses this list for direct marketing of its products. Since initial recognition, about 2,000 customer addresses have been deleted from the list and 3,000 new customer addresses added to it. The enterprise is determining the value in use of the customer list.
Under the proposal (rejected by IASC) that an enterprise should reflect only future cash inflows relating to the asset that was initially recognised, the enterprise would consider only those future cash inflows generated by the remaining 8,000 (10,000 less 2,000) customers from the list acquired.
Under IAS 36, an enterprise considers the future cash inflows generated by the customer list in its current condition, ie by all 11,000 customers (8,000 plus 3,000).

---

19   IASC approved an International Accounting Standard on intangible assets in 1998.

Value in use estimated in a foreign currency (paragraph 54)

BCZ46   In response to comments from field test participants, paragraph 54 of IAS 36 includes guidance on calculating the value in use of an asset that generates future cash flows in a foreign currency. IAS 36 indicates that value in use in a foreign currency is translated into the reporting currency[20] using the spot exchange rate at the balance sheet date.

BCZ47   If a currency is freely convertible and traded in an active market, the spot rate reflects the market's best estimate of future events that will affect that currency. Therefore, the only available unbiased estimate of a future exchange rate is the current spot rate, adjusted by the difference in expected future rates of general inflation in the two countries to which the currencies belong.

BCZ48   A value in use calculation already deals with the effect of general inflation since it is calculated either by:

(a)   estimating future cash flows in nominal terms (ie including the effect of general inflation and specific price changes) and discounting them at a rate that includes the effects of general inflation; or

(b)   estimating future cash flows in real terms (ie excluding the effect of general inflation but including the effect of specific price changes) and discounting them at a rate that excludes the effect of general inflation.

BCZ49   To use a forward rate to translate value in use expressed in a foreign currency would be inappropriate. This is because a forward rate reflects the market's adjustment for the differential in interest rates. Using such a rate would result in double-counting the time value of money (first in the discount rate and then in the forward rate).

BCZ50   Even if a currency is not freely convertible or is not traded in an active market —with the consequence that it can no longer be assumed that the spot exchange rate reflects the market's best estimate of future events that will affect that currency—IAS 36 indicates that an enterprise uses the spot exchange rate at the balance sheet date to translate value in use estimated in a foreign currency. This is because IASC believed that it is unlikely that an enterprise can make a more reliable estimate of future exchange rates than the current spot exchange rate.

BCZ51   An alternative to estimating the future cash flows in the currency in which they are generated would be to estimate them in another currency as a proxy and discount them at a rate appropriate for this other currency. This solution may be simpler, particularly where cash flows are generated in the currency of a hyperinflationary economy (in such cases, some would prefer using a hard currency as a proxy) or in a currency other than the reporting currency. However, this solution may be misleading if the exchange rate varies for reasons other than changes in the differential between the general inflation rates in the two countries to which the currencies belong. In addition, this

---

20   In IAS 21 *The Effects of Changes in Foreign Exchange Rates*, as revised by the IASB in 2003, the term 'reporting currency' was replaced by 'functional currency'.

solution is inconsistent with the approach under IAS 29 *Financial Reporting in Hyperinflationary Economies*, which does not allow, if the reporting currency[21] is the currency of a hyperinflationary economy, translation into a hard currency as a proxy for restatement in terms of the measuring unit current at the balance sheet date.

Discount rate (paragraphs 55–57 and A15–A21)

BCZ52 The purpose of discounting future cash flows is to reflect the time value of money and the uncertainties attached to those cash flows:

(a) assets that generate cash flows soon are worth more than those generating the same cash flows later. All rational economic transactions will take account of the time value of money. The cost of not receiving a cash inflow until some date in the future is an opportunity cost that can be measured by considering what income has been lost by not investing that money for the period. The time value of money, before consideration of risk, is given by the rate of return on a risk-free investment, such as government bonds of the same duration.

(b) the value of the future cash flows is affected by the variability (ie the risks) associated with the cash flows. Therefore, all rational economic transactions will take risk into account.

BCZ53 As a consequence IASC decided:

(a) to reject a discount rate based on a historical rate—ie the effective rate implicit when an asset was acquired. A subsequent estimate of recoverable amount has to be based on prevailing interest rates because management's decisions about whether to keep the asset are based on prevailing economic conditions. Historical rates do not reflect prevailing economic conditions.

(b) to reject a discount rate based on a risk-free rate, unless the future cash flows have been adjusted for all the risks specific to the asset.

(c) to require that the discount rate should be a rate that reflects current market assessments of the time value of money and the risks specific to the asset. This rate is the return that investors would require if they were to choose an investment that would generate cash flows of amounts, timing and risk profile equivalent to those that the enterprise expects to derive from the asset.

BCZ54 In principle, value in use should be an enterprise-specific measure determined in accordance with the enterprise's own view of the best use of that asset. Logically, the discount rate should be based on the enterprise's own assessment both of the time value of money and of the risks specific to the future cash flows from the asset. However, IASC believed that such a rate could not be verified objectively. Therefore, IAS 36 requires that the enterprise

---

21 In IAS 21 *The Effects of Changes in Foreign Exchange Rates*, as revised by the IASB in 2003, the term 'reporting currency' was replaced by 'functional currency'.

should make its own estimate of future cash flows but that the discount rate should reflect, as far as possible, the market's assessment of the time value of money. Similarly, the discount rate should reflect the premium that the market would require from uncertain future cash flows based on the distribution estimated by the enterprise.

BCZ55 IASC acknowledged that a current asset-specific market-determined rate would rarely exist for the assets covered by IAS 36. Therefore, an enterprise uses current market-determined rates for other assets (as similar as possible to the asset under review) as a starting point and adjusts these rates to reflect the risks specific to the asset for which the cash flow projections have not been adjusted.

Additional guidance included in the Standard in 2004

Elements reflected in value in use (paragraphs 30–32)

BC56 The Exposure Draft of Proposed Amendments to IAS 36 proposed, and the revised Standard includes, additional guidance to clarify:

(a) the elements that are reflected in an asset's value in use; and

(b) that some of those elements (ie expectations about possible variations in the amount or timing of future cash flows, the price for bearing the uncertainty inherent in the asset, and other factors that market participants would reflect in pricing the future cash flows the entity expects to derive from the asset) can be reflected either as adjustments to the future cash flows or as adjustments to the discount rate.

The Board decided to include this additional guidance in the Exposure Draft in response to a number of requests from its constituents for clarification of the requirements in the previous version of IAS 36 on measuring value in use.

BC57 Respondents to the Exposure Draft generally agreed with the proposals. Those that disagreed varied widely in their views, arguing that:

(a) IAS 36 should be amended to permit entities to measure value in use using methods other than discounting of future cash flows.

(b) when measuring the value in use of an intangible asset, entities should be required to reflect the price for bearing the uncertainty inherent in the asset as adjustments to the future cash flows.

(c) it is inconsistent with the definition of value in use to reflect in that measure the other factors that market participants would reflect in pricing the future cash flows the entity expects to derive from the asset—this element refers to market pricing of an asset rather than to the value to the entity of the asset. Other factors should be reflected in value in use only to the extent that they affect the cash flows the entity can achieve from the asset.

BC58 In considering (a) above, the Board observed that the measure of recoverable amount in IAS 36 (ie higher of value in use and fair value less costs to sell) stems from IASC's decision that an asset's recoverable amount should reflect the likely behaviour of a rational management, with no preference given to the market's expectation of the recoverable amount of an asset (ie fair value less costs to sell) over a reasonable estimate performed by the entity that controls the asset (ie value in use) or vice versa (see paragraph BCZ23). In developing the Exposure Draft and revising IAS 36, the Board concluded that it would be inappropriate to modify the measurement basis adopted in the previous version of IAS 36 for determining recoverable amount until the Board considers and resolves the broader question of the appropriate measurement objective(s) in accounting. Moreover, IAS 36 does not preclude the use of other valuation techniques in estimating fair value less costs to sell. For example, paragraph 27 of the Standard states that 'If there is no binding sale agreement or active market for an asset, fair value less costs to sell is based on the best information available to reflect the amount that an entity could obtain, at the balance sheet date, from the disposal of the asset in an arm's length transaction between knowledgeable, willing parties, after deducting the costs of disposal.'[22]

BC59 In considering (b) above, the Board observed that the previous version of IAS 36 permitted risk adjustments to be reflected either in the cash flows or in the discount rate, without indicating a preference. The Board could see no justification for amending this approach to require risk adjustments for uncertainty to be factored into the cash flows, particularly given the Board's inclination to avoid modifying the requirements in the previous version of IAS 36 for determining recoverable amount until it considers and resolves the broader question of measurement in accounting. Additionally, the Board as part of its consultative process conducted field visits and round-table discussions during the comment period for the Exposure Draft.[23] Many field visit participants indicated a preference for reflecting such risk adjustments in the discount rate.

BC60 In considering (c) above, the Board observed that the measure of value in use adopted in IAS 36 is not a pure 'entity-specific' measure. Although the cash flows used as the starting point in the calculation represent entity-specific cash flows (ie they are derived from the most recent financial budgets/forecasts approved by management and represent management's best estimate of the set of economic conditions that will exist over the remaining useful life of the asset), their present value is required to be determined using a discount rate that reflects current market assessments of the time value of

---

22 IFRS 13, issued in May 2011, contains the requirements for measuring fair value. As a consequence paragraph 27 of IAS 36 has been deleted.

23 The field visits were conducted from early December 2002 to early April 2003, and involved IASB members and staff in meetings with 41 companies in Australia, France, Germany, Japan, South Africa, Switzerland and the United Kingdom. IASB members and staff also took part in a series of round-table discussions with auditors, preparers, accounting standard-setters and regulators in Canada and the United States on implementation issues encountered by North American companies during first-time application of US Statements of Financial Accounting Standards 141 *Business Combinations* and 142 *Goodwill and Other Intangible Assets*, and the equivalent Canadian Handbook Sections, which were issued in June 2001.

money and the risks specific to the asset. Paragraph 56 of the Standard (paragraph 49 of the previous version of IAS 36) clarifies that 'A rate that reflects current market assessments of the time value of money and the risks specific to the asset is the return that investors would require if they were to choose an investment that would generate cash flows of amounts, timing and risk profile equivalent to those that the entity expects to derive from the asset.' In other words, an asset's value in use reflects how the market would price the cash flows that management expects to derive from that asset.

BC61   Therefore, the Board concluded that:

(a)   it is consistent with the measure of value in use adopted in IAS 36 to include in the list of elements the other factors that market participants would reflect in pricing the future cash flows the entity expects to derive from the asset.

(b)   all of the elements proposed in the Exposure Draft (and listed in paragraph 30 of the revised Standard) should be reflected in the calculation of an asset's value in use.

Estimates of future cash flows (paragraphs 33, 34 and 44)

BC62   The Exposure Draft proposed requiring cash flow projections used in measuring value in use to be based on reasonable and supportable assumptions that take into account both past actual cash flows and management's past ability to forecast cash flows accurately.

BC63   Many respondents to the Exposure Draft disagreed with this proposal, arguing that:

(a)   the reasons for past cash flow forecasts differing from actual cash flows may be irrelevant to the current projections. For example, if there has been a major change in management, management's past ability to forecast cash flows might not be relevant to the current projections. Additionally, a poor record of forecasting cash flows accurately might be the result of factors outside of management's control (such as the events of September 11, 2001), rather than indicative of management bias.

(b)   it is unclear how, in practice, the assumptions on which the cash flow projections are based could take into account past differences between management's forecasts and actual cash flows.

(c)   the proposal is inconsistent with the requirement to base cash flow projections on the most recent financial budgets/forecasts approved by management.

BC64   The Board observed that, as worded, the proposal would have *required* the assumptions on which the cash flow forecasts are based to be adjusted for past actual cash flows and management's past ability to forecast cash flows accurately. The Board agreed with respondents that it is not clear how, in practice, this might be achieved, and that in some circumstances past actual cash flows and management's past ability to forecast cash flows accurately might not be relevant to the development of current forecasts. However, the

Board remained of the view that in developing the assumptions on which the cash flow forecasts are based, management should remain mindful of, and when appropriate make the necessary adjustments for, an entity's actual past performance or previous history of management consistently overstating or understating cash flow forecasts.

BC65 Therefore, the Board decided not to proceed with the proposal, but instead to include in paragraph 34 of the Standard guidance clarifying that management:

(a) should assess the reasonableness of the assumptions on which its current cash flow projections are based by examining the causes of differences between past cash flow projections and actual cash flows; and

(b) should ensure that the assumptions on which its current cash flow projections are based are consistent with past actual outcomes, provided the effects of subsequent events or circumstances that did not exist when those actual cash flows were generated make this appropriate.

BC66 In finalising the Standard the Board also considered two issues identified by respondents to the Exposure Draft and referred to the Board by the International Financial Reporting Interpretations Committee. Both issues related to the application of paragraphs 27(b) and 37 of the previous version of IAS 36 (now paragraphs 33(b) and 44). The Board did not reconsider those paragraphs when developing the Exposure Draft.

BC67 Paragraph 27(b) required the cash flow projections used to measure value in use to be based on the most recent financial budgets/forecasts that have been approved by management. Paragraph 37, however, required the future cash flows to be estimated for the asset [or cash-generating unit] in its current condition and excluded estimated future cash inflows or outflows that are expected to arise from: (a) a future restructuring to which an enterprise is not yet committed; or (b) future capital expenditure that will improve or enhance the asset [or cash-generating unit] in excess of its originally assessed standard of performance.[24]

BC68 The first issue the Board considered related to the acquisition of a cash-generating unit when:

(a) the price paid for the unit was based on projections that included a major restructuring expected to result in a substantial increase in the net cash inflows derived from the unit; and

(b) there is no observable market from which to estimate the unit's fair value less costs to sell.[25]

---

24 The requirement to exclude future capital expenditure that will improve or enhance the asset in excess of its originally assessed standard of performance was amended in 2003 as a consequential amendment arising from the revision of IAS 16 *Property, Plant and Equipment*. Paragraph 44 of IAS 36 now requires estimates of future cash flows to exclude future cash inflows or outflows that are expected to arise from improving or enhancing the asset's performance.

25 IFRS 13, issued in May 2011, contains the requirements for measuring fair value.

Respondents expressed concern that if the net cash inflows arising from the restructuring were not reflected in the unit's value in use, comparison of the unit's recoverable amount and carrying amount immediately after the acquisition would result in the recognition of an impairment loss.

BC69   The Board agreed with respondents that, all else being equal, the value in use of a newly acquired unit would, in accordance with IAS 36, be less than the price paid for the unit to the extent that the price includes the net benefits of a future restructuring to which the entity is not yet committed. However, this does not mean that a comparison of the unit's recoverable amount with its carrying amount immediately after the acquisition will result in the recognition of an impairment loss. The Board observed that:[26]

(a)   recoverable amount is measured in accordance with IAS 36 as the higher of value in use and fair value less costs to sell. Fair value less costs to sell is defined in the Standard as 'the amount obtainable from the sale of an asset or cash-generating unit in an arm's length transaction between knowledgeable, willing parties, less the costs of disposal.'

(b)   paragraphs 25–27 of the Standard provide guidance on estimating fair value less costs to sell. In accordance with that guidance, the best evidence of a recently acquired unit's fair value less costs to sell is likely to be the arm's length price the entity paid to acquire the unit, adjusted for disposal costs and for any changes in economic circumstances between the transaction date and the date at which the estimate is made.

(c)   if the unit's fair value less costs to sell were to be otherwise estimated, it would also reflect the market's assessment of the expected net benefits any acquirer would be able to derive from restructuring the unit or from future capital expenditure on the unit.

BC70   Therefore, all else being equal, the unit's recoverable amount would be its fair value less costs to sell, rather than its value in use. As such, the net benefits of the restructuring would be reflected in the unit's recoverable amount, meaning that an impairment loss would arise only to the extent of any material disposal costs.

BC71   The Board acknowledged that treating the newly acquired unit's fair value less costs to sell as its recoverable amount seems inconsistent with the reason underpinning a 'higher of fair value less costs to sell and value in use' recoverable amount measurement objective. Measuring recoverable amount as the higher of fair value less costs to sell and value in use is intended to reflect the economic decisions that are made when an asset becomes impaired: is it better to sell or keep using the asset?

---

26 IFRS 13, issued in May 2011, contains the requirements for measuring fair value. As a consequence paragraphs 25–27 of IAS 36 have been deleted.

BC72   Nevertheless, the Board concluded that:

    (a)   amending IAS 36 to include in value in use calculations the costs and benefits of future restructurings to which the entity is not yet committed would be a significant change to the concept of value in use adopted in the previous version of IAS 36. That concept is 'value in use for the asset in its current condition'.

    (b)   the concept of value in use in IAS 36 should not be modified as part of the Business Combinations project, but should be reconsidered only once the Board considers and resolves the broader question of the appropriate measurement objectives in accounting.

BC73   The second issue the Board considered related to what some respondents suggested was a conflict between the requirements in paragraphs 27(b) and 37 of the previous version of IAS 36 (now paragraphs 33(b) and 44). Paragraph 27(b) required value in use to be based on the most recent forecasts approved by management—which would be likely to reflect management's intentions in relation to future restructurings and future capital expenditure—whereas paragraph 37 required value in use to exclude the effects of a future restructuring to which the enterprise is not yet committed and future capital expenditure that will improve or enhance the asset in excess of its originally assessed standard of performance.[27]

BC74   The Board concluded that it is clear from the Basis for Conclusions on the previous version of IAS 36 that IASC's intention was that value in use should be calculated using estimates of future cash inflows for an asset in its current condition. The Board nevertheless agreed with respondents that the requirement for value in use to be based on the most recent forecasts approved by management could be viewed as inconsistent with paragraph 37 of the previous version of IAS 36 when those forecasts include either future restructurings to which the entity is not yet committed or future cash flows associated with improving or enhancing the asset's performance.

BC75   Therefore, the Board decided to clarify, in what is now paragraph 33(b) of the revised Standard, that cash flow projections should be based on the most recent financial budgets/forecasts that have been approved by management, but should exclude any estimated future cash inflows or outflows expected to arise from future restructurings or from improving or enhancing the asset's performance. The Board also decided to clarify that when a cash-generating unit contains assets with different estimated useful lives (or, similarly, when an asset comprises components with different estimated useful lives), the replacement of assets (components) with shorter lives is considered to be part of the day-to-day servicing of the unit (asset) when estimating the future cash flows associated with the unit (asset).

---

27   The requirement to exclude future capital expenditure that will improve or enhance the asset in excess of its originally assessed standard of performance was amended in 2003 as a consequential amendment arising from the revision of IAS 16 *Property, Plant and Equipment*. Paragraph 44 of IAS 36 now requires estimates of future cash flows to exclude future cash inflows or outflows that are expected to arise from improving or enhancing the asset's performance.

Using present value techniques to measure value in use (paragraphs A1–A14)

BC76   The Exposure Draft proposed additional application guidance on using present value techniques in measuring value in use. The Board decided to include this additional guidance in the Exposure Draft in response to requests for clarification of the requirements in the previous version of IAS 36 on measuring value in use.

BC77   Respondents to the Exposure Draft were generally supportive of the additional guidance. Those that were not varied in their views, suggesting that:

(a)   limiting the guidance to a brief appendix to IAS 36 is insufficient.

(b)   although the guidance is useful, it detracts from the main purpose of IAS 36, which is to establish accounting principles for impairment testing assets. Therefore, the guidance should be omitted from the Standard.

(c)   entities should be required to use an expected cash flow approach to measure value in use.

(d)   an expected cash flow approach is not consistent with how transactions are priced by management and should be prohibited.

BC78   In considering (a) and (b) above, the Board noted that the respondents that commented on the additional guidance generally agreed that it is useful and sufficient.

BC79   In considering (c) and (d) above, the Board observed that the previous version of IAS 36 did not require value in use to be calculated using an expected cash flow approach, nor did it prohibit such an approach. The Board could see no justification for requiring or prohibiting the use of an expected cash flow approach, particularly given the Board's inclination to avoid modifying the requirements in the previous version of IAS 36 for determining recoverable amount until it considers and resolves the broader measurement issues in accounting. Additionally, in relation to (d), some field visit participants said that they routinely undertake sensitivity and statistical analysis as the basis for using an expected value approach to budgeting/forecasting and strategic decision-making.

BC80   Therefore, the Board decided to include in the revised Standard the application guidance on using present value techniques that was proposed in the Exposure Draft.

Income taxes

Consideration of future tax cash flows

BCZ81   Future income tax cash flows may affect recoverable amount. It is convenient to analyse future tax cash flows into two components:

(a)   the future tax cash flows that would result from any difference between the tax base of an asset (the amount attributed to it for tax purposes) and its carrying amount, after recognition of any impairment loss. Such differences are described in IAS 12 *Income Taxes* as 'temporary differences'.

(b)   the future tax cash flows that would result if the tax base of the asset were equal to its recoverable amount.

BCZ82   For most assets, an enterprise recognises the tax consequences of temporary differences as a deferred tax liability or deferred tax asset in accordance with IAS 12. Therefore, to avoid double-counting, the future tax consequences of those temporary differences—the first component referred to in paragraph BCZ81—are not considered in determining recoverable amount (see further discussion in paragraphs BCZ86–BCZ89).

BCZ83   The tax base of an asset on initial recognition is normally equal to its cost. Therefore, net selling price[28] implicitly reflects market participants' assessment of the future tax cash flows that would result if the tax base of the asset were equal to its recoverable amount. Therefore, no adjustment is required to net selling price to reflect the second component referred to in paragraph BCZ81.

BCZ84   In principle, value in use should include the present value of the future tax cash flows that would result if the tax base of the asset were equal to its value in use—the second component referred to in paragraph BCZ81. Nevertheless it may be burdensome to estimate the effect of that component. This is because:

(a)   to avoid double-counting, it is necessary to exclude the effect of temporary differences; and

(b)   value in use would need to be determined by an iterative and possibly complex computation so that value in use itself reflects a tax base equal to that value in use.

For these reasons, IASC decided to require an enterprise to determine value in use by using pre-tax future cash flows and, hence, a pre-tax discount rate.

Determining a pre-tax discount rate

BCZ85   In theory, discounting post-tax cash flows at a post-tax discount rate and discounting pre-tax cash flows at a pre-tax discount rate should give the same result, as long as the pre-tax discount rate is the post-tax discount rate adjusted to reflect the specific amount and timing of the future tax cash

---

28   In IFRS 5 *Non-current Assets Held for Sale and Discontinued Operations*, issued by the IASB in 2004, the term 'net selling price' was replaced in IAS 36 by 'fair value less costs to sell'.

flows. The pre-tax discount rate is not always the post-tax discount rate grossed up by a standard rate of tax.

Example

This example illustrates that a post-tax discount rate grossed-up by a standard rate of tax is not always an appropriate pre-tax discount rate.

At the end of 20X0, the carrying amount of an asset is 1,757 and its remaining useful life is 5 years. The tax base in 20X0 is the cost of the asset. The cost is fully deductible at the end of 20X1. The tax rate is 20%. The discount rate for the asset can be determined only on a post-tax basis and is estimated to be 10%. At the end of 20X0, cash flow projections determined on a pre-tax basis are as follows:

		20X1	20X2	20X3	20X4	20X5
(1)	Pre-tax cash flows (CF)	800	600	500	200	100

Value in use determined using post-tax cash flows and a post-tax discount rate

End of 20X0		20X1	20X2	20X3	20X4	20X5
(2)	Deduction of the cost of the asset	(1,757)	–	–	–	–
(3)	Tax CF [((1) – (2)) × 20%]	(191)	120	100	40	20
(4)	Post-tax CF [(1) – (3)]	991	480	400	160	80
(5)	Post-tax CF discounted at 10%	901	396	301	109	50
Value in use [Σ(5)] =						1,757

Value in use determined using pre-tax cash flows and a pre-tax discount rate (determined by grossing-up the post-tax discount rate)

Pre-tax discount rate (grossed-up) [10%/(100% – 20%)] 12.5%

End of 20X0		20X1	20X2	20X3	20X4	20X5
(6)	Pre-tax CF discounted at 12.5%	711	475	351	125	55
Value in use [Σ(6)] =						1,717

continued...

...continued

Example

Determination of the 'real' pre-tax discount rate

A pre-tax discount rate can be determined by an iterative computation so that value in use determined using pre-tax cash flows and a pre-tax discount rate equals value in use determined using post-tax cash flows and a post-tax discount rate. In the example, the pre-tax discount rate would be 11.2%.

End of 20X0		20X1	20X2	20X3	20X4	20X5
(7) Pre-tax CF discounted at 11.2%		718	485	364	131	59
Value in use [Σ(7)] =						1,757

The 'real' pre-tax discount rate differs from the post-tax discount rate grossed-up by the standard rate of tax depending on the tax rate, the post-tax discount rate, the timing of the future tax cash flows and the useful life of the asset. Note that the tax base of the asset in this example has been set equal to its cost at the end of 20X0. Therefore, there is no deferred tax to consider in the balance sheet.

Interaction with IAS 12

BCZ86   IAS 36 requires that recoverable amount should be based on present value calculations, whereas under IAS 12 an enterprise determines deferred tax assets and liabilities by comparing the carrying amount of an asset (a present value if the carrying amount is based on recoverable amount) with its tax base (an undiscounted amount).

BCZ87   One way to eliminate this inconsistency would be to measure deferred tax assets and liabilities on a discounted basis. In developing the revised version of IAS 12 (approved in 1996), there was not enough support to require that deferred tax assets and liabilities should be measured on a discounted basis. IASC believed there was still not consensus to support such a change in existing practice. Therefore, IAS 36 requires an enterprise to measure the tax effects of temporary differences using the principles set out in IAS 12.

BCZ88   IAS 12 does not permit an enterprise to recognise certain deferred tax liabilities and assets. In such cases, some believe that the value in use of an asset, or a cash-generating unit, should be adjusted to reflect the tax consequences of recovering its pre-tax value in use. For example, if the tax rate is 25 per cent, an enterprise must receive pre-tax cash flows with a present value of 400 in order to recover a carrying amount of 300.

BCZ89   IASC acknowledged the conceptual merit of such adjustments but concluded that they would add unnecessary complexity. Therefore, IAS 36 neither requires nor permits such adjustments.

Comments by field visit participants and respondents to the December 2002 Exposure Draft

BC90   In revising IAS 36, the Board considered the requirement in the previous version of IAS 36 for:

    (a)   income tax receipts and payments to be excluded from the estimates of future cash flows used to measure value in use; and

    (b)   the discount rate used to measure value in use to be a pre-tax rate that reflects current market assessments of the time value of money and the risks specific to the asset for which the future cash flow estimates have not been adjusted.

BC91   The Board had not considered these requirements when developing the Exposure Draft. However, some field visit participants and respondents to the Exposure Draft stated that using pre-tax cash flows and pre-tax discount rates would be a significant implementation issue for entities. This is because typically an entity's accounting and strategic decision-making systems are fully integrated and use post-tax cash flows and post-tax discount rates to arrive at present value measures.

BC92   In considering this issue, the Board observed that the definition of value in use in the previous version of IAS 36 and the associated requirements on measuring value in use were not sufficiently precise to give a definitive answer to the question of what tax attribute an entity should reflect in value in use. For example, although IAS 36 specified discounting pre-tax cash flows at a pre-tax discount rate—with the pre-tax discount rate being the post-tax discount rate adjusted to reflect the specific amount and timing of the future tax cash flows—it did not specify *which* tax effects the pre-tax rate should include. Arguments could be mounted for various approaches.

BC93   The Board decided that any decision to amend the requirement in the previous version of IAS 36 for pre-tax cash flows to be discounted at a pre-tax discount rate should be made only after the Board has resolved the issue of what tax attribute should be reflected in value in use. The Board decided that it should not try to resolve this latter issue as part of the Business Combinations project—decisions on the treatment of tax in value in use calculations should be made only as part of its conceptual project on measurement. Therefore, the Board concluded it should not amend as part of the current revision of IAS 36 the requirement to use pre-tax cash flows and pre-tax discount rates when measuring value in use.

BC94   However, the Board observed that, conceptually, discounting post-tax cash flows at a post-tax discount rate and discounting pre-tax cash flows at a pre-tax discount rate should give the same result, as long as the pre-tax discount rate is the post-tax discount rate adjusted to reflect the specific amount and timing of the future tax cash flows. The pre-tax discount rate is generally not the post-tax discount rate grossed up by a standard rate of tax.

Recognition of an impairment loss (paragraphs 58–64)

BCZ95   IAS 36 requires that an impairment loss should be recognised whenever the recoverable amount of an asset is below its carrying amount. IASC considered various criteria for recognising an impairment loss in the financial statements:

(a)   recognition if it is considered that the impairment loss is permanent ('permanent criterion');

(b)   recognition if it is considered probable that an asset is impaired, ie if it is probable that an enterprise will not recover the carrying amount of the asset ('probability criterion'); and

(c)   immediate recognition whenever recoverable amount is below the carrying amount ('economic criterion').

Recognition based on a 'permanent' criterion

BCZ96   Supporters of the 'permanent' criterion argue that:

(a)   this criterion avoids the recognition of temporary decreases in the recoverable amount of an asset.

(b)   the recognition of an impairment loss refers to future operations; it is contrary to the historical cost system to account for future events. Also, depreciation (amortisation) will reflect these future losses over the expected remaining useful life of the asset.

This view was supported by only a few commentators on E55 *Impairment of Assets*.

BCZ97   IASC decided to reject the 'permanent' criterion because:

(a)   it is difficult to identify whether an impairment loss is permanent. There is a risk that, by using this criterion, recognition of an impairment loss may be delayed.

(b)   this criterion is at odds with the basic concept that an asset is a resource that will generate future economic benefits. Cost-based accrual accounting cannot reflect events without reference to future expectations. If the events that led to a decrease in recoverable amount have already taken place, the carrying amount should be reduced accordingly.

Recognition based on a 'probability' criterion

BCZ98   Some argue that an impairment loss should be recognised only if it is considered probable that the carrying amount of an asset cannot be fully recovered. Proponents of a 'probability' criterion are divided between:

(a)   those who support the use of a recognition trigger based on the sum of the future cash flows (undiscounted and without allocation of interest costs) as a practical approach to implementing the 'probability' criterion; and

(b)   those who support reflecting the requirements in IAS 10 (reformatted 1994) *Contingencies and Events Occurring After the Balance Sheet Date*.[29]

Sum of undiscounted future cash flows (without interest costs)

BCZ99   Some national standard-setters use the 'probability' criterion as a basis for recognition of an impairment loss and require, as a practical approach to implementing that criterion, that an impairment loss should be recognised only if the sum of the future cash flows from an asset (undiscounted and without allocation of interest costs) is less than the carrying amount of the asset. An impairment loss, when recognised, is measured as the difference between the carrying amount of the asset and its recoverable amount measured at fair value (based on quoted market prices or, if no quoted market prices exist, estimated considering prices for similar assets and the results of valuation techniques, such as the sum of cash flows discounted to their present value, option-pricing models, matrix pricing, option-adjusted spread models and fundamental analysis).[30]

BCZ100   One of the characteristics of this approach is that the bases for recognition and measurement of an impairment loss are different. For example, even if the fair value of an asset is lower than its carrying amount, no impairment loss will be recognised if the sum of undiscounted cash flows (without allocation of interest costs) is greater than the asset's carrying amount. This might occur, especially if an asset has a long useful life.

BCZ101   Those who support using the sum of undiscounted future cash flows (without allocation of interest costs) as a recognition trigger argue that:

(a)   using a recognition trigger based on undiscounted amounts is consistent with the historical cost framework.

(b)   it avoids recognising temporary impairment losses and creating potentially volatile earnings that may mislead users of financial statements.

(c)   net selling price[31] and value in use are difficult to substantiate — a price for the disposal of an asset or an appropriate discount rate is difficult to estimate.

(d)   it is a higher threshold for recognising impairment losses. It should be relatively easy to conclude that the sum of undiscounted future cash flows will equal or exceed the carrying amount of an asset without incurring the cost of allocating projected cash flows to specific future periods.

This view was supported by a minority of commentators on E55 *Impairment of Assets*.

---

29 The requirements relating to contingencies in the 1994 version of IAS 10 were replaced in 1998 with the requirements in IAS 37 *Provisions, Contingent Liabilities and Contingent Assets*.

30 IFRS 13, issued in May 2011, contains the requirements for measuring fair value.

31 In IFRS 5 *Non-current Assets Held for Sale and Discontinued Operations*, issued by the IASB in 2004, the term 'net selling price' was replaced in IAS 36 by 'fair value less costs to sell'.

BCZ102   IASC considered the arguments listed above but rejected this approach because:

(a)   when it identifies that an asset may be impaired, a rational enterprise will make an investment decision. Therefore, it is relevant to consider the time value of money and the risks specific to an asset in determining whether an asset is impaired. This is particularly true if an asset has a long useful life.

(b)   IAS 36 does not require an enterprise to estimate the recoverable amount of each [depreciable] asset every year but only if there is an indication that an asset may be materially impaired. An asset that is depreciated (amortised) in an appropriate manner is unlikely to become materially impaired unless events or changes in circumstances cause a sudden reduction in the estimate of recoverable amount.

(c)   probability factors are already encompassed in the determination of value in use, in projecting future cash flows and in requiring that recoverable amount should be the higher of net selling price and value in use.

(d)   if there is an unfavourable change in the assumptions used to determine recoverable amount, users are better served if they are informed about this change in assumptions on a timely basis.

Probability criterion based on IAS 10 (reformatted 1994)

BCZ103   IAS 10 required the amount of a contingent loss to be recognised as an expense and a liability if:

(a)   it was probable that future events will confirm that, after taking into account any related probable recovery, an asset had been impaired or a liability incurred at the balance sheet date; and

(b)   a reasonable estimate of the amount of the resulting loss could be made.

BCZ104   IASC rejected the view that an impairment loss should be recognised based on the requirements in IAS 10 because:

(a)   the requirements in IAS 10 were not sufficiently detailed and would have made a 'probability' criterion difficult to apply.

(b)   those requirements would have introduced another unnecessary layer of probability. Indeed, as mentioned above, probability factors are already encompassed in estimates of value in use and in requiring that recoverable amount should be the higher of net selling price and value in use.

Recognition based on an 'economic' criterion

BCZ105   IAS 36 relies on an 'economic' criterion for the recognition of an impairment loss—an impairment loss is recognised whenever the recoverable amount of an asset is below its carrying amount. This criterion was already used in many International Accounting Standards before IAS 36, such as IAS 9 *Research and*

Development Costs, IAS 22 *Business Combinations*, and IAS 16 *Property, Plant and Equipment*.

BCZ106   IASC considered that an 'economic' criterion is the best criterion to give information which is useful to users in assessing future cash flows to be generated by the enterprise as a whole. In estimating the time value of money and the risks specific to an asset in determining whether the asset is impaired, factors, such as the probability or permanence of the impairment loss, are subsumed in the measurement.

BCZ107   The majority of commentators on E55 supported IASC's view that an impairment loss should be recognised based on an 'economic' criterion.

Revalued assets: recognition in the income statement versus directly in equity

BCZ108   IAS 36 requires that an impairment loss on a revalued asset should be recognised as an expense in the income statement[32] immediately, except that it should be recognised directly in equity[33] to the extent that it reverses a previous revaluation on the same asset.

BCZ109   Some argue that, when there is a clear reduction in the service potential (for example, physical damage) of a revalued asset, the impairment loss should be recognised in the income statement.

BCZ110   Others argue that an impairment loss should always be recognised as an expense in the income statement. The logic of this argument is that an impairment loss arises only where there is a reduction in the estimated future cash flows that form part of the business's operating activities. Indeed, according to IAS 16, whether or not an asset is revalued, the depreciation charge is always recognised in the income statement. Supporters of this view question why the treatment of an impairment loss on a revalued asset should be different to depreciation.

BCZ111   IASC believed that it would be difficult to identify whether an impairment loss is a downward revaluation or a reduction in service potential. Therefore, IASC decided to retain the treatment used in IAS 16 and to treat an impairment loss of a revalued asset as a revaluation decrease (and similarly, a reversal of an impairment loss as a subsequent revaluation increase).

BCZ112   For a revalued asset, the distinction between an 'impairment loss' ('reversal of an impairment loss') and another 'revaluation decrease' ('revaluation increase') is important for disclosure purposes. If an impairment loss that is material to the enterprise as a whole has been recognised or reversed, more information on how this impairment loss is measured is required by IAS 36 than for the recognition of a revaluation in accordance with IAS 16.

---

32   IAS 1 *Presentation of Financial Statements* (as revised in 2007) requires an entity to present all income and expense items in one statement of comprehensive income or in two statements (a separate income statement and a statement of comprehensive income).

33   As a consequence of the revision of IAS 1 (revised 2007) an impairment loss is recognised in other comprehensive income.

Cash-generating units (paragraphs 66–73)

BCZ113   Some support the principle of determining recoverable amount on an individual asset basis only. This view was expressed by a few commentators on E55. They argued that:

(a)   it would be difficult to identify cash-generating units at a level other than the business as a whole and, therefore, impairment losses would never be recognised for individual assets; and

(b)   it should be possible to recognise an impairment loss, regardless of whether an asset generates cash inflows that are independent from those of other assets or groups of assets. Commentators quoted examples of assets that have become under-utilised or obsolete but that are still in use.

BCZ114   IASC acknowledged that identifying the lowest level of independent cash inflows for a group of assets would involve judgement. However, IASC believed that the concept of cash-generating units is a matter of fact: assets work together to generate cash flows.

BCZ115   In response to requests from commentators on E55, IAS 36 includes additional guidance and examples for identifying cash-generating units and for determining the carrying amount of cash-generating units. IAS 36 emphasises that cash-generating units should be identified for the lowest level of aggregation of assets possible.

Internal transfer pricing (paragraph 70)

BC116   The previous version of IAS 36 required that if an active market exists for the output produced by an asset or a group of assets:

(a)   that asset or group of assets should be identified as a cash-generating unit, even if some or all of the output is used internally; and

(b)   management's best estimate of the future market prices for the output should be used in estimating:

(i)   the future cash inflows that relate to the internal use of the output when determining the value in use of this cash-generating unit; and

(ii)   the future cash outflows that relate to the internal use of the output when determining the value in use of the entity's other cash-generating units.

BC117   The requirement in (a) above has been carried forward in the revised Standard. However, some respondents to the Exposure Draft asked for additional guidance to clarify the role of internal transfer pricing versus prices in an arm's length transaction when developing cash flow forecasts. The Board decided to address this issue by amending the requirement in (b) above to deal more broadly with cash-generating units whose cash flows are affected by internal transfer pricing, rather than just cash-generating units whose internally consumed output could be sold on an active market.

BC118   Therefore, the Standard clarifies that if the cash inflows generated by *any* asset or cash-generating unit are affected by internal transfer pricing, an entity should use management's best estimate of future prices that could be achieved in arm's length transactions in estimating:

(a)   the future cash inflows used to determine the asset's or cash-generating unit's value in use; and

(b)   the future cash outflows used to determine the value in use of other assets or cash-generating units affected by the internal transfer pricing.

Testing indefinite-lived intangibles for impairment

BC119   As part of the first phase of its Business Combinations project, the Board concluded that:

(a)   an intangible asset should be regarded as having an indefinite useful life when, based on an analysis of all relevant factors (eg legal, regulatory, contractual, competitive and economic), there is no foreseeable limit on the period over which the asset is expected to generate net cash inflows for the entity; and

(b)   an indefinite-lived intangible should not be amortised, but should be tested regularly for impairment.

An outline of the Board's deliberations on each of these issues is provided in the Basis for Conclusions on IAS 38 *Intangible Assets*.

BC120   Having reached these conclusions, the Board then considered the form that the impairment test for indefinite-lived intangibles should take. The Board concluded that:

(a)   an indefinite-lived intangible should be tested for impairment annually, or more frequently if there is any indication that it may be impaired; and

(b)   the recoverable amounts of such assets should be measured, and impairment losses (and reversals of impairment losses) in respect of those assets should be accounted for, in accordance with the requirements in IAS 36 for assets other than goodwill.

Paragraphs BC121–BC126 outline the Board's deliberations in reaching its conclusion about the frequency and timing of impairment testing indefinite-lived intangibles. Paragraphs BC129 and BC130 outline the Board's deliberations in reaching its conclusions about measuring the recoverable amount of such assets and accounting for impairment losses and reversals of impairment losses.

Frequency and timing of impairment testing (paragraphs 9 and 10(a))

BC121   In developing the Exposure Draft, the Board observed that requiring assets to be remeasured when they are impaired is a valuation concept rather than one of cost allocation. This concept, which some have termed 'the recoverable cost concept', focuses on the benefits to be derived from the asset in the future, rather than on the process by which the cost or other carrying amount of the asset should be allocated to particular accounting periods. Therefore, the purpose of an impairment test is to assess whether the carrying amount of an asset will be recovered through use or sale of the asset. Nevertheless, allocating the depreciable amount of an asset with a limited useful life on a systematic basis over that life provides some assurance against the asset's carrying amount exceeding its recoverable amount. The Board acknowledged that non-amortisation of an intangible asset increases the reliance that must be placed on impairment reviews of that asset to ensure that its carrying amount does not exceed its recoverable amount.

BC122   Accordingly, the Exposure Draft proposed that indefinite-lived intangibles should be tested for impairment at the end of each annual reporting period. The Board concluded, however, that testing such assets annually for impairment is not a substitute for management being aware of events occurring or circumstances changing between annual tests that indicate a possible impairment. Therefore, the Exposure Draft also proposed that an entity should be required to test such assets for impairment whenever there is an indication of possible impairment, and not wait until the next annual test.

BC123   The respondents to the Exposure Draft generally supported the proposal to test indefinite-lived intangibles for impairment annually and whenever there is an indication of possible impairment. Those that disagreed argued that requiring an annual impairment test would be excessively burdensome, and recommended requiring an impairment test only when there is an indication that an indefinite-lived intangible might be impaired. After considering these comments the Board:

    (a)   reaffirmed its view that non-amortisation of an intangible asset increases the reliance that must be placed on impairment reviews of that asset to ensure that its carrying amount does not exceed its recoverable amount.

    (b)   concluded that IAS 36 should require indefinite-lived intangibles to be tested for impairment annually and whenever there is an indication of possible impairment.

BC124   However, as noted in paragraph BC122, the Exposure Draft proposed that the annual impairment tests for indefinite-lived intangibles should be performed at the end of each annual period. Many respondents to the Exposure Draft disagreed that IAS 36 should mandate the timing of the annual impairment tests. They argued that:

(a)   it would be inconsistent with the proposal (now a requirement) that the annual impairment test for a cash-generating unit to which goodwill has been allocated may be performed at any time during an annual period, provided the test is performed at the same time every year. There is no justification for providing less flexibility in the timing of the annual impairment test for indefinite-lived intangibles.

(b)   if the impairment test for an indefinite-lived intangible is linked to the impairment test for goodwill (ie if the indefinite-lived intangible is assessed for impairment at the same cash-generating unit level as goodwill, rather than individually or as part of a smaller cash-generating unit), the requirement to measure its recoverable amount at the end of the annual period could result in the cash-generating unit to which it (and the goodwill) belongs being tested for impairment at least twice each annual period, which is too burdensome. For example, assume a cash-generating unit contains goodwill and an indefinite-lived intangible, and that the indefinite-lived intangible is assessed for impairment at the same cash-generating unit level as goodwill. Assume also that the entity reports quarterly, has a December year-end, and decides to test goodwill for impairment at the end of the third quarter to coincide with the completion of its annual strategic planning/budgeting process. The proposal that the annual impairment test for an indefinite-lived intangible should be performed at the end of each annual period would mean that the entity would be required:

       (i)   to calculate at the end of each September the recoverable amount of the cash-generating unit, compare it with its carrying amount, and, if the carrying amount exceeds the recoverable amount, recognise an impairment loss for the unit by reducing the carrying amount of goodwill and allocating any remaining impairment loss to the other assets in the unit, including the indefinite-lived intangible.

       (ii)   to perform the same steps again each December to test the indefinite-lived intangible for impairment.

       (iii)   to perform the same steps again at any other time throughout the annual period if there is an indication that the cash-generating unit, the goodwill or the indefinite-lived intangible may be impaired.

BC125   In considering these comments, the Board indicated a preference for requiring entities to perform the recoverable amount calculations for both goodwill and indefinite-lived intangibles at the end of the annual period. However, the Board acknowledged that, as outlined in paragraph BC124(b), impairment tests for indefinite-lived intangibles will sometimes be linked to impairment tests for goodwill, and that many entities would find it difficult to perform all those tests at the end of the annual period.

BC126   Therefore, consistently with the annual impairment test for goodwill, the
         Standard permits the annual impairment test for an indefinite-lived intangible
         to be performed at any time during an annual period, provided it is performed
         at the same time every year.

Carrying forward a recoverable amount calculation (paragraph 24)

BC127   The Standard permits the most recent detailed calculation of the recoverable
         amount of an indefinite-lived intangible to be carried forward from a
         preceding period for use in the current period's impairment test, provided all
         of the criteria in paragraph 24 of the Standard are met.

BC128   Integral to the Board's decision that indefinite-lived intangibles should be
         tested for impairment annually was the view that many entities should be
         able to conclude that the recoverable amount of such an asset is greater than
         its carrying amount without actually recomputing recoverable amount.
         However, the Board concluded that this would be the case only if the last
         recoverable amount determination exceeded the carrying amount by a
         substantial margin, and nothing had happened since then to make the
         likelihood of an impairment loss other than remote. The Board concluded
         that, in such circumstances, permitting a detailed calculation of the
         recoverable amount of an indefinite-lived intangible to be carried forward
         from the preceding period for use in the current period's impairment test
         would significantly reduce the costs of applying the impairment test, without
         compromising its integrity.

Measuring recoverable amount and accounting for impairment losses and reversals of impairment losses

BC129   The Board could see no compelling reason why the measurement basis
         adopted for determining recoverable amount and the treatment of
         impairment losses and reversals of impairment losses for one group of
         identifiable assets should differ from those applying to other identifiable
         assets. Adopting different methods would impair the usefulness of the
         information provided to users about an entity's identifiable assets, because
         both comparability and reliability, which rest on the notion that similar
         transactions are accounted for in the same way, would be diminished.
         Therefore, the Board concluded that the recoverable amounts of
         indefinite-lived intangibles should be measured, and impairment losses and
         reversals of impairment losses in respect of those assets should be accounted
         for, consistently with other identifiable assets covered by the Standard.

BC130   The Board expressed some concern over the measurement basis adopted in the
         previous version of IAS 36 for determining recoverable amount (ie higher of
         value in use and net selling price) and its treatment of impairment losses and
         reversals of impairment losses for assets other than goodwill. However, the
         Board's intention in revising IAS 36 was *not* to reconsider the general approach
         to impairment testing. Accordingly, the Board decided that it should address
         concerns over that general approach as part of its future re-examination of
         IAS 36 in its entirety, rather than as part of its Business Combinations project.

Testing goodwill for impairment (paragraphs 80–99)

BC131   [Deleted]

BC131A   The Board concluded that goodwill should not be amortised and instead should be tested for impairment annually, or more frequently if events or changes in circumstances indicate that it might be impaired. IAS 22 *Business Combinations* required acquired goodwill to be amortised on a systematic basis over the best estimate of its useful life. There was a rebuttable presumption that its useful life did not exceed twenty years from initial recognition. If that presumption was rebutted, acquired goodwill was required to be tested for impairment in accordance with the previous version of IAS 36 at least at each financial year-end, even if there was no indication that it was impaired.

BC131B   In considering the appropriate accounting for acquired goodwill after its initial recognition, the Board examined the following three approaches:

    (a)   straight-line amortisation but with an impairment test whenever there is an indication that the goodwill might be impaired;

    (b)   non-amortisation but with an impairment test annually or more frequently if events or changes in circumstances indicate that the goodwill might be impaired; and

    (c)   permitting entities a choice between approaches (a) and (b).

BC131C   The Board concluded, and the respondents to ED 3 *Business Combinations* that expressed a clear view on this issue generally agreed, that entities should not be allowed a choice between approaches (a) and (b). Permitting such choices impairs the usefulness of the information provided to users of financial statements because both comparability and reliability are diminished.

BC131D   The respondents to ED 3 who expressed a clear view on this issue generally supported approach (a). They put forward the following arguments in support of that approach:

    (a)   acquired goodwill is an asset that is consumed and replaced by internally generated goodwill. Therefore, amortisation ensures that the acquired goodwill is recognised in profit or loss and no internally generated goodwill is recognised as an asset in its place, consistently with the general prohibition in IAS 38 on the recognition of internally generated goodwill.

    (b)   conceptually, amortisation is a method of allocating the cost of acquired goodwill over the periods it is consumed, and is consistent with the approach taken to other intangible and tangible fixed assets that do not have indefinite useful lives. Indeed, entities are required to determine the useful lives of items of property, plant and equipment, and allocate their depreciable amounts on a systematic basis over those useful lives. There is no conceptual reason for treating acquired goodwill differently.

(c)   the useful life of acquired goodwill cannot be predicted with a satisfactory level of reliability, nor can the pattern in which that goodwill diminishes be known. However, systematic amortisation over an albeit arbitrary period provides an appropriate balance between conceptual soundness and operationality at an acceptable cost: it is the only practical solution to an intractable problem.

BC131E   In considering these comments, the Board agreed that achieving an acceptable level of reliability in the form of representational faithfulness while striking some balance with what is practicable was the primary challenge it faced in deliberating the subsequent accounting for goodwill. The Board observed that the useful life of acquired goodwill and the pattern in which it diminishes generally are not possible to predict, yet its amortisation depends on such predictions. As a result, the amount amortised in any given period can be described as at best an arbitrary estimate of the consumption of acquired goodwill during that period. The Board acknowledged that if goodwill is an asset, in some sense it must be true that goodwill acquired in a business combination is being consumed and replaced by internally generated goodwill, provided that an entity is able to maintain the overall value of goodwill (by, for example, expending resources on advertising and customer service). However, consistently with the view it reached in developing ED 3, the Board remained doubtful about the usefulness of an amortisation charge that reflects the consumption of acquired goodwill, when the internally generated goodwill replacing it is not recognised. Therefore, the Board reaffirmed the conclusion it reached in developing ED 3 that straight-line amortisation of goodwill over an arbitrary period fails to provide useful information. The Board noted that both anecdotal and research evidence supports this view.

BC131F   In considering respondents' comments summarised in paragraph BC131D(b), the Board noted that although the useful lives of both goodwill and tangible fixed assets are directly related to the period over which they are expected to generate net cash inflows for the entity, the expected physical utility to the entity of a tangible fixed asset places an upper limit on the asset's useful life. In other words, unlike goodwill, the useful life of a tangible fixed asset could never extend beyond the asset's expected physical utility to the entity.

BC131G   The Board reaffirmed the view it reached in developing ED 3 that if a rigorous and operational impairment test could be devised, more useful information would be provided to users of an entity's financial statements under an approach in which goodwill is not amortised, but instead tested for impairment annually or more frequently if events or changes in circumstances indicate that the goodwill might be impaired. After considering respondents' comments to the exposure draft of proposed amendments to IAS 36 on the form that such an impairment test should take, the Board concluded that a sufficiently rigorous and operational impairment test could be devised.

BC132   Paragraphs BC133–BC177 outline the Board's deliberations on the form that the impairment test for goodwill should take:

(a)   paragraphs BC137–BC159 discuss the requirements relating to the allocation of goodwill to cash-generating units and the level at which goodwill is tested for impairment.

(b)   paragraphs BC160–BC170 discuss the requirements relating to the recognition and measurement of impairment losses for goodwill, including the frequency of impairment testing.

(c)   paragraphs BC171–BC177 discuss the requirements relating to the timing of goodwill impairment tests.

BC133   As a first step in its deliberations, the Board considered the objective of the goodwill impairment test and the measure of recoverable amount that should be adopted for such a test. The Board observed that recent North American standards use fair value as the basis for impairment testing goodwill, whereas the previous version of IAS 36 and the United Kingdom standard are based on an approach under which recoverable amount is measured as the higher of value in use and net selling price.

BC134   The Board also observed that goodwill acquired in a business combination represents a payment made by an acquirer in anticipation of future economic benefits from assets that are not capable of being individually identified and separately recognised. Goodwill does not generate cash flows independently of other assets or groups of assets and therefore cannot be measured directly. Instead, it is measured as a residual amount, being the excess of the cost of a business combination over the acquirer's interest in the net fair value of the acquiree's identifiable assets, liabilities and contingent liabilities. Moreover, goodwill acquired in a business combination and goodwill generated after that business combination cannot be separately identified, because they contribute jointly to the same cash flows.[34]

BC135   The Board concluded that because it is not possible to measure separately goodwill generated internally after a business combination and to factor that measure into the impairment test for acquired goodwill, the carrying amount of goodwill will always be shielded from impairment by that internally generated goodwill. Therefore, the Board took the view that the objective of the goodwill impairment test could at best be to ensure that the carrying amount of goodwill is recoverable from future cash flows expected to be generated by both acquired goodwill and goodwill generated internally after the business combination.

BC136   The Board noted that because goodwill is measured as a residual amount, the starting point in any goodwill impairment test would have to be the recoverable amount of the operation or unit to which the goodwill relates, regardless of the measurement basis adopted for determining recoverable amount. The Board decided that until it considers and resolves the broader

---

34   In the second phase of its business combinations project, the Board revised the definition and measurement of goodwill in IFRS 3. See paragraph 32 and Appendix A of IFRS 3 (as revised in 2008).

question of the appropriate measurement objective(s) in accounting, identifying the appropriate measure of recoverable amount for that unit would be problematic. Therefore, although the Board expressed concern over the measurement basis adopted in IAS 36 for determining recoverable amount, it decided that it should not depart from that basis when measuring the recoverable amount of a unit whose carrying amount includes acquired goodwill. The Board noted that this would have the added advantage of allowing the impairment test for goodwill to be integrated with the impairment test in IAS 36 for other assets and cash-generating units that include goodwill.

Allocating goodwill to cash-generating units (paragraphs 80–87)

BC137　The previous version of IAS 36 required goodwill to be tested for impairment as part of impairment testing the cash-generating units to which it relates. It employed a 'bottom-up/top-down' approach under which the goodwill was in effect tested for impairment by allocating its carrying amount to each of the smallest cash-generating units to which a portion of that carrying amount could be allocated on a reasonable and consistent basis.

BC138　Consistently with the previous version of IAS 36, the Exposure Draft proposed that:

(a)　goodwill should be tested for impairment as part of impairment testing the cash-generating units to which it relates; and

(b)　the carrying amount of goodwill should be allocated to each of the smallest cash-generating units to which a portion of that carrying amount can be allocated on a reasonable and consistent basis.

However, the Exposure Draft proposed additional guidance clarifying that a portion of the carrying amount of goodwill should be regarded as capable of being allocated to a cash-generating unit on a reasonable and consistent basis only when that unit represents the lowest level at which management monitors the return on investment in assets that include the goodwill. That cash-generating unit could not, however, be larger than a segment based on the entity's primary reporting format determined in accordance with IAS 14 *Segment Reporting*.

BC139　In developing this proposal, the Board noted that because acquired goodwill does not generate cash flows independently of other assets or groups of assets, it can be tested for impairment only as part of impairment testing the cash-generating units to which it relates. However, the Board was concerned that in the absence of any guidance on the precise meaning of 'allocated on a reasonable and consistent basis', some might conclude that when a business combination enhances the value of all of the acquirer's pre-existing cash-generating units, any goodwill acquired in that business combination should be tested for impairment only at the level of the entity itself. The Board concluded that this should not be the case. Rather, there should be a link between the level at which goodwill is tested for impairment and the level of internal reporting that reflects the way an entity manages its operations and with which the goodwill naturally would be associated. Therefore, it was important to the Board that goodwill should be tested for impairment at a level at which information about the operations of an entity and the assets that support them is provided for internal reporting purposes.

BC140   In redeliberating this issue, the Board noted that respondents' and field visit participants' comments indicated that the Board's intention relating to the allocation of goodwill had been widely misunderstood, with many concluding that goodwill would need to be allocated to a much lower level than that intended by the Board. For example, some respondents and field visit participants were concerned that the proposal to allocate goodwill to such a low level would force entities to allocate goodwill arbitrarily to cash-generating units, and therefore to develop new or additional reporting systems to perform the test. The Board confirmed that its intention was that there should be a link between the level at which goodwill is tested for impairment and the level of internal reporting that reflects the way an entity manages its operations. Therefore, except for entities that do not monitor goodwill at or below the segment level, the proposals relating to the level of the goodwill impairment test should *not* cause entities to allocate goodwill arbitrarily to cash-generating units. Nor should they create the need for entities to develop new or additional reporting systems.

BC141   The Board observed from its discussions with field visit participants that much of the confusion stemmed from the definition of a 'cash-generating unit', when coupled with the proposal in paragraph 73 of the Exposure Draft for goodwill to be allocated to each 'smallest cash-generating unit to which a portion of the carrying amount of the goodwill can be allocated on a reasonable and consistent basis'. Additionally, field visit participants and respondents were unclear about the reference in paragraph 74 of the Exposure Draft to 'the lowest level at which management monitors the return on investments in assets that include goodwill', the most frequent question being 'what level of management?' (eg board of directors, chief executive officer, or segment management).

BC142   The Board noted that once its intention on this issue was clarified for field visit participants, they all, with the exception of one company that believes goodwill should be tested for impairment at the entity level, supported the level at which the Board believes goodwill should be tested for impairment.

BC143   The Board also noted the comment from a number of respondents and field visit participants that for some organisations, particularly those managed on a matrix basis, the proposal for cash-generating units to which the goodwill is allocated to be no larger than a segment based on the entity's *primary* reporting format could result in an outcome that is inconsistent with the Board's intention, ie that there should be a link between the level at which goodwill is tested for impairment and the level of internal reporting that reflects the way an entity manages its operations. The following example illustrates this point:

A company managed on a matrix basis is organised primarily on a geographical basis, with product groups providing the secondary basis of segmentation. Goodwill is acquired as part of an acquisition of a product group that is present in several geographical regions, and is then monitored on an ongoing basis for internal reporting purposes as part of the product group/secondary segment. It is feasible that the secondary segment might, depending on the definition of 'larger', be 'larger' than a primary segment.

BC144   Therefore, the Board decided:

(a)   that the Standard should require each unit or group of units to which goodwill is allocated to represent the lowest level within the entity at which the goodwill is monitored for internal management purposes.

(b)   to clarify in the Standard that acquired goodwill should, from the acquisition date, be allocated to each of the acquirer's cash-generating units, or groups of cash-generating units, that are expected to benefit from the combination, irrespective of whether other assets or liabilities of the acquiree are assigned to those units or groups of units.

(c)   to replace the proposal for cash-generating units or groups of units to which goodwill is allocated to be no larger than a segment based on the entity's *primary* reporting format, with the requirement that they be no larger than a segment based on either the entity's primary or the entity's secondary reporting format. The Board concluded that this amendment is necessary to ensure that entities managed on a matrix basis are able to test goodwill for impairment at the level of internal reporting that reflects the way they manage their operations.[35]

BC145   Some respondents to the Exposure Draft raised the following additional concerns on the allocation of goodwill for impairment testing purposes:

(a)   mandating that goodwill should be allocated to at least the segment level is inappropriate — it will often result in arbitrary allocations, and entities would need to develop new or additional reporting systems.

(b)   for convergence reasons, the level of the goodwill impairment test should be the same as the level in US Financial Accounting Standards Board Statement of Financial Accounting Standards No. 142 *Goodwill and Other Intangible Assets* (SFAS 142) (ie the reporting unit level).

(c)   cash-generating units that constitute businesses with similar characteristics should, as is required by SFAS 142, be aggregated and treated as single units, notwithstanding that they may be monitored independently for internal purposes.

BC146   In relation to (a), the Board reaffirmed the conclusion it reached when developing the Exposure Draft that requiring goodwill to be allocated to at least the segment level is necessary to avoid entities erroneously concluding that, when a business combination enhances the value of all of the acquirer's pre-existing cash-generating units, any goodwill acquired in that combination could be tested for impairment only at the level of the entity itself.

---

35 In 2006 IAS 14 was replaced by IFRS 8 *Operating Segments*. IFRS 8 does not require disclosure of primary and secondary segment information. See paragraph BC150A.

BC147   In relation to (b), the Board noted that SFAS 142 requires goodwill to be tested for impairment at a level of reporting referred to as a 'reporting unit'. A reporting unit is an operating segment (as defined in SFAS 131 *Disclosures about Segments of an Enterprise and Related Information*[36]) or one level below an operating segment (referred to as a component). A component of an operating segment is a reporting unit if the component constitutes a business for which discrete financial information is available and segment management regularly reviews the operating results of that component. However, two or more components of an operating segment must be aggregated and deemed a single reporting unit if the components have similar economic characteristics. An operating segment is deemed to be a reporting unit if all of its components are similar, if none of its components is a reporting unit, or if it comprises only a single component.

BC148   Therefore, unlike IAS 36, SFAS 142 places a limit on how far goodwill can be 'pushed down' for impairment testing (ie one level below an operating segment).

BC149   In deciding not to converge with SFAS 142 on the level of the goodwill impairment test, the Board noted the following findings from the field visits and North American round-table discussions:

(a)   most of the US registrant field visit participants stated that the Board's proposals on the level of the goodwill impairment test would result, in practice, in goodwill being tested for impairment at the same level at which it is tested in accordance with SFAS 142. However, several stated that under the Board's proposals, goodwill would be tested for impairment at a lower level than under SFAS 142. Nevertheless, they believe that the Board's approach provides users and management with more useful information.

(b)   several round-table participants stated that they (or, in the case of audit firm participants, their clients) manage and have available information about their investments in goodwill at a lower level than the level of the SFAS 142 impairment test. They expressed a high level of dissatisfaction at being prevented by SFAS 142 from recognising goodwill impairments that they knew existed at these lower levels, but which 'disappeared' once the lower level units were aggregated with other units containing sufficient 'cushions' to offset the impairment loss.

---

36 The basis for identifying 'operating segments' under SFAS 131 differs from the basis for identifying segments based on the entity's primary reporting format under IAS 14. SFAS 131 defines an operating segment as a component of an enterprise (a) that engages in business activities from which it may earn revenues and incur expenses, including revenues and expenses relating to transactions with other components of the enterprise; (b) whose operating results are regularly reviewed by the enterprise's chief operating decision maker to make decisions about resources to be allocated to the segment and assess its performance; and (c) for which discrete financial information is available. IAS 14 was replaced by IFRS 8 in 2006. See paragraph BC150A.

BC150   In considering suggestion (c) in paragraph BC145, the Board observed that aggregating units that constitute businesses with similar characteristics could result in the disappearance of an impairment loss that management *knows* exists in a cash-generating unit because the units with which it is aggregated contain sufficient cushions to offset the impairment loss. In the Board's view, if, because of the way an entity is managed, information about goodwill impairment losses is available to management at a particular level, that information should also be available to the users of the entity's financial statements.

BC150A   In 2006 IFRS 8 replaced IAS 14 and changed the basis for identifying segments. Under IAS 14, two sets of segments were identified—one based on related products and services, and the other on geographical areas. Under IFRS 8, operating segments are identified on the basis of internal reports that are regularly reviewed by the entity's chief operating decision maker in order to allocate resources to the segment and assess its performance. The objective of the change was to improve the disclosure of segment information, not to change the requirements of IAS 36 relating to the allocation of goodwill for impairment testing. The previous wording of the requirement in IAS 36 that each unit or group of units to which goodwill is allocated shall 'not be larger than a segment based on either the entity's primary or the entity's secondary reporting format determined in accordance with IAS 14' has been amended by IFRS 8 to 'not be larger than an operating segment determined in accordance with IFRS 8'. The arguments set out above in support of the original requirement based on segments determined in accordance with IAS 14 support the revised requirements based on segments determined in accordance with the requirements in IFRS 8.

BC150B   Entities adopting IFRS 8 must reconsider the allocation of goodwill to cash-generating units because of the definition of operating segment introduced by IFRS 8. That definition affects the determination of the largest unit permitted by paragraph 80 of IAS 36 for testing goodwill for impairment. In 2008 the Board was made aware that divergent views had developed regarding the largest unit permitted by IAS 36 for impairment testing of goodwill. One view was that the unit is the operating segment level as defined in paragraph 5 of IFRS 8 *before* the aggregation permitted by paragraph 12 of IFRS 8. The other view was that the unit is the operating segment level as defined in paragraph 5 of IFRS 8 *after* the aggregation permitted by paragraph 12 of IFRS 8. The Board noted that the lowest level of the entity at which management monitors goodwill as required in paragraph 80(a) is the same as the lowest level of operating segments at which the chief operating decision maker regularly reviews operating results as defined in IFRS 8. The Board also noted that the linkage of the entity's goodwill monitoring level with the entity's internal reporting level is intentional, as described in paragraph BC140. The Board noted that aggregating operating segments for goodwill impairment testing into a unit larger than the level at which goodwill is monitored contradicts the rationale underlying IAS 36, as set out in paragraphs BC145–BC150. In addition, meeting the aggregation criteria of similar economic characteristics permitted in IFRS 8 does not automatically result in groups of cash-generating units that are expected to benefit from the synergies of allocated goodwill. Similarly, the aggregated segments do not necessarily represent business operations that are economically interdependent or work in concert to recover the goodwill being assessed for impairment. Therefore, in *Improvements to IFRSs* issued in April 2009, the Board amended paragraph 80(b) to state that the required unit for goodwill impairment in IAS 36 is not larger than the operating segment level as defined in paragraph 5 of IFRS 8 before the permitted aggregation.

Completing the initial allocation of goodwill (paragraphs 84 and 85)

BC151 If the initial allocation of goodwill acquired in a business combination cannot be completed before the end of the annual period in which the business combination is effected, the Exposure Draft proposed, and the revised Standard requires, that the initial allocation should be completed before the end of the first annual period beginning after the acquisition date. In contrast, ED 3 proposed, and IFRS 3 requires, that if the initial accounting for a business combination can be determined only provisionally by the end of the period in which the combination is effected, the acquirer should:

(a) account for the combination using those provisional values; and

(b) recognise any adjustments to those provisional values as a result of completing the initial accounting within twelve months of the acquisition date.[37]

BC152 Some respondents to the Exposure Draft questioned why the period to complete the initial allocation of goodwill should differ from the period to complete the initial accounting for a business combination. The Board's view is that acquirers should be allowed a longer period to complete the goodwill allocation, because that allocation often might not be able to be performed until after the initial accounting for the combination is complete. This is because the cost of the combination or the fair values at the acquisition date of the acquiree's identifiable assets, liabilities or contingent liabilities, and therefore the amount of goodwill acquired in the combination, would not be finalised until the initial accounting for the combination in accordance with IFRS 3 is complete.

Disposal of a portion of a cash-generating unit containing goodwill (paragraph 86)

BC153 The Exposure Draft proposed that when an entity disposes of an operation within a cash-generating unit to which goodwill has been allocated, the goodwill associated with that operation should be:

(a) included in the carrying amount of the operation when determining the gain or loss on disposal; and

---

37 In the second phase of its business combinations project, the Board clarified that adjustments to provisional values should be made only to reflect new information obtained about facts and circumstances that existed as of the acquisition date that, if known, would have affected the measurement of the amounts recognised as of that date. Such adjustments should be made within the measurement period, which shall not exceed one year from the acquisition date.

(b)   measured on the basis of the relative values of the operation disposed of and the portion of the cash-generating unit retained.

BC154   This proposal has been carried forward in the Standard with one modification. The Standard requires the goodwill associated with the operation disposed of to be measured on the basis of the relative values of the operation disposed of and the portion of the cash-generating unit retained, unless the entity can demonstrate that some other method better reflects the goodwill associated with the operation disposed of.

BC155   In developing the Exposure Draft, the Board concluded that the proposed level of the impairment test would mean that goodwill could not be identified or associated with an asset group at a level lower than the cash-generating unit to which the goodwill is allocated, except arbitrarily. However, the Board also concluded that when an operation within that cash-generating unit is being disposed of, it is appropriate to presume that some amount of goodwill is associated with that operation. Thus, an allocation of the goodwill should be required when the part of the cash-generating unit being disposed of constitutes an operation.

BC156   Some respondents to the Exposure Draft suggested that although in most circumstances goodwill could not be identified or associated with an asset group at a level lower than the cash-generating unit or group of cash-generating units to which it is allocated for impairment testing, there may be some instances when this is not so. For example, assume an acquiree is integrated with one of the acquirer's pre-existing cash-generating units that did not include any goodwill in its carrying amount. Assume also that almost immediately after the business combination the acquirer disposes of a loss-making operation within the cash-generating unit. The Board agreed with respondents that in such circumstances, it might reasonably be concluded that no part of the carrying amount of goodwill has been disposed of, and therefore no part of its carrying amount should be derecognised by being included in the determination of the gain or loss on disposal.

Reorganisation of reporting structure (paragraph 87)

BC157   The Exposure Draft proposed that when an entity reorganises its reporting structure in a way that changes the composition of cash-generating units to which goodwill has been allocated, the goodwill should be reallocated to the units affected using a relative value approach similar to that used when an entity disposes of an operation within a cash-generating unit.

BC158   In developing the Exposure Draft, the Board concluded that a reorganisation that changes the composition of a cash-generating unit to which goodwill has been allocated gives rise to the same allocation problem as disposing of an operation within that unit. Therefore, the same allocation methodology should be used in both cases.

BC159　　As a result, and consistently with the Board's decision to modify its proposal on allocating goodwill when an entity disposes of an operation, the revised Standard requires an entity that reorganises its reporting structure in a way that changes the composition of one or more cash-generating units to which goodwill has been allocated:

(a)　　to reallocate the goodwill to the units affected; and

(b)　　to perform this reallocation using a relative value approach similar to that used when an entity disposes of an operation within a cash-generating unit (group of cash-generating units), unless the entity can demonstrate that some other method better reflects the goodwill associated with the reorganised units (groups of units).

Recognition and measurement of impairment losses (paragraphs 88–99 and 104)

Background to the proposals in the Exposure Draft

BC160　　The Exposure Draft proposed a two-step approach for impairment testing goodwill. The first step involved using a screening mechanism for identifying potential goodwill impairments, whereby goodwill allocated to a cash-generating unit would be identified as potentially impaired only when the carrying amount of the unit exceeded its recoverable amount. If an entity identified the goodwill allocated to a cash-generating unit as potentially impaired, an entity would then determine whether the goodwill allocated to the unit was impaired by comparing its recoverable amount, measured as the 'implied value' of the goodwill, with its carrying amount. The implied value of goodwill would be measured as a residual, being the excess of:

(a)　　the recoverable amount of the cash-generating unit to which the goodwill has been allocated, over

(b)　　the net fair value of the identifiable assets, liabilities and contingent liabilities the entity would recognise if it acquired the cash-generating unit in a business combination on the date of the impairment test (excluding any identifiable asset that was acquired in a business combination but not recognised separately from goodwill at the acquisition date).

BC161　　In developing the Exposure Draft, the Board's discussion focused first on how the recoverable amount of goodwill allocated to a cash-generating unit could be separated from the recoverable amount of the unit as a whole, given that goodwill generated internally after a business combination could not be measured separately. The Board concluded that a method similar to the method an acquirer uses to allocate the cost of a business combination to the net assets acquired could be used to measure the recoverable amount of goodwill after its initial recognition. Thus, the Board decided that some measure of the net assets of a cash-generating unit to which goodwill has been allocated should be subtracted from the recoverable amount of that unit to determine a current implied value for the goodwill. The Board concluded that the measure of the net assets of a cash-generating unit described in paragraph BC160(b) would result in the best estimate of the current implied value of the goodwill, given that goodwill generated internally after a business combination could not be measured separately.

BC162 Having decided on the most appropriate measure of the recoverable amount of goodwill, the Board then considered how often an entity should be required to test goodwill for impairment. Consistently with its conclusions about indefinite-lived intangibles, the Board concluded that non-amortisation of goodwill increases the reliance that must be placed on impairment tests to ensure that the carrying amount of goodwill does not exceed its recoverable amount. Accordingly, the Board decided that goodwill should be tested for impairment annually. However, the Board also concluded that the annual test is not a substitute for management being aware of events occurring or circumstances changing between annual tests indicating a possible impairment of goodwill. Therefore, the Board decided that an entity should also be required to test goodwill for impairment whenever there is an indication of possible impairment.

BC163 After the Board decided on the frequency of impairment testing, it expressed some concern that the proposed test would not be cost-effective. This concern related primarily to the requirement to determine the fair value of each identifiable asset, liability and contingent liability within a cash-generating unit that would be recognised by the entity if it had acquired the cash-generating unit in a business combination on the date of the impairment test (to estimate the implied value of goodwill).

BC164 Therefore, the Board decided to propose as a first step in the impairment test for goodwill a screening mechanism similar to that in SFAS 142. Under SFAS 142, goodwill is tested for impairment by first comparing the fair value of the reporting unit to which the goodwill has been allocated for impairment testing purposes with the carrying amount of that unit. If the fair value of the unit exceeds its carrying amount, the goodwill is regarded as not impaired. An entity need estimate the implied fair value of goodwill (using an approach consistent with that described in paragraph BC160) only if the fair value of the unit is less than its carrying amount.

The Board's redeliberations

BC165 Many respondents disagreed with the proposal to adopt a two-step approach to impairment testing goodwill. In particular, the second step of the proposed impairment test and the method for measuring any impairment loss for the goodwill caused considerable concern. Respondents provided the following conceptual arguments against the proposed approach:

(a) by drawing on only some aspects of the SFAS 142 two-step approach, the result is a hybrid between fair values and value in use. More particularly, not measuring goodwill's implied value as the difference between the unit's fair value and the net fair value of the identifiable net assets in the unit, but instead measuring it as the difference between the unit's recoverable amount (ie higher of value in use and fair value less costs to sell) and the net fair value of the identifiable net assets in the unit, results in a measure of goodwill that conceptually is neither fair value nor recoverable amount. This raises questions about the conceptual validity of measuring goodwill impairment losses as the difference between goodwill's implied value and carrying amount.

(b)   it seems inconsistent to consider goodwill separately for impairment testing when other assets within a unit are not considered separately but are instead considered as part of the unit as a whole, particularly given that goodwill, unlike many other assets, cannot generate cash inflows independently of other assets. The previous version of IAS 36 is premised on the notion that if a series of independent cash flows can be generated only by a group of assets operating together, impairment losses should be considered only for that group of assets as a whole—individual assets within the group should not be considered separately.

(c)   concluding that the recoverable amount of goodwill—which cannot generate cash inflows independently of other assets—should be measured separately for measuring impairment losses makes it difficult to understand how the Board could in the future reasonably conclude that such an approach to measuring impairment losses is also not appropriate for other assets. In other words, if it adopts the proposed two-step approach for goodwill, the Board could in effect be committing itself to an 'individual asset/fair value' approach for measuring impairments of all other assets. A decision on this issue should be made only as part of a broad reconsideration of the appropriate measurement objective for impairment testing generally.

(d)   if goodwill is considered separately for impairment testing using an implied value calculation when other assets within a unit are considered only as part of the unit as a whole, there will be asymmetry: unrecognised goodwill will shield the carrying value of other assets from impairment, but the unrecognised value of other assets will not shield the carrying amount of goodwill from impairment. This seems unreasonable given that the unrecognised value of those other assets cannot then be recognised. Additionally, the carrying amount of a unit will be less than its recoverable amount whenever an impairment loss for goodwill exceeds the unrecognised value of the other assets in the unit.

BC166   Additionally, respondents, field visit participants and North American round-table participants raised the following concerns about the practicability and costs of applying the proposed two-step approach:

(a)   many companies would be required regularly to perform the second step of the impairment test, and therefore would need to determine the fair values of each identifiable asset, liability and contingent liability within the impaired unit(s) that the entity would recognise if it acquired the unit(s) in a business combination on the date of the impairment test. Although determining these fair values would not, for some companies, pose significant practical challenges (because, for example, fair value information for their significant assets is readily available), most would need to engage, on a fairly wide scale and at significant cost, independent valuers for some or all of the unit's assets. This is particularly the case for identifying and measuring the fair values of unrecognised internally generated intangible assets.

(b) determining the fair values of each identifiable asset, liability and contingent liability within an impaired unit is likely to be impracticable for multi-segmented manufacturers that operate multi-product facilities servicing more than one cash-generating unit. For example, assume an entity's primary basis of segmentation is geographical (eg Europe, North America, South America, Asia, Oceania and Africa) and that its secondary basis of segmentation is based on product groups (vaccinations, over-the-counter medicines, prescription medicines and vitamins/dietary supplements).[38] Assume also that:

(i) the lowest level within the entity at which the goodwill is monitored for internal management purposes is one level below primary segment (eg the vitamins business in North America), and that goodwill is therefore tested for impairment at this level;

(ii) the plants and distribution facilities in each geographical region manufacture and distribute for all product groups; and

(iii) to determine the carrying amount of each cash-generating unit containing goodwill, the carrying amount of each plant and distribution facility has been allocated between each product group it services.

If, for example, the recoverable amount of the North American vitamins unit were less than its carrying amount, measuring the implied value of goodwill in that unit would require a valuation exercise to be undertaken for *all* North American assets so that a portion of each asset's fair value can then be allocated to the North American vitamins unit. These valuations are likely to be extremely costly and virtually impossible to complete within a reasonable time period (field visit participants' estimates ranged from six to twelve months). The degree of impracticability will be even greater for those entities that monitor, and therefore test, goodwill at the segment level.

BC167 In considering the above comments, the Board noted that:

(a) all of the US registrant field visit participants and North American round-table participants that have had to perform the second step of the SFAS 142 impairment test were compelled to engage, at significant cost, independent valuers.

(b) the impairment model proposed in the Exposure Draft, although based on the two-step approach in SFAS 142, differed from the SFAS 142 test and would be unlikely to result in convergence for the following reasons:

---

38 In 2006 IAS 14 was replaced by IFRS 8 *Operating Segments* which does not require disclosure of primary and secondary segment information. See paragraph BC150A.

(i)   the recoverable amount of a unit to which goodwill is allocated in accordance with IAS 36 would be the higher of the unit's value in use and fair value less costs to sell, rather than fair value. Many of the US registrant field visit participants stated that the measure of recoverable amount they would use under IAS 36 would differ from the fair value measure they would be required to use under SFAS 142.

(ii)   the level at which goodwill is tested for impairment in accordance with SFAS 142 will often be higher than the level at which it would be tested under IAS 36. Many of the US registrant field visit participants stated that goodwill would be tested for impairment in accordance with IAS 36 at a lower level than under SFAS 142 because of either: (1) the limit SFAS 142 places on how far goodwill can be 'pushed down' for impairment testing (ie one level below an operating segment); or (2) the requirement in SFAS 142 to aggregate components with similar economic characteristics. Nevertheless, these participants unanimously agreed that the IAS 36 approach provides users and management with more useful information. The Board also noted that many of the North American round-table participants stated that they (or, in the case of audit firm participants, their clients) manage and have available information about their investments in goodwill at a level lower than a reporting unit as defined in SFAS 142. Many of these participants expressed a high level of dissatisfaction at being prevented by SFAS 142 from recognising goodwill impairments that they knew existed at these lower levels, but 'disappeared' once the lower level units were aggregated with other units containing sufficient 'cushions' to offset the impairment loss.

BC168   The Board also noted that, unlike SFAS 142, it had as its starting point an impairment model in IAS 36 that integrates the impairment testing of *all* assets within a cash-generating unit, including goodwill. Unlike US generally accepted accounting principles (GAAP), which use an undiscounted cash flow screening mechanism for impairment testing long-lived assets other than goodwill, IAS 36 requires the recoverable amount of an asset or cash-generating unit to be measured whenever there is an indication of possible impairment. Therefore, if at the time of impairment testing a 'larger' unit to which goodwill has been allocated there is an indication of a possible impairment in an asset or 'smaller' cash-generating unit included in that larger unit, an entity is required to test that asset or smaller unit for impairment first. Consequently, the Board concluded that it would be reasonable in an IAS 36 context to presume that an impairment loss for the larger unit would, after all other assets and smaller units are assessed for impairment, be likely to relate to the goodwill in the unit. Such a presumption would not be reasonable if an entity were following US GAAP.

BC169   The Board considered converging fully with the SFAS 142 approach. However, although supporting convergence, the Board was concerned that the SFAS 142 approach would not provide better information than an approach under which goodwill is tested for impairment at a lower level (thereby removing many of the 'cushions' protecting the goodwill from impairment) but with the amount of any impairment loss for goodwill measured in accordance with the one-step approach in the previous version of IAS 36.

BC170   The Board concluded that the complexity and costs of applying the two-step approach proposed in the Exposure Draft would outweigh the benefits of that approach. Therefore, the Board decided to retain the approach to measuring impairments of goodwill included in the previous version of IAS 36. Thus, the Standard requires any excess of the carrying amount of a cash-generating unit (group of units) to which goodwill has been allocated over its recoverable amount to be recognised first as an impairment loss for goodwill. Any excess remaining after the carrying amount of goodwill has been reduced to zero is then recognised by being allocated to the other assets of the unit pro rata with their carrying amounts.

Changes as a result of 2008 revisions to IFRS 3 (Appendix C)

BC170A   As a result of the changes to IFRS 3 (as revised in 2008), the requirements in Appendix C of the Standard and the related illustrative examples have been amended to reflect the two ways of measuring non-controlling interests: at fair value and as a proportion of the identifiable net assets of the acquiree. Appendix C has also been modified to clarify the requirements of the Standard.

Timing of impairment tests (paragraphs 96–99)

BC171   To reduce the costs of applying the test, and consistently with the proposals in the Exposure Draft, the Standard permits the annual impairment test for a cash-generating unit (group of units) to which goodwill has been allocated to be performed at any time during an annual period, provided the test is performed at the same time every year. Different cash-generating units (groups of units) may be tested for impairment at different times. However, if some or all of the goodwill allocated to a unit (group of units) was acquired in a business combination during the current annual period, that unit (group of units) must be tested for impairment before the end of the current annual period.

BC172   The Board observed that acquirers can sometimes 'overpay' for an acquiree, resulting in the amount initially recognised for the business combination and the resulting goodwill exceeding the recoverable amount of the investment. The Board concluded that the users of an entity's financial statements are provided with representationally faithful, and therefore useful, information about a business combination if such an impairment loss is recognised by the acquirer in the annual period in which the business combination occurs.

BC173   The Board was concerned that it might be possible for entities to delay recognising such an impairment loss until the annual period after the business combination if the Standard included only a requirement to impairment test cash-generating units (groups of units) to which goodwill has been allocated on an annual basis at any time during a period. Therefore, the Board decided to include in the Standard the added requirement that if some or all of the goodwill allocated to a unit (group of units) was acquired in a business combination during the current annual period, the unit (group of units) should be tested for impairment before the end of that period.

Sequence of impairment tests (paragraph 97)

BC174   The Standard requires that if the assets (cash-generating units) constituting the cash-generating unit (group of units) to which goodwill has been allocated are tested for impairment at the same time as the unit (group of units) containing the goodwill, those other assets (units) should be tested for impairment before the unit (group of units) containing the goodwill.

BC175   The Board observed that assets or cash-generating units making up a unit or group of units to which goodwill has been allocated might need to be tested for impairment at the same time as the unit or group of units containing the goodwill when there is an indication of a possible impairment of the asset or smaller unit. The Board concluded that to assess whether the unit or group of units containing the goodwill, and therefore whether the goodwill, is impaired, the carrying amount of the unit or group of units containing the goodwill would need first to be adjusted by recognising any impairment losses relating to the assets or smaller units within that unit or group of units.

Carrying forward a recoverable amount calculation (paragraph 99)

BC176   Consistently with the impairment test for indefinite-lived intangibles, the Standard permits the most recent detailed calculation of the recoverable amount of a cash-generating unit (group of units) to which goodwill has been allocated to be carried forward from a preceding period for use in the current period's impairment test, provided all of the criteria in paragraph 99 are met.

BC177   Integral to the Board's decision that goodwill should be tested for impairment annually was the view that many entities should be able to conclude that the recoverable amount of a cash-generating unit (group of units) to which goodwill has been allocated is greater than its carrying amount without actually recomputing recoverable amount. However, again consistently with its conclusions about indefinite-lived intangibles, the Board concluded that this would be the case only if the last recoverable amount determination exceeded the carrying amount of the unit (group of units) by a substantial margin, and nothing had happened since that last determination to make the likelihood of an impairment loss other than remote. The Board concluded that in such circumstances, permitting a detailed calculation of the recoverable amount of a cash-generating unit (group of units) to which goodwill has been allocated to be carried forward from the preceding period for use in the current period's impairment test would significantly reduce the costs of applying the impairment test, without compromising its integrity.

Allocating an impairment loss between the assets of a cash-generating unit (paragraphs 104–107)

BCZ178 IAS 36 includes requirements for the allocation of an impairment loss for a cash-generating unit that differ from the proposals in E55. In particular, E55 proposed that an impairment loss should be allocated:

(a)   first, to goodwill;

(b)   secondly, to intangible assets for which no active market exists;

(c)   thirdly, to assets whose net selling price[39] is less than their carrying amount; and

(d)   then, to the other assets of the unit on a pro-rata basis based on the carrying amount of each asset in the unit.

BCZ179 The underlying reasons for making this proposal were that:

(a)   an impairment loss for a cash-generating unit should be allocated, in priority, to assets with the most subjective values. Goodwill and intangible assets for which there is no active market were considered to be in that category. Intangible assets for which there is no active market were considered to be similar to goodwill (IASC was thinking of brand names, publishing titles etc).

(b)   if the net selling price of an asset is less than its carrying amount, this was considered a reasonable basis for allocating part of the impairment loss to that asset rather than to other assets.

BCZ180 Many commentators on E55 objected to the proposal on the grounds that:

(a)   not all intangible assets for which no active market exists are similar to goodwill (for example, licences and franchise rights). They disagreed that the value of intangible assets is always more subjective than the value of tangible assets (for example, specialised plant and equipment).

(b)   the concept of cash-generating units implies a global approach for the assets of the units and not an asset-by-asset approach.

In response to these comments, IASC decided to withdraw E55's proposal for the allocation of an impairment loss to intangible assets and assets whose net selling price is less than their carrying amount.

BCZ181 IASC rejected a proposal that an impairment loss for a cash-generating unit should be allocated first to any obviously impaired asset. IASC believed that if the recoverable amount of an obviously impaired asset can be determined for the individual asset, there is no need to estimate the recoverable amount of the asset's cash-generating unit. If the recoverable amount of an individual asset cannot be determined, it cannot be said that the asset is obviously impaired because an impairment loss for a cash-generating unit relates to all of the assets of that unit.

---

39 In IFRS 5 *Non-current Assets Held for Sale and Discontinued Operations*, issued by the IASB in 2004, the term 'net selling price' was replaced in IAS 36 by 'fair value less costs to sell'.

Reversing impairment losses for assets other than goodwill (paragraphs 110–123)

BCZ182   IAS 36 requires that an impairment loss for an asset other than goodwill should be reversed if, and only if, there has been a change in the estimates used to determine an asset's recoverable amount since the last impairment loss was recognised.

BCZ183   Opponents of reversals of impairment losses argue that:

(a)   reversals of impairment losses are contrary to the historical cost accounting system. When the carrying amount is reduced, recoverable amount becomes the new cost basis for an asset. Consequently, reversing an impairment loss is no different from revaluing an asset upward. Indeed, in many cases, recoverable amount is similar to the measurement basis used for the revaluation of an asset. Hence, reversals of impairment losses should be either prohibited or recognised directly in equity as a revaluation.

(b)   reversals of impairment losses introduce volatility in reported earnings. Periodic, short-term income measurements should not be affected by unrealised changes in the measurement of a long-lived asset.

(c)   the result of reversals of impairment losses would not be useful to users of financial statements since the amount of a reversal under IAS 36 is limited to an amount that does not increase the carrying amount of an asset above its depreciated historical cost. Neither the amount reversed nor the revised carrying amount have any information content.

(d)   in many cases, reversals of impairment losses will result in the implicit recognition of internally generated goodwill.

(e)   reversals of impairment losses open the door to abuse and income 'smoothing' in practice.

(f)   follow-up to verify whether an impairment loss needs to be reversed is costly.

BCZ184   IASC's reasons for requiring reversals of impairment losses were the following:

(a)   it is consistent with the *Framework*[40] and the view that future economic benefits that were not previously expected to flow from an asset have been reassessed as probable.

(b)   a reversal of an impairment loss is not a revaluation and is consistent with the historical cost accounting system as long as the reversal does not result in the carrying amount of an asset exceeding its original cost less amortisation/depreciation, had the impairment loss not been

---

40   References to the *Framework* in this Basis for Conclusions are to the IASC's *Framework for the Preparation and Presentation of Financial Statements*, adopted by the Board in 2001 and in effect when the Standard was developed and revised.

recognised. Accordingly, the reversal of an impairment loss should be recognised in the income statement and any amount in excess of the depreciated historical cost should be accounted for as a revaluation.

(c) impairment losses are recognised and measured based on estimates. Any change in the measurement of an impairment loss is similar to a change in estimate. IAS 8 *Net Profit or Loss for the Period, Fundamental Errors and Changes in Accounting Policies*[41] requires that a change in accounting estimate should be included in the determination of the net profit or loss in (a) the period of the change, if the change affects the period only, or (b) the period of the change and future periods, if the change affects both.

(d) reversals of impairment losses provide users with a more useful indication of the potential for future benefits of an asset or group of assets.

(e) results of operations will be more fairly stated in the current period and in future periods because depreciation or amortisation will not reflect a previous impairment loss that is no longer relevant. Prohibition of reversals of impairment losses may lead to abuses such as recording a significant loss one year with the resulting lower amortisation/depreciation charge and higher profits in subsequent years.

BCZ185 The majority of commentators on E55 supported IASC's proposals for reversals of impairment losses.

BCZ186 IAS 36 does not permit an enterprise to recognise a reversal of an impairment loss just because of the unwinding of the discount. IASC supported this requirement for practical reasons only. Otherwise, if an impairment loss is recognised and recoverable amount is based on value in use, a reversal of the impairment loss would be recognised in each subsequent year for the unwinding of the discount. This is because, in most cases, the pattern of depreciation of an asset is different from the pattern of value in use. IASC believed that, when there is no change in the assumptions used to estimate recoverable amount, the benefits from recognising the unwinding of the discount each year after an impairment loss has been recognised do not justify the costs involved. However, if a reversal is recognised because assumptions have changed, the discount unwinding effect is included in the amount of the reversal recognised.

Reversing goodwill impairment losses (paragraph 124)

BC187 Consistently with the proposal in the Exposure Draft, the Standard prohibits the recognition of reversals of impairment losses for goodwill. The previous version of IAS 36 required an impairment loss for goodwill recognised in a previous period to be reversed when the impairment loss was caused by a specific external event of an exceptional nature that was not expected to

---

41 IAS 8 *Net Profit or Loss for the Period, Fundamental Errors and Changes in Accounting Policies* was superseded in 2003 by IAS 8 *Accounting Policies, Changes in Accounting Estimates and Errors*.

recur, and subsequent external events had occurred that reversed the effect of that event.

BC188 Most respondents to the Exposure Draft agreed that reversals of impairment losses for goodwill should be prohibited. Those that disagreed argued that reversals of impairment losses for goodwill should be treated in the same way as reversals of impairment losses for other assets, but limited to circumstances in which the impairment loss was caused by specific events beyond the entity's control.

BC189 In revising IAS 36, the Board noted that IAS 38 *Intangible Assets* prohibits the recognition of internally generated goodwill. Therefore, if reversals of impairment losses for goodwill were permitted, an entity would need to establish the extent to which a subsequent increase in the recoverable amount of goodwill is attributable to the recovery of the acquired goodwill within a cash-generating unit, rather than an increase in the internally generated goodwill within the unit. The Board concluded that this will seldom, if ever, be possible. Because the acquired goodwill and internally generated goodwill contribute jointly to the same cash flows, any subsequent increase in the recoverable amount of the acquired goodwill is indistinguishable from an increase in the internally generated goodwill. Even if the specific external event that caused the recognition of the impairment loss is reversed, it will seldom, if ever, be possible to determine that the effect of that reversal is a corresponding increase in the recoverable amount of the acquired goodwill. Therefore, the Board concluded that reversals of impairment losses for goodwill should be prohibited.

BC190 The Board expressed some concern that prohibiting the recognition of reversals of impairment losses for goodwill so as to avoid recognising internally generated goodwill might be viewed by some as inconsistent with the impairment test for goodwill. This is because the impairment test results in the carrying amount of goodwill being shielded from impairment by internally generated goodwill. This has been described by some as 'backdoor' capitalisation of internally generated goodwill.

BC191 However, the Board was not as concerned about goodwill being shielded from the recognition of impairment losses by internally generated goodwill as it was about the direct recognition of internally generated goodwill that might occur if reversals of impairment losses for goodwill were permitted. As discussed in paragraph BC135, the Board is of the view that it is not possible to devise an impairment test for acquired goodwill that removes the cushion against the recognition of impairment losses provided by goodwill generated internally after a business combination.

Disclosures for cash-generating units containing goodwill or indefinite-lived intangibles (paragraphs 134 and 135)

Background to the proposals in the Exposure Draft

BC192   The Exposure Draft proposed requiring an entity to disclose a range of information about cash-generating units whose carrying amounts included goodwill or indefinite-lived intangibles. That information included:

(a)   the carrying amount of goodwill and the carrying amount of indefinite-lived intangibles.

(b)   the basis on which the unit's recoverable amount had been determined (ie value in use or net selling price).

(c)   the amount by which the unit's recoverable amount exceeded its carrying amount.

(d)   the key assumptions and estimates used to measure the unit's recoverable amount and information about the sensitivity of that recoverable amount to changes in the key assumptions and estimates.

BC193   If an entity reports segment information in accordance with IAS 14 *Segment Reporting*, the Exposure Draft proposed that this information should be disclosed in aggregate for each segment based on the entity's primary reporting format. However, the Exposure Draft also proposed that the information would be disclosed separately for a cash-generating unit when:

(a)   the carrying amount of the goodwill or indefinite-lived intangibles allocated to the unit was significant in relation to the total carrying amount of goodwill or indefinite-lived intangibles; or

(b)   the basis for determining the unit's recoverable amount differed from the basis used for the other units within the segment whose carrying amounts include goodwill or indefinite-lived intangibles; or

(c)   the nature of, or value assigned to the key assumptions or growth rate on which management based its determination of the unit's recoverable amount differed significantly from that used for the other units within the segment whose carrying amounts include goodwill or indefinite-lived intangibles.

BC194   In deciding to propose these disclosure requirements in the Exposure Draft, the Board observed that non-amortisation of goodwill and indefinite-lived intangibles increases the reliance that must be placed on impairment tests of those assets to ensure that their carrying amounts do not exceed their recoverable amounts. However, the nature of impairment tests means that the carrying amounts of such assets and the related assertion that those carrying amounts are recoverable will normally be supported only by management's projections. Therefore, the Board decided to examine ways in which the reliability of the impairment tests for goodwill and indefinite-lived intangibles could be improved. As a first step, the Board considered including a subsequent cash flow test in the revised Standard, similar to that included in

UK Financial Reporting Standard 11 *Impairment of Fixed Assets and Goodwill* (FRS 11).

Subsequent cash flow test

BC195   FRS 11 requires an entity to perform a subsequent cash flow test to confirm, ex post, the cash flow projections used to measure a unit's value in use when testing goodwill for impairment. Under FRS 11, for five years following each impairment test for goodwill in which recoverable amount has been based on value in use, the actual cash flows achieved must be compared with those forecast. If the actual cash flows are so much less than those forecast that use of the actual cash flows in the value in use calculation could have required recognition of an impairment in previous periods, the original impairment calculations must be re-performed using the actual cash flows, but without revising any other cash flows or assumptions (except those that change as a direct consequence of the occurrence of the actual cash flows, for example where a major cash inflow has been delayed for a year). Any impairment identified must then be recognised in the current period, unless the impairment has reversed and the reversal of the loss satisfies the criteria in FRS 11 regarding reversals of impairment losses for goodwill.

BC196   The Board noted the following arguments in support of including a similar test in the revised Standard:

(a)   it would enhance the reliability of the goodwill impairment test by preventing the possibility of entities avoiding the recognition of impairment losses by using over-optimistic cash flow projections in the value in use calculations.

(b)   it would provide useful information to users of an entity's financial statements because a record of actual cash flows continually less than forecast cash flows tends to cast doubt on the reliability of current estimates.

BC197   However, the subsequent cash flow test is designed only to prevent entities from avoiding goodwill write-downs. The Board observed that, given current trends in 'big bath' restructuring charges, the greater risk to the quality of financial reporting might be from entities trying to write off goodwill without adequate justification in an attempt to 'manage' the balance sheet. The Board also observed that:

(a)   the focus of the test on cash flows ignores other elements in the measurement of value in use. As a result, it does not produce representationally faithful results in a present value measurement system. The Board considered incorporating into the recalculation performed under the test corrections of estimates of other elements in the measurement of value in use. However, the Board concluded that specifying which elements to include would be problematic. Moreover, adding corrections of estimates of those other elements to the test would, in effect, transform the test into a requirement to perform a comprehensive recalculation of value in use for each of the five annual reporting periods following an impairment test.

(b)   the amount recognised as an impairment loss under the test is the amount of the impairment that would have been recognised, provided changes in estimates of remaining cash flows and changes in discount and growth rates are ignored. Therefore, it is a hypothetical amount that does not provide decision-useful information – it is neither an estimate of a current amount nor a prediction of ultimate cash flows.

(c)   the requirement to perform the test for each of the five annual reporting periods following an impairment test could result in an entity having to maintain as many as five sets of 5-year computations for each cash-generating unit to which goodwill has been allocated. Therefore, the test is likely to be extremely burdensome, particularly if an entity has a large number of such units, without producing understandable or decision-useful information.

BC198   Therefore, the Board decided not to propose a subsequent cash flow test in the Exposure Draft. However, the Board remained committed to finding some way of improving the reliability of the impairment tests for goodwill and indefinite-lived intangibles, and decided to explore improving that reliability through disclosure requirements.

Including disclosure requirements in the revised Standard

BC199   In developing the Exposure Draft, the Board observed that the *Framework* identifies reliability as one of the key qualitative characteristics that information must possess to be useful to users in making economic decisions. To be reliable, information must be free from material error and bias and be able to be depended upon to represent faithfully that which it purports to represent. The *Framework* identifies relevance as another key qualitative characteristic that information must possess to be useful to users in making economic decisions. To be relevant, information must help users to evaluate past, present or future events, or confirm or correct their past evaluations.

BC200   The Board observed that information that assists users in evaluating the reliability of other information included in the financial statements is itself relevant, increasing in relevance as the reliability of that other information decreases. For example, information that assists users in evaluating the reliability of the amount recognised for a provision is relevant because it helps users to evaluate the effect of both a past event (ie the economic consequences of the past event giving rise to the present obligation) and a future event (ie the amount of the expected future outflow of economic benefits required to settle the obligation). Accordingly, IAS 37 *Provisions, Contingent Liabilities and Contingent Assets* requires an entity to disclose, for each class of provision, information about the uncertainties surrounding the amount and timing of expected outflows of economic benefits, and the major assumptions concerning future events that may affect the amount required to settle the obligation and have been reflected in the amount of the provision.

BC201   The Board concluded that because information that assists users in evaluating the reliability of other information is itself relevant, an entity should disclose information that assists users in evaluating the reliability of the estimates used by management to support the carrying amounts of goodwill and indefinite-lived intangibles.

BC202   The Board also concluded that such disclosures would provide users with more useful information for evaluating the reliability of the impairment tests for goodwill and indefinite-lived intangibles than the information that would be provided by a subsequent cash flow test.

BC203   The Board then considered how some balance might be achieved between the objective of providing users with useful information for evaluating the reliability of the estimates used by management to support the carrying amounts of goodwill and indefinite-lived intangibles, and the potential magnitude of those disclosures.

BC204   The Board decided that a reasonable balance might be achieved between the objective of the disclosures and their potential magnitude by requiring:

(a)   information to be disclosed on an aggregate basis for each segment based on the entity's primary reporting format that includes in its carrying amount goodwill or indefinite-lived intangibles; but

(b)   information for a particular cash-generating unit within that segment to be excluded from the aggregate information and disclosed separately when either:

(i)   the basis (ie net selling price or value in use), methodology or key assumptions used to measure its recoverable amount differ from those used to measure the recoverable amounts of the other units in the segment; or

(ii)   the carrying amount of the goodwill or indefinite-lived intangibles in the unit is significant in relation to the total carrying amount of goodwill or indefinite-lived intangibles.

The Board's redeliberations

BC205   After considering respondents' and field visit participants' comments, the Board confirmed its previous conclusion that information that assists users in evaluating the reliability of other information is itself relevant, increasing in relevance as the reliability of that other information decreases. Therefore, entities should be required to disclose information that assists users in evaluating the reliability of the estimates used by management to support the carrying amounts of goodwill and indefinite-lived intangibles. The Board noted that almost all field visit participants and many respondents expressed explicit support of its conclusion that, because non-amortisation of goodwill and indefinite-lived intangibles increases the reliance that must be placed on impairment tests of those assets, some additional disclosure is necessary to provide users with information for evaluating the reliability of those impairment tests.

BC206   However, it was clear from field visit participants' responses that the proposed disclosures could not be meaningfully aggregated at the segment level to the extent the Board had hoped might be the case. As a result, the proposal to require the information to be disclosed on an aggregate basis for each segment, but with disaggregated disclosures for cash-generating units in the circumstances set out in paragraph BC193 would not result in a reasonable balance between the objective of the disclosures and their potential magnitude.

BC207   The Board was also sympathetic to field visit participants' and respondents' concerns that the proposed disclosures went beyond their intended objective of providing users with relevant information for evaluating the reliability of the impairment tests for goodwill and indefinite-lived intangibles. For example, field visit participants and respondents argued that:

(a)   it would be extremely difficult to distil the recoverable amount calculations into concise but meaningful disclosures because those calculations typically are complex and do not normally result in a single point estimate of recoverable amount—a single value for recoverable amount would normally be determined only when the bottom-end of the recoverable amount range is less than a cash-generating unit's carrying amount. These difficulties make it doubtful that the information, particularly the sensitivity analyses, could be produced on a timely basis.

(b)   disclosing the proposed information, particularly the values assigned to, and the sensitivity of, each key assumption on which recoverable amount calculations are based, could cause significant commercial harm to an entity. Users of financial statements might, for example, use the quantitative disclosures as the basis for initiating litigation against the entity, its board of directors or management in the highly likely event that those assumptions prove less than accurate. The increased litigation risk would either encourage management to use super-conservative assumptions, thereby resulting in improper asset write-downs, or compel management to engage independent experts to develop all key assumptions and perform the recoverable amount calculations. Additionally, many of the field visit participants expressed concern over the possible impact that disclosing such information might have on their ability to defend themselves in various legal proceedings.

BC208   Therefore, the Board considered the following two interrelated issues:

(a)   if the proposed disclosures went beyond their intended objective, what information *should* be disclosed so that users have sufficient information for evaluating the reliability of impairment tests for goodwill and indefinite-lived intangibles?

(b)   how should this information be presented so that there is an appropriate balance between providing users with information for evaluating the reliability of the impairment tests, and the potential magnitude of those disclosures?

BC209   As a result of its redeliberations, the Board decided:

     (a)   not to proceed with the proposal to require information for evaluating the reliability of the impairment tests for goodwill and indefinite-lived intangibles to be disclosed in aggregate for each segment and separately for cash-generating units within a segment in specified circumstances. Instead, the Standard requires this information to be disclosed only for each cash-generating unit (group of units) for which the carrying amount of goodwill or indefinite-lived intangibles allocated to that unit (group of units) is significant in comparison with the entity's total carrying amount of goodwill or indefinite-lived intangibles.

     (b)   not to proceed with the proposal to require an entity to disclose the amount by which the recoverable amount of a cash-generating unit exceeds its carrying amount. Instead, the Standard requires an entity to disclose this information only if a reasonably possible change in a key assumption on which management has based its determination of the unit's (group of units') recoverable amount would cause the unit's (group of units') carrying amount to exceed its recoverable amount.

     (c)   not to proceed with the proposal to require an entity to disclose the value assigned to each key assumption on which management based its recoverable amount determination, and the amount by which that value must change, after incorporating any consequential effects of that change on the other variables used to measure recoverable amount, in order for the unit's recoverable amount to be equal to its carrying amount. Instead, the Standard requires an entity to disclose a description of each key assumption on which management has based its recoverable amount determination, management's approach to determining the value(s) assigned to each key assumption, whether those value(s) reflect past experience or, if appropriate, are consistent with external sources of information, and, if not, how and why they differ from past experience or external sources of information. However, if a reasonably possible change in a key assumption would cause the unit's (group of units') carrying amount to exceed its recoverable amount, the entity is also required to disclose the value assigned to the key assumption, and the amount by which that value must change, after incorporating any consequential effects of that change on the other variables used to measure recoverable amount, in order for the unit's (group of units') recoverable amount to be equal to its carrying amount.

     (d)   to require information about key assumptions to be disclosed also for any key assumption that is relevant to the recoverable amount determination of multiple cash-generating units (groups of units) that individually contain insignificant amounts of goodwill or indefinite-lived intangibles, but contain, in aggregate, significant amounts of goodwill or indefinite-lived intangibles.

Changes as a result of *Improvements to IFRSs* (2008)[42]

BC209A   The Board noted that the disclosures that IAS 36 requires when value in use is used to determine recoverable amount differ from those required when fair value less costs to sell is used. These differing requirements appear inconsistent when a similar valuation methodology (discounted cash flows) has been used. Therefore, as part of *Improvements to IFRSs* issued in May 2008, the Board decided to require the same disclosures for fair value less costs to sell and value in use when discounted cash flows are used to estimate recoverable amount.

Changes as a result of IFRS 13 *Fair Value Measurement*

BC209B   In developing IFRS 13, issued in May 2011, the Board was asked by users of financial statements to minimise the differences between the disclosures made about impaired assets in IFRSs and in US GAAP (which requires assets to be tested for impairment by comparing their carrying amount with their fair value). The Board noted that the disclosure requirements in IAS 36 were developed specifically to ensure consistency in the disclosure of information about impaired assets so that the same type of information is provided whether the recoverable amount was determined on the basis of value in use or fair value less costs of disposal. Consequently, the Board did not think it would be appropriate to require an entity to provide information when the recoverable amount is determined on the basis of fair value less costs of disposal (ie those required in IFRS 13) that is significantly different from what the entity would provide when the recoverable amount is determined on the basis of value in use.

BC209C   Although IFRSs and US GAAP have different impairment models, the Board concluded that requiring the following information (in addition to what IAS 36 currently requires) about impaired assets measured at fair value less costs of disposal would improve comparability between entities applying IFRSs and those applying US GAAP as well as increase the convergence of IFRSs and US GAAP:

(a)   the fair value less costs of disposal;

(b)   the level of the fair value hierarchy within which the fair value less costs of disposal is categorised in its entirety (Level 1, 2 or 3);

(c)   if applicable, changes to valuation techniques and reasons for those changes; and

(d)   quantitative information about significant inputs used when measuring fair value less costs of disposal (along with a conforming amendment to the disclosures about value in use).

BC209D   In addition, those disclosures are consistent with the disclosures required for non-recurring fair value measurements in IFRS 13 and in US GAAP.

---

42   This heading and paragraph BC209A were added by *Improvements to IFRSs* issued in May 2008.

Recoverable Amount Disclosures for Non-Financial Assets

BC209E   As a consequence of issuing IFRS 13, the IASB amended some of the disclosure requirements in IAS 36 for the recoverable amount of impaired assets. As described in paragraphs BC209B–BC209D, those amendments resulted from the IASB's decision to require the disclosure of the recoverable amount of impaired assets and additional disclosures about the measurement of the recoverable amount of impaired assets when the recoverable amount was based on fair value less costs of disposal. The IASB also intended to retain a balance between the disclosures about fair value less costs of disposal and the disclosures about value in use.

BC209F   After issuing IFRS 13, the IASB was made aware that one of the amendments that that Standard had made to IAS 36 resulted in the disclosure requirements being more broadly applicable than the IASB had intended. Instead of requiring the disclosure of the recoverable amount for impaired assets, that amendment required the disclosure of the recoverable amount of each cash-generating unit for which the carrying amount of goodwill or intangible assets with indefinite useful lives allocated to that unit is significant when compared to an entity's total carrying amount of goodwill or intangible assets with indefinite useful lives.

BC209G   Consequently, the IASB decided to publish, in January 2013, the Exposure Draft ED/2013/1 *Recoverable Amount Disclosures for Non-Financial Assets* ('Exposure Draft ED/2013/1'), which proposed to amend paragraphs 130 and 134 of IAS 36 to make clear its intention about the scope of the disclosure requirements. For the same reason, the IASB also proposed to amend paragraph 130(f) to require additional information about the fair value measurement when the recoverable amount of impaired assets is based on fair value less costs of disposal, consistently with the disclosure requirements for impaired assets in US GAAP. As mentioned in paragraph BC209C, although IFRS and US GAAP have different impairment models, the IASB had concluded that requiring that additional information about impaired assets measured at fair value less costs of disposal would improve comparability between the disclosures presented in the financial statements of entities applying IFRS and the disclosures presented in the financial statements of those applying US GAAP.

BC209H   One of the consequential amendments made by IFRS 13 amended paragraph 134(e) of IAS 36 that relates to fair value less costs of disposal for each cash-generating unit for which the carrying amount of goodwill or intangible assets with indefinite useful lives allocated to that unit is significant in comparison with an entity's total carrying amount of goodwill or intangible assets with indefinite useful lives. That amendment required the disclosure of the level of the fair value hierarchy in which the measurement is categorised, and whether (and if so why) there has been a change in the valuation technique used to measure fair value less costs of disposal for such cash-generating units. In developing Exposure Draft ED/2013/1, the IASB did not consider it necessary to amend those disclosure requirements because they were consistent with its intention of aligning the disclosures about fair value less costs of disposal in IAS 36 with the fair value disclosures in IFRS 13.

Consequently, the IASB decided to retain the disclosure requirements in paragraph 134(e) and to add, as mentioned in paragraph BC209G, requirements for similar disclosures in paragraph 130(f).

BC209I   When developing Exposure Draft ED/2013/1, the IASB considered whether there should be consistency between the wording of the disclosure requirements in IAS 36 (which uses the term 'assumptions') with the wording of the measurement requirements in IFRS 13 (which uses the term 'inputs'). The IASB concluded that it was unlikely that those terms could have different meanings because IFRS 13 defines 'inputs' as "the assumptions that market participants would use when pricing the asset or liability…". In addition, the IASB wanted to make clear that the proposed amendments did not change the meaning of the information that is required to be disclosed in accordance with IAS 36. On the basis of that analysis and given that the use of the term 'assumptions' was not questioned by the respondents to Exposure Draft ED/2013/1, the IASB decided to retain that term in the final amendments.

BC209J   When developing Exposure Draft ED/2013/1, the IASB also noted that its proposed amendments overlapped with an amendment to paragraph 130(f) of IAS 36 that had been proposed in the Exposure Draft ED/2012/1 *Annual Improvements to IFRSs 2010–2012 Cycle* ('Exposure Draft ED/2012/1') published in May 2012. The intention behind the proposal in Exposure Draft ED/2012/1 was to harmonise the disclosure requirements for fair value less costs of disposal and value in use by adding to paragraph 130(f) the requirement to disclose the discount rates that were used in the current and previous measurements if the recoverable amount of impaired assets, determined on the basis of fair value less costs of disposal, was measured using a present value technique. A total of 64 respondents commented on that proposal, with nearly all of those respondents supporting it. Consequently, the IASB decided to incorporate that proposal into Exposure Draft ED/2013/1, but did not request comments in response to this topic.

BC209K   A total of 74 respondents commented on Exposure Draft ED/2013/1. Even though the vast majority of the respondents supported the proposed amendments, a few respondents believed that, when impairment losses were calculated by reference to the recoverable amount determined on the basis of fair value less costs of disposal, the amendments would result in the disclosure requirements being broader than the disclosures that would be required if the same impairment losses were calculated by reference to the recoverable amount determined on the basis of value in use. The IASB noted that it had already taken the decision to require this incremental disclosure when it first amended IAS 36 as a result of issuing IFRS 13. As mentioned in paragraph BC209G, that decision had been taken on the grounds that those amendments would improve comparability between the disclosures presented in the financial statements of entities applying IFRS and the disclosures presented in the financial statements of those applying US GAAP.

BC209L   During the development of IFRS 13, the IASB also noted that not all of the additional disclosure requirements for the recoverable amount determined on the basis of fair value less costs of disposal would be applicable for the recoverable amount determined on the basis of value in use. The requirement of disclosing the level of the fair value hierarchy within which the fair value measurement of the impaired asset is categorised would, for example, not be applicable to a measurement based on value in use. In addition, the IASB noted that the amendments to paragraph 130(f) would help to align the disclosure requirements for fair value less costs of disposal for impaired assets with the disclosure requirements in paragraph 134(e) for fair value less costs of disposal for each cash-generating unit for which the carrying amount of goodwill or intangible assets with indefinite useful lives allocated to that unit is significant in comparison with an entity's total carrying amount of goodwill or intangible assets with indefinite useful lives.

BC209M   Exposure Draft ED/2013/1 also proposed to remove the term 'material' from paragraph 130. When developing these proposals, the IASB concluded that it was unnecessary to state explicitly that the disclosure requirements in paragraph 130 relate to assets (including goodwill) or cash-generating units, for which a material impairment loss has been recognised or reversed during the period, because all IFRSs are governed by the concept of materiality as described in IAS 1 *Presentation of Financial Statements* (see paragraph 31 of IAS 1) and IAS 8 *Accounting Policies, Changes in Accounting Estimates and Errors*. Some respondents to Exposure Draft ED/2013/1 were opposed to removing this term because they thought that, by removing it, it would become unclear whether the disclosure requirements in paragraph 130 apply only when a material impairment loss has been recognised or reversed during the period. They were also concerned that the elimination of the term 'material' in paragraph 130 could impact the understanding of the requirements in paragraph 131 that deal with the disclosure of immaterial items on an aggregate basis.

BC209N   The IASB had not intended to change the scope of the disclosure requirements in paragraph 130. In addition, the IASB concluded that the removal of the term 'material' in paragraph 130 should not impact the disclosure requirements in paragraph 131. Consequently, the IASB concluded that the rationale for removing the term 'material', as presented in Exposure Draft ED/2013/1, was still valid and, as a result, the IASB confirmed the removal of that term in the final amendments.

BC209O   The IASB decided not to retain in the final amendments the last sentence of paragraph 130(f), as proposed in Exposure Draft ED/2013/1. That sentence stated that an "... entity is not required to provide the disclosures required by IFRS 13". The IASB noted that IFRS 13 already excludes from the scope of its disclosure requirements assets for which the recoverable amount is fair value less costs of disposal in accordance with IAS 36. As a result, the IASB concluded that that sentence in paragraph 130(f) was redundant and could cause confusion and therefore decided to remove it from the final amendments.

BC209P   Exposure Draft ED/2013/1 proposed to include an illustrative example of the requirements in paragraph 130(b) and the proposed requirements in paragraph 130(f)(ii). Some respondents questioned the usefulness of that illustrative example, which did not illustrate all of the disclosures that are required for the recoverable amount of impaired assets based on fair value less costs of disposal. In their view, such an illustrative example could be misleading rather than helpful, because it might suggest that no other disclosures are required. On the basis of these comments, and because the IASB noted that Illustrative Example 15 to IFRS 13 includes similar disclosures to the ones included in the proposed illustrative example, it decided not to incorporate the proposed example in the final amendments.

BC209Q   On the basis of the respondents' comments, the IASB decided to proceed with the final amendments subject to only minor drafting modifications.

Transitional provisions (paragraphs 138–140)

BC210   If an entity elects to apply IFRS 3 from any date before the effective dates outlined in IFRS 3, it is also required to apply IAS 36 from that same date. Paragraphs BC181–BC184 of the Basis for Conclusions on IFRS 3 outline the Board's deliberations on this issue.[43]

BC211   Otherwise, IAS 36 is applied:

(a)   to goodwill and intangible assets acquired in business combinations for which the agreement date is on or after 31 March 2004; and

(b)   to all other assets prospectively from the beginning of the first annual period beginning on or after 31 March 2004.

BC212   In developing the requirements set out in paragraph BC211, the Board considered whether entities should be required:

(a)   to apply retrospectively the revised impairment test for goodwill; and

(b)   to apply retrospectively the requirement prohibiting reversals of impairment losses for goodwill and therefore eliminate any reversals recognised before the date the revised Standard was issued.

BC213   The Board concluded that retrospective application of the revised impairment test for goodwill would be problematic for the following reasons:

(a)   it was likely to be impossible in many cases because the information needed may not exist or may no longer be obtainable.

(b)   it would require the determination of estimates that would have been made at a prior date, and therefore would raise the problem of how the effect of hindsight could be separated from the factors existing at the date of the impairment test.

BC214   The Board also noted that the requirement for goodwill to be tested for impairment annually, irrespective of whether there is any indication that it may be impaired, will ensure that by the end of the first period in which the Standard is effective, all recognised goodwill acquired before its effective date would be tested for impairment.

---

43   The Board issued a revised IFRS 3 in 2008. This paragraph relates to IFRS 3 as issued in 2004.

BC215 In the case of reversals of impairment losses for goodwill, the Board acknowledged that requiring the elimination of reversals recognised before the revised Standard's effective date might seem appropriate, particularly given the Board's reasons for prohibiting reversals of impairment losses for goodwill (see paragraphs BC187–BC191). The Board concluded, however, that the previous amortisation of that goodwill, combined with the requirement for goodwill to be tested for impairment at least annually, ensures that the carrying amount of the goodwill does not exceed its recoverable amount at the end of the reporting period in which the Standard is effective. Therefore, the Board concluded that the Standard should apply on a prospective basis.

Transitional impairment test for goodwill

BC216 Given that one of the objectives of the first phase of the Business Combinations project was to seek international convergence on the accounting for goodwill, the Board considered whether IAS 36 should include a transitional goodwill impairment test similar to that included in SFAS 142. SFAS 142 requires goodwill to be tested for impairment annually, and between annual tests if an event occurs or circumstances change and would be more likely than not to reduce the fair value of a reporting unit below its carrying amount. The transitional provisions in SFAS 142 require the impairment test for goodwill to be applied prospectively. However, a transitional goodwill impairment test must be performed as of the *beginning* of the fiscal year in which SFAS 142 is applied in its entirety. An impairment loss recognised as a result of a transitional test is recognised as the effect of a change in accounting principle, rather than as an impairment loss. In addition to the transitional test, SFAS 142 requires an entity to perform the required annual goodwill impairment test in the year that SFAS 142 is initially applied in its entirety. In other words, the transitional goodwill impairment test may not be regarded as the initial year's annual test unless an entity designates the beginning of its fiscal year as the date for its annual goodwill impairment test.

BC217 The FASB concluded that goodwill that was not regarded as impaired under US GAAP before SFAS 142 was issued could be determined to be impaired if the SFAS 142 impairment test was applied to that goodwill at the date an entity initially applied SFAS 142. This is because, under previous US GAAP, entities typically tested goodwill for impairment using undiscounted estimates of future cash flows. The FASB further concluded that:

(a) the preponderance of any transitional impairment losses was likely to result from the change in methods and treating those losses as stemming from changes in accounting principles would therefore be more representationally faithful.

(b) given that a transitional impairment loss should be reported as a change in accounting principle, the transitional goodwill impairment test should ideally apply as of the date SFAS 142 is initially applied.

BC218　The Board observed that under the previous version of IAS 36, goodwill that was amortised over a period exceeding 20 years was required to be tested for impairment at least at each financial year-end. Goodwill that was amortised over a period not exceeding 20 years was required to be tested for impairment at the balance sheet date if there was an indication that it might be impaired. The revised Standard requires goodwill to be tested for impairment annually or more frequently if there is an indication the goodwill might be impaired. It also carries forward from the previous version of IAS 36 (a) the indicators of impairment, (b) the measure of recoverable amount (ie higher of value in use and fair value less costs to sell), and (c) the requirement for an impairment loss for a cash-generating unit to be allocated first to reduce the carrying amount of any goodwill allocated to the unit.

BC219　Therefore, goodwill tested for impairment in accordance with the previous version of the revised Standard immediately before the beginning of the reporting period in which the revised Standard becomes effective (because it was being amortised over a period exceeding 20 years or because there was an indicator of impairment) could not be identified as impaired under IAS 36 at the beginning of the period in which it becomes effective. This is because application of the Standard results in a goodwill impairment loss being identified only if the carrying amount of the cash-generating unit (group of units) to which the goodwill has been allocated exceeds its recoverable amount, and the impairment test in the previous version of IAS 36 ensures that this will not be the case.

BC220　The Board concluded that there would be only one possible situation in which a transitional impairment test might give rise to the recognition of an impairment loss for goodwill. This would be when goodwill being amortised over a period not exceeding 20 years was, immediately before the beginning of the period in which the revised Standard becomes effective, impaired in the absence of any indicator of impairment that ought reasonably to have been considered by the entity. The Board concluded that this is likely to be a rare occurrence.

BC221　The Board observed that any such impairment loss would nonetheless be recognised as a consequence of applying the requirement in IAS 36 to test goodwill for impairment at least annually. Therefore, the only benefit of applying a transitional impairment test would be, in those rare cases, to separate the impairment loss arising before the period in which the revised Standard is effective from any impairment loss arising after the beginning of that period.

BC222　The Board concluded that given the rare circumstances in which this issue would arise, the benefit of applying a transitional goodwill impairment test would be outweighed by the added costs of the test. Therefore, the Board decided that the revised Standard should not require a transitional goodwill impairment test.

Transitional impairment test for indefinite-lived intangibles

BC223   SFAS 142 also requires a transitional impairment test to be applied, as of the beginning of the fiscal year in which that Standard is initially applied, to intangible assets recognised before the effective date of SFAS 142 that are reassessed as having indefinite useful lives. An impairment loss arising from that transitional impairment test is recognised as the effect of a change in accounting principle rather than as an impairment loss. As with goodwill:

(a)   intangible assets that cease being amortised upon initial application of SFAS 142 are tested for impairment in accordance with SFAS 142 using a different method from what had previously applied to those assets. Therefore, it is possible that such an intangible asset not previously regarded as impaired might be determined to be impaired under SFAS 142.

(b)   the FASB concluded that the preponderance of any transitional impairment losses would be likely to result from the change in impairment testing methods. Treating those losses as stemming from changes in accounting principles is therefore more representationally faithful.

BC224   The Board considered whether IAS 36 should include a transitional impairment test for indefinite-lived intangibles similar to that in SFAS 142.

BC225   The Board observed that the previous version of IAS 38 *Intangible Assets* required an intangible asset being amortised over a period exceeding 20 years to be tested for impairment at least at each financial year-end in accordance with the previous version of IAS 36. An intangible asset being amortised over a period not exceeding 20 years was required, under the previous version of IAS 36, to be tested for impairment at the balance sheet date only if there was an indication the asset might be impaired. The revised Standard requires an indefinite-lived intangible to be tested for impairment at least annually. However, it also requires that the recoverable amount of such an asset should continue to be measured as the higher of the asset's value in use and fair value less costs to sell.

BC226   As with goodwill, the Board concluded that the revised Standard should not require a transitional impairment test for indefinite-lived intangibles because:

(a)   the only circumstance in which a transitional impairment test might give rise to the recognition of an impairment loss would be when an indefinite-lived intangible previously being amortised over a period not exceeding 20 years was, immediately before the beginning of the period in which the revised Standard is effective, impaired in the absence of any indicator of impairment that ought reasonably to have been considered by the entity.

(b)   any such impairment loss would nonetheless be recognised as a consequence of applying the requirement in the Standard to test such assets for impairment at least annually. Therefore, the only benefit of such a test would be to separate the impairment loss arising before the period in which the revised Standard is effective from any impairment loss arising after the beginning of that period.

(c)   given the extremely rare circumstances in which this issue is likely to arise, the benefit of applying a transitional impairment test is outweighed by the added costs of the test.

Early application (paragraph 140)

BC227   The Board noted that the issue of any Standard demonstrates its opinion that application of the Standard will result in more useful information being provided to users about an entity's financial position, performance or cash flows. On that basis, a case exists for permitting, and indeed encouraging, entities to apply IAS 36 before its effective date. However, the Board also considered that permitting a revised Standard to be applied before its effective date potentially diminishes comparability between entities in the period(s) leading up to that effective date, and has the effect of providing entities with an option.

BC228   The Board concluded that the benefit of providing users with more useful information about an entity's financial position, performance and cash flows by permitting early application of IAS 36 outweighs the disadvantages of potentially diminished comparability. Therefore, entities are encouraged to apply the requirements of IAS 36 before its effective date. However, given that the revision of IAS 36 is part of an integrated package, IAS 36 requires IFRS 3 and IAS 38 (as revised in 2004) to be applied at the same time.

Transitional provision for *Improvements to IFRSs* (2009)

BC228A   The Board considered the transition provisions and effective date of the amendment to paragraph 80(b). The Board noted that the assessment of goodwill impairment might involve the use of hindsight in determining the fair values of the cash-generating units at the end of a past reporting period. Considering practicability, the Board decided that the effective date should be for annual periods beginning on or after 1 January 2010 although the Board noted that the effective date of IFRS 8 is 1 January 2009. Therefore, the Board decided that an entity should apply the amendment to paragraph 80(b) made by *Improvements to IFRSs* issued in April 2009 prospectively for annual periods beginning on or after 1 January 2010.

Transition provisions for *Recoverable Amount Disclosures for Non-Financial Assets*

BC228B   In Exposure Draft ED/2013/1, the IASB proposed retrospective application and to permit earlier application of the amendments. The vast majority of the respondents supported those proposals.

BC228C   The IASB decided to retain in the final amendments the transition requirements proposed in Exposure Draft ED/2013/1 that meant that entities should not provide comparative information for the prior period if they are not also applying IFRS 13 in that period. The objective of such transition requirements is to make these amendments have the same effect as if they had been issued when the IASB issued IFRS 13.

Summary of main changes from the Exposure Draft

BC229   The following are the main changes from the Exposure Draft:

(a)   the Exposure Draft proposed that an intangible asset with an indefinite useful life should be tested for impairment at the end of each annual period by comparing its carrying amount with its recoverable amount. The Standard requires such an intangible asset to be tested for impairment annually by comparing its carrying amount with its recoverable amount. The impairment test may be performed at any time during an annual period, provided it is performed at the same time every year, and different intangible assets may be tested for impairment at different times. However, if such an intangible asset was initially recognised during the current annual period, the Standard requires that intangible asset to be tested for impairment before the end of the current annual period.

(b)   the Exposure Draft proposed that the cash flow projections used to measure value in use should be based on reasonable and supportable assumptions that take into account both past actual cash flows and management's past ability to forecast cash flows accurately. This proposal has not been included in the Standard. Instead, the Standard includes guidance clarifying that management:

(i)   should assess the reasonableness of the assumptions on which its current cash flow projections are based by examining the causes of differences between past cash flow projections and actual cash flows; and

(ii)   should ensure that the assumptions on which its current cash flow projections are based are consistent with past actual outcomes, provided the effects of subsequent events or circumstances that did not exist when those actual cash flows were generated make this appropriate.

(c)   the Exposure Draft proposed that if an active market exists for the output produced by an asset or a group of assets, that asset or group of assets should be identified as a cash-generating unit, even if some or all of the output is used internally. In such circumstances, management's best estimate of future market prices for the output should be used in estimating the future cash flows used to determine the unit's value in use. The Exposure Draft also proposed that when estimating future cash flows to determine the value in use of cash-generating units using the output, management's best estimate of future market prices for the output should be used. The Standard similarly requires that if an active market exists for the output produced by an asset or a group of assets, that asset or group of assets should be identified as a cash-generating unit, even if some or all of the output is used internally. However, the Standard clarifies that if the cash inflows generated by *any* asset or cash-generating unit are affected by internal transfer pricing, an entity should use management's best estimate of future price(s) that could be achieved in arm's length transactions in estimating:

(i) the future cash inflows used to determine the asset's or cash-generating unit's value in use; and

(ii) the future cash outflows used to determine the value in use of other assets or cash-generating units affected by the internal transfer pricing.

(d) the Exposure Draft proposed that goodwill acquired in a business combination should be allocated to one or more cash-generating units, with each of those units representing the smallest cash-generating unit to which a portion of the carrying amount of the goodwill could be allocated on a reasonable and consistent basis. The Exposure Draft also proposed that:

(i) a portion of the carrying amount of goodwill should be regarded as capable of being allocated to a cash-generating unit on a reasonable and consistent basis only when that unit represents the lowest level at which management monitors the return on investment in assets that include the goodwill.

(ii) each cash-generating unit should not be larger than a segment based on the entity's primary reporting format determined in accordance with IAS 14 *Segment Reporting*.

The Standard requires goodwill acquired in a business combination to be allocated to each of the acquirer's cash-generating units, or groups of cash-generating units, that are expected to benefit from the synergies of the combination, irrespective of whether other assets or liabilities of the acquiree are assigned to those units or groups of units. The Standard also requires each unit or group of units to which the goodwill is so allocated: (1) to represent the lowest level within the entity at which the goodwill is monitored for internal management purposes; and (2) to be not larger than a segment based on either the entity's primary or the entity's secondary reporting format determined in accordance with IAS 14.

(e) the Exposure Draft proposed that when an entity disposes of an operation within a cash-generating unit to which goodwill has been allocated, the goodwill associated with that operation should be:

(i) included in the carrying amount of the operation when determining the gain or loss on disposal; and

(ii) measured on the basis of the relative values of the operation disposed of and the portion of the cash-generating unit retained.

This proposal has been included in the Standard with one modification. The Standard requires the goodwill associated with the operation disposed of to be measured on the basis of the relative values of the operation disposed of and the portion of the cash-generating unit retained, unless the entity can demonstrate that some other method better reflects the goodwill associated with the operation disposed of.

(f) the Exposure Draft proposed that when an entity reorganises its reporting structure in a way that changes the composition of cash-generating units to which goodwill has been allocated, the goodwill should be reallocated to the units affected using a relative value approach similar to that used when an entity disposes of an operation within a cash-generating unit. The Standard similarly requires an entity that reorganises its reporting structure in a way that changes the composition of one or more cash-generating units to which goodwill has been allocated to reallocate the goodwill to the units (groups of units) affected. However, the Standard requires this reallocation to be performed using a relative value approach similar to that used when an entity disposes of an operation within a cash-generating unit, unless the entity can demonstrate that some other method better reflects the goodwill associated with the reorganised units (groups of units).

(g) the Exposure Draft proposed a two-step approach for impairment testing goodwill. The first step involved using a screening mechanism for identifying potential goodwill impairments, whereby goodwill allocated to a cash-generating unit would be identified as potentially impaired only when the carrying amount of the unit exceeded its recoverable amount. If an entity identified the goodwill allocated to a cash-generating unit as potentially impaired, an entity would then determine whether the goodwill allocated to the unit was impaired by comparing its recoverable amount, measured as the implied value of the goodwill, with its carrying amount. The implied value of goodwill would be measured as a residual, being the excess of the recoverable amount of the cash-generating unit to which the goodwill has been allocated, over the net fair value of the identifiable assets, liabilities and contingent liabilities the entity would recognise if it acquired the cash-generating unit in a business combination on the date of the impairment test. The Standard requires any excess of the carrying amount of a cash-generating unit (group of units) to which goodwill has been allocated over its recoverable amount to be recognised first as an impairment loss for goodwill. Any excess remaining after the carrying amount of goodwill has been reduced to zero is then recognised by being allocated to the other assets of the unit pro rata with their carrying amounts.

(h)   the Exposure Draft proposed requiring an entity to disclose information about cash-generating units whose carrying amounts included goodwill or indefinite-lived intangibles. That information included the carrying amount of goodwill and the carrying amount of indefinite-lived intangibles, the basis on which the unit's recoverable amount had been determined (ie value in use or net selling price), the amount by which the unit's recoverable amount exceeded its carrying amount, the key assumptions and estimates used to measure the unit's recoverable amount and information about the sensitivity of that recoverable amount to changes in the key assumptions and estimates. If an entity reports segment information in accordance with IAS 14, the Exposure Draft proposed that this information should be disclosed in aggregate for each segment based on the entity's primary reporting format. However, the Exposure Draft also proposed that the information would be disclosed separately for a cash-generating unit if specified criteria were met. The Standard:

(i)   does not require information for evaluating the reliability of the impairment tests for goodwill and indefinite-lived intangibles to be disclosed in aggregate for each segment and separately for cash-generating units within a segment when specified criteria are met. Instead, the Standard requires this information to be disclosed for each cash-generating unit (group of units) for which the carrying amount of goodwill or indefinite-lived intangibles allocated to that unit (group of units) is significant in comparison with the entity's total carrying amount of goodwill or indefinite-lived intangibles.

(ii)   does not require an entity to disclose the amount by which the recoverable amount of a cash-generating unit exceeds its carrying amount. Instead, the Standard requires an entity to disclose this information only if a reasonably possible change in a key assumption on which management has based its determination of the unit's (group of units') recoverable amount would cause the unit's (group of units') carrying amount to exceed its recoverable amount.

(iii)   does not require an entity to disclose the value assigned to each key assumption on which management has based its recoverable amount determination, and the amount by which that value must change, after incorporating any consequential effects of that change on the other variables used to measure recoverable amount, in order for the unit's recoverable amount to be equal to its carrying amount. Instead, the Standard requires an entity to disclose a description of each key assumption on which management has based its recoverable amount determination, management's approach to determining the value(s) assigned to each key assumption, whether those value(s) reflect past experience or, if appropriate, are consistent with external sources of information, and, if not, how and why they differ from past experience or external sources of information. However, if a reasonably possible change in a key assumption would cause the unit's (group of units') carrying amount to exceed its recoverable amount, the entity is also required to disclose the value assigned to the key assumption, and the amount by which that value must change, after incorporating any consequential effects of that change on the other variables used to measure recoverable amount, in order for the unit's (group of units') recoverable amount to be equal to its carrying amount.

(iv)   requires information about key assumptions to be disclosed for any key assumption that is relevant to the recoverable amount determination of multiple cash-generating units (groups of units) that individually contain insignificant amounts of goodwill or indefinite-lived intangibles, but which contain, in aggregate, significant amounts of goodwill or indefinite-lived intangibles.

History of the development of a standard on impairment of assets

BCZ230   In June 1996, IASC decided to prepare an International Accounting Standard on Impairment of Assets. The reasons for developing a Standard on impairment of assets were:

(a)   to combine the requirements for identifying, measuring, recognising and reversing an impairment loss in one Standard to ensure that those requirements are consistent;

(b)   the previous requirements and guidance in International Accounting Standards were not detailed enough to ensure that enterprises identified, recognised and measured impairment losses in a similar way, eg there was a need to eliminate certain alternatives for measuring an impairment loss, such as the former option not to use discounting; and

(c)   IASC decided in March 1996 to explore whether the amortisation period of intangible assets and goodwill could, in certain rare circumstances, exceed 20 years if those assets were subject to detailed and reliable annual impairment tests.

BCZ231   In April 1997, IASC approved Exposure Draft E55 *Impairment of Assets*. IASC received more than 90 comment letters from over 20 countries. IASC also performed a field test of E55's proposals. More than 20 companies from various business sectors and from 10 different countries participated in the field test. About half of the field test participants prepared their financial statements using International Accounting Standards and the other half reported using other Standards. Field test participants completed a detailed questionnaire and most of them were visited by IASC staff to discuss the results of the application of E55's proposals to some of their assets. A brief summary of the comment letters received on E55 and the results of the field test was published in IASC *Insight* in December 1997.

BCZ232 In October 1997, IASC, together with the Accounting Standards Boards in Australia, Canada, New Zealand, the United Kingdom and the United States, published a discussion paper entitled *International Review of Accounting Standards Specifying a Recoverable Amount Test for Long-Lived Assets* (Jim Paul, from the staff of the Australian Accounting Research Foundation, was the principal author). This discussion paper resulted from the discussions of a 'working group' consisting of some Board members and senior staff members from the standard-setting bodies listed above and IASC. The paper:

(a) noted the key features of the working group members' existing or proposed accounting standards that require an impairment test, and compared those standards; and

(b) proposed the views of the working group on the major issues.

BCZ233 In April 1998, after considering the comments received on E55 and the results of the field test, IASC approved IAS 36 *Impairment of Assets*.

Dissenting opinions

Dissent of Anthony T Cope, James J Leisenring and Geoffrey Whittington

DO1   Messrs Cope and Leisenring and Professor Whittington dissent from the issue of IAS 36.

DO2   Messrs Cope and Leisenring and Professor Whittington dissent because they object to the impairment test that the Standard requires for goodwill.

DO3   Messrs Cope and Leisenring agree with the prohibition, in paragraph 54 of IFRS 3 *Business Combinations*, of amortisation of goodwill.[44] Research and experience have demonstrated that the amortisation of goodwill produces data that is meaningless, and perhaps even misleading. However, if goodwill is not amortised, its special nature mandates that it should be accounted for with caution. The Basis for Conclusions on IAS 36 (paragraph BC131) states that 'if a rigorous and operational impairment test [for goodwill] could be devised, more useful information would be provided to users of an entity's financial statements under an approach in which goodwill is not amortised, but instead tested for impairment annually or more frequently if events or changes in circumstances indicate that the goodwill might be impaired.' Messrs Cope and Leisenring agree with that statement. However, they believe that the impairment test to which a majority of the Board has agreed lacks the rigour to satisfy that condition.

DO4   Messrs Cope and Leisenring share the reservations of some Board members, as noted in paragraph BC130 of the Basis for Conclusions on IAS 36, about an impairment test based on measuring the recoverable amount of an asset, and particularly an asset with an indefinite life, as the higher of fair value less costs to sell or value in use. Messrs Cope and Leisenring are content, however, for the time being to defer consideration of that general measurement issue, pending more research and debate on measurement principles. (They note that the use of fair value would achieve significant convergence with US GAAP.) But a much more rigorous effort must be made to determine the recoverable amount of goodwill, however measured, than the Board's revised impairment test. The 'two-step' method originally proposed by the Board in the Exposure Draft of Proposed Amendments to IAS 36 and IAS 38 was a more useful approach to determining the 'implied value' of goodwill. That test should have been retained.

DO5   Messrs Cope and Leisenring recognise that some constituents raised objections to the complexity and potential cost of the requirements proposed in the Exposure Draft. However, they believe that many commentators misunderstood the level at which the Board intended impairment testing to be undertaken. This was demonstrated during the field-testing of the Exposure Draft. Furthermore, the provisions of paragraph 99 of IAS 36, specifying when impairment testing need not be undertaken, provide generous relief from the

---

44   The Board issued a revised IFRS 3 in 2008. The amortisation of goodwill is prohibited, but the paragraph reference no longer exists in IFRS 3 (as revised in 2008).

necessity of making frequent calculations. They would have preferred to meet those objections by specifying that the goodwill impairment test should be at the level set out in US Financial Accounting Standards Board's Statement of Financial Accounting Standards No. 142 *Goodwill and Other Intangible Assets*.

DO6 Professor Whittington believes that there are two aspects of the proposed impairment test that are particularly unsatisfactory. First, the failure to eliminate the shield from impairment provided by the internally generated goodwill of the acquiring entity at acquisition. This is discussed in paragraph DO7. Second, the lack of a subsequent cash flow test. This is discussed in paragraphs DO8–DO10. The inability to eliminate the shield from impairment provided by internally generated goodwill accruing after the acquisition date is also a problem. However, there is no obvious practical way of dealing with this problem within the framework of conventional impairment tests.

DO7 When an acquired business is merged with an acquirer's existing operations, the impairment test in IAS 36 does not take account of the acquirer's pre-existing internally generated goodwill. Thus, the pre-existing internally generated goodwill of the acquirer provides a shield against impairment additional to that provided by subsequent internally generated goodwill. Professor Whittington believes that the impairment test would be more rigorous if it included a requirement similar to that in UK Financial Reporting Standard 11 *Impairment of Fixed Assets and Goodwill*, which recognises, for purposes of impairment testing, the implied value of the acquirer's goodwill existing at the time of acquisition.

DO8 The subsequent cash flow test is discussed in paragraphs BC195–BC198 of the Basis for Conclusions on IAS 36. A subsequent cash flow test substitutes in past impairment tests the cash flows that actually occurred for those that were estimated at the time of the impairment tests, and requires a write-down if the revised estimates would have created an impairment loss for goodwill. It is thus a correction of an estimate. Such a test is incorporated in FRS 11.

DO9 The Board's reasons for rejecting the subsequent cash flow test are given in paragraph BC197(a)–(c). The preamble to paragraph BC197 claims that the subsequent cash flow test is misdirected because excessive write-downs of goodwill may be a problem that should be prevented. However, the subsequent cash flow test requires only realistic write-downs (based on actual outcomes), not excessive ones. If the statement in paragraph BC197 is correct, this may point to another deficiency in the impairment testing process that requires a different remedy.

DO10 Paragraph BC197(a) asserts that 'it does not produce representationally faithful results' because it ignores other elements in the measurement of value in use. As explained above, it merely substitutes the outcome cash flow for the estimate, which should have a clear meaning and provides a safeguard against over-optimism in the estimation of cash flows. If corrections of estimates of other elements, such as variations that have occurred in interest rates, were considered important in this context, they could be incorporated in the calculation. Paragraph BC197(b) seems to raise the same point as paragraph BC197(a), as to the meaning of the impairment loss under the test. Paragraph BC197(c) complains about the excessive burden that a subsequent cash flow test might impose. Professor Whittington notes that the extent of the burden depends, of course, upon the frequency with which the test is applied. He also notes that the extensive disclosure requirements currently associated with the impairment test might be reduced if the subsequent cash flow test were in place.

IASB documents published to accompany

IAS 37

Provisions, Contingent Liabilities and Contingent Assets

The text of the unaccompanied standard, IAS 37, is contained in Part A of this edition. Its effective date when issued was 1 July 1999. The text of the Accompanying Guidance on IAS 37 is contained in Part B of this edition. This part presents the following document:

BASIS FOR CONCLUSIONS

Contents

Basis for Conclusions on
IAS 37 *Provisions, Contingent Liabilities and Contingent Assets*

This Basis for Conclusions accompanies, but is not part of, IAS 37. IAS 37 was issued by the International Accounting Standards Committee in 1998 and was not accompanied by a Basis for Conclusions. This Basis for Conclusions summarises the considerations of the International Accounting Standards Board (Board) in developing amendments to IAS 37. Individual Board members gave greater weight to some factors than to others.

Onerous Contracts—Cost of Fulfilling a Contract (paragraph 68A)

BC1　In May 2020 the Board added paragraph 68A to IAS 37. Paragraph 68A specifies which costs an entity includes in determining the cost of fulfilling a contract for the purpose of assessing whether the contract is onerous. The Board added this clarification in response to a recommendation from the IFRS Interpretations Committee, whose research indicated that:

　(a)　differing views on which costs to include could lead to material differences in the financial statements of entities that enter into some types of contracts.

　(b)　the need for clarification was urgent. Following the withdrawal of IAS 11 *Construction Contracts*, entities are required to apply IAS 37 instead of IAS 11 to assess whether construction contracts are onerous. IAS 11 specified which costs to include, but IAS 37 did not.

The cost of fulfilling a contract

BC2　Views differed on what an entity should include in the cost of fulfilling a contract when assessing whether the contract is onerous—whether to include:

　(a)　only the incremental costs of fulfilling the contract—for example, the cost of materials and labour required to construct a building; or

　(b)　all costs that relate directly to the contract—both the incremental costs and an allocation of other costs that relate directly to fulfilling contracts—for example, an allocation of the depreciation charge for an item of property, plant and equipment used in fulfilling the contract among others, or an allocation of the costs of management and supervision of contracts.

BC3　The Board decided to require an entity to include all costs that relate directly to a contract. The Board concluded that:

　(a)　including all such costs provides more useful information to users of the entity's financial statements (paragraphs BC4–BC7);

　(b)　the benefits of providing that information are likely to outweigh the costs (paragraphs BC8–BC9); and

　(c)　a requirement to include all costs that relate directly to a contract is consistent with other requirements in IAS 37 and requirements in other IFRS Standards (paragraphs BC10–BC13).

Useful information

BC4 An entity may obtain the resources it needs to fulfil a contract in different ways. For example, if an entity needs equipment to fulfil a contract to manufacture goods or provide services, it may either hire the equipment for use only on that contract, or buy the equipment and use it on several contracts. The Board concluded that to provide a faithful representation of the effect of a contract on an entity's financial position, the entity should identify the resources needed to fulfil the contract and include the cost of those resources, regardless of how it expects to obtain them. Including only incremental costs in that assessment—for example, the costs of hiring equipment but not an allocation of the depreciation of purchased equipment—would fail to recognise the costs of resources shared with other contracts.

BC5 The Board considered contracts an entity will fulfil using existing assets with idle capacity. If the income from such a contract will exceed the incremental cost of fulfilling it, the contract will improve the entity's financial position and performance. But, unless the income will fully cover the cost of the capacity used, including that cost in assessing whether the contract is onerous might suggest otherwise because the entity will recognise an onerous contract provision and a loss when it incurs a present obligation by entering into the contract. If that capacity were not used to fulfil the contract, such a loss would not be recognised.

BC6 The Board concluded that, even for a contract that will be fulfilled using existing idle capacity, including all costs that relate directly to the contract (that is, including the cost of the capacity used) provides useful information. By entering into a contract at a price that does not fully cover the cost of the capacity used, the entity has committed itself to using that capacity to provide goods or services at a price that would not be sustainable if all contracts were similarly priced. The entity has effectively committed itself to making a loss on that capacity for the life of the contract. In the Board's view, including the cost of the capacity used in assessing whether a contract is onerous provides information that is relevant to users of financial statements and faithfully represents the effect of the contract on the entity's financial position and performance. The Board noted that an entity would disclose additional information about the contract if such information is relevant to an understanding of the entity's financial statements.

BC7 The Board also considered requirements in other IFRS Standards. Several IFRS Standards—such as IAS 2 *Inventories*—specify the costs to include in measuring a non-monetary asset. Although their detailed requirements differ, they all require an entity to include both the incremental costs of purchasing or constructing the asset, and an allocation of other directly related or directly attributable costs, such as production overheads. The Board concluded that, in assessing whether a contract to deliver goods is onerous, the way an entity determines the cost of fulfilling the contract should be broadly consistent with the way it measures the cost of the goods when it holds them. Such consistency leads to more useful information.

Cost of applying the requirements

BC8   The Board discussed suggestions that it might be costly for a manufacturing entity to estimate and allocate all the costs that relate directly to a contract if the entity has not yet manufactured the goods it will deliver under the contract.

BC9   The Board noted that IAS 2 requires an entity to measure the cost of manufactured inventories at an amount that includes both the incremental costs of production and an allocation of production overheads. Further, a manufacturing entity that enters into contracts to supply inventory is likely to need information about these costs to make pricing decisions. Therefore, the entity is likely to have already the information it needs to estimate and allocate the costs that will relate directly to contracts into which it has entered. The Board therefore concluded that a requirement to estimate and allocate costs that relate directly to a contract would not impose costs that outweigh the usefulness of the information provided.

Consistency with other requirements in IAS 37 and requirements in other IFRS Standards

BC10   IAS 37 defines an onerous contract as 'a contract in which the unavoidable costs of meeting the obligations under the contract exceed the economic benefits expected to be received under it'. The Board concluded that the unavoidable costs of fulfilling a contract are the costs an entity cannot avoid because it *has* the contract (as opposed to the costs the entity could avoid if it *did not have* the contract). The costs an entity cannot avoid because it has a contract include both the incremental costs of that contract and an allocation of other costs that relate directly to fulfilling contracts, including that contract.

BC11   The Board discussed whether including costs other than the incremental costs of fulfilling a contract would be inconsistent with other requirements in IAS 37. Those holding this view suggested that, because an entity will incur those other costs regardless of whether it fulfils the contract under consideration, the costs are not costs of 'fulfilling the contract' — they are costs of operating the business. Paragraph 18 of IAS 37 specifies that no provision is recognised for costs that need to be incurred to operate in the future, and paragraph 63 prohibits recognition of future operating losses.

BC12   However, the Board concluded that a requirement to include all costs that relate directly to a contract in assessing whether the contract is onerous is consistent with other requirements in IAS 37. It concluded that:

    (a)   in recognising an onerous contract provision, an entity would not be recognising a provision for the costs themselves — that is, it would not be identifying those costs as present obligations in their own right. Instead, the entity would be recognising its present obligation to deliver goods or provide services in exchange for other economic benefits, measuring that obligation at an amount that includes the cost of all the resources to be used to fulfil the obligation.

(b)   paragraph 63 of IAS 37 prohibits an entity from recognising future operating losses because such losses are not liabilities; in other words, the entity does not have a present obligation to incur those losses. In contrast, in assessing whether a contract is onerous, an entity determines the cost of fulfilling its present obligation under an existing contract. Therefore, including all costs that relate directly to a contract in assessing whether the contract is onerous does not result in an entity recognising future operating losses.

BC13   The Board noted that a requirement to include all costs that relate directly to a contract is consistent with IFRS 17 *Insurance Contracts*. IFRS 17 requires insurers to include all costs that relate directly to the fulfilment of a contract in assessing whether an insurance contract is onerous. These costs include an allocation of fixed and variable overheads directly attributable to fulfilling insurance contracts.

Examples

BC14   When it exposed draft amendments for comment, the Board proposed to include a list of examples of costs that do and do not relate directly to a contract. These examples were based on paragraphs 97–98 of IFRS 15 *Revenue from Contracts with Customers*.

BC15   Some respondents to the Board's draft amendments noted differences between the examples proposed and those in other IFRS Standards that specify which costs to include in measuring the cost of non-monetary assets. Those respondents asked the Board to clarify whether some costs mentioned in those other IFRS Standards would be regarded as costs that relate directly to the contract by an entity applying IAS 37. Respondents also asked the Board to provide examples of costs that relate directly to contracts other than contracts to deliver goods or provide services.

BC16   In response to this feedback, the Board decided to replace the list of examples with a more general description of the types of costs that relate directly to a contract—that is, the incremental costs of fulfilling the contract and an allocation of other costs that relate directly to fulfilling contracts. The Board concluded that the more general description:

(a)   can be applied to all types of contract, rather than only to contracts to deliver goods or provide services;

(b)   avoids unintended consequences of slight differences in the wording of examples in different IFRS Standards; and

(c)   provides a framework within which an entity can judge whether a particular cost relates directly to a contract.

Interaction with requirements for impaired assets

BC17   Paragraph 69 of IAS 37 requires that, before an entity establishes a provision for an onerous contract, the entity recognises any impairment loss that has occurred on assets 'used in fulfilling the contract'. Paragraph 69 originally referred to assets 'dedicated to that contract'. However, the term 'dedicated' could be read to apply only to assets used solely on that contract, and not used on other contracts. The Board amended the terminology in paragraph 69 to clarify that the requirement to recognise any impairment loss before establishing an onerous contract provision applies to all assets whose cost would be considered in assessing whether the contract is onerous.

Scope

BC18   Some respondents to the Board's draft amendments asked the Board to expand the scope of the project to clarify other aspects of the onerous contract requirements in IAS 37, such as:

(a)   measuring onerous contracts—whether an entity would consider the same costs in measuring a provision for an onerous contract as it would consider in assessing whether that contract is onerous.

(b)   selecting a unit of account—whether, and if so when, an entity should combine groups of similar contracts or segment contracts into components when applying the onerous contract requirements.

BC19   The Board decided not to consider other aspects of the onerous contract requirements in IAS 37 because doing so would have prolonged the project, delaying the issue of amendments regarded as urgent (see paragraph BC1(b)). The amendments therefore do not change the requirements in IAS 37 beyond clarifying the costs an entity is required to include in assessing whether a contract is onerous.

Transitional provisions

BC20   On transition entities are required to apply the amendments only to contracts for which the entity has not fulfilled all its obligations at the date of initial application, without restating comparative amounts. The Board concluded that it may be difficult and costly for an entity to obtain the information needed to restate comparative amounts, and the information provided by doing so was unlikely to be sufficiently useful to justify the costs that the entity might incur.

BC21   The Board decided not to provide entities with an option to restate comparative amounts—that is, not to provide the option of retrospective application, as defined in IAS 8 *Accounting Policies, Changes in Accounting Estimates and Errors*. The Board concluded that the benefits of providing that option would be limited, and would be outweighed by the complexity and possible loss of comparability between the financial statements of entities applying the amendments at their effective date.

IASB documents published to accompany

IAS 38

Intangible Assets

The text of the unaccompanied standard, IAS 38, is contained in Part A of this edition. Its effective date when issued was 31 March 2004. The text of the Accompanying Guidance on IAS 38 is contained in Part B of this edition. This part presents the following documents:

BASIS FOR CONCLUSIONS

DISSENTING OPINIONS

CONTENTS

Basis for Conclusions on
IAS 38 *Intangible Assets*

The International Accounting Standards Board revised IAS 38 as part of its project on business combinations. It was not the Board's intention to reconsider as part of that project all of the requirements in IAS 38.

The previous version of IAS 38 was accompanied by a Basis for Conclusions summarising the former International Accounting Standards Committee's considerations in reaching some of its conclusions in that Standard. For convenience the Board has incorporated into its own Basis for Conclusions material from the previous Basis for Conclusions that discusses (a) matters the Board did not reconsider and (b) the history of the development of a standard on intangible assets. That material is contained in paragraphs denoted by numbers with the prefix BCZ. Paragraphs describing the Board's considerations in reaching its own conclusions are numbered with the prefix BC.

Introduction

BC1   This Basis for Conclusions summarises the International Accounting Standards Board's considerations in reaching the conclusions in IAS 38 *Intangible Assets*. Individual Board members gave greater weight to some factors than to others.

BC2   The International Accounting Standards Committee (IASC) issued the previous version of IAS 38 in 1998. It has been revised by the Board as part of its project on business combinations. That project has two phases. The first has resulted in the Board issuing simultaneously IFRS 3 *Business Combinations* and revised versions of IAS 38 and IAS 36 *Impairment of Assets*. Therefore, the Board's intention in revising IAS 38 as part of the first phase of the project was not to reconsider all of the requirements in IAS 38. The changes to IAS 38 are primarily concerned with:

   (a)   the notion of 'identifiability' as it relates to intangible assets;

   (b)   the useful life and amortisation of intangible assets; and

   (c)   the accounting for in-process research and development projects acquired in business combinations.

BC3   With the exception of research and development projects acquired in business combinations, the Board did not reconsider the requirements in the previous version of IAS 38 on the recognition of internally generated intangible assets. The previous version of IAS 38 was accompanied by a Basis for Conclusions summarising IASC's considerations in reaching some of its conclusions in that Standard. For convenience, the Board has incorporated into this Basis for Conclusions material from the previous Basis for Conclusions that discusses the recognition of internally generated intangible assets (see paragraphs BCZ29–BCZ46) and the history of the development of a standard on intangible assets (see paragraphs BCZ104–BCZ110). The views expressed in paragraphs BCZ29–BCZ46 and BCZ104–BCZ110 are those of IASC.

Definition of an intangible asset (paragraph 8)

BC4　An intangible asset was defined in the previous version of IAS 38 as 'an identifiable non-monetary asset without physical substance held for use in the production or supply of goods or services, for rental to others, or for administrative services'. The definition in the revised Standard eliminates the requirement for the asset to be held for use in the production or supply of goods or services, for rental to others, or for administrative services.

BC5　The Board observed that the essential characteristics of intangible assets are that they:

(a)　are resources controlled by the entity from which future economic benefits are expected to flow to the entity;

(b)　lack physical substance; and

(c)　are identifiable.

The Board concluded that the purpose for which an entity holds an item with these characteristics is not relevant to its classification as an intangible asset, and that all such items should be within the scope of the Standard.

Identifiability (paragraph 12)

BC6　Under the Standard, as under the previous version of IAS 38, a non-monetary asset without physical substance must be identifiable to meet the definition of an intangible asset. The previous version of IAS 38 did not define 'identifiability', but stated that an intangible asset could be distinguished from goodwill if the asset was separable, but that separability was not a necessary condition for identifiability. The revised Standard requires an asset to be treated as meeting the identifiability criterion in the definition of an intangible asset when it is separable, or when it arises from contractual or other legal rights, regardless of whether those rights are transferable or separable from the entity or from other rights and obligations.

Background to the Board's deliberations

BC7　The Board was prompted to consider the issue of 'identifiability' as part of the first phase of its Business Combinations project as a result of changes during 2001 to the requirements in Canadian and United States standards on the separate recognition of intangible assets acquired in business combinations. The Board observed that intangible assets comprise an increasing proportion of the assets of many entities, and that intangible assets acquired in a business combination are often included in the amount recognised as goodwill, despite the requirements in IAS 22 *Business Combinations* and IAS 38 for them to be recognised separately from goodwill. The Board agreed with the conclusion reached by the Canadian and US standard-setters that the usefulness of financial statements would be enhanced if intangible assets acquired in a business combination were distinguished from goodwill. Therefore, the Board concluded that the IFRS arising from the first phase of the Business Combinations project should provide a definitive basis for identifying and recognising intangible assets acquired in a business combination separately from goodwill.

BC8   In revising IAS 38 and developing IFRS 3, the Board affirmed the view in the previous version of IAS 38 that identifiability is the characteristic that conceptually distinguishes other intangible assets from goodwill. The Board concluded that to provide a definitive basis for identifying and recognising intangible assets separately from goodwill, the concept of identifiability needed to be articulated more clearly.

Clarifying identifiability (paragraph 12)

BC9   Consistently with the guidance in the previous version of IAS 38, the Board concluded that an intangible asset can be distinguished from goodwill if it is separable, ie capable of being separated or divided from the entity and sold, transferred, licensed, rented or exchanged. Therefore, in the context of intangible assets, separability signifies identifiability, and intangible assets with that characteristic that are acquired in a business combination should be recognised as assets separately from goodwill.

BC10   However, again consistently with the guidance in the previous version of IAS 38, the Board concluded that separability is not the only indication of identifiability. The Board observed that, in contrast to goodwill, the values of many intangible assets arise from rights conveyed legally by contract or statute. In the case of acquired goodwill, its value arises from the collection of assembled assets that make up an acquired entity or the value created by assembling a collection of assets through a business combination, such as the synergies that are expected to result from combining entities or businesses. The Board also observed that, although many intangible assets are both separable and arise from contractual-legal rights, some contractual-legal rights establish property interests that are not readily separable from the entity as a whole. For example, under the laws of some jurisdictions some licences granted to an entity are not transferable except by sale of the entity as a whole. The Board concluded that the fact that an intangible asset arises from contractual or other legal rights is a characteristic that distinguishes it from goodwill. Therefore, intangible assets with that characteristic that are acquired in a business combination should be recognised as assets separately from goodwill.

Non-contractual customer relationships (paragraph 16)

BC11   The previous version of IAS 38 and the Exposure Draft of Proposed Amendments to IAS 38 stated that 'An entity controls an asset if the entity has the power to obtain the future economic benefits flowing from the underlying resource and also can restrict the access of others to those benefits'. The documents then expanded on this by stating that 'in the absence of legal rights to protect, or other ways to control, the relationships with customers or the loyalty of the customers to the entity, the entity usually has insufficient control over the economic benefits from customer relationships and loyalty to consider that such items meet the definition of intangible assets'.

BC12　However, the Draft Illustrative Examples accompanying ED 3 *Business Combinations* stated that 'If a customer relationship acquired in a business combination does not arise from a contract, the relationship is recognised as an intangible asset separately from goodwill if it meets the separability criterion. Exchange transactions for the same asset or a similar asset provide evidence of separability of a non-contractual customer relationship and might also provide information about exchange prices that should be considered when estimating fair value.' Whilst respondents to the Exposure Draft generally agreed with the Board's conclusions on the definition of identifiability, some were uncertain about the relationship between the separability criterion for establishing whether a non-contractual customer relationship is identifiable, and the control concept for establishing whether the relationship meets the definition of an asset. Additionally, some respondents suggested that non-contractual customer relationships would, under the proposal in the Exposure Draft, be separately recognised if acquired in a business combination, but not if acquired in a separate transaction.

BC13　The Board observed that exchange transactions for the same or similar non-contractual customer relationships provide evidence not only that the item is separable, but also that the entity is able to control the expected future economic benefits flowing from that relationship. Similarly, if an entity separately acquires a non-contractual customer relationship, the existence of an exchange transaction for that relationship provides evidence both that the item is separable, and that the entity is able to control the expected future economic benefits flowing from the relationship. Therefore, the relationship would meet the intangible asset definition and be recognised as such. However, in the absence of exchange transactions for the same or similar non-contractual customer relationships, such relationships acquired in a business combination would not normally meet the definition of an 'intangible asset'—they would not be separable, nor would the entity be able to demonstrate that it controls the expected future economic benefits flowing from that relationship.

BC14　Therefore, the Board decided to clarify in paragraph 16 of IAS 38 that in the absence of legal rights to protect customer relationships, exchange transactions for the same or similar non-contractual customer relationships (other than as part of a business combination) provide evidence that the entity is nonetheless able to control the future economic benefits flowing from the customer relationships. Because such exchange transactions also provide evidence that the customer relationships are separable, those customer relationships meet the definition of an intangible asset.

Criteria for initial recognition

BC15　In accordance with the Standard, as with the previous version of IAS 38, an intangible asset is recognised if, and only if:

(a)　it is probable that the expected future economic benefits that are attributable to the asset will flow to the entity; and

(b)　the cost of the asset can be measured reliably.

In revising IAS 38 the Board considered the application of these recognition criteria to intangible assets acquired in business combinations. The Board's deliberations on this issue are set out in paragraphs BC16–BC25.

Acquisition as part of a business combination (paragraphs 33–38)

BC16   [Deleted]

BC16A   The Board observed that in a business combination both criteria, the probability criterion and the reliability of measurement criterion, will always be met.

Probability recognition criterion

BC17   In revising IAS 38, the Board observed that the fair value of an intangible asset reflects market expectations about the probability that the future economic benefits associated with the intangible asset will flow to the acquirer. In other words, the effect of probability is reflected in the fair value measurement of an intangible asset.[1] Therefore, the probability recognition criterion is always considered to be satisfied for intangible assets acquired in business combinations.

BC18   The Board observed that this highlights a general inconsistency between the recognition criteria for assets and liabilities in the *Framework*[2] (which states that an item meeting the definition of an element should be recognised only if it is probable that any future economic benefits associated with the item will flow to or from the entity, and the item can be measured reliably) and the fair value measurements required in, for example, a business combination. However, the Board concluded that the role of probability as a criterion for recognition in the *Framework* should be considered more generally as part of a forthcoming Concepts project.

Reliability of measurement recognition criterion

BC19   [Deleted]

BC19A   In developing IFRS 3, the IASB noted that the fair values of identifiable intangible assets acquired in a business combination are normally measurable with sufficient reliability to be recognised separately from goodwill. The effects of uncertainty because of a range of possible outcomes with different probabilities are reflected in measuring the asset's fair value;[3] the existence of such a range does not demonstrate an inability to measure fair value reliably. IAS 38 (as revised in 2004) included a rebuttable presumption that the fair value of an intangible asset with a finite useful life acquired in a business combination can be measured reliably. The Board had concluded that it might

---

1   IFRS 13 *Fair Value Measurement*, issued in May 2011, defines fair value and contains the requirements for measuring fair value.

2   References to the *Framework* in this Basis for Conclusions are to the IASC's *Framework for the Preparation and Presentation of Financial Statements*, adopted by the Board in 2001 and in effect when the Standard was developed and revised.

3   IFRS 13, issued in May 2011, contains the requirements for measuring fair value.

not always be possible to measure reliably the fair value of an asset that has an underlying contractual or legal basis. However, IAS 38 (revised 2004) provided that the only circumstances in which it might not be possible to measure reliably the fair value of an intangible asset acquired in a business combination that arises from legal or other contractual rights were if it either:

(a)   is not separable; or

(b)   is separable, but there is no history or evidence of exchange transactions for the same or similar assets, and otherwise estimating fair value would depend on immeasurable variables.

BC19B   In developing the 2005 Business Combinations exposure draft, the Board concluded that separate recognition of intangible assets, on the basis of an estimate of fair value, rather than subsuming them in goodwill, provides better information to the users of financial statements even if a significant degree of judgement is required to estimate fair value. For this reason, the Board decided to propose consequential amendments to IAS 38 to remove the reliability of measurement criterion for intangible assets acquired in a business combination. In redeliberating the proposals in the 2005 Business Combinations exposure draft, the Board affirmed those amendments to IAS 38.

BC19C   When the Board developed IFRS 3 (as revised in 2008), it decided that if an intangible asset acquired in a business combination is separable or arises from contractual or other legal rights, sufficient information exists to measure the fair value of the asset reliably. The Board made related amendments to IAS 38 to reflect that decision. However, the Board identified additional amendments that were needed to reflect clearly its decisions on the accounting for intangible assets acquired in a business combination. Consequently, in *Improvements to IFRSs* issued in April 2009, the Board amended paragraphs 36 and 37 of IAS 38 to clarify the Board's intentions.

BC19D   Additionally, in *Improvements to IFRSs* issued in April 2009, the Board amended paragraphs 40 and 41 of IAS 38 to clarify the description of valuation techniques commonly used to measure intangible assets at fair value[4] when assets are not traded in an active market. The Board also decided that the amendments should be applied prospectively because retrospective application might require some entities to remeasure fair values associated with previous transactions. The Board does not think this is appropriate because the remeasurement might involve the use of hindsight in those circumstances.

BC20–   [Deleted]
BC25

Separate acquisition (paragraphs 25 and 26)

BC26   Having decided to include paragraphs 33–38 in IAS 38, the Board also decided that it needed to consider the role of the probability and reliability of measurement recognition criteria for separately acquired intangible assets.

---

4   IFRS 13, issued in May 2011, contains the requirements for measuring fair value. As a consequence paragraphs 40 and 41 of IAS 38 have been deleted.

BC27   Consistently with its conclusion about the role of probability in the recognition of intangible assets acquired in business combinations, the Board concluded that the probability recognition criterion is always considered to be satisfied for separately acquired intangible assets. This is because the price an entity pays to acquire separately an intangible asset normally reflects expectations about the probability that the expected future economic benefits associated with the intangible asset will flow to the entity. In other words, the effect of probability is reflected in the cost of the intangible asset.

BC28   The Board also concluded that when an intangible asset is separately acquired in exchange for cash or other monetary assets, sufficient information should exist to measure the cost of that asset reliably. However, this might not be the case when the purchase consideration comprises non-monetary assets. Therefore, the Board decided to carry forward from the previous version of IAS 38 guidance clarifying that the cost of a separately acquired intangible asset can usually be measured reliably, particularly when the purchase consideration is cash or other monetary assets.

Internally generated intangible assets (paragraphs 51–67)

BCZ29   The controversy relating to internally generated intangible assets surrounds whether there should be:

(a)   a requirement to recognise internally generated intangible assets in the balance sheet whenever certain criteria are met;

(b)   a requirement to recognise expenditure on all internally generated intangible assets as an expense;

(c)   a requirement to recognise expenditure on all internally generated intangible assets as an expense, with certain specified exceptions; or

(d)   an option to choose between the treatments described in (a) and (b) above.

Background on the requirements for internally generated intangible assets

BCZ30   Before IAS 38 was issued in 1998, some internally generated intangible assets (those that arose from development expenditure) were dealt with under IAS 9 *Research and Development Costs*. The development of, and revisions to, IAS 9 had always been controversial.

BCZ31   Proposed and approved requirements for the recognition of an asset arising from development expenditure and other internally generated intangible assets had been the following:

(a)   in 1978, IASC approved IAS 9 *Accounting for Research and Development Activities*. It required expenditure on research and development to be recognised as an expense when incurred, except that an enterprise had the option to recognise an asset arising from development expenditure whenever certain criteria were met.

(b)   in 1989, Exposure Draft E32 *Comparability of Financial Statements* proposed retaining IAS 9's option to recognise an asset arising from development expenditure if certain criteria were met and identifying:

     (i)   as a preferred treatment, recognising all expenditure on research and development as an expense when incurred; and

     (ii)   as an allowed alternative treatment, recognising an asset arising from development expenditure whenever certain criteria were met.

The majority of commentators on E32 did not support maintaining an option or the proposed preferred treatment.

(c)   in 1991, Exposure Draft E37 *Research and Development Costs* proposed requiring the recognition of an asset arising from development expenditure whenever certain criteria were met. In 1993, IASC approved IAS 9 *Research and Development Costs* based on E37.

(d)   in 1995, consistently with IAS 9, Exposure Draft E50 *Intangible Assets* proposed requiring internally generated intangible assets — other than those arising from development expenditure, which would still have been covered by IAS 9 — to be recognised as assets whenever certain criteria were met.

(e)   in 1997, Exposure Draft E60 *Intangible Assets* proposed:

     (i)   retaining E50's proposals for the recognition of internally generated intangible assets; but

     (ii)   extending the scope of the Standard on intangible assets to deal with all internally generated intangible assets — including those arising from development expenditure.

(f)   in 1998, IASC approved:

     (i)   IAS 38 *Intangible Assets* based on E60, with a few minor changes; and

     (ii)   the withdrawal of IAS 9.

BCZ32   From 1989, the majority view at IASC and from commentators was that there should be only one treatment that would require an internally generated intangible asset — whether arising from development expenditure or other expenditure — to be recognised as an asset whenever certain recognition criteria are met. Several minority views were strongly opposed to this treatment but there was no clear consensus on any other single treatment.

Combination of IAS 9 with the Standard on intangible assets

BCZ33   The reasons for not retaining IAS 9 as a separate Standard were that:

(a)   IASC believed that an identifiable asset that results from research and development activities is an intangible asset because knowledge is the primary outcome of these activities. Therefore, IASC supported treating expenditure on research and development activities similarly to expenditure on activities intended to create any other internally generated intangible assets.

(b) some commentators on E50, which proposed to exclude research and development expenditures from its scope,

(i) argued that it was sometimes difficult to identify whether IAS 9 or the proposed Standard on intangible assets should apply, and

(ii) perceived differences in accounting treatments between IAS 9 and E50's proposals, whereas this was not IASC's intent.

BCZ34 A large majority of commentators on E60 supported including certain aspects of IAS 9 with the proposed Standard on intangible assets and the withdrawal of IAS 9. A minority of commentators on E60 supported maintaining two separate Standards. This minority supported the view that internally generated intangible assets should be dealt with on a case-by-case basis with separate requirements for different types of internally generated intangible assets. These commentators argued that E60's proposed recognition criteria were too general to be effective in practice for all internally generated intangible assets.

BCZ35 IASC rejected a proposal to develop separate standards (or detailed requirements within one standard) for specific types of internally generated intangible assets because, as explained above, IASC believed that the same recognition criteria should apply to all types of internally generated intangible assets.

Consequences of combining IAS 9 with IAS 38

BCZ36 The requirements in IAS 38 and IAS 9 differ in the following main respects:

(a) IAS 9 limited the amount of expenditure that could initially be recognised for an asset arising from development expenditure (ie the amount that formed the cost of such an asset) to the amount that was probable of being recovered from the asset. Instead, IAS 38 requires that:

(i) all expenditure incurred from when the recognition criteria are met until the asset is available for use should be accumulated to form the cost of the asset; and

(ii) an enterprise should test for impairment, at least annually, an intangible asset that is not yet available for use. If the cost recognised for the asset exceeds its recoverable amount, an enterprise recognises an impairment loss accordingly. This impairment loss should be reversed if the conditions for reversals of impairment losses under IAS 36 *Impairment of Assets* are met.

(b) IAS 38 permits an intangible asset to be measured after recognition at a revalued amount less subsequent amortisation and subsequent impairment losses. IAS 9 did not permit this treatment. However, it is highly unlikely that an active market (the condition required to revalue intangible assets) will exist for an asset that arises from development expenditure.

(c) IAS 38 requires consideration of residual values in determining the depreciable amount of an intangible asset. IAS 9 prohibited the consideration of residual values. However, IAS 38 sets criteria that make it highly unlikely that an asset that arises from development expenditure would have a residual value above zero.

BCZ37 IASC believed that, in practice, it would be unlikely that the application of IAS 38 would result in differences from the application of IAS 9.

Recognition of expenditure on all internally generated intangible assets as an expense

BCZ38 Those who favour the recognition of expenditure on all internally generated intangible assets (including development expenditure) as an expense argue that:

(a) internally generated intangible assets do not meet the *Framework*'s requirements for recognition as an asset because:

(i) the future economic benefits that arise from internally generated intangible assets cannot be distinguished from future economic benefits that arise from internally generated goodwill; and/or

(ii) it is impossible to distinguish reliably the expenditure associated with internally generated intangible assets from the expenditure associated with enhancing internally generated goodwill.

(b) comparability of financial statements will not be achieved. This is because the judgement involved in determining whether it is probable that future economic benefits will flow from internally generated intangible assets is too subjective to result in similar accounting under similar circumstances.

(c) it is not possible to assess reliably the amount that can be recovered from an internally generated intangible asset, unless its fair value can be determined by reference to an active market.[5] Therefore, recognising an internally generated intangible asset for which no active market exists at an amount other than zero may mislead investors.

(d) a requirement to recognise internally generated intangible assets at cost if certain criteria are met results in little, if any, decision-useful or predictive information because:

---

5 IFRS 13, issued in May 2011, defines an active market.

(i)   demonstration of technological feasibility or commercial success in order to meet the recognition criteria will generally not be achieved until substantial expenditure has been recognised as an expense. Therefore, the cost recognised for an internally generated intangible asset will not reflect the total expenditure on that asset.

(ii)   the cost of an internally generated intangible asset may not have any relationship to the value of the asset.

(e)   in some countries, users are suspicious about an enterprise that recognises internally generated intangible assets.

(f)   the added costs of maintaining the records necessary to justify and support the recognition of internally generated intangible assets do not justify the benefits.

Recognition of internally generated intangible assets

BCZ39   Those who support the mandatory recognition of internally generated intangible assets (including those resulting from development expenditure) whenever certain criteria are met argue that:

(a)   recognition of an internally generated intangible asset if it meets the definition of an asset and the recognition criteria is consistent with the *Framework*. An enterprise can, in some instances:

(i)   determine the probability of receiving future economic benefits from an internally generated intangible asset; and

(ii)   distinguish the expenditure on this asset from expenditure on internally generated goodwill.

(b)   there has been massive investment in intangible assets in the last two decades. There have been complaints that:

(i)   the non-recognition of investments in intangible assets in the financial statements distorts the measurement of an enterprise's performance and does not allow an accurate assessment of returns on investment in intangible assets; and

(ii)   if enterprises do not track the returns on investment in intangible assets better, there is a risk of over- or under-investing in important assets. An accounting system that encourages such behaviour will become an increasingly inadequate signal, both for internal control purposes and for external purposes.

(c)   certain research studies, particularly in the United States, have established a cost-value association for research and development expenditures. The studies establish that capitalisation of research and development expenditure yields value-relevant information to investors.

(d)   the fact that some uncertainties exist about the value of an asset does not justify a requirement that no cost should be recognised for the asset.

(e)   it should not matter for recognition purposes whether an asset is purchased externally or developed internally. Particularly, there should be no opportunity for accounting arbitrage depending on whether an enterprise decides to outsource the development of an intangible asset or develop it internally.

IASC's view in approving IAS 38

BCZ40   IASC's view—consistently reflected in previous proposals for intangible assets—was that there should be no difference between the requirements for:

(a)   intangible assets that are acquired externally; and

(b)   internally generated intangible assets, whether they arise from development activities or other types of activities.

Therefore, an internally generated intangible asset should be recognised whenever the definition of, and recognition criteria for, an intangible asset are met. This view was also supported by a majority of commentators on E60.

BCZ41   IASC rejected a proposal for an allowed alternative to recognise expenditure on internally generated intangible assets (including development expenditure) as an expense immediately, even if the expenditure results in an asset that meets the recognition criteria. IASC believed that a free choice would undermine the comparability of financial statements and the efforts of IASC to reduce the number of alternative treatments in International Accounting Standards.

Differences in recognition criteria for internally generated intangible assets and purchased intangible assets

BCZ42   IAS 38 includes specific recognition criteria for internally generated intangible assets that expand on the general recognition criteria for intangible assets. It is assumed that these criteria are met implicitly whenever an enterprise acquires an intangible asset. Therefore, IAS 38 requires an enterprise to demonstrate that these criteria are met for internally generated intangible assets only.

Initial recognition at cost

BCZ43   Some commentators on E50 and E60 argued that the proposed recognition criteria in E50 and E60 were too restrictive and that they would prevent the recognition of many intangible assets, particularly internally generated intangible assets. Specifically, they disagreed with the proposals (retained in IAS 38) that:

(a)   an intangible asset should not be recognised at an amount other than its cost, even if its fair value can be determined reliably; and

(b)   expenditure on an intangible asset that has been recognised as an expense in prior periods should not be reinstated.

They argued that these principles contradict the *Framework* and quoted paragraph 83 of the *Framework*, which specifies that an item that meets the definition of an asset should be recognised if, among other things, its '*cost or value* can be measured with reliability'. These commentators supported recognising an intangible asset – an internally generated intangible asset – at its fair value, if, among other things, its fair value can be measured reliably.

BCZ44   IASC rejected a proposal to allow the initial recognition of an intangible asset at fair value (except if the asset is acquired in a business combination, in exchange for a dissimilar asset[6] or by way of a government grant) because:

(a)   this is consistent with IAS 16 *Property, Plant and Equipment*. IAS 16 prohibits the initial recognition of an item of property, plant or equipment at fair value (except in the specific limited cases as those in IAS 38).

(b)   it is difficult to determine the fair value of an intangible asset reliably if no active market exists for the asset.[7] Since active markets with the characteristics set out in IAS 38 are highly unlikely to exist for internally generated intangible assets, IASC did not believe that it was necessary to make an exception to the principles generally applied for the initial recognition and measurement of non-financial assets.

(c)   the large majority of commentators on E50 supported the initial recognition of intangible assets at cost and the prohibition of the reinstatement of expenditure on an intangible item that was initially recognised as an expense.

Application of the recognition criteria for internally generated intangible assets

BCZ45   IAS 38 specifically prohibits the recognition as intangible assets of brands, mastheads, publishing titles, customer lists and items similar in substance that are internally generated. IASC believed that internally generated intangible items of this kind would rarely, and perhaps never, meet the recognition criteria in IAS 38. However, to avoid any misunderstanding, IASC decided to set out this conclusion in the form of an explicit prohibition.

BCZ46   IAS 38 also clarifies that expenditure on research, training, advertising and start-up activities will not result in the creation of an intangible asset that can be recognised in the financial statements. Whilst some view these requirements and guidance as being too restrictive and arbitrary, they are based on IASC's interpretation of the application of the recognition criteria in IAS 38. They also reflect the fact that it is sometimes difficult to determine

---

6   IAS 16 *Property, Plant and Equipment* (as revised in 2003) requires an entity to measure an item of property, plant and equipment acquired in exchange for a non-monetary asset or assets, or a combination of monetary and non-monetary assets, at fair value unless the exchange transaction lacks commercial substance. Previously, an entity measured such an acquired asset at fair value unless the exchanged assets were similar. The IASB concluded that the same measurement criteria should apply to intangible assets acquired in exchange for a non-monetary asset or assets, or a combination of monetary and non-monetary assets.

7   IFRS 13, issued in May 2011, defines an active market.

whether there is an internally generated intangible asset distinguishable from internally generated goodwill.

2008 Amendments[8]

BC46A   Paragraph 68 states that expenditure on an internally developed intangible item shall be recognised as an expense when it is incurred. The Board noted that it was unclear to some constituents how this should be interpreted. For example, some believed that an entity should recognise expenditure on advertising and promotional activities as an expense when it received the goods or services that it would use to develop or communicate the advertisement or promotion. Others believed that an entity should recognise an expense when the advertisement or promotion was delivered to its customers or potential customers. Therefore, the Board decided to amend paragraph 69 to clarify the meaning of 'incurred'.

BC46B   The Board noted that advertising and promotional activities enhance or create brands or customer relationships, which in turn generate revenues. Goods or services that are acquired to be used to undertake advertising or promotional activities have no other purpose than to undertake those activities. In other words, the only benefit of those goods or services is to develop or create brands or customer relationships, which in turn generate revenues. Internally generated brands or customer relationships are not recognised as intangible assets.

BC46C   The Board concluded that it would be inconsistent for an entity to recognise an asset in respect of an advertisement that it had not yet published if the economic benefits that might flow to the entity as a result of publishing the advertisement are the same as those that might flow to the entity as a result of the brand or customer relationship that it would enhance or create. Therefore, the Board concluded that an entity should not recognise as an asset goods or services that it had received in respect of its future advertising or promotional activities.

BC46D   In reaching this conclusion the Board noted that, if an entity pays for advertising goods or services in advance and the other party has not yet provided those goods or services, the entity has a different asset. That asset is the right to receive those goods and services. Therefore, the Board decided to retain paragraph 70, which allows an entity to recognise as an asset the right to receive those goods or services. However, the Board did not believe that this paragraph should be used as a justification for recognising an asset beyond the point at which the entity gained a right to access the related goods or received the related services. Therefore, the Board decided to amend the paragraph to make clear that a prepayment may be recognised by an entity only until that entity has gained a right to access to the related goods or has received the related services.

---

8   This heading and paragraphs BC46A–BC46I were added by *Improvements to IFRSs* issued in May 2008.

BC46E   The Board noted that when the entity has received the related goods or services, it ceases to have the right to receive them. Because the entity no longer has an asset that it can recognise, it recognises an expense. However, the Board was concerned that the timing of delivery of goods should not be the determinant of when an expense should be recognised. The date on which physical delivery is obtained could be altered without affecting the commercial substance of the arrangement with the supplier. Therefore, the Board decided that an entity should recognise an expense for goods when they have been completed by the supplier in accordance with a contract to supply them and the entity could ask for delivery in return for payment—in other words, when the entity had gained a right to access the related goods.

BC46F   A number of commentators on the exposure draft of proposed *Improvements to International Financial Reporting Standards* published in 2007 thought that it was unclear when the Board intended an expense to be recognised. In response to those comments, the Board added paragraph 69A to clarify when entities would gain a right to access goods or receive services.

BC46G   The Board also received a number of comments arguing that mail order catalogues are not a form of advertising and promotion but instead give rise to a distribution network. The Board rejected these arguments, believing that the primary objective of mail order catalogues is to advertise goods to customers. To avoid confusion, the Board decided to include mail order catalogues in the Standard as an example of advertising activities.

BC46H   Some respondents who argued that the cost of mail order catalogues should be capitalised suggested that making an analogy to web site costs in SIC-32 *Intangible Assets—Web Site Costs* would be appropriate. The Board agreed and concluded that its proposed amendments would result in accounting that is almost identical to that resulting from the application of SIC-32. In particular, SIC-32 requires the cost of content (to the extent that it is developed to advertise and promote products and services) to be recognised as an expense as it is incurred. The Board concluded that in the case of a mail order catalogue, the majority of the content is intended to advertise and promote products and services. Therefore, permitting the cost of catalogues to be capitalised while at the same time requiring the cost of developing and uploading web site content used to advertise and promote an entity's products to be recognised as an expense would base the accounting on the nature of the media (paper or electronic) used to deliver the content rather than the nature of the expenditure.

BC46I   The Board also noted that SIC-32 permits expenditure on an internally developed web site to be capitalised only in the 'application and infrastructure development stage'. It requires costs associated with developing the functionality and infrastructure that make a web site operate to be capitalised. In the Board's view, the electronic infrastructure capitalised in accordance with SIC-32 is analogous to the property, plant and equipment infrastructure—for example, a sign—that permits advertising to be displayed to the public not the content that is displayed on that sign.

Subsequent accounting for intangible assets

BC47 The Board initially decided that the scope of the first phase of its Business Combinations project should include a consideration of the subsequent accounting for intangible assets acquired in business combinations. To that end, the Board initially focused its attention on the following three issues:

(a) whether an intangible asset with a finite useful life and acquired in a business combination should continue to be accounted for after initial recognition in accordance with IAS 38.

(b) whether, and under what circumstances, an intangible asset acquired in a business combination could be regarded as having an indefinite useful life.

(c) how an intangible asset with an indefinite useful life (assuming such an asset exists) acquired in a business combination should be accounted for after initial recognition.

BC48 However, during its deliberations of the issues in (b) and (c) of paragraph BC47, the Board decided that any conclusions it reached on those issues would equally apply to recognised intangible assets obtained other than in a business combination. The Board observed that amending the requirements in the previous version of IAS 38 only for intangible assets acquired in business combinations would create inconsistencies in the accounting for intangible assets depending on how they are obtained. Thus, similar items would be accounted for in dissimilar ways. The Board concluded that creating such inconsistencies would impair the usefulness of the information provided to users about an entity's intangible assets, because both comparability and reliability (which rests on the notion of representational faithfulness, ie that similar transactions are accounted for in the same way) would be diminished. Therefore, the Board decided that any amendments to the requirements in the previous version of IAS 38 to address the issues in (b) and (c) of paragraph BC47 should apply to all recognised intangible assets, whether generated internally or acquired separately or as part of a business combination.

BC49 Before beginning its deliberations of the issues identified in paragraph BC47, the Board noted the concern expressed by some that, because of the subjectivity involved in distinguishing goodwill from other intangible assets as at the acquisition date, differences between the subsequent treatment of goodwill and other intangible assets increases the potential for intangible assets to be misclassified at the acquisition date. The Board concluded, however, that adopting the separability and contractual or other legal rights criteria provides a reasonably definitive basis for separately identifying and recognising intangible assets acquired in a business combination. Therefore, the Board decided that its analysis of the accounting for intangible assets after initial recognition should have regard only to the nature of those assets and not to the subsequent treatment of goodwill.

Accounting for intangible assets with finite useful lives acquired in business combinations

BC50   The Board observed that the previous version of IAS 38 required an intangible asset to be measured after initial recognition:

(a)   at cost less any accumulated amortisation and any accumulated impairment losses; or

(b)   at a revalued amount, being the asset's fair value, determined by reference to an active market,[9] at the date of revaluation less any subsequent accumulated amortisation and any subsequent accumulated impairment losses. Under this approach, revaluations must be made with such regularity that at the balance sheet date the carrying amount of the asset does not differ materially from its fair value.

Whichever of the above methods was used, the previous version of IAS 38 required the depreciable amount of the asset to be amortised on a systematic basis over the best estimate of its useful life.

BC51   The Board observed that underpinning the requirement for all intangible assets to be amortised is the notion that they all have determinable and finite useful lives. Setting aside the question of whether, and under what circumstances, an intangible asset could be regarded as having an indefinite useful life, an important issue for the Board to consider was whether a departure from the above requirements would be warranted for intangible assets acquired in a business combination that have finite useful lives.

BC52   The Board observed that any departure from the above requirements for intangible assets with finite lives acquired in business combinations would create inconsistencies between the accounting for recognised intangible assets based wholly on the means by which they are obtained. In other words, similar items would be accounted for in dissimilar ways. The Board concluded that creating such inconsistencies would impair the usefulness of the information provided to users about an entity's intangible assets, because both comparability and reliability would be diminished.

BC53   Therefore, the Board decided that intangible assets with finite useful lives acquired in business combinations should continue to be accounted for in accordance with the above requirements after initial recognition.

Impairment testing intangible assets with finite useful lives (paragraph 111)

BC54   The previous version of IAS 38 required the recoverable amount of an intangible asset with a finite useful life that is being amortised over a period of more than 20 years, whether or not acquired in a business combination, to be measured at least at each financial year-end.

---

9   IFRS 13, issued in May 2011, defines an active market.

BC55   The Board observed that the recoverable amount of a long-lived tangible asset needs to be measured only when, in accordance with IAS 36 *Impairment of Assets*, there is an indication that the asset may be impaired. The Board could see no conceptual reason for requiring the recoverable amounts of some identifiable assets being amortised over very long periods to be determined more regularly than for other identifiable assets being amortised or depreciated over similar periods. Therefore, the Board concluded that the recoverable amount of an intangible asset with a finite useful life that is amortised over a period of more than 20 years should be determined only when, in accordance with IAS 36, there is an indication that the asset may be impaired. Consequently, the Board decided to remove the requirement in the previous version of IAS 38 for the recoverable amount of such an intangible asset to be measured at least at each financial year-end.

BC56   The Board also decided that all of the requirements relating to impairment testing intangible assets should be included in IAS 36 rather than in IAS 38. Therefore, the Board relocated to IAS 36 the requirement in the previous version of IAS 38 that an entity should estimate at the end of each annual reporting period the recoverable amount of an intangible asset not yet available for use, irrespective of whether there is any indication that it may be impaired.

Residual value of an intangible asset with a finite useful life (paragraph 100)

BC57   In revising IAS 38, the Board considered whether to retain for intangible assets with finite useful lives the requirement in the previous version of IAS 38 for the residual value of an intangible asset to be assumed to be zero unless:

(a)   there is a commitment by a third party to purchase the asset at the end of its useful life; or

(b)   there is an active market[10] for the asset and:

(i)   the asset's residual value can be determined by reference to that market; and

(ii)   it is probable that such a market will exist at the end of the asset's useful life.

BC58   The Board observed that the definition in the previous version of IAS 38 (as amended by IAS 16 when revised in 2003) of residual value required it to be estimated as if the asset were already of the age and in the condition expected at the end of the asset's useful life. Therefore, if the useful life of an intangible asset was shorter than its economic life because the entity expected to sell the asset before the end of that economic life, the asset's residual value would not be zero, irrespective of whether the conditions in paragraph BC57(a) or (b) are met.

---

10   IFRS 13, issued in May 2011, defines an active market.

BC59 Nevertheless, the Board observed that the requirement for the residual value of an intangible asset to be assumed to be zero unless the specified criteria are met was included in the previous version of IAS 38 as a means of preventing entities from circumventing the requirement in that Standard to amortise all intangible assets. Excluding this requirement from the revised Standard for finite-lived intangible assets would similarly provide a means of circumventing the requirement to amortise such intangible assets — by claiming that the residual value of such an asset was equal to or greater than its carrying amount, an entity could avoid amortising the asset, even though its useful life is finite. The Board concluded that it should not, as part of the Business Combinations project, modify the criteria for permitting a finite-lived intangible asset's residual value to be other than zero. However, the Board decided that this issue should be addressed as part of a forthcoming project on intangible assets.

Useful lives of intangible assets (paragraphs 88–96)

BC60 Consistently with the proposals in the Exposure Draft of Proposed Amendments to IAS 38, the Standard requires an intangible asset to be regarded by an entity as having an indefinite useful life when, based on an analysis of all of the relevant factors, there is no foreseeable limit to the period over which the asset is expected to generate net cash inflows for the entity.

BC61 In developing the Exposure Draft and the revised Standard, the Board observed that the useful life of an intangible asset is related to the expected cash inflows that are associated with that asset. The Board observed that, to be representationally faithful, the amortisation period for an intangible asset generally should reflect that useful life and, by extension, the cash flow streams associated with the asset. The Board concluded that it is possible for management to have the intention and the ability to maintain an intangible asset in such a way that there is no foreseeable limit on the period over which that particular asset is expected to generate net cash inflows for the entity. In other words, it is conceivable that an analysis of all the relevant factors (ie legal, regulatory, contractual, competitive, economic and other) could lead to a conclusion that there is no foreseeable limit to the period over which a particular intangible asset is expected to generate net cash inflows for the entity.

BC62 For example, the Board observed that some intangible assets are based on legal rights that are conveyed in perpetuity rather than for finite terms. As such, those assets may have cash flows associated with them that may be expected to continue for many years or even indefinitely. The Board concluded that if the cash flows are expected to continue for a finite period, the useful life of the asset is limited to that finite period. However, if the cash flows are expected to continue indefinitely, the useful life is indefinite.

BC63 The previous version of IAS 38 prescribed a presumptive maximum useful life for intangible assets of 20 years. In developing the Exposure Draft and the revised Standard, the Board concluded that such a presumption is inconsistent with the view that the amortisation period for an intangible asset should, to be representationally faithful, reflect its useful life and, by extension, the cash flow streams associated with the asset. Therefore, the Board decided not to include in the revised Standard a presumptive maximum useful life for intangible assets, even if they have finite useful lives.

BC64   Respondents to the Exposure Draft generally supported the Board's proposal to remove from IAS 38 the presumptive maximum useful life and instead to require useful life to be regarded as indefinite when, based on an analysis of all of the relevant factors, there is no foreseeable limit to the period of time over which the intangible asset is expected to generate net cash inflows for the entity. However, some respondents suggested that an inability to determine clearly the useful life of an asset applies equally to many items of property, plant and equipment. Nonetheless, entities are required to determine the useful lives of those items of property, plant and equipment, and allocate their depreciable amounts on a systematic basis over those useful lives. Those respondents suggested that there is no conceptual reason for treating intangible assets differently.

BC65   In considering these comments, the Board noted the following:

(a)   an intangible asset's useful life would be regarded as indefinite in accordance with IAS 38 only when, based on an analysis of all of the relevant factors, there is no foreseeable limit to the period of time over which the asset is expected to generate net cash inflows for the entity. Difficulties in accurately determining an intangible asset's useful life do not provide a basis for regarding that useful life as indefinite.

(b)   although the useful lives of both intangible and tangible assets are directly related to the period during which they are expected to generate net cash inflows for the entity, the expected physical utility to the entity of a tangible asset places an upper limit on the asset's useful life. In other words, the useful life of a tangible asset could never extend beyond the asset's expected physical utility to the entity.

The Board concluded that tangible assets (other than land) could not be regarded as having indefinite useful lives because there is always a foreseeable limit to the expected physical utility of the asset to the entity.

Useful life constrained by contractual or other legal rights (paragraphs 94–96)

BC66   The Board noted that the useful life of an intangible asset that arises from contractual or other legal rights is constrained by the duration of those rights. The useful life of such an asset cannot extend beyond the duration of those rights, and may be shorter. Accordingly, the Board concluded that in determining the useful life of an intangible asset, consideration should be given to the period that the entity expects to use the intangible asset, which is subject to the expiration of the contractual or other legal rights.

BC67   However, the Board also observed that such rights are often conveyed for limited terms that may be renewed. It therefore considered whether renewals should be assumed in determining the useful life of such an intangible asset. The Board noted that some types of licences are initially issued for finite periods but renewals are routinely granted at little cost, provided that licensees have complied with the applicable rules and regulations. Such licences are traded at prices that reflect more than the remaining term, thereby indicating that renewal at minimal cost is the general expectation. However, renewals are not assured for other types of licences and, even if they are renewed, substantial costs may be incurred to secure their renewal.

BC68 The Board concluded that because the useful lives of some intangible assets depend, in economic terms, on renewal and on the associated costs of renewal, the useful lives assigned to those assets should reflect renewal when there is evidence to support renewal without significant cost.

BC69 Respondents to the Exposure Draft generally supported this conclusion. Those that disagreed suggested that:

(a) when the renewal period depends on the decision of a third party and not merely on the fulfilment of specified conditions by the entity, it gives rise to a contingent asset because the third-party decision affects not only the cost of renewal but also the probability of obtaining it. Therefore, useful life should reflect renewal only when renewal is not subject to third-party approval.

(b) such a requirement would be inconsistent with the basis used to measure intangible assets at the date of a business combination, particularly contractual customer relationships. For example, it is not clear whether the fair value of a contractual customer relationship includes an amount that reflects the probability that the contract will be renewed. The possibility of renewal would have a fair value regardless of the costs required to renew. This means the useful life of a contractual customer relationship could be inconsistent with the basis used to determine the fair value of the relationship.[11]

BC70 In relation to (a) above, the Board observed that if renewal by the entity is subject to third-party (eg government) approval, the requirement that there be evidence to support the entity's ability to renew would compel the entity to make an assessment of the likely effect of the third-party approval process on the entity's ability to renew. The Board could see no conceptual basis for narrowing the requirement to situations in which the contractual or legal rights are not subject to the approval of third parties.

BC71 In relation to (b) above, the Board observed the following:

(a) the requirements relating to renewal periods address circumstances in which *the entity* is able to renew the contractual or other legal rights, notwithstanding that such renewal may, for example, be conditional on the entity satisfying specified conditions, or subject to third-party approval. Paragraph 94 of the Standard states that '... the useful life of the intangible asset shall include the renewal period(s) only if there is evidence to support renewal *by the entity* [emphasis added] without

---

11 IFRS 13, issued in May 2011, contains the requirements for measuring fair value.

significant cost.' The ability to renew a customer contract normally rests with the customer and not with the entity.

(b)   the respondents seem to regard as a single intangible asset what is, in substance, two intangible assets—one being the customer contract and the other being the related customer relationship. Expected renewals by the customer would affect the fair value of the customer relationship intangible asset, rather than the fair value of the customer contract. Therefore, the useful life of the customer contract would not, under the Standard, extend beyond the term of the contract, nor would the fair value of that customer contract reflect expectations of renewal by the customer. In other words, the useful life of the customer contract would not be inconsistent with the basis used to determine its fair value.

BC72   However, in response to respondents' suggestions, the Board included paragraph 96 in the Standard to provide additional guidance on the circumstances in which an entity should be regarded as being able to renew the contractual or other legal rights without significant cost.

Intangible assets with finite useful lives (paragraph 98)[12]

BC72A   The last sentence of paragraph 98 previously stated, 'There is rarely, if ever, persuasive evidence to support an amortisation method for intangible assets with finite useful lives that results in a lower amount of accumulated amortisation than under the straight-line method.' In practice, this wording was perceived as preventing an entity from using the units of production method to amortise assets if it resulted in a lower amount of accumulated amortisation than the straight-line method. However, using the straight-line method could be inconsistent with the general requirement of paragraph 38 that the amortisation method should reflect the expected pattern of consumption of the expected future economic benefits embodied in an intangible asset. Consequently, the Board decided to delete the last sentence of paragraph 98.

Amortisation method (paragraphs 97–98C)

BC72B   The IASB decided to amend IAS 38 to address concerns regarding the use of a revenue-based method for amortising an intangible asset. The IASB's decision was in response to a request to clarify the meaning of the term 'consumption of the expected future economic benefits embodied in the asset' when determining the appropriate amortisation method for intangible assets of service concession arrangements (SCA) that are within the scope of IFRIC 12 *Service Concession Arrangements*. The issue raised is related to the application of paragraphs 97–98 of IAS 38, although the IASB decided to address the issue broadly, rather than limit it only to intangible assets arising in an SCA.

---

12   This heading and paragraph BC72A were added by *Improvements to IFRSs* issued in May 2008.

BC72C   A revenue-based amortisation method is one that allocates an asset's amortisable amount based on revenues generated in an accounting period as a proportion of the total revenues expected to be generated over the asset's useful economic life. The total revenue amount is affected by the interaction between units (ie quantity) and price and takes into account any expected changes in price. The IASB observed that the price component of revenue may be affected by inflation and noted that inflation has no bearing upon the way in which the asset is consumed.

BC72D   The IASB observed that paragraph 97 of IAS 38 states that the amortisation method used shall reflect the pattern in which the intangible asset's future economic benefits are expected to be consumed by the entity.

BC72E   On the basis of the guidance in IAS 38 the IASB proposed to clarify in the Exposure Draft *Clarification of Acceptable Methods of Depreciation and Amortisation* (Proposed amendments to IAS 16 and IAS 38) (the 'ED') that a method of amortisation that is based on revenue generated from an activity that includes the use of an asset is not appropriate, because it reflects a pattern of economic benefits being generated from operating the business (of which the asset is part) rather than the economic benefits being consumed through the use of the asset.

BC72F   During its redeliberations of the ED the IASB decided to include a rebuttable presumption that revenue is generally presumed to be an inappropriate basis for measuring the consumption of the economic benefits embodied in the intangible asset. The IASB also considered the question of whether there could be circumstances in which revenue could be used to reflect the pattern in which the future economic benefits of the intangible asset are expected to be consumed.

BC72G   In finalising the proposed amendments to IAS 38, the IASB decided to make clear in the Standard that the presumption precluding the use of revenue as a basis for amortisation could be overcome in two circumstances. One of those circumstances is when it can be demonstrated that revenue is highly correlated with the consumption of the economic benefits embodied in an intangible asset. The IASB also noted that another circumstance in which revenue could be used is when the right embodied by an intangible asset is expressed as a total amount of revenue to be generated (rather than time, for example), in such a way that the generation of revenue is the measurement used to determine when the right expires. The IASB noted that, in this case, the pattern of consumption of future economic benefits that is embodied in the intangible asset is defined by reference to the total revenue earned as a proportion of the contractual maximum and, consequently, the amount of revenue generated contractually reflects the consumption of the benefits that are embodied in the asset.

BC72H   The IASB also analysed situations in which an intangible asset is used in multiple activities to provide multiple revenue streams. Some respondents commented that the application of a units of production method did not seem practicable, because the units of production were not homogeneous. For example, the producer of a motion picture will typically use the intellectual property embodied in the film to generate cash flows through exhibiting the film in theatres, licensing the rights to characters to manufacturers of toys and other goods, selling DVDs or digital copies of the film and licensing broadcast rights to television broadcasters. Some respondents thought that the best way to amortise the cost of the intellectual property embodied in the film was to use a revenue-based method, because revenue was considered a common denominator to reflect a suitable proxy of the pattern of consumption of all the benefits received from the multiple activities in which the intellectual property could be used.

BC72I   The IASB acknowledged that determining an appropriate amortisation method for situations in which an intangible asset is used in multiple activities, and generates multiple cash flow streams in different markets, requires judgement. The IASB considered suggestions that an intangible asset should be componentised for amortisation purposes in circumstances in which the asset is used to generate multiple cash flow streams. It observed that separating an asset into different components is not a new practice in business or in IFRS—it is routinely done for property, plant and equipment and IAS 16 provides guidance in this respect—but refrained from developing guidance in this respect for intangible assets.

BC72J   The IASB also decided to provide guidance on how an entity could identify an amortisation method in response to some respondents who observed that further guidance was required in the application of paragraph 98 of IAS 38, which is limited to providing a description of the amortisation methods most commonly used. During its deliberations the IASB determined that, when choosing an amortisation method, an entity could determine the predominant limiting factor for the use of the intangible asset. For example, a contract could be limited by a number of years (ie time), a number of units produced or an amount of revenue to be generated. The IASB clarified that identifying such a predominant limiting factor is only a starting point for the identification of the amortisation method and an entity may apply another basis if the entity determines that it more closely reflects the expected pattern of consumption of economic benefits.

BC72K   In the ED the IASB proposed to provide guidance to clarify the role of obsolescence in the application of the diminishing balance method. In response to the comments received about the proposed guidance, the IASB decided to change the focus of this guidance to explain that expected future reductions in the selling price of an item that was produced using an intangible asset could indicate the expectation of technological or commercial obsolescence of the asset, which, in turn, might reflect a reduction of the future economic benefits embodied in the asset. The IASB noted that the expectation of technical or commercial obsolescence is relevant for estimating both the pattern of consumption of future economic benefits and the useful life of an asset. The IASB noted that the diminishing balance method is an accepted amortisation methodology in paragraph 98 of IAS 38, which is capable of reflecting an accelerated consumption of the future economic benefits embodied in the asset.

BC72L   Some respondents to the ED suggested that the IASB should define the notion of 'consumption of economic benefits' and provide guidance in this respect. During its redeliberations the IASB decided against doing so, noting that explaining the notion of consumption of economic benefits would require a broader project.

Consistency in the use of the phrase 'units of production'

BC72M   The IASB decided to make consistent the phrase 'units of production method' and has therefore amended the instances of the phrase 'unit of production method'.

Accounting for intangible assets with indefinite useful lives (paragraphs 107–110)

BC73   Consistently with the proposals in the Exposure Draft, the Standard prohibits the amortisation of intangible assets with indefinite useful lives. Therefore, such assets are measured after initial recognition at:

(a)   cost less any accumulated impairment losses; or

(b)   a revalued amount, being fair value determined by reference to an active market[13] less any accumulated impairment losses.

Non-amortisation

BC74   In developing the Exposure Draft and the revised Standard, the Board observed that many assets yield benefits to an entity over several periods. Amortisation is the systematic allocation of the cost (or revalued amount) of an asset, less any residual value, to reflect the consumption over time of the future economic benefits embodied in that asset. Thus, if there is no foreseeable limit on the period during which an entity expects to consume the future economic benefits embodied in an asset, amortisation of that asset over, for example, an arbitrarily determined maximum period would not be representationally faithful. Respondents to the Exposure Draft generally supported this conclusion.

BC75   Consequently, the Board decided that intangible assets with indefinite useful lives should not be amortised, but should be subject to regular impairment testing. The Board's deliberations on the form of the impairment test, including the frequency of impairment testing, are included in the Basis for Conclusions on IAS 36. The Board further decided that regular re-examinations should be required of the useful life of an intangible asset that is not being amortised to determine whether circumstances continue to support the assessment that the useful life is indefinite.

---

13   IFRS 13, issued in May 2011, defines an active market.

Revaluations

BC76   Having decided that intangible assets with indefinite useful lives should not be amortised, the Board considered whether an entity should be permitted to carry such assets at revalued amounts. The Board could see no conceptual justification for precluding some intangible assets from being carried at revalued amounts solely on the basis that there is no foreseeable limit to the period over which an entity expects to consume the future economic benefits embodied in those assets.

BC77   As a result, the Board decided that the Standard should permit intangible assets with indefinite useful lives to be carried at revalued amounts.

Revaluation method—proportionate restatement of accumulated amortisation when an intangible asset is revalued

BC77A   The IFRS Interpretations Committee reported to the Board that practice differed in calculating the accumulated depreciation for an item of property, plant and equipment that is measured using the revaluation method in cases in which the residual value, the useful life or the depreciation method has been re-estimated before a revaluation.

BC77B   The reasons for making the change are further explained in paragraphs BC25A–BC25G of IAS 16.

BC77C   The Board noted that the issue in paragraphs BC25A–BC25G of IAS 16 regarding accumulated depreciation upon revaluation could also occur when revaluing an intangible asset under IAS 38, because both IAS 16 and IAS 38 have the same requirements for accumulated depreciation/amortisation when revaluing items of property, plant and equipment/intangible assets. Differences in the revaluation models for items of property, plant and equipment and intangible assets do not result in different models for restating accumulated depreciation/amortisation. For example, IAS 38 requires that the fair value of an intangible asset is measured by reference to an active market. Otherwise, the revaluation model cannot be applied. However, IAS 38 requires fair value measurement by reference to an active market only for the carrying amount of an intangible asset in contrast to its gross carrying amount.

BC77D   Consequently, the Board decided to amend paragraph 80(a) to state that:

(a)   the gross carrying amount is adjusted in a manner that is consistent with the revaluation of the carrying amount; and

(b)   the accumulated amortisation is calculated as the difference between the gross carrying amount and the carrying amount after taking into account accumulated impairment losses.

The Board also decided to amend paragraph 80(b) to be consistent with the wording used in those amendments.

BC77E   The Board decided to include wording in paragraph 80(a) to require an entity to take into account accumulated impairment losses when adjusting the amortisation on revaluation. This was to ensure that when future revaluation increases occur, the correct split according to paragraph 85 of IAS 38 and paragraph 119 of IAS 36 is made between profit or loss and other comprehensive income when reversing prior accumulated impairment losses.

Research and development projects acquired in business combinations

BC78   The Board considered the following issues in relation to in-process research and development (IPR&D) projects acquired in a business combination:

(a)   whether the proposed criteria for recognising intangible assets acquired in a business combination separately from goodwill should also be applied to IPR&D projects;

(b)   the subsequent accounting for IPR&D projects recognised as assets separately from goodwill; and

(c)   the treatment of subsequent expenditure on IPR&D projects recognised as assets separately from goodwill.

The Board's deliberations on issue (a), although included in the Basis for Conclusions on IFRS 3, are also, for the sake of completeness, outlined below.

BC79   The Board did not reconsider as part of the first phase of its Business Combinations project the requirements in the previous version of IAS 38 for internally generated intangibles and expenditure on the research or development phase of an internal project. The Board decided that a reconsideration of those requirements is outside the scope of this project.

Initial recognition separately from goodwill

BC80   The Board observed that the criteria in IAS 22 *Business Combinations* and the previous version of IAS 38 for recognising an intangible asset acquired in a business combination separately from goodwill applied to all intangible assets, including IPR&D projects. Therefore, in accordance with those Standards, any intangible item acquired in a business combination was recognised as an asset separately from goodwill when it was identifiable and could be measured reliably, and it was probable that any associated future economic benefits would flow to the acquirer. If these criteria were not satisfied, the expenditure on the cost or value of that item, which was included in the cost of the combination, was part of the amount attributed to goodwill.

BC81   The Board could see no conceptual justification for changing the approach in IAS 22 and the previous version of IAS 38 of using the same criteria for all intangible assets acquired in a business combination when assessing whether those assets should be recognised separately from goodwill. The Board concluded that adopting different criteria would impair the usefulness of the information provided to users about the assets acquired in a combination because both comparability and reliability would be diminished. Therefore,

IAS 38 and IFRS 3 require an acquirer to recognise as an asset separately from goodwill any of the acquiree's IPR&D projects that meet the definition of an intangible asset. This will be the case when the IPR&D project meets the definition of an asset and is identifiable, ie is separable or arises from contractual or other legal rights.

BC82   Some respondents to the Exposure Draft of Proposed Amendments to IAS 38 expressed concern that applying the same criteria to all intangible assets acquired in a business combination to assess whether they should be recognised separately from goodwill results in treating some IPR&D projects acquired in business combinations differently from similar projects started internally. The Board acknowledged this point, but concluded that this does not provide a basis for subsuming those acquired intangible assets within goodwill. Rather, it highlights a need to reconsider the conclusion in the Standard that an intangible asset can never exist in respect of an in-process research project and can exist in respect of an in-process development project only once all of the Standard's criteria for deferral have been satisfied. The Board decided that such a reconsideration is outside the scope of its Business Combinations project.

Subsequent accounting for IPR&D projects acquired in a business combination and recognised as intangible assets

BC83   The Board observed that the previous version of IAS 38 required all recognised intangible assets to be accounted for after initial recognition at:

(a)   cost less any accumulated amortisation and any accumulated impairment losses; or

(b)   revalued amount, being the asset's fair value, determined by reference to an active market,[14] at the date of revaluation less any subsequent accumulated amortisation and any subsequent accumulated impairment losses.

Such assets included: IPR&D projects acquired in a business combination that satisfied the criteria for recognition separately from goodwill; separately acquired IPR&D projects that satisfied the criteria for recognition as an intangible asset; and recognised internally developed intangible assets arising from development or the development phase of an internal project.

BC84   The Board could see no conceptual justification for changing the approach in the previous version of IAS 38 of applying the same requirements to the subsequent accounting for all recognised intangible assets. Therefore, the Board decided that IPR&D projects acquired in a business combination that satisfy the criteria for recognition as an asset separately from goodwill should be accounted for after initial recognition in accordance with the requirements applying to the subsequent accounting for other recognised intangible assets.

---

14   IFRS 13, issued in May 2011, defines an active market.

Subsequent expenditure on IPR&D projects acquired in a business combination and recognised as intangible assets (paragraphs 42 and 43)

BC85 The Standard requires subsequent expenditure on an IPR&D project acquired separately or in a business combination and recognised as an intangible asset to be:

(a) recognised as an expense when incurred if it is research expenditure;

(b) recognised as an expense when incurred if it is development expenditure that does not satisfy the criteria for recognition as an intangible asset in paragraph 57; and

(c) added to the carrying amount of the acquired IPR&D project if it is development expenditure that satisfies the recognition criteria in paragraph 57.

BC86 In developing this requirement the Board observed that the treatment required under the previous version of IAS 38 of subsequent expenditure on an IPR&D project acquired in a business combination and recognised as an asset separately from goodwill was unclear. Some suggested that the requirements in the previous version of IAS 38 relating to expenditure on research, development, or the research or development phase of an internal project should be applied. However, others argued that those requirements were ostensibly concerned with the initial recognition and measurement of internally generated intangible assets. Instead, the requirements in the previous version of IAS 38 dealing with subsequent expenditure should be applied. Under those requirements, subsequent expenditure on an intangible asset after its purchase or completion would have been recognised as an expense when incurred unless:

(a) it was probable that the expenditure would enable the asset to generate future economic benefits in excess of its originally assessed standard of performance; and

(b) the expenditure could be measured and attributed to the asset reliably.

If these conditions were satisfied, the subsequent expenditure would be added to the carrying amount of the intangible asset.

BC87 The Board observed that this uncertainty also existed for separately acquired IPR&D projects that satisfied the criteria in the previous version of IAS 38 for recognition as intangible assets.

BC88 The Board noted that applying the requirements in the Standard for expenditure on research, development, or the research or development phase of an internal project to subsequent expenditure on IPR&D projects acquired in a business combination and recognised as assets separately from goodwill would result in such subsequent expenditure being treated inconsistently with subsequent expenditure on other recognised intangible assets. However, applying the subsequent expenditure requirements in the previous version of IAS 38 to subsequent expenditure on IPR&D projects acquired in a business combination and recognised as assets separately from goodwill would result in research and development expenditure being accounted for differently depending on whether a project is acquired or started internally.

BC89   The Board concluded that until it has had the opportunity to review the requirements in IAS 38 for expenditure on research, development, or the research or development phase of an internal project, more useful information will be provided to users of an entity's financial statements if all such expenditure is accounted for consistently. This includes subsequent expenditure on a separately acquired IPR&D project that satisfies the Standard's criteria for recognition as an intangible asset.

Transitional provisions (paragraphs 129–132)

BC90   If an entity elects to apply IFRS 3 from any date before the effective dates outlined in IFRS 3, it is also required to apply IAS 38 prospectively from that same date. Otherwise, IAS 38 applies to the accounting for intangible assets acquired in business combinations for which the agreement date is on or after 31 March 2004, and to the accounting for all other intangible assets prospectively from the beginning of the first annual reporting period beginning on or after 31 March 2004. IAS 38 also requires an entity, on initial application, to reassess the useful lives of intangible assets. If, as a result of that reassessment, the entity changes its useful life assessment for an asset, that change is accounted for as a change in an accounting estimate in accordance with IAS 8 *Accounting Policies, Changes in Accounting Estimates and Errors*.

BC91   The Board's deliberations on the transitional issues relating to the initial recognition of intangible assets acquired in business combinations and the impairment testing of intangible assets are addressed in the Basis for Conclusions on IFRS 3 and the Basis for Conclusions on IAS 36, respectively.

BC92   In developing the requirements outlined in paragraph BC90, the Board considered the following three questions:

(a)   should the useful lives of, and the accounting for, intangible assets already recognised at the effective date of the Standard continue to be determined in accordance with the requirements in the previous version of IAS 38 (ie by amortising over a presumptive maximum period of twenty years), or in accordance with the requirements in the revised Standard?

(b)   if the revised Standard is applied to intangible assets already recognised at its effective date, should the effect of a reassessment of an intangible asset's useful life as a result of the initial application of the Standard be recognised retrospectively or prospectively?

(c)   should entities be required to apply the requirements in the Standard for subsequent expenditure on an acquired IPR&D project recognised as an intangible asset retrospectively to expenditure incurred before the effective date of the revised Standard?

BC93   In relation to the first question above, the Board noted its previous conclusion that the most representationally faithful method of accounting for intangible assets is to amortise those with finite useful lives over their useful lives with no limit on the amortisation period, and not to amortise those with indefinite useful lives. Thus, the Board concluded that the reliability and comparability of financial statements would be diminished if the Standard was not applied to intangible assets recognised before its effective date.

BC94   On the second question, the Board observed that a reassessment of an asset's useful life is regarded throughout IFRSs as a change in an accounting estimate, rather than a change in an accounting policy. For example, in accordance with the Standard, as with the previous version of IAS 38, if a new estimate of the expected useful life of an intangible asset is significantly different from previous estimates, the change must be accounted for as a change in accounting estimate in accordance with IAS 8. IAS 8 requires a change in an accounting estimate to be accounted for prospectively by including the effect of the change in profit or loss in:

(a)   the period of the change, if the change in estimate affects that period only; or

(b)   the period of the change and future periods, if the change in estimate affects both.

BC95   Similarly, in accordance with IAS 16 *Property, Plant and Equipment*, if a new estimate of the expected useful life of an item of property, plant and equipment is significantly different from previous estimates, the change must be accounted for prospectively by adjusting the depreciation expense for the current and future periods.

BC96   Therefore, the Board decided that a reassessment of useful life resulting from the initial application of IAS 38, including a reassessment from a finite to an indefinite useful life, should be accounted for as a change in an accounting estimate. Consequently, the effect of such a change should be recognised prospectively.

BC97   The Board considered the view that because the previous version of IAS 38 required intangible assets to be treated as having a finite useful life, a change to an assessment of indefinite useful life for an intangible asset represents a change in an accounting policy, rather than a change in an accounting estimate. The Board concluded that, even if this were the case, the useful life reassessment should nonetheless be accounted for prospectively. This is because retrospective application would require an entity to determine whether, at the end of each reporting period before the effective date of the Standard, the useful life of an intangible asset was indefinite. Such an assessment requires an entity to make estimates that would have been made at a prior date, and therefore raises problems in relation to the role of hindsight, in particular, whether the benefit of hindsight should be included or excluded from those estimates and, if excluded, how the effect of hindsight can be separated from the other factors existing at the date for which the estimates are required.

BC98   On the third question, and as noted in paragraph BC86, it was not clear whether the previous version of IAS 38 required subsequent expenditure on acquired IPR&D projects recognised as intangible assets to be accounted for:

(a)   in accordance with its requirements for expenditure on research, development, or the research or development phase of an internal project; or

(b)   in accordance with its requirements for subsequent expenditure on an intangible asset after its purchase or completion.

The Board concluded that subsequent expenditure on an acquired IPR&D project that was capitalised under (b) above before the effective date of the Standard might not have been capitalised had the Standard applied when the subsequent expenditure was incurred. This is because the Standard requires such expenditure to be capitalised as an intangible asset only when it is development expenditure and all of the criteria for deferral are satisfied. In the Board's view, those criteria represent a higher recognition threshold than (b) above.

BC99   Thus, retrospective application of the revised Standard to subsequent expenditure on acquired IPR&D projects incurred before its effective date could result in previously capitalised expenditure being reversed. Such reversal would be required if the expenditure was research expenditure, or it was development expenditure and one or more of the criteria for deferral were not satisfied at the time the expenditure was incurred. The Board concluded that determining whether, at the time the subsequent expenditure was incurred, the criteria for deferral were satisfied raises the same hindsight issues discussed in paragraph BC97: it would require assessments to be made as of a prior date, and therefore raises problems in relation to how the effect of hindsight can be separated from factors existing at the date of the assessment. In addition, such assessments could, in many cases, be impossible: the information needed may not exist or no longer be obtainable.

BC100   Therefore, the Board decided that the Standard's requirements for subsequent expenditure on acquired IPR&D projects recognised as intangible assets should not be applied retrospectively to expenditure incurred before the revised Standard's effective date. The Board noted that any amounts previously included in the carrying amount of such an asset would, in any event, be subject to the requirements for impairment testing in IAS 36.

Revaluation method—proportionate restatement of accumulated amortisation when an intangible asset is revalued

BC100A *Annual Improvements to IFRSs 2010–2012 Cycle*, issued in December 2013, amended paragraph 80. The Board also decided that the amendment should be required to be applied to all revaluations occurring in annual periods beginning on or after the date of initial application of the amendment and in the immediately preceding annual period. The Board was concerned that the costs of full retrospective application might outweigh the benefits.

Early application (paragraph 132)

BC101   The Board noted that the issue of any Standard reflects its opinion that application of the Standard will result in more useful information being provided to users about an entity's financial position, performance or cash flows. On that basis, a case exists for permitting, and indeed encouraging, entities to apply the revised Standard before its effective date. However, the Board also considered the assertion that permitting a revised Standard to be applied before its effective date potentially diminishes comparability between entities in the period(s) leading up to that effective date, and has the effect of providing entities with an option.

BC102   The Board concluded that the benefit of providing users with more useful information about an entity's financial position and performance by permitting early application of the Standard outweighs the disadvantages of potentially diminished comparability. Therefore, entities are encouraged to apply the requirements of the revised Standard before its effective date, provided they also apply IFRS 3 and IAS 36 (as revised in 2004) at the same time.

Summary of main changes from the Exposure Draft

BC103   The following are the main changes from the Exposure Draft of Proposed Amendments to IAS 38:

(a)   The Standard includes additional guidance clarifying the relationship between the separability criterion for establishing whether a non-contractual customer relationship is identifiable, and the control concept for establishing whether the relationship meets the definition of an asset. In particular, the Standard clarifies that in the absence of legal rights to protect customer relationships, exchange transactions for the same or similar non-contractual customer relationships (other than as part of a business combination) provide evidence that the entity is nonetheless able to control the future economic benefits flowing from the customer relationships. Because such exchange transactions also provide evidence that the customer relationships are separable, those customer relationships meet the definition of an intangible asset (see paragraphs BC11–BC14).

(b)   The Exposure Draft proposed that, except for an assembled workforce, an intangible asset acquired in a business combination should always be recognised separately from goodwill; there was a presumption that sufficient information would always exist to measure reliably its fair value. The Standard states that the fair value of an intangible asset acquired in a business combination can *normally* be measured with sufficient reliability to qualify for recognition separately from goodwill. If an intangible asset acquired in a business combination has a finite useful life, there is a rebuttable presumption that its fair value can be measured reliably (see paragraphs BC16–BC25).

(c)   The Exposure Draft proposed, and the Standard requires, that the useful life of an intangible asset arising from contractual or other legal rights should not exceed the period of those rights. However, if the rights are conveyed for a limited term that can be renewed, the useful life should include the renewal period(s) only if there is evidence to support renewal by the entity without significant cost. Additional guidance has been included in the Standard to clarify the circumstances in which an entity should be regarded as being able to renew the contractual or other legal rights without significant cost (see paragraphs BC66–BC72).

History of the development of a standard on intangible assets

BCZ104   IASC published a Draft Statement of Principles on Intangible Assets in January 1994 and an Exposure Draft E50 *Intangible Assets* in June 1995. Principles in both documents were consistent as far as possible with those in IAS 16 *Property, Plant and Equipment*. The principles were also greatly influenced by the decisions reached in 1993 during the revisions to the treatment of research and development costs and goodwill.

BCZ105   IASC received about 100 comment letters on E50 from over 20 countries. Comment letters on E50 showed that the proposal for the amortisation period for intangible assets—a 20-year ceiling for almost all intangible assets, as required for goodwill in IAS 22 (revised 1993)—raised significant controversy and created serious concerns about the overall acceptability of the proposed standard on intangible assets. IASC considered alternative solutions and concluded in March 1996 that, if an impairment test that is sufficiently robust and reliable could be developed, IASC would propose deleting the 20-year ceiling on the amortisation period for both intangible assets and goodwill.

BCZ106   In August 1997, IASC published proposals for revised treatments for intangible assets and goodwill in Exposure Drafts E60 *Intangible Assets* and E61 *Business Combinations*. This followed the publication of Exposure Draft E55 *Impairment of Assets* in May 1997, which set out detailed proposals for impairment testing.

BCZ107   E60 proposed two major changes to the proposals in E50:

(a)   as explained above, revised proposals for the amortisation of intangible assets; and

(b)   combining the requirements relating to all internally generated intangible assets in one standard. This meant including certain aspects of IAS 9 *Research and Development Costs* in the proposed standard on intangible assets and withdrawing IAS 9.

BCZ108   Among other proposed changes, E61 proposed revisions to IAS 22 to make the requirements for the amortisation of goodwill consistent with those proposed for intangible assets.

BCZ109   IASC received about 100 comment letters on E60 and E61 from over 20 countries. The majority of the commentators supported most of the proposals in E60 and E61, although some proposals still raised significant controversy. The proposals for impairment tests were also supported by most commentators on E55.

BCZ110   After considering the comments received on E55, E60 and E61, IASC approved:

(a)   IAS 36 *Impairment of Assets* (April 1998);

(b)   IAS 38 *Intangible Assets* (July 1998);

(c)   a revised IAS 22 *Business Combinations* (July 1998); and

(d)   withdrawal of IAS 9 *Research and Development Costs* (July 1998).

Dissenting opinions

Dissent of Geoffrey Whittington from IAS 38 issued in March 2004

DO1   Professor Whittington dissents from the issue of this Standard because it does not explicitly require the probability recognition criterion in paragraph 21(a) to be applied to intangible assets acquired in a business combination, notwithstanding that it applies to all other intangible assets.

DO2   The reason given for this (paragraphs 33 and BC17) is that fair value is the required measurement on acquisition of an intangible asset as part of a business combination, and fair value incorporates probability assessments. Professor Whittington does not believe that the *Framework*[15] precludes having a prior recognition test based on probability, even when subsequent recognition is at fair value. Moreover, the application of probability may be different for recognition purposes: for example, it may be the 'more likely than not' criterion used in IAS 37 *Provisions, Contingent Liabilities and Contingent Assets*, rather than the 'expected value' approach used in the measurement of fair value.

DO3   This inconsistency between the recognition criteria in the *Framework* and fair values is acknowledged in paragraph BC18. In Professor Whittington's view, the inconsistency should be resolved before changing the recognition criteria for intangible assets acquired in a business combination.

---

15 References to the *Framework* in this Dissent are to the IASC's *Framework for the Preparation and Presentation of Financial Statements*, adopted by the Board in 2001 and in effect when the Standard was revised.

Dissent of James J Leisenring from amendments issued in May 2008

DO1   Mr Leisenring dissents from the amendments to IAS 38 *Intangible Assets* made by *Improvements to IFRSs* issued in May 2008.

DO2   Mr Leisenring believes that the Board's amendments introduce a logical flaw into IAS 38. Paragraph 68 states that 'expenditure on an intangible item shall be recognised as an expense when it is incurred unless' specific conditions apply. The amendments to paragraph 69 include guidance on the accounting for expenditure on a tangible rather than an intangible item and therefore the amendment to paragraph 69 is inconsistent with paragraph 68.

DO3   Extending the application of IAS 38 to tangible assets used for advertising also raises application concerns. Are signs constructed by a restaurant chain at their location an advertising expense in the period of construction? Would the costs of putting an entity's name on trucks, airplanes and buildings be an advertising expense in the year incurred? The logic of this amendment would suggest an affirmative answer to these questions even though the result of the expenditure benefits several periods.

DO4   Mr Leisenring believes that if an entity acquires goods, including items such as catalogues, film strips or other materials, the entity should determine whether those goods meet the definition of an asset. In his view, IAS 38 is not relevant for determining whether goods acquired by an entity and which may be used for advertising should be recognised as an asset.

DO5   Mr Leisenring agrees that the potential benefit that might result from having advertised should not be recognised as an intangible asset in accordance with IAS 38.

Dissent of Mary Tokar from *Clarification of Acceptable Methods of Depreciation and Amortisation* (Amendments to IAS 16 and IAS 38) as issued in May 2014

DO1   Ms Tokar is dissenting from the publication of this amendment. She does not object to the IASB's objective of clarifying acceptable methods of depreciation and amortisation, nor to its conclusions to preclude revenue-based depreciation and nor to the introduction of a rebuttable presumption that revenue cannot be used as a basis for amortisation of intangibles. She also agrees that expectations of obsolescence should be considered when determining the useful life of an asset and selecting an amortisation or depreciation method that reflects the pattern of consumption of the asset. However, she is concerned that the amendments will not fully resolve the practice issue that was originally raised with the IFRS Interpretations Committee. She believes that the amendments are not sufficiently clear regarding what evidence is required to overcome the presumption and instead support the use of revenue as the basis for amortisation of an intangible asset. She believes that further guidance should be included to explain when the pattern of consumption of economic benefits is the same as the pattern in which revenue is generated.

IASB documents published to accompany

IAS 39

Financial Instruments: Recognition and Measurement

The text of the unaccompanied standard, IAS 39, is contained in Part A of this edition. Its effective date when issued was 1 January 2005. The text of the Accompanying Guidance on IAS 39 is contained in Part B of this edition. This part presents the following documents:

BASIS FOR CONCLUSIONS

DISSENTING OPINIONS

CONTENTS

© IFRS Foundation

Basis for Conclusions on
IAS 39 *Financial Instruments: Recognition and Measurement*

This Basis for Conclusions accompanies, but is not part of, IAS 39.

In this Basis for Conclusions the terminology has not been amended to reflect the changes made by IAS 1 Presentation of Financial Statements *(as revised in 2007).*

References to the Framework are to IASC's Framework for the Preparation and Presentation of Financial Statements, adopted by the IASB in 2001. In September 2010 the IASB replaced the Framework with the Conceptual Framework for Financial Reporting.

IFRS 9 Financial Instruments *replaced IAS 39. However, the Board did not reconsider most of the requirements of IAS 39 relating to scope, classification and measurement of financial liabilities or derecognition of financial assets and financial liabilities. Accordingly the following were relocated to IFRS 9: paragraphs BC11C, BC15–BC24Y, BC30–BC79A and BC85–BC104.*

BC1   This Basis for Conclusions summarises the International Accounting Standards Board's considerations in reaching the conclusions on revising IAS 39 *Financial Instruments: Recognition and Measurement* in 2003. Individual Board members gave greater weight to some factors than to others.

BC2–   [Deleted]
BC130

Hedging

BC131   The Exposure Draft proposed few changes to the hedge accounting guidance in the original IAS 39. The comments on the Exposure Draft raised several issues in the area of hedge accounting suggesting that the Board should consider these issues in the revised IAS 39. The Board's decisions with regard to these issues are presented in the following paragraphs.

Consideration of the shortcut method in SFAS 133

BC132   SFAS 133 *Accounting for Derivative Instruments and Hedging Activities* issued by the FASB allows an entity to assume no ineffectiveness in a hedge of interest rate risk using an interest rate swap as the hedging instrument, provided specified criteria are met (the 'shortcut method').

BC133   The original IAS 39 and the Exposure Draft precluded the use of the shortcut method. Many comments received on the Exposure Draft argued that IAS 39 should permit use of the shortcut method. The Board considered the issue in developing the Exposure Draft, and discussed it in the round-table discussions that were held in the process of finalising IAS 39.

BC134   The Board noted that, if the shortcut method were permitted, an exception would have to be made to the principle in IAS 39 that ineffectiveness in a hedging relationship is measured and recognised in profit or loss. The Board agreed that no exception to this principle should be made, and therefore concluded that IAS 39 should not permit the shortcut method.

BC135   Additionally, IAS 39 permits the hedging of portions of financial assets and financial liabilities in cases when US GAAP does not. The Board noted that under IAS 39 an entity may hedge a portion of a financial instrument (eg interest rate risk or credit risk), and that if the critical terms of the hedging instrument and the hedged item are the same, the entity would, in many cases, recognise no ineffectiveness.

Hedges of portions of financial assets and financial liabilities (paragraphs 81, 81A, AG99A and AG99B)

BC135A   IAS 39 permits a hedged item to be designated as a portion of the cash flows or fair value of a financial asset or financial liability. In finalising the Exposure Draft *Fair Value Hedge Accounting for a Portfolio Hedge of Interest Rate Risk*, the Board received comments that demonstrated that the meaning of a 'portion' was unclear in this context. Accordingly, the Board decided to amend IAS 39 to provide further guidance on what may be designated as a hedged portion, including confirmation that it is not possible to designate a portion that is greater than the total cash flows of the asset or liability.

Expected effectiveness (paragraphs AG105–AG113)

BC136   Qualification for hedge accounting is based on expectations of future effectiveness (prospective) and evaluation of actual effectiveness (retrospective). In the original IAS 39, the prospective test was expressed as 'almost fully offset', whereas the retrospective test was 'within a range of 80–125 per cent'. The Board considered whether to amend IAS 39 to permit the prospective effectiveness to be within the range of 80–125 per cent rather than 'almost fully offset'. The Board noted that an undesirable consequence of such an amendment could be that entities would deliberately underhedge a hedged item in a cash flow hedge so as to reduce recognised ineffectiveness. Therefore, the Board initially decided to retain the guidance in the original IAS 39.

BC136A   However, when subsequently finalising the requirements for portfolio hedges of interest rate risk, the Board received representations from constituents that some hedges would fail the 'almost fully offset' test in IAS 39, including some hedges that would qualify for the shortcut method in US GAAP and thus be assumed to be 100 per cent effective. The Board was persuaded that the concern described in the previous paragraph that an entity might deliberately underhedge would be met by an explicit statement that an entity could not deliberately hedge less than 100 per cent of the exposure on an item and designate the hedge as a hedge of 100 per cent of the exposure. Therefore, the Board decided to amend IAS 39:

    (a)   to remove the words 'almost fully offset' from the prospective effectiveness test, and replace them by a requirement that the hedge is expected to be 'highly effective'. (This amendment is consistent with the wording in US GAAP.)

(b) to include a statement in the Application Guidance in IAS 39 that if an entity hedges less than 100 per cent of the exposure on an item, such as 85 per cent, it shall designate the hedged item as being 85 per cent of the exposure and shall measure ineffectiveness on the basis of the change in the whole of that designated 85 per cent exposure.

BC136B Additionally, comments made in response to the Exposure Draft *Fair Value Hedge Accounting for a Portfolio Hedge of Interest Rate Risk* demonstrated that it was unclear how the prospective effectiveness test was to be applied. The Board noted that the objective of the test was to ensure there was firm evidence to support an expectation of high effectiveness. Therefore, the Board decided to amend the Standard to clarify that an expectation of high effectiveness may be demonstrated in various ways, including a comparison of past changes in the fair value or cash flows of the hedged item that are attributable to the hedged risk with past changes in the fair value or cash flows of the hedging instrument, or by demonstrating a high statistical correlation between the fair value of cash flows of the hedged item and those of the hedging instrument. The Board noted that the entity may choose a hedge ratio of other than one to one in order to improve the effectiveness of the hedge as described in paragraph AG100.

Hedges of portions of non-financial assets and non-financial liabilities for risk other than foreign currency risk (paragraph 82)

BC137 The Board considered comments on the Exposure Draft that suggested that IAS 39 should permit designating as the hedged risk a risk portion of a non-financial item other than foreign currency risk.

BC138 The Board concluded that IAS 39 should not be amended to permit such designation. It noted that in many cases, changes in the cash flows or fair value of a portion of a non-financial hedged item are difficult to isolate and measure. Moreover, the Board noted that permitting portions of non-financial assets and non-financial liabilities to be designated as the hedged item for risk other than foreign currency risk would compromise the principles of identification of the hedged item and effectiveness testing that the Board has confirmed because the portion could be designated so that no ineffectiveness would ever arise.

BC139 The Board confirmed that non-financial items may be hedged in their entirety when the item the entity is hedging is not the standard item underlying contracts traded in the market. In this context, the Board decided to clarify that a hedge ratio of other than one-to-one may maximise expected effectiveness, and to include guidance on how the hedge ratio that maximises expected effectiveness can be determined.

Loan servicing rights

BC140 The Board also considered whether IAS 39 should permit the interest rate risk portion of loan servicing rights to be designated as the hedged item.

BC141　　The Board considered the argument that interest rate risk can be separately identified and measured in loan servicing rights, and that changes in market interest rates have a predictable and separately measurable effect on the value of loan servicing rights. The Board also considered the possibility of treating loan servicing rights as financial assets (rather than non-financial assets).

BC142　　However, the Board concluded that no exceptions should be permitted for this matter. The Board noted that (a) the interest rate risk and prepayment risk in loan servicing rights are interdependent, and thus inseparable, (b) the fair values of loan servicing rights do not change in a linear fashion as interest rates increase or decrease, and (c) concerns exist about how to isolate and measure the interest rate risk portion of a loan servicing right. Moreover, the Board expressed concern that in jurisdictions in which loan servicing right markets are not developed, the interest rate risk portion may not be measurable.

BC143　　The Board also considered whether IAS 39 should be amended to allow, on an elective basis, the inclusion of loan servicing rights in its scope provided that they are measured at fair value with changes in fair value recognised immediately in profit or loss. The Board noted that this would create two exceptions to the general principles in IAS 39. First, it would create a scope exception because IAS 39 applies only to financial assets and financial liabilities; loan servicing rights are non-financial assets. Second, *requiring* an entity to measure loan servicing rights at fair value through profit or loss would create a further exception, because this treatment is optional (except for items that are held for trading). The Board therefore decided not to amend the scope of IAS 39 for loan servicing rights.

Whether to permit hedge accounting using cash instruments

BC144　　In finalising the amendments to IAS 39, the Board discussed whether an entity should be permitted to designate a financial asset or financial liability other than a derivative (ie a 'cash instrument') as a hedging instrument in hedges of risks other than foreign currency risk. The original IAS 39 precluded such designation because of the different bases for measuring derivatives and cash instruments. The Exposure Draft did not propose a change to this limitation. However, some commentators suggested a change, noting that entities do not distinguish between derivative and non-derivative financial instruments in their hedging and other risk management activities and that entities may have to use a non-derivative financial instrument to hedge risk if no suitable derivative financial instrument exists.

BC145　　The Board acknowledged that some entities use non-derivatives to manage risk. However, it decided to retain the restriction against designating non-derivatives as hedging instruments in hedges of risks other than foreign currency risk. It noted the following arguments in support of this conclusion:

(a) The need for hedge accounting arises in part because derivatives are measured at fair value, whereas the items they hedge may be measured at cost or not recognised at all. Without hedge accounting, an entity might recognise volatility in profit or loss for matched positions. For non-derivative items that are not measured at fair value or for which changes in fair value are not recognised in profit or loss, there is generally no need to adjust the accounting of the hedging instrument or the hedged item to achieve matched recognition of gains and losses in profit or loss.

(b) To allow designation of cash instruments as hedging instruments would diverge from US GAAP: SFAS 133 precludes the designation of non-derivative instruments as hedging instruments except for some foreign currency hedges.

(c) To allow designation of cash instruments as hedging instruments would add complexity to the Standard. More financial instruments would be measured at an amount that represents neither amortised cost nor fair value. Hedge accounting is, and should be, an exception to the normal measurement requirements.

(d) If cash instruments were permitted to be designated as hedging instruments, there would be much less discipline in the accounting model because, in the absence of hedge accounting, a non-derivative may not be selectively measured at fair value. If the entity subsequently decides that it would rather not apply fair value measurement to a cash instrument that had been designated as a hedging instrument, it can breach one of the hedge accounting requirements, conclude that the non-derivative no longer qualifies as a hedging instrument and selectively avoid recognising the changes in fair value of the non-derivative instrument in equity (for a cash flow hedge) or profit or loss (for a fair value hedge).

(e) The most significant use of cash instruments as hedging instruments is to hedge foreign currency exposures, which is permitted under IAS 39.

Whether to treat hedges of forecast transactions as fair value hedges

BC146 The Board considered a suggestion made in some of the comment letters received on the Exposure Draft that a hedge of a forecast transaction should be treated as a fair value hedge, rather than as a cash flow hedge. Some argued that the hedge accounting provisions should be simplified by having only one type of hedge accounting. Some also raised concern about an entity's ability, in some cases, to choose between two hedge accounting methods for the same hedging strategy (ie the choice between designating a forward contract to sell an existing asset as a fair value hedge of the asset or a cash flow hedge of a forecast sale of the asset).

BC147　The Board acknowledged that the hedge accounting provisions would be simplified, and their application more consistent in some situations, if the Standard permitted only one type of hedge accounting. However, the Board concluded that IAS 39 should continue to distinguish between fair value hedge accounting and cash flow hedge accounting. It noted that removing either type of hedge accounting would narrow the range of hedging strategies that could qualify for hedge accounting.

BC148　The Board also noted that treating a hedge of a forecast transaction as a fair value hedge is not appropriate for the following reasons: (a) it would result in the recognition of an asset or liability before the entity has become a party to the contract; (b) amounts would be recognised in the balance sheet that do not meet the definitions of assets and liabilities in the *Framework*; and (c) transactions in which there is no fair value exposure would be treated as if there were a fair value exposure.

Hedges of firm commitments (paragraphs 93 and 94)

BC149　The previous version of IAS 39 required a hedge of a firm commitment to be accounted for as a cash flow hedge. In other words, hedging gains and losses, to the extent that the hedge is effective, were initially recognised in equity and were subsequently 'recycled' to profit or loss in the same period(s) that the hedged firm commitment affected profit or loss (although, when basis adjustment was used, they adjusted the initial carrying amount of an asset or liability recognised in the meantime). Some believe this is appropriate because cash flow hedge accounting for hedges of firm commitments avoids partial recognition of the firm commitment that would otherwise not be recognised. Moreover, some believe it is conceptually incorrect to recognise the hedged fair value exposure of a firm commitment as an asset or liability merely because it has been hedged.

BC150　The Board considered whether hedges of firm commitments should be treated as cash flow hedges or fair value hedges. The Board concluded that hedges of firm commitments should be accounted for as fair value hedges.

BC151　The Board noted that, in concept, a hedge of a firm commitment is a fair value hedge. This is because the fair value of the item being hedged (the firm commitment) changes with changes in the hedged risk.

BC152　The Board was not persuaded by the argument that it is conceptually incorrect to recognise an asset or liability for a firm commitment merely because it has been hedged. It noted that for all fair value hedges, applying hedge accounting has the effect that amounts are recognised as assets or liabilities that would otherwise not be recognised. For example, assume an entity hedges a fixed rate loan asset with a pay-fixed, receive-variable interest rate swap. If there is a loss on the swap, applying fair value hedge accounting requires the offsetting gain on the loan to be recognised, ie the carrying amount of the loan is increased. Thus, applying hedge accounting has the effect of recognising a part of an asset (the increase in the loan's value attributable to interest rate movements) that would otherwise not have been recognised. The only difference in the case of a firm commitment is that, without hedge accounting, none of the commitment is recognised, ie the carrying amount is zero. However, this difference merely reflects that the historical cost of a firm commitment is usually zero. It is not a fundamental difference in concept.

BC153   Furthermore, the Board's decision converges with SFAS 133, and thus eliminates practical problems and eases implementation for entities that report under both standards.

BC154   However, the Board clarified that a hedge of the foreign currency risk of a firm commitment may be treated as either a fair value hedge or a cash flow hedge because foreign currency risk affects both the cash flows and the fair value of the hedged item. Accordingly a foreign currency cash flow hedge of a forecast transaction need not be re-designated as a fair value hedge when the forecast transaction becomes a firm commitment.

Basis adjustments (paragraphs 97–99)

BC155   The question of basis adjustment arises when an entity hedges the future purchase of an asset or the future issue of a liability. One example is that of a US entity that expects to make a future purchase of a German machine that it will pay for in euro. The entity enters into a derivative to hedge against possible future changes in the US dollar/euro exchange rate. Such a hedge is classified as a cash flow hedge under IAS 39, with the effect that gains and losses on the hedging instrument (to the extent that the hedge is effective) are initially recognised in equity.[1] The question the Board considered is what the accounting should be once the future transaction takes place. In its deliberations on this issue, the Board discussed the following approaches:

(a)   to remove the hedging gain or loss from equity and recognise it as part of the initial carrying amount of the asset or liability (in the example above, the machine). In future periods, the hedging gain or loss is automatically recognised in profit or loss by being included in amounts such as depreciation expense (for a fixed asset), interest income or expense (for a financial asset or financial liability), or cost of sales (for inventories). This treatment is commonly referred to as 'basis adjustment'.

(b)   to leave the hedging gain or loss in equity. In future periods, the gain or loss on the hedging instrument is 'recycled' to profit or loss in the same period(s) as the acquired asset or liability affects profit or loss. This recycling requires a separate adjustment and is not automatic.

BC156   It should be noted that both approaches have the same effect on profit or loss and net assets for all periods affected, so long as the hedge is accounted for as a cash flow hedge. The difference relates to balance sheet presentation and, possibly, the line item in the income statement.

---

1   As a consequence of the revision of IAS 1 *Presentation of Financial Statements* in 2007 such gains and losses are recognised in other comprehensive income.

BC157 In the Exposure Draft, the Board proposed that the 'basis adjustment' approach for forecast transactions (approach (a)) should be eliminated and replaced by approach (b) above. It further noted that eliminating the basis adjustment approach would enable IAS 39 to converge with SFAS 133.

BC158 Many of the comments received from constituents disagreed with the proposal in the Exposure Draft. Those responses argued that it would unnecessarily complicate the accounting to leave the hedging gain or loss in equity when the hedged forecast transaction occurs. They particularly noted that tracking the effects of cash flow hedges after the asset or liability is acquired would be complicated and would require systems changes. They also pointed out that treating hedges of firm commitments as fair value hedges has the same effect as a basis adjustment when the firm commitment results in the recognition of an asset or liability. For example, for a perfectly effective hedge of the foreign currency risk of a firm commitment to buy a machine, the effect is to recognise the machine initially at its foreign currency price translated at the forward rate in effect at the inception of the hedge rather than the spot rate. Therefore, they questioned whether it is consistent to treat a hedge of a firm commitment as a fair value hedge while precluding basis adjustments for hedges of forecast transactions.

BC159 Others believe that a basis adjustment is difficult to justify in principle for forecast transactions, and also argue that such basis adjustments impair comparability of financial information. In other words, two identical assets that are purchased at the same time and in the same way, except for the fact that one was hedged, should not be recognised at different amounts.

BC160 The Board concluded that IAS 39 should distinguish between hedges of forecast transactions that will result in the recognition of a *financial* asset or a *financial* liability and those that will result in the recognition of a *non-financial* asset or a *non-financial* liability.

Basis adjustments for hedges of forecast transactions that will result in the recognition of a financial asset or a financial liability

BC161 For hedges of forecast transactions that will result in the recognition of a financial asset or a financial liability, the Board concluded that basis adjustments are not appropriate. Its reason was that basis adjustments cause the initial carrying amount of acquired assets (or assumed liabilities) arising from forecast transactions to move away from fair value and hence would override the requirement in IAS 39 to measure a financial instrument initially at its fair value.

BC161A If a hedged forecast transaction results in the recognition of a financial asset or a financial liability, paragraph 97 of IAS 39 required the associated gains or losses on hedging instruments to be reclassified from equity to profit or loss as a reclassification adjustment in the same period or periods during which the hedged item affects profit or loss (such as in the periods that interest income or interest expense is recognised).

BC161B   The Board was informed that there was uncertainty about how paragraph 97 should be applied when the designated cash flow exposure being hedged differs from the financial instrument arising from the hedged forecast cash flows.

BC161C   The example below illustrates the issue:

> An entity applies the guidance in the answer to Question F.6.2 of the guidance on implementing IAS 39.[a] On 1 January 20X0 the entity designates forecast cash flows for the risk of variability arising from changes in interest rates. Those forecast cash flows arise from the repricing of existing financial instruments and are scheduled for 1 April 20X0. The entity is exposed to variability in cash flows for the three-month period beginning on 1 April 20X0 attributable to changes in interest rate risk that occur from 1 January 20X0 to 31 March 20X0.
>
> The occurrence of the forecast cash flows is deemed to be highly probable and all the other relevant hedge accounting criteria are met.
>
> The financial instrument that results from the hedged forecast cash flows is a five-year interest-bearing instrument.

(a)   IFRS 9 *Financial Instruments* deletes the guidance in IAS 39.

BC161D   Paragraph 97 required the gains or losses on the hedging instrument to be reclassified from equity to profit or loss as a reclassification adjustment in the same period or periods during which the asset acquired or liability assumed affected profit or loss. The financial instrument that was recognised is a five-year instrument that will affect profit or loss for five years. The wording in paragraph 97 suggested that the gains or losses should be reclassified over five years, even though the cash flows designated as the hedged item were hedged for the effects of interest rate changes over only a three-month period.

BC161E   The Board believes that the wording of paragraph 97 did not reflect the underlying rationale in hedge accounting, ie that the gains or losses on the hedging instrument should offset the gains or losses on the hedged item, and the offset should be reflected in profit or loss by way of reclassification adjustments.

BC161F   The Board believes that in the example set out above the gains or losses should be reclassified over a period of three months beginning on 1 April 20X0, and not over a period of five years beginning on 1 April 20X0.

BC161G   Consequently, in *Improvements to IFRSs* issued in April 2009, the Board amended paragraph 97 of IAS 39 to clarify that the gains or losses on the hedged instrument should be reclassified from equity to profit or loss during the period that the hedged forecast cash flows affect profit or loss. The Board also decided that to avoid similar confusion paragraph 100 of IAS 39 should be amended to be consistent with paragraph 97.

Basis adjustments for hedges of forecast transactions that will result in the recognition of a non-financial asset or a non-financial liability

BC162   For hedges of forecast transactions that will result in the recognition of a non-financial asset or a non-financial liability, the Board decided to permit entities a choice of whether to apply basis adjustment.

BC163   The Board considered the argument that changes in the fair value of the hedging instrument are appropriately included in the initial carrying amount of the recognised asset or liability because such changes represent a part of the 'cost' of that asset or liability. Although the Board has not yet considered the broader issue of what costs may be capitalised at initial recognition, the Board believes that its decision to provide an option for basis adjustments in the case of non-financial items will not pre-empt that future discussion. The Board also recognised that financial items and non-financial items are not necessarily measured at the same amount on initial recognition, because financial items are measured at fair value and non-financial items are measured at cost.

BC164   The Board concluded that, on balance, providing entities with a choice in this case was appropriate. The Board took the view that allowing basis adjustments addresses the concern that precluding basis adjustments complicates the accounting for hedges of forecast transactions. In addition, the number of balance sheet line items that could be affected is quite small, generally being only property, plant and equipment, inventory and the cash flow hedge line item in equity. The Board also noted that US GAAP precludes basis adjustments and that applying a basis adjustment is inconsistent with the accounting for hedges of forecast transactions that will result in the recognition of a financial asset or a financial liability. The Board acknowledged the merits of these arguments, and recognised that by permitting a choice in IAS 39, entities could apply the accounting treatment required by US GAAP.

Hedging using internal contracts

BC165   IAS 39 does not preclude entities from using internal contracts as a risk management tool, or as a tracking device in applying hedge accounting for external contracts that hedge external positions. Furthermore, IAS 39 permits hedge accounting to be applied to transactions between entities in the same group in the *separate reporting* of those entities. However, IAS 39 does not permit hedge accounting for transactions between entities in the same group in consolidated financial statements. The reason is the fundamental requirement of consolidation that the accounting effects of internal contracts should be eliminated in consolidated financial statements, including any internally generated gains or losses. Designating internal contracts as hedging instruments could result in non-elimination of internal gains and losses and have other accounting effects. The Exposure Draft did not propose any change in this area.

BC166 To illustrate, assume the banking book division of Bank A enters into an internal interest rate swap with the trading book division of the same bank. The purpose is to hedge the net interest rate risk exposure in the banking book of a group of similar fixed rate loan assets funded by floating rate liabilities. Under the swap, the banking book pays fixed interest payments to the trading book and receives variable interest rate payments in return. The bank wants to designate the internal interest rate swap in the banking book as a hedging instrument in its consolidated financial statements.

BC167 If the internal swap in the banking book is designated as a hedging instrument in a cash flow hedge of the liabilities, and the internal swap in the trading book is classified as held for trading, internal gains and losses on that internal swap would not be eliminated. This is because the gains and losses on the internal swap in the banking book would be recognised in equity[2] to the extent the hedge is effective and the gains and losses on the internal swap in the trading book would be recognised in profit or loss.

BC168 If the internal swap in the banking book is designated as a hedging instrument in a fair value hedge of the loan assets and the internal swap in the trading book is classified as held for trading, the changes in the fair value of the internal swap would offset both in total net assets in the balance sheet and profit or loss. However, without elimination of the internal swap, there would be an adjustment to the carrying amount of the hedged loan asset in the banking book to reflect the change in the fair value attributable to the risk hedged by the internal contract. Moreover, to reflect the effect of the internal swap the bank would in effect recognise the fixed rate loan at a floating interest rate and recognise an offsetting trading gain or loss in the income statement. Hence the internal swap would have accounting effects.

BC169 Some respondents to the Exposure Draft and some participants in the round-tables objected to not being able to obtain hedge accounting in the consolidated financial statements for internal contracts between subsidiaries or between a subsidiary and the parent (as illustrated above). Among other things, they emphasised that the use of internal contracts is a key risk management tool and that the accounting should reflect the way in which risk is managed. Some suggested that IAS 39 should be changed to make it consistent with US GAAP, which allows the designation of internal derivative contracts as hedging instruments in cash flow hedges of forecast foreign currency transactions in specified, limited circumstances.

BC170 In considering these comments, the Board noted that the following principles apply to consolidated financial statements:

(a) financial statements provide financial information about an entity or group as a whole (as that of a single entity). Financial statements do not provide financial information about an entity as if it were two separate entities.

---

2 As a consequence of the revision of IAS 1 *Presentation of Financial Statements* in 2007 such gains and losses are recognised in other comprehensive income.

(b)   a fundamental principle of consolidation is that intragroup balances and intragroup transactions are eliminated in full. Permitting the designation of internal contracts as hedging instruments would require a change to the consolidation principles.

(c)   it is conceptually wrong to permit an entity to recognise internally generated gains and losses or make other accounting adjustments because of internal transactions. No external event has occurred.

(d)   an ability to recognise internally generated gains and losses could result in abuse in the absence of requirements about how entities should manage and control the associated risks. It is not the purpose of accounting standards to prescribe how entities should manage and control risks.

(e)   permitting the designation of internal contracts as hedging instruments violates the following requirements in IAS 39:

(i)   the prohibition against designating as a hedging instrument a non-derivative financial asset or non-derivative financial liability for other than foreign currency risk. To illustrate, if an entity has two offsetting internal contracts and one is the designated hedging instrument in a fair value hedge of a non-derivative asset and the other is the designated hedging instrument in a fair value hedge of a non-derivative liability, from the entity's perspective the effect is to designate a hedging relationship between the asset and the liability (ie a non-derivative asset or non-derivative liability is used as the hedging instrument).

(ii)   the prohibition on designating a net position of assets and liabilities as the hedged item. To illustrate, an entity has two internal contracts. One is designated in a fair value hedge of an asset and the other in a fair value hedge of a liability. The two internal contracts do not fully offset, so the entity lays off the net risk exposure by entering into a net external derivative. In that case, the effect from the entity's perspective is to designate a hedging relationship between the net external derivative and a net position of an asset and a liability.

(iii)   the option to fair value assets and liabilities does not extend to portions of assets and liabilities.

(f)   the Board is considering separately whether to make an amendment to IAS 39 to facilitate fair value hedge accounting for portfolio hedges of interest rate risk. The Board believes that that is a better way to address the concerns raised about symmetry with risk management systems than permitting the designation of internal contracts as hedging instruments.

(g)   the Board decided to permit an option to measure any financial asset or financial liability at fair value with changes in fair value recognised in profit or loss. This enables an entity to measure matching asset/liability positions at fair value without a need for hedge accounting.

BC171   The Board reaffirmed that it is a fundamental principle of consolidation that any accounting effect of internal contracts is eliminated on consolidation. The Board decided that no exception to this principle should be made in IAS 39. Consistently with this decision, the Board also decided not to explore an amendment to permit internal derivative contracts to be designated as hedging instruments in hedges of some forecast foreign currency transactions, as is permitted by SFAS 138 *Accounting for Certain Derivative Instruments and Certain Hedging Activities*.

BC172   The Board also decided to clarify that IAS 39 does not preclude hedge accounting for transactions between entities in the same group in individual or separate financial statements of those entities because they are not internal to the entity (ie the individual entity).

BC172A   Previously, paragraphs 73 and 80 referred to the need for hedging instruments to involve a party external to the reporting entity. In doing so, they used a segment as an example of a reporting entity. However, IFRS 8 *Operating Segments* requires disclosure of information that is reported to the chief operating decision maker even if this is on a non-IFRS basis. Therefore, the two IFRSs appeared to conflict. In *Improvements to IFRSs* issued in May 2008 and April 2009, the Board removed from paragraphs 73 and 80 references to the designation of hedging instruments at the segment level.

Eligible hedged items in particular situations (paragraphs AG99BA, AG99E, AG99F, AG110A and AG110B)

BC172B   The Board amended IAS 39 in July 2008 to clarify the application of the principles that determine whether a hedged risk or portion of cash flows is eligible for designation in particular situations. This followed a request by the IFRIC for guidance.

BC172C   The responses to the exposure draft *Exposures Qualifying for Hedge Accounting* demonstrated that diversity in practice existed, or was likely to occur, in two situations:

(a)   the designation of a one-sided risk in a hedged item

(b)   the designation of inflation as a hedged risk or portion in particular situations.

Designation of a one-sided risk in a hedged item

BC172D   The IFRIC received requests for guidance on whether an entity can designate a purchased option in its entirety as the hedging instrument in a cash flow hedge of a highly probable forecast transaction in such a way that all changes in the fair value of the purchased option, including changes in the time value, are regarded as effective and would be recognised in other comprehensive income. The exposure draft proposed to amend IAS 39 to clarify that such a designation was not allowed.

BC172E   After considering the responses to the exposure draft, the Board confirmed that the designation set out in paragraph BC172D is not permitted.

BC172F   The Board reached that decision by considering the variability of future cash flow outcomes resulting from a price increase of a forecast commodity purchase (a one-sided risk). The Board noted that the forecast transaction contained no separately identifiable risk that affects profit or loss that is equivalent to the time value of a purchased option hedging instrument (with the same principal terms as the designated risk). The Board concluded that the intrinsic value of a purchased option, but not its time value, reflects a one-sided risk in a hedged item. The Board then considered a purchased option designated in its entirety as the hedging instrument. The Board noted that hedge accounting is based on a principle of offsetting changes in fair value or cash flows between the hedging instrument and the hedged item. Because a designated one-sided risk does not contain the time value of a purchased option hedging instrument, the Board noted that there will be no offset between the cash flows relating to the time value of the option premium paid and the designated hedged risk. Therefore, the Board concluded that a purchased option designated in its entirety as the hedging instrument of a one-sided risk will not be perfectly effective.

Designation of inflation in particular situations

BC172G   The IFRIC received a request for guidance on whether, for a hedge of a fixed rate financial instrument, an entity can designate inflation as the hedged item. The exposure draft proposed to amend IAS 39 to clarify that such a designation was not allowed.

BC172H   After considering the responses to the exposure draft, the Board acknowledged that expectations of future inflation rates can be viewed as an economic component of nominal interest. However, the Board also noted that hedge accounting is an exception to normal accounting principles for the hedged item (fair value hedges) or hedging instrument (cash flow hedges). To ensure a disciplined use of hedge accounting the Board noted that restrictions regarding eligible hedged items are necessary, especially if something other than the entire fair value or cash flow variability of a hedged item is designated.

BC172I   The Board noted that paragraph 81 permits an entity to designate as the hedged item something other than the entire fair value change or cash flow variability of a financial instrument. For example, an entity may designate some (but not all) risks of a financial instrument, or some (but not all) cash flows of a financial instrument (a 'portion').

BC172J   The Board noted that, to be eligible for hedge accounting, the designated risks and portions must be separately identifiable components of the financial instrument, and changes in the fair value or cash flows of the entire financial instrument arising from changes in the designated risks and portions must be reliably measurable. The Board noted that these principles were important in order for the effectiveness requirements set out in paragraph 88 to be applied in a meaningful way. The Board also noted that deciding whether designated risks and portions are separately identifiable and reliably measurable requires judgement. However, the Board confirmed that unless the inflation portion is a contractually specified portion of cash flows and other cash flows of the financial instrument are not affected by the inflation portion, inflation is not separately identifiable and reliably measurable and is not eligible for designation as a hedged risk or portion of a financial instrument.

Fair value hedge accounting for a portfolio hedge of interest rate risk

Background

BC173   The Exposure Draft of proposed improvements to IAS 39 published in June 2002 did not propose any substantial changes to the requirements for hedge accounting as they applied to a portfolio hedge of interest rate risk. However, some of the comment letters on the Exposure Draft and participants in the round-table discussions raised this issue. In particular, some were concerned that portfolio hedging strategies they regarded as effective hedges would not have qualified for fair value hedge accounting in accordance with previous versions of IAS 39. Rather, they would have either:

(a)   not qualified for hedge accounting at all, with the result that reported profit or loss would be volatile; or

(b)   qualified only for cash flow hedge accounting, with the result that reported equity would be volatile.

BC174   In the light of these concerns, the Board decided to explore whether and how IAS 39 could be amended to enable fair value hedge accounting to be used more readily for portfolio hedges of interest rate risk. As a result, in August 2003 the Board published a second Exposure Draft, *Fair Value Hedge Accounting for a Portfolio Hedge of Interest Rate Risk*, with a comment deadline of 14 November 2003. More than 120 comment letters were received. The amendments proposed in this second Exposure Draft were finalised in March 2004. Paragraphs BC135A–BC136B and BC175–BC220 summarise the Board's considerations in reaching conclusions on the issues raised.

Scope

BC175   The Board decided to limit any amendments to IAS 39 to applying fair value hedge accounting to a hedge of interest rate risk on a portfolio of items. In making this decision it noted that:

(a)   implementation guidance on IAS 39[3] explains how to apply cash flow hedge accounting to a hedge of the interest rate risk on a portfolio of items.

---

3   IFRS 9 *Financial Instruments* deleted the guidance on implementing IAS 39.

(b)   the issues that arise for a portfolio hedge of interest rate risk are different from those that arise for hedges of individual items and for hedges of other risks. In particular, the three issues discussed in paragraph BC176 do not arise in combination for such other hedging arrangements.

The issue: why fair value hedge accounting was difficult to achieve in accordance with previous versions of IAS 39

BC176   The Board identified the following three main reasons why a portfolio hedge of interest rate risk might not have qualified for fair value hedge accounting in accordance with previous versions of IAS 39.

(a)   Typically, many of the assets that are included in a portfolio hedge are prepayable, ie the counterparty has a right to repay the item before its contractual repricing date. Such assets contain a prepayment option whose fair value changes as interest rates change. However, the derivative that is used as the hedging instrument typically is not prepayable, ie it does not contain a prepayment option. When interest rates change, the resulting change in the fair value of the hedged item (which is prepayable) differs from the change in fair value of the hedging derivative (which is not prepayable), with the result that the hedge may not meet IAS 39's effectiveness tests.[4] Furthermore, prepayment risk may have the effect that the items included in a portfolio hedge fail the requirement[5] that a group of hedged assets or liabilities must be 'similar' and the related requirement[6] that 'the change in fair value attributable to the hedged risk for each individual item in the group shall be expected to be approximately proportional to the overall change in fair value attributable to the hedged risk of the group of items'.

(b)   IAS 39[7] prohibits the designation of an overall net position (eg the net of fixed rate assets and fixed rate liabilities) as the hedged item. Rather, it requires individual assets (or liabilities), or groups of similar assets (or similar liabilities), that share the risk exposure equal in amount to the net position to be designated as the hedged item. For example, if an entity has a portfolio of CU100 of assets and CU80 of liabilities, IAS 39 requires that individual assets or a group of similar assets of CU20 are designated as the hedged item. However, for risk management purposes, entities often seek to hedge the net position. This net position changes each period as items are repriced or derecognised and as new items are originated. Hence, the individual items designated as the hedged item also need to be changed each period. This requires de- and redesignation of the individual items that constitute the hedged item, which gives rise to significant systems needs.

---

4   see IAS 39, paragraph AG105
5   see IAS 39, paragraph 78
6   see IAS 39, paragraph 83
7   see IAS 39, paragraph AG101

(c) Fair value hedge accounting requires the carrying amount of the hedged item to be adjusted for the effect of changes in the hedged risk.[8] Applied to a portfolio hedge, this could involve changing the carrying amounts of many thousands of individual items. Also, for any items subsequently de-designated from being hedged, the revised carrying amount must be amortised over the item's remaining life.[9] This, too, gives rise to significant systems needs.

BC177 The Board decided that any change to IAS 39 must be consistent with the principles that underlie IAS 39's requirements on derivatives and hedge accounting. The three principles that are most relevant to a portfolio hedge of interest rate risk are:

(a) derivatives should be measured at fair value;

(b) hedge ineffectiveness should be identified and recognised in profit or loss;[10] and

(c) only items that are assets and liabilities should be recognised as such in the balance sheet. Deferred losses are not assets and deferred gains are not liabilities. However, if an asset or liability is hedged, any change in its fair value that is attributable to the hedged risk should be recognised in the balance sheet.

Prepayment risk

BC178 In considering the issue described in paragraph BC176(a), the Board noted that a prepayable item can be viewed as a combination of a non-prepayable item and a prepayment option. It follows that the fair value of a fixed rate prepayable item changes for two reasons when interest rates move:

(a) the fair value of the contracted cash flows to the contractual repricing date changes (because the rate used to discount them changes); and

(b) the fair value of the prepayment option changes (reflecting, among other things, that the likelihood of prepayment is affected by interest rates).

BC179 The Board also noted that, for risk management purposes, many entities do not consider these two effects separately. Instead they incorporate the effect of prepayments by grouping the hedged portfolio into repricing time periods based on *expected* repayment dates (rather than contractual repayment dates). For example, an entity with a portfolio of 25-year mortgages of CU100 may expect 5 per cent of that portfolio to repay in one year's time, in which case it schedules an amount of CU5 into a 12-month time period. The entity schedules all other items contained in its portfolio in a similar way (ie on the basis of expected repayment dates) and hedges all or part of the resulting overall net position in each repricing time period.

---

8   see IAS 39, paragraph 89(b)

9   see IAS 39, paragraph 92

10 Subject to the same materiality considerations that apply in this context as throughout IFRSs.

BC180　The Board decided to permit the scheduling that is used for risk management purposes, ie on the basis of expected repayment dates, to be used as a basis for the designation necessary for hedge accounting. As a result, an entity would not be required to compute the effect that a change in interest rates has on the fair value of the prepayment option embedded in a prepayable item. Instead, it could incorporate the effect of a change in interest rates on prepayments by grouping the hedged portfolio into repricing time periods based on expected repayment dates. The Board noted that this approach has significant practical advantages for preparers of financial statements, because it allows them to use the data they use for risk management. The Board also noted that the approach is consistent with paragraph 81 of IAS 39, which permits hedge accounting for a portion of a financial asset or financial liability. However, as discussed further in paragraphs BC193–BC206, the Board also concluded that if the entity changes its estimates of the time periods in which items are expected to repay (eg in the light of recent prepayment experience), ineffectiveness will arise, regardless of whether the revision in estimates results in more or less being scheduled in a particular time period.

BC181　The Board also noted that if the items in the hedged portfolio are subject to different amounts of prepayment risk, they may fail the test in paragraph 78 of being similar and the related requirement in paragraph 83 that the change in fair value attributable to the hedged risk for each individual item in the group is expected to be approximately proportional to the overall change in fair value attributable to the hedged risk of the group of items. The Board decided that, in the context of a portfolio hedge of interest rate risk, these requirements could be inconsistent with the Board's decision, set out in the previous paragraph, on how to incorporate the effects of prepayment risk. Accordingly, the Board decided that they should not apply. Instead, the financial assets or financial liabilities included in a portfolio hedge of interest rate risk need only share the risk being hedged.

Designation of the hedged item and liabilities with a demand feature

BC182　The Board considered two main ways to overcome the issue noted in paragraph BC176(b). These were:

(a)　to designate the hedged item as the overall net position that results from a portfolio containing assets and liabilities. For example, if a repricing time period contains CU100 of fixed rate assets and CU90 of fixed rate liabilities, the net position of CU10 would be designated as the hedged item.

(b)　to designate the hedged item as a portion of the assets (ie assets of CU10 in the above example), but not to require individual assets to be designated.

BC183　Some of those who commented on the Exposure Draft favoured designation of the overall net position in a portfolio that contains assets and liabilities. In their view, existing asset-liability management (ALM) systems treat the identified assets and liabilities as a natural hedge. Management's decisions about additional hedging focus on the entity's remaining net exposure. They observe that designation based on a portion of either the assets or the liabilities is not consistent with existing ALM systems and would entail additional systems costs.

BC184   In considering questions of designation, the Board was also concerned about questions of measurement. In particular, the Board observed that fair value hedge accounting requires measurement of the change in fair value of the hedged item attributable to the risk being hedged. Designation based on the net position would require the assets and the liabilities in a portfolio each to be measured at fair value (for the risk being hedged) in order to compute the fair value of the net position. Although statistical and other techniques can be used to estimate these fair values, the Board concluded that it is not appropriate to assume that the change in fair value of the hedging instrument is equal to the change in fair value of the net position.

BC185   The Board noted that under the first approach in paragraph BC182 (designating an overall net position), an issue arises if the entity has liabilities that are repayable on demand or after a notice period (referred to below as 'demandable liabilities'). This includes items such as demand deposits and some types of time deposits. The Board was informed that, when managing interest rate risk, many entities that have demandable liabilities include them in a portfolio hedge by scheduling them to the date when they *expect* the total amount of demandable liabilities in the portfolio to be due because of net withdrawals from the accounts in the portfolio. This expected repayment date is typically a period covering several years into the future (eg 0–10 years hence). The Board was also informed that some entities wish to apply fair value hedge accounting based on this scheduling, ie they wish to include demandable liabilities in a fair value portfolio hedge by scheduling them on the basis of their expected repayment dates. The arguments for this view are:

(a)   it is consistent with how demandable liabilities are scheduled for risk management purposes. Interest rate risk management involves hedging the interest rate margin resulting from assets and liabilities and not the fair value of all or part of the assets and liabilities included in the hedged portfolio. The interest rate margin of a specific period is subject to variability as soon as the amount of fixed rate assets in that period differs from the amount of fixed rate liabilities in that period.

(b)   it is consistent with the treatment of prepayable assets to include demandable liabilities in a portfolio hedge based on expected repayment dates.

(c)   as with prepayable assets, expected maturities for demandable liabilities are based on the historical behaviour of customers.

(d)   applying the fair value hedge accounting framework to a portfolio that includes demandable liabilities would not entail an immediate gain on origination of such liabilities because all assets and liabilities enter the hedged portfolio at their carrying amounts. Furthermore, IAS 39 requires the carrying amount of a financial liability on its initial recognition to be its fair value, which normally equates to the transaction price (ie the amount deposited).[11]

(e) historical analysis shows that a base level of a portfolio of demandable liabilities, such as chequing accounts, is very stable. Whilst a portion of the demandable liabilities varies with interest rates, the remaining portion—the base level—does not. Hence, entities regard this base level as a long-term fixed rate item and include it as such in the scheduling that is used for risk management purposes.

(f) the distinction between 'old' and 'new' money makes little sense at a portfolio level. The portfolio behaves like a long-term item even if individual liabilities do not.

BC186 The Board noted that this issue is related to that of how to measure the fair value of a demandable liability. In particular, it interrelates with the requirement in IAS 39 that the fair value of a liability with a demand feature is not less than the amount payable on demand, discounted from the first date that the amount could be required to be paid.[12] This requirement applies to all liabilities with a demand feature, not only to those included in a portfolio hedge.

BC187 The Board also noted that:

(a) although entities, when managing risk, may schedule demandable liabilities based on the expected repayment date of the total balance of a portfolio of accounts, the deposit liabilities included in that balance are unlikely to be outstanding for an extended period (eg several years). Rather, these deposits are usually expected to be withdrawn within a short time (eg a few months or less), although they may be replaced by new deposits. Put another way, the balance of the portfolio is relatively stable only because withdrawals on some accounts (which usually occur relatively quickly) are offset by new deposits into others. Thus, the liability being hedged is actually the forecast replacement of existing deposits by the receipt of new deposits. IAS 39 does not permit a hedge of such a forecast transaction to qualify for fair value hedge accounting. Rather, fair value hedge accounting can be applied only to the liability (or asset) or firm commitment that exists today.

(b) a portfolio of demandable liabilities is similar to a portfolio of trade payables. Both comprise individual balances that usually are expected to be paid within a short time (eg a few months or less) and replaced by new balances. Also, for both, there is an amount—the base level—that is expected to be stable and present indefinitely. Hence, if the Board were to permit demandable liabilities to be included in a fair value hedge on the basis of a stable base level created by expected replacements, it should similarly allow a hedge of a portfolio of trade payables to qualify for fair value hedge accounting on this basis.

---

11   IFRS 9 *Financial Instruments* replaced IAS 39.
12   IFRS 9 *Financial Instruments* replaced IAS 39.

(c)   a portfolio of similar core deposits is not different from an individual deposit, other than that, in the light of the 'law of large numbers', the behaviour of the portfolio is more predictable. There are no diversification effects from aggregating many similar items.

(d)   it would be inconsistent with the requirement in IAS 39 that the fair value of a liability with a demand feature is not less than the amount payable on demand, discounted from the first date that the amount could be required to be paid, to schedule such liabilities for hedging purposes using a different date. For example, consider a deposit of CU100 that can be withdrawn on demand without penalty. IAS 39 states that the fair value of such a deposit is CU100. That fair value is unaffected by interest rates and does not change when interest rates move. Accordingly, the demand deposit cannot be included in a fair value hedge of interest rate risk—there is no fair value exposure to hedge.

BC188   For these reasons, the Board concluded that demandable liabilities should not be included in a portfolio hedge on the basis of the expected repayment date of the *total balance of a portfolio* of demandable liabilities, ie including expected rollovers or replacements of existing deposits by new ones. However, as part of its consideration of comments received on the Exposure Draft, the Board also considered whether a demandable liability, such as a demand deposit, could be included in a portfolio hedge based on the expected repayment date of the *existing balance of individual deposits*, ie ignoring any rollovers or replacements of existing deposits by new deposits. The Board noted the following.

(a)   For many demandable liabilities, this approach would imply a much earlier expected repayment date than is generally assumed for risk management purposes. In particular, for chequing accounts it would probably imply an expected maturity of a few months or less. However, for other demandable liabilities, such as fixed term deposits that can be withdrawn only by the depositor incurring a significant penalty, it might imply an expected repayment date that is closer to that assumed for risk management.

(b)   This approach implies that the *fair value* of the demandable liability should also reflect the expected repayment date of the existing balance, ie that the fair value of a demandable deposit liability is the present value of the amount of the deposit discounted from the expected repayment date. The Board noted that it would be inconsistent to permit fair value hedge accounting to be based on the expected repayment date, but to measure the fair value of the liability on initial recognition on a different basis. The Board also noted that this approach would give rise to a difference on initial recognition between the amount deposited and the fair value recognised in the balance sheet. This, in turn, gives rise to the issue of what the difference represents. Possibilities the Board considered include (i) the value of the depositor's option to withdraw its money before the expected maturity, (ii) prepaid servicing costs or (iii) a gain. The Board did not reach a conclusion on what the difference represents, but agreed that if it were to require such differences to be recognised, this would apply to all demandable liabilities, not only to those included in a portfolio hedge. Such a requirement would represent a significant change from present practice.

(c)   If the fair value of a demandable deposit liability at the date of initial recognition is deemed to equal the amount deposited, a fair value portfolio hedge based on an expected repayment date is unlikely to be effective. This is because such deposits typically pay interest at a rate that is significantly lower than that being hedged (eg the deposits may pay interest at zero or at very low rates, whereas the interest rate being hedged may be LIBOR or a similar benchmark rate). Hence, the fair value of the deposit will be significantly less sensitive to interest rate changes than that of the hedging instrument.

(d)   The question of how to fair value a demandable liability is closely related to issues being debated by the Board in other projects, including Insurance (phase II), Revenue Recognition, Leases and Measurement. The Board's discussions in these other projects are continuing and it would be premature to reach a conclusion in the context of portfolio hedging without considering the implications for these other projects.

BC189   As a result, the Board decided:

(a)   to confirm the requirement in IAS 39 that 'the fair value of a financial liability with a demand feature (eg a demand deposit) is not less than the amount payable on demand, discounted from the first date that the amount could be required to be paid',[13] and

(b)   consequently, that a demandable liability cannot qualify for fair value hedge accounting for any time period beyond the shortest period in which the counterparty can demand payment.

The Board noted that, depending on the outcome of its discussions in other projects (principally Insurance (phase II), Revenue Recognition, Leases and Measurement), it might reconsider these decisions at some time in the future.

BC190   The Board also noted that what is designated as the hedged item in a portfolio hedge affects the relevance of this issue, at least to some extent. In particular, if the hedged item is designated as a portion *of the assets* in a portfolio, this issue is irrelevant. To illustrate, assume that in a particular repricing time period an entity has CU100 of fixed rate assets and CU80 of what it regards as fixed rate liabilities and the entity wishes to hedge its net exposure of CU20. Also assume that all of the liabilities are demandable liabilities and the time period is later than that containing the earliest date on which the items can be repaid. If the hedged item is designated as CU20 of *assets*, then the demandable *liabilities* are not included in the hedged item, but rather are used only to determine how much of the assets the entity wishes to designate as being hedged. In such a case, whether the demandable liabilities can be

---

13   IFRS 9 *Financial Instruments* replaced IAS 39.

designated as a hedged item in a fair value hedge is irrelevant. However, if the overall net position were to be designated as the hedged item, because the net position comprises CU100 of assets and CU80 of demandable liabilities, whether the demandable liabilities can be designated as a hedged item in a fair value hedge becomes critical.

BC191 Given the above points, the Board decided that a portion of assets or liabilities (rather than an overall net position) may be designated as the hedged item, to overcome part of the demandable liabilities issue. It also noted that this approach is consistent with IAS 39,[14] whereas designating an overall net position is not. IAS 39[15] prohibits an overall net position from being designated as the hedged item, but permits a similar effect to be achieved by designating an amount of assets (or liabilities) equal to the net position.

BC192 However, the Board also recognised that this method of designation would not fully resolve the demandable liabilities issue. In particular, the issue is still relevant if, in a particular repricing time period, the entity has so many demandable liabilities whose earliest repayment date is before that time period that (a) they comprise nearly all of what the entity regards as its fixed rate liabilities and (b) its fixed rate liabilities (including the demandable liabilities) exceed its fixed rate assets in this repricing time period. In this case, the entity is in a net liability position. Thus, it needs to designate an amount of the *liabilities* as the hedged item. But unless it has sufficient fixed rate liabilities other than those that can be demanded before that time period, this implies designating the demandable liabilities as the hedged item. Consistently with the Board's decision discussed above, such a hedge does not qualify for fair value hedge accounting. (If the liabilities are non-interest bearing, they cannot be designated as the hedged item in a cash flow hedge because their cash flows do not vary with changes in interest rates, ie there is no cash flow exposure to interest rates. However, the hedging relationship may qualify for cash flow hedge accounting if designated as a hedge of associated assets.)

What portion of assets should be designated and the impact on ineffectiveness

BC193 Having decided that a portion of assets (or liabilities) could be designated as the hedged item, the Board considered how to overcome the systems problems noted in paragraph BC176(b) and (c). The Board noted that these problems arise from designating individual assets (or liabilities) as the hedged item. Accordingly, the Board decided that the hedged item could be expressed as an *amount* (of assets or liabilities) rather than as individual assets or liabilities.

BC194 The Board noted that this decision—that the hedged item may be designated as an amount of assets or liabilities rather than as specified items—gives rise to the issue of how the amount designated should be specified. The Board considered comments received on the Exposure Draft that it should not specify any method for designating the hedged item and hence measuring

---

14 see IAS 39, paragraph 84
15 see IAS 39, paragraph AG101

effectiveness. However, the Board concluded that if it provided no guidance, entities might designate in different ways, resulting in little comparability between them. The Board also noted that its objective, when permitting an amount to be designated, was to overcome the systems problems associated with designating individual items whilst achieving a very similar accounting result. Accordingly, it concluded that it should require a method of designation that closely approximates the accounting result that would be achieved by designating individual items.

BC195   Additionally, the Board noted that designation determines how much, if any, ineffectiveness arises if actual repricing dates in a particular repricing time period vary from those estimated or if the estimated repricing dates are revised. Taking the above example of a repricing time period in which there are CU100 of fixed rate assets and the entity designates as the hedged item an amount of CU20 of assets, the Board considered two approaches (a layer approach and a percentage approach) that are summarised below.

Layer approach

BC196   The first of these approaches, illustrated in figure 1, designates the hedged item as a 'layer' (eg (a) the bottom layer, (b) the top layer or (c) a portion of the top layer) of the assets (or liabilities) in a repricing time period. In this approach, the portfolio of CU100 in the above example is considered to comprise a hedged layer of CU20 and an unhedged layer of CU80.

Figure 1: Illustrating the designation of an amount of assets as a layer

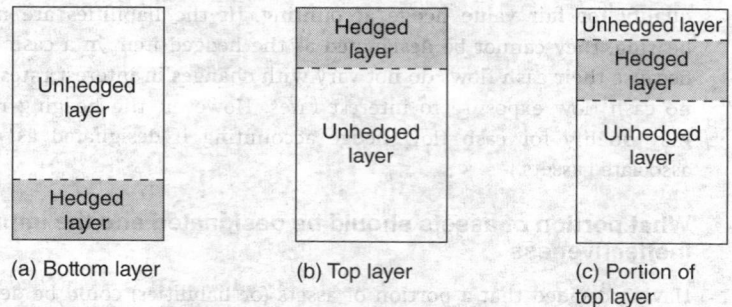

(a) Bottom layer   (b) Top layer   (c) Portion of top layer

BC197   The Board noted that the layer approach does not result in the recognition of ineffectiveness in all cases when the estimated amount of assets (or liabilities) changes. For example, in a bottom layer approach (see figure 2), if some assets prepay earlier than expected so that the entity revises downward its estimate of the amount of assets in the repricing time period (eg from CU100 to CU90), these reductions are assumed to come first from the unhedged top layer (figure 2(b)). Whether any ineffectiveness arises depends on whether the downward revision reaches the hedged layer of CU20. Thus, if the bottom layer is designated as the hedged item, it is unlikely that the hedged (bottom) layer will be reached and that any ineffectiveness will arise. Conversely, if the top layer is designated (see figure 3), any downward revision to the estimated amount in a repricing time period will reduce the hedged (top) layer and ineffectiveness will arise (figure 3(b)).

Figure 2: Illustrating the effect on changes in prepayments in a bottom layer approach

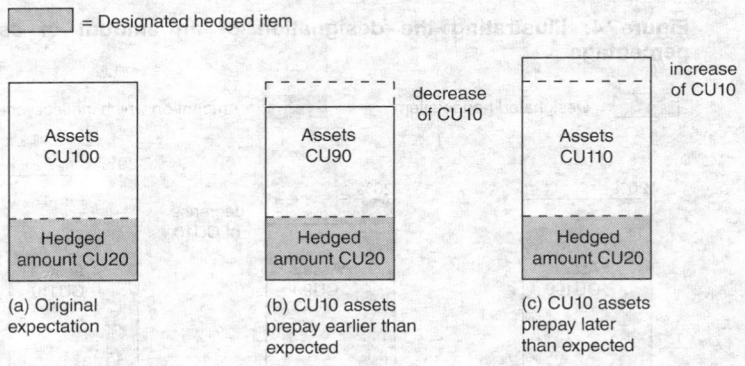

Figure 3: Illustrating the effect on changes in prepayments in a top layer approach

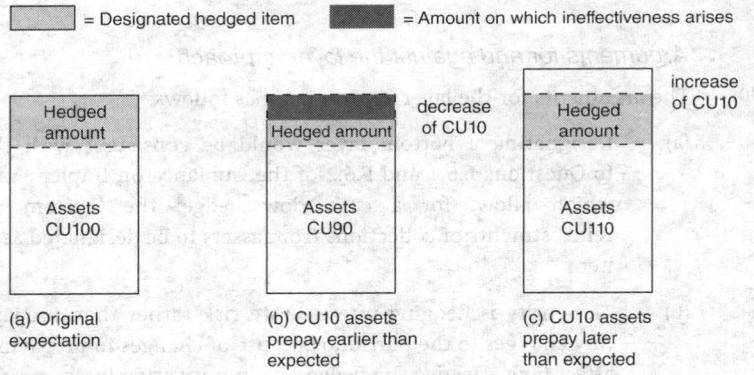

BC198   Finally, if some assets prepay *later* than expected so that the entity revises *upwards* its estimate of the amount of assets in this repricing time period (eg from CU100 to CU110, see figures 2(c) and 3(c)), no ineffectiveness arises no matter how the layer is designated, on the grounds that the hedged layer of CU20 is still there and that was all that was being hedged.

Percentage approach

BC199   The percentage approach, illustrated in figure 4, designates the hedged item as a percentage of the assets (or liabilities) in a repricing time period. In this approach, in the portfolio in the above example, 20 per cent of the assets of CU100 in this repricing time period is designated as the hedged item (figure 4(a)). As a result, if some assets prepay *earlier* than expected so that the entity revises *downwards* its estimate of the amount of assets in this repricing time period (eg from CU100 to CU90, figure 4(b)), ineffectiveness arises on 20 per cent of the decrease (in this case ineffectiveness arises on CU2). Similarly, if some assets prepay *later* than expected so that the entity revises *upwards* its estimate of the amount of assets in this repricing time period (eg from CU100 to CU110, figure 4(c)), ineffectiveness arises on 20 per cent of the increase (in this case ineffectiveness arises on CU2).

Figure 4: Illustrating the designation of an amount of assets as a percentage

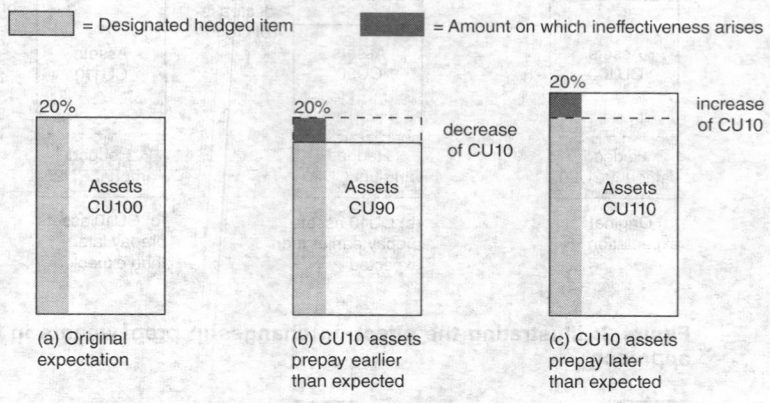

Arguments for and against the layer approach

BC200   The arguments for the layer approach are as follows:

(a)   Designating a bottom layer would be consistent with the answers to Questions F.6.1 and F.6.2 of the Guidance on Implementing IAS 39, which allow, for a cash flow hedge, the 'bottom' portion of reinvestments of collections from assets to be designated as the hedged item.[16]

(b)   The entity is hedging interest rate risk rather than prepayment risk. Any changes to the portfolio because of changes in prepayments do not affect how effective the hedge was in mitigating interest rate risk.

(c)   The approach captures all ineffectiveness on the hedged portion. It merely allows the hedged portion to be defined in such a way that, at least in a bottom layer approach, the first of any potential ineffectiveness relates to the unhedged portion.

(d)   It is correct that no ineffectiveness arises if changes in prepayment estimates cause more assets to be scheduled into that repricing time period. So long as assets equal to the hedged layer remain, there is no ineffectiveness and upward revisions of the amount in a repricing time period do not affect the hedged layer.

(e)   A prepayable item can be viewed as a combination of a non-prepayable item and a prepayment option. The designation of a bottom layer can be viewed as hedging a part of the life of the non-prepayable item, but none of the prepayment option. For example, a 25-year prepayable mortgage can be viewed as a combination of (i) a non-prepayable, fixed term, 25-year mortgage and (ii) a written prepayment option that

---

16   IFRS 9 *Financial Instruments* deleted the guidance on implementing IAS 39.

allows the borrower to repay the mortgage early. If the entity hedges this asset with a 5-year derivative, this is equivalent to hedging the first five years of component (i). If the position is viewed in this way, no ineffectiveness arises when interest rate changes cause the value of the prepayment option to change (unless the option is exercised and the asset prepaid) because the prepayment option was not hedged.

BC201 The arguments against the layer approach are as follows:

(a) The considerations that apply to a fair value hedge are different from those that apply to a cash flow hedge. In a cash flow hedge, it is the cash flows associated with the reinvestment of probable future collections that are hedged. In a fair value hedge it is the fair value of the assets that currently exist.

(b) The fact that no ineffectiveness is recognised if the amount in a repricing time period is re-estimated upwards (with the effect that the entity becomes underhedged) is not in accordance with IAS 39. For a fair value hedge, IAS 39 requires that ineffectiveness is recognised both when the entity becomes overhedged (ie the derivative exceeds the hedged item) and when it becomes underhedged (ie the derivative is smaller than the hedged item).

(c) As noted in paragraph BC200(e), a prepayable item can be viewed as a combination of a non-prepayable item and a prepayment option. When interest rates change, the fair value of both of these components changes.

(d) The objective of applying fair value hedge accounting to a hedged item designated in terms of an amount (rather than as individual assets or liabilities) is to obtain results that closely approximate those that would have been obtained if individual assets or liabilities had been designated as the hedged item. If individual prepayable assets had been designated as the hedged item, the change in both the components noted in (c) above (to the extent they are attributable to the hedged risk) would be recognised in profit or loss, both when interest rates increase and when they decrease. Accordingly, the change in the fair value of the hedged asset would differ from the change in the fair value of the hedging derivative (unless that derivative includes an equivalent prepayment option) and ineffectiveness would be recognised for the difference. It follows that in the simplified approach of designating the hedged item as an amount, ineffectiveness should similarly arise.

(e) *All* prepayable assets in a repricing time period, and not just a layer of them, contain a prepayment option whose fair value changes with changes in interest rates. Accordingly, when interest rates change, the fair value of the hedged assets (which include a prepayment option whose fair value has changed) will change by an amount different from that of the hedging derivative (which typically does not contain a prepayment option), and ineffectiveness will arise. This effect occurs regardless of whether interest rates increase or decrease — ie regardless of whether re-estimates of prepayments result in the amount in a time period being more or less.

(f) Interest rate risk and prepayment risk are so closely interrelated that it is not appropriate to separate the two components referred to in paragraph BC200(e) and designate only one of them (or a part of one of them) as the hedged item. Often the biggest single cause of changes in prepayment rates is changes in interest rates. This close relationship is the reason why IAS 39 prohibits a held-to-maturity asset[17] from being a hedged item with respect to either interest rate risk or prepayment risk. Furthermore, most entities do not separate the two components for risk management purposes. Rather, they incorporate the prepayment option by scheduling amounts based on expected maturities. When entities choose to use risk management practices — based on not separating prepayment and interest rate risk — as the basis for designation for hedge accounting purposes, it is not appropriate to separate the two components referred to in paragraph BC200(e) and designate only one of them (or a part of one of them) as the hedged item.

(g) If interest rates change, the effect on the fair value of a portfolio of prepayable items will be different from the effect on the fair value of a portfolio of otherwise identical but non-prepayable items. However, using a layer approach, this difference would not be recognised — if both portfolios were hedged to the same extent, both would be recognised in the balance sheet at the same amount.

BC202 The Board was persuaded by the arguments in paragraph BC201 and rejected layer approaches. In particular, the Board concluded that the hedged item should be designated in such a way that if the entity changes its estimates of the repricing time periods in which items are expected to repay or mature (eg in the light of recent prepayment experience), ineffectiveness arises. It also concluded that ineffectiveness should arise both when estimated prepayments decrease, resulting in more assets in a particular repricing time period, and when they increase, resulting in fewer.

Arguments for a third approach—measuring directly the change in fair value of the entire hedged item

BC203 The Board also considered comments on the Exposure Draft that:

(a) some entities hedge prepayment risk and interest rate risk separately, by hedging to the expected prepayment date using interest rate swaps, and hedging possible variations in these expected prepayment dates using swaptions.

(b) the embedded derivatives provisions of IAS 39 require some prepayable assets to be separated into a prepayment option and a non-prepayable host contract (unless the entity is unable to measure separately the prepayment option, in which case it treats the entire asset as held for

---

17 IFRS 9 eliminated the category of held-to-maturity.

trading). This seems to conflict with the view in the Exposure Draft that the two risks are too difficult to separate for the purposes of a portfolio hedge.[18]

BC204   In considering these arguments, the Board noted that the percentage approach described in paragraph AG126(b) is a proxy for measuring the change in the fair value of the *entire* asset (or liability) — including any embedded prepayment option — that is attributable to changes in interest rates. The Board had developed this proxy in the Exposure Draft because it had been informed that most entities (a) do not separate interest rate risk and prepayment risk for risk management purposes and hence (b) were unable to value the change in the value of the entire asset (including any embedded prepayment option) that is attributable to changes in the hedged interest rates. However, the comments described in paragraph BC203 indicated that in some cases, entities may be able to measure this change in value directly. The Board noted that such a direct method of measurement is conceptually preferable to the proxy described in paragraph AG126(b) and, accordingly, decided to recognise it explicitly. Thus, for example, if an entity that hedges prepayable assets using a combination of interest rate swaps and swaptions is able to measure directly the change in fair value of the entire asset, it could measure effectiveness by comparing the change in the value of the swaps and swaptions with the change in the fair value of the entire asset (including the change in the value of the prepayment option embedded in them) that is attributable to changes in the hedged interest rate. However, the Board also decided to permit the proxy proposed in the Exposure Draft for those entities that are unable to measure directly the change in the fair value of the entire asset.

Consideration of systems requirements

BC205   Finally, the Board was informed that, to be practicable in terms of systems needs, any approach should not require tracking of the amount in a repricing time period for multiple periods. Therefore it decided that ineffectiveness should be calculated by determining the change in the estimated amount in a repricing time period between one date on which effectiveness is measured and the next, as described more fully in paragraphs AG126 and AG127. This requires the entity to track how much of the change in each repricing time period between these two dates is attributable to revisions in estimates and how much is attributable to the origination of new assets (or liabilities). However, once ineffectiveness has been determined as set out above, the entity in essence starts again, ie it establishes the new amount in each repricing time period (including new items that have been originated since it last tested effectiveness), designates a new hedged item, and repeats the procedures to determine ineffectiveness at the next date it tests effectiveness. Thus the tracking is limited to movements between one date when effectiveness is measured and the next. It is not necessary to track for multiple periods. However, the entity will need to keep records relating to each repricing time period (a) to reconcile the amounts for each repricing time

---

18   IFRS 9 replaced IAS 39.

period with the total amounts in the two separate line items in the balance sheet (see paragraph AG114(f)), and (b) to ensure that amounts in the two separate line items are derecognised no later than when the repricing time period to which they relate expires.

BC206　The Board also noted that the amount of tracking required by the percentage approach is no more than what would be required by any of the layer approaches. Thus, the Board concluded that none of the approaches was clearly preferable from the standpoint of systems needs.

The carrying amount of the hedged item

BC207　The last issue noted in paragraph BC176 is how to present in the balance sheet the change in fair value of the hedged item. The Board noted the concern of respondents that the hedged item may contain many—even thousands of—individual assets (or liabilities) and that to change the carrying amounts of each of these individual items would be impracticable. The Board considered dealing with this concern by permitting the change in value to be presented in a single line item in the balance sheet. However, the Board noted that this could result in a decrease in the fair value of a financial asset (financial liability) being recognised as a financial liability (financial asset). Furthermore, for some repricing time periods the hedged item may be an asset, whereas for others it may be a liability. The Board concluded that it would be incorrect to present together the changes in fair value for such repricing time periods, because to do so would combine changes in the fair value of assets with changes in the fair value of liabilities.

BC208　Accordingly, the Board decided that two line items should be presented, as follows:

(a)　for those repricing time periods for which the hedged item is an asset, the change in its fair value is presented in a single separate line item within assets; and

(b)　for those repricing time periods for which the hedged item is a liability, the change in its fair value is presented in a single separate line item within liabilities.

BC209　The Board noted that these line items represent changes in the fair value of the hedged item. For this reason, the Board decided that they should be presented next to financial assets or financial liabilities.

Derecognition of amounts included in the separate line items

Derecognition of an asset (or liability) in the hedged portfolio

BC210　The Board discussed how and when amounts recognised in the separate balance sheet line items should be removed from the balance sheet. The Board noted that the objective is to remove such amounts from the balance sheet in the same periods as they would have been removed had individual assets or liabilities (rather than an amount) been designated as the hedged item.

BC211   The Board noted that this objective could be fully met only if the entity schedules individual assets or liabilities into repricing time periods and tracks both for how long the scheduled individual items have been hedged and how much of each item was hedged in each time period. In the absence of such scheduling and tracking, some assumptions would need to be made about these matters and, hence, about how much should be removed from the separate balance sheet line items when an asset (or liability) in the hedged portfolio is derecognised. In addition, some safeguards would be needed to ensure that amounts included in the separate balance sheet line items are removed from the balance sheet over a reasonable period and do not remain in the balance sheet indefinitely. With these points in mind, the Board decided to require that:

(a)   whenever an asset (or liability) in the hedged portfolio is derecognised —whether through earlier than expected prepayment, sale or write-off from impairment—any amount included in the separate balance sheet line item relating to that derecognised asset (or liability) should be removed from the balance sheet and included in the gain or loss on derecognition.

(b)   if an entity cannot determine into which time period(s) a derecognised asset (or liability) was scheduled:

(i)   it should assume that higher than expected prepayments occur on assets scheduled into the first available time period; and

(ii)   it should allocate sales and impairments to assets scheduled into all time periods containing the derecognised item on a systematic and rational basis.

(c)   the entity should track how much of the total amount included in the separate line items relates to each repricing time period, and should remove the amount that relates to a particular time period from the balance sheet no later than when that time period expires.

Amortisation

BC212   The Board also noted that if the designated hedged amount for a repricing time period is reduced, IAS 39[19] requires that the separate balance sheet line item described in paragraph 89A relating to that reduction is amortised on the basis of a recalculated effective interest rate. The Board noted that for a portfolio hedge of interest rate risk, amortisation based on a recalculated effective interest rate could be complex to determine and could demand significant additional systems requirements. Consequently, the Board decided that in the case of a portfolio hedge of interest rate risk (and only in such a hedge), the line item balance may be amortised using a straight-line method when a method based on a recalculated effective interest rate is not practicable.

---

19   see paragraph 92

The hedging instrument

BC213 The Board was asked by commentators to clarify whether the hedging instrument may be a portfolio of derivatives containing offsetting risk positions. Commentators noted that previous versions of IAS 39 were unclear on this point.

BC214 The issue arises because the assets and liabilities in each repricing time period change over time as prepayment expectations change, as items are derecognised and as new items are originated. Thus the net position, and the amount the entity wishes to designate as the hedged item, also changes over time. If the hedged item decreases, the hedging instrument needs to be reduced. However, entities do not normally reduce the hedging instrument by disposing of some of the derivatives contained in it. Instead, entities adjust the hedging instrument by entering into new derivatives with an offsetting risk profile.

BC215 The Board decided to permit the hedging instrument to be a portfolio of derivatives containing offsetting risk positions for both individual and portfolio hedges. It noted that all of the derivatives concerned are measured at fair value. It also noted that the two ways of adjusting the hedging instrument described in the previous paragraph can achieve substantially the same effect. Therefore the Board clarified paragraph 77 to this effect.

Hedge effectiveness for a portfolio hedge of interest rate risk

BC216 Some respondents to the Exposure Draft questioned whether IAS 39's effectiveness tests[20] should apply to a portfolio hedge of interest rate risk. The Board noted that its objective in amending IAS 39 for a portfolio hedge of interest rate risk is to permit fair value hedge accounting to be used more easily, whilst continuing to meet the principles of hedge accounting. One of these principles is that the hedge is highly effective. Thus, the Board concluded that the effectiveness requirements in IAS 39 apply equally to a portfolio hedge of interest rate risk.

BC217 Some respondents to the Exposure Draft sought guidance on how the effectiveness tests are to be applied to a portfolio hedge. In particular, they asked how the prospective effectiveness test is to be applied when an entity periodically 'rebalances' a hedge (ie adjusts the amount of the hedging instrument to reflect changes in the hedged item). The Board decided that if the entity's risk management strategy is to change the amount of the hedging instrument periodically to reflect changes in the hedged position, that strategy affects the determination of the term of the hedge. Thus, the entity needs to demonstrate that the hedge is expected to be highly effective only for the period until the amount of the hedging instrument is next adjusted. The Board noted that this decision does not conflict with the requirement in paragraph 75 that 'a hedging relationship may not be designated for only a portion of the time period during which a hedging instrument remains outstanding'. This is because the entire hedging instrument is designated (and not only some of its cash flows, for example, those to the time when the hedge

---

20 see paragraph AG105

is next adjusted). However, expected effectiveness is assessed by considering the change in the fair value of the entire hedging instrument only for the period until it is next adjusted.

BC218　A third issue raised in the comment letters was whether, for a portfolio hedge, the retrospective effectiveness test should be assessed for all time buckets in aggregate or individually for each time bucket. The Board decided that entities could use any method to assess retrospective effectiveness, but noted that the chosen method would form part of the documentation of the hedging relationship made at the inception of the hedge in accordance with paragraph 88(a) and hence could not be decided at the time the retrospective effectiveness test is performed.

Transition to fair value hedge accounting for portfolios of interest rate risk

BC219　In finalising the amendments to IAS 39, the Board considered whether to provide additional guidance for entities wishing to apply fair value hedge accounting to a portfolio hedge that had previously been accounted for using cash flow hedge accounting. The Board noted that such entities could apply paragraph 101(d) to revoke the designation of a cash flow hedge and re-designate a new fair value hedge using the same hedged item and hedging instrument, and decided to clarify this in the Application Guidance. Additionally, the Board concluded that clarification was not required for first-time adopters because IFRS 1 already contained sufficient guidance.

BC220　The Board also considered whether to permit retrospective designation of a portfolio hedge. The Board noted that this would conflict with the principle in paragraph 88(a) that 'at the inception of the hedge there is formal designation and documentation of the hedging relationship' and accordingly, decided not to permit retrospective designation.

Novation of derivatives and continuation of hedge accounting

BC220A　The IASB received an urgent request to clarify whether an entity is required to discontinue hedge accounting for hedging relationships in which a derivative has been designated as a hedging instrument in accordance with IAS 39 when that derivative is novated to a central counterparty (CCP) due to the introduction of a new law or regulation.[21]

BC220B　The IASB considered the derecognition requirements of IAS 39 to determine whether the novation in such a circumstance leads to the derecognition of an existing derivative that has been designated as a hedging instrument. The IASB noted that a derivative should be derecognised only when it meets both the derecognition criteria for a financial asset and the derecognition criteria

---

21　In this context, the term 'novation' indicates that the parties to a derivative agree that one or more clearing counterparties replace their original counterparty to become the new counterparty to each of the parties. For this purpose, a clearing counterparty is a central counterparty or an entity or entities, for example, a clearing member of a clearing organisation or a client of a clearing member of a clearing organisation, that are acting as counterparty in order to effect clearing by a central counterparty.

for a financial liability in circumstances in which the derivative involves two-way payments between parties (ie the payments are or could be from and to each of the parties).

BC220C   The IASB observed that paragraph 17(a) of IAS 39 requires that a financial asset is derecognised when the contractual rights to the cash flows from the financial asset expire. The IASB noted that through novation to a CCP, a party (Party A) to the original derivative has new contractual rights to cash flows from a (new) derivative with the CCP, and this new contract replaces the original contract with a counterparty (Party B). Thus the original derivative with Party B has expired and as a consequence the original derivative through which Party A has engaged with Party B shall meet the derecognition criteria for a financial asset.[22]

BC220D   The IASB also observed that paragraph AG57(b) of IAS 39 states that a financial liability is extinguished when the debtor is legally released from primary responsibility for the liability. The IASB noted that the novation to the CCP would release Party A from the responsibility to make payments to Party B and also would oblige Party A to make payments to the CCP. Consequently, the original derivative through which Party A has transacted with Party B also meets the derecognition criteria for a financial liability.[23]

BC220E   Consequently, the IASB concluded that the novation of a derivative to a CCP would be accounted for as the derecognition of the original derivative and the recognition of the (new) novated derivative.

BC220F   Taking into account the conclusion of the assessment on the derecognition requirements, the IASB considered paragraphs 91(a) and 101(a) of IAS 39, which require an entity to discontinue hedge accounting prospectively if the hedging instrument expires or is sold, terminated or exercised. The IASB noted that novation to a CCP would require the entity to discontinue hedge accounting because the derivative that was designated as a hedging instrument has been derecognised and consequently the hedging instrument in the existing hedging relationship no longer exists.

BC220G   The IASB, however, was concerned about the financial reporting effects that would arise from novations that result from new laws or regulations. The IASB noted that the requirement to discontinue hedge accounting meant that although an entity could designate the new derivative as the hedging instrument in a new hedging relationship, this could result in more hedge ineffectiveness, especially for cash flow hedges, compared to a continuing hedging relationship. This is because the derivative that would be newly designated as the hedging instrument would be on terms that would be different from a new derivative, ie it was unlikely to be 'at-market' (for example, a non-option derivative such as a swap or forward might have a significant fair value) at the time of the novation. The IASB also noted that there would be an increased risk that the hedging relationship would fail to fall within the 80–125 per cent hedge effectiveness range required by IAS 39.

---

22   IFRS 9 replaced IAS 39.
23   IFRS 9 replaced IAS 39.

BC220H The IASB, taking note of these financial reporting effects, was convinced that accounting for the hedging relationship that existed before the novation as a continuing hedging relationship, in this specific situation, would provide more useful information to users of financial statements. The IASB also considered the feedback from outreach that involved the members of the International Forum of Accounting Standard Setters (IFASS) and securities regulators and noted that this issue is not limited to a specific jurisdiction because many jurisdictions have introduced, or are expected to mandate, laws or regulations that encourage or require the novation of derivatives to a CCP.

BC220I The IASB noted that the widespread legislative changes across jurisdictions were prompted by a G20 commitment to improve transparency and regulatory oversight of over-the-counter (OTC) derivatives in an internationally consistent and non-discriminatory way. Specifically, the G20 agreed to improve OTC derivatives markets so that all standardised OTC derivatives contracts are cleared through a CCP.

BC220J The IASB also considered the draft requirements of the forthcoming hedge accounting chapter of IFRS 9. The IASB noted that those draft requirements also would require hedge accounting to be discontinued if the novation to a CCP occurs.

BC220K Consequently, the IASB decided to publish, in January 2013, the Exposure Draft *Novation of Derivatives and Continuation of Hedge Accounting* ('ED/2013/2'), which proposed amendments to IAS 39 and IFRS 9. In ED/2013/2, the IASB proposed to amend paragraphs 91(a) and 101(a) of IAS 39 to provide relief from discontinuing hedge accounting when the novation to a CCP is required by new laws or regulations and meets certain criteria. The IASB decided to set the comment period for those proposals to 30 days. The IASB noted that the reduced comment period was necessary because the amendments should be completed urgently because the new laws or regulations to effect CCP clearing of OTC derivatives would come into force within a short period; the contents of the proposed amendments were short; and there was likely to be a broad consensus on the topic.

BC220L When developing ED/2013/2, the IASB tentatively decided that the terms of the novated derivative should be unchanged other than the change in counterparty, however, the IASB noted that, in practice, other changes may arise as a direct consequence of the novation. For example, in order to enter into a derivative with a CCP it may be necessary to make adjustments to the collateral arrangements. Such narrow changes that are a direct consequence of or are incidental to the novation were acknowledged in the proposed amendments. However, this would not include changes to, for example, the maturity of the derivatives, the payment dates, or the contractual cash flows or the basis of their calculation, except for charges that may arise as a consequence of transacting with a CCP.

BC220M When developing ED/2013/2, the IASB also discussed whether to require an entity to disclose that it has been able to continue hedge accounting by applying the relief provided by these proposed amendments to IAS 39 and IFRS 9. The IASB tentatively decided that it was not appropriate to mandate specific disclosure in this situation because, from the perspective of a user of financial statements, the hedge accounting would be continuing.

BC220N   A total of 78 respondents commented on ED/2013/2. The vast majority of respondents agreed that the proposed amendments are necessary. However, a few respondents expressed disagreement with the proposal on the basis that they disagreed with the IASB's conclusion that hedge accounting would be required to be discontinued as a result of such novations. In expressing such disagreement some noted that IAS 39 expressly acknowledges that certain replacements or rollovers of hedging instruments are not expirations or terminations for the purposes of discontinuing hedge accounting. The IASB noted that this exception applies if '[a] replacement or rollover is part of the entity's documented hedging strategy' (IAS 39.91(a) and IAS 39.101(a)). The IASB questioned whether replacement of a contract as a result of unforeseen legislative changes (even if documented) fits the definition of a replacement that is part of a 'documented hedging strategy'.

BC220O   Even though the vast majority of respondents agreed with the proposal, a considerable majority of respondents disagreed with the scope of the proposed amendments. They believed that the proposed scope of 'novation required by laws or regulations' is too restrictive and that the scope therefore should be expanded by removing this criterion. In particular, they argued that voluntary novation to a CCP should be provided with the same relief as novation required by laws or regulations. A few respondents further requested that the scope should not be limited to novation to a central counterparty and that novation in other circumstances should also be considered.

BC220P   In considering respondents' comments, the IASB noted that voluntary novation to a CCP could be prevalent in some circumstances such as novation in anticipation of regulatory changes, novation due to operational ease, and novation induced but not actually mandated by laws or regulations as a result of the imposition of charges or penalties. The IASB also noted that many jurisdictions would not require the existing stock of outstanding historical derivatives to be moved to CCPs, although this was encouraged by the G20 commitment.

BC220Q   The IASB observed, however, that for hedge accounting to continue voluntary novation to a CCP should be associated with laws or regulations that are relevant to central clearing of derivatives. The IASB noted that while a novation need not be required by laws or regulations for hedge accounting to be allowed to continue, allowing all novations to CCPs to be accommodated was broader than the IASB had intended. In addition, the IASB agreed that hedge accounting should continue when novations are performed as a consequence of laws or regulations or the introduction of laws of regulations but noted that the mere possibility of laws or regulations being introduced was not a sufficient basis for the continuation of hedge accounting.

BC220R   Some respondents were concerned that restricting the relief to novation directly to a CCP was too narrow. In considering respondents' comments, the IASB noted that in some cases a CCP has a contractual relationship only with its 'clearing members', and therefore an entity must have a contractual relationship with a clearing member in order to transact with a CCP; a clearing member of a CCP provides a clearing service to its client who cannot access a CCP directly. The IASB also noted that some jurisdictions are introducing a so-called 'indirect clearing' arrangement in their laws or regulations to effect clearing with a CCP, by which a client of a clearing member of a CCP provides a (indirect) clearing service to its client in the same way as a clearing member of a CCP provides a clearing service to its client. In addition, the IASB observed that an intragroup novation also can occur in order to access a CCP; for example, if only particular group entities can transact directly with a CCP.

BC220S On the basis of respondents' comments, the IASB decided to expand the scope of the amendments by providing relief for novations to entities other than a CCP if such novation is undertaken with the objective of effecting clearing with a CCP rather than limiting relief to situations in which novation is directly to a CCP. The IASB decided that in these circumstances the novation had occurred in order to effect clearing through a CCP, albeit indirectly. The IASB thus decided also to include such novations in the scope of the amendments because they are consistent with the objective of the proposed amendments—they enable hedge accounting to continue when novations occur as a consequence of laws or regulations or the introduction of laws or regulations that increase the use of CCPs. However, the IASB noted that when parties to a hedging instrument enter into novations with different counterparties (for example, with different clearing members), these amendments only apply if each of those parties ultimately effects clearing with the same central counterparty.

BC220T Respondents raised a concern about the phrase 'if and only if' that was used in ED/2013/2 when describing that the relief is provided 'if and only if' the criteria are met. In considering respondents' comments, the IASB noted that ED/2013/2 was intended to address a narrow issue—novation to CCPs—and therefore changing the phrase 'if and only if' to 'if' would target the amendment on the fact patterns that the IASB sought to address. The IASB noted that this would have the effect of requiring an analysis of whether the general conditions for continuation of hedge accounting are satisfied in other cases (for example, as was raised by some respondents, in determining the effect of intragroup novations in consolidated financial statements).

BC220U The IASB decided to make equivalent amendments to the forthcoming chapter on hedge accounting that will be incorporated into IFRS 9, as proposed in ED/2013/2; no respondents opposed this proposal.

BC220V ED/2013/2 did not propose any additional disclosures. The vast majority of respondents agreed with this. The IASB confirmed that additional disclosures are not required. However, the IASB noted that an entity may consider disclosures in accordance with IFRS 7 *Financial Instruments: Disclosures*, which requires qualitative and quantitative disclosures about credit risk.

BC220W   The IASB also decided to retain in the final amendments the transition requirements proposed in ED/2013/2 so that the amendments should apply retrospectively and early application should be permitted. The IASB noted that even with retrospective application, if an entity had previously discontinued hedge accounting, as a result of a novation, that (pre-novation) hedge accounting relationship could not be reinstated because doing so would be inconsistent with the requirements for hedge accounting (ie hedge accounting cannot be applied retrospectively).

BC221–   [Deleted]
BC222

Amendments for Interest Rate Benchmark Reform (September 2019)

BC223   Interest rate benchmarks such as interbank offered rates (IBORs) play an important role in global financial markets. These interest rate benchmarks index trillions of dollars and other currencies in a wide variety of financial products, from derivatives to residential mortgages. However, cases of attempted market manipulation of some interest rate benchmarks, together with the post-crisis decline in liquidity in interbank unsecured funding markets, have undermined confidence in the reliability and robustness of some interest rate benchmarks. Against this background, the G20 asked the Financial Stability Board (FSB) to undertake a fundamental review of major interest rate benchmarks. Following the review, the FSB published a report setting out its recommended reforms of some major interest rate benchmarks such as IBORs. Public authorities in many jurisdictions have since taken steps to implement those recommendations. In some jurisdictions, there is already clear progress towards the reform of interest rate benchmarks, or the replacement of interest rate benchmarks with alternative, nearly risk-free interest rates that are based, to a greater extent, on transaction data (alternative benchmark rates). This has in turn led to uncertainty about the long-term viability of some interest rate benchmarks. In these amendments, the term 'interest rate benchmark reform' refers to the market-wide reform of an interest rate benchmark including its replacement with an alternative benchmark rate, such as that resulting from the FSB's recommendations set out in its July 2014 report 'Reforming Major Interest Rate Benchmarks' (the reform).[24]

BC224   In 2018 the Board noted the increasing levels of uncertainty about the long-term viability of some interest rate benchmarks and decided to address as a priority the issues affecting financial reporting in the period before the reform (referred to as pre-replacement issues).

BC225   As part of the pre-replacement issues, the Board considered the implications for specific hedge accounting requirements in IFRS 9 and IAS 39, which require forward-looking analysis. As a result of the reform, contractual cash flows of hedged items and hedging instruments based on an existing interest rate benchmark will likely change when that interest rate benchmark is

---

24   The report, 'Reforming Major Interest Rate Benchmarks', is available at http://www.fsb.org/wp-content/uploads/r_140722.pdf.

subject to the reform—in these amendments, contractual cash flows encompass both contractually specified and non-contractually specified cash flows. The same uncertainty arising from the reform regarding the timing and the amount of future cash flows will likely affect the changes in fair value of hedged items and hedging instruments in a fair value hedge of the interest rate benchmark exposure. Until decisions are made about what the alternative benchmark rate is, and when and how the reform will occur, including specifying its effects on particular contracts, uncertainties will exist regarding the timing and the amount of future cash flows of the hedged item and the hedging instrument.

BC226   The Board noted that the hedge accounting requirements in IFRS 9 and IAS 39 provide a clear basis for accounting for such uncertainties. In applying these requirements, the uncertainties about the timing and the amount of future cash flows could affect an entity's ability to meet those specific forward-looking hedge accounting requirements in the period when uncertainty is created by the reform. In some cases, solely due to such uncertainties, entities could be required to discontinue hedge accounting for hedging relationships that would otherwise qualify for hedge accounting. Also, because of the uncertainties arising from the reform, entities may not be able to designate new hedging relationships that would otherwise qualify for hedge accounting applying IFRS 9 and IAS 39. In some cases, discontinuation of hedge accounting would require an entity to recognise gains or losses in profit or loss.

BC227   In the Board's view, discontinuation of hedge accounting solely due to such uncertainties before the reform's economic effects on hedged items and hedging instruments are known would not provide useful information to users of financial statements. Therefore, the Board decided to publish in May 2019 the Exposure Draft *Interest Rate Benchmark Reform* (2019 Exposure Draft), which proposed exceptions to IFRS 9 and IAS 39 to provide relief during this period of uncertainty.

BC228   The 2019 Exposure Draft proposed exceptions to specific hedge accounting requirements such that entities would apply those requirements assuming the interest rate benchmark on which the hedged risk and/or cash flows of the hedged item or of the hedging instrument are based is not altered as a result of the reform. The proposed exceptions applied only to the hedge accounting requirements specified in that Exposure Draft and were not intended to provide relief from all consequences arising from the reform.

BC229   Almost all respondents to the 2019 Exposure Draft agreed with the Board's decision to address pre-replacement issues. Many highlighted the urgency of these issues, especially in some jurisdictions where there is already clear progress towards the reform or replacement of interest rate benchmarks with alternative benchmark rates.

BC230   In September 2019 the Board amended IFRS 9, IAS 39 and IFRS 7 by issuing *Interest Rate Benchmark Reform*, which confirmed with modifications the proposals in the 2019 Exposure Draft. In the amendments issued in September 2019, the Board added paragraphs 102A–102N and 108G to IAS 39.

BC231   The Board decided to propose amendments to IAS 39 as well as IFRS 9 because when entities first apply IFRS 9, they are permitted to choose as an accounting policy to continue to apply the hedge accounting requirements of IAS 39. The Board understands that a significant number of IFRS preparers—financial institutions in particular—have made such an accounting policy choice.

Scope of the exceptions

BC232   In the 2019 Exposure Draft, the Board noted that the hedge accounting issues being addressed arise in the context of interest rate benchmark reform, and, therefore, the proposed exceptions would apply only to hedging relationships of interest rate risk that are affected by the reform. However, some respondents expressed the view that the scope of the exceptions, as set out in the 2019 Exposure Draft, would not include other types of hedging relationships that may be affected by uncertainties arising from the reform such as hedging relationships in which an entity designates cross-currency interest rate swaps to hedge its exposure to both foreign currency and interest rate risk. These respondents asked the Board to clarify whether the scope of the exceptions was meant to include such hedging relationships.

BC233   In its redeliberations on the 2019 Exposure Draft, the Board clarified that it did not intend to exclude from the scope of the amendments hedging relationships in which interest rate risk is not the only designated hedged risk. The Board agreed with respondents that other hedging relationships could be directly affected by the reform when the reform gives rise to uncertainties about the timing or the amount of interest rate benchmark-based cash flows of the hedged item or of the hedging instrument. Therefore, the Board confirmed that the exceptions would apply to the interest rate benchmark-based cash flows in these situations. The Board noted that many derivatives, designated in hedging relationships in which there is no uncertainty about the timing or the amount of interest rate benchmark-based cash flows, could be indirectly affected by the reform. For example, this would be the case when the valuation of the derivatives is affected by general uncertainty in the market caused by the reform. The Board confirmed that the exceptions do not apply to these hedging relationships, despite the indirect effect the uncertainties arising from the reform could have on the valuation of derivatives.

BC234   Consequently, the Board clarified the wording in paragraph 102A of IAS 39 to refer to all hedging relationships that are directly affected by interest rate benchmark reform. Paragraph 102A of IAS 39 explains that a hedging relationship is directly affected by interest rate benchmark reform only if the reform gives rise to uncertainties about the interest rate benchmark (contractually or non-contractually specified) designated as a hedged risk and/or the timing or the amount of interest rate benchmark-based cash flows of the hedged item or of the hedging instrument. The scope of the exceptions does not exclude hedging relationships in which interest rate risk is not the only hedged risk.

Highly probable requirement

BC235 The Board noted that if an entity designates a forecast transaction as the hedged item in a cash flow hedge, applying paragraph 88(c) of IAS 39, that transaction must be highly probable (highly probable requirement). This requirement is intended to ensure that changes in the fair value of designated hedging instruments are recognised in other comprehensive income only for those hedged forecast transactions that are highly probable to occur. This requirement is an important discipline in applying hedge accounting to forecast transactions. The Board noted that the requirements in IAS 39 provide a clear basis to account for the effects of the reform—that is, if the effects of the reform are such that the hedged cash flows are no longer highly probable, hedge accounting should be discontinued. As set out in paragraph BC227, in the Board's view, discontinuing all affected hedging relationships solely due to such uncertainty would not provide useful information to users of financial statements.

BC236 Therefore, the Board amended IAS 39 to provide an exception to the highly probable requirement that would provide targeted relief during this period of uncertainty. More specifically, applying the exception, if the hedged future cash flows are based on an interest rate benchmark that is subject to the reform, an entity assumes that the interest rate benchmark on which the hedged cash flows are based is not altered when assessing whether the future cash flows are highly probable. If the hedged future cash flows are based on a highly probable forecast transaction, by applying the exception in paragraph 102D of IAS 39 when performing the assessment of the highly probable requirement for that forecast transaction, the entity would assume that the interest rate benchmark on which the hedged cash flows are based will not be altered in the future contract as a result of the reform. For example, for a future issuance of a London Interbank Offered Rate (LIBOR)-referenced debt instrument, the entity would assume that the LIBOR benchmark rate on which the hedged cash flows are based will not be altered as a result of the reform.

BC237 The Board noted that this exception does not necessarily result in an entity determining that the hedged cash flows are highly probable. In the example described in paragraph BC236, the entity assumed that the interest rate benchmark in the future contract would not be altered as a result of the reform when determining whether that forecast transaction is highly probable. However, if the entity decides not to issue the debt instrument because of uncertainty arising from the reform or for any other reason, the hedged future cash flows are no longer highly probable (and are no longer expected to occur). The exception would not permit or require the entity to assume otherwise. In this case, the entity would conclude that the LIBOR-based cash flows are no longer highly probable (and are no longer expected to occur).

BC238 The Board also included an exception for discontinued hedging relationships. Applying this exception, any amount remaining in other comprehensive income when a hedging relationship is discontinued would be reclassified to profit or loss in the same period(s) during which the hedged cash flows affect profit or loss, based on the assumption that the interest rate benchmark on which the hedged cash flows are based is not altered as a result of the reform. If, however, the hedged future cash flows are no longer expected to occur for other reasons, the entity is required to immediately reclassify to profit or loss any amount remaining in other comprehensive income. In addition, the exception would not exempt entities from reclassifying the amount that is not expected to be recovered into profit or loss as required by paragraph 97 of IAS 39.

Effectiveness assessment

BC239   Applying IAS 39, a hedging relationship qualifies for hedge accounting only if the conditions in paragraph 88 are met. Two of the conditions in that paragraph — the prospective assessment and the retrospective assessment — require that the hedging relationship is highly effective in achieving offsetting changes in fair value or cash flows attributable to the hedged risk. If either of these conditions is not met, paragraphs 91(b) and 101(b) require the entity to discontinue hedge accounting prospectively.

Prospective assessment

BC240   When applying paragraph 88(b) of IAS 39, demonstrating that a hedging relationship is expected to be highly effective requires the estimation of future cash flows because the assessment is prospective in nature. Interest rate benchmark reform could affect this assessment for hedging relationships that may extend beyond the timing of the reform. That is because entities would have to consider possible changes to the fair value or future cash flows of hedged items and hedging instruments in determining whether a hedging relationship is expected to be highly effective. Consequently, at some point in time, it is possible that entities would not be able to meet the condition in paragraph 88(b) of IAS 39 solely because of uncertainties arising from the reform.

BC241   The Board considered the usefulness of the information that would result from the potential discontinuation of hedge accounting for affected hedging relationships and decided to amend the requirement in IAS 39 to provide an exception for the prospective assessment for the same reasons as discussed in paragraph BC227.

BC242   Applying this exception, an entity shall assess whether the hedge is expected to be highly effective in achieving offsetting as required by IAS 39, based on the assumption that the hedged risk or the interest rate benchmark on which the hedged item or the hedging instrument is based is not altered as a result of the reform. Similarly, if an entity designates a highly probable forecast transaction as the hedged item, the entity shall perform the prospective assessment based on the assumption that the interest rate benchmark on which the hedged cash flows are based will not change as a result of the reform.

BC243   The Board noted that an offset between the hedged item and the hedging instrument is a fundamental principle of the hedge accounting model in IAS 39 and, therefore, the Board considered it critical to maintain this principle. The exception addresses only the uncertainties arising from the reform. Therefore, if an entity is unable to demonstrate that a hedging relationship is expected to be highly effective for other reasons, the entity shall discontinue hedge accounting as required by IAS 39.

Retrospective assessment

BC244   When developing the 2019 Exposure Draft, the Board decided not to propose an exception to the retrospective assessment required by paragraph 88(e) and AG105(b) of IAS 39 for the effects of the reform. As described in the 2019 Exposure Draft, that assessment is based on the actual results of the hedging relationship based on the extent to which hedging gains or losses on the hedged item attributable to the hedged risk offset changes in the fair value of the hedging instrument. The Board noted that existing IFRS Standards already provide an adequate basis for measuring ineffectiveness.

BC245   Most respondents disagreed with the Board's decision not to propose an exception to the retrospective assessment. Respondents noted that due to the inherent interaction between the assessment of the forward-looking cash flows of the hedged item and its effect on both prospective and retrospective assessments, the proposed amendments would not achieve their intended effect unless an exception is also provided for the retrospective assessment.

BC246   Furthermore, these respondents expressed the view that the discontinuation of hedge accounting because hedging relationships do not meet the requirements in paragraph AG105(b) of IAS 39, as a result of the temporary ineffectiveness caused by the reform, would not reflect an entity's risk management strategy and, therefore, would not provide useful information to users of financial statements.

BC247   In its redeliberations on the amendments to IAS 39, the Board considered the feedback received. The Board discussed three approaches that it could apply for providing an exception to the retrospective assessment for the impact of the uncertainty arising from the reform.

BC248   The Board observed that one possible approach would be to require entities to assume that the interest rate benchmark is not altered similar to the prospective assessment. Applying this approach would require entities to separate the assessment of retrospective effectiveness from the measurement of hedge ineffectiveness. More specifically, the Board considered that the objective of this approach would be to exclude the uncertainty arising from the reform from the assessment of whether a hedge is considered to be highly effective and that hedge accounting is continued when the results of this assessment are within the range of 80–125 per cent as required in paragraph AG105(b) of IAS 39, even if the measurement of actual ineffectiveness is outside that range. The Board was of the view that even though this approach is consistent with the other exceptions provided in the amendments to IAS 39, the requirement to perform two effectiveness calculations based on different assumptions could be burdensome on preparers. The Board therefore rejected this approach.

BC249   The Board also considered an approach that was recommended by respondents to the 2019 Exposure Draft, in which entities would be required, for the purposes of the retrospective assessment, to demonstrate the existence of an economic relationship between the hedged item and hedging instrument similar to the requirements in IFRS 9. However, the Board noted that the existence of an economic relationship between the hedged item and the hedging instrument, is only one of the requirements in IFRS 9 for a hedging relationship to be highly effective. The Board considered that the requirements in paragraph 6.4.1(c) of IFRS 9 are inherently linked and the application of the economic relationship in isolation might not achieve the intended objective and could result in unintended consequences. The Board therefore rejected this approach.

BC250   The Board decided on an approach whereby an entity could continue to apply hedge accounting for hedging relationships directly affected by the reform, even if the actual results of the hedging relationship do not meet the requirements in paragraph AG105(b) of IAS 39, if the ineffectiveness arose from uncertainty arising from the reform or other sources, subject to satisfying the other conditions in paragraph 88 of IAS 39, including the prospective assessment (as amended by paragraph 102F of IAS 39).

BC251   The Board acknowledged that such an approach might provide less discipline compared to the approach described in paragraph BC248, which would introduce additional requirements to mitigate the risk of continuing hedge accounting for hedging relationships that failed the retrospective assessment for reasons other than the reform. However, the Board noted that its approach still maintains a level of discipline around the application of the IAS 39 hedge accounting model through the prospective assessment and neither imposes additional costs or burden for preparers nor introduces new requirements in IAS 39.

BC252   The Board noted that any exception to the retrospective assessment will apply only to a well-defined population of hedging relationships during the period of uncertainty on the hedged items and hedging instruments arising from the reform. Furthermore, the Board noted that the risk of allowing hedge accounting to be applied for hedging relationships that would not otherwise qualify for hedge accounting is mitigated by the required prospective assessment as only the uncertainty arising from the reform is excluded from that assessment. Any other sources of ineffectiveness would continue to be included in the assessment of whether the hedge is expected to be highly effective in future periods. The Board noted that any high level of ineffectiveness arising in a hedging relationship is expected to be captured by the prospective assessment. The Board also noted that all ineffectiveness would be recognised and measured and thus be transparent in financial reporting. The Board, therefore, decided to provide an exception from the requirement to discontinue hedge accounting as a result of paragraph 88(e) of IAS 39 because the actual results of the hedge do not meet the requirements in paragraph AG105(b) of IAS 39.

Measurement of ineffectiveness

BC253   The Board noted that the exceptions were not intended to change the requirement that entities measure and recognise hedge ineffectiveness. The Board considered that the actual results of the hedging relationships would provide useful information to users of financial statements during the period of uncertainty arising from the reform. Therefore, the Board decided that entities should continue to measure and recognise hedge ineffectiveness as required by IFRS Standards.

BC254   The Board also considered whether any exceptions should be made to the measurement of hedged items or hedging instruments because of the uncertainty arising from the reform. However, the Board noted that such an exception would be inconsistent with the decision not to change the requirements to measure and recognise hedge ineffectiveness in the financial statements. Therefore, the Board decided not to provide an exception from the measurement of hedging instruments and hedged items. This means that the fair value of a derivative designated as the hedging instrument should continue to be measured using the assumptions that market participants would use when pricing that derivative as required by IFRS 13 *Fair Value Measurement*.

BC255   For a hedged item designated in a fair value hedge, IAS 39 requires an entity to remeasure the hedged item for changes in fair value attributable to the hedged risk and recognise the gain or loss related to that fair value hedge adjustment in profit or loss. In doing so, the entity uses the assumptions that market participants would use when pricing the hedged item for changes in fair value attributable to the hedged risk. This would include a risk premium for uncertainty inherent in the hedged risk that market participants would consider. For example, to measure changes in fair value attributable to the hedged risk such as the IBOR component of a fixed-rate loan, an entity needs to reflect the uncertainty caused by the reform. When applying a present value technique to calculate the changes in fair value attributable to the designated risk component, such measurement should reflect market participants' assumptions about the uncertainty arising from the reform.

BC256   When an entity designates interest rate benchmark-based cash flows as the hedged item in a cash flow hedge, to calculate the change in the value of the hedged item for the purpose of measuring hedge ineffectiveness, the entity may use a derivative that would have terms that match the critical terms of the designated cash flows and the hedged risk (this is commonly referred to as a 'hypothetical derivative'). As the Board decided that entities should continue to measure and recognise hedge ineffectiveness as required by IFRS Standards, entities should continue to apply assumptions that are consistent with those applied to the hedged risk of the hedged item. For example, if an entity designated interest rate benchmark-based cash flows as the hedged item in a cash flow hedge, the entity would not assume for the purpose of measuring hedge ineffectiveness that the expected replacement of the interest rate benchmark with an alternative benchmark rate will result in zero cash flows after the replacement. The hedging gain or loss on the hedged item should be measured using the interest rate benchmark-based cash flows (that is, the cash flows on which the hypothetical derivative is based) when applying a present value technique, discounted at a market-based discount rate that reflects market participants' assumptions about the uncertainty arising from the reform. The Board concluded that reflecting market participants' assumptions when measuring hedge ineffectiveness provides useful information to users of financial statements about the effects of the uncertainty arising from the reform on an entity's hedging relationships. Therefore, the Board decided that no exceptions are needed for the measurement of actual ineffectiveness.

Hedges of designated portions

BC257   The Board noted that in accordance with IAS 39 an entity may designate an item in its entirety or only a portion thereof, as the hedged item in a hedging relationship. For example, an entity that issues a 5-year floating-rate debt instrument that bears interest at 3-month LIBOR + 1%, could designate as the hedged item either the entire debt instrument (that is, all of the cash flows) or only the 3-month LIBOR portion of the floating-rate debt instrument. Specifically, paragraphs 81 and AG99F of IAS 39 allow entities to designate only changes in the cash flows or fair value of an item attributable to a specific risk or risks (designated portion), provided that the designated portion is separately identifiable and reliably measurable.

BC258   The Board observed that an entity's ability to conclude that an interest rate benchmark is a separately identifiable designated portion in accordance with paragraph 81 of IAS 39 requires a continuous assessment over the duration of the hedging relationship and could be affected by the reform. For example, if the outcome of the reform affects the market structure of an interest rate benchmark, it could affect an entity's assessment of whether a non-contractually specified LIBOR portion is separately identifiable and, therefore, an eligible hedged item in a hedging relationship. The Board considered only those designated portions that are implicit in the fair value or the cash flows of an item of which they are a part (referred to as non-contractually specified) because the same issue does not arise for designated portions that are explicitly specified in the contract.

BC259   For the reasons outlined in paragraph BC227, the Board noted that discontinuing hedging relationships due to uncertainty arising from the reform would not provide useful information. Consequently, the Board decided to propose amending IAS 39 so that entities would not discontinue hedge accounting solely because the designated portion is no longer separately identifiable as a result of the reform. In the 2019 Exposure Draft, the Board proposed that the separately identifiable requirement for hedges of the benchmark portion of interest rate risk be applied only at the inception of those hedging relationships affected by the reform.

BC260   The Board proposed not to extend the relief to allow entities to designate the benchmark portion of interest rate risk as the hedged item in a new hedging relationship if the designated portion is not separately identifiable at the inception of the hedging relationship. In the Board's view, allowing hedge accounting for designated portions that are not separately identifiable at the inception would be inconsistent with the objective of the exception. The Board noted that such circumstances are different from allowing continued designation as the hedged item for designated portions that had met the requirement at the inception of the hedging relationship.

BC261 Furthermore, the Board did not propose any exception from the requirement that changes in the fair value or cash flows of the designated portion must be reliably measurable. As noted in paragraph BC243, in the Board's view, an offset between the hedged item and the hedging instrument is a fundamental principle of the hedge accounting model in IAS 39 and, therefore, the Board considered reliable measurement of the hedged item and the hedging instrument to be critical to maintain this principle.

BC262 Almost all respondents agreed with the exception proposed in the 2019 Exposure Draft to apply the separately identifiable requirement only at the inception of a hedging relationship. However, some respondents noted that the proposed exception did not provide equivalent relief to hedging relationships that frequently reset (ie discontinue and restart). In those hedging relationships both the hedging instrument and the hedged item frequently change (ie the entity uses a dynamic process in which both the hedged items and the hedging instruments used to manage that exposure do not remain the same for long). As hedging instruments and hedged items are being added or removed from a portfolio, entities are de-designating and redesignating hedging relationships regularly to adjust the exposure. If each redesignation of the hedging relationship is considered to be the inception of a new hedging relationship (even though it is still the same hedging strategy), then the separately identifiable requirement would need to be assessed for all hedged items at each redesignation even if they have been assessed previously. For the same reasons as those noted in paragraph BC258, this could affect an entity's ability to conclude that a non-contractually specified risk component remains separately identifiable and, therefore, an eligible hedged item for hedge accounting purposes.

BC263 The Board noted that the exception proposed in the 2019 Exposure Draft has the effect that if a non-contractually specified designated portion meets the separately identifiable requirement at the inception of a hedging relationship, then that requirement would not be reassessed subsequently. Hence, providing a similar exception for hedging relationships that frequently reset (ie discontinue and restart) would be consistent with the objective of the exception originally provided in the 2019 Exposure Draft.

BC264 Thus, the Board confirmed the proposal that a designated portion is only required to be separately identifiable at the inception of the hedging relationship. In addition, to respond to the feedback described in paragraph BC262, the Board added the exception in paragraph 102I of IAS 39 for hedging relationships that, consistent with an entity's hedge documentation, frequently reset (ie discontinue and restart) because both the hedging instrument and the hedged item frequently change. Applying that paragraph, an entity shall determine whether the designated portion is separately identifiable only when it initially designates an item as a hedged item in the hedging relationship. The hedged item is not reassessed at any subsequent redesignation in the same hedging relationship.

BC265 In reaching its decision for the exception in paragraph 102I of IAS 39 the Board considered an example when an entity applies hedge accounting for a portfolio hedge of interest rate risk under IAS 39 and designates the LIBOR portion of floating-rate loans as the hedged risk. At the inception of the relationship, the entity assesses whether LIBOR is a separately identifiable designated portion for all loans designated within the hedging relationship. As the entity updates the risk position with the origination of new loans and the maturity or repayment of existing loans, the hedging relationship is adjusted by de-designating the 'old' hedging relationship and redesignating a 'new' hedging relationship for the updated amount of the hedged items. Applying the exception in paragraph 102I of IAS 39 requires the entity to assess whether LIBOR is a separately identifiable designated portion only for the new loans added to the hedging relationship. The entity would not reassess the separately identifiable requirement for the loans that have been redesignated.

Mandatory application

BC266 The Board decided to require entities to apply the exceptions in paragraphs 102D–102N of IAS 39 to all hedging relationships to which the exceptions are applicable. In other words, the Board decided that an entity is required to apply the exceptions to all hedging relationships that are directly affected by the uncertainties arising from the reform and continue to apply the exceptions until required to cease their application as specified in paragraphs 102J–102N of IAS 39.

BC267 The Board considered but rejected alternatives that would have allowed entities to apply the exceptions voluntarily. In the Board's view, voluntary application of these exceptions could give rise to selective discontinuation of hedge accounting and selective reclassification of the amounts recorded in other comprehensive income related to previously discontinued hedging relationships. The Board does not expect that requiring entities to apply the exceptions would entail significant cost for preparers and other affected parties because the exceptions require entities to assume that the interest rate benchmark, on which the hedged risk and the hedged cash flows and cash flows of the hedging instrument are based, is not altered as a result of the reform.

BC268 In addition, the Board observed that in some circumstances the exceptions in paragraphs 102D–102N of IAS 39 may not be applicable. For example, for a particular interest rate benchmark not subject to the reform or replacement with an alternative benchmark rate, there is no uncertainty affecting the timing or the amount of the interest rate benchmark-based cash flows arising from a hedged item or a hedging instrument. The exceptions set out in paragraphs 102D–102N of IAS 39 would not be applicable to such a hedging relationship.

BC269   Furthermore, for a particular hedging relationship the exceptions may be applicable to some but not all aspects of the hedging relationship. For example, if an entity designates a hedged item that is based on LIBOR against a hedging instrument that is already referenced to an alternative benchmark rate (assuming the entity can demonstrate that hedging relationship meets the qualifying criteria for hedge accounting in IAS 39), the exceptions in paragraphs 102D and 102F of IAS 39 would apply for the hedged item because there is uncertainty related to its future cash flows. However, there is no uncertainty regarding how the reform would impact the cash flows of the hedging instrument and, therefore, the exception in paragraph 102F of IAS 39 is not applicable for the hedging instrument. Similarly, the exception applicable to non-contractually specified designated portions would not be relevant for hedging relationships that do not involve the designation of non-contractually specified portions.

End of application

BC270   As described in paragraph BC227, the Board decided to amend IAS 39 to address specific aspects of hedge accounting affected by uncertainties in relation to the hedged items and hedging instruments about when the interest rate benchmarks will change to alternative benchmark rates, when any spread adjustment between the interest rate benchmark and the alternative benchmark rate will be determined (collectively, timing) and what the cash flows based on the alternative benchmark rate will be, including their frequency of reset, and any spread adjustment between the interest rate benchmark and the alternative benchmark rate (collectively, amount). Therefore, the Board intended the exceptions set out in paragraphs 102D–102N of IAS 39 to be available only while these uncertainties are present.

BC271   The Board considered whether to provide an explicit end date for the exceptions but decided not to do so. The reform is following different timelines in different markets and jurisdictions and contracts are being modified at different times and, therefore, at this stage, it is not possible to define a period of applicability for the exceptions.

BC272   The Board decided that an entity ceases applying the exceptions at the earlier of (a) when the uncertainty regarding the timing and the amount of interest rate benchmark-based cash flows is no longer present as it relates to a hedged item and/or hedging instrument (depending on the particular exception) and (b) the discontinuation of the hedging relationship.[25] The exceptions require entities to apply specific hedge accounting requirements assuming the interest rate benchmark on which the hedged risk, hedged cash flows or the cash flows of the hedging instrument are based is not altered as a result of the reform. The end of applicability of the exceptions means that entities would

---

25   For the purpose of applying the exception in paragraph 102E of IAS 39 to a discontinued hedging relationship, the amendments require an entity to cease applying the exception at the earlier of (a) as described above and (b) when the entire amount that had been recognised in other comprehensive income with respect to the hedging relationship has been reclassified to profit or loss. See paragraph 102K of IAS 39.

from that date apply all hedge accounting requirements in IAS 39 without applying these exceptions.

BC273　In the Board's view, for uncertainty regarding the timing and the amount of cash flows arising from a change in an interest rate benchmark to be eliminated, the underlying contracts are generally required to be amended to specify the timing and the amount of cash flows based on the alternative benchmark rate (and any spread adjustment between the interest rate benchmark and the alternative benchmark rate). The Board noted that, in some cases, a contract may be amended to include reference to the alternative benchmark rate without actually altering the interest rate benchmark-based cash flows in the contract. Such an amendment may not eliminate the uncertainty regarding the timing and the amount of interest rate benchmark-based cash flows in the contract. The Board considered the following scenarios to assess the robustness of the end of application requirements. However, these scenarios are not exhaustive and other scenarios may exist in which the uncertainties arising from the reform regarding the timing and the amount of cash flows would no longer be present.

BC274　Scenario A—a contract is amended to include a clause that specifies (a) the date the interest rate benchmark will be replaced by an alternative benchmark rate and (b) the alternative benchmark rate on which the cash flows will be based and the relevant spread adjustment between the interest rate benchmark and the alternative benchmark rate. In this case, the uncertainty regarding the timing and the amount of cash flows for this contract is eliminated when the contract is amended to include this clause.

BC275　Scenario B—a contract is amended to include a clause that states modifications of contractual cash flows will occur due to the reform but that specifies neither the date that the interest rate benchmark will be replaced nor the alternative benchmark rate on which the amended cash flows will be based. In this case, the uncertainty regarding the timing and the amount of cash flows for this contract has not been eliminated by amending the contract to include this clause.

BC276　Scenario C—a contract is amended to include a clause which states that conditions specifying the amount and timing of interest rate benchmark-based cash flows will be determined by a central authority at some point in the future. But the clause does not specify those conditions. In this case, the uncertainty regarding the timing and the amount of the interest rate benchmark-based cash flows for this contract has not been eliminated by including this clause in the contract. Uncertainty regarding both the timing and the amount of cash flows for this contract will be present until the central authority specifies when the replacement of the benchmark will become effective and what the alternative benchmark rate and any related spread adjustment will be.

BC277　Scenario D—a contract is amended to include a clause in anticipation of the reform that specifies the date the interest rate benchmark will be replaced and any spread adjustment between the interest rate benchmark and the alternative benchmark rate will be determined. However, the amendment does not specify the alternative benchmark rate or the spread adjustment between the interest rate benchmark and the alternative benchmark rate on which the cash flows will be based. In this scenario, by amending the contract to include this clause, uncertainty regarding the timing has been eliminated but uncertainty about the amount remains.

BC278　Scenario E—a contract is amended to include a clause in anticipation of the reform that specifies the alternative benchmark rate on which the cash flows will be based and the spread adjustment between the interest rate benchmark and the alternative benchmark rate but does not specify the date from which the amendment to the contract will become effective. In this scenario, by amending the contract to include this clause, uncertainty about the amount has been eliminated but uncertainty with respect to timing remains.

BC279　Scenario F—in preparation for the reform, a central authority in its capacity as the administrator of an interest rate benchmark undertakes a multi-step process to replace an interest rate benchmark with an alternative benchmark rate. The objective of the reform is to cease the publication of the current interest rate benchmark and replace it with an alternative benchmark rate. As part of the reform, the administrator introduces an interim benchmark rate and determines a fixed spread adjustment based on the difference between the interim benchmark rate and the current interest rate benchmark. Uncertainty about the timing or the amount of the alternative benchmark rate-based cash flows will not be eliminated during the interim period because the interim benchmark rate (including the fixed spread adjustment determined by the administrator) represent an interim measure in progressing towards the reform but it does not represent the alternative benchmark rate (or any related spread adjustment agreed between parties to the contract).

BC280　For reasons similar to those described in paragraph BC269, the Board noted that there could be situations in which the uncertainty for particular elements of a single hedging relationship could end at different times. For example, assume an entity is required to apply the relevant exceptions to both the hedged item and the hedging instrument. If the hedging instrument in that hedging relationship is subsequently amended through market protocols covering all derivatives in that market, and will be based on an alternative benchmark rate such that the uncertainty about the timing and the amount of interest rate benchmark-based cash flows of the hedging instrument is eliminated, the relevant exceptions would continue to apply to the hedged item but would no longer apply to the hedging instrument.[26]

BC281　The Board observed that continuing to apply the exception after the uncertainty was resolved would not faithfully represent the actual characteristics of the elements of the hedging relationship in which the uncertainty arising from the reform is eliminated. The Board considered whether it should extend the relief provided such that the exceptions would apply at the hedging relationship level for as long as any element of that

---

26　In this scenario, the entity would first consider the accounting consequences of amending the contractual terms of the hedging instrument. The Board will consider the accounting consequences of the actual amendment of financial instruments as a result of interest rate benchmark reform in the next phase of this project (ie the replacement phase).

hedging relationship was affected by the uncertainties arising from the reform. The Board agreed that doing so would be beyond the objective of addressing only those issues directly affected by the uncertainty arising from the reform. This is also because the exceptions in paragraphs 102D–102N of IAS 39 and the respective requirements in IAS 39 apply to the same elements of the hedging relationship. Therefore, applying each exception at the hedging relationship level would be inconsistent with how the underlying requirements are applied.

BC282　The Board decided that the end of application requirement would also apply to hedges of a forecast transaction. The Board noted that IAS 39 requires an entity to identify and document a forecast transaction with sufficient specificity so that, when the transaction occurs, the entity is able to determine whether the transaction is the hedged transaction. For example, if an entity designates a future issuance of a LIBOR-based debt instrument as the hedged item, although there may be no contract at the time of designation, the hedge documentation would refer specifically to LIBOR. Consequently, the Board concluded that entities should be able to identify when the uncertainty regarding the timing and the amount of the resulting cash flows of a forecast transaction is no longer present.

BC283　In addition, the Board decided not to require end of application with respect to the exception for the separately identifiable requirements set out in paragraphs 102H and 102I of IAS 39. Applying these exceptions, entities would continue applying hedge accounting when an interest rate benchmark meets the separately identifiable requirement at the inception of the hedging relationship (assuming all other hedge accounting requirements continue to be met). If the Board included an end date for these exceptions, an entity may be required to immediately discontinue hedge accounting because, at some point, as the reform progresses, the designated portion based on the interest rate benchmark may no longer be separately identifiable (for example, as the market for the alternative benchmark rate is established). Such immediate discontinuation of hedge accounting would be inconsistent with the objective of the exception. The Board noted that linking the end of application for these exceptions to contract amendments would not achieve the Board's intention either because, by definition, non-contractually specified designated portions are not explicitly stated in a contract and, therefore, these contracts may not be amended for the reform. This is particularly relevant for fair value hedges of a fixed-rate debt instrument. Therefore, the Board decided that an entity should cease applying the exceptions to a hedging relationship only when the hedging relationship is discontinued applying IAS 39.

BC284　Some respondents to the 2019 Exposure Draft noted that the Board had not addressed when an entity ceases applying the proposed exceptions to a group of items designated as the hedged item or a combination of financial instruments designated as the hedging instrument. Specifically, when assessing whether the uncertainty arising from the reform is no longer present, these respondents asked whether that assessment should be performed on an individual basis (that is, for each individual item within the group or financial instrument within the combination) or on a group basis (that is, for all items in the group or all financial instruments in the combination until there is no uncertainty surrounding any of the items or financial instruments).

BC285 Consequently, the Board decided to add paragraph 102N of IAS 39 to clarify that, when designating a group of items as the hedged item or a combination of financial instruments as the hedging instrument, entities assess when the uncertainty arising from the reform with respect to the hedged risk and/or the timing and amount of the interest rate benchmark-based cash flows of that item or financial instrument is no longer present on an individual basis — that is, for each individual item in the group or financial instrument in the combination.

Effective date and transition

BC286 The Board decided that entities shall apply the amendments for annual periods beginning on or after 1 January 2020, with earlier application permitted.

BC287 The Board decided that the amendments apply retrospectively. The Board highlighted that retrospective application of the amendments would not allow reinstating hedge accounting that has already been discontinued. Nor would it allow designation in hindsight. If an entity had not designated a hedging relationship, the exceptions, even though applied retrospectively, would not allow the entity to apply hedge accounting in prior periods to items that were not designated for hedge accounting. Doing so would be inconsistent with the requirement that hedge accounting applies prospectively. Retrospective application of the exceptions would enable entities to continue hedge accounting for a hedging relationship that the entity had previously designated and that qualifies for hedge accounting applying IAS 39.

BC288 Many respondents to the 2019 Exposure Draft commented on the clarity of the proposed retrospective application and suggested that further explanation be provided in the Standard. Consequently, the Board amended the transition paragraph to specify that retrospective application applies only to those hedging relationships that existed at the beginning of the reporting period in which an entity first applies these amendments or were designated thereafter, and to the gain or loss recognised in other comprehensive income that existed at the beginning of the reporting period in which an entity first applies these amendments. The Board used this wording to permit an entity to apply the amendments from the beginning of the reporting period in which an entity first applies these amendments even if the reporting period is not an annual period.

Amendments for *Interest Rate Benchmark Reform—Phase 2* (August 2020)

Background

BC289 In 2014, the Financial Stability Board recommended the reform of specified major interest rate benchmarks such as interbank offered rates (IBORs). Since then, public authorities in many jurisdictions have taken steps to implement interest rate benchmark reform and have increasingly encouraged market participants to ensure timely progress towards the reform of interest rate benchmarks, including the replacement of interest rate benchmarks with alternative, nearly risk-free interest rates that are based, to a greater extent, on transaction data (alternative benchmark rates). The progress towards interest rate benchmark reform follows the general expectation that some major interest rate benchmarks will cease to be published by the end of 2021. The term 'interest rate benchmark reform' refers to the market-wide reform of an interest rate benchmark as described in paragraph 102B of IAS 39 (the reform).

BC290 In September 2019, the Board amended IFRS 9, IAS 39 and IFRS 7, to address as a priority issues affecting financial reporting in the period before the reform of an interest rate benchmark, including the replacement of an interest rate benchmark with an alternative benchmark rate (Phase 1 amendments). The Phase 1 amendments provide temporary exceptions to specific hedge accounting requirements due to the uncertainty arising from the reform. Paragraphs BC223–BC288 discuss the background to the Phase 1 amendments.

BC291 After the issuance of the Phase 1 amendments, the Board commenced its Phase 2 deliberations. In Phase 2 of its project on the reform, the Board addressed issues that might affect financial reporting during the reform of an interest rate benchmark, including changes to contractual cash flows or hedging relationships arising from the replacement of an interest rate benchmark with an alternative benchmark rate (replacement issues).

BC292 The objective of Phase 2 is to assist entities in providing useful information to users of financial statements and to support preparers in applying IFRS Standards when changes are made to contractual cash flows or hedging relationships because of the transition to alternative benchmark rates. The Board observed that for information about the effects of the transition to alternative benchmark rates to be useful, the information has to be relevant to users of financial statements and faithfully represent the economic effects of that transition on the entity. This objective assisted the Board in assessing whether it should amend IFRS Standards or whether the requirements in IFRS Standards already provided an adequate basis to account for such effects.

BC293 In April 2020 the Board published the Exposure Draft *Interest Rate Benchmark Reform – Phase 2* (2020 Exposure Draft), which proposed amendments to specific requirements in IFRS 9, IAS 39, IFRS 7, IFRS 4 *Insurance Contracts* and IFRS 16 *Leases* to address replacement issues.

BC294   Almost all respondents to the 2020 Exposure Draft welcomed the Board's decision to address replacement issues and agreed that the proposed amendments would achieve the objective of Phase 2. Many respondents highlighted the urgency of these amendments, especially in some jurisdictions that have progressed towards the reform or the replacement of interest rate benchmarks with alternative benchmark rates.

BC295   In August 2020 the Board amended IFRS 9, IAS 39, IFRS 7, IFRS 4 and IFRS 16 by issuing *Interest Rate Benchmark Reform—Phase 2* (Phase 2 amendments). The Phase 2 amendments, which confirmed with modifications the proposals in the 2020 Exposure Draft added paragraphs 102O–102Z3 and 108H–108K of IAS 39. Paragraph 102M was amended.

Amendments to hedging relationships

BC296   The Phase 2 amendments relating to the hedge accounting requirements in IAS 39 apply to hedging relationships directly affected by the reform as and when the requirements in paragraphs 102D–102I of IAS 39 cease to apply to a hedging relationship (see paragraphs 102J–102O of IAS 39). Therefore, an entity is required to amend the hedging relationship to reflect the changes required by the reform as and when the uncertainty arising from the reform is no longer present with respect to the hedged risk or the timing and the amount of interest rate benchmark-based cash flows of the hedged item or of the hedging instrument. The scope of the hedging relationships to which the Phase 2 amendments apply is therefore the same as the scope to which the Phase 1 amendments apply, except for the amendment to the separately identifiable requirement, which also applies to the designation of new hedging relationships (see paragraph 102Z3 of IAS 39).

BC297   As part of the Phase 1 amendments, the Board acknowledged that, in most cases, for uncertainty regarding the timing and the amount of interest rate benchmark-based cash flows arising from the reform to be resolved, the underlying financial instruments designated in the hedging relationship would have to be changed to specify the timing and the amount of alternative benchmark rate-based cash flows.

BC298   The Board noted that, applying the hedge accounting requirements in IAS 39, changes to the basis for determining the contractual cash flows of a financial asset or a financial liability (see paragraphs 5.4.6–5.4.9 of IFRS 9) that are designated in a hedging relationship would affect the designation of such a hedging relationship in which an interest rate benchmark was designated as a hedged risk.

BC299   The Board observed that amending the formal designation of a hedging relationship to reflect the changes required by the reform would result in the discontinuation of the hedging relationship. This is because, as part of the qualifying criteria for hedge accounting to be applied, IAS 39 requires the formal designation of a hedging relationship to be documented at inception. The hedge documentation includes identification of the hedging instrument, the hedged item, the nature of the risk being hedged and how the entity will assess hedge effectiveness.

BC300 The Board therefore concluded that, in general, the hedge accounting requirements in IAS 39 are sufficiently clear about how to account for hedging relationships directly affected by the reform after the Phase 1 exceptions set out in paragraphs 102D–102I of IAS 39 cease to apply. However, consistent with the Board's objective for Phase 2 (see paragraph BC292) and its objective for Phase 1 (see paragraph BC227), the Board considered that discontinuing hedge accounting solely due to the effects of the reform would not always reflect the economic effects of the changes required by the reform on a hedging relationship and therefore would not always provide useful information to users of financial statements.

BC301 Accordingly, the Board decided that if the reform requires a change to a financial asset or a financial liability designated in a hedging relationship (see paragraphs 5.4.6–5.4.8 of IFRS 9), it would be consistent with the Board's objective for Phase 2 to require the hedging relationship to be amended to reflect such a change without requiring discontinuation of that hedging relationship. For these reasons, in the 2020 Exposure Draft, the Board proposed that an entity would be required to amend the formal designation of the hedging relationship as previously documented to make one or more of these changes:

(a) designating the alternative benchmark rate (contractually or non-contractually specified) as a hedged risk;

(b) amending the description of the hedged item so it refers to the alternative benchmark rate;

(c) amending the description of the hedging instrument so it refers to the alternative benchmark rate; or

(d) amending the description of how the entity will assess hedge effectiveness.

BC302 Respondents to the 2020 Exposure Draft agreed with the proposed amendments because those proposals would generally result in an entity continuing to apply hedge accounting to hedging relationships directly affected by the reform. Respondents also said that changes to the hedge designation necessary to reflect changes required by the reform are not expected to represent a change in an entity's risk management strategy or risk management objective for hedging their exposure to interest rate risk. Therefore, the Board concluded that continuing to apply hedge accounting to the affected hedging relationships when making changes required by the reform would correspond with the Board's objective for issuing the Phase 1 amendments in September 2019.

BC303 However, notwithstanding their general agreement with the proposed amendments, some respondents asked the Board to clarify the scope and timing of the required changes to the affected hedging relationships.

BC304 Regarding the scope of the required changes to the affected hedging relationships, the Board acknowledged it may be necessary to amend the designated hedged portion of the cash flows or fair value being hedged when the hedging relationship is amended to reflect the changes required by the reform. The Board also noted that the changes required by the reform described in paragraphs 5.4.6–5.4.8 of IFRS 9 were implicit in the required amendments to the hedging relationships as proposed in the 2020 Exposure Draft. In considering the timing of when entities are required to amend an affected hedging relationship, the Board sought to balance the operational effort needed to amend the hedging relationships with maintaining the required discipline in the amendments to hedging relationships. Specifically, it sought to address the challenges associated with specifying the timing of when entities have to amend hedging relationships as required in paragraph 102P of IAS 39 — particularly in the context of the large volume of changes that entities may need to make in a relatively short time — while also ensuring that the amendments to hedging relationships are accounted for in the applicable reporting period.

BC305   In response to respondents' requests, the Board revised the proposed wording in paragraph 102P of IAS 39 so that:

(a)   amending the description of the hedged item includes amending the description of the designated portion of the cash flows or fair value being hedged;

(b)   the changes required by the reform described in paragraphs 5.4.6–5.4.8 of IFRS 9 are relevant when amending the formal designation of a hedging relationship; and

(c)   amendments to hedging relationships are required to be made by the end of the reporting period during which the respective changes to the hedged item, hedged risk or hedging instrument are made.

BC306   The Board noted that the Phase 1 amendments may cease to apply at different times to directly affected hedging relationships and to the different elements within a hedging relationship. Therefore, an entity may be required to apply the applicable Phase 2 exceptions in paragraphs 102P–102Z2 of IAS 39 at different times, which may result in the designation of a particular hedging relationship being amended more than once. The Phase 2 amendments to the hedge accounting requirements in IAS 39 apply only to the requirements specified in these paragraphs. All other hedge accounting requirements in IAS 39, including the qualifying criteria in paragraph 88 of IAS 39, apply to hedging relationships directly affected by the reform. In addition, consistent with the Board's decision for the Phase 1 amendments (see paragraph BC254), the Phase 2 amendments also do not provide an exception from the measurement requirements for a hedging relationship. Therefore, entities apply the requirements in paragraphs 89 or 96 of IAS 39 to account for any changes in the fair value of the hedged items or hedging instruments (also see paragraphs BC315–BC320).

BC307   As set out in paragraph BC5.318 of the Basis for Conclusions on IFRS 9, the Board considered that changes might be made to a financial asset or a financial liability, or to the formal designation of a hedging relationship, in addition to those changes required by the reform. The effect of such additional changes to the formal hedge designation on the application of the hedge accounting requirements would depend on whether those changes result in the derecognition of the underlying financial instrument (see paragraph 5.4.9 of IFRS 9).

BC308   The Board therefore required an entity first to apply the applicable requirements in IAS 39 to determine if those additional changes result in discontinuation of hedge accounting, for example, if the financial asset or financial liability designated as a hedged item no longer meets the qualifying criteria to be an eligible hedged item as a result of changes in addition to those required by the reform. Similarly, if an entity amends the hedge designation to make a change other than the changes described in paragraph 102P of IAS 39 (for example, if it extends the term of the hedging relationship), the entity would first determine if those additional changes to the hedge designation result in the discontinuation of hedge accounting. If the additional changes do not result in the discontinuation of hedge accounting, the designation of the hedging relationship would be amended as required by paragraph 102P of IAS 39.

BC309   Some respondents to the 2020 Exposure Draft said that entities may change a hedging relationship as a result of the reform, but such a change is not necessary as a direct consequence of the reform. This could include, for example, designating a basis swap as a new hedging instrument to mitigate ineffectiveness arising from the difference between the compounding of the alternative benchmark rates used for cash products and derivatives. These respondents asked the Board to permit such changes to be in the scope of the required changes to the hedging relationship set out in paragraph 102P of IAS 39. The Board however decided not to extend the scope of paragraph 102P of IAS 39 to other changes an entity makes as a result of the reform. The Board considered that its objective for the Phase 2 amendments is not only to support entities in applying the IFRS requirements during the transition to alternative benchmark rates, but also to provide users of financial statements with useful information about the effect of the reform on an entity's financial statements. To balance achieving this objective with maintaining the discipline that exists in the hedge accounting requirements in IAS 39, the Board limited the scope of the changes required to the designation of hedging relationships to only those changes that are necessary to reflect the changes required by the reform (as described in paragraphs 5.4.6–5.4.8 of IFRS 9).

Replacement of hedging instruments in hedging relationships

BC310   Respondents to the 2020 Exposure Draft said that, instead of changing the contractual terms of a derivative designated as a hedging instrument, counterparties may facilitate the transition to alternative benchmark rates using approaches that result in outcomes that are equivalent to changing the contractual terms of the derivative. These respondents asked whether using such an approach would be within the scope of the Phase 2 amendments—ie whether paragraph 102P(c) of IAS 39 would apply—if the approach results in an economic outcome that is similar to changing the basis for determining the contractual cash flows of the derivative.

BC311   The Board confirmed that, consistent with the rationale in paragraph BC5.298 of the Basis for Conclusions on IFRS 9, it is the substance of an arrangement, rather than its form, that determines the appropriate accounting treatment. The Board considered that the conditions in paragraph 5.4.7 of IFRS 9—ie the change is necessary as a direct consequence of the reform and is done on economically equivalent basis—are helpful in analysing the amendments to the contractual terms of derivatives described in paragraph BC310. In this context, the Board noted that if these other approaches result in derivatives with substantially different terms from those of the original derivative, the change may not have been made on an economically equivalent basis. The Board also noted that if a hedging instrument is derecognised, hedge accounting is required to be discontinued. Therefore, the Board decided that for hedge accounting to continue it is also necessary that the original hedging instrument would not be derecognised.

BC312   The Board considered these approaches described by respondents:

(a)   *close-out and replace on the same terms (ie off-market terms)*—An entity applying this approach would enter into two new derivatives with the same counterparty. These two would be, a new derivative that is equal and offsetting to the original derivative (so both contracts are based on the interest rate benchmark to be replaced), and a new alternative benchmark-based derivative with the same terms as the original derivative so its fair value at initial recognition is equivalent to the fair value—on that date—of the original derivative (ie the new derivative is off-market). Under this approach the counterparty to the new derivatives is the same as to the original derivative, the original derivative has not been derecognised and the terms of the alternative benchmark rate derivative are not substantially different from that of the original derivative. The Board therefore concluded that such an approach could be regarded as consistent with the changes required by the reform as required in paragraph 102P of IAS 39.

(b)   *close-out and replace on substantially different terms (eg on-market terms)*—An entity applying this approach would terminate (close-out) the existing interest rate benchmark-based derivative with a cash settlement. The entity then enters into a new on-market alternative benchmark rate derivative with substantially different terms, so that the new derivative has a fair value of zero at initial recognition. Some respondents to the 2020 Exposure Draft were of the view that since this approach does not result in any gain or loss recognised in profit or loss, it suggests the exchange was done on an economically equivalent basis. The Board disagreed with this view because the original derivative is extinguished and replaced with an alternative benchmark rate derivative with substantially different contractual terms. Therefore, this approach is not considered consistent with the changes required by the reform as required in paragraph 102P of IAS 39.

(c) *add a new basis swap*—An entity applying this approach would retain the original interest rate benchmark-based derivative but enter into a basis swap that swaps the existing interest rate benchmark for the alternative benchmark rate. The combination of the two derivatives is equivalent to modifying the contractual terms of the original derivative to replace the interest rate benchmark with an alternative benchmark rate. The Board noted that, in principle, the combination of an interest rate benchmark-based derivative and an interest rate benchmark-alternative benchmark rate swap could achieve an outcome economically equivalent to amending the original interest rate benchmark-based derivative. However, the Board observed that, in practice, basis swaps are generally entered into on an aggregated basis to economically hedge an entity's net exposure to basis risk, rather than on an individual derivative basis. The Board therefore noted that for this approach to be consistent with the changes required by the reform as described in paragraph 102P of IAS 39, the basis swap must be coupled or linked with the original derivative, ie done on an individual derivative basis. This is because a change to the basis for determining the contractual cash flows of a hedging instrument is made to an individual instrument and, to achieve the same outcome, the basis swap would need to be coupled with an individual derivative.

(d) *novating to a new counterparty*—An entity applying this approach would novate the original interest rate benchmark-based derivative to a new counterparty and subsequently change the contractual cash flows on the novated derivative to replace the interest rate benchmark with an alternative benchmark rate. The Board noted that novation of a derivative would result in the derecognition of the original derivative and thus would require hedge accounting to be discontinued in accordance with paragraph 101 of IAS 39 (see further paragraphs BC220E–BC220G). Therefore, this approach is not consistent with the changes required by the reform as set out in paragraph 102P of IAS 39.

BC313 The Board therefore added paragraph 102Q of IAS 39 so that, an entity also applies paragraph 102P(c) of IAS 39 if these three conditions are met:

(a) the entity makes a change required by the reform using an approach other than changing the basis for determining the contractual cash flows of the hedging instrument (as described in paragraph 5.4.6 of IFRS 9);

(b) the original hedging instrument is not derecognised; and

(c) the chosen approach is economically equivalent to changing the basis for determining the contractual cash flows of the original hedging instrument (as described in paragraphs 5.4.7 and 5.4.8 of IFRS 9).

BC314 The Board decided not to add further amendments or provide application guidance because IAS 39 as amended provides an adequate basis for analysing the accounting requirements in context of the approaches described in paragraph BC312.

Remeasurement of the hedged item and hedging instrument

BC315 In paragraph BC254, the Board explained that no exceptions were made in Phase 1 to the measurement requirements for hedged items or hedging instruments. The Board concluded that the most useful information would be provided to users of financial statements if requirements for recognition and measurement of hedge ineffectiveness remain unchanged (see paragraph BC253). This is because recognising ineffectiveness in the financial statements based on the actual results of a hedging relationship faithfully represents the economic effects of the reform, thereby providing useful information to users of financial statements.

BC316 Applying the hedge accounting requirements in IAS 39, a gain or loss arising from the remeasurement of the hedged item attributable to the hedged risk or from remeasuring the hedging instrument is reflected in profit or loss when measuring and recognising hedge ineffectiveness.

BC317 When deliberating the Phase 2 amendments, the Board considered that changes in the fair value of the hedged item or hedging instrument could arise when the formal designation of a hedging relationship is amended.

BC318 The Board considered whether to provide an exception from the requirement to include in hedge ineffectiveness such fair value changes when they arise. The Board considered, but rejected, these approaches:

(a) *recognising the measurement adjustment in profit or loss over time* — An entity applying this approach would recognise the measurement adjustment in profit or loss over time (ie amortised) as the hedged item affects profit or loss. The Board rejected this approach because it would require an offsetting entry to be recognised either in the statement of financial position or as an adjustment to the carrying amount of the hedged item or hedging instrument. Such an offsetting entry would fail to meet the definition of an asset or a liability in the *Conceptual Framework*. Adjusting the carrying amount of the hedged item or hedging instrument would result in the recognition of a net measurement adjustment of zero and would be inconsistent with the Board's decision that no exceptions would be made to the measurement of hedged items or hedging instruments. The Board also noted that such an approach would likely result in increased operational complexity because an entity would need to track adjustments that occur at different times for the purpose of amortising the adjustments in the period(s) in which the hedged item affects profit or loss.

(b) *recognising the measurement adjustment as an adjustment to retained earnings* — An entity applying this approach would recognise the measurement adjustment as an adjustment to retained earnings during the period in which the measurement difference arises. However, the Board rejected this approach because the changes to the hedged risk might be driven by amendments to hedging relationships that may occur in different reporting periods. Therefore, recognising adjustments to retained earnings over time would be inconsistent with the Board's previous decisions (throughout IFRS Standards) that an adjustment to retained earnings only applies on transition to new requirements in IFRS Standards. Furthermore, the Board noted that the measurement adjustment would meet the definition of income or expense in the *Conceptual Framework* and therefore should be recognised in the statement of profit or loss. The Board also noted that recognising measurement adjustments directly in retained earnings would be inconsistent with the decision that no exceptions should be made to the measurement of hedged items or hedging instruments.

BC319 Some respondents to the 2020 Exposure Draft said they would not expect any significant changes in fair value to arise from the remeasurement of a hedged item or hedging instrument based on the alternative benchmark rate. That is because these amendments would apply only when the conditions in paragraph 5.4.7 of IFRS 9 are met, which require that changes are made on an economically equivalent basis. The Board acknowledged these comments noting that, applying paragraph 102P of IAS 39, a significant change in fair value arising from the remeasurement of the hedged item or the hedging instrument indicates that the changes were not made on an economically equivalent basis. Furthermore, the Board observed that the requirement in paragraph 102P(b) of IAS 39 which requires the description of the designated portion for the cash flows or fair value being hedged enables entities to amend a hedging relationship to minimise fair value changes on the remeasurement of the hedged item or the hedging instrument.

BC320 The Board therefore confirmed its previous decision not to provide an exception from the requirements in IAS 39 regarding the measurement and recognition of hedge ineffectiveness. Therefore, an entity would apply the requirements in paragraphs 89 (for a fair value hedge) and 96 (for a cash flow hedge) of IAS 39 for the measurement and recognition of hedge ineffectiveness. The Board considered that accounting for such fair value changes in any other way would be inconsistent with the decision to continue applying hedge accounting for such amended hedging relationships (see paragraph 102P of IAS 39). In the Board's view, applying the requirements in IAS 39 for the recognition and measurement of ineffectiveness reflects the economic effects of the amendments to the formal designation of a hedging relationship and therefore, provides useful information to users of financial statements.

Accounting for qualifying hedging relationships

Retrospective effectiveness assessment

BC321 Applying the Phase 1 exception in paragraph 102G of IAS 39, an entity is not required to discontinue a hedge accounting relationship because the actual results of the hedge do not meet the requirements in paragraph AG105(b) of IAS 39. Applying paragraph 102M of IAS 39, an entity is required to cease applying this exception when the uncertainty is no longer present with respect to the hedged risk and the timing and the amount of the interest rate benchmark-based cash flows of the hedged item and hedging instrument, unless the hedging relationship is discontinued before that date. As with the other Phase 1 amendments, at the date the exception in paragraph 102G of IAS 39 ceases to apply, an entity must apply the requirements in IAS 39 (as amended by the Phase 2 amendments). Therefore, at that time, an entity would apply paragraph AG105(b) of IAS 39 to assess whether the actual results of the hedge are within a range of 80–125 per cent and, if the results are outside that range, discontinue hedge accounting.

BC322　The Board considered that when paragraph 102G of IAS 39 ceases to apply and an entity first applies the requirement in paragraph AG105(b) of IAS 39 to assess the retrospective effectiveness of a hedging relationship, the hedging relationship could fail the retrospective assessment if the entity assesses hedge effectiveness on a cumulative basis. In the Board's view, this outcome would be inconsistent with the Board's objective for Phase 1. Specifically, it would be inconsistent with the objective of the exception to prevent the discontinuation of hedge accounting solely due to the effects of the uncertainties arising from the reform on the actual results of a hedge while recognising all ineffectiveness in the financial statements.

BC323　To address the issue described in paragraph BC322, the 2020 Exposure Draft proposed an amendment to IAS 39 that would require an entity, only for the purpose of applying the retrospective assessment, to reset to zero the cumulative fair value changes of the hedged item and the hedging instrument when the exception from the retrospective assessment ceases to apply. This proposed amendment would apply only when an entity assesses retrospective effectiveness on a cumulative basis (ie using the dollar offset method on a cumulative basis). As required by IAS 39, the entity would continue to measure and recognise hedge ineffectiveness by comparing the actual gains or losses on the hedged item to those on the hedging instrument.

BC324　Respondents to the 2020 Exposure Draft agreed with the objective of this proposed amendment but identified particular circumstances in which it could unintentionally cause some hedging relationships to fail the retrospective effectiveness assessment. For example, this could be the case when there is market volatility during the initial period following the transition to an alternative benchmark rate. Such volatility could cause the retrospective effectiveness assessment to breach the 80-125 per cent threshold because an entity would be precluded from assessing effectiveness based on data prior to the reset date even if that data would show that the hedging relationship actually is effective over a longer time horizon. The Board agreed with these comments and therefore, amended paragraph 102V of IAS 39 so that it permits, rather than requires, entities (ie entities may elect) to reset to zero the cumulative fair value changes for the purpose of assessing the retrospective effectiveness of a hedging relationship on a cumulative basis. Considering the nature of this amendment, the Board decided this election is made on an individual hedging relationship basis.

Prospective assessments

BC325   The Phase 1 exception in paragraph 102F of IAS 39 requires an entity to assume that, for the purpose of the prospective effectiveness assessment as required by paragraphs 88(b) and AG105(a) of IAS 39, the interest rate benchmark on which the hedged cash flows and/or the hedged risk (contractually or non-contractually specified) are based, is not altered as a result of the reform. As noted in paragraph 102L of IAS 39, this exception ceases to apply to the hedged item and the hedging instrument, respectively, at the earlier of, when there is no longer uncertainty about the hedged risk or the timing and the amount of the interest rate benchmark-based cash flows; and when the hedging relationship that the hedged item and the hedging instrument are a part of is discontinued.

BC326   Consistent with the Board's considerations on the highly probable requirement (see paragraphs BC327–BC328), the Board considered that, when the formal designation of a hedging relationship has been amended (see paragraph 102P of IAS 39), the prospective assessment should be performed based on the alternative benchmark rate on which the hedged cash flows and/or the hedged risk will be based. The Board therefore provided no exceptions from the prospective assessment for the period after the Phase 1 exception in paragraph 102F of IAS 39 ceases to apply.

Amounts accumulated in the cash flow hedge reserve

BC327   During the period in which a hedging relationship is affected by uncertainty arising from the reform, paragraph 102D of IAS 39 requires an entity to assume that the interest rate benchmark on which the hedged cash flows (contractually or non-contractually specified) are based is not altered for the purpose of determining whether a forecast transaction (or a component thereof) is highly probable. An entity is required to cease applying this exception at the earlier of the date the uncertainty arising from the reform is no longer present with respect to the timing and the amount of the interest rate benchmark-based cash flows of the hedged item; and the date the hedging relationship of which the hedged item is a part of is discontinued.

BC328   The Board considered that uncertainty about the timing and the amount of the hedged cash flows would no longer be present when the interest rate benchmark on which the hedged cash flows are based is altered as required by the reform. In other words, uncertainty would no longer be present when an entity amends the description of the hedged item, including the description of the designated portion of the cash flows or fair value being hedged, applying paragraph 102P(b) of IAS 39. Thereafter, applying the requirement in paragraph 88(c) of IAS 39, the assessment of whether the hedged cash flows are still highly probable to occur would be based on the contractual cash flows determined by reference to the alternative benchmark rate.

BC329   The Board noted that the amendment in paragraph 102P(b) of IAS 39 for amending the formal designation of a hedging relationship could lead to changes in the hedged item. Therefore, if an entity uses a hypothetical derivative—that is, a derivative that would have terms matching the critical terms of the designated cash flows and the hedged risk, commonly used in cash flow hedges to represent the forecast transaction—the entity may need to change the hypothetical derivative to calculate the change in the value of the hedged item to measure hedge ineffectiveness.

BC330　Consequently, as hedge accounting would not be discontinued when a hedging relationship is amended for changes required by the reform (see paragraph 102P of IAS 39), the Board decided that an entity would deem the amount accumulated in the cash flow hedge reserve at that point to be based on the alternative benchmark rate on which the hedged future cash flows are determined. Therefore, in applying paragraph 97 of IAS 39, the amount accumulated in the cash flow hedge reserve would be reclassified to profit or loss in the same period(s) during which the hedged cash flows based on the alternative benchmark rate affect profit or loss.

BC331　The approach described in paragraph BC330 is consistent with the Board's view that, when a hedging relationship is amended for changes required by the reform, more useful information is provided to users of financial statements if hedge accounting is not discontinued and amounts are not reclassified to profit or loss solely due to the changes required by the reform. This is because such an approach will more faithfully reflect the economic effects of changes required by the reform.

BC332　Consistent with the requirements in paragraphs 102E and 102K of IAS 39, the Board considered whether to provide similar relief for any discontinued hedging relationships in which the previously designated hedged item is subject to the reform. The Board observed that although a hedging relationship may have been discontinued, the amount accumulated in the cash flow hedge reserve arising from that hedging relationship remains in the reserve if the hedged future cash flows are still expected to occur. The Board noted that if the hedged future cash flows are still expected to occur, the previously designated hedged item will be subject to a change required by the reform, even if the hedging relationship has been discontinued.

BC333　The Board therefore decided that, for the purpose of applying paragraph 101(c) of IAS 39, an entity deems the cumulative gain or loss recognised in the other comprehensive income for a discontinued hedging relationship, to be based on the alternative benchmark rate on which the contractual cash flows will be based, which is similar to the amendment in paragraph 102W of IAS 39. That amount is reclassified to profit or loss in the same period(s) in which the hedged future cash flows based on the alternative benchmark rate affect profit or loss.

BC334　Some respondents to the 2020 Exposure Draft asked the Board to clarify whether the requirements in paragraphs 102W–102X of IAS 39 require the retrospective measurement of the hedged item based on the alternative benchmark rate-based cash flows—in other words, whether an entity would be required to recalculate what the cumulative gain or loss recognised in other comprehensive income would have been if the hedged item was based on the alternative benchmark rate since inception.

BC335   The Board considered that the cumulative gain or loss recognised in other comprehensive income is adjusted as required by paragraph 96 of IAS 39 (ie the cumulative gain or loss recognised in other comprehensive income is not subject to separate measurement requirements, but instead is derived from the cumulative changes in the fair value of the hedged item (present value) and hedging instrument). The Phase 2 amendments do not include an exception from the measurement requirements in IFRS 9. Accordingly, the fair value of the hedging instrument or of the hedged item (ie the present value of the cumulative changes in the hedged expected future cash flows) is determined at the measurement date based on the expected future cash flows and assumptions that market participants would use. In other words, the fair values are not determined retrospectively. The Board therefore considered that the cumulative gain or loss recognised in other comprehensive income is not remeasured as if it had been based on the alternative benchmark rate since inception of the hedging relationship.

BC336   The Board confirmed that the amendments in paragraphs 102W–102X of IAS 39 extend to cash flow hedges, regardless of whether the cash flow hedge is for an open or closed hedged portfolio. The general reference to cash flow hedges in these paragraphs reflects such scope, therefore, the Board considered that explicitly addressing open or closed hedged portfolios was unnecessary.

Groups of items

BC337   The Board considered that for groups of items designated as hedged items in a fair value or cash flow hedge, the hedged items could consist of items still referenced to the interest rate benchmark as well as items already referenced to the alternative benchmark rate. Therefore, an entity could not amend the description of the hedged risk or the hedged item, including the designated portion of the cash flows or fair value being hedged with reference only to an alternative benchmark rate for the whole group. The Board also considered that it would be inconsistent with the objectives of the Phase 2 amendments to require the discontinuation of such a hedging relationship solely because of the effects of the reform. In the Board's view, the same requirements and relief that apply to other hedging relationships should apply to groups of items designated as hedged items, including dynamic hedging relationships.

BC338   Paragraphs 102Y–102Z of IAS 39 therefore require an entity to allocate the individual hedged items to subgroups based on the benchmark rate designated as the hedged risk for each subgroup and to apply the requirements in paragraphs 78 and 83 of IAS 39 to each subgroup separately. The Board acknowledged that this approach is an exception to the hedge accounting requirements in IAS 39 because other hedge accounting requirements, including the requirements in paragraphs 89 and 96 of IAS 39, are applied to the hedging relationship in its entirety. However, in the Board's view, the robustness of the hedge accounting requirements is maintained because if any subgroup fails to meet the requirements in paragraphs 78 and 83 of IAS 39, the entity is required to discontinue hedge accounting for that entire hedging relationship. The Board concluded this accounting outcome is appropriate because the basis for designating the hedged item on a group basis is that the entity is managing the designated hedge for the group as a whole.

BC339   The Board acknowledged that preparers may incur additional costs to assess each subgroup in a hedging relationship separately, and to track items moving from one subgroup to another. However, the Board concluded that an entity is likely to have such information available because IAS 39 already requires it to identify and document hedged items designated within a hedging relationship with sufficient specificity. Therefore, the Board concluded that the benefits of avoiding the discontinuation of hedge accounting and the resulting accounting impacts outweigh the associated costs of this exception.

BC340   Respondents to the 2020 Exposure Draft asked the Board whether the requirement for groups of items applies to dynamic hedges of interest rate benchmark-based items when the items mature and are replaced with alternative benchmark rate-based items. The Board considered that although the objective of the Phase 2 amendments is to provide relief when individual items transition to an alternative benchmark rate, the replacement of items that have expired with items that reference the alternative benchmark rate is a natural consequence of a dynamic hedging relationship. Therefore, the Board observed that new items designated as part of the group to replace interest rate benchmark-based items that have matured would be allocated to the relevant subgroup based on the benchmark rate being hedged.

BC341   Respondents also asked the Board to clarify how the requirements in paragraphs 102Y–102Z of IAS 39 apply to the hypothetical derivative in a cash flow hedge, specifically, whether the hypothetical derivative could be amended (and therefore measured) based on the alternative benchmark rate if the actual hedged item (such as a floating rate loan) has not yet transitioned to the alternative benchmark rate. The Board considered that IAS 39 does not include specific requirements for the hypothetical derivative because it is one possible way of calculating the change in the value of the hedged item to measure ineffectiveness. Therefore, the terms on which the hypothetical derivative is constructed replicate the hedged risk and the hedged cash flows of the hedged item an entity is hedging. The hypothetical derivative cannot include features in the value of the hedged item that exist only in the hedging instrument (but not in the hedged item). The Board therefore decided that the identification of an appropriate hypothetical derivative is based on the requirements to measure hedge ineffectiveness and it would not be appropriate to include specific amendments for applying the requirements in paragraphs 102Y–102Z to the hypothetical derivative.

Designating financial items as hedged items

End of application of the Phase 1 exception

BC342   An entity may designate an item in its entirety or a portion of an item as the hedged item in a hedging relationship. Paragraphs 81 and AG99F of IAS 39 allow entities to designate only changes in the cash flows or fair value of an item attributable to a specific risk or risks (risk portion).

BC343   When developing the Phase 1 amendments, the Board decided not to set an end date for applying the exception for the separately identifiable requirement (see paragraphs 102H–102I of IAS 39). The Board considered that including an end date for that exception could require an entity to immediately discontinue hedge accounting at a point in time because, as the reform progresses, a risk portion based on the interest rate benchmark may no longer be separately identifiable (for example, as the market for the alternative benchmark rate is established). As noted in paragraph BC283, in the Board's view, such an immediate discontinuation of hedge accounting would be inconsistent with the objective of this exception in Phase 1. Therefore, when issuing the Phase 1 amendments, the Board decided that an entity should cease applying the Phase 1 exception from the separately identifiable requirement to a hedging relationship only when that hedging relationship is discontinued applying the requirements in IAS 39.

BC344   Having considered the interaction between the Phase 1 exception from the separately identifiable requirement and the Phase 2 amendments to the hedge accounting requirements in IAS 39, the Board decided it is necessary to specify that an entity is required to cease applying the Phase 1 exception from the separately identifiable requirement when the uncertainty arising from the reform, which led to that exception, is no longer present.

BC345   The Board considered that continuing to apply the Phase 1 amendments after the uncertainty arising from the reform is no longer present would not faithfully represent the actual characteristics of the elements of the hedging relationship in which the uncertainty has been eliminated nor the economic effects of the reform. The Board therefore added paragraph 102O to IAS 39 so the Phase 1 exception from the separately identifiable requirement ceases to apply at the earlier of:

(a)   when changes required by the reform are made to the non-contractually specified risk portion as set out in paragraph 102P of IAS 39; or

(b)   when the hedging relationship in which the non-contractually specified risk portion was designated is discontinued.

Application of the 'separately identifiable' requirement to an alternative benchmark rate

BC346   In developing the Phase 2 amendments, the Board was aware that considerations similar to those discussed in paragraphs BC342–BC345 apply to designating an alternative benchmark rate as a non-contractually specified risk portion in either a cash flow hedge or a fair value hedge. This is because an entity's ability to conclude that the alternative benchmark rate meets the requirements in paragraphs 81 and AG99F of IAS 39 that a risk portion must be separately identifiable and reliably measurable could be affected in the early stages of the reform.

BC347 Specific requirements on the separately identifiable requirement are already set out in paragraph 81 of IAS 39. However, the Board considered that an entity might expect an alternative benchmark rate to meet the separately identifiable requirement in IAS 39 within a reasonable period of time even though the alternative benchmark rate does not meet the requirement when it is designated as a risk portion.

BC348 The amendment in paragraph 102Z1 of IAS 39 applies to different set of instruments from the Phase 1 exception. For items within the scope of paragraph 102Z1 of IAS 39, the separately identifiable requirement has never been satisfied. In contrast, the population of hedging relationships to which the Phase 1 relief applied had already satisfied the qualifying criteria for hedge accounting to be applied. The Board therefore considered that any relief from the separately identifiable requirement in Phase 2 should be temporary.

BC349 Consequently, in the 2020 Exposure Draft, the Board proposed that an alternative benchmark rate that does not meet the requirement to be separately identifiable at the date it is designated as a non-contractually specified risk portion would be deemed to have met the requirement at that date if, and only if, an entity reasonably expects that the alternative benchmark rate will be separately identifiable within 24 months from the date it is designated as a risk portion.

BC350 Respondents to the 2020 Exposure Draft agreed with this proposed amendment but asked the Board to clarify the date from which the 24-month period applies. The Board acknowledged respondents' concerns, and considered whether the 24-month period applies:

(a) on a hedge-by-hedge basis—that is, to each hedging relationship individually, beginning from the date an alternative benchmark rate is designated as a risk portion in that relationship; or

(b) on a rate-by-rate basis—that is to, each alternative benchmark rate separately, beginning from the date when an entity first designates an alternative benchmark rate as a hedged risk for the first time.

BC351 The Board acknowledged that applying the 24-month period to each hedging relationship individually (as proposed in the 2020 Exposure Draft)—that is, on a hedge-by-hedge basis—is consistent with the basis on which hedging relationships are designated. For each new hedge designation, an entity is required to assess whether the qualifying criteria to apply hedge accounting, including the separately identifiable requirement, have been met. However, the Board also considered that applying the 24-month period to different hedging relationships (with the same alternative benchmark rate designated as a risk portion) at different times, could add an unnecessary operational burden as the period would end at different times and thus would need to be monitored over different periods, for different hedging relationships. For example, if an entity designates the alternative benchmark rate as the risk portion in two hedging relationships—the first designated on 31 March 20X1 and the second on 30 June 20X1—the 24-month period for each hedge would begin and end at different dates, although the designated risk is the same in both hedging relationships.

BC352   Therefore, the Board decided that the requirement in paragraph 102Z1 would apply on a rate-by-rate basis so the 24-month period applies to each alternative benchmark rate separately and hence, starts from the date that an entity designates an alternative benchmark rate as a non-contractually specified risk portion for the first time (but see also paragraph 108J of IAS 39). The Board considered that if an entity concludes for one hedging relationship that it no longer has a reasonable expectation that the alternative benchmark rate would meet the requirements within the 24-month period, it is likely that the entity would reach the same conclusion for all other hedging relationships in which that particular alternative benchmark rate has been designated. Applying this requirement to the example in paragraph BC351, the 24-month period will begin on 31 March 20X1 for that alternative benchmark rate.

BC353   Despite the requirement to apply the 24-month period to each alternative benchmark rate separately, the requirement to assess whether an alternative benchmark rate is separately identifiable continues to separately apply to each hedging relationship. In other words, an entity is required to assess, for each hedge designation, whether the qualifying criteria to apply hedge accounting, including the separately identifiable requirement, are met for the remainder of the 24-month period (ie until 31 March 20X3 following from the example in paragraph BC351).

BC354   Consistent with the requirement in IAS 39 to continuously assess the separately identifiable requirement, an entity's ability to conclude that an alternative benchmark rate is a separately identifiable component requires assessment over the life of the hedging relationship including during the 24-month period discussed in paragraph BC352. However, the Board decided that to avoid the complexity of detailed judgements during the 24-month period, an entity is required to cease applying the requirement during the 24-month period if, and only if, the entity reasonably expects that the alternative benchmark rate will not meet the separately identifiable requirement within that period. If an entity reasonably expects that an alternative benchmark rate will not be separately identifiable within 24 months from the date the entity designates it as a non-contractually specified risk portion for the first time, the entity is required to cease applying the requirement in paragraph 102Z1 of IAS 39 to that alternative benchmark rate and discontinue applying hedge accounting prospectively from the date of that reassessment to all hedging relationships in which the alternative benchmark rate was designated as a non-contractually specified risk portion.

BC355   The Board acknowledged that 24 months is an arbitrary period. However, in the Board's view, a clearly defined end point is necessary because of the temporary nature of the amendment. The exception described in paragraphs 102Z1–102Z3 of IAS 39 is a significant relief from one of the requirements that is a basis for the robustness of the hedge accounting requirements, therefore the relief is intentionally short-lived. The Board considered that a period of 24 months will assist entities in applying the hedge accounting requirements in IAS 39 particularly during the early stages of the transition to alternative benchmark rates. Therefore, the Board decided that a period of 24 months from the date an entity first designates an alternative benchmark rate as a non-contractually specified risk portion, is a reasonable period and would enable entities to implement the reform and comply with any regulatory requirements, while avoiding potential short-term disruption as the market for an alternative benchmark rate develops.

BC356   While developing the proposals in the 2020 Exposure Draft, the Board considered proposing alternative periods for the requirement in paragraph 102Z1 of IAS 39, including a period of 12 months or a period longer than 24 months. However, the Board acknowledged the diversity in the approaches to the reform or replacement of interest rate benchmarks and the timing of the expected completion across various jurisdictions. The Board was concerned that 12 months would not provide sufficient time across all jurisdictions. At the same time, the Board considered that entities may not be able to have a reasonable expectation that an alternative benchmark rate would satisfy the separately identifiable requirement over a period longer than 24 months.

BC357   The Board emphasised that the amendments apply only for the separately identifiable requirement and not the reliably measurable requirement. Therefore, if the risk portion is not reliably measurable, either when it is designated or thereafter, the alternative benchmark rate would not meet the qualifying criteria to be designated as a risk portion in a hedging relationship. Similarly, if the hedging relationship fails to meet any other qualifying criteria set out in IAS 39 to apply hedge accounting, either at the date the alternative benchmark rate is designated or during the 24-month period, the entity is required to discontinue hedge accounting prospectively from that date. The Board decided that providing relief only for the separately identifiable requirement would achieve the objective described in paragraph BC292.

Mandatory application

BC358   The Board decided to require application of the Phase 2 amendments. The Board considered that allowing voluntary application of these amendments (ie except for the amendment in paragraph 102V of IAS 39 which is permitted, but not required) could lead to selective application to achieve specific accounting results. The Board also noted that the amendments are, to a large extent, interlinked and need to be applied consistently. Voluntary application, even if only possible by area or type of financial instruments, would reduce comparability of information provided in the financial statements between entities. The Board also does not expect that mandatory application of these amendments would result in significant additional costs for preparers and other affected parties because these amendments are designed to ease the operational burden on preparers, while providing useful information to users of financial statements, and would not require significantly more effort by preparers in addition to what is already required to implement the changes required by the reform.

End of application

BC359   The Board did not add specific end of application requirements for the Phase 2 amendments because the application of these amendments is associated with the point at which changes to financial instruments or hedging relationships occur as a result of the reform. Therefore, by design, the application of these amendments has a natural end.

BC360   The Board noted that, in a simple scenario, the Phase 2 amendments will be applied only once to each financial instrument or element of a hedging relationship. However, the Board acknowledged that because of differences in the approach to the reform applied in different jurisdictions and differences in timing, implementing the reform could require more than one change to the basis for determining the contractual cash flows of a financial asset or a financial liability.

BC361   As noted in paragraph 102R of IAS 39, the Board considered that an entity may be required to amend the formal designation of its hedging relationships at different times, or to amend the formal designation of a hedging relationship more than once. For example, an entity may first make changes required by the reform to a derivative designated as a hedging instrument, while only making changes required by the reform to the financial instrument designated as the hedged item later. In applying the amendments, the entity would be required to amend the hedge documentation to amend the description of the hedging instrument. The hedge documentation of the hedging relationship would then have to be amended again to change the description of the hedged item and/or hedged risk as required in paragraph 102P of IAS 39.

BC362   The amendment for hedges of risk portions in paragraph 102Z1 of IAS 39 applies only at the date an entity first designates a particular alternative benchmark rate as a non-contractually specified risk portion for the first time if an entity's ability to conclude that an alternative benchmark rate is separately identifiable is directly affected by the reform. Thus, an entity could not apply this amendment in other circumstances in which the entity is not able to conclude that an alternative benchmark rate is a separately identifiable risk portion.

BC363   The Board developed the amendment in paragraph 102V of IAS 39 to address the potential effect in hedge accounting at the date the Phase 1 exception from the retrospective assessment in paragraph 102G of IAS 39 ceases to apply. Therefore, the amendment in paragraph 102V of IAS 39 only applies at that date ie the date that the exception from the retrospective assessment in paragraph 102G of IAS 39 ceases to apply.

Effective date and transition

BC364   Acknowledging the urgency of the amendments, the Board decided that entities must apply the Phase 2 amendments for annual periods beginning on or after 1 January 2021, with earlier application permitted.

BC365   The Board decided that the amendments apply retrospectively in accordance with IAS 8 (except as discussed in paragraphs BC367–BC370) because prospective application would have resulted in entities applying the amendments only if the transition to alternative benchmark rates occurred after the effective date of the amendments.

BC366   The Board acknowledged that there could be situations in which an entity amended a hedging relationship as specified in paragraph 102P of IAS 39 in the period before the entity first applied the Phase 2 amendments; and in the absence of the Phase 2 amendments, IAS 39 would require the entity to discontinue hedge accounting. The Board noted that the reasons for the amendment in paragraph 102P of IAS 39 (see paragraphs BC300–BC301), apply equally in such situations. The Board therefore considered that discontinuation of hedge accounting solely because of amendments an entity made in hedge documentation to reflect appropriately the changes required by the reform, regardless of when those changes occurred, would not provide useful information to users of financial statements.

BC367   The Board acknowledged that the reinstatement of discontinued hedging relationships is inconsistent with the Board's previous decisions about hedge accounting in IAS 39. This is because hedge accounting is applied prospectively and applying it retrospectively to discontinued hedging relationships usually requires the use of hindsight. However, the Board considered that in the specific circumstances of the reform, an entity would typically be able to reinstate a discontinued hedging relationship without the use of hindsight. The Board noted that this reinstatement of discontinued hedging relationships would apply to a very targeted population for a short period—that is, for hedging relationships which would not have been discontinued if the Phase 2 amendments relating to hedge accounting had been applied at the point of discontinuation. The Board therefore proposed in the 2020 Exposure Draft that an entity would be required to reinstate hedging relationships that were discontinued solely due to changes required by the reform before an entity first applies the proposed amendments.

BC368   Respondents to the 2020 Exposure Draft generally supported and welcomed the transition proposals but asked the Board to reconsider a specific aspect of the proposal that would require entities to reinstate particular discontinued hedging relationships. Specifically, these respondents highlighted circumstances in which reinstating discontinued hedging relationships would be challenging or have limited benefit—for example, when:

   (a)   the hedging instruments or the hedged items in the discontinued hedging relationships have been subsequently designated into new hedging relationships;

   (b)   the hedging instruments in the discontinued hedging relationships no longer exist at the date of initial application of the amendments—eg they have been terminated or sold; or

   (c)   the hedging instruments in the discontinued hedging relationships are now being managed within a trading mandate with other trading positions and reported as trading instruments.

BC369　The Board noted that the transition requirements as proposed in the 2020 Exposure Draft to apply the amendments retrospectively in accordance with IAS 8—including the requirement to reinstate particular discontinued hedging relationships—would be subject to impracticability applying IAS 8. However, the Board agreed with respondents' concerns that there could be other circumstances in which it would not be impracticable to reinstate the hedging relationship, but such reinstatement would be challenging or would have limited benefit. For example, if the hedging instrument or hedged item has been designated in a new hedging relationship, it appears inappropriate to require entities to reinstate the 'old' (original) hedging relationship and discontinue or unwind the 'new' (valid) hedging relationship. Consequently, the Board added paragraph 108I(b) to IAS 39 to address these concerns.

BC370　In addition, the Board concluded that if an entity reinstates a discontinued hedging relationship applying paragraph 108I(b) of IAS 39, for the purpose of applying paragraphs 102Z1–102Z2 of IAS 39, the 24-month period for the alternative benchmark rate designated as a non-contractually specified risk portion begins from the date of initial application of the Phase 2 amendments (ie it does not begin from the date the entity designated the alternative benchmark rate as a non-contractually specified risk portion for the first time in the original hedging relationship).

BC371　Consistent with the transition requirements for Phase 1, the Board decided that an entity is not required to restate comparative information. However, an entity may choose to restate prior periods if, and only if, it is possible without the use of hindsight.

Dissenting opinions

Dissent of John T Smith from the issue in March 2004 of *Fair Value Hedge Accounting for a Portfolio Hedge of Interest Rate Risk* (Amendments to IAS 39)

DO1   Mr Smith dissents from these Amendments to IAS 39 Financial Instruments: Recognition and Measurement—*Fair Value Hedge Accounting for a Portfolio Hedge of Interest Rate Risk*. He agrees with the objective of finding a macro hedging solution that would reduce systems demands without undermining the fundamental accounting principles related to derivative instruments and hedging activities. However, Mr Smith believes that some respondents' support for these Amendments and their willingness to accept IAS 39 is based more on the extent to which the Amendments reduce recognition of ineffectiveness, volatility of profit or loss, and volatility of equity than on whether the Amendments reduce systems demands without undermining the fundamental accounting principles.

DO2   Mr Smith believes some decisions made during the Board's deliberations result in an approach to hedge accounting for a portfolio hedge that does not capture what was originally intended, namely a result that is substantially equivalent to designating an individual asset or liability as the hedged item. He understands some respondents will not accept IAS 39 unless the Board provides still another alternative that will further reduce reported volatility. Mr Smith believes that the Amendments already go beyond their intended objective. In particular, he believes that features of these Amendments can be applied to smooth out ineffectiveness and achieve results substantially equivalent to the other methods of measuring ineffectiveness that the Board considered when developing the Exposure Draft. The Board rejected those methods because they did not require the immediate recognition of all ineffectiveness. He also believes those features could be used to manage earnings.

IASB documents published to accompany

IAS 40

Investment Property

The text of the unaccompanied standard, IAS 40, is contained in Part A of this edition. Its effective date when issued was 1 January 2005. This part presents the following documents:

IASB BASIS FOR CONCLUSIONS ON IAS 40 (AS REVISED IN 2003)

IASC BASIS FOR CONCLUSIONS ON IAS 40 (2000)

Basis for Conclusions on
IAS 40 *Investment Property*

This Basis for Conclusions accompanies, but is not part of, IAS 40.

Introduction

BC1 This Basis for Conclusions summarises the International Accounting Standards Board's considerations in reaching its conclusions on revising IAS 40 *Investment Property* in 2003. Individual Board members gave greater weight to some factors than to others.

BC2 In July 2001 the Board announced that, as part of its initial agenda of technical projects, it would undertake a project to improve a number of Standards, including IAS 40. The project was undertaken in the light of queries and criticisms raised in relation to the Standards by securities regulators, professional accountants and other interested parties. The objectives of the Improvements project were to reduce or eliminate alternatives, redundancies and conflicts within Standards, to deal with some convergence issues and to make other improvements. In May 2002 the Board published its proposals in an Exposure Draft of *Improvements to International Accounting Standards*, with a comment deadline of 16 September 2002. The Board received over 160 comment letters on the Exposure Draft.

BC3 Because the Board's intention was not to reconsider the fundamental approach to the accounting for investment property established by IAS 40, this Basis for Conclusions does not discuss requirements in IAS 40 that the Board has not reconsidered. The IASC Basis for Conclusions on IAS 40 (2000) follows this Basis.

Scope

Property interests held under an operating lease

BC4 Paragraph 14 of IAS 17 *Leases* requires a lease of land with an indefinite economic life to be classified as an operating lease, unless title is expected to pass to the lessee by the end of the lease term. Without the provisions of IAS 40 as amended, this operating lease classification would prevent a lessee from classifying its interest in the leased asset as an investment property in accordance with IAS 40. As a result, the lessee could not remeasure its interest in the leased asset to fair value and recognise any change in fair value in profit or loss. However, in some countries, interests in property (including land) are commonly — or exclusively — held under long-term operating leases. The effect of some of these leases differs little from buying a property outright. As a result, some contended that such leases should be accounted for as finance leases or investment property, or as both.

BC5   The Board discussed possible solutions to this issue. In particular, it considered deleting paragraph 14 of IAS 17, so that a long-term lease of land would be classified as a finance lease (and hence could qualify as an investment property) when the conditions for finance lease classification in paragraphs 4–13 of IAS 17 are met. However, the Board noted that this would not resolve all cases encountered in practice. Some leasehold interests held for investment would remain classified as operating leases (eg leases with significant contingent rents), and hence could not be investment property in accordance with IAS 40.

BC6   In the light of this, the Board decided to state separately in paragraph 6 (rather than amend IAS 40's definition of investment property) that a lessee's interest in property that arises under an operating lease could qualify as investment property. The Board decided to limit this amendment to entities that use the fair value model in IAS 40, because the objective of the amendment is to permit use of the fair value model for similar property interests held under finance and operating leases. Put another way, a lessee that uses the cost model for a property would not be permitted to recognise operating leases as assets. The Board also decided to make the change optional, ie a lessee that has an interest in property under an operating lease is allowed, but not required, to classify that property interest as investment property (provided the rest of the definition of investment property is met). The Board confirmed that this classification alternative is available on a property-by-property basis.

BC7   When a lessee's interest in property held under an operating lease is accounted for as an investment property, the Board decided that the initial carrying amounts of that interest and the related liability are to be accounted for as if the lease were a finance lease. This decision places such leases in the same position as investment properties held under finance leases in accordance with the previous version of IAS 40.

BC8   In doing so, the Board acknowledged that this results in different measurement bases for the lease asset and the lease liability. This is also true for owned investment properties and debt that finances them. However, in accordance with IAS 39 *Financial Instruments: Recognition and Measurement*,[1] as revised in 2003, an entity can elect to measure such debt at fair value, but lease liabilities cannot be remeasured in accordance with IAS 17.

BC9   The Board considered changing the scope of IAS 39, but concluded that this would lead to a fundamental review of lease accounting, especially in relation to contingent rentals. The Board decided that this was beyond the limited revisions to IAS 40 to facilitate application of the fair value model to some operating leases classified as investment properties. The Board did, however, indicate that it wished to revisit this issue in a later project on lease accounting. The Board also noted that this was the view of the Board of the

---

1   IFRS 9 *Financial Instruments* replaced IAS 39. IFRS 9 applies to all items that were previously within the scope of IAS 39. This paragraph refers to matters relevant when IAS 40 was issued.

former IASC as expressed in its Basis for Conclusions, in paragraphs B25 and B26.[2]

BC10 Finally, the Board noted that the methodology described in paragraphs 40 and 50(d) of IAS 40, whereby a fair valuation of the property that takes all lease obligations into account is adjusted by adding back any liability that is recognised for these obligations, would, in practice, enable entities to ensure that net assets in respect of the leased interest are not affected by the use of different measurement bases.[3]

IFRS 16 *Leases*

BC10A IFRS 16 *Leases* amended the scope of IAS 40 by defining investment property to include both owned investment property and investment property held by a lessee as a right-of-use asset. A summary of the IASB's considerations in developing the amendments to the scope of IAS 40 are set out in paragraphs BC178–BC181 of IFRS 16.

The choice between the cost model and the fair value model

BC11 The Board also discussed whether to remove the choice in IAS 40 of accounting for investment property using a fair value model or a cost model.

BC12 The Board noted that IASC had included a choice for two main reasons. The first was to give preparers and users time to gain experience with using a fair value model. The second was to allow time for countries with less-developed property markets and valuation professions to mature. The Board decided that more time is needed for these events to take place (IAS 40 became mandatory only for periods beginning on or after 1 January 2001). The Board also noted that requiring the fair value model would not converge with the treatment required by most of its liaison standard-setters. For these reasons, the Board decided not to eliminate the choice as part of the Improvements project, but rather to keep the matter under review with a view to reconsidering the option to use the cost model at a later date.

BC13 The Board did not reconsider IAS 40 in relation to the accounting by lessors. The definition of investment property requires that such a property is held by the owner or a lessee under a finance lease. As indicated above, the Board agreed to allow a lessee under an operating lease, in specified circumstances, also to be a 'holder'. However, a lessor that has provided a property to a lessee under a finance lease cannot be a 'holder'. Such a lessor has a lease receivable, not an investment property.

---

2 These paragraphs in the IASC Basis are no longer relevant and have been deleted.

3 Subsequently, the Board concluded that the drafting of paragraph 50(d) was misleading because it implied that the fair value of an investment property asset held under a lease was equal to the net fair value plus the carrying amount of any recognised lease liability. Therefore, in *Improvements to IFRSs* issued in May 2008 the Board amended paragraph 50(d) to clarify the intended meaning.

BC14　The Board did not change the requirements for a lessor that leases property under an operating lease that is classified and accounted for by the lessee as investment property. The Board acknowledged that this would mean that two parties could both account as if they 'hold' interests in the property. This could occur at various levels of lessees who become lessors in a manner consistent with the definition of an investment property and the election provided for operating leases. Lessees who use the property in the production or supply of goods or services or for administrative purposes would not be able to classify that property as an investment property.

Scope

Investment property under construction

BC15　In response to requests for guidance, the Board revisited the exclusion of investment property under construction from the scope of IAS 40. The Board noted that investment property being redeveloped remained in the scope of the Standard and that the exclusion of investment property under construction gave rise to a perceived inconsistency. In addition, the Board concluded that with increasing experience with the use of fair value measures since the Standard was issued, entities were more able to measure reliably the fair value of investment property under construction. Therefore, in the exposure draft of proposed *Improvements to International Financial Reporting Standards* published in 2007 the Board proposed amending the scope of the Standard to include investment property under construction.

BC16　Many respondents supported the Board's proposal. However, many expressed concern that including in IAS 40 investment property under construction might result in fewer entities measuring investment property at fair value. This was because the fair value model in the Standard requires an entity to establish whether fair value can be determined reliably when a property first becomes an investment property. If not, the property is accounted for using the cost model until it is disposed of. In some situations, the fair value of investment property under construction cannot be measured reliably but the fair value of the completed investment property can. In these cases, including in the Standard investment property under construction would have required the properties to be accounted for using the cost model even after construction had been completed.

BC17　Therefore, the Board concluded that, in addition to including investment property under construction within the scope of the Standard, it would also amend the Standard to allow investment property under construction to be measured at cost if fair value cannot be measured reliably until such time as the fair value becomes reliably measurable or construction is completed (whichever comes earlier).

Classification of property as investment property or owner-occupied property

Acquisition of investment property: interrelationship with IFRS 3

BC18   The IFRS Interpretations Committee (the 'Interpretations Committee') reported to the Board that practice differed in delineating the scope of IFRS 3 *Business Combinations* and IAS 40:

(a)   some considered both Standards as mutually exclusive if investment property with associated insignificant ancillary services, as specified in paragraph 11 of IAS 40, is acquired. They view property, together with any associated insignificant ancillary services, as being a single 'unit of account' and they consider this unit of account to be one asset called 'investment property'.

(b)   others did not view IFRS 3 and IAS 40 as being mutually exclusive if investment property with associated insignificant ancillary services, as specified in paragraph 11 of IAS 40, is acquired; nor did they view the definitions of a business as defined in Appendix A of IFRS 3 and investment property as defined in paragraph 5 of IAS 40 as being interrelated. They think that an entity that acquires investment property has to determine whether it meets both definitions.

BC19   The Board noted that paragraphs 7–14 of IAS 40 have been developed to differentiate investment property from owner-occupied property and to define the scope of IAS 40 to distinguish it from the scope of IAS 16 *Property, Plant and Equipment*. In addition, neither IFRS 3 nor IAS 40 contains a limitation in its scope that restricts its application when the other Standard applies, ie there is nothing within the scope of each Standard to suggest that they are mutually exclusive. The Board also noted that the wording of IAS 40 is not sufficiently clear about the interrelationship between the two Standards.

BC20   The Board agreed with the proponents of the view presented in paragraph BC18(b) that IFRS 3 and IAS 40 are not mutually exclusive. It amended IAS 40 to state explicitly that judgement is also needed to determine whether the transaction is the acquisition of an asset or a group of assets or is a business combination within the scope of IFRS 3. That judgement is not based on paragraphs 7–14 of IAS 40 but is instead based on the guidance in IFRS 3. Only the judgement needed to distinguish investment property from owner-occupied property is based on those paragraphs.

BC21   Consequently, the Board clarified the interrelationship between the two Standards by adding paragraph 14A and a heading before paragraph 6 to IAS 40.

Effective date and transition

BC22 *Annual Improvements Cycle 2011–2013* issued in December 2013 added headings before paragraph 6 and after paragraph 84 and added paragraphs 14A, 84A and 85D to clarify the interrelationship between IFRS 3 and IAS 40. It considered the provisions for transition and the effective date of the amendment to IAS 40. The Board noted that applying IFRS 3 to transactions that have previously been accounted for as the acquisition of an asset or a group of assets might involve the use of hindsight when determining the fair values, at acquisition date, of the identifiable assets acquired and of the liabilities assumed as part of the business combination transaction. However, it also noted that the amendment is only a clarification of the interrelationship between IFRS 3 and IAS 40. Consequently, it decided that an entity would apply the amendments to IAS 40 prospectively for annual periods beginning on or after 1 July 2014, but an entity may choose to apply the amendment to individual transactions that occurred prior to the beginning of the first annual period occurring on or after the effective date only if the information needed is available to the entity.

Transfers of investment property

BC23 The Board received a question regarding the application of paragraph 57, which specifies requirements on transfers to, or from, investment property. The question asked whether an entity transfers property under construction or development previously classified as inventory to investment property when there is evidence of a change in use, even if that evidence is not specifically listed in paragraph 57(a)–(d).

BC24 Paragraph 57 requires transfers to, or from, investment property when, and only when, there is a change in use of property supported by evidence. The Board noted that the words 'when, and only when' in this paragraph are important to ensure that a transfer is limited to situations in which a change in use has occurred. The Board observed that the list of circumstances that provide evidence of a change in use specified in paragraph 57(a)–(d) of IAS 40 was drafted such that it was exhaustive (as shown by the references to 'when and only when' and 'evidenced by' in that paragraph).

BC25 The Board decided, however, to amend paragraph 57 so that it reflects the principle that a change in use would involve (a) an assessment of whether a property meets, or has ceased to meet, the definition of investment property; and (b) supporting evidence that a change in use has occurred. Applying this principle, an entity transfers property under construction or development to, or from, investment property when, and only when, there is a change in the use of such property, supported by evidence.

BC26 The Board also re-characterised the list of circumstances in paragraph 57(a)–(d) as a non-exhaustive list of examples to be consistent with the principle described in paragraph BC25.

BC27 Respondents to the Board's proposals asked whether management's intended use of a property would provide sufficient evidence of a change in use of a property under construction or development. The Board decided to confirm in paragraph 57 that, in isolation, a change in management's intentions would not be enough to support a transfer of property. This is because management's intentions, alone, do not provide evidence of a change in use — an entity must have taken observable actions to support such a change.

BC28 Some other respondents asked the Board to explain what provides substantive evidence of a change in use. The Board decided that such explanation is not needed. An entity assesses the specific facts and circumstances when applying paragraph 57, and paragraph 14 notes that judgement is needed to determine whether a property qualifies as investment property.

BC29 Respondents agreed with the Board's decision to re-characterise the list of circumstances in paragraph 57(a)–(d). However, some respondents were concerned that this list appeared to apply only to completed properties and, thus, they suggested that the Board add examples for a change in use of properties under construction or development. In response, the Board decided to amend paragraph 57(a) (ie to include 'commencement of development with a view to owner-occupation') and paragraph 57(d) (ie to refer to 'inception' of an operating lease, because at this point the construction of the related property might not be complete).

Transition

BC30 The Board proposed that an entity apply the amendments retrospectively. However, some respondents disagreed. They said that retrospective application might be impossible for some entities without the use of hindsight, or could be complex and burdensome in some situations — for example, in determining the exact point at which there was evidence of a change in use in prior periods, or in obtaining fair values at transfer dates in the past. Those respondents suggested either prospective application or, alternatively, retrospective application with some practical expedients.

BC31 In considering the comments, the Board observed the following:

(a) the amounts recognised on the date of initial application would be unaffected by the transition approach for some previous changes in use, for example, transfers between investment property and owner-occupied property for entities that use the cost model.

(b) applying the amendments retrospectively could be complex or may require the use of hindsight for some previous changes in use, for example, transfers from investment property measured using the fair value model to owner-occupied property that occurred some considerable time ago.

(c)   a prospective approach would require entities to apply the amendments only to changes in use that occur on or after the date of initial application. Such an approach might prevent an entity from reclassifying some property to reflect the conditions that exist on the date of initial application.

BC32   To address the concerns raised, the Board developed the transition method in paragraph 84C to ease the burden of applying the amendments retrospectively and to ensure that, on transition, an entity classifies property consistently with the amended Standard. If an entity uses this transition method, the Board decided to require specific disclosure of any reclassification of property at the date of initial application as part of the reconciliation of the carrying amount of investment property that is already required to be provided. This disclosure informs users of financial statements about changes to the carrying amount of investment property at the date of transition that do not reflect an underlying change in use of the property at that date.

BC33   The Board also noted that, depending on the properties held and previous changes in use that occurred, an entity may be able to apply the amendments retrospectively without the use of hindsight. If that is the case, the Board decided that the entity should not be prevented from doing so.

Contents

Basis for Conclusions on
IAS 40 (2000) *Investment Property*

This Basis for Conclusions accompanies, but is not part of, IAS 40. It was issued by the Board of the former International Accounting Standards Committee (IASC) in 2000. Apart from the deletion of paragraphs B10–B20, B25 and B26, this Basis has not been revised by the IASB — those paragraphs are no longer relevant and have been deleted to avoid the risk that they might be read out of context. However, cross-references to paragraphs in IAS 40 as issued in 2000 have been marked to show the corresponding paragraphs in IAS 40 as revised by the IASB in 2003 (superseded references are struck through and new references are underlined). Paragraphs are treated as corresponding if they broadly address the same matter even though the guidance may differ. In addition, the text has been annotated where references to material in other standards are no longer valid, following the revision of those standards. Reference should be made to the IASB's Basis for Conclusions on the amendments made in 2003.

Background

B1   The IASC Board (the "Board") approved IAS 25 *Accounting for Investments* in 1986. In 1994, the Board approved a reformatted version of IAS 25 presented in the revised format adopted for International Accounting Standards from 1991. Certain terminology was also changed at that time to bring it into line with then current IASC practice. No substantive changes were made to the original approved text.

B2   IAS 25 was one of the standards that the Board identified for possible revision in E32 *Comparability of Financial Statements*. Following comments on the proposals in E32, the Board decided to defer consideration of IAS 25, pending further work on Financial Instruments. In 1998, the Board approved IAS 38 *Intangible Assets* and IAS 39 *Financial Instruments: Recognition and Measurement*,[1] leaving IAS 25 to cover investments in real estate, commodities and tangible assets such as vintage cars and other collectors' items.

B3   In July 1999, the Board approved E64 *Investment Property*, with a comment deadline of 31 October 1999. The Board received 121 comment letters on E64. Comment letters came from various international organisations, as well as from 28 individual countries. The Board approved IAS 40 *Investment Property* in March 2000. Paragraph B67 below summarises the changes that the Board made to E64 in finalising IAS 40.

B4   IAS 40 permits entities to choose between a fair value model and a cost model. As explained in paragraphs B47–B48 below, the Board believes that it is impracticable, at this stage, to require a fair value model for all investment property. At the same time, the Board believes that it is desirable to permit a fair value model. This evolutionary step forward will allow preparers and users to gain greater experience working with a fair value model and will allow time for certain property markets to achieve greater maturity.

---

1   IFRS 9 *Financial Instruments* replaced IAS 39. IFRS 9 applies to all items that were previously within the scope of IAS 39. This paragraph refers to matters relevant when IAS 40 was issued.

Need for a Separate Standard

B5   Some commentators argued that investment property should fall within the scope of IAS 16 *Property, Plant and Equipment*, and that there is no reason to have a separate standard on investment property. They believe that:

(a)   it is not possible to distinguish investment property rigorously from owner-occupied property covered by IAS 16 and without reference to management intent. Thus, a distinction between investment property and owner-occupied property will lead to a free choice of different accounting treatments in some cases; and

(b)   the fair value accounting model proposed in E64 is not appropriate, on the grounds that fair value is not relevant and, in some cases, not reliable in the case of investment property. The accounting treatments in IAS 16 are appropriate not only for owner-occupied property, but also for investment property.

B6   Having reviewed the comment letters, the Board still believes that the characteristics of investment property differ sufficiently from the characteristics of owner-occupied property that there is a need for a separate Standard on investment property. In particular, the Board believes that information about the fair value of investment property, and about changes in its fair value, is highly relevant to users of financial statements. The Board believes that it is important to permit a fair value model for investment property, so that entities can report fair value information prominently. The Board tried to maintain consistency with IAS 16, except for differences dictated by the choice of a different accounting model.

Scope

Investment Property Entities

B7   Some commentators argued that the Standard should cover only investment property held by entities that specialise in owning such property (and, perhaps, also other investments) and not cover investment property held by other entities. The Board rejected this view because the Board could find no conceptual and practical way to distinguish rigorously any class of entities for which the fair value model would be less or more appropriate.

Investment Property Reportable Segments

B8   Some commentators suggested that the Board should limit the scope of the Standard to entities that have a reportable segment whose main activity is investment property. These commentators argued that an approach linked to reportable segments would require an entity to adopt the fair value model when the entity considers investment property activities to be an important element of its financial performance and would allow an entity to adopt IAS 16 in other cases.

B9   An approach linked to reportable segments would lead to lack of comparability between investment property held in investment property segments and investment property held in other segments. For this reason, the Board rejected such an approach.

B10–B20 [Deleted]

Property Occupied by Another Entity in the Same Group

B21   In some cases, an entity owns property that is leased to, and occupied by, another entity in the same group. The property does not qualify as investment property in consolidated financial statements that include both entities, because the property is owner-occupied from the perspective of the group as a whole. However, from the perspective of the individual entity that owns it, the property is investment property if it meets the definition set out in the Standard.

B22   Some commentators believe that the definition of investment property should exclude properties that are occupied by another entity in the same group. Alternatively, they suggest that the Standard should not require investment property accounting in individual financial statements for properties that do not qualify as investment property in consolidated financial statements. They believe that:

(a)   it could be argued (at least in some such cases) that the property does not meet the definition of investment property from the perspective of a subsidiary whose property is occupied by another entity in the same group—the subsidiary's motive for holding the property is to comply with a directive from its parent and not necessarily to earn rentals or to benefit from capital appreciation. Indeed, the intragroup lease may not be priced on an arm's length basis;

(b)   this requirement would lead to additional valuation costs that would not be justified by the limited benefits to users. For groups with subsidiaries that are required to prepare individual financial statements, the cost could be extensive as entities may create a separate subsidiary to hold each property;

(c)   some users may be confused if the same property is classified as investment property in the individual financial statements of a subsidiary and as owner-occupied property in the consolidated financial statements of the parent; and

(d)   there is a precedent for a similar exemption (relating to disclosure, rather than measurement) in paragraph 4(c) of IAS 24 Related Party Disclosures, which does not require disclosures in a wholly-owned subsidiary's financial statements if its parent is incorporated in the same country and provides consolidated financial statements in that country.[2]

---

2   IAS 24 Related Party Disclosures as revised by the IASB in 2003 no longer provides the exemption mentioned in paragraph B22(d).

B23   Some commentators believe that the definition of investment property should exclude property occupied by any related party. They argue that related parties often do not pay rent on an arm's length basis, that it is often difficult to establish whether the rent is consistent with pricing on an arm's length basis and that rental rates may be subject to arbitrary change. They suggest that fair values are less relevant where property is subject to leases that are not priced on an arm's length basis.

B24   The Board could find no justification for treating property leased to another entity in the same group (or to another related party) differently from property leased to other parties. Therefore, the Board decided that an entity should use the same accounting treatment, regardless of the identity of the lessee.

B25–B26   [Deleted]

Government Grants

B27   IAS 20 *Accounting for Government Grants and Disclosure of Government Assistance* permits two methods of presenting grants relating to assets—either setting up a grant as deferred income and amortising the income over the useful life of the asset or deducting the grant in arriving at the carrying amount of the asset. Some believe that both of those methods reflect a historical cost model and are inconsistent with the fair value model set out in this Standard. Indeed, Exposure Draft E65 *Agriculture*, which proposes a fair value model for biological assets, addresses certain aspects of government grants, as these are a significant factor in accounting for agriculture in some countries.

B28   Some commentators urged IASC to change the accounting treatment of government grants related to investment property. However, most commentators agreed that IASC should not deal with this aspect of government grants now. The Board decided not to revise this aspect of IAS 20 in the project on Investment Property.

B29   Some commentators suggested that IASC should begin a wider review of IAS 20 as a matter of urgency. In early 2000, the G4+1 group of standard setters published a Discussion Paper *Accounting by Recipients for Non-Reciprocal Transfers, Excluding Contributions by Owners: Their Definition, Recognition and Measurement*. The Board's work plan does not currently include a project on the accounting for government grants or other forms of non-reciprocal transfer.

Definition of Investment Property

B30   The definition of investment property excludes:

(a)   owner-occupied property—covered by IAS 16 *Property, Plant and Equipment*. Under IAS 16, such property is carried at either depreciated cost or revalued amount less subsequent depreciation. In addition, such property is subject to an impairment test; and

(b)   property held for sale in the ordinary course of business – covered by IAS 2 *Inventories*. IAS 2 requires an entity to carry such property at the lower of cost and net realisable value.

B31   These exclusions are consistent with the existing definitions of property, plant and equipment in IAS 16 and inventories in IAS 2. This ensures that all property is covered by one, and only one, of the three Standards.

B32   Some commentators suggested that property held for sale in the ordinary course of business should be treated as investment property rather than as inventories (covered by IAS 2). They argued that:

(a)   it is difficult to distinguish property held for sale in the ordinary course of business from property held for capital appreciation; and

(b)   it is illogical to require a fair value model for land and buildings held for long-term capital appreciation (investment property) when a cost model is still used for land and buildings held for short-term sale in the ordinary course of business (inventories).

B33   The Board rejected this suggestion because:

(a)   if fair value accounting is used for property held for sale in the ordinary course of business, this would raise wider questions about inventory accounting that go beyond the scope of this project; and

(b)   it is arguably more important to use fair value accounting for property that may have been acquired over a long period and held for several years (investment property) than for property that was acquired over a shorter period and held for a relatively short time (inventories). With the passage of time, cost-based measurements become increasingly irrelevant. Also, an aggregation of costs incurred over a long period is of questionable relevance.

B34   Some commentators suggested requiring (or at least permitting) entities, particularly financial institutions such as insurance companies, to use the fair value model for their owner-occupied property. They argued that some financial institutions regard their owner-occupied property as an integral part of their investment portfolio and treat it for management purposes in the same way as property leased to others. In the case of insurance companies, the property may be held to back policyholder liabilities. The Board believes that property used for similar purposes should be subject to the same accounting treatment. Accordingly, the Board concluded that no class of entities should use the fair value model for their owner-occupied property.[3]

B35   Some commentators suggested that the definition of investment property should exclude property held for rentals, but not for capital appreciation. In their view, a fair value model may be appropriate for dealing activities, but is inappropriate where an entity has historically held rental property for many

---

3   IFRS 17 *Insurance Contracts* amended the subsequent measurement requirements in IAS 16 by permitting entities to elect to measure owner-occupied properties in specified circumstances as if they were investment properties measured at fair value through profit or loss in accordance with IAS 40. The Board's considerations in providing that exemption are set out in paragraph BC65(c) of the Basis for Conclusions on IFRS 17.

years and has no intention of selling it in the foreseeable future. They consider that holding property for long-term rental is a service activity and the assets used in that activity should be treated in the same way as assets used to support other service activities. In their view, holding an investment in property in such cases is similar to holding "held-to-maturity investments", which are measured at amortised cost under IAS 39.[4]

B36 In the Board's view, the fair value model provides useful information about property held for rental, even if there is no immediate intention to sell the property. The economic performance of a property can be regarded as being made up of both rental income earned during the period (net of expenses) and changes in the value of future net rental income. The fair value of an investment property can be regarded as a market-based representation of the value of the future net rental income, regardless of whether the entity is likely to sell the property in the near future. Also, the Standard notes that fair value is determined without deducting costs of disposal—in other words, the use of the fair value model is not intended as a representation that a sale could, or should, be made in the near future.[5]

B37 The classification of hotels and similar property was controversial throughout the project and commentators on E64 had mixed views on this subject. Some see hotels essentially as investments, while others see them essentially as operating properties. Some requested a detailed rule to specify whether hotels (and, perhaps, other categories of property, such as restaurants, bars and nursing homes) should be classified as investment property or as owner-occupied property.

B38 The Board concluded that it is preferable to distinguish investment property from owner-occupied property on the basis of general principles, rather than have arbitrary rules for specific classes of property. Also, it would inevitably be difficult to establish rigorous definitions of specific classes of property to be covered by such rules. Paragraphs 9–11 11–13 of the Standard discuss cases such as hotels in the context of the general principles that apply when an entity provides ancillary services.

B39 Some commentators requested quantitative guidance (such as a percentage) to clarify whether an "insignificant portion" is owner-occupied (paragraph 8 10) and whether ancillary services are "significant" (paragraphs 9–11 11–13 of the Standard). As for similar cases in other Standards, the Board concluded that quantitative guidance would create arbitrary distinctions.

Subsequent Expenditure

B40 Some believe that there is no need to capitalise subsequent expenditure in a fair value model and that all subsequent expenditure should be recognised as an expense. However, others believe—and the Board agreed—that the failure to capitalise subsequent expenditure would lead to a distortion of the reported

---

4   IFRS 9 *Financial Instruments* eliminated the held-to-maturity category. This paragraph discusses matters relevant when IAS 40 was issued.

5   IFRS 13 *Fair Value Measurement*, issued in May 2011, defines fair value and contains the requirements for measuring fair value.

components of financial performance. Therefore, the Standard requires that an entity should determine whether subsequent expenditure should be capitalised using a test similar to the test used for owner-occupied property in IAS 16.

B41   Some commentators suggested that the test for capitalising subsequent expenditure should not refer to the originally assessed standard of performance. They felt that it is impractical and irrelevant to judge against the originally assessed standard of performance, which may relate to many years in the past. Instead, they suggested that subsequent expenditure should be capitalised if it enhances the previously assessed standard of performance —for example, if it increases the current market value of the property or is intended to maintain its competitiveness in the market. The Board saw some merit in this suggestion.

B42   Nevertheless, the Board believes that a reference to the previously assessed standard of performance would require substantial additional guidance, might not change the way the Standard is applied in practice and might cause confusion. The Board also concluded that it was important to retain the existing reference to the originally assessed standard of performance[6] to be consistent with IAS 16 and IAS 38.

Subsequent Measurement

Accounting Model

B43   Under IAS 25, an entity was permitted to choose from among a variety of accounting treatments for investment property (depreciated cost under the benchmark treatment in IAS 16 *Property, Plant and Equipment*, revaluation with depreciation under the allowed alternative treatment in IAS 16, cost less impairment under IAS 25 or revaluation under IAS 25).[7]

B44   E64 proposed that all investment property should be measured at fair value. Supporters of the fair value model believe that fair values give users of financial statements more useful information than other measures, such as depreciated cost. In their view, rental income and changes in fair value are inextricably linked as integral components of the financial performance of an investment property and measurement at fair value is necessary if that financial performance is to be reported in a meaningful way.

B45   Supporters of the fair value model also note that an investment property generates cash flows largely independently of the other assets held by an entity. In their view, the generation of independent cash flows through rental or capital appreciation distinguishes investment property from owner-occupied property. The production or supply of goods or services (or

---

6   IAS 16 *Property, Plant and Equipment* as revised by the IASB in 2003 requires all subsequent costs to be covered by its general recognition principle and eliminated the requirement to reference the originally assessed standard of performance. IAS 40 was amended as a consequence of the change to IAS 16.

7   IAS 16 *Property, Plant and Equipment* as revised by the IASB in 2003 eliminated all references to 'benchmark' treatment and 'allowed alternative' treatments. They are replaced with cost model and revaluation model.

the use of property for administrative purposes) generates cash flows that are attributable not merely to property, but also to other assets used in the production or supply process. Proponents of the fair value model for investment property argue that this distinction makes a fair value model more appropriate for investment property than for owner-occupied property.

B46 Those who oppose measurement of investment property at fair value argue that:

(a) there is often no active market for investment property (unlike for many financial instruments). Real estate transactions are not frequent and not homogeneous. Each investment property is unique and each sale is subject to significant negotiations. As a result, fair value measurement will not enhance comparability because fair values are not determinable on a reliable basis, especially in countries where the valuation profession is less well established. A depreciated cost measurement provides a more consistent, less volatile, and less subjective measurement;

(b) IAS 39[8] does not require fair value measurement for all financial assets, even some that are realised more easily than investment property. It would be premature to consider extending the fair value model until the Joint Working Group on financial instruments has completed its work;

(c) a cost basis is used for "shorter term" assets (such as inventories) for which fair value is, arguably, more relevant than for "held for investment" assets; and

(d) measurement at fair value is too costly in relation to the benefits to users.

B47 This is the first time that the Board has proposed requiring a fair value accounting model for non-financial assets. The comment letters on E64 showed that although many support this step, many others still have significant conceptual and practical reservations about extending a fair value model to non-financial assets, particularly (but not exclusively) for entities whose main activity is not to hold property for capital appreciation. Also, some entities feel that certain property markets are not yet sufficiently mature for a fair value model to work satisfactorily. Furthermore, some believe that it is impossible to create a rigorous definition of investment property and that this makes it impracticable to require a fair value model at present.

B48 For those reasons, the Board believes that it is impracticable, at this stage, to require a fair value model for investment property. At the same time, the Board believes that it is desirable to permit a fair value model. This evolutionary step forward will allow preparers and users to gain greater experience working with a fair value model and will allow time for certain property markets to achieve greater maturity.

---

8   IFRS 9 *Financial Instruments* replaced IAS 39. IFRS 9 applies to all items that were previously within the scope of IAS 39. This paragraph refers to matters relevant when IAS 40 was issued.

B49 IAS 40 permits entities to choose between a fair value model and a cost model. An entity should apply the model chosen to all its investment property. [This choice is not available to a lessee accounting for an investment property under an operating lease as if it were a finance lease—refer to the IASB's Basis for Conclusions on the amendments made in 2003.] The fair value model is the model proposed in E64: investment property should be measured at fair value and changes in fair value should be recognised in the income statement. The cost model is the benchmark treatment[9] in IAS 16 *Property, Plant and Equipment*: investment property should be measured at depreciated cost (less any accumulated impairment losses). An entity that chooses the cost model should disclose the fair value of its investment property.

B50 Under IAS 8 *Net Profit or Loss for the Period, Fundamental Errors and Changes in Accounting Policies*,[10] a change in accounting policies from one model to the other model should be made only if the change will result in a more appropriate presentation of events or transactions.[11] The Board concluded that this is highly unlikely to be the case for a change from the fair value model to the cost model and paragraph 25 31 of the Standard reflects this conclusion.

B51 The Board believes that it is undesirable to permit three different accounting treatments for investment property. Accordingly, if an entity does not adopt the fair value model, the Standard requires the entity to use the benchmark treatment in IAS 16 and does not permit the use of the allowed alternative treatment. However, an entity may still use the allowed alternative for other properties covered by IAS 16.[12]

Guidance on Fair Value[13]

B52 The valuation profession will have an important role in implementing the Standard. Accordingly, in developing its guidance on the fair value of investment property, the Board considered not only similar guidance in other IASC literature, but also International Valuation Standards (IVS) issued by the International Valuation Standards Committee (IVSC). The Board understands that IVSC intends to review, and perhaps revise, its Standards in the near future.

B53 The Board believes that IASC's concept of fair value is similar to the IVSC concept of market value. IVSC defines market value as "the estimated amount for which an asset should exchange on the date of valuation between a willing buyer and a willing seller in an arm's length transaction after proper marketing wherein the parties had each acted knowledgeably, prudently and without compulsion". The Board believes that the guidance in

---

9 IAS 16 *Property, Plant and Equipment* as revised by the IASB in 2003 eliminated all references to 'benchmark' treatment and 'allowed alternative' treatments.

10 revised by the IASB in 2003 as IAS 8 *Accounting Policies, Changes in Accounting Estimates and Errors*

11 The IASB conformed the terminology used in paragraph 31 to the terminology used in IAS 8 by *Improvements to IFRSs* issued in May 2008.

12 IAS 16 *Property, Plant and Equipment* as revised by the IASB in 2003 eliminated all references to 'benchmark' treatment and 'allowed alternative' treatments.

13 IFRS 13, issued in May 2011, contains the requirements for measuring fair value.

paragraphs ~~29–30~~ 36, 37 and ~~32–38~~ 39–44 of the Standard is, in substance (and largely in wording as well), identical with guidance in IVS 1.[14]

B54   Paragraphs ~~31~~ 38 and ~~39–46~~ 45–52 have no direct counterpart in the IVSC literature. The Board developed much of this material in response to commentators on E64, who asked for more detailed guidance on determining the fair value of investment property. In developing this material, the Board considered guidance on fair value in other IASC Standards and Exposure Drafts, particularly those on financial instruments (IAS 32 and IAS 39[15]), intangible assets (IAS 38) and agriculture (E65).[16]

Independent Valuation

B55   Some commentators believe that fair values should be determined on the basis of an independent valuation, to enhance the reliability of the fair values reported. Others believe, on cost-benefit grounds, that IASC should not require (and perhaps not even encourage) an independent valuation. They believe that it is for preparers to decide, in consultation with auditors, whether an entity has sufficient internal resources to determine reliable fair values. Some also believe that independent valuers with appropriate expertise are not available in some markets.

B56   The Board concluded that an independent valuation is not always necessary. Therefore, as proposed in E64, the Standard encourages, but does not require, an entity to determine the fair value of all investment property on the basis of a valuation by an independent valuer who holds a recognised and relevant professional qualification and who has recent experience in the location and category of the investment property being valued. This approach is consistent with the approach to actuarial valuations in IAS 19 *Employee Benefits* (see IAS 19, paragraph 57).[17]

Inability to Measure Fair Value Reliably

B57   E64 included a rebuttable presumption that an entity will be able to determine reliably the fair value of property held to earn rentals or for capital appreciation. E64 also proposed a reliability exception: IAS 16 should be applied if evidence indicates clearly, when an entity acquires or constructs a property, that fair value will not be determinable reliably on a continuing basis.

---

14 The requirements for measuring fair value in IFRS 13, issued in May 2011, differ in some respects from the guidance for measuring market value in accordance with IVS 1. IFRS 13 deleted paragraphs 36, 37 and 42–44 of IAS 40.

15 IFRS 9 *Financial Instruments* replaced IAS 39. IFRS 9 applies to all items that were previously within the scope of IAS 39. This paragraph refers to matters relevant when IAS 40 was issued.

16 IFRS 13, issued in May 2011, defines fair value and contains the requirements for measuring fair value. As a consequence paragraphs 38, 45–47, 49 and 51 of IAS 40 have been deleted.

17 Paragraph 57 was renumbered as paragraph 59 when IAS 19 was amended in 2011.

B58   Some commentators opposed various aspects of this proposal, on one or more of the following grounds:

(a)   the rebuttable presumption underestimates the difficulties of determining fair value reliably. This will often be impossible, particularly where markets are thin or where there is not a well-established valuation profession;

(b)   the accounting model under IAS 16 includes an impairment test under IAS 36. However, it is illogical to rely on an impairment test when fair value cannot be determined using cash flow projections, because an impairment test under IAS 36 is also difficult in such cases;

(c)   where fair value cannot be determined reliably, this fact does not justify charging depreciation. Instead, the property in question should be measured at cost less impairment losses; and

(d)   to avoid the danger of manipulation, all efforts should be made to determine fair values, even in a relatively inactive market. Even without an active market, a range of projected cash flows is available. If there are problems in determining fair value, an entity should measure the property at the best estimate of fair value and disclose limitations on the reliability of the estimate. If it is completely impossible to determine fair value, fair value should be deemed to be zero.

B59   The Board concluded that the rebuttable presumption and the reliability exception should be retained, but decided to implement them in a different way. In E64, they were implemented by excluding a property from the definition of investment property if the rebuttable presumption was overcome. Some commentators felt that it was confusing to include such a reliability exception in a definition. Accordingly, the Board moved the reliability exception from the definition to the section on subsequent measurement (paragraphs 47–49 53–55).

B60   Under E64, an entity should not stop using the fair value model if comparable market transactions become less frequent or market prices become less readily available. Some commentators disagreed with this proposal. They argued that there may be cases when reliable estimates are no longer available and that it would be misleading to continue fair value accounting in such cases. The Board decided that it is important to keep the E64 approach, because otherwise entities might use a reliability exception as an excuse to discontinue fair value accounting in a falling market.[18]

B61   In cases where the reliability exception applies, E64 proposed that an entity should continue to apply IAS 16 until disposal of the property. Some commentators proposed that an entity should start applying the fair value model once the fair value becomes measurable reliably. The Board rejected this proposal because it would inevitably be a subjective decision to determine

---

18   IFRS 13, issued in May 2011, discusses the measurement of fair value when the volume or level of activity for an asset has significantly decreased.

when fair value has become measurable reliably and this subjectivity could lead to inconsistent application.

B62   E64 proposed no specific disclosure where the reliability exception applies. Some commentators felt that disclosure would be important in such cases. The Board agreed and decided to include disclosures consistent with paragraph 170(b) of IAS 39[19] (see paragraphs ~~68 and 69(e)~~ 78 and 79(e) of IAS 40). Paragraph 170(b) of IAS 39 requires disclosures for financial assets whose fair value cannot be reliably measured.

Gains and Losses on Remeasurement to Fair Value

B63   Some commentators argued that there should be either a requirement or an option to recognise changes in the fair value of investment property in equity, on the grounds that:

(a)   the market for property is not liquid enough and market values are uncertain and variable. Investment property is not as liquid as financial instruments and IAS 39 allows an option for available-for-sale investments;[20]

(b)   until performance reporting issues are resolved more generally, it is premature to require recognition of fair value changes in the income statement;

(c)   recognition of unrealised gains and losses in the income statement increases volatility and does not enhance transparency, because revaluation changes will blur the assessment of an entity's operating performance. It may also cause a presumption that the unrealised gains are available for distribution as dividends;

(d)   recognition in equity is more consistent with the historical cost and modified historical cost conventions that are a basis for much of today's accounting. For example, it is consistent with IASC's treatment of revaluations of property, plant and equipment under IAS 16 and with the option available for certain financial instruments under IAS 39;[21]

(e)   for properties financed by debt, changes in the fair value of the properties resulting from interest rate changes should not be recognised in the income statement, since the corresponding changes in the fair value of the debt are not recognised under IAS 39;

---

19   In August 2005, the IASB relocated all disclosures relating to financial instruments to IFRS 7 *Financial Instruments: Disclosures*.

20   IFRS 9 *Financial Instruments* eliminated the category of available-for-sale financial assets.

21   IFRS 9 *Financial Instruments* replaced IAS 39. IFRS 9 applies to all items that were previously within the scope of IAS 39. This paragraph refers to matters relevant when IAS 40 was issued.

(f)   under paragraphs 92 and 93 of the *Framework*,[22] income should be recognised only when it can be measured with sufficient certainty. For example, IAS 11 *Construction Contracts*[23] requires certain conditions before an entity can use the percentage-of-completion method. These conditions are not normally met for investment property; and

(g)   results from operations should be distinguished from changes in values. For example, under IAS 21, unrealised exchange differences on a foreign entity[24] are recognised in equity.

B64   Some commentators suggested that increases should be recognised in equity and decreases should be recognised in profit or loss. This is similar to the revaluation model that forms the allowed alternative treatment[25] in IAS 16 (except for the lack of depreciation).

B65   As proposed in E64, the Board concluded that, in a fair value model, changes in the fair value of investment property should be recognised in the income statement as part of profit or loss for the period. The arguments for this approach include the following:

(a)   the conceptual case for the fair value model is built largely on the view that this provides the most relevant and transparent view of the financial performance of investment property. Given this, it would be inconsistent to permit or require recognition in equity;

(b)   recognition of fair value changes in equity would create a mismatch because net rental income would be recognised in the income statement, whereas the related consumption of the service potential (recognised as depreciation under IAS 16) would be recognised in equity. Similarly, maintenance expenditure would be recognised as an expense while related increases in fair value would be recognised in equity;

(c)   using this approach, there is no need to resolve some difficult and controversial issues that would arise if changes in the fair value of investment property were recognised in equity. These issues include the following:

(i)   should fair value changes previously recognised in equity be transferred ("recycled") to profit or loss on disposal of investment property; and

---

22 The reference to the *Framework* is to the IASC's *Framework for the Preparation and Presentation of Financial Statements*, adopted by the Board in 2001 and in effect when the Standard was developed.

23 IFRS 15 *Revenue from Contracts with Customers*, issued in May 2014, replaced IAS 11 *Construction Contracts*.

24 In IAS 21 *The Effects of Changes in Foreign Exchange Rates*, as revised by the IASB in 2003, the term 'foreign entity' was replaced by 'foreign operation'.

25 IAS 16 *Property, Plant and Equipment* as revised by the IASB in 2003 eliminated all references to 'benchmark' treatment and 'allowed alternative' treatments.

(ii)   should fair value changes previously recognised in equity be transferred ("recycled") to profit or loss when investment property is impaired? If so, how should such impairment be identified and measured; and

(d)   given the difficulty in defining investment property rigorously, entities will sometimes have the option of applying the investment property standard or either of the two treatments in IAS 16. It would be undesirable to include two choices in the investment property standard, as this would give entities a choice (at least occasionally) between four different treatments.

Transfers

B66   When an owner-occupied property carried under the benchmark treatment under IAS 16 becomes an investment property, the measurement basis for the property changes from depreciated cost to fair value. The Board concluded that the effect of this change in measurement basis should be treated as a revaluation under IAS 16 at the date of change in use. The result is that:

(a)   the income statement excludes cumulative net increases in fair value that arose before the property became investment property. The portion of this change that arose before the beginning of the current period does not represent financial performance of the current period; and

(b)   this treatment creates comparability between entities that had previously revalued the property under the allowed alternative treatment in IAS 16 and those entities that had previously used the IAS 16 benchmark treatment.[26]

Summary of Changes to E64

B67   The most important change between E64 and the final Standard was the introduction of the cost model as an alternative to the fair value model. The other main changes are listed below.

(a)   The guidance on determining fair value was expanded, to clarify the following:[27]

(i)   the fair value of investment property is not reduced by transaction costs that may be incurred on sale or other disposal (paragraph ~~30~~ 37 of the Standard). This is consistent with the measurement of financial assets under paragraph 69 of IAS 39.[28] E64 was silent on the treatment of such costs;

---

26   IAS 16 *Property, Plant and Equipment* as revised by the IASB in 2003 eliminated all references to 'benchmark' treatment and 'allowed alternative' treatments.

27   IFRS 13, issued in May 2011, contains the requirements for measuring fair value and for disclosing information about fair value measurements. As a consequence paragraphs 37, 38, 45–47, 49, 51 and 75(d) of IAS 40 have been deleted.

28   Paragraph 69 was replaced by paragraph 46 when the Board revised IAS 39 in 2003. IFRS 9 *Financial Instruments* deleted paragraph 46 of IAS 39.

(ii)   measurement is based on valuation at the balance sheet date (paragraph ~~31~~ 38);

(iii)   the best evidence of fair value is normally given by current prices on an active market for similar property in the same location and condition and subject to similar lease and other contracts (paragraph ~~39~~ 45). In the absence of such evidence, fair value reflects information from a variety of sources and an entity needs to investigate reasons for any differences between the information from different sources (paragraphs ~~40–41~~ 46 and 47);

(iv)   market value differs from value in use as defined in IAS 36 *Impairment of Assets* (paragraph ~~43~~ 49);

(v)   there is a need to avoid double counting of investment property and separately recognised assets and liabilities. Integral equipment (such as elevators or air-conditioning) is generally included in the investment property, rather than recognised separately (paragraph ~~44~~ 50);

(vi)   the fair value of investment property does not reflect future capital expenditure that will improve or enhance the asset and does not reflect the related future benefits from this future expenditure (paragraph ~~45~~ 51);

(vii)   an entity uses IAS 37 to account for any provisions associated with investment property (paragraph ~~46~~ 52); and

(viii)   in the exceptional cases when fair value cannot be determined reliably, measurement is under the IAS 16 benchmark treatment[29] only (in such cases, revaluation under IAS 16 would also not be reliable) and residual value is assumed to be zero (given that fair value cannot be determined reliably) (paragraphs ~~47–48~~ 53 and 54).

(b)   In relation to the scope of the Standard and the definition of investment property:

(i)   paragraph ~~3~~ 4 now clarifies that the Standard does not apply to forests and similar regenerative natural resources and to mineral rights, the exploration for and extraction of minerals, oil, natural gas and similar non-regenerative resources. This wording is consistent with a similar scope exclusion in IAS 16 *Property, Plant and Equipment*. The Board did not wish to prejudge its decision on the treatment of such items in the current projects on Agriculture and the Extractive Industries;

---

29 IAS 16 *Property, Plant and Equipment* as revised by the IASB in 2003 eliminated all references to 'benchmark' treatment and 'allowed alternative' treatments.

(ii)   land held for a currently undetermined future use is a further example of investment property (paragraph 6(b) 8(b)), on the grounds that a subsequent decision to use such land as inventory or for development as owner-occupied property would be an investment decision;

(iii)   new examples of items that are not investment property are: property held for future use as owner-occupied property, property held for future development and subsequent use as owner-occupied property, property occupied by employees (whether or not the employees pay rent at market rates) and owner-occupied property awaiting disposal (paragraph 7(c) 9(c));

(iv)   property that is being constructed or developed for future use as investment property is now covered by IAS 16 and measured at cost, less impairment losses, if any (paragraph 7(d) 9(d)). E64 proposed that investment property under construction should be measured at fair value; and

(v)   the reference to reliable measurement of fair value (and the related requirements in paragraphs 14–15 of E64) was moved from the definition of investment property into the section on subsequent measurement (paragraphs 47–49 53–55).

(c)   New paragraph 20 23 deals with start up costs, initial operating losses and abnormal wastage (based on paragraphs 17 and 18 of IAS 16[30]). The Board considered adding guidance on the treatment of incidental revenue earned during the construction of investment property. However, the Board concluded that this raised an issue in the context of IAS 16 and decided that it was beyond the scope of this project to deal with this.

(d)   There is an explicit requirement on determining gains or losses on disposal (paragraph 62 69). This is consistent with IAS 16, paragraph 56.[31] There are also new cross-references to:

(i)   IAS 17 *Leases* and IAS 18 *Revenue*,[32] as guidance for determining the date of disposal (paragraph 61 67); and

(ii)   IAS 37 *Provisions, Contingent Liabilities and Contingent Assets*, for liabilities retained after disposal (paragraph 64 71).

(e)   The Standard states explicitly that an entity should transfer an investment property to inventories when the entity begins to develop the property for subsequent sale in the ordinary course of business (paragraphs 51(b) and 52 57(b) and 58). E64 proposed that all transfers from investment properties to inventories should be prohibited. The

---

30   In IAS 16 *Property, Plant and Equipment* as revised by the IASB in 2003, paragraphs 17 and 18 were replaced by paragraphs 19–22.

31   In IAS 16 *Property, Plant and Equipment* as revised by the IASB in 2003, paragraph 56 was replaced by paragraphs 68 and 71.

32   IFRS 15 *Revenue from Contracts with Customers*, issued in May 2014, replaced IAS 18 *Revenue* and amended paragraph 67 of IAS 40 for consistency with the requirements in IFRS 15.

Standard also deals more explicitly than E64 with certain other aspects of transfers.

(f)　New disclosure requirements include:[33]

    (i)　extension of the required disclosure on methods and significant assumptions, which are now to include disclosure of whether fair value was supported by market evidence, or whether the estimate is based on other data (which the entity should disclose) because of the nature of the property and the lack of comparable market data (paragraph 66(b) 75(d));

    (ii)　disclosures of rental income and direct operating expenses (paragraph 66(d) 75(f)); and

    (iii)　disclosures in the exceptional cases when fair value is not reliably determinable (paragraphs 68 and 69(e) 78 and 79(e)).

(g)　E64 proposed a requirement to disclose the carrying amount of unlet or vacant investment property. Some commentators argued that this disclosure was impracticable, particularly for property that is partly vacant. Some also felt that this is a matter for disclosure in a financial review by management, rather than in the financial statements. The Board deleted this disclosure requirement. It should be noted that some indication of vacancy levels may be available from the required disclosure of rental income and from the IAS 17 requirement to disclose cash flows from non-cancellable operating leases (split into less than one year, one to five years and more than five years).

(h)　E64 included no specific transitional provisions, which means that IAS 8 would apply. There is a risk that restatement of prior periods might allow entities to manipulate their reported profit or loss for the period by selective use of hindsight in determining fair values in prior periods. Accordingly, the Board decided to prohibit restatement in the fair value model, except where an entity has already publicly disclosed fair values for prior periods (paragraph 70 80).

33　IFRS 13, issued in May 2011, contains the requirements for measuring fair value and for disclosing information about fair value measurements. As a consequence paragraphs 37, 38, 45–47, 49, 51 and 75(d) of IAS 40 have been deleted.

IASB documents published to accompany

IAS 41

Agriculture

The text of the unaccompanied standard, IAS 41, is contained in Part A of this edition. Its effective date when issued was 1 January 2003. The text of the Accompanying Guidance on IAS 41 is contained in Part B of this edition. This part presents the following documents:

BASIS FOR CONCLUSIONS

BASIS FOR IASC'S CONCLUSIONS ON IAS 41

DISSENTING OPINIONS

Basis for Conclusions on IAS 41 *Agriculture*

This Basis for Conclusions accompanies, but is not part of, IAS 41.

Introduction

BC1　This Basis for Conclusions summarises the International Accounting Standards Board's considerations in reaching its conclusions on amending IAS 41 *Agriculture*, including by issuing *Agriculture: Bearer Plants* (Amendments to IAS 16 and IAS 41)[1] in June 2014. Individual Board members gave greater weight to some factors than to others.

BC2　Because the Board's intention was not to reconsider the fundamental approach to the accounting for agriculture established by IAS 41, this Basis for Conclusions does not discuss requirements in IAS 41 that the Board has not reconsidered. The IASC Basis for Conclusions on IAS 41 follows this Basis.

Scope (2008 and 2014 amendments)

Costs to sell (paragraph 5) – 2008 amendments

BC3　Before the *Improvements to IFRSs* issued in May 2008, IAS 41 used the term 'point-of-sale costs'. This term was not used elsewhere in IFRSs. The term 'costs to sell' is used in IFRS 5 *Non-current Assets Held for Sale and Discontinued Operations* and IAS 36 *Impairment of Assets*. The Board decided that 'point-of-sale costs' and 'costs to sell' meant the same thing in the context of IAS 41. The word 'incremental' in the definition of 'costs to sell' excludes costs that are included in the fair value measurement of a biological asset, such as transport costs. It includes costs that are necessary for a sale to occur but that would not otherwise arise, such as commissions to brokers and dealers, levies by regulatory agencies and commodity exchanges, and transfer taxes and duties. Both terms relate to transaction costs arising at the point of sale.

BC4　Therefore, the Board decided to replace the terms 'point-of-sale costs' and 'estimated point-of-sale costs' with 'costs to sell' to make IAS 41 consistent with IFRS 5 and IAS 36.

1　*Agriculture: Bearer Plants* (Amendments to IAS 16 and IAS 41), issued in June 2014, introduced a definition of a bearer plant. The amendments require biological assets meeting the definition of a bearer plant to be accounted for as property, plant and equipment in accordance with IAS 16 *Property, Plant and Equipment* and as such the amendments are more comprehensively discussed in paragraphs BC38–BC117 of IAS 16. The produce growing on the bearer plants is within the scope of IAS 41. A summary of the specific changes to IAS 41 are discussed in paragraphs BC4A–BC4E of this Standard.

Produce growing on bearer plants – 2014 amendments

BC4A   Before *Agriculture: Bearer Plants* (Amendments to IAS 16 and IAS 41) was issued in June 2014, IAS 41 required all biological assets related to agricultural activity to be measured at fair value less costs to sell. However, the Board observed that there is a class of biological assets, bearer plants, that are held by an entity solely to grow produce over their productive life. The Board's principal decision underlying the 2014 amendments is that bearer plants should be treated as property, plant and equipment. Accordingly, the Board decided to account for bearer plants as property, plant and equipment in accordance with the requirements in IAS 16 *Property, Plant and Equipment*.

BC4B   Nevertheless the Board noted that the same argument is not true for the produce growing on the bearer plants that is undergoing biological transformation until it is harvested (for example, grapes growing on a grape vine). The Board observed that the produce is a consumable biological asset growing on the bearer plant and the growth of the produce directly increases the expected revenue from the sale of the produce. Consequently, fair value measurement of the growing produce provides useful information to users of financial statements about future cash flows that an entity is expected to realise. In contrast the bearer plants themselves are not sold and the changes in the fair value of the bearer plants do not directly influence the entity's future cash flows. The Board also observed that produce will ultimately be detached from the bearer plants and is normally sold separately, meaning it has a market value on its own. This is in contrast to many bearer plants that are unlikely to have an observable market value on their own because they can only be sold while attached to the land.

BC4C   The Board acknowledged that measuring produce growing on bearer plants at fair value less costs to sell sometimes might be difficult to apply in practice. However, it was noted that similar difficulties are encountered when measuring the fair value less costs to sell of the produce growing in the ground. Consequently, the Board decided that it would be inconsistent to provide additional relief from fair value measurement for produce growing on a bearer plant and not also for other biological assets within the scope of IAS 41. The Board observed that if preparers encounter significant practical difficulties on initial measurement of produce, they should consider whether they meet the requirements of the exemptions in paragraphs 10(c) and 30 of IAS 41.

BC4D   Consequently, the Board decided to reaffirm that produce is a biological asset within the scope of IAS 41 and should be measured at fair value less costs to sell with changes recognised in profit and loss as the produce grows. This would maintain consistency of accounting for produce growing in the ground and produce growing on a bearer plant. Consequently, the Board decided to keep the produce within the scope of IAS 41.

BC4E   The Board noted that most of the areas for which respondents asked for additional guidance were specific to a particular type of bearer plant or produce. The Board decided that because of the specialised nature and diversity of bearer plants and produce it would be too difficult for the Board to develop additional guidance on measuring the fair value of produce.

Recognition and measurement

Discount rate (paragraph 20) – 2008 amendments

BC5   As part of the annual improvements project begun in 2007, the Board reconsidered whether it is appropriate to require a pre-tax discount rate in paragraph 20 when measuring fair value.[2] The Board noted that a fair value measurement should take into account the attributes, including tax attributes, that a market participant would consider when pricing an asset or liability.

BC6   The Board noted that a willing buyer would factor into the amount that it would be willing to pay the seller to acquire an asset (or would receive to assume a liability) all incremental cash flows that would benefit that buyer. Those incremental cash flows would be reduced by expected income tax payments using appropriate tax rates (ie the tax rate of a market participant buyer). Accordingly, fair value takes into account future income taxes that a market participant purchasing the asset (or assuming the liability) would be expected to pay (or to receive), without regard to an entity's specific tax situation.[3]

BC7   Therefore, the Board decided to keep the requirement to use a current market-based discount rate but in *Improvements to IFRSs* issued in May 2008 removed the reference to a pre-tax discount rate in paragraph 20.

Additional biological transformation (paragraph 21) – 2008 amendments

BC8   Sometimes the fair value of an asset in its current location and condition is estimated using discounted cash flows. Paragraph 21 could be read to exclude from such calculations increases in cash flows arising from 'additional biological transformation'. Diversity in practice had developed from different interpretations of this requirement. The Board decided that not including these cash flows resulted in a carrying amount that is not representative of the asset's fair value. The Board noted that an entity should consider the risks associated with cash flows from 'additional biological transformation' in determining the expected cash flows, the discount rate, or some combination of the two. Therefore, the Board decided to amend IAS 41 to remove the prohibition on an entity taking into account the cash flows resulting from

---

2   IFRS 13 *Fair Value Measurement*, issued in May 2011, defines fair value and contains the requirements for measuring fair value.

3   IFRS 13, issued in May 2011, defines fair value and contains the requirements for measuring fair value.

'additional biological transformation' when estimating the fair value of a biological asset.[4]

BC9 In its exposure draft of proposed *Improvements to International Financial Reporting Standards* published in 2007, the Board proposed changing the definition of biological transformation to include harvest. This was because the Board wished to make clear that harvest altered the condition of a biological asset. Some commentators objected to this change on the basis that harvest is a human activity rather than a biological transformation. The Board agreed with this argument and decided not to include the harvest in the definition of biological transformation. Instead, the Board amended the Standard to refer to biological transformation or harvest when applicable to make clear that harvest changes the condition of an asset.

BC10 Because applying the changes discussed in paragraphs BC8 and BC9 retrospectively might require some entities to remeasure the fair value of biological assets at a past date, the Board decided that these amendments should be applied prospectively.

Taxation in Fair Value Measurements – 2020 amendment

BC11 The 2008 amendments removed the requirement for entities to use a pre-tax discount rate to discount cash flows when measuring fair value (see paragraphs BC5–BC7). At that time the Board did not amend paragraph 22 of IAS 41 to delete the reference to cash flows for taxation. Consequently, before *Annual Improvements to IFRS Standards 2018–2020*, IAS 41 had required an entity to use pre-tax cash flows when measuring fair value but did not require the use of a pre-tax discount rate to discount those cash flows.

BC12 In 2020, the Board amended paragraph 22 to remove the requirement to exclude cash flows for taxation when measuring fair value because:

(a) doing so aligns the requirements in IAS 41 on fair value measurement with those in IFRS 13 *Fair Value Measurement*. When measuring fair value, IFRS 13 neither prescribes the use of a single present value technique nor limits the use of present value techniques to only those discussed in that Standard. However, when using a present value technique, paragraph B14 of IFRS 13 requires assumptions about cash flows and discount rates to be internally consistent. Depending on the particular facts and circumstances, an entity applying a present value technique might measure fair value by discounting after-tax cash flows using an after-tax discount rate or pre-tax cash flows at a rate consistent with those cash flows.

(b) it would appear the Board's intention in amending IAS 41 in 2008 was to permit entities to include tax cash flows in measuring fair value (see paragraph BC6). Removing 'taxation' from paragraph 22 is consistent with that intent.

---

4 IFRS 13, issued in May 2011, contains the requirements for measuring fair value. As a consequence, paragraph 21 of IAS 41 has been deleted.

CONTENTS

Basis for IASC's Conclusions on IAS 41 *Agriculture*

This Basis for Conclusions accompanies, but is not part of, IAS 41. It was prepared by the IASC Staff in 2000 but was not approved by the IASC Board. It summarises the Board's reasons for:

(a)   *initiating and proposing an International Accounting Standard on agriculture; and*

(b)   *accepting or rejecting certain alternative views.*

Individual Board members gave greater weight to some factors than to others.

This Basis has not been revised by the IASB and the terminology has not been amended to reflect the changes made by Improvements to IFRSs *issued in May 2008.*

Background

B1   In 1994, the IASC Board (the 'Board') decided to develop an International Accounting Standard on agriculture and appointed a Steering Committee to help define the issues and develop possible solutions. In 1996, the Steering Committee published a Draft Statement of Principles ('DSOP') setting out the issues, alternatives, and the Steering Committee's proposals for resolving the issues and inviting public comment. In response, 42 comment letters were received. The Steering Committee reviewed the comments, revised certain of its recommendations, and submitted them to the Board.

B2   In July 1999, the Board approved Exposure Draft E65 *Agriculture* with a comment deadline of 31 January 2000. The Board received 62 comment letters on E65. They came from various international organisations, as well as from 28 individual countries. In April 2000, the IASC Staff sent a questionnaire to entities that undertake agricultural activity in an attempt to determine the reliability of the fair value measurement proposed in E65 and received 20 responses from 11 countries. In December 2000, after considering the comments on E65 and responses to the questionnaire, the Board approved IAS 41 *Agriculture* (the Standard). Paragraph B82 below summarises the changes that the Board made to E65 in finalising the Standard.

The need for an International Accounting Standard on agriculture

B3   A main objective of the IASC is to develop International Accounting Standards that are relevant in the general purpose financial statements of all businesses. While most International Accounting Standards apply to entities in all activities, some International Accounting Standards, for example IAS 30 *Disclosures in the Financial Statements of Banks and Similar Financial Institutions*[1] and IAS 40 *Investment Property*, deal with issues that arise in particular activities. IASC has also undertaken industry-specific projects on insurance and extractive industries.

---

1   In August 2005, IFRS 7 *Financial Instruments: Disclosures* superseded IAS 30.

B4   Diversity in accounting for agricultural activity has occurred because:

(a)   prior to the development of the Standard, assets related to agricultural activity and changes in those assets were excluded from the scope of International Accounting Standards:

(i)   IAS 2 *Inventories* excluded 'producers' inventories of livestock, agricultural and forest products... to the extent that they are measured at net realisable value in accordance with well established practices in certain industries';

(ii)   IAS 16 *Property, Plant and Equipment* did not apply to 'forests and similar regenerative natural resources';

(iii)   IAS 18 *Revenue*[2] did not deal with revenue arising from 'natural increases in herds, and agricultural and forest products'; and

(iv)   IAS 40 *Investment Property* did not apply to 'forests and similar regenerative natural resources';

(b)   accounting guidelines for agricultural activity developed by national standard setters have, in general, been piecemeal, developed to resolve a specific issue related to a form of agricultural activity of significance to that country; and

(c)   the nature of agricultural activity creates uncertainty or conflicts when applying traditional accounting models, particularly because the critical events associated with biological transformation (growth, degeneration, production, and procreation) that alter the substance of biological assets are difficult to deal with in an accounting model based on historical cost and realisation.

B5   Most business organisations involved in agricultural activity are small, independent, cash and tax focused, family-operated business units, often perceived as not being required to produce general purpose financial statements. Some believe that because of this an International Accounting Standard on agriculture would not have widespread application. However, even small agricultural entities seek outside capital and subsidies, particularly from banks or government agencies, and these capital providers increasingly request financial statements. Moreover, an international trend towards deregulation, an increasing number of cross-border listings and more investment have resulted in increasing scale, scope, and commercialism of agricultural activity. This has created a greater need for financial statements based on sound and generally accepted accounting principles. For the above reasons, in 1994 the Board added to its agenda a project on agriculture.

B6   The DSOP specifically asked for views on the feasibility of developing a comprehensive International Accounting Standard on agriculture. Some commentators felt that the diversity of agricultural activity prevents the development of a single International Accounting Standard on accounting for

---

2   IFRS 15 *Revenue from Contracts with Customers*, issued in May 2014, replaced IAS 18 *Revenue*. IFRS 15 also does not address revenue arising from 'natural increases in herds, and agricultural and forest products'.

all agricultural activities. Others said that different principles should attach to agricultural activity with short and long production cycles. Some cited the need to develop International Accounting Standards that are simple to apply and broad in application. Commentators on the DSOP also noted that agriculture is a significant industry in many countries, particularly in developing and newly industrialised countries. In many such countries it is the most important industry.

B7   After considering the comments on the DSOP, the Board reaffirmed its conclusion that an International Accounting Standard is needed. The Board believes that the principles set forth in the Standard have wide application and provide a clear set of principles.

Scope

B8   The Standard prescribes, among other things, the accounting treatment for biological assets and for the initial measurement of agricultural produce harvested from an entity's biological assets at the point of harvest. However, the Standard does not deal with the processing of agricultural produce after harvest, since the Board did not consider it appropriate to undertake a partial revision of IAS 2 *Inventories* which deals with the accounting treatment for inventories under the historical cost system.[3] The processing after harvest is accounted for under IAS 2 or another applicable International Accounting Standard (for example, if an entity harvests logs[4] and decides to use them for constructing its own building, IAS 16 *Property, Plant and Equipment* is applied in accounting for the logs).

B9   Some may think of such processing as agricultural activity, particularly if it is done by the same entity that developed the agricultural produce (for example, the processing of grapes into wine by a vintner who has grown the grapes). While such processing may be a logical and natural extension of agricultural activity, and the events taking place may bear some similarity to biological transformation, such processing is not included within the definition of agricultural activity in the Standard.

B10   In particular, the Board considered whether to include circumstances where there is a long ageing or maturation process after harvest (for example, for wine production from grapes and cheese production from milk) in the scope of the Standard. Those who believe that the Standard should cover such processing argue that:

(a)   such a long ageing or maturation process is similar to biological transformation and fundamental to assessing the performance of an entity; and

(b)   many agricultural entities are vertically integrated and involved in, for example, producing both grapes and wine.

---

3   The term 'historical cost system' is no longer applicable owing to revisions made to IAS 2 in December 2003.

4   As the result of an amendment by the IASB, contained in *Improvements to IFRSs* issued in May 2008, 'logs' is an example of produce that has been processed rather than an example of unprocessed produce.

B11   The Board decided not to include such circumstances in the scope of the Standard because of concerns about difficulties in differentiating them from other manufacturing processes (such as conversion of raw materials into marketable inventories as defined in IAS 2). The Board concluded that the requirements in IAS 2 or another applicable International Accounting Standard would be suited to accounting for such processes.

B12   The Board also considered whether to deal with contracts for the sale of a biological asset or agricultural produce and government grants related to agricultural activity in the Standard. These issues are discussed below (see paragraphs B47–54 and B63–73).

Measurement

Biological assets

Fair value versus cost

B13   The Standard requires an entity to use a fair value approach in measuring its biological assets related to agricultural activity as proposed in the DSOP and E65, except for cases where the fair value cannot be measured reliably on initial recognition.

B14   Those who support fair value measurement argue that the effects of changes brought about by biological transformation are best reflected by reference to the fair value changes in biological assets. They believe that fair value changes in biological assets have a direct relationship to changes in expectations of future economic benefits to the entity.

B15   Those who support fair value measurement also note that the transactions entered into to effect biological transformation often have only a weak relationship with the biological transformation itself and, thus, a more distant relationship to expected future economic benefits. For example, patterns of growth in a plantation forest directly affect expectations of future economic benefits but differ markedly, in timing, from patterns of cost incurrence. No income might be reported until first harvest and sale (perhaps 30 years) in a plantation forestry entity using a transaction-based, historical cost accounting model. On the other hand, income is measured and reported throughout the period until initial harvest if an accounting model is used that recognises and measures biological growth using current fair values.

B16   Further, those who support fair value measurement cite reasons for concluding that fair value has greater relevance, reliability, comparability, and understandability as a measurement of future economic benefits expected from biological assets than historical cost, including:

     (a)   many biological assets are traded in active markets with observable market prices. Active markets for these assets provide a reliable measure of market expectations of future economic benefits. The presence of such markets significantly increases the reliability of market value as an indicator of fair value;

(b)   measures of the cost of biological assets are sometimes less reliable than measures of fair value because joint products and joint costs can create situations in which the relationship between inputs and outputs is ill-defined, leading to complex and arbitrary allocations of cost between the different outcomes of biological transformation. Such allocations become even more arbitrary if biological assets generate additional biological assets (offspring) and the additional biological assets are also used in the entity's own agricultural activity;

(c)   relatively long and continuous production cycles, with volatility in both the production and market environment, mean that the accounting period often does not depict a full cycle. Therefore, period-end measurement (as opposed to time of transaction) assumes greater significance in deriving a measure of current period financial performance or position. The less significant current year harvest is in relation to total biological transformation, the greater the significance of period-end measures of asset change (growth and degeneration). In relatively high turnover, short production cycle, highly controlled agricultural systems (for example, broiler chicken or mushroom production) in which the majority of biological transformation and harvesting occurs within a year, the relationship between cost and future economic benefits appears more stable. This apparent stability does not alter the relationship between current market value and future economic benefits, but it makes the difference in measurement method less significant; and

(d)   different sources of replacement animals and plants (home-grown or purchased) give rise to different costs in a historical cost approach. Similar assets should give rise to similar expectations with regard to future benefits. Considerably enhanced comparability and understandability result when similar assets are measured and reported using the same basis.

B17   Those who oppose measuring biological assets at fair value believe there is superior reliability in cost measurement because historical cost is the result of arm's length transactions, and therefore provides evidence of an open-market value at that point in time, and is independently verifiable. More importantly, they believe fair value is sometimes not reliably measurable and that users of financial statements may be misled by presentation of numbers that are indicated as being fair value but are based on subjective and unverifiable assumptions. Information regarding fair value can be provided other than in a single number in the financial statements. They believe the scope of the Standard is too broad. They also argue that:

(a)   market prices are often volatile and cyclical and not appropriate as a basis of measurement;

(b)   it may be onerous to require fair valuation at each balance sheet date, especially if interim reports are required;

(c)   the historical cost convention is well established and commonly used. The use of any other basis should be accompanied by a change in the IASC *Framework for the Preparation and Presentation of Financial Statements*[5] (the '*Framework*'). For consistency with other International Accounting Standards and other activities, biological assets should be measured at their cost;

(d)   cost measurement provides more objective and consistent measurement;

(e)   active markets may not exist for some biological assets in some countries. In such cases, fair value cannot be measured reliably, especially during the period of growth in the case of a biological asset that has a long growth period (for example, trees in a plantation forest);

(f)   fair value measurement results in recognition of unrealised gains and losses and contradicts principles in International Accounting Standards on recognition of revenue; and

(g)   market prices at a balance sheet date may not bear a close relationship to the prices at which assets will be sold, and many biological assets are not held for sale.

B18   The *Framework* is neutral with respect to the choice of measurement basis, identifying that a number of different bases are employed to different degrees and in varying combinations, though noting that historical cost is most commonly adopted. The alternatives specifically identified are historical cost, current cost, realisable value, and present value. Precedents for fair value measurement exist in other International Accounting Standards.

B19   The Board concluded that the Standard should require a fair value model for biological assets related to agricultural activity because of the unique nature and characteristics of agricultural activity. However, the Board also concluded that, in some cases, fair value cannot be measured reliably. Some respondents to the questionnaire, as well as some commentators on E65, expressed significant concern about the reliability of fair value measurement for some biological assets, arguing that:

(a)   active markets do not exist for some biological assets, in particular for those with a long growth period;

(b)   present value of expected net cash flows is often an unreliable measure of fair value due to the need for, and use of, subjective assumptions (for example, about weather); and

(c)   fair value cannot be measured reliably prior to harvest.

Some commentators on E65 suggested that the Standard should include a reliability exception for cases where no active market exists.

---

5   References to the *Framework* in this Basis for Conclusions are to the IASC's *Framework for the Preparation and Presentation of Financial Statements*, adopted by the Board in 2001 and in effect when the Standard was developed.

B20   The Board decided there was a need to include a reliability exception for cases where market-determined prices or values are not available and alternative estimates of fair value are determined to be clearly unreliable. In those cases, biological assets should be measured at their cost less any accumulated depreciation and any accumulated impairment losses. In determining cost, accumulated depreciation and accumulated impairment losses, an entity considers IAS 2 *Inventories*, IAS 16 *Property, Plant and Equipment* and IAS 36 *Impairment of Assets*.

B21   The Board rejected a benchmark treatment of fair value and an allowed alternative treatment of historical cost because of the greater comparability and understandability achieved by a mandatory fair value approach in the presence of active markets. The Board is also uncomfortable with options in International Accounting Standards.

Treatment of point-of-sale costs

B22   The Standard requires that a biological asset should be measured at its fair value less estimated point-of-sale costs. Point-of-sale costs include commissions to brokers and dealers, levies by regulatory agencies and commodity exchanges, and transfer taxes and duties. Point-of-sale costs exclude transport and other costs necessary to get assets to a market. Such transport and other costs are deducted in determining fair value (that is, fair value is a market price less transport and other costs necessary to get an asset to a market).[6]

B23   E65 proposed that pre-sale disposal costs that will be incurred to place an asset on the market (such as transport costs) should be deducted in determining fair value, if a biological asset will be sold in an active market in another location. However, E65 did not specify the treatment of point-of-sale costs. Some commentators suggested that the Standard should clarify the treatment of point-of-sale costs, as well as pre-sale disposal costs.

B24   Some argue that point-of-sale costs should not be deducted in a fair value model. They argue that fair value less estimated point-of-sale costs would be a biased estimate of markets' estimate of future cash flows, because point-of-sale costs would in effect be recognised as an expense twice if the acquirer pays point-of-sale costs on acquisition; once related to the initial acquisition of biological assets and once related to the immediate measurement at fair value less estimated point-of-sale costs. This would occur even when point-of-sale costs would not be incurred until a future period or would not be paid at all for a bearer biological asset that will not be sold.

B25   On the other hand, some believe that point-of-sale costs should be deducted in a fair value model. They believe that the carrying amount of an asset should represent the economic benefits that are expected to flow from the asset. They argue that fair value less estimated point-of-sale costs would represent the markets' estimate of the economic benefits that are expected to flow to the entity from that asset at the balance sheet date. They also argue that failure to

---

6   IFRS 13, issued in May 2011, describes how transport costs are factored into a fair value measurement.

deduct estimated point-of-sale costs could result in a loss being deferred until a sale occurs.

B26 The Board concluded that fair value less estimated point-of-sale costs is a more relevant measurement of biological assets, acknowledging that, in particular, failure to deduct estimated point-of-sale costs could result in a loss being deferred.

Hierarchy in fair value measurement[7]

B27 The Standard requires that, if an active market exists for a biological asset, the quoted price in that market is the appropriate basis for determining the fair value of that asset. If an active market does not exist, an entity uses market-determined prices or values (such as the most recent market transaction price) when available. However, in some circumstances, market-determined prices or values may not be available for a biological asset in its present condition. In these circumstances, the Standard indicates that an entity uses the present value of expected net cash flows[8] from the asset.

B28 E65 proposed that, if an active market exists for a biological asset, an entity should use the market price in the active market. If an active market does not exist, E65 proposed that an entity should consider other measurement bases such as the price of the most recent transaction for the same type of asset, sector benchmarks, and present value of expected net cash flows. E65 did not set a hierarchy in cases where no active market exists; that is, E65 did not indicate which basis is preferable to the other bases.

B29 The Board considered setting an explicit hierarchy in cases where no active market exists. Some believe that using market-determined prices or values; for example, the most recent market transaction price, would always be preferable to present value of expected net cash flows. On the other hand, some believe that market-determined prices or values would not necessarily be preferable to present value of expected net cash flows, especially when an entity uses market prices for similar assets with adjustment to reflect differences.

B30 The Board concluded that a detailed hierarchy would not provide sufficient flexibility to appropriately deal with all the circumstances that may arise and decided not to set a detailed hierarchy in cases where no active market exists. However, the Board decided to indicate that an entity uses all available market-determined prices or values since otherwise there is a possibility that entities may opt to use present value of expected net cash flows from the asset even when useful market-determined prices or values are available. Of the 20 companies that responded to the questionnaire, six companies used present value of expected net cash flows as a basis of fair value measurement and, in addition, two companies indicated that it was impossible to measure their

---

7 IFRS 13, issued in May 2011, defines an active market and contains a three-level fair value hierarchy for the inputs used in the valuation techniques used to measure fair value.

8 Paragraph 20 of the previous version of IAS 41 required entities to use a pre-tax discount rate when measuring fair value. The IASB decided to maintain the requirement to use a current market-based discount rate but removed the reference to a pre-tax discount rate by *Improvements to IFRSs* issued in May 2008.

biological assets reliably since the present value of expected net cash flows would not be reliable (as they would need to use present value as a basis).

B31   When an entity has access to different markets, the Standard indicates that the entity uses the most relevant one. For example, if an entity has access to two active markets, it uses the price existing in the market expected to be used. Some believe that the most advantageous price in the accessible markets should be used. The Standard reflects the view that the most relevant measurement results from using the market expected to be used.

Frequency of fair value measurement

B32   Some argue that less frequent measurement of fair value should be permitted because of concerns about burdens on entities. The Board rejected this approach because of the:

(a)   continuous nature of biological transformation;

(b)   lack of direct relationships between financial transactions and the outcomes of biological transformation; and

(c)   general availability of reliable measures of fair value at reasonable cost.

Independent valuation

B33   A significant number of commentators on the DSOP indicated that, if present value of expected net cash flows is used to determine fair value, an external independent valuation should be required. The Board rejected this proposal since it believes that external independent valuations are not commonly used for certain agricultural activity and it would be burdensome to require an external independent valuation. The Board believes that it is for entities to decide how to determine fair value reliably, including the extent to which independent valuers need to be involved.

Inability to measure fair value reliably

B34   As noted previously, the Board decided to include a reliability exception in the Standard for cases where fair value cannot be measured reliably on initial recognition. The Standard indicates a presumption that fair value can be measured reliably for a biological asset. However, that presumption can be rebutted only on initial recognition for a biological asset for which market-determined prices or values are not available and for which alternative estimates of fair value are determined to be clearly unreliable. In such a case, that biological asset should be measured at its cost less any accumulated depreciation and any accumulated impairment losses. Once the fair value of such a biological asset becomes reliably measurable, the Standard requires that an entity should start measuring the biological asset at its fair value less estimated point-of-sale costs.

B35   Some believe that, if an entity was previously using the reliability exception, the entity should not be allowed to start fair value measurement (that is, an entity should continue to use a cost basis). They argue that it could be a subjective decision to determine when fair value has become reliably measurable and that this subjectivity could lead to inconsistent application and, potentially, abuse. The Board noted, however, that in agricultural activity, it is likely that fair value becomes measurable more reliably as biological transformation occurs and that fair value measurement is preferable to cost in those cases. Thus, the Board decided to require fair value measurement once fair value becomes reliably measurable.

B36   If an entity has previously measured a biological asset at its fair value less estimated point-of-sale costs, the Standard requires that the entity should continue to measure the biological asset at its fair value less estimated point-of-sale costs until disposal. Some argue that reliable estimates may cease to be available. The Board believed that this would rarely, if ever, occur. Accordingly, the Board decided to prohibit entities from changing their measurement basis from fair value to cost, because otherwise an entity might use a reliability exception as an excuse to discontinue fair value accounting in a falling market.

B37   If an entity uses the reliability exception, the Standard requires additional disclosures. The additional disclosures include information on biological assets held at the end of the period such as a description of the assets and an explanation of why fair value cannot be measured reliably. The additional disclosures also include the gain or loss recognised for the period on disposal of biological assets measured at cost less any accumulated depreciation and any accumulated impairment losses, even though those biological assets are not held at the end of the period.

Gains and losses

B38   The Standard requires that a gain or loss arising on initial recognition of a biological asset and from a change in fair value less estimated point-of-sale costs of a biological asset should be included in net profit or loss[9] for the period in which it arises. Those who support this treatment argue that biological transformation is a significant event that should be included in net profit or loss because:

(a)   the event is fundamental to understanding an entity's performance; and

(b)   this is consistent with the accrual basis of accounting.

B39   Some commentators on the DSOP and E65 argued that fair value changes should be included directly in equity, through the statement of changes in equity, until realised, arguing that:

(a)   the effects of biological transformation cannot be measured reliably and, therefore, should not be reported as income;

(b)   fair value changes should only be included in net profit or loss when the earnings process is complete;

---

9   IAS 1 *Presentation of Financial Statements* (revised in 2003) replaced the term 'net profit or loss' with 'profit or loss'.

(c) recognition of unrealised gains and losses in net profit or loss increases volatility of earnings;

(d) the results of biological transformation may never be realised, particularly given the risks to which biological assets are exposed; and

(e) it is premature to require recognition of fair value changes in net profit or loss, until performance reporting issues are resolved.

B40 The Board rejected requiring changes in fair value to be included directly in equity since it is difficult to find any conceptual basis for reporting any portion of the changes in fair value of biological assets related to agricultural activity directly in equity. No distinction is made in the *Framework* between recognition in the balance sheet and recognition in the income statement.

Agricultural produce

B41 The Standard requires that agricultural produce harvested from an entity's biological assets should be measured at its fair value less estimated point-of-sale costs at the point of harvest. Such measurement is the cost at that date when applying IAS 2 *Inventories* or another applicable International Accounting Standard.

B42 The Board noted that the same basis of measurement should generally be applied to agricultural produce on initial recognition and to the biological asset from which it is harvested. Because the fair value of a biological asset takes into account the condition of the agricultural produce that will be harvested from the biological asset, it would be illogical to measure the agricultural produce at cost when the biological asset is measured at fair value. For example, the fair value of a sheep with half fleece will differ from the fair value of a similar sheep with full fleece. It would be inconsistent and distort reporting of current period performance if, upon shearing, the shorn fleece is measured at its cost when the fair value of the sheep is reduced by the fair value of the fleece.

B43 As noted previously, certain biological assets are measured at their cost less any accumulated depreciation and any accumulated impairment losses, if the reliability exception is applied. Some argue that a reliability exception should exist for measurement of agricultural produce. The Board rejected this view because many of the arguments for a reliability exception do not apply to agricultural produce. For example, markets more often exist for agricultural produce than for biological assets. The Board also noted that it is generally not practicable to reliably determine the cost of agricultural produce harvested from biological assets.

B44 With regard to measurement after harvest, some argue that agricultural produce should be measured at its fair value both at the point of harvest and at each balance sheet date until sold, consumed, or otherwise disposed of. They argue that this approach would ensure that all agricultural produce of a similar type is measured similarly irrespective of date of harvest, thus enhancing comparability and consistency.

B45   The Board concluded that fair value less estimated point-of-sale costs at the point of harvest should be the cost when applying IAS 2 or another applicable International Accounting Standard, since this is consistent with the historical cost accounting model applied to manufacturing processes in general and other types of inventory.

B46   In reaching the above conclusion, the Board noted that entities undertaking agricultural activity sometimes purchase agricultural produce for resale, and other entities often engage in processing purchased agricultural produce into consumable products. If agricultural produce would be measured at its fair value after harvest, a desire for consistency would suggest revaluing purchased inventories as well, and such a treatment would be inconsistent with IAS 2. The Board did not consider it appropriate to undertake a partial revision of IAS 2.

Sales contracts

B47   Entities often enter into contracts to sell at a future date their biological assets or agricultural produce. The Standard indicates that contract prices are not necessarily relevant in determining fair value and that the fair value of a biological asset or agricultural produce is not adjusted because of the existence of a contract.

B48   E65 did not propose how to account for a contract for the sale of a biological asset or agricultural produce. Some commentators suggested prescribing the treatment of sales contracts since such sales contracts are common in certain agricultural activity. Some commentators also pointed out that certain sales contracts are not within the scope of IAS 39 *Financial Instruments: Recognition and Measurement*[10] and that no other International Accounting Standards deal with those contracts.

B49   Some argue that contract prices should be used in measuring the related biological assets when an entity expects to settle the contract by delivery and believe this would result in the most relevant carrying amount for the biological asset. Others argue that contract prices are not necessarily relevant in measuring the biological assets at fair value since fair value reflects the current market in which a willing buyer and seller would enter into a transaction.[11]

B50   The Board concluded that contract prices should not be used in measuring related biological assets, because contract prices do not necessarily reflect the current market in which a willing buyer and seller would enter into a transaction and therefore do not necessarily represent the fair value of assets. The Board wished to maintain a consistent approach to the measurement of assets. The Board instead considered whether it might require that sales contracts be measured at fair value. It is logical to measure a sales contract at fair value to the extent that a related biological asset is also measured at fair value.

---

10   IFRS 9 *Financial Instruments* replaced IAS 39. IFRS 9 applies to all items that were previously within the scope of IAS 39.

11   IFRS 13, issued in May 2011, contains the requirements for measuring fair value.

B51   However, the Board noted that to achieve symmetry between the measurement of a biological asset and a related sales contract the Standard would have to carefully restrict the sales contracts to be measured at fair value. An entity may enter into a contract to sell agricultural produce to be harvested from the entity's biological assets. The Board concluded that it would not be appropriate to require fair value measurement for a contract to sell agricultural produce that does not yet exist (for example, milk to be harvested from a cow), since no related asset has yet been recognised or measured at fair value and to do so would be beyond the scope of the project on agriculture.

B52   Thus, the Board considered restricting the sales contracts to be measured at fair value to those for the sale of an entity's existing biological assets and agricultural produce. However, the Board noted that it is difficult to differentiate existing agricultural produce from agricultural produce that does not exist. For example:

(a)   if an entity enters into a contract to sell fully-grown wheat at a future date and has half-grown wheat at a balance sheet date, it seems clear that the wheat to be delivered under the contract does not yet exist at the balance sheet date; but

(b)   on the other hand, if an entity enters into a contract to sell mature cattle at a future date and has mature cattle at a balance sheet date, it could be argued that the cattle exist in the form in which they will be sold at the balance sheet date. However, it could also be argued that the cattle do not yet exist in the form in which they will be sold at the balance sheet date since further biological transformation will occur between the balance sheet date and the date of delivery.

B53   The Board also noted that the Standard would have to require an entity to stop fair value measurement for sales contracts once agricultural produce to be sold under the contract is harvested from an entity's biological assets, since accounting for agricultural produce is not dealt with in the Standard except for initial measurement and IAS 2 *Inventories* or another applicable International Accounting Standard applies after harvest. It would be illogical to continue fair value measurement when the agricultural produce is measured at historical cost. The Board noted that it would be anomalous to require an entity to start measuring a contract at fair value once the related asset exists and to stop doing that at a later date.

B54   The Board concluded that no solution is practicable without a complete review of the accounting for commodity contracts that are not within the scope of IAS 39.[12] Because of the above difficulties, the Board concluded that the Standard should not deal with the measurement of sales contracts that are not within the scope of IAS 39. Instead, the Board decided to include an observation that those sales contracts may be onerous contracts under IAS 37 *Provisions, Contingent Liabilities and Contingent Assets*.

---

12   IFRS 9 *Financial Instruments* replaced IAS 39. IFRS 9 applies to all items that were previously within the scope of IAS 39.

Land related to agricultural activity

B55   The Standard does not establish any new principles for land related to agricultural activity. Rather, an entity follows IAS 16 *Property, Plant and Equipment* or IAS 40 *Investment Property* depending on which standard is appropriate in the circumstances. IAS 16 requires land to be measured either at its cost less any accumulated impairment losses, or at a revalued amount. IAS 40 requires land that is investment property to be measured at its fair value, or cost less any accumulated impairment losses.

B56   Some argue that land attached to biological assets related to agricultural activity should also be measured at its fair value. They argue that fair value measurement of land results in consistency of measurement with the fair value measurement of biological assets. They also argue that it is sometimes difficult to measure the fair value of such biological assets separately from the land since an active market often exists for the combined assets (that is, land and biological assets; for example, trees in a plantation forest).

B57   The Board rejected this approach, primarily because requiring the fair value measurement of land related to agricultural activity would be inconsistent with IAS 16.

Intangible assets

B58   The Standard does not establish any new principles for intangible assets related to agricultural activity. Rather, an entity follows IAS 38 *Intangible Assets*. IAS 38 requires an intangible asset, after initial recognition, to be measured at its cost less any accumulated amortisation and impairment losses, or at a revalued amount.

B59   E65 proposed that an entity should be encouraged to follow the revaluation alternative in IAS 38 for intangible assets related to agricultural activity, to enhance consistency of measurement with the fair value measurement of biological assets. Some commentators on E65 disagreed with having the encouragement. They argued that a unique treatment for intangible assets related to agricultural activity is not warranted.

B60   The Board did not include the encouragement in E65 in the Standard. The Board concluded that IAS 38 should be applied to intangible assets related to agricultural activity, as it is to intangible assets related to other activities.

Subsequent expenditure

B61   The Standard does not explicitly prescribe how to account for subsequent expenditure related to biological assets. E65 proposed that costs of producing and harvesting biological assets should be charged to expense when incurred and that costs that increase the number of units of biological assets owned or controlled by the entity should be added to the carrying amount of the asset.

B62   Some believe that there is no need to capitalise subsequent expenditure in a fair value model and that all subsequent expenditure should be recognised as an expense. Some also argue that it would sometimes be difficult to prescribe which costs should be recognised as expenses and which costs should be capitalised; for example, in the case of vet fees paid for delivering a calf. The Board decided not to explicitly prescribe the accounting for subsequent expenditure related to biological assets in the Standard, because it believes to do so is unnecessary with a fair value measurement approach.

Government grants

B63   The Standard requires that an unconditional government grant related to a biological asset measured at its fair value less estimated point-of-sale costs should be recognised as income when, and only when, the government grant becomes receivable. If a government grant is conditional, including where a government grant requires an entity not to engage in specified agricultural activity, an entity should recognise the government grant as income when, and only when, the conditions attaching to the government grant are met.

B64   The Standard requires a different treatment from IAS 20 *Accounting for Government Grants and Disclosure of Government Assistance* in the circumstances described above. IAS 20 is to be applied only to government grants related to biological assets measured at cost less any accumulated depreciation and any accumulated impairment losses.

B65   IAS 20 requires that government grants should not be recognised until there is reasonable assurance that:

(a)   the entity will comply with the conditions attaching to them; and

(b)   the grants will be received.

IAS 20 also requires that government grants should be recognised as income over the periods necessary to match them with the related costs that they are intended to compensate, on a systematic basis. In relation to the presentation of government grants related to assets, IAS 20 permits two methods—setting up a government grant as deferred income or deducting the government grant from the carrying amount of the asset.

B66   The latter method of presentation—deducting a government grant from the carrying amount of the related asset—is inconsistent with a fair value model in which an asset is measured and presented at its fair value. Using the deduction from carrying value approach, an entity would first deduct the government grant from the carrying amount of the related asset and then measure that asset at its fair value. In effect, an entity would recognise a government grant as income immediately, even for a conditional government grant. This conflicts with the requirement in IAS 20 that government grants should not be recognised until there is reasonable assurance that the entity will comply with the conditions attaching to them.

B67 Because of the above, the Board concluded that there was a need to deal with government grants related to biological assets measured at their fair value. Some argued that IASC should begin a wider review of IAS 20 rather than provide special rules in individual International Accounting Standards. The Board acknowledged that this might be a more appropriate approach, but concluded that such a review would be beyond the scope of the project on agriculture. Instead, the Board decided to deal with government grants in the Standard, since the Board noted that government grants related to agricultural activity are common in some countries.

B68 E65 proposed that, if an entity receives a government grant in respect of a biological asset that is measured at its fair value and the grant is unconditional, the entity should recognise the grant as income when the government grant becomes receivable. E65 also proposed that, if a government grant is conditional, the entity should recognise it as income when there is reasonable assurance that the conditions are met.

B69 The Board noted that, if a government grant is conditional, an entity is likely to have costs and ongoing obligations associated with satisfying the conditions attaching to the government grant. It may be possible that the inflow of economic benefits is much less than the amount of the government grant. Given that possibility, the Board acknowledged that the criterion for recognising income from a conditional government grant in E65, when there is reasonable assurance that the conditions are met, may give rise to income recognition that is inconsistent with the *Framework*. The *Framework* indicates that income is recognised in the income statement when an increase in future economic benefits related to an increase in an asset or a decrease in a liability has arisen that can be measured reliably. The Board also noted that it would inevitably be a subjective decision as to when there is reasonable assurance that the conditions are met and that this subjectivity could lead to inconsistent income recognition.

B70 The Board considered two alternative approaches:

(a) an entity should recognise a conditional government grant as income when it is probable that the entity will meet the conditions attaching to the government grant; and

(b) an entity should recognise a conditional government grant as income when the entity meets the conditions attaching to the government grant.

B71 Proponents of approach (a) argue that this approach is generally consistent with the revenue recognition requirements in IAS 18 *Revenue*.[13] IAS 18 requires that revenue should be recognised, among other things, when it is probable that the economic benefits associated with the transaction will flow to the entity.

---

13 IFRS 15 *Revenue from Contracts with Customers*, issued in May 2014, replaced IAS 18 *Revenue*.

B72 Proponents of approach (b) believe that, until the conditions attaching to the government grant are met, a liability should be recognised under the *Framework* rather than income since an entity has a present obligation to satisfy the conditions arising from past events. They also argue that income recognition under approach (a) would still be subjective and inconsistent with the recognition criteria indicated in the *Framework*.

B73 The Board concluded that approach (b) is more appropriate. The Board also decided that a government grant that requires an entity not to engage in specified agricultural activity should also be accounted for in the same way as a conditional government grant related to a biological asset measured at its fair value less estimated point-of-sale costs.

Disclosure

Separate disclosure of physical and price changes

B74 The Standard encourages, but does not require, separate disclosure of the effects of the factors resulting in changes to the carrying amount of biological assets, physical change and price change, when there is a production cycle of more than one year. Physical change is attributable to changes in the assets themselves while price change is attributable to changes in unit fair values.

B75 Some argue that the separate disclosure should be required since it is useful in appraising current period performance and future prospects in relation to production from, and maintenance and renewal of, biological assets. Others argue that it may be impracticable to separate these elements and the two components cannot be separated reliably.

B76 The Board concluded that the separate disclosure should not be required because of practicability concerns. However, the Board decided to encourage the separate disclosure, given that such disclosure may be useful and practically determinable in some circumstances. The separate disclosure is not encouraged when the production cycle is less than one year (for example, when raising broiler chickens or growing cereal crops) since that information is less useful in that circumstance.

B77 Some argue that physical changes should be included in net profit or loss and that price changes should be included directly in equity, through the statement of changes in equity. The Board rejected this approach because both components are indicative of management's performance.

Disaggregation of the gain or loss

B78 The Standard requires that an entity should disclose the aggregate gain or loss arising during the current period on initial recognition of biological assets and agricultural produce and from the change in fair value less estimated point-of-sale costs of biological assets. The Standard does not require or encourage disaggregating the gain or loss, except that the Standard encourages separate disclosure of physical changes and price changes as discussed above.

B79   The Board considered requiring, or encouraging, disclosure of the gain or loss on a disaggregated basis; for example, requiring separate disclosure of the gain or loss related to biological assets and the gain or loss related to agricultural produce. Those who supported disaggregating the gain or loss believe that such information is useful in appraising current period performance in relation to biological transformation. Others argued that disaggregation would be impracticable and require a subjective procedure.

Other disclosures

B80   E65 proposed disclosing the:

(a)   extent to which the carrying amount of biological assets reflects a valuation by an external independent valuer, or if there has been no valuation by an external independent valuer, that fact;

(b)   activities that are unsustainable with an estimated date of cessation of the activities;

(c)   aggregate carrying amount of an entity's agricultural land and the basis (cost or revalued amount) on which the carrying amount was determined under IAS 16 *Property, Plant and Equipment*; and

(d)   carrying amount of agricultural produce either on the face of the balance sheet or in the notes.

B81   The Board did not include the above disclosures in the Standard. The Board noted that requiring item (a) above would not be appropriate since external independent valuations are not commonly used for assets related to agricultural activity, unlike for certain other assets such as investment property. The Board also noted that item (b) is not required in other International Accounting Standards and a unique disclosure requirement is not warranted for agricultural activity. Items (c) and (d) would be outside the scope of the Standard and covered by other International Accounting Standards (IAS 16 or IAS 2 *Inventories*).

Summary of changes to E65

B82   The Standard made the following principal changes to the proposals in E65:

(a)   The Standard includes a reliability exception for biological assets on initial recognition. If the exception is applied, the biological asset should be measured at its cost less any accumulated depreciation and any accumulated impairment losses (paragraph 30 of the Standard). As a consequence, the Standard includes disclosure requirements consistent with paragraph 170(b) of IAS 39 *Financial Instruments: Recognition and Measurement*[14] and paragraph 68 of IAS 40 *Investment Property*[15] (paragraphs 54(a)–(c) and 55 of the Standard), and consistent

---

14   Paragraph 170(b) of IAS 39 was replaced by paragraph 90 of IAS 32 *Financial Instruments: Disclosure and Presentation* when the IASB revised those standards in 2003. In 2005, the IASB relocated all disclosures relating to financial instruments to IFRS 7 *Financial Instruments: Disclosures*.

15   Paragraph 68 of IAS 40 was replaced by paragraph 78 when the IASB revised IAS 40 in 2003.

with paragraphs 60(b)–(d) and 60(e)(v)–(vii) of IAS 16 *Property, Plant and Equipment*[16] (paragraphs 54(d)–(f) and 55).

(b) If the reliability exception is applied but fair value subsequently becomes reliably measurable and, therefore, an entity has started measuring the biological assets at their fair value less estimated point-of-sale costs, the Standard requires the entity to disclose a description of the biological assets, an explanation of why fair value has become reliably measurable, and the effect of the change (paragraph 56).

(c) E65 did not specify how to account for point-of-sale costs (such as commissions to brokers). The Standard requires that biological assets and agricultural produce should be measured at their fair value less estimated point-of-sale costs (paragraphs 12–13).

(d) E65 included net realisable value as one of the measurement bases in cases where no active market exists. Net realisable value was deleted from the bases since it is not a market-determined value.

(e) The Standard indicates that market-determined prices or values are used when available. The Standard also indicates that, in some circumstances, market-determined prices or values may not be available for an asset in its present condition. In these circumstances, an entity uses the present value of expected net cash flows (paragraphs 18–20).

(f) Guidance on the performance of present value calculations was added (paragraphs 21–23).

(g) E65 did not specify how to account for contracts for the sale of a biological asset or agricultural produce. The Standard indicates that the fair value of a biological asset or agricultural produce is not adjusted because of the existence of a sales contract (paragraph 16).

(h) E65 did not explicitly indicate that a gain or loss may arise on initial recognition of agricultural produce. The Standard clarifies that a gain or loss may arise on initial recognition of agricultural produce; for example, as a result of harvesting and that such a gain or loss should be included in net profit or loss[17] for the period in which it arises (paragraphs 28–29).

(i) E65 proposed that costs of producing and harvesting biological assets should be charged to expense when incurred, and that costs that increase the number of units of biological assets owned or controlled by the entity should be added to the carrying amount of the asset. The Standard does not explicitly prescribe how to account for subsequent expenditure related to biological assets.

---

16 Paragraph 60 of IAS 16 was replaced by paragraph 73 when IAS 16 was revised in 2003.

17 IAS 1 *Presentation of Financial Statements* (revised in 2003) replaced the term 'net profit or loss' with 'profit or loss'.

(j) E65 proposed that an entity should recognise a conditional government grant as income when there is reasonable assurance that the conditions are met. The Standard requires that a conditional government grant related to a biological asset measured at its fair value less estimated point-of-sale costs, including where a government grant requires an entity not to engage in specified agricultural activity, should be recognised as income when, and only when, the conditions attaching to the government grant are met. The Standard also indicates that IAS 20 *Accounting for Government Grants and Disclosure of Government Assistance* is applied to a government grant related to a biological asset measured at its cost less any accumulated depreciation and any accumulated impairment losses (paragraphs 34–35 and 37).

(k) E65 provided the following encouragements specific to agricultural activity with regard to alternative treatments allowed in other International Accounting Standards, to achieve consistency with the accounting treatment of activities covered by E65:

(i) analysing expenses by nature, as set out in IAS 1 *Presentation of Financial Statements*; and

(ii) revaluing certain intangible assets used in agricultural activity if an active market exists, as set out in IAS 38 *Intangible Assets*.

The Board did not include these encouragements in the Standard. The Board noted that IAS 1 and IAS 38 apply to entities that undertake agricultural activity, as well as to those in other activities.

(l) New disclosure requirements include disclosing the:

(i) basis for making distinctions between consumable and bearer biological assets or between mature and immature biological assets, when an entity provides a quantified description of each group of biological assets (paragraph 43);

(ii) methods and significant assumptions applied in determining the fair value of each group of agricultural produce at the point of harvest (paragraph 47);

(iii) fair value less estimated point-of-sale costs of agricultural produce harvested during the period, determined at the point of harvest (paragraph 48);

(iv) increases resulting from business combinations in the reconciliation of the carrying amount of biological assets (paragraph 50(e)); and

(v) significant decreases expected in the level of government grants related to agricultural activity covered by the Standard (paragraph 57(c)).

(m)   E65 proposed disclosing the:

(i)   extent to which the carrying amount of biological assets reflects a valuation by an external independent valuer or, if there has been no valuation by an external independent valuer, that fact;

(ii)   activities that are unsustainable with an estimated date of cessation of the activities;

(iii)   aggregate carrying amount of an entity's agricultural land and the basis (cost or revalued amount) on which the carrying amount was determined under IAS 16; and

(iv)   carrying amount of agricultural produce either on the face of the balance sheet or in the notes.

The Standard does not include the above disclosures.

(n)   The amendment to IAS 17 *Leases* now clarifies that IAS 17 should not be applied to the measurement by:

(i)   lessees of biological assets held under finance leases; and

(ii)   lessors of biological assets leased out under operating leases.

Biological assets held under finance leases and those leased out under operating leases are measured under the Standard rather than IAS 17. A lease of a biological asset is classified as a finance lease or operating lease under IAS 17. If a lease is classified as a finance lease, the lessee recognises the leased biological asset under IAS 17 and thereafter measures and presents it under the Standard. In that case, the lessee makes disclosures both under the Standard and IAS 17. A lessor of a biological asset under an operating lease measures and presents the biological asset under the Standard, and makes disclosures both under the Standard and IAS 17.

Dissenting Opinions

Dissent of Patrick Finnegan and Patricia McConnell

DO1   Mr Finnegan and Ms McConnell voted against the publication of *Agriculture: Bearer Plants* (Amendments to IAS 16 and IAS 41) issued in June 2014 (the 'June 2014 Amendment') because they believe that including bearer plants within the scope of IAS 16 *Property, Plant and Equipment* instead of IAS 41 *Agriculture* will eliminate information about the fair value changes in bearer plants and the underlying assumptions used to estimate those changes. Information about the fair values of all biological assets including bearer plants is critical both to managing agricultural activities and to investing in entities that engage in those activities. Without such information, investors are unable to assess changes in expectations of future net cash inflows for an entity engaged in agricultural activity. The fact that published price quotations have developed throughout the world for orchards and plantations that include bearer plants demonstrates the importance of fair value information to those who invest in agricultural activities.

DO2   IAS 41 prescribes the accounting for agricultural activity, that is, the management by an entity of the biological transformation of living animals or plants (biological assets) for sale, into agricultural produce or into additional biological assets. The underlying principle of IAS 41 is that fair value measurement best reflects the biological transformation of biological assets. It requires measurement at fair value less costs to sell (referred to hereafter as fair value) from initial recognition of biological assets up to and including the point of harvest, other than when fair value cannot be measured reliably on initial recognition.

DO3   The June 2014 Amendment changes the measurement for one subset of biological assets, bearer plants, from fair value to a cost-based measure. Bearer plants are plants that are used only in the production or supply of agricultural produce and are expected to bear produce for more than one period. The June 2014 Amendment includes bearer plants within the scope of IAS 16. Consequently, entities would be permitted to choose either the cost model or the revaluation model for bearer plants. All other biological assets related to agricultural activity will remain under the fair value model in IAS 41, including bearer animals.

The importance of fair value information for biological assets

DO4   Fundamentally, IAS 41 is a Standard on accounting for biological transformation. Biological transformation of bearer assets occurs both prior to maturity and after maturity. A cost model ignores biological transformation when it occurs. That is why IAS 41 requires fair value measurement. The Basis for Conclusions of IAS 41 states:

> "Those who support fair value measurement argue that the effects of changes brought about by biological transformation are best reflected by reference to the fair value changes in biological assets. They believe that fair value changes in biological assets have a direct relationship to changes in expectations of future economic benefits to the entity."

Mr Finnegan and Ms McConnell see no reason to abandon that principle with respect to bearer plants. Consequently, they do not agree that prior to maturity, bearer plants should be measured at accumulated cost. They do not believe that accounting for bearer plants in the same way as for self-constructed items of property, plant and equipment will provide users of financial statements with information that is useful to an understanding of the agricultural entity's performance for the period or of its productive capacity at a point in time.

DO5   While maturing, bearer plants are undergoing biological transformation. Mr Finnegan and Ms McConnell continue to believe that fair value measurement for the biological transformation process provides the best information about bearer assets' quality and quantitative changes during their growth period. They also believe that the fair value of bearer plants at maturity provides the best measure of an entity's resources being placed into the production of produce at maturity. Investors need that information to assess management's stewardship of the resources invested in the production process and the performance of the entity using those resources. Consequently, they believe that bearer plants must be measured at fair value while maturing because fair value provides users of financial statements with the best information about an important aspect of an agricultural entity's performance and management stewardship.

DO6   They also reject the view that biological transformation of bearer assets is no longer a key element for understanding the future net cash flows to an entity once such assets reach maturity. By definition, biological transformation is not limited to merely the growth process to maturity, but also includes the cycles of production and degeneration, which are critical phases in the life cycle of bearer assets. Fair value measurements of bearer assets throughout their lives provide information about the effectiveness and efficiency of the production process, and about the capability of such assets to generate net cash inflows into the future. In contrast, depreciation of the cost of a mature bearer asset only approximates the biological transformation of a bearer asset throughout its productive life and has only an indirect relationship, at best, to changes in future net cash inflows.

Effects of the use of fair value measurement

DO7   Mr Finnegan and Ms McConnell acknowledge that measuring bearer plants at fair value may sometimes be difficult. In particular, the Board has been told that the fair value of bearer plants is particularly subjective during the early years of their life cycle. However, Mr Finnegan and Ms McConnell note that IAS 41 contains an exception from fair value for biological assets for which quoted market prices are not available and for which alternative fair value measurements are determined to be clearly unreliable on initial recognition. They believe that this exception is sufficient to deal with the concerns about the reliability of fair value measures of bearer plants during the early years of their life cycle. They also note that entities throughout the world have been applying IAS 41 in a wide variety of agricultural activities since 2003. In fact, some national accounting standards required or recommended measurement of bearer assets at fair values even before IAS 41 was issued. They do not believe that measuring fair value of bearer plants, in general, is any more difficult than measuring fair value for other biological assets such as bearer animals. Furthermore, they believe that applying a cost measure to bearer plants may be equally as difficult in some situations. Fair value measurements are required in assessing bearer plants for impairment, and surely those who are urging a reversion to a cost model for bearer assets would not suggest that impairment should be ignored because fair value measurement may sometimes be difficult. Moreover, the June 2014 Amendment would permit fair value measurements as a pure accounting policy choice. Mr Finnegan and Ms McConnell believe that accounting should reflect underlying economic circumstances and should not merely be left to choice. The existing fair value exception in IAS 41 is based on circumstances (measurement reliability), and is not an accounting policy choice.

DO8   In addition to concerns about the reliability of fair value measures, entities with bearer assets expressed concern about the volatility that arises from recognising changes in the fair value of the bearer plants in profit or loss and said that users of financial statements adjust reported profit or loss to eliminate the effects of changes in fair values of bearer biological assets. Mr Finnegan and Ms McConnell accept the view that the use of fair value for bearer assets makes the analysis of profit or loss and financial position more difficult. At the same time, they note that price volatility is an indicator of risk, and risk assessment is part of an analyst's job. Mr Finnegan and Ms McConnell note that sound financial statement analysis will always adjust reported profit or loss and financial position for the effects of unusual or non-recurring changes in reported information. However, if critical information about changes in the economic benefits arising in an agricultural operation is not reported, such analysis is impaired or not possible at all.

DO9   Mr Finnegan and Ms McConnell believe that instead of ignoring the fair value volatility, which a cost model does, volatility should be addressed as a matter of financial statement presentation—such as by putting the fair value changes in other comprehensive income. They note that under the June 2014 Amendment, the bearer assets will be within the scope of IAS 16 and revaluation will be permitted. If an entity were to choose revaluation, the change in the revaluation amount (which approximates fair value) would be reported in other comprehensive income. Consequently, they believe that requiring fair value measurement during the entirety of the bearer plant's life cycle with the fair value changes reported in other comprehensive income would be consistent with permitting revaluation of the bearer asset. Furthermore, Mr Finnegan and Ms McConnell believe that such a change would preserve relevant information for investors through prominent display in the primary financial statements, while addressing the concerns of those who believe that fair value changes distort profit or loss.

Current proposals are not improvements to IFRS

DO10   Mr Finnegan and Ms McConnell believe that if bearer assets are measured at accumulated cost, then at a minimum, the fair value of the bearer plants should be a required disclosure, including information about the valuation techniques and key inputs/assumptions used. However, the 2014 Amendment is not requiring disclosure of fair value. Consequently, critical information is being eliminated from the financial statements of entities engaged in agricultural activities using bearer assets. Mr Finnegan and Ms McConnell do not believe that this is an improvement to financial reporting. In January 2013, the Trustees of the IFRS Foundation approved a new *Due Process Handbook* that specifies, among other things, the criteria for new Standards or major improvements. The main criteria (in addition to pervasiveness of the issue) are (a) whether there is a deficiency in the way particular types of transactions or activities are reported in financial reports, and (b) the importance of the matter to those who use financial reports. Mr Finnegan and Ms McConnell believe that, from a user perspective, there is no deficiency in the accounting for, and disclosures about, bearer assets in IAS 41 and that fair value information is important (indeed essential) to those who use the financial reports of entities engaged in agricultural activity.

DO11   In the user outreach performed by the staff, most investors and analysts said that fair value information about bearer plants is of either limited or no use to them *without* fair value information about the related land, agricultural machinery, etc. Instead of meeting the needs of users by providing this additional fair value information to make the fair value of bearer plants more useful, the Board has chosen to withdraw the requirement to provide the fair value of bearer plants. In the view of Mr Finnegan and Ms McConnell this solution does not adequately address the needs of users of financial statements.

DO12   A better solution would have been for the Board to require the fair value of bearer plants in combination with the fair value of the land to which such plants are attached. One of the weaknesses in IAS 41 is that it does not require the use of fair value to measure land to which bearer plants are attached. This is a weakness because the value of bearer plants is inextricably tied to the value of the land. By understanding the value of the bearer plants and the land, investors know the true potential of an entity's future net cash inflows. A historical cost model for either or both is incapable of providing such information.

DO13   As just discussed, Mr Finnegan and Ms McConnell do not believe the June 2014 Amendment represents an improvement to IFRS and, in fact, represents a step towards lowering the quality of the information available in the financial statements of entities engaged in agricultural activities. The June 2014 Amendment therefore fails to meet the Board's own criteria for a new or amended Standard.

Documents published to accompany

IFRIC 1

Changes in Existing Decommissioning, Restoration and Similar Liabilities

The text of the unaccompanied Interpretation, IFRIC 1, is contained in Part A of this edition. Its effective date when issued was 1 September 2004. The text of the Accompanying Guidance on IFRIC 1 is contained in Part B of this edition. This part presents the following document:

BASIS FOR CONCLUSIONS

Basis for Conclusions on
IFRIC Interpretation 1 *Changes in Existing Decommissioning, Restoration and Similar Liabilities*

This Basis for Conclusions accompanies, but is not part of, IFRIC 1.

The original text has been marked up to reflect the revision of IAS 1 Presentation of Financial Statements *in 2007: new text is underlined and deleted text is struck through.*

Introduction

BC1   This Basis for Conclusions summarises the IFRIC's considerations in reaching its consensus. Individual IFRIC members gave greater weight to some factors than to others.

Background

BC2   IAS 16 *Property, Plant and Equipment* requires the cost of an item of property, plant and equipment to include the initial estimate of the costs of dismantling and removing an asset and restoring the site on which it is located, the obligation for which an entity incurs either when the item is acquired or as a consequence of having used the item during a particular period for purposes other than to produce inventories during that period.

BC3   IAS 37 *Provisions, Contingent Liabilities and Contingent Assets* requires that the measurement of the liability, both initially and subsequently, should be the estimated expenditure required to settle the present obligation at the ~~balance sheet date~~ end of the reporting period and should reflect a current market-based discount rate. It requires provisions to be reviewed at ~~each balance sheet date~~ the end of each reporting period and adjusted to reflect the current best estimate. Hence, when the effect of a change in estimated outflows of resources embodying economic benefits and/or the discount rate is material, that change should be recognised.

BC4   The IFRIC was asked to address how to account for changes in decommissioning, restoration and similar liabilities. The issue is whether changes in the liability should be recognised in current period profit or loss, or added to (or deducted from) the cost of the related asset. IAS 16 contains requirements for the initial capitalisation of decommissioning costs and IAS 37 contains requirements for measuring the resulting liability; neither specifically addresses accounting for the effect of changes in the liability. The IFRIC was informed that differing views exist, resulting in a risk of divergent practices developing.

BC5   Accordingly, the IFRIC decided to develop guidance on accounting for the changes. In so doing, the IFRIC recognised that the estimation of the liability is inherently subjective, since its settlement may be very far in the future and estimating (a) the timing and amount of the outflow of resources embodying economic benefits (eg cash flows) required to settle the obligation and (b) the discount rate often involves the exercise of considerable judgement. Hence, it is likely that revisions to the initial estimate will be made.

Scope

BC6   The scope of the Interpretation addresses the accounting for changes in estimates of existing liabilities to dismantle, remove and restore items of property, plant and equipment that fall within the scope of IAS 16 and are recognised as a provision under IAS 37. The Interpretation does not apply to changes in estimated liabilities in respect of costs that fall within the scope of other IFRSs, for example, inventory or production costs that fall within the scope of IAS 2 *Inventories*. The IFRIC noted that decommissioning obligations associated with the extraction of minerals are a cost either of the property, plant and equipment used to extract them, in which case they are within the scope of IAS 16 and the Interpretation, or of the inventory produced, which should be accounted for under IAS 2.

Basis for Consensus

BC7   The IFRIC reached a consensus that changes in an existing decommissioning, restoration or similar liability that result from changes in the estimated timing or amount of the outflow of resources embodying economic benefits required to settle the obligation, or a change in the discount rate, should be added to or deducted from the cost of the related asset and depreciated prospectively over its useful life.

BC8   In developing its consensus, the IFRIC also considered the following three alternative approaches for accounting for changes in the outflow of resources embodying economic benefits and changes in the discount rate:

(a)   capitalising only the effect of a change in the outflow of resources embodying economic benefits that relate to future periods, and recognising in current period profit or loss all of the effect of a change in the discount rate.

(b)   recognising in current period profit or loss the effect of all changes in both the outflow of resources embodying economic benefits and the discount rate.

(c)   treating changes in an estimated decommissioning, restoration and similar liability as revisions to the initial liability and the cost of the asset. Under this approach, amounts relating to the depreciation of the asset that would have been recognised to date would be reflected in current period profit or loss and amounts relating to future depreciation would be capitalised.

BC9   The IFRIC rejected alternative (a), because this approach does not treat changes in the outflow of resources embodying economic benefits and in the discount rate in the same way, which the IFRIC agreed is important, given that matters such as inflation can affect both the outflow of economic benefits and the discount rate.

BC10   In considering alternative (b), the IFRIC observed that recognising all of the change in the discount rate in current period profit or loss correctly treats a change in the discount rate as an event of the present period. However, the IFRIC decided against alternative (b) because recognising changes in the estimated outflow of resources embodying economic benefits in current period profit or loss would be inconsistent with the initial capitalisation of decommissioning costs under IAS 16.

BC11   Alternative (c) was the approach proposed in draft Interpretation D2 *Changes in Decommissioning, Restoration and Similar Liabilities*, published on 4 September 2003. In making that proposal, the IFRIC regarded the asset, from the time the liability for decommissioning is first incurred until the end of the asset's useful life, as the unit of account to which decommissioning costs relate. It therefore took the view that revisions to the estimates of those costs, whether through revisions to estimated outflows of resources embodying economic benefits or revisions to the discount rate, ought to be accounted for in the same manner as the initial estimated cost. The IFRIC still sees merit in this proposal, but concluded on balance that, under current standards, full prospective capitalisation should be required for the reasons set out in paragraphs BC12–BC18.

IAS 8 and a change in accounting estimate

BC12   IAS 8 *Accounting Policies, Changes in Accounting Estimates and Errors* requires an entity to recognise a change in an accounting estimate prospectively by including it in profit or loss in the period of the change, if the change affects that period only, or the period of the change and future periods, if the change affects both. To the extent that a change in an accounting estimate gives rise to changes in assets or liabilities, or relates to an item of equity, it is required to be recognised by adjusting the asset, liability or equity item in the period of change.

BC13   Although the IFRIC took the view that the partly retrospective treatment proposed in D2 is consistent with these requirements of IAS 8, most responses to the draft Interpretation suggested that IAS 8 would usually be interpreted as requiring a fully prospective treatment. The IFRIC agreed that IAS 8 would support a fully prospective treatment also, and this is what the Interpretation requires.

IAS 16 and changes in accounting estimates for property, plant and equipment

BC14   Many responses to the draft Interpretation argued that the proposal in D2 was inconsistent with IAS 16, which requires other kinds of change in estimate for property, plant and equipment to be dealt with prospectively. For example, as IAS 8 also acknowledges, a change in the estimated useful life of, or the expected pattern of consumption of the future economic benefits embodied in, a depreciable asset affects depreciation expense for the current period and for each future period during the asset's remaining useful life. In both cases, the effect of the change relating to the current period is recognised in profit or loss in the current period. The effect, if any, on future periods is recognised in profit or loss in those future periods.

BC15 Some responses to the draft Interpretation noted that a change in the estimate of a residual value is accounted for prospectively and does not require a catch-up adjustment. They observed that liabilities relating to decommissioning costs can be regarded as negative residual values, and suggested that the Interpretation should not introduce inconsistent treatment for similar events. Anomalies could result if two aspects of the same change are dealt with differently—for example, if the useful life of an asset was extended and the present value of the decommissioning liability reduced as a result.

BC16 The IFRIC agreed that it had not made a sufficient case for treating changes in estimates of decommissioning and similar liabilities differently from other changes in estimates for property, plant and equipment. The IFRIC understood that there was no likelihood of the treatment of other changes in estimate for such assets being revisited in the near future.

BC17 The IFRIC also noted that the anomalies that could result from its original proposal, if other changes in estimate were dealt with prospectively, were more serious than it had understood previously, and that a fully prospective treatment would be easier to apply consistently.

BC18 The IFRIC had been concerned that a fully prospective treatment could result in either unrealistically large assets or negative assets, particularly if there are large changes in estimates toward the end of an asset's life. The IFRIC noted that the first concern could be dealt with if the assets were reviewed for impairment in accordance with IAS 36 *Impairment of Assets*, and that a zero asset floor could be applied to ensure that an asset did not become negative if cost estimates reduced significantly towards the end of its life. The credit would first be applied to write the carrying amount of the asset down to nil and then any residual credit adjustment would be recognised in profit or loss. These safeguards are included in the final consensus.

Comparison with US GAAP

BC19 In reaching its consensus, the IFRIC considered the US GAAP approach in Statement of Financial Accounting Standards No. 143, *Accounting for Asset Retirement Obligations* (SFAS 143). Under that standard, changes in estimated cash flows are capitalised as part of the cost of the asset and depreciated prospectively, but the decommissioning obligation is not required to be revised to reflect the effect of a change in the current market-assessed discount rate.

BC20 The treatment of changes in estimated cash flows required by this Interpretation is consistent with US GAAP, which the proposal in D2 was not. However, the IFRIC agreed that because IAS 37 requires a decommissioning obligation to reflect the effect of a change in the current market-based discount rate (see paragraph BC3), it was not possible to disregard changes in the discount rate. Furthermore, SFAS 143 did not treat changes in cash flows and discount rates in the same way, which the IFRIC had agreed was important.

The interaction of the Interpretation and initial recognition under IAS 16

BC21 In developing the Interpretation, the IFRIC considered the improvements that have been made to IAS 16 by the Board and agreed that it would explain the interaction of the two.

BC22 IAS 16 (as revised in 2003) clarifies that the initial measurement of the cost of an item of property, plant and equipment should include the cost of dismantling and removing the item and restoring the site on which it is located, if this obligation is incurred either when the item is acquired or as a consequence of having used the item during a particular period for purposes other than to produce inventories during that period. This is because the Board concluded that whether the obligation is incurred upon acquisition of the item or as a consequence of using it, the underlying nature of the cost and its association with the asset are the same.

BC23 However, in considering the improvements to IAS 16, the Board did not address how an entity would account for (a) changes in the amount of the initial estimate of a recognised obligation, (b) the effects of accretion of, or changes in interest rates on, a recognised obligation or (c) the cost of obligations that did not exist when the entity acquired the item, such as an obligation triggered by a change in a law enacted after the asset is acquired. The Interpretation addresses issues (a) and (b).

The interaction of the Interpretation and the choice of measurement model under IAS 16

BC24 IAS 16 allows an entity to choose either the cost model or the revaluation model for measuring its property, plant and equipment, on a class-by-class basis. The IFRIC's view is that the measurement model that an entity chooses under IAS 16 would not be affected by the Interpretation.

BC25 Several responses to the draft Interpretation sought clarification of how it should be applied to revalued assets. The IFRIC noted that:

(a) if the entity chooses the revaluation model, IAS 16 requires the valuation to be kept sufficiently up to date that the carrying amount does not differ materially from that which would be determined using fair value at the balance sheet date.[1] This Interpretation requires a change in a recognised decommissioning, restoration or similar liability generally to be added to or deducted from the cost of the asset. However, a change in the liability does not, of itself, affect the *valuation* of the asset for financial reporting purposes, because (to ensure that it is not counted twice) the separately recognised liability is excluded from its valuation.

---

1 IAS 1 *Presentation of Financial Statements* (revised 2007) replaced the term 'balance sheet date' with 'end of the reporting period'.

(b) rather than changing the valuation of the asset, a change in the liability affects the difference between what would have been reported for the asset under the cost model, under this Interpretation, and its valuation. In other words, it changes the revaluation surplus or deficit that has previously been recognised for the asset. For example, if the liability increases by CU20, which under the cost model would have been added to the cost of the asset, the revaluation surplus reduces (or the revaluation deficit increases) by CU20. Under the revaluation model set out in IAS 16, cumulative revaluation surpluses for an asset are accounted for in equity,[2] and cumulative revaluation deficits are accounted for in profit or loss. The IFRIC decided that changes in the liability relating to a revalued asset should be accounted for in the same way as other changes in revaluation surpluses and deficits under IAS 16.

(c) although a change in the liability does not directly affect the value of the asset for financial reporting purposes, many events that change the value of the liability may also affect the value of the asset, by either a greater or lesser amount. The IFRIC therefore decided that, for revalued assets, a change in a decommissioning liability indicates that a revaluation may be required. Any such revaluation should be taken into account in determining the amount taken to profit or loss under (b) above. If a revaluation is done, IAS 16 requires all assets of the same class to be revalued.

(d) the depreciated cost of an asset (less any impairment) should not be negative, regardless of the valuation model, and the revaluation surplus on an asset should not exceed its value. The IFRIC therefore decided that, if the reduction in a liability exceeds the carrying amount that would have been recognised had the asset been carried under the cost model, the excess reduction should always be taken to profit or loss. For example, if the depreciated cost of an unimpaired asset is CU25, and its revalued amount is CU100, there is a revaluation surplus of CU75. If the decommissioning liability associated with the asset is reduced by CU30, the depreciated cost of the asset should be reduced to nil, the revaluation surplus should be increased to CU100 (which equals the value of the asset), and the remaining CU5 of the reduction in the liability should be taken to profit or loss.

The unwinding of the discount

BC26 The IFRIC considered whether the unwinding of the discount is a borrowing cost for the purposes of IAS 23 *Borrowing Costs*. This question arises because if the unwinding of the discount rate were deemed a borrowing cost for the purposes of IAS 23, in certain circumstances this amount might be capitalised

---

2 As a consequence of the revision of IAS 1 *Presentation of Financial Statements* in 2007 the increase is recognised in other comprehensive income and accumulated in equity under the heading of revaluation surplus.

under the allowed alternative treatment of capitalisation.[3] The IFRIC noted that IAS 23 addresses funds borrowed specifically for the purpose of obtaining a particular asset. It agreed that a decommissioning liability does not fall within this description since it does not reflect funds (ie cash) borrowed. Hence, the IFRIC concluded that the unwinding of the discount is not a borrowing cost as defined in IAS 23.

BC27   The IFRIC agreed that the unwinding of the discount as referred to in paragraph 60 of IAS 37 should be reported in profit or loss in the period it occurs.

Disclosures

BC28   The IFRIC considered whether the Interpretation should include disclosure guidance and agreed that it was largely unnecessary because IAS 16 and IAS 37 contain relevant guidance, for example:

(a)   IAS 16 explains that IAS 8 requires the disclosure of the nature and effect of changes in accounting estimates that have an effect in the current period or are expected to have a material effect in subsequent periods, and that such disclosure may arise from changes in the estimated costs of dismantling, removing or restoring items of property, plant and equipment.

(b)   IAS 37 requires the disclosure of:

(i)   a reconciliation of the movements in the carrying amount of the provision for the period.

(ii)   the increase during the period in the discounted amount arising from the passage of time and the effect of any change in the discount rate.

(iii)   a brief description of the nature of the obligation and the expected timing of any resulting outflows of economic benefits.

(iv)   an indication of the uncertainties about the amount or timing of those outflows, and where necessary the disclosure of the major assumptions made concerning future events (eg future interest rates, future changes in salaries, and future changes in prices).

BC29   However, in respect of assets measured using the revaluation model, the IFRIC noted that changes in the liability would often be taken to the revaluation surplus. These changes reflect an event of significance to users, and the IFRIC agreed that they should be given prominence by being separately disclosed and described as such in the statement of changes in equity.[4]

---

3   In March 2007, IAS 23 was revised to require the previously allowed alternative treatment of capitalisation. Capitalisation of borrowing costs for a qualifying asset becomes the only accounting treatment. That revision does not affect the reasoning set out in this Basis for Conclusions.

4   As a consequence of the revision of IAS 1 *Presentation of Financial Statements* in 2007 such changes are presented in the statement of comprehensive income.

Transition

BC30 The IFRIC agreed that preparers that already apply IFRSs should apply the Interpretation in the manner required by IAS 8, which is usually retrospectively. The IFRIC could not justify another application method, especially when IAS 37 requires retrospective application.

BC31 The IFRIC noted that, in order to apply the Interpretation retrospectively, it is necessary to determine both the timing and amount of any changes that would have been required by the Interpretation. However, IAS 8 specifies that:

(a) if retrospective application is not practicable for all periods presented, the new accounting policy shall be applied retrospectively from the earliest practicable date; and

(b) if it is impracticable to determine the cumulative effect of applying the new accounting policy at the start of the current period, the policy shall be applied prospectively from the earliest date practicable.

BC32 The IFRIC noted that IAS 8 defines a requirement as impracticable when an entity cannot apply it after making every reasonable effort to do so, and gives guidance on when this is so.

BC33 However, the provisions of IAS 8 on practicability do not apply to IFRS 1 *First-time Adoption of International Financial Reporting Standards*. Retrospective application of this Interpretation at the date of transition to IFRSs, which is the treatment required by IFRS 1 in the absence of any exemptions, would require first-time adopters to construct a historical record of all such adjustments that would have been made in the past. In many cases this will not be practicable. The IFRIC agreed that, as an alternative to retrospective application, an entity should be permitted to include in the depreciated cost of the asset at the date of transition an amount calculated by discounting the liability at that date back to, and depreciating it from, when it was first incurred. This Interpretation amends IFRS 1 accordingly.

Documents published to accompany

IFRIC 2

Members' Shares in Co-operative Entities and Similar Instruments

The text of the unaccompanied Interpretation, IFRIC 2, is contained in Part A of this edition. Its effective date when issued was 1 September 2004. This part presents the following document:

BASIS FOR CONCLUSIONS

Basis for Conclusions on
IFRIC Interpretation 2 *Members' Shares in Co-operative Entities and Similar Instruments*

This Basis for Conclusions accompanies, but is not part of, IFRIC 2.

Introduction

BC1 This Basis for Conclusions summarises the IFRIC's considerations in reaching its consensus. Individual IFRIC members gave greater weight to some factors than to others.

Background

BC2 In September 2001, the Standing Interpretations Committee instituted by the former International Accounting Standards Committee (IASC) published Draft Interpretation SIC D-34 *Financial Instruments – Instruments or Rights Redeemable by the Holder*. The Draft Interpretation stated: 'The issuer of a Puttable Instrument should classify the entire instrument as a liability.'

BC3 In 2001 the International Accounting Standards Board (IASB) began operations in succession to IASC. The IASB's initial agenda included a project to make limited amendments to the financial instruments standards issued by IASC. The IASB decided to incorporate the consensus from Draft Interpretation D-34 as part of those amendments. In June 2002 the IASB published an exposure draft of amendments to IAS 32 *Financial Instruments: Disclosure and Presentation* that incorporated the proposed consensus from Draft Interpretation D-34.

BC4 In their responses to the Exposure Draft and in their participation in public round-table discussions held in March 2003, representatives of co-operative banks raised questions about the application of the principles in IAS 32 to members' shares. This was followed by a series of meetings between IASB members and staff and representatives of the European Association of Co-operative Banks. After considering questions raised by the bank group, the IASB concluded that the principles articulated in IAS 32 should not be modified, but that there were questions about the application of those principles to co-operative entities that should be considered by the IFRIC.

BC5 In considering the application of IAS 32 to co-operative entities, the IFRIC recognised that a variety of entities operate as co-operatives and these entities have a variety of capital structures. The IFRIC decided that its proposed Interpretation should address some features that exist in a number of co-operatives. However, the IFRIC noted that its conclusions and the examples in the Interpretation are not limited to the specific characteristics of members' shares in European co-operative banks.

Basis for consensus

BC6   Paragraph 15 of IAS 32 states:

> The issuer of a financial instrument shall classify the instrument, or its component parts, on initial recognition as a financial liability, a financial asset or an equity instrument in accordance with the *substance of the contractual arrangement* and the definitions of a financial liability, a financial asset and an equity instrument. [Emphasis added]

BC7   In many jurisdictions, local law or regulations state that members' shares are equity of the entity. However, paragraph 17 of IAS 32 states:

> With the exception of the circumstances described in paragraphs 16A and 16B or paragraphs 16C and 16D, a critical feature in differentiating a financial liability from an equity instrument is *the existence of a contractual obligation of one party to the financial instrument (the issuer) either to deliver cash or another financial asset to the other party (the holder)* or to exchange financial assets or financial liabilities with the holder under conditions that are potentially unfavourable to the issuer. Although the holder of an equity instrument may be entitled to receive a pro rata share of any dividends or other distributions of equity, the issuer does not have a contractual obligation to make such distributions because it cannot be required to deliver cash or another financial asset to another party. [Emphasis added]

BC8   Paragraphs cited in the examples in the Appendix and in the paragraphs above show that, under IAS 32, the terms of the contractual agreement govern the classification of a financial instrument as a financial liability or equity. If the terms of an instrument create an unconditional obligation to transfer cash or another financial asset, circumstances that might restrict an entity's ability to make the transfer when due do not alter the classification as a financial liability. If the terms of the instrument give the entity an unconditional right to avoid delivering cash or another financial asset, the instrument is classified as equity. This is true even if other factors make it likely that the entity will continue to distribute dividends or make or other payments. In view of those principles, the IFRIC decided to focus on circumstances that would indicate that the entity has the unconditional right to avoid making payments to a member who has requested that his or her shares be redeemed.

BC9   The IFRIC identified two situations in which a co-operative entity has an unconditional right to avoid the transfer of cash or another financial asset. The IFRIC acknowledges that there may be other situations that may raise questions about the application of IAS 32 to members' shares. However, it understands that the two situations are often present in the contractual and other conditions surrounding members' shares and that interpretation of those two situations would eliminate many of the questions that may arise in practice.

BC10   The IFRIC also noted that an entity assesses whether it has an unconditional right to avoid the transfer of cash or another financial asset on the basis of local laws, regulations and its governing charter in effect at the date of classification. This is because it is local laws, regulations and the governing charter in effect at the classification date, together with the terms contained in the instrument's documentation that constitute the terms and conditions of the instrument at that date. Accordingly, an entity does not take into account expected future amendments to local law, regulation or its governing charter.

The right to refuse redemption (paragraph 7)

BC11　An entity may have the unconditional right to refuse redemption of a member's shares. If such a right exists, the entity does not have the obligation to transfer cash or another financial asset that IAS 32 identifies as a critical characteristic of a financial liability.

BC12　The IFRIC considered whether the entity's history of making redemptions should be considered in deciding whether the entity's right to refuse requests is, in fact, unconditional. The IFRIC observed that a history of making redemptions may create a reasonable expectation that all future requests will be honoured. However, holders of many equity instruments have a reasonable expectation that an entity will continue a past practice of making payments. For example, an entity may have made dividend payments on preference shares for decades. Failure to make those payments would expose the entity to significant economic costs, including damage to the value of its ordinary shares. Nevertheless, as outlined in IAS 32 paragraph AG26 (cited in paragraph A3), a holder's expectations about dividends do not cause a preferred share to be classified as a financial liability.

Prohibitions against redemption (paragraphs 8 and 9)

BC13　An entity may be prohibited by law or its governing charter from redeeming members' shares if doing so would cause the number of members' shares, or the amount of paid-in capital from members' shares, to fall below a specified level. While each individual share might be puttable, a portion of the total shares outstanding is not.

BC14　The IFRIC concluded that conditions limiting an entity's ability to redeem members' shares must be evaluated sequentially. Unconditional prohibitions like those noted in paragraph 8 of the consensus prevent the entity from *incurring a liability* for redemption of all or some of the members' shares, regardless of whether it would otherwise be able to satisfy that financial liability. This contrasts with conditional prohibitions that prevent payments being made only if specified conditions—such as liquidity constraints—are met. Unconditional prohibitions prevent a liability from coming into existence, whereas the conditional prohibitions may only defer the payment of a liability already incurred. Following this analysis, an unconditional prohibition affects classification when an instrument subject to the prohibition is issued or when the prohibition is enacted or added to the entity's governing charter. In contrast, conditional restrictions such as those described in paragraphs 19 and AG25 of IAS 32 do not result in equity classification.

BC15　　The IFRIC discussed whether the requirements in IAS 32 can be applied to the classification of members' shares as a whole subject to a partial redemption prohibition. IAS 32 refers to 'a financial instrument', 'a financial liability' and 'an equity instrument'. It does not refer to groups or portfolios of instruments. In view of this the IFRIC considered whether it could apply the requirements in IAS 32 to the classification of members' shares subject to partial redemption prohibitions. The application of IAS 32 to a prohibition against redeeming some portion of members' shares (eg 500,000 shares of an entity with 1,000,000 shares outstanding) is unclear.

BC16　　The IFRIC noted that classifying a group of members' shares using the individual instrument approach could lead to misapplication of the principle of 'substance of the contract' in IAS 32. The IFRIC also noted that paragraph 23 of IAS 32 requires an entity that has entered into an agreement to purchase its own equity instruments to recognise a financial liability for the present value of the redemption amount (eg for the present value of the forward repurchase price, option exercise price or other redemption amount) even though the shares subject to the repurchase agreement are not individually identified. Accordingly, the IFRIC decided that for purposes of classification there are instances when IAS 32 does not require the individual instrument approach.

BC17　　In many situations, looking at either individual instruments or all of the instruments governed by a particular contract would result in the same classification as financial liability or equity under IAS 32. Thus, if an entity is prohibited from redeeming any of its members' shares, the shares are not puttable and are equity. On the other hand, if there is no prohibition on redemption and no other conditions apply, members' shares are puttable and the shares are financial liabilities. However, in the case of partial prohibitions against redemption, the classification of members' shares governed by the same charter will differ, depending on whether such a classification is based on individual members' shares or the group of members' shares as a whole. For example, consider an entity with a partial prohibition that prevents it from redeeming 99 per cent of the highest number of members' shares ever outstanding. The classification based on individual shares considers each share to be potentially puttable and therefore a financial liability. This is different from the classification based on all of the members' shares. While each member's share may be redeemable individually, 99 per cent of the highest number of shares ever outstanding is not redeemable in any circumstances other than liquidation of the entity and therefore is equity.

Measurement on initial recognition (paragraph 10)

BC18　　The IFRIC noted that when the financial liability for the redemption of members' shares that are redeemable on demand is initially recognised, the financial liability is measured at fair value in accordance with paragraph 49 of IAS 39 *Financial Instruments: Recognition and Measurement*.[1] Paragraph 49 states:

1　　IFRS 9 *Financial Instruments* replaced IAS 39. Paragraph 49 of IAS 39 was ultimately relocated to paragraph 47 of IFRS 13 *Fair Value Measurement*. Paragraph BC18 refers to matters relevant when IFRIC 2 was issued.

'The fair value of a financial liability with a demand feature (eg a demand deposit) is not less than the amount payable on demand, discounted from the first date that the amount could be required to be paid'. Accordingly, the IFRIC decided that the fair value of the financial liability for redemption of members' shares redeemable on demand is the maximum amount payable under the redemption provisions of its governing charter or applicable law. The IFRIC also considered situations in which the number of members' shares or the amount of paid-in capital subject to prohibition against redemption may change. The IFRIC concluded that a change in the level of a prohibition against redemption should lead to a transfer between financial liabilities and equity.

Subsequent measurement

BC19   Some respondents requested additional guidance on subsequent measurement of the liability for redemption of members' shares. The IFRIC noted that the focus of this Interpretation was on clarifying the classification of financial instruments rather than their subsequent measurement. Also, the IASB has on its agenda a project to address the accounting for financial instruments (including members' shares) that are redeemable at a pro rata share of the fair value of the residual interest in the entity issuing the financial instrument. The IASB will consider certain measurement issues in this project. The IFRIC was also informed that the majority of members' shares in co-operative entities are not redeemable at a pro rata share of the fair value of the residual interest in the co-operative entity thereby obviating the more complex measurement issues. In view of the above, the IFRIC decided not to provide additional guidance on measurement in the Interpretation.

Presentation

BC20   The IFRIC noted that entities whose members' shares are not equity could use the presentation formats included in paragraphs IE32 and IE33 of the Illustrative Examples with IAS 32.

Alternatives considered

BC21   The IFRIC considered suggestions that:

(a)   members' shares should be classified as equity until a member has requested redemption. That member's share would then be classified as a financial liability and this treatment would be consistent with local laws. Some commentators believe this is a more straightforward approach to classification.

(b)   the classification of members' shares should incorporate the probability that members will request redemption. Those who suggest this view observe that experience shows this probability to be small, usually within 1–5 per cent, for some types of co-operative. They see no basis for classifying 100 per cent of the members' shares as liabilities on the basis of the behaviour of 1 per cent.

BC22　The IFRIC did not accept those views. Under IAS 32, the classification of an instrument as financial liability or equity is based on the 'substance of the contractual arrangement and the definitions of a financial liability, a financial asset and an equity instrument.' In paragraph BC7 of the Basis for Conclusions on IAS 32, the IASB observed:

> Although the legal form of such financial instruments often includes a right to the residual interest in the assets of an entity available to holders of such instruments, the inclusion of an option for the holder to put the instrument back to the entity for cash or another financial asset means that the instrument meets the definition of a financial liability. The classification as a financial liability is independent of considerations such as when the right is exercisable, how the amount payable or receivable upon exercise of the right is determined, and whether the puttable instrument has a fixed maturity.

BC23　The IFRIC also observed that an approach similar to that in paragraph BC21(a) is advocated in the Dissenting Opinion of one Board member on IAS 32. As the IASB did not adopt that approach its adoption here would require an amendment to IAS 32.

Transition and effective date (paragraph 14)

BC24　The IFRIC considered whether its Interpretation should have the same transition and effective date as IAS 32, or whether a later effective date should apply with an exemption from IAS 32 for members' shares in the interim. Some co-operatives may wish to amend their governing charter in order to continue their existing practice under national accounting requirements of classifying members' shares as equity. Such amendments usually require a general meeting of members and holding a meeting may not be possible before the effective date of IAS 32.

BC25　After considering a number of alternatives, the IFRIC decided against any exemption from the transition requirements and effective date in IAS 32. In reaching this conclusion, the IFRIC noted that it was requested to provide guidance on the application of IAS 32 when it is first adopted by co-operative entities, ie from 1 January 2005. Also, the vast majority of those who commented on the draft Interpretation did not object to the proposed effective date of 1 January 2005. Finally, the IFRIC observed that classifying members' shares as financial liabilities before the date that the terms of these shares are amended will affect only 2005 financial statements, as first-time adopters are not required to apply IAS 32 to earlier periods. As a result, any effect of the Interpretation on first-time adopters is expected to be limited. Furthermore, the IFRIC noted that regulators are familiar with the accounting issues involved. A co-operative entity may be required to present members' shares as a liability until the governing charter is amended. The IFRIC understands that such amendments, if adopted, could be in place by mid-2005. Accordingly, the IFRIC decided that the effective date for the Interpretation would be annual periods beginning on or after 1 January 2005.

Documents published to accompany

IFRIC 5

Rights to Interests arising from Decommissioning, Restoration and Environmental Rehabilitation Funds

The text of the unaccompanied Interpretation, IFRIC 5, is contained in Part A of this edition. Its effective date when issued was 1 January 2006. This part presents the following document:

BASIS FOR CONCLUSIONS

Basis for Conclusions on
IFRIC Interpretation 5 *Rights to Interests arising from Decommissioning, Restoration and Environmental Rehabilitation Funds*

This Basis for Conclusions accompanies, but is not part of, IFRIC 5.

The original text has been marked up to reflect the revision of IAS 1 Presentation of Financial Statements *in 2007: new text is underlined and deleted text is struck through.*

Introduction

BC1 This Basis for Conclusions summarises the IFRIC's considerations in reaching its consensus. Individual IFRIC members gave greater weight to some factors than to others.

Background (paragraphs 1–3)

BC2 The IFRIC was informed that an increasing number of entities with decommissioning obligations are contributing to a separate fund established to help fund those obligations. The IFRIC was also informed that questions have arisen in practice over the accounting treatment of interests in such funds and that there is a risk that divergent practices may develop. The IFRIC therefore concluded that it should provide guidance to assist in answering the questions in paragraph 6, in particular on the accounting for the asset of the right to receive reimbursement from a fund. On the issue of whether the fund should be consolidated or equity accounted, the IFRIC concluded that the normal requirements of IAS 27 *Consolidated and Separate Financial Statements*, SIC-12 *Consolidation – Special Purpose Entities*, IAS 28 *Investments in Associates*[1] or IAS 31 *Interests in Joint Ventures*[2] apply and that there is no need for interpretative guidance.[3] The IFRIC published its proposed Interpretation on 15 January 2004 as D4 *Decommissioning, Restoration and Environmental Rehabilitation Funds*.

BC3 Paragraphs 1–3 describe ways in which entities might arrange to fund their decommissioning obligations. Those that are within the scope of the Interpretation are specified in paragraphs 4–6.

Scope (paragraphs 4 and 5)

BC4 D4 did not precisely define the scope because the IFRIC believed that the large variety of schemes in operation would make any definition inappropriate. However, some respondents to D4 disagreed and commented that the absence of any definition made it unclear when the Interpretation should be applied.

---

1 In May 2011, the Board amended IAS 28 and changed its title to *Investments in Associates and Joint Ventures*.

2 IFRS 11 *Joint Arrangements*, issued in May 2011, replaced IAS 31.

3 The consolidation requirements in IAS 27 and SIC-12 were superseded by IFRS 10 *Consolidated Financial Statements* issued in May 2011.

As a result, the IFRIC has specified the scope by identifying the features that make an arrangement a decommissioning fund. It has also described the different types of fund and the features that may (or may not) be present.

BC5   The IFRIC considered whether it should issue a wider Interpretation that addresses similar forms of reimbursement, or whether it should prohibit the application of the Interpretation to other situations by analogy. The IFRIC rejected any widening of the scope, deciding instead to concentrate on the matter referred to it. The IFRIC also decided that there was no reason to prohibit the application of the Interpretation to other situations by analogy and thus the hierarchy of criteria in paragraphs 7–12 of IAS 8 *Accounting Policies, Changes in Accounting Estimates and Errors* would apply, resulting in similar accounting for reimbursements under arrangements that are not decommissioning funds, but have similar features.

BC6   The IFRIC considered comments from respondents that a contributor may have an interest in the fund that extends beyond its right to reimbursement. In response, the IFRIC added clarification that a residual interest in a fund, such as a contractual right to distributions once all the decommissioning has been completed or on winding up the fund, may be an equity instrument within the scope of IAS 39 *Financial Instruments: Recognition and Measurement*.[4]

Basis for consensus

Accounting for an interest in a fund (paragraphs 7–9)

BC7   The IFRIC concluded that the contributor should recognise a liability unless the contributor is not liable to pay decommissioning costs even if the fund fails to pay. This is because the contributor remains liable for the decommissioning costs. Additionally, IAS 37 *Provisions, Contingent Liabilities and Contingent Assets* provides that:

(a)   when an entity remains liable for expenditure, a provision should be recognised even where reimbursement is available; and

(b)   if the reimbursement is virtually certain to be received when the obligation is settled, then it should be treated as a separate asset.

BC8   In concluding that the contributor should recognise separately its liability to pay decommissioning costs and its interest in the fund, the IFRIC also noted the following:

(a)   There is no legally enforceable right to set off the rights under the decommissioning fund against the decommissioning liabilities. Also, given that the main objective is reimbursement, it is likely that settlement will not be net or simultaneous. Accordingly, treating these rights and liabilities as analogous to financial assets and financial

---

4   IFRS 9 *Financial Instruments* replaced IAS 39. IFRS 9 applies to all items that were previously within the scope of IAS 39.

liabilities would not result in offset because the offset criteria in IAS 32 *Financial Instruments: Disclosure and Presentation*[5] are not met.

(b) Treating the decommissioning obligation as analogous to a financial liability would not result in derecognition through extinguishment. If the fund does not assume the obligation for decommissioning, the criteria in IAS 39[6] for derecognition of financial liabilities through extinguishment are not met. At best, the fund acts like an in-substance defeasance that does not qualify for derecognition of the liability.

(c) It would not be appropriate to treat decommissioning funds as analogous to pension funds, which are presented net of the related liability. This is because, in allowing a net presentation for pension plans in IAS 19 *Employee Benefits*, the International Accounting Standards Board's predecessor organisation, IASC, stated that it believed the situation is 'unique to employee benefit plans and [it did] not intend to permit this net presentation for other liabilities if the conditions in IAS 32 and IAS 39[7] are not met' (IAS 19, Basis for Conclusions paragraph BC68I).[8]

BC9 As to the accounting for the contributor's interest in the fund, the IFRIC noted that some interests in funds would be within the scope of IAS 27, IAS 28, IAS 31[9] or SIC-12. As noted in paragraph BC2, the IFRIC concluded that, in such cases, the normal requirements of those Standards would apply and there is no need for interpretative guidance.

BC10 Otherwise, the IFRIC concluded that the contributor has an asset for its right to receive amounts from the fund.

The right to receive reimbursement from a fund and amendment to the scope of IAS 39[10]

BC11 The IFRIC noted that under existing IFRSs, there are two forms of rights to reimbursement that would be accounted for differently:

(a) A contractual right to receive reimbursement in the form of cash. This meets the definition of a financial asset and is within the scope of IAS 39. Such a financial asset would be classified as an available-for-sale financial asset[11] (unless accounted for using the fair value option) because it does not meet the definitions of a financial asset held for trading, a held-to-maturity investment or a loan or receivable.

---

5 In August 2005, IAS 32 was amended as IAS 32 *Financial Instruments: Presentation*.

6 IFRS 9 *Financial Instruments* replaced IAS 39. IFRS 9 applies to all items that were previously within the scope of IAS 39.

7 IFRS 9 *Financial Instruments* replaced IAS 39. IFRS 9 applies to all items that were previously within the scope of IAS 39.

8 Paragraph BC68I was renumbered as paragraph BC186 when IAS 19 was amended in 2011.

9 IFRS 11 *Joint Arrangements*, issued in May 2011, replaced IAS 31.

10 IFRS 9 *Financial Instruments* replaced IAS 39. IFRS 9 applies to all items that were previously within the scope of IAS 39.

11 IFRS 9 *Financial Instruments* eliminated the categories of available-for-sale and held-to-maturity financial assets.

(b) A right to reimbursement other than a contractual right to receive cash. This does not meet the definition of a financial asset and is within the scope of IAS 37.

BC12 The IFRIC concluded that both these forms of reimbursement have economically identical effects. Therefore accounting for both forms in the same way would provide relevant and reliable information to a user of the financial statements. However, the IFRIC noted that this did not appear possible under existing IFRSs because some such rights are within the scope of IAS 39, and others are not. Therefore, it asked the Board to amend the scope of IAS 39 to exclude rights to reimbursement for expenditure required to settle:

(a) a provision that has been recognised in accordance with IAS 37; and

(b) obligations that had been originally recognised as provisions in accordance with IAS 37, but are no longer provisions because their timing or amount is no longer uncertain. An example of such a liability is one that was originally recognised as a provision because of uncertainty about the timing of the cash outflow, but subsequently becomes another type of liability because the timing is now certain.

BC13 This amendment was approved by the Board and is set out in the Appendix of IFRIC 5.[12] As a result, all such rights to reimbursement are within the scope of IAS 37.

BC14 The IFRIC noted that paragraph 53 of IAS 37 specifies the accounting for rights to receive reimbursement. It requires this right to reimbursement to be separately recognised when it is virtually certain that reimbursement will be received if the contributor settles the obligation. The IFRIC also noted that this paragraph prohibits the recognition of an asset in excess of the recognised liability. For example, rights to receive reimbursement to meet decommissioning liabilities that have yet to be recognised as a provision are not recognised. Accordingly, the IFRIC concluded that when the right to reimbursement is virtually certain to be received if the contributor settles its decommissioning obligation, it should be measured at the lower of the amount of the decommissioning obligation recognised and the reimbursement right.

BC15 The IFRIC discussed whether the reimbursement right should be measured at:

(a) the contributor's share of the fair value of the net assets of the fund attributable to contributors, taking into account any inability to access any surplus of the assets of the fund over eligible decommissioning costs (with any obligation to make good potential defaults of other contributors being treated separately as a contingent liability); or

(b) the fair value of the reimbursement right (which would normally be lower than (a) because of the risks involved, such as the possibility that the contributor may be required to make good defaults of other contributors).

---

12 The amendment has been incorporated into the text of IAS 39 as published in this volume.

BC16   The IFRIC noted that the right to reimbursement relates to a decommissioning obligation for which a provision would be recognised and measured in accordance with IAS 37. Paragraph 36 of IAS 37 requires such provisions to be measured at 'the best estimate of the expenditure required to settle the present obligation at the ~~balance sheet date~~ <u>end of the reporting period</u>'. The IFRIC noted that the amount in paragraph BC15(a)—ie the contributor's share of the fair value of the net assets of the fund attributable to contributors, taking into account any inability to access any surplus of the assets of the fund over eligible decommissioning costs—is the best estimate of the amount available to the contributor to reimburse it for expenditure it had incurred to pay for decommissioning. Thus, the amount of the asset recognised would be consistent with the amount of the liability recognised.

BC17   In contrast, the IFRIC noted that the amount in paragraph BC15(b)—ie the fair value of the reimbursement right—would take into account the factors such as liquidity that the IFRIC believed to be difficult to measure reliably. Furthermore, this amount would be lower than that in paragraph BC15(a) because it reflects the possibility that the contributor may be required to make potential additional contributions in the event of default by other contributors. The IFRIC noted that its decision that the obligation to make potential additional contributions should be treated as a contingent liability in accordance with IAS 37 (see paragraphs BC22–BC25) would result in double-counting of the risk of the additional contribution being required if the measure in paragraph BC15(b) were to be used.

BC18   Consequently, the IFRIC concluded that the approach in paragraph BC15(a) would provide the most useful information to users.

The asset cap

BC19   Many respondents to D4 expressed concern about the 'asset cap' that is imposed by the requirement in paragraph 9. This asset cap limits the amount recognised as a reimbursement asset to the amount of the decommissioning obligation recognised. These respondents argued that rights to benefit in excess of this amount give rise to an additional asset, separate from the reimbursement asset. Such an additional asset may arise in a number of ways, for example:

(a)   the contributor has the right to benefit from a repayment of any surplus in the fund that exists once all the decommissioning has been completed or on winding up the fund.

(b)   the contributor has the right to benefit from reduced contributions to the fund or increased benefits from the fund (eg by adding new sites to the fund for no additional contributions) in the future.

(c)   the contributor expects to obtain benefit from past contributions in the future, based on the current and planned level of activity. However, because contributions are made before the decommissioning obligation is incurred, IAS 37 prevents recognition of an asset in excess of the obligation.

BC20   The IFRIC concluded that a right to benefit from a repayment of any surplus in the fund that exists once all the decommissioning has been completed or on winding up the fund may be an equity instrument within the scope of IAS 39,[13] in which case IAS 39 would apply. However, the IFRIC agreed that an asset should not be recognised for other rights to receive reimbursement from the fund. Although the IFRIC had sympathy with the concerns expressed by constituents that there may be circumstances in which it would seem appropriate to recognise an asset in excess of the reimbursement right, it concluded that it would be inconsistent with paragraph 53 of IAS 37 (which requires that 'the amount recognised for the reimbursement should not exceed the amount of the provision') to recognise this asset. The IFRIC also noted that the circumstances in which this additional asset exists are likely to be limited, and apply only when a contributor has restricted access to a surplus of fund assets that does not give it control, joint control or significant influence over a fund. The IFRIC expects that most such assets would not meet the recognition criteria in the *Framework*[14] because they are highly uncertain and cannot be measured reliably.

BC21   The IFRIC also considered arguments that there should not be a difference between the treatment of a surplus when a fund is accounted for as a subsidiary, joint venture or associate, and when it is not. However, the IFRIC noted that, under IFRSs, restrictions on assets in subsidiaries, joint ventures or associates do not affect recognition of those assets. Hence it concluded that the difference in treatment between funds accounted for as subsidiaries, joint ventures or associates and those accounted for as a reimbursement right is inherent in IFRSs. The IFRIC also concluded that this is appropriate because, in the former case, the contributor exercises a degree of control not present in the latter case.

Obligations to make additional contributions (paragraph 10)

BC22   In some cases, a contributor has an obligation to make potential additional contributions, for example, in the event of the bankruptcy of another contributor.

BC23   The IFRIC noted that by 'joining' the fund, a contributor may assume the position of guarantor of the contributions of the other contributors, and hence become jointly and severally liable for the obligations of other contributors. Such an obligation is a present obligation of the contributor, but the outflow of resources associated with it may not be probable. The IFRIC noted a parallel with the example in paragraph 29 of IAS 37, which states that 'where an entity is jointly and severally liable for an obligation, the part of the obligation that is expected to be met by other parties is treated as a contingent liability.' Accordingly, the IFRIC concluded that a liability would be recognised

---

13 IFRS 9 *Financial Instruments* replaced IAS 39. IFRS 9 applies to all items that were previously within the scope of IAS 39.

14 The reference to the *Framework* is to the IASC's *Framework for the Preparation and Presentation of Financial Statements*, adopted by the Board in 2001 and in effect when the Interpretation was developed.

by the contributor only if it is probable that it will make additional contributions. The IFRIC noted that such a contingent liability may arise both when the contributor's interest in the fund is accounted for as a reimbursement right and when it is accounted for in accordance with IAS 27, IAS 28, IAS 31[15] or SIC-12.

BC24   The IFRIC considered the argument that an obligation to make good potential shortfalls of other contributors is a financial instrument (ie a financial guarantee) as defined in IAS 32 and hence should be accounted for in accordance with IAS 39.[16] The grounds for this point of view are that the contributor has an obligation to deliver cash to the fund, and the fund has a right to receive cash from the contributor if a shortfall in contributions arises. However, the IFRIC noted that:

(a)   a contractual obligation to make good shortfalls of other contributors is a financial guarantee. Financial guarantee contracts that provide for payments to be made if the debtor fails to make payment when due are excluded from the scope of IAS 39.

(b)   when the obligation is not contractual, but rather arises as a result of regulation, it is not a financial liability as defined in IAS 32 nor is it within the scope of IAS 39.

BC25   Therefore, the IFRIC concluded that an obligation to make additional contributions in the event of specified circumstances should be treated as a contingent liability in accordance with IAS 37.

Disclosure (paragraphs 11–13)

BC26   The IFRIC noted that the contributor may not be able to access the assets of the fund (including cash or cash equivalents) for many years (eg until it undertakes the decommissioning), if ever. Therefore, the IFRIC concluded that the nature of the contributor's interest and the restriction on access should be disclosed. The IFRIC also concluded that this disclosure is equally relevant when a contributor's interest in a fund is accounted for by consolidation, proportional consolidation[17] or using the equity method because the contributor's ability to access the underlying assets may be similarly restricted.

Effective date and transition (paragraphs 14 and 15)

BC27   D4 proposed that the Interpretation should be effective for annual periods beginning on a date set at three months after the Interpretation was finalised. The IFRIC considered the view of some respondents that the Interpretation should apply from 1 January 2005 (an earlier date) on the grounds that this is the date from which many entities will adopt IFRSs, and hence adopting the

---

15 IFRS 11 *Joint Arrangements*, issued in May 2011, replaced IAS 31.

16 IFRS 9 *Financial Instruments* replaced IAS 39. IFRS 9 applies to all items that were previously within the scope of IAS 39.

17 IFRS 11 *Joint Arrangements*, issued in May 2011, replaced IAS 31. IFRS 11 does not permit an entity to use 'proportional consolidation' for accounting for interests in joint ventures.

Interpretation at that time would promote comparability between periods. However, the IFRIC noted its general practice is to allow at least three months between finalising an Interpretation and its application, to enable entities to obtain the Interpretation and implement any necessary systems changes. In addition, the IFRIC considered the Board's concern that the amendment to IAS 39[18] issued as part of the Interpretation would change the 'stable platform' of Standards that are in force for entities that will apply IFRSs for the first time in 2005. Therefore, the IFRIC decided to require that the Interpretation should be applied for annual periods beginning on or after 1 January 2006, with earlier application encouraged.

BC28 The IFRIC observed that the implementation of the Interpretation is not expected to be problematic. Therefore, the IFRIC concluded that IAS 8 should apply. Respondents to D4 did not disagree with this conclusion.

---

18 IFRS 9 *Financial Instruments* replaced IAS 39. IFRS 9 applies to all items that were previously within the scope of IAS 39.

Documents published to accompany

IFRIC 6

Liabilities arising from Participating in a Specific Market — Waste Electrical and Electronic Equipment

The text of the unaccompanied Interpretation, IFRIC 6, is contained in Part A of this edition. Its effective date when issued was 1 December 2005. This part presents the following document:

BASIS FOR CONCLUSIONS

Basis for Conclusions on
IFRIC Interpretation 6 *Liabilities arising from Participating in*
a Specific Market—Waste Electrical and Electronic
Equipment

This Basis for Conclusions accompanies, but is not part of, IFRIC 6.

BC1   This Basis for Conclusions summarises the IFRIC's considerations in reaching its consensus. Individual IFRIC members gave greater weight to some factors than to others.

BC2   The IFRIC was informed that the European Union's Directive on Waste Electrical and Electronic Equipment (WE&EE) had given rise to questions about when a liability for the decommissioning of WE&EE for certain goods should be recognised. The IFRIC therefore decided to develop an Interpretation that would provide guidance regarding what constitutes an obligating event in the circumstances created by the Directive.

BC3   The IFRIC's proposals were set out in Draft Interpretation D10 *Liabilities arising from Participating in a Specific Market—Waste Electrical and Electronic Equipment*, which was published in November 2004. The IFRIC received 22 comment letters on the proposals.

BC4   The Directive indicates that it is participation in the market during the measurement period that triggers the obligation to meet the costs of waste management.

BC5   For example, an entity selling electrical equipment in 20X4 has a market share of 4 per cent for that calendar year. It subsequently discontinues operations and is thus no longer in the market when the waste management costs for its products are allocated to those entities with market share in 20X7. With a market share of 0 per cent in 20X7, the entity's obligation is zero. However, if another entity enters the market for electronic products in 20X7 and achieves a market share of 3 per cent in that period, then that entity's obligation for the costs of waste management from earlier periods will be 3 per cent of the total costs of waste management allocated to 20X7, even though the entity was not in the market in those earlier periods and has not produced any of the products for which waste management costs are allocated to 20X7.

BC6   The IFRIC concluded that the effect of the cost attribution model specified in the Directive is that the making of sales during the measurement period is the 'past event' that requires recognition of a provision under IAS 37 *Provisions, Contingent Liabilities and Contingent Assets* over the measurement period. Aggregate sales for the period determine the entity's obligation for a proportion of the costs of waste management allocated to that period. The measurement period is independent of the period when the cost allocation is notified to market participants. The timing of the obligating event may also be independent of the particular period in which the activities to perform the waste management are undertaken and the related costs incurred. Incurring costs in the performance of the waste management activities is a separate matter from incurring the obligation to share in the ultimate cost of those activities.

BC7 Some constituents asked the IFRIC to consider the effect of the following possible national legislation: the waste management costs for which a producer is responsible because of its participation in the market during a specified period (for example 20X6) are not based on the market share of the producer during that period but on the producer's participation in the market during a previous period (for example 20X5). The IFRIC noted that this affects only the measurement of the liability and that the obligating event is still participation in the market during 20X6.

BC8 The IFRIC considered whether its conclusion is undermined by the principle that the entity will continue to operate as a going concern. If the entity will continue to operate in the future, it treats the costs of doing so as future costs. For these future costs, paragraph 18 of IAS 37 emphasises that 'Financial statements deal with the financial position of an entity at the end of its reporting period and not its possible position in the future. Therefore, no provision is recognised for costs that need to be incurred to operate in the future.'

BC9 The IFRIC considered an argument that manufacturing or selling products for use in private households constitutes a past event that gives rise to a constructive obligation. Allocating waste management costs on the basis of market share would then be a matter of measurement rather than recognition. Supporters of this argument emphasise the definition of a constructive obligation in paragraph 10 of IAS 37 and point out that in determining whether past actions of an entity give rise to an obligation it is necessary to consider whether a change in practice is a realistic alternative. These respondents believed that when it would be necessary for an entity to take some unrealistic action in order to avoid the obligation then a constructive obligation exists and should be accounted for.

BC10 The IFRIC rejected this argument, concluding that a stated intention to participate in a market during a future measurement period does not create a constructive obligation for future waste management costs. In accordance with paragraph 19 of IAS 37, a provision can be recognised only in respect of an obligation that arises independently of the entity's future actions. For historical household equipment the obligation is created only by the future actions of the entity. If an entity has no market share in a measurement period, it has no obligation for the waste management costs relating to the products of that type which it had previously manufactured or sold and which otherwise would have created an obligation in that measurement period. This differentiates waste management costs, for example, from warranties (see Example 1 in the guidance on implementing IAS 37), which represent a legal obligation even if the entity exits the market. Consequently, no obligation exists for the future waste management costs until the entity participates in the market during the measurement period.

Documents published to accompany

IFRIC 7

Applying the Restatement Approach under IAS 29 Financial Reporting in Hyperinflationary Economies

The text of the unaccompanied Interpretation, IFRIC 7, is contained in Part A of this edition. Its effective date when issued was 1 March 2006. The text of the Accompanying Guidance on IFRIC 7 is contained in Part B of this edition. This part presents the following document:

BASIS FOR CONCLUSIONS

Basis for Conclusions on
IFRIC Interpretation 7 *Applying the Restatement Approach under IAS 29 Financial Reporting in Hyperinflationary Economies*

This Basis for Conclusions accompanies, but is not part of, IFRIC 7.

In this Basis for Conclusions the terminology has not been amended to reflect the changes made by IAS 1 Presentation of Financial Statements *(as revised in 2007).*

Introduction

BC1   This Basis for Conclusions summarises the IFRIC's considerations in reaching its consensus. Individual IFRIC members gave greater weight to some factors than to others.

Background

BC2   The IFRIC was asked for guidance on how an entity should restate its financial statements when it starts to apply IAS 29 *Financial Reporting in Hyperinflationary Economies*. There was uncertainty whether the opening balance sheet at the beginning of the reporting period should be restated to reflect changes in prices before that date.

BC3   In addition, there was uncertainty about the measurement of comparative deferred tax items in the opening balance sheet. IAS 29 states that at the balance sheet date deferred tax items of the restated financial statements should be measured in accordance with IAS 12 *Income Taxes*. However, it was not clear how an entity should account for the corresponding deferred tax figures.

BC4   In response, the IFRIC developed and published Draft Interpretation D5 *Applying IAS 29* Financial Reporting in Hyperinflationary Economies *for the First Time* for public comment in March 2004. It received 30 letters in response to the proposals.

Basis for consensus

The restatement approach

BC5   In developing D5, the IFRIC observed that the purpose of restating financial statements in hyperinflationary economies in accordance with IAS 29 is to reflect the effect on an entity of changes in general purchasing power. Paragraph 2 of IAS 29 states:

> In a hyperinflationary economy, reporting of operating results and financial position in the local currency without restatement is not useful. Money loses purchasing power at such a rate that comparison of amounts from transactions and other events that have occurred at different times, even within the same accounting period, is misleading.

This purpose applies to the financial statements of the first reporting period in which an entity identifies the existence of hyperinflation in the economy of its functional currency as well as to subsequent reporting periods (if the criteria for a hyperinflationary economy are still met).

BC6   The IFRIC considered the meaning of paragraph 4 of IAS 29, which states:

> ... this Standard applies to the financial statements of any entity from the beginning of the reporting period in which it identifies the existence of hyperinflation in the country in whose currency it reports.

The IFRIC noted that some may interpret this provision as restricting the restatement of an entity's opening balance sheet in the reporting period in which it identifies the existence of hyperinflation. Consequently, the opening balance sheet should be restated to reflect the change in a general price index for the reporting period only and not for changes in a general price index before the beginning of the reporting period, even though some balance sheet items may have been acquired or assumed before that date. However, the IFRIC also noted that paragraph 34 of IAS 29 requires:

> *Corresponding figures for the previous reporting period*, whether they were based on a historical cost approach or a current cost approach, are restated by applying a general price index so that the comparative financial statements are *presented in terms of the measuring unit current at the end of the reporting period*. Information that is disclosed in respect of earlier periods is also expressed in terms of the measuring unit current at the end of the reporting period ... [emphasis added]

BC7   The IFRIC considered a possible inconsistency between the restriction in paragraph 4 of IAS 29 and the requirement in paragraph 34. The IFRIC noted that paragraph 4 is a scope paragraph, which identifies when an entity has to comply with the Standard. The paragraph clarifies that an entity applies the requirements of the Standard to its financial statements from the beginning of the reporting period to the balance sheet date and not only from the date when it identifies the existence of hyperinflation. However, paragraph 4 does not deal with the restatement and presentation of the financial statements (either at the balance sheet date or in relation to the comparative figures). Hence, paragraph 4 of IAS 29 does not exclude from the restatement of an entity's opening balance sheet changes in the general price level before the beginning of the reporting period in which the entity identifies the existence of hyperinflation.

BC8   The IFRIC concluded that, in the context of the purpose of the Standard, the restatement of the financial statements for the reporting period in which an entity identifies the existence of hyperinflation should be consistent with the restatement approach applied in subsequent reporting periods.

BC9   Some respondents to D5 expressed concerns about whether the restatement approach in IAS 29 was always practicable for preparers and whether it provided decision-useful information to users. Though the IFRIC understood those concerns, the IFRIC observed that such concerns reflected broader aspects related to the accounting for hyperinflation in general, rather than how an entity has to apply the current Standard.

BC10   Nevertheless, the IFRIC considered how an entity should apply the Standard if, for example, detailed records of the acquisition dates of items of property, plant and equipment are not available. The IFRIC noted that, in those circumstances, paragraph 16 of IAS 29 states:

> ... In these rare circumstances, it may be necessary, in the first period of application of this Standard, to use an independent professional assessment of the value of the items as the basis for their restatement.

The IFRIC also noted that a similar exemption exists when a general price index may not be available. Paragraph 17 of IAS 29 states:

> ... In these circumstances, it may be necessary to use an estimate based, for example, on the movements in the exchange rate between the functional currency and a relatively stable foreign currency.

BC11   The IFRIC observed that, in developing IFRS 1 *First-time Adoption of International Financial Reporting Standards*, the International Accounting Standards Board discussed whether IFRS 1 should exempt first-time adopters of IFRSs from the effects of restatement in their first IFRS financial statements. Paragraph BC67 of IFRS 1 states:

> Some argued that the cost of restating financial statements for the effects of hyperinflation in periods before the date of transition to IFRSs would exceed the benefits, particularly if the currency is no longer hyperinflationary. However, the Board concluded that such restatement should be required, because hyperinflation can make unadjusted financial statements meaningless or misleading.

BC12   However, the IFRIC also observed that first-time adopters of IFRSs could use, for example, the fair value at transition date as deemed cost for property, plant and equipment, and, in some instances, also for investment property and intangible assets. Hence, if a first-time adopter that would otherwise have to apply IAS 29 at its transition to IFRSs applies the fair value measurement exemption of IFRS 1, it would apply IAS 29 to periods only after the date for which the fair value was determined. Such remeasurements would therefore reduce the need for a first-time adopter to restate its financial statements.

BC13   The IFRIC noted that the exemptions from the general restatement approach for preparers that already apply IFRSs, as stated in paragraph BC10 above, apply only in specific circumstances, whereas a first-time adopter may always elect to use the fair value remeasurement exemption for property, plant and equipment in IFRS 1. Nevertheless, the IFRIC concluded that the application of the exemptions in the Standards is clear and, therefore, extending the exemptions in IAS 29 to permit preparers that already apply IFRSs to elect fair value remeasurement of property, plant and equipment when applying the restatement approach under IAS 29 would require amendments of the Standard itself, rather than an Interpretation.

BC14   Respondents to D5 also argued that the procedures, as proposed to be clarified, are inconsistent with the accounting for a change in functional currency under IAS 21 *The Effect of Changes in Foreign Exchange Rates*, which in their view is comparable to moving into a state of hyperinflation. Moreover, they noted that retrospective application is also inconsistent with the

US GAAP approach, which accounts for a change in hyperinflation status prospectively.

BC15   In relation to the reference to a change in functional currency, the IFRIC observed that the existence of hyperinflation may (but not necessarily should) initiate such a change. The IFRIC noted that a change in functional currency is a change in the currency that is normally used to determine the pricing of an entity's transactions. As clarified in paragraph BC5 above, the purpose of restatement for the effects of hyperinflation is to reflect the effect of changes in purchasing power in the economy of an entity's functional currency. Therefore, the IFRIC did not believe that the application of accounting for hyperinflation should be based on the accounting for the change in an entity's functional currency.

BC16   The IFRIC also observed that respondents' reference to prospective application under US GAAP reflects requirements only for investments in foreign entities in hyperinflationary economies. In this case, paragraph 11 of SFAS 52 *Foreign Currency Translation* states:

> The financial statements of a foreign entity in a highly inflationary economy shall *be remeasured as if the functional currency were the reporting currency.* Accordingly, the financial statements of those entities shall be remeasured into the reporting currency according to the requirements of paragraph 10 ... [emphasis added]

Therefore, under US GAAP a foreign entity's financial statements are remeasured into its investor's functional currency. The IFRIC noted that this approach is different from the restate/translate approach under IFRSs. US GAAP provides different guidance for reporting entities operating with a hyperinflationary functional currency. APB Statement No. 3 *Financial Statements Restated for General Price-Level Changes* is also based on a restatement approach, and would require retrospective application, as under IAS 29. The IFRIC observed that for the purpose of presenting comparative amounts in a different presentation currency under IFRSs paragraphs 42(b) and 43 of IAS 21 apply. In such instances, an entity will have relief from the required restatement of comparatives under IAS 29. Paragraph BC22 of IAS 21 explains the reasoning for this specific exemption as follows:

> ... If exchange rates fully reflect differing price levels between the two economies to which they relate, the SIC-30 approach will result in the same amounts for the comparatives as were reported as current year amounts in the prior year financial statements. Furthermore, the Board noted that in the prior year, the relevant amounts had been already expressed in the non-hyperinflationary presentation currency, and there was no reason to change them.

BC17   D5 proposed that applying the restatement approach under IAS 29 should be regarded as a change in circumstances, rather than a change in accounting policy. Some respondents to D5 believed this was inconsistent. This is because IAS 8 *Accounting Policies, Changes in Accounting Estimates and Errors*, paragraph 16, states that a change in circumstances is not a change in accounting policy and an entity would not apply IAS 29 retrospectively. However, the IFRIC observed that IAS 29 contains specific requirements on this point, as noted in paragraphs BC5–BC16 above. The IFRIC concluded that the opening balance sheet for the reporting period in which an entity identifies the existence of hyperinflation ought to be restated as if the entity had always applied the restatement approach under IAS 29. The IFRIC reconfirmed its view that this treatment is similar to the retrospective application of a change in accounting policy described in IAS 8.

Deferred tax items

BC18 The IFRIC was asked for guidance on the accounting for deferred tax items when an entity restates its financial statements according to IAS 29. In particular, the IFRIC was asked for guidance on measuring deferred tax items in the opening balance sheet for the reporting period in which an entity identifies the existence of hyperinflation.

BC19 The IFRIC observed that paragraph 32 of IAS 29 states:

> The restatement of financial statements in accordance with this Standard may give rise to differences between the carrying amount of individual assets and liabilities in the balance sheet and their tax bases. These differences are accounted for in accordance with IAS 12 *Income Taxes*.

Therefore, at the closing balance sheet date of the reporting period an entity remeasures its deferred tax items on the basis of the restated financial statements, rather than by applying the general restatement provisions for monetary items or non-monetary items. However, the IFRIC noted that it was not clear how an entity should account for its comparative deferred tax items.

BC20 In developing D5, the IFRIC considered the following options:

(a) restatement of deferred tax items as monetary items;

(b) restatement of deferred tax items as non-monetary items; or

(c) remeasurement of deferred tax items as if the economy of the entity's functional currency had always been hyperinflationary.

BC21 D5 proposed clarifying that deferred tax items are neither clearly monetary nor non-monetary in nature. This was because deferred tax items are determined by the assets' (and liabilities') relative carrying amounts and tax bases. However, some respondents to D5 objected to that view, for various reasons. Some argued that deferred tax items, by nature, are received or paid in a fixed or determinable number of units of currency, and so should be considered as monetary items in accordance with paragraph 8 of IAS 21. Others noted that general practice is to classify deferred taxes as non-monetary items.

BC22 When considering respondents' comments the IFRIC confirmed that its conclusion in paragraph BC17 above should also apply to deferred tax items. In other words, the deferred tax items in the opening balance sheet for the reporting period in which an entity identifies the existence of hyperinflation should be calculated as if the environment had always been hyperinflationary, ie option (c) in paragraph BC20. Although the IFRIC acknowledged that deferred tax items may meet the definition of monetary items it noted that the purposes of option (c) would not be achieved if opening deferred tax items were restated in the same manner as applied generally for monetary items.

BC23　The IFRIC observed that some respondents to D5 suggested that deferred tax items in the opening balance sheet should be remeasured after restating the opening balance sheet with the measurement unit current at the closing balance sheet date of the reporting period. In the IFRIC's view, that proposal would (in case of a deferred tax liability) overstate the deferred tax item recognised in the opening balance sheet and, accordingly, understate the costs recognised in the reporting period. This is because the loss on the tax base caused by the inflation in the reporting period would be recognised directly in opening equity. The IFRIC illustrated this by the following example:

> At the end of Year 1, a non-monetary asset is restated at the measurement unit current at that date. Its restated amount is CU1,000[1] and its tax base is CU500. If the tax rate is 30 per cent, the entity would remeasure a deferred tax liability of CU150. In Year 2 inflation is 100 per cent. Assuming that nothing has changed the entity would, in its restated financial statements, recognise an asset of CU2,000 (both at the closing balance sheet date of the reporting period and in the comparative figures). At the closing balance sheet date, the deferred tax liability is remeasured at CU450 ((CU2,000 − CU500) × 0.3). However, if the comparative deferred tax liability is remeasured after restating the asset by the measuring unit current at the closing balance sheet date of the reporting period, the entity should recognise an opening deferred tax liability of CU450, and there would be no impact on profit or loss (CU450 − CU450). On the other hand, if the comparatives are stated as proposed in D5, the restated opening deferred tax liability would be CU300 ((CU1,000 − CU500) × 0.3) × 100% + CU150). Accordingly, the entity should recognise a loss of CU150 (CU450 − CU300), which is the loss of purchasing power on the tax base in the reporting period.

BC24　The IFRIC observed that paragraph 18 of Appendix A to IAS 12 explains:[2]

> Non-monetary assets are restated in terms of the measuring unit current at the balance sheet date (see IAS 29 *Financial Reporting in Hyperinflationary Economies*) and no equivalent adjustment is made for tax purposes. *(notes: (1) the deferred tax is charged in the income statement;[3] and (2) if, in addition to the restatement, the non-monetary assets are also revalued, the deferred tax relating to the revaluation is charged to equity[4] and the deferred tax relating to the restatement is charged in the income statement.)*

1　In this example monetary amounts are denominated in 'currency units (CU)'.

2　Paragraph 18 has been amended as a consequence of the changes made by IAS 1 *Presentation of Financial Statements* (as revised in 2007).

3　IAS 1 (revised 2007) requires an entity to present all income and expense items in one statement of comprehensive income or in two statements (a separate income statement and a statement of comprehensive income).

4　Under IAS 1 (revised 2007), such effect is recognised in other comprehensive income.

BC25 Consequently, the IFRIC confirmed its conclusion that restatement of comparative deferred tax items would require an entity, first, to remeasure its deferred tax items on the basis of the financial statements of the previous reporting period, which have been restated by applying a general price index reflecting the price level at the end of that period. Secondly, the entity should restate those calculated deferred tax items by the change in the general price level for the reporting period.

Documents published to accompany

IFRIC 10

Interim Financial Reporting and Impairment

The text of the unaccompanied Interpretation, IFRIC 10, is contained in Part A of this edition. Its effective date when issued was 1 November 2006. This part presents the following document:

BASIS FOR CONCLUSIONS

Basis for Conclusions on
IFRIC Interpretation 10 *Interim Financial Reporting and*
Impairment

This Basis for Conclusions accompanies, but is not part of, IFRIC 10.

BC1   This Basis for Conclusions summarises the IFRIC's considerations in reaching its consensus. Individual IFRIC members gave greater weight to some factors than to others.

BC2   IAS 34 requires an entity to apply the same accounting policies in its interim financial statements as it applies in its annual financial statements. For annual financial statements, IAS 36 prohibits an entity from reversing an impairment loss on goodwill that it recognised in a prior annual period. Similarly, IAS 39[1] prohibits an entity from reversing in a subsequent annual period an impairment loss on an investment in an equity instrument or in a financial asset carried at cost. These requirements might suggest that an entity should not reverse in a subsequent interim period an impairment loss on goodwill or an investment in an equity instrument or in a financial asset carried at cost that it had recognised in a prior interim period. Such impairment losses would not be reversed even if no loss, or a smaller loss, would have been recognised had the impairment been assessed only at the end of the subsequent interim period.

BC3   However, IAS 34 requires year-to-date measures in interim financial statements. This requirement might suggest that an entity should reverse in a subsequent interim period an impairment loss it recognised in a prior interim period. Such impairment losses would be reversed if no loss, or a smaller loss, would have been recognised had the impairment been assessed only at the end of the subsequent interim period.

BC4   The IFRIC released Draft Interpretation D18 *Interim Financial Reporting and Impairment* for public comment in January 2006. It received more than 50 letters in response.

BC5   The IFRIC noted that many of the respondents believed that in attempting to address contradictions between standards, D18 was beyond the scope of the IFRIC. Some believed that the issue addressed could be better resolved by amending IAS 34. Before finalising its views, the IFRIC asked the International Accounting Standards Board to consider this point. The Board, however, did not wish to amend IAS 34 and asked the IFRIC to continue with its Interpretation.

BC6   Respondents to D18 were divided on whether the proposed Interpretation should prohibit the reversal of impairment losses on goodwill or investments in equity instruments or in financial assets carried at cost that had been recognised in interim periods. The IFRIC considered these responses but maintained its view that such losses should not be reversed in subsequent

---

1   IFRS 9 *Financial Instruments* replaced IAS 39. IFRS 9 applies to all items that were previously within the scope of IAS 39.

financial statements. The IFRIC observed that the wide divergence of views evident from respondents' letters underlined the need for additional guidance and it therefore decided to issue the Interpretation with few changes from D18.

BC7　The IFRIC considered the example of Entity A and Entity B, which each hold the same equity investment with the same acquisition cost. Entity A prepares quarterly interim financial statements and Entity B prepares half-yearly financial statements. The entities have the same year-end. The IFRIC noted that if there was a significant decline in the fair value of the equity instrument below its cost in the first quarter, Entity A would recognise an impairment loss in its first quarter interim financial statements. However, if the fair value of the equity instrument subsequently recovered, so that by the half-year date there had not been a significant decline in fair value below cost, Entity B would not recognise an impairment loss in its half-yearly financial statements if it tested for impairment only at its half-yearly reporting dates. Therefore, unless Entity A reversed the impairment loss that had been recognised in an earlier interim period, the frequency of reporting would affect the measurement of its annual results when compared with Entity B's approach. The IFRIC also noted that the recognition of an impairment loss could similarly be affected by the timing of the financial year-ends of the two entities.

BC8　The IFRIC noted that the illustrative examples accompanying IAS 34 provide examples of applying the general recognition and measurement principles of that standard, and that paragraph B36 states that IAS 34 requires an entity to apply the same impairment testing, recognition, and reversal criteria at an interim date as it would at the end of its financial year.

BC9　The IFRIC concluded that the prohibitions on reversals of recognised impairment losses on goodwill in IAS 36 and on investments in equity instruments and in financial assets carried at cost in IAS 39[2] should take precedence over the more general statement in IAS 34 regarding the frequency of an entity's reporting not affecting the measurement of its annual results.

BC10　Furthermore, the IFRIC concluded that the rationale for the non-reversal of impairment losses relating to goodwill and investments in equity instruments, as set out in paragraph BC189 of IAS 36 and paragraph BC130 of IAS 39, applies at both interim and annual reporting dates.

BC11　The IFRIC considered a concern that this conclusion could be extended to other areas of potential conflict between IAS 34 and other standards. The IFRIC has not studied those areas and therefore has not identified any general principles that might apply both to the Interpretation and to other areas of potential conflict. The IFRIC therefore added a prohibition against extending the consensus by analogy to other areas of potential conflict between IAS 34 and other standards.

2　In November 2009 and October 2010 the Board amended some of the requirements of IAS 39 and relocated them to IFRS 9 *Financial Instruments*. IFRS 9 applies to all items within the scope of IAS 39.

BC12   D18 proposed fully retrospective application. A number of comment letters stated that this could be read as being more onerous than the first-time adoption requirements of IAS 36. The IFRIC revised the wording of the transition requirements to make clear that the Interpretation should not be applied to periods before an entity's adoption of IAS 36 in the case of goodwill impairments and IAS 39 in the case of impairments of investments in equity instruments or in financial assets carried at cost.

Documents published to accompany

IFRIC 12

Service Concession Arrangements

The text of the unaccompanied Interpretation, IFRIC 12, is contained in Part A of this edition. Its effective date when issued was 1 January 2008. The text of the Accompanying Guidance on IFRIC 12 is contained in Part B of this edition. This part presents the following document:

BASIS FOR CONCLUSIONS

Basis for Conclusions on
IFRIC Interpretation 12 *Service Concession Arrangements*

This Basis for Conclusions accompanies, but is not part of, IFRIC 12.

Introduction

BC1　This Basis for Conclusions summarises the IFRIC's considerations in reaching its consensus. Individual IFRIC members gave greater weight to some factors than to others.

Background (paragraphs 1–3)

BC2　SIC-29 *Service Concession Arrangements: Disclosures* (formerly *Disclosure — Service Concession Arrangements*) contains disclosure requirements in respect of public-to-private service arrangements, but does not specify how they should be accounted for.

BC3　There was widespread concern about the lack of such guidance. In particular, operators wished to know how to account for infrastructure that they either constructed or acquired for the purpose of a public-to-private service concession arrangement, or were given access to for the purpose of providing the public service. They also wanted to know how to account for other rights and obligations arising from these types of arrangements.

BC4　In response to this concern, the International Accounting Standards Board asked a working group comprising representatives of the standard-setters of Australia, France, Spain and the United Kingdom (four of the countries that had expressed such concern) to carry out initial research on the subject. The working group recommended that the IFRIC should seek to clarify how certain aspects of existing accounting standards were to be applied.

BC5　In March 2005 the IFRIC published for public comment three draft Interpretations: D12 *Service Concession Arrangements — Determining the Accounting Model*, D13 *Service Concession Arrangements — The Financial Asset Model* and D14 *Service Concession Arrangements — The Intangible Asset Model*. In response to the proposals 77 comment letters were received. In addition, in order to understand better the practical issues that would have arisen on implementing the proposed Interpretations, IASB staff met various interested parties, including preparers, auditors and regulators.

BC6　Most respondents to D12–D14 supported the IFRIC's proposal to develop an Interpretation. However, nearly all respondents expressed concern with fundamental aspects of the proposals, some urging that the project be passed to the Board to develop a comprehensive standard.

BC7　In its redeliberation of the proposals the IFRIC acknowledged that the project was a large undertaking but concluded that it should continue its work because, given the limited scope of the project, it was by then better placed than the Board to deal with the issues in a timely way.

Terminology

BC8   SIC-29 used the terms 'Concession Provider' and 'Concession Operator' to describe, respectively, the grantor and operator of the service arrangement. Some commentators, and some members of the IFRIC, found these terms confusingly similar. The IFRIC decided to adopt the terms 'grantor' and 'operator', and amended SIC-29 accordingly.

Scope (paragraphs 4–9)

BC9   The IFRIC observed that public-to-private service arrangements take a variety of forms. The continued involvement of both grantor and operator over the term of the arrangement, accompanied by heavy upfront investment, raises questions over what assets and liabilities should be recognised by the operator.

BC10   The working group recommended that the scope of the IFRIC's project should be restricted to public-to-private service concession arrangements.

BC11   In developing the proposals the IFRIC decided to address only arrangements in which the grantor (a) controlled or regulated the services provided by the operator, and (b) controlled any significant residual interest in the infrastructure at the end of the term of the arrangement. It also decided to specify the accounting treatment only for infrastructure that the operator constructed or acquired from a third party, or to which it was given access by the grantor, for the purpose of the arrangement. The IFRIC concluded that these conditions were likely to be met in most of the public-to-private arrangements for which guidance had been sought.

BC12   Commentators on the draft Interpretations argued that the proposals ignored many arrangements that were found in practice, in particular, when the infrastructure was leased to the operator or, conversely, when it was held as the property, plant and equipment of the operator before the start of the service arrangement.

BC13   In considering these comments, the IFRIC decided that the scope of the project should not be expanded because it already included the arrangements most in need of interpretative guidance and expansion would have significantly delayed the Interpretation. The scope of the project was considered at length during the initial stage, as indicated above. The IFRIC confirmed its view that the proposed Interpretation should address the issues set out in paragraph 10. Nonetheless, during its redeliberation the IFRIC considered the range of typical arrangements for private sector participation in the provision of public services, including some that were outside the scope of the proposed Interpretation. The IFRIC decided that the Interpretation could provide references to relevant standards that apply to arrangements outside the scope of the Interpretation without giving guidance on their application. If experience showed that such guidance was needed, a separate project could be undertaken at a later date. Information Note 2 contains a table of references to relevant standards for the types of arrangements considered by the IFRIC.

Private-to-private arrangements

BC14   Some respondents to the draft Interpretations suggested that the scope of the proposed Interpretation should be extended to include private-to-private service arrangements. The IFRIC noted that addressing the accounting for such arrangements was not the primary purpose of the project because the IFRIC had been asked to provide guidance for public-to-private arrangements that meet the requirements set out in paragraph 5 and have the characteristics described in paragraph 3. The IFRIC noted that application by analogy would be appropriate under the hierarchy set out in paragraphs 7–12 of IAS 8 *Accounting Policies, Changes in Accounting Estimates and Errors*.

Grantor accounting

BC15   The Interpretation does not specify the accounting by grantors, because the IFRIC's objective and priority were to establish guidance for operators. Some commentators asked the IFRIC to establish guidance for the accounting by grantors. The IFRIC discussed these comments but reaffirmed its view. It noted that in many cases the grantor is a government body, and that IFRSs are not designed to apply to not-for-profit activities in the private sector, public sector or government, though entities with such activities may find them appropriate (see *Preface to IFRSs* paragraph 9).[1]

Existing assets of the operator

BC16   The Interpretation does not specify the treatment of existing assets of the operator because the IFRIC decided that it was unnecessary to address the derecognition requirements of existing standards.

BC17   Some respondents asked the IFRIC to provide guidance on the accounting for existing assets of the operator, stating that the scope exclusion would create uncertainty about the treatment of these assets.

BC18   In its redeliberations the IFRIC noted that one objective of the Interpretation is to address whether the operator should recognise as its property, plant and equipment the infrastructure it constructs or to which it is given access. The accounting issue to be addressed for existing assets of the operator is one of derecognition, which is already addressed in IFRSs (IAS 16 *Property, Plant and Equipment*). In the light of the comments received from respondents, the IFRIC decided to clarify that certain public-to-private service arrangements may convey to the grantor a right to use existing assets of the operator, in which case the operator would apply the derecognition requirements of IFRSs to determine whether it should derecognise its existing assets.

---

1   *Preface to International Financial Reporting Standards* renamed *Preface to IFRS Standards*, December 2018.

The significant residual interest criterion

BC19   Paragraph 5(b) of D12 proposed that for a service arrangement to be within its scope the residual interest in the infrastructure handed over to the grantor at the end of the arrangement must be significant. Respondents argued, and the IFRIC agreed, that the significant residual interest criterion would limit the usefulness of the guidance because a service arrangement for the entire physical life of the infrastructure would be excluded from the scope of the guidance. That result was not the IFRIC's intention. In its redeliberation of the proposals, the IFRIC decided that it would not retain the proposal that the residual interest in the infrastructure handed over to the grantor at the end of the arrangement must be significant. As a consequence, 'whole of life' infrastructure (ie where the infrastructure is used in a public-to-private service arrangement for the entirety of its useful life) is within the scope of the Interpretation.

Treatment of the operator's rights over the infrastructure (paragraph 11)

BC20   The IFRIC considered the nature of the rights conveyed to the operator in a service concession arrangement. It first examined whether the infrastructure used to provide public services could be classified as property, plant and equipment of the operator under IAS 16. It started from the principle that infrastructure used to provide public services should be recognised as property, plant and equipment of the party that controls its use. This principle determines which party should recognise the property, plant and equipment as its own. The reference to control stems from the *Framework*:[2]

(a)   an asset is defined by the *Framework* as 'a resource controlled by the entity as a result of past events and from which future economic benefits are expected to flow to the entity.'

(b)   the *Framework* notes that many assets are associated with legal rights, including the right of ownership. It goes on to clarify that the right of ownership is not essential.

(c)   rights are often unbundled. For example, they may be divided proportionately (undivided interests in land) or by specified cash flows (principal and interest on a bond) or over time (a lease).

BC21   The IFRIC concluded that treatment of infrastructure that the operator constructs or acquires or to which the grantor gives the operator access for the purpose of the service arrangement should be determined by whether it is controlled by the grantor in the manner described in paragraph 5. If it is so controlled (as will be the case for all arrangements within the scope of the Interpretation), then, regardless of which party has legal title to it during the arrangement, the infrastructure should not be recognised as property, plant

---

2   References to the *Framework* in this Basis for Conclusions are to the IASC's *Framework for the Preparation and Presentation of Financial Statements*, adopted by the Board in 2001 and in effect when the Interpretation was developed.

and equipment of the operator because the operator does not control the use of the public service infrastructure.

BC22   In reaching this conclusion the IFRIC observed that it is control of the right to use an asset that determines recognition under IAS 16 and the creation of a lease under IAS 17 *Leases*. IAS 16 defines property, plant and equipment as tangible items that 'are held for use in the production or supply of goods or services, for rental to others or for administrative purposes ...'. It requires items within this definition to be recognised as property, plant and equipment unless another standard requires or permits a different approach. As an example of a different approach, it highlights the requirement in IAS 17 for recognition of leased property, plant and equipment to be evaluated on the basis of the transfer of risks and rewards. That standard defines a lease as 'an agreement whereby the lessor conveys to the lessee in return for a series of payments the right to use an asset' and it sets out the requirements for classification of leases. IFRIC 4 *Determining whether an Arrangement contains a Lease* interprets the meaning of right to use an asset as 'the arrangement conveys the right to control the use of the underlying asset.'

BC23   Accordingly, it is only if an arrangement conveys the right to control the use of the underlying asset that reference is made to IAS 17 to determine how such a lease should be classified. A lease is classified as a finance lease if it transfers substantially all the risks and rewards incidental to ownership. A lease is classified as an operating lease if it does not transfer substantially all the risks and rewards incidental to ownership.

BC24   The IFRIC considered whether arrangements within the scope of IFRIC 12 convey 'the right to control the use of the underlying asset' (the public service infrastructure) to the operator. The IFRIC decided that, if an arrangement met the conditions in paragraph 5, the operator would not have the right to control the use of the underlying asset and should therefore not recognise the infrastructure as a leased asset.

BC25   In arrangements within the scope of the Interpretation the operator acts as a service provider. The operator constructs or upgrades infrastructure used to provide a public service. Under the terms of the contract the operator has access to operate the infrastructure to provide the public service on the grantor's behalf. The asset recognised by the operator is the consideration it receives in exchange for its services, not the public service infrastructure that it constructs or upgrades.

BC26   Respondents to the draft Interpretations disagreed that recognition should be determined solely on the basis of control of use without any assessment of the extent to which the operator or the grantor bears the risks and rewards of ownership. They questioned how the proposed approach could be reconciled to IAS 17, in which the leased asset is recognised by the party that bears substantially all the risks and rewards incidental to ownership.

BC27   During its redeliberation the IFRIC affirmed its decision that if an arrangement met the control conditions in paragraph 5 of the Interpretation the operator would not have the right to control the use of the underlying asset (public service infrastructure) and should therefore not recognise the infrastructure as its property, plant and equipment under IAS 16 or the creation of a lease under IAS 17. The contractual service arrangement between the grantor and operator would not convey the right to use the infrastructure to the operator. The IFRIC concluded that this treatment is also consistent with IAS 18 *Revenue*[3] because, for arrangements within the scope of the Interpretation, the second condition of paragraph 14 of IAS 18 is not satisfied. The grantor retains continuing managerial involvement to the degree usually associated with ownership and control over the infrastructure as described in paragraph 5.

BC28   In service concession arrangements rights are usually conveyed for a limited period, which is similar to a lease. However, for arrangements within the scope of the Interpretation, the operator's right is different from that of a lessee: the grantor retains control over the use to which the infrastructure is put, by controlling or regulating what services the operator must provide, to whom it must provide them, and at what price, as described in paragraph 5(a). The grantor also retains control over any significant residual interest in the infrastructure throughout the period of the arrangement. Unlike a lessee, the operator does not have a right of use of the underlying asset: rather it has access to operate the infrastructure to provide the public service on behalf of the grantor in accordance with the terms specified in the contract.

BC29   The IFRIC considered whether the scope of the Interpretation might overlap with IFRIC 4. In particular, it noted the views expressed by some respondents that the contractual terms of certain service arrangements would be regarded as leases under IFRIC 4 and would also be regarded as meeting the scope criterion set out in paragraph 5 of IFRIC 12. The IFRIC did not regard the choice between accounting treatments as appropriate because it could lead to different accounting treatments for contracts that have similar economic effects. In the light of comments received the IFRIC amended the scope of IFRIC 4 to specify that if a service arrangement met the scope requirements of IFRIC 12 it would not be within the scope of IFRIC 4.

---

3   IFRS 15 *Revenue from Contracts with Customers*, issued in May 2014, replaced IAS 18 *Revenue*.

Recognition and measurement of arrangement consideration (paragraphs 12 and 13)

BC30　The accounting requirements for construction and service contracts are addressed in IAS 11 *Construction Contracts*[4] and IAS 18[5]. They require revenue to be recognised by reference to the stage of completion of the contract activity. IAS 18 states the general principle that revenue is measured at the fair value of the consideration received or receivable. However, the IFRIC observed that the fair value of the construction services delivered may in practice be the most appropriate method of establishing the fair value of the consideration received or receivable for the construction services. This will be the case in service concession arrangements, because the consideration attributable to the construction activity often has to be apportioned from a total sum receivable on the contract as a whole and, if it consists of an intangible asset, may also be subject to uncertainty in measurement.

BC31　The IFRIC noted that IAS 18[6] requires its recognition criteria to be applied separately to identifiable components of a single transaction in order to reflect the substance of the transaction. For example, when the selling price of a product includes an identifiable amount for subsequent servicing, that amount is deferred and is recognised as revenue over the period during which the service is performed. The IFRIC concluded that this requirement was relevant to service arrangements within the scope of the Interpretation. Arrangements within the scope of the Interpretation involve an operator providing more than one service, ie construction or upgrade services, and operation services. Although the contract for each service is generally negotiated as a single contract, its terms call for separate phases or elements because each separate phase or element has its own distinct skills, requirements and risks. The IFRIC noted that, in these circumstances, IAS 18 paragraphs 4 and 13 require the contract to be separated into two separate

---

4　IFRS 15 *Revenue from Contracts with Customers*, issued in May 2014, replaced IAS 11 *Construction Contracts* and IAS 18 *Revenue*. IFRS 15 requires revenue to be recognised when (or as) an entity satisfies a performance obligation by transferring a promised good or service to a customer. IFRS 15 measures the revenue by (a) determining the amount of consideration to which an entity expects to be entitled in exchange for transferring promised goods or services to a customer; and (b) allocating that amount to the performance obligations.

5　IFRS 15 *Revenue from Contracts with Customers*, issued in May 2014, replaced IAS 11 *Construction Contracts* and IAS 18 *Revenue*. IFRS 15 requires revenue to be recognised when (or as) an entity satisfies a performance obligation by transferring a promised good or service to a customer. IFRS 15 measures the revenue by (a) determining the amount of consideration to which an entity expects to be entitled in exchange for transferring promised goods or services to a customer; and (b) allocating that amount to the performance obligations.

6　IFRS 15 *Revenue from Contracts with Customers*, issued in May 2014, replaced IAS 11 *Construction Contracts* and IAS 18 *Revenue*. IFRS 15 requires revenue to be recognised when (or as) an entity satisfies a performance obligation by transferring a promised good or service to a customer. IFRS 15 measures the revenue by (a) determining the amount of consideration to which an entity expects to be entitled in exchange for transferring promised goods or services to a customer; and (b) allocating that amount to the performance obligations.

phases or elements, a construction element within the scope of IAS 11[7] and an operations element within the scope of IAS 18. Thus the operator might report different profit margins on each phase or element. The IFRIC noted that the amount for each service would be identifiable because such services were often provided as a single service. The IFRIC also noted that the combining and segmenting criteria of IAS 11 applied only to the construction element of the arrangement.

BC32   In some circumstances, the grantor makes a non-cash payment for the construction services, ie it gives the operator an intangible asset (a right to charge users of the public service) in exchange for the operator providing construction services. The operator then uses the intangible asset to generate further revenues from users of the public service.

BC33   Paragraph 12 of IAS 18[8] states:

> When goods are sold or services are rendered in exchange for dissimilar goods or services, the exchange is regarded as a transaction which generates revenue. The revenue is measured at the fair value of the goods or services received, adjusted by the amount of any cash or cash equivalents transferred. When the fair value of the goods or services received cannot be measured reliably, the revenue is measured at the fair value of the goods or services given up, adjusted by the amount of any cash or cash equivalents transferred.

BC34   The IFRIC noted that total revenue does not equal total cash inflows. The reason for this outcome is that, when the operator receives an intangible asset in exchange for its construction services, there are two sets of inflows and outflows rather than one. In the first set, the construction services are exchanged for the intangible asset in a barter transaction with the grantor. In the second set, the intangible asset received from the grantor is used up to generate cash flows from users of the public service. This result is not unique to service arrangements within the scope of the Interpretation. Any situation in which an entity provides goods or services in exchange for another dissimilar asset that is subsequently used to generate cash revenues would lead to a similar result.

BC35   Some IFRIC members were uncomfortable with such a result, and would have preferred a method of accounting under which total revenues were limited to the cash inflows. However, they accepted that it is consistent with the treatment accorded to a barter transaction, ie an exchange of dissimilar goods or services.

---

7   IFRS 15 *Revenue from Contracts with Customers*, issued in May 2014, replaced IAS 11 *Construction Contracts* and IAS 18 *Revenue*. IFRS 15 requires revenue to be recognised when (or as) an entity satisfies a performance obligation by transferring a promised good or service to a customer. IFRS 15 measures the revenue by (a) determining the amount of consideration to which an entity expects to be entitled in exchange for transferring promised goods or services to a customer; and (b) allocating that amount to the performance obligations.

8   IFRS 15 *Revenue from Contracts with Customers*, issued in May 2014, replaced IAS 18 *Revenue*. IFRS 15 requires an entity to measure non-cash consideration at fair value, unless the entity cannot reasonably estimate the fair value of the non-cash consideration. In such cases, IFRS 15 requires the entity to measure the consideration indirectly by reference to the stand-alone selling price of the goods or services promised to the customer in exchange for the consideration.

Consideration given by the grantor to the operator (paragraphs 14–19)

BC36   The IFRIC observed that the contractual rights that the operator receives in exchange for providing construction services can take a variety of forms. They are not necessarily rights to receive cash or other financial assets.

BC37   The draft Interpretations proposed that the nature of the operator's asset depended on who had the primary responsibility to pay the operator for the services. The operator should recognise a financial asset when the grantor had the primary responsibility to pay the operator for the services. The operator should recognise an intangible asset in all other cases.

BC38   Respondents to the draft Interpretations argued that determining which accounting model to apply by looking at who has the primary responsibility to pay the operator for the services, irrespective of who bears demand risk (ie ability and willingness of users to pay for the service), would result in an accounting treatment that did not reflect the economic substance of the arrangement. Respondents were concerned that the proposal would require operators with essentially identical cash flow streams to adopt different accounting models. This would impair users' understanding of entities involved in providing public-to-private service concession arrangements. Several gave the example of a shadow toll road and a toll road, where the economics (demand risk) of the arrangements would be similar, pointing out that under the proposals the two arrangements would be accounted for differently. In the light of comments received on the proposals, the IFRIC decided to clarify (see paragraphs 15–19) the extent to which an operator should recognise a financial asset and an intangible asset.

BC39   Responses to the draft Interpretations provided only limited information about the impact of the proposals. To obtain additional information, IASB staff arranged for discussions with preparers, auditors and regulators. The consensus of those consulted was that the identity of the payer has no effect on the risks to the operator's cash flow stream. The operator typically relies on the terms of the service arrangement contract to determine the risks to its cash flow stream. The operator's cash flows may be guaranteed by the grantor, in which case the grantor bears demand risk, or the operator's cash flows may be conditional on usage levels, in which case the operator bears demand risk.

BC40   The IFRIC noted that the operator's cash flows are guaranteed when (a) the grantor agrees to pay the operator specified or determinable amounts whether or not the public service is used (sometimes known as take-or-pay arrangements) or (b) the grantor grants a right to the operator to charge users of the public service and the grantor guarantees the operator's cash flows by way of a shortfall guarantee described in paragraph 16. The operator's cash flows are conditional on usage when it has no such guarantee but must obtain its revenue either directly from users of the public service or from the grantor in proportion to public usage of the service (road tolls or shadow tolls for example).

A financial asset (operator's cash flows are guaranteed by the grantor)

BC41   Paragraph 11 of IAS 32 *Financial Instruments: Presentation* defines a financial asset to include 'a contractual right to receive cash or another financial asset from another entity'. Paragraph 13 of that standard clarifies that 'contractual' refers to 'an agreement between two or more parties that has clear economic consequences that the parties have little, if any, discretion to avoid, usually because the agreement is enforceable by law.'

BC42   The IFRIC decided that a financial asset should be recognised to the extent that the operator has an unconditional present right to receive cash from or at the direction of the grantor for the construction services; and the grantor has little, if any, discretion to avoid payment, usually because the agreement is enforceable by law. The operator has a contractual right to receive cash for the construction services if the grantor contractually guarantees the operator's cash flows, in the manner described in paragraph 16. The IFRIC noted that the operator has an unconditional right to receive cash to the extent that the grantor bears the risk (demand risk) that the cash flows generated by the users of the public service will not be sufficient to recover the operator's investment.

BC43   The IFRIC noted that:

(a)   an agreement to pay for the shortfall, if any, between amounts received from users of the service and specified or determinable amounts does not meet the definition of a financial guarantee in paragraph 9 of IAS 39 *Financial Instruments: Recognition and Measurement*[9] because the operator has an unconditional contractual right to receive cash from the grantor. Furthermore, the amendments made to IAS 39 in August 2005 by *Financial Guarantee Contracts* do not address the treatment of financial guarantee contracts by the holder. The objective of the amendments was to ensure that issuers of financial guarantee contracts recognise a liability for the obligations the guarantor has undertaken in issuing that guarantee.

(b)   users or the grantor may pay the contractual amount receivable directly to the operator. The method of payment is a matter of form only. In both cases the operator has a present, unconditional, contractual right to receive the specified or determinable cash flows from or at the direction of the grantor. The nature of the operator's asset is not altered solely because the contractual amount receivable may be paid directly by users of the public service. The IFRIC observed that accounting for these contractual cash flows in accordance with IASs 32 and 39 faithfully reflects the economics of the arrangements, which is to provide finance to the operator for the construction of the infrastructure.

---

9   IFRS 9 *Financial Instruments* replaced IAS 39. IFRS 9 applies to all items that were previously within the scope of IAS 39.

Operator's cash flows are contingent on the operator meeting specified quality or efficiency requirements

BC44　The IFRIC concluded that the definition of a financial asset is met even if the contractual right to receive cash is contingent on the operator meeting specified quality or efficiency requirements or targets. Before the grantor is required to pay the operator for its construction services, the operator may have to ensure that the infrastructure is capable of generating the public services specified by the grantor or that the infrastructure is up to or exceeds operating standards or efficiency targets specified by the grantor to ensure a specified level of service and capacity can be delivered. In this respect the operator's position is the same as that of any other entity in which payment for goods or services is contingent on subsequent performance of the goods or service sold.

BC45　Therefore IFRIC 12 treats the consideration given by the grantor to the operator as giving rise to a financial asset irrespective of whether the contractual amounts receivable are contingent on the operator meeting levels of performance or efficiency targets.[10]

An intangible asset (operator's cash flows are conditional on usage)

BC46　IAS 38 *Intangible Assets* defines an intangible asset as 'an identifiable non-monetary asset without physical substance'. It mentions licences as examples of intangible assets. It describes an asset as being identifiable when it arises from contractual rights.

BC47　The IFRIC concluded that the right of an operator to charge users of the public service meets the definition of an intangible asset, and therefore should be accounted for in accordance with IAS 38. In these circumstances the operator's revenue is conditional on usage and it bears the risk (demand risk) that the cash flows generated by users of the public service will not be sufficient to recover its investment.

BC48　In the absence of contractual arrangements designed to ensure that the operator receives a minimum amount (see paragraphs BC53 and BC54), the operator has no contractual right to receive cash even if receipt of the cash is highly probable. Rather, the operator has an opportunity to charge those who use the public service in the future. The operator bears the demand risk and hence its commercial return is contingent on users using the public service. The operator's asset is a licence, which would be classified as an intangible asset within the scope of IAS 38. And, as clarified in paragraph AG10 of the application guidance in IAS 32:

10　IFRS 15 *Revenue from Contracts with Customers*, issued in May 2014, replaced IAS 18 *Revenue*. IFRS 15 requires an entity to recognise a financial asset to the extent that it has an unconditional contractual right to receive cash or another financial asset. This is also discussed in paragraph 16 of IFRIC 12.

Physical assets (such as inventories, property, plant and equipment), leased assets and intangible assets (such as patents and trademarks) are not financial assets. Control of such physical and intangible assets creates an opportunity to generate an inflow of cash or another financial asset, but it does not give rise to a present right to receive cash or another financial asset.

BC49   The IFRIC considered whether a right to charge users unsupported by any shortfall guarantee from the grantor could be regarded as an indirect right to receive cash arising from the contract with the grantor. It concluded that although the operator's asset might have characteristics that are similar to those of a financial asset, it would not meet the definition of a financial asset in IAS 32: the operator would not at the balance sheet date have a contractual right to receive cash from another entity. That other entity (ie the user) would still have the ability to avoid any obligation. The grantor would be passing to the operator an opportunity to charge users in future, not a present right to receive cash.

Contractual arrangements that eliminate substantially all variability in the operator's return

BC50   The IFRIC considered whether agreements incorporating contractual arrangements designed to eliminate substantially all variability in the operator's return would meet the definition of a financial asset, for example:

(a)   the price charged by the operator would be varied by regulation designed to ensure that the operator received a substantially fixed return; or

(b)   the operator would be permitted to collect revenues from users or the grantor until it achieved a specified return on its investment, at which point the arrangement would come to an end.

BC51   The IFRIC noted that, as a result of such contractual arrangements, the operator's return would be low risk. Only if usage were extremely low would the contractual mechanisms fail to give the operator the specified return. The likelihood of usage being that low could be remote. Commercially, the operator's return would be regarded as fixed, giving its asset many of the characteristics of a financial asset.

BC52   However, the IFRIC concluded that the fact that the operator's asset was low risk did not influence its classification. IAS 32 does not define financial assets by reference to the amount of risk in the return—it defines them solely by reference to the existence or absence of an unconditional contractual right to receive cash. There are other examples of licences that offer the holders of the rights predictable, low risk returns, but such licences are not regarded as giving the holder a contractual right to cash. And there are other industries in which price regulation is designed to provide the operators with substantially fixed returns—but the rights of operators in these other industries are not classified as financial assets as a result. The operator's asset is a variable term licence, which would be classified as an intangible asset within the scope of IAS 38.

A financial asset and an intangible asset

BC53   The IFRIC concluded that if the operator is paid for its construction services partly by a financial asset and partly by an intangible asset it is necessary to account separately for each component of the operator's consideration. The IFRIC included the requirement to account separately for each component (sometimes known as a bifurcated arrangement) of the operator's consideration in response to a concern raised on the draft Interpretations. The concern was that, in some arrangements, both parties to the contract share the risk (demand risk) that the cash flows generated by users of the public service will not be sufficient to recover the operator's investment. In order to achieve the desired sharing of risk, the parties often agree to arrangements under which the grantor pays the operator for its services partly by a financial asset and partly by granting a right to charge users of the public service (an intangible asset). The IFRIC concluded that in these circumstances it would be necessary to divide the operator's consideration into a financial asset component for any guaranteed amount of cash or other financial asset and an intangible asset for the remainder.

BC54   The IFRIC concluded that the nature of consideration given by the grantor to the operator is determined by reference to the contract terms and when it exists, relevant contract law. The IFRIC noted public-to-private service agreements are rarely if ever the same; technical requirements vary by sector and country. Furthermore, the terms of the contractual agreement may also depend on the specific features of the overall legal framework of the particular country. Public-to-private service contract laws, where they exist, may contain terms that do not have to be repeated in individual contracts.

Contractual obligations to restore the infrastructure to a specified level of serviceability (paragraph 21)

BC55   The IFRIC noted that IAS 37 *Provisions, Contingent Liabilities and Contingent Assets* prohibits an entity from providing for the replacement of parts of its own property, plant and equipment. IAS 16 requires such costs to be recognised in the carrying amount of an item of property, plant and equipment if the recognition criteria in paragraph 7 are met. Each part of an item of property, plant and equipment with a cost that is significant in relation to the total cost of the item is depreciated separately. The IFRIC concluded that this prohibition would not apply to arrangements within the scope of the Interpretation because the operator does not recognise the infrastructure as its own property, plant and equipment. The operator has an unavoidable obligation that it owes to a third party, the grantor, in respect of the infrastructure. The operator should recognise its obligations in accordance with IAS 37.

BC56   The IFRIC considered whether the Interpretation should contain guidance on the timing of recognition of the obligations. It noted that the precise terms and circumstances of the obligations would vary from contract to contract. It concluded that the requirements and guidance in IAS 37 were sufficiently clear to enable an operator to identify the period(s) in which different obligations should be recognised.

Borrowing costs (paragraph 22)

BC57   IAS 23 *Borrowing Costs* permits borrowing costs to be capitalised as part of the cost of a qualifying asset to the extent that they are directly attributable to its acquisition, construction or production until the asset is ready for its intended use or sale. That Standard defines a qualifying asset as 'an asset that necessarily takes a substantial period of time to get ready for its intended use or sale'.

BC58   For arrangements within the scope of the Interpretation, the IFRIC decided that an intangible asset (ie the grantor gives the operator a right to charge users of the public service in return for construction services) meets the definition of a qualifying asset of the operator because generally the licence would not be ready for use until the infrastructure was constructed or upgraded. A financial asset (ie the grantor gives the operator a contractual right to receive cash or other financial asset in return for construction services) does not meet the definition of a qualifying asset of the operator. The IFRIC observed that interest is generally accreted on the carrying value of financial assets.

BC59   The IFRIC noted that financing arrangements may result in an operator obtaining borrowed funds and incurring associated borrowing costs before some or all of the funds are used for expenditure relating to construction or operation services. In such circumstances the funds are often temporarily invested. Any investment income earned on such funds is recognised in accordance with IAS 39,[11] unless the operator adopts the allowed alternative treatment, in which case investment income earned during the construction phase of the arrangement is accounted for in accordance with paragraph 16 of IAS 23.[12]

Financial asset (paragraphs 23–25)[13]

BC60   Paragraph 9 of IAS 39 identifies and defines four categories of financial asset: (i) those held at fair value through profit or loss; (ii) held-to-maturity investments; (iii) loans and receivables; and (iv) available-for-sale financial assets.

---

11   IFRS 9 *Financial Instruments* replaced IAS 39. IFRS 9 applies to all items that were previously within the scope of IAS 39.

12   In March 2007, IAS 23 was revised to require the previously allowed alternative treatment of capitalisation. Therefore, an entity is required to capitalise borrowing costs as part of the cost of a qualifying asset to the extent that they are directly attributable to its acquisition, construction or production until the asset is ready for its intended use or sale. That revision does not affect the reasoning set out in this Basis for Conclusions.

13   IFRS 9 *Financial Instruments* replaced IAS 39. IFRS 9 applies to all items that were previously within the scope of IAS 39.

BC61   Paragraph 24 of IFRIC 12 assumes that public-to-private service arrangement financial assets will not be categorised as held-to-maturity investments. Paragraph 9 of IAS 39 states that a financial asset may not be classified as a held-to-maturity investment if it meets the definition of a loan or receivable. An asset that meets the definition of a held-to-maturity investment will meet the definition of a loan or receivable unless:

(a)   it is quoted in an active market; or

(b)   the holder may not recover substantially all of its initial investment, other than because of credit deterioration.

It is not envisaged that a public-to-private service arrangement financial asset will be quoted in an active market. Hence the circumstances of (a) will not arise. In the circumstances of (b), the asset must be classified as available for sale (if not designated upon initial recognition as at fair value through profit or loss).

BC62   The IFRIC considered whether the contract would include an embedded derivative if the amount to be received by the operator could vary with the quality of subsequent services to be provided by the operator or performance or efficiency targets to be achieved by the operator. The IFRIC concluded that it would not, because the definition of a derivative in IAS 39 requires, among other things, that the variable is not specific to a party to the contract. The consequence is that the contract's provision for variations in payments does not meet the definition of a derivative and, accordingly, the requirements of IAS 39 in relation to embedded derivatives do not apply. The IFRIC observed that if the amount to be received by the operator is conditional on the infrastructure meeting quality or performance or efficiency targets as described in paragraph BC44, this would not prevent the amount from being classified as a financial asset. The IFRIC also concluded that during the construction phase of the arrangement the operator's asset (representing its accumulating right to be paid for providing construction services) should be classified as a financial asset when it represents cash or another financial asset due from or at the direction of the grantor.

Intangible asset (paragraph 26)

BC63   The Interpretation requires the operator to account for its intangible asset in accordance with IAS 38. Among other requirements, IAS 38 requires an intangible asset with a finite useful economic life to be amortised over that life. Paragraph 97 states that 'the amortisation method used shall reflect the pattern in which the asset's future economic benefits are expected to be consumed by the entity.'

BC64   The IFRIC considered whether it would be appropriate for intangible assets under paragraph 26 to be amortised using an 'interest' method of amortisation, ie one that takes account of the time value of money in addition to the consumption of the intangible asset, treating the asset more like a monetary than a non-monetary asset. However, the IFRIC concluded that there was nothing unique about these intangible assets that would justify use of a method of depreciation different from that used for other intangible assets. The IFRIC noted that paragraph 98 of IAS 38 provides for a number of amortisation methods for intangible assets with finite useful lives. These methods include the straight-line method, the diminishing balance method and the units of production method. The method used is selected on the basis of the expected pattern of consumption of the expected future economic benefits embodied in the asset and is applied consistently from period to period, unless there is a change in the expected pattern of consumption of those future economic benefits.

BC65　The IFRIC noted that interest methods of amortisation are not permitted under IAS 38. Therefore, IFRIC 12 does not provide exceptions to permit use of interest methods of amortisation.

BC66　The IFRIC considered when the operator should first recognise the intangible asset. The IFRIC concluded that the intangible asset (the licence) received in exchange for construction services should be recognised in accordance with general principles applicable to contracts for the exchange of assets or services.

BC67　The IFRIC noted that it is current practice not to recognise executory contracts to the extent that they are unperformed by both parties (unless the contract is onerous). IAS 37 describes executory contracts as 'contracts under which neither party has performed any of its obligations or both parties have partially performed their obligations to an equal extent'. Paragraph 91 of the *Framework* states:

> In practice, obligations under contracts that are equally proportionately unperformed (for example, liabilities for inventory ordered but not yet received) are generally not recognised as liabilities in the financial statements.

BC68　Therefore, the IFRIC concluded that contracts within the scope of the Interpretation should not be recognised to the extent that they are executory. The IFRIC noted that service concession arrangements within the scope of the Interpretation are generally executory when the contracts are signed. The IFRIC also concluded that during the construction phase of the arrangement the operator's asset (representing its accumulating right to be paid for providing construction services) should be classified as an intangible asset to the extent that it represents a right to receive a right (licence) to charge users of the public service (an intangible asset).

Items provided to the operator by the grantor (paragraph 27)

BC69　For service arrangements within the scope of the Interpretation, pre-existing infrastructure items made available to the operator by the grantor for the purpose of the service arrangement are not recognised as property, plant and equipment of the operator.

BC70   However, different considerations apply to other assets provided to the operator by the grantor if the operator can keep or deal with the assets as it wishes. Such assets become assets of the operator and so should be accounted for in accordance with general recognition and measurement principles, as should the obligations undertaken in exchange for them.

BC71   The IFRIC considered whether such assets would represent government grants, as defined in paragraph 3 of IAS 20 *Accounting for Government Grants and Disclosure of Government Assistance*:

> Government grants are assistance by government in the form of transfers of resources to an entity in return for past or future compliance with certain conditions relating to the operating activities of the entity. They exclude those forms of government assistance which cannot reasonably have a value placed upon them and transactions with government which cannot be distinguished from the normal trading transactions of the entity.

The IFRIC concluded that if such assets were part of the overall consideration payable by the grantor on an arms' length basis for the operator's services, they would not constitute 'assistance'. Therefore, they would not meet the definition of government grants in IAS 20 and that standard would not apply.

Transition (paragraphs 29 and 30)

BC72   IAS 8 *Accounting Policies, Changes in Accounting Estimates and Errors* states that an entity shall account for a change in accounting policy resulting from initial application of an Interpretation in accordance with any specific transitional provisions in that Interpretation. In the absence of any specific transitional provisions, the general requirements of IAS 8 apply. The general requirement in IAS 8 is that the changes should be accounted for retrospectively, except to the extent that retrospective application would be impracticable.

BC73   The IFRIC noted that there are two aspects to retrospective determination: reclassification and remeasurement. The IFRIC took the view that it will usually be practicable to determine retrospectively the appropriate classification of all amounts previously included in an operator's balance sheet, but that retrospective remeasurement of service arrangement assets might not always be practicable.

BC74   The IFRIC noted that, when retrospective restatement is not practicable, IAS 8 requires prospective application from the earliest practicable date, which could be the start of the current period. Under prospective application, the operator could be applying different accounting models to similar transactions, which the IFRIC decided would be inappropriate. The IFRIC regarded it as important that the correct accounting model should be consistently applied.

BC75   The Interpretation reflects these conclusions.

Amendments to IFRS 1

BC76   The amendments to IFRS 1 *First-time Adoption of International Financial Reporting Standards* are necessary to ensure that the transitional arrangements are available to both existing users and first-time adopters of IFRSs. The IFRIC believes that the requirements will ensure that the balance sheet will exclude any items that would not qualify for recognition as assets and liabilities under IFRSs.

Summary of changes from the draft Interpretations

BC77   The main changes from the IFRIC's proposals are as follows:

(a)   The proposals were published in three separate draft Interpretations, D12 *Service Concession Arrangements – Determining the Accounting Model*, D13 *Service Concession Arrangements – The Financial Asset Model* and D14 *Service Concession Arrangements – The Intangible Asset Model*. In finalising IFRIC 12, the IFRIC combined the three draft Interpretations.

(b)   By contrast with IFRIC 12 the draft Interpretations did not explain the reasons for the scope limitations and the reasons for the control approach adopted by the IFRIC in paragraph 5. The IFRIC added Information Note 2 to IFRIC 12 to provide references to standards that apply to arrangements outside the scope of the Interpretation.

(c)   The scope of the proposals did not include 'whole of life infrastructure' (ie infrastructure used in a public-to-private service arrangement for its entire useful life). IFRIC 12 includes 'whole of life infrastructure' within its scope.

(d)   Under the approach proposed, an entity determined the appropriate accounting model by reference to whether the grantor or the user had primary responsibility to pay the operator for the services provided. IFRIC 12 requires an entity to recognise a financial asset to the extent that the operator has an unconditional contractual right to receive cash from or at the direction of the grantor. The operator should recognise an intangible asset to the extent that it receives a right to charge users of the public service.

(e)   By contrast with IFRIC 12, the draft Interpretations implied that the nature of asset recognised (a financial asset or an intangible asset) by the operator as consideration for providing construction services determined the accounting for the operation phase of the arrangement.

(f)   Under the approach proposed in the draft Interpretations, an entity could capitalise borrowing costs under the allowed alternative treatment in IAS 23. IFRIC 12 requires borrowing costs to be recognised as an expense in the period in which they are incurred unless the operator has a contractual right to receive an intangible asset (a right to charge users of the public service), in which case borrowing costs attributable to the arrangement may be capitalised in accordance with the allowed alternative treatment under IAS 23.[14]

(g)   In finalising IFRIC 12, the IFRIC decided to amend IFRIC 4.

---

14 In March 2007, IAS 23 was revised to require the previously allowed alternative treatment of capitalisation. Therefore, an entity is required to capitalise borrowing costs as part of the cost of a qualifying asset to the extent that they are directly attributable to its acquisition, construction or production until the asset is ready for its intended use or sale. That revision does not affect the reasoning set out in this Basis for Conclusions.

Documents published to accompany

IFRIC 14

IAS 19 – The Limit on a Defined Benefit Asset, Minimum Funding Requirements and their Interaction

The text of the unaccompanied Interpretation, IFRIC 14, is contained in Part A of this edition. Its effective date when issued was 1 January 2008. The text of the Accompanying Guidance on IFRIC 14 is contained in Part B of this edition. This part presents the following document:

BASIS FOR CONCLUSIONS

Basis for Conclusions on IFRIC Interpretation 14 *IAS 19—The Limit on a Defined Benefit Asset, Minimum Funding Requirements and their Interaction*

This Basis for Conclusions accompanies, but is not part of, IFRIC 14.

The original text has been marked up to reflect the revision of IAS 1 Presentation of Financial Statements *in 2007: new text is underlined and deleted text is struck through.*

BC1 This Basis for Conclusions summarises the IFRIC's considerations in reaching its consensus. Individual IFRIC members gave greater weight to some factors than to others.

BC2 The IFRIC noted that practice varies significantly with regard to the treatment of the effect of a minimum funding requirement on the limit placed by paragraph 64 of IAS 19 *Employee Benefits* on the amount of a defined benefit asset. The IFRIC therefore decided to include this issue on its agenda. In considering the issue, the IFRIC also became aware of the need for general guidance on determining the limit on the measurement of the defined benefit asset, and for guidance on when that limit makes a minimum funding requirement onerous.

BC3 The IFRIC published D19 *IAS 19 — The Asset Ceiling: Availability of Economic Benefits and Minimum Funding Requirements* in August 2006. In response, the IFRIC received 48 comment letters.

BC3A In November 2009 the International Accounting Standards Board amended IFRIC 14 to remove an unintended consequence arising from the treatment of prepayments in some circumstances when there is a minimum funding requirement (see paragraphs BC30A–BC30D).

Definition of a minimum funding requirement

BC4 D19 referred to statutory or contractual minimum funding requirements. Respondents to D19 asked for further guidance on what constituted a minimum funding requirement. The IFRIC decided to clarify that for the purpose of the Interpretation a minimum funding requirement is any requirement for the entity to make contributions to *fund* a post-employment or other long-term defined benefit plan.

Interaction between IAS 19 and minimum funding requirements

BC5 Funding requirements would not normally affect the accounting for a plan under IAS 19. However, paragraph 64 of IAS 19 limits the amount of the net defined benefit asset to the available economic benefit. The interaction of a minimum funding requirement and this limit has two possible effects:

(a) the minimum funding requirement may restrict the economic benefits available as a reduction in future contributions, and

(b) the limit may make the minimum funding requirement onerous because contributions payable under the requirement in respect of services already received may not be available once they have been paid, either as a refund or as a reduction in future contributions.

BC6 These effects raised general questions about the availability of economic benefits in the form of a refund or a reduction in future contributions.

Availability of the economic benefit

BC7 One view of 'available' would limit the economic benefit to the amount that is realisable immediately at the <u>end of the reporting period</u> ~~balance sheet date~~.

BC8 The IFRIC disagreed with this view. The *Framework*[1] defines an asset as a resource 'from which future economic benefits are expected to flow to the entity'. Therefore, it is not necessary for the economic benefit to be realisable immediately. Indeed, a reduction in future contributions cannot be realisable immediately.

BC9 The IFRIC concluded that a refund or reduction in future contributions is available if it could be realisable at some point during the life of the plan or when the plan liability is settled. Respondents to D19 were largely supportive of this conclusion.

BC10 In the responses to D19, some argued that an entity may expect to use the surplus to give improved benefits. Others noted that future actuarial losses might reduce or eliminate the surplus. In either case there would be no refund or reduction in future contributions. The IFRIC noted that the existence of an asset at the <u>end of the reporting period</u> ~~balance sheet date~~ depends on whether the entity has the right to obtain a refund or reduction in future contributions. The existence of the asset at that date is not affected by possible future changes to the amount of the surplus. If future events occur that change the amount of the surplus, their effects are recognised when they occur. Accordingly, if the entity decides to improve benefits, or future losses in the plan reduce the surplus, the consequences are recognised when the decision is made or the losses occur. The IFRIC noted that such events of future periods do not affect the existence or measurement of the asset at the <u>end of the reporting period</u> ~~balance sheet date~~.

The asset available as a refund of a surplus

BC11 The IFRIC noted that a refund of a surplus could potentially be obtained in three ways:

(a) during the life of the plan, without assuming that the plan liabilities have to be settled in order to get the refund (eg in some jurisdictions, the entity may have a right to a refund during the life of the plan, irrespective of whether the plan liabilities are settled); or

---

1 The reference to the *Framework* is to the IASC's *Framework for the Preparation and Presentation of Financial Statements*, adopted by the Board in 2001 and in effect when the Interpretation was developed.

(b)   assuming the gradual settlement of the plan liabilities over time until all members have left the plan; or

(c)   assuming the full settlement of the plan liabilities in a single event (ie as a plan wind-up).

BC12   The IFRIC concluded that all three ways should be considered in determining whether an economic benefit was available to the entity. Some respondents to D19 raised the question of when an entity controls an asset that arises from the availability of a refund, in particular if a refund would be available only if a third party (for example the plan trustees) gave its approval. The IFRIC concluded that an entity controlled the asset only if the entity has an unconditional right to the refund. If that right depends on actions by a third party, the entity does not have an unconditional right.

BC13   If the plan liability is settled by an immediate wind-up, the costs associated with the wind-up may be significant. One reason for this may be that the cost of annuities available on the market is expected to be significantly higher than that implied by the IAS 19 basis. Other costs include the legal and other professional fees expected to be incurred during the winding-up process. Accordingly, a plan with an apparent surplus may not be able to recover any of that surplus on wind-up.

BC14   The IFRIC noted that the available surplus should be measured at the amount that the entity could receive from the plan. The IFRIC decided that in determining the amount of the refund available on wind-up of the plan, the amount of the costs associated with the settlement and refund should be deducted if paid by the plan.

BC15   The IFRIC noted that the costs of settling the plan liability would be dependent on the facts and circumstances of the plan and it decided not to issue any specific guidance in this respect.

BC16   The IFRIC also noted that the present value of the defined benefit obligation and the fair value of assets are both measured on a present value basis[2] and therefore take into account the timing of the future cash flows. The IFRIC concluded that no further adjustment for the time value of money needs to be made when measuring the amount of a refund determined as the full amount or a proportion of the surplus that is realisable at a future date.

The asset available in the form of a future contribution reduction

BC17   The IFRIC decided that the amount of the contribution reduction available to the entity should be measured with reference to the amount that the entity would have been required to pay had there been no surplus. The IFRIC concluded that is represented by the cost to the entity of accruing benefits in the plan, in other words by the future IAS 19 service cost. Respondents to D19 broadly supported this conclusion.

---

2   IFRS 13 *Fair Value Measurement*, issued in May 2011, defines fair value and contains the requirements for measuring fair value. IFRS 13 does not specify a particular valuation technique for measuring the fair value of plan assets.

BC18   When the issue of the availability of reductions in future contributions was first raised with the IFRIC, some expressed the view that an entity should recognise an asset only to the extent that there was a formal agreement between the trustees and the entity specifying contributions payable lower than the IAS 19 service cost. The IFRIC disagreed, concluding instead that an entity is entitled to assume that, in general, it will not be required to make contributions to a plan in order to maintain a surplus and hence that it will be able to reduce contributions if the plan has a surplus. (The effects of a minimum funding requirement on this assumption are discussed below.)

BC19   The IFRIC considered the assumptions that underlie the calculation of the future service cost. In respect of the discount rate, IAS 19 requires the measurement of the present value of the future contribution reduction to be based on the same discount rate as that used to determine the present value of the defined benefit obligation.

BC20   The IFRIC considered whether the term over which the contribution reduction should be calculated should be restricted to the expected future working lifetime of the active membership. The IFRIC disagreed with that view. The IFRIC noted that the entity could derive economic benefit from a reduction in contributions beyond that period. The IFRIC also noted that increasing the term of the calculation has a decreasing effect on the incremental changes to the asset because the reductions in contributions are discounted to a present value. Thus, for plans with a large surplus and no possibility of receiving a refund, the available asset will be limited even if the term of the calculation extends beyond the expected future working lifetime of the active membership to the expected life of the plan. This is consistent with paragraph BC77 of the Basis for Conclusions on IAS 19,[3] which states that 'the limit [on the measurement of the defined benefit asset] is likely to come into play *only* where … the plan is very mature and has a very large surplus that is more than large enough to eliminate *all* future contributions and cannot be returned to the entity' (emphasis added). If the contribution reduction were determined by considering only the term of the expected future working lifetime of the active membership, the limit on the measurement of the defined benefit asset would come into play much more frequently.

BC21   Most respondents to D19 were supportive of this view. However, some argued that the term should be the shorter of the expected life of the plan and the expected life of the entity. The IFRIC agreed that the entity could not derive economic benefits from a reduction in contributions beyond its own expected life and has amended the Interpretation accordingly.

BC22   Next, the IFRIC considered what assumptions should be made about a future workforce. D19 proposed that the assumptions for the demographic profile of the future workforce should be consistent with the assumptions underlying the calculation of the present value of the defined benefit obligation at the end of the reporting period balance sheet date. Some respondents noted that the calculation of service costs for future periods requires assumptions that are not required for the calculation of the defined benefit obligation. In

---

3   As a result of the amendments to IAS 19 in June 2011, paragraph BC77 was deleted.

particular, the assumptions underlying the present value of the defined benefit obligation calculation do not include an explicit assumption for new entrants.

BC23 The IFRIC agreed that this is the case. The IFRIC noted that assumptions are needed in respect of the size of the future workforce and future benefits provided by the plan. The IFRIC decided that the future service cost should be based on the situation that exists at the end of the reporting period ~~balance sheet date~~ determined in accordance with IAS 19. Therefore, increases in the size of the workforce or the benefits provided by the plan should not be anticipated. Decreases in the size of the workforce or the benefits should be included in the assumptions for the future service cost at the same time as they are treated as curtailments in accordance with IAS 19.

The effect of a minimum funding requirement on the economic benefit available as a refund

BC24 The IFRIC considered whether a minimum funding requirement to make contributions to a plan in force at the end of the reporting period ~~balance sheet date~~ would restrict the extent to which a refund of surplus is available. The IFRIC noted that there is an implicit assumption in IAS 19 that the specified assumptions represent the best estimate of the eventual outcome of the plan in economic terms, while a requirement to make additional contributions is often a prudent approach designed to build in a risk margin for adverse circumstances. Moreover, when there are no members left in the plan, the minimum funding requirement would have no effect. This would leave the IAS 19 surplus available. To the extent that the entity has a right to this eventual surplus, the IAS 19 surplus would be available to the entity, regardless of the minimum funding restrictions in force at the end of the reporting period ~~balance sheet date~~. The IFRIC therefore concluded that the existence of a minimum funding requirement may affect the timing of a refund but does not affect whether it is ultimately available to the entity.

The effect of a minimum funding requirement on the economic benefit available as a reduction in future contributions

BC25 The entity's minimum funding requirements at a given date can be analysed into the contributions that are required to cover (a) an existing shortfall for past service on the minimum funding basis and (b) future service.

BC26 Contributions required to cover an existing shortfall may give rise to a liability, as discussed in paragraphs BC31–BC37 below. But they do not affect the availability of a reduction in future contributions for future service.

BC27 In contrast, future contribution requirements in respect of future service do not generate an additional liability at the end of the reporting period ~~balance sheet date~~ because they do not relate to past services received by the entity. However, they may reduce the extent to which the entity can benefit from a reduction in future contributions. Therefore, the IFRIC decided that the available asset from a contribution reduction should be calculated as the present value of the IAS 19 future service cost less the minimum funding contribution requirement in respect of future service in each year.

BC28 If the minimum funding contribution requirement is consistently greater than the IAS 19 future service cost, that calculation may be thought to imply that a liability exists. However, as noted above, an entity has no liability at the end of the reporting period ~~balance sheet date~~ in respect of minimum funding requirements that relate to future service. The economic benefit available from a reduction in future contributions can be nil, but it can never be a negative amount.

BC29 The respondents to D19 were largely supportive of these conclusions.

BC30 The IFRIC noted that future changes to regulations on minimum funding requirements might affect the available surplus. However, the IFRIC decided that, just as the future service cost was determined on the basis of the situation existing at the end of the reporting period ~~balance sheet date~~, so should the effect of a minimum funding requirement. The IFRIC concluded that when determining the amount of an asset that might be available as a reduction in future contributions, an entity should not consider whether the minimum funding requirement might change in the future. The respondents to D19 were largely supportive of these conclusions.

Prepayments of a minimum funding requirement

BC30A If an entity has prepaid future minimum funding requirement contributions and that prepayment will reduce future contributions, the prepayment generates economic benefits for the entity. However, to the extent that the future minimum funding requirement contributions exceeded future service costs, the original version of IFRIC 14 did not permit entities to consider those economic benefits in measuring a defined benefit asset. After issuing IFRIC 14, the Board reviewed the treatment of such prepayments. The Board concluded that such a prepayment provides an economic benefit to the entity by relieving the entity of an obligation to pay future minimum funding requirement contributions that exceed future service cost. Therefore, considering those economic benefits in measuring a defined benefit asset would convey more useful information to users of financial statements. In May 2009 the Board published that conclusion in an exposure draft *Prepayments of a Minimum Funding Requirement*. After considering the responses to that exposure draft, the Board amended IFRIC 14 by issuing *Prepayments of a Minimum Funding Requirement* in November 2009.

BC30B Some respondents noted that the amendments increase the effect of funding considerations on the measurement of a defined benefit asset and liability and questioned whether funding considerations should ever affect the measurement. However, the Board noted that the sole purpose of the amendments was to eliminate an unintended consequence in IFRIC 14. Thus, the Board did not re-debate the fundamental conclusion of IFRIC 14 that funding is relevant to the measurement when an entity cannot recover the additional cost of a minimum funding requirement in excess of the IAS 19 service cost.

BC30C   Many respondents noted that the proposals made the assessment of the economic benefit available from a prepayment different from the assessment for a surplus arising from actuarial gains. Most agreed that a prepayment created an asset, but questioned why the Board did not extend the underlying principle to other surpluses that could be used to reduce future payments of minimum funding requirement contributions.

BC30D   The Board did not extend the scope of the amendments to surpluses arising from actuarial gains because such an approach would need further thought and the Board did not want to delay the amendments for prepayments. However, the Board may consider the matter further in a future comprehensive review of pension cost accounting.

Onerous minimum funding requirements

BC31   Minimum funding requirements for contributions to cover an existing minimum funding shortfall create an obligation for the entity at the <u>end of the reporting period</u> ~~balance sheet date~~ because they relate to past service. Nonetheless, usually minimum funding requirements do not affect the measurement of the defined benefit asset or liability under IAS 19. This is because the contributions, once paid, become plan assets and the additional net liability for the funding requirement is nil. However, the IFRIC noted that the limit on the measurement of the defined benefit asset in paragraph 64 of IAS 19 may make the funding obligation onerous, as follows.

BC32   If an entity is obliged to make contributions and some or all of those contributions will not subsequently be available as an economic benefit, it follows that when the contributions are made the entity will not be able to recognise an asset to that extent. However, the resulting loss to the entity does not arise on the payment of the contributions but earlier, at the point at which the obligation to pay arises.

BC33   Therefore, the IFRIC concluded that when an entity has an obligation under a minimum funding requirement to make additional contributions to a plan in respect of services already received, the entity should reduce the ~~balance sheet~~ asset or increase the liability <u>recognised in the statement of financial position</u> to the extent that the minimum funding contributions payable to the plan will not be available to the entity either as a refund or a reduction in future contributions.

BC34   Respondents to D19 broadly supported this conclusion. But some questioned whether the draft Interpretation extended the application of paragraph 64 of IAS 19 too far. They argued that it should apply only when an entity has a defined benefit asset. In particular, it should not be used to classify a funding requirement as onerous, thereby creating an additional liability to be recognised beyond that arising from the other requirements of IAS 19. Others agreed that such a liability existed, but questioned whether it fell within the scope of IAS 19 rather than IAS 37 *Provisions, Contingent Liabilities and Contingent Assets.*

BC35   The IFRIC did not agree that the Interpretation extends the application of paragraph 64 of IAS 19. Rather, it applies the principles in IAS 37 relating to onerous contracts in the context of the requirements of IAS 19, including paragraph 64. On the question whether the liability falls within the scope of IAS 19 or IAS 37, the IFRIC noted that employee benefits are excluded from the scope of IAS 37. The IFRIC therefore confirmed that the interaction of a minimum funding requirement and the limit on the measurement of the defined benefit asset could result in a decrease in a defined benefit asset or an increase in a defined benefit liability.

BC36–   [Deleted]
BC37

Transitional provisions

BC38   In D19, the IFRIC proposed that the draft Interpretation should be applied retrospectively. The draft Interpretation required immediate recognition of all adjustments relating to the minimum funding requirements. The IFRIC therefore argued that retrospective application would be straightforward.

BC39   Respondents to D19 noted that paragraph 58A[4] of IAS 19 causes the limit on the defined benefit asset to affect the deferred recognition of actuarial gains and losses. Retrospective application of the Interpretation could change the amount of that limit for previous periods, thereby also changing the deferred recognition of actuarial gains and losses. Calculating these revised amounts retrospectively over the life of the plan would be costly and of little benefit to users of financial statements.

BC40   The IFRIC agreed with this view. The IFRIC therefore amended the transitional provisions so that IFRIC 14 is to be applied only from the beginning of the first period presented in the financial statements for annual periods beginning on or after the effective date.

Summary of changes from D19

BC41   The Interpretation has been altered in the following significant respects since it was exposed for comment as D19:

   (a)   The issue of when an entity controls an asset arising from the availability of a refund has been clarified (paragraphs BC10 and BC12).

   (b)   Requirements relating to the assumptions underlying the measurement of a reduction in future contributions have been clarified (paragraphs BC22 and BC23).

   (c)   The transitional requirements have been changed from retrospective application to application from the beginning of the first period presented in the first financial statements to which the Interpretation applies (paragraphs BC38–BC40).

---

4   IAS 19 (as amended in June 2011) eliminated deferred recognition of actuarial gains and losses and deleted paragraph 58A.

(d)   In November 2009 the Board amended IFRIC 14 to require entities to recognise as an economic benefit any prepayment of minimum funding requirement contributions. At the same time, the Board removed references to 'present value' from paragraphs 16, 17, 20 and 22 and 'the surplus in the plan' from paragraph 16 because these references duplicated references in paragraph 64 of IAS 19. The Board also amended the term 'future accrual of benefits' to 'future service' for consistency with the rest of IAS 19.

(e)   In June 2011 the Board issued an amended IAS 19 that eliminated the deferred recognition of actuarial gains and losses. As a consequence of that amendment, the Board deleted paragraphs 25 and 26, amended paragraphs 1, 6, 17, 24 and amended Examples 1–4 in the illustrative examples accompanying IFRIC 14. As a result of those changes paragraphs BC36 and BC37 of this Basis for Conclusions were deleted and paragraph BC5 was amended. Lastly, cross-references to IAS 19 were updated.

Documents published to accompany

IFRIC 16

Hedges of a Net Investment in a Foreign Operation

The text of the unaccompanied Interpretation, IFRIC 16, is contained in Part A of this edition. Its effective date when issued was 1 October 2008. The text of the Accompanying Guidance on IFRIC 16 is contained in Part B of this edition. This part presents the following document:

BASIS FOR CONCLUSIONS

Basis for Conclusions on
IFRIC Interpretation 16 *Hedges of a Net Investment in a Foreign Operation*

This Basis for Conclusions accompanies, but is not part of, IFRIC 16.

Introduction

BC1   This Basis for Conclusions summarises the IFRIC's considerations in reaching its consensus. Individual IFRIC members gave greater weight to some factors than to others.

Background

BC2   The IFRIC was asked for guidance on accounting for the hedge of a net investment in a foreign operation in the consolidated financial statements. Interested parties had different views of the risks eligible for hedge accounting purposes. One issue is whether the risk arises from the foreign currency exposure to the functional currencies of the foreign operation and the parent entity, or whether it arises from the foreign currency exposure to the functional currency of the foreign operation and the presentation currency of the parent entity's consolidated financial statements.

BC3   Concern was also raised about which entity within a group could hold a hedging instrument in a hedge of a net investment in a foreign operation and in particular whether the parent entity holding the net investment in a foreign operation must also hold the hedging instrument.

BC4   Accordingly, the IFRIC decided to develop guidance on the accounting for a hedge of the foreign currency risk arising from a net investment in a foreign operation.

BC5   The IFRIC published draft Interpretation D22 *Hedges of a Net Investment in a Foreign Operation* for public comment in July 2007 and received 45 comment letters in response to its proposals.

Consensus

Hedged risk and hedged item

Functional currency versus presentation currency (paragraph 10)

BC6   The IFRIC received a submission suggesting that the method of consolidation can affect the determination of the hedged risk in a hedge of a net investment in a foreign operation. The submission noted that consolidation can be completed by either the direct method or the step-by-step method. In the direct method of consolidation, each entity within a group is consolidated directly into the ultimate parent entity's presentation currency when preparing the consolidated financial statements. In the step-by-step method, each intermediate parent entity prepares consolidated financial statements, which are then consolidated into its parent entity until the ultimate parent entity has prepared consolidated financial statements.

BC7 The submission stated that if the direct method was required, the risk that qualifies for hedge accounting in a hedge of a net investment in a foreign operation would arise only from exposure between the functional currency of the foreign operation and the presentation currency of the group. This is because each foreign operation is translated only once into the presentation currency. In contrast, the submission stated that if the step-by-step method was required, the hedged risk that qualifies for hedge accounting is the risk between the functional currencies of the foreign operation and the immediate parent entity into which the entity was consolidated. This is because each foreign operation is consolidated directly into its immediate parent entity.

BC8 In response to this, the IFRIC noted that IAS 21 *The Effects of Changes in Foreign Exchange Rates* does not specify a method of consolidation for foreign operations. Furthermore, paragraph BC18 of the Basis for Conclusions on IAS 21 states that the method of translating financial statements will result in the same amounts in the presentation currency regardless of whether the direct method or the step-by-step method is used. The IFRIC therefore concluded that the consolidation mechanism should not determine what risk qualifies for hedge accounting in the hedge of a net investment in a foreign operation.

BC9 However, the IFRIC noted that its conclusion would not resolve the divergence of views on the foreign currency risk that may be designated as a hedge relationship in the hedge of a net investment in a foreign operation. The IFRIC therefore decided that an Interpretation was needed.

BC10 The IFRIC considered whether the risk that qualifies for hedge accounting in a hedge of a net investment in a foreign operation arises from the exposure to the functional currency of the foreign operation in relation to the presentation currency of the group or the functional currency of the parent entity, or both.

BC11 The answer to this question is important when the presentation currency of the group is different from an intermediate or ultimate parent entity's functional currency. If the presentation currency of the group and the functional currency of the parent entity are the same, the exchange rate being hedged would be identified as that between the parent entity's functional currency and the foreign operation's functional currency. No further translation adjustment would be required to prepare the consolidated financial statements. However, when the functional currency of the parent entity is different from the presentation currency of the group, a translation adjustment will be included in other comprehensive income to present the consolidated financial statements in a different presentation currency. The issue, therefore, is how to determine which foreign currency risk may be designated as the hedged risk in accordance with IAS 39 *Financial Instruments:*

Recognition and Measurement[1] in the hedge of a net investment in a foreign operation.

BC12   The IFRIC noted the following arguments for permitting hedge accounting for a hedge of the presentation currency:

(a)   If the presentation currency of the group is different from the ultimate parent entity's functional currency, a difference arises on translation that is recognised in other comprehensive income. It is argued that a reason for allowing hedge accounting for a net investment in a foreign operation is to remove from the financial statements the fluctuations resulting from the translation to a presentation currency. If an entity is not allowed to use hedge accounting for the exposure to the presentation currency of the group when it is different from the functional currency of the parent entity, there is likely to be an amount included in other comprehensive income that cannot be offset by hedge accounting.

(b)   IAS 21 requires an entity to reclassify from equity to profit or loss as a reclassification adjustment any foreign currency translation gains and losses included in other comprehensive income on disposal of a foreign operation. An amount in other comprehensive income arising from a different presentation currency is therefore included in the amount reclassified to profit or loss on disposal. The entity should be able to include the amount in a hedging relationship if at some stage it is recognised along with other reclassified translation amounts.

BC13   The IFRIC noted the following arguments for allowing an entity to designate hedging relationships solely on the basis of differences between functional currencies:

(a)   The functional currency of an entity is determined on the basis of the primary economic environment in which that entity operates (ie the environment in which it generates and expends cash). However, the presentation currency is an elective currency that can be changed at any time. To present amounts in a presentation currency is merely a numerical convention necessary for the preparation of financial statements that include a foreign operation. The presentation currency will have no economic effect on the parent entity. Indeed, a parent entity may choose to present financial statements in more than one presentation currency, but can have only one functional currency.

(b)   IAS 39 requires a hedging relationship to be effective in offsetting changes in fair values or cash flows attributable to the hedged risk. A net investment in a foreign operation gives rise to an exposure to changes in exchange rate risk for a parent entity. An economic exchange rate risk arises only from an exposure between two or more functional currencies, not from a presentation currency.

---

1   IFRS 9 *Financial Instruments* replaced the hedge accounting requirements in IAS 39. However, the requirements regarding hedges of a net investment in a foreign operation were retained from IAS 39 and relocated to IFRS 9.

BC14   When comparing the arguments in paragraphs BC12 and BC13, the IFRIC concluded that the presentation currency does not create an exposure to which an entity may apply hedge accounting. The functional currency is determined on the basis of the primary economic environment in which the entity operates. Accordingly, functional currencies create an economic exposure to changes in cash flows or fair values; a presentation currency never will. No commentators on the draft Interpretation disagreed with the IFRIC's conclusion.

Eligible risk (paragraph 12)

BC15   The IFRIC considered which entity's (or entities') functional currency may be used as a reference point for the hedged risk in a net investment hedge. Does the risk arise from the functional currency of:

(a)   the immediate parent entity that holds directly the foreign operation;

(b)   the ultimate parent entity that is preparing its financial statements; or

(c)   the immediate, an intermediate or the ultimate parent entity, depending on what risk that entity decides to hedge, as designated at the inception of the hedge?

BC16   The IFRIC concluded that the risk from the exposure to a different functional currency arises for any parent entity whose functional currency is different from that of the identified foreign operation. The immediate parent entity is exposed to changes in the exchange rate of its directly held foreign operation's functional currency. However, indirectly every entity up the chain of entities to the ultimate parent entity is also exposed to changes in the exchange rate of the foreign operation's functional currency.

BC17   Permitting only the ultimate parent entity to hedge its net investments would ignore the exposures arising on net investments in other parts of the entity. Conversely, permitting only the immediate parent entity to undertake a net investment hedge would imply that an indirect investment does not create a foreign currency exposure for that indirect parent entity.

BC18   The IFRIC concluded that a group must identify which risk (ie the functional currency of which parent entity and of which net investment in a foreign operation) is being hedged. The specified parent entity, the hedged risk and hedging instrument should all be designated and documented at the inception of the hedge relationship. As a result of comments received on the draft Interpretation, the IFRIC decided to emphasise that this documentation should also include the entity's strategy in undertaking the hedge as required by IAS 39.

Amount of hedged item that may be hedged (paragraphs 11 and 13)

BC19   In the draft Interpretation the IFRIC noted that, in financial statements that include a foreign operation, an entity cannot hedge the same risk more than once. This comment was intended to remind entities that IAS 39 does not permit multiple hedges of the same risk. Some respondents asked the IFRIC to clarify the situations in which the IFRIC considered that the same risk was being hedged more than once. In particular, the IFRIC was asked whether the same risk could be hedged by different entities within a group as long as the amount of risk being hedged was not duplicated.

BC20   In its redeliberations, the IFRIC decided to clarify that the carrying amount of the net assets of a foreign operation that may be hedged in the consolidated financial statements of a parent depends on whether any lower level parent of the foreign operation has hedged all or part of the net assets of that foreign operation and that accounting has been maintained in the parent's consolidated financial statements. An intermediate parent entity can hedge some or all of the risk of its net investment in a foreign operation in its own consolidated financial statements. However, such hedges will not qualify for hedge accounting at the ultimate parent entity level if the ultimate parent entity has also hedged the same risk. Alternatively, if the risk has not been hedged by the ultimate parent entity or another intermediate parent entity, the hedge relationship that qualified in the immediate parent entity's consolidated financial statements will also qualify in the ultimate parent entity's consolidated financial statements.

BC21   In its redeliberations, the IFRIC also decided to add guidance to the Interpretation to illustrate the importance of careful designation of the amount of the risk being hedged by each entity in the group.

Hedging instrument

Location of the hedging instrument (paragraph 14) and assessment of hedge effectiveness (paragraph 15)

BC22   The IFRIC discussed where in a group structure a hedging instrument may be held in a hedge of a net investment in a foreign operation. Guidance on the hedge of a net investment in a foreign operation was originally included in IAS 21. This guidance was moved to IAS 39 to ensure that the hedge accounting guidance included in paragraph 88 of IAS 39 would also apply to the hedges of net investments in foreign operations.

BC23   The IFRIC concluded that any entity within the group, other than the foreign operation being hedged, may hold the hedging instrument, as long as the hedging instrument is effective in offsetting the risk arising from the exposure to the functional currency of the foreign operation and the functional currency of the specified parent entity. The functional currency of the entity holding the instrument is irrelevant in determining effectiveness.

BC24   ~~The IFRIC concluded that the foreign operation being hedged could not hold the hedging instrument because that instrument would be part of, and denominated in the same currency as, the net investment it was intended to hedge. In this circumstance, hedge accounting is unnecessary. The foreign exchange differences between the parent's functional currency and both the hedging instrument and the functional currency of the net investment will automatically be included in the group's foreign currency translation reserve~~

as part of the consolidation process. The balance of the discussion in this Basis for Conclusions does not repeat this restriction.[2]

BC24A Paragraph 14 of IFRIC 16 originally stated that the hedging instrument could not be held by the foreign operation whose net investment was being hedged. The restriction was included in draft Interpretation D22 (from which IFRIC 16 was developed) and attracted little comment from respondents. As originally explained in paragraph BC24, the IFRIC concluded, as part of its redeliberations, that the restriction was appropriate because the foreign exchange differences between the parent's functional currency and both the hedging instrument and the functional currency of the net investment would automatically be included in the group's foreign currency translation reserve as part of the consolidation process.

BC24B After IFRIC 16 was issued, it was brought to the attention of the International Accounting Standards Board that this conclusion was not correct. Without hedge accounting, part of the foreign exchange difference arising from the hedging instrument would be included in consolidated profit or loss. Therefore, in *Improvements to IFRSs* issued in April 2009, the Board amended paragraph 14 of IFRIC 16 to remove the restriction on the entity that can hold hedging instruments and deleted paragraph BC24.

BC24C Some respondents to the exposure draft *Post-implementation Revisions to IFRIC Interpretations* (ED/2009/1) agreed that a parent entity should be able to use a derivative held by the foreign operation being hedged as a hedge of the net investment in that foreign operation. However, those respondents recommended that the amendment should apply only to derivative instruments held by the foreign operation being hedged. They asserted that a non-derivative financial instrument would be an effective hedge of the net investment only if it were issued by the foreign operation in its own functional currency and this would have no foreign currency impact on the profit or loss of the consolidated group. Consequently, they thought that the rationale described in paragraph BC24B to support the amendment did not apply to non-derivative instruments.

BC24D In its redeliberations, the Board confirmed its previous decision that the amendment should not be restricted to derivative instruments. The Board noted that paragraphs AG13–AG15 of IFRIC 16 illustrate that a non-derivative instrument held by the foreign operation does not need to be considered to be part of the parent's net investment. As a result, even if it is denominated in the foreign operation's functional currency a non-derivative instrument could still affect the profit or loss of the consolidated group. Consequently, although it could be argued that the amendment was not required to permit non-derivative instruments to be designated as hedges, the Board decided that the proposal should not be changed.

---

2 Paragraph BC24 was deleted and paragraphs BC24A–BC24D and paragraph BC40A added as a consequence of *Improvements to IFRSs* issued in April 2009.

BC25   The IFRIC also concluded that to apply the conclusion in paragraph BC23 when determining the effectiveness of a hedging instrument in the hedge of a net investment, an entity computes the gain or loss on the hedging instrument by reference to the functional currency of the parent entity against whose functional currency the hedged risk is measured, in accordance with the hedge documentation. This is the same regardless of the type of hedging instrument used. This ensures that the effectiveness of the instrument is determined on the basis of changes in fair value or cash flows of the hedging instrument, compared with the changes in the net investment as documented. Thus, any effectiveness test is not dependent on the functional currency of the entity holding the instrument. In other words, the fact that some of the change in the hedging instrument is recognised in profit or loss by one entity within the group and some is recognised in other comprehensive income by another does not affect the assessment of hedge effectiveness.

BC26   In the draft Interpretation the IFRIC noted Question F.2.14 in the guidance on implementing IAS 39, on the location of the hedging instrument, and considered whether that guidance could be applied by analogy to a net investment hedge. The answer to Question F.2.14 concludes:

> IAS 39 does not require that the operating unit that is exposed to the risk being hedged be a party to the hedging instrument.

This was the only basis for the IFRIC's conclusion regarding which entity could hold the hedging instrument provided in the draft Interpretation. Some respondents argued that the Interpretation should not refer to implementation guidance as the sole basis for an important conclusion.[3]

BC27   In its redeliberations, the IFRIC considered both the International Accounting Standards Board's amendment to IAS 21 in 2005 and the objective of hedging a net investment described in IAS 39 in addition to the guidance on implementing IAS 39.

BC28   In 2005 the Board was asked to clarify which entity is the reporting entity in IAS 21 and therefore what instruments could be considered part of a reporting entity's net investment in a foreign operation. In particular, constituents questioned whether a monetary item must be transacted between the foreign operation and the reporting entity to be considered part of the net investment in accordance with IAS 21 paragraph 15, or whether it could be transacted between the foreign operation and any member of the consolidated group.

BC29   In response the Board added IAS 21 paragraph 15A to clarify that 'The entity that has a monetary item receivable from or payable to a foreign operation described in paragraph 15 may be any subsidiary of the group.' The Board explained its reasons for the amendment in paragraph BC25D of the Basis for Conclusions:

> The Board concluded that the accounting treatment in the consolidated financial statements should not be dependent on the currency in which the monetary item is denominated, nor on which entity within the group conducts the transaction with the foreign operation.

---

3   IFRS 9 replaced IAS 39.

In other words, the Board concluded that the relevant reporting entity is the group rather than the individual entity and that the net investment must be viewed from the perspective of the group. It follows, therefore, that the group's net investment in any foreign operation, and its foreign currency exposure, can be determined only at the relevant parent entity level. The IFRIC similarly concluded that the fact that the net investment is held through an intermediate entity does not affect the economic risk.

BC30   Consistently with the Board's conclusion with respect to monetary items that are part of *the net investment*, the IFRIC concluded that monetary items (or derivatives) that are *hedging instruments* in a hedge of a net investment may be held by any entity within the group and the functional currency of the entity holding the monetary items can be different from those of either the parent or the foreign operation. The IFRIC, like the Board, agreed with constituents who noted that a hedging item denominated in a currency that is not the functional currency of the entity holding it does not expose the group to a greater foreign currency exchange difference than arises when the instrument is denominated in that functional currency.

BC31   The IFRIC noted that its conclusions that the hedging instrument can be held by any entity in the group and that the foreign currency is determined at the relevant parent entity level have implications for the designation of hedged risks. As illustrated in paragraph AG5 of the application guidance, these conclusions make it possible for an entity to designate a hedged risk that is not apparent in the currencies of the hedged item or the foreign operation. This possibility is unique to hedges of net investments. Consequently, the IFRIC specified that the conclusions in the Interpretation should not be applied by analogy to other types of hedge accounting.

BC32   The IFRIC also noted that the objective of hedge accounting as set out in IAS 39 is to achieve offsetting changes in the values of the *hedging instrument* and of the *net investment* attributable to the hedged risk. Changes in foreign currency rates affect the value of the entire *net investment* in a foreign operation, not only the portion IAS 21 requires to be recognised in profit or loss in the absence of hedge accounting but also the portion recognised in other comprehensive income in the parent's consolidated financial statements. As noted in paragraph BC25, it is the total change in the hedging instrument as result of a change in the foreign currency rate with respect to the parent entity against whose functional currency the hedged risk is measured that is relevant, not the component of comprehensive income in which it is recognised.

Reclassification from other comprehensive income to profit or loss (paragraphs 16 and 17)

BC33   In response to requests from some respondents for clarification, the IFRIC discussed what amounts from the parent entity's foreign currency translation reserve in respect of both the hedging instrument and the foreign operation should be recognised in profit or loss in the parent entity's consolidated financial statements when the parent disposes of a foreign operation that was hedged. The IFRIC noted that the amounts to be reclassified from equity to profit or loss as reclassification adjustments on the disposition are:

(a)   the cumulative amount of gain or loss on a hedging instrument determined to be an effective hedge that has been reflected in other comprehensive income (IAS 39 paragraph 102), and

(b)   the cumulative amount reflected in the foreign currency translation reserve in respect of that foreign operation (IAS 21 paragraph 48).

BC34   The IFRIC noted that when an entity hedges a net investment in a foreign operation, IAS 39 requires it to identify the cumulative amount included in the group's foreign currency translation reserve as a result of applying hedge accounting, ie the amount determined to be an effective hedge. Therefore, the IFRIC concluded that when a foreign operation that was hedged is disposed of, the amount reclassified to profit or loss from the foreign currency translation reserve in respect of the hedging instrument in the consolidated financial statements of the parent should be the amount that IAS 39 requires to be identified.

Effect of consolidation method

BC35   Some respondents to the draft Interpretation argued that the method of consolidation creates a difference in the amounts included in the ultimate parent entity's foreign currency translation reserve for individual foreign operations that are held through intermediate parents. These respondents noted that this difference may become evident only when the ultimate parent entity disposes of a second tier subsidiary (ie an indirect subsidiary).

BC36   The difference becomes apparent in the determination of the amount of the foreign currency translation reserve that is subsequently reclassified to profit or loss. An ultimate parent entity using the direct method of consolidation would reclassify the cumulative foreign currency translation reserve that arose between its functional currency and that of the foreign operation. An ultimate parent entity using the step-by-step method of consolidation might reclassify the cumulative foreign currency translation reserve reflected in the financial statements of the intermediate parent, ie the amount that arose between the functional currency of the foreign operation and that of the intermediate parent, translated into the functional currency of the ultimate parent.

BC37   In its redeliberations, the IFRIC noted that the use of the step-by-step method of consolidation does create such a difference for an *individual* foreign operation although the aggregate net amount of foreign currency translation reserve for all the foreign operations is the same under either method of consolidation. At the same time, the IFRIC noted that the method of consolidation *should not* create such a difference for an individual foreign operation, on the basis of its conclusion that the economic risk is determined in relation to the ultimate parent's functional currency.

BC38   The IFRIC noted that the amount of foreign currency translation reserve for an individual foreign operation determined by the direct method of consolidation reflects the economic risk between the functional currency of the foreign operation and that of the ultimate parent (if the parent's functional and presentation currencies are the same). However, the IFRIC noted that IAS 21 does not require an entity to use this method or to make adjustments to produce the same result. The IFRIC also noted that a parent entity is not precluded from determining the amount of the foreign currency translation reserve in respect of a foreign operation it has disposed of as if the direct method of consolidation had been used in order to reclassify the appropriate amount to profit or loss. However, it also noted that making such an adjustment on the disposal of a foreign operation is an accounting policy choice and should be followed consistently for the disposal of all net investments.

BC39   The IFRIC noted that this issue arises when the net investment disposed of was not hedged and therefore is not strictly within the scope of the Interpretation. However, because it was a topic of considerable confusion and debate, the IFRIC decided to include a brief example illustrating its conclusions.

Transition (paragraph 19)

BC40   In response to respondents' comments, the IFRIC clarified the Interpretation's transitional requirements. The IFRIC decided that entities should apply the conclusions in this Interpretation to existing hedging relationships on adoption and cease hedge accounting for those that no longer qualify. However, previous hedge accounting is not affected. This is similar to the transition requirements in IFRS 1 *First-time Adoption of International Financial Reporting Standards* paragraph 30,[4] for relationships accounted for as hedges under previous GAAP.

Effective date of amended paragraph 14

BC40A   The Board amended paragraph 14 in April 2009. In ED/2009/01 the Board proposed that the amendment should be effective for annual periods beginning on or after 1 October 2008, at the same time as IFRIC 16. Respondents to the exposure draft were concerned that permitting application before the amendment was issued might imply that an entity could designate hedge relationships retrospectively, contrary to the requirements of IAS 39. Consequently, the Board decided that an entity should apply the amendment to paragraph 14 made in April 2009 for annual periods beginning on or after 1 July 2009. The Board also decided to permit early application but noted that early application is possible only if the designation, documentation and effectiveness requirements of paragraph 88 of IAS 39 and of IFRIC 16 are satisfied at the application date.

---

4   Paragraph B6 in the revised version of IFRS 1 issued in November 2008.

Summary of main changes from the draft Interpretation

BC41 The main changes from the IFRIC's proposals are as follows:

(a) Paragraph 11 clarifies that the carrying amount of the net assets of a foreign operation that may be hedged in the consolidated financial statements of a parent depends on whether any lower level parent of the foreign operation has hedged all or part of the net assets of that foreign operation and that accounting has been maintained in the parent's consolidated financial statements.

(b) Paragraph 15 clarifies that the assessment of effectiveness is not affected by whether the hedging instrument is a derivative or a non-derivative instrument or by the method of consolidation.

(c) Paragraphs 16 and 17 and the illustrative example clarify what amounts should be reclassified from equity to profit or loss as reclassification adjustments on disposal of the foreign operation.

(d) Paragraph 19 clarifies transitional requirements.

(e) The appendix of application guidance was added to the Interpretation. Illustrative examples accompanying the draft Interpretation were removed.

(f) The Basis for Conclusions was changed to set out more clearly the reasons for the IFRIC's conclusions.

Documents published to accompany

IFRIC 17

Distributions of Non-cash Assets to Owners

The text of the unaccompanied Interpretation, IFRIC 17, is contained in Part A of this edition. Its effective date when issued was 1 July 2009. The text of the Accompanying Guidance on IFRIC 17 is contained in Part B of this edition. This part presents the following document:

BASIS FOR CONCLUSIONS

Basis for Conclusions on IFRIC Interpretation 17 *Distributions of Non-cash Assets to Owners*

This Basis for Conclusions accompanies, but is not part of, IFRIC 17.

Introduction

BC1　This Basis for Conclusions summarises the IFRIC's considerations in reaching its consensus. Individual IFRIC members gave greater weight to some factors than to others.

BC2　At present, International Financial Reporting Standards (IFRSs) do not address how an entity should measure distributions to owners acting in their capacity as owners (commonly referred to as dividends). The IFRIC was told that there was significant diversity in practice in how entities measured distributions of non-cash assets.

BC3　The IFRIC published draft Interpretation D23 *Distributions of Non-cash Assets to Owners* for public comment in January 2008 and received 56 comment letters in response to its proposals.

Scope (paragraphs 3–8)

Should the Interpretation address all transactions between an entity and its owners?

BC4　The IFRIC noted that an asset distribution by an entity to its owners is an example of a transaction between an entity and its owners. Transactions between an entity and its owners can generally be categorised into the following three types:

(a)　exchange transactions between an entity and its owners.

(b)　non-reciprocal transfers of assets by owners of an entity to the entity. Such transfers are commonly referred to as contributions from owners.

(c)　non-reciprocal transfers of assets by an entity to its owners. Such transfers are commonly referred to as distributions to owners.

BC5　The IFRIC concluded that the Interpretation should not address exchange transactions between an entity and its owners because that would probably result in addressing all related party transactions. In the IFRIC's view, such a scope was too broad for an Interpretation. Instead, the IFRIC concluded that the Interpretation should focus on distributions of assets by an entity to its owners acting in their capacity as owners.

BC6　In addition, the IFRIC decided that the Interpretation should not address distributions in which owners of the same class of equity instrument are not all treated equally. This is because, in the IFRIC's view, such distributions might imply that at least some of the owners receiving the distributions indeed gave up something to the entity and/or other owners. In other words, such distributions might be more in the nature of exchange transactions.

Should the Interpretation address all types of asset distributions?

BC7 The IFRIC was told that there was significant diversity in the measurement of the following types of non-reciprocal distributions of assets by an entity to its owners acting in their capacity as owners:

(a) distributions of non-cash assets (eg items of property, plant and equipment, businesses as defined in IFRS 3, ownership interests in another entity or disposal groups as defined in IFRS 5 *Non-current Assets Held for Sale and Discontinued Operations*) to its owners; and

(b) distributions that give owners a choice of receiving either non-cash assets or a cash alternative.

BC8 The IFRIC noted that all distributions have the same purpose, ie to distribute assets to an entity's owners. It therefore concluded that the Interpretation should address the measurement of all types of asset distributions with one exception set out in paragraph 5 of the Interpretation.

A scope exclusion: a distribution of an asset that is ultimately controlled by the same party or parties before and after the distribution

BC9 In the Interpretation, the IFRIC considered whether it should address how an entity should measure a distribution of an asset (eg an ownership interest in a subsidiary) that is ultimately controlled by the same party or parties before and after the distribution. In many instances, such a distribution is for the purpose of group restructuring (eg separating two different businesses into two different subgroups). After the distribution, the asset is still controlled by the same party or parties.

BC10 In addition, the IFRIC noted that dealing with the accounting for a distribution of an asset within a group would require consideration of how a transfer of any asset within a group should be accounted for in the separate or individual financial statements of group entities.

BC11 For the reasons described in paragraphs BC9 and BC10, the IFRIC concluded that the Interpretation should not deal with a distribution of an asset that is ultimately controlled by the same party or parties before and after the distribution.

BC12 In response to comments received on the draft Interpretation, the IFRIC redeliberated whether the scope of the Interpretation should be expanded to include a distribution of an asset that is ultimately controlled by the same party or parties before and after the distribution. The IFRIC decided not to expand the scope of the Interpretation in the light of the Board's decision to add a project to its agenda to address common control transactions.

BC13 The IFRIC noted that many commentators believed that most distributions of assets to an entity's owners would be excluded from the scope of the Interpretation by paragraph 5. The IFRIC did not agree with this conclusion. It noted that in paragraph B2 of IFRS 3 *Business Combinations* (as revised in 2008), the Board concluded that a group of individuals would be regarded as controlling an entity only when, as a result of contractual arrangements, they collectively have the power to govern its financial and operating policies so as to obtain benefits from its activities. In addition, in *Cost of an Investment in a Subsidiary, Jointly Controlled Entity or Associate* in May 2008, the Board clarified in the amendments to IAS 27 *Consolidated and Separate Financial Statements* that the distribution of equity interests in a new parent to shareholders in exchange for their interests in the existing parent was not a common control transaction.[1]

BC14 Consequently, the IFRIC decided that the Interpretation should clarify that unless there is a contractual arrangement among shareholders to control the entity making the distribution, transactions in which the shares or the businesses of group entities are distributed to shareholders outside the group (commonly referred to as a spin-off, split-off or demerger) are not transactions between entities or businesses under common control. Therefore they are within the scope of the Interpretation.

BC15 Some commentators on D23 were concerned about situations in which an entity distributes some but not all of its ownership interests in a subsidiary and retains control. They believed that the proposed accounting for the distribution of ownership interests representing a non-controlling interest in accordance with D23 was inconsistent with the requirements of IAS 27 (as amended in 2008). That IFRS requires changes in a parent's ownership interest in a subsidiary that do not result in a loss of control to be accounted for as equity transactions. The IFRIC had not intended the Interpretation to apply to such transactions so did not believe it conflicted with the requirements of IAS 27. As a result of the concerns expressed, the IFRIC amended the Interpretation to make this clear.

BC16 Some commentators on D23 were also concerned about situations in which a subsidiary with a non-controlling interest distributes assets to both the parent and the non-controlling interests. They questioned why only the distribution to the controlling entity is excluded from the scope of the Interpretation. The IFRIC noted that when the parent controls the subsidiary before and after the transaction, the entire transaction (including the distribution to the non-controlling interest) is not within the scope of the Interpretation and is accounted for in accordance with IAS 27.

BC17 Distributions to owners may involve significant portions of an entity's operations. In such circumstances, sometimes referred to as split-off, some commentators on D23 were concerned that it would be difficult to determine which of the surviving entities had made the distribution. They thought that it might be possible for each surviving entity to recognise the distribution of

---

1 The consolidation guidance was removed from IAS 27 and the Standard was renamed *Separate Financial Statements* by IFRS 10 *Consolidated Financial Statements* issued in May 2011. The accounting requirements for transactions between owners did not change.

the other. The IFRIC agreed with commentators that identifying the distributing entity might require judgement in some circumstances. However, the IFRIC concluded that the distribution could be recognised in only one entity's financial statements.

When to recognise a dividend payable (paragraph 10) and amendment to IAS 10

BC18   D23 did not address when an entity should recognise a liability for a dividend payable and some respondents asked the IFRIC to clarify this issue. The IFRIC noted that in IAS 10 *Events after the Reporting Period* paragraph 13 states that 'If dividends are declared (ie the dividends are appropriately authorised and no longer at the discretion of the entity) after the reporting period but before the financial statements are authorised for issue, the dividends are not recognised as a liability at the end of the reporting period because no obligation exists at that time.'

BC19   Some commentators stated that in many jurisdictions a commonly held view is that the entity has discretion until the shareholders approve the dividend. Therefore, constituents holding this view believe a conflict exists between 'declared' and the explanatory phrase in the brackets in IAS 10 paragraph 13. This is especially true when the sentence is interpreted as 'declared by *management but before the shareholders' approval*'. The IFRIC concluded that the point at which a dividend is appropriately authorised and no longer at the discretion of the entity will vary by jurisdiction.

BC20   Therefore, as a consequence of this Interpretation the IFRIC decided to recommend that the Board amend IAS 10 to remove the perceived conflict in paragraph 13. The IFRIC also noted that the principle on when to recognise a dividend was in the wrong place within the IASB's authoritative documents. The Board agreed with the IFRIC's conclusions and amended IAS 10 as part of its approval of the Interpretation. The Board confirmed that this Interpretation had not changed the principle on when to recognise a dividend payable; however, the principle was moved from IAS 10 into the Interpretation and clarified but without changing the principle.

How should an entity measure a dividend payable? (paragraphs 11–13)

BC21   IFRSs do not provide guidance on how an entity should measure distributions to owners. However, the IFRIC noted that a number of IFRSs address how a liability should be measured. Although IFRSs do not specifically address how an entity should measure a dividend payable, the IFRIC decided that it could identify potentially relevant IFRSs and apply their principles to determine the appropriate measurement basis.

Which IFRSs are relevant to the measurement of a dividend payable?

BC22   The IFRIC considered all IFRSs that prescribe the accounting for a liability. Of those, the IFRIC concluded that IAS 37 *Provisions, Contingent Assets and Contingent Liabilities* and IAS 39 *Financial Instruments: Recognition and Measurement*[2] were the most likely to be relevant. The IFRIC concluded that other IFRSs were not applicable because most of them addressed only liabilities arising from exchange transactions and some of them were clearly not relevant (eg IAS 12 *Income Taxes*). As mentioned above, the Interpretation addresses only non-reciprocal distributions of assets by an entity to its owners.

BC23   Given that all types of distributions have the purpose of distributing assets to owners, the IFRIC decided that all dividends payable should be measured the same way, regardless of the types of assets to be distributed. This also ensures that all dividends payable are measured consistently.

BC24   Some believed that IAS 39 was the appropriate IFRS to be used to measure dividends payable. They believed that, once an entity declared a distribution to its owners, it had a contractual obligation to distribute the assets to its owners. However, IAS 39 would not cover dividends payable if they were considered to be non-contractual obligations. In addition, IAS 39 covers some but not all obligations that require an entity to deliver non-cash assets to another entity. It does not cover a liability to distribute non-financial assets to owners. The IFRIC therefore concluded that it was not appropriate to conclude that all dividends payable should be within the scope of IAS 39.

BC25   The IFRIC then considered IAS 37, which is generally applied in practice to determine the accounting for liabilities other than those arising from executory contracts and those addressed by other IFRSs. IAS 37 requires an entity to measure a liability on the basis of the best estimate of the expenditure required to settle the present obligation at the end of the reporting period. Consequently, in D23 the IFRIC decided that it was appropriate to apply the principles in IAS 37 to all dividends payable (regardless of the types of assets to be distributed). The IFRIC decided that to apply IAS 37 to measure a liability for an obligation to distribute non-cash assets to owners, an entity should consider the fair value of the assets to be distributed. The fair value of the assets to be distributed is clearly relevant no matter which approach in IAS 37 is taken to determine the best estimate of the expenditure required to settle the liability.

BC26   However, in response to comments received on D23, the IFRIC reconsidered whether the Interpretation should specify that all dividends payable should be measured in accordance with IAS 37. The IFRIC noted that many respondents were concerned that D23 might imply that the measurement attribute in IAS 37 should always be interpreted to be fair value. This was not the intention of D23 as that question is part of the Board's project to amend IAS 37. In addition, many respondents were not certain whether measuring the dividend payable 'by reference to' the fair value of the assets to be

---

2   IFRS 9 *Financial Instruments* replaced IAS 39. IFRS 9 applies to all items that were previously within the scope of IAS 39.

distributed required measurement at their fair value or at some other amount.

BC27   Therefore, the IFRIC decided to modify the proposal in D23 to require the dividend payable to be measured at the fair value of the assets to be distributed, without linking to any individual standard its conclusion that fair value is the most relevant measurement attribute. The IFRIC also noted that if the assets being distributed constituted a business, its fair value could be different from the simple sum of the fair value of the component assets and liabilities (ie it includes the value of goodwill or the identified intangible assets).

Should any exception be made to the principle of measuring a dividend payable at the fair value of the assets to be distributed?

BC28   Some are concerned that the fair value of the assets to be distributed might not be reliably measurable in all cases. They believe that exceptions should be made in the following circumstances:

(a)   An entity distributes an ownership interest of another entity that is not traded in an active market and the fair value of the ownership interest cannot be measured reliably. The IFRIC noted that IAS 39[3] does not permit investments in equity instruments that do not have a quoted market price in an active market[4] and whose fair value cannot be measured reliably to be measured at fair value.

(b)   An entity distributes an intangible asset that is not traded in an active market and therefore would not be permitted to be carried at a revalued amount in accordance with IAS 38 *Intangible Assets*.

BC29   The IFRIC noted that in accordance with IAS 39 paragraphs AG80 and AG81,[5] the fair value of equity instruments that do not have a quoted price in an active market[6] is reliably measurable if:

---

3   IFRS 9 *Financial Instruments* requires all investments in equity instruments to be measured at fair value.

4   IFRS 13 *Fair Value Measurement*, issued in May 2011, defines fair value and contains the requirements for measuring fair value. IFRS 13 defines a Level 1 input as a quoted price in an active market for an identical asset or liability. Level 2 inputs include quoted prices for identical assets or liabilities in markets that are not active. As a result IFRS 9 refers to such equity instruments as 'an equity instrument that does not have a quoted price in an active market for an identical instrument (ie a Level 1 input)'.

5   IFRS 9 *Financial Instruments* deleted paragraphs AG80 and AG81 of IAS 39. IFRS 13 *Fair Value Measurement*, issued in May 2011, defines fair value and contains requirements for measuring fair value. IFRS 13 defines a Level 1 input as a quoted price in an active market for an identical asset or liability. Level 2 inputs include quoted prices for identical assets or liabilities in markets that are not active. As a result IFRS 9 refers to such equity instruments as 'an equity instrument that does not have a quoted price in an active market for an identical instrument (ie a Level 1 input)'.

6   IFRS 13 *Fair Value Measurement*, issued in May 2011, defines fair value and contains requirements for measuring fair value. IFRS 13 defines a Level 1 input as a quoted price in an active market for an identical asset or liability. Level 2 inputs include quoted prices for identical assets or liabilities in markets that are not active. As a result IFRS 9 refers to such equity instruments as 'an equity instrument that does not have a quoted price in an active market for an identical instrument (ie a Level 1 input)'.

(a) the variability in the range of reasonable fair value estimates is not significant for that instrument, or

(b) the probabilities of the various estimates within the range can be reasonably assessed and used in estimating fair value.

BC30 The IFRIC noted that, when the management of an entity recommends a distribution of a non-cash asset to its owners, one or both of the conditions for determining a reliable measure of the fair value of equity instruments that do not have a quoted price in an active market is likely to be satisfied. Management would be expected to know the fair value of the asset because management has to ensure that all owners of the entity are informed of the value of the distribution. For this reason, it would be difficult to argue that the fair value of the assets to be distributed cannot be determined reliably.

BC31 In addition, the IFRIC recognised that in some cases the fair value of an asset must be estimated. As mentioned in paragraph 86 of the *Framework for the Preparation and Presentation of Financial Statements*,[7] the use of reasonable estimates is an essential part of the preparation of financial statements and does not undermine their reliability.

BC32 The IFRIC noted that a reason why IAS 38 and IAS 39[8] require some assets to be measured using a historical cost basis is cost-benefit considerations. The cost of determining the fair value of an asset not traded in an active market at the end of each reporting period could outweigh the benefits. However, because an entity would be required to determine the fair value of the assets to be distributed only once at the time of distribution, the IFRIC concluded that the benefit (ie informing users of the financial statements of the value of the assets distributed) outweighs the cost of determining the fair value of the assets.

BC33 Furthermore, the IFRIC noted that dividend income, regardless of whether it is in the form of cash or non-cash assets, is within the scope of IAS 18 *Revenue*[9] and is required to be measured at the fair value of the consideration received. Although the Interpretation does not address the accounting by the recipient of the non-cash distribution, the IFRIC concluded that the Interpretation did not impose a more onerous requirement on the entity that makes the distribution than IFRSs have already imposed on the recipient of the distribution.

BC34 For the reasons described in paragraphs BC28–BC33, the IFRIC concluded that no exceptions should be made to the requirement that the fair value of the asset to be distributed should be used in measuring a dividend payable.

---

7 References to the *Framework* in this Basis for Conclusions are to the IASC's *Framework for the Preparation and Presentation of Financial Statements*, adopted by the Board in 2001 and in effect when the Interpretation was developed.

8 IFRS 9 *Financial Instruments* eliminated the requirement in IAS 39 for some assets to be measured using a historical cost basis.

9 IFRS 15 *Revenue from Contracts with Customers*, issued in May 2014, replaced IAS 18 *Revenue*. IFRS 15 does not address dividends. Dividends should be accounted for in accordance with IFRS 9, or IAS 39 if applicable.

Whether an entity should remeasure the dividend payable (paragraph 13)

BC35   The IFRIC noted that paragraph 59 of IAS 37 requires an entity to review the carrying amount of a liability at the end of each reporting period and to adjust the carrying amount to reflect the current best estimate of the liability. Other IFRSs such as IAS 19 *Employee Benefits* similarly require liabilities that are based on estimates to be adjusted each reporting period. The IFRIC therefore decided that the entity should review and adjust the carrying amount of the dividend payable to reflect its current best estimate of the fair value of the assets to be distributed at the end of each reporting period and at the date of settlement.

BC36   The IFRIC concluded that, because any adjustments to the best estimate of the dividend payable reflect changes in the estimated value of the distribution, they should be recognised as adjustments to the amount of the distribution. In accordance with IAS 1 *Presentation of Financial Statements* (as revised in 2007), distributions to owners are required to be recognised directly in the statement of changes in equity. Similarly, adjustments to the amount of the distribution are also recognised directly in the statement of changes in equity.

BC37   Some commentators argued that the changes in the estimated value of the distribution should be recognised in profit or loss because changes in liabilities meet the definition of income or expenses in the *Framework*. However, the IFRIC decided that the gain or loss on the assets to be distributed should be recognised in profit or loss when the dividend payable is settled. This is consistent with other IFRSs (IAS 16, IAS 38, IAS 39[10]) that require an entity to recognise in profit or loss any gain or loss arising from derecognition of an asset. The IFRIC concluded that the changes in the dividend payable before settlement related to changes in the estimate of the distribution and should be accounted for in equity (ie adjustments to the amount of the distribution) until settlement of the dividend payable.

When the entity settles the dividend payable, how should it account for any difference between the carrying amount of the assets distributed and the carrying amount of the dividend payable? (paragraph 14)

BC38   When an entity distributes the assets to its owners, it derecognises both the assets distributed and the dividend payable.

BC39   The IFRIC noted that, at the time of settlement, the carrying amount of the assets distributed would not normally be greater than the carrying amount of the dividend payable because of the recognition of impairment losses required by other applicable standards. For example, paragraph 59 of IAS 36 *Impairment of Assets* requires an entity to recognise an impairment loss in profit or loss when the recoverable amount of an asset is less than its carrying amount. The recoverable amount of an asset is the higher of its fair value less costs to sell and its value in use in accordance with paragraph 6 of IAS 36. When an entity

---

10   IFRS 9 *Financial Instruments* replaced IAS 39. IFRS 9 applies to all items that were previously within the scope of IAS 39.

has an obligation to distribute the asset to its owners in the near future, it would not seem appropriate to measure an impairment loss using the asset's value in use. Furthermore, IFRS 5 requires an entity to measure an asset held for sale at the lower of its carrying amount and its fair value less costs to sell. Consequently, the IFRIC concluded that when an entity derecognises the dividend payable and the asset distributed, any difference will always be a credit balance (referred to below as the credit balance).

BC40 In determining how the credit balance should be accounted for, the IFRIC first considered whether it should be recognised as an owner change in equity.

BC41 The IFRIC acknowledged that an asset distribution was a transaction between an entity and its owners. The IFRIC also observed that distributions to owners are recognised as owner changes in equity in accordance with IAS 1 (as revised in 2007). However, the IFRIC noted that the credit balance did not arise from the distribution transaction. Rather, it represented the cumulative unrecognised gain associated with the asset. It reflects the performance of the entity during the period the asset was held until it was distributed.

BC42 Some might argue that, since an asset distribution does not result in the owners of an entity losing the future economic benefits of the asset, the credit balance should be recognised directly in equity. This view would be based upon the proprietary perspective in which the reporting entity does not have substance of its own separate from that of its owners. However, the IFRIC noted that the *Framework* requires an entity to consider the effect of a transaction from the perspective of the entity for which the financial statements are prepared. Under the entity perspective, the reporting entity has substance of its own, separate from that of its owners. In addition, when there is more than one class of equity instruments, the argument that all owners of an entity have effectively the same interest in the asset would not be valid.

BC43 For the reasons described in paragraphs BC41 and BC42, the IFRIC concluded that the credit balance should not be recognised as an owner change in equity.

BC44 The IFRIC noted that, as explained in the Basis for Conclusions on IAS 1, the Board explicitly prohibited any income or expenses (ie non-owner changes in equity) from being recognised directly in the statement of changes in equity. Any such income or expenses must be recognised as items of comprehensive income first.

BC45 The statement of comprehensive income in accordance with IAS 1 includes two components: items of profit or loss, and items of other comprehensive income. The IFRIC therefore discussed whether the credit balance should be recognised in profit or loss or in other comprehensive income.

BC46 IAS 1 does not provide criteria for when an item should be recognised in profit or loss. However, paragraph 88 of IAS 1 states: 'An entity shall recognise all items of income and expense in a period in profit or loss unless an IFRS requires or permits otherwise.'

BC47   The IFRIC considered the circumstances in which IFRSs require items of income and expense to be recognised as items of other comprehensive income, mainly as follows:

(a)   some actuarial gains or losses arising from remeasuring defined benefit liabilities provided that specific criteria set out in IAS 19 are met.

(b)   a revaluation surplus arising from revaluation of an item of property, plant and equipment in accordance with IAS 16 or revaluation of an intangible asset in accordance with IAS 38.

(c)   an exchange difference arising from the translation of the results and financial positions of an entity from its functional currency into a presentation currency in accordance with IAS 21 *The Effects of Changes in Foreign Exchange Rates*.

(d)   an exchange difference arising from the translation of the results and financial position of a foreign operation into a presentation currency of a reporting entity for consolidation purposes in accordance with IAS 21.

(e)   a change in the fair value of an available-for-sale[11] investment in accordance with IAS 39.

(f)   a change in the fair value of a hedging instrument qualifying for cash flow hedge accounting in accordance with IAS 39.[12]

BC48   The IFRIC concluded that the requirement in IAS 1 prevents any of these items from being applied by analogy to the credit balance. In addition, the IFRIC noted that, with the exception of the items described in paragraph BC47(a)–(c), the applicable IFRSs require the items of income and expenses listed in paragraph BC47 to be reclassified to profit or loss when the related assets or liabilities are derecognised. Those items of income and expenses are recognised as items of other comprehensive income when incurred, deferred in equity until the related assets are disposed of (or the related liabilities are settled), and reclassified to profit or loss at that time.

BC49   The IFRIC noted that, when the dividend payable is settled, the asset distributed is also derecognised. Therefore, given the existing requirements in IFRSs, even if the credit balance were recognised as an item of other comprehensive income, it would have to be reclassified to profit or loss immediately. As a result, the credit balance would appear three times in the statement of comprehensive income — once recognised as an item of other comprehensive income, once reclassified out of other comprehensive income to profit or loss and once recognised as an item of profit or loss as a result of the reclassification. The IFRIC concluded that such a presentation does not faithfully reflect what has occurred. In addition, users of financial statements were likely to be confused by such a presentation.

---

11   IFRS 9 *Financial Instruments* eliminated the category of available-for-sale financial assets.

12   IFRS 9 *Financial Instruments* replaced the hedge accounting requirements in IAS 39.

BC50   Moreover, when an entity distributes its assets to its owners, it loses the future economic benefit associated with the assets distributed and derecognises those assets. Such a consequence is, in general, similar to that of a disposal of an asset. IFRSs (eg IAS 16, IAS 38, IAS 39[13] and IFRS 5) require an entity to recognise in profit or loss any gain or loss arising from the derecognition of an asset. IFRSs also require such a gain or loss to be recognised when the asset is derecognised. As mentioned in paragraph BC42, the *Framework* requires an entity to consider the effect of a transaction from the perspective of an entity for which the financial statements are prepared. For these reasons, the IFRIC concluded that the credit balance and gains or losses on derecognition of an asset should be accounted for in the same way.

BC51   Furthermore, paragraph 92 of the *Framework* states: 'Income is recognised in the income statement when an increase in future economic benefits related to an increase in an asset or *a decrease of a liability* has arisen that can be measured reliably' (emphasis added). At the time of the settlement of a dividend payable, there is clearly a decrease in a liability. Therefore, the credit balance should be recognised in profit or loss in accordance with paragraph 92 of the *Framework*. Some might argue that the entity does not receive any additional economic benefits when it distributes the assets to its owners. As mentioned in paragraph BC41, the credit balance does not represent any additional economic benefits to the entity. Instead, it represents the unrecognised economic benefits that the entity obtained while it held the assets.

BC52   The IFRIC also noted that paragraph 55 of the *Framework* states: 'The future economic benefits embodied in an asset may flow to the entity in a number of ways. For example, an asset may be: (a) used singly or in combination with other assets in the production of goods or services to be sold by the entity; (b) exchanged for other assets; (c) used to settle a liability; or (d) *distributed to the owners of the entity* [emphasis added].'

BC53   In the light of these requirements, in D23 the IFRIC concluded that the credit balance should be recognised in profit or loss. This treatment would give rise to the same accounting results regardless of whether an entity distributes non-cash assets to its owners, or sells the non-cash assets first and distributes the cash received to its owners. Most commentators on D23 supported the IFRIC's conclusion and its basis.

BC54   Some IFRIC members believed that it would be more appropriate to treat the distribution as a single transaction with owners and therefore recognise the credit balance directly in equity. This alternative view was included in D23 and comments were specifically invited. However, this view was not supported by commentators. To be recognised directly in equity, the credit balance must be considered an owner change in equity in accordance with IAS 1. The IFRIC decided that the credit balance does not arise from the distribution transaction. Rather, it represents the increase in value of the assets. The increase in the value of the asset does not meet the definition of an owner

---

13 IFRS 9 *Financial Instruments* replaced IAS 39. IFRS 9 applies to all items that were previously within the scope of IAS 39.

change in equity in accordance with IAS 1. Rather, it meets the definition of income and should be recognised in profit and loss.

BC55 The IFRIC recognised respondents' concerns about the potential 'accounting mismatch' in equity resulting from measuring the assets to be distributed at carrying amount and measuring the dividend payable at fair value. Consequently, the IFRIC considered whether it should recommend that the Board amend IFRS 5 to require the assets to be distributed to be measured at fair value.

BC56 In general, IFRSs permit remeasurement of assets only as the result of a transaction or an impairment. The exceptions are situations in which the IFRSs prescribe current measures on an ongoing basis as in IASs 39 and 41 *Agriculture*, or permit them as accounting policy choices as in IASs 16, 38 and 40 *Investment Property*. As a result of its redeliberations, the IFRIC concluded that there was no support in IFRSs for requiring a remeasurement of the assets because of a decision to distribute them. The IFRIC noted that the mismatch concerned arises only with respect to assets that are not carried at fair value already. The IFRIC also noted that the accounting mismatch is the inevitable consequence of IFRSs using different measurement attributes at different times with different triggers for the remeasurement of different assets and liabilities.

BC57 If a business is to be distributed, the fair value means the fair value of the business to be distributed. Therefore, it includes goodwill and intangible assets. However, internally generated goodwill is not permitted to be recognised as an asset (paragraph 48 of IAS 38). Internally generated brands, mastheads, publishing titles, customer lists and items similar in substance are not permitted to be recognised as intangible assets (paragraph 63 of IAS 38). In accordance with IAS 38, the carrying amounts of internally generated intangible assets are generally restricted to the sum of expenditure incurred by an entity. Consequently, a requirement to remeasure an asset that is a business would contradict the relevant requirements in IAS 38.

BC58 Furthermore, in addition to the lack of consistency with other IFRSs, changing IFRS 5 this way (ie to require an asset held for distribution to owners to be remeasured at fair value) would create internal inconsistency within IFRS 5. There would be no reasonable rationale to explain why IFRS 5 could require assets that are to be sold to be carried at the lower of fair value less costs to sell and carrying value but assets to be distributed to owners to be carried at fair value. The IFRIC also noted that this 'mismatch' would arise only in the normally short period between when the dividend payable is recognised and when it is settled. The length of this period would often be within the control of management. Therefore, the IFRIC decided not to recommend that the Board amend IFRS 5 to require assets that are to be distributed to be measured at fair value.

Amendment to IFRS 5

BC59   IFRS 5 requires an entity to classify a non-current asset (or disposal group) as held for sale if its carrying amount will be recovered principally through a sale transaction rather than through continuing use. IFRS 5 also sets out presentation and disclosure requirements for a discontinued operation.

BC60   When an entity has an obligation to distribute assets to its owners, the carrying amount of the assets will no longer be recovered principally through continuing use. The IFRIC decided that the information required by IFRS 5 is important to users of financial statements regardless of the form of a transaction. Therefore, the IFRIC concluded that the requirements in IFRS 5 applicable to non-current assets (or disposal groups) classified as held for sale and to discontinued operations should also be applied to assets (or disposal groups) held for distribution to owners.

BC61   However, the IFRIC concluded that requiring an entity to apply IFRS 5 to non-current assets (disposal groups) held for distribution to owners would require amendments to IFRS 5. This is because, in the IFRIC's view, IFRS 5 at present applies only to non-current assets (disposal groups) held for sale.

BC62   The Board discussed the IFRIC's proposal at its meeting in December 2007. The Board agreed with the IFRIC's conclusion that IFRS 5 should be amended to apply to non-current assets held for distribution to owners as well as to assets held for sale. However, the Board noted that IFRS 5 requires an entity to classify a non-current asset as held for sale when the sale is highly probable and the entity is *committed* to a plan to sell (emphasis added). Consequently, the Board directed the IFRIC to invite comments on the following questions:

(a)   Should an entity apply IFRS 5 when it is committed to make a distribution or when it has an obligation to distribute the assets concerned?

(b)   Is there a difference between those dates?

(c)   If respondents believe that there is a difference between the dates and that an entity should apply IFRS 5 at the commitment date, what is the difference? What indicators should be included in IFRS 5 to help an entity to determine that date?

BC63   On the basis of the comments received, the IFRIC noted that, in many jurisdictions, shareholders' approval is required to make a distribution. Therefore, in such jurisdictions there could be a difference between the commitment date (ie the date when management is committed to the dividend) and the obligation date (ie the date when the dividend is approved by the shareholders). On the other hand, some commentators think that, when a distribution requires shareholders' approval, the entity cannot be committed until that approval is obtained: in that case, there would be no difference between two dates.

BC64   The IFRIC concluded that IFRS 5 should be applied at the commitment date at which time the assets must be available for immediate distribution in their present condition and the distribution must be *highly probable*. For the distribution to be highly probable, it should meet essentially the same conditions required for assets held for sale. Further, the IFRIC concluded that the probability of shareholders' approval (if required in the jurisdiction) should be considered as part of the assessment of whether the distribution is highly probable. The IFRIC noted that shareholder approval is also required for the sale of assets in some jurisdictions and concluded that similar consideration of the probability of such approval should be required for assets held for sale.

BC65   The Board agreed with the IFRIC's conclusions and amended IFRS 5 as part of its approval of the Interpretation.

Summary of main changes from the draft Interpretation

BC66   The main changes from the IFRIC's proposals in D23 are as follows:

(a)   Paragraphs 3–8 were modified to clarify the scope of the Interpretation.

(b)   Paragraph 10 clarifies when to recognise a dividend payable.

(c)   Paragraphs 11–13 were modified to require the dividend payable to be measured at the fair value of the assets to be distributed without linking the IFRIC's conclusion that fair value is the most relevant measurement attribute to any individual standard.

(d)   Illustrative examples were expanded to set out clearly the scope of the Interpretation.

(e)   The Interpretation includes the amendments to IFRS 5 and IAS 10.

(f)   The Basis for Conclusions was changed to set out more clearly the reasons for the IFRIC's conclusions.

Documents published to accompany

IFRIC 19

Extinguishing Financial Liabilities with Equity Instruments

The text of the unaccompanied Interpretation, IFRIC 19, is contained in Part A of this edition. Its effective date when issued was 1 July 2010. This part presents the following document:

BASIS FOR CONCLUSIONS

Basis for Conclusions on
IFRIC Interpretation 19 *Extinguishing Financial Liabilities with Equity Instruments*

This Basis for Conclusions accompanies, but is not part of, IFRIC 19.

Introduction

BC1   This Basis for Conclusions summarises the IFRIC's considerations in reaching its consensus. Individual IFRIC members gave greater weight to some factors than to others.

BC2   The IFRIC received a request for guidance on the application of IAS 39 *Financial Instruments: Recognition and Measurement*[1] and IAS 32 *Financial Instruments: Presentation* when an entity issues its own equity instruments to extinguish all or part of a financial liability. The question is how the entity should recognise the equity instruments issued.

BC3   The IFRIC noted that lenders manage loans to entities in financial difficulty in a variety of ways including one or more of the following:

(a)   selling the loans in the market to other investors/lenders;

(b)   renegotiating the terms of the loan (eg extension of the maturity date or lower interest payments); or

(c)   accepting the creditor's equity instruments in full or partial settlement of the liability (sometimes referred to as a 'debt for equity swap').

BC4   The IFRIC was informed that there was diversity in practice in how entities measure the equity instruments issued in full or partial settlement of a financial liability following renegotiation of the terms of the liability. Some recognise the equity instruments at the carrying amount of the financial liability and do not recognise any gain or loss in profit or loss. Others recognise the equity instruments at the fair value of either the liability extinguished or the equity instruments issued and recognise a difference between that amount and the carrying amount of the financial liability in profit or loss.

BC5   In August 2009 the IFRIC published draft Interpretation D25 *Extinguishing Financial Liabilities with Equity Instruments* for public comment. It received 33 comment letters in response to the proposals.

Scope

BC6   The IFRIC concluded that its Interpretation should address only the accounting by an entity when the terms of a financial liability are renegotiated and result in the entity issuing equity instruments to a creditor of the entity to extinguish part or all of the liability. It does not address the

---

1   IFRS 9 *Financial Instruments* replaced IAS 39. IFRS 9 applies to all items that were previously within the scope of IAS 39.

accounting by the creditor because other IFRSs already set out the relevant requirements.

BC7   The IFRIC considered whether to provide guidance on transactions in which the creditor is also a direct or indirect shareholder and is acting in its capacity as an existing direct or indirect shareholder. The IFRIC concluded that the Interpretation should not address such transactions. It noted that determining whether the issue of equity instruments to extinguish a financial liability in such situations is considered a transaction with an owner in its capacity as an owner would be a matter of judgement depending on the facts and circumstances.

BC8   In its redeliberations, the IFRIC clarified that transactions when the creditor and the entity are controlled by the same party or parties before and after the transaction are outside the scope of the Interpretation when the substance of the transaction includes an equity distribution by, or contribution to, the entity. The IFRIC acknowledged that the allocation of consideration between the extinguishment of all or part of a financial liability and the equity distribution or contribution components may not always be reliably measured.

BC9   Some respondents questioned whether the Interpretation should be applied to transactions when the extinguishment of the financial liability by issuing equity shares is in accordance with the original terms of the liability. In its redeliberations the IFRIC decided that these transactions should be excluded from the scope of the Interpretation, noting that IAS 32 includes specific guidance on those financial instruments.

Are an entity's equity instruments 'consideration paid'?

BC10   The IFRIC noted that IFRSs do not contain specific guidance on the measurement of an entity's equity instruments issued to extinguish all or part of a financial liability. Paragraph 41 of IAS 39[2] requires an entity to recognise in profit or loss the difference between the carrying amount of the financial liability extinguished and the consideration paid. That paragraph describes 'consideration paid' as including non-cash assets transferred, or liabilities assumed, and does not specifically mention equity instruments issued. Consequently, some are of the view that equity instruments are not 'consideration paid'.

BC11   Holders of this view believe that, because IFRSs are generally silent on how to measure equity instruments on initial recognition (see paragraph BC15), a variety of practices has developed. One such practice is to recognise the equity instruments issued at the carrying amount of the financial liability extinguished.

---

2   IFRS 9 *Financial Instruments* replaced IAS 39. IFRS 9 applies to all items that were previously within the scope of IAS 39.

BC12   However, the IFRIC observed that both IFRS 2 *Share-based Payment* and IFRS 3 *Business Combinations* make it clear that equity instruments are used as consideration to acquire goods and services as well as to obtain control of businesses.

BC13   The IFRIC also observed that the issue of equity instruments to extinguish a financial liability could be analysed as consisting of two transactions — first, the issue of new equity instruments to the creditor for cash and second, the creditor accepting payment of that amount of cash to extinguish the financial liability.

BC14   As a result of its analysis, the IFRIC concluded that the equity instruments issued to extinguish a financial liability are 'consideration paid' in accordance with paragraph 41 of IAS 39.

How should the equity instruments be measured?

BC15   The IFRIC observed that although IFRSs do not contain a general principle for the initial recognition and measurement of equity instruments, guidance on specific transactions exists, including:

(a)   *initial recognition of compound instruments* (IAS 32). The amount allocated to the equity component is the residual after deducting the fair value of the financial liability component from the fair value of the entire compound instrument.

(b)   *cost of equity transactions and own equity instruments ('treasury shares') acquired and reissued or cancelled* (IAS 32). No gain or loss is recognised in profit or loss on the purchase, sale, issue or cancellation of an entity's own equity instruments. These are transactions with an entity's owners in their capacity as owners.

(c)   *equity instruments issued in share-based payment transactions* (IFRS 2). For equity-settled share-based payment transactions, the entity measures the goods or services received, and the corresponding increase in equity, directly, at the fair value of the goods or services received, unless that fair value cannot be estimated reliably. If the entity cannot estimate reliably the fair value of the goods or services received (eg transactions with employees), the entity measures their value, and the corresponding increase in equity, indirectly, by reference to the fair value of the equity instruments granted.

(d)   *consideration transferred in business combinations* (IFRS 3). The total consideration transferred in a business combination is measured at fair value. It includes the acquisition-date fair values of any equity interests issued by the acquirer.

BC16   The IFRIC noted that the general principle of IFRSs is that equity is a residual and should be measured initially by reference to changes in assets and liabilities (the *Framework*[3] and IFRS 2). IFRS 2 is clear that when goods or services are received in return for the issue of equity instruments, the increase in equity is measured directly at the fair value of the goods or services received.

BC17   The IFRIC decided that the same principles should apply when equity instruments are issued to extinguish financial liabilities. However, the IFRIC was concerned that entities might encounter practical difficulties in measuring the fair value of both the equity instruments issued and the financial liability, particularly when the entity is in financial difficulty. Therefore, the IFRIC decided in D25 that equity instruments issued to extinguish a financial liability should be measured initially at the fair value of the equity instruments issued or the fair value of the liability extinguished, whichever is more reliably determinable.

BC18   However, in response to comments received on D25, the IFRIC reconsidered whether the entity should initially measure equity instruments issued to a creditor to extinguish all or part of a financial liability at the fair value of the equity instruments issued or the fair value of the liability extinguished. The IFRIC noted that many respondents proposed that a preferred measurement basis should be determined to avoid an 'accounting choice' developing in practice, acknowledging that both measurement approaches would need to be used to identify which was more reliably determinable.

BC19   Therefore the IFRIC decided to modify the proposal in D25 and identify a preferred measurement basis. In identifying this preferred measurement basis, the IFRIC noted that many respondents considered that the principles in IFRS 2 and the *Framework* referred to in paragraph BC16 support a measurement based on the fair value of the liability extinguished.

BC20   However, some respondents argued that the fair value of the equity issued should be the proposed measurement basis. They pointed out that this approach would be consistent with the consensus that the issue of an entity's equity instruments is consideration paid in accordance with paragraph 41 of IAS 39.[4] They also argued that the fair value of the equity issued best reflects the total amount of consideration paid in the transaction, which may include a premium that the creditor requires to renegotiate the terms of the financial liability.

BC21   The IFRIC considered that the fair value of the equity issued should be the proposed measurement basis for the reasons described in paragraph BC20. Consequently the IFRIC concluded that an entity should initially measure equity instruments issued to a creditor to extinguish all or part of a financial liability at the fair value of the equity instruments issued, unless that fair

---

3   References to the *Framework* in this Basis for Conclusions are to the IASC's *Framework for the Preparation and Presentation of Financial Statements*, adopted by the Board in 2001 and in effect when the Interpretation was developed.

4   IFRS 9 *Financial Instruments* replaced IAS 39. IFRS 9 applies to all items that were previously within the scope of IAS 39.

value cannot be reliably measured. If the fair value of the equity instruments issued cannot be reliably measured then these equity instruments should initially be measured to reflect the fair value of the liability extinguished.

BC22　In redeliberations, the IFRIC noted that these transactions often take place in situations when the terms of the financial liability are breached and the liability becomes repayable on demand. The IFRIC agreed with comments received that paragraph 49 of IAS 39 is not applied in measuring the fair value of all or part of a financial liability extinguished in these situations.[5] This is because the extinguishment transaction suggests that the demand feature is no longer substantive.

BC23　In response to comments, the IFRIC also clarified that the equity instruments issued should be recognised initially and measured at the date the financial liability (or part of that liability) is extinguished. This is consistent with paragraphs BC341 and BC342 of the Basis for Conclusions on IFRS 3, which discuss the views on whether equity instruments issued as consideration in a business combination should be measured at fair value at the agreement date or acquisition date, concluding that measurement should be at the acquisition date.

How should a difference between the carrying amount of the financial liability and the consideration paid be accounted for?

BC24　In accordance with paragraph 41 of IAS 39,[6] the entity should recognise a gain or loss in profit or loss for any difference between the carrying amount of the financial liability extinguished and the consideration paid. This requirement is consistent with the *Framework*'s discussion of income:

(a)　Income is increases in economic benefits during the accounting period in the form of inflows or enhancements of assets or *decreases of liabilities that result in increases in equity*, other than those relating to contributions from equity participants. (paragraph 70(a)) (emphasis added)

(b)　Gains represent other items that meet the definition of income and may, or may not, arise in the course of the ordinary activities of an entity. Gains represent increases in economic benefits ... (paragraph 75)

(c)　Income may also result from the settlement of liabilities. For example, an entity may provide goods and services to a lender in settlement of an obligation to repay an outstanding loan. (paragraph 77)

5　IFRS 9 *Financial Instruments* replaced IAS 39. Paragraph 49 of IAS 39 was ultimately relocated to paragraph 47 of IFRS 13 *Fair Value Measurement*. Paragraph BC22 refers to matters relevant when IFRIC 19 was issued.

6　IFRS 9 *Financial Instruments* replaced IAS 39. IFRS 9 applies to all items that were previously within the scope of IAS 39.

Full extinguishment

BC25 The IFRIC noted that, as discussed in paragraph BC13, a transaction in which an entity issues equity instruments to extinguish a liability can be analysed as first, the issue of new equity instruments to the creditor for cash and second, the creditor accepting payment of that amount of cash to extinguish the financial liability. Consistently with paragraph BC24, when the creditor accepts cash to extinguish the liability, the entity should recognise a gain or loss in profit or loss.

BC26 Similarly, the IFRIC noted that, in accordance with IAS 32, when an entity amends the terms of a convertible instrument to induce early conversion, the entity recognises in profit or loss the fair value of any additional consideration paid to the holder. Thus, the IFRIC concluded that when an entity settles an instrument by issuing its own equity instruments and that settlement is not in accordance with the original terms of the financial liability, the entity should recognise a gain or loss in profit or loss.

BC27 As a result of its conclusions, the IFRIC decided that the entity should recognise a gain or loss in profit or loss. This gain or loss is equal to the difference between the carrying amount of the financial liability and the fair value of the equity instruments issued, or fair value of the liability extinguished if the fair value of the equity instruments issued cannot be reliably measured.

Partial extinguishment

BC28 The IFRIC also observed that the restructuring of a financial liability can involve both the partial settlement of the liability by the issue of equity instruments to the creditor and the modification of the terms of the liability that remains outstanding. Therefore, the IFRIC decided that the Interpretation should also apply to partial extinguishments. In the case of a partial extinguishment, the discussion in paragraphs BC25–BC27 applies to the part of the liability extinguished.

BC29 Many respondents requested clarification of the guidance on partial extinguishment included in D25. During its redeliberations, the IFRIC acknowledged that the issue of an entity's equity shares may reflect consideration paid for both the extinguishment of part of a financial liability and the modification of the terms of the part of the liability that remains outstanding.

BC30 The IFRIC decided that to reflect this, an entity should allocate the consideration paid between the part of the liability extinguished and the part of the liability that remains outstanding. The entity would consider this allocation in determining the profit or loss to be recognised on the part of the liability extinguished and in its assessment of whether the terms of the remaining liability have been substantially modified.

BC31   The IFRIC concluded that providing additional guidance on determining whether the terms of the part of the financial liability that remains outstanding has been substantially modified in accordance with paragraph 40 of IAS 39[7] was outside the scope of the Interpretation.

Presentation

BC32   The IFRIC decided that an entity should disclose the gain or loss on the extinguishment of the financial liability by the issue of equity instruments as a separate line item in profit or loss or in the notes. This requirement is consistent with the *Framework* and the requirements in other IFRSs, for example:

(a)   When gains are recognised in the income statement, they are usually displayed separately because knowledge of them is useful for the purpose of making economic decisions. (paragraph 76 of the *Framework*)

(b)   An entity shall present additional line items, headings and subtotals in the statement of comprehensive income and the separate income statement (if presented), when such presentation is relevant to an understanding of the entity's financial performance. (paragraph 85 of IAS 1 *Presentation of Financial Statements*)

(c)   An entity shall disclose net gains or net losses on financial liabilities either in the statement of comprehensive income or in the notes. (paragraph 20 of IFRS 7 *Financial Instruments: Disclosures*)

Transition

BC33   The IFRIC decided that the Interpretation should be applied retrospectively even though it acknowledged that determining fair values retrospectively may be problematic. The IFRIC noted that IAS 8 *Accounting Policies, Changes in Accounting Estimates and Errors* provides guidance on circumstances in which retrospective application might be impracticable. The IFRIC concluded that it was preferable to require entities that could apply the Interpretation retrospectively to do so, rather than requiring all entities to apply it prospectively to future transactions. However, to simplify transition, the IFRIC also concluded that it should require retrospective application only from the beginning of the earliest comparative period presented because application to earlier periods would result only in a reclassification of amounts within equity.

Summary of main changes from the draft Interpretation

BC34   The main changes from the IFRIC's proposals in D25 are as follows:

(a)   Paragraph 3 was added because the IFRIC identified specific transactions that are outside of the scope of the Interpretation.

---

7   IFRS 9 *Financial Instruments* replaced IAS 39. IFRS 9 applies to all items that were previously within the scope of IAS 39.

(b)   Paragraph 6 was modified to state that measurement should be based on the fair value of the equity instruments issued, unless that fair value cannot be reliably measured.

(c)   Paragraph 7 was added to reflect the modification to paragraph 6. It also clarifies the intention of the IFRIC that in measuring the fair value of a financial liability extinguished that includes a demand feature (eg a demand deposit), paragraph 49 of IAS 39[8] is not applied.

(d)   Paragraph 8 was added, and paragraph 10 was modified, to clarify how the Interpretation should be applied when only part of the financial liability is extinguished by the issue of equity instruments.

(e)   Paragraph 9 was modified to state when the equity instruments issued should be initially measured.

---

8   IFRS 9 *Financial Instruments* replaced IAS 39. Paragraph 49 of IAS 39 was ultimately relocated to paragraph 47 of IFRS 13 *Fair Value Measurement*. Paragraph BC22 refers to matters relevant when IFRIC 19 was issued.

Documents published to accompany

IFRIC 20

Stripping Costs in the Production Phase of a Surface Mine

The text of the unaccompanied Interpretation, IFRIC 20, is contained in Part A of this edition. Its effective date when issued was 1 January 2013. The text of the Accompanying Guidance on IFRIC 20 is contained in Part B of this edition. This part presents the following document:

BASIS FOR CONCLUSIONS

Basis for Conclusions on
IFRIC Interpretation 20 *Stripping Costs in the Production Phase of a Surface Mine*

This Basis for Conclusions accompanies, but is not part of, IFRIC 20.

Introduction

BC1   This Basis for Conclusions summarises the IFRS Interpretations Committee's considerations in reaching its consensus. Individual Committee members gave greater weight to some factors than to others.

Background

BC2   The Committee received a request to issue guidance on the accounting for waste removal ('stripping') costs incurred in the production phase of a surface mine ('production stripping costs'). Accounting for production stripping costs is challenging, because the costs that are incurred may benefit both future and current period production, and there is no specific guidance in IFRSs that addresses this issue.

BC3   Consequently, there is diversity in practice in accounting for production stripping costs—some entities recognise production stripping costs as an expense (a cost of production), some entities capitalise some or all production stripping costs on the basis of a 'life-of-mine ratio' calculation or some similar basis, and some capitalise the costs associated with specific betterments. The Committee decided to develop an Interpretation in response to this diversity in practice.

Scope

BC4   This Interpretation gives guidance on the accounting for stripping costs incurred in the production phase of a surface mine. In developing the Interpretation, the Committee decided to focus only on surface mining activities and not on underground mining activities. This Interpretation applies to the activity of surface mining and therefore to all types of natural resources that are extracted using this process. Where this Interpretation refers to 'extraction of mineral ore', it applies equally to surface mining activities used to extract other natural resources that may not be embedded in an ore deposit but are nevertheless extracted using a surface mining activity, for example coal. However, the Committee decided not to address oil and natural gas extraction, including the question of whether oil sands extraction was a surface mining activity, when it determined the scope of this Interpretation.

BC5   The Committee decided not to include stripping costs incurred during the development phase of a surface mine because there is no significant diversity in practice in accounting for such costs. During the development phase of a surface mine (before production begins), stripping costs are usually capitalised as part of the depreciable cost of building, developing and constructing the mine if it is probable that these costs will be recovered through future mining activity. These capitalised costs are depreciated or amortised on a systematic basis, usually by using the units of production method, once production begins.

Consensus

Recognition of production stripping costs as an asset

BC6 The Committee decided that an entity may create two benefits by undertaking stripping activity (and incurring stripping costs). These benefits are the extraction of the ore in the current period and improved access to the ore body for a future period. The result of this is that the activity creates an inventory asset and a non-current asset.

BC7 The asset recognition criteria included in paragraph 9 of this Interpretation are those referred to in paragraph 4.44 of the *Conceptual Framework for Financial Reporting*.[1] An additional criterion is, however, also included in this Interpretation for recognising the stripping activity asset—that the entity can specifically identify the 'component' of the ore body for which access is being improved. All three criteria must be met for the costs to qualify for recognition as an asset. If the criteria are not met, a stripping activity asset will not be recognised.

BC8 'Component' refers to the specific volume of the ore body that is made more accessible by the stripping activity. The identified component of the ore body would typically be a subset of the total ore body of the mine. A mine may have several components, which are identified during the mine planning stage. As well as providing a basis for measuring the costs reliably at recognition stage, identification of components of the ore body is necessary for the subsequent depreciation or amortisation of the stripping activity asset, which will take place as that identified component of the ore body is mined.

BC9 Identifying components of the ore body requires judgement. The Committee understands that an entity's mine plan will provide the information required to allow these judgements to be made with reasonable consistency.

BC10 This Interpretation also states that the stripping cost asset should be recognised as 'part' of an existing asset. 'Part' refers to the addition to, or enhancement of, the existing asset that relates to the stripping activity asset. The Committee took the view that the stripping activity asset was more akin to being a part of an existing asset, rather than being an asset in its own right. The stripping activity asset might add to or improve a variety of existing assets, for example the mine property (land), the mineral deposit itself, an intangible right to extract the ore or an asset that originated in the mine development phase.

---

1 The reference is to the *Conceptual Framework for Financial Reporting*, issued in 2010 and in effect when the Interpretation was developed.

BC11   The Committee decided that it is not necessary for the Interpretation to define whether the benefit created by the stripping activity is tangible or intangible in nature — this will be determined from the nature of the related underlying existing asset.

Initial measurement of the stripping activity asset

BC12   IAS 16 paragraph 16(b) states that the cost of an item of property, plant and equipment includes 'any costs directly attributable to bringing the asset to the location and condition necessary...'. Examples of the types of costs that the Committee would expect to be included as directly attributable overhead costs (paragraph 12 of the Interpretation) would include an allocation of salary costs of the mine supervisor overseeing that component of the mine, and an allocation of rental costs of any equipment that was hired specifically to perform the stripping activity.

BC13   The Committee thought that it was important to be guided by the principle contained in paragraph 21 of IAS 16 when addressing incidental operations in the Interpretation. The Committee is aware that a number of activities are carried out simultaneously in a mine operation, and it thought that it was important for the entity to be aware of what constitutes production stripping activity, and what does not, when considering the measurement of the stripping activity asset. An example of such an incidental operation would be building an access road in the area in which the stripping campaign is taking place.

BC14   The Committee noted that, when inventory is produced at the same time as the stripping activity asset is created, it may be difficult in practice to measure the separate cost of each benefit directly. The Committee agreed that an allocation basis would be needed in order to differentiate between the cost of the inventory produced and the cost of the stripping activity asset.

BC15   In its discussions of the most appropriate allocation basis, the Committee rejected any basis that was based on sales values. The Committee considered that such a basis in the context of stripping costs would be inappropriate because it was not closely linked to the activity taking place. Furthermore, if the current sales price of the relevant mineral was used in determining the allocation basis, the same current sales price would be applied to the volume of the mineral in both the extracted ore and the identified component. Hence the relevant variable would be the volume of mineral in both the extracted ore and the identified component, ie the current sales price would not change the allocation basis. The Committee understood that applying a future sales price basis would involve practical difficulties and that it would be costly in comparison to the benefit that it would provide. From the outreach performed by the staff, the Committee understood that identifying a future sales price for ore that will be mined in the future can be difficult, given the volatility of market prices for many minerals. Further complexities may arise when more than one mineral is present (whether by-products or joint products) when the ore is extracted.

BC16   The Committee decided to require an allocation approach that was based on a relevant production measure, because a production measure was considered to be a good indicator of the nature of the benefits that are generated for the activity taking place in the mine. The production measure basis requires an entity to identify when a level of activity has taken place beyond what would otherwise be expected for the inventory production in the period, and that may have given rise to a future access benefit.

Subsequent measurement of the stripping activity asset

BC17   The Committee decided that the cost of the stripping activity asset should be depreciated or amortised over the expected useful life of the identified component of the ore body that is made more accessible by the activity, on a basis that best reflects the consumption of economic benefits. The units of production method is commonly used, and would be focused only on the identified component of the ore body, the access to which has been improved by the stripping activity. Because the life of the identified component is expected to be only a part of the entire life of the mine, the stripping activity asset will be depreciated or amortised over a shorter period than the life of the mine, unless the stripping activity provides improved access to the whole of the remaining ore body, for example, towards the end of a mine's useful life when the identified component represents the final part of the ore body to be extracted.

BC18   The Committee decided that the principles of this Interpretation would also be applicable to an entity that subsequently accounts for its mine assets at revaluation, although the Committee noted that this method was seldom used. The Committee decided that the subsequent measurement basis of the stripping activity asset should follow that of the existing asset of which it is a part, that is, if the existing asset is measured using a cost basis, then the stripping activity asset would also be measured using a cost basis. The Committee also decided that there was no need for specific impairment guidance to be given and expects that the principles in IAS 36 *Impairment of Assets* would be applied to the existing asset of which the stripping activity asset is a part, and not at the level of the stripping activity asset itself.

Transition

BC19   Because of the complex and lengthy nature of many mining operations, and the past diversity of practice in respect of this issue, the Committee concluded that the cost of applying the change in accounting policy retrospectively would exceed the benefit that would be gained from doing so. The Committee therefore decided that this Interpretation shall require prospective application to production stripping costs incurred on or after the beginning of the earliest period presented.

BC20   The Committee decided to follow the principles in IAS 8 *Accounting Policies, Changes in Accounting Estimates and Errors* on transition. It decided to require recognition of any predecessor stripping asset balances (see paragraph A3) as at the beginning of the earliest period presented, in opening retained earnings at that date, if such balances could not be identified with a remaining component of the ore body that was made more accessible by the stripping activity.

BC21   The Committee noted that any liability balances resulting from prior production stripping activity that existed at the transition date would not be recognised under the principles described in the Interpretation. The Committee understood from the comments received on the draft Interpretation that such balances were uncommon, and therefore did not think that it needed to provide any guidance on recognition of liability balances, because constituents may find it confusing.

Documents published to accompany

IFRIC 21

Levies

The text of the unaccompanied Interpretation, IFRIC 21, is contained in Part A of this edition. Its effective date when issued was 1 January 2014. The text of the Accompanying Guidance on IFRIC 21 is contained in Part B of this edition. This part presents the following document:

BASIS FOR CONCLUSIONS

Basis for Conclusions on
IFRIC Interpretation 21 *Levies*

This Basis for Conclusions accompanies, but is not part of, IFRIC 21.

Introduction

BC1   This Basis for Conclusions summarises the considerations of the IFRS Interpretations Committee (the Interpretations Committee) in reaching its consensus. The Interpretations Committee received a request to clarify whether, under certain circumstances, IFRIC 6 *Liabilities arising from Participating in a Specific Market—Waste Electrical and Electronic Equipment* should be applied by analogy to identify the obligating event that gives rise to the recognition of a liability for other levies imposed by governments on entities. The question relates to when to recognise a liability to pay a levy that is accounted for in accordance with IAS 37 *Provisions, Contingent Liabilities and Contingent Assets*.

BC2   In particular, the request was for the Interpretations Committee to clarify how an entity should account for levies when the calculation for the levies is based on financial data that relates to a period before the period that contains the activity that triggers the payment of the levy. This is the case if, for example, the activity that triggers the payment of the levy, as identified by the legislation, occurs in 20X1 and the calculation of the levy is based on financial data for 20X0 (see Illustrative Example 2).

BC3   The Interpretations Committee was informed that there was diversity in practice in how entities account for the obligation to pay such a levy.

Scope

BC4   One of the questions that was submitted was how to account for levies whose calculation basis uses data such as the gross amount of revenue, assets or liabilities. The Interpretations Committee noted that those levies do not meet the definition of income taxes provided in IAS 12 *Income Taxes* because they are not based on taxable profit. In two Agenda Decisions (published in March 2006 and May 2009), the Interpretations Committee (then called the IFRIC) noted that the term 'taxable profit' implies a notion of a net rather than a gross amount. In those Agenda Decisions, the Interpretations Committee also observed that any taxes that are not within the scope of other Standards (such as IAS 12) are within the scope of IAS 37. The Interpretations Committee further observed that IAS 37 contains a definition of a liability and that a provision is defined in IAS 37 as a liability of uncertain timing or amount. The Interpretations Committee noted that the same recognition requirements should apply to provisions to pay a levy and to liabilities to pay a levy whose timing and amount is certain. Consequently, this Interpretation also addresses the accounting for a liability to pay a levy whose timing and amount is certain.

BC5   The Interpretations Committee noted that IAS 37 does not apply to executory contracts unless they are onerous, so the Interpretations Committee decided that this Interpretation should therefore not apply to executory contracts unless they are onerous.

BC6   The Interpretations Committee decided that, for the purposes of this Interpretation, a levy is an outflow of resources embodying economic benefits that is imposed by governments on entities in accordance with legislation (ie laws and/or regulations), other than those outflows of resources that are within the scope of other Standards (such as income taxes that are within the scope of IAS 12). Amounts that are collected by entities on behalf of governments (such as value added taxes) and remitted to governments are not outflows of resources embodying economic benefits for the entities that collect and remit those amounts. The Interpretations Committee decided to use the definition of the term 'government' provided in IAS 20 *Accounting for Government Grants and Disclosure of Government Assistance* and IAS 24 *Related Party Disclosures*.

BC7   The Interpretations Committee noted that a payment made by an entity for the acquisition of an asset, or for the rendering of services under a contractual agreement with a government, does not meet the definition of a levy. For the purposes of this Interpretation, levies are imposed by governments and therefore do not arise from contractual agreements. Similarly, the Interpretations Committee noted that this Interpretation does not apply to the accounting for trade discounts and volume rebates agreed between a seller and a purchaser under a contractual agreement.

BC8   The Interpretations Committee decided that this Interpretation should not address the accounting for fines and other penalties. Fines and penalties are paid as a consequence of the breach of laws and/or regulations, whereas levies are paid as a consequence of complying with laws and/or regulations.

BC9   The Interpretations Committee decided that an entity should not be required to apply this Interpretation to liabilities that arise from emissions trading schemes. The IASB decided in 2011 to add a project on this topic to its research agenda. The Interpretations Committee thinks that it would be better to address the accounting for liabilities that arise from emissions trading schemes in a comprehensive project on all recognition and measurement issues related to emissions trading schemes.

BC10   The Interpretations Committee decided not to withdraw IFRIC 6 because it provides useful information on the accounting for liabilities within its scope. The Interpretations Committee noted that the consensus in IFRIC 6 is consistent with the consensus in this Interpretation, and concluded that a scope exclusion for liabilities for waste management within the scope of IFRIC 6 is not necessary.

BC11   The Interpretations Committee decided that this Interpretation should provide guidance on applying IAS 37 to a liability to pay a levy and should not address the accounting for the costs arising from recognising the liability to pay a levy. The Interpretations Committee observed that other Standards would determine whether the recognition of a liability to pay a levy gives rise to an asset or an expense.

What is the obligating event that gives rise to the recognition of a liability to pay a levy?

BC12   According to the definition in paragraph 10 of IAS 37, an obligating event is an event that creates a legal or constructive obligation that results in an entity having no realistic alternative to settling the obligation. According to paragraph 14(a) of IAS 37, a provision should be recognised only when an entity has a present obligation as a result of a past event. The Interpretations Committee noted that the main consequence of these requirements is that there can be only one single obligating event. The Interpretations Committee acknowledged that, in some circumstances, an obligating event can occur only if other events have occurred previously. For example, for some levies, the entity paying the levy must have undertaken an activity both in the previous and in the current periods in order to be obliged to pay the levy. The Interpretations Committee noted that the activity undertaken in the previous period is necessary, but not sufficient, to create a present obligation.

BC13   Consequently, the Interpretations Committee concluded that the obligating event that gives rise to a liability to pay a levy is the activity that triggers the payment of the levy, as identified by the legislation. In other words, the liability to pay a levy is recognised when the activity that triggers the payment of the levy occurs, as identified by the legislation. For example, if the activity that triggers the payment of the levy is the generation of revenue in 20X1 and the calculation of that levy is based on the revenue generated in 20X0, the obligating event for that levy is the generation of revenue in 20X1 (see Illustrative Example 2). The date on which the levy is paid does not affect the timing of recognition of the liability to pay a levy, because the obligating event is the activity that triggers the payment of the levy (and not the payment of the levy itself).

BC14   The Interpretations Committee noted that some respondents to the draft Interpretation think that the result of the proposed accounting does not provide a fair representation of the economic effects of recurring levies when the liability is recognised at a point in time and gives rise to an expense, although these respondents acknowledged that the proposed accounting in the draft Interpretation is a technically correct interpretation of the requirements in IAS 37. Those respondents think that the substance of a recurring levy is that it is an expense associated with a specific period (and not an expense triggered on a specific date). The Interpretations Committee concluded that this Interpretation is needed to address the diversity in practice and that it provides consistent information about an entity's obligations to pay levies. The Interpretations Committee also observed that this Interpretation does not address the accounting for the costs arising from recognising a liability to pay a levy and that other Standards would determine whether the recognition of the liability to pay a levy gives rise to an asset or an expense. Some respondents to the draft Interpretation asked the Interpretations Committee to consider the effect of economic compulsion to continue to operate in a future period and of going concern assumption on the accounting for levies. The Interpretations Committee's conclusions are set out below.

Does economic compulsion to continue to operate in a future period create a constructive obligation to pay a levy that will be triggered by operating in that future period?

BC15 The Interpretations Committee considered an argument that, if it would be necessary for an entity to take unrealistic action in order to avoid an obligation to pay a levy that would otherwise be triggered by operating in the future, then a constructive obligation to pay the levy exists and a liability should be recognised. For example, if the activity that triggers the payment of the levy occurs in 20X1 and the calculation of the levy is based on financial data for 20X0 (as in Illustrative Example 2), some argue that a liability should be recognised in 20X0. Supporters of this argument point to the definition of a constructive obligation in paragraph 10 of IAS 37 and conclude that an entity might have no realistic alternative other than to continue to operate in the next period (ie 20X1). For example, they note that an entity may operate in a regulated market and may not be able to stop operating without a long period of run-off.

BC16 The Interpretations Committee rejected this argument, noting that if this rationale were applied, many types of future expenditure within the scope of IAS 37 would be recognised as liabilities. Indeed, in many cases, entities have no realistic alternative but to pay expenditures to be incurred in the future. The Interpretations Committee noted that, in accordance with paragraphs 18–19 of IAS 37:

(a) no provision is recognised for costs that need to be incurred to operate in the future; and

(b) it is only those obligations arising from past events existing independently of an entity's future conduct of its business that are recognised as provisions.

BC17 As a result, the Interpretations Committee concluded that, when an entity is economically compelled to incur operating costs that relate to the future conduct of the business, that compulsion does not create a constructive obligation and thus does not lead to the entity recognising a liability. This point is illustrated in the examples accompanying IAS 37.

BC18 The Interpretations Committee noted that a levy is triggered as a result of undertaking an activity in a specified period, as identified by the legislation. As a result, the Interpretations Committee concluded that there is no constructive obligation to pay a levy that relates to the future conduct of the business, even if:

(a) it is economically unrealistic for the entity to avoid the levy if it has the intention of continuing in business;

(b)   there is a legal requirement to incur the levy if the entity does continue in business;

(c)   it would be necessary for an entity to take unrealistic action to avoid paying the levy, such as to sell, or stop operating, property, plant and equipment;

(d)   the entity made a statement of intent (and has the ability) to operate in the future period(s); or

(e)   the entity has a legal, regulatory or contractual requirement to operate in the future period(s).

BC19   Consequently, the Interpretations Committee concluded that an entity does not have a constructive obligation at a reporting date to pay a levy that will be triggered by operating in a future period as a result of the entity being economically compelled to continue to operate in that future period.

Does the going concern assumption imply that an entity has a present obligation to pay a levy that will be triggered by operating in a future period?

BC20   The Interpretations Committee noted that this issue is related to the basis of preparation of financial statements. Some question whether the going concern assumption affects the timing of the recognition of the liability to pay a levy.

BC21   The Interpretations Committee observed that IAS 1 *Presentation of Financial Statements* sets out general features for the financial statements, including the accrual basis of accounting and the going concern assumption. The Interpretations Committee noted that, when an entity prepares financial statements on a going concern basis, it shall also comply with all the recognition and measurement requirements of IFRS. Consequently, the Interpretations Committee concluded that the going concern assumption cannot lead to the recognition of a liability that does not meet the definitions and recognition criteria set out in IAS 37.

BC22   Specifically, the Interpretations Committee concluded that the preparation of financial statements under the going concern assumption does not imply that an entity has a present obligation to pay a levy that will be triggered by operating in a future period. Paragraphs 18–19 of IAS 37 specify that no provision is recognised in that case.

Does the recognition of a liability to pay a levy arise at a point in time or does it, in some circumstances, arise progressively over time?

BC23   The Interpretations Committee observed that most of the liabilities in IAS 37 and in the Illustrative Examples accompanying IAS 37 are recognised at a point in time, that is, when the obligating event occurs. Nevertheless, they noted that, in one example accompanying IAS 37, the liability is recognised progressively over time.

BC24 In Illustrative Example 3 accompanying IAS 37, an entity operates an offshore oilfield and is required to restore the seabed because of damage caused by the extraction of oil. According to this example, the restoration costs that arise through the extraction of oil are recognised as a liability when the oil is extracted. The Interpretations Committee noted that in this example, the damage is directly caused by the extraction of oil, and that more damage occurs when more oil is extracted. Thus, the outcome is that the liability for damage caused over time is recognised progressively over time as the entity extracts oil and causes damage to the environment.

BC25 The Interpretations Committee discussed whether this outcome is linked to a recognition issue or to a measurement issue and concluded that this is a recognition issue, because the obligating event (ie the damage caused by the extraction of oil) occurs progressively over a period of time. In accordance with paragraph 19 of IAS 37, the Interpretations Committee noted that a present obligation exists only to the extent of the damage caused to date to the environment, because the entity has no present obligation to rectify the damage that will result from the extraction of oil in the future (ie the future conduct of its business).

BC26 Consequently, the Interpretations Committee concluded that the liability to pay a levy is recognised progressively if the obligating event (ie the activity that triggers the payment of the levy, as identified by the legislation) occurs over a period of time. For example, if the obligating event is the generation of revenue over a period of time, the corresponding liability is recognised as the entity generates that revenue (see Illustrative Example 1).

What is the obligating event that gives rise to the recognition of a liability to pay a levy that is triggered if a minimum threshold is reached?

BC27 The draft Interpretation did not address the accounting for levies that are triggered if a minimum revenue threshold is reached. However, many respondents to the draft Interpretation emphasised the importance of providing guidance on this issue. The Interpretations Committee agreed with the respondents' comments and concluded that this Interpretation should provide guidance on the accounting for levies with minimum thresholds. The Interpretations Committee decided that the accounting for the liability to pay such levies should be consistent with the principles established in paragraphs 8 and 11 of this Interpretation.

BC28 For example, if a levy is triggered when a minimum activity threshold is reached (such as a minimum amount of revenue or sales generated or outputs produced), the obligating event is the reaching of that activity threshold. If a levy is triggered as the entity undertakes an activity above a minimum level of activity (such as revenue or sales generated or outputs produced in excess of the minimum amount specified in the legislation), the obligating event is the activity that is undertaken after the threshold is reached (see Illustrative Example 4). If a levy is triggered if an entity operates on a specified date, as identified by the legislation, provided that a minimum threshold is reached in a previous period (such as a minimum amount of revenue, a minimum number of employees, or a minimum amount of assets and liabilities), the obligating event is the entity operating on the specified date as identified by the legislation after having reached the threshold in the previous period. In that case, the reaching of the threshold in the previous period is necessary, but not sufficient, to create a present obligation.

Are the principles for recognising a liability to pay a levy in the annual financial statements and in the interim financial report the same?

BC29   IAS 34 *Interim Financial Reporting* (paragraph 29) states that the same recognition principles should be applied in the annual financial statements and in the interim financial report. By applying the requirements of IAS 34 (paragraphs 31–32 and 39, as illustrated by paragraphs B2, B4 and B11 of the Illustrative Examples accompanying IAS 34), no liability would be recognised at the end of an interim reporting period if the obligating event has not yet occurred. For example, an entity does not have an obligation at the end of an interim reporting period if the present obligation arises only at the end of the annual reporting period. Similarly, if a present obligation to pay a levy exists at the end of an interim reporting period, the liability should be recognised.

BC30   The Interpretations Committee observed that paragraph 16A of IAS 34 requires the disclosure of explanatory comments about the nature and amount of items affecting liabilities that are unusual because of their nature, size or incidence and about the events after the interim period that have not been reflected in the financial statements for the interim period. If necessary, an entity would therefore provide disclosures about levies that are recognised in the interim financial report or that will be recognised in future interim financial reports.

Documents published to accompany

IFRIC 22

Foreign Currency Transactions and Advance Consideration

The text of the unaccompanied Interpretation, IFRIC 22, is contained in Part A of this edition. Its effective date when issued was 1 January 2018. The text of the Accompanying Guidance on IFRIC 22 is contained in Part B of this edition. This part presents the following document:

BASIS FOR CONCLUSIONS

Basis for Conclusions on IFRIC 22 *Foreign Currency Transactions and Advance Consideration*

This Basis for Conclusions accompanies, but is not part of, IFRIC 22.

Introduction

BC1   This Basis for Conclusions summarises the considerations of the IFRS Interpretations Committee (the Interpretations Committee) in reaching its consensus.

Background

BC2   The Interpretations Committee received a question asking how to determine the exchange rate to use in applying IAS 21 *The Effects of Changes in Foreign Exchange Rates* when recognising revenue. The question addressed a circumstance in which an entity receives advance consideration in a foreign currency. IAS 21 does not specifically address such a circumstance.

BC3   The Interpretations Committee noted that the feedback from its outreach on the question indicated that:

    (a)   the issue affects a number of jurisdictions, and particularly affects the construction industry.

    (b)   diverse reporting methods are applied. Some entities recognise revenue using the spot exchange rate between the functional currency and the foreign currency at the date of the receipt of the advance consideration and others use the exchange rate at the date that revenue is recognised.

BC4   To address the issue, in October 2015 the Interpretations Committee published a draft Interpretation *Foreign Currency Transactions and Advance Consideration* for public comment. It received 45 comment letters. The Interpretations Committee considered the comments received in developing this Interpretation.

Scope

Foreign currency transactions other than revenue transactions

BC5   The question received related specifically to revenue transactions. However, in discussing the issue, the Interpretations Committee noted that a similar question arises for other transactions when consideration is denominated in a foreign currency and is paid or received in advance. For example:

    (a)   purchases and sales of property, plant and equipment;

    (b)   purchases and sales of intangible assets;

(c)   purchases and sales of investment property;

(d)   purchases of inventory;

(e)   purchases of services;

(f)   entering into lease contracts; and

(g)   receipt of some government grants.

BC6   In addition, the Interpretations Committee noted that IAS 21 applies to all foreign currency transactions, not only to revenue transactions in a foreign currency. Consequently, the Interpretations Committee decided that the Interpretation applies to a foreign currency transaction (or part of it) when an entity recognises a non-monetary asset or non-monetary liability arising from the payment or receipt of advance consideration. Respondents to the draft Interpretation generally supported the scope proposed by the Interpretations Committee.

Income taxes and insurance contracts

BC7   The Interpretations Committee decided that an entity is not required to apply the Interpretation to income taxes, or to insurance contracts (including reinsurance contracts) that it issues or reinsurance contracts that it holds.

BC8   The Interpretations Committee concluded that it is important to avoid unintended consequences for income taxes because of the complexities that arise from the interplay with deferred tax. Similarly, the Interpretations Committee concluded that it is important to avoid unintended consequences for insurance contracts. The International Accounting Standards Board's project on Insurance Contracts is at an advanced stage and it would be inappropriate to require a change in accounting before the application of the forthcoming insurance contracts Standard.[1]

Non-cash consideration

BC9   Advance consideration may be denominated in a foreign currency, but in a form other than cash. For example, an entity may receive equity instruments, or an item of inventory that has a fair value determined in a foreign currency, in exchange for the provision of services.

BC10   IAS 21 applies to both cash and non-cash foreign currency transactions. Accordingly, the Interpretations Committee determined that the Interpretation applies to both cash and non-cash transactions when an entity recognises a non-monetary asset or non-monetary liability arising from advance consideration in a foreign currency.

---

1   The Board completed its insurance project with the issuance of IFRS 17 *Insurance Contracts* in May 2017. When applying IAS 21, a group of insurance contracts is treated as a monetary item.

Transactions measured at fair value on initial recognition

BC11 Paragraph 23(c) of IAS 21 requires an entity to translate non-monetary items measured at fair value in a foreign currency using the exchange rate at the date when the fair value was measured. Consequently, the Interpretations Committee decided that the Interpretation does not apply to foreign currency transactions for which the related asset, expense or income is initially measured at fair value.

BC12 The Interpretations Committee also decided the Interpretation does not apply to foreign currency transactions for which the related asset, expense or income is initially measured at the fair value of the consideration paid or received at a date other than the date of the transaction specified in this Interpretation. This is because the date of measurement of the fair value used to measure the asset, expense or income on initial recognition would determine the date of the transaction.

Monetary and non-monetary items

BC13 The payment or receipt of advance consideration generally gives rise to the recognition of a non-monetary asset or non-monetary liability. However, an advance payment or receipt could give rise to a monetary asset or liability instead of a non-monetary asset or liability.

BC14 When the asset or liability is a monetary item, paragraphs 28–29 of IAS 21 require an entity to recognise an exchange difference in profit or loss for any change in the exchange rate between the transaction date and the date of settlement of that asset or liability. Consequently, the question about which exchange rate to use on initial recognition of the related asset, expense or income arises only when the advance consideration gives rise to the recognition of a non-monetary asset or non-monetary liability. Accordingly, the Interpretations Committee decided that this Interpretation applies only in circumstances in which an entity recognises a non-monetary asset or non-monetary liability arising from advance consideration.

BC15 Some respondents to the draft Interpretation requested guidance in determining whether the payment or receipt of advance consideration gives rise to a monetary or non-monetary asset or liability. These respondents said that, for some transactions, this assessment can be difficult.

BC16 In considering the request, the Interpretations Committee noted that the Interpretation is not adding a new requirement to determine whether an item is monetary or non-monetary—this requirement already exists in IAS 21. The Interpretation simply clarifies which exchange rate to use for particular transactions. The Interpretations Committee decided that it was outside the scope of this Interpretation to provide application guidance on the definition of monetary and non-monetary items.

BC17   Nonetheless, the Interpretations Committee acknowledged that an entity may need to apply judgement in determining whether an item is monetary or non-monetary. It also noted references in Standards and *The Conceptual Framework for Financial Reporting* (the *Conceptual Framework*)[2] that may be helpful in determining whether an item is monetary or non-monetary. These references include:

    (a)   paragraph 16 of IAS 21;

    (b)   paragraph AG11 of IAS 32 *Financial Instruments: Presentation*; and

    (c)   paragraph 4.17 of *The Conceptual Framework*.

Consensus

The date of the transaction

BC18   Paragraph 22 of IAS 21 defines the date of the transaction for the purpose of determining the exchange rate to use on initial recognition of a foreign currency transaction as 'the date on which the transaction first qualifies for recognition in accordance with IFRSs'.

BC19   The Interpretations Committee observed that there could be two ways of identifying 'the transaction' for the purpose of determining the exchange rate to use on initial recognition:

    (a)   the 'one-transaction' approach—the receipt or payment of consideration and the transfer of the goods or services are all considered to be part of the same transaction. Thus, the date of the transaction is determined by the date on which the first element of the transaction qualifies for recognition applying the relevant Standards.

    (b)   the 'multi-transaction' approach—the receipt or payment of consideration and the transfer of the goods or services are considered to be separate transactions, each of which has its own 'date of the transaction' when it first qualifies for recognition applying the relevant Standards.

BC20   The one-transaction approach is consistent with the notion that purchases and sales represent exchange transactions, and the payment and transfer of goods or services are inherently interdependent. Accordingly, if the first element of the transaction to be recognised is a non-monetary asset or non-monetary liability, that would determine the date of the transaction for the purpose of recognising the related asset, expense or income (or part of it).

BC21   The multi-transaction approach treats the transfer of goods or services and the receipt or payment of consideration as two separate transactions. This approach would result in a date of the transaction that is the same as the date of recognition of the related asset, expense or income (or part of it), regardless of the timing of the payment or receipt of consideration.

---

2   References to the *Conceptual Framework for Financial Reporting* in this Basis for Conclusions are to the *Conceptual Framework for Financial Reporting*, issued in 2010 and in effect when the Interpretation was developed.

BC22   The Interpretations Committee decided that the one-transaction approach is a more appropriate interpretation of IAS 21 when the payment or receipt of advance consideration gives rise to a non-monetary asset or non-monetary liability. This is because:

(a)   it reflects that an entity is typically no longer exposed to foreign exchange risk in respect of the transaction to the extent that it has received or paid advance consideration. After receipt of advance consideration in a foreign currency, the entity can decide whether to hold the foreign currency consideration and be exposed to foreign exchange risk. After payment of advance consideration in a foreign currency, the entity is no longer exposed to foreign exchange risk in respect of that amount.

(b)   the obligation to perform (reflected in the recognition of a non-monetary liability) and the subsequent fulfilment of that obligation (which gives rise to income) are interdependent and are part of the same transaction.

(c)   the right to receive assets, goods or services (reflected in the recognition of a non-monetary asset) and the receipt of those assets, goods or services are inherently interdependent.

(d)   it is consistent with the treatment of non-monetary assets and non-monetary liabilities applying paragraph 23(b) of IAS 21, because an entity does not subsequently update the translated amounts of such items.

BC23   In addition, considering paragraph 22 of IAS 21, the Interpretations Committee concluded that, for a transaction to qualify for recognition in accordance with the Standards, an entity must record the transaction in its financial statements with a value. The Interpretations Committee observed that paragraph 4.46 of the *Conceptual Framework* notes that 'in practice, obligations under contracts that are equally proportionately unperformed (for example, liabilities for inventory ordered but not yet received) are generally not recognised as liabilities in the financial statements'. Consequently, the Interpretations Committee concluded the date on which an entity first recognises the transaction in its financial statements with a value determines the date of the transaction. If an entity recognises a non-monetary asset or non-monetary liability arising from advance consideration, the date of initial recognition of that asset or liability is the date of the transaction. The date of initial recognition of the non-monetary asset or non-monetary liability is generally the date on which the entity pays or receives the advance consideration.

Multiple payments

BC24   If only part of the consideration is received or paid in advance, then an entity has initially recognised only part of the transaction as a non-monetary asset or non-monetary liability. In that case, applying this Interpretation, an entity determines the date of the transaction for only that part of the related asset, expense or income for which consideration has been received or paid in advance. If there are subsequent advance payments or receipts, the date(s) of the transaction for the remaining part(s) of the related asset, expense or income will be the date(s) on which the entity recognises those subsequent advance receipts or payments. Correspondingly, if part of the consideration is paid in arrears, the date(s) of the transaction for the remaining part(s) of the related asset, expense or income will be the date(s) on which the entity initially recognises that (those) part(s) of the asset, expense or income in its financial statements applying applicable Standards.

BC25 The Interpretations Committee observed that this treatment reflects that an entity typically has no foreign exchange risk in respect of foreign currency amounts already paid or received, but is still exposed to foreign exchange risk in respect of any unpaid consideration.

Embedded derivatives

BC26 The Interpretations Committee was asked to clarify how the Interpretation applies to an embedded derivative that requires separation at contract inception. The Interpretations Committee decided it was not necessary to clarify this matter in the Interpretation. The Interpretation Committee noted that paragraph 24 of IAS 21 requires an entity to determine the carrying amount of an item in conjunction with other relevant Standards. Consequently, an entity first evaluates transactions for embedded derivatives that require separation at contract inception before applying the requirements in IAS 21 or this Interpretation.

BC27 The Interpretations Committee further noted that, if an entity separately accounts for an embedded derivative, the requirements of the Interpretation apply to a remaining host contract denominated in a foreign currency when consideration has been paid or received in advance as they do to other such foreign currency transactions.

Illustrative examples

BC28 Some respondents to the draft Interpretation suggested including an example to illustrate how the Interpretation applies to transactions with a significant financing component. The Interpretations Committee decided not to include an example because it concluded that any such example would interpret other Standards.

Interaction with the presentation of exchange differences arising on monetary items

BC29 The Interpretations Committee considered the interaction of the Interpretation with the presentation of exchange differences on the settlement or retranslation of monetary items that, applying paragraphs 28–29 of IAS 21, an entity recognises in profit or loss in the period in which they arise.

BC30 The Interpretations Committee decided that presentation of exchange differences in profit or loss is outside the scope of the issue being addressed in the Interpretation. This is because the Interpretation addresses only how to determine the 'date of the transaction' for the purpose of determining the exchange rate to use on initial recognition of the related asset, expense or income on the derecognition of a non-monetary asset or non-monetary liability arising from advance consideration in a foreign currency.

Transition

BC31 The Interpretations Committee observed that retrospective application of the Interpretation may be burdensome, in particular for foreign currency transactions involving purchases of assets. Consequently, the Interpretations Committee decided that, on initial application, entities should have the option not to retrospectively adjust assets, expenses and income (or parts of them) that had been recognised before the beginning of the reporting period in which the Interpretation is first applied or the beginning of a prior reporting period presented as comparative information in the period in which the Interpretation is first applied.

BC32 If an entity uses this option and applies the Interpretation prospectively as permitted in paragraph A2(b), the entity does not restate amounts recognised before either the beginning of the reporting period in which the entity first applies the Interpretation (if paragraph A2b(i) is applied) or the beginning of a prior reporting period presented as comparative information in the period in which the entity first applies the Interpretation (if paragraph A2b(ii) is applied).

First-time adopters

BC33 The Interpretations Committee received feedback that first-time adopters of IFRS Standards may also find retrospective application burdensome. Consequently, the Interpretations Committee decided that first-time adopters should not be required to apply the Interpretation to assets, expenses and income initially recognised before the date of transition to IFRS Standards. Accordingly, this Interpretation amends IFRS 1 *First-time Adoption of International Financial Reporting Standards*.

Documents published to accompany

IFRIC 23

Uncertainty over Income Tax Treatments

The text of the unaccompanied Interpretation, IFRIC 23, is contained in Part A of this edition. Its effective date when issued was 1 January 2019. The text of the Accompanying Guidance on IFRIC 23 is contained in Part B of this edition. This part presents the following document:

BASIS FOR CONCLUSIONS

Basis for Conclusions on
IFRIC 23 *Uncertainty over Income Tax Treatments*

This Basis for Conclusions accompanies, but is not part of, IFRIC 23. It summarises the considerations of the IFRS Interpretations Committee (the Committee) in reaching its consensus.

Background

BC1   The Committee received a question asking when it is appropriate for entities to recognise a current tax asset if tax laws require entities to make payments in respect of a disputed tax treatment. In the circumstance the question described, the entity intended to appeal a tax ruling.

BC2   IAS 12 *Income Taxes* includes requirements on recognition and measurement of tax assets and liabilities, but does not specify how to reflect uncertainty. The Committee observed that entities apply diverse reporting methods when the application of tax law is uncertain.

BC3   Accordingly, in October 2015 the Committee published a draft Interpretation *Uncertainty over Income Tax Treatments* for public comment. It received 61 comment letters. The Committee considered the comments received in developing this Interpretation.

Scope

BC4   The question that the Committee received related to a particular circumstance in which an entity is required to make a payment to a taxation authority in respect of a disputed income tax treatment. However, in discussing the issue, the Committee noted that a similar question could arise in other circumstances in which there is uncertainty over income tax treatments. Consequently, the Committee decided that the Interpretation should address the accounting for income taxes whenever tax treatments involve uncertainty that affects the application of IAS 12. Respondents to the draft Interpretation generally supported the scope that the Committee proposed.

BC5   Uncertainty over income tax treatments may affect both current and deferred tax. For example, the timing of deductibility of the cost of an intangible asset under tax law may be uncertain and this may affect both taxable profit and the tax base of the asset, which in turn affects the determination of current and deferred tax respectively. The Committee decided to require a consistent approach to reflecting the effect of uncertainty for both current and deferred tax; therefore, the Interpretation applies in determining both current and deferred tax.

BC6   The Committee developed the Interpretation as an interpretation of IAS 12, ie the requirements in the Interpretation add to, and complement, the requirements in IAS 12. The Committee decided not to expand the scope of the Interpretation to taxes or levies outside the scope of IAS 12 because it was concerned that a wider scope might create conflicts within IFRS Standards.

Interest and penalties

BC7   IAS 12 does not explicitly refer to interest and penalties payable to, or receivable from, a taxation authority, nor are they explicitly referred to in other IFRS Standards.

BC8   A number of respondents to the draft Interpretation suggested that the Interpretation explicitly include interest and penalties associated with uncertain tax treatments within its scope. Some said that entities account for interest and penalties differently depending on whether they apply IAS 12 or IAS 37 *Provisions, Contingent Liabilities and Contingent Assets* to those amounts.

BC9   The Committee decided not to add to the Interpretation requirements relating to interest and penalties associated with uncertain tax treatments. Rather, the Committee noted that if an entity considers a particular amount payable or receivable for interest and penalties to be an income tax, then that amount is within the scope of IAS 12 and, when there is uncertainty, also within the scope of this Interpretation. Conversely, if an entity does not apply IAS 12 to a particular amount payable or receivable, then this Interpretation does not apply to that amount, regardless of whether there is uncertainty.

Consensus

Whether an entity considers uncertain tax treatments separately

BC10   The amount of a tax asset or liability could be affected by whether an entity considers each uncertain tax treatment separately or together with one or more other uncertain tax treatments. Consequently, the Committee decided to include the requirement in paragraph 6 of the Interpretation in this respect. The Committee noted that an entity may need to use judgement in applying that requirement.

Examination by taxation authorities

BC11   The Committee decided that an entity should assume a taxation authority will examine amounts it has a right to examine and have full knowledge of all related information. In making this decision, the Committee noted that paragraphs 46–47 of IAS 12 require an entity to measure tax assets and liabilities based on tax laws that have been enacted or substantively enacted.

BC12   A few respondents to the draft Interpretation suggested that an entity consider the probability of examination, instead of assuming that an examination will occur. These respondents said such a probability assessment would be particularly important if there is no time limit on the taxation authority's right to examine income tax filings.

BC13   The Committee decided not to change the examination assumption, nor create an exception to it for circumstances in which there is no time limit on the taxation authority's right to examine income tax filings. Almost all respondents to the draft Interpretation supported the examination assumption. The Committee also noted that the assumption of examination by the taxation authority, in isolation, would not require an entity to reflect the effects of uncertainty. The threshold for reflecting the effects of uncertainty is whether it is probable that the taxation authority will accept an uncertain tax treatment. In other words, the recognition of uncertainty is not determined based on whether a taxation authority examines a tax treatment.

Determination of taxable profit (tax loss), tax bases, unused tax losses, unused tax credits and tax rates

When to reflect the effect of uncertainty

BC14   Paragraph 24 of IAS 12 requires the recognition of deferred tax assets to the extent that it is probable that an entity will be able to use deductible temporary differences against taxable profit. The objective of IAS 12 also refers to a probable threshold in the context of deferred tax. In addition, although IAS 12 does not include an explicit recognition threshold for current tax, paragraph 14 of IAS 12 implies that a probable threshold applies to current tax assets arising from a tax loss.

BC15   Consequently, the Committee decided that an entity should reflect the effect of uncertainty in accounting for current and deferred tax when the entity concludes it is not probable that the taxation authority will accept an uncertain tax treatment (and thus, it is probable that the entity will receive or pay amounts relating to the uncertain tax treatment).

BC16   The Committee concluded that setting this explicit threshold for the recognition of the effect of uncertainty will increase comparability among entities and reduce some of the costs of measurement.

How to reflect the effect of uncertainty

BC17   To reflect the effect of uncertainty, the Committee decided that an entity should use the expected value or the most likely amount, whichever method better predicts the resolution of the uncertainty. This approach is similar to the approach used in IFRS 15 *Revenue from Contracts with Customers* to estimate the amount of variable consideration in a revenue contract.

BC18   The Committee considered whether to permit or require the use of a third measurement method, such as a 'cumulative-probability approach' (ie the measurement method used to reflect uncertainty over income tax treatments in US Generally Accepted Accounting Principles). The Committee observed that the inclusion of a third method would have complicated the judgements that need to be made in applying the Interpretation. This is because an entity would have had to assess which of three measurement methods best predicts the resolution of the uncertainty. The Committee also noted that IFRS Standards do not use the cumulative-probability approach, whereas the expected value and the most likely amount are used elsewhere in the Standards. Including a measurement method not used elsewhere in the Standards might have reduced comparability.

BC19   Consequently, the Committee decided not to permit or require a third measurement method to reflect the effects of uncertainty.

Changes in facts and circumstances

BC20 Considering uncertainty over income tax treatments means it is necessary to make estimates, and such estimation involves judgements based on available information. The information available to an entity about uncertain tax treatments can change over time. Consequently, the Committee decided that an entity should reassess a judgement or estimate required by the Interpretation when related facts and circumstances change.

BC21 The Committee also decided that an entity should reflect the effect of any changes in its judgements or estimates consistently with the requirements in IAS 8 *Accounting Policies, Changes in Accounting Estimates and Errors* for changes in accounting estimates.

Disclosure

BC22 IAS 1 *Presentation of Financial Statements* and IAS 12 provide disclosure requirements that may be relevant when there is uncertainty over income tax treatments. Consequently, instead of introducing new disclosure requirements, the Committee decided to highlight those existing requirements in the Interpretation.

Business combinations

BC23 The Committee considered whether the Interpretation should address the accounting for tax assets and liabilities acquired or assumed in a business combination when there is uncertainty over income tax treatments. The Committee noted that IFRS 3 *Business Combinations* applies to all assets acquired and liabilities assumed in a business combination. Consequently, the Committee concluded that the Interpretation should not explicitly address tax assets and liabilities acquired or assumed in a business combination.

BC24 Nonetheless, paragraph 24 of IFRS 3 requires an entity to account for deferred tax assets and liabilities that arise as part of a business combination applying IAS 12. Accordingly, the Interpretation applies to such assets and liabilities when there is uncertainty over income tax treatments that affect deferred tax.

Transition

BC25 The Committee observed that retrospective application of the Interpretation without the use of hindsight would often be impossible for entities. Consequently, the Committee decided not to require the restatement of comparative information when an entity first applies the Interpretation. However, the Committee concluded that an entity should not be prevented from applying the Interpretation retrospectively if it is able to do so without the use of hindsight. Consequently, the Committee decided to permit retrospective application if that is possible without the use of hindsight.

First-time adopters

BC26 The Committee observed that if a first-time adopter's date of transition to IFRSs is before the date the Interpretation is issued, the first-time adopter may face the same hindsight difficulties as entities that already apply IFRS Standards. Consequently, the Committee decided not to require first-time adopters whose date of transition to IFRSs is before 1 July 2017 to present in their first IFRS financial statements comparative information that reflects this Interpretation.

Material published to accompany

SIC-7

Introduction of the Euro

The text of the unaccompanied Interpretation, SIC-7, is contained in Part A of this edition. Its effective date when issued was 1 June 1998. This part presents the following document:

BASIS FOR CONCLUSIONS

Basis for Conclusions on
SIC Interpretation 7 *Introduction of the Euro*

This Basis for Conclusions accompanies, but is not part of, SIC-7.

[The original text has been marked up to reflect the revision of IAS 21 in 2003 and IAS 1 in 2007 and the amendment of IAS 27 in 2008:[1] new text is underlined and deleted text is struck through.]

5   IAS 21.23~~11~~(a) requires that foreign currency monetary items (as defined by IAS 21.~~8~~07) be reported using the closing rate at ~~each balance sheet date~~ the end of each reporting period. According to IAS 21.28~~15~~, exchange differences arising from the translation of monetary items generally should be recognised as income or as expenses in the period in which they arise. The effective start of the EMU after the reporting period ~~balance sheet date~~ does not change the application of these requirements at the end of the reporting period ~~balance sheet date~~; in accordance with IAS 10.10~~28~~[2] it is not relevant whether or not the closing rate can fluctuate after the ~~balance sheet date~~ reporting period.

6   IAS 21.5~~14~~ states that the Standard does not apply to ~~deal with~~ hedge accounting~~, except in restricted circumstances~~. Therefore, this Interpretation does not address how foreign currency hedges should be accounted for. IAS 8.~~42~~ would allow such a change in accounting policy only if the change would result in a more appropriate presentation of events or transactions.[3] The effective start of EMU, of itself, does not justify a change to an entity's established accounting policy related to ~~anticipatory~~ hedges of forecast transactions because the changeover does not affect the economic rationale of such hedges. Therefore, the changeover should not alter the accounting policy where gains and losses on financial instruments used as ~~anticipatory~~ hedges of forecast transactions are ~~currently deferred~~ initially recognised in ~~equity~~ other comprehensive income and matched with the related income or expense in a future period.

7   IAS 21.48~~37~~ requires the cumulative amount of exchange differences relating to the translation of the financial statements of a foreign operation ~~entity~~ ~~which~~ that have been ~~deferred in equity~~ recognised in other comprehensive income and accumulated in a separate component of equity in accordance with IAS 21.~~17,~~ ~~19 or 30~~32 or 39(c) to be ~~recognised as income or expenses~~ reclassified from equity to profit or loss in the same period in which the gain or loss on disposal or partial disposal of the foreign operation ~~entity~~ is recognised. The fact that the cumulative amount of exchange differences will be fixed under EMU does not justify immediate recognition as income or

---

1   The consolidation requirements in IAS 27 were superseded, and IAS 27 was renamed *Separate Financial Statements*, by IFRS 10 *Consolidated Financial Statements* issued in May 2011.

2   ~~IAS 10 (revised in 1999), paragraph 20, contains similar requirements.~~

3   As SIC-7 was issued before IAS 39, the previous version of this Interpretation could refer only to the entity's own accounting policies on the matter. The accounting for hedges was subsequently covered under IAS 39 *Financial Instruments: Recognition and Measurement*. In November 2013 the Board replaced the hedge accounting requirements in IAS 39 and relocated them to IFRS 9 *Financial Instruments*.

expenses ~~since~~ <u>because</u> the wording and the rationale of IAS 21.<u>48</u>~~37~~ clearly preclude such a treatment.

8 ~~Under the Allowed Alternative Treatment of IAS 21.21, exchange differences resulting from severe devaluations of currencies are included in the carrying amount of the related assets in certain limited circumstances. Those circumstances do not apply to the currencies participating in the changeover since the event of severe devaluation is incompatible with the required stability of participating currencies.~~

Material published to accompany

SIC-10

Government Assistance—No Specific Relation to Operating Activities

The text of the unaccompanied Interpretation, SIC 10, is contained in Part A of this edition. Its effective date when issued was 1 August 1998. This part presents the following document:

BASIS FOR CONCLUSIONS

Basis for Conclusions on
SIC Interpretation 10 *Government Assistance—No Specific Relation to Operating Activities*

This Basis for Conclusions accompanies, but is not part of, SIC-10.

4   IAS 20.03 defines government grants as assistance by the government in the form of transfers of resources to an entity in return for past or future compliance with certain conditions relating to the operating activities of the entity. The general requirement to operate in certain regions or industry sectors in order to qualify for the government assistance constitutes such a condition in accordance with IAS 20.03. Therefore, such assistance falls within the definition of government grants and the requirements of IAS 20 apply, in particular paragraphs 12 and 20, which deal with the timing of recognition as income.

Material published to accompany

SIC-25

Income Taxes — Changes in the Tax Status of an Entity or its Shareholders

The text of the unaccompanied Interpretation, SIC 25, is contained in Part A of this edition. Its effective date when issued was 15 July 2000. This part presents the following document:

BASIS FOR CONCLUSIONS

Basis for Conclusions on
SIC Interpretation 25 *Income Taxes—Changes in the Tax Status of an Entity or its Shareholders*

This Basis for Conclusions accompanies, but is not part of, SIC-25.

[The original text has been marked up to reflect the amendment to IAS 12 in 2003, and the revision of IAS 38 Intangible Assets in 2004 and IAS 1 Presentation of Financial Statements in 2007: new text is underlined and deleted text is struck through.]

5   IAS 12.58 requires current and deferred tax to be included in ~~the net~~ profit or loss for the period, except to the extent the tax arises from a transaction or event that is recognised <u>outside profit or loss either in other comprehensive income or</u> directly in equity, in the same or a different period, (or arises from a business combination ~~that is an acquisition~~). IAS 12.61A requires ~~that~~ current and deferred tax <u>to</u> be <u>recognised outside profit or loss</u> ~~charged or credited directly to equity~~ if the tax relates to items that are <u>recognised</u> ~~credited or charged~~, in the same or a different period, <u>outside profit or loss</u> ~~directly to equity~~.

5A   <u>IAS 12.62 identifies examples of circumstances in which a transaction or event is recognised in other comprehensive income as permitted or required by another IFRS. All of these circumstances result in changes in the recognised amount of equity through recognition in other comprehensive income.</u>

6   IAS 12.62<u>A</u> identifies examples of circumstances in which a transaction or event is recognised directly in equity as ~~is~~ permitted or required by another <u>IFRS</u> ~~International Financial Reporting Standard~~. All of these circumstances result in changes in the recognised amount of equity through recognition of a credit or charge directly to equity.

7   IAS 12.65 explains that where the tax base of a revalued asset changes, any tax consequence is recognised <u>in other comprehensive income</u> ~~directly in equity~~ only to the extent <u>that</u> a related accounting revaluation was or is expected to be recognised <u>in other comprehensive income</u> ~~directly in equity~~ (revaluation surplus).

8   Because tax consequences recognised <u>outside profit or loss, whether in other comprehensive income or</u> directly in equity<u>,</u> must relate to a transaction or event recognised <u>outside profit or loss</u> ~~directly in equity~~ in the same or a different period, the cumulative amount of tax ~~charged or credited directly to equity~~ <u>recognised outside profit or loss</u> can be expected to be the same amount that would have been <u>recognised outside profit or loss</u> ~~charged or credited directly to equity~~ if the new tax status had applied previously. IAS 12.63(b) acknowledges that determining the tax consequences of a change in the tax rate or other tax rules that affects a deferred tax asset or liability and relates to an item previously <u>recognised outside profit or loss</u> ~~charged or credited to equity~~ may prove to be difficult. Because of this, IAS 12.63 suggests that an allocation may be necessary.

Material published to accompany

SIC-29

Service Concession Arrangements: Disclosures

The text of the unaccompanied Interpretation, SIC 29, is contained in Part A of this edition. Its effective date when issued was 31 December 2001. This part presents the following document:

BASIS FOR CONCLUSIONS

Basis for Conclusions on
SIC Interpretation 29 *Service Concession Arrangements: Disclosures*

This Basis for Conclusions accompanies, but is not part of, SIC-29.

[The original text of paragraphs 8 and 9 has been marked up to reflect the revision of IAS 1 in 2003 and 2007 and the issue of IFRIC 12 in 2006: new text is underlined and deleted text is struck through.]

8   Paragraph 15 of the *Framework*[1] states that the economic decisions taken by users of financial statements require an evaluation of the ability of the entity to generate cash and cash equivalents and of the timing and certainty of their generation. Paragraph 21 of the *Framework* states that financial statements also contain notes and supplementary schedules and other information. For example, they may contain additional information that is relevant to the needs of users about the items in the statement of financial position balance sheet and statement of comprehensive income statement. They may also include disclosures about the risks and uncertainties affecting the entity and any resources and obligations not recognised in the statement of financial position balance sheet.

9   A service concession arrangement often has provisions or significant features that warrant disclosure of information necessary to assist in assessing the amount, timing and certainty of future cash flows, and the nature and extent of the various rights and obligations involved. The rights and obligations associated with the services to be provided usually involve a high level of public involvement (eg to provide electricity to a city). Other obligations could include significant acts such as building an infrastructure asset (eg power plant) and delivering that asset to the Concession Provider grantor at the end of the concession period.

The text of paragraph 10 has been marked up to reflect the revision of IAS 1 in 2007. Previous amendments to the paragraph, reflecting the revision of IAS 1 in 2003, have been incorporated into the text to avoid confusion with the new amendments in 2007.

10   IAS 1.112(c)103(c) requires an entity's notes to provide additional information that is not presented elsewhere in the financial statements on the face of the balance sheet, income statement, statement of changes in equity or cash flow statement, but is relevant to an understanding of any of them. The definition of notes in IAS 1.711 indicates that notes provide narrative descriptions or disaggregations of items disclosed in the statement of financial position balance sheet, statement of comprehensive income, separate income statement (if presented), statement of changes in equity and statement of cash flows statement, as well as information about items that do not qualify for recognition in those statements.

---

1   References to the *Framework* in this Basis for Conclusions are to the IASC's *Framework for the Preparation and Presentation of Financial Statements*, adopted by the IASB in 2001 and in effect when the Interpretation was developed.

Material published to accompany

SIC-32

Intangible Assets — Web Site Costs

The text of the unaccompanied Interpretation, SIC-32, is contained in Part A of this edition. Its effective date when issued was 25 March 2002. The text of the Accompanying Guidance on SIC-32 is contained in Part B of this edition. This part presents the following document:

BASIS FOR CONCLUSIONS

Basis for Conclusions on
SIC Interpretation 32 *Intangible Assets—Web Site Costs*

This Basis for Conclusions accompanies, but is not part of, SIC-32.

[The original text has been marked up to reflect the revision of IAS 16 in 2003 and the subsequent issue of IFRS 3: new text is underlined and deleted text is struck through.]

11   An intangible asset is defined in IAS 38.87 as an identifiable non-monetary asset without physical substance held for use in the production or supply of goods or services, for rental to others, or for administrative purposes. IAS 38.9 provides computer software as a common example of an intangible asset. By analogy, a web site is another example of an intangible asset.

12   IAS 38.68 requires expenditure on an intangible item to be recognised as an expense when incurred unless it forms part of the cost of an intangible asset that meets the recognition criteria in IAS 38.18–.67. IAS 38.69 requires expenditure on start-up activities to be recognised as an expense when incurred. An entity developing its own web site for internal or external access is not undertaking a start-up activity to the extent that an internally generated intangible asset is created. The requirements and guidance in IAS 38.52–.67 in addition to the general requirements described in IAS 38.21 for recognition and initial measurement of an intangible asset, apply to expenditure incurred on the development of an entity's own web site. As described in IAS 38.65–.67, the cost of a web site recognised as an internally generated intangible asset comprises all expenditure that can be directly attributed, or allocated on a reasonable and consistent basis, and is necessary to creating, producing and preparing the asset for it to be capable of operating in the manner intended by management its intended use.

13   IAS 38.54 requires expenditure on research (or on the research phase of an internal project) to be recognised as an expense when incurred. The examples provided in IAS 38.56 are similar to the activities undertaken in the Planning stage of a web site's development. Consequently, expenditure incurred in the Planning stage of a web site's development is recognised as an expense when incurred.

14   IAS 38.57 requires an intangible asset arising from the development phase of an internal project to be recognised only if an entity can demonstrate fulfilment of the six criteria specified. One of the criteria is to demonstrate how a web site will generate probable future economic benefits (IAS 38.57(d)). IAS 38.60 indicates that this criterion is met by assessing the economic benefits to be received from the web site and using the principles in IAS 36 *Impairment of Assets*, which considers the present value of estimated future cash flows from continuing use of the web site. Future economic benefits flowing from an intangible asset, as stated in IAS 38.17, may include revenue from the sale of products or services, cost savings, or other benefits resulting from the use of the asset by the entity. Therefore, future economic benefits from a web site may be assessed when the web site is capable of generating revenues. A web site developed solely or primarily for

advertising and promoting an entity's own products and services is not recognised as an intangible asset, because the entity cannot demonstrate the future economic benefits that will flow. Consequently, all expenditure on developing a web site solely or primarily for promoting and advertising an entity's own products and services is recognised as an expense when incurred.

15   Under IAS 38.~~21~~19, an intangible asset is recognised if, and only if, it meets specified criteria. IAS 38.65~~53~~ indicates that the cost of an internally generated intangible asset is the sum of expenditure incurred from the date when the intangible asset first meets the specified recognition criteria. When an entity acquires or creates content for purposes other than to advertise and promote an entity's own products and services, it may be possible to identify an intangible asset (eg a licence or a copyright) separate from a web site. However, a separate asset is not recognised when expenditure is directly attributed, ~~or allocated on a reasonable and consistent basis,~~ to creating, producing, and preparing the web site for <u>it to be capable of operating in the manner intended by management</u> ~~its intended use~~ – the expenditure is included in the cost of developing the web site.

16   IAS 38.69~~57~~(c) requires expenditure on advertising and promotional activities to be recognised as an expense when incurred. Expenditure incurred on developing content that advertises and promotes an entity's own products and services (eg digital photographs of products) is an advertising and promotional activity, and consequently recognised as an expense when incurred ~~in accordance with IAS 38.57(c)~~.

17   ~~Once development of a web site is complete, an enterprise begins the activities described in the Operating stage. Subsequent expenditure to enhance or maintain an enterprise's own web site is recognised as an expense when incurred unless it meets the recognition criteria in IAS 38.60. IAS 38.61 explains that if the expenditure is required to maintain the asset at its originally assessed standard of performance, then the expenditure is recognised as an expense when incurred.[1]__ <u>Once development of a web site is complete, an entity begins the activities described in the Operating stage. Subsequent expenditure to enhance or maintain an entity's own web site is recognised as an expense when incurred unless it meets the recognition criteria in IAS 38.18. IAS 38.20 explains that most subsequent expenditures are likely to maintain the future economic benefits embodied in an existing intangible asset rather than meet the definition of an intangible asset and the recognition criteria set out in IAS 38. In addition, it is often difficult to attribute subsequent expenditure directly to a particular intangible asset rather than to the business as a whole. Therefore, only rarely will subsequent expenditure – expenditure incurred after the initial recognition of a purchased intangible asset or after completion of an internally generated intangible asset – be recognised in the carrying amount of an asset.[2]</u>

---

1   ~~IAS 16 Property, Plant and Equipment as revised by the IASB in 2003 requires all subsequent costs to be covered by its general recognition principle and eliminated the requirement to reference the originally assessed standard of performance. IAS 38 was amended as a consequence of the change to IAS 16 and the paragraphs specifically referred to were eliminated. This paragraph has been struck through to avoid any confusion.~~

2   <u>The new text was added by IFRS 3 Business Combinations in 2004.</u>

18   An intangible asset is measured after initial recognition by applying the requirements of IAS 38.~~72–.87~~63–.78. The <u>revaluation model</u> ~~Allowed Alternative Treatment~~ in IAS 38.~~75~~64 is applied only when the fair value of an intangible asset can be determined by reference to an active market.[3] However, as an active market is unlikely to exist for web sites, the <u>cost model</u> ~~Benchmark Treatment~~ applies. Additionally, ~~since IAS 38.84 states that an intangible asset always has a finite useful life, a web site that is recognised as an asset is amortised over the best estimate of its useful life under IAS 38.79. As~~ <u>as</u> indicated in IAS 38.~~92~~81, many intangible assets are susceptible to technological obsolescence, and given the history of rapid changes in technology, the useful life of web sites will be short.

Amended reference to the *Conceptual Framework*

19   Following the issue of the revised *Conceptual Framework for Financial Reporting* in 2018 (2018 *Conceptual Framework*), the Board issued *Amendments to References to the Conceptual Framework in IFRS Standards*. In SIC-32, that document replaced a reference in paragraph 5 to the *Framework for the Preparation and Presentation of Financial Statements* adopted by the Board in 2001 (*Framework*) with a reference to the 2018 *Conceptual Framework*. The Board does not expect that replacement to have a significant effect on the application of the Interpretation. Paragraph 5 describes the accounting for expenditure excluded from the scope of the Interpretation. That paragraph also states that this type of expenditure — expenditure on an Internet service provider hosting the entity's web site — is recognised as an expense, so the amendment will not affect the accounting treatment.

---

3   IFRS 13 *Fair Value Measurement*, issued in May 2011, defines fair value and contains the requirements for measuring fair value. IFRS 13 defines an active market.

IFRS Practice Statement 1

Management Commentary
A framework for presentation

IFRS Practice Statement 1 *Management Commentary* was issued in December 2010 for application from 8 December 2010. The text of Practice Statement 1 is contained in Part B of this edition. This part presents the following accompanying document:

BASIS FOR CONCLUSIONS

This Basis for Conclusions accompanies, but is not part of, the Practice Statement.

Introduction

BC1 This Basis for Conclusions summarises the International Accounting Standard Board's considerations in developing the IFRS Practice Statement *Management Commentary*. Individual Board members gave greater weight to some factors than to others.

BC2 The Practice Statement was approved by the Board for issue as non-binding guidance, after considering the responses to its public consultation on the discussion paper *Management Commentary* and the exposure draft *Management Commentary*.

BC3 The purpose of financial statements is to provide information about the financial position, financial performance and cash flows of an entity that is useful to a wide range of users in making economic decisions (paragraph 9 of IAS 1 *Presentation of Financial Statements*). Financial statements prepared for that purpose meet the common needs of most users. However, financial statements do not provide all the information that users need to make economic decisions because the financial statements largely portray the financial effects of past events and do not provide non-financial measures of performance or a discussion of future prospects and plans.

BC4 Management commentary supplements and complements the financial statements. The Board's objective in issuing the Practice Statement is to improve the usefulness of the information provided in an entity's management commentary so that, when it is provided in conjunction with the financial statements, users are better able to make decisions about providing resources to the entity.

BC5 Governments, securities regulators, stock exchanges and professional accountancy bodies often require entities whose debt or equity securities are publicly traded to publish management commentary. Management commentary encompasses reporting that jurisdictions may describe as management's discussion and analysis (MD&A), operating and financial review (OFR), business review or management's report.

BC6 This Basis for Conclusions discusses the following matters:

(a) background (paragraphs BC7–BC11);

(b) objective (paragraphs BC12–BC14);

(c) scope (paragraphs BC15–BC17);

(d) identification of management commentary (paragraphs BC18–BC21);

(e) users of management commentary (paragraphs BC22–BC25);

(f) purpose of management commentary (paragraphs BC26–BC28);

(g) principles for the presentation of management commentary (paragraphs BC29–BC44);

(h)   presentation (paragraphs BC45 and BC46);

(i)   elements of management commentary (paragraphs BC47–BC49); and

(j)   placement of disclosure within the financial reports (paragraphs BC50–BC53).

Background

BC7   In late 2002 the Board set up a project team comprising representatives from the national standard-setters in Germany, New Zealand and the United Kingdom and from the Canadian Institute of Chartered Accountants. The project team examined the potential for issuing a standard or guidance on management commentary. In October 2005 the Board published the results of the project team's research in a discussion paper *Management Commentary*.

BC8   In the discussion paper, the project team presented its views on the users, objective and qualitative characteristics of management commentary. The project team also described essential elements (described as 'content elements' in the discussion paper) of management commentary and a possible framework for use by standard-setters in distinguishing between information that would appear in management commentary and information that would appear in the notes to the financial statements.

BC9   In 2009 the Board published an exposure draft *Management Commentary*. The exposure draft took into account the proposals contained in the discussion paper and respondents' comments on those proposals. It also reflected developments in narrative reporting at the regulatory level in a variety of jurisdictions and the Board's recent work on the *Conceptual Framework for Financial Reporting*, specifically the work on the exposure draft *An improved Conceptual Framework for Financial Reporting: Chapter 1: The Objective of Financial Reporting* and *Chapter 2: Qualitative Characteristics and Constraints of Decision-useful Financial Reporting Information* (May 2008). Importantly, the exposure draft *Management Commentary* included a proposal to publish the proposals in the exposure draft as non-binding guidance, not as an International Financial Reporting Standard (IFRS).

BC10   Most respondents supported the Board's proposal in the exposure draft to issue guidance. In developing the Practice Statement, the Board considered responses to this proposal and on other issues such as applying the qualitative characteristics to information in management commentary, including application guidance and illustrative examples in the Practice Statement and whether forecasts must be included in management commentary as forward-looking information.

BC11   The Board observed that management commentary meets the definition of 'other financial reporting' described in paragraph 7 of the *Preface to International Financial Reporting Standards*.[1] Thus the Board decided that management commentary is within the boundaries of financial reporting and

---

1   *Preface to International Financial Reporting Standards* renamed *Preface to IFRS Standards* in December 2018. The reference to paragraph 7 remains unchanged.

within the scope of the *Conceptual Framework*.[2] Consequently, management commentary is also within the scope and authority of the Board.

Objective

BC12 The Practice Statement sets out a non-binding framework to guide the presentation of management commentary. The Board's intention in issuing the Practice Statement is to foster good practice in management commentary reporting by permitting an entity's management to exercise discretion in tailoring its commentary to the entity's particular circumstances.

BC13 Although the Practice Statement is not an IFRS and is not binding, the Board believes the Statement will promote comparability across all entities that present management commentary to accompany their IFRS financial statements, thereby improving the usefulness of the financial reports to users.

BC14 The Board considered the view that a non-binding practice statement would not result in improvements in financial reporting. However, the Board decided that a practice statement would provide useful guidance for entities, and its flexible application would benefit entities in jurisdictions that have local requirements or regulations. Furthermore, the Board believes that a practice statement might encourage entities that are not accustomed to presenting management commentary to provide it for users. The existence of a practice statement might also encourage jurisdictions to adopt it as their own.

Scope

BC15 The Board believes that the Practice Statement may prove useful to entities that are not accustomed to presenting management commentary. It may also be useful for entities that are already accustomed to presenting reports setting out commentary by management because of local requirements or regulations imposed by the public exchanges on which their securities are listed, provided the Practice Statement does not contradict those requirements or regulations. Thus, the Board decided that the Practice Statement could be applied by entities that present management commentary that relates to financial statements that have been prepared in accordance with IFRSs.

BC16 The Board decided to provide guidance on the content of management commentary in the form of a non-binding practice statement, rather than an IFRS, because it believes it is up to individual jurisdictions to make their own judgements on:

(a) whether entities should be required to include management commentary in addition to their IFRS financial statements and whether inclusion is necessary to assert compliance with IFRSs;

(b) the level of assurance to which management commentary should be subjected;

---

2 References to the *Conceptual Framework* in this Basis for Conclusions are to the *Conceptual Framework for Financial Reporting*, issued in 2010 and in effect when the Practice Statement was developed.

(c)   the necessity of 'safe harbour' provisions in relation to the inclusion of forward-looking information;[3] and

(d)   the type of entity that should present management commentary.

BC17   The Board's decision to issue a practice statement and not an IFRS means that entities applying IFRSs are not required to comply with the Practice Statement, unless specifically required by their jurisdiction. Furthermore, non-compliance with the Practice Statement does not prevent the entity's financial statements from complying with IFRSs, if they otherwise do so. Additionally, the entity's financial statements may comply with IFRSs if an entity has not provided management commentary during a particular financial year.

Identification of management commentary

BC18   The positioning of management commentary relative to the financial statements varies among jurisdictions that require management commentary. In some jurisdictions, management commentary accompanies the annual financial statements in a printed report to shareholders. In others, management commentary is contained within separate annual regulatory filings.

BC19   The Board considered whether it would be desirable to incorporate management commentary within the financial statements, perhaps by adding textual material and other information within the notes to the financial statements. The Board rejected this idea on the ground that management commentary should supplement and complement the financial statements. Consequently, the Board concluded that management commentary should not be placed within the financial statements themselves.

BC20   The Board also decided to link management commentary to the financial statements because, as noted in paragraph BC33, management commentary is designed to supplement and complement information provided in a related set of financial statements. The Board observed that providing management commentary without (at minimum) identifying the related financial statements might be misleading for users. Consequently, the Board decided that when an entity presents management commentary that relates to IFRS financial statements, it should either make the financial statements available with the commentary or identify the financial statements to which the commentary relates. The Board noted that because the Practice Statement does not require entities to prepare management commentary, IFRS financial statements can be made available for use without a corresponding management commentary.

BC21   In the Board's view, it is important for users of the financial reports to be able to distinguish information contained in the reports using the Practice Statement from information that is prepared using IFRSs and from information that may be useful to users but is neither the subject of the

---

3   A safe harbour is a provision of a statute or a regulation that reduces or eliminates a party's liability under the law, on the condition that the party performed its actions in good faith.

Practice Statement nor the requirements in IFRSs. While the Board concluded that preparers should not be required to include a formal confirmation that they have complied with the Practice Statement, because the Statement is not binding, it did agree that it would be helpful if preparers included in management commentary an explanation of the extent to which the Practice Statement has been followed. The Board also concluded that it would be misleading if preparers were to assert compliance with the Practice Statement if they did not comply with the Practice Statement in its entirety.

Users of management commentary

BC22   In September 2010 the Board published two chapters of the *Conceptual Framework*: Chapter 1: *The objective of general purpose financial reporting* and Chapter 3: *Qualitative characteristics of useful financial information*. In the Board's view, management commentary is within the scope of the *Conceptual Framework*. The two aspects of the Practice Statement most affected by the *Conceptual Framework* are the definition of users and the qualitative characteristics (see paragraphs BC41–BC43) of management commentary.

BC23   In most jurisdictions, the requirements or guidance on management commentary specify that the information should be directed to meeting the needs of investors, or a narrower group such as existing shareholders. In some jurisdictions there has been debate about which users should be the focus of management commentary—with many constituents taking the view that management commentary should meet the needs of all stakeholders.

BC24   The Board reasoned that given that management commentary forms a part of financial reporting and is within the scope of the *Conceptual Framework*, it follows that information provided by management commentary should focus on the same users as do general purpose financial reports.

BC25   Therefore, the Board concluded that the primary users of management commentary are those identified in paragraph OB2 of Chapter 1 of the *Conceptual Framework*: 'existing and potential investors, lenders and other creditors'.

Purpose of management commentary

BC26   The Board agreed that the purpose of management commentary is to provide, from management's perspective, context for the financial statements. This is consistent with the objectives stated in regulations and guidance in many jurisdictions. For example, guidance issued by the US Securities and Exchange Commission (SEC) in December 2003 states that the purpose of Management's Discussion and Analysis (MD&A) is 'not complicated'. It is to provide users with information 'necessary to an understanding of [a company's] financial condition, changes in financial condition and results of operations' (SEC, Regulation S–K, Item 303).

BC27   The content of management commentary is not necessarily bound to the reporting period described by the financial statements to which it relates. Some information within management commentary looks to the future. The Board concluded that the inclusion of forward-looking information within management commentary helps users of the financial reports assess whether past performance is indicative of future performance and whether the progress of the entity is in line with management's stated objectives.

BC28   The Board defined the term 'progress' in the Appendix on the basis of the usage of the term 'development' in the European Union's requirement for 'at least a fair review of the development of the company's business and of its position' (Article 46 of the Fourth Council Directive on the annual accounts of certain types of companies (78/660/EEC)). The Board did not use the term 'development' in the Practice Statement, because it is already defined in IFRSs.

Principles for the presentation of management commentary

Management's view

BC29   The principle in paragraph 12(a) raises the issue of what is meant by 'management'. The term 'key management personnel' is defined in IAS 24 *Related Party Disclosures* to mean 'those persons having authority and responsibility for planning, directing and controlling the activities of the entity, directly or indirectly, including any director (whether executive or otherwise) of that entity' (paragraph 9 of IAS 24).

BC30   The Board noted that determining who presents and approves management commentary may not be limited to 'key management personnel' and is likely to depend on jurisdictional requirements. For example, in the United Kingdom the Companies Act 2006 requires a business review as part of the directors' report. For quoted companies, the requirements are reflected in the UK Accounting Standards Board's (ASB's) OFR Reporting Statement, which recommends that an OFR should be the analysis by the directors. Furthermore, it is the directors who are responsible for approving the business review or OFR. There are similar requirements in Canada, France and Germany. Therefore, the Board determined that referring to 'management' would enable entities to apply the principle in paragraph 12(a) given their jurisdictional requirements.

BC31   The Board observed that the principle that management commentary should describe management's view of the financial statements has its roots in regulation. For example, the first of the SEC objectives requires that MD&A:

> ... provide a narrative explanation of a company's financial statements that enables investors to see the company through the eyes of management. [SEC, Regulation S–K, Item 303]

That requirement has also been enshrined in securities regulation in Canada and in the UK ASB's OFR Reporting Statement.

BC32　The Board noted a study that suggests that, with few exceptions, the information important to management in managing the business is the same information that is important to capital providers in assessing performance and prospects. Consequently, the Board decided that management commentary should derive from the same information that is important to management.

Supplement and complement the financial statements

BC33　Paragraph BC11 points out that the Board observed that management commentary meets the definition of 'other financial reporting' in the Preface. In addition, the Board noted that the principle of providing information to supplement and complement the financial statements in effect formalises the statement in paragraph 7 of the *Preface* that:

> Other financial reporting comprises information provided outside financial statements that assists in the interpretation of a complete set of financial statements or improves users' ability to make efficient economic decisions.

BC34　To provide context for the principle of supplementing and complementing the financial statements is the example of commentary for a defined benefit pension plan that has a deficit. In this example, management could supplement and complement the disclosure in the financial statements by providing a narrative explanation of the nature of the deficit and the conditions and events that led to the deficit (eg poor returns on plan assets or the demographics of those covered by the plan). Furthermore, management could provide helpful information related to the plan that is not otherwise disclosed in the financial statements, but is important to the management of the plan (eg changing investment managers or focusing on specific investment opportunities).

Forward-looking information

BC35　The Board observed that in many jurisdictions, requirements relating to management commentary focus on information that helps users of the financial reports to assess the entity's prospects. These requirements have their roots in regulation, specifically in the MD&A requirements of the SEC. The third of the SEC objectives for MD&A reporting is:

> … to provide information about the quality of, and potential variability of, a company's earnings and cash flow, so that investors can ascertain the likelihood that past performance is indicative of future performance. [SEC, Regulation S-K, Item 303]

BC36　This US regulatory requirement for the inclusion of information that helps investors assess prospects is found in both Canadian securities regulations and the European Modernisation Directive. The Directive has in turn been transposed into legislation in EU Member States.

BC37　The Board agreed with the inclusion of forward-looking information in management commentary for the reasons specified in the SEC MD&A requirements.

BC38   Many respondents to the exposure draft were concerned about the focus on forward-looking information. However, the Board decided that forward-looking information is important. Explanations of management's perspective of the entity's direction, targets and prospects, in addition to explanations of past events, can help users of the financial reports to develop expectations about the entity from its past performance and current state. Furthermore, the Board observed that the Practice Statement allows flexibility for management in determining to what extent management commentary includes forward-looking information. In particular, the Board observed that the Practice Statement clearly indicates that the extent of forward-looking information will be influenced by the regulatory and legal environment within which the entity operates. Moreover, although disclosure of forward-looking information is encouraged in many jurisdictions, this does not necessarily mean providing forecasts or projections. The Board notes that in some jurisdictions there are safe harbour provisions to restrict liability claims or regulatory provisions, or both, for forward-looking information. However, those safe harbour provisions require cautionary statements to be included with the forward-looking information.

BC39   The Board considered the view that forward-looking information might present an over-optimistic picture of the entity. However, the Board observes that forward-looking information must possess the qualitative characteristics, including faithful representation, and thus must be neutral. Furthermore, management must disclose its assumptions used in providing the forward-looking information, thus enabling users to evaluate the reasonableness of the assumptions.

BC40   An example of what the Board envisages as forward-looking information that does not include forecasts or projections is again the commentary that could be provided for a defined benefit pension plan that has a deficit (described in paragraph BC34). In that example, management could provide forward-looking information by explaining management's objectives and strategies for remedying the plan deficit. These strategies might include a planned future increase in contributions, changes in investment strategy or changes to the plan. Management could also provide an explanation of how general market trends or other risks might affect the deficit and the strategies of management for remedying the deficit. This disclosure could include some quantitative information, but it is not necessarily a forecast or a projection.

BC41   In developing the exposure draft, the Board considered the view that detailed application guidance or illustrative examples are necessary to put into operation the guidance around forward-looking information included in the Practice Statement. However, the Board decided not to include such detailed guidance because there is a risk that undue emphasis could be placed on the application guidance or illustrative examples. Furthermore, the Board observed that such guidance or examples could be misinterpreted and thus reduce the flexibility in applying the framework. Many respondents to the exposure draft supported the Board's decision not to include detailed application guidance or illustrative examples.

Qualitative characteristics

BC42   As a result of the Board concluding that management commentary is within the scope of the *Conceptual Framework*, the Practice Statement specifies that the appropriate qualitative characteristics are those identified in Chapter 3 of the *Conceptual Framework* (see paragraph BC22). The qualitative characteristics in Chapter 3 will therefore be applied to both financial statements and management commentary.

BC43   In discussing the application of the qualitative characteristics to management commentary, the Board considered how the concept of balance (ie the inclusion of both bad news and good news) relates to the qualitative characteristics in general and the application of the qualitative characteristic of verifiability in particular. The Board decided that balance is equivalent to neutrality, in the context described in Chapter 3 of the *Conceptual Framework*. Consequently, the Board reasoned that because neutrality is a characteristic of faithful representation, balance is subsumed within faithful representation.

BC44   Furthermore, the Board decided that information in management commentary, including forward-looking information, can possess the qualitative characteristic of verifiability as it is described in Chapter 3. Paragraph QC26 of Chapter 3 indicates that 'verifiability means that different knowledgeable and independent observers could reach consensus'. Expressed differently, the information presented is capable of being tested, either by observation or experiment. The Board observed that for forward-looking information, the test to ensure verifiability may be one of reasonableness: do the assumptions that support the forward-looking information in financial reports make sense?

Presentation

BC45   The Board agreed that it should be management's responsibility to decide both the content of its management commentary and the best way to present that content (ie the form). The Board observed that providing flexibility in both the content and form of management commentary reduces the risk that management will adopt a boilerplate approach to the presentation of management commentary.

BC46   Because management commentary supplements and complements the financial statements, the Board decided that management commentary should be consistent with the financial statements, particularly in terms of its presentation of segment information. The Board noted that, if the financial statements include segment information, the information presented in the management commentary should reflect that segmentation. The Board observed that this information is relevant for understanding the entity as a whole.

Elements of management commentary

BC47   The Board noted that specifying disclosures for management commentary may be more difficult than specifying information to be disclosed in the notes to the financial statements. The types of activities that are critical to an entity are specific to that entity. As a consequence, regulators have tended to identify the elements that reflect the type of content that they expect to see in management commentary rather than defining the elements themselves. The Board decided that following a similar approach would generate more meaningful disclosures, because entities can discuss those matters most relevant to their individual circumstances. Some Board members requested that the Practice Statement should include a detailed list of items (eg critical accounting estimates), even though they recognise that the elements and the framework would lead to discussion of those items. However, the Board wishes to avoid a checklist-compliance mentality, which might result from specifying a detailed list.

User needs

BC48   The Board decided to include the five elements described in paragraphs 24–40 of the Practice Statement as based upon the needs of existing and potential investors, lenders and other creditors as the primary users of management commentary information. The table below relates the five elements to the Board's assessment of the needs of the primary users of management commentary.

Elements	User needs
Nature of the business	The knowledge of the business in which an entity is engaged and the external environment in which it operates.
Objectives and strategies	To assess the strategies adopted by the entity and the likelihood that those strategies will be successful in meeting management's stated objectives.
Resources, risks and relationships	A basis for determining the resources available to the entity as well as obligations to transfer resources to others; the ability of the entity to generate long-term, sustainable net inflows of resources; and the risks to which those resource-generating activities are exposed, both in the near term and in the long term.
Results and prospects	The ability to understand whether an entity has delivered results in line with expectations and, implicitly, how well management has understood the entity's market, executed its strategy and managed the entity's resources, risks and relationships.

continued...

...continued

Elements	User needs
Performance measures and indicators	The ability to focus on the critical performance measures and indicators that management uses to assess and manage the entity's performance against stated objectives and strategies.

BC49 The Board observed that information in management commentary will be of interest to users other than the primary users described in paragraph 8 of the Practice Statement. As a result, the Board noted that management may need to consider the extent to which commenting on issues relevant to a wider user group may be appropriate given the degree of those issues' influence on the performance of the entity and its value. The Board also noted that management commentary should not, however, be seen as a replacement for other forms of reporting addressed to a wider stakeholder group.

Placement of disclosure within the financial reports

BC50 The Board noted that neither IFRSs nor the *Conceptual Framework* include principles to guide the Board's approach for establishing disclosure requirements. Thus, it is not always clear whether information belongs in the notes to the financial statements or in management commentary.

BC51 In December 2007 the Board decided to defer its work on a framework for disclosure and instead wait for the phase *Boundaries of financial reporting, and presentation and disclosure* (phase E) of the conceptual framework project. The Board noted that phase E includes the development of disclosure principles. Consequently, the Board views phase E of the conceptual framework as the appropriate project to resolve questions about the placement of disclosures in the financial reports.

BC52 The Board acknowledges that until phase E is completed, overlap will exist between the type of information that is disclosed in the notes to the financial statements and the type of information that is disclosed in management commentary. In the light of this overlap, the Board decided that it was important to establish management commentary as a disclosure tool, before resolving questions of placement.

BC53 The Board acknowledges that some entities already present management commentary and it has addressed this overlap in one area, which is the risk disclosures required by IFRS 7 *Financial Instruments: Disclosures*. IFRS 7 permits management to provide required risk disclosures either in the financial statements or in management commentary, if the disclosure in management commentary is cross-referenced in the financial statements and management commentary is provided at the same time and under the same terms as the financial statements. However, IFRS 7 and the Practice Statement do not address auditing matters related to the location of those disclosures.

IFRS Practice Statement 2

Making Materiality Judgements

IFRS Practice Statement 2 *Making Materiality Judgements* was issued in September 2017 for application from 14 September 2017. The text of Practice Statement 2 is contained in Part B of this edition. This part presents the following accompanying document:

BASIS FOR CONCLUSIONS

IFRS Practice Statement 2 *the Making Materiality Judgements*

This Basis for Conclusions accompanies, but is not part of, the IFRS Practice Statement 2 Making Materiality Judgements *(Practice Statement). It summarises the considerations of the International Accounting Standards Board (Board) when developing the Practice Statement. Individual Board members gave greater weight to some factors than to others.*

Background

BC1   The Board was informed at the Discussion Forum on Financial Reporting Disclosure in January 2013, through feedback on the 2014 Exposure Draft of proposed amendments to IAS 1 *Presentation of Financial Statements* and from other sources, that entities experience difficulties making materiality judgements when preparing financial statements. Some entities are unsure how to make materiality judgements and tend to use disclosure requirements in IFRS Standards as if they were items on a checklist, rather than using judgement when deciding what information to provide in financial statements. Some stakeholders stated that these difficulties and practices contribute to a disclosure problem—namely, entities provide too much irrelevant information and not enough relevant information in their financial statements.

BC2   Some stakeholders suggested that one of the factors contributing to these difficulties was the lack of guidance on materiality in IFRS Standards, particularly on how entities should make materiality judgements about information disclosed in the notes to the financial statements. In the light of this feedback, the Board decided to provide further guidance. The aim of the Board is to promote a behavioural change in the way entities prepare their financial statements, encouraging a greater exercise of judgement when determining what information to include or not to include in those statements.

BC3   In October 2015, the Board published the Exposure Draft IFRS Practice Statement *Application of Materiality to Financial Statements* (Practice Statement ED). The Board developed the Practice Statement ED after considering the input obtained from outreach and consultations with the IFRS Advisory Council; the Accounting Standards Advisory Forum (ASAF); the World Standard-Setters; the Global Preparers Forum (GPF); the Capital Markets Advisory Committee (CMAC); representatives of the International Auditing and Assurance Standards Board and the International Organization of Securities Commissions; and a number of other accounting professionals, academics and representatives of other regulatory bodies.[1]

---

1   The IFRS Advisory Council, the Accounting Standards Advisory Forum (ASAF), the Global Preparers Forum (GPF) and the Capital Markets Advisory Committee (CMAC) are the Board's advisory bodies. The World Standard-Setters is a meeting of accounting standard-setters organised by the Board.

BC4 The Board received 95 comment letters in response to the Practice Statement ED. The Board also conducted outreach on the proposals in the Practice Statement ED, including consultation with the ASAF, the CMAC and the GPF. Responses to the Practice Statement ED indicated widespread support for the Board to issue practical guidance on making materiality judgements in the preparation of financial statements. The Board considered the input it received on the Practice Statement ED when developing this Practice Statement.

Form of the guidance

BC5 The Practice Statement sets out non-mandatory guidance with the aim of assisting entities in making materiality judgements when preparing general purpose financial statements. Entities applying IFRS Standards are not required to comply with the Practice Statement to state compliance with those Standards. Nevertheless, the Board expects the Practice Statement to help promote a greater understanding of the role of materiality in applying IFRS Standards and of how judgement should be exercised to assess materiality in preparing financial statements. The Board expects that better understanding of the role of materiality will ultimately make financial statements more useful and easier to understand.

BC6 The Board decided to provide guidance on how to make materiality judgements in the form of a non-mandatory Practice Statement because:

(a) issuing mandatory requirements in a Standard could risk appearing prescriptive, which could undermine the emphasis on entities applying their judgement in the assessment of materiality; and

(b) issuing guidance as a separate non-mandatory document, rather than as non-mandatory implementation guidance supporting a specific Standard, such as IAS 1, would help to emphasise that the concept of materiality is pervasive throughout IFRS Standards.

BC7 Moreover, the Board was told that adding mandatory requirements in a Standard could risk creating conflicts with local legal or regulatory frameworks. Nevertheless, the Board observed that even though some jurisdictions might have legal or regulatory requirements that interact with IFRS materiality requirements, this should not result in a conflict with the guidance in the Practice Statement, provided that those local requirements do not prevent an entity from applying the requirements in IFRS Standards. No respondents to the Practice Statement ED and no participants in the outreach organised by the Board reported such a circumstance.

BC8 Furthermore, this Practice Statement does not change any requirements in IFRS Standards or introduce any new requirements. The Board decided that non-mandatory status was more appropriate.

BC9 Finally, the Board issued a Practice Statement rather than asking the IFRS Foundation staff to develop educational material because a Practice Statement is subject to full due process, including public consultation, and is more accessible than educational material.

BC10   Responses to the Practice Statement ED indicated widespread agreement with the considerations that led the Board to include its guidance in a non-mandatory Practice Statement.

Scope

BC11   The objective of this Practice Statement is to provide entities with guidance on making materiality judgements when preparing general purpose financial statements in accordance with IFRS Standards. The Board discussed whether to broaden the audience of the Practice Statement by also addressing it to other parties involved in financial reporting, but concluded that the Practice Statement should only be addressed to those involved in the preparation of the financial statements. The Board noted, however, that the Practice Statement is also likely to help other parties, such as auditors, users of financial statements, regulators and enforcers, understand the approach an entity follows in making materiality judgements when preparing its financial statements.

BC12   The Board discussed whether the Practice Statement should also be addressed to entities applying the *IFRS for SMEs*® Standard. However, the *IFRS for SMEs* Standard is a separate and stand-alone accounting framework based on full IFRS Standards with modifications to reflect cost-benefit considerations specific to small and medium sized entities and the need of users of the financial statements of such entities. The *IFRS for SMEs* Standard does not refer to the concept of primary users as included in the *Conceptual Framework for Financial Reporting (Conceptual Framework)* and does not include recent changes to full IFRS Standards (eg that an entity shall not reduce the understandability of its financial statements by obscuring material information with immaterial information). Therefore, the Board decided that the Practice Statement is not intended for entities applying the *IFRS for SMEs* Standard. The *IFRS for SMEs* Standard permits, but does not require, entities to refer to guidance available in full IFRS Standards. Those entities may therefore refer to the guidance in the Practice Statement in the same way they consider the requirements and guidance in full IFRS Standards dealing with similar and related issues in developing and applying accounting policies when the *IFRS for SMEs* Standard does not specifically address a transaction, other event or condition.

BC13   Materiality is a general concept widely used for financial reporting and other purposes. For example, auditors usually assess materiality when making judgements about the nature, timing and extent of the work to be done to express an opinion as to whether the financial statements are prepared, in all material respects, in accordance with an applicable financial reporting framework. Some respondents to the Practice Statement ED noted that preparers and auditors of financial statements assess materiality using a comparable approach—they both focus on information that could reasonably be expected to influence decisions of the users of an entity's financial statements. The Board discussed whether to include in the Practice Statement a reference to the assessment of materiality for auditing or other purposes, but decided to focus its guidance on the preparation of financial statements

only. Assessing materiality for purposes other than the preparation of financial statements is beyond the scope of this Practice Statement. Moreover, referring to different applications of the concept of materiality might cause confusion.

General characteristics of materiality

Definition of material

BC14 The Board has discussed the definition of 'material' and whether to change or clarify that definition in its Principles of Disclosure project. In September 2017, on the basis of those discussions, the Board published the Exposure Draft *Definition of Material (Proposed amendments to IAS 1 and IAS 8)* (Definition of Material ED). The Definition of Material ED proposes refining the definition of material by incorporating the existing description of material information in paragraph 7 of IAS 1[2] and emphasising the need to ensure material information is not obscured, as described in paragraph 30A of IAS 1. IFRS Standards already include both concepts; consequently, the Practice Statement includes these notions. The Board considered whether to postpone issuing this Practice Statement until the completion of the Definition of Material project. However, the Board concluded that providing guidance on making materiality judgements as quickly as possible would be useful and responded to requests for guidance.

BC15 Moreover, the Board observed that, since the proposed amendments in the Definition of Material ED do not constitute substantive changes to the existing requirements in IFRS Standards, they are unlikely to result in a change in practice for most entities or to significantly affect entities' financial statements. Therefore, the guidance in this Practice Statement would not be affected by the proposed amendments, other than by the possible need to update the definition of material quoted in the document.

Materiality judgements are pervasive

BC16 The Board discussed whether to focus the guidance in the Practice Statement on IFRS presentation and disclosure requirements only, but concluded that the need for materiality judgements is pervasive in the preparation of financial statements, also encompassing recognition and measurement requirements. Consequently, the Board provided, throughout the Practice Statement, guidance on how to make materiality judgements in the context of recognition and measurement as well as of presentation and disclosure.

Primary users and their information needs

BC17 The Practice Statement explains that, when making its materiality assessments, an entity should consider the primary users of its financial statements — its primary users — as defined by the *Conceptual Framework*, that is, existing and potential investors, lenders and other creditors. The Board

---

2 '... the assessment needs to take into account how users [...] could *reasonably* be expected to be influenced in making economic decisions' [emphasis added].

discussed whether it would be appropriate to emphasise the existence, among those primary users, of different subsets of users whose information needs might differ. However, the Board concluded that requiring an entity to identify different subsets of primary users, or focusing on any special information needs and expectations those users might have, could create a tension with the definition of general purpose financial statements, which focuses on the common information needs of a wide range of users. Consequently, the Practice Statement refers to the three categories of primary users identified in the *Conceptual Framework* — existing and potential investors, lenders and other creditors.

BC18 Furthermore, the Board decided to emphasise in the Practice Statement that the primary users of an entity's financial statements include potential investors, lenders and other creditors, as well as existing ones. The Board concluded this would address concerns some stakeholders expressed about an inappropriate focus on specific existing users; the Board decided to make clear that an entity cannot narrow the information provided in its financial statements by focusing only on its existing users' information needs.

BC19 An entity considers decisions its primary users make on the basis of the financial statements when deciding what information to include in those statements. Consequently, the Board decided the Practice Statement should describe primary users' decisions and related information needs as set out in the *Conceptual Framework*. Primary users' decisions depend on the returns they expect from the resources they provide to an entity. Expectations about returns, in turn, depend on primary users' assessment of the amount, timing and uncertainty of the future cash inflows to the entity, as well as on the assessment of management's stewardship of the entity's resources.

BC20 The Board further considered the *Conceptual Framework* when developing its guidance on the information needs of primary users an entity should consider when making materiality judgements. Providing all the information existing and potential investors, lenders and other creditors need is not the objective of general purpose financial statements. The Board clarified that an entity is not required to address information needs that respond to unique or individual information requests. An entity should aim to meet primary users' common information needs. In developing its guidance, the Board clarified that, to avoid losing information relevant to one category of primary users (among the three identified in the *Conceptual Framework*), the common information needs are not limited to the information needs simultaneously shared across all categories of primary users. An entity separately identifies the common information needs for each of the three categories, and meets the total of these needs.

Interaction with local laws and regulations

BC21 The Board discussed the interaction of materiality requirements in IFRS Standards with local laws and regulations in the light of stakeholders' comments relating to potential conflicts between the guidance in the Practice Statement ED and local legal or regulatory requirements. The Board noted that the Practice Statement provides guidance on making materiality judgements when preparing financial statements in accordance with IFRS Standards; it does not provide guidance on how to apply local legal or regulatory requirements.

BC22 Nevertheless, the Board acknowledged that local requirements might affect information provided in the financial statements. In these circumstances, an entity must comply with the materiality requirements in IFRS Standards, but the Standards do not prohibit the disclosure of additional information required by local laws or regulations, even if that information is not material according to IFRS Standards. A conflict would only occur if local laws or regulations prohibit the inclusion of information that is material for the purpose of IFRS Standards. No respondents to the Practice Statement ED and no participants in the outreach organised by the Board reported such a circumstance.

BC23 When information in addition to that required by IFRS Standards is provided in the financial statements, paragraph 30A of IAS 1 requires an entity to ensure that material information required by the Standards is not obscured. The Board observed that the appropriate organisation of information in the financial statements would allow an entity to meet that requirement.

Making materiality judgements

BC24 Respondents commenting on the Practice Statement ED welcomed the fact it gathered guidance on materiality from multiple IFRS Standards. However, some respondents suggested it would be useful to also describe the practical steps an entity follows when making materiality judgements in the preparation of its financial statements. The Board developed a four-step process (materiality process) in consultation with the ASAF, the CMAC and the GPF. The description of the materiality process illustrates the role materiality plays in the preparation of financial statements and clarifies how a materiality judgement is made. The materiality process also identifies the factors an entity should consider when making materiality judgements.

BC25 Consistent with the non-mandatory status of the Practice Statement, the Board developed the materiality process as an example of the approach an entity may follow in making materiality judgements, but clarified that the materiality process includes the materiality requirements an entity must apply to state compliance with IFRS Standards.

BC26 The Board considered whether to focus its guidance on the application of judgement or to illustrate the overall process of which materiality judgements are a part. However, as some respondents to the Practice Statement ED noted, describing the overall process helps an entity understand how materiality judgements can influence the preparation of its financial statements, as well as how the various materiality decisions are connected with each other.

BC27   The Board included Step 1 (identify) to provide an entity with a clear starting point for its assessments. Stakeholders largely agreed that an entity should use the requirements in IFRS Standards to identify information that primary users might need to make decisions about providing resources to the entity. When using the requirements in IFRS Standards, an entity benefits from the assessment the Board makes when developing IFRS Standards—when developing a Standard the Board identifies information it expects will meet the needs of a broad range of primary users. The Board also considered that some information not specified in IFRS Standards might be necessary to enable primary users to understand the impact of an entity's transactions, other events and conditions on the entity's financial position, financial performance and cash flows. Therefore, the Board decided that the entity's knowledge about its primary users' common information needs should be an additional input to Step 1. On the basis of that knowledge, an entity should consider whether to include additional information not specified by IFRS Standards in its financial statements.

BC28   Step 2 (assess) describes factors an entity should consider in identifying whether an item of information is material. The Board concluded that the application of judgement in assessing whether information is material involves both quantitative and qualitative considerations. Respondents to the Practice Statement ED also agreed that, in making materiality judgements, an entity should consider both quantitative and qualitative factors. The Practice Statement includes some examples of materiality factors. However, the Board decided to describe a limited number of factors rather than provide an exhaustive list of considerations to be taken into account.

BC29   The Board decided to include some guidance in the materiality process on the way an entity should reflect its materiality judgements. Step 3 (organise) deals with the output of an entity's materiality judgements and provides guidance the entity might want to consider to make its financial statements easier to understand. The Board recommends that an entity considers the different roles of the primary financial statements and the notes in deciding whether to present an item of information separately in the primary financial statements, to aggregate it with other information and/or to disclose the information in the notes. However, the Board decided not to provide further guidance on those topics in the Practice Statement. A discussion of the roles of the different components of the financial statements, as well as of the implications of those roles, has been included in the *Principles of Disclosure* Discussion Paper, which the Board published in March 2017.

BC30   Step 4 (review) gives an entity the opportunity to 'step back', once it has prepared its draft financial statements, and consider the information from an aggregated perspective. The Board discussed whether this step duplicates the assessment performed in Step 2 and clarified that an entity makes its materiality judgements in Step 2, but then reviews these judgements once a draft of the financial statements is available. In Step 2, an entity based its assessment on the expected financial statements as a whole, while it was still preparing its draft. In Step 4, an entity checks its assessment against the actual draft financial statements—this review may lead the entity to revisit the assessment performed in Step 2, provide additional information in the financial statements, remove immaterial information or reorganise existing information.

Specific topics

Prior-period information

BC31　When discussing materiality judgements about prior-period information included in financial statements, the Board acknowledged some legal or regulatory requirements might set out the amount of prior-period information to include in the financial statements. However, the Board decided that providing guidance on making materiality judgements about prior-period information in the Practice Statement would be necessary to promote behavioural change consistently across all parts of the financial statements and to encourage entities to exercise greater judgement when determining what information to include or not to include in financial statements.

BC32　The Board developed the guidance in the Practice Statement in the light of the minimum comparative information required by IAS 1. However, the Board acknowledged that an entity needs to consider any legal or regulatory requirements when making materiality judgements about prior-period information. Consequently, the Board decided to explain that, in its current-period financial statements, an entity may summarise prior-period information, compared to the way it was included in prior-period financial statements, except when local laws or regulations demand otherwise. The Board also clarified that an entity that wishes to state compliance with IFRS Standards cannot provide less information than the information required by the Standards, even if local laws and regulations permit otherwise.

BC33　The Board also emphasised that, when providing prior-period information in addition to the minimum comparative information required by IFRS Standards, information has to be provided in accordance with those Standards and should not obscure material information. Some stakeholders asked whether providing prior-period information at the same level of detail as current-period information could be seen as obscuring material information in the current-period financial statements. The Board does not expect that such prior-period information would obscure current-period material information.

Errors

BC34　The Board discussed whether to include in the Practice Statement guidance to help entities determine whether an error is material. The Board noted that the assessment of whether an error could reasonably be expected to influence primary users' decisions is an integral part of the preparation of the financial statements, and therefore concluded that the Practice Statement should address this topic. The Board noted that the materiality factors an entity would apply to conclude whether an error is material are the same as those described in the materiality process. Consequently, there is no need to provide any specific additional guidance. In the 'Errors' section, the Practice Statement suggests that an entity refer to the considerations described in the materiality process.

BC35 Respondents to the Practice Statement ED asked the Board to also address the situation in which an entity faces errors generated by the accumulation over several periods of errors that were immaterial both in individual prior periods and cumulatively over all prior periods (sometimes called 'cumulative errors'). The Board concluded it would be helpful to clarify that, in such circumstances:

(a) materiality judgements about cumulative errors that an entity made at the time the prior-period financial statements were authorised for issue need not be revisited in the current period, provided those judgements were reasonable at the time they were made and the entity considered information that was available, or was reasonably expected to be available, at that time; however

(b) an entity needs to assess whether cumulative errors have become material to the current-period financial statements.

BC36 The Board decided to include a statement in the Practice Statement to remind an entity that a cumulative error must be corrected if it becomes material to the current-period financial statements. The Board discussed whether to provide further guidance on how to correct such an error, but concluded that the Practice Statement should focus on how to make materiality judgements, instead of dealing with the consequences of these judgements. IAS 8 contains the requirements on the correction of errors.

BC37 The Practice Statement ED included some wording implying that if an entity intentionally misstates or omits information to achieve a particular presentation or result, such an error is always material. Respondents to the Practice Statement ED commented that the wording appears inconsistent with paragraph 41 of IAS 8 *Accounting Policies, Changes in Accounting Estimates and Errors*. Paragraph 41 of IAS 8 does not characterise such errors as material, however, it requires the correction of all errors made intentionally to achieve a particular presentation of an entity's financial position, financial performance or cash flows. The Board decided to align the wording in the Practice Statement with the wording of paragraph 41 of IAS 8.

Information about covenants

BC38 When discussing whether the existence of a covenant, or similar contractual terms, could influence materiality judgements, the Board identified two concerns:

(a) do any specific considerations apply in making materiality judgements on information about the existence and terms of a covenant, or a covenant breach?

(b)   does the existence of a covenant influence materiality judgements about information other than about the existence of the covenant, or a covenant breach, included in the financial statements?

BC39   In respect of the first concern, the Board concluded that, in addition to the materiality factors described in the materiality process, materiality judgements are specifically influenced by the consequences of a breach occurring and the likelihood of that breach occurring. In particular, the Board clarified that, regardless of the significance of the consequences of a breach occurring, information about the covenant is not material if the likelihood of the breach occurring is remote. In providing this clarification, the Board applied the disclosure threshold set in paragraph 28 of IAS 37 *Provisions, Contingent Liabilities and Contingent Assets* regarding the disclosure of contingent liabilities.

BC40   In respect of the second concern, the Board discussed including in the Practice Statement guidance stating that the existence of a covenant should not influence an entity's assessment of the materiality of other information in the financial statements. In other words, an entity is not required to reperform its materiality assessments the closer it gets to breaching a covenant. However, some stakeholders observed that such guidance would conflict with existing guidance developed by other parties on the assessment of the materiality of errors. To avoid creating any confusion among preparers and others involved in financial reporting, the Board decided not to include in the Practice Statement guidance on the impact of covenants on materiality assessments.

Materiality judgements for interim reporting

BC41   The Board discussed whether to provide guidance on how to make materiality judgements when preparing an interim financial report. The Board concluded that, when preparing an interim financial report, an entity should consider the same materiality factors it considers in preparing its annual financial statements. However, the Board also noted that it would be helpful to explain any additional considerations relevant to making a materiality judgement in the preparation of an interim financial report. In particular, the Board noted that it would be helpful to explain how the different time period and purposes of an interim financial report, compared to the annual financial statements, affect materiality judgements, as well as to address some practical concerns raised by respondents to the Practice Statement ED.

Likely effects of this Practice Statement

BC42   The Board is committed to assessing and sharing knowledge about the likely costs of implementing proposed new requirements and guidance—the costs and benefits are collectively referred to as 'effects'. The Practice Statement is designed to provide guidance on how to make materiality judgements in the preparation of financial statements. The Practice Statement does not change any requirements in IFRS Standards or introduce any new requirements. With no changes in existing requirements and given that the application of the

Practice Statement is not required to state compliance with IFRS Standards, the Board concluded that a separate effects analysis was not necessary.

BC43 The expected effects of the Practice Statement have been considered as part of the Board's discussions. The Board expects the Practice Statement will:

(a) enhance awareness of the role of materiality in helping to promote positive changes in behaviour (such as to discourage rigid adherence to checklists by an entity preparing financial statements);

(b) encourage an entity to exercise judgement to a greater extent when preparing financial statements, which should lead to a reduction in boilerplate disclosures and redundant information and provide a framework for assessing the need in the financial statements for information that is additional to disclosure requirements specified by IFRS Standards; and

(c) provide a useful reference point for discussions between an entity, its auditors and regulators on the assessment of materiality, which could help facilitate agreement.

BC44 The Board does not expect any significant costs associated with the application of the Practice Statement because it introduces no new requirements nor is the application of the Practice Statement mandatory. However, some implementation costs might be faced by an entity that has previously relied on a checklist approach when preparing its financial statements. The Board expects such an entity would apply more judgement when deciding what information to include in the financial statements, if it follows the guidance in the Practice Statement. The Board concluded that the benefits of higher-quality disclosures and easier access to information for primary users of financial statements exceed the implementation costs required when entities apply judgement in preparing financial statements, rather than following a checklist. Conversely, an entity already applying appropriate judgement in the preparation of its financial statements would incur no additional implementation costs and could benefit from the issue of the Practice Statement in its interaction with auditors and other stakeholders.

BC45 The effects the Board expects from the Practice Statement were assessed against the comments received on the Practice Statement ED. Overall, respondents confirmed the Board's expectations and welcomed the proposal to issue the Practice Statement.

Interaction with the Board's other projects

BC46 The Board decided to issue this Practice Statement before the finalisation of the Principle of Disclosures project, for which a Discussion Paper was published in March 2017; the Definition of Material project, for which an Exposure Draft was published in September 2017; or the *Conceptual Framework* project—the revised *Conceptual Framework* is expected to be issued in 2018.[3] The

3 In 2018 the Board issued a revised *Conceptual Framework*. References to the *Conceptual Framework* in this Practice Statement were updated to refer to the revised *Conceptual Framework*.

Board considered whether to postpone issuing this Practice Statement until the completion of one or more of those projects; however, it concluded that it would be useful to provide guidance on making materiality judgements as quickly as possible, to respond to requests for guidance. Moreover, the Board concluded that the finalisation of these projects would be unlikely to affect the guidance in the Practice Statement.

Approvals by the Board of Annual Improvements to IFRS Standards

Approval by the Board of *Improvements to IFRSs* issued in May 2008

In May 2008 the International Accounting Standards Board issued *Improvements to IFRSs*. The document contained miscellaneous amendments to International Financial Reporting Standards (IFRSs) and the related Bases for Conclusions and guidance made in the Board's first annual improvements project.

The annual improvements project provides a vehicle for making non-urgent but necessary amendments to IFRSs. The amendments have been incorporated into the text of the IFRSs set out in this edition.

Improvements to IFRSs was approved for issue by the thirteen members of the International Accounting Standards Board, except that:

- Mr Yamada dissented from one of the amendments to IAS 28 *Investments in Associates*.

- Mr Leisenring dissented from one of the amendments to IAS 38 *Intangible Assets*.

The dissenting opinions of those Board members are set out after the Basis for Conclusions on the IFRSs affected.

Sir David Tweedie	Chairman
Thomas E Jones	Vice-Chairman
Mary E Barth	
Stephen Cooper	
Philippe Danjou	
Jan Engström	
Robert P Garnett	
Gilbert Gélard	
James J Leisenring	
Warren J McGregor	
John T Smith	
Tatsumi Yamada	
Wei-Guo Zhang	

Approval by the Board of *Improvements to IFRSs* issued in April 2009

In April 2009 the International Accounting Standards Board issued *Improvements to IFRSs*. The document contained miscellaneous amendments to International Financial Reporting Standards (IFRSs) and the related Bases for Conclusions and guidance made in the Board's second annual improvements project.

The annual improvements project provides a vehicle for making non-urgent but necessary amendments to IFRSs. The amendments have been incorporated into the text of the IFRSs set out in this edition.

Improvements to IFRSs was approved for issue by the fourteen members of the International Accounting Standards Board, except that:

- Mr Cooper dissented from the amendment to IFRS 8 *Operating Segments*.

- Mr Leisenring dissented from the amendment to IAS 17 *Leases*.

The dissenting opinions of those Board members are set out after the Basis for Conclusions on the IFRSs affected.

Sir David Tweedie	Chairman
Thomas E Jones	Vice-Chairman
Mary E Barth	
Stephen Cooper	
Philippe Danjou	
Jan Engström	
Robert P Garnett	
Gilbert Gélard	
Prabhakar Kalavacherla	
James J Leisenring	
Warren J McGregor	
John T Smith	
Tatsumi Yamada	
Wei-Guo Zhang	

Approval by the Board of *Improvements to IFRSs* issued in May 2010

In May 2010 the International Accounting Standards Board issued *Improvements to IFRSs*. The document contained miscellaneous amendments to International Financial Reporting Standards (IFRSs) and the related Bases for Conclusions and guidance made in the Board's third annual improvements project.

The annual improvements project provides a vehicle for making non-urgent but necessary amendments to IFRSs. The amendments have been incorporated into the text of the IFRSs set out in this edition.

Improvements to IFRSs was approved for issue by the fifteen members of the International Accounting Standards Board.

Sir David Tweedie   Chairman

Stephen Cooper

Philippe Danjou

Jan Engström

Patrick Finnegan

Robert P Garnett

Gilbert Gélard

Amaro Luiz de Oliveira Gomes

Prabhakar Kalavacherla

James J Leisenring

Patricia McConnell

Warren J McGregor

John T Smith

Tatsumi Yamada

Wei-Guo Zhang

Approval by the Board of *Annual Improvements 2009–2011 Cycle* published in May 2012

Annual Improvements 2009–2011 Cycle was approved for publication by the fourteen members of the International Accounting Standards Board.

Hans Hoogervorst	Chairman
Ian Mackintosh	Vice-Chairman
Stephen Cooper	
Philippe Danjou	
Jan Engström	
Patrick Finnegan	
Amaro Luiz de Oliveira Gomes	
Prabhakar Kalavacherla	
Patricia McConnell	
Takatsugu Ochi	
Paul Pacter	
Darrel Scott	
John T Smith	
Wei-Guo Zhang	

Approval by the Board of *Annual Improvements to IFRSs 2010–2012 Cycle* published in December 2013

Annual Improvements to IFRSs 2010–2012 Cycle was approved for publication by the sixteen members of the International Accounting Standards Board.

Hans Hoogervorst	Chairman
Ian Mackintosh	Vice-Chairman
Stephen Cooper	
Philippe Danjou	
Martin Edelmann	
Jan Engström	
Patrick Finnegan	
Amaro Luiz de Oliveira Gomes	
Gary Kabureck	
Prabhakar Kalavacherla	
Patricia McConnell	
Takatsugu Ochi	
Darrel Scott	
Chungwoo Suh	
Mary Tokar	
Wei-Guo Zhang	

Approval by the Board of *Annual Improvements to IFRSs 2011–2013 Cycle* published in December 2013

Annual Improvements to IFRSs 2011–2013 Cycle was approved for publication by the sixteen members of the International Accounting Standards Board.

Hans Hoogervorst	Chairman
Ian Mackintosh	Vice-Chairman
Stephen Cooper	
Philippe Danjou	
Martin Edelmann	
Jan Engström	
Patrick Finnegan	
Amaro Luiz de Oliveira Gomes	
Gary Kabureck	
Prabhakar Kalavacherla	
Patricia McConnell	
Takatsugu Ochi	
Darrel Scott	
Chungwoo Suh	
Mary Tokar	
Wei-Guo Zhang	

Approval by the Board of *Annual Improvements to IFRSs 2012–2014 Cycle* issued in September 2014

Annual Improvements to IFRSs 2012–2014 Cycle was approved for issue by the fourteen members of the International Accounting Standards Board.

Hans Hoogervorst	Chairman
Ian Mackintosh	Vice-Chairman
Stephen Cooper	
Philippe Danjou	
Amaro Luiz de Oliveira Gomes	
Martin Edelmann	
Patrick Finnegan	
Gary Kabureck	
Suzanne Lloyd	
Takatsugu Ochi	
Darrel Scott	
Chungwoo Suh	
Mary Tokar	
Wei-Guo Zhang	

Approval by the Board of *Annual Improvements to IFRS Standards 2014–2016 Cycle* issued in December 2016

Annual Improvements to IFRS Standards 2014–2016 Cycle was approved for issue by the 11 members of the International Accounting Standards Board.

Hans Hoogervorst	Chairman
Suzanne Lloyd	Vice-Chair
Stephen Cooper	
Martin Edelmann	
Amaro Gomes	
Gary Kabureck	
Takatsugu Ochi	
Darrel Scott	
Chungwoo Suh	
Mary Tokar	
Wei-Guo Zhang	

Approval by the Board of *Annual Improvements to IFRS Standards 2015–2017 Cycle* issued in December 2017

Annual Improvements to IFRS Standards 2015–2017 Cycle was approved for issue by 11 of 14 members of the International Accounting Standards Board (Board). Messrs Anderson and Lu and Ms Tarca abstained in view of their recent appointments to the Board.

Hans Hoogervorst	Chairman
Suzanne Lloyd	Vice-Chair
Nick Anderson	
Martin Edelmann	
Françoise Flores	
Amaro Luiz de Oliveira Gomes	
Gary Kabureck	
Jianqiao Lu	
Takatsugu Ochi	
Darrel Scott	
Thomas Scott	
Chungwoo Suh	
Ann Tarca	
Mary Tokar	

Approval by the Board of *Annual Improvements to IFRS Standards 2018–2020* issued in May 2020

Annual Improvements to IFRS Standards 2018–2020 was approved for issue by all 14 members of the International Accounting Standards Board.

Hans Hoogervorst	Chairman
Suzanne Lloyd	Vice-Chair
Nick Anderson	
Tadeu Cendon	
Martin Edelmann	
Françoise Flores	
Gary Kabureck	
Jianqiao Lu	
Darrel Scott	
Thomas Scott	
Chungwoo Suh	
Rika Suzuki	
Ann Tarca	
Mary Tokar	

IFRS Foundation

Constitution

CONTENTS

Preface

This *Constitution* was approved in its original form by the former International Accounting Standards Committee (the IASC) in March 2000 and by the members of the IASC at a meeting in Edinburgh on 24 May 2000.

At its meeting in December 1999, the IASC had appointed a Nominating Committee to select the first Trustees. Those Trustees were nominated on 22 May 2000 and took office on 24 May 2000 as a result of the approval of the *Constitution*. In execution of their duties under the *Constitution*, the Trustees formed the International Accounting Standards Committee Foundation (the IASC Foundation) on 6 February 2001. As a consequence of a resolution by the Trustees, Part C of the revised *Constitution*, approved on 24 May 2000, ceased to have effect and was deleted.

Reflecting the Trustees' decision to create the IFRS Interpretations Committee, and following public consultation, the *Constitution* was revised on 5 March 2002. Subsequently the Trustees amended the *Constitution*, which came into effect from 8 July 2002, to reflect other changes that had taken place since the formation of the IASC Foundation.

The *Constitution* requires the Trustees to review the *Constitution* every five years. The Trustees initiated the first review in November 2003 and following extensive consultation completed the review in June 2005. The changes were adopted and approved by the Trustees on 21 June 2005 and came into effect on 1 July 2005. Further amendments were adopted and approved by the Trustees on 31 October 2007 and came into immediate effect.

The Trustees formally initiated their second five-yearly review of the organisation's constitutional arrangements in February 2008. The first part of that review, which focused on public accountability and the composition and size of the International Accounting Standards Board (the Board), led to changes that were approved by the Trustees on 15 January 2009 and came into effect on 1 February 2009. This version reflects further changes made at the conclusion of the review. The Trustees approved the changes on 26 January 2010 and they came into effect on 1 March 2010. In 2010, the IASC Foundation changed its name to the IFRS Foundation[1].

Following the recommendations of the Trustees' 2011 Strategy Review *IFRSs as the Global Standards: Setting a Strategy for the Foundation's Second Decade* and the Monitoring Board's Governance Review of the IFRS Foundation *Final Report on the Review of the IFRS Foundation's Governance*, the Trustees amended the Constitution to reflect the separation of the role of the Chair of the Board from that of the Executive Director. The Trustees approved the changes on 23 January 2013 when they took immediate effect.

In July 2015, the Trustees launched a review of the Structure and Effectiveness of the IFRS Foundation. This review commenced by way of a 120-day public consultation document entitled: *Request for Views — Trustees' Review of Structure and Effectiveness — Issues for the Review*. The Trustees reviewed stakeholder feedback and in May 2016 concluded that it was necessary to further consult, by way of an Exposure Draft, on all the proposed changes to the *Constitution* arising from the review. The Trustees reviewed stakeholder

---

1   The steps necessary to give legal effect to the IFRS Foundation's change of name were completed in mid-2010.

feedback on this further consultation and in October 2016 agreed to amend the *Constitution* with immediate effect.

In October 2018, the Trustees approved a narrow-scope amendment to Section 10 of the Foundation's Constitution to extend the term of the Trustee Chair and Vice-Chairs up to a maximum of nine years, taking into account any previous term already served as Trustee, Vice-Chair or Chair, as the case may be. The Trustees also approved an amendment to allow for the Trustee Chair to be appointed from among the Trustees or to be recruited externally. These changes came into effect on 1 December 2018.

The Foundation's trade marks and editorial style have also been updated in this document, for example, IFRSs is now written as IFRS Standards; the defined term for the International Accounting Standards Board is 'the Board'; and an Interpretation by the IFRS Interpretations Committee is an 'IFRIC® Interpretation'.

In August 2020, resulting from the amendments to the *Due Process Handbook*, the Trustees amended paragraphs 43, 44 and 45 of the IFRS Foundation *Constitution*. These amendments reflect that the Advisory Council advises the Board (and Trustees) on strategic matters and no longer functions as a technical consultative body.

IFRS® Foundation *Constitution*

(Approved by the members of the IASC at a meeting in Edinburgh, Scotland on 24 May 2000 and revised by the Trustees of the IFRS Foundation (formerly the IASC Foundation) on 5 March and 8 July 2002, 21 June 2005, 31 October 2007, 15 January 2009, 26 January 2010, 23 January 2013, 13 October 2016 and 1 December 2018).

Name and objectives

1   The name of the organisation shall be the IFRS Foundation, a name which shall be put into legal effect as soon as practical and then shall replace the name the International Accounting Standards Committee Foundation (the IASC Foundation). The International Accounting Standards Board (the Board), whose structure and functions are laid out in sections 24–37, shall be the standard-setting body of the IFRS Foundation.

2   The objectives of the IFRS Foundation are:

(a)   to develop, in the public interest, a single set of high quality, understandable, enforceable and globally accepted financial reporting standards based upon clearly articulated principles. These standards should require high quality, transparent and comparable information in financial statements and other financial reporting to help investors, other participants in the world's capital markets and other users of financial information make economic decisions.

(b)   to promote the use and rigorous application of those standards.

(c)   in fulfilling the objectives associated with (a) and (b), to take account of, as appropriate, the needs of a range of sizes and types of entities in diverse economic settings.

(d)   to promote and facilitate adoption of the IFRS Standards, being the Standards and IFRIC® Interpretations issued by the Board, through the convergence of national accounting standards and IFRS Standards.

Governance of the IFRS Foundation

3   The governance of the IFRS Foundation shall primarily rest with the Trustees and such other governing organs as may be appointed by the Trustees in accordance with the provisions of this *Constitution*. A Monitoring Board (described further in sections 18–23) shall provide a formal link between the Trustees and public authorities. The Trustees shall use their best endeavours to ensure that the requirements of this *Constitution* are observed; however, they may make minor variations in the interest of feasibility of operation if such variations are agreed by 75 per cent of the Trustees.

Trustees

4   The Trustees shall comprise 22 individuals.

5   The Monitoring Board (described further in sections 18–23) shall be responsible for the approval of all Trustee appointments and reappointments. In approving such selection, the Monitoring Board shall be bound by the criteria set out in sections 6 and 7. The Trustees and the Monitoring Board shall agree a nomination process that will entitle the Monitoring Board to recommend candidates and provide other help. In administering the nomination process and putting forward nominations to the Monitoring Board for approval, the Trustees shall consult the international organisations set out in section 7.

6   All Trustees shall be required to show a firm commitment to the IFRS Foundation and the Board as a high quality global standard-setter, to be financially knowledgeable, and to have an ability to meet the time commitment. Each Trustee shall have an understanding of, and be sensitive to, the challenges associated with the adoption and application of high quality global accounting standards developed for use in the world's capital markets and by other users. The mix of Trustees shall broadly reflect the world's capital markets and diversity of geographical and professional backgrounds. The Trustees shall be required to commit themselves formally to acting in the public interest in all matters. In order to ensure a broad international basis, there shall be:

   (a)   six Trustees appointed from the Asia-Oceania region;

   (b)   six Trustees appointed from Europe;

   (c)   six Trustees appointed from the Americas;

   (d)   one Trustee appointed from Africa; and

   (e)   three Trustees appointed from any area, subject to maintaining overall geographical balance.

7   The Trustees shall comprise individuals that, as a group, provide a balance of professional backgrounds, and have an interest in promoting and maintaining transparency in corporate reporting globally. This includes individuals with global experience at a senior level in securities market regulators, firms representing investors, international audit networks, preparers, users, academics and officials serving the public interest. To achieve such a balance, Trustees should be selected after consultation with the accounting and audit profession, the securities market and other public interest bodies, regulators, investors, preparers, users and academics. The Trustees shall establish procedures for inviting suggestions for appointments from these relevant organisations and for allowing individuals to put forward their own names, including advertising vacant positions.

8   Trustees shall normally be appointed for a term of three years, renewable once.

9   Subject to the voting requirements in section 14, the Trustees may terminate the appointment of an individual as a Trustee on grounds of poor performance, misbehaviour or incapacity.

10   The Chair and up to two Vice-Chairs of the Trustees shall be appointed by the Trustees, subject to the approval of the Monitoring Board:

    (a)   The Chair may be appointed from among the Trustees or recruited externally. With the agreement of the Trustees, a Chair that is appointed from among the Trustees may serve as Chair for a term of three years, renewable twice, from the date of appointment as Chair, but may not exceed nine consecutive years in total length of service, whether in the capacity of Trustee, Vice-Chair and/or Chair. If the Chair is appointed through an external recruitment process, he or she may serve as Chair for a term of three years, renewable twice, up to a maximum of nine consecutive years in total length of service as Chair. The appointment of a Chair should be made with regard to maintaining a geographical balance.

    (b)   Vice-Chairs shall only be appointed from among the Trustees. Their role shall be to chair meetings of the Trustees in the absence of the Chair or to represent the Chair in external contacts. With the agreement of the Trustees, a Vice-Chair may serve for a term of three years, renewable twice, from the date of appointment as Vice-Chair, but may not exceed nine consecutive years in total length of service as a Trustee. The appointment of a Vice-Chair(s) should be made with regard to maintaining a geographical balance.

11   The Trustees shall meet at least twice each year and shall be remunerated by the IFRS Foundation with an annual fee, commensurate with the responsibilities assumed, such fee to be determined by the Trustees. Expenses of travel on IFRS Foundation business shall be met by the IFRS Foundation.

12   In addition to the powers and duties set out in section 13, the Trustees may make such operational commitments and other arrangements as they deem necessary to achieve the organisation's objectives, including, but without limitation, leasing premises and agreeing contracts of employment with Board members.

13   The Trustees shall:

    (a)   assume responsibility for establishing and maintaining appropriate financing arrangements;

    (b)   establish or amend operating procedures for the Trustees;

    (c)   determine the legal entity under which the IFRS Foundation shall operate, provided always that such legal entity shall be a foundation or other body corporate conferring limited liability on its members and that the legal documents establishing such legal entity shall incorporate provisions to achieve the same requirements as the provisions contained in this *Constitution*;

(d)   review in due course the location of the IFRS Foundation, as regards both its legal base and its operating location;

(e)   investigate the possibility of seeking charitable or similar status for the IFRS Foundation in those countries where such status would assist fundraising;

(f)   open their meetings to the public but may, at their discretion, hold certain discussions (normally only about selection, appointment and other personnel issues, and funding) in private; and

(g)   publish an annual report on the IFRS Foundation's activities, including audited financial statements and priorities for the coming year.

14   There shall be a quorum for meetings of the Trustees if 60 per cent of the Trustees are present in person or by telecommunications: Trustees shall not be represented by alternates. Each Trustee shall have one vote, and a simple majority of those voting shall be required to take decisions on matters other than termination of the appointment of a Trustee, amendments to the *Constitution*, or minor variations made in the interest of feasibility of operations, in which cases a 75 per cent majority of all Trustees shall be required. Voting by proxy shall not be permitted on any issue. In the event of a tied vote, the Chair shall have an additional casting vote.

15   In addition to the duties set out above, the Trustees shall:

(a)   appoint the members of the Board and establish their contracts of service and performance criteria;

(b)   appoint the Executive Director, in consultation with the Chair of the Board, and establish his or her contract of service and performance criteria;

(c)   appoint the members of the IFRS Interpretations Committee (the Interpretations Committee) and the IFRS Advisory Council (the Advisory Council);

(d)   review annually the strategy of the IFRS Foundation and the Board and its effectiveness, including consideration, but not determination, of the Board's agenda;

(e)   approve annually the budget of the IFRS Foundation and determine the basis for funding;

(f)   review broad strategic issues affecting financial reporting standards, promote the IFRS Foundation and its work and promote the objective of rigorous application of our Standards, provided that the Trustees shall be excluded from involvement in technical matters relating to financial reporting standards;

(g)   establish and amend operating procedures, consultative arrangements and due process for the Board, the Interpretations Committee and the Advisory Council;

(h)   review compliance with the operating procedures, consultative arrangements and due process as described in (g);

(i)   approve amendments to this *Constitution* after following a due process, including consultation with the Advisory Council and publication of an Exposure Draft for public comment and subject to the voting requirements given in section 14;

(j)   exercise all powers of the IFRS Foundation except for those expressly reserved to the Board, the Interpretations Committee and the Advisory Council; and

(k)   foster and review the development of educational programmes and materials that are consistent with the IFRS Foundation's objectives.

16   The Trustees may terminate the appointment of a member of the Board, the Interpretations Committee or the Advisory Council, on grounds of poor performance, misbehaviour, incapacity or other failure to comply with contractual requirements, and the Trustees shall develop procedures for such termination.

17   The accountability of the Trustees shall be ensured, inter alia, through:

(a)   a commitment made by each Trustee to act in the public interest;

(b)   their commitment to report to and engage with the Monitoring Board according to the terms described in sections 18–23;

(c)   a review of the strategy of the IFRS Foundation and its effectiveness, such review to include consideration of the structure of the organisation (if appropriate) and changing the geographical distribution of Trustees in response to changing global economic conditions, and publishing the proposals of that review for public comment at the latest every five years after the conclusion of the most recent review; and

(d)   a similar review subsequently every five years.

The Monitoring Board

18   The Monitoring Board will provide a formal link between the Trustees and public authorities. This relationship seeks to replicate, on an international basis, the link between accounting standard-setters and those public authorities that have generally overseen accounting standard-setters. A Memorandum of Understanding will be agreed between the Monitoring Board and the Trustees describing the interaction of the Monitoring Board with the Trustees. This Memorandum of Understanding will be made available to the public.

19   The responsibilities of the Monitoring Board shall be:

(a)   to participate in the process for appointing Trustees and to approve the appointment of Trustees according to the guidelines in sections 5–8.

(b)   to review and provide advice to the Trustees on their fulfilment of the responsibilities set out in sections 13 and 15. The Trustees shall make an annual written report to the Monitoring Board.

(c)   to meet with the Trustees or a subgroup of the Trustees at least once annually, and more frequently as appropriate. The Monitoring Board shall have the authority to request meetings with the Trustees or separately with the Chair of the Trustees (or with the Chair of the Board as appropriate) about any area of work of either the Trustees or the Board. These meetings may include discussion of issues that the Monitoring Board has referred for timely consideration by the IFRS Foundation or the Board, and of any proposed resolution of those issues by the IFRS Foundation or the Board.

20   The Monitoring Board shall develop a charter that sets out its organisational, operating and decision-making procedures. The charter shall be made public.

21   Initially, the Monitoring Board shall comprise:

(a)   the responsible member of the European Commission;

(b)   the Chair of the International Organization of Securities Commissions (IOSCO) Emerging Markets Committee;

(c)   the Chair of the IOSCO Technical Committee (or Vice-Chair or designated securities commission Chair in cases where either the Chair of an EU securities regulator, commissioner of the Japan Financial Services Agency or Chair of the US Securities and Exchange Commission is the Chair of the IOSCO Technical Committee);

(d)   the Commissioner of the Japan Financial Services Agency;

(e)   the Chair of the US Securities and Exchange Commission; and

(f)   as an observer, the Chair of the Basel Committee on Banking Supervision.

22   The Monitoring Board shall reconsider its composition from time to time relative to its objectives.

23   The Monitoring Board shall reach decisions to approve the appointment of Trustees and establish any common positions by consensus.

The Board

24   The International Accounting Standards Board (the Board) shall normally comprise 14 members. The members of the Board are appointed by the Trustees under section 15(a). Up to three members may be part-time members (the expression 'part-time' meaning that the members concerned commit most of their time to paid employment by the IFRS Foundation) and shall meet appropriate guidelines of independence established by the Trustees. The remaining members shall be full-time members (the expression 'full-time' meaning that the members concerned commit all of their time to paid employment by the IFRS Foundation). The work of the Board shall not be

invalidated by its failure at any time to have a full complement of members, although the Trustees shall use their best endeavours to achieve a full complement.

25   The main qualifications for membership of the Board shall be professional competence and recent relevant professional experience. The Trustees shall select members of the Board, consistently with the 'Criteria for Board members' set out in the Annex to the *Constitution*, so that it will comprise a group of people representing, within that group, the best available combination of technical expertise and diversity of international business and market experience, including auditors, preparers, users, academics and market and/or financial regulators, in order that the Board as a group can contribute to the development of high quality, global financial reporting standards. The members of the Board shall be required to commit themselves formally to acting in the public interest in all matters. No individual shall be both a Trustee and a member of the Board at the same time.

26   In a manner consistent with the 'Criteria for Board members' as set out in the Annex to the *Constitution* and in order to ensure a broad international basis, there shall normally be:

   (a)   four members from the Asia-Oceania region;

   (b)   four members from Europe;

   (c)   four members from the Americas;

   (d)   one member from Africa; and

   (e)   one member appointed from any area, subject to maintaining overall geographical balance.

   The work of the Board shall not be invalidated by its failure at any time to have a full complement of members according to the above geographical allocation, although the Trustees shall use their best endeavours to achieve the geographical allocation.

27   The Board will, in consultation with the Trustees, be expected to establish and maintain liaison with national standard-setters, other standard-setters, and other official bodies with an interest in accounting standard-setting in order to assist in the development of IFRS Standards and to promote the convergence of national accounting standards and our Standards.

28   Each full-time and part-time member of the Board shall agree contractually to act in the public interest and to have regard to the Board's *Framework*[2] (as amended from time to time) in deciding on and revising the Standards.

29   The Trustees shall appoint one of the full-time members as the Chair of the Board. Up to two of the full-time members of the Board may also be designated by the Trustees as a Vice-Chair, whose role shall be to chair meetings of the Board in the absence of the Chair or to represent the Chair in external contacts. The appointment of the Chair and the designation as Vice-

---

2   The reference to the *Framework* is to the Board's *Conceptual Framework for Financial Reporting*, which was issued in March 2018.

Chair shall be for such term as the Trustees decide. The title of Vice-Chair would not imply that the member (or members) concerned is (or are) the Chair elect. The appointment of a Chair and Vice-Chair(s) should be made with regard to maintaining a geographical balance.

30 Members of the Board appointed before 2 July 2009 shall be appointed for a term of five years, renewable once for a further term of five years. Members of the Board appointed after 2 July 2009 shall be appointed initially for a term of five years. Terms may be renewable for a further term of three years, with the possibility of renewal up to a maximum of five years, in line with procedures developed by the Trustees for such renewals. The terms may not exceed 10 years in total length of service as a member of the Board.

31 The Trustees shall develop rules and procedures to ensure that the Board is, and is seen to be, independent, and, in particular, on appointment, full-time members of the Board shall sever all employment relationships with current employers and shall not hold any position giving rise to economic incentives that might call into question their independence of judgement in setting financial reporting Standards. Secondments and any rights to return to an employer would therefore not be permitted. Part-time members of the Board would not be expected to sever all other employment arrangements.

32 Full-time and part-time members of the Board shall be remunerated at rates commensurate with the respective responsibilities assumed: such rates shall be determined by the Trustees. Expenses of travel on Board business shall be met by the IFRS Foundation.

33 The Board shall meet at such times and locations as it determines: meetings of the Board shall be open to the public, but certain discussions (normally only about selection, appointment and other personnel issues) may be held in private at the discretion of the Board.

34 Each member of the Board shall have one vote. On both technical and other matters, proxy voting shall not be permitted nor shall members of the Board be entitled to appoint alternates to attend meetings. In the event of a tied vote, on a decision that is to be made by a simple majority of the members of the Board present at a meeting in person or by telecommunications, the Chair shall have an additional casting vote.

35 The publication of an Exposure Draft, or an IFRS Standard (including an IAS® Standard or an IFRIC Interpretation of the Interpretations Committee) shall require approval by eight members of the Board, if there are 13 members or fewer, or by nine members if there are 14 members. Other decisions of the Board, including the publication of a Discussion Paper, shall require a simple majority of the members of the Board present at a meeting that is attended by at least 60 per cent of the members of the Board, in person or by telecommunications.

36   The Board shall:

- (a) have complete responsibility for all Board technical matters, including the preparation and issuing of IFRS Standards (other than IFRIC Interpretations) and Exposure Drafts, each of which shall include any dissenting opinions, and the approval and issuing of IFRIC Interpretations developed by the Interpretations Committee.

- (b) publish an Exposure Draft on all projects and normally publish a discussion document for public comment on major projects in accordance with procedures approved by the Trustees.

- (c) in exceptional circumstances, and only after formally requesting and receiving prior approval from 75 per cent of the Trustees, reduce, but not dispense with, the period for public comment on an Exposure Draft below that is described as the minimum in the IFRS Foundation *Due Process Handbook*.

- (d) have full discretion in developing and pursuing its technical agenda, subject to the following:

  - (i) consulting the Trustees (consistently with section 15(d)) and the Advisory Council (consistently with section 43(a)); and

  - (ii) carrying out a public consultation every five years from the date of the most recent public agenda consultation.

- (e) have full discretion over project assignments on technical matters: in organising the conduct of its work, the Board may outsource detailed research or other work to national standard-setters or other organisations.

- (f) establish procedures for reviewing comments made within a reasonable period on documents published for comment.

- (g) normally form working groups or other types of specialist advisory groups to give advice on major projects.

- (h) consult the Advisory Council on major projects, agenda decisions and work priorities.

- (i) normally publish a Basis for Conclusions with a Standard or an Exposure Draft.

- (j) consider holding public hearings to discuss proposed Standards, although there is no requirement to hold public hearings for every project.

- (k) consider undertaking field tests (both in developed countries and in emerging markets) to ensure that proposed Standards are practical and workable in all environments, although there is no requirement to undertake field tests for every project.

- (l) give reasons if it does not follow any of the non-mandatory procedures set out in (b), (g), (i), (j) and (k).

37   The authoritative text of any Exposure Draft, draft Interpretation or Standard shall be that published by the Board in the English language. The Board may publish authorised translations or give authority to others to publish translations of the authoritative text of Exposure Drafts, draft Interpretations and Standards.

IFRS Interpretations Committee (the Interpretations Committee)

38   The Interpretations Committee, formerly called the International Financial Reporting Interpretations Committee, shall comprise 14 voting members, appointed by the Trustees under section 15(c) for renewable terms of three years. The Trustees shall select members of the Interpretations Committee so that it comprises a group of people representing, within that group, the best available combination of technical expertise and diversity of international business and market experience in the practical application of IFRS Standards and analysis of financial statements prepared in accordance with the Standards. Expenses of travel on Interpretations Committee business shall be met by the IFRS Foundation.

39   The Trustees shall appoint a member of the Board, the Director of Technical Activities or another senior member of the Board staff, or another appropriately qualified individual, to chair the Interpretations Committee. The Chair has the right to speak to the technical issues being considered but not to vote. The Trustees, as they deem necessary, shall appoint as non-voting observers representatives of regulatory organisations, who shall have the right to attend and speak at meetings.

40   The Interpretations Committee shall meet as and when required and 10 voting members present in person or by telecommunications shall constitute a quorum: one or two Board members shall be designated by the Board and shall attend meetings as non-voting observers; other members of the Board may attend and speak at the meetings. On exceptional occasions, members of the Interpretations Committee may be allowed to send non-voting alternates, at the discretion of the Chair of the Interpretations Committee. Members wishing to nominate an alternate should seek the consent of the Chair in advance of the meeting concerned. Meetings of the Interpretations Committee shall be open to the public, but certain discussions (normally only about selection, appointment and other personnel issues) may be held in private at the Interpretations Committee's discretion.

41   Each member of the Interpretations Committee shall have one vote. Members vote in accordance with their own independent views, not as representatives voting according to the views of any firm, organisation or constituency with which they may be associated. Proxy voting shall not be permitted. Approval of draft or final IFRIC Interpretations shall require that not more than four voting members vote against that draft or final Interpretation.

(h)   The Exposure Draft proposed that a financial instrument that is an equity instrument of a subsidiary should be eliminated on consolidation when held by the parent, or presented in the consolidated balance sheet within equity when not held by the parent (as a minority interest[11] separate from the equity of the parent). The Standard requires all terms and conditions agreed between members of the group and the holders of the instrument to be considered when determining if the group as a whole has an obligation that would give rise to a financial liability. To the extent there is such an obligation, the instrument (or component of the instrument that is subject to the obligation) is a financial liability in consolidated financial statements.

(i)–(j)   [deleted]

(k)   In August 2005, the IASB issued IFRS 7 *Financial Instruments: Disclosures*. As a result, disclosures relating to financial instruments, if still relevant, were relocated to IFRS 7.

Amendments for some puttable instruments and some instruments that impose on the entity an obligation to deliver to another party a pro rata share of the net assets of the entity only on liquidation

Amendment for puttable instruments

BC50   As discussed in paragraphs BC7 and BC8, puttable instruments meet the definition of a financial liability and the Board concluded that all such instruments should be classified as liabilities. However, constituents raised the following concerns about classifying such instruments as financial liabilities if they represent the residual claim to the net assets of the entity:

(a)   On an ongoing basis, the liability is recognised at not less than the amount payable on demand. This can result in the entire market capitalisation of the entity being recognised as a liability depending on the basis for which the redemption value of the financial instrument is calculated.

(b)   Changes in the carrying value of the liability are recognised in profit or loss. This results in counter-intuitive accounting (if the redemption value is linked to the performance of the entity) because:

(i)   when an entity performs well, the present value of the settlement amount of the liabilities increases, and a loss is recognised.

---

11   In January 2008 the IASB issued an amended IAS 27 *Consolidated and Separate Financial Statements*, which amended 'minority interest' to 'non-controlling interests'. The consolidation requirements in IAS 27 were superseded by IFRS 10 *Consolidated Financial Statements* issued in May 2011. The term 'non-controlling interests' and the requirements for non-controlling interests were not changed.

42 The Interpretations Committee shall:

    (a)   interpret the application of IFRS Standards and provide timely guidance on financial reporting issues not specifically addressed in the Standards, in the context of the Board's *Framework*,[3] and undertake other tasks at the request of the Board;

    (b)   in carrying out its work under (a) above, have regard to the Board's objective of working actively with national standard-setters to bring about convergence of national accounting standards and IFRS Standards to high quality solutions;

    (c)   publish, after clearance by the Board, draft Interpretations for public comment and consider comments made within a reasonable period before finalising an IFRIC Interpretation; and

    (d)   report to the Board and obtain the approval of eight of its members for final IFRIC Interpretations if there 13 members or fewer, or by nine of its members if there are 14 members.

IFRS Advisory Council (the Advisory Council)

43 The Advisory Council, formerly called the Standards Advisory Council, whose members shall be appointed by the Trustees under section 15(c), provides a forum for participation by organisations and individuals, with an interest in international financial reporting, having diverse geographical and functional backgrounds.

The Advisory Council provides broad strategic advice to the Trustees and the Board and can provide views that are supplemental to other consultative processes.

44 The Advisory Council shall comprise 30 or more members, having a diversity of geographical and professional backgrounds, appointed for renewable terms of three years. The Chair of the Advisory Council shall be appointed by the Trustees and shall not be a member of the Board or a member of staff. The Trustees shall invite the Chair of the Advisory Council to attend and participate in the Trustees' meetings, as appropriate.

45 The Advisory Council shall normally meet at least twice a year. Meetings shall be open to the public. The matters on the agenda for the Advisory Council's meetings will include those strategic matters and other priorities identified through consultation among the Chair of the Advisory Council and representatives of the Trustees and the Board. The Advisory Council shall also be consulted by the Trustees in advance of any proposed changes to this *Constitution*.

---

3   The reference to the *Framework* is to the Board's *Conceptual Framework for Financial Reporting*, which was issued in March 2018.

Executive Director and staff

46 An Executive Director of the IFRS Foundation, appointed by the Trustees and the Chair of the Board, shall be responsible for overseeing operational decisions affecting the day-to-day management of the IFRS Foundation and staff. The Executive Director shall report to the Chair of the Board on matters relating to the Board's standard-setting activities and to the Trustees on all other matters.

47 The Chair of the Board shall be responsible for establishing the senior technical team of the Board, in consultation with the Trustees, and will be responsible for the supervision of this team and their staff.

Administration

48 The administrative office of the IFRS Foundation shall be located in such location as may be determined by the Trustees in accordance with section 13(d).

49 The IFRS Foundation shall be a legal entity as determined by the Trustees and shall be governed by this *Constitution* and by any laws that apply to such legal entity, including, if appropriate, laws applicable because of the location of its registered office.

50 The IFRS Foundation shall be bound by the signature(s) of such person or persons as may be duly authorised by the Trustees.

ANNEX
IFRS Foundation

Criteria for Board members

The following would represent criteria for Board membership:

1   **Demonstrated technical competence and knowledge of financial accounting and reporting.** All members of the Board, regardless of whether they are from the accounting profession, preparers, users or academics, should have demonstrated a high level of knowledge and technical competence in financial accounting and reporting. The credibility of the Board and its individual members and the effectiveness and efficiency of the organisation will be enhanced by members who have such knowledge and skills.

2   **Ability to analyse.** Members of the Board should have demonstrated the ability to analyse issues and consider the implications of that analysis for the decision-making process.

3   **Communication skills.** Effective oral and written communication skills are necessary. These skills include the ability to communicate effectively in private meetings with members of the Board, in public meetings, and in written materials such as financial reporting standards, speeches, articles, memos and external correspondence. Communication skills also include the ability to listen to and consider the views of others. While a working knowledge of English is necessary, there should not be discrimination in selection against those for whom English is not their first language.

4   **Judicious decision-making.** Members of the Board should be capable of considering varied viewpoints, weighing the evidence presented in an impartial fashion, and reaching well-reasoned and supportable decisions in a timely fashion.

5   **Awareness of the financial reporting environment.** High quality financial reporting will be affected by the financial, business and economic environment. Members of the Board should have an understanding of the global economic environment in which the Board operates. This global awareness should include awareness of business and financial reporting issues that are relevant to, and affect the quality of, transparent financial reporting and disclosure in the various capital markets worldwide, including those using IFRS Standards.

6   **Ability to work in a collegial atmosphere.** Members should be able to show respect, tact and consideration for one another's views and those of third parties. Members must be able to work with one another in reaching consensus views based on the objective of the Board to develop high quality and transparent financial reporting. Members must be able to put the objective of the Board above individual philosophies and interests.

7   **Integrity, objectivity and discipline.** The credibility of members should be demonstrated through their integrity and objectivity. This includes intellectual integrity as well as integrity in dealing with fellow members of the Board and others. Members should demonstrate an ability to be objective in reaching decisions. Members also should demonstrate an ability to show rigorous discipline and carry a demanding workload.

8   **Commitment to the IFRS Foundation's mission and public interest.** Members should be committed to achieving the objective of the IFRS Foundation of establishing international financial reporting standards that are of high quality, comparable and transparent. A candidate for the Board should also be committed to serving the public interest through a private standard-setting process.

IFRS Foundation

Due Process Handbook

This handbook sets out the due process principles that apply to the International Accounting Standards Board and the IFRS Interpretations Committee. The Trustees of the IFRS Foundation have a Due Process Oversight Committee that is responsible for monitoring compliance with due process.

The DPOC oversaw a major overwrite of the Due Process Handbook in 2012, with the final changes being published in February 2013. The DPOC oversaw a review of the IFRS Taxonomy due process in 2015–2016. In May 2016, the DPOC approved the staff proposals for the final IFRS Taxonomy due process as an appendix to the Due Process Handbook. The DPOC oversaw a review of the Due Process Handbook in 2019–2020, with the final changes being published in August 2020.

CONTENTS

1. Introduction

1.1 The foremost objective of the IFRS Foundation is to develop, in the public interest, a single set of high-quality, understandable, enforceable and globally accepted financial reporting standards based on clearly articulated principles. The IFRS Foundation Trustees (Trustees) believe that, in carrying out the IFRS Foundation's mission as its standard-setting body, the International Accounting Standards Board (Board) should develop financial reporting standards that result in an entity providing useful information about its financial position and performance in its financial statements. Those standards should serve investors and other primary users of financial statements[1] in making informed resource allocation and other economic decisions. The confidence of all users of financial statements in the transparency and integrity of those statements is critically important for the effective functioning of capital markets, efficient capital allocation, global financial stability and sound economic growth.

1.2 The IFRS Foundation *Constitution* (*Constitution*) gives the Board full discretion in developing and pursuing its technical programme and in organising the conduct of its work. The Trustees and the Board have established consultative procedures with the objective of ensuring that, in exercising its independent decision-making, the Board conducts its standard-setting in a transparent manner, considering a wide range of views from interested parties throughout all stages of the development of International Financial Reporting Standards (*IFRS Standards*). (Note that when this document refers to the development of an IFRS Standard or an amendment to an IFRS Standard, the same process also applies to the development of an *IFRS for SMEs* Standard or an amendment to the *IFRS for SMEs* Standard.) The Board uses these procedures to gain a better understanding of different accounting alternatives and the potential effect of the proposals on affected parties. A comprehensive and effective due process is essential to developing high-quality IFRS Standards that serve investors and other primary users of financial statements.

1.3 The IFRS Interpretations Committee (Interpretations Committee) assists the Board in improving financial reporting through timely assessment, discussion and resolution of financial reporting issues identified to it within the IFRS framework.

1.4 The Board, the Interpretations Committee and the Trustees are assisted by the staff of the IFRS Foundation. References to 'IFRS Foundation staff' in this document cover all staff. The staff who assist the work of the Board and the Interpretations Committee are referred to in this document as the 'technical staff'. The staff who assist the work of the Trustees are referred to as the 'Trustee staff'.

---

[1] The terms 'primary users' and 'users' refer to those existing and potential investors, lenders and other creditors who must rely on general purpose financial statements for much of the financial information they need.

1.5   The *Due Process Handbook* (*Handbook*) describes the due process requirements of the Board and the Interpretations Committee relating to their standard-setting activities, the development of materials to support the consistent application of IFRS Standards, and the *IFRS Taxonomy*. The requirements reflect and further the due process that is laid out in the *Constitution*.

1.6   The due process requirements are built on the principles of transparency, full and fair consultation – considering the perspectives of those affected by IFRS Standards globally – and accountability. The Board and the Interpretations Committee will often perform steps and procedures over and above those described here because they are continually striving to improve how they consult and operate. From time to time the Board and the Trustees' Due Process Oversight Committee (DPOC) (see section 2) review how the Board and the Interpretations Committee are operating to determine whether some of these new and additional steps should be embedded into their due process. Similarly, such reviews could remove or amend due process steps that impede, rather than enhance, the efficient and effective development of the Standards and material to support the consistent application of the Standards. The DPOC seeks to ensure that the *Handbook* achieves a balance between timely development of high-quality Standards and a thorough due process.

1.7   The formal due process for the Board and the Interpretations Committee:

(a)   specifies the minimum steps to be taken to ensure that their activities have benefited from a thorough and effective consultation process;

(b)   identifies the non-mandatory steps to be considered, the 'comply or explain' approach, meaning that the non-mandatory steps in the process were still recommended, so non-compliance with them would require an explanation; and

(c)   identifies other, optional, steps available to them to help improve the quality of IFRS Standards and related documents.

1.8   The formal due process relating to the IFRS Taxonomy is described in the Annex to this *Handbook*. References to the IFRS Taxonomy also appear in the main body of this *Handbook* when applicable.

2. Oversight

Mission

2.1   The Trustees oversee the operations of the Board and the Interpretations Committee.

2.2   The Trustees have a committee – the DPOC – that is responsible for overseeing the due process of the Board and the Interpretations Committee. The DPOC operates in a manner that is timely and enhances rather than hinders the efficient operation of the Board and the Interpretations Committee, and the timely development of IFRS Standards and material to support the consistent application of IFRS Standards.

2.3 The DPOC is accountable to the Trustees and is responsible for ensuring that the Board and the Interpretations Committee follow due process procedures that reflect the requirements set out in this *Handbook*. Improvements to due process, including those to reflect good practice, are made on a timely basis when the DPOC considers it to be necessary.

2.4 The DPOC provides ongoing oversight over the due process of the Board and the Interpretations Committee throughout the development of an IFRS Standard, the IFRS Taxonomy or an *IFRIC Interpretation*, including agenda-setting and *post-implementation reviews*.

2.5 The DPOC achieves oversight through the defined and transparent steps it follows in its ongoing and regular activities, as well as by responding to matters raised by stakeholders about the standard-setting process.

2.6 Activities of the DPOC are limited to matters of due process. The DPOC does not review or consider technical financial reporting matters that have been decided on by the Board or the Interpretations Committee. As the *Constitution* makes clear, these decisions are solely the responsibility of the Board.

2.7 The DPOC is supported by a member of the Trustee staff who is responsible for managing Trustee activities and who is independent of the technical staff.

Areas of responsibility

2.8 The DPOC is responsible for:

(a) reviewing regularly, and in a timely manner, together with the Board and the IFRS Foundation staff, the due process activities of the Board and the Interpretations Committee, including standard-setting, the development of materials to support the consistent application of IFRS Standards, and the IFRS Taxonomy;

(b) reviewing, and proposing updates to, the procedures in the *Handbook* so as to ensure that they reflect good practice;

(c) reviewing the composition of *consultative groups* to ensure an appropriate balance of perspectives and overseeing the monitoring by the Board and the technical staff of the effectiveness of those groups;

(d) responding to correspondence from third parties about due process matters, in collaboration with the Trustee staff and the technical staff; and

(e) making recommendations to the Trustees about constitutional changes related to the composition of committees that are integral to due process, as appropriate.

Process

2.9 The DPOC operates throughout the development of an IFRS Standard, the IFRS Taxonomy or an IFRIC Interpretation, including agenda-setting and post-implementation reviews. This is achieved through periodic reporting by, and dialogue with, representatives of the Board, the Interpretations Committee and IFRS Foundation staff.

2.10 For each technical project, the Board assesses whether it has complied with its due process requirements, on the basis of a technical staff report that:

(a) includes a summary of any matters raised about due process, the extent of stakeholder engagement and the areas in a proposed IFRS Standard or IFRIC Interpretation that are likely to be controversial;

(b) provides evidence and evaluation of the process that was undertaken;

(c) outlines the reasons why the Board decided not to undertake a non-mandatory 'comply or explain' step for a given project (see paragraphs 3.45–3.46); and

(d) concludes whether, in the technical staff's opinion, applicable due process steps have been complied with.

Any such reports are communicated to the DPOC, giving it sufficient time to review them and to react in a timely manner.

2.11 These reports are posted on the IFRS Foundation website.

2.12 The DPOC reviews and evaluates the evidence provided by the Board and IFRS Foundation staff of compliance with the established due process. The conclusions of that review and evaluation, including whether due process concerns are identified or not, are included in the reports referred to in paragraph 2.15(d). Before any new or amended IFRS Standard is finalised, the DPOC will confirm that it has completed its review of the due process. In reaching its decisions, the DPOC operates on a simple majority basis.

2.13 The DPOC, through its contact with stakeholders, responds when appropriate to matters raised about the due process of the Board or the Interpretation Committee and ensures that such matters are addressed satisfactorily (see section 9).

2.14 Although the DPOC is assisted in its activities by Trustee staff, there is currently no intention to verify the information provided by the Board, because of the transparent manner in which the Board and the DPOC operate. However, the DPOC can request a review by Trustee staff of any of the information provided to it.

Communication

2.15 The DPOC operates transparently and with fair consideration of the matters raised by stakeholders. The DPOC:

(a) meets in public, ensuring that meeting papers and recordings of the meeting are made available on the IFRS Foundation website.

(b)   updates the Trustees on its activities at regularly scheduled Trustee meetings and on an ad-hoc basis as required.

(c)   on behalf of the Trustees, provides updates to the Monitoring Board at regularly scheduled joint sessions with the Trustees and on an ad-hoc basis as required.

(d)   provides reports of its conclusions and discussions on the IFRS Foundation website. The reports include details of all the matters discussed, including compliance with due process on each of the technical activities. Such reports should be provided promptly after the DPOC meetings.

(e)   prepares an annual report of its activities for the Trustees.

(f)   ensures that its operating protocol, together with this document and any other DPOC governance documents, are available on the IFRS Foundation website.

3. Principles

3.1   The due process requirements are built on the following principles:

(a)   transparency—the Board and the Interpretations Committee conduct their activities in a transparent manner;

(b)   full and fair consultation—considering the perspectives of stakeholders globally; and

(c)   accountability—the Board analyses the potential effects of its proposals on affected parties and explains the rationale for the decisions it reached in developing or amending an IFRS Standard.

Transparency

Public meetings, voting and balloting

Public meetings

3.2   Meetings of the Board and the Interpretations Committee are open to the public who may attend meetings as observers. Meetings are recorded and, when possible, webcast live. Recordings of meetings are made available on the IFRS Foundation website. The Board and the Interpretations Committee can meet privately to discuss administrative and other non-technical matters. Acknowledging that the boundary between technical and non-technical matters is sometimes difficult to define, the Board and the Interpretations Committee use their best endeavours not to undermine the principle that full and open consideration of technical matters needs to take place during public meetings.

3.3   A summary of the decisions reached in each Board meeting is published in a meeting summary called *IASB Update* and decisions of the Interpretations Committee are published in a meeting summary called *IFRIC Update*. These summaries are also made available on the IFRS Foundation website.

3.4 The regular meetings of the Board and the Interpretations Committee are planned as far in advance as is practicable to help the technical staff, Board and Interpretations Committee members, and stakeholders prepare for those meetings.

3.5 The meetings schedule is published on the IFRS Foundation website. Occasionally, the Board will need to hold a meeting at short notice. The Chair of the Board can convene such meetings at any time. The Board will make its best efforts to announce forthcoming meetings, usually via the IFRS Foundation website, giving a minimum of 24 hours' notice in all but exceptional circumstances.

Papers and observer access

3.6 The technical staff is responsible for developing technical staff papers with recommendations and supporting analysis for consideration by the Board or the Interpretations Committee in their public meetings.

3.7 The objective of staff papers is to provide sufficient information for Board or Interpretations Committee members to make informed decisions on technical matters. In developing papers, the technical staff is expected to conduct research, including seeking advice from Board members. However, recommendations ultimately reflect technical staff's views, after consideration of the information obtained.

3.8 Technical staff papers are normally distributed 10–14 days before they are scheduled for discussion to allow Board and Interpretations Committee members sufficient time to consider and assess the recommendations.

3.9 Sometimes it is necessary to distribute technical staff papers much closer to the meeting date, sometimes even on the day of the meeting. Board or Interpretations Committee members may, for example, ask for additional analysis during a meeting, which the technical staff prepares and distributes at a later session of that meeting.

3.10 It is the responsibility of Board and Interpretations Committee members to assess whether they have sufficient information and sufficient time to be able to make decisions on the technical staff recommendations.

3.11 All material discussed by Board or Interpretations Committee members in their public meetings, including papers that are prepared by technical staff, is usually made available to observers via the IFRS Foundation website. The Chair or Vice-Chair of the Board or the Executive Director of Technical Activities have the discretion to withhold papers, or parts of papers, from observers if they determine that making the material publicly available would be harmful to individual parties, for example, if releasing that information could breach securities disclosure laws. The DPOC expects that withholding material in such circumstances would be rare and that most papers of the Board and the Interpretations Committee will be publicly available in their entirety.

3.12   The technical staff is required to report to the Board and the DPOC at least annually on the extent to which material discussed by the Board or the Interpretations Committee has not been made available to observers and the main reasons for doing so. In addition, the technical staff is required to include in that report the number of meeting papers that have been distributed less than five working days in advance and the main reasons for doing so.

3.13   Notwithstanding the importance of technical staff papers, the technical staff may supplement the papers orally at a Board or Interpretations Committee meeting, drawing from research, consultations with consultative groups and other interested parties, and comments and information gained from *public hearings*, *fieldwork*, education sessions and *comment letters*.

Publications, meetings and the ballot process

3.14   There are minimum voting requirements for all important Board decisions:

Publications	
Request for information (paragraph 4.16)	Simple majority in a public meeting attended by at least 60% of the Board members.
Research paper (paragraph 4.16)	
Discussion paper (paragraph 4.16)	Simple majority, by way of ballot.
Exposure draft (paragraph 6.9)	Supermajority, by way of ballot.
Proposed *IFRS for SMEs* Standard (paragraph 6.9)	
IFRS Standard (paragraph 6.23)	
IFRS for SMEs Standard (paragraph 6.23)	
Practice guidance (paragraph 6.39)	Supermajority, by way of ballot.
Conceptual Framework for Financial Reporting (paragraph 4.21)	Supermajority, by way of ballot.
Draft IFRIC Interpretation (paragraph 7.8)	No more than four members of the Interpretations Committee object, by way of ballot.

continued...

...continued

Publications	
IFRIC Interpretation (paragraphs 7.18 and 7.23)	No more than four members of the Interpretations Committee object, by way of ballot.
	Ratification by the Board requires a supermajority, in a public meeting.
Proposed IFRS Taxonomy update (paragraph A16)	Supermajority, by way of ballot.
IFRS Taxonomy update (paragraph A16)	

3.15   A *supermajority* of the Board requires that eight members ballot in favour of the publication of a document if the Board has 13, or fewer, appointed members, and nine members in favour if the Board has 14 appointed members. Abstaining is equivalent to voting against a proposal.

3.16   In addition to the publications noted in paragraph 3.14, adding a standard-setting project to the Board's work plan and decisions about consultative groups, fieldwork and other due process matters such as not to establish a consultative group, require the support of a *simple majority* of the Board in a public meeting attended by at least 60% of the Board members in person or by telecommunications.

Meetings

3.17   Board members are expected to attend meetings in person. However, meetings may be held using teleconference, videoconference or any other similar communication facilities. A Board quorum is 60% of the appointed members. Proxy voting by members of the Board is not permitted.

3.18   The Interpretations Committee also meets in public and follows procedures similar to the Board's general policy for its Board meetings. A minimum of 10 voting members present in person or by telecommunications constitutes a quorum of the Interpretations Committee. Each voting member of the Interpretations Committee has one vote. Members vote in accordance with their own independent views, not as representatives of any firm, organisation or constituency with which they may be associated. Proxy voting is not permitted by members of the Interpretations Committee.

3.19   The Chairs of the Board and the Interpretations Committee may invite others to attend meetings as advisors when specialised input is required. A member of the Interpretations Committee, or an appointed observer, may also, with the prior consent of the Chair, bring to a meeting an advisor who has specialised knowledge of a topic that is being discussed. Such invited advisors have the right to speak.

3.20   During the development stage of technical documents such as *discussion papers*, *exposure drafts* and IFRS Standards, the Board discusses technical matters in public meetings. During such meetings Board members are often asked to indicate to the staff which technical alternative they support. These tentative votes on particular technical matters provide the technical staff with direction from the Board to develop the relevant due process document, but are not part of the formal approval process. Individual Board members may prefer an alternative financial reporting treatment to that supported by a majority of the Board, but nevertheless consider that the project proposals as a whole would improve financial reporting.

3.21   A simple majority in favour of a technical alternative is generally sufficient to guide the technical staff in developing the project. In the event of a tied vote on a decision to be made by a simple majority of the members present at a meeting in person or by telecommunications, the Chair has an additional casting vote. The technical staff will need to determine whether any Board members who disagree with a tentative decision might dissent from the whole proposal because of that decision.

Balloting

3.22   Balloting is the formal process by which Board members assent to the publication of a document, as listed in the table at paragraph 3.14, or Interpretations Committee members assent to the publication of a draft IFRIC Interpretation or the finalisation of an IFRIC Interpretation, before it is sent to the Board for ratification. Balloting takes place outside of meetings.

3.23   In its public meetings, the Board or the Interpretations Committee makes technical decisions that relate to recognition, measurement and disclosure matters. The technical staff is responsible for ensuring that the final publication reflects those decisions.

3.24   When a document is in the process of being balloted, Board or Interpretations Committee members review it to confirm that the drafting is consistent with their technical decisions. Any dissenting opinions are incorporated into the pre-ballot and ballot drafts for other Board members to see before balloting is completed.

3.25   Before the formal ballot procedure begins, the technical staff usually prepares one or more pre-ballot drafts, in response to which Board or Interpretations Committee members provide drafting comments.

3.26   Sometimes the drafting process reveals an uncertainty about a technical matter because the decision reached is not as clear as first thought. In other cases, the drafting process may highlight inconsistencies between sections of an IFRS Standard or other matters that were not discussed at a Board or Interpretations Committee meeting. Such technical matters are usually resolved by having the technical staff prepare a technical staff paper and taking it to a public meeting of the Board or the Interpretations Committee as a *sweep issue*, where the matter can be resolved by a simple majority of the Board or the Interpretations Committee. Taking a sweep issue to the Board or the Interpretations Committee does not cause the balloting process to start again.

3.27 To support the consistent application of IFRS Standards internationally, the Board aims to develop Standards that are clear, understandable and enforceable. In addition, it provides the necessary implementation guidance and illustrative examples to accompany the Standards, consistent with a principle-based approach.

3.28 In drafting new IFRS Standards, the Board is conscious that many of those applying or using the Standards work with translated versions of the English Standards. As part of the balloting process the technical staff liaises with the IFRS Foundation Translations and IFRS Taxonomy staff to ensure that the proposed document can be translated into other languages and incorporated easily into the IFRS Taxonomy. All documents undergo editorial review.

3.29 Once the technical staff has assessed that the document is ready for formal voting, it circulates a ballot draft. Board or Interpretations Committee members vote on this document. The Board or the Interpretations Committee can determine how voting should be carried out, but may use paper or electronic means.

3.30 Even after balloting it is not uncommon for the technical staff to make drafting changes to improve the clarity of the document. Such changes are permitted as long as the technical decisions are unaffected. The technical staff reports to the Board or the Interpretations Committee after the ballot or prepares and circulates to the Board or the Interpretations Committee a post-ballot draft showing the final changes.

Drafts for editorial review

3.31 The Board normally seeks input on the drafting of IFRS Standards, IFRIC Interpretations as well as major exposure drafts and discussion papers from people outside of the IFRS Foundation. For convenience, a draft of such documents is referred to as a *draft for editorial review*. A draft for editorial review might be distributed to a selected group of reviewers, such as members of a consultative group, the Interpretations Committee, other standard-setters or parties that have provided feedback on the project. It may also be made available on the IFRS Foundation website while it is with the selected group of reviewers.

3.32 A draft for editorial review has a limited purpose. It does not constitute, nor is it a substitute for, a formal step in the due process. Rather, it is an editorial review in which reviewers are asked for feedback on whether the document contains any internal inconsistencies or inconsistencies with other IFRS Standards, and whether it clearly describes:

(a) the requirements for an IFRS Standard or IFRIC Interpretation;

(b) the proposed requirements for an exposure draft; and

(c) the matters considered by the Board and the Board's preliminary views for a discussion paper.

Because reviewers are conveying their personal views rather than those of their organisations, their comments are not usually made public.

3.33 It is not a mandatory step to use reviewers from outside of the IFRS Foundation.

Information on the IFRS Foundation website

3.34 The IFRS Foundation website is the platform that communicates the activities and due process of the Board and the Interpretation Committee.

3.35 All public materials, including those related to due process, are freely available on the IFRS Foundation website. These materials include: the Board and the Interpretations Committee work plan, meeting schedules and agendas; public papers; summaries and recordings of meetings; consultation documents; comment letters; and material that supports the consistent application of IFRS Standards. The work plan is updated periodically to reflect estimated project time lines based on recent Board and Interpretations Committee decisions. The IFRS Foundation website also includes materials relating to consultative group meetings.

3.36 Each project has its own project page to communicate progress on that project.

3.37 Information related to the DPOC's work is freely available on the IFRS Foundation website.

Education sessions, small group meetings and assigned Board members

3.38 In addition to public decision-making meetings, the Board sometimes holds education sessions and small group meetings.

Education sessions

3.39 Education sessions are sometimes held before Board meetings to give Board members a chance to seek clarification about points in the papers and discuss details of approaches or disagreements with the technical staff in advance of the decision-making meeting. Education sessions are open to the public and follow the same principles of transparency that apply to a normal Board meeting.

Private and small group meetings

3.40 Board members may meet privately to discuss technical matters, sometimes at the request of the technical staff. Small group meetings cannot undermine the principle that full and open consideration of technical matters take place during public meetings. The number of Board members attending a small group meeting is restricted to ensure that the Board members attending could not form a potential blocking minority for balloting (see paragraph 3.14).

Board advisors

3.41 All Board and Interpretations Committee members are responsible for the decisions they make in developing and issuing IFRS Standards and IFRIC Interpretations. For major projects, specific Board members are typically assigned to the project as Board advisors. Board advisors provide strategic and technical advice on the project to the technical staff. However, the recommendations made in staff papers do not necessarily reflect the views of the Board advisors and the technical staff has ultimate responsibility for the staff papers and their recommendations. The number of Board advisors is restricted to ensure that the Board members so assigned could not form a potential blocking minority for balloting (see paragraph 3.14).

Full and fair consultation

3.42 The Board and the Interpretations Committee operate on the principle that wide consultation with their stakeholders enhances the quality of IFRS Standards. This consultation can be carried out through various means including, but not limited to, invitations to comment, individual meetings or fieldwork. Some consultation procedures are mandatory. Other procedures are not mandatory but are considered by the Board and, if it is decided that the process is not necessary, the Board gives the DPOC its reasons for not taking that step.

Minimum safeguards

3.43 The Board and the Interpretations Committee are required to follow some steps before they can issue an IFRS Standard or an IFRIC Interpretation. These steps are designed to be the minimum safeguards to ensure the integrity of the standard-setting.

3.44 The due process steps that are mandatory include:

(a) debating any proposals in one or more public meetings;

(b) exposing for public comment a draft of any proposed new IFRS Standard, proposed amendment to a Standard or proposed IFRIC Interpretation—with minimum comment periods;

(c) considering in a timely manner comment letters received on the proposals;

(d) considering whether the proposals should be exposed again;

(e) consulting the Accounting Standards Advisory Forum (ASAF) and the *IFRS Advisory Council* (Advisory Council) on the work plan, major projects, project proposals and work priorities; and

(f) deciding in a public Board meeting whether to ratify an Interpretation.

'Comply or explain' steps

3.45 Other steps specified in the *Constitution* are not mandatory. They include:

(a) publishing a discussion document for major projects (for example, a discussion paper) before an exposure draft is developed;

     (b)   establishing consultative groups or other types of specialist advisory groups for major projects;

     (c)   holding public hearings; and

     (d)   undertaking fieldwork.

3.46   If the Board decides not to undertake those non-mandatory steps, it informs the DPOC of its decision and reasons for not undertaking the steps.

Investors

3.47   The Board is responsible for developing IFRS Standards that serve investors and other primary users of financial statements in making informed resource allocation and other economic decisions.

3.48   Investors, and investment intermediaries such as analysts, tend to be under-represented as submitters of comment letters and, therefore, the Board takes additional steps to consult investors throughout standard-setting. These additional steps could include surveys, private meetings, webcasts and meetings with representative groups, such as the Capital Markets Advisory Committee. Feedback from this consultation with investors is summarised in a staff paper and is considered and assessed along with comment letters. The reporting of this feedback is as transparent as possible, while respecting requests for confidentiality.

3.49   As a project progresses, the Board reports on how it has consulted with investors, and their intermediaries, in staff papers, the project pages on the IFRS Foundation website and in reports to the DPOC. The DPOC receives this information in the periodic technical update report and the review of due process at the end of a project (see paragraph 2.12). The Board needs to be satisfied that it has gathered sufficient information from investors to make informed decisions about the proposed new requirements.

A national and regional network

3.50   The Board is supported by a network of national accounting standard-setting bodies and regional bodies. In addition to performing functions within their mandates, such bodies can undertake research, provide guidance on the Board's priorities, facilitate or co-operate on outreach, encourage stakeholder input from their own jurisdictions into the Board's due process and identify emerging issues.

3.51   The Board shares information with and consults ASAF. In addition, it shares information with and consults international and regional bodies such as the International Forum of Accounting Standard Setters, the Asian-Oceanian Standard-Setters Group, the Group of Latin American Standard Setters, the European Financial Reporting Advisory Group and the Pan African Federation of Accountants as well as jurisdictional (national) standard-setters. Board members meet with representatives of these regional and national bodies. Close co-ordination between the Board's due process and the due process of other accounting standard-setters is important to achieving the Board's objectives.

3.52   Consultation activities extend beyond interaction with accounting standard-setters. The Board interacts with a wide range of interested parties throughout a project, which can include practical business analysis by way of fieldwork. The Board also liaises with the International Auditing and Assurance Standards Board, which comments on matters relating to the auditability of proposed new IFRS Standards and amendments to Standards. Board members and technical staff also regularly hold educational sessions, attend meetings and conferences of interested parties, invite interested organisations to voice their views, and announce major events of the IFRS Foundation on the IFRS Foundation website.

3.53   The Board consults throughout standard-setting, to promote cooperation and communication between the Board and parties interested in standard-setting.

IFRS Advisory Council

3.54   The Advisory Council provides broad strategic advice to the Board and the Trustees on the Board's work plan, project priorities and strategic matters related to the consistent application of IFRS Standards. The Advisory Council also serves as a sounding board for the Board and can be used to gather views that supplement the normal consultative process. When the Board is considering adding a major project to the work plan not contemplated in the previous consultation on the work plan, it consults the Advisory Council (see paragraph 4.6). The Board also presents updates to the Advisory Council on the work plan periodically.

Securities and other regulators

3.55   The Board is responsible for developing high-quality, understandable and enforceable IFRS Standards that improve the transparency and integrity of financial statements. The Board is also responsible for an IFRS Taxonomy that can support securities regulators in facilitating digital access to general purpose financial reports.

3.56   To achieve this the Board maintains a dialogue with securities regulators, usually by establishing regular meetings. In addition, members of regulatory bodies are invited to act as observers to Interpretations Committee meetings.

3.57   Financial information prepared in accordance with IFRS Standards is used by other regulators, including prudential supervisors.

3.58   In that context the Board maintains an enhanced dialogue with such authorities, particularly through the Financial Stability Board and the Bank for International Settlements.

Consultative groups

3.59   The IFRS Foundation usually establishes a consultative group for each of the Board's major projects, such as a specialist or expert advisory group. Consultative groups give the Board access to additional practical experience and expertise.

3.60 Once a major project is added to the Board's standard-setting programme the Board considers whether a consultative group should be established for that project. It is not mandatory to have such a group, but if the Board decides not to do so, it explains that decision on the project page and informs the DPOC. The composition of a consultative group reflects the purpose for which the group is being formed, bearing in mind the need to ensure that it draws on a diverse and geographically balanced membership. The composition of a consultative group may change over time, reflecting the need for different types of expertise at different stages of a project.

3.61 The IFRS Foundation may also establish or host specialist advisory groups whose membership reflects a particular sector, such as investors or preparers, that meet regularly to provide advice on a wide range of topics rather than on a specific project.

3.62 The IFRS Foundation normally advertises for nominations and applications to its consultative groups (whether a project-specific consultative group or a specialist advisory group) via its website, but it may also approach parties directly. The DPOC reviews the proposed composition of each group to ensure an appropriate balance of perspectives, including geographical balance.

3.63 Each consultative group has terms of reference, setting out the objectives of the group, the Board's expectations of the members and the responsibilities of the Board to that group. The Board could have more than one consultative group on a project, for example, to provide advice on a particular aspect of a proposed IFRS Standard or post-implementation review.

3.64 Once work on a project starts, the consultative group for that project is consulted when doing so would benefit the project. The technical staff provides group members with regular updates on the progress of the project and provides the Board with feedback on the group's work.

3.65 Meetings of consultative groups are normally open to the public and chaired by a Board member or by a member of the technical staff, however consultative groups may meet in private. Papers discussed by the consultative group are made publicly available. Meetings are recorded and, when possible, webcast live. Recordings of meetings are made available on the IFRS Foundation website. If the Board were to decide that a particular meeting of a consultative group should be private, a summary of each such meeting would usually be posted on the relevant project page.

3.66 All consultative groups are reviewed by the IFRS Foundation staff each year to assess whether each group is continuing to serve the function for which it was established and whether the membership should remain the same. The outcome of the review is presented to the Board and the DPOC.

Comment letters

3.67 Comment letters play a pivotal role in Board and Interpretations Committee deliberations because the letters provide considered and public responses to a formal consultation.

3.68 All comment letters received by the Board and the Interpretations Committee are available on the IFRS Foundation website. Portions of a comment letter may be withheld from the public if publication would be harmful to the submitting party, for example, if the letter potentially breached securities disclosure laws.

3.69 When considering comment letters, the Board and the Interpretations Committee assesses the matters raised and the related explanations and evidence provided by respondents. It is the strength of the analysis provided in comment letters, and the evidence supporting the analysis, that is important. An analysis of the type of respondent and their geographical origin can help the Board assess whether there are any areas or types of respondent for which additional outreach might be appropriate. For some technical matters it can be helpful if the technical staff provides the Board with an analysis of the extent to which the views of particular sectors are shared or divided — for example, the extent to which investors have a common view or whether views differ between the types of respondent or regions.

Fieldwork

3.70 The Board and the technical staff sometimes use fieldwork to gain a better understanding of how a proposal is likely to affect those who use and apply IFRS Standards.

3.71 Fieldwork can be undertaken in different ways, including one-to-one visits or interviews with preparers, auditors, regulators or users of financial statements who are likely to be affected by the proposals. It can also include workshops in which several such parties are brought together or experiments are undertaken to assess how the proposals might be interpreted or applied.

3.72 Fieldwork may include:

(a) asking participants to assess how the proposals would apply to actual transactions or contracts;

(b) asking preparers or users to complete case studies;

(c) assessing how users process information; or

(d) assessing how systems are likely to be affected.

Fieldwork may also include gathering examples to help the Board gain a better understanding of industry practices and how proposed IFRS Standards could affect them. It is likely that some fieldwork will be undertaken on each standard-setting project, except for minor or narrow-scope amendments. The Board and the technical staff will need to assess which, if any, activities are appropriate and proportionate for a project, weighing the costs of the activity and what the Board is likely to learn from the fieldwork.

3.73 Undertaking fieldwork is not mandatory but, if the Board decides not to do so, it explains why to the DPOC and on the project page on the IFRS Foundation website.

3.74 Feedback from any fieldwork, public hearings or other outreach is summarised in a technical staff paper and assessed by the Board along with the comment letters.

Public hearings

3.75 In addition to inviting comment letters to seek views and suggestions, the Board may hold public hearings with interested organisations to listen to, and exchange views on, specific topics. Public hearings include round-table meetings and discussion forums. Round-table meetings are primarily consultative, providing participants with the opportunity to present and discuss their analysis of Board proposals. Discussion forums tend to have more of an educational focus, with Board members or technical staff explaining the Board's proposals before discussing them with the participants.

Accountability

Effect analysis

3.76 The Board is committed to assessing and explaining its views about the likely costs of implementing proposed new requirements and the likely ongoing associated costs and benefits of each new IFRS Standard—the costs and benefits are collectively referred to as *effects*. The Board gains insight on the likely effects of the proposals for new or amended Standards through its formal exposure of proposals and through its fieldwork, analysis and consultations with relevant parties. The likely effects are assessed:

(a)   in the light of the Board's objective of financial reporting transparency; and

(b)   in comparison to the existing financial reporting requirements.

3.77 The process of assessing the likely effects is intrinsic to the development of financial reporting requirements. Therefore, the Board assesses the likely effects throughout the development of a new or amended IFRS Standard, tailoring its assessment to the stage of development of the new or amended Standard. For example, at the research phase, the Board focuses on assessing the nature of the financial reporting deficiency being addressed, seeks to define the problem and proposes possible solutions, focusing particularly on the likely benefits of developing new financial reporting requirements. At the standard-setting phase, the Board is developing a specific proposal for a new or amended Standard. Accordingly, the Board focuses on assessing the potential costs and benefits of implementing that proposal, and on assessing any alternatives. The Board tailors the level of analysis to the nature of the proposed change to financial reporting. The format of the analysis is also tailored to the type of due process document being published.

3.78 When the Board undertakes a post-implementation review it has an opportunity to understand the effects of the change in financial reporting by comparison to those identified by the Board when it issued the new requirements.

3.79 In assessing the likely effects, the Board focuses on assessing how financial statements are likely to change because of the new financial reporting requirements, whether those changes will improve the quality of financial statements and whether those changes are justifiable. The Board considers matters such as:

(a) how the proposed changes are likely to affect the reporting of activities in the financial statements of those applying IFRS Standards.

(b) how those proposed changes are likely to affect the comparability of financial information between different reporting periods for an individual entity and between different entities in a particular reporting period.

(c) how the proposed changes are likely to affect the ability of a user of financial statements to assess the future cash flows of an entity.

(d) how the proposed changes to financial reporting are likely to affect economic decision-making.

(e) the likely effect on compliance costs for preparers, both on initial application and on an ongoing basis.

(f) the likely effects on the costs of analysis for users of financial statements (including any costs of extracting data, identifying how the data has been measured and adjusting data for the purposes of including them in, for example, a valuation model). The Board also considers the costs incurred by users of financial statements when information is not available and the comparative advantage that preparers have in developing information, when compared with the costs that users would incur to develop surrogate information.

3.80 IFRS Standards specify requirements for entities to provide high-quality, transparent and comparable financial information that can enhance financial stability in the global economy. The Board has regard to the effects on financial stability when assessing the effects of new financial reporting requirements to the extent appropriate and when relevant. For example, in explaining to a broad stakeholder audience the expected benefits of a new Standard, the Board may consider it useful to explain the link between increased transparency in financial reporting and a potential positive effect on financial stability. The introduction by an IFRS Standard of a current value measurement basis could, for instance, be a circumstance in which the Board concludes such explanation is appropriate and relevant. In addition, while it is generally impossible to quantitively assess the possible broader economic consequences of new financial reporting requirements, the Board may assess specific economic effects when relevant. The Board is not required to make a formal quantitative assessment of the overall effect of a new or amended IFRS Standard. Initial and ongoing costs and benefits are likely to affect different parties in different ways.

Reporting the effects

3.81 The Board explains its views on the likely effects at each stage of the development of a new or amended IFRS Standard. The level and format of the analysis is tailored to and reflects the nature of the change to financial reporting and the stage of development of the new or amended Standard. For instance, in the research phase, an analysis of the perceived financial reporting shortcoming being addressed and the possible solutions are an integral part of the discussion paper. In the standard-setting phase, the Board explains why it is proposing a particular change to financial reporting requirements, including referring to the evidence it has collected and any outreach it has undertaken, in the basis for conclusions accompanying the exposure draft. When a major Standard is issued, the Board publishes a separate effect analysis report that summarises the likely effects and how the Board made its assessments. This report is included as part of the documents accompanying the Standard balloted by the Board. For other new requirements, the Board presents its views as part of the basis for conclusions accompanying the new requirements.

Basis for conclusions and dissenting opinions

3.82 In the basis for conclusions the Board explains the rationale behind the decisions it reached in developing or amending an IFRS Standard. The basis for conclusions also includes the Board's responses to comments received when the proposals were exposed.

3.83 The Board does not operate as a consensus body. A decision to publish an exposure draft or issue an IFRS Standard requires a supermajority (see paragraph 3.14). Board members who disagree with the proposals or the final Standard are required to explain why they have a dissenting opinion. Such dissenting opinions are published with the basis for conclusions.

3.84 When a Board member dissents, they are voting against the exposure draft or IFRS Standard as a whole. A Board member cannot dissent from one part of a document but still vote to issue that document.

3.85 Throughout the development of an IFRS Standard there may be decisions with which individual Board members disagree. However, disagreeing on a matter does not mean the Board member will dissent from the whole document. The test for Board members is whether they think that the new requirements will improve financial reporting, taking into account the likely effects of those requirements. The hurdle to dissenting is deliberately high.

3.86 The dissent itself should address only those matters that caused the Board member to vote against the document as a whole. Board members should avoid using the dissent to express dissatisfaction with other parts of the document that, taken on their own, would not have caused the Board member to vote against issuing the document.

4. Technical work plan

4.1   The technical work plan is the group of projects the Board and the Interpretations Committee manage. The technical work plan focuses on projects and activities that are steps toward possible publications by the Board and the Interpretations Committee, including *research papers*, discussion papers, *requests for information*, exposure drafts, an IFRS Standard, a draft IFRIC Interpretation, an IFRIC Interpretation, an agenda decision and a report for a post-implementation review. The technical work plan is updated regularly and is available on the IFRS Foundation website, which also includes estimates of project time lines reflecting recent Board decisions.

4.2   Board technical activities incorporate a wide range of activities, and may also include financial reporting research, updates and revisions to the *Conceptual Framework for Financial Reporting* (*Conceptual Framework*), the maintenance and consistent application of IFRS Standards, post-implementation reviews, and the IFRS Taxonomy.

Five-yearly consultation on the Board's work plan (technical agenda)

4.3   The Board undertakes a public consultation on the work plan every five years by way of a public request for information. The Board normally allows a minimum of 120 days for comment on a work plan (agenda) consultation request for information. The primary objective of the review is to seek formal public input on the strategic direction and balance of the Board's work plan, including the criteria for assessing projects that may be added to the Board's work plan. The review could also seek views on financial reporting matters that respondents think should be given priority by the Board, together with any proposals to withdraw from the Board's work plan any projects that have not proceeded as planned or for which the prospects for progress are limited. The Board's discussion of potential projects to be added to or withdrawn from the work plan takes place in public Board meetings.

4.4   As part of this public consultation, the Board consults the Advisory Council.

4.5   In line with paragraphs 36(d) and 15(d) of the *Constitution*, the Board consults with the Trustees regarding the work plan and, through the DPOC, keeps the Trustees informed of its process in respect of its five-yearly consultation, including how it expects to respond to the input it has received. The next consultation should commence at the latest five years after the current consultation has been completed.

4.6   While the five-yearly consultations are the principal means of determining the Board's work plan, the Board can add projects to the work plan or change its priorities between consultations in response to changing circumstances. However, before adding a major project to the work plan that was not contemplated in the previous consultation, the Board consults the Advisory Council and ASAF on the potential project. The Board's discussion of potential projects to be added to the work plan takes place in public Board meetings.

4.7　　　　For minor or narrow-scope amendments to IFRS Standards, including *annual improvements*, the Board is not required to consult the Advisory Council or ASAF before adding a project to the work plan because such amendments are part of the maintenance and consistent application of the Standards.

Research programme

4.8　　　　New financial reporting requirements developed by the Board should address problems identified with the existing requirements. Sometimes a problem identified with current financial reporting can be remedied with a relatively minor amendment to an IFRS Standard. In other cases, the problem might require a more significant change to financial reporting requirements, such as a major change to a Standard or the development of a new Standard. Consequently, the first step in developing a new financial reporting requirement is to assess and define the problem within the existing reporting practice. For how the Board assesses the likely effects at this stage of a project see paragraph 3.77.

4.9　　　　The purpose of the Board's research programme is to analyse possible financial reporting problems by collecting evidence on the nature and extent of the perceived shortcoming and assessing potential ways to improve financial reporting or to remedy a deficiency. This analysis will help the Board decide whether it should undertake a standard-setting project to develop a proposal for a new IFRS Standard or to amend or replace a Standard. The research programme might also include the consideration of broader financial reporting matters, such as how financial reporting is evolving, to encourage international debate on financial reporting matters.

4.10　　　To help the Board in developing the work plan, the technical staff is asked to identify, review and raise matters that might warrant the Board's attention. New matters may arise from the five-yearly consultation on the technical work plan or a change to the Board's *Conceptual Framework*. In addition, the Board raises and discusses potential topics in the light of comments from the Advisory Council, ASAF, other standard-setters and other interested parties, and the Interpretations Committee, as well as technical staff research and other recommendations.

4.11　　　The Board and the technical staff are not expected to undertake all of the activities on its research programme. The Board may ask others, such as national accounting standard-setting bodies and regional bodies associated with accounting standard-setting or regional financial reporting bodies, academics and other interested parties, to participate in these activities. The Board will, however, need to provide clear direction on the matters on which to focus and on its expectations of the parties with whom it consults.

Research papers, discussion papers and requests for information

4.12　　　The main output of the research programme is expected to be discussion papers and research papers. Discussion papers and research papers are designed to elicit comments from interested parties that can help the Board decide whether to add a standard-setting project to the work plan. Discussion papers and research papers typically include a comprehensive overview of the issues, possible approaches to addressing the issues, the preliminary views of the Board and an *invitation to comment*.

4.13 Discussion papers are issued by the Board and present the analysis and collective views of the Board on a particular topic, although the discussion will reflect and convey any significant differences in Board members' views. The matters presented will have been discussed in public meetings of the Board.

4.14 Research papers are also issued by the Board but are prepared by the technical staff. Research papers may also be prepared by other accounting standard-setters or bodies, normally at the request of the Board. A research paper published by the Board includes a clear statement of the extent of the Board's involvement in the development or endorsement of that paper. In some cases, the Board will not have discussed the paper in a public meeting and will not, therefore, have developed any views on the matters set out in the paper.

4.15 Requests for information are formal requests by the Board for information or feedback on a matter related to technical projects or broader consultations. Examples of appropriate topics for a request for information include seeking comment on the Board's work plan every five years, post-implementation reviews, or help in assessing the practical implications of a potential financial reporting requirement.

Publication of discussion papers, requests for information and research papers

4.16 The Board ballots discussion papers. Before the Board asks the technical staff to prepare a discussion paper for ballot, the Board confirms that it has completed all of the steps necessary to ensure that the discussion paper is likely to meet its purpose. Research papers and requests for information require the support of a simple majority of the Board, with approval given in a public meeting.

4.17 The Board normally allows at least 120 days for comment on a discussion paper, a research paper, and requests for information on the work plan (see paragraph 4.3) or a post-implementation review (see paragraph 6.54). For other requests for information, the Board normally allows a minimum of 60 days for comment. If the information request is narrow in scope and urgent the Board may set a shorter period and need not consult the DPOC before doing so.

4.18 Discussion papers, requests for information and research papers are posted on the IFRS Foundation website.

4.19 Once the comment period for a discussion paper ends the technical staff analyses and summarises the comment letters and provides that analysis and summary to the Board.

Conceptual Framework for Financial Reporting

4.20   The Board maintains the *Conceptual Framework*. The *Conceptual Framework* describes the objective of and concepts for general purpose financial reporting. It is a practical tool that helps the Board to develop requirements in IFRS Standards based on consistent concepts.

4.21   Proposals to change the *Conceptual Framework* are developed and exposed by the Board in the same way that it exposes proposed changes to IFRS Standards, with similar comment periods.

4.22   The Board might decide to publish a discussion paper as a first step to revising part of the *Conceptual Framework*, although this is not a requirement.

4.23   The Board might need to consider whether any IFRS Standards should be amended to reflect revisions to the *Conceptual Framework*. However, amending a Standard is not an automatic consequence of such revisions. Changes to Standards address deficiencies in financial reporting. Any changes to the *Conceptual Framework* that highlight inconsistencies in the Standards are considered by the Board in the light of other priorities when developing or modifying the work plan.

5. Standards-setting projects

5.1   In considering whether to add a standard-setting project to the work plan, the Board or the Interpretations Committee requires the development of a specific project proposal and an assessment against the project criteria outlined in paragraph 5.4. That consideration will include whether the proposal is for a comprehensive project to develop a new IFRS Standard or major amendment to a Standard (see paragraphs 5.4–5.12), or a narrow-scope project for the purposes of maintenance and consistent application (see paragraphs 5.13–5.19).

5.2   The primary objective of a project proposal is to help the Board to manage its resources effectively and to prioritise its standard-setting work. The Board distinguishes between major and narrow-scope projects in its planning to help reduce the risk of committing resources to a project when other projects should have a higher priority.

5.3   A proposed new IFRS Standard, an amendment to a Standard, or an IFRIC Interpretation are exposed for public comment. Accordingly, if stakeholders believe that the Board has failed to establish the need for improvements to an area of financial reporting, they will have the opportunity to express their views during the consultation process.

Criteria for new IFRS Standards or major amendments

5.4   The Board evaluates the merits of adding a potential project to the work plan primarily on the basis of the needs of users of financial reports, while also taking into account the costs of preparing the information in financial reports. When deciding whether a proposed agenda item will address users' needs, the Board considers:

(a)   whether there is a deficiency in the way particular types of transactions or activities are reported in financial reports;

(b)   the importance of the matter to those who use financial reports;

(c)   the types of entities likely to be affected by any proposals, including whether the matter is more prevalent in some jurisdictions than others; and

(d)   how pervasive or acute a particular financial reporting issue is likely to be for entities.

5.5   The Board considers adding a standard-setting project to the work plan after considering any research it has undertaken on the topic. The Board would normally propose to develop a new IFRS Standard or to make major amendments to a Standard only after it has published a discussion paper and considered the comments it receives from that consultation. Publishing a discussion paper before adding a major standard-setting project to the work plan is not a requirement. However, to proceed without a discussion paper, the Board needs to be satisfied that it has sufficient information and understands the problem and the potential solutions well enough. The Board might conclude that a discussion paper is not necessary because it has sufficient input from a research paper, request for information or other research to proceed directly to an exposure draft. The reasons for not publishing a discussion paper need to be set out by the Board and reported to the DPOC.

5.6   The Board's discussion of potential projects and its decisions to adopt new projects take place in public Board meetings. The Board's decision to add standard-setting projects to the work plan, as well as its decisions on their priority, is by a simple majority vote at a Board meeting.

5.7   The Board adds a project to the work plan only if it concludes that the benefits of the improvements to financial reporting will outweigh the costs.

Matters referred by the Monitoring Board

5.8   The Monitoring Board may refer technical financial reporting matters to the Trustees and the Chair of the Board. The Monitoring Board's consensus-based decision-making limits such actions to extremely rare and urgent cases in which all Monitoring Board members agree that a technical financial reporting matter warrants referral.

5.9   The Trustees and the Chair of the Board are required to ensure that any such referral is addressed in a timely manner. Such referrals do not need to follow the formal consultation process set out in paragraph 4.6 and paragraphs 5.1–5.7.

5.10   The Board, together with the Trustees, reports to the Monitoring Board, usually within 30 days but sooner if the matter is more urgent, those steps it is taking to consider the referral.

5.11 If the Board decides not to take up the referred matter, the Board explains to the Trustees and the Monitoring Board why addressing the matter by amending an IFRS Standard would be inconsistent with the standard-setting responsibilities established in the *Constitution*.

5.12 In all cases, it is understood that the Monitoring Board will neither influence the decision-making nor challenge the decisions made by the Board with regard to its standard-setting.

Maintenance and consistent application

Identification of matters

5.13 The Board and the Interpretations Committee work together in supporting the consistent application of IFRS Standards. They do so by, among other things, issuing narrow-scope amendments to the Standards, issuing IFRIC Interpretations and publishing agenda decisions to address application questions. The Board and Interpretations Committee seek to achieve a balance between maintaining the principle-based nature of the Standards and adding or changing requirements in response to emerging application questions.

5.14 Some Board members attend each Interpretations Committee meeting and a report of each Interpretations Committee meeting is presented to the Board at a public meeting.

5.15 Stakeholders are encouraged to submit application questions to the Interpretations Committee when they view it as important that the Board or the Interpretations Committee address the matter. Such matters could include cases of doubt about the required accounting for a particular circumstance or transaction, or concerns expressed by investors about the application of specified disclosure requirements. The Interpretations Committee often consults on questions submitted to it with national accounting standard-setting bodies and regional bodies involved with accounting standard-setting.

5.16 The Interpretations Committee decides a standard-setting project should be added to the work plan, either by recommending that the Board develop a narrow-scope amendment or by deciding to develop an IFRIC Interpretation, when all of the following criteria are met:

(a) the matter has widespread effect and has, or is expected to have, a material effect on those affected;

(b) it is necessary to add or change requirements in IFRS Standards to improve financial reporting—that is, the principles and requirements in the Standards do not provide an adequate basis for an entity to determine the required accounting;

(c) the matter can be resolved efficiently within the confines of the existing Standards and the *Conceptual Framework*; and

(d)   the matter is sufficiently narrow in scope that the Board or the Interpretations Committee can address it in an efficient manner, but not so narrow that it is not cost-effective for the Board or the Interpretations Committee and stakeholders to undertake the due process required to change a Standard.

5.17   A simple majority of Interpretations Committee members present decides, after a debate in a public meeting, whether a standard-setting project should be added to the work plan.

5.18   If the Interpretations Committee recommends that the Board should develop a narrow-scope amendment, it refers the matter to the Board. If the Interpretations Committee decides to develop an IFRIC Interpretation, it follows the process described in section 7. The Board can also decide to make narrow-scope amendments (which include annual improvements) to the Standards, following the process described in paragraphs 6.4–6.15. The Board may seek the assistance of the Interpretations Committee in developing such narrow-scope amendments, drawing on the Interpretations Committee's experience of the application of IFRS Standards.

5.19   If the Interpretations Committee decides that a standard-setting project should not be added to the work plan to address a question submitted, it explains why in an agenda decision (see paragraphs 8.2–8.7).

6. New or amended IFRS Standards

Exposure drafts

6.1   Publication of an exposure draft is a mandatory step in the due process before a new IFRS Standard can be issued or an existing Standard can be amended.

6.2   An exposure draft sets out a specific proposal in the form of a proposed IFRS Standard (or amendment to a Standard) and is therefore generally set out in the same way as, and has all of the components of, a Standard. The main differences are that:

(a)   the basis for conclusions is written to explain the Board's rationale for the proposal, and is not a draft of the rationale for the final IFRS Standard or final amendments to the Standard; and

(b)   the consequential amendments need not be set out in as much detail as they would be in a final IFRS Standard, particularly where such amendments are changes to cross-references or terminology and other matters that are more editorial.

6.3   An exposure draft is the Board's main vehicle for consulting the public and therefore includes an invitation to comment, setting out the issues that the Board has identified as being of particular interest. Although it is normally included with the ballot draft, it is not necessary for the Board to ballot the invitation to comment.

Developing an exposure draft

6.4 The development of an exposure draft takes place in public meetings. The technical staff prepares papers for the Board to consider on the matters to be addressed.

6.5 Development of an exposure draft normally begins with the Board considering the issues on the basis of technical staff research and recommendations. The Board also considers the comments received on any discussion paper, research paper or request for information, suggestions made by consultative groups and accounting standard-setters, and suggestions arising from consultation with other stakeholders.

6.6 When the Board has reached general agreement on the technical matters in the project and has considered the likely effects of the proposals (see paragraphs 3.76–3.81), the technical staff presents a paper to the Board:

    (a) summarising the steps that the Board has taken in developing the proposals, including a summary of when the Board discussed the project in public meetings, public hearings held, outreach activities and meetings of consultative groups;

    (b) if applicable, reaffirming why the Board has decided that it was not necessary to have a consultative group or to have conducted fieldwork; and

    (c) recommending a comment period for the exposure draft.

6.7 The Board normally allows a minimum period of 120 days for comment on an exposure draft. If the matter is narrow in scope and urgent the Board may set a comment period of less than 120 days but no less than 30 days after consulting and obtaining approval from the DPOC.

6.8 In exceptional circumstances, and only after requesting and receiving approval from 75% of the Trustees, the Board may reduce the period for public comment on an exposure draft to below 30 days but may not dispense with a comment period.

6.9 If the Board is satisfied that it has addressed all of these matters it votes to have the technical staff prepare the exposure draft for balloting. Board members who intend to dissent from the proposals in the exposure draft make their intentions known at this time.

Exposing annual improvements

6.10 Some proposed amendments to IFRS Standards that are sufficiently minor or narrow in scope can be packaged together and exposed in one document even though the amendments are unrelated. Such amendments are called 'annual improvements'. Annual improvements follow the same due process as other amendments to the Standards, except that annual improvements consist of unrelated amendments that are exposed together, rather than separately.

6.11   The justification for exposing unrelated improvements in one package is that such amendments are limited to changes that either clarify the wording in an IFRS Standard or correct relatively minor unintended consequences, oversights or conflicts between existing requirements of the Standards. Because of their nature, it is not necessary to undertake consultation or outreach for annual improvements beyond the comment letter process. The Board needs to be cautious and avoid including in the annual improvements package an amendment that merits separate consultation and outreach.

6.12   Clarifying an IFRS Standard involves either replacing unclear wording in existing Standards or providing requirements where an absence of requirements is causing concern. Such an amendment maintains consistency with the existing principles within the applicable Standard and does not propose a new principle or change an existing principle.

6.13   Resolving a conflict between existing requirements of IFRS Standards includes addressing oversights or relatively minor unintended consequences that have arisen as a result of the existing requirements of the Standards. Such amendments do not propose a new principle or change an existing principle.

6.14   Proposed annual improvements should be well defined and narrow in scope. The Board assesses proposed annual improvements against the criteria set out in paragraphs 6.10–6.13 before they are published in an exposure draft. As a guide, if the Board takes several meetings to reach a conclusion it is an indication that the cause of the issue is more fundamental than can be resolved within the annual improvements process.

6.15   The Board normally allows a minimum period of 90 days for comment on annual improvements.

Publication

6.16   The publication of an exposure draft is accompanied by a news release.

6.17   Depending on the nature of the exposure draft, the Board and the technical staff might also develop, and make available, a project *snapshot*, podcast, webcast, question and answer pack or presentation (speech) pack. The more significant the exposure draft the more comprehensive the related communications package is likely to be.

6.18   All exposure drafts and related publications are freely available on the IFRS Foundation website.

Consideration of comments received and consultations

6.19   After the comment period ends, the Board reviews the comment letters and the results of the other consultations, such as the investor consultation. The technical staff provides a summary of the comment letters, giving a general overview of the comments received and the major points raised in the letters. The analysis helps the Board to identify the main topics for consideration during the deliberations—or whether the Board should even proceed with the project.

6.20   The development of an IFRS Standard is carried out during Board meetings.

6.21   As a means of exploring the issues further, and seeking further comments and suggestions, the Board may conduct fieldwork, or arrange public hearings and round-table meetings. The Board also maintains contact with its consultative groups.

Completion of the deliberations

6.22   When the Board has reached general agreement on the technical matters in the project and has considered the likely effects of the new IFRS Standard (see paragraphs 3.76–3.81), the technical staff presents a paper to the Board:

(a)   summarising the steps that the Board has taken in developing the Standard, including a summary of when the Board discussed this project in public meetings, public hearings held, outreach activities and meetings of consultative groups;

(b)   if applicable, reaffirming why the Board has decided that it was not necessary to have a consultative group or to have conducted fieldwork; and

(c)   assessing whether the proposals can be finalised or whether they should be re-exposed.

6.23   If the Board is satisfied that it has addressed all of these matters it votes to have the technical staff prepare the IFRS Standard for balloting. Board members who intend to dissent from the proposals of the Standard make their intentions known at this time.

6.24   The Board informs the DPOC of its decision to proceed to the ballot stage for an IFRS Standard, explaining why it is satisfied that *re-exposure* is not necessary, before the Standard or major amendment is issued.

Re-exposure criteria

6.25   In considering whether there is a need for re-exposure, the Board:

(a)   identifies substantial issues that emerged during the comment period on the exposure draft and that it had not previously considered;

(b)   assesses the evidence that it has considered;

(c)   determines whether it has sufficiently understood the issues, implications and likely effects of the new requirements and actively sought the views of interested parties; and

(d)   considers whether the various viewpoints were appropriately aired in the exposure draft and adequately discussed and reviewed in the basis for conclusions.

6.26   It is inevitable that the final proposals will include changes from those originally proposed. The fact that there are changes does not compel the Board to re-expose the proposals. The Board needs to consider whether the revised proposals include any fundamental changes on which respondents have not had the opportunity to comment because they were not contemplated or discussed in the basis for conclusions accompanying the exposure draft. The Board also needs to consider whether it will learn anything new by re-exposing the proposals. If the Board is satisfied that the revised proposals respond to the feedback received and that it is unlikely that re-exposure will reveal any new concerns, it should proceed to finalise the proposed requirements.

6.27 The more extensive and fundamental the changes from the exposure draft and current practice the more likely the proposals should be re-exposed. However, the Board needs to weigh the cost of delaying improvements to financial reporting against the relative urgency for the need to change and what additional steps it has taken to consult since the exposure draft was published. The use of consultative groups or targeted consultation can give the Board information to support a decision to finalise a proposal without the need for re-exposure.

6.28 The Board should give more weight to changes in recognition and measurement than disclosure when considering whether re-exposure is necessary.

6.29 The Board's decision on whether to publish its revised proposals for another round of comment is made in a Board meeting. If the Board decides that re-exposure is necessary, the due process to be followed is the same as for the first exposure draft. However, because it is not the first exposure of the proposed IFRS Standard, it may be appropriate to have a shortened comment period, particularly if the Board is seeking comments on only specific aspects of the revised exposure draft, while recognising that respondents may not limit their comments to these aspects. The public comment period for such documents will normally be at least 90 days.

Finalising an IFRS Standard

6.30 The mandatory parts of an IFRS Standard are:

(a) the principles and the related application guidance;

(b) the defined terms; and

(c) the effective date and transition paragraphs.

6.31 When a new IFRS Standard, or amendment to a Standard, is issued, it is also accompanied by amendments to other Standards that are a consequence of the new requirements—these are called 'consequential amendments'.

6.32 Each IFRS Standard usually has accompanying material that is not an integral part of the Standard:

(a) a table of contents;

(b) an introduction;

(c) illustrative examples;

(d) the basis for conclusions (including the Board's analysis of the likely effects if not presented as a separate report);

(e)   an effect analysis report (for a major Standard); and

(f)   dissenting opinions.

6.33   Sometimes the accompanying material will include a table that shows the relationship between paragraphs in the old and the new requirements and a brief history of the IFRS Standard. In all cases the documents will state clearly whether the material is an integral part of the Standard or whether it accompanies it but is not integral. Material that is integral to a Standard is provided to governments, or the relevant authorities, that have adopted the Standards and have an agreement with the IFRS Foundation to receive such material.

6.34   As a principle, IFRS Standards should be able to be applied without the accompanying material.

Effective date and transition

6.35   An IFRS Standard, or an amendment to a Standard, has an effective date and transition requirements. The mandatory effective date is set so that jurisdictions have sufficient time to incorporate the new requirements into their legal systems and those applying the Standards have sufficient time to prepare for the new requirements.

6.36   The Board also considers how first-time adopters of IFRS Standards should apply the Standard, or an amendment to a Standard, and whether any amendments are needed to IFRS 1 *First-time Adoption of International Financial Reporting Standards*.

Publication

6.37   The publication of a new IFRS Standard, or an amendment to a Standard, is accompanied by a news release.

6.38   The publication of a new IFRS Standard or a major amendment to a Standard, is also accompanied by a project summary and *feedback statement*. Depending on the nature of the new requirements, the Board and the IFRS Foundation staff might also develop, and make available, a podcast, webcast, question and answer pack or presentation (speech) pack. The more significant the changes to the Standards, the more comprehensive the related communications package is likely to be.

Practice guidance

6.39   The Board may produce non-mandatory *practice guidance*, normally on a topic not addressed by an IFRS Standard (such as the Practice Statement on management commentary), if it considers that doing so would improve financial reporting. The Board follows the same procedures used for the development of a Standard, including the balloting of documents.

Post-publication procedures and maintenance

6.40 After an IFRS Standard is issued, the IFRS Foundation undertakes various activities to support its implementation and consistent application. These might include publishing educational materials, such as articles and webcasts (see paragraphs 8.8–8.10). Board members and technical staff may also hold meetings with interested parties, including other standard-setting bodies, to help understand unexpected matters that have arisen from the implementation of the Standard and the potential effect of its requirements.

6.41 Technical staff may make editorial corrections to technical documents to remedy drafting errors that are made when writing or typesetting the document, provided that the corrections do not alter the technical meaning of the text. Editorial corrections normally fix spelling errors, grammatical mistakes or incorrectly marked consequential amendments.

Translation

6.42 Translations of IFRS Standards are initiated by the IFRS Foundation staff as a response to requests from jurisdictions adopting or developing an interest in the Standards.

6.43 The translations policy allows for only one translation per language, to ensure that all users of a particular language use the same translation. The two-stage translation procedure, consisting of the initial translation followed by a review by a committee of accounting experts, is designed to produce a high-quality translation that accurately renders the meaning of IFRS Standards in English into another language.

6.44 Review committee members are native speakers of the language and experts in the field of financial reporting. Review committees typically comprise representatives from major accounting firms, national accounting bodies, academics, appropriate government bodies and specialist industries, such as banking and insurance.

6.45 The review committee has one person designated as the co-ordinator. In addition to managing the review process, the co-ordinator has the final responsibility for the content of the translation, and has a casting vote if consensus in the committee cannot be reached.

6.46 When a language is spoken and used in more than one country, participation in the review committee is encouraged from all countries using that language to ensure that the resulting translation aids the consistent application of IFRS Standards.

IFRS Taxonomy (see the Annex)

6.47 The implications for the IFRS Taxonomy are considered during the development and drafting of new or amended IFRS Standards. The publication of the *proposed IFRS Taxonomy update* normally happens at the same time as, or shortly after, the final Standard or amendment to a Standard is published.

Post-implementation review

6.48　The Board is required to conduct a post-implementation review of each new IFRS Standard or major amendment. A post-implementation review normally begins after the new requirements have been applied internationally for two years, which is generally about 30–36 months after the effective date.

6.49　In addition to post-implementation reviews that respond to a new IFRS Standard or major amendment to a Standard, the Board may decide to conduct a post-implementation review in response to changes in the financial reporting environment and regulatory requirements, or in response to concerns about the quality of a Standard that have been expressed by the Advisory Council, the Interpretations Committee, standard-setters or interested parties.

6.50　Each review has two phases. The first involves an initial identification and assessment of the matters to be examined, which are then the subject of a public consultation by the Board in the form of a request for information. In the second phase, the Board considers the comments it has received from the request for information along with the information it has gathered through other consultative activities. On the basis of that information, the Board presents its findings and sets out the steps it plans to take, if any, as a result of the review.

Initial assessment and public consultation

6.51　The goal of improving financial reporting underlies any new IFRS Standard. A post-implementation review is an opportunity to assess the effect of the new requirements on investors, preparers and auditors following the issuance and application of a Standard. The review considers the issues that were important or contentious during the development of the publication (which should be identifiable from the basis for conclusions, project summary, feedback statement and effect analysis of the relevant Standard), as well as issues that have come to the attention of the Board after the document was published. The Board and the technical staff also consult stakeholders to help the Board identify areas where possible unexpected costs or implementation problems were encountered.

6.52　This initial assessment should draw on the broad network of IFRS Standards-related bodies and interested parties, such as the Interpretations Committee, the Board's consultative groups, securities regulators, national accounting standard-setting bodies, regional bodies involved with accounting standard-setting, preparers, auditors and investors. The purpose of these consultations is to inform the Board so that it can establish an appropriate scope for the review. How extensive the consultations need to be in this phase will depend on the Standard being reviewed and on what the Board already knows about the implementation of that Standard. The Board needs to be satisfied that it has sufficient information to establish the scope of the review.

6.53   The Board publishes a request for information, setting out the matters for which it is seeking feedback by means of a formal public consultation. In the request for information, the Board explains why it is seeking feedback on the matters specified and includes any initial assessment by the Board of the IFRS Standard or major amendment that is being reviewed. The request for information will also set out the process that the Board followed in establishing the scope of the review.

6.54   The Board normally allows a minimum of 120 days for comment on a request for information that is part of a post-implementation review. The Board will only set a period of less than 120 days after consulting and obtaining approval from the DPOC.

6.55   The Board may decide, on the basis of its initial assessment, that it would be premature to undertake a post-implementation review at that time. The Board informs the DPOC of its intention to defer a post-implementation review, explaining why it has reached this conclusion and indicating when it expects to resume the review.

Consideration of evidence and presentation of findings

6.56   The Board considers whether it is necessary to supplement the responses to the request for information with other information or evidence, such as by undertaking:

(a)   an analysis of financial statements or of other financial information;

(b)   a review of academic and other research related to the implementation of the IFRS Standard being reviewed; and

(c)   surveys, interviews and other consultations.

6.57   The extent to which further information is gathered will depend on the IFRS Standard being reviewed and the feedback from the request for information.

6.58   The Board considers the comments that it has received from the request for information along with the evidence and information that it has obtained from any additional analysis. When the Board has completed its deliberations, it presents its findings in a public report. The Board may consider making minor amendments to the IFRS Standard or preparing an agenda proposal for a broader revision of the Standard. There is no presumption that a post-implementation review will lead to any changes to a Standard. The Board may recommend to the DPOC that the Board should make changes to its procedures, such as how effects of a Standard are assessed or additional steps that should be taken during the development of a Standard.

6.59   The Board reports regularly to the DPOC during the period of a post-implementation review and informs the DPOC when it has completed its review and provides the DPOC with a draft of the report. When the DPOC is satisfied that the Board has completed the review satisfactorily, the report can be finalised.

7. IFRIC Interpretations

7.1   IFRIC Interpretations are developed by the Interpretations Committee but, because they are part of IFRS Standards, they are ratified by the Board.

Draft IFRIC Interpretation

7.2   Publication of a draft IFRIC Interpretation is a mandatory step in the due process before an IFRIC Interpretation can be issued.

7.3   A draft IFRIC Interpretation sets out a specific proposal in the form of a proposed Interpretation and is therefore generally set out in the same way as, and has all of the components of, an Interpretation. The main difference is that the basis for conclusions is written to explain the Interpretations Committee's rationale for the proposal, rather than a draft of the rationale for the final IFRIC Interpretation.

7.4   A draft IFRIC Interpretation is the Interpretations Committee's main vehicle for consulting the public and therefore includes an invitation to comment, setting out the matters that have been identified as being of particular significance. Although it is normally included with the ballot draft, it is not necessary for the Interpretations Committee to ballot the invitation to comment.

Developing a draft IFRIC Interpretation

7.5   The development of a draft IFRIC Interpretation takes place in public meetings. The technical staff prepares papers about the matters being addressed for the Interpretations Committee to consider.

7.6   The Interpretations Committee applies a principle-based approach founded on the *Conceptual Framework*. It considers the principles established in the relevant IFRS Standards to develop an interpretation and to determine that the interpretation does not change or conflict with the Standards. If the Interpretations Committee concludes that the requirements of a Standard differ from the *Conceptual Framework*, it obtains direction from the Board. In developing IFRIC Interpretations, the Interpretations Committee is not seeking to create an extensive rule-oriented environment, nor does it act as an urgent issues group.

7.7   The solution developed by the Interpretations Committee should be effective for a reasonable period of time. Accordingly, the Interpretations Committee would not normally develop an IFRIC Interpretation if the topic is being addressed in a forthcoming IFRS Standard. However, this does not prevent the Interpretations Committee from acting on a particular matter if the short-term improvements can be justified.

7.8   If the Interpretations Committee is satisfied that it has addressed all of the technical matters it votes to see whether there is general agreement that the technical staff should prepare the draft IFRIC Interpretation for balloting. General agreement is reached when no more than four members have voted against the proposal. Because Interpretations are developed on the basis of the Interpretations Committee reaching general agreement on the particular matter, a draft Interpretation does not include any dissenting opinions. However, the invitation to comment and the basis for conclusions identifies whether any members do not agree with the draft Interpretation.

7.9   When Interpretations Committee members generally agree on the technical matters, the technical staff presents a paper to the Board summarising the steps that have been taken in developing the proposals and recommending a comment period for the draft IFRIC Interpretation.

7.10   Board members receive ballot drafts of the draft IFRIC Interpretation. If four or more Board members object to the release of the draft Interpretation during the balloting process, the draft Interpretation is not released. If a draft Interpretation is not released because of Board members' objections, the Board decides whether the draft Interpretation should be published with amendments, whether the matter should be referred back to the Interpretations Committee or considered further by the Board, or if there should be no further action.

7.11   The Board and the Interpretations Committee normally allow a minimum period of 90 days for comment on a draft IFRIC Interpretation. If the matter is narrow in scope and urgent the Board may set a comment period of less than 90 days but no less than 30 days after consulting and obtaining approval from the DPOC.

Publication

7.12   All draft IFRIC Interpretations are accompanied by a news release.

7.13   All draft IFRIC Interpretations are freely available on the IFRS Foundation website.

Consideration of comments received

7.14   After the comment period ends, the Interpretations Committee reviews the comment letters received.

7.15   The development of an IFRIC Interpretation is carried out during Interpretations Committee meetings, when Interpretations Committee members consider the comments received on the draft Interpretation and decide whether to proceed with the project.

7.16   When the Interpretations Committee decides that it has reached general agreement on the technical matters in the IFRIC Interpretation, the technical staff presents a paper to the Interpretations Committee summarising the steps that have been taken in developing the Interpretation and assessing whether the proposals can be finalised or if they should be re-exposed.

7.17   In considering whether there is a need for re-exposure, the Interpretations Committee applies the same criteria as set out for the Board in paragraphs 6.25–6.28. If the Interpretations Committee decides that re-exposure is necessary, the due process to be followed is the same as for the first draft IFRIC Interpretation, with a minimum comment period determined in accordance with paragraph 7.11.

Finalising an IFRIC Interpretation

7.18 If the Interpretations Committee is satisfied that it has addressed all of the technical matters it votes to see whether there is general agreement that the technical staff should prepare the IFRIC Interpretation for balloting. General agreement is reached when no more than four members have voted against the Interpretation.

7.19 An IFRIC Interpretation includes:

(a) requirements specifying the accounting for the transactions or other events within its scope;

(b) references to relevant IFRS Standards and parts of the *Conceptual Framework* that have been drawn upon in the IFRIC Interpretation; and

(c) the effective date and transition paragraphs.

7.20 The basis for conclusions states the reasons for the IFRIC Interpretation. An IFRIC Interpretation does not include any dissenting opinions of Interpretations Committee members. However, when the IFRIC Interpretation is submitted to the Board for ratification, the technical staff paper accompanying the request for ratification identifies how many Interpretations Committee members objected to the IFRIC Interpretation and their reasons for doing so.

Effective date and transition

7.21 As with any change to IFRS Standards, an IFRIC Interpretation includes effective date and transition paragraphs. The mandatory effective date is set so that jurisdictions have sufficient time to incorporate the new requirements into their legal systems and those applying the Standards have sufficient time to prepare for the new requirements. Interpretations generally address matters of a narrower scope than a major amendment to a Standard so the time necessary to prepare for the new requirements is also likely to be shorter.

7.22 The Interpretations Committee also considers how first-time adopters of IFRS Standards should apply the IFRIC Interpretation, and whether to recommend that the Board amend IFRS 1 *First-time Adoption of International Financial Reporting Standards*.

Agreement and ratification by the Board

7.23 When the Interpretations Committee has balloted the IFRIC Interpretation, it is submitted to the Board for ratification together with a staff paper summarising the steps that have been taken in developing the IFRIC Interpretation. The Board votes to ratify an IFRIC Interpretation in a public meeting. Ratification requires a supermajority, the same level of support by Board members as is required for a new or amended IFRS Standard.

7.24 Board members may dissent from the ratification of an IFRIC Interpretation. The fact that one or more Board members dissented is stated in the approvals section of the IFRIC Interpretation along with their reasons for doing so.

7.25 The Board votes on the IFRIC Interpretation as submitted by the Interpretations Committee. If an Interpretation is not ratified by the Board, the Board provides the Interpretations Committee with reasons for the objection. On the basis of these reasons, the Board will decide whether to refer the matter back to the Interpretations Committee, whether to consider it further or whether to take no further action. The Board may make editorial changes to the IFRIC Interpretation or change the effective date, and it informs the Interpretations Committee of any changes it makes.

7.26 Ratified IFRIC Interpretations are issued by the Board.

Publication

7.27 All IFRIC Interpretations are accompanied by a news release.

8. Supporting consistent application

8.1 The objective of the material described in this section is to improve consistency of application of IFRS Standards.

Agenda decisions

Interpretations Committee agenda decisions

8.2 If the Interpretations Committee decides that a standard-setting project should not be added to the work plan to address a question submitted (see paragraphs 5.13–5.19), it explains why in a tentative agenda decision in IFRIC Update and on the IFRS Foundation website. The Interpretations Committee requests comments on tentative agenda decisions, the comment period for which is normally 60 days. After considering those comments, the Interpretations Committee will:

(a) confirm its decision and publish an agenda decision (subject to the Board not objecting—see paragraph 8.7);

(b) revise its decision and re-expose for comment a revised tentative agenda decision (when the Interpretations Committee decides that re-exposure is necessary, after applying the re-exposure criteria in paragraphs 6.25–6.28);

(c) decide that a standard-setting project should be added to the work plan; or

(d) refer the matter to the Board.

8.3 An agenda decision explains why a standard-setting project has not been added to the work plan and, in many cases, includes explanatory material. The objective of including such explanatory material is to improve the consistency of application of IFRS Standards. An agenda decision typically includes explanatory material when the reason for not adding a standard-setting project to the work plan is the Interpretations Committee's conclusion that the principles and requirements in the Standards provide an adequate basis for an entity to determine the required accounting. Explanatory material included as part of a tentative agenda decision is subject to comment.

8.4 Agenda decisions (including any explanatory material contained within them) cannot add or change requirements in IFRS Standards. Instead, explanatory material explains how the applicable principles and requirements in IFRS Standards apply to the transaction or fact pattern described in the agenda decision.

8.5 Explanatory material derives its authority from the Standards themselves. Accordingly, an entity is required to apply the applicable IFRS Standard(s), reflecting the explanatory material in an agenda decision (subject to it having sufficient time to implement that accounting—see paragraph 8.6).

8.6 Explanatory material may provide additional insights that might change an entity's understanding of the principles and requirements in IFRS Standards. Because of this, an entity might determine that it needs to change an accounting policy[2] as a result of an agenda decision. It is expected that an entity would be entitled to sufficient time to make that determination and implement any necessary accounting policy change (for example, an entity may need to obtain new information or adapt its systems to implement a change). Determining how much time is sufficient to make an accounting policy change is a matter of judgement that depends on an entity's particular facts and circumstances. Nonetheless an entity would be expected to implement any change on a timely basis and, if material, consider whether disclosure related to the change is required by IFRS Standards.

8.7 Before an agenda decision is published, the Board is asked—at its first public meeting at which it is practicable to present the agenda decision—whether it objects to the agenda decision. Specifically, Board members are asked whether they object to (a) the Interpretations Committee's decision that a standard-setting project should not be added to the work plan, and (b) the Interpretations Committee's conclusion that the agenda decision does not add or change requirements in IFRS Standards. If four or more Board members object, the agenda decision is not published and the Board decides how to proceed.

Educational material

8.8 The IFRS Foundation sometimes publishes educational material related to IFRS Standards on its website, including webcasts, articles, presentations for conferences and *IFRS for SMEs* training material. Educational material is not part of the Standards and cannot add or change requirements in the Standards.

8.9 The development of educational material does not take place in public meetings and is not subjected to the public scrutiny that is given to the development of IFRS Standards. Nonetheless, educational material is subject to quality assurance processes reflecting the nature and complexity of the

---

2   IAS 8 *Accounting Policies, Changes in Accounting Estimates and Errors* addresses accounting policies, accounting estimates and prior period errors.

material, and to ensure that the material does not add or change requirements in the Standards and is clearly distinguished from the Standards.

8.10 In order to meet the assurances in paragraph 8.9, educational material is subjected to at least the following level of review:

(a) high-level summaries of the requirements in an IFRS Standard, such as introductory webcasts on a new Standard, are reviewed by a Board member;

(b) more detailed materials explaining the requirements in a Standard, such as a webcast on specific aspects of a Standard, are reviewed by two Board members; and

(c) material explaining or illustrating how the requirements in a Standard might be applied to particular transactions or other circumstances, such as a new example demonstrating how the requirements might be applied to a particular fact pattern, are reviewed by three Board members.

8.11 The DPOC receives periodic reports on educational material published by the IFRS Foundation. The reports identify the nature of the material and the level of review undertaken, and state the IFRS Foundation staff's conclusion as to whether the required level of review has been undertaken.

9. Protocol for Trustee action for perceived breaches of due process

9.1 Any alleged breaches of due process will be considered within the context of the DPOC's ongoing oversight of the Board's and the Interpretations Committee's due process. Alleged breaches could be raised by external parties (including media reports), internal parties, the DPOC or other Trustees. All parties are encouraged to raise any concerns as soon as they perceive that an alleged breach of due process has occurred.

9.2 The DPOC will consider the alleged breach and the evidence provided by the complainant, IFRS Foundation staff, the Board and the Interpretations Committee. The alleged breach will also be assessed in the light of the reporting measures set out in this *Handbook*.

9.3 Complaints to the DPOC are made by using the procedures set out on the IFRS Foundation website. Each complaint, together with the name and contact details of the complainant, is posted on the IFRS Foundation website.

9.4 The Trustee staff member responsible for managing Trustee activities is responsible for ensuring that the DPOC receives a report from the appropriate technical staff in response to the complaint. This report is posted on the IFRS Foundation website and is then considered by the DPOC at one of its meetings at which the Chair and/or the Vice-Chair of the Board are present. The DPOC may request additional information from the Trustee staff member before finalising a response. The response of the DPOC, usually in the form of a letter to the complainant, is also posted on the IFRS Foundation website.

9.5   Although the Board and the Interpretations Committee are required to adhere to these policies and to inform the DPOC of their actions, a limited failure does not render a pronouncement invalid. Retrospective steps can be taken to remedy such a situation if it arises and the DPOC may decide that no additional action is required if it concludes that no harm has been done as a result of the breach. In this circumstance the DPOC will make public its conclusions and discussions in line with the reporting requirements set out in paragraph 2.15.

9.6   If the majority of the DPOC concludes that the Board or the Interpretations Committee has breached due process, the DPOC will request that the Board or the Interpretations Committee take action to remedy the breach either within the current phase of the project to which the breach relates, or by taking some additional steps in a future phase of that project.

9.7   If the DPOC and the Board or the Interpretations Committee cannot resolve differences of opinion as to whether due process has been breached, or cannot agree on the action to remedy a breach as identified in paragraph 9.6, the matter will be brought to the attention of the Trustees, who will then resolve it (see paragraph 9.9). The Trustees may need to convene a meeting to consider the matter. Such a meeting may be held by telephone or video conference if a prompt response is required.

9.8   If a due process complaint relates to a project for which the Board has yet to issue a new IFRS Standard, an amendment to an IFRS Standard or an IFRIC Interpretation, the Board or the Interpretations Committee will not be permitted to complete that particular phase of the project until the due process complaint has been addressed by the DPOC or the Trustees. As stated in paragraph 9.5, a breach of due process does not invalidate a pronouncement issued by the Board. Accordingly, if the matter relates to a Standard, an amendment to a Standard or an IFRIC Interpretation that has been issued by the Board, that pronouncement shall remain valid in all respects until the due process complaint has been addressed by the DPOC or the Trustees. In such cases the DPOC or the Trustees should address the complaint as expeditiously as possible, taking into consideration the effective date of the pronouncement.

9.9   If differences of opinion between the DPOC and the Board or the Interpretations Committee cannot be resolved, or they cannot agree on the action to remedy a breach (see paragraph 9.7), the Trustee staff member responsible for managing Trustee activities, in consultation with the DPOC Chair, will prepare a full brief for consideration by the Trustees. If the majority of Trustees attending the meeting conclude that the Board or the Interpretations Committee is in breach of its due process, the Board or the Interpretations Committee follows whatever the Trustees decide is necessary to be satisfied that due process is remedied.

9.10   The DPOC and the Trustees cannot raise technical accounting considerations as evidence of a breach of due process.

Annex

The IFRS Taxonomy due process

The IFRS Taxonomy and its objectives

A1 The IFRS Taxonomy is a structured classification system. It encompasses the elements (including their descriptions, properties, relationships and the data model) that can be used to tag quantitative and qualitative information presented and disclosed in financial reports that are prepared in accordance with IFRS Standards (including the *IFRS for SMEs* Standard).

A2 The main purpose of the IFRS Taxonomy is to support the consistent tagging of information prepared applying IFRS Standards. In doing so, the IFRS Foundation is assisting those preparers and users of financial statements that are required to or prefer to report and receive information in a structured electronic format.

A3 The IFRS Taxonomy represents the presentation and disclosure requirements in IFRS Standards. However, it is not an integral part of the Standards. Development and publication of the IFRS Taxonomy by the Board and the IFRS Foundation helps to ensure that the IFRS Taxonomy is consistent with, and does not interpret, the requirements in the Standards.

The components of the IFRS Taxonomy

A4 The IFRS Taxonomy can be described as having two components:

    (a) the IFRS Taxonomy **content**: this is the set of elements (including associated descriptions, properties, relationships and the data model) that is used to reflect:

        (i) IFRS Standards, specifically disclosures and presentation requirements that are explicitly referred to in the Standards (including IFRIC Interpretations) and the accompanying materials to the Standards (implementation guidance, illustrative examples);

        (ii) IFRS reporting practice (common practice);

        (iii) general improvements; and

        (iv) other taxonomy content not referred to explicitly in IFRS Standards or their accompanying materials to Standards.

    (b) the IFRS Taxonomy **technology**: refers to taxonomy features including, but not limited to, the syntax employed to publish and express the content of the IFRS Taxonomy and the taxonomy architecture used. The architecture relates to taxonomy characteristics such as, for example, how the IFRS Taxonomy content is organised into files and naming protocols. The IFRS Taxonomy technology does not include the internal systems used by the IFRS Foundation to manage and generate the *IFRS Taxonomy files* and documents.

The objectives of the IFRS Taxonomy due process

A5   The content and technology are both important features of a taxonomy that supports high-quality and consistent application of IFRS Standards and are interrelated. The IFRS Taxonomy due process is designed to protect the integrity of both its content and technology, in particular to ensure that:

(a)   the IFRS Taxonomy content:

(i)   does not conflict with, and does not represent an interpretation of or additional application guidance on, IFRS Standards or the *Conceptual Framework*; and

(ii)   assists with the effective and efficient communication, dissemination and analysis of IFRS disclosures.

(b)   the IFRS Taxonomy technology:

(i)   adheres to the specifications of the technical syntax used to deliver and express the IFRS Taxonomy content; and

(ii)   reflects best practices in order to facilitate adoption by current and future users of the IFRS Taxonomy and to remain relevant and up to date.

The IFRS Taxonomy due process publications

A6   The two IFRS Taxonomy due process publications are the *IFRS Taxonomy update* and the IFRS Taxonomy files.

IFRS Taxonomy updates

A7   A proposed IFRS Taxonomy update is used to describe and consult on proposed updates to the content or technology of the IFRS Taxonomy. An IFRS Taxonomy update is published for the final changes to the IFRS Taxonomy.

A8   The IFRS Taxonomy update contains information in a human-readable form, including:

(a)   the questions on which feedback is sought (this applies only to a proposed IFRS Taxonomy update);

(b)   the proposed (or final) amendments being made; for example, the elements being added or removed from the IFRS Taxonomy; and

(c)   the reasons behind these changes and, when alternative options exist, the reasoning as to why a specific option is preferred.

IFRS Taxonomy files

A9   These are the files used to express and deliver the IFRS Taxonomy content employing a taxonomy delivery mechanism, such as the eXtensible Business Reporting Language (XBRL) syntax. These files allow computers to process the IFRS Taxonomy and to render its content using various software applications.

A10   The *proposed IFRS Taxonomy files* expose the proposed updates to the IFRS Taxonomy whereas the IFRS Taxonomy files represent the final updates.

A11   The IFRS Foundation may also publish IFRS Taxonomy supporting and educational materials, such as files that provide the IFRS Taxonomy content in human-readable form. These materials do not constitute a formal due process publication.

The IFRS Taxonomy Review Panel

A12   A designated group, the IFRS Taxonomy Review Panel, exists to provide oversight over IFRS Taxonomy content not referred to explicitly by IFRS Standards reflecting new or amended IFRS Standards (including the accompanying materials to the Standards). The IFRS Taxonomy Review Panel consists of at least three, but not more than five, Board members. At least one senior member of the technical staff is also a member of this panel.

The IFRS Taxonomy Consultative Group

A13   The Board has a consultative group for its taxonomy related activities, called the IFRS Taxonomy Consultative Group (ITCG).

A14   The ITCG operates under the general principles set out for consultative groups as described in paragraphs 3.59–3.66 of this *Handbook*. The ITCG also has terms of reference that set out its objectives and its workings.

A15   The technical staff consults the ITCG during the development of IFRS Taxonomy changes.

Review and approval of the IFRS Taxonomy

Reviews and approval by the Board

A16   Approval of the proposed IFRS Taxonomy updates and the IFRS Taxonomy updates for IFRS Taxonomy content reflecting new or amended IFRS Standards (including the accompanying materials to the Standards) requires the support of a supermajority of the Board, by means of a ballot.

A17   General improvements and changes to IFRS Taxonomy common practice and any other content not referred to explicitly in IFRS Standards reflecting new or amended IFRS Standards (including the accompanying materials to the Standards) are subject to review—but not approval—by the IFRS Taxonomy Review Panel. These changes are normally not discussed or reviewed by the Board. However, if considered appropriate, any member of the IFRS Taxonomy Review Panel may decide to raise a specific issue for general discussion and review at a public Board meeting.

A18   The IFRS Taxonomy Review Panel also reviews technical staff proposals for the initiation of a new IFRS Taxonomy common practice or general improvements projects or any other projects that affect the content of the IFRS Taxonomy but that do not directly result from the release of a new or amended IFRS Standard. This includes any content amendments that have been triggered as a result of a change to the technology of the IFRS Taxonomy.

A19   Changes affecting solely the technology of the IFRS Taxonomy are not approved or reviewed by either the Board or the IFRS Taxonomy Review Panel, but are assessed by the ITCG (see paragraphs A38–A40).

Reviews by the ITCG

A20   The Board does not review or approve the proposed IFRS Taxonomy files or the IFRS Taxonomy files. However, the ITCG reviews the proposed IFRS Taxonomy files and the IFRS Taxonomy files to help ensure the technical integrity of the IFRS Taxonomy. The ITCG also reviews the proposed IFRS Taxonomy updates and the IFRS Taxonomy updates and may also be asked to review IFRS Taxonomy educational and supporting materials.

A21   For new or amended IFRS Standards, the ITCG review period is normally aligned with the editorial review period of the related Standard (the process for editorial reviews of the Standards is described in paragraphs 3.31–3.33 of this *Handbook*). For other reviews, and in cases in which no editorial review of the related Standard takes place, the ITCG normally has a 14-day period in which to conduct its reviews. If the matter is considered narrow in scope or urgent, the period may be reduced, but may not be less than seven days.

A22   Because reviewers convey their personal views, rather than those of their organisations, their comments are not made public, unless specifically agreed with the ITCG member providing the comment. The technical staff normally summarises the ITCG comments received at a public meeting of the ITCG.

Review processes for proposed IFRS Taxonomy updates and IFRS Taxonomy updates

A23   The tables below tabulate the review and approval for proposed IFRS Taxonomy updates and IFRS Taxonomy updates:

	Proposed IFRS Taxonomy update		IFRS Taxonomy update	
	Board approval	ITCG	Board approval	ITCG
New or amended IFRS Standards	Required paragraph A16	Optional paragraph A31	Required paragraph A16	Optional paragraph A51

	Proposed IFRS Taxonomy update		IFRS Taxonomy update	
	IFRS Taxonomy Review Panel	ITCG	IFRS Taxonomy Review Panel	ITCG
Common practice	Required paragraphs A17 and A35	Optional paragraph A37	Required paragraph A17	Optional paragraph A51
General improvements	Required paragraphs A17 and A35	Optional paragraph A37	Required paragraph A17	Optional paragraph A51
Technology	Not required paragraph A19	Required paragraph A40	Not required paragraph A19	Optional paragraph A51

DPOC oversight of IFRS Taxonomy due process

A24 At each of its meetings, the DPOC is informed about IFRS Taxonomy due process publications in the period and, when applicable, the date that publication was approved by the Board. The DPOC also receives the report of the IFRS Foundation staff's review of the ITCG annually (see paragraph 3.66).

Initiating a proposal to update the IFRS Taxonomy

A25 Updates may relate to a change to the content or technology of the IFRS Taxonomy. In some circumstances, an update may affect both the content and the technology of the IFRS Taxonomy. The IFRS Taxonomy due process that is applied then combines the process followed for the content and the technology, respectively, of the IFRS Taxonomy.

Content changes reflecting new or amended IFRS Standards

A26 The IFRS Taxonomy content should reflect new or amended IFRS Standards in a timely manner. This ensures that the IFRS Taxonomy is an accurate reflection of the Standards at any moment in time.

A27 IFRS Standards must be articulated clearly and consistently enough to enable appropriate representation through the IFRS Taxonomy. Consequently, the implications of the Standards on the IFRS Taxonomy are considered during the development of a new or amended Standard. The technical staff prepares papers for the Board to consider at public meetings. These papers may incorporate IFRS Taxonomy content-related matters if review or approval by the Board on a specific topic is required.

A28 The IFRS Foundation may also make available, on its website, IFRS Taxonomy materials depicting the presentation and disclosure requirements of an exposure draft or a draft IFRIC Interpretation. These materials do not constitute a proposed IFRS Taxonomy update and therefore do not need to be approved by the Board. Their aim is to facilitate the understanding of the proposed presentation and disclosure requirements. A proposed IFRS Taxonomy update is developed for the final IFRS Standard only.

A29 The Board approval of the proposed IFRS Taxonomy update normally takes place concurrently with the approval of the ballot of the related final IFRS Standard. The Board may decide that the approval of the proposed IFRS Taxonomy update should take place at a later time if:

(a) its concurrent publication with the related Standard risks delaying the publication of the Standard; or

(b) the proposed amendments to the IFRS Taxonomy are sufficiently narrow in scope and consequently can be combined with future proposed amendments into one proposed IFRS Taxonomy update.

A30 Proposed IFRS Taxonomy files for content amendments reflecting a new or amended IFRS Standard are prepared if considered appropriate. In assessing whether such files should be prepared, the technical staff reviews the scope of the proposed changes and the likely impact of these changes on users of the IFRS Taxonomy.

A31   The technical staff normally provides a draft outline of the proposed IFRS Taxonomy update and, if they have been prepared, the proposed IFRS Taxonomy files, for review by members of the ITCG. Members of the ITCG are asked to review whether the proposed changes to the content of the IFRS Taxonomy reflect the amendments to the IFRS Standard accurately and in the most appropriate way.

General improvements, new common practice and other content changes

A32   General improvements may include, for instance, changes to data models to better support consistent tagging or new elements to better reflect presentation and disclosure requirements in IFRS Standards. *IFRS Taxonomy common practice content* relates to disclosures that are commonly reported by entities in practice when applying IFRS Standards but are not explicitly referred to in the Standards (including the accompanying materials to the Standards) reflecting new or amended Standards. Other content changes may include for example IFRS Taxonomy element definitions or IFRS Taxonomy implementation guidance.

A33   The technical staff and the IFRS Taxonomy Review Panel consider adding topics to the IFRS Taxonomy work plan based, primarily, on the needs of the users of the IFRS Taxonomy.[3] For example, a new common practice project may arise from a post-implementation review of an IFRS Standard or feedback from regulators and other users of the IFRS Taxonomy.

A34   The process followed to develop the proposed content changes to the IFRS Taxonomy that do not respond to a new or amended IFRS Standard depends on the type and the purpose of the content change. For example, for a common practice project, the technical staff may perform an empirical analysis of financial statements and may set specific benchmark criteria to identify and select proposed new taxonomy elements. The IFRS Foundation makes publicly available materials that document the specific development process being followed.

A35   Review of the proposed content changes by the IFRS Taxonomy Review Panel is a required step. Provided the IFRS Taxonomy Review Panel has not highlighted any issues that require further investigation, the technical staff proceeds with the drafting of the proposed IFRS Taxonomy update.

A36   The proposed IFRS Taxonomy files are prepared if considered appropriate. In assessing whether such files should be prepared, the technical staff reviews the scope of the proposed changes and the likely impact of these changes on users of the IFRS Taxonomy.

A37   The technical staff normally provides a draft outline of the proposed IFRS Taxonomy update and, if they have been prepared, the proposed IFRS Taxonomy files, for review by members of the ITCG.

---

3   This only relates to the work plan for IFRS Taxonomy content not referred to explicitly by IFRS Standards. The work plan for IFRS Taxonomy content reflecting a new or amended Standard is determined by the standard-setting work plan of the Board.

Technology changes

A38   IFRS Taxonomy technology changes may affect the way in which the IFRS Taxonomy has been implemented by its users. The technical staff assesses the necessity of any planned changes and develop any such required changes in consultation with the ITCG while also conducting targeted outreach, for example with regulators and software vendors. When the changes are expected to be substantial or alternative options exist, it may be appropriate to issue a request for information before finalising a proposal to change the IFRS Taxonomy.

A39   A proposed IFRS Taxonomy update describing the technology changes and the proposed IFRS Taxonomy files are prepared and exposed for public comment.

A40   The technical staff provides the ITCG with a draft outline of the proposed IFRS Taxonomy update, a draft of the proposed IFRS Taxonomy files and, when published, any draft of the request for information for their review prior to publication and consultation.

Publication and consultation

A41   Proposed IFRS Taxonomy updates and, when prepared, proposed IFRS Taxonomy files are the subject of public consultation. The comment period will normally be at least 60 days. The comment period can be reduced, but not to less than 30 days, if the matter is urgent or narrow in scope:

(a)   for a proposed change that is narrow in scope, a reduced comment period does not need approval from the DPOC. For proposed content changes the Board or when appropriate the IFRS Taxonomy Review Panel can consider a comment period of no less than 30 days. For proposed technology changes, the technical staff can consider a comment period of no less than 30 days after consulting the ITCG.

(b)   for a proposed change that is not narrow in scope but urgent, a reduced comment period needs approval from the DPOC.

A42   In the case of a taxonomy update reflecting a new or amended IFRS Standard, the proposed IFRS Taxonomy update is released at the same time or shortly after the final Standard is published, except as described in paragraph A29.

A43   Paragraphs A30 and A36 state that the preparation of the proposed IFRS Taxonomy files that reflect proposed content updates is an optional step. No public consultation on these files is required for content updates, because the updated files merely capture the proposed content changes set out in the proposed IFRS Taxonomy update. If these files are prepared, they are published at the same time or shortly after the publication of the related proposed IFRS Taxonomy update.

A44   An IFRS Taxonomy release may include multiple and unrelated updates to the IFRS Taxonomy, for example an update resulting from the publication of a new IFRS Standard and an update resulting from a change to the IFRS Taxonomy technology or a common practice addition. However, the IFRS

Foundation will normally only publish one set of proposed IFRS Taxonomy files, including all proposed updates.

A45 When developing a proposed IFRS Taxonomy update, the Board and the technical staff will consider whether they need to take additional steps to consult stakeholders on the proposed changes. These additional steps could include, for example, private meetings with regulators and other IFRS Taxonomy users, field testing of proposed technology changes by software vendors or the setting up of a taskforce to test tag proposed content changes. Feedback from this additional consultation is considered and assessed along with public comment letters.

Finalising updates to the IFRS Taxonomy

Consideration of comments received and consultations

A46 All public comment letters received on the proposed IFRS Taxonomy updates and, when published, the proposed IFRS Taxonomy files are posted on the IFRS Foundation website. The technical staff analyses the comments received and evaluates whether to recommend changes to the original proposals and whether any revised proposals should be re-exposed.

A47 The technical staff discusses the comments received and the changes to the original proposals, including any proposal to re-expose, with:

(a) the Board at a public meeting (for new or amended IFRS Standards);

(b) the IFRS Taxonomy Review Panel, with a public summary of these discussions being prepared by the staff when relevant (for general improvements, common practice and other taxonomy content reflecting new or amended Standards not referred to explicitly by Standards); and

(c) the ITCG at a public meeting (for changes to the technology of the IFRS Taxonomy).

A48 The DPOC is informed about the due process steps that have been undertaken prior to the finalisation of substantive changes to the IFRS Taxonomy technology.

Drafting, review and publication

A49 After comments have been considered and discussed, the technical staff proceeds with the drafting, Board approval (for content amendments reflecting new or amended IFRS Standards) and the publication of the IFRS Taxonomy update.

A50 The preparation and publication of the IFRS Taxonomy files is a mandatory step for final updates to both the content and the technology of the IFRS Taxonomy.

A51   A review by the ITCG of the IFRS Taxonomy files and the IFRS Taxonomy updates is optional. When assessing whether such a review would be useful, the technical staff considers the substance of any changes made to the final IFRS Taxonomy as a result of comments received during public consultation.

IFRS Taxonomy compilations, translations and editorial corrections

A52   The IFRS Foundation makes available a compiled IFRS Taxonomy using content and technology that has previously been subjected to full due process. Consequently, no public consultation is required prior to the release of a compiled IFRS Taxonomy. A compiled IFRS Taxonomy should be made available at least annually.

A53   Translations of the IFRS Taxonomy content are initiated in response to requests from jurisdictions that have adopted or are developing an interest in, the IFRS Taxonomy. The same procedures followed for translations of IFRS Standards apply to translations of the IFRS Taxonomy.

A54   The technical staff may make editorial corrections to the IFRS Taxonomy after publication, to remedy any errors that have been made. Editorial corrections do not alter the intended accounting meaning of IFRS Taxonomy elements or change the technology of the IFRS Taxonomy. For example, editorial corrections may fix specific XBRL attributes such as debit or credit or element label spelling errors. The technical staff may also make maintenance-type changes to the IFRS Taxonomy, such as, for example, an update to the effective and expiry dates of the IFRS Taxonomy elements to reflect the passage of time. Editorial corrections and maintenance-type amendments are considered post-publication procedures, and do not need to be approved, reviewed or exposed for public consultation.

Glossary of terms

Annual improvements: narrow-scope or minor amendments to IFRS Standards that are packaged together and exposed in one document even though the amendments are unrelated.

Comment letter: a letter or a formal submission received by the Board in response to a consultation document. All comment letters are made public and can be viewed on the IFRS Foundation website.

Consultative group: a group which the Board or the Interpretations Committee consults. Such groups provide the Board with feedback based on research, experience or background, for example, in order to offer different perspectives on a given topic. Consultative groups have their membership reviewed and endorsed by the DPOC. For each of its major projects, the Board considers whether it should establish a consultative group. If the Board decides not to establish a consultative group it explains its reasons in a public meeting.

Discussion paper: a paper issued by the Board that presents the analysis and collective views of the Board on a particular topic. The matters presented will have been discussed in public meetings of the Board. Discussion papers are issued for public comment, the feedback from which informs the Board and helps it to assess whether and how to develop a new or amended IFRS Standard.

Draft for editorial review: a draft of a due process document that the Board and the technical staff use to gather drafting feedback. A draft for editorial review might be distributed to selected groups or be made available more generally on the IFRS Foundation website, or both. Reviewers are asked whether the draft document is clear and contains any inconsistencies. A draft for editorial review does not include an invitation to comment because the purpose of such a review is not to question the technical decisions. A draft for editorial review is not a mandatory step.

Effect analysis: a process for assessing the likely effects of a proposed IFRS Standard, which is undertaken as the new requirements are developed, culminating in an analysis presented as part of, or with, the basis for conclusions published with a new IFRS Standard that summarises the Board's assessment of the likely effects of the new requirements.

Exposure draft: a draft of a proposed IFRS Standard, amendment to a Standard or IFRIC Interpretation. An exposure draft sets out a specific proposal and includes a basis for conclusions and, if relevant, alternative views. An exposure draft is a mandatory due process step.

Feedback statement: a document that gives direct feedback to the comments that were submitted on the exposure draft. It identifies the most significant matters raised in the comment process and explains how the Board responded to those matters.

Fieldwork: work conducted with stakeholders to help the Board assess the likely effects of a proposed IFRS Standard. Fieldwork might include experimentally applying new proposals to individual transactions or contracts as if the proposed Standard was already in effect, asking for feedback on the proposed wording of a particular proposal or assessing the extent of system changes that would be required if a proposed Standard was implemented. Fieldwork also includes gathering examples from practice to help the

Board gain a better understanding of industry practices and how proposed Standards could affect them.

IASB Update: a summary of decisions made at a public meeting of the Board.

IFRIC Update: a summary of decisions made at a public meeting of the Interpretations Committee.

IFRIC Interpretations: Interpretations are developed by the Interpretations Committee before being ratified and issued by the Board. IFRIC Interpretations are part of IFRS Standards.

IFRS Advisory Council: an advisory body that provides a formal vehicle through which organisations and individuals with an interest in international financial reporting can participate. The participants have diverse geographical and functional backgrounds. The Advisory Council's objective is to provide broad strategic advice to the Trustees and the Board. The members of the Advisory Council are appointed by the Trustees.

IFRS Standards: Standards and Interpretations issued by the Board. They comprise International Financial Reporting Standards, International Accounting Standards, IFRIC Interpretations and SIC Interpretations.

Invitation to comment: a document that accompanies a discussion paper or exposure draft and sets out the matters on which the Board is seeking feedback.

Post-implementation review: a review of an IFRS Standard or major amendment to a Standard. It is undertaken by the Board.

Practice guidance: non-mandatory guidance developed by the Board, normally on a topic not addressed by an IFRS Standard — such as guidance on management commentary.

Public hearing: a meeting with interested organisations to listen to, and exchange views on, specific topics. Public hearings include round-table meetings and discussion forums.

Re-exposure: a formal request for comments on a revised version of an exposure draft.

Request for information: a formal consultation step that the Board undertakes to receive feedback and information on a specific aspect of one of its projects. A request for information normally helps the Board to prepare an exposure draft or finalise an IFRS Standard. A request for information is not a mandatory due process step.

Research paper: a paper issued by the Board that was not developed in public meetings, thereby distinguishing it from a discussion paper. Research papers may be prepared by the technical staff. Research papers may also be prepared by other standard-setters or bodies, normally at the request of the Board. A research paper is not a mandatory due process step.

Simple majority: for the Board, a simple majority is achieved when more than half of the Board members vote in favour of a decision in a public meeting attended by at least 60% of the Board members or when more than half of the Board members vote in favour of issuing a document by way of ballot. Abstaining is equivalent to voting against a proposal.

Snapshot: a high-level and simplified summary of the main aspects of a discussion paper or exposure draft.

Supermajority: for the Board, a supermajority is achieved when eight members ballot in favour of the publication of a document if the Board has 13, or fewer, appointed members, and nine in favour if the Board has 14 appointed members. Abstaining is equivalent to voting against a proposal.

Sweep issue: a technical matter identified during the balloting of a document that needs to be resolved by a discussion by the Board or the Interpretations Committee in a public meeting.

IFRS Taxonomy terms

IFRS Taxonomy: a structured classification system of IFRS disclosures. It encompasses the elements (including their descriptions, properties, relationships and the data model) that can be used to tag quantitative and qualitative information presented and disclosed in financial reports that are prepared in accordance with IFRS Standards (including *IFRS for SMEs* Standard).

IFRS Taxonomy common practice content: these are IFRS Taxonomy elements (including their descriptions, properties, relationships and data model) to reflect IFRS disclosures that are commonly disclosed in practice by entities when applying IFRS Standards. They are not referred to explicitly in the Standards or the accompanying materials to the Standards.

IFRS Taxonomy files: these are the files used to express and deliver the IFRS Taxonomy content employing a taxonomy delivery mechanism, such as the eXtensible Business Reporting Language (XBRL) syntax. They allow computers to automatically process the IFRS Taxonomy and to render its content using various software applications.

IFRS Taxonomy update: a document that describes in human-readable form the changes that are being made to the IFRS Taxonomy, why these changes are made and, when alternative options exist, the reasoning as to why a particular option is preferred.

Proposed IFRS Taxonomy files: these are the files that are used to express and deliver proposed updates to both the content and the technology of the IFRS Taxonomy employing a taxonomy delivery mechanism, such as the eXtensible Business Reporting Language (XBRL) syntax. They allow computers to automatically process the IFRS Taxonomy and to render its content using various software applications.

Proposed IFRS Taxonomy update: a document that exposes the changes to the technology or content of the IFRS Taxonomy for public comment. It describes in human-readable form the proposed changes, why these changes are made and, when alternative options exist, the reasoning as to why a particular option is preferred. It also includes the questions on which feedback is sought.

Appendix—History and approval

This appendix summarises the development of the IFRS Foundation *Due Process Handbook*. Although the appendix accompanies the *Handbook*, it is not an integral part of the *Handbook* and may be updated from time to time.

In establishing its consultative arrangements, the Board originally drew upon, and expanded the practices of, national standard-setters and other regulatory bodies. The Board sought to enhance its procedures in 2004 and proposed a series of steps to improve transparency. Those steps, after public consultation, were incorporated into practice.

In **March 2006** the Trustees published the *Due Process Handbook* for the first time.

In **October 2008** the Trustees added Appendix IV (Trustees' oversight role).

In **July 2009** the following major changes were made to the IFRS Foundation *Due Process Handbook*:

- the group tasked with regularly reviewing Board procedures changed from the Trustees' Procedures Committee to the Trustees' Due Process Oversight Committee;

- the sections describing project summaries and feedback statements were added;

- the cost/benefit analysis section was renamed 'Impact analysis'; and

- a section describing post-implementation reviews was added and combined with segments of the previous section that referenced the initiation of studies post-publication.

In **December 2010**, as a consequence of the Trustees' second five-yearly review of the *Constitution*, the *Handbook* was amended to:

- reflect the change of the name of the IASC Foundation to the IFRS Foundation.

- reflect the change of the name of the International Financial Reporting Interpretations Committee (IFRIC) to the IFRS Interpretations Committee (Interpretations Committee).

- reflect the change of the name of the Standards Advisory Council (SAC) to the IFRS Advisory Council.

- include the objective of the IFRS Foundation. These changes were approved in December 2010.

In **February 2011** the Trustees:

- introduced a three-yearly public review of the Board's technical work programme, in response to comments received during the second Constitution Review of the IFRS Foundation; and

- added enhanced criteria for deciding whether a matter could be exposed as part of the annual improvements process.

In **May 2012** the DPOC oversaw a major re-write of the due process handbooks of the Board and Interpretations Committee to:

- combine the separate Board and Interpretations Committee handbooks into one document. This reflected the recommendation by the Trustees, after their review of the Interpretations Committee, that the Board and its Interpretations Committee should work more closely together. In addition, the new *Handbook* incorporated the due process protocol developed by the DPOC. The DPOC also took the opportunity to redraft existing requirements in a more principled way and using plain English.

- describe the three-yearly public review of the Board work programme. The *Handbook* clarified that the focus of the review was strategic and was not designed to add individual projects to the Board's work programme. Instead, the focus was on seeking formal, public input on the strategic direction and balance of the Board's work programme.

- reflect the enhancements of the DPOC's role. The DPOC's responsibilities in overseeing the due process of the Board and the Interpretations Committee were outlined. This section also described the protocols for the action that the Trustees could take in the event of a perceived breach of due process.

- no longer refer to the liaison roles that the Board had with individual standard-setters when the Board was first set up. The section became broader and anticipated the likely steps that the Board would take to develop a more formal network of standard-setters and others.

- include a more extensive discussion of the process of assessing the likely effects of a Standard. More importantly, the *Handbook* reflected the fact that the Board had begun the process of embedding this assessment throughout the development of a Standard rather than simply having an assessment document at the end of the process.

The other more substantive changes were:

- the description of a research programme, which would become the development base from which potential standards-level projects would be identified. The use of a discussion paper as the first external due process document was moved into this research programme and would precede a proposal to add a major standards-level project to the Board work programme. Previously, a discussion paper was required as a step after a project had been added to the standards-level programme.

- the addition of a new section that described the oversight of the *Conceptual Framework* as a standing activity of the Board.

- the addition of a new section on maintenance, which formalised the practice that the Board and Interpretations Committee had been following for addressing matters that were narrow in scope. It clarified that the more formal project proposal processes, such as prior consultation with the Advisory Council, were always intended to apply to new Standards and major amendments. The Board was given the discretion to initiate changes that were narrow in scope as part of the general maintenance of Standards. The new section also explained how the activities of the Board and its Interpretations Committee were closely related.

- the expansion of the sections that explained post-implementation reviews—these described in more detail how the Board expected to develop each review. This section included an explanation of the related public consultation.

- the increase in the minimum comment period for exposing the draft of a rejection of a request for an Interpretation from 30 days to 60 days. This change responded to concerns that the Interpretations Committee was not receiving sufficient feedback on draft rejection notices.

- the reduction in comment period for documents that the Board planned to re-expose. Some re-exposure documents were intended to focus on a narrow aspect of an exposure draft, rather than being a fundamentally different document. A minimum 120-day comment period may not have been necessary in some cases and may had led to an undue delay in the publication of a final Standard. A minimum comment period of 60 days would be permitted.

The redrafted *Handbook* was also updated to reflect actual practice and includes expanded discussions of some matters that seem not to be well understood:

- references to observer notes were replaced by a simple principle that all Board papers were made available for observers. A clearer basis for withholding material and an example of such an instance was provided.

- the Board used a request for information document to seek feedback on many topics, for example, the three-yearly agenda consultation and a targeted request for input on the practical implications and approach to impairment. The *Handbook* explained the purpose of this type of consultation and the process for issuing such a request.

- the process for correcting typographical and other editorial errors was explained.

- the nature of technical votes in meetings was explained, as well as how they related to the ballot process. The balloting process was also set out, including the role of review drafts in this process. This section replaced references to fatal flaw reviews, and provided an explanation of the scope of such reviews.

- the nature and purpose of education sessions and small group sessions was explained, along with a description of the role of assigned Board members.

- the purpose of staff papers was explained, including the relative responsibilities of Board members and staff.

- the different types of consultative groups that the Board used, such as working groups and expert advisory panels, were explained. This section also clarified which types of meeting had to be held in public and which groups had their membership ratified by the DPOC.

- the manner in which the Board uses fieldwork to support the development of Standards (which the current *Handbook* refers to as 'field testing' and 'field visits') was explained. Fieldwork can include components of field tests and field visits, but may also include other methods of collecting information to assess the feasibility and cost of a potential Standard.

- the fact that Board members could dissent from the ratification of an Interpretation. The dissent of a Board member, along with their reasons, is published in the approvals section of the Interpretation.

- the purpose of the annual improvements criteria was clarified as helping the Board to decide whether it would be appropriate to expose several unrelated proposals to amend Standards in a single document rather than separately.

The draft *Due Process Handbook* was issued for public comment for 120 days. A summary of the comments received, and how the IFRS Foundation responded to them in finalising the 2013 edition of the *Due Process Handbook*, was set out in a feedback statement which could be accessed on the DPOC section of the IFRS Foundation website.

In **October 2015**, the DPOC considered and approved the issue of an invitation to comment on the IFRS Taxonomy due process (published in November 2015), which proposed an enhanced due process for the development and maintenance of the IFRS Taxonomy. The proposed changes entailed giving the Board a role in reviewing and approving the content of the IFRS Taxonomy.

In **May 2016**, the DPOC considered the feedback to the November 2015 invitation to comment and considered and approved the staff proposals for the final version of the IFRS Taxonomy due process as an annex to the *Due Process Handbook*. As a consequence, the former XBRL Handbook was withdrawn. The DPOC also approved a number of consequential amendments to the main text of the *Due Process Handbook*. A summary of the comments received, and how the IFRS Foundation responded to them in finalising the 2016 edition of the *Due Process Handbook*, was set out in a feedback statement which could be accessed on the DPOC section of the IFRS Foundation website.

The DPOC also approved a further consequential amendment to the *Due Process Handbook* to extend the interval between agenda consultations by the Board from three years to five years. This change had been proposed by the Board in Request for Views: *2015 Agenda Consultation*, issued for comment in August 2015.

In **November 2017** the DPOC commenced a review of the *Handbook*. The objectives of the review were to update the *Handbook* in line with the Board's and the Interpretations Committee's developing due process conventions. The main changes were to:

- reflect developments in the Board's effects analysis process;

- clarify the role of agenda decisions;

- enhance the due process associated with Interpretation Committee agenda decisions by giving the Board a role in their finalisation;

- refine the consultation required before the Board adds major projects to its work plan;

- update the level of review required for educational material published by the IFRS Foundation;

- clarify the DPOC's oversight of the due process associated with IFRS Taxonomy content; and

- clarify the remit of the Advisory Council reflecting that it now advises the Board (and Trustees) on strategic matters.

The DPOC published an exposure draft of proposed amendments to the *Handbook* in April 2019.

Due Process Handbook

In **June 2020** the DPOC approved the publication of the updated *Handbook* reflecting the amendments. A summary of the comments received on the exposure draft, and how the DPOC responded to them, is set out in a feedback statement which can be accessed on the DPOC section of the IFRS Foundation website.

© IFRS Foundation

NOTES

NOTES

NOTES

NOTES

NOTES

NOTES

the use of the assets created a sufficiently strong link with the employee benefit obligations that a net presentation was more relevant than a gross presentation, even if the entity retained a direct obligation to the employees.

BC186   IASC believed that such restrictions were unique to employee benefit plans and did not intend to permit this net presentation for other liabilities if the conditions then in IAS 32 and IAS 39 were not met. Accordingly, condition (a) in the new definition refers to the reason for the existence of the fund. IASC believed that an arbitrary restriction of this kind was the only practical way to permit a pragmatic exception to IASC's general offsetting criteria without permitting an unacceptable extension of this exception to other cases.

BC187   In some plans in some countries, an entity is entitled to receive a reimbursement of employee benefits from a separate fund, but the entity has discretion to delay receipt of the reimbursement or to claim less than the full reimbursement. Some argue that this element of discretion weakens the link between the benefits and the reimbursement so much that a net presentation is not justifiable. They believe that the definition of plan assets should exclude assets held by such funds and that a gross approach should be used in such cases. IASC concluded that the link between the benefits and the reimbursement was strong enough in such cases that a net approach was still appropriate.

BC188   IASC's proposal for extending the definition of plan assets was set out in exposure draft E67 *Pension Plan Assets*, published in July 2000. The vast majority of the 39 respondents to E67 supported the proposal.

BC189   A number of respondents to E67 proposed a further extension of the definition to include particular insurance policies that have similar economic effects to funds whose assets qualify as plan assets under the revised definition proposed in E67. Accordingly, IASC extended the definition of plan assets to include some insurance policies (described in IAS 19 as qualifying insurance policies) that satisfy the same conditions as other plan assets. These decisions were implemented in amendments to IAS 19 approved by IASC in October 2000.

BC190   A qualifying insurance policy is not necessarily an insurance contract as defined in IFRS 4 *Insurance Contracts*.[13]

Plan assets—measurement

BC191   IAS 19 before its revision in 1998 stated that plan assets are valued at fair value, but did not define fair value. However, other International Accounting Standards defined fair value as 'the amount for which an asset could be exchanged or a liability settled between knowledgeable, willing parties in an arm's length transaction'.[14] This might be taken to imply that no deduction is made for the estimated costs that would be necessary to sell the asset (in other words, it is a mid-market value, with no adjustment for transaction costs).

---

13 IFRS 17 *Insurance Contracts*, issued in May 2017, replaced IFRS 4.

14 IFRS 13 *Fair Value Measurement*, issued in May 2011, defines fair value, describes the effect transaction costs have on a fair value measurement and addresses the application of bid and ask prices when measuring fair value.

BC4.234   that are calculated using such a simple measurement technique and could suggest that fair value measurement would provide more useful information.

BC4.234   Consequently, the IASB proposed a second eligibility condition in the 2017 Negative Compensation Exposure Draft. That eligibility condition would have required that the fair value of the prepayment feature is insignificant when the entity initially recognises the financial asset. The objective of that proposed eligibility condition was to limit further the scope of the amendments so that financial assets would be eligible to be measured at amortised cost only if it is unlikely that prepayment, and thus negative compensation, would occur.

BC4.235   While some respondents agreed with that proposed eligibility condition, others disagreed and expressed concerns about matters such as how difficult the condition would be to apply, whether it would unduly restrict the scope of the amendments and whether it would achieve the IASB's stated objective. Most of the respondents that disagreed with the second eligibility condition said the first eligibility condition (discussed above in paragraphs BC4.222–BC4.232) was sufficient. They expressed the view that the requirements in paragraph B4.1.11(b) of IFRS 9 should accommodate reasonable negative compensation for the early termination of the contract without additional restrictions; ie an entity should be required to assess negative compensation for the early termination of the contract in the same way as it assesses additional compensation for the early termination of the contract. Some respondents suggested alternatives that they thought would better achieve the IASB's objective. Those suggestions included assessing the probability that prepayment, or negative compensation, will occur.

BC4.236   During its redeliberations, the IASB observed that the second eligibility condition proposed in the 2017 Negative Compensation Exposure Draft would, in some cases, achieve its objective. That is because the fair value of the prepayment feature would take into account the likelihood that prepayment will occur. Accordingly, if it is very unlikely that prepayment will occur, then the fair value of the prepayment feature will be insignificant. The IASB also reconfirmed its view that the scope of the amendments must be limited to financial assets for which the effective interest method, and thus amortised cost, can provide useful information, and observed that a second eligibility condition would be helpful to precisely identify the relevant population.

BC4.237   However, the IASB acknowledged the concerns expressed by respondents. The Board agreed with the concern that the fair value of a prepayment feature would reflect not only the probability that reasonable negative compensation will occur, but it would also reflect the probability that reasonable additional compensation (as accommodated by paragraph B4.1.11(b) of IFRS 9 (as issued in 2014)) will occur. In some circumstances, the fair value of the prepayment feature may be more than insignificant due largely, or entirely, to the latter. In such circumstances, the financial asset would not meet the second eligibility condition even if the holder determined that it was very unlikely that negative compensation will occur.